TV Times FILM & VIDEO GUIDE

1995

TV Times FILM & VIDEO GUIDE

1995

David Quinlan

MANDARIN

First published in Great Britain 1994
by Mandarin Paperbacks
an imprint of Reed Consumer Books Limited
Michelin House, 81 Fulham Road, London SW3 6RB
and Auckland, Melbourne, Singapore and Toronto

The author has asserted his moral rights

A CIP catalogue record for this title
is available from the British Library

ISBN 0 7493 18872

Printed and bound in Great Britain

Editor: Julian Brown
Designer: Bryan Dunn
Jacket Designer: Rabab Adams
Production Controller: Michelle Thomas

Introduction

Welcome to the second edition of *The TVTimes Film and Video Guide* which comprises a collection of more than 6,000 reviews from the *TVTimes* Film Archives, together with assessments of many recent films yet to appear on television or even video.

As before, we have kept the reviews mainly to major American and British films to obtain a greater coverage of these markets, particularly in terms of the last 10 years. Thus you will find few continental films, silent movies or TV movies, although a few may have crept in for a variety of reasons.

Reviews often have to be shortened in *TVTimes*, according to how many films are being shown on all channels in a particular week. But most appear here in their full versions (the writer's cut). Any lists of films that readers would like to see included in future editions of this book will be most welcome, and can be sent to me c/o the publishers.

RATINGS

The rating system is straightforward, with one minor addition from last time:

★★★★	excellent
★★★	good film of its type
★★	fair to middling
★	poor or worse

You may also occasionally encounter RB. This stands for 'Really Bad' or, if you prefer 'Rock Bottom'. Don't say that we didn't warn you about the few films that get this rating!

VIDEO

Following numerous requests, we have also included the symbol ⓥ to indicate that a film is available to buy and/or rent on video.

FAMILY VIEWING

The family viewing guide symbols that appear by the film's titles translate as follows:

⊙ Suitable for children to watch alone

○ Family fare

◑ Elements of sex, violence, bad language or adult themes may make the film unsuitable for youngsters to watch

● Adults only

DATES/RUNNING TIMES

Dates of films should correspond with those on the credits of the movie, and running times indicate the original length of the film. Please bear in mind that films run one minute in every 25 shorter on television and video than they did in cinemas.

ALTERNATIVE TITLES

Aka (also known as) denotes any alternative titles by which the film may be known.

The majority of the film reviews here were written by me, but there are also pieces by *TVTimes* writers of past years, as well as by my present colleagues Diana Hall, Judith Jacobs (whose video reviews have made a valuable contribution to this edition), Steven Bunney and Kevin Wilson.

Whether your tastes run to *Citizen Kane* and *Cinderella*, or *Shadowlands* and *Schindler's List*, you will find most of your personal favourites in the pages that follow. Happy viewing!

David Quinlan, London
1994

A

Abandon Ship ○
1957, UK, 100 mins, b/w
Dir: Richard Sale
Stars: Tyrone Power, Mai Zetterling, Lloyd Nolan, Stephen Boyd
Rating: ★★★

Gripping sea adventure where survivors from a sunken luxury liner crowd a small boat commanded by Tyrone Power. A telling portrait of survivors in crisis; not for the squeamish.

ABBA the Movie ⊙ Ⓥ
1977, Sweden/Australia, 95 mins, colour
Dir: Lasse Hallstrom
Stars: Anni-Frid Lyngstad, Agnetha Faltskog, Benny Andersson, Bjorn Ulvaeus
Rating: ★★★

If the first half of this concert film-cum-musical portrait doesn't tell you why the Swedish group ABBA became the biggest world pop stars since The Beatles, then nothing will. Photogenic, melodious, happy and professional – the quartet is all of these. Its two girls are both strong singers and the lyrics of their songs, too few of which can be heard here, are highly original. Somewhere around the middle of the film, though, things start to go a bit wrong. Blame a too-loud soundtrack (which you can turn down a bit on TV!), the monotonously slender plot, and the lack of insight into the group without which an otherwise glorious finale can't quite take wing. At the end, though, such a film stands or falls by its stars. And their joy of living and innate talent see it through with ease.

Abbott and Costello Go to Mars ⊙
1953, US, 76 mins, b/w
Dir: Charles Lamont
Stars: Bud Abbott, Lou Costello, Mari Blanchard
Rating: ★

Actually, they go to Venus, so somebody slipped up somewhere. The inhabitants of that far-off planet turn out to be the Miss Universe beauties, though they're armed to the shoulders. The team was past its sell-by date by now and this is one of their least tolerable ventures.

Abbott and Costello in the Foreign Legion ⊙
1950, US, 80 mins, b/w
Dir: Charles Lamont
Stars: Bud Abbott, Lou Costello, Patricia Medina
Rating: ★★

A hundred lashes to the slapdash scripters who made this one of the weaker entries in the Abbott and Costello comedy career. Bud and Lou are beaux of the desert and the jests are enough to make a camel blush. Still, Patricia Medina sparkles behind her yashmak and a good collection of bad guys includes Walter Slezak, Douglass Dumbrille, Marc Lawrence and Tor Johnson. On second thoughts, failure with a cast like that deserves a thousand lashes.

Abbott and Costello Meet Captain Kidd ⊙
1952, US, 70 mins, colour
Dir: Charles Lamont
Stars: Bud Abbott, Lou Costello, Charles Laughton, Leif Erickson
Rating: ★★

This was Bud Abbott's pet project – but he never thought he'd get Charles Laughton to agree to do it. 'I never have been able to do a double-take,' Laughton explained. 'If I do a picture with Lou Costello, I can learn.' Laughton hams it up in style in a historical romp that's fun rather than funny. One of the few films made in the rather bizarre Supercinecolor.

Abbott and Costello Meet Dr Jekyll and Mr Hyde ○
1953, US, 77 mins, b/w
Dir: Charles Lamont
Stars: Bud Abbott, Lou Costello, Boris Karloff
Rating: ★★

This slapstick comedy was one of a series in which Abbott and Costello met every Hollywood monster from Dracula to the Mummy. In this adventure-comedy-horror, they're American policemen in London at the turn of the century, hindering British bobbies in their attempts to solve the 'mad beast' murders. One critic remarked that the make-up and cameraman's tricks were clever, but the worst monsters were some of the jokes in the script. Be that as it may, parents should be reminded that, thanks to Boris Karloff's performance as Jekyll and Hyde, the film originally had an 'X' certificate. On the other hand, that was more than 40 years ago.

Abbott and Costello Meet Frankenstein ○
1948, US, 83 mins, b/w
Dir: Charles Barton
Stars: Bud Abbott, Lou Costello, Bela Lugosi, Lon Chaney Jr
Rating: ★★★

In 1948, Universal decided to end its 20-year horror series with a bang. Abbott and Costello, its top box-office stars, would be pitted against *all* the monsters. The title, of course, is a misnomer. Bud and Lou meet everybody *but* Frankenstein. At least the British distributors called it *Abbott and Costello Meet the Ghosts*. Lon Chaney Jr is again Lawrence Talbot the Wolf Man, while Bela Lugosi plays Dracula for the first time since 1930. Efforts were made to persuade Boris Karloff to return as Frankenstein's monster, but they were unsuccessful. So Glenn Strange, former Western villain who had played the creature before, was again encased in monster make-up. There's even a guest 'appearance' from the Invisible Man. The result is alarmingly successful, with chills and cackles coming in balanced proportions.

Abbott and Costello Meet the Invisible Man ⊙
1951, US, 82 mins, b/w
Dir: Charles Lamont
Stars: Bud Abbott, Lou Costello, Nancy Guild, Adele Jurgens
Rating: ★★★

This is the best of several films that veteran Hollywood director Charles Lamont made with the comedy team of Bud Abbott and Lou Costello. A lot of intelligent fun is had with the invisibility gimmick, especially in a hilarious boxing match in which tubby Lou Costello has more than a little invisible help. His opponent is John Day, a good-looking ex-boxer turned actor, who found himself back in the ring several times during his film career! Incidentally, Abbott and Costello almost never played characters actually called Bud and Lou – but they do here.

Abbott and Costello Meet the Keystone Cops ⊙
(aka: Abbott and Costello Meet the Keystone Kops)
1954, US, 79 mins, b/w
Dir: Charles Lamont
Stars: Bud Abbott, Lou Costello, Mack Sennett, Lyn Bari
Rating: ★★★

A

Certainly the best Abbott and Costello comedy of the Fifties, if only because such genuine slapstick men as Mack Sennett, Heinie Conklin, Hank Mann and Roscoe Ates are around to provide atmosphere and a little fun. The film is set in 1912, and the heroine is Lynn Bari, who had a 20-year Hollywood career and was once described as 'the Paulette Goddard of the B-picture'. Most of the jokes here are pretty tired, and the film's not really funny until the final chase sequence, which really whips up the pace.

Abbott and Costello Meet the Killer Boris Karloff ⊙
1949, US, 84 mins, b/w
Dir: Charles T Barton
Stars: Bud Abbott, Lou Costello, Boris Karloff
Rating: ★

More mayhem and comedy capers from Bud and Lou who were in the process of meeting all the famous film 'frighteners' when this murder lark was made. Having just co-starred with Lon Chaney Jr and Bela Lugosi, to say nothing of the Invisible Man, the boys now had as guest star the master chiller himself. Karloff plays an evil old Indian (the turbaned variety), who chases little Lou through the Lost Caverns in a hair-raising climax. Overall, though, it's a lukewarm and lacklustre dose of chuckles and chills.

Abbott and Costello Meet the Mummy ⊙
1955, US, 79 mins, b/w
Dir: Charles Lamont
Stars: Bud Abbott, Lou Costello, Marie Windsor
Rating: ★

The only screen monster that Bud Abbott and Lou Costello hadn't previously met gets a grip on them in this typical A and C comedy. Marie Windsor, raven-haired actress from the Forties and Fifties, who never got the parts her talents deserved, plays the villainess to the hilt, in the finest Gale Sondergaard tradition. The humour is tried and true, but by and large the lads are in fair form, Costello in particular making the most of a scene where a medallion is slipped into his food. After crunching it up, he is given an X-ray examination so that the villainess can read the inscription! There's even something for jazz enthusiasts in a night-club spot by Peggy King.

ABC Murders, The
See: The Alphabet Murders

Abilene Town ○
1946, US, 89 mins, b/w
Dir: Edwin L Marin
Stars: Randolph Scott, Ann Dvorak
Rating: ★★★

Tough-skinned, fast-moving Western – the first of a whole run of Randolph Scott action films made by director Edwin L Marin, a series that was stopped short by Marin's early death in 1951. Rhonda Fleming, who had made her debut in another Scott Western, *In Old Oklahoma*, three years earlier, was upped to the second female lead in this one, below Ann Dvorak, who has a Marlene Dietrich-style role as a singing saloon queen. Based on Ernest Haycox's novel *Trail Town*.

Abominable Dr Phibes, The ● Ⓥ
1971, UK, 93 mins, colour
Dir: Robert Fuest
Stars: Vincent Price, Joseph Cotten, Virginia North
Rating: ★★★

Spoof horror piece with delightful Thirties decor, a series of grisly deaths and a plot about a disfigured madman (Vincent Price) who, from the depths of his grandiose mansion, vows to kill the 10-man surgical team 'responsible' for the death of his wife. Phibes' massive cinema organ, which graces the beginning and the end, is rather splendid and, as the dead wife he keeps preserved, you may just recognise the delectable Caroline Munro, later a star of such action spectaculars as *The Golden Voyage of Sinbad*.

A Bout de Souffle
See: Breathless (1959)

About Last Night . . . ● Ⓥ
1986, US, 113 mins, colour
Dir: Edward Zwick
Stars: Rob Lowe, Demi Moore, James Belushi
Rating: ★

No surprises here: boy meets girl, boy beds girl, girl moves in, boy fights with girl, girl moves out, boy gets girl. Rob Lowe and Demi Moore bare a lot of body in the cause of simulated passion but the dialogue, although it has moments of truth, tends to the raucous and doesn't convey much real tenderness. Acting honours go to

plainish Elizabeth Perkins and plumpish James Belushi, who both sketch in deftly the qualities that make them loners. Just a word about that fake snow in the winter scenes: it was *terrible*.

About Mrs Leslie ○
1954, US, 104 mins, b/w
Dir: Daniel Mann
Stars: Shirley Booth, Robert Ryan
Rating: ★★★

That highly watchable actress Shirley Booth, who notched up an Academy Award for her performance in *Come Back, Little Sheba*, actually gets a chance to look a little glamorous in this downbeat love story. She plays a woman who runs a rather ordinary boarding house but treasures memories of a middle-age love affair. Not that hers is the only good performance. All the characters are sharply delineated and well written, in particular that of Pixie, the obnoxious teenage girl whom Mrs Leslie (Booth) has to look after. She's played for all she's worth by 16-year-old Eilene Janssen, who makes her every bit as mean and objectionable as screenplay writers Ketti Frings and Hal Kanter intended. One critic described the resulting character as 'deliciously revolting'. Alex Nicol as a youth who falls in love with the pretty lodger (Marjie Millar) also does good work; and Robert Ryan gives a fine performance as the world-weary aircraft designer lost in the history of the American Civil War, who becomes Booth's part-time lover. The film's tightly written sentiments and absorbing drama are admirably suited for transference to the TV screen.

Above Suspicion ○
1943, US, 90 mins, b/w
Dir: Richard Thorpe
Stars: Joan Crawford, Fred MacMurray, Basil Rathbone
Rating: ★★★

A fast-moving comedy-thriller made when tales of espionage and adventure were all the rage (even Hitchcock joined in with *Foreign Correspondent* and *Saboteur*). This one is crammed with brash, flag-waving Hollywood dialogue (mostly for Fred MacMurray) and enough twists to keep any mystery fan guessing until the last reel.

Above the Law ● Ⓥ

(aka: Nico)
1988, US, 99 mins, colour
Dir: Andrew Davis
Stars: Steven Seagal, Sharon Stone, Henry Silva, Pam Grier, Thalmus Rasasula
Rating: ★★

Steven Seagal's debut is a numbingly violent thriller that offers us gratuitous blood and bone for the sake of a gasp from the audience. Seagal is a cop who, naturally, doesn't so much arrest his suspects as take them apart at the seams. He bulldozes his way into something big that involves master hit-men and a senatorial assassination at the end of the line, upsets authority – 'Nico', whispers his wife (Sharon Stone), 'why is the CIA calling you at two in the morning?' – and finally demolishes the entire china shop. Dislikeable characters throughout make it hard to want to stick around and see what happens to them and the film is dull in between its bursts (or should I say spurts) of violent action. Seagal looked a little long in the tooth to be starting a movie career but, as events proved, both he and director Davis (who made *Under Siege* and *The Fugitive*) were to go on to better things.

Above Us the Waves ○ Ⓥ

1955, UK, 99 mins, b/w
Dir: Ralph Thomas
Stars: John Mills, John Gregson, Donald Sinden
Rating: ★★★

One of director Ralph Thomas's best films, this is also among the most exciting he ever made. It's the true-to-life story of an assault by midget submarines on a giant German battleship that threatened Allied shipping during World War Two. The photography by Ernest Seward is praiseworthy, and the climax will have even non-war film fans on the edges of their seats.

Absence of Malice ◑ Ⓥ

1981, US, 116 mins, colour
Dir: Sydney Pollack
Stars: Paul Newman, Sally Field, Bob Balaban, Melinda Dillon
Rating: ★★★

Paul Newman is close to his best here as an innocent man whose life is virtually wrecked – because hotheads at the DA's office believe he *may* be someone who could help crack a months-old investigation into the dis-

appearance of a prominent union leader. So the news of his possible complicity is leaked to a hard-headed newsgirl (Sally Field) who duly splashes it all over the front page. Subsequent developments lead almost inevitably to tragedy before Newman, by now romantically involved with the contrite reporter, decides to get his own back. Although the ways and means of this are not presented in quite the hard-hitting manner they might be, it's nice to see the bad guys get their come-uppance at the end. Bob Balaban's coldly sneaky investigator also catches the eye in a smooth and thought-provoking entertainment.

Absent-Minded Professor, The ⊙ Ⓥ

1961, US, 97 mins, b/w
Dir: Robert Stevenson
Stars: Fred MacMurray, Nancy Olson, Keenan Wynn
Rating: ★★★

A riotous comedy from the Disney stable, made by the studio's best director, Robert Stevenson, who did *Mary Poppins* for them three years later. Fred MacMurray, as the prof of the title, accidentally invents a rubbery substance that makes things fly. Things from then on happen at breakneck speed, with some very funny chase sequences and wonderful comic support from James Westerfield as a continually bewildered cop, and from Keenan Wynn, making the first of several appearances in Disney comedies as the crooked financier Alonzo Hawk, a role he was still playing as late as 1974 in *Herbie Rides Again*. One of the funniest scenes of all in this film involves Wynn bounding uncontrollably up and down on his lawn. Wynn's real-life father Ed is very droll as the local fire chief.

Absent-Minded Professor, The ⊙

1988, US, 94 mins, colour
Dir: Bob Sweeney
Stars: Harry Anderson, Mary Page Keller
Rating: ★

If this Disney comedy seems to change direction about halfway through, it's because it was actually made as two entirely separate one-hour stories! Based on the characters in the 1961 film, it finds Harry Anderson stepping uncomfortably into Fred MacMurray's shoes as the professor.

But this Disney sideshoot from a comedy classic lacks all the joy and wonderment of the original.

Absolute Beginners ◑ Ⓥ

1986, UK, 107 mins, colour
Dir: Julien Temple
Stars: David Bowie, Patsy Kensit, Eddie O'Connell, James Fox
Rating: ★★★

Certainly the biggest British musical in a couple of decades, and not half as bad as some critics avowed. Julien Temple's film re-creates the summer of 1958 when 'teenagers started' and so, he contends, did modern Britain, with all its racial warts and sores. It's a pity the film doesn't have the courage to go all the way with its approach of the first 15 minutes which vividly evokes nostalgia for the environments of Soho and Notting Hill in a slightly surrealistic and kaleidoscopic way, creating its atmosphere through a flurry of images, off-camera lines and surreptitiously prowling cameras. The clean exhilaration of all this, however, is sullied not only by the Notting Hill riots that form the climax but by a sub-plot (involving heroine Patsy Kensit) straight out of a British pop musical of the Sixties.

Abyss, The ◑ Ⓥ

1989, US, 134 mins, colour
Dir: James Cameron
Stars: Ed Harris, Mary Elizabeth Mastrantonio, Michael Biehn
Rating: ★★★

'He's losing it,' cry the crew of the stranded 'submersible' as skipper Ed Harris starts babbling at about 12,000 feet down, while diving to disarm a nuclear warhead. The film, too, starts to lose it at about this point, after a fine first two hours whose urgency and excitement is what James Cameron, who made *Aliens* and the *Terminator* films, is all about. But the whole 'alien' involvement in the later stages could conveniently have been ditched into the abyss of the title, to say nothing of the money the producers could have saved on special effects. Cameron is also responsible for a script that disintegrates when asked to express human emotion, but which drives the drama along in fine style as long as the action is strong and virile. The excitement in the main body of the film is supercharged, with racing tracking shots and an agonising resuscitation scene adding to the tension. Mary Elizabeth Mastrantonio is along for the dive as Harris's estranged

A

scientist wife, and Cameron favourite Michael Biehn enjoys himself as the naval lieutenant who 'loses it' in style and prepares to blow up nothing less than the entire world.

Accident ◐ ⓥ
1967, UK, 105 mins, colour
Dir: Joseph Losey
Stars: Dirk Bogarde, Stanley Baker, Jacqueline Sassard, Michael York
Rating: ★★

Casts and credits came no more fashionable in 1967 than in this flashback drama, which caused highbrow critics to reach for such adjectives as 'elliptical', 'seminal' and 'schematic' in describing director Joseph Losey's approach to the story of three men involved with the same woman. The script by Harold Pinter, from the novel by Nicholas Mosley (both of whom play cameo roles in the film), breaks down the characters' thoughts, actions and motives to clearly reveal their personalities. There are skilful portraits from Dirk Bogarde, Stanley Baker, Michael York and Vivien Merchant. Only Jacqueline Sassard as the girl at the centre of things seems to fall below this level of excellence.

Accidental Hero ◐ ⓥ
(aka: Hero)
1992, US, 117 mins, colour
Dir: Stephen Frears
Stars: Dustin Hoffman, Geena Davis, Andy Garcia, Chevy Chase, Joan Cusack
Rating: ★★★

Petty thief Dustin Hoffman, about to go to prison for receiving stolen property, saves 54 people from a burning plane, but homeless Andy Garcia takes the credit – and the one million dollars that goes with it. Previously unwilling to step into the limelight, Hoffman belatedly tries to grab the glory (despite having robbed the people he was rescuing). But, as is traditionally the case in this kind of social comedy, the fates conspire against him, and under the guidance of survivor and crusading reporter Gale Galey (a super-sexy performance by Geena Davis) and her scoop-hungry editor (Chevy Chase, unbilled and unwigged), Garcia becomes a national celebrity. What's more he's a nice guy (who starts doing good deeds) and Hoffman isn't – so hasn't justice been done? Well, you'll know the answers to that. The spirit of Frank Capra lives in this modern-day story quite rightly given an old-fashioned (save the language) treatment. After you've shed

a tear or two, the film neatly sends you off with a laugh in the final scene. All the performances are good.

Accidental Tourist, The ◐ ⓥ
1988, US, 121 mins, colour
Dir: Lawrence Kasdan
Stars: William Hurt, Kathleen Turner, Geena Davis, Bill Pullman, Ed Begley Jr
Rating: ★★

Acted with great care, this long, drawn-out and sometimes boring romantic drama reveals that the same pacing and tactics director Lawrence Kasdan used to such effect on *Body Heat* don't necessarily work when used with such little variation on a different kind of film. William Hurt is the central character, a tour-book writer and walking iceberg who has become zombiefied since the death of his only son a year earlier. No wonder wife Kathleen Turner wants to leave this member of an extremely eccentric family who play weird card games and never answer the phone. For some reason, dog trainer Geena Davis is attracted to Hurt, setting up the triangular motif that dominates the film. You can't think that either woman is getting much of a bargain and the path to Hurt's choice between them is not exactly fun. Davis's performance, though, is a knockout and won her an Oscar.

Accused, The ○
(aka: Strange Deception)
1948, US, 101 mins, b/w
Dir: William Dieterle
Stars: Loretta Young, Wendell Corey
Rating: ★★★

A taut psychological thriller with some pretty complex characters as well as moments of suspense and a good story. Director William Dieterle handles it all with confident visual flair, and compels attention as the varying characters approach their dates with destiny. Loretta Young handles an unusual part well, but Wendell Corey's role is the most interesting in the film.

Accused, The ● ⓥ
1988, US, 111 mins, colour
Dir: Jonathan Kaplan
Stars: Jodie Foster, Kelly McGillis
Rating: ★★★★

Jodie Foster deservedly won an Oscar in this brutal, uncompromising drama about the battle to prosecute onlookers at a gang rape after the actual

attackers get off on reduced charges. Foster couldn't be better as the far-from-squeaky-clean victim, betrayed by the justice system, who fights her corner like an alleycat. And not since *Fatal Attraction* had a film engendered so much press coverage, ensuring that it was one of the biggest box-office earners of the year. The film itself is a real time-bomb of a drama that provides both graphic, unpalatable food for thought and excellent courtroom dramatics, especially when attorney Kelly McGillis, mortified by her failure to represent Foster to the best of her ability, fights for self-redemption under threat of dismissal from her firm. McGillis is driven on by the realisation that, in the unlikely event of her prosecuting the jeering crowd successfully, the original rapists will be forced to serve the full term of the light five-year sentence they had been given and have their crime reclassified from 'reckless endangerment' to rape. There is, of course, a missing witness to be found, and much trauma in court before the case is closed. Mighty powerful, hyper-emotive stuff and engrossing entertainment too.

Ace in the Hole ○
(aka: The Big Carnival)
1951, US, 112 mins, b/w
Dir: Billy Wilder
Stars: Kirk Douglas, Jan Sterling, Robert Arthur
Rating: ★★★★

An expertly turned out study of a brutal sensation monger – produced, directed and partly written by Billy Wilder. Although the story may leave a sour taste, it is packed with tension, high drama and first-rate acting. Kirk Douglas offers another of his callous, hard-driving portrayals as the ruthless reporter out to make a sensation from the story of a man trapped by a rock fall. Jan Sterling is subtly sluttish and sullen as the trapped man's wife. Repulsive as the leading character is, you may be even more appalled by the dreadful crowd which congregates around the scene, full of glee at being in on a cheap thrill, as a man's tragedy is quickly turned into a circus.

Aces High ○ ⓥ
1976, UK, 114 mins, colour
Dir: Jack Gold
Stars: Malcolm McDowell, Christopher Plummer, Simon Ward, Peter Firth
Rating: ★★

R C Sherriff's classic play about life in the trenches during World War One, *Journey's End*, was reworked as a drama of fliers in the Royal Flying Corps by screenwriter Howard Barker. Fine aerial sequences (directed by Derek Cracknell) but the dramatics on the ground soar rather less and the characters tend towards cliché. A solid roster of guest stars includes John Gielgud, Ray Milland and Richard Johnson.

Ace Ventura, Pet Detective ● Ⓥ
1993, US, 86 mins, colour
Dir: Tom Shadyac
Stars: Jim Carrey, Sean Young, Courteney Cox
Rating: ★★

Although it has only one or two big laughs, this is quite a jolly lowbrow jape with a neat central idea. New comedian Jim Carrey, who looks like Jim Dale on speed, mugs madly in the title role. Missing animals are this hunter's bag all right, although naturally he's an ace at the formula stuff as well. After solving the mystery of a missing shih-tzu dog, Ace is hired to investigate the poolnapping of a dapper dolphin who's the ball-playing mascot of the local Miami football team. Ace soon gets in the hair of lady lieutenant Einhorn (Sean Young) as well as the bed of the dolphin's PR girl (Courteney Cox). There are one or two pleasant incidentals: the menagerie Ace keeps at his apartment disappears at the mere sound of the landlord; and he drives his car sideways as a result of an earlier fracas with another petnapper. No, Ace won't bore you and you might even get a chuckle or two – especially at Carrey's dead-on impersonation of Sean Connery as James Bond.

Across the Great Divide ☉ Ⓥ
1977, US, 101 mins, colour
Dir: Stewart Raffill
Stars: Robert Logan, Heather Rattray
Rating: ★★★★

If you've forgotten how much fun films used to be, take a look at this, the best of the *Wilderness Family*-style adventures. Director Stewart Raffill has taken his own story, of how two children, a teenage girl and a boy about 10, trek across the American wilderness to Oregon over desolate plain and icy mountain, with the help of a roguish frontier gambler, and has told it cleanly and strongly, with never

a drop in pace and barely a concession to sentimentality. There isn't even a hint of a romance between the gambler and the girl, who is allowed to be entirely her own character. The animal footage is fabulous, as deer and lion-cubs romp with the children and a bear convincingly menaces the gambler, who hides in a beaver's lodge as the tenant exits hastily by the back door. Look: no stuntmen and no doubles, either, especially as the trio take a tumble in the rapids. Robert Logan, in his best screen performance, is almost faultless as the gambler: the charm never seems forced and the ending promises no guarantee of his redemption. Heather Rattray, too, is excellent as Holly: one of those rare sub-teen portrayals whose strength and truth she is unlikely to equal again. The story is absolutely packed with incident, but never over-stresses its own simplicity.

Across the Pacific ○
1942, US, 99 mins, b/w
Dir: John Huston
Stars: Humphrey Bogart, Mary Astor, Sydney Greenstreet
Rating: ★★

A rugged action thriller from the same team – star Humphrey Bogart, director John Huston – that had just made *The Maltese Falcon*. Bogart's role in many ways foreshadows the world-weary adventurer – also called Rick – that he played in his next film, *Casablanca*. In the cast of this film: two oriental actors, Sen Young (later Victor Sen Young of *Bonanza*) and Keye Luke, who was world-famous in the late Thirties as Charlie Chan's son.

Across the Wide Missouri ○
1951, US, 78 mins, colour
Dir: William A Wellman
Stars: Clark Gable, Ricardo Montalban, Maria Elena Marques
Rating: ★★

Unusual Western, oddly reminiscent of Oliver Reed's *The Trap*. Clark Gable, radiating sincerity, gives one of his best performances as the rugged trapper, and Maria Elena Marques, who only made one other Hollywood film, is enchanting as the girl.

Action in the North Atlantic ○
1943, US, 127 mins, b/w
Dir: Lloyd Bacon
Stars: Humphrey Bogart, Raymond Massey, Alan Hale
Rating: ★★★

And the action is everything in this all-guns-firing Warner Brothers tribute to the American marines. Excellent battle scenes involving submarines and surface vessels and fine performances. It is outside Humphrey Bogart's usual metier, but he gives a rugged portrayal that complements the inner steel of Raymond Massey as his captain. And there's a peach of a performance from that perennial Hollywood blonde, Iris Adrian, here seen as Alan Hale's domineering wife.

Act of Violence ○
1948, US, 92 mins, b/w
Dir: Fred Zinnemann
Stars: Van Heflin, Robert Ryan, Janet Leigh
Rating: ★★★

This thriller bursts into action without so much as a single credit appearing on the screen (they're left to the end). Commonplace, nowadays, but when director Fred Zinnemann pulled the stunt in an effort to hold the audience's interest from start to finish, it was regarded as something of an innovation – and a welcome one at that. Originally, Gregory Peck and Humphrey Bogart were set to play the roles finally filled by Van Heflin and Robert Ryan.

Ada ○
1961, US, 109 mins, colour
Dir: Daniel Mann
Stars: Susan Hayward, Dean Martin, Ralph Meeker
Rating: ★★

Intriguing and colourful drama about a strong-willed woman urging her husband on to political power in the southern states of America. Interesting performance from Britain's Wilfrid Hyde White, abandoning his normal chintzy image for that of an unscrupulous political manipulator.

Adam's Rib ○
1949, US, 100 mins, b/w
Dir: George Cukor
Stars: Spencer Tracy, Katharine Hepburn, Judy Holliday, Tom Ewell, David Wayne
Rating: ★★★★

Spencer Tracy and Katharine Hepburn are in sparkling form as lawyers whose marriage comes under strain when they find themselves on opposing sides in court, but they face stiff opposition from Judy Holliday as the lady accused of shooting her husband. Strong support, too, from Tom Ewell as the man

A

winged by Holliday's shot and David Wayne as a songwriter with none-too-honourable designs on Hepburn. George Cukor has the comedy under perfect control; Ruth Gordon and Garson Kanin supplied the smart screenplay.

Addams Family, The ◑ ⓥ
1991, US, 101 mins, colour
Dir: Barry Sonnenfeld
Stars: Anjelica Huston, Raul Julia, Christopher Lloyd, Christina Ricci
Rating: ★★

This living horror comic (from the famous newspaper strip and subsequent TV series) looks great. Doubtless its cobwebs are the finest money can buy. Here is the familiar gallery of ghouls led by Morticia, a symphony in black, white and blood-red, matriarch to a gothic family whose pet is Thing, a severed hand. And yet something is missing. It's flair, imagination, or whatever magic ingredient is needed to make the Addamses (if they'll pardon the expression) spring to life. A dance sequence at a party almost does it, but most of the characters stubbornly stay cardboard comic cut-outs. Honourable exceptions are Christopher Lloyd as long-lost brother Fester, a shaven demon with a wonderful idiot grin; and Christina Ricci as the Addams daughter, a perfectly poker-faced malevolent child. The dialogue is meticulously keyed to the Addams' love of the dark side of life. 'Imagine if Fester did come back,' muses Morticia's husband (Raul Julia). 'Half-human and a rotting shell.' 'Don't tease,' she replies. Big laughs, however, are notably missing, and most gags are heavily signposted.

Addams Family Values ○ ⓥ
1993, US, 92 mins, colour
Dir: Barry Sonnenfeld
Stars: Anjelica Huston, Raul Julia, Christopher Lloyd, Joan Cusack, Carol Kane
Rating: ★★

More of the same, only less. The gleefully ghoulish Addamses are back, with Morticia (Anjelica Huston) having a baby and Fester (Christopher Lloyd) in love with the Black Widow (Joan Cusack), a notorious husband-killer posing as the Addamses' new nanny. Like Cusack's initially amusing performance, the whole thing wears thin in quite a short time, with few really funny lines to keep it going. Huston has almost nothing to

do and she and Raul Julia (as her husband) get little room for improvisation under Barry Sonnenfeld's head-on direction. Christina Ricci is still good as Wednesday but, like Jimmy Workman as Pugsley, already a little too old for the part. Lloyd does what he can with Fester, grinning idiotically (visually he's perfect) and pining for love. 'Some day,' he's told, 'you'll meet someone very special . . . someone who won't press charges.' Like this, most of the funny stuff comes at the start. 'He has my father's eyes,' coos Julia, looking at the baby. 'Gomez,' chides Huston, 'take them out of his mouth.' It may be pinched from *Hot Shots!*, but it's still the best line in the film.

Admirable Crichton, The ○
(aka: Paradise Lagoon)
1957, UK, 93 mins, colour
Dir: Lewis Gilbert
Stars: Kenneth More, Diane Cilento, Cecil Parker, Sally Ann Howes, Martita Hunt, Jack Watling
Rating: ★★★

Director Lewis Gilbert took a break from making such distinguished war films as *Reach for the Sky* and *Carve Her Name with Pride* to create J M Barrie's famous comedy story about a noble family marooned on a desert island. Kenneth More enjoys himself immensely as the butler who gradually but inevitably takes over. Cecil Parker offers splendidly pompous support as Lord Loam and Diane Cilento is delightful as Tweeny.

Adolf Hitler – My Part in His Downfall ○
1972, UK, 102 mins, colour
Dir: Norman Cohen
Stars: Jim Dale, Bill Maynard, Spike Milligan, Windsor Davies, Arthur Lowe
Rating: ★★

This film version of Spike Milligan's best-selling account of his wartime army days is a funny-sad black comedy enriched by the comic talents of Bill Maynard, Windsor Davies and Arthur Lowe. Jim Dale makes a brave try at playing Spike, even though he's clearly too old for the part, but Spike himself steals the show playing his own father. Although the film undergoes some changes of mood, the underlying wit of the original sees it through.

Adventure ○
1945, US, 125 mins, b/w
Dir: Victor Fleming
Stars: Clark Gable, Greer Garson, Joan Blondell
Rating: ★★

This was Clark Gable's first film after war service and the publicity ran: 'Gable's back and Garson's got him!' Gable plays a tough sailor who falls for a staid librarian: both he and Greer Garson were then among America's top 10 moneymakers at the box office. The film rounded off a notable 10 years for director Victor Fleming – a decade in which he directed such films as *Captains Courageous*, *Dr Jekyll and Mr Hyde* and *The Wizard of Oz*, as well as *Gone With the Wind*, for which he won an Oscar. This one's humdrum by his standards.

Adventure of Sherlock Holmes' Smarter Brother, The ○ ⓥ
1975, UK, 91 mins, colour
Dir: Gene Wilder
Stars: Gene Wilder, Madeline Kahn, Marty Feldman
Rating: ★★

Gene Wilder made his name as a funny man in Mel Brooks' films, and his first film as star-director turns out to be a typically Brooksian curate's egg of a helter-skelter farce, fussily set in Victorian times, but with some nice scenes involving Roy Kinnear. These are mostly played for laughs, but include one piece of calculated excitement which really stirs the blood, as he and Wilder swing at each other with giant-sized boot and glove from the tops of speeding carriages.

Adventures in Babysitting
See: A Night on the Town

Adventures of Baron Munchausen, The ○ ⓥ
1988, UK, 131 mins, colour
Dir: Terry Gilliam
Stars: John Neville, Eric Idle, Sarah Polley, Uma Thurman, Ray D Tutto (Robin Williams)
Rating: ★★

This fantasy adventure is a work of considerable visual imagination, but not a little tedium too – very much like the good baron's stories themselves. You'll remember that he was the tall tale-teller from the past (the opening title states: 'Late 18th Century. The Age of Reason. Wednesday') who assured his listeners that he had visited the Moon (and bested its king), visited the inside of the volcano of the gods (and fallen for Venus) and been swallowed into the belly of a gigantic whale – each time accompanied by his faithful companions, a strong man, a dwarf who can blow men over and an idiot whose feet move faster than sound. All of these tales are woven into the film's central story, the siege of a mythical European town by a Turkish army whose caliph is after Munchausen's head. The film succeeds in fits and starts, but its screenplay is couched in much too high-flown terms, and the ending doesn't play fair, even by its own standards. A feast for the eyes, then, but a mixed blessing for the mind.

Adventures of Buckaroo Banzai Across the Eighth Dimension, The ○ ⓥ
1984, US, 102 mins, colour
Dir: W D Richter
Stars: Peter Weller, John Lithgow, Ellen Barkin, Jeff Goldblum, Christopher Lloyd
Rating: ★

A Marvel comic book hero-type film that shows even less regard for its audience than for logic. Familiar elements are thrown into the 'plot' in haphazard fashion by director W D Richter (who would do better work later), while neuro-surgeon super-hero Banzai, played uncharismatically by Peter Weller, takes on aliens from outer space who want to . . . well, who knows or cares . . . something to do with an overthruster that can take you through mountains . . . I think. Matt Clark, at that time a welcome character star with his disgruntled, hangdog looks, plays the senator who tries to keep track of it all, while John Lithgow as the villain looks as though he enjoyed himelf rather more than I did. Great cast, though, and brilliant Metrocol photography by Fred Koenekamp. The ending threatens a sequel that mercifully never happened.

Adventures of Bullwhip Griffin, The ○ ⓥ
1965, US, 110 mins, colour
Dir: James Neilson
Stars: Roddy McDowall, Suzanne Pleshette, Karl Malden
Rating: ★★

This Disney adventure caper was the film in which Tony Hancock was to have made his Hollywood debut. But the deal fell through and Hancock's role as a down-at-heel actor with a

treasure map was taken over by Richard Haydn. Roddy McDowall gives one of his sprightlier performances as the 1890 Bostonian butler at large in the Far West, where he achieves an accidental reputation as a prizefighter. The script makes clever use of the material it parodies and Karl Malden is an amiably shifty villain. A lively and quite zany couple of hours; a pity Hancock missed out.

Adventures of Don Juan ○ ⓥ
(aka: The New Adventures of Don Juan)
1948, US, 110 mins, colour
Dir: Vincent Sherman
Stars: Errol Flynn, Viveca Lindfors, Robert Douglas, Raymond Burr, Alan Hale, Ann Rutherford
Rating: ★★★

Flynn's final glorious fling. This was the last major swashbuckler mounted by Warner Brothers for its superstar of sword and swagger, Errol Flynn. Richly costumed in splendid Technicolor, the film is no masterpiece, but made with immense confidence by director Vincent Sherman and so crammed with action there hardly seems to be a sequence that doesn't begin or end with a fight. Flynn is still very nearly at his most deft and agile, and finds a worthy fencing adversary in the British actor Robert Douglas as the treacherous Duc de Lorca. And, although Flynn may be playing Don Juan, love is pretty much shunted to the sidelines for most of the plot. Viveca Lindfors is forthright as the queen who, like Bette Davis before her, secretly loves her champion, while Romney Brent as King Philip seems to have an idea this is a subtle picture: he's too good for the role. It was, alas, all downhill for Flynn after this. But, with the mass battle royal at the end, and the final romantic gesture for the fadeout, he certainly gave his fans something to remember him by.

Adventures of Huckleberry Finn, The ○
1939, US, 91 mins, b/w
Dir: Richard Thorpe
Stars: Mickey Rooney, Walter Connolly, William Frawley
Rating: ★★★

Solidly entertaining MGM version of the Mark Twain classic, with Mickey Rooney giving a breezy but controlled account of the title role. The scene-stealing characters, though, are two Mississippi conmen, delightfully

played in this version by Walter Connolly and William Frawley. One of the first big MGM films entrusted to their reliable contract director, Richard Thorpe, who later made such hits for the studio as *The Great Caruso*, *Ivanhoe* and *Jailhouse Rock*.

Adventures of Marco Polo, The ○ ⓥ
1938, US, 100 mins, b/w
Dir: Archie Mayo
Stars: Gary Cooper, Sigrid Gurie, Basil Rathbone
Rating: ★★★

Don't expect historical accuracy from this light-hearted epic which casts an understandably uneasy-looking Gary Cooper as the famed 13th-century Venetian explorer. The producer, Samuel Goldwyn, was more concerned with offering lavish entertainment than factual information and he succeeded, with a cast of some 5,000, headed by Cooper, Basil Rathbone (who replaced originally cast John Carradine as the villain of the piece) and Sigrid Gurie, billed in the advertising for the film as having been 'discovered by Samuel Goldwyn in Norway'. In fact, by the time the picture was released, it had been discovered that Gurie hailed from the rather less exotic land of Brooklyn. Director Archie Mayo (who replaced John Cromwell after a few days) sees to it that the pageant moves at a lively clip. Look out for Lana Turner in her sixth film, making a short appearance as a slave girl.

Adventures of Mark Twain, The ○
1944, US, 130 mins, b/w
Dir: Irving Rapper
Stars: Fredric March, Alexis Smith
Rating: ★★

Well-acted and entertaining, if a bit rambling, this lavish biography of Mark Twain and his adventurous life has picturesque black and white photography by Sol Polito who shot many of Errol Flynn's earlier films. The plot as a whole fails to grip, but does have a number of felicitous moments and the riverboat scenes are splendid. Fredric March's Twain is on the dull side.

Adventures of Mark Twain, The ○ ⓥ
1985, US, 86 mins, colour
Dir: Will Vinton
Voice star: James Whitmore
Rating: ★★★

A

Ever seen an entire feature film made in moving plasticene? You could be in for a pleasant surprise. This labour of love, peppered with the wit and wisdom of Mark Twain, is a sight more imaginative and entertaining than some live-action films. It supposes that Twain, born and dying in the years of Halley's Comet, builds a fantastic flying machine from which he hopes to be engulfed in the flaming comet that he believes gave birth to him. With him on the voyage go several of his most famous fictional characters – Tom Sawyer, Huckleberry Finn, Becky Thatcher and Homer, the famous jumping frog. On board they discover a mysterious door, which admits them to numerous Twain characters and stories. A space Satan is chillingly frightening, the story of Adam and Eve touching and amusing; there's even a sequence on varying kinds of heaven. 'Is there a Heaven or a Hell?' muses Twain. 'I wouldn't like to express an opinion. I have friends in both places.'

Adventures of Milo and Otis, The ⊙
(Koneko Monogatari)
1986, Japan, 80 mins, colour
Dir: Masanori Hata
Stars: Narrated by Dudley Moore
Rating: ★★★

You won't believe some of the scenes in this amazing animal adventure with great appeal for kids – especially a dog riding through the sea on a giant turtle, and the same dog pulling a cat out of a pit on the end of a rope. Encounters between the cat and a snake, the cat and a deer and the cat and an owl, or the cat sitting on a pig, are commonplace by comparison. Reminiscent of *The Incredible Journey*, this Japanese film (with English narration by Dudley Moore) relates the adventures of a pug-dog, Otis, and a ginger cat, Milo, when they stray from their farm, after the cat has been washed down-river in a wooden box. The kind of film that modern cinema has sadly missed, and this one's all the more welcome for that.

Adventures of Quentin Durward, The ○
(aka: Quentin Durward)
1955, US, 101 mins, colour
Dir: Richard Thorpe
Stars: Robert Taylor, Kay Kendall, Robert Morley
Rating: ★★★

The third in a splendid trilogy of films which Robert Taylor made for MGM in England (the others were *Ivanhoe* and *The Knights of the Round Table*). This one has a fast pace, splendid Technicolor photography and an exciting confrontation in a bell tower as its climax.

Adventures of Robin Hood, The ⊙ ⓥ
1938, US, 102 mins, colour
Dir: Michael Curtiz
Stars: Errol Flynn, Olivia de Havilland, Basil Rathbone, Claude Rains
Rating: ★★★★

Forget Kevin Costner, forget Richard Greene, Errol Flynn is the definitive bandit of Sherwood Forest in this, the Robin Hood film by which all others should be judged. All the elements that go to make a classic film are here: perfect casting, lots of vigorous action, a strong story and rousing music by Eric Wolfgang Korngold. Flynn is perfectly cast as Robin, Olivia de Havilland is a winsome Maid Marian, Claude Rains is a delightfully rascally King John and Basil Rathbone sneers as only he can as the evil Guy of Gisbourne. Even the most minor of supporting roles is well scripted and observed. Director Michael Curtiz, a master of action and adventure films, pulled out all the stops with this one. It confirmed Flynn as the cinema's greatest swashbuckling hero and no-one to this day has bettered him. Much against the studio's wishes, he did all his own stunts, including the classic swordfight with Rathbone, complete with huge dancing shadows.

Adventures of Sadie, The
See: Our Girl Friday

Adventures of Sherlock Holmes, The ○
1939, US, 83 mins, b/w
Dir: Alfred Werker
Stars: Basil Rathbone, Nigel Bruce, Ida Lupino
Rating: ★★★

To a generation of cinemagoers, Basil Rathbone *was* Sherlock Holmes. Tall, supercilious and ascetic, he fitted the role as surely as a Savile Row deerstalker fitted the character. And Nigel Bruce, another British actor, made a superb bumbling, stumbling Watson. In this, the second of their film adventures together, they encounter Holmes' arch-enemy Moriarty, splendidly portrayed by a third British actor, the sepul-

chral-toned George Zucco. Rathbone and Bruce subsequently made a dozen further Holmes adventures to thrill and delight audiences of the Forties.

Adventures of Tartu, The ○
(aka: Tartu)
1943, UK, 103 mins, b/w
Dir: Harold S Bucquet
Stars: Robert Donat, Valerie Hobson, Walter Rilla, Glynis Johns
Rating: ★★

Robert Donat's smart performance gives a lift to this familiar, but carefully, briskly made wartime thriller. Donat plays Capt Stevenson, linguist, chemical engineer and explosives expert, with a panache that would have done credit to James Bond. Whether smoothing the lapel of his over-padded suit, passing his hand over a headful of waves that could be plotted on graph paper, or simply bursting into action, Donat fits the part of the debonair Stevenson like a glove. There's also a heart-rending performance from Glynis Johns, then only 19, as a badly-frightened young girl whose patriotism drives her to deeds of desperate courage.

Adventures of Tom Sawyer, The ○ ⓥ
1938, US, 77 mins, colour
Dir: Norman Taurog
Stars: Tommy Kelly, Jacky Moran, May Robson
Rating: ★★★

The original Selznick classic, with Tommy Kelly and Ann Gillis making sparky leads and Victor Jory frightening as the villainous Injun Joe. It moves fluently from one incident to another and is always most attractive to look at, thanks to the art direction of William Cameron Menzies (who two years earlier had directed *Things to Come*) and the photography of another Oscar-winner, James Wong Howe. Howe's colour camerawork brought a nightmare quality to the film's most exciting scenes – in a graveyard and a network of caverns. But little more was heard of young Tommy Kelly, who plays Tom, in subsequent years.

Adventuress, The
See: I See a Dark Stranger

Affair in Trinidad ○
1952, US, 98 mins, b/w
Dir: Vincent Sherman
Stars: Rita Hayworth, Glenn Ford
Rating: ★★

Echoes of *Gilda*, but, alas, only echoes, in this 'comeback' vehicle prepared for Rita Hayworth by her studio Columbia after her four years away (she married and divorced Aly Khan), along the lines of her past successes there. Leading man Glenn Ford is back, as is chubby character player Steven Geray, but the handling no longer has the confidence to carry such a tuppence-coloured plot. Rita sings a couple of numbers, 'Trinidad' and 'I've Been Kissed Before', but the fires that burned so bright in *Gilda* are noticeably lower here.

Affair to Remember, An ○
1957, US, 115 mins, colour
Dir: Leo McCarey
Stars: Cary Grant, Deborah Kerr, Richard Denning
Rating: ★★

Four-star, four-handkerchief remake of the classic weepie which originally saw the light of day in 1939 as *Love Affair*, with Irene Dunne. A couple fall in love and make a tryst for six months later on top of the Empire State Building to see if their feelings have changed. Elegantly steered on its tearful way by the performances of the stars and Leo McCarey, who also made the original and won an Oscar for its screenplay. Remade again in 1994 with Warren Beatty, under the original title.

Affair with a Stranger ○
1953, US, 89 mins, b/w
Dir: Roy Rowland
Stars: Jean Simmons, Victor Mature
Rating: ★★

A mediocre dose of suds and tears about an item in a gossip column that sets off a chain reaction among the friends of a writer (Victor Mature) and his wife (Jean Simmons, sold short by Hollywood again). It's directed with no great style by Roy Rowland, who cut his teeth on the *Crime Does Not Pay* and *Pete Smith Specialities* series of shorts, and was generally more at home with action films.

Afraid of the Dark ● ⓥ
1991, UK, 91 mins, colour
Dir: Mark Peploe
Stars: Ben Keyworth, Fanny Ardant, James Fox, Paul McGann, Clare Holman, Robert Stephens
Rating: ★

For all those who love a good anti-climax, director Peploe has a whole string of them ready for you in this psychological chiller-drama. Young Lucas (Ben Keyworth) is going blind and needs a sight-saving operation. He is also going out of his tiny little mind and fearsomely jealous of the new baby his blind mother (Fanny Ardant) is about to have. Meanwhile, a slasher is stalking the district cutting the faces of blind people. Lucas, a born peeper, steals a telescope and starts seeing fragments of murder. His blind sister seems about to fall victim to the killer. But wait . . . all is not what it seems, as Peploe gives us the first of several 'But waits . . .' which only end when the final credits roll before what seems to have been set up as the final chill. It's slightly stiffly performed by a cast who seem to have been instructed to act as enigmatically as possible. Still, if you want to be sold short at ever-decreasing intervals, Peploe is undoubtedly your man . . .

African Fury
See: Cry, the Beloved Country

African Queen, The ○ ⓥ
1951, US/UK, 105 mins, colour
Dir: John Huston
Stars: Katharine Hepburn, Humphrey Bogart, Robert Morley
Rating: ★★★★

Not-to-be-missed John Huston film made on location under testing conditions. Humphrey Bogart at last won the Oscar he deserved, for his portrayal of the dissolute, vulgar and cowardly riverboat captain who is persuaded to take a stern lady missionary on a dangerous voyage down African rivers in World War One to try to sink a German gunboat. Richly characterised and a thoroughly enjoyable film. Katharine Hepburn was also nominated for an Academy Award for her portrayal of the rasp-tongued spinster who gradually develops mellower feelings towards her rugged companion, but lost out to Vivien Leigh in *A Streetcar Named Desire*.

African Rage
See: Tigers Don't Cry

Africa Screams ⊙
1949, US, 79 mins, b/w
Dir: Charles Barton
Stars: Bud Abbott, Lou Costello, Hillary Brooke
Rating: ★★

Bud Abbott and Lou Costello are up to no good in the jungles of Africa in this underrated comedy. Famous lion tamers Frank Buck (inspiration for the series *Bring 'Em Back Alive*) and Clyde Beatty join in the mayhem alongside one-time 'Stooges' Shemp Howard and Joe Besser. Howard was actually physically sick in the studio tank at United Artists (standing in for a swirling jungle river) during production. Real-life heavyweight prizefighters, the Baer brothers, add muscle as the formidable Hillary Brooke's henchmen.

Africa Texas Style ⊙
1967, US, 106 mins, colour
Dir: Andrew Marton
Stars: Hugh O'Brian, John Mills, Tom Nardini, Nigel Green, Adrienne Corri
Rating: ★★

A likeable animal adventure with good performances from John Mills (the central figure in the film's best sequence, when he demonstrates the lie of the land instead of controlling his plane) and Tom Nardini. The action is thunderingly well shot by director Andrew Marton and his unit, and one skirmish with a dyspeptic rhinoceros is especially engaging. There's a fleeting appearance, as a girl at an airport, by Hayley Mills.

After Dark, My Sweet ● ⓥ
1990, US, 111 mins, colour
Dir: James Foley
Stars: Jason Patric, Rachel Ward, Bruce Dern, George Dickerson
Rating: ★★

If it had been 30 minutes shorter and had a different director and leading actress, this doomy *film noir* could have been a cracker. That might sound drastic, but there was a lot of potential here if a tighter overall grip had been exercised on the project, which emerges as an occasionally fascinating but too often slow and soporific suspenser. Jason Patric is pretty good as the no-hoper who forms the axis of the plot: an ex-boxer escaped from a psychiatric hospital only to wander into a bizarre plot to kidnap the diabetic son of rich parents. Bruce Dern is always watchable as the ex-cop who dreams up the scheme, but Rachel Ward is less than adequate as the seductive alcoholic who draws Patric into the plot. The story – the title has no relevance whatsoever – is nicely rounded off, but by that time you may have lost interest, which is frankly a real shame. Jane Greer, where are you when we need you most?

A

After Hours ◐ ⓥ
1985, US, 97 mins, colour
Dir: Martin Scorsese
Stars: Griffin Dunne, Rosanna Arquette,
Verna Bloom, Linda Fiorentino, Teri Garr
Rating: ★★

A comedy that proves that ace director
Martin Scorsese is not at his best in
lighter mood. The idea is great: cuddly
Griffin Dunne, a taller version of
Dudley Moore, goes chasing after a
girl downtown and lurches from disaster to disaster in a series of events
that somehow contrive to interlock.
The chill and still of the early hours
on deserted city streets seem to seep
into the bones of the plot, which
staggers on in staccato fashion,
amusing us with its developments
(Cheech and Chong are actually
funny!) but muffling them in
Scorsese's execution.

After the Fox ◐
(Caccia alla Volpe)
1966, UK/Italy, 103 mins, colour
Dir: Vittorio De Sica
Stars: Peter Sellers, Victor Mature, Britt
Ekland, Martin Balsam
Rating: ★★

For those who like to see Peter Sellers
in a number of disguises, this Vittorio
De Sica-directed comedy should be a
beanfeast. Mainly, Sellers plays an
Italian master crook who foils the police with a series of wild schemes. The
opening sequence – a gallery of the
world's most inept criminals – gets the
film off with a bang. Thereafter, this is
a mild comedy whose good ideas
mostly fire on only one cylinder, and
whose director and cast seem largely
not to be on the same comedy wave-
length as the star. Still, Victor Mature
sends up his own film image nicely as
a fading screen idol and Martin Balsam
scores as his agent.

Against All Odds ◐ ⓥ
1984, US, 128 mins, colour
Dir: Taylor Hackford
Stars: Jeff Bridges, Rachel Ward, James
Woods, Alex Karras, Richard Widmark
Rating: ★★

A loose remake of the 1947 Robert
Mitchum thriller *Out of the Past*
(shown in Britain as *Build My Gallows
High*). Not at all bad on the whole,
laced with contemporary sex and violence as well as miles of footage of
lovely Mexican beaches and a final
shoot-out (a long time coming) that's
like the gangster equivalent of a Sergio
Leone Western. Veteran Richard

Widmark easily steals the acting honours from Jeff Bridges, underplaying,
James Woods, overplaying, and Rachel Ward, hardly playing at all. The
music provides the intensity the
offbeat drama badly needs elsewhere.
Jane Greer and Paul Valentine,
co-stars in the Mitchum original,
make cameo appearances here.

Against the Wind ◯
1947, UK, 96 mins, b/w
Dir: Charles Crichton
Stars: Simone Signoret, Robert Beatty,
Jack Warner, Gordon Jackson
Rating: ★★★

Charles Crichton directed this Ealing
spy thriller. Jack Warner is untypically
cast as a traitor working alongside
British and Belgian agents who are
sent to France to work with the resistance. Simone Signoret makes her
British film debut, and Robert Beatty
and a host of character actors play out
their roles in the force. A well-made
war drama.

Agent 8 3/4
See: Hot Enough for June

Age of Consent ◐
1969, Australia, 103 mins, colour
Dir: Michael Powell
Stars: James Mason, Helen Mirren
Rating: ★★★

Michael Powell's Australian idyll in
which Helen Mirren, nude and nubile, raised the temperatures of
cinemagoing males the world over,
but subsequently decided to go back
to the sterner stuff of the Royal
Shakespeare Company, for whom she
made a remarkable Lady Macbeth.
James Mason still manages to register
well as the artist trying to find himself
and there are some breathtaking
locations on and around the Great
Barrier Reef.

Age of Innocence, The ◯ ⓥ
1993, US, 139 mins, colour
Dir: Martin Scorsese
Stars: Michelle Pfeiffer, Daniel
Day-Lewis, Winona Ryder
Rating: ★★★

An amazingly elegant, exquisitely
made period romance, paced in stately
but never tedious style, and marred
(considerably) only by its complete
inability to surprise. In fashionable
New York of the 1870s, Archer
(Daniel Day-Lewis), a handsome
young lawyer, is to be married to
beautiful, impeccably mannered

airhead May (Winona Ryder), but falls
in love with the intelligent and
ever-so-slightly dangerous Countess
Olenska (Michelle Pfeiffer), who has a
messy marriage behind her and is advised to avoid a divorce action which
would offend the closed New York
society which has, with mixed
enthusiasms, taken her back. Given
the bulwark of this initial setback, the
writers contrive to thwart the
would-be lovers' happiness at every
remaining step of the story, to an
irritating degree. The performances
are excellent, though: Pfeiffer has
come a long way since her early days
and this is as good as anything she's
done. Even so, she doesn't entirely
overshadow Ryder, who is truly
admirable in a difficult subordinate
role. Supporting cameos are rolled off
the tongue with relish by Alec
McCowen, Miriam Margoyles, Michael Gough, Ian Phillips and Richard
E Grant. Certainly a film to win the
impeccable taste award of its year.

Agnes of God ● ⓥ
1985, US, 98 mins, colour
Dir: Norman Jewison
Stars: Jane Fonda, Anne Bancroft, Meg
Tilly
Rating: ★★★

A sort of ecclesiastical whodunnit
about a young novitiate nun who
seems to have strangled the baby
no-one knew she was having, and the
investigative psychiatrist determined
to find out the truth. Meg Tilly is the
nun, Jane Fonda the shrink, and Anne
Bancroft the hip-talking Mother Superior who tries to come between
them: all are excellent. The ending is
logically the only possible one, but
can't help but lend a sense of
anti-climax to an otherwise absorbing
adult tale that almost entirely escapes
its stage origins.

Agony and the Ecstasy, The ◯
1965, US, 140 mins, colour
Dir: Carol Reed
Stars: Charlton Heston, Rex Harrison,
Diane Cilento
Rating: ★★

Carol Reed's careful study of the
painter Michelangelo and his work on
the Sistine Chapel. Rex Harrison is
unexpectedly good as the warrior
Pope who all too often opposes the
painter's ideas, while Charlton Heston,
though physically completely miscast,
is surprisingly good as the artist. The
first half is dreadfully uninteresting,

but there's much more human development in the second, even though Harrison gets some pretty trite dialogue from Philip Dunne's script, which has him saying, on viewing the finished ceiling, 'This work is so much greater than both of us,' when what he reputedly said was, 'Sprinkle a little gold paint on it – it will make it look much better.' Although there are one or two moving moments, this is, on the whole, a missed opportunity.

Aguirre: The Wrath of God ◐
(Aguirre, der Zorn Gottes)
1972, West Germany, 95 mins, colour
Dir: Werner Herzog
Stars: Klaus Kinski, Ruy Guerra
Rating: ★★★

Chilling, hypnotic adventure down the Amazon river with Klaus Kinski getting madder by the second as he and his raft-borne team of conquistadors search for the Inca city of El Dorado. West German director Werner Herzog hits every nerve-end right on the button, showing Hollywood just how to do it in terms of tension as the Spaniards get whittled down one by one by headhunting Indians.

A-Haunting We Will Go ☉
1942, US, 68 mins, b/w
Dir: Alfred Werker
Stars: Stan Laurel, Oliver Hardy
Rating: ★★

Laurel and Hardy are assigned to deliver a coffin – which has a live gangster inside. One of their later films, made away from the auspices of Hal Roach with whom they had worked for so long. Henry Morgan and Elisha Cook Jr crop up as gangsters.

Air America ◐ ⓥ
1990, US, 112 mins, colour
Dir: Roger Spottiswoode
Stars: Mel Gibson, Robert Downey Jr, Nancy Travis, Lane Smith
Rating: ★★

Perhaps the noisiest film of its year, if not the easiest to follow (not unconnected aspects perhaps), this is the story of a CIA-backed US air company in 1969 Laos, running food to the villagers and drugs and guns for the local warlord to help him fight against the communists. The motto of the pilots is 'Anything, anywhere, anytime'. Gene (Mel Gibson) is storing a nest-egg of guns for his imminent retirement. Billy (Robert

Downey Jr) is the newcomer, regarded as a maverick in America but a greenhorn in Laos. Their hair-raising flights together – and separately – form the core of the story, which is one long succession of explosions, crash-landings, drunken sprees and shouted conversations. The climax is heavily contrived but balanced by some witty captions at the very end dealing with the ultimate fates of the various characters involved. Gibson holds centre of the picture with easy grace, Nancy Travis scarcely gets a look in, and Lane Smith scores as a seemingly gullible US senator on a fact-finding mission that Air America hopes will be a blind alley.

Air Force ☉ ⓥ
1943, US, 145 mins, b/w
Dir: Howard Hawks
Stars: John Garfield, Gig Young, Arthur Kennedy, Charles Drake, John Ridgley, Harry Carey
Rating: ★★★

If you can ignore the flag-waving American sentiment and occasional truculence, and concentrate on its action sequences and effective quieter moments, this Howard Hawks production is a hell of a war film. John Garfield, John Ridgley (a character player in a rare leading role) and Harry Carey give fiercely well-defined portrayals of men under stress. And plum-nosed George Tobias, who starred in *Captains of the Clouds*, is aloft again, though you may wince at his victorious yell of 'Fried Jap going down', a rare lapse in Dudley Nichols' purposeful and believable screenplay. Hawks' direction is masterly in its pace, economy and power.

Airplane! ☉ ⓥ
1980, US, 86 mins, colour
Dir: David Zucker
Stars: Robert Hays, Julie Hagerty, Lloyd Bridges, Peter Graves, Leslie Nielsen, Robert Stack
Rating: ★★★

The spoof of disaster movies that set millions rocking with laughter, thanks to an inventive script and wonderfully poker-faced playing by a starstrewn cast. Loosely based on an Arthur Hailey novel originally filmed as *Zero Hour!*

Airplane II – The Sequel ☉ ⓥ
1982, US, 85 mins, colour
Dir: Ken Finkleman

Stars: Robert Hays, Julie Hagerty, Lloyd Bridges, Chuck Connors, William Shatner, Peter Graves
Rating: ★★★

Those *Airport* spoofers are at it again, with Robert Hays once more (barely) at the controls, this time of a disaster-bound space shuttle headed for the moon. Keep an eye on what's going on in the background of the scenes: it's often funnier than what's happening up front. We especially liked the poster with an aged boxer, advertising *Rocky XXVIII*.

Airport ☉ ⓥ
1969, US, 137 mins, colour
Dir: George Seaton
Stars: Burt Lancaster, Dean Martin, Jacqueline Bisset, Jean Seberg, George Kennedy, Helen Hayes
Rating: ★★★

The prototype airborne disaster movie of modern times, with Burt Lancaster and Dean Martin at the controls, Van Heflin as the man with the bomb, George Kennedy making the first of his several appearances in such films, and Helen Hayes taking an Oscar as a little old lady on board.

Airport 1975 ☉
1974, US, 106 mins, colour
Dir: Jack Smight
Stars: Charlton Heston, Karen Black, George Kennedy
Rating: ★★★

The second in the series of airborne suspensers derived from the Arthur Hailey bestseller finds another star-studded cast facing death in the skies as stewardess Karen Black finds herself in charge of a crippled airliner and ever-reliable Charlton Heston flies to the rescue. Director Jack Smight racks up the tension commendably and, among those strapped into their seats and exhibiting varying degrees of aplomb and hysteria, are Gloria Swanson, playing herself, the regulation nuns, Helen Reddy and Martha Scott, Myrna Loy, Sid Caesar and Linda (*The Exorcist*) Blair. Back in 1957 in *Zero Hour!* (also from a Hailey story and memorably sent up in *Airplane!*), Dana Andrews was the troubled former pilot who saves the day when the crew of an airliner are struck down by food poisoning. Here he's the cause of all the trouble when he crashes his private plane into the trans-continental Boeing.

A

Airport '77 ○ ⓥ

(aka: Airport III)
1977, US, 113 mins, colour
Dir: Jerry Jameson
Stars: Jack Lemmon, Lee Grant
Rating: ★★

After two *Airplane!* spoofs, it's hard
to take any of the four *Airport* films
seriously for a minute. This third
entry has a novel idea at its core – a
plane surviving a crash with an oil rig
and having to be rescued from the sea
bed before it is crushed by water
pressure – but its passenger list is the
usual motley crew of deadbeats and
adulterers. The crash and subsequent
rescue bid are well handled, but the
tension would have been all the
greater had the script made you care
about any of the victims. Christopher
Lee does the honourable thing in the
mould of Oates of the Arctic and takes
an early bath. The rest of the cast look
as though they wish they'd done the
same!

Airport '80 . . . ◑

(aka: The Concorde – Airport '79)
1979, US, 123 mins, colour
Dir: David Lowell Rich
Stars: Alain Delon, Susan Blakely,
Robert Wagner, Sylvia Kristel, George
Kennedy, Eddie Albert
Rating: ★

Airport meets James Bond, and the result is very superior hokum. As the
Concorde takes off, the second thread
of the plot is already in motion.
Power-mad Robert Wagner, who
runs a missile plant, has been caught
selling arms to the bad guys of the
world, and his reporter-mistress Susan
Blakely is the girl with the evidence.
And what is she travelling on? That's
right! 'It's still amazing to me, only
three and a half hours ago we were in
Paris,' muses Capt Alain Delon just
before Wagner launches an attack
missile against the plane. The plot
then develops into Tom and Jerry
stuff, and one can visualise Wagner
jumping up and down with rage as
each new attempt fails. 'I'd love to see
what my horoscope said for the
morning,' yells co-pilot George
Kennedy (simply running away with
the film) as he banks to avoid two of
Wagner's fighter planes. The dialogue
is hilarious, the photography magnificent, the pace unflagging; it's what
Hollywood movie-making used to be
all about.

Airport III

See: Airport '77

Aladdin ⊙ ⓥ

1992, US, 91 mins, colour
Dir: John Musker, Ron Clements
Voice stars: Robin Williams, Scott
Weinger, Linda Larkin, Jonathan
Freeman
Rating: ★★★

More from modern Disneyland, a kaleidoscope of adventures that's always
doing the unexpected – blink and you
miss a visual joke – and makes Robin
Williams the star voice of the piece as
a show-off, non-stop genie of the
lamp, who does everything but say
'Good Morning, Baghdad!' 'Getting
kinda fond of you,' he confides to
Aladdin at one point, ' . . . not that I
want to pick out curtains.' Set in an
eastern city where the traders sell
Dead Sea tupperware, the film is full
of semi-adult humour that's bound to
please parents, as much as the story,
visual delights and animal supporting
characters (including a performing
monkey who sounds like Donald
Duck) will please the children. On the
musical front, the Menken-Ashman
score is on the thin side, its big number, 'Brand New World', sounding
very much like a mixture of ballads
from the duo's previous *Beauty and the
Beast* and *The Little Mermaid.* A small
quibble at a big, colourful show that's
more consistently entertaining than
any pantomime.

Alamo, The ○

1960, US, 193 mins, colour
Dir: John Wayne
Stars: John Wayne, Richard Widmark,
Laurence Harvey, Frankie Avalon,
Richard Boone, Linda Cristal
Rating: ★★

John Wayne's first film as director and
star, an epic Western about the state of
Texas' fight for independence, is a
troubled affair. Wearing one expression – that of a man with a $12
million budget weighing heavy on his
conscience – his character of Davy
Crockett spouts endless pompous and
gratuitous homilies to a better way
of life. It's not until the rip-roaring,
crushing climax of total massacre
(with a large part of the credit going
to second unit director Cliff Lyons and
uncredited assistance from Wayne's
friend John Ford) that the film comes
alive at all.

Alamo Bay ● ⓥ

1985, US, 98 mins, colour
Dir: Louis Malle
Stars: Ed Harris, Amy Madigan, Ho
Nguyen, Donald Moffat
Rating: ★★

There's a Western struggling to get
out of this present-day account of
Texas redneck shrimp fishermen and
their conflict with the Vietnamese
boat people whose determination to
earn a living invades their territorial
waters. It leads not only to outright
warfare but also to the Texans' enlistment of the Ku Klux Klan. The
film has some fresh and valid social
statements to make and it puts them
across forcibly, even if the script fails
to raise the events above the level of
routine drama which, while
interesting, lacks dramatic punch. Ed
Harris, almost unrecognisable beneath
a bushy beard, has an interesting role
as a 'hero' whom circumstances turn
villain. He and real-life wife Amy
Madigan give dour, downbeat performances that probably reflect the
bitterness involved but fail to do much
for the film itself.

Albert RN ○

(aka: Break to Freedom)
1955, UK, 88 mins, b/w
Dir: Lewis Gilbert
Stars: Anthony Steel, Jack Warner,
Robert Beatty, Anton Diffring
Rating: ★★

One of a long line of good British
'escape' films, started by *The Wooden
Horse,* and carried on by such gems as
The Colditz Story and *Danger Within.*
PoW's create a dummy – the Albert
RN of the title – as a cover up for
an absentee prisoner. Its director is
Lewis Gilbert, who should have got a
medal for his services to the war film,
with such successes as *The Sea Shall
Not Have Them, Reach for the Sky, Sink
the Bismarck!* and *Carve Her Name with
Pride.*

Alexander the Great ○

1956, US, 141 mins, colour
Dir: Robert Rossen
Stars: Richard Burton, Fredric March,
Claire Bloom, Harry Andrews, Stanley
Baker
Rating: ★★★

A much underrated epic, with stunningly staged battle scenes, Richard
Burton at his stormy best and a script
that keeps sentiment (if not philosophy) to the minimum. The overall cast
is remarkable, the 'middle order'

players including Harry Andrews, Stanley Baker, Peter Cushing, Niall MacGinnis, Michael Hordern, Peter Wyngarde, Helmut Dantine and that delightful French actress Danielle Darrieux. The film was written, produced and directed by Robert Rossen, whose work might be thought variable; but at his best – for example in *All the King's Men*, which won an Oscar, and *The Hustler* – he was brilliant.

Alfie ● Ⓥ
1966, UK, 114 mins, colour
Dir: Lewis Gilbert
Stars: Michael Caine, Shelley Winters, Millicent Martin, Julia Foster, Jane Asher, Shirley Anne Field
Rating: ★★★

Bill Naughton wrote the screen adaptation of his own highly successful stage play and the result was one of the British cinema's biggest comedy hits of the mid-Sixties. Michael Caine scores as the totally amoral anti-hero who remains engaging and likeable, a girl-chaser de luxe. And there's a remarkable supporting cast in which the females – especially Vivien Merchant – are all very good.

Alf's Button Afloat ☉
1938, UK, 89 mins, b/w
Dir: Marcel Varnel
Stars: Bud Flanagan, Chesney Allen, Alistair Sim
Rating: ★★★

There had already been a couple of versions of W A Darlington's famous farce (one featuring Anton Dolin and the Royal Ballet!) before the Crazy Gang got hold of it and made it their own. They play six buskers serving in the Marines. They discover a magic button which, when rubbed, produces a genie (magnificently played by Alastair Sim) who tends to stripe everything pink.

Alias Bulldog Drummond
See: Bulldog Jack

Alias Jesse James ☉
1959, US, 92 mins, colour
Dir: Norman Z McLeod
Stars: Bob Hope, Rhonda Fleming, Wendell Corey
Rating: ★★★

The last of Bob Hope's really funny comedies, pitching him once again into *Paleface* territory as an inept insurance man who sells a policy to Jesse James. 'Ain't a-Hankerin' is a cute novelty song in the best 'Buttons and Bows' tradition, and it's nicely delivered by Hope and leading lady Rhonda Fleming. The action and fun come fast and furious under the direction of Norman Z McLeod, who directed Hope in *Road to Rio*, *The Paleface*, *My Favorite Spy* and *Casanova's Big Night*. Stay tuned for the ending in which Hope receives a few unexpected helping hands when besieged by outlaw gunmen.

Alice ❶ Ⓥ
1990, US, 105 mins, colour
Dir: Woody Allen
Stars: Mia Farrow, Joe Mantegna, William Hurt, Judy Davis, Cybill Shepherd, Alec Baldwin
Rating: ★★

Another Woody Allen film that will delight his fans and further irritate those who can't stand his work. Mia Farrow has the Woody-type role (and the Woody-type dialogue) as the mousy, well-to-do housewife who starts a whole new cycle in her life when she suddenly experiences an attraction to another man (Joe Mantegna) and visits Dr Yang (a last screen role for character actor Keye Luke), discovering his marvellous potions, one of which can make her invisible. Using her new-found 'gift', she soon finds out what a slimebag her husband (William Hurt) is – which the rest of us could see from the start – and discovers herself in the process. All this is told in typically Allen style, with some brilliantly witty lines (though not enough), much overlapping dialogue (monotonous after a while) and a plot that's fun but gets a bit too silly towards the end, even if its fable-like qualities see it through. Farrow is excellent.

Alice Doesn't Live Here Anymore ❶ Ⓥ
1974, US, 113 mins, colour
Dir: Martin Scorsese
Stars: Ellen Burstyn, Kris Kristofferson, Billy Green Bush, Diane Ladd, Harvey Keitel
Rating: ★★★★

Seldom was an Academy Award more deserved than that won by Ellen Burstyn, who gives one of the cinema's great female performances as the attractive if dumpy widow who falteringly sets out to make a new life for herself and her 11-year-old son after her husband dies in an accident. Although Burstyn dominates the film, the action that swirls around her is crammed with laughs and truths that deserve almost equal praise. Characters along the way include the dozy waitress (Valerie Curtin) at the cafe where Alice works who reads 'The Bride Screamed Murder' and tells the boy, 'You can colour it if you want to'; the older, loud-mouthed waitress (Diane Ladd) who proves a feet-on-the-ground friend; and the 12-year-old girl (Jodie Foster), going on 24, who tunes the boy into shoplifting. Alice enjoys a unique, just-right relationship with her son. 'Don't look back,' she tells him, as they leave their old home, 'or you might turn into a pillar of shit.' Alice's four-letter words are so rare that they're a delightful part of the wry, anything-goes humour that keeps her afloat on the bilge of the world. Robert Getchell's screenplay never opts entirely for the soft centre, and Scorsese's direction rightly and sensibly just pays homage to it, seeing that it gets its full justice. A completely original screen classic.

Alice in Wonderland ○
1951, US, 75 mins, colour
Dir: Hamilton Luske, Wilfred Jackson
Rating: ★★★

This Disney adaption of Lewis Carroll's classic children's story was miserably underrated in its time, mainly by people who objected to the studio's 'Americanisation' of the story's characters. In fact, the Disney animation team is on top form, especially with the Caterpillar, the Cheshire Cat, the March Hare, the Mad Hatter and Bill the Lizard. And the Queen of Hearts is a formidable adversary in best Peggy Mount style. Besides the dreamy title number, the catchy songs include 'I'm Late' and 'A Very Merry Unbirthday to You'.

Alice's Restaurant ❶
1969, US, 111 mins, colour
Dir: Arthur Penn
Stars: Arlo Guthrie, Pat Quinn
Rating: ★★★

Kaleidoscopic, attractive patchwork of a film about the early life of singer Arlo Guthrie, son of the legendary Woody Guthrie. The deconsecrated church at which Arlo and his hippie friends gather has real atmosphere, there are some funny and touching moments, catchy theme music by Arlo himself and an outstanding performance by Pat Quinn as Alice.

A

Alien ● ⓥ
1979, US, 117 mins, colour
Dir: Ridley Scott
Stars: Tom Skerritt, Sigourney Weaver,
Ian Holm, John Hurt, Harry Dean
Stanton, Veronica Cartwright
Rating: ★★★

A silly but very exciting slice of science-fiction — it broke box office
records all over the world — about a
monster from another planet loose
aboard a spaceship, devouring the
crew one by one. Directed with force
if not finesse by Ridley Scott, it has a
performance by Sigourney Weaver as
Lt Ripley that could and should have
made her a star. She was little seen
subsequently but went on to make
the sequel, *Aliens*, *Working Girl* and
Gorrilla's in the Mist. A dominant actress with a Jane Fonda voice and a
mass of dark curls, it is she who is left
to face the alien after it has erupted
from the stomach (faint-hearts should
get ready to close their eyes at this sequence) of one of the crew who has
been unwise enough to investigate
egg-like things on another planet. The
hardware is imposing, and the alien
itself mostly horrifyingly convincing,
although the film's vein of foolishness
persists in scenes of characters creeping
around alone in search of the ship's cat
when they're all aware that the alien
may be slithering around waiting.

Alien Nation ● ⓥ
1988, US, 94 mins, colour
Dir: Graham Baker
Stars: James Caan, Mandy Patinkin,
Terence Stamp
Rating: ★★★

A science-fiction thriller that welds an
old plot to a new concept. Cops, drug
dealer, the old cop with the new
partner — you could see this story
every night on the box. What gives it
the sci-fi twist is that it's set in the future. A few years previously, a vast
shipload of aliens has landed in
America, and its occupants, vaguely
human in appearance, have been as-
similated into the general population.
In effect, they have taken the place of
blacks as ghetto-dwellers, living in a
kind of unholy Toontown amid the
slag of the city. When veteran cop
(James Caan) sees his partner killed by
alien hitmen, revenge drives him to
volunteer for the job nobody wants —
partner to America's first alien
detective (Mandy Patinkin). The film
mistakenly underplays the alien factor
in its search for the plot and a spec-

tacular climax. Even so, it remains
edgily exciting: pretty good entertainment in a minor key.

Aliens ● ⓥ
1986, US, 137 mins, colour
Dir: James Cameron
Stars: Sigourney Weaver, Michael Biehn,
Carrie Henn, Lance Henriksen, Paul
Rieser
Rating: ★★★★

Flight Officer Ripley (Sigourney
Weaver, repeating her role from *Alien*)
is the living proof that, when the going gets tough, the tough get going.
Somehow, after 57 years in hyper
space (she hasn't changed a bit), she's
induced to go back to the alien planet
where it all started. The aliens have
taken over from human colonists and
a little girl's the sole survivor. And
Weaver's Ripley really gets the bit
between her teeth when the kid's in
danger. Like the bad guys who incur
Clint Eastwood's wrath when they
mess with his dog, you know the aliens are in deep trouble when the girl
disappears. You can almost hear John
Wayne shouting: 'Fill your hands, you
sons of a bitch', as Ripley charges to
the rescue armed with what seems like
half her spaceship's arsenal. It's a tremendous part for any actress, and
Weaver responds by bruisingly giving
it all she's got. She's helped in the
impact she makes by the fact that the
film has 300 per cent more action than
its predecessor once it gets going and
100 per cent more logic. Crisis follows
crisis as director James Cameron
hammers away at your nerve-ends
(and your fingernails), enormously
aided by the urgently pounding score
of James Horner. Aliens to the left of
you, aliens to the right of you: it never
lets up.

Alien 3 ● ⓥ
1992, US/UK, 115 mins, colour
Dir: David Fincher
Stars: Sigourney Weaver, Charles
Dance, Charles S Dutton, Brian Glover,
Lance Henriksen
Rating: ★★

Too much talk and not enough action
cripple this muddled end to the *Alien*
trilogy. Sigourney Weaver, in the least
of her three performances in these
films, is still Lt Ripley, cast adrift from
her homebound vessel by an alien intruder, and the only human survivor
of a subsequent crash on to a prison
planet whose few inhabitants are the
shaven-headed scum of the galaxy —
and have no weapons. The alien, re-

generating itself via a dog, is soon
scuttling into slobbery, heavy-headed,
tombstone-toothed action. Similar in
structure to the first film, with people
creeping around in the dark after an
unknown force, the film has too many
scenes with the prisoners shouting
obscenities about their condition, and
not enough cohesion in its story
which moves, when at all, in fits and
starts. There is less of a sense of evil,
and more of a simpler science-fiction
menace. Naturally, there are still
some spine-tingling moments, and
James Cameron's pulsating second film
was a hard act to follow. Addicts will
doubtless embrace the creature
whole.

Al Jennings of Oklahoma ○
1951, US, 79 mins, colour
Dir: Ray Nazarro
Stars: Dan Duryea, Gale Storm, Dick
Foran
Rating: ★★★

This colourful Western followed hard
on those which glorified the exploits
of the James Brothers and the
Younger Brothers. It tries to do the
same thing for Al Jennings, played by
Dan Duryea in one of his two 'true
life' adventure roles of the late Forties
(the other being *Black Bart* – *Highwayman*). This too is about brothers,
Al and Frank Jennings, lawyers gone
to the bad who eventually tired of the
outdoor life and were said to have
lived to a ripe old age.

All About Eve ○ ⓥ
1950, US, 138 mins, b/w
Dir: Joseph L Mankewicz
Stars: Bette Davis, Anne Baxter, George
Sanders, Gary Merrill
Rating: ★★★★

Bette Davis received her eighth
Academy Award nomination in 16
years for this brilliant dissection of
Broadway life. Anne Baxter,
magnificently hateful as the insidious
Eve (you want to jump into the screen
and throttle her before she does any
more damage), was also nominated for
an Oscar. Twelve further 'nods' to the
Academy board made the film the
most Oscar-nominated picture in his-
tory. It actually won six: Best Picture,
Best Director (Joseph L Mankiewicz),
Best Script (Mankiewicz again), Best
Supporting Actor (George Sanders),
Best Sound and Best Costume Design.
All this, and Marilyn Monroe in an
eye-catching supporting role. Barbara

Bates, as a new 'Eve', is also worthy of note in a film laced with razor-sharp acting and caustic, witty phrases.

All Creatures Great and Small ○
1974, US/UK, 92 mins, colour
Dir: Claude Whatham
Stars: Simon Ward, Anthony Hopkins, Lisa Harrow, Freddie Jones
Rating: ★★★

An enjoyable little trifle (except for those squeamish about things happening to animals) as newly qualified vet Simon Ward comes to work at a Yorkshire practice where he very soon learns the facts of country life. Acting honours are wholly stolen by Anthony Hopkins as Ward's senior partner, who is exactly as one would imagine a country doctor or vet to be. Jiggling his pipe noisily between his teeth, brushing recalcitrant hair away from his eyes, or trying desperately to remember to do his accounts, Hopkins makes this inconsequential film entirely his own.

Allegheny Uprising
See: The First Rebel

All Hands on Deck ○
1961, US, 98 mins, colour
Dir: Norman Taurog
Stars: Pat Boone, Dennis O'Keefe, Barbara Eden, Buddy Hackett
Rating: ★★

An energetic musical romp with a plot that wouldn't disgrace a Marx Brothers film. Pat Boone has the Zeppo role as the romantic lead (and sings some Ray Evans-Jay Livingston songs), while Buddy Hackett and a turkey called Owasso lead the farceurs. There's also a pelican, an egg, a newshen and an admiral, none of whom, in the best tradition of farce, are supposed to encounter one another. Snappy editing by Frederick Y Smith keeps it moving pretty well.

All I Desire ○
1953, US, 79 mins, b/w
Dir: Douglas Sirk
Stars: Barbara Stanwyck, Richard Carlson
Rating: ★★

Barbara Stanwyck is perfectly cast as the strong but tormented woman who reluctantly returns to her hometown years after a bitter divorce. She dominates the tear-stained plot but, under Douglas Sirk's sensitive direction, Universal starlets Marcia

Henderson and Lori Nelson do their best screen work as her contrasting daughters; Lyle Bettger is also distinctive as the merchant who fancies the returning prodigal.

Alligator ● ⓥ
1980, US, 94 mins, colour
Dir: Lewis Teague
Stars: Robert Forster, Robin Riker, Henry Silva, Dean Jagger
Rating: ★★★

A cross between *Jaws* and *Them!*, with a 40-foot alligator loose in the sewers of Chicago. If anyone so much as sets foot in these murky waters, it's snap! crackle! pop! and out come bits of body to the surface, to the consternation of detective Robert Forster and pretty herpetologist Robin Riker, whose own pet alligator was flushed down the loo by her father 10 years before (yes, you've guessed it). Ramon, for such is our scaly slayer's name, munches up pretty well all the cast before the end, including Henry Silva, enjoying himself as a big game hunter who tries to bring his methods to the backstreets of Chicago. Altogether this is a film of some style, with all the expected storm-drain excitements and a personable hero and heroine in the beleagered Forster and the piquant Riker. Just be careful where you stand the next time you flush the loo.

Alligator Named Daisy, An ○
1955, UK, 88 mins, colour
Dir: J Lee Thompson
Stars: Donald Sinden, Diana Dors, Margaret Rutherford, Jean Carson
Rating: ★★

Enjoyable frolic (though its song-and-dance routines aren't up to much) with a brilliant cast headed by Donald Sinden, Diana Dors and Margaret Rutherford and a winsome alligator for good measure.

All I Want for Christmas ⊙ ⓥ
1992, US, 92 mins, colour
Dir: Robert Lieberman
Stars: Harley Jane Kozak, Jamey Sheridan, Thora Birch, Ethan Randall, Leslie Nielsen, Lauren Bacall
Rating: ★★

Films suitable for children to watch alone are rare birds these days outside of Disney's cartoon features, so it's well that the personal charm of little Thora Birch just about keeps this cardboard cracker from sinking in its

own saccharine. Christmas is coming, and all seven-year-old Hallie (Birch) wants is for her divorced parents to reunite. To this end, she enlists the help of her brother (Ethan Randall) and his pals, who hatch an elaborate plan. There's lots of artificial heart in this family film, plus Lauren Bacall (as the kids' granny) and Leslie Nielsen as guest stars. If you enjoy watching precocious children work their manipulative wiles, while the filmmakers try to do the same thing with your emotions, this could be for you, even if it's really as empty as a stocking on Christmas Eve. Bring back *The Parent Trap!*

All Night Long ◖
1981, US, 89 mins, colour
Dir: Jean-Claude Tramont
Stars: Barbra Streisand, Gene Hackman, Diane Ladd, Dennis Quaid
Rating: ★★★

This is quite a nice little comedy in its gently quirky way. Gene Hackman is a middle-aged, minor executive who can't take being trodden on any more, and throws a chair out of the (closed) window. His marriage follows it when he falls in love with his son's mistress (Barbra Streisand), the nutty nymphomaniac wife of his cousin. Hackman's demotion to nightstore manager results in some amusing encounters with shoplifters and assorted felons and there are elements of *The Graduate* in there somewhere. Hackman is very good in a rare comedy role.

All of Me ◖ ⓥ
1984, US, 93 mins, colour
Dir: Carl Reiner
Stars: Steve Martin, Lily Tomlin, Victoria Tennant
Rating: ★★★

This madcap, crazy comedy has shades of *Heaven Can Wait*, *Here Comes Mr Jordan*, the *Topper* films and even *Tootsie*, with its story of a wealthy woman's soul trapped by mistake after her death in the body of her oddball lawyer (Steve Martin). In the hands of Martin's ofttime collaborator and director Carl Reiner (they also made *The Jerk*, *The Man With Two Brains* and *Dead Men Don't Wear Plaid* together) the action moves swiftly through the usual uneasy blend of side-splitting visual gags and juvenile vulgarity. Martin, a comic actor who is at his best with physical comedy, has rarely been funnier on film. He delivers a tour-de-force performance

A

as the legal eagle who has to battle constantly with the very vocal soul of crotchety millionairess Lily Tomlin, over everything from going to the toilet to sex. Although it seems unbearably silly at first, its sense of humour creeps up on you.

All Quiet on the Western Front ○ ⓥ
1930, US, 130 mins, b/w
Dir: Lewis Milestone
Stars: Lew Ayres, Louis Wolheim
Rating: ★★★★

The doyen of sound war films, this is a vivid and consistently involving version of Erich Maria Remarque's famous pacifist novel about the progressive disillusionment of young German soldiers (and one in particular) during World War One. The ending is now one of the movies' immortal moments and Academy Awards went to the picture itself, and to director Lewis Milestone.

All That Heaven Allows ○
1955, US, 89 mins, colour
Dir: Douglas Sirk
Stars: Jane Wyman, Rock Hudson
Rating: ★★

A follow-up for the stars, Jane Wyman, Rock Hudson, and director Douglas Sirk after *Magnificent Obsession*, this romantic weepie looks very artificial today, like a woman's magazine story of the Fifties sprung to life. But the lush Technicolor photography of Russell Metty still looks as good now as it did then.

All That Jazz ● ⓥ
1979, US, 123 mins, colour
Dir: Bob Fosse
Stars: Roy Scheider, Jessica Lange, Ann Reinking, Leland Palmer, John Lithgow, Keith Gordon
Rating: ★★★

Bob Fosse's acerbic musical, red in tooth and claw, has a lot to offer in one way or another, not least Roy Scheider as you have never seen him before – singing, jumping, clowning, being allowed to react a lot visually and generally to dominate a film in such a way as he's rarely had elsewhere. The film itself is quasi-autobiographical in that it deals with a dance director who suffers a heart attack, but Fosse has only used his own experiences as a starting point for a dazzling display of cinematic pyrotechnics that resemble one of those fragmented patterns you

see at the bottom of a kaleidoscope. It's almost impossible to realise such a project without being self-indulgent at one stage or another or making the occasional miscalculation (the open-heart surgery at the end is massively difficult to watch) but it's entertaining, imaginative and, at its highpoints, thrilling stuff. The girls all excel in the dance numbers, which have the exhilaration of Fosse's all-out sweatgland-bursting snap without ever becoming ragged.

All the Brothers Were Valiant ○
1953, US, 101 mins, colour
Dir: Richard Thorpe
Stars: Robert Taylor, Stewart Granger, Ann Blyth, Betta St John, Keenan Wynn
Rating: ★★

This rousing sea adventure was one of the most colourful films that MGM ever made. A trio of rather stuffy leading performances (Robert Taylor, Stewart Granger, Ann Blyth) is amply compensated by an amazing in-depth cast, and some full-blooded action scenes. The ending comes over as a trifle unlikely, but all in all it's a well-plotted yarn, based on a book by Ben Ames Williams.

All the King's Men ○
1949, US, 109 mins, b/w
Dir: Robert Rossen
Stars: Broderick Crawford, Joanne Dru, John Ireland, John Derek, Mercedes McCambridge
Rating: ★★★

Hard-hitting, true-life dramas come no stronger than this story of the rise and fall of a power-hungry politician. Robert Penn Warren's novel, inspired by ruthless, corrupt Louisiana state governor Huey Long, has been brilliantly realised as a film by screen-writer Robert Rossen, who also directed. It won the best picture Oscar in its year, as well as best actor for burly Broderick Crawford (who captures the ambitious 'Willie Stark' to the last shady scowl) and best supporting actress for Mercedes McCambridge on her film debut. A raw, shocking portrait of the misuse of power.

. . . All the Marbles
See: California Dolls

All the President's Men ○ ⓥ
1976, US, 138 mins, colour
Dir: Alan J Pakula

Stars: Dustin Hoffman, Robert Redford, Jack Warden, Martin Balsam, Hal Holbrook, Jason Robards
Rating: ★★★★

Director Alan J Pakula shapes this gripping story of the Watergate scandals with his usual emphasis on urban paranoia. The star charisma of Dustin Hoffman and Robert Redford, as *Washington Post* journalists Woodward and Bernstein, never detracts from the considerable documentary detail which, despite its many excellences, would have been better with a more audible dialogue track, less murky photography and a clearer introduction of the characters concerned. The acting, however, is a treat.

All the Right Moves ◑ ⓥ
1983, US, 91 mins, colour
Dir: Michael Chapman
Stars: Tom Cruise, Lea Thompson
Rating: ★★★

An excellent youth-oriented film which, thanks to its theme of American football, was undeservedly denied a screening over here on its first appearance. Former cinematographer Michael Chapman made an impressive directorial debut, and Tom Cruise took another stride towards superstardom as the high school senior struggling to escape the environment of a depressed steel town. A gritty script by Michael Kane gives Cruise ample opportunities to demonstrate his growing range as an actor, especially in scenes with Charles Cioffi as his father, and with Craig T Nelson, giving a superb performance as the hard-nosed coach who wants the big time as much as Cruise. Lea Thompson is also impressive as Cruise's girlfriend and the love scenes between them are low-key and dramatically responsible.

All Through the Night ○
1942, US, 107 mins, b/w
Dir: Vincent Sherman
Stars: Humphrey Bogart, Conrad Veidt, Kaaren Verne, Peter Lorre
Rating: ★★

A light-hearted, rough-and-tumble wartime thriller, with Humphrey Bogart rooting out a nest of spies. There is rather too much comedy relief from Frank McHugh, but a simply marvellous supporting cast that includes Conrad Veidt, Peter Lorre, William Demarest, Judith Anderson,

Jackie Gleason, Wallace Ford, Jane Darwell, Barton MacLane and Phil Silvers.

Almost an Angel ○ Ⓥ
1990, US, 95 mins, colour
Dir: John Cornell
Stars: Paul Hogan, Elias Koteas, Linda Kozlowski
Rating: ★★

This comedy about a criminal who believes he has been saved from death by God to become a worker of good deeds has a few nice set pieces and quite a few smart one-liners, but it could have been a whole lot better. The film leans heavily on star Paul Hogan's easygoing charm and it's a credit to Hogan's persona that it works as well as it does. Believing himself charmed, Hogan gets into all sorts of scrapes knowing nothing can happen to him. He is given competent support by Linda Koslowski, his co-star in the *Crocodile Dundee* films (and in real life). Not a bad film; Hogan fans will enjoy seeing their hero again, but one does get the sneaking suspicion that he peaked early with *Crocodile Dundee*.

Along Came Jones ○
1945, US, 90 mins, b/w
Dir: Stuart Heisler
Stars: Gary Cooper, Loretta Young, William Demarest, Dan Duryea
Rating: ★★

Enjoyable Western about a mild-mannered cowpoke who impersonates a notorious badman – with dire consequences. Nunnally Johnson's screenplay has a strong vein of humour which enables Gary Cooper and Dan Duryea to enjoy themselves hugely as goodie and baddie respectively.

Along the Great Divide ○
1950, US, 88 mins, colour
Dir: Raoul Walsh
Stars: Kirk Douglas, Virginia Mayo, John Agar, Walter Brennan
Rating: ★★

Blazing colour photography (by Sid Hickox), an unusual detective element to the plot, a spectacular desert backdrop and storm, and a hard-driving performance by Kirk Douglas are the key factors that lift this Warners Western above the ordinary. Direction is in the capable hands of Raoul Walsh, who ensures that the pace is surprisingly good and the action scenes hit hard.

Alphabet Murders, The ○
(aka: The ABC Murders)
1966, UK, 93 mins, b/w
Dir: Frank Tashlin
Stars: Tony Randall, Anita Ekberg, Robert Morley
Rating: ★★

Having completed their quartet of Miss Marple thrillers, MGM turned their attention to Agatha Christie's other famous detective, Hercule Poirot. Here he investigates a series of murders whose victims' initials are AA, BB and so forth. Madcap comedy expert Frank Tashlin seemed an odd choice to direct Agatha's famous story of suspense and sudden death. But he had a good ally in Tony Randall who, despite previously being best known as a light comedian, proved a natural for the part of Poirot.

Altered States ● Ⓥ
1980, US, 102 mins, colour
Dir: Ken Russell
Stars: William Hurt, Blair Brown
Rating: ★★

The Jeykll and Hyde story brought up to date. Jekyll (William Hurt) is now Jessop, a scientist; Hyde, the hairy other self he releases when dabbling in secret potions prepared by South American medicine men from lizards, human blood and psychedelic mushrooms. This psychological twaddle is dressed up in pounding, eye-hurting, top-of-the-pops style by Ken Russell, who seems to have told his cast to jabber their dialogue so fast that the audience won't have time to take in all its latest absurdities. Russell certainly drums the shock value home at a good 95 per cent, with the aid of some superb special effects. But the ending, spectacular though it is, finally reveals this as a film with nowhere to go.

Alvarez Kelly ○
1966, US, 116 mins, colour
Dir: Edward Dmytryk
Stars: William Holden, Richard Widmark, Janice Rule
Rating: ★★

Based on a true incident during the American Civil War when a vast herd of cattle see-sawed between equally hungry opposing forces, this Western packs plenty of colourful action. William Holden and Richard Widmark play vigorously in the leads, but are out-acted by Patrick O'Neal, as an egotistic Union commander, and Richard Rust, as a leering Confed-

erate sergeant. The best moment comes when one side digs a massive tunnel towards the cattle, only to come, in an unnerving moment, face to face with the enemy underground. Director Edward Dmytryk quite rightly likes this bizarre confrontation and lets his camera linger on the scene. The theme song is a bit of a hoot.

Always ○ Ⓥ
1989, US, 122 mins, colour
Dir: Steven Spielberg
Stars: Richard Dreyfuss, Holly Hunter, Audrey Hepburn, John Goodman, Brad Johnson
Rating: ★★

You could call this pretty dopey romance, about an airborne fire-fighter who dies and goes to Heaven in a remake of 1943's *A Guy Named Joe*), a pancake landing from whizzbang director Steven Spielberg. Thank goodness it picks up in the last half hour; otherwise there could have been wreckage strewn everywhere. The problem is, of course, the script, which is partly responsible (but only partly) for making the film seem so wrongly cast. Although the dialogue gives him a bumpy ride throughout, Richard Dreyfuss keeps control pretty well most of the time as the daredevil pilot who takes one too many risks and leaves his flying-controller girlfriend (a strident Holly Hunter) grief-striken on the ground. Up in the fire-fighters' heaven, though, guardian angel Audrey Hepburn tells Dreyfuss to get back down there and straighten Hunter's life out. And so he does. Most of the cast are better actors than you'd guess from watching this. But the fire-fighter scenes are spot-on, even though some of the footage is 'pinched' from a real forest blaze in Yellowstone Park.

Amadeus ● Ⓥ
1984, US, 158 mins, colour
Dir: Milos Forman
Stars: F Murray Abraham, Tom Hulce, Elizabeth Berridge, Simon Callow
Rating: ★★★

Adapted from the giant theatrical hit, this eight-Oscar film spotlights the clash of wills in 18th century Vienna between two composers: Mozart (Tom Hulce), a vulgar, licentious popinjay with a hyena laugh, but kissed with genius, and Salieri (F Murray Abraham), the court composer whose work Mozart mocks and who, even while he plots his tormentor's destruction, is tortured

A

himself by the knowledge that Mozart is the greatest composer he has ever heard. Looking at the story through Salieri's envy-green eyes is a clever ploy by writer Peter Shaffer and one that works. Mozart is so awful, so much a crass vulgarian, that our instinctive wish is for him to get what he deserves – obscurity. Like Salieri, however, we are pulled both ways by the beauty of his music, so that Shaffer compels us to follow developments attentively to their horrifying conclusion. Salieri is played in masterly style throughout by Abraham (winning one of the film's Academy Awards), conveying inner feelings by eyes, mouth or gesture rather than words. Even so, the film is almost stolen by Jeffrey Jones, six-inch thick but inch-perfect as the emperor. The opera scenes are well-staged and shot – especially the extracts from Don Giovanni – though non opera lovers may find them a mite lengthy. Despite the original PG certificate, this is not entirely suitable for younger children.

Amarcord ●
1973, Italy/France, 123 mins, colour
Dir: Federico Fellini
Stars: Puppela Maggio, Magali Noel
Rating: ★★

Director Federico Fellini's award-winner is a grab-bag of fragmentary boyhood memories: crude pranks at school; the death of the mother; the first encounter with sex. The best episode concerns a loony uncle who climbs to the top of an enormous tree and won't come down. All in all, though, even with such moments of pictorial beauty as a huge liner looming up through the fog, ablaze with light, and despite its Academy Award as best foreign film, this project is likely to prove less than gripping for today's average viewer.

Amazing Dr Clitterhouse, The ○
1938, US, 87 mins, b/w
Dir: Anatole Litvak
Stars: Edward G Robinson, Claire Trevor, Humphrey Bogart
Rating: ★★★

A consistently enjoyable pre-war Warners gangster romp, with Edward G Robinson and Humphrey Bogart as hero and villain, just as they had been in the studio's *Bullets or Ballots*. Robinson plays a criminologist who joins a gang of thieves (headed by Bogart as a character called Rocks) to study the criminal mind. Claire Trevor oozes

class in the female lead and the supporting cast is positively stuffed with familiar faces – and one familiar voice. Needing a good speaker for the voice of an unseen radio announcer, the studio picked on one of their young contract players: Ronald Reagan.

Amazing Mr Beecham, The
See: The Chiltern Hundreds

Amazing Mr Blunden, The ○
1972, UK, 98 mins, colour
Dir: Lionel Jeffries
Stars: Laurence Naismith, Lynne Frederick, Garry Miller
Rating: ★★★

Lionel Jeffries' second venture into direction: although not as overwhelmingly popular as his first film, *The Railway Children*, this is every bit as good. The remarkable self-assured performance by Lynne Frederick, as the elder of two children involved with ghosts from a century before, is better than anything else in either film.

Amazing Mr Forrest, The
See: The Gang's All Here [1939]

Amazing Mrs Holliday, The ○
1943, US, 96 mins, b/w
Dir: Bruce Manning
Stars: Deanna Durbin, Edmond O'Brien, Barry Fitzgerald
Rating: ★★

Deanna Durbin goes to war in a film that starts off looking like a forerunner to *The Inn of the Sixth Happiness*. A pity the plot didn't stay in the Far East, for it gets sillier as it goes along, leaving Durbin's lovely song interludes as the main interest. The only film that Bruce Manning, otherwise a producer, directed.

Amazon Women on the Moon ◐ ▽
1986, US, 81 mins, colour
Dir: Joe Dante, Carl Gottlieb, John Landis, Robert K Weiss, Peter Horton
Stars: Rosanna Arquette, Steve Guttenberg, Michelle Pfeiffer, Carrie Fisher, Griffin Dunne
Rating: ★★

Don't be too attracted by the cast: this is a quite often mildly amusing, but rarely hilarious compendium of comedy sketches in the still-current American 'rude' vein, punctuated by a black-and-white take-off of an old science-fiction movie that probably looked funnier in its original form. A

class cast which, besides the above, includes Sybil Danning, Andrew Dice Clay, Ralph Bellamy, Steve Forrest, Kelly Preston, Arsenio Hall, Ed Begley Jr and (briefly) hulking veteran Mike Mazurki, at least keeps boredom at bay in the main. Most of the directors involved took lessons from this slapdash slapstick, 'adult'-style, to move on to better things.

Ambassador, The ○
1984, US, 90 mins, colour
Dir: J Lee Thompson
Stars: Robert Mitchum, Ellen Burstyn, Rock Hudson
Rating: ★★★

This political thriller retains a hint of topicality in its Middle East crisis setting. Robert Mitchum plays the title role with monumental calm; he's the US ambassador to Israel, caught in the middle of the fierce conflict between Zionist and extremist Palestinian factions. His determined efforts to seek a solution to the fighting are somewhat complicated by his wife's affair with a high-ranking PLO official. Veteran British director J Lee Thompson efficiently glosses over the plot's implausible moments and the scenes between Mitchum and Ellen Burstyn (as his wife) possess adult wit and realistic weariness.

Ambassador's Daughter, The ○
1956, US, 106 mins, colour
Dir: Norman Krasna
Stars: Olivia de Havilland, John Forsythe, Myrna Loy, Adolphe Menjou
Rating: ★★

Pleasant comedy of mistaken identity, whose chief charms lay in allowing Olivia de Havilland, Myrna Loy and Adolphe Menjou to make screen comebacks. Romantic froth.

Ambush ○
1949, US, 89 mins, b/w
Dir: Sam Wood
Stars: Robert Taylor, John Hodiak, Arlene Dahl, Jean Hagen, Don Taylor
Rating: ★★

This looks like an ordinary Western on the surface – until one takes a closer look at its credentials. The director is Sam Wood, one of MGM's most experienced men, and the screenplay is by Marguerite Roberts, who wrote John Wayne's Oscar-winning Western, *True Grit*. Robert Taylor plays impassively as the

Cavalry scout hero, but there's a dynamic, throat-clutching action climax.

Ambush at Tomahawk Gap ○
1953, US, 73 mins, colour
Dir: Fred F Sears
Stars: John Derek, John Hodiak, Maria Elena Marques, David Brian
Rating: ★★★

Remarkably rough, tough, gripping and well-characterised Western about four desperadoes, with an Indian girl in tow, hunting for buried gold. It was one of a series of Columbia Westerns made in the early Fifties, but it differs from its contemporaries in that its script was attentive enough to character to attract three star players to act in it. John Hodiak and Maria Elena Marques had co-starred before – with Clark Gable in Across the Wide Missouri – and here, as there, they give tough, realistic portrayals.

Ambush Bay ○
1966, US, 109 mins, colour
Dir: Ron Winston
Stars: Hugh O'Brian, Mickey Rooney, James Mitchum, Tisa Chang
Rating: ★★

Explosive action film about a group of Marines on a top secret mission in the Far East during World War Two. Mickey Rooney is in typically pugnacious form as a tough little sergeant.

American Anthem ○
(aka: Take It Easy)
1986, US, 101 mins, colour
Dir: Albert Magnoli
Stars: Mitch Gaylord, Janet Jones, Michael Pataki
Rating: RB

There can't be too many films featuring Olympic gymnasts and, if this is anything to judge by, there may not be too many more. Mitch Gaylord is, for an athlete, a reasonable actor but the mistakes lie in a) asking him to play a gymnast and b) saddling him with a perfectly ludicrous script that must have come out of the Ark. 'I guess,' says leggy contender Janet Jones (well done on the gym work Janet), 'this place is going to be a lot different from Park Avenue, huh?' You bet Jan, as Mitch finds out too. He's dropped out once after attempting a quadruple twist and smashing his face up. Now his trophies have cobwebs on them (yes, they really have). His Russian coach

(Michael Pataki who, on this form, needs more acting lessons than the star) gruffly takes him back. 'Work on your compulsories!' he barks – advice we could all bear in mind. Does Gaylord bring off the quadruple wotsit at the end? Will his unloving dad make a last-minute appearance on the spectators' balcony? Can a duck swim?

American Flyers ◑ ⓥ
1985, US, 114 mins, colour
Dir: John Badham
Stars: Kevin Costner, David Grant, Rae Dawn Chong
Rating: ★★

Made before he hit the big time in *The Untouchables*, this cycling drama about two brothers who untangle their mixed emotions as they compete in a gruelling race, has a striking performance by Kevin Costner. But, ultimately, the film makes too many big statements and attempts to career in too many directions. It's not a patch on screenwriter Steve Tesich's earlier cycle movie, *Breaking Away*, which managed to keep all its themes and ideas in proportion. The women's roles in particular are hopelessly underwritten. The director – who should be shot for the clumsy instances of product placement – is John Badham of *Saturday Night Fever* and *WarGames* fame.

American Friends ○ ⓥ
1991, UK, 96 mins, colour
Dir: Tristram Powell
Stars: Michael Palin, Connie Booth, Trini Alvarado, Alfred Molina
Rating: ★★

Based on a fragment from the diary of Michael Palin's great-great-grandfather, this is an unexpected film from the former Monty Python star: a gentle, leisurely romantic anecdote with moments of comedy and wry observation, and a final delicate balance between tragedy and happiness. It's performed in rather studied style by Palin himself as the academic, and by Connie Booth and Trini Alvarado as aunt and niece, the 'American friends' he meets on holiday in the Alps, who both fall in love with him. Pleasant and watchable, even if it doesn't make us feel much for the characters, the film abounds in delicious satirical studies of Oxford dons. The screenplay, by Palin and director Tristram Powell, is literate and even has its poetic moments. Somehow, though, it remains

inconsequential, a vignette of depth but no weight and, in the end, of curiosity value only.

American Gigolo ● ⓥ
1980, US, 117 mins, colour
Dir: Paul Schrader
Stars: Richard Gere, Lauren Hutton, Hector Elizondo, Nina Van Pallandt, Bill Duke
Rating: ★★★

Another strong, dark social thriller from Paul Schrader, writer of *Taxi Driver* and *Rolling Thunder* and *The Hardcore Life*. The environment is redolent of Raymond Chandler, while the constant night-time scenes of Richard Gere driving around poor and rich areas of a coastal city to grating, doomy music (by Giorgio Moroder) remind us that we're not that far removed from *Taxi Driver* itself. Gere's 'hero' is the all-American cowboy made good: he pleases rich women for rich rewards. Where he comes unstuck – in a typical Schrader touch – is in accepting an 'unusual' assignment, one that leads to his being framed for murder. Although the film rather loses its grip in the last two reels this is, on the whole, an impressive piece of work. Gere copes quite well with a difficult role even if his dialogue is sometimes a bit difficult to hear.

American Graffiti ○ ⓥ
1973, US, 110 mins, colour
Dir: George Lucas
Stars: Richard Dreyfuss, Ron Howard, Paul Le Mat, Charles Martin Smith
Rating: ★★★

Part-financed by Francis Ford Coppola, and written and directed by George Lucas. This is the high school nostalgia classic which, made while Americans were still dying in Vietnam, looks back towards the rock 'n' roll, juke-box, drive-in and soda-fountain America of the not-so-distant past. It's a film about rebels without causes and the pop culture of the early 60s.

American Guerilla in the Philippines, An ○
(aka: I Shall Return)
1950, US, 105 mins, colour
Dir: Fritz Lang
Stars: Tyrone Power, Micheline Presle, Tom Ewell, Jack Elam
Rating: ★★

Noisy but vaguely dull Hollywood war film with a taciturn performance

A

by Tyrone Power in the lead. There are eye-catching portrayals from Tom Ewell and Jack Elam, but it's a strange film to come from German expatriate Fritz Lang. British title (they obviously didn't approve of such Yankee flag-waving!): *I Shall Return.*

American Heart ● Ⓥ
1992, US, 114 mins, colour
Dir: Martin Bell
Stars: Jeff Bridges, Edward Furlong
Rating: ★

You've seen more depressing films than this, but not many. Jeff Bridges is fresh out of jail and reunited with his 14-year-old son (Edward Furlong). Their accommodation is grubby and the landlady dubious about their ability to pay. Still, Bridges gets a job as a window-cleaner and the kid has to enrol in school. It's the filmmakers rather than society who decree these people have no chance. Happy endings were well out of style when this was made, so Bridges loses all his earnings to a vengeful ex-partner-in-crime and the kid is soon consorting with junkies, pushers, strippers and hookers. It gets so that you can't wait for Bridges to go back to crime so that you can all go home. It takes nearly two hours, though, and in all that time not one of the performers reaches our emotions.

American in Paris, An ☉ Ⓥ
1951, US, 115 mins, colour
Dir: Vincente Minnelli
Stars: Gene Kelly, Leslie Caron, Oscar Levant
Rating: ★★★

Vincente Minnelli's enchanting musical raised standards to a new level, with Gene Kelly and Leslie Caron forming a brilliant dancing partnership. Minnelli's direction was full of vivid, imaginative touches. And George Gershwin's music was the perfect background for a Paris which really sprang to life. The film won eight Oscars, including one for best picture; one for story and screenplay (by Alan Jay Lerner); and a special award to Kelly for his superb choreography, topped by his roller-skate routine and the final 'ballet'.

American Tail, An ☉
1986, US, 80 mins, colour
Dir: Don Bluth
Voice stars: Dom DeLuise, Madeline Kahn, Nehemiah Persoff, Christopher Plummer
Rating: ★★★

This faintly off-beat cartoon feature from independent director Don Bluth outpointed anything the rival Disney studio had produced since *The Jungle Book* almost 20 years earlier. There certainly can't be many animated features that would dare start their story in 1885 Russia. Beneath the Moscowitz family, fleeing repression to start a new life in America, live the Mousekewitzes, fleeing their own oppression to the States because they think, in the words of the film's catchiest song 'There are no cats in America'! The grim voyage of the immigrants is nicely caught by the animators without any recourse to over-sombre detail. The Mousekewitz son, Fievel, is washed overboard, arrives in America in a bottle and sets out to find his family. From here on, the film slips into slightly more routine cat-and-mouse stuff, but there are two or three excellent characters, including a calculating cockroach; Henri le Pigeon, busy decorating the Statue of Liberty; and a fat orange cat (voiced by Dom DeLuise) who's vegetarian (apart from the occasional fish), a thicko and a softie and becomes Fievel's friend. Although the film drifts on a bit at the end, the body of its story bulges with invention and bright ideas.

American Way, The ◖
(aka: Riders of the Storm)
1986, US, 105 mins, colour
Dir: Maurice Phillips
Stars: Dennis Hopper, Michael J Pollard, Eugene Lipinski, James Aubrey
Rating: ★★

'Boy, there's some incredibly weird people out there,' exclaims skipper Dennis Hopper as he leads his crew of spaced-out Vietnam veterans, manning a pirate TV station aboard an old bomber plane. Among his men are Michael J Pollard as the resident electronics wizard, dodging all the missiles an enraged US military can launch, and an oriental sitting astride a massive bomb. And these are the quieter members of a crew that soon becomes dedicated to blocking the nomination of one Willa Westinghouse, a presidential candidate planning to start another war somewhere, somehow. This is a bitter black comedy constantly battling to shrug off an ordinary plot and working best when it succeeds. Hopper and Pollard offer their familiar 'eccentric'

characterisations, but the central 'surprise' of the plot is rather obvious throughout.

American Werewolf in London, An ● Ⓥ
1981, UK, 103 mins, colour
Dir: John Landis
Stars: David Naughton, Griffin Dunne, Jenny Agutter, John Woodvine
Rating: ★★

A joky horror film that's even funnier than it thinks it is. David Naughton and Griffin Dunne are two Americans adrift on English country moors until they come across The Slaughtered Lamb, an inn where the Hammer Bit-Part Union clam up like camels in a sandstorm when asked about the five-pointed star on the wall. 'Beware the Moon, lads,' warns purse-lipped Brian Glover, 'and stick to the road.' Ooh-aah, lads. But of course they leave the road and wander blithely across the moors in the thrashing rain (are we actually supposed to *believe* this?), where they say a few four-letter words as they're in for an adult rating anyway for having their throats torn out in the next scene. Naughton survives(!) and, before bedding Nurse Jenny Agutter, has a visitation from his dead friend. Dr Woodvine pooh-poohs all this. 'If there were a monster roaming around the north of England, we'd have seen it on the telly,' he protests. How right. Not like *News at Ten* to miss out on anything like that. Imagine Trevor Mcdonald's eyebrows. There's a lot more of this before Naughton metamorphosises in a really impressive scene and eats up half the population of London. It's a howl!

Amityville Horror, The ● Ⓥ
1979, US, 117 mins, colour
Dir: Stuart Rosenberg
Stars: James Brolin, Margot Kidder, Rod Steiger, Don Stroud
Rating: ★★★

This film carries a unique disclaimer that 'certain events and characters have been altered to heighten dramatic effect'. It forms a disturbing coda to an allegedly true story about a house haunted by victims and killer from a previous mass murder there, and by evil spirits from a long-distant (Red Indian) past. It is certainly most persuasively done, with James Brolin and Margot Kidder suitably fraught as the young couple who do well to stay three weeks in a neighbourhood where thunder and lightning are the order of the night – quite apart from what oozes out of the boards of their home.

Amityville II: The Possession ● Ⓥ
1982, US, 104 mins, colour
Dir: Damiano Damiani
Stars: Burt Young, James Olson, Rutanya Alda
Rating: ★★

The now-familiar ride up the dark stairways of a haunted house to meet whatever horrors the special effects experts can dream up. Although not stated anywhere in this film, this is, in fact, a prequel to *The Amityville Horror*, dealing with events that (might have) happened before that film. Demonic possession is soon in the air, especially when slobby father Burt Young tells a visitor: 'This is my first-born, Sonny. He hasn't been feeling well lately'. Unsympathetic characters give us plenty of chance to cheer for the demons.

Amityville 4: The Evil Escapes ◐ Ⓥ
1989, US, 100 mins, colour
Dir: Sandor Stern
Stars: Patty Duke, Jane Wyatt
Rating: ★★

The fourth of six films to date about the possessed house in Amityville comes up with the pretty dotty idea of having the evil of the Amityville house 'transmigrate' into a peculiar-looking lamp – something which can be transferred from house to house and from family to family, thereby giving prospective Amityville film-makers as many angles as they could wish, and condemning audiences to interminable variations on a theme. At least we can consider ourself brighter than the beleaguered family here. Finding her pet parrot done to a turn in the toaster oven, Alice (Jane Wyatt) blames herself for leaving the bird's cage open, never wondering how the bird managed to incinerate itself. Nancy (Patty Duke) asks her kids if they feel 'comfortable' in the house after one of them has gone berserk with a chain-saw. And no-one at all seems to remember the poor plumber who by this time has been engulfed by a disgustingly gooey sewer demon. The cast (which includes Norman Lloyd, who once fell from the Statue of Liberty in Hitchcock's *Saboteur*) is better than the

material and the special effects are convincingly done. But it's just all so *silly*.

Amongst Friends ● Ⓥ
1993, US, 88 mins, colour
Dir: Rob Weiss
Stars: Steve Parlavecchio, Joseph Lindsay, Mira Sorvino
Rating: ★★

Three teenage boys from well-to-do families enjoy a privileged childhood in Long Island. But, instead of going on to high school and sedate suburban lives, they turn to crime. This is a rather jerkily-paced story of twentysomething gangsters who fall out over the inevitable girl, but it does throw up a couple of charismatic performers in Steve Parlavecchio (who looks like James Dean) and Joseph Lindsay (who looks like Rob Lowe). Mira Sorvino, who also executive-produced, is a good-looking and appealing heroine, and presumably related to actor Paul Sorvino, who is 'thanked' at the end of the film. Not always as interesting as it gets in the last half-hour, the film does exercise a certain fascination as its (clichéd) storyline approaches the inevitable confrontational conclusion.

Amorous Adventures of Moll Flanders, The ◐
1965, UK, 126 mins, colour
Dir: Terence Young
Stars: Kim Novak, Richard Johnson, Angela Lansbury, George Sanders, Leo McKern, Vittorio De Sica
Rating: ★★

A film much after the style of *Tom Jones*, with bags of colour and incident. Kim Novak is the female Tom, chased around every bedchamber in London town. Although Hugh Griffith, memorable in *Tom Jones*, is here also, this time as a prison governor, the film misses some of the lip-smacking period relish with which the earlier film (and the age) so distinguished itself.

Amorous Prawn, The ○
1962, UK, 89 mins, b/w
Dir: Anthony Kimmins
Stars: Ian Carmichael, Joan Greenwood, Cecil Parker, Dennis Price
Rating: ★★

A film adaptation of the riotously successful stage farce about an army headquarters that gets turned into a luxury hotel. And the screen version has a cast more starry than almost any

stage play could hope to muster. It was directed by the redoubtable Anthony Kimmins, who had made almost all of George Formby's smash hit comedies, before moving on to such other comic successes as *Who Goes There!*, *The Captain's Paradise* and *Aunt Clara*.

Amsterdamned ● Ⓥ
1987, Holland, 113 mins, colour
Dir: Dick Maas
Stars: Huub Stapel, Monique van de Ven
Rating: ★★

This facile but fast-paced Dutch film is a kind of Creature from the Black Canal. 'There's something fishy going on here,' mutters one character early on, just before being disembowelled by the Demon Diver. How right he is. Nothing clever about what follows, either, just a speedy mix of commercial elements that includes cuties dangling their toes from lilos in the deadly waters and the inevitable speedboat chase towards the end. Connoisseurs of subtitling, as well as bosses of the well-known fast-food chain, will be delighted to see a 'McDonalds' translated as 'top quality beef'.

Anastasia ○
1956, US, 105 mins, colour
Dir: Anatole Litvak
Stars: Ingrid Bergman, Yul Brynner, Helen Hayes, Akim Tamiroff, Martita Hunt, Felix Aylmer
Rating: ★★★

The film in which Ingrid Bergman returned to Hollywood and won an Oscar all in one swoop. However, she is out-acted by that dowager duchess of actresses, Helen Hayes, in a good strong story about an attempt to pass off a young woman as the surviving daughter of the last Czar of Russia.

Anatomy of a Murder ○
1959, US, 160 mins, b/w
Dir: Otto Preminger
Stars: James Stewart, Lee Remick, Ben Gazzara, Arthur O'Connell, Eve Arden
Rating: ★★★

Otto Preminger's highly watchable courtroom drama, with James Stewart foreshadowing his Hawkins television series as the slow-talking lawyer picking his way determinedly through a tangle of rape and murder. It was explosive stuff in its time, with most of the controversy centring on the scenes in which the prosecution (a striking early appearance by George C

A

Scott) is trying to establish that Lee Remick was not raped at all, but only too willing. Joseph N Welch, a real-life judge, performs nobly in the only acting role of his career as the judge in charge of this high-tension trial – Miss Remick's husband (Ben Gazzara) is accused of killing the man who allegedly ravished her – and there are two fine supporting performances from Arthur O'Connell and Eve Arden as Stewart's dog-eared assistant and wisecracking secretary, both creating characters that are instantly likeable.

Anchors Aweigh ⊙ Ⓥ

1945, US, 140 mins, colour
Dir: George Sidney
Stars: Gene Kelly, Frank Sinatra, Kathryn Grayson
Rating: ★★★★

This lively and colourful musical was a triumph for Gene Kelly and made him a major star at MGM. He and Frank Sinatra are two sailors on leave in Hollywood and Kelly is chasing Kathryn Grayson, an aspiring singer. The plot's pretty thin, but that doesn't matter – the songs, written by Jule Styne and Sammy Kahn, are great and Kelly's dancing is spectacular. A particular high point is a routine he does with cartoon mouse Jerry (of Tom and Jerry fame). Beautifully done and highly entertaining. Kelly, who did all the choreography, really put his mark on this musical, and it shows. Great stuff.

Anderson Tapes, The ◐ Ⓥ

1971, US, 98 mins, colour
Dir: Sidney Lumet
Stars: Sean Connery, Dyan Cannon, Martin Balsam, Alan King, Ralph Meeker, Christopher Walken
Rating: ★★★

Despite its heavy undertones of satire, irony and social comment, this entertaining film from Sidney Lumet, who has made a string of critical hits from *Twelve Angry Men* to *Network*, is basically a 'caper' thriller. Sean Connery gives a fine study of bullet-headed aggressiveness as a professional safe-cracker who is as far removed from James Bond as it's possible to imagine. Still, he does have a bedmate worthy of 007 in the sinuous shape of Dyan Cannon, and the robbery itself provides a thrilling, if black-edged, climax.

. . . And God Created Woman ●

1956, France, 92 mins, colour
Dir: Roger Vadim
Stars: Brigitte Bardot, Curt Jurgens, Jean-Louis Trintignant
Rating: ★★

Roger Vadim's first film as a director created quite a stir when it first arrived in Britain in 1957, on account of its sexiness and its exploitation of the physical charms of a semi-nude Brigitte Bardot. It was cut by four minutes from the original version, and clearly exception was taken to the title which was changed in Britain to *And Woman . . . Was Created* – evidently to keep God out of it. When the film was reissued there in 1967, it was under the proper title and with a couple of deleted minutes restored.

And God Created Woman ● Ⓥ

1988, US, 94 mins, colour
Dir: Roger Vadim
Stars: Rebecca DeMornay, Vincent Spano, Frank Langella, Donovan Leitch, Judith Chapman
Rating: ★★

Roger Vadim returns to the title if not the story of his greatest hit with Brigitte Bardot but the best you can say is that there have been worse Vadim films in the past couple of decades. Rebecca DeMornay and Vincent Spano do help as the couple who undergo a marriage of convenience to get her out of jail. Frank Langella is the gubernatorial candidate who keeps a friendly eye on her progress and you can pretty well guess the rest, given that Vadim is such a romantic at heart. DeMornay does take her clothes off but for all that it's a naive, innocent, almost primitive film. Quite entertaining, if you're really stuck with nothing to do for an hour and a half.

. . . And Justice for All ◐ Ⓥ

1979, US, 117 mins, colour
Dir: Norman Jewison
Stars: Al Pacino, Jack Warden, John Forsythe, Christine Lahti, Sam Levene, Craig T Nelson
Rating: ★

Difficult-to-like black satire with an unattractive central performance by Al Pacino, who's supposed to be the only sane lawyer in a legal world gone mad. His judges include one who lets off robbers and rapists with probation, another with a suicide complex

during recesses (a wildly overdone performance from Jack Warden) and a third, an ultra-hardliner (John Forsythe doing his best with a ludicrous role) who comes up himself for rape and assault. Pacino's own cases seem doomed to tragedy: two of his clients are sent unnecessarily to jail through no fault of his own; one hangs himself, the other takes hostages and is shot. If this is comedy, it is of the very blackest kind. But director Jewison ensures that it's far too overblown to succeed as comedy or drama. The pace is leaden, mainly because individual scenes are time and again stretched beyond breaking point, but without fleshing out any of the background – even to the central and climactic story. Everyone shouts a lot.

And Now for Something Completely Different ○

1971, UK, 89 mins, colour
Dir: Ian MacNaughton
Stars: Graham Chapman, John Cleese, Terry Gilliam, Michael Palin, Eric Idle, Terry Jones
Rating: ★★

Early Monty Python film intended for the US market, which explains the fact that most of the sketches appeared here in their TV series. John Cleese enjoys his classic encounter with a pet-shop owner over a deceased parrot.

. . . And Now the Screaming Starts! ● Ⓥ

1973, UK, 87 mins, colour
Dir: Roy Ward Baker
Stars: Peter Cushing, Stephanie Beacham, Herbert Lom, Patrick Magee, Ian Ogilvy
Rating: ★★

Family curses and malevolent ghosts make up the brew for this grisly horror film, which becomes pretty sinister towards the end. Denys Coop's remarkably skilled camerawork is rather negated by strange colour, as putrescent-looking as the severed hand which hovers on the edges of the film.

And Now Tomorrow ○

1944, US, 86 mins, b/w
Dir: Irving Pichel
Stars: Alan Ladd, Loretta Young, Susan Hayward
Rating: ★★

Hollywood works in mysterious ways and thus Raymond Chandler, esteemed author of hard-boiled detective fiction, was assigned by Paramount to co-script this romantic drama from Rachel Field's sentimental bestseller. Spirited playing from Loretta Young and Susan Hayward as warring sisters, the more stolid Alan Ladd and Barry Sullivan completing the romantic quadrangle.

Androcles and the Lion ⊙
1952, US, 98 mins, b/w
Dir: Chester Erskine
Stars: Jean Simmons, Alan Young, Victor Mature, Robert Newton, Elsa Lanchester
Rating: ★★

Gabriel Pascal had made an impression with his British-made film adaptations of plays by George Bernard Shaw, above all *Pygmalion*. But *Androcles and the Lion* is a trifle heavy-handed where a lighter touch is required and perhaps because of one or two instances of debatable casting. Nevertheless, it is reasonably faithful to the original and does contain some good performances by its star-studded cast. Victor Mature, as the captain, took over the role which was to have been played by James Donald who dropped out of the cast.

Android ○
1982, US, 80 mins, colour
Dir: Aaron Lipstadt
Stars: Klaus Kinski, Brie Howard, Don Opper, Kendra Kirchner
Rating: ★★★

A unique combination of elements from Frankenstein, *Metropolis* and Frank Capra films sparks this science-fiction film, the best new movie from a first-time director (Aaron Lipstadt) since John Carpenter burst on the cinema scene with *Dark Star*. Klaus Kinski is the mad doctor to the life (though even he may not be quite what he seems) while Don Opper (who also co-scripted) will bring a tear to your eye as the android Max – especially when tentatively trying to make a date with a female fugitive who has invaded his space station. You'll be hoping that this robot hero can, like Pinocchio, 'beat the system'!

Andromeda Strain, The ○
1970, US, 127 mins, colour
Dir: Robert Wise
Stars: Arthur Hill, James Olson, Kate Reid
Rating: ★★★

The combination of writer Nelson Gidding and director Robert Wise has

often been at its best in providing chills and thrills. Together they made *The Haunting* and *Audrey Rose*. This science fiction yarn has the benefit of special effects co-directed by Douglas Trumbull (who did *2001: A Space Odyssey* and *Blade Runner*) and is at its best in the eerie beginning and in the hair-raising climax. The ending, in fact, is worthy of a James Bond film: you'll perch on the very edge of the armchair as James Olson fights against time (assailed by poison gas and deadly laser beams) to disarm a self-destruct device before it can trigger itself off.

And Soon the Darkness ◐
1970, UK, 98 mins, colour
Dir: Robert Fuest
Stars: Pamela Franklin, Michele Dotrice, Sandor Eles
Rating: ★★

Carrying uncomfortable contemporary resonance, this is a rather protracted chiller from the pen of Brian Clemens, which seems to take a long time to get around to its suspenseful final reel. At least, however, the script succeeds in keeping you guessing as to the identity of the pervert pursuing two pretty English nurses cycling in France, which is what it has seemed determined at all costs to do.

And Then There Were None ○
(aka: Ten Little Niggers)
1945, US, 98 mins, b/w
Dir: Rene Clair
Stars: Barry Fitzgerald, Louis Hayward, Walter Huston, June Duprez, C Aubrey Smith, Roland Young
Rating: ★★★★

Rene Clair's atmospheric version of Agatha Christie's classic thriller (once known as *Ten Little Niggers*) is one of the best mystery films you are ever likely to see, as well as being one of the creepiest – thanks to Clair's edgy direction and Charles Previn's doom-filled music. If you haven't seen the ending coming, you will find it quite shattering. And the beginning, with the victims travelling to the unknown island on a storm-swept boat, is a masterpiece of mood-setting. Among those meeting ingenious deaths are Sir C Aubrey Smith, Richard Haydn, Roland Young and Mischa Auer. Forget other versions – this is the one to watch.

Andy Hardy Comes Home ○
1958, US, 77 mins, b/w
Dir: Howard W Koch

Stars: Mickey Rooney, Patricia Breslin
Rating: ★★

Twelve years after the last film in the Andy Hardy series proper, Mickey Rooney, having fallen from public favour in the intervening years, before making a comeback as a pugnacious character star, put together this affectionate farewell to the characters from the series. Lewis Stone had died (from a heart attack chasing vandals from his property), so there was now Judge Hardy to offer words of wisdom. And negotiations fell through for Ann Rutherford (formerly perennial girlfriend Polly) to return as Andy's wife, so newcomer Patricia Breslin was chosen. Otherwise the cast was complete as before, and Andy was in trouble as usual, this time falling foul of a local landowner who tries to turn everyone against our diminutive hero. The results were unexceptional, but a pleasant dose of nostalgia.

Andy Hardy Gets Spring Fever ○
1939, US, 85 mins, b/w
Dir: W S Van Dyke II
Stars: Lewis Stone, Mickey Rooney
Rating: ★★

More fun with amorous teenager Andy Hardy, once again in this episode falling for the attraction of an older woman to the discomfort of his steady date, peppy Polly Benedict. As Andy, Mickey Rooney turns on his infectious impersonation of a lovestruck duck, and Cecilia Parker is once more his equally gullible sister Marian. Although the part she plays is that of a 19-year-old, the youthful-looking Cecilia was incredibly 34 at the time that *Andy Hardy Gets Spring Fever* was made. She continued playing the role off and on until the end of the series proper in 1946, even returning for the one-off 1958 nostalgia piece *Andy Hardy Comes Home*, making nonsense of her 53 years.

Andy Hardy Meets Debutante ○
1940, US, 89 mins, b/w
Dir: George B Seitz
Stars: Mickey Rooney, Judy Garland, Lewis Stone, Fay Holden
Rating: ★★

Familiar leaves from the Hardy family scrapbook. We've seen Andy fall for society girls before, but Mickey Rooney, Lewis Stone and company still manage to squeeze some amuse-

A

ment out of the little fellow's inevitable come-uppance, and there's always Judy Garland, who's given two songs in this episode: 'Alone' and 'Nobody's Baby'. Rooney's usual series girlfriend, Ann Rutherford, is in it too, as is Diana Lewis (in real life, Mrs William Powell for 44 years) as the debutante of the title. 'My', says Rooney in the course of the capers, 'how one's women do mount up.' He couldn't know at the time, of course, that he himself would be married eight times!

Andy Hardy's Blonde Trouble O
1944, US, 107 mins, b/w
Dir: George B Seitz
Stars: Mickey Rooney, Lewis Stone, Bonita Granville
Rating: ★★

One of the later Andy Hardy frolics, more like an MGM college musical of the Forties than the usual Hardy family comedy-drama. Dean Herbert Marshall soothes the fevered (Mickey) Rooney brow, while Bronita Granville, Jean Porter and the Wilde Twins are lively college girls. Song-and-dance interludes includes 'You'd Be So Easy to Love'.

Andy Hardy's Double Life O
1942, US, 92 mins, b/w
Dir: George B Seitz
Stars: Mickey Rooney, Lewis Stone, Esther Williams
Rating: ★★

Small wonder that MGM decided to build swim champion Esther Williams into a big star after this debut appearance. She was never better or more delightful, and gets a chance to play the comedy vamp with a talent that was rarely exploited in her subsequent aqua-musicals. This well-balanced concoction of home-spun sentiment, humour and romance proved that the Hardy series still had plenty of life.

Andy Hardy's Private Secretary O
1941, US, 101 mins, b/w
Dir: George B Seitz
Stars: Lewis Stone, Mickey Rooney, Fay Holden
Rating: ★★

The 10th film in the Hardy series finds the likeable family caught up in the preparations for Andy's high school graduation. The story is routine but the film is notable for the acting debut

of singing star Kathryn Grayson as Andy's secretary. Mickey Rooney, Lewis Stone and Fay Holden give their usual solid performances with a good supporting cast headed by Ian Hunter and Todd Karns.

Angel O
1937, US, 91 mins, b/w
Dir: Ernst Lubitsch
Stars: Marlene Dietrich, Herbert Marshall, Melvyn Douglas
Rating: ★★★

This Marlene Dietrich film has a dash of polish and sophistication given to a risque romantic comedy by that old master of the genre, Ernst Lubitsch. The title song by Frederick Hollander and Leo Robin sets the mood for a light fantastic Parisian romp in which Dietrich wears a wardrobe of clothes that few other actresses would, or could, get away with.

Angel ●
1982, UK, 90 mins, colour
Dir: Neil Jordan
Stars: Stephen Rea, Alan Devlin,Veronica Quilligan, Honor Heffernan, Marie Kean, Ray McAnally
Rating: ★★★

Although set in Ireland this film is more of a contemporary black thriller than a comment on the present-day Irish troubles. Stephen Rea, as the musician who swaps his saxophone for a submachine gun to avenge the dance hall murder of two acquaintances, is firmly in the tradition of lone-wolf heroes established by Alan Ladd in Hollywood 40 years earlier. And Chris Menges' imaginative photography exactly matches the mood of the film. It was a formidable cinematic debut for Sligo-born Neil Jordan, both as writer and director – a slice of Raymond Chandler, if you like, within a particularly abrasive and desperate Irish context.

Angel Face O
1952, US, 91 mins, b/w
Dir: Otto Preminger
Stars: Robert Mitchum, Jean Simmons, Mona Freeman, Herbert Marshall
Rating: ★★★

This moody and rather unsettling RKO *noir* thriller looks as though it were written with studio contractees Jane Greer or Faith Domergue in mind. But Greer had just left the studio and, when Jean Simmons arrived from England, studio boss Howard

Hughes, after months of not knowing what to do with her, gave her the disturbed murderess in *Angel Face*. Icily effective she is too, ensnaring poor Robert Mitchum who was at one time or another the fall guy for pretty well all the studio's formidable stock of femmes fatales.

Angel Heart ● Ⓥ
1987, US, 113 mins, colour
Dir: Alan Parker
Stars: Mickey Rourke, Robert De Niro, Charlotte Rampling
Rating: ★★★

A surrealist detective story or a modern reworking of an old legend? Alan Parker's powerful thriller certainly has bags of style and it flaunts it too. You get lots of clues along the way as to what it's all about, amid a welter of blood and voodoo, but they may not be enough unless you have your wits about you. Mickey Rourke gives a startled, shuffling performance as a seedy private eye in 1955 whose precarious living has earned him little apart from a permanent designer stubble. Summoned by the mysterious Louis Cyphre (smoothly played by Robert De Niro), he is commanded, money no object, to find an obscure crooner, Johnny Favorite, who vanished in 1943 after being injured in the war. Every contact he talks to seems to end up dead, but gradually the fantastic truth begins to dawn... Thumped along by doomy music, the film treads a bloody path to its inexorable conclusion, against meancing backgrounds that sometimes seem to have a life of their own. It's something a little different for those with strong stomachs.

Angel in Exile O
1948, US, 90 mins, b/w
Dir: Charles Lawson
Stars: John Carroll, Adele Mara
Rating: ★★★

This unusual, well-handled movie melodrama was made by Republic when they were trying hard to build themselves up as realistic rivals to the major Hollywood studios. It's a modest but effective semi-Western about a bad man who undergoes a change of heart when hailed as a miracle man by Mexican peasants. The assured direction is from the experienced hands of Allan Dwan. Adele Mara's fiery Raquel catches the eye.

Angels One Five ○ Ⓥ
1951, UK, 98 mins, b/w
Dir: George More O'Ferrall
Stars: Jack Hawkins, Michael Denison, John Gregson, Dulcie Gray
Rating: ★★★

This much-praised film tribute to The Few received no greater acclaim than from Group Capt Douglas Bader, legless air ace of the Battle of Britain. 'I went to see it with my tongue in my cheek,' Bader commented. 'I came out amazed. I could not fault it.' Moving and inspiring, the film is set in a Royal Air Force base in the summer of 1940. With their roles in it, Jack Hawkins and John Gregson took giant strides towards stardom.

Angel Street
See: Gaslight

Angels with Dirty Faces ○ Ⓥ
1938, US, 97 mins, b/w
Dir: Michael Curtiz
Stars: James Cagney, Pat O'Brien, Humphrey Bogart, Ann Sheridan
Rating: ★★★

Three of Warners' 'big five' gangster stars (the other two were George Raft and Edward G Robinson) came together in this classic of the genre. James Cagney and Pat O'Brien, in their familiar roles of likeable gangster and priest respectively, are the boys from the slums who grow up on opposite sides of the law. Humphrey Bogart has his usual part, too, as a humourless crook with whom Cagney is clearly destined to fall out. Add Ann Sheridan, bursting to stardom as the girl involved, and the Dead End Kids (later, among other things, the Bowery Boys) as the little toughs with whom Cagney and O'Brien have different ways of dealing, and the mixture is irresistible, encapsulating the whole spectrum of Warners thrillers and crime dramas of the Thirties in one potent dose.

Angry Silence, The ○
1959, UK, 95 mins, b/w
Dir: Guy Green
Stars: Richard Attenborough, Pier Angeli, Michael Craig
Rating: ★★★★

One of the great post-war films: a poignant, moving and extremely penetrating portrait of the pressure, both physical and mental, put upon a man who refuses to strike, by members of his union. Richard

Attenborough is hauntingly true as the 'black-leg', Pier Angeli delicate and moving as his wife – her best screen work since *Somebody Up There Likes Me*. It can't have pleased the unions or the militants, but nonetheless much of it remains engraved in the mind – especially Brian Bedford's repellent bully and Alfred Burke's magnificent dog-eared and hateful Communist organiser. Easily director Guy Green's most memorable film.

Animal Crackers ☉ Ⓥ
1930, US, 98 mins, b/w
Dir: Victor Heerman
Stars: Groucho Marx, Harpo Marx, Chico Marx, Zeppo Marx, Margaret Dumont, Lillian Roth
Rating: ★★★

The film in which Groucho sings 'Hooray for Captain Spaulding' and Harpo turns out to have stolen half the house when forced to open his capacious raincoat. Yes, The (four) Marx Brothers in full flow, with Groucho propositioning the incomparable Margaret Dumont by rolling up his trouser leg and then going down on the other knee. The plot has something to do with a stolen painting but don't let it bother you; it certainly doesn't seem to bother the four stars.

Animal Farm ○
1955, UK, 72 mins, colour
Dir: Joy Batchelor
Rating: ★★★

Still Britain's best feature cartoon: a brilliantly animated, strongly dramatic version of George Orwell's classic allegory. The makers can even be excused for altering the ending in the cause of dramatic effect. Extraordinary voice work by Maurice Denham as all the animals. A few comic episodes are justifiably inserted to lighten the strong and sombre tone of the whole.

Anna ◑ Ⓥ
1986, US, 95 mins, colour
Dir: Yurek Bogayevicz
Stars: Sally Kirkland, Paulina Porizkova, Robert Fields, Stefan Schnabel, Larry Pine
Rating: ★★

A more modern-day cousin of *All About Eve*. Sally Kirkland's Oscar-nominated title role sees her convincingly playing a Czech film star who can find no work in America after escaping her homeland to follow a director-husband who no longer wants anything to do with her. Get-

ting a $200-a-week understudy role in a off-Broadway show enables her to take under her wing the waiflike Paulina Porizkova as Krystyna, a teenage Czech refugee who, with teeth capped and face made up, proves to look just like Audrey Hepburn. Krystyna soon attracts the attention of showbiz scouts Anna meets in her quest for work and, when the older woman offers her protégé her identity and her life, Krystyna takes her up on it. Good performances and an interesting milieu should add up to a class movie here, but somehow the piece fails to entertain, even though the director shies away from a seemingly inevitable tragic ending. Lack of proper plot development is the root cause although, like Krystyna in the film, it could have also have done with another set of teeth.

Anna and the King of Siam ☉
1946, US, 128 mins, b/w
Dir: John Cromwell
Stars: Irene Dunne, Rex Harrison, Linda Darnell, Lee J Cobb, Gale Sondergaard
Rating: ★★★

A film unlike any Hollywood had made before, this romantic drama was such a success on its appearance in 1946 that, inside 10 years, Rodgers and Hammerstein had produced smash-hit stage and screen musical versions of the story. The film is a songless but charming and very moving version of the story of Anna Owens and her friendship with the King of Siam.

Anna Christie ○
1930, US, 90 mins, b/w
Dir: Clarence Brown
Stars: Greta Garbo, Charles Bickford, Marie Dressler
Rating: ★★

'Give me a whisky, with ginger ale on the side – and don't be stingy, baby'. Imagine that in a gruff Swedish accent, and you have Greta Garbo's first words for the screen, in the morality drama for which MGM proudly announced: 'Garbo speaks!' *Anna Christie*, which is taken from Eugene O'Neill's play, has Garbo in less sophisticated mood as a prostitute trying to start life afresh in a fishing community. Her deep-felt (not to say deep-voiced) performance gives the hackneyed venture some validity. Veteran actress Marie Dressler also made the most of her big emotional moments to set herself up with a wonderful last few years at MGM in

A

the twilight of her career. The film's a must for collectors of a complete Garbo catalogue of superior screen suffering.

Anna Karenina ○
1935, US, 95 mins, b/w
Dir: Clarence Brown
Stars: Greta Garbo, Fredric March, Freddie Bartholomew, Basil Rathbone, Maureen O'Sullivan
Rating: ★★★

Beautifully crafted MGM version of Tolstoy's famous novel of illicit romance at the court of Russia in the 19th century. A haunting portrayal by Greta Garbo in the title role and a piercing performance by Basil Rathbone as her husband are the things that stand out in the foreground of one's memory, against the back-cloth of some distinguished black and white photography.

Anna Karenina ○ ⓥ
1947, UK, 123 mins, b/w
Dir: Julien Duvivier
Stars: Vivien Leigh, Ralph Richardson, Kieron Moore
Rating: ★★

Julien Duvivier's elegant but rather stuffy version of Tolstoy's novel, immortalised in two film versions by Garbo (*Love* in 1927 and, the more famous *Anna Karenina* in 1935). Vivien Leigh makes a wistful doomed heroine and Ralph Richardson is in cuttingly splendid form as her cuckolded husband. Attention to detail in costumes and settings is immaculate, and the camerawork of distinguished French cinematographer Henri Alekan achieves some fine effects in black and white. It did not, however, restore the fortunes of its producer, the famous Alexander Korda, to their pre-war glory.

Anne of the Indies ○
1951, US, 81 mins, colour
Dir: Jacques Tourneur
Stars: Jean Peters, Louis Jourdan, Debra Paget, Herbert Marshall
Rating: ★★★

Jean Peters, sadly lost to the screen when she married millionaire-recluse Howard Hughes, cuts a dashing figure as the lady buccaneer in this rousing action movie. Talented director Jacques Tourneur packs in enough action for half-a-dozen pirate films.

Anne of the Thousand Days ○ ⓥ
1969, US, 145 mins, colour
Dir: Charles Jarrott
Stars: Richard Burton, Genevieve Bujold, Irene Papas, Anthony Quayle, Michael Hordern
Rating: ★★★

This sumptuous costume drama won Oscar nominations for best picture, best actor (Richard Burton as Henry VIII) and best actress (Genevieve Bujold as Anne Boleyn). In the event, it clinched only one Academy Award that year – the one for costume design. Engrossing, well-crafted drama, even if Burton was to have unfair competition in the Henry VIII stakes a couple of years later from Sidney James in *Carry On Henry*!

Annie ○ ⓥ
1982, US, 128 mins, colour
Dir: John Huston
Stars: Albert Finney, Carol Burnett, Aileen Quinn, Tim Curry
Rating: ★★

A huge-scale musical that starts tremendously well, but goes relentlessly downhill. What with Columbia paying a record $9.5 million for the screen rights to the Broadway smash-hit musical about little orphan Annie and costs escalating to $52 million during shooting, the film faced a near-impossible task of earning $150 millon just to break even. Quite why veteran director John Huston allowed himself to be wooed to direct it as his first (and last) musical we shall never know. Just one of the giant street sets cost a million dollars, and that kind of expenditure was carried through into the stunning costumes (by Theoni V Aldredge) and big production numbers. Albert Finney shaved his head as munitions millionaire Daddy Warbucks, Aileen Quinn (chosen after a nationwide talent search) is a touch too cute as the moppet of the title, and Carol Burnett stole the show as gin-swigging orphanage crone Miss Hannigan. The highlights are the show-stopping numbers 'Hard Knock Life for Us' and 'Tomorrow'.

Annie Get Your Gun ☉
1950, US, 107 mins, colour
Dir: George Sidney
Stars: Betty Hutton, Howard Keel, Louis Calhern, J Carroll Naish, Edward Arnold, Keenan Wynn
Rating: ★★★

Blockbuster musical Western about a lady sharpshooter. Betty Hutton took over the role of Annie Oakley, to which Judy Garland had been assigned before falling ill, and turned it into a personal triumph. She and her co-star Howard Keel put over Irving Berlin's lively songs in great style.

Annie Hall ◐ ⓥ
1977, US, 94 mins, colour
Dir: Woody Allen
Stars: Woody Allen, Diane Keaton, Tony Roberts, Carol Kane, Paul Simon
Rating: ★★★

Woody Allen's first commercial success and his fourth collaboration with his then-girlfriend, Diane Keaton. It's easy to speculate that it was also his most autobiographical to date, with the theme of the main character living in a house built under a rollercoaster followed through into his later *Radio Days*. This assured comedy deals with the shifting sands of a new relationship. The humour comes from banal day-to-day situations and dialogue, which American audiences lapped up to the tune of $19 million at the box-office. The Oscar voters were similarly impressed and awarded the film statuettes for Best Picture, Director and Screenplay (co-written by Allen with his regular collaborator, Marshall Brickman). Sigourney Weaver fans should keep their eyes peeled for her brief debut film appearance as Woody's date outside a cinema.

Annie Oakley ○
1935, US, 88 mins, b/w
Dir: George Stevens
Stars: Barbara Stanwyck, Preston Foster, Melvyn Douglas, Moroni Olsen
Rating: ★★★

The historical story, more or less, of the lady later immortalised in *Annie Get Your Gun*, Barbara Stanwyck was surely born to play the spunky sharpshooter character of Annie Oakley. George Stevens presents her story as a bumper bundle of comedy, romance and Wild West stuntwork. Lively semi-Western with good dialogue, this love story was one of Stevens's earliest successes, made when Stanwyck was at the height of her early career.

Ann Vickers ○
1933, US, 73 mins, b/w
Dir: John Cromwell
Stars: Irene Dunne, Walter Huston
Rating: ★

Almost a pocket version of Sinclair Lewis' novel, with Irene Dunne breathlessly chasing from affair to affair, pregnancy to pregnancy, while becoming a prominent social worker and industrial reformer, and all in the space of 75 minutes. Doctor friend Edna May Oliver has it about right when she says that 'Ann's going to make the world over if it takes her all winter.' RKO proclaimed that the picture would 'inflame the nation like a purifying fire'. Alas, these were the straitlaced Thirties and all the film did was burn the studio's fingers.

Another Country ● ⊙
1984, UK, 90 mins, colour
Dir: Marek Kanievska
Stars: Rupert Everett, Colin Firth, Anna Massey, Betsy Brantley, Cary Elwes, Michael Jenn
Rating: ★★

Based on the true-life story of Guy Burgess, this is a study of homosexuality at a public school in the Thirties and how persecution led ultimately to one of the young men involved defecting to the Russians from the Diplomatic Corps. The ritual of public school life is hideously well observed, even if the story's grip is hardly vicelike. Rupert Everett is exceptionally good as the languorous 'Bennett' who flouts school conventions to his eventual cost. Selected for the 1984 Cannes Film Festival, where it received an award for Best Artistic Contribution (specifically cinematographer Peter Biziou), the film also won Everett a BAFTA nomination the following year.

Another 48 HRS ● ⊙
1990, US, 95 mins, colour
Dir: Walter Hill
Stars: Eddie Murphy, Nick Nolte, Brion James, Kevin Tighe, Ed O'Ross
Rating: ★★

Sequel to smash-hit films really should have something better than this to offer the paying public. This is an utterly routine slam-bang action comedy packed with familiar and predictable scenes and elements culled from dozens of similar films. The shoot-out in the strip club, the flight down the fire escape, the villain discovered with a naked woman, the saloon-bar brawl, the crooked cops – absolutely no prizes for guessing the identity of Mr Big the Ice-Man – and virtually no wisecracking lines from Eddie Murphy and Nick Nolte, who just take the money and run. Directed in

tired but efficient style by Walter Hill, this would be completely dismissed without its star names.

Another Man, Another Chance ○
(aka: Another Man, Another Woman)
1977, France/US, 132 mins, colour
Dir: Claude Lelouch
Stars: James Caan, Genevieve Bujold, Francis Huster
Rating: ★★

Another of French director Claude Lelouch's finally-they-met convergent romances, this time set in the old west. In this picturesque setting a French immigrant (Genevieve Bujold) is destined to meet a veterinarian, played by James Caan. Going through the tragedies that bring this about would give away too much of the plot; suffice to say that the film has quite an amount of charm, if perhaps not quite enough to see it through its lengthy running time. Caan fans will enjoy the sight of their hero doing some unexpected things, such as playing billiards on horseback, and feeding (and changing) a baby. They may object though, to the director's insistence on shooting everything through a yellow lens to convey a sense of period, a device that proves rather trying to the eyes.

Another Man, Another Woman
See: Another Man, Another Chance

Another Man's Poison ○
1951, UK, 89 mins, b/w
Dir: Irving Rapper
Stars: Bette Davis, Gary Merrill, Anthony Steel
Rating: ★★

The lightning flashes match those in Bette Davis's eyes as she laughs in the face of death in this all-stops-out melodrama about a woman with a penchant for poisoning those who get in her way. Directed by Irving Rapper, who made some of Bette's most notable successes, including *Now, Voyager.*

Another Stakeout ○ ⊙
1993, US, 109 mins, colour
Dir: John Badham
Stars: Richard Dreyfuss, Emilio Estevez, Rosie O'Donnell, Madeleine Stowe
Rating: ★

There's lots of shouting and very little plot in this unbearably tedious sequel to the entertaining original. Embarrassments and

misunderstandings far outweigh the action in this story and, although Richard Dreyfuss and Emilio Estevez are back on duty (minus their moustaches), it just goes to show what a difference a well-constructed script will make to a movie. Rosie O'Donnell is squirmingly strident at the assistant D.A. who sets up the stakeout to find a missing witness, and only Cathy Moriarty as the witness does anything to contribute to the film, although Madeleine Stowe (unwisely) reprises her role, unbilled (wisely) as Dreyfuss' love. And can you believe Miguel Ferrer failing to pick up his 'accidental' Las Vegas jackpot at the beginning of the film? No way: even hit-men gotta live.

Another Time, Another Place ○
1958, US, 98 mins, b/w
Dir: Lewis Allen
Stars: Lana Turner, Barry Sullivan, Sean Connery
Rating: ★★

A love story which gave Sean Connery (in a pre-James Bond role) his first real chance in a big star part. He was chosen by the leading lady herself, Lana Turner. Connery seized the opportunity to show his worth, and the American actress had no regrets about her choice.

Another Woman ◐ ⊙
1988, US, 81 mins, colour
Dir: Woody Allen
Stars: Gena Rowlands, Mia Farrow, Ian Holm, Blythe Danner, Gene Hackman, Martha Plimpton
Rating: ★★

Impeccably acted, though sometimes as dry and dusty as an old Latin primer, Woody Allen's Bergmanesque drama is basically Scrooge for highbrows. Gena Rowlands is the college professor who, reaching 50, sets to work on a new book at her hideaway writing flat (we should all afford such luxuries), where she begins to hear voices through the ventilation, ostensibly from the psychiatrist's next door. The problems of a pregnant woman (Mia Farrow) on the couch there mirror her own. She begins to see herself in a different light, more as others see her. Are the voices ghostly, or are they really there? By the end, they have helped Rowlands cast off the old and bring on the new. Allen's writing here is often perceptive (if occasionally shallow), but certainly for minority audiences only. Mainline

A

moviegoers may agree with the character half-way through who says that: 'We've talked this to death'.

Another You ● Ⓥ

1991, US, 98 mins, colour
Dir: Maurice Phillips
Stars: Gene Wilder, Richard Pryor, Mercedes Ruehl, Stephen Lang, Vanessa Williams, Kevin Pollak
Rating: ★

The in-and-out partnership of Gene Wilder and Richard Pryor has come a long way down from the dizzy heights of *Silver Streak* and hits a new low with this formula farce about a small-time conman (Pryor) enlisted to look after a mental patient and pathological liar (Wilder) as part of his punishment of community service. Staunch fibbing ensues in a zany but wafer-thin plot that soon sees the duo in deep trouble in more ways than one. Pryor piles up the wisecracks, albeit in subdued style (symptoms of his real-life illness are all too evident), while Wilder twitches nervously as only he can. A wince-worthy comedy for devoted fans of the two stars only. On second thoughts, settle for a re-run of *Silver Streak.*

Any Number Can Play ○

1949, US, 112 mins, b/w
Dir: Mervyn LeRoy
Stars: Clark Gable, Alexis Smith, Wendell Corey, Audrey Totter
Rating: ★★

Clark Gable is at his debonair best here as an honest gambler. It's just as well, as this is a lacklustre drama by his own demanding standards. Even the cast doesn't have a polished MGM look about it, except for the presence in the supporting cast of Frank Morgan (his last film role) and Mary Astor. Mervyn LeRoy does keep it moving well, and Richard Brooks' slightly off-beat dialogue occasionally rises above a sloppy sub-plot that threatens to swamp the film.

Anything Can Happen ○

1952, US, 107 mins, b/w
Dir: George Seaton
Stars: Jose Ferrer, Kim Hunter
Rating: ★★

In complete contrast to his memorable roles as Toulouse-Lautrec in *Moulin Rouge* and Cyrano de Bergerac in the film of that name, Jose Ferrer here starred in an amusingly off-beat if over-sentimental film about the adventures of a Georgian emigre

(Georgia in Russia, that is) in the great United States of America. Ferrer's portrayal is fresh, vital and entertaining, carrying off every comic situation with irresistible verve. He is supported by a rich array of ethnic 'types', including Nuri Bey, a Turk, played by plump-cheeked Kurt Kasznar; Ferrer's uncle, a successful chef, portrayed by snake-eyed Oscar Beregi; and, best of all, the formidable Natasha Lytess.

Anything Goes ○

1956, US, 106 mins, colour
Dir: Robert Lewis
Stars: Bing Crosby, Donald O'Connor, Mitzi Gaynor, Jeanmaire
Rating: ★★

Lively and very colourful musical in which Bing Crosby sets up what must be an all-time record: he played the same part that he had played in the first version of the film 20 years earlier! At that time Ethel Merman filled the part now sparklingly played by Mitzi Gaynor. Cole Porter wrote the score that includes what was an overwhelming hit of the Thirties – the title song. Too many flat spots, thought: the original's still better.

Any Wednesday ○

1966, US, 109 mins, colour
Dir: Robert Ellis Miller
Stars: Jane Fonda, Jason Robards, Dean Jones, Rosemary Murphy, Ann Prentiss
Rating: ★★★

One of the great fun films of the Sixties, and in its original uncut form, as opposed to the mutilated version which appeared in this country's cinemas under the title *Bachelor Girl Apartment.* It's a warm, wise and witty adaptation of Muriel Resnik's hit stage play, scripted by the author herself. Good performances from all the principals, and from Ann Prentiss, sister of Paula, as a too-bright secretary. And there's a memorably hilarious sequence as the three stars and Rosemary Murphy (as Jason Robards' wife) play word games in Robards' car.

Any Which Way You Can ◑ Ⓥ

1980, US, 116 mins, colour
Dir: Buddy Van Horn
Stars: Clint Eastwood, Sondra Locke, Geoffrey Lewis, Ruth Gordon
Rating: ★★

This zany romp is a shade more agreeable and entertaining than its predecessor *Every Which Way But Loose.* The best thing is that the streak of malice carried by the earlier film has been largely ironed out, leaving us with the antics of Clyde the orang-utan, some crude but sometimes quite effective gags and a bruising bare-knuckle fight at the end. William Smith is a personable opponent for Clint Eastwood, whose fans will lap it up.

Anzio ○ Ⓥ

(aka: Battle for Anzio)
1967, Italy, 117 mins, colour
Dir: Edward Dmytryk
Stars: Robert Mitchum, Arthur Kennedy, Peter Falk, Robert Ryan, Earl Holliman, Mark Damon
Rating: ★★★

A big Italian-American co-production based on the famous Wynford Vaughan-Thomas book on the subject and how decisions were allegedly taken in 1944 that cost thousands of Allied lives. The screenplay takes an hour or so to get down to brass tacks but then enlivens the film with a dangerous passage through a minefield and a sharp shootout between snipers before the moral is brought home (and not overstated either).

Apache ○

1954, US, 91 mins, colour
Dir: Robert Aldrich
Stars: Burt Lancaster, Jean Peters, John McIntire, Charles Buchinsky (Bronson)
Rating: ★★

Much-heralded but unexceptional Western with Burt Lancaster playing a blue-eyed Indian as the last of the great Apache warriors. The approach is too reverent, perhaps because the story is solidly based on fact. Nonetheless there are exciting and suspenseful moments and good acting from Jean Peters as Lancaster's squaw. Based on the book *Bronco Apache* by Paul I Wellman.

Apache Rifles ○

1964, US, 92 mins, colour
Dir: William H Witney
Stars: Audie Murphy, Michael Dante, Linda Lawson
Rating: ★★

A latter-day Audie Murphy Western that goes great guns for several reels and loses its original fire only in the last half an hour. For 60 minutes or so, it's a handsome Cavalry Western, with blue and yellow uniforms dashing everywhere, some really bad white miners, and Indian-hating Murphy being converted to peace-loving ways by the most beautiful white missionary ever to tread desert. Some early shots, both indoor and outdoor, are remarkably well composed by director William H Witney. Action is bang on target. And there's some nice, slack-jawed villainy from L Q Jones. But this Audie Murphy sure was a hard man to kill in his Westerns. Here, he gets an Indian lance smack-dab through the chest and he's back on duty 'three weeks later' with his arm in a sling.

Apache Uprising ○
1966, US, 90 mins, colour
Dir: R G Springsteen
Stars: Rory Calhoun, Corinne Calvet, John Russell, Lon Chaney Jr, DeForrest Kelley
Rating: ★★

Indian arrows fly again in this Sixties' action film that's a treasury of stars from the past. Johnny Mack Brown, husky cowboy actor who once starred with Greta Garbo, turns up as the sheriff. And there's a nostalgic reunion for Richard Arlen and Jean Parker, who co-starred in a number of adventure films in the Forties.

Apartment, The ○ ⓥ
1960, US, 125 mins, b/w
Dir: Billy Wilder
Stars: Jack Lemmon, Shirley MacLaine, Fred MacMurray, Ray Walston, Edie Adams, Jack Kruschen
Rating: ★★★★

Whether fast-talking his way out of a tight situation, straining spaghetti through a tennis racket, or saving Shirley MacLaine from a suicide attempt, Jack Lemmon is totally watchable throughout this black-edged romantic comedy from Billy Wilder. It won five Academy Awards, including best film, and clocked up numerous other nominations, including acting awards for Lemmon, MacLaine and Jack Kruschen as Lemmon's doctor neighbour.

Apartment for Peggy ○
1948, US, 99 mins, colour
Dir: George Seaton
Stars: Jeanne Crain, William Holden, Edmund Gwenn
Rating: ★★★

Old-timer Edmund Gwenn scoops up the acting honours in this warm, sentimental comedy about an old university professor, contemplating a quiet suicide, who is given new interest in life through the problems of two young students who move into his attic. Plump-cheeked Gene Lockhart is almost as good as another professor, and Jeanne Crain quite charming as the girl.

Apocalypse Now ● ⓥ
1979, US, 150 mins, colour
Dir: Francis Coppola
Stars: Marlon Brando, Robert Duvall, Martin Sheen, Frederic Forrest, Dennis Hopper, Harrison Ford
Rating: ★★★

Many thought this would be the Vietnam film to end them all. Unfortunately it isn't, in any sense. Parts of this long film, though, are so brilliant – the opening sequences are stunningly atmospheric – that you long for a better whole. Vittorio Storraro's amazing colour photography shows the Far Eastern landscape in far greater clarity than you would have thought possible. And Martin Sheen's voice-over narration a la Humphrey Bogart is another successful ingredient of the film. But, in spite of its impact, its sound and its fury, the movie is also often slow and pretentious. Its action throws in every possible atrocity to shock the viewer: in words as well as pictures Francis Ford Coppola plays heavily for effect. Marlon Brando's renegade Colonel – Sheen's attempts to assassinate him form the hub of the story – cannot be despatched with a bullet, but must be hacked to pieces with a machete to symbolise the simultaneous slaughter of a sacrificial bull. Coppola does attempt to balance his elements with injections of some horrifically black humour, including a superbly-choreographed attack by helicopters to the music of 'Ride of the Valkyrie'. In the end, though, the stage-manager in him wins, while the director loses.

Apple Dumpling Gang, The ⊙
1974, US, 100 mins, colour
Dir: Norman Tokar
Stars: Bill Bixby, Susan Clark, Don Knotts, Tim Conway
Rating: ★★★

Although this Western comedy doesn't quite fire on all six-shooters, it's the best Disney romp since *Snowball Express* two years earlier. Susan Clark, more usually seen in

ladylike roles, revels in her unexpected casting as Dusty, part-time stagecoach owner and full-time wildcat, who becomes involved with a footloose gambler (Bill Bixby), three orphan kids (the gang of the title), two incompetent outlaws (Don Knotts, Tim Conway) and a gang of desperados headed by Slim Pickens. Hard-core film fans will be delighted by the supporting cast which includes such stalwarts as David Wayne (as Clark's bombastic father), Marie Windsor, John McGiver and Iris Adrian. There's also the grizzled, melancholy Harry Morgan as the sheriff, who gets the film's best line when he tells Knotts and Conway: 'With you two, it's always "attempted" robbery!'

Apple Dumpling Gang Rides Again, The ⊙
1979, US, 88 mins, colour
Dir: Vincent McEveety
Stars: Tim Conway, Don Knotts, Tim Matheson
Rating: ★★

A broad Western farce from Disney, full of comic character actors who can be relied on to go over the top, like Jack Elam (as Big Mac), Kenneth Mars (as Woolly Bill) and Ruth Buzzi (as Tough Kate). Fish-eyed Don Knotts is rather funnier than his partner Tim Conway, but kids will enjoy the simple slapstick and the uncomplicated storyline and cheer as our goofy heroes ride off into the sagebrush sunset.

Appointment in Honduras ○
1953, US, 79 mins, colour
Dir: Jacques Tourneur
Stars: Glenn Ford, Ann Sheridan, Zachary Scott
Rating: ★★

Colourful thrills in Central America, brimming with revolutionary fervour at the turn of the century. The action, handsomely shot in Technicolor by Joseph Biroc, reinforces a novelettish story of an affair between one of the protagonists and the wife of an acquaintance. Strong performances by Glenn Ford and Ann Sheridan counter-balance the cliches in the script, but Zachary Scott is wasted in the role of the husband. Rodolfo Acosta and Jack Elam add bite and character to the cast.

Appointment in London ○
1952, UK, 96 mins, b/w
Dir: Philip Leacock

A

Stars: Dirk Bogarde, Dinah Sheridan, Bill Kerr, Bryan Forbes, Ian Hunter
Rating: ★★★

A war film which does for Bomber Command what *Angels One Five* did for the Spitfire boys – and does it just as well. Director Philip Leacock makes an excellent job of depicting the strain and stress that the bomber crews had to endure. The climactic raid is about the best thing of its kind seen on screen to that date, thanks partly to the bomber experts who were attached to the production unit, assigned the task of giving advice at every stage. Dirk Bogarde gives one of the best of his early performances as the young wing commander on the verge of cracking up.

Appointment with Danger ○
1949, US, 89 mins, b/w
Dir: Lewis Allen
Stars: Alan Ladd, Phyllis Calvert, Paul Stewart, Jan Sterling, Henry Morgan
Rating: ★★

At the height of her film career in Britain, Phyllis Calvert went to Hollywood to star with Alan Ladd in this Paramount thriller. The film, though not completely successful, has some crisp, tough dialogue, as well as an early appearance by Jack Webb, as a hired killer. It was three years before Webb began his famous *Dragnet* series on TV, and he was beginning to make a name for himself in prominent supporting roles, mostly as cunning, chicken-hearted crooks. Paul Stewart, that slim, steely-eyed purveyor of menace, plays his boss.

Appointment with Death ◖
1988, US, 108 mins, colour
Dir: Michael Winner
Stars: Peter Ustinov, Lauren Bacall, Carrie Fisher, John Gielgud
Rating: ★

Peter Ustinov stars once more as ace Belgian detective 'Hercuool Pwarow', as he pronounces it, but neither he nor glitz can lift the picture from an impression of little more than a routine whodunit. Michael Winner's direction is only lacklustre, the script and characterisations bland and there simply are not enough murders to sustain the interest of even the most avid Agatha Christie fan. Christie stories somehow induce even the best of actors to stand around stiffly and give stilted performances, as if they felt their chief function in the film was to behave suspiciously by sounding

vaguely unconvincing. Piper Laurie, though miscast as the ogress bumped off in the midst of the Palestinian desert, does have her moments.

Appointment with Venus ○
(aka: Island Rescue)
1951, UK, 89 mins, b/w
Dir: Ralph Thomas
Stars: David Niven, Glynis Johns, Kenneth More
Rating: ★★★

A delightful comedy, directed by Ralph Thomas, which has nothing to do with space opera but centres on a prize cow. It was scripted by Nicholas Phipps, who had earlier worked on some of the famous Anna Neagle romances of the Forties such as *Piccadilly Incident* and *Spring in Park Lane*. And two or three years after making *Appointment with Venus*, he and director Ralph Thomas collaborated again on the hilarious *Doctor in the House*. A capital trio of principals is supplemented by a splendid supporting cast which includes George Coulouris, Barry Jones, Noel Purcell and Bernard Lee.

April Fools, The ○
1969, US, 95 mins, colour
Dir: Stuart Rosenberg
Stars: Jack Lemmon, Catherine Deneuve, Peter Lawford, Jack Weston, Myrna Loy, Charles Boyer
Rating: ★★

Catherine Deneuve's international ventures have been consistently less successful than her films in her native France, and she's out of luck again with this forced and unbelievable romantic comedy that also suffers from being particularly modish, which dates it rather badly. A tremendous cast, though, is still worth watching, including Jack Lemmon, as professional and funny as ever, Myrna Loy, Charles Boyer, Sally Kellerman, Melinda Dillon, Peter Lawford, Jack Weston and Harvey Korman.

April in Paris ⊙ Ⓥ
1952, US, 101 mins, colour
Dir: David Butler
Stars: Doris Day, Ray Bolger, Claude Dauphin
Rating: ★★★

Frothy, light and witty musical romp. Doris Day and Ray Bolger don't exactly go together like Laurel and Hardy, but they do strike sparks in the film's best musical sequence, a riotous song-and-dance session in the galley of

an ocean liner. Day sings the title number and several more, while Bolger's effortless dancing (as a romantic leading man he's a strain) is a delight.

April Showers ○
1948, US, 94 mins, b/w
Dir: James V Kern
Stars: Jack Carson, Ann Sothern, Robert Alda
Rating: ★★

Typical Hollywood musical backstage drama of the Forties. Jack Carson and Ann Sothern lend their likeable personalities to the leading roles, and there are plenty of tunes from the era depicted (1912) to set you humming. Shot in black and white for reasons known only to the studio.

Arabesque ○
1966, US, 105 mins, colour
Dir: Stanley Donen
Stars: Gregory Peck, Sophia Loren, Alan Badel, Kieron Moore
Rating: ★★★

From the opening credits, it's plain that director Stanley Donen is prepared to resort to all the tricks in the cinematic trade to make this as rivetting a thriller as his earlier *Charade*. Donen's enthusiasm for making the best of his material lends pace and sustained interest to a rather fatuous tale about a university professor involved in sinister goings-on around a Middle East oil state. Gregory Peck is amusingly bewildered, if surprisingly tough, as the professor and Sophia Loren provides the glamorous mystery element in the plot. Perhaps the biggest mystery is how she manages to change her Dior dresses (sometimes in the same sequence) at a rate bordering on the miraculous. Good (but not that good), it makes relaxing entertainment.

Arabian Adventure ⊙
1979, UK, 98 mins, colour
Dir: Kevin Connor
Stars: Christopher Lee, Oliver Tobias
Rating: ★★

The Thief of Baghdad this isn't, but director Kevin Connor's movie is nonetheless a star-spangled exotic adventure complete with handsome prince, beautiful princess, a magic carpet and all manner of evil schemers and mechanical monsters, lavishly mounted and well photographed. Christopher Lee is suitably formidable as the dictator, Oliver Tobias makes a handsome prince, Mickey Rooney scurries and gibbers as the guardian of the sacred rose and beetle-browed Milo O'Shea glowers purposefully as the dictator's double-dealing minion. Look out for some joyous cameos from such cinematic luminaries as Elizabeth Welch, Art Malik (before his leap to stardom in *The Jewel in the Crown*), Peter Cushing, Capucine and John Ratzenberger, better known as know-all Cliff in TV's *Cheers*.

Arabian Nights ☉

1942, US, 86 mins, colour
Dir: John Rawlins
Stars: Jon Hall, Maria Montez, Leif Erickson, Sabu, John Qualen, Turhan Bey
Rating: ★★

Universal's follow-up to *Ali Baba and the Forty Thieves* finds the studio less happy with their control of the early Technicolor. The crowd and pitched-battle scenes are elaborate, but messy because director John Rawlins seems to have no proper control over colour contrasts (or crowds). The cast is full of fascinating people, including Leif Erickson and Thomas Gomez as the bad guys, Norwegian character actor John Qualen as Aladdin (!) and comedy stars Shemp Howard (later one of The Three Stooges) and Billy Gilbert in character roles.

Arachnophobia ◑ ⓥ

1990, US, 106 mins, colour
Dir: Frank Marshall
Stars: Jeff Daniels, Harley Jane Kozak, John Goodman, Julian Sands
Rating: ★★★

This is not the film to see if you're scared of spiders. In fact its disadvantage as a chiller is that it's nothing but spiders. One scene of spider scares may prove memorable in a story, but a complete film of them proves a touch monotonous. On the whole, though, this is a tense and exciting (if humourless) movie, especially at the end, when chief arachnophobe Jeff Daniels has to tackle the lethal insects in their lair. The spiders have a little help here from the special effects department, but it all makes for a thrilling final tableau. On the debit side, the film is dully scripted and directed with rather too much camera movement by *Indiana Jones* producer Frank Marshall. There's also lots of low-angle shots of people hanging around waiting to get bitten by spiders, but good performances – especially from Daniels and from

Harley Jane Kozak as his wife. John Goodman pops in towards the end as an insect exterminator with 'Bug-B-Ware' embroidered on his cap.

Arise My Love ○

1940, US, 113 mins, b/w
Dir: Mitchell Leisen
Stars: Claudette Colbert, Ray Milland, Walter Abel
Rating: ★★★

Claudette Colbert is elegantly at home in this freewheeling comedy-thriller. Splendidly directed by Mitchell Leisen, the film treads a delicate path between love, humour and war with considerable success. Charles Brackett and Billy Wilder sprinkle some sparkling lines in their script, several of them going to Walter Abel as the heroine's editor, who has his celebrated speech about not being happy at all.

Armed and Dangerous ◑ ⓥ

1986, US, 88 mins, colour
Dir: Mark L Lester
Stars: John Candy, Eugene Levy, Meg Ryan, Robert Loggia
Rating: ★★

Roly-poly US comedy actor John Candy always seemed too big for the material Hollywood provides him with. His films, notably *Uncle Buck*, *The Great Outdoors* and *Who's Harry Crumb?*, were usually little more than a series of chases and misunderstandings as his character blunders from one disaster to another, usually in a variety of outlandish male and female disguises. The formula is much the same here, with Candy as a sacked cop confronting the Mafia almost single-handedly. The most outrageous scene has him trussed up in a blue tuxedo with a ruffled shirt that makes his enormous bulk look like a wrapped Christmas present. The hit-and-miss script is by Harold Ramis, star and co-writer of *Ghost Busters*, and James Keach, brother of Stacy.

Army of Darkness: The Medieval Dead ● ⓥ

1992, US, 89 mins, colour
Dir: Sam Raimi
Stars: Bruce Campell, Embeth Davidtz, Marcus Gilbert, Ian Abercrombie
Rating: ★★

More literally a horror comic sprung to life than any episode of a *Creepshow* film, this is the third film in director

Sam Raimi's *Evil Dead* trilogy. This time, the medieval dead rise (and ride) as Bruce Campbell's Ash, sucked back in time to the 13th century, fails to recite the sacred words correctly in his quest for the Necronomicon (Book of the Dead) and raises all the old bones in the graveyard. Crudely acted and scripted, but with some invention and visual splendours, the film isn't actually as good as its excellent trailer makes it look. You can almost see the dialogue balloons as in the comics, but that doesn't make the words in them more than occasionally amusing. Still fans of such games as Demonworld, Dungeons and Dragons and Heroquest should relish this, while film buffs can groan at the dialogue and its delivery and congratulate themselves on spotting Bridget Fonda, who appears very briefly at the start.

Around the World in 80 Days ☉ ⓥ

1956, US, 167 mins, colour
Dir: Michael Anderson
Stars: David Niven, Robert Newton, Cantinflas, Shirley MacLaine, Charles Boyer, Ronald Colman
Rating: ★★★

Mike Todd's glistening film adaptation of Jules Verne's famous extravaganza was overwhelmingly voted Best Picture at the 1956 Oscar's ceremony. The screenplay, music and photography also took Academy Awards. More than 40 guest stars appear in cameo roles, and Robert Newton takes his last film role as the intrepid Inspector Fix.

Around the World Under the Sea ☉

1966, US, 117 mins, colour
Dir: Andrew Marton
Stars: Lloyd Bridges, Shirley Eaton, David McCallum, Keenan Wynn
Rating: ★★

David McCallum, then box-office hot from the *Man from Uncle* series, and Lloyd Bridges lead a fundamentally TV and B-Picture cast in this 'Boy's Own' saga of underwater testing for earthquakes. The real stars are the special effects.

Arouse and Beware
See: The Man from Dakota

Arrowhead ○

1953, US, 105 mins, colour
Dir: Charles Marquis Warren

A

Stars: Charlton Heston, Jack Palance, Katy Jurado, Brian Keith
Rating: ★★

A vigorous, well-photographed Cavalry versus Indians Western, climaxed by one of the best hand-to-hand fights ever seen on film, between Charlton Heston and Jack Palance, who give intense, muscle-ripping performances. *Arrowhead* was written and directed by Charles Marquis Warren, who has written many fine Western novels, including *Only the Valiant*.

Arthur ◐ ⓥ

1980, US, 97 mins, colour
Dir: Steve Gordon
Stars: Dudley Moore, Liza Minnelli, John Gielgud, Geraldine Firzgerald, Jill Eikenberry
Rating: ★★★

John Gielgud won an Oscar and Dudley Moore was nominated for one in this side-splitting comedy about a tiny, near-40, cosseted billionaire whose drunken, girl-laden life is menaced by a family who threaten to cut him off without a penny unless he marries a socially acceptable milk-and-water heiress. Heiress's father is a self-made homicidal maniac who will put a knife through Arthur if he doesn't sway up to the altar. So what's the poor little chap, who loves a sassy shoplifter, to do? The answer makes for a comedy that gleams with wisecracks. Moore perfectly captures a state of permanent inebriation, while Gielgud plainly relishes the butler whose tongue rolls deliciously round rude insults that belie his primness.

Arthur 2: On the Rocks ○ ⓥ

1988, US, 113 mins, colour
Dir: Bud Yorkin
Stars: Dudley Moore, Liza Minnelli, John Gielgud, Geraldine Fitzgerald, Jack Gilford
Rating: ★★

We'll say this for Dudley Moore's Arthur: it's nice to see him again, but he was a lot more fun when he was filthy rich. Not that there aren't quite a few fun moments in this sequel, but its real problem is that none of it is even remotely believable. It's not the situations and development, however. Characters themselves change quite suddenly, without the slightest justification. When we first meet Arthur, he's still rich, perennially tipsy and married to his Linda (still Liza Minnelli, who's the best thing in the

film when she's allowed to be). Then his ex-fiancée's dad does a deal (one of the film's many weak plotlines) which leaves Arthur penniless. 'Don't you feel a little relieved?' asks Liza. 'Yes,' gulps Dudley. 'Relieved of 750 million dollars.' Does Arthur take it all lying down? You bet. Face down in the gutter of life, until the ghost of his dead butler (John Gielgud) comes down to sort him out. Then Arthur does battle with his enemies in a finale that's just as unconvincing as everything else in the film.

Article 99 ● ⓥ

1991, US, 96 mins, colour
Dir: Howard Deutch
Stars: Ray Liotta, Kiefer Sutherland, Kathy Baker, Lea Thompson, Forest Whitaker, Eli Wallach
Rating: ★★★

Let's hear a cheer one more time for the good guys against harsh and self-serving authorities. And, despite a story that runs along as bumpily as a hospital trolley, the urge to watch the underdogs win sees this one through in an emotive conclusion. A slightly more serious sideshoot of *M*A*S*H* and *The Hospital*, the story centres on a forces veterans hospital where patients, if they can get treatment at all, are shunted out before they are ready, thanks to reams of red tape that bond all but the most maverick members of staff, led by rebel surgeon by Ray Liotta, a constant thorn in the side of administrator John Mahoney, who runs the hospital to his convenience and profit rather than those of the patients. Enter Kiefer Sutherland as the new surgeon on the block, add a dash of romance behind those operating doors, cap it all off with a mutiny after Liotta is framed and suspended and you have a surefire recipe that leaves you wishing the film had picked up its pace, and the body of its plot, a bit earlier on. Never mind, its heart (ouch, a reminder that there are some gruesome ops here) is in the right place.

Artists and Models ☉

1955, US, 109 mins, colour
Dir: Frank Tashlin
Stars: Dean Martin, Jerry Lewis, Shirley MacLaine, Dorothy Malone
Rating: ★★★

The zany touch of writer-director Frank Tashlin, responsible for some of Hollywood's most side-splitting comedies in the 1946-66 period, is stamped all over this Dean Martin and

Jerry Lewis extravaganza. Lewis excels as the nincompoop whose dreams are used by cartoonist Martin for adventure ideas. The supporting cast glitters with talent, including Eddie Mayehoff, superior stooge of so many Martin and Lewis romps, Shirley MacLaine (then right at the start of her career), Anita Ekberg, Jack Elam, Dorothy Malone, Kathleen Freeman and Eva Gabor.

Ashanti ◐ ⓥ

1979, US, 117 mins, colour
Dir: Richard Fleischer
Stars: Michael Caine, Peter Ustinov, Beverly Johnson, Omar Sharif, Rex Harrison
Rating: ★

Top model Beverly Johnson made her screen debut as Michael Caine's wife in this pot-boiler about African slave-traders. Peter Ustinov and Omar Sharif go through familiar characterisations as the villains, while Rex Harrison and William Holden have little more than cameo roles. The action is in the safe hands of veteran director Richard Fleischer, and fans of vintage films will identify the swarthily portly figure of Eric Pohlmann in one of his last film performances.

Ash Wednesday ◐

1973, US, 90 mins, colour
Dir: Larry Peerce
Stars: Elizabeth Taylor, Henry Fonda, Helmut Berger, Keith Baxter
Rating: ★

A film for the very rich. With a subtler script, it could well have been made 40 years earlier with tremendous success. Elizabeth Taylor is the woman who undergoes cosmetic surgery – the operation scenes are dauntingly painful. Henry Fonda is her husband, and he behaves like a man who knows he's fighting a losing battle with the script, but is still determined to act everyone off the screen. He does.

Ask a Policeman ☉

1939, UK, 82 mins, b/w
Dir: Marcel Varnel
Stars: Will Hay, Graham Moffatt, Moore Marriott
Rating: ★★★

It's an idyllic life for Sgt Dudfoot, Albert and Harbottle (Will Hay, Graham Moffatt and Moore Marriott). They are the three policemen charged with protecting the village of Turnbotham

Round from crime. But there hasn't been a crime for ten years. Pressure from the Chief Constable forces them to try to drum up a bit of business. Although it's showing its age a bit now, this delightfully dotty comedy is one of Will Hay's best and is still good for a chuckle or two.

As Long as They're Happy ○
1955, UK, 91 mins, colour
Dir: J Lee Thompson
Stars: Jack Buchanan, Janette Scott, Jean Carson
Rating: ★★★

Made at a time when the major British studios, Rank and Associated-British, were spreading their musical wings and tentatively imitating Hollywood, this is a good-natured romp with tuneful songs and vigorous choreography. Jean Carson and Janette Scott give vivacious performances, while Jack Buchanan as their harassed father (he had also starred in the stage version) is as suave and debonair as ever. Guest stars include Diana Dors and Norman Wisdom and the frolics (satirising the escapades of a 'crying' crooner) are nicely photographed in Eastman Colour by Gilbert Taylor.

Asphalt Jungle, The ○ ⓥ
1950, US, 112 mins, b/w
Dir: John Huston
Stars: Sterling Hayden, Louis Calhern, Sam Jaffe, Jean Hagen
Rating: ★★★★

John Huston's classic crime caper is a taut, realistic thriller that concentrates on the intricate plotting of a jewel robbery and the subsequent undoing of the thieves. First-rate roles for Sterling Hayden, Louis Calhern and Sam Jaffe are rewarded with performances to match. Marilyn Monroe makes an impression in a small but showy 'bit'. Remade three times and copied countless others, the film remains a model of its kind.

Asphyx, The ●
1973, UK, 99 mins, colour
Dir: Peter Newbrook
Stars: Robert Powell, Robert Stephens, Jane Lapotaire
Rating: ★

Although it features such distinguished British performers as Robert Powell, Robert Stephens and Jane Lapotaire, this horror film about a man who tries to trap the spirit of death does take some believing, even by the standards

of this extravagant genre. The beginning, with its glimpses into Victorian 'psychological research', is fascinating.

Assassin, The ● ⓥ
(aka: Point of No Return)
1993, US, 108 mins, colour
Dir: John Badham
Stars: Bridget Fonda, Gabriel Byrne, Dermot Mulroney, Anne Bancroft, Harvey Keitel, Miguel Ferrer
Rating: ★★★

Slightly better than the French original, this remake of *La Femme Nikita* has much the same vices and virtues. It starts strongly, sags in the middle, but fires on all cylinders again in the last reel. In the Hollywood version, it's thin lipped Bridget Fonda as a more acceptably vulnerable 'heroine', a criminal junkie who kills a policeman in a drug induced haze during a narcotics raid shoot-out between her cohorts and and the police. Sentenced to death, and seemingly executed, she wakes up to find herself locked away but targeted for a secret government programme that trains assassins to melt into the world, and carry out their occasional assignments at the ring of a telephone. Fonda is on the money in the training sequences, but mid-section, which has her falling for photographer Dermot Mulroney, is not only soppy but three-quarters redundant. Byrne is solid, though, as the 'trainer' who develops a sneaking regard (and desire) for his protege. Harvey Keitel makes a brief guest appearance at the end as the 'cleaner' called in to eliminate everyone when Fonda's toughest job goes awry.

Assassination Bureau, The ○
1968, UK, 110 mins, colour
Dir: Basil Dearden
Stars: Oliver Reed, Diana Rigg, Telly Savalas, Curt Jurgens
Rating: ★★★

This is a pleasingly idiotic, mildly funny comedy-thriller about the attempts of an inept group of assassins to murder their own boss back in 1906. Diana Rigg, in her first big cinema role, plays a militant feminist reporter out to scoop the world. Brilliant writer Wolf Mankowitz added some biting dialogue to the original screenplay which was written by the film's producer, Michael Relph. Basically it is a welcome attempt to hark back to the Ealing style of somewhat sly comedy, and certainly Oliver

Reed's witty performance in the lead suggests that you shouldn't believe a word of it.

Assault ◐
1970, UK, 91 mins, colour
Dir: Sidney Hayers
Stars: Suzy Kendall, Frank Finlay, Lesley Anne-Down, Freddie Francis
Rating: ★★★

The hunt for a maniac who is raping and killing schoolgirls is the harsh subject of this grim detection drama with a well-concealed surprise ending. Frank Finlay plays the investigating police superintendent and Suzy Kendall is the schoolteacher who places her own life in jeopardy in an attempt to uncover the identity of the murderer. The film was made by Stanley Hayers, a specialist in thrillers and chillers, who makes suspenseful use of the camera-as-murderer technique.

Assault on a Queen ○
1966, US, 106 mins, colour
Dir: Jack Donohue
Stars: Frank Sinatra, Tony Franciosa, Virna Lisi
Rating: ★

This sloppy adventure film about a group of hijackers who aim to hold up the *Queen Mary* on the high seas, is an unusual movie to come from the pen of Rod Serling, who wrote *Seven Days in May* and *Planet of the Apes*. Here Serling settles for pure escapist entertainment, without a hidden meaning in sight. Alas, the results resemble a Crosby-Hope-Lamour *Road* film without the laughs. Frank Sinatra, Virna Lisi and Tony Franciosa do little more than go through the motions in this tired enterprise.

Assault on Precinct 13 ● ⓥ
1976, US, 90 mins, colour
Dir: John Carpenter
Stars: Austin Stoker, Laurie Zimmer, Darwin Joston
Rating: ★★★

A super-tense story of a siege directed by John Carpenter, who later made *Halloween*, *The Fog* and *The Thing*, but whose first hit this was. There's just no let-up in this well-written film about a police station in a ghetto district which finds itself surrounded by gangs of heavily-armed youths. The attackers have sworn blood vengeance on the killer of one of their members, now inside the station. The catch is that the station, due for demolition, is

A

manned only by a skeleton staff. Carpenter milks the maximum suspense from the subsequent attempts by the police and their prisoners to escape or survive. Thanks to drily humorous dialogue, all the characters come across as real and human, eliciting our sympathy in their desperate attempts to avoid seemingly inevitable ends.

Assignment K ○
1967, UK, 97 mins, colour
Dir: Val Guest
Stars: Stephen Boyd, Camilla Sparv, Leo McKern, Michael Redgrave
Rating: ★★

Routine British espionage thriller from the prolific hand of writer/ director Val Guest. Leads Stephen Boyd and Camilla Sparv play with only marginal interest, and the sparks only fly from the supporting players, notably Leo McKern, Michael Redgrave and John Alderton. But the film's technical credits are first-rate, especially the crisp Technicolor camerawork by Ken Hodges, who makes the most out of the film's interesting variety of locations.

Assignment to Kill ○
1967, US, 102 mins, colour
Dir: Sheldon Reynolds
Stars: Patrick O'Neal, Joan Hackett, Herbert Lom
Rating: ★★

Noted radio producer Sheldon Reynolds made only two movies, of which this is the second (the other was *Foreign Intrigue* with Robert Mitchum in 1956). Patrick O'Neal stars as an insurance investigator and Sir John Gielgud makes one of his then-rare film appearances in a supporting role, although one which assumes considerable importance towards the end of the film. Like *Foreign Intrigue*, this is a pleasingly literate and well-plotted thriller. The screenplay, written by Reynolds himself, is more than usually intelligent and makes room for some abrasively amusing exchanges between O'Neal and that attractive actress Joan Hackett, who once again proves herself a talent to be reckoned with in the Jane Fonda/ Katharine Hepburn style. Oscar Homolka's all too brief appearance as a cunning police inspector is also a nice bonus to this intriguing film.

Assisi Underground, The ○ Ⓥ
1984, US, 115 mins, colour
Dir: Alexander Ramati

Stars: Ben Cross, James Mason, Irene Papas, Maximilian Schell, Karl-Heinz Hackl
Rating: ★★

Brilliantly photographed in colour by Giuseppe Rotunno, this is in some ways a bigger-scale version of the 1960 British film *Conspiracy of Hearts*, in that it deals with the efforts of the religious communities in Italian towns in World War Two to help Jewish refugees escape from the Nazis. The treatment is resolutely superficial, but Ben Cross, James Mason (in his last film) and especially German actor Karl-Heinz Hackl do their best to make the characters spring to life.

Astonished Heart, The ○
1949, UK, 89 mins, b/w
Dir: Antony Darnborough
Stars: Noel Coward, Celia Johnson, Margaret Leighton
Rating: ★★

If you don't like this unusually literate romantic comedy, it should be easy to find a scapegoat. For Noel Coward not only stars in it, he also wrote the screenplay and composed the background music into the bargain. It was in fact the last film of which the Master was really in charge.

Asylum ●
1972, UK, 92 mins, colour
Dir: Roy Ward Baker
Stars: Robert Powell, Charlotte Rampling, Peter Cushing, Britt Ekland, Patrick Magee, Herbert Lom
Rating: ★★★

Compilation horror movies from Amicus Films abounded in the British cinema of the Sixties and Seventies, but this is about the best – and has suitably sombre performances from Robert Powell and Patrick Magee at its centre, a framework story more chillingly effective than any other Amicus film. The direction by Roy Ward Baker is calculated to be bad news for anyone trying to give up biting their nails; and a good cast, including Herbert Lom (in fine form as a maker of living dolls), Peter Cushing and Charlotte Rampling, gives their director grim-faced support. Excellent colour work and lighting effects by Denys Coop also play a prominent role in evoking the horror.

At Close Range ● Ⓥ
1985, US, 115 mins, colour
Dir: James Foley
Stars: Sean Penn, Christopher Walken, Mary Stuart Masterson, Millie Perkins, Christopher Penn, Candy Clark
Rating: ★

Brat-packer Sean Penn's promising career looked set to take off with this violent downbeat father/son drama. The omens were good. The theme song was performed by Madonna. And the script presented Penn for once with a well-drawn character, a rough kid drawn towards a world of violence by his murdering crook of a father (yet another chilling, smiling psychopath from Christopher Walken), but held teetering on the edge by his love for a spunky 16-year-old girl (a rare tiresome performance from Mary Stuart Masterson). The bad news is partly the jerky direction of James Foley, partly dialogue which seems to have been subjected to some primitive form of recording, with Tennessee accents an additional problem. Instead of letting the situations speak for themselves, Foley has his actors laboriously spell things out, so some scenes seem to drag on for an eternity. It is, in short, a film that one way or another sorely tries our patience. Such reliable screen veterans as Millie Perkins and Candy Clark have little to do here but stand around and watch.

At Gunpoint ○
(aka: Gunpoint)
1955, US, 81 mins, colour
Dir: Alfred Werker
Stars: Fred MacMurray, Dorothy Malone, Walter Brennan, Tommy Rettig
Rating: ★★★

One of several sturdy Westerns Fred MacMurray made in the Fifties. This one bristles with the tension engendered by the casting of MacMurray as a mild storekeeper whose accidental shooting of a bank robber makes him the town outcast when the outlaw's gang threatens to come back and take revenge. Excellent support from Walter Brennan, Dorothy Malone, surly Skip Homeier and little Tommy Rettig. Rich pastures for Western fans.

Atlantic City ○
1944, US, 87 mins, b/w
Dir: Ray McCarey
Stars: Brad Taylor, Constance Moore
Rating: ★★

Hollywood musicals were never more popular than with wartime audiences, and 36 of them were made in 1944 alone. Many, like this one, used slim storylines and forgettable leading players, but boosted their chances at the box-office by injecting 'guest spots' from well-known singers and musicians of the day. Those featured here included Paul Whiteman and his orchestra, Louis Armstrong and his orchestra, Jerry Colonna, Buck and Bubbles, Dorothy Dandridge and Belle Baker. Singer-actress Constance Moore is a personable and graceful leading lady, but little more was ever heard of her co-star, Brad Taylor, who turned up decades later in a list of 'lost' actors whose whereabouts no one had been able to trace.

Atlantic City ◑ ⓥ
1980, France/Canada, 104 mins, colour
Dir: Louis Malle
Stars: Burt Lancaster, Susan Sarandon, Michel Piccoli
Rating: ★★

Louis Malle's drama about small-time crooks with big-time dreams finds the director on foreign soil, but still getting fine performances from his actors, who include Burt Lancaster, splendidly cast as the ageing gangster, Susan Sarandon and Michel Piccoli. Despite winning five Oscar nominations, including Best Actor (Lancaster), Best Actress (the delightful Sarandon), Best Director and Best Picture, the movie emerged from the year's Oscar ceremonies empty-handed and, in spite of its carefully conceived style and deeply-etched portraits, it does leave a faintly unpleasant aftertaste.

Atlantis, the Lost Continent ☉
1961, US, 90 mins, colour
Dir: George Pal
Stars: Anthony Hall, Joyce Taylor, John Dall
Rating: ★

A lurid and cheap-looking George Pal mythical fantasy. For John Dall (here the villain) it was a long way down from Hitchcock's *Rope* of 12 years earlier, in which he was one of the murderers. The dialogue is as stiff as the scenery.

At Long Last Love ○
1975, US, 118 mins, colour
Dir: Peter Bogdanovich

Stars: Burt Reynolds, Cybill Shepherd, Madeline Kahn
Rating: ★

Peter Bogdanovich's tribute to the Fred-and-Ginger musicals of the Thirties follows Hollywood's still-current theory of hiring actors who can sing and dance a bit rather than singers and dancers who can act a bit. And Burt Reynolds, Cybill Shepherd, Madeline Kahn and Duilio Del Prete all show some nice touches – especially when they let themselves go a little. For all that, they remain actors in unfamiliar guise, all of their deficiences exposed by the glaring spotlight of the cinema. But the Cole Porter score to this scatty romp is pure delight.

At Play in the Fields of the Lord ● ⓥ
1991, US, 187 mins, colour
Dir: Hector Babenco
Stars: Tom Berenger, Daryl Hannah, Kathy Bates, Aidan Quinn, John Lithgow, Tom Waits
Rating: ★★

Hollywood was going green in a big way in the early Nineties, but this contribution to the cycle is about as weird and studied as you might expect from director Hector Babenco, who made *Kiss of the Spider Woman*. A visually stunning drama about the fate of a tribe of Amazonian Indians, Babenco's film follows their destruction through the well-meaning but deadly interference of a group of American missionaries and a half Cheyenne Indian (Tom Berenger, down in the jungle yet again) who decides to go native and live in their community. A thoughtful but massively overlong epic which does pick up considerably towards the end to help drive its message home.

At Sword's Point
See: Sons of the Musketeers

Attack! ○
1956, US, 107 mins, b/w
Dir: Robert Aldrich
Stars: Jack Palance, Eddie Albert, Lee Marvin, Robert Strauss, Richard Jaekel
Rating: ★★★

A look at the cast suggests that this tough, bitter war drama is another *Dirty Dozen*. And it has the same director – Robert Aldrich. There the similarity ends. *Attack!* is a war film so frank and un-American that when it was shown at the Venice festival, a US

ambassador walked out in protest. Eddie Albert dominates the film with a tremendously impressive performance as the cowardly captain, even over Jack Palance's snarling ferocity as the revengeful lieutenant.

Attack of the 50ft Woman ◑
1958, US, 72 mins, b/w
Dir: Nathan Hertz
Stars: Allison Hayes, William Hudson
Rating: ★

Never mind the quality – see the height! Bizarre science-fiction nonsense which appears on many all-time worst film lists, with Allison Hayes as neurotic Nancy who meets a giant alien in the desert. Having pinched her priceless diamond, the monster makes her radioactive, which causes her to grow and grow and eventually go on the rampage. Remade in 1993 with Daryl Hannah!

At the Circus ☉
1939, US, 87 mins, b/w
Dir: Edward Buzzell
Stars: Groucho Marx, Chico, Marx, Harpo Marx, Margaret Dumont, Eve Arden
Rating: ★★★

The film in which Groucho Marx, as J Cheever Loophole, sang 'Lydia the Tattooed Lady' long before it was immortalised by the Muppets. He also woos statuesque Margaret Dumont for the penultimate time. 'That night,' he tells her, 'I drank champagne from your slipper – two quarts. It would have held more but you were wearing inner soles.' Memorable moments include the search of the strongman's apartment, ending in a snowstorm of feathers, and the finale, with an entire orchestra being towed out to sea still playing the Prelude to Act III of Wagner's *Lohengrin*.

At the Earth's Core ○ ⓥ
1976, UK, 90 mins, colour
Dir: Kevin Connor
Stars: Doug McClure, Peter Cushing, Caroline Munro
Rating: ★★★

Another ripping yarn from the makers of *The Land That Time Forgot* and *The People That Time Forgot* which, like them, is based on a novel by Edgar Rice Burroughs. Here the burrowing is done by Peter Cushing's splendid 'iron mole' and more conventional muscle is supplied by the amiable hero, Doug McClure. Cushing steals the film with a hugely enjoyable performance as an absent minded

A

Professor Challenger-like scientist who is delighted to be at the centre of the earth and cheerfully unaware of the dangers surrounding him. While the special effects are sometimes shaky and most of the monsters are all too clearly men in rubber suits, the zest of the performances and Kevin Connor's brisk direction make for a light hearted slice of adventure hokum.

Attila the Hun ○
1955, Italy/France, 83 mins, colour
Dir: Pietro Francisci
Stars: Anthony Quinn, Sophia Loren
Rating: ★★

With a cast of Hollywood (Anthony Quinn, Eduardo Ciannelli), Italian (Sophia Loren, Ettore Manni), French (Henri Vidal, Claude Laydu) and Greek (Irene Papas) players, producers Carlo Ponti and Dino De Laurentiis were heavily reliant on the dubbing for the international version of this, one of their first big epics. The 'cast of thousands' of fur-clad extras looks impressive thundering across the screen and Quinn plays the title role, according to one contemporary reviewer, 'with simple, uncomplicated vigour'.

At War with the Army ⊙
1950, US, 100 mins, b/w
Dir: Hal Walker
Stars: Dean Martin, Jerry Lewis, Polly Bergen, Mike Kellin
Rating: ★

Paramount's first solo vehicle for Dean Martin and Jerry Lewis set them on a fabulous seven-year roll of film success before they went their separate ways. Their stereotypes were already established: Martin the smooth-talking girl-chaser, Lewis as what, in today's parlance, would be called the nerd. Not their most wonderful: there are still some rough edges, but a few mildly funny comedy routines in the stagy and stodgy whole. The film's big song hit was 'The Navy Gets the Gravy and the Army Gets the Beans'.

Audrey Rose ● ⓥ
1977, US, 113 mins, colour
Dir: Robert Wise
Stars: Marsha Mason, Anthony Hopkins, John Beck
Rating: ★★

Be prepared for two highly charged hours with this gripping drama about a 12-year-old girl called Ivy who's possessed by the soul of another (Audrey Rose of the title) who died the mo-

ment Ivy was born. It's one of those films about children that is definitely not for young viewers. The possessed girl is most convincingly played by a young lady called Susan Swift, and her agonised parents by Marsha Mason and John Beck. A pivotal role goes to Britain's popular Anthony Hopkins as the dead girl's distraught father who insists on communicating with his daughter through Ivy. While director Robert Wise won Oscars for *The Sound of Music* and *West Side Story*, he is at his best with sinister subjects, of which *Audrey Rose* is a good example.

Auntie Mame ○
1958, US, 143 mins, colour
Dir: Morton DaCosta
Stars: Rosalind Russell, Forrest Tucker, Coral Browne
Rating: ★★

Re-creating her smash Broadway performance as Auntie Mame, the high-class Bohemian, Rosalind Russell won the fourth and last Best Actress Oscar nomination of her career. She was a hit all over again as big-spending society hostess Mame Dennis, who believes that 'Life is a banquet – and most poor suckers are starving to death'. Not even the Depression that wipes out her fortune can depress Mame for long. Infinitely superior to the musical remake, with Lucille Ball and Bea Arthur, this film was tailor-made for Miss Russell's talents and she delivers 110 per cent. Melbourne-born actress Coral Browne, whose later life inspired the hit Alan Bennett-scripted *An Englishman Abroad*, provides solid support as Mame's alcoholic actress friend, Vera Charles.

Aunt Julia and the Scriptwriter ○ ⓥ
1990, US, 107 mins, colour
Dir: Jon Amiel
Stars: Peter Falk, Barbara Hershey, Keanu Reeves, Patricia Clarkson, Bull McCutcheon
Rating: ★★★

This is for sure no ordinary film. Set in 1951, in the world of radio, its combination of romance, lunacy and bitter-sweet humour centres on Pedro (Peter Falk), a brilliant, controversial soap-opera writer, who feeds on the intrigues of those about him, and creates ratings and havoc at the same time. His number one target for material at the WXBU station in New Orleans is rookie newswriter Martin (Keanu Reeves) and his infatuation for

his sort-of aunt Julia, 15 years his senior (Barbara Hershey, at 43 passing for 36 with years to spare). The soap opera that results on radio, riddled with incest, hatred of rats and persecution of Albanians, is ludicrous enough to be fun, although it wears a bit thin towards the end when the whole enterprise threatens to turn sour. Falk frequently verges on being the whole show, but Hershey and Reeves are good enough to make you care about their romance, and the distinguished 'soap' cast includes Elizabeth McGovern, Peter Gallagher, Hope Lange and John Larroquette.

Author! Author! ○
1982, US, 110 mins, colour
Dir: Arthur Hiller
Stars: Al Pacino, Dyan Cannon, Tuesday Weld, Alan King
Rating: ★★

A marriage-go-round comedy about a Broadway playwright (Al Pacino) trying to tie up all the loose ends of two failed marriages, cope with various troublesome offspring and deliver urgently needed re-writes for his latest play. It seeks to dig deeper than Neil Simon, whose territory this clearly is, but emerges as a bland confection. It is left to the sparkling playing of Dyan Cannon and Tuesday Weld, as the women in his life, to give the film a vitality that's sadly missing in the script. The career of Pacino was really on the skids at this time, following the tedious love story *Bobby Deerfield* and the seedy murder thriller *Cruising*, with the mega-turkey *Revolution* just around the corner. It would be another seven years before *Sea of Love* put him back in the ranks of Hollywood's leading men for keeps.

Autumn Sonata ◐
1978, Sweden, 97 mins, colour
Dir: Ingmar Bergman
Stars: Ingrid Bergman, Liv Ullmann
Rating: ★★

The great Ingrid Bergman deliberately made this first collaboration with her distinguished namesake, director Ingmar Bergman, her last work for the cinema. In it, she plays a pianist whose almost total absence on concert tours has left her daughter (Liv Ullmann) an emotional cripple. When the prodigal mother returns after the death of her lost lover, Ullmann lets her have it in a verbal battering that goes on all through the night. This grim, unrelenting tirade is harrowingly well enacted by the two stars. It's sad that two people with so much in common refuse to stop looking for a fight with each other, especially the daughter – and the film may strike chords in our own lives that we'd rather leave unstruck. But, as a portrait of two fine actresses digging deep into their own emotional resources to play their parts, it has rarely been bettered.

Avalanche ○
1978, US, 91 mins, colour
Dir: Corey Allen
Stars: Rock Hudson, Mia Farrow
Rating: ★

As disaster movies go, this one is pretty disastrous – although making the avalanche scene at the end is a triumph of editing over matter. A number of major stars battle gamely against prevailing wintry conditions. And they all read the script?

Avalanche Express ○
1979, US, 88 mins, colour
Dir: Mark Robson
Stars: Robert Shaw, Lee Marvin, Linda Evans, Maximilian Schell, Horst Buchholz
Rating: ★★★

The late Mark Robson – he died just before this film was finished and it was completed by Monte Hellman – must have thought he was back at his old studio, RKO, in its final mid-Fifties years while making *Avalanche Express*. For this fast and frenetic thriller has all the hallmarks of the colourful SuperScope 'cheapies' that the studio churned out in its bid to survive. A top Russian defector must be got to America by transcontinental express – for no other apparent reason than it makes for an incident-filled story. It's what used to be called a cloak-and-dagger: the train exteriors, as the express rushes through nigh-time, snowbound country, arouse some atmosphere, the regulation shootouts provide some routine excitement and the avalanche scenes are quite spectacular. The acting is barely serviceable, and Robert Shaw stridently overplays – but Jack Cardiff's thoughtful colour photography is a delight to the eye, and adds to the enjoyment of the film.

Avanti! ◑
1972, US, 144 mins, colour
Dir: Billy Wilder
Stars: Jack Lemmon, Juliet Mills
Rating: ★★★

Billy Wilder's last completely successful comedy, *Avanti!* neatly combines the two halves of Jack Lemmon's screen persona – frenzied young comic and angst-ridden middle-aged man – in the story of a dyspeptic millionaire seduced by continental sunshine, his late father's lifestyle and the charms of Juliet Mills. She's never been better, more attractive or more relaxed in this fun-filled comedy whose only problem is a touch of overlength.

Awakenings ◑ ⓥ
1990, US, 117 mins, colour
Dir: Penny Marshall
Stars: Robert De Niro, Robin Williams, Julie Kavner, John Heard, Penelope Ann Miller, Max Von Sydow
Rating: ★★★

In 1969, under a new treatment, a dozen patients who had been catatonic since surviving encephalitis 30 to 40 years earlier, were revived temporarily by a caring doctor and a new drug. This heartwarming and heartbreaking film is their story. It focuses on the first patient to be 'awakened' – Leonard, miraculously and agonizingly re-created by Robert De Niro. Dramatically, the film is hampered by the fact that its high-point, the 're-awakening' itself, occurs half-way through the story and the downbeat aspects set in from then on. But there is still much to admire and touch the emotions throughout the film. Robin Williams captures exactly the withdrawn nature of the neurologist who finds it easier to communicate with a catatonic patient than with his fellow man. Julia Kavner, as his faithful nurse, and John Heard as the sceptical chief of medicine, are also excellent, and there are painfully poignant portraits from many of those playing the other patients, whose reflex reactions to things being thrown at them first alert Williams and his staff that there is still a functioning mind inside the helpless body.

Away All Boats! ○
1956, US, 118 mins, colour
Dir: Joseph Pevney
Stars: Jeff Chandler, George Nader, Julie Adams
Rating: ★★

Universal-International made mainly double-feature fodder for the mass market in the Fifties, but this was one of their most prestigious projects, based on a best-selling book by Kenneth M Dodson and featuring half the studio's contract stars. But the studio was so used to making colourful, shallow entertainments at this period that *Away All Boats!* comes out as much like any other assembly-line action film, under the uninspired direction of Joseph Pevney. Jeff Chandler is well cast as the aloof naval commander trying to weld his inexperienced crew into a fighting unit, and the supporting cast is pretty interesting, including George Nader, David Janssen, Julie Adams, Richard Boone, Keith Andes, ex-Tarzan Lex Barker and future Tarzan Jock Mahoney. Clint Eastwood, here in his earliest Hollywood days, also has a miniscule role but you'll have to keep your eyes peeled to spot him.

Awful Truth, The ○
1937, US, 92 mins, b/w
Dir: Leo McCarey
Stars: Cary Grant, Irene Dunne, Ralph Bellamy, Robert Allen
Rating: ★★★

A very funny romantic comedy. Screenwriter Vina Delmar, with assistance from director Leo McCarey himself, took a 15-years-old stage farce and brought it up as fresh as paint. Cary Grant and Irene Dunne play with pleasure and consummate timing as the divorcing couple who are clearly going to survive any amount of madcap antics and hair's-breadth escapes from embarrassment to get back together in the end. As those who nearly come between them, Ralph Bellamy and Molly Lamont, the latter an English actress who never quite made Hollywood stardom, play difficult roles with considerable panache.

AWOL
See: Lionheart

A

B

Babe, The ○ ⓥ
1992, US, 115 mins, colour
Dir: Arthur Hiller
Stars: John Goodman, Kelly McGillis, Bruce Boxleitner, J C Quinn, Trini Alvarado, Peter Donat
Rating: ★★★

George Herman 'Babe' Ruth is one of America's greatest sporting legends, a burly baseball hero who also had a passion for wine, women and food. Thankfully this old-fashioned but gritty biopic (which never saw the light of day in British cinemas) doesn't completely whitewash the off-field life of the great man. *Roseanne* star John Goodman fills out every inch of the big basher, truculently dominating the film, and, thanks to great make-up, is a dead ringer for the Babe too. Kelly McGillis is quietly competent as Ruth's second wife. You don't have to be a complete baseball nut to enjoy this film — but it does help. For that kind of fan, at least, *The Babe* hits a home run.

Babes in Arms ⊙
1939, US, 93 mins, b/w
Dir: Busby Berkeley
Stars: Mickey Rooney, Judy Garland
Rating: ★★★

This is probably the original 'Hey kids, let's put on a show' musical. Mickey Rooney and Judy Garland star in a fast and furious piece of fun based rather loosely on the original Rodgers and Hart stage show of the same name. Rooney dominates the whole picture; he's five feet of pure energy and eagerness. To a generation brought up on how to be cool and laconic, such in-your-face cheerfulness can doubtless be deeply irritating. Still, there's no denying the lad's talent and energy. Rumour had it that Garland had trouble keeping up with Rooney and she was already swallowing pills like they were Smarties. The exuberance of the whole thing is infectious, though, with Busby Berkeley weaving his directorial magic to create a box office smash.

Babes in Toyland ⊙
(aka: March of the Wooden Soldiers)
1934, US, 73 mins, b/w
Dir: Charles Rogers
Stars: Stan Laurel, Oliver Hardy, Charlotte Henry
Rating: ★★★★

This magical fantasy was said to have been one of Oliver Hardy's favourite films; he and Stan portray Dum and Dee, who work at the toy factory, and Charlotte Henry, who plays Bo-Peep, was also Alice in the original film of *Alice in Wonderland*. The toytown settings are quite fantastic, and the land of the villainous bogeymen, who live down a well, is a really imaginative creation, without being too frightening for today's tough-guy kids — who will also appreciate the excitement of the final battle between the hairy bogeymen, and Stan's army of life-size toy soldiers. The villain is played by Henry Kleinbach who, as Henry Brandon, starred in the cinema hit *When the North Wind Blows* 40 years later.

Babes in Toyland ⊙
1961, US, 105 mins, colour
Dir: Jack Donohue
Stars: Ray Bolger, Tommy Sands, Annette Funicello
Rating: ★★

Though it's not as good as the Laurel and Hardy original (what could be?) of Victor Herbert's fairytale operetta, there were few brighter, more colourful films in the whole of the decade than this Disney version. Henry Calvin and Gene Sheldon take Stan and Ollie's roles, Tommy Sands and Annette Funicello (here billed as 'Annette') are attractive leads with decent singing voices, and Ray Bolger makes one of his infrequent film appearances as the villainous Barnaby. The camera trickery is ahead of its time and the toy soldiers' attack at the end gives splendid value. Bland, perhaps, but never dull.

Babes on Broadway ⊙
1941, US, 118 mins, b/w
Dir: Busby Berkeley
Stars: Mickey Rooney, Judy Garland, Richard Quine, Fay Bainter
Rating: ★★★

This was to have been a three-star musical, but 20th Century-Fox wouldn't loan Shirley Temple to MGM as the third prong of this Judy Garland-Mickey Rooney fiesta and so a fascinating idea never materialised. Virginia Weidler takes the Temple role, Garland and Rooney prove they can keep the show afloat by themselves and the songs include 'FDR Jones' and the Oscar-nominated 'How About You?' It was an immensely popular film with its wartime public.

Baby Boom ○ ⓥ
1987, US, 103 mins, colour
Dir: Charles Shyer
Stars: Diane Keaton, Harold Ramis, Sam Shepard, Sam Wanamaker, James Spader
Rating: ★★★

One of the warmest, least complicated and most likeable of Diane Keaton's performances. She has never looked better, either, than here, playing a fearsome businesswoman nicknamed 'The Tiger Lady', who is all at sea when suddenly lumbered with her dead cousin's baby. Survive a first half hour that's alternately daft and embarrassing, in fact, and you're in for a treat. Just when the film seems about to become sloppy and sentimental in the second half, it really picks up its skirts and flies, just as Keaton does from the city. Usurped at work by a young pretender (James Spader at his smarmiest), she high-tails it for the hills, buying a mansion in the country that proves, behind its lovely facade, to be as rot-ridden as the one Tom Hanks bought in *The Money Pit*. Subsequent developments are not only very enjoyable, but quite in keeping with the character's abilities as a dynamic business lady. Sunny and funny.

Baby Doll ● ⓥ
1956, US, 114 mins, b/w
Dir: Elia Kazan
Stars: Carroll Baker, Karl Malden, Eli Wallach, Mildred Dunnock
Rating: ★★★

When this explosive and provocative drama was first released in the mid-Fifties, *Time* magazine claimed it as 'just possibly the dirtiest American picture ever legally exhibited' and the Catholic Legion of Decency condemned it for 'dwelling upon carnal suggestiveness'. Compared to Hollywood's sexual excesses of later times, that condemnation now looks a little OTT but there is still no denying the power of some of the sexual imagery here, particularly a torrid love scene on a swing. Without one kiss exchanged between Carroll Baker and Eli Wallach, there is more heat coming off the screen than from a roaring coal fire. The Oscar-nominated screenplay was adapted for the screen by Tennessee Williams from *27 Wagons Full of Cotton*, his big stage success of the previous year, and rarely has the American Deep South been portrayed as more depressing or sleazy. The film also garnered Oscar nominations for star Baker (in only her second film) as the under-age and over-developed wife who stirs the sexual embers in wily Sicilian Wallach; Mildred Dunnock as Aunt Rose Comfort; and Boris Kaufman's handsome black-and-white photography.

Baby Face ○
1933, US, 70 mins, b/w
Dir: Alfred E Green
Stars: Barbara Stanwyck, George Brent, Donald Cook
Rating: ★★★

Super-fast essay on how to succeed in business by pure sexual smoulder, as Barbara Stanwyck vamps her way from the bottom of a firm to the top via every seducible male employee. The notorious Hays Code threw a fit at all this, and Warners had to shoot a new ending giving Stanwyck a re-formatory change of heart before the censor would allow it a certificate. George Brent and a young John Wayne are two of 'Baby Face's' hypnotised victims.

Baby Face Nelson ◑
1957, US, 85 mins, b/w
Dir: Don Siegel
Stars: Mickey Rooney, Carolyn Jones, Cedric Hardwicke
Rating: ★★★

A harsh, uncompromising gangster film featuring a Mickey Rooney far removed from his MGM musical days. Snarling defiance and bile, Rooney dominates a cheap-looking but action-packed movie whose tasty cast also includes Carolyn Jones, Sir Cedric Hardwicke, Elisha Cook Jr, Leo Gordon, Ted de Corsia, John Hoyt, Jack Elam, Emile Meyer, Lisa Davis (as the 'lady in red') and Anthony Caruso. Don Siegel directs in his toughest vein.

Baby, It's You ●
1982, US, 105 mins, colour
Dir: John Sayles
Stars: Rosanna Arquette, Vincent Spano
Rating: ★★

Back in the days when Rosanna Arquette was still making decent movies, she joined a whole crowd of young actors who would soon become better known in this flavoursome period piece about high-school lovers

who go together like oil and water. Although sharp in its observation of (young) human behaviour, the film's raucous, high-throttle approach becomes tiresome towards the end and it doesn't quite fulfil its initial promise. When interest in the story flags, though, you can while away the time spotting people like Tracy Pollan, Fisher Stevens, Caroline Aaron, Matthew Modine, Robert Downey Jr and Robin Johnson. Arquette and Vincent Spano are both excellent in the leading roles.

Baby on Board ○ ⓥ
1992, US, 95 mins, colour
Dir: Frankie Schaeffer
Stars: Judge Reinhold, Carol Kane, Geza Kovacs
Rating: ★

Judge Reinhold, who must be one of the poorest choosers of scripts in Hollywood history, strikes out again with this romantic caper thriller featuring curly Carol Kane as Maria, a widow on the run from the Mafia, along with her charmingly precocious four-year-old daughter. The likeable Reinhold is Ernie, the luckless cab driver sucked into the feud. The rest of the movie consists more or less of one long chase scene, and will be okay for undemanding families who like this sort of thing, although occasionally a bit violent for sensitive toddlers. In fact, if you've ever wondered what New York looks like as seen from inside a taxi cab at high speed then this is the movie for you – but keep the travel sickness pills handy.

Baby – Secret of the Lost Legend ◑
1985, US, 95 mins, colour
Dir: B W L Norton
Stars: William Katt, Sean Young, Patrick McGoohan
Rating: ★

This overly cute, muddily coloured dinosaur picture about a young American couple rescuing a new-born prehistoric animal from the African rain forest suffers from lurching violently in tone. It would have been perfect family fare but for semi-nudity and implied lovemaking between the two leads, William Katt and Sean Young. Katt comes off better in the acting stakes, but both have an uphill struggle with the unconvincing models. Patrick McGoohan, making a rare film appearance, is a suitably evil foil.

Bachelor and the Bobby-Soxer, The
See: Bachelor Knight

Bachelor Knight ○
(aka: The Bachelor and the Bobby-Soxer)
1947, US, 95 mins, b/w
Dir: Irving Reis
Stars: Cary Grant, Myrna Loy, Shirley Temple, Rudy Vallee
Rating: ★★★★

Screamingly funny comedy, superbly structured and scripted by Sidney Sheldon, with the incomparable Cary Grant at the top of his form as a 40-ish lecturer forced to squire the young girl who has a crush on him, to the extent of competing for her with her younger admirers. Myrna Loy – who has the famous 'man of power' running dialogue with Grant – Rudy Vallee, Shirley Temple, Ray Collins and Harry Davenport all play with pleasure. Scenes at an athletics meeting and a nightclub table are just riotous. Enjoy.

Bachelor of Hearts ○
1958, UK, 100 mins, colour
Dir: Wolf Rilla
Stars: Hardy Kruger, Sylvia Syms, Ronald Lewis
Rating: ★★

A pleasant, sunny, incident-filled romantic comedy of university life, this film brought Hardy Kruger back to Britain after his runaway success here as the escaped prisoner-of-war in *The One That Got Away*. The supporting cast is packed with stars-to-be, including Barbara Steele (the 'queen of horror') in her first role, and John Richardson, later to become leading man to Ursula Andress and Raquel Welch.

Bachelor Party ● ⓥ
1984, US, colour
Dir: Neal Israel
Stars: Tom Hanks, Tawny Kitaen
Rating: ★

A very lowbrow comedy considerably enhanced by the presence of Tom Hanks as the happy-go-lucky guy whose decision to get married provides the momentum for the action. If you loved *Porky's* and *National Lampoon's Animal House*, then you should like this one. The easily offended, however, should approach with caution.

B

Backbeat ● ⓥ

1994, UK, 100 mins, colour
Dir: Iain Softley
Stars: Sheryl Lee, Stephen Dorff, Ian Hart
Rating: ★★

I always thought of Pete Best as the fifth Beatle, but before Best, or at least at the same time, there was Stuart Sutcliffe. Torn between his desire to paint and his love of music, Sutcliffe also had an uncertain relationship with John Lennon, and an affair with the enigmatic Kirchherr during the bands Hamburg days that brought the frictions within the group to a head. The impressions of real people seem spot-on here, but there's a certain lack of chemistry between leads Sheryl Lee (as Kirchherr) and Stephen Dorff (as Sutcliffe) that prevents you becoming too involved with their problems. It's left to Ian Hart to steal the show as Lennon, a role he had already played two years earlier in a rather obscure offering called *The Hours and the Times*. The Beatle's music, as ever, is great, and director Iain Softley moves the story along fast enough to keep all but the occasional patch of tedium at bay.

Backdraft ● ⓥ

1991, US, 131 mins, colour
Dir: Ron Howard
Stars: Kurt Russell, William Baldwin, Robert De Niro, Donald Sutherland, Jennifer Jason Leigh, Scott Glenn, Rebecca DeMornay
Rating: ★★

Although it's long, drawn-out and often spectacular, this is no *Towering Inferno*. Unintelligible dialogue, sometimes indistinct, sometimes drowned out by the fires or the music, renders the complex arson plot virtually incomprehensible. William Baldwin mumbles huskily like a man talking through a mouthful of apple; the rest of a distinguished cast falls victim to Ron Howard's poor direction and the general soundtrack noise. Only Donald Sutherland, as a jailbird who is to fire what Anthony Hopkins is to murder in *The Silence of the Lambs*, really stamps his authority on the role. The fire scenes are superb, with special effects going off all over the place, and the backdrafts (freak fireballs) claiming their victims like something out of a horror film. Take along a heat shield and a hearing aid.

Back from Eternity ○

1956, US, 97 mins, b/w
Dir: John Farrow
Stars: Robert Ryan, Anita Ekberg, Rod Steiger, Phyllis Kirk, Gene Barry
Rating: ★★

This adventure is the familiar chestnut about a plane crash landing in the jungle and the survivors having to fight off natives to survive. The crippled plane is repaired but will only carry five of the passengers to safety! It was familiar to director/producer John Farrow, too, who first used the story 17 years earlier in *Five Came Back*. Despite a bigger budget and therefore better production values, this version doesn't eclipse the orginal. It's also about 20 minutes longer, most of which is merely padding. Nevertheless, it's quite exciting and has strong performances by Robert Ryan, Rod Steiger, Phyllis Kirk and Gene Barry.

Background to Danger ○

1943, US, 80 mins, b/w
Dir: Raoul Walsh
Stars: George Raft, Sydney Greenstreet, Peter Lorre, Brenda Marshall
Rating: ★★★

This very fast-moving Warners wartime espionage drama gets through a mighty lot of plot in its actual 80-minute running time, with hero George Raft having to extract himself from one tricky situation after another. Raft (for the Americans), Sydney Greenstreet (for the Germans) and Peter Lorre (for the Russians) are all after the same envelope which contains details of a phoney plan along similar lines to *The Man Who Never Was*. Lovely Brenda Marshall (who, in real life, was married to William Holden for 30 years) is the heroine, but a much sharper image is registered by the Danish-born actress Osa Massen, who performs much the same function in the plot as the mystery woman at the beginning of *The 39 Steps*.

Backlash ○

1956, US, 84 mins, colour
Dir: John Sturges
Stars: Richard Widmark, Donna Reed
Rating: ★★★

Set in the wilds of Arizona, this tough John Sturges Western, about a gunman out to find his father's killer, includes good helpings of hard-riding outlaws, Apache raiders, duels to the death and range warfare. Sterling

supporting cast includes Barton MacLane who found his 'ugly mug' his fortune as he played the villain in dozens of crime thrillers. The plot is unusually well worked-out for a Western, and contains one or two first-rate surprises in the closing reel. 'If they ever get around to giving Oscars for the busiest Western of the year,' remarked one contemporary critic, 'this one would be a certain winner'.

Back Room Boy ⊙

1942, UK, 82 mins, b/w
Dir: Herbert Mason
Stars: Arthur Askey, Googie Withers, Moore Marriott, Graham Moffatt
Rating: ★★

It became the standard thing for Britain's top radio comics to tilt with the Nazis on screen in wartime, and this Arthur Askey farce is no exception. He's packed off to the Scottish coast after scrambling the BBC news 'pips'. Those institutions of British comedy films of the era, wheezy Moore Marriott and tubby Graham Moffatt, add to the fun.

Back to Bataan ○ ⓥ

1945, US, 97 mins, b/w
Dir: Edward Dymtryk
Stars: John Wayne, Anthony Quinn, Beulah Bondi
Rating: ★★

Big John Wayne takes on the Japs, aided by Anthony Quinn and a small army of Filipino resistance fighters in this rousing action saga. The Japanese army has overrun the Philipines, sending General MacArthur packing, promising to return. Meanwhile it's down to the Duke to hold the fort. The Japanese are all evil and nasty and there's a fair bit of flag-waving, but that was just what was needed when the film was made. Director Edward Dmytryk handles it all (especially the battle scenes) with vigor and flair. Wayne's character is based on a real-life American who fought with the resistance movement. It may not be a classic, but this is an exciting and well made war epic.

Back to School ◑ ⓥ

1986, US, 96 mins, colour
Dir: Alan Metter
Stars: Rodney Dangerfield, Sally Kellerman
Rating: ★★

An outrageous gag-a-minute comedy that's the most successful cinema showcase to date for oversized American comic Rodney Dangerfield. He's the millionaire owner of the Tall and Fat chain of discount clothes stores, who enrols at his son's school as a (very) mature student by greasing the palms of the education authorities. The comedy rarely rises above the belt – 'Maybe you can help me straighten out my Longfellow,' he asks a blonde student in his English class – but despite the cliched characters, it's hard not to laugh along at the humour arising from the ridiculous scenario. Sally Kellerman is particularly good as the hands-on literature teacher who recites Dylan Thomas with breathless perfection and teaches in the same seductive way. Look out for Robert Downey Jr.

Back to the Beach ○ ⓥ
1987, US, 92 mins, colour
Dir: Lyndall Hobbs
Stars: Frankie Avalon, Annette Funicello, Lori Loughlin, Connie Stevens, Don Adams, Edd Byrnes, Pee-wee Herman
Rating: ★★★

This lampoon of the beach party movies of the Sixties, complete with Annette Funicello (hardly changed at all), Connie Stevens and Frankie Avalon (changed but looking incredibly good) in such a sweetie of a film and such fun for most of the time that you can forgive its shortcomings (it's a shade lacking in directorial professionalism). Frankie bores everyone with his surfing stories, Annette confesses she always wanted to be the bad girl, and everything is much as it was way back when, with Annette leading beachniks in a musical number, numbing her teenage son with peanut butter sandwiches and holding a pyjama party when she's down in the dumps. Possibly funniest of all is the teenage son everyone hates and whose head Avalon uses as a battering ram to break down a door.

Back to the Future ○ ⓥ
1985, US, 115 mins, colour
Dir: Robert Zemeckis
Stars: Michael J Fox, Christopher Lloyd, Lea Thompson, Crispin Glover, Thomas F Wilson
Rating: ★★★

The collision of past, present and future has long fascinated Hollywood, and here's a time-travel movie that not only gets golden boy Steven Spielberg's seal of approval (he's executive producer), but has spawned two sequels. The youthful Michael J

Fox puts his good looks to good use as teenager Marty McFly, who travels from 1985 back to 1955 in a time machine made from a DeLorean car. While in the past, he accidentally stops his parents from meeting and falling in love, with dire consequences for his own future. How Marty patches up the history he has changed is shown in complex but thoroughly entertaining fashion by director Robert Zemeckis (director of all three *Future* films), and the year 1955 is re-created with nostalgia and humour. Christopher Lloyd stands out with an exceptionally zany performance as Dr Emmett Brown, the eccentric inventor of the DeLorean time machine, in an ingenious and ultimately charming time-travel jaunt. Look out for Huey Lewis, who sings the hit song from the film, 'The Power of Love', in a small role as a teacher.

Back to the Future Part II ○ ⓥ
1989, US, 107 mins, colour
Dir: Robert Zemeckis
Stars: Michael J Fox, Christopher Lloyd, Lea Thompson, Thomas F Wilson, Elizabeth Shue
Rating: ★★

The biggest box-office hit of 1985, *Back to the Future* was an exhilarating switchback of a movie that zipped along between thrills and comedy and deserved every bit of its enormous success. The sequel, unfortunately, is more steamroller than roller-coaster, relentlessly grinding its way from one putative cliff-hanger to the next with little variation of pace and no time at all for the quirky characterisation that made the first film a delight.

Back to the Future Part III ☉ ⓥ
1990, US, 112 mins, colour
Dir: Robert Zemeckis
Stars: Michael J Fox, Christopher Lloyd, Mary Steenburgen, Lea Thompson, Thomas F Wilson, Elisabeth Shue
Rating: ★★★★

It's quite a journey. And for once the publicity is right. They have saved the best for last. Zemeckis' adventures of Marty McFly (Michael J Fox) in a Western setting of 1885 move like the De Lorean time machine of Doc Brown (Christopher Lloyd). That is to say, like a thunderbolt, with flames burning up the edges of the film. When Marty discovers the doctor's name on a tombstone – shot in the back in 1885 – he has to go back in

time to stop it happening. Adopting the name Clint Eastwood, McFly jets back from 1955 to 1885, where he evades an Indian charge and finds the good doctor reluctant to come back since he's fallen in love with schoolteacher Clara, with whom he shares a love of science and Jules Verne. Mary Steenburgen, terrific in the part, was presumably chosen for her experience in time-travel in *Time after Time*! Things move very fast indeed from then on, proceeding to a traditional gun duel in Main Street which happens to coincide with the time for our heroes' journey back to the future. Zemeckis constantly plays amusing variations on Western traditions and wraps things up tidily at the end.

Bad and the Beautiful, The ○ ⓥ
1952, US, 118 mins, b/w
Dir: Vincente Minnelli
Stars: Lana Turner, Kirk Douglas, Walter Pidgeon, Dick Powell, Barry Sullivan, Gloria Grahame
Rating: ★★★

Hollywood stabs itself in the back (with the help of some of its biggest stars) in this dark and penetrating look at the fluctuating fortunes of an egomaniac mogul, played with silky power by Kirk Douglas. Gloria Grahame won a best supporting actress Oscar as an ambitious wife. Although the film was not as popular as it might have been, probably because of its theme, Charles Schnee's screenplay is full of insight and biting humour and deservedly made him another of the film's Oscar winners. Much better than the same director's later stab at Hollywood, *Two Weeks in Another Town*.

Bad Behaviour ● ⓥ
1992, UK, 103 mins, colour
Dir: Les Blair
Stars: Stephen Rea, Sinead Cusack, Philip Jackson, Phil Daniels, Saira Todd
Rating: ★★★

Gently amusing, this is an improvised film and really quite nicely so, about a mild crisis in the state of a modern marriage of two Irish people (Stephen Rea, Sinead Cusack) living in London's semi-fashionable Kentish Town. Most centrally, it concerns the arrival in their life of a wheeler-dealer shark (Philip Jackson), forever on his mobile phone, offering them advice on the builders to get for their bathroom renovation, and then charging them for it. The builders turn out to be

B

twins (both played by Phil Daniels) who create a barrage of noise that plays havoc with Rea's neighbours. On and off Cusack is also beset by: their two children; a deserted and slightly loopy wife with all the troubles in the world; a chatty but empty friend; and various relatives of the above. All of the performances are good, with a nice natural feel, but pride of place undoubtedly goes to Jackson's Howard, with a meaningless phrase for every occasion, a predatory air and a tendency to turn nasty at the hint of non-payment of one of his specious bills. Fun.

Bad Company ◑
1972, US, 92 mins, colour
Dir: Robert Benton
Stars: Jeff Bridges, Barry Brown, John Savage
Rating: ★★

Charming, likeable American Civil War drama with a clutch of personable performances from the ragamuffin bunch of youngsters on the run from Union Army conscription. Barry Brown is amusingly prim as the small town boy who joins forces with Jeff Bridges' ramshackle group of runaways, while David Huddleston's bear-like presence as outlaw Big Joe Simmons casts a menacing shadow over the autumnal landscapes (lovingly photographed by Gordon Willis). An immensely assured work from first-time director Robert Benton (he went on to make *Kramer vs Kramer* and *Places in the Heart*), who co-wrote the screenplay with his *Bonnie and Clyde* partner David Newman.

Bad Day at Black Rock ○
1954, US, 81 mins, colour
Dir: John Sturges
Stars: Spencer Tracy, Robert Ryan, Anne Francis, Dean Jagger, Walter Brennan
Rating: ★★★

Too much talk and too little action slows down this 'modern' Western, although the material is good – and very original – and the situations at times crackle with suspense. There are convincing performances from some of Hollywood's best actors, including Spencer Tracy as the one-armed war veteran coming to a township that seems to be nursing a guilty secret.

Bad For Each Other ○
1953, US, 83 mins, b/w
Dir: Irving Rapper
Stars: Charlton Heston, Lizabeth Scott
Rating: ★★

Here's medicine and romance again proving a bad mix for the doctor, just as they did in *The Citadel* and *Green Fingers*. Charlton Heston and sultry Lizabeth Scott (as the girl who's no good for him) had been teamed before on his first major film, *Dark City*. But the actor who was to make his name in epics went home at nights with another member of the cast. Her name was Lydia Clarke, and she was already Mrs Charlton Heston. The film's not very good though. Nobody looks as though they're having a good time and neither does the audience.

Bad Girl ●
1992, UK, 75 mins, colour
Dir: George Case
Stars: Jane Horrocks
Rating: ★★★

The Social Services people take a right bashing in this timely realist drama that, perhaps unintentionally, somewhat undercuts its own case by showing that they may have taken the right decisions, albeit for the wrong reasons. Jane Horrocks is right on the mark as the single mum whose battle for the custody of her own son is bedevilled by bad luck and her temperament, although you may find the film's relentless pursuit of a downbeat ending a trifle depressing. Food for thought, though, unlike the heroine's cockroach-laced cake.

Bad Influence ● Ⓥ
1990, US, 102 mins, colour
Dir: Curtis Hanson
Stars: James Spader, Rob Lowe, Lisa Zane, Kathleen Wilhoite
Rating: ★★

More 'sex, lies and videotape' for James Spader in this satanic sideshoot from *Strangers on a Train*. Spader plays a brainy computer boffin, anxious both for a top job and a way out of getting hitched to a beautiful and wealthy socialite. When he runs into evil thrill-seeker Alex (played by Rob Lowe, looking much more mature than in his Brat Pack days), Spader sees a man who makes things happen by his own rules. Lowe soon gets him what he wants – but the price is sky-high and soul-deep. The acting of the leading duo is good but the writing isn't always worthy of their efforts in this interesting but flawed little shocker. Several endings were contemplated and the one the film eventually got seems truncated – and told an entirely different story from

the one on the distributors' handout. Another case, perhaps, for a director's cut?

Bad Lands ○
1939, US, 70 mins, b/w
Dir: Lew Landers
Stars: Noah Beery Jr, Robert Barrat, Paul Hurst
Rating: ★★

Curious Western remake of the classic *The Lost Patrol*. There are no stars in the story (which transfers easily from the African desert to the Arizona wilderness), but it provides rare acting meat for some great Hollywood character actors, including Noah Beery Jr, Robert Barrat, Paul Hurst and Andy Clyde.

Badlands ● Ⓥ
1973, US, 94 mins, colour
Dir: Terrence Malick
Stars: Martin Sheen, Sissy Spacek, Warren Oates
Rating: ★★★

This grim drama about a couple who go on a murderous spree across the midwest of America, killing ten innocent people, is based on a true incident and has become something of a cult classic. Debut director/writer Terrence Malick gave early starring roles to Martin Sheen and Sissy Spacek. Sheen is the vengeful and socially maladjusted Kit and Spacek is his mindless teenaged girlfriend Holly. Warren Oates makes a strong impression as Holly's father, but he ends up as Kit's first victim. Despite fine portrayals, the main charaters are totally unlikeable which mean you watch as a fascinated observer without becoming involved with them or their motives. The film is visually impressive but ultimately depressing.

Bad Lieutenant ●
1992, US, 98 mins, colour
Dir: Abel Ferrara
Stars: Harvey Keitel, Frankie Thorn, Victor Argo
Rating: ★

Youv'e heard of feelgood films: here's a feelbad one. Director Abel Ferrara's study of a totally corrupt cop contains almost every adult certificate element you could think of: drugs and needles of all kinds, the rape of a nun, prostitution, three-in-a-room brothel frolics, brutal murders and sexual humiliation. Despite (or perhaps because of) all this, it remains practically unwatchable. Harvey Keitel gives a performance of typically fierce intensity, as the cop headed straight for hell, but briefly sidetracked both by the nun's rape, which gnaws at his Catholic guts, and by a world baseball series that stands to win him a fortune. There's no let up here, as Ferrara's prowling camera brings every element of the film down to street level and below; and it's all too much, turning the audience off instead of on to the problems illustrated in the film.

Bad Man of Brimstone ○
1938, US, 90 mins, b/w
Dir: J Walter Ruben
Stars: Wallace Beery, Virginia Bruce, Dennis O'Keefe, Bruce Cabot
Rating: ★★

Beefy, swaggering Wallace Beery was still a big noise at MGM (he had won an Oscar earlier in the decade for *The Champ*) when he made this rugged comedy-Western that the studio hoped might emulate the success of *Viva Villa!*. The producers surrounded the rough-hewn star with a glittering array of talent – Virginia Bruce, Charley Grapewin, Dennis O'Keefe, Joseph Calleia, Lewis Stone, Guy Kibbee and Bruce Cabot. A guest role was even found for the star's brother, Noah Beery. If only more trouble had been taken with the script, the studio might have had a top-grade Western on its hands.

Bad Man's River ○
1972, Spain/Italy, 90 mins, colour
Dir: Gene Martin
Stars: Lee Van Cleef, James Mason, Gina Lollobrigida
Rating: ★

Although Lee Van Cleef was doubtless pleased to get away from a run of grim Western killers, he and his co-stars, Gina Lollobrigida and James Mason, seem ill-at-ease with the vein of comedy that runs rather too close to the surface of this Spanish-Italian action romp. Screenwriters Gene Martin and Philip Yordan keep their plot writhing like a snake with every variety of cross and double-cross they can lay their pens on, but the odds are that you won't believe a word of it.

Bad News Bears, The ○
1976, US, 100 mins, colour
Dir: Michael Ritchie
Stars: Walter Matthau, Tatum O'Neal, Vic Morrow
Rating: ★★★

Wonderfully likeable and entertaining feelgood movie about a team of ragamuffin, semi-delinquent, abrasive kids somehow licked into shape as a baseball team by grouchy old Walter Matthau. Marvellous script by Bill Lancaster hits home in all the right places without you even noticing your emotions are being ruthlessly manipulated. The baseball action is exciting, there are lots of funny lines and Tatum O'Neal as the team's girl star has never been better. Two sequels were made in the hope that lightning might strike twice. They just struck out instead.

Bad Timing ● Ⓥ
(aka: Bad Timing: A Sensual Obsession)
1979, US, 135 mins, colour
Dir: Nicholas Roeg
Stars: Art Garfunkel, Theresa Russell, Harvey Keitel, Denholm Elliott
Rating: ★★★

In the creation of Alex Linden, director Nicolas Roeg and his screenwriter Yale Udoff have come up with a psychopath to set alongside Norman Bates in Psycho. At the start, the story runs like a suicide attempt by a girl after a tiff with her boyfriend. But gradually, horrifyingly, Roeg prises the relationship apart until you realise the truth. One can't go further into the plot without touching on the final, nasty twists to a very unpalatable if well-made story. Theresa Russell, here coming over as a kind of young Gloria Grahame, is very good as the girl. But actor-singer Art Garfunkel is only barely equal to the demands of her analyst lover.

Ball of Fire ○
1941, US, 111 mins, b/w
Dir: Howard Hawks
Stars: Gary Cooper, Barbara Stanwyck, Oscar Homolka, Dana Andrews, Dan Duryea
Rating: ★★★

A sparkling Billy Wilder-Charles Brackett script provides Barbara Stanwyck with a rare comedy glamour role as showgirl Sugarpuss O'Shea in an amusing and inventive modern reworking of the Snow White theme. Howard Hawks, usually found making action films, is the director, displaying an unexpectedly deft comedy touch. And some of the early Forties slang is as fascinating as it is baffling. Producer Samuel Goldwyn, never one to waste

good material, revamped the whole thing a few years later as a vehicle for Danny Kaye called *A Song Is Born*.

Bambi ⊙ Ⓥ
1942, US, 69 mins, colour
Dir: David Hand
Rating: ★★★★

One of Walt Disney's most enduring classics only released on video in 1994. A brilliant depiction of forest life, the changing seasons and weather conditions (notably leading to the exquisitely animated song 'Little April Shower'), it's a heart-warming and sometimes heart-rending tale of a young fawn growing up in the forest and his friendship with an equally young rabbit and skunk. Superbly realised action scenes and sometimes witty dialogue combine to give the film an overwhelming appeal, with Thumper the ground-drumming rabbit unexpectedly proving the star of the show. Tinies should have an adult standing by for their reactions to the fate of Bambi's mother. Made with great dignity, the film is still an altogether enchanting experience.

Bananas ◑ Ⓥ
1971, US, 82 mins, colour
Dir: Woody Allen
Stars: Woody Allen, Louise Lasser
Rating: ★★

Hilarity slips into vulgarity rather too often in this typically in-an-out early Woody Allen comedy which embroils the little man in a South American revolution. Like the revolutionaries, the gags fire off in all directions – there are spoof TV commercials and even a Battleship Potemkin joke for buffs. Jacob Morales has many of the best moments as the rebel leader especially when, drunk with power, he declares Swedish to be the new national language. Woody's life as a human guinea pig at the start of the film is funny enough to make you wish there were more of it, but you'll have to keep your eyes peeled to spot Sylvester Stallone (in his second film) as a hoodlum.

Bandit of Sherwood Forest, The ⊙
1946, US, 87 mins, colour
Dir: Henry Levin
Stars: Cornel Wilde, Anita Louise, Jill Esmond, Edgar Buchanan, George Macready
Rating: ★★

B

A kind of *Twenty Years After*, Sherwood Forest style, and actually based on a novel called *Son of Robin Hood*. Following in the footsteps of such distinguished Old Sherwoodians as Douglas Fairbanks and Errol Flynn, Cornel Wilde cuts a dashing figure as Hood's scion in this spectacular adventure film. It was one of the few to take advantage of Wilde's real-life prowess as an international fencer.

Bandit of Zhobe, The ○
1959, UK, 81 mins, colour
Dir: John Gilling
Stars: Victor Mature, Anne Aubrey, Anthony Newley
Rating: ★★

A fiery 19th century adventure yarn that makes little sense but bulges with action that keeps coming at you. It's one of several exotic action films made in Britain in the Fifties with such Hollywood stars as Victor Mature (as here) and Robert Taylor. Co-producer of these ventures was 'Cubby' Broccoli, soon to turn his attention to the James Bond films.

Band of Angels ○
1957, US, 127 mins, colour
Dir: Raoul Walsh
Stars: Clark Gable, Yvonne De Carlo, Sidney Poitier
Rating: ★★

This big, expensive action film, adapted from a best-seller by Robert Penn Warren, tended to acquire the reputation of a poor man's *Gone With the Wind*, set as it is in the southern states at the time of the American Civil War, and with Gable as its star. Acting honours, however, are stolen by Sidney Poitier as a rebellious negro overseer. Lucien Ballard's WarnerColor photography sets off the action in handsome fashion, especially in a chase scene through swamplands.

Bandolero ○
1968, US, 106 mins, colour
Dir: Andrew V Mclaglen
Stars: James Stewart, Dean Martin, Raquel Welch, George Kennedy
Rating: ★★★

It's remarkable that all Andrew McLaglen's best Westerns have been made with James Stewart as star. Stewart's integrity, plus a gritty performance from Dean Martin and striking colour photography, go a long way to making *Bandolero!* above average as a fiery adventure yarn. All

the action is well staged, especially the opening rescue of Martin and his gang from the hangman (a bouquet to Guy Raymond who believes that there is 'nothing worse than a sloppy hanging') and film fans will recognise Jack Mahoney, once the Range Rider and Tarzan, as a rancher who gets killed off in the first reel.

Band Waggon ⊙
1939, UK, 85 mins, b/w
Dir: Marcel Varnel
Stars: Arthur Askey, Richard Murdoch, Pat Kirkwood
Rating: ★★★

A rare chance to catch up on the film version of radio's first-ever comedy series, which won enormous popularity in its time. Arthur Askey and Richard Murdoch are once again to be discovered in their flat on the roof of Broadcasting House, but the nearness of war demanded that in the film they get involved with spies as well. The radio show itself, broadcast on Sunday evenings, was so popular in late Thirties' Britain that it was said church services were cancelled because of it.

Band Wagon, The ⊙ ⓥ
1953, US, 112 mins, colour
Dir: Vincente Minnelli
Stars: Fred Astaire, Cyd Charisse, Jack Buchanan
Rating: ★★★★

With the line, 'Gosh, with all this raw talent around, why can't us kids get together and put ourselves on a show,' this musical is a sophisticated tribute to all the innocent backstage musicals that preceded it. Twenty years after Fred Astaire made his debut in *Dancing Lady*, this film gave him perhaps his best role in one of the best movies of his career, as a fading Hollywood musical star pursuaded to make a comeback. Cyd Charisse (in her first starring role and dubbed by India Adams) plays a ballet dancer, and Ava Gardner makes a guest appearance. Out of all the film's songs, only one was new – 'That's Entertainment', written in just 30 minutes by Arthur Schwartz and Howard Dietz.

Bang the Drum Slowly ○
1973, US, 97 mins, colour
Dir: John Hancock
Stars: Michael Moriarty, Robert De Niro, Vincent Gardenia
Rating: ★★★

This is the best of four good films made by the American director John Hancock (the others are *Let's Scare Jessica to Death*, *California Dreaming*, *Blue Marine* and *Baby*), none of which have been widely seen on this side of the Atlantic. The reason here is fairly obvious, for the theme is baseball. But the playing of Michael Moriarty and Robert De Niro sweeps aside all sentiment attached to the theme of a dying baseball player, makes the most of the script's moments of abrasive humour and generally raises the film far above the average weepie, into the class reached by the classic TV film *Brian's Song*.

Banjo on My Knee ○
1936, US, 95 mins, b/w
Dir: John Cromwell
Stars: Barbara Stanwyck, Joel McCrea, Walter Brennan
Rating: ★★★

This rather delightful musical works well despite having very few musical stars in it! Down the cast there's Tony Martin (billed as Anthony) and Buddy Ebsen (a pretty fair hoofer in his younger days). But the two stars, Barbara Stanwyck and Joel McCrea, weren't obvious musical material. Stanwyck sings surprisingly well – surprising that is until you realise she started off as a song and dance girl in the Ziegfeld Follies. The story, about McCrea going on the run after killing a man, is of little consequence, so don't worry too much about it. Just enjoy the film for what it is – a lightweight piece of fun, with some very entertaining individual scenes. Stanwyck fans will love watching her letting her hair down.

Bank Detective, The
See: The Bank Dick

Bank Dick, The ⊙
(aka: The Bank Detective)
1940, US, 74 mins, b/w
Dir: Edward Cline
Stars: W C Fields, Cora Witherstone, Una Merkel, Grady Sutton
Rating: ★★★★

W C Fields' last comedy classic in which he emerges from the mass henpecking of a family of females to become the hero of his local town. Fields' screenplay, written under the pseudonym of Mahatma Kane Jeeves, is a happy amalgam of themes and characters from other, earlier Fieldsian romps – including the hat that won't go on the Fields head for the very good reason that he's lifting it in the air with his own čane.

Bank Holiday ○
1938, UK, 86 mins, b/w
Dir: Carol Reed
Stars: Margaret Lockwood, Hugh Williams, John Lodge
Rating: ★★★

This was director Carol Reed's first big success, starring Margaret Lockwood, who had appeared for him in *Midshipman Easy*. Here she plays a nurse who is poignantly torn between two men. Hers is just one of the stories which, in similar fashion to the later *Holiday Camp*, capture a long-gone era of the British middle- and working-classes on holiday. Strangely, Kathleen Harrison plays a cockney mum in both films.

Barabbas ○
1961, Italy/US, 134 mins, colour
Dir: Richard Fleischer
Stars: Anthony Quinn, Silvana Mangano, Arthur Kennedy, Jack Palance
Rating: ★★★

Sombre Italian-American epic with a good deal to recommend it thanks to a thoughtful performance by Anthony Quinn as the man set free when Jesus was crucified and to a quality script by Christopher Fry. There's also a ferocious piece of over-acting from Jack Palance as a sadistic gladiator.

Barbarella ● ⓥ
1967, France/Italy, 98 mins, colour
Dir: Roger Vadim
Stars: Jane Fonda, John Phillip Law, David Hemmings, Anita Pallenberg, Milo O'Shea
Rating: ★★

The film that Jane Fonda is reputedly least fond of – it portrays her as a space maiden and general sex object, a far cry from the liberated ladies she portrays today. It's great fun, though, with John Phillip Law – in films since childhood – as the winged hero.

Barbarian and the Geisha, The ○ ⓥ
1958, US, 105 mins, colour
Dir: John Huston
Stars: John Wayne, Eiko Ando, Sam Jaffe
Rating: ★★

John Huston's pictorially beautiful film about the first American ambassador to Japan, a role for which John Wayne seems odd casting.

Barbarosa ○
1981, US, 90 mins, colour
Dir: Fred Schepisi
Stars: Willie Nelson, Gary Busey, Isela Vega, Gilbert Roland
Rating: ★★

A Western by the Australian director Fred Schepisi. This saga of revenge and banditry in the old West makes effective landscape use of Rio Grande scenery and Western singer Willie Nelson (in the title part of a notorious outlaw), with Gary Busey (who made such an early hit in *The Buddy Holly Story*) as a Texan of German descent who becomes his partner in robbery and pillage.

Barbary Coast ○
1935, US, 91 mins, b/w
Dir: Howard Hawks
Stars: Edward G Robinson, Miriam Hopkins, Joel McCrea
Rating: ★★★

Ben Hecht and Charles MacArthur wrote Edward G Robinson a rich 'rascal' role for the rip-roaring epic of the San Francisco waterfront in the 1850s, which cast him as a kind of gold rush equivalent of Little Caesar. When a society swell ignores him, Robinson snarls: 'I'll fix him – and that horseface he calls his wife!'

Barbary Coast Gent ○
1944, US, 87 mins, b/w
Dir: Roy Del Ruth
Stars: Wallace Beery, Binnie Barnes, John Carradine, Noah Beery Jr
Rating: ★★

Big Wallace Beery blusters his way through another of the rough and ready comedy adventures that he made with such regularity for MGM. Despite a good supporting cast in this tall tale of a Western bandit trying to go straight, Beery's really the whole show.

Barefoot Contessa, The ○ ⓥ
1954, US, 128 mins, colour
Dir: Joseph L Mankiewicz
Stars: Humphrey Bogart, Ava Gardner, Edmund O'Brien, Marius Goring, Rossano Brazzi
Rating: ★★

A star-studded if rather stolid drama about a stunning Spanish gipsy dancer and her rise and fall in the dizzy world of stardom. Humphrey Bogart is at his most world-weary as a disillusioned, cynical Hollywood writer, but it was Edmond O'Brien's portrayal of a loud-mouthed press agent that took the acting honours and won him an Academy Award. Writer-director Joseph L Mankiewicz, who had already won Oscars for *A Letter for Three Wives* and the even more highly esteemed *All About Eve*, faltered somewhat on the script of this one, which is rather over-sardonic in tone. The cast also includes Elizabeth Sellars, Rossano Brazzi, Marius Goring, Valentina Cortesa and, in a small role, ex-ballet dancer Mari Aldon, who was a star in her first film (*Distant Drums*) but failed to stay at the top.

Barefoot in the Park ○ ⓥ
1967, US, 105 mins, colour
Dir: Gene Saks
Stars: Robert Redford, Jane Fonda, Charles Boyer, Mildred Natwick
Rating: ★★★

A spicy, dry and often hilariously-scripted comedy about two honeymooners. It achieves both warm, human relationships, and comic lines that are set against one another with precision balance, never overloading the laughs, but rattling them out at a consistent pace. 'I think I'm going to be a lousy wife,' Jane Fonda tells Robert Redford at the door of their honeymoon hotel. 'But I'm very sexy.' After six days and night, he's convinced. 'I have to go to work,' he gasps, staggering out on the seventh. 'I don't do this for a living.' Alas in their new flat (top floor) comes the dawn. The radiator won't radiate, the bed (to Jane's horror) fails to arrive for the first night and snow comes through the skylight. It's a film cocktail that never fails to sparkle.

Barfly ● ⓥ
1987, US, 100 mins, colour
Dir: Barbet Schroeder
Stars: Mickey Rourke, Faye Dunaway, Alice Krige, J C Quinn
Rating: ★★

This is a vignettes-from-the-early-life-of-the-writer-type movie. You know, you've seen 'em: the writer getting all nostalgic about his slum beginnings in garret rooms, and the rich characters of the poor people he knew. *Barfly* plays a variation on this theme in that it homes in on the slurred, blurred lives of downtown alcoholics, frequenting cheap bars whenever and wherever they can get cheap credit. Mickey Rourke, coming on like a male Mae West, gives another of his low-life, designer-stubble studies as the writer. Faye Dunaway is

B

good, too, as the slightly higher-class lush who takes him under her wing and occasionally beats his brains out. He takes on the bartender (Sylvester Stallone's brother Frank) in a nightly brawl, and his seedy, smelly lifestyle is captured by the director down to the last peeling flap on the wallpaper. Some of this is entertaining, some indulgent, some merely tedious. About what you'd expect from leaves from the author's – in this case Charles Bukowski – early days.

Barkleys of Broadway, The ○ Ⓥ
1949, US, 105 mins, colour
Dir: Charles Walters
Stars: Fred Astaire, Ginger Rogers, Oscar Levant, Billie Burke
Rating: ★★★

Let's face it, any film with Fred and Ginger above the titles has got to be good. Add a screenplay by Adolph Green and Betty Comden, music by Harry Warren and Ira Gershwin, and Oscar Levant third billed and this should be a classic. But it isn't. This tale of a dancing couple who split because she wants to be a serious actress starts well and ends well, but loses its way in the middle. Ginger was brought in to renew the partnership that had lapsed for a decade when first choice Judy Garland backed out due to illness. Whatever its shortcomings, Fred and Ginger together again were ample compensations, as were Fred singing 'They Can't Take That Away From Me' and Oscar doing his own version of 'Sabre Dance'.

Barnacle Bill ☉
1957, UK, 87 mins, b/w
Dir: Charles Frend
Stars: Alec Guinness, Irene Browne
Rating: ★★★

This rib-tickling comedy film – although muted by Ealing standards – was the last collaboration from the fantastically successful team of Ealing Studios and Alec Guinness. It was written by T E B Clarke, who also scripted *Hue and Cry*, *Passport to Pimlico*, *The Blue Lamp* and *The Lavender Hill Mob*. And Guinness' talents for comedy and disguise were rarely better displayed than in a witty story that pokes fun at local government and other institutions. Playing Captain Ambrose, who has the sea in his blood but is the world's worst sailor, Guinness also portrays the hero's six ancestors, all of whom die hilariously heroic naval deaths.

Barretts of Wimpole Street, The ○
1934, US, 109 mins, b/w
Dir: Sidney Franklin
Stars: Norma Shearer, Charles Laughton, Fredric March, Maureen O'Sullivan
Rating: ★★★

A well-acted, slightly staid, but handsomely produced version of the romance between Elizabeth Barrett and Robert Browning under the eagle eye of her martinet father. Norma Shearer was never better cast than as Elizabeth and consequently gives her finest film performance, even though she is only one year younger than Charles Laughton, who gives a striking portrayal of the intractable Mr Barrett. Fredric March is poorly cast as Browning, but struggles hard to make something of the role. Director Sidney Franklin must have had a great affection for this most romantic of true stories: 23 years later he remade it for the same studio, this time with Jennifer Jones and Bill Travers.

Barricade ○
1950, US, 75 mins, colour
Dir: Peter Godfrey
Stars: Ruth Roman, Dane Clark, Raymond Massey
Rating: ★★

A gripping little Technicolor thriller with plenty of action. Raymond Massey, so expert a villain, here plays a character so evil that few will forget him. The plot, a landbound remake of *The Sea Wolf*, is unusual and takes several unexpected turnings.

Barton Fink ● Ⓥ
1991, US, 117 mins, colour
Dir: Joel Coen
Stars: John Turturro, John Goodman, Judy Davis, Michael Lerner, John Mahoney, Jon Polito
Rating: ★★

An interesting black joke from the Coen brothers, who gave us *Raising Arizona* and *Miller's Crossing*. Here they dump a much-lauded young Jewish playwright (John Turturro) into the entertainment-oriented Hollywood of 1941. But the film's not only a satire of life in a poverty row studio of the war years, but a dark little number about Fink's run-down hotel, whose wallpaper peels obscenely in the heat from cardboard-thin walls, and whose only inhabitants are a red-eyed bellboy (Steve Buscemi, clearly auditioning for

Renfield in the next Dracula) and an aged liftman who never says anything but the number of the floor. Here Fink meets writer's block, as well as a moose of a man (John Goodman) in the room next door. He's also due to encounter violent death, a towering inferno and, maybe, a head in a hatbox. It's a black comedy that doesn't actually give you much to laugh about, just a shade too clever and perverse for its own good.

Basic Instinct ● Ⓥ
1992, US, 128 mins, colour
Dir: Paul Verhoeven
Stars: Michael Douglas, Sharon Stone, George Dzundza, Jeanne Tripplehorn, Denis Arnt, Leilani Sarelle
Rating: ★★★

Credit director Paul Verhoeven with a keen cinematic brain. He only has about 70 minutes of plot here, so he packs it (cynics might say pads it) with gory murders, hot sex scenes, death defying car chases and lots of lovely California scenery. The result may be flaky tripe, but it goes out and grabs you from the start. The curtain rises on a violent love scene involving a sumptuously built blonde (whose body doesn't quite resemble any one of the three main suspects) who pounds up and down on her lover, ties his hands to the bed posts and pounds up and down on his head with an ice-pick. Gets your attention, right? Enter detective Michael Douglas who interviews the victim's mistress (Sharon Stone), a foul-mouthed, done-it-all millionaire authoress who's just written a book detailing just such a murder. Double bluff? Maybe. But you won't need two guesses to forecast Douglas falling heavily for his shapely suspect. You may not even be sure who dunnit at the end, for the film is pretty good when it remembers to concentrate on the plot. Douglas, Stone and Co snap, snarl, smoulder, smooch and keep straight faces in the cause of melodrama.

Basil The Great Mouse Detective
See: *The Great Mouse Detective*

Bataan ○
1943, US, 114 mins, b/w
Dir: Tay Garnett
Stars: Robert Taylor, George Murphy, Thomas Mitchell
Rating: ★★

A big money-maker and immensely popular in its time, this war film now looks sadly dated with its studio jungles and *10 Little Niggers* plot, as American soldiers defending a Pacific island go off and do silly things so that they keep the plot rolling by getting killed off one by one. In 1943 this was inspiring stuff, and there are still occasional excitements, even though Robert Taylor looks miscast as the sergeant left in charge when the patrol's officer is killed.

Bathing Beauty ○
1944, US, 101 mins, colour
Dir: George Sidney
Stars: Red Skelton, Esther Williams
Rating: ★★

'Hollywood's Mermaid' Esther Williams was launched to stardom in this elaborate aquatic extravaganza. The plot hardly held water, but escapist entertainment was the name of the game and MGM had picked a winner in the form of the champion swimmer who looked just dreamy in a swimsuit and peachy in glorious Technicolor. Good trouper that he is, Red Skelton provides some great comedy, including tripping tutu-clad into a ballet class. Director George Sidney and choreographer John Murray Anderson have a field day with the aquatic climax that mixes fire and water to the strains of Strauss's 'Blue Danube' waltz.

Batman ☉ ⓥ
1966, US, 105 mins, colour
Dir: Leslie H Martinson
Stars: Adam West, Burt Ward, Burgess Meredith, Lee Merriwether, Cesar Romero, Frank Gorshin
Rating: ★★

Colourful film based on the famous television series. Fine fun for children (an perhaps some adults!), with a great performance from Burgess Meredith who squawks splendidly as The Penguin, waddling rings round his fellow-villains.

Batman ☾ ⓥ
1989, US, 126 mins, colour
Dir: Tim Burton
Stars: Michael Keaton, Jack Nicholson, Kim Basinger, Robert Wuhl, Pat Hingle, Billy Dee Williams
Rating: ★★★

This dark and *film noir*-influenced update of the comic-strip hero smashed records left, right and centre. Jack Nicholson's bravura performance as The Joker, with his grotesque acid-scarred clown face and green

hair, takes top honours even if his camp becomes too high before the end. Michael Keaton struggled manfully to bring a human personality to the man in the rubber suit, but it really was The Joker's show. Mick Jagger's girlfriend, Jerry Hall, has a cameo, and Kim Basinger won the role of reporter Vicki Vale only after first choice Sean Young broke her arm during rehearsals. The dark and brooding Prince soundtrack adds to the Gothic atmosphere. The special effects are good, the fight scenes are well done and the Batmobile's pretty impressive, too. There's an almost gothic look to Gotham City at night (like something out of *Metropolis*) and the final confrontation with The Joker atop a skyscraper provides a fitting climax. And remember, the phrase of the season was: 'Never rub another man's rhubarb!'

Batman Returns ☾ ⓥ
1992, US, 127 mins, colour
Dir: Tim Burton
Stars: Michael Keaton, Danny DeVito, Michelle Pfeiffer, Christopher Walken, Michael Gough
Rating: ★★

Amazing in conception, with sets reminiscent of German expressionist movies of the Twenties and Thirties, Batman's joust with The Penguin, Catwoman and Max Schreck is rather less in execution and effect. There's not much story to speak of, resulting in the film falling victim to its own set design. And animal rights protesters are likely to be up in arms at the apparent cruelty to whole hordes of penguins. Michael Keaton's Batman is even more taciturn than before, leading you to wonder from Christopher Walken's Schreck whether he might not have made a better stab at the role. Things start brilliantly, with The Penguin as a baby being dispatched by his father (Paul Rubens, aka Pee-wee Herman) to what he believes is a watery grave. This, like most of the story, takes place against a bleak and snowy backcloth. Saved by penguins and reared in sewers beneath their pool in Gotham Zoo, The Penguin (now Danny DeVito) wreaks havoc in the city with the help of an army of freaks. Walken is a businessman who has been sucking Gotham dry, and 'kills' secretary Michelle Pfeiffer (more fun when she's being ditzy) who is revived by cats and somehow transformed into Catwoman. She and DeVito certainly

look their roles and emote fiercely; even so, the film's darkness works against it where the action is concerned, and you may be looking at your bat watches some time before the end.

*Batteries Not Included ☉ ⓥ
1987, US, 105 mins, colour
Dir: Matthew Robbins
Stars: Hume Cronyn, Jessica Tandy, Frank McRae, Elizabeth Pena
Rating: ★★★★

Elderly apartment owners are hiding out in fear from developers' enforcers with baseball bats. It looks like a case for the A-Team. But wait. The B-Team is at hand, in the form of tiny, living spaceships from a galaxy far, far away. And, after being befriended by old Hume Cronyn and his fellow-fogeys, the aliens will do *anything* to help. This is a very silly film of great charm, whose most engaging scenes are those in which the aliens help Cronyn make a fresh go of his cafe. Though little girls may shed a tear at the appropriate moments, it's perfect viewing for the very young, and a refreshing tonic for the rest of us.

Battle Beneath the Earth ○
1967, UK, 92 mins, colour
Dir: Montgomery Tully
Stars: Viviane Ventura, Kerwin Matthews
Rating: ★

Don't look now but those fiendish Chinese are burrowing under the Pacific with their atom bombs again. 'My God, they're everywhere,' says the Allied supreme commander. Never fear, sir, Professors Kerwin Mathews and Viviane Ventura, in unzipped red boiler suit, will soon put an end to the devils. A film that qualifies for the term 'fantastic' in every sense of the word.

Battle Beyond the Stars ○
1980, US/Japan, 104 mins, colour
Dir: Jimmy T Murakami
Stars: Robert Vaughn, Richard Thomas, George Peppard, John Saxon
Rating: ★★★

A cheeky, colourful science-fiction remake of *The Magnificent Seven*, with Robert Vaughn, looking no different 20 years on, actually returning to his original task as one of the avenging septet. The rest of the space seven include George Peppard as an inter-galactic cowboy and Richard

B

Thomas, once John-Boy of *The Waltons*. Effects are well up to the new par established by such blockbusters as *Star Wars*, and there are some ingenious touches (though not quite enough) like the severed arm that carries on a life of its own. Heroine Darlanne Fluegel is rather put in the shade by the magnificent Sybil Danning as the Valkyrie warrior St Exmin.

Battle Circus ○
1953, US, 90 mins, b/w
Dir: Richard Brooks
Stars: Humphrey Bogart, June Allyson, Keenan Wynn, Robert Keith
Rating: ★★

This Korean War story brings together the sweet and the sour: hard-shelled Humphrey Bogart as a cynical major and girl-next-door June Allyson as the nursing officer who loves him. Bogey and Juney go together like chalk and cheese, but even so the film has its moments, thanks to Richard Brooks' direction, which is superior to his script.

Battle Cry ○
1954, US, 149 mins, colour
Dir: Raoul Walsh
Stars: Van Heflin, Aldo Ray, Tab Hunter, Nancy Olson, Dorothy Malone
Rating: ★★

A long slog through the loves of US Marines en route to battle in World War Two, scripted by Leon M Uris from his own massive novel. The ladies come off best. Anne Francis and Nancy Olson exude warmth, and Dorothy Malone appears in a dry run for the series of fading blondes that would culminate in her Academy Award for *Written on the Wind*.

Battle for Anzio
See: Anzio

Battle for the Planet of the Apes ○ ⓥ
1973, US, 92 mins, colour
Dir: J Lee Thompson
Stars: Roddy McDowall, Claude Akins
Rating: ★★

John Huston's distinctive features prove to be recognisable even under John Chambers' marvellous ape make-up in this, the 'final chapter' of the Apes saga that had begun five years earlier. Much of its force and originality is now blurred but Roddy McDowall's strong performance, he

plays here the son of the character he first created, provides the sturdy central pivot the film sorely needs.

Battleground ○
1949, US, 118 mins, colour
Dir: William Wellman
Stars: Van Johnson, John Hodiak, Ricardo Montalban
Rating: ★★★

War-film fans will like this vivid action film about the Battle of the Bulge, and of American troops fighting against huge odds towards the end of World War Two in Europe. The strong vein of humour is very welcome, and director William Wellman loses no chance to make real human beings out of the characters on the battlefield. He is helped by a talented supporting cast that includes Ricardo Montalban, Richard Jaeckel, Jerome Courtland, Marshall Thompson, Don Taylor, James Whitmore, Denise Darcel, Leon Ames and James Arness.

Battle Hymn ○
1957, US, 108 mins, colour
Dir: Douglas Sirk
Stars: Rock Hudson, Dan Duryea, Anna Kashfi
Rating: ★★★

Rock Hudson's third modern-day adventure in the East (the others were *Spiral Road* and *Thunder of the Gods*) is an exciting and sometimes moving story of a chaplain whose wartime bravery earns him a string of honours. The strong supporting cast includes veteran bad man Dan Duryea, doing well in a rare sympathetic role as Hudson's army sergeant companion.

Battle of Britain ○ ⓥ
1969, UK, 131 mins, colour
Dir: Guy Hamilton
Stars: Michael Caine, Kenneth More, Laurence Olivier, Susannah York, Robert Shaw, Christopher Plummer
Rating: ★★

Reverential, all-star treatment of the famous period of conflict which turned the tide of World War Two. The film comes spectacularly alive in the skies, even though the dialogue remains rooted to the tarmac: watch out for the exchange between Ralph Richardson (British minister) and Curt Jurgens (German baron) which is particularly priceless. Michael Caine is excellent at the head of the all-star cast. On the whole, though, a doomed venture, made at the wrong time.

Battle of Midway, The ○ ⓥ
1976, US, 130 mins, colour
Dir: Jack Smight
Stars: Charlton Heston, Henry Fonda, James Coburn, Glenn Ford
Rating: ★★★

Some of the drama and impact of the mighty World War Two naval battle still emerges from under the weight of a star-studded cast in this blockbuster spectacular which mingles actual wartime footage, sterling star performances and soap-opera subplots. Originally released in Sensurround, the film is now kinder to the eardrums, and will allow you to concentrate on spotting the many stars – including *Magnum*'s Tom Selleck – in minor roles.

Battle of Powder River
See: Tomahawk

Battle of the Bulge ○ ⓥ
1965, US, 163 mins, colour
Dir: Ken Annakin
Stars: Henry Fonda, Robert Shaw, Robert Shaw, Dana Andrews, George Montgomery, Ty Hardin
Rating: ★★★

Blockbuster war film about the Germans' last serious attempt to win the war by making a determined thrust with an army of Tiger tanks in order to gain time to build enough jet planes to blast the Allies out of the sky. Robert Shaw is the fanatical tank commander, blue eyes blazing, Henry Fonda earnest and true as the American officer who pin-points the coming attack and finds the tanks' vital attacking position by gliding through fog in a reconnaisance plane. In the supporting cast James MacArthur catches well the transformation from boy-to-man as the young lieutenant who's the sole survivor of a machine-gun massacre of prisoners; and George Montgomery is particularly noteworthy as a battle-hungry sergeant. Technicolor photography by Jack Hildyard is fresh and clear. Indeed, some of the scenery would be striking enough to grace a Flemish painting if it weren't blighted by war. And the American sense of humour is ever present, never more so than when Fonda and pilot are gliding through the fog. 'We'll pick up a landmark,' says Fonda. 'Sure,' replies the pilot, 'We'll pick up a landmark – right in the kisser.' It's nice to think war was like that as well.

Battle of the River Plate, The ○
(aka: Pursuit of the Graf Spee)
1956, UK, 115 mins, colour
Dir: Michael Powell, Emeric Pressburger
Stars: John Gregson, Anthony Quayle,
Peter Finch, Ian Hunter, Jack Gwillim,
Bernard Lee
Rating: ★★★

A Royal Command Performance film
which aroused a certain amount of
criticism from those who thought
that the war movie was too outdated a
genre in 1956 to set before a queen.
Anthony Quayle is the man to watch
for acting honours in this excellently
made story of how the British finally
caught up with the German battleship
Graf Spee.

Battle of the Sexes, The ○
1960, UK, 83 mins, b/w
Dir: Charles Crichton
Stars: Peter Sellers, Robert Morley,
Constance Cummings
Rating: ★★★

A very funny, often brilliant comedy,
which raises laughs by pitting Scots
canniness (personified by Peter
Sellers) against American efficiency,
embodied by Constance Cummings.
Sellers has rarely been more insidiously
hilarious, and Robert Morley,
wearing what must be one of the
biggest kilts ever made, makes his
tweed magnate boss a fine figure of
pompous fun. The stars are supported
in the ensuing shenanigans by some of
Scotland's finest character players of
the period.

Battle of the V1 ○
(aka: V1)
1958, UK, 109 mins, b/w
Dir: Vernon Sewell
Stars: Michael Rennie, Patricia Medina,
Milly Vitale, David Knight
Rating: ★★

A factually-based wartime drama made
by the veteran and prolific British director Vernon Sewell. Michael
Rennie and David Knight immerse
themselves completely in a thrilling
quantity of cloak-and-dagger work in
the story of a hunt, helped by the
Polish underground, for one of
Hitler's deadliest secret weapons, the
V1 rocket. Actual shots of Royal Air
Force bombing raids heighten the atmosphere of realism.

Battlestar Galactica ○ ⊛
1978, US, 125 mins, colour
Dir: Richard A Colla

Stars: Lorne Greene, Richard L Hatch,
Dirk Benedict, Ray Milland, Ed Begley Jr,
John Colicos
Rating: ★★

Television's answer to *Star Wars*, made
for more than $10 million by Uni-
versal in an attempt to emulate rival
20th Century-Fox's cinema success.
Lorne Greene is an intergalactic Moses, leading a band of fugitives from
across space to a promised land –
Earth. It's more or less a reworking of
Wagon Train, with deadly robots (the
Cylons) substituting for hostile Indians. All good fun, and the effects are
above par, but several shots – in particular the launching of fighter jets –
seem to be repeated endlessly. Dirk
Benedict went on to greater success
as *The A-Team*'s Faceman.

Battle Stations ○
1956, US, 81 mins, b/w
Dir: Lewis Seiler
Stars: John Lund, William Bendix, Keefe
Brasselle, Richard Boone
Rating: ★★

A rather unusual war film about frayed
relationships aboard a 'ghost' US
aircraft carrier, which the Japanese
believe (wrongly) they have sunk.
Director Lewis Seiler came to films via
a flurry of silent Westerns in the early
1920s. But his penchant for war films
soon made itself apparent. *Air Circus*
was his first big one, in 1928, and his
best, the superb *Guadalcanal Diary*,
appeared in 1943. Seiler died in 1964,
after a lifetime in films. This one has a
strong cast of familiar film 'faces'.

Battle Taxi ○
1955, US, 82 mins, b/w
Dir: Herbert L Strock
Stars: Sterling Hayden, Arthur Franz,
Marshall Thompson
Rating: ★★

An all-male war adventure about the
work of the US helicopter rescue service during the Korean conflict. The
action involves some magnificent
stunts with helicopters, and Hollywood stunt pilots had to take some
genuinely alarming risks when the film
was shot.

Bat*21 ● ⊛
1988, US, 105 mins, colour
Dir: Peter Markle
Stars: Gene Hackman, Danny Glover,
Jerry Reed
Rating: ★★★★

This has to be the first Vietnam film to
get the balance right between the

old-style combat movie and the
Platoon bloodbath. And it mixes rugged action and dialogue with
continuous suspense. It laments the
loss of life and the agony involved,
without losing sight of the
continuation of its exciting storyline
or of the necessities of war. Lovers of
action, compassionate thinkers and
pacifists will all find satisfaction here.
On top of that, the true story of a
Lieutenant-Colonel (Gene
Hackman) stranded deep in
Viet-Cong territory with knowledge
vital to the enemy, and his friendship
through radio with the reconnaissance
pilot (Danny Glover) who becomes
determined to save him, works on all
levels. The actors are terrific, the
action exciting and unsparing and the
script rarely puts a foot wrong.
Poignant vignettes punctuate the
tension without breaking it. Good? As
Glover would say, that's a copy!

Beachcomber, The ○
1954, UK, 90 mins, colour
Dir: Muriel Box
Stars: Glynis Johns, Robert Newton,
Donald Sinden, Paul Rogers, Donald
Pleasence
Rating: ★★★

Robert Newton is beautifully cast as
Somerset Maugham's drunken South
Seas vagabond, the Honourable Ted.
This part was first played by Charles
Laughton in the 1938 film *Vessel of
Wrath* in which Newton, strangely,
had a supporting role. Glynis Johns
proves more than a match as the mis-
sionary who first loathes him, then
loves him.

Beaches ◐ ⊛
1988, US, 123 mins, colour
Dir: Garry Marshall
Stars: Bette Midler, Barbara Hershey,
John Heard, Spalding Gray, Lainie
Kazan
Rating: ★★★★

There hasn't been a double-girl bawler
like this since *Old Acquaintance*. Two
11-year-old girls from disparate
backgrounds meet accidentally on a
holiday beach and form a bond of
exceptional friendship that somehow
holds, in spite of long periods apart
and occasional blazing rows, down the
years, through to a tremendous weepie
climax you will need at least two
handkerchiefs to even see. Mary
Agnes Donoghue's script, as adept at
funny one-liners – the film isn't all
tears – as at dramatic confrontations,
pulls all the right emotional strings and

B

Bette Midler and Barbara Hershey, both first-rate, give it full value. Generally it's Hershey's character who has the crises in life and the ebullient Midler who's always on hand with a well-padded shoulder. Besides the stars, mention should be made of Garry Marshall's unobtrusive direction, a couple of bright and entertaining musical numbers, and little Mayim Bialik – who's an 11-year-old Midler to the life – and Marcie Leeds. Basically, though, this is just a terrific script that makes you realise the value of friendship. There aren't too many of those around these days.

Beach Party ⊙
1964, US, 101 mins, colour
Dir: William Asher
Stars: Bob Cummings, Dorothy Malone, Frankie Avalon, Annette Funicello
Rating: ★★★

This teenage surfing comedy musical, about a group of holidaying youngsters 'studied' by a professor and his glamorous assistant, is great fun. Director William Asher swings it along nicely on a slender story and a few songs, and the performances he gets from his actors are uniformly good. The hit of the show is undoubtedly Harvey Lembeck's Eric Von Zipper, the leader of a motorcycle gang, for whom things somehow just won't go right. Watch out for a surprise, unbilled guest star right at the end.

Bear Island ◐ ⓥ
1979, UK/Canada, 118 mins, colour
Dir: Don Sharp
Stars: Donald Sutherland, Vanessa Redgrave, Richard Widmark, Christopher Lee, Lloyd Bridges
Rating: ★★

The usual Alistair MacLean combination of exciting action, rugged far-flung locations, foolish dialogue and positive performances, the exception here being Vanessa Redgrave, whose Norwegian accent makes her sound like Inspector Clouseau. The Arctic settings, beautifully photographed by Ian Hume, give the highly-coloured adventure an additional boost and Don Sharp, who made the sizzling speedboat sequence in another MacLean-inspired film, *Puppet on a Chain*, this time offers us a snowboat chase guaranteed to warm the iciest blood.

Beast from 20,000 Fathoms, The ◐
1953, US, 80 mins, b/w
Dir: Eugene Lourie
Stars: Paul Christian, Paula Raymond, Cecil Kellaway, Lee Van Cleef
Rating: ★★

A science fiction adventure, based on a tale by Ray Bradbury, about a gigantic monster, this has some fine special effects from Ray Harryhausen, and an early featured role for Lee Van Cleef, who's allowed to take a pot shot at the creature loose in the city. Many of the sets in the film were built at enormous expense – only to be quickly destroyed as part of the plot. A costly routine, but the effect is convincing. One of the props was a huge mock iceberg. For the base of the model technicians packed together 40 tons of plaster, 30 tons of salt and – to make it crackle realistically under the actors' feet – 500lbs of cornflakes. To complete the structure, they crushed 70 tons of real ice and sprayed it over the cornflakes. It was the biggest helping of frosted flakes Hollywood had ever seen!

Beast of the City ○
1932, US, 87 mins, b/w
Dir: Charles Brabin
Stars: Walter Huston, Jean Harlow, Wallace Ford, Jean Hersholt, Mickey Rooney
Rating: ★★★

Strong gangster drama which was one of the first films to tell the crime battle from the policeman's point of view. Jean Harlow is at her best as the blonde who tempts the police chief's brother (Wallace Ford) off the straight and narrow, and the film ends, as one contemporary reviewer put it, 'in the biggest massacre in years.'

Beasts of Marseilles, The
See: Seven Thunders

Beast with Five Fingers, The ◐
1946, US, 88 mins, b/w
Dir: Curt Siodmak
Stars: Peter Lorre, Robert Alda, Andrea King
Rating: ★★★

William Fryer Harvey's classic story of the macabre is brought to the screen, with Peter Lorre giving an eye-popping, memorable performance as the man haunted by the beast of the title (a severed hand with a life of its own). Directed with a bravura touch

by Robert Florey (he made his first great horror film, *The Murders in the Rue Morgue*, back in 1932), endowing the scary proceedings with a unique nightmare quality.

Beat Street ◐
1984, US, 107 mins, colour
Dir: Stan Lathan
Stars: Rae Dawn Chong, Guy Davis, Jon Chardiet, Leon W Grant
Rating: ★★★★

Or: Street Beat. For this emotive musical, centred round the shortlived breakdancing craze, takes us right down to street level. Here are ghettoes that look like ghettoes, subways that look like subways and housing conditions made to appear genuinely cramped – both a disgrace to humanity and credit to those who rise above them. And, despite its story thread of lovers from different sides of the tracks, this is a film totally lacking in pretentiousness; rarely does it go over the top. Semi-allegorical elements are woven with surprising grace into the fabric of a beat musical, and give it an emotive bite not seen in this kind of entertainment since *West Side Story*. The rap music, with its easy-to-hear jive talk, is well done by the performers, while its characters, and certainly the lower-life ones, seem real and not contrived and the climax will bring tears to your eyes as well as taps to your toes. Grab this beat: it makes *Flashdance* seem like a damp squib.

Beat the Devil ○
1953, US/UK, 100 mins, b/w
Dir: John Huston
Stars: Humphrey Bogart, Gina Lollobrigida, Peter Lorre, Jennifer Jones, Robert Morley
Rating: ★★★

This offbeat comedy-thriller may be the strangest of the several films made together by Humphrey Bogart and John Huston. With its African setting and curious mix of ill-assorted people, it's always a treat to look at, but sometimes odd to listen to. Huston's script (co-written with the somewhat eccentric Truman Capote) is full of peculiar asides and little in-jokes. Of the splendidly cosmopolitan cast, Gina Lollobrigida looks the most uncomfortable and Peter Lorre comes off the best. An indispensable part of many of Bogart's successes in the Forties, Lorre was persuaded to return to the screen after ill-health had forced him into retirement. This new, plumper Lorre went on to take scene-stealing parts in several horror spoofs before his eventual death in 1964. Here, his expressive face and courtly manner with dialogue provide many quiet chuckles in an erratically entertaining film.

Beau Brummell ○
1954, US/UK, 111 mins, colour
Dir: Curtis Bernhardt
Stars: Stewart Granger, Elizabeth Taylor, Peter Ustinov, Robert Morley, James Donald
Rating: ★★★

One of the most colourful and convincing slices of history that MGM ever produced, *Beau Brummell* inevitably courted controversy when it was chosen as the Royal Command Performance film of its year. Some thought that it distorted historical facts, while others protested that it wasn't cricket to present royalty with a portrait of, to say the least, an eccentric ancestor in George III. Some said that the film wasn't good enough; others raved. But the Regency atmosphere is marvellously well caught in this portrait of the scandalous Brummell (Stewart Granger) – leader of fashion in his day, spendthrift and scoundrel. The impact of the film is heightened by the magnificent performance of Peter Ustinov as the Prince of Wales. The actor reveals the prince as a man not to be laughed at, but sympathised with. Together, he and Granger make the final scene a moving movie moment. And Elizabeth Taylor, portraying Lady Patricia, never looked more beautiful, under the loving gaze of Oswald Morris's colour camera.

Beau Geste ○
1939, US, 114 mins, b/w
Dir: William A Wellman
Stars: Gary Cooper, Ray Milland, Robert Preston, Susan Hayward, Brian Donlevy, J Carrol Naish
Rating: ★★★

Like Robert Mitchum, Gary Cooper had a deceptively lazy delivery that endeared him to millions, although he had a gentler style than Mitchum, and there was nearly always a twinkle of humour behind the eyes. Here he is Beau (of course) in the best screen version of P C Wren's classic yarn of three brothers who join the Foreign Legion. The climax at the fort littered with dead men gave rise to a thousand comedy skits, and Brian Donlevy

gave one of his most memorable screen portrayals as the scarred and sadistic sergeant.

Beau James ○
1957, US, 107 mins, colour
Dir: Melville Shavelson
Stars: Bob Hope, Vera Miles, Paul Douglas, Alexis Smith
Rating: ★★★

Quite a pleasant excursion into romantic nostalgia, made at a time when Bob Hope was trying to widen the range of his appeal. The drama lacks bite, but the period atmosphere has a melancholy charm and there are some bright guest spots.

Beautiful Blonde from Bashful Bend, The ○
1949, US, 77 mins, colour
Dir: Preston Sturges
Stars: Betty Grable, Cesar Romero, Rudy Vallee, Olga San Juan, Sterling Holloway
Rating: ★★

The last of a long string of comedy hits that made their writer-director, Preston Sturges, something of a cult figure in the film world. This story of a lady sharpshooter might have been merrier with another Betty (Hutton) in the lead but a supporting cast to delight all vintage-film fans includes Margaret Hamilton (the green-faced witch from *The Wizard of Oz*), Sterling Holloway, Olga San Juan, and three stars of 1930s two-reeler comedies: Hugh Herbert, El Brendel and Chester Conklin. Sturges' fortunes were well on the wane by this time, and critics slammed the film. By most directors' standards, however, it remains a pretty enjoyable romp.

Beauty and the Beast ⊙ ⓥ
1991, US, 85 mins, colour
Dir: Gary Trousdale, Kirk Wise
Voice stars: Paige O'Hara, Robby Benson, Gerry Orbach, Angela Lansbury, Jo Anne Worley
Rating: ★★★★

A classic Disney cartoon feature, very much in the tradition of *Sleeping Beauty*, but with slightly more wit and innovation in the minor characters, and with 'big' Broadway-style songs rather than 'novelty' numbers. Beauty is not *too* beautiful and the Beast not *too* beastly, but even so they're outshone by the servants at the Beast's castle, all of whom have been turned into things like clocks, candlesticks, wardrobes and teapots. Hit of the show is undoubtedly a Chevalier-style

candelabra called Lumiere, who also leads off the most enjoyable musical number, when all the utensils launch into a Ziegfeld Follies routine while inviting Beauty to 'Be Our Guest'. But the film is also poignant, scary, exciting and invigorating when it needs to be: no doubt about it, Disney Studios are still well ahead in this tricky field. And remember, in the words of the clock: 'If it ain't Baroque, don't fix it!'

Beauty Jungle, The ○
(aka: Contest Girl)
1963, UK, 114 mins, colour
Dir: Val Guest
Stars: Janette Scott, Ian Hendry, Ronald Fraser, Edmund Purdom
Rating: ★★

Val Guest's eminently watchable portrait of the in-fighting behind the plastic smiles and pneumatic busts of the beauty contest world. Janette Scott is the no-claws-barred beauty queen and Ian Hendry is as excellent as ever as the manager who moulds her to his ideal.

Because of Him ⊙
1945, US, 88 mins, b/w
Dir: Richard Wallace
Stars: Deanna Durbin, Charles Laughton, Franchot Tone
Rating: ★★★

This musical, pleasantly centred on a series of amusing absurdities, isn't quite up to the standard of Deanna Durbin and Charles Laughton's previous venture together, *It Started with Eve* four years earlier. But Deanna's millions of fans will enjoy her singing 'Danny Boy' and Laughton steals the show as a conceited stage star. Franchot Tone, too, as a Broadway playwright, shows a fine sense of the ridiculous.

Because You're Mine ○
1952, US, 103 mins, colour
Dir: Alexander Hall
Stars: Mario Lanza, Doretta Morrow, James Whitmore
Rating: ★★

Mario Lanza (alias Alfred Cocozza from Philadelphia) got a new co-star in the curvy Doretta Morrow (alias Doretta Marano from Brooklyn) in the fourth of his musicals for MGM, which saw the real beginning of the weight problems (he had shed almost five stones, rather too much, since *The Great Caruso*) that would help to undermine his sensational film career.

B

Here he anticipated Elvis Presley eight years later by playing a popular singer drafted to the army. Besides the title song, the hits included 'Be My Love' (revised from *The Toast of New Orleans*), 'All the Things You Are' and Lanza's own smash rendition of 'The Lord's Prayer'. Seven years later he was dead, from a heart attack after yet another crash diet. It was the lovely Morrow's only film and she, too, was not destined for a long life, dying from cancer aged 42.

Becket ○
1966, US/UK, 148 mins, colour
Dir: Peter Glenville
Stars: Richard Burton, Peter O'Toole, John Gielgud, Donald Wolfit, Martita Hunt
Rating: ★★★

Superior entertainment in a powerful story of the friendship-turned-sour between Henry II (a flamboyantly eye-catching performance by Peter O'Toole) and his one-time fellow adventurer Thomas Becket. British director Peter Glenville splashes the exciting slice of history convincingly across his colour canvas. And the dialogue is studded with sparkling phrases. One particularly remembers Becket's description of the shedding of his worldly goods as 'the clumsy gesture of a spiritual gatecrasher.'

Bedazzled ◑
1967, UK, 107 mins, colour
Dir: Stanley Donen
Stars: Peter Cook, Dudley Moore, Eleanor Bron, Raquel Welch, Barry Humphries
Rating: ★★

After their success on British TV, this was Peter Cook and Dudley Moore's biggest attempt to break into the world of mainline film comedy. But the most successful sequence in this story of a little man (Dud) who sells his soul to the Devil (Pete) in return for seven wishes, is the 'leaping nuns', itself a direct transference from television. And, despite several tries since at re-teaming, both of these funny men proved most successful with solo ventures. Raquel Welch puts in a guest appearance here as one of the seven deadly sins. Yes, she's Lust.

Bedelia ○
1946, UK, 90 mins, b/w
Dir: Lance Comfort

Stars: Margaret Lockwood, Ian Hunter, Barry K Barnes, Anne Crawford
Rating: ★★

Margaret Lockwood proved in such epics as *The Wicked Lady* and *The Man in Grey* that she can bring an immaculate polish to the parts of evil women. She does it once more in this tale of a bewitching murderess who disposes of one husband after another for their insurance money.

Bedford Incident, The ○ ⊙
1965, US, 105 mins, b/w
Dir: James B Harris
Stars: Richard Widmark, Sidney Poitier, James MacArthur, Martin Balsam
Rating: ★★★

James Poe, best known for his adaptations of Tennessee Williams' plays for the screen (*Cat on a Hot Tin Roof, Summer and Smoke*), here contributes a concise, brittle screenplay which does a lot to build up the tension in the story of an American nuclear warship tracking a Russian atomic submarine, as both steer an uneasy course through icebergs off the coast of Greenland. Richard Widmark is superb as the insanely patriotic warship skipper who takes his men to the limits of their endurance and his country to the brink of war.

Bedknobs and Broomsticks ⊙
1971, US, 117 mins, colour
Dir: Robert Stevenson
Stars: Angela Lansbury, David Tomlinson, Roddy McDowall, Sam Jaffe, Bruce Forsyth
Rating: ★★★

Disney follow-up to *Mary Poppins*, with some enchanting cartoon segments (directed by Ward Kimball) inserted into its live-action story about a trio of evacuee children who undergo some remarkable adventures in 1940 with the assistance of a down-to-earth witch (personably portrayed by *Murder She Wrote*'s Angela Lansbury). The undersea sequences, with their accompanying song – 'Bobbing Along on the Bottom of the Beautiful Briny Sea' – will delight younger viewers. It was artfully reissued by Disney with the selling line 'You'll believe a woman can fly!'

Bedlam ●
1946, US, 80 mins, b/w
Dir: Mark Robson
Stars: Boris Karloff, Anna Lee
Rating: ★★★

Addicts of the macabre should on no account miss this. The last of the famous Val Lewton/RKO horror classics of the Forties, this has a fine sense of period atmosphere, filling one with revulsion for the conditions in which unfortunate asylum inmates are forced to exist. Anna Lee gives one of her best performances as the intrepid heroine.

Bedroom Window, The ● ⓥ
1987, US, 115 mins, colour
Dir: Curtis Hanson
Stars: Steve Guttenberg, Elizabeth McGovern, Isabelle Huppert, Paul Shenar
Rating: ★★★

A silly but entertaining thriller which follows some unexpected paths to reach a familiar chase-and-rescue, trap-the-killer climax. Steve Guttenberg fairly convincingly takes a change of pace as the yuppie executive whose affair with the boss's wife (Isabelle Huppert, not very good) leads them to the edge of a whirlpool of circumstance when, just after sex, she witnesses a psycho attacking a young girl (Elizabeth McGovern). Knowing she can't tell the police because of their affair, Guttenberg volunteers to be the witness; when, through a hazardous chain of events, Guttenberg himself becomes a suspect, Huppert refuses to come to his aid. Although it gets nowhere near Hitchcock's black logic, the film's hook of suspense works well enough to keep us snapping at the bait until an undeniably tense and exciting climax, worked out in fairly formula fashion by director Curtis Hanson. Not even Hitch, though, could have helped McGovern, otherwise solid, bring off a bar-room sequence in which she has to 'lure' the killer into following her.

Bedtime for Bonzo ⊙
1951, US, 83 mins, b/w
Dir: Norman Taurog
Stars: Ronald Reagan, Diana Lynn, Walter Slezak
Rating: ★★

Ronald Reagan stars in a bright comedy that's often cited as the lowpoint of his career, presumably on the grounds that it teamed him with a chimp. But it's certainly better than one or two other films he made at this time, and shows him to be a relaxed comedy player undeterred by the inevitability of being upstaged by an animal. Diana Lynn is a delightful heroine and the chimpanzee (who died tragically in a fire soon after the film had been completed) is hilarious.

Bedtime Story ○
1941, US, 85 mins, b/w
Dir: Alexander Hall
Stars: Fredric March, Loretta Young, Robert Benchley
Rating: ★★★

A sparkling, racy romantic comedy with the accent on laughs, made by director Alexander Hall hard on the heels of his classic fantasy-farce, *Here Comes Mr Jordan*. Wittily scripted by Richard Flournoy, who cut his writing teeth on the earliest (and best) of the *Blondie* comedies, the plot's developments keep stars Fredric March and Loretta Young on their toes – just as well since they're confronted by a battery of supporting scene-stealers, including Eve Arden, Robert Benchley, Helen Westley and Joyce Compton. And, thanks in part to Joseph Walker's top-grade photography, Loretta has never looked lovelier.

Bedtime Story ○
1964, US, 99 mins, colour
Dir: Ralph Levy
Stars: Marlon Brando, David Niven, Shirley Jones
Rating: ★★★

'But isn't there a name for men who get money from women?', says David Niven to Marlon Brando in this smoothly-crafted entertainment. 'Yeah,' replies Brando. 'Smart!' Both men are confidence tricksters – in very different circles, Niven being an upper-crust devil – but Brando's upstart learns fast. Soon the rivals are battling it out for the rogues' kingdom of the Riviera. Both Brando and Niven give excellent performances in this polished, pleasant comedy that's enjoyable without being uproarious and shot in terrific Technicolor. Remade in 1988 with Steve Martin and Michael Caine, as *Dirty Rotten Scoundrels*.

Beethoven ○
1992, US, 87 mins, colour
Dir: Brian Levant
Stars: Charles Grodin, Bonnie Hunt, Stanley Tucci, Dean Jones Oliver Platt, David Duchovny
Rating: ★★

If you love oversized, slobbering pooches then this mutt comedy will be right up your kennel. The title character is a 185lb Saint Bernard

dog. Stolen as a puppy he stumbles into the lives of the Newton family – much to the annoyance of father (Charles Grodin). The human cast, a pretty good one by the standards of this sort of romp, all contribute well, but even so are constantly upstaged by their massive four-legged co-star. The surprise comedy hit of its year, *Beethoven* has already spawned one sequel and more are promised. Good, clean family fun, thank goodness, with a particularly good role for Dean Jones, well at home in Disney-style romps in his days as a star but here enjoying himself hugely as the villain.

Beethoven's 2nd ○ ⓥ
1993, US, 89 mins, colour
Dir: Rod Daniel
Stars: Charles Grodin, Bonnie Hunt, Debi Mazar
Rating: ★

A pretty basic doggy comedy with a bit of plot-pinching from *101 Dalmatians*. Beethoven the Saint Bernard falls in love with Missy, a lady dog owned by the monstrous Regina, and Missy subsequently (after a lot of romantic music and twosome shots) has four puppies which the children of Beethoven's reluctant master (Charles Grodin) hide in the basement. Since the family is broke, it would seem to be easier to sell the pups. But no. Even father agrees to keep them, thus setting the rest of the plot in motion in which Regina (Debi Mazar), in true Cruella De Vil style, decides to get the profit-making litter for herself. The rest of the story is very simple fun that will keep young children amused while dad does a crossword. Best scene: Beethoven pulling down half a holiday cabin (thus saving his teenage mistress from rape) and dowsing its partying occupants in the adjoining lake.

Beetlejuice ○ ⓥ
1988, US, 92 mins, colour
Dir: Tim Burton
Stars: Alec Baldwin, Geena Davis, Michael Keaton, Jeffrey Jones, Winona Ryder, Sylvia Sidney
Rating: ★★★

A wild comic fantasy from the director of *Batman* and *Edward Scissorhands*. Tim Burton's unstructured but visually delightful live-action cartoon provides Michael Keaton, looking like Ken Dodd after an accident, with a non-star-billed but definitely star part as the raucous and repulsive 'bio-exorciser' Betelgeuse, who can

only be contacted when his name is pronounced (correctly) three consecutive times. Among those who feel the need to contact him are Mr and Mrs Maitland (Alec Baldwin and Geena Davis), a couple of newly-deads who are confined to a living hell in their own home which is being destroyed by its obnoxious new owners, a city couple with a daughter (Winona Ryder) majoring in weirdness. Burton's quirky vision of the afterlife springs into life only when the grotesque Keaton's on screen. But, although it needed to be a bit sharper, this witches' brew is still free and easy fun.

Before Winter Comes ○
1968, UK, 102 mins, colour
Dir: J Lee Thompson
Stars: David Niven, Topol, Anna Karina, John Hurt, Anthony Quayle
Rating: ★

One of the films that Israeli star Topol made on the strength of his stage success (later repeated in the film version) in *Fiddler on the Roof*. Here he plays a kind-of-jack-of-all-trades at a camp for displaced persons in Austria just after World War Two. Pretty Technicolor photography by Gilbert Taylor almost compensates for the non-emergence of any positive storyline, and there's a good performance by John Hurt as an eager but inexperienced junior officer.

Beggar's Opera, The ○
1952, UK, 94 mins, colour
Dir: Peter Brook
Stars: Laurence Olivier, Stanley Holloway, George Devine, Dorothy Tutin
Rating: ★★★

John Gay's colourful musical play eventually begot the memorable *Threepenny Opera*. But here's the original version of the story of the scoundrel awaiting execution, and the women who create his lifeline. Laurence Olivier (as Macheath) and Stanley Holloway sing their own songs, the rest of the cast is superbly dubbed by operatic experts. Vivid, vigorous and stimulating, if perhaps never quite true cinema. Brilliant Technicolor photography by Guy Green, who could always be relied on for a first-class job, and a small early role for Kenneth Williams.

Beguiled, The ○ ⓥ
1970, US, 109 mins, colour
Dir: Don Siegel

Stars: Clint Eastwood, Geraldine Page, Elizabeth Hartman
Rating: ★★★

'Guess you're drying up like the rest of us women round here,' murmurs the housekeeper to the milkless cow – a comment which encapsulates the content of this, perhaps the strangest yet most spellbinding film that the *Dirty Harry* combination of Clint Eastwood and director Don Siegel ever made. Ostensibly a close-knit drama with a background of the American Civil War, the story soon develops into a kind of full blooded Southern states melodrama, smouldering with supressed passions, at which Geraldine Page excels. Once again she's a fading Southern belle, brooding over the past, and here in charge of a seminary for young ladies which is turned into a hotbed of intrigue with the arrival of a wounded Unionist soldier who soon reveals his opportunist nature. It's a haunting film, frequently near the edge of credibility and self-parody, but held back by Siegel's teasingly ambiguous direction and the often dream-like qualities of Bruce Surtees' colour camerawork.

Behemoth the Sea Monster ◑
1959, UK, 70 mins, colour
Dir: Eugene Lourie, Douglas Hickox
Stars: Gene Evans, Andre Morell, Leigh Madison
Rating: ★★★

Monster-from-the-depths film co-directed by Eugene Lourie – once production designer for director Jean Renoir – and Douglas Hickox. Hickox, then only 30, later made *Sitting Target* and *Brannigan*, with John Wayne. Hickox was only 59 when he died in 1988. Brisk, punchy and good of its kind.

Behind the Mask ○
1958, UK, 99 mins, colour
Dir: Brian Desmond Hurst
Stars: Michael Redgrave, Tony Britton, Carl Mohner
Rating: ★★

Vanessa Redgrave made a low-key screen debut in this serious-minded hospital drama made as a vehicle for her distinguished father, Michael Redgrave, who plays a wealthy, deeply-caring surgeon constantly at odds with dispassionate associates. Brian Desmond Hurst's busy direction keeps our interest going, and there's

sharp Eastman Colour photography along those white corridors by the Oscar-winning Robert Krasker.

Behold a Pale Horse ◑
1964, US, 118 mins, b/w
Dir: Fred Zinnemann
Stars: Gregory Peck, Anthony Quinn, Omar Sharif
Rating: ★

Made just after *Lawrence of Arabia*, in which Omar Sharif scored a great personal success, this very slow adventure film has him as a priest caught between an ex-guerilla leader and the police chief who has sworn to catch him. The director is the distinguished Fred Zinnemann, and the journey on film before the adversaries finally clash, though long, is often pictorially beautiful. But, in the acting clash, the stars are all put in the shade by Raymond Pellegrin's portrait of an informer – drawn to the life.

Being There ○
1979, US, 130 mins, colour
Dir: Hal Ashby
Stars: Peter Sellers, Shirley MacLaine, Melvyn Douglas, Jack Warden, Richard Basehart
Rating: ★★★

If you like comedies of embarrassment, then this simple-minded black farce will delight you. Peter Sellers was nominated for an Academy Award as the illiterate middle-aged gardener who, in a few days, moves from a sheltered existence through a ludicrously improbable series of misunderstandings to candidacy for the United States presidency. But it was Melvyn Douglas who took the film's Oscar as his benefactor.

Believers, The ●
1987, US, 113 mins, colour
Dir: John Schlesinger
Stars: Martin Sheen, Helen Shaver, Robert Loggia, Harris Yulin, Jimmy Smits
Rating: ★

An unfortunate title for a nasty voodoo chiller so full of improbabilities and implausibilities. A pity, for a lot of it is excitingly made by director John Schlesinger; it is events rather than script that torpedo this one amidships. A good cast does its best to lend credibility to the story of a psychotherapist (Martin Sheen) who has lost his wife in an accident in the home and moves with his small son (engagingly played by Harley Cross) to another city where he finds that boys

are being slaughtered in the cause of some obscure and evil sideshoot of a tribal religion. Sheen, Helen Shaver, Robert Loggia and others have undoubtedly registered better elsewhere, even though they give *The Believers* all that their producer and director could ask.

Bell, Book and Candle ○
1958, US, 103 mins, colour
Dir: Richard Quine
Stars: James Stewart, Kim Novak, Jack Lemmon, Hermione Gingold, Elsa Lanchester
Rating: ★★★

This delightful witchcraft comedy is fun all the way and allows James Stewart, Jack Lemmon and Kim Novak to let their hair down in no uncertain fashion, Lemmon in particular having a great time as an impish warlock. The film is almost stolen from all of them by a talented Siamese cat called Pyewacket.

Bell Bottom George ○
1943, UK, 97 mins, b/w
Dir: Marcel Varnel
Stars: George Formby
Rating: ★★

George Formby's film career was dipping into decline when he made this wartime caper which has three scriptwriters trying to think up new things for the lad from Lancashire to do. Comedy expert Marcel Varnel makes the most of what they devise and George sings the title song and 'Swim Little Fish' among others.

Belle de Jour ● ⓥ
1967, France/Italy, 100 mins, colour
Dir: Luis Buñuel
Stars: Catherine Deneuve, Jean Sorel, Michel Piccoli
Rating: ★★★

A surrealistic voyage into the mind of a bored, wealthy housewife (Catherine Deneuve) who leads the double life of afternoon prostitution. Director Luis Buñuel blends memory, fantasy and reality seamlessly, and it is never certain if what is seen is reality or fantasy. An exquisite and spellbinding film whose moral tone (Buñuel refuses to judge his character's actions) shocked Mary Whitehouse and her supporters into a vocal campaign against the BBC on its first TV screening.

Belle of New York, The ☉
1952, US, 82 mins, colour
Dir: Charles Walters
Stars: Fred Astaire, Vera-Ellen, Marjorie Main, Keenan Wynn
Rating: ★★★

A lighter-than-air MGM musical which producer Arthur Freed had originally intended as a Fred Astaire-Judy Garland vehicle in 1946. Garland dropped out, however, and the film went in front of the cameras in June 1951 with Vera-Ellen as the nimble Fred's leading lady. An attractive score by Harry Warren and Johnny Mercer includes 'Seeing's Believing' (well-named, since the stars literally dance on air to it) and one that became something of an Astaire trademark, 'I Wanna Be a Dancin' Man'. Alice Pearce, who scored such a hit in another MGM musical, *On the Town* (as Gene Kelly's wallflower date), raises more laughs here as a sassy Salvation Army girl.

Belle of the Nineties ○
1934, US, 73 mins, b/w
Dir: Leo McCarey
Stars: Mae West, Roger Pryor, John Mack Brown
Rating: ★★

Mae West in full flood (or, at least, in as full a flood as contemporary censorship allowed) in a typical vehicle scripted by her and thus giving her the chance to use all her co-stars as stooges off whom to bounce her memorable one-liners. If her screenplay owes more to vaudeville melodramas than anything else, it does allow her to sing 'My Old Flame', 'American Beauty' and 'Troubled Waters', with Duke Ellington's Orchestra in nifty support. Villainy comes from John Miljan. Roger Pryor and Johnny Mack Brown are among those caught up in the whirlwind from the West and director Leo McCarey knows what he is doing.

Belles of St Trinian's, The ☉
1954, UK, 91 mins, b/w
Dir: Frank Launder
Stars: Alastair Sim, Joyce Grenfell, George Cole, Hermione Baddeley
Rating: ★★★

The first and best of the crazy comedies devoted to the merry, madcap, mayhem-bent misses of St Trinian's School, created by cartoonist Ronald Searle. Alastair Sim, helped by witty dialogue that one can almost see him savour, is a riot in the dual roles of a headmistress of dubious honesty and her brother, a bookmaker of even more dubious morals.

Belle Starr ○ ⓥ
1941, US, 87 mins, colour
Dir: Irving Cummings
Stars: Gene Tierney, Randolph Scott, Dana Andrews, John Sheppard, Elizabeth Patterson
Rating: ★★★

Back in the days when the Technicolor Western was big and broad, they made films like the original *Belle Starr*. Ernest Palmer and Ray Rennahan's colour photography is as lush as it comes, the action is just sufficient and doesn't intrude on the well-handled love interest. Gene Tierney, always at her best as tough cookies, is just right as the gun-toting heroine, while Randolph Scott would have to wait more than 15 years for comparable hard-hitting roles. This certainly arouses an unusual amount of emotion for a film of its kind, with its excellent story and superior supporting performances from Dana Andrews, John Sheppard (later Shepperd Strudwick) and Louise Beavers.

Belle Starr ○
1980, US, 97 mins, colour
Dir: John A Alonzo
Stars: Elizabeth Montgomery, Cliff Potts, Fred Ward
Rating: ★★

Elizabeth Montgomery hits the Western trail she trod six years previous in the TV movie *Mrs Sundance*, a follow-up to the successful cinema hit *Butch Cassidy and the Sundance Kid*. And once again she plays the wife of a desperado, this time the legendary Belle Starr, Queen of the Old West. It's a pity that the script fails to deliver the goods and not even this highly-talented actress can make much of an impression. Director/ cinematographer John A Alonzo, however, comes up trumps in the atmosphere department, with a series of wonderful rustic, golden-lit scenes.

Bell for Adano, A ○
1945, US, 104 mins, b/w
Dir: Henry King
Stars: Gene Tierney, John Hodiak, William Bendix, Richard Conte
Rating: ★★★

John Hodiak never realised his full potential in Hollywood films – except in the leading role of this touching, human account of an American army unit in charge of a small Italian town during World War Two. The many characters are vividly coloured in, and Henry King's sensitive direction is in tune with his subject throughout.

Bellman and True ●
1987, UK, 122 mins, colour
Dir: Richard Loncraine
Stars: Bernard Hill, Derek Newark, Kieran O'Brien, Richard Hope, Frances Tomelty, Ken Bones
Rating: ★★

Deliberately doomy and tortuously long (with lots of shots of people in rooms thinking), this is a crime film with distinct ambitions in the direction of stature. The lugubrious Bernard Hill can scarcely raise a smile as the alcoholic computer gadgets expert reluctantly drawn into a big-time caper of increasing complexity. The first half of the film concerns his entrapment (via the stepson who lives with him, running from lodging to lodging), the second the planning and execution of the raid (on a major holding bank) itself. There's too little of such crustily amusing dialogue as the gang boss (Derek Newark) employs with his tunnellers ('Thanks lads. If you hurry you might just catch the last tube') and just too much gloom and doom. The slow motion at the beginning is maddening although it does set the film's Bellstately pace in which the bursts of action towards the end come as a welcome relief.

Bells Are Ringing ○
1960, US, 127 mins, colour
Dir: Vincente Minnelli
Stars: Judy Holliday, Dean Martin, Fred Clark
Rating: ★★

This musical-comedy romp was the last film made by Judy Holliday before she died of throat cancer a few years later. Here she's her usual dizzy self as a girl who runs a telephone answering service and gets involved in the lives of her customers. The voice she falls in love with belongs to Dean Martin. This fast-moving piece was originally a stage hit for Judy and it was adapted for the screen by Betty Comden and Adolph Green, who wrote the play with Jule Styne. Good fun, with some good songs, too, including 'Just in Time' and 'The Party's Over'. Jazz fans will spot baritone sax player Gerry Mulligan in a minor role. He was married to Judy at the time of her death.

B

Bells of St Mary's, The ○ Ⓥ

1945, US, 126 mins, b/w
Dir: Leo McCarey
Stars: Bing Crosby, Ingrid Bergman, Henry Travers, Ruth Donnelly, Rhys Williams
Rating: ★★★

Bing Crosby stars again as Father O'Malley in a sequel to *Going My Way*, for which he had won an Oscar in the previous year. Both films, which are among his best-remembered, blend pathos and humour with perfect professionalism. Here he teams delightfully with Ingrid Bergman, who plays a nun running a school on a shoestring. Both *Going My Way* and *The Bells of St Mary's* were directed by Leo McCarey, who also won an Oscar for the former film. McCarey had worked with Laurel and Hardy, The Marx Brothers and Mae West before winning his first two Oscars in the late Thirties for *The Awful Truth* and *Love Affair*. The title song, sung by Bing, was a huge hit at the time, and the film was at the top of the box-office for its year, grossing nearly $4 million in America alone, on a budget of little more than a million.

Belly of an Architect, The ●

1987, UK/Italy, 118 mins, colour
Dir: Peter Greenaway
Stars: Brian Dennehy, Chloe Webb
Rating: ★★

After years of contributing memorable supporting performances to a wide variety of films (from *Butch and Sundance: The Early Days* to *Gorky Park* and *Cocoon*), heavyweight American character actor Brian Dennehy achieved star status in this art-house work from Peter Greenaway, director of *The Draughtsman's Contract*. Dennehy is the architect of the title, mounting a prestigious exhibition in Rome but obsessed by intestinal problems which may, or may not, be phantom symptoms parallelling his much younger wife's pregnancy. Despite Dennehy's imposing presence and the excellent use of ravishing Roman locations, the film fails to engage the emotions because of the director's typically cool approach and his reluctance to confront the drama head-on. As a succession of visually pleasing sequences, however, it works well enough.

Beloved Infidel ○

1959, US, 123 mins, colour
Dir: Henry King
Stars: Gregory Peck, Deborah Kerr, Eddie Albert, Philip Ober
Rating: ★★

F Scott Fitzgerald, on whose novel the films of *The Great Gatsby* were based, gets the Hollywood biopic treatment in this tear-jerker. Directed in a curiously tired fashion by Henry King, who has such excellent films as *Wait 'Til the Sun Shines, Nellie, In Old Chicago, The Gunfighter, Twelve O'Clock High* (both the last two with Gregory Peck) and *Carousel* to his credit.

Ben ●

1972, US, 95 mins, colour
Dir: Phil Karlson
Stars: Lee Harcourt Montgomery, Joseph Campanella
Rating: ★★

Restored to the big city by night – the surroundings in which he has always worked best – director Phil Karlson made a belated return to something like form with this no-frills, no-nonsense sequel to *Willard*, relating the further adventures of Ben, the rat who walked by himself. The pursuit of Ben by police through the city's storm drains could, in fact, just as easily be a manhunt as a rat-hunt. Karlson directs his action – and its integral if familiar elements of harassed policeman, sympathetic child who befriends rat, and fast-talking, cynical reporter – with a brusque intensity against sombre, low-key settings, building steadily to the fiery climax.

Bend of the River

See: Where the River Bends

Beneath the Planet of the Apes ◑ Ⓥ

1970, US, 95 mins, colour
Dir: Ted Post
Stars: James Franciscus, Charlton Heston, Kim Hunter
Rating: ★★★

Although it lacks the impact of the actual premise of the original *Planet of the Apes*, this first sequel is in many ways more exciting and visually stylish than the original, with a good script and some particularly suspenseful and striking scenes in the overgrown ruins of what was once the New York subway. James Franciscus takes over the reins of the principal role from Charlton Heston, who makes a crucial cameo appearance towards the end of the film. This is, incidentally, the only Ape film in which Roddy McDowall

does not appear. His role as Cornelius is here played by David Watson.

Beneath the Twelve-Mile Reef ○

1953, US, 102 mins, colour
Dir: Robert D Webb
Stars: Robert Wagner, Terry Moore, Richard Boone, Gilbert Roland, J Carrol Naish, Peter Graves
Rating: ★★

The vogue for underwater photography was still at its height when director Robert D Webb decided to dip below the waves for this swimsuited love story. Robert Wagner and Terry Moore (female) are the children of rival families of Greek sponge fishermen and the fleets' constant quarrelling provides the cue for plenty of underwater adventure, all stunningly well photographed with the Florida coastline standing in amazingly well for Greece. The cameraman's achievements reach their peak in a fierce underwater fight at the climax of the film, as two young divers battle each other and the ocean kelp that threatens to strangle them.

Benefit of the Doubt ●

1992, US, 89 mins, colour
Dir: Jonathan Heap
Stars: Donald Sutherland, Amy Irving
Rating: RB

A lethally silly thriller that gets worse as it goes on. We all know that softly spoken, chillingly smiling Donald Sutherland is a bad guy who has done 22 years for killing his wife and, presently released, aims to revenge himself on the now 34-year-old daughter (Amy Irving) who put him away. The film's job is to make us believe that Irving and her 10-year-old son could be so taken in as to restore her father to their lives, believing him innocent. It fails miserably – especially as Sutherland is never sympathetic, and soon starts bumping off other people in Irving's life. Performances are not good and the movie was bad for Irving's faltering career; have a good laugh towards the end – it's the only emotion you'll be able to summon up. Badly directed by Jonathan Heap, whose action is so unconvincing as to rob proceedings of any menace.

Bengal Brigade ○

1954, US, 87 mins, colour
Dir: Laslo Benedek
Stars: Rock Hudson, Arlene Dahl, Ursula Thiess, Dan O'Herlihy, TorinThatcher
Rating: ★★

This adventure story was an unusual subject for Laslo Benedek to direct, so soon after making Marlon Brando's *The Wild One*. One suspects he saw more nuances in Hall Hunter's original novel than Universal-International envisaged in the finished film, which they saw as just a Rock Hudson action adventure. Hudson plays with some sensitivity the young man court-martialled in India in 1856, for disobeying a superior's order – even though his action led to the capture of a rebel-held fort. Arlene Dahl and Ursula Thiess are merely decorative, but there are strong performances from Dan O'Herlihy and Torin Thatcher as two other officers.

Ben-Hur ○ ⓥ
1959, US, 212 mins, colour
Dir: William Wyler
Stars: Charlton Heston, Jack Hawkins, Stephen Boyd, Haya Harareet, Hugh Griffith, Sam Jaffe
Rating: ★★★★

Despite the spectacular success of such action set-pieces as the chariot race, you may find that it is the moving moments that remain the most permanent memories of William Wyler's truly magnificent film of the hoary old story by General Lew Wallace, which was filmed several times in silent days, but hadn't been remade since 1926. The dialogue (restructured by Christopher Fry from Karl Tunberg's original screenplay), photography and direction combine to cast a potent spell – movie magic, indeed, completely overwhelming one's resistance to the Victorian-style sentiments of the original material. Charlton Heston is a tower of strength, as always, but perhaps has never before or since expressed so eloquently the dignity of the human spirit, surviving the impossible. Haya Harareet is tender and true as Esther, Stephen Boyd sharply and magnetically evil as Messala. For the record, the 11 Oscars won by this uplifting and exciting cinematic experience were: Best Picture, director, actor (Heston), supporting actor (Hugh Griffith), colour photography, costume design, music (by Miklos Rozsa), art direction, editing, sound effects and sound recording. The screenplay (because of disputed authorship) was the only one of its 12 nominations that was not a winner.

Benji ☉
1974, US, 86 mins, colour
Dir: Joe Camp
Stars: Edgar Buchanan, Peter Breck, Patsy Garrett
Rating: ★★★

A doggie film for youngsters, much along the lines of the *Lassie* movies of the Forties. Benji (a very talented dog actor) is a mongrel stray who becomes a hero after two children to whom he's attached succumb to kidnappers. Although there's rather too much slow motion in the film, the kidnap section of its story engenders an amount of tension and should prove thrilling for younger viewers.

Benji the Hunted ☉
1987, US, 88 mins, colour
Dir: Joe Camp
Stars: Frank Inn, Red Steagall
Rating: ★★★

Humans get pushed well into the background in the fourth adventure of filmland's most popular pooch since *Lassie*. Benji is obviously superbly trained and many of his stunts are truly amazing, during a story that has him shipwrecked and caring for an orphan brood of cougar cubs. There's a big bad wolf and mercifully a minimum of script as Benji's usual director, Joe Camp, tells the story almost entirely without people or dialogue. Fascinating, colourful stuff, and so cleanly shot in the wilds of Washington and Oregon that you can almost smell the country air.

Benny & Joon ◑ ⓥ
1993, US, 98 mins, colour
Dir: Jeremiah Chechick
Stars: Johnny Depp, Mary Stuart Masterson, Aidan Quinn, Julianne Moore
Rating: ★★

This romance is offbeat all right, but pretty sad too: its lovers don't stand a chance of anything permanent in the world. Joon (Juniper) – Mary Stuart Masterson – is a mentally unbalanced (?schizophrenic) young woman living, on the edge of tantrums and rages, in the care of her brother Benny (Aidan Quinn) who has just lost their latest housekeeper to one of Joon's fits. Into their lives comes Sam (Johnny Depp), a semi-literate simpleton who dresses like Buster Keaton, has an intimate mastery of silent-film comedy technique and toasts bread with a steam iron. Joon falls heavily: Benny throws Sam out. The lovers run away but Joon is overcome by noises in her

head and ends up in a psychiatric hospital. There's a happy ending – of sorts. Delicately played by its leading trio, but especially by Aidan Quinn in the most difficult of the three roles, this is an admirable, but unenjoyable and pretty despairing film

Benny Goodman Story, The ○
1955, US, 117 mins, colour
Dir: Valentine Davies
Stars: Steve Allen, Donna Reed
Rating: ★★★

Bright, lively musical biopic, confidently made by Universal-International hard on the heels of its success with *The Glenn Miller Story*. Steve Allen is no James Stewart, it's true, but the film is riddled with jazz greats, including Kid Ory, Lionel Hampton, Martha Tilton and Gene Krupa. Donna Reed gets a chance to show her warmer side as Goodman's wife and oozes charm – but the music makes the film; it includes clarinet solos dubbed by Goodman himself.

Bernadette ☉
1987, France, 118 mins, colour
Dir: Jean Delannoy
Stars: Sydney Penny, Jean-Marc Bory, Michel Simonnet, Roland Lesaffre
Rating: ★★★

A solid, sincere version of the 19th century visions of Bernadette at Lourdes, told in an affecting but straightforward manner and, almost unbelievably, with scarcely a tedious moment. Credit this to the storytelling skills of director Jean Delannoy and to the hypnotic performance of teenage American actress Sydney Penny, who avoids all temptations to embellish her role to its detriment, yet shows sufficient feeling to make us believe in Bernadette as a person. Told with patent belief in its subject, the film falters occasionally with minor characters, but shows the same feel for French peasant life (if perhaps understating its hardships) that so distinguished *Jean de Florette* and *Manon des Sources*. The results are likely to bring more than one lump to the throat before Bernadette's tale is told.

Berserk ◑
1967, UK, 96 mins, colour
Dir: Jim O'Connolly
Stars: Joan Crawford, Ty Hardin, Diana Dors, Michael Gough
Rating: ★★

La Crawford queens it in style over a series of grisly murders at a circus. Red herrings abound, and, like Superintendent Robert Hardy, you may have a little trouble in spotting the killer.

Bert Rigby, You're a Fool ◐

1989, US, 94 mins, colour
Dir: Carl Reiner
Stars: Robert Lindsay, Anne Bancroft, Corbin Bernsen, Robbie Coltrane
Rating: ★★

Rather uneasily dedicated to Gene Kelly, this is a ramshackle comedy-musical with a ragbag of ingredients that just don't hang together. Everything in this film seems to be operating at half-cock, with the exception of its leading man, the sparkling Robert Lindsay, who gets some chance, though not enough, to demonstrate the song-and-dance talents that took him to stardom on the London and New York stages in *Me and My Girl*. He lights up the screen every time the music plays, but the film itself just runs like a recipe hastily cobbled together for a rising star, with a few four-letter words thrown into the stew. Lindsay's a miner who dreams of stardom and turning his tatty British north country bingo hall into a glittering palace of entertainment. His subsequent misadventures on the road and then in California raise a few smiles, but are pretty rough-and-ready stuff, a criticism that could never be levelled at the elegant Mr L, doing his imitations of Keaton, Chaplin, Astaire and Kelly with uncanny style.

Best Defense ◐ ⊛

1984, US, 94 mins, colour
Dir: Willard Huyck
Stars: Dudley Moore, Eddie Murphy, Kate Capshaw, George Dzundza, Helen Shaver
Rating: ★

Dudley Moore teamed with Eddie Murphy sounds a mouth-watering prospect, but in fact the Murphy sequences were added on at a later date to try and save a not-very-funny slapstick comedy. Dudley is an engineer working on America's new Supertank who gets involved with industrial spies and Eddie comes in as the luckless lieutenant who has to field-test the new weapon, managing to get lost behind enemy lines in the middle of a war. One of Dud's duds which not even Murphy at his most strident and frenetic can rescue.

Best Friends ○

1982, US, 116 mins, colour
Dir: Norman Jewison
Stars: Burt Reynolds, Goldie Hawn, Jessica Tandy, Barnard Hughes
Rating: ★★

There are a few good laughs in this rather muffled comedy of marital discord, most of them provided by the interplay between Goldie Hawn and Burt Reynolds as two live-together screenwriters who decide on (his) impulse to get married. A honeymoon spent at her and his parents' homes – his mother tucks him up in a single bed at night and asks him if he'd like her to leave the light on – is such a total disaster that it seems the marriage is wrecked. Finally torrential storms wreck their apartment and wash away his car. 'That's not fair', wails Reynolds. 'That's heaven relieving itself on my bed'. What else can happen? Only a contrived happy ending, that's what.

Best Little Whorehouse in Texas, The ◐ ⊛

1982, US, 110 mins, colour
Dir: Colin Higgins
Stars: Burt Reynolds, Dolly Parton, Dom DeLuise, Charles Durning
Rating: ★★

A zingy little musical stretched out rather uncomfortably over two hours with a couple of hummable songs and hardly enough plot to cover a whorehouse customer's embarrassment in a police raid. Like June, Dolly Parton is bustin' out all over as the madame of a bordello, established in 1910 and happily accepted by the local county, which suddenly becomes the centre of a morals storm. Burt Reynolds gets the chance to sing a zippy duet with Dolly ('Sneakin' Around') as the sheriff who shares her bed and turns a blind eye to the others all around him. And bulky Charles Durning enjoys a few blithe musical moments as the state governor who enjoys 'side-stepping' and sitting on a fence of his own skilful making.

Best Man, The ○

1964, US, 104 mins, b/w
Dir: Franklin Schaffner
Stars: Henry Fonda, Cliff Robertson, Edie Adams, Kevin McCarthy
Rating: ★★★★

If you would bet that it was impossible to make a thrilling drama out of an American presidential nomination campaign, this biting film would see

you losing your money. As the contrasting candidates, Henry Fonda and Cliff Robertson both slip quickly into their characters, and there's a wealth of supporting talent, notably Kevin McCarthy as Fonda's agent, veteran Lee Tracy in an acid performance as the retiring president, and humorist Shelley Berman in a telling little role. The film is excellently lit by cameraman Haskell Wexler, and director Franklin Shaffner keeps a tight grip on the flow of the action, right up to one of the most surprising surprise endings you are likely to encounter.

Best of Enemies, The ○ ⊛

1962, UK/Italy, 104 mins, colour
Dir: Guy Hamilton
Stars: David Niven, Alberto Sordi, Michael Wilding, Harry Andrews
Rating: ★★

An elegantly sardonic comedy about the wartime prison-camp friendship between two officers from opposing sides – one British, one Italian. Even the credits to the film are shared: it was directed by a Briton, Guy Hamilton, and written by Italian Luciano Vincenzoni. The British acting contingent is a stalwart one: beside David Niven and Michael Wilding, there are Harry Andrews, promoted from his normal sergeant-major to captain, Duncan Macrae, Michael Trubshawe, Ronald Fraser and Bernard Cribbins.

Best of Everything, The ○

1959, US, 122 mins, colour
Dir: Jean Negulesco
Stars: Hope Lange, Robert Evans, Joan Crawford, Stephen Boyd
Rating: ★★★

Slick, opulent and overly complex, this soap-opera has no less than six stories going on at once. That's the nub of the problem, with too little time for deep characterisation everyone ends up as just thumbnail sketches. It's sad to see Joan Crawford billed fifth, but she relishes every minute of her role as an embittered typing-pool scourge. Her career may have been in decline, but a year later she would triumph alongside her rival of old, Bette Davis, in *What Ever Happened to Baby Jane?* Co-star Robert Evans would find bigger fame in years to come as a successful producer, notably with Roman Polanski's *Chinatown*. The theme song, sung by Johnny Mathis, won an Oscar nomination for Alfred Newman and Sammy Cahn.

Best of the Badmen ○

1951, US, 84 mins, colour
Dir: William D Russell
Stars: Robert Ryan, Claire Trevor, Robert Preston, Walter Brennan, Bruce Cabot
Rating: ★★

Too much jaw-jaw and not enough war-war hamper this Western that proves to be yet another post-Civil War story featuring the James Brothers and Younger Brothers. Though it shows signs of promise in its opening scenes, it doesn't rise too far above stereotyped mediocrity thereafter, in spite of a first-rate cast that includes Robert Ryan, Robert Preston, Claire Trevor and Walter Brennan, with Lawrence Tierney making a fierce Jesse James. First-class Technicolor photography, too (by the great Edward Cronjager), of the burnished brand so seldom seen today. There's some witty dialogue for Brennan and Bruce Cabot, and another smiling Western villain for Preston, to go with those he played in *Blood on the Moon* and *Whispering Smith*. Preston soon tired of such roles and repaired to Broadway, returning to Hollywood a major star a decade later in *The Music Man*.

Best of the Best ◐ ♥

1989, US, 100 mins, colour
Dir: Bob Radler
Stars: Eric Roberts, Christopher Penn, Sally Kirkland, James Earl Jones
Rating: ★

You've seen this chop-socky film before, but the surprising thing about it is that, despite an all-star cast, with seven Oscar nominations between them, it's just as badly acted as any Jean-Claude Van Damme film. 'Yes, but what about your shoulder?', asks Roberts' mum (Louise Fletcher with nothing to do) when he's chosen for the American team against Korea. Well, that's his part of the plot taken care of. Rhee's (Roberts) brother was killed by the Korean he's fighting, so that's the usual revenge motif accounted for. The others (led by Penn) don't really matter, since we can see they're not going to figure in the final outcome. Kirkland and Jones (who comes closest, but not that close, to coping with the risible dialogue) are the coaches as Roberts goes emotionally way over the top with the help of a screenplay that pulls every cliched weepie string in the book. The fights are good, but with all these minus factors who cares?

Best of Times, The ◐ ♥

1986, US, 103 mins, colour
Dir: Roger Spottiswoode
Stars: Robin Williams, Kurt Russell, Pamela Reed, Holly Palance, M Emmet Walsh, Margaret Whitton
Rating: ★★★

Haunted by his failure to catch a ball that would have given his college a football victory over neighbouring giants, Robin Williams manoeuvres a re-staging of the entire game in this affectionate comedy about small-town life and ambitions gone sour. Though it's a film whose appeal to the gut emotions wins through in the end, its leading characters (Williams, Kurt Russell) do get a bit tiresome at times and are more than matched by the warmly sexy Holly Palance and chirpily spicy Pamela Reed who play their loving but long-suffering wives. Fans of character actors past and present, though, have a feast in store. M Emmet Walsh, Kathleen Freeman, R G Armstrong (inevitably as a Bible-spouting coach) and Dub Taylor are all in there slugging for the home team. Its subject may not be dearest to the hearts of British audiences, but its sentiments are universal. At times, it's a trudge towards the big game at the end, but it proves to be worth it.

Best Seller ● ♥

1987, US, 110 mins, colour
Dir: John Flynn
Stars: James Woods, Brian Dennehy, Victoria Tennant
Rating: ★★

James Woods, he of the flick-knife cheekbones and bullet-hole eyes, gets another chance to play a man you'll love to hate in this well-begun but spottily developed thriller. Woods is a discarded hitman who, with the help of a cop (Brian Dennehy) who writes bestsellers, aims to nail the magnate for whom he eliminated business rivals. Dennehy is as tough as ever as the cop, but it's Woods's film. Like the similar Henry Silva two decades before, it's to his credit that you get a jolt of guilty pleasure from watching him dispatch his victims. The ending, incidentally, depends heavily on the contrivance of a teenage girl hostage leaving a safe place against instructions, and then running down a stairway where she can see a killer at bay!

Best Shot ◐ ♥

(aka: Hoosiers)
1986, US, 115 mins, colour
Dir: David Anspaugh
Stars: Gene Hackman, Barbara Hershey, Dennis Hopper
Rating: ★★★

It's not often that sports films challenge for a four-star rating, but this one comes mighty close. Only an over-the-top last few minutes from the script and a surfeit of slow-motion that stops the adrenaline flowing cost David Anspaugh's basketball hymn-to-the-underdog a gold medal. Otherwise, folks (to home in on the film's own tone), this is a real top-notcher which does all the right things by its familiar elements. And it has the inestimable Gene Hackman, as the long-banned sports coach called back from pasture by an old friend, the headmaster of tiny Hickory High. Everying goes wrong at first: firebrand Hackman kicks one player off his already small squad, upsets the acting coach and gets himself thrown off the touchbench for yelling at the referee. Last year's star refuses to play, and one of the team's fathers (Dennis Hopper, Oscar-nominated), an ex-basketball coach, turns out to be the town drunk. You could jot down some of the subsequent developments before you see them but, thanks to some crafty editing and sensible camera coverage of Hackman's fevered touchline participation, foreknowledge won't stop you getting to your feet to cheer the Hickory team on. Poor processing takes the edge off Fred Murphy's colour photography, but performances are whole-hearted and team members nicely individualised. Best shot is right.

Best Things in Life Are Free, The ○

1956, US, 99 mins, colour
Dir: Michael Curtiz
Stars: Gordon MacRae, Dan Dailey, Ernest Borgnine, Sheree North
Rating: ★★★

Sheree North's vitality-packed dancing, to 'The Black Bottom' and 'The Birth of the Blues', steals the spotlight from stars Gordon MacRae, Dan Dailey and Ernest Borgnine in this gaily-coloured and enjoyable musical biopic of the songwriters De Sylva, Brown and Henderson. Forget the plot, although Tony Galento is fun as a Kansas City gangster, and concentrate on a score (put across with panache by choreographer Rod Al-

B

exander and veteran director Michael Curtiz) that includes 'Button Up Your Overcoat', 'Sonny Boy', 'Sunny Side Up', 'Broken Hearted', 'If I Had a Talking Picture of You' and many more. Song-packed? You've got it. Gordon MacRae, who plays De Sylva, had shot to screen stardom as the hero of *Oklahoma!* and *Carousel*. But the fashion for musicals was fading fast, and this was to be MacRae's last film of any note.

Best Years of Our Lives, The ○
1946, US, 175 mins, b/w
Dir: William Wyler
Stars: Myrna Loy, Fredric March, Dana Andrews, Teresa Wright, Harold Russell
Rating: ★★★

William Wyler's powerful story of American servicemen returning from World War Two and fighting to adjust to civilian life. It was a box office colossus and won Academy Awards for Sam Goldwyn (as producer), director William Wyler, star Fredric March, and handless war veteran Harold Russell. Myrna Loy, never nominated for an Oscar in a long and distinguished Hollywood career, was unjustly neglected here.

Betrayal from the East ○
1945, US, 83 mins, b/w
Dir: William Burke
Stars: Lee Tracy, Nancy Kelly
Rating: ★★

A typical WW2 gung-ho story of love and honour that is pure fiction but has the ring of authenticity thanks to serious-toned narration and an epilogue by Drew Pearson. The former GI who gives his all in the defence of the Panama Canal is played by Lee Tracy, who went on to star on TV as *Martin Kane – Private Eye*, as well as being nominated for as Oscar for his role in *The Best Man* in the Sixties.

Betrayed ○
(aka: When Strangers Marry)
1944, US, 67 mins, b/w
Dir: William Castle
Stars: Kim Hunter, Dean Jagger, Robert Mitchum, Neil Hamilton
Rating: ★★★

This black little drama wastes not a second of its running time and is far superior to the horror films for which its director, William Castle, later became better known. Kim Hunter,

Dean Jagger and Robert Mitchum are all very effective as the three points of a deadly triangle.

Betrayed ○
1953, US, 108 mins, colour
Dir: Gottfried Reinhardt
Stars: Clark Gable, Lana Turner, Victor Mature, Louis Calhern
Rating: ★★

Clark Gable was looking tired and jaded when he made this rather lacklustre action drama of the wartime resistance movement in Holland, threatened by a mysterious traitor. It was shot mostly on location in Holland, far from his usual stamping grounds. But to the local people Gable was still the 'king' of stars. During shooting in a small Dutch town, director Gottfried Reinhardt asked for 800 extras. Over 3,000 turned up – most of them just to catch a glimpse of Gable. Victor Mature, however, takes what acting honours are going, as a resistance leader with a mother fixation.

Betrayed ● ⓥ
1988, US, 127 mins, colour
Dir: Costa-Gavras
Stars: Debra Winger, Tom Berenger, John Heard, Betsy Blair, John Mahoney
Rating: ★★

Strong and scary stuff, this tough romantic thriller becomes progressively less believable as the plot goes along. Debra Winger plays another of her wry loners as a Department of Justice agent sent to investigate a Mid-West widower farmer (Tom Berenger), suspected of carrying out a contract killing. In so doing, she not only falls in love with him but uncovers a vast nest of rats in the shape of an Aryan supremacy movement akin to the Ku Klux Klan, with a network of agents all over America. Solid performances all round: a pity about that credibility gap.

Betsy's Wedding ① ⓥ
1990, US, 94 mins, colour
Dir: Alan Alda
Stars: Alan Alda, Molly Ringwald, Ally Sheedy, Joe Pesci, Madeline Kahn, Joey Bishop, Anthony LaPaglia
Rating: ★★★

There hasn't been so much flimsy fun spun round a film marriage since Bette Davis's *Wedding Breakfast*. Alan Alda is the harassed father, determined to stage a grand affair for daughter Molly Ringwald, even though all she wants

is a quiet affair at and after the registry office. Strange man Alda. He has wild dreams which end with him wrestling with, or trying to throttle his hapless wife (Madeline Kahn). But then his whole family, a traditional American mix of Jews and Italians, is a little mad. Ringwald is at a fashion design college and wears clothes that make her look, as her future in-laws term it, 'like an explosion in a dress factory'. Second daughter Ally Sheedy is a cop. 'So glad you brought your gun,' remarks mother, 'you never know who's going to break in.' She falls for the dim gangster offspring of daddy's shady business associate (Burt Young). There's lots of gently wisecracking dialogue, courtesy Alda himself, before Betsy is finally married off in a second-class tent (provided by Young) that is rapidly succumbing to a rainstorm of tropical proportions.

Better Off Dead ① ⓥ
1985, US, 97 mins, colour
Dir: Savage Steve Holland
Stars: John Cusack, David Ogden Stiers, Kim Darby, Diane Franklin
Rating: ★★

Although admittedly nutty – almost like a strip from *Mad* magazine come to life – this is a mostly gross and wickedly unfunny teenage comedy that runs like a dream sequence from some other film. John Cusack comes on like a vague teenage second cousin to Woody Allen as the youth who tries to get over the loss of his girlfriend to the school ski champ, while his mother wears reindeer heads at Christmas and serves up green goo for dinner. His father scuttles in and out in his aardvark coat trying to mend windows broken by the paper boy and his little brother constructs laser beams from cereal packets and studies how to build your own space shuttle from household items (he does it in the end). The trouble is that this manic brew's constituents are too heavily underlined to be funny, and its overdrawn characters asked to mug to an alarming degree. But Diane Franklin has impish charm as the French girl who helps Cusack forget and the film grows on you a little as it goes on.

Betty Blue ● ⓥ
(aka: 37°2 le Matin)
1986, France, 120 mins, colour
Dir: Jean-Jacques Beineix
Stars: Béatrice Dalle, Jean-Hugues Anglade, Consuelo de Haviland, Gérard

Darmon, Clementine Celarié
Rating: ★★★

Imagine a Bardot film for the Eighties, from the man who made *Diva*, then streak it with tinges of Gallic low-life, *Love Story* and the Marx Brothers. You probably still haven't caught the flavour (which is everything) but it's the best we can do! Out by the sea in a setting that could only be in the south of France, a would-be writer and presently general handyman lives in a bungalow on stilts and gets involved with Betty (then-newcomer Béatrice Dalle), who engages in a passionate and uninhibited affair before burning his bungalow down in a gentle hint to him to pursue his writing ambitions in Paris. It isn't long in Paris before poor BB starts getting those strange headaches and the last thread of the plot begins to unravel. Young Dalle, then only 21, a looker with great gappy teeth, jutting lower lip and provocative figure (the wardrobe mistress couldn't have been over-employed on this one) handles her big scenes well towards the end and could have become the next continental sex symbol had such an outmoded position still existed. As it is, she's been able to find a range of roles Bardot would have envied. The film itself is gorgeous to look at, nicely paced and hauntingly scored. A curiosity rather than a masterpiece, but one from a director whose sense of cinema never seems less than at one with his subject.

Between Two Women ○
1944, US, 83 mins, b/w
Dir: Willis Goldbeck
Stars: Lionel Barrymore, Van Johnson
Rating: ★★

Handsome doctor Randall Adams (Van Johnson), called 'Red' in this episode of the Gillespie series, is torn between the charms of wealthy Marilyn Maxwell and ailing Gloria DeHaven. Johnson had become a major star at MGM in the war years, and this was his farewell to Blair Hospital after four films there. It was almost the end of the series too. But three years later, the studio allowed Lionel Barrymore one further gallop as Gillespie in *Dark Delusion* before finally closing the hospital doors.

Between Two Worlds ○
1944, US, 112 mins, b/w
Dir: Edward A Blatt

Stars: John Garfield, Paul Henreid, Sydney Greenstreet, Eleanor Parker
Rating: ★★★

The Warner Brothers repertory company is present in something approaching full strength (although it was a pity no room could be found for Peter Lorre) in this doughtily-cast version of Sutton Vane's play *Outward Bound*, in which a shipload of dead or dying souls travels between limbo and eternity. Sydney Greenstreet is in his usual formidable form as the 'examiner' (who decides who goes to Heaven and Hell), but John Garfield has so little to do that he hardly justifies his top billing over Paul Henreid and Eleanor Parker, who provide the main thrust of the story as a refugee couple hovering bewteen suicide and redemption.

Beverly Hills Cop ● ⓥ
1984, US, 105 mins, colour
Dir: Martin Brest
Stars: Eddie Murphy, Judge Reinhold, Lisa Eilbacher, John Ashton, Ronny Cox, Steven Berkoff
Rating: ★★★

Eddie Murphy's biggest hit, and the one that confirmed his position as a top international star. He fires on all cylinders here, as a tough Detroit cop who decides to track down the man responsible for the murder of an admittedly shady friend. The trail leads to Beverly Hills where Murphy makes friends and enemies and wreaks havoc on the way. He's fast, flip, flash and ahead of the game.

Beverly Hills Cop II ● ⓥ
1987, US, 102 mins, colour
Dir: Tony Scott
Stars: Eddie Murphy, Judge Reinhold, Jurgen Prochnow, John Ashton, Ronny Cox, Brigitte Neilsen
Rating: ★★★

This new crime caper for Eddie Murphy's Axel Foley keeps up the standard set by the first, providing fast and furious adult entertainment. Although Murphy's fast talking steals most of the big laughs, Judge Reinhold, as his seemingly-gentle sidekick who proves to have developed a Rambo complex, also makes the most of his opportunities. Villainess Brigitte Nielsen memorably orders her adversaries to 'Eat the floor!' in one of the many memorable lines (screenplay by

Larry Ferguson and Warren Skaaren) from perhaps the most-quoted film of the Eighties.

Beyond a Reasonable Doubt ○ ⓥ
1956, US, 80 mins, b/w
Dir: Fritz Lang
Stars: Dana Andrews, Joan Fontaine, Sidney Blackmer
Rating: ★★

One of director Fritz Lang's last Hollywood films, this twisty thriller has improved with age, although it still doesn't grip as it should. Dana Andrews is well cast in a role originally intended for Joseph Cotten, but Joan Fontaine seems a little long in the tooth as his fiancee, in a role that called for more sparkle. Steve McQueen is supposed to have a tiny role somewhere in this, though you may have to look hard to find him.

Beyond the Blue Horizon ⊙
1942, US, 76 mins, colour
Dir: Alfred Santell
Stars: Dorothy Lamour, Richard Denning, Jack Haley, Patricia Morison
Rating: ★★

Dorothy Lamour was so popular as the maiden bursting into sarong in wartime South Seas adventures that Paramount was actually encouraged to splash out with Technicolor on such tropical escapades as *Aloma of the South Seas*, *Typhoon* and *Rainbow Island*. Dorothy swims with a tiger, ambles with an ape, and tangles (in more ways than one) with jungle boy Richard Denning. The familiar flat features of Abner Biberman (who later turned director on similar spectacular fare) crops up as one of the natives. There's a welcome tongue-in-cheek tone to the proceedings, and cinematographer Charles Boyle at least justifies the studio's outlay on colour.

Beyond the Forest ○
1949, US, 96 mins, b/w
Dir: King Vidor
Stars: Bette Davis, Joseph Cotten, David Brian, Ruth Roman
Rating: ★★

Supposedly the film that led to the final break between Bette Davis and Warner Brothers, this melodrama, cleverly described by one critic as 'fiercely trashy', looks a whole lot better today. Directed by King Vidor with one eye on symbolism and another on the intensity of the Davis performance, it has a European feel,

B

tensions and innuendoes galore, a classic Davis line in 'What a dump!' and a sensational ending. Davis fans will love it.

Beyond the Limit
See: The Honorary Consul

Beyond the Poseidon Adventure ○
1979, US, 122 mins, colour
Dir: Irwin Allen
Stars: Michael Caine, Sally Field, Telly Savalas, Peter Boyle, Jack Warden, Karl Malden
Rating: ★

Like its predecessor, this disaster epic is very well acted and excitingly shot. Michael Caine and the perky Sally Field both give their best performances for some time and there are respectable showings from Karl Malden, Shirley Jones and Telly Savalas. There the resemblance to the earlier film, alas, ends. For the script (though written by the capable Nelson Gidding) and situations are really so silly as to make further comparisons futile. The action, though, is all one would expect from producer-director Irwin Allen, and the film will prove rewarding for undemanding adventure fans.

Beyond Therapy ●
1986, US/France, 93 mins, colour
Dir: Robert Altman
Stars: Julie Hagerty, Jeff Goldblum, Glenda Jackson, Tom Conti, Genevieve Page, Christopher Guest
Rating: ★

Perhaps director Robert Altman should himself have taken to the psychiatrist's couch after this adults-only version of *The Goon Shows*. All of its characters are burblingly bonkers, from the therapists themselves to the several flakebrains pouring out disconnected thoughts in their consulting-rooms. Yet even with a starry cast, a fair share of funny one-liners and a nice music score by Gabriel Yared, Altman has managed to turn their comic capers into a painfully boring film. The elegance of the cast and their costumes contrasts uneasily enough with the often foul-mouthed dialogue but the film's chief stumbling block is its director's lack of timing. So used to meaningful drama, Altman stamps a ponderous touch all over the gossamer thread of this thinking man's porno comedy. The result is a bit like one of those X certificate Peter Sellers comedies of the

early Seventies: it thinks its clever – and it means to make you laugh – but it just doesn't work.

Beyond the Stars ○ ⓥ
1989, US, 88 mins, colour
Dir: David Saperstein
Stars: Martin Sheen, Christian Slater, Sharon Stone, Robert Foxworth
Rating: ★★★

The James Dean-like Christian Slater plays rocket-mad teenager Eric Michaels who, after launching a home-built, miniature rocket that causes damage at school, gets punished by being sent to stay with his father, who now lives with a girlfriend. While lonely Eric kicks his heels in the new community, he discovers that one of its inhabitants happens to be his all-time hero – ex-astronaut Andrews (Martin Sheen), now an alcoholic near-hermit. As Eric and his new girlfriend (Maryam D'Abo) piece together the mystery of Andrews' bitterness and the secret of his long-ago trip to the moon, there unravels a quality small-town drama with a strong message for peace. F Murray Abraham has a small but dynamic role as a whale-watching fanatic, and Sheen gives a touching performance as the peace-seeking space hero. For the curious, there's also Sharon Stone, in a role far removed from her raunchy *Basic Instinct*, as Slater's possible future mother-in-law!

B F's Daughter ○
1948, US, 108 mins, b/w
Dir: David Z Leonard
Stars: Barbara Stanwyck, Van Heflin, Charles Coburn, Richard Hart
Rating: ★★★

A typically tempestuous role for La Stanwyck as the headstrong daughter of a tycoon. Not surprisingly, the British distributors didn't think much of the title (B F doesn't carry the same double-meaning in Britain). So the film was rechristened *Polly Fulton* for its British release. The men in Polly's life are played by Van Heflin, as a stubborn young political economist, and Richard Hart, as a stuffy socialite who becomes a war hero. Hart is one of the saddest figures in Hollywood history. After several films, he became one of television's first superstars in the title role of a 1950 detective series, *The Adventures of Ellery Queen*. Suave, good-looking Hart was perfect casting. Two months later he was dead – killed by a heart attack at the age of 35.

Bhowani Junction ○
1956, US/UK, 110 mins, colour
Dir: George Cukor
Stars: Ava Gardner, Stewart Granger, Bill Travers
Rating: ★★

Filmed on location in Pakistan, this screen translation of John Master's meaty novel of unrest, violence and love in pre-independence India gave Ava Gardner and her co-stars a strenuous time. Ava was trampled on by more than 100 native extras, then bruised and shaken in a staged fight with a soldier. Years later, she declared it 'the toughest film I ever worked on'. Britain's Francis Matthews, later famous as TV's Paul Temple, got one of his earliest screen chances – as an Indian.

Bible . . . in the Beginning, The ○
1966, US/Italy, 174 mins, colour
Dir: John Huston
Stars: Michael Parks, Richard Harris, George C Scott, Ava Gardner, Stephen Boyd, John Huston
Rating: ★★

The retelling of the whole of the Old Testament by a number of famous directors – the original idea of this project – predictably proved too daunting a task, and John Huston was eventually entrusted with simply telling the story up to Abraham and Isaac. He also plays Noah in the film's best episode, which comes complete with an impressive flood sequence.

Bicycle Thieves ○
1948, Italy, 90 mins, b/w
Dir: Vittorio De Sica
Stars: Lamberto Maggiorani, Enzo Staiola, Lianella Carell
Rating: ★★★★

Delicate, moving, post-war Italian film, with a director (Vittorio de Sica) right at his peak, and an entrancing performance from the urchin Enzo Staiola. An honest, beautifully told story of the search by a workman and his little son for a stolen bicycle that is life or death to their family, this is a film of rare humanity that took an Academy Award in its year.

Biddy ○
1983, UK, 86 mins, colour
Dir: Christine Edzard
Stars: Celia Bannerman
Rating: ★★★

The obverse side of *Mary Poppins* – the story of a real Victorian nursemaid, whose microcosmic world hides what her constant chatter reveals – a vivid imagination that seeks escape in literary flights of fancy to vary her well-ordered life. Celia Bannerman gives a perfectly controlled portrait of this caring, yet in a way frustrated soul. Biddy gives so much to the children in her care that she ought really to be invited to the big event of their lives 'downstairs' – but clearly would be embarrassed were it to happen. In this quiet, leisurely, but engrossing film (provided you give it time to come to terms with with you) she ends up in a room stuffed – almost horrifyingly – full of memories – but with her essential essence distilled into those whose lives she has helped to form. Christine Edzard's direction of her own script tracks and sometimes traps this fascinating character in her own, tightly packed doll's house existence, forever forsaking the projection of self.

Big ○ ⓥ
1988, US, 102 mins, colour
Dir: Penny Marshall
Stars: Tom Hanks, Elizabeth Perkins, Robert Loggia, John Heard
Rating: ★★★

The most successful in the rash of age-reversal comedies that assailed us in the late 80s. Two-thirds genuine fun and one-third slightly squirmy embarrassment, the film has a couple of truly delightful scenes, where the boy-turned-man (Tom Hanks, nominated for an Oscar) makes his adult acquaintances behave like children again. Other situations are standard for the course, including the heroine (the personable Elizabeth Perkins), who inevitably falls for the hero's boyish charm, and the adult business protagonists who are confounded by his innocence. Probably Hanks' greatest personal success before *Philadelphia*.

Bigamist, The ○
1953, US, 83 mins, b/w
Dir: Ida Lupino
Stars: Edmond O'Brien, Joan Fontaine, Ida Lupino
Rating: ★★★

Edmond O'Brien, who had become stuck in a series of Westerns and low-budget crime stories at this stage in his Hollywood career, eagerly seized upon the meaty acting opportunities offered by Collier Young's script in this story of a salesman with wives in each of two neighbouring

American cities. Young's then-wife, actress Ida Lupino, directs the film as well as playing one of the women involved. And she brings out all the poignancy of the situation, as well as providing it with a vital backbone of credibility.

Big Blue, The ◑ ⓥ
1988, France/US, 110 mins, colour
Dir: Luc Besson
Stars: Rosanna Arquette, Jean-Marc Barr, Jean Reno, Paul Shenar, Griffin Dunne
Rating: ★

Having gone underground in *Subway*, director Luc Besson went underwater. And there sure is a lot of the big blue (sea, that is) in this story of the lifelong rivalry between two deep-sea divers. The tragic ending is obvious always and pretty silly at that. Still, Rosanna Arquette is as engagingly buck-toothed and shapely as ever and does a pretty good level best to hold it all together for nigh on two hours. She gets little help from Jean-Marc Barr as the haunted diver who just wants to go off and play with the dolphins, and Griffin Dunne is in all too briefly as her New York boss. With locations in Greece, Sicily, New York, Peru and the French Riviera, this film may make you long for a holiday in more ways than one.

Big Broadcast of 1936, The ○
1935, US, 97 mins, b/w
Dir: Norman Taurog
Stars: Jack Oakie, George Burns, Gracie Allen, Bing Crosby, Ethel Merman
Rating: ★★★

This sequel to the 1932 film *The Big Broadcast*, which had George Burns and Gracie Allen as radio station owners, sees them this time as potty inventors, while Jack Oakie is the radio station man to whom they try to sell crazy ideas about 'radio eyes'. As with all the series, it's a kaleidoscope of unconnected speciality turns, somehow kept in some kind of shape by director Norman Taurog. Highlights include a comedy sketch by Mary Boland and Charlie Ruggles, the stunning dancing of the Nicholas Brothers, and Ethel Merman singing 'It's the Animal in Me', to the accompaniment of a troupe of dancing elephants. This number was deleted from *We're Not Dressing* the previous year, but happily resurrected here.

Big Broadcast of 1938, The ○
1938, US, 90 mins, b/w
Dir: Mitchell Leisen
Stars: W C Fields, Bob Hope, Martha Raye, Dorothy Lamour, Shirley Overman
Rating: ★★

The American showbusiness paper *Variety* once offered $10,000 to anyone who could fathom the plot of this all-star extravaganza, typical of many such offerings from Hollywood studios in the Thirties. Bonuses here include W C Fields in a dual role as bumbling brothers and doing his classic billiards routine; and Bob Hope and Shirley Ross with the original version of the song that became Hope's theme tune – 'Thanks for the Memory'. That plot, incidentally, has something to do with sabotage on a race across the Atlantic between two giant liners. But as far as we know, no-one has ever collected the $10,000.

Big Bus, The ○
1976, US, 85 mins, colour
Dir: James Frawley
Stars: Joseph Bologna, Stockard Channing, John Beck, Ned Beatty, Jose Ferrer
Rating: ★★★

Fancy a ride? This one is quite a laugh. The driver (Joseph Bologna) of the monster bus in this spoof disaster epic is under suspicion of once having eaten 116 passengers (his co-driver was responsible). New co-driver Shoulders (John Beck) suffers blackouts at high speed. The villain (Stuart Margolin), intent on sabotaging bus HQ, turns the lights out so that he can flash his torch. There are a lot more characters; these are only the sane ones. Although this journey runs out of ideas before the end, even its asides and background lines are funny while it still has a full head of steam. Satires on scenes and climaxes from a dozen other films are crammed into it. It's *Hellzapoppin* on wheels.

Big Business ○ ⓥ
1988, US, 97 mins, colour
Dir: Jim Abrahams
Stars: Bette Midler, Lily Tomlin, Fred Ward, Edward Herrmann
Rating: ★★★

There's some brilliant trick camerawork in the later stages of this fairly funny farce as one mismatched set of Bette Midler-Lily Tomlin twins bumps into the other. The story goes like this: the girls are muddled at birth when the millionaire father of one twinset is forced to buy the town of Jupiter Hollow to get his wife into its hospital. Thirty years later, predatory big businesswoman Bette 'A' and daffy-dilly sister Lily 'A' are set to close down the industry they've inherited in Jupiter Hollow, while the two Hollow residents, strong-willed Lily 'B' and starry-eyed sister Bette 'B', set out from the cornfields to stop them! The film doesn't waste much time at all and, being directed by Jim Abrahams of *Airplane!* fame, sets up some good gags on the side, including the tramp outside the Waldorf Hotel who keeps seeing double. It's Abrahams' deft touch that keeps the helter-skelter of changing partners – baffling husbands, boyfriends, lovers and colleagues alike – from becoming tiresome. And the trickwork when the foursome meets in the ladies' loo is worth the price of admission alone.

Big Carnival, The
See: Ace in the Hole

Big Chill, The ● ⓥ
1983, US, 115 mins, colour
Dir: Lawrence Kasdan
Stars: Tom Berenger, Glenn Close, Jeff Goldblum, William Hurt, JoBeth Williams, Kevin Kline
Rating: ★★★

Reminiscent of *Return of the Secaucus Seven*, this is a film with many nice touches, human moments and fragments of natural comic dialogue. Eight people reunite for the funeral of one of their friends from a close-knit group of a few years back when their set-the-world-to-rights fervour burned more brightly. Glenn Close, William Hurt and Meg Tilly give stand-out performances in an excellent star cast. The dead friend was originally played by Kevin Costner in flashback scenes, but his role ended up on the cutting-room floor.

Big Circus, The ○ ⓥ
1959, US, 109 mins, colour
Dir: Joseph M Newman
Stars: Victor Mature, Rhonda Fleming, Red Buttons, Vincent Price
Rating: ★★

One of the semi-blockbusters made by minor studio Allied Artists (formerly Monogram) when trying to break into the better-quality market in the 1950s. Irwin Allen, later a king of disaster movies, is the power behind this one, and there are a few disasters for circus owner Victor Mature (well cast for

once although improbably called Hank Whirling!) to overcome. A good cast of semi-star names includes Red Buttons, Vincent Price, Rhonda Fleming, Gilbert Roland, Kathryn Grant and – especially worth watching – Peter Lorre as a clown.

Big Clock, The ○
1947, US, 95 mins, b/w
Dir: John Farrow
Stars: Ray Milland, Charles Laughton, Maureen O'Sullivan, George Macready
Rating: ★★★★

Terrific thriller full of memorable scenes and images. Charles Laughton scores as the megalomaniac publisher whose strange speech pattern reflects the giant clock of the title in the lobby of his headquarters. Laughton's wife Elsa Lanchester is treasurable as an extremely talented but totally zany painter with a string of ex-husbands. Ray Milland and Maureen O'Sullivan are also good as the hero and heroine caught up in a web of violence and jealousy, and George Macready contributes another of his hissable snakes-in-the-grass. Director John Farrow tops it off with an exciting chase climax. Vaguely remade in 1987 as *No Way Out*.

Big Combo, The ◐ ⓥ
1954, US, 90 mins, b/w
Dir: Joseph Lewis
Stars: Cornel Wilde, Richard Conte, Brian Donlevy, Jean Wallace
Rating: ★★★

It seems as something of a surprise to find that this tough low-budget crime thriller was made in the mid-Fifties, since it has all the hallmarks of the archetypal Forties *film noir* – laconic dialogue, a pervading sense of fatalism, flawed characters who are trapped in hells of their own making and perverse (for the time) sexuality. All of which are to be expected, however, from director Joseph Lewis, one of the best (and most underrated) exponents of 'B' feature film-making in the Forties. Here he is very well served by the low-key monochrome cinematography of John Alton and his key actors, Cornel Wilde, Richard Conte, Brian Donlevy and Jean Wallace, while Lee Van Cleef and Earl Holliman contribute chilling cameos as a couple of sadistic hoods.

Big Country, The ○ ⓥ
1958, US, 165 mins, colour
Dir: William Wyler

Stars: Gregory Peck, Jean Simmons, Carroll Baker, Charlton Heston, Burl Ives, Charles Bickford
Rating: ★★★

The sweeping music, by Jerome Moross, is the thing most people remember today from this big-scale Western, which marked Gregory Peck's debut as a producer. This story of an easterner out West cost $3 million to make, and took five months to film. One of its highlights is a desperate fight, in mud and murk, between those two big men of the screen, Peck and Charlton Heston. But Jean Simmons gives the outstanding performance as a schoolteacher caught in the centre of a land dispute, between two embittered old ranchers (played to the hilt by Burl Ives and Charles Bickford). Miss Simmons has a ranch and – equally importantly – the water which is coveted by her neighbours. William Wyler directs with a suitable sense of occasion.

Big Deal at Dodge City ○
1966, US, 95 mins, colour
Dir: Fielder Cook
Stars: Henry Fonda, Joanne Woodward, Jason Robards, Kevin McCarthy
Rating: ★★★

A different, absorbing and richly rewarding Western about a huge game of poker (actually played at Laredo, whatever the title says). The character played with distinction by Joanne Woodward assumes considerable importance towards the climax – besides accounting for the movie's original title, *A Big Hand for the Little Lady* – and the twist ending is devastating. Lovers of vintage films will spot Chester Conklin and Mae Clarke (the lady who got a grapefruit in the face from James Cagney in *Public Enemy* in 1931) in minor roles.

Big Easy, The ● ⓥ
1986, US, 108 mins, colour
Dir: Jim McBride
Stars: Dennis Quaid, Ellen Barkin, Ned Beatty, John Goodman
Rating: ★★★

Dennis Quaid is the tough detective and Ellen Barkin the even tougher assisstant district attorney in this well-paced and slightly different thriller. The steamy New Orleans backdrop adds colour to the drama of murder, drugs and police corruption, making this an absorbing watch. Quaid is very good as the cool detective and Barkin rises above her stereotyped straight-laced legal eagle character to produce a performance of real passion. Although the story may not be startlingly original, dirctor Jim McBride packages it into a fast-moving and stylish thriller.

Bigfoot and the Hendersons ○ ⓥ
(aka: Harry and the Hendersons)
1987, US, 110 mins, colour
Dir: William Dear
Stars: John Lithgow, Melinda Dillon
Rating: ★★★

Known in the US as *Harry and the Hendersons*, and spawning the hit TV sitcom series of the same name, this is the sweet and sentimental story of how a yeti-type creature comes to live with an ordinary family in suburban Seattle and how it teaches them the lessons of love and peace. Reminiscent at times of *E.T.* (and, in fact, co-produced by an uncredited Steven Spielberg), it's full of amusing, touching images – like the gentle Bigfoot mourning the death of a mink stole and the family roast, and burying them in a shallow grave. Inside the bulky Bigfoot suit is six-feet-seven actor Kevin Peter Hall, who was later typecast as the very tall alien in both *Predator* movies. Bigfoot's excellent creature effects, by award-winning make-up expert Rick Baker, were Oscar-nominated.

Biggest Bank Robbery, The ○
(aka: A Nightingale Sang in Berkeley Square)
1980, UK, 95 mins, colour
Dir: Ralph Thomas
Stars: Richard Jordan, David Niven, Gloria Grahame, Elke Sommer
Rating: ★★

The Thomas brothers, Ralph and Gerald, have done much over the last three decades to keep the nation laughing and cinema tills ringing, with the highly-successful *Doctor* and *Carry On* films. Ralph Thomas stayed with comedy for this robbery caper TV movie. David Niven plays a ruthless leader of a big London gang, Hollywood's Gloria Grahame appears as a semi-retired American musical-comedy star, and glamorous Elke Sommer is splendidly cast as a bank manager's sexy secretary. In the supporting cast is Dicken Ashworth, for long a regular in the British soap opera *Brookside*.

Big Girls Don't Cry . . . They Get Even
See: Stepkids

Biggles ○ ⓥ
1986, UK, 108 mins, colour
Dir: John Hough
Stars: Neil Dickson, Alex Hyde-White, Fiona Hutchinson
Rating: ★

The much-loved World War One heroics of Biggles, the pilot from Captain W E Johns' series of books, are updated to 1986 Manhattan via a time-travel gimmick. Neil Dickson as Biggles is the best thing in the so-so film that hardly plays fair with fans of the original. A huskier, younger version of Peter O'Toole, he has a genteel streak that conceals the viciousness required in war. But the big drawback is Alex Hyde-White as his time-travelling American buddy, whose acting is as wooden as a Stalag vaulting horse. A bold idea ruined in the execution.

Big Heart, The
See: Miracle on 34th Street

Big Heat, The ① ⓥ
1953, US, 90 mins, b/w
Dir: Fritz Lang
Stars: Glenn Ford, Gloria Grahame, Lee Marvin, Jocelyn Brando
Rating: ★★★

A classic *film noir*, decorated by director Fritz Lang's stylish handling of what could have been a routine cops-and-robbers story and by stunning monochrome camerawork from Charles Lang Jr. Glenn Ford gives a strong, concentrated performance as a policeman but it is Lee Marvin – crystallising his villainous screen image – who sears into the memory as he throws scalding coffee into Gloria Grahame's face.

Big House USA ①
1955, US, 82 mins, b/w
Dir: Howard W Koch
Stars: Broderick Crawford, Ralph Meeker
Rating: ★★

Tough thriller about five men determined to break out of jail. Cast also includes such regular 'heavies' as Lon Chaney Jnr, William Talman and Charles Bronson.

Big Jake ○ ⓥ
1971, US, 110 mins, colour
Dir: George Sherman

Stars: John Wayne, Richard Boone, Maureen O'Hara, Patrick Wayne, Bruce Cabot
Rating: ★★

John Wayne corralled old friends, family and regular associates to help make this kidnap Western, but it's a major disappointment. Fashionable violence has been tacked on to a familiar story of a rugged father overcoming hostility with his sons to nail the bad guys, and a mediocre script doesn't help matters. Maureen O'Hara sets the tone as Wayne's wife, who calls on his help when their grandson is grabbed and held for ransom by raiders. 'It will require an extremely harsh and unpleasant kind of man to deal with,' she says, as the camera cuts to a gigantic close-up of The Duke, squinting down the barrel of a gun. It was directed in pedestrian fashion by George Sherman, who worked previously with Wayne when he was a rising star at Republic in the *Three Mesquiteers* series of the late 1930s.

Big Jim McLain ○
1953, US, 76 mins, b/w
Dir: Edward Ludwig
Stars: John Wayne, Nancy Olsen, James Arness, Alan Napier
Rating: ★

John Wayne, that most patriotic of Americans, put up the money for this film himself, as it was among the first to point out the 'dangers' of the Communist menace to the Americans in their own outposts. It's the rough, tough story of a US special agent's attempts to expose a nest of Communist agents in Hawaii. Fists fly faster than the dialogue as Big Jim – that's Wayne – tracks the Commies down. But even Big John is dwarfed by James Arness, who plays his assistant. Wayne, at 6ft 4in, was three inches shorter. Nancy Olson, that prettiest of Fifties heroines, calms Wayne's brow for the film's few tender moments.

Big Knife, The ①
1955, US, 110 mins, b/w
Dir: Robert Aldrich
Stars: Jack Palance, Ida Lupino, Wendell Corey, Shelley Winters, Jean Hagen, Rod Steiger
Rating: ★★★

Based on Clifford Odets' claustrophobic play, this systematic carve-up job on Hollywood caused quite a sensation when it burst on the film

B

scene. Director Robert Aldrich was always a bit of a maverick and here he clinically dissects the star-building machine, producing a bitterly tawdry portrait of the movie world's capital. The man in the spotlight is Charlie Castle (Jack Palance, so tense you expect him to literally explode), a top box-office star who leads a tormented, drink-sodden private life. The acting is rivetingly powerful, particularly from a disturbingly blond Rod Steiger, Wendell Corey (as Steiger's sinister hatchet-man) and, as one of Charlie's few remaining friends, Wesley Addy.

Big Land, The ○
(aka: Stampeded!)
1956, US, 92 mins, colour
Dir: Gordon Douglas
Stars: Alan Ladd, Virginia Mayo, Edmond O'Brien
Rating: ★★

Known in Britain as *Stampeded!*, this latter-day Alan Ladd Western packs plenty of action, has some good acting from Edmond O'Brien, and introduces Ladd's own son David in a supporting role. Some faces from the Forties in lesser roles include Julie Bishop and Don Castle.

Big Man, The ● ⓥ
1990, UK, 119 mins, colour
Dir: David Leland
Stars: Liam Neeson, Joanna Whalley-Kilmer, Ian Bannen, Billy Connolly
Rating: ★★

A tough British drama about an ex-miner, jailed during the great mine strike, and now out of work, who accepts the offer of a bare-knuckle fight from a shady businessman. This, incidentally, seems rather an odd reason for his wife to leave him. It takes an awful long time for the fight to come about and this, despite the surface brutality, is, like the rest of the film's fistfights, not exactly convincing, the punches visibly missing. However, the make-up of beaten boxers is agonisingly, excruciatingly good, and there are dogged, personable performances from Liam Neeson, Joanne Whalley-Kilmer, Ian Bannen and Billy Connolly. The doom-laden atmosphere, too, is quite well achieved by director David Leland. If only he'd made the whole thing shorter: this story doesn't have the plot development to carry it easily to two hours.

Big Noise, The ⊙
1944, US, 74 mins, b/w
Dir: Malcolm St Clair
Stars: Stan Laurel, Oliver Hardy
Rating: ★★

One of Laurel and Hardy's last comedies, this one has some inventive ideas, but was rather hampered by studio insistence on using old Stan-and-Ollie routines without any new variations. The duo's fans may spot a small appearance by Edgar Dearing who was the hopping-mad motorcycle cop in their classic *Two Tars*. Here, he's a . . . motorcycle cop.

Big Picture, The ● ⓥ
1988, US, 100 mins, colour
Dir: Christopher Guest
Stars: Kevin Bacon, Emily Longstreth, Jennifer Jason Leigh, Michael McKean
Rating: ★★

At least the constant appearances of famous guest stars will keep you from dropping off in this story of a film school prize winner who soon loses his sense of values in Tinseltown. Unable to make up its mind whether to be a satire, an out-and-out comedy or a morality tale, the film ends up as the kind of bastardised entertainment to which the young film-maker himself (Kevin Bacon) falls victim. In Hollywood he agrees to make any changes to his script in order to make a start, ditches his girlfriend for a starlet, gets an effete agent and neglects those who have his best interests at heart. It's as difficult to feel much sympathy for him as it is to give the 'film of his dreams' any chance of success. Still, Martin Short is hilarious as the agent, and J T Walsh as unctuous as ever as a mogul with a penchant for lesbian angles. You may also spot, if you're quick, Eddie Albert, Elliott Gould, Roddy McDowall, Stephen Collins, June Lockhart and John Cleese. Alas, they've all been in bigger and better pictures.

Big Red One, The ● ⓥ
1980, US, 113 mins, colour
Dir: Sam Fuller
Stars: Lee Marvin, Mark Hamill, Robert Carradine
Rating: ★★★

After remaining inactive for nearly a decade, cult writer-director Samuel Fuller came up with, despite its Eighties blood and violence, a film that is curiously old-fashioned and harks back in its style and attitudes to his Fifties pictures like *Fixed Bayonets*

and *The Steel Helmet*. Lee Marvin dominates the movie as a tough, grizzled sergeant leading a rifle squad through the European theatre of war from 1942 to 1945. Fuller's episodic script concentrates to good effect on four members of Marvin's squad, giving, in particular, a chance for *Star Wars*' Mark Hamill to abandon his interstellar swashbuckling for some realistic 'war is hell' acting. And Robert Carradine (who doubles as narrator) etches a neat performance as a would-be novelist, a character probably serving as Fuller's alter ego.

Big Shot, The ○
1942, US, 82 mins, b/w
Dir: Lewis Seiler
Stars: Humphrey Bogart, Irene Manning
Rating: ★★★

Interesting and rare Humphrey Bogart gangster film, one of the first following his breakthrough to big stardom with *The Maltese Falcon* and *High Sierra*. A weaker than usual supporting cast means that Bogart is virtually the whole show as the ex-big shot trapped by his own reputation after he has decided to opt out of a major robbery which could land him with a life sentence. The film, especially in its action sequences, is largely well handled by Lewis Seiler, an experienced Warners' director whose biggest hit came the year later with *Guadalcanal Diary*.

Big Show, The ○
1960, US, 113 mins, colour
Dir: James B Clark
Stars: Esther Williams, Cliff Robertson, Robert Vaughn
Rating: ★★

Circus sagas petered out after the Sixties and this was one of the last big ones, Esther Williams in her last film – a rare role as a dramatic actress – was teamed with two up-and-coming stars, Cliff Robertson and Robert Vaughn, who played brothers at their father's circus. Director James B Clark shows all the Hollywood skill at tightening the tension on tightrope and trapeze, in a story which runs oddly parallel to the Biblical tale of Joseph and his Brethren. An unusual item is a troupe of performing polar bears, which also has a vital part to play in the story.

Big Sky, The ○
1952, US, 122 mins, b/w
Dir: Howard Hawks
Stars: Kirk Douglas, Dewey Martin
Rating: ★★

After a dynamic start to his movie career, Kirk Douglas suffered his first major flops in 1952 with two Westerns, *The Big Trees* and *The Big Sky*. *The Big Sky* is certainly the more ambitious of the two, originally premiered at two hours 20 minutes, but later cut to just over two hours. Even at the shorter length, it's still a leisurely saga that badly needs Technicolor and a lot more action to give gusto to its story of three Kentuckian frontiersmen at the turn of the 19th century. Jim Davis, later Jock Ewing in Dallas, plays a villain, one-film wonder Elizabeth Threatt is striking as an Indian princess, Dmitri Tiomkin contributed a typically haunting score, and the scenery (largely shot in Grand Teton National Park) is imposing even in black and white.

Big Sleep, The ○ ⓥ
1946, US, 114 mins, b/w
Dir: Howard Hawks
Stars: Humphrey Bogart, Lauren Bacall, John Ridgely, Martha Vickers, Dorothy Malone
Rating: ★★★★

The archetypal private eye thriller, with Humphrey Bogart, as Philip Marlowe, trying to unravel a plot so fiendish that even the writers and director didn't understand all of it, whilst bandying words with Lauren Bacall in some of the raciest exchanges that ever got past the censors in the immediate post-war years. A supporting cast to treasure includes Elisha Cook Jr with another of his little guys who are life's losers, former Western star Bob Steele as a cold-blooded killer and a bespectacled Dorothy Malone as a bookstore proprietress keen to show Bogart her complete stock. The plot thunders along and, like Bogart, barely seems to stop for breath between one confrontation and another.

Big Sleep, The ◖
1978, UK, 95 mins, colour
Dir: Michael Winner
Stars: Robert Mitchum, Sarah Miles, Richard Boone, Candy Clark, Joan Collins, Edward Fox
Rating: ★

Raymond Chandler's tangled web of deception, murder and blackmail – immortalised in the 1946 Humphrey Bogart version – is here unhappily transferred by director Michael Winner to an English seaside setting. Star Robert Mitchum is an unusually elegant Philip Marlowe, while James Stewart and Joan Collins are the best of a supporting cast that also includes Candy Clark, Sarah Miles, Richard Boone, Edward Fox (spectacularly miscast as a shady bookie), John Mills, Oliver Reed and Richard Todd.

Big Steal, The ○
1949, US, 72 mins, b/w
Dir: Don Siegel
Stars: Robert Mitchum, Jane Greer, William Bendix, Ramon Novarro
Rating: ★★

Don Siegel made this hectic comedy-thriller early in his career, after winning Oscars for his first two films. The accent is on the thrills, as the plot soon develops into an odd-looking creation. Robert Mitchum and William Bendix are amusingly well matched in the leading roles.

Big Store, The ⊙
1941, US, 80 mins, b/w
Dir: Charles Reisner
Stars: Groucho Marx, Chico Marx, Harpo Marx, Tony Martin, Virginia Grey
Rating: ★★★

This film, the last of the five the Marx Brothers made for MGM, has them as store detectives, headed by Groucho in an incredibly moth-eaten fur coat. The best scene comes early on, with Groucho entertaining Margaret Dumont in his office, despite clouds of smoke emanating from his desk. The slapstick finale is uncharacteristic, but pretty funny nonetheless. Also the film in which Tony Martin made a big hit singing 'Tenement Symphony'.

Big Street, The ○
1942, US, 88 mins, b/w
Dir: Irving Reis
Stars: Lucille Ball, Henry Fonda, Agnes Moorehead, Barton MacLane, Eugene Pallette, Sam Levene
Rating: ★★

Based on Damon Runyon's story *Little Pinks*, this morality tale set in Runyon's famous world of guys and dolls offered a big chance to Lucille Ball, who grabbed all her opportunities as the grasping Gloria who remains spoiled and self-centred even when tragedy strikes her down. They gave Lucy a quality leading man too, and it's just a pity that Henry Fonda is so badly miscast as the 'busboy' who worships Lucy's glitzy singer from afar. Director Irving Reis, who died young, was one of Hollywood's most under-rated film-makers, turning out some good *Falcon* thrillers, as well as such gems as *Crack-up*, *The Bachelor and the Bobby-Soxer* and *Enchantment*. Here he conjures up a climax that has few parallels in the art of making an audience cry.

Big Top Pee-wee ○
1988, US, 86 mins, colour
Dir: Randal Kleiser
Stars: Pee-wee Herman, Kris Kristofferson, Valeria Golino, Penelope Ann Miller
Rating: ★

Paul Reubens' Pee-wee Herman is certainly an odd-looking creation. Dressed in a suit several sizes too small, and sporting a white face and silly walk and voice, he's one of America's top children's entertainers. His first feature film, *Pee-wee's Big Adventure*, was a monster hit, but this overblown sequel was a damp squib. The Pee-wee bubble had burst.

Big Town, The ● ⓥ
1987, US, 109 mins, colour
Dir: Ben Bolt
Stars: Matt Dillon, Tommy Lee Jones, Diane Lane, Tom Skerritt, Bruce Dern, Suzy Amis, Lee Grant
Rating: ★

This is the cinematic equivalent of a dime novel. It has the whiff of Mickey Spillane about it, although even Spillane would have disowned plot developments that ignore all logic. Set in 1957, the film looks as though it could been made then, too, apart from the nudity and occasional expletive. Matt Dillon plays the ace dice player who arrives in Chicago to become an 'arm', coming under the wing of gambling entrepreneurs Bruce Dern and Lee Grant and becoming involved with sweet, child-tied Suzy Amis and sassy stripper Diane Lane, married to the crooked gambler (Tommy Lee Jones, with hair raked back) he has just taken for $14,000. 'You think I can make it in Chicago?' he asks his mentor. No contest. There's a simple-minded sub-plot of sorts which involves Dern's thirst for revenge on the gambler who blinded him years before and who has a small red heart tattooed on his right wrist. Gee, wonder if they'll ever find him? Dillon strikes poses, Tom Skerritt lends his wry charm to a too-brief part and Don Lake scores as a very nervous dice salesman. It isn't boring, but that's about all you can say.

B

Big Trees, The ○

1952, US, 89 mins, colour
Dir: Felix Feist
Stars: Kirk Douglas, Eve Miller, Patrice Wymore
Rating: ★★

Made three times before, in 1919, 1927 and 1938 (under the title *Valley of the Giants*), this action yarn was revamped by Warner Brothers as a vehicle for Kirk Douglas. He's excellent as an unscrupulous charmer and the vigorous action is sharply captured in Technicolor by Bert Glennon. The plot is skilfully constructed and the dialogue boasts a welcome vein of humour. But it lacks the driving force a top director might have given it.

Big Trouble in Little China ① ⓥ

1986, US, 100 mins, colour
Dir: John Carpenter
Stars: Kurt Russell, Kim Cattrall, Dennis Dun, James Hong
Rating: ★★

The title could easily refer to the final state of director John Carpenter's spoof of an *Indiana Jones*-style adventure that manages to misfire on most cylinders, even while boasting some spectacular action and inventive fantasy sequences. Kurt Russell does a reprise of the John Wayne accent that served him so well in *Escape from New York*, but looks faintly harassed, as well he might, as a philosophising CB trucker, played as a cross between a swaggering Wayne, adventurous Harrison Ford and wacky Bill Murray. Virtually every Asian actor in Hollywood appears to have been signed up for this story of kidnap and Triad gangs, crossed with a black fantasy about a seven-foot tall Chinese magician controlling an evil empire deep beneath San Francisco's Chinatown district. Carpenter has more success composing the music for the film which is rousing stuff. Easy entertainment, but disappointingly thin.

Bill & Ted's Bogus Journey ○ ⓥ

1991, US, 93 mins, colour
Dir: Pete Hewitt
Stars: Keanu Reeves, Alex Winter, William Sadler, Joss Ackland
Rating: ★★★

At the Bill and Ted University in the 27th century (motto: Party On, Dudes), there's trouble afoot. Science students dressed like citizens of Oz are devastated by the arrival of wicked superbrain Joss Ackland who has created robot Bill-and-Teds to go back in time to destroy their predecessors. Far out man! If you haven't seen *Bill and Ted's Excellent Adventure*, you're lost from now on, as Bill and Ted (still Alex Winter, doubling as his own granny, and Keanu Reeves) are bumped off by their metal doubles, and end up in a quite bodaciously imaginative Hell, where they encounter Devil-Dude and Death Dude. Their one chance of returning is to beat the Grim Reaper, who has never lost, at a game. Naturally Death (William Sadler) expects this to be something like chess. But Bill and Ted choose Battleships! This is no great movie, but definitely a cult in the making: good fun and non-heinous to boot. Party on!

Bill & Ted's Excellent Adventure ○ ⓥ

1988, US, 91 mins, colour
Dir: Stephen Herek
Stars: Keanu Reeves, Alex Winter, Geroge Carlin, Bernie Caseie
Rating: ★★★

Though it takes time to warm to, this fantasy comedy is just daft enough to be engaging. Bill and Ted are two 17-year-olds whose minds are more on music than schooling. So much so that they're in danger of failing a vital history course, which will get Ted sent off to military academy and break up their band. This, for reasons best known to the Guardians of the Future, is not on. So they enable Bill and Ted to travel back through time in a telephone box (someone's seen *Doctor Who*), where they collect a series of historical figures who'll help them through the exam. Keanu Reeves and Alex Winter are well into the spirit of the thing as scapegrace Bill and Ted and, after seeing their excellent (well, moderately amusing) adventures, you may never want to pronounce Socrates any other way than 'Sew-crayts'.

Billion Dollar Brain ①

1967, UK, 111 mins, colour
Dir: Ken Russell
Stars: Michael Caine, Karl Malden, Francoise Dorleac
Rating: ★★

This is Ken Russell's Harry Palmer spy thriller with its memorable icebound climax. Among the villains of the piece: the dependable Karl Malden and blustering Ed Begley, who clearly relishes his role as a mad general. The principal feminine role is taken by Francoise Dorleac (Catherine Deneuve's sister) who was such an attractive figure on the international film scene before her tragic death in 1967, the year before this film was released. Yet another famous figure in the cast is Oscar Homolka, that gruff, wickedly humorous, always immensely enjoyable character actor who was first seen in Palmer-land in *Funeral in Berlin*, again with Michael Caine, a year earlier.

Billy Bathgate ● ⓥ

1991, US, 106 mins, colour
Dir: Robert Benton
Stars: Dustin Hoffman, Nicole Kidman, Loren Dean, Bruce Willis
Rating: ★★★

Taken from the best-seller by E L Doctorow, and with a tightly written screenplay by playwright Tom Stoppard, this compelling exploration of the world of 1930s gangsters centres on the activities of murderous mobster Dutch Schultz (edgily played by Dustin Hoffman). The story is told as seen through the eyes of young Billy Bathgate (Loren Dean), an opportunist street kid who, seduced by the glamour of power, money and the life of crime, works his way up to become one of Dutch's most trusted flunkies. In an explosive opening, we get a glimpse of the unpredictable Dutch's raging insanity as he sets out to dispose of his once-trusted sidekick, Bo Weinberg (Bruce Willis). Thereafter, events take a turn for the more romantic and less violent as Billy is entrusted with looking after the late Bo's lady friend, Drew (Nicloe Kidman), who is now Dutch's lover – and before long , daring Billy is both dallying with Drew and dicing with disaster. A grim and glossy drama from director Robert (*Kramer vs Kramer*) Benton, *Billy Bathgate* captures well the seedy gangster underworld atmosphere but, while the eyes can feast on lush period detail and lavish, expensive-looking sets, there is ultimately not enough story to absorb the mind.

Billy Budd ○

1962, US/UK, 112 mins, b/w
Dir: Peter Ustinov
Stars: Peter Ustinov, Robert Ryan, Melvyn Douglas, Terence Stamp, Ronald Lewis, David McCallum
Rating: ★★★

Fine performances distinguish this solid version of Herman Melville's stern allegory of good versus evil on board a British navy ship in 1797, headed by Terence Stamp's Oscar-nominated portrayal of the naive and incorruptible seaman whose clash with sadistic master-at-arms Robert Ryan ends in tragedy. Peter Ustinov co-wrote the screenplay with Robert Rossen and stars as Captain Vere. While his direction is somewhat unambitious (the focus is more often than not on his players in a manner more suited to television than to the cinema), there is no denying the film's cumulative power.

Billy Liar ○
1963, UK, 96 mins, b/w
Dir: John Schlesinger
Stars: Tom Courtenay, Julie Christie, Wilfred Pickles, Mona Washbourne
Rating: ★★★

This 'kitchen-sink' answer to *The Secret Life of Walter Mitty* provides a welcome comedy role for Tom Courtenay as the young north countryman who lives entirely in a dream world. He has strong competition, though, from the female contingent, especially Mona Washbourne as his down-to-earth mum, Julie Christie, well in character as his 'dream' girl and Helen Fraser, charming in an irksome role. The superb photography by Denys Coop includes one marvellous shot of a runner on the skyline.

Billy Rose's Diamond Horseshoe ○ ⓥ
(aka: Diamond Horshoe)
1945, US, 104 mins, colour
Dir: George Seaton
Stars: Betty Grable, Dick Haymes, Phil Silvers
Rating: ★★★

Betty Grable's fans will be delighted by her vivacious performance (even Grable-haters will find her livelier than usual) in this dazzling, very expensive-looking musical which has a lively script full of unforced humour, some tuneful songs and both Dick Haymes and Phil Silvers at their best. The most popular number was 'The More I See You', but the score also includes 'You'll Never Know', 'Let Me Call You Sweetheart', 'Aba Daba Honeymoon' (featuring guest star Willie Solar) and 'Melancholy Baby'. Choreographer Hermes Pan makes the most of his chances to interrupt the action by staging some swinging dance routines, especially 'Cooking Up a Show'. Even the formula plot is

so persuasively done as to bring a lump to the throat of the unwary towards the end.

Billy Rose's Jumbo
See: *Jumbo*

Billy the Kid ○
1940, US, 95 mins, colour
Dir: David Miller
Stars: Robert Taylor, Brian Donlevy, Ian Hunter, Mary Howard
Rating: ★★

The West's most famous outlaw has been dead since 1881, but the film-makers won't let him lie down. Since 1930 he has been reincarnated by actors ranging from Wallace Beery to Paul Newman. There's even been a *Billy the Kid Versus Dracula*, which no one took very seriously. This production was an entirely different kettle of fish. Based on a novel giving a fairly romantic account of the outlaw, it stars Robert Taylor. Action fans will find there's no shortage of gunplay.

Billy the Kid and the Green Baize Vampire ●
1985, UK, 93 mins, colour
Dir: Alan Clark
Stars: Phil Daniels, Alun Armstrong, Louise Gold
Rating: ★★

The streetwise British film of the Eighties collides head-on with the pop video, and the result is a musical about a Cockney snooker superstar who takes on a world champion whose vampiric aspect must surely be based on Ray Reardon! The music sounds great, the singers are good and the staging imaginative within an obviously limited budget. What a pity the orchestral backing is so deafening that you can't hear too many of the words in the songs – so vital in a film like this where the songs not only tell practically the whole story, but provide the atmosphere as well. Phil Daniels (as the kid), Alun Armstrong (as the vampire), Bruce Payne (as the kid's manager) and Louise Gold (the muppeteer, here as the girl reporting the title clash) give it mega-effort. The whole thing would probably look terrific on stage – apart from the snooker effects which are purely cinematic; both Daniels and Armstrong demonstrate some mighty potting power which must have taken a lot of practice.

Biloxi Blues ◐ ⓥ
1987, US, 106 mins, colour
Dir: Mike Nichols
Stars: Matthew Broderick, Christopher Walken, Penelope Ann Miller
Rating: ★★★

The second part of playwright Neil Simon's autobiographical trilogy, this relates with candour and ripe service humour, but above all with affection, Simon's months of training at an army boot camp in Mississippi for a war that was over before he could get to it. Matthew Broderick is just right as the young Simon, but Christopher Walken is a shade too emotional (if interesting) as the eccentric sergeant with a plate in his head who drills his platoon to distraction. Though well told, this ends up very much the standard recruit-training yarn, even if it is infused with Simon's unique humour, often surprisingly well delivered in Broderick's narrative to the story.

Bingo ○ ⓥ
1991, US, 87 mins, colour
Dir: Matthew Robbins
Stars: Cindy Williams, David Rasche, Robert J Steinmiller, David French, Kurt Fuller
Rating: ★

After Benji, but before there was Beethoven, along came Bingo. He wasn't nearly as successful as the other two, and little wonder. An unbelievably resourceful collie dog in the Lassie mould, Bingo runs away from mistreatment in a circus and straight into the heart of a young boy. When the boy's footballer father gets transferred, Bingo is left behind – but he decides to travel across country to be reunited with his young friend. Someone has obviously seen *Lassie Come Home* and *The Incredible Journey* here, and easily-moved children may be weeping buckets at the end of this facile frolic. No sequels, though: not so much bow-wow as bow out.

Bird ● ⓥ
1988, US, 160 mins, colour
Dir: Clint Eastwood
Stars: Forest Whitaker, Diane Venora, Michael Zelniker
Rating: ★★★

'Male, about 65' is said to have been the medical report on the death of jazz musician Charlie 'Bird' Parker. Parker was in fact 34, a big man, but a hulk as full of drugs and drink as he could lay hands on. Director Clint Eastwood's account of his career, told

B

in flashback fashion, is a caring film that tells us Parker was a gentle, genial giant, blessed with a musical genius that kept sparking his career even when he could hardly stay on his feet long enough to fulfil an engagement. Forest Whitaker and Diane Venora live the roles of Parker and his wife Chan to a remarkable degree, but the film drifts on too long and is very darkly photographed. No matter, there's always the music – Bird's own amazingly complex jazz renditions of standards which still take some beating today.

Birdman of Alcatraz ○ ⓥ
1962, US, 148 mins, b/w
Dir: John Frankenheimer
Stars: Burt Lancaster, Karl Malden, Thelma Ritter, Neville Brand, Telly Savalas, Edmund O'Brien
Rating: ★★★★

The now famous story of Robert Stroud, the 'life' prisoner who took up the study of birds, and became a leading authority on the subject, makes a memorable and moving film which Burt Lancaster himself considers among his finest, alongside *Sweet Smell of Success*. Lancaster's Stroud is a moving portrait of a man who suddenly finds hope in an unexpected quarter, and there's a good performance from Neville Brand as the warder who befriends the bird man.

Bird on a Wire ◐ ⓥ
1990, US, 110 mins, colour
Dir: John Badham
Stars: Mel Gibson, Goldie Hawn, David Carradine, Bill Duke, Joan Severance
Rating: ★★

For a mainline megastar movie, this is uncomfortably unconvincing. Ruthlessly formulaic, predictable and empty-headed, it raises very little chemistry between Mel Gibson and Goldie Hawn, whose hearts don't seem to be in it, and completely wastes David Carradine as the villain, not giving him a single decent scene. Nothing somehow seems real, and we never quite figure out why Mel is on the run after spending 15 years as a relocated witness (equally difficult to work out the reason for this in the first place). The final shootout in a zoo begins very promisingly but goes on too long. One of those action-comedy-romances that sometimes work a treat, this one suffers under the uncharacteristically jerky direction of John Badham and

characters who aren't given dialogue that will supply the vital dimensions of life.

Birds, The ◐ ⓥ
1963, US, 118 mins, colour
Dir: Alfred Hitchcock
Stars: Rod Taylor, Tippi Hedren, Suzanne Pleshette, Jessica Tandy
Rating: ★★★

Alfred Hitchcock's sensational version of the Daphne Du Maurier story has the same key elements as his previous film *Psycho*, suspense, horror and tremendous impact. Thanks to skilful direction and almost flawless special effects, this tale of birds turning against humans and attacking them in multitudes is chillingly effective. Tippi Hedren responds perfectly to the demands of her director, and her performance is matched by Suzanne Pleshette's glowing, bitter-sweet portrayal of the local schoolteacher, still in love with hero Rod Taylor. Jessica Tandy adds another keenly-etched character, but the outstanding memory from this savage film is still the evil of the birds themselves. The final scenes are grimly magnetic, frighteningly foreboding. Child actress Veronica Cartwright is now the adult star of such TV series as *LA Law*.

Birds and the Bees, The ○
1956, US, 94 mins, colour
Dir: Norman Taurog
Stars: George Gobel, Mitzi Gaynor, David Niven
Rating: ★★★

A charming remake, fizzingly photographed in Technicolor, of Preston Sturges' famous comedy film *The Lady Eve*, about a naive young man who is conned by a trio of card sharps aboard a luxury liner. The song-and-dance interludes between the buzzy George Gobel and vivacious Mitzi Gaynor (presumably the bee and the bird) are quite delightful. The delectable supporting cast includes Clinton Sundberg (fine as a snooty purser), Fred Clark, Reginald Gardiner and Hans Conried.

Birdy ● ⓥ
1984, US, 120 mins, colour
Dir: Alan Parker
Stars: Matthew Modine, Nicolas Cage, John Harkins, Karen Young, Bruno Kirby
Rating: ★★

For such a highly rated film this proves to be rather dull when you actually come to see it. You can appreciate,

though, the commercial factors that hyped up Alan Parker's movie about a youth who becomes obsessed with birds (the feathered variety) and the idea that he has to fly. This doesn't look too possible, especially as he's kept in a schizophrenically silent condition in an army hospital after his experiences in Vietnam. It's well-acted, especially by Nicolas Cage as Birdy's buddy, a sensitive performance worthy of the Oscar nomination it didn't get. But the story simply hasn't the dramatic strength to sustain its slim theme towards its impending, yet ever-elusive (anti) climax. Parker directs with attention to the more exploitable aspects around the film's perimeters and the bird scenes are amazing, particularly those involving a talented canary. In the end, though, it just doesn't add up to cohesive entertainment or, for that matter, to much else.

Birthday Present, The ○
1957, UK, 100 mins, b/w
Dir: Pat Jackson
Stars: Tony Britton, Sylvia Syms, Jack Watling
Rating: ★★★

Small-scale but neatly-scripted, well-acted and effective drama about a man whose life is almost ruined through his attempt to smuggle a watch through customs. There are no big stars, but the performances are solid.

Bishop's Wife, The ○
1947, US, 130 mins, b/w
Dir: Henry Koster
Stars: Cary Grant, Loretta Young, David Niven, Monty Woolley
Rating: ★★★

Hollywood magic (in more ways than one) at its sentimental best. Cary Grant is in wonderful form as the freewheeling, ice-skating angel sent down from Heaven to put a few decent people back on the road to happiness from which they seem to have stumbled. Although, with its snow-covered ending, it should ideally be seen at Christmas, the film is perfect entertainment at any time.

Bite the Bullet ○
1975, US, 131 mins, colour
Dir: Richard Brooks
Stars: Gene Hackman, James Coburn, Candice Bergen, Ben Johnson
Rating: ★★★

Director Richard Brooks makes sure that this story of an endurance race on horseback across south-west America in 1908 keeps going at a gallop, crammed with action and incident. For once, Gene Hackman, as the sensitive man who loves horses more than he wants to win the race, seems slightly at sea – perhaps at having to express so much humanity in one soul. But James Coburn and Candice Bergen sit more easily in the saddle. Menacing actor Paul Stewart, familiar from such Hollywood films as *The Window* and *Champion*, makes a welcome film appearance as the man behind the race. The best performance of all, though, comes from craggy, Oscar-winning character star Ben Johnson, as the veteran rider of the group. He has a magnificent final scene that tops anything else in this hell-for-leather film.

Bitter Harvest ◑
1963, UK, 96 mins, colour
Dir: Peter Graham Scott
Stars: Janet Munro, John Stride, Anne Cunningham, Alan Badel
Rating: ★★★

Ted Willis wrote this haunting little parable about a country girl who moves to London, and discards true love in favour of what she thinks are the bright, inviting lights. Janet Munro makes one feel genuinely sorry for this silly but tragic figure.

Bitter Moon ●
1992, US/France, 135 mins, colour
Dir: Roman Polanski
Stars: Peter Coyote, Emmanuelle Seignier, Hugh Grant, Kristin Scott Thomas
Rating: RB

'I say chaps, Nigel and Fiona are in trouble. Taking this cruise to Istanbul on their seventh anniversary, they were bally well accosted by this deviant American cripple and his nymphomaniac wife. Dashed bad luck, or what? If only Nigel hadn't said, "It's bad for an old married couple to be seen together all the time," it might never have happened. This chap told his whole bally life story; bally tedious it was, too, but poor old Nigel was besotted by his wife, don't you see, so he had to stay and listen to the whole load of poppycock!' If you insist on doing the same as poor old Nigel, at least you'll be able to build up a treasury of ludicrous lines from what must be Roman Polanski's worst film. Top of the dunghill is probably

disabled Peter Coyote's estimation of his then-mistress (Emmanuelle Seignier): 'I loved her too. But our credit was running out. We were headed for sexual bankruptcy.' A seemingly endless voyage into perversion and banality.

Bitter Victory ○
1957, FR, 82 mins, b/w
Dir: Nicholas Ray
Stars: Richard Burton, Curt Jurgens, Ruth Roman
Rating: ★★

Nicholas Ray's bleak war film about retribution that turns sour in the desert. As with most Ray films, this one split the critics, though most gave a thumbs down to Ray's efforts to enliven what is basically a tedious combination of war and romance, top-heavy with dialogue and stock characters. Richard Burton, Curt Jurgens and Ruth Roman labour mightily to make something of the affair; among those miscast in support are Alfred Burke (as a major) and Christopher Lee (as a sergeant), roles you would have thought better cast the other way round.

Black Angel ○
1946, US, 80 mins, b/w
Dir: Roy William Neill
Stars: Dan Duryea, June Vincent, Peter Lorre, Broderick Crawford
Rating: ★★★

This was director Roy William Neill's last film before his early death at 60. Neill was the man responsible for most of Universal's Sherlock Holmes films with Basil Rathbone. Here he creates a splendidly grating atmosphere for a doomy story about an alcoholic searching for his wife's killer in order to clear an innocent man. Dan Duryea remains compellingly watchable in this role and, although Peter Lorre is rather wasted as a slug-like nightclub-manager, the heroine is played by the fascinating June Vincent, a silky blonde who never quite made it in Hollywood, but who here gives full value to such smoochy songs as 'Heartbreak' and 'Time Will Tell'.

Black Arrow, The ○
(aka: The Black Arrow Strikes)
1948, US, 76 mins, b/w
Dir: Gordon Douglas
Stars: Louis Hayward, Janet Blair
Rating: ★★★

Although based on Robert Louis Stevenson's famous adventure novel,

this film was called *The Black Arrow Strikes* in Britain, to avoid confusion with a cowboys-and-Indians serial called *The Black Arrow*, made two years earlier. Louis Hayward, although a little old for for the part, makes a dashing hero, while George Macready is an excellent malevolent Sir Daniel. The ending is somewhat changed but exciting nonetheless, and Charles Lawton's sparkling photography is another factor in the film's favour. First-class entertainment for children of all ages.

Black Arrow Strikes, The
See: The Black Arrow

Black Bart ○
(aka: Black Bart – Highwayman)
1948, US, 80 mins, colour
Dir: George Sherman
Stars: Yvonne De Carlo, Dan Duryea
Rating: ★★★

This colourful Western was made at a time when Dan Duryea was getting most of his best roles. He plays a hold-up bandit who falls in love with the famous entertainer Lola Montez. Frank Lovejoy and John McIntire make film early film appearances.

Blackbeard's Ghost ☉ ⓥ
1967, US, 107 mins, colour
Dir: Robert Stevenson
Stars: Peter Ustinov, Suzanne Pleshette, Dean Jones
Rating: ★★★

The Walt Disney studio at its most inventive and amusing, with all sorts of fun being had from the invisibility of Blackbeard the Pirate's ghost as he helps athletes and gamblers alike past the winning post. Peter Ustinov enjoys himself engagingly in the title role, Dean Jones is a likeably harassed hero, and heroine Suzanne Pleshette also has her moments, especially when she's winning at a casino and refuses to quit while she's ahead.

Blackbeard the Pirate ☉
1952, US, 100 mins, colour
Dir: Raoul Walsh
Stars: Robert Newton, Linda Darnell, Keith Andes, William Bendix
Rating: ★★

Rolling his eyes wildly, and charging up and down the deck like a bearded Bligh, Robert Newton revels in this, his second pirate picture, following his immortal portrayal of Long John Silver two years before.

B

Black Beauty ○
1971, UK, 106 mins, colour
Dir: James Hill
Stars: Mark Lester, Walter Slezak, Peter Lee Lawrence, Ursula Glas, Patrick Mower
Rating: ★★

James Hill, director of such beguiling animal stories as *Born Free*, *An Elephant Called Slowly* and *The Belstone Fox*, here wove an appealing adventure story from Anna Sewell's novel about a black horse that undergoes various hardships, moving from one owner to another. Then-popular child star Mark Lester tugs at the heart-strings in the lead.

Blackboard Jungle ◑
1955, US, 101 mins, b/w
Dir: Richard Brooks
Stars: Glenn Ford, Anne Francis, Sidney Poitier, Vic Morrow, Louis Calhern, Margaret Hayes
Rating: ★★★★

Nominated for four Oscars but coming away empty-handed on the night, this uncompromising drama about race and violent confrontation in the classroom propelled Richard Brooks (one-time husband of Jean Simmons) to the front rank of American directors. It also marked the screen debut of Vic Morrow (the actor killed in a helicopter stunt accident on the set of *Twilight Zone – The Movie* in 1982) as a sadistic troublemaker, and gave a huge boost to Sidney Poitier's meteoric rise as Hollywood's leading black actor. The film was something of a landmark, being the first in Hollywood to feature rock music, with Bill Haley's 'Rock Around the Clock' playing over the opening credits. It was cut by five minutes on its first release in British cinemas.

Black Castle, The ○
1952, US, 81 mins, b/w
Dir: Nathan Juran
Stars: Richard Greene, Boris Karloff, Paula Corday
Rating: ★★

Paula Corday, the heroine of this cloak and dagger adventure, began her career in such films as *The Body Snatcher* – also with Boris Karloff. It's strange to find Karloff cast as a goodie, in this tale of an evil Austrian nobleman who roams the catacombs of his cavernous castle, where he holds his lovely wife against her will. But Stephen McNally, as the callous count and Lon Chaney, as his hulking body-

guard, have a high old time dispensing the sneers and the scowls. Richard Greene is every bit as dashing a hero as fans of his would expect.

Black Cat, The ◑
1934, US, 65 mins, b/w
Dir: Edgar G Ulmer
Stars: Boris Karloff, Bela Lugosi
Rating: ★★★

Boris Karloff and Bela Lugosi gave two of their best performances in this strong horror film with effectively bizarre settings, in which both were rather cast against type. Karloff plays suave and ruthless devil-worshipper without a sympathetic bone in his body, while Lugosi's a basically kindly but vengeance-obsessed doctor. Appealing heroine Jacqueline Wells enjoyed a career resurgence a few years later with a new studio (Warners) and a new name – Julie Bishop. Incidentally the film has virtually nothing in common with the Edgar Allan Poe short story on which it is supposedly based.

Black Cat, The ◑
1941, US, 70 mins, b/w
Dir: Albert S Rogell
Stars: Basil Rathbone, Broderick Crawford, Bela Lugosi, Gale Sondergaard
Rating: ★

This horror whodunit is a disappointment, especially as it boasts a rare gathering of ghoulish character stars, including Basil Rathbone, Bela Lugosi and Gale Sondergaard. Gladys Cooper, Anne Gwynne and Alan Ladd – in one of his last roles before stardom – look perturbed, possibly by the comedy antics of Hugh Herbert and Broderick Crawford, which dissipate too many of the chills.

Black Cauldron, The ○ ⓥ
1985, US, 80 mins, colour
Dir: Ted Berman, Richard Rich
Voice stars: Grant Bardsley, Susan Sheridan, John Byner, John Hurt
Rating: ★★★

The Disney contribution to the sword-and-sorcery cycle turns out to be an artful combination of Disney and Tolkien, but with no truly memorable characters to turn it into an animation classic. Some of the peripheral characters, indeed, like the cat at the beginning, recoiling in horror from the proffered slops, and the dogs and dragons whose prey forever eludes their slavering jaws by a width

of cloth, could do with expansion into major characters in the plot. Based (very freely) on a series of books by Lloyd Alexander, the plot tells of an oracular pig (a rather wet character) whose vision is required by the evil Horned King to find the location of the Black Cauldron. But the teenage pig-keeper, Taran, is determined that no such thing will happen. Packed with plot, the film, although a bit too spooky in parts for little ones, will delight six- to twelve-year-olds appreciative of a bit more bite.

Black Dakotas, The ○
1954, US, 64 mins, colour
Dir: Ray Nazarro
Stars: Gary Merrill, Wanda Hendrix, John Bromfield
Rating: ★

Well-photographed Western that packs more action into its hour's running time than many films of twice its length. Would that the acting and screenplay had the same strength.

Black Fury ○
1935, US, 92 mins, b/w
Dir: Michael Curtiz
Stars: Paul Muni, Karen Morley, William Gargan, Barton MacLane
Rating: ★★★

This hard-hitting tale of industrial action and brutal strike-breaking in a Pennsylvania mining town was pretty tough stuff in its day and indeed is still tense and watchable today. It's dominated by Paul Muni's powerful central performance as the striking miner whose colleague is killed by thug Barton MacLane. Muni captures MacLane and barricades himself and his prisoner inside the mine – becoming a nationwide news story. Long before Robert De Niro, Muni would go to great lengths to research a part. For this film he worked for weeks with miners, learning their job, accents and mannerism. The results were worth the effort and gave Muni another portrayal to add to an impressive collection of fine roles. He also had gritty support from MacLane, J Carrol Naish and John Qualen. Despite being sharply directed by Michael Curtiz and given a healthy budget by Warners, the film failed at the box office, deemed too dreary and realistic by public and critics alike. In spite of this, it has stood the test of time and plays better now than many of 1935's bigger successes.

Black Hand ○
1950, US, 93 mins, b/w
Dir: Richard Thorpe
Stars: Gene Kelly, J Carrol Naish
Rating: ★★

Even though he doesn't dance a step, Gene Kelly still treads nimbly through this story of one man's vendetta against the Mafia. Nowadays, no doubt, it would have a tragic ending. But even so, it didn't do too well at the box-office in its day. Perhaps MGM would have improved its chances by changing the title to that of Kelly's character: Johnny Columbo. The cast list seems to contain almost the entire gallery of Hollywood's 'Italian' actors of the Forties. Besides J Carrol Naish, there's Frank Puglia, Peter Brocco, Marc Lawrence and Mario Siletti. Lawrence, who plays an especially nasty Mafia chief, was a one-time opera singer (you would never guess it from his slight build) who found a more lucrative career in American films of the Thirties and Forties, mainly in gangster roles.

Black Hole, The ○ ⓥ
1979, US, 97 mins, colour
Dir: Gary Nelson
Stars: Maximilian Schell, Anthony Perkins, Robert Forster, Yvette Mimieux, Joseph Bottoms, Ernest Borgnine
Rating: ★★

Robust, robotic space opera, even if the story is compounded of familiar motifs from a variety of fantasy and science-fiction favourites. Even the central figure belongs to the familiar 'mad scientist' school of villains. In respect of its robots and its space-travel hardware, it's something of a cousin to *Star Wars*, though it lacks that film's sheer panache. But there's plenty going on most of the time and no doubt all space-minded youngsters will revel in it.

Black Horse Canyon ⊙
1954, US, 81 mins, colour
Dir: Jesse Hibbs
Stars: Joel McCrea, Mari Blanchard
Rating: ★★

The story of various people trying to capture a magnificent black stallion. Not so much a Western, more of an alfresco adventure, this refreshingly different film gave Joel McCrea one of the best of his later roles as the worldly-wise drifter who helps a hot-headed ranch girl (the fiery Mari Blanchard, never better) to capture the stallion. Murvyn Vye and Bill Williams scowl effectively as the bad guys.

Black Jack ○
1979, UK, 110 mins, colour
Dir: Ken Loach
Stars: Stephen Hirst, Louise Cooper, Jean Franval
Rating: ★★

Vaguely reminiscent of the Tommy Steele vehicle *Where's Jack?*, this period adventure (set in 1750) marked a considerable departure for British director Ken Loach, whose previous credits include *Kes* and *Family Life*. The narrative is stylised with some skill, but some of the performances are less than persuasive (the fact that the film carries no script credit may have a bearing) and the accents are variable. But the film certainly is colourful and, under the talented Chris Menges' camera lens, the adventures of Black Jack and his cohorts sometimes resemble a Brueghel painting sprung to life.

Black Knight, The ○
1953, UK, 85 mins, colour
Dir: Tay Garnett
Stars: Alan Ladd, Peter Cushing, Patricia Medina
Rating: ★

Third, last and very much worst of a trio of action films that Alan Ladd made in Britain in the early Fifties. This frightful foray into early English history is set in Arthurian times, with Ladd, as a swordmaker out to avenge his dead master, given such dialogue as: 'Lemme speak, sire. You gotta lissen. England's gonna be invaded.' The battle scenes are impressively organised, but it's not enough.

Black Legion ○
1936, US, 83 mins, b/w
Dir: Archie Mayo
Stars: Humphrey Bogart, Ann Sheridan, Erin O'Brien-Moore, Dick Foran
Rating: ★★★

One of Humphrey Bogart's earliest bona-fide roles and he's terrific, even if the ending of this Ku Klux Klan drama is never totally convincing. But there are some quite grim and frightening sequences in what was a bold film for its time.

Black Magic ○
1949, US, 105 mins, b/w
Dir: Gregory Ratoff
Stars: Orson Welles, Nancy Guild, Akim Tamiroff
Rating: ★★

Orson Welles, an enthusiastic conjuror in his own right – remember him sawing Marlene Deitrich in half in *Follow the Boys?* – must have been greatly attracted to the role of Cagliostro, 18th century magician, mesmerist and general all-round scoundrel. Unfortunately, Welles, encouraged by an over-ripe script, clambers all over the role and just about spits out the pieces as well. The film certainly has its own florid atmosphere and pretty Nancy Guild, who made too few films, is effective in a dual role.

Blackmail ○ ⓥ
1929, UK, 78 mins, b/w
Dir: Alfred Hitchcock
Stars: Anny Ondra (voice Joan Barry), John Longden, Sara Allgood
Rating: ★★★

Britain's first part-talkie, directed by Alfred Hitchcock (who makes his usual small appearance, this time on a tube train), is still amazingly hypnotic to watch today, with several sequences that remain genuinely striking. The atmosphere reeks with the feeling that something nasty is going to happen any second, a sign that Hitchcock's expertise at tightening tension was already building up. Future directors Ronald Neame and Michael Powell were clapper boy and stills cameraman respectively in this landmark thriller.

Blackmail ○
1939, US, 90 mins, b/w
Dir: H C Potter
Stars: Edward G Robinson, Ruth Hussey, Guinn Williams
Rating: ★★

A rarely seen but serviceable Edward G Robinson thriller which carries echoes of *I Am a Fugitive from a Chain Gang*, the classic realist drama from Robinson's old studio, Warner Bros. This was made over at MGM and there's a certain lack of toughness in the script and supporting cast, although Edward G comfortably snarls his way through hell and high water as he is framed, sentenced to a chain gang, escapes, is blackmailed, jailed again, and brings the plot to a fiery conclusion.

B

Black Narcissus O
1946, UK, 100 mins, colour
Dir: Michael Powell, Emeric Pressburger
Stars: Deborah Kerr, Sabu, David Farrar, Jean Simmons, Flora Robson
Rating: ★★★★

Ravishingly photographed in Technicolor, this is an unusual but palpable hit from the Powell and Pressburger team, masters of the offbeat, who shot it in between making *A Matter of Life and Death* and *The Red Shoes*. Deborah Kerr heads the group of nuns who are overtaken by worldly pleasures that shatter their lives at a remote convent in lush Himalayan jungles. Kathleen Byron, as another of the nuns, gives a brilliant portrayal of approaching madness.

Black Orchid O
1952, UK, 60 mins, b/w
Dir: Charles Saunders
Stars: John Bentley, Olga Edwardes, Ronald Howard
Rating: ★★

Following his success in the title parts of the *Paul Temple* and *Toff* films, John Bentley starred in this murder melodrama, which is very typical of British second feature production of the period. Also to be seen is the screen's most adept exponent of Scotland Yard investigators, Russell Napier.

Black Orchid, The O
1958, US, 95 mins, b/w
Dir: Martin Ritt
Stars: Sophia Loren, Anthony Quinn, Mark Richman, Ina Balin
Rating: ★★★

The first of Anthony Quinn's 'European' roles leading up to his triumph five years later in *Zorba the Greek*. In this unexpectedly tender love story he plays an Italian wooing a gangster's widow. The film also established Sophia Loren's claim as an actress of some worth and paved the way for her Oscar-winning triumph three years later in *Two Women*.

Blackout
See: Contraband

Black Rain ● ⓥ
1989, US, 125 mins, colour
Dir: Ridley Scott
Stars: Michael Douglas, Andy Garcia, Kate Capshaw, Ken Takakura
Rating: ★★

Despite its Japanese background (very picturesquely shot) and high level of violence, this is a routine crime thriller with a gun-barrel-load of familiar ingredients. Michael Douglas, looking wearier and older, is the slightly crooked, rule-bending cop sent to Japan with an oriental master crook captured in America. No prizes for guessing what happens at Tokyo Airport, nor any of the plot's other developments, given that Andy Garcia is Douglas's happy-go-lucky, honest partner, Ken Takakura the Japanese associate reluctant to go out on a limb for Douglas, and Kate Capshaw the club hostess who tells him to leave town. The only twist in the tale lies in the methods Douglas finally employs to get close to his quarry, leading to a chase climax in which another motorcycle is conveniently parked next to the one stolen by the bad guy. The performances are solid, if hardly spectacular, though Yusaka Matsuda makes rather a good job of the lithe, sneering villain.

Black Rainbow ● ⓥ
1989, US, 101 mins, colour
Dir: Mike Hodges
Stars: Rosanna Arquette, Jason Robards, Tom Hulce
Rating: ★★

Not content with being an okay if overlong straight thriller about a medium who finds herself seeing deaths – a theme used before, although not all that often – *Black Rainbow* finally makes it through to the supernatural proper in the last reel. This aspect seems rather 'tacked on' and not entirely relevant to the main theme of a moderately written but well acted and directed thriller, with some doomy *film noir* music by John Scott to back its trance of death. Rosanna Arquette's childlike voluptuousness is quite effective as the visionary in white who suddenly starts foreseeing events of purest black. The variable Jason Robards is for once on form as her father, who doesn't believe a word of it, and Tom Hulce somewhat caught between the two as the reporter on the scent of a decidedly unusual story. The action is tracked with taut edginess by director Mike Hodges, although some scenes could have been edited down a bit, and the scene where a hit-man susses out Arquette's gospel theatre omitted entirely. Chances are, though, that the element of the unknown will keep you hanging in there to the end.

Black Robe ● ⓥ
1991, Canada, 100 mins, colour
Dir: Bruce Beresford
Stars: Lothaire Bluteau, Aden Young, Sandrine Holt, August Schellenberg
Rating: ★★

This beautifully-photographed Canadian film is a cross between *The Mission* and *Dances With Wolves*, – a sort of *Dance With Moose*, perhaps. Those films showed how to portray early communion with native inhabitants as exciting, enthralling cinema. Beresford's film, while shimmering to look at and earnest of intent, shows how all too easy it is to bore your audience stiff with the same subject matter. There's lots of mud and snow and the atmosphere of primitivism is quite well caught. Only occasionally, however, does the story catch fire: a scene in which Lothaire Bluteau as the Jesuit priest (the black robe of the title) translates writing for native Indians who have never seen it is one of the few to generate genuine warmth and interest, and afford brief amusement.

Black Room, The ⓒ
1935, US, 67 mins, b/w
Dir: Roy William Neill
Stars: Boris Karloff, Marian Marsh
Rating: ★★

A period chiller with Boris Karloff on the rampage as twin brothers, in the first of numerous films he made for Columbia after his big successes at Universal in the early Thirties. A gruesomely spectacular climax and imaginative direction by Roy William Neill, who made many of Basil Rathbone's Sherlock Holmes films.

Black Rose, The O
1950, US/UK, 120 mins, colour
Dir: Henry Hathaway
Stars: Tyrone Power, Orson Welles, Jack Hawkins, Cecile Aubry, Michael Rennie, Herbert Lom
Rating: ★★★

Spectacular adventure with outstanding colour photography by Jack Cardiff, who later turned director with such films as *The Mercenaries* and <*Girl On a Motorcycle*. At the helm here is Hollywood veteran Henry Hathaway, imperiously putting his imposing cast through its paces in an enjoyably fanciful Far Eastern saga. Tyrone Power and Jack Hawkins are solidly teamed as the adventuresome friends falling foul of Orson Welles' Mongol chieftain.

Black Sheep of Whitehall, The ☉
1941, UK, 80 mins, b/w
Dir: Basil Dearden
Stars: Will Hay, John Mills, Basil Sydney, Felix Aylmer
Rating: ★★★

This is the Will Hay comedy that has the ferociously fast and funny motorcycle and sidecar chase as its climax, with Hay and John Mills on the bike, to which is attached a bath chair with an aged professor aboard. Partly done by back projection, of course, but the children should fall off the armchairs laughing. Hay plays a bumbling professor who thwarts a dastardly Nazi plot.

Black Shield of Falworth, The ○
1954, US, 100 mins, colour
Dir: Rudolph Mate
Stars: Tony Curtis, Janet Leigh, Daniel O'Herlihy, Barbara Bush
Rating: ★★★

Exuberant, spectacular Hollywood version of Merrie England, filled with battling bodies, wonderful mangling of the English language by Tony Curtis and attractive supporting performances by Daniel O'Herlihy, Barbara Rush and Herbert Marshall. Janet Leigh is a stunning heroine and the whole fast-moving thing has an invigorating comic-strip vitality running through it. Hang your brain in the hall, sit back and let this one flow over you.

Black Spurs ○
1965, US, 81 mins, colour
Dir: R G Springsteen
Stars: Rory Calhoun, Terry Moore, Scott Brady, Linda Darnell
Rating: ★

A ragged Western about a crisis in the life of an embittered bounty hunter, this features the last screen appearance of Linda Darnell. A few weeks later, she was killed in a fire. It's all decked out with one of those rousing Western theme songs. And fans of vintage film stars will recognise Bruce Cabot, Lon Chaney Jr, Richard Arlen and James Best in the supporting cast.

Black Stallion, The ○
1979, US, 117 mins, colour
Dir: Carroll Ballard
Stars: Mickey Rooney, Kelly Reno, Teri Garr
Rating: ★★★

A 1941 children's classic (by Walter Farley) about a boy's adventures with his Arabian horse from shipwreck to racing championship. Beautifully filmed by director Carroll Ballard and photographer Caleb Deschanel for Francis Coppola's Zoetrope studios, with Kelly Reno as the admirable hero. Mickey Rooney turns in a lovely, restrained performance as a wise old horse trainer. It gets a bit slow in patches, but remains stunningly shot throughout. The brilliant opening sequences contain material that may be distressing to sensitive younger children.

Black Sunday ◐
1976, US, 140 mins, colour
Dir: John Frankenheimer
Stars: Robert Shaw, Bruce Dern, Marthe Keller
Rating: ★★

This is an over-expanded 50-minute story, but director John Frankenheimer keeps the tension massively high throughout the last fifth of a chilling tale of a Black September-style plot to wipe out 80,000 Americans at the Super Bowl. Robert Shaw, Bruce Dern, Marthe Keller and Fritz Weaver all stand up well as personalities against the action.

Black Swan, The ☉
1942, US, 85 mins, colour
Dir: Henry King
Stars: Tyrone Power, Maureen O'Hara, Laird Cregar, George Sanders, Anthony Quinn
Rating: ★★★

Spirited pirate fare, made in rousing Technicolor. George Sanders doesn't seem too happy as the red-bearded villain and can't offer Tyrone Power, whose good looks and swordsmanship were both at their peak, much competition in the swashbuckling stakes. More stylish villainy is provided by a black-patched Anthony Quinn, the stoutly suave Laird Cregar and oily sophisticate George Zucco.

Black Tent, The ○
1956, UK, 93 mins, colour
Dir: Brian Desmond Hurst
Stars: Anthony Steel, Donald Sinden, Andre Morrell, Donald Pleasence
Rating: ★★

Exotic adventure yarn from the Rank factory, with Anthony Steel as the British officer who joins the bedouin during the African campaign and marries the sheikh's daughter. Pleasantly shot romantic drama, all very stiff upper lip.

Black Widow ○
1955, US, 95 mins, colour
Dir: Nunnally Johnson
Stars: Van Heflin, Ginger Rogers, Gene Tierney, George Raft
Rating: ★★

Flashback thriller that turns out to be a faintly uninteresting whodunnit. Van Heflin is first-rate as the Broadway producer trying to prove he didn't murder the girl found dead in his flat. Nunnally Johnson's witty script keeps things buzzing – despite some unexpectedly poor performances.

Black Widow ◐ ⓥ
1987, US, 103 mins, colour
Dir: Bob Rafelson
Stars: Debra Winger, Theresa Russell, Dennis Hopper, Sami Frey, Nicol Williamson, Diane Ladd
Rating: ★★★

It's refreshing these days to find a thriller with so much plot, although this one is a bit too complex for its own good, even if it does just enough to keep you engrossed to the end. The admirable Debra Winger has a tough time coping with the difficult role of the workaholic Department of Justice investigator whose beady brains detect a link between the seemingly natural deaths of wealthy middle-aged men. No-one is prepared to follow up her suspicions, but naturally she's right or we wouldn't have a film. Doing the matching, catching and dispatching is the picture's other female star, Theresa Russell, as the black widow of the title. Like the spider, you see, she mates and she kills. The investigator's Achilles heel is that she envies her suspect's lifestyle, and even becomes involved with one of the husbands-to-be. These weaknesses make the character oddly dislikeable. We can never quite take to her, any more than viewers may take to a film which asks them to do so much of the spadework themselves.

Black Windmill, The ◐
1974, UK, 106 mins, colour
Dir: Don Siegel
Stars: Michael Caine, Joseph O'Conor, Donald Pleasence, John Vernon
Rating: ★★

This espionage thriller is slick and craftsmanlike but runs along familiar lines and is packed with such veterans of the genre as John Vernon, Donald Pleasence, Clive Revill and Joss Ackland. Michael Caine, as usual, gives full value as the intelligence

B

agent whose pursuit of gun runners ultimately threatens his own family. But the film remains uncharacteristic of its distinguished director, Don Siegel, who also made the original *Invasion of the Body Snatchers* as well as *Riot in Cell Block 11*, *Madigan*, *Two Mules for Sister Sara*, *Dirty Harry* and *The Shootist*.

Black Zoo ☾

1963, US, 88 mins, colour
Dir: Robert Gordon
Stars: Michael Gough, Jeanne Cooper, Rod Lauren, Virginia Grey
Rating: ★★

Michael Gough's only American film is a horror story which casts him as a carnival owner who uses his big cats to kill his enemies, a situation used 30 years previously in *Murders in the Zoo*. This version includes some chilly set-pieces. In the supporting cast you will find Jerome Cowan and Elisha Cook Jr who on the face of it do not seem to have much in common. But vintage film-fans will remember that Cowan played Sam Spade's murdered partner, and Cook did his memorable portrait of the would-be tough gun-man, both in John Huston's 1941 classic *The Maltese Falcon*.

Blade Runner ☾ ⓥ

1982, US, 130 mins, colour
Dir: Ridley Scott
Stars: Harrison Ford, Rutger Hauer, Sean Young, Edward James Olmos, M Emmett Walsh, Darryl Hannah
Rating: ★★

The special effects and sets of the 21st century detective yarn are brilliant, even if the storyline takes some fol-lowing. If you aren't lost after the first 15 minutes, you score high marks on the genius IQ computer bank file. Harrison Ford is the monosyllabic hero hunting down deadly replicants (human duplications) amid breath-taking visuals that even surpass those in director Ridley Scott's previous film *Alien*.

Blade Runner – the Director's Cut ☾ ⓥ

1982, US, 117 mins, colour
Dir: Ridley Scott
Stars: Harrison Ford, Rutger Hauer, Sean Young, Edward James Olmos, M

Emmett Walsh, Darryl Hannah
Rating: ★★★

Preview audiences for this futuristic *film noir* classic in 1982 were confused by its storyline of a former cop in the next century tracking down mutinous replicants who had escaped to Earth from space. Executives at Warners had what they thought was the perfect answer: get British director Ridley Scott to re-edit certain sequences, add an upbeat ending and a hard-boiled voiceover from star Harrison Ford to explain the actions and motivation of his character. Almost a decade later, Scott was given the chance to look again at the film, and the result, here, is the cut he would have preferred to be released originally. And it marks the elevation of a flawed cult film to true classic status. Out goes the much maligned narration and the silly ending and the film now flows better with a moody and languid pace and its groundbreaking score by Vangelis tinkered with to awesome effect. Rarely in Hollywood does a director get two bites at the same cherry, but this print of *Blade Runner* now stands as a masterpiece of the sci-fi genre and one of the great visually visionary films of its decade. Not suitable for children of junior school age.

Blame It on Rio ● ⓥ

1983, US, 100 mins, colour
Dir: Stanley Donen
Stars: Michael Caine, Joseph Bologna, Michelle Johnson, Demi Moore, Valerie Harper
Rating: ★★★

A rarity: a sex comedy that at times is both sexy and funny – though not, you should be warned, all of the time. At least Stanley Donen's cameras catch the authentic Brazilian atmosphere, as Michael Caine and Joseph Bologna, both with marriage problems, go for a tropic holiday with their daughters – and Caine embarks on an affair with his friend's (very nubile) 'little girl'. Much of what follows is quite funny, particularly when Bologna finds out but proves to have an amorous secret of his own. Caine and Bologna play the shenanigans in commendably re-laxed style and, while Michelle Johnson can't act for toffee, she cer-tainly is an apple of a dish: must be why Caine falls in love with her! Even in the less showy role, though, you'd have put your money on Demi Moore for stardom out of the two girls in-volved.

Blame It on the Bellboy ☾ ⓥ

1991, UK, 78 mins, colour
Dir: Mark Herman
Stars: Dudley Moore, Bryan Brown, Richard Griffiths, Patsy Kensit, Alison Steadman, Penelope Wilton
Rating: ★★

Just a moderately amusing comedy of mistaken identity, this, but at least you can't accuse it of being too long. Picturesquely set in Venice, it all stems from the confusion surrounding the names Horton, Orton and Lawton, three guests at a hotel. One (Dudley Moore) is there to buy a villa, the second (Bryan Brown) is a hired assassin and the third (tubby Richard Griffiths) a north country mayor out for a dirty weekend. All the expected complications with sex and gangsters ensue, but the dialogue has its occa-sionally happy moments: 'You don't meet many people when you're an assassin', growls Brown to Penelope Wilton, there for a blind date with Griffiths. Neatly constructed and wound up by first-time director Mark Herman, the script mixes titters and tedium in about equal proportions. Of the cast, Wilton steals the show as the spinster whose toothy exterior conceals a spine of steel.

Blanche Fury ☾

1948, UK, 95 mins, colour
Dir: Marc Allegret
Stars: Valerie Hobson, Stewart Granger, Walter Fitzgerald, Michael Gough, Maurice Denham
Rating: ★★★

A lavish slice of gloom and doom, set in period, wonderfully photographed in Technicolor by Guy Green and Geoffrey Unsworth (both Os-car-winners) and altogether typical of Rank's splash-out policy of post-war years which nearly bankrupted the company. The story is pure melodrama, a sort of *Jane Eyre* meets *The Gypsy and the Gentleman*, with passions running high up at t'Hall. But Valerie Hobson never looked lovelier or more alluring under the smouldering direction of Frenchman Marc Allegret, who also added lustre to the careers of Brigitte Bardot, Hedy Lamarr, Jeanne Moreau and Danielle Darrieux.

Blaze ● ⓥ

1989, US, 121 mins, colour
Dir: Ron Shelton

Stars: Paul Newman, Lolita Davidovich, Jerry Hardin
Rating: ★★

If shot as a TV movie, this free-wheeling biopic would probably have been called *The Governor and the Strip Queen*, and passed on the sex scenes. Here it's recrafted as a vehicle for its star (Paul Newman with a quiff) and provides, with a top-notch production, quite good if somewhat protracted entertainment. Senator Earl K Long (an actorly portrait by Newman), first seen declaring 'I have a weakness for tough-willed, iron-minded, independent women with big hooters', gets all of that and more in Blaze Starr (red-haired Lolita Davidovich, good if not outstanding), a girl from a backwoods family who has become top cat at a plush New Orleans strip joint. She also loves him, in her own way, and the scandal of their affair rocks the governor's seat in more ways than one. Interesting rather than great, this hasn't the sort of script that makes for great cinema, but should still provide Newman fans with much to admire.

Blazing Saddles ◑ ⓥ
1974, US, 90 mins, colour
Dir: Mel Brooks
Stars: Cleavon Little, Gene Wilder, Slim Pickens, David Huddleston, Mel Brooks, Madeline Kahn
Rating: ★★★

Arguably Mel Brooks' funniest film, *Blazing Saddles* is without doubt his most successful. Daft situations, zany sight gags and a smattering of toilet humour are thrown together to lampoon every Western you've ever seen. Cleavon Little plays a black sheriff sent to protect a small town from land developers. Of course he's not exactly welcomed with open arms and his only ally is the lone prisoner in his new jail (Gene Wilder). The gags come thick and fast, like the pellets from a scattergun and some of them miss their target. But you will be too busy laughing at the ones that hit the target to notice. It's all extremely silly, but great fun even if you've seen it before. Interesting footnote: for many years this spoof was the high-est-grossing Western ever, until *Dances With Wolves* comfortably overtook it.

Bless This House ○
1972, UK, 89 mins, colour
Dir: Gerald Thomas

Stars: Sidney James, Diana Coupland, Terry Scott, June Whitfield
Rating: ★★

Or, to be more precise, *Bless This House* meets *Happy Ever After*, as the Abbots' new neighbours prove to be none other than Terry Scott and June Whitfield. Scott's old sparring partner Bill Maynard is also in the cast, and regular *Carry On* director Gerald Thomas is at the helm of a series of familiar slapstick scenes involving fire, water and DIY decorating.

Blind Alley ○
1939, US, 75 mins, b/w
Dir: Charles Vidor
Stars: Chester Morris, Ralph Bellamy, Ann Dvorak, Melville Cooper
Rating: ★★

A classic *film noir* with shades of *The Desperate Hours* as a group of escaped convicts hold a family hostage. An above-par offering from German-born director Charles Vidor, who was also responsible for that evergreen of Hollywood erotica, *Gilda*. It's a taut story (scripted by three writers based in turn on a hit play) with great moody black and white photography from Lucien Ballard, a part-Cherokee Indian cameraman who was married to Merle Oberon between 1944 and 1949. It was remade as *The Dark Past*, starring William Holden, in 1948.

Blind Corner ○
1963, UK, 76 mins, b/w
Dir: Lance Comfort
Stars: William Sylvester, Barbara Shelley, Elizabeth Shepherd
Rating: ★★★

A minor British thriller but an above average one, thanks to a tight script and William Sylvester's performance as a blind man in danger. Barbara Shelley is in fine form too, given a chance for once to play a sexy dramatic lady instead of her usual frightened (or frightening) Hammer heroine.

Blind Date ○
1959, UK, 95 mins, b/w
Dir: Joseph Losey
Stars: Stanley Baker, Hardy Kruger, Micheline Presle, Gordon Jackson
Rating: ★★★

Intriguing, if slightly obtuse, suspense thriller which proved a big boost to director Joseph Losey's career in Britain after he had been blacklisted in his native America by the Un-American Activities Committee. Intelligent, sardonic dialogue, a skilful dovetailing

of flashbacks and present action, and a clever performance by Stanley Baker as a class-conscious policeman bitter about his own status and the corruption he knows exists in the Force, overcome the improbabilities of the plot to make the film a big success by its own unambitious standards.

Blind Date ◑ ⓥ
1987, US, 93 mins, colour
Dir: Blake Edwards
Stars: Kim Basinger, Bruce Willis, John Larroquette
Rating: ★★

Some date! Nebbish third-grade businessman Bruce Willis, a scruffy workaholic failure desperate for a date at a big do, accepts his brother's offer of Nadia (Kim Basinger), a shy southern belle who mustn't be allowed to drink. So what does he do? Right! The man clearly hasn't seen any *Gremlins* films. What's more , he buys a bottle of champagne to take the girl along to the recording studio where he used to play guitar. Is this credible or what? Moreover, this opening sequence underlines the film's whole basic problem. Comedy like this urgently needs to be rooted in reality. But *Blind Date* is so totally unbelievable from start to finish that it just isn't funny. A witty script would help, but this one is pretty moderate, and it's only when director Blake Edwards manages to string a set of sight gags together towards the end that the film shows signs of breaking out of its laughter vacuum. Willis is about the best thing in it, but his fans shouldn't necessarily take that as a recommendation to reach for the 'On' switch.

Blind Fury ● ⓥ
1989, US, 87 mins, colour
Dir: Phillip Noyce
Stars: Rutger Hauer, Terrance O'Quinn, Brandon Call, Lisa Blount, Meg Foster
Rating: ★★★

This is a chop-their-limbs-off action film but, to its credit, it's one that tries hard, and often successfully, to keep a sense of humour running through its mayhem. Rutger Hauer is the blind Vietnam vet with quite impossible prowess with a sword, handed an equally impossible assignment in escorting a nine-year-old boy to his father. The boy's also wanted by Nevada gangsters who have just killed his mother and need the boy to force his chemist father (Terrance O'Quinn) into the drugs business. Director

B

Phillip Noyce keeps the action-packed journey as lively as you could wish and sword firmly in cheek. Two of the villains are called Lyle and Tector (after the brothers in *The Wild Bunch*) and the gangsters' secret weapon at the end turns out to be master screen swordsman Sho Kosugi. 'I'm gonna put that blind man in a wheelchair,' grinds Tector. No chance!

Blind Terror ◐ ⓥ

(aka: See No Evil)
1971, UK, 89 mins, colour
Dir: Richard Fleischer
Stars: Mia Farrow, Robin Bailey, Dorothy Alison, Paul Nicholas
Rating: ★★★★

A virtuoso performance by Mia Farrow, and powerhouse direction by Richard Fleischer, makes this spiral staircase-type thriller (blind girl menaced by unknown killer) one of the best of its kind. Fleischer's gradual build-up of the tension is an object lesson on how to make this kind of suspense work to the maximum effect. Farrow's delicate, sympathetic and later agonising performance remains one of the best of her career to date.

Blink ● ⓥ

1994, US, 106 mins, colour
Dir: Michael Apted
Stars: Madeleine Stowe, Aidan Quinn, Bruce A Young
Rating: ★★

This is the one about the cop who falls in love with a beautiful witness to murder and tries to protect her from the killer. The formula stuff is given a twist by making the witness (Madeleine Stowe) the recipient of newly-grafted eyes following 20 years of blindness. This leads to 'perceptual delay', which means that objects that are blurred to her now can crop up before her eyes, crystal-clear, 24 hours after. Strung out beyond its story, the plot takes too long to get going, although Stowe's unexpected visions make for some jumpy moments to begin with. Although the actress herself is remarkably good, she has too much shouting, screaming and romancing to do in scenes that inter-relate her with cop Aidan Quinn, whose behaviour, like hers, is none too logical at times. And why, as a violinist with a folk group, does she not wear dark glasses for the glare of the stage lights? Easy – cos then she wouldn't spot the killer in the audience! Dana Stevens' screenplay,

though, does have a few good lines, mostly for Bruce A Young as Quinn's boss, and some routine excitements.

Bliss ● ⓥ

1985, Australia, 111 mins, colour
Dir: Ray Lawrence
Stars: Barry Otto, Lynette Curran, Miles Buchanan, Helen Jones, Gia Carides
Rating: ★★

A black fantasy that blends rule-bending ideas with box-office elements in a crude, outrageous, often repulsive mix that at the same time offers a sentimental overview of a story that moves in zigzag fashion towards a happy ending. Harry (Barry Otto) is a fortyish ad executive with a comely, but faithless wife. Their snooty son and buxom daughter are both steeped in drugs and perversion. Affable enough in himself, Harry suffers a heart attack and 'dies' for four minutes before a prolonged spell in hospital and open heart surgery. Afterwards, he becomes convinced he sees visions of hell and resolves to purify his soul. His family have him locked away, but not before he has met Honey (Helen Jones), a hooker from the outback and all-round child of nature; their destinies become inextricably involved, even after Henry is freed from the asylum and falls prey to the great demon Advertising again. The ending takes the film into the realms of green fable rather than black farce. A definite oddity.

Bliss of Mrs Blossom, The ○

1968, UK, 93 mins, colour
Dir: Joseph McGarth
Stars: Shirley MacLaine, Richard Attenborough, James Booth, Freddie Jones, Willie Rushton, Bob Monkhouse
Rating: ★★★

There's a high percentage of fun in this crazy comedy about a wife (Shirley MacLaine) whose lover (James Booth) came to mend her sewing machine, stayed for four years and now lives in the attic. Her husband (Richard Attenborough) is a bra-manufacturer (known as Orpheus in the Undie-world) whose ambitions to invent an expanding bra come to grief in spectacular fashion. Director Joseph McGrath converts the lives of these people – played with beautifully straight faces by the trio of stars – into a kaleidoscope of colour, noise and fun, in a superb series of visual jokes. Not least of these is Freddie Jones' acutely comic detective, and Bob

Monkhouse puts in an appearance as a maniac psychiatrist. Only in the last 15 minutes does the fun flag.

Blithe Spirit ○ ⓥ

1945, UK, 96 mins, colour
Dir: David Lean
Stars: Rex Harrison, Constance Cummings, Kay Hammond
Rating: ★★★★

Another happy Noel Coward/David Lean collaboration to follow their success with *In Which We Serve* and *This Happy Breed*. Superbly shot in Technicolor by Ronald Neame, it gave the honey-voiced Kay Hammond one of her best film roles, as the ghost of Rex Harrison's late wife, who turns up to haunt his new bride. Margaret Rutherford also scores heavily as an eccentric medium.

Blob, The ● ⓥ

1988, US, 95 mins, colour
Dir: Chuck Russell
Stars: Shawnee Smith, Kevin Dillon
Rating: ★★

Thirty years after the camp, low budget horror film that launched the film career of Steve McQueen, this big-budget remake, starring Matt Dillon's brother Kevin, attempted to better it with the latest state-of-the-art special effects. While these are certainly eye-popping in scenes as an aggressive pink glue ball from outer space devours victims in a small American town, the script is full of holes, the dialogue is sub-standard and the ending is a tacked-on cop-out.

Blockade ○

1938, US, 85 mins, b/w
Dir: William Dieterle
Stars: Madeleine Carroll, Henry Fonda, Leo Carrillo
Rating: ★★

Banned in some American cities in its day since, although it doesn't take sides, it is unmistakeably set against the background of the Spanish Civil War. *Blockade* can be seen today as an exciting action film with well organised crowd and battle scenes. Much of the dialogue for the film was supplied (uncredited) by the novelist James M Cain, who wrote *The Postman Always Rings Twice*.

Block-Heads ⊙

1938, US, 60 mins, b/w
Dir: John G Blystone

Stars: Stan Laurel, Oliver Hardy, Patricia Ellis
Rating: ★★★★

One of the last great Laurel and Hardy feature comedies, made before a change of studio two years later hastened their decline. There are some splendid scenes of typical Stan-inspired cataclysmic disaster, two of which leave Ollie firstly buried up to his neck in sand and then ditto, in the remains of his own garage. Some of the dialogue exchanges are held in great affection by aficionados, and justifiably so.

Blonde Fist ● ⓥ
1991, UK, 102 mins, colour
Dir: Frank Clarke
Stars: Margi Clarke, Carroll Baker
Rating: ★

No wonder the British film industry has all but died out if this inane comedy, which sets out to emulate the harmless fun of the classic Ealing movies, is the best we can come up with. The omens were certainly good, with the writing chores in the capable hands of Frank Clarke, who penned *Letter to Brezhnev*, and the starring role, of a working class woman making good with her fists as a female boxer, going to his sister, the pneumatic blonde bombshell Margi Clarke – from BBCs *Making Out* and the wisecracking co-female lead from *Brezhnev*. But thanks to Frank Clarke's own ponderous direction and a script that proves not so much intelligent and humorous as a patronising fairytale of working-class life, it sinks quickly into a domestic drama comprising an endless stream of unfunny one-liners delivered at a snail's pace and hammered home visually with all the subtlety of a sledgehammer cracking a nut. It's also particularly sad to see Carroll Baker taking part in such mindless drivel.

Blonde Venus ○
1932, US, 97 mins, b/w
Dir: Josef von Sternberg
Stars: Marlene Dietrich, Herbert Marshall, Cary Grant
Rating: ★★★

A star vehicle for the moody and magnetic Marlene Dietrich, here shimmeringly photographed by Bert Glennon. It's a fairly daft story, a melodrama of love and jealousy, in which producer-director Josef von Sternberg foists upon Dietrich the chance to sing 'Hot Voodoo' in a go-

rilla suit (how many actresses can count that among their golden opportunities?). A bizarre mixture of campy excess and soapy drama.

Blondie ☉
1938, US, 68 mins, b/w
Dir: Frank R Strayer
Stars: Penny Singleton, Arthur Lake, Gene Lockhart, Ann Doran
Rating: ★★★

With Penny Singleton and Arthur Lake perfectly cast as the bothered and bewildered Bumsteads of Chic Young's strip cartoon, this filmed marked the beginning of one of the longest movie series in Hollywood history. The *Blondie* films ran from 1938 to 1950 and their millions of fans watched Larry Simms (as Baby Dumpling) stay and grow up with the series. Daisy, the incorrigible dog, and Mr Beasley, the long suffering mailman (played by prolific character actor Irving Bacon), were other regulars during the early years of a series which kept its popularity to the end.

Blood Alley ○
1955, US, 115 mins, colour
Dir: William Wellman
Stars: John Wayne, Lauren Bacall, Paul Fix
Rating: ★★

John Wayne as a seafaring soldier of fortune. Having already disposed of all unfriendly Japanese in the Second World War, this marked the start of Wayne's new campaign against any Orientals with Communist leanings. Only Wayne could get away with a line like this . . . Lauren Bacall asks him in one scene why he killed a Chinese soldier. He replies: 'Seemed like a good idea.'

Blood and Sand ○ ⓥ
1941, US, 123 mins, colour
Dir: Rouben Mamoulian
Stars: Tyrone Power, Linda Darnell, Rita Hayworth, Anthony Quinn, John Carradine
Rating: ★★★

Tyrone Power followed in the fancy footwork of Rudolph Valentino with this lavish remake of the silent star's 1922 classic saga of a matador's rise from rags to riches to retribution and won himself quite a few critical ears and tails in the process. For it, he was reunited with Linda Darnell (in the last of their four films together) and director Rouben Mamoulian, who had put Power through his paces in

The Mark of Zorro. The role of the second female lead was turned down by Carole Landis who refused to dye her hair red. Maria Montez and Lynn Bari were considered and rejected, although Bari ended up in the film as Power's sister. The part finally went to Rita Hayworth who made a fine, sensuous job of it and came near to stealing the picture from Power with a steamy (for the time) tango with Anthony Quinn. Mamoulian's sumptuous direction was attractively complemented by the Oscar-winning cinematography of Ernest Palmer and Ray Rennahan, and the Academy Award-nominated art direction by Richard Day, Joseph L Wright and Thomas Little.

Blood Beach ●
1980, US, 90 mins, colour
Dir: Jeffrey Bloom
Stars: David Huffman, Mariana Hill, John Saxon
Rating: ★★★

Jack Arnold, who made *The Creature from the Black Lagoon* and *The Incredible Shrinking Man*, would have been proud of this one. People are getting sucked through the sand like nobody's business in Southern California . 'Just when you know it's safe to go into the water,' growls police chief John Saxon, 'you can't get to it!' Something's under there all right and the creature's no anti-climax when it appears at the end: a sort of giant octopus without tentacles, but with an extended Venus fly trap mounted on top. Ugh! Intelligence gapes from every pore of this monster movie, and director Jeffrey Bloom builds suspense uncomfortably well as his camera lurks at a distance like some prowling predator. Bloom cleverly uses all sorts of little things to build up the atmosphere of menace and you can sense the stuffy stench of the monster's lair when it's finally invaded. Individual performances are almost all good: a group of interesting actors obviously sniffed a solid script and a marketable product.

Blood from the Mummy's Tomb ●
1971, UK, 87 mins, colour
Dir: Seth Holt
Stars: Andrew Keir, Valerie Leon, James Villiers
Rating: ★★

One of Hammer's most striking horror films, directed by the talented Seth Holt, who died before it was finished.

B

Holt (and Michael Carreras, who completed the film) revive the old story of the mummy's revenge on those who have defiled its tomb and make it seem chillingly fresh. And the imposing Valerie Leon, in by far her best role, makes the most of her chances in the dual roles of Egyptian queen of darkness and professor's daughter.

Bloodline ◑
1979, US, 116 mins, colour
Dir: Terence Young
Stars: Audrey Hepburn, Ben Gazzara, James Mason
Rating: ★

Frantically overheated thriller from Harold Robbins country, with Audrey Hepburn continuing her screen comeback as the heiress to 'an international pharmaceutical empire' desperately dodging various attempts on her life.

Blood Money ◑
(aka: Requiem for a Heavyweight)
1962, US, 100 mins, b/w
Dir: Ralph Nelson
Stars: Anthony Quinn, Jackie Gleason, Mickey Rooney, Julie Harris
Rating: ★★★

Gripping, tragic story of a fading boxer. Based on the powerful television play, *Requiem for a Heavyweight*, by Rod Serling, who also wrote the screenplay (Sean Connery played the lead in the British television version). Quinn is painfully real as the boxer, Mountain Rivera, and strong support comes from Mickey Rooney, Jackie Gleason and Harry Bellaver. Appearing as one of Mountain's opponents, a 21-year-old Cassius Clay, before he himself became World Heavyweight Champion. And another former world title holder, the legendary Jack Dempsey, makes an appearance.

Blood Oath ● ⊗
(aka: Prisoners of the Sun)
1990, Australia, 108 mins, colour
Dir: Stephen Wallace
Stars: Bryan Brown, George Takei, Jason Donovan, Tetsu Watanabe
Rating: ★★★

A sturdy combination of 'blood island' prison-camp film and court-martial drama, this war atrocities story, based on real facts, runs along familiar lines, but grips most of the way through. Bryan Brown, who once portrayed the victim of a court-martial in *Breaker*

Morant, is the prosecuting officer who must try to convict Japanese officers from the island where 300 Australian soldiers have been found butchered and buried. But he has no witnesses, no evidence and defendants who merely insist that no massacres ever took place. There is evidence, to be sure, but certain Allied factions withhold it from the prosecutor for political reasons. In the end, a breakthrough comes, though it provides neither side with much satisfaction. Well put together, the film throws up an interesting new actress in Canadian-born Aussie Deborah Unger, and carries a 'special appearance' by Jason Donovan, who has half-a-dozen close-ups, but only one line.

Blood of the Vampire ●
1958, UK, 85 mins, colour
Dir: Henry Cass
Stars: Donald Wolfit, Barbara Shelley, Vincent Ball
Rating: ★★

This gory horror film, played with enormous enthusiasm by a cast led by Donald Wolfit, is not, for once, a Hammer film, although it was scripted by Jimmy Sangster, who was to become a Hammer stalwart for more than a decade. Full-blooded support from Victor Maddern as a one-eyed hunchback and from the first lady of British horror, Barbara Shelley. You'll also spot a number of familiar 'character' faces, among them Bernard Bresslaw, John Le Mesurier, Denis Shaw, Hal Osmond, John Stuart and George Murcell. The excellent colour photography is the work of co-producer Monty Berman.

Blood on My Hands
See: Kiss the Blood Off My Hands

Blood on Satan's Claw ●
(aka: Satan's Skin)
1971, UK, 93 mins, colour
Dir: Piers Haggard
Stars: Patrick Wymark, Linda Hayden, Barry Andrews, Michele Dotrice
Rating: ★★

This very shuddery horror film is a demon offspring from *Children of the Damned* out of Vincent Price's *Witchfinder-General*. Some very nasty things happen to Simon Williams, remembered as James Bellamy from *Upstairs, Downstairs*. And Linda Hayden gives her best screen performance as the leader of the devil children behind some gruesome goings-on in a 17th century village.

Blood on the Arrow ○
1964, US, 91 mins, colour
Dir: Sidney Salkow
Stars: Dale Robertson, Martha Hyer, Wendell Corey
Rating: ★

Dale Robertson is the strong silent hero of this fast-paced but poorly-scripted Western, in which he outdraws what looks like the slowest gunfighter in the west. Martha Hyer is a traditional heroine in long, blonde tresses and off-the-shoulder blouse, while two of the villains are Ted de Corsia and Elisha Cook Jr, two familiar faces from Hollywood crime films of the Forties and Fifties.

Blood on the Moon ○
1948, US, 88 mins, b/w
Dir: Robert Wise
Stars: Robert Mitchum, Barbara Bel Geddes, Robert Preston, Walter Brennan
Rating: ★★★

Excellent dark Western, sturdily directed by Robert Wise, and featuring a strong performance by Robert Mitchum in the middle of a great period for him at RKO that also included *Crossfire* and *Build My Gallows High*. A fight in a darkened bar-room is only one of numerous memorable moments from this most powerful and atmospheric of post-war Westerns, to which Robert Preston, Barbara Bel Geddes, Phyllis Thaxter and Walter Brennan all make striking contributions.

Blood on the Sun ○ ⊗
1945, US, 98 mins, b/w
Dir: Frank Lloyd
Stars: James Cagney, Sylvia Sidney, Wallace Ford, Robert Armstrong
Rating: ★★★

Never-say-die James Cagney battles fiendish orientals plotting world domination in 1928, with the help of beautiful double agent Sylvia Sidney appearing in her first film for four years. Premier Tanaka (ironically also the name of a Japanese Prime Minister) was a real-life bad guy who allied with war lords and industrialists to further his own ends. Also suffering the slit-eyed treatment as villainous Colonel Tojo is burly Robert Armstrong, memorable as Denham in *King Kong*, *Son of Kong* and *Mighty Joe Young*.

Blood Red ◑ ⊗
1988, US, 91 mins, colour
Dir: Peter Masterson

Stars: Eric Roberts, Giancarlo Giannini, Dennis Hopper, Burt Young, Susan Anspach, Michael Madsen
Rating: ★

You've heard of spaghetti action films, now meet the vino Western. Sicilian immigrants to old California are muscled off their vineyards by railroad bully-boys, who murder the leader of the farmers' resistance. His son Marco (Eric Roberts, in plunging neckline and posy leather trousers) takes to the hills as a galloping avenger, cutting down his enemies one by one. Hollywood used to be able to make this kind of thing standing on its head, but alas no more. This is not so much *The Mark of Zorro* as *The Snore of Marco*, with drippy romantic interludes in between bursts of inconclusive action. Under Peter Masterson's direction, an all-too-distinguished cast rises to new heights of ineptitude. Pick of this curdled vintage of over-acting is Dennis Hopper's railroad boss, a role for which the actor was extremely unwise to attempt an Irish accent. Julia Roberts, in her first film, has only about three lines, which she may remember in retrospect as three too many.

Blood Simple ● ⓥ
1983, US, 96 mins, colour
Dir: Joel Coen
Stars: John Getz, Frances McDormand, M Emmet Walsh, Dan Hedeya
Rating: ★★★

A real *film noir* for the Eighties. There probably hasn't been a thriller as minimal as this since *Detour* in 1945. But director Joel Coen, making an impact with his very first film, has taken the accepted elements of adulterous couple, vengeful, dislikeable husband and corruptible private eye and moved them slowly and deliberately towards their own destinies. Blood is black, fear and agony are real. You may doze off in the exposition, but you'll sure as hell stay awake for the climax, as the story moves inexorably towards its pre-planned conclusion. M Emmet Walsh, after years of tiny and largely unrewarding roles, is brilliant as the wholly seedy Texas private eye whose perfect crime turns sour. An impressive first feature, if a shade too calculated to make the topmost bracket.

Bloodsport ● ⓥ
1987, US, 92 mins, colour
Dir: Newt Arnold

Stars: Jean-Claude Van Damme, Leah Ayres, Bolo Young, Donald Gibb, Forest Whitaker
Rating: ★

Or, more appropriately, *Bloodspurt*. The kind of movie that made you wonder where the industry was going, it takes us back 15 years to the kung fu rage, only with more blood and bone. People are getting killed out there, but Frank Dux (Jean-Claude Van Damme) wants to become world karate champion. There are a lot of preliminary bouts which really waste our time, since we know that Dux will fight and annihilate Chong Li, a Korean who flexes big pectorals a lot, in the final reel. This begets the kind of primitive violence that Van Damme was soon to demonstrate would drag 'em at the box-office. The direction lacks intelligence, the acting lacks talent. And what is Forest Whitaker, the big black actor from *Bird* and *The Crying Game*, doing in all this? Only he could tell us.

Bloody Mama ●
1969, US, 90 mins, colour
Dir: Roger Corman
Stars: Shelley Winters, Don Stroud, Robert De Niro, Bruce Dern, Pat Hingle
Rating: ★★★

One of the last films to date to be directed by Roger Corman (who made the 'Edgar Allan Poe' horror films of the Sixties), this is a kind of second-cousin to *Bonnie and Clyde*, except that there are no redeeming features about the appalling Ma Barker (Shelley Winters) and her brood of homicidal sons, which includes Robert De Niro in one of his earliest roles. A violent, unpleasant story that captures the right primitive backwoods feel.

Blossoms in the Dust ⊙
1941, US, 99 mins, colour
Dir: Mervyn Leroy
Stars: Greer Garson, Walter Pidgeon
Rating: ★★★

The first film (it's about orphan children) that Greer Garson and Walter Pidgeon made together started a box-office bonanza unseen at MGM since the peak years of Jeanette MacDonald and Nelson Eddy. The studio teamed them together seven more times in the next 12 years – years that included such highly praised hits as *Madame Curie* and *Mrs Miniver*.

Blowing Wild ○
1953, US, 90 mins, b/w
Dir: Philip Yordan
Stars: Gary Cooper, Barbara Stanwyck, Anthony Quinn, Ruth Roman, Ward Bond
Rating: ★★

Even with the writing talents of Philip Yordan, the star power of Gary Cooper, Barbara Stanwyck, Anthony Quinn and Ruth Roman, and one of those rolling ballads by Frankie Laine ('Marina mine – free from black gold; our love never can be'), this drama of desire in the oilfields of Mexico in the 1930s fails to strike many sparks. Stanwyck has the most interesting character and the film could do with more of her. But there's some (literally) dynamite action towards the end.

Blow Out ● ⓥ
1981, US, 108 mins, colour
Dir: Brian De Palma
Stars: John Travolta, Nancy Allen, John Lithgow, Dennis Franz
Rating: ★★★

John Travolta is a movie sound man who discovers that a car tyre blowout on a bridge was really a gunshot, followed by the car going over the side. He gamely rescues a prostitute in the car with a male politician (a neat flip of the Chappaquiddick scandal) and then his troubles start! Director Brian De Palma split the critics with this homage to Hitchcock by way of Michelangelo Antonioni's *Blow-Up* and Francis Coppola's *The Conversation*. The opening scenes are a nice tongue-in-cheek indication of the shocks that are to follow.

BlowUp ●
1966, UK, 110 mins, colour
Dir: Michelangelo Antonioni
Stars: David Hemmings, Vanessa Redgrave, Sarah Miles, Peter Bowles, Verushka, Jane Birkin
Rating: ★★★

Michelangelo Antonioni's much-discussed film about a trendy photographer who comes to believe he may have photographed a murder. The boldly sexual role played by Vanessa Redgrave, the exuberant nude sequence involving a group of young models, and the music score, which combined rock and modern-jazz idioms, were all among the factors that contributed to the film's success. How you interpret its story is part of the fascination.

Blue Angel, The ◐ ⓥ

1930, Germany, 102 mins, b/w
Dir: Joseph von Sternberg
Stars: Emil Jannings, Marlene Dietrich
Rating: ★★★★

The Marlene Dietrich classic about a middle-aged professor who becomes infatuated with a nightclub singer. Shot in an atmosphere of stifling sexuality, the film remains one of the most harrowing depictions of human degradation on record. Dietrich's appearance as Lola-Lola, in sheer stockings, silk topper, high heels and garter belt, remains one of the unshatterable images of cinema history. The film made her a world star, and she went to Hollywood later in the year. In the English language version of the film, it's interesting to compare Dietrich's rather guttural English with the seductive, all-purpose continental accent she soon developed in Hollywood.

Bluebeard ●

1972, US/Italy, 125 mins, b/w
Dir: Edward Dmytryk
Stars: Richard Burton, Raquel Welch
Rating: ★

This is what I suppose you could call high Gothic camp, with Richard Burton not as the Landru or Gilles de Retz of history but, would you credit it, a ficticious Austrian aristocrat with a blue-tinged beard, who does away with six wives, sundry hangers-on and a cat. All his brides, being played by some of the world's loveliest actresses, try to use their shapely wiles to turn our hero on. But he, sterile soul, remains singularly aloof, apart from struggling with some unspeakable dialogue. The results are fine, perhaps, for girl-starved males, but Burton fans are likely to find themselves demanding more in the way of drama.

Bluebeard's Eighth Wife ○

1938, US, 85 mins, b/w
Dir: Ernst Lubitsch
Stars: Claudette Colbert, Gary Cooper, David Niven, Edward Everett Horton
Rating: ★★★

Gary Cooper, who had previously starred for Ernst Lubitsch, master director of naughty-but-nice comedies, in *Design for Living*, is perfect casting for this later Lubitsch romp, as a millionaire who can handle money but not wives. Claudette Colbert is the girl who aims to be his eighth (but not last: she's after his alimony) wife, and there's astringent support from David Niven, Edward Everett Horton and Warren Hymer, plus Franklin Pangborn in his typecast but delightful running role of the snooty manager.

Bluebeard's 10 Honeymoons ○

1960, UK, 93 mins, colour
Dir: W Lee Wilder
Stars: George Sanders, Corinne Calvert, Patricia Roc, Jean Kent
Rating: ★★

Unlike the Richard Burton film, this chiller really is based on the case of Henri 'Bluebeard' Landru, the murderous monsieur who disposed of 10 wives. Among those getting the final curtain call from suave George Sanders are Greta Gynt, Maxine Audley, Corinne Calvet and Jean Kent.

Blue Bird, The ☉

1940, US, 80 mins, colour
Dir: Walter Lang
Stars: Shirley Temple, Johnny Russell, Gale Sondergaard, Eddi Collins
Rating: ★★

This much-neglected fantasy was Shirley Temple's present from 20th Century-Fox for their not allowing her to do *The Wizard of Oz*. Like Judy Garland in that film, Shirley also sets out on an incredible journey – to find the bluebird of happiness, searching for it in the past, the future and the Land of Luxury. The photography and art direction perfectly capture the sometimes quite creepy mood of Maeterlinck's original fairy-tale play, and the sole sadness is that the only existing versions of this film now run 20 minutes shorter than the original. Gale Sondergaard as a cat and Eddie Collins as a dog offer first-class class, if faintly sinister, supporting contributions. Bits, though, are just too twee.

Blue Chips ● ⓥ

1994, US, 108 mins, colour
Dir: William Friedkin
Stars: Nick Nolte, Mary McDonnell, J T Walsh, Shaquille O'Neal, Louis Gossett
Rating: ★

An intimate knowledge of the rules of basketball might help you a little here; but not much. This is a fairly uninteresting sports drama about the 'buying' of star students for university teams, with an over-the-top performance from Nick Nolte as the true-blue coach who sinks to corruption in order to assemble a winning team. J T Walsh is his usual loathsome self as the brains behind the bribes, and Mary McDonnell uncharacteristically damp as Nolte's supportive ex-wife. Basketball fans may be encouraged to go along by the presence of several junior greats (including the mighty Shaquille O'Neal) as members of Nolte's squad, and all of them prove serviceable actors. For the rest of us, though, there's little to cheer for here. Give us *Beau Chumps* any day.

Blue Dahlia, The ○

1945, US, 99 mins, b/w
Dir: George Marshall
Stars: Alan Ladd, Veronica Lake, William Bendix, Howard da Silva
Rating: ★★★

The last great Forties crime film to star Alan Ladd and Veronica Lake – creatures of the Hollywood night. And what music they made together. This one also has war veteran William Bendix complaining about the 'monkey music' in his head, a lean and laconic screenplay by Raymond Chandler, and a rare fat part for that lugubrious character actor Will Wright, here as a hotel detective. They reshot the original ending – now the odds are you'll never guess 'whodunnit'.

Blue Gardenia, The ○

1953, US, 90 mins, b/w
Dir: Fritz Lang
Stars: Anne Baxter, Richard Conte, Ann Sothern, Raymond Baxter, Nat 'King' Cole
Rating: ★★★

Solid Fritz Lang-directed thriller released in the same year as his classic *The Big Heat*. The characters are riddled with neuroses and blunder through a world of glossy nightspots and sudden death, all photographed evocatively in light and shade by the high priest of *film noir* cameramen, Nicholas Musuraca. His best effects come with rain-streaked windows – and a murder reflected in the shards of a shattered mirror. Lang's tracking shots that harry the characters emphasise their entrapment in circumstances largely of their own making, especially Norah, plaintively played by Anne Baxter, who believes she may have killed a man who attacked her.

Blue Hawaii ☉ ⓥ

1961, US, 103 mins, colour
Dir: Hal Kanter

Stars: Elvis Presley, Joan Blackman, Nancy Walters, Angela Lansbury
Rating: ★★

Angela Lansbury has always excelled at playing characters much older than herself – here she was only 10 years older than Elvis Presley but was picked to play his mother! This picture-postcard romp is little more than an Hawaiian tourist board film, padded out with 14 songs from the King, including the title song, first crooned by Bing Crosby in the 1937 film *Waikiki Wedding*. As lightweight as a lei, but it all looks splendid in Panavision and Technicolor.

Blue Heat ● Ⓥ
(aka: The Last of the Finest)
1990, US, 106 mins, colour
Dir: John MacKenzie
Stars: Brian Dennehy, Joe Pantoliano, Jeff Fahey, Bill Paxton
Rating: ★★

The city's finest are after a drugs bust again, and this time it's a big one. Nationwide, in fact. It's the involvement of the US government that lends an edge to this well-made but basically routine tale of four cops who turn vigilante when one is killed and their leader thrown off the force – while in pursuit of said druglords. The cops are quite nicely drawn by the star quartet, there's a lot of pseudo-smart dialogue, action in which the bullets fly thicker than the four-letter words and an ironic sideplot in which the super-honest cops are tempted to head for Mexico when they come into possession of $23 million worth of tainted money. Overall, though, it's a by-the-numbers job. 'You're slipping over the edge,' Brian Dennehy's superior (Henry Darrow) tells him. 'Well,' replies Dennehy, 'that's where we live. We're cops, remember.' It's an exchange that sums up the intrinsically familiar nature of the venture.

Blue Ice ● Ⓥ
1992, UK, 106 mins, colour
Dir: Russell Mulcahy
Stars: Michael Caine, Sean Young
Rating: ★★

Former MI6 agent Harry Anders (Michael Caine in a Harry Palmer type character 25 years on) just wants a quiet life running a backstreets jazz club. The trouble with Harry is that intrigue and murder dogs his every move. When beautiful American Stacy (Sean Young) prangs his prize car, Harry finds himself plunged back into the world of espionage. It's a shallow thriller but with a stylish feel, thanks to the stunning visuals conjured up by *Highlander* director Mulcahy. Silly dialogue, though, finally sinks it.

Blue Jean Cop ● Ⓥ
(aka: Shakedown)
1988, US, 90 mins, colour
Dir: James Glickenhaus
Stars: Peter Weller, Sam Elliott, Patricia Charbonneau
Rating: ★★★

A fast-moving thriller where actions speak louder than words. That's just as well, since director James Glickenhaus has filled the soundtrack with so much background noise that 30 per cent of the dialogue flies by before you can grasp it. It takes about 20 minutes before you accept this in the spirit that it doesn't matter. Then you can settle down to a rough, tough, spectacularly action-packed story that's not to be taken at all seriously. *Robocop*'s Peter Weller is a legal aid lawyer who teams up with shaggy undercover cop Sam Elliott, to prove a disreputable client innocent of murder – and clear up police corruption and a city-wide drugs ring for good measure. The girls involved are nothing much, but both Weller and Elliott bring a little more to their dialogue than other actors might have done, and that's to their credit. Action is certainly in the 'terrific' league, especially a shootout in Times Square that careers on to a crash in New York harbour. Very good stuff if you've had a hard day decorating the kitchen and want to be consistently well entertained without having to concentrate too much.

Blue Lagoon, The ○
1949, UK, 103 mins, colour
Dir: Frank Launder
Stars: Jean Simmons, Donald Houston
Rating: ★★★

Spectacular, colourful adventure film, adapted much more effectively than the recent remake – from H de Vere Stacpoole's famous novel of the same title, about two children facing the perils of nature on a desert island. The director of the stunning Technicolor photography – the film was shot on location in Fiji – was a young cameraman called Geoffrey Unsworth, who many years later was to win an Academy Award for *Cabaret*.

Blue Lamp, The ○ Ⓥ
1949, UK, 84 mins, b/w
Dir: Basil Dearden

Stars: Jack Warner, Jimmy Hanley, Dirk Bogarde, Robert Flemyng
Rating: ★★★

A now classic slice of British post-war cinema realism from Ealing Studios, with Jack Warner creating the character of kindly copper George Dixon that was to serve him so well. He made some 430 episodes of *Dixon of Dock Green* for television between 1955 and 1976, when he finally hung up his truncheon and retired. Other plus factors include a truculent young Dirk Bogarde as the villain, glimpses of actual police work and an exciting factual account of a murder hunt.

Blue Max, The ◑ Ⓥ
1966, US, 156 mins, colour
Dir: John Guillermin
Stars: George Peppard, James Mason, Ursula Andress, Jeremy Kemp
Rating: ★★

This isn't war, but it certainly is entertainment. With that proviso safely out of the way, one can definitely award a medal to director John Guillermin (later to make the *Towering Inferno*) and his cameraman on as riveting, bloody and thoroughly convincing series of World War One aerial dogfights as you are ever likely to see – to which a throbbing music score by Jerry Goldsmith gives additional excitement. Perhaps Guillermin's utter concentration on the aerial drama explains why his ground scenes are so unworthy in comparison. But James Mason does manage to make an impression as the suavely convincing Count Von Klugerman and Jeremy Kemp has one of his best film roles as his ruthless pilot nephew. There is also a famous love scene between Ursula Andress and George Peppard in which Ursula, although naked to the waist, remains miraculously covered by a towel around her neck.

Blue Murder at St Trinian's ☉
1957, UK, 85 mins, b/w
Dir: Frank Launder
Stars: Terry-Thomas, George Cole, Joyce Grenfell, Lionel Jeffries
Rating: ★★★

The little horrors of this infamous school give way to the nubile nymphets of the sixth form in this further catalogue of the girls' farcical adventures. The school song at the start is especially funny, and the busty beauty leading the girls into one catastrophe after another really is

B

Sabrina. It's a pity that such talented and funny people as Terry-Thomas and Joyce Grenfell have so little to do, but Lionel Jeffries waltzes away with the comedy honours. Other familiar faces in the supporting cast belong to Kenneth Griffith, Terry Scott, Eric Barker, Thorley Walters and Richard Wattis, while Alastair Sim appears briefly at the beginning of affairs as the imprisoned Miss Fritton.

Blues Brothers, The ● ⓥ
1980, US, 135 mins, colour
Dir: John Landis
Stars: John Belushi, Dan Aykroyd, James Brown, Ray Charles, Carrie Fisher, Aretha Franklin
Rating: ★★

One of the highest-grossing films of all time in America (although its cost was astronomical). A cataclysmic orgy of noise and destruction, it saw tubby John Belushi and big Dan Aykroyd shoot to stardom as the adult Abbott and Costello of the Eighties. Alas, two years later Belushi was dead, from an accidental overdose of drugs.

Blue Steel ● ⓥ
1989, US, 103 mins, colour
Dir: Kathryn Bigelow
Stars: Jamie Lee Curtis, Ron Silver, Clancy Brown, Elizabeth Pena
Rating: ★

The role of a cop fighting to find a serial killer in the city would seem tailor-made for Jamie Lee Curtis' tough-tender personality. Sadly, the character is helplessly adrift in a ludicrous psycho-thriller that needs at least four (equally silly) climaxes before it can stagger to a conclusion. Badly scripted, packed with giggle-prone dialogue and events that go on too long and just hold up the story, the film's stuck from the start with the audience knowing who the killer is. That negates any impact the plot might have derived from having him strike up a romantic relationship with the central character. Her subsequent entanglement with a detective (Clancy Brown) is equally unacceptable, as the killer's appearances in her (surely quadruple-locked) flat, in her parents' house or, come to that, wherever she goes. No one will believe her as to his identity, just as they failed to believe her about a gun (which the killer has stolen) held by a holdup man she shot. You'll feel embarrassed for the actors who simply can't make any of this seem credible.

Blue Thunder ● ⓥ
1982, US, 108 mins, colour
Dir: John Badham
Stars: Roy Scheider, Malcolm McDowell, Warren Oates, Candy Clark, Daniel Stern
Rating: ★★★

Director John Badham comes up trumps here: this is a good helicopter action thriller and no messing about. Maverick police chopper flier Roy Scheider gets a new assignment to fly an ultra-sophisticated, fully-armed helicopter to be used in emergency riot control. When the man in overall charge of the proect (Malcolm McDowell) turns out to be Scheider's old nemesis from 'Nam (Oh! Those headaches again!), you know he's in trouble. You also know he's going to find out something that isn't good for him, that everyone around him is liable to be killed, and that he'll end up aboard Blue Thunder taking on the bad guys single-handed: but that's half the fun. Apart from the subsequent action being in the top bracket, the script is also a winner, giving out with some nice laconic lines, especially for Warren Oates (to whom the film is dedicated) as Scheider's long-suffering supervisor. 'The moral of this story,' he tells Scheider, grounding him for some new exploit, 'is if you're walking on eggs – don't hop!'

Blue Velvet ● ⓥ
1986, US, 120 mins, colour
Dir: David Lynch
Stars: Kyle MacLachlan, Isabella Rossellini, Dennis Hopper, Laura Dern, Dean Stockwell
Rating: ★★

David Lynch's nightmare thriller lurches uncertainly between *film noir* and film bizarre. Even so, it certainly commands attention. It's reminiscent of one of those 'drug gang', darkly coloured movies of the late Sixties that the British censor would never pass, a feeling underlined by the presence of Dean Stockwell and Dennis Hopper, survivors from just that cycle of films. Here they hover dangerously on the edges of a story which centres on Kyle MacLachlan (Lynch's *Twin Peaks* star), whose gruesome discovery of a human ear in a field leads him to a sensual Italian torch singer (Isabella Rossellini). From here to the end of an actually not too complicated plot, direction and music help a great deal in creating a highly-charged atmosphere which helps offset deficiencies in the script and some of the performances. But MacLachlan is suitably

mesmerised as the youth, while Hopper and Rossellini charge with frenzied abandon at their psychosexual deviates.

Blume in Love ◖
1973, US, 117 mins, colour
Dir: Paul Mazursky
Stars: George Segal, Susan Anspach, Kris Kristofferson, Shelley Winters, Marsha Mason
Rating: ★★★

One of the wryest, most individual adult comedies to emerge from Hollywood in the Seventies. George Segal's hangdog expression and harassed humour are perfectly suited to the character of Blume, a lawyer much beset by life and especially by passionate memories of the ex-wife who threw him out on his ear after he had a fling with his secretary. Segal himself has never been better. But there are also outstanding contributions from Marsha Mason (just before she hit stardom) as his mistress and Shelley Winters as a plump matron. Director Paul Mazursky's sardonic and perceptive script makes the characters much more likeable than those in his previous hit *Bob & Carol & Ted & Alice*. This time, the humour is both warmer and more biting. It goes on too long, though.

Bob & Carol & Ted & Alice ◖
1969, US, 105 mins, colour
Dir: Paul Mazursky
Stars: Natalie Wood, Robert Culp, Elliott Gould, Dyan Cannon
Rating: ★★

Highly influential sex comedy which, under the direction of Paul Mazursky, was a tremendous hit at the box-office tills, and made stars out of Elliott Gould and the plastic Dyan Cannon. Especially noteworthy for the brilliant opening helicopter shots of a car making its way to the mountain hideaway where the group talk-in subsequently ensues, and the much-publicised four-in-a-bed sequence at the end. It was also very nice to see the delectable Natalie Wood back on the screen after an absence of three years.

Bobo, The ○
1967, UK, 105 mins, colour
Dir: Robert Parrish
Stars: Peter Sellers, Britt Ekland, Rossano Brazzi, Adolfo Celi
Rating: ★★

One of two comedies that then-married Peter Sellers and Britt Ekland made together casts him as a singing matador, and her as a famous courtesan whom he must conquer in order to assure his future as a troubador. Hattie Jacques, John Wells and Ferdy Mayne brighten up the supporting cast, although director Robert Parrish seems to be trying hard to give the impression that he wasn't really cut out to be making Sellers comedies.

Bob Roberts ◐
1992, US, 103m mins, colour
Dir: Tim Robbins
Stars: Tim Robbins, Giancarlo Esposito, Ray Wise, Susan Sarandon, Alan Rickman
Rating: ★★

Writer/director/star Tim Robbins almost gives us a telling political satire – but not quite. As played by the imposingly bland 6ft 5in Robbins, Roberts is a singer who would be senator. And the story shows him and his cronies as fiendishly clever manipulators of the public in their quest for power. Despite his clean-cut, Kennedy-style image, Roberts is clearly a sham, with a murky past involving drugs and the exploitation of housing for the poor – well up to the dirty tricks of the political scene that will put the opposition out of the running. We can see it; but Joe Public worships him; and the coup de grace in Roberts' campaign is a fake assassination attempt, with his chief journalistic opponent as the fall guy. None of this, though, quite works because its central device – the tracking camera of a documentary filmmaker – doesn't quite work either, drifting into tedium and disinterest when Roberts himself isn't centreshot. The result, though still frightening, isn't as tight or hard-hitting as it might have been, even though the film's heart is in the right place – firmly on its sleeve.

Body Double ● ⊗
1984, US, 109 mins, colour
Dir: Brian De Palma
Stars: Craig Wasson, Gregg Henry, Melanie Griffith, Deborah Shelton
Rating: ★★

A second-rate actor, played by Craig Wasson, witnesses a brutal slaying, but can he trust the evidence of his own eyes? This suspense thriller from Brian De Palma is a violent and voyeuristic re-working of Hitchcock's *Rear Window* and *Vertigo*. An interesting frisson is supplied by the casting (as a porn star) of Melanie Griffith, the daughter of one of Hitchcock's favourite blondes, Tippi Hedren, star of *Marnie* and *The Birds*.

Bodyguard, The ● ⊗
1992, US, 124 mins, colour
Dir: Mick Jackson
Stars: Kevin Costner, Whitney Houston, Gary Kemp
Rating: ★★

Kevin Costner has a lot on his plate here. Not only must he protect a singer/actress (Whitney Houston) from a threatening-letter writer *and* an unknown hit-man, he also has to contend with an entire supporting cast whose acting is at best moderate. The ordinary dialogue does no one any favours, either, but director Mick Jackson stages some tense action scenes when the plot is allowed to follow its natural course. Costner comes over as a cross between Steve McQueen and Gary Cooper in a movie that sorely needs his star presence. Houston sings distinctively, but seems unlikely ever to collect the Oscar which her character receives at the end of the film.

Body Heat ● ⊗
1981, US, 113 mins, colour
Dir: Lawrence Kasdan
Stars: William Hurt, Kathleen Turner, Richard Crenna, Ted Danson, Mickey Rourke
Rating: ★★★★

A real *film noir* for the Eighties. Writer-director Lawrence Kasdan has fired the ashes of *Double Indemnity* and fashioned a new wife-and-lover-plot-to-kill-husband story that has only that basic situation in common with its carnal forefather. The twists and triple twists that follow the actual murder are ingenious in the extreme. As the lovers and with the liberty adult certificates give today, William Hurt and Kathleen Turner genuinely capture the idea of an overriding passion that outstrips all other moral considerations. Hurt, with his bruised, laconic voice, and Turner, an updated Lauren Bacall with a slinky look from under the eyelids, became hot Hollywood properties following these performances. At the back of it all is the motif of heat: a fire, a fryer in a cafe and, of course, the weather and the love/lust affair. The dialogue between Hurt and Turner is terse, loaded and beautifully delivered by the stars. As for the director, he's made the kind of film where nothing is superfluous and the clue to the denouement might pass by in a trice under your very nose. John Barry's music evokes the scores of the Forties without aping them and is a great aid to the impact of the drama.

Body of Evidence ● ⊗
1993, US, 100 mins, colour
Dir: Ulid Edel
Stars: Madonna, Willem Dafoe, Anne Archer, Joe Mantegna, Jurgen Prochnow, Julianne Moore
Rating: ★

It's not often that Hollywood blows it with a courtroom thriller, but the trouble here is that the body of evidence isn't substantial enough to fill an episode of *L.A. Law*. If only it had as many curves as its star Madonna (dramatic actress – Not!), the daft dialogue wouldn't matter too much. As it is, the lack of plot is only underlined by the slowness of a film in which the story is irrelevant to sex scenes that are supposedly daring, but in fact pretty much as boring as the rest of the movie. Madonna's a 'gallery owner' (!) who seduces men with weak hearts who fall so heavily for her intense style of lovemaking that they writer her into their wills. The plot, as such it is, doesn't hang together for a moment, but you'll probably be too busy trying to stay awake to think about it. A lot of good people are involved: Willem Dafoe, Joe Mantegna, Anne Archer, Julianne Moore and Frank Langella, and have very little to do but spotlight the star (whose performance is inferior to any of theirs), take the money and run. It's a bit of a trial in more ways than one.

Body Snatchers ● ⊗
1993, US, 84 mins, colour
Dir: Abel Ferrara
Stars: Gabrielle Anwar, Billy Wirth, Meg Tilly, Forest Whitaker, Terry Kinney
Rating: ★★

An apocalyptic update of *Invasion of the Body Snatchers*, with no Kevin McCarthy, but most other elements intact. The aliens are now shown to need some time to take over the bodies of humans and substitute them with blank replicas, via invasion by tendrils from the pods which bend people to their will. Director Abel

Ferrara, in a switch from his usual mean-streets beat, cunningly casts a set of fairly blank-looking actors, so that the deceptions may be more chillingly accomplished. Once more, two survivors escape at the end, but with nowhere to go. Slow to start, it certainly has its moments near the end and is, if nothing else, a dire warning not to go to sleep in the bath. Mel Tilly, in and out of alienation, gives the best performance. Not a patch on the original, but not a waste of your time either.

Boeing Boeing ○
1965, US/UK, 102 mins, colour
Dir: John Rich
Stars: Tony Curtis, Jerry Lewis, Damu Saval, Suzanna Leigh, Thelma Ritter
Rating: ★★

A creaky stage play, about two bachelors trying to keep various air stewardess girlfriends apart in the face of the arrival of faster Boeing jet planes, is transformed into a creaky film. But the frantic playing of Tony Curtis and Jerry Lewis, dispensing double-takes with disarming energy, at least papers over the cracks. The Parisian location of Curtis' bachelor flat is conjured up via several fuzzy exterior shots and a pseudo-Maurice Chevalier voice-over. But despite all the frantic attempts at deception, why does Curtis have different bedrooms for each of his three fiancees?

Bofors Gun, The ●
1968, UK, 106 mins, colour
Dir: Jack Gold
Stars: Nicol Williamson, Ian Holm
Rating: ★★

Director Jack Gold, best known for his television movies such as *The Naked Civil Servant* and *Praying Mantis*, made an impressive feature film debut with this compelling drama which charts the brutalizing effects of military life through the experiences of seven soldiers who are given the futile task of guarding an obsolete World War Two Bofors anti-craft gun at a British army camp in Germany in 1954. His skill with actors was superbly demonstrated: showy roles went to David Warner and, in particular, Nicol Williamson, but the contributions from a near-perfect cast which includes Ian Holm, Peter Vaughan, John Thaw and Richard O'Callaghan, are similarly well-performed. And National Service survivors will get a

special identification with the situation! The film, however, gets far too oppressive towards the end and will be no one's idea of light entertainment.

Boiling Point ● ⊚
1993, US, 93 mins, colour
Dir: James B Harris
Stars: Wesley Snipes, Dennis Hopper, Valerie Perrine, Viggo Mortensen
Rating: ★★

An odd choice of title for a strange, offbeat, low-key crime thriller in which neither the heroes nor the villains exactly ooze menace. These are by and large people making the best of a short straw on either side of the law. Their plans for the future are short-term and without much prospect. Wesley Snipes is the cop who is near quitting after shedding both a partner and a wife; Dennis Hopper is the long-time loser hoping that the acquisition of a cold-blooded hitman partner (Viggo Mortensen) will give him a last chance of reconciliation with his wife (Valerie Perrine) and comfortable retirement. The paths of the men cross several times – a gents loo, a coffee-stall, a dance floor – without them realising it. At the end, as a sop to Hollywood happy endings, law and order prevail. Too downbeat to be exciting, the film's fascination is its mood, and the background of the dance hall – tiny lives played out in slow tempo; though there are slower patches, the melancholy of this may stay with you longer than the latest macho blockbuster shoot-'em-up.

Bolero ●
1934, US, 83 mins, b/w
Dir: Wesley Ruggles
Stars: George Raft, Carole Lombard, Frances Drake, Ray Milland
Rating: ★★

Despite a general critical thumbs-down, this dance-drama was so popular with the public that stars George Raft (who started his career as a dancer) and Carole Lombard were rushed into a follow-up called *Rumba*. Added attractions include famous fan-dancer Sally Rand, a fiery performance from Frances Drake as one of Raft's partners, Ray Milland (here billed as Raymond) five years before *French Without Tears*, and top-notch art direction and costume design. Never mind the story – watch the terrific dance routines.

Bombsite Stolen
See: *Cottage to Let*

Bond Street ○
1948, UK, 108 mins, b/w
Dir: Gordon Parry
Stars: Jean Kent, Roland Young, Kathleen Harrison, Derek Farr
Rating: ★★

The first of the 'portmanteau' films made by playwright Terence Rattigan with writer/producer Anatole de Grunwald. These would later become very grand and include *The VIPs* and *The Yellow Rolls Royce*. There's already a touch of class in the setting for this one, whose events revolve round the preparations for a posh wedding. And a veritable pot-boiler it proves: there's a crisis at the dressmakers, blackmail at the invisible menders and murder at the jewellers. The script is pretty variable in quality, but a good cast – Jean Kent, Roland Young, Kathleen Harrison, Derek Farr, Hazel Court, Ronald Howard, Patricia Plunkett, Kenneth Griffith – gives the vehicle the surface gloss it needs.

Bonjour Tristesse ○
1957, UK, 93 mins, colour
Dir: Otto Preminger
Stars: David Niven, Deborah Kerr, Jean Seberg
Rating: ★★

This ostensibly stylish melodrama set on the French Riviera is about a rakish Frenchman who falls for a repressed American beauty, an affair which has tragic consequences. In tow is his 17-year-old daughter who seems to be turning into a chip off the old block. Superficial is a good word to describe this whole picture and credibility isn't helped by the unfortunate casting. David Niven is as perfectly English as ever as the Parisian womaniser and Jean Seberg is totally unconvincing as his daughter. Deborah Kerr tries her best as the tragic Anne, but even she is hampered by a poor script. Director Otto Preminger should have known better, especially when casting Seberg. Only a year previously she had made a dog's dinner of the lead role in *Saint Joan*, also directed by Preminger.

Bonnie and Clyde ◐ ⊚
1967, US, 108 mins, colour
Dir: Arthur Penn
Stars: Warren Beatty, Faye Dunaway, Michael J Pollard, Gene Hackman, Estelle Parsons
Rating: ★★★★

One of the most exciting discoveries of its time. Director Arthur Penn shows all the dirt, sweat and above all desperation of the trade – outlawry – whose members lived by the very ends of shreds of nerves, knowing that death, sudden and painful, was never further away than a knock on a shuttered door in the night. The disreputable, edgy, unreal atmosphere of the times and the disregard for the life that still remains precious is very well conveyed, with Warren Beatty keeping a tight grip on the moody Clyde, who robs banks (and kills as a result of it) only because he knows no other way of life. But the real find of the film was Faye Dunaway, giving a slow-burning fusebox of a performance as Bonnie, with one stand-out moment – mistily photographed against a yellow cornfield – when she realises she can never go back to her old life.

Bonnie Prince Charlie ○
1948, UK, 113 mins, colour
Dir: Anthony Kimmins
Stars: David Niven, Margaret Leighton, Jack Hawkins, Finlay Currie
Rating: ★★

British film spectacular about the Young Pretender and the rising of '45. It boasts fine colour photography, in many cases in the actual locations where Charles' adventures and battles took place. David Niven takes the title role – an unusual piece of casting and one that, in the opinion of many, didn't work too well. Hardly the fault of this versatile actor, just that in this role he was somewhat out of his element. And the film's stately pace didn't help him, either.

Bonnie Scotland ⊙
1935, US, 80 mins, b/w
Dir: James W Horne
Stars: Stan Laurel, Oliver Hardy, June Lang, Jimmy Finlayson
Rating: ★★★

One of the most delightful of Stan Laurel and Oliver Hardy's vintage comedies from their golden Thirties period. This one includes some hilarious tomfoolery in Scotland (where Stan travels from America only to discover he has inherited not a fortune but a set of bagpipes) and India, as well as one of their famous dance routines. This one evolves from an order by their sergeant (the pop-eyed Jimmy Finlayson) to pick up a mass of litter with spikes – an operation which L and H gradually transform

into an impromptu soft-shoe shuffle. The film also includes the classic scene where Stan, hopelessly out of time on the march, gradually transfers his own step to the entire squad.

Boomerang ○
1946, US, 88 mins, b/w
Dir: Elia Kazan
Stars: Dana Andrews, Jane Wyatt, Lee J Cobb, Arthur Kennedy
Rating: ★★★★

Dana Andrews, an actor very much in the forefront of 20th Century-Fox's realist dramas, is in crisp, hard-hitting form in this true-life story as the politically ambitious attorney who is unconvinced of the guilt of a vagrant who has 'confessed' to the broad-daylight murder of a priest. The location filming, night-time shots and the fine details of the attorney's battle to establish the validity of his case all serve to give the film a unique grip.

Boomerang ● ⓥ
1992, US, 116 mins, colour
Dir: Reginald Hudlin
Stars: Eddie Murphy, Robin Givens, Halle Berry, Grace Jones, Eartha Kitt
Rating: ★★

There aren't many good things in this Eddie Murphy equivalent of a Rock Hudson-Doris Day comedy, set in a (fashion) world almost entirely populated with black people, and with photography dedicated to the worship of one E Murphy. The wittily barbed exchanges between Hudson and Day (and Tony Randall) are replaced with four-letter words and a dinner party scene rife with references to sex, one that ends with the parents of a prospective boyfriend having sex in the bathroom for an hour. Funny, huh? It's as glossy as those comedies of yesteryear, but without any of the finesse. So who expects finesse in an Eddie Murphy film? Halle Berry is an attractive heroine, but all in all this is another step on the slope downwards for this particular five-minute wonder.

Boom Town ○
1940, US, 120 mins, b/w
Dir: Jack Conway
Stars: Clark Gable, Spencer Tracy, Claudette Colbert, Hedy Lamarr
Rating: ★★

Clark Gable and Spencer Tracy pal up and break up, and get rich and go broke so many times in this oil-drilling saga that it's hard to keep track. But,

while Gable and Tracy got dirty making it, the film itself cleaned up at the box-office. It was the last of what Tracy called 'my three Gable pictures' (the others being *San Francisco* and *Test Pilot*). The two men got along well, but Tracy reckoned enough was enough, and never conceded top billing for a major role again.

Boost, The ● ⓥ
1988, US, 100 mins, colour
Dir: Harold Becker
Stars: James Woods, Sean Young, Steven Hill
Rating: ★★

If you had to cast one actor as a hyper-tense, high-flying salesman with a quick temper and a vulnerability to cocaine, it would have to be James Woods. And Woods it is, in this cautionary tale about the effects of demon drugs. Its melodramatic, over-the-top approach explains why it lay on the shelf for two years before a cinema release. Woods gives his usual 100 per cent and Sean Young has some appealing vulnerable moments as his wife, but they never come across as real people in this sad and harrowing but rarely affecting story. Woods is such an unsympathetic character to begin with, and gives such an unvarying performance, that sympathy is hard to muster and he and Young lack that vital spark of warmth that would make their plight easier to reach out to.

Border, The ●
1980, US, 107 mins, colour
Dir: Christopher Leitch
Stars: Telly Savalas, Danny De La Paz, Eddie Albert
Rating: ★★

Made originally as *The Border – USA*, this is a hard-hitting action film highlighting the unlawful smuggling of cheap Mexican labour across the Mexican/American border. It attempts to expose the corrupt element in the American border police (here in the form of a Commander played by screen veteran Eddie Albert) that lets traffickers get away with it. Telly Savalas stars as a very different lawman from the lollipop-sucking crook-seeker he portrayed in *Kojak*; he's a rugged US patrolman whose refusal of bribery has led to his transfer from the city to the no-man's-land which separates Mexico and the United States. Danny De La Paz, the young actor who made such an impression in *Boulevard Nights*

B

and *Cuba*, plays the friend who finally drives Savalas to take sides – and action – by his involvement in the refugee racket.

Border, The ●

1981, US, 108 mins, colour
Dir: Tony Richardson
Stars: Jack Nicholson, Harvey Keitel, Valerie Perrine, Warren Oates
Rating: ★★

Far from his famous Sixties films *Tom Jones* and *The Charge of the Light Brigade*, British director Tony Richardson casts a suitably severe eye on the serious problem of illegal immigration on the Texas-Mexico border. Heading a first-rate cast, Jack Nicholson is reckless enough to appear with a dangerously receding hairline and a hint of a pot-belly as the former cop who refuses to become involved in the wholesale corruption rife amongst his fellow border patrolmen. Even so, his character is no saint and it's hard to care too deeply about the fates of these unfortunate people trapped in the brutally depicted squalor of a Tex-Mex hell.

Border Incident ○

1949, US, 92 mins, b/w
Dir: Anthony Mann
Stars: Ricardo Montalban, George Murphy, Howard da Silva
Rating: ★★★

This tight-knit crime film, the forerunner of many others about 'wetbacks' – illegal immigrants scuttling across the border from Mexico to the United States – is similar in structure to another good thriller also directed by Anthony Mann: *T-Men*. One particular death scene is most uncompromising for the 1940s, and tension is kept on high throughout by the director and his formidable cast.

Borderline ◑

1980, US, 104 mins, colour
Dir: Jerrold Freedman
Stars: Charles Bronson, Bruno Kirby, Ed Harris
Rating: ★★

Another variation on what used to be called a social-conscience thriller, showing Hollywood's concern at the traffickers in human cargo who operate along the US-Mexico border. Charles Bronson is in trenchant form as the border patrolman out to put a stop to it, while the charismatic and later star-billed Ed Harris makes his

first major film appearance as the villain. Bulky Wilford Brimley also scores in a supporting role.

Border River ○

1954, US, 80 mins, colour
Dir: George Sherman
Stars: Joel McCrea, Yvonne De Carlo, Pedro Armendariz
Rating: ★★

A rugged 'A' class Western, set in the time of the American Civil War, with Joel McCrea battling Pedro Armendariz for Yvonne De Carlo and a fortune in arms, all in aid of the Confederacy. There's plenty of tough action, with McCrea continuing his image as the quietely-spoken but grimly determined man whom it's dangerous to double-cross. Miss De Carlo puts personality into the heroine, while fine Mexican actor Armendariz makes as greasy and smiling a villain as any Western fan could possibly want. An excellent climactic fight between him and McCrea in quicksand territory must have left both men needing a bath several times over. The director is the prolific Western man George Sherman, who made dozens of horse-operas between *Wild Horse Rodeo* (1937) and John Wayne's *Big Jake* (1971).

Bordertown ○

1934, US, 80 mins, b/w
Dir: Archie Mayo
Stars: Bette Davis, Paul Muni, Margaret Lindsay, Robert Barrat,Eugene Pallette
Rating: ★★★

Paul Muni received top billing but the dramatic garlands were easily snatched from him by Bette Davis, who gave a spirited, no-holds-barred performance as the wife of border town casino owner Eugene Pallette whom she murders to clear the way for her amorous pursuit of Muni. She succeeds, too, in overcoming Archie Mayo's somewhat flabby direction. The film served as the basis for 1940's *They Drive By Night*, with Ida Lupino in the reworked Davis role.

Born Free ⊙

1965, UK, 95 mins, colour
Dir: James Hill
Stars: Virginia McKenna, Bill Travers
Rating: ★★★★

If you thought that animal weepies had had their day when Lassie retired, then pad along and have a good cry at this one, magnificently transferred to the screen from Joy Adamson's

best-selling story of Elsa the lioness. Big bonuses, apart from the lions themselves, are the clear, sunny Technicolor photography, John Barry's marvellous wide-open spaces music, and the near-miraculous way that stars Virginia McKenna and Bill Travers romp as to the manner born with the three lionesses who play Elsa at various stages of her growth, as the Adamsons rear Elsa from a cub after her mother has been killed. The desperately difficult process of getting Elsa to fend for herself, taking months of effort (after they decide to return her to the wild) is painstakingly, heartbreakingly reconstructed. The story – true, of course – is the real winner. The film's a little slow in its later stages, but these do come directly after some particularly wonderful scenes of the two principals playing 'piggy in the middle' with Elsa in the sea. Otherwise, when the music rises to a crescendo, and Elsa strikes again at the heart by being happy, or playful, or naughty, or beaten in a fight, you'll be quite lost. Only hardened animal-haters will avoid blubbering almost all the way through.

Born on the Fourth of July ● ⓥ

1989, US, 145 mins, colour
Dir: Oliver Stone
Stars: Tom Cruise, Bryan Larkin, Raymond J Barry, Kyra Sedgwick, Willem Dafoe
Rating: ★★

No wonder Tom Cruise's Vietnam veteran finds it hard to come to terms with himself on his return to civilian life in this harrowing film that leaves absolutely no visceral aspect of his physical and mental plight unstated. He's not only gunned down a village full of women and babies, but one of his own men as well. Shot up himself, his spine severed, he makes desperate efforts to walk again, but then suffers a terrible accident that leaves him a paraplegic for life. How he comes to a sort of peace takes a grossly overlong 145 minutes, which includes all kinds of unnecessary scenes and parts of scenes – a tragedy that such an emotive subject should drain itself in such a self-destructive way. This one-note descent into a private hell puts an immense strain on our innate sympathy for the character, even though Cruise (Oscar-nominated) is pretty nearly as good as the circumstances will allow. It's full of director Stone's oft-vented bile at the Vietnam conflict; but that alone isn't enough to make a great movie.

Born to Dance ○
1936, US, 108 mins, b/w
Dir: Roy Del Ruth
Stars: Eleanor Powell, James Stewart, Virginia Bruce, Una Merkel
Rating: ★★★

Eleanor Powell, perhaps the most positive, confident and devastating female dancer the screen ever saw, became a star with this Cole Porter/MGM musical whose score includes 'Easy to Love', 'I've Got You Under My Skin' and the spectacular climactic number 'Swingin' the Jinx Away'. James Stewart sings (just about) as her co-star, almost as embarrassing a musical experience for him as his appearance on skates in *Ice Follies of 1939*.

Born to Kill
See: Lady of Deceit

Born Yesterday ○
1950, US, 103 mins, b/w
Dir: George Cukor
Stars: Judy Holliday, William Holden, Broderick Crawford
Rating: ★★★★

The punchy protagonists in this film adaptation of the stage comedy success turn it into a boxing match played out with words, wit and wisdom instead of fists. Judy Holliday's brilliant performance as the seemingly dumb blonde won her an Academy Award and set her up for a run of bright comedies at the studio (Columbia) through the Fifties. Broderick Crawford is also delightful as the shady tycoon (whose mistress she is) who determines to 'educate' her, to his cost.

Born Yesterday ○ Ⓥ
1993, US, 101 mins, colour
Dir: Luis Mandoki
Stars: Melanie Griffith, Don Johnson, John Goodman, Edward Herrmann
Rating: ★★

The film fan's tendency is to resist a remake of a classic. And indeed, the first 40 minutes of this one gives us every cause. The old magic exercises its spell in the last hour, even in diluted form, so that we cheer once again as bimbo mistress Billie Dawn, as she 'gets learning' and turns the tables on her gangster lover. Melanie Griffith is ideally cast as the hapless

showgirl taught the facts of American life by journalist Don Johnson, but the lighting is unflattering to her, so that she looks too old for the role. Johnson is completely nebulous as the journalist/teacher originally played by William Holden, and Goodman is quite effective as the blustery blowhard immortalised by Broderick Crawford. But all the plays on our emotions work because of writer Garson Kanin's original Broadway ideas and not this new treatment of his stage and film original. Have a look, then wait for the Judy Holliday version to come around: this is the real class.

Bostonians, The ○ Ⓥ
1984, UK, 122 mins, colour
Dir: James Ivory
Stars: Christopher Reeve, Vanessa Redgrave, Madeline Potter, Jessica Tandy
Rating: ★★

After filming Henry James's *The Europeans*, it was perhaps natural for the prolific producer-director team of Ismail Merchant and James Ivory to tackle his anti-feminist tract, *The Bostonians*. It's an uneven affair that manages to take all the fire out of its central fight over a young and impressionable girl by a handsome smooth-talking lawyer (Christopher Reeve) and a spinster (Vanessa Redgrave) who makes her promise never to marry. Reeve fails to exorcise the ghost of Superman in the central role, but richer pickings are to be had in the supporting roles, notably Jessica Tandy's feminist pensioner Miss Birdseye and Linda Hunt's Dr Prance. As expected, the period and social detail is overwhelmingly good and the photography of Walter Lassally exquisite. But *The Bostonians* is really little more than a catalogue of lost opportunities.

Botany Bay ○
1952, US, 90 mins, colour
Dir: John Farrow
Stars: Alan Ladd, James Mason, Patricia Medina, Cedric Hardwicke
Rating: ★★

Rugged and exciting if only skin-deep adventure film, splendidly shot in colour, about a cargo-load of convicts bound for Australia's Botany Bay. It is adapted from the novel by Charles Nordhoff and James Norman Hall, who wrote *Mutiny on the Bounty*. Director John Farrow's sea sequences are stirring, the action is tough and

uncompromising, and James Mason's performance as Gilbert, sadistic captain of the convict ship, is impeccable.

Both Ends of the Candle ○
(aka: The Helen Morgan Story)
1957, US, 118 mins, b/w
Dir: Michael Curtiz
Stars: Ann Blyth, Paul Newman, Richard Carlson
Rating: ★★

Another Hollywood biopic, the genre at which they were so good, and a real breakaway for Ann Blyth, used almost exclusively in 'sweet' parts throughout her career. Here cast in a really meaty part as Helen Morgan, disturbed and disturbing torch singer of the late 1920s and early 1930s, Miss Blyth's attempt to convey the complexities of the character is a brave try. And the free-for-all atmosphere of roaring Chicago is well captured by Oscar-winning director Michael Curtiz. Miss Blyth's singing voice was ironically too operatic for the role, and her songs were 'ghosted' by Gogi Grant.

Bottoms Up! ○
1959, UK, 89 mins, b/w
Dir: Mario Zampi
Stars: Jimmy Edwards, Arthur Howard, Martita Hunt, Sydney Tafler, Vanda Hudson
Rating: ★★

A full-blown film version of the radio and TV series 'Whack-O!', with Jimmy Edwards blustering away splendidly as the school head whose accountant is turf rather than chartered. Arthur Howard is the dithering deputy head, Pettigrew, and Vanda Hudson makes a delectable matron. The plot, which shouldn't be paid too much attention, is something about an oriental prince coming to the school as a pupil.

Bound for Glory ○
1976, US, 146 mins, colour
Dir: Hal Ashby
Stars: David Carradine, Ronny Cox, Melinda Dillon
Rating: ★★★

The story of homespun philosopher-singer-guitarist Woody Guthrie and his travels during the Depression years of the 1930s. David Carradine does well (and performs all his own songs) in the leading role, and the film's compositions – especially of a dust-storm or a 'squatters' camp in the

B

rain – are often impressive. But the story is rather too long and tends to be repetitive. Robert Getchell's screenplay comes as something of a disappointment after the heights of *Alice Doesn't Live Here Anymore*. Still, director Hal Ashby does show a remarkable feel for time and place, and there are early appearances by a number of now-familiar character players, among them Randy Quaid, M Emmet Walsh, Robert Ginty and Brion James.

Bounty, The ◐ ⊙
1984, New Zealand, 133 mins, colour
Dir: Roger Donaldson
Stars: Mel Gibson, Anthony Hopkins, Laurence Olivier, Edward Fox, Daniel Day Lewis, Bernard Hill
Rating: ★★

This third version of the classic story of mutiny and betrayal was to have marked David Lean's return to film directing after a 10-year semi-retirement, but along the way he left the project. Roger Donaldson (later to hit the target with Kevin Costner's thriller *No Way Out*) picked up the pieces and turned in a competent if uninspired adventure yarn. In a revisionist version that sets out to put the record straight, Anthony Hopkins' Captain Bligh bears little relation to Charles Laughton's earlier strutting, arrogant monster. And Mel Gibson's Fletcher Christian is portrayed less as a champion of the underdog than as an unreliable friend who prefers to go native with a coloured wife than do his duty and return with the ship to England. Beautiful to look at and with another typically haunting score in the *Chariots of Fire* mould from Vangelis, *The Bounty* suffers from problems of structure and climax that come two thirds of the way through, leaving it adrift with the horizon too distant. Daniel Day Lewis and Liam Neeson have supporting roles.

Bowery, The ○
1933, US, 90 mins, b/w
Dir: Raoul Walsh
Stars: Wallace Beery, George Raft, Jackie Cooper, Fay Wray, George Walsh
Rating: ★★★

One of the first films to break away from the stagy studio confines, and portray the people, streets and characters of the city. Big, gruff Wallace Beery and little, pouty-mouthed Jackie Cooper were already big box-office together when director Raoul Walsh teamed them with

slit-eyed George Raft and lovely Fay Wray in this bruising story of life in New York's East Side. The (real-life) names of the two leading characters – Steve Brodie and Chuck Connors – were both adopted by Hollywood actors in later years. The vigour of the direction placed the film well ahead of its time, and its portrait of the poorer quarter of New York in the 1890s fairly teems with life. Watch out for a super performance from feisty Pert Kelton as Beery's saloon soubrette girlfriend.

Boy, Did I Get a Wrong Number! ○
1966, US, 97 mins, colour
Dir: George Marshall
Stars: Bob Hope, Elke Sommer, Phyllis Diller
Rating: ★★

Here is Bob Hope, brighter, funnier and a lot less sentimental than in some of his early Sixties films, as an estate agent accidentally involved with a runaway actress. Hope's scriptwriters, too, are back to something like their old form. 'Coffee?', he asks his son. 'You want to stay awake in class?' In addition to glamorous Elke Sommer as a bubble bath queen, there are two more dotty females around in the shape of Phyllis Diller as Hope's maniacal maid and squeaky-voiced Joyce Jameson as the telephone operator who gives Hope the original wrong number. The plot and dialogue are just the kind that used to have Hope fans rolling in the aisles in the Forties and everything culminates in a frantic freeway chase in which Hope starts off being chased by three police cars but finishes up by following them. The director George Marshall was behind some of Hope's best films, including *The Ghost Breakers*, *Monsieur Beaucaire* and *Fancy Pants*.

Boy from Oklahoma, The ○
1953, US, 88 mins, colour
Dir: Michael Curtiz
Stars: Will Rogers Jr, Nancy Olson, Lon Chaney Jr, Anthony Caruso
Rating: ★★★

After his tremendous success as his rope-twirling, comedian father in *The Story of Will Rogers*, Warners put young Will Rogers Jr straight into this gentle, amusing, fast-paced Western. He gets good support from sunny Nancy Olson as a fiery lass called Katie Brannigan who's handier with a gun than the hero.

Boy on a Dolphin ○
1957, US, 111 mins, colour
Dir: Jean Negulesco
Stars: Alan Ladd, Sophia Loren, Clifton Webb
Rating: ★★

A plot about sunken treasure is the flimsy excuse for a brilliant travelogue around the isles of Greece and the contours of Sophia Loren. Alan Ladd is an unlikely archaeologist, the diving scenes are picturesque, and Clifton Webb (for once the bad guy) puts across his lines with his customary astringency. He plays a character called Mr Parmalee. A little in-joke: Parmalee was Webb's middle name.

Boys, The ○
1962, UK, 123 mins, b/w
Dir: Sidney Furie
Stars: Richard Todd, Robert Morley
Rating: ★★★

A courtroom whodunnit which poses the question: are we all inclined to prejudge people because of the way they look and dress, especially when they're members of the younger generation? Good, tense, well-constructed stuff.

Boys from Brazil, The ◐
1978, US, 123 mins, colour
Dir: Franklin J Schaffner
Stars: Gregory Peck, Laurence Olivier, James Mason, Steve Guttenberg, Denholm Elliott, Uta Hagen
Rating: ★★

Ira Levin's compulsively readable book about Nazi resurgence in South America is turned into a film which tends to underline its latent absurdities. It contains excellent visuals by French photographer Henry Decae and good supporting portrayals by Lilli Palmer and Denholm Elliott, outsmarting the three principals, Gregory Peck, Laurence Olivier and James Mason, all of whom seem rather uneasily cast.

Boys in Brown ○
1949, UK, 85 mins, b/w
Dir: Montgomery Tully
Stars: Jack Warner, Richard Attenborough, Dirk Bogarde, Michael Medwin, Jimmy Hanley, Alfie Bass
Rating: ★★★

A film about Borstal Boys which broke new ground when it was first released (hard to believe now that it was then considered daring) and provides the film buff with intriguing glimpses of stars when they were young. Here are Dirk Bogarde and Richard Attenborough, still playing juvenile delinquents in their late twenties. And Jimmy Hanley doing the same at 32! As the governor, Jack Warner epitomises considerate authority as thoroughly as he had represented the kindlier arm of the law in *The Blue Lamp*.

Boys' Town ○
1938, US, 96 mins, b/w
Dir: Norman Taurog
Stars: Spencer Tracy, Mickey Rooney, Henry Hull, Leslie Fenton
Rating: ★★★

Said to have been Louis B Mayer's favourite film, this true-ish story is blazingly effective sentiment, with Spencer Tracy winning his second consecutive Oscar, this time as the priest who founded a sanctuary for wayward boys. He and Mickey Rooney were among the world's five most popular stars at the time and the public flocked to see the film. But Tracy decided that the Academy Award he had won (which had in any case, been erroneously inscribed to 'Dick Tracy'!) really belonged to the real-life Flanagan. He sent it along to the priest with a new inscription that read 'To Father Edward J Flanagan, whose great human qualities, kindly simplicity and inspiring courage were strong enough to shine through my humble effort: Spencer Tracy.' An (inferior) sequel, *Men of Boys' Town*, with the same cast, appeared three years later.

Boys Will Be Boys ⊙ ⓥ
1935, UK, 75 mins, b/w
Dir: William Beaudine
Stars: Will Hay, Gordon Harker, Jimmy Hanley,
Rating: ★★★

Will Hay really hit his film stride in this school comedy, in which he appears for the first time in a feature film in his famous characterisation of a down-at-heel and distinctly inefficient schoolmaster. Hay himself helped write the screenplay, from characters played by J B Morton, alias 'Beachcomber'. How the famous Dorking necklace enters the story, and how it gets inside the ball to be used as the famous Narkoverian rugby match makes for a wildly hilarious conclusion. Directed by Hollywood's William Beaudine, fresh from his stint on one of W C Fields' most famous comedies, *The Old Fashioned Way*.

Several plot elements from *Boys Will Be Boys* turned up again years later in *Blue Murder at St Trinian's*.

Boy 10 Feet Tall, A
See: Sammy Going South

Boy Who Could Fly, The ○
1986, US, 114 mins, colour
Dir: Nick Castle
Stars: Lucy Deakins, Jay Underwood, Bonnie Bedelia, Fred Savage, Fred Gwynne, Louise Fletcher
Rating: ★★★

A well-intentioned film that tackles the subjects of mental illness and suicide head-on. But for much of its running time, it's pretty heavy going. Lucy Deakins as a new girl in town and Jay Underwood, as her neighbour, a mute, autistic boy who dreams of flying, handle their difficult roles with amazing grace, but they have an uphill battle with sombre material. The supporting cast of well-known faces, including Colleen Dewhurst as a sympathetic teacher, Fred Gwynne as the boy's alcoholic uncle, and Louise Fletcher as a soft-spoken psychiatrist, all turn in terrific portrayals. Look out for Jason Priestly from *Beverly Hills 90210* in a very early performance.

Boy Who Had Everything, The ◑
1984, Australia, 94 mins, colour
Dir: Stephen Wallace
Stars: Jason Connery, Diane Cilento, Laura Williams, Lewis Fitz-Gerald, Ian Gilmour
Rating: ★★

Jason Connery's first star role came in this penetrating look at the childish and almost barbaric rites that apparently still existed in Australia in 1965 for unfortunate first-year 'freshers' at some universities and colleges of further education. Certainly a more dislikeable set of characters in any film would be tough to find. It's not easy to understand anyone surviving three whole terms under their jurisdiction. The trouble is that, given this premise, the film never seems to go anywhere, especially in not sending Jason off to Vietnam, when the plot keeps dropping hints that that's what's most likely to happen. Connery has a definite raw-boned charisma and proves a most convincing runner in some of the most realistic race sequences yet filmed. Laura Williams also does well as his suburban girlfriend and a lot of

good Australian actors have fun trying to look young enough to be graduates and nasty at the same time.

Boyz N the Hood ● ⓥ
1991, US, 111 mins, colour
Dir: John Singleton
Stars: Cuba Gooding Jr, Larry Fishburne, Ice Cube, Nia Long, Angela Bassett
Rating: ★★★

Amid so much that's dross and inconsequential in this genre, it's good to find a film that's so relevant to modern living. To be accurate, black modern living in the poor quarter of L.A., where children grow up (if they grow up) trying to concentrate on their homework against background noises of police helicopters patrolling the district and the machine-gun fire of rival neighbourhood gangs exchanging mutual murder. If the outcome of this particular story is fairly predictable, that's not to deny the strength in its telling – an amazing first-time effort from its 23-year-old director. His portrait of growing up comes across as real and affects us all.

Brainstorm ○
1965, US, 114 mins, b/w
Dir: William Conrad
Stars: Jeffrey Hunter, Anne Francis, Dana Andrews, Viveca Lindfors
Rating: ★★

William (*Cannon*) Conrad directed this thriller about a man caught in a series of violent events that seem to be fashioned to drive him out of his mind. The actors try hard, but the plot takes some swallowing.

Brainstorm ◑ ⓥ
1983, US, 106 mins, colour
Dir: Douglas Trumbull
Stars: Christopher Walken, Natalie Wood, Louise Fletcher, Cliff Robertson
Rating: ★★

Completed with difficulty after the death of one of its stars, Natalie Wood, in a drowning tragedy, Douglas Trumbull's sci-fi drama has at least the core of an interesting idea, successfully carried out in spasms, and most notably so the nearer it approaches the realms of the straight thriller. Wood, Christopher Walken, Louise Fletcher and others are working on a project which enables brain waves to be transferred from one head to another, so that ultimately 'experiences' can be recorded. The government soon has its beady eyes on the project for its armed forces and

B

when Fletcher dies from a heart attack (which she 'records' on tape) it's up to Walken and Wood to destroy the programme before the warmongers can put it to use. Personal relationships of the characters tend to intrude on the central drama without affecting it, but maybe this is the result of Wood's untimely death. At times, the film is exciting, tense and amusing in turn. But not, alas, all of the time.

Bramble Bush, The ○
1960, US, 105 mins, colour
Dir: Daniel Petrie
Stars: Richard Burton, Barbara Rush, Jack Carson, Angie Dickinson
Rating: ★★

Emotion-charged drama, with Richard Burton adding weight to a *Peyton Place*-type story of a young doctor faced with a crisis of principles through his love for a married woman. This was Burton's first American film after his success in *Look Back in Anger*, and he lent authority to a difficult role. The story is taken from Charles Mergendahl's best-seller.

Bram Stoker's Dracula ● ⊘
1992, US/UK, 123 mins, colour
Dir: Francis Ford Coppola
Stars: Gary Oldman, Winona Ryder, Anthony Hopkins, Keanu Reeves, Tom Waits, Richard E Grant
Rating: ★★

An Oscar winner for costume design and nominated for production design, this new version of the vampire legend flaunts its sense of style with some justification, the opening sequence showing Dracula's origins being particularly breathtaking. The scenes in Edwardian England are pretty good too, and Gary Oldman's count proves an evil and convincing seducer, making this one of the sexiest Draculas in memory. There's lots of blood-letting, too, but what is missing is any sense of fear or real horror. The down side includes Anthony Hopkins' unexpectedly camp performance as Van Helsing and Keanu Reeves' embarrassing attempt at an English accent. Chuckles and creeps here, then, but nary a chill.

Branded ○
1950, US, 94 mins, colour
Dir: Rudolph Maté
Stars: Alan Ladd, Mona Freeman, Charles Bickford
Rating: ★★

A fairly gripping Western from Alan Ladd and Paramount to follow their first, *Whispering Smith*. 'They call me Choya,' says Ladd in this one, and proves to be as tough as his name, as someone obligingly explains in the course of the action, choya is Spanish for cactus. When asked if he has any friends, this impassive hombre replies, through gritted teeth: 'My guns'. This is fair stuff for Western fans, with as complex a plot as you could expect in a horse-opera, the prettiest of heroines in feisty Mona Freeman and lots of exciting action up and down the picturesque valley of the Rio Grande. Veteran actors Charles Bickford and Tom Tully give the stars solid support.

Brandy for the Parson ○
1951, UK, 79 mins, b/w
Dir: John Eldridge
Stars: James Donald, Kenneth More, Jean Lodge
Rating: ★★

The second film from Group Three, the 1950s production unit headed by John Grierson and John Baxter, is an amiable Ealing-style comedy. James Donald and Jean Lodge find themselves inadvertently involved with smuggler Kenneth More, whose bright and breezy performance gave him another leg up the ladder to stardom. A large roster of familiar character actors decorate the edges of the movie, among them Alfie Bass, Charles Hawtrey, Reginald Beckwith and the almost inevitable Sam Kydd. Director John Eldridge's pacing is leisurely but he displays an attractive narrative style and makes excellent use of some well-chosen locations.

Brannigan ○ ⊘
1975, UK, 111 mins, colour
Dir: Douglas Hickox
Stars: John Wayne, Richard Attenborough, Judy Geeson, Mel Ferrer
Rating: ★★★

The British director of this tough crime drama, Douglas Hickox, was quoted at the time as saying that he 'just wanted to make a John Wayne movie'. Well, he did it. Even more old-fashioned than the star's previous police drama, *McQ*, *Brannigan* is also more fun. Hickox was an expert at blazing action scenes and his style and Wayne's dovetail perfectly. The script doesn't exactly match other departments, but it has its moments, mainly in the reactions of Britishers ridden roughshod over by Wayne's Chicago cop. 'I was only here for the beer,'

protests a bowler-hatted type after being punched three times in a superb London pub brawl. And another, horrifed at Wayne's commandeering of his car and 'flying' it over an opening Tower Bridge, protests: 'I waited a year for delivery.'

Brasher Doubloon, The
See: The High Window

Bravados, The ◐ ⊘
1958, US, 98 mins, colour
Dir: Henry King
Stars: Gregory Peck, Joan Collins, Stephen Boyd, Albert Salmi
Rating: ★★★

The credentials of this tough Western are first-rate: written by the prolific Philip Yordan, from a novel by that fine western writer Frank O'Rourke, and directed by Henry King, one of the best of Hollywood's veteran directors (he began in early silent days). Here, King sustains the tensions, aroused by Gregory Peck's crazed hunt for the bandits who murdered his wife, at a remarkable pitch.

Brave Don't Cry, The ○
1952, UK, 90 mins, b/w
Dir: Philip Leacock
Stars: John Gregson, Meg Buchanan, John Rae, Fulton Mackay
Rating: ★★★

This stark, harrowing and suspense-packed story of a group of miners trapped down a Scottish pit was based on a real-life disaster (at Knockshinnock) and produced by the famous director of documentaries John Grierson. It was one of the biggest successes of the short-lived British state-backed film company, Group Three Productions, and is flawlessly acted by a cast who were then all virtually unknown. Its people are full of character, the dialogue crackles with the wit and courage of men facing death, and the rescue attempts will leave many fingernails in shreds. A sincere and moving film that did credit to all concerned. John Gregson heads the cast, which also includes Fulton Mackay and Jean Anderson.

Brazil ● ⊘
1985, UK/US, 142 mins, colour
Dir: Terry Gilliam
Stars: Jonathan Pryce, Robert De Niro, Michael Palin, Bob Hoskins, Kim Greist, Ian Holm
Rating: ★★★

Director Terry Gilliam's film is clearly influenced by his work as director and animator with the Monty Python team, even if it is perhaps rather more than a Pythonesque version of *1984*. The net result too is more of an entertainment than the Orwell tale, if only because the terror is leavened with streaks of surrealist humour and because Sam (Jonathan Pryce) does have his moments of triumph on the way to inevitable doom at the hands of the State. Working at Information Retrieval, Sam is a faceless cipher who dreams of flying through the sky as a bird, rescuing his ideal girl. Then she materialises, in the form of subversive Jill (Kim Greist) who's wanted by the State. While his private world (and his flat) is disintegrating, save for his friendship with an outlawed, crusading heating engineer (Robert De Niro), Sam's infatuation with Jill and his determination to save her leads him down nightmare corridors from which there's no escape. These are only half the facets of an imaginative plot which also involves Michael Palin, as Sam's friend who turns out to be the State Exterminator. If it seems long at times, the action, when it does come, is fast and furious.

Breaker Morant ◐ ⓥ
1979, Australia, 107 mins, colour
Dir: Bruce Beresford
Stars: Edward Woodward, Jack Thompson, Bryan Brown
Rating: ★★★

This is the true story of three Australian soldiers put on trumped-up court marshall charges for political reasons during the Boer War. Edward Woodward is effective in the title role, one of the accused, and Jack Thompson gives a powerful performance as his defence lawyer. The action scenes in the first third of the film are well done and the courtroom scenes that follow are tense. Writer/director Bruce Beresford builds a powerful drama that will have you raging against injustice.

Breakfast at Tiffany's ○ ⓥ
1961, US, 106 mins, colour
Dir: Blake Edwards
Stars: Audrey Hepburn, George Peppard, Mickey Rooney, Patricia Neal, Buddy Ebsen, Martin Balsam
Rating: ★★★★

One of the great film successes of the Sixties, containing possibly the best performance of Audrey Hepburn's career. Warm-hearted, tragic and

extraordinarily funny in turn, this bitter-sweet, scatterbrained entertainment pulls pretty well every emotional string. The wandering spirit of this wonderful, invigorating picture is enchantingly captured by Hepburn, at her wistful best, and George Peppard, whose offbeat romance makes director Blake Edwards' castings seem perfection. Among other highlights: Hepburn, as the kooky Holly Golightly, using her own voice to sing 'Moon River' (which won an Oscar for the best song); the final chase in the rain after the beloved Cat; and the fresh and delightfully relaxed scene in the jeweller's shop. Mickey Rooney, John McGiver (as the deadpan jewellery salesman) and Buddy Ebsen also score well; but this is Hepburn's show.

Breakfast Club, The ● ⓥ
1984, US, 97 mins, colour
Dir: John Hughes
Stars: Emilio Estevez, Judd Nelson, Molly Ringwald, Ally Sheedy, Anthony Michael Hall, Paul Gleason
Rating: ★★

This dialogue film about five angry young people trapped in an all-day detention at an American high school reaches high but only gets so-so far. There are times when the character piece almost catches fire, though, mostly in the humorous shafts that cut through the social barriers dividing the characters. But ultimately the film proves too facile, merely reflecting commonplace attitudes and opting for a tidy, cop-out ending with the boys getting the girls they've been angled away from all along. Too much bad language and shouting, underlined by over-emotional playing – compensation, perhaps, for the inconsistency of the characters.

Breakheart Pass ○ ⓥ
1975, US, 90 mins, colour
Dir: Tom Gries
Stars: Charles Bronson, Ben Johnson, Jill Ireland, Richard Crenna, Charles Durning
Rating: ★★★

A rare and consistently enjoyable combination of Western and whodunnit, set aboard a train carrying vital medicine in 1873. People on the train start dying mysteriously, one by one. The obvious suspect is Charles Bronson, as a killer under arrest. Fans of this sort of plot will know that's too easy, but the problem is that, as soon as someone comes under suspicion, he gets bumped off. Director Tom Gries

and his experienced second-unit aide Yakima Canutt keep the action tumbling across the screen. Cameraman Lucien Ballard shines when he's given the chance and the train itself is magnificent, charging along to some of the best film music Jerry Goldsmith has written. Here's one tuppence-coloured pot-boiler that's seldom off the boil.

Breaking Away ○
1979, US, 100 mins, colour
Dir: Peter Yates
Stars: Dennis Christopher, Dennis Quaid, Daniel Stern, Barbara Barrie
Rating: ★★★

This engaging film was, perhaps surprisingly and less than predictably, a success. Fundamentally, it's about four teenagers in Indiana who are, for various reasons, uncertain of their futures after they leave high school. But the development and the film's treatment make it far more entertaining than the basic material might suggest. In addition, a largely unfamiliar but accomplished cast make it the more convincing. Foremost among the players are Barbara Barrie (deservedly nominated for an Oscar) and Paul Dooley as the bewildered parents of Dennis Christopher, a youngster who yearns to be an Italian bicycle racing champion and speaks in pidgin Italian to boot. Peter Yates' direction and the film itself were also nominated for Academy Awards, although in the end its only major Oscar was for Steve Tesich's screenplay.

Breaking In ● ⓥ
1989, US, 94 mins, colour
Dir: Bill Forsyth
Stars: Burt Reynolds, Casey Siemaszko, Sheila Kelley, Albert Salmi
Rating: ★★

A gentle, almost inconsequential crime comedy-thriller about a young burglar's brief but fruitful apprenticeship in the hands of an old pro. Burt Reynolds is faintly uneasy as the sexagenarian safecracker, a part to which he does bring a certain faded charm as well as a new toupee that permits him to look slightly thin on top – but carefully coiffed, as would befit a man meticulous about both his appearance and his felonious profession. Scottish director Bill Forsyth certainly brings a fresh approach to American crime: the action, such as it is, is hardly dynamic and the emphasis decidedly on character. Unfortunately, neither Reynolds nor

B

Casey Siemaszko, as Reynolds' apprentice safecracker, really live their parts, and the more down-to-earth impression is made by *L.A. Law*'s Sheila Kelley as Siemaszko's prostitute girlfriend.

Breaking Point, The ○
1951, US, 97 mins, b/w
Dir: Michael Curtiz
Stars: John Garfield, Patricia Neal, Phyllis Thaxter
Rating: ★★

This is one of three Hollywood versions of Ernest Hemingway's *To Have and to Have Not*. The others are the Humphrey Bogart film of the same name, in which Lauren Bacall made her debut, and Audie Murphy's *The Gun Runners*. This one has taciturn John Garfield in the lead. Director Michael Curtiz charges it with as much tension as he can muster.

Breaking the Sound Barrier
See: The Sound Barrier

Break in the Circle ○
1955, UK, 92 mins, colour
Dir: Val Guest
Stars: Forrest Tucker, Eva Bartok, Marius Goring, Eric Pohlmann
Rating: ★★★

A neatly plotted spy yarn with an abundance of shady characters, kidnappings, gunfire, fisticuffs and heroics. Forrest Tucker is a rugged hero and Eva Bartok a provocative heroine. Val Guest's workmanlike handling of his own script and Walter Harvey's appropriately low-key Eastman Colour photography make this a cut above most British thick-ear thrillers of its time.

Breakout ◐
1975, US, 96 mins, colour
Dir: Tom Gries
Stars: Charles Bronson, Robert Duvall, Jill Ireland, John Huston, Randy Quaid, Sheree North
Rating: ★★

The producers of this thriller use a foreword to tell us that the prison escape method shown in the film has actually been used. At least that serves to scotch one of the many implausibilities in their story, which gets by on its exciting action sequences and a rich variety of supporting characters. Hard to tell at times, in fact, whether director Tom Gries is playing it all in light-hearted

vein, although the bloody events of the last few reels seem to contradict the theory, and the escape itself is full of tension. But a key part of the action involves Randy Quaid convincing prison guards that he's a girl. Mr Quaid is about six-feet-five and weighs 200 pounds!

Breakthrough ○
1950, US, 91 mins, b/w
Dir: Lewis Seiler
Stars: David Brian, John Agar, Frank Lovejoy
Rating: ★★

The D-Day landings and battle of the Normandy hedgerows as seen through the eyes of a platoon of American infantrymen led by David Brian and John Agar, a former husband of Shirley Temple. Insertion of actual newsreel clippings adds realism to some of the gripping battle scenes. A minor film, but war addicts will enjoy it.

Breakthrough ◐
1979, West Germany, 111 mins, colour
Dir: Andrew V Mclaglen
Stars: Richard Burton, Robert Mitchum, Rod Steiger, Curt Jurgens
Rating: ★★

This blockbuster wartime action film is in fact a kind of sequel to Sam Peckinpah's *Cross of Iron*, with the same leading character, here played by Richard Burton. The director Andrew V McLaglen was responsible in recent years for other big-budget, multi-national screen-blasters like *The Wild Geese*, *The Sea Wolves* and *The Dirty Dozen: Next Mission*.

Break to Freedom
See: Albert RN

Breathless ● ⊙
(aka: A Bout de Souffle)
1959, France, 90 mins, b/w
Dir: Jean-Luc Godard
Stars: Jean-Paul Belmondo, Jean Seberg
Rating: ★★★

Director Jean-Luc Godard's debut film was a trend-setter and the hit of the 1959 Cannes Film Festival. Jean-Paul Belmondo, in his first major film success, plays a casually ruthless and amoral small-time crook who, en route to Paris in a stolen car, shoots and kills a traffic cop. Keeping just one step ahead of the law, he meets up with his American girlfriend (Jean Seberg) in Paris and suggests a trip to Italy. But he has two problems: she

doesn't really want to go and he has no money. Belmondo's persona as a Gallic Bogart is entirely intentional, even down to mimicking some of Bogie's gestures, as Godard made the film as a homage to American gangster films. Belmondo's character is the most colourful and well-rounded in the film, while Seberg's is rather thin and insubstantial. The film jumps from scene to scene, giving it pace and mirroring the erratic personality of Belmondo's character. It all looks a little dated now, but is still entertaining and original – and a great deal better than the 1983 American remake.

Breathless ● ⊙
1983, US, 101 mins, colour
Dir: Jim McBride
Stars: Richard Gere, Valerie Kaprisky
Rating: ★

The camera-worship of Richard Gere reached new heights with a full-frontal shower scene in this vulgarisation of the classic French thriller *A Bout de Souffle*. The original film, directed by Jean-Luc Godard and written by François Truffaut, was a landmark of the French New Wave for its style and direct-to-camera monologues. But it was a mistake to transfer the story of a cop-killing amoral punk to Los Angeles and making Gere's kinetic character a self-obsessed loser hooked on Jerry Lee Lewis music and *Silver Surfer* comics. Naked for most of the time, semi-naked for the rest, constantly snapping fingers and forever stopping by any available mirror to wiggle his hips and preen, Gere ends up irritating rather than sympathetic. Most of the blame for the film's many failings belongs to director Jim McBride, who hit the mark four years later with Dennis Quaid in the steamy, erotic *The Big Easy* but was way off here.

Breed Apart, A ◐
1984, US, 101 mins, colour
Dir: Phillipe Mora
Stars: Rutger Hauer, Kathleen Turner, Powers Boothe
Rating: ★

Shot in North Carolina, this conservation drama – centring on a recluse's battle to protect the eggs of a rare eagle on the island where he lives – is absolutely stunning to look at. But the plot is strictly for the birds. Cool, blond, deep-voiced Rutger Hauer takes a break from cold-eyed killers to play the independent-minded conservationist. But he, Powers Boothe (familiar to TV viewers as Philip Marlowe) and that feisty actress Kathleen Turner, also a fictional detective, the *V I Warshawski* of film and radio fame, cannot do anything to sustain this thin and disjointed story.

Brewster's Millions ☉
1945, US, 84 mins, b/w
Dir: Allan Dwan
Stars: Dennis O'Keefe, Helen Walker, June Havoc
Rating: ★★

Perennial farce about a man who can't get rid of his millions. It's interesting to look at this, one of the most successful renditions of the theme in the five attempts to date. After a slow beginning, director Allan Dwan takes it along at a rampaging pace, with amusing performances from Eddie 'Rochester' Anderson and Mischa Auer in the supporting cast.

Brewster's Millions ○ ⓥ
1985, US, 97 mins, colour
Dir: Walter Hill
Stars: Richard Pryor, John Candy, Lonette McKee
Rating: ★

This oft-filmed story of a man who must spend several millions of dollars to inherit several million more always seems a tedious tale, and certainly doesn't improve in this uneventful re-working for Richard Pryor, directed in lackluster fashion by Walter Hill.

Bribe, The ○
1948, US, 105 mins, b/w
Dir: Robert Z Leonard
Stars: Robert Taylor, Ava Gardner, Vincent Price, Charles Laughton, John Hodiak
Rating: ★★★

Director Robert Z Leonard, king of lightness and brightness at MGM for 30 years, seems an unusual choice to direct what amounts to a *film noir* although, as one would expect from the studio, this is a glossier example than usual. Leonard dresses it up in swirling mists, mirror images and rain-streaked windows. Robert Taylor seems not entirely at his ease as the drug-busting agent besotted by femme fatale Ava Gardner, but Charles Laughton and Vincent Price as the villains revel in their surroundings. Bits of footage from this film later turned up in Steve Martin's *Dead Men Don't Wear Plaid*.

Bride, The ●
1985, US, 119 mins, colour
Dir: Franc Roddam
Stars: Sting, Jennifer Beals, Anthony Higgins, Clancy Brown, David Rappaport, Geraldine Page
Rating: ★

A trite and flat remake of the Boris Karloff/Elsa Lanchester *Bride of Frankenstein*. It's not helped by having two of the least animated actors – pop singer Sting as Dr Frankenstein and Jennifer Beals as his gauze-wrapped creation – in the leading roles. It's left for an electrifying scene in which a cat crosses Beals' path and the girl snarls back like a lion to suggest the sort of punch the rest of the film so badly lacks. At the end of the day, dwarf actor David Rappaport steals the film from the principals.

Bride Came C.O.D., The ○
1941, US, 92 mins, b/w
Dir: William Keighley
Stars: James Cagney, Bette Davis, Stuart Erwin, Jack Carson, Eugene Pallette, George Tobias
Rating: ★★

The unlikely team of James Cagney and Bette Davis in a comedy that could just as well have been called *Headstrong Heiress*. Miss Davis works hard, but is plainly not at home in comedy and after this and *The Man Who Came To Dinner*, returned to the headier realms of melodrama. It's left to Cagney and Jack Carson, reunited from *The Strawberry Blonde*, to raise the laughs in a comedy that's consistently amusing without ever becoming uproarious.

Bride of Frankenstein ◐
1935, US, 75 mins, b/w
Dir: James Whale
Stars: Boris Karloff, Colin Clive, Elsa Lanchester, Ernest Thesinger
Rating: ★★★★

Without doubt the best of all the Universal horror films, in which Frankenstein creates a bride for the monster, with tragic results. Director James Whale tells the story swiftly and incisively, with fluid camerawork, elegant settings, clever lighting and some weirdly effective theme music. In this film Boris Karloff's monster reaches full flower. Scenes of his friendship with a blind hermit, and his being chained up for the townsfolk to ogle, provide genuinely moving moments. The plot also introduces Dr Praetorious, who forces Frankenstein

to collaborate in his schemes. As played by Ernest Thesiger (with intense relish), Praetorious is a masterly portrait of madness. He lives in a draughty castle, full of endless stairs, mending the miniature beings he has 'bottled' away (a splendid piece of trick photography) and swigging gin, which he also uses to calm the monster. Spot if you can Walter Brennan and John Carradine among the villagers.

Brides of Dracula ●
1960, UK, 85 mins, colour
Dir: Terence Fisher
Stars: Peter Cushing, Yvonne Monlaur, David Peel, Martita Hunt
Rating: ★★

A follow-up to the highly successful remake of Bram Stoker's classic vampire story. Peter Cushing is again Van Helsing and David Peel as handsome a villain as one could wish. The finale is splendidly staged against the flapping sails of a windmill.

Bridge, The ● ⓥ
1991, UK, 110 mins, colour
Dir: Syd Macartney
Stars: Saskia Reeves, David O'Hara, Anthony Higgins, Rosemary Harris, Joss Ackland
Rating: ★★

Vaguely in *Lady Chatterley's Lover* country, this is a very prettily set story of a repressed Victorian mother of 29 or so who falls madly, passionately in love with an artist on his annual Suffolk holiday, and he with her. Saskia Reeves pants attractively and inevitably sheds all her clothes as the lovers consummate their mutual lust in the artist's beach hut (cor!). Alas, hubby (Anthony Higgins) returns, tells her that he can 'forgive everything, Isobel, except melodrama', and it ends in tears or, in the artist's case, the painting of his greatest work. Joss Ackland has too little to do, although he does it well, but the couple themselves, Reeves and David O'Hara (with glum countenance and Sean Connery voice), do very little to gain your sympathy at their ultimate betrayal. It is, however, beautifully shot in Fujicolor.

Bridge at Remagen, The ○
1968, US, 116 mins, colour
Dir: John Guillermin
Stars: George Segal, Robert Vaughn, Ben Gazzara, Bradford Dillman, E G Marshall, Peter Van Eyck
Rating: ★★

B

Talented director John Guillermin
shows the facility for explosive action
scenes that carried him through *The
Blue Max* and *The Towering Inferno*. A
virile cast, including George Segal,
Ben Gazzara, Robert Vaughn and
Bradford Dillman, grits its teeth and
gives the film its all. This war film has
a routine plot, but crisp photography
and tense action scenes more than
compensate.

**Bridge on the River Kwai,
The** ○ ⓥ
1957, UK, 161 mins, colour
Dir: David Lean
Stars: William Holden, Alec Guinness,
Jack Hawkins, Sersue Hayakawe
Rating: ★★★★

Anti-war classic starring Alec Guinness
as a British officer who raises the mo-
rale of his captured regiment in a PoW
camp in Burma by building a bridge
but in doing so is unwittingly helping
the Japanese war effort. William
Holden is the American escapee who
returns to destroy the bridge. An intelligent, ironic and deeply stirring
film, directed on an epic scale by David Lean. Based on the novel by Pierre
Boulle, who was credited for the
screenplay in the place of blacklisted
writers Carl Foreman and Michael
Wilson. The film won Oscars for Best
Picture, Director, Actor (Alec
Guinness), Script, Photography (Jack
Hildyard) and Music (Malcolm Arnold).

Bridges at Toko-Ri, The ○
1954, US, 103 mins, colour
Dir: Mark Robson
Stars: William Holden, Fredric March,
Grace Kelly, Mickey Rooney
Rating: ★★★

A war film of the type Hollywood
does so well. Packed with incident and
spectacular flying scenes, it's the
story of a pilot who is reluctant to fly
on a near-impossible mission. This
tricky decision is tied up with a
touching love story that may have
you reaching for a handkerchief before
the end. In an excellent cast, which
helps make this a superior production
of its kind, Mickey Rooney stands out
with his brave-as-a-bantam portrait of
a helicopter rescue pilot.

Bridge Too Far, A ◐ ⓥ
1977, UK, 175 mins, colour
Dir: Richard Attenborough
Stars: Dirk Bogarde, Sean Connery,
Robert Redford, James Caan, Michael

Caine, Edward Fox, Gene Hackman
Rating: ★★★

Richard Attenborough's re-creation of
the Second World War Arnhem
landings and their aftermath is almost
exactly the long blockbuster action
film one would have expected from
the director of *Oh! What a Lovely War*
and *Young Winston*. The preamble is
lengthy and the action and special effects are ruthlessly efficient. One tank
battle early on vividly expresses the
violence of war, although the lesson
is needlessly rubbed home in later
sequences. But the really impressive
performances come from Edward
Fox (as Lt.-General Horrocks) and
Sean Connery (as Major-General
Urquhart) – and from Frank Grimes in
a minor role.

Brief Encounter ○ ⓥ
1945, UK, 86 mins, b/w
Dir: David Lean
Stars: Celia Johnson, Trevor Howard,
Stanley Holloway, Joyce Carey
Rating: ★★★★

Amazingly atmospheric, touchingly
understated true love story adapted by
Noel Coward and others from Coward's play *Still Life*. Married Celia
Johnson meets a young doctor (Trevor
Howard) on her weekly shopping trip
to town, and their friendship gradually
turns to a love that they know has no
future. Director David Lean never
puts a foot wrong, neither do the actors, the agony of their frustrated
feelings etched on their faces for all to
see. Brilliantly photographed by
Robert Krasker, especially in the railway scenes, and deft supporting
playing from Stanley Holloway, Joyce
Carey, Cyril Raymond and young
Margaret Barton. The final scene involving Johnson is particularly
poignant and speaks volumes with almost no dialogue.

Brigadoon ○ ⓥ
1954, US, 108 mins, colour
Dir: Vincente Minnelli
Stars: Gene Kelly, Van Johnson, Cyd
Charisse
Rating: ★★

Audiences for big screen musicals
were waning when MGM put this
production of Lerner and Loewe's
stage hit before the cameras. Even so,
it was a fatal mistake to penny-pinch
on this one and shoot it entirely in the
studio on artificial-looking sets that
only emphasised its stagebound origins. Director Vincente Minnelli also

experienced difficulty with using
Ansco Color rather than his favoured
Technicolor stock and with filling
the rectangular frame in his first encounter with CinemaScope. As for
the cast, Cyd Charisse moves exquisitely but Gene Kelly is
uncharacteristically sluggish in yet another of his more whimsical roles. In
all, the film offers disappointingly few
pleasures except for the most ardent
fan of the pretty if bland score.

Brigand, The ○
1952, US, 92 mins, colour
Dir: Phil Karlson
Stars: Anthony Dexter, Anthony Quinn,
Jody Lawrance, Gale Robbins
Rating: ★★★

Swashbuckling adventure film, handsomely mounted in Technicolor, and
with more than a few echoes of *The
Prisoner of Zenda*. Anthony Dexter,
the debonair leading man whose previous film had been the starring role
in *Valentino*, plays the dual role of king
and commoner and shows a neat
touch in the swordplay. But he's no
match at acting for Anthony Quinn,
who smoothly walks off with the film
as the villain.

Brigand of Kandahar, The ○
1965, UK, 81 mins, colour
Dir: John Gilling
Stars: Ronald Lewis, Oliver Reed,
Yvonne Romain
Rating: ★★★

Rally round the flag, men. Those
dastardly tribesmen are killing off our
chaps at the Khyber Pass again. Here
at least is a film which makes no bones
about its intentions. It's more or less
one long round of battles, duels and
skirmishes. And some of the battle
scenes are pretty good, too. Oliver
Reed overacts like mad as a fierce native chieftain.

Brigham Young ○
1940, US, 114 mins, b/w
Dir: Henry Hathaway
Stars: Tyrone Power, Linda Darnell,
Dean Jagger, Brian Donlevy, Jane
Darwell, John Carradine
Rating: ★★★

Big-scale depiction of the Mormons'
epic trek from Illinois to their new
home state, Utah. Dean Jagger is
forthright in the title role, but has to
concede top billing to the romantic
leads, Tyrone Power and Linda
Darnell. They don't, however, match
his fire in a performance that

revitalised his own career but couldn't, alas, make this stirring film a box-office success.

Bright Eyes ☉
1934, US, 83 mins, b/w
Dir: David Butler
Stars: Shirley Temple, James Dunn, Jane Darwell
Rating: ★★★

Shirley Temple got her first solo billing above the title in this sentimental drama in which she plays the orphan daughter of a pilot, and brings joy into the life of an old man who doesn't believe in Father Christmas. Sounds gooey, but it's actually enchanting stuff, thanks to Shirley's own talented, down-to-earth approach to the story. She also sings 'On the Good Ship Lollipop'.

Bright Leaf ○
1950, US, 110 mins, b/w
Dir: Michael Curtiz
Stars: Gary Cooper, Lauren Bacall, Patricia Neal, Jack Carson, Donald Crisp
Rating: ★★

A rare unsympathetic role for Gary Cooper in this highly dramatic film about a ruthlessly ambitious man determined to monopolise the American tobacco industry. Cooper does well, and Karl Freund's black-and-white photography admirably captures the turn of the century feel. But the film's best performance comes from Patricia Neal, as the girl who marries the tobacco tycoon to exact a bitter-sweet revenge.

Bright Lights, Big City ● ⓥ
1988, US, 103 mins, colour
Dir: James Bridges
Stars: Michael J Fox, Kiefer Sutherland, Phoebe Cates, Swoozie Kurtz, Frances Sternhagen
Rating: ★★

Though it's good to see Michael J Fox attempting something different and deeper, this film is certainly not much fun. To be sure, it's a downbeat subject – a young New Yorker drowning in drugs and depression – but it never really goes anywhere. None of its few plot lines develop into anything substantial. Dramas of character need strong writing to grip the attention, and here the script is only average: Fox's personality holds it together for a while, but none of the other younger cast members is very effective, and the girls, Phoebe Cates, Tracy Pollan (soon to become Mrs

Fox in real life) and Swoosie Kurtz, don't amount to much at all. Jason Robards is more tolerable as a boozy veteran researcher with Fox's firm, and Dianne Wiest acts her socks off as Fox's dying mother. But, in a film that doesn't affect our emotions, she's fighting a lost cause. Fox's own brightness and snappy delivery aren't really suited to his role, however much he wanted to play it; yet another crash for the clown wanting to play Hamlet.

Brighton Beach Memoirs ① ⓥ
1986, US, 108 mins, colour
Dir: Gene Saks
Stars: Blythe Danner, Bob Dishy, Jonathan Silverman
Rating: ★★

It's hard to believe that this Neil Simon story won the New York Drama Critics' award as the best new play of 1983. All the more discredit to director Gene Saks for making such a dull film out of it. It's partly based on Simon's own life but, since Jonathan Silverman is actually rather obnoxious as the Simon character, there's nothing very endearing or nostalgic about the piece. It concentrates almost entirely on the boy's leering introduction to sex and misses out on the simple emotional appeal that should be the cornerstone of such fare. The entire cast is unmemorable.

Brighton Rock ○ ⓥ
1947, UK, 91 mins, b/w
Dir: John Boulting
Stars: Richard Attenborough, Hermione Baddeley, William Hartnell, Carol Marsh
Rating: ★★★

Richard Attenborough was almost always unexpectedly good when asked to portray menace and he's very good indeed in this story of a psychotic petty hoodlum at large in post-war Brighton. Sordid for its time, but strong, tense and realistic, with good support for the star from William Hartnell, Carol Marsh, Nigel Stock, Alan Wheatley and especially Hermione Baddeley as a raddled end-of-pier entertainer. Graham Greene's novel is intelligently adapted for the screen by Greene himself and Terence Rattigan, a formidable writing duo that supplies crisp, threatening, unpleasant dialogue.

Bringing Up Baby ☉
1938, US, 102 mins, b/w
Dir: Howard Hawks

Stars: Cary Grant, Katharine Hepburn, May Robson
Rating: ★★★★

A delightful screwball comedy of the very best vintage, with Cary Grant and Katharine Hepburn on glittering form: he a mild-mannered, orderly paleontologist painstakingly reconstructing a priceless dinosaur skeleton, she a batty heiress with a wilful dog (the one and only Asta from the Thin Man series) who grabs a vital bone from Grant's masterpiece. In case you thought the name 'Baby' belonged to this canine, you should know that 'Baby' is another troublesome animal in Hepburn's possession: a Brazilian leopard. Glorious chaos ensues from the encounter between scientist and heiress, the dialogue sparkles and director Howard Hawks presides over the whirling insanity with evident glee. There are also wonderful contributions from the support cast, in particular Charles Ruggles as Major Applegate, May Robson as Aunt Elizabeth and Fritz Feld as the psychiatrist.

Bring On the Night ① ⓥ
1985, UK, 97 mins, colour
Dir: Michael Apted
Stars: Sting, Omar Hakim, Darryl Jones, Kenny Kirkland, Trudie Styler, Miles Copeland
Rating: ★★★

If you're a fan of the particular brand of rock jazz played by Sting's ensemble here, there's no doubt you're in for a feast of it with this film, as well as an informative insight into the weeks of rehearsal that lead to a single concert performance. We're less sure that you'll want to watch the graphic filming of Sting's baby, but shut your eyes if you don't fancy that sort of thing and just listen to the music – as well as a few wild moments of pleasure in the interviews given by the extremely talented black American musicians who make up the band. To his credit, Sting fits in with these like a glove – another tribute to those long hours of rehearsal.

Britannia Hospital ● ⓥ
1982, UK, 105 mins, colour
Dir: Lindsay Anderson
Stars: Malcolm McDowell, Leonard Rossiter, Joan Plowright, Robin Askwith, Fulton Mackay, Alan Bates
Rating: ★★

Director Lindsay Anderson's first film in eight years is a bitter, black and

B

bloody satire on hospitals, unions, snobbery, spare-part surgery and society itself: indeed, anything within its reach. Anger drips from its jaws like the blood from the stitches of the composite creature mad surgeon Graham Crowden hopes to unveil to visiting royalty. Malcolm McDowell again returns to the role of Mick Travis (previously seen in Anderson's *if. . .* and *O Lucky Man!*), now an investigative reporter seeking to unmask the 'Frankenstein' surgeon. Leonard Rossiter is the senior hospital administrator who will stop at nothing (even murder) to see that the royal visit goes ahead. Meanwhile, demonstrators gather outside the hospital gates, and the whole unstable brew explodes in a final reel that ultimately lapses into pretentiousness.

Broadcast News ◑ ⓥ

1987, US, 131 mins, colour
Dir: James L Brooks
Stars: William Hurt, Albert Brooks, Holly Hunter, Joan Cusack, Lois Chiles, Jack Nicholson
Rating: ★★★

This immensely entertaining comedy-romance set in the Washington bureau of a TV news network has three excellent, Oscar-nominated performances from William Hurt, Albert Brooks and Holly Hunter as the central triangle of characters. All the daily drama of a hectic newsroom is there – last-minute changes, missing tapes, large egos and difficult bosses – beautifully put together by writer-director James L Brooks (who made the Oscar-winning *Terms of Endearment*). William Hurt is exactly right as the charming, although actually rather vulnerable ex-sportscaster whose ability to succeed without the requisite brain-power is a source of huge irritation to Holly Hunter's workaholic TV producer, convincingly torn between the professional and the personal life. And Albert Brooks is perfect as the best friend (who of course harbours deeper affections for Hunter's character). In the end, the satire takes second place to the romance, but it is a story that has a refreshingly realistic conclusion.

Broadway Danny Rose ◑ ⓥ

1984, US, 84 mins, b/w
Dir: Woody Allen
Stars: Woody Allen, Mia Farrow, Nick Apollo Forte, Milton Berle
Rating: ★★★

A quirky Woody Allen film in which the comedy is of a gentle variety. Allen both directs and stars as Danny Rose, a theatrical manager with a collection of no-hope acts. His luck changes when an overweight singer comes into fashion again thanks to a nostalgia boom. But he has Mafia connections – and Danny's involvement with his mistress Tina (Mia Farrow, brilliant if almost unrecognisable in a ridiculous bubble wig) lands him in hot water. It's the by-now-familiar Allen theme of a loser triumphing against unbelievable adversity, but the little maestro brings it up fresh and funny. Most hilarious scene: Allen and Farrow running through a warehouse storing gas containers that when hit by their pursuers' bullets, leave everyone talking in high-pitched voices. A little gem.

Broadway Melody of 1936, The ○

1935, US, 110 mins, b/w
Dir: Roy Del Ruth
Stars: Jack Benny, Eleanor Powell, Robert Taylor
Rating: ★★★

Second and best of this series of musical comedies, with Jack Benny on top form as a waspish Broadway theatre critic. Eleanor Powell has never danced better and a very young Robert Taylor was never lovelier! The Arthur Freed-Nacio Herb Brown songs include 'You Are My Lucky Star' and 'Broadway Rhythm'.

Broadway Melody of 1938 ○

1937, US, 110 mins, b/w
Dir: Roy Del Ruth
Stars: Robert Taylor, Eleanor Powell, George Murphy, Judy Garland
Rating: ★★

Eleanor Powell's dazzling dancing is the most eye-catching thing in this typical MGM musical from the late Thirties. The juvenile leads are a gangling Buddy Ebsen (long before Davy Crockett or Barnaby Jones) and Judy Garland, making her first big impact with her famous 'Dear Mr Gable' song.

Broadway Melody of 1940 ○

1940, US, 102 mins, b/w
Dir: Norman Taurog
Stars: Fred Astaire, Eleanor Powell, George Murphy, Frank Morgan
Rating: ★★★

The last of the great *Broadway Melody* series of musicals from MGM has the wonderful Eleanor Powell (billed at the time as 'the world's greatest tap dancer') partnered by none other than Fred Astaire in a thinnish story of an aspiring dance duo (Astaire and George Murphy) aiming for stage stardom. Powell and Astaire should have been absolute dance dynamite, but the chemistry didn't always quite fizz. However, this is a minor quibble when the film is scored by Cole Porter and there are such wonderful numbers as the glittering 'Begin the Beguine', 'I've Got My Eyes on You' and the great ship-board number featuring Powell, 'I Am the Captain'.

Broken Arrow ○

1950, US, 93 mins, colour
Dir: Delmer Daves
Stars: James Stewart, Jeff Chandler, Debra Paget
Rating: ★★★

This exciting and moving Western, beautifully shot in Technicolor, was a landmark film in Hollywood history. For the first time since silent days, the Red Indian was depicted as a human being, rather than a brute savage merely in the film to bite the dust at the hands of the US Cavalry. It was adapted from a big social-consience novel by Elliott Arnold, and marked the first step out West by director Delmer Daves after a series of thrillers, although he subsequently made *Jubal*, *Drum Beat*, *The Last Wagon*, *3:10 to Yuma*, *The Hanging Tree* and *Cowboy*. James Stewart's sincerity gives stature to the role of the frontier scout who tries to keep the peace. Jeff Chandler made his name with his strong and dignified portrait of the famous Indian chief Cochise, whom he would play in two further films – *Battle at Apache Pass* and *Taza, Son of Cochise*.

Broken Hearts and Noses

See: Crimewave

Broken Journey ○

1947, UK, 89 mins, b/w
Dir: Ken Annakin
Stars: Phyllis Calvert, James Donald, Margot Grahame, Francis L Sullivan
Rating: ★★

A British entry to the aircraft–crashed-in-the-middle-of-nowhere stakes. Mostly par for the crash course, but with Sonia Holm and Grey Blake forming a touching relationship as a nurse and her iron-lung patient. Director Ken Annakin later got aloft in more jocular vein with *Those Magnificent Men in Their Flying Machines*.

Broken Lance ○ ⓥ
1954, US, 96 mins, colour
Dir: Edward Dmytryk
Stars: Spencer Tracy, Robert Wagner, Jean Peters, Richard Widmark, Katy Jurado, Earl Holliman
Rating: ★★★★

A magnificent performance by a white-haired Spencer Tracy dominates everything else in this strong Fox Western remake of the Edward G Robinson drama *House of Strangers* – with echoes of King Lear for good measure. Only Katy Jurado, as Tracy's 'woman', even gets near to the star's crackling sincerity and abrasive authority in spite of a supporting cast that includes Richard Widmark, Robert Wagner, Hugh O'Brian, Earl Holliman (as Tracy's sons) and Jean Peters. Philip Yordan, who wrote the screenplay for the Robinson original, was rather oddly given an Oscar for 'best motion picture story' on *Broken Lance*. Good roughhouse duel at the end, but spectacular Cinemascope scenery will be a bit lost on TV.

Bronco Billy ◐ ⓥ
1980, US, 119 mins, colour
Dir: Clint Eastwood
Stars: Clint Eastwood, Sondra Locke, Geoffrey Lewis, Scatman Crothers, Sam Bottoms
Rating: ★★★

A holiday for the Clint Eastwood gang from all that heavy stuff like *Dirty Harry* and *The Gauntlet*. It tries entertainingly to mix the Eastwood Western myth, straitjacketed into a modern rodeo show, with a Thirties' screwball comedy that might well have been called *Footloose Heiress*. The film's heart is certainly in the right place and there are some good moments along the trail, especially when the rodeo's motley crew, including two native Americans, visit a mental institution (an inmate of which happens to be Lewis, sent there for the 'murder' of his disappeared wife). The chief physician tells them: 'You can take your meals with the staff or the patients, whichever you feel most comfortable with.'

Bronx Tale, A ● ⓥ
1993, US, 122 mins, colour
Dir: Robert De Niro

Stars: Robert De Niro, Chazz Palminteri, Lilli Brancato
Rating: ★★★

Somewhere between *GoodFellas*, *Grease* and *West Side Story*, Robert De Niro's directorial debut is full of Brooklyn flavour that even overcomes its lack of excitement and pace. If you can survive its torrent of bad language, there's a lot to savour in this story of a Bronx boy who worships a lethal gangster, played with charm by Chazz Palminteri (who also wrote it), despite the efforts of the boy's father (De Niro) to keep him on the straight and narrow. In spite of the gangster's viciousness and ruthlessness, he's also like a father to the boy, restricting him to sideline activities, not allowing him to become a gun-toting hoodlum 'like me' and even offering some laconic advice on his love life. The boy's well played (at nine) by Francis Capra, who must have the longest eyelashes in films and, at 17, by throaty Lillo Brancato, whose romance with a black schoolmate enables the film to raise a few pertinent issues that go beyond its ghetto portrait. Joe Pesci turns up in a cameo role, one of many colourful characters who include Mush, a losing gambler so abysmal that 'the racecourse touts gave him tickets already torn up'.

Brother Orchid ⊙
1940, US, 91 mins, b/w
Dir: Lloyd Bacon
Stars: Edward G Robinson, Humphrey Bogart, Ann Sothern, Donald Crisp
Rating: ★★★

Possibly the most charming crime comedy ever made. Edward G Robinson is perfect as the racketeer, forever looking for 'the real class', who seeks refuge in a monastery when shot in a gang war. Humphrey Bogart is a wonderful snarling villain and Ann Sothern delightful as Robinson's long-suffering moll. If you're looking for 'the real class' in Warner gangster classics, this is it.

Brothers-in-Law ○
1956, UK, 94 mins, b/w
Dir: Roy Boulting
Stars: Richard Attenborough, Ian Carmichael, Terry-Thomas
Rating: ★★★

The Boulting brothers strike at the legal profession in the second of their successful comedy series of the Fifties.

Ian Carmichael is fine as the embryo barrister for whom no case is open and shut.

Browning Version, The ○
1951, UK, 90 mins, b/w
Dir: Anthony Asquith
Stars: Michael Redgrave, Jean Kent, Wilfrid Hyde White, Bill Travers
Rating: ★★★

One of the 'prestige' British productions of its time, this is a fine film version of Terence Rattigan's stage play of marital discord against a background of school life. Michael Redgrave gave one of the best screen performances of his career as the hapless schoolmaster whose loveless existence and professional humiliation have given him a defensive armour of coldness and even, at times, brutality. How this armour is pierced makes for dramatic entertainment. There are good performances, too, from Jean Kent as the cold-blooded wife, Nigel Patrick as her science-master lover, and Wilfrid Hyde White somewhat untypically cast as the headmaster. Remade in 1994.

Brubaker ● ⓥ
1980, US, 130 mins, colour
Dir: Stuart Rosenberg
Stars: Robert Redford, Yaphet Kotto, Jane Alexander, Murray Hamilton, Morgan Freeman
Rating: ★★★

An old-fashioned but hearteningly entertaining prison film, with Robert Redford winning new haloes as the crusading prison governor determined to reform the vilest and most violent jail farm in the whole of the US. Naturally, there are those for him and those agin, and thereby hangs the nub of the tale. If Redford is sometimes too good to be true, this does sustain audience sympathy throughout, and ensures that the final scene is as moving as it is intended to be. Jane Alexander offers another of her strong human portrayals.

Brute Force ◐
1947, US, 96 mins, b/w
Dir: Jules Dassin
Stars: Burt Lancaster, Hume Cronyn, Charles Bickford, Yvonne De Carlo
Rating: ★★★

A brilliant, blackly violent expose of the worst kind of American prison life. Writer (later director) Richard Brooks and director Jules Dassin rarely did

B

better work than in this unrelenting portrait of sadistic guards driving their captives to a desperate attempted breakout. Stand-out performances from Burt Lancaster, Hume Cronyn, Howard Duff, Whit Bissell and John Hoyt.

Buccaneer, The ○
1958, US, 121 mins, colour
Dir: Anthony Quinn
Stars: Yul Brynner, Claire Bloom, Charlton Heston, Charles Boyer, Inger Stevens
Rating: ★★★

Cecil B DeMille's last film – he died while it was being made. His long-time associate Henry Wilcoxon took over as producer, and the direction of the film went to actor Anthony Quinn, who made such a good job of this splendid adventure yarn that one wonders why it was the only film he directed. A number of interesting items emerged from the $2 million epic. But the most newsworthy was a humble hairpiece, described as a 'sensitive blend of Bonaparte, Presley and a well-kept Irish setter'. Why was the hair so important? It adorned the most famous bald plate in the world – that of Yul Brynner. Among the cast, Claire Bloom wields a spirited sword as a tough talking pirate girl, and there are sizeable roles for such television stars of today as E G Marshall and Lorne Greene. The battle scenes – DeMille hired 12,000 extras – are immense.

Buchanan Rides Alone ○
1958, US, 78 mins, colour
Dir: Budd Boetticher
Stars: Randolph Scott, Craig Stevens, Jennifer Holden
Rating: ★★

Randolph Scott takes on almost an entire town in this example of director Budd Boetticher's tough, individual and highly rated Westerns of the 1950s. The bad guys department is, as usual, a happy hunting ground for spotters of those familiar figures who never turn up their toes. Here they include stout, menacing Barry Kelley, the angular and shifty L Q Jones and big, blustering Peter Whitney. The settings at times seem a little cramped, but the colour photography is razor sharp and the plot and dialogue need no alibis.

Buck and the Preacher ○
1971, US, 102 mins, colour
Dir: Sidney Poitier

Stars: Sidney Poitier, Harry Belafonte, Ruby Dee
Rating: ★★

Sidney Poitier starred in and directed this lively Western, giving it all the traditional elements of entertainment – shootouts, ambushes, battles with Indians and the like – while at the same time inserting a smattering of accusatory comment on the ill-treatment of Negroes 'whose graves are as unmarked as their place in history'. Poitier the actor seems content to stand back and let the limelight fall on Harry Belafonte's showy performance. The idea of having the Indians come to the rescue of the wagon train besieged by outlaws is a gem.

Buck Privates ⊙
(aka: Rookies)
1941, US, 84 mins, b/w
Dir: Arthur Lubin
Stars: Bud Abbott, Lou Costello, Jane Frazee
Rating: ★★

Although Bud Abbott and Lou Costello were nominally billed third and fourth on the cast list, this army comedy was their first starring vehicle – a reward for doing so well as supporting comedians in the previous year's *One Night in the Tropics*. It's loud, lively and one of their better films, and the fact that they aren't on screen all of the time means that they don't have to strain to pull in the laughs. In the supporting cast are Nat Pendleton, here a dumb sergeant instead of his usual dumb police officer, and Shemp Howard, later to become one of The Three Stooges. Jane Frazee is a breezy heroine, and the Andrews Sisters sing 'Boogie Woogie Bugle Boy from Company B'.

Buck Rogers in the 25th Century ○
1979, US, 89 mins, colour
Dir: Daniel Haller
Stars: Gil Gerard, Erin Gray, Pamela Hensley
Rating: ★★★

Enter the sci-hero with the James Bond sense of humour. This film, originally intended as the pilot for the TV series, but subsequently shown in the cinemas, may be more loony than moony. But at least it's a lot more fun than the po-faced *Battlestar Galactica* films, especially with the deft playing of Gil Gerard at the helm. And he has two sexy leading ladies in Pamela Hensley as the villainous en-

emy princess, and Erin Gray as the earth commander whose icy exterior soon melts under Buck's offbeat charm. Sometimes the film's audacity overreaches itself, as where Buck 'teaches' a 25th-century musician 20th-century music – the lesson is far too peremptory to convince. But mostly its approach (propositioned by the glamorous Erin, Buck confesses that after 500 years in space, he isn't quite ready for that kind of action) comes as a breath of fresh air in the force field. The consequent TV series always seemed as likely a candidate as it proved welcome.

Bud Abbott and Lou Costello in Hollywood ○
1945, US, 80 mins, b/w
Dir: S Sylvan Simon
Stars: Bud Abbott, Lou Costello, Jean Porter
Rating: ★★

One of Abbott and Costello's funniest comedies, with inspired direction from S Sylvan Simon and a riotous rollercoaster ride for the climax. The setting provides MGM with the opportunity for guest appearances by such studio contract players of the time as Lucille Ball, little Jackie 'Butch' Jenkins, Preston Foster and 'Rags' Ragland.

Buddy, Buddy ◐ ⓥ
1981, US, 96 mins, colour
Dir: Billy Wilder
Stars: Jack Lemmon, Walter Matthau, Paula Prentiss, Klaus Kinski
Rating: ★

The saddest episode in Billy Wilder's glittering career, *Buddy, Buddy* shows the full extent of the 20-year decline in the standards of the Austrian-born director and his regular collaborator, writer I A L Diamond, from the dizzy heights of *Sabrina* and *The Apartment* to little more than a mass of crass ideas, poor timing and four-letter words. This is an attempt at a re-run of *The Odd Couple* by teaming Jack Lemmon and Walter Matthau as, respectively, a jilted husband intent on committing suicide and a professional hitman unlucky enough to have an adjoing hotel room. But the material is almost non-existent and it's left to the mugging of the stars to carry the sorry affair.

Buddy Holly Story, The ○ ⓥ
1978, US, 113 mins, colour
Dir: Steve Rash

Stars: Gary Busey, Don Stroud, Charles Martin Smith, Maria Richwine
Rating: ★★★★

More shots in the arm like this were what biopics needed in the 1970s. This really is a remarkable re-creation of a singer whose skill with music placed him in the same category as The Beatles a few years later. The film benefits from the fact that the stars, Gary Busey (as Buddy), Don Stroud and Charlie Martin Smith not only look like Holly and The Crickets, but sound like them, generating all their own excitement on stage. And their performances are very good, too. The story is fluently told and, if one could have wished for more of the romantic ballads that, sung in Holly's highly individual manner, were such a significant part of his output, the whole film is so much better than you might imagine, that this is a minor grumble.

Buffalo Bill ○

1944, US, 90 mins, colour
Dir: William Wellman
Stars: Joel McCrea, Maureen O'Hara
Rating: ★★★

There are some simply tremendous scenes of hundreds of animals on the move in this crowd-pleasing, dust-rousing, spectacularly colourful account of the noted frontier scout and buffalo hunter's life. Factually something of a disgrace, but emotionally right on the mark, the film has one of Joel McCrea's most solid performances in the title role. Director William Wellman, who drives the film along in fine style, wanted to portray the old Westerner in more truthful, critical light, but studio boss Darryl F Zanuck insisted on preserving the myth of a great hero, down to a sentimental, beautifully staged ending. Zanuck was right.

Buffalo Bill and the Indians ◐ ⓥ

1976, US, 118 mins, colour
Dir: Robert Altman
Stars: Paul Newman, Joel Grey, Burt Lancaster
Rating: ★

Robert Altman's elaboration of Arthur Kopit's play *Indians* was given a rough ride by many critics though it's made with the director's customary flourish and oddball humour.

Buffy the Vampire Slayer ◐ ⓥ

1992, US, 86 mins, colour
Dir: Fran Rubel Kuzui
Stars: Kristy Swanson, Donald Sutherland, Rutger Hauer, Luke Perry
Rating: ★★

Somewhere between *Prom Night* and *Dracula* without any real sense of menace, this vampire comedy fails on most counts. Buffy (Kristy Swanson), a high school cheerleader, is the latest in a centuries-old line of nubile vampire-slayers trained by a mystery man (Donald Sutherland) who comes to call. At first, thanks to Sutherland's sober and delicately balanced performance, this works quite well, as Buffy moves from boy-mad airhead to vampire-mad airhead, even if the chunky, busty Swanson is only barely up to the high kicks and seems to get a considerable assist in the stuntwork and gymnastics. The vampires, however, are relentlessly comic, with fancy-dress fangs, never conveying the idea of an endangered heroine. And the film entirely falls apart with the arrival of Rutger Hauer at his worst, as an effete king vampire who says 'Oops!' when staked through the heart. The art of the comedy-chiller, once so neatly captured in early Bob Hope classics, now seems to have fallen by the wayside.

Bug ◐

1975, US, 101 mins, colour
Dir: Jeannot Szwarc
Stars: Bradford Dillman, Joanna Miles, Richard Gilliland, Patty McCormack
Rating: ★★

A nasty and, at least at first, believable horror film in which fire-making insects erupt from cracks in the ground after an earthquake. Even then, things might have been relatively okay, had not potty professor Bradford Dillman (there's always one) decided to meddle in things best left alone. The story developments get less credible later on, but there are some disgustingly good special effects and neat direction of the human stars by Jeannot Szwarc.

Bugles in the Afternoon ○

1952, US, 85 mins, colour
Dir: Roy Rowland
Stars: Ray Milland, Hugh Marlowe, Forrest Tucker, Barton MacLane, Helena Carter
Rating: ★★

Rousing Warner Bros. Western with a central character called Kern Shafter (they don't make up names like that any more) who re-enlists in the Cavalry after being dishonourably discharged. Ray Milland is suitably impassive as the wronged cavalryman, and the encounters between white man and Indian are among the most exciting action scenes ever shot. George Reeves, screen portrayer of Superman, appears as Lt Smith.

Bugs Bunny/Road Runner Movie, The ⊙

1979, US, 92 mins, colour
Dir: Chuck Jones, Phil Monroe
Rating: ★★★

The lunacy's pretty non-stop in this feature-length compilation of animation director Chuck Jones' best Warner cartoons. Bugs battles with Martians (well, er, just one, actually) and Daffy Duck tries to prove he's the Errol Flynn of Duckdom. Meanwhile, Wile E Coyote is still trying to make a meal of the Road Runner using a wild collection of highly unlikely and uniformly unsuccessful traps. Great fun for kids of all ages.

Bugsy ● ⓥ

1991, US, 135 mins, colour
Dir: Barry Levinson
Stars: Warren Beatty, Annette Bening, Harvey Keitel, Ben Kingsley, Elliott Gould, Joe Mantegna
Rating: ★★

Bugsy Siegel was a gangster as dangerous as he was debonair. In Hollywood of the early Forties, he saw himself as a patriot – and maybe a star. He also had a dream: to build a gambling casino in Las Vegas that would create a city. This film attempts to tell the story of that dream, and Bugsy's obsessive relationship with good time girl Virginia Hill. At the same time, it cannot escape the criminal origins of its story; and it lacks the urgency of the best gangster films, despite Warren Beatty's dynamic portrayal of Siegel, a man who could ooze charm and be subject to savage fits of anger in the same hour. Ida Lupino-lookalike Annette Bening does solid work as Virginia, as do Ben Kingsley as Bugsy's partner and an overweight Elliott Gould as a squealer. Long, stylish and sombre, it prowls on towards an end that even those who don't know the history of this true story will see coming a mile off.

B

Bugsy Malone ○ ⓥ
1976, UK, 93 mins, colour
Dir: Alan Parker
Stars: Scott Baio, Jodie Foster, Dexter
Fletcher, Bonnie Langford
Rating: ★★★

The first big-screen impact by Alan
Parker, the British director who has
since confirmed his status as a major
force in Hollywood through the success of films like *Midnight Express*,
Mississippi Burning and *The
Commitments*. It's a gangster movie
pastiche, a world populated by
children masquerading as mobsters and
molls, who 'drive' pedal cars and
where the deadliest weapon to hand is
a gun that fires 'splurge' bullets that
resemble custard pie mix. Future
household names to look for include
Scott Baio (*Happy Days*) as the hero,
Jodie Foster (*The Silence of the Lambs*)
as the speakeasy vamp, Dexter
Fletcher (*Press Gang*) as the aptly
named Baby Face, and Bonnie
Langford (billed as Bonita) as a
would-be child singing star. Foster was
furious when her big number 'My
Name is Tallulah' was dubbed by a
professional singer.

Bulldog Breed, The ○
1960, UK, 97 mins, b/w
Dir: Robert Asher
Stars: Norman Wisdom, Edward
Chapman, Ian Hunter, David Lodge
Rating: ★★

Norman Wisdom joins the navy and is
volunteered for rocket duty as
Britain's first astronaut. Even though
(or perhaps because) he co-wrote the
script himself, this simple sea-going
comedy is not one of the little man's
better efforts by any means, and he
retorts to vigorous mugging and slapstick to keep the film afloat. Still, there
is the odd funny moment and strong
support from a gallery of well-known
names, including Edward Chapman,
Peter Jones, John Le Mesurier,
Sydney Tafler and Liz Fraser.

Bulldog Drummond ○
1929, US, 86 mins, b/w
Dir: F Richard Jones
Stars: Ronald Colman, Joan Bennett,
Lilyan Tashman, Claud Allister
Rating: ★★★

Sapper's famous gentleman adventurer
was featured in silent pictures, but this
was the first talkie about the redoubtable Bulldog Drummond. To
this day, Ronald Colman's account of
the title role (which he repeated five

years later in *Bulldog Drummond Strikes
Back*) is considered by many to be
unsurpassed. Among incidental
pleasures is the comic relief supplied
by Claud Allister, doing his 'Silly
Englishman' act as Algy. And the
role of the heroine received spirited
playing from the 19-year-old Joan
Bennett, whose first great success this
was.

Bulldog Jack ○
(aka: Alias Bulldog Drummond)
1934, UK, 72 mins, b/w
Dir: Walter Forde
Stars: Jack Hulbert, Ralph Richardson,
Fay Wray
Rating: ★★★

Chills and chuckles galore as Jack
Hulbert (aided by the beautiful Fay
Wray of *King Kong* fame) takes the
place of the injured Bulldog
Drummond on the chase after the
Morelle gang of dastardly jewel
thieves. Splendid climax in London's
Underground system.

Bull Durham ● ⓥ
1988, US, 108 mins, colour
Dir: Ron Shelton
Stars: Kevin Costner, Susan Sarandon,
Tim Robbins
Rating: ★★

Susan Sarandon's squirrel eyes and
wild performance steal all the attention
going (even from Kevin Costner and
Tim Robbins) in this exceptionally
foul-mouthed baseball drama, 20 per
cent of which you won't understand,
and a further 20 per cent of which
disappears down a muffled sound
track. Still, the colour photography is
just fine, and there are moments when
the film's attempted bittersweet feel
does come across, as old pro Costner
(looking faintly like Paul Newman in
this one) eventually gets a hot-headed
young pitcher (Robbins) to do as he's
told – and become a major league star.
And then there's always Sarandon as
the film's axis, a baseball-mad local
lady who picks a likely new player to
shack up with every season – until
Costner, who wants her himself, tells
Robbins he'll lose his lucky streak
unless he lays off sex. 'This is the
darndest thing,' wails Sarandon in
consequence. 'The Durham Bulls
can't lose and I can't get laid.' She's a
delight.

Bullet for a Badman ○
1964, US, 80 mins, colour
Dir: R G Springsteen

Stars: Audie Murphy, Darren McGavin,
Ruta Lee
Rating: ★★

One of the last of the long series of
Westerns Audie Murphy made at the
Universal studios. The Eastman
Colour photography by Joseph Biroc
is a cut above the routine and the
supporting cast as strong as ever in
these rousing little films. The players
here include Ruta Lee, George
Tobias, Alan Hale Jr, Skip Homeier,
Edward C Platt and, as Murphy's
principal protagonist, Darren
McGavin, the latter giving a particularly forceful performance.

Bullet for Joey, A ○
1955, US, 85 mins, b/w
Dir: Lewis Allen
Stars: Edward G Robinson, George Raft,
Audrey Totter
Rating: ★★★

A throwback to Hollywood's golden
era, with two great gangster stars in
one film, which is about a to plot to
kidnap a scientist. Such old crime
stalwarts as George Dolenz, Peter Van
Eyck and Kaaren Verne add to the
Forties feel.

Bullets or Ballots ○ ⓥ
1936, US, 81 mins, b/w
Dir: William Keighley
Stars: Edward G Robinson, Humphrey
Bogart, Joan Blondell, Barton MacLane
Rating: ★★★

One of the best of the Warner
Brothers racketeering dramas of the
Thirties, with Edward G Robinson
and Humphrey Bogart snapping and
snarling at each other in a series of
confrontations that end in a memorable shoot-out, vividly staged by
cameraman Hal Mohr and director
William Keighley. Bogart employs
some memorable pieces of dramatic
'business' to show himself to be a
thinking actor, and outshine
fellow-baddie Barton MacLane.

Bullitt ○ ⓥ
1968, US, 106 mins, colour
Dir: Peter Yates
Stars: Steve McQueen, Robert Vaughn,
Jacqueline Bisset, Don Gordon, Robert
Duvall
Rating: ★★★★

Besides being a taut suspense drama in
its own right, *Bullitt* possesses the now
legendary car chase through the
streets and hills of San Francisco that
opened up a whole new box-office
bonanza for producers of crime

thrillers. Philip D'Antoni, who produced *Bullitt*, hit the jackpot again three years later in similar vein with *The French Connection*, which has a classic chase sequence of its own. In the title role Steve McQueen's charismatic, hard-hitting performance established him as the world's number one pin-up, while Jacqueline Bisset's strikingly warm portrayal of his girlfriend made the English girl a top Hollywood star. The third star is the city of San Francisco, never used to greater advantage than here by director Peter Yates and photographer William A Fraker, who later turned director himself. You can almost feel the sunshine and smell the California coast air. As for the plot, suffice to say that it will keep you guessing right up to the end.

Bullseye! ① ⊛
1990, UK, 90 mins, colour
Dir: Michael Winner
Stars: Michael Caine, Roger Moore, Sally Kirkland, Deborah Barrymore
Rating: RB

As a comedy, this doesn't even hit the dartboard. Michael Caine and Roger Moore play unscrupulous scientists and their doubles, two British con men. The resultant chase between the four over a nuclear fusion formula for producing cheap energy is handled heavily by the director – but the chief culprit is the script, something without which Moore in particular can't operate. Some of it is nearly passable, but not quite, and Caine's American accent as the 'bad' double is atrocious. Guest appearances by Jenny Seagrove, John Cleese, Alexandra Pigg and Patsy Kensit, but all to little avail in this numbingly unfunny and occasionally unpalatable experience.

Bullwhip ○
1958, US, 80 mins, colour
Dir: Harmon Jones
Stars: Guy Madison, Rhonda Fleming, James Griffith
Rating: ★★

Hardly as vigorous as the title implies, this is rather a slow romantic Western with Guy Madison ideally cast as the laconic westerner who escapes the hangman by agreeing to an arranged marriage with firebrand (or, at least, she's meant to be) Rhonda Fleming. James Griffith makes a highly original villain with a nice line in humour, but he's given too little to do. Pleasant if uninspired entertainment at a jog-trot.

Bunny Lake Is Missing ○
1965, UK, 107 mins, b/w
Dir: Otto Preminger
Stars: Laurence Olivier, Carol Lynley, Keir Dullea, Noel Coward, Martita Hunt, Finaly Currie
Rating: ★★★

A thriller that really thrills. Bunny Lake is a little American girl alleged to have disappeared on a visit to London. The problem the police, led by a puzzled Laurence Olivier, soon face is: does the child really exist? John and Penelope Mortimer's screenplay is full of pleasing incidentals which happily bring in Finlay Currie as a surgeon at a macabre dolls' hospital, Martita Hunt as an old lady who records children's fantasies, and Noel Coward as a boozy old intellectual with a vast collection of sadistic-looking objets d'art.

Buona Sera, Mrs Campbell ○
1968, US, 113 mins, colour
Dir: Melvin Frank
Stars: Gina Lollobrigida, Phil Silvers, Telly Savalas
Rating: ★★★

Unexpectedly delightful comedy about an Italian housewife (Gina Lollobrigida) whose life of ease at the expense of three Americans, all of whom assume they fathered her wartime child, is threatened by an Air Force reunion. The screenplay by Melvin Frank, Denis Norden and Sheldon Keller is full of funny lines and a good cast includes Lee Grant, Phil Silvers and Janet Margolin.

'burbs, The ① ⊛
1988, US, 103 mins, colour
Dir: Joe Dante
Stars: Tom Hanks, Bruce Dern, Carrie Fisher, Rick Ducommun, Corey Feldman, Henry Gibson
Rating: ★★

A bizarre comedy in which assorted American suburbanites (thus the title) become obsessed with the idea that a family of mad scientists has moved in across the road. From being occupied with nothing more unlawful than neigbour's dogs pooping on their lawns, Ray (Tom Hanks), Art (Rick Ducommun) and all-American ex-Vietnam psycho Mack (Bruce Dern) find themselves drawn to the mysterious old house on the corner, where the Klopeks have moved in. Hanks, seemingly perfectly cast in everything he does, has just the right width of manic streak in this comedy of edges, in which everything is just a

little bit larger (or more eccentric) than it would be in real life. Funny, in its observation of the 'burbs' various foibles, yet at the same time you have the feeling that Dana Olsen's screenplay is saying that this comedy could have been a tragedy had our heroes been wrong about the Klopeks. There are barbs in these 'burbs.

Burning Hills, The ○
1956, US, 94 mins, colour
Dir: Stuart Heisler
Stars: Tab Hunter, Natalie Wood, Skip Homeier
Rating: ★★

A rather naive 'pop' Western about a ruthless cattle baron and a young man trying to avenge his brother's death. It features the then-hot romantic duo Tab Hunter and Natalie Wood as the couple who manage to fall in love in spite of the violence around them. Ray Teal, so often the sheriff in Westerns, gets a meatier role on the other side of the law. He's the cattle baron.

Burnt Offerings ①
1976, US, 115 mins, colour
Dir: Dan Curtis
Stars: Karen Black, Oliver Reed, Bette Davis, Lee Montgomery, Burgess Meredith
Rating: ★★

A predecessor of *The Amityville Horror*, about a house (and a ghost upstairs?) which takes possession of its inhabitants. Director Dan Curtis' skilful direction helps disguise the basic silliness of the affair, and adds effectiveness to some of the shock set-pieces, notably a sequence in a swimming pool. Karen Black is quite good as the possessed wife, especially when she becomes involved in the inevitable *Psycho*-style twist at the end, but the rest of the players – Oliver Reed, Bette Davis and Burgess Meredith in particular – have far too high a time for the film's own good.

Burn, Witch, Burn
See: Night of the Eagle

Bushbaby, The ☉
1968, UK, 100 mins, colour
Dir: John Trent
Stars: Margaret Brooks, Louis Gossett, Donald Houston
Rating: ★★★

An African adventure drama, filmed on location in Tanzania in the lush jungles and in the shadow of the fa-

B

mous Mount Kilimanjaro. Featured in
the cast is Louis Gossett, the formidable black actor who won an
Academy Award in 1982 for his role
as the sergeant in *An Officer and a
Gentleman.*

Business As Usual ●
1987, UK, 90 mins, colour
Dir: Lezli-An Barrett
Stars: Glenda Jackson, John Thaw,
Cathy Tyson, Eamon Boland, Buki
Armstrong
Rating: ★

A film with its heart on its sleeve. Its
heart is notably with right-wing radical causes. And, in exploring themes
raised by its story of sexual harassment
at work it flies the flag for militancy as
a surefire method for achieving justice.
Scenes of police brutality may be gratuitous, but they are certainly not
foreign to the ideals of debutant feminist director Lezli-An Barrett if this is
anything to judge by. But her film is
so far over the top, in spite of caring
performances from Glenda Jackson
and John Thaw, that it soon forfeits
any claim to credibility. Little sense of
building to a climax is achieved here,
as would once have been the case with
a film made by that simplistic,
but so much more skilful crusader
against injustice, Frank Capra.
Barrett's overtly political Mrs Deeds
may conquer her enemies but not, I
fear, the audience.

Busman's Honeymoon ○
(aka: Haunted Honeymoon)
1940, UK, 95 mins, b/w
Dir: Arthur B Woods
Stars: Robert Montgomery, Constance
Cummings, Leslie Banks
Rating: ★★★

MGM described this Lord Peter
Wimsey whodunnit as 'a love story
with detective interruptions'.
Americans Robert Montgomery and
Constance Cummings aroused some
national ire when cast as such an essentially British couple as Lord Peter
and his bride. But they acquitted
themselves well enough, even though
some of their thunder was stolen by a
colourful supporting cast that
includes a glum Robert Newton and
Sir Seymour Hicks as a resourceful
butler.

Bus Stop ○ Ⓥ
1956, US, 96 mins, colour
Dir: Joshua Logan
Stars: Marilyn Monroe, Don Murray,
Arthur O'Connell, Betty Field, Eileen

Heckart, Hope Lange
Rating: ★★★★

Always on the brink of embarrassment, but never quite falling in, this
film-with-a-heart was one of the best
sentimental wallows of its year.
Marilyn Monroe, so awkward in some
scenes, can be infuriatingly just as
brilliant in others. Don Murray is
perfect as the gauche young cowboy
who pursues Monroe's world-weary
singing southern belle during his
one-day trip to the city for the annual
rodeo. Even so, both are out-scored
by Arthur O'Connell as a hoary old
cowpoke on the sidelines.

Buster ● Ⓥ
1988, UK, 102 mins, colour
Dir: David Green
Stars: Phil Collins, Julie Walters, Larry
Lamb, Stephanie Lawrence
Rating: ★★★

A glamorised treatment, in a comedy-drama setting, of the great train
robber Buster Edwards. Phil Collins is
unexpectedly good as Buster, but
Julie Walters as his wife, although she
delivers a lively performance, never
quite escapes her own image. Despite
a few dead patches, the film's content
grips the attention through to its conclusion; the robbery itself is handled
in low-key fashion, and the film
glosses over the less savoury aspects of
the £2-million crime which pitched
Edwards and 14 others into the headlines in 1963. Though the story hasn't
quite enough dramatic structure to
sustain its length, the dialogue is a
constant help. 'Hardly bleedin' Clacton, is it?' mutters Buster's partner
Bruce Reynolds, as he and Edwards
swat at tropical flies in Acapulco. 'If
we was in Clacton,' snarls Buster,
'we'd get some TCP from the chemist's.'

Busting ●
1973, US, 92 mins, colour
Dir: Peter Hyams
Stars: Elliott Gould, Robert Blake
Rating: ★★★★

A fast, tough, funny thriller about two
unconventional cops, personably
played by Robert Blake and Elliott
Gould before they fell from grace with
cinema audiences: this was a last
highpoint for both of them for quite a
while. Director Peter Hyams drives it
along in fine, clean, confident style,
with some tremendous chase
sequences, including a hair-raising
pursuit in a supermarket. Good

hard-nut jokes, strong action, clear-cut
characters and a bleak but
atmospheric city feel: great entertainment value from Hyams in his
first cinema feature.

Butch and Sundance – The Early Days ○
1979, US, 110 mins, colour
Dir: Richard Lester
Stars: William Katt, Tom Berenger, Jeff
Corey, Brian Dennehy
Rating: ★★

Given his success with the Musketeer
films, Richard Lester was perhaps the
obvious director to entrust with this
'prequel' to the famous Oscar-winning
Butch Cassidy and the Sundance Kid.
Once again, Lester's amusingly inventive touches are everywhere,
although his handling of the overall
pace is less sure. Tom Berenger and
William Katt, the two young actors
who play the roles created by Paul
Newman and Robert Redford, do
well enough, with Katt particularly
engaging as Sundance, even looking
at times just like a younger version of
Redford himself. The dialogue lacks
the witty spark of the original but the
action comes in dynamic bursts, with
Brian Dennehy making a fearsome O
C Hanks, forever trying to drill our
heroes full of holes.

Butch Cassidy and The Sundance Kid ○ Ⓥ
1969, US, 112 mins, colour
Dir: George Roy Hill
Stars: Paul Newman, Robert Redford,
Katharine Ross, Strother Martin, Jeff
Corey, Cloris Leachman
Rating: ★★★★

Perhaps the greatest Western of the
Sixties and certainly the most likeable,
with Paul Newman and Robert
Redford at their most charismatic as
the eponymous outlaws. The dialogue
shines with constant wit, the action
spot-on, the photography Conrad
Hall's best-ever. Even the supporting
players are beautifully drawn:
Katharine Ross as Etta, Strother Martin as Percy, Henry Jones as the bike
salesman, Timothy Scott as News
Carver (forever searching for a
mention of himself in the gang's exploits) and a glimpse of the young Sam
Elliott (years later to marry Ms Ross)
as a card player. Academy Awards for
screenplay, cinematography, music
score and the song 'Raindrops Keep
Fallin' on My Head'. And it still looks
good more than twenty years on.

Butcher's Wife, The ◐ ⓥ
1991, US, 107 mins, colour
Dir: Terry Hughes
Stars: Demi Moore, Jeff Daniels, George Dzundza, Mary Steenburgen, Frances McDormand
Rating: ★★★

It's always a vibrant surprise when players you've been watching for years as dramatic talents suddenly blossom forth as singers. Such is the case here with the Oscar-winning Mary Steenburgen who, with a supporting role in this feelgood film, proves herself a blues singer of grace, warmth and talent. She's one of the characters within a few blocks who come under the influence of Marina (Demi Moore), a clairvoyant from a lighthouse, who has moved to the neighbourhood because she felt fated to marry Leo (George Dzundza), a butcher as plump as his loin chops. That's part of a greater destiny for Marina, involving Leo, Dr Tremor (Jeff Daniels), a psychiatrist who feels 'uncomfortable' being called a shrink, his aggressive girlfriend (Margaret Colin), Grace (Frances McDormand), a neurotic clothes-shop assistant, and others whose lives Marina touches and enriches. Steenburgen has the best lines as well as the best songs. 'I'm looking,' she tells McDormand, 'for something dowdy and plain.' It's a romantic fantasy that's never juvenile, and, for her fey and fetching Cassandra of the tenements, Moore might well have been Oscar-nominated had not this nice little film been a flop at the box-office.

But Not For Me ○
1958, US, 105 mins, b/w
Dir: Walter Lang
Stars: Clark Gable, Carroll Baker, Lilli Palmer
Rating: ★★★

This was something of a landmark in comedy films. For the first time, Clark Gable, the uncrowned king of Hollywood, allowed people to poke fun at his age – and got the bird from the bird he fancied. He plays an ageing Broadway wolf who makes a last pass only to find that he's got a better knowledge of plays than of playing around with women. Lilli Palmer is gorgeous, Carroll Baker rather lost.

Buttercup Chain, The ◐
1970, UK, 95 mins, colour
Dir: Robert Ellis Miller
Stars: Hywel Bennett, Leigh Taylor-Young, Jane Asher, Sven-Bertil

Taube
Rating: ★★

The sights, sense, colours and atmosphere of a long, sun-filled summer have rarely been better captured than by the ravishing Technicolor photography of Douglas Slocombe in this sex fantasy about two loving couples. The four young leading players, Hywel Bennett, Jane Asher, Leigh Taylor-Young and Sven-Bertil Taube, all do well, and Clive Revill is also very good as a 'kind and unexpected' millionaire in love with Ms Taylor-Young. The music score, by Richard Rodney Bennett, gives the film an extra-special lift.

Butterfield 8 ◐
1960, US, 108 mins, colour
Dir: Daniel Mann
Stars: Elizabeth Taylor, Laurence Harvey, Eddie Fisher, Dina Merrill
Rating: ★★

Elizabeth Taylor won her first Oscar for her performance as the nymphomaniac Gloria Wandrous in this glossy romantic drama based on John O'Hara's bestselling novel. In its time it was something of a trend-setter as regards its frank, outspoken dialogue, plus just a dash of semi-nudity. Director Daniel Mann gave it plenty of old-style Hollywood sophistication as well. Some saw Liz Taylor's Oscar as a sympathy award for having just missed after being nominated in the previous three years. But her portrayal of the self-destructive Gloria is never less than compulsively watchable.

Butterflies Are Free ◐
1972, US, 104 mins, colour
Dir: Milton Katselas
Stars: Goldie Hawn, Edward Albert, Paul Michael Glaser, Eileen Heckart
Rating: ★★

The delightful Goldie Hawn here plays a free-living girl who guides a restricted young blind man (played by Edward Albert, real-life son of Eddie Albert) to his freedom. Also featured is Paul Michael Glaser, alias David Starsky from *Starsky and Hutch*. Eileen Heckart won an Academy Award (best supporting actress) for her wasp-tongued portrayal of the hero's over-protective mother.

Bye Bye Birdie ○
1963, US, 112 mins, colour
Dir: George Sidney

Stars: Janet Leigh, Dick Van Dyke, Ann-Margret, Maureen Stapleton
Rating: ★★★

This lively musical about a pop idol called up for service in the Army is shamelessly aimed at Elvis Presley and casts some sharp satirical shafts in that direction. Janet Leigh, struggling under the handicap of a black wig, still manages to outshine rival Ann-Margret. But the film is completely stolen by tombstone-toothed Paul Lynde, superbly harassed as the father of the small-town girl on whom the idol has chosen to bestow his last civilian kiss.

By Hook or By Crook
See: I Dood It

By the Light of the Silvery Moon ⊙
1953, US, 101 mins, colour
Dir: David Butler
Stars: Doris Day, Gordon MacRae, Leon Ames, Rosemary De Camp
Rating: ★★★

Doris Day back in tomboy mood, in a sequel to the earlier *On Moonlight Bay*. It looks a bit more dated now than the average Warners/Day musical, but still the small-town atmosphere is nicely built up, and supporting players Leon Ames, Mary Wickes and Rosemary deCamp, all repeating their assignments from the earlier film, are a pleasure to watch. Besides the title number, songs include 'Ain't We Got Fun', 'Be My Little Baby Bumble Bee' and (in the brightest production number) 'King Chanticleer'.

By the Sword ◐ ⓥ
1991, US, 91 mins, colour
Dir: Jeremy Paul Kagan
Stars: Eric Roberts, F Murray Abraham
Rating: ★

Fencing films have not exactly been plentiful and this one shows you why. Errol Flynn and Basil Rathbone may have thrilled us to the core in *The Adventures of Robin Hood*, but there's little excitement to be had in the training of fencers for Olympic glory. And a dire script is no help. 'How,' asks one female student of another, 'do you seriously expect to find a man where guys play with long, pointy objects?' And, having had his advances rejected, a male fencer complains, 'I was just being myself,' to which the girl comes back with the devastating riposte, 'Why don't you

B

try being someone else for a change?' Touché! F Murray Abraham is the old janitor who's an ace from years gone by, but seems to do little cleaning apart from ineffectually flicking a feather duster. Eric Roberts is as ludicrous as ever as the 'salle' maestro haunted by the achievements of his dead father. It's unlikely that you'll be as haunted by this film.

C

Cabaret ◐ ⓥ
1972, US, 128 mins, colour
Dir: Bob Fosse
Stars: Liza Minnelli, Michael York, Joel Grey, Marisa Berenson
Rating: ★★★

The musical sequences are razor-sharp under ex-dancer Bob Fosse's direction in this hugely successful film version of John Kander and Fred Ebb's throat-gripping, adrenalin-charging stage show. While singing and dancing, at least, Liza Minnelli, as Sally Bowles, and Joel Grey as the painted emcee of Berlin's Kit Kat Klub of the Thirties, give the performances of their lives, and it was no surprise when they and Fosse collected three of the film's eight Academy Awards. Dramatically, the film is often unsure of itself, but its dynamic, often devastating songs carry the day.

Cactus ◐
1986, Australia, 96 mins, b/w
Dir: Paul Cox
Stars: Isabelle Huppert, Robert Menzies
Rating: ★★

This romantic drama is a challenging piece of work from Dutch-born Paul Cox, one of Australia's most innovative directors, with French actress Isabelle Huppert giving a typically strong performance as the Frenchwoman escaping a bad marriage and, while staying with friends in Australia, partially blinded in a car accident. Her guilt-ridden friends introduce her to a neighbour, Robert, a shy, spiky individual who has been blind since birth and is a cactus fanatic. The two find friendship and eventually more. Cox mixes real-life footage into his narrative, such as, would you believe, a meeting of an actual cactus society. The many quirky asides and peripheral characters tend to get in the way of the narrative, but there's fine camerawork by Yuri Sokol, and the soundtrack is full of fascinating, eerie noises from the Australian bush. This makes the film reminiscent of Peter Weir's *Picnic at Hanging Rock*, although Cox is a director whose style and preoccupations are more in the Truffaut or Malle mould.

Cactus Flower ○ ⓥ
1969, US, 103 mins, colour
Dir: Gene Saks
Stars: Ingrid Bergman, Walter Matthau, Goldie Hawn, Rick Lenz
Rating: ★★★

Despite the cynicism inevitable in approaching such a romantic story these days, you'll find that this adaptation of a stage success is wise, witty and altogether welcome. Ingrid Bergman is a delight as the staid secretary (blooming rarely, like the cactus) who is at one time unkindly described as 'sort of like a large Band-Aid'. And Goldie Hawn, as her rival for Walter Matthau, won an Oscar in this, only her second film appearance.

Cactus Jack ○
(aka: The Villain)
1979, US, 89 mins, colour
Dir: Hal Needham
Stars: Kirk Douglas, Ann-Margret, Arnold Schwarzenegger
Rating: ★

This comic Western is a sort of live-action equivalent of the cartoon series featuring The Road Runner and his disaster-prone adversary Wile E Coyote. Here it's Kirk Douglas as the inept outlaw of the title whose attempts to stop the hero (Arnold Schwarzenegger) and heroine (Ann-Margret) from getting some vital cash to its destination only rebound on himself. Paul Lynde and Robert Tessier score as two Indians called Anxious Elk and Nervous Beaver, while the director of the farcical mayhem is comedy-action specialist Hal Needham, whose previous films include *Hooper* and *Smokey and the Bandit*. Here one could do without his attempts to 'lift' the comedy with quick-motion sequences when one would have thought editing skills would have sufficed.

Caddyshack ◐ ⓥ
1980, US, 95 mins, colour
Dir: Harold Ramis
Stars: Chevy Chase, Rodney Dangerfield, Bill Murray
Rating: ★★★

This zany, low-brow, knockabout comedy is fast-moving, juvenile and in the worst possible taste. In other words, it's a hoot! Its comic chaos centres on a golf club upon which boorish, tasteless Rodney Dangerfield descends. Ted Knight is the snobbish club captain, Chevy Chase its insincerely modest golf pro and Bill

Murray the groundsman obsessed with ridding the course of gophers. The woefully underused Dangerfield is wonderful as the kind of person right-thinking people run and hide from – the kind you always find yourself sitting next to you on a long air flight. The most humorously disgusting scene is where the club pool is emptied because a floating chocolate bar is assumed to be something quite different!

Cadillac Man ● Ⓥ
1990, US, 98 mins, colour
Dir: Roger Donaldson
Stars: Robin Williams, Tim Robbins, Annabella Sciorra, Pamela Reed, Elaine Stritch, Lori Petty
Rating: ★★★

Would you buy a car from Joey Walsh? Joey (Robin Williams) is banking that you will, especially as he owes $20,000 to gangsters, has promised his ex-wife $500 a month for his daughter's education, has two mistresses (at least) and gets two days to sell 12 cars or lose his job. All of Joey's troubles disappear, though, from the moment a new one crashes right through the window of his showroom in the shape of bemused, enraged Larry (Tim Robbins), wielding a machine-gun and with half a ton of explosives strapped to his bike. Larry is convinced that half the showroom staff has been having his wife (a secretary there) and it's Joey (ironically one of the few who hasn't) who becomes the front-man in a nationwide hostage drama. Although the film is occasionally heavy-handed and sometimes wearing (a lot of people shout at each other a lot of the time), you can forgive it a lot for tieing up its plot threads so neatly at the end after a splendid last reel. Williams oozes fake charm – which is just what the character (and situation) demands.

Caesar and Cleopatra ○ Ⓥ
1945, UK, 138 mins, colour
Dir: Gabriel Pascal
Stars: Vivien Leigh, Claude Rains, Flora Robson, Stewart Granger
Rating: ★★

Stunning Technicolor photography by four of the best in the business – Freddie Young, Jack Cardiff, Robert Krasker and Jack Hildyard – and a moody performance by Flora Robson are the main bonuses to this leisurely, expensive adaption of Shaw's play. Britain's most expensive film at the

time it was made, it failed to persuade cinemagoers to see it, and accounted for a large slice of the Rank Organisation's dismaying loss of £1.7 million on film production for 1945/46. Imposing sets, lavish costumes and stars by the handful failed to disguise the ponderous nature of Gabriel Pascal's direction, although Claude Rains' wonderful, civilised Caesar is pretty well director-proof. Vivien Leigh could have been the perfect Cleopatra had she been induced to produce a livelier performance and the crowd scenes are teeming with embryo stars strumming lutes, carrying spears and the like. You'll be hard-pushed, though, to spot Kay Kendall and Roger Moore among the hundreds of crowd players.

Caged ○
1950, US, 96 mins, b/w
Dir: John Cromwell
Stars: Eleanor Parker, Agnes Moorehead, Jan Sterling
Rating: ★★★

The transformation of a young, essentially innocent girl into a self-assured but embittered woman is depicted with perceptive realism, in this story of a sweet, innocent young girl who is sent to prison for unwittingly being involved in a bank robbery. There, brutal treatment by a sadistic wardress (played by 6ft 2in, 16st Hope Emerson, who was Oscar-nominated) and the evil influence of other inmates, turns her into a hard-boiled brassy woman. Eleanor Parker, devoid of make-up and wearing only an old dress of Shirley Temple's plus prison overalls, was also nominated for an Oscar for her vivid, painful performance as the girl who endures everything from loneliness to having her hair shorn off. A follow-up to *The Snake Pit*, which took a look at life in mental institutions, the film is taken from the real-life experiences of scriptwriter Virginia Kellogg, who had herself been incarcerated in a women's jail in the interests of truth and realism.

Cage of Gold ○
1950, UK, 53 mins, b/w
Dir: Basil Dearden
Stars: Jean Simmons, David Farrar, James Donald
Rating: ★★

This romantic thriller was one of the last films Jean Simmons made in England before going off to Hollywood, and her class shows, in comparison

with the rest of the cast. Good location shots of Paris and a strong whodunnit plot.

Cahill, United States Marshal ● Ⓥ
1973, US, 103 mins, colour
Dir: Andrew V Mclaglen
Stars: John Wayne, George Kennedy, Gary Grimes, Neville Brand
Rating: ★★★

If an award were to be given for the most underrated John Wayne Western of post-war years, there's no doubt that *Cahill* would get the vote. In some ways it is a companion film to the previous year's *The Cowboys*, which also involved Wayne with children. In this case the boys are his character's own two sons (the elder of whom is Gary Grimes, the teenager from *Summer of '42*), two wild minors who become involved in robbery and murder. Wayne has to round up the 'galoots' responsible, to help the boys out of what becomes a very scary scrape, and the results make thundering entertainment. The action is slightly stylised – an unusual departure for the director, Andrew V McLaglen – with George Kennedy in one of his meatiest roles as the villain who might well have stepped straight out of theatrical high melodrama. Joseph Biroc's camerawork is highly skilled, especially since much of the action takes place at night, and never sacrifices clarity in the cause of realism. And you'll love both the thunder and lightning finale and the performances of Neville Brand as Wayne's half-breed friend. Perhaps the action is a shade savage in places, but well in keeping with Wayne's character. Of particular note is the selling line to *Cahill*: 'Break the law and he's the last man you want to see. And the last you ever will.'

Caine Mutiny, The ○ Ⓥ
1954, US, 120 mins, colour
Dir: Edward Dmytryk
Stars: Humphrey Bogart, Jose Ferrer, Van Johnson, Fred MacMurray, Robert Francis, Lee Marvin
Rating: ★★★

You'll end up liking none of the characters in this famous sea story, in which Humphrey Bogart received an Oscar nomination as the unbalanced, ballbearing-clicking Captain Queeg, mutinied against, then finally destroyed in the memorable climactic courtroom scene. Tremendous Technicolor photography by Franz

C

Planer complements Stanley Roberts' bitter, corrosive screenplay which takes its characters apart and pares them down to their rawest emotions. There are worthy contributions from Robert Francis (killed shortly afterwards in an air crash), Fred MacMurray, always at his best when being sneaky, Jose Ferrer, scathing but with a glimpse of compassion as a lawyer, E G Marshall, Lee Marvin and Claude Akins. But it's Bogart you'll remember. The film deserved at least one Oscar (it was nominated for eight), for Planer's flawless colour camerawork, particularly effective in the sequence of storm at sea, and surely superior to the photography in *Three Coins in the Fountain*, which actually picked up the award.

Cairo ○
1963, UK, 91 mins, b/w
Dir: Wolf Rilla
Stars: George Sanders, Richard Johnson, Eric Pohlmann
Rating: ★★

A workmanlike if a trifle mechanical rehash of John Huston's *The Asphalt Jungle*. It's neat and well-characterised, with the role of the mastermind (formerly played by Sam Jaffe) now tailored to measure exactly up to George Sanders' inimitable brand of insolent charm.

Cairo Road ○
1950, UK, 95 mins, b/w
Dir: David Macdonald
Stars: Eric Portman, Laurence Harvey
Rating: ★★★

A grim, documentary-style production which spotlights the efforts of Cairo's police chief (Eric Portman) and his (sometimes too) eager assistant (played with inappropriately poker-faced coolness by Laurence Harvey) in laying traps for drugs traffickers along Egypt's frontiers. Many of the actors who became familiar playing suspicious characters in British films of the Fifties, including Marne Maitland, Harold Lang, Karel Stepanek, Gregoire 'Coco' Aslan and Abraham Sofaer, make early screen appearances. The Middle Eastern feel is well maintained by direction that otherwise keeps to the rudimentary. A perceptive performance by Portman stands head and shoulders above the rest of the cast.

Cal ○ ⓥ
1984, UK, 102 mins, colour
Dir: Pat O'Connor

Stars: Helen Mirren, John Lynch, Donal McCann, John Cavanagh, Ray McAnally
Rating: ★★

Although this well-made British film is ostensibly about the Irish Question, the only question most viewers are likely to find themselves asking is how long it will take mournful, guilt-obsessed John Lynch to get into farm widow Helen Mirren's bed. He drove the car, you see, for the assassin who killed her husband, and thereby hangs the irony. Outside this central issue, the film paints a probably justifiably bleak view of Belfast in the present-day troubles. Alas, it can offer no answer, only at best a cry of anguish in an abrasively-scripted film which remains watchable even if all concerned seem to be having a thoroughly miserable time.

Calamity Jane ○ ⓥ
1953, US, 100 mins, colour
Dir: David Butler
Stars: Doris Day, Howard Keel, Philip Carey
Rating: ★★★★

From the opening shots of Doris Day singing 'Whipcrackaway' on top of the Deadwood stagecoach, this film is pure delight. Calamity Jane sets out to show that anything a man can do, she can do better. Only Wild Bill Hickok, played by Howard Keel, seems unimpressed. It takes a whole string of songs and dances before Jane can convince him that under her tough exterior there is a woman's heart that is his for the asking. Breeze-fresh and full of get-up-and-go, the film contains one of the best original scores ever written for the screen, the hit song from which, 'Secret Love', won an Academy Award.

Calamity Jane and Sam Bass ○
1949, US, 85 mins, colour
Dir: George Sherman
Stars: Yvonne De Carlo, Howard Duff, Lloyd Bridges
Rating: ★★

Yvonne De Carlo was given a chance to break away from her sultry Eastern image with this portrait of the famous frontier wildcat. And she certainly puts plenty of fire into the role. A cast full of Hollywood stalwarts includes Lloyd Bridges, Marc Lawrence, Milburn Stone and, as Jim Murphy, Norman Lloyd, best remembered as the man who fell from the Statue of Liberty at the end of Hitchcock's *Saboteur*.

Calcutta ○
1945, US, 83 mins, b/w
Dir: John Farrow
Stars: Alan Ladd, Gail Russell, William Bendix, June Duprez
Rating: ★★★

Shot in 1945 when its star, Alan Ladd, was still at the peak of his laconic powers, this dark thriller, eventually released in 1947, has a Chandleresque screenplay by Seton I Miller that brims with memorable man–woman exchanges between Ladd and Gail Russell, who's a little too soft for a role that needed a Donna Reed, a Ruth Roman or even a Hedy Lamarr. Reliable support comes from Ladd's oft-time co-star William Bendix (they're hunting the killers of their partner), and the villains are as sneaky as can be. And remember (as Ladd has cause to): 'Man who trust woman walks on duckweed over pond'.

California Conquest ○
1952, US, 79 mins, colour
Dir: Lew Landers
Stars: Cornel Wilde, Teresa Wright, Alfonso Bedoya
Rating: ★★

This Western about Spanish Californians trying to escape the yoke of Mexican rule was made by Lew Landers, one of Hollywood's most prolific directors. Its fast pace can be attributed to Landers' training in the Thirties, when he began with such horror 'quickies' as *The Raven*, subsequently turning out scores of horror, action and adventure films, not one of them over 80 minutes in length. *California Conquest* is, at 79 minutes, his longest film and, like the rest of them, moves along like an express train.

California Dolls, The ◑
(aka: . . . All the Marbles)
1981, US, 115 mins, colour
Dir: Robert Aldrich
Stars: Peter Falk, Vicki Frederick, Laurene Landon, Burt Young, Richard Jaekel
Rating: ★★★

Released in the US as . . . *All the Marbles*, Robert Aldrich's bleakly humorous survival movie transfers Peter Falk from a crumpled mac to a crumbling Cadillac as he ferries his two-girl wrestling team around some of the less attractive venues of America's industrial Mid-West, their goal being the tacky neon glitter of Reno, where the climactic championship is held. *California Dolls* turned out to be Aldrich's last film, and the familiar cynicism is all there: life is a violent arena where your protective layers are ripped to shreds. Peter Falk is on top form as the seedy wheeler-dealer promoter and you don't have to be a wrestling fan to enjoy the film, which is extremely funny at times. The final wrestling bout will have you on the edge of your seat.

California Holiday ○ ⓥ
(aka: Spinout)
1966, US, 93 mins, colour
Dir: Norman Taurog
Stars: Elvis Presley, Shelley Fabares, Deborah Walley
Rating: ★★

Some fizzy songs and a cracking motor race are the highlights of this Elvis Presley musical produced by Joe Pasternak. Dodie Marshall's hip-waving dancer is the best of the quartet of curvy cuties surrounding the star, while such stalwart veterans as Cecil Kellaway, Una Merkel and Carl Betz bring up the rear.

California Man ◑ ⓥ
(aka: Encino Man)
1992, US, 89 mins, colour
Dir: Les Mayfield
Stars: Sean Astin, Brandon Farley, Pauly Shore, Megan Ward, Mariette Hartley, Richard Masur
Rating: ★★

An unexpected summer hit in America in 1992, this Disney romp is just like the kind of novelty teen comedy the studio was making 20 years ago. In fact, substitute Brandon Farley here for Jan-Michael Vincent and this could almost be a re-working of *The World's Greatest Athlete*. Sean Astin plays a chubby teenager, striking out with the girls and victimised by the school bully. While excavating for a swimming pool, he finds a caveman frozen in ice 12 feet below the ground. 'Link' is soon the hit of Astin's school, where he masquerades as an Estonian and helps him win the heart of the school prom queen (Megan Ward). All this is pepped up a bit (but not much) by Pauly Shore's mumblespeak as Astin's zombie-like friend. Old-stagers Mariette Hartley and Richard Masur are hardly in it as Astin's parents, and all the developments are par for the genre. Don't see this expecting anything new or meaningful.

California Split ◑
1974, US, 108 mins, colour
Dir: Robert Altman
Stars: George Segal, Elliott Gould, Ann Prentiss, Gwen Welles
Rating: ★

There are some very funny lines in this Robert Altman film about two compulsive gamblers who will bet on anything. Perhaps one can forgive the fact that the gambling scenes themselves generate little tension, as this was presumably not the director's primary intention. He concentrates more on overlapping dialogue, an improvised air and individual performances. Ann Prentiss and Gwen Welles as a couple of pushy but sympathetic hookers, with whom the boys become involved, are a treat to watch.

California Suite ○ ⓥ
1978, US, 103 mins, colour
Dir: Herbert Ross
Stars: Alan Alda, Michael Caine, Jane Fonda, Maggie Smith, Walter Matthau, Richard Pryor, Bill Cosby
Rating: ★★★

The famous Beverly Hills Hotel in Los Angeles is the setting for this omnibus-type film of several stories. Written by Neil Simon, it is much in the Simon mould with a delicious blend of comedy and touches of straight drama. Among the star cast are Maggie Smith, as a British actress who has been nominated for an Academy Award (she actually won an Oscar for this film!), Michael Caine, as her antiques-dealer husband, Walter Matthau, as a businessman from Philadelphia, Jane Fonda, as a wisecracking divorcee from New York, Alan Alda, as her screenwriter ex-husband, and Bill Cosby and Richard Pryor as two Chicago doctors who are close friends.

Call Harry Crown ◑
(aka: 99⁴⁴/₁₀₀ % Dead)
1974, US, 98 mins, colour
Dir: John Frankenheimer
Stars: Richard Harris, Edmond O'Brien, Ann Turkel, Bradford Dillman, Chuck Connors
Rating: ★★★

A smooth and not too serious thriller about a gang war and the gunman (Richard Harris) who is called in to end it. Ann Turkel and Kathrine Baumann are pretty newcomers with splendidly impressive figures. There are some good shoot-ups for the un-

demanding and a personable villain (Chuck Connors) with a hook hand – and other attachments – to be bested. It moves, it amuses and it entertains. Director John Frankenheimer steers the mayhem along like a well-oiled and happily-tuned motor.

Calling Bulldog Drummond ○
1951, UK, 80 mins, b/w
Dir: Victor Saville
Stars: Walter Pidgeon, Margaret Leighton, Robert Beatty, Peggy Evans, David Tomlinson
Rating: ★★

Sapper's famous fictional detective has been seen in films for over 50 years. Here he's played by Walter Pidgeon, but acting honours go to Margaret Leighton as an attractive and resourceful policewoman. David Tomlinson is ideally cast as Bulldog's sidekick Algy. Silly plot, though.

Call Me ●
1987, US, 96 mins, colour
Dir: Sollace Mitchell
Stars: Patricia Charbonneau, Patti D'Arbanville, Sam Freed, Stephen McHattie, Steve Buscemi, David Strathairn
Rating: ★★

This may be the first movie in which the hero is an obscene phone caller. Anna (Patricia Charbonneau), mistakenly thinking the caller's her boyfriend, goes to a sleazy bar to meet 'him' and witnesses a murder there. As the murderer's a cop, she's not sure what to do, and gradually finds her only solace in the seductive voice on the other end of the line. It's an interesting concept, but the execution of it is only mediocre and the film's enthusiasm for 'dirty talk' rather overwhelms the central story thread. Still, if you pay *Call Me* a visit, you may never view oranges in quite the same light again . . .

Call Me Bwana ⊙
1963, UK, 103 mins, colour
Dir: Gordon Douglas
Stars: Bob Hope, Anita Ekberg, Edie Adams, Lionel Jeffries
Rating: ★★

Gleefully scatty Bob Hope comedy – one of the last reasonably good ones he made – which finds our hero well at home tossing out wisecracks to the natives in the depths of the African jungle. Lionel Jeffries helps to keep it rolling zanily along.

c

Call Me Genius

See: *The Rebel*

Call Me Madam ○

1953, US, 117 mins, colour
Dir: Walter Lang
Stars: Ethel Merman, Donald O'Connor, Vera-Ellen, George Sanders
Rating: ★★★

The best thing about this rather flat Irving Berling musical was that it brought Ethel Merman back to Hollywood for a leading role for the first time since the Thirties. You'll get restless between the musical numbers, but these are almost all outstanding, from the dancing of Vera-Ellen and Donald O'Connor to such songs as 'It's A Lovely Day Today', 'You're Just In Love', 'The Best Thing For You', 'Hostess with the Mostest' and 'International Rag'. It's directed by 20th Century-Fox's king of musicals, Walter Lang, who topped off his musical career with an Oscar nomination for *The King and I*.

Call Northside 777 ○

1947, US, 111 mins, b/w
Dir: Henry Hathaway
Stars: James Stewart, Richard Conte, Lee J Cobb, Helen Walker
Rating: ★★★★

Documentary-style thriller based on the actual case of a reporter who ferreted around until he found out the truth about a 12-year-old murder case. Absorbing every step of the way – thanks to Henry Hathaway's pacy direction of an incident-filled script and another very fine performance from James Stewart – right up to the final agonising attempts to prove the innocence of the man sent down for a murder he didn't commit. Fine cinema.

Camelot ○ ⊙

1967, UK, 178 mins, colour
Dir: Joshua Logan
Stars: Richard Harris, Vanessa Redgrave, Franco Nero, David Hemmings, Lionel Jeffries
Rating: ★★

This famous musical is really a technicians' triumph: the music and lyrics, by Frederick Loewe and Alan Jay Lerner, the photography of Richard Kline, and John Truscott's costume designs are all very pleasing indeed. Of the performances, that of Richard Harris – who also does his own singing – stands out with his forthright and sympathetic King

Arthur. But Vanessa Redgrave, perhaps not beautiful enough from the start, is not a notable success as Guinevere. Incidentally, Richard Burton and Julie Andrews had played the original Broadway stage roles. The score includes 'If Ever I Would leave You', 'C'est Moi' and 'Camelot'.

Campbell's Kingdom ○

1957, UK, 100 mins, colour
Dir: Ralph Thomas
Stars: Dirk Bogarde, Stanley Baker, Michael Craig, Barbara Murray, James Robertson Justice
Rating: ★★★

Creditable British attempt to make a rousing adventure story in the best Hollywood tradition, based on a novel by Hammond Innes. Dirk Bogarde is a forthright hero, but Stanley Baker steals the film by making Morgan a truly villainous figure. The Eastman Colour photography of mountain locations is most attractive, and Ralph Thomas's direction gives the movie plenty of pace and urgency. The film's only weak point is its script, which has more than its share of silly lines. Once it moves into action, however, it's a different picture altogether.

Canadian Pacific ○

1949, US, 95 mins, colour
Dir: Edwin L Marin
Stars: Randolph Scott, Jane Wyatt, Victor Jory, Nancy Olson
Rating: ★★

A tired old Western plot, about bad hats out to stop the building of the railroad, is given a lift by the performances in this action adventure, especially those of Jane Wyatt, as an intrepid frontier doctor, and Nancy Olson, spirited in her screen debut as a tomboy French-Canadian. It's hard to believe that craggy old Randolph Scott could be fancied by both of these feisty young females, but Hollywood Westerns do tend to ignore normal logic. Nicely shot in Cinecolor, partly on location in the Canadian Rockies, although the colour work falls down when it leaves the countryside. A bit on the long side, but that allows room for snarling Victor Jory to properly etch one of his rasping-voiced villains. J Carrol Naish is the (very expendable) comic relief.

Canadians, The ○

1961, US, 85 mins, colour
Dir: Burt Kennedy

Stars: Robert Ryan, John Dehner, Torin Thatcher
Rating: ★★

Movies about those Mounties who always get their man have been few and far between. Here's an exciting manhunt story written and directed by Burt Kennedy, later to become one of America's foremost directors of Westerns. Robert Ryan, incidentally, played a Mountie in his very first film – De Mille's *North West Mounted Police*.

Can Can ○

1960, US, 131 mins, colour
Dir: Walter Lang
Stars: Frank Sinatra, Shirley MacLaine, Maurice Chevalier, Louis Jourdan, Juliet Prowse
Rating: ★

Less Ooo-La-La than Oh! No! No! Just how 20th Century-Fox allowed the hit Broadway musical to transfer to the screen as an unmitigated bore is a tragedy of the modern film musical. It had everything going for it – an all-star cast, fantastic Cole Porter songs, including 'C'est Magnifique', 'Let's Do It' and 'It's All Right With Me', and great dance numbers – but ended up with ponderous direction, dull performances and a tiresome screenplay. Even the dance numbers struck a wrong note, posing the question: just why did the can-can prove so scandalous? Shirley MacLaine's brassy central performance as the cafe owner facing prosecution for allowing the dance to be staged illegally, is one-dimensional, while Maurice Chevalier and Louis Jourdan can do little more than walk through their parts with much the same charm they brought to the earlier *Gigi*. In fact, the only good thing in the production is Juliet Prowse as Claudine, the snake, whose dancing at least has class.

Candleshoe ⊙

1977, UK, 101 mins, colour
Dir: Norman Tokar
Stars: David Niven, Helen Hayes, Jodie Foster, Leo McKern
Rating: ★★★

Disney rarely missed with its British films and this is another winner. Jodie Foster is the tough American 14-year-old whom a crooked detective plans to foist off as the heiress to an English fortune. Naturally, once in England, Jodie's cynical exterior soon breaks down to reveal a heart of pure

Disney, especially when the marchioness (Helen Hayes) proves all but broke and the butler (David Niven) appears in a number of disguises to help keep up appearances. Things develop well from here, with some lovely photography of the English countryside not allowed to interfere with a rattling good pace. The film is splendidly edited, presentably written in faintly *Just William* vein by David Swift and Rosemary Anne Sisson, and has some charming child performers.

Candy ●
1968, US/Italy, 115 mins, colour
Dir: Christian Marquand
Stars: Marlon Brando, Richard Burton, James Coburn, Walter Matthau, Charles Aznavour, Ewa Aulin
Rating: ★

The famous (and famously bad) comedy saga about a nubile nymphet who gives herself to mankind for any amount of charitable reasons. Marlon Brando and Walter Matthau offer amusing evidence that they are good enough to surmount any number of deficiencies in a script.

Candyman ● ● ⓥ
1992, US, 101 mins, colour
Dir: Bernard Rose
Stars: Virginia Madsen, Tony Todd, Xander Berkerley, Kasi Simmons, Vanessa Williams
Rating: ★★★

A good modern horror film, full of guts and gore, but scary enough to make you fight shy of the bathroom cabinet mirror before you go to bed. Virginia Madsen again demonstrates her amazing range in an anguished role far from her sometime glamour image. She's a mature student who opens up a particularly disgusting can of worms when she calls up the vast black phantom known as Candyman who guts his victims, well, from ear to there. British director Bernard Rose ensures there are not too many uncalled-for giggles in the blood-soaked but (by the standards of the genre) logical developments that follow.

Cannonball
See: *Carquake*

Cannonball Run, The ○ ⓥ
1980, US, 95 mins, colour
Dir: Hal Needham
Stars: Burt Reynolds, Dom DeLuise, Farrah Fawcett, Roger Moore, Dean

Martin, Sammy Davis Jr
Rating: ★

An amazingly star-studded cast, Burt Reynolds' then-popularity and a continuing catalogue of chaotic car chases were presumably the ingredients that pulled the American public in, and (in its own country at least) made this embarrassingly witless comedy a huge box-office success. Encouraged by its success, Reynolds made far too many similar smash-em-up-on-the-road romps in the next decade, hastening the decline of his film career.

Cannonball Run II ○
1983, US, 108 mins, colour
Dir: Hal Needham
Stars: Burt Reynolds, Dom DeLuise, Dean Martin, Sammy Davis Jr, Telly Savalas, Shirley MacLaine
Rating: ★★

Even more daft than its less-than-illustrious predecessor, this car chase caper is knee-deep in second-rate stars and some surprising appearances from some first-rate stars (Frank Sinatra, Dean Martin and Sammy Davis Jr for example). Amiable Burt Reynolds has a thoroughly enjoyable time doing his good ole boy act again (as in previous *Cannonball* and *Smokey and the Bandit* movies) as one of the host of ill-assorted drivers who dash at highly-illegal speeds across America. The best thing in the film is Dom DeLuise who, as the schitzophrenic Victor, turns in moments of stress into tubby superhero Captain Chaos! Quite fun if you switch your brain off, but perhaps offensively moronic if you don't!

Cannon for Cordoba ○
1970, US, 104 mins, colour
Dir: Paul Wendkos
Stars: George Peppard, Raf Vallone
Rating: ★★

Also known as *Dragon Master*, this is a pretty average Western, notable only for beautiful on-location filming in Spain. George Peppard is an intelligence captain called upon to quell a marauding band of Mexican outlaws. Look out for the late Pete Duel (of *Alias Smith and Jones* fame). Elmer Bernstein's stirring music adds to the atmosphere.

Can't Buy Me Love ◑
1987, US, 94 mins, colour
Dir: Steve Rash

Stars: Patrick Dempsey, Amanda Peterson, Courtney Gains, Seth Green
Rating: ★★

High school nerd Patrick Dempsey sees a way to buy himself into popularity (with the money he's saved for a telescope) when the obscure object of his desires, cheerleader queen Cindy (Amanda Peterson), desperately needs $1,000 to replace a ruined dress she's 'borrowed' from her mother. He loans her the money in return for her dating him for a month. She's beginning to fall for him at the end of the period, but the poor sap is too blinded by the 'stardom' she's given him to see it. Around about here, the plot isn't too logical. But, although the film is overly simplistic and paints a pretty appalling picture of American girlhood at every turn, the two young leads involve us sufficiently in their lives to make us feel irritated and angry with them when they blow it. As in *The Buddy Holly Story*, director Stever Rash proves that the most moderate material can work quite well provided you can conjure up persuasive and personable performances to hold it together.

Canterbury Tale, A ○ ⓥ
1944, UK, 124 mins, b/w
Dir: Michael Powell
Stars: Eric Portman, Sheila Sim
Rating: ★★

And a bizarre tale this is too, mystical and alienating even by that often brilliant director Michael Powell's standards. A dangerous crank is on the loose in a southern English village in wartime, pouring glue on local girls' hair when they go out at night. Photographer Erwin Hillier contrives to catch the atmosphere of the English countryside in summer in black and white – no mean feat – while there are early career appearances by Dennis Price and Sheila Sim, both to rise to prominence in post-war British cinema. Long and languorous, this strange kettle of fish finally drifts away into its own heat haze.

Canterville Ghost, The ○
1943, US, 96 mins, colour
Dir: Jules Dassin
Stars: Charles Laughton, Margaret O'Brien, Robert Young, William Gargan, Rags Ragland, Peter Lawford
Rating: ★★★

An absolutely charming piece of film whimsy about a tired old ghost who is

C

doomed to roam his ancestral home until one of his descendants performs a deed brave enough to lift the curse of cowardice from his family. With Charles Laughton in top comedy form as the ghost, and the delightfully un-sugary Margaret O'Brien – even making a passing attempt at an English accent! – as the little girl who befriends him, it's a rich piece of escapist entertainment. The director's identity is a surprise, though: it's Jules Dassin, later to make *The Naked City*, *Brute Force*, *Never on Sunday* and *Rififi*.

Can't Help Singing ○
1944, US, 89 mins, colour
Dir: Frank Ryan
Stars: Deanna Durbin, Robert Paige, Akim Tamiroff
Rating: ★★

Three Hollywood foreigners, Akim Tamiroff, Leonid Kinskey and Thomas Gomez, help enliven this Forties' musical, which offers Deanna Durbin out west, and in Technicolor too. The Jerome Kern songs include 'More and More', which was nominated for an Academy Award.

Can't Stop the Music ○
1980, US, 124 mins, colour
Dir: Nancy Walker
Stars: Valerie Perrine, Steve Guttenberg, Bruce Jenner, Tammy Grimes, June Havoc, Jack Weston
Rating: ★★

Curiously old-fashioned youth musical featuring the Village People and their massive hit 'YMCA'. Grisly rehash of the 'let's put on a show' plotline, all high spirited noise, lights, slogans, movement and dazzle. All of the acting, though, has a rather strained air.

Canyon Crossroads ○
1955, US, 83 mins, b/w
Dir: Alfred Werker
Stars: Richard Basehart, Phyllis Kirk, Stephen Elliott
Rating: ★★★

A modern-style Western concerning the quest for uranium, this is as much an adventure thriller as a horse opera. Phyllis Kirk, that slimmest and prettiest of Fifties' heroines, and Richard Basehart both mould characters one cares about.

Canyon Pass ○
(aka: Raton Pass)
1950, US, 84 mins, b/w
Dir: Edwin L Marin

Stars: Dennis Morgan, Patricia Neal, Steve Cochran
Rating: ★★

Oscar-winning actress Patricia Neal enjoys herself hugely as a bad girl in this off-beat Western. The film whips up a fair ration of excitement, even though Warner Bros. didn't rate it highly enough to splash out on Technicolor. But then Miss Neal always seemed at her best in black and white. She only made one colour film between 1948 and 1968, her peak period, and that was *Breakfast at Tiffany's*.

Canyon Passage ○
1946, US, 92 mins, colour
Dir: Jacques Tourneur
Stars: Dana Andrews, Susan Hayward, Brian Donlevy, Lloyd Bridges, Patricia Roc, Andy Devine
Rating: ★★★

A full-blooded Western with some spectacular action and scenery, strikingly shot in colour. There's a pulsating battle against Indians, and a fist-fight between Dana Andrews and Ward Bond that took days to shoot. Hoagy Carmichael, that ubiquitous piano player of the Forties, appears as a top-hatted character aptly named Linnet, chirping one or two tuneful melodies that include the memorable and catchy 'Buttermilk Sky'.

Cape Fear ◑ ⓥ
1962, US, 106 mins, b/w
Dir: J Lee Thompson
Stars: Gregory Peck, Robert Mitchum, Polly Bergan, Martin Balsam, Lori Martin, Telly Savalas
Rating: ★★★

Robert Mitchum can be frighteningly evil when he puts his mind to it and the two best examples are *The Night of the Hunter* and this tense and chilling thriller. He plays Max Cady, a psychopath recently released from prison. He's after the man who put him there, lawyer Sam Bowden (Gregory Peck). Cady terrorises the family in various ways, but is smart enough to keep the law at arm's length. Eventually, Bowden realises he'll have to deal with Cady himself. If you've seen the 1991 Robert De Niro/Nick Nolte version, this is still worth seeing because it's even better. Mitchum is grimly realistic, Peck powerful as the family man backed into a corner and there are excellent supporting performances from Polly Bergan, Martin Balsam and Telly

Savalas in a very early role. Striking black and white photography heightens the sense of menace and J Lee Thompson's direction doesn't allow the tension to slacken for a moment.

Cape Fear ● ⓥ
1991, US, 128 mins, colour
Dir: Martin Scorsese
Stars: Robert De Niro, Nick Nolte, Jessica Lange, Juliette Lewis, Joe Don Baker, Illeana Douglas
Rating: ★★★

Max Cady (Robert De Niro) is a maniac with a mission. And he's harder to kill than The Terminator. Max walks through fire, water and brutal beatings to exact his revenge on the lawyer (Nick Nolte) who suppressed evidence that would have saved him from 14 years in jail – because of the intense brutality of the rape of which Cady was guilty. Now Cady's back, to teach the lawyer and his family 'something about loss'. Like their dog, the lawyer's friend, their maid and the detective they hire. He traps the daughter, menaces the wife. And finally catches up with the whole family on a houseboat in a storm. Even nastier than the 1962 version, but not quite as good.

Capricorn One ○
1978, US, 128 mins, colour
Dir: Peter Hyams
Stars: Elliott Gould, James Brolin, Brenda Vaccaro, Sam Waterston, O J Simpson, Hal Holbrook
Rating: ★★★★

This pounding action drama is completely original, but many of its situations are worked by director Peter Hyams in tried and trusted Hollywood fashion. Elliott Gould stars as the reporter who gets wind of the fact that the first manned mission to Mars may be a giant hoax. James Brolin leads the trio of astronauts who are told that their families' lives depend on their co-operation. You could virtually write the plot developments yourself from then on, but they're shunted along with such verve by Hyams that you won't much care, especially in a nerve-crunching last 20 minutes as Brolin and Gould desperately flee from the baddies, with the help of a telling guest appearance from Telly Savalas as a crop-duster pilot.

Captain America ○ ⓥ
1989, US, 95 mins, colour
Dir: Albert Pyun

Stars: Matt Salinger, Ned Beatty, Scott Paulin
Rating: ★★★

Rising from the dead just when the world really needs a superhero, Captain America returns to save the day in this fast-moving comic-book saga. The *Marvel* comics hero is played with just the right level of humour and two-dimensional gravitas by Matt Salinger. Scott Paulin enjoys himself being irredeemably evil as the villain, The Red Skull, and there's a strong supporting cast that includes Ned Beatty, Ronny Cox, Melinda Dillon and Michael Nouri. It's all pure hokum, of course, but entirely in the spirit of the comics and enormous fun.

Captain Apache ○
1971, US/Spain, 94 mins, colour
Dir: Alexander Singer
Stars: Lee Van Cleef, Carroll Baker, Stuart Whitman
Rating: ★★

A Western made in the Continental style, this stars Lee Van Cleef in the title role of an Indian serving with US Army Intelligence. Captain Apache's assignment is to track down the killer of an Indian Commissioner named Collier, whose dying words were mysterious and enigmatic – 'April morning'. Van Cleef is no stranger to this type of film, since he rose to major fame during the vogue for 'spaghetti Westerns'. Less usually, in this Western, he is heard as a vocalist in a couple of songs. Not too surprisingly, one of these is called 'Captain Apache', the other 'April Morning'.

Captain Blood ○ Ⓥ
1935, US, 119 mins, b/w
Dir: Michael Curtiz
Stars: Errol Flynn, Olivia de Havilland, Basil Rathbone, Lionel Atwill, Guy Kibbee
Rating: ★★★

The film in which Tasmanian-born Errol Flynn, following just a couple of small Hollywood roles, burst upon the world as a new star. (Britain's Robert Donat was unable to accept the part of swashbuckling doctor Peter Blood.) The action scenes are choreographed with a surge and unity of which even Busby Berkeley would have been proud. Stirring stuff.

Captain Boycott ○
1947, UK, 93 mins, b/w
Dir: Frank Launder

Stars: Stewart Granger, Cecil Parker, Alastair Sim, Mervyn Johns
Rating: ★★★

This lusty historical drama has plenty of pace and punch, as well as integrity, in its story of how badly landowners treated their tenant farmers in the Ireland of the 19th century. Stewart Granger revels in his hero's role; and Robert Donat's brief and uncredited guest appearance leaves one gasping for more.

Captain Caution ○
1940, US, 85 mins, b/w
Dir: Richard Wallace
Stars: Victor Mature, Louise Platt, Leo Carrillo, Bruce Cabot
Rating: ★★

The 'hunk' legend about Victor Mature started around this film, which gave the beefcake star his first major leading role as a husky man of action on the seven seas in the early 19th century. His leading lady in this fast-moving period piece is pretty Louise Platt, whose spirited character is in marked contrast to her weepy wife in John Ford's *Stagecoach*. In 1942, however, she married and retired from acting aged just 27.

Captain Clegg
See: Night Creatures

Captain Eddie ○
1945, US, 107 mins, b/w
Dir: Lloyd Bacon
Stars: Fred MacMurray, Lloyd Nolan, Charles Bickford
Rating: ★★

A gently nostalgic look at the life of American air ace Captain Eddie Rickenbacker. The action spans a quarter of a century as Rickenbacker, marooned at sea after being shot down in World War Two, looks back at his life. Fred MacMurray gets sympathetic support from Thomas Mitchell, Charles Bickford and James Gleason, while a young Richard Conte can be seen as one of Rickenbacker's shipmates in distress.

Captain from Castile ○
1947, US, 140 mins, colour
Dir: Henry King
Stars: Tyrone Power, Jean Peters, Cesar Romero, Lee J Cobb, John Sutton
Rating: ★★★

A spectacular adventure film which introduced the fiery Jean Peters to the screen, this slice of 16th century history was among the first of its kind to

be made largely on location. Ostensibly a story of a Spanish adventurer, played by Tyrone Power, it is mainly concerned with Hernan Cortez and his conquest of the Aztec Empire. Lots of duels and battle scenes should please the action fans, and the colour photography by Charles Clarke and Arthur Arling is clarity itself.

Captain Horatio Hornblower RN ○
1951, UK, 117 mins, colour
Dir: Raoul Walsh
Stars: Gregory Peck, Virginia Mayo, Robert Beatty, James Robertson Justice, Stanley Baker
Rating: ★★★

The brightest bits of three C S Forester novels rolled into one omnibus edition of thrills. The awesome battle scenes in this rousing seafaring epic of the Napoleonic Wars were among the most expensive ever shot in Britain. But the dialogue scenes often run aground.

Captain January ☉
1936, US, 75 mins, b/w
Dir: David Butler
Stars: Shirley Temple, Guy Kibbee, Slim Summerville, June Lang
Rating: ★★★

This Shirley Temple film finds the most famous child star looked after by a lighthousekeeper. Authorities, of course, break into their idyll, giving rise to one of Shirley's best remembered lines: 'Cap! Cap! Cap! I don't want to go!' It's not all tears though. Shirley finds time to dance a step or two, and sing 'Early Bird', 'At the Codfish Ball' and 'The Right Somebody to Love'.

Captain Kronos – Vampire Hunter ●
1972, UK, 91 mins, colour
Dir: Brian Clemens
Stars: Horst Janson, Caroline Munro, Ian Hendry
Rating: ★★★

Not at all typical of Hammer's output, this atmospheric fantasy chiller comes from the fertile brain of writer Brian Clemens, who on this occasion sat in the director's chair as well. The camera is at times both narrator and predator, as the hero, a sort of Gothic Superman, stalks or is stalked by his prey. And there are good roles for Horst Janson, as Kronos, John Cater, John Carson, Ian Hendry and the fetching Caroline Munro.

c

Captain Nemo and the Underwater City ⊙

1968, UK, 106 mins, colour
Dir: James Hill
Stars: Robert Ryan, Chuck Connors, Nanette Newman
Rating: ★★

Silly but enjoyable schoolboy adventure with some fine sets inside the submarine *Nautilus* and an exciting undersea battle against a giant squid. Britain's Bill Fraser and Kenneth Connor provide light relief as a pair of not-too-clever gun-runners. Robert Ryan, Chuck Connors, Nanette Newman and Luciana Paluzzi have to grit their teeth, clench their jaws and play it for real.

Captain Pirate ⊙

(aka: Captain Blood, Fugitive)
1952, US, 85 mins, colour
Dir: Ralph Murphy
Stars: Louis Hayward, Patricia Medina, John Sutton, Ted de Corsia
Rating: ★★

Plenty of action and swordplay in the sequel to *The Fortunes of Captain Blood*, with Louis Hayward, one of the best swordsmen Hollywood (well, actually South Africa) ever produced, making the fencing seem easy in the title role. His gossamer touch with a line, and smooth personality, make a lot more of the character than exists in the script. Patricia Medina once agains partners him – as indeed she did in several other films – while Malu Gatica, as a tavern singer, has a pleasing voice and attractive enough personality to make one wonder why she wasn't seen more often in films. The fine Technicolor photography by Charles Lawson Jr helps to make this, despite a scrappy start, a good action package, full of battles of all kinds. Its British title was *Captain Blood, Fugitive*.

Captain Ron ℭ ⓥ

1992, US, 100 mins, colour
Dir: Thom Eberhardt
Stars: Kurt Russell, Martin Short, Mary Kay Place, Benjamin Salisbury, J A Preston
Rating: ★★

A colourful and largely inoffensive Disney romp starring the manic Martin Short as an executive who inherits a yacht, decides to take the family on the trip of a lifetime, then makes the mistake of hiring Captain Ron (Kurt Russell) to skipper the boat. Russell, unexpectedly handed the comic role instead of his co-star, steals every scene with his dime-store impersonation of Robert Newton, as the drunken, one-eyed lecher with dubious nautical skills and no sense of direction. But, while the film cruises for laughs, the outcome is more a series of soggy comic adventures set within a Caribbean travelogue. Like Russell's next film, *Tombstone*, though, this was an unexpected box-office success in the States.

Captains Courageous ○ ⓥ

1937, US, 115 mins, b/w
Dir: Victor Fleming
Stars: Spencer Tracy, Freddie Bartholomew, Melvyn Douglas, Lionel Barrymore, Mickey Rooney
Rating: ★★★

The original, and certainly the best version of Rudyard Kipling's famous story about the spoiled rich kid who learns about the real values of life when he falls (literally) into the hands of a group of earthy Portuguese fishermen. Spencer Tracy claimed the first of what was to be two consecutive Academy Awards as one of the fishermen, and Freddie Bartholomew is the boy. A heart-breaking ending ensures there won't be too many dry eyes in your sitting-rooms.

Captain Sinbad ○

1963, US/West Germany, 80 mins, colour
Dir: Byron Haskin
Stars: Guy Williams, Heidi Bruhl, Pedro Armendariz
Rating: ★★★

American director Byron Haskin, who made *The War of the Worlds*, shot this spellbinding film in Bavaria with a largely British cast. It has a cyclone, a tidal wave, a wizard with a pet ocelot, a superb nine-headed monster – and even dancing girls. The Technicolor photography is jewel-bright and the only sad note is that the great Mexican actor Pedro Armendariz died shortly after completing his role as the villain.

Captains of the Clouds ○

1942, US, 125 mins, colour
Dir: Michael Curtiz
Stars: James Cagney, Dennis Morgan, Alan Hale, Brenda Marshall
Rating: ★★

An at-times inspiring story of the Royal Canadian Air Force, full of fascinating technical detail, and with James Cagney, fresh from his Oscar for *Yankee Doodle Dandy*. Cagney is in fine form as the irresponsible 'bush pilot' who steals his best friend's girl but, in true Hollywood fashion, shows his true worth when lives are in danger. All a bit melodramatic, perhaps, for today's tastes, but the director (the formidable Michael Curtiz) creates some good action scenes, and there's richly rounded support from Alan Hale, George Tobias and Reginald Gardiner. It's all topped off with the vividly attractive Technicolor which typified the period.

Captain's Paradise, The ○ ⓥ

1953, UK, 89 mins, b/w
Dir: Anthony Kimmins
Stars: Alec Guinness, Yvonne De Carlo, Celia Johnson
Rating: ★★★

Very popular comedy from the Fifties with a gentle touch of Ealing about it (although it was made by Alexander Korda's London Films) and a witty script co-written by actor-author Nicholas Phipps, who also penned himself a part in the fun and frolics. He provides a very seaworthy vehicle for Alec Guinness, as a steamer captain with a wife on either side of the Mediterranean. In North Africa, there's exotic dancer Yvonne De Carlo, who yearns to be a conventional housewife; in Gibraltar, prim Celia Johnson secretly wants to kick over the traces. Captain Guinness, steaming contentedly back and forth between the two, gets his comeuppance in the end, of course, but not before you've had a chance to enjoy the cruise.

Captain's Table, The ○

1958, UK, 89 mins, colour
Dir: Jack Lee
Stars: John Gregson, Peggy Cummins, Donald Sinden, Reginald Beckwith, Nadia Gray
Rating: ★★★

Jack Lee is such a recognised director of rugged action (*A Town Like Alice*, *Robbery Under Arms*) that it comes as a surprise to find him at the helm of this pleasant little comedy about a skipper who steps from a grimy steamer to the bridge of a luxury liner. John Whiting, Bryan Forbes and Nicholas Phipps (who also takes a cameo role) wrote the script from a book by Richard Gordon, author of the *Doctor* books.

Captive City, The ○
1952, US, 91 mins, b/w
Dir: Robert Wise
Stars: John Forsythe, Joan Camden, Harold J Kennedy
Rating: ★★★

John Forsythe, later trapped in the profitable mediocrity of *Dynasty*, had his first major role in this taut, torn-from-the-headlines thriller, and gave a strong and convincing performance as the crusading newspaper editor fighting small-town corruption. At least two contemporary critics compared him to Henry Fonda. Director Robert Wise (who made the film for the production company Aspen he founded with fellow director Mark Robson) maintains excellent suspense and employs the deep focus camera of his cinematographer, Lee Garmes, to considerable dramatic effect.

Captive Heart, The ○
1946, UK, 108 mins, b/w
Dir: Basil Dearden
Stars: Michael Redgrave, Rachel Kempson, Mervyn Johns, Jack Warner, Basil Radford, Gordon Jackson
Rating: ★★★

A moving drama about a group of PoW's, their life in captivity and the lives of their loved ones back home. The settings cannot be faulted: all the camp scenes were shot at Marlag Milag Nord, in Germany, only six weeks after it was liberated from the Nazis. Nor does the script lack realism. One of the co-writers, Guy Morgan, was a Marlag inmate. Michael Redgrave plays a Czech officer who has assumed a dead Briton's identity to escape the Nazis. And Jimmy Hanley is excellent, among a battery of familiar British actors, as Private Matthews, a cockney wide boy who keeps up his friends' spirits with his stories of girls he has known.

Car, The ●
1976, US, 98 mins, colour
Dir: Elliot Silverstein
Stars: James Brolin, Kathleen Lloyd, John Marley
Rating: ★★

A combination of *Duel*, *Jaws* and *The Exorcist* as a demon car goes on the rampage. The theme was originally surveyed more tightly in a *Twilight Zone* episode and later reprised with some impact by director John Carpenter with Stephen King's *Christine*.

Caravaggio ● Ⓥ
1986, UK, 97 mins, colour
Dir: Derek Jarman
Stars: Nigel Terry, Sean Bean, Tilda Swinton
Rating: ★★★

Considering that one might describe maverick filmmaker Derek Jarman and the Italian artist Michelangelo Caravaggio as blood-brothers almost 400 years apart, it always seemed that Jarman was the ideal director to film the painter's tortured life story. As Caravaggio painted portraits of young men with his brushes, so Jarman does with his camera – skilfully aided by the colourwork of cinematographer Gabriel Beristain. Of the merits of the film's anachronistic content, one is less sure, but there are measured portrayals in the required vein by Nigel Terry, Sean Bean and Tilda Swinton.

Caravan ○
1946, UK, 122 mins, b/w
Dir: Arthur Crabtree
Stars: Stewart Granger, Anne Crawford, Jean Kent
Rating: ★★

Those who like romantic novels will probably enjoy this period drama with Stewart Granger. Here is in his customary handsome hero guise, with Dennis Price as the dastardly villain and – a surprising bit of casting – Robert Helpmann, at the time best known as a dancer, playing a gentleman's gentleman. Granger loves a beauty called Oriana, but after an abortive attempt on his life engineered by his rival, he loses his memory and marries a gypsy girl who has nursed him back to health. Florid escapism from Gainsborough which kept people's spirits up amid the austerities of post-war Britain.

Caravans ○
1978, US, 123 mins, colour
Dir: James Fargo
Stars: Anthony Quinn, Michael Sarrazin, Jennifer O'Neill, Christopher Lee, Joseph Cotten
Rating: ★★★

An unusual adventure story, set in the Middle East in 1948 and concerning an American emissary (Michael Sarrazin) sent to find a senator's daughter (Jennifer O'Neill). After unsuccessfully marrying a native army officer, she has joined a nomadic caravan travelling across the desert. Douglas Slocombe's photography and Mike Batt's distinctive music are the

real stars of this film, which also features Anthony Quinn as a kind of Zorba the Sheik. Apart from varying blue and grey skies over a desert ghost town, in fact, Slocombe's glowing colour work is well up to his usual high standards. The size of the drama is not sufficient to make this a great film but it remains in many ways an exhilarating, fascinating experience.

Caravan to Vaccares ○
1974, UK/France, 98 mins, colour
Dir: Geoffrey Reeve
Stars: Charlotte Rampling, David Birney, Michael Lonsdale, Michael Bryant
Rating: ★★

Alistair MacLean adventure romp which leans heavily on its action, the colour of its (Spanish) settings and the ultra-cool performances of David Birney and Charlotte Rampling. Geoffrey Reeve's direction is mechanically efficient.

Carbine Williams ○
1952, US, 91 mins, b/w
Dir: Richard Thorpe
Stars: James Stewart, Jean Hagen, Wendell Corey
Rating: ★★

By British standards American jails seem to be extraordinarily tough. Yet, paradoxically, prisoners in the US are occasionally afforded facilities they would never get over here. An example of this is the case of Robert Stroud, the *Bird Man of Alcatraz*. He was allowed all the books and equipment he needed to become an expert on birds while he was serving a life sentence. And here is the case of David Marshall Williams who, while serving 30 years for manslaughter, was allowed to make a revolutionary type of gun. His story is authentic in almost every detail, for the real-life Williams worked on the film as a technical adviser. Playing the film Williams, James Stewart gives a predictably sturdy, sincere performance.

Carbon Copy ◑
1981, US, 90 mins, colour
Dir: Michael Schultz
Stars: George Segal, Susan Saint James, Jack Warden, Denzel Washington
Rating: ★★

Although this comedy about a white businessman who finds he has a black son is embarrassing at times, there are moments when it is unexpectedly and uncommonly funny. For this, we can thank not just the shafts of wit in

c

Stanley Shapiro's violently variable script, but especially the star, George Segal. He reacts with superb timing and an immense range of facial grimaces as the hen-pecked, boss-pecked executive whose offspring (a young Denzel Washington) descends on him from the 20-year past.

Card, The ○
(aka: The Promoter)
1952, UK, 91 mins, b/w
Dir: Ronald Neame
Stars: Alec Guinness, Petula Clark, Glynis Johns, Valerie Hobson
Rating: ★★★

Made at a time when Alec Guinness could do no wrong in the British cinema, this is a cleverly commercial adaption of Arnold (*Clayhanger*) Bennett's Potteries novel about a poor-born opportunist who becomes mayor of his local town. Many fine little individual scenes build up to make an enchanting whole. Guinness has never been better, and Glynis Johns, Valerie Hobson and Petula Clark are finely contrasted as the ladies in his life.

Cardboard Cavalier ○
1948, UK, 95 mins, b/w
Dir: Walter Forde
Stars: Sid Field, Margaret Lockwood
Rating: ★★

This British farce, set in the days of Cavaliers and Roundheads, was popular comedian Sid Field's third and last film. Two years later he died at the age of 46. Margaret Lockwood enjoys herself as Nell Gwynne, and Field's trusty sidekick Jerry Desmonde is on hand to play Col Lovelace to Field's barrow-boy hero, who rejoices in the name of Sidcup Buttermeadow (get it?). Pretty mild fun, but better than Field's other two stabs at screen stardom.

Cardinal Richelieu ○
1935, US, 83 mins, b/w
Dir: Rowland V Lee
Stars: George Arliss, Maureen O'Sullivan, Edward Arnold, Cesar Romero
Rating: ★★

Briskly-paced account of Cardinal Richelieu's intrigues at the court of King Louis XIII. George Arliss dominates the film in the title role, bringing out different shades of the Cardinal's character with considerable skill. Photographer J Peverall Marley

and director Rowland V Lee combine to give the film a lavish and authentic period facade.

Care Bears Movie, The ☉
1985, US, 75 mins, colour
Dir: Arna Selznick
Rating: ★

Candy floss philosophy and pretty pastel colours dominate this cartoon adventure with the animated soft-toy teddies. Harry Dean Stanton and Mickey Rooney are among those lending their voices to a story designed for a very young audience.

Career ○
1959, US, 105 mins, b/w
Dir: Joseph Anthony
Stars: Dean Martin, Anthony Franciosa, Shirley MacLaine, Carolyn Jones
Rating: ★★★

A sombre, bitter account of a young actor's fight to reach the top, and of a cynical producer who tramples over everyone in sight. The well-constructed script is by James Lee, who wrote the original play. The best performance comes from the sharp-faced Carolyn Jones as a talent agent who's all brightness on the outside, and shrieking loneliness within.

Carefree ○
1938, US, 85 mins, b/w
Dir: Mark Sandrich
Stars: Fred Astaire, Ginger Rogers, Ralph bellamy, Luella Gear, Jack Carson, Hattie McDaniel
Rating: ★★★

The shortest and perhaps least popular of the ten Fred Astaire-Ginger Rogers musicals, this was an attempt to combine a Howard Hawks-type wacky comedy with music and dancing. But it failed to ignite the box office and the duo slipped out of the list of ten top box office draws – a list they had topped just two years earlier. It was Astaire's idea to play a psychiatrist ('shrinks' were as popular then in Hollywood as now) but RKO was experiencing severe financial difficulties so the film has a penny-pinching look. Ginger was badly photographed and the public felt cheated by the lack of big budget spectacular numbers. The highlight is when they dance 'The Yam'.

Cargo of Innocents ○
(aka: Stand by for Action!)
1943, US, 109 mins, b/w
Dir: Robert Z Leonard

Stars: Robert Taylor, Charles Laughton, Brian Donlevy, Walter Brennan
Rating: ★★

Salty, dramatic American World War Two action drama, set almost entirely aboard an old, but still combat-worthy warship. The story is a bit of a paradox: a rather crass war yarn containing a few well-filmed battle sequences. The object, apparently, is to show that the wartime US Navy was composed of spoilt playboys, as portrayed by Robert Taylor, as well as tough, hard-working commanders of the type played by Brian Donlevy. Taylor and Donlevy are at daggers drawn until their ship picks up a lifeboat packed with women and babies and becomes a floating nursery-cum-maternity unit. Watching over all this with a fiery but friendly eye is a senior officer played by Charles Laughton. There's some good below-decks humour, but too many lulls between the action.

Cargo to Capetown ○
1951, US, 80 mins, b/w
Dir: Earl McEvoy
Stars: Broderick Crawford, John Ireland, Ellen Drew, Edgar Buchanan, Ted de Corsia
Rating: ★★

This tough thriller about trouble aboard an oil tanker was the follow-up for its two stars, John Ireland and Broderick Crawford, to their Oscar-winning success *All the King's Men*. In *Cargo to Capetown*, he again gets the chance to pull out all the acting stops as a rugged engineer. The action, rough and raw, compares in ferocity with some of today's western films. Highlights include a hurricane at sea, and a tremendous fist-fight between the two principals.

Carlito's Way ● ⓥ
1993, US, 145 mins, colour
Dir: Brian De Palma
Stars: Al Pacino, Sean Penn, Penelope Ann Miller, Viggo Mortensen, John Leguizamo
Rating: ★★

Stars Al Pacino and director Brian De Palma are on numbingly familiar ground here with this real grind of a movie about a legendary gangster determined to go straight after being released from a long stretch in prison. The odds are well against him, of course, just as the odds are long against our finding any originality in such a theme. The results are predictably violent and depressing but what saves the film is its acting: Pacino, surely more deserving of an Oscar here than for his overrated performance in *Scent of a Woman*, is quite riveting as this doomed and tormented man. But even so he is matched by an almost unrecognisable Sean Penn as a slimy, frizzy-haired Jewish lawyer mesmerised by the criminal world. More and more, Penn's decision to concentrate on direction at this stage of his career was looking a regrettable one for cinemagoers.

Carlton-Browne of the F.O. ○ Ⓥ
(aka: Man in a Cocked Hat)
1958, UK, 88 mins, b/w
Dir: Roy Boulting
Stars: Terry-Thomas, Peter Sellers, Luciana Paluzzi, Thorely Walters, Ian Bannen
Rating: ★★★

Sometimes explosively funny Boulting Brothers satire on the diplomatic service, with Peter Sellers scoring as the oily prime-minister of an unnamed eastern Mediterranean country, and Terry-Thomas ideally cast as the hapless diplomat who achieves a 'brilliant series of disasters'. Co-directed by the lesser-known Jeffrey Dell, who had worked with the Boultings on many of their biggest successes, as far back as *Thunder Rock*, in 1942.

Carmen Jones ○
1954, US, 105 mins, colour
Dir: Otto Preminger
Stars: Dorothy Dandridge, Harry Belafonte, Olga James
Rating: ★★★

Full of ringing tunes and emotive power, *Carmen Jones* was a triumphant filming by Otto Preminger of Oscar Hammerstein's all-black Broadway adaption of Bizet's *Carmen*. It seems a shame that Dorothy Dandridge and Harry Belafonte, both reputable singers, were not allowed to use their own voices, but their performances are right on the ball and the songs are excitingly staged – particularly 'That's Love' (originally 'Habanera') and 'Stand Up and Fight Until You Hear the Bell' (from the 'Toreador's Song'). The dynamic Pearl Bailey as Frankie enjoys her finest film hour.

Carnal Knowledge ◑ Ⓥ
1971, US, 96 mins, colour
Dir: Mike Nichols

Stars: Jack Nicholson, Candice Bergen, Art Garfunkel, Ann-Margret, Cynthia O'Neal, Rita Moreno
Rating: ★★★

The cynical undertones director Mike Nichols hinted at in *The Graduate* are fully matured in this thought-provoking study of the developing sexual attitudes of two men, from their student days to middle-age, celebrated at the time of its release for its sexual frankness in language and gesture. A fine performance, as you would expect, from Jack Nicholson as the maverick, uncaring bachelor; less expected at the time was the warmth and emotion projected by Ann-Margret, hitherto just a sexy musical-comedy star, as the girl whose voluptuous sexuality brings her only despair. She was deservedly nominated for an Academy Award as best supporting actress and was unlucky to lose to one of the best-ever performances in that category – Cloris Leachman's in *The Last Picture Show*.

Carnival ○
1946, UK, 93 mins, b/w
Dir: Stanley Haynes
Stars: Sally Gray, Michael Wilding, Bernard Miles, Stanley Holloway, Jean Kent
Rating: ★★

Heavily tragic melodrama based on Compton Mackenzie's famous novel. Sally Gray, one of the loveliest and most durable British actresses through the Thirties and Forties, plays the ballet dancer heroine, in the late 19th century, who treads the steady downhill slope after her lover deserts her. The prolific Eric Maschwitz adapted Mackenzie's book and the result raised a good few tears in its time. The supporting cast includes those two formidable doyennes of the English cinema, Nancy Price and Catherine Lacey, as well as several up-and-coming young actresses, including Jean Kent, Brenda Bruce and Hazel Court. The evocative photography is by Guy Green, a young British cinematographer who in the same year won an Academy Award for his work on *Great Expectations*, and later became the much-praised director of such films as *Sea of Sand*, *The Angry Silence* and *A Patch of Blue*. This film, however, has few patches of blue: it's dull and dismal.

Carnival Story ○
1954, US, 90 mins, colour
Dir: Kurt Neumann

Stars: Anne Baxter, Steve Cochran, Lyle Bettger, George Nader
Rating: ★★★

Lurid tale of circus chicanery chiefly notable for offering a rare sympathetic role to that excellent movie villain Lyle Bettger. He's very good and so is Anne Baxter as the fellow high-wire star he marries. Their efforts, and those of Steve Cochran as an oily carnival barker, make this a colourful melodrama with a tang of realism. And the love scenes are handled with rare feeling and conviction for a Hollywood film of the early Fifties. The melodrama that accompanies them sometimes becomes as taut as a highwire braced to the point of snapping, with the innate danger of the character's occupations adding a tingle to the emotional suspense.

Carousel ○ Ⓥ
1956, US, 123 mins, colour
Dir: Henry King
Stars: Gordon MacRae, Shirley Jones, Cameron Mitchell, Gene Lockhart
Rating: ★★★

Full of warmth and colour, and some of the most lilting music Oscar Hammerstein ever wrote, this is an almost totally successful version of the stage smash. Gordon MacRae and Shirley Jones, the sweethearts from *Oklahoma!* are fortuitously re-teamed as Billy Bigelow, the irresponsible fairground barker, and Julie Jordan. Frank Sinatra had been cast as Billy, but he dropped out when he found he had to shoot all the scenes twice, once in widescreen and once in normal ratio. MacRae was rushed into the role and produced the performance of a lifetime. So did Barbara Ruick, as the girl who falls for fisherman Mr Snow, and Cameron Mitchell is also excellent as the rascally Jigger. Both Ruick and Mitchell sing remarkably well, and indeed one of the bonuses of this particular musical is that all of the players do their own singing. And what songs! Look almost anywhere in this score and you'll find a hit: 'If I Loved You', 'My Boy Bill', 'June is Busting Out All Over', 'A Real Nice Clambake', 'When I Marry Mr Snow', 'When the Children Are Asleep', 'What's the Use of Wondrin' and, even though it's now been annexed by Merseyside football crowds, 'You'll Never Walk Alone'. Sinatra made a big hit record of that later on, perhaps regretting that he could have been terrific in the part.

C

Carpetbaggers, The ○
1964, US, 150 mins, colour
Dir: Edward Dmytryk
Stars: George Peppard, Alan Ladd, Bob Cummings, Martha Hyer, Carroll Baker
Rating: ★★★

One of the earliest adaptations of a Harold Robbins novel for the big screen. Despite patches of silly dialogue and sub-standard technical qualities, the film makes good entertainment through the sheer weight of its production, by the expanse of its subject – Hollywood between the two world wars – the magnitude of its story, and its insight into those roaring free-for-all days when everything and everybody was there for the taking. It's one of those films where the (anti) hero's hair gets greyer as the story progresses, but his stony expression never changes. Carroll Baker is truly awful as the glamorous star drinking her way to oblivion, but Alan Ladd is impressive in his last film, and Bob Cummings even better, giving the performance of the film as a glib, slimy ten-per-center.

Carquake ○
(aka: Cannonball)
1976, US, 93 mins, colour
Dir: Paul Bartel
Stars: David Carradine, Bill McKinney, Veronica Hamel
Rating: ★★

A film for action fans about the ultimate car race across America. There are no rules and all the contestants are out to win the $100,000 prize at any cost – including life itself. From the moment the drivers rev their engines, the action is practically relentless: skids, swerves, smashes and crashes. Famous film director Roger Corman has a small role as the District Attorney, and an even stranger piece of casting has *Hill Street Blues* favourite Veronica Hamel as a voracious contestant.

Carrie ○
1952, US, 120 mins, b/w
Dir: William Wyler
Stars: Laurence Olivier, Jennifer Jones, Miriam Hopkins, Edie Albert, Basil Ruysdael, Ray Teal
Rating: ★★★

Based on a famous first novel by Theodore Dreiser which was banned at the beginning of the century for being too daring, this is the tragic story of a young girl corrupted by big city life. Reminiscent of *The Blue Angel*, it is given remarkable depth and poignancy by the acting of Jennifer Jones, as the girl, Miriam Hopkins and, in particular, Laurence Olivier. Director William Wyler's streets of Chicago at the turn of the century are teeming with life. And he also captures the atmosphere of the intangible moral code that hovers over, and dominates, the entire film. Olivier's once-prosperous restaurant manager, willing to go to any lengths for the young girl he loves although he is already married, is a pitiable creature portrayed with restraint and understanding. It's as fine a performance as he ever contributed to the cinema, and ensures that the final scenes are deeply moving. If tragedy can still be good entertainment without being Shakespeare, then this was the film that proved it so. A remarkably adult work to come from the American cinema at the time.

Carrie ● ⓥ
1976, US, 94 mins, colour
Dir: Brian De Palma
Stars: Sissy Spacek, Piper Laurie, John Travolta, Amy Irving, William Katt, Nancy Allen
Rating: ★★

Thunderously overwrought piece of Grand Guignol horror from the modern master of bloodstained mayhem, Brian De Palma. It stars sensitive actress Sissy Spacek who gives an anguished performance as the high-school girl whose sheltered upbringing (by a religious fanatic mother) has in no way prepared her to deal with the supernormal gift of telekinesis. Piper Laurie was nominated for an Academy Award for her performance as the mother, and John Travolta is also in there somewhere among the guts and gore. If you succeed in surviving the ensuing blood-feast, be prepared for the ending, which is one of the great shocks of the cinema.

Carrington VC ○
(aka: Court Martial)
1954, UK, 106 mins, b/w
Dir: Anthony Asquith
Stars: David Niven, Margaret Leighton, Allan Cuthbertson, Laurence Naismith, Clive Morton, Noelle Middleton
Rating: ★★★

David Niven gives a fine central performance as a highly decorated army officer wrongly brought up on three court-martial charges in an absorbing drama which transferred successfully from stage to celluloid. Allan Cuthbertson is effective as the jealous superior officer who trumps up the charges and Margaret Leighton is shrewish as the wife who stabs Carrington, metaphorically, in the back. The courtroom scenes are tense and filled with sharp, terse dialogue. Director Anthony Asquith extracts top performances from the cast and creates a powerful drama from Carrington's crisis.

Carry On Abroad ○ ⓥ
1972, UK, 89 mins, colour
Dir: Gerald Thomas
Stars: Sidney James, Kenneth Williams, Charles Hawtrey, Joan Sims, Kenneth Connor, Bernard Bresslaw
Rating: ★★

One of the strongest casts ever put together for a Seventies Carry On comedy – it includes Sidney James, Kenneth Williams, Charles Hawtrey, Joan Sims, Kenneth Connor, Bernard Bresslaw, Barbara Windsor and Hattie Jacques – sallies forth to the island of Elsbels for a week of fun, games and double-entendres. There are some amusing jibes at the expense of catchpenny Mediterranean hotels.

Carry On Admiral ○ ⓥ
(aka: The Ship Was Loaded)
1957, UK, 82 mins, b/w
Dir: Val Guest
Stars: David Tomlinson, Peggy Cummins, Ronald Shiner, Joan Sims
Rating: ★★

Not, in fact, one of the *Carry On* series (it just preceded the first of them) but in the more restrained vein of farce to which fans of David Tomlinson had become accustomed in the Fifties. Much of the hilarity in this navy lark stems from the performance of A E Matthews, then 87, as a muddled old admiral.

Carry On Again Doctor ○ ⓥ
1969, UK, 88 mins, colour
Dir: Gerald Thomas
Stars: Kenneth Williams, Sidney James, Barbara Windsor, Charles Hawtrey, Joan Sims, Jim Dale
Rating: ★★

Subtitled *The Bowels Are Ringing*, this medicinal mayhem offers Sid James as a Pacific island hospital orderly with a harem of wives. Despite the fact that they have not been among the best in the series, the hospital farces proved the most popular of the *Carry Ons*.

Carry On Behind ○ ⓥ
1975, UK, 90 mins, colour
Dir: Gerald Thomas
Stars: Elke Sommer, Kenneth Williams, Joan Sims, Kenneth Connor
Rating: ★★

The team had already done *Carry on Camping*, so this later romp, set on a caravan site, has as good a title as any. And guest star Elke Sommer's archaeological Ninotchka is a real and unexpected bonus. 'Vot is called de place,' she asks Kenneth Williams (as the stuffy Professor Crump) 'vere Roman soldiers are vor drinking and vor women and . . .' 'The NAAFI?,' suggests Williams hopefully. And her delightfully fractured English even manages to make such old lines as 'Iz bleeding terrible' sound funny.

Carry On Cabby ○ ⓥ
1963, UK, 95 mins, b/w
Dir: Gerald Thomas
Stars: Sidney James, Hattie Jacques, Kenneth Connor, Charles Hawtrety, Esma Cannon, Liz Fraser
Rating: ★★

One of the few *Carry On* films without the redoubtable Kenneth Williams in the cast. A lively entry in the famous series, this story of a fleet of taxis driven by glamorous cabbies managed to raise more chuckles than either of its immediate predecessors (*Carry On Regardless* and *Carry On Cruising*) and heralded an upsurge in the standard of *Carry Ons* that was to continue over the next three or four years.

Carry On Camping ○ ⓥ
1968, UK, 88 mins, colour
Dir: Gerald Thomas
Stars: Sidney James, Kenneth Williams, Joan Sims, Terry Scott, Peter Butterworth, Dilys Laye
Rating: ★★

An appropriate title if ever there were one. But the cast had to work hard to keep their spirits up this time, as the film was made not in the sunniest of weeks of the summer but in a field adjacent to Pinewood Studios during a particularly wet week in November. The publicists made much mileage out of the notable keep-fit sequence in which Barbara Windsor's bikini top flies off during one of the more vigorous physical jerks. The supporting cast is full of all the best *Carry On* people, including Joan Sims, Terry Scott, Peter Butterworth, Dilys Laye

and Bernard Bresslaw, plus Kenneth Williams' old sparring partner from *Beyond Our Ken* – Betty Marsden.

Carry On Cleo ○ ⓥ
1964, UK, 90 mins, colour
Dir: Gerald Thomas
Stars: Sidney James, Amanda Barrie, Kenneth Williams, Kenneth Connor, Joan Sims, Charles Hawtrey
Rating: ★★★

Encouraged by *Cleopatra*, the *Carry On* team invaded ancient Rome, hitting the usual targets ('Equality or Bust' state the Women's Lib placards: 'Blimus' cries Sid James). Lively playing; one of the best. Relish Kenneth Williams as Caesar, whether feeling sick *en voyage* ('Just a little sic in transit, Gloria') or being stabbed by conspirators ('Infamy! Infamy! They've all got it in for me!').

Carry On Constable ○ ⓥ
1960, UK, 86 mins, b/w
Dir: Gerald Thomas
Stars: Sidney James, Kenneth Connor, Kenneth Williams, Hattie Jacques, Eric Barker, Shirley Eaton
Rating: ★★

Farce in the force in this early entrant to the *Carry On* series, with the British bobby painted a bluer shade of blue in a cheerful series of vignettes. Such stalwarts as Eric Barker, Terence Longdon, Hattie Jacques and Irene Handl loom up in support, but funniest of all are Sidney James as the station sergeant and Joan Sims as WPC Passworthy.

Carry On Cowboy ○ ⓥ
1965, UK, 95 mins, colour
Dir: Gerald Thomas
Stars: Sidney James, Kenneth Williams, Jim Dale, Charles Hawtrey, Joan Sims, Angela Douglas
Rating: ★★★

The big bad Rumpo Kid (Sid James) has taken over Stodge City in the wild west, so the mayor (Kenneth Williams) sends for someone to clean up the town. Unfortunately, the state sends Marshall P Nutt (Jim Dale), who is really a sanitary inspector! The usual asinine antics you would expect from the *Carry On* team, with the lowbrow laughs coming thick and fast. By no means the best of the series that some people seem to think, but good for a few near-the-knuckle chuckles. For instance, Sid James complaining about

peace negotiations with the Indians: 'First it's peace on, then it's peace off!' Twas ever thus.

Carry On Cruising ○ ⓥ
1962, UK, 85 mins, colour
Dir: Gerald Thomas
Stars: Sidney James, Kenneth Williams, Liz Fraser, Kenneth Connor, Dilys Laye, Lance Percival
Rating: ★★

The first of the series to be made in colour, which means that the ocean waves are as blue as the jokes. Skippered by Sidney James, the men all have their eyes on the main chance, while the girls all have their eyes on the men.

Carry On Dick ○ ⓥ
1974, UK, 89 mins, colour
Dir: Gerald Thomas
Stars: Sidney James, Kenneth Williams, Barbara Windsor, Hattie Jacques, Bernard Bresslaw, Joan Sims
Rating: ★★★

Perhaps the last of the really funny *Carry Ons*, almost inevitably in period costume, as were all the best in this comedy series, and with the invaluable Sidney James in the dual role of Dick Turpin and the Reverend Mr Flasher.

Carry On Doctor ○ ⓥ
1968, UK, 90 mins, colour
Dir: Gerald Thomas
Stars: Sidney James, Frankie Howerd, Kenneth Williams, Jim Dale, Barbara Windsor, Charles Hawtrey
Rating: ★★

Probably the best of the four *Carry On* visits to a hospital, subtitled 'a bedpanorama of hospital life'. Jim Dale and Anita Harris bring a touch of freshness to the time-honoured, highly farcical situations.

Carry On – Don't Lose Your Head ○ ⓥ
1966, UK, 90 mins, colour
Dir: Gerald Thomas
Stars: Sidney James, Kenneth Williams, Joan Sims, Dany Robin, Peter Butterworth, Jim Dale
Rating: ★★★

Ribald revolution romp from the *Carry On* gang. The Scarlet Pimpernel becomes the Black Fingernail; and such names as Rodney Ffing and Citizen Bidet give rise to predictable but much-relished jokes.

C

Carry on Emmannuelle ◐ ⊗
1978, UK, 85 mins, colour
Dir: Gerald Thomas
Stars: Suzanne Danielle, Kenneth
Williams, Kenneth Connor, Jack Douglas
Rating: ★

Despite its leering lewdness and heavy
reliance on the word 'up' the laughs,
this does represent a small step *up* from
the depths of *Carry On England.* Its
few moments of genuine humour are
unfortuneately nearly all in the first
reel. But it's good to see Kenneth
Williams in full flow (bringing the
house down with 'I can't straighten
anything; I'm completely bent') and
new girl Suzanne Danielle tries hard
(another overworked *Carry On* word),
affecting an interesting French
accent. If only it weren't so sloppily
paced and edited, in fact, this might be
a great deal funnier.

Carry On . . . Follow That Camel ○ ⊗
1967, UK, 90 mins, colour
Dir: Gerald Thomas
Stars: Kenneth Williams, Phil Silvers,
Jim Dale, Charles Hawtrey, Anita Harris,
Peter Gilmore
Rating: ★★★

Jim Dale is Bertram Oliphant West
(B.O. to his friends), while such names
as Sergeant Nocker and Captain Le
Pice give rise to predictable double-entendres from the other ranks,
and the gang gaily mix-up *Morocco*
with *Beau Geste* in this sledgehammer
satire on all Foreign Legion adventure
films. Phil Silvers' conniving sergeant
is Bilko in all but name. And Anita
Harris personable enough as Corktip
(you'll remember Claudette Colbert
played Cigarette in *Under Two Flags*)
to make one wonder why she didn't
earn more than two *Carry On* roles.

Carry On Henry ○ ⊗
1971, UK, 89 mins, colour
Dir: Gerald Thomas
Stars: Sidney James, Kenneth Williams,
Joan Sims, Barbara Windsor, Charles
Hawtrey, Terry Scott
Rating: ★★★

Sid James enjoys himself hugely as
Henry VIII, a role that – in comedy at
any rate – he might have been born to
play. Richly costumed and inventively
scripted, this is one of the most
enjoyable of the Seventies *Carry Ons.*
A running gag about Charles Hawtrey
undergoing various forms of torture
to make him sign a document is particularly funny.

Carry On Jack ○ ⊗
(aka: Carry On Venus)
1964, UK, 85 mins, colour
Dir: Gerald Thomas
Stars: Bernard Cribbins, Kenneth
Williams, Juliet Mills, Donald Houston
Rating: ★★

The first *Carry On* comedy in period
costume, this nautical jaunt is an
amalgam of skits on *Mutiny on the
Bounty* and *Billy Budd.* This one
certainly has its moments, especially in
an early scene involving Jim Dale and
Ian Wilson as 'carriers' and in a sequence where the ship's cannon
backfires on Bernard Cribbins, Charles
Hawtrey and Percy Herbert. No
Sidney James, Joan Sims, Kenneth
Connor, Barbara Windsor or Hattie
Jacques this time around, but Kenneth
Williams, for once given a character to
work on, has some pricelessly funny
moments as the inappropriately
named Captain Fearless.

Carry On Loving ○ ⊗
1970, UK, 90 mins, colour
Dir: Gerald Thomas
Stars: Sidney James, Kenneth Williams,
Charles Hawtrey, Joan Sims, Hattie
Jacques, Terry Scott
Rating: ★

Little more than warmed-over 'double
entendres' from earlier films, delivered
by a cast of regulars past their sell-by
date. The subject may be sex, set
around the antics of the Wedded Bliss
Marriage Agency, but there's no
danger of anyone actually getting
down to the real thing. This one is
strictly for die-hard fans.

Carry On Matron ○ ⊗
1972, UK, 89 mins, colour
Dir: Gerald Thomas
Stars: Sidney James, Kenneth Williams,
Hattie Jacques, Charles Hawtrey,
Barbara Windsor, Terry Scott
Rating: ★★

Another series of low jinks in hospital
wards filled with characters that could
only have come from a *Carry On*film,
to follow in the footsteps of *Carry On
Nurse* and *Carry On Doctor.*

Carry On Nurse ○ ⊗
1959, UK, 85 mins, b/w
Dir: Gerald Thomas
Stars: Kenneth Connor, Kenneth
Williams, Shirley Eaton, Joan Sims,
Charles Hawtrey, Leslie Phillips
Rating: ★★

The second of the famous comedy
series, and the first of several *Carry*

Ons to be set in a hospital. Bedpan
jokes are almost as overworked as the
nurses, who are continually fending
off the advances of the patients. The
usual repertory company of stalwarts is
joined by Leslie Phillips, Joan Hickson
and Shirley Eaton.

Carry On Regardless ○ ⊗
1961, UK, 85 mins, b/w
Dir: Gerald Thomas
Stars: Sidney James, Kenneth Connor,
Charles Hawtrey, Joan Sims, Kenneth
Williams, Liz Fraser
Rating: ★

A series of farcical episodes, rather
than one story, make up this, the fifth
in the *Carry On* series. Our friends
form a 'Helping Hands' agency, and
predictably chaos ensues five times
over, with extra help from that queen
of ditherers, Esma Cannon.

Carry On Screaming ○ ⊗
1966, UK, 95 mins, colour
Dir: Gerald Thomas
Stars: Harry H Corbett, Kenneth
Williams, Jim Dale, Fenella Fielding,
Peter Butterworth, Joan Sims
Rating: ★★★

This horror comic proves to be one of
the *Carry On* gang's finest hours. Even
the worst of its corny jokes take on a
new amusement in a turn-of-the-
century setting and a mock horror
story. And the *Carry On* stock
company is perfectly cast and in irrepressible form: Jim Dale as the
dithering Potter, doing a little impromptu jig in bare feet during a
police investigation; Fenella Fielding
as Valeria, with alabaster cleavage and
a face straight from a chalk quarry;
Peter Butterworth, plump and droll as
Sgt Harry H Corbett's assistant; Joan
Sims, in fine fettle as Corbett's harridan wife; and Kenneth Williams as the
mad, reincarnated Dr Watt, who has
one final glorious moment as he falls
into his own cauldron. Best scene:
when Corbett comes home transformed into a wolfman, and Sims is
too busy nagging him to notice the
difference.

Carry On Sergeant ○ ⊗
1959, UK, 80 mins, b/w
Dir: Gerald Thomas
Stars: William Hartnell, Bob Monkhouse,
Shirley Eaton, Eric Barker, Dora Bryan
Rating: ★★

This was the one that started it all,
back in 1958. A low-budget comedy
about the army, it rang the box-office

bell with such vigour that a sequel had to follow. And a sequel to that. And . . .

Carry On Spying ○ ⓥ
1964, UK, 85 mins, b/w
Dir: Gerald Thomas
Stars: Kenneth Williams, Barbara Windsor, Bernard Cribbins, Charles Hawtrey, Eric Pohlmann, Eric Barker
Rating: ★★

Many of the *Carry On* regulars were missing for this sub-Bond caper, although bubbly Barbara Windsor makes a welcome addition to the gang in this, her first *Carry On* film. The pace is faster than before, but the whole enterprise is totally lacking in subtlety, something the series surprised us all by occasionally providing in subsequent outings. The last of the series in black-and-white.

Carry On Teacher ○ ⓥ
1959, UK, 86 mins, b/w
Dir: Gerald Thomas
Stars: Ted Ray, Kenneth Connor, Kenneth Williams, Joan Sims, Charles Hawtrey, Hattie Jacques
Rating: ★★

Third in the famous series, with Ted Ray showing how good he might have been as a second Will Hay. Here he's an acting headmaster hoping to move on to better things. But with a staff that includes Kenneth Williams, Kenneth Connor, and Charles Hawtrey, it's a pound to a pinch of itching powder that it will all end in disaster.

Carry On Up the Jungle ○ ⓥ
1970, UK, 89 mins, colour
Dir: Gerald Thomas
Stars: Frankie Howerd, Sidney James, Charles Hawtrey, Joan Sims, Terry Scott, Kenneth Connor
Rating: ★★★

The *Carry On* gang revert to the period costume in which their antics always seem funniest: here they are in darkest Africa, circa 1900, searching for the rare Oozulum bird. Jackie Piper, Valerie Leon and Edwina Carroll are the birds of a different feather. Terry Scott plays Jungle Boy. Kenneth Williams is the only member of the original gang not on parade, but Frankie Howerd, as a professor rejoicing in the name of Inigo Tinkle, is a more than adequate replacement. The jungle jokes come as thick and fast as the Pinewood undergrowth,

through which strides Bernard Bresslaw as Upsidasi, perhaps the least likely native warrior on record.

Carry On Up the Khyber ○ ⓥ
1968, UK, 85 mins, colour
Dir: Gerald Thomas
Stars: Sidney James, Kenneth Williams, Charles Hawtrey, Roy Castle, Joan Sims, Bernard Bresslaw
Rating: ★★★

Perhaps the highpoint of the *Carry On* films, with the series' only classic sequence – the dinner-party at the Governor's residence which continues despite the fact that the place is under siege from hostile tribesmen and the ceiling is falling in on the meal. Sid James cackles while Kenneth Williams schemes to undermine both Sid and his protectors, the Third Foot and Mouth regiment. Bernard Bresslaw looms large in the background as native chief Bungdit Din. Vintage stuff.

Carry On Venus
See: *Carry On Jack*

Carson City ○
1952, US, 87 mins, colour
Dir: Andre De Toth
Stars: Randolph Scott, Raymond Massey, Lucille Norman, Richard Webb
Rating: ★★★

A definitely upper-class Randolph Scott Western, this was well received when it first appeared, not least for Raymond Massey's sneering, leering performance as Big Jack Davis, as cultured as he is treacherous, given equally to popping champagne corks and shooting adversaries in the back. Scott is a sturdy hero and singer Lucille Norman a pallid heroine (as well she might be without a note to sing). The first film in WarnerColor.

Cars That Ate Paris, The ◐
1974, Australia, 91 mins, colour
Dir: Peter Weir
Stars: John Meillon, Melissa Jaffa, Terry Camilleri
Rating: ★★

Director Peter Weir's monstrous fantasy is set not in Paris, France, but Paris, Australia, where the townsfolk lay traps for unwary night-time motorists. The good people of Paris 'treat' the survivors of the resulting crashes and make their living from the pickings from the wrecks. A good idea, uncertainly acted by its Australian cast, but full of inventive touches.

Carve Her Name with Pride ○ ⓥ
1958, UK, 119 mins, b/w
Dir: Lewis Gilbert
Stars: Virginia McKenna, Paul Scofield, Jack Warner, Billie Whitelaw
Rating: ★★★

Inspiring, moving and exciting account of the wartime heroism of Violette Szabo, with a vivid account of her commando-type training, and solid performances from Paul Scofield, Jack Warner, Virginia McKenna and Billie Whitelaw.

Casablanca ○ ⓥ
1942, US, 102 mins, b/w
Dir: Michael Curtiz
Stars: Humphrey Bogart, Ingrid Bergman, Paul Henreid, Claude Rains, Sydney Greenstreet, Conrad Veidt
Rating: ★★★★

You must remember this: perhaps Hollywood's best-loved movie. Warners wanted Ronald Reagan and Ann Sheridan for the leads; what they got was Humphrey Bogart, Ingrid Bergman and immortality. Director Michael Curtiz, who brilliantly caught *Casablanca*'s raffish atmosphere in a Hollywood studio, won an Oscar. And the film itself was voted Best Picture. It's so much Bogart and Bergman's film that you tend to forget that Claude Rains, Paul Henreid, Conrad Veidt, Sydney Greenstreet and Peter Lorre were in it too. They're all gone now, but you get the feeling that somewhere in the great cinema in the sky, Rick's Cafe Americain is still open for business.

Casanova Brown ○
1944, US, 92 mins, b/w
Dir: Sam Wood
Stars: Gary Cooper, Teresa Wright, Frank Morgan
Rating: ★★

Frank Morgan, the crusty character actor who won lasting fame as the Wizard of Oz in the Judy Garland version, only made two films away from his home lot at MGM between 1937 and his death in 1949. This richly humorous production from RKO Radio was one of them. It offers viewers a rare treat of seeing Gary Cooper holding a baby. Not only holding it, but changing it, feeding it and generally doting on it like any proud father. Cooper, in fact, shows a real flair for comedy – especially in the scene where he accidentally burns down his in-laws' glossy maga-

c

zine-type home. Sam Wood, another refugee from MGM, directs with relish.

Casanova's Big Night ⊙
1953, US, 86 mins, colour
Dir: Norman Z McLeod
Stars: Bob Hope, Joan Fontaine, Basil Rathbone, Vincent Price, John Carradine, Lon Chaney Jr
Rating: ★★★

Inspired extravagant nonsense in the steps of Bob Hope's many other costume frolics. The novel setting of Venice in the 18th century gives him all sorts of opportunities for gags – as when he dips his finger in the Venetian waters, sniffs and remarks: 'Ah, must be Canal Number Five.' This dithering, disarming romp has Hope forced to impersonate the great lover Casanova. The supporting cast which, including Basil Rathbone, Vincent Price, Lon Chaney and John Carradine, looks like a horror film director's dream, cunningly amplify the star's comedy by taking themselves and their roles in deadly earnest. Stay tuned for the ending in which Hope rebels against Paramount's idea that his character be given the chop.

Casbah ○
1948, US, 94 mins, b/w
Dir: John Berry
Stars: Yvonne De Carlo, Tony Martin, Marta Toren, Peter Lorre
Rating: ★★

The classic Charles Boyer-Hedy Lamarr romantic adventure *Algiers*, itself based on a French original, is uncomfortably revamped as a musical in this version. Despite the fact that the songs are tolerable in an Arabian Nights sort of way, and Tony Martin sings them well, it's the plot elements which work the best. And, although Martin can be hardly anyone's idea of the romantic thief Pepe Le Moko, Peter Lorre is excellent as the wily inspector determined to bring him to book.

Casino de Paree
See: Go into Your Dance

Cassandra Crossing, The ○
1976, US, 129 mins, colour
Dir: George Pan Cosmatos
Stars: Sophia Loren, Richard Harris, Ava Gardner, Burt Lancaster, Martin Sheen, Ingrid Thulin
Rating: ★★★

Disaster strikes again! This time it's plague on board the Trans-Continental Express in a film that moves always with a sense of urgency. The script runs the full gamut of Hollywood cliches, but parts of the journey are tremendously exciting. The plague is carried by a saboteur trying to escape his pursuers. Of course, there are convenient babies, children, food, dogs, and drinking water for him to touch before he expires, transmitting the disease (maybe) to an assortment of typical Hollywood characters. These include a nun, a pop singer, a clergyman, a billionairess, a gigolo/mountaineer, a knowing child and a rascally con-man. A sinister note is provided by the Intelligence colonel (a very serious Burt Lancaster) who may be out to re-route the whole plague-ridden train to disaster. It's all immense hokum, of course, but done with great dash and panache, with some pulsating action. The director is the Greek George Pan Cosmatos, who keeps the suspense well on the rails.

Cass Timberlane ○
1947, US, 119 mins, b/w
Dir: George Sidney
Stars: Spencer Tracy, Lana Turner, Zachary Scott, Mary Astor, Tom Drake, Albert Dekker
Rating: ★★

A sincere adaptation from a Sinclair Lewis' novel, about a respectable mid-western judge who marries a beautiful but immature bride and has trouble keeping pace with her youth. Solid, if uninspired. The usual commanding performance from Spencer Tracy.

Cast a Dark Shadow ○
1955, UK, 82 mins, b/w
Dir: Lewis Gilbert
Stars: Margaret Lockwood, Dirk Bogarde, Kay Walsh, Kathleen Harrison, Mona Washborne
Rating: ★★★

This shivery thriller with a touch of graveyard humour came too late to revive Margaret Lockwood's fading film career, and she marched off to success in other fields. Actually, she gives her best performance in some years as the razor-tongued ex-barmaid in danger of being murdered for her money by shady young fortune-hunter Dirk Bogarde. Ten years earlier it was more likely to have been Lockwood doing the killing off!

Cast a Giant Shadow ○
1966, US, 141 mins, colour
Dir: Melville Shavelson
Stars: Kirk Douglas, Senta Berger, Angie Dickinson, John Wayne, Frank Sinatra, Yul Brynner
Rating: ★★

Big action film (with the famous line: 'This has got to be the biggest blow-up since falsies!') stars Kirk Douglas as the daredevil soldier of fortune who's in every military action ('I knew they wouldn't start D-Day without you,' says his wife, and they don't), culminating in the Israeli War of 1948. Douglas is rather disappointing, but there's a warmly glowing portrait of the 'war widow' from Angie Dickinson, and the ending, with its cleverly underplayed sentiment, is the most moving moment in the film.

Cast a Long Shadow ○
1958, US, 82 mins, colour
Dir: Thomas Carr
Stars: Audie Murphy, Terry Moore, John Dehner, James Best
Rating: ★★

America's most decorated Second World War serviceman, Audie Murphy, is the star of this unusual Western. Unusual, because it shows that even in the Wild West illegitimacy was regarded as a stigma. The film doesn't harp too much upon the subject, however. Guns blaze to good effect and there's a splendid cattle stampede.

Castaway ● ⑰
1986, UK, 117 mins, colour
Dir: Nicolas Roeg
Stars: Oliver Reed, Amanda Donohoe, Georgina Hale
Rating: ★★

Guys, if you advertised in the classified columns for a 'wife' to accompany you for a year on a deserted tropical island and Amanda Donohoe replied and said 'yes', it would presumably sound like real paradise. Girls, if you went along with the above scheme, planned a year out of your life and then found out you were to be paired with a bellicose chauvinist in the shape of burly Oliver Reed, how would you feel? This is the scenario created by Nicolas Roeg as he stylishly commits Lucy Irvine's soapy best-seller to the screen. As these two disparate characters struggle to adapt to the rigours of living in 'paradise', let alone coping with each other, the fragile bond of mutual dependence soon begins to fray. Roeg's treatment of this latter-day Robinson Crusoe story is full of luscious imagery and a preoccupation with shape, surrealism and symbolism which perhaps only the director can fully understand. Reed is as resistible as he's probably supposed to be but, handed a thankless task by the screenwriter, Donohoe almost makes a winning character out of her castaway.

Castle Keep ◑
1969, US, 107 mins, colour
Dir: Sydney Pollack
Stars: Burt Lancaster, Peter Falk, Patrick O'Neal, Bruce Dern, Jean Pierre Aumont
Rating: ★★

This film is certainly off the beaten track, as one might expect from its source – a very bizarre novel by William Eastlake that hovers between fantasy and reality. Burt Lancaster plays the one-eyed American major who billets his few remaining men at an Ardennes castle filled with priceless art treasures. It is also in the direct line of the German advance. The ensuing proceedings add up to distinctive entertainment and, in case you should be thinking this might be a war film without battles, there are skirmishes throughout and a really colossal holocaust at the end, when the Germans throw everything at the castle and its occupants.

Castle on the Hudson ○
(aka: Years Without Days)
1940, US, 77 mins, b/w
Dir: Anatole Litvak
Stars: John Garfield, Ann Sheridan, Pat O'Brien, Burgess Meredith, Jerome Cowan
Rating: ★★★

The castle of the title is no romantic pile, but the tough jail 'up the river' known as 'Sing Sing'. This is in fact a re-working of the Spencer Tracy film *20,000 Years in Sing Sing*, based on the book of the same title by real-life Sing Sing warden Lewis Lawes. John Garfield's portrayal of the wisecracking crook added to his growing list of chip-on-the-shoulder rebel roles, while Ann Sheridan provides a strong portrayal of resilient girlfriend Kay (and proves a far better gangster's moll than Bette Davis in the 1933 movie). Pat O'Brien is excellent as the sympathetic warden in charge of Garfield and Burgess Meredith attacks with

gusto his role as the leader of a breakout. It's all directed with pace by Anatole Litvak.

Casualties of War ● ⓥ
1989, US, 113 mins, colour
Dir: Brian De Palma
Stars: Michael J Fox, Sean Penn, Don Harvey, Sam Robards
Rating: ★★★

The approach of this Vietnam drama, about the deliberate rape and murder of a local girl by four US servicemen while a fifth stood helplessly by, seems unimpeachable, its heart undoubtedly in the right place. Sean Penn and Michael J Fox are uncommonly well cast as the brutish sergeant (who leads the rape) and the conscience-stricken PFC and both do the roles impassioned justice. However, you wouldn't expect De Palma to understate anything and he doesn't (except perhaps the rape itself); in many places the drama suffers from directorial overkill. And the ending, striving to satisfy its audience, is far too pat. But it's a strong piece of film-making, filled with the restless camerawork for which its director is noted, and which finds its niche in the hurly-burly desperation of jungle warfare.

Cat and the Canary, The ○
1939, US, 72 mins, b/w
Dir: Elliot Nugent
Stars: Bob Hope, Paulette Goddard, John Beal
Rating: ★★★★

From Bob Hope's best period (1939-48), this is the classic comedy-chiller that really gave his career a very big boost. One of the earliest of 'old dark house' mysteries, first filmed in 1927, it is tailored here to Hope's brightest comedy style, although his wisecracks seem just a pace away from panic as a shadowy killer stalks his victims around an old mansion in the swamps. In the first of several films with Hope, Paulette Goddard proves herself an ideal spirited-but-frightened heroine. Commented one contemporary American reviewer: 'Miss Goddard's screams would put a traffic snarl in Times Square'. Made before in a rarely-seen silent version of 1927. Remade in 1978.

Cat and the Canary, The ◑ ⓥ
1978, US, 98 mins, colour
Dir: Radley Metzger

Stars: Honor Blackman, Edward Fox, Michael Callan, Wendy Hiller
Rating: ★★

This is a decent enough remake of the old Bob Hope comedy-chiller about an heiress in peril in a creepy old house. It has a good cast too: Honor Blackman, Edward Fox, Michael Callan, Peter McEnery, Wendy Hiller, Olivia Hussey, Carol Lynley and Wilfrid Hyde White. An entertaining blend of gasps and chuckles, mildly recommended if you haven't seen the original.

Cat Ballou ○ ⓥ
1965, US, 96 mins, colour
Dir: Elliot Silverstein
Stars: Jane Fonda, Lee Marvin, Michael Callan, Tom Nardini, Nat 'King' Cole
Rating: ★★★

Pleasurable spoof Western about a shy young college miss who tilts her pretty nose at outlawry after her father has been killed by a hired gunfighter. Her 'gang' consists of two pusillanimous outlaws who never fire guns on principle, and an all-American Indian. 'It's no use blaming me,' he keeps saying, 'for what the Indians did to Custer.' But the Ballou band is not complete. And its real centrepiece is Kid Shelleen, as drunk a gunman as ever fell off his horse. The Kid turns out to be a glorious character study which won an Oscar for Lee Marvin. Not a lurch, not a sway, not a whisky-soaked blotch on the face are missed in Marvin's performance. 'Your eyes,' exclaims the Indian, 'they're all bloodshot.' Growls Marvin: 'You oughta see them from my side.' The music is nicely in keeping, including Nat 'King' Cole and Stubby Kaye as two 'almost' poker-faced minstrels who tell the story. You can have fun working out which is the Sundance Kid and which Professor Sam Shade. Effective is the rattle-snake noise the soundtrack uses whenever the villain, also played by Marvin (he has a silver nose because someone bit off his real one in a fight), is around. The colour photography is gorgeously keyed to every scene, and one piece, where the reflection of a tree dapples the leaves on the actors' faces, is masterly.

Cat Chaser ● ⓥ
1989, US, 90 mins, colour
Dir: Abel Ferrara
Stars: Peter Weller, Kelly McGillis, Charles Durning, Frederic Forrest, Juan

c

Hernandez
Rating: ★★

This does the job as a violent thriller, but it hasn't half the subtlety its first ten minutes promise, running more like Hank Jansen than Elmore Leonard, on whose crime novel the film is based. Kelly McGillis obviously fancied some sort of cathartic experience after *The Accused.* Here she seems happy just to show off her body as the wayward wife of De Boya, an ex-secret policeman in Latin America, a woman only too eager to resume an affair with her former lover George (Peter Weller). He's an ex-Marine who now owns a Florida hotel where the clientele are outnumbered by the staff. Other characters are involved in all this, all of them with an eye to the $2 million De Boya is said to have stashed away. But they are rootlessly written people, given more substance than the screenplay deserves by the actors, especially Charles Durning, Frederic Forrest and Juan Hernandez.

Catch Me a Spy ○
1971, US, 94 mins, colour
Dir: Dick Clement
Stars: Kirk Douglas, Marlene Jobert, Trevor Howard, Tom Courtenay, Patrick Mower
Rating: ★★

Writer-director Dick Clement and actor Tom Courtenay, who combined to such good effect on *Otley,* are together again in a not dissimilar but less effective spy comedy-thriller. Clement and his long-time collaborator Ian La Frenais have fashioned an ingenious plot, full of nice little comic flashes, with double agents everywhere and the hero and heroine dodging spies in Scotland in a manner reminiscent of *The 39 Steps.* Kirk Douglas and the appealing Marlene Jobert both offer attractive performances, but it's sad to see Trevor Howard wasted in an unworthy role and, for all its merits, the caper is never quite credible.

Catch-22 ● Ⓥ
1970, US, 115 mins, colour
Dir: Mike Nichols
Stars: Alan Arkin, Martin Balsam, Paula Prentiss, Jon Voight, Richard Benjamin, Art Garfunkel
Rating: ★★★

Joseph Heller's stunning and surreal black comedy about services life in World War Two is a novel that could never really be transferred to the screen and satisfy its thousands of devotees. That said, Buck Henry's screen adaptation, while inevitably having to leave out characters and favourite incidents, is a remarkable piece of work which largely succeeds in capturing the spirit of the original while hardly sticking to the letter. And Mike Nichols' direction is clever enough to bring out both the humour and the bitterness, focusing on Alan Arkin's impressive Captain Yossarian and a lavish array of lesser characters.

Catered Affair, The ○
(aka: The Wedding Breakfast)
1956, US, 93 mins, b/w
Dir: Richard Brooks
Stars: Bette Davis, Ernest Borgnine, Debbie Reynolds, Barry Fitzgerald, Rod Taylor
Rating: ★★★

After the success of *Marty,* film-makers rushed to the work of writer Paddy Chayefsky. This story is another of his looks at the lower strata of American life. Ernest Borgnine and Bette Davis play a Bronx couple whose quiet life runs into all sorts of troubled waters when their daughter (Debbie Reynolds) decides to get married. Borgnine gives a subdued performance that's just right.

Cat from Outer Space, The ☉
1978, US, 103 mins, colour
Dir: Norman Tokar
Stars: Ken Berry, Sandy Duncan, Harry Morgan
Rating: ★★★

Lots of winningly realised fun and games in this Disney comedy, a sort of close encounter of the furred kind as the alien moggy of the title foils a space-energy spy plot with the help of the powers that emanate from his illuminated collar. The film benefits enormously from the relationship between the wisecracking (talking) cat and the eccentric doctor (sympathetically played by Ken Berry) who becomes his sidekick. Roddy McDowall is rather too far over the top as the bad guy, but more laid-back support comes from Sandy Duncan, Harry Morgan, Jesse White, Alan Young and Hans Conried. [TVT]

Catlow ◐
1971, Spain, 101 mins, colour
Dir: Sam Wanamaker
Stars: Yul Brynner, Richard Crenna, Daliah Lavi, Leonard Nimoy
Rating: ★

Another Western from the pen of Louis L'Amour, the author of *Hondo.* Like the star's Sabata Westerns, this was filmed in Spain, with some splendid scenery getting the full treatment from Ted Scaife's Metrocolor camerawork. Daliah Lavi is a spitfire bandit girl in the finest Raquel Welch tradition, but too little is seen of Leonard (Mr Spock) Nimoy as the bounty killer: it hardly seemed worth the trek back from the stars for this role.

Cat on a Hot Tin Roof ○
1958, US, 108 mins, colour
Dir: Richard Brooks
Stars: Elizabeth Taylor, Paul Newman, Burl Ives, Jack Carson, Judith Anderson
Rating: ★★★

A favourite critical complaint is that Hollywood 'emasculated' the endings of Tennessee Williams' works such as this one and *Sweet Bird of Youth.* But that certainly will not spoil your enjoyment of this powerful film. And while the original Williams' themes and climaxes would be acceptable screen fare by today's standards, whether the average member of the public would rather see them this way is another thing. In this case, the theme that has been 'toned down' is homosexuality and the alcoholism of Brick (Paul Newman), who prefers the bottle to his lovely wife (a glowingly beautiful Elizabeth Taylor), is played up accordingly. But the important thing is that the spirit and highly-charged atmosphere of the original have been retained. Burl Ives repeats his stage triumph as the dying Big Daddy, and the strong performances of Newman and Miss Taylor were rewarded with Academy Award nominations. But no one tops Jack Carson's brilliant supporting portrayal of the sneaky Gooper – a masterly piece of acting.

Cat People ◐
1942, US, 73 mins, b/w
Dir: Jacques Tourneur
Stars: Simone Simon, Kent Smith
Rating: ★★★

The film that started a great cycle of fantasy-horror films in the mid-Forties. It became famous as the first film not to show its monster, and to prove that the power of suggestion was just as likely to scare the daylights out of an audience as actually seeing some fiendish creation. Brilliantly photographed and recommended – but not for the nervous.

Cat's Eye 🌓 Ⓥ
1984, US, 90 mins, colour
Dir: Lewis Teague
Stars: James Woods, Alan King, Drew
Barrymore, Kenneth McMillan
Rating: ★★

In contrast to other chillers by
Stephen King, this fantasy from the
King brain is on the light-hearted side
and rather fun. Drew Barrymore is
quite likeable as the girl whose tele-
pathic call for help alerts a stray cat
that she's in danger, and causes it to
use up quite a percentage of its nine
lives, with the *pièce de resistance* coming
as the cat does battle with an evil troll
threatening to steal Drew's breath
away. The trick work involved is
good enough to draw the viewer into
the fray, and the cat actors are intelligently deployed at all times.

Cattle Annie and Little Britches ○
1979, US, 95 mins, colour
Dir: Lamont Johnson
Stars: Burt Lancaster, John Savage, Rod
Steiger, Scott Glenn, Amanda Plummer,
Diane Lane
Rating: ★★

It should be pointed out that burly
Burt Lancaster plays neither of the title
roles in this pleasant, slightly spoof
action Western. It refers to the two
teenage tearaway girls who batten
themselves on to his tattered bandit
gang in the 1890s, and inspire them to
hit the outlaw trail again. The girls are
played by Amanda Plummer (daughter
of Christopher Plummer and Tammy
Grimes) and personable Diane Lane,
first noticed in *A Little Romance* and
later to star in *The Cotton Club*.

Cattle Drive ○
1950, US, 77 mins, colour
Dir: Kurt Neumann
Stars: Joel McCrea, Dean Stockwell,
Chill Wills
Rating: ★★

Photographed in beautiful colour, this
pleasing Western has a vigorous
performance from the young Dean
Stockwell – as a spoiled teenager along
on a huge cattle drive – whose enthusiasm spurs Joel McCrea to one of
the best of his latter-day performances
as the old hand who teaches him
about life and the tricks of the trail.

Cattle King
See: Guns of Wyoming

Cattle Queen of Montana ○
1955, US, 88 mins, colour
Dir: Allan Dwan
Stars: Barbara Stanwyck, Ronald
Reagan, Gene Evans, Jack Elam
Rating: ★★

A presentable Western with marvellous Technicolor photography by
John Alton. Barbara Stanwyck does
well as, unusually, a nice, uncomplicated lady with the super name of
Sierra Nevada Jones, and Ronald
Reagan is for once ideal as the mysterious gunfighter with whom she
falls in love. The story is of a higher
than usual calibre for a horse opera
and the scenery really superb. The
gutsy Stanwyck as usual did her own
stuntwork, so impressing the local
Blackfoot Indians that they named her
Princess Many Victories and made her
an honorary member of the tribe.

Caught ○
1948, US, 88 mins, b/w
Dir: Max Ophuls
Stars: James Mason, Barbara Bel
Geddes, Robert Ryan
Rating: ★★

This sometimes tense morality tale
about a shopgirl who believes that
marrying a rich man is the route to
happiness too often lapses into tiresome soap opera that proves a waste of
a good cast. Barbara Bel Geddes is the
girl, Robert Ryan the neurotic millionaire she marries and James Mason
(in his first American film) is the
young, intelligent doctor she falls for.
It all ends better for the heroine than
she deserves, but not without a fair bit
of pointless angst in between and no
small amount of scene-stealing competition between the stars. On the
whole it's stylish but also slow-moving
and depressing: you can't help feeling
Bel Geddes deserves all the suffering
for being so damn silly in the first
place.

Caught in the Draft ☉
1941, US, 82 mins, b/w
Dir: David Butler
Stars: Bob Hope, Dorothy Lamour, Eddie
Bracken
Rating: ★★★

Now one of the rarest of Bob Hope's
comedy films, this contemporary
romp finds the great man in good
form as a movie hero who's such a
coward in real life that he'll 'jump

when someone cracks their knuckles'.
While in pursuit of Dorothy Lamour
he finds himself in the army, and
thereby hangs the title – and the fun.
Panicky little Eddie Bracken made
some of his first strides towards the top
at Paramount as the star's minion who
finds himself also enlisting.

Cavalcade ○
1933, UK, 120 mins, b/w
Dir: Frank Lloyd
Stars: Diana Wynyard, Clive Brook,
Herbert Mundin, Una O'Connor
Rating: ★★★

Noel Coward's down-through-the-
years family saga lifted almost bodily
from the London stage (Fox even
imported a genuine London taxi) and
the winner of three Oscars, including
best picture and a best director trophy
for Frank Lloyd, whose second Academy Award it was. His standing began
to slip soon after *Mutiny on the Bounty*
two years later and he is little remembered today.

Cease Fire ● Ⓥ
1985, US, 97 mins, colour
Dir: David Nutter
Stars: Don Johnson, Lisa Blount, Robert
F Lyons, Chris Noel, Richard Chaves
Rating: ★★★

Director David Nutter's only major
film to date is a moving account of
mid-Eighties America that's interesting
on two counts. One, in that it's a very
serious look at the recurrent
nightmares that haunted the lives of
the country's Vietnam veterans and
two, in that it takes two players whose
looks might otherwise limit them, and
really gives them a chance to act.
Neither Don Johnson nor Lisa Blount
lets their director down. Their anguished performances in a key scene
almost rival those of Jane Fonda and
Jon Voight in *Coming Home*. The film
itself is slow to take a grip on you,
but its sincerity shines through, even
in the uncomfortably handled scenes
of the separate psychiatric clinics attended by the veterans and their
wives. Dialogues between Johnson
and fellow vet Robert F Lyons are less
successful at grabbing our attention,
although the Vietnam flashback
sequences are more rather than less
effective for obviously being shot on
a fairly minimal budget. It's a decent
attempt to make a valid social
statement within an entertainment
framework, without stepping too far
into the bog of maudlin depression
that lies beyond.

C

Ceiling Zero ○
1935, US, 95 mins, b/w
Dir: Howard Hawks
Stars: James Cagney, Pat O'Brien, June Travis, Stuart Erwin, Barton MacLane
Rating: ★★

An interesting film concerning World War One aviators who find it hard to come down from their combative 'high' and settle again to civilian life. This one carries its own charge of tension, plus a clever and complex performance by James Cagney and an intelligent and effective portrayal by Isabel Jewell in a difficult minor role. Director Howard Hawks, who made *The Air Circus* and the 1931 version of *The Dawn Patrol*, brings both excitement and realism to his shooting and editing of the flying scenes.

Cemetary Club, The ❶ ⓥ
1992, US, 106 mins, colour
Dir: Bill Duke
Stars: Ellen Burstyn, Olympia Dukakis, Diane Ladd, Danny Aiello, Lainie Kazan, Christina Ricci
Rating: ★★

'You're never too old to have some fun' is the message of this gentle romantic comedy. Our feisty, fiftysomething heroines (Olympia Dukakis, Ellen Burstyn and Diane Ladd), a trio of grey-haired, sharp-tongued Jewish widows (strange that the casting director should choose three non-Jewish actresses for these roles), meet each week to visit the graves of their husbands – until the day a stranger (Danny Aiello) appears at the cemetery. There's lots of *Golden Girls*-type squabbles in this one, with the quality cast rolling waspish tongues round some acid-sharp lines. Burstyn is wonderful in the side of the movie that becomes a touching sweet-natured romance, but some of the other performances are too self-indulgent at times, creating something of an imbalance in the final result. On the whole though, worth a look.

Century ● ⓥ
1993, UK, 112 mins, colour
Dir: Stephen Poliakoff
Stars: Charles Dance, Miranda Richardson, Clive Owen, Robert Stephens, Liza Walker, Joan Hickson
Rating: ★★

A bizarre, pretentious but sometimes quite absorbing arthouse movie which mixes its period medical drama with a dash of romance, and tops it off with some beautiful photography and a loving evocation of an era long past. At the turn of the century when much medicine was still considered quackery, Paul Reisner (Clive Owen) emerges as the star pupil of the mysterious Prof Mandry (Charles Dance). But Reisner lands in big trouble when he falls in love with Clara (Miranda Richardson), a laboratory assistant with a mysterious past. The performances here are suitably enigmatic, but, under Stephen Poliakoff's arty direction, the film annoyingly takes a long time getting nowhere fast.

Chad Hanna ○
1940, US, 86 mins, colour
Dir: Henry King
Stars: Henry Fonda, Dorothy Lamour, Linda Darnell, Guy Kibbee
Rating: ★★

Pretty unusual for a Hollywood film of its time, this is a heated romantic melodrama set against a travelling circus in the 1840s. It almost works, but not quite, despite the right touch of nostalgic affection by director Henry King and vivid Technicolor photography by Ernest Palmer.

Chains of Gold ● ⓥ
1990, US, 94 mins, colour
Dir: Rod Holcomb
Stars: John Travolta, Marilu Henner, Bernie Casey, Hector Elizondo
Rating: ★★

In between episodes in the *Look Who's Talking* comedy saga, John Travolta ventured into *Miami Vice* territory, but the territory and change of pace don't altogether suit him. Playing an idealistic social worker and ex-alcoholic, he becomes involved with a vicious Florida crack gang through his efforts to rescue a 13-year-old boy from a life of crime. The gang itself has a whole army of such boys, supplying crack to the nation. And the penalty for defection is, naturally, death. Travolta swears a lot, sweats a lot and goes without a shave, but can't convince us that all this is quite his cup of tea, especially the serial-like developments that leave him dangling over a pit of alligators. Although based on true events and people, which puts its heart firmly in the right place, the slack treatment the film gets makes it definitely a second-class citizen in the genre.

Chalk Garden, The ○
1964, UK, 106 mins, colour
Dir: Ronald Neame
Stars: Hayley Mills, Deborah Kerr, John Mills, Edith Evans, Felix Aylmer
Rating: ★★

Someone – most likely Ross Hunter, expert producer of Hollywood 'glossies' – has put a soft centre of sticky sentimentality in the bitter almonds of Enid Bagnold's play about a teenage girl who lives in a world of lies because she lacks love and understanding. As the girl, Hayley Mills gestures a lot but sounds unconvinced by the dialogue. Edith Evans gives a brilliant portrayal of the possessive old lady with no more ability to give love to the girl than life to the plants in her garden of chalk. It's a performance as impressive in close-up as it is at long range. Deborah Kerr and John Mills round out the cast.

Challenge, The ●
1982, US, 112 mins, colour
Dir: John Frankenheimer
Stars: Scott Glenn, Toshiro Mifune
Rating: ★★

Director John Frankenheimer tries to combine the action of a chop-socky film with the scale and spirit of a Kurosawa epic and falls heavily between the two stools. Scott Glenn is well in character as the cynical backstreets battler who foolishly accepts an obviously murky assignment to take two ancient swords back to Japan and in no time at all has been beaten up, knifed and left for dead. With dialogue that sounds as if it comes from a sword-and-sandal movie of 30 years earlier, action is clearly called for to save the day, and it's sharply done, too, though the spurts of it are rather too sparsely spaced. But you'll enjoy the devastating final battle, which appears to do no good at all to the Kyoto Conference Centre, let alone the actors who get bits of them sliced all over it.

Chamber of Horrors ❶
1966, US, 121 mins, colour
Dir: Hy Averback
Stars: Patrick O'Neal, Cesare Danova, Laura Devon, Patrice Wymore
Rating: ★★

A dose of Rue Morguery, set in Maryland of the 1890s where a madman is on the loose. Watch for the 'fear flasher' and the 'horror horn' which enable one to take evasive action at the film's 'four supreme fright points', as suggested by the original publicity. Patrick O'Neal has a field day as the madman, humming softly to himself as he screws an axe blade on to his hook hand while contemplating his next victim. There's also a special guest star. You'll have to be sharp to catch him, as he's on screen for all of two and a half seconds.

Champ, The ○ ⓥ
1979, US, 123 mins, colour
Dir: Franco Zeffirelli
Stars: Jon Voight, Faye Dunaway, Ricky Schroder, Jack Warden, Arthur Hill, Joan Blondell
Rating: ★

Those in charge of the casting for this updated version of MGM's classic Oscar-winning sudser deserve a nifty right upper-cut. Never for one moment does Faye Dunaway gain our sympathy for her efforts to get a larger share of the boy whom she deserted seven years before, nor is Jon Voight anyone's idea of an ageing ex-world champion boxer who has looked after the kid since she left. Voight mugs frantically as the champ – at least it's a performance in the Wallace Beery tradition. And we can say the same for Ricky Schroder as his son. Dunaway struggles Ms-fully with a part that just isn't hers. But none of them can do anything about the pace, and the film bobs and weaves like a punch-drunk punk until it falls asleep on its feet. Get your fellow-viewer to wake you up at the end in time for the final fight – it's well worth a look. At least Hollywood remembers how to do some things well.

Champagne Charlie ○
1944, UK, 100 mins, b/w
Dir: Alberto Cavalcanti
Stars: Tommy Trinder, Stanley Holloway, Jean Kent
Rating: ★★★

Described at the time as 'one of the best musical-comedies made in this country to date', this boisterous and invigorating period piece recreates (impressively, considering wartime exigencies) gaslit London of the 1860s for its farcical story of the 'drinking song' rivalry of two of the foremost music-hall personalities of the day – roles in which Tommy Trinder and Stanley Holloway prove perfectly cast. The sharp-eyed may also spot Guy Middleton, Harry Fowler, Hazel Court, Kay Kendall and James Robertson Justice.

Champagne for Caesar ○
1950, US, 95 mins, b/w
Dir: Richard Whorf
Stars: Ronald Colman, Celeste Holm, Vincent Price
Rating: ★★★

Mad but fun, this is a delightfully idiotic Hollywood comedy that was badly handled by its studio, adored by the critics and shunned by the public. Ronald Colman, as the unemployed genius seeking to win a fortune on a radio quiz (for reasons of revenge, not personal gain), shows himself a farceur with the lightest of touches, while Vincent Price is a wild-eyed delight as the nasty 'soap magnate' forever going into one of his 'trances'. And Caesar? He's a parrot who happens to like champagne, and he's voiced by Mel Blanc of Bugs Bunny fame. It's a sustained squawk that's full of fizz from beginning to end.

Champion ○
1949, US, 99 mins, b/w
Dir: Mark Robson
Stars: Kirk Douglas, Marilyn Maxwell, Arthur Kennedy
Rating: ★★★★

Kirk Douglas slugged his way to fame in this gruelling boxing story that was not overtaken for face-smashing realism until *Raging Bull* came along 31 years later. Douglas delivers a knockout *tour de force* performance as a ruthless, merciless, sadistic man who destroys anything or anyone who stands in the way of his ambition. It shocked audiences of the day and still retains that power today. Douglas seized the role gladly after being shown Carl Foreman's blistering script and he was promised top billing. It was the wisest decision of his early career, turning him into an overnight sensation and earning him a Best Actor Oscar nomination to boot. But he lost out on awards night to Broderick Crawford in *All the King's Men*. Arthur Kennedy is also superb as Douglas's trusting, loving brother while Ruth Roman, in one of her earliest roles, is utterly captivating as the victimised wife.

Champions ○ ⓥ
1983, UK, 115 mins, colour
Dir: John Irvin
Stars: John Hurt, Edward Woodward, Jan Francis, Ben Johnson, Peter Barkworth, Kirstie Alley
Rating: ★★★

It's difficult to be as thrilled by a winner when you know the outcome, but you just have to cheer for Bob Champion, the jockey who was not only cured of the cancer which, without treatment, would have killed him in months, but went on to win the Grand National on a horse which, a few months before, had nearly been put down after snapping a tendon. John Hurt is perhaps a little too expert at anguish (there are times when he looks like a dying crow) to be cast as Champion but, apart from a few obvious doubles in the Grand National, he does a splendid job in and out of the saddle. Champion himself obviously insisted that the film should not show him as a saint; and so it presents his weaknesses and vices along with his strengths and virtues. Jan Francis is all warmth and sympathy as the girl who chases and catches him; in fact all the women in the cast are good, from Alison Steadman as his sister, through Ann Bell as the horse's owner's wife, to the assortment of nurses who help pull Champion through.

Chances Are ○ ⓥ
1989, US, 108 mins, colour
Dir: Emile Ardolino
Stars: Cybill Shepherd, Robert Downey Jr, Ryan O'Neal, Mary Stuart Masterson, Christopher McDonald
Rating: ★★

In this fantasy Cybill Shepherd's dead husband comes back to Earth in the (much younger) shape of Robert Downey Jr, who initially remembers nothing of his previous life. Romantic complications ensue because Shepherd's daughter (Mary Stuart Masterson) fancies Downey and Ryan O'Neal carries a torch for Shepherd. By the generally high standards of such whimsy, this film is highly improbable – mainly because you don't believe in the characters, or the situations in which they find themselves, even though the treatment remains quite winningly sweet-natured throughout. Downey tries hard with what he's given and occasionally rises above it, but the rest of the cast copes less well with the uphill struggle. The classic *Here Comes Mr Jordan*, from which this film has stolen the basic plot premise, is infinitely superior.

Changeling, The ●
1979, US, 107 mins, colour
Dir: Peter Medak

c

Stars: George C Scott, Trish Van Devere, Melvyn Douglas, John Colicos
Rating: ★★★★

A very superior example of the haunted-house thriller, whose horrors are never (well, only in flashback) seen. There's the obligatory dire warning, of course, from a member of the historical society that sold George C Scott the house in question after his wife and daughter have been killed in an accident. 'That house isn't fit to live in,' she hisses. 'It doesn't want people.' People, unfortunately, are just what it does want, and Mr Scott in particular, his own loss making him a potent force for spirits to communicate with. The ghost lurks in narrow, confined spaces and age-old cobwebbed rooms, and director Peter Medak's camera tracks relentlessly through these claustrophobic environs like an invader in some old and murky painting stirred almost to life. The result is quite the most frightening film since *The Haunting*, much aided by the super-naturalistic portrayal of the star. Scenes at the end involving a wheel-chair may crunch you right into your armchair. Most horror films these days are not for the squeamish. *The Changeling* is old-fashioned in that respect: it's not for the nervous.

Chant of Jimmie Blacksmith, The ●
1978, Australia, 124 mins, colour
Dir: Fred Schepisi
Stars: Tommy Lewis, Freddy Reynolds
Rating: ★★★

A very violent true story about an Australian half-breed at the turn of the century who, ill-treated beyond belief by a succession of white masters, went berserk and killed two of the families that had caused him so much pain. Fred Schepisi's film of these events is beautifully composed and skilfully made, even if it doesn't entirely avoid dull spots and is sometimes hard to follow. Tommy Lewis is extraordinarily naturalistic as the much-abused Jimmie, and there are other good performances from Freddy Reynolds as his blood brother, and from Angela Punch as his ever-suffering wife.

Chaplin ◐ ⓥ
1992, US, 158 mins, colour
Dir: Richard Attenborough
Stars: Robert Downey Jr, Kevin Kline, Dan Aykroyd, Marisa Tomei, Anthony Hopkins, Geraldine Chaplin
Rating: ★★

Long and caring, the outcome of Richard Attenborough's ambitious biography of Charlie Chaplin was perhaps inevitable: bits of film history dully stuck together with famous actors striking poses as other famous actors – but no real life, not even from Robert Downey Jr's carefully considered and visually very good Chaplin. Slowly the Chaplin history unfolds: its facts *are* interesting, but their presentation sadly lacks the persuasive qualities necessary to attract us to them. Although beautifully dressed and set and professionally made, this remains a pageant rather than a picture, and could signal the end of such ambitious biopics for some time to come.

Charade ○ ⓥ
1963, US, 114 mins, colour
Dir: Stanley Donen
Stars: Cary Grant, Audrey Hepburn, Walter Matthau, James Coburn, George Kennedy
Rating: ★★★★

Thrillers like *Charade* lean heavily on character and directorial flair to make them work, and seldom has one worked better than this. Director Stanley Donen – previously best-known for his Gene Kelly musicals – doesn't miss a trick in keeping the action moving at a furious rate, spinning madly from one red herring to another, disclosure upon disclosure. Sometimes he goes for deadpan comedy, at others his camera is trained all out for thrills. But the two moods never clash. *Charade* is constantly intriguing, with its combination of wit and directness. And when it thrills, it really is a seat-gripper. One scene especially, a rooftop fight between Cary Grant and George Kennedy, is skillfully exciting. And a tracking shot of a villain firing at the hero through a forest of marble pillars is coolly calculated to set the pulses racing.

Charge at Feather River, The ○
1953, US, 96 mins, colour
Dir: Gordon Douglas
Stars: Guy Madison, Frank Lovejoy, Helen Westcott, Vera Miles
Rating: ★★★

Arrows to the left of you, arrows to the right of you. And if you weren't careful, you might have got one in the eye when you first saw this pulsating, personable action film, for it was originally released in 3-D. Guy Madison and Frank Lovejoy make forthright leads, while the supporting cast is full of gritty humour – notably Dick Wesson, a 'scat' comedian who should have gone further in films, Steve Brodie, Onslow Stevens, Neville Brand and Henry Kulky. As the girls kidnappped by Indians, both Helen Westcott and Vera Miles prove more than mere ciphers in the story. Max Steiner's music skillfully underscores some of the best action scenes that director Gordon Douglas ever shot.

Charge is Murder, The ○
(aka: Twilight of Honor)
1964, US, 116 mins, b/w
Dir: Boris Sagal
Stars: Richard Chamberlain, Claude Rains, Joan Blackman, Nick Adams
Rating: ★★

Richard Chamberlain's first big film role after his success as *Dr Kildare* casts him as a knight-in-armour lawyer defending a young hothead (Nick Adams) accused of murdering his wife's lover. As the wayward teenage wife, Joey Heatherton gives off strong echoes of the early Marilyn Monroe; while veteran Claude Rains scores as a wise and witty legal eagle on the hero's side. Veteran cowboy star Pat Buttram (remember him as Gene Autry's partner in countless minor Westerns?) has a most unusual role, giving him a chance to reveal genuine acting ability beneath that homely grin.

Charge of the Light Brigade, The ○
1936, US, 115 mins, b/w
Dir: Michael Curtiz
Stars: Errol Flynn, Olivia de Havilland, Patric Knowles, Donald Crisp, David Niven
Rating: ★★★

This legendary Hollywood epic has little to do with historical fact and everything to do with thrilling action featuring legendary swashbuckler Errol Flynn. The picture has everything: glamour, excitement, romance (with Olivia de Havilland – Flynn's romantic partner in many an adventure), incredibly realistic battle scenes and some breathtaking stunts. Director Michael Curtiz keeps the whole thing moving at break-neck speed – regardless of the suffering of either human or animal. In fact, Flynn said that this film was 'the toughest picture I ever made'. During the fatal charge, dozens of horses were seriously injured. Thanks to Flynn secretly tipping off the Society for the Prevention of Cruelty to Animals, the outrage was such that legislation was passed establishing firm rules for the treatment of animals in films. If you want to know what actually happened at Balaclava, you should refer to Tony Richardson's meticulously researched 1968 version, but it's not half as exciting.

Charge of the Light Brigade, The ○ ⓥ
1968, UK, 141 mins, colour
Dir: Tony Richardson
Stars: Trevor Howard, Vanessa Redgrave, David Hemmings
Rating: ★★★

The Michael Curtiz/Errol Flynn version of the famous suicidal charge was an almost impossible act to follow but director Tony Richardson's version of the events is an engrossing, if not vigorously exciting film. For a start, he sticks to the facts of the battle and the events that led up to it, something Hollywood didn't bother to do. Having said that, those facts are tinged by Richardson's inevitable knock at British imperialism and the arrogance of the upper classes, but given the period this seems fair comment. Acting honours go to John Gielgud as Lord Raglan and Trevor Howard as Lord Cardigan although there are uniformly fine performances from a gallery of British acting talent. The battle scenes don't compare with the Flynn version, but Richardson wasn't simply attempting a remake. If you want gung-ho thrills and adventure, stick with Errol; if you want to feel that history is being relived, this is the version to watch.

Chariots of Fire ○ ⓥ
1981, UK, 120 mins, colour
Dir: Hugh Hudson
Stars: Ben Cross, Ian Charleson, Nigel Havers, Alice Krige, Ian Holm, John Gielgud
Rating: ★★★★

Winner of four Academy Awards – writer Colin Welland took the occasion to warn Hollywood (rather prematurely, as it proved) that 'the British are coming' – and nominated for four others, this stirring story of the battle between two Olympic runners from different social and ethnic backgrounds is an unexpected box-office bullseye. Director Hugh Hudson had a solid background in shooting commercials, but this was his

auspicious feature film debut. John Gielgud and Lindsay Anderson have wonderful cameos as anti-semitic Cambridge officials, but many considered that Ian Holm, as a professional coach, was robbed of his best supporting actor Oscar when it was awarded to Gielgud for *Arthur*. Patriotic flag-waving, pretty photography and a memorable score by Vangelis.

Charley Moon ⊙
1956, UK, 92 mins, colour
Dir: Guy Hamilton
Stars: Max Bygraves, Dennis Price, Shirley Eaton
Rating: ★★

This British showbusiness musical from the Fifties, directed by Guy Hamilton, is often phoney and frequently embarrassing, with a poor script and cardboard characters. However, there are redeeming features: Max Bygraves, who is thoroughly likeable in the title role of the ex-national serviceman who goes into variety and, reluctantly leaving his less talented friend Harold behind, leaps up the ladder to stardom; a good cast – Dennis Price (as Harold), Shirley Eaton, Michael Medwin, Eric Sykes and Bill Fraser among them; one good song – 'Out of Town'; and some nice photography by the distinguished Jack Hildyard, who had shot *Summer Madness* and *Anastasia* and would go on to win an Oscar for *The Bridge on the River Kwai* a year later.

Charley's Aunt ○
1941, US, 81 mins, b/w
Dir: George Seaton
Stars: Jack Benny, Anne Baxter, Kay Francis, James Ellison, Laird Cregar, Edmund Gwenn
Rating: ★★★

Jack Benny enjoys one of his finest screen hours in this rollicking, fast-paced version of Brandon Thomas's oft-filmed play. Playing with enthusiasm, and romping crazily along his laughter route as an over-aged Oxford undergraduate in 1890, forced to masquerade as a rich Brazilian lady, Benny takes the fullest advantage of the chance to handle a straight farcical assignment without recourse to his radio retinue of writing wisecrackers. A marvellous supporting cast includes one or two players on the brink of Hollywood stardom.

Charley's Big-hearted Aunt ○
1940, UK, 76 mins, b/w
Dir: Walter Forde
Stars: Arthur Askey, Richard Murdoch, Phyllis Calvert, Graham Moffatt
Rating: ★★

Brandon Thomas's famous farce about an undergraduate forced to invent, and imitate, a South American aunt was retailored to the talents of the two stars, on the strength of their great success in the hit radio series *Band Waggon*. Stalwarts of the British comedy film, between1935 and 1945, plump Graham Moffatt and doddery Moore Marriott, are on hand to add to the fun, and the heroine is Phyllis Calvert, who was appearing in her second film.

Charley Varrick ◑
1973, US, 111 mins, colour
Dir: Don Siegel
Stars: Walter Matthau, Joe Don Baker, Felicia Farr, Andy Robinson, Sheree North
Rating: ★★★

This highly-rated Don Siegel-directed thriller pulled off the rare double of delighting critics and public alike. Walter Matthau – how pleasurable to see him break away from comedy for a change – brings his own laconic brand of charm to Charley Varrick, a small-time bank robber who suddenly and, to him unexpectedly, hits it big to the tune of more than $750,000. The drawback is it's Mafia money, and Charley and his young partner soon have a syndicate hit-man on their trail. Matthau's gift with throw-away lines is too good to be wasted altogether and Siegel (who makes a cameo appearance himself) ensures that humour isn't completely neglected. And the minor characters are all fully rounded people, from Joe Don Baker's fastidious killer (faintly reminiscent of Richard Widmark in *Kiss of Death*) called Molly, through Marjorie Bennnett's eccentric old dear ('that's mine: an obscene call, I expect') to Sheree North's blackmailing nymphomaniac photographer.

Charlotte's Web ⊙
1972, US, 100 mins, colour
Dir: Charles A Nichols, Iwao Takamoto
Rating: ★★★

A feature cartoon of some charm chronicling the adventures of a pig, Wilbur, and his friend Charlotte the spider, whose magic web-weaving not only saves him from being

c

chopped into streaky bacon, but makes him famous throughout the land. The scene-stealer is a rat called Templeton, voiced by Paul Lynde, who has all the best lines.

Charly ○ ⓥ
1968, US, 106 mins, colour
Dir: Ralph Nelson
Stars: Cliff Robertson, Claire Bloom, Leon Janney
Rating: ★★★

Too much science, like crime, it seems, doesn't pay. Thus Charly, a moron converted to near-genius by a brain operation, finds he must revert in a short time to his former self. Meanwhile, he has fallen in love with the teacher who has set the cycle in motion. Although director Ralph Nelson's treatment of this tricky theme verges on the pedestrian, first-rate performances by Cliff Robertson and Claire Bloom bring out all the heartbreak and frustration involved and turn the film into a near-classic of its kind. Robertson won an Best Actor Oscar for his portrayal, and the film was an unexpected winner with the public as well as critics.

Chase, The ◖
1966, US, 135 mins, colour
Dir: Arthur Penn
Stars: Marlon Brando, Jane Fonda, Robert Redford
Rating: ★★

Arthur Penn, who later made *Bonnie and Clyde* and *Little Big Man*, treads a gory, brutal path in this high-powered look at the warped, evil inhabitants of an American town, and the comparatively clean convict on the run they seek to destroy. Although basically unbelievable, the film remains utterly holding throughout, extremely well made and beautifully photographed in colour, especially in one scene where an escaped prisoner runs across an irrigated field at sunset. The acting is often very good, particularly from James Fox, getting an amazingly natural American accent for a British actor. And Richard Bradford, once of TV's *Man in a Suitcase*, has his biggest film role as the kill-crazy Damon. Others in a powerhouse cast include Marlon Brando, Jane Fonda, Robert Redford, Miriam Hopkins, Martha Hyer, Robert Duvall, Janice Rule, Angie Dickinson, Bruce Cabot and veteran character actor Henry Hull.

Chase, The ● ⓥ
1994, US, 89 mins, colour
Dir: Adam Rifkin
Stars: Charlie Sheen, Kristy Swanson
Rating: ★★

There are some good moments but lots of chances missed in this action comedy which at least lives up to its title by spending 95 per cent of its footage on one car chase. Charlie Sheen, convicted of an armed robbery he was nowhere near, flees from justice, is unluckily trapped by two local cops and grabs the nearest bystander (Kristy Swanson) as hostage, finding out later that she's the daughter of the richest man in the state. The chase starts well with lots of incident, but really needs to sustain the serio-comic mayhem on the freeway at a blood-surging rate if it's to carry us along for the ride. Nor do we believe for a moment kidnapper and hostage making love at the wheel at 80 miles an hour after she has fallen for his innocence – quite apart from it putting the brake on the thrills and spills. Given the stop-go pace, credibility takes a back seat long before the end, despite a personable performance by Sheen himself. You might also spot a guest shot from Cary Elwes as a newscaster to whom spontaneity is a complete stranger.

Chase a Crooked Shadow ◖
1957, UK, 87 mins, b/w
Dir: Michael Anderson
Stars: Anne Baxter, Richard Todd, Herbert Lom
Rating: ★★★

Probably director Michael Anderson's best film, this is one of those marvellous Fifties mysteries in which nothing and no-one is quite what they seem. You may have a hard time sorting out the plot twists before the final solution arrives, especially as Anderson and stars Anne Baxter, Richard Todd and Herbert Lom do their best to mislead us at every twist and turn.

Chato's Land ●
1971, US/Spain, 100 mins, colour
Dir: Michael Winner
Stars: Charles Bronson, Jack Palance, Richard Basehart, James Whitmore
Rating: ★

An excessively unpleasant Western on a revenge theme, with Charles Bronson as the half-Apache stalking the posse who are supposed to be hunting him, after they rape his woman and burn his friend. One of

Bronson's victims is knifed in the neck, another scalped, a third lassoed with a rattlesnake and a fourth clubbed to death with a rock. Gratuitous violence is certainly not to be sniffed at by director Michael Winner but, to his credit, he does get veteran bad guy Jack Palance to give his best performance in quite a while as the ex-Confederate officer who leads the posse.

Chattahoochee ●
1989, US, 97 mins, colour
Dir: Mick Jackson
Stars: Gary Oldman, Dennis Hopper, Frances McDormand, Pamela Reed, Ned Beatty
Rating: ★★

Disregard the upbeat-sounding title. This is a grim and harrowing docu-drama, slowly steered along by its director, about the horrendous treatment of inmates at an institution for the criminally insane. Gary Oldman is just fine (as is his – localised – American accent) as Emmett, a Korean War veteran who is sent to Chattahoochee after going berserk and shooting up the neighbourhood. Gradually coming to his senses inside, he befriends another 'patient' (Dennis Hopper) and begins a furtive campaign of letters to his sister (Pamela Reed) to try to get publicity of the weekly beatings and torture to which the inmates have to submit at the hands of sadistic guards. It's horrifying to realise that something out of medieval times could still exist as recently as 1955 (Emmett didn't get out until 1959). But the film perhaps over-emphasises these conditions, making the catalogue of filth and ill-treatment too much for the eye.

Cheap Detective, The ○
1978, US, 92 mins, colour
Dir: Robert Moore
Stars: Peter Falk, James Coco, Louise Fletcher, John Houseman, Nicol Williamson, Dom DeLuise
Rating: ★★

Everybody thinks they can do a parody of Humphrey Bogart movies and writer Neil Simon is no exception. But the magic of the original material is strong and resists in stubborn style, making this no more than a mild and genial parody of both *Casablanca* and *The Maltese Falcon*. Peter Falk lays on the Bogey stuff as thick as treacle, and a formidable cast contributes some good laughs along the way, not least John Houseman who settles well into the Sydney Greenstreet tradition.

Cheaper by the Dozen ○
1950, US, 85 mins, colour
Dir: Walter Lang
Stars: Clifton Webb, Jeanne Crain, Myrna Loy, Edgar Buchanan
Rating: ★★★

Warm, tender, human and funny and very much along the lines of the famous *Life With Father* (although this is even better), this is the real-life story, set in 1921, of an eccentric time and motion expert, his 12 children and his Victorian-style household run with all the precision of his office. First-rate performances by Clifton Webb and Myrna Loy as father and mother shine like jewels in the midst of Leon Shamroy's glowing colour photography. Few cameramen were as adept at capturing the nostalgic glow of a time gone by. *Cheaper by the Dozen*, which was based on a book by two of the leading characters' children, Ernestine Carey and Frank Gilbreth, was so popular that it gave rise to a sequel two years later, *Belles on Their Toes*, again with Myrna Loy.

Checking Out ◑
1989, US, 98 mins, colour
Dir: David Leland
Stars: Jeff Daniels, Melanie Mayron, Michael Tucker, Ann Magnuson
Rating: ★

A lightweight black comedy about the American obsession with death, which was examined decades earlier with sharper and funnier humour in *Send Me No Flowers*. This has a couple of good chuckles, but is mostly pretty weak. Jeff Daniels takes the Rock Hudson part as the young executive who sees his best friend keel over with a heart attack and panics himself into thinking he's about to follow suit. Covering himself with more tubes and plastic than a hospital operating theatre, he can no longer think about making love to his wife, getting on with his job or taking care of his children: he is preoccupied with 'checking out'. Daniels lacks the controlled panic of the hypochondriac and director David Leland over-paces it all, injecting it with shots from wide-angle lenses to emphasise its surreal and comic qualities. Chances are you'll fall asleep before Daniels comes to his senses.

Cheers for Miss Bishop ○
1941, US, 95 mins, b/w
Dir: Tay Garnett
Stars: Martha Scott, William Gargan, Edmund Gwenn, Sterling Holloway, Sidney Blackmer
Rating: ★★★

Martha Scott has to age 50 years in this nicely-directed chronicle of a schoolma'am's life. It comes out as a sort of *Goodbye Miss Chips*, strong on the atmosphere of a small mid-western town in the late 19th century, and with excellent music by Edward Ward (who was nominated for an Oscar) and photography by Hal Mohr. In a supporting role is Ralph Bowman, who soon changed his name to John Archer and became a minor star (actress Anne Archer is his daughter).

Cheyenne Social Club, The ◐
1973, US, 103 mins, colour
Dir: Gene Kelly
Stars: James Stewart, Henry Fonda, Shirely Jones, Sue Anne Langdon
Rating: ★★★

A comedy-Western of great charm, mainly because of its two stars. James Stewart and Henry Fonda are the two wandering cowboys who rub their hands in glee at the prospect of inheriting The Cheyenne Social Club, and then rub their heads in despair as they discover the truth that the Club is the town's bordello. There's some nice exchanges of dialogue between Stewart and Fonda, especially during their long trek to Cheyenne, but director Gene Kelly flexes fewer muscles than he perhaps should to make this gentle entertainment dynamic.

Chicago Joe and the Showgirl ◐ ⓥ
1989, UK, 103 mins, colour
Dir: Bernard Rose
Stars: Kiefer Sutherland, Emily Lloyd, Patsy Kensit, Keith Allen, Liz Fraser, Alexandra Pigg
Rating: ★★

An almost surrealistic treatment of a grim and fascinating real-life murder case. It could have worked too, but severe script problems and a rare dud performance from Emily Lloyd are damaging minus factors that undermine director Bernard Rose's imagination at every turn. The dialogue is studded with lines that either raise a nervous titter or simply don't advance the drama. And Lloyd's impish portrayal of the showgirl who

eggs on an American soldier to murder never captures the vicious, unbalanced nature you expect to see in a character who is clearly meant to revel in the blood and guts of it all. The baby-faced Kiefer Sutherland is convincing by comparison as the gang-connected lieutenant who may not be what he seems; and Patsy Kensit even better as his English rose on the side. By use of glitzy images, Rose emphasises the glamour the girl sees in crime, and the fact that the two central characters live in fantasy worlds that help make their crimes possible. And his re-creation of the (wartime) period and its atmosphere is the perfection we've – unfairly – come to take for granted in recent times.

Chief Crazy Horse ○
(aka: Valley of Fury)
1955, US, 88 mins, colour
Dir: George Sherman
Stars: Victor Mature, Suzan Ball, John Lund, Ray Danton, Dennis Weaver
Rating: ★★

Director George Sherman holds one's interest in this Western, which tells the story of one of the greatest Indian chiefs and his ultimately doomed alliance with the white man. The large cast includes David Janssen, in the days before he became one of television's busiest actors, John Lund, memorable as Grace Kelly's stuffy fiance in in *High Society*, Dennis Weaver, also to become a TV star, and Ray Danton, later regularly directing for the small screen.

Children of a Lesser God ◑ ⓥ
1986, US, 110 mins, colour
Dir: Randa Haines
Stars: William Hurt, Marlee Matlin, Piper Laurie, Philip Bosco
Rating: ★★★

Although it struggles a bit when William Hurt has to 'verbalise' deaf-mute co-star Marlee Matlin's dialogue, this is otherwise a throat-grippingly successful love story of a distinctly unconventional nature. Matlin's wonderfully expressive face enables her to give a performance that won her an Academy Award, while Hurt and Piper Laurie (who plays Matlin's mother) were also nominated for Oscars. Based on the equally triumphant play, this film version benefits from sensitive direction by Randa Haines that brings out both the comic and tragic aspects of the affair between

c

teacher Hurt and his 'special pupil'
and from glistening Metrocolor photography of the coldly beautiful
Canadian landscape by John Seale.

Children of the Corn ● ⊙
1984, US, 93 mins, colour
Dir: Fritz Kiersch
Stars: Peter Horton, Linda Hamilton,
John Franklin, R G Armstrong
Rating: ★

This expansion of a short story by ace
horror writer Stephen King calls for a
firm suspension of logic on the part of
its audience and plants its mayhem on
familiar ground. Somewhere in
Nebraska, a band of psychotic children
have killed all adults and established a
religious community worshipping a
mysterious deity of the corn fields.
You'll cull some chills and nervous
chuckles from subsequent goings-on
which carry echoes of *The Dark Secret
of Harvest Home* and *The Wicker Man*.
The real star of the film is Craig
Stearns' art direction, which suggests a
hidden evil around every corner.

Children's Hour, The ◐
(aka: The Loudest Whisper)
1961, US, 107 mins, b/w
Dir: William Wyler
Stars: Audrey Hepburn, Shirley
MacLaine, James Garner, Miriam
Hopkins, Fay Bainter
Rating: ★★★★

The relaxation of censorship codes
meant that Hollywood could really do
justice to Lillian Hellman's famous
play about the effects that a child's
malicious whispers about two
teachers' alleged lesbian relationship
have on the lives of the people concerned. And, with William Wyler at
the helm (he'd directed a wa-
tered-down version, *These Three*,
nearly 30 years earlier), a superb film
resulted. Five Oscar nominations
resulted in nothing from a film industry still slightly sensitive about
giving awards to films with such
themes. Audrey Hepburn is excellent
and Shirley MacLaine unbearably
touching. One of their pupils is
portrayed by Veronica Cartwright,
who grew up to play neurotic D.A.
Margaret Callaghan in *L. A. Law*. The
moving ending is perfectly handled
by the director.

Child's Play ● ⊙
1988, US, 91 mins, colour
Dir: Tom Holland

Stars: Catherine Hicks, Chris Sarandon,
Brad Dourif, Alex Vincent
Rating: ★

Horror films almost always ask us to
suspend our disbelief for the chills to
bite. But here's a would-be chiller
that's just too silly for that to happen.
A crazed killer, with some belief in
occult powers, transfers his soul to the
body of a doll before he dies. Quite
why the doll doesn't come to life before it's bought by a child's mother
from a tramp is only one of the mysteries of this film but, under the name
of Chuckie, he then sets out to revenge himself on the partner who
betrayed him and the cop who
gunned him down. There's actually
more to the plot, but it's even more
preposterous, culminating in the doll
gradually becoming human, thus giving the heroes a chance to kill it.
Director Tom Holland finally brings
this lame nag home via several false
climaxes as it staggers towards the
90-minute mark. Chuckie's worth a
chuckle here: no more. Better,
though, than the sequels that followed.

Chiltern Hundreds, The ○
(aka: The Amazing Mr Beecham)
1949, UK, 84 mins, b/w
Dir: John Paddy Carstairs
Stars: Cecil Parker, A E Matthews, David
Tomlinson, Lana Morris
Rating: ★★★

A classic film comedy with an Ealing
touch, about a young viscount (David
Tomlinson) who attempts to get out
of service in the Army and marry his
American fiancee by announcing that
he is standing as a candidate for Parliament. There's a rich
characterisation from A E Matthews as
Lord Lister and a brief glimpse of
Anthony Steel as an adjutant.

China Girl ● ⊙
1987, US, 90 mins, colour
Dir: Abel Ferrara
Stars: James Russo, Richard
Panebianco, Sari Chang, David Caruso,
Russell Wong
Rating: ★

This ludicrously overpumped melodrama emerges as a pop promo video
cross between *The Godfather* and *East
Side Story*. Young lovers from the opposite sides of the Chinese-Italian
tracks meet meltingly at one of those
ghetto discos where everybody seems
to wear vests, and are promptly
engulfed in gang warfare whose
hot-headed elements are supposed to

be kept in check by their own side.
The characters do little but scream and
shout at each other, beat each other
with heavy metal or blast each other
bloodily with heavier artillery.
However viciously beaten, though,
they all get up and run away when the
cops arrive. Director Ferrara tops it off
with overdone lighting effects and
portentous close-ups of inanimate
objects. His film, very slow for its
running time, is dedicated to the
people of Chinatown and Little Italy,
but we should think they'd want to
give it back.

China Seas ○
1935, US, 90 mins, b/w
Dir: Tay Garnett
Stars: Clark Gable, Jean Harlow,
Wallace Beery, Rosalind Russell, Robert
Benchley, Akim Tamiroff
Rating: ★★★

The stars are an entertainment in
themselves in this rousing romantic
adventure with Cap'n Clark Gable
trying to hang on to his cargo of gold
against China Seas pirates, as well as
dealing with contrasting women on
board. Film-maker, traveller and
sometime round-the-world
yachtsman Tay Garnett directs with a
good sense of atmosphere and locale.
The sea scenes are rousingly done, and
such big names as Gable, Jean Harlow,
Wallace Beery, Rosalind Russell,
Robert Benchley and Akim Tamiroff
all catch the eye. Acting honours,
however, go to veteran MGM star
Lewis Stone.

China Syndrome, The ◐ ⊙
1979, US, 122 mins, colour
Dir: James Bridges
Stars: Jane Fonda, Jack Lemmon,
Michael Douglas, Scott Brady, James
Hampton
Rating: ★★★

What went wrong at the nuclear
power plant? What caused the 'second
shudder' when a valve stuck and a
crisis occurred? Chief technician Jack
Lemmon, radical photographer Michael Douglas and TV reporter Jane
Fonda are determined to find out. The
ensuing developments form a social
concience thriller along the lines of a
nuclear *Coma*. Even if you have
difficulty in following what's going
on, the tension propels the story along
by itself and the climax, although
contrived and drawn out, is
unbearably suspenseful.

Chinatown ● ⓥ

1974, US, 131 mins, colour
Dir: Roman Polanski
Stars: Jack Nicholson, Faye Dunaway, John Huston, Perry Lopez, John Hillerman, Diane Ladd
Rating: ★★★

Roman Polanski's tough, downbeat contribution to the private eye thriller cycle. Jack Nicholson brings his own brand of cynical integrity to the role of a small-time detective in Los Angeles, 1937, who takes on a small matrimonial case, only to find it inevitably escalating into something that involves corruption on a city-wide scale. Polanski keeps his film scrupulously in period, not only in looks, but the way it's made as a whole, the only concessions to the Seventies being the rugged dialogue, and some fringe violence – our hero has his nose slit to warn him off. Watch out for the director himself in a small but memorable role as the vicious, knife-wielding hood. And John Huston brings his own brand unique of affable corruption to the role of a millionaire with much to hide.

Chisum ○ ⓥ

1970, US, 110 mins, colour
Dir: Andrew V McLaglen
Stars: John Wayne, Forrest Tucker, Ben Johnson, Bruce Cabot, Christopher George, Richard Jaekel
Rating: ★★

All action but not much heart, this is a routine latter-day John Wayne Western in which women hardly get a look in. Sideline attractions include rousing music by Dominic Frontiere (with the title song by Merle Haggard) and more Hollywood Western veterans than we have space to list! But a sense of danger is missing, robbing the film of any edge, even though it's set in the 1870s against the complex and fascinating history of the Lincoln County wars.

Chitty Chitty Bang Bang ⊙ ⓥ

1968, US/UK, 145 mins, colour
Dir: Ken Hughes
Stars: Dick Van Dyke, Sally Ann Howes, Lionel Jeffries, Gert Frobe, Anna Quayle, Benny Hill
Rating: ★★

A rather weak British musical despite being produced by the James Bond team, co-scripted by Roald Dahl, and based on a collection of stories by Ian Fleming. It includes such familiar 007

faces as Desmond Llewellyn and Gert Frobe, but in contrast to the James Bond films, the special effects are wobbly and the score a hit and miss affair. The story is a sugar-coated piece of whimsy about an amazing vintage car – a 'fine four-fendered friend' to chirpy Dick Van Dyke and two precocious kids – that can take to water or the air with the greatest of ease. The best thing about the film are the amazing sets and the bizarre mechanical contraptions of Rowland Emmett, especially the sausage and egg machine. In the human cast, Frobe and Anna Quayle make the most of their roles as villians. The whole thing passes the finishing flag six minutes later than *Mary Poppins*, from whom the producers borrowed the male star, choreographers and song writers.

Choirboys, The ●

1977, US, 119 mins, colour
Dir: Robert Aldrich
Stars: Charles Durning, Louis Gossett Jr, Perry King, Randy Quaid, James Woods, Don Stroud
Rating: ★★

Imagine turning over a stone in some dark corner of the *Hill Street Blues* precinct, and what crawls from underneath might well be the 'choirboys'. The title refers to ten maverick policemen on night duty in Los Angeles; and, from the start, shock, horror and melodrama run rampant as some of Hollywood's most abrasive modern 'tough guy' actors, including Charles Durning, Burt Young, James Woods, Don Stroud, Robert Webber, Louis Gossett, Perry King and Randy Quaid, lend their talents to a series of darkly eccentric character studies. Also in the cast: *Hill Street* alumnus Charles Haid, who plays a sergeant.

Chorus Line, A ◑

1985, US, 111 mins, colour
Dir: Richard Attenborough
Stars: Michael Douglas, Terrence Mann, Alyson Reed
Rating: ★★

They should have got Bob Fosse to make this one. Instead, they hired Britain's Oscar-winning Richard Attenborough, who had never made a musical before and the result is, well, just unexciting. Attenborough takes the show that set the stage alight and, in this curiously flat version, dampens its spirit. Talented directors often miss out on the sheer adrenalin-pumping verve of a hit musical – think of John

Huston and *Annie* – and, in the treatment here, the performances seem oddly muffled. The success of the insipid Cassie (Alyson Reed) is even less fair than in the stage show; frankly she's a bit of a pain. In the show's big number, 'What I Did for Love', the camera angles make you fear more for her safety in high heels on a high iron stairway than attentive to the lyrics of the song.

Chorus of Disapproval, A ○ ⓥ

1988, UK, 100 mins, colour
Dir: Michael Winner
Stars: Anthony Hopkins, Jeremy Irons, Richard Briers, Patsy Kensit, Jenny Seagrove, Sylvia Sims
Rating: ★★★

Any seaside rep would give its eye teeth to have a company like this: Jeremy Irons, Jenny Seagrove, Patsy Kensit, Richard Briers, Gareth Hunt, Prunella Scales, Lionel Jeffries, Sylvia Syms and Alexandra Pigg. The company's director is none other than Anthony Hopkins, sporting an impeccable Welsh accent (as well he might) in this adaptation of Alan Ayckbourn's play which, under Michael Winner's direction, provides pretty good fun and proves, perhaps, that Winner's real talent lies in comedy. Hopkins is superb as the little Welsh Hitler, Irons vastly amusing as the shy Yorkshire widower turned local Lothario. But no-one can take the film away from Prunella Scales as Hopkins' pudding wife, having a late, late fling with Irons. Occasionally, the film's characters grow too large for life, but overall the writer and director's affection for the subject shines through. No great movie, but very British and Winner's best effort in ages.

Chosen, The ◑

See: Holocaust 2000

Christine ● ⓥ

1983, US, 111 mins, colour
Dir: John Carpenter
Stars: John Stockwell, Alexandra Paul, Harry Dean Stanton, Robert Prosky, Christine Belford, Keith Gordon
Rating: ★★

This is the one about the demon car and it may make you wary of walking the streets at night. Christine is a beauty all right. Red as the devil, all gleaming chrome and dazzling headlamps, playing tunes on the radio to express her thoughts. But woe be-

C

tide anyone who comes between her and her young master Arnie. This is a film that believes strongly in action, and its scenario never misses a chance to aim for the lowest common denominator. But, after a longish period of delineating Arnie's many enemies that Christine will eventually take to the grinder's, there are few dull spots in the film's lengthy running time, although the final duel between Christine and the excavator doesn't have quite the variation of excitement that it might have done. Arnie is well played by Keith Gordon, who splendidly creates two quite separate characters.

Christmas Carol, A
See: Scrooge [1951]

Christmas Holiday ○
1944, US, 92 mins, b/w
Dir: Robert Siodmak
Stars: Deanna Durbin, Gene Kelly, Richard Whorf, Gale Sondergaard
Rating: ★★★

With a title like this, and Gene Kelly co-starring with Deanna Durbin, this has to be, you would think, a warm and happy musical. Well you would be wrong, especially with director Robert Siodmak, king of Forties' *film noir*, at the helm, working from a source novel by Somerset Maugham. Kelly is excellent as the smooth rotten apple obsessed with Durbin's cabaret singer. Pretty unusual.

Christmas in Connecticut ○
1945, US, 101 mins, b/w
Dir: Peter Godfrey
Stars: Barbara Stanwyck, Dennis Morgan, Sydney Greenstreet, Reginald Gardiner, S Z Sakall, Una O'Connor
Rating: ★★

A nostalgic if corny treat. Barbara Stanwyck is the lady with the double life – the chic spinster newspaper columnist who, when ordered by her boss to entertain a war hero at Christmas with her family at home on a Connecticut farm, must then rustle up aforementioned family and home. 'I don't have a farm,' she admits from her New York apartment. 'I don't even have a window box!' And thereby hangs the comic thread of this festive fable.

Christmas in July ☉
1940, US, 67 mins, b/w
Dir: Preston Sturges

Stars: Dick Powell, Ellen Drew, Raymond Walburn, Al Bridge, William Demarest
Rating: ★★★

Ace comedy writer-director Preston Sturges may have got the germ of the idea for this fun-feast from The Three Stooges' short *Healthy, Wealthy and Dumb*. There, of course, the resemblance ends. This is a joyously scripted, helter-skelter, occasionally talky but by-and-large hilarious tale of a man who thinks he's won a fortune in a competition and proceeds to go on the spending spree to end them all. Dick Powell took further steps away from his image as a song-and-dance man, while such Sturges regulars as Raymond Walburn, William Demarest and Franklin Pangborn provide characteristic support.

Christmas Martian, The ○
1971, Canada, 63 mins, colour
Dir: Bernard Gosselin
Rating: ★★★

Charming Canadian film about two small children who befriend a Martian stranded in the snow, and help him mend his spaceship. Shades of *E.T.*

Christmas Story, A ☉ ⓥ
1983, US, 98 mins, colour
Dir: Bob Clark
Stars: Melinda Dillon, Darren McGavin, Peter Billinglsly
Rating: ★★★

Director Bob Clark, best known for his offensive, juvenile sex comedies *Porky's* and *Porky's II: The Next Day*, turned in quite a sweet festive family film here. Set around the misadventures of an American family in the 1940s as Christmas approaches, its cast is wonderful (especially Darren McGavin as a father battling with a smoke-belching furnace) and the laughs come non-stop, in wry, very American fashion. A classic of its kind.

Christmas Tree, The ○
1969, US, 110 mins, colour
Dir: Terence Young
Stars: William Holden, Virna Lisi, Brook Fuller
Rating: ★

Terence Young, who made several of the James Bond action films, got right away from all that when he wrote and directed this king-sized weepie about a young boy dying from radiation poisoning. The child acquires two tame wolves to ease him through his dying days, and they're very

appealing. The script, however, could have been stiffened by draining away some of its unnecessary sentiment.

Christopher Columbus ○
1948, UK, 104 mins, colour
Dir: David Macdonald
Stars: Fredric March, Francis L Sullivan, Florence Eldridge, Kathleen Ryan, Derek Bond, Felix Aylmer
Rating: ★★

A lavishly-mounted, British-made account of Columbus' efforts in the late 15th century to prove that the world is round. There's too much talk and not enough action until near the end, but sterling performances come from Fredric March, Derek Bond, Felix Aylmer and that 200-pound master of menace, Francis L Sullivan. Director David Macdonald was one of Britain's brightest young directing hopes in pre-war years, with a series of comedy-thrillers in *Thin Man*-style, usually starring Barry K Barnes. But both star and director lost their popularity in the years following the end of World War Two, and this Technicolor epic fared no better at the box-office than the two financial flops made of the Columbus story in more recent times.

Christopher Columbus: The Discovery ◑ ⓥ
1992, US, 121 mins, colour
Dir: John Glen
Stars: George Corraface, Rachel Ward, Marlon Brando, Robert Davi, Tom Selleck, Catherine Zeta Jones
Rating: ★★

Halfway between a history lesson and a Sinbad film, this harks back to the days when Hollywood sailed the seven seas every other week. Never dull, John Glen's film hurtles through history at a rate of knots. Marlon Brando mumbles in his finest Fifties' fashion as Torquemada. A grumpy Tom Selleck gets a laugh just by coming on in a crown as the Spanish king. A girlish Rachel Ward is Queen Isabella and George Corraface flashes his teeth a lot as Columbus, going through such violent mood and personality changes (one minute dashing adventurer, the next ranting zealot) as to make you think there must have been more of the film than appears in this version. 'She's a fine vessel,' he tells his bride (a skittish Catherine Zeta Jones), 'but not too top heavy or narrow of beam. A little like someone I know.' Not that Zeta Jones' bust compares with that of the Indian chieftain's half-naked daughter who was of course chosen for her facial mobility. Rather more credibility is lent by Oliver Cotton (CC's right-hand man), Nigel Terry (a scowling bad guy) and Robert Davi as CC's fellow-captain; Davi's last line is worth staying in your seats for.

Chuka ◐
1967, US/UK, 105 mins, colour
Dir: Gordon Douglas
Stars: Rod Taylor, Ernest Borgnine, John Mills, Luciana Paluzzi, Louis Hayward
Rating: ★★

An intense, if rather slow-moving Western. The ever-reliable suspense of impending Indian attack on a fort becomes stronger as the climax of the film draws near.

Chump at Oxford, A ⊙
1940, US, 63 mins, b/w
Dir: Alfred Goulding
Stars: Stan Laurel, Oliver Hardy
Rating: ★★★★

In 1940 Laurel and Hardy returned to producer Hal Roach, with whom they'd made their best films, for two short features, *A Chump at Oxford* and *Saps at Sea*. A burlesque on *A Yank at Oxford*, this joyous comedy finds the boys given the chance of an Oxford education after foiling a gang of bank robbers. But they soon become the butt of endless practical jokes from a gang of bullies led by Peter Cushing, in one of his earliest screen roles. The material is delightful in both sections and even touching at the end. Certainly the last great Laurel and Hardy comedy.

Cimarron ○
1960, US, 142 mins, colour
Dir: Anthony Mann
Stars: Glenn Ford, Maria Schell
Rating: ★★

This is another case of a remake being a pale shadow of the original. The 1931 version had a huge budget, thousands of extras and won a trio of Oscars and although it looks a bit dated now, it's still a better film than this one. Set around the time of the Oklahoma land rush, Glenn Ford is the homesteader who, cheated out of his land, becomes sheriff of a new town and also runs the local newspaper. Despite a strong cast that includes Ford, Maria Schell, Anne Baxter, Russ Tamblyn and Vic Morrow and direction from Anthony Mann, this is a formula cowboy film that does little

justice to the original novel. It also offers no threat to its Oscar-winning predecessor.

Cimarron Kid, The ○
1951, US, 83 mins, colour
Dir: Budd Boetticher
Stars: Audie Murphy, James Best, Yvette Dugay, Hugh O'Brian
Rating: ★★

The story of Bill Doolin and the Daltons – one of the most exciting true tales in Western history – has been filmed several times, notably with Randolph Scott in 1949. Alas, in real-life Doolin came to a less happy end than the one depicted here. Not one of director Budd Boetticher's best westerns, but there is some efficiently-staged excitement and blazing Technicolor photography. Alas, that didn't save it from playing second fiddle to an Abbott and Costello comedy on double-bills in the year it came out.

Cincinnati Kid, The ○ ⓥ
1966, US, 113 mins, colour
Dir: Norman Jewison
Stars: Steve McQueen, Edward G Robinson, Ann-Margret, Karl Malden, Tuesday Weld, Joan Blondell
Rating: ★★★

If you're a card-playing fanatic, or a gambler of any kind, this Thirties' drama will probably wind up your nerves, bring all your sweat glands into action, rivet you to the screen and give you no end of enjoyment. Despite the starry cast, though, the human element to the drama is largely missing. The atmosphere is there, but seems to have gone stale on us. The actors do their best without really shining, but director Norman Jewison, who does keep the action moving at a steady clip, seems to have no overall hold on his subject, giving us no theme to get involved with. Steve McQueen is the poker-playing kid, but he gets a raw deal from the script. Cutting a few more aces are Tuesday Weld (as McQueen's quiet country mistress) and Joan Blondell, while Edward G Robinson lords over all in more ways than one as 'The Man', whom McQueen has to beat to get to the top of the red-hot poker tree. The final game between them is worth anybody's stake to an armchair view.

Cinderella ⊙ ⓥ
1950, US, 75 mins, colour
Dir: Wilfred Jackson, Hamilton Luske, Clyde Geronimi

Voice stars: Ilene Woods, William Phipps, Eleanor Sudley, Verna Felton
Rating: ★★★

Too many human characters and not enough of Disney's delightful animals are the downside to this generally enjoyable Disney version of the fairytale classic. Never mind, every time the mice Gus and Jacques and the ferocious cat Lucifer hold centre stage, the film blazes into life. And there's a toe-tapping score that includes the title song and the famous 'Bibbidi-Bobbidi-Boo'. The wicked stepmother and two repulsive ugly sisters (complete with Olive Oyl-type arms and legs, and huge feet) are well up to the Disney tradition for formidable female villains. What was it that Uncle Walt had against women?

Cinderfella ⊙ ⓥ
1960, US, 91 mins, colour
Dir: Frank Tashlin
Stars: Jerry Lewis, Anna Maria Alberghetti, Ed Wynn, Henry Silva
Rating: ★★

Colourful Jerry Lewis pantomime romp, with Jerry as a male Cinders, and a dazzling princess, beautifully played and sung by Anna Maria Alberghetti. Henry Silva also scores as Fella's polo-playing stepbrother, but the comedy routines are sometimes overdone to the verge of tedium. Providing the music at the ball: Count Basie and his band. You'll probably get tired of this, though, long before midnight comes.

Circle of Deception ○
1960, UK, 100 mins, b/w
Dir: Jack Lee
Stars: Bradford Dillman, Suzy Parker, Harry Andrews, Robert Stephens
Rating: ★★

An agonisingly intense performance from Bradford Dillman as an Allied officer captured by the Gestapo in France and subjected to unedifying interrogation techniques highlights this tense drama. Director Jack Lee sacrifices some of the suspense by using a flashback framework but the ironic ending is worth waiting for.

Circus, The ⊙
1928, US, 72 mins, b/w
Dir: Charles Chaplin
Stars: Charlie Chaplin, Merna Kennedy
Rating: ★★

Although this Charlie Chaplin film has some joyous comedy moments along the way, its pathos undoubtedly works

c

less well than in previous Chaplin classics, such as *The Kid*. Nonetheless, the industry felt moved to offer Chaplin a special Oscar that year 'for versatility and genius in writing, directing and producing *The Circus*'. Chaplin himself, as the tramp who becomes a star clown, is still in vintage form, but there is no Mack Swain or Eric Campbell for him to play against, and the supporting cast is undeniably weaker than in many of his films. But Chaplin was to bounce back with one of his greatest films, *City Lights*.

Circus of Horrors ●
1960, UK, 91 mins, colour
Dir: Sidney Hayers
Stars: Anton Diffring, Yvonne Monlaur, Erika Remberg, Jane Hylton, Donald Pleasence, Conrad Phillips
Rating: ★★

There's a whole parade of lovely young actresses for power-mad Anton Diffring to bump off at his circus, when they get a bit grumpy at their billing on the big top marquee, in this lively shocker. These unlikely circus stars include Vanda Hudson, Erika Remberg, Yvonne Romain and Yvonne Monlaur. The gorilla gets Donald Pleasence and, indeed, there can't be many of the cast left by the time policemen Conrad Phillips and Jack Gwillim close in on Diffring in an exciting last reel.

Circus World
See: The Magnificent Showman

Cisco Pike ●
1972, US, 94 mins, colour
Dir: Bill L Norton
Stars: Kris Kristofferson, Karen Black, Gene Hackman, Harry Dean Stanton
Rating: ★★★

This gripping thriller earned an 'X' certificate from the British film censor on release in 1972 thanks to its drug-related theme and hero who's a drug pusher. Kris Kristofferson – in a role that reflects in some ways his own personality – is a singer/songwriter whose star faded with the end of the swinging Sixties. At the barrel of a gun he is forced back into the drugs scene by the bitter cop (Gene Hackman) who once arrested him, and now wants a personal pension to cushion his retirement from the force. Kristofferson adds five of his own songs to the soundtrack, including 'Lovin' Her Was Easier'.

Citadel, The ○
1938, UK, 110 mins, b/w
Dir: King Vidor
Stars: Robert Donat, Rosalind Russell, Ralph Richardson, Rex Harrison, Emlyn Williams, Francis L Sullivan
Rating: ★★★★

Star Robert Donat, director King Vidor and the film itself were all nominated for Academy Awards. In the event, the only major award taken by this fine version of A J Cronin's medical saga was the New York Film Critics' award for best film. Extremely well adapted by a bevy of screen-writers, who included co-star Emlyn Williams, the film grips and entertains throughout, frequently touching the emotions with its skilful dialogue and persuasive direction. Ralph Richardson gives a memorable portrayal of Donat's stalwart friend, Denny, in a story peppered effectively with mini-climaxes.

Citizen Kane ○ ⓥ
1941, US, 119 mins, b/w
Dir: Orson Welles
Stars: Orson Welles, Joseph Cotten, Ray Collins, Everett Sloane, Dorothy Comingore
Rating: ★★★★

Still on most critics' lists of the best ten films ever made, Orson Welles' towering, brilliantly-edited and hypnotically entertaining jigsaw of a film is a trailblazing masterpiece that advanced the cinema by light years. Full of scenes that could be shown on their own and have the same impact, the film uses settings, light and shade (and, unusually, ceiling on its sets), to achieve realism and mood. Despite critical raves, the industry treated the movie, which surveys the rise and fall of a newspaper magnate, with considerable indifference. They gave it only one Academy Award (for the screenplay) and ignored Dudley Nichols' wonderful, innovative deep-focus photography in favour of Arthur Miller's more conventional work on *How Green Was My Valley*. You'll find a journey through the gates of Xanadu brings fresh rewards with each visit.

Citizens Band ○
(aka: Handle With Care)
1977, US, 100 mins, colour
Dir: Jonathan Demme
Stars: Paul Le Mat, Candy Clark
Rating: ★★★★

Director Jonathan Demme has been feted in recent years for *Married to the Mob* and *The Silence of the Lambs*, but this early comedy equals anything he's ever done. Reminiscent of the films of Frank Capra with its multitude of characters and incident, and wonderfully emotive ending, it gives the underrated and versatile Paul Le Mat his best role to date as the small-town guy who tries to hold several threads of his life together while trying to cope with wildcat broadcasters threatening to wreck his emergency rescue service. Demme directs with a great feeling of affection for his characters, creating the kind of film which leaves you with a warm feeling at the end.

City Beneath the Sea ○
1953, US, 87 mins, colour
Dir: Budd Boetticher
Stars: Robert Ryan, Mala Powers, Anthony Quinn, Susan Ball
Rating: ★★

This potboiler stars Robert Ryan and Anthony Quinn as rival deep sea divers on the hunt for treasure in the sunken city of Port Royal. The action bubbles along and is enlivened by an undersea earthquake, but is strictly studio conveyor-belt fodder.

City Beneath the Sea
See: One Hour to Domesday

City for Conquest ○
1940, US, 101 mins, b/w
Dir: Anatole Litvak
Stars: James Cagney, Ann Sheridan, Frank Craven, Donald Crisp, Arthur Kennedy, George Tobias
Rating: ★★★

A typical James Cagney role as (to quote the publicity): 'a slum newsboy who rises to fame by the power of his chunky fists, in a city peopled with hoodlums, frustrated do-gooders and a few geniuses.' Actually, it's a bit more sentimental than that, with Cagney sacrificing everything to help his brainy brother. This role is played by Arthur Kennedy (in his first film), foreshadowing his classic portrayal of Kirk Douglas' brother in *Champion* nine years later. The supporting cast is full of surprises, from a slick-haired Anthony Quinn, through character star Blanche Yurka, to Elia Kazan, who went on to become an Oscar-winning director. The whole film is immensely entertaining in the typical Warner Brothers manner of the day.

City Heat ◐ Ⓥ
1984, US, 97 mins, colour
Dir: Richard Benjamin
Stars: Clint Eastwood, Burt Reynolds,
Jane Alexander, Madeline Kahn, Rip
Torn, Richard Rountree
Rating: ★★

A crime romp within whose framework Clint Eastwood and Burt
Reynolds can exercise their familiar
film characters. The word 'framework'
just about sums up the plot, which is
set in the early 1930s and concerns the
demise of private eye Reynolds'
partner and the subsequent battle by
Reynolds and cop Eastwood (his
former police colleague) to corner the
two gang leaders involved. Jane Alexander is very good as the
wisecracking secretary, Madeline Kahn
plays Reynolds' high-society moll and
Irene Cara is a frightened witness.
Reynolds displays his agility,
Eastwood walks down Main Street in
the open while others fire at him from
cover, there's a lot of fairly
inconsequential gunfire and a running
gag about a suitcase loaded with dynamite, and it's all pretty enjoyable.
Just don't expect any surprises.

City Is Dark, The ○
(aka: Crime Wave)
1954, US, 74 mins, b/w
Dir: Andre De Toth
Stars: Gene Nelson, Sterling Hayden,
Phyllis Kirk, Ted De Corsia, Charles
Bronson
Rating: ★★★

Tough little *film noir* from Warner
Brothers, grittily directed by Andre
de Toth and full of Hollywood's
shadiest underworld types, including
Jay Novello, Ted De Corsia, James
Bell, Timothy Carey and Charles
Bronson (billed as Charles Buchinsky).
Gene Nelson, best known as a dancer,
turns in a decent job of straight acting,
and Phyllis Kirk is attractively plucky
as his wife. You may have trouble
following detective Sterling Hayden's
dialogue, as he talks with a toothpick
in his mouth for most of the film!

City Jungle, The ○
(aka: The Young Philadelphians)
1959, US, 136 mins, b/w
Dir: Vincent Sherman
Stars: Paul Newman, Barbara Rush,
Alexis Smith, Brian Keith, Robert Vaughn
Rating: ★★★

A much better title for a movie that
started life as *The Young Philadelphians*.
Paul Newman gives another of his

intense, exhilarating performances as
the young legal eagle on the make
(just how his alcoholic lawyer in *The
Verdict* might have started out) and he
gets sensitive support from lovely
Barbara Rush. The friend he defends
on a murder charge is played by
Robert (*Man from UNCLE*) Vaughn
who gives an outstanding performance
that won him an Oscar nomination.

City Lights ☉ Ⓥ
1931, US, 85 mins, b/w
Dir: Charles Chaplin
Stars: Charlie Chaplin, Virginia Cherrill,
Florence Lee
Rating: ★★★

Charlie Chaplin didn't always achieve
the difficult double of successful
comedy and successful pathos for
which he often strove, but this film,
released silent after almost three years
in the making, was a triumph for him
on both fronts. His scenes with the
blind flower girl are genuinely touching, and the sequence in the boxing
ring one of the most hilarious in all
Chaplin's distinguished contributions
to the cinema. Chaplin personally
composed and conducted the music
for this, his first film with a soundtrack
score.

City of Bad Men ○
1953, US, 82 mins, colour
Dir: Harmon Jones
Stars: Jeanne Crain, Dale Robertson,
Richard Boone, Lloyd Bridges
Rating: ★★

Large-scale, off-beat Western about
gangs planning to run off with the
proceeds from the Fitzsimmons-
Corbett heavyweight fight. John Day,
the young actor who plays Corbett,
was well used to sparring for the
cameras. He also 'fought' Kirk
Douglas in *Champion* and Tony Curtis
in *The Square Jungle*. This is ambitious
but lacks inspiration and there's no
central drive in the script.

City of Joy ○ Ⓥ
1992, UK/US/India, 134 mins, colour
Dir: Roland Joffe
Stars: Patrick Swayze, Pauline Collins,
Art Malik, Shabana Azmi, Om Puri
Rating: ★★★★

Director Roland Joffe scores an emotional bullseye with this far-away
movie. Poor as they are, the peasants
of Calcutta are still oppressed by a local godfather, who controls their work
and takes their protection money.
Newly arrived in the City of Joy, one

of the slum villages where the poor
live, is Hassan Pal (Om Puri), who
becomes a rickshaw driver to provide
for his family. Then there is Dr Max
(Patrick Swayze), an American surgeon on the run from personal ghosts
and disasters on the operating table. In
spite of his intentions of not becoming
involved, Max, after initial rough
handling from the godfather's vicious
son and his thugs, soon finds himself
drawn to the problems of the local
clinic run by Sister Joan (a plumply
reassuring Pauline Collins). Though
necessarily simplistic, the film brings
home something of the poverty of the
city, and Swayze is good enough to
overcome his somewhat uneasy
casting. The native contingent is notably fine, with Puri eliciting sympathy
for the tubercular rickshaw man,
Shabana Azmi warmly dignified as his
wife and Art Malik as a really despicable villain who cuts people up with
razor blades. The children are engaging and the local characters all
well-drawn. A winner.

City Slickers ◐ Ⓥ
1991, US, 114 mins, colour
Dir: Ron Underwood
Stars: Billy Crystal, Daniel Stern, Bruno
Kirby, Patricia Wettig, Helen Slater, Jack
Palance
Rating: ★★★★

Though it has lots of funny lines, this
is basically a poignant and sometimes
exciting story about three urban
work-hacks, each basically dissatisfied
with his life who, at the age of 39
apiece, take a two-week 'holiday' together on an arranged cattle drive.
Almost all of the subsequent developments work well, and so do the
guys – Billy Crystal, Daniel Stern and
Bruno Kirby – though the picture is
stolen from all of them by the
Oscar-winning performance of Jack
Palance as the veteran trail boss who
(literally) teaches them the ropes.
Great colour photography along the
trail by Dean Semler and a climax that
will have you cheering for the city
cowboys, wraps up this unusual but
rewarding entertainment package.

City Streets ☉
1931, US, 82 mins, b/w
Dir: Rouben Mamoulian
Stars: Gary Cooper, Sylvia Sidney, Paul
Lukas, William Boyd, Guy Kibbee
Rating: ★★★

Although its characters are killers and
bootleggers, this innovative film is not
so much a crime drama as a romance

c

with gangster embellishments. And, though there are ten killings in the film, the audience isn't actually shown one of them. Today's directors, obsessed with graphic violence, would have a fit, but in 1931 Rouben Mamoulian was more concerned with the overall style of the film, using the symbolism of various kinds of bars to express the plight of the trapped central characters. Gary Cooper is well at home as the taciturn sharpshooter, but he's matched by Sylvia Sidney, in her first major film role, as the pathetic yet resolute Nan. Paul Lukas is miscast as the gang leader (George Bancroft would have been better) but plump Guy Kibbee triumphantly overcomes casting against type as a mob killer.

Clairvoyant, The ○
1935, UK, 73 mins, b/w
Dir: Maurice Elvey
Stars: Claude Rains, Fay Wray, Mary Clare, Felix Aylmer
Rating: ★★★

Claude Rains and Fay Wray came to England (where British-born Rains had been a stage actor long before he tried his luck in Hollywood) to make this unusual and absorbing drama. Rains plays a fake clairvoyant called Maximus, who tours the halls with his wife as 'stooge' in the audience, then suddenly finds he has a real gift for foretelling the future. This is fine as long as he is forecasting Derby winners, but threatens to wreck his life when he foresees accidents and disasters. Rains gives a masterly performance, which carries the film through its slower patches to reach a most exciting underground climax.

Clan of the Cave Bear, The ● Ⓥ
1985, US, 99 mins, colour
Dir: Michael Chapman
Stars: Daryl Hannah, James Remar, Pamela Reed, Thomas G Waites, Curtis Armstrong
Rating: ★★★

A hefty blow for cavegirl's lib is struck by this film of Jean M Auel's monster bestseller. And, even as you giggle at some of the subtitles imposed on the Neanderthal dialogue, you'll be rooting for Daryl Hannah to come through in the end. She's one of the 'Others', a blond Cro-Magnon orphan adopted by the regressive Neanderthals, and a pretty wimpish six-year-old who grows up rather unbelievably to be tall and leggy Daryl. Forced to submit by the tribe's

embryo leader Brond, who likes nothing if not his own way, Daryl bears his child but at the same time secretly learns the hunting arts forbidden to women – which gets her expelled even after her slingshot saves a child from the jaws of a wolf. Resourcefully surviving the winter to the astonishment of the tribe, she is granted the title 'Woman Who Hunts'. This, as you can imagine, goes down like a lead balloon with Brond, and you know that a day of reckoning will have to come. Nicely pitched between the erotic fantasy of *One Million Years BC* and the ultra-realism of *Quest for Fire*, it's thoroughly enjoyable.

Clara's Heart ◑ Ⓥ
1988, US, 108 mins, colour
Dir: Robert Mulligan
Stars: Whoopi Goldberg, Michael Ontkean, Kathleen Quinlan, Neil Patrick Harris, Spalding Gray
Rating: ★★

A real tear-jerker with Whoopi Goldberg as a Jamaican maid with a big heart who comes to look after a 12-year-old American boy. His baby sister has just died and this finally cracks apart his parents' faltering marriage. Whoopi, with an immaculate Jamaican accent, teaches him all about life and how to grow up, in a story that makes for a very slow and cumbersome journey towards understanding. Clara the maid also has a dark secret which seems to take forever to come tumbling out of the closet. Nonetheless, there are some telling moments. Whoopi is well on form and Neil Patrick Harris very good as the boy. An emotionally powerful ending provides us with a rather better memory of the film than its overall pace perhaps deserves.

Clarence, the Cross-eyed Lion ☉
1965, US, 98 mins, colour
Dir: Andrew Marton
Stars: Marshall Thompson, Betsy Drake, Richard Haydn
Rating: ★★

Charming animal adventure featuring the stars of the television series *Daktari*. The director is Andrew Marton, who should be well at home with animals and the jungle – he was the man who directed the sensational second-unit action scenes in the 1951 version of *King Solomon's Mines* (and, incidentally, the chariot racing part of the 1959 *Ben-Hur*). Betsy Drake,

the charming actress who was at one time married to Cary Grant, plays an anthropologist.

Clash of the Titans ○ Ⓥ
1981, UK, 118 mins, colour
Dir: Desmond Davis
Stars: Laurence Olivier, Harry Hamlin, Judi Bowker
Rating: ★★

Some formidable acting talents were notably under-employed in this visually spectacular fantasy based on the Greek legend of Perseus, the mortal son of the god Zeus. Laurence Olivier, Claire Bloom, Maggie Smith, Burgess Meredith and Sian Phillips are an impressive group of acting heavyweights but they are let down by a lightweight, nay featherweight, script. Harry (*L.A. Law*) Hamlin makes a handsome Perseus and Judi Bowker a winsome Andromeda, but they are overshadowed by pretty much the rest of the cast. Mind you, everyone is overshadowed by the special effects, created by that master of the grand illusion Ray Harryhausen. These are what make the film worth watching and indeed it looks great, even if it doesn't really amount to much.

Class ●
1983, US, 98 mins, colour
Dir: Lewis John Carlino
Stars: Jacqueline Bisset, Rob Lowe, Andrew McCarthy
Rating: ★

Overloaded with sex scenes and bad language, this is one of those million-to-one scenarios in which unlikelihood is piled on improbability – well-enough made by director Lewis John Carlino but never communicating in genuine emotional terms. Andrew McCarthy is a virginal student who just happens to be picked up by stunning Jacqueline Bisset in a bar (exceptionally unlikely in view of the character's looks) who just happens to be filthy-rich roommate Rob Lowe's discontented mother. Coincidences continue to pile up in a comedy that has some class (courtesy Bisset) but no credibility at all. Writers Jim Kouf and David Greenwalt do give us a few very funny lines, but it isn't nearly enough. Up-and-comers Virginia Madsen, Casey Siemaszko and Joan Cusack have supporting roles.

Class Action 🌓 Ⓥ
1990, US, 109 mins, colour
Dir: Michael Apted
Stars: Gene Hackman, Mary Elizabeth
Mastrantonio, Colin Friels, Larry
Fishburne, Donald Moffatt
Rating: ★★★

Another successful Hollywood courtroom drama, solid all the way, but
familiar in construction apart from the
fact that the cross-bench protagonists
are a father (Gene Hackman) and
daughter (Mary Elizabeth
Mastrantonio). No matter how many
times you tell it, though, the triumph
of good over evil works with an audience as jury every time you try the
case. All you need is a decent script
(and this is more than that) and the
little detail that unhinges the bad guys
towards the end. In this instance,
Hackman's the idealistic lawyer whose
courtroom triumphs have to be set
against his failure as a family man, a
failure that has alienated his daughter,
now a smart corporate counsel. The
case over which they clash concerns
deaths caused by a faulty car, and
entails such time-honoured elements
as the records that go back years,
double-dealing behind the scenes and
– no surprise! – the final 'surprise
witness'. It's expertly handled by
director Michael Apted and a classy
cast. Pay up for this action and you
won't be suing for your money back.

Clean and Sober ⚫ Ⓥ
1988, US, 125 mins, colour
Dir: Glenn Gordon Caron
Stars: Michael Keaton, Kathy Baker,
Morgan Freeman, M Emmet Walsh,
Claudia Christian, Brian Benben
Rating: ★★★

This well-written, involving drama of
drug and alcohol addiction is a little
overlong but illuminated by its actors
and their personalities. Not as downbeat as you might expect, it features a
whole cluster of telling portrayals,
from Michael Keaton (who went
straight from the drugs clinic here to
the asylum of *The Dream Team*), Kathy
Baker, Morgan Freeman and M
Emmet Walsh (his best in years).
There are no dud performances in this
film. Baker, in particular, is
heart-rending. A bit heavy on
expletives, perhaps, but in a film with
so much anger to expend, it's perhaps
understandable.

Clean State 🌓 Ⓥ
1994, US, 107 mins, colour
Dir: Mick Jackson

Stars: Dana Carvey, Valeria Golino,
Michael Gambon, James Earl Jones,
Kevin Pollack
Rating: ★

A misbegotten comedy vehicle for
Dana Carvey, the less funny half of the
Wayne-and-Garth duo from *Wayne's
World*. Dana's a private eye in a plot
that might even have worked a bit
better played straight, but is pretty
much a non-starter on any level.
Carvey's character's problem is that
each morning he forgets what's gone
the day before. There are echoes of
Groundhog Day in this but, alas, only
echoes. A talented dog called Barkley
keeps proceedings afloat for the first
few minutes: his character has a 'depth
perception' problem which tends to
lead to him sailing wide of his targets.
Make the most of Barkley, though, as
he's the only good thing in the film.
The chief crime here is the running
time.

Cleopatra ◯
1934, US, 101 mins, b/w
Dir: Cecil B DeMille
Stars: Claudette Colbert, Warren
William, Henry Wilcoxon
Rating: ★★

The sumptuous spectacle, especially
the scenes aboard Cleopatra's barge,
dwarfs everything else in this Cecil B
DeMille version of the Antony and
Cleopatra saga, which has the considerable advantage of being less
than half the length of the disastrous
Elizabeth Taylor epic of almost 30
years later. A minxish Cleo is created
by Claudette Colbert, the French-
born Hollywood star.

Cleopatra ◯ Ⓥ
1963, US, 243 mins, colour
Dir: Joseph Mankiewicz
Stars: Elizabeth Taylor, Richard Burton,
Rex Harrison, Roddy MacDowall, Martin
Landau, Hume Cronyn
Rating: ★★

The casting of Hollywood's most
glamorous couple of the day as
famous lovers Antony and Cleopatra
must have seemed a dream ticket for
20th Century-Fox. But even Elizabeth
Taylor and Richard Burton could not
make this turkey fly. It was a $43
million yawn-inducing slice of
indigestible history. And with its
budget adjusted for inflation, the film
still ranks as the most expensive ever
made, dwarfing *Terminator 2: The
Judgment Day*'s $104 million budget at
$186 million at 1990 prices. Every

statistic about the film is colossal,
including Miss Taylor's wardrobe,
which even featured a dress of
24-carat-gold cloth. At $194,000, it
still ranks as the highest sum ever spent
on costumes for a single performer in
any one film. One anonymous critic
of the day hilariously summed up the
gaudy, opulent mess as: 'Elizabeth
Taylor is the first Cleopatra to sail
down the Nile to Las Vegas.'

Cliffhanger 🌓 Ⓥ
1993, US, 112 mins, colour
Dir: Renny Harlin
Stars: Sylvester Stallone, John Lithgow,
Janine Turner, Michael Rooker, Ralph
Waite, Craig Fairbrass
Rating: ★★★

From its dizzying opening thrills, as a
girl climber plunges to her death when
a mountain rescue goes wrong, this
action film delivers on adventure if
not logic. Months later, Sylvester
Stallone, who may have been at fault,
has quit the rescue service when a
crisis occurs. Unknown to him, it
involves desperate criminals whose
mid-air hijack has gone wrong, leaving them crashed in the snow in bad
weather, with suitcases containing
millions somewhere on the mountain.
'If you don't do this now,' yells
Stallone's girl (Janine Turner), 'you're
gonna be stuck on a ledge for the rest
of your life.' Well, a man can't turn
his back on that kind of cliche, and
Sly's soon up there battling evil mastermind John Lithgow and his gang.
Lithgow tries to look viciously invincible, but shoots his trustiest ally
in the back for no good reason, fails to
kill the good guys when he should and
lets a hostage go without collecting
the ransom first! Never mind, director
Renny Harlin gives us a thrill a minute with some hair-raising stunts and
one scene not for anyone who remotely dislikes bats. Stallone and Co
look the part and you can even hear
the howling winds, echoing gunshots
and Dolby Stereo. Lots of fraying
ropes, fingertip holds, avalanches and
collapsing bridges. Hang on! – to
everything but your thinking cap.

Clock, The
See: Under the Clock

Clockwise ◯ Ⓥ
1985, UK, 97 mins, colour
Dir: Christopher Morahan
Stars: John Cleese, Alison Steadman,
Penelope Wilton, Stephen Moore, Joan

C

Hickson
Rating: ★★★

It was a long wait to see John Cleese in his first starring role for the cinema but worth it. Cleese, with his Hitler moustache, grasshopper run and madman's eyes, is on top manic form as the punctilious headmaster of a mixed comprehensive from whose basilisk gaze no miscreant or misdemeanour escapes. Chosen to chair a headmasters' conference, he sets off cross-country by train. Betrayed by Basil Fawlty's favourite word – 'Right!' – he has a convoluted conversation with a ticket collector that results in him missing his connection – the prelude to a pattern of disasters that build to a patch-work-quilt catastrophe of giant proportions. The ensuing escapades evoke about the number of laughs you might expect from an average *Fawlty Towers* – still not bad for a 90-minute movie, if not quite Cleese at full throttle. Funniest scenes: Cleese vandalising a phone box in a paroxysm of Fawlty fury; and Cleese kicking a car stuck in a field only to fall in the mud himself.

Close Encounters of the Third Kind ○ ⓥ

1977, US, 127 mins, colour
Dir: Steven Spielberg
Stars: Richard Dreyfuss, Francois Truffaut, Teri Garr, Melinda Dillon, Bob Balaban
Rating: ★★★★

For those who happen not to know, a 'close encounter of the third kind' is defined as actual contact with the occupants on an Unidentified Flying Object. Set mainly in an Indiana town (though some sequences take place as far afield as India), Steven Spielberg's dazzling film is a story of ordinary people confronted by the extraordinary. The film is especially outstanding for the staggering and imaginative special effects of its spectacular concluding scenes.

Close My Eyes ● ⓥ

1991, UK, 108 mins, colour
Dir: Stephen Poliakoff
Stars: Clive Owen, Saskia Reeves, Alan Rickman
Rating: ★★

The once-taboo theme of sex between a brother and sister is tackled at full tilt by director Stephen Poliakoff in a film that's a visual stunner, yet awkward in its portrayal of human relationships,

and hampered by two central performances, by Saskia Reeves and Clive Owen, that aren't terribly good. So, while the exchanges between the two are making the audience shuffle and occasionally giggle, it's the happenings and characters in the margins of the film that prove most interesting. The hangdog-looking Alan Rickman is right on the money as Reeves' cuckolded husband and the events involving Owen's AIDS-infected boss (Karl Johnson) are touching and notably well contrived. And, while the naked flesh of our illicit lovers lurches off screen for another breather, Poliakoff finds time to capture the unique qualities of a particularly hot summer in the English countryside. More than a bit silly, *Close My Eyes* has enough of these beguiling incidentals and well-drawn supporting roles to hold your interest to the end.

Close to Eden ○ ⓥ

(aka: A Stranger Among Us)
1992, US, 111 mins, colour
Dir: Sidney Lumet
Stars: Melanie Griffith, Eric Thal, Tracy Pollan, John Pankow, Mia Sara
Rating: ★★

For most of us, Hasidic Jewry is a closed world, so Sidney Lumet's window on to a warm, loving if totally tradition-bound community is more than welcome. Unfortunately, there's rather too much concentration on the Hasidic world and too little on the plot, leaving cop Emily Eden (Melanie Griffith) to make her final breathless deductions even as she's finally failing to seduce the Hasidic Ariel (Eric Thal) from his intended bride. There are a few good thrills, but a few titters too, as the miscast but gallant Griffith (in a role for which Debra Winger would have been better suited) pursues the murderer of a Hasidic diamond dealer. Andrzej Bartkowiak's photography makes an excellent contrast between the enclosed Hasidic world – browns and golds – and the bleak red-white-and-blue brightness of the outside world.

Clown, The ○

1952, US, 92 mins, b/w
Dir: Robert Z Leonard
Stars: Red Skelton, Jane Greer, Tim Considine
Rating: ★★

All screen comics seem to want to play for pathos at some stage of their career, and here it was Red Skelton's

turn to go for Pagliacci, with moderate success, as a drunken has-been who once toplined in the Ziegfeld Follies. Jane Greer plays his divorced wife with feeling, and Tim Considine is charmingly natural as his adoring son, but otherwise the film suffers from a weak supporting cast and the feeling that Skelton's studio, MGM, weren't convinced that the film would make any money. As it happens, they were right, and Skelton's film career slipped into decline. Watch out for Charles Bronson as a dice player.

Clue ◐

1985, US, 90 mins, colour
Dir: Jonathan Lynn
Stars: Eileen Brennan, Tim Curry, Madeline Kahn, Christopher Lloyd, Michael McKean, Lesley Ann Warren
Rating: ★

Despite all the frantic running around and shouting (principally from Tim Curry as a hyperactive butler), this comedy murder-mystery doesn't amount to much. Inspired by the game 'Cluedo' – known in the US as 'Clue' – it is in fact a pale imitation of the earlier and more satisfying sleuthing spoof *Murder By Death*. Christopher Lloyd, since a star in the *Back to the Future* films, is a suitably eccentric Professor Plum. There were three different endings shot, each identifying a different killer, but this British print has only one, which is enough. With jokes about French maids with short skirts and big breasts, director Jonathan Lynn reveals his early TV origins on sitcoms like *On the Buses* and *Doctor at Large*. If only he had taken a lead from his later *Yes, Minister*.

Cluny Brown ○

1946, US, 100 mins, b/w
Dir: Ernst Lubitsch
Stars: Jennifer Jones, Charles Boyer, Peter Lawford, Reginald Owen, C Aubrey Smith
Rating: ★★★

Jennifer Jones gives one of her most delightful performances in this, the last great Ernst Lubitsch comedy: he died a year later aged only 55. Miss Jones plays a plumber's niece following in the footsteps of her uncle. She meets a penniless Czech boffin (Charles Boyer) in 1938 London and together they make some amusing assaults on the English caste system. Richard Haydn steals the film as a stuttering village chemist, but there's also excellent character work from Una O'Connor, Ernest Cossart, Reginald Owen and C Aubrey Smith.

Coal Miner's Daughter ○
1980, US, 119 mins, colour
Dir: Michael Apted
Stars: Sissy Spacek, Tommy Lee Jones, Beverly D'Angelo, Levon Helm
Rating: ★★★★

Sissy Spacek's southern accent, singing voice and admirable naturalistic acting all merit ten out of ten in this moving musical biopic about Loretta Lynn, a poor-born Tennessee girl who married at 13, had seven children and became America's number one female Country and Western star. Sissy deservedly scooped the year's Best Actress Oscar from under the noses of more fancied nominees. Other Oscar nominations went to the film itself, to Tom Rickman for his screenplay, to cinematographer Ralf D Bode and to the editor and art directors. The direction of Britain's Michael Apted is exemplary in its feel for time and place, and Tommy Lee Jones provides fine support as Lynn's unfeeling husband, the driving force behind her fortunes. If the film glosses over some of the less savoury aspects of the true story – drugs, nervous breakdowns etc – the treatment is in keeping with Spacek's wholesome portrait of the singing mum. She can be our number one lady of Country and Western any day.

Coast of Skeletons ◖
1964, UK/South Africa, 90 mins, colour
Dir: Robert Lynn
Stars: Richard Todd, Dale Robertson, Marianne Koch
Rating: ★★

The first of two films that Richard Todd made in the character of investigator Harry Sanders. The photography, both underwater and along the coastline of South-West Africa (now Namibia), is remarkably clear and there's an explosive climax.

Coast to Coast ○
1980, US, 90 mins, colour
Dir: Joseph Sargent
Stars: Dyan Cannon, Robert Blake
Rating: ★★★

The basic idea of this picture is so good that it would be a hell of a film if it fired on all cylinders all of the time. Dyan Cannon is its driving force as a wife who escapes from the asylum to which her grasping husband has had

her committed to avoid an expensive divorce. She teams up with a trucker (Robert Blake) who has problems of his own and plans to turn her in for the husband's reward money. Zany incidentals liven up the story as it rolls along the highway, and both leads seem to be doing all their own stuntwork. It looks hairy enough to give the film that little extra boost.

Cobra ● ⓥ
1986, US, 87 mins, colour
Dir: George Pan Cosmatos
Stars: Sylvester Stallone, Brigitte Nielsen, Reni Santoni
Rating: ★★

Comic-book stuff about the modern American equivalent of a sect of Kali-worshippers, hell-bent on creating a new world by chopping up nubile young things with axes and switchknives – which seems a strange way to achieve such ambitions. Still, if crime is a disease, then Marion Cobretti (Sylvester Stallone), a lone-wolf cop who chews long matches, is the self-proclaimed cure. He's a member of the Zombie Squad, a group for which Stallone's performance here eminently qualifies him, who track down and exterminate 'psychos' (Norman Bates beware). He locates a vital witness, and then has to protect her from the efforts of the bad guys. The leggy, busty Brigitte Nielsen is okay as the witness, and Reni Santoni, a sort of tall Robert Blake, is the Stallone sidekick you're rather siurprised to see survive to the end. The villains are encouraged to overact, which they do without much flair, save for Lee Garlington, a dead ringer for Stockard Channing, as the pawky policewoman secretly in league with the killers.

Cobweb, The ○
1955, US, 135 mins, colour
Dir: Vincente Minnelli
Stars: Richard Widmark, Lauren Bacall, Charles Boyer, Gloria Grahame, Lillian Gish, John Kerr
Rating: ★★

A sombre story of rising tension between patients and administration at an American psychiatric clinic. A strange film to come from ex-director of musicals, Vincente Minnelli – although he gets a splendid performance from veteran Lillian Gish, unusually cast as an old battleaxe. The cast-list is a treasure-house of experienced Hollywood performers, from the smooth charm of Charles Boyer as a psychi-

atrist, to the mature loveliness of Fay Wray – of *King Kong* fame – as his wife.

Coca Cola Kid, The ● ⓥ
1984, Australia, 94 mins, colour
Dir: Dusan Makaveyev
Stars: Eric Roberts, Gret Scacchi, Bill Kerr, Chris Haywood, Kris McQuade
Rating: ★★★

If you want to see a truly nutty film, this is probably about as close these days as you'll get. Imagine a sort of Ealing plot, with Goonish humour and adult trimmings, and you're only within hailing distance of what's a typical film from its director. Two very photogenic leads, Eric Roberts and Greta Scacchi, who also give decent performances, provide the sexual spark to a wild tale of an American whiz-kid coca-cola salesman out to rope in the last diehard fizz-making independent (Bill Kerr) from the Australian outback. As usual in a Makaveyev film you get all the trimmings, which means every exploitative angle he can lay his hands on – in the case of the delectable Scacchi, she of the challenging gaze, there are quite a number – diced with his own form of devilish satire. Bill Kerr adds another to his gallery of character portrayals as the outback independent, although it's not too clear what happens to him at the end.

Cockleshell Heroes ○ ⓥ
1955, UK, 94 mins, colour
Dir: Jose Ferrer
Stars: Jose Ferrer, Trevor Howard, Dora Bryan, Anthony Newley, David Lodge
Rating: ★★★

A rattling good war film on an unusual theme: the blowing-up of enemy battleships by a highly-trained group of men in cockleshell canoes. It was one of the first British war films to be made in Technicolor, and the photography is first-rate, as are the performances of Jose Ferrer (who also directed), Trevor Howard and then-newcomer Percy Herbert. The training of the men is even more entertaining than the raid itself.

Cocktail ● ⓥ
1988, US, 103 mins, colour
Dir: Roger Donaldson
Stars: Tom Cruise, Bryan Brown, Elisabeth Shue, Laurence Luckinbill, Kelly Lynch
Rating: ★★

C

While waiting for the script for *Rain Man* to be rewritten for the umpteenth time, Tom Cruise signed up for this lightweight concoction about an ex-Army buddy who becomes the hottest thing behind a Manhattan bar. And despite the weak and derivative material, Cruise's ear-to-ear grin still managed to light up the box office to the tune of $80 million. The storyline, which has him tutored in the art of pouring the niftiest cocktails in the sexiest fashion by craggy Bryan Brown and then fighting each other over pulling the same girls, is nothing more than an excuse for displaying acres of flesh. And there are no concessions to the AIDS epidemic in the sleep-around antics. Look closely for goose-pimples and blue lips in Cruise's waterfall seduction of Elisabeth Shue – the water was freezing.

Cocktails in the Kitchen
See: For Better, For Worse

Cocoanuts, The ⊙
1929, US, 89 mins, b/w
Dir: Robert Florey
Stars: Groucho Marx, Harpo Marx, Chico Marx, Zeppo Marx, Margaret Dumont
Rating: ★★★

'Just think, tonight, when the moon is sneaking around the clouds, I'll be sneaking around you . . . Oh, I can see you now. You and the moon . . . You wear a necktie so I'll know you.' Yes, it's Groucho Marx, propositioning the galleon-like Margaret Dumont in the Marx Brothers' earliest released film comedy. Groucho's the manager of a Florida hotel devoid of guests, or much else. The telephone rings. Groucho picks it up. 'Ice water in room 412?' he asks. 'Where did you get it?'

Cocoon ○ ⓥ
1985, US, 117 mins, colour
Dir: Ron Howard
Stars: Don Ameche, Jessica Tandy, Steve Guttenberg, Hume Cronyn, Brian Dennehy, Wilford Brimley
Rating: ★★★

A heartwarming and very unusual fantasy about an alien spacecraft that returns to earth after an absence of 10,000 years (the visitors seem to live more or less forever) to pick up 20 crewmen they left in 'pods' at the bottom of the sea centuries before. They take them to a deserted swimming pool, failing to realise that the lifeforce with which they energise the water to revive their comrades is in turn rejuvenating three old fogeys from a nearby retirement home who bathe there every day. All this takes rather a long while to get going, and one could do with more of the hot-blooded antics of the elderly trio and the women who share their secret. That said, Don Ameche, Hume Cronyn and Wilford Brimley (who, at 50, had to be set for another 20 years of crusty old men) have very winning ways, and their ladies, Jessica Tandy (the real-life Mrs Cronyn), Gwen Verdon and Maureen Stapleton, are not far behind. You'll especially enjoy Ameche's demonstration of breakdancing! If Ron Howard's direction is less sure in its pacing, he does bring the human element warmly to the fore – this extending particularly to Brian Dennehy's chief alien. Special effects in this sci-fi Indian summer are discreetly excellent without trying to be too spectacular.

Cocoon: the Return ○ ⓥ
1988, US, 130 mins, colour
Dir: Daniel Petrie
Stars: Don Ameche, Wilford Brimley, Courteney Cox, Hume Cronyn, Steve Guttenberg, Jessica Tandy
Rating: ★★

All the old cast is back for this lesser sequel to *Cocoon*, in which the old stagers made young by alien contact return to planet Earth with predictably dramatic consequences. The first hour or so is fairly tedious, but the latter stages are pretty good with some affecting moments, especially the scene where Hume Cronyn visits injured wife Jessica Tandy in hospital. Their poignant portrayals make this second trip just about worthwhile.

Codename Wildgeese ◖
1984, US/West Germany, 101 mins, colour
Dir: Anthony M Dawson
Stars: Lewis Collins, Lee Van Cleef, Ernest Borgnine, Mimsy Farmer, Klaus Kinski
Rating: ★★

A sort of *Dirty Dozen* meets *The Wild Geese*, with an international cast on a mission to destroy an opium depot deep in the jungles of Thailand. Lewis Collins, Ernest Borgnine and Lee Van Cleef assume the required grim expressions, Klaus Kinski is dubbed into Oxford English and thousands of oriental stuntmen bite honourable dust.

Code of Silence ○ ⓥ
1985, UK, 101 mins, colour
Dir: Andrew Davis
Stars: Chuck Norris, Henry Silva, Bert Remsen
Rating: ★★

This Chuck Norris film could just as easily have been called 'A Force of One', if Chuck and his cohorts hadn't already used it for a previous fist-feast. The Bronson-style plot involves the poker-faced Norris obliterating the South American branch of the Mafia (led by Henry Silva) single-handed after they have kidnapped the innocent daughter of a stateside mobster. If it's only action you want, the movie should satisfy in its 18-certificate way, and there's even an attempt at a story in the sub-plot of the corrupt policeman for whom Norris refuses to cover. But all the bone-crunching mayhem and Chicago location shooting help disguise the fact that director Andrew Davis is padding his film in *Miami Vice* style to reach its feature length.

Cold Feet ◖
1989, US, 94 mins, colour
Dir: Robert Dornhelm
Stars: Keith Carradine, Sally Kirkland, Tom Waits, Bill Pullman, Rip Torn
Rating: ★★

This quirky comedy, dipped in various shades of grey and black (with a dash of red for the blood it spills), is off the beaten track in more ways than one. For a start, it's set in the wilds of Montana. That's where crooked Monte (Keith Carradine) heads, with a fortune in emeralds hidden inside the horse he's riding, having ditched his associates, demented psycho Tom Waits and voracious blonde Sally Kirkland. Carradine's destination is the ranch of his brother (Bill Pullman), where he aims to – well, it's never clear what Monte aims to do 'ceptin' he never gits around to doin' it. Meanwhile, the gruesome twosome pursue some. And one of the twists to this strange, beautifully-photographed film is that Waits is a real psycho who actually kills people. Full of half-funny comic touches and off-kilter dialogue, the film is stolen from all the stars (including Rip Torn, tombstone-toothed Vincent Schiavelli and a guest shot from Jeff Bridges) by the natural warmth of Kathleen York as Pullman's wife.

Colditz Story, The ○ Ⓥ
1954, UK, 97 mins, b/w
Dir: Guy Hamilton
Stars: John Mills, Eric Portman, Christopher Rhodes, Lionel Jeffries, Bryan Forbes, Ian Carmichael
Rating: ★★★

The British really couldn't go wrong with prisoner-of-war escape stories in the early Fifties. And this one, a first major success for its young director, Paris-born Guy Hamilton, is firmly in the tradition of *The Wooden Horse*. Episodic, but personably acted by all concerned, especially Eric Portman as the senior officer.

Cold Sweat ◐
1970, France/Italy, 94 mins, colour
Dir: Terence Young
Stars: Charles Bronson, Liv Ullmann, James Mason, Jill Ireland
Rating: ★★

Terence Young, who directed the Bond films *Dr No*, *From Russia with Love* and *Thunderball*, made this thriller on location in France. The script does not do justice to the tension of the original novel – *Ride the Nightmare* by Richard Matheson, himself a prolific screenplay-writer – but Charles Bronson does all that can be expected of him, and Liv Ullmann's anguished performance as his wife will reward her legions of fans.

Cold Turkey ○
1970, US, 101 mins, colour
Dir: Norman Lear
Stars: Dick Van Dyke, Pippa Scott, Bob Newhart, Edward Everett Horton, Vincent Gardenia, Jean Stapleton
Rating: ★★

A bit of a curate's egg is this satirical comedy aimed at American middle-class attitudes, which was the first feature film from TV sitcom supremo Norman Lear. It stars Dick Van Dyke in a strange role as the self-seeking small-town reverend seizing the chance to get his town's name on the map when Edward Everett Horton's tobacco king offers a $25 million prize to any town that can give up smoking for 30 days. Bob Newhart is the oily publicity executive responsible for the stunt and there is a succession of entertaining character turns from a good cast: Bob Elliott and Ray Goulding as TV newscasters; Jean Stapleton's mayor's wife who can't stop eating; redneck patriot Graham Jarvis policing the town for contraband, Judith Lowry taking pot shots at potential commies, Tom Poston's disreputable cad, Barnard Hughes' doctor – all human life is there down to the minutest (sometimes fairly unpleasant!) detail. There is quite a lot of laughter along the way, but Lear gets cornered into a cop-out ending and remains really more at home with the TV screen.

Colorado Territory ○
1949, US, 94 mins, b/w
Dir: Raoul Walsh
Stars: Joel McCrea, Virginia Mayo, John Archer, Dorothy Malone, Henry Hull
Rating: ★★★

A cracking Western remake of *High Sierra*, with Joel McCrea lending a granite authority to the Humphrey Bogart role as the outlaw escaped from prison who dreams of one last holdup. Director Raoul Walsh, who also made the original, supplies an atmosphere heavy with tension, and writers John Twist and Edmund H North back his efforts with intelligent dialogue. They draw their characters with hard-etched but not unsympathetic lines. The rugged scenery is beautifully captured by Sid Hickox, a Western specialist.

Color of Money, The ● Ⓥ
1986, US, 119 mins, colour
Dir: Martin Scorsese
Stars: Paul Newman, Tom Cruise, Mary Elizabeth Mastrantonio, Helen Shaver, John Turturro, Bill Cobbs
Rating: ★★★

'Fast Eddie' Felson is back – and playing pool again. That's the good news, and fans of the sport and Paul Newman, who won a long-delayed Oscar for his role, will revel in this sequel to *The Hustler*. Richard Price's hard-boiled, if not too well structured screenplay concentrates this time on the sporting angles, by-passing the tragic drama of the original. Newman is superb, while Tom Cruise, as the young pool hustler he takes under his wing, hasn't much to do but 'strut his stuff', though he does it with great confidence. Martin Scorsese directs with polish and a feel for the right angle at the right time, while the snooker itself is effectively choreographed, both stars potting their set-up shots with masterly aplomb. Watch for John Turturro and Forest Whitaker in supporting roles.

Color Purple, The ◐ Ⓥ
1985, US, 152 mins, colour
Dir: Steven Spielberg
Stars: Danny Glover, Whoopi Goldberg, Margaret Avery, Oprah Winfrey
Rating: ★★★

This manipulative mixture of familiar elements from *Roots* and similar dramas is what you might call a six-handkerchief movie. It does go on a long time, but a lot of it works very well, even if you resent director Steven Spielberg, in a big Oscar try, allowing you to see him pull the strings while you sit there trying to restrain a tear. Whoopi Goldberg gives a moving performance as the girl who goes through more trials and perils than a silent serial heroine (Desreta Jackson, who plays the younger Celie, is also very good). Oprah Winfrey and Danny Glover make early marks, too, and the film was nominated for 11 Academy Awards. When it came to the ceremonies, though, the Academy saw right through Spielberg's intentions, and didn't give it one.

Colors ● Ⓥ
1988, US, 121 mins, colour
Dir: Dennis Hopper
Stars: Sean Penn, Robert Duvall, Maria Conchita Alonso, Randy Brooks
Rating: ★★

Or: *Hill Street Blues* with an adult certificate. This realist thriller about the police's attempted crack-down on ghetto gang warfare even has Trinidad Silva as one of the gang heads, a function he performed similarly as Jesus on *Hill Street*. That series perhaps first made the outside world aware of the armed street gangs – bloods and royals and the like – bossing the backstreets of cities like Los Angeles. Dennis Hopper turns this situation into a slam-bang action film with dramatic shootouts that recall gangster films of the Thirties. Robert Duvall is the wily veteran cop and Sean Penn (yes, he is given the chance to pump iron) his cocky, aggressive young partner. Their relationship follows a predictable pattern down to the final scene, but then this, unlike *Hill Street Blues*, is a movie where action always speak louder than words.

Colt 45 ○
1950, US, 74 mins, colour
Dir: Edwin L Marin
Stars: Randolph Scott, Zachary Scott, Ruth Roman, Lloyd Bridges
Rating: ★★★

This lively Western, distinguished by the forthright playing of the two

C

Scotts, Randolph and Zachary, as goodie and baddie, is an 'A' feature horse-opera in every respect except its brief running-time. The conflict between the two men roars across the western plains – and the pace of the action, tightly edited, never drops. Coincidence note: Ian MacDonald plays a Westerner called Miller, just as he does (to even greater effect) in the Western classic *High Noon*.

Column South ○
1953, US, 85 mins, colour
Dir: Frederick De Cordova
Stars: Audie Murphy, Joan Evans, Robert Sterling
Rating: ★★

A Western made at the height of Audie Murphy's career with Universal-International. It features an unusual role for Robert Sterling, as a bigoted cavalry captain. It's unusual because Sterling was, for many years, one of Hollywood's best 'good guys'. Dennis (*McCloud*) Weaver gets in some good acting training by playing an Indian; and two heroes of Hollywood cowboy films of the Thirties, Bob Steele and Johnny Downs, appear in supporting roles.

Coma ◑ ⓥ
1977, US, 113 mins, colour
Dir: Michael Crichton
Stars: Genevieve Bujold, Michael Douglas, Elizabeth Ashley, Rip Torn, Richard Widmark, Lois Chiles
Rating: ★★★

There hasn't been a heroine like Genevieve Bujold's Sue Wheeler in quite a while. In fact the intrepid girl detective had seemed a theme of the past until *Coma* came along. It gets revived with a vengeance in this story of a doctor who uncovers a racket in spare-part surgery at her own hospital. The perils of Pauline subsequently have nothing on our Sue: scaling to dizzy heights up air shafts; being pursued at length by a hired killer, on whom she ultimately turns the tables in gruesome fashion; beating off security guards and fleeing through a sinister institute; clambering along ventilation systems above a kaleidoscope of dangling corpses; clinging to the top of a speeding ambulance; until finally cornered by the big villain, who turns out to be none other than . . . but ah! That would be going too far. Would that the script were less comatose stuff, sounding at times like an episode of *Nurse Norton's Affair* from the film

version of *The National Health*. Fortunately, the action prevails and makes this film for most of its running time a real gripper. Bujold's exploits are such that, under the circumstances, co-stars Michael Douglas and company can only stand and gasp. Tom Selleck has a very early role as one of the patients in danger.

Comancheros, The ○ ⓥ
1961, US, 107 mins, b/w
Dir: Michael Curtiz
Stars: John Wayne, Stuart Whitman, Ina Balin, Lee Marvin
Rating: ★★★

John Wayne in action – and how! The explosive action scenes are the best things about this rumbustious Western, as one would expect from the Hungarian-born director Michael Curtiz, whose last film this was. Curtiz made almost all of Errol Flynn's best action films, including *Captain Blood*, *The Charge of the Light Brigade*, *The Adventures of Robin Hood* and *The Sea Hawk*. Wayne, of course, remains largely impervious to direction, although the story goes that he was called for a spectacular ad-lib during shooting when a pack of horses, affected by the heat, bolted forward in the direction of a group of children. Big John, sharper than anyone, broke away from the scene he was playing and flung himself on the nearest horse, preventing a tragedy. Well, that's the story . . . For the rest, Lee Marvin makes a fine swaggering, half-scalped bad guy but disappears all too soon.

Comanche Station ○
1960, US, 74 mins, colour
Dir: Budd Boetticher
Stars: Randolph Scott, Nancy Gates, Claude Akins, Skip Homeier
Rating: ★★

A typically tough Randolph Scott Western from his later years in films, directed by Budd Boetticher, with whom he made several films in the Fifties. Nancy Gates is a pretty heroine and no mean actress, while character villainy is in the capable hands of a trio of excellent 'uglies', Claude Akins, Skip Homeier and Richard Rust.

Come and Get It ○
1936, US, 99 mins, b/w
Dir: William Wyler
Stars: Edward Arnold, Joel McCrea, Frances Farmer, Walter Brennan
Rating: ★★★

Another epic drama from the works of Edna Ferber, whose massive novels proved irresistible film fodder to the Hollywood of the Thirties. Frances Farmer does her best screen work in a dual role, Joel McCrea is a stalwart hero and Walter Brennan took the first of his three 'best supporting actor' Oscars as a Swedish immigrant. Magnificent scenery amid the forests of Wisconsin is filmed with documentary clarity.

Come Back, Little Sheba ○
1952, US, 99 mins, b/w
Dir: Daniel Mann
Stars: Burt Lancaster, Shirley Booth, Terry Moore, Richard Jaeckel
Rating: ★★★

It's a tribute to the talents of director Daniel Mann (who also directed the hit play) and his veteran Hollywood screenwriter Ketti (real name: Katherine) Frings that such a seemingly unattractive subject should prove so engrossing throughout. Credit, too, the performances, notably Shirley Booth, the distinguished stage actress winning an Oscar in her first film, as the drudge, Burt Lancaster, in one of the first of his quieter performances, as her alcoholic husband, Terry Moore (also Oscar-nominated) and Richard Jaeckel. Little Sheba, by the way, who never does come back, is the leading character's lost dog.

Come Back to the 5 & Dime Jimmy Dean, Jimmy Dean ● ⓥ
1982, US, 105 mins, colour
Dir: Robert Altman
Stars: Cher, Sandy Dennis, Karen Black, Sudie Bond, Marta Heflin, Kathy Bates
Rating: ★★

We're close to Tennessee Williams country here, with country accents rising high in the film version of a successful Broadway play. Half-a-dozen middle-aged women gather for the 20th anniversary meeting of a rather seedy James Dean remembrance club in a small Texas town. True to form in this kind of thing, skeletons are soon cascading from cupboards as decades-old lies are stripped away to reveal less palatable truths beneath. Although the film can't quite escape its stage origins, it's very skilfully made by director Robert Altman, especially where the past is reflected in a huge mirror behind the bar of the 5 & Dime store. Sandy Dennis twitches in her familiar bird-like style as the frump who says her son is James Dean's, Cher is quite affecting as the fading belle of the town and Karen Black suitably enigmatic as an at-first-unrecognised stranger. Most impressive of all, however, is Marta Heflin's understated portrait of the pregnant mother-of-six who is happy with her lot.

Come Blow Your Horn ○
1962, US, 112 mins, colour
Dir: Bud Yorkin
Stars: Frank Sinatra, Lee J Cobb, Tony Bill, Barbara Rush
Rating: ★★

Frank Sinatra revels in the witticisms of this very Jewish comedy – and watch for *Bonanza*'s Dan Blocker, very funny in the cameo role of an irate Texan. On the whole, though, a slightly disappointing version of the Neil Simon play.

Comedians, The ○
1967, US/Bermuda/France, 160 mins, colour
Dir: Peter Glenville
Stars: Richard Burton, Elizabeth Taylor, Alec Guinness, Peter Ustinov, Lillian Gish, Cicely Tyson
Rating: ★★

Graham Greene's famous story, adapted for the cinema by Greene himself, about a group of people in strife-torn Haiti, all of whom find that they have, in modern parlance, to make some sort of commitment. The story suffers from the central casting of Richard Burton and Elizabeth Taylor, who are essentially 'stars,' but Alec Guinness is particularly good as the strange Major Jones – just as much at home in Greeneland here as he had been eight years earlier in *Our Man in Havana*. Lillian Gish and Paul Ford are consistently enjoyable as archetypal innocent Americans abroad, caught up in events beyond their comprehension. A very strong supporting cast includes the talented Cicely Tyson, winner of an Emmy Award for her performance in the TV film *The Autobiography of Miss Jane Pittman*.

Comedy of Terrors ◐ ⓥ
1963, US, 85 mins, colour
Dir: Jacques Tourneur
Stars: Vincent Price, Boris Karloff, Peter Lorre, Basil Rathbone, Joe E Brown
Rating: ★★★

Perhaps the most successful horror-farce ever made, this gleeful gallery of ghoulishness is a delight from the start to finish. In the depths of a cobwebbed funeral parlour lurk two lugubrious undertakers, Waldo (Vincent Price) and his frog-like underling Felix (Peter Lorre). Waldo's chalky-white father-in-law (Boris Karloff) is also there, aged about 100 by the look of him, but refusing to die off and leave Price the business, in spite of the fact that the medicine bottle Price gives him has a skull and crossbones on it. To add to Price's problems, business is so bad that he and Lorre have to go out and boost trade by helping a few of the sicklier local residents to meet their maker. A black comedy, rich in pace, invention and atmosphere: Price, Lorre and Basil Rathbone (as their landlord) play to the audience in glorious fashion. And Karloff's Aged Parent is the funniest thing around.

Come Fill the Cup ○
1952, US, 113 mins, b/w
Dir: Gordon Douglas
Stars: James Cagney, Phyllis Thaxter, Raymond Massey, Gig Young, James Gleason
Rating: ★★

An untypical James Cagney film in that the human dynamo has a battle with the bottle before he starts tangling with gangsters. Cagney's sustained brilliance gives this tough, raw story of a newspaperman who crashes his way back to the top, after drinking costs him his job and girlfriend, some of the kick of the classic film about alcoholism, *The Lost Weekend*. Look out for the arch-villain here. It was one of the last big-screen appearances by Sheldon Leonard, later producer and director of the *I Spy* series on TV, in which he occasionally cropped up as Public Enemy No 1.

Come Next Spring ○
1955, US, 92 mins, colour
Dir: R G Springsteen
Stars: Ann Sheridan, Steve Cochran, Walter Brennan, Sherry Jackson
Rating: ★★★

A sentimental rural drama that no-one at Republic Studios expected to amount to much, although its script had attracted Ann Sheridan, Steve Cochran, Sonny Tufts, Walter Brennan and Edgar Buchanan. When it came out, word of mouth soon spread about the 'nice little picture' that had resulted, and the studio found itself with a nice little profit on its hands. The events of the movie seem so real, in fact, that they make its appealing storyline seem almost dull. Miss Sheridan gives her best performance in ages in a down-to-earth role; Cochran is a gallant second as the errant husband who now returns to their farm seemingly a changed man. Great care was obviously taken in the making of this movie, and it pays off; even Trucolor seems muted in this very pleasing yarn.

Come On George! ⊙
1939, UK, 88 mins, b/w
Dir: Anthony Kimmins
Stars: George Formby, Pat Kirkwood, Joss Ambler, Ronald Shiner
Rating: ★★★

Formby in rollicking form as a lad who longs to be a jockey, and naturally ends up by climbing aboard the fiercest racehorse that ever broke a rider's collar-bone. He also finds time for several songs in his inimitable style.

Comes a Horseman ◐ ⓥ
1978, US, 113 mins, colour
Dir: Alan J Pakula
Stars: James Caan, Jane Fonda, Jason Robards, Richard Farnsworth
Rating: ★★★

A romantic Western directed (by Alan J Pakula) and photographed (by Gordon Willis) with a real feel for time and period – the ranchland of Montana in 1945. It's an elaborate but persuasive treatment of a familiar theme. Jane Fonda holds it together with another magnificent performance as the rancher fighting to make it on her own and not have to sell out to the local cattle baron (Jason Robards), whose affair with her as a girl had been the death of her father. James Caan is effective as the 'horseman' who proves her one helper and the blazing climax, in which they and Robards are involved, brings an interesting film to a highly satisfactory conclusion.

Come See the Paradise ● ⓥ
1990, US, 131 mins, colour
Dir: Alan Parker
Stars: Dennis Quaid, Tamlyn Tomita, Sab Shimono, Pruitt Taylor Vince
Rating: ★★

The 'rounding up' of Japanese-Americans who were herded together in US confinement camps was one of the war's most scandalous injustices. Only in recent times has compensation for the surviving victims been agreed. Alan Parker's

c

story about this ignoble episode in American history, and the mixed marriage caught up in it, runs a bit like a glowingly photographed TV mini-series, but nonetheless has some fine moments. These chiefly stem from the loving relationship between Lily (Tamlyn Tomita), daughter of a Japanese, and Jack (Dennis Quaid), an Irish-American forever in trouble for helping strikers in one form or another. Historically, the film will be an eye-opener for those of us who were hardly aware such a side to World War Two existed: understandable but still deplorable. As a story, the film is pretty long and slow in the telling: its best moments tend to be spaced too far apart for the comfort of constant attention.

Come September ○
1961, US, 112 mins, colour
Dir: Robert Mulligan
Stars: Rock Hudson, Gina Lollobrigida, Sandra Dee, Bobby Darin, Walter Slezak
Rating: ★★

When he wasn't being a rugged hero, Rock Hudson could turn a very effective hand at light comedy and produced some very enjoyable romps during the Sixties. *Come September* is not one of his more memorable efforts, but it's not his fault. Blame falls on the lack of a witty script and indifferent support from Bobby Darin and Sandra Dee. Gina Lollobrigida, on the other hand, gives as good a performance as her part allows. It's a farce about Hudson's villa in Italy being used as a guest house while he isn't there. The film's problem is that it tries to be witty and sophisticated, which it isn't. Hudson's comedies with Doris Day were a whole lot better.

Come to the Stable ○
1949, US, 94 mins, b/w
Dir: Henry Koster
Stars: Loretta Young, Celeste Holm, Hugh Marlowe, Elsa Lanchester, Thomas Gomez
Rating: ★★★

Nuns, churches, Christmas: all the best ingredients of the Hollywood tear-jerker are included in this likeable, if head-in-the-clouds story of two nuns from France trying to raise a large sum of money in America. Heart-warming stuff, so delicately and charmingly played by Loretta Young and Celeste Holm (especially good as a nun who turns out to be a whizz at tennis), that they were both

nominated for Academy Awards. Thomas Gomez is a riot as the Italian-bred Brooklyn gangster whom the nuns wind round their little fingers.

Comfort and Joy ○ ⓥ
1984, UK, 115 mins, colour
Dir: Bill Forsyth
Stars: Bill Paterson, Eleanor David, Clare Grogan, Alex Norton, Patrick Malahide, Rikki Fulton
Rating: ★★

A mellow comedy-drama from director Bill Forsyth, about a local radio deejay (Bill Paterson), who has little time to feel sorry for himself over his girlfriend walking out when he becomes involved in an 'ice-cream war' on the streets of Glasgow. The anecdote is sweet but lacks spice – exactly the ingredient for which the rival ice-cream 'families' are looking. Forsyth's cameras close in on the homely face of Paterson for their best effects, and he's equal to the test.

Comic, The ◐
1969, US, 90 mins, colour
Dir: Carl Reiner
Stars: Dick Van Dyke, Michele Lee, Mickey Rooney, Cornel Wilde, Carl Reiner
Rating: ★★★

Surprisingly denied a theatrical release in Britain, this is a fine tragi-comic look at the life of a silent screen comedian with a self-destructive ego, beautifully played by Dick Van Dyke whose film character is a fascinating amalgam of several real-life movie mirth-makers. Also first rate are Mickey Rooney, Cornel Wilde and Michele Lee, with Pert Kelton scoring strongly in a vignette role. The recreation of silent films is excellently done and the Hollywood atmosphere of the times seems so authentic that one can almost smell the excitement. The cherry on the cake is the apt script and direction of Carl Reiner, the man behind the original Van Dyke television series.

Coming Home ● ⓥ
1978, US, 121 mins, colour
Dir: Hal Ashby
Stars: Jane Fonda, Jon Voight, Bruce Dern, Robert Ginty, Penelope Milford, Robert Carradine
Rating: ★★★

Jane Fonda, Jon Voight and Bruce Dern is a pretty high-powered acting trio by anyone's standards, and their

superior performances dominate this story of a Vietnam officer's wife who falls in love with a paraplegic just returned from the war. Despite the acting – especially by Fonda and Voight, who both won Academy Awards – this is essentially an old plot in new dressing. It's high-class Vietnam soap opera, in fact, with few surprises. One wonders if the heavy use of four-letter words in the script might have been more effective if confined to Voight's final speech which, as he drifts helplessly into a state of anguish, represents the high point of the actor's career to date. The film also benefits from the use on soundtrack of music from the period, notably by The Beatles and Rolling Stones.

Coming to America ● ⓥ
1988, US, 116 mins, colour
Dir: John Landis
Stars: Eddie Murphy, James Earl Jones, Arsenio Hall, John Amos
Rating: ★★★

Almost every black actor in Hollywood seems to appear in this rude but funny Eddie Murphy comedy about an African prince who travels to the Queens district of New York – where else? – to find a bride. It's directed by John Landis, who steered Murphy to success in *Trading Places*. The adult script is peppered with risqué one-liners and there's some nudity. But by far the greatest fun is to be had trying to spot the different characters played by Murphy and Arsenio Hall. The make-up disguises are by Rick Baker, who won an Oscar for the special effects in Landis's *An American Werewolf in London*, and the best has Murphy as an elderly white Jew. The opening titles capture the fun element as the camera zooms in on the Paramount mountain logo and continues into the jungle below to Murphy's homeland.

Command, The ○
1954, US, 94 mins, colour
Dir: David Butler
Stars: Guy Madison, Joan Weldon, James Whitmore
Rating: ★★★

An action-packed Western in which a Cavalry officer is saddled with the dangerous assignment of steering a wagon train through hostile Indian territory. This was the first Cinema-Scope Western, and the first 'scope film of any kind from Warner Brothers, a studio previously committed to the 3-D process. Not surprisingly, they threw everything but the kitchen sink into *The Command* – not forgetting the panoramic shots that showed the new process off to its best effect. Guy Madison was one of the most popular Western stars at the time (he had also starred in the first 3-D Western, *The Charge at Feather River*), and he and James Whitmore both give splendidly forthright performances. Leading lady Joan Weldon was a stage musical star who proved herself a good actress during her six years with Warners – even though they never gave her the lead in a musical!

Command Decision ○
1948, US, 112 mins, b/w
Dir: Sam Wood
Stars: Clark Gable, Walter Pidgeon, Van Johnson, Brian Donlevy, Charles Bickford, John Hodiak
Rating: ★★★

Clark Gable, Walter Pidgeon and Van Johnson have the plum roles in this grim-faced but fascinating study of the emotions of top brass who, faced with the choice of sacrificing a few lives to save many, elect to send American air crews to their deaths. With its all-male cast and a script bristling with cynicism and irony, the film was hailed by critics as the first serious Hollywood attempt at a thinking man's World War Two film. The film's moments of humour are very welcome.

Commando ● Ⓥ
1985, US, 95 mins, colour
Dir: Mark L Lester
Stars: Arnold Schwarzenegger, Rae Dawn Chong, Dan Hedaya
Rating: ★★

If violent action is your favourite thing in films, then come on down. There is probably more per square foot of it here then in any other film. The mayhem is largely wrought by mighty Arnold Schwarzenegger (the film opens on a close-up of his biceps) who never delivers one blow or bullet where three will do. To set off this human H-bomb, the film-makers fall back on the old story of the quiet strong-man stung into action by a threat to something he loves – in this case his young daughter. To get her back, Arnie's army consists of himself and a stewardess (Rae Dawn Chong) he hijacks into helping – but it's more than enough for the bad guys, most of whom are Arnie's size to even the odds a little. Arnie just straps on his arsenal and it's all over bar the

shooting, not to mention the throat-cutting, limb-hacking and head-chopping, with the most spectacular death of all reserved for the chief villain, who fails to shoot our hero when he has the chance. As many cliches are turned over as bodies and at one stage one of the bad guys even says: 'Take her below!'

Commitments, The ● Ⓥ
1991, US/UK, 118 mins, colour
Dir: Alan Parker
Stars: Robert Arkins, Angeline Ball, Maria Doyle, Bronagh Gallagher, Andrew Strong
Rating: ★★★

Like other factual or fictional stories of bands on the rise, Alan Parker's film gets a tremendous boost from the dynamic performance of its songs by the motley crew of actors and musicians who make up Dublin's The Commitments – 'Saviours of Soul'. You could quite happily watch this well-drilled, adrenaline-throbbing lot all night, and maybe the film would be even more enjoyable if you did. Parker's script piles contrivance on contrivance to make the story go the way he wants, and you can still hardly believe the band breaking up at the end when in reality they'd be high on success. And would even the conceited lead singer pick a fight with the 'animal' drummer known for breaking noses and crushing bones? Not with his eye on fame he wouldn't. The whole constant four-letter wrangling among the band, in fact, gets a bit wearing, although the script contains a good quota of smile-inducing lines. 'The piano's me granny's,' explains the latest recruit. 'She doesn't know I took it. But she doesn't use the front room very often.' Such occasional gems, the authentic Dublin backstreets feel and the music – this band would be a hit anywhere – make this gig worth a visit.

Communion ◑
1989, US, 105 mins, colour
Dir: Philippe Mora
Stars: Christopher Walken, Lindsay Crouse, Frances Sternhagen, Andreas Katsulas
Rating: ★★

A literate, intelligent and delicate (but not completely successful) 'true life' story of an American writer who really did see little blue men from outer space and eventually found other people who had seen exactly the same creatures (including his own son).

Christopher Walken's performance as the writer is remarkable, and Lindsay Crouse is almost as good as his wife. The dialogue has a strange, improvised quality which only intermittently comes off and the film tells its interesting story at rather too great a length. The end product needs patience but makes mainly absorbing viewing for the discerning. Not your average dose of gore, slime and schlock, that's for sure.

Company of Wolves, The ◑ Ⓥ
1984, UK
Dir: Neil Jordan
Stars: Angela Lansbury, David Warner, Sarah Patterson, Stephen Rea, Tusse Silberg, Graham Crowden
Rating: ★★

A bold fantasy horror tale from director Neil Jordan (it could hardly be more different from his previous *Angel*) that crosses *Legend of the Werewolf* with *Red Riding Hood*. That it fails by the highest standards of its kind is perhaps due to an inconsistent pace that is sometimes as torpid as the bizarre, almost medieval background music, and because not all the acting matches that of Angela Lansbury's Granny in quality, as she fills the heroine's head with grim stories of wolves and is doomed, as in the fairy tale, to come to a sticky end. The special effects are gruesomely vivid, and the film is uncommonly successful at creating a fairytale horror environment inhabited by wolves, snakes, polecats, owls, and toads, hopping, prowling and slithering round the crooked houses of the forest. An early sequence, with the heroine's sister being pursued by wolves through a nightmare toyland, is the most fully realised in the film, although the settings throughout are vividly, if gloomily imaginative in the *Caligari* style.

Compromising Positions ○
1985, US, 98 mins, colour
Dir: Frank Perry
Stars: Susan Sarandon, Raul Julia, Edward Herrmann, Judith Ivey, Mary Beth Hurt, Joe Mantegna
Rating: ★★★

A pleasant surprise: an old-fashioned comedy-thriller-whodunnit whose comic overtones gradually give way to the plot in as painless a way as possible. A lothario dentist in a wealthy area is bumped off. The heroine, an ex-journalist and mother-of-two to

C

whom he had made the standard passing pass, finds her inquisitive nose twitching when several of her friends turn out to have been involved with the victim. In this role, which may look at first glance like a Goldie Hawn reject, Susan Sarandon gave one of 1985's best performances – and that's not easy in this kind of lightweight entertainment. Whether wisecracking, vulnerable, can't-leave-it-alone curious or sick-to-the-stomach brave, Sarandon uses her wide eyes and expressive face to get it just right in a highly intelligent performance.

Compulsion ◐
1959, US, 103 mins, b/w
Dir: Richard Fleischer
Stars: Orson Welles, Dean Stockwell, Bradford Dillman
Rating: ★★★

Although the names have been changes, this is a fairly faithful telling of the infamous Loeb and Leopold case, in which two wealthy college students were brought to trial for the murder of a collegue in 1924. Dean Stockwell and Bradford Dillman are excellent as the two utterly amoral killers but they are overshadowed by Orson Welles, who gives a grandstanding bravura performance as their defence lawyer. It's a tense and absorbing drama and full of suspense even for those familiar with the case and its outcome. Director Richard Fleischer keeps a firm grip on the story, which is well scripted from Meyer Levin's original novel by Richard Murphy. The courtroom scenes, especially, are electrifying.

Computer Wore Tennis Shoes, The ⊙
1969, US, 91 mins, colour
Dir: Robert Butler
Stars: Kurt Russell, Cesar Romero, Joe Flynn
Rating: ★★

High jinks at Medfield College, where, under the auspices of the Disney Studios, various madcap technical and medical misadventures flourished during the late Sixties and early Seventies. Several of these romps starred the studios' perennial juvenile lead, Kurt Russell, who later went on to adult stardom. The studio's touch for screwball comedy was beginning to fade at this time, but the entertainment is amiable enough, especially in the knockabout finale. Cesar Romero and Richard Bakalyan, as the

crooks, and Joe Flynn and William Schallert, as the academics, run acting rings round their younger co-stars.

Comrades ◐
1987, UK, 178 mins, colour
Dir: Bill Douglas
Stars: William Gaminara, Robin Soans, Ismelda Staunton, Philip Davis, Keith Allen, John Hargeaves
Rating: ★★

Long stretches without dialogue. Lingering close-ups of faces and objects. Carefully composed images. An impeccable attention to period detail. Mud and grime. A passionate care for the oppression of the poor. Yes, this story of the Tolpuddle Martyrs and their adventures after deportation to Australia is British film-making at its most concerned. The first half of this epic seems at time wilfully deliberate to the point that it's hard to keep one's attention on what is (sometimes not) going on. Once in Australia the film picks up, both in pace and incident and gains strength from the charismatic performance of John Hargreaves as a convict. Pretty good ensemble playing from little-known players as the Martyrs; and some ripe cameos from such familiar actors as Michael Hordern, James Fox, Barbara Windsor, Freddie Jones, Vanessa Redgrave and Robert Stephens.

Comrade X ○
1940, US, 87 mins, colour
Dir: King Vidor
Stars: Clark Gable, Hedy Lamarr, Oskar Homolka, Felix Bressart, Eve Arden
Rating: ★★★

Fast and funny farce, made by MGM on the heels of *Ninotchka*, with a racy script by Ben Hecht and Charles McArthur, who wrote *The Front Page*. Like that, this has a newspaperman hero, played at the double by Clark Gable, who is faced with the problem of getting the world's most glamorous tram-driver, Hedy Lamarr, out of her native Russia. The fact that Hedy doesn't want to go is the least of his problems. Director King Vidor keeps it going at the pace of a runaway tram and the chase climax is hilarious. Good satire, good fun.

Conan the Barbarian ◐ ⓥ
1981, US, 129 mins, colour
Dir: John Milius
Stars: Arnold Schwarzenegger, James Earl Jones, Max Von Sydow
Rating: ★★

Grim, taciturn and monosyllabic, big Arnold Schwarzenegger is perfectly cast as Robert E Howard's classic fantasy hero. An unsubtle tale of blood, death and revenge set in a mythical primitive age, this film holds to the spirit of the original stories without actually drawing directly on any of them. Again, this is entirely in keeping with Howard's vision of his improbably-muscled hero. He once said: 'Whenever I found I had written him into a tight corner, I just let him carve his way out again with his broadsword!' Arnie (thankfully) says very little, but then he isn't really expected to. What is slightly surprising is that an intelligent actor like James Earl Jones should chose to play the baddie in such sword-and-sandal hokum. Still, it's very well realised. Just slip the brain into neutral and enjoy the action.

Conan the Destroyer ○ ⓥ
1984, US, 103 mins, colour
Dir: Richard Fleischer
Stars: Arnold Schwarzenegger, Grace Jones, Wilt Chamberlain, Mako, Sarah Douglas, Olivia D'Abo
Rating: ★★

This *Conan* sequel is a sort of comic-strip adventure with the accent on the comic. 'Back to the crypt' is a typical sample of its dialogue, and the acting is rudimentary to say the least. Unfortunately comedy needs talent and there's very little evidence of much of that in front of these cameras, although Grace Jones does at least perform with enthusiasm as a formidable female warrior. So, in the end, we're left with the action which, thanks to the professionalism of veteran director Richard Fleischer is, although formula stuff, brilliantly presented and edited to offer the maximum impact. Further *Conan* sequels were threatened, but Arnold Schwarzenegger, who here has fun with a drunk scene, moved on to subtler stuff.

Concierge, The
See: For Love or Money

Concorde – Airport '80, The
See: Airport '79

Concrete Jungle, The
See: The Criminal

Condorman ⊙
1981, UK, 90 mins, colour
Dir: Charles Jarrott

Stars: Michael Crawford, Oliver Reed, Barbara Carrera
Rating: ★★★

In enlivening this action-comedy from the Disney studio, Michael Crawford reminds us how much he is missed since he defected to theatre and TV. He's a cartoonist (with a convincing American accent) who gets the chance to play his own creation, Condorman, when the CIA hires him to bring back doe-eyed defector Barbara Carrera from Russia. The action is efficient throughout, especially in a speedboat battle in which the Condorcraft with its laser gun takes on the KGB's five black boats with machine guns.

Cone of Silence ○
(aka: Trouble in the Sky)
1960, UK, 92 mins, b/w
Dir: Charles Frend
Stars: Michael Craig, Bernard Lee, Peter Cushing, Elizabeth Seal, George Sanders, Andrew Jackson
Rating: ★★

Buckle your seat-belts for a sweat-inducing slice of airborne suspense. Undervalued character actor Bernard Lee (best known as 'M' in the early Bond films) is here thrust into the spotlight usually reserved for stars. He's a pilot under pressure, a careful, steady type who inexplicably starts crashing planes. The manufacturers are far from pleased and all-too eager to lay the blame at his feet. To give the story extra impetus, a couple of nasty sorts are thrown in: George Sanders as a snide executive and Peter Cushing as a pompous pilot.

Coney Island ☉
1943, US, 96 mins, colour
Dir: Walter Lang
Stars: Betty Grable, George Montgomery, Cesar Romero, Phil Silvers
Rating: ★★★

Just the sort of colourful, tune-filled tonic of which wartime audiences were in so much need, this confirmed peaches-and-cream Betty Grable's reputation as Fox's biggest musical star. As well as such oldies as 'Pretty Baby', 'Cuddle Up a Little Closer' and 'Put Your Arms Around Me Honey', Betty warbles songs by Ralph Rainger (killed in an air crash while the film was being made) and Leo Robin that include 'Take It from There' and 'Lulu from Louisville'. Perhaps the acting is as over-bright as the colour, but Walter Lang's direction, the mul-

titude of songs and the choreography of the famous Hermes Pan (who stages a splendid finale with 'There's Danger in a Dance') swing it along with all the gaiety of the fairground of the title. The studio and star were so fond of the film that they actually reworked it only seven years later under the title *Wabash Avenue*.

Confession ○
1937, US, 90 mins, b/w
Dir: Joe May
Stars: Kay Francis, Ian Hunter, Basil Rathbone, Jane Bryan, Donald Crisp
Rating: ★★★

Although it's set in Warsaw, the actors all speak perfect English in this tear-jerking drama that calls for a full box of tissues to get through the highly emotional storyline. Kay Francis is well cast as a cabaret singer who kills a philandering concert pianist when she learns he's been performing with her daughter. A top-notch cast and special attention is paid to the film's musical content.

Confessions of a Nazi Spy ○
1939, US, 102 mins, b/w
Dir: Anatole Litvak
Stars: Edward G Robinson, George Sanders, Paul Lukas, Lya Lys
Rating: ★★★

Edward G Robinson is in quietly authoritative mood in this well-paced, fascinating story of the bid by American G-men to break up a worldwide nazi spy ring. Director Anatole Litvak's sober approach is reminiscent of the surge of documentary-style thrillers which began some six years later with *The House on 92nd Street*. Here, he draws especially good performances from Robinson himself and from Paul Lukas as a propaganda agent.

Confidential Agent ○
1945, US, 122 mins, b/w
Dir: Herman Shumlin
Stars: Charles Boyer, Lauren Bacall, Wanda Hendrix, Katina Paxinou, Peter Lorre, George Colouris
Rating: ★★★

Written by Robert Buckner, a man responsible, as writer-producer, for some of Hollywood's most polished and persuasive action films, *Confidential Agent* is typical of the many black thrillers turned out by Warners in the Forties – exciting and splendidly paced. Charles Boyer does well in a role that sounds as if it were

written for Humphrey Bogart. And the line-up of featured players now seems hardly less than dazzling.

Confidentially Connie ○
1953, US, 74 mins, b/w
Dir: Edward Buzzell
Stars: Janet Leigh, Van Johnson, Louis Calhern, Walter Slezak, Gene Lockhart
Rating: ★★

This classy MGM second-feature is a bright, light and lively frolic about the efforts of an expectant mum to satisfy her craving for prime steak. Bubbly Janet Leigh makes the most of her material as Connie and bluff Louis Calhern is at the top of his form as her cantankerous Texas father-in-law. Very good, too, is Gene Lockhart as the college dean who regards dinners given to him by promotion-seeking staff as one of the perks of his office.

Confidential Report ○ ⓥ
(aka: Mr Arkadin)
1955, UK, 99 mins, b/w
Dir: Orson Welles
Stars: Orson Welles, Michael Redgrave, Akim Tamiroff, Patricia Medina, Paola Mori, Robert Arden
Rating: ★★

Orson Welles' first film since *Othello*, three years earlier, has a complicated flashback structure reminiscent of *Citizen Kane* and a leading character who's the mythical figure of a dominating financier, again with shades of Welles' Kane. *Confidential Report* was filmed in Spain and bears all the Welles trademarks – tilted camera angles, heavy atmospheric shots, overlapping dialogue. But as a result of a low budget and some pretty amateurish acting, the film rarely touches base with reality and is a monument to talent being squandered.

Confirm or Deny ○
1941, US, 78 mins, b/w
Dir: Archie Mayo
Stars: Don Ameche, Joan Bennett, Roddy McDowall, Arthur Shields
Rating: ★★

Set in wartime London, this romantic drama has some quite realistic scenes of the Blitz, but otherwise proves largely uninteresting. Don Ameche is not entirely at home as the American correspondent, although more so than is Joan Bennett as the teletype operator at the Ministry of Information who falls for him. The supporting cast, though, includes a very young Roddy McDowall and

C

that delightful comic character actor Eric Blore, more familiar to buffs for his regular appearances in Fred Astaire and Ginger Rogers musicals.

Conflict ○ ⓥ
1945, US, 86 mins, b/w
Dir: Curtis Bernhardt
Stars: Humphrey Bogart, Sydney Greenstreet, Alexis Smith, Charles Drake
Rating: ★★★

It's fascinating to see Humphrey Bogart and Sydney Greenstreet cast against type – as a man who wants to kill his wife and the psychiatrist who tries to trap him respectively. The casting, and the performances that result, give a whole new edge to a stock movie plot. Director Curtis Bernhardt – aided by the menacingly dark cinematography of Merritt Gerstad – displays intelligent use of a mobile camera to add shivers to the thrills. The film was actually completed in 1943 but not released until two years later, presumably so as not to spoil Bogart's 'hero' image at the height of the war.

Conflict of Wings ⊙
(aka: Fuss Over Feathers)
1954, UK, 84 mins, colour
Dir: John Eldridge
Stars: John Gregson, Muriel Pavlow, Kieron Moore
Rating: ★★★

Just about the best film to come from the short-lived Group Three Productions enterprise. This story of a battle between villagers and the RAF over a bird sanctuary is extremely well thought out by screenplay writers Don Sharp and John Pudney, has a string of likeable performances headed by John Gregson and Muriel Pavlow and the bonus of delightful Eastman Colour photography by Arthur Grant and Martin Curtis. A credit mark to all concerned.

Congo Crossing ○
1956, US, 85 mins, colour
Dir: Joseph Pevney
Stars: George Nader, Virginia Mayo, Peter Lorre
Rating: ★

A colourful and unusual adventure story with some picturesque settings. *Congo Crossing* was Peter Lorre's third film on his comeback to the screen after a five-year absence brought on mainly by illness. He returned weightier, but more astringent than

ever. Alas, his is about the only enthusiastic performance from a tired-looking cast that also includes Virginia Mayo and George Nader.

Connecticut Yankee in King Arthur's Court, A ⊙
1949, US, 106 mins, colour
Dir: Tay Garnett
Stars: Bing Crosby, Rhonda Fleming, William Bendix, Sir Cedric Hardwicke, Henry Wilcoxon
Rating: ★★★★

This remake of Mark Twain's fantasy that had once provided a hit role for Will Rogers is perfectly tailored to Bing Crosby's laid-back charm. Peppered with inventive incident and photographed so ravishingly in colour by Ray Rennahan that you almost forget Rhonda Fleming can't act, the film also has attractive characters and a winning score by James Van Heusen and Johnny Burke. Pick of the songs is the immortal 'Busy Doin' Nothin' which, shared by Crosby with such unlikely vocalists as William Bendix and Sir Cedric Hardwicke, became one of the Old Groaner's most enduring hits.

Connecticut Yankee in King Arthur's Court, A ○
1989, US, 100 mins, colour
Dir: Mel Damski
Stars: Keshia Knight Pulliam, Jean Marsh, Michael Gross, Emma Samms
Rating: ★

A sorry remake of the Bing Crosby musical about a modern-day American whisked back in time to King Arthur's Camelot. Here the central character is a child of the MTV generation, 10-year-old Keshia Knight Pulliam, from *The Cosby Show*, who gets to cause mayhem in ye olde England. In Camelot she meets a lot of other familiar TV faces, including Michael Gross (from *Family Ties*) as Kingh Arthur, Emma Samms (*Dynasty*) as Queen Guenevere, and Jean Marsh (*Upstairs Downstairs*) as the wicked Morgana, but it's a pity that old Merlin couldn't magic up a half-decent script. It's hard to believe that this film used the original Mark Twain novel as source material because seldom do the Twain meet.

Connecting Rooms ○
1969, UK, 99 mins, colour
Dir: Franklin Gollings
Stars: Bette Davis, Michael Redgrave, Alexis Kanner, Kay Walsh
Rating: ★★

An old-fashioned story of love blooming in middle-age, set against a background of pop music and student riots. Michael Redgrave is quite touching as the unwanted and unemployed school-teacher who rents a room next to Bette Davis, as a seedy cellist. Somewhat underrated in its time, the film has an interesting supporting cast, which includes Alexis Kanner, French actress Olga Georges-Picot, British veterans Leo Genn and Kay Walsh, and American singing star Richard Wyler (formerly known as Richard Stapley) in a rare straight acting role.

Conquest of Cochise ○
1953, US, 70 mins, colour
Dir: William Castle
Stars: Robert Stack, John Hodiak, Joy Page
Rating: ★★

Briskly-told, plainly-acted Western, pleasantly shot in colour and set against some stunning scenery. The many strings to the plot are quickly gathered up, and tied securely during director William Castle's rousing finale. Better casting would have made this a grade 'A' horse opera.

Conquest of Space ○
1955, US, 78 mins, colour
Dir: Byron Haskin
Stars: Walter Brooke, Eric Fleming, Mickey Shaughnessy
Rating: ★★

First-rate acting from the entire cast enlivens this now-dated but fun story of a trip to Mars. The Martian landscapes weren't too brilliant even then, but the action sequences are good and the film doesn't have a single dud performance. One of the first large-scale, documentary-style space films, it was one of several famous special effects sagas produced by George Pal for Paramount in the Fifties. The first of these was *Destination Moon* which appeared in 1950. *When Worlds Collide* followed in 1951, and Pal's version of H G Wells' *War of the Worlds* in 1953: all three won Oscars. Eric Fleming, then an unknown, but later to win fame as Gil Favor of *Rawhide*, plays the young second-in-command.

Conquest of the Planet of the Apes ○ ⓥ
1972, US, 95 mins, colour
Dir: J Lee Thompson

Stars: Roddy McDowall, Don Murray, Ricardo Montalban, Natalie Trundy
Rating: ★★

The fourth episode of the Apes saga, full of sound and fury, providing a field day for the colour cameras of Bruce Surtees, who did such a good job on *The Outlaw Josey Wales*. Here, he makes colour by De Luxe seem more vivid than ever before, especially in the final fierce battle between apes and men, when the screen is filled with flickering, flaming reds, yellows and browns. Although various elements of the plot strain credibility to the limit – would you believe a circus owner who champions animal emancipation, or that apes could really be trained to do such sophisticated things as filing and cooking in the next 20 years? – Roddy McDowall is again on hand as Caesar to sustain our interest and anticipation.

Conspiracy of Hearts ○
1960, UK, 110 mins, b/w
Dir: Ralph Thomas
Stars: Lilli Palmer, Sylvia Syms, Yvonne Mitchell
Rating: ★★

A wartime escape story with a difference, about a group of nuns who help Jewish children to escape from Italy and Nazi persecution. The villains are rather theatrical, but Ernest Steward's vivid black-and-white photography makes the most of the escape sequences, which contain some tense, exciting and moving moments. The best performance comes from Megs Jenkins, who also makes by far the most convincing nun. Directed by Ralph Thomas in the middle of the most prolific and rewarding period of his career, years which also included *Doctor in the House*, *Above Us the Waves*, *A Tale of Two Cities*, *The Wind Cannot Read*, *The Clouded Yellow*, *Appointment with Venus* and *No Love for Johnnie*.

Constant Husband, The ○
1955, UK, 88 mins, colour
Dir: Sidney Gilliat
Stars: Rex Harrison, Kay Kendall, Margaret Leighton
Rating: ★★★

Sparkling Launder and Gilliat comedy about a man who has lost his memory, then finds he's the perfect husband – six times over. Cecil Parker and George Cole are excellent in their wittily-written roles as a psychiatrist and a tempestuous Italian, respectively. It's bright, saucy and at times a riot.

Consuming Passions ◐
1988, US, 98 mins, colour
Dir: Giles Foster
Stars: Tyler Butterworth, Vanessa Redgrave, Jonathan Pryce, Sammi Davis, Prunella Scales
Rating: ★★★

The equivalent of a minor Ealing comedy, Eighties style. Ian Littleton, played by tiny Tyler Butterworth as a cross between Norman Wisdom and Ian Carmichael, enrols at Chunley's Chocolate Factory with little hope of success as he has two left everything. Little hope that is until he accidentally plummets three workmen on a trestle into a giant chocolate vat, which devours them noisily within seconds. Sacked on the spot, Ian's reinstated when it's discovered that people hate the chox being marketed by whizzkid Jonathan Pryce and love the new variety. 'Quite unusual,' offers one tester. 'Got a lot of body in it.' Toss in (but, please, not the chocolate vat) Vanessa Redgrave enjoying herself immensely as the predatory Maltese widow of a 'victim' – a veritable falcon of a woman who sinks her talons into Ian for all she can get – and you have a surefire recipe for a tasty black comedy morsel.

Contest Girl
See: *The Beauty Jungle*

Contraband ○
(aka: Blackout)
1940, UK, 92 mins, b/w
Dir: Michael Powell
Stars: Conrad Veidt, Valerie Hobson, Esmond Knight
Rating: ★★★

Conrad Veidt plays a Danish sea captain who finds himself unwittingly involved in a British spy ring in this fast-moving and enjoyable thriller directed by Michael Powell. Veidt is brilliant in the central role, although after seeing him so often as the nasty Nazi Major Strasser in *Casablanca*, it's hard to accept him as a goodie. There are also good performances from Valerie Hobson and Esmond Knight. Look out, too, for early appearances by British actors Peter Bull and Leo Genn.

Contraband Spain ○
1956, UK, 82 mins, colour
Dir: Lawrence Huntington
Stars: Richard Green, Michael Denison, Anouk Aimee,
Rating: ★

It makes a change to see Richard Greene casting aside his swashbuckling gear, and here he and Michael Denison, as a British customs officer (Greene's an FBI agent), have a busy time following a tortuous trail of smuggling, blackmail and general skulduggery along the Franco-Spanish border. The beautiful Anouk Aimee is rather wasted in the midst of such thick-ear thrills. The action often drags and the supporting cast is poor.

Conversation, The ◐
1974, US, 113 mins, colour
Dir: Francis Ford Coppola
Stars: Gene Hackman, John Cazale
Rating: ★★★

Shattering revelations can often be the garland round the neck of the well-made thriller. But when they occur in five-second flashbacks, you'd better be sharp to keep up. To say more would be going unfairly into the ingenious plot of this Francis Ford Coppola film, which features Gene Hackman as a professional eavesdropper haunted by the time his 'bugging' cost the lives of three people and terrified that it's happening again. Hackman is excellent as the 'tapper', and the mood of his loneliness and isolation is well established. But don't blink during the last reel. A pre-stardom Teri Garr and Harrison Ford appear in minor roles.

Convicted ○
1950, US, 91 mins, b/w
Dir: Henry Levin
Stars: Glenn Ford, Broderick Crawford, Dorothy Malone, Ed Begley
Rating: ★★★

Enticing vintage film about prison life, featuring a really splendid cast. Glenn Ford has the hero's part as a man sent to prison for a killing, accidental of course, as any fan of Ford's will assume. Broderick Crawford plays the prison governor and Millard Mitchell gives one of his inimitable character portrayals as a 'con'.

Convict 99 ☉
1938, UK, 91 mins, b/w
Dir: Marcel Varnel
Stars: Will Hay, Moore Marriott, Graham Moffatt, Googie Withers
Rating: ★★★

Another relishable British Thirties comedy classic, with Will Hay as a

C

prison governor who turns his cells into homes from home, complete with armchairs, electric fires, radios and curtains. For once, bewhiskered Moore Marriott steals the show from under Hay's pince-nez, as a would-be escapee called Jerry the Mole, forever tunnelling his way to nowhere. Hay's other constant cohort, tubby Graham Moffatt, is also on hand in this richly funny comedy.

Convoy ○
1978, UK, 110 mins, colour
Dir: Sam Peckinpah
Stars: Kris Kristofferson, Ali MacGraw, Ernest Borgnine, Burt Young
Rating: ★★

A Western with trucks instead of gunmen, Sam Peckinpah's film works well on and off, but could have done with the overall drive of the C W McCall record on which it's based. Peckinpah gives Kris Kristofferson little chance to endow the major character, Rubber Duck (leader of a convoy of trucks running for Mexico after a fracas with police), with the charisma of which he's capable. The movie certainly has its moments; the problem is that they all belong, as it were, to different films. It also has some nice lines. A film of contrasting pleasures and annoyances, then, and, being a Peckinpah vehicle, one that's also peppered with slow-motion.

Coogan's Bluff ◑
1968, US, 94 mins, colour
Dir: Don Siegel
Stars: Clint Eastwood, Lee J Cobb, Susan Clark, Tisha Sterling, Don Stroud
Rating: ★★★

This rough-and-tumble Clint Eastwood cop thriller, containing some really excitingly-shot chase sequences, can be seen now as a kind of dry run for Dennis Weaver's famous *McCloud* series on TV. Don Stroud is outstanding as Eastwood's quarry, and Tisha Sterling also shines in the strong supporting cast. Good action fare.

Cookie ● ⓥ
1989, US, 98 mins, colour
Dir: Susan Seidelman
Stars: Peter Falk, Dianne Wiest, Emily Lloyd, Jerry Lewis
Rating: ★

Take a dozen surefire box-office elements, cast Peter Falk as a wily Mafioso, Emily Lloyd as his streetwise daughter by mistress Dianne Wiest,

Brenda Vaccaro as his raucous wife and sundry other talented players, and what do you get? You get a turkey, that's what! The script isn't too bad, so you have to lay most of the blame at the feet of director Suan Seidelman, who did wonders with similar material in *Smithereens* and *Desperately Seeking Susan*, but here displays little sense of the timing or pacing needed for a good comedy. This has only one pace and we're here to tell you it's not fast. Falk and Lloyd at least emerge with decent performances that left their reputations relatively unscathed. Others, like Wiest, Lewis and Michael V Gazzo, seem either to give it too much or too little, and are probably still licking their wounds.

Cook, the Thief, His Wife and Her Lover, The ● ⓥ
1989, UK/France, 120 mins, colour
Dir: Peter Greenaway
Stars: Richard Bohringer, Michael Gambon, Helen Mirren, Alan Howard, Tim Roth, Gary Olsen
Rating: ★★

Trust director Peter Greenaway, who made *The Draughtsman's Contract* and *Drowning by Numbers*, to produce a film that was at once the most stylish and repellent of its year. Vulgarity is the keynote and no opportunity is missed to underline it, from the continuous sex and violence, to the crass opulence of the restaurant where it all takes place. Michael Gambon, who in real life and not this Restoration equivalent of the Eighties, would be guaranteed to empty for weeks any restaurant at which he ate, is a disgusting gangster who 'dines' at the Hollandais (which he owns) with his much-beaten wife (Helen Mirren). When she spies a bookseller (Alan Howard) across the vomit on the red plush, it's lust at first sight. When Gambon finds out, the film finally fulfils its promise of something to offend everyone. Michael Nyman's score is his best to date, Greenaway takes it all full-tilt and head-on and Mirren and Howard, who have to perform most their scenes in the nude, give service above and beyond the call of duty. Don't eat anything for 24 hours before you see it.

Cool Hand Luke ◑ ⓥ
1967, US, 126 mins, colour
Dir: Stuart Rosenberg
Stars: Paul Newman, George Kennedy, J D Cannon, Strother Martin, Jo Van Fleet,

Dennis Hopper
Rating: ★★★★

Stuart Rosenberg's deservedly popular film has Paul Newman ideally cast as the carefree guy sentenced to two years on a chain gang. He becomes known as Cool Hand Luke because of his devil-may-care attitude and determination to escape. Grittily acted (George Kennedy won an Oscar as another prisoner) and powerfully made, the film also became famous for its phrase, 'Put him in the Box' – the diabolical sentence for prisoners who have incurred the wrath of the guards. Watch also for the memorable egg-eating sequence. Several of the cast went on to become well-known in the cinema. Strother Martin, who plays the brutal captain, later rose to co-star status, while Dennis Hopper (here reunited with *East of Eden* co-stars Jo Van Fleet and Richard Davalos) turned producer and director with *Easy Rider*. J D Cannon, who plays the prisoner known as Society Red, soon became familiar as Chief Clifford in the *McCloud series*. The aggressive features of Anthony Zerbe and Joe Don Baker are also around.

Cool Runnings ○ ⓥ
1993, US, 99 mins, colour
Dir: Jon Turtletaub
Stars: Leon, Doug E Doug, John Candy
Rating: ★★

A modest, old-fashioned, one-joke film about the first Jamaican bobsled team to compete in the Olympic Games. The script does its best to jazz the subject up, and there are a few (doubtless fictitious) spanners in the works before the team – consisting of a pushcart champion and three sprinters who fell in the Olympic trials – makes it on to the ice of the Winter Olympics. Coach John Candy does everything but implore his guys to win one for the Gipper and, although the ending is a bit of an anti-climax, the odds are that you'll be in there cheering and crying for the troupe from the tropics.

Cool World ◑ ⓥ
1992, US, 102 mins, colour
Dir: Ralph Bakshi
Stars: Gabriel Byrne, Kim Basinger, Brad Pitt
Rating: ★★

The British certificate (12) really said it all for this mixture of live-action and animation that falls between two stools. Despite strong language it isn't really an adult attraction and the language and sexual references make it not at all suitable for younger children. Once again, though, the actors do yeoman service in the cause of cartoon fun, especially Kim Basinger as the curvy embodiment of Holli Would, a 'doodle' who longs to be real and 'experience it all'. Gabriel Byrne is the cartoonist who finds himself trapped in his own creation and Brad Pitt the other sort-of human inhabitant of a world where, apart from one or two main characters, the animation is fluid and skilful but uninteresting. Director Ralph Bakshi partially keeps the excesses of *Fritz the Cat* in check, but this failed to restore him to the big league which seemed within his grasp with *Wizards* and *Lord of the Rings*.

Cop ●
1987, US, 110 mins, colour
Dir: James B Harris
Stars: James Woods, Lesley Ann Warren, Charles Durning
Rating: ★★

You've got to hand it to James Woods. You can't take your eyes off this lethal actor, even in a mediocre movie like this crime thriller, which runs like a Clint Eastwood reject of a few years earlier. No matter: Woods dead-set in pursuit of the bad guys is still a fearsome sight. With tender moments he's less secure, though he's on his own with this dialogue. Spitting out four-letter words like spent bullets and slitting his eyes in search of any clue, Woods is the last man you'd care to have on your tail, as a maverick cop who can't even be dragged off the scent by his superiors after getting wind of a serial killer who inflicts appalling injuries on his victims. Even though Eastwood and Charles Bronson have been down these mean and blood-soaked streets before, Woods, as a man who does nothing by half-measures, makes them his own. The film's implicit anti-feminism may restrict the numbers of those who respond to it.

Copacabana ☉
1947, US, 91 mins, b/w
Dir: Alfred C Green
Stars: Groucho Marx, Carmen Miranda, Steve Cochran
Rating: ★★

The very idea of teaming Groucho Marx with Carmen Miranda makes

the mouth water, but don't expect too much from this moth-eaten, very cheap-looking black-and-white comedy-musical, which has both funsters straining for laughs as they strive to carry the show on their own shoulders without a decent script to support them. A few light chuckles, but overall about as mangy as the legendary lover of Groucho's memoirs.

Cop and a ½ ○ Ⓥ
1993, US, 93 mins, colour
Dir: Henry Winkler
Stars: Burt Reynolds, Norman D Golden II, Ray Sharkey, Ruby Dee, Marc Macaulay
Rating: ★

Burt Reynolds' biggest hit in years, though it's no better than most of his woeful output since 1980. It's a knowingly performed, strenuously overplayed comedy about a veteran cop (Reynolds) forced to take an eight-year-old black kid (Norman D Golden II) on shift with him in order to prise out information the boy has on a drugs deal. The kid wants to be a cop and his price for the info is a stint on patrol. Henry Winkler's direction of their subsequent encounters with the crooks encourages his cast to overact and their larger-than-life performances consequently lack any conviction. The stupid comic criminals are a completely outmoded conception, sad in view of the fact that some of them, notably Ray Sharkey (whose last film this was), and Marc Macaulay, are obviously capable of genuine menace. Robbed of any real sense of danger, the chase scenes come across as routine rather than exciting, and Reynolds' feelings for his 'partner' whether hostile or tender, never seems genuine. Golden is okay if, like the rest of the movie, pretty much OTT.

Copper Canyon ○
1950, US, 83 mins, colour
Dir: Jonathan Latimer
Stars: Ray Milland, Hedy Lamarr, Macdonald Carey, Mona Freeman, Harry Carey Jr
Rating: ★★

Star Ray Milland has described this Western – which boasts some magnificent colour photography – as one of the films he most enjoyed making. He plays a trick-sharpshooter who may or may not be a famous gunman. Good supporting cast includes Harry Carey Jr, Ian Wolfe, Peggy Knudsen, Hope Emerson and

Frank Faylen. As an expert horseman and marksman, Milland was at home on the Hollywood range, despite this being only his second Western in 57 films. And none of the ten top stuntmen hired for the production was required to stand in for him in the man-sized rough-and-tumble action sequences.

Cornered ○
1945, US, 102 mins, b/w
Dir: Edward Dmytryk
Stars: Dick Powell, Walter Slezak, Luther Adler, Micheline Cheirel
Rating: ★★★

This high-tension *film noir* is one of Edward Dmytryk's best pictures. Dick Powell's tough guy hero is the equal of his Philip Marlowe in *Farewell, My Lovely* – adept at quick action and cynical dialogue, but romantic enough to cry at the memory of his dead first wife. After several writers had had a go at the script, John Paxton, who wrote Powell's version of *Farewell, My Lovely*, was called in, and did a brilliant job of tightening the whole film up, adding suspense and action scenes to create a *noir* spy classic. Thoroughly decadent studies of villainy from Walter Slezak, Luther Adler and Steven Geray add flavour to the picture.

Corn Is Green, The ○
1945, US, 118 mins, b/w
Dir: Irving Rapper
Stars: Bette Davis, John Dall, Nigel Bruce, Joan Lorring
Rating: ★★★

Irving Rapper, who directed Bette Davis on two of her other great Forties hits, *Now, Voyager* and *Deception*, assists her to give another telling performance in this fine adaptation of Emlyn Williams' famous play. Welsh actor Rhys Williams, who plays Mr Jones, also acted as technical adviser on the film.

Corn Is Green, The ○
1979, US, 93 mins, colour
Dir: George Cukor
Stars: Katharine Hepburn, Ian Saynor, Bill Fraser, Anna Massey
Rating: ★★

In her tenth (and final) teaming with veteran Hollywood director George Cukor, Katharine Hepburn gives a typically proud performance as the devoted teacher in a small Welsh mining town, coming to terms with the school's solitary gifted pupil.

c

Emlyn Williams' play was originally brought to the screen as a sturdy vehicle for Bette Davis in 1945. Here, the lush location photography is a mite too swish, emphasising the sentimental side of the story. And, while Miss Hepburn's acting is always worth watching, Ian Saynor struggles to make much of an impression as her talented protege.

Corridors of Blood ◑
1958, UK, 95 mins, b/w
Dir: Robert Day
Stars: Boris Karloff, Betta St John, Christopher Lee, Finlay Currie
Rating: ★★★

This film laudably brought back Boris Karloff to films after three years 'retirement' and gave him a far more interesting part to play than the ones that had driven him away in the early Fifties. It's grisly but literate, an interesting period horror thriller, highlighted by Karloff's own compassionate performance as the surgeon who becomes a drug addict when he experiments on himself in bids to find an anaesthetic. Christopher Lee and Francis de Wolff enjoy themselves thoroughly as two evil bodysnatchers called Resurrection Joe and Black Ben. In a much smaller role, you'll spot tubby Welsh character actor Roddy Hughes, a good servant to British film since the early days of sound. The title refers to the primitive conditions that existed in hospitals at the time.

Corsican Brothers, The ○
1941, US, 111 mins, b/w
Dir: Gregory Ratoff
Stars: Douglas Fairbanks Jr, Ruth Warrick, Akim Tamiroff, J Carroll Naish
Rating: ★★★

Surprisingly, this lively costume adventure was the first sound version of Alexandre Dumas' famous swashbuckling tale. Twin brothers seek revenge on an evil nobleman (a plum role for swarthy Akim Tamiroff) who has wiped out their family. Director Gregory Ratoff, more familiar in character roles as excitable foreigners, sets a hot pace throughout, and gets excellent performances from fellow character players Tamiroff, J Carrol Naish and H B Warner, as well as from Douglas Fairbanks Jr as the twins of the title.

Cottage to Let ○
(aka: Bombsite Stolen)
1941, UK, 90 mins, b/w
Dir: Anthony Asquith
Stars: Leslie Banks, John Mills, Alastair Sim, Carla Lehmann, George Cole
Rating: ★★★

Anthony Asquith's vigorous comedy-thriller, about Nazi agents on the loose in Scotland, is a splendid piece of fiction of its time. George Cole makes his screen debut at the age of 16 as a cockney evacuee; John Mills is chillingly cast against type as the leading Nazi; and there are splendid climactic scenes at an old mill and a carnival hall of mirrors.

Cotton Club, The ◑ Ⓥ
1984, US, 127 mins, colour
Dir: Francis Coppola
Stars: Richard Gere, Gregory Hines, Diane Lane, Bob Hoskins, Nicolas Cage
Rating: ★★

Cornet player Richard Gere finds himself caught in the middle of mobster rivalry in the 1920s in Francis Coppola's stylish gangster film. He gets a job in Harlem's famous Cotton Club, run by gangland overlord Owney Madden (Bob Hoskins), while his brother gets a job as Dutch Schultz's bodyguard. Threads of three different stories intertwine to reach an exciting climax, involving dancer Gregory Hines, Gere, Dutch Schultz (James Remar) and Hoskins. The film looks great and, despite a script that is a little too bumpy, keeps on the boil right to the end. Hoskins and sidekick Fred Gwynne are excellent as is Gregory Hines, who dances up a storm with his brother Maurice. In fact the only problem is Gere, whose performance is flat and uninteresting. He apparently did all his own cornet solos for the film. Maybe he should have concentrated on the acting rather than blowing his own trumpet. The music is great – all Duke Ellington and Cab Calloway numbers. Particularly good is Larry Marshall who, playing Cab Calloway, does a brilliant version of 'Minnie the Moocher'.

Couch Trip, The ◑
1988, US, 98 mins, colour
Dir: Michael Ritchie
Stars: Dan Aykroyd, Walter Matthau, Charles Grodin, Donna Dixon
Rating: ★★

Remember the remarks about the lunatics taking over the asylum? What about the saying: 'Physician heal thy-

self?' And of course you've heard the story about the imposter who makes a bigger success of his role than the man whose personality he's stolen. All three familiar themes are rolled into one story in this solo vehicle for Dan Aykroyd as the escaped mental patient who ends up taking over the practice (and radio show) of a Beverly Hills psychiatrist (Charles Grodin in a typical role) who is himself headed for the couch. (C)rude in the modern American manner, the film moves along well, and is good for a few chuckles, notably at the end when one of Aykroyd's patients (a bogus cleric played by Walter Matthau) climbs on to the top of the famous 'Hollywood' sign and threatens to jump off. 'How does this reflect on your treatment of him,' a reporter asks Aykroyd. 'Badly,' he replies. 'But maybe he won't live to tell about it.' Never riotous (more frantic editing was needed) but amusing enough to watch, especially if you've had a hard day at the office.

Countdown ○
1967, US, 101 mins, colour
Dir: Robert Altman
Stars: James Caan, Robert Duvall, Joanna Moore
Rating: ★★

The three major talents connected with this science-fiction thriller were all on the threshold of hugely successful careers. James Caan and Robert Duvall went on to appear together in Francis Coppola's *The Godfather* and Sam Peckinpah's *Killer Elite*, while director Robert Altman went on to make *M*A*S*H*, *McCabe and Mrs Miller*, *Nashville*, *The Player* and *Short Cuts*. An exciting space saga with a bone-crushing last reel that will leave you breathless, *Countdown* is most uncharacteristic of its director and the ethereal qualities of his later work.

Counterfeit Killer, The ○
1968, US, 95 mins, colour
Dir: Josef Leytes
Stars: Jack Lord, Shirely Knight
Rating: ★★

Hawaii Five-O's Jack Lord has a rough time as an undercover man in this thriller about a ring of counterfeiters. He's shot at, beaten up and thrown in jail for two months – and that's just for openers. To be seen in cameo roles are Charles Drake, Oscar-winning actress Mercedes McCambridge and angular, menacing L Q Jones.

Counterfeit Traitor, The ○
1962, US, 140 mins, colour
Dir: George Seaton
Stars: William Holden, Lilli Palmer, Hugh Griffith, Eva Dahlbeck
Rating: ★★

Long but frequently fascinating – and sometimes agonisingly suspenseful – true-life espionage story about a businessman who lives dangerously as a double agent for the Allies during World War Two. There's a tremendous performance from classic beauty Lilli Palmer, still haunting here in her late 40's.

Countess Dracula ● Ⓥ
1970, UK, 94 mins, colour
Dir: Peter Sasdy
Stars: Ingrid Pitt, Nigel Green, Lesley-Anne Down
Rating: ★★

Director Peter Sasdy (who also made the underrated *Hands of the Ripper* for the same studio, Hammer) and star Ingrid Pitt combine well here to suggest the air of total corruption that pervades the castle of the Hungarian countess who bathes in the blood of virgins to preserve her youth. Ken Talbot's rich photography should provide a test of how your colour television copes with varying shades of red. Indeed, in retrospect the film seems to have been all browns, reds and golds, indicating director and cinematographer's determination to paint a portrait of decay that could have come from the canvasses of Goya. A lot of the supporting acting is of variable quality, but time and again Miss Pitt pulls it all together with her fierce portrait of a bitter woman's determination to hang on to an unexpected, if grisly, new lease of life at all costs. The sequence where she sees herself begin to age in the mirror behind the head of her handsome young lover is made particularly frightening by the ferocity, fear and passion in the face of the actress.

Count Five and Die ○
1957, UK, 92 mins, b/w
Dir: Victor Vicas
Stars: Jeffrey Hunter, Nigel Patrick, Anne-Marie Duringer
Rating: ★★★

The Franco-Russian director Victor Vicas only made a handful of films, of which this tense war drama and the contrasting *The Wayward Bus* are the best. Here he builds the suspense with terse assurance towards a strikingly

shot climax. The convincing espionage fiction is helped by a strong star trio: Jeffrey Hunter's stolid, gullible American is neatly contrasted with Nigel Patrick's jaunty, quick-witted major in charge – not personality traits that one would readily associate with the actors – and the suspected radio operator of Anne-Marie Duringer, a West German actress little seen in English-speaking films, but still active in the continental cinema today.

Count of Monte Cristo, The ○
1934, US, 119 mins, b/w
Dir: Rowland V Lee
Stars: Robert Donat, Elissa Landi, Louis Calhern, Sidney Blackmer
Rating: ★★★

Still the outstanding version of Dumas' classic tale of revenge for unjust imprisonment. It's a notable director's triumph for Rowland V Lee, who made outstanding use of black and white throughout the Thirties, a period in which he also made *Zoo in Budapest*, *Son of Frankenstein* and *Tower of London*. Here he creates a Chateau d'If with dungeons so dingy, dusty and dirty that they almost make you cough.

Country Girl, The ○
1954, US, 104 mins, b/w
Dir: George Seaton
Stars: Bing Crosby, Grace Kelly, William Holden
Rating: ★★★★

Bing Crosby, in a rare dramatic role, gives the finest performance of his screen career as Frank Elgin, a middle-aged Broadway has-been. This tremendously powerful and moving film version of Clifford Odet's play won Oscars for Grace Kelly, as Best Actress, and writer-director George Seaton, for Best Screenplay. Bing was ironically only nominated for an Oscar, having won the award for a much lesser performance ten years earlier in *Going My Way*.

Count the Hours ○
1953, US, 74 mins, b/w
Dir: Don Siegel
Stars: Teresa Wright, Macdonald Carey
Rating: ★★

Despite an indifferent script and uneven acting, director Don Siegel makes this low-budget RKO thriller quite a tense and exciting drama. Macdonald Carey plays a lawyer who risks private life and career in a race

against time to prove the innocence of a man due to be condemned to death. Carey is authoritative in the role and Teresa Wright works hard as the troubled and hysterical wife of the man so close to execution. But it's Siegel's skills that keep the pot boiling and it's the film's pace that carries it through, in spite of its deficiencies.

Count Yorga, Vampire ●
1970, US, 91 mins, colour
Dir: Bob Kelljan
Stars: Robert Quarry, Michael Murphy, Roger Perry
Rating: ★★★

The film that pumped new blood into the vampire cycle, if only for a while. A succession of highly effective and sometimes very gruesome shock moments – the sight of the vampire count rushing at the screen as if from nowhere is really very scary – is capped by the shock twist in the final few feet of film. Director Bob Kelljan, a former actor, made nothing better than this rough-hewn contemporary version of the ancient legend.

Count Your Blessings ○
1959, US, 102 mins, colour
Dir: Jean Negulesco
Stars: Deborah Kerr, Rossano Brazzi, Maurice Chevalier, Patricia Medina
Rating: ★★

Jean Negulesco, one of Hollywood's most romantic-minded directors, made this melodrama that's faintly reminiscent of another Deborah Kerr film, *Perfect Strangers* (1946). Again, Deborah plays a wartime bride who finds difficulty in adjusting to post-war married life, in this case with Rossano Brazzi. Martin Stephens, the minor menace from *The Innocents* and *Children of the Damned*, contributes an amusing portrayal of the boy who tries to keep his parents' marriage where he thinks it belongs – on the rocks.

Courage Mountain ○ Ⓥ
1989, UK, 98 mins, colour
Dir: Christopher Leitch
Stars: Juliette Caton, Charlie Sheen, Leslie Caron
Rating: ★★★

Three yodels for this spirited sequel to earlier Heidi adventures in which Heidi is a teenager whose days at boarding school prove all too short when the boots of war stomp all over the school and she is thrown into an orphanage. Escaping with four

c

tremulous companions, she faces the same means of escape as Julie Andrews in *The Sound of Music* – over the Alps. When Heidi's grandfather (Jan Rubes) bids her goodbye with the line: 'The mountain is inside you. It will always be there,' we fear the worst. But the adventure that follows proves quite strong and stirring, even if it can't quite make up its mind between the Shirley Temple approach and 1989 realism. But there are some good bits, especially the flight over the mountains and a horrendous orphanage which rivals the one from *The Wolves of Willoughby Chase*. One of the other girls, Joanna Clarke, proves rather more than a match for Juliette Caton's slightly halting Heidi. Magnificent Alpine photography wraps up a sturdy little package that grown-ups can enjoy as well as kids.

Courage of Kavik, the Wolf Dog, The ○
1978, Canada/US, 90 mins, colour
Dir: Peter Carter
Stars: Ronny Cox, John Ireland, Linda Sorenson, John Candy
Rating: ★★

This is the sort of animal adventure story, shot in glorious colour and packed with incident, that has been popular with children since the days of Lassie. The hero is a sled-race dog called Kavik who is bought by a wealthy man for exhibition purposes. Kavik will have none of his new owner, however, and embarks on a 2,000 mile journey to rejoin the boy who saved his life. Keep a handkerchief handy for the end.

Courage of Lassie ⊙
1946, US, 89 mins, colour
Dir: Fred M Wilcox
Stars: Lassie, Elizabeth Taylor
Rating: ★★★

One of the best investments MGM ever made was to pay five dollars for a collie dog in the early 1940s. Eventually the dog brought the studio back more than $45 million. The dog, of course, was Lassie, and the success of *Lassie Come Home* and *Son of Lassie* meant there just had to be a third film. Throughout the film, the shaggy hero is referred to as Bill. But such was the box-office pull of Lassie that the studio insisted the name remain in the title of the picture.

Courier, The ● ⓥ
1987, Ireland, 85 mins, colour
Dir: Joe Lee, Frank Deasy

Stars: Gabriel Byrne, Ian Bannen, Cait O'Riordan, Padraig O'Loingsigh, Patrick Bergin
Rating: ★★

This is Dublin imitating Hollywood circa 1948. No bad thing, either, even on as low a budget as this. As a thriller, it's ultra-simplistic, but faster-paced than many, with hardly a dull moment. Padraig O'Loingsigh and Cait O'Riordan are personable leads with talent to spare, while Gabriel Byrne provides what Hollywood would call the marquee attraction as a sadistic drugs dealer who enforces loyalty with violence, rewards treachery with death and seems to spread his evil shadow over half the city. When the hero's girl's brother becomes Byrne's latest victim, the scene is set for a naive but seemingly effective vendetta which has the heroine justifiably asking her lover if he thinks he's Clint Eastwood. Frank Deasy and Joe Lee certainly know how to direct a film though, and their story is full of terse and suspenseful sequences, with Ian Bannen contributing a grumpy, rat-trap policeman only half a jump behind the villain.

Court Jester, The ⊙ ⓥ
1955, US, 101 mins, colour
Dir: Melvin Frank
Stars: Danny Kaye, Glynis Johns, Basil Rathbone, Angela Lansbury
Rating: ★★★★

Magnificent, madcap, medieval romp with Danny Kaye at the top of his form whether performing one of his tongue-twisting songs or fighting a duel with villainous Basil Rathbone. Best of all: the sequence where Kaye is forced to joust with the most fearsome knight in the land. One of them will have to drink from a tankard which contains a poison pellet, but each has trouble remembering whether it is in 'the chalice from the palace, the flagon with the dragon, or the vessel with the pestle'.

Court Martial
See: *Carrington VC*

Court-Martial of Billy Mitchell, The ○
(aka: One Man Mutiny)
1955, US, 100 mins, colour
Dir: Otto Preminger
Stars: Gary Cooper, Charles Bickford, Ralph Bellamy, Rod Steiger, Elizabeth Montgomery
Rating: ★★★

A fine, blazing courtroom drama, with Gary Cooper as the visionary and much-maligned Billy Mitchell who stood trial in 1925 in secret for bucking the Army and fighting for a separate Air Force, as well as correctly predicting that one day the US would have to fight Japan. But even 'Coop' is acted off the screen by Rod Steiger as a truly hateful prosecutor. Although he only makes a late appearance in the film, Steiger's ruthless portrayal makes a powerful impact on the proceedings. The film's script, good but not that good, was a surprising choice as an Oscar nominee.

Courtneys of Curzon Street, The ○
1947, UK, 120 mins, b/w
Dir: Herbert Wilcox
Stars: Anna Neagle, Michael Wilding, Gladys Young, Coral Browne
Rating: ★★★

Very successful through-the-years saga whose sentiments never ring false. Anna Neagle plays the maid who marries her aristocratic employer. It was her second success in a row opposite Michael Wilding (a late choice for her leading man in the previous year's *Piccadilly Incident*) and established them as Britain's leading post-war romantic team.

Courtship of Eddie's Father, The ○
1963, US, 117 mins, colour
Dir: Vincente Minnelli
Stars: Glenn Ford, Shirley Jones, Stella Stevens, Dina Merrill
Rating: ★★★

Director Vincente Minnelli had the right light touch for this bright, entertaining comedy-drama about a little boy trying to pick his widower dad a new wife. The boy is played with charm by Ron Howard who appeared in a string of films after his success in *The Music Man* (also with Shirley Jones), carved out an adult career for himself in such films as *American Graffiti* and *Smoke*, and went on to similar success behind the camera as director of *Splash* and *Cocoon*.

Cousins ◐ ⓥ
1989, US, 110 mins, colour
Dir: Joel Schumacher
Stars: Ted Danson, Isabella Rossellini, Sean Young, William Petersen, Lloyd Bridges
Rating: ★★★

A lushly romantic Hollywood adaptation of the French hit *Cousin Cousine*. There are no surprises in the plot, so director Joel Schumacher opts for sweepingly lyrical music with a touch of the Italian, and for making immensely nice, sympathetic characters out of dance master Ted Danson and legal secretary Isabella Rossellini, both of whose marital partners (Sean Young, William Petersen) bed anything in sight at the droop of an eyelid. When Ted's dad (Lloyd Bridges) tells Isabella that his son is 'a failure in everything but life,' you know Ted's a nice guy. The central relationship is nicely developed over a period of months, leaving you in no doubt as to the outcome, but things do go on rather a long time, even if some balance is struck by the insertion of some funny wisecracks. 'Did you let it breathe?' snaps Petersen to the waiter, receiving the (house) wine. 'Sir,' replies the waiter, taking his measure in an instant. 'I personally gave it mouth-to-mouth.' Rossellini, looking amazingly like her mother Ingrid Bergman in certain shots, gives a skilfully diffident portrayal, but is given a run for her money by tall Sean Young, who manages to make Danson's wife both flighty and dislikeable, but full of personality and odd redeeming features too.

Cover Girl ⊙ ⓥ
1944, US, 100 mins, colour
Dir: Charles Vidor
Stars: Rita Hayworth, Gene Kelly, Phil Silvers, Lee Bowman, Otto Kruger
Rating: ★★★★

Flushed with the success of two musicals teaming their biggest star, Rita Hayworth, with Fred Astaire, Columbia decided to mount a really major musical for her. When they took a chance on little-proved MGM contract dancer Gene Kelly as her co-star, the studio hit the jackpot. Kelly brought his friend Stanley Donen from MGM with him as co-choreographer and the two men worked out a routine that foreshadowed all their innovative work together over the next ten years. This was the 'alter ego' dance that Kelly performs with his mirror image (which turns into his conscience) in a store window. Stunningly costumed and shot in Technicolor, the film also has a hit score by Jerome Kern and Ira Gershwin that includes 'The Show Must Go On', 'Who's Complaining?',

'Make Way For Tomorrow' and 'Long Ago and Far Away'. Hayworth, Kelly and Phil Silvers are all on top form and the dances have an irresistible sweep and vitality. Nominated for a hatful of Academy Awards, the film won only one (for musical direction) in the face of competition from *Going My Way* and the prestigious *Wilson*. Columbia's acerbic chief Harry Cohn complained that 'it took two priests and a president to beat us'.

Cowboy ○
1958, US, 90 mins, colour
Dir: Delmer Daves
Stars: Glenn Ford, Jack Lemmon, Brian Donlevy, Anna Kashfi, Richard Jaeckel
Rating: ★★★

This genial Western is based on the true experiences of Frank Harris, who found that the lure of life on the range was too strong to ignore. Jack Lemmon considers it one of his favourite films and certainly his comedy-flecked study of a raw novice on a cattle drive is most attractive. 'Raw' is the word – for Lemmon, who's no horseman, claims he had to have his saddle-soreness cured by local anointment with whisky by the unit wranglers! Glenn Ford is impressive as the leathery cattleman who accepts Harris into partnership and then proceeds to teach him the business the hard way. Delmer Daves' direction achieves a happy balance of action and quizzical humour.

Cowboy and the Girl, The
See: Lady Takes a Chance

Cowboys, The ◐ ⓥ
1972, US, 128 mins, colour
Dir: Mark Rydell
Stars: John Wayne, Roscoe Lee Browne, Colleen Dewhurst, Bruce Dern
Rating: ★★★

Still unmistakeably a legendary figure of the west, even when wet-nursing an entire crew of sub-teenagers on a cattle drive, John Wayne's image remains impervious to the over-sentimentality inherent in the project. He strides through the story like a dinosaur that has triumphantly survived its own era.

Crackers ○
1984, US, 92 mins, colour
Dir: Louis Malle
Stars: Donald Sutherland, Jack Warden, Sean Penn
Rating: ★

You can have a great cast (Donald Sutherland, Jack Warden, Sean Penn) and a good director (Louis Malle) and an idea that worked well before (*Big Deal on Madonna Street*) and still end up with a stinker. Supposedly an 'off-beat comedy caper', this certainly misses every beat it can. Its criminals may be inept, but even so they're yards ahead of the script and direction! A gang of deadbeats decides to rob the big safe in the local pawn shop, owned by legendary meanie Jack Warden. That's it, really. With a tight script and a bit of pace, it could have been fun, guys. As it is, this must be one that everyone involved would prefer to forget. You would be wise to do the same.

Crack in the Mirror ○
1960, US, 97 mins, b/w
Dir: Richard Fleischer
Stars: Orson Welles, Juliette Greco, Bradford Dillman
Rating: ★★

Orson Welles, Juliette Greco and Bradford Dillman all play dual roles in this Paris-based, ingenious thriller-drama with a courtroom climax. Dillman, the young actor with a mean look (though in an appropriate part he can be just as pleasant), had co-starred with Welles before in another powerful courtroom drama called *Compulsion*.

Craig's Wife ○
1936, US, 75 mins, b/w
Dir: Dorothy Arzner
Stars: Rosalind Russell, John Boles, Billie Burke, Jane Darwell
Rating: ★★

This was the film that established Rosalind Russell both as an actress of forcefulness and substance, and as a 'name above the title'. When Dorothy Arzner, Hollywood's foremost woman director of the Thirties, undertook to make a fresh film of George Kelly's play about a fastidious wife who alienates all those around her, she insisted that Columbia borrow Russell from MGM for the title role. Russell did not let her down, giving a performance of icy dominance. The role of Mrs Craig's walked-over husband cried out for a dull actor, and it certainly got one in John Boles, who performed similar services in other 'women's pictures' (such as *Stella Dallas* and *Back Street*) during the course of the decade. The story had

c

been filmed before as a silent and would be made again in 1950, with Joan Crawford and Wendell Corey.

Crash Dive ○
1943, US, 105 mins, colour
Dir: Archie Mayo
Stars: Tyrone Power, Dana Andrews, Anne Baxter, James Gleason, Henry Morgan
Rating: ★★

One of those super-efficient American war films from the Forties. This one has the bonus of Oscar-winning actress Anne Baxter as the girl loved by two naval officers serving aboard the same submarine. Good action, skilfully shot in colour by master cameraman Leon Shamroy, who had three Academy Awards to his name by 1945.

Crash of Silence, The
See: Mandy

Crazy House
See: The House in Nightmare Park

Crazy People ◐ ⓥ
1990, US, 93 mins, colour
Dir: Tony Bill
Stars: Dudley Moore, Darryl Hannah, Paul Reiser, Mercedes Ruehl, J T Walsh, David Paymer
Rating: ★★★

Slight, silly, but quite engaging, this is a sideshoot of *The Dream Team*. Here, though, the field of the team is not adventure but advertising, as inmates of an asylum design best-selling ads by trying an amazing new concept: honesty. Spearheading their efforts is Emory (Dudley Moore), a frazzled ad executive who got institutionalised after thinking up original posters along the same lines. Within a week, thanks to his campaigns being distributed by accident, his firm is trying to get him out again or, failing that, employing him and his fellow jaybirds from art therapy class as an advertising unit. It all explodes, of course, when everyone gets too greedy. But, this being that kind of film, there's a happy ending, as well as one or two quite sharp barbs of satire along the way. The actual ads themselves are by and large too lewd to commit to print but they, like the film, are good black comedy fun.

Creature from the Black Lagoon, The ◐
1955, US, 79 mins, b/w
Dir: Jack Arnold
Stars: Richard Carlson, Julie Adams
Rating: ★★

This horror shocker created quite a stir when it first came out, and the initial appearance of its monster – one scaly claw clutching at the shore on emergence from the water – is a splendid piece of stage-management by director Jack Arnold (who made *Tarantula!* and *The Incredible Shrinking Man* in the same period). Julie Adams, in unscientific brief shorts, is a screaming heroine in the most vulnerable tradition of Fay Wray. Ricou Browning who plays the 'creature', later became a specialist in underwater direction – on such diverse entertainments as *Thunderball* and *Flipper*.

Creeping Flesh, The ●
1972, UK, 88 mins, colour
Dir: Freddie Francis
Stars: Peter Cushing, Christopher Lee
Rating: ★★★

This impressive Tigon horror movie is very much a return in class and style to the early Hammer films. Peter Cushing plays the scientist with a skeleton in the cupboard (his mad ex-wife) as well as one on the slab, the remains of a giant prehistoric man which develops new flesh when water drops on the bones. A great deal of scientific mumbo-jumbo is handled with sufficient flair to keep us from pondering its latent absurdities. But the film's real secret lies in its style, never flashy, but knitting together its complicated plot with considerable skill. Cushing's customary cultured performance looks even better in a strong storyline, while Lorna Heilbron is excellent as the repressed daughter to whom he administers an 'anti-evil' serum with perhaps inevitable results.

Creeping Unknown, The
See: The Quatermass Experiment

Creepshow ● ⓥ
1981, US, 120 mins, colour
Dir: George A Romero
Stars: Hal Holbrook, Adrienne Barbeau, Leslie Nielsen, Ted Danson, Ed Harris
Rating: ★★

This collaboration between one of America's greatest horror directors (George A Romero of *The Night of the Living Dead* fame) and top horror novelist Stephen King promises much with its five stories-in-one format. But despite supplying shocks in all the right places, it leaves you thinking 'so what?' at the end. King himself turns up in *The Lonesome Death of Jordy Verrill* episode, but his appearance only emphasises that he should stick to

what he does best. Watch for early appearances by Ed Harris and Ted Danson. A lot better, incidentally, than *Creepshow 2*.

Creepshow 2 ● ⓥ
1987, US, 90 mins, colour
Dir: Michael Gornick
Stars: Lois Chiles, George Kennedy, Dorothy Lamour, Tom Savini, Page Hannah, Stephen King
Rating: ★

Only three stories for comic-book horror fans in this second compendium of creepies – and all of them good for more chuckles than chills under the direction of Michael Gornick, who was well advised to stick to his career as cinematographer after this. In the first story a wooden Indian comes to life to destroy those who have killed the owners of the store outside which it stands. In the second, a floating tarpaulin devours 'sinful' holidaying teenagers on a lake. The third, concerning a hit-and-run victim who comes back to haunt his killer, has the best of George A Romero's dialogue and the best performance (Lois Chiles), but simply doesn't know how to round off its story with any ending other than the sickeningly conventional. Gornick's direction has no idea of how to shock an audience other than with head-on or overt horror; it's almost as sad as the appearance of a much-aged Dorothy Lamour in episode one.

Crime and Punishment ○
1935, US, 88 mins, b/w
Dir: Josef von Sternberg
Stars: Peter Lorre, Edward Arnold, Marian Marsh, Tala Birell
Rating: ★★★

One of the most interesting films made by the fascinating, bug-eyed, Hungarian-born Hollywood star Peter Lorre – a cold but strangely compelling version of Dostoevsky's novel. Predictably, and even with Josef von Sternberg in the director's chair, the film's writers kicked out most of the psychological undertones of the original, making Lorre's murderer's descent into guilt-ridden anguish rather too peremptory for total belief. Both von Sternberg and Lorre, however, had carefully read the original book and their interpretation, if confined by the demands of melodrama, is full of masterly touches and unexpected flashes of sardonic humour.

Crime of Passion ○
1956, US, 86 mins, b/w
Dir: Gerd Oswald
Stars: Barbara Stanwyck, Sterling Hayden, Raymond Burr, Fay Wray
Rating: ★★

Barbara Stanwyck, queen of movie melodrama, is in her element in this dramatic story of a wife who will stop at nothing – even murder – to further her husband's career. Although she dominates the film, her thunder is almost stolen at times by Fay Wray, giving a compellingly understated portrayal.

Crimes and Misdemeanors ◑ Ⓥ
1989, US, 104 mins, colour
Dir: Woody Allen
Stars: Martin Landau, Woody Allen, Mia Farrow, Anjelica Huston, Alan Alda, Claire Bloom
Rating: ★★★

One of Woody Allen's better movies, this blends his three themes – comedy, drama and personal angst – in almost as seamless a way as in *Hannah and Her Sisters*. As in *Hannah*, the action is bathed in a golden glow. But there's nothing golden about the predicament of Judah (Martin Landau), faced with a neurotic, quasi-blackmailing mistress (Anjelica Huston) and a gangster brother (Jerry Orbach) who offers him the devil's way out of the mess. Allen himself stars in the film's second plot, as a twitchy documentary film-maker whose marriage is falling apart. He fears his love for TV girl Mia Farrow may not be reciprocated and is surrounded by people more successful than himself. In a well-worked ending, the two leading characters only meet each other at a wedding in the final scene, where everything is resolved not as in a Hollywood happy ending, but as it might be in real life. Though a little top heavy with philosophical talk, the film and its doomy mood are lightened by some typical Woody one-liners.

Crimes of Passion ● Ⓥ
1984, US, 115 mins, colour
Dir: Ken Russell
Stars: Kathleen Turner, Anthony Perkins, John Laughlin, Annie Potts, Bruce Davison
Rating: ★★★

Originally called *China Blue*, a rather better title, this is a heady psycho-thriller from Ken Russell, dripping

with strong dialogue and graphic sex and photographed almost entirely in pastel neon shades. Anthony Perkins, entering into the gaudy spirit of the thing with total commitment, superbly dominates the film as the Peeping Tom priest who haunts the strip joints of the city and alternately longs to save or have (using fevered epithets that amalgamate the Bible and the gutter) a ritzy prostitute called China Blue (Kathleen Turner), who's a better actress in the bedroom than most Hollywood starlets on screen. Enter unhappily married Bobby (John Laughlin), sent to spy on CB in her daytime capacity of draughtsperson for a garment firm, and the scene is ultimately set for a *Klute*-type finale. The direction makes the most of what the film has and the raunchy music thickens its atmosphere; but it's Perkins' frenzied strength that gives this hemlock cocktail its lethal kick.

Crimes of the Heart ◑ Ⓥ
1986, US, 105m mins, colour
Dir: Bruce Beresford
Stars: Diane Keaton, Jessica Lange, Sissy Spacek, Sam Shepard, Tess Harper
Rating: ★★

Diane Keaton, Sissy Spacek and Jessica Lange in the same film seems too good to be true. And so, in a way, it proves. Even though the ladies are all as luminous as you'd expect (as three sisters living on the edge of madness with an inheritance of same), this anecdote is far too slight for the talents involved. The sisters, all eccentric and subject to violent outbursts in which they hardly know what they are doing, are brought together again by the terminal illness of their grandfather (Hurd Hatfield: Dorian Gray trying in vain to look ancient), but more urgently by the fact that the youngest, Babe (Sissy Spacek), has just shot her husband close to death. Occasionally too dull even for these three to redeem, the film is glowingly, if faintly gloomily shot in colour by Dante Spinotti, and has some felicitous comic moments, mostly from Spacek. Overall, though, it doesn't amount to very much.

Crime Wave
See: The City Is Dark

Crimewave ◑
(aka: Broken Hearts and Noses)
1985, US, 85 mins, colour
Dir: Sam Raimi

Stars: Brion James, Louise Lasser, Sheree J Wilson, Paul Smith
Rating: ★★

This confusing and undisciplined thriller has, on the face of it, a good pedigree, with Sam Raimi directing and he together with Joel and Ethan Coen (*Miller's Crossing*, *Barton Fink*) writing the script. But the end result, a tale of murder, mayhem and mistaken identity, fails to hit the target. To describe the film as cartoon-like gives you an idea but that description isn't being fair to most cartoons which, within their own terms of reference, at least make some sort of crazy sense.

Criminal, The ●
(aka: The Concrete Jungle)
1960, UK, 97 mins, b/w
Dir: Joseph Losey
Stars: Stanley Baker, Sam Wanamaker, Margit Saad, Patrick Magee, Jill Bennett
Rating: ★★★

Stanley Baker's rugged performance and a really top-notch supporting cast make this thriller live up to its reputation as one of the toughest films ever made in Britain. Joseph Losey's direction is fast-paced and uncompromising, and the action is raw, shocking in parts, always compelling. And be prepared for a script (by Alun Owen) that takes a hard look at Britain's prison system. Among the familiar faces in minor roles are Tom Bell, Rupert Davies, Nigel Green, Patrick Wymark and Kenneth Cope.

Criminal Law ● Ⓥ
1988, US, 118 mins, colour
Dir: Martin Campbell
Stars: Gary Oldman, Kevin Bacon, Karen Young, Joe Doe Baker, Tess Harper
Rating: ★★

Not half as bad as its two-year wait for a cinema release might suggest, this serial killer thriller is overlong and rather sonorously presented. It does, however, have good performances from Kevin Bacon as the criminal and Gary Oldman as the law, a very smart legal eagle who gets Bacon off the hook on an especially grisly murder/ rape/ mutilation charge, only to realise that a) Bacon's guilty b) he's gleefully killing to some kind of rote and c) is toying with Oldman by asking him to represent him again.

c

There's some eye-closing suspense, and good support from Karen Young and Elizabeth Shepherd, but the film comes close to being silly at times and lets its last scene go on too long. With this cast and a good story (not the same as a good script!) it could have been excellent. One imagines the two leading actors could just as easily have played each other's roles, but no doubt both were appreciative of the change of pace.

Criminals
See: Once Upon a Crime

Crimson Cult
See: Curse of the Crimson Altar

Crimson Pirate, The ○
1952, UK, 100 mins, colour
Dir: Robert Siodmak
Stars: Burt Lancaster, Nick Cravat, Eva Bartok, Torin Thatcher
Rating: ★★★

Burt Lancaster made this British swashbuckler in the midst of his man-of-action period that also included *The Flame and the Arrow*. This adventure story is played relentlessly tongue-in-cheek; a burlesque, in fact, with Lancaster poking fun at his own acrobatic ability, ably assisted by little, bearded Nick Cravat, in real life his former circus partner. Good colour photography by Otto Heller and loads of battles at sea complement skilful direction by Robert Siodmak. Christopher Lee has a small role and gets to fight a duel with the star.

Cripple Creek ○
1952, US, 77 mins, colour
Dir: Ray Nazarro
Stars: George Montgomery, Karin Booth, Jerome Courtland, Richard Egan
Rating: ★★

One of a whole posse of Technicolor Westerns George Montgomery made at Columbia in the early Fifties, all of them chock-full with action and gunplay, and setting a rousing pace from the opening scenes. Some interesting names cropped up in the supporting casts of these vigorous movies, and here there's William Bishop, Richard Egan, Don Porter and John Dehner to back up the stars in a story of two federal agents working undercover to bring to book a big gang of bullion raiders.

Crisis ○
1950, US, 95 mins, b/w
Dir: Richard Brooks
Stars: Cary Grant, Jose Ferrer, Paula Raymond, Signe Hasso, Ramon Novarro, Gilbert Roland
Rating: ★★

An often tense Richard Brooks film, set in one of those South American republics where, as in Central America today, the government could change at any second and a rifle barrel peers from every corner. Cary Grant is unusually cast as the surgeon held hostage so that he can operate on the current dictator, a very similar situation to that found in *State Secret*, which was being made in Britain at more or less the same time. Two Hollywood veterans from the Latin lover bracket, Antonio Moreno and Ramon Novarro, make valuable contributions to the suspense, and the riot scenes are spectacularly staged. The pace is a bit stately at times away from the action scenes.

Criss Cross ○
1948, US, 87 mins, b/w
Dir: Robert Siodmak
Stars: Burt Lancaster, Yvonne De Carlo, Dan Duryea
Rating: ★★★

Another moody, doom-laden crime thriller from the Forties directed by Robert Siodmak, who directed the brilliant 1945 version of *The Spiral Staircase*. The American-born, German-raised Siodmak came to Hollywood in the war years and, throughout the Forties, created his own world of dark action films, a world of night, of desperation, of menace, of murder and of despair. Most of those elements are present in *Criss Cross*, a rarely-seen but classic example of *film noir*. Burt Lancaster, all sub-surface menace, rarely allows himself a smile as the man whose obsession with his ex-wife (a well-cast Yvonne De Carlo) drags him ever deeper into a mire of secrecy and crime. Dan Duryea is a splendidly flashy villain and Tony Curtis makes his film debut in a tiny role as a young gigolo.

CrissCross ● ⓥ
1992, US, 101 mins, colour
Dir: Chris Menges
Stars: Goldie Hawn, Keith Carradine, Arliss Howard, J C Quinn, James Gammon, Steve Buscemi
Rating: ★

For all of those who can't believe there's a Goldie Hawn film that wasn't worth releasing, here's the proof. Goldie makes another stab at serious drama here, following the rather more successful *Deceived*. But this shallow story of a woman's struggle in the Sixties to make a better life for herself and her 12-year-old son is slow and over-saturated with melodrama. The plot sees Hawn taking a job as a stripper to make ends meet after her soldier husband (Keith Carradine), a mixed-up Vietnam vet, has left her for life in a monastery. Even Goldie's fiercest fans will have to fight to enjoy this one or, for that matter, to even stay awake.

Critical Condition ● ⓥ
1986, US, 100 mins, colour
Dir: Michael Apted
Stars: Richard Pryor, Rachel Ticotin, Ruben Blades, Joe Mantegna
Rating: ★

The talents of comedian Richard Pryor are wasted in this supposedly madcap mixture of medical mayhem, as are those of director Michael Apted. Writers Denis and John Hamill are to blame for a script that even Pryor's comic gifts can't salvage. All in all, there's too much going on to too little comic effect. Apted hasn't had too many flops in a distinguished career, but this was certainly one of them.

Critters ◐ ⓥ
1986, US, 86 mins, colour
Dir: Stephen Herek
Stars: Dee Wallace Stone, M Emmet Walsh, Billy Green Bush
Rating: ★★

A group of aliens escape from a prison in space and ends up causing chaos in Kansas. Looking like oversized hairballs, the Krites (hence critters) are no real danger to mankind, although the bounty hunters sent to catch or destroy them are a bit heavy-handed. All done with tongues firmly in cheeks, *Critters* is enjoyable enough, if ultimately rather predictable. A fun idea is having translations of the critters' gobbledegook chattering coming up as subtitles in colloquial English.

Crocodile Dundee ○ ⓥ
1986, Australia, 102 mins, colour
Dir: Peter Faiman
Stars: Paul Hogan, Linda Kozlowski, John Meillon
Rating: ★★★

A pleasant surprise and no mistake. Expect a broad, vulgar farce from Aussie comic Paul Hogan on his major film debut? Think again, cobber. Hogan projects an endearing image that, for veteran filmgoers, will land somewhere between Chips Rafferty and Dick Bentley, as a tall tale-telling outback man whose flip chat cloaks a tough and experienced hide. To be sure, there are many funny lines – but always within the context of the story. The first half of the film is taken almost straight, with a streak of quirky, natural wit, as Dundee shows an inquisitive American reporter (Linda Kozlowski) the wild regions where he had a (much-embroidered) narrow escape from a crocodile. His subsequent exploits in New York are more predictable and less relaxed, but still enjoyable. Kozlowski, with her Esther Rantzen looks and Jane Fonda voice, is perfectly cast as the amorous scribe, and Hogan's subtle, inch-perfect underplaying is a revelation.

Crocodile Dundee II ○ ⊗
1988, Australia, 111 mins, colour
Dir: John Cornell
Stars: Paul Hogan, Linda Kozlowski, John Meillon
Rating: ★★

A largely disappointing sequel to the original box office smash, with Aussie charmer Paul Hogan again as Mick 'Crocodile' Dundee, so called because of his infamous battle with a giant croc. Hogan's real-life partner, Linda Kozlowski, is still the heroine and still helpless, and it's left to Hogan as the irreverant, amiable Aussie to carry the movie on his charisma alone. The budget was doubled for *Croc II*, but the results were only half as good.

Cromwell ○ ⊗
1970, UK, 141 mins, colour
Dir: Ken Hughes
Stars: Richard Harris, Alec Guinness, Robert Morely, Dorothy Tutin, Frank Finlay, Timothy Dalton
Rating: ★★

Some folk have said that Oliver Cromwell was the last person to enter Parliament with honourable intentions. They might be right. But here we see a rather laboured and grinding version of his rise to puritanical power, directed by Ken Hughes, who had made such a good historical job of *The Trials of Oscar Wilde* in 1960. The

Lord Protector and pretender to the throne vacated by Charles I (Alec Guinness) is played by Richard Harris who does a splendid job in convincing us that, perhaps, Cromwell was just a pretender.

Crooks and Coronets ○
(aka: Sophie's Place)
1969, UK, 120 mins, colour
Dir: Jim O'Connolly
Stars: Telly Savalas, Edith Evans, Warren Oates, Cesar Romero
Rating: ★★

Kojak is a crook! Well, at any rate, before his famous cop characterisation was thought of, Telly Savalas came to Britain to make this daft comedy about some American crooks trying to rob an English stately home. It was a profitable trip for Warren Oates (later to play Dillinger) as well. For he met and married his female co-star Vickery Turner. At times, the pace is as sedate as the English aristocracy portrayed: but the magnificently lunatic climax is worth waiting for, as crooks fall out on the final assault on Great Friars, and are finally repulsed by a concerted counter-attack involving crossbows, a lion, and Edith Evans at the controls of a vintage German plane. It has to be said that Dame Edith has no trouble in beating the Americans at the acting game, either.

Crooks Anonymous ○
1962, UK, 87 mins, b/w
Dir: Ken Annakin
Stars: Leslie Phillips, Stanley Baxter, Wilfrid Hyde White, Julie Christie
Rating: ★★
A quite amusing comedy, one of a successful series from producers Julian Wintle and Leslie Parkyn, which gave Julie Christie her first starring role in pictures. Brisk direction by Ken Annakin carries the film triumphantly through its stickier patches.

Cross Creek ○ ⊗
1983, US, 122 mins, colour
Dir: Martin Ritt
Stars: Mary Steenburgen, Rip Torn, Peter Coyote, Alfre Woodard
Rating: ★★★★

Definitely an old-fashioned film, and very nearly an exceptional one. Director Martin Ritt goes back to the Deep South he lovingly surveyed in *Sounder* and *Conrack* and digs up a true story about a 30-year-old failed

woman writer, Marjorie Kinnan Rawlings who, in 1928, left her husband and went to live in an obscure part of the Florida Everglades to continue writing her 'Gothic romances'. Inevitably the lives of the dirt-poor people of the Creek became her life and she began to write about them instead. Her memoir, *Cross Creek*, was published in 1942 and, ironically, the weakest parts of this warm and gentle film are where her actual words are used. When Ritt relies on the screenplay written for him by Dalene Young, the movie is often a real heartbreaker. Not a lot happens to Marjorie in Cross Creek, yet you are never bored. And the performance of Mary Steenburgen as Marjorie, shamefully ignored in the Oscar race that year, is exactly the blend of femininity and strength that the role requires. Ritt pushes the lyricism a bit too hard at the end, but you could almost forgive him for over-dwelling on the lovely colour photography by John A Alonzo. The music (by Leonard Rosenman) is also excellent – and notably un-derivative.

Crossfire ○
1947, US, 85 mins, b/w
Dir: Edward Dmytryk
Stars: Robert Young, Robert Mitchum, Robert Ryan, Gloria Grahame, Sam Levene
Rating: ★★★

Probably Edward Dmytryk's best film, and a milestone in the history of the American crime thriller. The script, by John Paxton and Richard Brooks, from Brooks' own novel *The Brick Foxhole*, was so adult, hard-hitting and entertaining at the same time, that it opened the door for a whole series of superior racial prejudice films. The three Roberts, Mitchum, Young and Ryan, are all excellent, with top honours perhaps going to Ryan, in this story of the murder of a Jewish ex-GI, well played by Sam Levene. A young Gloria Grahame made such a striking impression in this film that she was nominated for an Academy Award.

Crossing Delancey ○
1988, US, 97 mins, colour
Dir: Joan Micklin Silver
Stars: Amy Irving, Peter Riegert, Reizl Bozyk, Jeroen Krabbe, Sylvia Miles
Rating: ★★★

C

In an unexpectedly enjoyable way, this mellow romantic drama addresses one of the great social issues of our day – the dilemma of how a thirtyish, attractive, successful, intelligent and unmarried female finds a mate she can be happy with. Under Joan Micklin Silver's easy direction, and Amy Irving's most attractive film performance, the story builds slowly to ensure you'll have your fingers crossed that the heroine makes all the 'right' decisions at the end.

Cross of Iron ● Ⓥ
1977, UK/West Germany, 119 mins, colour
Dir: Sam Peckinpah
Stars: James Coburn, James Mason, Maximilian Schell, Senta Berger, David Warner
Rating: ★★

This grim war film set during the German army's disastrous Russian campaign in 1943 is a more thoughtful film than director Sam Peckinpah's ususal fare, although it's still up to his usual bloody and violent standard. It not only deals with the German/Russian battle, but with the conflict between an arrogant Prussian officer (Maximilian Schell) and a more pragmatic, battle-weary sergeant (James Coburn). As a story of men suffering the pressures of war, the film has a worthy air, but harsh realism stops it being an enjoyable film, even though at times it is admittedly engrossing. Schell fills the role of the upper class officer well, but Coburn seems less at ease as the intelligent, philosophic but tough sergeant.

Crossplot ○
1969, UK, 92 mins, colour
Dir: Alvin Rakoff
Stars: Roger Moore, Martha Hyer, Alexis Kanner, Francis Matthews, Bernard Lee
Rating: ★★

Roger Moore and Bernard Lee are ironically cast as an advertising executive (innocently entangled in an assassination attempt) and his client in this thriller, four years before they met again as James Bond and his boss 'M'. Apart from its tense finale, the plot is commonplace, but there's some nice Eastman Colour photography of London locations by Brendan J Stafford, a veteran (and one time director) of films whose career went back to the earliest days of British sound cinema.

Crossroads ◑
1986, US, 96 mins, colour
Dir: Walter Hill
Stars: Ralph Macchio, Joe Seneca, Jami Gertz
Rating: ★★

For anyone except the most die-hard traditional blues aficionado, the music is the thread that holds this film together. Ralph Macchio, seen in the *Karate Kid* role, of which this is a sort of musical version, is a brilliant young musician who finds Willie, an aged survivor of the blues era, and takes him on the road back to the Mississippi delta, where he and other blues legends had lived and played. This could have been a more intelligent film, but for the fact that it obviously wanted to keep *Karate Kid* fans watching. Nevertheless, it remains an entertaining tale. Joe Seneca is enjoyable as Willie and Macchio, as the 'lightnin'' kid', looks a convincing guitarist. And there are some satisfying slices of old-time philosophy. 'Blues,' explains Seneca to his young travelling companion, 'ain't nothin' but a good man feelin' bad.' The only slightly jarring note is Eugene's climactic guitar duel with a heavy metal player which doesn't seem to have much to do with the blues.

Crow, The ● Ⓥ
1994, US, 110 mins, colour
Dir: Alex Proyas
Stars: Brandon Lee
Rating: ★★

The sad thing about this impressively-staged comic-strip action movie in the ultra-violent mould, as far as being a tribute to its deceased star, is that Lee's presence doesn't add anything to it. His part could be played by Dolph Lundgren or any other action star without changing the impact of the film. As it is, Lee is rock star Eric Draven, who meets a violent death on the eve of his wedding and returns from the grave a year later to wreak vengeance on those who also raped and killed his bride-to-be. Accompanied by the crow that has brought his soul back to earth, he sets about an orgy of death and destruction. The result is a bit like one of director Michael Winner's bloodbaths of the Seventies with a horror-film slant, although overhead travelling shots of the dark city, whether set ablaze by arsonists on Devil's Night

(Hallowe'en Eve), or rising sullenly from the ground, are undeniably impressive. The crow's good too.

Crowded Sky, The ○
1960, US, 104 mins, colour
Dir: Joseph Pevney
Stars: Dana Andrews, Efrem Zimbalist Jr, Rhonda Fleming, Anne Francis, Keenan Wynn
Rating: ★★

This nail-biting story may remind some viewers of John Wayne's *The High and the Mighty*, to which, especially with its star-studded cast, it bears a more than coincidental resemblance. Suspenseful if superficial, it matches the dramatic talents of old TV favourite, Efrem Zimbalist Jr, against those of the more screen-seasoned Dana Andrews. Rhonda Fleming, Anne Francis, John Kerr and Keenan Wynn are among others gripping their seats for the bumpy ride ahead.

Crowd Roars, The ○
1932, US, 85 mins, b/w
Dir: Howard Hawks
Stars: James Cagney, Joan Blondell, Eric Linden, Ann Dvorak, Guy Kibbee, Frank McHugh
Rating: ★★

James Cagney is in the typical form of his early years as a cocky and aggressive racing-driver. This was how the public were beginning to want to see him, and Warners lost no time in supplying him with a brisk number of appropriate star vehicles. Eric Linden scores as his younger brother, and Joan Blondell and Ann Dvorak are strong as the girls in their life. Some good racing locations were shot for the movie, which turned up again when Warners remade the film as *Indianapolis Speedway* in 1939 with Pat O'Brien and John Payne as the racing brothers.

Crowd Roars, The ○
1938, US, 92 mins, b/w
Dir: Richard Thorpe
Stars: Robert Taylor, Edward Arnold, Maureen O'Sullivan, Frank Morgan
Rating: ★★

Robert Taylor trained hard for his role in this solid, typical Hollywood boxing film, and it shows in the fights in the ring. It also cost him a broken finger, but the star felt it was worth it to help him escape the pretty-boy label with which he had been tagged after co-starring with Greta Garbo in *Camille*. The film was remade by MGM in 1947 as *Killer McCoy*, with the leading role scaled down to of it the dynamic but diminutive talents of Mickey Rooney.

Cruel Sea, The ○ ⓥ
1952, UK, 120 mins, b/w
Dir: Charles Frend
Stars: Jack Hawkins, Donald Sinden, John Stratton, Denholm Elliott, Virginia McKenna, Stanley Baker
Rating: ★★★★

A grimly realistic account, given in semi-documentary fashion, of the Battle of the Atlantic and of a corvette's crew who found that their worst enemy was the sea. Ealing Studios' brilliant adaptation of the famous Nicholas Monsarrat novel was the film which turned Jack Hawkins, Donald Sinden, Stanley Baker and Virginia McKenna into stars. It was Sinden's major screen debut and he turned in what still ranks as the finest performance of his career. To meet the demands of early Fifties' cinema, Ealing, whose fortunes had already suffered a downturn after the comedy heydays of a couple of years earlier, were forced to bowdlerise the book in many respects, yet, to their great credit, emerged with a first-rate film. It's dignified, thoughtful and always exciting to look at. It has moments of high tension and nervy anxiety, as when the ship ploughs through survivors in its determination to sink the enemy or presents itself as a sitting target in the full glare of a burning tanker. And the suspense is constantly accentuated by the pips of the asdic apparatus pinging on the soundtrack with menacing melody, a harbinger of imminent danger. At the centre of everything is Jack Hawkins' portrait of the skipper, intense, authoritative, tautly controlled yet not unemotional.

Cruisin' Down the River ○
1952, US, 80 mins, colour
Dir: Richard Quine
Stars: Dick Haynes, Billy Daniels, Audrey Totter, Cecil Kellaway
Rating: ★★

One of the Blake Edwards-Richard Quine musicals of the Fifties that bulged music and colour, and were all the better for their brevity. Alas, both men allowed their pretensions to run away with them later, when budgets permitted, although Edwards did

make the priceless *Breakfast at Tiffany's*, *The Pink Panther* and *A Shot in the Dark*. Quine's later credits as director include *Bell, Book and Candle*, *The Notorious Landlady* and *Sex and the Single Girl*. This is one of their few early musicals not to star Frankie Laine, but it does have Billy Daniels, with his old black magic on board a riverboat that crooning gambler Dick Haymes wants to turn into a floating night-club. Undemanding entertainment all the way.

Cry-Baby ○ ⓥ
1990, US, 85 mins, colour
Dir: John Waters
Stars: Johnny Depp, Amy Locane, Ricki Lake, Kim McGuire, Polly Bergen, Iggy Pop
Rating: ★★

Cult director John Waters makes another foray into mainline cinema with this pastiche of Fifties rock 'n' rebel movies, which is great fun up to a point, with more than a touch of the old Waters outrageousness. About 50 percent of it is wonderful, while the other half, especially when the songs go on a bit, only serves to remind us how awful some of the original movies were. The colour is exactly the right shade of garishness, the direction is as snappy as hell and the supporting cast of grotesques a mine of half-forgotten faces from every decade: Susan Tyrrell, Joey Heatherton, Troy Donahue, Iggy Pop, David Nelson, Polly Bergen, Patricia Hearst, Willem Dafoe and more. Stars Johnny Depp and Amy Locane have fun as the boy from The Drapes and the girl from The Squares whose hormone-driven love affair sparks the film. At 85 minutes of ghoulish glee, the film just about manages not to outstay its welcome. Kim McGuire is a notable addition to Waters gallery of gargoyles as an awful Drape woman who even scares convicts watching *The Creature from the Black Lagoon*.

Cry for Happy ○
1961, US, 110 mins, colour
Dir: George Marshall
Stars: Glenn Ford, Donald O'Connor
Rating: ★★

The promising combination of Irving Brecher, who wrote for the Marx Brothers on *At the Circus* and *Go West*, and director George Marshall, who worked with Bob Hope, W C Fields and Martin and Lewis, doesn't quite deliver the goods in this *Teahouse of the August Moon*-style

comedy about a group of US combat cameramen at large in a geisha house. Still, it's good-natured fun, with Glenn Ford giving an uncharacteristically relaxed performance in the lead role.

Cry Freedom ○ ⓥ
1987, UK, 157 mins, colour
Dir: Richard Attenborough
Stars: Kevin Kline, Penelope Wilton, Denzel Washington, John Hargreaves, John Thaw
Rating: ★★★

Although wordy and occasionally long-winded, Richard Atteborough's film about doomed South African activist Steve Biko (a role that consolidated stardom for Denzel Washington) is, on the whole, a very eloquent cry for freedom. And, despite a running time that seems profligate, the story keeps moving at quite a good pace as it changes from an exposé to a combination of tear-jerker and escape movie. It's in the escape section at the end that the director makes his only really false step, inserting flashbacks into a flight from authority that seriulsy undcuts the emotional impact of the climax. Elsewhere, Attenborough is content to let the events speak for themselves and they do so with sickening effect. And, although the South African law enforcers are portrayed as one-dimensional brutes, this does give the film a necessary balance. There are charismatic performances from Washington and from John Hargreaves as the Australian reporter friend of central character Donald Woods (Kevin Kline). For all its minor faults, one has to stand and applaud the fact that this eye-opening film got made at all.

Cry Havoc ○
1943, US, 97 mins, b/w
Dir: Richard Thorpe
Stars: Margaret Sullavan, Joan Blondell, Ann Sothern, Fay Bainter, Marsha Hunt
Rating: ★★★

Hollywood wartime heroism of the feminine variety, as a bunch of volunteer nurses at a Pacific base hospital stand by their patients while the Japanese close in. Margaret Sullavan dominates the film in a role originally planned for Joan Crawford, but having the similar Ann Sothern and Joan Blondell in the same film (and sometimes side by side) proves to be a little too much of a good thing.

c

Crying Game, The ●
1992, UK, 108 mins, colour
Dir: Neil Jordan
Stars: Stephen Rea, Forest Whitaker, Miranda Richardson, Jaye Davidson
Rating: ★★

The IRA thriller gets a few new twists here, but ironically it's the twists that fragment the film until it falls apart. Things start strongly: black British soldier (Hollywood's Forest Whitaker with a fair London accent) is captured by IRA men Stephen Rea, Adrian Dunbar and Miranda Richardson, and held hostage. Subsequent developments, after Rea and Whitaker become almost-friends, hit home hard and it's only when Rea tracks down Whitaker's girlfriend (Jaye Davidson) in London that the film starts to go to pieces. It's not only in the relationship between Rea and Davidson that credibility takes a beating, but in several other key plot developments, to which Jordan's own dialogue can't lend conviction. Rea looks miserable about people of different sexes throwing themselves at him, as well he might and there are some strange wobbles in the lighting towards the end as well as in the script. Richardson is fine and her Belfast accent sounds right., Davidson is almost convincing but (despite the Oscar nomination) not quite. A strange hybrid that's a cinematic curio.

Cry in the Dark, A ● Ⓥ
1988, Australia, 121 mins, colour
Dir: Fred Schepisi
Stars: Meryl Streep, Sam Neill, Bruce Myles, Nick Tate, Charles Tingwell
Rating: ★★★

The facts behind Australia's Lindy Chamberlain case are so extraordinary that they easily survive director Fred Schepisi's laborious treatment, to provide a movie that sticks in the mind and should set you arguing for weeks. It seems unbelievable, given the total lack of proof, not to mention motive, weapon or body, that any jury could have convicted Chamberlain of the murder of her baby daughter. Yet, just a few years ago this is exactly what took place. Camping at night, Lindy heard the baby cry and returned to her tent to glimpse a dingo fleeing and her baby gone. The film makes us believe that, even if the theory of the animal carrying off the child is an unproved possibility, the murder of the baby by her mother is even less likely. Meryl

Streep (whose Australian accent sounds fine to the untutored ear) and Sam Neill are certainly fine as the distraught parents, and the film finally does good emotive work at the end, even if it's a long haul. But the final question you'll be asking is not how good a film this is, but how could this happen?

Cry in the Wilderness, A ○
1974, UK, 73 mins, colour
Dir: Gordon Hessler
Stars: George Kennedy, Joanna Pettet
Rating: ★★

A 'disaster' movie of a more intimate nature, as farmer George Kennedy chains himself up to protect his family, fearing madness from the bite of a rabid skunk – then hears of an impending flood. If this all sounds a bit laughable, then the taut direction of Gordon Hessler and fevered performances from Kennedy and Joanna Pettet (as his wife) ensure that you'll be hanging on by the fingernails for a good chunk of the film's running time. But when Miss Pettet is threatened with rape by a passing motorist, you might be forgiven for thinking enough is enough. Made for TV.

Cry of the Banshee ◑
1970, UK, 87 mins, colour
Dir: Gordon Hessler
Stars: Vincent Price, Elisabeth Bergner, Patrick Mower
Rating: ★★

Thirties' screen star Elisabeth Bergner made a comeback to the screen in this beautifully photographed (John Coquillon using colour by Movielab) horror film, as the high priestess of a coven in 16th century England, who summons up an avenging spirit to destroy her enemies. Also in the cast, in her only British film, is Swedish actress Essy Persson, who attracted international attention as the nymphomaniac nurse in *I a Woman*. The ending is likely to both surprise and shock.

Cry Terror ○
1958, US, 96 mins, b/w
Dir: Andrew L Stone
Stars: James Mason, Rod Steiger, Inger Stevens, Angie Dickinson, Jack Klugman
Rating: ★★★

Eye-catching performances by the trio of 'baddies' – Rod Steiger, Angie Dickinson and Jack Klugman – steal the honours in this tightly-paced, tension-laden tale of a family held

hostage by a psychopath planning an extortion coup. Inger Stevens is also good as James Mason's wife, while director Andrew L Stone makes a fine job of cramming on the suspense.

Cry, the Beloved Country ○ Ⓥ
(aka: African Fury)
1951, UK, 96 mins, b/w
Dir: Zoltan Korda
Stars: Canada Lee, Sidney Poitier, Joyce Carey, Charles Carson
Rating: ★★★

Zoltan Korda, one of the three famous Korda brothers (the others were Alexander and Vincent), always shot his movies in far-off exotic locations, evoking a strong sense of period and locale. They could also often be ounted upon to have a secondary meaning and give an audience food for thought on their way home. This drama, filmed in South Africa, was no exception. The film scores highly because of its attention to detail and it keeps undue sentiment at bay. Star Canada Lee (born Lionel Canegata) only made four movies and died at the age of 45. Co-star Sidney Poitier was, of course, rather luckier.

Culpepper Cattle Co, The ◑
1972, US, 92 mins, colour
Dir: Dick Richards
Stars: Gary Grimes, Billy Green Bush, Bo Hopkins
Rating: ★★

Another tough-talking Western that tries to show America's wild days as they were. It was the debut of director Dick Richards, who subsequently made *Farewell My Lovely* and *March or Die*, both of which displayed a similar obsession for de-glamourising familiar film genres. Here the grime and gore are counter-balanced by the director's treatment as, helped by the photography, he contrived to bring something of the quality of old sepia photographs to his view of the west. Although the film never quite seems sure of what it wants to do – it starts off as a poetic treatment of a cattle drive and ends in the style of *The Magnificent Seven* – interest in its developments is sustained by the performances of the four tough cowboys who befriend greenhorn Gary Grimes on the drive – Luke Askew, Bo Hopkins, Wayne Sutherlin and especially Geoffrey Lewis as Russ Caldwell.

Curly Sue ○ Ⓥ
1991, US, 101 mins, colour
Dir: John Hughes
Stars: James Belushi, Alisan Porter, Kelly Lynch, John Getz, Fred Dalton Thompson
Rating: ★★

Just to prove that occasionally they do make 'em like they used to, here's a sort of Shirley Temple film for the Nineties. Although the formula never really works in today's terms, the movie was a big popular hit which must prove something. Bill Dance (James Belushi) and his cute but sassy nine-year-old sidekick Curly Sue (Alisan Porter) are hoboes. When Bill is hit by a car driven by Kelly Lynch, as an attorney as wealthy as she's beautiful and intense, things start looking up for our footloose, four-flushing friends. Down-to-earth playing by Belushi and Porter (as engaging a moppet as the cinema's thrown up in quite a while) stop this from oozing pure saccharine even if it never engages our emotions.

Curly Top ○
1935, US, 75 mins, b/w
Dir: Irving Cummings
Stars: Shirley Temple, John Boles, Rochelle Hudson, Jane Darwell
Rating: ★★★

Shirley Temple attempts to bring sweetness and light to an orphanage, much to the displeasure of the grumpy superintendent, played by pop-eyed Rafaela Ottiano. This is the one in which Shirley has a pony and a pet duck, and sings 'Animal Crackers in My Soup', one of her greatest hits.

Curse of Frankenstein, The ●
1957, UK, 83 mins, colour
Dir: Terence Fisher
Stars: Peter Cushing, Christopher Lee
Rating: ★★

Contemporary critics pursed their lips and were shocked at the full-frontal gore and spare-part surgery in this gaudy shocker but audiences had no such lily-livered inhibitions and flocked to see the bold, bad Baron and his do-it-yourself creature in vivid colour for the first time. Terence Fisher's unflinching depiction of horror and his skill as a storyteller established him as the best post-war maker of screen chillers, made international stars of Peter Cushing (in his first outing as *Frankenstein*) and Christopher Lee, in his one-and-only appearance as the Creature, and set

Hammer films on their profitable way to box-office bonanzas all over the world.

Curse of the Cat People, The ❍
1944, US, 70 mins, b/w
Dir: Robert Wise
Stars: Simone Simon, Kent Smith, Jane Randolph
Rating: ★★★

An indirect sequel to *Cat People* and, amazingly, just as good. Ann Carter gives a quite unnerving performance as the little girl who lives in a night-mare world of her own imagination. This chilling continuation of the story of the Smiths was the first directorial assignment for Robert Wise, hitherto an editor (on such films as *Citizen Kane*). Later he made a number of significant films and won two Academy Awards.

Curse of the Crimson Altar ○
(aka: Crimson Cult)
1968, UK, 88 mins, colour
Dir: Vernon Sewell
Stars: Boris Karloff, Christopher Lee, Barbara Steele, Rupert Davies
Rating: ★★

With such a superb cast, this should have been the horror film to end them all. It isn't quite – perhaps too many ghouls spoil the broth. Still, this witchcraft thriller contains some lurid shock moments, very sexy love scenes, and commendable underplaying from Boris Karloff, whizzing about in a wheelchair, in one of his last major films. The raven-haired Barbara Steele, the 'queen of horror films', is rather wasted in a smallish part of a long-dead witch. A far cry from the central roles in such Italian horror films as *Black Sunday* in which she made her name.

Curse of the Demon
See: The Night My Number Came Up

Curse of the Fly, The ●
1964, UK, 86 mins, b/w
Dir: Don Sharp
Stars: Brian Donlevy, Carole Gray
Rating: ★★

This British film completed the 'fly' trilogy about a family's obsession with the transference of matter through space, the first two with Vincent Price. Price's mantle as senior member of the family is here assumed by screen veteran Brian Donlevy, on his third visit to post-war Britain following *The*

Quatermass Experiment and *Quatermass II*. Carole Gray is startlingly effective as the heroine, although her career was by now faltering after a meteoric start as Cliff Richard's leading lady in *The Young Ones*.

Curse of the Mummy's Tomb, The ● Ⓥ
1964, UK, 80 mins, colour
Dir: Michael Carreras
Stars: Terence Morgan, Ronald Howard, Fred Clark, Jeanne Roland
Rating: ★

The beat of the cloth-wrapped feet sounds again, this time along the cobblestones of fog-enshrouded Victorian London. 'See where he goes,' cries Inspector John Paul to his men, after the mummy has committed murder in the drawing room before their eyes, 'but keep your distance.' Too true. Indeed, fans of the traditional B-grade horror film are likely to be happy all round, as the madman cries, 'Kill Her!' to the monster, while the scantily clad heroine lies draped picturesquely across a block of stone. A Hammer horror in more ways than one.

Curse of the Werewolf ●
1961, UK, 92 mins, colour
Dir: Terence Fisher
Stars: Oliver Reed, Yvonne Romain, Clifford Evans, Anthony Dawson
Rating: ★★

Hammer's fourth 'original copy', after their versions of the Frankenstein, Dracula and Mummy sagas. Guy Endore's novel *The Werewolf of Paris* was an obvious source of material, and Hammer producer Anthony Hinds, using his pseudonym of John Elder, provided a very serviceable screenplay from it, giving full rein to director Terence Fisher's natural talent for period flavour and a well-knit storyline. The role of the werewolf was difficult to cast. But the choice finally fell to an unknown young actor who had been confined to playing minor bullies. His name was Oliver Reed.

Curtain Call at Cactus Creek ○
(aka: Take the Stage)
1950, US, 86 mins, colour
Dir: Charles Lamont
Stars: Donald O'Connor, Gale Storm, Vincent Price, Walter Brennan
Rating: ★★★

This Western comedy is a kind of sideshoot from W C Fields' famous

C

comedy, *The Old Fashioned Way*, in that it deals with a travelling repertory company in 19th century America, with an awful old ham (in this case played by Vincent Price, who thoroughly enjoys himself) as its leading player. Three-time Oscar-winner Walter Brennan is also in good form as the hoary old outlaw who joins the troupe, while Donald O'Connor and the improbably-named Gale Storm (real name: Josephine Cottle) keep the flag flying for the younger generation.

Custer of the West ○
1966, US/Spain, 140 mins, colour
Dir: Robert Siodmak
Stars: Robert Shaw, Mary Ure, Robert Ryan, Jeffrey Hunter, Ty Hardin
Rating: ★★

Shot mainly in Spain, this epic Western was the last major film from Robert Siodmak, the American-born, German-trained director who made his name in Hollywood with a clutch of powerful thrillers that include *Phantom Lady*, *The Spiral Staircase* and *The Killers*. With the help of Robert Shaw's vivid portrayal of Custer, Siodmak keeps the action here rolling at a thunderingly good pace considering the film's length. Among the rest of the cast, Robert Ryan scores well as a gold-hungry deserter. It doesn't quite have the intimate feel of the 1941 Errol Flynn version, *They Died with Their Boots On*, which made that film such a classic, but in compensation provides plenty of colourful adventure – from a runaway train and the shooting of treacherous rapids leading inevitably to the famous Custer's 'last stand'.

Cutting Edge, The ○ ⓥ
1992, US, 101 mins, colour
Dir: Paul Michael Glaser
Stars: D B Sweeney, Moira Kelly, Roy Dotrice, Dwier Brown, Terry O'Quinn
Rating: ★

This is a wondrously bad film about ice skating with a script and situations that seem to have been stitched together from bad movies of 60 years ago. The chances are that you'll enjoy every minute of this even while spluttering uncontrollably into your coke or coffee as ex-ice hockey star D B Sweeney and 'ice queen' Moira Kelly feud their way to the world pairs championships and each other's arms. 'For 20 years I've been working on this,' exclaims their Russian coach (Roy Dotrice), describing the 'Panicenko' movement

that you know they'll refuse to do and then bring off at the last. Everyone except Sweeney and Kelly is excruciatingly bad, small wonder spouting lines that crash like lead pucks on to the ice. Puerile, silly and very enjoyable.

Cyrano de Bergerac ○ ⓥ
1990, France, 138 mins, colour
Dir: Jean-Paul Rappeneau
Stars: Gerard Depardieu, Jacques Weber, Anne Brochet
Rating: ★★★★

This French film of Rostand's classic play was highly successful and deservedly so, as it has everything – wit, drama, unrequited love and lots of swashbuckling action. Gerard Depardieu fills the role of the swaggering chevalier with the prominent proboscis with lusty vigour. He also manages to convey Cyrano's self-conscious insecurities because of his love for Roxane (luminously portrayed by Anne Brochet). The balcony love scene is wittily done, as is the sequence in which Cyrano creates a fracas in a theatre and the final scene is poignant in the extreme. The film looks spectacular. Even the subtitles aren't the usual irritating necessity, and they're also well-written – not suprising as they were the work of novelist Anthony Burgess. On a par (though very different) with the 1950 version starring Jose Ferrer.

D

Da ○ ⓥ
1988, US, 102 mins, colour
Dir: Matt Clark
Stars: Barnard Hughes, Martin Sheen, William Hickey, Doreen Hepburn, Hugh O'Conor
Rating: ★★

Despite the occasional abrasiveness of its protagonists, this is a sweet-natured picture about memories, and about the relationship down the years between a talented Irish boy and the father who seemed unruffled by time (or much else) and rooted in the past. It's also the story of all middle-aged men and their fathers in our time, a post-war legacy in which the generation gap has yawned wider than before or since. Unfortunately sweetness and nostalgia, like the film, only grip in fits and starts, but it is acted to perfection by Martin Sheen as the son who went to America and by Barnard Hughes as the blustery old man who stayed in Ireland and whose ghost comes to make its peace after his own funeral. This leads to often humorous flashbacks to the past, highlighted by attempts to drown the family dog, and by the old man's ruining his son's big chance with the local floozy.

Dad ○ ⓥ
1989, US, 116 mins, colour
Dir: Gary David Goldberg
Stars: Jack Lemmon, Ted Danson, Olympia Dukakis, Kathy Baker, Kevin Spacey, Ethan Hawke
Rating: ★★

This is an actors' showcase, and Jack Lemmon, with the help of prosthetic makeup that's a touch over the top (do many 78-year-old Americans actually look about 90?), does everything anyone could to make this story of senility and belated filial concern just as gut-wrenching as possible. He's already proved himself a wow at this sort of thing and does so again here. And, although the film is virtually a two-hander between Lemmon and Ted Danson as his son, it's full of good performances and emotive moments. Alas, the story itself seems to reach an end several times, only to go off at a tangent, until it finally seems about four hours long. The makers might argue that life's a bit like that – just one darn thing after another – but it doesn't make for very fluent entertainment in a film whose highpoints all seem to occur in the middle. The best section is the part where Danson rehabilitates Lemmon after the latter's suffocating wife has had a heart attack. It's downhill from here on, but, if you cry easily at the movies, you'll cry a lot at this one.

Daddy Long Legs ○
1955, US, 126 mins, colour
Dir: Jean Negulesco
Stars: Fred Astaire, Leslie Caron, Terry Moore, Thelma Ritter, Fred Clark
Rating: ★★★

When an irresible force meets an old immovable object then, to quote Fred Astaire in this musical's Os-car-nominated song, 'Somethings Gotta Give'. And what gives here is entertainment of the most elegant and sophisticated variety, especially when Astaire and Leslie Caron get anywhere near the dance floor. She's a waif without means, he's a man without a wife, and the twain shall eventually meet via a delightfully convoluted plot which has Fred 'adopting' Leslie to pay for her edu-cation in America. The world's most graceful old fogey gets hep with 'The Sluefoot' and Mmlle Caron makes a charming partner. The only fly in the ointment is 20th Century-Fox's dreadful Fifties colour by De Luxe. Not even the great cinematographer Leon Shamroy can do anything with its blue and green rinses.

Dakota Incident ○
1956, US, 88 mins, colour
Dir: Lewis R Foster
Stars: Linda Darnell, Dale Robertson, John Lund, Ward Bond
Rating: ★★

A Western that only springs to life in its periodic bursts of full-blooded ac-tion. Even a good cast that, in cricketing terms, bats right down to number 11, can do little with stodgy Frederic Louis Fox's stodgy dialogue; to add insult to injury they get killed one by one as the plot casts them as stranded stagecoach passsengers at the mercy of rampaging Indians. Os-car-winning photographer Ernest Haller, though, is to be congratulated on making the Trucolor process for once acceptable.

Dallas ○
1950, US, 94 mins, b/w
Dir: Stuart Heisler

Stars: Gary Cooper, Ruth Roman, Raymond Massey, Steve Cochran
Rating: ★★

A typical Gary Cooper Western with the tall, tanned and taciturn cowboy providing the firepower and fighting capability of a modern regiment as he wages a lone battle against carpetbaggers. The climax, in which he duels with Raymond Massey, is a spellbinder. Overall, though, competent rather than inspired.

Damage ● Ⓥ
1992, UK, 111 mins, colour
Dir: Louis Malle
Stars: Jeremy Irons, Juliette Binoche, Rupert Graves, Miranda Richardson, Ian Bannen, Leslie Caron
Rating: ★

A slow, grim, melodramatic and strangely unemotional portrait of the decay caused by obsessive love. Jeremy Irons plays an up-an-coming gov-ernment minister who falls hopelssly and passionately in love with his son's girlfriend (Juliette Binoche), a young woman happy both to supply his needs and remain engaged to his son. Tragedy inevitably strikes, and viewers so inclined can stay to watch the destruction of the lives of nearly all those involved. Irons' and particularly Binoche's hearts don't seem to be in this; but you may well feel the same way in rather less time. The valuable Miranda Richardson gives the only good performance in the film as Irons' discarded wife.

Dam Busters, The ○ Ⓥ
1954, UK, 125 mins, b/w
Dir: Michael Anderson
Stars: Richard Todd, Michael Redgrave, Ursula Jeans, Derek Farr
Rating: ★★★★

Inspired film-making from a British film industry still brimming with confidence before the bubble burst in the late Fifties. Michael Redgrave is superb as the scientist who invents the famous 'bouncing bomb' and Richard Todd at his best as the squad-ron-leader picked to lead the team that delivers it to the German dams it must destroy. The tremendously popular march theme by Eric Coates became a standard for all brass bands. And there's a star in almost every uniform.

Dames ○
1934, US, 90 mins, b/w
Dir: Ray Enright

Stars: Joan Blondell, Dick Powell, Ruby Keiler, ZaSu Pitts, Guy Kibbee
Rating: ★★★

The 'gold-digger'-style musicals never had the strongest of stories and de-pended on their songs and Busby Berkeley dance routines to bring in the paying public. This plot must be the thinnest of all but within its gos-samer framework are housed such classic numbers as 'The Girl at the Ironing Board', 'When You Were a Smile on Your Mother's Lips' and 'I Only Have Eyes for You', in which jigsaw puzzle pieces on dancing girls' backs form a giant portrait of Ruby Keeler.

Damien – Omen II ● Ⓥ
1978, US, 107 mins, colour
Dir: Don Taylor
Stars: William Holden, Lee Grant, Jonathan Scott-Taylor
Rating: ★★

The only drawback to the splen-didly-made *Omen* films is that the good guys so seldom even look like winning. Thus the results of their encounters with Damien are such a foregone conclusion that the chief excitement lies in seeing what new and spectacular deaths can be dreamt up by the special effects wizards. The most dazzling effect here involves slicing a man in two. Meanwhile Jonathan Scott-Taylor does very nicely as the teenage Damien (son of the Devil, you'll remember) and seems to dispatch some new victim every few seconds of the film. It's all fright-eningly entertaining.

Damnation Alley ○
1977, US, 91 mins, colour
Dir: Jack Smight
Stars: Jan-Michael Vincent, George Peppard, Dominique Sanda
Rating: ★★

This science-fiction thriller gets off to a spectacular start with the world rav-aged by a searing nuclear holocaust. Of course, the dangers are not over for a band of intrepid Americans who set out across their country in search of a small pocket of civilisation thought to have survived the horror. Tidal waves, ceaseless storms and other freak weather conditions, allied with such fearsome threats as giant scorpions and carnivorous cockroaches, are just some of the hazards in their way. As an imaginative, action-filled adventure yarn, it has some splendid moments, even if the script is not up to the scale

D

of the story. As well as men of action George Peppard and Jan-Michael Vincent, Jackie Earle Haley – the little tough guy from the *Bad News Bears* films – is also in the cast.

Damned Don't Cry, The ○
1950, US, 100 mins, b/w
Dir: Vincent Sherman
Stars: Joan Crawford, David Brian, Steve Cochran, Kent Smith
Rating: ★★

A typical Joan Crawford crime vehicle, allowing her to run the gamut from laughter to tears, from poverty to power, and pitching her up to her mink in crime and corruption. Her fans will love every melodramatic minute. A young Richard Egan appears as her husband in the opening scenes.

Damn the Defiant
See: HMS Defiant

Dance Hall ○
1950, UK, 90 mins, b/w
Dir: Charles Crichton
Stars: Natasha Parry, Jane Hylton, Diana Dors, Petula Clark
Rating: ★★

Ealing Studios took a look at another British tradition – the palais de danse – with a film whose conventional, relatively shapeless story uses the local palais as a background to examine the experiences of a quartet of factory girls who spend their evenings searching for relaxation and excitement. You might notice the same extras in scene after scene, but nostalgia is well catered for by Geraldo and His Orchestra and Ted Heath and His Music. You may spot Kay Kendall, Eunice Gayson and Dandy Nichols in minor roles.

Dance Little Lady ○
1954, UK, 105 mins, colour
Dir: Val Guest
Stars: Terence Morgan, Mai Zetterling, Guy Rolfe, Mandy Miller
Rating: ★★

Terence Morgan makes the best impression as a sponger as smooth as he is nasty, in this ballet-orientated story, tailored to the talents of Britian's then screen wonder child, Mandy Miller. It bases its appeal on its blend of small-girl sentiment, highly coloured melodramatics and ballet (the dance ensembles are very well done). Mai Zetterling and Guy Rolfe provide ra-

ther limp support to Mandy's undeniable charm, but the story's fiery climax is most effective.

Dance of the Vampires ◐
(aka: The Fearless Vampire Killers)
1967, UK, 110 mins, colour
Dir: Roman Polanski
Stars: Jack MacGowran, Roman Polanski, Sharon Tate, Ferdy Mayne, Alfie Bass
Rating: ★★★

Perhaps Polanski's most bizarre film – a spoof horror movie that turns out to be more horror than spoof. Alfie Bass is very funny as a Jewish vampire for whom a crucifix holds no fear. 'Boy,' he cries, advancing on a maiden shielding herself with a cross, 'have you got the wrong vampire!'

Dances with Wolves ◐ ⓥ
1990, US, 179 mins, colour
Dir: Kevin Costner
Stars: Kevin Costner, Mary McDonnell, Graham Greene, Rodney A Grant
Rating: ★★★★

It's rare that a film lives up to its rave reviews, but Kevin Costner's debut as director does just that. He plays Dunbar, an American lieutenant of the 1860s who escapes the horror of the Civil War (and, narrowly, the amputation of his foot) to live in peace and tranquillity in the far frontier. Here, at his outpost, and by no real design of his own, he comes to befriend, then live among the local Sioux Indians. Overcoming initial hostility, he learns their language, fights for them and falls in love with a white woman captured by them as a child. In one of the film's most telling snatches of dialogue, Dunbar records that he has 'never known people so eager to laugh, so close as a family, so dedicated to each other. The only word is harmony.' Shadows close across this harmony and happiness before the end but no matter: Dunbar has had his day in the sun. He also makes the acquaintance of a timber wolf which becomes almost tame; his playful game with the animal earns him his Indian name: Dances with Wolves. Costner's film really has everything: action, emotion, romance, laughter and an insight, admittedly superficial, into a half-lost culture. A remarkable first movie.

Dance with a Stranger ● ⓥ
1984, UK, 101 mins, colour
Dir: Mike Newell

Stars: Rupert Everett, Miranda Richardson, Ian Holm, Stratford Johns, Joanne Whalley
Rating: ★★

Stylish, biting retelling of the story of Ruth Ellis, the last woman to be hanged in Britain, shot in appropriately harsh colours by Peter Hannan. Though one can understand filmmakers' obsession with Ellis, first played 28 years earlier by Diana Dors in *Yield to the Night*, the events of the case are perilously close to the monotonous for the sustainment of the a full-length movie. One row, reconciliation, love-making session or beating between Ellis and her lover are, after all, very much like another, despite the excellent performances of Miranda Richardson (who conjures up a remarkable physical resemblance) and Rupert Everett. Ian Holm offers his customary skilled support as Ruth's oft rejected older suitor, and Stratford Johns also scores in a role far removed from his old image as Chief Inspector Barlow. The film's finally a narrow victory for style over content.

Dancing Lady ○
1933, US, 95 mins, b/w
Dir: Robert Z Leonard
Stars: Joan Crawford, Clark Gable, Franchot Tone
Rating: ★★★

You wouldn't usually associate Clark Gable and Joan Crawford with musicals, but here they have plenty of classy support to help carry the score of this back-stage saga of a poor-born but honest dancer (Crawford!) struggling to make it to Broadway without compromising her ideals. Fred Astaire makes his feature debut with a couple of dance routines.

Dancing with Crime ○
1946, UK, 83 mins, b/w
Dir: John Paddy Carstairs
Stars: Richard Attenborough, Sheila Sim, Barry K Barnes
Rating: ★★

A crime thriller about two Army mates who become involved with a criminal gang operating from a dance hall. The action moves briskly, and the film provides some fascinating insights into the British way of relaxation in the immediate post-war years. Bill Rowbotham, who plays hero Richard Attenborough's friend, later became better known as Bill Owen. Watch out for a brief appearance by Dirk Bogarde as a policeman – his first acting role in films.

Dancing Years, The ○
1949, UK, 96 mins, colour
Dir: Harold French
Stars: Dennis Price, Patricia Dainton, Gilese Preville, Olive Gilbert
Rating: ★★

Pleasant, lightweight Ivor Novello musical about a poor young pianist who becomes a famous composer. Elegant playing from Dennis Price complements some fine singing by Olive Gilbert and Martin Ross.

Dangerous Corner ○
1935, US, 65 mins, b/w
Dir: Phil Rosen
Stars: Melvyn Douglas, Virginia Bruce
Rating: ★★

This murder thriller is based on a successful stage play by J B Priestley and rather shows up its theatrical origins. Some government bonds are stolen and the principal suspect apparently commits suicide. In an unusual attempt to find the truth, those close to the dead man are invited to a seance. Despite its stage-bound limitations, sound performances from Melvyn Douglas, Conrad Nagel and Virginia Bruce and an interesting plot create a mystery that's a little different.

Dangerous Crossing ○
1953, US, 76 mins, b/w
Dir: Joseph M Newman
Stars: Jeanne Crain, Michael Rennie
Rating: ★★

A suspense thriller about a frightened bride whose husband disappears on their honeymoon voyage. Adapted by Leo Townsend from a story by master mystery writer John Dickson Carr, the plot of this one is guaranteed to keep you guessing to the very end.

Dangerous Liaisons ● Ⓥ
1988, US, 120 mins, colour
Dir: Stephen Frears
Stars: Glenn Close, John Malkovich, Michelle Pfeiffer, Swoozie Kurtz, Uma Thurman
Rating: ★★★

British director Stephen Frears' first American film is an elegant portrayal of the jaded decadence of the 18th century French aristocracy on the eve of the French Revolution. The film is based on Christopher Hampton's acclaimed stage version of Choderlos de Laclos' novel *Les Liaisons Dangereuses*, a scandalous success when it first appeared in 1782. The story concerns two aristocratic libertines, played by Glenn Close and John Malkovich, who embark on a cruel intrigue to spread corruption and dismay around them wherever they can. Michelle Pfeiffer plays a devout and faithful bourgeois wife who becomes one of their victims. The decision to cast American actors in the leading roles caused some controversy but is vindicated by the finished film. And the title was slightly changed, from that of the stage play and novel, as it was feared that the American audience would otherwise think it a French production! Without being absurdly anachronistic, the cast bring an immediacy and modernity to their roles that reveals the depth of feeling that exists beneath the powdered wigs and elegant language.

Dangerous Mission ○
1954, US, 75 mins, colour
Dir: Louis King
Stars: Victor Mature, Piper Laurie, William Bendix, Vincent Price
Rating: ★★

This adventure thriller really had everything going for it: a dazzling snowbound setting, Technicolor photography and a strong cast that includes Victor Mature, Piper Laurie, William Bendix and Vincent Price, though they prove *film noir* people adrift in these outdoor locales. That said, it must be added that director Louis King overplays his hand a bit on the thrills quite needlessly. And shame on the scriptwriters for giving the talented Piper Laurie so little to do. Watch for Dennis (*McCloud*) Weaver in a small role.

Dangerous Moonlight ○
(aka: Suicide Squadron)
1941, US, 95 mins, b/w
Dir: Brian Desmond Hurst
Stars: Anton Walbrook, Sally Grey
Rating: ★★★

The romantic film drama that sent Richard Addinsell's 'Warsaw Concerto' soaring into the wartime pop charts. It's a splendidly-acted story of a Polish pianist who joins the Royal Air Force to avenge himself on the country that has ravaged his own native land. Tight direction, excellent aerial combat scenes.

Dangerous When Wet ○
1953, US, 90 mins, colour
Dir: Charles Walters
Stars: Esther Williams, Fernando Lamas, Jack Carson
Rating: ★★★

Director Charles Walters was a former dancer and dance director who made too few films on his own. Almost all of his solo work behind the camera was good, resulting in some of the happiest and most heart-warming musicals of the Forties, Fifties and Sixties. Walters' films in this period include *Good News*, *Easter Parade*, *Lili*, *The Tender Trap*, *High Society*, *The Unsinkable Molly Brown* and a non-musical, <I>Walk Don't Run, a list which gives you some idea of his quality and consistency. Unsurprisingly, then, this is one of Esther Williams' best aqua-musicals, with the star as a reluctant Channel swimmer who falls in love with a French nobleman (Fernando Lamas, in real life her husband-to-be). A sequence combining live-action with some inventive animation, in which Esther swims with Tom and Jerry, is quite delightful, and Jack Carson, Charlotte Greenwood and Donna Corcoran all score well in a strong supporting cast. The title is so perfect for an Esther Williams movie that they must have thought of it before they made the picture.

Dangerous Woman, A ● Ⓥ
1993, US, 107 mins, colour
Dir: Stephen Gyllenhaal
Stars: Debra Winger, Gabriel Byrne, Barbara Hershey, David Strathairn
Rating: ★

Sometimes good actors see a story that's a little different and sniff a masterpiece in the making. All too often, alas, they're wrong, and so it proves in this rather fey story about a slightly-retarded 30-year-old who lives with an aunt six years older, whose husand has died. Debra Winger is just marvellous as the girl who can't lie but, against the naivety of the dialogue and the sluggishness of the direction, she's fighting a lost cause. Gabriel Byrne's a bore as the boozy Irish handyman who becomes sexually involved with both women, but Barbara Hershey just about keeps the giggles at bay in a thankless role as the glamorous aunt. Connoisseurs of bad dialogue will have a field day here and, to be fair to him, Byrne gets the worst of it. 'Sometimes we have to tell lies to get at the truth' or 'You're a

D

wonder, like a primitive thing that's never been spoiled. You might as well live in a glass cocoon' would defeat a string of Oscar-winners. Not even the wonderful Winger can save this one.

Danger Route ○

1967, UK, 92 mins, colour
Dir: Seth Holt
Stars: Richard Johnson, Carol Lynley, Barbara Bouchet
Rating: ★★

Richard Johnson gets four leading ladies – Carol Lynley, Barbara Bouchet, Sylvia Syms and Diana Dors – for the price of one in this thriller about a government hit man who wants to give it all up. Of course, his bosses won't let him and thereby hangs a routine but exciting tale.

Danger Within ○

1959, UK, 101 mins, b/w
Dir: Don Chaffey
Stars: Richard Todd, Michael Wilding, Richard Attenborough, Bernard Lee
Rating: ★★

A whodunnit with a difference, in the style of *Stalag 17*. Can you spot the traitor in the PoW camp before Col Richard Todd and his investigators? Todd is cast as the head of the Escape Committee, and Bernard Lee has one of his best roles as senior British officer in the camp. Dennis Price also scores as a captain whose interest centres on his forthcoming presentation of *Hamlet* at the camp theatre.

Danny the Champion of the World ⊙

1989, UK, 94 mins, colour
Dir: Gavin Millar
Stars: Jeremy Irons, Samuel Irons, Robbie Coltrane, Jean Marsh
Rating: ★★★

The heroes and villains are engagingly whiter than white and blacker than black in this charming adaptation of Roald Dahl's story about a father and son (real-life father and son Jeremy and Samuel Irons) who hold out against scheming landgrabbers. Robbie Coltrane and Jean Marsh score well as the obnoxious developer and the child welfare agent. Master Irons is a real charmer, and the beautiful colour photography lends a warm glow to this winning tale.

Dante's Inferno ○

1935, US, 88 mins, b/w
Dir: Harry Lachman

Stars: Spencer Tracy, Claire Trevor
Rating: ★★★

This heady concoction is one of Hollywood's more remarkable 'folies de grandeur' in which Spencer Tracy's power-hungry carnival man, evil streaming from his maniacal eyes, vies for attention with the inferno itself. This is the fairground sideshow to end them all: a monstrous pit of hell entered through the belly of a giant figure of Satan, and littered with infernal paintings and tableaux. Rita Hayworth has (under her real name, Rita Cansino) a supporting role in this remarkable cinematic curiosity which climaxes in a spectacular sequence set on board a floating casino.

Darby O'Gill and the Little People ⊙

1959, UK, 93 mins, colour
Dir: Robert Stevenson
Stars: Jimmy O'Dea, Sean Connery, Janet Munro, Albert Sharpe, Kieron Moore
Rating: ★★★

Although this vigorous Disney fantasy lays on its Oirish blarney with a trowel, the special effects are far ahead of their time and director Robert Stevenson rampages through the incident-filled plot in the smartest possible order. Jimmy O'Dea is totally beguiling as the king of the leprechauns, while Sean Connery and Kieron Moore make a virile hero and villain.

Daring Game ○

1968, US, 100 mins, colour
Dir: Laslo Benedek
Stars: Lloyd Bridges, Joan Blackman
Rating: ★★

Hungarian-born director Laslo Benedek is most famous for his Marlon Brando film *The Wild One*. But, in his later years, he seemed to develop a liking for seagoing adventure yarns. This typical Sixties pot-boiler has Lloyd Bridges back in *Sea Hunt* territory as the leader of a team of scuba divers out to rescue a professor held captive by revolutionaries.

Dark Angel ● ⓥ

1990, US, 92 mins, colour
Dir: Craig R Baxley
Stars: Dolph Lundgren, Brian Benben, Betsy Brantley, Matthias Hues, Michael J Pollard
Rating: ★★★

Or: Drug Dealer from Outer Space. With the help of modern technology, the results are nasty but quite fun, with massive Dolph Lundgren amusingly teamed with tiny Brian Benben as an FBI man who would surely have failed the physical. Alien Hues, already 6ft 6in without his build-up shoes, lumbers around killing his victims with a razor sharp compact disc, or extracting bodily fluids from them to form an inter-galactic drug. He's pursued not only by earthly cop Lundgren but by an alien law-enforcer who looks even more ghastly than him. The aliens also have flame-guns that almost never hit people, but blow up things just behind them. Director Craig R Baxley, who also made *Action Jackson*, knows how to stage this kind of thing all right, and makes sure we hardly have time to pause for breath or to consider how silly it all is. The result is what you might call a blast.

Dark Angel, The ○

1935, US, 110 mins, b/w
Dir: Sidney Franklin
Stars: Fredric March, Merele Oberon, Herbert Marshall, Janet Beecher
Rating: ★★★

This revival of a silent film weepie was rehashed yet again some years later as *Tomorrow is Forever*, with Claudette Colbert and Orson Welles. Here it's Merle Oberon and Fredric March sensitively portraying the woman and man torn by war, he being posted missing and she marrying another. A polished script by Lillian Hellman and Mordaunt Shairp gives the stars every assistance in ensuring you'll need a handkerchief or two for the later stages of the film.

Dark Avenger, The ○

(aka: The Warriors)
1955, UK, 85 mins, colour
Dir: Henry Levin
Stars: Errol Flynn, Joanne Dru, Peter Finch, Yvonne Furneaux, Michael Hordern
Rating: ★★

Just about the last cinematic buckle Errol Flynn ever swashed. Made only four years before Flynn's death in 1959, this is a dashing costume piece about an audacious English prince who foils a dastardly French plot to keep France for the French. Peter Finch is a fine, cruel villain.

Dark City ○

1950, US, 88 mins, b/w
Dir: William Dieterle

Stars: Charlton Heston, Lisabeth Scott, Dean Jagger, Viveca Lindfors, Ed Begley
Rating: ★★★

The high-tension thriller which introduced to the screen a Bogart-style newcomer in Charlton Heston who, for his own protection, would probably have been glad of one of the suits of armour he was to wear in his later films. Also starring are the *Dragnet* team of Jack Webb and Henry Morgan, and there's a gem of a performance from Ed Begley as a bookie with ulcers.

Dark Command ○
1940, US, 92 mins, b/w
Dir: Raoul Walsh
Stars: John Wayne, Claire Trevor, Roy Rogers, Walter Pidgeon
Rating: ★★

After *Stagecoach*, Republic Studios swiftly realised it had a major new star in John Wayne on its hands and immediately mounted a special vehicle for him, in what turned out to be the Studio's most expensive film to date. The darkly-photographed story proved to be the familiar one of 'Bloody' Bill Cantrell and his post-Civil War raiders. Possibly hoping for the emergence of a second Wayne in quick succession, Republic cast their young cowboy star Roy Rogers as his younger brother but Rogers, though a popular Western hero for another 12 years, proved not to quite have the stature for big-budget films.

Dark Corner, The ○
1946, US, 98 mins, b/w
Dir: Henry Hathaway
Stars: Mark Stevens, Lucille Ball, Clifton Webb, William Bendix
Rating: ★★★

The dark corner in the title of this archetypal Hollywood *film noir* of the Forties represents the predicament of the hero (a private eye just out of jail after being framed), who is just as surely alienated from the world as the returning ex-servicemen in *The Best Years of Our Lives*, released the same year. His insecurity is underlined when it seems someone is trying to frame him anew. 'I'm backed up in a dark corner,' mutters Mark Stevens as the detective, 'and I don't know who's hitting me.' All this and William Bendix as the mysterious White Suit, Clifton Webb as a cultured vulture, claustrophobic direction by Henry Hathaway, and bril-

liantly-shaded photography by Joe MacDonald. What more could any self-respecting fan of the genre want?

Dark Crystal, The ○ ⓥ
1982, US, 94 mins, colour
Dir: Frank Oz
Rating: ★★★

Jim Henson and his Muppet workshops caught everyone hopping with this brilliantly detailed and ultra-dark children's fantasy that was a million miles removed from the primary coloured brilliance of *The Muppet Show*. No Kermit or Miss Piggy in this universe, just monstrous flesh-eating Skeksis and their counterparts, the Mystics. They battle over possession of the shattered Dark Crystal, which will give ultimate power to the holder, unless it is restored to its rightful resting place. A young Gelfling has the task of saving the planet, but he's a real wimp and no mistake. A warning for children under 10: just like the best Disney good-versus-evil tale, the dark side is here represented by the sort of distressing creatures that could cause nightmares.

Darker than Amber ○
1970, US, 96 mins, colour
Dir: Robert Clouse
Stars: Rod Taylor, Suzy Kendall, Theodore Bikel, Jane Russell
Rating: ★★

Films and TV movies have made several attempts at capturing the world of John McDonald's houseboat-bound detective Travis McGee. This is as good as any, with striking location photography in Florida and the Caribbean, rugged Rod Taylor as McGee, and some excellent cameos from the supporting cast, notably Ahna Capri, and Janet MacLachlan, plus terrifyingly authentic performances of vicious thugs from William Smith and Robert Phillips.

Dark Eyes ○ ⓥ
1987, Italy, 117 mins, colour
Dir: Nikita Mikhalkov
Stars: Marcello Mastroianni, Silvana Mangano, Marthe Keller, Elena Sofonova
Rating: ★★★

Lush music by Francis Lai announces a return by Marcello Mastroianni to *Sunflower* country. In an unquenchably romantic piece, based mostly on Chekhov's *Lady With a Little Dog*, Mastroianni makes dazzling use of his entire repertoire as a working-class

Romeo seduced by riches into a life of opulent idleness within an increasingly barren marriage. Until he conquers the 'lady with a little dog', a Russian woman who falls in love with him but flees back to her husand in Moscow. It's one of those films full of scenes that conjure up old paintings, in many of which you can feel an atmosphere of sunshine, or heavy mists, or simply sumptuous emptiness. Despite some stretches that touch tedium, the director's skill keeps the piece alive until the (you guessed it) romantic ending.

Dark Eyes of London, The ○
1939, UK, 76 mins, b/w
Dir: Walter Summers
Stars: Bela Lugosi, Hugh Williams, Greta Gynt
Rating: ★★★

Hollywood chillmonger Bela Lugosi, the original Dracula, crossed the Atlantic to net an 'H' certificate for this British thriller about a series of gruesome murders. Based on a story by prolific purveyor of suspense, Edgar Wallace, it boasts several creepy characters – but none so awesome as Lugosi's sinister Dr Orloff. Although the film came out in 1939, sharp eyes will notice that all its references (newspapers etc) are to 1936. A mystery perhaps, deeper, than the one in the film.

Darkman ● ⓥ
1990, US, 95 mins, colour
Dir: Sam Raimi
Stars: Liam Neeson, Frances McDormand, Colin Friels, Larry Drake
Rating: ★

An unintentionally laughable modern sex clone of *Phantom of the Opera*, directed by Sam Raimi (of *Evil Dead* fame) on a wing and a prayer, with a little help from an unseen organist in the background. You'd never guess the four stars were all fine players from their painful efforts to bring any credibility to a non-script that Raimi and four other people cobbled together from old clichés, clattering banalities and fragments of better films. Liam Neeson is the scientist ready to perfect artificial skin that can be used as a mask. He's almost there (cue cliché: 'I can feel it. God, I can almost taste it.') when horribly disfigured in his laboratory by thugs hired to get a document he may have in his possession. The rest of the plot doesn't take much guessing. Congratulate Aussie Friels on his American accent, marvel

D

at how different Larry Drake is from his retard on *LA Law*, spot *Evil Dead* star Bruce Campbell in a cameo, and Jenny Agutter unbilled, wince at the poor process work, and you've seen it, done it. Find something better to do.

Dark Mirror, The ○
1946, US, 80 mins, b/w
Dir: Robert Siodmak
Stars: Olivia de Havilland, Lew Ayres, Thomas Mitchell, Richard Long
Rating: ★★★

Fine actress Olivia de Havilland gives a tour-de-force performance as identical twin sisters, one of whom is a murderess, in this complex, *film noir*-style psychological thriller, directed from Nunnally Johnson's script by Robert Siodmak the year after his best film, *The Spiral Staircase*. The special effects by J Devereaux Jennings and Paul Lerpae are brilliantly done, enabling de Havilland to play opposite herself and appear totally convincingly as two people. Fresh-faced Lew (Dr Kildare) Ayres acquits himself well as the psychologist brought in to help establish the truth – and whose life is endangered when he becomes the object of the twins' affections. It has a satisfactorily upbeat ending but de Havilland said of her roles: 'The technical problems involved in playing a dual role were extremely difficult to solve, and that horrible Terry I had to play haunts me to this day.'

Dark Obsession
See: Diamond Skulls

Dark Page, The
See: Scandal Sheet

Dark Passage ○ ⓥ
1947, US, 106 mins, b/w
Dir: Delmer Daves
Stars: Humphrey Bogart, Lauren Bacall, Bruce Bennett, Agnes Moorehead
Rating: ★★★

Humphrey Bogart is an escaped convict, wrongly jailed for the murder of his wife in this gripping and unusual thriller. For the first 40 minutes you don't see the star, only hear his voice – the camera sees through his eyes: a neat cinematic trick that was used to equally good effect a year later in *Lady in the Lake*. It's only after Bogart has plastic surgery that the camera turns on his 'new' face. Lauren Bacall is as cool as ever as the girl who hides him from the authorities but Agnes

Moorehead, given an unusually glamorous role, overacts shrilly. The Bogart/Bacall scenes are a delight, though, even if they are underplayed compared to those they shared in *To Have and to Have Not*. This film is less of a partnership because Bogart is very much the star and very much in his element. Unusually for the time, the film was shot on location in San Francisco. It's a good yarn with enough twists and turns to keep you guessing.

Dark Victory ○ ⓥ
1939, US, 100 mins, b/w
Dir: Edmund Goulding
Stars: Bette Davis, George Brent, Humphrey Bogart, Geraldine Fitzgerald, Ronald Reagan
Rating: ★★★

A very superior soap opera which might almost have won its star, Bette Davis, her third Academy Award: she was nominated but lost to Vivien Leigh's Scarlett O'Hara in *Gone with the Wind*. This story of a society woman dying from a brain tumour, but offered a brief chance of happiness, was lovingly directed by Edmund Goulding, also Miss Davis' director on *That Certain Woman*, *The Old Maid* and *The Great Lie*.

Dark Waters ○
1944, US, 90 mins, b/w
Dir: Andre De Toth
Stars: Merle Oberon, Franchot Tone, Thomas Mitchell, Fay Bainter
Rating: ★★★

Deep in the bayou someone is menacing Merle Oberon, trying to drive her out of her mind, in this notable study in fear. John Qualen, Thomas Mitchell, Elisha Cook and Fay Bainter make a formidably grotesque quartet of conspirators and the stage management of the swampland scenes at night is splendid. Watch it in the dark to appreciate its full power.

Dark Wind, The ● ⓥ
1991, US, 112 mins, colour
Dir: Errol Morris
Stars: Lou Diamond Phillips, Gary Farmer, Fred Ward, Guy Boyd
Rating: ★★

This may be the first native American *film noir*. Slow to get going, this murky desert murder thriller has an unfathomable plot, and Lou Diamond Phillips as Jim Chee, a Navajo policeman who finds his dead-end assignment unexpectedly enlivened by

mysterious happenings in the night. A light aircraft is seemingly mis-guided into crashing. The pilot dies. A passenger is shot. A note is left in his mouth about a deal. And maybe a third party makes off. Investigating a local burglary which may in some way be connected, Chee finds himself warned off by his chief (Fred Ward) and roughed up by an FBI man (Guy Boyd) who seems to think Chee knows where the plane's vanished cargo went. When he thinks about it, Phillips does know too. There's another body, and things begin to fall into place a bit, although the odds are that no-one in the audience will know exactly what's going on. Exciting towards the end, this is slightly pretentious stuff, with soporific narration by Phillips, who's otherwise okay.

Darling ◐
1965, UK, 125 mins, b/w
Dir: John Schlesinger
Stars: Dirk Bogarde, Julie Christie, Laurence Harvey
Rating: ★★

The film that won Julie Christie an Oscar and established her as the spirit of the swinging Sixties now looks very outmoded. Even at the time it seemed crammed with clever-clever chat and 'in' dialogue, though the acting from Dirk Bogarde, Roland Curram and the misty Miss Christie was so brilliant it hardly appeared to matter. Time, however, has fortified the remark of one contemporary critic who observed that: 'The characters aren't noticeably human beings of the sort whom one might actually meet.' Christie, though, is still magnetic in her best screen performance as the girl who, trapped in a gilded cage of her own charms, drifts from one man to another gaining what she fondly calls 'experience'. It isn't difficult to see that this little social moth is destined to get her wings burned by the end.

Darling Lili ○
1969, US, 106 mins, colour
Dir: Blake Edwards
Stars: Julie Andrews, Rock Hudson, Jeremy Kemp
Rating: ★★

Rather underrated at the time of its initial release, when both Julie Andrews and Rock Hudson were beginning to lose their box-office magic, this is an entertaining war spoof with some tuneful music and Julie enjoining herself as a German spy. A bit long, but always good fun.

D.A.R.Y.L. ○ ⓥ
1985, US, 99 mins, colour
Dir: Simon Wincer
Stars: Barret Oliver, Mary Beth Hurt, Michael McKean, Colleen Campk, Josef Sommer, Kathryn Walker
Rating: ★★★

This lively fantasy adventure about a 'robot' boy, the product of artificial insemination and a computerised brain, is just like a Disney film of the Fifties with the addition of computers and scientific hardware. Escaping into the outside world with the help of a sympathetic and soon-despatched scientist, Daryl (nicely played by Barret Oliver) soon lands in the laps of foster-parents Mary Beth Hurt and Michael McKean. Their fondness for such a well-behaved boy is somewhat tempered by the fact that he doesn't seem to need their friendship and is ultra-good at everything from maths to baseball. Australian director Simon Wincer makes sure that the obvious possibilities of all this are as enjoyable as they should be, before science intervenes to retrieve its youthful project, and the film is able to slip a gear into the obvious, but equally enjoyable chase sequences for its final 20 minutes. Filmmaking by numbers, perhaps, but none the worse for that.

Date with Judy, A ○
1948, US, 113 mins, colour
Dir: Richard Thorpe
Stars: Jane Powell, Wallace Beery, Elizabeth Taylor, Robert Stack, Carment Miranda
Rating: ★★★

An MGM 'teen swing' musical that's the perfect mirror of its time, with teenagers bopping away to the music of Xavier Cugat and his Orchestra, and veteran screen tough-guy Wallace Beery doing an incredible rumba with Carmen Miranda. Elizabeth Taylor's singing voice is not, alas, her own, but Jane Powell's is, and she uses it delightfully.

Daughter of Rosie O'Grady, The ⊙
1950, US, 104 mins, colour
Dir: David Butler
Stars: June Haver, Gordon MacRae, Gene Nelson, Debbie Reynolds
Rating: ★★

A switch of studios for the O'Grady family. Rosie O'Grady's original exploits in *Sweet Rosie O'Grady* were made at 20th Century-Fox, but, although one-time Fox contractee June Haver replaces another Fox blonde musical star, Betty Grable, as leading lady, this sequel was made over at Warner Brothers. Haver gets formula Warners backing from Gordon MacRae, S Z Sakall, Debbie Reynolds and Gene Nelson (whose dancing steals the show) and there's a good selection of turn-of-the-century melodies.

Daughters Courageous ○
1939, US, 102 mins, b/w
Dir: Michael Curtiz
Stars: Claude Rains, John Garfield, Jeffrey Lynn, Fay Bainter, Priscilla Lane
Rating: ★★★

Something of a rehash of the previous year's *Four Daughters*, again with John Garfield, Claude Rains, the Lane sisters and Gale Page providing enough sincerity to cut through the sentiment. It couldn't be a sequel – as Garfield's character had been killed off at the end of the previous film (which itself would be remade in 1955 as *Young at Heart*). The film became known for a while for Garfield's novel approach to courting Priscilla Lane, eyeing her up and down and then saying 'Wanna buy me a beer?'

Dave ◑ ⓥ
1993, US, 110 mins, colour
Dir: Ivan Reitman
Stars: Kevin Kline, Sigourney Weaver, Frank Langella, Ben Kingsley, Charles Grodin, Ving Rhames
Rating: ★★★★

Director Ivan Reitman lives up to his name by getting everything right in this triumphant treatment of the old dual identity theme. Gary Ross's magic screenplay never puts a foot wrong in its development of the story of a presidential impersonator Dave (Kevin Kline) who runs a temp agency one moment, and the White House the next. Dave's ascendancy to the Oval office is the brainchild of chief of staff Frank Langella, who seems to have the nation's interests at heart when Dave's double, the Prez himself, has a stroke while bedding a White House secretary. The vice-president (Ben Kingsley) apparently has a screw loose, so it's Dave for the hot seat. You'd never think that Dave would fool his staff, never mind the first lady (Sigourney Weaver). But he has a double edge: he's polished his presidential act to studied perfection, and Weaver hates 'his' guts and want nothing to do with him. It soon turns out that Langella's the second biggest crook around after the old president, and has had Kingsley put out of the way on an eastern tour to further his plans to inherit the presidency for himself. It won't surprise you to find that things don't work out the way the bad guys expect, but you'll get constant pleasure from the way it's done.

David and Bathsheba ○
1951, US, 111 mins, colour
Dir: Henry King
Stars: Gregory Peck, Susan Hayward, Raymond Massey, Kieron Moore, James Robertson Justice
Rating: ★★

Good crowd scenes and costumes compensate for some casting weaknesses in this Hollywood slice of *The Bible*. But Gregory Peck is fine as King David, and Leon Shamroy's colour photography is another plus factor. King Saul is played by silent screen star Francis X Bushman (at the age of 68). Bushman is best remembered as the evil Messala in Fred Niblo's great 1926 silent version of *Ben Hur*. Watch also for the the girl performing an exotic dance. She's Gwyneth Verdon, who later, as Gwen Verdon, became a big musical star on Broadway, repeating her biggest hit on film – in *Damn Yankees*.

David Copperfield ⊙ ⓥ
1934, US, 130 mins, b/w
Dir: George Cukor
Stars: W C Fields, Freddie Bartholomew, Lionel Barrymore, Frank Lawton, Edna May Oliver, Roland Young
Rating: ★★★★

This masterfully-cast version of the Dickens classic remained the best example of the author's work on screen until the post-war British versions of *Great Expectations* and *Oliver Twist*. W C Fields (replacing an uneasily-cast Charles Laughton), Roland Young, Basil Rathbone and Edna May Oliver might have been born to play the roles of Micawber, Uriah Heep, Murdstone and Aunt Betsey Trotwood. Fields especially is quite brilliant (even though director George Cukor had to restrain him from working his traditional juggling into the role) and the young British actor Freddie Bartholomew is extremely appealing as the boy David. Co-screenwriter Hugh Walpole also plays a small cameo role as a clergyman.

D

David Copperfield ○
1970, UK, 110 mins, colour
Dir: Delbert Mann
Stars: Robin Phillips, Susan Hampshire, Laurence Olivier, Edith Evans, Michael Redgrave, Ralph Richardson
Rating: ★★

Originally produced for American TV, but shown in cinemas here, this is the most star-studded version of Dickens' famous novel yet made, with such stalwarts as Laurence Olivier and Richard Attenborough in minor roles. The most welcome performances come from Ralph Richardson (Micawber) and Edith Evans' definitive portrayal of Aunt Betsey Trotwood.

Davy ⊙
1957, UK, 85 mins, colour
Dir: Michael Relph
Stars: Harry Secombe, Bill Owen, Adele Leigh, Ron Randell, Susan Shaw, Alexander Knox
Rating: ★★

William Rose, who scripted entertainment is as diverse as *Genevieve* and *Guess Who's Coming to Dinner?*, wrote this comedy-musical as Harry Secombe's first big feature film. Secombe sings well, especially in company with Adele Leigh, and Joan Sims and Liz Fraser can be glimpsed as waitresses.

Davy Crockett and the River Pirates ⊙
1956, US, 81 mins, colour
Dir: Norman Foster
Stars: Fess Parker, Buddy Ebsen
Rating: ★★

Second Davy Crockett film is, like the first, spun together from two TV shows but none the worse for it. Vigorous, colourful fun, packed with action, including a tremendous free-for-all on board a sinking keel boat. Fess Parker again dons the coonskin cap as a virile Crockett.

Davy Crockett – King of the Wild Frontier ⊙
1954, US, 93 mins, colour
Dir: Norman Foster
Stars: Fess Parker, Buddy Ebsen
Rating: ★★★

Originally conceived as episodes for a television series, the Crockett project was quickly converted to a feature film (with a sequel to follow) when the Disney studio saw what a winner it had on its hands. Fess Parker, a taciturn, slow-spoken actor

with only minor film appearances to his credit, became a national figure with his presentation of the intrepid frontier scout as a powerful, determined figure, with a welcome wry wit. The action is presented in short, sharp episodes as colourful and explicit as a comic-book story. A handsome vigorous Western adventure.

Dawn at Socorro ○
1954, US, 79 mins, colour
Dir: George Sherman
Stars: Rory Calhoun, Piper Laurie, David Brian, Alex Nicol, Edgar Buchanan, Kathleen Hughes
Rating: ★★

Big, dramatic Western on the theme of the ace gunslinger who tries to hang up his holsters. Action and direction constantly come to the rescue of a rather poor screenplay (from which Piper Laurie suffers most), and the final shoot-out is staged with some imagination by director George Sherman.

Dawning, The ○ ⓥ
1988, UK, 97 mins, colour
Dir: Robert Knights
Stars: Anthony Hopkins, Rebecca Pidgeon, Jean Simmons, Trevor Howard, Hugh Grant
Rating: ★★★

Not a popular film in Britain in its time, dealing as it does with the gunning down of British officers by Irish terrorists, albeit in 1920. It is, however, a good one, photographed in crystal-clear colour and solidly crafted. Although not always gripping, it's well acted by a distinguished cast, plus Rebecca Pidgeon as the 18-year-old girl who befriends fugitive terrorist Anthony Hopkins. She certainly looked to have more talent than most actresses of her age, although in subsequent years her career has not progressed as it might have done. Jean Simmons has a telling tipsy scene in which she confesses to have been 'happy, calm and useless most of my life'.

Dawn Patrol, The ○
1938, US, 103 mins, b/w
Dir: Edmund Goulding
Stars: Errol Flynn, David Niven, Basil Rathbone
Rating: ★★★

This WW1 aviation drama, directed by Edmund Goulding, puts over its anti-war message with considerable

skill. A remake of Howard Hawks' 1930 version, it uses much of that film's aerial footage. Errol Flynn and David Niven are very good indeed in the roles taken in the original by Richard Barthelmess and Douglas Fairbanks Jr; and Basil Rathbone, playing the commander of a Royal Flying Corps squadron in 1914 France, gives one of his finest performances. The strong British cast includes Donald Crisp and Melville Cooper and Tony Gaudio's fine monochrome cinematography is exemplary.

Day at the Races, A ⊙ ⓥ
1937, US, 107 mins, b/w
Dir: Sam Wood
Stars: Groucho Marx, Chico Marx, Harpo Marx, Maureen O'Sullivan, Allan Jones, Margaret Dumont
Rating: ★★★

Vintage Marx Brothers comedy in which a failing sanatarium hires Dr Hackenbush (Groucho) to restore its flagging fortunes. Alas, Groucho is a horse doctor and sees no reason to change his treatments. 'The last patient I gave one of these,' he leers, brandishing an enormous pill, 'won the Kentucky Derby.' Groucho pursues Margaret Dumont – 'Marry me and I'll never look at any other horse'; Chico is devoted to Maureen O'Sullivan – 'If she wants a Hackenbush, she's gonna get a Hackenbush'; and Harpo plays Pied Piper with an enchanting group of black children (who include Dorothy Dandridge). All this and the 'tutsy fruitsy' ice cream routine too.

Daydreamer, The ⊙
1966, US, 98 mins, colour
Dir: Jules Bass
Stars: Cyril Ritchard, Paul O'Keefe
Rating: ★★★

Charming Hans Christian Andersen musical which combines live action with puppet animation, with very entertaining results. The 'voice cast' includes such well-known film names as Boris Karloff, Tallulah Bankhead, Burl Ives, Hayley Mills and Terry-Thomas.

Day of the Badman ○
1958, US, 81 mins, colour
Dir: Harry Keller
Stars: Fred MacMurray, Joan Weldon, John Ericson, Robert Middleton
Rating: ★★

Well-acted, skilfully-mounted Western, with Fred MacMurray turning in yet another reliably good performance as the frontier judge who loses his girlfriend to a coward. Oily Robert Middleton is the villain.

Day of the Dolphin, The ○ ⓥ
1973, US, 104 mins, colour
Dir: Mike Nichols
Stars: George C Scott, Trish Van Devere, Paul Sorvino
Rating: ★★

Despite George C Scott's convincing portrayal of a marine biologist, this is a cumbersome mixture of science-fiction, spy thriller and heavy-handed comedy. The political misuse of talking dolphins seems an odd choice of subject for writer Buck Henry and director Mike Nichols (the team responsible for *The Graduate* and *Catch-22*) and the film comes alive only in the underwater sequences, superbly photographed by William A Fraker.

Day of the Evil Gun ○
1968, US, 93 mins, colour
Dir: Jerry Thorpe
Stars: Glenn Ford, Arthur Kennedy, Dean Jagger
Rating: ★★

Downbeat Western about two men in love with the same woman, forced to band together when she is kidnapped by Indians. Glenn Ford and Arthur Kennedy build up a tense relationship, and a stout supporting cast includes Dean Jagger and John Anderson.

Day of the Jackal, The ◑ ⓥ
1973, UK/France, 142 mins, colour
Dir: Fred Zinnemann
Stars: Edward Fox, Michael Lonsdale, Alan Badel, Tony Britton, Cyril Cusack, Delphine Seyrig
Rating: ★★★

Director Fred Zinnemann's otherwise excellent and highly successful version of Frederick Forsyth's best-selling novel has just two intrinsic weaknesses. One is that the leading character, an ace assassin, is so passionless that any audience would have difficulty in identifying with him (despite Edward Fox's fine performance) through his many hair-raising adventures. The other is that the ultimate outcome is inevitable, since the assassin's target is General de Gaulle. Zinnemann's strategy is to

counter these deficiencies by cramming his plot with as much incident as possible to keep it buzzing. Thus the police manhunt for the Jackal is counterpointed by his own immaculate and sometimes frighteningly unemotional preparations. And the director's final triumph is that the climax really will have you on the edge of your seat, forgetting even that the target must survive. Fox's authoritative portrayal is solidly backed by an international cast, in which Franco-British actor Michael Lonsdale is outstanding as his chief pursuer.

Day of the Locust, The ●
1974, US, 145 mins, colour
Dir: John Schlesinger
Stars: Donald Sutherland, Karen Black, Burgess Meredith, William Atherton, Geraldine Page
Rating: ★★

A daddy longlegs of a film, sprawling all over its story of life at the wrong end of Hollywood in the late Thirties, and finally finding its *raison d'etre* in a long and bloody riot scene at the end. William Atherton, then a fresh-faced newcomer, has the role on which all the action turns, as the young sketch artist who moves in with an old vaudevillian turned drunken salesman (Burgess Meredith) and his silly, virginal daughter (Karen Black). Director John Schlesinger lovingly recreates the period (as he was to do with *Yanks*), much of it in soft focus, intending to lend a glow of nostalgia to this adaptation of the bestseller by Nathanael West, but neglecting the most important element of all: discipline.

Day of the Triffids, The ◑
1962, UK, 95 mins, colour
Dir: Steve Sekely
Stars: Howard Keel, Kieron Moore, Janette Scott
Rating: ★★

John Wyndham's powerful, doomy novels, mainly about human beings caught up in events outside their natural experience, have translated better on the whole to radio than to the visual media. This is one of the best known of his stories and the only surprise was that no one had filmed it before (it was written in 1946). The director is Hungarian Steve Sekely, who made many low-budget thrillers in the Hollywood of the Forties. This is probably his best film, with some quite frightening sequences.

Days of Heaven ○ ⓥ
1978, US, 95 mins, colour
Dir: Terrence Malick
Stars: Richard Gere, Brooke Adams, Sam Shepard, Linda Manz
Rating: ★★

A ravishingly shot (by Nestor Almendros) story of immigrants to the Texas Panhandle in 1916. Director Terrence Malick really captures the feeling of time and place, although he fails to build up the story's relationships well enough to sustain his own obvious ambitions, despite charismatic acting by Richard Gere, Linda Manz and Sam Shepard. But it was no surprise on Oscar night when Almendros stepped up to receive his well-deserved Academy Award.

Days of Thunder ◑ ⓥ
1990, US, 107 mins, colour
Dir: Tony Scott
Stars: Tom Cruise, Nicole Kidman, Robert Duvall, Randy Quaid, Michael Rooker, Cary Elwes
Rating: ★★

Or: Top Car. This noisy popcorn movie has the same director (Tony Scott) and star (Tom Cruise) as the mindless mega-hit *Top Gun* but, instead of jets, our ears are assaulted by the roar of stock car engines. This is a peculiarly American form of racing where it seems the object is to push the other driver into the wall and where the race is stopped every few minutes for fresh tyres, with the drivers resuming the race in the same positions. Developments on the track remain predictable (down to the final freeze frame), but somewhat less than credible, as cocky young driver Cruise sets out to grab his share of stock car glory. 'I'm more afraid of bein' nothin' than I am of bein' hurt,' he tells his girlfriend, brain surgeon Nicole Kidman, whose (unsuccessful) attempts to conceal her Australian accent damage her performance. Cruise's rivals include another 'ice-man' in cool Russ (Cary Elwes) and Rowdy (Michael Rooker), a bozo who crashes, giving Cruise the one good line in the film: 'Any surgery around his brain is bound to be minor.'

Days of Wine and Roses ◑
1962, US, 117 mins, b/w
Dir: Blake Edwards
Stars: Jack Lemmon, Lee Remick, Charles Bickford, Jack Klugman
Rating: ★★★

D

The title song, sung by Andy Williams, earned an Oscar, but lent a rather misleading rosy glow to this study of alcoholism that was very direct and uncompromising (and almost unpalatable) for its time. Jack Lemmon, then still best known for his comic roles, and Lee Remick are uncomfortably convincing as the couple on a downward spiral into oblivion. Made by director Blake Edwards in the middle of his best period.

Day the Earth Caught Fire, The ●

1961, UK, 99 mins, b/w
Dir: Val Guest
Stars: Janet Munro, Leo McKern, Edward Judd
Rating: ★★★

Unbearably tense and uncomfortably realistic science-fiction thriller, directed (and co-written) by Val Guest in the middle of his most productive period. Guest builds his suspense flawlessly, as the population of Europe wilts under tropical temperatures-plus, and two diligent journalists uncover alarming reasons behind it all. Well worth stopping in for. Spot, if you can, the young Michael Caine as a policeman.

Day the Earth Stood Still, The ○ Ⓥ

1951, US, 90 mins, b/w
Dir: Robert Wise
Stars: Michael Rennie, Patricia Neal, Hugh Marlowe, Sam Jaffe
Rating: ★★★★

As relevant now as on the day of its release, this landmark science-fiction film delivers its anti-nuclear message with dignity and restraint. Edmund H North's literate script is performed beautifully by an excellent cast led by Michael Rennie as the Christ-like alien, and Patricia Neal, enormously affecting as the proprietress of the boarding house in which Rennie seeks shelter. There's much else to savour in this Hollywood classic, from Robert Wise's superbly controlled direction and Bernard Herrmann's haunting score to the imposing presence of Rennie's giant robot companion Gort. Not only did 'Klaatu barada nikto!' become a cult catch-phrase in the Fifties (see the film to find out why) but it was this movie's portrayal of an alien race as benign emissaries – rather than as the monstrous mutant war-mongerers that were the norm – which had such a

profound effect on a young man called Steven Spielberg, who grew up to make his own famous films about kindly extra-terrestrials.

Dead, The ○ Ⓥ

1987, UK, 82 mins, colour
Dir: John Huston
Stars: Anjelica Huston, Donal McCann, Dan O'Herlihy, Donal Donnelly, Marie Kean
Rating: ★★★

John Huston's last film could be termed an Irish indulgence. But it gives us a chance to hear some of James Joyce's most penetrating prose, spoken by people who know what it's all about. Thus Anjelica Huston and Donal McCann give full value, and get our total attention, from their big speeches at the end, while allowing Donal Donnelly (taking over Jack MacGowran's niche as the dishevelled Irishman) and Dan O'Herlihy to steal the major part of the film as the drunken revellers at an annual Dublin feast at the home of spinster sisters in the winter of 1904. Despite occasional sags, the piece remains a little hymn to nostalgic memories, and a fitting climax to the cinematic career of such an avowed Hibernophile.

Dead Again ● Ⓥ

1991, US, 105 mins, colour
Dir: Kenneth Branagh
Stars: Kenneth Branagh, Emma Thompson, Andy Garcia, Derek Jacobi, Hanna Schygulla
Rating: ★

For those who have their doubts about Kenneth Branagh's talents, this ludicrous thriller provides further ammunition. To start with, the title should have a question mark after it. Is Emma Thompson really going to meet the same fate at the end of this life as she did in the last? She's an amnesiac given into the charge of detective Mike Church (Branagh) and seems to be having nightmares about her past life. Hypnotist Derek Jacobi appears from nowhere to take her back into a past that involves a composer murdering his wife with scissors, a scenario that Branagh soon establishes happened 40 years before. It gets a lot sillier.

Dead Bang ● Ⓥ

1989, US, 108 mins, colour
Dir: John Frankenheimer
Stars: Don Johnson, Penelope Ann Miller, William Forsythe, Bob Balaban
Rating: ★★

It's always a flaw of the James Bond movies that the bad guys never kill 007 off when they have him dead to rights. The flaw becomes a gaping hole in this otherwise proficient thriller. The villains – American white supremists – who gun everyone else down in the blink of an eye, have hero Don Johnson looking down a gun barrel on several separate occasions, but they never pull the trigger. Johnson himself, a man who transforms his face when he smiles, is well at home as an LA cop, battling alcoholism and summonses from his ex-wife, who rides roughshod over prissier associates when he becomes involved in a case of cop-killing that escalates into an inter-state hunt. The film's 'surprise' at the end should be guessed at an early stage by fans of these hard-boiled thrillers, though they'll be highly satisfied by the vividly staged underground shootout.

Dead Calm ● Ⓥ

1988, Australia, 96 mins, colour
Dir: Phillip Noyce
Stars: Sam Neill, Nicole Kidman, Billy Zane
Rating: ★★★

Director Phillip Noyce takes three actors, two boats, a dog and an ocean and conjures up some spine-tingling suspense and plenty of shocks. Events take a turn for the worse when Sam Neill and Nicole Kidman encounter psycopath Billy Zane while in the middle of the Pacific Ocean. The happily married couple get separated and the unstable young killer sets to work terrorizing Kidman on her yacht. True, there are several moments that defy belief, when Kidman could escape her ordeal, but Noyce does a good job of keeping the pace and tension cranked up. The screenplay was based on the same Charles Williams novel that Orson Welles used for his never-completed film *The Deep.*

Dead Can't Lie, The ● Ⓥ

1988, US, 97 mins, colour
Dir: Lloyd Fonvielle
Stars: Tommy Lee Jones, Virginia Madsen, Colin Bruce, Frederic Forrest
Rating: ★★

This modern *film noir* is the kind of movie that book compilers give 2½ stars to because they don't quite know what to make of it. It's strange, almost ludicrous, but never quite of a kind and that's for sure. Tommy Lee Jones is a run-down private eye who's hired by a (literally) haunted man to find the ghost of his dead wife (she's been trailing him) and buy her off with the jewels he stole from her grave. At least, I think this is what happens. No mistaking what happens when Jones meets steamy Virginia Madsen and can't believe she's a ghost. The poor sap falls heavily. Then he finds out the truth . . . but is it the whole truth? Although you may not understand it all, there's lots of emotional power in the exchanges between Jones and a voluptuous Madsen – shot by the director in tight, glossy closeup (it was originally made for cable TV) with dark backgrounds. 'And you had the best of her,' she whispers, 'all the best of her.' But does he? Even though this one loses its drive three-quarters of the way through, it remains different. And Jones and Madsen *are* both good. How do I rate it? Oh, say 2½ stars.

Dead Cert O
1974, UK, 99 mins, colour
Dir: Tony Richardson
Stars: Scott Antony, Judi Dench, Michael Williams
Rating: ★

The career of British director Tony Richardson went off the boil after early success with *The Entertainer, Look Back in Anger, A Taste of Honey, The Loneliness of the Long-Distance Runner* and *Tom Jones,* for which he won a well-deserved Oscar in 1963. This murder-thriller set against the world of horse-racing came a decade later and is decidedly inferior work. Despite the fact that the film is based on a cracking good novel by Dick Francis and the production team went to the trouble of staging its own Grand National race, it is a plodding affair that lurches from drama to crisis instead of building momentum to a gripping climax. One amusing continuity slip that will tickle racing fans: Lord Oaksey is listed on the number-board as riding in a race, is simultaneously heard giving the race commentary, then pops up only minutes later in a small, uncredited role as a racecourse vet.

Dead End O
1937, US, 93 mins, b/w
Dir: William Wyler
Stars: Joel McCrea, Sylvia Sidney, Humphrey Bogart
Rating: ★★★

William Wyler's strong film about ghetto life in the America of the Thirties is rather obviously studio-set, but sparks to life with the appearance of Humphrey Bogart as a gangster who's a hero to the local youngsters, a group of teenagers who later made films as the Dead End Kids, the East Side Kids and the Bowery Boys.

Deadfall ①
1968, UK, 120 mins, colour
Dir: Bryan Forbes
Stars: Michael Caine, Giovanna Ralli, Eric Portman, Nanette Newman
Rating: ★★

Michael Caine is a master jewel thief in a Bryan Forbes thriller. Best sequence: Caine bringing off a daring cat burglary at great risk to life and limb, intercut with clips from the concert attended by the owners of the house he is robbing. Otherwise, the thrills are undernourished.

Deadlier Than the Male O
1966, UK, 101 mins, colour
Dir: Ralph Thomas
Stars: Richard Johnson, Elke Sommer, Sylva Koscina, Nigel Green
Rating: ★★

Bulldog Drummond updated to the Bond era. Richard Johnson makes a brave attempt to keep up with Sapper's original concept of the character, amid a mass of hardly-clad girls and exploding gadgets. Drummond has two formidable female adversaries in the shapes of Elke Sommer and Sylva Koscina in a violent thriller whose best moments come in a human chess game between Drummond and his arch-enemy Petersen, played in sinister style by Nigel Green. Collaborating on the screenplay is Jimmy Sangster, most famed as a specialist in horror-film scripts for Hammer.

Deadly Advice ● ⓥ
1993, UK, 97 mins, colour
Dir: Mandie Fletcher
Stars: Jane Horrocks, Brenda Fricker, Imedla Staunton, John Mills, Edward Woodward, Billie Whitelaw
Rating: ★★

A mildly amusing black comedy about a repressed Welsh librarian (didn't Peter Sellers once play one of those?) who, rebelling against her nearest and dearest, receives help in bumping them off from the ghosts of some of Britain's most famous murderers. Jane Horrocks, fast developing into a latter-day Rita Tushingham, plays this lethal lady, beset at the outset by an impossibly puritan mother (Brenda Fricker), who even drags her out of the local pub at lunchtime (what she's doing there herself is anyone's guess). Mummy clearly has to go and, though Jane's asthmatic, secretly scarlet sister (Imelda Staunton) helps her dump the corpse in the river, she's soon jealous of the attention her bisexual Chippendale boyfriend is giving Jane, and threatens to turn her in . . . Where will it all end? Horrocks is quite beguiling and Ian Abbey (the only convincing Welsh accent) excellent as the male stripper. But it's rather a raucous film with little room for subtlety. Not bad, though, in a sub-Ealing manner.

Deadly Affair, The ①
1966, UK, 107 mins, colour
Dir: Sidney Lumet
Stars: James Mason, Simone Signoret, Harriet Andersson, Maximilian Schell
Rating: ★★★★

Downbeat but totally absorbing espionage drama in typical John Le Carre style. The impressive low-key photography of Freddie Young sets the mood of bleakness, blackness and danger into which hard-pressed security agent James Mason must probe. He's out to break an espionage ring that lies behind a murder that most people thought was suicide. Director Sidney Lumet offers set pieces of nail-biting excitement.

Deadly Game, The
See: *Third Party Risk*

Deadly Is the Female
See: *Gun Crazy*

Deadly Pursuit ①
(aka: *Shoot to Kill*)
1988, US, 110 mins, colour
Dir: Roger Spottiswoode
Stars: Sidney Poitier, Tom Berenger, Kirstie Alley
Rating: ★★★

A picturesquely-shot chase thriller that runs like a high-class TV movie. A maniac has mercilessly killed a ransom victim after his demands have been met, and must be tracked down by a city-wise law enforcer (Sidney Poitier) and a mountain guide (Tom Berenger). Meanwhile the killer, identity unknown, joins an adventure tour planning to seize its guide (Kirstie Alley) and force her to take him to Canada. Packed with as much taut action as the plot will allow, but let down by silly situations, the film draws

D

gasps and giggles in about equal number. Poitier, looking scarcely older on his return to acting after 10 years away, gives a majestic performance as the obsessed FBI agent. And the script does have a few much-appreciated amusing lines. 'Maybe we could give it some food,' mutters Poitier, as he and Berenger face a grizzly bear up in the mountains. Berenger gives him a quick but withering glance. 'We *are* the food,' he replies.

Dead Men Don't Wear Plaid ○ ⓥ

1981, US, 95 mins, b/w
Dir: Carl Reiner
Stars: Steve Martin, Rachel Ward, Reni Santoni, Carl Reiner
Rating: ★★★★

This supremely funny and inventive parody of the *film noir* thrillers of the Forties has a gimmick: director Carl Reiner has edited into his story a series of carefully chosen clips from Hollywood films of the period. Steve Martin (never before as likeable as this) is the detective trying to solve what must be the most baffling case any Chandleresque private eye can have faced. Around every corner of the twisted trail await (literally) Alan Ladd, Bette Davis, James Cagney, Barbara Stanwyck and more. The plot vaguely concerns Nazis on a South American island but don't listen to a word of it. Wallow instead in the splendid pastiche music by Miklos Rosza, the costumes of Edith Head (her last film work) and the use of Humphrey Bogart as the hero's confidant and leg-man. Rachel Ward has bags of class as femme fatale Juliet and the script displays a delightfully zany sense of humour.

Dead of Night ◑

1945, UK, 95 mins, b/w
Dir: Alberto Cavalcanti, Robert Hamer, Basil Dearden, Charles Crichton
Stars: Mervyn Johns, Michael Redgrave, Googie Withers, Sally Ann Howes
Rating: ★★★★

Mervyn Johns' finest film: a must for chiller addicts and still revered as the greatest piece of ghost-story telling ever to come from the British cinema. Its *piece de resistance* is the final story, in which Michael Redgrave unnervingly plays a ventriloquist who appears to be exchanging personalities with his demonic dummy, Hugo. But the final scene is, in its unsettling way, more frightening than many of the tales

told to Johns by the inhabitants of a dark old cottage, most of which reach shattering climaxes thanks to knife-edge direction by Robert Hamer, Basil Dearden and Alberto Cavalcanti. A story directed by Charles Crichton, intended as comic relief, is somewhat less successful.

Dead or Alive ◑

1968, Italy/US, 89 mins, colour
Dir: Franco Giraldi
Stars: Alex Cord, Robert Ryan, Arthur Kennedy, Nicoletta Macchiavelli
Rating: ★★

This spaghetti Western is better than most, and certainly better-paced than the 'Dollars' films it followed. The ending might be rather too bitterly ironic for most tastes, but Alex Cord gives one of his best performances as the bounty hunter, and the whole thing has a downbeat flavour which suits its mood very well.

Dead Poets Society ○ ⓥ

1989, US, 126 mins, colour
Dir: Peter Weir
Stars: Robin Williams, Robert Sean Leonard, Ethan Hawke, Josh Charles, Norman Lloyd
Rating: ★★

Undermined by a series of improbabilities, this is a nonetheless often emotive film showcasing the considerable talents of Robin Williams as an innovative and eccentric English teacher arriving at a stuffy and expensive public school in Vermont. Indeed so extraordinary and incendiary are his methods – his subject is life, the English is incidental – that you wonder how teacher and school ever accepted each other in the first place. Nor is it easy for us to accept parents who react to their son's brilliance on stage by packing him off to a military academy. And would any teacher be allowed to rip up textbooks and parade his class around various corners of the school? An unlikely story, though you may think Williams' engaging personality sufficiently forceful to put it across. The performances are uniformly good, from Williams and his septet of poetry students to Norman Lloyd (once Hitchcock's 'Saboteur', falling from the Statue of Liberty) as the martinet headmaster who seeks to protect not the truth but the good name of the school.

Dead Pool, The ● ⓥ

1988, US, 91 mins, colour
Dir: Buddy Van Horn
Stars: Clint Eastwood, Patricia Clarkson, Liam Neeson
Rating: ★★

Dead in the water might be a better description of this fifth *Dirty Harry* cop thriller for Clint Eastwood. At least the blame can be shifted from the star to writer Steve Sharon and director Buddy Van Horn, who also put Clint through his paces in *Any Which Way You Can*. The villains always pause long enough to allow Clint to unholster his .44 Magnum, utter a witty one-liner and despatch them to oblivion. But Liam Neeson (with the strangest accent ever) as a film company boss who is supposed to be the No1 suspect isn't the remotest bit suspicious. The one stand-out scene that'll have you on the edge of your seat comes when the killer sends a bomb onto the streets of San Francisco strapped to a remote control toy car. This time, Clint fails to make anyone's day. For diehard fans only.

Dead Reckoning ○

1946, US, 97 mins, b/w
Dir: John Cromwell
Stars: Humphrey Bogart, Lizabeth Scott
Rating: ★★★

One of Humphrey Bogart's more successful ventures outside the walls of Warner Studios, not least because it gave him a strong vis-a-vis in the sultry shape of Lizabeth Scott (on loan from across the way at Paramount). Investigating the disappearance of an army pal, Bogart's character becomes both the hunter and the hunted as director John Cromwell creates a web of intrigue seen through low-key lighting and unusual camera angles. Both the characters and the plot are tough and tender at the same time, in this too-seldom-seen thriller.

Dead Ringers ● ⓥ

1988, Canada, 118 mins, colour
Dir: David Cronenberg
Stars: Jeremy Irons, Genevieve Bujold, Heidi von Palleske
Rating: ★

Preposterous, humourless psycho-horror (supposedly based on a true story!) from director David Cronenberg that represents a sad come-down for the Canadian schlock-horror director after the dizzy heights of *The Fly*. Although well-performed in a dual role by

Jeremy Irons, who stands alone in keeping unintentional mirth at bay for three-quarters of the plot, the film's unconvincing script and lack of light and shade eventually does for it more effectively than could be managed by either of Irons' twin surgeons, the battier of whom (by a whisker) craves to create steel implements for operating on mutant women (really!). All the elements that have kept laughter at bay in previous Cronenberg gore-feasts seem to desert him at once here. And most of all, few will care about the fates of any of the characters involved in this ludicrous and deeply unpleasant farrago.

Dead Zone, The ● ⓥ
1983, US, 90 mins, colour
Dir: David Cronenberg
Stars: Christopher Walken, Brooke Adams, Tom Skerritt, Herbert Lom, Anthony Zerbe, Martin Sheen
Rating: ★★★

Christopher Walken is a car crash victim who wakes from a five-year coma to find that he has strange psychic powers and can see into the future, in this gripping psychological thriller based on Stephen King's best-selling novel. By simply touching hands with someone, he can see their fate and this ability helps him rescue a child from a burning house and solve a series of murders. But then he realises he has the power to change the future. When he presses palms with cynical politician Martin Sheen, he realises Sheen, as president of the US, is capable of pushing the button. Without doubt, this is the most faithful screen adaption of a King story. Having said that, it gets bogged down a bit in the middle with the murder mystery, but picks up again in the final third and there's a nice twist at the climax. Walken, always seemingly a man on the edge, is well cast as the central character and there are fine performances from Sheen, Herbert Lom and Anthony Zerbe.

Dear Brigitte ○
1965, US, 100 mins, colour
Dir: Henry Koster
Stars: James Stewart, Glynis Johns, Fabian, Billy Mumy, Brigitte Bardot
Rating: ★★

Made by James Stewart in his 'family comedy' period of the early Sixties, this farce, about a literary-minded professor with a mathematical genius called Erasmus for a son, has some screamingly funny moments. Best of

these is when Erasmus, asked to divide one prodigious number by another, solemnly pronounces that it won't go. Nothing daunted, the scientists feed the problem into their computer which gets a nasty case of the tilts.

Dear Heart ○
1965, US, 114 mins, b/w
Dir: Delbert Mann
Stars: Glenn Ford, Geraldine Page, Angela Lansbury
Rating: ★★★

Warm, old-fashioned, genuine sort of film, about two middle-aged people who almost miss their chance of happiness together, because time has sapped their confidence in love, and made them want to settle for security. Glenn Ford and Geraldine Page play it so well together that, even though we've seen it all before, the old story still works. The old-time atmosphere is heightened by the appearance of Alice Pearce, memorable as the toothy spinster miss with the braying voice in *On the Town*. In *Dear Heart* she plays . . . a spinster miss.

Dear Mr Prohack ○
1949, UK, 91 mins, b/w
Dir: Thornton Freeland
Stars: Cecil Parker, Hermione Baddeley, Glynis Johns, Dirk Bogarde, Sheila Sim
Rating: ★★

An adaptation of a story by Arnold Bennett, this comedy features Cecil Parker in one of his best performances as a Treasury official who comes into a fortune, but has less success with his own finances than those of the nation. The supporting cast is very strong, including such names as Denholm Elliott, Henry Edwards, Frederick Valk, James Hayter, Ian Carmichael and Bryan Forbes, later to become a director. The amusing central situation gradually wears thin.

Dear Murderer ○
1947, UK, 94 mins, b/w
Dir: Arthur Crabtree
Stars: Eric Portman, Greta Gynt, Dennis Price, Maxwell Reed, Jack Warner
Rating: ★★★

What a revelation Oslo-born blonde glamour girl Greta Gynt was in this complex and grim crime melodrama from the Gainsborough studio. And her thrilling performance as a footloose wife whose lovers pay the ultimate price at the hands of her husband was more than matched by Eric Portman as her jealous, murder-

ous spouse. In fact, every one of the unpleasant characters get their just desserts in the intelligent script by the ever-reliable team of Muriel and Sydney Box and Peter Rogers, the latter of whom would later mine a lucrative vein with the *Carry On* comedy films.

Dear Wife ○
1949, US, 87 mins, b/w
Dir: Richard Haydn
Stars: William Holden, Joan Caulfield, Mona Freeman
Rating: ★★

Continuing the lighthearted saga of Bill and his Ruth, begun in an earlier film, *Dear Ruth* (and continued later in *Dear Brat*). Here, as in the later film, the spotlight is on Ruth's tomboy teenage sister Miriam, played by pretty Mona Freeman. What a change of pace this was for William Holden. The following year he started a film dead, shot and drowned, in a swimming-pool, in *Sunset Boulevard*.

Death at Broadcasting House ○
1934, UK, 71 mins, b/w
Dir: Reginald Denham
Stars: Ian Hunter, Austin Trevor, Jack Hawkins
Rating: ★★★

Advanced photography techniques help make the studios of the BBC appropriately sinister as ham actor Donald Wolfit 'gets his' in this early British whodunnit with a starry list of suspects and intriguing glimpses of popular radio personalities of the time. You're unlikely to spot the killer.

Death Becomes Her ◑ ⓥ
1992, US, 103 mins, colour
Dir: Robert Zemeckis
Stars: Meryl Streep, Goldie Hawn, Bruce Willis, Isabella Rossellini
Rating: ★★★

A triumph of prosthetic, state-of-the-art effects over a *Man from UNCLE*-style plot, this is the story of a potion that restores eternal youth – at a price (in more ways than one). Meryl Streep is every inch the glamour-puss Broadway star, who feels age gripping her by the throat when she sees dowdy Goldie Hawn, from whom she had stolen plastic surgeon Bruce Willis, looking exquisite at 50. She rushes off to mystery woman Isabella Rossellini, who walks around in nothing much but who claims to be 71. Offered The Potion, the dispirited

D

and dilapidated Meryl coughs up and becomes young again. But Goldie, having re-entered the picture, is intent on enlisting Willis, now sunk to embalming, into her plan to bump the long-hated Meryl off. This is a cue for a whole barrage of special effects which have already started when Goldie blows up to 20 stone after Willis has deserted her. Heads swivel on limbs, limbs stick out at awkward angles but still function, and — in an FX man's masterstroke — a see-through hole can be made in the middle of a body. The pace is a bit slow sometimes for a comedy, but there's always the next effect to look forward to.

Death Hunt ◑

1981, US, 97 mins, colour
Dir: Peter Hunt
Stars: Charles Bronson, Lee Marvin, Angie Dickinson, Carl Weathers, Ed Lauter
Rating: ★★

A glacial Western, with Charles Bronson as the man on the run across the Arctic and Lee Marvin as the battle-weary Mountie who always get his man. Various stereotypes around them are quite well presented by director Peter Hunt to spice the plot. There's Angie Dickinson as the woman who turns up for little apparent reason except to wait for Marvin; Carl Weathers — Apollo Creed from the Rocky films — as the Mountie's (obviously expendable) right-hand man; Ed Lauter, smiling and sneering in the same gesture as the real bad guy responsible for Bronson's plight; and Andrew Stevens as the obligatory rookie constable undergoing his baptism of fire.

Death in Venice ◑

1971, Italy, 130 mins, colour
Dir: Luchino Visconti
Stars: Dirk Bogarde, Silvana Mangano, Bjorn Andresen, Marisa Berenson
Rating: ★★★

This elegant and beautiful story about an ageing composer's unrequited passion for a young boy, set against the crumbling decadence of pre-Great War Venice, has a dark side, with the threat of disease cutting through the city. It also has a very fine central performance from Dirk Bogarde, whose obsession with the 14-year-old boy and the embodiment of beauty he represents, threatens to overwhelm him. Director Luchino Visconti has lovingly transferred Thomas Mann's

haunting novel to the screen but although visually stunning, it is ultimately rather empty. The story only really has enough strength to take up an hour of screen time at most so the film's pace is leisurely at best. Although he sticks pretty faithfully to the book, Visconti has proved that, despite the best efforts of a master, not all fine novels will make great films. Nevertheless, the film has much to commend it and will amply reward those patient enough to accept the story's slow unfolding.

Death on the Nile ○ Ⓥ

1978, UK, 140 mins, colour
Dir: John Guillermin
Stars: Peter Ustinov, Bette Davis, David Niven, Mia Farrow, Angela Lansbury, Maggie Smith
Rating: ★★★

It was to be expected after the success of *Murder on the Orient Express* that the same production team would launch a whole series of sleuthing films based on Agatha Christie stories. And the setting could not be grander than the temples and pyramids of the Nile, where love, lust, revenge and murder sit well with centuries-old curses and mysticism. Peter Ustinov takes over from Albert Finney as the rotund Belgian detective, Hercule Poirot, but the case of murder aboard a Nile cruise ship doesn't tax his 'little grey cells' too much. This overlong film will, however, tax your patience as the final scenes are taken up with endless re-runs of the crime from the viewpoint of everyone on board. Even so, there are a number of individual performances to enjoy, notably those of Mia Farrow, Bette Davis, Angela Lansbury and (especially) Maggie Smith. Antony Powell's gorgeous costumes rightly won an Oscar, and the main music theme by Nino Rota is excellent.

Death Race 2000 ◑ Ⓥ

1975, US, 90 mins, colour
Dir: Paul Bartel
Stars: David Carradine, Simone Griffeth, Sylvester Stallone
Rating: ★★

A truly anarchic, blow-them-all-to-bits fantasy caper that fires on all cylinders except the script. The cars are hot, the acting's not, though you may enjoy a pre-Rocky Sylvester Stallone as a competitor called Machine Gun Joe Viterbo. The violence

of the action leaves the Road Runner and Wile E Coyote with more than a little to answer for.

Death Ship ●

1979, Canada, 90 mins, colour
Dir: Alvin Rakoff
Stars: George Kennedy, Richard Crenna, Nick Mancuso
Rating: ★

The characters in this ingenious horror film do such silly things that your sympathies may well be with the mysterious black ship (with a lifeforce of its own) that seems to be trying to bump them off. A star studded cast seems to do its best to manoeuvre its members into situations least likely to ensure their survival. It's a familiar Hollywood horror framework, although in this case both the film and its director (Alvin Rakoff) are Canadian.

Death Takes a Holiday ○

1934, US, 78 mins, b/w
Dir: Mitchell Leisen
Stars: Fredric March, Evelyn Venable
Rating: ★★★

An absorbing, well-played film drama based on a play by Italian Alberto Casella. Fredric March is outstanding as Prince Sirki, alias Death. It is stylish and dreamlike, but a bit slow even in its brief running time.

Deathtrap ◑ Ⓥ

1982, US/UK, 112 mins, colour
Dir: Sidney Lumet
Stars: Michael Caine, Christopher Reeve, Dyan Cannon
Rating: ★★★

Even an improvement on the long-running play, this spine-chilling charade has good performances from Dyan Cannon, Christopher Reeve and especially Michael Caine, as the once wildly-popular playwright fallen on hard times whose eyes light up when he receives a superb new play from an untried writer through the post. From here on in the plot merely trifles with its audience, deliberately changing course so often that you are finally unprepared to accept anything at face value and conditioned to expect the unexpected. No plot of one of the protagonists can be certain of success, no corpse guaranteed dead. It is, of course, all too far-fetched to have anything to do with real life, but simply what the French call a *divertissement*; very ingeniously, writer Jay Presson Allen (from Ira Levin's play) has diverted us too.

Death Wheelers, The
See: Psychomania

Death Wish ● ⓥ
1974, US, 89 mins, colour
Dir: Michael Winner
Stars: Charles Bronson, Hope Lange, Vincent Gardenia
Rating: ★★★

It's getting so that a mugger's not safe on the streets of New York any more. Especially so when Charles Bronson is the one-man vigilante committee who cuts the city's hoodlum population down to size after three of them have killed his wife (Hope Lange) and reduced his daughter (Kathleen Tolan) to a living vegetable. A variable script is heftily combatted by skilful action scenes and good night-time photography on city streets. It's certainly exciting, though the morality may be questionable, even in this day and age. The public were clearly on the vigilante's side, and made the film a big hit: small wonder that Bronson subsequently made four further *Death Wish* films, all of them inferior.

Death Wish 2 ● ⓥ
1981, US, 93 mins, colour
Dir: Michael Winner
Stars: Charles Bronson, Jill Ireland, Vincent Gardenia
Rating: ★

Nothing succeeds like excess, it seems, as Charles Bronson reprises his role as the vigilante architect, bumping off every mugger in sight in Los Angeles, having already laid waste to the ungodly in New York in the first of the crime thrillers, which Michael Winner also directed. And with a cast list that contains such characters as Stomper, Punkcut and Cutter it's very much the recipe as before (and after). Winner went to make his third *Death Wish*, before other hands took over the directorial reins for further entries.

Death Wish 4: The Crackdown ● ⓥ
1987, US, 96 mins, colour
Dir: J Lee Thompson
Stars: Charles Bronson, Kay Lenz, John P Ryan, Perry Lopez

Once a vigilante, always a vigilante. Charles Bronson is wheeled out again (not quite yet in his bathchair) as the

righter of wrongs, this time wiping out half the drug dealers in Los Angeles. More a case of *Death Wish Fulfilment*. With veteran J Lee Thompson at the helm, you might expect this episode to herald a slight upsurge in the series. Instead the film, apart from action scenes, which are mechanically efficient, is a complete and utter disaster, a woeful script driving some of its actors to desperate lengths. As the two detectives tracking Bronson, Soon Teck-Oh and George Dickerson seem to be competing for the worst supporting actor of the year award. John P Ryan as Bronson's mysterious ally is hardly better, surely the worst performance this distinctive actor has ever given. Bronson himself contributes very little, apart from knocking people out with ridiculous ease.

Decadence ● ⓥ
1993, UK, 95 mins, colour
Dir: Steven Berkoff
Stars: Steven Berkoff, Joan Collins
Rating: RB

A so-called black comedy in which writer–director–star Steven Berkoff spews up bile against the aristocratic ruling classes in an attack far more vituperative and wider of the mark than anything you'll see in *Spitting Image*. No bodily function is left unturned, few scenes of (rhyming!) dialogue fail to contain offensive language or suggestions of the most foul behaviour imaginable. Joan Collins joins the 'fun' by spitting out more four-letter words than you'd find on the pages of one her sister Jackie's books. Just as well Mary Whitehouse has retired: this coarse course on sledgehammer satire would have finished her off. Let's see them try to edit this odious offering for television.

Deceived ◑ ⓥ
1991, US, 105 mins, colour
Dir: Damian Harris
Stars: Goldie Hawn, John Heard, Ashley Peldon, Robin Bartlett, Amy Wright
Rating: ★★★

As the title implies, this is Goldie Hawn in dramatic vein. A well-made thriller with an iffy script, especially towards the end when it often contributes the wrong line at the wrong moment, it casts Goldie as a businesswoman who becomes involved through a quirk of fate with Jack (John Heard), whom she marries. Six years into the marriage, little un-

explained events, like her husband being seen in New York when he said he was going to Boston, cast doubts in her mind. After an old museum curator is murdered, and Jack killed in a car crash, it becomes apparent to Goldie that her husband was leading some kind of double life. A devious criminal, perhaps, but, thanks to that script, a very careless one, leaving incriminating evidence around all over the place. When it comes to keeping the suspense hopping, though, closing mysteriously in on people and objects and frightening the audience almost as much as Goldie, director Damian Harris proves himself an expert. Hawn and Heard are good when the script allows them to be, but it's the scenes without dialogue where this film is at its considerable best.

Deceivers, The ◐
1988, UK, 103 mins, colour
Dir: Nicholas Meyer
Stars: Pierce Brosnan, Saeed Jaffrey, Shashi Kapoor, Helena Michell, Keith Michell
Rating: ★★★

Boasting a cast packed with real Indian actors, it's guaranteed that this lavish update on *The Stranglers of Bombay* will carry a ruthlessly authentic touch. Mixing the vogue for portraits of colonialism with a horrific if rousing true-life adventure, the film tells one more time the story of the T'huggee cult. Followers of the devil goddess Kali, they throttled and robbed rich travellers and buried the bodies of their victims. Much in the mould of *The Four Feathers* (our hero browns up and travels as a T'huggee to crack the cult), the plot stretches credulity at times, especially when the 'sugar gourd' of Kali is supposed to infuse our upright hero (Pierce Brosnan) with a lust for blood. But Brosnan is no mean actor as well as prime beefcake, and he pulls the story through in good style to its bloody conclusion. Shashi Kapoor and Saeed Jaffrey offer variations on their familiar (in this case murderous) rascals, but Helena Michell is only just adequate as Brosnan's wife.

Deception ○ ⓥ
1947, US, 112 mins, b/w
Dir: Irving Rapper
Stars: Bette Davis, Paul Henreid, Claude Rains
Rating: ★★★

A remarkable example of how to transform a trite story from within by

D

sheer force of acting personality. Paul
Henreid, Claude Rains and Bette
Davis, three of Warners' glittering
stock company of stars, never earned
their keep more than on this screenplay, which perhaps would never have
got off the ground in today's cinematic climate. The result was such
absorbing entertainment that, as one
contemporary critic put it: 'I
wouldn't have missed it for the
world.'

Decision at Sundown ○
1959, US, 77 mins, colour
Dir: Budd Boetticher
Stars: Randolph Scott, John Carroll,
Karen Steele
Rating: ★★

Another of the Westerns Randolph
Scott made with director Budd
Boetticher, which is rather hampered
by its small-town setting. Scott plays a
man who comes a-looking for the
hombre who caused the death of his
wife, only to have his vengeful ideals
compromised by finding that she was
worthless. Very much an adult
Western, with Scott splendidly grim in
the lead, and full of little incidentals
which mark it as a thinking man's action film.

Decision Before Dawn ○
1951, US, 119 mins, b/w
Dir: Anatole Litvak
Stars: Ricvhard Basehart, Oskar Werner,
Hildegarde Neff, Gary Merrill
Rating: ★★★

Many cinemagoers think of Oskar
Werner's screen career beginning with
Jules et Jim and then going on to such
English-speaking films as *Ship of Fools*
and *Interlude.* But here's a film that
proves the baby-faced Werner (who
died in 1984) was giving excellent
performances before Jules and Jim
were thought of. Here he is on screen
almost all of the time as Happy, a
German prisoner of war who agrees to
spy against his own country for the
Allies. And a very fine job he makes
of it, too, creating a likeable and
sympathetic character with whom
one lives through a series of
hairsbreadth escapes on a dangerous
mission. The excitement is well
sustained by director Anatole Litvak,
and the climax very moving.

Decline and Fall ◐
(aka: Decline and Fall of a Birdwatcher)
1968, UK, 113 mins, colour
Dir: John Krish

Stars: Colin Blakely, Robert Harris, Leo
McKern, Robin Phillips
Rating: ★★

In spite of the general impossibility of
transferring Evelyn Waugh from
page to screen (remember *The Loved
One?*), this starts out promisingly.
However, despite a splendid
supporting cast, which includes
Donald Wolfit, things go downhill
mainly because nobody had the faith
or sense to leave a comedy classic as
originally written.

Decoy
See: Mystery Submarine

Deep, The ◐ Ⓥ
1977, US, 123 mins, colour
Dir: Peter Yates
Stars: Robert Shaw, Jacqueline Bisset,
Nick Nolte, Eli Wallach, Lou Gossett Jr
Rating: ★★

Although rightly compared unfa-
vourably to *Jaws* when it first
appeared, this film is lively, spirited
and at times rather frightening light
entertainment. Part-scripted by
Peter Benchley, the author of *Jaws*,
and based on another of his sea-going
novels, it's again an adventure in
which the ocean depths figure prominently, although this time guarding
sunken treasure. Robert Shaw plays a
rugged ocean-wise recluse who is also
a treasure-hunter – and light-
house-keeper. The personable Eli
Wallach scores as an old seadog. The
action is plentiful, with undersea
excitement, a battle with a giant mo-
ray eel – in a terrifying sequence – and
even an element of voodoo.

Deep Cover ● Ⓥ
1992, US, 112 mins, colour
Dir: Bill Duke
Stars: Larry Fishburne, Jeff Goldblum,
Victoria Dillard, Charles Martin Smith,
Gregory Sierra
Rating: ★★★

There are some good sequences in this
backstreets thriller which allies elements of an old-fashioned *film noir* (the
undercover, cut-off cop; the deep,
monotone narration) to a more
modern, if familiar story about said
cop's attempts to bust a nationwide
narcotics organisation. Naturally he
becomes dazzled by the ease of his
new life as a drug dealer (his father
was a criminal junkie) and, kept
largely in the dark by superiors
themselves at the mercy of government whim, sinks deeper into the life

of the underworld. The dialogue between dope-dealers who never seem
to trust each other has the ring of
truth and the story is incisively told by
director Bill Duke, who made *A
Rage in Harlem.* Writers Henry Bean
and Michael Tolkin seem less able,
however, to write convincing
dialogue for women which, coupled
with a weakish performance by Victoria Dillard, leads to the least
satisfactory passages in the film. Larry
Fishburne rightly allows himself few
smiles as the cop who's never quite on
top of his own destiny, while Jeff
Goldblum is pretty well on the mark
as the dope-dealing bigtime lawyer
whose life and mind hover on the
brink of explosive violence.

Deep in My Heart ○
1954, US, 132 mins, colour
Dir: Stanley Donen
Stars: Jose Ferrer, Merle Oberon, Walter
Pidgeon, Paul Henreid
Rating: ★★★

There are any number of reasons why
you should put up with the cardboard
storyline of this MGM biopic about
Sigmund Romberg. But the foremost
has to be Jose Ferrer's side-splitting,
15-minute musical comedy burlesque
buried in the soggy depths of this
mammoth musical. The skit is a
take-off of all the old cliche-ridden
operettas you've ever suffered
through. It's the fastest, cleverest thing
in the film. And there are some sizzling numbers from an array of guest
stars, notably 'I Love to Go Swimmin'
with Women', by Gene Kelly and his
brother Fred. And Cyd Charisse,
dancing 'One Alone' in form-fitting
white satin, gives the old number a
whole new vibrancy. For the rest, it's
the mixture as before in Hollywood
musical biographies: poverty,
struggle, success, failure, and final triumph. Opera star Helen Traubel
makes a hit every time she appears.

Deep in the Heart
See: Handgun

Deep Six, The ○
1957, US, 106 mins, colour
Dir: Rudolph Mate
Stars: Alan Ladd, Dianne Foster, William
Bendix, Keenan Wynn, James Whitmore
Rating: ★★

It's surprising to find tough-guy Alan
Ladd cast as a reluctant hero. But here
he's a Quaker serving on a destroyer
in World War Two. Director
Rudolph Mate, a former cameraman,

ensures that the action is lively, especially in the climactic raid on a Japanese-held island. Canadian Dianne Foster has the solitary female role, and the cast also has Ladd's old Paramount punching partner, William Bendix, plus those penetrating character actors Keenan Wynn and James Whitmore, reunited here for the first time since *Kiss Me Kate*, in which they sang a memorable duet.

Deep Valley ○
1947, US, 104 mins, b/w
Dir: Jean Negulesco
Stars: Ida Lupino, Dane Clark, Fay Bainter, Henry Hull
Rating: ★★★

This film suffered in its day after being unfavourable compared with *High Sierra*. Ida Lupino gives a superb performance as the repressed farm girl finding love (at least temporarily) with an escaped prisoner. And director Jean Negulesco (*How to Marry a Millionaire*, *Three Coins in the Fountain*) was helped greatly by location shooting in Big Sur and Big Bear due to a strike at the Warners studio which prevented him working on the backlot.

Deer Hunter, The ● ⓥ
1978, US, 183 mins, colour
Dir: Michael Cimino
Stars: Robert De Niro, John Cazale, John Savage, Christopher Walken, Meryl Streep, George Dzundza
Rating: ★★★★

A richly-detailed, angry picture, for many 'the' Vietnam war film, but one that also deals with such subjects as American small-town life, rites of passage, love and death in a way that haunts the memory. Director Michael Cimino trained as an architect and he has constructed *The Deer Hunter* like a mighty building where every stone has a function: here every frame has a tale to tell. He extracted convincing portrayals from Robert De Niro, John Cazale and John Savage and a marvellous dominating performance from Christopher Walken, which established his star status and won him an Oscar. Other Academy Awards included Best Picture and Best Editor for Peter Zinner and Cimino. Meryl Streep, in one of her earliest roles, plays the girl who turns from Walken to De Niro in the numbingly poignant later stages of the film.

Defence of the Realm ◑ ⓒ ⓥ
1985, UK, 96 mins, colour
Dir: David Drury

Stars: Greta Scacchi, Gabriel Byrne, Denholm Elliott, Ian Bannen, Bill Paterson, Robbie Coltrane
Rating: ★★★

This is an excellent British political thriller which not only entertains, but also kicks against the governmental establishment of the 1980s. Ambitious newsman Nick Mullen, played by then-newcomer Gabriel Byrne, latches onto a Profumoesque exposé, and a prominent Labour MP (Ian Bannen) resigns. There's a story bigger than Watergate ripe for the writing but can Mullen survive to tell the tale? Director David Drury keeps the plot on a tight rein. In the acting stakes the excellent Byrne is edged out by Denholm Elliott as a dandruffed, alcoholic war-horse of the newsroom (he won a BAFTA award for his work). Although the filmmakers were uncertain of the ending, and shot two different equally dramatic finales, this David Puttnam-produced film is a home product to be proud of.

Defending Your Life ○ ⓥ
1991, US, 114 mins, colour
Dir: Albert Brooks
Stars: Albert Brooks, Meryl Streep, Rip Torn, Lee Grant, Buck Henry, Shirley MacLaine
Rating: ★

The cinema hasn't had too much luck with fantasy in recent times, and this film about death is on the whole pretty turgid stuff that only, if you'll pardon the expression, comes to life at the end. Albert Brooks, you see, is dead, and the story is about his 'processing' in Judgement City to see whether he goes on to a higher place, or back to earth to try again. This sort of thing always sounds good on paper, but Brooks barely gives it a chance, wearing too many hats as star, director (the biggest mistake) and writer. The segments with Meryl Streep (we should all meet Meryl in Heaven) are the best, but the scenes of Brooks' 'trial', with Rip Torn and Lee Grant as the opposing lawyers, are almost completely unsuccessful, with too little tightness in the telling. The emotive ending works pretty well, but it's almost too late: Brooks has already squeezed all but the last gasp of life out of his 'fantastic' project.

Defenseless ● ⓥ
1992, US, 104 mins, colour
Dir: Martin Campbell
Stars: Barbara Hershey, Sam Shepard, Mary Beth Hurt, J T Walsh, Jay O

Sanders, Sheree North
Rating: ★★

Here's yet another hot-shot lady lawyer having an affair with one of her clients. It was never like this on *LA Law*! Still, not many legal eagles are as finely feathered as Barbara Hershey, but she's up to her gorgeous beak in trouble when she becomes involved with a man accused of involvement in a porno racket. She thinks he is innocent, you see – but we know better. Or do we? At any rate, when the shady suitor turns up stiffer than yesterday's British Rail sandwich, nosy copper Sam Shepard is sent to investigate. There are few surprises from here on as the murder mystery plot attempts to thicken – but the quality acting of the cast, from Hershey and from Mary Beth Hurt in, for her, an offbeat role, ensures that this hits the par for the courtroom thriller course.

Defiant Ones, The ○ ⓥ
1958, US, 96 mins, b/w
Dir: Stanley Kramer
Stars: Tony Curtis, Sidney Poitier
Rating: ★★★

One of the earliest and best films on racial intolerance, this tale of two convicts on the run planted Sidney Poitier firmly at the top as the only big negro box-office star since Paul Robeson. It also gave Tony Curtis another chance to break away from his beefcake image, and confirmed the promise as a serious actor that he had shown in *Sweet Smell of Success*. Brilliantly directed by Stanley Kramer, whose constant switching between pursuers and pursued gives the piece an insistent rhythm, the film won well-deserved Academy Awards for its screenplay (by Nathan E Douglas and Harold Jacob Smith) and the dazzling black-and-white photography of Sam Leavitt.

Delicate Delinquent, The ⊙
1956, US, 101 mins, b/w
Dir: Don McGuire
Stars: Jerry Lewis, Darren McGavin, Martha Hyer
Rating: ★★★

This uneven but largely winning spoof on the then-Hollywood vogue for juvenile delinquent films was Jerry Lewis's first feature film without regular partner Dean Martin. In fact, the role of the cop assigned to keep an eye on Lewis's shy and cowardly janitor who is mistaken for a hoodlum was

D

actually written for Martin, but went in the end to Darren McGavin. It's an agreeable mix of social satire and knockabout comedy, and even its sentiment works quite well. World heavyweight boxing champ Rocky Marciano appears as himself. The studio was taking no chances on Lewis as a solo attraction, and made the film on the cheap in black-and-white. In the event, they needn't have worried.

Delirious ○ ⓥ

1990, US, 95 mins, colour
Dir: Tom Mankiewicz
Stars: John Candy, Mariel Hemingway, Emma Samms, Raymond Burr, Jerry Orbach
Rating: ★★★

An engagingly silly John Candy comedy about a TV scriptwriter who has an accident and falls into his own daily soap. The nice thing is that he finds he can control developments in the serial by typing them in his dreams, contrary to the real-life wishes of the guy who's been called in to rewrite his stuff. You'll like, too, the idea of Robert Wagner turning up as an unwanted guest star – 'But you're Robert Wagner, you don't do daytime soap,' Candy tells the bemused actor, who is supposed to be in character, just before Wagner blasts him with a shotgun for sending him to Cleveland. Candy exercises his own brand of personal charm and, if the comedy basically isn't up to much, and falls apart at the end, it's mainly thanks to the star that it proves at least a useful antidote to those daytime office blues.

Deliverance ● ⓥ

1972, US, 109 mins, colour
Dir: John Boorman
Stars: Jon Voight, Burt Reynolds, Ned Beatty, Ronny Cox, Billy McKinney
Rating: ★★★

This harsh, brutal adventure story with hints of significance divided the critics when first shown, but undoubtedly established the international reputation of its director, John Boorman, who received one of the film's several Oscar nominations. Burt Reynolds and Jon Voight did all their own dangerous stuntwork riding the rapids, as two of the four central characters, businessmen on a survival-against-nature holiday. They soon find that nature isn't all they have to combat, and thereby hang some of the film's less savoury aspects. The final image is as haunting as it is unexpected, and may disturb your

dreams. The film is based on a story by American poet James Dickey, who also wrote the screenplay, and has a small role.

Delta Force, The ◑ ⓥ

1986, US, 129 mins, colour
Dir: Menahem Golan
Stars: Chuck Norris, Lee Marvin, Martin Balsam
Rating: ★★

After a career as a solo attraction, Chuck Norris joined the all-star brigade in this prolonged hijack thriller, which pits America's Delta Force – a cross between the Marines and Britain's SAS – against Arab terrorists and their hostages aboard a Boeing 707. Both Robert Forster and David Menahem are realistically menacing as the hijackers and it's their acting that catches the eye rather than the stars – Chuck, as an independent major called in for this vital mission, Lee Marvin, looking very tired in his last film as Chuck's immediate superior, and George Kennedy, once again on a disaster-fraught plane, this time as a priest. The action – when it comes – is right out of James Bond's textbook, especially Chuck's motorcycle with its mini-rocket launchers. But, though you admire Chuck for doing almost all his own stunts, no plus factors can conceal the fact that this film is achingly overlong. Some measure of the fear and panic among ordinary people caught in such a situation is, however, conveyed, and for this, and for some of its acting (Martin Balsam adds quality to his role as a hostage), it's marginally more worth your attention than most Chuck Norris movies.

Delta Force 2 ● ⓥ

1990, US, 111 mins, colour
Dir: Aaron Norris
Stars: Chuck Norris, Billy Drago
Rating: ★★

Chuck Norris plays the US colonel who leads an American SAS-style unit into action against Latin American drug barons. His brother Aaron directs. It's an all-action drama that calls on Chuck's famed skills as a stuntman rather than on any in-depth acting. There's some humour in the *Dirty Harry* vein, the hint of a question about America's rights ('If America accuses us of being a nation of drug pushers, then we accuse America of being a nation of drug addicts,' says the fictional Latin-American president) and tons of explosive action.

Demetrius and the Gladiators ○ ⓥ

1954, US, 101 mins, colour
Dir: Delmer Daves
Stars: Victor Mature, Susan Hayward, Michael Rennie, Anne Bancroft
Rating: ★★

A sequel to Fox's first big Cinema-Scope success *The Robe*, with Victor Mature again as Demetrius, the Greek who is given charge of the robe of Christ at the Crucifixion. There are some good battles in the arena – when the stars are not doing battle with the script.

Demolition Man ● ⓥ

1993, US, 114 mins, colour
Dir: Marco Brambilla
Stars: Sylvester Stallone, Wesley Snipes, Sandra Bullock, Nigel Hawthorne
Rating: ★★★

A real blast of an action comedy largely set in 2032, when a nightmare psycho Simon Phoenix (Wesley Snipes) breaks out after 30 years frozen in the CryoPenitentiary and proceeds to terrorise the good people of San Angeles (as LA has become), which has outlawed nicotine, caffeine, fluid transfer activities (sex) and violations of verbal morality (swearing) and has no defence against such a man. None, that is, except Sgt John Spartan (Sylvester Stallone), similarly frozen 30 years before for being a cop who threw away the rule book and cost lives. Dominated by its amazing special effects and searing action, the film still finds room for a quite witty script which Snipes handles rather better than Stallone, although in most other respects they're well-matched in a ruthlessly entertaining bombshell of a film which squarely hits its box-office target.

Dennis

See: Dennis the Menace

Dennis the Menace ○ ⓥ

(aka: Dennis)
1993, US, 97 mins, colour
Dir: Nick Castle
Stars: Mason Gamble, Walter Matthau, Joan Plowright, Christopher Lloyd
Rating: ★

This is a laugh and a half. Well, about half a laugh actually. I think it came when villain Christopher Lloyd coughed after being set on fire and smoke poured out of his mouth. Yes, that must have been it. There's nothing wrong with the premise here: an angelic-looking but awful five-year-old kid torments his elderly neighbour and can't resist touching things that lead to escalating disaster. The two themes join forces when the elderly couple-next-door (Walter Matthau and Joan Plowright) agree to look after the little monster (Mason Gamble) while his parents are away. Under the treatment of director Nick Castle, however, this becomes a clodhopping affair that's never in touch with reality and is mostly unbearable to watch. The director seems to have little idea how to create comedy that will actually get you laughing. Oh well, it is at least wonderfully well shot in glowing Technicolor, and half a laugh is better than none.

Dentist in the Chair ○
1960, UK, 84 mins, b/w
Dir: Don Chaffey
Stars: Bob Monkhouse, Peggy Cummins, Kenneth Connor, Eric Barker
Rating: ★★

There must be a twist in the British sense of humour, when film-makers have turned out so many broad comedies with a medical background; films like *Carry On Nurse, Carry On Doctor, Carry On Again Doctor,* Carry On Matron, *the Richard Gordon*Doctor<I> series and this farce (and the following entry) about dentistry. Bob Monkhouse, Kenneth Connor and Eric Barker are guaranteed to make your ribs ache rather than your gums; Peggy Cummins, as pretty as ever, is the young student who makes patients forget all about their pains and dentists' drills.

Dentist on the Job ○
(aka: Get on with It)
1961, UK, 88 mins, b/w
Dir: C M Pennington-Richards
Stars: Bob Monkhouse, Kenneth Connor
Rating: ★★

You'll give that white, white smile to those blue, blue jokes in this *Carry On*-style farce. Star Bob Monkhouse also had a hand in the script (one of his fellow-writers was Hazel Adair, original co-ordinator of *Crossroads*). And such experienced exponents of farce as Charles Hawtrey, Kenneth Connor, Eric Barker and Richard Wattis need no laughing gas to help them out.

Denver and Rio Grande ○
1952, US, 89 mins, colour
Dir: Jerry Hopper

Stars: Edmond O'Brien, Laura Elliott, Sterling Hayden, Dean Jagger
Rating: ★★★

One of the rousing outdoor adventures that producers William Pine and William Thomas made with such regularity at Paramount in the Fifties. Many of them were set in exotic places, and carried such titles as *Jamaica Run, Hong Kong, Crosswinds, Hell's Island, Tripoli, The Eagle and the Hawk, Caribbean Gold* and *Captain China*. This one is a Western with fine Technicolor photography, good villains (especially Lyle Bettger) and a really spectacular head-on train crash.

Desert Attack
See: Ice Cold in Alex

Desert Bloom ○ ⓥ
1985, US, 106 mins, colour
Dir: Eugene Corr
Stars: Jon Voight, JoBeth Williams, Annabeth Gish, Ellen Barkin
Rating: ★★★

An intelligent family drama observing the story of a girl's growing pains in an emotionally deprived and politically warped environment, set in Las Vegas in 1950. Jon Voight plays a World War II veteran devoted more to his shortwave radio and military rumours than he is to his family. Stupidly compensating for feelings of inadequacy and impotency he mistreats his stepdaughters, takes to the bottle and makes a play for his wife's sexually provocative sister – nicely played by Ellen Barkin. But the focus is on the family's teenage daughter, glowingly captured by Annabeth Gish, who is also the film's narrator. Altogether a powerful drama which handles the emotional problems and situations of a lower-class family in ways that are entirely recognizable to any audience.

Desert Fox, The
See: Rommel – Desert Fox

Desert Hawk, The ○
1950, US, 77 mins, colour
Dir: Frederick De Cordova
Stars: Yvonne De Carlo, Richard Greene, George Macready, Jackie Gleason, Rock Hudson
Rating: ★★

A capital cast graced this Oriental extravaganza, the kind which Universal were adept at making. Indeed, these sword and sandal pictures were practically a studio speciality. Great fun, if

you have a taste for such colourful escapist entertainment. Rock Hudson has a supporting role.

Desert Hearts ○ ⓥ
1985, US, 93 mins, colour
Dir: Donna Deitch
Stars: Helen Shaver, Patricia Charbonneau, Audra Lindley
Rating: ★★★

There are some scorching scenes in this first feature from Donna Deitch (who also plays a tiny role in the film as a Hungarian gambler). The opening is reminiscent of the 1939 Hollywood classic *The Women*, as would-be divorcees stay at a ranch near Reno waiting for their 'freedom' to come through. But Deitch's mind is on more searching issues, and the film soon develops into a love affair between two of the women there. Sound film-making and excellent acting from the leading players (Helen Shaver, Patricia Charbonneau, Audra Lindley) ensures the film touches the emotions, even though it makes little concession in terms of costume to the late 1950s setting. Many viewers will recognise Jeffrey Tambor, who for so long played the transvestite judge in *Hill Street Blues*.

Desert Mice ○
1959, UK, 82 mins, b/w
Dir: Michael Relph
Stars: Alfred Marks, Sidney James, Dora Bryan
Rating: ★★

An entertaining double-edged tribute to ENSA – the bands of gallant entertainers who, during World War Two, travelled around entertaining our armed forces. Here the mobile entertainers are headed by an enjoyable roster of familiar British character actors, including Sid James, Dora Bryan, Reginald Beckwith, Irene Handl and Dick Bentley.

Desert Patrol
See: Sea of Sand

Desert Rats, The ○ ⓥ
1953, US, 88 mins, b/w
Dir: Robert Wise
Stars: Richard Burton, Robert Newton, James Mason, Robert Douglas, Chips Rafferty
Rating: ★★★

This reconstruction of a phase in the battle for Tobruk ranks as one of the best and most realistic of Fifties Hollywood war films. And its acting

D

brings the desert conflict vividly to life. Richard Burton gives the most sensitive of his early performances as the harsh, disciplinarian officer sent to bring order to a raw division of Australian troops fighting a desperate rearguard action against overwhelming odds. And Robert Newton is at his most disciplined and persuasive as an alcoholic schoolmaster turned reluctant soldier.

Desert Song, The ○ ⓥ
1953, US, 110 mins, colour
Dir: Bruce Humberstone
Stars: Kathryn Grayson, Gordon MacRae, Steve Cochran, Raymond Massey, Dick Wesson
Rating: ★★

Third screen version of Sigmund Romberg's melodious desert musical, awash with action and colour, and with the original score practically intact. Leading songsters Kathryn Grayson and Gordon MacRae seem so ill-at-ease with their roles that such attractive performers as Dick Wesson, Allyn McLerie (reunited from *Calamity Jane*) and Raymond Massey have no difficulty in diverting one's attention throughout.

Design for Living ○
1933, US, 90 mins, b/w
Dir: Ernst Lubitsch
Stars: Gary Cooper, Fredric March, Miriam Hopkins, Edward Everett Horton, Franklin Pangborn
Rating: ★★★

Delightfully described by one reviewer as 'chic fluff', this is a light and witty adaptation for the screen of the Noel Coward play about two men who find a free-spirited girl moving in to make a platonic menage-a-trois to ensure that they fulfil their respective artistic potentials. Although writer Ben Hecht had to remove most of Coward's sexual sting from the dialogue, he admirably preserved the general feel of the piece, and Hans Dreier's art direction is in a class by itself.

Desire ○
1936, US, 96 mins, b/w
Dir: Frank Borzage
Stars: Marlene Dietrich, Gary Cooper
Rating: ★★★

Marlene Dietrich never looked lovelier than in this elegant romantic drama in which she plays a glamorous jewel thief and sings 'Awake in a Dream'. Gary Cooper's innocent abroad is a perfect foil for her worldly

wisdom and there are confident character studies from Akim Tamiroff and William Frawley.

Desiree ○ ⓥ
1954, US, 110 mins, colour
Dir: Henry Koster
Stars: Marlon Brando, Jean Simmons, Merle Oberon, Michael Rennie
Rating: ★

A lavish but ultimately disappointing historical drama detailing the tangled love life of Napoleon Bonaparte. Marlon Brando never wanted to play the emperor but owed Fox a movie and so reluctantly agreed to add star power to the overblown soap opera. His performance is the only good thing about the finished product, which relies on pure fiction for its plot.

Desire Me ○
1947, US, 91 mins, b/w
Dir: Jack Conway
Stars: Greer Garson, Robert Mitchum, Richard Hart, George Zucco
Rating: ★★

Rather misleading title for this Greer Garson melodrama, about a man who leaves his friend to die when they escape from a PoW camp, then heightens the crime by trying to seduce his friend's wife. Of Miss Garson's two leading men, Robert Mitchum was to go on to a star career. But the unfortunate Richard Hart died four years later, aged 35.

Desire Under the Elms ○
1958, US, 114 mins, b/w
Dir: Delbert Mann
Stars: Sophia Loren, Anthony Perkins, Burl Ives
Rating: ★★

The screenplay of this brooding drama, adapted from Eugene O'Neill's play, is by Irwin Shaw, who wrote *The Young Lions*. Sophia Loren infuses the story with her own brand of sexual smoulder; also in the cast, in a supporting role, is Pernell Roberts, who was for many years Adam Cartwright in the popular *Bonanza* series.

Despair ●
1978, West Germany/France, 119 mins, colour
Dir: Rainer Werner Fassbinder
Stars: Dirk Bogarde, Andrea Ferreol
Rating: ★★

After a good start, in which the cutting wit of Tom Stoppard's screenplay is heard at its best, director Rainer

Werner Fassbinder exerts an increasingly heavy hand on this screen version of Vladimir Nabokov's delicate fantasy about a German chocolate manufacturer on the brink of madness. Playing another of Nabokov's double-named characters (like James Mason's Humbert Humbert in *Lolita*), Dirk Bogarde gives a civilised and credible portrait of paranoia as Hermann Hermann. It's a fascinating failure.

Desperadoes, The ○
1943, US, 85 mins, colour
Dir: Robert Carson
Stars: Randolph Scott, Glenn Ford, Claire Trevor, Evelyn Keyes
Rating: ★★★

Glenn Ford completed this Western just before leaving Hollywood to join the US Marines. Here he's a gunfighter framed for murder and he certainly managed to put in a lot of target practice for the real thing. The film, based on a novel by Max Brand, is packed with gun-battles and fist-fights. It even finds room for a double female interest; and a strong vein of humour in the heroine's rascally father. Richly photographed in Technicolor.

Desperados, The ●
1969, UK/Spain, 90 mins, colour
Dir: Henry Levin
Stars: Vince Edwards, Jack Palance, George Maharis, Sylvia Syms
Rating: ★

American Civil War (and after) adventure drama with grim-faced Vince Edwards unable to escape his murderous past, despite the (at one time) topless charms of Sylvia Syms. Nice restrained performance from Neville Brand but Jack Palance goes over the top. There's lots of explosive, tough action in this Spanish-made western, with a strong supporting cast which includes George Maharis, plus such British actors as Kenneth Cope, Christian Roberts, Patrick Holt, John Paul and the lovely Kate O'Mara.

Desperate Hours, The ○
1955, US, 113 mins, b/w
Dir: William Wyler
Stars: Humphrey Bogart, Fredric March, Arthur Kennedy, Martha Scott, Gig Young
Rating: ★★★

In the early Fifties, Humphrey Bogart's tough-guy characters were generally a bit soft-hearted. But on the release of this film version of a successful play, the word went round: Bogey's back. So he was. And deadlier than ever as the leader of a trio of escaped criminals holed up in a private house. The result is a taut, suspenseful thriller, made with a marvellous cast and all the power and expertise at director William Wyler's command. It never looks like a play and the last reel is gripping, exciting, explosive stuff with a memorable confrontation between Bogart and Fredric March.

Desperate Hours ● Ⓥ
1990, US, 105 mins, colour
Dir: Michael Cimino
Stars: Mickey Rourke, Anthony Hopkins, Mimi Rogers, Kelly Lynch, Shawnee Smith
Rating: ★★★

Not as good as the Bogart original, this new, slightly opened-out version of Joseph Hayes' play still generates enough action and emotion to make it work. Mickey Rourke has the Bogart role as the psychopath who, in this adaptation, seduces his leggy lawyer (Kelly Lynch: all lawyers should look like this) and, with her help, sets up an escape from custody that sees him first team up with two confederates, then hole up at a private house. Holding the occupants – Anthony Hopkins, his estranged wife Mimi Rogers and their two children, a foul-mouthed teenager (Shawnee Smith) and a querulous kid (Danny Garrett) – as terrified hostages, Rourke waits for Hopkins to collect enough money from the bank to help him make a getaway. If you've seen the original, you'll know what happens in the end, but, though it's pitched on too hysterical a level (with the screeching music score joining in), the acting and Michael Cimino's furious-paced direction just about keep the old stager going. The plot is not too fluidly constructed, but there are times when the action cancels this out.

Desperately Seeking Susan ◐ Ⓥ
1985, US, 104 mins, colour
Dir: Susan Seidelman
Stars: Rosanna Arquette, Aidan Quinn, Madonna, Robert Joy, Laurie Metcalf
Rating: ★★

A gaudy, trendy, comic jumble which caught the imagination of the public in '85, but is beginning to date. It gave a boost to the careers of Rosanna Arquette and Madonna that neither was quite able to sustain in the fol-

lowing years. Really amusing at first, the film becomes wearisome (and seemingly louder!) as it goes on: Arquette takes centre stage as a bored suburban wife who, drawn to free-living Madonna's lifestyle, ends up switching identities with her after a crack on the head brings on a severe case of amnesia. This gives director Susan Seidelman all the plot complications she could possibly wish, yet somehow she fails to make the most of them, relying on the photogenic and attractive leading trio to keep the movie going as long as they do. You'll be entertained, but don't expect too much.

Desperate Moment ○
1953, UK, 88 mins, b/w
Dir: Compton Bennett
Stars: Dirk Bogarde, Mai Zetterling, Philip Friend, Albert Lieven
Rating: ★★

Made at a time when Dirk Bogarde seemed to be forever playing men on the run, this Rank product again casts him as a fugitive, fighting to right past wrongs. The plot lacks tension and takes some believing too, but Bogarde and Mai Zetterling make the most of their roles, and the authentic post-war Berlin settings give the chase an atmosphere of chilling urgency when the dialogue and situations allow.

Destination Gobi ○
1952, US, 91 mins, colour
Dir: Robert Wise
Stars: Richard Widmark, Don Taylor, Murvyn Vye
Rating: ★★★

Gutsy American war film about a marathon trek through the Gobi desert by a small US naval detachment. Well directed by Robert Wise, who never lets the interest sag. Richard Widmark's sound acting gives the film authority and he's backed by an excellent cast that includes Earl Holliman in his screen debut. The plot packs good-humoured excitement with the laughs in the right places; and Charles G Clarke's Technicolor photography is highly commendable.

Destination Inner Space ◐
1966, US, 83 mins, colour
Dir: Francis D Lyon
Stars: Scott Brady, Sheree North, Gary Merrill, John Howard
Rating: ★★

Diving belle Sheree North and a rather splendid amphibian monster compete for attention in this fast and lively piece of underwater science-fiction, which passes 83 minutes away in no time. The thing, about whose menacing attentions the scientists look surprisingly unconcerned, is as imaginative as it is many-splendoured, with a blue-mottled scaly body, iridescent red and orange fins, and comb-like attachments. And the underwater photography (by Brick Marquard) is clarity itself: seldom has Eastman Colour looked so attractive.

Destination Tokyo ○ Ⓥ
1943, US, 135 mins, colour
Dir: Delmer Daves
Stars: Cary Grant, John Garfield, John Ridgely, Dane Clark
Rating: ★★★

This good war film was the first movie directed by Delmer Daves, who subsequently turned out such films as *Dark Passage*, *Broken Arrow* and *3:10 to Yuma*. Here he is lucky in having the immense presence of Cary Grant as the commander of a submarine, the crew of which is full of now-familiar faces; among them are John Garfield, Dane Clark, John Forsythe and Robert Hutton.

Destroyer ○
1942, US, 99 mins, b/w
Dir: William A Seiter
Stars: Edward G Robinson, Glenn Ford, Marguerite Chapman
Rating: ★★

Wartime action film about a ship's crew who have as many battles among themselves as they do with the enemy. Watch for fast-talking little Hollywood tough guy, Leo Gorcey. As Seaman Sarecky, he plays one of his few roles outside his character of Slip, leader of the Bowery Boys.

Destry ○
1954, US, 96 mins, colour
Dir: George Marshall
Stars: Audie Murphy, Thomas Mitchell, Mari Blanchard, Lyle Bettger, Lori Nelson, Wallace Ford
Rating: ★★★

Remake of the famous James Stewart Western classic, with Audie Murphy ideally cast as the milksop cowboy who cleans up a town. George Marshall directed two versions of this classic action yarn and this one comes (a respectable) second, despite its ace cast.

D

Destry Rides Again ○

1939, US, 94 mins, b/w
Dir: George Marshall
Stars: Marlene Dietrich, James Stewart, Charles Winninger, Mischa Auer, Brian Donlevy
Rating: ★★★★

After *Angel* in 1937, Marlene Dietrich was labelled 'box-office poison' by American exhibitors but her lively performance as the hard-boiled saloon girl in this broad, brawling and bawdy Western turned her film career around and made her a hot property again, as well as allowing her to show a delicious flair for comedy. Fortunately for filmgoers, she won the part of Frenchy from Universal's original choice, Paulette Goddard. The merry mixture of action and comedy never flags under George Marshall's spirited direction and the casting of James Stewart as the mild but crusading sheriff was inspired. Tom Mix had played the part in 1932, Audie Murphy would have a stab at it in 1954 but Stewart's is the definitive portrayal.

Detective, The ●

1968, US, 114 mins, colour
Dir: Gordon Douglas
Stars: Frank Sinatra, Lee Remick, Ralph Meeker, Jacqueline Bisset, Jack Klugman
Rating: ★★★★

Ignore the awkwardness of the first 20 minutes; this is a film that builds up as it goes along and, for all its brutality and brutally lurid depiction of homosexuality, one that is based on real values. As a thriller, it is superbly constructed (although rather well less written in parts) and directed with great single-mindedness by Hollywood veteran Gordon Douglas. It's the best work of his career. The acting, too, is excellent, particularly from Frank Sinatra, those world-weary eyes never put to greater effect, and from Lee Remick as his sad nymphomaniac wife. Their scenes together carry a genuine emotional charge, making this high-class adult entertainment.

Detective, The

See: *Father Brown*

Devil and Miss Jones, The ○

1941, US, 97 mins, b/w
Dir: Sam Wood
Stars: Jean Arthur, Robert Cummings, Charles Coburn, Edmund Gwenn, S Z Sakall, Spring Byington
Rating: ★★★

Eccentric millionaire Charles Coburn goes undercover to find out how the workers in one of his department stores tick in this delightful comedy. Shopgirl Jean Arthur takes pity on him when he is transferred by the harsh store management to the shoe department. Obviously, Coburn sees the error of his selfish ways, the store managers get their comeuppance and everyone else lives happily ever after. Director Sam Wood, who directed The Marx Brothers in *A Day at the Races* and *A Night at the Opera*, keeps the comedy sparkling and Arthur makes the most of her central role. Not to be outdone, Coburn, Spring Byington and Robert Cummings all put in fine, fun performances. Hugely enjoyable.

Devil at 4 O'Clock, The ○

1961, US, 126 mins, colour
Dir: Mervyn LeRoy
Stars: Spencer Tracy, Frank Sinatra, Kerwin Matthews, Jean-Pierre Aumont
Rating: ★★

Frank Sinatra and Spencer Tracy have a battle royal for acting honours in this story of a Pacific island threatened by volcanic eruption. The characters are reminiscent of Graham Greene's. Most of the film was made on location in Hawaii, but the volcanic explosion was shot in California. The 'island' you'll see in the blast was really a 200 foot long, 45 foot high pile of landscaped mud, filled with explosive. Of such common clay are movie miracles made!

Devil Dogs of the Air ○

1935, US, 86 mins, b/w
Dir: Lloyd Bacon
Stars: James Cagney, Pat O'Brien, Margaret Lindsay, Frank McHugh
Rating: ★★

Hardly back in the hangar after *Ceiling Zero*, made the same year, James Cagney and Pat O'Brien take to the skies again in this all-flags-waving tribute to the US Marine Flying Corps. As usual, Cagney is the cocky guy who needles everyone else, but proves his worth in the end, O'Brien his slightly stuffy friend who makes him see the light. Somehow the two actors, great personal friends, managed to sustain these images to the benefit of the box-office, throughout the Thirties. In this action film, there's some superb stunt flying to back the cornball plot, and memorable special effects. Plenty of humour in the script

helps too, with Frank McHugh getting one of the best of his many comedy relief roles.

Devil on Horseback ○

1954, UK, 89 mins, b/w
Dir: Cyril Frankel
Stars: Googie Withers, John McCallum, Jeremy Spenser
Rating: ★★

Husband and wife team Googie Withers and John McCallum star in this film about a boy jockey (Jeremy Spenser) whose head swells along with his list of winners. The racing scenes make exciting viewing.

Devil's Brigade, The ○

1968, US, 126 mins, colour
Dir: Andrew V McLaglen
Stars: William Holden, Cliff Robertson, Vince Edwards, Claude Akins, Richard Jaekel
Rating: ★★

Noisy, flag-waving, relentlessly routine all-action sideshoot from *The Dirty Dozen*, with William Holden leading the troop of misfits who find themselves in Italy after training for combat in Norway. An immense all-star cast is largely wasted on this script but, on the action front, director Andrew V McLaglen got in some useful practice for his later hits *The Wild Geese* and *The Sea Wolves*.

Devil's Canyon ○

1953, US, 88 mins, colour
Dir: Alfred Werker
Stars: Dale Robertson, Virginia Mayo, Stephen McNally, Arthur Hunnicutt
Rating: ★★

This grim Western has a pretty extraordinary cast, but no more remarkable than the plot and screenplay, both of which are hard to swallow, especially when captured bandit queen Virginia Mayo is assigned to an all-male prison. Despite the fact that you might be tempted to term the result 'She's Working Her Way Back to Prison', the actual depiction of life in jail seems depressingly accurate, apart from Mayo's presence, and Nicholas Musuraca's sombre lighting keeps Technicolor well under control. Best scene: grizzled Arthur Hunnicutt's hilarious account of the poker game with his mother-in-law that led to his 99-year sentence.

Devil's Disciple, The ○
1959, UK, 83 mins, b/w
Dir: Guy Hamilton
Stars: Burt Lancaster, Kirk Douglas, Laurence Olivier, Janette Scott
Rating: ★★★

Burt Lancaster and Kirk Douglas star in a real blockbuster based on George Bernard Shaw's play about the American War of Independence. The excellence of the action is equalled by the dialogue, Laurence Olivier, in particular, having a wonderful time spouting caustic witticisms as the strutting, sneering, smirking General Burgoyne. Might have been even more rousing (and earned a lot more money) if they'd shot in colour.

Devil's Doorway ○
1950, US, 84 mins, b/w
Dir: Anthony Mann
Stars: Robert Taylor, Louis Calhern, Paula Raymond, Marshall Thompson
Rating: ★★

By the time this film appeared, Robert Taylor was thoroughly launched into the Westerns that were to dominate his later years at MGM. The unusual thing about *Devil's Doorway* is that he plays not a gunfighter but a full-blooded Shoshone Indian who owns rich grassland coveted by the white man. The first of a notable series of Westerns for director Anthony Mann.

Devils of Darkness ●
1964, UK, 90 mins, colour
Dir: Lance Comfort
Stars: William Sylvester, Tracy Reed, Hubert Noel
Rating: ★★

There are plenty of lovely actresses for vampire Hubert Noel to get his teeth into in this horror film, including South African leading lady Carole Gray, who starred with Cliff Richard in *The Young Ones*, Tracy Reed, Diana Decker and Rona Anderson, heroine of Fifties' British thrillers, and still busy today on the stage. In private life, she was married to actor Gordon Jackson.

Diagnosis: Murder ○
1974, UK, 95 mins, colour
Dir: Sidney Hayers
Stars: Christopher Lee, Jon Finch, Judy Geeson
Rating: ★★

World-famous for his portrayal of Dracula, Christopher Lee is still in sinister vein in this thriller. The film tries to vary its familiar plot – husband out to bump off wife so that he can marry attractive mistress – by making the wife (Dilys Hamlett) unusually resourceful, and the inspector on the case (Jon Finch) a surly, oddball character with problems of his own.

Dial M for Murder ○ Ⓥ
1954, US, 105 mins, colour
Dir: Alfred Hitchcock
Stars: Ray Milland, Grace Kelly, Robert Cummings
Rating: ★★★

Jumpy, suspenseful Alfred Hitchcock thriller, with Grace Kelly as a woman convicted of murdering a man who broke into her house, and Ray Milland as the husband who had paid the man to kill her. Most of the suspense in this, one of Hitchcock's most famous films, falls into the will-he-won't-he, edge-of-the-seat variety. Will she escape the hangman? Will he ever give himself away? It doesn't look like it. But the inspector (John Williams) has a breathtaking trick up his sleeve. Milland is suitably impassive, Miss Kelly suitably frightened-out-of-her-wits. Robert Cummings has the role of the wife's best friend, and Anthony Dawson is impressively sinister as the public school black sheep who will do anything for money.

Dial 999 ○
1955, UK, 87 mins, b/w
Dir: Montgomery Tully
Stars: Gene Nelson, Mona Freeman, John Bentley, Michael Goodliffe
Rating: ★★★

A gem of a thriller, one of the best co-features British studios ever made. Director Montgomery Tully keeps the action moving and the tension as tight as a bowstring. Gene Nelson, the ex-dancer from *Oklahoma!*, gives his finest acting performance as a man on the run. And a self-effacing portrayal from Michael Goodliffe provides first-rate support.

Diamond Head ○
1963, US, 107 mins, colour
Dir: Guy Green
Stars: Charlton Heston, Yvette Mimieux, George Chakiris, France Nyen
Rating: ★★

Charlton Heston gets plenty of meat into which to sink his acting teeth in this film – as the ruthless head of a modern agricultural dynasty in Hawaii, whose self-righteous attitude conceals the skeletons in his own cupboard. Director Guy Green went on to make the moving *A Patch of Blue*. Here, he gets an unexpectedly fine and sensitive portrayal from France Nuyen as Heston's half-caste mistress. The developments, though, are pure soap-opera.

Diamond Horseshoe
See: Billy Rose's Diamond Horseshoe

Diamonds ○
1975, US/Israel, 101 mins, colour
Dir: Menahem Golan
Stars: Robert Shaw, Robert Shaw, Richard Roundtree, Barbara Seagull, Shelley Winters
Rating: ★★

The trouble with 'caper' films is that it always takes a long time to get round to the main event (the robbery itself) and the supporting bouts tend to be of lesser interest. Such is the case here, in which it's Robert Shaw and Richard Roundtree who go clambering through ventilators and across ceilings to steal a fortune in jewels. The actual robbery sequence, when it comes, is likely to keep most viewers near the edges of their seats.

Diamonds Are Forever ○ Ⓥ
1971, US, 119 mins, colour
Dir: Guy Hamilton
Stars: Sean Connery, Jill St John, Charles Gray, Lana Wood, Bruce Cabot
Rating: ★★★

One of Sean Connery's best films as James Bond. This is a sparkling action adventure, pocked only by a few double-entendres so dubious that only Connery, purring like a sated leopard, could handle them. Guy Hamilton's stylish direction exudes confidence and he is brilliantly backed by the crystal-clear photography of Ted Moore (equalled by the second unit camerawork of Harold Wellman). The action set-pieces really deliver the goods, and Jill St John proves both sexy and endearingly goofy as the heroine. Lana Wood, sister of Natalie, is another of the female decorations.

Diamond Skulls ● Ⓥ
(aka: Dark Obsession)
1989, UK, 87 mins, colour
Dir: Nick Broomfield
Stars: Gabriel Byrne, Amanda Donohoe, Michael Hordern, Judy Parfitt, Sadie Frost
Rating: ★★

D

There's not much to this one, although if you like pretty actresses with no clothes on there's quite a bit of that. Gabriel Byrne is the distinctly unstable nobleman tortured by the past peccadilloes of a wife (Amanda Donohoe) who now appears to be trying to stay faithful. Driving home in one of his preoccupied states, after a military reunion, he runs over a girl who turns out to be the cook at another noble household. The sensitive member of the party (Douglas Hodge), horrified by the revelation that the girl lived 17 hours after Byrne's evil influential friend (Struan Rodger) insisted she was dead, suffers almost as many crises of conscience as the noble Byrne. You may not have trouble guessing the rest, and the acting is just okay (save for Michael Hordern who's marvellously roguish as Byrne's doddering father), but the flimsy story, which never quite makes up its mind what kind of movie it wants to be, at least has the decency not to outstay its welcome.

Diamonds on Wheels ☉
1972, UK, 85 mins, colour
Dir: Jerome Courtland
Stars: Patrick Allen, Peter Firth
Rating: ★★

Perfect entertainment for children, this is Disney's equivalent of a Children's Film Foundation thriller. Peter Firth made his screen debut as the leader of a trio of teenagers unaware that their rally car contains a fortune in stolen diamonds. The resultant thrills and spills are directed with supreme efficiency by former Hollywood actor Jerome Courtland.

Diane ○
1955, US, 110 mins, colour
Dir: David Davies
Stars: Lana Turner, Roger Moore, Pedro Armendariz, Cedric Hardwicke, Marisa Pavan
Rating: ★★

A richly-costumed prowl down the 16th century corridors of power at the French court, with Lana Turner as the scheming femme fatale Diane de Poitiers. Christopher Isherwood wrote the script, and a formidable supporting cast includes Torin Thatcher, Taina Elg, Geoffrey Toone, John Lupton and Henry Daniell.

Diary of a Chambermaid, The ○
1946, US, 86 mins, b/w
Dir: Jean Renoir

Stars: Paulette Goddard, Burgess Meredith, Francis Lederer, Hurd Hatfield, Judith Anderson
Rating: ★★★

Paulette Goddard goes blonde and gives one of her best film performances as a vixenish 19th-century French chambermaid in this unsettling screen version of the famous novel by Octave Mirbeau. The script was by co-star Burgess Meredith, then Goddard's husband. It's not at all like most post-war Hollywood offerings, which is what you might expect from the work of famous French director Jean Renoir.

Diary of a Madman ●
1963, US, 95 mins, colour
Dir: Reginald Le Borg
Stars: Vincent Price, Nancy Kovack, Elaine Derry
Rating: ★

Vincent Price fans, but few others, will get good value from this grisly horror film about demonic possession. Male viewers can keep an eye on red-haired Nancy Kovack who, at 6 feet, was Hollywood's tallest leading lady at the time. Not that she lasts very long once Price is possessed by the Horla which shines a green filter in his eyes and makes him do the most terrible things which he knows little about: only a trail of blood that would make a bloodhound turn and run in sheer disbelief leads Price up to the attic. There's even a gory daub on the banisters to make sure he doesn't lose his way where he finds the head of one his victims neatly tucked away. Despite Price's enthusiasm as the involuntary madman, Reginald Le Borg's direction is styleless and shows a total lack of imagination. The many conversational close-ups, for example, only go to make the dialogual scenes more tedious. It's comic-strip horror at its worst.

Dick Tracy ◑ ♥
1990, US, 103 mins, colour
Dir: Warren Beatty
Stars: Warren Beatty, Al Pacino, Madonna, Dustin Hoffman, Mandy Patinkin, Dick Van Dyke
Rating: ★★★

This comic-strip sprung to life would make a wow of a stage musical. There's so much music in the film, mostly from Madonna and Mandy Patinkin, that the storyline seems like a series of dramatic interruptions. If it lacks emotive impact, that's the effect

of the makers' own intentions in brilliantly constructing the film as a comic-book sprung to life. The bad guys all have exaggerated features (a shade too much so) and they and the reporters and police all wear different coloured coats to correspond to the drawings in the original Dick Tracy police detective strip, so faithfully re-created here. Still, we can appreciate the performance of Warren Beatty, an admirable Tracy, Madonna, doing her best screen work to date as a singing siren, and especially Al Pacino, perfectly cast as the ranting Big Boy Caprice, looking like a caricaturist's impression of Sylvester Stallone.

Die, Die, My Darling
See: Fanatic

Die Hard ● ♥
1988, US, 131 mins, colour
Dir: John McTiernan
Stars: Bruce Willis, Bonnie Bedelia, Alan Rickman, Alexander Godunov, Reginald VelJohnson, Paul Gleason
Rating: ★★★★

This is some spectacular action film and you'd better believe it. Director John McTiernan and his technicians fairly blast the screen apart after a group of highly trained ex-terrorists hijack a vast company building at Christmas with even vaster sums of money in its vaults. Would you believe $640 million? Don't stop to count it: you won't have time. Enter lone wolf cop Bruce Willis, whose wife is a terrorist hostage. He becomes a one-man army, fighting desperately to bring help and stay alive. Although he tears the building to shreds doing it, this is no Stallone or Schwarzenegger cutting down the baddies with ease. Willis barely escapes the bad guys time and again. He's scratched, scorched, shot, stunned, strangled, throws himself down lift shafts or the side of the building and finds time to make friends with a street cop (Reginald VelJohnson) down below on a two-way radio. The bad guys are brimful of menace, the story throws in some unexpected twists and the action is explosive, painful and dynamically staged. You'll wince at Willis picking glass out of his feet in an eye-shutting scene and be too shellshocked to guess the final piece of action before it comes.

Die Hard 2 ● Ⓥ
1990, US, 118 mins, colour
Dir: Renny Harlin
Stars: Bruce Willis, Bonnie Bedelia, William Atherton, Franco Nero, William Sadler, Reginald VelJohnson
Rating: ★★★

Even if it takes a while getting up a head of steam, and lacks the claustrophobic dynamism of *Die Hard*, this is still a power-house action thriller, with Bruce Willis again as John McClane, 'the wrong guy in the wrong place at the wrong time'. The wrong place this time is an airport paralysed by terrorists who will resort even to causing the crash of passenger planes to free a Central American dictator (Franco Nero) on his way to the US to face drug charges. One of the planes hovering over the airport contains Willis' wife (Bonnie Bedelia), not that he has much time to think of her as he tackles hostile airport police (led by Dennis Franz), a SWAT squad and an army special missions force, not to mention the terrorists. Once again Willis bears a charmed life, even making like James Bond when he takes to a motor-bike on ice treads. The dialogue's not important (just as well since you often can't hear it): no, the action's the thing and the second half contains enough of it to send fans of the first film home happy. Sensational stunts, with Willis doing most of the rough work himself, put the icing on the cake.

Die Monster Die ●
(aka: Monster of Terror)
1965, UK, 80 mins, colour
Dir: Daniel Haller
Stars: Boris Karloff, Nick Adams, Suzan Farmer
Rating: ★★

This Grand Guignol chiller is based on a story by master horror writer H P Lovecraft, called *The Colour Out of Space*. It's one of only a handful of films (another is *The Dunwich Horror*, also based on a Lovecraft story) to have been directed by Daniel Haller, who was art director on all of Roger Corman's Edgar Allan Poe stories made in America in the Sixties.

Digby – the Biggest Dog in the World ○
1973, UK, 88 mins, colour
Dir: Joseph McGrath
Stars: Jim Dale, Spike Milligan, Angela Douglas, Milo O'Shea, Dinsdale Landen,

Victor Spinetti
Rating: ★★

The film is about an old English sheepdog who grows to enormous size after drinking a new super-growth chemical by mistake. It's good to see such a truly family film, even though children might not appreciate all of its funniest moments, such as most of Spike Milligan's dialogue (the great man is well on form as a mad doctor) or the scene in which Jim Dale learns how to eat in a transport cafe with a knife, fork and spoon chained to the table.

Diggstown
See: Midnight Sting

Dillinger ○ Ⓥ
1944, US, 100 mins, b/w
Dir: Max Nosseck
Stars: Lawrence Tierney, Edmund Lowe, Anne Jeffreys, Elisha Cook Jr
Rating: ★★★

This sombre reconstruction of the rise and fall of America's one-time public enemy number one dates from the Forties when, unlike the Thirties, few first-rate gangster movies were being made. This harsh and atmospheric look at the famous gangster's career is a happy exception, its bullet-strewn edges being decorated by such stalwarts of racketeer romps as Elisha Cook Jnr, Eduardo Ciannelli and Marc Lawrence. It also brought Lawrence Tierney, real-life brother of Scott Brady, fame in the title role.

Dillinger ●
1973, US, 107 mins, colour
Dir: John Milius
Stars: Warren Oates, Ben Johnson, Michelle Phillips, Cloris Leachman, Harry Dean Stanton, Richard Dreyfuss
Rating: ★★★

The first film made by the American director John Milius, whose subsequent output has included *The Wind and The Lion* and *Conan the Barbarian*. Milius pushes along his bullet-strewn narrative in the best *Untouchables* style, graphically illustrating the violence and self-glorification that bubbles beneath his characters on both sides of the legal fence. The acting is first-rate, with exception of a wild performance by Richard Dreyfuss (as Baby Face Nelson) which provides little hint of the Oscar-winning splendours to come in his career. The tailpiece will hit you hard.

Dime Box
See: Kid Blue

Dimples ○
1935, US, 78 mins, b/w
Dir: William A Seiter
Stars: Shirley Temple, Frank Morgan
Rating: ★★★

Another Civil War setting for little Shirley Temple in a plot which teams her with loveable Frank Morgan as her grandfather. Shirley plays a street entertainer, which gives her a chance to sing 'Picture Me Without You', 'He Was a Dandy', 'What Did the Blue Jay Say?' and 'Dixie Anna'. The last reel won't leave a dry eye in the sitting-room.

Diner ● Ⓥ
1982, US, 110 mins, colour
Dir: Barry Levinson
Stars: Daniel Stern, Steve Guttenberg, Mickey Rourke, Kevin Bacon, Ellen Barkin, Michael Tucker
Rating: ★★★

This nostalgia-and-reminiscence piece is a well-observed and affectionate portrait of American youth in 1959, and in particular of five guys in their early 20s who still hang out at the same riverside diner they've sat in for years, even though one of them is now married. Of these sharply contrasted characters, the standouts are Boogie (Mickey Rourke), who tries to make his own rules but finds life's not like that, and Fenwick (Kevin Bacon), an embittered loner who drinks too much, has dropped out of college and is brighter than he would care to admit to any of his friends. The fabric of the picture (written as well as directed by Barry Levinson) results in a portrait rather than a story, but one that's frequently rewarding. The Metrocolor photography of Peter Sova is spot-on and the use of contemporary pop music on the soundtrack provides the final nostalgic glow.

Dingaka ○
1964, South Africa, 98 mins, colour
Dir: Jamie Uys
Stars: Stanley Baker, Juliet Prowse, Ken Gampu
Rating: ★★

An unusual adventure film, made in South Africa, about a tribesman who has to venture into a big city that bewilders him, in order to exact revenge. The first 40 minutes of the film have such good, atmospheric moments, with brown figures swarming

D

across the screen, that it seems almost like a folk-odyssey, or fable with a documentary flavour, doing for the African something similar to the most subjective of the pre-Black Power Southern American Negro stories. Bertha Egnos' special tribal songs, and Basil Gray's music, together with Jamie Uys' sympathetic direction, go a long way towards achieving this. And Ken Gampu brings great strength and dignity to the African who must avenge the death of his wife, even if it means slaying a local witch doctor.

Dinner at Eight ○ ⓥ
1933, US, 113 mins, b/w
Dir: George Cukor
Stars: Marie Dressler, John Barrymore, Wallace Beery, Jean Harlow, Lionel Barrymore, Lee Tracy
Rating: ★★★★

A star-studded portmanteau picture, made with supreme confidence by director George Cukor at an MGM riding high in the early Thirties. Cinemagoers got full value from the performances of John Barrymore, foreshadowing his own last years as a fading, alcoholic matinee idol; from Lionel Barrymore, wheezing convincingly as the shipping magnate whose fortune and health alike are ailing; from Jean Harlow and Wallace Beery as a feuding nouveau riche couple; from Edmund Lowe as the caring doctor trying to back out of his affair with Harlow; from Billie Burke as Lionel Barrymore's selfish, fluttering wife; and from the great Marie Dressler as a stage star on hard times. There's even the classic device of film fiction, the key character (in this case two) who never appears. And the closing duologue between Harlow and Dressler is still an exchange to relish.

Diplomatic Courier ○
1952, US, 98 mins, b/w
Dir: Henry Hathaway
Stars: Tyrone Power, Patricia Neal, Stephen McNally, Hildegarde Neff, Karl Malden
Rating: ★★★

First class espionage thriller that is liable to put a little strain on your nervous system. Tyrone Power is the American agent dodging danger behind the Iron Curtain, and, with the help of crisply natural dialogue, Patricia Neal and Hildegarde Neff put personality into the female roles. Spot Lee Marvin in a small role as a military policeman. The film was the

latest (and in fact the last) in a line of actuality thrillers from director Henry Hathaway, all made at 20th Century-Fox and including such classics as *The House on 92nd Street*, *13 Rue Madeleine*, *Kiss of Death*, *Call Northside 777* and *Fourteen Hours*, all made between 1945 and 1951. In this one, the sense of constant danger is heightened by Lucien Ballard's heavily shadowed photography.

Dirigible ○
1931, US, 93 mins, b/w
Dir: Frank Capra
Stars: Fay Wray, Jack Holt, Ralph Graves
Rating: ★★

A rare treat for lovers both of Frank Capra films and of the work of the queen of screen screamers, Fay Wray. Its action sequences still look exciting today, even if the dialogue scenes are static and boring. Look hard at the snow scenes in this story of early aviators battling to make it to the South Pole. The film was actually shot at the height of summer and the actors, sweating in fur parkas, are being bombarded by wind machines blowing bleached cornflakes into their faces in 90-degree heat. The film itself launched both Capra and his studio, Columbia, into the big time, there to stay.

Dirty Dancing ● ⓥ
1987, US, 96 mins, colour
Dir: Emile Ardolino
Stars: Jennifer Grey, Patrick Swayze, Jerry Orbach
Rating: ★★

This extraordinarily successful film, which rocketed Patrick Swayze to stardom – he dances with grace and also sings one of the soundtrack's songs – is like an adult version of a pop musical from the mid-Sixties. The amazing thing is that, although its dated script and illogical plot hurt the film badly, a great deal of it still works. The dancing's good and so is the music, and even the script has odd lines that hit home, as when Max (Jack Weston), the ageing proprietor of the film's glamorous holiday camp, confesses on closing night that he feels 'like it's all slipping away'. The dialogue does, however, also contain Swayze's classic exclamation: 'Nobody leaves Baby in the corner!'

Dirty Dingus Magee ○
1970, US, 90 mins, colour
Dir: Burt Kennedy

Stars: Frank Sinatra, George Kennedy, Anne Jackson, Jack Elam
Rating: ★

A slapstick Western from the hands of director Burt Kennedy, who also made *Support Your Local Sheriff* and *Support Your Local Gunfighter*. Jack Elam, who played such an important part in the success of those two films, contributes an amusing cameo here as a would-be fearsome western outlaw, John Wesley Hardin (whose real-life story was allegedly told in a highly-coloured adventure yarn called *The Lawless Breed*, with Rock Hudson as Hardin). The supporting cast is full of faces from Kennedy's own little stock company of excellent character players, including John Dehner, Henry Jones, Don 'Red' Barry, Harry Carey Jr, Kathleen Freeman and Paul Fix. Sinatra tries to sink himself into the role of the grubby, unscrupulous small-time outlaw of the title – although, quite honestly, it isn't his scene.

Dirty Dozen, The ① ⓥ
1967, US, 150 mins, colour
Dir: Robert Aldrich
Stars: Lee Marvin, Ernest Borgnine, Robert Ryan, Charles Bronson, John Cassavetes, Telly Savalas
Rating: ★★★

Although unthinkable now, Donald Sutherland, one of the 12 men of the title, then never even got his name on the posters for the film, because he wasn't considered a strong enough draw. Mind you, there was no lack of other major star names in this rugged World War Two actioner about a team of GI murderers and thugs given the stark choice of the firing squad or a suicide mission to wipe out Hitler's top generals. If the mission is a success it will lead to their release from military custody with a clean slate. It's a typical vehicle from director Robert Aldrich, filled with frantic action sequences, and bucket-loads of explosive action and violence. The acting is uniformly good, with John Cassavetes and Lee Marvin especially deserving of a mention in dispatches. It was followed 20 years later by a rash of inferior TV movie sequels and rip-offs, which featured Marvin, Ernest Borgnine and Telly Savalas in varying combinations.

Dirty Harry ① ⓥ
1971, US, 103 mins, colour
Dir: Don Siegel

Stars: Clint Eastwood, Harry Guardino, Reni Santoni, John Vernon, Andy Robinson
Rating: ★★★

All tough and violent cop thrillers today, both good and bad, have a common ancestor, *Dirty Harry*. Harry Callahan (Clint Eastwood) strides grimly through San Francisco in pursuit of a psychopath, paying little heed to the formal niceties of the law. So little heed, in fact, that when he catches him, the killer is soon released again, thanks to Harry's unorthodox arrest procedure. Knowing the killer will strike again, Harry is soon back on his tail. Panned for being too violent and amoral by some critics when it was released, it pales by comparison with some present-day offerings. Nevertheless, it's still pretty tough. Eastwood is tall and taciturn in this modern-dress Western – his Magnum .44 pistol doing most of his talking for him. Andy Robinson is marvellous as the gibbering maniacal psychopath. Whatever your reservations about Harry's methods, one look at the killer and you know whose side you're on.

Dirty Knight's Work
See: Trial by Combat

Dirty Rotten Scoundrels ○ ⓥ
1988, US, 110 mins, colour
Dir: Frank Oz
Stars: Steve Martin, Michael Caine, Glenne Headly, Anton Rodgers, Barbara Harris
Rating: ★★★

This cheerful comedy about confidence tricksters at large on the French Riviera is an ingenious remake of the 1963 film *Bedtime Story*. Suave Lawrence Jamieson (Michael Caine in the David Niven role) is the one who has it all: silver-rinsed American matriarchs with enough money to walk lopsided are easy prey and supply him with that to which he has become accustomed: wealth. Freddy Benton (Steve Martin in the Marlon Brando part) isn't yet in that league. All that he lacks is class. After a brush with Lawrence, Freddy decides that this is the man to teach him. Lawrence's price is to hand Freddy a humiliating role as his idiot brother and do him out of any share in the profits while grooming him for sharpster stardom. Before long, though, the rivals are locked in battle to see who can squeeze $50,000 from an American 'soap queen' (Glenne Headly) – the

loser to leave the arena. There are some gleaming barbs in the duel of wits that follows, with touches of Tom and Jerry supplied by Martin's lunatic sense of humour – especially funny as the idiot. Both stars, in fact, are very good, laughs come at regular intervals, the script is almost too sophisticated to contain a swear-word (good grief!) and you may be surprised at how it all turns out. A highly civilised comedy.

Dirty Weekend ● ⓥ
1992, UK, 102 mins, colour
Dir: Michael Winner
Stars: Lia Williams, David McCallum, Rufus Sewell, Michael Cule
Rating: RB

Director Michael Winner attempts a female *Death Wish*, and the result is a deeply, deeply unattractive, even despicable movie. Lia Williams, a distinguished stage actress, makes a conspicuously inauspicious starring film debut as Bella, who falls victim in turn to a contemptuously faithless lover and a Peeping Tom heavy breather across the way from her Brighton flat. She decides she has 'had enough', flips, and does the peeper in with a hammer. Acquiring a knife and a gun, she dons a tight-fitting dress and goes out in search of perverts anonymous, which she finds swarming around Brighton like flies. Swatting them dead, and polishing off a mass murderer while strolling along the pier, she moves on to some other town. Ludicrous and thoroughly distasteful, this is clumsily directed and inexcusably violent exploitation without any redeeming features. Not only a waste of your time, but offensive (and badly acted) in the extreme.

Dishonored Lady ○
1947, US, 85 mins, b/w
Dir: Robert Stevenson
Stars: Hedy Lamarr, John Loder, Dennis O'Keefe, William Lundigan
Rating: ★

Director Robert Stevenson blotted an honourable Hollywood record – all the way from *Jane Eyre* to *Mary Poppins* – with his soporific treatment of what sounded like an interesting story, until you saw it. If it had been more sharply done, it could have been a suspenseful psychological thriller with elements of murder and blackmail thrown in.

Disorderly Orderly, The ☉
1963, US, 89 mins, colour

Dir: Frank Tashlin
Stars: Jerry Lewis, Glenda Farrell, Everett Sloane
Rating: ★★★

One of Jerry Lewis' funniest solo comedies, in which the unexpected is always happening. Take the scene where Jerry comes charging down the hospital corridor with a trolleyful of laundry bags. In the other direction, a doctor, carrying two glasses balanced on a tray. You close your eyes and wait for the crash. When you open them again, nothing has happened. Jerry has missed him. Kathleen Freeman makes a splendid comic foil as the horse-faced nurse who has to put up with Jerry's frantic antics, and Frank Tashlin's direction is a model of precision.

Disorganized Crime ◑
1989, US, 101 mins, colour
Dir: Jim Kouf
Stars: Hoyt Axton, Corbin Bernsen, Ruben Blades, Fred Gwynn, Ed O'Neill, Lou Diamond Phillips
Rating: ★★

Laughs are a bit thin on the ground in this weak crime comedy unless you are the sort of person who can cope with ill-timed slapstick and finds people swearing at each other funny for the sake of watching an admittedly excellent cast. For the rest of us, it's sad to see so many talented players wasted on a dumb cops 'n' robbers chase film. Hoyt Axton, Fred Gwynne, Lou Diamond Phillips, Ruben Blades, Ed O'Neill and Corben Bernsen try hard, but without a script worthy of the name, it's all largely down to vigorous mugging in the hopes of raising a smile. It's doubly sad when you realise that it was scripted and directed by Jim Kouf, who wrote the excellent *StakeOut*, made two years earlier, with Richard Dreyfuss and Emilio Estevez.

Distant Drums ○
1951, US, 99 mins, colour
Dir: Raoul Walsh
Stars: Gary Cooper, Mari Aldon, Richard Webb, Ray Teal, Arthur Hunnicutt
Rating: ★★

Fairly straightforward cowboys versus Indians Western, except that the setting is the Florida everglades. Director Raoul Walsh makes the most of the plentiful action scenes, the familiar bearded features and coonskin hat of Arthur Hunnicutt are promi-

D

nent and former ballerina Mari Aldon makes an impressive debut as a girl rescued from Redskin captivity.

Distant Trumpet, A ○

1964, US, 116 mins, colour
Dir: Raoul Walsh
Stars: Troy Donahue, Suzanne Pleshette, James Gregory
Rating: ★★

This Cavalry vs Indians horse opera has noble intentions, as the Indians are seen as real people and a negotiated peace ends the film. Nevertheless, it still ends up treating the subject in rather one-dimensional 'cowboys 'n' Injuns' fashion. This isn't helped much by a colourless hero (Troy Donahue as Lt Matt Hazard!) and a rather irrelevant love interest (Suzanne Pleshette). Still it's a fairly good yarn and the battle scenes between cavalry and Indians are exciting and well-staged. There's some rousing cavalry music by Max Steiner, good villainy from Claude Akins and spirited direction by veteran action man Raoul Walsh to help the threadbare story along.

Distant Voices, Still Lives ◐ ⓥ

1988, UK, 85 mins, colour
Dir: Terence Davies
Stars: Freda Dowie, Peter Postlethwaite, Angela Walsh
Rating: ★★★

'Most families come to terms with their history either by talking about or not talking about it – I make a public statement.' Director Terence Davies, arguably one of the most ambitious and most painstaking craftsmen at work in British films of the Eighties and Nineties, has turned personal memories of his family upbringing in Liverpool of the Forties and Fifties into a remarkable debut feature that won plaudits wherever it was shown. Christenings, weddings and a funeral are the highlights for a family dominated by a brutal patriarch, who turns the lives of his wife and children into a bleak, endless nightmare. 'Some of my family have seen the film. It opened up a lot of wounds and they cried,' says Davies. 'But my mother said, "He's told the truth," which I have.' It's actually two films in one, with *Still Lives* shot two years after *Distant Voices*, with the same cast but different technicians. But they run together as a seamless labour of love.

Distinguished Gentleman, The ◐ ⓥ

1992, US, 112 mins, colour
Dir: Jonathan Lynn
Stars: Eddie Murphy, Victoria Rowell, Joe Don Baker, Lane Smith, Kevin McCarthy, James Garner
Rating: ★★★

Quite a jolly if inconsequential vehicle for Eddie Murphy as a con-man elected to Congress where he finds himself, natch, perfectly at home. Lane Smith's impersonation of Richard Nixon (his character name actually is Dick, and much is made of it) is equally in its natural setting as the big white self-serving shark on whose major committee Murphy soon contrives to get – with the intention of pocketing as many back-handers as possible in the shortest time. Alas, it's not long before a pretty face (Victoria Rowell) and a good cause (cancer in children) steady Eddie, and he rounds on the rogues responsible (headed by Smith) with a 'sting' in the tail of the film. The ending really sums up the enterprise: at the final wisecrack, Rowell reacts while Murphy just mugs to the camera. They'll make a black Bob Hope of him yet.

Divided Heart, The ○

1954, UK, 89 mins, b/w
Dir: Charles Crichton
Stars: Cornell Borchers, Yvonne Mitchell, Armin Dahlen, Michel Ray
Rating: ★★★

Yvonne Mitchell won a British Academy Award for her role as a Yugoslavian mother fighting to get back her son from foster-parents. Another of the Academy's awards – for the Best Foreign Actress – went to Berlin-born Cornell Borchers, who plays the boy's foster-mother. The actor who will have many people reaching for their handkerchiefs is dark-eyed Michel Ray, who plays the boy pathetically torn between two worlds.

Divine Madness ◐ ⓥ

1980, US, 95 mins, colour
Dir: Michael Ritchie
Stars: Bette Midler
Rating: ★★★

Bette Midler is almost at full throttle in this film record of the singer's sensational, perpetual motion stage show. For those who have been to the Moon and don't know, the divine Ms M is a sort of non-stop Lenny Bruce, telling the foulest possible jokes in

between singing soulful, but gutsy ballads. The woman is so outrageous you wonder what she can possibly do next. Then she does it!

Dixie ○

1943, US, 89 mins, colour
Dir: A Edward Sutherland
Stars: Bing Crosby, Dorothy Lamour, Marjorie Reynolds
Rating: ★★★

Bing Crosby looks even more doleful than usual in blackface in this potted biography of showman Dan Emmett, who is credited with the idea of starting black-and-white minstrel shows. But there's a dash of liveliness about the climax, which purports to show how Dixie was born. Bing also sings 'Sunday, Monday or Always' and 'I'm from Missouri', but co-star Dorothy Lamour doesn't sing a note. Shame on you, Paramount.

D.O.A. ○

1950, US, 83 mins, b/w
Dir: Rudolph Maté
Stars: Edmond O'Brien, Pamela Britton, Luther Adler, Neville Brand, Beverly Campbell
Rating: ★★

Loosely remade with Dennis Quaid and Meg Ryan, this is a typically morose Hollywood *film noir* of the post-war years, shot mostly at night, and featuring a pugnacious performance by Edmond O'Brien as the man who, poisoned by unknown hands, has only a short time to find his own murderer. Screen debuts for Neville Brand, very effective as a psychotic thug, and Beverly Garland, here billed as Beverly Campbell. Not quite as good as its reputation, this is, all the same, pretty hypnotic stuff with spurts of quite savage action.

D.O.A. ● ⓥ

1988, US, 100 mins, colour
Dir: Rocky Morton, Annabel Jankel
Stars: Dennis Quaid, Meg Ryan, Charlotte Rampling, Daniel Stern
Rating: ★★

'Drop dead,' says Meg Ryan to Dennis Quaid in the course of this thriller. Poor guy – that's just what he's in the process of doing, trying to find his own killer after falling victim to a slow-acting poison. So what's it all about, Dennis? The answers would still run like the remake of an old *film noir* (which this is), even without the black-and-white 'bookends' that top and tail the film. The side of the plot that involves Charlotte Rampling is, without giving too much away, much more interesting than the part that pops its head up at the end, almost as if to confound the viewer for presuming to beat Quaid to the answers. Quaid himself, coming on here like a combination Jack Nicholson and Alan Ladd, is really pretty good and Ryan just great as the student who reluctantly helps Prof Quaid root out the truth. Directors Rocky Morton and Annabel Jankel fill the screen with too many unnecessary shots, but the thriller aspects of the film are well handled.

Doc Hollywood ◐ ⓥ
1991, US, 105 mins, colour
Dir: Michael Caton-Jones
Stars: Michael J Fox, Julie Warner, Woody Harrelson, George Hamilton, Bridget Fonda
Rating: ★★

A throwback to Forties-style stories has to be something special to make it in today's Schwarzenegger, sci-fi-oriented film world. This nothing-much-happens number certainly isn't that. Michael J Fox is the brash city doctor headed to Los Angeles for a career in plastic surgery, but sidelined into a small country town, Grady, en route. That's where he crashes his car, has to do 32 hours community service as a doctor, and falls for the local ambulance driver (Julie Warner). There's not enough of Fox's involvement with the locals to make an emotive story out of all this, and it remains a lightweight, faintly unbelievable tale. Director Michael Caton-Jones' handling is competent and assured, although he has several sizes to go to fill the boots of the great Frank Capra, to whose work this film has been compared. Though in somewhat similar vein, it lacks both the richness of detail and the heart that so distinguished Capra's work.

Doc Savage – The Man of Bronze ○
1975, US, 100 mins, colour
Dir: Michael Anderson
Stars: Ron Ely, Paul Gleason
Rating: ★★

This rather too unambitious cartoon-style adventure, light on action and special effects, was one of the few box-office misses for films based on comic-strip heroes. A cross between Superman and Indiana Jones, the mighty Doc Savage first appeared in 1933 in a monthly comic strip maga-

zine created by Lester Dent, who wrote under the pen name of Kenneth Robeson. The film is set in 1936, and any parody is affectionately offered, almost as a reverence to the character involved. Subtleties in the treatment, however, are notably lacking, and the sequel promised at the end of the movie never arrived.

Doctor, The ◐ ⓥ
1991, US, 123 mins, colour
Dir: Randa Haines
Stars: William Hurt, Christine Lahti, Elizabeth Perkins, Mandy Patinkin, Adam Arkin, Charlie Korsmo
Rating: ★★

It's debatable if William Hurt was good casting for the central role of this film about a doctor who gets cancer. It gets so you care little more about his character at the end than you did at the start — indeed, he doesn't seem to have changed that much. Supposedly a meeting with a dying cancer patient (Elizabeth Perkins) softens his outlook on life, turning him into more of a human being who cares about his fellows. But on Hurt, it doesn't show. Much more accessible is Christine Lahti as his wife. It's not a particularly good, nor consistent role, but Lahti enriches it with sincerity and warmth. Otherwise, the pace is slow and the heart only occasionally uplifted. Those who dislike seeing surgery on screen are given plenty of opportunity to look the other way.

Doctor at Large ○
1957, UK, 104 mins, colour
Dir: Ralph Thomas
Stars: Dirk Bogarde, Muriel Pavlow, Donald Sinden, James Robertson Justice, Shirley Eaton
Rating: ★★

Third in the series of *Doctor* comedy films gives Dirk Bogarde a piquant new partner in Muriel Pavlow (reintroduced from the first film), and still manages to raise quite a few genuine laughs from its corny catalogue of venerable medical jokes. The studio years of British films were drawing to a close and this was one of the last of Rank's films able to command such a brilliant supporting cast of comedy stalwarts.

Doctor at Sea ○
1955, UK, 93 mins, colour
Dir: Ralph Thomas
Stars: Dirk Bogarde, Brigitte Bardot, James Robertson Justice, Maurice

Denham
Rating: ★★★

Actually an improvement on its predecessor, *Doctor in the House*, with a long succession of amusing moments as one crazy situation after another rings the bell. Especially the final, glorious shipboard chaos that ensues when the captain mixes whisky with nerve pills. Dirk Bogarde is a likeable hero and his leading lady is none other than Brigitte Bardot, complete with the famous shower scene and most attractive French accented English. James Robertson Justice fares even better as the martinet ship's captain than as the irascible surgeon Sir Lancelot Spratt in the previous film, but the outstanding contribution in the supporting cast comes from Maurice Denham, who's in tremendous form. And Ernest Steward can pin a 'highly commended' riband on his sparkling Technicolor photography. If ever there were a laugh on the ocean wave, this is it.

Doctor Blood's Coffin ◐
1961, UK, 92 mins, colour
Dir: Sidney J Furie
Stars: Kieron Moore, Hazel Court
Rating: ★★

A grisly blend of horror and science fiction, as strange disappearances terrorise the inhabitants of a small Cornish village. The director is the young Canadian Sidney J Furie, who went on to make *Southwest to Sonor*, *The Ipcress File* and *Lady Sings the Blues*.

Doctor Dolittle ☉ ⓥ
1968, US/UK, 144 mins, colour
Dir: Richard Fleischer
Stars: Rex Harrison, Samantha Eggar, Anthony Newley, Richard Attenborough
Rating: ★★

A simplistic musical version of Hugh Lofting's tales of the eccentric doctor who talks to animals. Rex Harrison's splendid Dolittle owes a fair amount to his Prof Higgins from *My Fair Lady*. There's also Anthony Newley, really letting a jaunty cockney tenor rip as Matt, and Richard Attenborough's brief appearance as a circus owner.

Doctor in Clover ○
1966, UK, 101 mins, colour
Dir: Ralph Thomas
Stars: Leslie Phillips, James Robertson Justice, Shirley Anne Field, Joan Sims, John Fraser
Rating: ★★★

D

It seems that in the Fifties and Sixties, as fast as Richard Gordon wrote a new *Doctor* comedy book, Rank had Jack Davies fashion a screenplay from it. Apart from the usual crop of medical jokes to try to make some less modest part of the anatomy sound like something else, Davies' script shows a nice line in invention. Hilarious scenes include Joan Sims trying to give patient Arthur Haynes a blanket bath (in which it looks as though she had a hard task keeping a straight face) and Leslie Phillips going Mod in Carnaby Street as part of a rejuvenation treatment. Phillips releasing laughing gas is also funny.

Doctor in Distress ○
1963, UK, 102 mins, colour
Dir: Ralph Thomas
Stars: Dirk Bogarde, Samantha Eggar, James Robertson Justice, Mylene Demongeot, Barbara Murray, Donald Houston
Rating: ★★

After Michael Craig had donned the white overall for the third *Doctor* comedy, to follow *Doctor in the House* and *Doctor at Sea*, the Rank Organisation pressed Dirk Bogarde back into service for this entry into the series, which plays more or less as series of revue sketches. Most of the old crew are back, including Bogarde and James Robertson Justice – both in more than usually amorous mood – and Donald Houston. The most effective scene is a marvellous send-up of a film producer and his glamorous star, by Leo McKern and Jill Adams. Mylene Demongeot appears brightly if briefly, but Samantha Eggar is disappointing, although she does wear a fabulous array of clothes that are almost a parade of early Sixties fashions.

Doctor in Love ○
1960, UK, 97 mins, colour
Dir: Ralph Thomas
Stars: Michael Craig, Virginia Maskell, Leslie Phillips, James Robertson Justice, Reginald Beckwith
Rating: ★★

More leaves from Richard Gordon's comic casebook, this time with the accent on girls, who include Virginia Maskell, Carole Lesley, Joan Sims, Liz Fraser and Fenella Fielding. Leslie Phillips is his usual foxy self as one of the two young doctors pursuing them.

Doctor in the House ○ ⓥ
1954, UK, 91 mins, colour
Dir: Ralph Thomas

Stars: Dirk Bogarde, Muriel Pavlow, Kenneth More, Donald Sinden, Donald Houston, Kay Kendall, James Robertson Justice
Rating: ★★★

The rumbustious hospital comedy which introduced the beer-swilling, rugger-playing, women-chasing students of Richard Gordon's best-selling book. This renowned, joke-a-minute British comedy film, a product of the team of producer Betty Box and director Ralph Thomas, was the first of the popular *Doctor* series. And few, one fancies, would argue that it wasn't one of the best. In its vastly amusing tale of medical students at a large hospital, Dirk Bogarde and Kenneth More both give engaging performances, and James Robertson Justice, as Sir Lancelot, created his medical autocrat role for the first time. Also featured, though all too briefly, was the delightful Kay Kendall, fresh from her triumph and trumpet-playing in that other British comedy success of the period, *Genevieve*. The gags are as numerous as they are funny, including one at the point where Sir Lancelot suddenly shoots a question at the otherwise preoccupied Simon (Bogarde): 'What's the bleeding time?' When the picture was first issued, a film critic, rather neatly, likened it to the last bus home – you simply couldn't afford to miss it.'

Doctor in Trouble ○
1970, UK, 90 mins, colour
Dir: Ralph Thomas
Stars: Leslie Phillips, Harry Secombe, Angela Scoular, Irene Handl, Robert Morley, James Robertson Justice
Rating: ★★

Leslie Phillips' doctor is in trouble, all right, in the last to date of the famous comedy series. In the course of an ocean voyage, he falls in the water, loses his trousers, has to dress up as a woman and nearly gets hung, drawn and quartered by a breeches-buoy.

Doctor No
See: Dr No

Doctor Rhythm ○
1938, US, 80 mins, b/w
Dir: Frank Tuttle
Stars: Bing Crosby, Mary Carlisle, Beatrice Lillie
Rating: ★★★

For some reason this wasn't very popular in its time, but it has worn

better than most of Bing Crosby's Paramount musicals of the Thirties. There are hummable songs, a pleasingly idiotic story (originally from O Henry) about a vet hired as a bodyguard, Andy Devine and Sterling Holloway competing in degrees of hoarseness – and the incomparable Beatrice Lillie almost at her most eccentric. All this and a scene-stealing parrot too.

Doctor's Dilemma, The ○
1959, UK, 99 mins, colour
Dir: Anthony Asquith
Stars: Leslie Caron, Dirk Bogarde, Alastair Sim, Robert Morley, Felix Aylmer, Michael Gwynn
Rating: ★★★

Colourful MGM film based on George Bernard Shaw's medical spoof about an unscrupulous artist in bad health, his devoted wife and the doctors she calls in. It's an unusual performance from Dirk Bogarde as the patient – considering he made his name as a doctor in the *Doctor* series. And it's an unusual one, too, from Leslie Caron as the wife – since the role was originally written for an older woman.

Doctor Zhivago ○ ⓥ
1965, US/UK, 192 mins, colour
Dir: David Lean
Stars: Omar Sharif, Julie Christie, Tom Courtenay, Geraldine Chaplin, Rod Steiger, Alec Guinness
Rating: ★★★★

Omar Sharif's face, bleak as the steppes; the desperation of those on a long, doom-laden train journey across the plains to the Urals; the last idyll in the midst of snowbound landscapes for Sharif and Julie Christie; a charge across ice and snow-sodden trenches in wartime; and guerilla warriors mowing down a group of white-clad youths in a field of golden corn. These are the images which haunt you from David Lean's lyrical, five-Oscar treatment of Boris Pasternak's epic novel of strife and love in early 20th century Russia.

Dodge City ○ ⓥ
1939, US, 104 mins, colour
Dir: Michael Curtiz
Stars: Errol Flynn, Olivia de Havilland, Ann Sheridan, Bruce Cabot, Frank McHugh, Alan Hale
Rating: ★★★

Vintage Warner Brothers Western which reunites Errol Flynn with

Olivia de Havilland, his co-star in the other Thirties action classics, *Captain Blood* and *The Adventures of Robin Hood*. Michael Curtiz, the Hungarian-born director who became one of Hollywood's top men at filming blood-stirring action, made all three. There's a wonderful bar-room brawl, an immense feeling of wide-open spaces and brilliant marshalling of crowd scenes, as well as glowing photography in soft, rich early Technicolor by Sol Polito and Ray Rennahan.

Dodsworth ○
1936, US, 101 mins, b/w
Dir: William Wyler
Stars: Walter Huston, Ruth Chatterton, Paul Lukas, Mary Astor, David Niven
Rating: ★★★★

This affecting film of Sinclair Lewis' novel was one of director William Wyler's first major triumphs. Walter Huston is marvellous as the businessman who retires early and takes an extended holiday in Europe with his selfish wife. And you'll be praying that he makes the right decisions in the end. David Niven and John Payne feature in minor roles.

Dog Day Afternoon ● ⓥ
1975, US, 130 mins, colour
Dir: Sidney Lumet
Stars: Al Pacino, John Cazale, Charles Durning, Chris Sarandon, Carol Kane, Lance Henriksen
Rating: ★★

There's a lot to admire in this account of an attempted bank heist by two inept young robbers and their subsequent attempts to get away despite the cordon of police surrounding them. The acting is excellent, at least on the surface; Frank Pierson's screenplay won an Oscar and the film is beautifully made by director Sidney Lumet with some stunning overhead shots. It's meant, I think, as a funny-sad black comedy, although most of its humour comes from its characters swearing repeatedly, which does wear thin after a while. The two robbers, although given full value by Al Pacino and John Cazale, also prove tiresome, unsympathetic people, and only in the last 20 minutes is any tension or excitement engendered by their plight. Most of it is too grating or abrasive to entertain and non-Pacino fans may be restless throughout.

Dog's Life, A ○
1918, US, 30 mins, b/w
Dir: Charles Chaplin
Stars: Charlie Chaplin, Edna Purvience
Rating: ★★★

Charlie Chaplin in his most famous guise – the little tramp – and an appealing dog called Scraps. How can we resist such a combination? The best sequences involve man and dog working together to scrounge food – an early example of the moral: united we stand, divided we fall. This, one of the longest of Charlie's early films, was his first 'Million Dollar' release and bore his autograph at the beginning, together with the legend: 'None genuine without this signature!'

Dogs of War, The ● ⓥ
1980, US, 113 mins, colour
Dir: John Irvin
Stars: Christopher Walken, Tom Berenger, Colin Blakely, JoBeth Williams
Rating: ★★

Director John Irvin certainly gets to grips with Frederick Forsyth's bestseller about mercenaries in Africa although, despite some explosively effective action sequences, the film is perhaps a shade too dispassionate to set the pulses racing. Christopher Walken is a charismatic lead and there's a very good supporting performance from Colin Blakely.

Dolly Sisters, The ○
1945, US, 114 mins, colour
Dir: Irving Cummings
Stars: Betty Grable, John Payne, June Haver S Z Sakall, Reginald Gardiner
Rating: ★★★

There shouldn't be a dry eye in the house at the end of this epic, song-filled musical which kept wartime audiences enraptured. Betty Grable and June Haver display four of the best legs in the business as the real-life sisters of the title, and prove they can both milk a sentimental song for its maximum effect. John Payne, in the last of his musical roles opposite Fox's singing blondes (Grable, Haver and Alice Faye), has his thunder largely stolen by the performing seal with which he is forced to share the spotlight in one scene. Irving Cummings directs with affection, and Ernest Palmer's bright and breezy Technicolor photography (he shot his first film in 1912) sets the seal on the film's considerable nostalgia value.

Dominique ◐
1978, UK, 100 mins, colour
Dir: Michael Anderson
Stars: Cliff Robertson, Jean Simmons, Jenny Agutter
Rating: ★★

Faintly reminiscent of *Diabolique* (alias *The Fiends*), this is also rather (a long way) after director Michael Anderson's previous entry in the baffling-thriller field, *Chase a Crooked Shadow*, made 20 years previously. Jean Simmons makes a welcome reappearance as the lady who may be the victim of a terror campaign by her husband, or may even be the perpetrator. A distinguished supporting cast includes Jenny Agutter, Simon Ward, Judy Geeson, Flora Robson, Ron Moody, Jack Warner and Michael Jayston.

Domino Killings, The
See: The Domino Principle

Domino Principle, The ◐
(aka: The Domino Killings)
1977, US, 100 mins, colour
Dir: Stanley Kramer
Stars: Gene Hackman, Candice Bergen, Richard Widmark, Mickey Rooney, Eli Wallach
Rating: ★★

Presumably the title has something to do with the escalation of events in this predictable thriller. Gene Hackman is the convict sprung by 'them' in order to carry out a special assignment, which is cloaked in mystery, although hardened thriller fans should have little trouble in guessing pretty well what's going on. Richard Widmark contributes the best portrayal in a distinguished cast, and Mickey Rooney offers his customarily pugnacious performance.

Donovan's Brain ○
1953, US, 83 mins, colour
Dir: Felix Feist
Stars: Lew Ayres, Nancy Davis, Gene Evans, Steve Brodie
Rating: ★★★

Second screen re-working of Curt Siodmak's science-fiction shocker about a scientist's attempt to keep a brain alive, that backfires when it starts to control the scientist. It was first made in 1944, with Erich von Stroheim, and again (as *Vengeance*) in 1962 with Peter Van Eyck. Thanks mainly to Lew Ayres' electrifying acting in a Jekyll-and-Hyde role, the film preserves all the psychological tension of the original.

D

Donovan's Reef ○
1963, US, 105 mins, colour
Dir: John Ford
Stars: John Wayne, Lee Marvin, Jack Warden, Dorothy Lamour, Elizabeth Allen, Cesar Romero
Rating: ★★

John Wayne and his favourite director John Ford swap the wide open spaces of the prairie for the wide open spaces of a Pacific island in this sprawling, brawling adventure story that's packed with many Ford regulars such as Edgar Buchanan and Mike Mazurki. Heroes John Wayne and Lee Marvin are two mighty tough guys who would break a beer bottle at an angry word. The acting class is supplied by Jack Warden as a doctor, and by Elizabeth Allen as his blue-stocking daughter. She has a talent for comic timing that was never properly exploited by Hollywood. Watch for the amusing continuity slip when she falls in the sea with stockings on, and emerges bare-legged.

Don't Bother to Knock ◑
1952, US, 76 mins, b/w
Dir: Roy Baker
Stars: Marilyn Monroe, Richard Widmark, Anne Bancroft
Rating: ★★

Richard Widmark doesn't appear as happy in this stop-go chiller as in most of his post-war films for Fox, but then he has high-powered female co-stars Marilyn Monroe and Anne Bancroft both intent on making early impressions. Good, no; interesting, certainly.

Don't Bother to Knock ○ Ⓥ
(aka: Why Bother to Knock?)
1961, UK, 89 mins, colour
Dir: Cyril Frankel
Stars: Richard Todd, Elke Sommer, June Thorburn, Nicole Maurey
Rating: ★★

Richard Todd's first film venture as an independent producer sees him as an amorous travel agent on a laugh-and-mishap-filled tour of Europe. Veteran Judith Anderson – so memorable as Mrs Danvers in *Rebecca* – easily takes the acting honours. Watch out for a group of 'American' girls appearing in the picture, and you may spot the faces of Angela Douglas, Amanda Barrie and Jane Merrow and in smaller parts Warren Mitchell and Ronald Fraser. It's an uneasy role for Todd, and stopped his glittering run of success in its tracks.

Don't Drink the Water ○
1969, US, 100 mins, colour
Dir: Howard Morris
Stars: Jackie Gleason, Estelle Parsons
Rating: ★★

Woody Allen's stage play adapted to the talents of portly Jackie Gleason in a comedy film that never reached these shores. Gleason plays a Jewish caterer who, accused of spying in a Communist country, takes refuge with his family in the American embassy. Former comic supporting actor Howard Morris is the director.

Don't Ever Leave Me ○
1948, UK, 85 mins, b/w
Dir: Arthur Crabtree
Stars: Jimmy Hanley, Petula Clark
Rating: ★★

This comedy about the kidnapping of a teenage girl is remarkable for its parade of stars past and present. Besides those in the bigger roles, watch for fleeting appearances from Anthony Steel, Patricia Dainton and Dandy Nichols. Petula Clark – in the days when her public still thought of her as an impish schoolgirl – plays the all-too-willing kidnap victim, while Hugh Sinclair, Anthony Newley, Barbara Murray, Brenda Bruce, Sandra Dorne and Maurice Denham offer sound support.

Don't Just Lie There, Say Something! ◑
1973, UK, 91 mins, colour
Dir: Bob Kellett
Stars: Brian Rix, Leslie Phillips, Joan Sims, Joanna Lumley
Rating: ★

A mere glance at the title and the three stars (Brian Rix, Leslie Phillips and Joan Sims) is sufficient to indicate the brand of entertainment – lively, saucy, broad, clothes-losing capers in the British tradition. It's based on the successful stage farce by Michael Pertwee who also wrote the screenplay for this much less successful film.

Don't Look Now ● Ⓥ
1973, UK, 110 mins, colour
Dir: Nicolas Roeg
Stars: Donald Sutherland, Julie Christie
Rating: ★★★

You'll either love or hate this supernatural Daphne du Maurier tale made even more inscrutable by director Nicolas Roeg. The Baxters (Donald Sutherland and Julie Christie) travel to Venice after the accidental death of their young daughter. They become involved with two odd sisters (Hilary Mason and Clelia Matania), one of whom is a psychic and claims she can help them contact their daughter. Nothing is what it seems in this strange film, which, with Roeg's fine camerawork and the Venice location, is stunning to watch. Sutherland and Christie give intense performances, but if you demand a logical plot with an equally logical conclusion, you'll find this film irritating. If you let its surreal magic seduce you, you'll understand why it has a strong cult following.

Don't Make Waves ○
1967, US, 96 mins, colour
Dir: Alexander Mackendrick
Stars: Tony Curtis, Claudia Cardinale, Robert Webber, Sharon Tate
Rating: ★

An unhappy experience in Hollywood for ace British comedy director Alexander Mackendrick, who had made such gems as *Whisky Galore!*, *The Man in the White Suit* and *The Ladykillers*. Mackendrick had hit it big on a previous visit to America to make *Sweet Smell of Success*. But this time he found himself saddled with two stars in Tony Curtis and Claudia Cardinale whose lustre on the international scene was beginning to wane, and a script much inferior to the material on which he'd been able to work previously. Studio interference rendered the results even less to the director's liking and the comedy was further hacked about in Britain, where it barely surfaced as a second feature. An unfortunate end to a distinguished directorial career.

Don't Take it to Heart ○
1944, UK, 91 mins, b/w
Dir: Jeffrey Dell
Stars: Richard Greene, Edward Rigby, Patricia Medina
Rating: ★★★

Richard Greene made a couple of good films in his native England after being invalided out of the war and before returning to Hollywood. This ghost comedy co-stars him with then-wife Patricia Medina and is worthy of *The Ghost Goes West* and *The Canterville Ghost*. Jeffrey Dell's direction gives the ingenious story many little embellishments that mark it out as way above average in the fantasy field.

Don't Tell Mom the Babysitter's Dead ◑ ⓥ

1991, US, 105 mins, colour
Dir: Stephen Herek
Stars: Christina Applegate, Joanna Cassidy, John Getz, Josh Charles, Concetta Tomei
Rating: ★★

The title betrays only one of the many chances that this not-bad comedy misses. Five kids, left behind when their mother goes on holiday to Australia for two months, get a sadistic old witch to look after them and the household while she's away. Given that few mothers would pass over a 17-year-old daughter (Christina Applegate) to leave in charge, this is an okay action-farce situation. Straight away, though, the writers make the minder drop dead, and pitch us right into another kind of film. Head daughter Christina has to get a job to support the family (the minder has been buried with the housekeeping). Faking a CV, she falls on her cute blonde Sandra Dee-type feet when given an executive assistant's job with a clothing company. Now if Tina were to use her teenage know-how to make her way in the company, this would be all right. But she doesn't do that for another hour, and in the meantime we get a sappy plot about teenage romance and the junior members of the family stealing thousands from the firm's petty cash Tina has borrowed for groceries (as if she'd take the whole cashbox home!). The last half hour contains some quite bright moments, until Mom comes home to spoil everything before the film has reached any sort of climax. Mom, the kids' report says this is okay but they could have done so much better.

Doomed Cargo

See: Seven Sinners

Doomwatch ◑

1972, UK, 92 mins, colour
Dir: Peter Sasdy
Stars: Ian Bannen, Judy Geeson
Rating: ★★

A chiller based on the famous TV series which made a star of Robert Powell before his character was killed off. In this adventure, series regulars John Paul, Simon Oates and Jean Trend take a back seat while 'guest stars' Ian Bannen and Judy Geeson investigate strange happenings on a far-flung island.

Doors, The ● ⓥ

1991, US, 141 mins, colour
Dir: Oliver Stone
Stars: Val Kilmer, Meg Ryan, Kevin Dillon, Kyle MacLachlan, Frank Whaley, Kathleen Quinlan
Rating: ★★

Director Oliver Stone turns his uncompromising gaze on the self destruction of a rock star. The Adonis-like (well, to begin with) Jim Morrison of The Doors died aged 28 and, if this account of his later life is to be relied on, the only wonder is that he lived that long. Deeply into drugs and booze, he was barely ever in his right mind, yet found time to write poetry and poetic lyrics to songs as well. As played by Val Kilmer here, Jim was a born exhibitionist with a death wish. 'Death turns you on?' asks his long-suffering girlfriend (Meg Ryan, ditzier than usual). 'Life,' he tells her, 'hurts a lot more. When you die, the pain is over.' This is one of the few coherent conversations between a cast of characters who becomes tiresome long before the film is over. Stone's movie is wonderfully well put together, but we never get to know Jim, or any of the others involved. Kilmer works tremendously hard, but it's difficult to care about a character with so few redeeming features.

Door to Door ○

1984, US, 88 mins, colour
Dir: Patrick Bailey
Stars: Ron Leibman, Arliss Howard
Rating: ★★★

This offbeat crime comedy rolls along at a steady lick and boasts a powerful central performance from Ron Leibman as a glib, smooth-talking travelling salesman whose sideline in con tricks puts him at odds with the law. Only Arliss Howard fails to shine as the no-hoper Leibman takes under his wing to learn the art of getting one's foot in the door and keeping it there.

Double Bunk ○

1961, UK, 92 mins, b/w
Dir: C M Pennington-Richards
Stars: Ian Carmichael, Janette Scott, Sidney James, Liz Fraser, Dennis Price
Rating: ★★

This naval lark was Sid James' last film before becoming one of the *Carry On* team. There are some nice bits of comic business on the voyage and some familiar names in the distinguished supporting cast. All told, an enjoyable comedy entertainment of the kind that British studios used to do so well.

Double Confession ○

1950, UK, 85 mins, b/w
Dir: Ken Annakin
Stars: Derek Farr, Joan Hopkins, Peter Lorre, William Hartnell
Rating: ★★

Director Ken Annakin showed in an earlier film, *Holiday Camp*, that he liked to be beside the seaside. But, in this superior crime drama, he makes the resort of 'Seagate' appear a very sinister place indeed. The whodunnit plot benefits enormously from Peter Lorre's almost apologetic menace.

Double Impact ● ⓥ

1991, US, 118 mins, colour
Dir: Sheldon Lettich
Stars: Jean-Claude Van Damme, Alonna Shaw, Geoffrey Lewis, Alan Scarfe
Rating: ★★

If you fancy two Jean-Claude Van Dammes for the price of one (and it isn't worth more), you may get both a smile and a thrill from this bonecrunching action yarn about twin brothers who are separated as babies when their parents are murdered by Chinese mobsters. Twenty-nine years later, they are reunited to seek revenge. This Cain and Abel story is really more like a brass-knuckles version of a Laurel and Hardy film with lethal-looking kickboxing throw in for good measure. Watching Jean-Claude trying to sketch out two different characters, though, is quite a hoot, and director Sheldon Lettich certainly shows a flair for action as well as convincingly presenting us with two Van Dammes on screen at the same time.

Double Indemnity ○

1944, US, 106 mins, b/w
Dir: Billy Wilder
Stars: Barbara Stanwyck, Fred MacMurray, Edward G Robinson
Rating: ★★★★

This excellent crime thriller, enveloped in an atmosphere of doom and tightly directed by Billy Wilder, has now become a classic of its kind. It's incisively written and impeccably structured by Wilder and Raymond Chandler from the novel by James M Cain. Barbara Stanwyck creates her most magnetic femme fatale as the smouldering blonde who seduces insurance man Fred MacMurray into

D

murdering her husband. Her entrance down a stairway is one of the great moments of sexual attraction in the cinema. Studio moguls rejected an original ending (actually shot) in which MacMurray went to the gas chamber for his crimes, and replaced it with the totally different conception retained in the film today.

Double Life, A ○
1947, US, 103 mins, b/w
Dir: George Cukor
Stars: Ronald Colman, Signe Hasso, Edmond O'Brien, Shelley Winters, Ray Collins, Philip Loeb
Rating: ★★★★

A terrific film from the opening frame to closing credits, this was Shelley Winters' first film break after a success on the stage, and it established her as a star. Ronald Colman stars as a gifted stage actor whose despair and murderous moods come from playing the lead in *Othello*. Winters is a buxom, sultry waitress, who is attracted to the married thespian, but soon discovers his propensity for violence. Colman's performance is absolutely riveting and deservedly won an Oscar. The icing on the cake is the literate and intelligent script by the husband and wife team Ruth Gordon and Garson Kanin.

Double Man, The ○
1967, US, 105 mins, colour
Dir: Franklin J Schaffner
Stars: Yul Brynner, Britt Ekland, Clive Revill, Anton Diffring
Rating: ★★★

Which Yul Brynner is which? That's the key to this ingenious and thoroughly absorbing espionage thriller, directed by Franklin Schaffner (*The Best Man, Planet of the Apes, The War Lord*) in the days before he went off the boil. The twists and turns of the plot, based on Henry S Maxfield's *Legacy of a Spy*, reward close watching, and lead to an exciting ski-lift climax, in which Brynner's clever performance reaches its suspenseful height. Even Britt Ekland is more mobile than usual and makes a likeable leading lady.

Double X ◐
1992, UK, 95 mins, colour
Dir: Shani S Grewal
Stars: Norman Wisdom, Gemma Craven, William Katt, Simon Ward, Bernard Hill
Rating: ★★

Consistently through the years, in spite of its efforts to improve its image,

the British cinema has been dogged by inept wooden thrillers that make you laugh (and inwardly cringe). Since the early Fifties, fading film presences have been tempted to appear in these. The lineup here includes Norman Wisdom as a safecracker, Bernard Hill imitating Peter Sellers as an Irish gangster, Simon Ward (trying to be nasty) and, of course, the visiting American 'star', in this case William Katt, who has grown up to look like Sterling Hayden. Deeply unpleasant in theme, the film tries to earn its adult certificate with a short scene of torture, but comes nowhere near. What hurts it more are its smug characterisations, the slaps in the face that are no more than pats, the unconvincing gunplay and actors who lurch through their roles like performers on stage at your local church play. Best line: 'Michael, I understand about the photocopying but – why did you want a piece of raw steak and a Bible?' Laughable.

Down and Out in Beverly Hills ● ⓥ
1986, US, 103 mins, colour
Dir: Paul Mazursky
Stars: Nick Nolte, Bette Midler, Richard Dreyfuss, Little Richard, Elizabeth Pena
Rating: ★★

Hugely successful Hollywood comedy based (yet again) on a French original, this the 1932 classic *Boudu Sauve des Eaux*. It totally revived the star careers of Richard Dreyfuss and Bette Midler, although the film is stolen from both of them by a dog called Mike.

Down Argentine Way ○
1940, US, 94 mins, colour
Dir: Irving Cummings
Stars: Betty Grable, Don Ameche, Carmen Miranda, J Carrol Naish
Rating: ★★

This was the film that launched 20th Century-Fox's dazzlingly-coloured series of musicals, often with vivid and imaginative choreography, that ran throughout the 1940s. The films paired any two from Alice Faye, Don Ameche, Betty Grable and John Payne, and this one stars Ameche with Grable (who actually replaced Faye when the latter went down with appendicitis). Carmen Miranda, of the whirling skirts, fruit-compote hats and delightfully fractured English, was also a part of the Fox musical scene and had a big hit here with *South American Way*. Other musical highlights are a sizzling dance specialty

from The Nicholas Brothers and an amusing novelty number, 'Sing to Your Senorita', from Charlotte Greenwood and Leonid Kinskey. Kinskey replaced Cesar Romero, who ended up in the same hospital as Faye!

Downhill Racer ○
1969, US, 101 mins, colour
Dir: Michael Ritchie
Stars: Robert Redford, Gene Hackman, Camilla Sparv
Rating: ★★★

Interesting and at times exciting story of a poor-born ski-ace trying to win an Olympic gold. The film has excellent colour photography on and off the ski slopes. Robert Redford not only set up the production company for the film, but did most of the dangerous downhill racing himself.

Down Three Dark Streets ○
1954, US, 85 mins, b/w
Dir: Arnold Laven
Stars: Broderick Crawford, Ruth Roman, Martha Hyer, Marisa Pavan
Rating: ★★★

Good thriller which holds together three story threads well and maintains its factual approach throughout. Broderick Crawford is first rate as the FBI agent investigating a colleague's death and director Arnold Laven keeps things tense, compact and plausible.

Down Went McGinty
See: The Great McGinty

Dracula ◐ ⓥ
1931, US, 84 mins, b/w
Dir: Tod Browning
Stars: Bela Lugosi, Edward Van Sloan, Dwight Frye, Helen Chandler
Rating: ★★★★

Tod Browning's original and sometimes very sinister story of a vengeful vampire. The opening sequence is still a brilliant example of how to make the flesh creep, photographed in black and white, always a horror film's best asset. For sheer flesh-creeping nastiness, the settings of the count's homes in England and Transylvania has only been equalled in Browning's own *Mark of the Vampire*, made five years later. Lugosi is a forbidding character as Dracula – but the outstanding performance comes from Dwight Frye, as Dracula's dupe. Cinema has few scenes to equal the first sight of his madness, standing gibbering in a ship filled with dead men.

Dracula ●
(aka: The Horror of Dracula)
1958, UK, 82 mins, colour
Dir: Terence Fisher
Stars: Peter Cushing, Christopher Lee,
Melissa Stribling, Michael Gough
Rating: ★★★★

Hammer's original vampire film, an excellent adaptation of Bram Stoker's classic book. Plush, glossy, but above all scarifying, with a devastatingly effective climax whose special effects were much imitated in subsequent years. Christopher Lee is definitely intimidating in the title role and the film is directed by Terence Fisher with drive and great single-mindedness. Many sequels followed, all with Lee as Dracula, but none of them are half as good as this one.

Dracula ●
1973, US, 100 mins, colour
Dir: Dan Curtis
Stars: Jack Palance, Simon Ward,
Penelope Homer
Rating: ★★★

Director Dan Curtis clearly has a yearning to make a great horror film out of Bram Stoker's classic novel. The brilliant opening scenes declare his ambition. Mists rise from a black Transylvanian lake, like the memory of some faded and forgotten painting. A pack of great dogs, ownerless, pounds helter-skelter along the dim lakeside and through the dark pines that line it. But words soon take over from images and Richard Matheson's screenplay is uncharacteristically flabby. Although Curtis has clearly been influenced more by Universal than by Hammer, his devotion to how things look makes too often for a very static film. Jack Palance restrains himself commendably from over-acting as the Count, but just misses on the menace. Penelope Horner's Mina is the one first-class performance: deep and penetrating.

Dracula ●
1979, US/UK, 109 mins, colour
Dir: John Badham
Stars: Frank Langella, Laurence Olivier,
Donald Pleasence, Kate Nelligan, Trevor
Eve
Rating: ★

Abandon ship! Drac is back. And Frank Langella is visually a perfect Count Dracula in this over-styled re-telling of the Bram Stoker original. He is more than a match for Trevor Eve's sheepish Jonathan Harker, Laurence Olivier's ripely sliced Van Helsing and Donald Pleasence's familiar wild-eyed doctor. Director John Badham seems more conscious in achieving striking visuals (sometimes very good – as in the sequence where a vampire girl is encountered underground) than in getting his technical details right: a victim's bitemarks appear on the opposite side to the bite, and a vampire reflects not in a mirror but does in water. A major disappointment.

Dracula [1993]
See: Bram Stoker's Dracula

Dracula AD 1972 ● ⓥ
1972, UK, 100 mins, colour
Dir: Alan Gibson
Stars: Christopher Lee, Peter Cushing,
Stephanie Beacham
Rating: ★

The old Hammer vampire legend sits rather uneasily in modern times, the dialogue suggesting that the studio had half-decided to play this one for laughs. But the final confrontation between Peter Cushing and Christoper Lee is a good one, and there is an above-average line-up of beauties for Dracula to sink his fangs into.

Dracula Has Risen from the Grave ● ⓥ
1968, UK, 92 mins, colour
Dir: Freddie Francis
Stars: Christopher Lee, Rupert Davies,
Veronica Carlson
Rating: ★★

Dracula's tears of blood are the most original touch in this film. However, director Freddie Francis manages to stage one or two nice tableaux amid the gore.

Dracula – Prince of Darkness ● ⓥ
1965, UK, 90 mins, colour
Dir: Terence Fisher
Stars: Christopher Lee, Barbara Shelley,
Andrew Keir, Francis Matthews
Rating: ★★

The first sequel to the fine original Hammer *Dracula* suffers from a less credible basic premise, and heroes and heroines so silly that it's difficult to sympathise with their plight. Never mind, Christopher Lee is as hissingly horrifying as ever as the master of darkness. It's not until the film is over that you realise he hardly has a word to say. A minor annoyance is provided by the crossed swords at Dracula's castle. You would have thought the Count would not have allowed anything in the shape of a cross in his domain.

Dracula Prisoner of Frankenstein ●
1972, UK/Spain, 90 mins, colour
Dir: Jesus Franco
Stars: Dennis Price, Howard Vernon,
Mary Francis
Rating: ★

Spanish director Jesus Franco took a break from making sex romps to stitch together this horror film that's reminiscent of the tail-end of the Hollywood horrors of the Forties, when all the monsters were thrown together in one ghoulish pot-pourri. Just like that, Franco mixes together all the standard ingredients of the genre, and comes up with a pretty indigestible brew. Vampires are out for blood, the monster drags his feet, the werewolf looks miserable, winds howl, hinges creak and candles flicker (although Frankenstein seems to have plenty of electricity for his laboratory). One almost expects Abbott and Costello to creep round the corner of the crypt. Britain's Dennis Price has the leading role, in one of his last films.

Dracula's Daughter ◐
1936, US, 70 mins, b/w
Dir: Lambert Hillyer
Stars: Otto Kruger, Gloria Holden,
Marguerite Churchill
Rating: ★★★

The best of the Universal Dracula series by some little way, tenuously adapted from Bram Stoker's short story. Lambert Hillyer, a director whose experience stretches back to the early silent days, keeps a very firm grip on the clammy atmosphere, and the two ladies are absolutely splendid. Marguerite Churchill makes a pretty and resourceful heroine, while London-born Gloria Holden creates a real figure of pity as the countess afflicted with the curse of the vampire.

Dragnet ○ ⓥ
1987, US, 106 mins, colour
Dir: Tom Mankiewicz
Stars: Dan Aykroyd, Tom Hanks,
Christopher Plummer, Harry Morgan
Rating: ★★

If they'd stuck to the style of the beginning, this pastiche on the old TV

D

cop series of the Fifties might have been a gem. It's still enjoyable old-fashioned entertainment, even if it does give way too soon to a plot that looks like a throwoff from the *Our Man Flint* or *Matt Helm* series. Dan Aykroyd is the modern-day nephew of the now-deceased Joe Friday, immortalised on TV by Jack Webb; like his uncle he goes strictly by the book – like, ma'am, he just wants the facts. Tom Hanks completes the star pairing as Friday's new partner, a maverick who gradually assumes some of Friday's identity as the latter becomes involved in pursuit of the 'virgin Connie Swale' (Alexandra Paul), who is herself hunted by the PAGAN sect, led by a sadly come-down Christopher Plummer, that's out to control the city. Aykroyd is suitably stolid, throwing his lighter moments into amusing relief, in what was his best work before *Driving Miss Daisy*. Director Tom Mankiewicz, who should have taken this performance as his keystone, has been quoted as saying, 'I believe good comedy should have a base in realism.' Right you are Tom: a pity you didn't apply the maxim here.

Dragon Seed ○

1944, UK, 145 mins, b/w
Dir: Jack Conway, Harold S Bucquet
Stars: Katharine Hepburn, Walter Huston, Akim Tamiroff, Turhan Bey, Aline MacMahon, Hurd Hatfield
Rating: ★★★

An interesting effort to follow the success of writer Pearl S Buck's *The Good Earth* (which won two Oscars when filmed in 1937). Two screenwriters, Marguerite Roberts and Jane Murfin, toiled mightily to compress another vast Buck novel about China into something under two and a half hours actual running time, but it still seems a bit unwieldy, even when controlled by two directors. Katharine Hepburn, emoting fiercely with eyelids taped down, is always worth watching, however, especially in the film's extraordinary final tableau. Walter Huston, Akim Tamiroff and particularly Agnes Moorehead also do good work.

Dragonslayer ◑

1981, US, 108 mins, colour
Dir: Matthew Robbins
Stars: Peter MacNicol, Caitlin Clarke, Ralph Richardson, John Hallam
Rating: ★★★

'Its talons tear, its breath burns, it is terror,' ran the publicity ads for this glossy Walt Disney medieval fantasy adventure, the studio's second co-production with another major studio (Paramount). And for once you can forget the twee medieval worlds conjured up in previous Disney offerings; Urland is a dark and pitiful place where young girls are regularly sacrificed to a mighty dragon. Young Peter MacNicol, who a year later would fight Kevin Kline for the love of Meryl Streep in *Sophie's Choice*, is the boy who dreams of becoming a dragonslayer. It's an extremely long and winding road to the final (admitedly exciting) David and Goliath showdown, but flying dragon Vermithrax Pejorative is a stunning creation from George Lucas' Industrial Light and Magic workshops. In fact, the special effects were Oscar-nominated, but lost out on the night to *Raiders of the Lost Ark*.

Dragon, The Bruce Lee Story ◑ Ⓥ

1993, US, 121 mins, colour
Dir: Rob Cohen
Stars: Jason Scott Lee, Lauren Holly, Robert Wagner
Rating: ★★

A biography that looks almost as ludicrous as any of its star's films, *Dragon* still works quite well as entertainment. And there are some chilly overtones involving Lee's son Brandon, killed earlier that year while filming, as the movie dwells at length on the nightmare 'demons' that pursued both father and son. Scenes where Lee is drawn into fights after coming to America, then starts a martial arts academy, may be authentic but fit less cosily into the scenario, while a sequence where Lee is attacked by restaurant staff wielding kitchen choppers may give rise to more laughs than thrills. Jason Scott Lee and Lauren Holly catch Lee and his wife well enough, and Rob Cohen's direction keeps the film moving at a pace that (apart from a very slow credit sequence) keeps us occupied without stretching our minds.

Dragonwyck ○

1946, US, 103 mins, b/w
Dir: Joseph L Mankiewicz
Stars: Gene Tierney, Vincent Price, Walter Huston, Glenn Langan, Anne Revere, Jessica Tandy
Rating: ★★★

Vincent Price's career as a merchant of menace really began to take off from 1946, in *Dragonwyck* and, to a lesser extent, *Shock*, in which he played a mad doctor. *Dragonwyck*, Joseph L Mankiewicz's first film as director (he also wrote the script from Anya Seton's novel), is an elegant chiller atmospherically set in an 1840s mansion wherein Price lurks down the years, trying to get rid of various wives. He's terrific, and Gene Tierney is beautiful as the newest endangered wife.

Dragoon Wells Massacre ○

1957, US, 88 mins, colour
Dir: Harold Schuster
Stars: Dennis O'Keefe, Barry Sullivan, Mona Freeman, Katy Jurado
Rating: ★★★

Exciting and moving by turns, this Western about a wagon train trying to survive in Apache territory is an action film with heart that finds outdoor adventure specialist Harold Schuster back to his best form. Its script by Warren Douglas (a former minor Hollywood star who also plays a supporting role) creates real people and attracted a good cast – Dennis O'Keefe, Barry Sullivan, Katy Jurado, Mona Freeman, Jack Elam (for once a sympathetic figure), Sebastian Cabot and more. Terrific photography by William Clothier, both in close-up and long shot, makes the most of the colour by De Luxe. A serious, exciting and emotionally effective example of its kind.

Draughtsman's Contract, The ◑

1982, UK, 103 mins, colour
Dir: Peter Greenaway
Stars: Anthony Higgins, Janet Suzman, Anne Louise Lambert
Rating: ★★

A fascinating – if not perhaps 'easy' film – which has acquired an appreciable reputation thanks to its premiere at the London Film Festival and successive screenings elsewhere. It became one of London's biggest box-office hits, and was the third film made by director Peter Greenaway for the British Film Institute Production Board (in this instance, in association with Channel Four). Greenaway himself has described it in these terms: 'It's a very literate film; the dialogue has been very carefully worked out for puns and conceits. The whole thing is an elaborate charade, a conceit, which the 17th century enjoyed doing.' You may enjoy seeing it if you're the patient kind.

Dr Crippen ◐
1962, UK, 98 mins, b/w
Dir: Robert Lynn
Stars: Donald Pleasence, Coral Browne, Samantha Eggar
Rating: ★★★

Although the film is overlong, Donald Pleasence is never less than compelling in the title role of this account of a notorious Edwardian murderer. A slow, sincere reconstruction of the famous murder case of 1910, it sets out to prove that Crippen killed his wife only by accident – although you may find writer Leigh Vance's version less than convincing. Coral Browne conveys well the mixed feelings of Crippen's coarse, but pitifully love-craving wife, while Samantha Eggar gives one of her best performances as Crippen's young mistress Ethel, giving the role depth and sensitivity, and fully exploring the gamut of the girl's emotions. Nicolas Roeg's black-and-white photography is very atmospheric.

Dr Cyclops ○
1940, US, 75 mins, colour
Dir: Ernest B Schoedsack
Stars: Albert Dekker, Janice Logan, Thomas Coley
Rating: ★★★

A mad scientist, conducting bizarre experiments in deepest Brazil, shrinks former colleagues and leaves them to struggle against now-gigantic insects, birds and small animals. Interesting to compare the effects with the similarly styled *The Incredible Shrinking Man.* Albert Dekker is splendidly sinister as the scientist, and there are some suspenseful shock moments, notably the group's efforts to train a rifle on their sleeping tormentor, and the nail-biting climax. Directed by Ernest B Schoedsack, co-director of *King Kong.*

Dreamboat ○
1952, US, 80 mins, b/w
Dir: Claude Binyon
Stars: Clifton Webb, Ginger Rogers, Jeffrey Hunter, Anne Francis
Rating: ★★★

A riotous comedy film about a crusty college professor whose students discover he was once an idolised silent movie star. There are some riotous glimpses of silent films Clifton Webb

and Ginger Rogers' characters are supposed to have made, as well as a hilarious scene from one of Webb's Forties' films, *Sitting Pretty.* Sheer joy, with Fred Clark and Elsa Lanchester given acidly witty supporting roles by director Claude Binyon's sparkling script. Look out for the girl in the commercials – she is Gwyneth Verdon, just before she scored on Broadway in *The Pajama Game* as Gwen Verdon: she went on to tempt Tab Hunter in *Damn Yankees.*

Dreamchild ◐
1985, UK, 94 mins, colour
Dir: Gavin Millar
Stars: Coral Browne, Peter Gallagher, Ian Holm, Jane Asher
Rating: ★★

An ambitious and gimmicky exploration of the relationship between the Rev Charles L Dodgson (aka Lewis Carroll) and the little girl who inspired him to write *Alice's Adventures in Wonderland.* The film, directed by Gavin Millar, sets out with the idea that Dodgson was unnaturally attracted to underage girls. But the presentation is clumsy, involving several long, lustful gazes between Ian Holm as Dodgson and newcomer Amelia Shankley as Alice. An amusing diversion is created by grotesque caricatures of characters from the Wonderland story, produced by Jim Henson's Muppet workshops and voiced by Alan Bennett, Julie Walters and Fulton Mackay.

Dream Demon ● ⓥ
1988, UK, 89 mins, colour
Dir: Harley Cokliss
Stars: Jemma Redgrave, Kathleen Wilhoite, Jimmy Nail, Timothy Spall, Annabelle Lanyon
Rating: ★★★

A pretty scary this-house-possessed horror film, hampered by an unconvincing central perfomance (from Jemma Redgrave) and unbelievable characters but conceptually fairly interesting. Bride-to-be Redgrave moves into a rented house on the run-up to her wedding and immediately starts experiencing the most horrendous nightmares that not only strike you as convincing, but tell her the truth about her fiancé and bring her face-to-face with the horrific past of the house itself. She's joined by Jenny (Kathleen Wilhoite – very good), an American who feels she may once have lived there. Together the girls confront a dream demon that

may destroy them both. Take a friend to this one, excitingly thought out by director Harley Cokliss who has perhaps retained some of his more livid nightmares and incorporated them in the story. Seat-clutching stuff.

Dream Lover ● ⓥ
1993, Us, 103 mins, colour
Dir: Nicholas Kazan
Stars: James Spader, Mädchen Amick
Rating: ★★

This is pretty offbeat, if not as tight or taut or effective as it might be. James Spader, becoming typecast as the yuppie who has it all, divorces his first wife and runs slap into wide-eyed brunette Mädchen Amick, who swiftly becomes Mrs Spader No 2. But when she says, 'Just because I'm half-way pretty, guys look into my eyes and think they know me,' and starts talking about peeling away the layers of an onion, you suspect there's something afoot. Spader finds she's changed her name and divorced herself from her parents. Still, he's willing to forget this, and they have two children together. But then she starts getting smoochy phone calls, and there are those unspecified bills from the Hotel Chanticleer. It's all a diabolical plot, of course, and not many of its later developments hold water. Even so, Spader takes centre stage rather well, which is more than can be said for his vacuous leading lady. And the ending is neatly worked out, even if you can't agree with the conclusions Spader draws from it. Hitchcock might have made us believe more of it.

Dream Team, The ◐ ⓥ
1989, US, 113 mins, colour
Dir: Howard Zieff
Stars: Michael Keaton, Christopher Lloyd, Peter Boyle, Stephen Furst, Lorraine Bracco, Dennis Boutsikaris
Rating: ★★★

Any film that comes up with an idea that's fairly new after nearly a century of the cinema deserves some kudos. *The Dream Team* deserves even more for eventually overcoming our apprehensions and making us laugh at its four escaped psychiatric patients who are accidentally left adrift in the New York. 'It's great to be young and insane,' gasps Michael Keaton as they set out to see a ball game. But he and his three comrades have to 'sane up' pretty fast if they're to rescue their psychiatrist (Dennis Boutsikaris) from the murderous intentions of two crooked cops (Philip Bosco, James

D

Remar). This isn't easy for twitchy Christopher Lloyd, who thinks he's the psychiatrist, the holy Joe (Peter Boyle), who likes taking his clothes off, and plumply catatonic Stephen Furst. Slow to hit its stride, and initially often as sad as you'd expect, the film gains momentum with the unwinding of the mainspring of its plot and proves frequently funny in its closing stages. Keaton is aces as the short-fused Billy: he ought to make more of this kind of fun.

Dream Wife ○
1952, US, 101 mins, b/w
Dir: Sidney Sheldon
Stars: Cary Grant, Deborah Kerr, Walter Pidgeon, Betta St John
Rating: ★

Cary Grant is given another opportunity to exercise his inimitable flair for comedy in this fluffy number. And he's perfectly in command of his role as a rather bewildered suitor in a woman's world. The dialogue and situations are occasionally fresh and funny, but the plot goes on too long for its own good. It showed at the time that Hollywood could still weave gossamer fancies – but not without straining a little.

Dr Ehrlich's Magic Bullet ◐
1940, US, 103 mins, b/w
Dir: William Dieterle
Stars: Edward G Robinson, Ruth Gordon, Otto Kruger, Donald Crisp, Maria Ouspenskaya, Montagu Love
Rating: ★★★

One of the best of the Warner medical biographies, with Edward G Robinson as the 19th century German chemical genius who eventually invented a cure for syphilis. Despite the tricky subject, this makes compelling, well-written drama, with Robinson outstanding in the title role.

Dressed to Kill ○
1946, US, 70 mins, b/w
Dir: William Neill
Stars: Basil Rathbone, Nigel Bruce, Patricia Morison
Rating: ★★

Basil Rathbone cracks his last case in the long Universal series, appropriately known in Britain as *Sherlock Holmes and the Secret Code*. Striking opera star Patricia Morison has the female lead.

Dressed to Kill ● ⓥ
1980, US, 100 mins, colour
Dir: Brian De Palma

Stars: Michael Caine, Angie Dickinson, Nancy Allen, Keith Gordon, Dennis Franz
Rating: ★★

A highly exploitative suspense story, recognisably from the blood-spattered hands of director Brian De Palma, who gave us *Carrie*, *Scarface* and *Body Double*. This is perhaps his most blatant homage to Hitchcock (and especially *Psycho*), though the master might shift uneasily in his grave at the long drawn-out tension, the flashy sex scenes and the four-letter words used for shock effect. Michael Caine, Angie Dickinson and Nancy Allen do sterling service above and beyond the call to keep the frenzied farrago ticking over. The mechanics of suspense are worked quite well by the director and may frighten the easily scared quite badly.

Dresser, The ○ ⓥ
1983, UK, 118 mins, colour
Dir: Peter Yates
Stars: Albert Finney, Tom Courtenay, Edward Fox, Zena Walker, Michael Gough
Rating: ★★★

Tom Courtenay repeats his West End stage success as the camp theatrical dresser who lives his life through the performances of his master, a larger-than-life 40s actor-manager (Albert Finney). Ronald Harwood's screenplay is an acutely observed character study (said to be based on actor/manager Donald Wolfit) and, while it remains a stagebound affair, the film recreates perfectly the atmosphere of wartime England and shambolic squalor of life for a touring theatre company.

Dressmaker, The ● ⓥ
1988, UK, 92 mins, colour
Dir: Jim O'Brien
Stars: Jane Horrocks, Joan Plowright, Billie Whitelaw
Rating: ★★

The British cinema of the late Eighties seemed too often to be rooted in the past, and here's another *Hope and Glory* meets *Yanks* set in the wartime years. With its multiplicity of period trimmings, it looks, to use the vernacular of the Liverpool where its rather grim story is set, 'dead expensive'. It's also a fairly good job of work all round. Jane Horrocks is Rita, a slightly repressed teenager looked after by two aunts (Joan Plowright, Billie Whitelaw) and soon pitched into an encounter with an American

soldier who wants what wartime Yanks were supposed to want. When she slaps him off regretfully, he turns to her fun-loving Aunt Billie instead. Capable, careful performances etch themselves into a reasonably interesting portrait of the times, authentic to almost the last detail – although I'd like to know what the coin was that Rita is given to buy 40 2½d stamps.

Drive a Crooked Road ○
1954, US, 82 mins, b/w
Dir: Richard Quine
Stars: Mickey Rooney, Dianne Foster, Kevin McCarthy
Rating: ★★

This role, as a cocky little mechanic who becomes involved in murder, marked another step towards recognition as a straight actor for pint-sized Mickey Rooney, star of many musicals and comedies of the early Forties. A year later, Rooney was being acclaimed for his fine performance in the war film, *The Bold and the Brave*.

Driver, The ○ ⓥ
(aka: Driver)
1978, US, 91 mins, colour
Dir: Walter Hill
Stars: Ryan O'Neal, Bruce Dern, Isabelle Adjani, Ronee Blakely
Rating: ★★★

This effective modern *film noir* crime drama stars Ryan O'Neal as a professional getaway driver and Bruce Dern as the obsessive detective determined to catch him. The fact that none of the characters in the film have proper names (they're only The Driver, The Detective, The Connection, etc) give it a disconnected existential feel and an air of mystery it otherwise wouldn't have. Rather than alienating the viewer, though, this device serves to make the film more fascinating. Dern takes the acting honours although O'Neal makes his taciturn character quite believable. Director-writer Walter Hill directs with pace and style to make this a crime film that's interesting and slightly different. The best scene is where O'Neal takes a carload of crooks who doubt his ability on a high-speed run around an underground car park, delicately using pillars and walls to rip off parts of their car as he goes.

Driving Miss Daisy ○ ⓥ
1989, US, 99 mins, colour
Dir: Bruce Beresford
Stars: Morgan Freeman, Jessica Tandy, Dan Aykroyd, Patti Lupone
Rating: ★★★★

It's really hard to see anyone disliking this sweet-natured, if sharp-tongued story of a 70-year-old southern American Jewish lady (Jessica Tandy, winning an Oscar), forced by her son (Dan Aykroyd) to take on a black chauffeur (Morgan Freeman) after she can no longer be trusted behind her own wheel. This is 1948 and the winds of change are only beginning to blow through the magnolias outside her Georgia mansion. Still, it's not his colour she objects to, merely his presence. At first, she refuses to be driven in her own car, but soon she's in the back seat, drawing him pro-gressively into her confidence. Both mistress and servant have a sardonic sense of humour and it's the beginning of a 20-year friendship, not admitted as such by the tradition-bound Miss Daisy until the end of the film. The movie (also an Oscar winner) gently probes the demeaning position of blacks in the south, but only in so far as it fits writer Alfred Uhry's policy of education by an entertaining kind of persuasion. What's more important is the relationship between the three main characters, and this is carefully, flawlessly sketched in by Tandy, Freeman and Aykroyd, the latter qui-etly effective in a different kind of assignment from his raunchy comedy roles.

Dr Jekyll and Mr Hyde ○
1931, US, 98 mins, b/w
Dir: Rouben Mamoulian
Stars: Fredric March, Miriam Hopkins
Rating: ★★★★

This is still the best version by far of Robert Louis Stevenson's macabre story, in which Fredric March deservedly won an Oscar for his ter-rifying portrayal of the Victorian doctor who develops a sinister double personality. Directed by Rouben Mamoulian and shot by the Os-car-nominated Karl Struss (who had photographed the 1920 silent version starring John Barrymore), the film is a powerfully imaginative piece, full of symbolism and spine-chilling atmosphere. The opening scene in which Jekyll goes to the lecture the-atre and the audience has its first view of March remains a classic of cine-matography, while the

transformations from Jekyll to Hyde and back again were achieved in one take by the inspired use of makeup and coloured filters. March's chilling, unforgettable performance proved that he was well capable of far, far more than light comedy roles, and Miriam Hopkins, cast somewhat against type, is effective as the sadistic slut, Ivy.

Dr Jekyll and Mr Hyde ○
1941, US, 120 mins, b/w
Dir: Victor Fleming
Stars: Spencer Tracy, Spencer Tracy, Ingrid Bergman, Lana Turner
Rating: ★★

Fredric March's Oscar for the 1931 version of the classic horror tale has undeservedly overshadowed Spencer Tracy's performance in this early Forties remake. Using a minimum of make-up, Tracy achieves the maxi-mum in horror in the transformation scenes with a combination of lighting and facial expression. At first set to play the roles in reverse, Ingrid Bergman and Lana Turner decided to play the bad and good girl respec-tively. But their decision was ill-advised – even to beat type-casting – for each had much more to offer the other role.

Dr Jekyll and Sister Hyde ●
1971, UK, 94 mins, colour
Dir: Roy Ward Baker
Stars: Martine Beswick, Ralph Bates, Gerald Sim
Rating: ★★★

A ridiculous idea, you might think, to travesty Stevenson's old chiller classic by turning Mr Hyde (and Dr Jekyll) into a woman. Strangely, though, the notion results in one of the best films to come out of Hammer studios since their peak period some ten years ear-lier. Director Roy Ward Baker turns in his best work in years and combines with Technicolor cameraman Norman Warwick to make the film visually magnetic in its own way. Martine Beswick makes a fetching Sister Hyde, positively radiating evil, and the transformation sequences are above average for this sort of thing.

Dr No ○ ⓥ
1962, UK, 111 mins, colour
Dir: Terence Young
Stars: Sean Connery, Ursula Andress, Joseph Wiseman, Jack Lord, Bernard Lee
Rating: ★★★

First, fastest and best of the James Bond films. Sean Connery is an agile, handsome and sardonic hero, Ursula Andress still the most delectable Bondswoman on record. The action moves swiftly enough to cover the holes in the plot, and the humour is of a standard not maintained in some of the later Bond extravaganzas. This is the one, to refresh your memory, in which Bond meets the gorgeous Honey, is singed by a flamethrower, tickled by a tarantula, dogged by bloodhounds, grilled by some electric fencing, drugged by coffee, swamped by seawater and nearly atomised in a nuclear pile.

Drop Dead, Darling ○
(aka: Arrivederci Baby!)
1966, UK, 105 mins, colour
Dir: Ken Hughes
Stars: Tony Curtis, Rosanna Schiaffino, Lionel Jeffries, Nancy Kwan
Rating: ★★

At times sparkling black comedy about a confidence trickster who marries, then murders, for money. There's one delightfully audacious sequence in which Tony Curtis appears as a young teenager, complete with lollipop and velvet shorts. Curtis skates happily over the thin ice of this idea, to make it an inspiration. There are too many flat spots, but some very funny mo-ments are topped by the last words of Fenella Fielding, which are worth waiting to hear.

Drowning by Numbers ● ⓥ
1988, UK, 118 mins, colour
Dir: Peter Greenaway
Stars: Joan Plowright, Juliet Stevenson, Joely Richardson, Bernard Hill
Rating: ★★

A series of 'moving paintings' that depicts three women from the same family who all drown their husbands. As a black comedy, this is a great idea by maverick British director Peter Greenaway but, although his images recall the paintings of Brueghel, Greenaway lingers too long in the telling of the tale, and gives it too little substance. Not that the whole thing doesn't have a certain consist-ency. The coroner (Bernard Hill), who fancies all three women and lies about the watery deaths, has a 13-year-old son who numbers deaths, animal and human, fires off fireworks for every victim and has such a yen for the 'skipping girl' that he circumcises himself for her. All very contrived and artificial, the film gradually sheds

D

its tedium as it develops. Cinema-tographer Sacha Vierney's colour images – the fashionable word is 'painterly' – should have been worth an Oscar nomination. An intellectual farce, the film fascinates throughout without actually raising a smile.

Drowning Pool, The ◐
1975, US, 108 mins, colour
Dir: Stuart Rosenberg
Stars: Paul Newman, Joanne Woodward, Anthony Franciosa, Murray Hamilton, Gail Strickland, Melanie Griffith
Rating: ★★

A lively follow-up to *The Moving Target*, in which Paul Newman first played detective Lew Harper. It's a woman who hires Harper again (in this case played by Newman's wife Joanne Woodward) and he's soon up to his shoulder-holster in a lethal tangle that's murkier than the bayou in which his client's mother (Coral Browne) is soon found floating. Director Stuart Rosenberg, after a slowish start, sticks to a brisk telling of the basic story. The dialogue is tough, but the acting (apart from Newman and Richard Jaeckel as a bullet-headed cop) mannered and not too convincing. Newman himself, though, is a huge consolation. Some of his individual scenes, in which he displays a subtly quirky sense of humour, make wonderfully successful conversation pieces. He alone emerges from *The Drowning Poo!* dripping with credit. Down the cast Melanie Griffith makes one of her earliest film appearances.

Dr Phibes Rises Again ●
1972, UK, 89 mins, colour
Dir: Robert Fuest
Stars: Vincent Price, Robert Quarry, Peter Cushing
Rating: ★★

Robert Quarry, alias Count Yorga, takes over from Joseph Cotten as the new adversary for a Dr Phibes reactivated by fresh blood to replace the embalming fluid which has preserved him since his last adventure. This time the sense of the ludicrous is not used so well to the film's own advantage, although there is a good quota of splendidly ingenious deaths, topped by Hugh Griffith being flung overboard from a liner in a giant gin bottle.

Dr Socrates ○
1935, US, 74 mins, b/w
Dir: William Dieterle

Stars: Paul Muni, Ann Dvorak, Barton MacLane, Ralph Bellamy
Rating: ★★★

Paul Muni, taking the title role of a small-town doctor forced to treat a wounded gangster, here worked for the first time with director William Dieterle, with whom he would subsequently make *The Story of Louis Pasteur*, *The Life of Emile Zola* and *Juarez*. The film was remade in 1939 as *King of the Underworld*: Kay Francis took the Muni role and Humphrey Bogart was the lead gangster, the part taken here by Barton MacLane.

Dr Strangelove or: How I Learned to Stop Worrying and Love the Bomb ○ ⓥ
1963, US, 93 mins, b/w
Dir: Stanley Kubrick
Stars: Peter Sellers, George C Scott, Sterling Hayden, Keenan Wynn, Slim Pickens, James Earl Jones
Rating: ★★★

With the possible exception of *2001: A Space Odyssey*, this is probably the most famous of the relatively infrequent but always original films produced by the controversial and highly individual director Stanley Kubrick. A black comedy on a nuclear theme, it has the inimitable Peter Sellers triumphant in a trio of roles (notably as Strangelove, the scientist whose artificial arm repeatedly makes a Heil Hitler sign as an involuntary reflex action) plus two splendid co-stars in George C Scott and Sterling Hayden, and an impressive supporting cast which includes Keenan Wynn, Slim Pickens and Tracy Reed. Sellers and Wynn share what is the film's funniest scene, involving a telephone call to the American President.

Dr Syn ○
1937, UK, 81 mins, b/w
Dir: Roy William Neill
Stars: George Arliss, Margaret Lockwood, John Loder
Rating: ★★★

Russell Thorndike's famous adventure novel about the smuggling clergyman at large in the 19th century was filmed almost simultaneously by Hammer and by Disney (with Peter Cushing and Patrick McGoohan) in the early Sixties. This is the first version and just as exciting and well-handled as any, weakened only by the central casting of aristocratic George Arliss as Dr Syn.

Dr Syn Alias the Scarecrow ○
1963, UK, 93 mins, colour
Dir: James Neilson
Stars: Patrick McGoohan, George Cole, Tony Britton, Geoffrey Keen, Kay Walsh, Patrick Wymark
Rating: ★★★

A rip-roaring, fast-paced, *Boy's Own*-style smuggling adventure from the Disney studio. Originally made in three parts for American TV, *Dr Syn* proved well worthy of the cinema showing it received in Britain. Patrick McGoohan is ideally cast as the imperturbable vicar, who is also the Scarecrow, the Robin Hood-style leader of the smugglers. A hand-picked cast of convincing ruffians backs him splendidly, especially George Cole as the sexton. The story constantly grips, and there are several moments of real tension, particularly a jailbreak, where McGoohan's knife-edge playing and the taut direction of James Nielson do much to tighten the audience stranglehold. The Scarecrow's mask is a splendid Hammer-style creation; it, and one or two other jumpy moments, make the film perhaps just a little scary for young children.

Dr Terror's House of Horrors ●
1964, UK, 98 mins, colour
Dir: Freddie Francis
Stars: Peter Cushing, Christopher Lee, Roy Castle, Donald Sutherland
Rating: ★★

Taking its cue from the popular portmanteau style of *Dead of Night* some 20 years previously, this was the first of Amicus' successful series of horror story compendiums. The five segments – featuring werewolves, vampires, voodoo, killer vines and a re-working of *The Beast with Five Fingers* – are of varying quality, but there's no doubting the authentic creepiness of the opening and closing sequences. These are dominated by Peter Cushing's genuinely sinister Dr Sandor Schreck, a dealer of death through his set of Tarot cards. And there are some surprising faces in the cast: Christopher Lee you expect to see (and he's very impressive as an overbearing art critic), but Roy Castle, Kenny Lynch and – gulp – Alan Freeman? Max Adrian has fun as a vampire and, in the same episode, a youthful Donald Sutherland makes one of his first film appearances. The child actress Sarah Nicholls later achieved adult stardom as Phoebe Nicholls.

Drugstore Cowboy ● Ⓥ
1989, US, 101 mins, colour
Dir: Gus Van Sant
Stars: Matt Dillon, Kelly Lynch, James Le Gros, Heather Graham, James Remar
Rating: ★★★

Quite skilfully made, apparently on a low budget, this rough-edged drama is a kind of *Bonnie and Clyde* of the drug generation. There's even an allusion to not wanting to end up like Bonnie and Clyde in a recurring song. Matt Dillon (as 'Bad' Bobby Hughes) and Kelly Lynch are young marrieds who, with two confederates, rob drug stores for their own fixes and supply to others. As Dillon's quite effective narrative explains it: 'We were just trying to stay high.' But the cops pursue, death rears its head and it all has to stop, for Dillon at least. 'I'm a junkie,' he says with resigned regretfulness. 'I liked the whole lifestyle. But it didn't pay off.' The film's nicely old-fashioned in construction and Dillon reminiscent of the gangsters of earlier film eras, with his paranoias about the mention of pets or hats on the bed. He gives his best performance in several years. The film's no masterpiece, but its effective little sermon does stick in the mind.

Drum, The ○
(aka: Drums)
1938, UK, 96 mins, colour
Dir: Zoltan Korda
Stars: Sabu, Roger Livesey, Valerie Hobson, Raymond Massey, Francis L Sullivan
Rating: ★★★

Rip-roaring adventure yarn about the British in India struggling to prevent rebel tribesmen from usurping a young prince's throne. The battle scenes are extraordinarily well done, and the Technicolor photography takes the breath away. As the little prince, Sabu followed solidly on his success in *Elephant Boy*; and the suavity and presence of Raymond Massey gives much power to the villainous Ghul. A favourite line comes from the sergeant-major instructing his men on how to behave at a Mohammedan party: 'It doesn't matter what the entertainment is, snakes or stomach-wiggling or whatnot. I want to see a look of rapture on every face.' Spot, if you can, Leo Genn (as

Massey's right-hand man) and Guy Rolfe beneath a mass of make-up, in minor roles.

Drum Beat ○
1954, US, 107 mins, colour
Dir: Delmer Daves
Stars: Alan Ladd, Audrey Dalton, Marisa Pavan, Robert Keith, Charles Bronson, Warner Anderson
Rating: ★★

Tough-guy star Charles Bronson enjoyed one of his first big roles in this Western, as a vicious renegade Indian terrorising the west in the late 19th century. Bronson, who had just changed his name (from his real one, Charles Buchinski), makes the most of his part as the formidable Captain Jack, over-shadowing Alan Ladd, playing in his first big Western since *Shane*. Another notable performance comes from Marisa Pavan (in real-life, sister of Pier Angeli) as the sister of a friendly Indian chief whose life the hero once saved. Director Delmer Daves' stern direction helps make the most of spectacular ambush and battle scenes, and J Peverell Marley's Warnercolor photography broke away from the conventional chocolate-box hues to drape the Western backdrop convincingly in golds and browns.

Drum Crazy ○
(aka: The Gene Krupa Story)
1960, US, 101 mins, colour
Dir: Don Weis
Stars: Sal Mineo, Susan Kohner, James Darren, Yvonne Craig
Rating: ★★

This biography of the late, great jazz drummer Gene Krupa should have been the big breakthrough for Sal Mineo. But he didn't quite make it. Perhaps he was still too young, at 21, and too slight of stature to sustain stardom beyond a teenage rave. A pity: he really has the joint jumping with a keenly-observed copy of the Krupa style, with backing from such real-life jazz greats as Shelly Manne, Loring 'Red' Nichols, Buddy Lester, Bobby Troup and Anita O'Day.

Drums Along the Mohawk ○
1939, US, 103 mins, colour
Dir: John Ford
Stars: Claudette Colbert, Henry Fonda, Edna May Oliver, Arthur Shields, Ward Bond, John Carradine
Rating: ★★★

One of John Ford's early Western successes, this 'pioneers versus Indians'

adventure romance has some remarkable colour photography by Bert Glennon, the expected scenes of Redskin siege and pioneer hardship, Claudette Colbert keeping her upper lip prettily stiff, and Henry Fonda's famous marathon footslog through an Indian gauntlet. Solid, cunningly crafted entertainment.

Dr X ◑
1932, US, 82 mins, colour
Dir: Michael Curtiz
Stars: Lionel Atwill, Fay Wray, Lee Tracy
Rating: ★★★

A splendid essay into the macabre from the same team – director Michael Curtiz, stars Lionel Atwill and Fay Wray and the Warner Studio – that made the classic *The Mystery of the Wax Museum*. Only the unwelcome intrusion of a fast-talking reporter, annoyingly played by Lee Tracy, mars the sinister atmosphere of this creepy thriller about a full-moon murderer who strangles his victims with something that seems too powerful to be a normal human arm. Curtiz's cultured direction has bags of flair and doesn't miss a trick. Wray is as touchingly vulnerable as ever as Dr X's daughter. The film was made in two-colour Technicolor.

Dry Rot ○
1956, UK, 87 mins, b/w
Dir: Maurice Elvey
Stars: Ronald Shiner, Brian Rix, Sidney James, Michael Shipley, Joan Sims, Peggy Mount
Rating: ★★

A formidable cast of farceurs has a wild time in this film adaptation of the famous Whitehall comedy hit about three itinerant bookmakers trying to earn an honest – well, almost honest – living. Heather Sears makes her screen debut and the charms of Shirley Ann Field can be very briefly glimpsed as a waitress at the Three Frogs Cafe. But Peggy Mount sweeps all else before her in a relatively short, but devastating appearance as the indomitable Sergeant Fire.

Dry White Season, A ● Ⓥ
1989, US, 107 mins, colour
Dir: Euzhan Palcy
Stars: Donald Sutherland, Winston Ntshona, Jurgen Prochnow, Janet Suzman, Marlon Brando, Susan Sarandon
Rating: ★★★

D

Richard Attenborough's *Cry Freedom* spawned a whole batch of films about South African atrocities, and here's another. Once again, there's the caring white man (Donald Sutherland) who gradually comes to realise the full horror of the apartheid regime (the film is set in 1976) and there's a showy role for Marlon Brando as the Orson Welles-like lawyer who tears government witnesses to pieces at an inquest on a murdered black, knowing that it won't make a jot of difference. 'Justice and law could be described as distant cousins,' he tells Sutherland. 'And, here in South Africa, they're not on speaking terms at all.' It's all well-made and depressingly familiar, easily arousing our resentment and anger, although the upbeat ending is not only highly fanciful but would surely carry horrendous consequences for all concerned. The acting is quite good, if with rather passing attempts at local accents by some prominent members of the cast.

Duck Soup ⊙

1933, US, 68 mins, b/w
Dir: Leo McCarey
Stars: Groucho Marx, Harpo Marx, Chico Marx, Zeppo Marx, Margaret Dumont, Louis Calhern
Rating: ★★★★

A Marx Brothers classic in which Groucho plays Rufus T Firefly and asks Margaret Dumont for a lock of her hair, adding: 'I'm letting you off lightly – I was going to ask for the whole wig.' Groucho (he plays the president of the postage-stamp republic of Freedonia) also has a miraculous scene in which Harpo plays his mirror image. Instead of feeling to see if the mirror were there – the obvious step – Groucho tries to outwit Harpo by making sudden movements, in a sequence which becomes a memorable example of the Marxes' comic invention.

Duck You Sucker

See: A Fistful of Dynamite

Duel ○ ⓥ

1971, US, 91 mins, colour
Dir: Steven Spielberg
Stars: Dennis Weaver
Rating: ★★★★

Originally made for television, this classic chase-and-suspense thriller was the first film to be directed by Steven Spielberg. The prolific Dennis Weaver gives one of his very best performances as a driver who is at first

harried and eventually terrified by a huge truck, the face of whose driver he cannot see. Spielberg maintains the whole nightmare situation at fever pitch.

Duel at Diablo ◐

1965, US, 103 mins, colour
Dir: Ralph Nelson
Stars: James Garner, Sidney Poitier, Bibi Anderson, Dennis Weaver, Bill Travers
Rating: ★★★

Cavalry-and-Indians Westerns were thin on the ground in the Sixties and this one must have come as an oasis of red meat and strong drink to fans of the genre. James Garner is much more effective here, as a memory-haunted squaw-widower, than in his lighter roles. Even so, he is unable to prevent Sidney Poitier from running away with the film as a sharp-dressing horse-breaker. The beginning is fine, with bold helicopter work over two lone figures in scrub country, and Ralph Nelson's direction keeps things going at a remorselessly good clip. The action itself is blood-and-thunder at its best. Seldom can arrows have thudded more convincingly into their victims. The picture is rounded off by Charles F Wheeler's stunningly pictorial use of the southern Utah locations, and Neal Hefti's unusual, stirring music, really just a series of chords strung together, but haunting in its way.

Duel in the Jungle ○

1954, UK, 101 mins, colour
Dir: George Marshall
Stars: Dana Andrews, Jeanne Crain, David Farrar
Rating: ★★

On safari in darkest Africa, gorgeous Jeanne Crain, in spite of the help of Dana Andrews, has a pretty tough time trying to escape the clutches of treacherous David Farrar. Much publicised at the time of making – Miss Crain's 'diary' was serialised in the magazine *Picturegoer* – but the excitement that seemed inherent in the script never quite came across.

Duel in the Sun ○ ⓥ

1946, US, 130 mins, colour
Dir: King Vidor
Stars: Jennifer Jones, Gregory Peck, Joseph Cotten, Lionel Barrymore, Lillian Gish, Walter Huston
Rating: ★★

David O Selznick spent almost $5 million on this epic Western (starring

his wife Jennifer Jones as a half-breed spitfire called Pearl), more than his outlay for *Gone With the Wind*. But the controversy the film aroused – US religious organisations protested about the morals and the amount of blood spilled – ensured it of box-office if not critical success. Stars Jones, Gregory Peck and Joseph Cotten (untypically cast as bad and good brothers respectively) includes Lillian Gish, Walter Huston, Lionel Barrymore, Herbert Marshall, Otto Kruger and Charles Bickford.

Duellists, The ● ⓥ

1977, UK, 101 mins, colour
Dir: Ridley Scott
Stars: Keith Carradine, Harvey Keitel, Cristina Raines, Edward Fox, Robert Stephens, Albert Finney
Rating: ★★

A tragi-comedy about the hate-love-hate relationship between two French officers in Napoleonic times, one of whom persists in fighting duels with the other over some obscure quarrel for the best part of 20 years. It's almost a 'ripping yarn', and director, Ridley Scott, of *Alien* fame, seems not to know quite what to do with it, except to make it almost absurdly beautiful, as if he had decided to settle for a bid for the best photography Oscar and let the theme of the story settle its own course. As a result, the duel scenes are quite dwarfed by the (sometimes bleak) beauty of the landscapes. A decided oddity.

Duffy ○

1968, US/UK, 101 mins, colour
Dir: Robert Parrish
Stars: James Coburn, James Mason, Susannah York, James Fox
Rating: ★★

Caper film in which twist piles on twist as four eccentric adventurers plan to relieve a millionaire of his money. John Alderton shines in a supporting role. And the plot has a strong twist to its tail.

Dulcimer Street

See: London Belongs to Me

Dumbo ⊙ ⓥ

1941, US, 64 mins, colour
Dir: Ben Sharpsteen
Rating: ★★★★

Brief but memorable Walt Disney feature cartoon about the little circus elephant whose ears were so big that he could fly. Full of vivid, colourful animation and memorable characters, including some wonderful crows. The score includes the Oscar-nominated 'Baby Mine' as well as 'Pink Elephants on Parade' (the centre of an imaginative nightmare sequence) and (sung by the crows) 'When I See an Elephant Fly'.

Dune 🔾 ⓥ
1984, US, 140 mins, colour
Dir: David Lynch
Stars: Francesca Annis, Brad Dourif, Kyle MacLachlan, Sian Phillips, Sting, Max von Sydow
Rating: ★★

A triumph of visual imagination, but a mishmash of storytelling, *Dune*, from the marvellous Frank Herbert novel, is cast in bold strokes, but seems in many parts to have been overtaken by George Lucas' *Star Wars* trilogy, especially *Return of the Jedi*. As might be expected from the director David Lynch, the monstrosities are amazing (especially the sandworms, and the Supreme Being, a cross between a giant millipede and a maggot), and dwelt upon with some relish. But you'll need your thinking caps on to follow the plot, and even who is doing what to whom. As for the opening narration by Virginia Madsen, as the princess, which is meant to explain it all, it makes less sense than one of Ronnie Barker's tongue-twisting monologues.

Dunkirk ◯
1958, UK, 135 mins, b/w
Dir: Leslie Norman
Stars: John Mills, Richard Attenborough, Bernard Lee, Robert Urquhart
Rating: ★★

One of the last films from Ealing Studios: a graphic reconstruction of the famous Allied retreat from the advancing Nazis in 1940. It was also one of the most expensive films Ealing had ever made, and it certainly has its excitement, while failing, apart from the beach evacuation, to provide anything that one hadn't seen before. There's the procession of refugees, the officer who sacrifices himself for the men, the wounded soldier who has to be left behind by his comrades: familiar types and situations all. Extremely well and carefully made in every detail. Of the actors, however, only Bernard Lee really gets his character to spring to life, in a highly sympathetic performance.

Dust Be My Destiny ◯
1939, US, 88 mins, b/w
Dir: Lewis Seiler
Stars: John Garfield, Priscilla Lane, Alan Hale, Frank McHugh
Rating: ★★★

Good-looking John Garfield was on familiar ground in this story of an ex-prisoner working on a farm and suspected of murdering the mean-minded boss. His youth was spent at a school for problem children on New York's tough Lower East Side and later, after drama school, he drifted, picking up casual farm labouring jobs before becoming a success on Broadway in 1936. Here, he gives a punchy, convincing performance. Pretty Priscilla Lane, as the boss's daughter, is miscast, but there are some fine character performances from Alan Hale as a truth-seeking newspaper editor, Charley Grapewin (best-known for his Grandpa Joad in *The Grapes of Wrath* in 1940) as a sympathetic brakeman, and Moroni Olsen as an idealistic defence attorney. Although the film was among director Lewis Seiler's most profitable, it's a shame that the script did not quite do justice to the fine cast.

Dying Young 🔾 ⓥ
1991, US, 111 mins, colour
Dir: Joel Schumacher
Stars: Julia Roberts, Campbell Scott, Vincent D'Onofrio, Colleen Dewhurst, Ellen Burstyn
Rating: ★

Without Julia Roberts as star, there isn't much doubt that this maudlin tear-jerker would have died in its infancy at the box-office. Looking here like a cross between Kay Kendall and Audrey Hepburn, there's not much even the 'Pretty Woman' can do with this unconvincing tale of a leukemia victim who hires the least qualified of the applicants as his nurse just because she's attractive. There's a lot of tealeaf-gazing thereafter by one of the characters but you don't need a crystal ball to guess the (few) subsequent developments of a film that gets more embarrassing and tedious by the minute. Director Joel Schumacher piles on the agony until it's so over the top you have to laugh. Julia gives her all, but the dialogue and general approach is too much. Opposite her, Campbell Scott has so little light and shade in his performance that he might have walked off the set of *Thunderbirds*. We all like a good cry but this is ridiculous.

Dynamite Man from Glory Jail ◯
(aka: Fool's Parade)
1971, US, 95 mins, colour
Dir: Andrew V Mclaglen
Stars: James Stewart, Anne Baxter, George Kennedy, Kurt Russell
Rating: ★★★

This differs from other Andrew McLaglen-directed Westerns in that it's set in 1935. Yet it still manages to retain more of the elements of a Western than those of a thriller. Mattie Appleyard, the grizzled ex-convict determined to claim his $25,000 prison savings against all the odds (the money is in the bank of the town that just outlawed him), is a part tailor-made for the sincerity and quiet heroism that James Stewart has projected so well throughout his career. In many ways, the character he created, with variations, in several Frank Capra films, comes to terms with Seventies cinema in *Dynamite Man* – bloody but unbowed.

D

E

Each Dawn I Die ○ Ⓥ
1939, US, 85 mins, b/w
Dir: William Keighley
Stars: James Cagney, George Raft, Jane
Bryan, George Bancroft, Victor Jory
Rating: ★★★

Hard-hitting, if progressively less likely
Warners prison drama, which gave
James Cagney plenty of acting opportunities as the reporter framed for
manslaughter when he gets too close
to the crooked activities of the district
attorney – played with splendidly
sinister scowl by Victor Jory. Inside
prison walls, Cagney soon gains the
support of kingpin hoodlum George
Raft by proving he's an okay guy and
from then on the plot moves predictably if always entertainingly to its
action-packed conclusion. Lean John
Wray also deserves a mention, as the
meanest guard in the prison.

Eagle Has Landed, The ◖ Ⓥ
1976, UK, 117 mins, colour
Dir: John Sturges
Stars: Michael Caine, Donald
Sutherland, Robert Duvall, Jenny
Agutter, Donald Pleasence, Anthony
Qualye
Rating: ★★

Tom Mankiewicz's spotty adaptation
of Jack Higgins' best-selling novel
lands somewhere between *Where
Eagles Dare* and *The Dirty Dozen*, except that the protagonists are a group
of Nazi infiltrators bent on kidnapping
Winston Churchill. The action
sequences (although late in coming)
are first-rate in the capable hands of
director John Sturges. The two best
performances – hardly surprising as the
stars (Michael Caine, Donald Sutherland, Robert Duvall, Jenny Agutter)
get the worst lines from Mankiewicz's
variable script – come from Jean
Marsh (as a German secret agent) and
John Standing (as the parish priest). If
the film's twist opening seems vaguely
familiar that could be because the
same device was used in Ealing's wartime drama *Went the Day Well*.

Eagle's Wing ◖
1978, UK, 111 mins, colour
Dir: Anthony Harvey
Stars: Martin Sheen, Sam Waterston,
Harvey Keitel, Stephane Audran,
Caroline Langrishe
Rating: ★★

A Western about endurance. Shot in
Mexico by British director Anthony
Harvey (a former actor and editor
whose best-known film is *The Lion in
Winter*), the film carries a feeling of
primitive times, accentuated by the
burnished colour photography of
Billy Williams. Martin Sheen and Sam
Waterston are impressive as the principal protagonists, each striving to
prove that there is nothing more likely
to make an ultimate winner than a bad
loser.

Earl Carroll Vanities ○
1945, US, 91 mins, b/w
Dir: Joseph Santley
Stars: Dennis O'Keefe, Constance
Moore, Eve Arden, Otto Kruyer
Rating: ★★

A feather-brained musical, but lavish
by Republic Studios' yardsticks, with
some great music from Woody
Herman and his boys and a hit song,
'Endlessly', sung here by Constance
Moore, which was to become a
standard. Eve Arden is on hand to
make with the wisecracks against settings that, typical of Republic, have a
faintly hand-me-down look.

Early Bird, The ⊙
1965, UK, 95 mins, colour
Dir: Robert Ash
Stars: Norman Wisdom, Edward
Chapman, Jerry Desmonde
Rating: ★★

Norman Wisdom was hitting new
depths with each film at the end of his
film career with Rank, and here his
tedious antics as a little milkman
fighting against a big dairy just never
get off the ground. The situations send
telegrams in advance. The jokes are
elaborately staged – and look it. The
only original slapstick moment comes
when Norman gets taken for a ride by
a runaway power-mower.

Earth Girls Are Easy ○ Ⓥ
1988, US, 100 mins, colour
Dir: Julien Temple
Stars: Geena Davis, Jeff Goldblum,
Damon Wayans, Julie Brown, Jim Carrey,
Michael McKean
Rating: ★★

This typically glitzy musical farce from
Julien *Absolute Beginners* Temple is a
throwback to the Sixties, when all
blondes were bimbos and beach bun-
nies fawned around smirking surfers.
Add a visit from a spacecraft and you
have a sort of *Beach Blanket Alien*. For
at least an hour the tackiness, although

intentional, is just overwhelming. It
does get a bit better towards the end,
though, thanks largely to the sympathetic efforts of Jeff Goldblum
(mysteriously billed fourth in the beginning credits) and then-wife Geena
Davis, a six-foot, liquid-lipped
charmer who was already proving
herself too good for this sort of thing.

Earthquake ○
1974, US, 129 mins, colour
Dir: Mark Robson
Stars: Charlton Heston, Ava Gardner,
George Kennedy, Lorne Greene, Barry
Sullivan, Richard Roundtree
Rating: ★★

One of the biggest disaster epics on
record. It provides escapist
entertainment on a vast scale with Los
Angeles reduced to rubble as
buildings sway, crack, totter and
tumble and a giant dam threatens to
crack and release billions of gallons of
water into an already devastated
countryside. Small wonder the brilliant visual effects by Frank Brendel,
Albert Whitlock and Glen Robinson
won one of the film's two Academy
Awards. Watch for the eye-catching
Victoria Principal (Pam Ewing of
Dallas) and the versatile talents of
Genevieve Bujold; spot Walter
Matthau's guest shot as a drunk; and
marvel at Charlton Heston's skill and
authority in a routine role, whether
saving his wife from yet another
suicide attempt or fearlessly risking
death among the debris.

Easter Parade ⊙ Ⓥ
1948, US, 110 mins, colour
Dir: Charles Walters
Stars: Judy Garland, Fred Astaire, Peter
Lawford, Ann Miller, Jules Munshin
Rating: ★★★

One of the most famous of all the
celebrated MGM musicals, this was
originally to have starred Gene Kelly.
But Kelly had an accident that broke
his ankle and Fred Astaire was persuaded to come out of early
retirement and take over the role. It
turned out to be a lucky 'break' for
Fred as the result, which includes the
famous 'drum' dance and the 'Couple
of Swells' duet with Judy Garland, was
one of his biggest ever hits.

East of Eden ○ Ⓥ
1955, US, 115 mins, colour
Dir: Elia Kazan
Stars: Julie Harris, James Dean,
Raymond Massey, Burl Ives
Rating: ★★★

Based on the powerful, brooding novel by the late Nobel Prize-winning author John Steinbeck, this sombre and moving story of rivalry between two brothers provided the now legendary James Dean with his first major and still most highly-regarded acting role. Jo Van Fleet, playing his mysterious mother, won an Academy Award.

East of Piccadilly ○
1940, UK, 79 mins, b/w
Dir: Harold Huth
Stars: Sebastian Shaw, Judy Campbell, Niall MacGinnis
Rating: ★★

Or: the case of the nylon stocking murders. This wartime British thriller, a densely atmospheric murder mystery, comes with good writing credits. The script was co-written by bestselling authoress Lesley Storm, and by J Lee Thompson, later to become a distinguished director (of such films as *Tiger Bay*). Silent screen idol Henry Edwards has a prominent supporting role.

East of Sudan ○
1964, UK, 84 mins, colour
Dir: Nathan Juran
Stars: Anthony Quayle, Sylvia Sims, Jenny Agutter
Rating: ★

Adventure story set in the Sudan late last century, with Anthony Quayle as a forthright soldier of fortune trying to steer a party of battle survivors to safety and the cast often playing against filmed backgrounds. A 12-year-old Jenny Agutter plays a native girl. If you think you've seen some of the more spectacular scenes somewhere else, you're right. The 'extra' footage is from the 1939 version of *The Four Feathers*. Alas, despite the addition of such spectacle, the film itself never matches the excitement of its opening few scenes.

East of Sumatra ○
1953, US, 85 mins, colour
Dir: Budd Boetticher
Stars: Jeff Chandler, Anthony Quinn, Suzan Ball, Marilyn Maxwell
Rating: ★★

It was while filming this action film, set on a Pacific island and about a mining engineer in conflict with the islanders, that the tragic Suzan Ball sustained the leg injury that was eventually to end her life aged 22. The director is Budd Boetticher, who has

since become a cult figure, and the tense climax is a fight with machetes and flaming torches.

East Side, West Side ○
1949, US, 108 mins, b/w
Dir: Mervyn LeRoy
Stars: Barbara Stanwyck, James Mason, Van Heflin, Ava Gardner
Rating: ★★

Glossy emotional drama, with a big star cast, and some interesting side slants on American high society. Half-way through, the film develops into a fast-moving murder thriller. James Mason stars as a playboy whose world is the New York 'smart set'. He is torn between the attractions of his West Side mistress, Isabel, and his wife, Jessie, a pillar of the fashionable East Side. Fans of Ava Gardner should be warned that the lady gets bumped off quite early on. But there's a fierce and unusual fist-fight between Van Heflin and six-foot actress Beverly Michaels. And Oscar-winning actress Gale Sondergaard, in her last screen performance for a long while (a brush with the Un-American Activities Committee signalled an early end to her major career), icily dominates every scene in which she appears. Often too stodgy though.

Easy Living ○
1937, US, 86 mins, b/w
Dir: Mitchell Leisen
Stars: Jean Arthur, Edward Arnold, Ray Milland, Luis Alberni
Rating: ★★★

This screwball romantic comedy wasn't much liked by some contemporary critics but now stands as a classic of the genre. With Preston Sturges scripting and Mitchell Leisen directing, the mood is one of elegant lunacy as a fur coat flung from a window changes Jean Arthur's life.

Easy Money ○
1947, UK, 94 mins, b/w
Dir: Bernard Knowles
Stars: Jack Warner, Petula Clark, Dennis Price, Greta Gynt
Rating: ★★

The British became very fond of multiple story films in the Forties – *Dead of Night*, *The Wallet*, *Holiday Camp* and the Maugham complications all spring to mind – but the vogue was killed off rather quickly by the advent of half-hour stories on television. This one is about the effect on four people, from varying walks of

life, of a massive win on the pools. Directed by Bernard Knowles, who proved himself a brilliant cinematographer on *The 39 Steps*, *Brown on Resolution* and *Gaslight*. His career as a director, however, never quite caught fire.

Easy to Love ○
1953, US, 95 mins, colour
Dir: Charles Walters
Stars: Esther Williams, Van Johnson, Tony Martin, John Bromfield
Rating: ★★★

Not much plot here – Esther Williams loves Van Johnson but he doesn't seem to notice her, so she has an affair with her swimming instructor, hoping Van will get jealous – but that shouldn't stop you enjoying this very tuneful (and colourful!) MGM musical. Esther is given plenty of opportunities to display her aquatic abilities and the musical numbers are spectacularly staged by veteran choreographer Busby Berkeley. The film's climax is the classic number involving dozens of motorboats towing dozens of skiers. Great fun. Carroll Baker's screen debut here went almost unnoticed, but three years later she got the role of *Baby Doll* and became a star.

Easy to Wed ○
1946, US, 110 mins, colour
Dir: Edward Buzzell
Stars: Van Johnson, Esther Williams, Lucille Ball, Keenan Wynn
Rating: ★★★

Lucille Ball and Keenan Wynn give show-stopping performances in this zany remake of the classic comedy *Libelled Lady*, with Esther Williams doing a minimum of swimming as the heiress who sues a newspaper for $2 million. Director Edward Buzzell was also responsible for a couple of Marx Brothers comedies.

Eating Raoul ◐
1982, US, 83 mins, colour
Dir: Paul Bartel
Stars: Paul Bartel, Mary Woronov, Robert Beltran
Rating: ★★★

A wild black comedy about a penurious couple who raise the money to buy a restaurant by murdering the perverts they lure into their house via the sex-ad columns. 'Do you think we could buy another frying pan?' the wife (Mary Woronov) asks her husband (Paul Bartel, who also directed

E

the film). 'I'm getting a little squeamish about using the one we use to kill people.' It's an uneven film (just not black enough perhaps) and its three leading players strangely all look like other people: Paul Bartel resembles British TV personality Clement Freud, Mary Woronov is like Sally Kellerman, and Robert Beltran (as Raoul) like Erik Estrada of *CHiPS* fame. Buck Henry comes on for a funny turn as a lascivious loan company manager appropriately called Leech.

Eat My Dust! ○
1976, US, 90 mins, colour
Dir: Charles Griffith
Stars: Ron Howard, Christopher Norris
Rating: ★

Hang on tight for this dust-rouser about two youngsters with a passion for speed – which develops into one long car chase. Star Ron Howard, a former child player, has since turned director with conspicuous success making *Splash*, *Cocoon*, *Backdraft* and *Far and Away*.

Echoes of a Summer ○
1975, US, 98 mins, colour
Dir: Don Taylor
Stars: Richard Harris, Jodie Foster, Lois Nettleton
Rating: ★★

It must have been every actor's greatest dread in the Seventies to be cast in a film with Jodie Foster, that precocious bundle of young talent. And imagine Jodie playing a girl with only a short time to live. Well, that's just what she does in this beautifully photographed weepie. She makes all her adult co-stars seem shallow by her mature understanding of the role and consequent understated performance – which goes a long way towards taking the stickiness out of the film's sentiment.

Eddie Cantor Story, The ○
1953, US, 116 mins, colour
Dir: Alfred E Green
Stars: Keefe Brasselle, Marilyn Erskine, Aline MacMahon, Will Rogers Jr
Rating: ★★

Despite having the same director (Alfred E Green) as *The Jolson Story*, this similar biopic on another of America's best-loved entertainers was nowhere near as successful with the public. If Keefe Brasselle's Cantor doesn't quite have the warmth of personality that Larry Parks brought

to Jolson, the production is on a similar lavish scale and the famous Cantor songs and routines are present in strength. The script, though, is totally lacking in flair.

Eddy Duchin Story, The ○
1956, US, 123 mins, colour
Dir: George Sidney
Stars: Tyrone Power, Kim Novak, Victoria Shaw, James Whitmore, Rex Thompson
Rating: ★★★

A musical tearbath about the triumph-and-tragedy life of American pianist Eddy Duchin. The film was a great personal success for Tyrone Power, whose fingering to the playing of Carmen Cavallaro is first-rate. The film is a little too over-emotional to make the topmost bracket, but Kim Novak acts with a very sure touch as Duchin's wife, and Australian actress Victoria Shaw, schoolgirl-awkward in ordinary scenes, is surprisingly powerful in the dramatic ones. James Whitmore provides solid support, and the film is sumptuously dressed, and opulently photographed in Technicolor by Harry Stradling.

Edge of Darkness ○
1943, US, 124 mins, b/w
Dir: Lewis Milestone
Stars: Errol Flynn, Ann Sheridan, Walter Huston, Judith Anderson, Helmut Dantine, Ruth Gordon
Rating: ★★★

Pretty downbeat for a Hollywood war film of 1943, this story of the resistance in Norway has a subdued and credible performance from Errol Flynn, even if his star presence in some ways hampers the film. With an opening uncannily reminiscent of *Beau Geste*, the movie carries remarkable intensity at times.

Edge of Doom ○
(aka: Stronger than Fear)
1950, US
Dir: Mark Robson
Stars: Dana Andrews, Farley Granger, Joan Evans, Robert Keith
Rating: ★★

Adapted from Catholic author Leo Brady's prizewinning novel, this sombre film examines the perverted thinking of a tormented youth nagged by the problems of poverty and a sense of guilt over the death of his pious mother. The consequences make for a powerful murder story with religious and psychological overtones. The darkly handsome Farley Granger

broods convincingly as the mixed-up kid and gaunt Robert Keith scores as a detective out to trap a killer.

Edge of Eternity ○
1959, US, 80 mins, colour
Dir: Don Siegel
Stars: Cornel Wilde, Victoria Shaw, Edgar Buchanan, Mickey Shaughnessy, Jack Elam
Rating: ★★

Don Siegel, who went on to make *Dirty Harry*, was already making colour crime thrillers like *Edge of Eternity* on location before most people had started to think about it. The location in this case is awesome – in and around the Grand Canyon – and Siegel uses it spectacularly in the climactic fist-fight, which takes place in a mining bucket hundreds of feet above ground level. Varying suspects are competently played by Jack Elam, Rian Garrick and Mickey Shaughnessy, and Cornel Wilde has the Clint Eastwood-type role as the tough-talking sheriff out to solve the case.

Edge of the City ○
(aka: A Man Is Ten Feet Tall)
1957, US, 85 mins, b/w
Dir: Martin Ritt
Stars: John Cassavetes, Sidney Poitier, Jack Warden, Kathleen Maguire
Rating: ★★★

Edge of the City was a landmark film in the careers of stars John Cassavetes and Sidney Poitier and director Martin Ritt. A punchy, dramatic *On the Waterfront*-style expose of both American union racketeering and working-class racial prejudice in the mid-Fifties, the film has a towering performance by Poitier, and others that fit the story like gloves. If you've seen this moralising kind of film before – excellent though this example is – you'll be able to predict the finish easily enough. But it still makes mighty powerful entertainment. The only thing that seems dated is the intrusive background score.

Edison, The Man ○
1940, US, 107 mins, b/w
Dir: Clarence Brown
Stars: Spencer Tracy, Rita Johnson, Lynn Overman, Charles Cobourn
Rating: ★★★

Solid, worthy follow-up to *Young Tom Edison*. Spencer Tracy is ideal as the adult Edison, and Rita Johnson, an actress who seldom got the breaks she deserved, enjoys her finest film hour as his wife – even though a temptation to alter the facts to suit the drama isn't always resisted.

Educating Rita ◐ ⓥ
1983, UK, 110 mins, colour
Dir: Lewis Gilbert
Stars: Michael Caine, Julie Walters, Michael Williams, Maureen Lipman
Rating: ★★★

As a lower-class British housewife hungering for an education, Julie Walters launched herself into the acting limelight, winning the Best Actress BAFTA Award and a Golden Globe in this surprisingly winning film version of Willy Russell's stage play. The story concerns a 26-year-old peroxide-blonde hairdresser who gets a drunken Oxford don for a tutor when she comes to open university to better herself. Michael Caine as the don also won a BAFTA award, although the film almost loses its way in his character's disillusionment, not only with life, but with the 'new woman' he seems to have created. In the end, the story reasserts itself thanks to a climax that's just right without being overtly happy and to extremely attractive performances by the two stars in virtually the only roles of any stature in the whole film.

Edward My Son ○
1949, UK, 112 mins, b/w
Dir: George Cukor
Stars: Spencer Tracy, Deborah Kerr, Ian Hunter, James Donald
Rating: ★★★

Towering performances from the stars in the drama of a man who is spurred by the birth of his son to elevate himself from obscurity to peerage, losing all his friends along the way. Based on the hit play by Robert Morley and Noel Langley, in which the son never actually appears, this was MGM's first production in Britain after World War II. The great George Cukor was brought over from Hollywood to direct, and Deborah Kerr came back to star as the wife, two years after leaving England for America.

Edward Scissorhands ◐ ⓥ
1990, US, 107 mins, colour
Dir: Tim Burton
Stars: Johnny Depp, Winona Ryder, Dianne Wiest, Kathy Baker, Vincent Price, Alan Arkin
Rating: ★★★

Director Tim Burton, of *Batman* and *Beetlejuice* fame, is obviously destined to become a master of the dark fairytale. Once upon a time . . . there was an everyday American town, with a spooky hilltop castle just around the corner. There lived Vincent Price, alias The Inventor, and he made a man, Edward (Johnny Depp), but died before his creation could be completed, leaving the hapless Edward with long scissor blades for hands. Burton's film takes up the story when Edward is discovered by the local Avon lady (Dianne Wiest), falls in love with her daughter (Winona Ryder) and becomes the rage of the neighbourhood. Edward snips and snaps away happily, creating horrendous haircuts, grotesque gardens and brighter, better poodles. Ere long, alas, with the inevitability of all good fairytales, Edward's hands (with which he can also unpick locks) get him into trouble. An enormous amount of vision and invention (not to mention expense) has gone into the staging of this story; and, if it hasn't quite the stature to measure up to the likes of Frankenstein, Depp is every inch the pitiable creature at the mercy of how his dead creator has left him.

Egg and I, The ☉
1947, US, 104 mins, b/w
Dir: Chester Erskine
Stars: Claudette Colbert, Fred MacMurray, Marjorie Main, Percy Kilbride
Rating: ★★★

The first film since the merger of the Universal studio with rival International, and the promise of Bill Goetz as head of production of only turning out 'A' product, was a memorable fizz-bang comedy. Claudette Colbert and Fred MacMurray work well together as newly-weds up to their necks in trouble on a poultry farm, but the film is more memorable for introducing Ma and Pa Kettle (Marjorie Main and Percy Kilbride), a pair of raucous rurals, who went on to feature in nine spin-off films.

Egyptian, The ○
1954, US, 139 mins, colour
Dir: Michael Curtiz
Stars: Edmund Purdom, Jean Simmons, Michael Wilding, Victore Mature, Gene Tierney, Peter Ustinov
Rating: ★★

Michael Curtiz's superb control of the crowd scenes, and Leon Shamroy's breathtaking colour photography, ensure that the spectacle saves this Hollywood slice of ancient history. Edmund Purdom takes the title role, and Peter Ustinov is excellent as Kaptah, his rascally servant. The story – set in Thebes, 1300 BC – tells of two men, a medical student called Sinuhe (played well by Purdom, despite some overlong speeches) and a low-born military cadet, Horemheb (played in let's-rip-up-the-scenery fashion by Victor Mature – his best line is 'More wine, you waddling toad!') and their adventures after they rescue the Pharaoh of Egypt from a lion. The cast is mightier than the film.

Eiger Sanction, The ◐ ⓥ
1975, US, 125 mins, colour
Dir: Clint Eastwood
Stars: Clint Eastwood, George Kennedy, Vonetta McGee
Rating: ★

Lovers of mountain climbing are in for a rare treat here, for the story is about an assassin who has to carry out his mission on one of three climbers with whom he shares an expedition to the perilous north face of the Eiger mountain in Switzerland. Lovers of the thriller are not in for such a good deal, as the story takes a long and slippery road up to the obvious conclusion. Clint Eastwood provides the star power (and direction); acting quality comes from Jack Cassidy as a gay, treacherous spy. Another Alpine disaster.

18 Again! ○ ⓥ
1988, US, 100 mins, colour
Dir: Paul Flaherty
Stars: George Burns, Charlie Schlatter, Jennifer Runyon, Tony Roberts
Rating: ★★

Yet another rejuvenation comedy, but a pretty affable one at that, with young Charlie Schlatter doing a very good impression of how George Burns would have been at 18 when he and the cigar-puffing old reprobate switch bodies during a car crash. Since the title is actually the reversal of numerals on a birthday cake and Burns was actually 91 or so at the time, maybe *19 Again* would have been a more appropriate title! But that would have taken our hero beyond the age of high school, where all the fun takes place. Burns himself gets the rough end of the deal with some smuttily shoddy lines, while young Schlatter laps up the best of the situations, swaying, smiling and stooping in the best Burns fashion as he outwits enemies who have previously flattened him mentally and physically. Though the film doesn't escape embarrassment, there are some good performances around here, notably from Schlatter, Tony Roberts as his downtrodden dad and Anthony Starke as the class bully. Genetically speaking, the son who's about a foot shorter than his father seems as likely as *18 Again!* itself.

Eight Iron Men ○
1952, US, 80 mins, b/w
Dir: Edward Dmytryk
Stars: Bonar Colleano, Lee Marvin, Arthur Franz, Richard Kiley
Rating: ★★★

The credentials of this war film are as high as they come: the producer is Stanley Kramer and the director Edward Dmytryk. It's about an eight-man squad, trapped in a ruined house by enemy machine-gun fire. Outside, another of their number lies pinned down in a shell-hole. Tension predictably rises rapidly between the men. Bonar Colleano makes a splendid job of his one and only Hollywood role, as the cocky Collucci, and his characterisation dominates the film. His dreams of a pin-up girl (Mary Castle) provide refreshing breaks of charm and humour in the sombre if exciting tale.

Eight Men Out ◐ ⓥ
1988, US, 120 mins, colour
Dir: John Sayles
Stars: John Cusack, John Mahoney, Charlie Sheen, D B Sweeney, Christopher Lloyd, David Strathairn
Rating: ★★

Although painstakingly reconstructed by writer-director John Sayles, this ends up as a dullish depiction of baseball's biggest scandal – the 'fix' of the World Series by the Chicago White Sox in 1919. Underpaid by their money-grabbing owner, who welshed on every promise, the ringleaders were easy prey for the gamblers and mobsters who brought financial incentive to bear, then proved just as unreliable as the players' bosses when it came to paying up. Some good actors, notably John Cusack, D B Sweeney, Charlie Sheen, David Strathairn and Michael Lerner, as crime kingpin Arnold Rothstein, couldn't be bettered. But Sayles' treatment is far too slow and cries out for editing down by 15 or 20 minutes. Such action as there is is confined to the baseball field and won't mean

much to non-American audiences. The period is observed to the last detail, although the dialogue ('Way to go, Joe!') strikes a few anachronistic notes.

Eight O'Clock Walk ○
1953, UK, 87 mins, b/w
Dir: Lance Comfort
Stars: Richard Attenborough, Cathy O'Donnell, Derek Farr
Rating: ★★

Almost a reprise for Richard Attenborough of his role in *London Belongs to Me*. Again he's a working-class lad involved in the murder of a girl, and again he faces the gallows. Attenborough tries to look harassed, but he's been through it all before. Cathy O'Donnell is very sympathetic as his young wife and Derek Farr and Ian Hunter ooze authority as the rival counsels on the case.

Eight on the Lam
See: Eight on the Run

Eight on the Run ○
(aka: Eight on the Lam)
1967, US, 106 mins, colour
Dir: George Marshall
Stars: Bob Hope, Shirley Eaton, Jill St John, Phyllis Diller
Rating: ★★

This spasmodically funny comedy about a widower with seven children (and a very large dog) marked something of a return to form for its star after such early-Sixties disasters as *A Global Affair* and *I'll Take Sweden*. Veteran director George Marshall – who had directed Hope seven times before, from *The Ghost Breakers* in 1940 to *Boy, Did I Get a Wrong Number* in 1966 – maintains a frenzied pace.

84 Charing Cross Road ○ ⓥ
1986, US, 97 mins, colour
Dir: David Jones
Stars: Anne Bancroft, Anthony Hopkins, Judi Dench, Mercedes Ruehl
Rating: ★★★

An unusual and delightful film, *84 Charing Cross Road* gave Anne Bancroft one of her most memorable roles. She plays Helene Hanff, a New York book collector and Anglophile. She starts up a correspondence with Frank Doel (Anthony Hopkins), who works in an antiquarian bookshop in London. The film, based on a true

story, spans 20 years of their written friendship. Despite the closeness generated by their letters the two never met, which, perhaps, is the ultimate sadness of the film. Hopkins plays the undemonstrative Doel with his usual understated skill, but has to take second place to Bancroft. Beautifully constructed, this gentle but absorbing drama shows its theatrical origins and does at times seem a little static, but still, it's a joy to watch.

80,000 Suspects ○
1963, UK, 113 mins, b/w
Dir: Val Guest
Stars: Richard Johnson, Claire Bloom, Cyril Cusack
Rating: ★★★

Thriller about an epidemic which threatens to sweep across a big city. Yolande Donlan, wife of the film's director, Val Guest, has a key role in the story.

El Cid ○ ⓥ
1962, US, 184 mins, colour
Dir: Anthony Mann
Stars: Charlton Heston, Sophia Loren, John Fraser, Raf Vallone
Rating: ★★★

You'll be impressed by the sweep and grandeur of this dignified epic, inevitably with Charlton Heston as the legendary 'lord' of 11th century Spain who, after being exiled from the Spanish courts, leads his followers to rid the country of the Moors, before riding into history. It's in the quieter moments – times of passion and tragedy – that *El Cid* is at its best and here Heston and Sophia Loren, giving a superb, warmly real performance as his wife, register really well as heroic characters. Fitting nicely into supporting roles are Raf Vallone, John Fraser, Herbert Lom and Gary Raymond, although Genevieve Page is rather a weak link as a heartless queen. The photography is superb and only the muddled quality of the battle scenes keeps this from the top rank of first-rate epics of the screen.

El Condor ◐
1970, US, 102 mins, colour
Dir: John Guillermin
Stars: Jim Brown, Lee Van Cleef
Rating: ★★

Slow Western set against some mightily imposing scenery. Heroes Jim Brown and Lee Van Cleef, both after a fortune in gold hidden in a far-off fortress, were hot in films at the time though, like the spaghetti Western this resembles, not for long. One critic remarked that leading lady Mariana Hill looked good even with her clothes on, which is sexist, but especially apt: she never gave a more striking performance.

El Dorado ○
1967, US, 127 mins, colour
Dir: Howard Hawks
Stars: John Wayne, Robert Mitchum, James Caan, Arthur Hunnicutt, Ed Asner
Rating: ★★★

Action abounds in this colourful Western whose characters are happily two sizes larger than life. The film is uproarious, lively and has character, swagger and style. Shoot-outs occur at regular intervals, and for no special reason, although one particular gun battle in a chapel is worth anyone's money. Stitched into the mayhem is a series of running gags guaranteed to break down the fiercest anti-Western resistance. Great stuff from director Howard Hawks.

Electric Dreams ○ ⓥ
1984, US, 97 mins, colour
Dir: Steve Barron
Stars: Lenny Von Dohlen, Virginia Madsen, Maxwell Caulfield, Bud Cort
Rating: ★★★

The story of the computer that develops human tendencies and tries to dominate its master is by now a familiar one and usually has a tragic ending. But, since this is a musical, or at least nearly one, it's a sure bet that the ending will be (literally) on an upbeat note – and, in this case, a good thing too. Lenny Van Dohlen is Miles, a bespectacled architect who buys a computer to wake him up in the morning and finds it does a lot more besides, apart from, through an initial mistype, calling him Moles. He falls in love with the cello player (Virginia Madsen) upstairs, but the sounds of her music wafting through the air vent brings a response from the computer, which ends in it composing songs she thinks are her lover's. The word 'love' has to be explained to the computer (the whole film is described as a fairy-tale for computers) before the affair can reach a logical conclusion. Bud Cort has both the pivotal and most difficult role as the voice of the computer, and it's his performance that gives the film its emotive viability. The driving disco score by Giorgio Moroder is an added plus. The odds are you'll like it.

Electric Horseman, The ○
1979, US, 114 mins, colour
Dir: Sydney Pollack
Stars: Robert Redford, Jane Fonda, Valerie Perrine, Willie Nelson, John Saxon
Rating: ★★★

Director Sydney Pollack and star Robert Redford had come close to making memorable movies before – but they really hit the jackpot with this one. Redford plays a has-been rodeo champion reduced to being on-air spokesman for a breakfast cereal. One night, the frayed elastic holding him to the purse-strings of society finally comes away and, hotly pursued by Jane Fonda as a slick TV reporter, he rides out into the desert. The encounters and subsequent adventures of newsgirl and cowboy provide the touching core of the film. The dialogue between them is beautifully written by Robert Garland, who gradually softens the edges of their hardened attitudes and brings them to fond togetherness in a most believable and persuasive way.

Eleni ○ ⓥ
1985, US, 117 mins, colour
Dir: Peter Yates
Stars: Kate Nelligan, John Malkovich, Linda Hunt, Ronald Pickup
Rating: ★

Although made with heartfelt sincerity, this is a grim and drab account of the repression of the Greek people in the post-war period. The story concerns a Greek-American newspaperman (John Malkovich) returning to his native land to hunt down those responsible for the unjust death by firing squad of his mother Eleni. In the title role, Kate Nelligan gives everything to a role that once would have been ideal for Sophia Loren or Irene Papas, and occasionally touches our hearts.

Elephant Boy ○
1937, UK, 80 mins, b/w
Dir: Zoltan Korda
Stars: Sabu, Walter Hudd, Wilfrid Hyde White
Rating: ★★★

Plagued by the monsoon season and the painstaking shooting schedule of master documentarist Robert Flaherty, this adventure story (some way) after Kipling was eventually completed by producer Alexander Korda's brother Zoltan. The result still made a star of former Indian stable

boy Sabu, and won a best director prize at the Venice Film Festival. Watch out for a young Wilfrid Hyde White as the Commissioner. He was then billed simply as Hyde White, as he had been since his film debut three years before. The photography by Osmond Borrodaile is quite superb.

Elephant Man, The ● ⓥ
1980, UK, 124 mins, b/w
Dir: David Lynch
Stars: Anthony Hopkins, John Hurt, Anne Bancroft, John Gielgud, Wendy Hiller, Freddie Jones
Rating: ★★★

Some may find this remarkable film difficult to watch, simply because of the subject: a grotesquely deformed man is rescued from a freak show and sheltered at a hospital in Victorian times by a brilliant surgeon. Although this theme teeters on the edge of embarrassment at odd moments, it always draws back from the brink, thanks to controlled performances from Anthony Hopkins (the surgeon), John Hurt (playing the title role under a mound of makeup, and really eliciting pity and sympathy), John Gielgud (the hospital chief), Hannah Gordon as Hopkins' wife and Wendy Hiller as the hospital's senior matron. Director David Lynch's treatment (magnificently shot in black and white by Freddie Francis) tends to the melodramatic, but the story is still affecting at most stages and even outstanding at times: see it and decide for yourself.

Elephant Walk ○
1954, US, 103 mins, colour
Dir: William Dieterle
Stars: Elizabeth Taylor, Dana Andrews, Peter Finch
Rating: ★★

You won't notice it, but the heroine in this film is played by two women – Vivien Leigh and Elizabeth Taylor. The latter took over after Vivien Leigh fell ill. Close-ups of Miss Taylor were then cut into the film already shot, leaving Miss Leigh, unrecognisable, in the long shots. Action fans will enjoy the climax, when a herd of thirsty elephants bulldoze their way through the old plantation house. An outbreak of cholera, a monsoon and an extraordinary game of bicycle polo (plus, of course, Miss Taylor) are among the film's extra added attractions. And there is some fine Sri Lankan scenery.

E

11 Harrowhouse ○

1974, US, 108 mins, colour
Dir: Aram Avakian
Stars: Charles Grodin, Candice Bergen, John Gielgud, Trevor Howard, James Mason
Rating: ★★★

An engagingly elaborate diamond heist caper is further enlivened by the nervous hero (the underrated Charles Grodin) interjecting an ironically deadpan narration at key moments throughout the film. The title is the London address of the world's clearing house for diamonds, and a stalwart British cast – James Mason, Trevor Howard, John Gielgud, Jack Watling – ensures that urbane underplaying wins out over the too-hectic car chase finale.

Elmer Gantry ○

1960, US, 146 mins, colour
Dir: Richard Brooks
Stars: Burt Lancaster, Jean Simmons, Dean Jagger, Arthur Kennedy, Shirley Jones
Rating: ★★★★

Critics applauded this prize-winning story of a discredited preacher, based on the controversial book by Sinclair Lewis. Burt Lancaster has rightly said that this was his best part ever. 'I would rather play one character as vital and exciting as Elmer Gantry than a dozen of those big, handsome heroes who always get the beautiful girl,' he said. The pessimists of Hollywood forecast doom for the story if it was made into a film. They pointed out that back in the 1920s, the book had been banned all over the world. They were proved wrong when *Elmer Gantry* won three Oscars: Burt Lancaster, as the salesman–turned–preacher, for Best Actor; Shirley Jones for Best Supporting Actress, as a deacon's daughter, and writer/director Richard Brooks for the best screenplay.

Elopement ○

1951, US, 82 mins, b/w
Dir: Henry Koster
Stars: Clifton Webb, Anne Francis, Charles Bickford, William Lundigan
Rating: ★★★

Splendidly written by Bess Taffel, this witty comedy, packed with incidents, provides plum roles for Clifton Webb and Charles Bickford as two irascible fathers chasing their eloping offspring through a rainy and muddy American countryside. Evelyn Varden and Margalo Gillmore add acid to the piquant brew as the two wives involved, and Tommy Rettig is a splendidly hateable kid. The kind of funny family film they just can't seem to write any more.

Elvira, Mistress of the Dark ○ ⓥ

1988, US, 96 mins, colour
Dir: James Signorelli
Stars: Cassandra Peterson, Morgan Sheppard, Daniel Greene, Susan Kellerman, Jeff Conaway, Edie McClurg
Rating: ★

Elvira is an American TV personality majoring in straight black dresses, extravagant eye makeup and gynormous cleavage. Elvira's cleavage (you've seen it, you're going to see in the first 10 seconds) is the *raison d'être* of a strident spoof horror film that's neither fish nor fowl. As comedy, horror or satire on small-town morals, it never gets going. Elvira herself is a would-be Mae West without the weight, physically or vocally, to measure up to Mae's shoulderpads; even if the script does give her the odd good line ('Tell 'em I never turned down a friend. I never turn down a stranger for that matter'), she delivers them at such a fast staccato that their impact is all but lost. I was with the townsfolk who try to burn her as a witch, chanting 'two, four, six, eight, who do we incinerate?' 'You don't fit in this town,' snarls one townswoman. 'You don't even fit in that dress.' Not in films, either, by the look of it. Elvira, go home!

Elvis: The Movie ○

1979, US, 104 mins, colour
Dir: John Carpenter
Stars: Kurt Russell, Shelley Winters, Season Hubley
Rating: ★★

A monster-size TV movie much praised in America, although a shortened version had a mixed reception when shown in cinemas elsewhere in the world. Anyone expecting a warts and all picture of 'The King's early life' should be reminded that this had a 'U' certificate in British cinemas and the tone, even with the formidable John Carpenter in the director's chair, is pretty reverential. Nonetheless, the film was immensely popular on American TV, and Kurt Russell (whose songs were dubbed by Ronnie McDowell) was effective enough as Elvis to be nominated for an Emmy. The star's own father, character actor Bing Russell, plays his father in the film, and you'll spot emerging leading men Ed Begley Jr and Joe Mantegna in supporting roles.

Embassy ○

1972, UK, 90 mins, colour
Dir: Gordon Hessler
Stars: Richard Roundtree, Chuck Connors, Max Von Sydow, Broderick Crawford, Ray Milland
Rating: ★

Extremely offbeat thriller about two American agents trying to get a Russian defector out of the US embassy in Beirut, while a KGB assassin tries to gun him down. The direction of Gordon Hessler, who had some stylish horror films already to his credit, ensures that the crucial action sequences are a cut above anything else in the film. The stalking of Chuck Connors by hero Richard Roundtree through a deserted and labyrinthine embassy building creates some rare moments of suspense.

Emerald Forest, The ① ⓥ

1985, US, 113 mins, colour
Dir: John Boorman
Stars: Powers Boothe, Meg Foster, Charley Boorman
Rating: ★★

An ecological thriller-cum-mystical adventure that was ahead of its time in highlighting the destruction of the South American rain forest. Based on an uncredited true story about a Peruvian whose son disappeared under similar circumstances, director John Boorman cast his own son Charley in the starring role. Grabbed by tribesmen whose community is facing destruction because of the construction of a massive dam, designed by his father (Powers Boothe), the boy spends the next 10 years living under jungle law and integrating into an alternative lifestyle. The lush cinematography by Philippe Rousselot is breathtaking and action scenes of in-fighting between bloodthirsty rival tribes – obviously shot under difficult conditions on location – generate a lot of excitement.

Emil and the Detectives ☉

1963, UK, 99 mins, colour
Dir: Peter Tewksbury
Stars: Walter Slezak, Bryan Russell, Roger Mobley
Rating: ★★

Erich Kastner's famous children's book about a horde of youngsters who tackle a gang of crooks has been itself tackled a number of times by film-makers. This is the Walt Disney version, amiably filmed on location in West Berlin. Walter Slezak and Heinz Schubert are both genially entertaining as the crooks and the fun sags a bit when they're not on screen.

Emperor of the North ◐
(aka: Emperor of the North Pole)
1973, US, 119 mins, colour
Dir: Robert Aldrich
Stars: Lee Marvin, Ernest Borgnine, Keith Carradine, Charles Tyner
Rating: ★★

Lee Marvin is the train-hopping, freeloading tramp who wants to become Emperor of the North Pole in this archetypal Robert Aldrich blood-and-guts action adventure. Ernest Borgnine is the brutal train guard, the setting is 1933 Oregon, and Keith Carradine is the disciple learning Marvin's easy-riding ways.

Emperor Waltz, The ○
1948, US, 106 mins, colour
Dir: Billy Wilder
Stars: Bing Crosby, Joan Fontaine, Roland Culver
Rating: ★★

Quite what the most abrasive of black comedy directors, Billy Wilder, was doing making the more romantic type of Bing Crosby musical is one of the mysteries of the age. Although Victor Young's background music was nominated for an Academy Award, this frothy Viennese frippery, revolving around a phonograph salesman of 1901, remains a strange choice for Crosby, Wilder, Joan Fontaine and all concerned.

Empire of the Ants ●
1977, US, 90 mins, colour
Dir: Bert I Gordon
Stars: Joan Collins, Robert Lansing
Rating: ★

It's Joan Collins – no mean maneater herself on the screen – versus a colony of giant ants in this science-fiction thriller. It's based (rather remotely) on the famous H G Wells story.

Empire of the Sun ◐ ⓥ
1987, US, 152 mins, colour
Dir: Steven Spielberg
Stars: Christian Bale, John Malkovich, Miranda Richardson, Nigel Havers, Joe Pantoliano, Leslie Phillips
Rating: ★★★

Steven Spielberg sometimes appears obsessed with telling his stories from a child's point of view. Here it's newcomer Christian Bale as an 11-year-old boy separated from his parents and having to survive an internment camp after the Japanese invade China during World War Two. There's no denying the power of the amazing set pieces (especially the evacuation of Shanghai) in this adaptation of the epic J G Ballard novel, but on a human level, the film is less happy. John Malkovich's opportunistic *King Rat* type threatens to become a fully developed character but never follows through. There's a strong British contingent – including Paul McGann in an early role, but it's Bale who takes most of the attention. His flight through swamp scrub outside the prison camp in which he spends most of his time is one of the film's few highlights.

Empire State ● ⓥ
1987, UK, 104 mins, colour
Dir: Ron Peck
Stars: Ian Sears, Emily Bolton, Ray McAnally, Cathryn Harrison, Martin Landau
Rating: ★

Reminiscent of a British exploitation film of 20 years earlier – dozens of characters, strobe lighting and a pop soundtrack, all in search of a plot. Pretty well every element an adult certificate could encompass is here – but no comprehensible narrative. Something seems to be going on at the Empire State, a gleaming nightclub with dolly hostesses upstairs and a gay bar downstairs – though we never really find out what. Most of the characters in fact are gay and the film does them few favours: they're all unpleasant or unsympathetic, except perhaps the wimpish reporter on an unlikely magazine sent down to get the story he's eventually killed for, though it hardly seemed worth the nightclub's trouble. Still, the film has style and energy in its fruitless search for content and charismatic performances from Ray McAnally as the State's proprietor and Lee Drysdale as a crisp young rent boy on the make. A bareknuckle fight at the end, though, is unforgivably violent.

Empire Strikes Back, The ○ ⓥ
1980, US, 124 mins, colour
Dir: Irvin Kershner
Stars: Harrison Ford, Mark Hamill, Carrie Fisher, Billy Dee Williams, Alec Guinness
Rating: ★★★

Second in the *Star Wars* trilogy. A masterpiece of special effects, it punctuates a tortuous storyline with bursts of swift and violent action. Mark Hamill, looking as though he really believed in it all, is back as Luke Skywalker, and romance blossoms between Leia (Carrie Fisher) and Han Solo (Harrison Ford). Although the awesome ice-planet Hoth is put to insufficient use, the swamp planet, with its weird little maharishi-type inhabitant (courtesy of Muppet-maker Frank Oz), makes up for it with fronds, gloom, mists and hidden horrors, all beautifully keyed in brown, green and grey.

Enchanted April ○ ⓥ
1991, UK, 99 mins, colour
Dir: Mike Newell
Stars: Miranda Richardson, Joan Plowright, Josie Lawrence, Michael Kitchen, Jim Broadbent, Alfred Molina
Rating: ★★

An archetypal British made-for-television movie – high on period detail and genteel to a point that makes one long for something really dramatic to happen and interrupt the almost incessant dialogue. Not that Peter (*The Ruling Class*) Barnes' dialogue is bad. Much of it has the air of a pretty good parody of the kind of Edwardian play that delighted middle-class matinees – polished, safe and, above all, not too witty. The performances, too, are exactly what one would expect, with the honours going to Jim Broadbent's not-quite-as-boring-as-he-seems husband. It's always a pleasure to see Joan Plowright deliver yet another variation on her now beautifully polished Beryl Reid impression (this one won her an Oscar nomination); and Polly Walker is right on target with her cool society vamp. But you are left with the (doubtless unworthy) feeling that the cast and crew had rather more fun making this film (since it involved a location trip to Italy) than audiences will have watching it.

Enchanted Cottage, The ○
1945, US, 92 mins, b/w
Dir: John Crowell
Stars: Dorothy McGuire, Robert Young
Rating: ★★

Robert Young plays a disfigured and embittered World War One veteran

E

and Dorothy McGuire is the plain girl with whom he finds true love in this incurably romantic story. They move into a secluded cottage which has been the venue for dozens of honeymooners, all of whom have found happiness. A small miracle happens: Young's disfigurement disappears and McGuire becomes a beautiful young woman . . . Despite a fine script from De Witt Bodeen and Herman J Mankiewicz and intelligent direction from John Cromwell, this looks a good deal less impressive today than when it first appeared, with very mannered acting and developments that, even given 'fantastic' licence, just aren't believable. Still, its heart is in the right place and it does offer sentiment without sentimentality.

Enchantment ○

1948, US, 101 mins, b/w
Dir: Irving Reis
Stars: David Niven, Teresa Wright, Farley Granger
Rating: ★★★

An unashamedly romantic story about a stately London house and the people who live – or have lived – in it. A typically lavish Sam Goldwyn production, it employs an interesting flashback technique, and the camerawork by Gregg Toland (winner of awards for *Citizen Kane* and *The Grapes of Wrath*) is outstanding. The screenplay by John Patrick and direction by the underrated Irving Reis both skilfully add to the film's effectiveness as a weepie of class and charm.

Encino Man

See: California Man

Encore ○

1951, UK, 88 mins, b/w
Dir: Pat Jackson
Stars: Nigel Patrick, Roland Culver, Kay Walsh, Glynis Johns
Rating: ★★★

Dramatisations of three more Somerset Maugham stories, this time introduced by the author himself. This was chronologically the third and last of the popular British compilation films from Maugham's works. A splendid British cast does the drily effective tales full justice, with Kay Walsh especially delightful in one episode as a chatterbox spinster – surrounded by some of Britain's best character players.

Enemies, A Love Story ●

1989, US, 120 mins, colour
Dir: Paul Mazursky
Stars: Ron Silver, Anjelica Huston, Lena Olin, Margaret Sophie Stein
Rating: ★★

No wonder Ron Silver wanders through this carnal, Jewish-slanted tragicomedy looking dazed, like Zeppo in a Marx Brothers film. Three wives yet he has – all of them pursuing him, or going round the bend, or both. You can almost hear the man muttering to himself as he turns his collar up against the snow in some Bronx backstreet of 1949, where the cameraman always has a sepia filter over his lens. *Enemies* takes a bit of getting into, but it has some rare, ripe moments in its second half, especially when two of the wives meet. You see, his wife was killed (but wasn't) during the war, so he marries the earthy servant who saved his life, whom he doesn't love (but makes pregnant), preferring the company of his fiery, red-haired mistress, whom he also makes pregnant (only she isn't). Silver seems numbed by it all, as well he might. Anjelica Huston, Lena Olin and Margaret Sophie Stein are all great as the women. The meal they serve up is overlong, but it does have some tasty moments.

Enemy Below, The ○

1957, US, 98 mins, colour
Dir: Dick Powell
Stars: Robert Mitchum, Curt Jurgens, Theodore Bikel, David Hedison
Rating: ★★★

German actor Curt Jurgens made his first major mark on the international film scene in this surprisingly tough and tense World War Two submarine chase drama, directed by former film star Dick Powell. Jurgens and Robert Mitchum are a beautifully balanced match as the skippers who gradually come to respect each other, and Harold Rosson's Technicolor photography vividly captures the claustrophobic undersea tension. The film won an Academy Award for its special effects, created by Walter Rossi.

Enemy from Space

See: Quatermass II

Enemy Mine ◑ ⓥ

1985, US, 108 mins, colour
Dir: Wolfgang Petersen
Stars: Dennis Quaid, Louis Gossett Jr, Brion James
Rating: ★★★

After several weeks shooting in almost inhuman conditions off the coast of Iceland, director Richard Loncraine (*The Missionary, Brimstone and Treacle*) was replaced by German Wolfgang Petersen, who had triumphed with a similar large-scale fantasy, *The NeverEnding Story*. The story has Dennis Quaid and Louis Gosset Jr (the latter unrecognisable under mountains of latex) as earthman and alien creature forgetting their differences to survive an inhospitable planet together. Everything about this film is spectacularly larger than life; the video version has a bonus of an extra 15 minutes of footage cut from the version seen in British cinemas, adding several key quieter moments and making the ending more comprehensible.

Enforcer, The ○ ⓥ

(aka: Murder Inc)
1950, US, 87 mins, b/w
Dir: Bretaigne Windust
Stars: Humphrey Bogart, Zero Mostel, Ted De Corsia, Everett Sloane
Rating: ★★★

One of the most gruelling of even Humphrey Bogart's gangster films. Faint-hearts should be warned that there are killings galore – murder by knife, by razor, by pick axe – all done with horrific but hypnotic realism. Gripping entertainment in semi-documentary style. The stars are backed by a host of good character studies, plus a script by Martin Rackin, and photography by Robert Burks, that add impact to the action.

Enforcer, The ● ⓥ

1976, US, 95 mins, colour
Dir: James Fargo
Stars: Clint Eastwood, Harry Guardino, Bradford Dillman, John Mitchum, Tyne Daly
Rating: ★★★

Clint Eastwood returns as unorthodox San Francisco *Dirty Harry* Callahan, in trouble as usual with his superiors because of his methods that tend to succeed but leave a pile of corpses in his wake. Here, in a complex story by Sterling Silliphant and Dean Reisner, he ends up with a female partner, well played by Tyne Daly, alias Lacey of *Cagney and Lacey*. Plenty of vivid action from first-time director James

Fargo, Eastwood has the character down to a 'T' and there is excellent use of locations.

England Made Me ◐
1972, UK, 100 mins, colour
Dir: Peter Duffell
Stars: Peter Finch, Michael York, Hildegarde Niel, Michael Hordern
Rating: ★★

Another of Peter Finch's towering performances, this time as a German industrialist, determined to preserve his mid-Thirties' empire at all costs. The costs may include marriage to the English girl (Hildegarde Neil, a shade too dispassionate) who is his strong right arm, and the possible dispatch of her worthless brother (Michael York) for whom she nurses an incestuous desire. Based on a novel by Graham Greene, this is stern and uncompromising stuff. But Michael Hordern contributes an amusing cameo as a penniless, seedy reporter, and Michael York turned in his best screen work to date.

Enid Is Sleeping
See: Over Her Dead Body

Ensign Pulver ○
1964, US, 104 mins, colour
Dir: Joshua Logan
Stars: Robert Walker, Burl Ives, Walter Matthau, Millie Perkins
Rating: ★★

Noted US film-maker Joshua Logan directed and co-wrote this ramshackle follow-up to his famous *Mister Roberts*. Robert Walker takes over the title role, which had won Jack Lemmon an Oscar, but he lacks the maniacal edginess that made Lemmon's Pulver so funny. The film, in fact, is more noteworthy for its cast, little-known then, of whom many went on to stardom: Walter Matthau, Diana Sands, James Farentino, Larry Hagman, James Coco and Jack Nicholson among them. Millie Perkins, who shot to short-lived fame in her first film, *The Diary of Anne Frank*, is an appealing female lead, and Burl Ives brings an amusing irascibility to The Captain which almost fills the gap left by James Cagney's departure from the role.

Entertainer, The ◐
1960, UK, 97 mins, b/w
Dir: Tony Richardson
Stars: Laurence Olivier, Brenda de Banzie, Joan Plowright, Alan Bates, Roger Livesey, Albert Finney
Rating: ★★★

Archie Rice, seedy seaside entertainer who is a failure in his career and as a man, is another in the memorable gallery of dramatic creations that only a Laurence Olivier could have brought so compellingly to life. He repeats his stage triumph in John Osbourne's play alongside a terrific cast including his wife, Joan Plowright, plus Roger Livesey, Brenda de Banzie, Alan Bates, Shirley Ann Field, Albert Finney, Thora Hird, and Daniel Massey. Years after seeing the film, his grotesque smile and dead eyes remain vivid in the memory.

Entertaining Mr Sloane ●
1969, UK, 94 mins, colour
Dir: Douglas Hickox
Stars: Beryl Reid, Peter McEnery, Harry Andrews
Rating: ★

A spasmodically successful adaptation of the Joe Orton play that makes a virtue of bad taste, but gets tedious before the end. Beryl Reid is unforgettable as a middle-aged, frumpy spinster – minus her false teeth and dressed in a see-through baby-doll nightie – trying to seduce young lodger Mr Sloane (a lean and muscular Peter McEnery, oozing sexual menace out of every pore). And Harry Andrews is every inch her predatory, seedy spiv brother, who wants to satisfy his own carnal lust with the blond stud he elevates to his leather-clad chauffeur. Douglas Hickox – at long last given the chance to shine at the helm of a full-length feature after years as an assistant director – has the measure of Orton's sourly outrageous humour, and is helped greatly by the gaudy, multi-coloured Gothic cemetery lodge set. Awarded an 'X' certificate on first release for its morally questionable tone and bisexual subject matter, it all looks rather more tame today.

Enter the Dragon ● ⓥ
1973, US, 97 mins, colour
Dir: Robert Clouse
Stars: Bruce Lee, John Saxon, Ahna Capri, Angela Mao
Rating: ★★

Bruce Lee's biggest international venture is a bit like a Universal B-picture of the Forties – on a million-dollar budget. Lee cleans up the white slave/narcotics market on an off-shore Chinese island, and he and co-star John Saxon polish off hundreds of kung-fu experts just before the US helicopter fleet arrives. Bits of the action are hysterically funny and bits of it – especially a pursuit through a maze of mirrors – are quite exciting. Personality-wise, honours go to little Angela Mao (a hapkido black belt champion) as Lee's sister – as demure as she is devastating.

Equinox ◐
1992, Canada, 103 mins, colour
Dir: Alan Rudolph
Stars: Matthew Modine, Lara Flynn Boyle, Fred Ward, Tyra Ferrell, Marisa Tomei, M Emmett Walsh
Rating: ★★★

A fascinating movie with a disappointing ending. It's a kind of surrealist *film noir* which opens with a destitute old woman dying on the street. From a letter found on her, a morgue attendant Tyra Ferrell begins to piece together the story of twin sons she gave away for adoption. Both have grown up to look like Matthew Modine; both hover dangerously on the edge of sanity. One is a mass of insecurities and strange aggression. The other is a gangster whose rarely controlled violence brings him to the attention of a local crime kingpin. Stunningly well constructed, and studded with apposite lines: 'My whole life seems to be taking place without me in it,' declares the baffled 'good' Modine, the film almost ascends the peaks of perfection before falling headlong into the pit of an 'I don't how to end this, so let's close with a stunningly enigmatic shot' ending. Pity.

Equus ◐ ⓥ
1977, UK, 132 mins, colour
Dir: Sidney Lumet
Stars: Richard Burton, Peter Firth, Colin Blakely, Jenny Agutter, Joan Plowright, Harry Andrews
Rating: ★★

This strange story was one of its decade's most magnetic stage plays. In this long film version all the cracks show, even though the wallpapering of director Sidney Lumet is as expert as can be. Richard Burton has one of the most demanding parts of his later years as the psychiatrist who has to find out why a strange youth (Peter Firth) blinded six horses. Firth is excellent, easily besting a distinguished supporting cast, most of whom give actorly performances whose mechanics show all too near the surface. Hokum

E

at heart, the story is exceptionally well done in places, especially in some of the scenes between psychiatrist and patient.

Erik the Viking ○ ⓥ
1989, UK, 108 mins, colour
Dir: Terry Jones
Stars: Tim Robbins, Mickey Rooney, Eartha Kitt, Terry Jones, John Cleese
Rating: ★

Monty Python meets Sinbad the Sailor without the laughs. Fashionably photographed, mainly in brown and white, this is the scattershot story of how Erik attempted to end the Age of Warfare by besting the dragon of the North Sea, blowing the Horn Resounding in the legendary island of Hy-Brasil (Atlantis), awakening the gods and getting them to release the sun that has been swallowed by Fenrir the wolf. Sounds fun, doesn't it? Alas, although there are a few chuckles (mainly provided by the dry delivery of John Cleese as villainous Halfdan the Black), the vehicle proves as unwieldy as a Viking sword, as cumbersome as the Viking clothing and as ramshackle as a Viking hut. Performances range from exaggerated to hysterical. And just what is Tim Robbins doing starring in this?

Ernest Saves Christmas ○
1988, US, 88 mins, colour
Dir: John Cherry
Stars: Jim Varney
Rating: ★★★

This was the second of (to date) five big screen adventures featuring well-meaning disaster Ernest P Worrell, a sort of American version of Mr Bean. After 151 years, Santa's magic powers are dimming and he wants to pass the torch on to a kindly but down-on-his-luck TV host, whose show has just been cancelled. Naturally, bungling Ernest gets involved with disastrous results, but all ends happily in time for Christmas Eve.

Errand Boy, The ⊙ ⓥ
1961, US, 92 mins, b/w
Dir: Jerry Lewis
Stars: Jerry Lewis, Brian Donlevy, Dick Wesson
Rating: ★★★

A wacky, way-out comedy, written and directed by its star, Jerry Lewis, with Jerry's home studio, Paramount, seeing service as the Paramutual Pictures of the story. The long string of gags that ensues rather lacks discipline, but it's good-natured fun, and the stars of the then-popular TV Western series *Bonanza* pop up in guest appearances. Jerry's character name, Morty S Tashman, is an in-joke referring to director Frank Tashlin who directed the comedian in numerous comedies.

Escapade ○
1955, UK, 88 mins, b/w
Dir: Philip Leacock
Stars: John Mills, Yvonne Mitchell, Alastair Sim
Rating: ★★

Delightful, relaxed performances from John Mills, Yvonne Mitchell and Alastair Sim in a sensitive comedy-drama about a father obsessed with his campaign for world peace, while his three sons are up to some strange tricks at their boarding school.

Escapade in Japan ○
1957, US, 95 mins, colour
Dir: Arthur Lubin
Stars: Teresa Wright, Cameron Mitchell
Rating: ★★

Japan has never been more lovingly presented, nor better photographed than in this Technicolor treat about two little boys who, surviving a plane crash, decide to trek to Tokyo on their own. Cameron Mitchell and Teresa Wright are just perfect as the anguished parents who try to track them down. The film is full of incidental pleasures, not least the boys' hilarious visit to a geisha house, leading to a tense climax with the boys at risk. Clint Eastwood has a tiny role.

Escape ○
1940, US, 104 mins, b/w
Dir: Mervyn LeRoy
Stars: Robert Taylor, Norma Shearer, Conrad Veidt
Rating: ★★★

A thriller set in pre-war Germany about a young American artist (Robert Taylor) desperately trying to rescue his sick mother from a concentration camp. It was one of the first Hollywood attempts to show what life was like in Germany in the early days of the Nazi regime, and captures well the fearful atmosphere in a country where people are polite – but speak only in generalities.

Escape by Night ○
1952, UK, 79 mins, b/w
Dir: John Gilling

Stars: Bonar Colleano, Sidney James, Andrew Ray, Ted Ray, Simone Silva
Rating: ★★

It's hard to think of the loveable wisecracking Sid James as a screen villain but his role here as a vicious gangster was his big break in the cinema world. Andrew Ray, still riding high on his success as *The Mudlark*, is featured with his real-life father Ted playing, for the only time in a film, his on-screen dad as well.

Escape from Alcatraz ◑ ⓥ
1979, US, 112 mins, colour
Dir: Don Siegel
Stars: Clint Eastwood, Patrick McGoohan, Fred Ward, Roberts Blossom
Rating: ★★★

A solid, old-fashioned prison movie, still a Clint Eastwood film for all that it's based on fact, but refreshingly free from excessive violence and four-letter words. Familiar elements of the genre – the prison gang leader, the martinet warden, the eventual break – are smoothly integrated with a downbeat approach that eschews making heroes out of the quartet of inmates bent on escape. Director Don Siegel is clearly having little truck with sideline issues and indeed, with a movie already running around two hours, he has little call for them. His actors, Eastwood included, sink themselves entirely in their roles, all problems are (perhaps too obviously) eased aside for the final bid for freedom and few of those who see the film are likely to find it below their expectations. Sharp eyes may spot Danny Glover in a very minor role.

Escape from Fort Bravo ○
1953, US, 98 mins, colour
Dir: John Sturges
Stars: William Holden, Eleanor Parker, John Forsythe, William Demarest
Rating: ★★★

Vigorous, he-man Cavalry Western, forcefully directed by the redoubtable John Sturges, who also made *The Magnificent Seven*. Here, he used MGM's new colour, Ansco Color, for the first time, achieving some striking visual effects. Slow-moving at the start, the story works up to a tense climax when the principal characters are trapped by Indians. Good acting all round from a cast headed by William Holden and John Forsythe.

Escape from New York ◐ ⓥ
1981, US, 95m mins, colour
Dir: John Carpenter
Stars: Kurt Russell, Lee Van Cleef, Ernest Borgnine, Donald Pleasence, Isaac Hayes, Harry Dean Stanton
Rating: ★★★

A stylish, extravagant and deliberately eye-catching John Carpenter enterprise set in 1997 on Manhattan Island, the whole of which is walled in to create one vast prison to which very bad boys are consigned for the rest of their lives. When the US president crash lands there, a master thief (played by Kurt Russell with a Clint Eastwood whisper) is given 24 hours to earn an amnesty by getting him out. His exciting and often fearsome adventures in the attempt form the body of the story. One scene of a boxing ring turned into a gladiatorial area is really imaginative both in conception and execution, as Russell and a massive opponent do battle with spiked clubs.

Escape from the Planet of the Apes ○ ⓥ
1971, US, 98 mins, colour
Dir: Don Taylor
Stars: Roddy McDowall, Kim Hunter, Bradford Dillman
Rating: ★★★

Not so much a sequel to the second film in the series, more a neat and ingenious re-working of Pierre Boulle's original premise. The intelligent script is by Paul Dehn, one-time film critic of *The News Chronicle*, who put theory into practice and won the 1951 Oscar for Best Screenplay for *Seven Days to Noon*. Here, the apes make off from their incinerated planet (it blew up at the end of *Beneath the Planet of the Apes*) in Charlton Heston's original spacecraft, to land in modern America. Bradford Dillman gives a superb performance as Dr Dixon, while Roddy McDowall and Kim Hunter are excellent as usual under the clever simian make-up. One of the best of the Apes movies – and it moves well all the way.

Escape Route ○
(aka: I'll Get You)
1952, UK, 79 mins, b/w
Dir: Peter Graham Scott
Stars: George Raft, Sally Gray, Clifford Evans
Rating: ★★

George Raft's second British film casts him as an FBI agent tracking down

the brains behind a huge kidnapping ring. Playing the brains: Clifford Evans, once famous in TV's *The Power Game*. It's pretty slow, but the climax is a terrific running fight through a riverside wharf.

Escape to Happiness
See: Intermezzo

Escape to Victory ○
1981, US/UK, 111 mins, colour
Dir: John Huston
Stars: Sylvester Stallone, Michael Caine, Pele, Bobby Moore, Max Von Sydow, Daniel Massey
Rating: ★

A really excruciating PoW camp escape film, so artificially contrived as to be only a pace ahead of a sketch from a variety show. The idea is that a team of footballing prisoners will take on the might of the Reich, win and escape at the same time. Takes some believing, doesn't it? Lots of famous soccer stars are in the cast, plus Sylvester Stallone in goal: one can hardly believe John Huston directed this, but he did. Bad luck John: you were the one who needed to escape.

Escape to Witch Mountain ○
1974, US, 74 mins, colour
Dir: John Hough
Stars: Eddie Albert, Ray Milland, Donald Pleasence
Rating: ★★

This Disney sci-fi spree may leave the less demanding child agog. The two children, Kim Richards and Ike Eisenmann, are excellent. But the last half-hour cheats them of their triumph by playing their adventures for laughs rather than thrills.

Esther Waters ○
1948, UK, 109 mins, b/w
Dir: Ian Dalrymple
Stars: Kathleen Ryan, Dirk Bogarde, Fay Compton
Rating: ★★

Gloom and doom became for some reason fashionable in British films of the post-war years, and in this 19th-century weepie Kathleen Ryan suffers spectacularly as a servant-girl who falls for a ne'er-do-well and pays for it down the years. The rascal is played by Dirk Bogarde at a time when his career was full of such shady, shallow characters.

Eternally Yours ○
1939, US, 95 mins, b/w
Dir: Tay Garnett
Stars: Loretta Young, David Niven, Broderick Crawford
Rating: ★★

Loretta Young deserts the more dependable charms of her society boyfriend Broderick Crawford for charismatic magician David Niven, but comes to have second thoughts about her decision in this interesting drama, typical of Hollywood's output at this period. A really strong supporting cast includes the film's director Tay Garnett as a pilot, as well as such hardened scene-stealers as ZaSu Pitts, Billie Burke, C Aubrey Smith and Eve Arden.

E.T. The Extra-Terrestrial ☉ ⓥ
1982, US, 115m mins, colour
Dir: Steven Spielberg
Stars: Dee Wallace, Peter Coyote, Henry Thomas
Rating: ★★★★

The most successful family film of all time, perhaps the most succesful film Walt Disney never made. Combining elements of *Peter Pan* and *The Bible*, director Steven Spielberg weaves a highly manipulative spell that is sure not to leave a dry eye in the house. Perhaps it was this sense of brazen manipulation or just sheer jealously at its monstrous box office success that led to its Oscars haul being restricted to technical awards for visual and audio effects, sound, and for John Williams' sweeping score. E.T.'s voice is supposedly by Debra Winger.

Eureka ● ⓥ
1982, UK/US, 129 mins, colour
Dir: Nicolas Roeg
Stars: Gene Hackman, Theresa Russell, Rutger Hauer, Jane Lapotaire
Rating: ★★

A sort of *Citizen Kane* on ice. Gene Hackman is (in flashback) a man who makes a fortune in Yukon gold, keeps a strange stone with a shape on it, and is finally beset by gangsters in the Caribbean. Sounds hard to follow? You've got it. But Nicolas Roeg's puzzle piece is also beautifully scored, skilfully shot and made deliberately in fragments, like the facets of a diamond showing a previously hidden face with a change of light.

E

Even Cowgirls Get the Blues ● Ⓥ

1993, US, A mins, colour
Dir: Gus Van Sant Jr
Stars: Uma Thurman, John Hurt, Rain Phoenix, Angie Dickinson
Rating: ★

This tedious film is like a flower power comedy of 25 years ago. Sissy (Uma Thurman), born with abnormally long thumbs, becomes a professional hitchhiker (she has to hitch every day when her thumbs get stiff and sore). Thanks to her activities as a part-time model for the transvestite Countess (John Hurt), she ends up at the Rubber Rose Ranch, a distinctly kinky establishment currently in danger of being taken over by the lesbian cowgirls who hover about its fringes. Sissy falls heavily for the leader, Bonanza Jellybean (Rain Phoenix – hard to know which name is sillier), consults The Chink (Pat Morita), a wise man from the hills who guards a giant clockworks in a cave, and helps the cowgirls in their fight to breed a flock of whooping cranes. A cross between any number of movies from the late Sixties, this is the kind of film where characters look at each other through a hole in a piece of toast and a string quartet plays in a field. As you'll have gathered, the thumb total of this foolish frolic is not very much.

Evergreen ○ Ⓥ

1934, UK, 91 mins, b/w
Dir: Victor Saville
Stars: Jessie Matthews, Sonnie Hale
Rating: ★★★

This enchanting musical was Jessie Matthews' greatest popular success, opening up the possibility of a Hollywood career – although, for personal reasons, she chose to remain in Britain. Playing mother-and-daughter stars of London's theatreland, Jessie, dazzlingly photographed by Glenn MacWilliams, sings 'Over My Shoulder', 'Dancing on the Ceiling' and more. The high-key lighting is reminiscent of the Astaire-Rogers musicals being made at the time on the other side of the Atlantic.

Everybody Does It ○

1949, US, 98 mins, b/w
Dir: Edmund Goulding
Stars: Paul Douglas, Celeste Holm, Linda Darnell
Rating: ★★★★

This vintage Hollywood comedy was lighter fare than usual for director Edmund Goulding, more often associated with such serious drama as the Bette Davis vehicles *Dark Victory*, *The Old Maid* and *The Great Lie*. Beetle-browed comedian Paul Douglas is boring businessman Leonard Borland, keen to promote wife Celeste Holm's operatic career – until her debut bombs and glamorous soprano Linda Darnell discovers that he has a splendid baritone voice himself. Douglas is a very amiable buffoon, Holm plays wittily (and sings prettily) and Darnell is fine as the catalyst for potential domestic disaster. The film is a remake of 1939's *Wife, Husband and Friend*, starring Warner Baxter, Loretta Young and Binnie Barnes; both were scripted by Nunnally Johnson. Contemporary critics sniffed at this remake, but when audiences reached for their handkerchiefs, it was to dry the tears of laughter from their eyes.

Everybody's All American

See: When I Fall in Love

Everybody Sing ○

1937, US, 80 mins, b/w
Dir: Edwin L Marin
Stars: Judy Garland, Allan Jones, Fanny Brice
Rating: ★★★

Although this was one of MGM's shorter-length musicals, they still managed to squeeze in a dozen songs, showcase a young Judy Garland, give Fanny Brice the chance to do her famous 'Baby Snooks' routine and get Allan Jones on to share the songs.

Every Girl Should Be Married ○

1948, US, 85 mins, b/w
Dir: Don Hartman
Stars: Cary Grant, Betsy Drake, Franchot Tone, Diana Lynn
Rating: ★★

Model Betsy Drake took most of the best reviews for this mild comedy in which she made her acting debut, complete with bubbly voice and cue-jumping delivery. A year later she married her co-star Cary Grant (she was the third of his four wives). Some of the lines are certainly funny, but the confection is overcooked by director Don Hartman.

Every Home Should Have One ○

(aka: Think Dirty)
1971, UK, 94 mins, colour
Dir: Jim Clark
Stars: Marty Feldman, Judy Cornwell, Shelley Berman, Julie Ege, Patrick Cargill
Rating: ★

This was Marty Feldman's first starring role after an appearance in Richard Lester's *The Bed Sitting Room* (1969) and the smutty script (by Feldman, Barry Took and Denis Norden) gives him plenty of opportunities to display his frenetic brand of Jerry Lewis-style mugging.

Everything You Always Wanted to Know About Sex, But Were Afraid to Ask ● Ⓥ

1972, US, 85 mins, colour
Dir: Woody Allen
Stars: Woody Allen, John Carradine, Anthony Quayle, Lynn Redgrave, Burt Reynolds, Gene Wilder
Rating: ★★★

Although parts of this seven-episode romp are admittedly too crude to be funny, with Woody Allen at the reins in his zaniest mood, you know you're in for a good few laughs. The best of the stories are the first, second and last, the opener being about a court jester (Woody) who tries to seduce the Queen (Lynn Redgrave) by spinning such 11th century lines as 'Lady, I hast the hots for thee' and slipping an aphrodisiac in her bedtime drink. Alas, the poor fool gets his hand stuck in the Queen's chastity belt, which enables Mr Allen to go around for the rest of the scene with his hand clasped to Miss Redgrave's bottom (yes, he did write the script). Best line, by the jester about the prowess of the King (Anthony Quayle): 'He's the only man I know who can swim the moat lengthwise.' In the second yarn, Gene Wilder is just superb as a doctor who falls in love with a sheep, while the last story (in which Burt Reynolds joins Woody) imagines all parts of the male body are populated by little men, and studies their reactions as they prepare for making love. For most of the way, an enjoyably rude jape.

Every Which Way But Loose ○ Ⓥ

1978, US, 114 mins, colour
Dir: James Fargo
Stars: Clint Eastwood, Sondra Locke, Geoffrey Lewis, Beverly D'Angelo, Ruth Gordon
Rating: ★

This is a very loose-limbed comedy of mayhem which its star Clint Eastwood (who also directed) intends no-one to take seriously. An orang-utan called Clyde steals practically every scene. It's so like an old biker movie of the Sixties, though, that you practically expect Peter Fonda and Dennis Hopper (or maybe even Frankie Avalon and Annette Funicello) to wander in at any minute. The story and the characters are really too silly even by the standards of this kind of romp, and the film's disparate elements hardly ever begin to gel. It still pulled 'em in at the box-office, though, and Eastwood's personal share of the profits was said to be more than $15 million. No wonder he made a sequel, *Any Which Way You Can*.

Evil Dead, The ● ⓥ
1983, US, 85 mins, colour
Dir: Sam Raimi
Stars: Bruce Campbell, Ellen Sandweiss, Betsy Baker, Hal Delrich, Sarah York
Rating: ★★★

This sensationally scary film from Sam Raimi cleaned up at the world's box-offices, returning vast profits on its $400,000 budget. Five young people seek shelter in a remote abandoned woodland cabin – and find pretty well everything except shelter. Following the discovery of an ancient Book of the Dead, they're soon being possessed by dormant woodland demons in *10 Little Niggers* style, giving rise to some special effects that are pretty breath-taking on such a low budget. Raimi's trademark black humour is already in evidence at this early stage of his career, and he's greatly aided by the moody photography of Tim Philo and Joshua M Becker, using the adaptable Color by Du Art, which suggests the menacing presence of the lurking de-mons even when they can't be seen. For those who demand rivers of gore, this one has that too; a bit of every-thing, in fact, and all done well.

Evil Dead II ● ● ⓥ
1987, US, 85 mins, colour
Dir: Sam Raimi
Stars: Bruce Campbell, Sarah Berry, Dan Hicks, Kassie Wesley
Rating: ★★

Good clean fun for those horror fans who demand nothing more than a welter of blood, swivelling zombies and non-stop action and don't ask for a story that makes any kind of sense. It's all, as the dialogue demonstrates,

tongue-in-cheek (well, chainsaw-in-cheek anyway) and director Sam Raimi probably has it about right when he claims that 'we're just trying to give the audience a good time'. As for the rest, Denise Bixler is far too dishy and talented to get killed in the first reel and the rest of the cast give it all they've got which isn't terribly much, but suffices for the occasion. That cabin in the woods is still in-fested with evil spirits and you may find their gruesome antics growing on you as the film goes on.

Evil Under the Sun ○ ⓥ
1981, UK, 115 mins, colour
Dir: Guy Hamilton
Stars: Peter Ustinov, Jane Birkin, Colin Blakely, James Mason, Maggie Smith, Roddy McDowall
Rating: ★★

There's another cast-to-treasure in this follow-up to the same producers' *Death on the Nile*. If only the film lived up to the accumulated talents of Peter Ustinov, Maggie Smith, Roddy McDowall, James Mason, Diana Rigg, Colin Blakely and the rest. Alas, too often director Guy Hamilton seems to let the plot almost go to sleep under the Adriatic sun of the title. However, the opening sequence is an excellent piece of scene-setting, and the pairing of Maggie Smith and Diana Rigg provides some delightfully bitchy moments.

Excalibur ● ⓥ
1981, UK, 140 mins, colour
Dir: John Boorman
Stars: Nigel Terry, Helen Mirren, Nicholas Clay, Nicol Williamson, Cheri Lunghi
Rating: ★★

Director John Boorman ambitiously romps through the entire Arthurian legend – from possession of the sword Excalibur by Uther Pendragon to the death of his son, King Arthur – in this gigantic slice of blood and sorcery which is not for the faint-hearted. The result is almost always the handsomest of films to behold. Dramatically, it has its moments, too, even if it never quite achieves that monstrously diffi-cult blend of grandeur and madness for which it strives. The battle scenes hold all the excitement and gore that modern wizardry will allow, but Boorman's quieter visual effects can bring gasps to the throat – and giggles, as in Helen Mirren's battle armour,

which might well be authentic but seems to have strayed from *Fire Maid-ens from Outer Space*.

Executive Suite ○
1954, US, 104 mins, b/w
Dir: Robert Wise
Stars: William Holden, June Allyson, Fredric March, Barbara Stanwyck, Walter Pidgeon, Shelley Winters
Rating: ★★★

One of those all-star films stemming from massive bestselling books, a genre of which Hollywood became particularly fond in the mid-Fifties. The world of big business becomes a battleground when a company chairman dies without naming his successor. The conflict between those fighting over the position is de-veloped with good character insight, their ambitions, dislikes and individual foibles presented with a distinctly hu-man touch. Punchy performances all round, especially from William Holden, Dean Jagger, Barbara Stanwyck and Nina Foch. Twenty-five years later the story was taken to a sequel in a short-lived TV series.

Exodus ○
1960, US, 220 mins, colour
Dir: Otto Preminger
Stars: Paul Newman, Eva Marie Saint, Ralph Richardson, Peter Lawford, Lee J Cobb, Sal Mineo
Rating: ★★

Otto Preminger's version of Leon Uris' vast novel about the birth of modern Israel split critics and public alike. Preminger, determined to make his own film, ditched Uris as screen-writer, let the story run to more than three and a half hours, and commented that: 'I think the result is closer to the truth than the book, and to the facts. It also avoids proaganada. It's an American picture, after all, that tries to tell the story giving both sides a chance to plead their case.' Paul Newman radiates sincerity as the young Israeli leader; scenes of the refugees escaping their Cyprus de-tention centre are the most suspenseful in the film; and Ernest Gold's stirring score won an Oscar. Humorist Mort Sahl implored at the preview, as the film entered its fourth hour: 'Otto, let my people go!'

Exorcist III, The ● ⓥ
1990, US, 109 mins, colour
Dir: William Peter Blatty

E

Stars: George C Scott, Brad Dourif, Jason Miller, Nicol Williamson, Viveca Lindfors
Rating: ★★

He's back! The devil, that is, in a Linda Blair-less sequel to the original, in which poor dead priest Jason Miller from the first film is resurrected and tossed in a lunatic asylum, wrapped round the body and mind of a serial killer. When the 'Gemini' killings start all over again, an incredulous George C Scott, as a police lieutenant involved in both cases, has to try to root out the truth – and the cure. The story begins well, with the horror element being lightened by the joky relationship between Scott and Ed Flanders, as the kind of priest who tells a sinner 'God loves you, everyone else thinks you're an asshole.' But as soon as Flanders is killed, the film begins to flounder in a welter of demonic talk, occasionally alleviated by the odd very effective shock moment. Brad Dourif (the serial killer) does his best with a pretty boring character with far too much to say.

Experiment in Terror
See: Grip of Fear

Explorers ○ ⓥ
1985, US, 109 mins, colour
Dir: Joe Dante
Stars: River Phoenix, Ethan Hawke, Jason Presson, Amanda Peterson
Rating: ★★★

This rather odd but interesting little picture is a cross between a teen angst film and a sci-fi adventure. In the beginning three young friends, a dreamer, an egghead and a misfit, decide to build their own spacecraft. This is mixed in with the usual schoolroom antics, bullies versus nerds, puppy love and parental troubles for the egghead. The big switch comes when they actually succeed in making a working spacecraft and set off for other worlds. Their ship is swallowed by a giant spaceship whose alien occupants have been watching American TV shows for the past 30 years. A bizarre but funny idea that works, providing you too have been an avid fan of American TV shows. Not a rip-roaring *Star Wars* adventure, but a quirky and entertaining tale told well by director Joe Dante, who also made *Gremlins*, *InnerSpace* and *Gremlins 2: The New Batch*. Ethan Hawke, River Phoenix and Jason Presson have fun as the teenage astronauts.

Expresso Bongo ◐ ⓥ
1959, UK, 111 mins, b/w
Dir: Val Guest
Stars: Laurence Harvey, Sylvia Syms, Cliff Richard, Yolande Donlan
Rating: ★

A film adaptation of the satirical musical that revolves around Soho and its thriving coffee bars in the late Fifties. The movie's main problem is that it never makes up its mind in which direction it's supposed to be travelling and ends up as an earthy, happy-go-lucky ramble. Laurence Harvey hams the part of the get-rich quick agent splendidly, but Sylvia Syms seems ill-at-ease as his stripper girlfriend.

Extreme Prejudice ◐ ⓥ
1987, US, 104 mins, colour
Dir: Walter Hill
Stars: Nick Nolte, Powers Boothe, Michael Ironside, Maria Conchita Alonso, Rip Torn, Clancy Brown
Rating: ★★

Shunned by the cinemagoing public for two decades, the Western has regrouped its forces and emerged in other guises. The modern action thriller, with its constant chases, killings and shootouts, provides an ideal cover and, with its 'Tex-Mex' border setting, and a Texas ranger hero in Nick Nolte, director Walter Hill's film comes closer to the old Hollywood shoot-em-ups. There are even the two old friends, now on opposite sides of the law, who must shoot it out in the end. Ostensibly, though, this is a thriller about six soldiers of fortune, all officially listed as dead, who home in on the border town where Nolte is having a tough time keeping the lid on the drugs trade run by his old chum Powers Boothe. Even with some crazy dialogue, Boothe has no problem walking off with the film, especially once Rip Torn's local sheriff has been eradicated from the scene too soon for the movie's own good. Michael Ironside and the chameleon Clancy Brown are the best of the military men; the action itself is formula stuff; and lots of extras, as well as most of the cast, bite the adobe dust. They sure have it tough down Mexico way.

Eye for an Eye, An ● ⓥ
1981, US, 106 mins, colour
Dir: Steve Carver
Stars: Chuck Norris, Christopher Lee, Richard Roundtree
Rating: ★★

The plot is no great strain on the brain – Martial Arts expert Chuck Norris (with a little help from his friends) takes on wicked Christopher Lee and his henchmen and demolishes them. But the movie is an expertly-crafted piece of kung foolery designed to showcase former world karate champion Chuck and director Steve Carver – a graduate of the New World School of exploitation film-making – displays a good eye for high-kicking action. He even succeeds in making the usually monolithic Mr Norris look dramatically quite lively.

Eye of the Cat ◐
1969, US, 102 mins, colour
Dir: David Lowell Rich
Stars: Michael Sarrazin, Gayle Hunnicutt, Eleanor Parker
Rating: ★★

Bizarre thriller about devious plotting in a house full of felines. Eleanor Parker enjoys herself in another cripple-in-a-wheelchair role but it's the cats, full of silky menace, who steal this offbeat thriller.

Eyes in the Night ○
1942, US, 80 mins, b/w
Dir: Fred Zinnemann
Stars: Edward Arnold, Ann Harding, Donna Reed, Stephen McNally
Rating: ★★★

This off-beat thriller about a blind detective trying to outwit a gang of spies was one of director Fred Zinnemann's earliest assignments, and provided an out-of-character role for Edward Arnold as the detective. Fans of vintage films will have a field day, recognising such stars as Steven Geray, Allen Jenkins, Reginald Denny, Barry Nelson, Milburn Stone and Mantan Moreland. The elegant Ann Harding seemed here to have stepped into mother roles too quickly.

Eyes of Laura Mars ● ⓥ
1978, US, 104 mins, colour
Dir: Irvin Kershner
Stars: Faye Dunaway, Tommy Lee Jones, Brad Dourif, Rene Auberjonois, Raul Julia
Rating: ★★

An old-fashioned creepie, rather unworthy of its Oscar-winning star, Faye Dunaway, although its murders are directed with a lot of flair by Irvin Kershner. Miss Dunaway plays a rather way-out fashion photographer who finds herself seeing the murders of her friends as they happen, via some nightmarish second sight. The plot needs her visions to pep it all up, but for an hour or so it careers along nastily but nicely. Whodunnit fans should be able to spot the killer.

Eyewitness ○
1956, UK, 82 mins, b/w
Dir: Muriel Box
Stars: Donald Sinden, Muriel Pavlow, Michael Craig, Belinda Lee
Rating: ★★

This pursuit thriller made a nice change of pace for Muriel Pavlow after a series of milk-and-water roles, although the role of a girl who witnesses murder and goes on the run for the rest of the film didn't really suit her. There's a fine performance, though, from Nigel Stock, who acts everyone else off the screen as an unwilling, deaf safebreaker. The story has too many threads but provides some excitement.

Eyewitness ◐ ⓥ
(aka: Sudden Terror)
1970, UK, 95 mins, colour
Dir: John Hough
Stars: Mark Lester, Lionel Jeffries, Susan George, Jeremy Kemp
Rating: ★★★

A breathlessly exciting thriller along the lines of the story of the boy who cried wolf. Mark Lester is the boy on a strife-torn Mediterranean island who witnesses a murder – then tries to get people to believe it while the murderer closes in on him. John Hough's furious direction in the final chase sequence will leave you gasping.

F

Fabulous Baker Boys, The ● ⓥ
1989, US, 113 mins, colour
Dir: Steve Kloves
Stars: Jeff Bridges, Michelle Pfeiffer, Beau Bridges, Jennifer Tilly
Rating: ★★★

No-one who has seen this romantic comedy can ever forget the sight of Michelle Pfeiffer in a blazing red dress crawling all over the top of a piano and crooning 'Makin' Whoopee'. She's pure dynamite in a role that takes full advantage of her natural singing talent and casts her as the saviour of a dying lounge saloon double act, played with great knowing charm by real-life brothers Jeff and Beau Bridges. You know where the story is heading after the initial set-up, but thanks to spot-on performances and a stellar script, the getting there is most enjoyable.

Face Behind the Mask, The ○
1941, US, 69 mins, b/w
Dir: Robert Florey
Stars: Peter Lorre, Evelyn Keyes, Don Beddoe
Rating: ★★★

Peter Lorre in a rare appearance as a man of his own nationality, Hungarian. This is about a man who, his face horribly disfigured in a fire, becomes a criminal mastermind beneath a rubber mask. Lorre wore no actual mask for the role, only chalk-white make-up and strips of tape to help him immobilise part of his features. 'If an actor can't make his body do what he wants it to do, he isn't an actor. If he needs mounds of make-up to create an illusion, he's a mere impressionist.' The scene where he first removes the bandages and sees his fire-ravaged face is genuinely harrowing.

Face in the Crowd, A ○
1957, US, 126 mins, b/w
Dir: Elia Kazan
Stars: Andy Griffith, Patricia Neal, Anthony Franciosa, Walter Matthau, Lee Remick
Rating: ★★★

A powerful drama about media exploitation, *A Face in the Crowd* is as pertinent today as when it was released. Andy (Matlock) Griffith is Lonesome Rhodes, a drunken down-and-out with a guitar and a wry sense of humour who is discovered by reporter Patricia Neal. He is given his own radio show and within weeks is the station's main asset. A move to television and national stardom soon follows. But the power and influence of stardom begins to corrupt and Rhodes becomes involved with a right-wing political group. Marcia (Neal) realises she has created a media monster. Griffith gives a powerful performance in this, his first film, and never quite reached these heights again. It was also the debut film for Lee Remick, who plays the cheerleader Rhodes marries. Director Elia Kazan and writer Budd Schulberg created a hard-hitting look at television and how it can be misused. It caused quite a stir when it was released and has lost little of its power since.

Face of a Fugitive ○
1958, US, 81 mins, colour
Dir: Paul Wendkos
Stars: Fred MacMurray, Lin McCarthy, Dorothy Green, James Coburn
Rating: ★★★

This film is small-scale, originally released as a second-feature, but one contemporary critic remarked that this taut Western, about a man running from his past, is 'worth going almost any distance to see.' It became the first minor Western to win four stars from *Picturegoer* (the top movie magazine of the time). Director Paul Wendkos puts impact into every scene right from the start. The credits unfold over a sketch of the wanted man. Across the face, one bar after another appears, creating a prison motif which is repeated throughout the film, with barred foregrounds, ruined buildings, a fence, an iron bedstead. With rare economy and truth, the powerful script refuses to be side-tracked into extraneous action, and sticks to its theme of the redemption of a man. Lin McCarthy is especially impressive as the green but fanatically fair sheriff. And Fred MacMurray creates a memorable figure as the fugitive. Down the cast list (in his second film): a rising star called James Coburn.

Faces ◐ ⓥ
1968, US, 130 mins, b/w
Dir: John Cassavetes
Stars: John Marley, Gena Rowlands, Lynn Carlin
Rating: ★★★

F

Although one of his best films, this is still very typical of director John Cassevetes' work. It deals with a very human and essentially ordinary problem (in this case a 14-year marriage that has gone stale), much of the acting is improvised and the feel almost documentary. The acting is very good. Also typical was the difficulty Cassevetes had getting it to the big screen, the race reviews the critics gave it and the lukewarm response from the public. John Marley and Lynn Carlin play the couple who look elsewhere for love: he with a prostitute (Gena Rowlands), she with an old beatnick (Seymour Cassel). Although it has its flat spots the film is ultmately rewarding for those who stick with it.

Fahrenheit 451 ○
1966, UK, 111 mins, colour
Dir: Francois Truffaut
Stars: Julie Chrisite, Oskar Werner, Cyril Cusack, Anton Diffring
Rating: ★★★

Underrated science-fiction film adapted from Ray Bradbury's novel. Set in a book-burning society of the future, it has haunting performances from Julie Christie and Oskar Werner and delicate colour photography by Nicolas Roeg, who was soon to become one of the major directors of the British cinema.

Fail Safe ○
1964, US, 111 mins, b/w
Dir: Sidney Lumet
Stars: Henry Fonda, Walther Matthau, Frank Overton, Dan O'Herlihy, Larry Hagman
Rating: ★★

The straight version of *Dr Strangelove*, tautly handled by Sidney Lumet, is a tension-fraught vision of a nightmare coming true. The film didn't receive its true recognition at the time, as *Strangelove*, which treated similar subject matter – nuclear war – as black comedy, had just been released. Henry Fonda offers another of his authoritative Americans, in the form of the President, and only Fritz Weaver's performance is over the top in a sober supporting cast. You'll sweat as the bombers keep on going towards Moscow: director Lumet ensures it's a masterly if leisurely lesson in suspense.

Fair Wind to Java ○
1953, US, 92 mins, colour
Dir: Joseph Kane

Stars: Fred MacMurray, Vera Ralston, Robert Douglas, Victor McLaglen
Rating: ★★

Somewhere in the gulf between Joseph Conrad and Douglas Fairbanks comes this lushly-coloured adventure yarn, one of a fistful of bigger-budgeted adventures from the pinchpenny Republic Studio in the Fifties. It could be better (and a lot worse) than it is, with lots of brawn (Fred MaMurray, Victor McLaglen, Buddy Baer), a better-than-usual performance from Vera Ralston (the studio boss's wife) as a Javanese dancer and a typically sneaky swash-buckling villain from Britain's Robert Douglas, who also took on Burt Lancaster in *The Flame and the Arrow* and Errol Flynn in *Adventures of Don Juan*. Awful backdrops, good volcanic eruption, credibility kept easily at arm's length. Rainy-day fare.

Falcon and the Co-eds, The ○
1943, US, 67 mins, b/w
Dir: William Clemens
Stars: Tom Conway, Jean Brooks
Rating: ★★★

Not until James Bond films surfaced was a screen sleuth surrounded by so many beautiful women as Tom Conway in this above-average *Falcon* murder thriller. Quite creepy in places, too – not surprising considering the script is largely the work of Ardel Wray, who worked on some of the Val Lewton chillers.

Falcon and the Snowman, The ●
1984, US, 130 mins, colour
Dir: John Schlesinger
Stars: Timothy Hutton, Sean Penn, David Suchet, Lori Singer
Rating: ★★

British director John Schlesinger's career has been uneven to say the least since his Oscar-winning triumph with *Midnight Cowboy*. Most of his films have tended to be disappointments, and this falls into that category. Routine, clichéd and ponderous, it's a spy story that offers no motivation for its real-life characters, two former altar boy childhood friends who end up spying against America for the Russians. Timothy Hutton and Sean Penn (in one of the best performances of his career) go through the required motions as a spy centre worker and a junkie drug dealer respectively, who both end up passing on top secrets.

But their fine acting is wasted by a poor script that fails to engage the emotions.

Falcon in Hollywood, The ○
1944, US, 65 mins, b/w
Dir: Gordon Douglas
Stars: Tom Conway, Barbara Hale
Rating: ★★

RKO cheated on the budget of this one – it's a murder mystery set in a film studio. That super blond Veda Ann Borg scores heavily as a wise-cracking taxi-driver, and the film also boasts a trio of Hollywood's most durable Forties' actresses. Barbara Hale, who went on to play Della Street in the *Perry Mason* series, is probably the best known, but also on view are Jean Brooks, whose speciality was smart girl-Friday secretaries and Rita Corday, a Swiss-born beauty who starred in other films under the names of Paula Corday and Paule Croset.

Falcon in Mexico, The ○
1944, US, 70 mins, b/w
Dir: William Berke
Stars: Tom Conway, Mona Maris
Rating: ★★

The Falcon heads south to solve a mystery involving the emergence of new paintings from a supposedly dead artist, giving RKO the opportunity to add flavour to the backgrounds by using some of Orson Welles' footage from his documentary *It's All True*. Tom Conway's sleuth looks ill-at-ease on unfamiliar ground; leading lady Martha MacVicar married Mickey Rooney and had a second career under the name Martha Vickers.

Falcon in San Francisco, The ○
1945, US, 66 mins, b/w
Dir: Joseph H Lewis
Stars: Tom Conway, Rita Corday
Rating: ★★

Director Joseph H Lewis was renowned for his classy 'B' movie thrillers, but he's batting on a sticky wicket here thanks to a sub-standard script that hinted that the *Falcon* series was reaching its sell-by date. Good locations and a bright child actor (Sharyn Moffett) are the only plus factors in this story of a smuggling racket.

Falcon Strikes Back, The ○
1943, US, 65 mins, b/w
Dir: Edward Dmytryk

Stars: Tom Conway, Harriet Hilliard
Rating: ★★★

A much-used style of title for the great detectives of novel and film, most of whom 'struck back' in their time. This adventure of the Falcon was directed by Edward Dmytryk (a young director on his way to the top) whose subsequent career would be hampered by the Communist witchhunts. The leading lady is former songstress Harriet Hilliard, and an excellent cast of Hollywood character players includes Edgar Kennedy, Wynne Gibson, Byron Foulger, Frank Faylen, Ed Gargan and perennial screen 'drunk' Jack Norton.

Fallen Angel ○
1945, US, 97 mins, b/w
Dir: Otto Preminger
Stars: Dana Andrews, Alice Faye, Linda Darnell, Charles Bickford, Anne Revere, Bruce Cabot
Rating: ★★

This dark thriller was a follow-up for director Otto Preminger to his tremendously successful *Laura*. It suffers by comparison, but time has lent it qualities of its own. The direction of the scenes in the cafe is particularly interesting, as it seems that Preminger is trying to lend sinister shafts to the narrative. Alice Faye is not really comfortable in these black surroundings, but the other members of an excellent cast all seem well at home: Dana Andrews as the con-man involved with two girls, one fair, one dark; Linda Darnell, as the sluttish Stella; and Bruce Cabot, Charles Bickford, Percy Kilbride and John Carradine as assorted bystanders and suspects in an eventual murder. There's even an oft-repeated theme song – 'Slowly' – which echoes the one in *Laura*.

Fallen Idol, The ○
1948, UK, 94 mins, b/w
Dir: Carol Reed
Stars: Ralph Richardson, Michele Morgan, Bobby Henrey, Jack Hawkins, Dora Bryan
Rating: ★★★★

One of Carol Reed's most subtly engrossing films, showing great understanding of character, and made in the middle of his best period (the movies he made on either side were *Odd Man Out* and *The Third Man*). Bobby Henrey responds perfectly to the demands of his director, as the lonely little boy at a foreign embassy

in London, who tries to protect his friend the butler (a magnetic and very sympathetic portrayal by Ralph Richardson) when the man is suspected of murder.

Falling Down ● ⓥ
1993, US, 115 mins, colour
Dir: Joel Schumacher
Stars: Michael Douglas, Robert Duvall, Barbara Hershey, Rachel Ticotin, Frederic Forrest, Tuesday Weld, Lane Smith
Rating: ★★★

Michael Douglas gives a gripping performance as a man pushed beyond his limits in this unnerving drama set in the sweltering heat of LA's urban jungle. It begins when shopkeeper refuses law-abiding citizen Douglas a simple request. Suddenly, Douglas snaps – and off he storms on a one-man crusade to crush the bullies and bureaucrats whom he feels are standing in his way. Robert Duvall is charismatic as the cop who, about to retire, finds himself on the trail of this white-collar vigilante but, for those who feel the iron claw of inner-city stress, it's Douglas's sad and misguided anti-hero who remains the pervading memory from this powerful if somewhat pointless film. But it does make you feel the claustrophobic pressure of those heat-hazed LA highways, and Douglas was once again spot-on with his sense of the kind of film that makes a box-office bombshell.

Falling in Love ○ ⓥ
1984, US, 107 mins, colour
Dir: Ulu Grosbard
Stars: Meryl Streep, Robert De Niro
Rating: ★★★

Robert De Niro in a romantic drama is as rare as a white Christmas, and his pairing here with Meryl Streep, as commuters who fall in love on their daily trip to Manhattan, is an unexpected delight. True, there are many coincidences for cynical viewers and New York's station platforms have never looked cleaner. But lovers of pulp fiction and anyone who harks back to the golden Douglas Sirk days of 1950s Hollywood melodrama, will be weeping uncontrollably into their Kleenex.

Fall of the House of Usher, The ● ⓥ
1960, US, 85 mins, colour
Dir: Roger Corman

Stars: Vincent Price, Mark Damon, Myrna Fahey
Rating: ★★★

A beautiful young girl's suitor comes to ask for her hand in marriage and meets her strange and gloomy older brother. Only then does the horror begin. This is the first of director Roger Corman's films based on Edgar Allan Poe's Gothic stories and an impresssive start to the series. Vincent Price is in gloriously obsessed form as the doomed brother and exudes menace and apprehension in just the right quantities. Is he dangerous or merely eccentric? The photography is marvellous and the whole production is a delight for fans of Gothic horror. Unlike later films in the genre, more horror is implied than seen, which leaves a lot to your imagination.

Fall of the Roman Empire, The ○ ⓥ
1964, US, 173 mins, colour
Dir: Anthony Mann
Stars: Sophia Loren, Stephen Boyd, Alec Guinness, James Mason, Christopher Plummer, Omar Sharif
Rating: ★★★

With its bleak settings and towering central story, which dwarfed personal relationships, it was inevitable that *Roman Empire* should emerge as a director's and photographer's film, rather than relying on acting for its impact. Robert Krasker's hard-edged photography brings an added magnetism to such scenes as a chariot race, a wintry funeral, a lovers tryst and a savage pitched battle in a cave. Sophia Loren, in the film's only substantial female role, looks stunning throughout, especially in one overhead shot of her sprawled on a couch in a flimsy, hyacinth-pink gown. Mann's handling of the tumultuous crowd scenes constantly makes one aware that this important period of history is being filmed with the care, and on the scale, it deserves. The battles are sufficiently muddled – as indeed they must have been – without depriving us of the knowledge of who is who. Especially memorable is a battle set in a stiflingly cramped German forest. And the final single combat between Livius (Stephen Boyd) and Commodus (Christopher Plummer), before thousands of Romans in the Forum, has Commodus making an impressive entry from a huge black hand made of stone. Despite the scale of the action, there are several performances to ad-

F

mire, too – especially from Alec Guinness as the warm, wise, dying Marcus Aurelius, gentle but firm, the last of the great Roman emperors, and from James Mason, articulating and acting impeccably as his Greek philosopher friend, Timonides.

False Witness 🌓
(aka: Zigzag)
1970, US, 105 mins, colour
Dir: Richard A Colla
Stars: George Kennedy, Anne Jackson, Eli Wallach
Rating: ★★★

We've seen this one before, even though this version plays an interesting variation on a well-worn theme. Facing death, a man launches an ingenious scheme to provide for his wife, involving, in this case, framing himself for an unsolved murder. Naturally, he's miraculously cured, and faces the horrendous task of escaping the fate he's prepared for himself. Nicely nervy performances by George Kennedy, Eli Wallach and Anne Jackson make this a good bet in the suspense stakes.

Fame Is the Spur ○
1947, UK, 116 mins, b/w
Dir: Roy Boulting
Stars: Michael Redgrave, Rosamund John, Bernard Miles, Carla Lehmann
Rating: ★★★

Although pretty engrossing stuff, this was not quite the great movie it might have been considering its credentials. The source novel, said to have been based on the career of Ramsey MacDonald, is by Howard Spring, and the screenplay written by Nigel Balchin. Michael Redgrave gives his usual strong, thoughtful performance as the politician whose quest for fame gradually alienates him from his ideals and friends alike, but Roy Boulting's direction perhaps just lacks the power to stir the blood. Skilful film-making though, and a major British film of its time.

Family Affair, A ○
1937, US, 69 mins, b/w
Dir: George B Seitz
Stars: Lionel Barrymore, Spring Byington, Cecilia Parker, Eric Linden, Mickey Rooney
Rating: ★★★

Little did MGM know that this small-scale comedy would turn into an absolute goldmine known as the Andy Hardy series. The Hardy films –

portraits of American small-town life in the pre-war and wartime years – made big money for the studio, principally on the popularity of Mickey Rooney, who played the Hardys' youngest son, always in and out of girl trouble. Within two years, Rooney would be America's most popular film star, and the running times of the Hardy films ballooned from 60-odd minutes towards the two-hour mark as the public flocked in. Through the years, MGM used the series as a training-ground for such young actresses as Judy Garland, Esther Williams, Kathryn Grayson, Donna Reed and Lana Turner.

Family Business 🌓 ⓥ
1989, US, 110 mins, colour
Dir: Sidney Lumet
Stars: Sean Connery, Dustin Hoffman, Matthew Broderick, Rosana DeSoto
Rating: ★★★

Pretty risky business, actually, in that the family tradition here through three generations is crime. Sean Connery, Dustin Hoffman and Matthew Broderick represent the generations involved, all three going on an exciting heist when the grandson feels he has to prove himself in the family way. It's quite enjoyable, although fairly lightweight by the standards of the talents involved, including director Sidney Lumet. And it's difficult to sympathise with the film's moral point of view. Still, Connery is at his roguish best as the grandpa and Broderick does well as the young sprig. Hoffman seems miscast as Broderick's dad, letting Connery steal all the best moments in the film.

Family Jewels, The ☉
1965, US, 95 mins, colour
Dir: Jerry Lewis
Stars: Jerry Lewis, Donna Butterworth, Sebastian Cabot, Robert Strauss
Rating: ★★

Watch out folks – Jerry Lewis is directing himself again, and that means half the usual quota of laughs. Even so, this comedy gets off to a bright start, with the first ten minutes containing some very good visual gags, plus the always useful scene where the apparently inept hero clears the table after taking on the biggest hustler in the poolroom. It all makes pretty good entertainment for children, with plenty of bright colour, and simple, straightforward humour, coupled with the fact that the central character (Donna Butterworth) is a 12-year-old

girl. When her father dies, she has to decide which of her six uncles is to be her legal guardian. The uncles, all dotty of course, are all played by Lewis, who also appears as the family chauffeur. Director Lewis, though, allows star Lewis too much self-indulgence, making the characters struggle to make us laugh, instead of laughing naturally at them – and allowing his fellow actors to tackle the dialogue at a creeping pace. All in all, another step on the downward path for a falling star.

Family Plot ○ ⓥ
1976, US, 120 mins, colour
Dir: Alfred Hitchcock
Stars: Karen Black, Bruce Dern, Barbara Harris, William Devane
Rating: ★★★

Hitchcock's last film is perhaps lightweight Hitch, but still an entertaining comedy-thriller in which the Master gets more chance than usual to display his sense of humour. Classic Hitchcock situations abound in the story of a fake spiritualist (Barbara Harris) and her cabbie lover (Bruce Dern) who are out to find the long-lost illegitimate nephew of a millionairess who wants to leave him all her money. It's not giving too much of the plot away to say that the nephew turns out to be a notorious kidnapper (William Devane). Trails cross, uncross and cross again in a typical Hitchcock finale. The stars all give good performances, while remaining subservient to the director's demands on the plot and especially such set pieces as a car chase and a funeral. There's even some serviceable suspense at the end with Harris's life in danger.

Family Way, The 🌓
1966, UK, 110 mins, colour
Dir: Roy Boulting
Stars: Hayley Mills, Hywel Bennett, John Mills
Rating: ★★★

John Mills turns the tables on daughter Hayley – who walked away with their earlier film *Tiger Bay* – by stealing every scene in which he appears in this story of a north country wedding and a young couple frustrated by the proximity of their in-laws. His is a fully-rounded portrayal of an old-school working man, well in the tradition of his other provincial portrayals in *Hobson's Choice* and the underrated *The History of Mr Polly*. It's also a performance that touches the heart, as do those of Hywel Bennett (in his screen debut) and Hayley Mills as the newly-weds.

Fanatic ◖

(aka: Die, Die, My Darling)
1964, UK, 97 mins, colour
Dir: Silvio Narizzano
Stars: Tallulah Bankhead, Stefanie Powers, Peter Vaughan, Yootha Joyce, Donald Sutherland
Rating: ★★

This fearsome dose of Grand Guignol from the house of Hammer horror was picturesquely re-titled by the Americans as *Die, Die, My Darling*. It features Tallulah Bankhead, in her last screen role, playing with all stops out as a religious fanatic who imprisons her dead son's fiancée – to the accompaniment of a screenplay by Richard Matheson, who wrote almost all the film adaptations of Edgar Allan Poe's work. One little annoyance: why does the fanatic leave the girl with a convenient ashtray in her attic prison, when she is a professed hater of smoking?

Fancy Pants ⊙

1950, US, 88 mins, colour
Dir: George Marshall
Stars: Bob Hope, Lucille Ball, Bruce Cabot
Rating: ★★★

Bob Hope reverts to almost pure Mack Sennett slapstick in this riotous, glowingly Technicolored comedy, a hectic remake of *Ruggles of Red Gap* that pokes fun at everything from Westerns to English gentlemen. Hope plays Humphrey, an actor hired to pose as an English butler by an adventurer who wants to marry Agatha, daughter of the wealthy Floud family. Agatha's social-climbing mother is so impressed that she drags Humphrey back west to teach the tearaway Agatha how to be a proper Eastern lady. Songs by Jay Livingston and Ray Evans and a vivacious performance by Lucille Ball round off a bright package.

Fandango ○

1984, US, 91 mins, colour
Dir: Kevin Reynolds
Stars: Kevin Costner, Judd Nelson, Elizabeth Daily
Rating: ★★

This was the film in which Kevin Costner first showed star quality – but then he had ended up on the cutting-room floor in his previous two

efforts, *The Big Chill* and *Frances*. He was to forge a good relationship with director Kevin Reynolds and chose him to direct him in *Robin Hood: Prince of Thieves* six years later. Costner is a dynamic presence at the heart of this rites-of-passage picture set in 1971 when the Vietnam war and the draft were still looming large in students' lives. The rest of the good cast are up to the material's demands if not the same assured confidence with the script as Costner. The film was only made at all thanks to Steven Spielberg, who agreed to finance a feature-length version of a short film made by Reynolds while he was a student at the USC film school.

Fanny ○

1960, US, 133 mins, colour
Dir: Joshua Logan
Stars: Leslie Caron, Maurice Chevalier, Charles Boyer, Horst Buchholz
Rating: ★★★

The bistros and fish stalls of the old Marseilles waterfront were the setting for Marcel Pagnol's salty 1930s trilogy (memorably filmed in France at the time) about Fanny, Cesar, Panisse and the other characters of the ancient Mediterranean port. Director Joshua Logan has taken his cameras back to the old haunts to tell the story once more, with feeling. Jack Cardiff's photography provides a glossy rinse to the old city. Leslie Caron gives a poignant performance as the girl who falls in love with a sailor (Horst Buchholz), then finds, after he has gone away to sea, that she is expecting his baby. Maurice Chevalier is touchingly true as the old man who marries the girl for the sake of the child.

Fanny by Gaslight ○

1944, UK, 108 mins, b/w
Dir: Anthony Asquith
Stars: Phyllis Calvert, James Mason, Wilfrid Lawson, Stewart Granger
Rating: ★★★

The Gainsborough Lady, who inclined her head so charmingly from the company's trademark, never smiled more radiantly than in the early Forties when, at their Shepherd's Bush and Islington studios, Gainsborough produced a crop of box-office winners. Among the most popular of these were a number of costume dramas featuring any or all of a quartet comprising James Mason, Stewart Granger, Margaret Lockwood and Phyllis Calvert who had all appeared together in *The Man in Grey*

(1943). With the advantage of a good script adapted from Michael Sadleir's novel and direction by Anthony Asquith, *Fanny by Gaslight* proved to be one of Gainsborough's best. And as the evil Lord Manderstoke, James Mason contributed one of his 'villainous cad' parts.

Fantasia ○ ⊗

1940, US, 117 mins, colour
Dir: Joe Grant, Dick Huemer
Rating: ★★★★

Probably the best and most imaginative Disney cartoon feast ever set before an audience. Eight pieces of music are set to cartoon images to create a wonderland of magic and charm; once entered, you are completely under its spell for close to two hours. Some of the colour work is still amazing today and so brilliant are the cartoons that it often seems that the music has been synchronised to the picture and not vice versa. All eight segments are excellent, but outstanding are the 'Nutcracker Suite' (the dance of the toadstools is a comic highlight never to be forgotten), 'The Rite of Spring' (a brilliantly impressionistic vision of the Dark Ages), Beethoven's 'Pastoral Symphony' (sentimental but possibly the most delightful of all) and 'A Night on a Bare Mountain' (a scary, eerie and lurid interpretation of Mussorgsky). All this, and Mickey Mouse as 'The Sorcerer's Apprentice' too. Such stuff as dreams are made of – outlasting the years.

Fantastic Voyage ○

1966, US, 100 mins, colour
Dir: Richard Fleischer
Stars: Stephen Boyd, Raquel Welch, Edmond O'Brien, Donald Pleasence, Arthur Kennedy
Rating: ★★

Fantastic is the word for it as five scientists are shrunk to pinpoint size and injected into the vein of a genius to try and save his life. The special effects are weirdly beautiful, and the same could be said for Raquel Welch in her first big starring role. The miniaturisation plot theme was resurrected by Steven Spielberg in his *InnerSpace* production.

Far and Away ◖ ⊗

1992, US, 140 mins, colour
Dir: Ron Howard
Stars: Tom Cruise, Nicole Kidman, Thomas Gibson, Robert Prosky, Barbara

F

Babcock
Rating: ★★★

There hadn't been such a sprawlingly old-fashioned romantic melodrama as this in quite a while. Even with a sprinkling of foolish moments, it must rate highly as a rousing, crowd-pleasing spectacle, pulling its participants through Ireland, over the Atlantic and across half the breadth of America. Tom Cruise, with an Irish accent good enough to pass muster unless you're Irish, is the son of a poor dirt farmer in 1890s western Ireland. Swearing vengeance for the death of his father and the burning of their home, he somehow ends up with the daughter (Nicole Kidman) of his sworn enemy finding that she is as eager to escape her environment as he is. They get to America posing as brother and sister, lodging in what turns out to be a brothel, where there is, but naturally, only one room for the both of them. Cruise takes out his frustrated love for her by earning money as an unorthodox boxer, but their unspoken affection proves their undoing and a tragedy or two ensues, before the story sweeps to a gloriously corny and excitingly shot finish in the midst of the great Oklahoma land rush of 1903. The film teems with detail in a relatively unobtrusive manner, in the fashion of films from a much earlier time.

Far Country, The ○
1954, US, 95 mins, colour
Dir: Anthony Mann
Stars: James Stewart, Ruth Roman, Corinne Calvet, Walter Brennan
Rating: ★★★

A rip-snorting Technicolor Western from the middle of director Anthony Mann's best period of work. Stars James Stewart and Ruth Roman have to give second-best to Walter Brennan (another of his grizzled westerners), Corinne Calvet as a winsome French-Canadian spitfire and John McIntire as the top-hatted villain. Solid value for fans of both Stewart and the Western.

Farewell Again ○
(aka: Troopship)
1937, UK, 81 mins, b/w
Dir: Tim Whelan
Stars: Leslie Banks, Flora Robson, Robert Newton
Rating: ★★★

Absorbing, well-directed British film which has worn remarkably well and remains well worth a view as the archetypal a-few-hours-ashore style drama. The photography – James Wong Howe, Hans Scheeburger and Wilkie Cooper all worked on the film – is first-rate, while director Tim Whelan pulls disparate elements together with consummate skill to create a richly human film.

Farewell, My Lovely ○
(aka: Murder, My Sweet)
1945, US, 95 mins, b/w
Dir: Edward Dmytryk
Stars: Dick Powell, Claire Trevor, Anne Shirley, Otto Kruger, Mike Mazurki
Rating: ★★★★

With one bound, Dick Powell leapt from baby-faced singer to tough-guy superstar in this remarkably faithful adaptation of Raymond Chandler's hard-boiled thriller. He plays detective Philip Marlowe, and chronicles his involvement with the massive Moose Malloy's search for his ex-girlfriend Velma, whose identity remains a mystery until near the end. Full of very punchy scenes (often aided by camera trickery) and an atmosphere of menace, the film has dry, laconic acting by Powell. The massive Mike Mazurki is perfectly cast as Moose, Claire Trevor and Anne Shirley supply the femmes fatale, and the movie's eye-opening centrepiece is Marlowe's imprisonment in a terrifying clinic, from whence, though drugged to the eyeballs, he eventually manages to escape, producing the classic piece of self-advice: 'Okay Marlowe, you're a tough guy: you've been sapped twice, choked, beaten silly with a gun, shot in the arm until you're as crazy as a couple of waltzing mice. Now let's see you do something really tough – like putting your pants on!' Chandler was so grateful to writer John Paxton for retaining the structure, flavour and much of the dialogue of the original novel that he wrote him a personal letter of thanks.

Farewell, My Lovely ◑
1975, US, 95 mins, colour
Dir: Dick Richards
Stars: Robert Mitchum, Charlotte Rampling, John Ireland, Sylvia Miles, Jack O'Halloran, Anthony Zerbe
Rating: ★★★

The best of the modern recreations of Forties' detective thrillers, and only a pace behind the Dick Powell original. Robert Mitchum is a serviceable Marlowe, even at 57, and lovers of the atmospheric thick-ear thriller won't complain about the action. Charlotte Rampling does quite a good imitation of Lauren Bacall as the society siren, handling the best of the throwaway dialogue with dry aplomb. And there's an early screen role for Sylvester Stallone as one of the bad guys. Director Dick Richards, whose best film this is, prowls his cameras menacingly through some marvellously seedy neo-Forties settings.

Farewell to Arms, A ○ Ⓥ
1957, US, 150 mins, colour
Dir: Charles Vidor
Stars: Rock Hudson, Jennifer Jones, Vittorio De Sica, Mercedes McCambridge
Rating: ★★

This epic combination of weepie and World War One action film was first brought to the screen in 1932 with Helen Hayes and Gary Cooper. This version encompasses much more of Ernest Hemingway's novel (the original was 78 minutes, this runs 150) and boasts a steady and occasionally inspired performance by Rock Hudson that ranks among his best. Jennifer Jones is rather less successful as the nurse with whom he falls in love, but the war scenes – including a colossal snowbound retreat reminiscent of Vidor's *War and Peace* – have a quite breathtaking impact.

Farewell to the King ◐ Ⓥ
1988, UK, 117 mins, colour
Dir: John Milius
Stars: Nick Nolte, Nigel Havers, James Fox, Frank McRae
Rating: ★★★

There's a lot of the spirit of Joseph Conrad in this wartime adventure. Set (and shot) in Borneo, it catches the imagination in much the same way as Conrad's flavoursome stories of wanderings and adventures in the Far East. Nick Nolte is impressive as Learoyd, an American deserter who becomes king of a Bornean tribe, and has much in common with Conrad's *Lord Jim*. Both stories contain blood brothers of different races, action in the jungle and a narrator who lives through at least part of the story, played in this case by Nigel Havers, giving his best film performance as the botanist turned officer whose mission is to enlist the jungle tribes for the fight against the Japanese. Some of the consequent battle scenes amid monsoon conditions are vividly, imaginatively staged, with an impression of the conflict often being given rather than the bloody details, though these are not ignored.

Far from the Madding Crowd ○

1967, UK, 169 mins, colour
Dir: John Schlesinger
Stars: Julie Christie, Terence Stamp, Peter Finch, Alan Bates
Rating: ★★★

Although never in quite the same league as Roman Polanski's *Tess*, John Schlesinger's attempt at confining the lush, sweeping narrative of Thomas Hardy to the screen is a worthy one. As the central character Bathsheba Everdene, Julie Christie is in imperious form – a strongly independent soul on the surface, but a victim of Hardy's obsessions with the fallibility of man and the cruel hand of fate underneath. The film is worth watching for Miss Christie alone. She is perhaps the only British actress of her day to combine stunning looks with real talent. The three men vying for her hand in marriage are played by an impressive trio – Alan Bates, Peter Finch and Terence Stamp, with Finch just edging out the others in the acting stakes.

Far Horizons, The ○

1955, US, 105 mins, colour
Dir: Rudolph Mate
Stars: Charlton Heston, Fred MacMurray, Donna Reed, Barbara Hale, William Demarest
Rating: ★★

Jump into your canoe for a refresher course in early American history. Opening up the west wasn't all done in covered wagons; sometimes they took to the boats. A splashing time is had by all in this colourful 'dramatisation' of classroom history, which was the biggest film ever produced by the action-minded unit of producers William Pine and William Thomas. The script hits a few rocks and shallow passages, but there's enough action to keep the going good. Charlton Heston and Fred MacMurray keep stiff jaws as the waterborne pioneers.

Farmer Takes a Wife, The ○

1953, US, 93 mins, colour
Dir: Henry Levin
Stars: Betty Grable, Dale Robertson, Thelma Ritter
Rating: ★★★

The blonde hair and million-dollar legs of Betty Grable – the idol of and sex symbol for the GI's of World War Two – can be seen in this breeze-fresh musical version of a much earlier film, with eight good tunes pepping up the plot. Thelma Ritter has a good comedy role. Betty's heyday, though, was clearly over: in Britain, the film was released as a second-feature.

Far North ◐ ⓥ

1988, US, 89 mins, colour
Dir: Sam Shepard
Stars: Jessica Lange, Charles Durning, Tess Harper, Donald Moffat, Patricia Arquette
Rating: RB

Well might the makers of this farrago thank the North American Loon Fund. Only they perhaps would have been loony enough to believe they could make any money from a story that revolves entirely around a not-quite-all-there family that can't make up its mind whether or not to shoot a horse. Personally, we'd have shot writer-director Sam Shepard instead, especially for giving us so many dingy shots of trees to pad his film out to an interminable hour and a half. He gets strident performances from Jessica Lange, Charles Durning, Tess Harper and Patricia Arquette, though he does give them dialogue that never manages to sound like things people would really say.

Far Off Place, A ○ ⓥ

1993, US, 105 mins, colour
Dir: Mikael Salomon
Stars: Reese Witherspoon, Ethan Randall, Maximilian Schell, Jack Thompson, Robert Burke, Patricia Kalember
Rating: ★★★

Although probably a bit too graphic at times for young children, and certainly red in tooth and claw, this is a superbly shot, old-fashioned Disney adventure that will please teenagers and pre-teens of a stern disposition. Nonnie (Reese Witherspoon), a game warden's daughter, and Harry (Ethan Randall), a visitor from the city, are two teenagers living on an African wildlife reserve. A brutal attack by a gang of ivory poachers leaves the kids orphaned and as the only witnesses to the murders of their parents, they are forced to flee into the barren Kalahari Desert. There they face hunger, exhaustion, sandstorms and wild animals, with the killers all the while hot on their trail. The trek's a shade on

the slow side, but pictorial qualities compensate, the acting is staunch, and the elephants nearly steal the show.

Fashions
See: Fashions of 1934

Fashions of 1934 ○

(aka: Fashions)
1934, US, 78 mins, b/w
Dir: William Dieterle
Stars: William Powell, Bette Davis, Frank McHugh, Verree Teasdale
Rating: ★★★

One doesn't expect much from Hollywood films with titles like this, but the presence of William Powell, as a dapper con-man, and Bette Davis, a devious designer, alerts you to the fact that there may be more than a parade of gowns on display here. And so it proves. An accompanying story of industrial chicanery is decked out with dance spectacle from Busby Berkeley, a witty script that allows room for a rollicking performance from Verree Teasdale as a fake duchess, a lively story and sophisticated good humour. Powell is at his most debonair, and even Frank McHugh is more bearable than usual as an enterprising photographer who carries a miniature camera in the handle of his cane.

Fast and Furious ○

1939, US, 70 mins, b/w
Dir: Busby Berkeley
Stars: Franchot Tone, Ann Sothern, Lee Bowman, Ruth Hussey
Rating: ★★★

One of several Hollywood comedy-mysteries spun around the sleuthing exploits of husband and wife team Joel and Garda Sloane (played here by Franchot Tone and Ann Sothern), whose wisecracks and light touch made their adventures obvious rivals to the *Thin Man* series. Busby Berkeley directs without a dance number in sight – although he does have a bevy of beauty contestants as part of the murder-strewn plot.

Fast and Loose ○

1939, US, 80 mins, b/w
Dir: Edwin L Marin
Stars: Robert Montgomery, Rosalind Russell, Ralph Morgan
Rating: ★★

There are lots of good actors to bolster one's enjoyment of this otherwise routine romantic mystery thriller from the MGM stable. Robert

F

Montgomery (in training for his next role as Lord Peter Wimsey) and Rosalind Russell are bright leads and the supporting cast is full of those familiar faces to whom one could never quite put the name.

Fast and Loose ○
1954, UK, 75 mins, b/w
Dir: Gordon Parry
Stars: Stanley Holloway, Kay Kendall, Brian Reece
Rating: ★

A romping bedroom farce of White-hall proportions. Ben Travers, who wrote many of the Whitehall successes in the Thirties, actually worked on the screenplay of this film, which is an inferior remake of the 1934 version of his play *A Cuckoo in the Nest*.

Fast Company ○
1938, US, 75 mins, b/w
Dir: Edward Buzzell
Stars: Melvyn Douglas, Florence Rice, Louis Calhern
Rating: ★★

Comedy mystery featuring the sleuthing book experts from *Fast and Loose*, Joel and Garda Sloane. Here they're played by Melvyn Douglas (the best Joel) and Florence Rice. The best Garda, Ann Sothern, didn't come along until the third adventure, *Fast and Furious*. Nostalgia fans will catch their breath at a list of suspects that includes some of Hollywood's most distinctive character actors of the day: Louis Calhern, Shepperd Strudwick, Dwight Frye, Douglass Dumbrille, Thurston Hall, George Zucco and Horace MacMahon among them.

Fastest Gun Alive, The ○
1956, US, 85 mins, b/w
Dir: Russell Rouse
Stars: Glenn Ford, Broderick Crawford, Jeanne Crain, Russ Tamblyn, Leif Erickson
Rating: ★★

A workmanlike, if not too inspired, airing for what must be one of the oldest Western plots around – the gunman who tries to retire but has to face yet another fast gun to whom the word has somehow got around. Director Russell Rouse ensures that the following events keep one guessing until the end of the last reel. Glenn Ford gives an edgy, carefully–considered performance as the man whose prowess with a gun hangs over him like the Sword of Damocles, but the most powerful portrayal comes

from Broderick Crawford, as the man hunting him, and such familiar faces as Russ Tamblyn, Allyn Joslyn, Leif Erickson and Noah Beery Jnr decorate the fringes of the action.

Fast Lady, The ○
1962, UK, 95 mins, colour
Dir: Ken Annakin
Stars: James Robertson Justice, Stanley Baxter, Leslie Phillips, Julie Christie
Rating: ★★★

The same team's follow-up to the hilarious success of *Very Important Person* and *Crooks Anonymous*. The fast lady of the title is not, as one might imagine, Julie Christie – here playing her first big role in a colour film – but a souped-up car. A formidable supporting cast of character comedians that includes Dick Emery, Eric Barker, Fred Emney and Frankie Howerd.

Fatal Attraction ● ⊙
1987, US, 120 mins, colour
Dir: Adrian Lyne
Stars: Michael Douglas, Glenn Close, Anne Archer, Fred Gwynne
Rating: ★★★

A rollercoaster thriller about a one-night stand that goes hideously wrong. Feminists were up in arms about the portrayal of the spurned lover (Glenn Close) who sets out to ruin married Michael Douglas' 'happy' home life. On a more superficial level, it's a cracking good white-knuckle ride, with plenty of shocks and heart-stopping moments, several of which are annoyingly telegraphed well ahead. The much-imitated ending would be more at home in a *Rambo* film, and the unreleased alternative 'suicide' ending for Japan, that implies Douglas will be charged with murder because his fingerprints are found on a knife used two-thirds of the way through the film, would have been an improvement. None of this fazed the paying public, who made the film an enormous popular hit.

Fat City ◑
1972, US, 100 mins, colour
Dir: John Huston
Stars: Stacy Keach, Jeff Bridges, Susan Tyrrell, Candy Clark
Rating: ★★★

John Huston's best film of the Seventies, this could easily have been called *The Misfits*, had the title not already been used so auspiciously by the same director 11 years earlier. The film's theme song, 'Help me Make it

Through the Night', composed and sung by Kris Kristofferson, is immensely appropriate, as the film is all about making it through the night – and day – getting a foothold on life, and coming to terms with failure. Stacy Keach and Jeff Bridges give career-best performances as two boxers in whom hope springs eternal, but leads, inevitably, to their continual disillusionment. And much underrated and under-used actress Susan Tyrrell gives a haunting performance as the sad Oma, using a voice that sounds thoroughly soaked in a mixture of gin and tears. Conrad Hall's photography – which seems, in recollection, an attractive mix of shades of brown and blue – rightly emphasises the non-existent glamour of the lower reaches of the boxing profession.

Father Brown ○
(aka: The Detective)
1954, UK, 90 mins, b/w
Dir: Robert Hamer
Stars: Alec Guinness, Joan Greenwood, Peter Finch, Cecil Parker, Bernard Lee, Sidney James
Rating: ★★★

This stylish comedy-thriller is probably director Robert Hamer's most successful film, apart from *Kind Hearts and Coronets*, and it reunited him with Alec Guinness. Guinness cleverly gets under the skin of G K Chesterton's priest-detective; his scenes with Peter Finch's suave master criminal Flambeau are a delight. In the course of the story, Hamer veers from high suspense, through near-melodrama to light comedy and, with the invaluable help of Guinness, he masters them all.

Father Came Too ○
1963, UK, 93 mins, colour
Dir: Peter Graham Scott
Stars: Stanley Baxter, Leslie Phillips, James Robertson Justice, Sally Smith
Rating: ★★

A comedy from the *Fast Lady* team that starts off promisingly with a Scotsman worrying about the size of the tip his bride has given the chambermaid on their honeymoon, before it trails off into a series of music-hall jokes about how not to decorate a house. People put their feet in paint buckets, get their faces painted when they open doors, fall through floorboards, tread on wallpaper they are about to put up, and generally behave in similar fashion to circus clowns. Stanley Baxter is the harassed husband, Sally Smith a delectable bride.

Father Goose ○ ⓥ
1964, US, 116 mins, colour
Dir: Ralph Nelson
Stars: Cary Grant, Leslie Caron, Trevor Howard, Jack Good
Rating: ★★★

Thank goodness for Cary Grant. He makes this naive family comedy seem at times the quintessence of wit, playing a sockless, unshaven, whisky-swilling beachcomber in the Pacific during World War Two, he's blackmailed into spying for the Allies by wily old officer Trevor Howard, who reveals the whereabouts of a bottle of whisky hidden on Grant's island for every snippet of information sent. What Grant doesn't bargain for are teacher Leslie Caron and her seven schoolgirl charges who get cast away on the island with him. As long as Grant has the upper hand in his running battle with the flock of females, the film remains funny. When it's the other way round, it's frequently embarrassing, thanks to a heavy performance by Caron that almost sinks the ship.

Father of the Bride ○ ⓥ
1950, US, 93 mins, b/w
Dir: Vincente Minnelli
Stars: Spencer Tracy, Joan Bennett, Elizabeth Taylor, Russ Tamblyn, Don Taylor
Rating: ★★★★

Famous comedy about the many crises leading up to an impending marriage. Spencer Tracy is superb as the harassed father, and there are some lovely set-piece comedy scenes. Elizabeth Taylor (at 17) and Rusty (Russ) Tamblyn (at 15) are his daughter and son. Great fun, which led to a sequel – *Father's Little Dividend* – with Tracy again as the star. Joan Bennett played the heartily domestic mother. The remake in 1991 with Steve Martin and Diane Keaton carried rather less warmth and bite.

Father of the Bride ○ ⓥ
1991, US, 105 mins, colour
Dir: Charles Shyer
Stars: Steve Martin, Diane Keaton, Kimberly Williams, Martin Short
Rating: ★★★

This glossy, slightly ruder remake of the Spencer Tracy-Joan Bennett classic is not far short of the original in warmth and humour, with Steve Martin superb as the doting father who careers off the rails at the news of his beloved daughter's impending wedding. The script hardly makes the most of Diane Keaton's talents as his wife, though, and Kimberly Williams not unexpectedly lacks Elizabeth Taylor's beauty and glow; at least for once they picked an actress the right height for her on-screen parents: not as tall as Martin, but taller than Keaton. Martin Short scores in a smartly-written cameo role, and the whole makes ideal, well-paced entertainment for reasonably broad-minded families.

Father's Doing Fine ○
1952, UK, 83 mins, colour
Dir: Henry Cass
Stars: Richard Attenborough, Heather Thatcher, Diane Hart
Rating: ★★★

A boisterous British comedy about a scatterbrained widow, her four equally dotty daughters, various offspring, and a life full of trouble and strife. There are more entrances and exits than in a Brian Rix farce and great fun is had by all, especially Richard Attenborough as the expectant father of one of the daughters.

Father's Little Dividend ○
1951, US, 82 mins, b/w
Dir: Vincente Minnelli
Stars: Spencer Tracy, Joan Bennett, Elizabeth Taylor, Russ Tamblyn, Don Taylor
Rating: ★★★

For once a sequel that's as good as the original. This is a sparkling comedy follow-up to *Father of the Bride*, with the same cast, writers and director. Spencer Tracy is magnificent, at first loathing the idea of grandfatherhood, then doting on the baby when it does arrive, even though it erupts in floods of tears whenever he gets near it. A model of how to make a superbly-constructed, constantly funny situation comedy.

Fathom ○
1967, UK, 99 mins, colour
Dir: Leslie H Martinson
Stars: Raquel Welch, Anthony Franciosa, Ronald Fraser, Richard Briers
Rating: ★★

Spy spoof, with Raquel Welch as a sky diver involved with an enigmatic Englishman and a Scot who claims to be a top security chief. Top-dressing from director Leslie Martinson (though not, fortunately, for Miss Welch) includes some remarkable colour effects.

Fat Man and Little Boy
See: Shadow Makers

Favour, the Watch and the Very Big Fish, The ◖ ⓥ
1991, UK/France, 89 mins, colour
Dir: Ben Lewin
Stars: Bob Hoskins, Jeff Goldblum, Natasha Richardson, Angela Pleasence, Jean-Pierre Cassel
Rating: ★

A surreal, stylised comedy that has some attractive elements, but one major fault: apart from one or two isolated moments, it just isn't funny. Bob Hoskins is Louis, a photographer of staged religious scenes who, through a favour to a friend, becomes involved with Sybil (Natasha Richardson), who runs a beauty parlour and doubles as a voice-over actress for porno movies. She in turn tells him about her affair with a glum pianist (Jeff Goldblum), whom she drove to madness and violence when seduced by a demon violinist. The pianist emerges from jail to be grabbed by Louis who wants him to pose as Jesus in a series of tableaux. The problem is that the pianist, who has vengeance on Sybil (who has disappeared) in mind, begins to live his role. Hoskins and Richardson both deliver strained, uncomfortable performances and director Ben Lewin signals the few funny moments heavily.

FBI Story, The ○
1958, US, 149 mins, colour
Dir: Mervyn LeRoy
Stars: James Stewart, Vera Miles, Murray Hamilton, Larry Pennell, Nick Adams
Rating: ★★★

The last crime story directed by Mervyn LeRoy, and made at Warners, scene of such great LeRoy successes as *Little Caesar*, *Five Star Final* and *I Am a Fugitive from a Chain Gang*. It rambles a bit from time to time, but James Stewart is a pillar of strength and integrity, and enough ammunition is expended in numerous thrill-a-minute segments about famous gangsters to make the average *Untouchables* story appear sedate by comparison.

F

Fear Inside, The ● ⓥ
1991, US, 115 mins, colour
Dir: Leon Ichaso
Stars: Christine Lahti, Dylan McDermott, Jennifer Rubin, David Ackroyd, Thomas Ian Nicholas
Rating: ★★

For three-quarters of its running time at any rate, this is a psychological thriller that's better than most. Pretty unpleasant most of the time, it features another good performance by Christine Lahti, as the lady trapped in her own home by agoraphobia, not to mention a psychopathic robber (Dylan McDermott) and his seemingly nice-as-pie killer girlfriend (Jennifer Rubin). Credibly etched characters rack up the tension in an often jumpy, scary thriller that unfortunately becomes increasingly unlikely and illogical in the last couple of reels. Extensive use of blue filters may prove a bit of an eyestrain here. Not released to cinemas, though certainly a lot better than many chillers that are.

Fear Is the Key ○ ⓥ
1972, UK, 108 mins, colour
Dir: Michael Tuchner
Stars: Barry Newman, Suzy Kendall, John Vernon, Ray McAnally
Rating: ★★★

During the 20-minute, no-holds-barred car chase that opens the thriller, it seems that Barry Newman is still carrying on the duel with death that he started in his previous film, *Vanishing Point*. In the event, *Fear Is the Key* proves to be a cleverly-plotted, helter-skelter, Alistair MacLean thriller, ideally suited to Newman's own high pressure, short-fuse style of acting. Here he's cast as a man out for revenge on those who killed his wife, child and brother, and his hard-driving portrayal of the obsessed Talbot carries the film excitingly through to an equally thrilling climax, 400 feet down on the seabed. In the featured cast, watch out for Ben Kingsley who, 10 years later, hit top stardom in Richard Attenborough's *Gandhi*.

Fearless ● ⓥ
1993, US, 122 mins, colour
Dir: Peter Weir
Stars: Jeff Bridges, Rosie Perez, Tom Hulce, Isabella Rossellini, John Turturro
Rating: ★

Director Peter Weir has made some impressive films in his time, but this isn't one of them. Jeff Bridges plays the survivor of an air crash who now has no fear of dying and gets up everyone's nose with his bizarre attitudes on his return to the living. It might be a bit more interesting if Bridges were a ghost but alas it's just a form of PCS (post-crash shock) and, though helpless to help himself, he does aid a fellow survivor (Rosie Perez) to come to terms with the loss of her baby. Such arrant nonsense needs to be a good deal faster of foot to be of interest and this turns out instead to be a deeply irritating (not to mention slow and boring) film which Weir's mystic, doomy treatment and Bridges' dishevelled mumbling do little to enliven. Perez was mysteriously Oscar-nominated for this, although much of her dialogue is unintelligible. 'I'm going to survive this!' one character exclaims. Your own resolve may be likewise tested.

Fearless Vampire Killers, The
See: Dance of the Vampire

Fedora ○
1978, West Germany, 115 mins, colour
Dir: Billy Wilder
Stars: Marthe Keller, William Holden, Jose Ferrer, Hildegarde Knef, Frances Sternhagen
Rating: ★★

Billy Wilder's puzzle picture co-written with his old partner-in-crime I A L Diamond and adapted from a short story by former actor Tom Tryon. Why should a seemingly ageless actress throw herself under a train for no apparent reason? You may well guess most of the answers before the end, but the fascination lies in the picture's sheer style, its contemplation of celebrity and its portrait of people trapped within their own images.

Feds ●
1988, US, 91 mins, colour
Dir: Dan Goldberg
Stars: Rebecca DeMornay, Mary Gross, Ken Marshall
Rating: ★

This film's executive producer, Ivan Reitman, has delivered some of Hollywood's greatest comedy hits as a director, including *Ghostbusters*, *Kindergarten Cop*, *Twins* and *Dave*. But this was a rare dud. Rebecca DeMornay and Mary Gross are the unhappy twosome enduring numerous vulgar jokes and considerable humiliation at the hands of male recruits at the FBI's training school. It's basically a rehash of ideas and gags that were already looking exceedingly ropey from the *Police Academy* films and *Private Benjamin*. There isn't an original idea or gag in Len Blum and Dan Goldberg's transparent screenplay. This is a turkey that the two stars must have hoped would sink without trace forever.

Fellow Traveller ◐ ⓥ
1989, UK, 97 mins, colour
Dir: Philip Saville
Stars: Ron Silver, Imogen Stubbs, Hart Bochner, Daniel J Travanti
Rating: ★★★

If there's an entertaining way of looking at the late Forties' Communist witchhunts and their effect on those artists pulled into their web, chewed over and spat into oblivion, then writer Michael Eaton comes close to it here. Ron Silver plays a blacklisted writer, an ex-Communist sympathiser forced to flee America sans famille before he can be subpoenaed to testify about his affiliations and associates. In Britain, he does pretty well for himself, quickly sliding into the bed of his best friend's ex-mistress (Imogen Stubbs) and getting a job as a writer (under a pseudonym) on TV's *Robin Hood*. But old ghosts return to haunt him. The back-and-forth flashback structure works to surprising effect, the settings are well in period, be it 1943, 1947 or 1954 and the performances, especially Daniel J Travanti's, flesh out the characters nicely. The *Robin Hood* interludes look very much like the real thing, with Silver's vengeful bile for past wrongs occasionally spilling out amusingly in scenes that will never see the light of screen.

Feminine Touch, The ○
1956, UK, 91 mins, colour
Dir: Pat Jackson
Stars: George Baker, Belinda Lee, Delphi Lawrence, Adrienne Corri
Rating: ★★

Sir Michael Balcon tries to do for the nursing profession what he had done for the policeman with *The Blue Lamp*. It's a sympathetic look at the lives and loves of five trainee nurses. Mostly credible, too though it's doubtful you would find five such attractive girls at the same hospital, a factor which tends to draw out the soap opera qualities lurking in the script. A very young George Baker provides a surgical shoulder to cry on.

FernGully: The Last Rainforest ☉ Ⓥ
1992, US, 76 mins, colour
Dir: Bill Kroyer
Voice stars: Tim Curry, Samantha Mathis, Christian Slater, Robin Williams, Jonathan Ward, Grace Zabriskie, Cheech Marin, Tommy Chong
Rating: ★★★

An ecologically friendly cartoon feature that's clean, green (very) and on your screen. The fairies of FernGully are horrified to learn that humans are near with their leveller: one of the humans, Zak, an Australian student (with an American accent) helping the tree-fellers, is accidentally instrumental in releasing Hexxus, evil spirit of the woods, from his tree prison. Shrunk to fairy size by the precocious Crysta (who has much the same fascination for humans that got *The Little Mermaid* into so much trouble), Zak helps the fairies try to fight both Hexxus and the leveller. Helping and hindering in the fight is Batty Koda (distinctively voiced by Robin Williams), a bat escaped from laboratory experiments (yes, all ecological protest is here). Lively enough when Batty and Hexxus are around, the film also has a successful line in humour – a singing iguana is good fun – but could do with rather more of it. The scenes between Zak and Crysta are typically drippy cartoon romance. Mostly excellent, though, for children of eight or less.

Ferris Bueller's Day Off ◐ Ⓥ
1986, US, 103 mins, colour
Dir: John Hughes
Stars: Matthew Broderick, Alan Ruck, Mia Sara, Jennifer Grey
Rating: ★★★

A teenage comedy demonstrating the great lengths to which the impressible Ferris Bueller (Matthew Broderick) will go to in order to hoodwink his parents and high school principal into thinking he's sick, when, in fact, all he wants to do is play truant for a day. Irreverent attitude, cast sassiness, tons of rock music and all the other expected ingredients are present and as always, teen film maestro John Hughes presents his teenagers' feeling of superiority to adults as being totally justified. In the adult camp, there's a pricelessly funny performance from Jeffrey Jones as the high school principal, driven nearly out of his mind in his frustrated pursuit of Ferris. Ferris's sister is played by Jennifer Grey, soon to reach brief stardom in *Dirty Danc-*

ing. And Charlie Sheen has a funny cameo as a drunken biker. He confessed that he didn't sleep for 48 hours to get the desired effect.

Ferry to Hong Kong ○
1958, UK, 113 mins, colour
Dir: Lewis Gilbert
Stars: Curt Jurgens, Orson Wells, Sylvia Syms
Rating: ★★

An adventure story offering a personality clash between Orson Welles and Curt Jurgens, as well as providing some very attractive and exotic shots of the mysterious Far East. Filmed on location at a cost of half a million pounds, it represented one of the first attempts by British film-makers to rival the opulent escapism that Hollywood was providing.

Few Good Men, A ◐ Ⓥ
1992, US, 138 mins, colour
Dir: Rob Reiner
Stars: Tom Cruise, Jack Nicholson, Demi Moore, Kiefer Sutherland, Kevin Bacon, Kevin Pollack
Rating: ★★★

This predictable but powerful courtroom drama is fuelled by the high-octane performances of Tom Cruise and Jack Nicholson, brandishing charisma as well as their acting credentials, as two men on opposite sides of the military fence. 'Why would a lawyer with nine months experience and a record of plea bargaining get a murder case?' muses naval lieutenant Cruise. 'Perhaps so it never sees the inside of a courtroom.' A marine has died after being attacked by two fellow marines; ostensibly, its a homicidal plot. But Cruise sniffs a Code Red, a rather harsher equivalent of public school ragging, under which the men have been ordered to carry out the attack to teach the weakling (a known informer) a severe lesson. Circumstantial evidence that the victim's possible heart condition may have been the cause of death is denied by the unit doctor and Cruise and hot-headed co-counsel Demi Moore's investigation soon falls foul of the rocks patrolled by the great white shark, Col Jack Nicholson himself. You'll know the outcome, of course, but be happy to stay the course and welcome it with a cheer when it comes.

ffolkes
See: North Sea Hijack

Fiddler on the Roof ○ Ⓥ
1971, US, 180 mins, colour
Dir: Norman Jewison
Stars: Topol, Norma Crane, Leonard Frey
Rating: ★★★

Topol's star quality doesn't burn quite so bright in this film version of the overwhelming musical success as it had in the original stage version, but it's still impossible to see anyone else in the role of the Jewish milkman with five marriageable daughters. Often rousing in its score, the film is less effective once the music stops, and goes on rather a long time. It's still well worth a look, though, if only for Topol's inspired performance of the big hit number 'If I Were a Rich Man'. Director Norman Jewison's treatment of the piece is perhaps over-ambitious, as underlined by Oswald Morris's sombre photography, full of browns ands golds, which surprisingly won him an Oscar although not really among his best work.

Fiddlers Three ○
1944, UK, 88 mins, b/w
Dir: Harry Watt
Stars: Tommy Trinder, Frances Day, Sonnie Hale
Rating: ★★

The idea of most British comedy films of the early Forties was to provide an escapist cure for the wartime blues. And this British sideshoot from Eddie Cantor's *Roman Scandals* certainly fitted the bill. Bright spark Diana Decker made her screen debut at the age of 17. More difficult to spot in their first film roles are Kay Kendall and James Robertson Justice.

Field, The ◐ Ⓥ
1990, UK, 110 mins, colour
Dir: Jim Sheridan
Stars: Richard Harris, John Hurt, Tom Berenger, Sean Bean, Frances Tomelty, Brenda Fricker
Rating: ★★★

Director Jim Sheridan (*My Left Foot*) presents another study of Irish familial tensions and stunted lives. The source of the family's problems here is not a crippling disease but an equally debilitating combination of festering family secret, stubborn patriarchy, blind obsession with land, and cruel history, one which hangs over their

F

entire community like a cold, damp mist. Richard Harris' great performance was nominated for an Oscar.

Field of Dreams ○ Ⓥ
1989, US, 106 mins, colour
Dir: Phil Alden Robinson
Stars: Kevin Costner, Amy Madigan, James Earl Jones, Ray Liotta, Burt Lancaster, Gaby Hoffman
Rating: ★★★★

This very winning fantasy is certainly one of a kind. Kevin Costner is an Iowa farmer, alienated from his baseball-mad father as a teenager, who hears voices that tell him to build a baseball field (at the cost of half his corn) in which a ghost team of legendary outlawed players then appears. Further voices drive him to locate a self-exiled author (James Earl Jones) and an obscure doctor (Burt Lancaster) who missed playing major league baseball by a whisker. The result is a bizarre movie but one which frequently touches the emotions in the manner of the finest Hollywood 'moonshine'. The film's endearing qualities are boosted by the wholesome performances of Costner, Amy Madigan (as his wife), Ray Liotta (as the ghost team's leader), Lancaster and Timothy Busfield as Costner's disbelieving brother-in-law. You may think this film is dumb to begin with, but if you're any sort of romantic, you'll soon be won over by its magic. Frank Capra would have approved.

Fiendish Plot of Dr Fu Manchu, The ○
1980, UK, 108 mins, colour
Dir: Piers Haggard
Stars: Peter Sellers, Helen Mirren, David Tomlinson
Rating: ★★

This is a typical latter-day film from Peter Sellers in that it's fun without actually being very funny (apart from the appearance of a clockwork tarantula) – painless enough and probably closer to pure Goonery than Sellers had been for some time. If they could have added Spike Milligan as Nayland Smith's aged servant (played here by John Le Mesurier), Harry Secombe as the keeper of the Crown Jewels, forced to take a cure for obesity (John Sharp), and Michael Bentine as the lunatic Harley Street specialist in elephants (Clement Harari) you could have had a sentimental reunion. Sellers acquits himself quite well as Nayland Smith and Fu Manchu while Simon

Williams is funny in support as a man from the ministry who is wet – usually in more ways than one. Helen Mirren adopts a stage cockney accent as the policewoman engaged to track Fu Manchu down in this pleasant lightweight lunacy.

Fifth Avenue Girl ○
1939, US, 79 mins, b/w
Dir: Gregory La Cava
Stars: Ginger Rogers, Walter Connolly
Rating: ★★

Ginger Rogers was the tops in musicals with Fred Astaire, but she lit no fires on her own until the early Forties. Top screwball comedy director Gregory La Cava was hired to boost the chances of this comedy about a workless girl hired to pose as a gold-digger, but he couldn't do much with its tiresome plot. Tim Holt steps down from the saddle to play the rich boy for whom Miss Rogers falls.

Fifth Musketeer, The ○
1978, US, 106 mins, colour
Dir: Ken Annakin
Stars: Beau Bridges, Sylvia Kristel, Ursula Andress, Cornel Wilde, Lloyd Bridges, Jose Ferrer
Rating: ★★

Yet another re-telling of Dumas' famous story *The Man in the Iron Mask*, with lavish production values, full-blooded fight sequences, two of the world's most beautiful actresses and a fascinating sense of romantic heroics. Beau Bridges proves more effective than one might expect in the dual role of the French king and his twin brother, while Jack Cardiff's lush Eastman Colour photography and Rex Harrison's engagingly crafty Colbert are other plus factors.

55 Days at Peking ○ Ⓥ
1962, US/UK, 154 mins, colour
Dir: Nicholas Ray
Stars: Charlton Heston, Ava Gardner, David Niven, Flora Robson, John Ireland
Rating: ★★★

Some time, there is a great film to be made about the Boxer Rebellion, that strange and violent piece of history when the embassies of five countries held out for 55 days against thousands of vicious Chinese Boxer warriors in the siege of Peking. Visually, and as far as exciting action can take it, this goes a long way to being that film. As a spectacle, it's fine value for money. Too much so-so dialogue slows it down, but every time that second-unit

director Andrew Marton takes over from Nicholas Ray, the picture springs to life with eye-catching action.

52 Pick Up ● Ⓥ
1986, US, 108 mins, colour
Dir: John Frankenheimer
Stars: Roy Scheider, Ann-Margret, Kelly Preston, John Glover, Vanity, Robert Trebor
Rating: ★★★

Very nasty but pretty effective, this shows just what can happen when a man takes a step out of line. Roy Scheider is the tough-talking, self-made businessman, enticed into an affair by a nubile blond as a prelude to blackmail. When he gives the crooks a figurative V sign, they steal his gun and clothing and kill the girl. Scheider, who has already swallowed his pride to tell his wife (Ann-Margret) everything, now has to track down the blackmailers to tell them that, despite a prospering business, he only currently has $52,000 (thus the title) to his name. From here on in, it's a game of bloody cat and mouse played to a violent end. Scheider grits his teeth and convinces throughout, while John Glover has a dream of a role in early Richard Widmark style as the photographer who runs the blackmail racket. For those who fancy a minor *film noir* in late Eighties fashion – even the photography seems full of blackness and death – this, with its believably seedy background of 'adult' videos, could fit the bill.

Fighter Squadron ○
1948, US, 96 mins, colour
Dir: Raoul Walsh
Stars: Edmond O'Brien, Robert Stack, Tom D'Andrea, Henry Hull
Rating: ★★

Under the vigorous direction of Raoul Walsh, an exciting, red-blooded action film has been woven around the grim realities of war in this stirring account of US fighter pilots battling the Luftwaffe in 1943–4. Edmond O'Brien is the commander of a small squadron, becoming grounded (like the script), while in the skies the thrilling music of Max Steiner takes over, providing a pounding accompaniment to dogfights, strafings, explosions and bomb raids, all awesomely well shot in Technicolor by Syd Wilcox and Wilfred M Kline. Rock Hudson is alleged to have required 38 takes before completing his one scene in this, his first film!

Fighting Back ○
1982, Australia, 98 mins, colour
Dir: Michael Caulfield
Stars: Lewis Fitz-Gerald, Paul Smith, Kris McQuade
Rating: ★★

A distant Australian relative of *The Miracle Worker*, as a dedicated teacher tries to win friendship of a violent and deeply disturbed 13-year-old boy, at the risk of the hatred of his fellow teachers and finally even his job. A bit unremitting in its punishing portrait of a difficult relationship, and ruthlessly cute in its depiction of happier times (teacher and boy on a camping/canoeing holiday). But still there are times when the film cuts right to the heart. The acting is generally competent and, in the case of Kris McQuade as the boy's mother, rather more.

Fighting Man of the Plains ○
1949, US, 94 mins, colour
Dir: Edwin L Marin
Stars: Randolph Scott, Jane Nigh, Victor Jory, Bill Williams
Rating: ★★★

This 'A' class Western was one of three made by star Randolph Scott for 20th Century-Fox when they were toying with the idea of using the cheap Cinecolor process for their major outdoor features. Treacherous looking Victor Jory was in all three; usually Jory played waistcoated villains, but here he heads a fine supporting cast as a gambler who befriends Scott (an outlaw posing as a marshal) and helps him when he can. Dale Robertson got his first major role with the studio here, as Jesse James, who has a short but key role to play in the action. Jane Nigh and Joan Taylor are weak as the women involved, but Barry Kelley and Bill Williams strongly supply tight-lipped and smiling villainy respectively.

Fighting Prince of Donegal, The ○
1966, UK, 104 mins, colour
Dir: Michael O'Herlihy
Stars: Peter McEnery, Susan Hampshire, Gordon Jackson
Rating: ★

With its cardboard castle and script that will have you chuckling at every other line, this is a 'penny dreadful' Disney historical epic, squarely aimed at children. Some of the performances are better than the film deserves, notably from Peter McEnery in the title role, and from Gordon Jackson, cast successfully against type as a smirking villain. But director Michael O'Herlihy makes the mistake of reckoning sheer noise a substitute for pace and action.

Fighting 69th, The ○ ⓥ
1940, US, 90 mins, b/w
Dir: William Keighley
Stars: James Cagney, Pat O'Brien, George Brent, Alan Hale, Frank McHugh
Rating: ★★

With the advent of war in Europe, the Warners stars who had been busy shooting it out in city streets suddenly presented a united front against a common enemy. Humphrey Bogart took on the Japanese in *Across the Pacific*, while Edward G Robinson dealt with infiltrators in *Confessions of a Nazi Spy* and George Raft tackled the Germans and Russians in *Background to Danger*. James Cagney, Pat O'Brien and George Brent were all piled in to *The Fighting 69th*, the studio's biggest war film to that date, about a World War One regiment also known as 'The Fighting Irish'. Its two most famous scions, both portrayed here, were the poet Joyce Kilmer and the priest Father Duffy, whose statue stands in Times Square. 'I don't go for that Holy Joe stuff,' snarls braggart Cagney to pious Pat at the beginning of the film. He does before the end, though, like all good Hollywood heroes should. There's action a-plenty and a supporting cast that, as in so many Warners films, is worth its weight in gold.

Fighting Sullivans, The ○
(aka: The Sullivans)
1944, US, 111 mins, b/w
Dir: Lloyd Bacon
Stars: Anne Baxter, Thomas Mitchell
Rating: ★★★

Pretty well all the right emotional strings were pulled by this wartime flagwaver about five brothers, devoted to one another, who broke all the rules by getting postings together on the same naval cruiser. Casting of virtually unknown actors as the brothers is a great help, and Thomas Mitchell offers another well-judged performance as the boys' father.

Figures in a Landscape ◑
1970, UK, 110 mins, colour
Dir: Joseph Losey
Stars: Robert Shaw, Malcolm McDowell
Rating: ★

Allegory is the name of the game in this dessicated thriller, in which two fugitives flee a nameless force across a nameless country. The ruggedness of the action, and Robert Shaw's abrasive performance (he also wrote the script) almost save it from boredom.

File of the Golden Goose, The ○
1969, UK, 102 mins, colour
Dir: Sam Wanamaker
Stars: Yul Brynner, Charles Gray, Edward Woodward, John Barrie
Rating: ★★

The performances of Yul Brynner and Edward Woodward distinguish this B-feature thriller in A-feature dressing about American and British undercover men after a counterfeiting ring. Typical of many thrillers coming from British studios at the time, this one is decorated at the edges by Adrienne Corri and Hilary Dwyer. Charles Gray offers another of his hedonistic villains; Karel Stepanek and Walter Gotell clamp their jaws and look grim; and Graham Crowden is successfully cast against type as a sadistic killer inseparable from his umbrella-knife.

File on Thelma Jordon, The ○
(aka: Thelma Jordan)
1949, US, 100 mins, b/w
Dir: Robert Siodmak
Stars: Barbara Stanwyck, Wendell Corey, Paul Kelly
Rating: ★★★

Another chance for Barbara Stanwyck to show that she could play the poor little bad girl just as well as Bette Davis or Joan Crawford. As the brittle and beautiful femme fatale with husky voice and gleaming lips, La Stanwyck had no equal. Here, as usual, she's involved in murder, in a movie that's slow on pace, but has bags of atmosphere and style. Directed by Robert Siodmak, who made the original version of *The Killers* and other atmospheric thrillers of the 1940s.

Filofax ◑ ⓥ
(aka: Taking Care of Business)
1990, US, 107 mins, colour
Dir: Arthur Hiller
Stars: James Belushi, Charles Grodin, Anne DeSalvo, Loryn Locklin, Veronica Hamel, Mako
Rating: ★★★

If you dislike 'nice' films, this is not for you. A variant on *Trading Places*, it casts (equally happily) James Belushi as a convict who escapes from prison to

F

see a baseball game, and Charles Grodin as the workaholic ad salesman into whose hands his Filofax falls. Grodin gets mugged and then thrown in jail, which is fortunate for Belushi who has taken over Grodin's lifestyle for an ad-pitch weekend, sinfully beating a powerful could-be client (Mako) at tennis, bedding the boss's daughter, and wining and dining in Grodin's best white suit. Grodin learns a lot, Belushi falls on his feet and everything is neatly tied up with a happy ending. Belushi and Grodin don't put a foot wrong, unlike Hector Elizondo, who overdoes his caricature of Belushi's hated warden. Veronica Hamel makes the most of her few chances as Grodin's wife.

Final Analysis ● Ⓥ
1992, US, 124 mins, colour
Dir: Phil Joanou
Stars: Richard Gere, Kim Basinger, Uma Thurman, Eric Roberts, Paul Guilfoyle
Rating: ★★★

This Hitchcock-style thriller has more twists than the steps of the lighthouse where, once it's introduced into the story, you just know the principal protagonists will end up. Once psychiatrist Richard Gere has taken on Uma Thurman as a disturbed patient, and been introduced to her seductive sister (Kim Basinger), the story continually dodges this way and that. You're never quite certain who's plotting what, or which combination of the characters is on which side of the law. Basinger has a hateful husband (Eric Roberts) whom she describes as a Greek Orthodox gangster. Perhaps she'll ensnare Gere into a plan to bump him off. But no. That's just one of the ways this devious drama doesn't work out. Ignore some fairly foolish goings-on in the court-room and throw yourself headlong into this intoxicating brew, shot through by flashes of lightning and screechingly scored in the Bernard Herrmann manner by George Fenton. Basinger makes as luscious a femme fatale as anyone could wish and her acting has improved by miles from earlier days. A polished, excitingly-paced piece of *film noir*.

Final Combination ● Ⓥ
1993, US, 93 mins, colour
Dir: Nigel Dick
Stars: Michael Madsen, Lisa Bonet, Gary Stretch
Rating: RB

A real grade Z movie this, in every sense, the kind of film that has no business going anywhere but straight to video. God knows what the title means, but the story has bimbo-happy cop Michael Madsen trying to track down a boxing serial killer (Gary Stretch), with the help of a reporter (Lisa Bonet) who's the first girl in ages not to actually lie down immediately before the cop's monolithic advances. Madsen is no second Kirk Douglas here, nor even William Bendix, but he's a lot better than Bonet and Stretch in what must be one of the worst-performed movies in quite a while. And, true to form, the serial killer escapes death only to come back for a final confrontation with the detective when you or I would be half-way to another continent.

Final Conflict, The
See: Omen III – The Final Conflict

Final Countdown, The ○
1980, US, 104 mins, colour
Dir: Don Taylor
Stars: Kirk Douglas, Martin Sheen, Katharine Ross, James Farentino, Charles Durning
Rating: ★★★

It can hardly be said that this is a science-fiction film. But for the foundation of its story it does borrow from a stock science-fiction theme, for it is essentially of the 'time travel' variety. An American aircraft carrier on routine duty in the Pacific encounters a storm of unprecedented violence. When it's all over, captain and crew find themselves back in time the day before the Japanese attack Pearl Harbor. The subsequent story developments are ingeniously worked out with sufficient logic to make them convincing and compelling. Quite an unusual, fascinating movie.

Finders Keepers ☉
1966, UK, 94 mins, colour
Dir: Sidney Hayers
Stars: Cliff Richard, Viviane Ventura, Robert Morley, Peggy Mount
Rating: ★★

For this musical comedy with a Spanish setting, a big search was made to find an actress to play the Spanish girl who falls for Cliff. The quest ended with the choice of 21-year-old Viviane Ventura, who was born in London, but spoke Spanish fluently. Here she sings a lively duet with Cliff, called 'Paella'. Peggy Mount and Robert Morley ('for £10,000, I'd

walk naked down Horse Guards Parade') provide formidable comedy support for the stars.

Finders Keepers ◐
1984, US, 96 mins, colour
Dir: Richard Lester
Stars: Michael O'Keefe, Beverly D'Angelo, Louis Gossett Jr
Rating: ★★

A light and agreeable train romp which starts really well, but ultimately fails as a film because, for all the energy with which director Richard Lester invests it, it simply isn't funny. Most of the unnecessary four-letter words in the script of this frenzied froth go to Beverly D'Angelo, so it's much to her credit that she's still the best thing in a film which defies the efforts of such experienced players as David Wayne, Ed Lauter, Brian Dennehy, Pamela Stephenson and Louis Gossett to get a laugh. Harmless enough, but totally lacking in comic distinction.

Find the Lady ○
1976, Canada, 79 mins, colour
Dir: John Trent
Stars: Lawrence Dane, John Candy, Peter Cook, Dick Emery
Rating: ★

A lot of bright comic stars from various countries got themselves involved in this ramshackle romp about a bizarre kidnap. Big John Candy, later a major star of Hollywood comedies, made his screen debut in a crazy misadventure never shown in cinemas outside its native Canada.

Fine Madness, A ◐
1966, US, 104 mins, colour
Dir: Irvin Kershner
Stars: Sean Connery, Joanne Woodward, Jean Seberg, Patrick O'Neal
Rating: ★★★

A nine-tenths hilarious comedy, with a few sinister undertones, about an amorous out-of-work poet called Samson Shillitoe (Sean Connery), who falls foul of one of his mistresses' husbands. Good performances from Joanne Woodward, screamingly funny as the poet's long-suffering and amusingly belligerent wife, and Sue Ane Langdon, as the chattiest of his 'victims', highlight this pleasing entertainment. Patrick O'Neal's satirical portrait of a psychiatrist is frighteningly droll until he catches Connery in the steam-bath with his wife (O'Neal's, that is) and consigns him to a gruesome brain operation – performed by a dotty scientist, played in best Peter Sellers style by Clive Revill.

Fine Romance, A ◐ ⓥ
(aka: Tchin Tchin; A Touch of Adultery)
1992, US/Italy, 83 mins, colour
Dir: Gene Saks
Stars: Julie Andrews, Marcello Mastroianni, Ian Fitzgibbon, Jean-Pierre Castaldi, Maria Machado
Rating: ★

A romantic comedy that echoes the style of continental movies from the Sixties, but lacks their class and *joie-de-vivre*. Unimaginative casting doesn't help, either, with Marcello Mastroianni as Cesareo, the archetypal incurably romantic Italian, and Julie Andrews as Pamela, a prim English rose. The pair discover they have both been jilted and romance blossoms between them as they set out to retrieve their errant spouses. Andrews, here in her late fifties, still looks fabulous, and the Paris settings are a delight. Gene Saks' heavy-handed direction at least keeps proceedings short enough to justify Andrews fans taking a look.

Finest Hour, The ● ⓥ
1991, US, 110 mins, colour
Dir: Shimon Dotan
Stars: Rob Lowe, Gale Hansen, Tracy Griffith, Eb Lottimer
Rating: ★★

What does it take to be a hero? Apparently, a spindly moustache, a crew cut, a sleepy look and a good casting agent. Rob Lowe stars as a tough raw recruit who becomes a SEAL – a member of the elite US navy commando fighting force – in this cheapie cash-in action thriller set during the Gulf War. Despite the shallowness of the main characters, there are some fine *Top Gun*-style heroics and an undercurrent of rivalry in love and war. If only it didn't go on so long, this might have been twice as effective.

Fingers at the Window ○
1942, US, 80 mins, b/w
Dir: Charles Lederer
Stars: Lew Ayres, Basil Rathbone, Laraine Day
Rating: ★★★

Neat and highly professional Hollywood crime thriller of its time, splendidly edited, with Lew Ayres giving good value to the role of the unemployed actor caught up in a deception which could cost him his life.

Director Charles Lederer was best known for his scripts – on such classics as *The Front Page* and *Kiss of Death*.

Finian's Rainbow ○ ⓥ
1968, US, 140 mins, colour
Dir: Francis Ford Coppola
Stars: Fred Astaire, Petula Clark, Tommy Steele, Keenan Wynn
Rating: ★★★

Directed by Francis Ford Coppola in stark contrast to his other big hits – the *Godfather* films and *Apocalypse Now* – this charming, colourful (fine Technicolor camerawork by Philip Lathrop) and at times bitingly satirical musical first saw light of day on stage in 1947, a peak period for the American musical. Coppola's casting gambles all come off: Fred Astaire is lovable but never fey as Finian, the Irish wanderer; Petula Clark (in the role created on Broadway by Ella Logan, aunt of Jimmy) is fresh and charming as his daughter; and Tommy Steele funny and tuneful as Og the leprechaun. The songs include 'Old Devil Moon'.

Fireball 500 ◐
1966, US, 92 mins, colour
Dir: William Asher
Stars: Frankie Avalon, Annette Funicello, Fabian, Chill Wills
Rating: ★★

Despite a spectacular fight and some hair-raising scenes of stock-car racing, this is pretty tough, chewy meat, showing the Frankie Avalon-Annette Funicello team away from the beach and near the end of the road. There are some sexy love scenes, not, of course, involving Annette, but Frankie, who harder and more professional than before, prefers a blonde who husks: 'I'm getting restless. You know how I am when I'm restless.' Good action, bad script? You've got it.

Fire Birds
See: Wings of the Apache

Firecreek ◐
1968, US, 104 mins, colour
Dir: Vincent McEveety
Stars: James Stewart, Henry Fonda, Inger Stevens, Gary Lockwood, Dean Jagger, Jack Elam
Rating: ★★★

Enjoyable, old-style Western with James Stewart as the mild-mannered farmer-cum-sheriff whose resolute core slowly but surely comes to the surface when five tough and vicious marauders invade his town. Vincent McEveety's direction is especially effective in the pulsating *High Noon*-style climax and the Technicolor photography exemplary, particularly in a night-time scene at a bizarre 'wake'. The performances of Stewart – radiating sincerity and determination – and Henry Fonda, as the tormented outlaw leader, lift a basically ordinary action yarn right out of the rut.

Fire Down Below ○
1957, UK, 116 mins, colour
Dir: Robert Parrish
Stars: Rita Hayworth, Robert Mitchum, Jack Lemmon, Herbert Lom, Bernard Lee, Anthony Newley
Rating: ★★

Although not quite as explosive as its advance notices had proclaimed, the teaming of Rita Hayworth, Robert Mitchum and Jack Lemmon gives this strange triangular melodrama quite a powerful kick. Lemmon comes off best, two years after his Academy Award for *Mr Roberts*, as a young Caribbean fisherman who becomes consumed with hatred after falling out with his partner (Mitchum) over a mystery woman (Hayworth) whom Mitchum seems to regard with contempt. Desmond Dickinson offers exciting colour camerawork on location in the West Indies, and a sterling company of home-based actors including Anthony Newley, Herbert Lom and Bernard Lee black up in best repertory style. The most exciting part of the film comes when Lemmon is trapped by a girder in the bow of a sinking Greek tramp steamer. The title song, quite a hit in its time, is scorched through by Shirley Bassey.

Firefox ◐ ⓥ
1982, US, 131 mins, colour
Dir: Clint Eastwood
Stars: Clint Eastwood, Freddi Jones, David Huffman, Warren Clarke
Rating: ★

Clint Eastwood takes a cold war espionage story that could have been knocking around 30 years ago and, as well as directing, lends his own abrasive personality to the leading role. He plays a Vietnam-haunted US pilot (a part that would have been perfectly suited to Errol Flynn) called on to sneak the Russians' latest top-secret aircraft from under their very noses. Every step of the way, his contacts assail him with 'You have not been told this, but . . .' as the assignment

F

becomes progressively less likely. Eastwood's British supporting cast labour mightily with their Russian accents and the special effects involved in showing the high-speed Firefox planes in action are often pretty good. Overall, though, this is Eastwood's slackest job in quite a while, with barely enough action, and stodgily-directed dialogue scenes that stretch the film away past the two-hour mark.

Fire Maidens from Outer Space ○
1956, UK, 80 mins, b/w
Dir: Cy Roth
Stars: Anthony Dexter, Susan Shaw
Rating: ★

Five space scientists in a cardboard craft land on Jupiter's 13th moon to find it inhabited by girls in bikinis in this supremely daft, if very entertaining British sci-fi romp. One of the cinema's great bad films of all time, and another step on the long road down for Hollywood's Anthony Dexter, who had started his career in the title role of *Valentino*.

Firm, The ● ⓥ
1993, US, 155 mins, colour
Dir: Sydney Pollack
Stars: Tom Cruise, Gene Hackman, Jeanne Tripplehorn, Holly Hunter, Hal Holbrook, Ed Harris
Rating: ★★

This is one of those get-yourself-out-of-this thrillers that Hollywood adores. Tom Cruise is the hotshot young lawyer just out of Harvard who signs up with a plush Tennessee law firm that provides him with a house, a car and a small fortune. Unfortunately it also offers him a prison cell: the Firm is the principal state legislator for the Mafia and no one ever leaves it. Not alive, at any rate. Cruise is contacted by FBI agent Ed Harris and told: 'Your life, as you know it, is over.' A witness protection programme is offered. Of course his career will be finished, and the Firm will almost certainly find him and kill him. In any case, they have a blackmail hold on him, with photos of a fleeting affair they can show his wife. So there's no way out. But hold on there, guys: this is a Tom Cruise film. A pretty slow Tom Cruise film at that, although the Hitchcock-style last 30 minutes is just about worth waiting for. A pity we didn't manage to mention Gene Hackman in all this, as Hackman gives the best performance in the movie by

some way as a cynical co-lawyer who fancies Jeanne Tripplehorn as Cruise's wife.

First a Girl ○ ⓥ
1935, UK, 94 mins, b/w
Dir: Victor Saville
Stars: Jessie Matthews, Sonnie Hale, Griffith Jones, Anna Lee
Rating: ★★★

This enchanting musical took the public (if not the critics) by storm, and proved Jessie Matthews' second most successful after *Evergreen*. The story is the original of the Eighties' Julie Andrews movie *Victor/Victoria*, with Jessie, as a girl impersonating a boy impersonating a girl, never sexier and singing 'Everything's in Rhythm with My Heart' and 'Say the Word and I'm Yours'. The finale, a sequence set in a gigantic bird cage, is quite extraordinary, although the reality was less exotic. The cage, 40 feet high, was built in open fields at Northolt in North London and filmed between two and five in the morning, while 52 chorus girls in feathers perched all over the bars. If Jessie looks doubtful in one or two shots, it's probably because her perch was 30 feet up!

First Blood ● ⓥ
1982, US, 93 mins, colour
Dir: Ted Kotcheff
Stars: Sylvester Stallone, Richard Crenna, Brian Dennehy, David Caruso
Rating: ★★★

An excitingly made blood-and-thunder film that pits a wronged Vietnam veteran against the redneck police force of a small mid-west town. Sylvester Stallone plays the muscular Medal of Honor winner picked up for vagrancy on the slightest of pretences by sheriff Brian Dennehy and subsequently beaten and humiliated by his deputy, before the inevitable happens: he goes berserk, escapes and takes to the wooded and rocky local countryside. From then on, it's only a question of spinning the film out as Stallone first picks off the pursuing posse one by one, then escapes from being trapped in a mine and comes lookin' for Dennehy and blasting apart practically his whole town. Pretty nearly the action film of its year, this gives its audience what they want: continual, violent and fluid action with a hero it's easy to identify with. The best scenes are probably those in the mine, where Stallone fights off a cave of rats to reach freedom. The weakest are the last few, which point

a moral, it's true, but make for anti-climax too, especially as most of Stallone's dialogue here is unintelligible.

First Deadly Sin, The ●
1980, US, 112 mins, colour
Dir: Brian Hutton
Stars: Frank Sinatra, Faye Dunaway, Brenda Vaccaro, James Whitmore
Rating: ★★

If you're squeamish about operations, prepare to close your eyes to the opening sequence of this city-streets thriller, which brings Frank Sinatra half-way between his own film *The Detective* and such vigilante cop thrillers as *10 to Midnight*. The screenplay is fatally flawed by a sub-plot which has Sinatra mooning over his dying wife (Faye Dunaway) and works best when he gets down to the main business of tracking down a particularly unpleasant psychopathic killer. A stalking pursuit around the flapping cellophane tunnels of a building site is splendidly staged by director Brian Hutton, while at police headquarters acting honours are solidly snaffled by doughty veteran James Whitmore as a pathologist. Sinatra himself looks a bit old but then so might anyone who had to read some of these lines.

First Great Train Robbery, The ◐
1978, US, 108 mins, colour
Dir: Michael Crichton
Stars: Sean Connery, Donald Sutherland, Lesley-Anne Down, Wayne Sleep, Michael Elphick
Rating: ★★★

Train robberies have provided a basic story ingredient for many a motion picture but where this one differs is that it is set in 1855. The film is rich in Victorian period detail, but it's the action that counts, in which respect the robbery sequence is effectively done. A bearded Sean Connery stars as the gentleman crook whose interest in perpetrating the robbery is more particularly a matter of fascination with crime. Donald Sutherland has a splendid character part as his accomplice. Good entertainment for anyone who enjoys a film in 'caper' style.

First Love ○
1939, US, 84 mins, b/w
Dir: Henry Koster

Stars: Deanna Durbin, Helen Parrish, Robert Stack
Rating: ★★★

Deanna Durbin goes to the ball in this romantic musical – but is warned she must leave by midnight. But there's a midnight kiss and she has to flee, dropping a slipper on the stairway. So, as you can see, this is very much a Cinderella-like affair – and absolutely intentionally so. It's full of charm and frothily directed by Henry Koster, always a dab hand at this sort of thing. It's the film in which Deanna's songs include the hit 'Amapola' and in which she received her first screen kiss – from Robert Stack.

First Men in the Moon ○
1964, UK, 99 mins, colour
Dir: Nathan Juran
Stars: Edward Judd, Lionel Jeffries, Martha Hyer
Rating: ★★★

Entertaining H G Wells yarn about a moon expedition in 1899, led by a professor who has invented a substance which defies gravity. Exciting special effects by Dynamation wizard Ray Harryhausen, who creates the Selenites, complement a super performance by Lionel Jeffries as the professor – all sudden ups and downs, snuffles and flashes of illuminating thought. The space vehicle comes equipped with all mod cons – even including its own livestock.

First Monday in October ◐
1981, US, 99 mins, colour
Dir: Ronald Neame
Stars: Jill Clayburgh, Walter Matthau, Jan Sterling, Barnard Hughes
Rating: ★★★

A comedy-drama that's sometimes caustic, sometimes likeable and sometimes as dry as the law books over which Jill Clayburgh and Walter Matthau wrangle. She's the first woman judge to be appointed to the American Supreme Court, he, naturally, is the recalcitrant rebel who opposes her but finally falls for her charm. The film seems a little short, but the stars play the limited situations wonderfully well together to make the cerebral mixture a feast for their fans.

First Power, The ● Ⓥ
1990, US, 96 mins, colour
Dir: Robert Resnikoff

Stars: Lou Diamond Phillips, Tracy Griffith, Jeff Kober, Mykel T Williamson
Rating: ★★

A silly and far-fetched but quite suspenseful chiller on the now-familiar theme of a serial killer's spirit returning after execution to possess the bodies of others and continue his killing spree. Lou Diamond Phillips is quite good as the detective who at first thinks he's going out of his mind, then follows a bloody trail with the help of beautiful red-haired psychic Tracy Griffith, real-life half-sister of Melanie. The action keeps the plot hopping, and it's well-orchestrated throughout by director Robert Resnikoff – though the final scene is unnecessary and stretches the whole plot too far.

First Rebel, The ○ Ⓥ
(aka: Allegheny Uprising)
1939, US, 81 mins, b/w
Dir: William A Seiter
Stars: John Wayne, Claire Trevor
Rating: ★★

After the success of *Stagecoach*, RKO hurriedly put their new cowboy star John Wayne and his leading lady Claire Trevor in other Western action dramas. This saga set in an America still under British rule, has Wayne battling against Brian Donlevy, who is selling guns to the Indians and George Sanders, a tyrannical British officer. A good cast, then, and plenty of action too. Not a bad film, but not a memorable one, either, in spite of its offbeat setting. A must for Wayne fans, though.

First Travelling Saleslady, The ○
1956, US, 92 mins, colour
Dir: Arthur Lubin
Stars: Ginger Rogers, Carol Channing, Barry Nelson, James Arness, Clint Eastwood
Rating: ★

Ginger Rogers and Carol Channing go west to sell barbed wire to ranchers in this lightweight comedy Western, one of the last films Rogers made for RKO. Both ladies appear to be having fun, but it's all pretty forgettable really. The only point of interest for the film buff is that Miss Channing's tall Texan boyfriend is played by Clint Eastwood! Even taller James Arness is also around, in one of his comparatively few big-screen roles; he had to be content with remaining the Clint Eastwood of the little screen.

First Yank into Tokyo ○
(aka: Mask of Fury)
1945, US, 82 mins, b/w
Dir: Gordon Douglas
Stars: Tom Neal, Barbara Hale, Richard Loo
Rating: ★★

RKO cashed in on the end of the war by adding newsreel footage to the end of this spy film, re-shaping its plot to involve the atomic bomb, and extending its running time to bring it up to 'A' feature level. It all looks a bit ludicrous today, save for Richard Loo's considered portrait of the Japanese officer who's quickly on to the fact that the 'oriental' hero (made to look that way with plastic surgeyry) is an American he used to know. The British understandably baulked at the flag-waving title and intelligently called the film *Mask of Fury*.

Fish Called Wanda, A ● Ⓥ
1988, UK, 108 mins, colour
Dir: Charles Crichton
Stars: John Cleese, Jamie Lee Curtis, Kevin Kline, Michael Palin, Tom Georgeson, Maria Aitken
Rating: ★★★

Monty Python meets Ealing comedy when a stuffy London barrister becomes involved with a double-crossing gang of jewel thieves. Writer-star John Cleese plays straight-man to the comic antics of Jamie Lee Curtis's coolly calculating vamp Wanda, Michael Palin's stuttering pet-lover and Oscar-winning Kevin Kline's dim-witted ex-CIA agent. Veteran Ealing director Charles Crichton handles the farce with aplomb and keeps the plot rattling along at a fair lick. Incidentally, there's an in-joke in the name of Cleese's uptight character (and in his status as romantic leading man). It's Archie Leach, the real name of Cary Grant.

Fisher King, The ● Ⓥ
1991, US, 137 mins, colour
Dir: Terry Gilliam
Stars: Robin Williams, Jeff Bridges, Amanda Plummer, Mercedes Ruehl
Rating: ★★★

A stylish and visionary emotional fantasy from director Terry Gilliam, this entwines the sorry life of former cult deejay Jack Lucas (Jeff Bridges) with that of former history professor Parry (Robin Williams) who has become a vagrant in the big city. How these two lost souls discover salvation and the meaning of life through each other

F

makes an excellent lark movie that merges moments of deep melodrama with sudden shafts of happiness. A real treat, with a career-best performance from Mercedes Ruehl as Bridges' girlfriend that won her the Oscar as best supporting actress.

F.I.S.T. ○
1978, US, 145 mins, colour
Dir: Norman Jewison
Stars: Sylvester Stallone, Rod Steiger, Peter Boyle, Melinda Dillon, David Huffman
Rating: ★★★

A sort of trucking version of *The Godfather*, this was one of Sylvester Stallone's first big efforts to strike out on his own after the success of *Rocky*. He co-wrote the screenplay of this turbulent if rather overlong drama, in which he plays an angry young workless man in late 1930s Chicago who becomes involved with thuggery in his efforts to help set up a workers' union. The moral of absolute power corrupting absolutely is a familiar one, but director Norman Jewison finds genuine excitement in the nocturnal clashes between strikers and company men, and real charm in Stallone's courtship of his Lithuanian wife-to-be (the invaluable Melinda Dillon) which recalls his scenes with Talia Shire in *Rocky*.

Fistful of Dollars, A ○ ◐ ⓥ
1964, Italy, 96 mins, colour
Dir: Sergio Leone
Stars: Clint Eastwood, Marianne Koch
Rating: ★★

The impact of the action in this trail-blazing adventure film opened the floodgates for the huge numbers of spaghetti Westerns that made fortunes for their producers in the Sixties and early Seventies. This one made an international star out of Clint Eastwood, up to then best-known for his running role in the TV series *Rawhide*. Eastwood doesn't have a lot to say, but then the most famous Western screen heroes rarely did. Dramatically staged shoot-outs occur on and off throughout a plot that's mainly cribbed from the Japanese samurai action classic *Yojimbo*.

Fistful of Dynamite, A ◐
(aka: Duck You Sucker)
1972, Italy, 150 mins, colour
Dir: Sergio Leone
Stars: Rod Steiger, James Coburn
Rating: ★★★

This wham-bam, rip-roaring adventure yarn set in revolutionary Mexico is lively fun, providing you don't examine the plot too closely and forgive the somewhat eccentric casting (Rod Steiger is a Mexican bandit, James Coburn an Irish explosives expert). In fact the American title of the film, *Duck, You Sucker*, accurately sums up the flavour of this tortilla Western. Sergio Leone, who directed all of Clint Eastwood's classic spaghetti Westerns, is at the helm and there's a much greater sense of broad humour. Steiger and Coburn seem to enjoy themselves immensely, Coburn flashing a devilishly pearly grin that's equal to Burt Lancaster at his best. Fast-moving, noisy action stuff.

Fitzwilly Strikes Back ○
1967, US, 102 mins, colour
Dir: Delbert Mann
Stars: Dick Van Dyke, Barbara Feldon, Edith Evans
Rating: ★★★

Not a sequel, curiously enough, but the very same film that was known in America simply as *Fitzwilly*; Dick Van Dyke is the butler who has to organise a Christmas Eve robbery in order to recue his employer's ailing fortunes. Edith Evans is in splendid dowager form, looking like some Ruritanian Queen Mother who has inadvertently wandered into the staff pantry during celebrations and is now doing her best to pretend that she's not really there at all.

5 Branded Women ○
1960, Italy/US, 106 mins, colour
Dir: Martin Ritt
Stars: Silvana Mangano, Van Heflin, Vera Miles, Barbara Bel Geddes, Jeanne Moreau, Richard Basehart
Rating: ★★

A tough but less than magnetic film about five girl guerillas in Yugoslavia during World War Two. The star line-up of actresses all give strong performances, almost eclipsing their male co-stars. The quintet of branded women (they actually have their hair shaved off for having had relations with Nazi soldiers: and the actresses really had to undergo just that indignity, although they all look rather striking) is completed by Carla Gravina, then only 20, who became a major star in her native Italy. Also from Italy is the fabulous Silvana Mangano, whose international fame dates from 1951. It was then that she

created something of a sensation as a sultry siren of the paddy fields in the film *Bitter Rice*.

Five Angles on Murder
See: The Woman in Question

Five Came Back ○
1939, US, 75 mins, b/w
Dir: John Farrow
Stars: Chester Morris, Lucille Ball, C Aubrey Smith, John Carradine
Rating: ★★★

This film about a small plane load of passengers crashing in South American jungle and threatened by headhunters was an unexpected big success and a boost for the career of its director, John Farrow. Its plot (the writing credits are distinguished to say the least) still carries some suspense, even if the eventual survivors are arranged in highly contrived fashion. Since remade twice – as *Back from Eternity* and *Valley of Mystery*.

Five Card Stud ◐
1968, US, 100 mins, colour
Dir: Henry Hathaway
Stars: Dean Martin, Robert Mitchum, Inger Stevens, Roddy McDowall, Yaphet Kotto
Rating: ★★★

A Western for Agatha Christie fans. Director Henry Hathaway takes a firm grip on the tension from the opening card game, that engenders a lynching, and never lets up – as the card players are killed one by one by a mysterious assassin. Robert Mitchum is perhaps larger than life as a gun-toting preacher, but Dean Martin is extremely good as the reluctant 'hero' and strong supporting work comes from Inger Stevens, Yaphet Kotto and Bill Fletcher. Excellent Technicolor photography ties up a first-rate thriller package.

Five Corners ● ⓥ
1987, US, 93 mins, colour
Dir: Tony Bill
Stars: Jodie Foster, Tim Robbins, Todd Graff, John Turturro, Elizabeth Berridge
Rating: ★

Set in 1964, this oddity could, apart from its four-letter words, have been made then too. The whole enterprise seems old-fashioned, its disparate elements coming across with curiously muffled effect, and its social sentiments getting swamped by a routine plot about the local psycho coming home from the pen and kidnapping the

Bronx belle, given the gamest of tries by Jodie Foster. Not that the plot helps her much: it certainly isn't too likely, for instance, that she would keep an appointment with a homicidal maniac by a deserted swimming-pool at midnight. But then none of the characters here is any too bright. Some of the dialogue is ludicrous, and some plain peculiar, while the supporting acting ranges from the eccentric to the bemused. The two penguins in the plot, though, are nice, and deeply talented.

Five Days One Summer ◑
1982, US, 108 mins, colour
Dir: Fred Zinnemann
Stars: Sean Connery, Betsy Brantley, Lambert Wilson
Rating: ★

The last film to come from the distinguished Austrian-born director Fred Zinnemann boasts superb location cinematography by Giuseppe Rotunno, which adds dimension to the story of the romance in the Alps between middle-aged Scottish doctor Sean Connery and Betsy Brantley, with emotional (and otherwise) intervention by guide Lambert Wilson. Solidly crafted in the tradition of movies from a more leisurely age of movie-making.

Five Easy Pieces ○ ⓥ
1970, US, 98 mins, colour
Dir: Bob Rafelson
Stars: Jack Nicholson, Susan Anspach, Karen Black
Rating: ★★★

Cult study of American alienation and one of the few US films to explore the question of class distinctions. Brilliantly acted by Jack Nicholson as the self-tormenting drifter who's in flight from middle-class rectitude and responsibility. 'I move around a lot,' he tells his paralysed father, 'not because I'm looking for anything but to get away from things that go bad if I stay. Auspicious beginnings.' The film earned Academy Award nominations for Best Film, Script (Adrien Joyce), Actor (Nicholson) and Actress (Karen Black).

Five Finger Exercise ○
1962, US, 109 mins, b/w
Dir: Daniel Mann
Stars: Rosalind Russell, Jack Hawkins, Maximilian Schell, Richard Beymer
Rating: ★★

Emotionally charged drama, based on Peter Shaffer's successful play, about a warring family for whom a young German tutor acts as an explosive catalyst. Director Daniel Mann came to films from Broadway, and was responsible for both stage and screen versions of *Come Back Little Sheba* and *The Rose Tattoo*. By way of contrast his later films included the shocker *Willard*.

Five Fingers ○
1952, US, 105 mins, b/w
Dir: Joseph L Mankiewicz
Stars: James Mason, Danielle Darrieux, Michael Rennie
Rating: ★★★

A thriller that's as smooth and steely as James Mason's central performance as the embassy valet who stole Allied secrets for the Nazis. Director Joseph L Mankiewicz masterminds the documentary approach that had already distinguished a number of Fox realist thrillers in post-war years. The result is a tension-filled winner all the way.

Five Golden Hours ○
1960, UK/Italy, 90 mins, b/w
Dir: Mario Zampi
Stars: Ernie Kovacs, Cyd Charisse, George Sanders, Kay Hammond
Rating: ★★

Off-beat but clumsy comedy about a professional mourner and con-man who has the wool pulled over his eyes by a beautiful widow. Watch for the captivating Kay Hammond, star of *Blithe Spirit*.

Five Graves to Cairo ○
1943, US, 96 mins, b/w
Dir: Billy Wilder
Stars: Franchot Tone, Erich von Stroheim, Anne Baxter, Akim Tamiroff
Rating: ★★★

This highly successful wartime adventure gave Erich von Stroheim one of his most famous roles (as Rommel) and confirmed Austrian-born Billy Wilder's standing in Hollywood following his initial success there the previous year with *The Major and the Minor*. He also collaborated on the script with Charles Brackett, which was based on a play by Lajos Biro.

Five Heartbeats, The ● ⓥ
1991, US, 120 mins, colour
Dir: Robert Townsend
Stars: Michael Wright, Harry J Lennix, Leon, Robert Townsend, Tico Wells,

Diahann Carroll
Rating: ★★

Although it makes a change from today's black crime movies, this is a long and sometimes incoherent account of the rise and fall of a black pop group, which starts up in 1965. A good-looking film, it charts the group's progression from small-time to big-time, along the way falling into the clutches of a shady shark who owns a record company, and losing the lead singer to a combination of drugs and booze. Besides overlength, the film suffers from the fact that its leading characters (and their women) are insufficiently defined – apart from its lyricist, played by Robert Townsend, who also directed the film. Chuck Patterson is good as the manager and it's nice to see Diahann Carroll again as his wife, as well as Harold Nicholas, once of the dazzling dancing Nicholas Brothers, as the group's aged choreographer.

Five Million Miles to Earth
See: Quatermass and the Pit

Five Pennies, The ○
1957, US, 117 mins, colour
Dir: Melville Shavelson
Stars: Danny Kaye, Barbara Bel Geddes, Louis Armstrong
Rating: ★★★

Danny Kaye tackles something akin to a straight acting role in this sentimentalised tribute to jazzman Red Nichols, whose traumatic private life was a natural for Hollywood treatment. Barbara Bel Geddes gives sympathetic support as Nichols' wife and several jazz greats are also in the film, including Louis Armstrong, whose duets with Kaye are the highspots of the film.

Five Star Final ○
1931, US, 89 mins, b/w
Dir: Mervyn LeRoy
Stars: Edward G Robinson, Marian Marsh, H B Warner, Aline MacMahon, Boris Karloff
Rating: ★★★

A scathing indictment of sensationalist journalism that pulls no punches on its way to an uncompromising ending. Edward G Robinson, who had just scored his first big film success with *Little Caesar*, creates a real character as a fast-talking big city editor. He gets strong support from Aline MacMahon, as a staunch secretary, and Boris Karloff, as an odious unfrocked min-

F

ister who now wheedles his way into people's confidence to get scandal material for the paper. Preview audiences found Karloff's character, T Vernon Isopod, so effectively repulsive that they complained about his being allowed to live!

Five Steps to Danger ○
1955, US, 80 mins, colour
Dir: Henry S Kesler
Stars: Sterling Hayden, Ruth Roman
Rating: ★★

Made towards the end of the Communist spy-scare era in America, this well-knit drama dwells less on the Red Menace than its predecessors, and more on action, suspense and intrigue. Ruth Roman and Sterling Hayden keep the plot moving well along its well-worn but very twisting road. And Werner Klemperer – later the familiar Colonel Klink from *Hogan's Heroes* – gives a good study in villainy, in the days before he was known as a funny-man. The story is a tangle of Hitchcockian proportions.

5,000 Fingers of Dr T, The ⊙
1953, US, 88 mins, colour
Dir: Roy Rowland
Stars: Hans Conried, Tommy Rettig, Peter Lind Hayes, Mary Healy
Rating: ★★★

A wild fantasy musical, so far ahead of its time that the distributors completely mishandled it, making it a flop at the box-office. The fingers in the title belong to the 500 boys imprisoned in the castle of the fiendish Dr T, condemned to play 500 pianos to eternity. Amazing Technicolor photography by Franz Planer, some pleasant songs and a 'dungeon ballet' that's a gem of imaginative thought and execution. Eccentric character star Hans Conried has himself a ball as Dr T, the piano teacher who becomes the subject of the youthful hero's nightmare visions. Conceived and part-written by the noted children's author Dr Seuss, the film was originally available in wide screen and stereophonic sound, unusual for its time.

Five Weeks in a Balloon ⊙
1962, US, 101 mins, colour
Dir: Irwin Allen
Stars: Red Buttons, Peter Lorre, Barbara Eden, Cedric Hardwicke, Fabian, Richard Haydn
Rating: ★★

Based on a novel by Jules Verne, this is a colourful, star-studded adventure story about a balloon expedition to Africa in the 19th century. Director and co-writer Irwin Allen's treatment is deliberately comic and fills the old vehicle with enough laughing gas to lift it clear off the ground. Children can goggle while adults giggle, and both will enjoy the antics of the balloon and of a chimp called Duchess, as well as Peter Lorre's throwaway line in sinister jokes, and plump Billy Gilbert's apoplectic slapstick. De Luxe colour never looked better than under the skilful hands of Oscar-winning cameraman Winton C Hoch.

Fixed Bayonets! ○
1951, US, 93 mins, b/w
Dir: Samuel Fuller
Stars: Richard Basehart, Gene Evans, Michael O'Shea, Richard Hylton
Rating: ★★★

Another in a long line of gritty war films directed by Samuel Fuller, running through 30 years from *Steel Helmet* to *The Big Red One*. Fuller's handling of the situation where a platoon is pinned down in a cave brings little relief from the pressures they are under, dispenses almost entirely with humour, and concentrates on the stress, mental and physical, that the soldiers face. Good performances from a cast headed by Richard Basehart, Gene Evans and Michael O'Shea. James Dean has a tiny role.

Flame and the Arrow, The ○
1950, US, 88 mins, colour
Dir: Jacques Tourneur
Stars: Burt Lancaster, Virginia Mayo, Robert Douglas
Rating: ★★★★

This brilliant adventure film established Burt Lancaster as the natural successor to Errol Flynn in Warner Brothers' swashbucklers. It also strengthened his credentials as a leading man and not just another tough guy; from then on he began to get a much wider range of roles. Recouping several times its original cost to the surprise of the studio (it was the 11th biggest grossing film in the world for the year), the film found underrated director Jacques Tourneur re-using sets from Flynn's *Adventures of Don Juan* in a joyous and action-filled story of derring-do in medieval Lombardy. Lancaster, teamed with his ex-circus partner Nick Cravat, does almost all his own stunts. As handy with a sword as with an arrow, Lancaster is here,

there and everywhere; Britain's Robert Douglas, once a national fencing champion, provides handsome, personable villainy.

Flame in the Streets ○
1961, UK, 93 mins, colour
Dir: Roy Baker
Stars: John Mills, Sylvia Sims
Rating: ★★★

Ted Willis wrote this sincere early screen look at the colour problem with the versatile John Mills as the 'liberal' unionist who finds his values called into question when his daughter falls for a coloured boy. There's an exciting Guy Fawkes night climax.

Flame of Araby ○
1951, US, 77 mins, colour
Dir: Charles Lamont
Stars: Jeff Chandler, Maureen O'Hara, Richard Egan, Susan Cabot
Rating: ★★

At one time, Universal was a studio quite noted for its Eastern or Oriental action-adventure extravaganzas. This one was made at a time when the grey-haired Jeff Chandler had won considerable popularity. And what better co-star could there have been than the fiery, red-haired Maureen O'Hara, one of the best swashbuckleresses in the business.

Flame of the Barbary Coast ○
1945, US, 97 mins, b/w
Dir: Joseph Kane
Stars: John Wayne, Ann Dvorak
Rating: ★★

A standard Republic 'gambling saloon' Western. The studio at least gave their regular action man, John Wayne, a decent leading lady in spitfire Ann Dvorak, and threw in the San Francisco earthquake for good measure. But an uncharacteristically slack script by Borden Chase hurts the film's efforts in other departments. A good supporting cast includes Virginia Grey, Joseph Schildkraut, William Frawley, Adele Mara (on her way up at the studio), Paul Fix and Marc Lawrence.

Flame Over India
See: North West Frontier

Flaming Feather ○
1951, US, 77 mins, colour
Dir: Ray Enright
Stars: Sterling Hayden, Forrest Tucker, Barbara Rush, Richard Arlen, Victory Jory
Rating: ★★

A lively Technicolor Western directed by Ray Enright, a man who knew Hollywood from top to bottom. He started in the early silent days as a Sennett gagman, then became an editor and finally director, one of his first assignments being a whole clutch of Rin Tin Tin silent shorts.

Flaming Star ○ ⓥ
1960, US, 92 mins, colour
Dir: Don Siegel
Stars: Elvis Presley, Steve Forrest, Barbara Eden, Dolores Del Rio
Rating: ★★★

Certainly a candidate for Elvis Presley's best film, virtually songless and made a couple of years before his film career started to slide into interchangeable milk-and-water musicals. A Western with echoes of classic tragedy, it's drivingly well directed by Don Siegel, who achieves some scenes of great beauty and others of stunning excitement, the two elements combining in the initial attack by Indians on a farmhouse. For once, the frontier land looks vast, rugged and just as it should.

Flashback ●
1990, US, 105 mins, colour
Dir: Franco Amurri
Stars: Dennis Hopper, Kiefer Sutherland
Rating: ★★

Flawed but underrated action comedy which works extremely well for the first hour but then begins to go off the rails. Until then, though, there are some sparkling exchanges of dialogue between Dennis Hopper as the ex-hippie hero now being escorted to justice and Kiefer Sutherland, as his young FBI captor. Hopper gently guys his own image, and Sutherland is in particularly sharp form at the beginning of the story: scenes between them on a train are the best in the film. There are also some nice comic moments later on, notably a sequence involving a Christmas tree. Once Sutherland's own hippie background comes into play, though, the film is never the same force.

Flashdance ◐ ⓥ
1983, US, 96 mins, colour
Dir: Adrian Lyne
Stars: Jennifer Beals, Michael Nouri, Lilia Skala
Rating: ★★

With a soundtrack that sounds like a *Fame* sequel, a stream of tough dialogue, sensational disco choreography

and a story about a girl who's a welder by day and a club dancer by night, this film rang the bell with the hardcore teen trade in a big way in spite of its absurdities. How unlikely that Jennifer Beals' boyfriend would anonymously arrange for her dreamed-of ballet audition, and then spill the beans! Then the whole thing is about half as close to life as *Saturday Night Fever*, but it has toe-tapping music and some emotive moments, like the impossibly happy ending, that work in spite of everything.

Flash Gordon ○ ⓥ
1980, US, 115 mins, colour
Dir: Michael Hodges
Stars: Sam J Jones, Melody Anderson, Topol, Max Von Sydow, Brian Blessed
Rating: ★★

Everything about this lavish film version of Alex Raymond's 1930s' comic strip is OTT, but especially Danilo Donati's impressive sets and a pounding rock score by Queen. Former American footballer and Playgirl magazine centrefold Sam J Jones is a rather bland Flash, but Max Von Sydow relishes every moment of his role as Ming the Merciless, plotting nothing less than world domination. Among the wealth of British talent in the supporting roles, look out for Robbie Coltrane (in his first feature film) as a man at the airport.

Flashpoint ◐ ⓥ
1985, US, 94 mins, colour
Dir: William Tannen
Stars: Kris Kristofferson, Treat Williams, Rip Torn, Tess Harper, Kevin Conway
Rating: ★

This action film with a vein of mystery threatens early on to settle down into being a lively thriller, but never really follows through. The source of the $800,000 found on a 20-year-dead corpse by two border patrolmen (Kris Kristofferson, Treat Williams) is fairly obvious from the beginning, but the film spells it out for you at the end in case you missed it. Tess Harper is, as usual, wasted, while Rip Torn overacts grindingly as the senior patrolman who helps our heroes in their investigations. William Tannen's direction is too flat to be much help, but then he doesn't have a lot to work on from the start.

Flatliners ● ⓥ
1990, US, 114 mins, colour
Dir: Joel Schumacher

Stars: Kiefer Sutherland, Julia Roberts, Kevin Bacon, William Baldwin, Oliver Platt, Kimberly Scott
Rating: ★★

Don't expect to learn too much about life after death from this horror-ish story of a quintet of medical students who take it in turns to stay 'dead' for as long as possible. Despite the stylish presentation, starry cast and two-hour running time, the result is a pile of old cobblers that will remind old-time film buffs and late horror show fans of some of those doomed medical ventures of the black and white Forties when zombies walked and ghoulies talked. Contrary to the film's publicity about the visions of briefly-dead people brought back to life, what happens to our heroes here is that they are haunted by images from the past, which return in the present. Kiefer Sutherland keeps getting beaten up by a malevolent child, Julia Roberts sees the ghost of her father who shot himself, William Baldwin is pursued by visions of the girls he videoed while making love to them, Kevin Bacon is taunted by the nine-year-old girl he tormented at school. Despite good performances from the cast, it gets more preposterous by the reel.

Fleet's In, The ○
1942, US, 93 mins, b/w
Dir: Victor Schertzinger
Stars: Dorothy Lamour, William Holden, Eddie Bracken, Betty Hutton
Rating: ★★

Zesty wartime musical with a string of Johnny Mercer hits including 'I Remember You', 'Somebody Else's Moon' and 'Tangerine'. Rather too much of minor dancers, comics and vocalists and not quite enough room for an all-star cast which, besides Dorothy Lamour, William Holden and Eddie Bracken, includes Betty Hutton and Cass Daley, both making bombshell film debuts. Jimmy Dorsey and His Band are also in there fighting for footage.

Flesh and Blood ● ⓥ
1985, US/Holland, 126 mins, colour
Dir: Paul Verhoeven
Stars: Rutger Hauer, Jennifer Jason Leigh, Tom Burlinson, Susan Tyrrell, Brion James, Bruno Kirby
Rating: ★

Pity Rutger Hauer in this 10th century mud and guts epic. I mean, here he is, a medieval rogue, thrown down

F

a castle well up to the neck in contaminated water, fireballs overhead, plague in the courtyard, a vengeful army outside and the only man who can rescue him chained to a wall. And what happens? It starts raining, that's what. At that point, you have to accept that it's one of those days and reach for your glass of Guinness or Hamlet cigar – if you could light it. Never mind, there's heaps of rape and pillage in this hideous but sometimes hilarious visceral variety show, performed with over-the-top relish by its motley cast. The dialogue is packed with clichés and modern anachronisms, and there are even prentensions to *El Cid*-style grandeur among the churning breasts, heaving buttocks and slicing flesh. 'Agnes, are you all right?' bellows her swain, besieging the castle to retrieve her from rascally Rutger's clutches. 'Yes,' shrieks the damsel, jumping up and down. 'Having a good time!'

Flesh and Fantasy ○
1943, US, 94 mins, b/w
Dir: Julien Duvivier
Stars: Edward G Robinson, Charles Boyer, Barbara Stanwyck, Betty Field, Robert Cummings, Thomas Mitchell
Rating: ★★★

A high-class trilogy of macabre tales, directed by Frenchman Julien Duvivier during his enforced wartime stay in Hollywood. The choicest of the trio involves Edward G Robinson as an attorney who scoffs at palmist Thomas Mitchell's prediction that the attorney's about to commit a murder. It's based on Oscar Wilde's classic story *Lord Arthur Savile's Crime*.

Fletch ○ ⓥ
1985, US, 96 mins, colour
Dir: Michael Ritchie
Stars: Chevy Chase, Joe Don Baker, Dana Wheeler-Nicholson, Tim Matheson, Geena Davis
Rating: ★★★★

An exceptionally enjoyable comedy *film noir* for which star Chevy Chase is ideally suited. Scriptwriter Andrew Bergman obviously has a weakness for Bob Hope films and the result of his collaboration with Chase and director Michael Ritchie is a sort of 'My Favourite Reporter', except that Chase's character is no coward, even if he does always seem to be on the spot or on the run. He's supercool reporter Irwin ('Don't call me Irwin') Fletcher; on the trail of a drugs ring, he finds that his comparatively low-profile

seashore hangout is the key to some very big men in drugs trafficking, when one of them hires Fletch the beach bum as an assassin. None of this need be taken any more seriously than in any Hope romp of the Forties, but Chase is ever ready with a wisecrack in the tightest of corners and you'll chuckle happily throughout. Such heavyweight character men as Joe Don Baker, M Emmet Walsh and Richard Libertini play up to the star with a refreshing lack of self-consideration, and you can't miss six-foot actress Geena Davis in one of her earliest roles.

Fletch Lives ○ ⓥ
1989, US, 95 mins, colour
Dir: Michael Ritchie
Stars: Chevy Chase, Julianne Phillips, Hal Holbrook, Cleavon Little, R Lee Ermey
Rating: ★

Much anticipated after the initial success of *Fletch*, this was a dismal disappointment, a lifeless sequel drained of every vital sign. The cliched characters are so cardboardd they could topple over at the touch of a finger, and the plot runs like an indifferent episode of *Moonlighting*. The identity of the villain must be 1989's worst kept secret and dunce's caps will be passed around for failing to pick him out. Chase sleepwalks through it and the occasional flashes of graveyard humour comes across as hearty but forced and laboured and his impersonations are unimpressive. An early scene in which Fletch sings 'Zippedee-Doo-Dah' with cartoon characters is quite endearingly tacky, but it's all downhill from then on.

Flight of the Doves ○
1971, UK, 97 mins, colour
Dir: Ralph Nelson
Stars: Ron Moody, Jack Wild, Dorothy McGuire, Stanley Holloway
Rating: ★★★

After presumably purging his system with *Soldier Blue*, director Ralph Nelson turned his talents completely in the opposie direction with this whimsical Irish fancy about two children (Jack Wild and the tiny, very appealing Helen Raye) searching for their equivalent of the crock of gold at the end of the rainbow. Photographed in pretty, postcard colours by Harry Waxman, the film has a song or two from Dana, and gives Ron Moody full scope for his flair for impersonations as the children's wicked Uncle Hawk.

During the course of the action, Moody turns up as, among other things, an officious police inspector, and an unlikely lady journalist called Heather Marblestone. That bewiskered Irish veteran, Noel Purcell, is an equally unlikely Rabbi. It's pleasant to see the delicate, charming actress Dorothy McGuire again, but rather sad to note her already taking on grandmother roles at the age of 50. Jack Wild, who was the original Artful Dodger in *Oliver!* and then featured in the television series *H R Pufnstuf*, was actually 19 when he made this film, although looking many years younger.

Flight of the Intruder ◑ ⓥ
1991, US, 113 mins, colour
Dir: John Milius
Stars: Danny Glover, Willem Dafoe, Brad Johnson
Rating: ★

'The most boring Vietnam war movie since *The Green Berets*,' said *Variety* of this unpleasant story about bored US pilots. Frustrated by the lack of action during the 1972 peace talks, one of their number decides on a private mission to wipe out the People's Resistance Park in Hanoi. The film's only redeeming feature is the raid itself – a tribute to special effects, model-makers and the generous contribution of the US military: on the ground, though, things look extremely static. Principal roles are played by Danny Glover, as the tough-talking commander, Willem Dafoe as a veteran flier and Brad Johnson as an ace pilot. Rosanna Arquette and Tom Sizemore are also in a good cast: presumably they did all read the script.

Flight of the Navigator ○ ⓥ
1986, US, 89 mins, colour
Dir: Randal Kleiser
Stars: Joey Cramer, Veronica Cartwright, Cliff De Young, Sarah Jessica Parker
Rating: ★★★

An engaging, if minor chunk of science-fantasy from the Disney studio. Despite a promising beginning, with a boy recovering from an accident to find strangers living at his home (could be anything, but in fact he's lost eight years from his life without himself ageing), the film simply can't follow through with enough incident. The boy has been (in 1978) on a mission to a distant planet, one of whose ships now (in 1986) needs his help. This leads the film into a brief section of its greatest charm, as the boy examines the specimens of alien life the spaceship has gathered from various planets, including a moving sludge of mud (with a cold) that eats anything. Parents of teenies should be aware that, despite the original 'U' certificate, the film does contain a sprinkling of mild bad language. More to the point, they may wonder about people (in the film) who let children of eight and 12 wander home through woods in the dark. Max the alien, for those struggling to recognise the voice, is played by Paul Reubens (alias Pee-wee Herman, here acting under the pseudonym of Paul Mall.

Flight of the Phoenix, The ○
1965, US, 149 mins, colour
Dir: Robert Aldrich
Stars: James Stewart, Richard Attenborough
Rating: ★★★

An ingenious variation on the Hollywood plot of the 'plane that crashes in the middle of nowhere'. In a high class acting battle, Richard Attenborough's navigator descended from RAF officer to near-alcoholic, wins the narrowest of points verdict over James Stewart's stubborn, veteran pilot. An outrageous piece of casting against character comes off in Dan Duryea's mincing, bespectacled Standish; and Ian Bannen, too, finds plenty to get his teeth into as a Scots engineer with a rasping wit. A good, entertaining film that packs quite a grip and offers a nail-biting climax.

Flight of the White Stallion
See: Miracle of the White Stallions

Flight to Tangier ○
1953, US, 90 mins, colour
Dir: Charles Marquis Warren
Stars: Joan Fontaine, Jack Palance, Corinne Calvet, Robert Douglas
Rating: ★★

This mystery thriller packed with action features one of the longest chase sequences ever filmed. Art director Hal Pereira is to be congratulated for capturing the sleazy atmosphere of Tangier without ever moving out of Hollywood. He turned the entire Paramount Studio into a facsimile of the city, complete with winding alleys and grubby bars. A pity the stars didn't 'front' his work with more inspired performances.

Flim-Flam Man, The ○
(aka: One Born Every Minute)
1967, US, 115 mins, colour
Dir: Irvin Kershner
Stars: George C Scott, Michael Sarrazin, Sue Lyon
Rating: ★★★★

A crazy character comedy that remains one of the most delightful films George C Scott has ever made. Almost buried under make-up, he's a rascally old con-man called Mordecai who takes an army deserter (Michael Sarrazin) under his wing and makes him his apprentice. Some of their con-tricks together are very funny and there's a marvellous, town-wrecking car chase staged by director Irvin Kershner and his veteran second-unit director Yakima Canutt. The screenplay, which helps the fun fairly whiz along, was provided by British comedy king William Rose (whose credits date back to *Genevieve* and *The Lady Killers*). Here Rose provides choice supporting roles for Harry Morgan and Albert Salmi as the sheriff and his deputy, forever one frustrating step behind the two 'flim-flam' men. Altogether a refreshing and likeable dose of laughter.

Flipper ☉
1963, US, 87 mins, colour
Dir: James B Clark
Stars: Chuck Connors, Luke Halpin
Rating: ★★

This wildlife adventure about a boy and his pet dolphin is highly recommended for young children. The script is intelligent, and director James B Clark has a real feel for the Florida Keys locations, wonderfully well captured in colour.

Flipper and the Pirates ☉
(aka: Flipper's New Adventure)
1964, US, 103 mins, colour
Dir: Leon Benson
Stars: Luke Halpin, Pamela Franklin
Rating: ★★

The second screen adventure of the dolphin who became a superstar of Sixties' television. Small children who liked the first film can here enjoy Flipper defeating a rather harmless trio of convicts who hold a prim English family to ransom. And co-star Luke Halpin seems to be genuinely fond of his dolphin friend, which will add to the realism of the thing for youngsters. Quite a few well-known people are involved in the escapade, with Helen Cherry giving it rather

better acting than it deserves as the children's mother. No doubt she, like the rest of the cast, had a great time shooting the movie in the sunshine and blue seas of the Bahamas. As for Flipper himself, he's acquired one or two new tricks – like butting his enemies in the midriff to knock them cold.

Flipper's New Adventure
See: Flipper and the Pirates

Floods of Fear ○
1958, UK, 84 mins, b/w
Dir: Charles Crichton
Stars: Howard Keel, Anne Heywood, Cyril Cusack, Harry H Corbett
Rating: ★★

Singer Howard Keel came to Britain after a run of Hollywood musicals to play a strong straight role as an escaped convict in this rugged and uncompromising thriller. Director Charles Crichton charges his atmosphere with latent violence as two prisoners and a warder in charge of them are trapped by floods at an isolated house whose only other occupant is an attractive woman. Characters are drawn with bold, sharply-defined lines (Crichton himself wrote the screenplay, from a novel by John and Ward Hopkins) and the forthright portraits of the star quartet grip audience attention throughout the film. The distinguished Irish character actor Cyril Cusack is cast as Keel's fellow convict and Harry H Corbett plays it straight in the role of the warder in charge of them.

Florian ○
1940, US, 91 mins, b/w
Dir: Edwin L Marin
Stars: Robert Young, Helen Gilbert, Charles Coburn, Lee Bowman
Rating: ★★

If you saw *Miracle of the White Stallions*, then you'll know all about the famous white Lipizzan horses from the Spanish riding stables in Vienna. Florian is one of those, a regal stallion of first-rate intelligence who virtually has to carry this whole film on his broad white shoulders. Ballerina Irina Baronova is the only other member of the cast to really get a look in. Despite her brilliant dancing, and the presence of co-stars Robert Young and Charles Coburn, it's Florian's show.

Flowers in the Attic ● Ⓥ
1987, US, 92 mins, colour
Dir: Jeffrey Bloom

F

Stars: Louise Fletcher, Victoria Tennant, Kristy Swanson, Jeb Stuart Adams
Rating: RB

Author Virginia Andrews must have spun around on her royalties at the sight of what the cinema had done to her bestselling book. Writer-director Jeffrey Bloom has turned her engrossing chiller (based on fact) into something that seems utterly preposterous. Bloom's flat, flairless direction and the poor performances he extracts from his players, together with his own hysterical script, ensure that giggles of derision far outweigh any suspense from the first reel onwards. Even as Victorian melodrama along *East Lynne* lines, you would be hard put to swallow this tale of four children, impoverished by their father's death, who are taken by their mother (Victoria Tennant) to the mansion of her invalid father and vengeful mother, religious fanatics bent on rooting out evil even where none exists. Lashed unmercifully in one of the film's more ludicrous sequences, the weak-willed mother (the man she married was technically her uncle) is soon indoctrinated into the ways of the house, whose inheritance she hopes will be restored to her, while her 'tainted' children are locked away in an attic lest grandad should get to know of them. Character names like Corrine, Bart and Cory hardly add to the quickly-disintergrating reality of the whole miserable enterprise.

Fly, The ● ⓥ
1958, US, 95 mins, colour
Dir: Kurt Neumann
Stars: David Hedison, Patricia Owens, Herbert Marshall, Vincent Price
Rating: ★★★

Despite the fact that the premise for this film is patently ridiculous (and indeed biologically impossible), it's fun and frightening in equal measure. Scientist Andre (Al Hedison) invents a matter transfer machine, but when he personally test drives it, a fly gets trapped in the chamber with him. At the other end, he comes out with an enormous fly's head, and the fly has his. Patricia Owens as his wife and Vincent Price as his brother deal with the problem in their own ways (say no more!). Gleefully gruesome, this film has become something of a cult classic. Even the superior remake starring Jeff Goldblum hasn't diminished the original's curious appeal.

Fly, The ● ⓥ
1986, US, 100 mins, colour
Dir: David Cronenberg
Stars: Jeff Goldblum, Geena Davis, John Getz, Joy Boushel
Rating: ★★★

Although its horrors get rather too much to take towards the end, this is an immensely superior remake of the 1958 horror classic about a scientist who tries to transport human matter from one machine to another, but gets his genes mixed with those of a fly accidentally locked in the teleportation machine with him. In his finest screen performance, Jeff Goldblum creates one of the most pitiable figures of the horror genre since Boris Karloff's creature in the Frankenstein films, even upstaging the Oscar-winning makeup effects by Chris Walas and Stephan Dupuis. Geena Davis, who was soon to be Mrs Goldblum for a while, is excellent as the reporter he falls for, one of several characters who engage our emotions by seeming to be real people. Well worth a look, this, even if you have to peep through your fingers at times to see it.

Fly II, The ● ⓥ
1989, US, 105 mins, colour
Dir: Chris Walas
Stars: Eric Stoltz, Daphne Zuniga, John Getz
Rating: ★★

A jolly cauldron of fly vomit and no mistake. The script – especially one unintentionally funny scene – is nowhere near the calibre of its ancestor, but this horror film does have some touching moments, lots of action and excitement and a passable stag-beetle monster, which is what you get if you cross a man and a fly. Eric Stoltz follows up his malformed teenager in *Mask* with another heavy-duty makeup job.

Flying Deuces, The ☉
1939, US, 67 mins, b/w
Dir: Edward Sutherland
Stars: Oliver Hardy, Stan Laurel, Jean Parker
Rating: ★★★

Laurel and Hardy return to the Foreign Legion, where they scored such a success in an earlier film *Beau Chumps*. They even have the same actor, Charles Middleton, playing the fort commander. And there's another of their charming song-and-dance num-

bers, this time joining the fort band in a rendition of 'Shine On, Harvest Moon'.

Flying Down to Rio ○ ⓥ
1933, US, 85 mins, b/w
Dir: Thornton Freeland
Stars: Dolores Del Rio, Gene Raymond, Raul Roulien, Fred Astaire, Ginger Rogers
Rating: ★★★

With this musical Fred Astaire and Ginger Rogers set RKO back on the road to solvency. It was their first screen teaming, and the result was pure Hollywood magic, packed with extraordinary dance numbers and unforgettable tunes. Bland Gene Raymond and exotic Dolores Del Rio were the nominal stars, but the public mainly flocked to see Astaire and Rogers doing the carioca. Everything about the production was lavish, from its stunning art deco sets to its armies of chorus girls, sometimes even on the wings of planes!

Flying Leathernecks ○ ⓥ
1951, US, 102 mins, colour
Dir: Nicholas Ray
Stars: John Wayne, Robert Ryan, Don Taylor, Janis Carter
Rating: ★★

A Howard Hughes war spectacular, made with the co-operation of the US Marines, which probably accounts for the brilliance of the photography of the Guadalcanal aerial dogfights, superbly captured in sharp bright Technicolor which today's colour processors never seem able to reproduce. John Wayne and Robert Ryan are the officers whose inevitable feud ranges from the wartime Pacific to peacetime America, and grizzled veteran Jay C Flippen provides stalwart support.

Flying Tigers ○ ⓥ
1942, US, 100 mins, b/w
Dir: David Miller
Stars: John Wayne, John Carroll, Anna Lee
Rating: ★★★

Rousing wartime propaganda that helped bolster the American spirit. It was the Republic studio's salute to the all-American Volunteer Group flying for China and Chiang Kai-Shek (long before Pearl Harbor) who received $500 for every Japanese plane shot down. John Wayne, in the first of his many war films, is the leader of one squadron of carefree pilots, and he displays a soft heart beneath the tough, blustering exterior. Virtually a straight lift from the story of Howard Hawks' *Only Angels Have Wings*, the film displays all the clichés that were becoming commonplace in Hollywood aerial combat films, including frequent shots of Japanese pilots dying horrible deaths in graphic close-up, bullets smashing through the canopies of their planes, and exploding in their faces, blood pouring from their mouths and eyes. It was left to Willie Fung, as Jim, the Chinese waiter who refuses to eat so-called Chinese food, to provide much-needed laughs in an otherwise grim drama.

Fog, The ● Ⓥ
1979, US, 90 mins, colour
Dir: John Carpenter
Stars: Adrienne Barbeau, Hal Holbrook, Janet Leigh, Jamie Lee Curtis
Rating: ★★

A splendid idea for a horror film turns out, in this treatment, to be ripe old sub-Roger Corman hokum about long-dead leper seamen returning to avenge themselves on the town that robbed them of their gold these 100 years before. The approach is very obvious, crushing the inventive theme beneath a ship load of standard horror cliches. But the ladies, Adrienne Barbeau, Jamie Lee Curtis and Janet Leigh, are all worth watching.

Fog Over Frisco ○
1934, US, 68 mins, b/w
Dir: William Dieterle
Stars: Bette Davis, Donald Woods, Margaret Lindsay, Lyle Talbot
Rating: ★★

Never mind the complex plot, which crams incident upon incident into the short running time. What makes this thriller a real treat is William Dieterle's frenetically fast direction which employs just about every trick in the cinematic book – dissolves, wipes and fades and the kind of editing that makes Richard Lester look like a sleepwalker. If there had been an Oscar for sheer speed, Dieterle would have won, hands down.

Folks! ● Ⓥ
1992, US, 109 mins, colour
Dir: Ted Kotcheff
Stars: Tom Selleck, Don Ameche, Anne Jackson, Michael Murphy, Christine Ebersole
Rating: ★

Tom Selleck's film career took a nosedive here; nor is it the kind of sign-off Don Ameche would have wished in films. Comedies come no blacker or battier (and not much worse, either) than this tale of the chaos caused when hapless Jon (Selleck) invites his parents to live with him because his father (Ameche) is suffering from senile dementia. Everyone suffers from then on, the audience especially, as, in the first half of the film, Selleck loses various parts of his anatomy to an assortment of slapstick accidents. The second half features Selleck trying to find ways to end the lives of his parents, at their request. Euthanasia would be a good solution to the whole film, a totally tasteless frolic that may invoke a few uncomfortable giggles.

Follow a Star ○
1959, UK, 103 mins, b/w
Dir: Robert Asher
Stars: Norman Wisdom, June Laverick
Rating: ★★

This Norman Wisdom comedy is on the maudlin side, with the unnecessary addition of a handicapped girlfriend for the star. But the supporting cast is one to treasure, with Jerry Desmonde, Richard Wattis, Charles Gray, Dick Emery and John Le Mesurier in its ranks. The main theme is more or less borrowed from *Singin' in the Rain*.

Follow Me, Boys! ☉
1966, US, 130 mins, colour
Dir: Norman Tokar
Stars: Fred MacMurray, Vera Miles, Lillian Gish, Charlie Ruggles
Rating: ★★★

This Disney saga doesn't dazzle you with cleverness; it has moments when charm tips over into nausea and it slows towards the end. Yet this was one of the nicest films of its year. With no megastar names and a spin-out piece of Americana to work with, the set-up can't have looked promising. Yet the actors rise to the occasion, the direction (by Norman Tokar) is care itself, the small-town atmosphere is never lost, and the corn becomes sweet, warm and human. Fred MacMurray, a tower of acting quality here, gives one of his best performances as the footloose musician who drops off at a tiny mid-West town because he has an eye for the banker's daughter (Vera Miles) and stays not only to marry her, but becomes the town's first scoutmaster and, of course, one of its best-loved

citizens. Miss Miles, as the wife who can't have children, washes away years of playing drab heroines. And Tokar sparks the film's slower second half with a couple of fine, throat-lumping scenes, including one in which MacMurray, who has always wanted to be a lawyer, defends an elderly lady (Lillian Gish) on a charge of insanity.

Follow That Dream ○ Ⓥ
1962, US, 105 mins, colour
Dir: Gordon Douglas
Stars: Elvis Presley, Anne Helm, Arthur O'Connell, Joanna Moore
Rating: ★★★

One of Elvis Presley's brightest films, this is an amusing comedy about a family of hillbillies. Tuneful songs, too.

Follow That Horse! ○
1959, UK, 80 mins, b/w
Dir: Alan Bromly
Stars: David Tomlinson, Mary Peach, Cecil Parker
Rating: ★★

A chance to savour one of the last of David Tomlinson's famous silly-ass characterisations for the cinema, here as a civil servant on the trail of a horse that has swallowed a top-secret micro-film. And there's also an opportunity to admire the permanently perplexed Cecil Parker

Follow the Fleet ○
1936, US, 110 mins, b/w
Dir: Mark Sandrich
Stars: Fred Astaire, Ginger Rogers, Randolph Scott, Harriet Hilliard, Betty Grable
Rating: ★★

A much overrated Fred Astaire musical, a couple of notches below *Top Hat* which it followed for RKO. Astaire and Ginger Rogers dance up a storm but Randolph Scott and Harriet Hilliard are woefully miscast as the film's comedy stars. Irving Berlin, who loved to write for Astaire more than any other singer, provides the toe-tapping tunes, including the classic 'Let's Face the Music and Dance'. If the plot looks familiar, it is. It first appeared in a 1925 silent film, *Shore Leave*, starring Richard Barthelmess and Dorothy Mackaill, then was dusted off for a 1930 musical, *Hit the Deck*.

Folly to be Wise ○
1952, UK, 91 mins, b/w
Dir: Frank Launder

F

Stars: Alastair Sim, Roland Culver, Elizabeth Allan
Rating: ★★★

The delightful talent of Alastair Sim helps glue together this film version of a James Bridie comedy play. Sim's a chaplain chairing a brains trust that turns into a catalogue of sexual scandal. Some of the other performances are amusing to, with Janet Brown making a rare appearance, and George Cole popping in as guest star.

Food of the Gods, The ◐

1976, US, 88 mins, colour
Dir: Bert I Gordon
Stars: Ida Lupino, Ralph Meeker, Marjoe Gortner, Pamela Franklin
Rating: ★

A pretty messy horror film whose special effects vary from wobbly to excellent as a farmload of monster animals goes on the rampage thanks to the food of the title, originally invented by H G Wells. The dialogue is treasurable for addicts of such late-night fare. 'Giant rats! Awful giant rats,' screeches Ida Lupino, running from her farm. 'But we're looking for Mr Skinner,' says her companion unimpressed. Britain's Pamela Franklin weighs in as the inevitable imperilled heroine. 'Why do you work for me?' asks industrialist Ralph Meeker. 'Well,' she muses, 'jobs for female bacteriologists are just not that easy to find.'

Fool for Love ◐

1985, US, 106 mins, colour
Dir: Robert Altman
Stars: Sam Shepard, Kim Basinger, Harry Dean Stanton, Randy Quaid
Rating: ★

Writer-star Sam Shepard's deliberately enigmatic play still runs like a play, in spite of direction by Robert Altman that alternately opens things out and focuses tightly on the drama. A grubby ranch in the New Mexico desert is run by Harry Dean Stanton, who may be father both to Kim Basinger, who works there, and Sam Shepard, who has come to win her back after past infidelities. Or then again, this may all be just a figment of their imaginations, told by all three to Kim's suitor Randy Quaid. The cast is good – Stanton, in particular, is always worth watching – but the piece itself is slow, symbolic and empty.

Fools of Fortune ◐

1990, UK, 109 mins, colour
Dir: Pat O'Connor
Stars: Mary Elizabeth Mastrantonio, Iain Glen, Julie Christie, Michael Kitchen
Rating: ★★

The Irish countryside is the real star of this historical saga that tends to melodrama. The Irish war of independence is the spark that destroys a family and kindles an unlikely love story. Iain Glenn plays a profoundly tortured soul who seeks retribution on the British army soldiers who murdered his family in rural Ireland. His performance is genuinely moving, as is that of Julie Christie as his mother, who relishes every minute of her descent into depression and alcoholism. American Mary Elizabeth Mastrantonio is a surprising choice as the young English woman who helps Glenn's character through his troubles, but her English accent is impeccable, and certainly far more convincing than when she played Maid Marian to Kevin Costner's *Robin Hood* the following year. The camerawork is top drawer, notably in the slow-motion sepia-coloured opening scenes of a summer high tea in the grounds of the family mansion with everyone dressed to the nines in their crisp, white Sunday best.

Fool's Parade

See: Dynamite Man from Glory Jail

Footlight Parade ○ ⓥ

1933, US, 100 mins, b/w
Dir: Busby Berkeley
Stars: James Cagney, Joan Blondell, Ruby Keeler, Dick Powell, Guy Kibbee
Rating: ★★★★

This James Cagney film is notable for two reason. Not only does it present the usually tough star in light vein, tripping the light fantastic, but it's also one of the best examples of one of those wonderful Warner Brothers musicals with numbers by Busby Berkeley. It has four big production numbers, though, because three of them don't come until the last half-hour. But when they do come, the wait has been worthwhile. The best is the fantastic 'By a Waterfall' in which scores of shapely girls go through their paces (or strokes) in a gigantic swimming pool. Another number, 'Shanghai Lil', gives Cagney the chance to do a dance as a sailor enamoured of an oriental girl (Ruby Keeler). The third, 'Honeymoon Hotel', presents Dick

Powell distracted on his wedding night by a bevy of beautiful brides. *Footlight Parade* was one of many popular films of the Thirties teaming Joan Blondell and Keeler with Powell. Powell and Blondell were later to marry and divorce.

Footlight Serenade ○

1942, US, 80 mins, b/w
Dir: Gregory Ratoff
Stars: Betty Grable, John Payne, Victor Mature, Jane Wyman
Rating: ★★

Victor Mature's third film in a row opposite Betty Grable, which casts him as a boxer making a career in showbiz and her as the chorus girl who takes over from the leading lady and becomes a star. A familiar, cosy musical framework, steered on its predictable but entertaining way by the Russian-born director (and character actor) Gregory Ratoff, who was improbably put in charge of several Fox musicals from the 1942-47 period. A quality supporting cast includes Phil Silvers, June Lang, Jane Wyman and James Gleason. Co-star John Payne is Mature's rival for the Grable attentions. Mysteriously made in black and white, as opposed to the gaudy Technicolor Fox used for most of their Forties' musicals.

Footloose ○ ⓥ

1984, US, 107 mins, colour
Dir: Herbert Ross
Stars: Kevin Bacon, Lori Singer, John Lithgow, Dianne Wiest, Christopher Penn, Sarah Jessica Parker
Rating: ★★

Disco dancing dug back into the rock 'n' roll era for this silly old plot, which runs like a cross between *Saturday Night Fever*, *Rock Around the Clock* and *Rebel Without a Cause*. Actually, the story of the town that bans music goes back 50 years or more, although it wouldn't seem today to have a place outside farce or comic opera. Young Ren (Kevin Bacon) finds himself a rebel without applause when he comes to the 'redneck' town of Boford where the good ol' boys have banned dancing and parties and all that awful teenage stuff. The local preacher (John Lithgow, who tries every which way to make something of the part) breathes fire and brimstone over the local congregation to such an extent that they're soon burning half the books in the local library. 'It's not that we don't talk,' he tells his wife (Dianne Wiest, in another performance that smacks of desperation). 'It's just that people sometimes run out of things to say.' It's hard to believe the average teenager will watch all this without falling about. But the film has a first-class pop soundtrack full of hit numbers, even if, as the storyline suggests, there's very little actual dancing.

Footsteps in the Dark ○
1941, US, 96 mins, b/w
Dir: Lloyd Bacon
Stars: Errol Flynn, Brenda Marshall, Ralph Bellamy, Alan Hale
Rating: ★★

A pretty unusual assignment for Errol Flynn, who's given a break from swashbucklers, as a mystery story writer dabbling in amateur detective work. Director Lloyd Bacon keeps it going nicely and there are scene-stealing supporting roles for Lee Patrick and William Frawley, only two of many familiar Hollywood characters from the period in the cast of this lightweight but polished piece of fun.

Footsteps in the Fog ○
1955, UK, 90 mins, colour
Dir: Arthur Lubin
Stars: Stewart Granger, Jean Simmons, Bill Travers, Belinda Lee
Rating: ★★★

The then-married Grangers returned to England from Hollywood to make this throwback to thrillers of the Thirties and Forties, with characters padding around in the pea-soupers trying to bump each other off. Jean Simmons gets the better of the acting duel as a minx of a maid who blackmails her murdering employer into making her first his housekeeper, then his wife. The Technicolor photography is quite excellent.

For a Few Dollars More ◑
1965, Italy, 130 mins, colour
Dir: Sergio Leone
Stars: Clint Eastwood, Lee Van Cleef, Klaus Kinski
Rating: ★★

The second in Clint Eastwood's alternately violent and ponderous Western trilogy, memorable for the scenes in which he and Lee Van Cleef shoot off each other's hats, and Van Cleef strikes a match on Klaus Kinski's neck.

For Better, For Worse ○
(aka: Cocktails in the Kitchen)
1954, UK, 84 mins, colour
Dir: J Lee Thompson
Stars: Dirk Bogarde, Susan Stephen, Cecil Parker, Dennis Price
Rating: ★★★

Arthur Watkyn's famous stage success has proved successful material for drama societies up and down the land – but still comes up like new in this bright little film version. Delightful performances from both Dirk Bogarde and Susan Stephen as the would-be happy couple, helped by a full compliment of British character comedians, ensure a fistful of chuckles. The simple plotline is packed full of amusing incident in this warm, human and charmingly funny domestic comedy, dressed up as fresh as paint by Guy Green's Eastman Colour camerawork.

Forbidden ○
1932, US, 83 mins, b/w
Dir: Frank Capra
Stars: Barbara Stanwyck, Adolphe Menjou
Rating: ★★

Sensitive, touching performances by Adolphe Menjou and Barbara Stanwyck lift this tragedy-laden romantic drama, more typical of such Thirties' weepies as *Back Street* than the average Frank Capra film. Not that Capra doesn't do a highly professional job on what he himself described as a '99.44% soap opera', especially in an understated scene in which the leading players engage in mock romantic dialogue while wearing Halloween masks.

Forbidden Planet ○ ⓥ
1956, US, 98 mins, colour
Dir: Fred M Wilcox
Stars: Walter Pidgeon, Anne Francis, Leslie Nielsen
Rating: ★★★

A science-fiction thriller that later became a cult classic. The climax is frighteningly well done, Leslie Nielsen keeps a straighter face than in any of his *Naked Gun* comedies, and the film's 'inhuman' star, Robby the Robot, proved so popular that MGM brought him back for a second appearance, in another fantasy, *The Invisible Boy*. Walter Pidgeon and Anne Francis head the human cast.

Force of Arms ○
1951, US, 100 mins, b/w
Dir: Michael Curtiz
Stars: William Holden, Frank Lovejoy, Nancy Olson, Gene Evans
Rating: ★★

Wartime love story enlivened by the injection of some fierce combat scenes. The dour William Holden and the ultra-pretty Nancy Olson were one of the most popular romantic teams of the early Fifties. Paramount had already teamed them three times, and they co-star again in this story of an infantry sergeant who falls in love with a WAC officer.

Force 10 from Navarone ○ ⓥ
1978, UK, 118 mins, colour
Dir: Guy Hamilton
Stars: Robert Shaw, Harrison Ford, Edward Fox, Barbara Bach, Franco Nero, Richard Kiel
Rating: ★★

Those *Guns of Navarone* saboteurs are at it again in this lively adventure film, trying to blow up a dam to stop the Germans 'cutting Yugoslavia in half'. The dialogue's a lot like that example and, with everyone saying 'the place is crawling with Krauts', it could well be a film of 20 years earlier. Still, there's Edward Fox around, doing splendid work as ever-so-British demolitions expert Miller (the part created by David Niven). What an incorrigible scene-stealer the man is! In comparison, Robert Shaw doesn't quite come across with his usual crackling fire, while Harrison Ford seems to be trying to imitate John Wayne. One expects him to shout 'shape up or ship out' at any moment. Barbara Bach and Richard Kiel renew their rivalry from *The Spy Who Loved Me*, with Kiel coming off best. The action and special effects are good enough to satisfy most fans of the genre, but the scriptwriters are the real saboteurs of this expedition.

Foreign Affair, A ○
1948, US, 116 mins, b/w
Dir: Billy Wilder
Stars: Jean Arthur, Marlene Dietrich, John Lund, Millard Mitchell
Rating: ★★★

Amusing Billy Wilder comedy, given a slightly rough edge by its war-torn Berlin backgrounds. Jean Arthur and Marlene Dietrich spar delightfully; John Lund had about his last decent movie role as the man in the middle.

F

As scabrously funny as all the best Wilder comedies (though less vicious than its contemporary reputation) the film also contains some delightful musical interludes, including Jean Arthur's 'Iowa State' song and two from Dietrich entitled 'Black Market' and 'Ruins of Berlin'. Millard Mitchell supplies some spiky wit at the head of the supporting cast.

Foreign Body ●
1986, UK, 111 mins, colour
Dir: Ronald Neame
Stars: Victor Banerjee, Warren Mitchell, Geraldine McEwan, Denis Quilley
Rating: ★

An oddity that unsurprisingly never found its public, this is like a Fifties' comedy caught in a time capsule and whisked three decades on. Victor Banerjee, all Asiatic earnestness, is the ever-smiling Calcutta refugee who comes to England and progresses from bus conductor to bogus Harley Street doctor in a remarkably short time. He becomes wildly successful and pretty girls flock for consultations. There's a lot of non-contact sex of the kind seen in old Norman Wisdom and Dirk Bogarde comedies, and even the old chestnut of boiling milk symbolising Banerjee's rising passion. A beautiful Indian girl called Sinitta Renet who's briefly in the film at the start knocks spots off the English competition (even Amanda Donohoe), who were all presumably numbed by having read a script which contains no laughs at all. However, Ken Howard's music is delightful and the whole prescription would probably have gone down quite well in 1954.

Foreign Correspondent ○
1940, US, 119 mins, b/w
Dir: Alfred Hitchcock
Stars: Joel McCrea, Laraine Day, Herbert Marshall, George Sanders, Edmund Gwenn
Rating: ★★★★

Alfred Hitchcock's plea to America to join the war, under the cover of a thriller about a reporter's bid to smash an espionage ring. It's memorable for the scene in a windmill where Joel McCrea's coat gets caught in moving machinery; Edmund Gwenn as a chillingly matter-of-fact assassin; and the drama of a crashing aeroplane, filmed head-on by the director, who ingeniously put his cameras inside the cabin. There was a transparency screen on the other side and, behind the screen, a huge water tank, which burst

apart (and through the screen, and into the cabin) at the touch of a button. Hitchcock himself makes his usual fleeting guest appearance, but had more trouble with the leading role. The director had at first wanted Gary Cooper to star. But Cooper thought the film 'just a thriller' and turned it down, Joel McCrea making an admirable replacement. Asked about it years later, Cooper was, as usual, candid, laconic and to the point. 'That was a mistake,' he said. 'I should have done it.'

Foreign Intrigue ○
1956, US/Italy, 97 mins, colour
Dir: Sheldon Reynolds
Stars: Robert Mitchum, Genevieve Page, Ingrid Thulin
Rating: ★★★

Strange to find a crime film of the mid-Fifties in colour, although the Eastman Colour photography of Vienna and Stockholm is extremely pleasing. It's a fast-paced thriller with press agent Robert Mitchum forever loping down alleys and shadowy by-ways trying to unravel an espionage mystery well knit together by writer-director Sheldon Reynolds, a radio specialist who only made two or three films. Ingrid Thulin, soon to become one of director Ingmar Bergman's favourite actresses, is seen in an early role as the dishy blonde in love with our lazy-lidded hero.

Foreman Went to France, The ○
(aka: Somewhere in France)
1942, UK, 87 mins, b/w
Dir: Charles Frend
Stars: Clifford Evans, Constance Cummings, Tommy Trinder, Robert Morley, Gordon Jackson
Rating: ★★★

An exciting re-creation of the incredible exploit of a civilian who went to France in 1940 to recover top-secret machinery in danger of falling into the hands of the advancing Germans. Humour, purveyed in the face of adversity by the wisecracking Tommy Trinder, provides a nice balance to the heroic adventures of the 'foreman', portrayed in forthright fashion by Clifford Evans. Based on a real-life character called Melbourne Johns, to whom the film is dedicated.

Forever Amber ○
1947, US, 140 mins, colour
Dir: Otto Preminger

Stars: Linda Darnell, Cornel Wilde, Richard Greene, George Sanders, Jessica Tandy, Ann Revere
Rating: ★★

Hollywood gave this historical melodrama an elaborate treatment, but inevitably bowdlerised Kathleen Winsor's runaway bestseller of sex and swashbuckling, the forerunner of a thousand coffee-table epics in similar vein. Britain's Peggy Cummins was at first picked to play the infamous Amber St Clair, but was later dropped from the film in favour of Hollywood's sultry Linda Darnell.

Forever and a Day ○
1943, US, 104 mins, b/w
Dir: Rene Clair, Edmund Goulding, Cedric Hardwicke, Frank Lloyd, Victor Saville, Robert Stephenson, Herbert Wilcox
Stars: Merle Oberon, Anna Neagle, Ray Milland, Claude Rains, Ida Lupino, Gladys Cooper, C Aubrey Smith
Rating: ★★

More than 100 stars of their day gave their services free for this film, the profit being shared between urgently needed cash for Britain's war effort and America's National Foundation for Infantile Paralysis. No less than 21 famous scriptwriters worked on the film, a blockbuster epic of English family life through 140 years. The tremendous cast includes every British-born actor in Hollywood at the time. One of them was Sir Cedric Hardwicke who shared the directing with six other famous names of the cinema and, in company with Buster Keaton, provides the most joyous scene in the film – a delicious few moments as two plumbers who try to instal a bathtub.

Forever Female ○
1954, US, 94 mins, b/w
Dir: Irving Rapper
Stars: William Holden, Ginger Rogers, Paul Douglas, Pat Crowley
Rating: ★★★

Biting comedy about an ageing actress fighting against both Old Father Time and competition from a young and peppy actress. As the youngster, 20-year-old Pat Crowley offers a sparkling performance in her first film role. Ginger Rogers gives an observant, beautifully calculated portrayal of the doyenne star, and all concerned revel in the acidly witty script by Oscar-winning writers Julius J and Philip G Epstein.

Forever Young ○ ⓥ
1992, US, 102 mins, colour
Dir: Steve Miner
Stars: Mel Gibson, Jamie Lee Curtis,
Isabel Glasser, Elijah Wood
Rating: ★★★

A quintuple handkerchief movie, this
silly but wildly engaging romance
works because Mel Gibson and Isabel
Glasser really do give a feeling of total
love as he roars across the skies testing
new fighter planes in 1939. Before he
can pluck up the courage to propose, a
road accident takes her out of his life
for ever, into a permanent coma. Utterly shattered, Gibson volunteers for a
cryogenic experience, to be frozen for
a year. He wakes up 50 years later,
seemingly no older. Somehow he
catapults out of the clutches of a disbelieving military, and into the life of
a divorcee nurse (Jamie Lee Curtis),
whose son (Elijah Wood) released him
from his ice prison. How Gibson sorts
out Curtis' and Wood's problems as
well as his own (which includes fits in
which he begins to age) make up the
bulk of the story which may provide a
titter or two, and certainly a tear or
two before a finale which may creep
up on you unawares. Swelling music
by Jerry Goldsmith lends further cre-
dence and impetus to the unlikely tale.

For Keeps?
See: Maybe Baby

For Love or Money ○ ⓥ
(aka: The Concierge)
1993, US, 94 mins, colour
Dir: Barry Sonnenfeld
Stars: Michael J Fox, Gabrielle Anwar,
Anthony Higgins
Rating: ★

Black marks to the film that starts off
with a great idea and then ditches it
after the first reel. Michael J Fox is
the concierge (day manager) at a swish
hotel, and he's a wheeler-dealer who
can do anything for anyone. He
bargains outside the premises with
street traders for theatre tickets, and
has his own cut-price shop where
(after he takes his cut) hotel customers
can save hundreds of dollars. There are
dozens of stories to be told here but
unfortunately the film jetisons almost
all of them after the first 15 minutes in
favour of by far the soppiest: Fox,
who's saving all his fat tips to buy his
own hotel, falls for perfume assistant/
singer Gabrielle Anwar, who just
happens to be the mistress of the
heartless shark (Anthony Higgins)
who's agreed to bankroll Fox for the

rest of his hotel. The film then devotes
90% of its running time to the increasingly drippy situation of Fox
organising Anwar and Higgins' love
life while falling ever deeper for the
girl but trying to keep his mind on the
money. Fox is good in his know-it-all
guise but less strong on sincerity.
Higgins is a lightweight substitute for
Alan Rickman and Anwar a disappointing blank who makes Fox's
infatuation against the odds not too
comprehensible.

For Me and My Gal ○
(aka: For Me and My Girl)
1942, US, 104 mins, b/w
Dir: Busby Berkeley
Stars: Judy Garland, Gene Kelly, George
Murphy, Marta Eggert, Richard Quine,
Keenan Wynn
Rating: ★★★

The Harry Palmer who's the central
character in this wartime musical has
nothing to do with Michael Caine,
but did provide a film debut for a
30-year-old Broadway musical star
called Gene Kelly. And what company
he found himself in – Judy Garland,
George Murphy and director Busby
Berkeley. Although the plot of the
film is pure Hollywood cornball, the
public were really grabbed by its
patriotic fervour, and made it a big hit
for MGM, setting Kelly up for a fabulous career at the studio. The songs
come at you in dozens, but among the
more memorable are 'Oh, You
Beautiful Doll', 'After You've Gone',
'Ballin' the Jack' and the Gar-
land-Kelly duet on the title song.

Formula, The ○
1980, US, 115 mins, colour
Dir: John G Avildsen
Stars: George C Scott, Marlon Brando,
Marthe Keller, John Gielgud
Rating: ★★

It's hard to work out what attracted
two actors who were then two of the
world's top stars to appear in a film
whose script is its weakest link. Formula is right, in fact, for this is a
standard high-finance thriller whose
roots cross with those of *Marathon Man*
and countless others where
implications are worldwide and stretch
up to men at the top of skyscrapers,
whose power the hero cannot break.
It starts well as a police investigation
thriller, but the trite screenplay soon
takes its grip. Marlon Brando has to
resort to a weird bag of tricks to
enliven a stereotyped villain who
could have been played by any effi-

cient Hollywood character star. Little
remains of the rest apart from another
limp performance by Marthe Keller
and a series of 'suspicious' minor
characters who are bumped-off in
sequence, presumably for bad acting.
George C Scott's frayed veteran cop is
the strongest element in a film whose
excitements are all too deliberate, and
there's good work too from Calvin
Jung as his Oriental sidekick.

Fort Algiers ○
1953, US, 78 mins, b/w
Dir: Lesley Selander
Stars: Yvonne De Carlo, Carlos
Thompson, Raymond Burr, Leif Erickson
Rating: ★★

This was the action film for which
Yvonne De Carlo brought Argentinian matinee idol Carlos Thompson
to Hollywood. Raymond Burr is a
turbanned villain, and some of the
battle scenes are genuine – fighting
between French Legionnaires and
Arab tribesmen was filmed by a location unit in North Africa.

Fort Apache ○ ⓥ
1947, US, 127 mins, b/w
Dir: John Ford
Stars: John Wayne, Henry Fonda, Shirley
Temple, John Agar, Pedro Armendariz,
Victor McLaglen
Rating: ★★★★

Fort Apache was the first of Ford's unofficial trilogy of Cavalry Westerns –
the others were *She Wore a Yellow
Ribbon* and *Rio Grande*. It possesses all
the sweep, grandeur and action of an
age long past. John Wayne gives one
of his best performances of his long
career.

Fort Apache the Bronx ◐
1981, US, 123 mins, colour
Dir: Daniel Petrie
Stars: Paul Newman, Edward Asner,
Danny Aiello, Ken Wahl, Rachel Ticotin
Rating: ★★

If you had to pick the archetypal, average American cop movie of the
Eighties, this would be a likely candidate. Set your story in a tough
neighbourhood, throw in an assortment of pimps, pushers and hookers,
add a veteran cop and his young partner, toss in the disciplinarian new
chief of the station and a story thread
involving murder and you have the
quintessential formula. The film never
rises above the sum total of those ingredients, although Paul Newman
and Ken Wahl work quite well to-

F

gether as the partners, and Rachel
Ticotin gives an interesting performance as the nurse with whom
Newman becomes involved. The
ending is inevitably part-tragic and
part-hopeful, cut to formula just like
the rest.

Fort Dobbs ○

1958, US, 90 mins, b/w
Dir: Gordon Douglas
Stars: Clint Walker, Virginia Mayo, Brian
Keith, Richard Eyer
Rating: ★★

Clint Walker, of *Cheyenne* fame, gets
into trouble through changing clothes
with another man. Clint is in fine
form in this vigorous Western, looking as gigantic as ever, riding what
appear to be Shetland ponies, rough-
ing it with Indians and white men
alike and winning the heart of Virginia
Mayo.

For the Boys ◐ ⓥ

1991, US, 146 mins, colour
Dir: Mark Rydell
Stars: Bette Midler, James Caan,
George Segal, Patrick O'Neal,
Christopher Rydell, Arye Gross
Rating: ★★

There's too little patter, singing and
dancing in this Bette Milder vehicle
which casts the dynamo dame as an
entertainer who, through her
partnership with another, finds herself
frequently involved in taking part in
shows 'for the boys' at war. It begins
well – the first 30 minutes are hugely
enjoyable – but grows increasingly
heavy as it (and the wars) go on. One
scene in particular, when James Caan
tries to persuade Midler, by now his
ex-partner, to go to Vietnam, is allowed by director Mark Rydell to
ramble on far too long. It might have
been better, in fact, if the scenario had
just been limited to one war, the Second World, which would still have
afforded enough tragedy and reality –
the loss of Midler's husband, the
bloody introduction of the touring
troupe to real war – to spice the mixture up without making it too lumpy.
As it is, the old age make-up that results from making this a 50-year saga
merely makes Caan and Midler (who
never really suggest, on stage, a
legendary partnership) look like
troglodytes. The ending touches the
right emotional chords for audiences
still with the characters after such a
long haul.

For the First Time ○

1959, US, 97 mins, colour
Dir: Rudolph Mate
Stars: Mario Lanza, Johanna von
Koczian, Zsa Zsa Gabor
Rating: ★★

This Mario Lanza extravaganza moves
from mawkish romance through
Technicolor European travelogue to
maudlin sentimentality. He plays a famous tenor who falls in love with a
deaf girl while on the Isle of Capri.
But she won't tie the knot until her
deafness is cured and she can hear him
sing. Mario's fund-raising concert tour
is the excuse for the travelogue bit and
for him to sing a lot of songs – from
operatic arias to one about a
pineapple! The climactic scene where
she hears him singing 'Ave Maria'
surrounded by a chorus of nuns will
either have you dewy-eyed or reaching for the nearest strong brown paper
bag. Sadly for his millions of fans, it
was Lanza's last film. A short while
after this film was completed he died
of a heart attack at the early age of 38.
He could have wished for a better
swan song than this.

For the Love of Benji ☉

1977, US, 84 mins, colour
Dir: Joe Camp
Stars: Peter Bowles, Bridget Armstrong,
Patsy Garrett
Rating: ★★★

More antics with the scruffy canine
who made his debut in *Benji*. This
romp, in which Benji goes to Greece,
was an enormous success in America,
where it grossed over $5 million.
Britain's Peter Bowles and
Hollywood's Ed Nelson (once Dr
Rossi in *Peyton Place*) are among those
being upstaged by our furry friend.

For the Love of Mary ○

1948, US, 90 mins, b/w
Dir: Frederick De Cordova
Stars: Deanna Durbin, Edmond O'Brien,
Don Taylor, Jeffrey Lynn
Rating: ★★

Deanna Durbin's last film, a lightweight romance which casts her as a
White House switchboard operator
whose romantic problems have to be
sorted out by no less than the
President! Songs include 'Moonlight
Bay', 'I'll Take You Home Again
Kathleen', 'On the Wings of a Song'
and 'Let Me Call You Sweetheart'.

For Them That Trespass ○

1949, UK, 95 mins, b/w
Dir: Alberto Cavalcanti
Stars: Richard Todd, Stephen Murray,
Patricia Plunkett
Rating: ★★

Richard Todd and Patricia Plunkett
(playing yet again a girl who tries to
clear a falsely accused man) made their
screen debuts in this gripping movie
drama which has a lot of high feeling
and style, although it is hampered by
some stagey-looking sets, particularly
when the camera moves inside a
'London pub'. Also, the Cockneys are
just a bit too Cockney.

Fort Osage ☉

1952, US, 72 mins, colour
Dir: Lesley Selander
Stars: Rod Cameron, Jane Nigh,
Douglas Kennedy, John Ridgely
Rating: ★★★

Minor but rousing entertainment,
with the West as wild you could wish.
There's a forthright performance in
the lead by Rod Cameron, a loping
six-footer in the Gary Cooper tradition, and a satisfying free-for-all
climax that leaves the sagebrush
carpeted with corpses. A vivid, action-packed adventure in above-par
Cinecolor.

Fortune, The ◐

1974, US, 85 mins, colour
Dir: Mike Nichols
Stars: Stockard Channing, Jack
Nicholson, Warren Beatty
Rating: ★★

It has to be said that the piquant
Stockard Channing deserves the top
billing of this comedy of kidnap and
murder. For her own unforced
clowning is a clear winner over the
heavily stylised performances of her
co-stars. Miss Channing plays a spirited heiress who runs away with a
married rogue (Warren Beatty) and
also becomes involved with his embezzling friend (Jack Nicholson).
Once she has discovered that their
interest in her is more pecuniary than
romantic, the hapless pair start a series
of bungled attempts to bump her off.
The fun that follows really calls for the
snappy treatment of Richard Lester or
the biting wit of Billy Wilder. Mike
Nichols, who made *The Graduate*,
settles for a modern variant on the
screwball comedy films of the Thirties.

Fortune Hunter, The
See: The Outcast

Fortune Is a Woman ○
(aka: She Played with Fire)
1956, UK, 95 mins, b/w
Dir: Sidney Gilliat
Stars: Jack Hawkins, Arlene Dahl,
Dennis Price, Ian Hunter
Rating: ★★★

This Launder-Gilliat thriller really has
the lot: a story in which there's a
chain reaction of blackmail, forgery,
fraud and murder. Good old Jack
Hawkins, as usual, makes you believe
that it's all happening. And Hollywood's Arlene Dahl, coolly enigmatic,
was never better cast. The supporting
cast boasts considerable strength in
depth, with room for Dennis Price,
Christopher Lee, Patrick Holt,
Michael Goodliffe and more.

Fort Worth ○
1951, US, 80 mins, colour
Dir: Edwin L Marin
Stars: Randolph Scott, David Brian,
Phyllis Thaxter
Rating: ★★

Veteran Western star Randolph Scott
once again proves that his characters
are hard men to kill or double-cross in
this bullet-a-minute Western about
outlaws trying to hold up the progress
of a railroad. David Brian is ideally
suited to the role of the hero's friend
who may or may not be on the side of
law and order. Sid Hickox's Technicolor photography is award-worthy on
its own. Director Edwin L Marin
made several attractively structured
Scott Westerns, but died in 1951 aged
only 50.

Forty Carats ○
1973, US, 110 mins, colour
Dir: Milton Katselas
Stars: Liv Ullmann, Edward Albert, Gene
Kelly, Billy 'Green' Bush, Binnie Barnes
Rating: ★

A jaded comedy film from the stage
success by the authors of *Cactus
Flower*. Liv Ullmann, unlike Ingrid
Bergman in the earlier film, has little
talent for this sort of light romantic
romp, and comes a distant fourth in
the female acting stakes, behind Binnie
Barnes (wife of the film's producer,
Mike Frankovich), Nancy Walker
(Mildred from *McMillan and Wife*) and
the sparkling young actress Deborah
Raffin, who has done nothing better
since. Edward Albert, who plays the
young man in love with Liv (hardly

looking the 40-year-old she is
supposed to be) is the son of veteran
character actor Eddie Albert.

48 Hours
See: Went Well the Day

48HRS ● ⓥ
1982, US, 97 mins, colour
Dir: Walter Hill
Stars: Nick Nolte, Eddie Murphy,
Annette O'Toole, Frank McRae, James
Remar
Rating: ★★

Overheated police thriller with some
sensational deep-driving music. It
teams a white redneck cop (Nick
Nolte) with a hip black convict (Eddie
Murphy) in the manhunt for the team
that has blown away two careless policemen. The action has some good
moments, especially towards the end,
and Murphy's swaggering performance
made him a movie megastar.

49th Parallel ○
(aka: The Invaders)
1941, UK, 123 mins, b/w
Dir: Michael Powell
Stars: Leslie Howard, Raymond Massey,
Laurence Olivier, Anton Walbrook, Glynis
Johns, Eric Portman
Rating: ★★

A very patriotic and slightly unreal
war film which was the top money-
maker in British cinemas in 1942.
Michael Powell's direction skilfully
skirts the obvious to create an
out-of-the-rut propaganda thriller.
Leslie Howard, Laurence Olivier, Eric
Portman, Anton Walbrook and Glynis
Johns all do their bit for the war effort,
and there's a forthright, telling performance from Raymond Massey
near the end.

Forty Pounds of Trouble ○
1962, US, 106 mins, colour
Dir: Norman Jewison
Stars: Tony Curtis, Suzanne Pleshette,
Phil Silvers, Stubby Kaye, Kevin
McCarthy
Rating: ★★

This comedy is bright enough and has
a sweet moppet star in Claire Wilcox,
but with all the talent involved and a
director like Norman Jewison, we
might have been entitled to expect
something extra-special. Still, the
casino and Disneyland backgrounds
couldn't be more colourful, and that
cast really is tasty: Tony Curtis,
Suzanne Pleshette, Kevin McCarthy,
Mary Murphy, Stubby Kaye and

funny bits from Larry Storch, Howard
Morris, Edward Andrews and espe-
cially Phil Silvers, on all too briefly as
Curtis' boss at the casino.

42nd Street ◐ ⓥ
1932, US, 86 mins, b/w
Dir: Lloyd Bacon
Stars: Warner Baxter, Bebe Daniels,
George Brent, Ruby Keeler
Rating: ★★★★

The film that totally revived the popularity of the musical, with the
archetypal story of the producer
struggling to put on a show and the
chorus girl who goes out there and
becomes a star when the leading lady
crashes out just before the show. The
action smoothly integrates the story
with the dances (masterminded by
Busby Berkeley) and songs – which
include '42nd Street', 'Shuffle Off to
Buffalo', 'Young and Healthy' and
'You're Getting to be a Habit with
Me'. Ginger Rogers is sheer joy as a
chorus girl with class called Anytime
Annie.

For Whom the Bell Tolls ○
1943, US, 160 mins, colour
Dir: Sam Wood
Stars: Gary Cooper, Ingrid Bergman,
Akim Tamiroff
Rating: ★★★

An effective if not totally memorable
film version of Ernest Hemingway's
adventure set during the Spanish
Civil War. Hemingway himself felt all
along that Gary Cooper and Ingrid
Bergman were the right actors to
portray Jordan and Maria. And when
the film was released the critics reserved special praise for the
performances of Bergman and Katina
Paxinou, who played the guerilla
leader's woman. You can also admire
the rich warmth of the Technicolor
photography, and keep your eyes
peeled for Yvonne De Carlo, who has
a tiny part in a crowd scene.

For Your Eyes Only ○ ⓥ
1981, UK, 127 mins, colour
Dir: John Glen
Stars: Roger Moore, Carole Bouquet,
Topol, Jill Bennett, Lois Maxwell,
Lynn-Holly Johnson
Rating: ★★★

Former editor John Glen, who had
served as second unit director on *On
Her Majesty's Secret Service* and *The Spy
Who Loved Me*, took over direction of
the 12th 007 epic and came up with a
near non-stop series of stunts and

F

smart special effects which rarely gave Roger Moore – or the audience – time to take breath in between bouts of action and suspense. Bernard Lee, who had been Bond's boss 'M' since 1962's *Dr No*, died before his scenes could be filmed, leaving Lois Maxwell as Miss Moneypenny the sole survivor of all 12 movies. Janet Brown and John Wells provide wicked cameos of Margaret and Denis Thatcher.

Foul Play ◐ ⓥ
1978, US, 112 mins, colour
Dir: Colin Higgins
Stars: Goldie Hawn, Chevy Chase, Burgess Meredith, Dudley Moore, Rachel Roberts, Brian Dennehy
Rating: ★★★

Full of delicious absurdities, this is a comedy-thriller in the *Charade* tradition, with wide-eyed Goldie Hawn who plays a librarian (the thought of Goldie as a librarian is amusing in itself) who finds herself pursued across town for no apparent reason by assassins called Stiltskin and Scarface. Television comedian Chevy Chase made his breakthrough to big-time Hollywood stardom in the co-starring role, while Dudley Moore came to the attention of American audiences for the first time as a star comic actor, with his manic portrait of a sex-starved Englishman who can't wait to put his plush 'swinger's apartment' to good use. Of the other actors, only veteran villain Marc Lawrence, looking more like a deadly snake than ever, plays it light enough to catch the mood intended by director Colin Higgins, who also made Gene Wilder's *Silver Streak*.

Four Desperate Men
See: The Siege of Pinchgut

Four Faces West ○
1948, US, 92 mins, b/w
Dir: Alfred E Green
Stars: Joel McCrea, Frances Dee, Charles Bickford
Rating: ★★★

There's another case for Pat Garrett in this Western, just to prove he did something else with his life apart from chasing Billy the Kid all over the landscape. The story, though, is well off the beaten trail, with thoughtful performances from Joel McCrea, Frances Dee (real-life husband and wife), Charles Bickford (as Garrett), Joseph Calleia and, as another sheriff,

William Conrad, already a bulky presence even at this early stage of his career.

Four Feathers, The ○ ⓥ
1939, UK, 130 mins, colour
Dir: Zoltan Korda
Stars: John Clements, Ralph Richardson, C Aubrey Smith, June Duprez
Rating: ★★★★

One of the finest ever British action films, concerning the efforts of a turn-of-the-century Englishman to disprove his cowardice, against a backcloth of Kitchener's war with the Arabs. Magnificent Technicolor photography by Osmond Borrodaile and Georges Perinal and an awe-inspiring performance by Ralph Richardson, as the hero's friend, especially when blinded and lost in the heat of the desert.

Four Feathers, The ○
1978, UK, 95 mins, colour
Dir: Don Sharp
Stars: Beau Bridges, Robert Powell, Jane Seymour
Rating: ★★★

The part of Jack Durrance in A E W Mason's storming saga of action and self-redemption in the heat of North Africa at the turn of the century is traditionally the juciest in this blood-raising story. In 1939 Ralph Richardson eclipsed all other versions of the part in a magnificent performance, and Laurence Harvey's tortured, if less forceful, Durrance stole *Storm Over the Nile*, the routine remake of 1955. So it's no surprise that Robert Powell walks away with the honours in this latest production of the tale. Jane Seymour is excellent as the heroine, her convincing, high-spirited performance besting such past Ethne's as Fay Wray, June Duprez and Mary Ure. And a word of praise, too, for David Robb.

Four for Texas ○
1963, US, 124 mins, colour
Dir: Robert Aldrich
Stars: Frank Sinatra, Dean Martin, Anita Ekberg, Ursula Andress, Charles Bronson, Victor Buono
Rating: ★★

Another contribution from the Frank Sinatra clan, following hard on the heels of *Ocean's Eleven* and *Sergeants Three*. In this lively comedy-Western, sharply shot in Technicolor, Sinatra and Dean Martin play a couple of

lovable crooks who make a last-ditch alliance to defeat even bigger crooks than themselves. The opening scenes are excellent: a stagecoach manned by Sinatra and Martin beats off bandits before crashing spectacularly into the dust. Unfortunately, only the ending comes up to this standard thereafter. Robert Aldrich directs the slight story at tortoise pace, and receives two performances of statuesque immobility from Ursula Andress and Anita Ekberg.

Four Girls in Town ○
1956, US, 85 mins, colour
Dir: Jack Sher
Stars: George Nader, Julie Adams, Marianne Cook, Elsa Martinelli, Gia Scala
Rating: ★★★

This Universal-International vehicle for four of its prettiest starlets provides a fascinating behind-the-scenes look at the studio itself. Of the girls, Marianne Cook (who had to change her name from Koch) provides the warmest personality. Alex North contributes one of his lushest and most melodic scores and the studio's top star, Rock Hudson, pops in to make a guest appearance.

Four Guns to the Border ○
1954, US, 85 mins, colour
Dir: Richard Carlson
Stars: Rory Calhoun, Walter Brennan, Colleen Miller, George Nader, Nina Foch
Rating: ★★★

One of a long series of action-packed double-features made at Universal-International studios in the Fifties – films which made stars out of Rock Hudson, Tony Curtis and Audie Murphy besides the stars of this Western, Rory Calhoun and George Nader. *Four Guns to the Border* was directed by another actor, Richard Carlson. Jay Silverheels, who plays a half-breed outlaw, was better known for his role as Tonto in the long-running *Lone Ranger* series on TV.

Four Jills in a Jeep ○
1944, US, 89 mins, b/w
Dir: William A Seiter
Stars: Carole Landis, Kay Francis, Martha Raye, Mitzi Mayfair, Phil Silvers, Dick Haymes
Rating: ★★

A fascinating look at USO tour groups, through the eyes of four showbiz ladies who actually made such a trip, and made palatable for wartime audiences by 20th Century-Fox presenting the story in the guise of a musical. The girls, including Kay Francis and Martha Raye, play themselves, and there are singing guest appearances by Betty Grable, Alice Faye and Carmen Miranda. Grable sings 'Cuddle Up a Little Closer' with a million GIs just dying for the chance. Black-and-white lends the film a feel of contemporary reality. Despite the star-spangled cast, the studio's usual Technicolor coating for such offerings would have been wrong.

Four Men and a Prayer ○
1938, US, 85 mins, b/w
Dir: John Ford
Stars: Loretta Young, Richard Greene, George Sanders, David Niven, C Aubrey Smith
Rating: ★★

One of John Ford's most vigorous films, this splashy production about four brothers trying to clear their father's name after a massacre in India gave a major movie debut role to a 19-year-old English actor as a raw as his name: Richard Greene. Forthright in the part, alongside such established names as David Niven and George Sanders, Greene went on to a 15-year Hollywood career, before becoming famous the world over as television's *Robin Hood*.

Four Musketeers: The Revenge of Milady, The ○
1974, UK, 105 mins, colour
Dir: Richard Lester
Stars: Oliver Reed, Raquel Welch, Richard Chamberlain, Michael York, Faye Dunaway, Frank Finlay
Rating: ★★★

The fun of *The Three Musketeers* is overturned to reveal the darker, more serious side of the coin in this sequel. But the action is still all dazzling stuff, from an epic sword battle in a nunnery to an eye-stunning duel on ice. Faye Dunaway, as the evil Milady, and Oliver Reed as Athos, playing a more prominent part in the plot in this sequel, are both in dominant form. The sweeping last 15 minutes and the triumphant ending almost make you forget that this is just a notch below the previous film in sheer *joie de vivre*.

Four Seasons, The ○
1981, US, 107 mins, colour
Dir: Alan Alda

Stars: Alan Alda, Carol Burnett, Len Cariou, Sandy Dennis, Rita Moreno, Jack Weston
Rating: ★★

The policy of the Hollywood superstars these days seems to be to alternate the films they really want to make with the movies they do for money. But *The Four Seasons* is a film in which Alan Alda, as star, screen-writer and director, believed in passionately. He must have been overjoyed when the film proved not only a critical success, but also a financial one. It's a comic but credible and lovingly-photographed portrait of three couples who take their holidays together, but who find the artificiality of their companionship cracking when one of the husbands decides on divorce. Though leisurely in development, the film has a certain charm, and Bess Armstrong, as the 'new' wife who proves the very slim end of the wedge, makes a strong impression.

Fourteen Hours ○
1951, US, 92 mins, b/w
Dir: Henry Hathaway
Stars: Paul Douglas, Richard Basehart, Barbara Bel Geddes, Agnes Moorehead, Robert Keith, Debra Paget
Rating: ★★★

Although it rather simplifies the issues at stake, this suspense thriller sustains remarkably well for over 90 minutes its central situation of a man threatening to jump off a ledge on a high building. A formidable cast includes Richard Basehart as the disturbed man, Paul Douglas, Agnes Moorehead (in a typically fierce role), Robert Keith, Barbara Bel Geddes, Debra Paget, Jeffrey Hunter, Howard da Silva, Frank Faylen and – in her screen debut – Grace Kelly.

1492: The Conquest of Paradise ○ ⒱
1992, US/UK/France/Spain, 145 mins, colour
Dir: Ridley Scott
Stars: Gerard Depardieu, Sigourney Weaver, Armand Assante, Frank Langella, Loren Dean, Fernando Rey
Rating: ★★

This was the third of three Christopher Columbus films released in the summer of 1992 to mark the 500th anniversary of the explorer's discovery of America. Although it was definitely a case of saving the best until last, even this spectacularly

mounted version is a deeply flawed film, not least in the way of pacing. Backed by millions of dollars from the Spanish government, it features French superstar Gerard Depardieu, visually in commanding form but mangling the English language a shade too far as Columbus, and director Ridley Scott delivering some stunning action visuals in his own distinctive style. But the acting honours are stolen from all and sundry by Michael Wincott, playing the blackest most sadistic villain seen in a major film for many a long day.

Fourth Protocol, The ○ ⒱
1987, UK, 119 mins, colour
Dir: John Mackenzie
Stars: Michael Caine, Pierce Brosnan, Ned Beatty, Joanna Cassidy, Ray McAnally, Ian Richardson
Rating: ★★

If you're expecting one of those ever-so-grim cold war thrillers where you could rustle a newspaper and miss a vital part of the plot, then go no further. If you like preposterous, well-acted, well-staged espionage yarns with big treatment, then this will be right up your pre-perestroika street. The two central characters are spycatcher Michael Caine and crack KGB officer Pierce Brosnan (once a potential James Bond!). Brosnan is to assemble a nuclear bomb in Britain from parts smuggled through customs (so much for bringing in too many bottles of wine). Caine is out to stop him. Throw in the sultry Joanna Cassidy as a colonel who's never so much as sipped a pink gin, and you're in for an evening of high entertainment. On a critical note, look out for a glaring continuity error (clue: it involves Mr Caine's jackets).

Four Weddings and a Funeral ● ⒱
1993, UK, 117 mins, colour
Dir: Mike Newell
Stars: Hugh Grant, Andie MacDowell, Simon Callow, James Fleet, Corin Redgrave, Rowan Atkinson
Rating: ★★★

A Boulting Brothers comedy brought up to date with bad language – hero Hugh Grant always swears several times in moments of crisis – and enough richly funny lines to sustain us through a rollicking 85 minutes. Unfortunately, the film runs rather more than 30 minutes longer than that, so it's not as uproarious as it might be. A comedy of embarrassments,

F

indiscretions and missed chances, it stars Grant (never better) as a sort of foul-mouthed Bertie Wooster always turning up late for friends' weddings, but avoiding one of his own. His friend Tom (James Fleet) disapproves. 'It worked for my parents,' he says, 'apart from the divorce.' The best of the dialogue here's a bit like that: a seemingly sincere line twisted by an endpiece that makes it funny. And the plot allows room for a funny turn by Rowan Atkinson as an inexperienced priest who refers to the Father, Son and Holy Goat. Grant eventually falls for Andie MacDowell, but finds it hard to break a lifetime habit that means never having to say 'I do' . . . and thereby hangs the rest of the story. Good performances from an enthusiastic cast, especially Simon Callow as a bachelor gay whose life is as vivid as his waistcoats.

Fox, The ●
1968, US, 110 mins, colour
Dir: Mark Rydell
Stars: Anne Heywood, Sandy Dennis, Keir Dullea
Rating: ★★★

Mark Rydell created quite a stir on his directorial debut with this very erotic account of two women living together on a farm, whose lesbian–inclined rapport is shattered by the arrival of a sharp, tough young man. Full of symbolism, with a very strong and sexy performance by Anne Heywood, and outstanding colour photography.

Foxhole in Cairo ○
1960, UK, 80 mins, b/w
Dir: John Moxey
Stars: James Robertson Justice, Adrian Hoven, Peter Van Eyck Albert Lieven, Fenella Fielding
Rating: ★★

British thriller about German agents detailed to get hold of the British plans for the counter-attack in the Libyan desert. Albert Lieven's Rommel is nicely played if underwritten, and Michael Caine makes an early film appearance as Weber.

Fragment of Fear ◐
1971, UK, 95 mins, colour
Dir: Richard C Sarafian
Stars: David Hemmings, Gayle Hunnicutt, Roland Culver, Daniel Massey
Rating: ★★

This psychological thriller is as fascinating a jigsaw puzzle as the screen

has ever presented: only the ending may disappoint you. But David Hemmings is fine as the baffled ex-drug addict hero. And there are enigmatic performances from such distinguished players as Dame Flora Robson, Roland Culver, Arthur Lowe, Yootha Joyce, Daniel Massey, Wilfred Hyde White and Mona Washbourne.

Framed ○
(aka: Paula)
1947, US, 82 mins, b/w
Dir: Richard Wallace
Stars: Glenn Ford, Janis Carter, Barry Sullivan
Rating: ★★★

Glacial blonde Janis Carter was always at her best as cool, calculating charmers, and here is one of her most deadly. Paula (her character) was also the British title of the film, and Miss Carter certainly holds centre stage in a magnetic portrayal of a girl whose goal is money and who certainly wouldn't dream of not casually murdering anyone who stood in her way.

Frances ● ⓥ
1982, US, 140 mins, colour
Dir: Graeme Clifford
Stars: Jessica Lange, Kim Stanley, Sam Shepard
Rating: ★★★

This is a grim and unrelenting biopic of beautiful Hollywood star Frances Farmer, all the more distressing because the horrific incidents featured are true. Jessica Lange really suffers in the title role, getting drunk, being raped and assaulted in a mental hospital (where she's been committed by her hateful, overbearing mother), and finally ending up undergoing a brain operation that ruins her life for ever. Not exactly a jolly night's entertainment, but a solidly crafted drama all the same. Veteran actor John Randolph has a small role as a judge. He scored a big success three years later as Jack Nicholson's Mafia father in *Prizzi's Honor*. Look fast for Kevin Costner as a character in an alley. He has one line.

Francis ☉
1950, US, 90 mins, b/w
Dir: Arthur Lubin
Stars: Donald O'Connor, Patricia Medina, ZaSu Pitts, Ray Collins, John McIntyre
Rating: ★★

Bright, brash farce that, with its sundry sequels, and together with the Ma and Pa Kettle series, kept Universal Studios afloat from 1949 to the late Fifties by taking enormous amounts of money on very low budgets. Francis was a talking mule and his master was Donald O'Connor (after Mickey Rooney, always a poor decision-maker, had turned the job down), who only quit the series after six escapades because the mule was getting more fan-mail than him. One compensation for O'Connor was that the films paired him with every pretty Universal starlet from Piper Laurie to Mamie Van Doren. In this first romp, the girl is Patricia Medina, while the voice of the mule is supplied by croaky Chill Wills, who carried on this asinine chore for the rest of the series. The films all date pretty badly and look a good deal more tiresome now than they did then. Tony Curtis has a 'bit' in this one.

Frankenstein ◐
1931, US, 71 mins, b/w
Dir: James Whale
Stars: Boris Karloff, Colin Clive, Mae Clark, John Boles
Rating: ★★★

James Whale's bizarre but almost poetic version of the most famous horror story of all. Notable among its best parts are the opening grave-snatching scene, with Frankenstein and the hunchback lurking behind silhouetted railings at a funeral; and the confrontation between the monster and a little girl which, with its tragic aftermath, remains a little masterpiece. The final hunt for the monster is frighteningly well realised, and Boris Karloff's pitiable creature, to reach full flower in the sequel, *Bride of Frankenstein*, remains one of the screen's most remarkable creations.

Frankenstein ◐
1973, US, 93 mins, colour
Dir: Glenn Jordan
Stars: Robert Foxworth, Susan Strasberg, Bo Svenson
Rating: ★★

In between directing *Dracula*, *Scream of the Wolf*, *Trilogy of Terror*, *The Night Strangler* and *The Night Stalker*, Dan Curtis, king of TV terror in the Seventies, found time to produce this version of Mary Shelley's classic chiller. Another TV expert, Glenn Jordan, who made a fine version of *Les Misérables* for the medium, actually directed here, getting a nice pitiable performance from the tree-like Bo Svenson as the Frankenstein monster, and a delicate one from Susan Strasberg as the neglected Elisabeth.

Frankenstein and the Monster from Hell ●
1973, UK, 99 mins, colour
Dir: Terence Fisher
Stars: Peter Cushing, Shane Briant, Madeline Smith
Rating: ★

'Ah, kidneys. Delicious.' It must be Baron Frankenstein, and it is. The country is recognisably Hammer-land. The Baron (Peter Cushing) has secreted a new creature in the depths of the asylum at which he is resident doctor. Alas, the monster (David Prowse, later Darth Vader in *Star Wars*) takes a turn for the nurse (Madeline Smith) which proves his undoing. The quality of Terence Fisher's direction slows the Hammer decline in this one, but the script is a touch too tongue-in-cheek, and the playing matches it.

Frankenstein Meets the Wolf Man ●
1943, US, 73 mins, b/w
Dir: Roy William Neill
Stars: Lon Chaney Jr, Ilona Massey, Bela Lugosi
Rating: ★★

With the death of Ludwig Frankenstein in *The Ghost of Frankenstein*, the Frankenstein series proper ended. But the public demanded more horror – and more monsters per film. So the Wolf Man, created two years previously by Lon Chaney Jr, was brought into the Frankenstein saga. Chaney, being strongly identified with the Wolf Man, was thus no longer available to portray the Monster. The death of Ygor in *Ghost* left Bela Lugosi free to have a stab at the part. The supporting cast includes great old lady and character actress of the screen, Maria Ouspenskaya, and Dwight Frye, who appeared to such chilling effect in the 1930 (Lugosi) version of *Dracula*.

Frankenstein Must Be Destroyed ● ⓥ
1969, UK, 97 mins, colour
Dir: Terence Fisher
Stars: Peter Cushing, Veronica Carlson, Freddie Jones, Simon Ward
Rating: ★★

First discovered under a skull-like mask, chasing after a burglar through

dismembered bodies after scything off a passerby's head, the bad baron is up to his old tricks again. Well, not quite – it's brain transplants that are uppermost in his mind, this time. Things go predictably on from then on (although Freddie Jones creates a pitiable creature) and everything ends in the inevitable conflagration.

Frankenstein Unbound ● ⓥ
1990, US, 87 mins, colour
Dir: Roger Corman
Stars: John Hurt, Raul Julia, Bridget Fonda, Jason Patric, Michael Hutchence, Nick Brimble
Rating: ★★

After a 19-year break, Roger Corman, the man who made the Edgar Allan Poe films in the Sixties, returned to direction with this version of a sci-fi novel that gives a futuristic topping and tailing to the old story. John Hurt plays a 21st century scientist, working on an implosion ray that will make its target disappear: no mess, no radiation. But there are side effects and, before Hurt can work to correct them, one 'side effect', a pulsating cloud that opens the door to time, seizes him and whisks him to the early 19th century, where he meets Byron and Shelley and realises to his horror that Mary Shelley drew her inspiration for *Frankenstein* from life. The creature is still terrorising the countryside but, this being a 1990 film, the call for gore demands that he rip the hearts out of his victims or, at the very least, decapitate them. These effects are dwelt on with some relish by the director, rather undercutting his visual achievements at other parts of the film, especially the icebound climax. Some of the traditional elements, though – like the electrical storm over the castle tower as Frankenstein prepares the monster's bride – are still intact.

Frankie and Johnny ○ ⓥ
1966, US, 87 mins, colour
Dir: Frederick De Cordova
Stars: Elvis Presley, Donna Douglas ·
Rating: ★★

Elvis Presley stars as a singing gambler on a Mississippi riverboat, presumably around the turn of the century, in an adaptation of the story of the classic song, with the ending altered so that Presley won't bite the dust. Brightly shot in Technicolor, with Donna Douglas (once of *The Beverly*

Hillbillies) a personable female lead, and some amusing hamming by Sue Ane Langdon and Joyce Jameson.

Frankie & Johnny ○ ⓥ
1991, US, 118 mins, colour
Dir: Garry Marshall
Stars: Al Pacino, Michelle Pfeiffer, Hector Elizondo, Kate Nelligan
Rating: ★★★

There are no big surprises in this story of a short-order cook falling for a lonely waitress at the fast-food joint where they both work. Just the pleasure of watching first-rate actors working away like mad to sink themselves into their roles. Johnny's been bad, but not that bad: after all he's Al Pacino. And how could he resist Frankie, particularly as she's played by Michelle Pfeiffer? There's some nice fooling around with their ages and their pasts, and director Garry Marshall decorates it with a bit of busy funny stuff going on half in the background. Pfeiffer's far too attractive for her role, though she's good, especially in her big breakdown scene. Pacino's sincere but never quite lovable. Kate Nelligan, usually so cool, makes a real but convincing switch as Pfeiffer's tarty colleague. And the hash house background is believably established. It's smooth, over-easy entertainment, even if it doesn't have too much real heart.

Frantic ● ⓥ
1988, US, 120 mins, colour
Dir: Roman Polanski
Stars: Harrison Ford, Emmanuelle Seigner, John Mahoney
Rating: ★★

Star Harrison Ford and director Roman Polanski suffered a rare misfire with this dreary thriller which, with its collection of oily foreigners and seedy settings, is reminiscent of one of those old British 'B' crime films done on an expensive budget. Ford, very low-key in this one, is the surgeon whose wife disappears on a trip to Paris. The stale brew that follows is full of swarthy Arabs, entrepreneurs with carnations in their buttonholes, bodies in empty rooms and a 'McGuffin' in the form of an atomic detonator. Disappointing.

Frauds ○ ⓥ
1992, Australia, 94 mins, colour
Dir: Stephan Elliott
Stars: Phil Collins, Hugo Weaving, Josephine Byrnes
Rating: ★

F

A combination of *Toys* and *An Inspector Calls*, if that's possible, this is an expensive looking surreal black comedy. Housewife Josephine Byrnes kills a burglar, only to discover he's her husband's friend and best man. Enter a weird insurance man (Phil Collins), who tumbles that hubby (Hugo Weaving) and friend planned an insurance scam that went wrong. Now Collins plans to bleed the couple dry. To fight back, they have to beard him in his toy-laden gadget-ridden lair. All about games and people who never grow up, this could have been a fascinating movie in hands other than those of debutant director Stephan Elliott. But the audience has to be gripped by the throat from the beginning by this sort of thing: here your inclination in the first hour is to nod off waiting for the nitty-gritty to get going. Weird but by no means wonderful, the result is a colourful, oddball misfire.

Fraulein Doktor ◑
1968, UK/Italy, 102 mins, colour
Dir: Alberto Lattuada
Stars: Suzy Kendall, Kenneth More, Capucine, James Booth
Rating: ★★★

Suzy Kendall's biggest role, as a German spy during World War One, and she's good enough to make one wonder why her career didn't catch fire more than it did. Period atmosphere is nicely captured by director Alberto Lattuada and his colour cameraman Luigi Kuveiller. A poison gas attack and graphic trench warfare are notable among some grippingly effective set pieces.

Freaks ●
1932, US, 64 mins, b/w
Dir: Tod Browning
Stars: Wallace Ford, Leila Hyams, Olga Baclanova
Rating: ★★★

Banned for 30 years, this horror classic remains largely undiluted by time. Once the mainspring of its plot swings into action, the atmosphere gradually clouds over with evil, reaching a climax as circus freaks crawl through mud clutching knives on a dark and stormy night. This scene is all the more effective for being revealed only in flashes of lightning by the director Tod Browning, whose direction of the freaks is quite brilliant, arousing our pity as well as our horror.

Freaky Friday ⊙
1976, US, 100 mins, colour
Dir: Gary Nelson
Stars: Jodie Foster, Barbara Harris, John Astin
Rating: ★★

Jodie Foster takes a Disney holiday from heavy dramatics in this comic forerunner of such recent successes as *Vice Versa* and *Big*. The complications from her swapping identities with mum Barbara Harris are happily endless (and endlessly happy), and there is some mild fun here, especially in a car chase at the end. The Disney process work is as abysmal as ever, but the sunny personalities of the two leading actresses see the project through with charm to spare.

Freddie as F.R.0.7. ⊙
1992, UK, 90 mins, colour
Dir: Jon Acevski
Stars: Voice stars: Ben Kingsley, Jenny Agutter, Brian Blessed, Sir Michael Hordern
Rating: ★

Everybody's doing it these days – making cartoon features that it. This one, with its largely disconnected story, and clodhopping sense of humour, is one step up from Saturday morning TV fare, with a French frog hero (yes, he did used to be a prince), a busty chop-socky heroine and a villainess who spends most of her time transformed into a snake. Most of the voicing is surprisingly clumsy, although Ben Kingsley's Freddie is acceptable enough, even if he does have trouble with the word camouflage (which, surely, is French), but the goodies are too po-faced, the sentiment too sickly and the songs not integrated with the story. Another problem is that the story itself isn't even vaguely believable, involving the 'stealing' of castles, palaces and monuments from Britain. Animation is fair, but the characters lack warmth, variation, likeability. Excruciating for adults, acceptable enough for small children.

Freddy's Dead: The Final Nightmare ● ⓥ
1991, US, 90 mins, colour
Dir: Rachel Talalay
Stars: Robert Englund, Lisa Zane, Yaphet Kotto
Rating: ★★

Gone for good? Who can say? At any rate this sixth dice (and slice) with the fiendish Freddy is a jolly horror romp that reveals Freddy's reasons for revenge and ties everything up neatly at the end. Cinemas even had a last reel in 3D, though the process, as ever, was hardly up to snuff. Robert Englund gives it his best shot as the scarred child murderer who halts the dreams of his victims, now after the last surviving teenager from Springwood, scene of the original Elm Street. He hopes that the youth will lead him to his nearest and dearest – the child that was taken away from him after his guilt was discovered. Effects, gory and otherwise, are adequately done, though they don't look too expensive and Freddy is permitted a nice last line by way of a curtain call.

Freedom Radio ○
(aka: A Voice in the Night)
1941, UK, 95 mins, b/w
Dir: Anthony Asquith
Stars: Clive Brook, Diana Wynyard, Raymond Huntley, Derek Farr
Rating: ★★★

Since eight people worked on the script of this wartime morale-booster, it's surprising it turned out so well. But it is gripping, strongly-cast and more subtle than most propaganda thrillers of its time. Clive Brook is convincing as the anti-Nazi Austrian doctor who founds the radio of the title, there's an early chance for Derek Farr as his comrade, and film buffs may spot Katie Johnson, later to win fame in *The Ladykillers* but here, 13 years earlier, already in granny roles!

Freejack ◑ ⓥ
1992, US, 111 mins, colour
Dir: Geoff Murphy
Stars: Emilio Estevez, Mick Jagger, Rene Russo, Anthony Hopkins, Amanda Plummer
Rating: ★★

Although its chases are spectacular and its futuristic settings have all the trimmings, this science-fiction thriller needs beefier actors, in more ways than one, than Emilio Estevez and Rene Russo as its leads. And the dialogue trips up every time it tries to step outside the strict boundaries of the action genre. Estevez is a racing-driver snatched at the moment of his death by a dying force, years in the future, which intends to swap his mind for its own. There's something shaky in the logic of all this if you think about it; so, maintaining a crunching pace, director Geoff Murphy hopes you won't have time to do so while you concentrate on Estevez's escape into the America of 2009, his flight from the armed guards intent on recapturing him and his battle to identify the man behind it all. The intentional thrills mix in with the unintentional chuckles in this vivid but uneasy blaster that runs like a super-budgeted story from *The Twilight Zone*.

Free Willy ☉ Ⓥ
1993, US, 111 mins, colour
Dir: Simon Wincer
Stars: Jason James Richter, Lori Petty, Jayne Atkinson, Michael Madsen, August Schellenberg
Rating: ★★★

There have been films about freeing marine creatures before, but few as successful as this, which builds to an exhilarating climax that will have you cheering or crying or both. Jason James Richter is the embryo juvenile delinquent sentenced to the American equivalent of community service for vandalising a marine amusement park. Doing 'time' at the park, the boy becomes attached to Willy, a killer whale and the park's star turn. When the boy learns that the owner plans to sacrifice Willy for the sake of some hefty insurance, there's only one decision he can make. Never over-sentimental, the film has more backbone than similar ventures would have done in past years and the whale (and his animatronic stand-ins) is a real scene-stealer. Warm, human and gutsy; good entertainment for intelligent children and families alike.

French Connection, The ● Ⓥ
1971, US, 104 mins, colour
Dir: William Friedkin
Stars: Gene Hackman, Fernando Rey, Roy Scheider, Tony LoBianco
Rating: ★★★★

Much imitated but rarely bettered, this fast-paced documentary-style thriller took Oscars for best film, actor (Gene Hackman), director (William Friedkin), screenplay (Ernest Tidyman), and editing (Jerry Greenberg). Greenberg's skill is superbly evident in the film's most exciting – and copied – sequence, a race between policeman Hackman's car and an overhead train carrying an escaping killer. Roy Scheider matches Hackman scene for scene as one of the cops involved in busting a multi-million-dollar drug-smuggling racket in New York. Fine location

shooting and muscular dialogue add to the overall impact. The two real-life cops on whom the leading characters are based, Eddie Egan and Sonny Grosso, both have sizeable supporting roles.

French Connection II ● Ⓥ
(aka: French Connection No. 2)
1975, US, 119 mins, colour
Dir: John Frankenheimer
Stars: Gene Hackman, Fernando Rey, Bernard Fresson
Rating: ★★★★

Although slow in the exposition, this thriller ultimately rates even better than the first *The French Connection* film, full of action and working up to some great individual scenes, as when American cop Gene Hackman, drying out after being doped by the narcotics ring he's chasing in Marseilles, gets drunk on cognac and has a hilarious conversation with his French opposite number about baseball and boxing. It's tough, but superior adult entertainment, with Hackman so good that it's hard to tell whether the rest of the film is routine or as riveting as he makes it seem. Even though the plot is hard to believe, the set-pieces are superbly staged and the action hard and violent. The chase leaves Hackman literally breathless and could do the same for you.

Frenchie ○
1950, US, 81 mins, colour
Dir: Louis King
Stars: Joel McCrea, Shelley Winters, Elsa Lanchester, Paul Kelly, Marie Windsor, John Russell
Rating: ★★

Vivid Western, with Joel McCrea standing small chance against such female opposition as Shelley Winters (a gamblin' gal out to avenge the death of her father), Elsa Lanchester and the delicious Marie Windsor. Some of Shelley's dialogue sounds as though it were written for Mae West; and there's a first-class bar-room brawl, no claws barred, between those two fiery ladies of films, Winters and Windsor.

French Lieutenant's Woman, The ● Ⓥ
1981, UK, 123 mins, colour
Dir: Karel Reisz
Stars: Jeremy Irons, Meryl Streep, David Warner, Leo McKern, Charlotte Mitchell
Rating: ★★

There's a romantic magic about times past that gives a lift to long-ago love affairs such as this even before they've begun. And the image of Meryl Streep watching the waves pound in at Lyme Regis with a haunted look in her eyes remains one of the most potent and enduring images from the cinema of the Eighties. Forever looking out to sea for the French lieutenant who abandoned her, Streep is bewitching in the title role, and her English accent is impeccable. The only drawback is that the modern story that frames the main action doesn't have the same strength as the central tale.

French Line, The ○
1953, US, 102 mins, colour
Dir: Lloyd Bacon
Stars: Jane Russell, Gilbert Roland, Arthur Hunnicutt
Rating: ★★★

Jane Russell's musical-comedy variations on Loos-living – *Gentlemen Prefer Blondes* and *Gentlemen Marry Brunettes* were based on shows by Anita Loos, and the film version of the latter was co-scripted by Anita's niece Mary – continued with *The French Line*, also co-written by Mary Loos (with Richard Sale). Considered pretty saucy in its day, the film had four minutes snipped out of Jane's bubble-bath and finale routines but is now shown in its original version. Made in 3D, it's a boisterous, entertaining and amusing semi-musical in which Mary McCarty as Jane's friend nearly (but not quite) steals the star's thunder. Kim Novak's in the chorus.

Frenchman's Creek ○
1944, US, 112 mins, colour
Dir: Mitchell Leisen
Stars: Joan Fontaine, Arturo de Cordova, Basil Rathbone, Nigel Bruce
Rating: ★★

Bolstered by its production values – the Technicolor is brilliant, the Victor Young score one of his best – if not by the script and acting, this lavish adaptation of a Daphne du Maurier story about a highborn lady who falls for a French pirate was said to have cost more than $3 million. Even so, its colourful escapism ensured it made a profit. Mitchell Leisen, whose speciality in direction was romantic comedy, was perhaps not the ideal director, but he gets a classy supporting performance from Basil Rathbone that steals the film.

F

French Mistress, A ○ ⓥ

1960, UK, 98 mins, b/w
Dir: Roy Boulting
Stars: Cecil Parker, James Robertson
Justice, Ian Bannen, Agnes Laurent
Rating: ★★★

Delectable French star Agnes Laurent made a couple of sparky comedies in Britain, this one for the Boulting Brothers as a French teacher who shatters the calm of an all-male school. The attractive young mistress from France parades on the tennis court in the shortest of shorts, displays her bikini at the school swimming pool and captures the heart of the headmaster's son. The headmaster is played by Cecil Parker with a splendid display of blustering pomposity. The fun runs down a little after the first hour, which contains some very amusing moments. You may recognise a very short-haired Michael Crawford as one of boys.

Frenzy ●

1972, UK, 120 mins, colour
Dir: Alfred Hitchcock
Stars: Jon Finch, Barry Foster, Anna Massey, Alec McCowen, Vivien Merchant
Rating: ★★★

Vintage Hitchcock, filled with the Master's touches, and marking a satisfying return to form after late Sixties lapses, as a killer roams round London strangling women with his old school tie. Our (tarnished) hero has a tough time clearing himself of suspicion. Anthony Shaffer's script provides Hitch with all he could want in the way of suspense and black comedy and, in a uniformly excellent cast, Barry Foster and Alec McCowen (as a wife-ridden policeman) stand out. In his first British film for many years, Hitchcock uses London locations to great effect, particularly in the Covent Garden scenes: after watching Barry Foster wrestling with a corpse buried in a sack of potatoes, you might not be able to look a spud in the eye for some time. Look out for Hitchcock himself, urbanely listening to a politician spouting on pollution and the cleanliness of the River Thames, just at the moment a corpse bobs to the surface.

Fresh Horses ◐

1988, US, 103 mins, colour
Dir: David Anspaugh
Stars: Molly Ringwald, Andrew McCarthy, Patti D'Arbanville, Ben Stiller
Rating: ★★★

One of those sudden love, will-he-won't-he hang on to her? romances at which Hollywood has been adept since the silent days. This one keeps you guessing right up to the last few seconds as to whether the central couple will end up together. Molly Ringwald, once again the gal from the wrong side of the tracks, and Andrew McCarthy, once again the college boy with everything, may not be the very brightest of the old Brat Pack, but here prove charismatic and thoughtful enough to carry the old framework over for a touchdown, and raise a tear or two along the way. Additional complications to their contrasting lifestyles are raised by the facts that he has to jilt a fiancee and she has to ditch a feckless husband. The dialogue has the occasional hiccup – '*Listen* to him. He's a fifth-year senior' – but is mostly sensible, even if it makes McCarthy's character the original Doubting Thomas. At the slightest hint of the scarlet in Ringwald's past he's ready to walk out: some great love. Under the circumstances, it's to the credit of the two leading players that you care to the end.

Freshman, The ○ ⓥ

1990, US, 102 mins, colour
Dir: Andrew Bergman
Stars: Matthew Broderick, Marlon Brando, Bruno Kirby, Penelope Ann Miller, Paul Benedict, Maximilian Schell
Rating: ★★★

Brando skates! Yes, Hollywood's heavyweight maverick genius takes to the ice like a moving waxwork of *The Godfather* in this pleasant comedy that runs like a classic American short story, complete with laconic background narration by Brando's co-star Matthew Broderick. There was once a running gag in the US stage production of *Arsenic and Old Lace* about an escapee (played by Boris Karloff) enraged to be told that he looked like Boris Karloff! It's repeated here, as characters are always about to tell Brando's influential 'importer' that he reminds them of *The Godfather*, but never quite spit it out. How Broderick comes to New York to study, comes into possession of a rare komodo dragon, falls into the clutches of the Mafia and ends up at a gourmet banquet where the guests pay $350,000 a head, is related to the dry humour of such vintage American story-tellers as O Henry and James Thurber. Brando's a delight, even when you

can't hear all the words, in this inconsequential but flavoursome little entertainment.

Friday the Thirteenth ○

1933, UK, 85 mins, b/w
Dir: Victor Saville
Stars: Sonnie Hale, Jessie Matthews, Emlyn Williams
Rating: ★★★

Not the more recent multi-murder bloodbath, but a successful early omnibus film which utilised most of the best British cinema talent of the time. Jessie Matthews, Edmund Gwenn and Ralph Richardson are particularly pleasing.

Frieda ○

1947, UK, 97 mins, b/w
Dir: Basil Dearden
Stars: David Farrar, Mai Zetterling, Glynis Johns, Flora Robson
Rating: ★★★

Swedish star Mai Zetterling made an outstanding impression with her haunting performance in this, her English-speaking debut. The film itself is a powerful drama from Ealing Studios just before they embarked on their famous series of comedies. The theme – a German girl married to an Englishman suffers the hostility of his family – was very relevant to the times. And the intelligent screenplay aims some well-timed darts at bigotry and race hatred.

Fried Green Tomatoes at the Whistle Stop Cafe ◐ ⓥ

(aka: Fried Green Tomatoes)
1991, US, 130 mins, colour
Dir: Jon Avnet
Stars: Kathy Bates, Jessica Tandy, Mary Stuart Masterson, Mary-Louise Parker, Cicely Tyson
Rating: ★★★

Southern States nostalgia is on the menu here, as well as the eponymous tomatoes. But for once the story is well enough told to grip the attention for almost all of what's a very long film. Kathy Bates plays a middle-ageing Alabama housewife whose encounter with elderly Ninny (Jessica Tandy) during a visit to an old folks' home unlocks the door to a lifetime of memories. We meet Idgie (Mary Stuart Masterson), a tomboy whose beloved brother is killed by a train, whose boyfriend is hard-won by his last girlfriend and who, after the girls go into partnership at the Whistle Stop Cafe, ends up accused of murder.

There are rather a lot of breaks from here on, for Tandy to reveal various bits of the story, which is a pity as the framing story is much weaker than Idgie's own saga, which is filmed in warmer, deeper colours to underline the difference. Tandy and Bates do as well as they can, but the film really belongs to the two younger actresses, Mary-Louise Parker being particularly good as the much-loved, much-abused, inherently good Ruth. Parker makes her sympathetic but never pious.

Friendly Persuasion ○
1956, US, 139 mins, colour
Dir: William Wyler
Stars: Gary Cooper, Dorothy McGuire, Anthony Perkins, Marjorie Main
Rating: ★★★★

Probably the best film ever to come out of a minor Hollywood studio (Allied Artists), *Friendly Persuasion* is the story of a Quaker family caught up in the American Civil War. Director William Wyler captures a tender mood which pervades the whole film, and totally catches up the audience in the family's problems. The De Luxe Colour photography is glowingly good, and the climax very moving.

Fright ●
1971, UK, 87 mins, colour
Dir: Peter Collinson
Stars: Honor Blackman, Susan George, George Cole, Dennis Waterman
Rating: ★★

Susan George's fine study in mounting hysteria is responsible for the edgy moments in this slightly nasty chiller. It concerns a homicidal psychotic (a wild performance by Ian Bannen) who returns to his family mansion to stalk the babysitter, while his wife is out for the evening. Director Peter Collinson piles on the suspense with a none-too-steady hand, but Miss George, cardigan asunder and eyes awry, really sustains the horror hokum at fever pitch.

Fright Night ● Ⓥ
1985, US, 105 mins, colour
Dir: Tom Holland
Stars: Chris Sarandon, Roddy McDowall, William Ragsdale, Traci Lin
Rating: ★★★

A vampire movie that for once breaks fresh earth. Naturally, no-one will believe Charley (William Ragsdale) when he tells them that a Count Dracula type (Chris Sarandon) has

moved into the spooky mansion next door and is seducing and murdering nubile maidens there. Well, would *you*? The miracle – and certainly the making of the film – is that Roddy McDowall, host of a late, late TV horror show, *does* come along to Hell House, lured by a $500 bait proffered by Charley's girlfriend, who happens to look like the vampire's long-lost love. McDowall wanders around in a state of total disbelief until he happens to notice Sarandon casts no reflection in a glass. From that moment, a confrontation is inevitable, and it's an exciting one at that, with special effects from the team who enlivened *Ghost Busters*. Sarandon is every inch the smoothly savage vampire, but the film's master-stroke is the casting of McDowall as the quivering questor. He provides the human element that adds the blood and guts to the acid bite of the effects men's work.

Fright Night II ● Ⓥ
1988, US, 104 mins, colour
Dir: Tommy Lee Wallace
Stars: Roddy McDowall, William Ragsdale, Traci Lin, Julie Carmen
Rating: ★★

The *Fright Night* gang are back and boy are they in trouble. Roddy McDowall is locked in a psychiatric hospital, William Ragsdale has been bitten and kidnapped by the chief lady vampire and Traci Lin is trapped with a vampire doctor next to a lonely railroad. Can they get themselves out of this? Fans needn't worry – worse is to come. This sequel is pretty lively once it gets going after a slow start. No wonder McDowall wanted to repeat his role as the horror-film telehost forced to turn genuine vampire-killer. It's his best opportunity for years, and he's aces in it. Lin's as nubile as an intrepid heroine as the genre's thrown up in ages and Jonathan Fries, as a goofy vampire–cum–werewolf, is the best of the baddies. Special makeup drips the requisite grot, goo and gore but isn't over-used. Not quite as good (or scary) as the original, this is nonetheless a spirited creep into the crypt.

Frogmen, The ○
1951, US, 96 mins, b/w
Dir: Lloyd Bacon
Stars: Richard Widmark, Gary Merrill, Dana Andrews, Jeffrey Hunter, Robert Wagner, Jack Warden
Rating: ★★★

Richard Widmark in one of his typically tough all-action film roles of the

early Fifties. As in *Red Skies of Montana, Halls of Montezuma, Destination Gobi* and *Hell and High Water*, Widmark plays an unpopular commander – this time of an underwater demolition team in World War Two. John Tucker Battle's virile screenplay finds no time for ladies, and the supporting cast includes Warren Stevens, Harvey Lembeck and William Bishop. Robert Wagner and Jeffrey Hunter appeared in a six films together.

Frogs ◐
1972, US, 91 mins, colour
Dir: George Mccowan
Stars: Ray Milland, Sam Elliott, Joan Van Ark
Rating: ★★★

Man took quite a battering from nature in the cinema of the Sixties and Seventies, what with *The Birds, Willard* and *Ben (rats), Sssnake,* and *Phase IV (ants). In* Squirm<1> even the worms got nasty. Here, it's the turn of the slimy brigade, in a very stylish and superior horror film. The air of menace hangs as heavily over proceedings as the atmosphere over the swamplands mansion in which Ray Milland and company find themselves under siege from a slimy army of frogs, toads, lizards, snakes, alligators, salamanders and even leeches. Skilful direction by George McCowan – which makes the most of a sharply satirical script and weaves the animal footage into the rest with complete conviction – complements some especially good night-time camerawork by Mario Tosi. There's a startling soundtrack, too, which comes up with a terrifying cacophony of rustling, slithering, hissing and croaking. The final scene, in which one of the characters gets croaked by his attackers, is a masterpiece of montage.

From Beyond ● Ⓥ
1986, US, 85 mins, colour
Dir: Stuart Gordon
Stars: Jeffrey Combs, Barbara Crampton, Ken Foree, Ted Sorel
Rating: RB

From the guys who gave you *Re-Animator,* this is a humourless and truly tacky horror film that relies entirely on yucky special effects for its impact. Plus a 'resonator' which acts as a sexual stimulant, turning the professor heroine into a lip-smacking bondage slave. Alas, she is neither sexy enough nor actress enough to add spice to this messy story of brain-eating fishes created by some Frankenstein machine.

F

Simply monstrous: one would suggest feeding it to its fish if it had enough intelligence to interest them.

From Beyond the Grave ●

1973, UK, 98 mins, colour
Dir: Kevin Connor
Stars: Peter Cushing, David Warner, Donald Pleasence, Ian Bannen, Diana Dors
Rating: ★★

Another quartet of horror stories from the gore-minded boys at Amicus Films. There's too many corpses and too little chilling atmosphere, but the second episode is good, with father and daughter Donald and Angela Pleasence complementing each other well as a sinister match seller and his daughter. Put an apron on to catch the blood at the end of this particular story.

From Hell to Texas ◐

(aka: Manhunt)
1957, US, 100 mins, colour
Dir: Henry Hathaway
Stars: Don Murray, Diane Varsi, Chill Wills, Dennis Hopper
Rating: ★★

Director Henry Hathaway did a useful job on this convincing Western, previously shown in Britain as Manhunt. But he had a good list of players, all type-cast but to great effect: R G Armstrong in typical fire-eating form as the vengeful rancher gunning for innocent Don Murray; Dennis Hopper as Armstrong's wild son; Rudolfo Acosta as a crafty Mexican and hoarse-voiced Chill Wills, bringing his own brand of homespun charm to the role of the heroine's father.

From Here to Eternity ○ ⊗

1953, US, 118 mins, b/w
Dir: Fred Zinnemann
Stars: Burt Lancaster, Montgomery Clift, Deborah Kerr, Donna Reed, Frank Sinatra, Ernest Borgnine
Rating: ★★★★

Its eight Oscars, its scorching love scenes between Burt Lancaster and Deborah Kerr and its raw, shocking portrayal of the oppressions and torments of American army life at the time of Pearl Harbor made this film a sure box-office hit. It also remade Frank Sinatra's career when he won one of the Oscars. Donna Reed (another Oscar-winner), Montgomery Clift, Ernest Borgnine (memorable as the sadistic sergeant who goes gunning

for Sinatra), Claude Atkins, Mickey Shaughnessy and Jack Warden all snapped up their chances.

From Noon Till Three ○

1975, US, 95 mins, colour
Dir: Frank D Gilroy
Stars: Charles Bronson, Jill Ireland
Rating: ★★

Strange is certainly the word for this black action fantasy romance starring Charles Bronson – although Bronson adventure fans may well not know what to make of this one. No synopsis could convey the flavour of a film that almost creates its own genre and even might have done so with Cary Grant and Irene Dunne in the roles taken by Bronson and his real-life wife Jill Ireland.

From Russia with Love ○ ⊗

1963, UK, 118 mins, colour
Dir: Terence Young
Stars: Sean Connery, Daniela Bianchi, Pedro Armendariz, Lotte Lenya, Robert Shaw, Bernard Lee
Rating: ★★★

This, the second in chronological order of the James Bond films, differs appreciably from its predecessor *Dr No* as regards pacing. With the same director and the same scriptwriters, the production team clearly learnt a lot from making *Dr No*, and subsequent 007 adventures were to concentrate on action-packed incident. *From Russia With Love* goes at at a spanking pace, beginning with a splendid opening sequence and the now famous credit titles presented on the curves of a belly dancer. Then it's a matter of one highlight, spectacle or thrill after another, with helicopters, trains, cars and speedboats figuring in some of the fast action. It was, too, the start of the vogue for gadgetry and sundry unorthodox lethal devices, ranging from venom-coated knives to exploding suitcases. And apart from various surprises and bizarre touches, there's the expected wide variety of glamorous females whom James invariably meets (with various degrees of informality). Also in the cast are Pedro Armendariz, who has an important role as an agent in Istanbul, the redoubtable Lotte Lenya, as a villainess de luxe, and Robert Shaw as a killer.

From the Mixed-Up Files of Mrs Basil E Frankweiler

See: The Hideaways

From the Terrace ○

1960, US, 144 mins, colour
Dir: Mark Robson
Stars: Paul Newman, Joanne Woodward, Myrna Loy, Ina Balin, Leon Ames, Felix Aylmer
Rating: ★★

This sprawling love story straddles big business, a family at war and a marriage made in hell, and marked the third screen collaboration between Paul Newman and his wife Joanne Woodward. It was an attempt to re-assemble the commercial elements of *Peyton Place*, an earlier hit for the same director, Mark Robson, but it is a glutinous, plodding affair. Woodward comes off best in the acting stakes with a portrait of a soulless, physically frustrated society girl, glinting as sharply as the tiara she appears to reserve for wearing solely in taxis. But in comparison, Newman displays only an inflexible, glum boorishness.

From This Day Forward ○

1946, US, 95 mins, b/w
Dir: John Berry
Stars: Joan Fontaine, Mark Stevens
Rating: ★★

Post-war RKO was no longer the glamour studio it had been in the Thirties and its films reflected that. There were hopes that *From This Day Forward* would make an important contribution to the contemporary problem of soldiers struggling with readjustment to civilian life, but not only did the film prove to be more of a flashback romantic drama than a social statement, but also woefully miscast the vaguely aristocratic Joan Fontaine as a Bronx tenement housewife. Chubby-cheeked little Bobby Driscoll, soon to rise to major moppet stardom, steals every scene he's in as Timmy.

Front, The ◐ ⊗

1976, US, 95 mins, colour
Dir: Martin Ritt
Stars: Woody Allen, Zero Mostel, Michael Murphy, Andrea Marcovicci
Rating: ★★

One of the most vicious forms of blacklisting in the cinema's history was the list compiled by the House Un-American Activities Committee in the years following the war. It put thousands of actors, writers, directors and technicians who were alleged to have had connections with communism in trouble, in prison, or just plain out-of-work. Star Woody Allen takes a straight role – although fragments of the Allen comedy persona keep breaking in, like Hyde occasionally getting the better of Jekyll – as a man who 'fronts' for three blacklisted writers; that is, they all work under his name. It may give you quite an insight into the incredible things that went on at the time (even a funeral is spied on to discern who the deceased Communist-sympathiser's friends were). But it's probably to the film's disadvantage that it should have been made by a writer and director (Walter Bernstein, Martin Ritt) who were themselves blacklisted. Perhaps they don't have as clear a perspective as they might on how this should work as a film. Never mind, Zero Mostel gives his best performance in many a day as an actor who finds even nightclub fees cut in half after suspicion clouds his horizon.

Front Page Story ○
1953, UK, 99 mins, b/w
Dir: Jay Lewis
Stars: Jack Hawkins, Elizabeth Allen, Eva Bartok, Derek Farr
Rating: ★★★

One of Britain's better newspaper dramas, this absorbing film benefits from two outstanding performances – from the experienced Jack Hawkins as the news editor, and 10-year-old Jenny Jones as the brave, bossy eldest of a bunch of cockney children. Hawkins – in a rare towering rage he's a sight to behold – is given reliable support from a convincing team of newspaper types: Derek Farr, as the editor's treacherous assistant; Michael Goodliffe, the office idealist; and Walter Fitzgerald as an alcoholic reporter assigned to a story of an atomic spy. Elizabeth Allan gives an appealing study of Hawkins' wife, and Eva Bartok brings sincere pathos to the role of a woman accused of murdering her dying husband. The office atmosphere is, for its time, remarkably plausible, in this solid slice of human drama.

Frozen Assets ◑ ⓥ
1992, US, 96 mins, colour
Dir: George Miller
Stars: Shelley Long, Corbin Bernsen, Larry Miller, Matt Clark, Gerrit Graham
Rating: ★

Shelley Long strikes out again in a writhingly embarrassing comedy whose very subject should have warned her off. Corbin Bernsen – whose real-life mother, Jeanne Cooper, has a cameo role – plays a chauvinistic corporate yuppie who gets tranferred to a small-town bank. Long is the feminist head of the business which, to Bernsen's horror, turns out to be a *sperm* bank! Is all this believable or what? The corny plot in which Bernsen clinches a mega-deal to sell 5,000 phials and, in a desperate attempt to attract depositors, hosts a 'Stud of the Year' contest, is lost among the allegedly comic *doubles entendres*. Still, the romantic among us who are still watching this after an hour and a half needn't worry – there's a nappy ending.

Frozen Limits, The ○
1939, UK, 84 mins, b/w
Dir: Marcel Varnel
Stars: Bud Flanagan, Chesney Allen
Rating: ★★★

One of several zany farces made by Bud Flanagan and his colleagues in the Crazy Gang in the late Thirties and early Forties. Most of them, like this one, which has the gang organising a new gold rush in the Yukon, were written by Marriott Edgar and Val Guest. Edgar wrote many of Stanley Holloway's famous monologues, including those about Albert and Sam, while Guest went on to become a director. Here the familiar face of Bernard Lee turns up as, of all things, a Western badman called Dangerous Bill McGrew!

Fugitive, The ○
1947, US, 104 mins, b/w
Dir: John Ford
Stars: Henry Fonda, Dolores Del Rio, Pedro Armendariz, J Carrol Naish, Robert Armstrong
Rating: ★★★

Director John Ford never tired over the years of telling Henry Fonda that his starring role here of a saintly priest, hunted in a south-of-the-border country that has outlawed the clergy, was the best performance of his career. Fonda is truly rivetting and compelling in a film (based on a Graham Greene novel) that sits nicely as a companion piece to Ford's marvellous *The Informer*, yet another tale of personal betrayal and challenged morality. *The Fugitive* was the first joint venture between RKO and Argosy Pictures, a company headed by Ford and Merian

C Cooper, but it was a dismal box-office failure. Years later it would be remade as *The Power and the Glory*, starring Laurence Olivier.

Fugitive, The ◑ ⓥ
1993, US, 127 mins, colour
Dir: Andrew Davis
Stars: Harrison Ford, Tommy Lee Jones, Jeroen Krabbe, Joe Pantoliano
Rating: ★★★

He's back after 30 years – and still on the run. The massively popular TV series of the mid-Sixties is exploded into a big screen adventure nearly three decades later, with Harrison Ford every bit as doggedly glum (and every bit as elusive) as David Jannsen was in the original. He has good reason too: arriving home to find himself battling a one-armed intruder who has shot and clubbed his wife. Dr Richard Kimble is soon accused and convicted of her murder. Inheriting an escape bid by other prisoners also on the way to Death Row, Kimble continues to evade pursuing police by a hairsbreadth as he tries to trace the real killer. This being a big-screen epic, the writers concoct a complex plot behind the one-armed man's break-in as well. None of this, though, stops dynamic Tommy Lee Jones, as the deputy marshall on Ford's trail, from stealing the film from under the star's nose. A bit too long (with too many setting scenes), the film has just enough action to sustain its momentum, and its only real fault is that the eventual bad guy *looks* villanous from the start, rather robbing the story of its element of surprise.

Fugitive Kind, The ○
1959, US, 135 mins, b/w
Dir: Sidney Lumet
Stars: Marlon Brando, Anna Magnani, Joanne Woodward
Rating: ★★

One of the strongest of all Tennessee Williams' works, *The Fugitive Kind*, based on his play *Orpheus Descending*, is reduced to elements overheated with everything except real emotions. A tempestuous performance by Anna Magnani in the female lead doesn't really save it.

Full House
See: O Henry's Full House

Full Metal Jacket ● ⓥ
1987, UK, 115 mins, colour
Dir: Stanley Kubrick

F

Stars: Matthew Modine, Lee Ermey,
Adam Baldwin, Vincent D'Onofrio, Arliss
Howard
Rating: ★★

The only surprise about this very average Vietnam war film is that it took
Stanley Kubrick more than a year to
make. The story falls into two halves,
both familiar staples of military films.
The training (in this case particularly
hard, of a group of Marine recruits)
and the combat action, in a slightly
stylised and sanitised Vietnam which,
as befits the English locations, seems
devoid of jungle, but full of glowing
skies and shattered villages and towns.
The feeling of these scenes is faintly
unreal. More realistic, indeed the best
thing about the film, is the drill
sergeant, although as the actor, Lee
Ermey, is an ex-drill NCO himself, his
dialogue is presumably ripped from
experience in all its crude but often
amusing colour. Of course there's a
closing homily on what it all means
but even *Platoon* had that; the
Americans, it seems, can't resist trying
to make some sense out of the whole
messy business.

Full Moon in Blue Water ●

1988, US, 94 mins, colour
Dir: Peter Masterson
Stars: Gene Hackman, Teri Garr,
Burgess Meredith, Elias Koteas
Rating: ★★

This is a 'chamber piece', the kind of
film actors love to do but nobody pays
to see. With fewer than 10 characters
and virtually a single location, this
off-centre comedy-drama is set in the
obscure Blue Water Grill, where the
owner (Gene Hackman), dolefully
watching home movies of his dead
wife, is sinking into debts, back taxes
and self-pity. He has a girlfriend (Teri
Garr), who's more of a concubine,
and a dim-witted assistant (Elias
Koteas) who looks after his senile,
wheelchair-bound father-in-law
(Burgess Meredith). Of course,
Hackman should marry Garr and accept her savings and a partnership, but
then we wouldn't have a movie, so
we must watch as businessmen,
knowing his land will soon be a
goldmine, exert a devious squeeze to
make him sell the Blue Water at a
rock-bottom price. Garr is excellent as
the 36-year-old still living with her
mother, but Hackman can't seem to
put a consistent character together in
this one.

Full of Life ○

1956, US, 91 mins, b/w
Dir: Richard Quine
Stars: Judy Holliday, Richard Conte
Rating: ★★

Likeable and well-scripted comedy
about a rather dizzy pregnant blonde
(Judy Holliday in good form) and her
misadventures after she and her husband move in with her Italian
father-in-law, a tremendous performance by plump Italian comedian
Salvatore Baccaloni. In the end,
though, it falls between comedy,
drama and embarrassment.

Fun and Fancy Free ⊙

1947, US, 73 mins, colour
Dir: Jack Kinney
Rating: ★★★

Fun it is, but slightly disappointing
too, for a major Disney cartoon that
occupies its second half with a
version of *Jack and the Beanstalk* that
casts Mickey Mouse, Donald Duck
and Goofy as the heroes. The first of
the two stories (framed by cartoon/
live action involving Jiminy Cricket
from *Pinocchio* with ventriloquist Edgar
Bergen) is a charming but very slight
affair about a little performing bear
who escapes from a circus. The
beanstalk bit is by far the best, with
Mickey, Donald and Goofy amusing
outside their normal environment and
plump comedian Billy Gilbert supplying the voice of Willie the Giant.
The animation in this sequence is
first-class, particularly when our intrepid trio is wending its way through
the jungle of the giant's garden.
Jiminy's song, 'I'm a Happy-Go-
Lucky Fellow', was originally written
for *Pinocchio*. Waste not, want not.

Funeral in Berlin ◖

1967, UK, 100 mins, colour
Dir: Guy Hamilton
Stars: Michael Caine, Paul Hubschmid,
Oscar Homolka, Eva Renzi
Rating: ★★★

The second screen adventure of
cockney spy Harry Palmer, the
creation of author Len Deighton.
Michael Caine again brings a
grudging, rebellious charm to the
character, but Evan Jones' screenplay
lacks the wealth of finely-observed
detail that made his first appearance
(in *The Ipcress File*) such a welcome
antithesis from super-human
Bondage. The Russian intelligence
officer in charge of the Berlin Wall
security (Oscar Homolka in fine,

spitting form) makes it known that he
is planning to defect and Palmer's assignment is warily to check the
authenticity of the rumour. Hugh
Burden steals the acting honours as
Hallam of the Foreign Office.

Funny About Love ◖

1990, US, 100 mins, colour
Dir: Leonard Nimoy
Stars: Gene Wilder, Christine Lahti,
Mary Stuart Masterson, Robert Prosky,
Anne Jackson
Rating: ★

When even such good actresses as
Christine Lahti and Mary Stuart
Masterson can't do anything with a
script that's meant to be a warm,
funny and occasionally sad look at
romance and heartbreak, you know
you're in trouble. You're even worse
off, though, when you have Gene
Wilder, trying too hard as the
impossible-to-live-with cartoonist
whose second fling at marriage (with a
lady chef) turns into an excruciatingly
embarrassing obsession about having
a baby. Wilder jokes a lot in between
outbursts of hysteria, and does James
Cagney impressions, but none of it is
amusing, or even touching, when it
should be. There is one funny line,
when a bimbo girlfriend is described as
'a little vague about her last name, but
this is usual for the witness protection
programme.' Otherwise, the only
good thing in it is Susan Ruttan, from
TV's *LA Law*, who brings real warmth
and personality to the woman Wilder's
father marries after his mother dies.

Funny Face ○ ▽

1956, US, 103 mins, colour
Dir: Stanley Donen
Stars: Audrey Hepburn, Fred Astaire,
Kay Thompson, Robert Flemyng
Rating: ★★★★

A delightful musical, mistily photographed in VistaVision and
Technicolor, that was never given its
due when it first appeared. The elfin
Audrey Hepburn combined with Fred
Astaire, still a Peter Pan of the dance
floor at 57, to happily revitalise an
enchanting pre-war Gershwin
musical romance about a photographer
who takes a thin, bookish girl to Paris
and transforms her looks and personality. If you need to be reminded that
Fred was still the best musical comedy
dancer in the business, watch his
bullfighting routine in 'Let's Kiss and
Make-Up', and his timing as he talks
his way through the songs, especially
the title number. One unexpected

pleasure: the real voice of Miss Hepburn (who didn't sing for herself in *My Fair Lady*) making a throat-catching vocal dream out of 'How Long Has this Been Going On?' She also dances divinely, providing Astaire with another gamine partner to follow Leslie Caron from *Daddy Long Legs*. Kay Thompson fizzes deliciously in and out of it as Astaire's editor, the dance routines are superbly staged and all the songs irresistible. As you'll have gathered it's a treat, even if the fashions have dated.

Funny Girl ○ ⓥ
1968, US, 169 mins, colour
Dir: William Wyler
Stars: Barbra Streisand, Omar Sharif, Kay Medford, Anne Francis, Walter Pidgeon
Rating: ★★★

This musical biography of unique singer-comedienne Fanny Brice goes on a bit too long, but still made a stunning debut for singer Barbra Streisand, who tied for that year's Best Actress Oscar with Katharine Hepburn. At her best when being goofily funny, Streisand has some memorable songs in this one, including 'Second Hand Rose', 'Funny Girl', 'People', ''My Man', 'I'd Rather Be Blue' and 'Don't Rain on My Parade'.

Funny Lady ○ ⓥ
1975, US, 138 mins, colour
Dir: Herbert Ross
Stars: Barbra Streisand, James Caan, Roddy McDowall, Omar Sharif, Ben Vereen
Rating: ★★★

A musical that continues the story of entertainer Fanny Brice, begun in *Funny Girl*. Barbra Streisand is so right for this role it's amazing, but the film is also illuminated by co-stars James Caan, excellent as the shambling showman Billy Rose, and Roddy McDowall, making a lot out of not very much screen time as Fanny's asexual acolyte.

Funny Thing Happened on the Way to the Forum, A ○ ⓥ
1966, UK, 99 mins, colour
Dir: Richard Lester
Stars: Michael Crawford, Phil Silvers, Zero Mostel, Michael Hordern, Buster Keaton, Jack Gilford
Rating: ★★★

The comic talents of five decades are pooled in this helter-skelter musical about capers in ancient Rome, directed by Richard Lester, following his two memorable Beatles films, and the equally popular *The Knack*. Buster Keaton, deservedly, has the funniest scene in the film. Keaton died soon after this film was completed and it was released after his death.

Fun with Dick and Jane ◖
1976, US, 95 mins, colour
Dir: Ted Kotcheff
Stars: Jane Fonda, George Segal, Ed McMahon
Rating: ★★★

Dick (George Segal) is a spend-spend-spend aerospace engineer who suddenly finds himself all spent when he is fired. Before they know it, and as soon as word is got around, he and his modish wife (Jane Fonda) are up to their neck in debt. Their ultimate solution is accidental but simple: they turn to crime. A scene where Segal tries to rob a drugstore and ends up being sold packets of contraceptives is really funny. So is the end of a sequence where they hold up a restaurant. The first half of the film is too stylised for its own good, but when Segal, Fonda and a swagbagful of incidents are allowed to take over, we really do have fun with Dick and Jane.

Furies, The ○
1950, US, 109 mins, b/w
Dir: Anthony Mann
Stars: Barbara Stanwyck, Wendell Corey, Walter Huston, Judith Anderson, Gilbert Roland
Rating: ★★★

Barbara Stanwyk, one of the grandes dames of the cinema, in a typical Stanwyck role. As the headstrong daughter of an equally iron-willed rancher, she falls in love with the son of his worst enemy. A tribute to her durability that she could still be convincing (and do all her own riding and stunting) in roles such as this, at the age of 43. A tigerish supporting cast includes Walter Huston, Judith Anderson, Thomas Gomez, Beulah Bondi, Wallace Ford, Wendell Corey and Blanche Yurka, but they all have to give best to Stanwyck in the end. Huston didn't even live to see the premiere: a few weeks after the film had finished shooting, he died from a heart attack.

Further Up the Creek ○
1958, UK, 91 mins, b/w
Dir: Val Guest

Stars: David Tomlinson, Frankie Howerd, Shirley Eaton, Thora Hird
Rating: ★★

Nautical comedy romp very much on a par with its predecessor, *Up the Creek*. Thora Hird strikes a welcome aggressive note to the soggy affair. Also featured are Frankie Howerd and Shirley Eaton, who both subsequently played comedy in similar vein in *Carry On* films.

Fury ○
1936, US, 89 mins, b/w
Dir: Fritz Lang
Stars: Spencer Tracy, Sylvia Sydney, Walter Abel, Bruce Cabot, Wlater Brennan
Rating: ★★★★

Fritz Lang's first American film is a savage and bitter indictment of mob violence, with a performance of fierce and sometimes brooding intensity by Spencer Tracy as the innocent man trapped in jail by a lynch mob baying for his blood. Still timely today.

Fuss Over Feathers
See: Conflict of Wings

Future Cop
See: Trancers

Futureworld ○
1976, US, 104 mins, colour
Dir: Richard T Heffron
Stars: Peter Fonda, Blythe Danner, Arthur Hill, Yul Brynner
Rating: ★★★

Westworld was a distinctive science-fiction film, full of edginess and shock moments, about a pleasure palace gone wrong. While this sequel is on a similar lavish scale, with a dazzling array of sets, its content is on a more serial-like level. Even so, it remains exciting in parts, the mechanical marvels are admirably amusing and Peter Fonda and Blythe Danner (as a heroine called Socks) acquit themselves capably in the leading roles. There's a rather touching sub-plot about a faceless robot that has to be left behind when its human partner tries to escape.

F/X – Murder by Illusion ◖ ⓥ
1985, US, 103 mins, colour
Dir: Robert Mandel
Stars: Bryan Brown, Brian Dennehy, Diane Venora, Cliff De Young, Mason Adams
Rating: ★★

F

A nice idea this: a film special effects ace (Bryan Brown) is recruited by US intelligence to stage a fake assassination and help protect a criminal witness. The scheme seems to go wrong and the 'FX' man goes on the run from police and assassins alike. The set pieces here are often ingenious, but at base this is a highly unlikely yarn whose characters remain remarkably dislikeable probably due both to Robert Mandel's untutored direction and a pedestrian script which somehow contrives to just miss the way real people might speak. The best performances is from Cliff De Young whose smile is as ready and shallow as it is treacherous. But even the effects aren't all that special in this crisp, impersonal thriller that, apart from its four-letter words, runs like the efficient pilot for an off-beat TV series.

F/X 2 – The Deadly Art of Illusion ◐ ⓥ
1991, US, 104 mins, colour
Dir: Richard Franklin
Stars: Bryan Brown, Brian Dennehy, Rachel Ticotin, Joanna Gleason, Philip Bosco
Rating: ★★

This sequel to *F/X* starts off as a dark thriller but evolves into something far more casual and lightweight. Bryan Brown is back as Rollie Tyler, the film special-effects man who now specialises only in high-tech toys, such as a clown whose movements obey its owners. He's asked by his wife's ex-husband, a cop, to help with illusory effects on a stakeout. Naturally it all goes wrong, the cop is killed unexpectedly by a second, unknown criminal, and Rollie becomes involved with the case. The first 20 minutes are gripping stuff, but credibility is soon as illusory as Rollie's bag of tricks, and the denouement of the plot looks more like something from a James Bond film, or a caper thriller from the Sixties. By the end, no-one, least of all Brian Dennehy as a policeman turned private eye, seems to be taking it too seriously. Pity.

G

Gaby ○
1958, US, 97 mins, colour
Dir: Curtis Bernhardt
Stars: Leslie Caron, John Kerr, Cedric Hardwicke, Taina Elg
Rating: ★★

Second remake of the classic weepie *Waterloo Bridge*, about a wartime love affair. Former ballerinas Leslie Caron and Taina Elg take over the parts played in former versions by Mae Clarke and Bette Davis (1931) and Vivien Leigh and Virginia Field (1940). The ending's different, but it's still a good cry.

Gaiety George ○
1946, UK, 98 mins, b/w
Dir: George King
Stars: Richard Greene, Ann Todd, Leni Lynn
Rating: ★★

This British musical, hardly seen since its initial appearance in post-war years, is really not at all bad, capturing much of the spirit of the era (London in the 1890s) in a biopic about an Irish-born showman of the times, and his up-and-down fortunes. American songtress Leni Lynn, a pretty little thing who made several sentimental musicals in Britain in the Forties, sings beautifully and there's an early role for the equally attractive Hazel Court. The very minor roles are supposed to include appearances by Kay Kendall, Maxwell Reed and Roger Moore, but you'll have to be sharp to spot them.

Gallant Hours, The ○ ⓥ
1959, US, 115 mins, b/w
Dir: Robert Montgomery
Stars: James Cagney, Dennis Weaver
Rating: ★★★

Although it has a shortage of battle scenes, this tense war drama about the battle for dominance of the Guadalcanal Canal is a fine, well-realised drama. This is largely due to James Cagney's impressive performance as Fleet Admiral 'Bull' Halsey, the man who masterminded the battle against the Japanese Admiral Yamamoto's fleet. An absorbing film that contains one of Cagney's finest portrayals.

Gallipoli ◐ ⓥ
1981, AUS, 111 mins, colour
Dir: Peter Weir
Stars: Mel Gibson, Mark Lee, Bill Kerr, Robert Grubb, Bill Hunter
Rating: ★★★

Certainly one of the most internationally popular of Eighties Australian movies, this much acclaimed account of the doomed Anzac World War One campaign turned out to be the passport to Hollywood for its director, Peter Weir. Powerful and moving, it's nonetheless a fashionably made and predictably ended film. Mel Gibson and Mark Lee play two champion runners, one from the country, the other from the city, who join forces on a countryside trek to join the Australian Light Horse and fight at Gallipoli. When they finally arrive, they find Gallipoli not a battlefield but cliffs and hills lit up like some deadly Golden Mile. Some of the film's best moments come in its humorous lines. There's the army doctor who, according to his sergeant, 'has had it all and cured it all'. And there's the outback prospector, who, told about the war with the Turks by our two young heroes – 'If we don't stop them there, they could end up here,' they tell him – offers them a withering glance. 'Yes mate,' he drawls, 'and they're welcome to it.'

Gal who Took the West, The ○
1949, US, 84 mins, colour
Dir: Frederick De Cordova
Stars: Yvonne De Carlo, Scott Brady, Charles Coburn, John Russell
Rating: ★★

Yvonne De Carlo queens it over a vigorous Western that casts her as an actress out west, entertaining the cowboy masses in the wilds of Arizona. Veteran actor Charles Coburn takes the honours with another in his rich gallery of character portrayals. And cameraman William Daniels deserves a special mention for his photography.

Gambit ○
1966, US, 109 mins, colour
Dir: Ronald Neame
Stars: Shirley MacLaine, Michael Caine, Herbert Lom
Rating: ★★★

Even though it leans heavily on *Topkapi* for inspiration, this is one of the tautest edge-of-seat thrillers the Sixties produced. The film starts with a robbery as it would be if the plan went off to perfection – so we know that it won't. Strangely, that doesn't take the edge away from the suspense. Ronald Neame's direction frays away the nerves, the cutting is commendable and the storyline keeps giving out with another twist to wind us back to fingernail level. Shirley MacLaine is delicious as the girl who slides between bars like a gymnastic eel.

Gambler, The ●
1974, US, 111 mins, colour
Dir: Karel Reisz
Stars: James Caan, Lauren Hutton, Paul Sorvino
Rating: ★

A grim and uncompromising account of a man who can't stop gambling even when he has won back what he lost and brought it home. James Caan brings a tightly-compressed fervour to the title role, but Karel Reisz' static direction unexpectedly fails to recognise the cinematic possibilities offered by the subject, and the story lacks the incident to sustain its length. Morris Carnovsky, best remembered as the bad guy in Humphrey Bogart's *Dead Reckoning*, makes one of his rare film appearances (as Caan's grandfather) since his Hollywood blacklisting in 1950.

Gambler from Natchez, The ○
1954, US, 88 mins, colour
Dir: Henry Levin
Stars: Dale Robertson, Debra Paget, Thomas Gomez, Kevin McCarthy
Rating: ★

Twentieth Century-Fox were trying to build Dale Robertson into a big star at the time this large-scale action film was made. After watching his stolid performance here, it's easy to see why he didn't quite make the Clark Gable grade in the end. There are far more colourful portrayals from the beautiful Debra Paget, from Thomas Gomez, from Kevin McCarthy as a slyly treacherous villain and from the giant negro actor Woody Strode, playing one of his earliest roles. The director Henry Levin throws in bags of local colour in this story of a gambling vendetta in the American South of the 1840s. Alas, it's still dull.

Gandhi ○ ⓥ
1982, UK, 188 mins, colour
Dir: Richard Attenborough
Stars: Ben Kingsley, Candice Bergen, Edward Fox, John Gielgud, Trevor

Howard, John Mills, Martin Sheen
Rating: ★★★★

Richard Attenborough's best film to date as director proves that he is capable of touching the heart as well as stirring the senses, and deservedly won an Oscar, as did Ben Kingsley: his portrayal of India's supreme man of peace is a stunning example of the master character actor's art. Even across more than three hours, this saga of 55 years' history is inevitably choppy in places, but to the untutored eye at least it seems that nothing essential has been missed. The atmosphere of India itself is captured all too well in all its splendour and poverty and the Indians, at least, involved in the story emerge as real characters. There are one or two small patches of mild tedium, but many more sequences that stir the imagination, blood and emotions, as a whole panoply of a life dedicated to peace and justice sweeps across the screen. All in all, a staggering achievement.

Gang's All Here, The ○
(aka: The Amazing Mr Forrest)
1939, UK, 77 mins, b/w
Dir: Thornton Freeland
Stars: Jack Buchanan, Googie Withers
Rating: ★★

Not the Busby Berkeley musical of the same name, but the second of two British Thirties' comedy-thrillers made by debonair Jack Buchanan in the character of John Forrest. In the previous film, *Smash and Grab*, Forrest was a carefree private eye with a weakness for model railways. In this later adventure, he has become a retired insurance investigator, with Googie Withers in the role of his wife, created in the first film by Buchanan's oft-time stage partner, Elsie Randolph. A stunning supporting cast includes British comedy specialists Syd Walker, Ronald Shiner and Robb Wilton, plus such American stars as Edward Everett Horton (again in his worried penguin act), Jack La Rue and Otto Kruger. Another experienced American, Thornton Freeland, was in the director's chair. The result, not surprisingly, was a box-office hit.

Gang's All Here, The ○
(aka: The Girls He Left Behind)
1943, US, 103 mins, colour
Dir: Busby Berkeley
Stars: Alice Faye, Carmen Miranda, James Ellison
Rating: ★★★

A later Busby Berkeley musical in Technicolor. It's the one with Carmen Miranda (and a parade of bananas) singing and dancing 'The Lady in the Tutti Frutti Hat'. Carmen, in fact, steals the show with some wonderful minced English ('I am spillink ze cat out of ze beans'), though it's also worth watching Charlotte Greenwood's high kicks, and looking out for up-and-coming Fox stars Sheila Ryan, June Haver and Jeanne Crain. Vulgar, colourful, tuneful and almost a complete delight.

Gangster, The ○
1947, US, 84 mins, b/w
Dir: Gordon Wiles
Stars: Barry Sullivan, Belita
Rating: ★★★

A rather curious *film noir*, this, with a gangster looking back on and agonsing over his life of crime. Barry Sullivan plays the curiously-named Shubunka, a mobster who has fought his way from petty thief to gang boss. Now at the top, he loses interest in everything but his girl Nancy (Belita), uncaring that rival mobster Cornell (Sheldon Leonard) is closing in on him. The film has an intellectual angle to it not usually associated with gangster films. Rumour has it that credited scriptwriter Daniel Fuchs was a front for the then-blacklisted Dalton Trumbo and the film was critically well received. Now the playing of Sullivan, Akim Tamiroff and John Ireland looks a bit mannered and the whole thing comes across as very stagey. Nevertheless it's something different and a must for students of the genre.

Garbo Talks ○
1984, US, 103 mins, colour
Dir: Sidney Lumet
Stars: Anne Bancroft, Ron Silver, Carrie Fisher, Hermione Gingold
Rating: ★

Not one of Sidney Lumet's most successful films, this off-beat comedy has its moments, even if it suffers from an excess of cuteness. But the central idea is a delightful one, the cast is tremendous, and Anne Bancroft is at her endearing best as the ageing eccentric forever in search of the elusive and reclusive Greta Garbo.

Garden of Allah, The ○
1936, US, 80 mins, colour
Dir: Richard Boleslawski

G

Stars: Marlene Dietrich, Charles Boyer,
Basil Rathbone, C Aubrey Smith
Rating: ★★★

Ravishingly shot in early Technicolor
by W Howard Green and Hal Rossen,
this is one of Hollywood's most lushly
romantic films. Marlene Dietrich's
exotic adventuress, riding off into the
desert with a man who turns out to
be a monk who has deserted his
monastery, is almost matched by the
extraordinary Austrian actress Tilly
Losch, whom one critic described as:
'In her bizarre costume . . . an embodiment of lust and decadence!'
The film established Charles Boyer's
reputation as a romantic lover of the
screen.

Garden of Evil ○
1954, US, 100 mins, colour
Dir: Henry Hathaway
Stars: Gary Cooper, Susan Hayward,
Richard Widmark, Hugh Marlowe
Rating: ★★

Leisurely, at times tense and exciting
Western whose storyline follows
well-trodden trails. It's considerably
boosted by the three stars, Gary
Cooper, Susan Hayward and Richard
Widmark, who add stature to the
routine plot about a desperate group
of men rescuing the husband of the
woman travelling with them, and then
being pursued by vengeful Indians.
No prizes for guessing in which order
the characters get killed off.

Gardens of Stone ○ ⓥ
1987, US, 111 mins, colour
Dir: Francis Coppola
Stars: James Caan, Anjelica Huston,
James Earl Jones, D B Sweeney, Dean
Stockwell, Mary Stuart Masterson
Rating: ★★

The title refers to the tombstones of
US soldiers buried at Arlington Cemetery in this impressively-cast but very
slightly dull and strangely uninvolving
film about a couple of unusually human sergeant-majors and their
youthful charges at the Arlington base.
There are good portrayals from all the
older players, particularly Anjelica
Huston (in a rare sympathetic role)
and Lonette McKee, and from the
much younger Mary Stuart Masterson,
whose real-life parents play her family
in the film. The central weakness is an
uncharismatic performance from D B
Sweeney in the film's pivotal role of
young soldier Jackie Willow. It's not

bad, with the odd effective emotional
moment, but hardly the last word on
any of the varying genres it touches.

Gas, Food, Lodging ◑ ⓥ
1991, US, 102 mins, colour
Dir: Allison Anders
Stars: Brooke Adams, Ione Skye, Fairuza
Balk, James Brolin, Donovan Leitch
Rating: ★★

Growing up fast in the New Mexico
desert town of Laramie are the two
teenage daughters of caravan dweller
Brooke Adams, long ago deserted by
her husband. The oldest (Ione Skye)
has sex with any boy that'll have her,
the younger, Shade (Fairuza Balk), still
has her dreams, mostly lived through
the films shown at a local Mexi-
can-speaking cinema. Older sister falls
for an English rock collector who
leaves her pregnant, Shade hitches up
with a local Mexican boy and mother
finds someone at last after years alone.
Not much to all this, but it's shot on
location with a sense of real camera
movement by Allison Anders. Although the too-long screenplay leaves
lengthy stretches of dullness that may
account for the inattentive viewer,
the performances are caring, especially
from the wide-awake Balk, seen not
so many years before as Dorothy in
Disney's *Return to Oz*.

Gaslight ○
(aka: Angel Street)
1939, UK, 88 mins, b/w
Dir: Thorold Dickinson
Stars: Anton Walbrook, Diana Wynyard
Rating: ★★★★

Chilling first version of the famous
mystery thriller, remade four years
later by Hollywood with Ingrid
Bergman and Charles Boyer. In this
earlier British film, with Diana
Wynyard and Anton Walbrook in the
leading roles, director Thorold
Dickinson achieves an atmosphere
alive with menace. Draw the curtains
and keep out the light to put yourself
in the right mood to be scared.

Gaslight ○
(aka: The Murder in Thornton Square)
1944, US, 114 mins, b/w
Dir: George Cukor
Stars: Charles Boyer, Ingrid Bergman,
Joseph Cotten
Rating: ★★★

Charming but evil Charles Boyer
pushes his wealthy new wife Ingrid
Bergman towards madness while
searching for her long dead aunt's

jewels in this glossy Hollywood melodrama. It's a remake of the 1940
Anton Walbrook/Diana Wynyard
film that MGM mogul Louis B Meyer
tried to destroy! Luckily for us, the
(better) British version survived. Despite an Oscar-winning performance
from Bergman, a fine debut portrayal
of a flirty chambermaid by an
18-year-old Angela Lansbury and a
lavish production under the direction
of George Cukor, this remake fails to
convey the air of menace that seeped
through the original. Nevertheless it's
a good film: it just had a very hard act
to follow.

Gathering of Eagles, A ○
1963, US, 115 mins, colour
Dir: Delbert Mann
Stars: Rock Hudson, Mary Peach, Rod
Taylor, Barry Sullivan
Rating: ★★

The *Twelve O'Clock High* story of
American airmen stationed in
Britain, here remade for peacetime
with Rock Hudson in the role created
by Gregory Peck. Unlike *Yanks* the
issue is not how the Americans
behave towards the British but how
they behave towards each other while
living at air bases over here, and in
that sense perhaps *Eagles* could equally
well have been set in Germany or
Hawaii. However, despite Delbert
Mann's strong casting, the story
somehow makes a lot less sense
without the war background.

Gator ◑
1976, US, 111 mins, colour
Dir: Burt Reynolds
Stars: Burt Reynolds, Jack Weston,
Lauren Hutton
Rating: ★★★

The most significant thing about this
vigorous thriller is that it marked the
directorial debut of its star, Burt
Reynolds. All through the film it is
evident that Reynolds is trying to do
a little something different with each
scene. Sometimes he can't prevent the
plot becoming bogged down in its
own routineness, and the violence of
the climax only just survives its jux-
taposition with the previous
humour, as characters we have come
to like become brutally killed off. But
the action scenes are first class, and
Reynolds gets uniformly good performances from his actors: Jack
Weston, stealing the film as a plump
and faintly incompetent federal agent;
Lauren Hutton, a cool, gap-toothed
heroine; Jerry Reed, a country and

western singer who lends real menace and evil to the rather cardboard vice king; Alice Ghostley as a cranky social crusader with a passion for cats; and by no means least, from himself. *Gator* chalked up a bright start for its budding director which he hasn't followed through enough.

Gauntlet, The ● ⓥ
1977, US, 108 mins, colour
Dir: Clint Eastwood
Stars: Clint Eastwood, Sondra Locke, Pat Hingle, William Prince
Rating: ★

If Clint Eastwood, again directing himself, wanted to prove that he could make a film tougher, uglier, faster-moving and more explosive than any other modern director of thrillers, then he did a pretty good job with *The Gauntlet*. Right from the start, with Eastwood a (rather unconvincing) drunken cop sent to shepherd a (female) witness back for a trial, to the deliberately ludicrous finale, in which the pair defy what seems like half the hardware in America, this is a slam-bang bloodbath aimed squarely at the box-office.

Gay Desperado, The ○
1936, US, 86 mins, b/w
Dir: Rouben Mamoulian
Stars: Nino Martini, Ida Lupino, Leo Carrillo
Rating: ★★★

This delightful comedy musical directed by Rouben Mamoulian was designed as a vehicle for opera star Nino Martini and has a pretty preposterous plot: crazy Mexican bandido models himself on American screen gangsters and decides to satisfy his love of music by kidnapping a famous tenor. He also manages to gather up heiress Ida Lupino on his first hold-up (more by luck than judgement). The songs – very operatic – are very lovely (although Mischa Auer, in a priceless shot, plainly doesn't think so) but slow up the wonderful comic 'business' going on, particularly Leo Carrillo's hilarious Hispanic; this film is where he really established the mad Mexican persona 'weez zee awfool Eengleesh' that was to delight cinemagoers, and then Fifties kids in the form of The Cisco Kid's trusty sidekick, Pancho. The film looks glorious as well, with great sweeping views of the landscape and bandidos in

the swirling dust, of cacti and buildings encrusted with crenellations. Magnifico amigo!

Gay Divorcee, The ○
1934, US, 107 mins, b/w
Dir: Mark Sandrich
Stars: Fred Astaire, Ginger Rogers
Rating: ★★★★

Fred Astaire's West End stage hit *The Gay Divorce* became *The Gay Divorcee* on screen because the censor ruled that divorce was no laughing matter. The story is just as fragile as ever but Astaire and Ginger Rogers dance up a storm, including a delightfully lengthy and complex sequence to the Oscar-winning 'The Continental'. The only song remaining from the original Cole Porter score was the immortal 'Night and Day'. Audiences flocked to see it and it turned the two stars into household names overnight.

Gay Impostors, The
See: Gold Diggers in Paris

Gazebo, The ○
1959, US, 100 mins, b/w
Dir: George Marshall
Stars: Glenn Ford, Debbie Reynolds, Carl Reiner, John McGiver
Rating: ★★★

A hit and miss but mostly delightful black comedy with Debbie Reynolds as a Broadway star whose husband is being blackmailed over a series of nude pictures from her cash-strapped past. He decides to bump off the villain and bury him under a piece of garden furniture, but he kills the wrong man. It's pretty amusing, well-directed fluff, although only when the murder is being planned is the film really funny. Based on a play by Alec Coppel, one of the film's highlights is Reynolds' rendition of 'Something Called Love'.

Geisha Boy, The ⊙
1958, US, 98 mins, colour
Dir: Frank Tashlin
Stars: Jerry Lewis, Marie MacDonald, Barton MacLane, Suzanne Pleshette
Rating: ★★

Wild Jerry Lewis comedy, full of rib-tickling touches thanks to the direction of Frank Tashlin, a former cartoonist. It was Suzanne Pleshette's first film, and Marie 'The Body' McDonald's last, as a film star involved with Jerry, who plays a third-rate magician. The jokes all work well, especially the one involving

hard-nosed major Barton MacLane, who can't wait for his own funeral because he loves hearing 'Taps'. Crystal-clear colour, too, thanks to the VistaVision process and ace cameraman Haskell Boggs.

Gene Krupa Story, The
See: Drum Crazy

General, The ⊙
1926, US, 74 mins, b/w
Dir: Clyde Bruckman
Stars: Buster Keaton, Marion Mack
Rating: ★★★★

Universally accepted as one of Buster Keaton's greatest feature films, this is based on a book called *The Great Locomotive Chase*, filmed under the title 30 years later by the Disney organisation. It's an action comedy with as many thrills as comic spills and lots of sight gags to embellish a fast-paced story based on true-life incidents in the American Civil War.

Generation
See: A Time for Giving

Genevieve ⊙
1953, UK, 86 mins, colour
Dir: Henry Cornelius
Stars: John Gregson, Dinah Sheridan, Kenneth More, Kay Kendall
Rating: ★★★★

'I'll show them how to play the plumpet.' With such an unlikely line did Kay Kendall shoot to stardom – something that should have happened much earlier – in this richly enjoyable comedy spun round the veteran car run to Brighton. It also made a star of Kenneth More and is greatly helped on its way by a gently funny and beautifully-knit screenplay from that king of comedy, William Rose. Ravishingly shot in colour by Christopher Challis, the film has memorable harmonica music by Larry Adler and was directed sympathetically by Henry Cornelius, who had already made *Passport to Pimlico* but was soon to die aged 45.

Genghis Khan ○ ⓥ
1965, US, 120 mins, colour
Dir: Henry Levin
Stars: Omar Sharif, Stephen Boyd, James Mason, Françoise Dorléac
Rating: ★★★

One of the best of the crop of epics produced in the mid-Sixties. Unlike some, it makes no attempt to hang out its story, and keeps the screen brimful

G

of action. The colour photography is exemplary, reaching a peak in the moving final scene. And director Henry Levin tells the full-blooded adventure story with dash, taste and a feel for real human beings. Telly (*Kojak*) Savalas can be seen far from New York City as a Mongol warrior. And his brother George Savalas has a minor role as Toktao.

Gentle Giant ○
1967, US, 93 mins, colour
Dir: James Neilson
Stars: Dennis Weaver, Vera Miles, Ralph Meeker
Rating: ★★★

Harmless, well-photographed story of the friendship between a boy and a bear. Dennis Weaver lends his customary authority to the role of the boy's father, but the principal interest for film fans will lie in the appearance of Huntz Hall, once famous as the gormless Satch in the Bowery comedy films. The film was made by James Neilson, a former war photographer turned motion picture director. He became associated particularly with family entertainment films for Walt Disney, including *Summer Magic, Bon Voyage* and *The Moon-Spinners*.

Gentleman Jim ○ ⓥ
1942, US, 104 mins, b/w
Dir: Raoul Walsh
Stars: Errol Flynn, Alexis Smith, Jack Carson, Alan Hale, John Loder, Ward Bond
Rating: ★★★

Errol Flynn got the chance to display his physique and give a robust performance in the fictionalised biography of prizefighter 'Gentleman Jim' Corbett who became the first heavyweight champion of the world under the Marquis of Queensberry rules. The film is played as much for comedy as drama, put over in particular by Jack Carson. The fight scenes are well staged by director Raoul Walsh and first-rate art direction adds to the impact of the movie.

Gentleman's Agreement ○ ⓥ
1947, US, 118 mins, b/w
Dir: Elia Kazan
Stars: Gregory Peck, Dorothy McGuire, John Garfield, Celeste Holm, Anne Rever, Dean Stockwell
Rating: ★★★

Winner of three Oscars and nominated for several more, this is Elia Kazan's clinical dissection of anti-Semitism in America. The direction (Kazan won one of the three Academy Awards) is tautly strung from beginning to end, and the sequence of events joined together with such skill and dramatic cohesion as to make each new development, and the final outcome, totally absorbing. Despite sincere performances from Gregory Peck and Dorothy McGuire, the outstanding portrayals lie in the supporting cast, notably from Celeste Holm (another Oscar-winner), June Havoc, Albert Dekker and Anne Revere.

Gentlemen Prefer Blondes ○ ⓥ
1954, US, 910 mins, colour
Dir: Howard Hawks
Stars: Jane Russell, Marilyn Monroe, Charles Coburn
Rating: ★★★★

How they got Jane Russell and Marilyn Monroe together to make this breeze-fresh comedy is one of the wonders of the age. It contains three of Marilyn's best numbers – 'Bye, Bye, Baby', 'Two Little Girls from Little Rock' and 'Diamonds Are a Girl's Best Friend' – and the girls sing wonderfully well together. Tommy Noonan, as the son of a millionaire infatuated with one of the girls, and George Winslow, the little boy with the foghorn voice, are the pick of a supporting cast, the rest of which is eclipsed by the stars. Howard Hawks directs with verve and the result is a champagne cocktail that could well have been called *Gold Diggers of 1954*. The wit and the humour are all there. Vastly enjoyable.

George in Civvy Street ○
1946, UK, 79 mins, b/w
Dir: Marcel Varnel
Stars: George Formby, Rosalyn Boulter, Ronald Shiner
Rating: ★★

The partnership of music hall favourite George Formby and director Marcel Varnel (who also turned out the best of the Will Hay and Arthur Askey comedies) was looking distinctly jaded after six movies in a row. And despite a formidable array of four new writers, this stale comedy about pub rivalry ended Formby's screen career on a low note.

George Raft Story, The
See: Spin of a Coin

Georgy Girl ◐ ⓥ
1966, UK, 100 mins, b/w
Dir: Silvio Narizzano
Stars: Lynn Redgrave, James Mason, Alan Bates, Charlotte Rampling
Rating: ★★★

That attractive actress Lynn Redgrave is both *raison d'être* and chief delight in this story of a tall, solid, 'glumpy' 22-year-old dancing teacher whom nobody loves. With its strange ending, which throws Georgy out of character, and its lack of any real objective, the film has a certain emptiness that even Lynn Redgrave's agonising, unbelievably close-to-life portrait of lumbering loneliness can't quite fill. Its most effective scenes are those in which she rather pathetically makes fun of her parents and, best of all, conducts a Joyce Grenfell-style dance class for children, complete with a gorgeous range of grunts, groans and gurgles.

Geronimo ○
1962, US, 101 mins, colour
Dir: Arnold Laven
Stars: Chuck Connors, Kamala Devi
Rating: ★★

Hatchet-faced Chuck Connors presides impassively over this actionful slice of Indian history. Connors' real-life wife, Kamala Devi, plays the beautiful Apache girl who loves the warrior chief. The cast also includes Adam West, alias television's Batman, and Denver Pyle. The film was made by Arnold Laven, an underrated director who also turned out *Without Warning, The Rack, The Glory Guys* and *Sam Whiskey*. The action moves briskly along and the night-time colour photography is impressive.

Getaway, The ◐ ⓥ
1972, US, 122 mins, colour
Dir: Sam Peckinpah
Stars: Steve McQueen, Ali MacGraw, Ben Johnson, Sally Struthers, Slim Pickens
Rating: ★★★

Steely-eyed Steve McQueen gives a memorably glowering performance as the ex-con mastermind behind a ruthlessly efficient bank heist in Sam Peckinpah's typically violent crime caper. Although Ali MacGraw's vacuous performance as McQueen's wife is a bit of a liability, there are enough colourful characters in the supporting cast to compensate. Particularly good are Al Lettieri as a treacherous hit-man and Bo Hopkins as his trigger-happy apprentice. Re-made in 1994.

Getaway, The ● Ⓥ
1994, US, 110 mins, colour
Dir: Roger Donaldson
Stars: Alec Baldwin, Kim Basinger, Michael Madsen, James Woods, Jennifer Tilly, Richard Farnsworth
Rating: ★★

Gun-blasting violence and graphic sex enliven an otherwise tiresome thriller about a freelance bank robber and general Mr Fixit (Alec Baldwin) who gets double-crossed more times than a British taxpayer in his efforts to pull one last heist, so that he and his gorgeous accomplice and wife (Kim Basinger) can retire in luxury. Baldwin is pretty anonymous in the old Steve McQueen role, James Woods is shunted out of the plot be-fore he has much chance to shine, and Michael Madsen is an unkempt and unpersonable villain. Basinger, how-ever, is much better than her partner and she and Jennifer Tilly (a vet's wife who gets hooked on the pursuing Madsen) are more interesting bodies than those mown down by the gun-fire. Veteran Richard Farnsworth scores in a little cameo right at the end, about the only time Donaldson's direction seems not to be on automatic pilot. Action fans will love the shoot-outs and get plenty of time to make the coffee in between. Oh yes, and Baldwin *does* say: 'This is gonna be our last job.' Yes, he does.

Get Carter ●
1971, UK, 112 mins, colour
Dir: Mike Hodges
Stars: Michael Caine, Ian Hendry, Britt Ekland, John Osborne
Rating: ★★★

The influx of directors from television brought a new harsh realism to the British cinema of the late Sixties and early Seventies – especially to the world of the crime thriller, of which this film and *Villain* are prime exam-ples. No principles, morals or good guys exist in these bleak portraits of underworld warfare. Michael Caine's Carter is as nasty as the rest of the racketeers portrayed here. If we sym-pathise with him, it is only because he is one man against the mob; the same sympathy received by Clint Eastwood, perhaps, in his efforts to earn a few dollars more. The chilly

Newcastle settings are splendidly converted by Wolfgang Suschitzky's steely Metrocolor photography, and both Caine and Ian Hendry are in cutting form.

Get on with It
See: Dentist on the Job

Getting it Right ◐
1989, UK, 102 mins, colour
Dir: Randal Kleiser
Stars: Jesse Birdsall, Helena Bonham Carter, Peter Cook, John Gielgud, Lynn Redgrave
Rating: ★★★

There are some sharp performances in this throwback to Sixties British cin-ema, notably from Helena Bonham Carter as a sad and lonely spaced-out teenage aristocrat and Lynn Redgrave as an equally sad and lonely 45-year-old who fears the dark and craves companionship. Hero Jesse Birdsall is sad and lonely, too, in his way. A 31-year-old hairdresser who lives with his parents (but isn't gay), he's only concerned with getting it right – difficult when he's painfully shy with girls. And there's aggro at work with the caustic tongue of his bewigged boss (Peter Cook) who, told by complaining staff 'I've only got one pair of hands', cracks back 'Don't dazzle me with mathematics.' Birdsall is perhaps a shade too diffident as the hero to whom everything starts to happen at once. But this is a pleasant comedy with the right feel about its settings, and some wickedly funny lines. Chances are you'll get a warm feeling when Jesse does eventually get it right.

Getting of Wisdom, The ○
1977, Australia, 101 mins, colour
Dir: Bruce Beresford
Stars: Susannah Fowle, Barry Humphries, Hilary Ryan
Rating: ★★★

Australian Bruce Beresford, now a major director on the international scene, scored his first big international success with this beautifully made and astutely observed story of the stulti-fying existence undergone by teenage girl students at an exclusive ladies' college in late 19th-century Melbourne. Not that Beresford's film is ever dull. Susannah Fowle, as the plain-Jane heroine who learns more about gamesmanship and cheating than wisdom itself, keeps the plot sparking with her escapades in and out of the classroom and on the sports

field. Sometimes things are over-emphasised, one of Beresford's faults in earlier films, but ironed out from this point in his career. Barry Humphries' stentorian portrait of the headmaster, for example, is over-the-top but a model of tact compared to his work in earlier Beresford films. It's all glowingly photographed by Donald McAlpine, who catches all the warmth and colour of an Antipodean summer, and con-tinued to work with Beresford when he moved to Hollywood.

Ghost ◐ Ⓥ
1990, US, 127 mins, colour
Dir: Jerry Zucker
Stars: Patrick Swayze, Demi Moore, Tony Goldwyn, Whoopi Goldberg
Rating: ★★★

It's hard to imagine virile, very-much-alive Patrick Swayze as a ghost. But that's what he becomes when shot by a mugger while walking home with lover Demi Moore. Swayze can't figure why he's been left to roam the earth, but it doesn't take him long to work out that he's there for a purpose and that's to protect Demi from those who had his killing rigged to look like a casual shoot-and-run affair. This isn't too easy (as Demi can't see or hear him and he can't move objects) until he latches on to a psychic (Whoopi Goldberg) and takes lessons in telekinesis from subway ghost Vin-cent Schiavelli. Goldberg isn't enthusiastic: 'Why don't you get some chains and find a house to haunt?' she complains. But Swayze makes himself a nuisance enough to force her hand. This could have made a first-rate off-beat romantic thriller (and even more money); for the reason it's only ef-fective in patches, look no further than the running time, far too much of which is spent in pseudo-erotic moonings. Never mind, enjoy the thriller plot (though the villain isn't difficult to spot), the special effects and Goldberg's lively, Oscar-winning performance.

Ghost and Mr Chicken, The ☉
1966, US, 90 mins, colour
Dir: Alan Rafkin
Stars: Don Knotts, Joan Staley
Rating: ★★

'Nervous' American comedian Don Knotts never really caught on outside America, despite having made several films, starting with an hilarious debut as the shoe salesman in Doris Day's

G

Move Over Darling. Here, he's a timid reporter assigned to spending a night in a haunted house.

Ghost and Mrs Muir, The ○
1947, US, 104 mins, b/w
Dir: Joseph L Mankiewicz
Stars: Gene Tierney, Rex Harrison, George Sanders, Edna Best, Natalie Wood
Rating: ★★★

A charming piece of whimsy about a beautiful but impoverished widow helped to fight grasping relations by the ghost of a rascally old sea-dog. The film is beautifully made and consistently entertaining, besides boasting an eye-catching performance by Natalie Wood, then only eight, as the widow's daughter. Twenty years later, the subject became a famous television series, with Hope Lange and Edward Mulhare (here it is Gene Tierney and Rex Harrison) as the widow and the ghost.

Ghost Breakers, The ○
1940, US, 85 mins, b/w
Dir: George Marshall
Stars: Bob Hope, Paulette Goddard, Paul Lukas, Richard Carlson, Anthony Quinn
Rating: ★★★

A follow-up to the success of co-stars Bob Hope and Paulette Goddard in *The Cat and the Canary* that both tickles the ribs and chills the spine. Directed at a rattling pace by a George Marshall brimming with confidence after his success the previous year with *Destry Rides Again*, the film bristles with wisecracks and mixes its chuckles and creepy bits with a facility rarely seen in this genre. Look fast for a young Robert Ryan as an intern near the start of the film.

Ghost Busters ○ Ⓥ
1984, US, 105 mins, colour
Dir: Ivan Reitman
Stars: Bill Murray, Dan Aykroyd, Sigourney Weaver, Harold Ramis, Rick Moranis, Ernie Hudson
Rating: ★★★

This modestly scary supernatural comedy, with some very funny individual lines and moments of visual hilarity thrown in, quite unexpectedly took the box-offices of the world by storm. Bill Murray, Dan Aykroyd and Harold Ramis play three university boffins who become private exorcisers after their college facility is whipped from under them.

After a slow start, business picks up, which isn't surprising as Doomsday itself appears to be at hand. Special effects in the apocalyptic finale are well up to par and admirably counterbalanced by the humour which is *National Lampoon* pleasantly tamed, and delivered with perfect deadpan timing, especially by the laconic Bill Murray. Ivan Reitman's direction is fairly sharp, only occasionally failing to drive the capers along at quite a wild enough speed.

Ghostbusters II ○ Ⓥ
1989, US, 99 mins, colour
Dir: Ivan Reitman
Stars: Bill Murray, Dan Aykroyd, Sigourney Weaver, Harold Ramis, Rick Moranis, Ernie Hudson
Rating: ★★★

Five years have passed and the ghost-busting exorcisers have fallen on hard times. Two of them (Dan Aykroyd, Ernie Hudson) are reduced to entertaining at children's parties. But help is at hand, in the form of a medieval madman who escapes from a painting and terrorises the city. All the cast from the first film (that means Bill Murray, Sigourney Weaver, Harold Ramis, Rick Moranis and sundry minor players) are reunited for this snappy sequel, which provides a serviceable, if highly unlikely dose of spooky fun. The special effects are perhaps not quite so spectacular as in the original, but this one does have a mobile Statue of Liberty to help clean up the bad guys, and a good sprinkling of laconic lines, of which, as usual, Murray makes the most in his deadpan fashion. Moranis, too, scores again as the nerdish assistant. A bit scary for younger children.

Ghost Catchers ○
1944, US, 68 mins, b/w
Dir: Edward F Cline
Stars: Ole Oslen, Chic Johnson, Leo Carrillo, Lon Chaney Jr, Gloria Jean, Andy Devine
Rating: ★★

Although it has some spooky moments, notably early on, and some funny ones too, this Olsen and Johnson comedy rather wastes its talented cast and shows that, with the success of Abbott and Costello, Universal was beginning to lose interest in the team. Ironically Olsen and Johnson get in a crack about the Abbott and Costello picture *Hold That Ghost* in one scene of a plot which also makes room for singers Gloria Jean, Ella Mae

Morse and Morton Downey and actor-bandleader Kirby Grant, who was killed in a car crash. Spot the drummer in Grant's band: it's Mel Torme.

Ghost Dad ○
1990, US, 84 mins, colour
Dir: Sidney Poitier
Stars: Bill Cosby
Rating: ★

Sidney Poitier teamed up to direct his old mate Bill Cosby on film for the third time (following *Uptown Saturday Night* and *Let's Do It Again*) in this lacklustre ghost comedy. Cosby is a family man who dies in a car crash but survives on earth as a spirit. The story outlives his demise 10 minutes into the film, but not for long and soon does a disappearing act of its own. There are plenty of laughs from the special effects as ghostly Cosby tries to tie up one last business deal to provide for his grieving family's future, but once the invisibility gag has been played a couple of times, the novelty wears off. Poitier directs with vitality and verve, but he's badly served by the tedious script.

Ghost Goes West, The ○
1935, UK, 85 mins, b/w
Dir: Rene Clair
Stars: Robert Donat, Jean Parker, Eugene Pallette, Elsa Lanchester
Rating: ★★★

Charming, amusing and eminently watchable ghost comedy, directed at a spanking pace by Rene Clair. Robert Donat plays both the Scottish hero and his ghostly double, and Jean Parker is quite delightful as the American girl with whom he falls in love. The Scottish scenes are atmospherically romantic – quite an achievement for a Frenchman who had never been north of the border. But Harold Rosson's elegant black-and-white photography undoubtedly helped him out a lot.

Ghost of Frankenstein, The ◐
1942, US, 68 mins, b/w
Dir: Erle C Kenton
Stars: Lon Chaney Jr, Cedric Hardwicke, Bela Lugosi, Lionel Atwill
Rating: ★★★

The son also rises, in this case the bold, bad Baron's second son Cedric Hardwicke, continuing his dad's pioneering work with the best of intentions, only to be sabotaged by evil Lionel Atwill and crazy Bela Lugosi, repeating his role from *Son of*

Frankenstein. Lon Chaney Jr takes over from Boris Karloff as the Creature in this sadly underrated film – the best of the Universal series after *Bride of Frankenstein*. Director Erle C Kenton, who ten years before had made the Charles Laughton horror classic *Island of Lost Souls*, creates some really chilling moments, especially when Ygor (Lugosi) is reborn within the Creature.

Ghost of St Michael's, The ○
1941, UK, 82 mins, b/w
Dir: Marcel Varnel
Stars: Will Hay, Charles Hawtrey
Rating: ★★★

Will Hay's last film in his famous role of the disreputable schoolmaster, this time in a comedy about a school evacuated to a sinister castle in wartime. Things go bump in the night and successive headmasters keep getting bumped off in a successful chiller comedy that gives Hay some hilarious tomfoolery with his schoolboys, as well as a very compatible new teammate in moon-faced Claude Hulbert.

Ghost Story ●
1981, US, 110 mins, colour
Dir: John Irwin
Stars: Fred Astaire, Melvyn Douglas, Douglas Fairbanks Jr, John Houseman
Rating: ★★★

A formidable quartet of veteran actors – Fred Astaire, Melvyn Douglas, Douglas Fairbanks Jr and John Houseman – is assembled for this story of a vengeful ghost. The plot has more loose ends than apparitions, which is going some, but the four old smoothies, Astaire especially, see it through.

Ghost Train, The ○
1941, UK, 85 mins, b/w
Dir: Walter Forde
Stars: Arthur Askey, Richard Murdoch, Kathleen Harrison
Rating: ★★★

The third film version of Arnold Ridley's famous play about a group of passengers stranded at a small and sinister rural railway station. It's loaded with chuckles, chills and thrills and tailored to the talents of its stars, Arthur Askey and Richard Murdoch. They share what was originally a single role, played in the 1931 version by Jack Hulbert.

Ghoul, The ◖
1933, UK, 79 mins, b/w
Dir: T Hayes Hunter

Stars: Boris Karloff, Cedric Hardwicke, Ernest Thesiger, Dorothy Hyson
Rating: ★★

Having left England as an unknown nearly a quarter of a decade before, Boris Karloff was welcomed back with a fanfare of trumpets for his first British starring role, a chiller piece specifically prepared with him in mind. Although visually stylish, the film has a cramped look that suggests a surprisingly low budget, and keeps it below the level of Karloff's best Thirties' work. But the photography, by Gunther Krampf, and make-up, by Heinrich Heitfield, is certainly on a par with his work for Universal. Poorly cut for the American market, the film is nowadays shown in its original version. Cedric Hardwicke scores nicely as a conniving solicitor and Ralph Richardson makes his film debut.

Giant ○ ⓥ
1956, US, 197 mins, colour
Dir: George Stevens
Stars: Elizabeth Taylor, Rock Hudson, James Dean
Rating: ★★★

Rock Hudson and James Dean were both nominated for an Oscar, in this sprawling, towering adaptation of Edna Ferber's novel of cattle and oil barons. The publicity described the film as 'bigger than Texas itself' and director George Stevens, who did win an Oscar, was able to endow the film with a wealth of personal detail. He also took a courageous stand over the exploitation of Mexican workers. The first two-thirds of the film are stirring stuff, but its grip relaxes rather too much towards the end, and Dean (whose last film this was before his death in a car crash) grapples rather unsteadily with his character once it has progressed to middle age.

Gideon of Scotland Yard ○
(aka: Gideon's Day)
1958, UK, 91 mins, colour
Dir: John Ford
Stars: Jack Hawkins, Dianne Foster, Anna Lee, Anna Massey
Rating: ★★★

An incident-packed account of life at Scotland Yard, driving home the point that a policeman's lot is not a happy one. A pleasing addition to the ranks of genteel crime thrillers. Homely fun, stocked with British stalwarts, touched with wry humour. Directed, astonishingly, by John Ford.

Gideon's Day
See: Gideon of Scotland Yard

Gidget ○
1959, US, 105 mins, colour
Dir: Paul Wendkos
Stars: Sandra Dee, James Darren, Cliff Robertson
Rating: ★★

Happy-go-lucky Sandra Dee became the role model of countless teenage girls in the 1950s. In this beach comedy that led to a slew of sequels and TV movies, she's Gidget (nickname for 'girl midget'), who falls in love with James Darren during a summer of sun and fun. The best of the series, but that's not saying very much!

Gift Horse, The ○
(aka: Glory at Sea)
1952, UK, 100 mins, b/w
Dir: Compton Bennett
Stars: Trevor Howard, Richard Attenborough, Joan Rice, Sonny Tufts
Rating: ★★★

The British seldom went wrong with war films, and this fine piece of craftmanship is in the tradition of *In Which We Serve*. It tells of an old destroyer – given by the Americans to the British navy – that's just about ready for the junkyard, its martinet skipper (Trevor Howard, excellent), its crew and the difficulties they overcome to weld a fighting partnership. Supporting roles are solidly well-acted by a cast that includes Richard Attenborough, glamour girl Joan Rice and American star Sonny Tufts, making his first film for three years.

Gigi ○ ⓥ
1958, US, 119 mins, colour
Dir: Vincente Minnelli
Stars: Leslie Caron, Maurice Chevalier, Louis Jourdan, Hermione Gingold, Eva Gabor
Rating: ★★★★

Delightful musical that took nine Academy Awards, equalling the record set by *Gone With the Wind*. Maurice Chevalier, as the old man with a twinkle in his eye for 'leetle girls', got a special Oscar 'for his contribution to the world of entertainment for more than half a century'. Among other award-winners were Vincente Minnelli for his direction, Cecil Beaton (costume design), Andre Previn (score), and Lerner and Loewe for their songs and lyrics. Miss Caron sang and danced in

G

effortless fashion as the heroine of the story, which was based on a tale by Colette.

Gilda ○
1946, US, 110 mins, b/w
Dir: Charles Vidor
Stars: Rita Hayworth, Glenn Ford, George Macready, Joseph Calleia
Rating: ★★★

Of all the femmes fatales of the Forties, Rita Hayworth's Gilda is perhaps the most vivid in the memory. First seen sitting on a bed, tossing back her long tawny hair, every man's image of the immediate post-war sex symbol par excellence, she glides sinuously through a story of deceit, danger and ambition for power. The ambition is that of her husband, magnetically played by George Macready, a scarred death's head of a man who runs a sumptuous gambling casino in Buenos Aires, and aims to become the world's most powerful tycoon. The fly in the ointment is Johnny (Glenn Ford), the tycoon's junior partner, who was once Gilda's lover. Director Charles Vidor had worked with all three principal actors in previous films, and here he uses them as a team to produce an atmosphere loaded with eroticism and menace. Macready's white house, a sort of Gatsby mansion gone to the devil, is, with the gambling casino it contains, an art director's dream. And cameraman Rudolph Mate, later to become a director, captures this and other settings in crisp, glossy black and white. The over-dark, shadowed streets contrast with the over-bright tycoon's palace of sin. Seldom has an atmosphere of decadence been so cleverly suggested. But it's Miss Hayworth you'll remember, in the film that made her *the* siren: whether singing 'Put the Blame on Mame, Boys' or stripping off long black gloves in an unforgettable night-club scene.

Girl Can't Help It, The ○ ⓥ
1956, US, 95 mins, colour
Dir: Frank Tashlin
Stars: Tom Ewell, Jayne Mansfield, Edmond O'Brien, Henry Jones
Rating: ★★★

Full of visual gags, as you'd expect from director Frank Tashlin, this good-natured comedy-musical full of harmlessly dubious humour has Tom Ewell as the out-of-work press agent trying to make voluptuous, but dumb, Jayne Mansfield into a star and thereby justify his engagement to

over-the-hill gangster Edmond O'Brien. In the event, the film did make Mansfield a star, albeit not for long; it also preserved on celluloid forever no less than 14 rock 'n' rollers of the period.

Girl Crazy ⊙
1943, US, 95 mins, b/w
Dir: Norman Taurog
Stars: Mickey Rooney, Judy Garland, 'Rags' Ragland, June Allyson
Rating: ★★★

Of all the Mickey Rooney-Judy Garland musicals made at MGM, this is the most fully realised. And hardly surprising, with a score by George and Ira Gershwin that includes 'But Not for Me', 'I Got Rhythm', 'Embraceable You' and 'Fascinatin' Rhythm' and the marvellously-staged 'Bidin' My Time' (by Charles Walters). All this, plus a finale masterminded by Busby Berkeley, who was originally set to direct the entire film. The story is tediously familiar – Rooney's a bad boy but comes good in the end – but the stars perform with enough energy for half a dozen musicals, and there's room in there somewhere for cameo performances from June Allyson, 'Rags' Ragland, Frances Rafferty and Nancy Walker.

Girl Happy ○ ⓥ
1965, US, 96 mins, colour
Dir: Boris Sagal
Stars: Elvis Presley, Shelley Fabares
Rating: ★★

One of Elvis' liveliest and funniest offerings. He plays a musician who finds himself chaperon to a vivacious teenage girl. The tunes – including 'Girl Happy', 'Do The Clam', 'Puppet on a String', 'She's Evil' and 'Do Not Disturb' – nearly all have that something extra; and Shelley Fabares is a cute little package who can even survive a sunset kiss. When she finds Elvis has been squiring her on orders, she gets drunk and starts doing a striptease in a local nightclub. Elvis saves her, and his U certificate, in the nick of time. Mary Ann Mobley, a former Miss America, is also sparky in support.

Girl in Room 17, The
See: Vice Squad

Girl in the Headlines ○
(aka: The Model Murder Case)
1963, UK, 93 mins, b/w
Dir: Michael Truman

Stars: Ian Hendry, Ronald Fraser
Rating: ★★★

Thriller fans can play spot-the-killer while film fans play spot-the-face in this cleverly plotted thriller with a gallery of 'second-line' stars to make up the suspects. Among those on Inspector Ian Hendry's list are Kieron Moore, Peter Arne, Jane Asher, Rosalie Crutchley, Patrick Holt, Zena Walker, James Villiers and Robert Harris. It's based on a novel called *The Nose On My Face* by another well known actor, Laurence Payne. Hendry and Fraser are in fine form as the two policemen on the case, and dominate the film.

Girl in the Picture, The ◐
1985, UK, 85 mins, colour
Dir: Cary Parker
Stars: John Gordon Sinclair, Irina Brook, David McCay, Gregor Fisher
Rating: ★★

We're back in the country mapped out by director Bill Forsyth in this Glasgow-set romantic comedy which is, if you like, *Gregory's Girl* five years on. John Gordon Sinclair gives young photographer Alan very much Gregory's character in this story in which he finds, like Judy Garland's Dorothy, that happiness may lie in your own backyard all the time. Sinclair can do wonders with words like 'Good', 'Great' and 'Nice' and his picaresque adventures in search of the girl of his dreams have a certain charm and are sometimes wryly funny in their observation of life as it is. It must also be admitted, though, that the film is much too slow and that Cary Parker's script and direction, though often wittily observant, aren't quite good enough to overcome that handicap altogether.

Girl in the Red Velvet Swing, The ○ ⓥ
1955, US, 109 mins, colour
Dir: Richard Fleischer
Stars: Ray Milland, Joan Collins, Farley Granger
Rating: ★★★

Here's an excellent film that relies more on the skills of its director, writer, photographer and designer for its impact than on the acting abilities of its stars. This is a first-class reconstruction by writers Walter Reisch and Charles Brackett of a cause celebre that rocked America just after the turn of the century. Joan Collins, acting with more depth than she had shown in British films, Ray Milland, and Farley Granger, giving his best performance since *Strangers on a Train*, provide the three points of an explosive eternal triangle which inevitably ends in murder. Polished direction by Richard Fleischer.

Girl on Approval ○
1962, UK, 75 mins, b/w
Dir: Charles Frend
Stars: Rachel Roberts, James Maxwell, Annette Whiteley
Rating: ★★

A penetrating low-budget film about the problems of being foster-parents to a 14-year-old girl angry with the world. Rachel Roberts, just after her triumph in *Saturday Night and Sunday Morning*, gives another fine performance in a very different role, as the suburban mum who finds her marriage under severe strain as she and her husband try to cope with – and love – their rebellious foster-daughter. Under Charles Frend's caring direction, the film pulls all the right emotional strings, as well as making you think.

Girl Rush, The ○
1955, US, 85 mins, colour
Dir: Robert Pirosh
Stars: Rosalind Russell, Fernando Lamas, Eddie Albert, Gloria de Haven
Rating: ★★

Scatter-brained musical comedy about a woman who inherits a share in a tumbledown Las Vegas hotel, and plans to turn it into a glittering nightclub. Rosalind Russell is enthusiasm itself, Fernando Lamas works hard at being the Latin lover, and Gloria de Haven shows again what a superb dancing star she could have been, if her kind of musical hadn't gone out of style.

Girls at Sea ○
1958, UK, 80 mins, colour
Dir: Gilbert Gunn
Stars: Guy Rolfe, Ronald Shiner, Alan White
Rating: ★

Locked doors, complex explanations, young women dashing around in their nightwear – in fact, all the usual ingredients of farce are the order of the day in this adaptation of the stage play *The Middle Watch*. Plunging headlong into the fun are Daniel Massey in a gauche lieutenant and, very briefly, old Alf Garnett himself, Warren Mitchell as Arthur.

Girls He Left Behind, The
See: The Gang's All Here [1943]

Girls of Pleasure Island, The ○
1953, US, 95 mins, colour
Dir: F Hugh Herbert
Stars: Leo Genn, Don Taylor, Audrey Dalton, Gene Barry
Rating: ★★★

Sentimental Hollywood sob-stuff at its very best, superbly scripted by F Hugh Herbert, who wrings the last tear out of a heart-rending ending. Fine acting from Audrey Dalton and Don Taylor brings these characters to life; and watch out in the supporting cast for Elsa Lanchester, giving us another in her catalogue of delightfully dotty females.

Give My Regards to Broad Street ○
1984, UK, 108 mins, colour
Dir: Peter Webb
Stars: Paul McCartney, Bryan Brown, Ringo Starr, Barbara Bach
Rating: ★★

Closer in spirit to The Beatles' own whimsical excesses in their 1967 *Magical Mystery Tour* TV film than the irreverent wit of the features they made with Richard Lester, Paul McCartney's big budget extravaganza is engagingly old-fashioned in outlook. The flimsy story line is subordinate to its artful selection of songs made famous by The Beatles and McCartney's own group, Wings. In fact, it's almost like a home movie: Paul's wife Linda is joined in the cast by Mr and Mrs Ringo Starr and George Martin, producer of the Beatles' hits. Ralph Richardson, in his last screen role, appears in an enigmatic cameo.

Give My Regards to Broadway ○
1948, US, 95 mins, colour
Dir: Lloyd Bacon
Stars: Dan Dailey, Charles Winninger, Nancy Guild, Charlie Ruggles
Rating: ★★★

Dan Dailey taps a relaxed dancing path through this pleasant musical about the dying days of vaudeville, and sings several standards, including the title song. Proceedings are additionally brightened both by screen veterans Charles Winninger and Sig Ruman, and by three of the loveliest aspiring actresses of the time, Nancy Guild, Barbara Lawrence and Jane Nigh.

Gladiator, The ● Ⓥ
1992, US, 101 mins, colour
Dir: Rowdy Herrington
Stars: James Marshall, Cuba Gooding Jr, Brian Dennehy, Robert Loggia, Ossie Davis, John Heard
Rating: ★★

A brutal backstreets boxing picture, with all the ingredients beloved of cinematic filmgoers down the years. The crooked promoter (Brian Dennehy) who blackmails our young hero (James Marshall) into staying in the (illegal) ring. The dirty fighter who blinds and kills Marshall's best friend. The loyal girlfriend, the promoter's moll, the feckless father, the promoter's hustler and the friend (Cuba Gooding Jr, mysteriously billed above Marshall) who must be fought and maybe killed in the ring. They're all here, residents from Hollywood's boxing hall of fame, with the twist that the promoter is an ex-light heavyweight champ who himself provides the final opponent when our hero makes his bid to break free and seek a college education. Not a punching cliche fails to land. As you reel out of the cinema, the producers hope you may be too punch-drunk to remember where you've seen it all before.

Glass Bottom Boat, The ○
1966, US, 110 mins, colour
Dir: Frank Tashlin
Stars: Doris Day, Rod Taylor, Arthur Godfrey
Rating: ★★★

Inventive, rib-tickling comedy about a girl who is chased by spies for secrets from the space laboratory where she works. Director Frank Tashlin brings a lunatic quality to his visual jokes. One remembers with particular affection Doris Day's vacuum cleaner: it looks like a dog and springs from its 'kennel' with alarming rapidity whenever a scrap of litter hits its beloved floor. The supporting cast includes Dom De Luise; the wolfish Paul Lynde; the plump and querulous John McGiver; Dick Martin, soon to find fame as the clean-shaven half of the famous *Laugh-In* comedy team; and apoplectic Edward Andrews.

Glass Key, The ◑
1942, US, 85 mins, b/w
Dir: Stuart Heisler
Stars: Alan Ladd, Veronica Lake, Brian Donlevy, William Bendix
Rating: ★★★

G

Tough, busy thriller in which a shady politician's sidekick just about keeps his boss out of trouble at some damage to life and limb. Jonathan Latimer's dialogue is memorably hard-boiled. William Bendix steals the show as a brutal heavy.

Glass Menagerie, The ○
1987, US, 130 mins, colour
Dir: Paul Newman
Stars: Joanne Woodward, John Malkovich
Rating: ★★★

Paul Newman wisely doesn't attempt to 'open up' Tennessee Williams' claustrophobic one-set play about a family suffering from its own delusions. Except for an occasional visit to the fire escape or a nearby tenement, the action is confined to the Wingfield family's apartment. John Malkovich, as the tormented son, Tom, speaks with a little, faint swish reminiscent of Williams himself, but the biggest surprise in the top-notch cast is Karen Allen, still best known as Harrison Ford's feisty sidekick in *Raiders of the Lost Ark*. Her interpretation of Laura, Tom's shy crippled sister, lifts Newman's adaptation from the category of well-meaning to memorable. Occasionally he will focus too long on things such as the lighting of a cigarette or the silly-looking portrait of a moustachioed Malkovich – meant to be his departed father – on the wall, but these are small irritations.

Glass Web, The ○
1953, US, 82 mins, b/w
Dir: Jack Arnold
Stars: Edward G Robinson, John Forsythe, Marcia Henderson, Richard Denning
Rating: ★★★

Creepy, brisk, tightly-knit thriller, in which the web is a frame-up for murder and the glass that of the television screen. Originally released as a second-feature to Norman Wisdom's first comedy, *The Glass Web* is much better than that would indicate. Ruthlessly professional acting from Edward G Robinson and John Forsythe, and compelling direction by Jack Arnold ensure that the suspense never sags.

Gleaming the Cube ○ Ⓥ
1988, US, 104 mins, colour
Dir: Graeme Clifford
Stars: Christian Slater, Steven Bauer, Min Luong, Micole Mercurio
Rating: ★★

This ho-hum thriller about a teenager out to revenge his brother's killing is taken slightly away from the ordinary by its skateboarding theme and by the involvement of its city's Vietnamese community. That said, the results are at least 20 minutes too long, with skateboarding and other slowing-down elements continually sidetracking the main plot. Full of incidents seemingly put in just to make striking moments in the plot – what teenager would really turn up half-way through his brother's funeral? – it's presentably acted, with Christian Slater parading an early variant on his 'alienated' personality, but tests the patience long before the end. The title means attaining the ultimate in skateboarding terms.

Glengarry Glen Ross ● Ⓥ
1992, US, 100 mins, colour
Dir: James Foley
Stars: Al Pacino, Jack Lemmon, Alec Baldwin, Alan Arkin, Ed Harris, Jonathan Pryce
Rating: ★★

With this adaptation of his own exceptionally foul-mouthed play, writer David Mamet attempts to make a giant-sized drama out of an anecdote about little men with little problems. Only the presence of an all-star cast saves the film version from being a complete grind to watch. Al Pacino, Jack Lemmon, Ed Harris and Alan Arkin are life-soured, short-fused real estate salesman given impossible 'leads' by their head office, with the threat of being fired if they don't sell property. Did anyone ever operate like this? Even if they did, it just seems so unlikely that you get almost as testy about the idea as the characters, one of whom is driven to break into his own office and steal 'good' leads that lie locked in a safe. It all seems pretty potty, but at least the actors give it 100 per cent spit and bile. Everything these characters do is a spiel, but, try as they might, even these driven salesmen can't sell this monotonous movie.

Glenn Miller Story, The ○ Ⓥ
1954, US, 116 mins, colour
Dir: Anthony Mann
Stars: James Stewart, June Allyson
Rating: ★★★★

One of the best and most enduring musical biographies ever to come out of Hollywood, packed to the gills with a clutch of hit tunes, from 'Little Brown Jug', 'Chattanooga Choo Choo' and 'In the Mood' to 'String of Pearls' and 'Pennsylvania 6-5000'. Not surprisingly, it was one of the top box office hits of the year. James Stewart looks every inch the trombonist who scrimped and saved and hocked his instrument over the years to make it as a big band composer. Pretty June Allyson had her best role in years as Miller's wife – although she does look younger in the tear-jerking final scenes than the start of the film, set 20 years previously. An added bonus is the appearance of Louis Armstrong and Gene Krupa, blowing up a storm in a Harlem night club scene. Stewart's miming is spot on to dubbing provided by Murray MacEachern.

Glory ◑ Ⓥ
1989, US, 122 mins, colour
Dir: Edward Zwick
Stars: Matthew Broderick, Denzel Washington, Cary Elwes, Morgan Freeman, Cliff DeYoung
Rating: ★★★★

A stirring war Western with some savage and striking battle scenes, this is the story of the first black regiment to fight for the Union during the American Civil War. Its young white commander, at first reluctant to be hard on his rag-tag troops, later sees that he has to be tough before he can be comradely and generous and eventually win the love of his men. This difficult role, an introverted young man determined not to flinch from duty or from leading his men into battle, is skilfully handled by Matthew Broderick in one of his best performances. Other soldiers are perhaps cut to type, but resourcefully drawn, notably by Morgan Freeman, a grave-digger who becomes a sergeant-major, by Cary Elwes as Broderick's second-in-command, and by Denzel Washington as a black racist, whose performance won him an Oscar. The script isn't quite emotive enough to make this a screen classic, but fortunately its actions, and action speak louder than words.

Glory Alley ○
1952, US, 77 mins, b/w
Dir: Raoul Walsh
Stars: Leslie Caron, Ralph Meeker, Gilbert Roland, Louis Armstrong
Rating: ★★

A good deal of good jazz decorates this story about a disgraced former boxer who finds renewed public glory as a Korean War hero. Louis Armstrong as the boxer's faithful trainer is like a double dose of fresh air each time he put in an appearance. And Leslie Caron appears in one of the earliest of her wholly dramatic roles. Tough-guy Ralph Meeker's the boxer. If the action scenes are the most convincing in the film, it should come as no surprise to film fans who know the work of the director Raoul Walsh, here spending an unaccustomed few weeks with MGM after working more than half his prolific career for Warner Brothers. No-one had more talent at shooting hard-hitting action than Walsh.

Glory at Sea
See: The Gift Horse

Glory Brigade, The ○
1953, US, 82 mins, b/w
Dir: Robert D Webb
Stars: Victor Mature, Lee Marvin, Richard Egan
Rating: ★★

This hard man's, Samuel Fuller-type war film was in fact directed by Robert D Webb, who gets strong performances from Victor Mature, Lee Marvin and Alexander Scourby, and keeps his action going at a fast pace, telling a good story in under 90 minutes. Outstanding black and white photography by Lucien Ballard and not a girl in sight! Good stuff for fans of Hollywood war movies, but don't expect too much subtlety.

Glory Guys, The ○
1965, US, 112 mins, colour
Dir: Arnold Laven
Stars: Tom Tryon, Harve Presnell, Senta Berger, James Caan
Rating: ★★★

One of the best examples of the Cavalry-and-Indians Westerns from the Sixties, this Sam Peckinpah-inspired, Arnold Laven-directed adventure film, full of action, colour, a gutsy music score and firm characterisation, is a story about the Cavalry as a master, rather than about individual people. Tom Tryon is a rugged hero, and there are well-grafted portrayals from Michael Anderson Jr, Slim Pickens, James Caan (as a garrulous Irishman) and Peter Breck. As the frontier scout, Harve Presnell's magnetically sincere acting exudes the quiet authority and natural casual humour that makes one instantly identify with the character. A cohesive, gripping, anti-war Western, with brilliant colour photography by veteran cinematographer James Wong Howe.

G Men ◑
1935, US, 85 mins, b/w
Dir: William Keighley
Stars: James Cagney, Ann Dvorak, Robert Armstrong, Margaret Lindsay, Lloyd Nolan, Barton MacLane
Rating: ★★★

Once again in the fore of Warners' thriller trends, James Cagney forsakes his famous gangster roles to play an equally dedicated 'G-Man' (Federal Government agent) hunting down public enemies. The film is constructed in swift, staccato scenes by Seton I Miller and directed at a cracking pace by William Keighley.

Godfather, The ● ⓥ
1971, US, 175 mins, colour
Dir: Francis Ford Coppola
Stars: Marlon Brando, Al Pacino, James Caan, Diane Keaton
Rating: ★★★★

The first part of Fancis Ford Coppola's Mafia trilogy is, perhaps, the ultimate modern Hollywood gangster opus. All the lead characters are sensational, but the enduring image is of Marlon Brando as the lethal, rasping Godfather of the central New York Mafia family, his cheeks stuffed with cotton wool and his throat jammed with colloquialisms. Brando made one of the biggest financial killings of his career with the role by cleverly accepting only $100,000 up front and a percentage of any future profits. The film stormed the world, taking $150 million, netting Brando a cool $16 million. Although the film is really the story of Brando's college-educated son, played by Al Pacino, it was Brando who won the second Oscar of his career. The film also took Academy Awards for screenplay and as best picture.

Godfather Part II, The ● ⓥ
1974, US, 200 mins, colour
Dir: Francis Ford Coppola
Stars: Al Pacino, Robert Duvall, Diane Keaton, Robert De Niro
Rating: ★★★★

An even more satisfying film than its much-lauded predecessor, this was the first sequel ever to win a Best Film Oscar – the same as the original film. Al Pacino is in commanding form as the head of the Corleone Mafia family, following the death of overweight Marlon Brando, but he is given a run for his money in an at first confusing sub-plot from Robert De Niro, who plays Brando's character as a young man, revealing his entry into crime from his arrival in America as a penniless immigrant. There is death and bloodshed by the bucketful, directed with an unmistakable flourish by Francis Ford Coppola, who in all three *Godfather* films juxtaposes the most stunning execution scenes with the calm and serenity of Church ceremonies, such as weddings, christenings and confirmations. The acting is flawless, particularly from De Niro, who even beat his acting teacher, Lee Strasberg, to an Oscar; and it's impossible not to be swept along by the exhilarating twists and turns of the plot.

Godfather Part III, The ● ⓥ
1990, US, 161 mins, colour
Dir: Francis Ford Coppola
Stars: Al Pacino, Diane Keaton, Talia Shire, Andy Garcia, Eli Wallach, Bridget Fonda
Rating: ★★

Parts I and II were long, but brilliant cinema. Part III, alas, is just long and very slow. Directorial flair and acting charisma are notably absent from this chapter (presumably the last), which deals more or less with a single episode in the later life of Michael Corleone (still Al Pacino). His bastard nephew (the faceless Andy Garcia) falls in love with Michael's daughter (Sofia Coppola) and, wanting out of his association with gangster Joey Zaza (Joe Bologna), sets in motion a chain of events which drags Michael back down from semi-respectability into high-profile gang wars and even the assassination of the Pope. Pacino, looking like a sawn-off Stallone, also sports a Brando hoarseness (presumably on purpose) which detracts from the magnetism of the performance. Shire is the personification of evil as Pacino's sister, but Keaton now seems out of place as his wife. There's no dynamism in Coppola's direction and the story shuffles along like a Sicilian peasant leading a donkey. After more than two-and-a-half hours, you echo Pacino's lament when he asks, 'Where the hell does it end?'

God's Little Acre ◑
1958, US, 110 mins, b/w
Dir: Anthony Mann
Stars: Robert Ryan, Tina Louise, Aldo Ray, Jack Lord, Buddy Hackett, Vic Morrow
Rating: ★★

G

Anthony Mann's earthy film adaptation of Erskine Caldwell's novel started a whole rash of inferior imitations after its appearance. Robert Ryan, long one of Hollywood's most underrated actors, gets right under the skin of the grizzled, free-living Ty Ty Walden, the Georgia farmer who believes he has gold hidden on his land. Aldo Ray and Tina Louise perspire with passion: nobody smiles much.

Godspell ○

1973, US, 103 mins, colour
Dir: David Greene
Stars: Victor Garber, David Haskell, Lynne Thigpen, Katie Hanley
Rating: ★★

Although it has the original Broadway cast aboard, this musical based on the Gospel according to St Matthew never quite bridges the gap between stage and screen. But the cast's vivacity is sometimes infectious, and the score includes 'Day By Day' (the show's big hit), 'Turn Back, O Man', 'All Good Gifts' and 'Beautiful City'. Updated parables include a version of The Prodigal Son illustrated by clips from silent films starring such comedians as Harold Lloyd, Billy Bevan and Larry Semon.

Go for a Take ○

1972, UK, 90 mins, colour
Dir: Harry Booth
Stars: Reg Varney, Norman Rossington, Sue Lloyd, Dennis Price
Rating: ★★

An above-average British comedy of its time, *Go for a Take* runs very much along the lines of a Norman Wisdom romp, giving rubber-faced Reg Varney the opportunity to run amok through a film studio as submarine officer, vampire victim, knight, gunman, prisoner, waiter, Tarzan and Viking warrior. It makes clean and pleasant comedy, although the apparent budget and shooting restrictions imposed on the film force its star from time to time into some desperate mugging that only his fans and younger children will find funny.

Going in Style ○

1979, US, 96 mins, colour
Dir: Martin Brest
Stars: George Burns, Art Carney
Rating: ★★★

Superb work by the three elderly stars (George Burns, Lee Strasberg and Art Carney) as a trio of old codgers who execute a bank robbery to relieve boredom, ensures that this comedy does indeed go in style. Also good are Charles Hallahan and Pamela Payton Wright as the young couple who eventually end up with the loot. Martin Brest moved on to direct the phenomenally successful *Beverly Hills Cop*.

Going My Way ○

1944, US, 126 mins, b/w
Dir: Leo McCarey
Stars: Bing Crosby, Barry Fitzgerald, Rise Stevens
Rating: ★★★

Leo McCarey's film about a down-to-earth priest who alters the lives of those around him seemed to skate more skilfully around its sentiment than it does to the more jaded view of today. But Bing Crosby was certainly never better, Barry Fitzgerald's older priest added a much-needed vein of saltiness, and the film swept all before it at the Academy Awards of its year: Oscars for best film, best director (McCarey), best actor (Crosby), best supporting actor (Fitzgerald) and three more, including one for its hit song, 'Swingin' on a Star'. A huge popular success, a sequel had to follow and it did: *The Bells of St Mary's*.

Goin' South ◐

1978, US, 109 mins, colour
Dir: Jack Nicholson
Stars: Jack Nicholson, Mary Steenburgen, John Belushi
Rating: ★★★

Although unusual in quality, this Western plays a variation on a familiar theme: the rough-hewn man who goes to work for a fiercely independent woman and ends up on her side, not to mention in her bed. The variation here is that our 'hero' is an especially disreputable outlaw (Jack Nicholson, who also directed) saved from the hangman's noose by a marriage of convenience to Mary Steenburgen, who works a useless goldmine (look out, here comes the plot) left to her by her father. Nicholson the director does just fine, but Nicholson the actor suffers from the strain of split responsibilities, his usual well-modulated performance often going over the top, leaving the film relying on the very appealing performance of Steenburgen to keep our sympathy and the story going. Its mood of romantic farce, with bursts of action and undertones of eroticism, is remarkably well sustained. Good support from Veronica Cartwright, previously seen simpering and whimpering at the *Alien*, but here as a 'baccy-chewing bandit hellcat'!

Go into Your Dance ○

(aka: Casino de Paree)
1935, US, 85 mins, b/w
Dir: Archie Mayo
Stars: Al Jolson, Ruby Keeler, Helen Morgan, Glenda Farrell, Barton MacLane, Akim Tamiroff
Rating: ★★

The only screen teaming of Al Jolson and his then-wife Ruby Keeler, heavy on histrionics and notable chiefly for a Harry Warren–Al Dubin score (the composers also appear briefly on screen together) that includes 'About a Quarter to Nine' (reprised in *The Jolson Story*), 'She's a Latin from Manhattan' and (sung by Helen Morgan) 'The Little Things You Used to Do'.

Gold ○

1974, UK, 124 mins, colour
Dir: Peter Hunt
Stars: Roger Moore, Susannah York, Ray Milland, Bradford Dillman
Rating: ★★

This action film starts like a sizzler, pitching you headlong into a dramatic story about treachery in high places which rebounds on those in low places – condemning hundreds of gold-miners to a watery grave. Roger Moore is the husky hero, immaculate in matching denims, white or blue. Susannah York is the husky-voiced heroine who conclusively out-acts an otherwise all-male cast. Away from its pulsating action scenes down the mine, the film has less substance to offer. But director Peter Hunt knows all about thrills, having also directed Moore in *Shout at the Devil*, Charles Bronson in *Death Hunt* and George Lazenby in *On Her Majesty's Secret Service*. He's less successful in a scene in which Moore and Miss York take a bath together, where both stars seem to be struggling hard to repress a fit of the giggles.

Gold Diggers in Paris ○

(aka: The Gay Imposters)
1938, US, 100 mins, b/w
Stars: Rudy Vallee, Rosemary Lane, Hugh Herbert, Allen Jenkins
Rating: ★★★

Fifth and last in the Warner *Gold Digger* series, which had started nine years earlier; this one is distinctly light on plot, but saved as usual by the Busby Berkeley musical numbers despite the fact that the great dance director was by now working on a severely restricted budget. Rudy Vallee at the height of his radio stardom still failed to make the transition to screen stardom, but there's a vintage score by Johnny Mercer plus Dubin and Warren.

Gold Diggers of 1933 ○
1933, US, 96 mins, b/w
Dir: Mervyn LeRoy
Stars: Warren Willian, Joan Blondell
Rating: ★★★★

Opening with the stunning number 'We're in the Money', with Ginger Rogers (as Fay Fortune!) clad from head to toe in silver dollars, this Depression musical scores in every department and proved that when it came to staging dance numbers, Busby Berkeley was peerless. Warners dusted off the 1929 play *Gold Diggers* of Broadway for the storyline but it was the song and dance numbers that make this film so memorable today. From the silhouetted (but clearly nude) dancers of 'Pettin' in the Park' to 60 violin-playing chorines in 'The Shadow Waltz' and the emotional climax, 'My Forgotten Man', which boasted 150 extras playing soldiers back from World War One with no hope of employment, the numbers boasted an atmosphere and personality all their own. It was exceedingly rare for such a piece of social comment to work within the context of popular musical entertainment. Look out for Berkeley himself as a call boy.

Gold Diggers of 1935 ○ Ⓥ
1935, US, 95 mins, b/w
Dir: Busby Berkeley
Stars: Dick Powell, Adolphe Menjou, Gloria Stuart, Wini Shaw, Glenda Farrell
Rating: ★★★

There's not a lot of plot in this Warners musical, but director Busby Berkeley pulls out all the stops on the choreography – culminating in the sensational 'Lullaby of Broadway', which remained his own personal favourite among all the numbers he staged for screen musicals. Look closely at the 56 moving miniature pianos in one scene and see if you can spot the 56 men who are concealed beneath them.

Gold Diggers of 1937 ○
1936, US, 101 mins, b/w
Dir: Lloyd Bacon

Stars: Dick Powell, Joan Blondell, Victor Moore, Glenda Farrell
Rating: ★★★

Based on Richard Maibaum's play *Sweet Mystery of Life*, this musical continued the fabulous *Gold Diggers* series, although perhaps the lustre was just beginning to dim. Joan Blondell is back partnering Dick Powell and they are the 'good guys' in this quite substantial story of an insurance fraud that does not quite turn out as planned. But of course it's all just an excuse for the lavish song and dance numbers. *42nd Street* director Lloyd Bacon here achieves attractive performances from the two stars and some delightful comedy from Victor Moore (as the elderly Broadway producer) and Glenda Farrell (as the gold-digger who pursues him) while choreographer Busby Berkeley provided some more of his stunning production numbers – notably 'Let's Put Our Heads Together', featuring 50 couples in huge rocking chairs, and a fabulous finale involving 70 young ladies marching across a glossy floor to Al Dubin and Harry Warren's 'All's Fair in Love and War'.

Golden Blade, The ☉
1953, US, 80 mins, colour
Dir: Nathan Juran
Stars: Rock Hudson, Pipie Laurie, George Macready, Kathleen Hughes, Gene Evans
Rating: ★★

Arabian Nights adventure, with brisk action and a story about a magic sword. Rock Hudson and Piper Laurie try not to look embarrassed: both, though, were soon to move on to better things.

Golden Boy ○
1939, US, 99 mins, b/w
Dir: Rouben Mamoulian
Stars: William Holden, Barbara Stanwyck, Adolphe Menjou
Rating: ★★★

Boxing gloves or a violinist's bow? That's the choice facing poor Joe in this Thirties drama from the play by Clifford Odets. The film made a star of the young William Holden, as the hero torn between two talents – boxing and music. Much feted in it day, but its lack of genuine emotive appeal has dated it.

Golden Child, The ○ Ⓥ
1986, US, 93 mins, colour
Dir: Michael Ritchie

Stars: Eddie Murphy, Charles Dance, Charlotte Lewis
Rating: ★★★

Much maligned but actually far more enjoyable than some Eddie Murphy ventures, this unashamed *Indiana Jones* style hokum casts Murphy as a child-finder called to Tibet to find the child of the title, capable of bringing peace to the earth, but now kidnapped by evil forces. Charles Dance will doubtless want to forget his role as the villain, but the proceedings are colourful, action-packed, inventive and punched along at powerhouse pace by director Michael Ritchie. With his usually salty language restricted by the need to make a 'family' entertainment, Murphy is actually quite likeable!

Golden Girl ○
1951, US, 108 mins, colour
Dir: Lloyd Bacon
Stars: Mitzi Gaynor, Dale Robertson, Dennis Day, James Barton
Rating: ★★★

Mitzi Gaynor turns in her best screen performance in this entertaining period mixture of music, action and sentiment. Lloyd Bacon, who directed most of the Thirties' musicals choreographed by Busby Berkeley, pulls out all his best tricks. If you cry easily at films, beware the ending of this one. The dazzling Technicolor photography is by Charles G Clarke.

Goldengirl ○
1979, US, 104 mins, colour
Dir: Joseph Sargent
Stars: Susan Anton, James Coburn, Robert Culp, Leslie Caron
Rating: ★

An athletics soap-opera! Susan Anton's *Goldengirl* of the title is skyscraper-tall, blonde, stunningly good-looking and not a natural athlete. Anton rises nicely to what acting challenges the script provides, but is clearly less at home on the running track, most of these scenes relying on clever editing and camera angles to suggest her rivals are getting thrashed. She does, however, prove herself a singer of more than usual promise with her rendition of the film's theme tune. Alas for such American wish fulfilment, the story was over-taken by events, with the United States boycotting the Moscow Olympics at which the climax is set.

G

Golden Hawk, The ☉
1952, US, 84 mins, colour
Dir: Sidney Salkow
Stars: Rhonda Fleming, Sterling Hayden,
Helena Carter, John Sutton
Rating: ★★

A swashbuckling tale of swordfights
and sea battles – the type no longer
made in Hollywood, but exhilarating
to watch. Dazzlingly photographed in
Technicolor, it has two exceptionally
photogenic leading ladies in Rhonda
Fleming and Helena Carter.
Clean-cut heroics, anachronistic script
and handsomely roguish villainy from
John Sutton.

Golden Mistress, The ○
1954, US, 83 mins, colour
Dir: Joel Judge
Stars: John Agar, Rosemarie Bowe,
Abner Biberman
Rating: ★★★

Thrill-a-minute adventure story about
a hunt for treasure in the jungles of
Haiti, and a threat of voodoo
vengeance after a golden idol is stolen.
Shot entirely in Haiti, this yarn boasts
some of the most striking scenery ever
recorded on film. Add a hunt for
treasure, gooseflesh-provoking voodoo ceremonies and fights with
horrific-looking tribesmen and you
have a film well worth viewing. Soon
after completing it, sultry leading lady
Rosemarie Bowe married Robert
Stack and retired. They're still married. The film was directed by featured
player Abner Biberman under the
pseudonym Joel Judge.

Golden Rendezvous ○
1977, US, 103 mins, colour
Dir: Ashley Lazarus
Stars: Richard Harris, Ann Turkel, David
Janssen
Rating: ★★★

Another adaptation from Alistair
MacLean and a good slice of hokum
too. Not much of it makes any sense
but the pace never stops. The story is
set aboard a ship peopled with characters so cardboard they could fall
over at a touch: the intrepid first officer (Richard Harris), the mystery
woman (Ann Turkel) who won't talk,
the tycoon (David Janssen) who drinks
too much, the captain (Robert
Flemyng) whose lip juts with determination, the faded blonde (Dorothy
Malone), the gambler (Burgess
Meredith) with a foolproof system, the
good doctor (Gordon Jackson) who
won't take arms (but naturally does).

The list is as long as a yardarm, with
Michael Howard scoring briefly as a
steward who gets killed off early on –
for scene-stealing, one presumes. On
the technical side, cameraman Ken
Higgins turns in a first-rate job in this
hugely enjoyable film.

Golden Salamander ○
1949, UK, 87 mins, b/w
Dir: Ronald Neame
Stars: Trevor Howard, Anouk Aimée,
Herbert Lom, Jacques Sernas
Rating: ★★★

Out-of-the-rut British adventure story
based on a tale by Victor Canning,
which keeps you guessing until the last
scenes. The direction by ex-
cameraman Ronald Neame is swift
and brilliant. The film marked the introduction to British films of the
beautiful French actress Anouk, later
Anouk Aimée. She was just 17 at the
time, and critics in this country raved
about her looks and her acting ability.

Golden Virgin
See: The Story of Esther Costello

Golden Voyage of Sinbad, The ○ ⓥ
1973, UK, 104 mins, colour
Dir: Gordon Hessler
Stars: John Phillip Law, Caroline Munro,
Tom Baker
Rating: ★★★

Special effects wizard Ray
Harryhausen here returned to the
scene of his first great triumph. For it
was in *The 7th Voyage of Sinbad* 15
years earlier that his process of
Dynamation first opened its magic box
of tricks to an eager paying public. In
this later venture, Harryhausen's famous stop-motion techniques enable
Sinbad to fight a gryphon, a centaur, a
six-armed goddess (each arm bearing a
sword) and various other weird and
wonderful opponents. Caroline
Munro is an eye-catching heroine,
even if she has little more to do than
cower in the face of some new horror.
Sinbad's human opponent is played by
Tom Baker, just before he became
TV's Dr Who.

Goldfinger ○ ⓥ
1964, UK, 111 mins, colour
Dir: Guy Hamilton
Stars: Sean Connery, Honor Blackman,
Gert Frobe, Shirely Eaton
Rating: ★★★

Another Bond cliffhanger (or in this
case, cobalt bomb-hanger), with agent

007 taking on Auric Goldfinger, a
master criminal who plans to plunder
the American gold reserves in Fort
Knox. Screenwriters Paul Dehn and
Richard Maibaum miss our on none
of the thrills of Ian Fleming's book. At
the same time they endow Bond with
a sense of humour that Fleming never
gave him. Sean Connery revels in this,
enjoying himself much more as a sort
of super-Saint than in the parts that are
pure Pearl White. German actor Gert
Frobe burst into international film
recognition with the title role, while
wrestler Harold Sakata enjoys fleeting
screen fame by making the Korean
Odd-Job a villain fraught with menace. Another star is the Bond-mobile,
in this case a 'modified' Aston Martin
which has a radar screen and an oil
slick, and fires machine guns to boot.
Naturally, it's bullet-proof as well.
Incidentally, don't miss the first 15
minutes of the film, which, as so
often in the series, contain the tail-end
of another Bond adventure for good
measure.

Gold of the Seven Saints ○
1961, US, 89 mins, colour
Dir: Gordon Douglas
Stars: Clint Walker, Roger Moore
Rating: ★★

Two trappers find gold – and an outlaw team hard on their heels. Clint
Walker and Roger Moore are strong
in stature in these roles, if not in his-
trionic abilities. The film was made in
temperatures of between 100 and 120
degrees. But the magnificent scenery
– the Arches National Monument
with its fantastic rock formations, the
dramatic Colorado River and the
mountains – made it all worthwhile.

Gold Rush, The ☉
1925, US, 70 mins, b/w
Dir: Charles Chaplin
Stars: Charlie Chaplin, Georgia Hale,
Mack Swain
Rating: ★★★★

Surely the funniest of Chaplin's feature films, this sublime saga of the
frozen North has the side-splitting,
beautifully worked-out scene in
which a starving Chaplin and Mack
Swain make a Thanksgiving feast out
of one of Chaplin's boots. Later, a
crazed Swain tries to eat Chaplin
himself, seeing him as a gigantic
chicken. And the scene where their
cabin totters on the edge of a precipice
is milked for all the laughs it's worth,
and then some more. The film was
mostly shot high in the Sierra Nevadas

at a cost of close to a million dollars but made a mint. Chaplin later said that it was the one by which he would most like to be remembered.

Goldwyn Follies, The ○
1938, US, 120 mins, colour
Dir: George Marshall
Stars: Adolphe Menjou, Vera Zorina, Ritz Brothers
Rating: ★★

You can dip in almost anywhere in this frantic compendium of comedy, dancing, ballet and song and pull out something worth watching, from the riotous routines of the Ritz Brothers (always at their best when not asked to carry a film on their own shoulders) to Alan Ladd as an audition singer (he doesn't get the job). Ventriloquist Edgar Bergen turns up with the treasurable Charlie McCarthy (Bergen was never the most brilliant of 'vents', but McCarthy was so memorable a doll it didn't matter) and comedian Bobby Clark makes his first film appearance since the suicide of his long-time partner, Paul McCullough, two years earlier. Highlight of it all is probably the Ritzes' maniac version of 'Serenade to a Fish'.

Go Naked in the World ○
1961, US, 100 mins, colour
Dir: Ranald MacDougall
Stars: Gina Lollobrigida, Anthony Franciosa, Ernest Borgnine
Rating: ★

An overheated and ultimately foolish melodrama with Nick (Anthony Franciosa) discovering that the girl he has fallen in love with (Gina Lollobrigida) is a prostitute. The fact that this piece of information is gleefully imparted to him by his domineering father doesn't help. So he leaves her; then he begs her to marry him; then they go to Mexico; then Nick's dad begs her to marry Nick. Yes, really. As you can see, the plot soon parts company with reality. This wouldn't be so bad if the film had wit, humour or style, but it's static and unimaginative. La Lollo looks gorgeous (of course), but that's about it and Franciosa seems about to emote himself into an early grave. Ernest Borgnine plays with the relish of a man determined at least to enjoy himself if he absolutely has to appear in tosh like this.

Gone to Earth
See: The Wild Heart

Gone With the Wind ○
1939, US, 220 mins, colour
Dir: Victor Fleming
Stars: Clark Gable, Vivien Leigh, Olivia de Havilland, Leslie Howard, Thomas Mitchell, Hattie McDaniel
Rating: ★★★

Although Hollywood's greatest epic, this is a film of memorable moments, rather than an outstanding whole. But the war scenes are magnificently impressive and the burning of Atlanta – handled by production designer William Cameron Menzies – a brilliant sequence by any standards. The performance of a lifetime from Vivien Leigh, pulsating with passion, was rightly rewarded with one of the film's nine Academy Awards.

Goodbye Charlie ○
1964, US, 116 mins, colour
Dir: Vincente Minnelli
Stars: Tony Curtis, Debbie Reynods, Pat Boone, Walter Matthau
Rating: ★★

A zany film comedy about a Romeo who turns into an equally amorous Juliet! The director is the Oscar-winning Vincente Minnelli, who made such happy movies as *Gigi* and *The Bells Are Ringing*; here he gets a stand-out performance from Walter Matthau, whose Sir Leopold is a comic creation of which Peter Sellers would have been proud.

Goodbye, Columbus ◑
1969, US, 105 mins, colour
Dir: Larry Peerce
Stars: Richard Benjamin, Ali MacGraw, Jack Klugman
Rating: ★★

Immensely successful, modish bitter-sweet romance, filled with dislikeable characters and superbly scripted by Arnold Schulman from Philip Roth's biting portrait of a successful suburban Jewish family. Watch for Michael Nouri, since the leading man of *Flashdance*, Jaclyn (here billed as Jackie) Smith as a model and a guest appearance from director Larry Peerce's opera singer father Jan Peerce. But the honours are stolen from everyone by Michael Meyers as heroine Ali MacGraw's brother.

Goodbye Girl, The ◑ ⓥ
1977, US, 110 mins, colour
Dir: Herbert Ross

Stars: Richard Dreyfuss, Marsha Mason, Quinn Cummings, Paul Benedict
Rating: ★★★

If you fancy both a good cry and a happy time, this is the film for you. Full of Neil Simon's wisest and wittiest dialogue, it's the story of an emotional divorcee (Marsha Mason) who's been 'duped' by two men, but still crumbles at the thought of living alone – alone, that is, except for her 10-year-old daughter (Quinn Cummings) with whom she shares an amusingly abrasive relationship. Enter out-of-work actor Elliott (Richard Dreyfuss) who seems to have first claim on their apartment and the three are thrown together by 'one of God's little jests'. They get on each other's nerves at first, but, well . . . it's an old-fashioned sort of film. If it perhaps lacks the warmth and spontaneity of the very best cat-and-dog encounters of the past, then be thankful for the frequent Simon gems, as when Dreyfuss, who won an Oscar, is thrown out of his own flat at first sight, and has to call up his tenant in the pouring rain. '873-5261,' he screeches in desperation. 'It's a flooded booth on 7th Avenue.'

Goodbye Mr Chips! ○
1939, US, 114 mins, b/w
Dir: Sam Wood
Stars: Robert Donat, Greer Garson, Paul Henreid
Rating: ★★★★

James Hilton's novel of a schoolmaster's life was sentimentalised for pre-war audiences, but brilliantly knit together by director Sam Wood, and memorably acted by Robert Donat (as Chips) whose performance won an Academy Award, succeeding against such competition as Clark Gable in *Gone With the Wind*. The last few minutes are guaranteed to move even the hardest of hearts.

Goodbye Mr Chips ○
1969, UK, 151 mins, colour
Dir: Herbert Ross
Stars: Peter O'Toole, Petula Clark, Michael Redgrave
Rating: ★★

To remake a much-loved film and one that had such a powerful central performance seems an act of madness. To then turn it into a musical just accentuates the lunacy. The best advice to anyone who loves the 1939 Robert Donat version is: watch something else. The story has been

G

messed about with, the music is limp and the songs are instantly forgettable. They even changed Mr Chips' Christian name from Charles to Arthur (Why? What's the point?). To be fair, Peter O'Toole is an engaging Mr Chips (but ignore his singing!) and it seems a shame his talents are largely wasted here. Petula Clark does a fair job as his wife, but Greer Garson she isn't.

Goodbye My Fancy ○
1951, US, 104 mins, b/w
Dir: Vincent Sherman
Stars: Joan Crawford, Robert Young, Frank Lovejoy, Eve Arden
Rating: ★★★

One for the romantics — although this off-beat love story has a bright line in humour, too. Joan Crawford is particularly good as a lady politician who picks up an old romance while digging up a juicy scandal or two at her old college at the same time. It's a slick comedy-drama which, with its talk of academic liberty and the importance of free education, should please the student community. Eve Arden, the comedienne whose acid wisecracks saved some Forties comedies, had no need to perform a rescue act in this one. Not with Joan Crawford around.

Good Companions, The ○
1957, UK, 104 mins, colour
Dir: J Lee Thompson
Stars: Eric Portman, Celia Johnson, Janette Scott, John Fraser
Rating: ★★★

This 1957 film of J B Priestley's famous back-stage story was made 25 years after the Matthews-Gielgud original. The tuneful score includes six songs with lyrics by Paddy Roberts, and the remarkable cast will keep starspotters busy. And, if Janette Scott is certainly no Jessie Matthews, her verve and enthusiasm, together with the sympathetic playing of the entire cast, more than make amends, as she and Paddy Stone dance up a storm while Celia Johnson and Eric Portman, back stage, make off with the acting honours. Excellent colour photography and fairly fizzy direction from J Lee Thompson.

Good Day for a Hanging ○
1958, US, 85 mins, colour
Dir: Nathan Juran
Stars: Fred MacMurray, Robert Vaughn, Maggie Hayes, James Drury
Rating: ★★

Dramatic, well-characterised Western, dealing with the relationship between a dedicated, but very human law officer, and a young ex-convict, in whom the lawman is continually trying to seek out good. Made by the same team (producer Charles Schneer and director Nathan Juran) that was, a year later, to get together with special effects man Ray Harryhausen to produce the SuperDynamation films *The 7th Voyage of Sinbad* and *The Three World of Gulliver* — and they made this Western as enthralling as their fantasies were later to be. Robert Vaughn made one of his first big impressions as the ex-convict, snarling his way to a memorable portrayal. Fred MacMurray is also impressive as the unpopular marshal.

Good Die Young, The ○
1954, UK, 94 mins, b/w
Dir: Lewis Gilbert
Stars: Laurence Harvey, Margaret Leighton, Gloria Grahame, Richard Basehart, Joan Collins
Rating: ★★

The women fare best in this all-star robbery thriller, whose grip would be tighter if only its basic situation were more believable. Gloria Grahame does her good-time girl act once again to perfection, while Joan Collins scores in an unexpectedly quiet role as a pregnant young wife. Freda Jackson's compelling study of selfishness, René Ray's loyal wife (whose brother loses her husband's savings and drives him to crime) and Margaret Leighton's poised sophisticate all make off with the goods while the men (led by Laurence Harvey, Stanley Baker and John Ireland) remain shadowy figures.

Good Earth, The ○
1937, US, 138 mins, b/w
Dir: Sidney Franklin
Stars: Paul Muni, Luise Rainer, Walter Connolly
Rating: ★★★★

Luise Rainer's portrayal of the indomitable wife of a Chinese peasant made her the first actress to win two Academy Awards (following her success in the previous year in *The Great Ziegfeld*) in this dogged MGM adaptation of Pearl Buck's vast best-selling novel. Fame was not to last for the Austrian actress, however, and she was out of Hollywood in just a few more years. Another Oscar went to distinguished cinematographer Karl Freund, for his work on the storm, the

famine and the locust sequence, which remains a timeless classic in miniature.

Good Father, The ○ ⓥ
1986, UK, 86 mins, colour
Dir: Mike Newell
Stars: Anthony Hopkins, Jim Broadbent, Harriet Walter, Simon Callow, Joanne Whalley
Rating: ★★

This is almost like a throwback to those abrasive Nicol Williamson films of the late Sixties, right down to the girl who rips off her top at one of those boring swinging parties that surely never were. This time it's the admirable Anthony Hopkins in the Williamson role, and it would be hard to find a character more embittered or full of suppressed rage than Bill Hooper, who has left his wife and young son for a reason that does not become apparant (even to Bill) until towards the end of the film. He finds himself channelling his anger into a friend's fight for the custody of his own child, whisked away from him by his lesbian wife. As the friend, Jim Broadbent gives the best performance in the film. Joanne Whalley and Harriet Walter are also good as the mistress and wife in Hooper's life, but the film finally ends in the middle with Hooper unable to decide what to do. As one might expect, though, there are some smart oneliners in between the angst and the four-letter words. 'Some judges,' confides oily legal eagle Simon Callow, knowing he's found the right magistrate for his case, 'are giving custody to lesbians. Kirby-Smith would rather have the child taken out and shot.'

GoodFellas ● ⓥ
1990, US, 143 mins, colour
Dir: Martin Scorsese
Stars: Robert De Niro, Ray Liotta, Joe Pesci, Lorraine Bracco, Paul Sorvino
Rating: ★★★

Robert De Niro back where he shows up best — in the world of guns and godfathers. Faster-talking than the average Mafia saga, this also has a blackly comic edge. Otherwise, the familiar elements of the genre are all violently and gratingly in place. Ray Liotta is Henry Hill, a war baby who grows up with gangsters and dreams only of being one. In his neighbourhood, it's easy. He soon has everything he needs and pities ordinary working guys. He makes dangerous friends like Jimmy the Gent

(De Niro) and Tommy DeVito (Joe Pesci), a frighteningly unpredictable hitman who only stops talking for long enough to shoot someone over some (often imagined) insult. These are all 'wiseguys' or 'goodfellas', but Henry's world of glittering nightclubs and easy cheating on his wife (Lorraine Bracco) starts to slide downhill after one of Jimmy and Tommy's maniac fits of fury results in a senseless death of far-reaching consequences. The film's a mite oppressive and certainly too long: you get the sense of having lived with gangsters, all right, but they all talk the same way in the same harsh, metallic voices, brown men with an aura of death hanging about them. Perfectly acted, though, especially by Liotta, De Niro and Oscar-winning Pesci, whose deliberately one-key performances make their characters seem all the more dangerous.

Good Guys and the Bad Guys, The ○
1969, US, 90 mins, colour
Dir: Burt Kennedy
Stars: Robert Mitchum, George Kennedy, David Carradine, Tina Louise
Rating: ★★

Burt Kennedy became an erratic director, after the highpoint of *Support Your Local Sheriff!*, but this is one of his better spoof Westerns. Robert Mitchum and George Kennedy score nicely off each other as the bad guys combining to tackle an even worse guy (David Carradine, sneering stonily in the days before *Kung Fu*). An excellent supporting cast includes such doughty Hollywood character actors as Martin Balsam, John Davis Chandler, Kathleen Freeman and John Carradine.

Good Guys Wear Black ◐ ♥
1977, US, 96 mins, colour
Dir: Ted Post
Stars: Chuck Norris, Anne Archer, James Franciscus
Rating: ★

A stillborn thriller about a group of Vietnam veterans, once an elite squad of assassins who were set up by a traitor. Now, in California five years later, the survivors are being bumped off in Agatha Christie fashion. The plot is quite preposterous and plays at times like a very old American 'B' movie. Chuck Norris acts mostly with his feet but even so is preferable to the rest of an all-too-distinguished cast, of whom Anne Archer especially is (as

she later proved) capable of much better work. The suspense sequences, although picturesquely shot on a variety of locations, have all the tension of sago pudding.

Good Humor Man, The ⊙
1950, US, 79 mins, b/w
Dir: Lloyd Bacon
Stars: Jack Carson, Lola Albright, Jean Wallace
Rating: ★★★★

One of several amusing postwar comedies to tandem the talents of zany young writer Frank Tashlin (later to become a director himself) and veteran Hollywood director Lloyd Bacon. Others were *Innocence Is Bliss*, *The Affairs of Sally* and *Kill the Umpire*, but this is probably the funniest of the lot. Jack Carson excels himself as an ice-cream salesman unwillingly involved with murder and a disappearing corpse. A scream from start to finish, this crams in enough laughs to leave you breathless.

Good Morning, Boys! ⊙
1936, UK, 79 mins, b/w
Dir: Marcel Varnel
Stars: Will Hay, Graham Moffatt, Lilli Palmer, Martita Hunt
Rating: ★★★

One of Will Hay's earliest film appearances in his famous character of a seedy schoolmaster. The cast includes the famous fat boy, Graham Moffatt, a young Charles Hawtrey and Hay's own son, Will Jr, as an unholy trio of schoolboys, as well as Lilli Palmer, also at the beginning of her career, as a kind of Mata Hari. Peter Godfrey, who plays Cliquot, later went on to Hollywood and became a successful director of Warner thriller films. The story, written by Hay himself (and remade 16 years later with Ronald Shiner as *Top of the Form*) concerns a gang of thieves planning to steal the Mona Lisa.

Good Morning, Vietnam ● ♥
1987, US, 120 mins, colour
Dir: Barry Levinson
Stars: Robin Williams, Forest Whitaker, Tung Thanh Trah, Bruno Kirby, J T Walsh
Rating: ★★★

After a handful of films that really didn't exploit his manic comic talents, Robin Williams exploded on to the screen and made this film a scatological one-man show. He plays a crazy over-the-top army DJ let loose at the

armed forces radio station in Vietnam during the 1960s. Director Barry Levinson gave Williams his head, so much of the dialogue was either changed or ad-libbed by the comedian to suit his own style and persona. The result is stream-of-conciousness lunacy and wicked one-liners delivered with machine-gun rapidity, and it earned Williams an Oscar nomination. It's only after the film has finished that you realise that there's very little storyline. But that doesn't matter; it's immensely enjoyable even if, ultimately, it's much ado about nothing.

Good Neighbour Sam ○
1964, US, 130 mins, colour
Dir: David Swift
Stars: Jack Lemmon, Romy Schneider, Edward G Robinson
Rating: ★★★

There's nothing better for a good situation comedy than complications. And this lively film has plenty of those. Jack Lemmon plays an advertising executive who has to live with his wife's best friend, so that the friend can inherit a fortune. Have you followed the plot so far? Some of the comedy is an embarrassing misfire. But it gets funnier as it goes along. Lemmon's expertise is constantly breathing new life into the film. And there's a very funny running joke about a cigarette advertising film that keeps going wrong. The sunny Dorothy Provine, in a Doris Day-style role, easily outshines continental import Romy Schneider, as the femme fatale, while a strong supporting cast includes such redoubtable character players as Edward Andrews, Anne Seymour, Joyce Jameson and Louis Nye. Michael Connors of *Mannix* fame is in there, too, while the whole flimsy whimsy is skilfully spun together by its director, David Swift, who had previously directed Lemmon to another virtuoso performance as the over-amorous landlord in *Under the Yum Yum Tree*.

Good News ○
1947, US, 95 mins, colour
Dir: Charles Walters
Stars: June Allyson, Peter Lawford, Patricia Marshall, Mel Torme
Rating: ★★★

Dance director Charles Walters made an impressive step up to the director's chair in a college-swing musical whose scarcely believable plot (especially the casting of ever-so-refined Peter Lawford as a brainless football hero)

G

was boosted to the skies by a knock-out De Sylva-Brown-Henderson score in which almost every number was a hit: 'Just Imagine', 'Lucky in Love', 'Good News', 'Ladies' Man', 'The Best Things in Life Are Free' and particularly the spirited final ensemble 'Varsity Drag', performed with truly infectious joie-de-vivre by Lawford (one of his most likeable screen performances) and especially by fizzy leading lady June Allyson. The pair also combine on 'The French Lesson', an ingenious song written for the film by Betty Comden, Adolph Green and Roger Edens. First staged on Broadway in 1927, and filmed before in 1930, but not half as well as this.

Good, the Bad and the Ugly, The ○
1966, Italy, 180 mins, colour
Dir: Sergio Leone
Stars: Clint Eastwood, Lee Van Cleef, Eli Wallach
Rating: ★★★

The third and last Sergio Leone/Clint Eastwood Western and arguably the best. It's long and rambling but always interesting and has a powerful trio of stars in Eastwood, Eli Wallach and Lee Van Cleef. They're all on the trail of a hoard of gold and they cross, double cross and cheat each other right up to the tense and exciting climax – a three-cornered shoot-out in a cemetery. A sprawling tale set during the American Civil War, the film looks very impressive (it was Leone's biggest-budget film at that time). Eastwood is the grim man with no name again but he's positively angelic compared to the ugly, grasping and amoral Wallach and the cold and sadistic Van Cleef. A classic Western that's always worth a second, third or fourth viewing.

Good Time Girl ○
1948, UK, 93 mins, b/w
Dir: David Macdonald
Stars: Jean Kent, Dennis Price, Griffith Jones, Herbert Lom
Rating: ★★★

Jean Kent's striking performance as the reform school refugee in this convincing and very successful British 'social conscience' thriller (based on a true story) got her typed in a kind of role she found hard to escape. Once hailed as one of Britain's most promising directors, David Macdonald

disappointed in postwar times, but this is one of his best films from the period.

Good Wife, The ● Ⓥ
(aka: The Umbrella Woman)
1986, Australia, 97 mins, colour
Dir: Ken Cameron
Stars: Rachel Ward, Bryan Brown, Sam Neill
Rating: ★

A very bizarre kettle of fish and no mistake. A story of sexual obsession in the Australian outback of 1939, it provides a change of step for husband-and-wife co-stars Rachel Ward and Bryan Brown. She plays the wife trying to escape her mother's reputation as a scarlet woman. He's the timber cutter she marries and who inexplicably releases her repressed passions by allowing his younger brother to make love to her. Ward has a stab at an Australian accent, Brown tries to sublimate his macho image and Sam Neill is so oily as the man who comes between them that you wonder why women are so attracted to him. It's unkind to suggest these roles are outside the range of these actors, since any star trio would struggle to make sense of them. Professionally directed, though, and beautifully photographed, technical credits that cannot make this overheated melodrama seem any less unlikely than it does.

Goonies, The ○ Ⓥ
1985, US, 111 mins, colour
Dir: Richard Donner
Stars: Sean Astin, Josh Brolin, Corey Feldman, Ke Huy Quan
Rating: ★★

Full of good ideas, if ultimately something of a likeable mess, this is an adventure story in the Spielberg tradition about a group of kids who hit on a labyrinth of underground tunnels and chambers while trying to find a centuries-old pirate treasure. The sets look like leftovers from an *Indiana Jones* movie, but provide plenty of jumpy moments, as the kids battle against ancient pirate booby traps, as well as a trio of rather too comic crooks, led by Anne Ramsey, later famous as the momma they couldn't throw from the train. You may need an interpreter for some of the children's dialogue, but the action speaks for itself – and there's lots of it. One of the boys is Corey Feldman, who later played adult roles; but juvenile honours go to the endearing fat boy of Jeff Cohen, especially when

he's blurting out the foul deeds of his past after being forced by Ramsey to 'tell everything'.

Goose Steps Out, The ○
1942, UK, 79 mins, b/w
Dir: Will Hay, Basil Dearden
Stars: Will Hay, Frank Pettingell, Charles Hawtrey, Peter Ustinov, Anne Firth
Rating: ★★

Good, fast fun, as comedian Will Hay (in a dual role as a schoolmaster and a German spy!) is parachuted into wartime Germany. Patchy by Hay's standards, though, with rather too much attention paid to the flag-waving plot.

Gorgo ◑
1960, UK, 78 mins, colour
Dir: Eugene Lourie
Stars: Bill Travers, William Sylvester
Rating: ★★★

Good special effects fantasy film as a mother monster comes charging up the Thames to rescue her offspring, which has been captured by mankind. Star Bill Travers obviously didn't believe in the famous piece of advice about never acting with children or animals: after being upstaged by the creatures here, he went on to make *Born Free* (lions), *Ring of Bright Water* (otters), *An Elephant Called Slowly* and *The Belstone Fox*. In its own category, this is certainly a moving and well-handled variation of a familiar theme.

Gorgon, The ●
1964, UK, 83 mins, colour
Dir: Terence Fisher
Stars: Peter Cushing, Christopher Lee, Barbara Shelley
Rating: ★★

Horror specialists Hammer had already ploughed their way through a redoubtable array of vampires, mummies and spare-part creatures by the time they came to this chiller about a snake-haired Medusa, the very sight of whom turns her victims to stone. Peter Cushing and Christopher Lee are bravely cast against type – Cushing as a resoundingly sinister and suspicious doctor, Lee as a sympathetic professor. Director Terence Fisher races through the action while investing the film with a sense of brooding menace. One poor character turns to stone and even loses his hair – which is what comes, perhaps, of actors wearing wigs.

Gorilla at Large ☺

1954, US, 84 mins, colour
Dir: Harmon Jones
Stars: Anne Bancroft, Cameron Mitchell, Charlotte Austin, Lee J Cobb, Lee Marvin, Raymond Burr
Rating: ★★

Formidable cast in carnival murder thriller originally made in 3-D. Oscar-winning Miss Bancroft upstages all but the 'gorilla', although Marvin has a few nice dry lines as a sardonic policeman.

Gorillas in the Mist ☺ ☺

1988, US, 124 mins, colour
Dir: Michael Apted
Stars: Sigourney Weaver, Bryan Brown, Julie Harris
Rating: ★★★

The amazing story of Dian Fossey, an intrepid American woman who studied, befriended and protected mountain gorillas in the wilds of Africa, doesn't have too many faults. Overlength and a slight over-emphasis on Fossey's affair with a wildlife photographer are two of them, but they are far outweighed by its virtues. Sigourney Weaver is perfectly cast as Fossey; you could imagine no more suitable actress to portray a dominant woman who fiercely defends (from poachers) property she regards as her own. The style of editing and the credit to ape makeup expert Rick Baker makes you doubt the authenticity of all the gorilla footage involved, but it cannot be questioned that Weaver was as courageous as her character in moving among the gorillas in their natural habitat. The story is full of drama, and she takes charge of it from the start. Bryan Brown, Julie Harris and Iain Cuthbertson (as her initial mentor) offer decent support, but the film is essentially Weaver and the gorillas; they come out as both winning and winners – and there's an emotional and inspiring ending.

Gorky Park ●

1983, US, 128 mins, colour
Dir: Michael Apted
Stars: William Hurt, Lee Marvin, Brian Dennehy, Joanna Pacula
Rating: ★★★

It certainly is an interesting idea to set a murder investigation in Moscow, where the KGB convolutions run deeper than if the CIA were involved in the States. Three bodies are discovered in Gorky Park, buried in snow with their faces, fingerprints and teeth stripped away. Nevertheless, the city's chief investigator (William Hurt) soon gets on the scent of a conspiracy which predictably involves those in high places, although the workings of the plot remain absorbing and the ending is exhilaratingly right. Hurt is on the mark as the top cop, and Lee Marvin characteristically baccy-spittin' forceful as a visiting American with an interest in sables. In a brief appearance, Alexei Sayle proves himself more interesting as a character actor than as a comedian, and Brian Dennehy is also good as an American lawman whose brother was one of the three victims. Quite a good two hours' worth, although strung out too far. Don't expect a masterpiece and you'll enjoy it.

Go Tell the Spartans ●

1977, US, 114 mins, colour
Dir: Ted Post
Stars: Burt Lancaster, Craig Wasson, Marc Singer
Rating: ★★

A very tough Vietnam war film made by director Ted Post, whose speciality is rugged films of all kinds: he also helmed Clint Eastwood's *Hang 'Em High* and *Magnum Force*. Post has made his movie in the form of a 'patrol' drama, much beloved by makers of Hollywood Westerns and war films and revived so successfully by Oliver Stone in his Oscar winning *Platoon*. Burt Lancaster is in typically uncompromising form as the veteran major and the predictably bloody ending reflects the bitterness and disillusion felt by most Americans as the war came to an end.

Gothic ● ☺

1986, UK, 87 mins, colour
Dir: Ken Russell
Stars: Gabriel Byrne, Natasha Richardson, Julian Sands, Miriam Cyr, Timothy Spall
Rating: ★

To frighten us, to fire our imagination, a nightmare must seem totally real. Ken Russell's tall (and expensive-looking) tale of Shelley, Byron and their ladies conjuring up demons of the mind all through a stormy night is quite plainly such arrant nonsense, like a pretentious surrealist painting come to life, that it never raises more than the occasional visual shudder at some grisly detail. We're bombarded in fact with so many horrific images, each intended to offend the sensibilities and revolt the eyes, that the director never gives the central idea the chance to grip. The cast do their best, though in the case of Julian Sands and Natasha Richardson, that isn't terribly good. Richardson's Scots accent came and went as regularly as the audience where we saw the film, who were perhaps supplying an answer to Timothy Spall's Dr Polidori's plea: 'Is there no escape from this madhouse?' No, this is no living nightmare. More like *Monty Python's Life of Byron*.

Go to Blazes ○

1962, UK, 84 mins, colour
Dir: Michael Truman
Stars: Dave King, Robert Morley, Maggie Smith, Daniel Massey
Rating: ★★

Fast and funny comedy about three crooks with a fire engine as their getaway car. The cast is packed with talent, right down to the minor roles, and includes Daniel Massey, Dennis Price, Coral Browne, Norman Rossington, Miles Malleson, Wilfrid Lawson, Finlay Currie, Arthur Lowe, David Lodge, James Hayter, John le Mesurier and Derek Nimmo! Judging by this, Dave King should have made more films.

Go West ☉

1925, US, 70 mins, b/w
Dir: Lex Neal
Stars: Buster Keaton
Rating: ★★★

Buster Keaton's sixth feature-length comedy provides him with one of his more unusual leading ladies, a Jersey cow named Brown Eyes, who Keaton himself trained for her screen debut. Here the bovine beauty vies for the star's affections with the rancher's daughter Kathleen Myers in one of the Wild West's odder romantic triangles, but as usual, love takes a back seat to Keaton's splendid roster of gags as he proves to be the greenest greenhorn ever to hit the Arizona trail. Roscoe 'Fatty' Arbuckle makes a bizarre appearance in drag.

Go West ☉ ☺

1940, US, 81 mins, b/w
Dir: Edward Buzzell
Stars: Groucho Marx, Chico Marx, Harpo Marx, John Carroll
Rating: ★★★

'Brake! The brake!' yelps Chico in the helter-skelter train-bound finale to this busy comedy lark. Smiling, Harpo

G

obliges by snapping the brake in two and throwing it off the train. It's this fast, furious and riotous visual finish that children will find funniest, while Marx purists will go for the scene at the start where 'greenhorns' Chico and Harpo take 'sharpster' Groucho to the cleaners with the help of a dollar bill on a piece of string.

Graduate, The ◐ ⓥ
1967, US, 105 mins, colour
Dir: Mike Nichols
Stars: Dustin Hoffman, Anne Bancroft, Katharine Ross, William Daniels, Murray Hamilton
Rating: ★★★★

Fast, funny, landmark sex comedy driven along with irresistible verve by Mike Nichols, whose Academy Award as best director was amazingly the only Oscar that the film won. Spot-on performances from Dustin Hoffman, Anne Bancroft and Katharine Ross, superbly sympathetic song score from Simon and Garfunkel and an agonising, cliffhanging ending. Look fast to spot a tiny cameo from Richard Dreyfuss in this great film entertainment.

Grand Canyon ● ⓥ
1991, US, 134 mins, colour
Dir: Lawrence Kasdan
Stars: Danny Glover, Kevin Kline, Steve Martin, Mary McDonnell, Mary-Louise Parker, Alfre Woodard
Rating: ★★

This moody study of American angst scratches the surfaces of several of the malaises of American society, but, like its characters, strikes poses rather than attitudes. Helicopters pound overhead, patrolling the city and especially the 'hood; everywhere is the evidence of bad things coming down. Mack (Kevin Kline), a lawyer, is rescued from a gang of street thugs by Simon (Danny Glover) and feels he must see him again to thank him and maybe do something for him. Claire (Mary McDonnell), Mack's wife, unaware he's had a one-night affair with his secretary (Mary-Louise Parker), finds an abandoned baby and is filled with a desire to adopt it. Simon's sister lives in fear in the bullet-riddled 'hood, while her son runs with its young gangs. Mack's filmmaker friend (Steve Martin) is shot in the thigh by a mugger after his watch. All of these people, Glover excepted, seem a little unhinged. The outlook is bleak. But director Lawrence Kasdan opts for a happy ending and a theory that

sometimes things come out right. Finally the film seems to have fewer teeth even than something like Hill Street Blues. Good performances, though, notably from McDonnell, and a few smartly funny lines here and there.

Grand Central Murder ○
1942, US, 73 mins, b/w
Dir: S Sylvan Simon
Stars: Van Heflin, Cecilia Parker, Sam Levene, Tom Conway
Rating: ★★★

Private eye Rocky Custer, under suspicion for murder, retaliates by taking on the case himself. Tight, fast, hard-hitting thriller that's a lot better than it sounds, if a bit cluttered, and very strongly cast for a 'B' Movie. Van Heflin makes a brashly gritty impression as the hero, and the killer is difficult to spot.

Grand Prix ○
1966, US, 180 mins, colour
Dir: John Frankenheimer
Stars: James Garner, Eva Marie Saint, Yves Montand, Toshiro Mifune
Rating: ★★

The highlight of this motor-racing drama about the lives and loves of drivers on the European racing circuit is undoubtedly a spectacular crash with one car driving up a cliff and another plunging into the sea. But, even with romantic and domestic interludes away from the track, the film remains stuck firmly in bottom gear. Aware that a gimmick is needed to relieve the monotony of race after race, director John Frankenheimer adopts a split-screen technique with the separate images complementary, or splitting it into three to convey simultaneous action. It worked well on the big screen (but is pretty meaningless on TV) and was taken up by Norman Jewison for The Thomas Crown Affair. But it has been little used since. James Garner and the international cast do what they can with the pulp-fiction roles, but their thunder is stolen by the sea of cars flying along at 100mph, with their engines growling like tigers.

Grand Tour: Disaster in Time
See: Timescape

Grandview USA ● ⓥ
1984, US, 97 mins, colour
Dir: Randal Kleiser
Stars: Jamie Lee Curtis, C Thomas Howell, Patrick Swayze, Jennifer Jason

Leigh, Troy Donahue
Rating: ★★

A tough little drama revolving around a demolition derby and teenagers' attempts to prove themselves their own people away from parental influence. The cast is full of such stars-to-be as Patrick Swayze, C Thomas Howell, Jennifer Jason Leigh, Jamie Lee Curtis and real-life brother and sister Joan and John Cusack.

Grapes of Wrath, The ○ ⓥ
1940, US, 128 mins, b/w
Dir: John Ford
Stars: Henry Fonda, Jane Darwell, John Carradine
Rating: ★★★★

Compelling, atmospheric story of a migratory family, their struggle to reach California after leaving their Oklahoma dustbowl homes, and the misfortunes that befall them when they arrive at their destination. Full of memorable moments, the film has magnificent performances from Henry Fonda and John Carradine. But it was another noteworthy portrayal, by Jane Darwell as the mother of the family, that won the Academy Award. Director John Ford also took an Oscar for his sensitive handling of a timeless classic, whose ending has haunted filmgoers down the years.

Graveyard Shift ●
1990, US, 87 mins, colour
Dir: Ralph S Singleton
Stars: David Andrews, Kelly Wolf, Stephen Macht, Brad Dourif
Rating: ★★

Though slow to develop and mostly composed of people creeping around after rats, this is rather a jolly horror film about a giant bat (with tentacles for good measure) that occupies the area beneath an old mill and the adjacent graveyard. When the bullying, lecherous foreman, played with relish, a Vincent Price gleam and a vaguely fake Scottish accent by Steven Macht, decides to clean out the old basement, the time has come for the sound of bat on bone. The Tom Berenger-like David Andrews is the strong and silent hero, and Brad Dourif steals all his scenes as the exterminator who declares himself to be 'not one of your wheedling types Bruce Dern plays' before disappearing all too soon from the action. It's old-fashioned stuff that horror fans should enjoy.

Gray Lady Down ○
1978, US, 111 mins, colour
Dir: David Greene
Stars: Charlton Heston, David Carradine
Rating: ★★★

When the crew of a damaged submarine in a film say, 'We'll be all right for a day and a half', and the captain replies, 'We won't be down here that long', you can bet your last fathom they're in trouble. With Charlton Heston at the con-ning-tower, the producers obviously figured out that this film had to be an epic of some sort. So they made it an epic of suspense. There are some tellingly harrowing moments, and the film is quite exceptionally well made. Christopher (Superman) Reeve makes his screen debut as one of the rescuers.

Grease ○ ⊗
1978, US, 110 mins, colour
Dir: Randal Kleiser
Stars: John Travolta, Olivia Newton-John, Stockard Channing, Jeff Conaway
Rating: ★★★

The story is trite, the dialogue equally so, but it's hard not to like this bouncy pastiche of Fifties teen musicals. All the predictable elements are here (young love, macho posing, hot rod racing and rock 'n' roll), but they're mixed to perfection. John Travolta is great as the high school tough who has a fling with nice Olivia Newton-John on holiday, but is embarrassed when she turns up at his school. Olivia is fine, too, as squeaky-clean Sandy. The songs are good – in fact, as many people bought the soundtrack album as watched the film – the production numbers really swing along.

Grease 2 ○ ⊗
1982, US, 115 mins, colour
Dir: Patricia Birch
Stars: Michelle Pfeiffer, Maxwell Caulfield
Rating: ★

A young and energetic cast attempt to recreate the box-office gold of the John Travolta/Olivia Newton-John Fifties musical, but choreographer and director Patricia Birch merely slips up on a slick of her own making. Where the original film had the high-school hero posing as an athlete to win a new girl's affections, here it is a new (English) boy at school posing as a black-clad biker to win over the heroine. British actor Maxwell Caulfield is not known for being animated on screen, preferring petulance and pouting to creating believable characters with any depth. But here his Chippendale-style pin-up looks serve the lacklustre material well. In the light of his later casting in the *Dynasty* spin-off *The Colbys*, his character name of Carrington appears a happy coincidence. But Michelle Pfeiffer must cringe in her stilettoes when she looks back on this early embarrassment. Fans of Fifties movies should enjoy spotting blasts from the past Tab Hunter, Connie Stevens and Eve Arden.

Great Balloon Adventure, The ⊙
(aka: Olly Olly Oxen Free)
1978, US, 89 mins, colour
Dir: Richard A Colla
Stars: Katharine Hepburn, Kevin McKenzie, Dennis Dimster
Rating: ★★

Katharine Hepburn enjoys herself as an old junk dealer in this refreshing and invigorating tale about two young boys who want to construct their own hot-air balloon. Kate slums it in style, and there's also a wonderful shaggy dog who shares the aerial adventures with this unlikely trio.

Great Balls of Fire! ◑ ⊗
1989, US, 102 mins, colour
Dir: Jim McBride
Stars: Dennis Quaid, Winona Ryder
Rating: ★★

Rock 'n' roller Jerry Lee Lewis was the wild man of Fifties rock, so you would expect a film about his life to be pretty over-the-top, too. And so it is, but unfortunately Dennis Quaid's manic protrayal does the performer little justice and is the driving force behind a very superficial film. The film focuses on a brief part of the man's career and how his marriage to his 13-year-old cousin Myra Gale (Winona Ryder) dented it irreparably. Quaid plays the part as if he's performing on stage all the time. Surely, whatever his faults, Lewis is a man of greater depth than this. On the plus side, the scenes of Jerry Lee in concert are well done and exciting but they only serve to show how awful the rest of the film is.

Great Caruso, The ○
1950, US, 109 mins, colour
Dir: Richard Thorpe
Stars: Mario Lanza, Ann Blyth
Rating: ★★★

The greatest hit of Mario Lanza's career, and one of MGM's biggest financial successes, this most cunningly crafted of all 'highbrow' musicals netted the studio close to five million dollars. The screenplay predictably played around with the truth, glossing over Caruso's first wife and going straight on to Ann Blyth as his second, but the running time was so full of music that the plot scarcely mattered. Despite the presence of arias from the works of Verdi, Puccini and Rossini, the film's biggest hits were 'The Loveliest Night of the Year' (first sung by Blyth to Lanza at a dance), 'Because' and the Bach/Gounod 'Ave Maria'. The tumultuous ending left not a dry eye in the house, but the film surprisingly won only one Oscar – for best sound recording.

Great Catherine ○
1968, UK, 98 mins, colour
Dir: Gordon Flemyng
Stars: Peter O'Toole, Jeanne Moreau
Rating: ★

Lifeless and laughless, this is a would-be comic extension of Shaw's playlet about the amorous adventures of Catherine the Great of Russia and an English officer. The supporting cast includes Zero Mostel, Jack Hawkins and Akim Tamiroff.

Great Day in the Morning ○
1955, US, 87 mins, colour
Dir: Jacques Tourneur
Stars: Robert Stack, Virginia Mayo, Ruth Roman, Raymond Burr
Rating: ★★★

This pre-Civil War Western is definitely superior of its kind. Its hero is another of those tough guys with big hearts, but in this case he's more real than most, and the strongly-written characterisation of this man is what allows Robert Stack to dominate the film against some fierce acting competition. There are good performances from Ruth Roman, Raymond Burr (as a villain called Jumbo Means) and Leo Gordon, but heroine Virginia Mayo, despite top billing, displays little of the fire her character needs. Thanks to cinematographer William Snyder, colour and photography are both excellent and the story has quite a few original twists.

Great Dictator, The ○ ⊗
1940, US, 129 mins, b/w
Dir: Charles Chaplin

G

Stars: Charlie Chaplin, Paulette Goddard, Jack Oakie, Reginald Gardiner
Rating: ★★★

Charlie Chaplin's satire on the Axis leaders was said to have so incensed Adolf Hitler that he thrust the little man to the top of his 'death list' after his proposed conquest of America. Hitler can't have exactly been pleased by the funny performances of Chaplin's co-stars, Jack Oakie as Napaloni (Mussolini), Henry Daniell as Garbitsch (Goebbels) and Billy Gilbert as Herring (Goering). Funniest scene is the one in which Chaplin and Oakie each tries to keep his head higher than the other in revolving barber's chairs.

Great Escape, The ○ ⓥ
1963, US, 173 mins, colour
Dir: John Sturges
Stars: Steve McQueen, James Garner, Richard Attenborough, James Donald, Charles Bronson, Donald Pleasence
Rating: ★★★

For its first 90 minutes, this is a truly great example of the POW film. By comparison, its second half is merely exciting. The screenplay, cuttingly well written by James Clavell and W R Burnett from Paul Brickhill's book, has all the bite of the best prison-camp humour and heartbreak too, especially when the first intricate escape tunnel, which has taken weeks to build, is discovered by the Germans. Although it perhaps lacks the emotional involvement to put it in the topmost class, *The Great Escape* still has much to offer in the way of thrills and entertainment. Of the many first-class actors taking part, the three who make the most impact are Steve McQueen as Hilts, who chalks up his 20th escape bid in the course of the film; John Leyton as Willie, the tunneller; and James Donald, giving an immaculate performance as the British commanding officer.

Greatest Show on Earth, The ○ ⓥ
1952, US, 153 mins, colour
Dir: Cecil B DeMille
Stars: Cornel Wilde, Betty Hutton, Charlton Heston, Dorothy Lamour, James Stewart
Rating: ★★★

Cecil B DeMille's circus blockbuster: it won an Academy Award as the best film of its year, and boasts a spectacular train crash besides thrills in the ring. Best performances come from James

Stewart, as the clown on the run from his past, and Lyle Bettger, as the insanely jealous Klaus. On the glamour side, it's nice to see Betty Hutton and Dorothy Lamour together again. Both had been stalwarts of Paramount pictures for some years. And, back in 1942, Betty Hutton's first film had starred Dorothy Lamour.

Great Expectations ○ ⓥ
1946, UK, 118 mins, b/w
Dir: David Lean
Stars: John Mills, Valerie Hobson, Bernard Miles, Alec Guinness, Jean Simmons
Rating: ★★★★

Director David Lean turned Charles Dickens's novel into a lavish but unostentatious screen masterpiece that has stood up well to the passage of time. Thanks for this is due, in no small way, to John Mills and Jean Simmons. Alec Guinness made his major screen debut in this film as the toffee-nosed Herbert Pocket and injected some dateless humour into his role. His finest moment comes when he challenges John Mills to a fight. Alec prances around like a ballet dancer. Very showy. But it is John who does all the scoring. The film also contains several pretty frightening sequences, the worst being that in which Finlay Currie, playing the convict Magwitch, jumps out of an eerie churchyard and grabs young Pip.

Great Gatsby, The ○
1949, US, 90 mins, b/w
Dir: Elliot Nugent
Stars: Alan Ladd, Betty Field, Macdonald Carey, Ruth Hussey, Shelley Winters, Barry Sullivan
Rating: ★★★

Second and best of the three film versions of F Scott Fitzgerald's famous story of a wealthy socialite gangster undone by love of a worthless woman. Errol Flynn wanted the title role, but it went to Alan Ladd, who was exactly right for it, and gave a sharply-shaded performance, probably his best. Betty Field doesn't seem so well-cast as Daisy (Susan Hayward, perhaps?), but there's a whole string of interesting supporting performances from Macdonald Carey, Shelley Winters, Barry Sullivan, Ed Begley, Carole Mathews, Henry Hull and Elisha Cook Jr. Together with Ladd, they infuse the picture with real life (which the subsequent Robert Redford version didn't have) and keep the viewer on nerve-edge hoping the

story will turn away from an impending tragic ending. Only the film's relatively small scale and lack of ambition pushes it down from the top level.

Great Gatsby, The ❶ ⓥ
1974, US, 146 mins, colour
Dir: Jack Clayton
Stars: Robert Redford, Mia Farrow, Bruce Dern, Karen Black, Scott Wilson, Sam Waterston
Rating: ★★

About every 25 years the cinema takes it into its head to have a go at Scott Fitzgerald's almost unfilmable story about the mysterious millionaire living in his Long Island mansion, staring out at the Sound and looking destiny enigmatically in the face. Successive generations of bland charmers – Warner Baxter in 1926, Alan Ladd in 1949 and Robert Redford here – have attempted the title role. The direction and production design perfectly capture the flavour of the post-World War One period in which the film is set. But they also tend to make the film so rarefied as to squeeze the life force out of it, setting the excellent supporting performances of Karen Black, Bruce Dern, Sam Waterston and Scott Wilson in isolation rather than as part of a whole. You'll also spot Howard Da Silva, who was in the 1949 version before being blacklisted for alleged Communist connections. Scott Wilson has Da Silva's old role this time. The costumes and set decorations are breathtaking.

Great Guns ⊙ ⓥ
1941, US, 74 mins, b/w
Dir: Monty Banks
Stars: Stan Laurel, Oliver Hardy
Rating: ★★

This is the first and best of Laurel and Hardy's films after they left Hal Roach and found control of their material rapidly running away from them. Watch out for Alan Ladd in a tiny part as a soldier buying gum in a store. A year later he was to become a star.

Great Locomotive Chase, The ○
1956, US, 86 mins, colour
Dir: Francis D Lyon
Stars: Fess Parker, Jeffrey Hunter
Rating: ★★

A good but not outstanding Western thriller from Walt Disney, based on the same story that inspired Buster Keaton's *The General*. Although the characters are never as clear-cut as they might be, the action moves along swiftly and the Technicolor photography is splendid, Fess Parker is appropriately rugged, but co-star Jeffrey Hunter has a less happy time on the acting front. Still, it's pretty rousing stuff for the younger viewer.

Great Manhunt, The
See: State Secret

Great McGinty, The ○
(aka: Down Went McGinty)
1940, US, 83 mins, b/w
Dir: Preston Sturges
Stars: Brian Donlevy, Muriel Angelus, Akim Tamiroff, William Demarest
Rating: ★★★

The film started director Preston Sturges' brief but giddy ascent to the ranks of cinema's immortals. A screenwriter with Paramount (after eventful early years as an inventor), Sturges offered the studio one of his scripts for 10 dollars on condition that they let him direct it himself. The result was this bitingly satirical comedy about a bird-brained down-and-out (Brian Donlevy) who rises to governorship thanks to quirks of fate. Full of wonderful moments and a marvellous ending.

Great Mouse Detective, The ○ ⓥ
(aka: Basil The Great Mouse Detective)
1986, US, 75 mins, colour
Dir: John Musker
Stars: Voice stars: Vincent Price, Val Bettin, Barrie Ingham, Candy Candido, Alan Young, Shani Wallis
Rating: ★★

Lesser Disney, but a veritable masterpiece of wit and action in comparison with such competition as the Care Bears and My Little Pony films. It's the broadness and crudeness of its outlines and general animation that betray it as no more than a mildly enjoyable diversion from the studio. Its good scenes are really limited to two or three – a toyshop battle and a waterfront dive among them – and, of the three musical numbers, only one shows the signs of due care and attention that would soon return to the studio. This is 'Let Me Be Good to You', which could have come straight out of Chicago and, raunchily voiced by Melissa Manchester as a mouse chanteuse, momentarily transports proceedings to a more lively dimension. Vincent Price enjoys himself much as one might expect as

the arch-fiend Ratigan, a murine relative of Dr Phibes, and some additional fun is afforded by the mouse queen, target of Ratigan's plot, who looks at the peg-legged bat Fidget dressed in yeoman's uniform and asks, 'Have you been with us long?' Not too frightening, and at least never cloying, it's a safe bet for under-twelves.

Great Muppet Caper, The ○ ⓥ
1981, UK, 95 mins, colour
Dir: Jim Henson
Stars: Charles Grodin, Diana Rigg, John Cleese, Robert Morley, Peter Ustinov, Jack Warden
Rating: ★★★

'Look, Dad, it's a bear.' 'No dear, it's a frog. Bears wear hats.' The muppets are hardly ever as bad as they might be and here they go on a spoof jewel caper with a full quota of asides to the audience and spoofs of movie legend. Miss Piggy takes part in a (rather good) take-off of an Esther Williams water ballet and a Busy Berkeley dance routine, Kermit and Fozzie pose as twins to foil the villains, and Charles Grodin is splendidly po-faced as the rascally brother of heroine Diana Rigg, falling in love with Miss Piggy with heart-rending sincerity. There are longueurs, of course, but also continuous reminders of an original humour at work. 'You know,' confides Fozzie to Kermit at a sleazy hotel, 'I may be mistaken, but the bellhops look like rats.' 'Humph,' says the proprietor, overhearing, 'you should see the chambermaids.'

Great Outdoors, The ○ ⓥ
1988, US, 90 mins, colour
Dir: Howard Deutch
Stars: Dan Aykroyd, John Candy
Rating: ★★

John Hughes, the writer of Home Alone, whose box-office takings have made it the biggest comedy money-spinner of all time, has had more hits than misses in his career. There are a few good belly laughs in this caper about a family holiday going disastrously wrong and the pairing of Dan Aykroyd (always better when playing an unsympathetic character) and John Candy works well, but the material is on the whole depressingly threadbare. Fans of up-and-coming star Annette Bening will recognise her in one of her earliest roles as Aykroyd's pampered wife. The distributors thought so little of the

movie's chances outside America that it didn't even get a British cinema release, going direct to video instead.

Great Santini, The ◐
1979, US, 111 mins, colour
Dir: Lewis John Carlino
Stars: Robert Duvall, Blythe Danner, Michael O'Keefe
Rating: ★★

Not exactly a run-of-the-mill film to come across these days, this story of a wildcat Marine Flying Corps colonel and his much put-upon family, with whom he shares a strident and sometimes amusing love-loathe relationship. Director Lewis John Carlino (who also wrote the film) hasn't the know-how to extract the skilful performances, especially from the youngsters, that the film needs, although one warms to the ugly daughter (Lisa Jane Persky) who, desperate for her macho father's attention, tells him she is pregnant by a cross-eyed negro pacifist.

Great Scout and Cathouse Thursday, The ◐
1976, US, 102 mins, colour
Dir: Don Taylor
Stars: Lee Marvin, Oliver Reed, Robert Culp, Elizabeth Ashley, Kay Lenz
Rating: ★

Careering comedy-Western with pantomime performances from Lee Marvin and Oliver Reed as bedraggled Westerner and overweight Indian respectively. The plot's situations come up with some nice ideas, especially Robert Culp's refusal to pay a ransom for his wife because he doesn't want her back, although director Don Taylor's treatment of them is not exactly subtle.

Great St Trinian's Train Robbery, The ○ ⓥ
1965, UK, 94 mins, colour
Dir: Sidney Gilliat
Stars: Frankie Howerd, Dora Bryan, George Cole, Reg Varney
Rating: ★★

St Trinian's listed as an ancient monument. Three hundred of its pupils awarded the MBE ('It's a diabolical liberty,' declares Ringo in a newspaper headline). Yes, those teenage tigresses are back, thwarting a gang of thieves led by Frankie Howerd and the voice of Stratford Johns. The fun is kept lively, and a little dialogue be-

G

tween Howerd and Leon Thau (as a Pakistani railwayman) towards the end is priceless.

Great Waldo Pepper, The ○ ⓥ
1975, US, 108 mins, colour
Dir: George Roy Hill
Stars: Robert Redford, Bo Svenson, Susan Sarandon
Rating: ★★★

Written by William Goldman, Oscar winner for *Butch Cassidy and the Sundance Kid*, this elegiac homage to World War One fliers who became barnstorming aerial stunt men in the Twenties reunited Robert Redford with George Roy Hill, director of his two hits *Butch Cassidy* and *The Sting*. Redford, as the disillusioned pilot reduced to defying death in an air circus, gives one of his best, least self-admiring performances and Susan Sarandon, as always, is superb. Stunning flying scenes and an intelligent screenplay are major assets, and it is genuinely surprising that the film failed to take off at the box-office.

Great Waltz, The ○
1938, US, 103 mins, b/w
Dir: Julien Duvivier
Stars: Luise Rainer, Fernand Gravet, Miliza Korjus, Lionel Atwill
Rating: ★★★

One of Hollywood's best reach-for-your-handkerchief biopics of great composers, in this case Johann Strauss. Never mind the story, feel the treatment: the film is full of the splendour of Strauss' lilting music, and the roaring spirit of the times, with French director Julien Duvivier achieving a bewitching blend of music and pictures. Crowd sequences and production numbers are thrillingly well organised and really stir the emotions. Double Oscar-winner Luise Rainer acts quite exquisitely as Strauss' devoted wife; Miliza Korjus sings brilliantly as the opera star he later falls in love with; Fernand Gravet makes Strauss believable both as a musical genius and a flesh-and-blood person.

Great Waltz, The ○
1972, US, 150 mins, colour
Dir: Andrew L Stone
Stars: Horst Buchholz, Mary Costa, Nigel Patrick
Rating: ★★

This great piece of schmaltz is an over-colourful musical biopic of the

Viennese composer Johann ('Blue Danube') Strauss Jr. It stars a highly energetic Horst Buchholz as the composer who became the 'Waltz King' despite the efforts of his father Johann Sr (probably best known for 'The Radetsky March') to prevent him from pursuing a musical career. The story is okay while the conflict between tempestuous Johann Sr and eager young Johann lasts. But after dad's demise, we are swept off into an indigestible whirl of chocolate-box romance and champagne-soaked parties — a sort of *Come Dancing* gone mad, with dialogue straight out of a second-feature Western. Director Andrew L Stone has done far, far better things (the Lena Horne/Bill Bojangles Robinson musical *Stormy Weather*, the disaster movie *The Last Voyage*). But then there is the music — 'The Blue Danube' (of course), the 'Tritsch-Tratsch Polka' and 'Thunder and Lightning' are just part of a generous selection of truly magnificent music, which also includes narration sung by Kenneth McKellar. Shame you can't turn the vision off and leave the sound on!

Great Ziegfeld, The ○
1936, US, 176 mins, b/w
Dir: Robert Z Leonard
Stars: William Powell, Myrna Loy, Luise Rainer, Frank Morgan
Rating: ★★★

This is a skilfully structured, extravagantly mounted look at the career of showman Florenz Ziegfeld (astutely played by William Powell) who gave his name to the Ziegfeld Follies. Luise Rainer's sympathetic portrait of Anna Held was rewarded with an Oscar, while the climax may have been remembered by Orson Welles when he came to make *Citizen Kane*. The singer on the revolving staircase in one of the biggest musical numbers will be recognised by some as Dennis Morgan, then still appearing under his real name, Stanley Morner. Strangely, he doesn't use his own (very respectable) singing voice. The tones that issue from his lips, singing about a pretty girl being like a melody, are those of Allan Jones. The film won the Academy Award for Best Film.

Greed ◑ ⓥ
1994, US, 113 mins, colour
Dir: Jonathan Lynn
Stars: Michael J Fox, Kirk Douglas, Nancy Travis, Olivia D'Abo, Ed Begley Jr, Jonathan Lynn

A deadeningly over-performed comedy about a group of grasping relatives all willing to go to any lengths to get their hands on the $25 million scrap metal fortune of their elderly wheelchaired Uncle Joe (Kirk Douglas). All, that is, except failed pro bowler Danny (Michael J Fox), who isn't interested — until the relatives drag him into the act. They're super-worried about the old man's nubile 'nurse' (Olivia D'Abo) whom they're afraid will inherit the lot. We never do find out if Olivia is after the old guy's money, but she's such a bad actress no one will care. Under director Jonathan Lynn's far from gentle persuasion, a whole cast of seasoned pros go further over the top than in a TV variety sketch: interest bites the dust quicker here than in almost any film in living memory. Incidentally, the family name is McTeague, the name of the principal character in the 1923 classic *Greed*: it's a little doubtful if anyone will get this in-joke, yet it's the only hint of subtlety around. Nancy Travis alone plays it all straight.

Green Berets, The ○ ⓥ
1968, US, 141 mins, colour
Dir: Ray Kellogg
Stars: John Wayne, David Janssen, Jim Hutton, Aldo Ray, Raymond St Jacques
Rating: ★★★

John Wayne's pro-America-in-Vietnam film is a fine piece of entertainment if one ignores the flag-waving and concentrates on it purely as an escapist war movie. Wayne also had a hand in the direction and his son Patrick had a featured role. In a small role: a then little-known comedian called Richard Pryor.

Green Card ◑ ⓥ
1990, US, 107 mins, colour
Dir: Peter Weir
Stars: Gerard Depardieu, Andie MacDowell, Bebe Neuwirth, Robert Prosky
Rating: ★★★

Following the success of *Pretty Woman*, romance was well in at Hollywood studios in 1990, and what better ally could they have to rally the cause than France's own incredible hulk, Gerard Depardieu! He plays an alien in America who enters into a marriage of convenience with horticulturist Andie MacDowell to obtain the precious Green Card that will enable him to stay in the country. She in turn can claim a marvellous apartment with refectory/greenhouse attached that is only available to married couples. They part as strangers, and everything is fine until immigration decides to investigate in depth. In an enforced weekend together, Depardieu and MacDowell discover what the rest of us have guessed from reel one: but that's romantic cinema for you. Very nicely done, all the same, with dialogue that smacks sweetly of ad-libbing, the same attention to supporting roles as in *Pretty Woman*, and an inspired sequence where the 'happy' couple invents a series of honeymoon snapshots. Depardieu adapts very well to the subtleties of English-speaking comedy, and even submits to some ribbing about his weight.

Green Dolphin Street ○
1947, US, 155 mins, b/w
Dir: Victor Saville
Stars: Lana Turner, Van Heflin, Donna Reed, Richard Hart
Rating: ★★

The great New Zealand earthquake of 1855 has been devastatingly recreated for this story of a young couple in the Antipodes. British director Victor Saville has used the Hollywood studio and the Californian redwood forests to film trees being tossed into the air; geysers spouting water and mud; houses collapsing and a mountain splitting down the middle. Even Lana Turner gets her hair mussed: nothing is missed in the cause of realism.

Green Fingers ○
1947, UK, 87 mins, b/w
Dir: John Harlow
Stars: Robert Beatty, Nova Pilbeam
Rating: ★★

A rare opportunity to see Nova Pilbeam, one of Britain's top stars in the Thirties (she made her debut as a teenager in 1934), whose film career stretched over 20 years. Here she's the society girl that poor-born osteopath Robert Beatty (here at the peak of his successful years of the Forties) loves in a plot remarkably similar to that used by the Americans for the Charlton Heston-Lizabeth Scott drama, *Bad for Each Other*. In the cast is Moore Marriott, best remembered now for his comedy character roles in the most popular of the Will Hay comedies.

Green Fire ○
1955, US, 95 mins, colour
Dir: Andrew Marton
Stars: Stewart Granger, Grace Kelly, Paul Douglas, John Ericson
Rating: ★★

A colourful film about romance, adventure and emerald mining in the Colombian jungles of South America – surely one of the most unusual settings in film history. During location filming in Colombia, Stewart Granger, Grace Kelly and others lived aboard a huge barge moored in a river. When the river suddenly went into spate, the barge broke loose and was drifting at speed down the river when the natives in canoes rescued the stars. Definitely not in the script.

Greengage Summer, The ○
(aka: Loss of Innocence)
1961, UK, 99 mins, colour
Dir: Lewis Gilbert
Stars: Kenneth More, Susannah York, Danielle Darrieux, Jane Asher, Maurice Denham
Rating: ★★★

A strange and most appealing film about the pains of growing up. Susannah York shines in her first demanding role in the cinema, as one of four youngsters stranded in France. And the colour photography of the French countryside is quite breathtaking. There's a very welcome appearance by the talented French star Danielle Darrieux, and the young Jane Asher is minxishly effective as Miss York's sister.

Green Grass of Wyoming ○
1948, US, 89 mins, colour
Dir: Louis King
Stars: Peggy Cummins, Charles Coburn, Lloyd Nolan, Robert Arthur
Rating: ★★

Dog-fever in the Hollywood of the Forties, after MGM had struck it rich with Lassie, was quickly followed by horse-fever. A colt called Flicka spearheaded a host of vigorous, colourful outdoor adventure stories, guaranteed to thrill animal lovers and wring a tear from the most hardened animal-hater. *My Friend Flicka*, *The Red Pony*, *Black Beauty* and *Thunderhead, Son of Flicka* were offspring of the idea. *Green Grass of Wyoming*, a sort of sequel to the last of these, is a folksy Western with some exciting trotting scenes towards the end.

Green Grow the Rushes ○
1950, UK, 80 mins, b/w
Dir: Derek Twist
Stars: Richard Burton, Honor Blackman, Roger Livesey
Rating: ★★★

Inspired by the success of *Whisky Galore!*, British filmmakers turned out so many similar comedies in the next few years that it seemed the entire English coast must be a seething nest of rum-runners and smugglers. The scene here is the Kent marsh country and the spirit in question is brandy. Although its brand of whimsy is rather far behind Ealing Studios, *Green Grow the Rushes* has amusing performances by Roger Livesey as Captain Biddle and Harcourt Williams as a chairman of the Bench. It was Richard Burton's last British film before he went to Hollywood the next year.

Green Hell ○
1940, US, 87 mins, b/w
Dir: James Whale
Stars: Douglas Fairbanks Jr, Joan Bennett, George Sanders, Alan Hale, George Bancroft, Vincent Price
Rating: ★★

A prime cast in one of the last films from the original master of the American sound horror film, British-born James Whale. Here he turned in an oddity among adventure stories, with Douglas Fairbanks Jr, Joan Bennett, George Sanders, Alan Hale, George Bancroft and Vincent Price all emoting madly in the depths of the South American jungle. The screenplay is by double Oscar-winner Frances Marion.

Green Man, The ○
1956, UK, 80 mins, b/w
Dir: Robert Day
Stars: Alastair Sim, George Cole, Terry-Thomas, Jill Adams
Rating: ★★★

A happy comedy film about a hired assassin – Alastair Sim – determined to bump off an inept politician (Raymond Huntley) who has come to a country inn for an illicit weekend. Sim's performance – especially when the character is seen in flashback, committing youthful assassinations – reminds one how much subtlety the British comedy film has lost in the past few decades, and how scandalously under-used Sim remained. This is written by the old and reliable firm of Frank Launder and Sidney Gilliat,

G

who also worked with Sim on such classics as *Waterloo Road, Green for Danger, The Happiest Days of Your Life* and *The Belles of St Trinian's.*

Gregory's Girl ○ Ⓥ

1980, UK, 91 mins, b/w
Dir: Bill Forsyth
Stars: John Gordon Sinclair, Dee Hepburn, Jake D'Arcy, Clare Grogan
Rating: ★★★

The freshest and funniest school comedy from Britain since *It's Great to be Young* 25 years earlier. The soccer team of an unnamed Scottish school is in trouble. 'Hear they were awarded a corner last week,' says a spectator at their latest debacle, 'and took a lap of honour.' But wait. There's a new star on the horizon. Her name is Dorothy (Dee Hepburn). She's beautiful. And deadly (with a futba' that is). The deposed striker Gregory (John Gordon Sinclair), demoted to goalie, falls heavily for her. In between his attempts to come to terms with this hopeless infatuation, the film is fiercely funny about school life . . . and so true you have to laugh. It's a personal triumph for writer–director Bill Forsyth, moving with one bound into the field of commercial hits without discarding any of his unique native talents. The two leads are both very good, but the film is stolen by tiny Allison Forster as Gregory's wiser-than-he sister – all of 10 years old.

Gremlins ○ Ⓥ

1984, US, 106 mins, colour
Dir: Joe Dante
Stars: Zach Galligan, Phoebe Cates, Hoyt Axton, Frances Lee McCain
Rating: ★★★★

Basically a children's film with horrific overtones, this is a vastly entertaining fantasy, directed by Joe (*InnerSpace*) Dante, who doesn't miss a trick from the moody opening in Chinatown when Papa (Hoyt Axton, whose narration and performance are both spot-on) buys a mogwai there. An endearing cross between a chihuahua and a bat-eared fox, the mogwai must not, Axton is told, be exposed to bright light, have water dropped on it or be fed after midnight. Of course, you don't need me to tell you that Axton and his family rapidly do all three, ending up with a whole pack of man-eating, three-feet high, slavering gremlins who, besides people, eat everything in sight, stop the traffic, smoke and gamble in the local bars

and enjoy a showing of *Snow White and the Seven Dwarfs.* The trick-work and technical skill involved in all this is immense, and the humour, sentiment, excitement and horror, although all pretty basic, are blended as well as one could reasonably expect. The highlight of the fun and grisly games is undoubtedly the ingenious scene in which Axton's wife disposes of several death-bent gremlins with the aid of various kitchen contrivances.

Gremlins 2: The New Batch ◐ Ⓥ

1990, US, 107 mins, colour
Dir: Joe Dante
Stars: Zach Galligan, Phoebe Cates, John Glover, Robert Prosky, Christopher Lee
Rating: ★★★

They're back and hyped to the hilt – singing, dancing, eating and even taking over the cinema. Everything is thrown into this one – from old-time 'B' stars like Kathleen Freeman, Dick Miller and Kenneth Tobey, to getting Daffy Duck to top and tail the movie. It's just as well, as the laughs and thrills are rather fewer this time around: Old Wing (Keye Luke) dies and Gizmo the mogwai, on the loose again, is soon doused with water and gives rise to the puffball creatures that quickly metamorphose into cackling, scaly, bat-eared, fang-baring gremlins. Some of them even take over the laboratory where mad scientist Christopher Lee is conducting all sorts of experiments. 'All a man wants,' he grumbles, 'are some fresh germs.' The gremlins he gets are fresh all right, enough to swallow all his potions and turn into anything from a talking gremlin-about-town to a monstrous cross between gremlin and spider.

Grey Fox, The ○

1982, Canada, 91 mins, colour
Dir: Phillip Borsos
Stars: Richard Farnsworth, Jackie Burroughs
Rating: ★★★★

This old-fashioned Western about an old-fashioned Westerner – the true-life character Bill Miner who robbed stagecoaches for 18 years before serving 26 years for doing it – is well-nigh flawless of its type. The film takes up Miner's story when he's released from prison in 1901 at 60. After an abortive two years trying to scratch a living, he turns to robbing trains instead of stages. Richard Farnworth, a

veteran Western stuntman turned featured player, makes the most of the role of a lifetime as Miner, with a reflective performance that stamps his own slow-burning and humorous personality on the character he's playing. He has admirable assistance from John Hunter's perfectly poised script which never overstates or supplies unnecessary embellishment, but always manages to catch the perfect phrase to fit the scene.

Greyfriars Bobby ☉

1961, UK, 91 mins, colour
Dir: Don Chaffey
Stars: Donald Crisp, Laurence Naismith, Kay Walsh, Andrew Cruikshank, Gordon Jackson
Rating: ★★★

The Disney version, to be taken with a wee drop of scotch, about the 19th century Edinburgh dog who kept a long and lonely vigil by his master's grave until he passed into legend. Donald Crisp, a hardened veteran of several *Lassie* films, is at his crusty best, and the film is cannily set and wonderfully well shot in Technicolor. The supporting cast includes a battery of familiar Scottish players of the time, and reunites many of the actors from that charming Ealing film *The Kidnappers*, including the littlest kidnapper himself, Vincent Winter. Have a handkerchief at the ready.

Greystoke – The Legend of Tarzan, Lord of the Apes ◐ Ⓥ

1984, US, 130 mins, colour
Dir: Hugh Hudson
Stars: Ralph Richardson, Ian Holm, Christopher Lambert, Andie MacDowell, James Fox, Cheryl Campbell
Rating: ★★★

As probably befits a movie that cost $33 million and took eight years to get to the screen, production on this mammoth Tarzan epic was a fraught affair. Respected scriptwriter Robert Towne removed his name and insisted on the pseudonym P H Vazak when he was taken off the film. Then, after casting fashion model and acting newcomer Andie MacDowell as Tarzan's girlfriend Jane, director Hugh Hudson took her voice off the soundtrack and had all her lines re-dubbed by Glenn Close. To her undying credit, MacDowell bounced back a couple of years later to become one of Hollywood's brightest young stars. Beautifully shot and impeccably acted, the film's main plus is that it sticks closer to the original Edgar Rice Burroughs' novel than all the previous chest-thumping, vine-swinging Hollywood versions. But for all that, it's a dramatically uneven picture. The first half works best, with the boy Tarzan being raised by a family of cute apes, and is on less sure ground when adult Tarzan (Christopher Lambert) is brought back to Edwardian England.

Grifters, The ● ⓥ
1990, US, 110 mins, colour
Dir: Stephen Frears
Stars: Anjelica Huston, John Cusack, Annette Bening
Rating: ★★

Con artist Roy Dillon (John Cusack) has a good front for his small-time but successful criminal activities and an attractive girlfriend (Annette Bening) in tow. Everything is fine until his mother (Anjelica Huston) shows up. She tries to come between him and his girl but all the while the Mob is after her. Despite sound performances from all the principals, this film is less satisfying than the novel by Jim Thompson upon which it is based. It's all a little uneven until all the pieces start coming together towards the end. Half the problem, perhaps, is that the characters don't really command our sympathy, making it difficult to care for or about them. Still, it's a fascinating tale in which the twists and turns keep your interest right to the end.

Grigsby
See: The Last Grenade

Grip of Fear, The ⓞ
(aka: Experiment in Terror)
1962, US, 122 mins, b/w
Dir: Blake Edwards
Stars: Glenn Ford, Lee Remick, Stefanie Powers, Ross Martin
Rating: ★★★

Hitchcock-style thriller tautly turned out by director Blake Edwards in between making such comedy gems as *Breakfast at Tiffany's* and *The Pink Panther*. Here, he coaxes a nicely-timed performance from the young Lee Remick as a cashier menaced by a frightened, wheezy killer (a solid start to Ross Martin's film career) who is out to rob her bank. Stefanie Powers is also very good as Remick's younger sister. There's a tense climax, in a stadium, to a film that's full of edgy moments.

Grip of the Strangler ⓞ
(aka: The Haunted Strangler)
1958, UK, 79 mins, b/w
Dir: Robert Day
Stars: Boris Karloff, Jean Kent, Elizabeth Allan
Rating: ★★

This literate horror thriller brought Boris Karloff back to British films after more than 20 years away. For the occasion, screenwriter Jan Read contributed a fascinating plot that involves a novelist investigating an old murder case. There's a splendidly atmospheric ending (heightened by Lionel Banes' vivid black-and-white photography), with Karloff in a graveyard, unravelling the mystery at last – to his own cost.

Groundhog Day ○ ⓥ
1992, US, 103 mins, colour
Dir: Harold Ramis
Stars: Bill Murray, Andie MacDowell, Chris Elliot, Stephen Tobolowsky
Rating: ★★★

Imagine how you would feel if you woke up at 6am and every day was the same. Well yes, okay we all feel that way. But for Bill Murray, a self-centred TV weatherman sullenly enduring his fourth annual visit to Punxsutawney on Feb 2 (Groundhog Day), every day from now really is the same. He's trapped in a 24-hour timelock in which most events – apart from those he affects – are exactly the same. It's surprising to find Murray at the head of the cast of this romantic comedy-fantasy, since it's almost a remake of his own *Scrooged*. At first, as each 'new' day dawns, Murray is angry, desperate to escape. He confides in his producer (Andie MacDowell) but naturally on the 'next' day their conversation never happened. Nor can he get her into bed, despite learning, day after day, all her whims and fancies. Passing through the 'I can do anything' stage, and past several days of committing suicide in different ways, Murray finally decides on a life of good deeds. Get the picture? So far, so sweet, but all this is inevitably, well, repetitive, so despite a few good laughs, necessity often gets the better of invention. In spurts, though, it's quirky fun in vaguely old-fashioned style.

Group, The ⓞ
1966, US, 152 mins, colour
Dir: Sidney Lumet

Stars: Candice Bergen, Joan Hackett, Elizabeth Hartman, Shirley Knight
Rating: ★★

This story of the lives of eight college girls from 1933 to 1939, is a pretty strong brew – with its elements of lesbianism, insanity, drunkenness, war, frigidity, death, beating-up and problems over contraception. The best episode is the lightest, as Polly puts up with the harmless and rather jolly eccentricities of her fat old father, who plays cunningly upon the fact that he is supposed to be mad. The fashions are fascinating, and the director, of course, is Sidney Lumet. But can you remember the rest of the group? They were Jessica Walter, Kathleen Widdoes, Joanna Pettet and (most difficult) Mary Robin-Redd, who plays Pokey.

Grumpy Old Men ⓞ ⓥ
1993, US, 100 mins, colour
Dir: Donald Petrie
Stars: Jack Lemmon, Walter Matthau, Ann-Margret, Burgess Meredith, Daryl Hannah, Kevin Pollack
Rating: ★★★

Despite a serious credibility deficiency, this is an undeniably lovable, rude (but not too rude) comedy with some very funny outtakes at the end that are guaranteed to send you off in a good mood. Ripely, if enjoyably over-acted by its largely veteran cast, the film top-stars those old sparring partners Jack Lemmon and Walter Matthau as two widowed old codgers whose feud and mutual insults seem as perpetual as the snow that clamps down on their Minnesota town. You won't really believe that a voluptuous 50-year-old red-headed widow (Ann-Margret) would move in opposite their adjoining houses, far less that she'd be likely to storm from her sauna in a leotard and roll about frenziedly in the snow, while they frost up the windows with their open mouths. Given such proclivities, however, it may not surprise you that she should throw herself into Lemmon's then Matthau's bed after Lemmon, beset by tax worries, has, well, thrown her out into the snow. Lemmon and Matthau enjoy themselves exchanging verbal and occasionally physical blows, setting traps for each other, torpedoing the other's TV and depositing dead fish in each other's cars.

Guadalcanal Diary ○
1943, US, 100 mins, b/w
Dir: Lewis Seiler

G

Stars: Preston Foster, Lloyd Nolan, William Bendix, Richard Conte, Anthony Quinn
Rating: ★★★

One of the best American films about the Pacific conflict in World War Two. Very patriotic, but immensely exciting, firmly characterised, and in places, very moving too. Richard Jaeckel, the little blond tough guy whose screen credits extend through 25 years to *The Dirty Dozen*, was working as a delivery boy in the 20th Century-Fox mail room when spotted, and signed for the role of Baby Marine. He was almost 17.

Guardian, The ●
1990, US, 90 mins, colour
Dir: William Friedkin
Stars: Jenny Seagrove, Dwier Brown, Carey Lowell, Brad Hall, Miguel Ferrer
Rating: ★

Although very well made, even by today's horror film standards, this is an extremely silly story, dragged out interminably to feature-length, about the spirit of an ancient tree which takes life in the form of a woman and steals new-born babies (in the guise of a child-minder) to feed to the tree. There's only enough material here for a half-hour *Twilight Zone* episode, and even experienced director Friedkin, who made *The Exorcist*, is pushed to keep our attention for more than a few minutes at a time before he can get cracking on the last-reel climax. Still, the cast plays it straight and gives all they've got and the story does give a new slant to the old phrase: 'The baby slept like a log'.

Guess Who's Coming to Dinner ○ Ⓥ
1967, US, 112 mins, colour
Dir: Stanley Kramer
Stars: Spencer Tracy, Katharine Hepburn, Sidney Poitier
Rating: ★★★

Intrinsically facile film about the dilemma facing the parents of a white girl wanting to marry a black man – but lifted onto an altogether higher plane by the magical acting (their last film together) of Katharine Hepburn and Spencer Tracy, the latter having a superbly delivered final speech that will bring tears to your eyes. Miss Hepburn took the third of her best actress awards, and William Rose was also given an Oscar for his screenplay.

Guide for the Married Man, A Ⓒ
1967, US, 91 mins, colour
Dir: Gene Kelly
Stars: Walter Matthau, Inger Stevens, Robert Morse
Rating: ★★★

Star-studded joke of a film directed by Gene Kelly, which surveys 'case histories' as an experienced adulterer (Robert Morse) teaches his friend (Walter Matthau) the art of cheating in marriage. Inger Stevens is too delicious a wife to ever dream of cheating on, but you'll have fun recognising the visitors from Hollywood's A-Z, who include Lucille Ball, Jack Benny, Sid Caesar, Jeffrey Hunter, Jayne Mansfield, Phil Silvers and Terry-Thomas.

Guilty As Sin ● Ⓥ
1993, US, 107 mins, colour
Dir: Sidney Lumet
Stars: Rebecca DeMornay, Don Johnson, Jack Warden
Rating: ★★

This okay thriller has good performances from Rebecca DeMornay and Don Johnson, both of which deserve rather better than this adequate but fairly humdrum script. Johnson in particular, oozing evil, does his best screen work in some time as a manipulative womaniser and maybe-murderer who lights on DeMornay's high-flying lawyer to defend him on a charge of killing his wife. The lady's intrigued. She takes the case – but soon realises that Johnson is not only guilty, but has been pulling the strings on her and the whole case. DeMornay's character, in fact, is the big weakness here. When Johnson says that 'You're not as tough or as smart as I thought you were,' he's right. She's illogical too but maybe we should give her the benefit of the doubt and say that, in the face of Johnson's prime evil, her logic flew out of the window. Later developments could well raise a few gasps from the nervously inclined, but most viewers will have no problems keeping two paces ahead of the plot.

Guilty by Suspicion Ⓒ Ⓥ
1990, US, 106 mins, colour
Dir: Irwin Winkler
Stars: Robert De Niro, Annette Bening, George Wendt, Sam Wanamaker, Martin Scorsese
Rating: ★★★

Hollywood's conscience showing again – and very effectively, too, even if there can't be many film-goers now unaware of the infamous activities of the communist witch-hunters of the post-war period, or the debilitating effects they had on the film industry. Robert De Niro plays a director whose attendance at a couple of communist meetings in the late Thirties – he was thrown out for arguing too much – jeopardises his whole career 12 years later. He finds himself blacklisted – blocked from working at even the smallest studio. The story is slight and seems to have nowhere much to go – indeed it comes to a stop rather than ends – but the performances make it watchable throughout; Annette Bening is admirable as the ex-wife to whom De Niro finds himself forced to turn. The film's sense of period is sometimes a bit fuzzy – surely *Gentlemen Prefer Blondes* wasn't being filmed as early as 1951? – but its values are all in the right place.

Guinea Pig, The ○
1948, UK, 97 mins, b/w
Dir: Roy Boulting
Stars: Richard Attenborough, Sheila Sim, Bernard Miles
Rating: ★★★

No one today could get away with casting a 25-year-old actor as a 14-year-old schoolboy, but Richard Attenborough's interpretation of the role here is so sensitive that there were few complaints when this film was released. The traumatic times of the elementary schoolboy sent to a public school as part of an education experiment provide touching, sometimes harrowing and often thought-provoking entertainment. Anthony Newley and Peter Reynolds also don schoolcaps.

Gumball Rally, The ○ Ⓥ
1976, US, 105 mins, colour
Dir: Chuck Bail
Stars: Michael Sarrazin, Gary Busey, Normann Burton
Rating: ★★

Here's the forerunner of all those *Cannonball Run* films, a painless panorama of pandemonium about an illegal car race across America. One or two performances even outshine the hardware, notably Tricia O'Neil, a curvy contestant with a fine range of facial expressions, and Harvey Jason as a manic Hungarian aboard a seemingly indestructible motor-cycle.

Gumshoe ◐ ⓥ
1972, UK, 85 mins, colour
Dir: Stephen Frears
Stars: Albert Finney, Billie Whitelaw, Frank Finlay, Janice Rule
Rating: ★★★

From the opening titles of *Gumshoe*, it's quite clear we are in for a treat. The opening music (by Tim Rice and Andrew Lloyd Webber, the *Evita* men) and credit titles are both superbly evocative of those Forties' detective thrillers which *Gumshoe* seeks to gently spoof and, at the same time raise a respectful hat. Director Stephen Frears never loses this mood, from the moment one first meets Eddie Ginley (a marvellous performance by Albert Finney), a small-time bingo caller and an even smaller-time private eye who dreams of being Humphrey Bogart, Elvis Presley and Dashiell Hammett rolled into one. His subsequent adventures on the trail of the Fat Man will delight any film fan with an affection for the kind of films whose atmosphere *Gumshoe* conjures up. All through the story (cleverly written and constructed by Neville Smith) characters play along with Eddie's fantasies of greatness partly because they know him, but partly because they find it difficult to resist. You'll find *Gumshoe* difficult to resist, too.

Gun Crazy ○
(aka: Deadly Is the Female)
1950, US, 87m mins, b/w
Dir: Joseph H Lewis
Stars: John Dall, Peggy Cummins
Rating: ★★★★

A moody minor masterpiece about a couple obsessed both with firearms and each other, and their inevitable flight from the law. Extremely well made, this is one 'cult' classic that justifies its reputation. Director Joseph H Lewis chooses all the right angles for his impact and never puts a foot wrong. Peggy Cummins (she frighteningly ecstatic at the thrill of the crime) and John Dall give their best film performances by a country mile. Certainly to be mentioned in the same breath as *Bonnie and Clyde*.

Guncrazy ● ⓥ
1992, US, 93 mins, colour
Dir: Tamra Davis
Stars: Drew Barrymore, James LeGros, Billy Drago
Rating: ★★★

Part love story, part thriller and part comedy, this is the *Bonnie and Clyde*-style story of two juvenile misfits on the run. He (James LeGros) is an ex-killer on parole, she (Drew Barrymore, all grown up after *E.T.*) is a poor, mixed-up teenager in a dead-end town. They share an obsession with guns, a passion for each other – and a background of murder soon develops. Barrymore does well with her character, a bored, sluttish 16-year-old who, desperate to be loved, starts corresponding with a prisoner (LeGros) and so begins a long-distance love affair. A touching study of loneliness and doomed love. Despite the modern adult themes, it's almost like an old-fashioned good-quality B-movie.

Gunfight at Comanche Creek ○
1963, US, 90 mins, colour
Dir: Frank Mcdonald
Stars: Audie Murphy, Colleen Miller
Rating: ★

Audie Murphy gets two heroines for the price of one in this grim-faced but lacklustre Western in which intrepid Audie takes on a whole gang of outlaws. The two girls, Colleen Miller (like Murphy, a refugee from Universal-International) and Susan Seaforth, both make the acting sparks fly. Ben Cooper is the best of the baddies.

Gunfight at Dodge City, The ○
1958, US, 81 mins, colour
Dir: Joseph M Newman
Stars: Joel McCrea, Julie Adams, John McIntire, Nancy Gates
Rating: ★★★

Better-than-average Western with Joel McCrea as the famous gunman and gambler Bat Masterson. Nancy Gates must have been used to the character, having previously played opposite a different Bat (George Montgomery) in the Western *Masterson of Kansas*.

Gunfight at the OK Corral ○
1956, US, 122 mins, colour
Dir: John Sturges
Stars: Burt Lancaster, Kirk Douglas, Rhonda Fleming, John Ireland, Jo Van Fleet, Earl Holliman
Rating: ★★★

Hollywood's obsession with the battle between the Earps and the Clantons at Tombstone's OK Corral in 1881 reached perhaps its peak (before the 1994 revamps) in this action film that pitched in most of the cinema's best bad guys against Burt Lancaster, earnest but excellent as Wyatt Earp, and Kirk Douglas, more flamboyant but just as good as Doc Holliday. It's amazing, in fact, that so many good actors – such excellent villains as Lyle Bettger, Jack Elam, Lee Van Cleef, Frank Faylen and Ted de Corsia among them – should consent to appear in what amount to very small roles. The lion's share of the acting meat deservedly goes to the Oscar-winning Jo Van Fleet, usually cast as characters much older than herself, who is allowed a rare touch of glamour as Holliday's mistress Kate Fisher. There is, in addition, Frankie Laine's catchy theme song, and the equally famous roaring climax. If you're a Western fan, you can't go far wrong with this.

Gunfighter, The ○
1950, US, 84 mins, b/w
Dir: Henry King
Stars: Gregory Peck, Helen Westcott, Millard Mitchell, Karl Malden
Rating: ★★★

Classic, humourless Western, with Gregory Peck (in a role originally sought by John Wayne) as the gunfighter trying (and inevitably failing) to run away from his past. It carries a surprising feeling of authenticity for a Western of this period and there are good supporting portrayals from Millard Mitchell, Karl Malden and (as two gun-happy punks) Richard Jaeckel and Skip Homeier. Studio executives at 20th Century-Fox are said to have blamed the film's indifferent box-office performance on the fact that Peck wore a moustache!

Gun for a Coward ○
1956, US, 88 mins, colour
Stars: Fred MacMurray, Jeffrey Hunter, Dean Stockwell, Janice Rule
Rating: ★★

The stars play three brothers in this strange, but entertaining Western, one of a clutch of good horse-operas made by MacMurray in the late Fifties. Here, all three are outscored by a peach of a performance from Chill Wills, as Loving.

Gun Fury ○
1953, US, 83 mins, colour
Dir: Raoul Walsh
Stars: Rock Hudson, Donna Reed, Phil Carey, Roberta Haynes
Rating: ★★★

G

Veteran director Raoul Walsh ensured plenty of action and strong performances in this 'A' class Western with a formidable cast. Rock Hudson and Donna Reed are certainly a notch above the conventional Western leads, and the bad guys include Phil Carey, Lee Marvin, Leo Gordon and Neville Brand. The blazing colour photography by Lester H White was originally slated to be shown in 3-D, but looks ravishing in any ratio.

Gunga Din ○
1939, US, 117 mins, b/w
Dir: George Stevens
Stars: Cary Grant, Douglas Fairbanks Jr, Victor McLagen, Joan Fontaine, Sam Jaffe
Rating: ★★★★

RKO's hugely entertaining North-West Frontier spectacular, with stalwart sergeants three Cary Grant, Victor McLaglen and Douglas Fairbanks Jr on top form. One of the most stirring and exciting action films ever made, with some wonderful bantering dialogue, a heart-rending ending and a performance by Sam Jaffe in the title role that all but steals the show. Ace entertainment.

Gung Ho ◑
1986, US, 105 mins, colour
Dir: Ron Howard
Stars: Michael Keaton, Mimi Rogers, Gedde Watanabe
Rating: ★★★

Michael Keaton is at the centre of a bad case of culture clash when a Japanese company reopens a car plant in Pennsylvania and runs it the way they would back home. Oddly, it's the American factory workers who come off worse here, portrayed largely as a bunch of lazy and inefficient backsliders. The Japanese work ethic means hard work and pride in their job. If all this sounds a little serious, don't be alarmed – it's a fast-moving comedy that provides a good deal of fun. Directed by Ron Howard, it shares some similarities with his hit comedy *Splash* and is lighter fare that its plot would imply. Keaton, in zany mood, dominates, but Gedde Watanabe, as the young Japanese executive in charge of the plant, is also very good.

Gun Glory ○
1957, US, 89 mins, colour
Dir: Roy Rowland
Stars: Stewart Granger, Rhonda Fleming
Rating: ★★

Although he was tops at Britain's box-office during the Forties, it took Hollywood and a whole posse of Westerns and other action films to turn Stewart Granger into an international star. This drama – about a gunfighter trying to settle down to ranch life – is one of the least exciting, although it's based on Phillip Yordan's novel *Man of the West*. The theme song is sung by Burl Ives.

Gun Hawk, The ○
1963, US, 92 mins, colour
Dir: Edward Ludwig
Stars: Rory Calhoun, Rod Cameron, Rod Lauren, Ruta Lee
Rating: ★★★

Uneven, but at times quite splendid Western about a dying gunfighter and the young man whom he is determined to steer clear of the outlaw trail. Rory Calhoun, not the sort one usually associates with great acting, gives a performance of almost Brando-like intensity as the bandit. The dialogue written for him seems particularly apposite to the character, with humour, pathos and the inner workings of the mind carefully interwoven. Jo Heims' screenplay rises to greatness by Western standards in the closing stages.

Gun in Betty Lou's Handbag, The ◑ ⓥ
1992, US, 89 mins, colour
Dir: Allan Moyle
Stars: Penelope Ann Miller, Eric Thal, Alfre Woodard, William Forsythe, Cathy Moriarty, Julianne Moore, Xander Berkeley
Rating: ★★

Great title, good supporting cast: if only the two stars had the charm required to carry the rest. Betty Lou (Penelope Ann Miller) is a meek and mousy librarian lady with a policeman husband (Eric Thal) who ignores her, a boss who bullies her and friends who think that she's just plain dull (on this showing, they've got a point). To grab their attention, she confesses to a murder she didn't commit – and, instantly, shy Betty Lou becomes a national celebrity. In the tradition of the best screwball farces things soon go hopelessly wrong, and the result is a sweet, if ultimately bland comedy romp.

Gunn ○
1966, US, 94 mins, colour
Dir: Blake Edwards

Stars: Craig Stevens, Laura Devon
Rating: ★★

There's plenty of action in this detective yarn, based on the TV series *Peter Gunn*, which was created by the director of the film, Blake Edwards. Edwards also co-wrote the screenplay with William Peter Blatty, who later turned his pen to *The Exorcist*.

Gunpoint
See: At Gunpoint)

Gun Runner, The ○
(aka: Santiago)
1956, US, 92 mins, colour
Dir: Gordon Douglas
Stars: Alan Ladd, Rossana Podesta, Lloyd Nolan, Chill Wills
Rating: ★★★

One of Alan Ladd's last big films, this adventure story cast him as an ex-military man running guns from Cuba to Florida during Cuba's war of independence. Stiff direction of the dialogue by Gordon Douglas is balanced by some tense action scenes.

Gun Runners, The ○
1958, US, 83 mins, b/w
Dir: Don Siegel
Stars: Audie Murphy, Patricia Owens, Eddie Albert, Everett Sloane
Rating: ★★

Don Siegel-directed third screen version of Ernest Hemingway's *To Have and Have Not*, with Audie Murphy as the man who gets involved in gun-running to Cuba. It's perhaps the most faithful of the three to the spirit of the book, with plenty of action and a supporting cast which guarantees interest, including the baby-faced Richard Jaeckel, thin-lipped Everett Sloane and Jack Elam, taking a well-earned breather from Western shoot-outs.

Guns at Batasi ○
1964, UK, 103 mins, b/w
Dir: John Guillermin
Stars: Richard Attenborough, Jack Hawkins, Mia Farrow, Flora Robson
Rating: ★★★

Richard Attenborough draws the regimental sergeant-major to life in this action drama of unrest in an emergent African state. 'On the parade ground a tyrant, in a hot spot a hero' – for once, the publicity said it all. John Leyton, a former pop singer, does well as the juvenile lead, although his haircut wouldn't do for the Army in 1964.

Guns in the Afternoon ○
(aka: Ride the High Country)
1961, US, 93 mins, colour
Dir: Sam Peckinpah
Stars: Randolph Scott, Joel McCrea,
Mariette Hartley, Edgar Buchanan,
Warren Oates
Rating: ★★★★

Director Sam Peckinpah was responsible for some of the most exciting
gun duels and shoot-outs ever seen on
the screen. This Western remains his
best film, despite the notoriety of his
later, blood-spattered work. And it
includes a final gunfight as fierce and
fine as anything the Western has given
us. From the opening shot, the
adrenaline is flowing, but Peckinpah
doesn't shortchange on the low-key
details that give the proceedings a
genuine whiff of life. Joel McCrea and
Randolph Scott (whose last film this
was before retiring on a fortune estimated at between 50 and 100 million
dollars) give career-best performances
as two ex-lawmen at loggerheads over
a consignment of gold. The final finishing touch is top-notch
photography courtesy of Peckinpah's
regular cinematographer Lucien
Ballard (himself part-Cherokee Indian)
who went on to make four further
films with Peckinpah, including the
infamous *The Wild Bunch.*

Gunsmoke ○
1953, US, 79 mins, colour
Dir: Nathan Juran
Stars: Audie Murphy, Susan Cabot
Rating: ★★

Nothing to do with James Arness and
his famous Western hero Matt Dillon,
who starred in the TV series of the
same name, but a spirited Technicolor
horse-opera about a hired gun (Audie
Murphy) who changes sides in a
range war. Directed by Nathan Juran
(who won an Academy Award for art
direction on *How Green Was My
Valley*), the film also features Murphy's
real-life friend, Charles Drake, and
pretty, raven-haired Susan Cabot,
whose operatic singing voice was
never put to use during her
Hollywood film career.

Guns of Darkness ○
1962, UK, 95 mins, b/w
Dir: Anthony Asquith
Stars: Leslie Caron, David Niven, James
Robertson Justice
Rating: ★★

Anthony Asquith directed this ad-
venture story, which has a colourful
backcloth of revolution in Central
America. The script is by John
Mortimer, who had written the film
adaptation of *The Innocents* the
previous year. For this source,
Mortimer had a best seller called *Act of
Mercy* by Francis Clifford, whose *The
Naked Runner* has also been filmed.
Both books deal with ordinary busi-
nessmen caught up in high adventure.
The atmospheric photography of
Robert Krasker is especially effective
during a tense battle for life in a
sinister swamp.

Guns of Fort Petticoat, The ○
1958, US, 82 mins, colour
Dir: George Marshall
Stars: Audie Murphy, Kathryn Grant
Rating: ★★★

Better-than-average Western, directed
by George Marshall, who made *Destry
Rides Again* and *When the Daltons
Rode.* Excitement mounts in the closing stages as the women (who have to
defend a cavalry fort while their
menfolk are away) begin to fall one
by one, and the Indians threaten to
overwhelm them.

Guns of Navarone, The ○ Ⓥ
1961, US/UK, 157 mins, colour
Dir: J Lee Thompson
Stars: Gregory Peck, David Niven,
Anthony Quinn, Anthony Quayle, Stanley
Baker
Rating: ★★★

This blazing adventure yarn pulled the
public into cinemas in droves when it
was first released. There are fights and
nail-biting action scenes galore as six
saboteurs scale massive cliffs in a daring attempt to destroy two enormous
German guns pointed firmly in the
direction of Allied shipping. Almost
overloaded with stars, the cast also
includes Anthony Quayle, Anthony
Quinn, Stanley Baker, Irene Papas,
Gia Scala, James Darren and Richard
Harris.

Guns of the Magnificent Seven ○
1968, US, 106 mins, colour
Dir: Paul Wendkos
Stars: George Kennedy, Monte
Markham, Joe Don Baker
Rating: ★★★

Next to the original, this is the best of
the *Seven* films. Despite the familiar
framework of the plot, director Paul
Wendkos, whose work remains undervalued in this country, actually
manages to raise some fresh excitement from the old story of the septet
of gunfighters riding to the rescue of
yet another group of downtrodden
Mexicans. George Kennedy's unexpectedly lithe and forceful
performance as Chris is a great help
and holds the film together when it
looks as though it might disintegrate
after a promising start, as did other
follow-ups in the series. Antonio
Macasoli's sharp DeLuxe Colour
photography helps highlight the
action in the thrilling climax, and the
gunfighters themselves are quite well
defined.

Guns of the Timberland ○
1959, US, 91 mins, colour
Dir: Robert D Webb
Stars: Alan Ladd, Jeanne Crain, Gilbert
Roland, Lyle Bettger
Rating: ★★

Jeanne Crain, Hollywood's sweetest
teenager in the Forties, played rather
a lot of bad girls in her later films, and
this Western proves no exception.
Rivalling her in the villainy stakes is
husky-voiced Lyle Bettger, who for
once does not bite the dust – one of
the few original touches in this busy
story of timber-men at loggerheads.
Alan Ladd and Gilbert Roland play
the logging partners who fall out with
predictably tragic results but more
fire is provided by Miss Crain and by
Noah Beery Jr. Pop singer Frankie
Avalon makes his acting debut.

Guns of Wyoming ○
(aka: Cattle King)
1963, US, 88 mins, colour
Dir: Tay Garnett
Stars: Robert Taylor, Joan Caulfield
Rating: ★★

Latter-day Robert Taylor Western,
pleasantly shot in Metrocolor, which
casts him as Sam Brassfield, owner of a
giant cattle ranch (the American title
of the film is, in fact, *Cattle King*). It's
nice to see powder-puff blonde Joan
Caulfield, again, and the villain – once
the hero's best friend – provides a
plum role for one of the screen's best
oily badmen, Robert Middleton.
Overall, though, this is a mighty slow
ride through familiar pastures.

Guy Named Joe, A ○
1943, US, 120 mins, b/w
Dir: Victor Fleming
Stars: Spencer Tracy, Van Johnson,
Irene Dunne
Rating: ★★

G

A draggy action-fantasy with Spencer Tracy's sincerity its major asset as an airman who, after getting killed, looks after the fortunes of his fellows. The supporting cast of MGM reliables includes Ward Bond, Lionel Barrymore, Henry O'Neill, Barry Nelson, James Gleason and Don DeFore. Right down the list, without a swimming pool in sight, there's the lovely Esther Williams. Remade by Steven Spielberg in 1989 as *Always*.

Guys and Dolls ○
1955, US, 150 mins, colour
Dir: Joseph L Mankiewicz
Stars: Marlon Brando, Jean Simmons, Frank Sinatra, Vivian Blaine
Rating: ★★★

Samuel Goldwyn's film version of the famous musical about the gambler who falls for the Salvation Army girl retains only Vivian Blaine from the original Broadway stars and she obliges by stealing every scene she is in. The individual song hit is undoubtedly Stubby Kaye with 'Sit Down, You're Rockin' the Boat'. Controversial choices Marlon Brando and Jean Simmons were all right on the night, but it's all a bit wearing.

Gypsy ○
1962, US, 149 mins, colour
Dir: Mervyn Le Roy
Stars: Rosalind Russell, Natalie Wood, Karl Malden
Rating: ★★★

Rosalind Russell played the stage mother to end them all in this richly entertaining musical about her two daughters, who became actress June Havoc and strip queen Gypsy Rose Lee. The Stephen Sondheim-Jule Stein score includes 'Everything's Coming Up Roses', 'Together Wherever We Go', 'Small World' and 'Let Me Entertain You'. Russell does her own singing, while Natalie Wood (as Rose) is dubbed (as she had been in *West Side Story*) by perennial 'ghost voice' Marni Nixon. Remade in 1994.

Gypsy and the Gentleman, The ○
1957, UK, 107 mins, colour
Dir: Jospeh Losey
Stars: Melina Mercouri, Keith Michell, Patrick McGoohan
Rating: ★★

By coincidence, this barnstorming melodrama, about a beautiful gypsy casing the downfall of a philandering rake, was the third film in the careers

of both Keith Michell (looking a little overweight) and scenery-chewing Greek actress Melina Mercouri (looking ravishing and playing the foot-stomping spitfire for all she was worth). In only three years she would be nominated for an Oscar and achieve worldwide fame in the enchanting *Never on Sunday*. Michell and Mercouri do well to rise above the somewhat silly story, and a big plus is cinematographer Jack Hildyard's striking use of Eastman Colour stock, which manages to evoke both the quality and look of old sporting prints in the numerous exterior scenes.

Gypsy Colt ⊙
1954, US, 72 mins, colour
Dir: Andrew Marton
Stars: Donna Corcoran, Ward Bond, Frances Dee
Rating: ★★★

A nice little remake of *Lassie Come Home*, using a horse in the story instead of a dog. Young Donna Corcoran was never more appealing, while Ward Bond and Frances Dee are believable country folk as her parents. Andrew Marton moves the story smoothly along to a tearstained conclusion, while the American outdoors is warmly, richly captured in Harold Lipstein's Ansco Color photography. A rock-solid MGM family film.

Gypsy Girl
See: Sky West and Crooked

Gypsy Moths, The ◖
1969, US, 110 mins, colour
Dir: John Frankenheimer
Stars: Burt Lancaster, Deborah Kerr, Gene Hackman
Rating: ★★★

Ebullient director John Frankenheimer and tough-guy star Burt Lancaster continued their association in this tale of three free-fall parachutists. The two collaborated to great effect in *The Young Savages*, *Birdman of Alcatraz* (for which Lancaster won an Oscar), *Seven Days in May* and *The Train*. Lancaster and Deborah Kerr renew their on-screen passion of *From Here to Eternity* but Gene Hackman quietly steals this disturbing and — at times — suspenseful film.

Hail the Conquering Hero ○
1944, US, 101 mins, b/w
Dir: Preston Sturges
Stars: Eddie Bracken, Ella Raines, William Demarest
Rating: ★★★

Writer-director Preston Sturges savagely swipes at some of America's most sacred cows — including small-town politics, patriotism and mother-love — in a classic comedy that contains some of his most sustained satire. It was his last totally effective film and it marked the high spot in the movie career of star Eddie Bracken whose shy, bumbling persona was ideal as a vehicle for Sturges' attacks. Here, he's rejected for army service, then hides out while the townsfolk believe him to be a hero in battle and prepare a triumphal return.

Hairspray ◐ ⓥ
1988, US, 96 mins, colour
Dir: John Waters
Stars: Ricki Lake, Divine, Debbie Harry, Sonny Bono
Rating: ★★★

Like film-maker John Waters' other comedy *Cry Baby*, this is an engagingly affectionate spoof of teen movies of the Fifties and Sixties that also draws on the director's own memories of the period. Marvellously tacky stuff, with Waters himself as a deranged psychiatrist, Pia Zadora in a cameo role, and Ricki Lake a total delight as the happily overweight teenage heroine who buys her clothes at the Hefty Hideaway dress shop.

Half Angel ○
1951, US, 77 mins, colour
Dir: Richard Sale
Stars: Loretta Young, Joseph Cotten
Rating: ★★

This romantic comedy about a girl with a split personality would probably be treated today as a sex comedy, and all the poorer for it. The evergreen Loretta Young — who started her career at 15 by answering a studio call intended for her sister — sparkles as the girl.

Half a Sixpence ⊙
1967, UK, 148 mins, colour
Dir: George Sidney

Stars: Tommy Steele, Julia Foster
Rating: ★★★

Until it runs out of steam towards the end, this enjoyable adaptation of H G Wells's novel is a flash-bang-wallop of a picture, all sweep and verve, with Tommy Steele and Julia Foster giving run-for-years performances in the leading roles. The song-and-dance routines have the explosive build-up of a combined fireworks display.

Half Moon Street ●
1986, US, 90 mins, colour
Dir: Bob Swaim
Stars: Sigourney Weaver, Michael Caine
Rating: ★

This one runs like an episode from the *Hammer House of Mystery and Suspense*, except that it would give even that series a bad name, filled with dialogue that has an unreal ring, and a cast that sound as though they're acting 99 per cent of the time. Sigourney Weaver, who is, with Michael Caine, one of the only two actors most people will recognise, is disturbed by her living conditions – she invites the landlord in to mend the plumbing while she's in the bath – and her low pay at a research institute. 'How do you manage on £150 a week?' she asks her upper-class twit colleague. 'I don't,' he replies. 'My parents own a small merchant bank.' Not having such essentials to fall back on, Sigourney joins an escort agency, wining, dining and bedding men at a rate sufficient to set her up in luxury in about a fortnight. That's where Caine comes in. He's a political 'fixer' who becomes interested in Siggy for herself. 'Don't put walls around me, Sam,' she warns. 'China was full of walls. I'm sick of them.' Still he goes ahead and the lurking camera, and music (changed from romantic to ominous) indicates that Someone Is Watching It All. Thereafter, the script never disappoints in its utter predictability. Good title, though. Perhaps the film-makers should have started again from that.

Hallelujah Trail, The ○ ⓥ
1965, US, 167 mins, colour
Dir: John Sturges
Stars: Burt Lancaster, Lee Remick, Jim Hutton, Donald Pleasance, Brian Keith
Rating: ★★★

A gloriously entertaining comedy-Western about the battle for a wagon train-load of whisky bound for Colorado. The Indians – only one of

the factions after the liquor – get all the best dialogue, and all the funniest visual gags. These include one scene where the Indians huddle terrified within a circle of wagons while the *Cavalry* ride whooping round them. There's a superb climax, and good-humoured playing from Burt Lancaster, Donald Pleasence and Brian Keith. Only Lee Remick is ill-served by her dialogue as the leader of a band of temperance women.

Halloween ● ⓥ
1978, US, 93 mins, colour
Dir: John Carpenter
Stars: Donald Pleasence, Jamie Lee Curtis, Nancy Loomis, P J Soles
Rating: ★★★

Jamie Lee Curtis, daughter of Tony Curtis and Janet Leigh, made an auspicious film debut in this shocker, in which a killer back from 15 years in the asylum stalks a trio of teenage girls with heavy breath and hand-held camera, and takes a heck of a while to get about his gory business. Director John Carpenter wracks up the suspense to breaking point thanks to ingenious use of tight-tracked camera shots around the rooms of a house. It spawned a clutch of sequels and bare-faced imitators but none was a patch on this spine-tingler.

Halloween II ● ⓥ
1981, US, 92 mins, colour
Dir: Rick Rosenthal
Stars: Jamie Lee Curtis, Donald Pleasence
Rating: ★★

The masked maniac from John Carpenter's stalk-and-slash classic is still on the loose and terrorising scream queen Jamie Lee Curtis once more. Co-scripted by Carpenter himself, but directed by Rick Rosenthal, the film picks up the action on the same night the original film ended.

Halloween III: Season of the Witch ●
1983, US, 98 mins, colour
Dir: Tommy Lee Wallace
Stars: Dan O'Herlihy, Tom Atkins, Stacey Nelkin
Rating: ★★

Quite a nice little horror story idea, even if it's nothing to do with *Halloween* or any of its other sequels. Something nasty is happening at America's Shamrock Halloween Masks factory, where all the staff are Irish, and it's all due to come to a head (!)

on pumpkin night. Genial evil genius Dan O'Herlihy is clearly plotting something foul with the aid of men in blue suits whom he has perhaps picked up as seconds at Futureworld. It all degenerates into standard grisly horror before the end, although you may also wonder why O'Herlihy couldn't content himself with just making a fortune from his factory.

Halls of Montezuma ○
1950, US, 113 mins, colour
Dir: Lewis Milestone
Stars: Richard Widmark, Jack Palance, Karl Malden, Robert Wagner
Rating: ★★★

An uncharacteristic war film from Lewis Milestone in that it's all flag-waving, glory-glory and martial music in the background. One expects quieter, grimmer stuff from the man who made *All Quiet on the Western Front* and *Pork Chop Hill*. It's powerfully acted by a strong cast which, besides stars Richard Widmark, Jack Palance, Karl Malden and Robert Wagner, includes Reginald Gardiner – in a rare dramatic role – Skip Homeier, Neville Brand and Richard Boone plus Jack (*Dragnet*) Webb as a war correspondent.

Hamburger Hill ● ⓥ
1987, US, 108 mins, colour
Dir: John Irvin
Stars: Anthony Barile, Michael Patrick Boatman, Don Cheadle, Dylan McDermott, Tim Quill, Steven Weber
Rating: ★★

The futility of war is again writ large before our eyes in this graphic Vietnam drama about a 10-day siege by US airborne troops (the 'Screaming Eagles') of a hill that no one really cared about and which was forgotten once the battle was over. Senator Edward Kennedy called it 'madness' and he was undoubtedly right. In writer Jim Carabatsos and director John Irvin's account of the battle, though, it seems to take us far too long to get to know the personalities involved. The film gathers pace in the last half hour, with the final assault, but by then its impetus is all but gone. Having said that, some individual scenes are nicely composed by any measure, and the ensemble performances are goodish while lacking in the individual charisma this kind of enterprise demands. The message is once again painfully driven home, however. Perhaps that's all that really matters, in a film that also in some repects is so old-

H

fashioned that you almost expect the strains of 'Halls of Montezuma' to thunder after the soldiers.

Hamlet ○
1948, UK, 142 mins, b/w
Dir: Laurence Olivier
Stars: Laurence Olivier, Jean Simmons, Eileen Herlie, Basil Sydney
Rating: ★★★

Laurence Olivier's film of the Shakespeare tragedy (cut by some two hours from the original's four and a half hours running time) was the first of his three screen adaptations of the Bard's plays and the first wholly British picture to win the Best Film Oscar. The star's fascinating interpretation of the role of the moody Dane was controversially received but always compelling, earning him the Oscar for Best Actor. There were Oscars, too, for the art direction and costumes. As director, Olivier made dramatic use of Desmond Dickinson's atmospheric monochrome cinematography and his generosity towards his fellow players resulted in attractive performances from, in particular, Jean Simmons (Ophelia), Eileen Herlie and Basil Sydney as the Queen and King, Felix Aylmer (Polonius) and Stanley Holloway as the Gravedigger. There was an enjoyably fey performance from Peter Cushing as Osric and the film marked the first time in which he and his later companion in terror, Christopher Lee, appeared in the same film.

Hamlet ○ ⊛
1990, UK, 133 mins, colour
Dir: Franco Zeffirelli
Stars: Mel Gibson, Glenn Close, Alan Bates, Paul Scofield, Ian Holm, Helena Bonham Carter
Rating: ★★★

Zeffirelli's version of Shakespeare's most famous play chalks quite clearly the line between what attracts in the cinema and the theatre. Think of the cast here: Paul Scofield (as the ghost), Alan Bates (as Claudius), Ian Holm (as Polonius), plus the casting coups of Glenn Close as the queen and Mel Gibson as Hamlet. Theatre-goers would pay a fortune to see them. And the production would run as long as its cast could be kept together. Yet cinemagoers, fed on a diet of special effects, might well pass by on the other side of the road. True, the film actually is a thing of rags and patches. There are too many boring bits in the first half, but Zeffirelli picks it up

half-way through and keeps it galloping along to its corpse-strewn finale. Gibson's good, especially in the key speeches, but occasionally falters when trying to lend too much lightness to the role. Close is perfect casting as the double-dealing Queen. Helena Bonham Carter is visually flawless as Ophelia but her reading of the dialogue leaves something to be desired. But it's got to be worth the price of admission, hasn't it, to hear Mad Mel recite 'To Be or Not to Be'? You'd better believe it.

Hammersmith Is Out ◑
1972, US, 108 mins, colour
Dir: Peter Ustinov
Stars: Elizabeth Taylor, Richard Burton, Beau Bridges
Rating: ★

One of Peter Ustinov's rare forays as a film director, in a bizarre story about an escaped madman who improbably becomes an all-powerful magnate. The script's shafts of wit are at their sharpest during the scenes in the asylum itself, while the supporting cast includes Ustinov himself, John Schuck, Leon Ames and that former gangster movie star, George Raft.

Hammett ◑
1982, US, 100 mins, colour
Dir: Wim Wenders
Stars: Frederic Forrest, Peter Boyle, Marilu Henner, Elisha Cook
Rating: ★★★

First scripted in 1976, shot in 1980 and reputedly largely reshot the following year by Francis Coppola, Wim *Paris, Texas* Wenders' first American film still turns out to be a stylistic treat. Frederic Forrest is superb as famed author Dashiell Hammett who gets caught up in a real-life *film noir* mystery. The Thirties' studio look is beautifully and authentically re-created and the sordid story of blackmail and murder grips to the end. Crime cultists will realise that several elements of the storyline appear in Hammett's later books.

Handful of Dust, A ○ ⊛
1988, UK, 118 mins, colour
Dir: Charles Sturridge
Stars: James Wilby, Kristin Scott Thomas, Rupert Graves, Alec Guinness
Rating: ★★

Evelyn Waugh's tragi-comic dissection of the indolent aristocracy in pre-war England is brought to the screen with all the loving attention to period detail

one might expect from Charles Sturridge, the director of the epic *Brideshead Revisited* series. In comparison, this is a chamber piece, brilliantly acted by its talented young leads – James Wilby as the kindly but dull cuckold, Rupert Graves as his smarmy upstart rival and, best of all, Kristin Scott Thomas as the adulterous wife – who more than hold their own, in illustrious company, against a string of eye-catching performances (Judi Dench, for example, won a Best Supporting Actress BAFTA award). The stately pacing works in the film's favour, lending resonance to a story which – for all the bizarre black humour of the climactic scenes involving Alec Guinness – has too many unsympathetic characters for its own good.

Handgun ● ⊛
(aka: Deep in the Heart)
1982, US, 100 mins, colour
Dir: Tony Garnett
Stars: Karen Young, Clayton Day
Rating: ★★★

Films about rape and the woman's attempts to fight back, pioneered by TV movies, gained momentum in the cinema of the Eighties, reaching a spectacular climax with *The Accused*. In this cleverly commercialised example, perky teacher Karen Young, hurt by a previous involvement, says 'No' to gun-crazy Texas boyfriend Clayton Day, following three dates and a sumptuous meal in his flat. Enraged, the macho man forces himself on her – and changes her life. Advised against prosecution, she takes up arms literally by becoming a crack sharpshooter. The final duel scene at the end is especially effective, not least as you just can't guess who's going to win. Young is very good in the two 'personalities' of her character: you can really believe in her both as a vulnerable girl and an ice-cool killer. It seemed that this was a star-making performance; but subsequent cinema roles for her brittle personality have proved hard to find.

Handle With Care
See: Citizens Band

Hands Across the Table ○
1935, US, 76 mins, b/w
Dir: Mitchell Leisen
Stars: Carole Lombard, Fred MacMurray, Ralph Bellamy
Rating: ★★★

One of the best examples of the brittle, pseudo-cynical style of Hollywood comedy of the 1934-1936 period, which led to the 'screwball' comedies of the end of the decade. Carole Lombard sparkles in a screenplay that steers perfectly the difficult course between reality, humour and sentimentality. Said one contemporary critic: 'The story is as slender as a young willow, but before the film comes to an end a bat has been made out of it which sends almost everything to the boundary.'

Hands of the Ripper ● Ⓥ
1971, UK, 85 mins, colour
Dir: Peter Sasdy
Stars: Angharad Rees, Eric Porter, Jane Merrow, Dora Bryan
Rating: ★★★

A sort of Hammer horror version of *Mamie*, with more people getting impaled on a greater variety of sharp weapons than in *Friday the 13th* and its sequels put together. Interesting pale colour photography, good performances and a nice period feel help counter-balance the disappointingly routine development of the plot.

Hand that Rocks the Cradle, The ● Ⓥ
1992, US, 110 mins, colour
Dir: Curtis Hanson
Stars: Annabella Sciorra, Rebecca DeMornay, Matt McCoy, Ernie Hudson, Julianne Moore
Rating: ★★★

Although it has its share of silly moments, this suspense thriller is well enough made to score points most of the time. When pregnant mum Clare (Annabella Sciorra) exposes her hospital doctor as a groper (and other women join in), he blows his brains out. His own pregnant wife (Rebecca DeMornay) has a miscarriage. Months later, DeMornay shows up at the Sciorra household offering her services as a nanny. Quite why she doesn't make off with Sciorra's daughter and baby to begin with is something of a mystery, but presumably she wants the other woman to suffer as much as possible. She breast-feeds the baby, alienating it from its mother. When the retarded handyman (Ernie Hudson) becomes suspicious, she has him tagged as a child-molester and dismissed. Sister-in-law rumbles her too, but is quickly dispatched in a trap originally set for Sciorra. Soon the scene is set for a climactic night of terror Hollywood can stage-manage

standing on its head. DeMornay is icy as the vengeful widow, outshining Sciorra, who does as well as she can with the wife, and Matt McCoy, who has the thankless role of the husband.

Hang 'Em High ● Ⓥ
1967, US, 114 mins, colour
Dir: Ted Post
Stars: Clint Eastwood, Inger Stevens, Ed Begley
Rating: ★★★

This was Clint Eastwood's first starring role in an American Western following his phenomenal success in Italy. It is a bitter film, an uneven one, and sometimes quite as violent as its Italian counterparts. But it's more deserving of serious consideration as a movie than Eastwood's work with Italian director Sergio Leone, not least for the fine, burnished colour photography of Leonard South and Richard Kline, and for an extraordinary supporting cast.

Hanging Tree, The ○
1958, US, 106 mins, colour
Dir: Delmer Daves
Stars: Gary Cooper, Maria Schell, Karl Malden, George C Scott
Rating: ★★

A typically brooding performance from Gary Cooper dominates this Western, directed with a keen eye for detail by Delmer Daves. Set in an unruly Montana gold mining township, the drama unfolds with carefully sustained suspense sequences. A strong supporting cast includes Karl Malden, King Donovan and, best of all, George C Scott, enjoying himself immensely as a phoney faith-healer.

Hangin' with the Homeboys ● Ⓥ
1991, US, 88 mins, colour
Dir: Joseph B Vasquez
Stars: Doug E Doug, Mario Joyner, John Leguizamo
Rating: ★★

A night on the town with four Bronx buddies, two black, two Puerto Rican. Although the film runs out of steam even before its shortish running time is up, there are some funny lines around and a chuckle or two, as one or two of the 'homeboys' learn a thing or two about the future. Comedian Doug E Doug is particularly good as the initially amusing, but finally pitiable Workshy Willie who sees everything as racist. As he tells the (black) employment clerk: 'You're

doing this to me because I'm black, right?' Tom's a black actor who finds out that acting is a steadier girlfriend than some women. Of the Puerto Ricans, Vinny's a compulsive womaniser who'll never learn, Johnny a pretty boy shop assistant who really ought to be thinking about going to college. Before you tire of their escapades you'll get enough smiles to justify your money.

Hangman, The ○
1958, US, 86 mins, b/w
Dir: Michael Curtiz
Stars: Robert Taylor, Fess Parker, Jack Lord, Tina Louise
Rating: ★★

A low-key, well-made Western from Oscar-winning director Michael Curtiz. Robert Taylor puts on his sternest face as the embittered lawman whose soubriquet provides the film's title and Jack Lord, later to star in *Hawaii Five-O*, has a featured role.

Hangman's Knot ○
1953, US, 81 mins, colour
Dir: Roy Huggins
Stars: Randolph Scott, Donna Reed, Richard Denning, Lee Marvin, Claude Jarman Jr
Rating: ★★★

Post-Civil War Western with an absolutely cracking cast, including three Oscar-winners: Donna Reed, Lee Marvin (in one of his earliest roles) and Claude Jarman Jr. Although the action is largely confined to four walls, there's plenty of it, and the fight between Marvin and upright Confederate major Randolph Scott is a corker. Despite its familiar plot, in fact, this carefully-made Western is well worth watching. Another plus factor: it has spot-on Technicolor photography by master lensman Charles Lawton Jr.

Hangmen Also Die ○
1943, US, 131 mins, b/w
Dir: Fritz Lang
Stars: Brian Donlevy, Anna Lee, Walter Brennan, Gene Lockhart, Dennis O'Keefe
Rating: ★★★

Fritz Lang's fiercely anti-Nazi suspense film about the aftermath of the assassination of Reinhardt Heydrich, 'Hitler's hangman', in Czechoslovakia. It has no really big star names, but there are outstanding performances from Gene Lockhart, Alexander Granach, Walter Brennan, Anna Lee

H

and Tonio Selwart. James Wong Howe again demonstrates his mastery of black and white photography and the film, though long, is always gripping in the telling and never outstays its welcome.

Hangover Square ○
1945, US, 77 mins, b/w
Dir: John Brahm
Stars: Laird Cregar, Linda Darnell, George Sanders
Rating: ★★★

That embryo Sydney Greenstreet, Laird Cregar, lumbers deliciously through his last film role before a crash diet – he aspired to romantic leading roles – killed him at just 28. The mists through which Cregar drifts before some new nefarious deed fortunately blur much of the 1903 Chelsea background which, architecturally and geographically, is typically wide of the Hollywood mark. Otherwise, this is a super dose of gaslit Grand Guignol. An early score by the prolific composer Bernard Herrmann, later to work for Alfred Hitchcock, screeches its own warnings to viewers already rendered apprehensive by Cregar's powerful, subtle and moving rendition of a role that could have drawn audience giggles in the hands of a lesser actor. An exuberant amalgam of murder, arson and music, with a spectacular, if overloaded, climax.

Hannah and Her Sisters ○ Ⓥ
1986, US, 103 mins, colour
Dir: Woody Allen
Stars: Woody Allen, Michael Caine, Mia Farrow, Carrie Fisher, Barbara Hershey, Dianne Wiest
Rating: ★★★

Another of Woody Allen's funny-sad slices of life with all its complications and anxieties. Abounding in warmth and humour, it marked a forward step from the relative failure and disappointments of Woody's *Interiors* and *Stardust Memories*. Here he returned in triple Oscar-winning form with a delicate romantic portrait of the tensions within family life. With more than a passing nod to Chekhov and *King Lear*, it's the story of three sisters whose upper class lives are interlinked over a two-year period. Allen is in top form as Mia Farrow's hypochondriac ex-husband, but it was Michael Caine who won the Best Supporting Actor Oscar, as the agent who secretly lusts after his wife's sexy sister, played by Barbara Hershey, and Dianne Wiest

the Best Supporting Actress as a poor woman who is always busy but has nothing to show for it. The acting is exemplary, as is the photography – for the first time in a decade not by Allen's regular collaborator Gordon Willis, but rather by Carlo Di Palma.

Hanna's War ●
1988, US, 148 mins, colour
Dir: Menahem Golan
Stars: Maruschka Detmers, Anthony Andrews, David Warner, Donald Pleasence, Ellen Burstyn
Rating: ★★

The Golan-Globus answer to *Carve Her Name with Pride*. That hit film, though, was made in 1958 and 30 years on the stories of such war heroines as Violette Szabo and, here, the young Hungarian writer Hanna Senesh seem, especially when told at such length, more appropriate to the format of a mini-series. Menahem Golan's film gets off to a pretty sticky start and only succeeds in spasms. Maruschka Detmers is quite good as Hanna, but, like the film, it's a variable performance that's not always totally convincing. Even more up and down is Anthony Andrews as her RAF instructor, with a Scottish accent that mostly stays, but occasionally goes altogether. David Warner and Donald Pleasence, mournfully and myopically respectively, parade their familiar baddies. Ellen Burstyn is adequate as Hanna's mother and Ingrid Pitt registers briefly as a fierce Yugoslav partisan. Action scenes are okay, but too few and far between.

Hannibal ○
1959, Italy, 103 mins, colour
Dir: Carlo Ludovico
Stars: Victor Mature, Rita Gam
Rating: ★

Italo-American action spectacle which loses no chance to spread its battle scenes all over the canvas of its screen, but doesn't convince for a minute as far as the dialogue is concerned. Victor Mature is ideally cast in the title role. No white elephant at the box-office, though: it made a mint.

Hannibal Brooks ○
1968, UK, 102 mins, colour
Dir: Michael Winner
Stars: Oliver Reed, Michael J Pollard
Rating: ★★★

World War Two adventure that veers unsteadily between farce and drama as British POW Oliver Reed attempts

to cross the Alps on the back of an elephant he's liberated from Munich Zoo. Snub-nosed American Michael J Pollard provides comic support and the elephant wins all hearts in the emotive ending.

Hannie Caulder ◑
1971, US, 85 mins, colour
Dir: Burt Kennedy
Stars: Raquel Welch, Robert Culp, Ernest Borgnine, Strother Martin, Jack Elam, Diana Dors
Rating: ★

With Raquel Welch as a female Clint Eastwood clad only in poncho and gunbelt, Ernest Borgnine, Jack Elam and Strother Martin virtually eating the scenery as the villains, and Robert Culp as a sardonic bounty hunter, this Western seemed to have it made. But its story, though riddled with fierce action, just never seems to get going. Stephen Boyd makes an unbilled appearance as a mysterious character called The Preacher and bizarre guest spots by Christopher Lee and Diana Dors heighten the air of unreality.

Hanover Street ◑ Ⓥ
1979, US, 108 mins, colour
Dir: Peter Hyams
Stars: Harrison Ford, Lesley-Anne Down, Christopher Plummer, Alec McCowen, Richard Masur, Patsy Kensit
Rating: ★★

Some effective and quite erotic love scenes add to the poignancy of Peter Hyams' attempt to make a *Brief Encounter*-style love story in a war-torn setting. But the passions and attitudes that made such movies are long gone, and their spirit proves too elusive for Hyams to grasp. Faced with such odds, Harrison Ford and Lesley-Anne Down (both of whose hairstyles make only a passing acknowledgement to the Forties) are not equal to the demands placed upon them. In the supporting cast, Michael Sacks, as the pilot's hero navigator, impresses most, while the exciting last 20 minutes underline the fact that Hyams' true vocation – he also made *Busting* and *Capricorn One* – is for fast-moving chase-and-action sequences. (Ford replaced originally-cast Kris Kristofferson in the leading role.)

Hans Christian Andersen ☉
1952, US, 120 mins, colour
Dir: Charles Vidor
Stars: Danny Kaye, Farley Granger, Zizi Jeanmaire
Rating: ★★★

It's a pity about the simple-minded story to this 'fairy-tale' about the great Danish storyteller, but never mind. You'll still enjoy Danny Kaye's gentle charm and one of the most tuneful scores that Frank Loesser ever wrote: 'The Ugly Duckling', 'Inchworm', 'I'm Hans Christian Andersen', 'The Emperor's New Clothes', 'Thumbelina', 'No Two People' and more – every one a hit. Pure magic.

Happiest Days of Your Life, The ☉
1950, UK, 81 mins, b/w
Dir: Frank Launder
Stars: Alastair Sim, Margaret Rutherford, Joyce Grenfell
Rating: ★★★★

No two players were ever more happily teamed than Alastair Sim and Margaret Rutherford in this riotous comedy about a boys' school forced to share its buildings with a girls' school. Dame Margaret quivers indignantly, while Sim dithers delightfully at each new crisis. Joyce Grenfell as the 'jolly hockey sticks' games mistress adds to the fun. Richly characterised, frantically paced and very funny.

Happiest Millionaire, The ☉
1967, US, 165 mins, colour
Dir: Norman Tokar
Stars: Fred MacMurray, Tommy Steele, Greer Garson, Geraldine Page
Rating: ★★★

Light, colourful, amusing Disney offering about an eccentric 1916 Boston household. The Sherman brothers contribute their best score outside *Mary Poppins* (it includes 'Fortuosity', 'Watch Your Footwork' and 'What's Wrong with That?') and the well-plotted script never deviates from the proven Disney formula of entertainment pure and simple. Tommy Steele is almost as engaging as the family's toothy Irish butler as a scene-stealing alligator, and doyenne actresses Geraldine Page and Gladys Cooper enjoy themselves with their caustic duet about the social graces. Lesley Ann Warren makes her screen debut.

Happy Ever After ☉ ⓥ
(aka: Tonight's the Night)
1954, UK, 87 mins, colour
Dir: Mario Zampi
Stars: David Niven, Yvonne De Carlo, A E Matthews, Barry Fitzgerald, Michael Shepley, George Cole
Rating: ★★★

Another comedy feather in the cap of director Mario Zampi is this rollicking, riotous romp about the new squire of an Irish village, and the locals' attempts to bump him off. Some of the sequences are really side-splitting, George Cole is especially funny as the village idiot and the film is superbly shot in Technicolor. Niven, A E Matthews, Barry Fitzgerald and Michael Shepley all help speed this drop of Irish fun along at a rattling pace.

Happy Go Lovely ○
1950, UK, 97 mins, colour
Dir: Bruce Humberstone
Stars: David Niven, Vera-Ellen, Cesar Romero, Bobby Howes
Rating: ★★★

Lightweight, amusing piece of musical candyfloss made as a semi-official contribution to the Festival of Britain. The plot is no *War and Peace* but it has some good dialogue from the then emerging Val Guest and some very fine song and dance routines. Let down by the lack of cinema techniques and natural locales, it is lifted again by the performances of its US-imported stars. *Variety* said at the time: 'At last a British musical that can face the world on its own merits and will not have to bear odious comparison with a Hollywood production.' Based on a Thirties British musical called *Paradise for Two*.

Happy Is the Bride! ☉
1957, UK, 85 mins, b/w
Dir: Roy Boulting
Stars: Ian Carmichael, Janette Scott, Cecil Parker
Rating: ★★★

Delightful and highly amusing domestic comedy (a remake of *Quiet Wedding*), directed and part-scripted by Roy Boulting. The fun centres on the trials and tribulations of a young engaged couple whose wedding arrangements become increasingly complicated and almost drive them to despair.

Happy Landing ○
1937, US, 102 mins, b/w
Dir: Roy Del Ruth
Stars: Sonja Henie, Don Ameche, Ethel Merman, Cesar Romero
Rating: ★★

Fortuitous would be the word, rather than happy, for the landing that triggers off the action in this ice-musical, particularly seeing that

Don Ameche and Cesar Romero contrive to land their Paris-bound plane just a few skating rinks from Sonja Henie's home in Norway. Subsequent proceedings include Ethel Merman belting out a couple of songs and a extraordinary galvanic tap-dance number by The Condos Brothers called 'War Dance of the Wooden Indians'.

Happy Thieves, The ○
1962, US, 88 mins, b/w
Dir: George Marshall
Stars: Rex Harrison, Rita Hayworth
Rating: ★★

The teaming of Rita Hayworth and Rex Harrison suggests light comedy of the Forties. But this is an up-to-date Sixties frolic about two elegant art thieves – a colourful caper through castles, casinos and conspiracies. An unusual film to come from veteran director George Marshall, more at home with Bob Hope comedies (he made seven) or such classic Westerns as *Destry Rides Again* and *When the Daltons Rode*. Including two-reelers, Marshall claimed to have directed more than 400 films.

Happytimes
See: The Inspector General

Hard Contract ◐
1969, US, 106 mins, colour
Dir: S Lee Pogostin
Stars: James Coburn, Lee Remick, Lilli Palmer, Burgess Meredith, Patrick Magee, Sterling Hayden
Rating: ★★

In this rather deliberately paced thriller, James Coburn stars as John Cunningham, an enigmatic American hired killer. The film is as much a morality play under its cover of murder thriller, and as such fails to be consistently involving, although certainly there are some good bursts of action. The cast includes Trevor Howard's widow Helen Cherry and the later star-billed Karen Black.

Hard Day's Night, A ☉ ⓥ
1964, UK, 85 mins, b/w
Dir: Richard Lester
Stars: John Lennon, Paul McCartney, George Harrison, Ringo Starr, Wilfred Brambell, Norman Rossington
Rating: ★★★

The Beatles make like Merseybeat Marx Brothers (with a touch of Mack Sennett) in this distinguished debut feature with an enjoyable line in witty

H

lunacy. All four flopheads show a deft touch with a throwaway joke, and examples of the boys' wry sense of humour are legion. Interviewer: 'How did you find America?' John: 'Left after Greenland.' Interviewer: 'What do you call that hairstyle?' George: 'Arthur.' With Richard Lester directing at an 80-mile-an-hour pace and a sharp script by Alun Owen, this is a very funny and entertaining film. Its two best sequences are a wacky, wild fling as the Beatles escape from it all for a few minutes in a field; and a chaotic press conference. It almost goes without saying that the songs are all very good too.

Harder They Fall, The ○
1956, US, 109 mins, b/w
Dir: Mark Robson
Stars: Humphrey Bogart, Rod Steiger, Jan Sterling, Mike Lane
Rating: ★★★

One of the most scathing indictments of boxing in film history, this rugged, almost merciless profile of the game featured Humphrey Bogart in his last role. It was one of his most memorable parts, as a once scrupulous sports reporter who has fallen on hard times, but he was already dying of cancer and the tough shooting schedule exhausted him. He also encountered difficulty acting with co-star Rod Steiger, as a manipulative Mob boss, who insisted on Method acting. By underplaying, though, Bogart steals the show, and his scene in a car with boxer Mike Lane towards the end remains one of the most emotive moments in Fifties' films. Director Mark Robson knew the degree of brutality he wanted to capture in the ring from his earlier experiences on *Champion*, starring Kirk Douglas. He got the gruelling results he wanted.

Hard, Fast and Beautiful ○
1951, US, 79 mins, b/w
Dir: Ida Lupino
Stars: Claire Trevor, Sally Forrest
Rating: ★★★

Ida Lupino directs this unusual melodrama revolving around the cut and thrust of the tennis world. Claire Trevor is on top form as the grasping mother pushing her daughter up the championship ladder.

Hard Man, The ○
1957, US, 80 mins, colour
Dir: George Sherman

Stars: Guy Madison, Valerie French, Lorne Greene
Rating: ★★

Very tough Western scripted by Leo Katcher from his own hard-hitting novel. Guy Madison is the Texas Ranger who believes in bringing more of 'em back dead than alive while Lorne Greene, TV's Ben Cartwright from *Bonanza*, expertly handles the role of an embittered cattle king.

Hard Target ● ⓥ
1993, US, 95 mins, colour
Dir: John Woo
Stars: Jean-Claude Van Damme, Yancy Butler, Lance Henriksen, Wilford Brimley
Rating: ★★

Yet another Jean-Claude Van Damme bloodbath, with a little more style than most (though not much), courtesy of Hong Kong director John Woo. Once again, Van Damme is wise enough to surround himself with actors no better than he is (especially heroine Yancy Butler), though he throws himself into the action with a will, demonstrating that one can always dodge a speeding bullet with sideways or upwards leaps, something the bad guys always neglect to do. Down in New Orleans, there's a police strike on, and men are being hunted for money, on 'safaris' organised by crazy, piano-playing Fouchon (Lance Henriksen) and his partner, ex-mercenary Van Cleaf, played by South African actor Arnold Vosloo. Henriksen is really the only member of the cast who can act, but this doesn't bother Van Damme who only has to share the final wordless confrontation with him anyway. Our hero is hunted through streets, bayous and old deserted buildings, but it makes no difference: with one bound he's free. Hard target? Make that impossible.

Hard Times
See: The Streetfighter

Hard Way, The ○
1942, US, 109 mins, b/w
Dir: Vincent Sherman
Stars: Ida Lupino, Dennis Morgan, Joan Leslie, Jack Carson
Rating: ★★★

One of the most neglected of the great Warner Brothers melodramas of the Forties. Ida Lupino was at the peak of her form, and dominates the story as the strong-willed poor-born woman who sees her chance of a new lifestyle

by maximising the limited show business talent of her younger sister, riding roughshod over the feelings of all who stand in their way. Lupino won the New York Film Critics award for that year as best actress, but amazingly was not even nominated for an Oscar. Equally surprising, her meaty role had been turned down by Bette Davis. Five years later, with her career faltering, Davis would have given her eye-teeth for the role. As one of those trodden on by Lupino, Jack Carson again demonstrates his ability to poignantly play good-hearted guys with sensitive feelings.

Hard Way, The ● ⓥ
1991, US, 111 mins, colour
Dir: John Badham
Stars: Michael J Fox, James Woods, Stephen Lang, Annabella Sciorra, LL Cool J
Rating: ★★★

Take a friendless cop with some kind of a death wish, on the trail of a serial killer and unable to attract women. 'Maybe it's something about my personality,' he surmises. Then take an egotistical, sawn-off movie star who has no idea about real life, but wants to make a film 'without a goddamn Roman numeral in it'. Cast James Woods and Michael J Fox in the parts, shake well around the before-mentioned serial killer and you have the mixture for a fairly sure-fire action comedy. Nick Lang (Fox) wants real police experience to help him with a new role, and John Moss (Woods) is the man he chooses to provide it. Stunts and chases abound in the ensuing developments of a film that might have been better but remains enjoyable for all that. Fox has a good time (including a running gag about his looking like Nick Lang, only shorter); Woods is as OTT in comedy as he is in drama and just as entertaining.

Hardys Ride High, The ○
1939, US, 80 mins, b/w
Dir: George B Seitz
Stars: Mickey Rooney, Lewis Stone, Cecilia Parker, Fay Holden, Ann Rutherford, Sara Haden
Rating: ★★

With the arrival of Sara Haden as spinster Aunt Milly, the Hardy films' cast was in place for the next seven years, as they consolidated their position as America's favourite screen family of the war years. Mickey Rooney, now America's number one box-office attraction, was given top billing for the first time, and is up to all his usual tricks panting after girls half a foot taller, as the family fancies it's about to come into a fortune.

Harem Holiday ☉ ⓥ
(aka: Harum Scarum)
1965, US, 86 mins, colour
Dir: Gene Nelson
Stars: Elvis Presley, Mary Ann Mobley, Fran Jeffries, Michael Ansara
Rating: ★★

Elvis Presley goes east (well, at any rate, as far as the Hollywood Hills) in a colourful comedy-musical about a pop singer kidnapped by a sheikh. Mary Ann Mobley, a one-time Miss America, is the heroine, and the score includes such desert-pop hybrids as 'It's Kismet', 'If You Love a Mirage', 'Go East Young Man' and 'Desert Serenade'. It is directed by former dancing star Gene Nelson, who brings a balletic quality to scenes of karate combat.

Harlem Nights ● ⓥ
1989, US, 115 mins, colour
Dir: Eddie Murphy
Stars: Eddie Murphy, Richard Pryor
Rating: ★

Eddie Murphy had reached the 'can do no wrong' stage of his career when he produced, directed and wrote this foul-mouthed disaster of a film – proving that he could do wrong and in a big way. Murphy's idea of wry wit and humour is a seemingly constant stream of invective and profanity and the derivative story (a cross between *The Sting* and *The Cotton Club*) holds no surprises. However much his vanity may tell him otherwise, Murphy doesn't showcase his own particular talents as well as other directors and writers have and this film also wastes the considerable comic talents of Richard Pryor and Redd Foxx. If this film has any redeeming virtues they're completely lost under the frantic mugging of the cast. Disbelief that Murphy can fall as flat on his face as anyone else may lead you to take a look at this, but *Harlem Nights* gets a Bronx cheer from me.

Harlequin ☉
1980, AUS, 96 mins, colour
Dir: Simon Wincer
Stars: Robert Powell, David Hemmings, Carmen Duncan, Broderick Crawford
Rating: ★★★

An enjoyable science-fiction tall tale about a faith healer and a political plot in Australia. The characters' names suggest a parallel with the Rasputin story but, while the protagonist retains his hypnotic and healing qualities, the plot veers away into something more devious. Robert Powell, blue eyes shining, is every bit as charismatic as the makers could wish as the 'healer' who infiltrates the home of a senator whose child has leukaemia, although, after his arrival, he behaves more like Dracula than Rasputin. David Hemmings keeps rather too low a profile as a senator, but Carmen Duncan is extraordinary as his wife, and Broderick Crawford most effective as the weasel in the political woodpile. It develops ultimately into a paranormal thriller, whose special effects occasionally wobble but whose other elements remain tight, tense and intriguing throughout.

Harold and Maude ●
1971, US, 92 mins, colour
Dir: Hal Ashby
Stars: Ruth Gordon, Bud Cort, Vivian Pickles, Cyril Cusack
Rating: ★★★

This extremely black comedy about the relationship between a death-obsessed young man and an elderly woman is often very funny and has something to offend almost everyone. The youth's series of staged suicides is particularly amusing, especially when dismissed by his harridan of a mother, who finds him hanging himself from the ceiling of his room and remarks, 'I suppose you think that's very funny.' It's one of a kind.

Harper ☉
(aka: The Moving Target)
1966, US, 121 mins, colour
Dir: Jack Smight
Stars: Paul Newman, Lauren Bacall, Julie Harris, Janet Leigh, Robert Wagner
Rating: ★★★

Paul Newman in a private-eye thriller (shown in British cinemas as *The Moving Target*) that was Hollywood's own tribute to those superb Bogart thrillers of the Forties. Newman plays the seedy, tough detective Lew Harper who is, as William Goldman's screenplay succinctly puts it, 'hired by a bitch to find scum'. The 'scum' is a missing millionaire, although his wife (played by Bogart's widow, Lauren Bacall) doesn't seem too upset when warned that he may already be dead. So who's the kidnapper? The flashy

playboy (Robert Webber), the chauffeur who seems to live above his means (Robert Wagner), the drug-addicted pianist (Julie Harris) or a film star who 'got fat' (Shelley Winters)? Or is it all of them? Not above suspicion are Harper's own estranged wife (Janet Leigh) and his lawyer friend (Arthur Hill). As might be expected from such a cast list, this is rather a thing of bits and pieces. But Newman and Bacall really strike sparks off each other in their too-few scenes together.

Harriet Craig ☉
1950, US, 94 mins, b/w
Dir: Vincent Sherman
Stars: Joan Crawford, Wendell Corey
Rating: ★★★

Joan Crawford was coming to the end of her sequence of black dramas after winning an Oscar for *Mildred Pierce* in 1945, when she made this one about a ruthlessly ambitious woman – a remake of the 1936 film *Craig's Wife*. Wendell Corey was an excellent foil for queens of the screen, fresh as he was from playing opposite Barbara Stanwyck (in *The Furies* and *The File on Thelma Jordon*).

Harry and Son ☉
1984, US, 117 mins, colour
Dir: Paul Newman
Stars: Paul Newman, Robby Benson, Ellen Barkin, Wilford Brimley, Joanne Woodward
Rating: ★★

A young, virtually unknown actor called Tom Cruise was originally lined up to play Paul Newman's son in this angst-ridden family drama. Robby Benson took the role instead and years later, when Newman had won his first Oscar alongside Cruise in *The Color of Money*, Newman joked: 'Boy did I save you from that one!' Directed, co-produced and co-written by Newman, *Harry and Son* is an underdeveloped hodgepodge that never makes up its mind what it wants to be. Newman is a widower who faces a crossroads in his life. He can either throw in the towel or make a fresh start. The tragedy of the thing is that he goes nowhere. His real-life wife, Joanna Woodward, pops up as an eccentric neighbour, but the overriding sense is of a waste of talent all round.

H

Harry and the Hendersons
See: Bigfoot and the Hendersons

Harry and Walter Go to New York ○
1976, US, 123 mins, colour
Dir: Mark Rydell
Stars: James Caan, Michael Caine, Elliott Gould, Diane Keaton, Lesley Ann Warren, Charles Durning
Rating: ★

A magnificent cast – James Caan, Michael Caine, Elliott Gould, Diane Keaton, Lesley Ann Warren, Charles Durning and Burt Young – and a talented director, Mark Rydell (*Cinderella Liberty*, *On Golden Pond*), are along for the ride in this colourful comedy about two vaudeville comedians and would-be bank robbers in and out of jail in 19th century America. Unfortunately, thanks to a disappointingly pallid script, almost none of it works.

Harry Black
See: Harry Black and the Tiger

Harry Black and the Tiger ○
(aka: Harry Black)
1958, UK, 107 mins, colour
Dir: Hugo Fregonese
Stars: Stewart Granger, Barbara Rush, Anthony Steel, Kamala Devi
Rating: ★★★

Jungle adventure of superior quality. Excellent colour photography and a cracking climax are bonus attractions to this story of a white hunter in India, a role that sits easily on Stewart Granger's shoulders. Anthony Steel gives one of his best performances as the figure from Black's past, a weakling who now turns up with his wife, while I S Johar is brilliant as Black's Indian helper.

Harum Scarum
See: Harem Holiday

Harvey ⊙ ⓥ
1950, US, 100 mins, b/w
Dir: Henry Koster
Stars: James Stewart, Josephine Hull, Charles Drake, Peggy Dow
Rating: ★★★

The smash-hit comedy that provides scores of impersonators with their standard James Stewart impression, as he totters drunkenly home in the company of a six-foot white rabbit (the Harvey of the title) which only he can see. Stewart's in marvellous form, but the film's acting Oscar went to little Josephine Hull, who plays his dithering sister.

Harvey Girls, The ⊙
1946, US, 101 mins, colour
Dir: George Sidney
Stars: Judy Garland, Ray Bolger, John Hodiak, Angela Lansbury
Rating: ★★★

A happy, colourful musical show which reunites Judy Garland with Ray Bolger (who played the scarecrow in *The Wizard of Oz*) and contains such toe-tapping tunes as 'Honky-Tonk' and the big show-stopper 'On the Atcheson, Topeka and Santa Fe'. There's also a memorable wistful trio, 'It's a Great Big World', sung and danced by Garland, Cyd Charisse and Virginia O'Brien and some rousing action scenes, especially towards the end. Angela Lansbury is a delight as a decadent dance-hall hostess.

Has Anybody Seen My Gal ⊙
1952, US, 92 mins, colour
Dir: Douglas Sirk
Stars: Piper Laurie, Charles Coburn, Rock Hudson, Lynn Bari
Rating: ★★★

A delightful comedy with music, set in the late Twenties and directed by Douglas Sirk before he made a different kind of reputation with such weepies as *Magnificent Obsession* and *Imitation of Life*. The romantic lead of a youthful Piper Laurie and Rock Hudson is irresistible, but even so it's really Charles Coburn who is not only at the centre of things, but also steals the film. Bright, diverting and warm-hearted entertainment, with a fleeting appearance by future superstar James Dean as a youth who orders an incredibly complicated ice cream special.

Hasty Heart, The ○
1949, UK, 107 mins, b/w
Dir: Vincent Sherman
Stars: Richard Todd, Ronald Reagan, Patricia Neal
Rating: ★★★

A great old tear-jerker with a fine performance from Richard Todd as the taciturn Scot in a Burmese war hospital who, unbeknown to him at first, has only a short time to live. It set Todd up for a 15-year career as a major cinema star.

Hatari! ○
1962, US, 159 mins, colour
Dir: Howard Hawks
Stars: John Wayne, Elsa Martinelli, Hardy Kruger
Rating: ★★

Not surprisingly Howard Hawks, the director with whom John Wayne made *Red River*, *Rio Bravo*, *El Dorado* and *Rio Lobo*, injected much of the spirit of the Western into this big, sprawling drama of a group of big-game trappers pursuing their African quarries in Landrovers. Wayne even wears a stetson to heighten the comparison. Hardy Kruger, the German actor so memorable in *The One That Got Away*, gives a deft portrayal of the ex-racing driver whose skill returns to him when he gets behind the wheel of a jeep, and Michele Girardon is notable as a girl called Brandy. Hawks crams in some exciting scenes of animals on the run.

Hatter's Castle ○
1941, UK, 102 mins, b/w
Dir: Lance Comfort
Stars: Robert Newton, Deborah Kerr, James Mason, Emlyn Williams
Rating: ★★★

Although not bearing too great a resemblance to the AJ Cronin novel on which it's based (most notably in the telescoping together of two of the main characters to make one), this story of a tyrannical Scottish businessman provided an acting tour-de-force for Robert Newton (as the almost-mad hatter of the title) that confirmed his newly won place at the forefront of British cinema.

Haunted Honeymoon ○
1986, US, 82 mins, colour
Dir: Gene Wilder
Stars: Gene Wilder, Gilda Radner, Dom DeLuise, Jonathan Pryce, Paul L Smith, Peter Vaughn
Rating: ★

This frantic comedy-chiller saw the last film appearance together of star-director Gene Wilder and real-life wife, comedienne Gilda Radner, who died from cancer in 1989. It's a send-up of old thunderstorm mystery films, but relentlessly overplayed. The main character, who has irrational fears that someone plans to cure him by literally scaring him to death, spends the entire story in his spooky ancestral home. The cast mug and scream enthusiastically, but the film only manages a few chuckles rather than belly laughs. Wilder's direction is brimming with good ideas, though his pacing is erratic and the chills catch the eye but not the throat. The vital difference between this and the similar Bob Hope classic *The Cat and the Canary* is the lack of feeling that any of this is for real. Only little Ann Way, as the fierce maid-of-all-trades, seems to have come from the old dark houses we used to know.

Haunted Honeymoon
See: *Busman's Honeymoon*

Haunted Palace, The ● ⊙
1964, US, 85 mins, colour
Dir: Roger Corman
Stars: Vincent Price, Debra Paget, Lon Chaney Jr
Rating: ★★★

Roger Corman's film, inspired by the stories of Edgar Allan Poe, leaves behind the light-heartedness of *The Raven* and returns to a sinister world of flickering candles, shadowy corridors and coffins whose inhabitants seem destined not to rest in peace. Vincent Price gives one of his most controlled performances as the man possessed by the evil spirit of his ancestor, and the final few feet contain a shock that will chill you to the bone. The colour photography by Floyd Crosby, shrill music composed by the redoubtable Les Baxter and restrained supporting performances all add to the sense of underlying horror. That frightened little man of the screen, Elisha Cook Jr, adds being burned alive to his gallery of film deaths.

Haunted Strangler, The
See: *The Grip of the Strangler*

Haunted Summer ●
1988, US, 115 mins, colour
Dir: Ivan Passer
Stars: Philip Anglim, Laura Dern, Alice Krige, Eric Stoltz, Alex Winter
Rating: ★

This story of Shelley and Byron is pretty (thanks to photographer Giuseppe Rotunno) and pretty boring too. Ken Russell made a hash of the same story in *Gothic* and here the only spark of interest in Ivan Passer's tedious treatment lies in how long it will take Byron (Anglim) to get Mary Shelley (Krige) into bed. The answer's 110 of the film's 115 minutes. The actors spout epigrams and strike poses. Bloodless and gutless, the film just lies there in the Swiss sunshine. Ironically, its most interesting scenes are the

closest it gets to the Russell treatment, as the protagonists are visited (in a cavern, in an opium-induced haze) by the monster of their worst nightmares.

Haunting, The ●
1963, UK, 112 mins, b/w
Dir: Robert Wise
Stars: Julie Harris, Claire Bloom, Richard Johnson, Russ Tamblyn, Lois Maxwell, Fay Compton
Rating: ★★★★

A young American, and three psychic research experts, come to investigate an allegedly haunted house that he has inherited. Faint hearts may not be up to this truly frightening ghost story about a house that was 'born bad' and claims the souls of those who enter it. The film's great strength lies in the fact that the 'thing' is never seen; and the infra-red camerawork makes the walls of the house – 'leprous' one of the characters call them – seem almost alive, and brings the horror right out of the screen. Director Robert Wise sets electricity crackling into the audience with a hair-raising opening, and rarely lets the chilling temperature rise. Julie Harris and Claire Bloom are both excellent, striking the right note of hysteria, and clinging together most convincingly when – well, whatever it is – is thundering its anger outside their bedroom door. Tamblyn's performance gradually gains authority and reaches a climax on the last line. And, just when the suspense seems to be slackening, a beautiful study of evil by Rosalie Crutchley sends the shivers racing down our spines again.

Havana ◐ ⊙
1991, US, 145 mins, colour
Dir: Sydney Pollack
Stars: Robert Redford, Lena Olin, Raul Julia
Rating: ★★

Robert Redford is a gambler looking for a big win in the dying days of Batista's Cuba and Lena Olin is the wealthy and married woman he falls for in this overlong drama which seems to be an attempt to make a *Casablanca* for the Nineties. Redford's seventh collaboration with director Sydney Pollack is arguably the team's least successful, especially compared with their previous outing – *Out of Africa*. It looks good and the feel of Cuba during the build-up to Castro's successful bid for power is well realised. But Redford seems too world-weary and disinterested and, at

145 minutes, the film is far too long. There are compensations, though, with fine supporting performances from Alan Arkin, Tomas Milan, Mark Rydell and an unbilled Raul Julia. Tighter editing, though, would have made a much more interesting film.

Having Wonderful Time ○
1938, US, 71 mins, b/w
Dir: Alfred Santell
Stars: Ginger Rogers, Douglas Fairbanks Jr, Peggy Conklin, Lucille Ball, Red Skelton
Rating: ★★★

A warmly human and richly amusing kind of American version of *Holiday Camp*. Miss Rogers strings it together in her most vivacious form: from the point where she backgammons a wealthy playboy to sleep, the film's humour really starts to take off. In the supporting cast are Red Skelton, making his debut and doing his famous 'doughnut dunking' routine; Ann Miller, Eve Arden; Allan 'Rocky' Lane, who later became a cowboy star; and Lee Bowman and Jack Carson, both especially good as two of Ginger's suitors whose luck is out.

Hawaii ○
1966, US, 155 mins, colour
Dir: George Roy Hill
Stars: Julie Andrews, Max Von Sydow, Richard Harris, Gene Hackman
Rating: ★★★

A rarity – a literate epic that also has plenty of action, and is a joy to look at. Dalton Trumbo and Daniel Taradash, who wrote the screenplay of this massive adventure story, have taken James A Michener's enormous novel, and compressed it into compact, intelligent scenes. Max Von Sydow excels as the bigoted minister sent to Hawaii in the 19th century to convert the natives: his portrayal clearly delineates the alternating torment and authority of a man unable to communicate his emotions. Julie Andrews hasn't quite the weight for the role of the consumptive wife who keeps him going through his darkest hours, but makes a game stab at it. While, talking of weight, there's a captivating performance from Jocelyn La Garde as the native ruler. Gene Hackman can be spotted in a minor role. It was his second film, some years before he went on to become a star in *The French Connection*. You'll have to concentrate harder to pick up Bette Midler as a seaside bride.

H

Hawk, The ● ⊚
1992, UK, 86 mins, colour
Dir: David Hayman
Stars: Helen Mirren, George Costigan,
Rosemary Leach, Owen Teale
Rating: ★★★

A gritty, keep-'em-guessing mystery
with TV's *Prime Suspect* star Helen
Mirren emoting strongly (perhaps a
shade too strongly at times) in the
central role of suburban housewife
Annie Marsh. A casual remark by
Annie's husband (George Costigan)
leads her to believe that he could be
perpetrator of a series of horrific
local murders. But Annie has a history
of mental illness and, before long, we
are wondering if she's imagining the
whole thing. A thoroughly convincing
and beautifully crafted British thriller
that only fails to stem its credibility
gaps towards the end, though the wall
of belief just about holds firm through
to the unlikely, but highly satisfying
ending.

Hawk the Slayer ◐ ⊚
1980, UK, 93 mins, colour
Dir: Terry Marcel
Stars: Jack Palance, John Terry, Annette
Crosbie, Cheryl Campbell, Bernard
Bresslaw, Catriona MacColl
Rating: ★

You might have thought that such
medieval romps had died the death
when Universal lost its International.
But lo! they live, in this ripely sliced
chunk of swords, sandals and sorcery.
In a land of swirling mists, a motley
crew of Equity reservists rides at the
shoulder of heroic Hawk (John
Terry) through an orange-skied landscape to Ennio Morricone-style music
adapted for rustic flute. They hope to
bring peace to the land; but Terrible
Jack Palance is a law unto himself as
Voltan the Unbelievable wearing a
scowl that would intimidate Giant
Haystacks as he over-and-out-acts a
understandably cowed crew of
minions, and guards his visage with a
semi-visor lest his black acne be revealed before the final reel. Methinks
there's a vein of satire to all this and
that references to 'legions of darkness
making savage cuts to the country'
are merely veiled jibes at the British
Government.

Hawmps! ⊙
1976, US, 120 mins, colour
Dir: Joe Camp
Stars: James Hampton, Christopher
Connelly, Slim Pickens
Rating: ★★

An elongated comic version of a remarkably nutty little chapter in U S
history already filmed (as a straightforward action film) 20 years earlier as
Camels West. It deals with a brief but
doomed attempt by the U S government just before the outbreak of Civil
War to introduce camels as a substitute
for horses for the U S Cavalry in desert conditions. The expected slapstick
involving Cavalrymen and their new
mounts is followed by a hilarious race
between camels and horses, in which
wall-eyed Western veteran Jack Elam
comes on for a splendid comic turn as
the bad hat who tries to sabotage the
race. Fellow film Westerners Slim
Pickens and Denver Pyle are also
along for the bumpy ride, and children
will adore a baby camel called Valentine.

Head Over Heels ○
1937, UK, 90 mins, b/w
Dir: Sonnie Hale
Stars: Jessie Matthews, Louis Borell,
Robert Flemyng
Rating: ★★★

Although this airy musical was popular
enough in its day, it does in retrospect
mark the beginning of the downswing
in star Jessie Matthews' career. For the
first time in the major part of her run
of success as Britain's foremost musical
star, Matthews was without the talents
of the incomparable director Victor
Saville. This time the man behind the
camera is her then-husband Sonnie
Hale and, although it's the best of
Hale's three efforts for her, Saville's
light touch and innate elegance are
already beginning to be missed. Still,
Jessie is a delight, as always, and her
numbers include 'Head Over Heels in
Love', 'May I Have the Next Romance with You?' and 'Looking
Around Corners for You'.

Hear My Song ◐ ⊚
1991, UK, 105 mins, colour
Dir: Peter Chelsom
Stars: Ned Beatty, Adrian Dunbar, David
McCallum, Tara Fitzgerald, Shirley Anne
Field, William Hootkins
Rating: ★★★

Chances are you'll be humming the
songs of Josef Locke after you leave
this one. Locke? Ask your parents. He
was an Irish tenor who ruled the halls
for nigh on 20 years in post-war times
until he had to flee the country on tax
evasion charges. Around this brief
thread, writer-director Peter Chelsom
has woven a decidedly different sort of
film. Rotund American actor Ned

Beatty enjoys his finest hour since
Deliverance as Locke, sought by seedy
young Irish-born impresario Micky
O'Neill (Adrian Dunbar) on a trip
back across the sea to Ireland. O'Neill,
pressed by creditors at his nightclub,
has tried to pass off a Locke impersonator, to the humiliation of his
girlfriend's mother (Shirley Anne
Field) who shared an affair with Locke
25 years before. Now Micky must
make amends, but finding Locke,
never mind persuading him back to
England and the vengeful arms of the
law (David McCallum) proves a tricky
thing. The film sags a bit around
half-way, and degenerates into farce at
the end, but its heart, definitely in the
right place, sees it through. Beatty,
unlike some of the cast, never
overplays. Field, in her late fifties, is
still ravishing.

Hear No Evil ◐ ⊚
1993, US, 99 mins, colour
Dir: Robert Greenwald
Stars: Marlee Matlin, D B Sweeney,
Martin Sheen
Rating: ★★

A peculiar little thriller, okay video
fare for the most part, which casts deaf
actress Marlee Matlin as the girl in
danger after a friend steals a priceless
coin and hides it in her apartment.
Matlin soon finds both a masked killer
and crooked police (led by Martin
Sheen) on her heels. The pace of the
story is sort of stop-go, not surprising
when you consider that parts of it are
padded out with scenery and
soundtrack music and parts of it are
almost elliptical, as if little bits of the
plot were missing, causing the action
to move unnecessarily quickly from
one scene to another. Matlin and D B
Sweeney (he obviously qualifying in
gloom as the Stephen Rea of the
Nineties Hollywood scene) are
adequate, Sheen quite interesting as a
bad guy for once, though his role ends
too tamely. Not bad.

Heart and Souls ○ ⊚
1993, US, 104 mins, colour
Dir: Ron Underwood
Stars: Robert Downey Jr, Charles
Grodin, Kyra Sedgwick, Tom Sizemore,
Alfre Woodard
Rating: ★★★

An initially iffy but often effective
fantasy that pulls relentlessly at our
emotions in its later stages. Four people, each with things in life to do, are
killed, along with the driver of their
bus, whose gaze strays too long on a

courting couple in the car speeding alongside. Also caught in the impact is a pregnant mother, whose baby, born there and then, finds himself with four guardian angels, as the dead people are 'missed' in the pick-up for Heaven. So is he there to help the lost souls achieve their ambitions? Or are they there to help him achieve his? Director Ron Underwood's answer is a bit of both in a film that largely endears itself, but occasionally embarrasses when the spirits step into Robert Downey Jr, as the grown boy, and take over his body. A string of good performances here, from Charles Grodin, Kyra Sedgwick, Tom Sizemore and Alfre Woodard as the quaint quartet, David Paymer as the bus driver and Elisabeth Shue, who makes more of Downey's long-suffering girlfriend than is really there. Only Downey himself seems less than at ease with it all.

Heartbreakers ● ⓥ
1984, US, 98 mins, colour
Dir: Bobby Roth
Stars: Peter Coyote, Nick Mancuso, Max Gail, Carole Laure, Carol Wayne, Kathryn Harrold
Rating: ★★★

On the surface an erotic comedy-drama, this is at heart a serious little number about two macho men adopting different stances to life, but both groping for some kind of meaning to it all which they find impossible to grasp. Peter Coyote and Nick Mancuso, two talented actors who deserved higher-profile careers, are both up to the emotional intricacies and subtleties of all this, although it's a pity that both have to play such un-sympathetic characters – men who wallow in self-pity and seem unwilling or unable to assert a pattern of stability in their lives. James Laurenson enjoys himself as the effete owner of a fashionable art gallery and, in so doing, comes across as about the most real character in the film. The girls remain little more than sexy ciphers in a story whose uneasy undertones you may find too unsettling for enjoyment. It's basically a film about insecurity – and that may strike too loud a chord in many people's lives.

Heartbreak Kid, The ◐ ⓥ
1972, US, 106 mins, colour
Dir: Elaine May
Stars: Charles Grodin, Cybill Shepherd, Jeannie Berlin
Rating: ★★★

This Neil Simon script is fun all through – in a biting kind of way. Charles Grodin (who's hardly seemed to age in the last 20 years) has the title role as Lenny, who deserts his talkative Jewish bride of a few days to pursue a beautiful blond (Cybill Shepherd) from Florida to Minnesota, just stopping off long enough on the way to get a quickie divorce. Lenny's wild fantasies deceive everyone but Shepherd's hard-headed father (Eddie Albert). By the end, though, the point has been well and truly made that Lenny isn't likely to be satisfied with anything for more than a few days at a time. Grodin is unnervingly accurate as the self-seeking hero and Jeannie Berlin brilliant as the bartered bride. Good entertainment.

Heartbreak Ridge ● ⓥ
1986, US, 130 mins, colour
Dir: Clint Eastwood
Stars: Clint Eastwood, Marsha Mason, Everett McGill, Moses Gunn, Bo Svenson
Rating: ★

Clint Eastwood was always destined to be John Wayne's heir when it came to upholding the American macho myth. As director and star of this drama about the Marines' invasion of Grenada, he turned in the most gung-ho Marine Corps movie since The Duke's *Sands of Iwo Jima*. Clint is a barking sergeant, cajoling and wet-nursing young recruits into battle readiness. It's thin material that appears to run even longer than the invasion itself, but then Hollywood was obviously pushed to find a recent confrontation that the Americans had actually won. Eastwood also wrote one of the film's background songs.

Heartburn ◐ ⓥ
1986, US, 109 mins, colour
Dir: Mike Nichols
Stars: Meryl Streep, Jack Nicholson, Jeff Daniels, Maureen Stapleton, Stockard Channing, Richard Masur
Rating: ★★

Hollywood heavyweights Jack Nicholson and Meryl Streep make this lightweight comedy about marriage and infidelity perhaps more enjoyable than it deserves. After a whirlwind romance political journalist Mark (Nicholson) proposes to food writer Rachel (Streep). But the marriage doesn't seem made in heaven when she suspects he is playing away . . . There's nothing here we haven't seen

before, but thanks to the charisma of the stars and assured and well-observed direction by Mike Nichols it's an enjoyable if rather predictable journey. There's also a good supporting cast in Jeff Daniels, Stockard Channing, Richard Masur and Catherine O'Hara.

Heart Condition ● ⓥ
1989, US, 103 mins, colour
Dir: James D Parriott
Stars: Bob Hoskins, Denzel Washington, Chloe Webb
Rating: ★★

Bob Hoskins must be used to acting with someone who isn't there. First a white cartoon rabbit, now a black ghost, in the form of a criminal lawyer whose heart he has. Hoskins is a cop who's had a heart attack, Denzel Washington the lawyer who wants him to solve a murder – his. Result: an okay movie, but one that doesn't exactly grip the attention throughout. Hoskins gives his familiar blustering, perspiring, hard-cursing performance; Washington is less effective than in some of his roles; and Chloe Webb is negligible as the girl they both love. When Hoskins is 'transformed' with the help of Washington's money, it's amusing that – even with hand-tailored suits and a toupee – he still looks the same old Hoskins.

Heart Is a Lonely Hunter, The ○
1968, US, 125 mins, colour
Dir: Robert Ellis Miller
Stars: Alan Arkin, Sondra Locke, Stacy Keach, Cicely Tyson
Rating: ★★★

Alan Arkin gives a deeply felt performance here as a deaf mute who moves to a small southern town to be near a similarly-affected friend who has been put in a nearby institution. Taking a room in a family home, he has a positive effect on the lives around him but does not cure his own loneliness. This is a brave attempt to bring Carson McCullers' moving and sensitive book to the screen. Brave, but not entirely successful, as the film tries to cover too much ground and most of the characters, save for Arkin's, are too thinly sketched. His performance is the force that moves the story and makes it worth watching. Making their debut appearances are Stacy Keach and Sondra Locke.

H

Heart Like a Wheel ○
1983, US, 110 mins, colour
Dir: Jonathan Kaplan
Stars: Beau Rossi, Bonnie Bedelia,
Loe Rossi, Hoyt Axton
Rating: ★★★

Despite a small (but devoted) following in this country, drag racing is a
peculiarly American sport. This film,
therefore, which is a biopic of the first
woman drag-racing champion Shirley
Muldowney, may not at first glance
appeal. Nevertheless it's a good solid
drama and the racing sequences are
loud and exciting, once you've figured
out what's going on. Miss
Muldowney's private life didn't run
on the smooth tarmac her racing career did, so there's plenty of off-track
drama, too. Bonnie Bedelia fills the
starring role so well it's suprising it
didn't give her career the boost it deserved. Beau Bridges is also effective as
the man she turns to after her divorce.
Pedal to the metal, good buddy

Heat and Dust ◐ Ⓥ
1982, UK, 133 mins, colour
Dir: James Ivory
Stars: Julie Christie, Christopher
Cazenove, Greta Scacchi, Julian Glover,
Susan Fleetwood, Shashi Kapoor
Rating: ★★★

Director James Ivory's vivid evocation
of the sights, sounds and feel of India
in the Twenties and the Eighties is
every bit as assured as the more expensive visits to the sub-continent in
The Jewel in the Crown and *A Passage to
India*. And, in many ways, it's rather
better, less like a tourist guide to the
country. One of the best of the
Merchant-Ivory films.

Heathers ● Ⓥ
1989, US, 102 mins, colour
Dir: Michael Lehmann
Stars: Winona Ryder, Christian Slater,
Shannen Doherty, Lisanne Falk
Rating: ★★★

Now there's weird, very weird and
major weird. But *Heathers*, described
by its makers as a teenage black comedy, is mega-weird, for at least 90
minutes that is, before descending to
conventionality (by its own
standards) in the final reel. There's a
queen bitch clique at Westerburg
High in Ohio and three of its four
members are called Heather. They
talk in a language all their own and
show no mercy to intruders. The
fourth member is Veronica (Winona
Ryder) who, rapidly becoming disil-

lusioned with the Heathers, is offered
a way out in the form of smiling J D
(Christian Slater), whose easy grin
hides a psychotic nature and whose
plans to 'kill' one of the Heathers and
a couple of school bullies with 'fake'
frightening schemes prove to
Veronica's horror to be all too real.
Most of the characters, especially the
parents, seem to have stepped from
surreal paintings, and provide a bizarre
backdrop to the stunning
performance of Ryder. Slater, too, is
most interesting as the martini-voiced
J D, a worthy successor to Norman
Bates. Come to think of it, this could
be Hollywood's answer to Lindsay
Anderson's *If . . .*

Heaven Can Wait ○
1943, US, 112 mins, colour
Dir: Ernst Lubitsch
Stars: Don Ameche, Gene Tierney,
Charles Coburn, Marjorie Main
Rating: ★★★

Not the early version of the Warren
Beatty film of the same title (that was
1941's *Here Comes Mr Jordan*), but a
highly original romantic comedy, this
was the great director Ernst Lubitsch's
last film classic. Don Ameche is
suavely tongue in cheek as the late
Lothario telling Satan his sins to engineer himself into the 'Lower
Regions' and Gene Tierney gorgeous
as his much-beset wife.

Heaven Can Wait ○
1978, US, 100 mins, colour
Dir: Buck Henry, Warren Beatty
Stars: Warren Beatty, Julie Christie,
James Mason, Jack Warden, Charles
Grodin, Dyan Cannon
Rating: ★★★★

It is to the great credit of Warren
Beatty (showing a delicate touch as a
star, producer, co-writer and
co-director) that this remake of a
classic fantasy film from the Forties is
every bit as memorable as the original.
Beatty (as the athlete 'taken' too soon
by Heaven), Julie Christie (as the girl
he falls for but can't keep), James
Mason – his best in ages – Jack
Warden and Charles Grodin are all
first-rate. But the film is almost stolen
by (Oscar-nominated) Dyan Cannon
as a tycoon's faithless wife.

Heaven Knows, Mr Allison ○
1957, US, 100 mins, colour
Dir: John Huston
Stars: Deborah Kerr, Robert Mitchum
Rating: ★★★★

Deborah Kerr's favourite film and one
of John Huston's best, a sort of
sideshoot from his own *The African
Queen*. Instead of a missionary and a
riverboat skipper, Huston gives us a
nun (Kerr's first appearance 'in habit'
since *Black Narcissus* 10 years before)
and a tough US Marine (Robert
Mitchum perfectly cast), shipwrecked
on a Pacific island during World War
Two. Virtually a duologue between
the two, with lots of action, adventure
and drama to hold the interest.
Huston's film has moments of high
pathos, excitement and tenderness, all
in superb settings, as the director and
his photographer (the great Oswald
Morris) skilfully convey the humid,
lush atmosphere of a small tropical island that might be a paradise in other
circumstances. The tensions between
Kerr and Mitchum are cleverly written
and their performances are first-class.
Ultimately, though, it's the unusual
qualities of the story that probably
contribute more than anything else
to the film's success.

Heavens Above! ◐
1963, UK, 118 mins, b/w
Dir: John Boulting
Stars: Peter Sellers, Eric Sykes, Bernard
Miles, Irene Handl, Miriam Karlin
Rating: ★★

After the hilarious goings-on of
Private's Progress, *Brothers-in-Law* and
Lucky Jim, this scathing satire about a
prison chaplain sent by mistake to the
living of a snooty country parish was
quite a departure for the Boulting
Brothers. One wonders whether
snobbery in church people, even if it
exists to the extent shown here, is of
the same outward kind. But no matter: Eric Sykes, Irene Handl, Miriam
Karlin and Roy Kinnear are splendidly
scurrilous as the gipsy family to
whom Peter Sellers' vicar unwisely
opens his home.

Heaven's Gate ◐ Ⓥ
1980, US, 219 mins, colour
Dir: Michael Cimino
Stars: Kris Kristofferson, Christopher
Walken, Isabelle Huppert, Sam
Waterston, John Hurt, Jeff Bridges
Rating: ★

After scooping five Oscars for *The
Deer Hunter*, this next film from writer/
director Michael Cimino was eagerly
awaited. Budgeted at $7.5 million, it
ballooned out of control to $36 mil-
lion, almost bankrupted its studio and
was an unmitigated disaster. The top
brass yanked it from American

cinemas as audiences were left bewildered by the events on screen, and
hacked it down from 205 minutes to
149. It was later shown in Britain in a
fractionally shorter format.
Ravishingly shot in luminous Technicolor by Vilmos Zsigmond, it is
basically a Western about the conflict
between immigrant settlers and the
ruthless empire builders who want
them eliminated. What it seriously
lacks is an understandable storyline,
and that's its ultimate undoing. The
prologue, set in Harvard, was actually
shot at Oxford, England.

Heidi ☉
1937, US, 88 mins, b/w
Dir: Allan Dwan
Stars: Shirley Temple, Jean Hersholt,
Arthur Treacher, Helen Westley
Rating: ★★★

Shirley Temple celebrated her ninth
birthday on the set of this cute but
un-sugary Hollywood version of
Johanna Spyri's children's classic about
a little Swiss girl living with her
grandfather. It was Shirley's third
consecutive year as top box-office attraction in America.

Heiress, The ◐
1949, US, 115 mins, b/w
Dir: William Wyler
Stars: Olivia De Havilland, Montgomery
Clift, Ralph Richardson, Miriam Hopkins
Rating: ★★★★

In post-war years, Olivia de Havilland
won an Oscar for *To Each His Own*
and was further nominated for *The
Snake Pit*. But *The Heiress*, which won
her a second Oscar, directed by William Wyler in studiously stylish
fashion, is surely Olivia's finest hour.
Your heart will go out to her as the
dowdy spinster Catherine Sloper and,
like her, you'll probably never be
quite sure as to whether or not handsome young Montgomery Clift is
genuinely in love with her or just a
fortune-hunter out for her money.
De Havilland was never more poignant, Clift never more charismatic. And
top-quality supporting performances
are given by Ralph Richardson as
Catherine's martinet father and by
Miriam Hopkins, one of Wyler's favourite actresses, as Lavinia. The
ending, splendidly acted and
stage-managed, is a real hammer blow
at the emotions – and exactly right
into the bargain.

He Laughed Last ○
1956, US, 77 mins, colour
Dir: Blake Edwards
Stars: Frankie Laine, Anthony Dexter,
Lucy Marlow, Richard Long
Rating: ★★

This Damon Runyon-style comedy,
with songs from Frankie Laine, was
one of several bright and breezy films
(most featuring Laine) made by Blake
Edwards before he moved on to such
films as *The Pink Panther* and *Breakfast
at Tiffany's*. Anthony Dexter is the
actor who shot to fame in *Valentino*
(1951), then fell away in a series of
increasingly silly costume charades.
Here, alas, he doesn't get much of a
look-in. Lucy Marlow sparkles as a
chorus girl who inherits a gangster's
millions, and character actor Jesse
White steals the happy show as gangster Max, tough as a plank – and twice
as thick.

Helen Morgan Story
See: Both Ends of the Candle

Helen of Troy ○
1955, US/UK, 118 mins, colour
Dir: Robert Wise
Stars: Rossana Podesta, Jack Sernas,
Cedric Hardwicke, Stanley Baker
Rating: ★★

Director Robert Wise (he made *West
Side Story*) picked two of the Continent's brightest young stars Rossana
Podesta and Jacques (here Jack) Sernas
to play the lovers in this spectacular
story of the Trojan War and what led
up to it. Down in a minor role, he
cast a teenage actress called Brigitte
Bardot. The producers, with an almost
unheard of £2 million budget for the
film, had gathered together a huge
all-star cast and almost 6,000 extras,
armed with 30,000 arrows, on some of
the most impressive sets ever built.
But from the moment the cameras
rolled at the studios in Rome, the film
was in trouble – trouble that almost
ended in it being scrapped. Accidents
put more than 200 extras in hospital.
One of its stars, Rossana Podesta,
sprained an ankle, holding up production. There was a switch of
directors mid-film and a £400,000
fire. After all this hell in Troy, the results were only fair to middling.

Hell and High Water ○
1954, US, 103 mins, colour
Dir: Samuel Fuller
Stars: Richard Widmark, Bella Darvi,
Cameron Mitchell, David Wayne
Rating: ★★★

Pure entertainment from Samuel
Fuller, better known as director of
such exploitation dramas as *Shock
Corridor* and *The Naked Kiss*.
Non-stop excitement in a story about
a submarine on a secret mission in the
Arctic Circle, with an explosive
climax as two submarines stalk each
other through the depths – one intent
on ramming the other. Heroine Bella
Darvi, along with Inger Stevens and
both Gia Scala and Pier Angeli, was
one of those tragic European actresses
who ended their own lives after tast-
ing success in Hollywood.

Hell Below Zero ○ ⓥ
1954, UK, 90 mins, colour
Dir: Mark Robson
Stars: Alan Ladd, Joan Tetzel, Basil
Sydney, Stanley Baker, Jill Bennett
Rating: ★★★

Exciting action film, set in the Antarctic, and directed at a cracking pace
by Mark Robson. Jill Bennett just has
time to take the acting honours as a
cool Scandinavian blonde, who's also
the skipper of a whaler. A fight with
axes between Alan Ladd and Stanley
Baker on an ice-floe is the highlight of
this adventure yarn, which is based on
a popular novel by Hammond Innes
called *The White South*, cleverly
adapted to the screen by Alec Coppel
and Max Trell. Storms at sea are convincingly realistic, and another acting
performance that earns full marks is
that of Niall MacGinnis as a drunken
ship's doctor. Fans of screen escapism
will be happy with this one, which
knocks spots off some of the film
adaptations of novels by Innes's rival
on the adventure front, Alistair
MacLean.

Hell Bent for Glory ○
(aka: Lafayette Escadrille)
1957, US, 93 mins, b/w
Dir: William A Wellman
Stars: Tab Hunter, Etchika Choureau,
Rating: ★★

Director William Wellman, who
made such aviation classics as *Wings*
(the first Oscar winning film, in 1927),
Men With Wings and *The High and the
Mighty*, continued his romance with
the air in this account of his own
World War One flying memoirs. Two
of the young aviators are played by
up-and-coming David Janssen and
Clint Eastwood, and Wellman's own
son Bill also has a featured role.

H

Hellbound: Hellraiser II ● ⓥ
1989, UK, 96 mins, colour
Dir: Tony Randel
Stars: Clare Higgins, Ashley Laurence, Kenneth Cranham, Ingrid Boorman
Rating: ★★

They're fiddling with that puzzle box again and addicts of gory horror films will be delighted to know that the results are even more disgusting (if less entertaining) than the first time around. What's missing, of course, is the originality of the first film, the second instalment more or less recycling familiar elements, only more so. It does add a mad doctor (Kenneth Cranham), who gives the whole enterprise a whiff of the classic B-movies of the 1940's. 'What is today's agenda?', he snarls. 'Ah yes, evisceration.' Ashley Laurence and Ingrid Boorman scream with conviction; Clare Higgins comes back (gorily) from the dead as the Lady Macbeth figure; there's a magic mirror and references to Snow White and excellent, imaginative sets – and a baffling ending. Now, if only they'd burnt that damned mattress, we might all have been saved from the inevitable *Hellraiser III*. Needless to add, this is totally unsuitable for children!

Hell Divers ○
1931, US, 113 mins, b/w
Dir: George Hill
Stars: Wallace Beery, Clark Gable, Dorothy Jordan
Rating: ★★★

Reminiscent of some of Wallace Beery's later Forties vehicles in its rough-and-ready boisterousness, this lively if overlong action film teams puffing Beery with a Clark Gable on the very edge of top stardom. The girl they're fighting over is pretty Dorothy Jordan, one of MGM's most popular leading ladies from the early Thirties, who was lost to the screen when she married explorer and *King Kong* co-director Merian C Cooper.

Hell Drivers ○
1957, UK, 108 mins, b/w
Dir: Cy Endfield
Stars: Stanley Baker, Peggy Cummins, Herbert Lom, Patrick McGoohan
Rating: ★★★

Rough, tough, no emotions barred story of daredevil lorry drivers who seem scarcely to pause for breath between the end of one fight and the beginning of another in their bid to make a fortune in their high-speed

vehicles. The love scenes have, courtesy of Stanley Baker and Peggy Cummins, more bite than in most British films of the time, while Herbert Lom, cast for once in a sympathetic role, gives a likeable performance as Gino. Patrick McGoohan has a tremendous time as the brutally villainous Red. Sean Connery and Sidney James have supporting roles.

Heller in Pink Tights ○
1960, US, 100 mins, colour
Dir: George Cukor
Stars: Sophia Loren, Anthony Quinn, Eileen Heckart, Ramon Novarro, Margaret O'Brien, Steve Forrest
Rating: ★

Old-time idols Edmund Lowe and Ramon Novarro prop up the cast of this unusual Western based on Louis L'Amour's novel, *Heller with a Gun*. Sympathetically directed by George Cukor, it features a bewigged Sophia Loren as the leading actress of a travelling rep company in the old West. The action includes amusing extracts from the plays (including *La Belle Hélène*) in the company's repertoire. By and large, though, the stars are uneasily cast, and the results are curiously tedious.

Hellfighters ○ ⓥ
1969, US, 120 mins, colour
Dir: Andrew V McLaglen
Stars: John Wayne, Katharine Ross, Jim Hutton
Rating: ★★★

Apart from the subject – red-suited firefighters quell large-scale oil and gas blazes all over the world – this is a typical John Wayne, move-it-along, take-it-or-leave-it movie – full of brawls, battles and blunt staccato dialogue, with a redundant love interest. Fragmentary but entertaining, it's based on the career of 'Red' Adair.

Hellfire Club, The ○
1960, UK, 93 mins, colour
Dir: Monty Berman
Stars: Keith Michell, Adrienne Corri, Peter Cushing
Rating: ★★

A hoary old melodrama in the Gainsborough tradition, played with enthusiasm and humour by most of the cast – commendably so in view of the tired nature of the whole Victorian enterprise. The background is interesting, although the activities of the infamous Hellfire Club seem ra-

ther jaded by today's standards. Especially sprightly performances by Keith Michell (good guy), Peter Arne (bad guy) and Adrienne Corri (bad girl) keep it going.

Hell in Korea
See: A Hill in Korea

Hell Is a City ◐
1959, UK, 100 mins, b/w
Dir: Val Guest
Stars: Stanley Baker, John Crawford, Donald Pleasence, Billie Whitelaw
Rating: ★★★

The tense, hard-hitting story of a city-wide manhunt. Stanley Baker is the hard-bitten cop in this kitchen-sink British thriller which makes no attempt to pull its punches or glamorise its characters. One of the finest performances is given by the city of Manchester. Its real-life buildings and settings – smoky pubs, back alleys, a Sunday-morning meeting of gamblers on a slag-heap – give the film a great deal of grim authenticity.

Hell Is for Heroes! ◐
1962, US, 90 mins, b/w
Dir: Don Siegel
Stars: Steve McQueen, Fess Parker, Bobby Darin, James Coburn, Nick Adams, Harry Guardino
Rating: ★★★

Tough, uncompromising war film from Don Siegel with a magnetic performance from Steve McQueen as the professional soldier who enjoys killing for its own sake.

Hello Again ○ ⓥ
1987, US, 96 mins, colour
Dir: Frank Perry
Stars: Shelley Long, Gabriel Byrne, Corbin Bernsen, Judith Ivey, Sela Ward
Rating: ★★

A not-so-hot first solo comedy vehicle for Shelley Long as a woman who is brought back from the dead by an occult incantation. Most of the comedy before and after death stems from the fact that her character has two left feet and Long is skilful in seeming to get entangled with things without meaning to. In other respects, however, things are less happy; ickily scripted and raucously directed, the film's performances seem unrelaxed. Gabriel Byrne and Corbin Bernsen are both uneasily cast, and the rest of the players are rather below par. One of

Long's better vehicles, though, from a so-far unlucky and unrewarding film career.

Hello, Dolly! ○ ⓥ

1969, US, 140 mins, colour
Dir: Gene Kelly
Stars: Barbra Streisand, Walter Matthau, Michael Crawford, Louis Armstrong
Rating: ★★★

Hollywood's last multi-million dollar musical in the grand tradition boasts lavish production design, splendid choreography by Michael Kidd and, of course, the clarion-voiced Barbra Streisand as matchmaker Dolly Levi. She was really too young for the role, played variously on stage by Mary Martin, Ginger Rogers, Pearl Bailey, Dora Bryan and, improbably, by Danny La Rue. But she was certainly in fine voice, making more of the songs by Jerry Herman than did Herman himself. Michael Crawford acquits himself commendably as a song-and-dance man under Gene Kelly's direction.

Hell on Frisco Bay ○

1955, US, 98 mins, colour
Dir: Frank Tuttle
Stars: Alan Ladd, Edward G Robinson, Joanne Dru, Paul Stewart, William Demarest
Rating: ★★★

Though the cast would place this crime thriller a good 10 years earlier, it was one of Warners' first big Cine-maScope films, based on a splendid novel by William P McGivern called *The Darkest Hour*. Under the direction of Frank Tuttle, who made Alan Ladd's first big hit, *This Gun for Hire*, Ladd and Edward G Robinson showed renewed relish for the genre, and there are excellent supporting portrayals from Paul Stewart as Robinson's battered sidekick, and Fay Wray, the frightened heroine of so many Thirties' horror films. Here, she adds bags of class to the tough proceedings, as Edward G's high-toned mistress. Rod Taylor and Jayne Mansfield have minor roles.

Hellraiser ● ⓥ

1987, UK, 92 mins, colour
Dir: Clive Barker
Stars: Andrew Robinson, Clare Higgins, Ashley Lawrence, Sean Chapman
Rating: ★★★

The advice proffered to TV quiz contestants of yore – 'Open the box!'

– would be well unheeded by the protagonists of this horror film which, as gore/slime/maggots/rending flesh feasts go, is distinctly above average. 'Every drop of blood you spill puts new flesh on my bones,' groans the reviving monster to his besotted female accomplice. Now where have we heard that before? Never mind, this is good stuff of its kind, well edited and directed by its writer Clive Barker about a man who seems to have made several pacts with the Devil before going into one of those Chinese dens seen at the beginning of *Gremlins*. Here he gets a mysterious box which comes apart and, when locked into a certain formation, can call forth skinhead beings from another dimension. These tear apart the man, who takes advantage of a few drops of blood and the handiness of the previously seduced wife of his brother to escape the destruction of the other world. Clare Higgins makes a splendid Lady Macbeth figure as the wife who does her slimy lover's bidding

Hell's Angels ○

1930, US, 127 mins, b/w
Dir: Howard Hughes
Stars: Jean Harlow, Ben Lyon, James Hall
Rating: ★★★

The classic World War One flying spectacular. The romantic element is the weakest in the movie, although Jean Harlow, in her first major film triumph, does her best to enliven it, especially when informing an understandably hypnotised Ben Lyon that she is 'just going to change into something more comfortable'. The scenes of aerial combat have hardly dated at all, remaining absorbing and exciting, especially in a dogfight between RAF and German planes, a sequence which lasts for almost half an hour.

Hellzapoppin' ⊙

1941, US, 84 mins, b/w
Dir: H C Potter
Stars: Ole Olsen, Chick Johnson, Mischa Auer, Martha Raye, Jane Frazee, Robert Paige
Rating: ★★★

Hollywood's craziest comedy this side of the Marx Brothers, only originally less madcap than the long-running stage show on which it was based. It revived the dormant cinema careers of Ole Olsen and Chic Johnson, who went on to make two other very funny and almost equally wacky

comedy films, *Crazy House* and *Ghost Catchers*. The projectionist (Shemp Howard of Three Stooges fame) tries to run the film while arguing with his girlfriend and the stars have to step out of it and remonstrate with him. A woman with a potted plant wanders through the movie looking for Mr Jones, a love song is interrupted for a card asking Stinky Miller to go home, a mad private eye (Hugh Herbert) keeps addressing the audience. These are only some of the saner moments in a unique Hollywood experience, directed in freewheeling fashion by H C Potter.

Help! ⊙ ⓥ

1965, UK, 92 mins, colour
Dir: Richard Lester
Stars: John Lennon, Paul McCartney, Ringo Starr, George Harrison, Leo McKern, Eleanor Bron
Rating: ★★★★

The second Beatles feature turned out to be a latter-day Goon Show with music. Although wholly sublimated to director Richard Lester's zany, fly-away comedy technique, the boys work with a will and great sense of fun at carrying out the gags the script had devised for them. After getting the story – a little thing about a sacrificial ring that ends up on one of Ringo's fingers – out of the way, the laughs come thick and fast. Lester's cutting and editing are models of timing, making things move along at a cracking pace, right up to the final glorious melée on the seashore with the ring passing frantically from one finger to another. And a sequence which starts with Eleanor Bron (an eastern princess on the Beatles' side) whistling a snatch of Beethoven's ninth to save Ringo from a music-loving tiger, and ends with practically the whole country singing the symphony, is a classic example of the sustained comedy gag – worthy of Laurel and Hardy at something near their best. A shame that the Beatles' career in this sort of film ended right here.

Henry V ○

1944, UK, 137 mins, colour
Dir: Laurence Olivier
Stars: Laurence Olivier, Robert Newton, Renée Asherson, Esmond Knight, Leo Genn, Felix Aylmer
Rating: ★★★★

Rousing and patriotic at a time when the English spirit needed lifting, Laurence Olivier's first stab at putting the bard on film was an artistic and commercial success. It also proved to be a stirring panoply of comedy, patriotic speeches and some enthrallingly original battle scenes. And it had the cream of the British stage in large and small roles. And not just the legitimate stage – music hall comic George Robey had a cameo role. Olivier starred, directed and had a hand in the screen adaptation, tasks Kenneth Branagh took on when he remade the film in 1989. Marvellous stuff and a tough act to follow. If you've seen the Branagh version, watch this to see if he succeeded.

Henry V ○ ⓥ
1989, UK, 137 mins, colour
Dir: Kenneth Branagh
Stars: Kenneth Branagh, Derek Jacobi, Simon Shepherd, Robbie Coltrane, Judi Dench, Emma Thompson
Rating: ★★★

A pity this version of Shakespeare's play doesn't grab us from the word go, like Laurence Olivier's in 1944. The comparison between the two is won and lost in those first few scenes. And the night before Agincourt seems to last an eternity, before the film picks up with the battle itself. This is staged with pace and imagination as well as mud and blood by director-star-adapter Kenneth Branagh, as is the pleasing endpiece dealing briefly but amusingly with the courtship of the French princess (Emma Thompson with a convincing accent) by the English king, with the assistance of Geraldine McEwan as a chaperon direct from the French quarter of Tilling. But the pace of earlier scenes seems slow and the low-life characters merely dull and objectionable, rather than colourful and full of life. A purist's *Henry*, perhaps, it serves to remind us how stunning, sweeping and daring was Olivier's film, making this a commoner in faint pursuit of a king.

Henry VIII and His Six Wives ○
1972, UK, 125 mins, colour
Dir: Waris Hussein
Stars: Keith Michell, Charlotte Rampling, Jane Asher, Lynne Frederick, Donald Pleasance
Rating: ★★★

There's pomp but no pomposity in this spin-off from the TV series *The Six Wives of Henry VIII*. As the change of title implies, this condensed version concentrates more on Keith Michell's splendid portrayal of Henry. From the array of wives, Charlotte Rampling's Anne Boleyn and Lynne Frederick as Catherine Howard shine the brightest.

Her Alibi ○ ⓥ
1989, US, 94 mins, colour
Dir: Bruce Beresford
Stars: Tom Selleck, Paulina Porizkova, William Daniels, James Farentino
Rating: ★★

Lightweight comedy fluff with Selleck in a Burt Reynolds–type role as a thriller writer whose claim to have modelled his suave fictitious sleuth upon himself is as empty as his typewriter since his wife left him four years before. Then Porizkova, a mysterious Romanian with a willowy figure and melting eyes, walks into a courtroom accused of murder and Selleck sniffs a story. Giving her an alibi, he takes her to his country house, lusts after her from afar, and writes a new novel based on the developing case, worrying all the time that's she's going to stick a knife in him. 'You fell in love with a murderess,' accused his family. 'It's tough to meet girls these days,' he grumbles apologetically. The dialogue has a few happy moments like this, but not enough to promote it far enough above an average TV segment in similar vein. Selleck tries hard with the grouchy charm, Porizkova is lovely (though raw as an actress) and William Daniels deservedly gets the best lines as Selleck's nagging agent.

He Ran All the Way ○
1951, US, 77 mins, b/w
Dir: John Berry
Stars: John Garfield, Shelley Winters, Wallace Ford
Rating: ★★★

John Garfield gives a haunting study of the hunted killer in this crime drama, charged with a burning intensity by director John Berry and his players. Garfield's portrayal of the cold and callous Nick was the last portrait in his cinematic gallery of men on the run: a year later he died, at 39. His work in this film went largely unappreciated, partly due to his own declining popularity, partly due to the film's short running-time, which got it released as a second feature outside the United States.

Herbie Goes Bananas ⊙
1980, US, 100 mins, colour
Dir: Vincent McEveety

Stars: Cloris Leachman, Charles Martin Smith, John Vernon
Rating: ★

A mild, harmless lark about the car with a mind of its own, which will look (a bit) better on TV than it did in cinemas. The local scenery is lovely, and, though the human cast is charmless, Herbie the Volkswagen makes up for them. The film's funniest line (from Harvey Korman) must almost have robbed it of its 'U' certificate! But it was worth keeping, as it's about the only laugh there is for mums and dads.

Herbie Goes to Monte Carlo ⊙
1977, US, 105 mins, colour
Dir: Vincent McEveety
Stars: Dean Jones, Don Knotts, Julie Sommars
Rating: ★★

The third 'Love Bug' adventure finds Dean Jones back in the driving seat as Herbie becomes involved with the Monte Carlo Rally and a stolen diamond. Jones is as good as ever, but director Vincent McEveety's poor pacing shows up his performance less well than before. Roy Kinnear is one of the comic villains, while Herbie himself falls for a lady Lancia.

Herbie Rides Again ⊙
1974, US, 88 mins, colour
Dir: Robert Stevenson
Stars: Helen Hayes, Ken Berry, Stefanie Powers, Keenan Wynn
Rating: ★★

Almost equally successful sequel to the Disney studio's *The Love Bug*, with Herbie the Volkswagen (and a few of his friends) taking on a ruthless property developer, played for all the part's worth by Keenan Wynn. Helen Hayes and Stefanie Powers personably lead the rest of the humans, but it's Herbie's show.

Here Comes Mr Jordan ○
1941, US, 93 mins, b/w
Dir: Alexander Hall
Stars: Robert Montgomery, Claude Rains, Evelyn Keyes, Edward Everett Horton
Rating: ★★★★

Delightfully droll fantasy about a man sent to hevan before his time that was an unexpected critical and commercial success in its day and won two Academy Awards for its story and screenplay. Director Alexander Hall never made anything so good again, but this was remade to surprisingly delightful effect in 1978 as *Heaven Can Wait*. Edward Everett Horton steals the show in this version as the dithering heavenly messenger 7013.

Here Comes the Groom ⊙
1951, US, 113 mins, b/w
Dir: Frank Capra
Stars: Bing Crosby, Jane Wyman, Alexis Smith, Franchot Tone
Rating: ★★★

Here's a chance to re-evaluate one of Frank Capra's later films, starring Bing Crosby. It mixes sentiment, comedy and songs, the hit number in this one being 'In the Cool, Cool, Cool of the Evening' by Hoagy Carmichael and Johnny Mercer, which won an Academy Award. Also popular was 'Misto Cristofo Columbo' which Bing sings on a plane, accompanied by numerous guest 'passengers', including Louis Armstrong, Cass Daley, Phil Harris and Dorothy Lamour. Crosby was reported to have been highly elated when asked to make the first film with Capra, *Riding High*. The two men, both fanatical golfers, were personal friends and welcomed the chance to work together, even if Bing was not quite the same type as Gary Cooper and James Stewart, who had starred so successfully for Capra in previous pictures. In a wedding scene in church, you may spot a number of silent comedy veterans (including Jimmy Finlayson and Chester Conklin) who had been especially gathered together by Capra for the occasion.

Here Come the Girls ⊙
1953, US, 78 mins, colour
Dir: Claude Binyon
Stars: Bob Hope, Tony Martin, Arlene Dahl, Rosemary Clooney
Rating: ★★★

A bright, amusing, likeable Bob Hope comedy-musical from the very end of the best period (1939–1953) of his Paramount romps. With three co-stars (Tony Martin, Rosemary Clooney and Arlene Dahl), a short running time and several songs to get through, it's not surprising that Hope is given too little scope for his own brand of 'cowardly comedy' in this story of the 'world's oldest chorus boy' on the run from a killer called Jack the Slasher. Playing Jack, and heading a cast of stalwart character players, is scowling Robert Strauss, the actor who won fame in his underwear as Animal in *Stalag 17*. Hope shares a really zippy duet with the delightful

Clooney called 'You Got Class'. Stay tuned for the closing Hope crack in an ending which leaves him up in the air!

Her Jungle Love ○
1938, US, 81 mins, colour
Dir: George Archainbaud
Stars: Dorothy Lamour, Ray Milland, Lynne Overman, J Carroll Naish
Rating: ★★

Dorothy Lamour was already well launched into her career as the star bursting into sarong when she made this tropical adventure about a jungle girl believed by the natives to be a goddess. Directed by George Archainbaud, who had been in Hollywood since the early silent days, and rather sadly ended his career making Gene Autry Westerns. Here, he is in splendid control of such attractions as a typhoon, a tidal wave and an earthquake. The two stars had previously made a big hit together in another South Sea bauble, *The Jungle Princess*.

Hero
See: Accidental Hero

Hero at Large ○ ⓥ
1980, US, 98 mins, colour
Dir: Martin Davidson
Stars: John Ritter, Anne Archer, Kevin McCarthy
Rating: ★★

Out-of-work actor Steve Nichols (John Ritter) earns rent money by making public appearances as comic book hero Captain Avenger. On the way home from an appearance (and still in costume) he foils a corner store hold-up, making everyone think there really is a Captain Avenger. Lightweight fun, with the underrated Ritter skimming merrily over the clichés. Anne (*Fatal Attraction*) Archer, in an early role, plays his girlfriend. Kevin McCarthy enjoys himself as one of the bad guys and a young Kevin Bacon can be glimpsed briefly in the supporting cast. It's engaging enough, but too simple-minded for complete success.

Heroes of Telemark, The ◐ ⓥ
1965, UK, 131 mins, colour
Dir: Anthony Mann
Stars: Kirk Douglas, Richard Harris, Ulla Jacobsson, Michael Redgrave, Anton Diffring, Eric Porter
Rating: ★★

A Second World War blockbuster that could be best described as *Operation Crossbow* on skis. It's in the action, sharp and telling when it comes, that the film's strength lies. The 'heroes' are lucky in fact that their dialogue is kept to a minimum, for most of it is sub-standard. The photography on the other hand is never less than excellent, from snowy nocturnal landscapes, beautifully captured, to red lamplight reflected on Germans' helmets. Unfortunately, its crystal clarity tends to heighten the effect of comic-strip war which the film often seems to do its best to give – an effect which is happily shattered in the last 15 minutes with a climactic sequence aboard a sabotaged ship, in which the suspense is really killing; Douglas organises a desperate 'game' to see which child can put a life jacket on first, as the floating death-trap beneath them nears explosion point. Richard Harris gives the best acting performance, and Jennifer Hilary's touching portrayal makes one of the minor roles spring vividly to life.

He Said, She Said ◐ ⓥ
1991, US, 104 mins, colour
Dir: Ken Kwapis, Marisa Silver
Stars: Kevin Bacon, Elizabeth Perkins, Anthony LaPaglia, Sharon Stone, Nathan Lane
Rating: ★★★

A sweet-natured romantic comedy in the old style, with nice old-fashioned music by Miles Goodman, but just not quite enough bite to take it into the super-hit class. Elizabeth Perkins and Kevin Bacon are rival columnists for a newspaper. Their competition for a leader column results in them being paired up in opposition. Newsprint leads to television, and in no time at all, they're debating topical subjects with each other on local TV. Of course, they also fall in love, but he's reluctant to commit, and that's where the two directors, Ken Kwapis and Marisa Silver, come in, each showing the course of the romance from their own sex's point of view. Most of it works, although some of it is merely repetitive. Perkins is adorable; Bacon, although miscast, gets by.

He Walked By Night ○
1948, US, 79 mins, b/w
Dir: Anthony Mann
Stars: Richard Basehart, Scott Brady, Jack Webb, Aldred Werker
Rating: ★★★

H

Although this atmospheric noir thriller is credited to Alfred Werker, a lot of it was directed, uncredited, by Anthony Mann, who had already made some striking thrillers, including *T-Men* and *Raw Deal* for the same studio, Eagle-Lion. Richard Basehart made a big impact as the killer whose only friend is a dog.

He Who Rides a Tiger ○
1965, UK, 103 mins, b/w
Dir: Charles Crichton
Stars: Tom Bell, Judi Dench, Paul Rogers, Kay Walsh
Rating: ★★★

Superlative acting by Tom Bell and Judi Dench, and skilful treatment by director Charles Crichton made this film an unexpected winner. Bell plays an habitual criminal whose story springs to vivid life under Crichton's taut direction, aided by photography from John von Kotze that's a treat to watch, and astute editing by Jack Harris and John Smith that never lets our eyes drop from the screen. Sideline highlights include some charming reactions from orphanage children, with whom Bell really does seem at home, and a realistically-staged fight between Bell and Edina Ronay that rivals the no-claws-barred scrap from *The Pumpkin Eater*. The film's only weakness is an improbable twist near the end when the police get on to Bell's biggest robbery. Otherwise it's excellent, compact entertainment.

Hey! Hey! USA ⊙
1938, UK, 92 mins, b/w
Dir: Marcel Varnel
Stars: Will Hay, Edgar Kennedy
Rating: ★★★

The incomparable Will Hay reprises his splendidly shifty Dr Benjamin Twist character (the incompetent headmaster of St Michael's) in this breezy British comedy set in a quaintly observed America full of gun-toting gangsters. Comic stalwart Edgar Kennedy provides slow-burning support under the direction of Marcel Varnel, the dapper Frenchman who made most of Hay's biggest successes. Sharp eyes will spot Roddy McDowall in one of several appearances he made in British films as a boy before shipping off to Hollywood to win fame and fortune with 20th Century-Fox.

Hickey & Boggs ◐
1972, US, 111 mins, colour
Dir: Robert Culp

Stars: Bill Cosby, Robert Culp
Rating: ★★★

Fans of Bill Cosby and Robert Culp from the hit comedy-thriller TV series *I Spy* were probably quite surprised to discover their favourites teamed in this Seventies *film noir* in which two shabby private eyes are hired to find a missing girl and find themselves caught up in bloody mayhem. Tautly directed by Culp himself, the hard-hitting results marked one of the first appearances on the movie scene of Walter Hill, here as a writer, but later to become a director of such similar blue-collar thrillers as *48 Hrs*, *Extreme Prejudice*, *Red Heat*, *Another 48 Hrs* and *Trespass*. In the supporting cast there were some actors whose names, like Hill's, would soon become better known, among them Ed Lauter, Vincent Gardenia, Michael Moriarty and James Woods.

Hidden Agenda ● ⓥ
1990, UK, 108 mins, colour
Dir: Ken Loach
Stars: Frances McDormand, Brian Cox, Brad Dourif, Mai Zetterling
Rating: ★★★

Ken Loach's political thriller hunted a British distributor for some time, and no wonder. For this Cannes Festival prizewinner is a very hot potato indeed. There's a distinctly anti-British and pro-IRA flavour to its powderkeg plot, which concerns the killing of an American lawyer (Brad Dourif) who formed part of an international team investigating infringements of civil liberties in Northern Ireland. A senior British detective (Brian Cox), sent to investigate the death, uncovers a past CIA plot to dump Edward Heath as prime minister, discredit Harold Wilson and wreck Labour's chances of winning the following election. But publishing his findings, despite the help of the IRA and the dead man's fiancée (Frances McDormand), is another matter. Loach describes the film as 'an important story that wasn't being told'. After the subsequent spate of miscarriages of justice, who is to say where fiction ends and the truth begins?

Hidden Eye, The ○
1945, US, 70 mins, b/w
Dir: Richard Whorf
Stars: Edward Arnold, Frances Rafferty
Rating: ★★

Portly Edward Arnold made his second appearance as the blind detective

Duncan Maclain (created by novelist Baynard Kendrick) in this good MGM second-feature with a twisty plot and a list of suspects that includes such shifty Hollywood character actors as Ray Collins, Byron Foulger, Morris Ankrum and Jack Lambert. Friday the dog, Arnold's 'seeing eye', is a real scene-stealer.

Hidden Room, The
See: Obsession [1948]

Hideaways, The ○
(aka: From the Mixed-Up Files of Mrs Basil E Frankweiler)
1973, US, 105 mins, colour
Dir: Fielder Cook
Stars: Ingrid Bergman, Sally Prager, Richard Mulligan, George Rose
Rating: ★★

A low-key fable about two bored American kids and their encounters with an eccentric recluse – a bizarre role for Ingrid Bergman in one of her last films, playing a woman about 15 years older herself. Highly suitable for children, although the younger ones will find it has too little action and too many stretches of tedium.

High and Dry
See: The Maggie

High Anxiety ○ ⓥ
1977, US, 94 mins, colour
Dir: Mel Brooks
Stars: Mel Brooks, Madeline Kahn, Cloris Leachman, Harvey Korman
Rating: ★★

This comic homage to Alfred Hitchcock is, like all of Mel Brooks' films, simply bubbling with ideas. More's the pity, then, that Brooks takes it all above and beyond its subtler comic possibilities. Under Brooks' own direction, he and the rest of his cast go high over the top together.

High Barbaree ○
1947, US, 91 mins, b/w
Dir: Jack Conway
Stars: Van Johnson, June Allyson, Thomas Mitchell
Rating: ★★★

Van Johnson and June Allyson were a hugely popular MGM romantic team who appeared in almost as many films together as Greer Garson and Walter Pidgeon. Johnson had been among the three most popular stars in the world for 1945 and 1946, but *High Barbaree* signalled the beginning of his decline. The story sounds promising – an airman, shot down in World War Two, makes, with a wounded companion, for an island he remembers from boyhood stories – but becomes ponderous in the telling. There isn't much anyone can have done with this script, but Johnson isn't the world's most interesting actor. Small wonder fellow-flier Cameron Mitchell seems to be dying – Johnson is boring him (and us) to death with a rambling account of his life.

High Commissioner, The
See: Nobody Runs Forever

High Heels ● ⓥ
1991, Spain, 114 mins, colour
Dir: Pedro Almodovar
Stars: Victoria Abril, Marisa Paredes, Miguel Bosé
Rating: ★★

Is it a black comedy? Is it an offbeat romance? Is it a murder thriller? Or an intimate drama about the relationship between a mother and a daughter down the years? This film from the fashionable Spanish director Pedro Almodovar is certainly his least boring so far – and will definitely keep you guessing to the end, even if it does go on a bit. And you can't wholly dislike a film where the female jailblock inmates go into a dance number while confessed murderess Victoria Abril awaits her fate. She's been reunited with her singing-star mother after many years of neglect on both sides, ditched by her loutish husband and seduced by a transvestite entertainer. But is she guilty? That will keep you guessing at least until a couple of reels before the end and even then Almodovar isn't finished with the twists – or is he? In between titillating and tantalising, the director occasionally loses his grip – so take care not to nod off in the middle.

Highlander ◐ ⓥ
1986, UK, 111 mins, colour
Dir: Russell Mulcahy
Stars: Christopher Lambert, Sean Connery, Roxanne Hart, Clancy Brown, Beatie Edney
Rating: ★★

Thanks to an indecisive and cliché-ridden script, this ambitious fantasy thriller emerges as a very curious film indeed. 'I've been alive for four and half centuries,' groans MacLeod (Christopher Lambert), one of the 'immortals' seeking 'the prize'. 'Well,' shrugs the heroine (Roxanne Hart), unfazed. 'Everyone's got their

problems.' True, true, but this film has a multitude of them. There are some well-staged duels from a director with a strong pictorial sense, and some noisy songs by Queen, before we get to the final clash between MacLeod and his deadly enemy The Kurgan (Clancy Brown), although what a Kurgan is (apart from a humanised dose of evil energy) is never properly explained. The rest of the movie, though, isn't exactly exciting, if often attractive to look at. The script is credited to three writers, and sounds as though one (or two) was playing for laughs, while the others were taking it all seriously. Thus Lambert, Hart, Brown and Sean Connery (as MacLeod's 18th century tutor) all have their moments, even if sometimes their roles seem more suited to members of the 'Carry On' team. Special effects, like the film, look jolly expensive and are often impressively done.

Highly Dangerous ○
1950, UK, 85 mins, b/w
Dir: Roy Baker
Stars: Margaret Lockwood, Dane Clark, Marius Goring, Naunton Wayne
Rating: ★★

A beautiful woman, a tough newspaperman, a sinister police chief and a box of deadly bugs all add up to a fast-moving thriller. Equality for women is one thing, but it really doesn't stretch to someone like Margaret Lockwood being sent by our Government to a Middle East country to probe the use of germs in warfare. One doesn't fancy her chances overmuch, even with the help of Dane Clark, a newspaper reporter, whose interest in Margaret is probably something more than insects. Still less would we bet on her success when we meet the menacing State Police Chief, played with a glint by Marius Goring. But Margaret, as well as being an entomologist, is an addict of the Dick Barton, Special Agent radio programmes. When Goring unchivalrously has her drugged she imagines that she's Barton, and dreams up a scheme so wildly impossible that it has to be seen to be believed. And, oddly enough, it comes off, which brightly rounds out this unabashed hokum.

High Noon ○ ⓥ
1952, US, 85 mins, b/w
Dir: Fred Zinnemann

Stars: Gary Cooper, Grace Kelly, Thomas Mitchell, Lloyd Bridges, Katy Jurado, Otto Kruger
Rating: ★★★★

Fred Zinnemann's now-classic Western, with its can't-miss ingredients of love, loyalty, duty and guns in the afternoon. Gary Cooper, at his grimmest and best, swept aside all opposition for the Best Actor Oscar, and the film won three other Academy Awards, including one for the famous title song, written by Ned Washington and Dmitri Tiomkin, and sung by Tex Ritter, which both sweeps along and intensifies the drama. Thomas Mitchell, Grace Kelly and Katy Jurado also make notable contributions, while one of the villains is the later-famous Lee Van Cleef, who has the film's striking opening image all to himself.

High Plains Drifter ○ ⓥ
1972, US, 105 mins, colour
Dir: Clint Eastwood
Stars: Clint Eastwood, Verna Bloom, Billy Curtis
Rating: ★★

Clint Eastwood's second outing as a director-star is a leisurely Western revenge story which pays homage to Sergio Leone – the director who contributed most to Eastwood's early career as an actor. As in the Leone 'Dollar' trilogy, Eastwood is an unidentified stranger who rides menacingly into a frontier town and exerts a God-like power over it, having been hired by its citizens to protect them against vengeful outlaws. Orchestrating plots and counter-plots, the stranger deals ruthlessly with the town's corrupt hierarchy and provides the story with an eerie, surrealistic climax. Alongside Eastwood's characteristically laconic performance, midget actor Billy Curtis is a great foil as Mordecai Fortune. Moody, self-conscious and off-beat, High Plains Drifter is more than anything an exercise in style that sees Eastwood's direction in imitative form before emerging in its own distinctive fashion with the masterfully made The Outlaw Josey Wales. Nevertheless it makes for compelling viewing.

High Sierra ○ ⓥ
1941, US, 96 mins, b/w
Dir: Raoul Walsh
Stars: Humphrey Bogart, Ida Lupino, Arthur Kennedy, Joan Leslie
Rating: ★★★★

H

Hold-up man Roy Earle is out of prison and in need of money, so goes back to what he does best and pulls a robbery job. But he is identified and has to go on the run. Earle is personified by Humphrey Bogart at his bad-guy best (seizing his first major role for six years after it had been rejected by several other Warner stars) before *Casablanca* made him a romantic hero, although even here he has a soft centre. The film's action is slowed somewhat by the scenes in which he befriends a hillbilly couple and their handicapped granddaughter (the soft centre bits), but the climax in the Sierra mountains of the title is the stuff that film legends are made of. Ida Lupino is the girl who falls for him and Henry Travers is delightfully folksy as the hillbilly grandpa.

High Society ○ ⓥ
1956, US, 107 mins, colour
Dir: Charles Walters
Stars: Bing Crosby, Frank Sinatra, Grace Kelly, Celeste Holm, John Lund, Louis Armstrong
Rating: ★★★

This musical remake of the Oscar-winning *The Philadelphia Story* united Bing Crosby and Frank Sinatra, the two top singers of their era. And what a memorable occasion it was. An abrasive script by John Patrick was complemented by a score that included 'True Love', 'Who Wants to Be a Millionaire?', 'Now You Has Jazz' and a show-stopping Crosby-Sinatra duet called 'Did You Evah?'

High Spirits ◑
1988, UK, 97 mins, colour
Dir: Neil Jordan
Stars: Peter O'Toole, Daryl Hannah, Steve Guttenberg, Beverly D'Angelo, Liam Neeson, Ray McAnally
Rating: ★★

An amiable Irish ghost comedy with a few giggles and a personable cast. It's a little low on incident, perhaps, but the sheer glee of the enterprise makes up for some of its shortcomings, which include an over-reliance on repetitious tracking shots by director Neil Jordan. At Castle Plunkett hotel, the rooms are guestless, the debts are endless and the good Lord Plunkett (Peter O'Toole) is legless, and at the end of his tether, when he gets the idea of a few ghosts to drum up trade. A coachload of Americans arrives, but the ghost night is a disaster, and doom beckons Lord Peter again before the

real castle ghosts, led by Ray McAnally, decide to bale him out. Generally, the idea, like most ghost comedies, sounds funnier than it is. But you'll find it lively enough (and brief enough) to get by with a smile. The special effects have an appealing low-tech cottage industry charm about them, but the script is little more than hot air.

High Tide at Noon ○
1957, UK, 111 mins, b/w
Dir: Philip Leacock
Stars: Betta St John, William Sylvester, Michael Craig, Patrick McGoohan
Rating: ★★

Packed with incident and magnificent scenery, this love story with a difference, set among fisherfolk, took director Philip Leacock back to Nova Scotia, scene of his earlier triumph, *The Kidnappers*. Its top-notch cast includes many of Britain's best young hopefuls of the time, including Michael Craig, Jill Dixon, Patrick McGoohan and Susan Beaumont. Appealing performances by Betta St John and William Sylvester in the leading roles are more than a match for a variable script. Bernard Bresslaw and Paul Massie may also be spotted by the sharp-eyed during the unravelling of Neil Paterson's screenplay, adapted from a very readable novel by Elizabeth Ogilvie. Leacock himself went on to make more black-and-white gems (*Innocent Sinners*, *Hand in Hand*, *The Rabbit Trap*, *Take a Giant Step*). This one is so fresh that you can almost catch a whiff of the sea air even if that, like the characters, remains at a tantalising distance.

High Time ○
1960, US, 103 mins, colour
Dir: Blake Edwards
Stars: Bing Crosby, Nicole Maurey, Tuesday Weld, Fabian, Richard Beymer
Rating: ★★

Here's a question to baffle the buffs. What has Bing Crosby got in common with Rodney Dangerfield? Answer: they both starred in versions of the same plot about a middle-aged millionaire deciding to embark on a belated college education. This is Crosby's film (Dangerfield's, 26 years later, was called *Back to School*) and the Old Crooner throws himself into the farce with a will, singing a couple of songs, perfectly timing his laughs, and even appearing in drag. The cast is the predictable Sixties Hollywood assortment: a pop star (Fabian), a teen

idol (Richard Beymer, soon to star in *West Side Story*), a French charmer (Nicole Maurey) and a blonde starlet (Tuesday Weld). Yvonne Craig is cute as one of the co-eds; a few years later she would play Batgirl in the *Batman* TV series.

High Vermilion
See: Silver City

Highway to Hell ●
1991, US, 94 mins, colour
Dir: Ate De Jong
Stars: Chad Lowe, Kristy Swanson, Patrick Bergin, Richard Farnsworth
Rating: ★★

There's lots of action going on in this horror fantasy, but not much of it strikes the same kind of note. Chad Lowe and girlfriend Kristy Swanson, eloping to Las Vegas, decide to take a back road. 'When you see two Joshua trees,' warns 'Last Chance' garageman Richard Farnsworth, 'and you're feeling sleepy, don't pull over 'til you pass the second.' Hah! So much for that part of the plot. In less time than it takes to yawn, Lowe (who looks nothing like brother Rob) duly pulls over, and Swanson is bagged by Hellcop (using two severed hands for handcuffs) who carts her off to Hell. Given advice by Farnsworth, Lowe follows on, and finds himself on a sort of yellow brick road, where references to Oz mix uneasily with a group of bikers, repulsive monsters, cardboard sets, people who explode into nothingness when shot, glimpses of the real Hell and an enigmatic figure called Beezle (Patrick Bergin). Bergin lends the film such much-needed charisma. Lowe displays enthusiasm but not much else. Swanson looks great but doesn't act much. It isn't dull but, frequently miscalculating the right tone, doesn't pull you along with the story either.

High Wind in Jamaica, A ○
1965, UK, 104 mins, colour
Dir: Alexander Mackendrick
Stars: Anthony Quinn, James Coburn, Dennis Price, Gert Frobe, Lila Kedrova, Nigel Davenport
Rating: ★★★★

Lusty, gutsy yarn of a disreputable group of pirates who become the very unwilling custodians of several spirited children. The flap of sail, the creak of boards and Douglas Slocombe's magnificent colour camerawork make the voyage so believable that you can almost taste the salt: and Deborah Baxter's portrayal is the finest piece of child acting since Hayley Mills in *Tiger Bay*. It's a film one doesn't want to end. Alexander Mackendrick had the knack of getting fine work from children, as he showed in *The Maggie* and *Sammy Going South*. Together, he and his technicians made an almost classic sea story.

High Window, The ○
(aka: The Brasher Doubloon)
1947, US, 72 mins, b/w
Dir: John Brahm
Stars: George Montgomery, Nancy Guild, Conrad Janis, Fritz Kortner
Rating: ★★

A dip into the world of Raymond Chandler's famous detective Philip Marlowe, full of shifty faces, weak-chinned rich boys and two-timing lovelies. A few liberties have been taken with the original, most notably with the key event, and both George Montgomery and Marlowe look unhappy with that moustache. Still, the story's grip remains considerable, and young Nancy Guild is a heroine in the best Bacall mould.

Hilda Crane ○
1956, US, 87 mins, colour
Dir: Philip Dunne
Stars: Jean Simmons, Guy Madison, Jean-Pierre Aumont
Rating: ★★

Tears and more tears, as Jean Simmons stumbles from one broken marriage to another in her search for happiness. Turgid emotional melodrama with minimal support for a star who deserves better. Still, at least it isn't long.

Hill, The ◑
1965, UK, 122 mins, colour
Dir: Sidney Lumet
Stars: Sean Connery, Harry Andrews, Ian Bannen, Ian Hendry, Michael Redgrave
Rating: ★★★

A hard, tough story of life in a military stockade that makes gripping viewing. Although its dialogue is often difficult to grasp, this powerful film leaves one with an indelible impression of primitive violence, for men's emotions have rarely been ripped as raw on screen. Sean Connery broke right away from the Bond image as the bullet-headed ex-sergeant-major who leads the ultimate revolt against authority. Ian Hendry's sneering sergeant is also a splendid piece of

character work. Sidney Lumet's determined direction ensures that no punches are pulled.

Hill in Korea, A ○
(aka: Hell in Korea)
1956, UK, 81 mins, b/w
Dir: Julian Amyes
Stars: George Baker, Harry Andrews, Stanley Baker, Michael Medwin, Stephen Boyd
Rating: ★★

Goodish British war film about the Korean conflict. George Baker gives a very carefully-observed portrait of the national-service officer, and there's some excellent black-and-white photography. In retrospect, however, the chief interest lies in the sweat-and-blood supporting roles – Stanley Baker as Cpl Ryker, Stephen Boyd as Pte Sims, Robert Shaw as L Cpl Hedge and – in his first film – Michael Caine as Pte Lockyer.

Hill's Angels ☉
(aka: The North Avenue Irregulars)
1978, US, 99 mins, colour
Dir: Bruce Bilson
Stars: Edward Herrmann, Barbara Harris, Cloris Leachman
Rating: ★★

A pleasant enough Disney comedy that starts well but soon reverts to formula, and even includes the standard obligatory car pile-up finale. The quality cast seems rather wasted in this clichéd story of a new priest in town who tries to unite the local women to form a crack crime-fighting unit. The screenplay is derived from a true story – Reverend Albert Fay Hill's novel, *The North Avenue Irregulars*.

Hills of Home, The ☉
(aka: Master of Lassie)
1948, US, 97 mins, colour
Dir: Fred M Wilcox
Stars: Edmund Gwenn, Donald Crisp, Janet Leigh, Tom Drake
Rating: ★★★

Edmund Gwenn as the Scottish doctor manages to outshine even Lassie, his co-star, here in one of her best scripts, which saddles her with a psychological fear of water. How this is eventually overcome will leave few dry eyes in the house. Gwenn and Donald Crisp exude cosy crustiness, while Janet Leigh, in her early contract days with MGM, is as pretty a heroine as you could wish for. Wonderful Techni-

color photography of the rolling Scottish (actually Californian) countryside by Charles Schoenbaum.

Hindenburg, The ○
1975, US, 130 mins, colour
Dir: Robert Wise
Stars: George C Scott, Anne Bancroft, William Atherton, Roy Thinnes, Gig Young, Burgess Meredith
Rating: ★

The fascinating idea that the 1937 *Hindenburg* disaster might have been an act of sabotage is rather overwhelmed by an all-star cast and a *Grand Hotel*-style plot structure. Burgess Meredith and Rene Auberjonois are good enough as a couple of cardsharps to merit more screen time than they get.

Hired Hand, The ◑
1971, US, 93 mins, colour
Dir: Peter Fonda
Stars: Peter Fonda, Warren Oates, Verna Bloom
Rating: ★★★

Although slow to start, this thinking man's Western about a cowboy's eternal longings for the wide open prairie has a splendid script by British writer Alan Sharp that comes into its own once the film gets under way. The acting, especially from Verna Bloom who blazes sincerity as the very real, much-put-upon wife, is first class. Peter Fonda's own performance, in fact, is rather better than his direction, which is perhaps the weakest element in this unusual and often rewarding film.

Hireling, The ◑
1973, US, 103 mins, colour
Dir: Alan Bridges
Stars: Robert Shaw, Sarah Miles
Rating: ★★

Another screen adaptation from the work of L P Hartley, who wrote *The Go-Between*. Although the glowing muted colour photography (Michael Reed) and sumptuous production design (Natasha Kroll) are the equal of the earlier film, they tend to overdominate things here, with the consequence that *The Hireling* is a less cleanly striking film than its predecessor. Sarah Miles gives another of her careful studies of repressed sexuality, but co-star Robert Shaw is never quite at ease as the chauffeur who sets his peaked cap at her, flouting all of the social conventions.

H

His Butler's Sister ⊙

1943, US, 88 mins, b/w
Dir: Frank Borzage
Stars: Deanna Durbin, Franchot Tone, Pat O'Brien
Rating: ★★★

Breezy is the word for this much-requested Deanna Durbin musical which seems to be the favourite of many of her fans. The sparkling songthrush sings a bar or two of Puccini, plus the popular songs 'While You're Away' and 'Spirit of the Moment' and a medley of 'Russian' ditties. This has probably the best supporting cast of any Durbin musical, including an on-form Pat O'Brien and Franchot Tone, plus such delightful 'below stairs' types as Sig Arno, Akim Tamiroff, Hans Conried, Frank Jenks, Franklin Pangborn and Alan Mowbray.

His Excellency ○

1951, UK, 80 mins, b/w
Dir: Robert Hamer
Stars: Eric Portman, Cecil Parker, Susan Stephen, Helen Cherry
Rating: ★★

This disappointing and rather condescending spotlights the dilemmas which must face many good trade unionists who suddenly find themselves controlling the destinies of their fellow-workers. Eric Portman plays the central character – an ex-docker who finds himself governor of a strife-torn West Indian island. Popular, though: another sucdess for Ealing Studios at the box-office.

His Girl Friday ○

1940, US, 89 mins, b/w
Dir: Howard Hawks
Stars: Cary Grant, Rosalind Russell, Ralph Bellamy, Gene Lockhart, John Qualen
Rating: ★★★★

Howard Hawks' rip-roaring remake of the classic newspaper comedy *The Front Page*, with the pivotal role assigned to a woman (Rosalind Russell) instead of a man. Charles Lederer's brilliantly tart script gives her and Cary Grant (as her managing editor and ex-husband) some memorable exchanges as Hawks overlaps scenes and dialogue to carry the black farce along at helter-skelter speed. Certainly the kind of film they can't make anymore, as Billy Wilder found when he tried to film the original with a

great cast but only moderate success in 1974. Meanwhile, don't miss this classic version.

His Majesty O'Keefe ○

1953, UK, 92 mins, colour
Dir: Byron Haskin
Stars: Burt Lancaster, Joan Rice, Andre Morell, Abraham Sofaer
Rating: ★★

The scenic qualities of the film are rather better than the disjointed plot in this high adventure made during star Burt Lancasters 'athletic action' period. Stunningly set against Hong Kong and Fijian backgrounds, the story concerns Cap'n Lancaster's attempts to make a fortune out of pearls, copra or anything else he can lay his hands on, when he's not fighting bands of pirates. Andre Morell is excellent as a disgruntled German trader; Abraham Sofaer scores as a friendly medicine man.

History Is Made at Night ○

1937, US, 93 mins, b/w
Dir: Frank Borzage
Stars: Jean Arthur, Charles Boyer, Colin Clive
Rating: ★★★

Strange mixture of romance, comedy-thriller and high drama, with an excellent sequence of disaster at sea near the end. It's primarily a vehicle for that delightful actress Jean Arthur, and she makes the most of her chances as an unhappily married lady who finds herself at the centre of a baffling and violent series of events in Paris. Charles Boyer is his usual elegant self, and shows a lighter touch than usual, in his interpretation of the man with whom she becomes romantically involved during the very intricate plot.

History of Mr Polly, The ⊙

1949, UK, 94 mins, b/w
Dir: Anthony Pelissier
Stars: John Mills, Sally Ann Howes, Finlay Currie, Edward Chapman, Megs Jenkins
Rating: ★★★

This vision of H G Wells' classic story of a little man's fight to be free of his wretched life was produced by its star, John Mills, and has immense charm. The original author would surely have been delighted with the performances of Mills, Megs Jenkins, Betty Ann Davies and Finlay Currie, and Desmond Dickinson's sunny photography exactly catches the leisurely pace and atmosphere of British rural

life. Wells' ingenious plot, crammed with incident, is treated remarkably faithfully by director Anthony Pelissier's screenplay, with a fire sequence and the final riverside battle between Mills and Currie coming out as the highlights. A memorable British success.

History of the World Part I ● ⓥ

1981, US, 92 mins, colour
Dir: Mel Brooks
Stars: Mel Brooks, Dom DeLuise, Madeline Kahn, Harvey Korman
Rating: ★

'You Romans have a god for everything,' says Comicus (Mel Brooks), 'except premature ejaculation. But I hear that's coming quickly.' You may not credit it, but this is the verbal highpoint of this Brooks gathering of historical excreta, to use a term of which he himself would approve: it's all downhill from there on. Brooks goes at it all with a will, leering at the camera, writing dozens of jokes about bodily functions and constructing whole scenes round single punchlines. He looks as though he's having a tremendous time and, if crude sledgehammer comedies are your bag, you may too. It makes a *Carry On* film resemble a tapestry of wit and understatement.

Hit, The ●

1984, UK, 98 mins, colour
Dir: Stephen Frears
Stars: John Hurt, Tim Roth, Laura Del Sol
Rating: ★★

Bleakly dramatic suspense film about a 'squealer' (Terence Stamp) who flees to Spain but finds that retribution eventually catches up with him. The dialogue is frequently amusing and the action red in tooth and claw. The delicious Laura del Sol is the girl improbably hauled along for a desert trek, giving rise to some lovely burnished photography of Spanish landscapes.

Hitcher, The ● ⓥ

1986, US, 97 mins, colour
Dir: Robert Harmon
Stars: C Thomas Howell, Rutger Hauer, Jennifer Jason Leigh, Jeffrey DeMunn
Rating: ★★

Both a road movie and a battle between good and evil, *The Hitcher* is thus a direct descendant from *Duel*. A psycho killer, Ryder (Rutger Hauer), who murders the drivers with whom he hitches lifts, seems to decide that teenager Jim (C Thomas Howell) is the man to end his torment. 'Stop me,' he grates, with a knife to Jim's cheek. When Jim's answer is to propel Ryder from the car, his nightmare begins. Ryder kills more hapless motorists, crimes for which Jim is eventually arrested and jailed. Always grim, unpleasant and visceral, the film's sometimes exciting as well. Howell delineates very well his desperate descent from normal teenager to hyped-up hunter, while Hauer does what he can to make his psycho memorable. The chase sequences are done with all the efficiency and damage we've come to expect from modern Hollywood. It isn't quite the nail-biter *Duel* was (and has a less logical ending too) but it won't bore you either.

Hitler – The Last Ten Days ◐ Ⓥ
1973, UK, 108 mins, colour
Dir: Ennio De Concini
Stars: Alec Guinness, Simon Ward, Adolfo Celli, Diane Cilento, Eric Porter
Rating: ★★

A flawless British cast, with a few distinguished Continental additions, act out the Fuhrer's last few tortured days in his underground bunker against a Berlin background of burnished browns and flickering reds, superbly captured by the Technicolor cameras of Ennio Guarnieri. Alec Guinness' portrayal in the title role is the perfection one would expect, at least on the surface, although the persuasive qualities of his performance are too often undermined by the uncertainties in the screenplay (based on Gerhardt Boldt's book *The Last Days of the Chancellery*) which never seems sure of its purpose. Boldt himself, one of Hitler's staff officers who escaped from the bunker in these last few days, acted as adviser on the film. He is said to have been quite shaken by some of the subtler aspects of Guinness' disturbing characterisation.

Hit the Ice ☉
1943, US, 82 mins, b/w
Dir: Charles Lamont
Stars: Bud Abbott, Lou Costello
Rating: ★★

Bud and Lou as wartime American papparazzi caught up with a gang of crooks while trying to snap some newspaper pictures; their great ice-skating rink routine is here, as is

Sheldon Leonard who later gave up acting to become one of the most successfull producers in American television.

H M Pulham Esq ○
1941, US, 120 mins, b/w
Dir: King Vidor
Stars: Hedy Lamarr, Robert Young, Ruth Hussey, Charles Coburn, Van Heflin, Leif Erickson
Rating: ★★★

The best of Robert Young's earlier work, starring as a staid Bostonian businessman looking back on the one magic period of his dull and respectable life. Hedy Lamarr has never been better, or looked lovelier, as the one fine fling of his youth. Here she finally gave the lie to those of her detractors who said that she couldn't act. Director King Vidor's adaptation (with Elizabeth Hill) of John P Marquand's fine novel glows with warmth, wit and wisdom. Sara Haden and Fay Holden take a vacation from the Hardy family series to play character parts, and you may also spot singer John Raitt and star-to-be Ava Gardner in very tiny roles.

HMS Defiant ○
(aka: Damn the Defiant)
1962, UK, 101 mins, colour
Dir: Lewis Gilbert
Stars: Alec Guinness, Dirk Bogarde, Anthony Quayle, Tom Bell, Maurice Denham
Rating: ★★★

A distinguished cast of British actors take to the sea for a spectacular tale of a British ship sailing against Napoleon. Action and mutiny abound, and director Lewis Gilbert makes a splendid job of capturing the period atmosphere. Firm characterisations from a talented cast – Dirk Bogarde has a field day as the sadistic First Lieutenant – ensure engrossing and exciting entertainment.

Hobson's Choice ○
1953, UK, 120 mins, b/w
Dir: David Lean
Stars: Charles Laughton, John Mills
Rating: ★★★★

The great British actor Charles Laughton produced another of his memorable, over-the-top tyrants in David Lean's splendid adaptation of Harold Brighouse's 1915 domestic comedy that gave the British language a metaphor. This Captain Bligh of the bootmaking trade is of course even-

tually outdone and Laughton is almost out-acted by fair-haired, slightly matronly Brenda de Banzie, who gives her all (and became a star as a result) as the tough-as-old-boots Maggie, a determined Lancashire lass who turns the tables on her despotic dad by marrying John Mills' wonderfully wimpish boothand and using his craftsmanship as a secret weapon in the family war. Lean is in Dickens mode with this carefully set and directed piece, which has some superb photography by Lean regular Jack Hildyard (who won an Oscar for his cinematography on *The Bridge on the River Kwai* three years later) – a particularly memorable scene being where Laughton lumbers through a series of puddles in pursuit of the moon's reflection. A classic period piece to cherish.

Hockey Night ○
1984, Canada, 77 mins, colour
Dir: Paul Shapiro
Stars: Megan Fellows, Rick Moranis, Sean McCann, Gail Youngs
Rating: ★★

A likeable, if not exceptional, Canadian film about a teenage girl, who, hockey-mad, determines to make the boys' team in her new home town when she finds there's no girls' team around. Megan Fellows is spunky as the girl goalie and the leading man is Rick Moranis, later to feature in *Ghost Busters, Honey, I Shrunk the Kids* and *The Flintstones.*

Hocus Pocus ○ Ⓥ
1993, US, 97 mins, colour
Dir: Kenny Ortega
Stars: Bette Midler, Sarah Jessica Parker, Kathy Najimy, Omri Katz, Vinessa Shaw
Rating: ★★★

Burnt at the stake by most critics, this jolly and juicy slice of witchery-pokery proves less than half as black as its reputation. Its cauldron bubbles with funny lines and sensationally good special effects and – eye of newt! – it has Bette Midler looking like a *Spitting Image* puppet of herself as the leader of a trio of Connecticut witches who return from the dead 300 years on, thanks to stupid teenager Max lighting the black candle at the museum that was once their home. If they can breathe in enough souls of children, the witches will live forever. Attempting to see that the tartar-tongued trio come to a bad end instead are Max (Omri Katz), his girl-

H

friend (Vinessa Shaw) and baby sister (Thora Birch), a vengeful 300-year-old cat and a zombie, resuscitated by Midler, who changes sides despite her exhortation to 'Follow those children, you maggot museum.' The ending goes too far into sentiment, but Sarah Jessica Parker and Kathy Najimy are right on the mark as the other witches: highlight of the action is their acting as raddled Ronettes to Bette's singing sorceress when the trio invade the local hop.

Hoffa ● ⓥ
1992, US, 140 mins, colour
Dir: Danny DeVito
Stars: Jack Nicholson, Danny DeVito, Armand Assante, J T Walsh, Kevin Anderson, Robert Prosky
Rating: ★★

A tough-talking American blue-collar drama about Jimmy Hoffa, a legendary union leader who jumped into bed with the Mafia early in his career and was eventually to pay for that with his life. Although impressively staged and set – especially in the major action sequences involving strikes by Hoffa's Teamsters – by director Danny DeVito (who also plays a key role), the film is surprisingly dully written by David Mamet. The lack of colour in the words is accentuated by the one-note performance of Jack Nicholson as Hoffa, even though this might reflect the man in real life. Mamet's scenario also gives little sense of the varying times in which the film is set, several years obviously having passed on occasions. Together with dialogue that tends to the repetitive, it leads your attention wandering from time to time. The inherent fascination of the subject just about carries it through; but, like a hot air balloon, *Hoffa* looks good, feels good, but hasn't much inside.

Holcroft Covenant, The ● ⓥ
1985, UK, 112 mins, colour
Dir: John Frankenheimer
Stars: Michael Caine, Anthony Andrews, Victoria Tennant, Lilli Palmer
Rating: ★

When three distinguished screen-writers have a go at the same best-selling novel and the result is a clumsy mess, you have to wonder what went wrong. As it is, the words that Edward Anhalt, George Axelrod and John Hopkins have provided make this film version of Robert Ludlum's race-along book run like a dubbed English version of the conti-

nental spy thrillers from two decades earlier. Thanks to a marvellously relaxed portrayal by Michael Caine, laughter is more or less kept at bay for about half an hour. But soon such lines as 'What a brilliant way to hide – just become a world-famous public figure' and 'You drive to Geneva taking the back roads – I'll take the train' stumble distressingly over one another. Anthony Andrews gives the impression that his performance might look quite good with different dialogue, but the dual purpose of Victoria Tennant's role is quite beyond her.

Hold That Blonde ○
1945, US, 76 mins, b/w
Dir: George Marshall
Stars: Eddie Bracken, Veronica Lake, Albert Dekker, George Zucco
Rating: ★★

Veronica Lake was never quite the same force without the peek-a-boo hairstyle that she was forced to change when 'peek-a-boo' factory girls started catching the style in machinery, and her studio, Paramount, began to lose interest in her, pitching her into comedy roles that didn't suit her slinky style. Here she's mismatched with firecracker Eddie Bracken in the story of a kleptomaniac who tries to reform a professional lady thief. Director George Marshall made several Bob Hope films, and this fast-moving farce is very much like them.

Hold That Co-ed ○
(aka: Hold That Girl)
1938, US, 80 mins, b/w
Dir: George Marshall
Stars: John Barrymore, George Murphy, Marjorie Weaver, Joan Davis
Rating: ★★

John Barrymore had one of the best roles of his later career as a scheming politician out to be elected to the US Senate and using state funds to finance a college football team as part of his campaign strategy. He makes the most – and sometimes more – of every scene in which he appears, leaving the song and dance chores in this satirical comedy-musical to George Murphy. Joan Davis almost steals the film as a goal-kicking lady footballer in a movie that cheerfully celebrates those two all-consuming American passions – politics and sport.

Hold That Ghost! ○
1941, US, 82 mins, b/w
Dir: Arthur Lubin

Stars: Bud Abbott, Lou Costello, Joan Davis, Mischa Auer, Evelyn Ankers, Richard Carlson
Rating: ★★★

Chuckle as you chill to the first of Abbott and Costello's many encounters with things that went bump in the night. This one was made soon after their initial impact on the cinemagoing public when Universal, their studio, was working its newest star team overtime. Bud and Lou find themselves in a haunted house and the laughs (and dead bodies) come thick and fast, with a great supporting cast working hard. Universal ditched the original ending, where Bud and Lou are running a health farm when a dead body (from the haunted house) falls into the room as they ring for dinner, in favour of a grand musical finale. At least they did leave in Lou's famous 'flickering candle' routine.

Hold That Girl
See: *Hold That Co-ed*

Hole in the Head, A ○
1959, US, 120 mins, colour
Dir: Frank Capra
Stars: Frank Sinatra, Edward G Robinson, Eleanor Parker
Rating: ★★

Comedy-cum-drama about a good time Charlie who suddenly finds that he is in danger of losing his most prized possession, his son. Directed by two-time Oscar winner Frank Capra, the film contains two big song hits from its star, Frank Sinatra: 'High Hopes' and 'All My Tomorrows'. The film, though, seems to have a hole in its heart, just not having the emotional pull that it should.

Holiday Camp ○
1947, UK, 97 mins, b/w
Dir: Ken Annakin
Stars: Flora Robson, Dennis Price, Jack Warner, Kathleen Harrison, Hazel Court, Jimmy Hanley
Rating: ★★

This entertaining portrait of the British enjoying themselves in the immediate post-war years started a flood of similar 'portmanteau' films, and Jack Warner and Kathleen Harrison scored such immense personal successes that a series was made around the Huggetts, the Cockney characters they play. The setting now seems a world away.

Holiday for Lovers ○
1959, US, 103 mins, colour
Dir: Henry Levin
Stars: Clifton Webb, Jane Wyman, Paul
Henreid, Carol Lynley
Rating: ★★

Clifton Webb actually contrives to
make some fairly tired humour sound
like waspish wit in this fiesta of a romp
that takes Webb, Jane Wyman and
their two daughters to South America.
Not that there's much suggestion that
they actually went there, as the lovely
footage of Brazil and Peru sits
uneasily behind the actors superim-
posed against it. Spanish dancer Jose
Greco fires things up towards the end
with a terrific speciality number.

Holiday Inn ⊙ ⓥ
1942, US, 101 mins, b/w
Dir: Mark Sandrich
Stars: Bing Crosby, Fred Astaire, Virginia
Dale, Marjorie Reynolds
Rating: ★★★

This Irving Berlin musical was directed by Mark Sandrich, who made
many of the best Astaire-Rogers
musicals of the Thirties. The score
includes 'Easter Parade', 'White
Christmas' and 'Be Careful, It's My
Heart'. Not much of a plot, but with
Bing Crosby singing and Fred Astaire
dancing, who needs such niceties?

Holiday on the Buses ○
1973, UK, 83 mins, colour
Dir: Bryan Izzard
Stars: Reg Varney, Queenie Watts,
Arthur Mullard
Rating: ★

Stan Butler (Reg Varney) and the
gang go to a holiday camp in Wales
where Stan blows up the toilet and
sewage system. While Stan and Jack
salvage a few cuties from the camp,
the indispensable Queenie Watts and
Arthur Mullard salvage themselves a
few laughs from the script.

Hollow Triumph ○
(aka: The Scar)
1948, US, 80 mins, b/w
Dir: Steve Sekely
Stars: Paul Henreid, Joan Bennett
Rating: ★★★

Paul Henreid plays a dual role as a
crook on the run and his psychologist
double in this well-paced and
beautifully shot piece of *film noir*. The
crook kills the doc to assume his
identity only to find the medic had a
guilty secret of his own . . . Henreid,
famed for his role as freedom fighter

Victor Laszlo in *Casablanca*, not only
starred in but also produced this tense
thriller with a twist in its tail. Joan
Bennett gives earnest support as the
girl embroiled in the criminal's
scheme. A rarely seen and unjustly
overlooked entry in the genre.

Holly and the Ivy, The ○
1952, UK, 83 mins, b/w
Dir: George More O'Ferrall
Stars: Ralph Richardson, Margaret
Leighton, Celia Johnson, John Gregson,
Denholm Elliott
Rating: ★★★

This adaptation of Wynyard Brown's
play about a country cleric at Christmas and the resolution of his own life
and those of his three children strikes
all the right emotional notes and is
acted with great understatement and
feeling for character, especially by
Ralph Richardson (as the clergyman)
and Celia Johnson and Margaret
Leighton as his daughters.

Hollywood Canteen ○
1944, US, 124 mins, b/w
Dir: Delmer Daves
Stars: Robert Hutton, Joan Leslie, Bette
Davis, John Garfield, Sydney
Greenstreet, Joan Crawford
Rating: ★★★

They don't – and indeed can't – make
'em like this any more. Warner
Brothers had already had one smash
wartime hit with *Stage Door Canteen*, a
star-studded musical compendium,
and aimed to repeat the trick with this
similar project, spun round an
eggshell-thin plot about a young soldier who dreams of meeting his
favourite film star. Just as well she
turns out to be Joan Leslie, who was
under contract to the studio. Pretty
well the whole Warner roster is on
parade (with the exception of
Humphrey Bogart) and any film that
has a violin duet of 'The Bee' from
Joseph Szigeti and Jack Benny has to
be worth watching. Roy Rogers pops
in (not forgetting Trigger) to warble
one of his greatest hits, 'Don't Fence
Me In'. Wartime audiences wept
buckets at the final scene in Union
Station, a hankie-inducing finish to a
dazzling show.

Hollywood Cavalcade ○
1939, US, 96 mins, colour
Dir: Irving Cummings
Stars: Alice Faye, Don Ameche, Buster
Keaton, Ben Turpin, Chester Conklin
Rating: ★★★

A thinly disguised biography of Mabel
Normand and Mack Sennett, this film
is also a potted history of Hollywood
silent films, funniest in its silent
comedy scenes. Buster Keaton appears
as himself and several of the original
Keystone Cops are on hand to join in
the fun. Alice Faye throws herself with
a will into slapstick scenes that seem
primarily designed to get her wet and
show off her figure. After all that
physical effort, she was probably not
best pleased when her three songs
(including the hit 'Whispering') were
cut from the film – although the plot
still slows down a lot in its later stages.
Wonderful Fox Technicolor as usual,
especially in the interior scenes.

Hollywood Hotel ○
1937, US, 109 mins, b/w
Dir: Busby Berkeley
Stars: Dick Powell, Rosemary Lane, Lola
Lane
Rating: ★★★

This lively musical is memorable for
its celebrated song 'Hooray for Hollywood' which immediately became
the movie capital's rousing theme
song. Ronald Reagan does an unbilled
cameo as a radio announcer, and other
stars glimpsed briefly include Carole
Landis (as a hat check girl) and Susan
Hayward (as a starlet sitting at a table).
Gossip columnist Louella Parsons
plays herself. It was the last of the cycle of Warner musicals that had started
with *42nd Street*. Once more Busby
Berkeley was at the helm.

Hollywood or Bust ○
1956, US, 95 mins, colour
Dir: Frank Tashlin
Stars: Dean Martin, Jerry Lewis, Anita
Ekberg, Pat Crowley
Rating: ★★

Hollywood was courtesy of Paramount and Anita Ekberg – playing
herself – supplied the bust for the last
of the Dean Martin-Jerry Lewis
comedies that had begun with *My
Friend Irma* in 1949. Fun and foolery
on the road to Los Angeles, with director Frank Tashlin (with whom
Lewis would make some of his best
solo films) keeping the pace brisk and
disguising the fact that Dean and
Jerry's double act had practically dis-
integrated and the stars weren't
speaking to each other off screen.

Holocaust 2000 ◑
(aka: The Chosen)
1977, UK/Italy, 105 mins, colour
Dir: Alberto De Martino

H

Stars: Kirk Douglas, Simon Ward
Rating: ★

Never mind the plot – a heady combination of *The AntiChrist* and *The Omen*, plus a few extra supernatural trimmings thrown in for good effect. There's plenty to hold your attention in this enjoyably awful film, including Kirk Douglas taking on the Devil, and Simon Ward dressed in white, named 'Angel' but turning out to be something rather nasty, along with a supporting cast that includes a wasted Virginia McKenna, Geoffrey Keen, Anthony Quayle and Alexander Knox. Some lively special effects add to the fun and Alberto de Martino (who directed *The AntiChrist*) stirs up his brew of hocus pocus with a commendably straight face.

Holy Matrimony ○
1943, US, 87 mins, b/w
Dir: John Stahl
Stars: Gracie Fields, Monty Woolley, Laird Cregar
Rating: ★★★

A thoroughly enjoyable comedy – based on Arnold Bennett's witty novel – about a shy artist, who, horrified by the fame a knighthood brings 'kills himself off', switches identities with his dead butler, marries and becomes involved in a public scandal. Easily the best of Gracie Fields' Hollywood ventures, blending well with an on-form Monty Woolley as the painter, and receiving rollicking support from a whole battery of the Forties' best character comedians.

Hombre ○
1966, US, 111 mins, colour
Dir: Martin Ritt
Stars: Paul Newman, Fredric March, Richard Boone, Diane Cilento,
Rating: ★★★

Director Martin Ritt's third film with Paul Newman, following *Hud* and *The Outrage*, this rugged Western has superb opening scenes. The stagecoach passengers gather together in a waiting-room so dry and dusty it almost makes one cough. Villain Richard Boone's entrance is a tremendous piece of histrionics, each syllable having a satisfying ring, culminating in his facing-down of a would-be passenger who's insulted him, merely by the use of a reflective pause followed by 'What'd you say?' Newman gets to grips with the enigmatic title role, Diane Cilento scores heavily as the too often loved-and-let-

down Jessie, and Fredric March grapples gallantly with the cardboard part of an embezzling Indian agent.

Home Alone ○ ⓥ
1990, US, 100 mins, colour
Dir: Chris Columbus
Stars: Macaulay Culkin, Joe Pesci, Daniel Stern, John Heard, Catherine O'Hara, John Candy
Rating: ★★★

Eighty minutes of medium amusement, capped by a side-splitting last 20 minutes, raising several of the biggest cinema laughs in ages: the formula for a box-office blaster from prolific writer John Hughes. And he just about gets away with the unlikely premise that triggers the story. After all, how do you adequately explain an eight-year-old boy being left alone by his parents when they fly off on a Christmas holiday to Paris? Well, you give his parents five kids, add brother-in-law's six, send little Kevin (Macauley Culkin) to bed for being naughty, throw in a power failure that leaves everyone asleep when the vans arrive from the airport, leave Kevin the sleeping victim of a 'head count' that accidentally takes in the kid next door, top it off with a desperate run for the airport, with the kids in third class and the adults in first class, and hope the viewer will believe it. After this, the story veers uneasily between France and America until burglars Joe Pesci and Daniel Stern come on to the scene to turn things up. Getting wise to their plans, Kevin decides to defend his home. How he does so leads to a series of violent jokes that make it no mere coincidence that a shaven-headed Pesci looks like a refugee from The Three Stooges. Be patient and, like Kevin, you'll have fun. A (too similar) sequel followed.

Home Alone 2 – Lost in New York ○ ⓥ
1992, US, 120 mins, colour
Dir: Chris Columbus
Stars: Macaulay Culkin, Joe Pesci, Daniel Stern, Catherine O'Hara, John Heard, Tim Curry, Brenda Fricker, Eddie Bracken
Rating: ★★

A repeat of the hugely successful *Home Alone* formula, except that, instead of being left at home when his family flies off on its Christmas holidays, young Kevin (Macaulay Culkin) takes the wrong plane – and gets stranded in New York. There, he encounters again the two bumbling burglars from

the first film (Joe Pesci and Daniel Stern) and with lots of slapstick comedy and yelps of 'Yikes!', it's up to Kevin to save the day with his home-made army assault course of obstacles – again. Not so much a sequel, more of an action replay but even more violent than the original – so perhaps a little too much for very small children. Britain's Brenda Fricker scores as a New York pigeon lady.

Home at Seven ○
(aka: Murder on Monday)
1952, UK, 82 mins, b/w
Dir: Ralph Richardson
Stars: Ralph Richardson, Margaret Leighton, Jack Hawkins
Rating: ★★★

A suspenseful adaptation of R C Sherriff's successful stage play, this makes dramatic enough mystery entertainment, thanks appreciably to its good cast. It stars Ralph Richardson who also directed in an intense and painstaking fashion that made you regret that it remained his only work in the latter capacity. It's difficult to believe that the film was made on virtually a shoestring budget and in only 15 days. The film's commendably tight and brief too, giving the viewer short, sharp scenes that make the plot intriguing every step of the way. The American distributors weren't keen on the cosy title, however: they changed it to *Murder on Monday*!

Homeboy ● ⓥ
1988, US, 112 mins, colour
Dir: Michael Seresin
Stars: Mickey Rourke, Debra Feuer, Christopher Walken, Thomas Quinn, Ruben Blades
Rating: ★★

This was Mickey Rourke's pet project, a boxing picture about a pug who's over the hill and so punchdrunk he's liable to die in the ring. The film's a bit slow, its pace rather emphasised by Eric Clapton's doomy guitar score (taken on its own, moodily fine) but with individual scenes nicely realised. Rourke, Debra Feuer (the fairground girl he falls for) and Christopher Walken – the small-time smoothie who tries to suck Rourke into crime – are all well in character, and the final boxing match is not for the squeamish. There's plenty of guts in this film in more ways than one.

Home of Our Own, A ○ Ⓥ
1992, US, 100 mins, colour
Dir: Tony Bill
Stars: Kathy Bates, Edward Furlong, Soon Teck-Oh, Tony Campisi
Rating: ★★★

A big family weepie about a big family. The 'Lacey tribe', Mom (Kathy Bates) and six kids, pull up roots in Los Angeles and end up in the wilds of Idaho, where they take a half-built house and, with a promise of work for the man who owns the land, make it their own. The resulting catalogue of hardships and tiny triumphs is nicely constructed, and only lacks that certain touch of class that the best Hollywood family pictures have. Performances are competent, especially so from Soon Teck-Oh as the oriental owner of the site, and Bates' real-life husband Tony Campisi makes a rare film appearance as the man who courts, then clouts her.

Home Sweet Homicide
See: What a Carve-Up!

Homeward Bound: The Incredible Journey ☉ Ⓥ
1992, US, 84 mins, colour
Dir: Dunwayne Dunham
Voice stars: Michael J Fox, Sally Field, Don Ameche
Rating: ★★★

Disney have dug up their Sixties family hit, *The Incredible Journey*, and given it a Nineties gloss in the style of *Look Who's Talking*. Three family pets face the perils of open, wild country in their character-forming quest to be reunited with their human beings: Shadow is a venerable golden retriever (voiced with suitable gravitas by Don Ameche), Sassy a well-named long-haired Himalayan cat (voiced by Sally Field) and Chance (voiced by Michael J Fox), a bouncy young American boxer, who also acts as narrator. The story is very much from the animals' point of view, with some witty dialogue and asides. As you would expect, there are some large doses of sentimentality and the humans are doomed to remain mere cyphers. But it's a charmer for all that, beautifully shot in Oregon, targeted at children but not without appeal to their parents.

Homicidal ●
1961, US, 87 mins, b/w
Dir: William Castle
Stars: Patricia Breslin, Glenn Corbett, Jean Arless
Rating: ★★

This is the film in which director William Castle, the self-styled 'showman of shock', introduced the 'fright break'. This was an interval of one minute, which allowed the audience time to get out of the cinema before the most frightening scene. You may use it either to make the hot chocolate or rush up to bed and quiver beneath the blankets. In this chiller about a girl in peril from a person unknown, Castle moved away from the more obvious *The House on Haunted Hill* and close to the territory explored by Hitchcock in *Psycho*, employing variations on the same kinds of suspense devices.

Homicide ● Ⓥ
1991, US, 102 mins, colour
Dir: David Mamet
Stars: Joe Mantegna, William H Macy, Rebecca Pidgeon, Ving Rhames, Natalija Nogulich
Rating: ★★

A slow, sad, low-key, cleverly put-together police detective story, with Joe Mantegna as the Jewish cop who considers himself expendable and an outsider; so he is ready meat for a group of Jewish activists when their organisation crops up in a murder case he's almost accidentally assigned to. The sombre classical music background tends to make you think this is about anti-semitism. But writer/director David Mamet is too cunning to leave it at that, and that proves merely a cloak for the real story – of how easily men can be manipulated and ruined by their own backgrounds. If only Mamet the writer had assigned somebody to direct who could have upped the pace, this might have been a little classic.

Honey, I Blew Up the Kid ☉ Ⓥ
1993, US, 89 mins, colour
Dir: Randal Kleiser
Stars: Rick Moranis, Marcia Strassman, Robert Oliveri, Lloyd Bridges, Gregory Sierra
Rating: ★★

The Disney formula works like a charm in this occasionally clumsy but consistently likeable sequel to *Honey, I Shrunk the Kids*. Rick Moranis again plays the scatty inventor who this time accidentally subjects his two-year-old son to the effects of a mat-ter-expanding machine. The toddler (played by twins Joshua and Daniel Shalikar) is impishly cute even as a naughty 50-footer, and the scenes where he rampages through Las Vegas are hilarious. A good old-fashioned family frolic whose tendency to get a bit repetitive and tiresome towards the end won't worry the kidlet audience at which it's aimed.

Honey, I Shrunk the Kids ☉ Ⓥ
1989, US, 93 mins, colour
Dir: Joe Johnston
Stars: Rick Moranis, Matt Frewer, Marcia Strassman, Kristine Sutherland
Rating: ★★★

Every now and again Hollywood produces an 'incredible shrinking people' film, and this hugely successful comedy is as much fun as any of them. Rick Moranis' personable performance makes a sturdy centre for the high jinks here as the scientist dad whose children accidentally turn his experimental ray gun on themselves, and shrink to microscopic size, soon finding themselves in the garden, where they encounter all the usual perils beloved of such films. This one's well-paced though, with one or two outstandingly funny scenes, pretty good trickwork and sparkling Technicolor photography. A sequel, *Honey I Blew Up the Kid*, followed somewhat less successfully three years later.

Honeymoon Hotel ○
1964, US, 89 mins, colour
Dir: Henry Levin
Stars: Robert Goulet, Robert Morse, Nancy Kwan, Jill St John
Rating: ★★★

Peppy Robert Morse gives a non-stop, Jerry Lewis-style performance in this racy comedy that even sees the statuesque Robert Goulet unbending at times. Morse has many of the Lewis qualities, including a little-boy-lost attitude that makes him instantly likeable. There's also a Jack Lemmon-ish quality to his delivery of a funny line. One dance-comedy scene between him and Nancy Kwan has no real part in the film, but is so good that it obviously had to stay. The comedy shows a remarkably delicate touch in risqué humour, and all its sex jokes are funny. It also gives Keenan Wynn a part that really allows him to spread his deft comedy talents liberally around him.

H

Honeymoon in Vegas ◐
1992, US, 96 mins, colour
Dir: Andrew Bergman
Stars: Nicolas Cage, James Caan, Sarah
Jessica Parker, Pat Morita, Peter Boyle,
Anne Bancroft
Rating: ★★

It's one of those situations that used to
be tailor-made for Hollywood screwball farce. Jack (Nicolas Cage),
haunted by his promise to his dying
mother (Anne Bancroft) never to wed,
goes to Vegas with his current squeeze
Betsy (Sarah Jessica Parker) to do the
deed after a year's dithering. Once in
the neon city, however, Jack falls prey
to millionaire gambler James Caan,
who's gobsmacked by Parker's being
the image of his dead wife. Taking a
still dallying Cage for $65,000 in a
poker game, Caan announces the
price for the debt is Betsy's spending
the weekend with him. The rest of
the film concerns Caan's wooing of
her in Hawaii and Cage's hot if penniless pursuit. This is all quite light
and not unenjoyable, but the film's
problems lie with its casting. Cage
shouts and sweats a lot; Caan's portrayal is too broad and lacking in
charm: you don't really want Parker
(who herself oozes curves rather than
charisma) to end up with either of
these guys. The film does literally
spread its wings, though, in a lunatic
climax that involves 34 Flying Elvises
skydiving on Las Vegas.

Honeymoon Machine, The ○
1961, US, 92 mins, colour
Dir: Richard Thorpe
Stars: Steve McQueen, Brigid Bazlen,
Jim Hutton, Paula Prentiss
Rating: ★★

Steve McQueen again shows (as he
did in *The Reivers*) what a dab hand he
could be at comedy, in this zany romp
about two sailors who get their hands
on an electronic brain, and plan to
win a fortune with it, at gambling casinos. On the distaff side, the
treacle-voiced Paula Prentiss adds immeasurably to the fun as does
veteran Dean Jagger in a rare comedy
film role.

Honeysuckle Rose ○
1980, US, 119 mins, colour
Dir: Jerry Schatzberg
Stars: Willie Nelson, Dyan Cannon, Amy
Irving, Slim Pickens
Rating: ★★

With all due respect to the pleasant
Amy Irving, it's hard to believe that

anyone in his right mind would risk
his marriage to the dynamic Dyan
Cannon for a fling with her – even if
the man in question is an ageing
country-and-western singer (Willie
Nelson) and Amy's his guitarist on the
road. Miss Cannon is tremendous –
easily the best thing in the film, in
fact – and one can't help thinking that
things might have worked better as a
whole if Nelson's wife had been
played by someone less sensational to
look at. It's hard to see what either
woman could see in this plain,
greying, long-haired, hard-drinking
man, although his readily strong, unusual singing voice gives him a certain
magnetism. Still, the music clangs
melodically away and veteran
character actor Slim Pickens wheezes
around happily in the background.

Honky Tonk ○
1941, US, 100 mins, b/w
Dir: Jack Conway
Stars: Clark Gable, Lana Turner, Frank
Morgan, Claire Trevor
Rating: ★★

The first screen meeting of Clark Gable and Lana Turner is a lively, glossy,
MGM drama that might well have
been called *The Con-Man and the Lady*.
Gable apart, the film is almost an
index of the actresses who played
those hard-hearted slinky blonde
temptresses of the Forties. Lana
Turner, Claire Trevor and Veda Ann
Borg are all here. Albert Dekker is a
splendidly nasty villain, and Turner's
father is played with witty affability by
that old MGM stalwart Frank Morgan.
The story assumes epic proportions
towards the end, giving Lana a chance
to show the talent for emotive acting
that she had already revealed in
Ziegfeld Girl.

Honkytonk Man ○ ⓥ
1982, US, 122 mins, colour
Dir: Clint Eastwood
Stars: Clint Eastwood, Kyle Eastwood,
John McIntire
Rating: ★★

Unfairly ignored at the box-office
(presumably because audiences would
only accept Clint Eastwood with a
magnum in his hand, gunning down
all and sundry), this is a charming
tragi-comedy with a subtle variation
by Eastwood on the kind of redneck
character usually played by Burt
Reynolds. And as director, he is as
generous as ever towards his co-stars,
in particularly getting a sharp and
sensitive portrayal from his real-life

son Kyle, here cast as his hero-
worshipping nephew. By no means a
typical Eastwood vehicle, but
satisfying enough if overlong.

Honolulu ○
1939, US, 83 mins, b/w
Dir: Edward Buzzell
Stars: Robert Young, Eleanor Powell,
George Burns, Gracie Allen, Rita
Johnson, Ruth Hussey
Rating: ★★

This MGM musical has a plot as ram-
shackle as a grass hut. The
compensations, however, are dazzling.
George Burns and Gracie Allen tie
everyone in verbal knots, and
Eleanor Powell storms to glory in the
dance routines, which include a bril-
liant hula number. Harry Warren and
Gus Kahn wrote the score, which in-
cludes 'The Night Was Made for
Dreaming', 'Honolulu', 'Hymn to the
Sun' and Gracie Allen doing a Mae
West on 'The Leader Doesn't Like
Music'.

Honorary Consul, The ● ⓥ
(aka: Beyond the Limit)
1983, US, 104 mins, colour
Dir: John Mackenzie
Stars: Michael Caine, Richard Gere, Bob
Hoskins
Rating: ★★★

Graham Greene's novels have often
made absorbing entertainment and this
is no exception, despite some
improbabilities in the plot development, particularly towards the end.
Richard Gere, with a faintly odd
English accent that baulks at 'a's, plays
the young doctor working around the
Argentine-Paraguay border who
allows himself to become involved in
two equally dangerous games: aiding
revolutionaries (who he thinks may
help him find his missing father) and
having a passionate affair with the
glamorous young wife of the boozy
British consul. Gere's battles with his
accent permit those wily old birds
Michael Caine (as the consul) and
Bob Hoskins (as the Argentine chief of
police) to sneak off with the acting
honours.

Hoodlum Empire ○
1952, US, 95 mins, b/w
Dir: Joseph Kane
Stars: Brian Donlevy, Claire Trevor,
Forrest Tucker, Vera Ralston, Luther
Adler, John Russell
Rating: ★★

A cold-blooded crime thriller featuring many of Hollywood's best gangster actors of the time, made in the pseudo-documentary style pioneered by 20th Century-Fox in post-war years. An unusual film to come from Republic who, like director Joseph Kane, were more used to turning out rousing adventure movies supposedly set in exotic locations.

Hoodlum Priest, The ○
1961, US, 101 mins, b/w
Dir: Irvin Kershner
Stars: Don Murray, Larry Gates, Keir Dullea
Rating: ★★★

Honest and gripping study of a young priest's attempts to save a delinquent youth from his own tragic destiny. Looked on by the critics as a 'sleeper' – a low-budget film of surprising quality – this drama gave Keir Dullea, later to star in *2001: A Space Odyssey*, his first motion picture role.

Hook ○ ⓥ
1991, US, 140 mins, colour
Dir: Steven Spielberg
Stars: Dustin Hoffman, Robin Williams, Julia Roberts, Bob Hoskins, Maggie Smith, Charlie Korsmo
Rating: ★★

You might guess it would take this Steven Spielberg fantasy a long time to get going and it does. But 100 minutes? That's how long it takes fortyish businessman Robin Williams to remember that he was once Peter Pan and get cracking into the core of the plot. Then there's some fun to be had, if of a somewhat heavy-handed variety, as Peter fights to free his children from the clutches of the evil Hook. Strenuously over-scored, over-dressed and over-populated, the film is for the most part a musical without the songs, parading its sets like carnival attractions. Dustin Hoffman makes quite a droll Hook, but Williams seems ill at ease and Bob Hoskins, Maggie Smith, Julia Roberts and others get little chance to shine under Spielberg's direction, which requires all the players, and particularly the junior ones, to be over-emphatic. Yes, the top dressing's here in abundance, but there's too little spring in the step of this particular *Peter Pan*.

Hooper ○
1978, US, 100 mins, colour
Dir: Hal Needham

Stars: Burt Reynolds, Jan-Michael Vincent, Sally Field, Brian Keith
Rating: ★★★

A light-hearted look (with serious undertones) at the life of an ageing Hollywood stuntman. Although the stuntmen do their stuff in ripsnorting style, the script lacks the insight and invention to give it the stature to rise above a formula action film. Burt Reynolds turns on the casual charm in the title role, and is involved in the film's best sequence – where Hooper rides alone round the corral outside his ranch-house at night.

Hoosiers
See: Best Shot

Hope and Glory ○ ⓥ
1987, UK, 113 mins, colour
Dir: John Boorman
Stars: Sarah Miles, David Hayman, Derrick O'Connor, Susan Wooldridge, Sammi Davis, Ian Bannen
Rating: ★★★

A slight but often flavoursome recollection of a wartime childhood, John Boorman's memoir is not a portrait of the working classes battling through the Blitz, rather a picture of the lower middle classes in their suburban semis. Sometimes it rings horrendously true, at others it doesn't seem at all the bombsite childhood of contemporary documentaries. The sight of a 15-year-old dancing round celebrating the house down the road being on fire might be a vignette from Boorman's boyhood, but is still likely to cause a few raised eyebrows. And young Sebastian Rice-Edwards certainly comes across more sins than most wartime kids will remember. Still, the gangs of boys are well-drawn, as is the grandfather figure, played with relish by Ian Bannen, who all but steals the film. Boorman's own dialogue provides some good chuckles, and there's a rollicking portrait of an absolute monster of a teacher from Barbara Pierson.

Hopscotch ○ ⓥ
1980, US, 104 mins, colour
Dir: Ronald Neame
Stars: Walter Matthau, Glenda Jackson, Ned Beatty
Rating: ★★★

Enjoyable, inconsequential stuff with Walter Matthau, in the sort of role Cary Grant once claimed as his own, in complete control as America's ace secret service agent who decides to

get his own back on the bull-headed bosses who relegated him to a desk job. The merry dance he leads them across the world is always enjoyable and contains several pleasant performances, not least from Matthau himself but also from Glenda Jackson (even if her dialogue is less acid than one might wish), Sam Waterston (as the admiring agent who pursues Matthau), Ned Beatty (as his perspiring, constantly ill-tempered chief) and, in a much smaller role, Jacqueline Hyde as a gabbly estate agent. Although the fun game of cat and mouse never reaches the sublime heights of comedy, one would be quite happy for it to go on a lot longer.

Horn Blows at Midnight, The ⊙
1945, US, 80 mins, b/w
Dir: Raoul Walsh
Stars: Jack Benny, Alexis Smith, Allyn Joslyn, Dolores Moran, Guy Kibbee, Reginald Gardiner
Rating: ★★★

This is a comedy-fantasy which Jack Benny always joked about on his radio and TV shows in the same way that Ben Lyon referred disparagingly to *Hell's Angels*. Not nearly as bad as Benny always pretended, it's an enjoyable entertainment with a wonderful comic supporting cast that includes Reginald Gardiner, Guy Kibbee, Margaret Dumont, Allyn Joslyn, Mike Mazurki and – best of all – snooty Franklin Pangborn as a hot-and-bothered hotel detective.

Hornets' Nest ○
1969, US, 110 mins, colour
Dir: Phil Karlson
Stars: Rock Hudson, Sylva Koscina
Rating: ★★

There's a moral here somewhere about the futility of war and its effect on children, but it's all lost amid a welter of blood-letting and admittedly well-staged action scenes, as Captain Rock Hudson leads a little army of war orphans in World War Two Italy. Hudson gets another Continental leading lady in the sultry Sylva Koscina (a rather unlikely German doctor) to follow Leslie Caron and Claudia Cardinale in previous films, but the mixture of accents and acting styles – the cast includes American, British, Italian, French, German and Yugoslav players – is a bit disconcerting. The kids' leader is well

H

played by Mark Colleano, son of Bonar Colleano, once a favourite face in British films.

Horror Express ●
1972, UK/Spain, 88 mins, colour
Dir: Gene Martin
Stars: Christopher Lee, Peter Cushing, Telly Savalas
Rating: ★★★

There's something very nasty aboard the train thundering its way across snowscapes in this turn-of-the century chiller, very good indeed by the rather low standards set in this genre in recent years. Peter Cushing, Christopher Lee and Telly Savalas are on hand to give horror enthusiasts an additional frisson of satisfaction.

Horror of Dracula
See: Dracula [1958]

Horse Feathers ⊙ ⓥ
1932, US, 69 mins, b/w
Dir: Norman Z McLeod
Stars: Groucho Marx, Harpo Marx, Chico Marx, Zeppo Marx, Thelma Todd
Rating: ★★★★

Sheer Marx Brothers mania: Chico helps to run a speakeasy; Harpo catches a dog-catcher; Groucho takes over a college and gives a lecture on the human body that is pure Ronnie Barker. All this and a riotous football match for the finale. Remember – the password is 'Swordfish'.

Horsemen, The ○
1970, US, 109 mins, colour
Dir: John Frankenheimer
Stars: Omar Sharif, Leigh Taylor-Young, Jack Palance
Rating: ★★

This drama of the wide open spaces of Afghanistan is an unusual film for director John Frankenheimer, more at home with thrillers (*The Manchurian Candidate, French Connection II*) or studies of small-town Americana (*All Fall Down, The Gypsy Moths*). Omar Sharif is a proud Afghan rider whose failure in a crucial contest forces him to set out on an epic journey across hazardous terrain in order to redeem himself. Although it never quite breaks free of its own pageantry, *The Horsemen* has some very striking and sometimes savage sequences, notably one in which riders battle each other with whips. Claude Renoir's highly competent colour photography conveys well the primitive power of such barbaric rites.

Horse's Mouth, The
See: The Oracle

Horse Soldiers, The ○ ⓥ
1959, US, 120 mins, colour
Dir: John Ford
Stars: John Wayne, William Holden, Constance Towers, Anna Lee
Rating: ★★

A typical John Ford Western, with splendid scenery, and an explosive conflict between two big men – John Wayne as a tough colonel and William Holden as the army surgeon who disagrees with his methods. In supporting roles, two interesting Gibsons. There's Althea, one-time Wimbledon tennis champion, in her only film role, and old-time cowboy star Hoot. And those reliable Western character actors, Strother Martin and Denver Pyle, play two disreputable deserters. Some effective action scenes are topped by a frighteningly well realised street siege.

Horse Without a Head, The ⊙
1963, UK, 89 mins, colour
Dir: Don Chaffey
Stars: Jean-Pierre Aumont, Herbert Lom, Leo McKern, Pamela Franklin
Rating: ★★★

A delightful film for children, all pitched on the same note of light but exciting comedy-thriller and full of marvellously inept and humorous crook characters. Leo McKern has a field day as a roguish pedlar whose plans to participate in a great train robbery are constantly at risk at the hands of a gang of children. Riotous climax in a disused novelty factory and excellent colour photography by Paul Beeson.

Hospital, The ●
1971, US, 103 mins, colour
Dir: Arthur Hiller
Stars: George C Scott, Diana Rigg, Barnard Hughes, Nancy Marchand
Rating: ★★★

Mordant black comedy starring Oscar-nominated George C Scott as the harassed chief of a large New York hospital, beset by disasters at work and in his private life. Paddy Chayefsky's sardonic, often hysterically funny script won an Oscar. Filmed on location at New York's Metropolitan Hospital where the crew took over two floors of a newly completed wing.

Hot Blood ○
1956, US, 85 mins, colour
Dir: Nicholas Ray
Stars: Jane Russell, Cornel Wilde, Luther Adler, Joseph Calleia
Rating: ★★

Director Nicholas Ray, who made this film just before *Rebel Without a Cause*, looks into the cause of modern American gipsies, whom he calls the 'original good-time Charlies', because, he feels, they wander about without taking on any real responsibilities. For star Cornel Wilde, *Hot Blood* was one of the last of his 'Hollywood' films as a dashingly romantic leading man. This one, however, is not as hot as the title suggests.

Hotel ○
1967, US, 124 mins, colour
Dir: Richard Quine
Stars: Rod Taylor, Karl Malden, Melvyn Douglas, Merle Oberon, Richard Conte
Rating: ★★

Hollywood can do this sort of thing standing on its head. It's the story of various stories played out on the several floors of a luxury hotel, and upstairs, in boardroom and penthouse suite a struggle for the control of the hotel is reaching its crucial moments. Only Quincy Jones' inapt score drags proceedings down to ground level. There are some very good performances: Rod Taylor, as the endearingly upright and shrewd young manager; Melvyn Douglas as the owner, grumbling about skyscrapers that threaten to obscure his view; Kevin McCarthy as an all-devouring tycoon with his own personal version of the Lord's Prayer; and especially, Karl Malden as Keycase, the sneak thief who is here, there and everywhere, chuckling gleefully to himself and loping along the corridors like Groucho Marx. Richard Conte plays the crooked hotel detective.

Hotel Berlin ○
1945, US, 98 mins, b/w
Dir: Peter Godfrey
Stars: Helmut Dantine, Andrea King, Raymond Massey, Peter Lorre
Rating: ★★

If Bogart and Bacall had done the leading roles, this could have been a top-notch movie. As it is, what seems like half the Warner Brothers repertory company puts in some tremendous work in support of second-string stars Helmut Dantine and Andrea King. Particularly vivid performances come from Raymond Massey, Peter Lorre, George Coulouris, Henry Daniell and Steve Geray. From a novel by Vicki Baum, who seemed to have a thing about such settings: she also wrote *Grand Hotel*.

Hotel New Hampshire, The ● ⓥ
1984, US, 110 mins, colour
Dir: Tony Richardson
Stars: Rob Lowe, Jodie Foster, Beau Bridges, Nastassja Kinski, Matthew Modine
Rating: ★★★

Considered by many to be Tony Richardson's best film since *Tom Jones*, this is a Herculean adaptation of John Irving's extraordinary novel surveying life, love and death through the eyes of an eccentric American family. A stunning cast includes Rob Lowe and Jodie Foster as a brother and sister with an unhealthy fascination for each other, Matthew Modine in a dual role, Beau Bridges as the idealistic father and Nastassja Kinski as a girl who spends her life inside a bear suit. Adult audiences with a taste for the bizarre will find this black tale exerts a strange fascination that makes it one of a kind. Joey Richardson appears ever so briefly as a waitress.

Hotel Paradiso ○
1966, UK, 96 mins, colour
Dir: Peter Glenville
Stars: Alec Guinness, Gina Lollobrigida, Robert Morley, Peggy Mount
Rating: ★

Skittish cinema version of Feydeau's farce, with Alec Guinness skipping lightly through the kind of role he was already playing with practised ease (and rather better dialogue) in the early Fifties. The fun takes a while to get going, but when it does, the ins and outs of the different characters through hotel bedrooms are amusing enough. Watch out for scene-stealing Leonard Rossiter as a police inspector.

Hotel Sahara ○
1951, UK, 96 mins, b/w
Dir: Ken Annakin
Stars: David Tomlinson, Yvonne De Carlo, Peter Ustinov, Roland Culver
Rating: ★★★

This amusing trifle was one of several bright films that Hollywood star Yvonne De Carlo made in Britain in the early Fifties. Although the idea –

an exotic wartime desert hotel switching its loyalties according to the forces occupying it – is rather more amusing than the execution, there are two very funny performances: by David Tomlinson as a stiff upper-lipped English officer called Puffin, and by the inimitable Peter Ustinov as the ever-panicking proprietor of the hotel.

Hot Enough for June ○
(aka: Agent 8¾)
1963, UK, 98 mins, colour
Dir: Ralph Thomas
Stars: Dirk Bogarde, Sylva Koscina, Robert Morley, Leo McKern, John Le Mesurier
Rating: ★★

A satirical spy thriller that fails to make the most of its opportunities, with Dirk Bogarde playing a reluctant spy behind the Iron Curtain, and sharing a steamy love scene with sultry Sylva Koscina, who gives the whole film a lift every time she appears. The most suspenseful moments come, so to speak, at the last knockings, with Bogarde beating at the door of his embassy at six in the morning, and the secret police closing in. But there's a lot of irrelevant and slow travelling around Prague (*The Russia House* suffered from the same documentary diarrhoea) before the chase hots up. Bogarde gives his usual polished performance, and Robert Morley is given some opportunity to demonstrate his mastery of irony. Overall, *Hot Enough* is just about lukewarm.

Hot Millions ○
1968, UK, 106 mins, colour
Dir: Eric Till
Stars: Peter Ustinov, Maggie Smith, Karl Malden, Bob Newhart, Robert Morley, Cesar Romero
Rating: ★★★

Three delightful people who all make too few films – Peter Ustinov, Bob Newhart and Maggie Smith – combine in the frequently hilarious story of an embezzler who sets out to outwit a massive computer. The script – by Ustinov and Ira Wallach – crackles with dry wit, and Newhart and Karl Malden are almost as funny as the star while playing two executives called Gnatpole and Klemper, who must also be confounded by the embezzler. Newhart, in particular, is a delight as the sneaky Gnatpole, always trying to prove something against Ustinov, but never quite able to succeed. And Robert Morley, too, is ideally cast as the real computer expert

(impersonated by Ustinov who sends his rival off on a wild butterfly chase to South America). Ken Higgins' pleasing use of Metrocolor rounds it off.

Hot Pursuit ◐ ⓥ
1987, US, 93 mins, colour
Dir: Steven Lisberger
Stars: John Cusack, Robert Loggia, Wendy Gazelle
Rating: ★★

This lightweight comedy is a cross between a teen movie and a road film, with student John Cusack rushing to catch up with his girlfriend and her family who are off on what for him should be a dream holiday. It's all pretty silly, really, but young Mr Cusack gives an engaging performance which makes it worth sticking with. Having said that, it's not as good as Cusack's earlier and superficially similar comedy *The Sure Thing*. The story is set at a fast pace by director Steven Lisberger, who tends to ride quite well over the many plot bumps along the way.

Hot Rock, The ○
(aka: How to Steal a Diamond in Four Uneasy Lessons)
1972, US, 105 mins, colour
Dir: Peter Yates
Stars: Robert Redford, George Segal, Zero Mostel
Rating: ★★

British-born director Peter Yates had already made such a reputation directing top stars in big films – Steve McQueen in *Bullitt*, Dustin Hoffman in *John and Mary* and Peter O'Toole in *Murphy's War* – that he really couldn't go wrong with Robert Redford *and* George Segal in a glossy comedy-thriller about a robbery that does keep going wrong. Although William Goldman's script is not one of his best (or most stylish), there are all sorts of compensations from the actors. Redford engagingly spoofs his own image as the ice-cool (but inwardly ulcer-prone) robber-in-chief, Ron Leibman is very funny as Murch, who claims he can 'drive anything' and Willaim Redfield contributes a marvellous cameo as the harassed, paranoid police lieutenant. Yates makes ingenious use of his New York surroundings, coming up with all sorts of new locations and new angles on old locations: very much the same sort of precision job, in fact as in

H

Bullitt, but allowing room for the comedy to amuse and the suspense to bite.

Hot Shots! ◗ ⓥ
1991, US, 85 mins, colour
Dir: Jim Abrahams
Stars: Charlie Sheen, Cary Elwes, Valeria Golino, Lloyd Bridges, Kevin Dunn, Kristy Swanson
Rating: ★★★

A genial *Top Gun* spoof from the *Airplane!* guys. Lloyd Bridges is along for the flight again, as an admiral whose body has almost completely been replaced by spare parts, while Charlie Sheen has the Cruise role as 'Topper' Harley who, though suffering from Paternal Conflict Syndrome, knows that 'All my life I've wanted to fly. Bomb stuff. Shoot people down.' The unit psychiatrist (Valeria Golino) is a sculpting equestrian for whom Sheen falls 'like a blind roofer'. She also has a 'sizzling stomach' he can fry eggs on. There's a dastardly villain (played by once-incorruptibly Efrem Zimbalist Jr), some (very mild) spoofs of other movies and an Indian called Dances with Bikers. But Sheen will come through. 'After all,' he pronounces, producing a little box. 'I've got my father's eyes.' It's the kind of film that even offers you recipes (presumably to be cooked on Golino's tum) with the credits.

Hot Shots! Part Deux ◗ ⓥ
1993, US, 89 mins, colour
Dir: Jim Abrahams
Stars: Charlie Sheen, Valeria Golino, Lloyd Bridges, Brenda Bakke, Richard Crenna, Miguel Ferrer
Rating: ★★

Well, it's not as funny as part Un, and that's for sure. But there are so many attempted gags in this Hollywood spoof that some of them are bound to hit your particular funny bone. 'Topper' Harley (Charlie Sheen) is back, sent in by a demented US president (Lloyd Bridges) to get the men who went in to get the men taken captive by Iraq. There's a remarkable Saddam Hussein lookalike as a lisping villain and mostly weak take-offs of other movies. Sheen, all beefed up as Rambo the second, keeps a straight face throughout, although Valeria Golino has the best lines, delivered beautifully deadpan. It seems that she is shot at the climax, but no: her lucky Topper charm has stopped the bullet. 'My God,' says Sheen, 'I thought you were . . .' 'Gabriella Sabatini?' she re-

plies. 'Yes, I know, it happens all the time.' There are subtle jokes (though not many), background jokes, lavatorial jokes (lots of these) non-stop to the final credits that assure us that 'Prosthetic animals were used where necessary.' They're pot shots rather than hot shots, but comedy fans are guaranteed a chuckle or two.

Hot Spell ○
1958, US, 86 mins, b/w
Dir: Daniel Mann
Stars: Shirley Booth, Anthony Quinn, Shirley MacLaine
Rating: ★★

Shirley Booth, that arch-portrayer of put-upon women (remember her in *Come Back, Little Sheba*?), turns up acting trumps again as a middle-aged wife who suddenly finds her husband is contemplating running off with a girl in her twenties. Director Daniel Mann does an admirable job of catching the sultry and oppressive atmosphere of a small Louisiana town; and the three Oscar-winners in the cast (Miss Booth, Anthony Quinn and Eileen Heckart) are given sterling competition by Shirley MacLaine (pert and likeable as Miss Booth's romantic daughter), Earl Holliman, Jody Lawrance and Warren Stevens.

Hot Spot, The ● ⓥ
1990, US, 130 mins, colour
Dir: Dennis Hopper
Stars: Don Johnson, Virginia Madsen, Jennifer Connelly, Charles Martin Smith, William Sadler
Rating: ★★★

A slow and steamy modern version of a *film noir* – and, despite its too-long running time, quite an effective one at that. Don Johnson is Harry, who drifts into a small Texas town ostensibly looking for work, gets it as a car salesman and promptly becomes involved with two gorgeous women, his boss's predatory wife and the demure 19-year-old receptionist at the showroom. Wifey soon has him wrapped in her web, but he finds himself attracted to the younger girl, despite the fact that she seems to have a dark past. Even when the wife horrifies Harry by suggesting something might happen to aggravate her hubby's weak heart, we can see that things might have worked out well for Harry. But there's one thing we haven't told you: Harry is a travelling bank robber. And this is about to complicate his life no end. Johnson's surly charisma is just right for this role, while both the girls, in

different ways, ooze sexual come-hither. The atmosphere created is so tangibly fascinating, that you hardly realise the story doesn't have much action (apart from the sexual kind). Nice ending, too: apt but not too downbeat. A winner, but only on points.

Hot Spot
See: *I Wake Up Screaming*

Houdini ○
1953, US, 106 mins, colour
Dir: George Marshall
Stars: Tony Curtis, Janet Leigh, Torin Thatcher, Angela Clarke
Rating: ★★

A vivid account of the life of Harry Houdini, the famous escapologist. It's the film Tony Curtis rates as his 'personal' picture. 'The one I would gladly do for nothing,' he said while it was being made. Curtis was a natural for the part: he'd always been interested in magic and illusions and bore a passing resemblance to Houdini himself. The highlights of this earnest biography are Houdini's escape from an 'impregnable' Scotland Yard jail, his arrest in Germany as a fraud and his acquittal after a courtroom demonstration of his techniques. Another good trick was getting Janet Leigh, then Mrs Curtis, to play Mrs Houdini.

Hound of the Baskervilles, The ○
1939, US, 80 mins, b/w
Dir: Sidney Lanfield
Stars: Richrd Greene, Basil Rathbone, Nigel Bruce, Lionel Atwill, John Carradine
Rating: ★★★

Sherlock Holmes found his finest interpreter in the skeletal shape of coolly calculating Basil Rathbone in this splendidly atmospheric version of Conan Doyle's most famous story. Mists swirl, hounds bay, bodies go bump in the night and the game's afoot. 'You surely don't believe in that ridiculous hound legend?' protests Richard Greene, which disqualifies his character from any further sympathy. With Nigel Bruce as Dr Watson, Rathbone went on to gallop through 13 further Holmes adventures, ending the series in 1946.

Hound of the Baskervilles, The ◗
1959, UK, 84 mins, colour
Dir: Terence Fisher

Stars: Peter Cushing, André Morell, Christopher Lee, Marla Landi
Rating: ★★

Hammer horror meets Sir Arthur Conan Doyle. And with Peter Cushing as Sherlock Holmes, the scene is well and truly set for a chilling film version of the most famous Baker Street mystery of all. The scenes on the moors, as the famous hound bays his way towards another killing, are just what Hammer's top director, Terence Fisher, ordered.

Hound of the Baskervilles, The ◐

1977, UK, 84 mins, colour
Dir: Paul Morrissey
Stars: Peter Cook, Dudley Moore, Joan Greenwood
Rating: ★

Peter Cook and Dudley Moore's own version of Sherlock Holmes' most famous adventure, full of trusty old jokes and frenziedly acted by an all-too-distinguished cast. The direction is almost non-existent, allowing Messrs Cook and Moore to run riot over the plot as well as the Devon moors. But one running gag involving Denholm Elliott's chihuahua is screamingly funny if only by dint of sheer persistence, and cleverly sustained to keep you chuckling for minutes.

Hour of Glory

See: The Small Back Room

Hour of the Gun ○

1967, US, 109 mins, colour
Dir: John Sturges
Stars: James Garner, Jason Robards Jr, Robert Ryan
Rating: ★★

One of the many films made about the Earp brothers and Doc Holliday, this was made by John Sturges, one of Hollywood's best directors of Westerns. His record includes *Bad Day at Black Rock*, *The Magnificent Seven* and that other film about the Earps, *Gunfight at the OK Corral*, whose story this film continues. Jon Voight can be seen in one of his earliest screen roles. There's a surging beginning, but the film's adrenalin gradually drains away.

Hour of the Pig, The ● ⓥ

1993, UK, 117 mins, colour
Dir: Leslie Megahey
Stars: Colin Firth, Ian Holm, Amina Annabi, Donald Pleasence, Nicol

Williamson, Lysette Anthony
Rating: ★★★

Bawdy, Breughelesque and bizarre, this is a good-looking, well-constructed black drama that crosses a medieval mystery with portraits of ignorance and fear. The setting is rural 15th century France. A city lawyer (Colin Firth) finds himself in a society where witches are still burnt at the stake, evil and superstition are kings, women drop their chemises at the merest hint of interest and an animal can be tried and condemned on the same charges as a human. When a pig is accused of killing a young Jewish boy, it seems to the lawyer that the accusation hides a more complex sequence of events involving the human population of the village, but the pig belongs to the Egyptian gypsy girl (Amina Annabi) to whom he has taken a fancy. Watchable and well-considered performances by Firth, Ian Holm, Donald Pleasence, Nicol Williamson and Lysette Anthony make this an interesting companion to films like *The Name of the Rose*. The squalor of medieval life is convincingly portrayed, while never being allowed to get in the way of the plot.

House ● ⓥ

1986, US, 93 mins, colour
Dir: Steve Miner
Stars: William Katt, George Wendt, Richard Moll, Kay Lenz
Rating: ★★

Successful but highly derivative horror film about a man who seems to have inherited a house full of demons. William Katt is the man with a monster in every closet. Kay Lenz is wasted in the too-brief role of his estranged wife.

House II: The Second Story ◐ ⓥ

1987, US, 88 mins, colour
Dir: Ethan Wiley
Stars: Arye Gross, Jonathan Stark, Royal Dano
Rating: ★★★

You can't believe this was the film the producers of *House* expected when they asked Ethan Wiley, who scripted it, to write and direct a sequel. You can forget about the guts and gore, because this is a horror comedy, with the emphasis on the latter – somewhat after the style of old Vincent Price films like *The Raven*, but much more zany.

Houseboat ○

1958, US, 110 mins, colour
Dir: Melville Shavelson
Stars: Cary Grant, Sophia Loren, Martha Hyer
Rating: ★★★

Sophia Loren's first Hollywood comedy was this winsome fable about a widower who falls for the Italian girl who looks after his three children. With Cary Grant as the widower, it's guaranteed to skate skilfully over the stickier patches.

House by the River ○

1950, US, 95 mins, b/w
Dir: Fritz Lang
Stars: Louis Hayward, Lee Bowman, Jane Wyatt
Rating: ★★★

In a story that may send a shiver or two up your spine, Louis Hayward accidentally kills his housemaid while trying to seduce her, then tries to blame her death on his brother. When his wife discovers the truth, he has to consider killing them both. This seemingly improbable melodrama is given a stylistic lift by the fact that it was directed by Fritz Lang, who makes the whole thing visually moody and intriguing. Stilted acting by Hayward, Lee Bowman and Jane Wyatt stops this thriller being any more than interesting, the film's undeniable style not disguising a lack of content. Keep tuned, though, for a chilling, eye-opening ending that will have video viewers freezing frames to see how the director did it.

House Calls ○

1978, US, 98 mins, colour
Dir: Howard Zieff
Stars: Walter Matthau, Glenda Jackson, Art Carney, Richard Benjamin
Rating: ★★★

This romantic comedy is very much in the Seventies style, and, thanks to the skills of Walter Matthau and Glenda Jackson, you'll laugh out loud at some parts of this story of a widowed doctor wooing a salty but lovable divorcee. And Art Carney is a scream as the head of surgery at Matthau's hospital. The funny bits, though, aren't strung together well enough to make a successful whole. The film attempts to be endearing, but only succeeds in spurts. Ronald Neame showed how to direct the tasty Jackson-Matthau pairing to rather better effect in *Hopscotch* a couple of years later.

H

House in Nightmare Park, The ◐
(aka: Crazy House)
1973, UK, 95 mins, colour
Dir: Peter Sykes
Stars: Frankie Howerd, Ray Milland
Rating: ★★★

It's just one darned thing after another for our hapless hero in this delightfully old-fashioned comedy thriller. Frankie Howerd revels in the chance to mix chuckles with chills as a fifth-rate entertainer invited out to a gloomy mansion by a weird collection of aristocrats. Things start to go bump in the night with hectic regularity on his arrival, and it isn't long before bodies begin to follow them. The proceedings are decked up in good style by director Peter Sykes, who stages his more gasp-provoking moments with considerable expertise. But the giggles hold their own in the midst of the mayhem. One look at Howerd's crabbed expression is likely to have you falling about. In the centre of a film such as this, he's invaluable. There's a hair-raising scene in a snake-pit, and other developments it wouldn't be fair to reveal. Ray Milland heads the would-be deadly relations.

Housekeeping ○
1987, US, 116 mins, colour
Dir: Bill Forsyth
Stars: Christine Lahti, Sara Walker, Andrea Burchill
Rating: ★★

As a change of pace from his Scottish comedies, director Bill Forsyth made this affectionate memoir of a girl's Canadian childhood, spent in the care – if that's the word – of an eccentric slattern of an aunt, who seems previously to have been some kind of hobo, and keeps crackers in her pockets for the runaway children who live in the frosty woods. The seasons are caught so well that we can almost smell and feel woodsmoke and winter chill. But the film is long and slow for its content, and only occasionally achieves the poignancy for which it strives. It lacks the charismatic spark that the original casting of Diane Keaton might have given it: Christine Lahti is a fine actress, but altogether too down-to-earth for this flaky character. The two girls, Sara Walker and Andrea Burchill, are entirely adequate without having quite the appeal to make their emotions ours.

House of Angels ● ⓥ
1992, Sweden, 121 mins, colour
Dir: Colin Nutley
Stars: Helena Bergstrom, Rikard Wolff, Ernst Gunther, Per Oscarsson
Rating: ★★

A Swedish manor house and the surrounding forest, much coveted by local farmers and businessmen, is left by her grandfather to a nightclub entertainer (Helena Bergstrom) of somewhat shady background. Together with her equally shady cohort, a devil-eyed fellow-entertainer with stubble and earrings, she arrives, leather-clad on a motor bike, to claim the inheritance – and tongues soon start wagging in the small village that adjoins the manor. Although ensuing developments do go on a bit, there is charm and perception in equal proportions as director Colin Nutley details the self-righteousness and prejudice among people who are often more perverted than the newcomers they talk about behind their hands. The story goes a bit awry with the arrival of the heiress's clubland friends, but rights itself again before the end, even if what remains is a film with not quite enough of the right stuff.

House of Bamboo ○
1954, US, 102 mins, colour
Dir: Samuel Fuller
Stars: Robert Ryan, Robert Stack, Cameron Mitchell, Shirley Yamaguchi, Brad Dexter
Rating: ★★

Twentieth Century-Fox went east to make this detective thriller – not to Hong Kong, but Japan, where some interesting backdrops make a welcome change from those of New York, Chicago or San Francisco. Robert Ryan delivers a cold, passionless and precise portrait of a greedy killer. Director Samuel Fuller went on to become something of a 'cult' discovery.

House of Dracula ◐
1945, US, 67 mins, b/w
Dir: Erle C Kenton
Stars: Lon Chaney Jr, John Carradine, Onslow Stevens, Glenn Strange
Rating: ★★

All the monsters get together for the last in the Universal series, before they met Abbott and Costello. The director of this shocker was Erle C Kenton, who directed innumerable horror films for the studio, including *Ghost of*

Frankenstein, *House Of Frankenstein* and *The Cat Creeps*. Probably, his most successful essay into the bizarre was the 1932 classic, *Island Of Lost Souls*, with Charles Laughton and Bela Lugosi.

House of Frankenstein ◐
1944, US, 71 mins, b/w
Dir: Erle C Kenton
Stars: Boris Karloff, John Carradine, Lon Chaney Jr, J Carroll Naish, Lionel Atwill, George Zucco
Rating: ★★

By the time this contribution to the Universal horror series came out, Hollywood audiences were no longer content with one monster, or even two. The producers reasoned that three monsters, a mad scientist and a hunchback should prove enough for even the most avid horror fan. They also threw in every available actor with a reputation in the genre. Not surprisingly things fuse here, there and everywhere in more ways than one. And it's rather unnerving to see Boris Karloff as the scientist working on the creature (now portrayed by ex-cowboy Glenn Strange) that Karloff had made immortal 15 years earlier.

House of Fright
See: The Two Faces of Dr Jekyll

House of Games ● ⓥ
1987, US, 102 mins, colour
Dir: David Mamet
Stars: Lindsay Crouse, Joe Mantegna, Mike Nussbaum, J T Walsh
Rating: ★★★

Fancy a psychological up-market version of *The Sting*? Then come with writer-director David Mamet to the con-man's kingdom, in a sleazy corner of the city, called the *House of Games*. Psychiatrist Lindsay Crouse enters its portals, to become enmeshed in a world where the swiftness of the lip deceives the ear. You, the viewer, may think yourself a step ahead of her, but be careful, as master-puppeteer Mamet is inclined to change the rules as he goes along. Clever it is, and fun too, with appropriately strange, stylised performances by players who seem almost under hypnosis.

House of Numbers ○
1957, US, 92 mins, b/w
Dir: Russell Rouse
Stars: Jack Palance, Barbara Lang, Harold J Stone
Rating: ★★

Much of this MGM production was filmed in San Quentin prison. And director Russell Rouse's search for realism did not end there, for he persuaded the authorities to allow him to use the prison warders and some of the inmates as 'extras'. It's a stark prison drama with Jack Palance giving a tougher-than-tough performance as a homicidal maniac – and playing the killer's brother in a softer key.

House of Rothschild, The ○
1933, US, 95 mins, b/w
Dir: Alfred Werker
Stars: George Arliss, Boris Karloff, Loretta Young, Robert Young, C Aubrey Smith
Rating: ★★★

A lavish historical drama with George Arliss – who won an Oscar in 1930 for his portrayal of Disraeli – giving an excellent account of himself in the dual role of patriarch Mayer Rothschild and his son Nathan. The screenplay, by director-to-be Nunnally Johnson, makes for compelling viewing and Alfred Werker's workmanlike direction gets the most out of it and out of his strong cast. Loretta Young is excellent as Arliss' daughter, Robert Young is sympathetic as her suitor and Boris Karloff, three years after his surge to stardom as the monster in *Frankenstein*, provides a highly enjoyable study in suave villainy. The last few minutes of this film are in colour.

House of Secrets ○
1956, UK, 95 mins, colour
Dir: Guy Green
Stars: Michael Craig, Julia Arnall, Brenda de Banzie, David Kossof
Rating: ★★

Enjoyed by critics and cinemagoers alike, this exciting crime drama about a gang of counterfeiters made a star of Michael Craig, a former extra who had been confined to minor roles in the early Fifties, and did very well at the box-office. It certainly raised the level of the British thriller to that of the best American 'B' movies, which was a considerable jump at the time. Craig punches well, and shaped up as a star with all the attack, confidence and charm of a British Robert Mitchum. American actress Barbara Bates, whose career would soon be ended by ill-health, is a pleasant heroine: she and Austrian-born Julia Arnall bring a welcome touch of warmth to the slam-bang thick-ear thrills. And that fine character actress

Brenda de Banzie revels in her casting as the mysterious and menacing Madame Ballu. The supporting cast is crammed with a fine selection of those European-born actors who made their careers largely in British films, including Anton Diffring, Eric Pohlmann, Jacques Brunius and Eugene Deckers.

House of Spirits, The ● ⓥ
1993, US/Germany/Denmark/Portugal, 147 mins, colour
Dir: Bille August
Stars: Jeremy Irons, Meryl Streep, Glenn Close, Winona Ryder, Antonio Banderas
Rating: ★

Here's ammunition for those who say that foreign directors these days shouldn't be allowed to make anything without subtitles. Bille August's *Best Intentions* was a deserved international success, but best intentions are not enough when it comes to this massive screen adaptation of Isabel Allende's epic novel. Rarely has 147 minutes seemed longer and the ironic thing is, in this telling of Allende's saga, there seems hardly enough plot for an hour and a half. Meryl Streep is the fey spirit who can move objects and foresee the future; she marries hopeful miner Jeremy Irons, attempting a downright peculiar accent. He becomes the ruthless patron of a hacienda, but his daughter (Winona Ryder) gets involved with a budding revolutionary (Antonio Banderas) who is the antithesis of everything Irons stands for. Somewhere in this is Glenn Close as Irons' sister, yearning after both her brother and his bride, but clearly auditioning for the role Mrs Danvers in the sequel to *Rebecca*. Most of the lines are delivered by the actors as if in a trance and, despite the occasional emotive moment, the film never reaches the epic scale to which it aspires.

House of Strangers ○
1949, US, 101 mins, b/w
Dir: Joseph L Mankiewicz
Stars: Edward G Robinson, Susan Hayward, Richard Conte, Efrem Zimbalist Jr
Rating: ★★★

Dynamic drama, told in the flashback form much favoured at the time, about a father's suffocating influence on his several sons. The style of the film makes it seem like a sort of *I Remember Papa*, but there's nothing very kindly about the character so vividly

etched by Edward G Robinson. Richard Conte and Luther Adler are effectively contrasted as the principal sons, and there are early screen appearances for Efrem Zimbalist Jr (later the star of numerous television series) and Debra Paget. The studio, Fox, remade the film five years later as a Western, *Broken Lance*, with Spencer Tracy memorable in the Robinson role.

House of the Long Shadows ●
1982, UK, 101 mins, colour
Dir: Pete Walker
Stars: Vincent Price, Peter Cushing, Christopher Lee, Desi Arnaz Jr, John Carradine, Julie Peasgood
Rating: ★★

Take care how you rate this one: it will throw all your judgments back in your face in the last reel. An American author (Desi Arnaz Jr) is sent to an isolated Welsh manor by his publisher (Richard Todd) to win a bet that he can write a book in 24 hours. The manor is alive with mystery, not to mention two caretakers (cadaverous John Carradine and glaze-eyed Sheila Keith), Vincent Price in a red bow-tie, Christopher Lee looking bad-tempered and Peter Cushing posturing madly. But remember, nothing in this old ghouls' reunion is what it seems, not even the story or the history behind the story. At the end two 'normal' twists are followed by two 'super-normal' twists and even a twist tailpiece, which is something of an anti-climax since by this time, we're conditioned to expect anything. Writer Michael Armstrong must have sat up for months thinking it all out and deserves credit for the plot if not most of the dialogue, only some of which is intentionally funny. 'Ah, piano wire,' muses Price, inspecting the throttled body of Ms Keith. 'He must have heard her sing.' We, too, have heard her sing . . .

House of the Seven Hawks, The ○
1959, US, 100 mins, b/w
Dir: Richard Thorpe
Stars: Robert Taylor, Nicole Maurey, Linda Christian
Rating: ★★

A thriller based on a Victor Canning novel which contains enough red herrings to fill a creel. Unfortunately, all these complications only bog the film down so that, despite its team of stars, it never rises much above the ordinary. Robert Taylor and Linda

H

Christian are the stars, but the biggest surprise in this film is David Kossoff's role. Usually cast as the mildest and most inoffensive of men, he plays Wilhelm Dekker who, from his first appearance on the screen, is obviously up to no good. He is one of the people who make life complicated for our hero.

House of Wax ◐
1953, US, 88 mins, colour
Dir: André De Toth
Stars: Vincent Price, Frank Lovejoy, Phyllis Kirk, Carolyn Jones, Charles Bronson
Rating: ★★★

Warner Brothers moved fast to cash in on the short-lived Fifties boom in 3-D films, remaking their 1933 chiller *Mystery of the Wax Museum* in under two weeks and cleaning up at the box office in the process. It retains most of its power, even when it's shown 'flat', due in great measure to Vincent Price's gleefully horrid performance as the mad wax museum proprietor who uses real bodies as a basis for his immobile exhibits. Phyllis Kirk makes an attractive heroine with a nice line in screams, Charles Bronson puts in an early screen appearance, here billed as Charles Buchinski, and most wondrous of all, the film was directed by André de Toth who, because he had only one eye, was unable to see in three dimensions!

House on Carroll Street, The ◐ ⓥ
1987, US, 101 mins, colour
Dir: Peter Yates
Stars: Kelly McGillis, Jeff Daniels, Mandy Patinkin, Jessica Tandy
Rating: ★★★

A decent looking thriller set in 1951 which actually achieves the effect of looking as if it were made at that time. Nothing much wrong with that, although the excitements and characters come across as a shade dated and the plot is made to develop from time to time with the benefit of rather improbable events. Kelly McGillis is strong in the central role of a girl who finds that the senate witchhunter probing her for Communist-affiliated activities is actually the power behind a rather more sinister plot to introduce illegal refugees into America by giving them the identities of dead men. Peter Yates' direction of these nefarious events brings one much in mind of Hitchcock and, although the Master would have hastened the pace

here and there, this is a very respectable job of work, with a nicely balanced plot in which characters make logical moves, bursts of action and a typical suspense-film climax in and around (and above) a huge railway station.

House on Haunted Hill ◐
1958, US, 76 mins, b/w
Dir: William Castle
Stars: Vincent Price, Carol Ohmart, Richard Long, Elisha Cook
Rating: ★★

Horror producer/director William Castle was well known for introducing gimmicks in the auditoria of cinemas showing his films. For this haunted house chiller he arranged for a full-size skeleton to 'leap' from the screen and descend on cinemagoers along a hidden wire – a gimmick dubbed 'emergo'. But word soon got around about the stunt and the skeleton was pelted with food and boxes from the concession kiosk each time it appeared. It's silly but good fun as Vincent Price arranges shocks for his house guests while his wife arranges to have him shot as an 'accident'. There are even a couple of genuine shocks among the floating sheets and banging windows.

House on 92nd Street, The ○
1945, US, 84 mins, b/w
Dir: Henry Hathaway
Stars: William Eythe, Lloyd Nolan, Signe Hasso, Gene Lockhart
Rating: ★★★★

This drama about a Nazi spy ring was one of the best thrillers that Hollywood ever made. Taut, tense, intricate and really suspenseful, with a superb climax, it set the fashion for a whole host of imitations. Advanced camera techniques, allied to a clever mystery plot, and a brisk, semi-documentary approach by director Henry Hathaway, produced a film worthy of Hitchcock at his best. Its hero, William Eythe, was among the foremost young leading men of the Forties. But his career was dogged by illness, and he died in 1957 at the age of 39. Making his screen debut in a small role: E G (then known as Everett G) Marshall.

House Party ● ⓥ
1990, US, 104 mins, colour
Dir: Reginald Hudlin
Stars: Christopher Reid, Christopher Martin, Robin Harris
Rating: ★

If this is black American teenage life, show us the door marked Exit. In downtown Blaxville, USA, a party is only a flop if the loo gets clogged or one of the partygoers ends in jail. A guy ain't got a prayer if he can't talk the lingo and a girl only respects a man if he asks her if she's on the pill before he pins her to the bed. British cinema goers will need subtitles and a phrase-book to even get to first base with this modern equivalent of the teenage pop musical. Modern black music can be served well, as *Beat Street* showed. But *House Party* is too concerned with its own image to tool its scenario towards some kind of entertainment. The only scene to break through the generations and amuse us all is when the scrawny hero desperately tries to rap-talk his way out of a cellblock gang bang.

Housesitter ○ ⓥ
1992, US, 102 mins, colour
Dir: Frank Oz
Stars: Steve Martin, Goldie Hawn, Dana Delany, Julie Harris
Rating: ★★

Not exactly the blast of laughter you'd expect from a teaming of Steve Martin and Goldie Hawn, this is an inconsequential romantic comedy that's good for a few chuckles but rather more yawns. Martin's a stuck-in-a-rut architect whose girlfriend (Dana Delany) turns him and his dream house down. Rebounding to a one-night stand with waitress Hawn, Martin arrives at the (empty) house one day to find that Hawn has moved in, having convinced his parents and the whole town that they're married. Martin and Hawn never convince you of their attraction for one another here, and you keep thinking he should marry Delany until the script makes her turn around into a bit of a bitch.

House That Dripped Blood, The ●
1970, UK, 101 mins, colour
Dir: Peter Duffell
Stars: Peter Cushing, Christopher Lee, Ingrid Pitt
Rating: ★★

Talented director Peter Duffell creates some good shock moments during this quartet of horror stories from the pen of Robert (*Psycho*) Bloch. Ingrid Pitt is in fine, fang-baring form with another of her vampire ladies, and the house – rich, dark and filled with shadows – is quite a character in itself. But the most chilling story is the third, with Chloe Franks (the teenage heroine of Disney's *Escape from the Dark*) as a devil-child more genuinely evil than anything out of *The Innocents*. The sombre and brooding atmosphere here is a welcome contrast to the comic-book horror of the other episodes.

Hoverbug, The ⊙
1970, UK, 57 mins, colour
Dir: Jan Darnley-Smith
Stars: Jill Riddick, John Trayhorn, Arthur Howard
Rating: ★★★

Dick Brewster and his sister Jenny build a hovercraft to enter in a race, but it keeps fallng apart. Luckily, Mr Watt, an eccentric inventor, has invented a high-powered glue, but is it the answer to their problems? An entertaining children's comedy, with the hovercraft race itself as an exciting climax. The Hoverbug of the title is a whimsical, Heath-Robinson-style creation. Character actor Arthur Howard enjoys himself as the dotty Mr Watt, and Jill Riddick and John Trayhorn are delightfully natural as Dick and Jenny.

Howard . . . A New Breed of Hero
See: Howard the Duck

Howards End ○ ⓥ
1991, UK, 142 mins, colour
Dir: James Ivory
Stars: Anthony Hopkins, Vanessa Redgrave, Helena Bonham Carter, Emma Thompson, James Wilby, Samuel West
Rating: ★★★★

The most successful adaptation of an E M Forster novel to date, and the best Merchant-Ivory film in quite a while. Vigorously shot and immaculately set, the story starts in 1910 when the fates of the conventional, upper-class Wilcox family and the free-thinking, upper middle-class Schlegels begin to intertwine. Several threads of the plot have already been set in motion when Mrs Wilcox (Vanessa Redgrave) leaves her house, Howards End, to the older Miss Schlegel (Emma Thompson), with whom she has developed a warm friendship. Because her wishes are written in pencil, and have no weight in law, the Wilcoxes decide to burn them, setting in motion a momentous, often tragic sequence of events that need never have happened. All this is related in terms of some feisty dialogue by Ruth Prawer Jhabvala,

intelligent stuff that sounds like the conversation of real people. Given this impetus, the players rise to the occasion. Anthony Hopkins' excellence under such circumstances tends to be taken for granted, but Thompson and Helena Bonham Carter are both better than one could possibly have imagined, and James Wilby, clearly relishing playing a nasty piece of work, is a more effective actor than heretofore. Tony Pierce-Roberts' mobile camera work makes the most of the settings, too, from the countryside, through St Pancras Station, to the dusty, cavernous offices of an insurance company. Thompson's subsequent Oscar was richly deserved.

Howard the Duck ○
(aka: Howard . . . A New Breed of Hero)
1986, US, 110 mins, colour
Dir: Willard Huyck
Stars: Lea Thompson, Jeffrey Jones, Tim Robbins

First shown as *Howard the Duck*, but soon dubbed 'Howard the Turkey', this tiresome and embarrassing fantasy adventure proved that *Star Wars* creator George Lucas didn't always have his finger on the pulse of popular taste. It was retitled *Howard . . . a New Breed of Hero* in Britain, presumably to disguise the fact that the star is a duck! Based on the adventures of a Marvel Comics character, it laid an egg that, far from being golden, cost Universal Studios millions.

How Green Was My Valley ○ ⓥ
1941, US, 118 mins, b/w
Dir: John Ford
Stars: Walter Pidgeon, Maureen O'Hara, Donald Crisp, Roddy McDowall, Barry Fitzgerald, Anna Lee
Rating: ★★★★

Award-winning John Ford tearjerker about life in a Welsh mining village at the end of the 19th century. Beautiful performances by Donald Crisp, Sara Allgood, Roddy McDowall and Barry Fitzgerald produce the maximum impact, especially in the climactic scenes. The Welsh village set, designed by Nathan Juran and Richard Day, is one of the best ever constructed in Hollywood, and turned up in several other films in subsequent years. Juran and Day deservedly took one of the production's many Oscars, which also included awards for Best Film (against strong competition) and Best Director.

How I Won the War ◐
1967, UK, 110 mins, colour
Dir: Richard Lester
Stars: Michael Crawford, John Lennon, Roy Kinnear, Lee Montague
Rating: ★★★

Richard Lester's surrealistic comedy about a small group of soldiers in World War Two is as black a film as you would ever wish to see in colour. The initial 20 minutes are hilarious in Goon Show style, with satire lurking somewhere to the rear, but the film soon develops into a bloodstrewn, charnel-house allegory about unnecessary blood-letting and blatant disregard for human life. The platoon of eight soldiers are, you may think, merely symbols. Six are expendable players in the 'game' of war. The seventh (Michael Crawford) may be Everyman. The eighth (Jack MacGowran) is, in my interpretation, Death. For all its underlying seriousness, the film contains glimpses of humour throughout the mayhem. Funniest of all is Michael Hordern's veteran campaigner, forever referring to 'the wily Pathan'.

Howling, The ● ⓥ
1980, US, 91 mins, colour
Dir: Joe Dante
Stars: Dee Wallace, Patrick Macnee, Dennis Dugan
Rating: ★★★

The special make-up effects by Rick Baker, later to amaze us on *An American Werewolf in London* and other modern horror films, give an extra dimension to this fang-in-cheek werewolf chiller in which many of the character names are those of directors associated with cinematic terror. Patrick Macnee has a field day as the psychologist involved in dangerous research into werewolves (it must have been almost like playing a villain from *The Avengers*), while ubiquitous character actor Dick Miller crops up as Walter Paisley, whom he originally created in *A Bucket of Blood* (whose director, Roger Corman, is another guest star). Director Joe Dante later enjoyed even more spectacular success with *Gremlins*. Five sequels followed, none of them anywhere near as much fun as this.

How Sweet It Is! ○
1968, US, 99 mins, colour
Dir: Jerry Paris
Stars: James Garner, Debbie Reynolds, Maurice Ronet
Rating: ★★★

H

This film springs a rare surprise: a Hollywood comedy about the generation gap that is actually very funny. Every character has a personality of its own. Only the sex jokes are sometimes clumsy. James Garner, friendly with his teenage son like never before (while Mum Debbie Reynolds is fending off the advances of a Riviera playboy), even takes to wearing his offspring's hippie neck-charm. The hotel clerk is horrified. 'It symbolises love and peace,' snarls Garner. 'Y'wanna make something of it?'

How the West was Won ○ ⓥ

1962, US, 162 mins, colour
Dir: John Ford, George Marshall
Stars: James Stewart, Henry Fonda, Gregory Peck, Debbie Reynolds, Richard Widmark, John Wayne
Rating: ★★★

The American West has a mighty and turbulent history, some of which is told, in story and folk song, in this epic movie, originally in Cinerama and photographed in gorgeous Metrocolor, which is somewhat dampened down in transition to wide screen – though some early scenes still rate with the best of the West. The storyline is inevitably somewhat bitty: the Civil War is the shortest section and the weakest, and somewhere or other there's a pocket version of every Western you ever saw. Not many of the actors have a chance to register (and certainly not Henry Fonda under a yard of beard), but Debbie Reynolds, surprisingly, is supreme here in a performance that epitomises the spirit of the early West – at least as Hollywood saw it.

How to Commit Marriage ○

1969, US, 95 mins, colour
Dir: Norman Panama
Stars: Bob Hope, Jane Wyman, Jackie Gleason
Rating: ★★

Bob Hope and the modern scene never did mix. His comedy technique belonged essentially to a world of fiendish oriental spies, mad doctors and anything that exposed a yellow streak running up the centre of his back. Thus it's not surprising that the most successful parts of this latter-day Bob Hope comedy are his exchanges with fellow-veteran Jackie Gleason as an alcoholic impresario. ('Your breath,' Hope tells him, 'could start the windmill on an old Dutch paint-

ing') and the occasionally very funny visual gags, especially the ending. Less successful are interludes with Hope as hippie or mystic, invading the world of his teenage daughter, who has decided to live with her fiancé, when her parents decide to divorce.

How to Get Ahead in Advertising ● ⓥ

1988, UK, 98 mins, colour
Dir: Bruce Robinson
Stars: Richard E Grant, Rachel Ward, Richard Johnson
Rating: ★★

A black horror-comic that might have emanated from Ealing Studios had they still been going 30 years on. Obsessed with the pressure of coming up with an advertising campaign for a boil cream, ad exec Bagley (Richard E Grant) freaks out. Himself having a boil, he imagines it having life (and voice) of it's own, representing the Hyde in him to his own Jekyll. Eventually the boil takes over . . . or did it all really happen? We'll never know because the film leaves us in no-mans-land. Grant never quite sounds as though he believes in all this, even with such prime lines as 'My Grandfather was caught molesting a wallaby in Sydney Zoo in 1919. He put his hand in its pouch . . .' Rachel Ward is okay as his long-suffering wife but, despite some good laughs, the film doesn't quite have the consistency, pace or bite to grip our attention (and funny-bone) throughout.

How to Marry a Millionaire ○ ⓥ

1953, US, 95 mins, colour
Dir: Jean Negulesco
Stars: Marilyn Monroe, Betty Grable, Lauren Bacall, David Wayne, Rory Calhoun, William Powell
Rating: ★★★

A familiar story of a trio of gold-diggers on the prowl in New York, this was the second CinemaScope feature. The three huntresses are attractively played by Betty Grable, Marilyn Monroe, who makes myopia entertaining, and Lauren Bacall, who has all the best lines and delivers them stylishly. The film has more good humour, perhaps, than real wit, but director Jean Negulesco makes it all very pleasing to watch, with William Powell scoring for the men, who include David Wayne, Cameron Mitchell and Rory Calhoun.

How to Murder a Rich Uncle ○

1957, UK, 80 mins, b/w
Dir: Nigel Patrick
Stars: Nigel Patrick, Charles Coburn, Wendy Hiller
Rating: ★★

Things going bump in the night are mostly the bodies resulting from bungled attempts to kill off old Uncle George in this British comedy of terrors. Michael Caine can be glimpsed carrying people around and uttering an occasional grunt; and that lovable little old lady, Katie Johnson, gives a rib-tickling performance as one of Uncle George's relatives. But stardom, which had found her suddenly with *The Ladykillers*, was not to last for long. She died later the same year at the age of 78.

How to Murder Your Wife ○ ⓥ

1964, US, 118 mins, colour
Dir: Richard Quine
Stars: Jack Lemmon, Virna Lisi, Terry-Thomas, Claire Trevor
Rating: ★★

Eddie Mayehoff, a jovial gent with black button eyes, steals what laughs there are going from under the noses of such experienced comedy stars as Jack Lemmon and Terry-Thomas in this black comedy. Unfortunately, like Lemmon, fed on a diet of pasta by an unwanted wife, it gets progressively more heavy. And if you had a wife as tiresome as Virna Lisi, you might want to drop her into a cement mixer, too. This was the film on which Lemmon had a brush with death when a fire escape stunt went wrong. Falling, he was able to hook his arm on to a steel pipe, sustaining arm, shoulder and chest strains that troubled him for months afterwards.

How to Steal a Diamond in Four Uneasy Lessons
See: The Hot Rock

How to Steal a Million ○

1966, US, 120 mins, colour
Dir: William Wyler
Stars: Audrey Hepburn, Peter O'Toole, Eli Wallach, Hugh Griffith, Charles Boyer
Rating: ★★★

Elegant Audrey Hepburn delivers the goods in more than one in this comedy about an attempt to steal a priceless statue. Director William Wyler also guided her through her Oscar-winning performance in

Roman Holiday, and this girl is such fun to watch – the voice, the face are ever-changing, completely individual. And it's not so much what Givenchy clothes do for Audrey as what she does for Givenchy. There's a sly joke about Givenchy, in fact, during the sleek proceedings, the pièce de resistance of which is the robbery itself, in which Topkapi-like safety precautions have to be overcome. Three French matinee idols of the thirties – Charles Boyer, Fernand Gravet and Marcel Dalio – appear in supporting roles, each in his 60s, but all as debonair as ever. And a fat comedian called Moustache is very funny as a museum guard.

How to Succeed in Business Without Really Trying ○
1967, US, 121 mins, colour
Dir: David Swift
Stars: Robert Morse, Michele Lee, Rudy Vallee
Rating: ★★★

Bright, colourful, zestful musical in the best Hollywood traditions. Robert Morse is most engaging as the young man who starts off in the post-room of a big firm, and succeeds so well that the executives eventually have to band together to stop him getting higher. Michele Lee is entrancing as the girl-friend who watches over him, and sings beautifully, especially in 'I Believe in You'. It's a crime that she was seen so seldom in films. Individual numbers are vividly staged with a zip only seen since in *Cabaret*. The gutsy score, organised, garish colour and fluid, physical camerawork all pay tribute to the heyday of the American musical.

Hucksters, The ○
1947, US, 115 mins, b/w
Dir: Jack Conway
Stars: Clark Gable, Deborah Kerr, Sydney Greenstreet, Ava Gardner
Rating: ★★★

Slick, sophisticated satire aimed squarely at the con-men and sharks of the immediate post-war American advertising world. Clark Gable is at his suave, fast-talking best as brash Vic Norman, who takes New York's ad-world by storm – then finds rough weather brewing when he clashes with a sadistic soap magnate, played to dictatorial perfection by Sydney Greenstreet. It was Deborah Kerr's first Hollywood film, but it was Ava Gardner who most boosted her Hol-

lywood stock, displaying a gift for satirical comedy which few suspected she possessed.

Hud ○
1963, US, 112 mins, b/w
Dir: Martin Ritt
Stars: Paul Newman, Patricia Neal, Melvyn Douglas, Brandon de Wilde
Rating: ★★★★

Martin Ritt's brilliant 'modern Western'. Paul Newman dominates the film as Hud, 'the man with the barbed wire soul', while Patricia Neal's sensitive portrayal as Alma won her an Academy Award. Other Oscars went to Melvyn Douglas as Best Supporting Actor, and to veteran cinematographer James Wong Howe (his second Academy Award) for his fine black-and-white camerawork. Director Ritt keeps a firm grip on the absorbing story about an amoral tearaway (Paul Newman) and the clash of old and new ideas on a huge Texas cattle ranch. Newman was also nominated for an Academy Award for his uncompromising portrayal but lost to Sidney Poitier, who won the Oscar for his performance in *Lilies of the Field*.

Hudson Hawk ● ⓥ
1991, US, 97 mins, colour
Dir: Michael Lehmann
Stars: Bruce Willis, Andie MacDowell, Danny Aiello, James Coburn, Richard E Grant, David Caruso
Rating: ★★

Wisecracking Hudson Hawk (Bruce Willis) is a cool cat burglar trying to go straight. But some incredibly over-the-top villains are insisting on his crooked help. And so begin a whole series of Keystone Kops-style slapstick adventures, in which Hawk brings off a series of daring art heists that bring back memories of *How to Steal a Million*, *Topkapi* and *Gambit*. This one isn't half as well written as any of those but fast-moving (if completely incoherent) with a few of the Willis wisecracks coming off here and there. Willis places his tongue rather too obviously in his cheek, and the result is glossy but irritatingly overblown entertainment.

Human Comedy, The ○
1943, US, 117 mins, b/w
Dir: Clarence Brown
Stars: Mickey Rooney, Frank Morgan, Marsha Hunt
Rating: ★★★

This was the favourite film of MGM mogul Louis B Mayer. Its story of an American town during World War II reduced the great man to tears whenever he read it. It contains what many regard as Mickey Rooney's finest screen performance, as the town telegram boy, who has the unenviable task of delivering messages on the days when a telegram can only mean that someone has been wounded or killed in action overseas. But his thunder is stolen whenever up-and-coming child star Jackie 'Butch' Jenkins appears on screen. Although Rooney went on to become a major teenage and adult star, 'Butch' developed a stutter and was forced to stop acting within five years. In the hands of Greta Garbo's regular director, Clarence Brown, *The Human Comedy* emerged as a sentimental celebration of the American way of life, and it marked the style for his later films, including *National Velvet* and *The Yearling*. Watch for early cameos from Robert Mitchum (billed as Bob), Barry Nelson and Don DeFore.

Human Factor, The ●
1975, UK/Italy, 96 mins, colour
Dir: Edward Dmytryk
Stars: George Kennedy, John Mills, Rita Tushingham
Rating: ★★★

This vendetta thriller is Edward Dmytryk's best piece of direction in his later years. George Kennedy, full of menace, is particularly good as the man who seeks out a terrorist group in Italy after his wife and children have been killed there.

Human Factor, The ●
1979, UK, 114 mins, colour
Dir: Otto Preminger
Stars: Richard Attenborough, John Gielgud, Derek Jacobi, Robert Morley, Ann Todd, Nicol Williamson
Rating: ★★

The prospect of Tom Stoppard adapting a Graham Greene novel promises more than the film actually offers, though this darkly ironic tale of Foreign Office treason still throws up delights: Richard Attenborough's comic introduction to Maltesers, for example, or the spectacle of fate catching the characters in a pincer grip. Director Otto Preminger's acting discovery, Iman, is perhaps an acquired taste, but the bulk of the cast is pleasantly familiar in this interesting if slow drama. Preminger's direction tends to lack passion, robbing what

H

should be a moving story of some of the human factor of the title – no fault of the formidable Nicol Williamson, who is billed eighth in alphabetical order, but quite clearly has the central part.

Humoresque ○

1947, US, 120 mins, b/w
Dir: Jean Negulesco
Stars: Joan Crawford, John Garfield
Rating: ★★★

A black romantic drama, typical of Hollywood in the mid-Forties, about a wealthy woman who falls for a musician. Joan Crawford makes the most of some pretty good dialogue, written by Clifford Odets and Zachary Gold. As with the contemporary Bette Davis film *Deception*, direction and music sequences are, like the performances, impeccable. To ensure absolute perfection visually, a real violinist's arm was passed through an opening in co-star John Garfield's jacket, the special effects men's magic concealing the deception.

Hunchback of Notre Dame, The ○ ⊗

1939, US, 117 mins, b/w
Dir: William Dieterle
Stars: Charles Laughton, Maureen O'Hara, Edmond O'Brien, Cedric Hardwicke
Rating: ★★★★

Superb, compelling version of Victor Hugo's famous tale. Charles Laughton's pity-inspiring, ugly-but-moving portrait of the hunchback is one of the screen's most fantastic achievements, and he dominates the film, despite stiff competition from Cedric Hardwicke, as the tight-lipped Prefet de Paris. And there's a neat little cameo, too, from Walter Hampden as the king. The action scenes are fine (and teem with staggering detail), the photography excellent. One of the most memorable movies Hollywood ever made.

Hunger, The ● ⊗

1983, US, 99 mins, colour
Dir: Tony Scott
Stars: Catherine Deneuve, David Bowie, Susan Sarandon
Rating: ★★

In the hands of former TV commercials director Tony Scott (brother of Ridley, director of *Blade Runner*, *Thelma and Louise* and *Someone to Watch Over Me*), Catherine Deneuve is quite the sexiest blood-

sucker ever to grace the screen. Her character has been around since the time of the pharaohs, while her partner in crime, David Bowie, is only 200 years old. But everything about this vampire story – dubbed 'chic trash' by the American critics – looks a million dollars thanks to elaborate art direction and shooting in permanently smoky rooms, creating a visual feast of light, colour and shadow. But where the Hammer vampire films took nudity no further than plunging cleavages, Susan Sarandon has to endure an explicit lesbian shower attack by Deneuve. The story tends towards silliness rather than creating a mood of terror, and the non-stop blood-letting appears excessive in the extreme. But it marks an astonishing debut from a master of visuals over content.

Hungry Hill ○

1946, UK, 109 mins, b/w
Dir: Brian Desmond Hurst
Stars: Margaret Lockwood, Cecil Parker
Rating: ★★

Daphne du Maurier helped write the script of this long and often engrossing film version of her own epic novel about a long-standing, bitter feud between two Irish families. The film also gave early screen chances to several promising young players, among them Michael Denison, Siobhan McKenna, Dermot Walsh, Dan O'Herlihy and Jean Simmons.

Hunted ○

(aka: The Stranger in Between)
1952, UK, 84 mins, b/w
Dir: Charles Crichton
Stars: Dirk Bogarde, Kay Walsh, Elizabeth Sellars, Jon Whiteley
Rating: ★★★

Suspenseful and decidedly different thriller. Dirk Bogarde has one of the best of his early screen roles as a murderer on the run – but no one really stands a chance against the brilliant performance of seven-year-old Jon Whiteley, later to win more laurels in *The Kidnappers*. Jon plays a little boy who runs away from home and meets up with a killer. The strange and fascinating relationship that springs up between the two fugitives makes compelling viewing.

Hunter, The ◑ ⊗

1980, US, 95 mins, colour
Dir: Buzz Kulik

Stars: Steve McQueen, Eli Wallach, Kathryn Harrold
Rating: ★★

Steve McQueen's last film is a likeable enough thriller that casts him as a true-life modern-day bounty hunter (the real Ralph Thorson makes a cameo appearance as a bartender) with a hankering after the old ways ('New things are no good,' he says). The action scenes are blazingly well presented by director Buzz Kulik, even if the plot has, as one contemporary critic put it, 'holes that Hannibal could have driven elephants through'. A sub-plot with Kathryn Harrold as the hero's pregnant girlfriend could comfortably have been dispensed with, leaving McQueen as his fans would like to remember him, as the man of constant action. The best sequence in the film takes McQueen to Chicago for the pursuit of a much-wanted fugitive.

Hunters, The ○

1958, US, 108 mins, colour
Dir: Dick Powell
Stars: Robert Mitchum, Robert Wagner, Richard Egan, May Britt
Rating: ★★

Nothing very relaxing about this strong, taut and noise-filled story of a special jet fighter squadron on a secret mission during the Korean War. Director Dick Powell – the former song-and-dance and tough guy star – inserts a backbone of steel into this strong action film, which boasts some spectacular flying sequences breathtakingly captured in colour. Robert Mitchum is thoroughly convincing as the squadron's leader. Dialogue is less believable.

Hunt for Red October, The ○ ⊗

1990, US, 135 mins, colour
Dir: John McTiernan
Stars: Sean Connery, Alec Baldwin, Scott Glenn, Sam Neill, James Earl Jones, Richard Jordan
Rating: ★★

There's no snap in submarine suspense films any more. Time was when you could have heard a ping! drop as the metal warriors stalked each other beneath the surface. Now the nuclear leviathans are so huge (and John McTiernan's direction so slow) that it's no longer just galleons that are stately. Not even Sean Connery can salvage this waterlogged plot as a Russian sub skipper planning to defect (or is he?) with a fistful of nuclear weapons aboard his prototype vessel. The Russians, naturally not wanting to lose such a prize, let the Americans think that Connery is a madman about to blow the US apart. Thus both sides could be seeking to eliminate him – until a wily American CIA researcher (Alec Baldwin) sees through it. All of this cruises through many a doldrum until, thank goodness, a saboteur crops up at the end on the Russian sub and we get an exciting chase and shootout, after one or two minor members of the crew have been gunned down, perhaps for bad acting. For underwater suspense freaks only.

Hurricane, The ○
1937, US, 110 mins, b/w
Dir: John Ford
Stars: Dorothy Lamour, Jon Hall, Mary Astor, Raymond Massey
Rating: ★★

At the then-hefty cost of two million dollars, producer Samuel Goldwyn spared little expence in putting the best-selling novel by Charles Nordhoff and James Norman Hall (authors of *Mutiny On The Bounty*) up there on the screen. Director John Ford and special effects chief James Basevi gave him a devastating hurricane for climax, this sequence alone taking 400,000 dollars out of the movie's budget. Basevi would undoubtedly have won an Academy Award for his work but the special effects Oscar didn't come into being until two years later. A master of disaster, Basevi also created the fire in *In Old Chicago* and the earthquake in *San Francisco*. Dorothy Lamour sings 'Moon Over Manukura' to solidify her growing reputation as the maiden bursting into sarong.

Hurricane Smith ○
1952, US, 89 mins, colour
Dir: Jerry Hopper
Stars: John Ireland, Yvonne De Carlo, James Craig, Lyle Bettger
Rating: ★★★

Glorious piece of escapism, all action and colour, about a group of thieves and soldiers of fortune who search for sunken treasure in the South Seas. Typical of the Pine-Thomas adventure films made at Paramount in the Forties and Fifties, but better than most, with a sturdy cast that includes John Ireland, Forrest Tucker, Yvonne de Carlo, James Craig, Richard Arlen and Lyle Bettger. Not to be confused with

a 1941 film of the same title. Oddly the 1952 film was based on a novel called *Hurricane Williams*!

Hurry Sundown ○
1967, US, 146 mins, colour
Dir: Otto Preminger
Stars: Michael Caine, Jane Fonda, John Phillip Law, Faye Dunaway, Burgess Meredith
Rating: ★

A laughable tale of racial bigotry that marked a low point in the career of director Otto Preminger. Despite a top-drawer cast, it is sunk by many factors, among them Michael Caine's inept attempt at an American Deep South accent, a tediously slow first hour and a crazy guns-blazing finale that suggests a pantomime version of Greek tragedy.

Husbands and Wives ○ ⓥ
1992, US, 107 mins, colour
Dir: Woody Allen
Stars: Woody Allen, Mia Farrow, Blythe Danner, Liam Neeson, Judy Davis, Juliette Lewis
Rating: ★★

As you'd expect, Mia Farrow and Woody Allen's last film together is way too close for comfort. A funny-sad look at the rocky state of marriage, it makes you laugh and smile wryly from time to time, but also gets on your nerves a bit, with characters repeating the same lines several times over (like in life, sure, but does this make it better?). And the bewildering hand-held camera will surely give you eyestrain. Woody tells Mia that he has 'always had this penchant for kamikaze women'. She retorts that, 'You use sex to express every emotion except love'. This is far from the ideal goofy romanticism of their first film *A Midsummer Night's Sex Comedy*, and their parting at the end, and Woody's falling for (but declining) a 20-year-old girl express, more than anywhere else, lives played out on screen over an 11-year period. Good supporting performances from Judy Davis, typically abrasive, Juliette Lewis (as Allen's younger flight of fancy) and especially Lysette Anthony, amazingly good as the astrological bimbo who takes up with one of the splitting husbands.

Hush . . . Hush, Sweet Charlotte ● ⓥ
1964, US, 133 mins, b/w
Dir: Robert Aldrich

Stars: Bette Davis, Olivia de Havilland, Joseph Cotten, Agnes Moorehead, Cecil Kellaway, Mary Astor
Rating: ★★★

A splendidly macabre film thriller (the same director's follow-up to *What Ever Happened to Baby Jane?*) that commits viewers to sit chewing their fingernails for more than two hours. Bette Davis and Olivia de Havilland are admirably enigmatic; and Agnes Moorehead, too, makes an indelible mark on the film as the weird house-keeper. Watch for Bruce Dern (as the murder victim at the start) and George Kennedy, both taking early film roles.

Hustle ●
1975, US, 120 mins, colour
Dir: Robert Aldrich
Stars: Burt Reynolds, Catherine Deneuve, Ben Johnson, Eddie Albert
Rating: ★

Not exactly a film that celebrates the finer qualities of the American cinema. In fact, Burt Reynolds' performance as the cynical police lieutenant at the centre of the story is the only saving grace of this routine, facile police thriller in which director Robert Aldrich never misses a chance to emphasise the sordid and the unnecessary. Catherine Deneuve, Eddie Albert, Ernest Borgnine and Ben Johnson are also involved, none of them to any great effect, with Johnson offering one of the few poor performances he has ever given. At the foot of the cast, a young Robert Englund, later Freddy Krueger in the *Elm Street* films, makes one of his earliest appearances, as a hold-up man.

Hustler, The ○ ⓥ
1961, US, 135 mins, b/w
Dir: Robert Rossen
Stars: Paul Newman, Jackie Gleason, Piper Laurie, George C Scott, Murray Hamilton
Rating: ★★★★

A grim, tragic drama in a low key, but terribly gripping, uplifting and moving in spite of the terrible personal tragedies it unfolds. And it has three magnetically lifelike performances. Paul Newman, as the young pool player determined to beat the great Minnesota Fats (Jackie Gleason at his most phlegmatic) is remarkably compelling, an all-too-vulnerable blue-eyed bombshell who draws one with him wherever he goes. Less expected, judging by her Universal

H

frivolities of the Fifties, is the brilliant portrayal by Piper Laurie of the crippled girl, desperate for a love that is more than ephemeral, and suicidal when she fails to obtain it. Completing a dynamic trio of real people is George C Scott's incisive, keen-edged performance as Newman's hawk-cruel, relentless manager. The final scene between Newman and Scott is a masterpiece in smouldering, if inert, intensity.

I Accuse! ○
1957, UK, 99 mins, b/w
Dir: Jose Ferrer
Stars: Jose Ferrer, Anton Walbrook, Viveca Lindfors, Emlyn Williams
Rating: ★★

L'Affaire Dreyfus was one of the most notorious scandals in the whole of French history and this film is one of several that have dealt with the subject. Jose Ferrer directed and took – with distinction – the central role of the Jewish-French army officer Alfred Dreyfus, convicted of treason on a trumped-up charge. With a screenplay by Gore Vidal, the result is a carefully detailed reconstruction of events that is honest, if sometimes a little too cold. However, some of the court-room scenes are compelling and the film comes complete with a highly distinguished cast: Anton Walbrook (as the real culprit, Esterhazy), Viveca Lindfors, Emlyn Williams (as the novelist Emile Zola, who famously took up Dreyfus's cause), David Farrar, Donald Wolfit, Herbert Lom, Harry Andrews, Felix Aylmer, Peter Illing, George Coulouris, Eric Pohlmann, Laurence Naismith and Michael Hordern. The film was photographed by Freddie Young, who worked with David Lean on such films as *Lawrence of Arabia* and *Doctor Zhivago*.

I Am a Camera ○
1955, UK, 98 mins, b/w
Dir: Henry Cornelius
Stars: Julie Harris, Laurence Harvey, Shelley Winters
Rating: ★★

Kaleidoscopic, atmospheric, but rather irritating nostalgia piece from the stories of Christopher Isherwood, later remade in musical form as *Cabaret*. Successfully creating a portrait of a nation falling into moral decay, the film has its grim moments, but there's also a lot to laugh about, especially in the sequences featuring the determinedly amoral Sally Bowles, played close to the edge of tragedy by America's Julie Harris.

I Am a Fugitive from a Chain Gang ○
1932, US, 93 mins, b/w
Dir: Mervyn LeRoy
Stars: Paul Muni, Glenda Farrell, Helen Vinson, Preston Foster
Rating: ★★★★

This harrowing prison drama caused great controversy when it was released in 1932, based as it was on the true-life memoirs of Robert E Burns. Warner Brothers, the only studio brave enough to take on such dramas, created a classic, elements of which have been freely borrowed by other film-makers ever since. Paul Muni gives a powerhouse central performance as the innocent man sentenced to 10 years hard labour. He escapes and starts to rebuild his life, but is betrayed by his shrewish wife. Persuaded he will be pardoned if he gives himself up, he goes back to the prison only to suffer brutally at the hands of the warders and have his sentence increased. The grim realism of *Chain Gang* (which was echoed in the later *Black Fury*) was at variance with the escapism offered by other Hollywood studios in the 1930s and, unlike *Black Fury*, was a great critical and commercial success. So much so, the state of Georgia banned the film (Burns' book, on which the film was based was called *I Am a Fugitive from a Georgia Chain Gang*). In fact a nervous and skittish Burns travelled incognito to Hollywood to collaborate on the film. At the howl of a sound-effect siren from a nearby sound stage he went to ground and didn't reappear until many hours later!

I Am the Law ○
1938, US, 83 mins, b/w
Dir: Alexander Hall
Stars: Edward G Robinson, Otto Kruger, John Beal, Wendy Barrie
Rating: ★★★

Edward G Robinson is on the right side of the law for once (he even dances!) in a story of a crusading law professor who sets out to expose racketeers operating in his city. Surprisingly from Columbia rather than Robinson's home studio, Warners, the plot is familiar stuff, but smoothly done and plausibly written by the prolific Jo Swerling.

I Believe in You ○
1952, UK, 91 mins, b/w
Dir: Basil Dearden
Stars: Cecil Parker, Celia Johnson, Joan Collins, Godfrey Tearle, Laurence Harvey
Rating: ★★★

Ace comedy studio Ealing went dramatic in this very popular film about

I'd Climb the Highest Mountain 343

the work of probation officers. Ealing were able to make much publicity mileage out of the fact that the film gave early chances to two young hopefuls – Joan Collins and Laurence Harvey. They, and Harry Fowler, are perfectly cast as a trio of young people in trouble, as are Cecil Parker and Celia Johnson as the probation officers. Despite the rather cosy view of probation work, the characters and situation spring to life and grip the attention throughout, the performances making us care about the fates of the characters. Cleverly made by director Basil Dearden, who also had a hand in the script.

Ice Cold in Alex ○ ⓥ
(aka: Desert Attack)
1958, UK, 129 mins, b/w
Dir: J Lee Thompson
Stars: John Mills, Sylvia Syms, Anthony Quayle, Harry Andrews
Rating: ★★★

Long but gripping war film, surprisingly based on true events. Much mileage was gained at the time by scenes of John Mills unbuttoning his stiff upper lip to do the same with nurse Sylvia Syms in the desert, but in fact the film's appeal leans more on the emotions and suspense stirred by the interrelationship of all four main characters, as they dice with death at the hands of Germans, minefields and sandstorms and dream of ice-cold beer in Alexandria.

Iceland ○
(aka: Katina)
1942, US, 79 mins, b/w
Dir: Bruce Humberstone
Stars: Sonja Henie, John Payne, Jack Oakie, Osa Massen
Rating: ★★

Wartime flag-waving and such tunes as 'Let's Bring New Glory to Old Glory' rather date this Sonja Henie ice-musical (known previously in Britain as *Katina*), although the star's Hawaiian hula routine is a hit, and the score does also include 'There Will Never Be Another You', 'It's a Lovers' Knot' and 'You Can't Say No to a Soldier', perhaps not the best advice for singing co-star Joan Merrill to give to the girls back home. John Payne and Jack Oakie, so often Alice Faye's co-stars, do good back-up work here for the star, whose skating sequences were staged by James Gonzales, with Sammy Kaye and His Band providing an enthusiastic backdrop. The director is Bruce

Humberstone, whose other Fox musicals include *Sun Valley Serenade* (also with Henie and Payne), *Pin Up Girl*, *Hello, Frisco, Hello* and *Three Little Girls in Blue*.

Ice Palace ○
1960, US, 143 mins, colour
Dir: Vincent Sherman
Stars: Richard Burton, Robert Ryan, Martha Hyer, Carolyn Jones
Rating: ★★

Edna Ferber's doorstep-sized novel, one of the first of the blockbusters, here filmed with Burton and Ryan as the two fishery tycoons slugging it out during Alaska's struggle to become a state of the Union. Burton comes up with a Welsh-American accent and some minor James Cagney impressions.

Ice Pirates, The ○
1984, US, 94 mins, colour
Dir: Stewart Raffill
Stars: Robert Urich, Mary Crosby, Anjelica Huston
Rating: ★★

This spoof on the *Star Wars* type of sci-fi spectacular suffers from an appallingly low budget that doesn't allow the special effects to be all that special. Robert (*Spenser for Hire*) Urich is our firm-jawed hero, a pirate who deals in the future's most precious commodity – water. The adventure starts when he agrees to help Mary Crosby, whose lost father has reportedly found a huge supply of water. It's a sort of low-buck *Robin Hood* of the spaceways and providing you can accept the low production values, okay. Your kids will love it, so set the video recorder! Oh yes, and Anjelica Huston has one of her pre-stardom roles in this one.

Ice Station Zebra ○ ⓥ
1968, US, 148 mins, colour
Dir: John Sturges
Stars: Rock Hudson, Ernest Borgnine, Patrick McGoohan, Jim Brown
Rating: ★★★

Intrigue and adventure come in equal measure in this exciting adaptation of Alastair MacLean's Arctic thriller. Rock Hudson stars as the leader of a submarine expedition to trace a downed Soviet satellite which contains photos of sensitive US and Russian missile sites. But the sub is damaged and it is clear there's a traitor on board. Is it Russian defector Ernest Borgnine, US captain Jim Brown or

British naval officer Patrick McGoohan? Things come to a head when they reach Ice Station Zebra, a weather station in the frozen wastes, only to find everyone there has been killed. Muscular playing by all the principals coupled with excellent photography and special effects make this a thrilling yarn even if the plot and counter-plot isn't up to John Le Carré standards. Watching McGoohan in one of his rare major film roles makes you realise how under-valued and under-used he has been. Possibly a little violent for younger children.

I Confess ○ ⓥ
1953, US, 94 mins, b/w
Dir: Alfred Hitchcock
Stars: Montgomery Clift, Anne Baxter, Brian Aherne, Karl Malden, O E Hasse
Rating: ★★

A rather slower than usual slice of suspense from Alfred Hitchcock, though the climax may still take you by surprise. The central situation isn't new: a murderer confesses to a priest and then refuses to give himself up to the police. But it's given intensity by the performances of Karl Malden, as a detective, and O E Hasse, as the refugee who confesses to the crime. More sober portrayals from Montgomery Clift (as the priest), Anne Baxter and Brian Aherne. Hitchcock himself makes his customary appearance. Whereabouts? Just watch the skyline!

I Could Go on Singing ○
1963, UK, 100 mins, colour
Dir: Ronald Neame
Stars: Judy Garland, Dirk Bogarde
Rating: ★★★

The critics clapped after a preview of this film, principally because of an emotional bomb of a performance by Judy Garland, cast in a role which sadly reflected her own life. Dirk Bogarde offers sympathetic support. The rest is nothing special, but Garland's singing is.

I'd Climb the Highest Mountain ○
1951, US, 89 mins, colour
Dir: Henry King
Stars: Susan Hayward, William Lundigan
Rating: ★★★

This story of a travelling preacher in the early 1900s provided William Lundigan with his biggest movie role. A strapping, fair-haired six-footer,

Lundigan came up the hard way –
supporting roles in the late Thirties,
war service, B-picture leads from the
mid-Forties. Here he's treated to a
first-rate supporting cast that includes
Alexander Knox, Lynn Bari, Barbara
Bates and Gene Lockhart.

Idiot's Delight ○

1939, US, 105 mins, b/w
Dir: Clarence Brown
Stars: Clark Gable, Norma Shearer,
Edward Arnold, Charles Coburn, Burgess
Meredith
Rating: ★★★

Nothing is more delightful in this
thoughtful adaptation of his own
pacifist play by Robert Sherwood than
the sight of old jug-ears himself, Clark
Gable, singing and dancing as the
front-man for a six-girl dance team.
Although softened for the screen,
Sherwood's Pulitzer Prize-winning
work still has enough bite to expose
the idiocy and pointlessness of mili-
tarism while keeping our interest in
its story of two of life's failures from
the more obscure corners of show
business. Good supporting
performances from Charles Coburn
and Laura Hope Crews (later that year
to play Aunt Pittypat in *Gone With the
Wind*), but it's Gable's deliberately
awful entertainer that you'll
remember.

I Don't Care Girl, The ○

1953, US, 78 mins, colour
Dir: Lloyd Bacon
Stars: Mitzi Gaynor, Bob Graham, David
Wayne, Oscar Levant
Rating: ★★

The sparkling Mitzi Gaynor series of
musicals for 20th Century-Fox –
Bloodhounds of Broadway, Golden Girl
and *Down Among the Sheltering Palms*
were others – didn't quite make her
into the star that they should have. This
one is a snappy, colourful biography of
torch singer Eva Tanguay, and its only
faults are that it's too short at only 78
minutes, and has a weak leading man
in Bob Graham. Oscar Levant tickles
the ivories in his own droll style, and
Miss Gaynor is enchanting in the title
role.

I Dood It ⊙

(aka: By Hook or By Crook)
1943, US, 102 mins, b/w
Dir: Vincente Minnelli
Stars: Red Skelton, Eleanor Powell, John
Hodiak, Lena Horne
Rating: ★★

If the title of this Red Skelton comedy
sounds unfamiliar, it was shown in
Britain as *By Hook or By Crook*. A
loose adaptation of Buster Keaton's
silent classic *Spite Marriage*, the film is
just a lengthy vehicle for the clowning
of Skelton and the dance artistry of
Eleanor Powell, whose climactic
number, 'Swinging the Jinx Away',
looks suspiciously like the big routine
from her earlier hit 'Born to Dance'.
Vincente Minnelli (his second film as
director) inherited the movie from
other hands, and got the most from
the musical greats in the cast, who also
include Lena Horne and Jimmy
Dorsey and His Orchestra.

If . . . ● ⓥ

1968, UK, 111 mins, colour
Dir: Lindsay Anderson
Stars: Malcolm McDowell, David Wood,
Christine Noonan, Richard Warwick
Rating: ★★★

Lindsay Anderson's weird but powerful indictment of the public school
system (and the country as a whole?)
made a star of Malcolm McDowell in
a role he recreated, a few years on, in
the same director's *O Lucky Man!* and
again for Anderson in *Britannia Hospital*. Here he plays a sixth form boy
in whose mind symbolism and fantasy
gradually take over from reality, as
they do in the film, the first half of
which is a kind of up-dated *Tom
Brown's Schooldays*, with public school
ritual being observed down to the last
hideous Stone-Age detail.

If He Hollers, Let Him Go! ◑

1968, US, 106 mins, colour
Dir: Charles Martin
Stars: Dana Wynter, Raymond St
Jacques, Kevin McCarthy
Rating: ★

Kevin McCarthy and Dana Wynter,
the stars of the brilliant science-fiction
classic *Invasion of the Body Snatchers* in
1956, were reunited in this intricately-plotted thriller with a racialist
slant. Lightning, alas, doesn't strike
twice for them, and film fans will find
most interest in the appearance of two
handsome ex-stars, John Russell and
James Craig, as a sheriff and police
chief respectively.

If I Had a Million ⊙

1932, US, 88 mins, b/w
Dir: Norman Taurog, Stephen Roberts,
Norman McLeod, James Cruze, William A
Seiter, H Bruce Humberstone
Stars: Charles Laughton, W C Fields,
Gary Cooper, Charlie Ruggles, George

Raft, Jackie Oakie
Rating: ★★★

Paramount pumped the considerable
might of their roster of stars and directors into this bitter-sweet (mostly
sweet) compilation of stories about
people who unexpectedly come into
a million dollars apiece. The Charles
Laughton and W C Fields stories are
delightful and you'll spot Gary
Cooper, George Raft, Jack Oakie,
Charles Ruggles, Frances Dee, Mary
Boland and many more familiar star
faces from the early Thirties.

If I Were King ○

1938, US, 97 mins, b/w
Dir: Frank Lloyd
Stars: Ronald Colman, Frances Dee,
Basil Rathbone, Ellen Drew
Rating: ★★★

One of Ronald Colman's least-seen
films, although it's by no means unattractive and, chronologically
speaking, follows two of his greatest
hits, *Lost Horizon* and *The Prisoner of
Zenda*. It's a remake of John
Barrymore's 1927 film *The Beloved
Rogue* and casts Colman as François
Villon, the 15th-century French adventurer and poet. The star
underlines his reputation as a swashbuckler in the action scenes, while
only Colman's velvet tones could get
away so well with speaking lines in
verse. An almost unrecognisable Basil
Rathbone matches him line for line as
the sly King Louis XI. In later years,
the story would be made into a musical (and filmed) as *The Vagabond
King*.

If Winter Comes ○

1947, US, 105 mins, b/w
Dir: Victor Saville
Stars: Deborah Kerr, Walter Pidgeon,
Janet Leigh, Angela Lansbury, Binnie
Barnes
Rating: ★★

Lucky Walter Pidgeon is surrounded
by female co-stars (headed by Deborah
Kerr), who no doubt helped to cheer
him up while making this sombre
story of a publisher accused of driving
a young girl to suicide. Lots of acting
class in the supporting cast which includes Dame May Whitty, Angela
Lansbury, Binnie Barnes, Janet Leigh,
Virginia Keiley and Rene Ray, who
appeared in scores of British films from
the beginning of sound before going
to America to make this one film.

I Know Where I'm Going! ○ Ⓥ
1945, UK, 91 mins, b/w
Dir: Michael Powell, Emeric Pressburger
Stars: Wendy Hiller, Roger Livesey, Pamela Brown, Petula Clark, Finlay Currie
Rating: ★★★

There are some very odd things about this romantic drama, as you might expect from the unconventional film-making team of Michael Powell and Emeric Pressburger. Their script abounds in wit, charm and eccentric characters. Most of these are female, including Wendy Hiller, terrific as the heroine who thinks she knows where she's going, Catherine Lacey, Petula Clark and particularly Pamela Brown who gets a gem of a role as a decidedly individual Scots lassie. Nicely shot on location in the Scottish islands: cameraman Erwin Hillier somehow makes it look as atmospheric in black-and-white as it undoubtedly would have been in colour.

I'll Be Seeing You ○
1944, US, 83 mins, b/w
Dir: William Dieterle
Stars: Ginger Rogers, Joseph Cotten, Shirley Temple
Rating: ★★★

This polished weepie could hardly fail to be a success: Shirley Temple was making her first picture as a teenager after a fabulous career as Hollywood's top child star; Ginger Rogers, too, had a string of successes behind her as a dramatic actress (including the Oscar-winning *Kitty Foyle*) after the great Astaire-Rogers musicals of the Thirties. And their director was William Dieterle, responsible for such literate entertainments as *The Story of Emile Zola, Juarez* and Laughton's *The Hunchback of Notre Dame*. Rogers skilfully understates her role as a woman convict falling in love (with Joseph Cotten) while on parole, and ensures audience sympathy every step of the tear-stained way.

I'll Be Your Sweetheart ○
1945, UK, 104 mins, b/w
Dir: Val Guest
Stars: Margaret Lockwood, Vic Oliver, Michael Rennie, Peter Graves
Rating: ★★★

A British musical on a theme much favoured by Hollywood – the lives of writers of popular songs – in this case three of them, at the turn of the century, named Le Brunn, Kahn and

Kelly: an unlikely-sounding trio. On a more serious note, the plot also concerns the fight to establish copyright and crush private publishers. Vic Oliver, that Jack Benny of the British halls, plays Kahn. Bewhiskered Moore Marriott, so often a figure of fun in British farces, typically with Will Hay, portrays the tragic figure of Le Brunn. Margaret Lockwood's role, as a songstress of the music-halls, gives her a chance to sing such favourites as 'The Honeysuckle and the Bee', 'Oh, Mr Porter', 'Little Wooden Hut' and 'Sooner or Later'. It was one of the earliest films to be directed by Val Guest, who had started his career writing Will Hay films.

Illegal ○
1955, US, 88 mins, b/w
Dir: Lewis Allen
Stars: Edward G Robinson, Nina Foch, Albert Dekker, Hugh Marlowe, Jayne Mansfield, Deforest Kelley
Rating: ★★★

There's an early glimpse of a 22-year-old Jayne Mansfield as the surprise winner in this remake of a 1932 gangster-courtroom drama originally filmed as *The Mouthpiece*, and then remade in 1940 as *The Man Who Talked Too Much*. Warners did all three versions, and this marked Edward G Robinson's return to their studio after 15 years away. Tough, no-nonsense stuff, but lacking the vital drive of the star's Thirties vehicles.

I'll Get You
See: Escape Route

I'll Get You for This ○
(aka: Lucky Nick Cain)
1951, UK, 83 mins, b/w
Dir: Joseph M Newman
Stars: George Raft, Coleen Gray
Rating: ★★

George Raft, more usually seen as a denizen of dark corners of the underworld, looks somewhat ill-at-ease in the open-air Italian locations of this James Hadley Chase thriller which casts him as an American gambler (hence the film's alternative title, *Lucky Nick Cain*) who gets involved with a counterfeit gang. Enzo Staiola, the little boy from *Bicycle Thieves*, is a lovable urchin, helping Raft round up the gang while effortlessly stealing scenes from under his nose.

Ill-Met by Moonlight ○
(aka: Night Ambush)
1956, UK, 100 mins, b/w
Dir: Michael Powell, Emeric Pressburger
Stars: Dirk Bogarde, Marius Goring, David Oxley, Cyril Cusack
Rating: ★★★

Slightly different from the usual run of war films, this British-made adventure has Dirk Bogarde as one of the British officers who engineer the wartime kidnapping of a German general (Marius Goring) who commands 30,000 enemy paratroopers in Crete. The film's strong vein of humour doesn't stop it whipping up plenty of excitement. It's a true story, and one of the more conventional films of maverick British film-making duo of Michael Powell and Emeric Pressburger.

I'll Never Forget What's 'is Name ◐
1967, UK, 99 mins, colour
Dir: Michael Winner
Stars: Orson Welles, Oliver Reed, Carol White, Wendy Craig
Rating: ★★

With its jump-cut pacing and frenetic camera motion, Michael Winner's savage satire on the swinging Sixties in general and the advertising industry in particular is clearly a film of its time. But even if it does show its age, it's true to say that Peter Draper's acerbic script offers plenty of wicked insights amidst the visual confusion. Most of the best lines are grabbed greedily by Orson Welles' towering advertising chief who tries to bully Oliver Reed's resentful whizzkid into working for him again. Carol White and Wendy Craig are touchingly vulnerable as prim secretary and ignored wife, and the climactic 'award-winning commercial' is a cleverly constructed monument to appalling taste.

Illustrated Man, The ◐
1969, US, 103 mins, colour
Dir: Jack Smight
Stars: Rod Steiger, Claire Bloom
Rating: ★★

A brave, and to some degree a successful attempt to transfer the imaginative fantasy of Ray Bradbury to the screen. Although not quite fulfilling the promise of its early scenes, it is by any standards a strange and compelling film, with a powerful virtuoso performance by Rod Steiger as the man entirely covered with beautiful tattoos, apart from one bare

I

patch. It marked something of a change of pace for its versatile director, Jack Smight, following such light-hearted diversions as *Kaleidoscope*, *The Secret War of Harry Frigg*, and *No Way to Treat a Lady*, also with Steiger.

I Love Melvin ⊙
1952, US, 77 mins, colour
Dir: Don Weis
Stars: Donald O'Connor, Debbie Reynolds, Una Merkel, Richard Anderson
Rating: ★★

A minor but fresh and enjoyable MGM musical, with good tunes, an entertaining and, for once, original story, and bouncy performances from Debbie Reynolds and Donald O'Connor, two of the youngest veterans (then 20 and 27 respectively) on the MGM lot. The characters are all likeable and well-drawn and the Technicolor photography by expert Hollywood cameraman Harold Rosson decorates the settings in gay, springlike colours. For such a short running time, it's strange that some of the film is so lacking in pace – a black mark to director Don Weis. But its people are such a pleasure to be with, that that's easily forgiven.

I Love My Wife ◐
1970, US, 95 mins, colour
Dir: Mel Stewart
Stars: Elliott Gould, Brenda Vaccaro
Rating: ★★

A sex-orientated comedy that varies from the serious to the satirical, and from whiplash comedy to flaccid farce. How anyone could leave the delicious Brenda Vaccaro, even with her hair in curlers, for the plastic Angel Tompkins, is quite beyond me. The script (by Robert Kaufman) does best with its incidental lines. One remembers especially Elliott Gould's *cri de coeur* as his wife and mother-in-law do battle around him: 'I have three weeks to live – four if I stay in bed.'

I Love You Again ○
1940, US, 110 mins, b/w
Dir: W S Van Dyke II
Stars: William Powell, Myrna Loy
Rating: ★★★

This delightful romantic comedy reunited William Powell, Myrna Loy and director W S Van Dyke II but was in a different vein from their classic *Thin Man* series together. Loy is about to divorce respectable, deadly dull Powell when an accident unlocks him

from nine years of amnesia and reveals a raffish Lothario with distinctly criminal tendencies. Highly entertaining confusion results, directed at a rattling pace by Van Dyke from a bubbly script spiced with some choice exchanges: Powell to Loy, 'You turn my head.' Loy's retort, 'I've often wished I could turn your head – on a spit over a slow fire.' The performances sparkle and Gene Ruggiero's editing keeps the film moving at a perfect pace.

I Love You, Alice B Toklas ◐
1968, US, 93 mins, colour
Dir: Hy Averback
Stars: Peter Sellers, Jo Van Fleet, Leigh Taylor-Young, Joyce Van Patten
Rating: ★★★

Spasmodic Peter Sellers comedy in which he plays a businessman inducted into the world of 'pot' parties by an attractive young hippie girl who bakes him Marijuana cookies. Joyce Van Patten is hilarious as Sellers' crow-voiced fiancée.

I Love You to Death ◐
1990, US, 97 mins, colour
Dir: Lawrence Kasdan
Stars: Kevin Kline, Tracey Ullman, Joan Plowright, William Hurt, Keanu Reeves, River Phoenix
Rating: ★★

Quirky, slow and as strange as the true-life case on which it's based, this is a star-studded study of a philandering, food-loving Italian (Kevin Kline) and the wife (Tracey Ullman) and mother-in-law (Joan Plowright) who decide to do away with him. Stir in River Phoenix as their helper, William Hurt and Keanu Reeves as stoned-out amateur assassins and unbilled Phoebe Cates (Kline's real-life wife) and you have a mixture that tickles the ribs but never produces a lethal dose of laughter. The succession of failed attempts on Kline's life should be absolutely hilarious, but the comedy is often too dark and/or flatly directed to be really funny.

I'm All Right, Jack ○ ⓥ
1959, UK, 105 mins, b/w
Dir: John Boulting
Stars: Ian Carmichael, Peter Sellers, Terry-Thomas, Richard Attenborough, Dennis Price, Margaret Rutherford
Rating: ★★★

The Boulting Brothers' greatest hit – an anarchic swipe at trade unions and their bosses. It contains Peter Sellers'

first unsympathetic portrayal, as the bigoted shop steward, and proved a tremendous box-office hit. A bit too serious and direct for its own good at times, but delightful performances from Ian Carmichael, Terry-Thomas, Irene Handl, and especially Liz Fraser as Cynthia Kite, the rave of the shop floor, who sets her cap at Carmichael.

Imitation General ○
1958, US, 88 mins, colour
Dir: George Marshall
Stars: Glenn Ford, Red Buttons, Taina Elg, Dean Jones
Rating: ★★

Veteran director George Marshall (he made *Destry Rides Again*) maintains a fast pace in this war comedy-drama about a sergeant who decides to 'promote' himself to general. Dean Jones, now a regular star of comedies from the Disney studio, is seen to advantage as a zestful corporal.

Imitation of Life ○
1959, US, 124 mins, colour
Dir: Douglas Sirk
Stars: Lana Turner, John Gavin, Dan O'Herlihy, Sandra Dee
Rating: ★★

Glossily presented but wholly unpersuasive, this is one of a series of weepies made by producer Ross Hunter during his years with Universal-International that also included *Magnificent Obsession*, *All That Heaven Allows*, *Portrait in Black* and *Back Street*. Lana Turner suffers in sable but her character, like the screenplay's appeal to our emotions, is almost entirely synthetic. Director Douglas Sirk does tremendous work under the circumstances and it was largely thanks to his efforts that the film was one of the top moneymakers of its year. A remake of the equally tear-soaked 1934 original with Claudette Colbert, which involved you more in its characters.

Immaculate Conception ● ⓥ
1991, UK, 120 mins, colour
Dir: Jamil Dehlavi
Stars: James Wilby, Melissa Leo, Shabana Azmi, Zia Mohyeddin
Rating: ★★

This culture-clash drama is as dry and arid as the acting of Merchant-Ivory favourite James Wilby at its core. He is a wildlife conservationist married to a Jewish-American daughter of a US Senator and living in 1988 Pakistan.

The couple are so desperate for a child of their own that they visit a eunuch-run shrine reputed to have a cure for infertility. But things take a rum turn when they're slipped the local equivalent of a Mickey Finn . . . Director Jamil Dehlavi, whose 1980 film *The Blood of Hussain* made him unwelcome in Pakistan in the eyes of the Junta leader General Zia, tries to place this story within the context of political upheaval and conflict. But despite the best intentions, it emerges as a fairly indigestible curate's egg.

Immortal Sergeant, The ○
1943, US, 91 mins, b/w
Dir: John M Stahl
Stars: Henry Fonda, Maureen O'Hara, Thomas Mitchell
Rating: ★★

Although not much liked by its star Henry Fonda ('It was a silly picture,' he told an interviewer testily. 'You wanna hear the plot? I won the war single-handed!'), this is actually quite a poetic war film (set in North Africa), as one might have expected from that great romantic director John M Stahl, who had previously made such classic weepies as *Back Street, Magnificent Obsession* and *Imitation of Life*. Not only do the film's emotive elements work well, but Lamar Trotti's screenplay supplies plenty of action into the bargain.

I'm No Angel ○
1933, US, 84 mins, b/w
Dir: Wesley Ruggles
Stars: Mae West, Cary Grant, Edward Arnold
Rating: ★★★★

The film in which Mae West really twisted the censor by the tail, as well as consolidating her first big success in *She Done Him Wrong*. She was never allowed quite the same freedom of dialogue (written by herself) after this, but mean time, there are many aphorisms to treasure as Mae plays a carnival dancer who tames lions – and men – as a sideline. 'I like sophisticated men to take me out,' she tells young society swell Kent Taylor. 'I'm not really sophisticated,' he tells her. Growls Mae: 'You're not really out yet, either.' And that's really her in the lions' cage, to the dismay of the film's producers, who went purple with anxiety at the thought of their high-priced star in the big cats' company.

I, Mobster ○①
1958, US, 80 mins, b/w
Dir: Roger Corman
Stars: Steve Cochran, Lita Milan, Robert Strauss, Grant Withers
Rating: ★★

A typically zestful film from director Roger Corman from the period when he was one of the most prolific (37 movies in 10 years) and best makers of low-budget exploitation pictures largely aimed at the young drive-in cinema audience. Here he revives the kind of gangster opus popular in the Thirties, executing it with pace and narrative drive and drawing from Steve Cochran in the title role one of his best later portrayals.

I, Monster ●
1970, UK, 75 mins, colour
Dir: Stephen Weeks
Stars: Christopher Lee, Peter Cushing, Richard Hurndall
Rating: ★★

Director Stephen Weeks was one of two young British film-makers to emerge in the horror field in the late Sixties (the other, Michael Reeves, died at 25). This was Weeks' second film – at the age of 22 – and it turns out to be a very intelligent and largely faithful re-working of *Dr Jekyll and Mr Hyde*. Christopher Lee gives one of his best performances in one of the best parts that the cinema of terror has offered him in a 30-year career. His portrayal and the director's very authentic-seeming Victorian settings, full of amusingly bizarre bric-a-brac, are both much in contrast to the lurid approach taken by most latter-day film makers to Stevenson's famous double-identity chiller.

Impact ○
1949, US, 111 mins, b/w
Dir: Arthur Lubin
Stars: Brian Donlevy, Ella Raines, Charles Coburn, Helen Walker
Rating: ★★

Very long and twisty thriller with a biting performance from the underrated Helen Walker, offering us another of her waspish wives, and stealing the distaff honours from the silky Ella Raines. Good background music and an ingenious plot boost this tale of a man who finds himself declared dead in mistake for the person who tried to kill him.

Importance of Being Earnest, The ○ ⓥ
1952, UK, 95 mins, colour
Dir: Anthony Asquith
Stars: Michael Redgrave, Michael Denison, Edith Evans, Dorothy Tutin, Margaret Rutherford, Joan Greenwood
Rating: ★★★

Oscar Wilde's timeless comic stage satire about the efforts of two men-about-town to get hitched was given top drawer treatment by director Anthony Asquith. He cast Michael Redgrave (who had given one of his finest performances the previous year in Asquith's *The Browning Version*) as one of the suitors, but it is Edith Evans' dragon of a Lady Bracknell who dominates the film. Her indignant cry of '. . . a handbag?' entered screen history as one of the all-time classic lines and her barn-storming performance still ranks as the one against which all future interpretations of the role are measured. Even Margaret Rutherford's quivering Miss Prism has to give her best.

Impossible Years, The ○
1968, UK, 92 mins, colour
Dir: Michael Gordon
Stars: David Niven, Lola Albright
Rating: ★

This film comedy is based on the Bob Fisher-Arthur Marx play which ran on Broadway for three years. The jokes are chiefly about virginity, and poor David Niven, saddled with an awful teenage daughter, and faced with such lines as 'Look, pumpkin, if you flunk gym, you won't graduate' retreats behind a bemused expression. Faring better are that warm actress Lola Albright, as his wife, and likeable Chad Everett, as a young professor at the girl's school. Everett later blossomed as a poet and singer. Cristina Ferrare is highly resistible as the pumpkin involved, in this nudging, all-too-knowing sex farce.

Impromptu ○① ⓥ
1990, UK, 107 mins, colour
Dir: James Lapine
Stars: Judy Davis, Hugh Grant, Mandy Patinkin, Bernadette Peters, Emma Thompson, Julian Sands
Rating: ★★

A capable international cast attempts the nearly impossible task of carrying off a light comedy about the relationship between George Sand, Chopin and other artists, writers and

I

musicians in 19th century Paris. A good try, too, although you have the uneasy feeling that some of the giggles are unsought and that not all the cast is playing on the same level. Judy Davis does a wicked impression of Glenda Jackson playing George Sand; Emma Thompson enjoys herself voraciously in a supporting but immensely showy part; Julian Sands almost attempts a foreign accent as Liszt; Bernadette Peters is occasionally embarrassing but sometimes very funny as his wife. Anton Rodgers restrains himself (just) from playing it as Restoration farce. Hugh Grant smiles shyly a lot as Chopin. Some of the dialogue is smartly written and you'll get a few chuckles for sure – though you may find it difficult afterwards to describe what kind of film you've just seen.

Impulse ○
1954, UK, 80 mins, b/w
Dir: Charles De La Tour
Stars: Arthur Kennedy, Constance Smith, Joy Shelton
Rating: ★★

One of two thrillers that the Hollywood actor Arthur Kennedy made in this country (the other was the Agatha Christie mystery *Murder She Said!*), this casts him as an estate agent in a sleepy Sussex town whose association with a shady lady tips him from the straight and narrow. An ordinary thriller, but it keeps you guessing, and Kennedy's presence seems to have inspired some pretty good performances.

Impulse ● ⓥ
1984, US, 99 mins, colour
Dir: Graham Baker
Stars: Meg Tilly, Tim Matheson, Hume Cronyn
Rating: ★

A very nasty chiller about a town where people are blowing their brains out but not dying. Confused, malevolent and definitely not for the squeamish, this could have been interesting if director Graham Baker, who made *Alien Nation*, had not chosen to go so far over the top. The delicate talents of Meg Tilly are wasted as the heroine.

Impulse ●
1990, US, 108 mins, colour
Dir: Sondra Locke
Stars: Theresa Russell, Jeff Fahey
Rating: ★★★

Despite solid performances from Theresa Russell, Jeff Fahey and George Dzundza, this thriller relies too heavily on coincidences for its plot twists and, with every startling development, its grip on believability weakens. Russell is an undercover cop whose life and career seem to be going nowhere. When her car breaks down on the way home, on impulse she goes into a bar and picks up a man who is subsequently murdered in his apartment while she is in the bathroom. Would you believe it: he just happened to be a witness she and her department were searching for. It's a hell of a long shot, even more improbable when you would think the police would have circulated a photo of him and that Russell would have seen it. The scenario may be poor, but the story is rattled along at a fair pace by director Sondra Locke, who was the frightened-rabbit heroine in many of Clint Eastwood's films. Judging by this and her previous effort *Ratboy*, she should stick to directing as she shows a talent never hinted at in her acting.

Inadmissible Evidence ◖
1968, UK, 96 mins, b/w
Dir: Anthony Page
Stars: Nicol Williamson, Jill Bennett, Peter Sallis
Rating: ★★

An agonisingly accurate and painful portrait of a man whose life is in a hopeless mess. Nicol Williamson is wretchedly riveting as the faded legal eagle whose sex drive is like a death wish. Even if you don't care about the character, you can't deny the power of the performance. Based on John Osborne's biting stage play (in which Williamson again took the leading role), this is a tense, strongly dramatic film, with good work from Eleanor Fazan, Jill Bennett and Gillian Hills as three of the ladies in Williamson's tangled life. Lindsay Anderson appears in a cameo role, as a barrister.

In a Lonely Place ○
1950, US, 93 mins, b/w
Dir: Nicholas Ray
Stars: Humphrey Bogart, Gloria Grahame, Frank Lovejoy
Rating: ★★★

One of Humphrey Bogart's most underrated movies. Bogart plays a scriptwriter whose violent temperament makes him a prime suspect when the body of a girl is found shortly after she had left his apartment. He also has a brittle and faintly bizarre

affair with the woman (Gloria Grahame) who provides him with a much-needed alibi. Bogart had wanted his wife Lauren Bacall to play the role, but Warners, who still had her under contract, refused. As it is, he still gives one of his most remarkable and intense performances.

Incendiary Blonde ○
1945, US, 113 mins, colour
Dir: George Marshall
Stars: Betty Hutton, Arturo de Cordova, Charles Ruggles, Albert Dekker, Barry Fitzgerald
Rating: ★★★

There can't be many more colourful showbusiness stories than that of 'Texas' Guinan, an American nightclub entertainer who packed more incident into her 48 years than many would have done in twice the time. Betty Hutton gives a typical all-stops-out performance as the gal who was queen of the rodeo, nightclubs, Broadway and even the underworld.

In Cold Blood ○
1967, US, 128 mins, b/w
Dir: Richard Brooks
Stars: Scott Wilson, Robert Blake
Rating: ★★★

In Cold Blood, Truman Capote's non-fiction novel-like account about two Kansas killers, is a probing, sensitive, tasteful, balanced and suspenseful documentary-drama. Heading the competent cast are Robert Blake and Scott Wilson, bearing a striking resemblance to the now-dead Kansas drifters who, in the course of a burglary on 15 November 1959, murdered four of a family. Almost six years later, after an exhausted appeal route, they were hanged. John Forsythe plays the chief investigator who broke the case.

In Country ● ⓥ
1989, US, 115 mins, colour
Dir: Ted Kotcheff
Stars: Bruce Willis, Emily Lloyd, Joan Allen, Kevin Anderson
Rating: ★★★

More American self-flagellation about Vietnam. This underrated film, though, is engagingly framed in the form of a weepie, with Britain's Emily Lloyd quirkily playing the nubile Kentucky teenager trying to find out more about the father who was killed in the war. Lloyd's certainly an actress to watch, whether or not you approve of her style. And the scenes between her and Bruce Willis (as her uncle) towards the end really hit home as he fills her in on what the war was truly like. Willis is almost unrecognisable – hair lightened and slicked back greasily, droop moustache and underlip beard – in a real character performance that ups his acting stock. This is a peculiarly American problem, but rather more of the deep emotions involved filter through here than is usual; it gets close to the nub of things but remains clear-headed throughout.

Incredible Journey, The ⊙ ⊙
1963, US, 80 mins, colour
Dir: Fletcher Markle
Stars: Emile Genest, John Drairie, Tommy Tweed, Sandra Scott
Rating: ★★★

The things done by the three animal stars of this exciting Disney adventure would put even Lassie to shame. All in all, Sheila Burnford's book about a retriever, an old bull terrier and a Siamese cat who trek 300 miles together to return home across mountain, river and forest was a sitter for the Disney album. I hope that dog-lovers will forgive me if I say that Tao, the cat, is the real star of film. For one thing, he has more to do than the two dogs. He fights a bear and a lynx (not at the same time!), is swept away in a raging torrent (and survives), and rescues the two dogs when they are locked up by a friendly trapper who thinks he's doing them a good turn. If only the humans and their dialogue were not so gooey, this would be a wonderful film all the way through. Remade by the studio in 1993.

Incredible Mr Limpet, The ⊙
1963, US, 102 mins, colour
Dir: Arthur Lubin
Stars: Don Knotts, Carole Cook, Jack Weston
Rating: ★★★

Delightful comedy-cartoon-musical about a man who wants to become a fish. The songs are tuneful, the comedy warmly amusing, and the cartoon creates a memorable character in a hermit crab with swivelling eyeballs. The human actors, the boggle-eyed Knotts, tubby Jack Weston, the late Larry Keating as an apoplectic admiral, and especially Carole Cook as a Shelley Winters-style wife, are all very likeable, creating believable characters that add to the film's charm.

Incredible Shrinking Man, The ◑
1957, US, 81 mins, b/w
Dir: Jack Arnold
Stars: Grant Williams, Randy Stuart, April Kent
Rating: ★★★

This classic science-fiction film has a compelling and literate script (from his novel) by Richard Matheson, sustained direction from Jack Arnold, excellent effects by Clifford Stine and really imaginative art direction by Alexander Golitzen and Robert Clatworthy. The fight between tiny Grant Williams and a spider is still a genuine chiller.

Incredible Shrinking Woman, The ⊙
1981, US, 88 mins, colour
Dir: Joel Schumacher
Stars: Lily Tomlin, Charles Grodin, Ned Beatty, Henry Gibson
Rating: ★★★

Universal's new sideshoot from its own 1957 classic *The Incredible Shrinking Man* is mainly for laughs. The same schoolboy enthusiasm for the project is still there, though, and special effects score neatly as Lily Tomlin shrinks towards nothingness. The entire project has a light touch that never allows sentimentality or drama to put a damper on the fun.

Indecent Proposal ● ⊙
1992, US, 117 mins, colour
Dir: Adrian Lyne
Stars: Robert Redford, Demi Moore, Woody Harrelson, Seymour Cassel, Billy Connolly
Rating: ★★

This is *Honeymoon in Vegas* without the laughs. Another couple heavily in debt: another billionaire with an eye for the wife. Here the twist is that the rich man (Robert Redford) offers the poor man (Woody Harrelson) a million dollars for one night with his wife (Demi Moore). Just about believable, perhaps, in Hollywood's world, and the couple vow to agree and forget it ever happened. No problems huh? Well, soon this totally devoted couple is at each other's throats, he yelling that he doesn't trust her anymore, and suspecting she's been sleeping with Redford all the time. Convincing? Well, hang on to the edge of that credibility chasm: worse is to follow. The casting, however, sustains you through the rest. Redford turns on the charm, Moore walks around showing

off her formidable bust, and Harrelson looks crestfallen and morose even when he's not supposed to be. Two of them end up together but you wouldn't give a plugged nickel for the relationship's survival. Hollywood tripe, this, glossily dished up. The 34 Flying Elvises are sadly missed.

Indiana Jones and the Last Crusade ○ ⊙
1989, US, 127 mins, colour
Dir: Steven Spielberg
Stars: Harrison Ford, Sean Connery, Denholm Elliott, Alison Doody, John Rhys-Davies, River Phoenix
Rating: ★★★

Villains in fezzes and Nazis after the Holy Grail. It could only be Indiana Jones (or Monty Python) and it is. Steven Spielberg had to have his arm twisted to cast Sean Connery as the crusty but benign father of Indiana Jones in this third – and many consider finest – of his action-packed adventures. After all, there are only 12 years separating him and Indy star Harrison Ford. But the casting was inspired, with Ford and Connery sparking off each other and the latter engaging in amusing sexual one-upmanship and a string of patronising putdowns. It is easily the best screen pairing since Robert Redford and Paul Newman joined forces. The Nazi villains are less comical and more menacing this time round – Indiana ('just there with a bullwhip to keep the world at bay') even comes face to face with Hitler – and the action set pieces are once again stunningly mounted. Preposterous, exciting and dynamically staged, it's perfect entertainment for all the family.

Indiana Jones and the Temple of Doom ○ ⊙
1984, US, 118 mins, colour
Dir: Steven Spielberg
Stars: Harrison Ford, Kate Capshaw, Ke Huy Kwan
Rating: ★★

Improbable is hardly the word for this billion-dollar 'B' movie which resurrects the spirit of Mr Moto from Thirties films, but adds an air of artificiality more appropriate to a James Bond movie to which, with its massive sets and thousands of yelling extras, this bears more than a passing resemblance. Highlights of the action include the opening sequence in the Obi-Wan (get it?) nightclub, a duel on a collapsed rope ladder and a running

I

gun battle on mining buckets careering along a kind of underground scenic railway that seems to run for miles. Everything is contrived for its effect on the audience and, although some scenes are not for squeamish kids, one can't help imagining that Crosby, Hope and Lamour are hiding round the next boulder.

Indiscreet ○ ⓥ
1958, UK, 100 mins, colour
Dir: Stanley Donen
Stars: Cary Grant, Ingrid Bergman, Cecil Parker, Phyllis Calvert, David Kossof, Megs Jenkins
Rating: ★★★

Entertaining and glossy, this frothy romantic comedy makes a shaky start but builds to a glorious final reel at the same pace as Cary Grant and Ingrid Bergman's relationship. A rarity in that the film is actually better than the play it was based on (with Norman Krasna adapting his own play, *Kind Sir*), its only real surprise was to reveal how deft a comedienne Bergman could be. It's a crying shame she was not offered more opportunity during her career to exploit this talent to the full.

Informer, The ○
1935, US, 91 mins, b/w
Dir: John Ford
Stars: Victor McLaglen, Heather Angel, Una O'Connor, Wallace Ford
Rating: ★★★

Teeming with danger-fraught life and with its angry action spilling across the screen, this stylised examination of the human soul, as seen through the Irish 'Troubles' of the 1920s, was so effectively, chillingly made by director John Ford that his Oscar for best director was only one of several the film won. Ford was so knocked out by the performance of Victor McLaglen (which also took an Academy Award) in the title role that he employed the ugly but loveable veteran actor for the rest of his career. Superb photography by Joseph August suggests menace around every cobbled Dublin corner.

Informers, The ◑
1963, UK, 104 mins, b/w
Dir: Ken Annakin
Stars: Nigel Patrick, Frank Finlay, Margaret Whiting, Colin Blakely
Rating: ★★

Quite vicious for its time, this is a crime thriller with a familiar plot, a story of coppers' narks, big bank raids and the detective (Nigel Patrick) who,

framed by crooks, vows to bring them to book and clear his name while out on bail. Unfortunately, we are asked to believe that his friendly superior and daughter's godfather (Harry Andrews) could be so taken in by a faked picture and money planted in our hero's house as to say, 'I helped make you – now I'll break you!' Still Patrick is always worth watching, there's a fine free-for-all at the end and Frank Finlay, as the chief crook, gives the best performance in the film.

In Harm's Way ○
1965, US, 167 mins, b/w
Dir: Otto Preminger
Stars: John Wayne, Kirk Douglas, Patricia Neal, Tom Tryon, Paula Prentiss, Henry Fonda
Rating: ★★★

Otto Preminger's epic war film about the Japanese devastation of Pearl Harbor, and the initial stages of the American fight back. The first half is at its best when the action is fiercest, but dwells too much on personal relationships. The second half is very much better, with Hollywood showing just how good it is at the war film. In a lengthy cast – it includes Patrick O'Neal, Franchot Tone and Stanley Holloway – John Wayne gives one of his best performances for some while, as a forceful admiral. Other particularly thoughtful portrayals come from Dana Andrews, Paula Prentiss and Burgess Meredith. Kirk Douglas seems slightly out of character as the bitter officer who dashes off on a convenient suicide mission after a young girl he has raped has taken her own life. But that action, from Pearl Harbor to the Pacific front line, packs a powerful punch.

Inherit the Wind ○
1960, US, 127 mins, b/w
Dir: Stanley Kramer
Stars: Spencer Tracy, Fredric March, Florence Eldridge, Gene Kelly
Rating: ★★★

Stanley Kramer's powerful drama, based on the true incident in which a school teacher faced prosecution for lecturing on Darwin's Theory of Evolution in America's Deep South. Spencer Tracy and Fredric March are well matched as the courtroom antagonists. Kramer makes an enthralling spectacle of the courtroom fireworks that take place between these giants of the cinema. Gene Kelly lurks, danceless, on the sidelines as a reporter.

In-Laws, The ○
1979, US, 103 mins, colour
Dir: Arthur Hiller
Stars: Peter Falk, Alan Arkin, Richard Libertini, Penny Peyser, Nancy Dussault, Ed Begley Jr
Rating: ★★★

Peter Falk and Alan Arkin co-star in made-to-measure roles in this zany comedy. Arkin plays a New Yorker dentist and family man who is about to meet his prospective son-in-law's parents for the first time. Little does he suspect that the father, Vince, quite unbeknown to anyone else, is an agent for the CIA. It's all too much for an unadventurous dentist! Arkin plays with what has been termed his 'brand of sub-hysterical panic' but many might well feel that, not for the first time, it's Falk who runs away with the entire film.

In Like Flint ○
1967, US, 114 mins, colour
Dir: Gordon Douglas
Stars: James Coburn, Lee J Cobb, Jean Hale, Andrew Duggan, Anna Lee
Rating: ★

If you like thrillers crammed to overflowing with pretty girls, this spy spoof does its best to please. James Coburn goes through his familiar motions of being Derek Flint, mechanical spy, in athletic style but the absence of any contact with reality, or the hero being in any real danger, brings it down to *Batman* level. Lee J Cobb, in a performance which includes a classic piece of drag, contributes a tinge of acting respect to the cocksure, cartoon-style charade.

In Name Only ○
1939, US, 100 mins, b/w
Dir: John Cromwell
Stars: Cary Grant, Carole Lombard, Kay Francis, Charles Coburn
Rating: ★★★

Cary Grant and Carole Lombard co-starring might lead you to expect something on the lighter side. But no. This is no zany comedy, rather a sombre drama about a frustrated marriage, though well made and handled with taste by director John Cromwell. Kay Francis gleams with venom as Grant's wife.

Inner Circle, The ◑ ⓥ
(aka: The Projectionist)
1992, US, 134 mins, colour
Dir: Andrei Konchalovsky

Stars: Tom Hulce, Lolita Davidovich, Bob Hoskins, Bess Meyer
Rating: ★★

A long, grim drama that comes at you head-on, set in Stalin's Russia and based on a true story. Tom Hulce is earnest but rather annoying as Ivan, a young cinema projectionist who is taken from his home one night by the KGB, and whisked to the inner sanctum of Society power where, thanks to Stalin's love of films, he becomes the Kremlin's private projectionist. Torn between his love for his hero, addiction to his new-found power, loyalty to his wife (Lolita Davidovich) and fear for his life, Ivan eventually has some terrible decisions to make. On-location filming here helps produce some spectacular individual scenes but the acting lacks subtlety with Bob Hoskins going spectacularly over the top as Beria.

InnerSpace ○ Ⓥ
1987, US, 119 mins, colour
Dir: Joe Dante
Stars: Dennis Quaid, Martin Short, Meg Ryan, Vernon Wells, Fiona Lewis, Kevin McCarthy
Rating: ★★★★

Remember the 1966 fantasy *Fantastic Voyage* in which a group of miniaturised scientists were injected into the bloodstream of a human being? Here the vivid imagination of director Joe Dante and his writing team creates brilliant entertainment from a sideshoot of that idea. Hard-drinking naval lieutenant Dennis Quaid is the only one crazy enough to be the guinea pig in a privately financed experiment to inject him into a rabbit. Enter the bad guys, and the chief scientist goes on the run with Quaid and capsule inside a syringe, which he ends up injecting into the backside of ineffectual hypochondriac Martin Short. The rest of this very entertaining film, which seamlessly blends science-fiction, comedy and thrills, involves Quaid contacting Short through the inner ear and trying to keep him clear of immediate extermination by the villains. Quaid and Short both deliver socko performances; and big Vernon Wells has a Jack Palance style menace as the deadly one-armed assassin with an engaging assortment of fake 'hands'.

Innocence Is Bliss ⊙
(aka: Miss Grant Takes Richmond)
1949, US, 87 mins, b/w
Dir: Lloyd Bacon

Stars: Lucille Ball, William Holden
Rating: ★★★

Lucille Ball is at her funniest in this wild farce as a dimwit secretary with William Holden as her bookmaker who's having trouble with the syndicate. They land up promoting low cost housing for the homeless when Ball thinks she's working for an estate agent. The original story is credited to Everett Freeman (older brother Devery helped write the screenplay) but there is a startling resemblance to the tales of Damon Runyon – the gambler with the heart of gold, the gal who's smarter than she looks, the characters who hang out with the bookie. Holden had, up to now, been known as a dramatic actor, but here displays a talent for comedy. He holds his own against seasoned veterans like James Gleason and Frank McHugh and this performance could have been the reason he was chosen to co-star with Judy Holliday in *Born Yesterday*, one of the best ever comedies, just one year later.

Innocent Blood ● Ⓥ
1992, US, 115 mins, colour
Dir: John Landis
Stars: Anne Parillaud, Anthony LaPaglia, Robert Loggia, Don Rickles
Rating: ★★

Round up the usual special effects suspects, there's another vampire movie in town. Though John Landis's modern stab at the dead is strictly fang-in-cheek, it throws in all the adult elements horror and video fans will enjoy: glowing eyes, gouts of blood, gorged throats, the dead come to life, topless dancers, a touch of vaguely kinky sex and enough four-letter words to make a vampire blush. Marie (Anne Parillaud) is the new lady bloodsucker on the block, but she only chomps on the bad guys. Since this is Mob territory and she likes to eat Italian, there's no lack of titbits. After dinner, she blows off the meal's head with a shotgun to ensure he doesn't roam the streets after death (and dark). Marie's problems come when she a) fails to behead mobster kingpin Sal the Shark (Robert Loggia) and b) falls in lust with a good cop (Anthony LaPaglia). The question is: can she resist sinking her teeth into his neck before he's sunk his teeth into the hunt for the crazed Sal? Formula stuff but fans will lap it up, complete with clips from old vampire movies.

Innocent Bystanders ◐
1972, UK, 111 mins, colour
Dir: Peter Collinson
Stars: Stanley Baker, Geraldine Chaplin, Donald Pleasence, Dana Andrews
Rating: ★

Stanley Baker's last major film, this is in the vein of the long list of hard, tough thrillers that established his rugged screen personality. Written by James Mitchell, the film – with its espionage theme and its confusing plot of double-cross – and triple-cross – could well be an extension of Mitchell's famous TV series *Callan*, the leading character here being a top British agent whose nerve has allegedly gone. Although the colour photography often seems as bleached as the desert settings, director Peter Collinson makes his way briskly through the complicated storyline, doing his best to live up to the standards established by this genre in the Seventies.

Innocent Man, An ● Ⓥ
1989, US, 114 mins, colour
Dir: Peter Yates
Stars: Tom Selleck, F Murray Abraham, Laila Robins, David Rasche
Rating: ★★

They could have called this prison drama-cum-revenge thriller *Each Dawn I Die* if Cagney hadn't 'nicked' the title 50 years before. Not that things have changed all that much, apart from the language. Selleck is an ordinary guy framed by two bent vice cops after they bust into his house by mistake and shoot him. Unlikely it all is, but no more so than in Cagney's day when, like Tom, Jimmy was dragged off to serve six years screaming his innocence. In prison, 'shivs' are passed around to do unwanted convicts in, and Selleck has to learn to stand up for himself, with the help of veteran con F Murray Abraham, before getting out in one piece, on parole, to seek a desperate (and again unlikely) revenge on the cops who are still – foolishly – harassing him and his wife. Not a very good movie, as you may have gathered, but certainly quite a watchable one, thanks to its gallery of familiar elements entertainingly put together. Oh yes, and Selleck even does '90 days in the hole', emerging with a stubble and slight cough. Like we said, some things never change, and perhaps it's not altogether a bad thing.

I

Innocents, The ◐
1961, UK, 99 mins, b/w
Dir: Jack Clayton
Stars: Deborah Kerr, Michael Redgrave,
Peter Wyngarde, Megs Jenkins
Rating: ★★★★

Jack Clayton's constantly eerie and finally terrifying version of Henry
James's *The Turn of the Screw*. Consistent performances by Deborah Kerr
and Megs Jenkins, and a briefly powerful one by Peter Wyngarde are
nicely counter-balanced by Martin
Stephens and Pamela Franklin, perfectly in character as the other-worldly
children. Preferably not one to watch
alone. And hold tight for the shattering climax.

Inn of the Sixth Happiness, The ○
1958, US/UK, 151 mins, colour
Dir: Mark Robson
Stars: Ingrid Bergman, Curt Jurgens,
Robert Donat
Rating: ★★★

A moving story of a lady missionary in
China. The film is made more
touching by being the last in which
the splendid Robert Donat was to
appear: he died shortly after
completing it, and his performance,
fine though it is, is sometimes painful
to watch.

In Old California ○
1942, US, 89 mins, b/w
Dir: William McGann
Stars: John Wayne, Binnie Barnes
Rating: ★★

Routine, rather dingy-looking John
Wayne Western from Republic, made
at a time when the studio should have
been doing rather better by their biggest star, following his leap to fame in
Stagecoach. Almost all of Wayne's best
films of the Forties were made on loan
out to other companies, and he didn't
get a decent movie from his home
studio until *Sands of Iwo Jima* in 1949,
which won him his first Oscar nomination. Wayne as a pharmacist takes
some swallowing on the law at the
time of the Gold Rush. Edgar Kennedy and Patsy Kelly supply some
predictably over-the-top light relief.

In Old Chicago ○
1938, US, 95 mins, b/w
Dir: Henry King

Stars: Tyrone Power, Alice Faye, Don
Ameche, Alice Brady, Brian Donlevy,
Andy Devine
Rating: ★★★

Fox's Darryl F Zanuck had wanted
Clark Gable and Jean Harlow for the
leading roles in this classic Thirties
disaster movie but had to settle for
Tyrone Power and Alice Faye, who
was to work memorably again with
Power in *Alexander's Ragtime Band* and
Rose of Washington Square. The story of
rivalry between brothers and Power's
romantic entanglement with Faye may
be strictly routine but it serves well
enough to showcase the still stunning
burning of Chicago in 1871. The fire
itself was staged on Fox's back lot
where it burned for three days under
the direction of H Bruce
Humberstone and the special effects
crew led by Fred Sersen. The rest of
the film was helmed competently by
Henry King and Alice Brady, playing
the owner of the cow that started the
blaze, won a Best Supporting Oscar.

In Old Oklahoma
See: War of the Wildcats

In Search of Gregory ◐
1969, UK, 90 mins, colour
Dir: Peter Wood
Stars: Julie Christie, Michael Sarrazin,
John Hurt, Adolfo Celi
Rating: ★★

Weird little film about a girl in pursuit
of a young man she has never met, but
by whose description she has been
magnetically intrigued. There are
some good individual scenes, including a spectacular game of 'autoball',
but they don't fit together in quite the
way that a cinematic jigsaw should. A
good supporting cast is headed by
Roland Culver.

In Search of the Castaways ☉
1961, US/UK, 100 mins, colour
Dir: Robert Stevenson
Stars: Maurice Chevalier, Hayley Mills,
George Sanders, Wilfrid Hyde White
Rating: ★★★

An absolutely spiffing time is had by
all when this jolly Jules Verne adventure from Disney gets going, and
once it does it hardly ever lets up.
Pinewood stands in nobly for South
America and ice caverns, giant trees,
waterspouts and volcanic eruptions are
all convincingly re-created there.
Hayley Mills, still fresh and exuberant
in her early days with the studio,
Maurice Chevalier and the rest all

give the impression of enjoying the
grand, if occasionally perilous adventure and Paul Beeson's crystal-clear
Technicolor photography puts an
added sparkle on the thrills. Beeson
even finds a touch of poetry in a tableau of four horses rearing in panic
against the steel grey of a gathering
storm.

Inside Daisy Clover ○ Ⓥ
1965, US, 128 mins, colour
Dir: Robert Mulligan
Stars: Natalie Wood, Christopher
Plummer, Robert Redford
Rating: ★★

A searching Hollywood self-
examination: the drama of a talented
teenage singing star almost destroyed
by the studio system, its standards and
its demands. Director Robert
Mulligan, who made *To Kill a Mockingbird* and *Summer of '42*, conducts us
chillingly through Daisy's life, from
success to disillusionment to rebellion.
Natalie Wood gives one of her best
performances, and Robert Redford is
seen in an early film role as the star she
marries. The screenplay tends to
hover around the grave of the Hollywood of 1936 without ever getting
out its shovel and really digging in.
But a few film moguls may still turn in
theirs.

Inside Moves ○
1980, US, 113 mins, colour
Dir: Richard Donner
Stars: John Savage, David Morse, Diana
Scarwid, Amy Wright
Rating: ★★

Here's a film scripted by the husband
and wife team of Valerie Curtin and
Barry Levinson (who also wrote *Best
Friends*). It takes the characters who
converge in a bar – a favourite
framework of Hollywood films since
The Time of Your Life – and follows
their fortunes. In Max's Bar, however,
the denizens are life's mental and
physical misfits. Still, the characters
are colourful, appealing and amusing
and their hearts, like that of the film,
are certainly in the right place. It
marks one of the rare screen appearances of real-life double amputee
Harold Russell, who won an Oscar in
1946 for *The Best Years of Our Lives*.

Insignificance ●
1985, UK, 105 mins, colour
Dir: Nicolas Roeg
Stars: Michael Emil, Theresa Russell,
Tony Curtis
Rating: ★★★

Don't be fooled by the character names in Nicolas Roeg's well-received, ironic and thought-provoking comedy drama. They may be called 'The Professor', 'The Actress', 'The Senator' and 'The Ballplayer' but screenplay and performances – particularly that of Theresa Russell who is seen standing over a subway grating while a gust of air blows her dress above her knees – make it quite clear who the protagonists really are – Albert Einstein, Marilyn Monroe, Senator Joseph McCarthy and Joe Di Maggio. Terry Johnson, ingeniously adapting his play for the screen, comes up with a fascinating proposition. The famous four meet in a New York hotel room one night in 1954 during which, among many strange delights, Monroe explains the Theory of Relativity to Einstein! Roeg has always been an ambitious filmmaker, both in terms of subject and style, as such films as *Walkabout*, *The Man Who Fell To Earth* and *Eureka* have demonstrated. Here subject and style are smartly integrated.

In Society ⊙
1944, US, 74 mins, b/w
Dir: Jean Yarbrough
Stars: Bud Abbott, Lou Costello, Kirby Grant, Ann Gillis
Rating: ★★

A typically frantic Forties vehicle for the slapstick talents of Bud Abbott and Lou Costello casts them as a couple of incompetent plumbers who run amok in a posh mansion. Highlights include the flooding of the bathroom, Lou out of control during a fox hunt and a wild climactic chase with the daffy duo pursuing villain Thomas Gomez in a fire engine. Director Jean Yarbrough, who put Bud and Lou through their comic paces in five features, handles the caper with brisk aplomb, even though some of their capers look little more than embarrassing now.

Inspector, The
See: Lisa

Inspector Clouseau ○ ⓥ
1968, UK, 92 mins, colour
Dir: Bud Yorkin
Stars: Alan Arkin, Delia Boccardo, Frank Finlay
Rating: ★

Alan Arkin took over from Peter Sellers for this one comedy, chronicling the further adventures of the

world's worst Sureté detective, called in to circumvent a robbery. The British supporting cast puts in some stout cameos, but Sellers proves a hard act to follow.

Inspector General, The ⊙
(aka: Happytimes)
1949, US, 102 mins, colour
Dir: Henry Koster
Stars: Danny Kaye, Barbara Bates, Walter Slezak, Elsa Lanchester
Rating: ★★★

Nikolai Gogol's play doesn't do badly as a vehicle for Danny Kaye, the Goldwyn gloss, some good quips and ditties and a colourful supporting cast making it brighter than it ever seemed on stage. Barbara Bates is a pretty heroine and Walter Slezak supremely oily as Kaye's sometime confidant.

Inspector Hornleigh ○
1938, UK, 87 mins, b/w
Dir: Eugene Forde
Stars: Gordon Harker, Alastair Sim
Rating: ★★★

The first of three popular British comedy-thrillers based on a successful radio series of the immediate pre-war days. Gordon Harker and Alastair Sim who, one imagines, could just as well have tackled each other's roles, are wonderfully well teamed as the inspector and sergeant on the trail of the men who stole the Chancellor of the Exchequer's bag! The results are a bit wordy but very entertaining. Followed by *Inspector Hornleigh on Holiday* and *Inspector Hornleigh Goes to It*: all three are well worth catching for Sim and Harker fans.

Interiors ◐
1978, US, 93 mins, colour
Dir: Woody Allen
Stars: Richard Jordan, Diane Keaton, Geraldine Page, Sam Waterston
Rating: ★

Described by some critics as Woody Allen's attempt to make a film in the style of Ingmar Bergman, this heavily-stylised tale of inter-familial bickering does finally get around to showing us the kind of film it might have been all along. As soon as dumpy, abrasive Maureen Stapleton steps on to the scene, as the new bride-to-be of the father of the film's three sisters, the movie not only tightens up, but brightens up, taking its cue from the colour of her dress. She gives the over-intense events a new dimension, a different ingredient

against which the other characters – all as neurotic as each other – can play. The performance was rightly rewarded with an Academy Award nomination for best supporting actress, an award she actually won three years later for *Reds*. The subtle cinematography of Allen's regular cameraman, Gordon Willis, complements the director's vision.

Interlude ◐
1968, UK, 113 mins, colour
Dir: Kevin Billington
Stars: Oskar Werner, Barbara Ferris, Virginia Maskell, Donald Sutherland, John Cleese
Rating: ★★

Justifiably high hopes were held for Barbara Ferris at the time of this skilful love story, and it's rather sad that she never made a complete breakthrough to stardom. Here she matches that excellent actor Oskar Werner emotion for emotion in a well photographed, if bleak, look at the affair between a young girl reporter and a famous conductor. Shafts of lunatic humour break up the sentimental moments, and John Cleese has a few deliciously acid lines as a public relations man.

Intermezzo ○ ⓥ
(aka: Escape to Happiness)
1939, US, 69 mins, b/w
Dir: Gregory Ratoff
Stars: Ingrid Bergman, Leslie Howard, Edna Best, John Halliday
Rating: ★★★

This Hollywood remake of Ingrid Bergman's sixth Swedish picture (also called *Intermezzo*) made her an international star. Playing a young pianist involved in an adulterous affair with violinist Leslie Howard, she garnered rave reviews, including one from Britain's Graham Greene who wrote of a 'performance which doesn't give the effect of acting at all but of living'. Impeccable black and white photography by Gregg Toland, and Oscar-nominated musical direction by Lou Forbes. British title: *Escape to Happiness*. One of the briefest Hollywood super-hits on record.

Internal Affairs ● ⓥ
1990, US, 117 mins, colour
Dir: Mike Figgis
Stars: Richard Gere, Andy Garcia, Nancy Travis, William Baldwin, Annabella Sciorra
Rating: ★★

I

Gere's brilliant performance as a very crooked cop who has no hesitation in getting people killed fires this otherwise overlong, overdone and directorially very flashy thriller. Taciturn Andy Garcia plays the newcomer to Internal Affairs (the cops' department that investigates cops) whose examination of one corrupt policeman, a former buddy, leads him to an obsession with the buddy's boss (Richard Gere). Garcia has a strange and unbelievable marriage with Nancy Travis that degenerates into abuse and foul-mouthed screaming matches at the drop of a few late nights and Garcia's acquisition of a female (lesbian) partner – Laurie Metcalf with the film's only other decent performance. No wonder Gere finds it easy to drive a wedge between them, although it's hard to see why he eventually presses the self-destruct button by meddling in Garcia's private life. This is all long, slow and spun out by its director from a straight action film to one with pretensions its plot and dialogue can't sustain. But it's kept alive by the spark of Gere's understated but lethal menace.

International Lady ○
1941, US, 100 mins, b/w
Dir: Tim Whelan
Stars: George Brent, Ilona Massey, Basil Rathbone, George Zucco, Gene Lockhart
Rating: ★★

Typical fast-moving, middle-budget American espionage thriller of the war years. George Brent and Basil Rathbone are well matched as the American and British agents on the track of a spy ring. In a small role: Clayton Moore, later to win TV fame as *The Lone Ranger*.

International Velvet ○
1978, UK, 127 mins, colour
Dir: Brian Forbes
Stars: Tatum O'Neal, Nanette Newman, Christopher Plummer, Anthony Hopkins
Rating: ★★

There was a 34-year wait for a sequel to the Elizabeth Taylor children's classic *National Velvet*, and after sitting through more than two hours of this inferior soap opera, you'll be wishing director/screenwriter Bryan Forbes had kept his hands off the story. Forbes' real-life wife, Nannette Newman, plays the grown-up Velvet character, now living in England, and looking after an orphaned American niece (Tatum O'Neal). Distrust and animosity on the part of the girl

soon melts away when they discover a mutual love of horses. But the film is marred by supremely banal dialogue, matched only by the direction.

Interpol ○
(aka: Pickup Alley)
1957, UK, 92 mins, b/w
Dir: John Gilling
Stars: Victor Mature, Trevor Howard, Anita Ekberg
Rating: ★★

Hollywood's original Mr Beefcake, Victor Mature, frowns and glowers his way through this story about an international crime chase, while Britain's Trevor Howard quietly acts him off the screen. Howard leads the police a merry dance (and runs rings round his fellow stars) as the villain.

Intersection ● ⓥ
1994, US, 99 mins, colour
Dir: Mark Rydell
Stars: Richard Gere, Sharon Stone, Lolita Davidovich, Martin Landau, Jenny Morrison
Rating: ★★

Richard Gere is torn between two women in this remake of a 1970 French film which opens, as does this, with the leading character hovering between life and death after a car crash. What happens between that and the final resolution is just barely interesting in a high-gloss kind of way. Gere turns on the charm, but occasionally goes over the top. Sharon Stone and Lolita Davidovich give it their best shot as the women involved, but they're not quite up to touching our emotions with their problems. Pretty 14-year-old Jenny Morrison makes a promising debut as Gere's daughter and old-stager Martin Landau gets the best bit of dialogue in the film when he tells Gere to get on with things and make a decision between estranged wife (Stone) and new lover (Davidovich). Real life, though, is kept resolutely at bay.

In the Doghouse ○
1961, UK, 84 mins, b/w
Dir: Michael Pertwee
Stars: Leslie Phillips, Peggy Cummins, Hattie Jacques
Rating: ★★

Fast and furious *Carry On*-style comedy about the misadventures of a hapless vet. It was pretty Peggy Cummins' last film to date in a career

which stretches back to a debut as a teenager in the Thirties. In the late Forties, she was put under contract by 20th Century-Fox, and starred in such films as *Moss Rose*, *The Late George Apley*, *Green Grass of Wyoming*, *Escape*, *That Dangerous Age* and – perhaps best of all – *Gun Crazy*.

In the French Style ◐
1963, US, 105 mins, b/w
Dir: Robert Parrish
Stars: Jean Seberg, Stanley Baker
Rating: ★★★

This touching, involving Anglo-French drama, about a girl called Christina fruitlessly in search of love, is remembered as the film in which Miss Seberg finally obliterated memories of her disastrous film debut in Saint Joan with a haunting performance that brilliantly reflects Christina in all her moods.

In the Good Old Summertime ☉
1949, US, 115 mins, colour
Dir: Robert Z Leonard
Stars: Judy Garland, Van Johnson, S Z Sakall, Buster Keaton
Rating: ★★★

A musical remake of the 1940 romance *The Shop Around The Corner*, with the location switched from Vienna to Chicago. Judy Garland is virtually the whole show and the songs include, besides the title number 'I Don't Care', 'Merry Christmas', 'Put Your Arms Around Me Honey' and 'Wait 'Til the Sun Shines, Nellie'. The three-year-old tot who appears with Judy and Van Johnson at the end of the picture is Judy's daughter Liza Minnelli.

In the Heat of the Night ◐ ⓥ
1967, US, 109 mins, colour
Dir: Norman Jewison
Stars: Sidney Poitier, Rod Steiger, Warren Oates, Lee Grant, Scott Wilson, Larry Gates
Rating: ★★★

This essentially simple whodunnit is raised far above the norm, thanks to a racially-charged sub-plot and powerful acting from Sidney Poitier and Rod Steiger. Woven together with tension and drama by director Norman Jewison, *In the Heat of the Night* scooped five Oscars. Big city policeman Virgil Tibbs (Poitier) comes up against a wall of prejudice when he tries to help bigoted but canny Police Chief Gillespie (Steiger) solve a murder case in a small Southern town. Tibbs finds he has to come to terms with his own prejudices as well as those of the people around him, which adds another dimension to the film. Steiger won an Oscar for Best Actor, while Poitier went on to reprise the role of Tibbs in two follow-ups – *They Call Me MISTER Tibbs!* and *The Organisation*. This was the original and best, though, and the intervening years haven't dated it.

In the Line of Fire ● Ⓥ
1993, US, 127 mins, colour
Dir: Wolfgang Peterson
Stars: Clint Eastwood, John Malkovich, Rene Russo, Dylan McDermott, Gary Cole
Rating: ★★

Clint Eastwood's back in smart-suited action, though as Frank Horrigan rather than Harry Callahan, and sensibly playing on his advancing years to add a few frayed edges to the character. Frank's a secret service man, a dinosaur from the Kennedy era, and now 'the only active agent who ever lost a president'. When a psycho assassin (John Malkovich) homes in on the current president, Frank demands back into the protection racket. Trouble is, jogging alongside the president's car, he now has problems keeping up. However, the assassin, realising that Frank was around at the Kennedy killing, begins a cat-and-mouse game with him, taunting him with the failures of his past life. When one of Clint's buddies gets shot in pursuit of the villain, the old-timer grits his teeth and you know the bad guy's in trouble. Despite a suspensefully edited ending, the film's a tad long, and efficient rather than exciting, especially in its treatment of a rooftop chase, which doesn't make the blood race the way it should.

In the Name of the Father ● Ⓥ
1993, UK, 133 mins, colour
Dir: Jim Sheridan
Stars: Daniel Day-Lewis, Pete Postlethwaite, Emma Thompson, Corin Redgrave
Rating: ★★

Considering it concerns one of the major miscarriages of justice this century – the wrongful conviction of the Guildford Four – it's a pity this isn't a more dramatically gripping film. Your attention may wander more than once en route to its explosive con-

clusion. The facts, of course, speak for themselves. Thanks to police suppression of defence evidence, not only were the Four, led by Gerry Conlon (Daniel Day-Lewis) sentenced to 30-year terms for the bombing of a Guildford pub in 1974, but their relatives, some of them hardly more than children, went to prison and detention centres too. Conlon's father, resolutely played by Pete Postlethwaite, served several years of a 12-year term before dying in prison. Against this background, director Jim Sheridan makes something of the father-son relationship but very little of the passing years in jail which, despite a few explosive incidents, convey boredom rather than suspense. The formidable Emma Thompson (barely in the film at all till near the end) seems miscast, and her final courtroom scenes rushed and misjudged, as the defence counsel who finally seized on the vital piece of evidence that won the Four their freedom. Day-Lewis does all you could expect as Conlon, and the film does make you wonder how many such miscarriages lurk in the darker corners of the British legal system.

In the Navy ☉
1941, US, 85 mins, b/w
Dir: Arthur Lubin
Stars: Bud Abbott, Lou Costello, Dick Powell, The Andrews Sisters
Rating: ★★★

A pretty funny Abbott and Costello comedy, which gives them a chance to include one or two of their best stage routines, including 'the old shell game', performed here with lemons. Not quite sure at this time of their new stars' pulling power, Universal asked Dick Powell to co-star to boost the film's box-office prospect (which, as it turned out, needed very little boosting). Powell, whose career was temporarily on the slide, agreed, provided he be given equal billing with the stars. And so it was 'Abbott & Costello and Dick Powell *In the Navy*' on the billboards. Powell was given a couple of songs and so were The Andrews Sisters, in what proved to be a breezy romp that stands the test of time better than most of the comedians' films.

In the Nick ○
1960, US, 105 mins, b/w
Dir: Ken Hughes
Stars: Anthony Newley, Anne Aubrey, Ian Hendry, Harry Andrews, Bernie Winters,

James Booth
Rating: ★★

Anthony Newley as a prison psychiatrist, with whom a gangster's moll falls in love. Quite a bright comedy with attractive characters and a script that's largely warm and witty. Sort of a sequel to *Jazzboat*, this has its embarrassing moments, but a believable villain in Ian Hendry.

In This Our Life ○
1942, US, 101 mins, b/w
Dir: John Huston
Stars: Bette Davis, Olivia de Havilland, George Brent, Dennis Morgan, Charles Coburn, Hattie McDaniel
Rating: ★★★

Only crusty old Charles Coburn proves a match for Bette Davis (both in the story and the acting department) as she rampages over the rest of the cast in this lurid melodrama about a self-willed hussy who ruins everyone's life including her own. 'There's a demon within Bette,' observed director John Huston afterwards, 'and I let the demon go on this one.' You're supposed to be able to spot the stars of Huston's *The Maltese Falcon* (including Humphrey Bogart and Peter Lorre) in a 'good luck' guest appearance in a bar scene, but you'll have to be mighty sharp to do it.

Into the Night ◐ Ⓥ
1985, US, 115 mins, colour
Dir: John Landis
Stars: Jeff Goldblum, Michelle Pfeiffer, Richard Farnsworth, Irene Papas, Paul Mazursky, David Bowie
Rating: ★★★

A foray into the madness of insomnia, directed by John Landis. The under-rated Jeff Goldblum is perfectly cast as the insomniac who becomes involved with damsel-in-distress Michelle Pfeiffer – and much more besides. The starry line-up also features David Bowie, Dan Aykroyd and Richard Farnsworth, as well as cameos from a host of Hollywood directors. The wonderful bluesy soundtrack features BB King. A delight for film buffs, blues fans and insomniacs alike.

Into the West ○ Ⓥ
1992, UK/Ireland, 102 mins, colour
Dir: Mike Newell
Stars: Gabriel Byrne, Ellen Barkin, Brendon Gleeson, David Kelly
Rating: ★★★

I

Partly a story about a boy and a horse, partly an allegory, and partly a story of finding yourself and leaving the past behind, this liltingly scored Irish movie has a good deal of charm, even if its pace, like that of the horse (white of course) varies from a trot to a gallop. The horse appears on the seashore, attaches itself to Grandpa Riley and clearly has a mission in life. Cottoning on to Riley's eight-year-old grandson Ossie, it settles into the family high-rise with Ossie's cool, protective older brother Tito and their father (Gabriel Byrne), an ex-traveller who has tried to settle to city life since the death of his wife and now lurches between odd jobs and the bottle. The horse's jumping prowess brings it to the attention of Byrne's arch-enemy, the local (crooked) police inspector, who sees to it that the horse ends up in the hands of an equally corrupt businessman. The rest of the film concerns the boys' seizure of the horse during a show-jumping event and their subsequent flight into the west. The film goes a bit precious on us in an over-sentimental ending, but incidentals along the way – especially when boys and horse break into a cinema and watch a Western eating popcorn – more than make up for it.

Intrigue ○
1947, US, 90 mins, b/w
Dir: Edwin L Marin
Stars: George Raft, June Havoc, Tom Tully
Rating: ★

Far from the days of Far Eastern settings heavy with atmosphere, this Shanghai-set thriller is a good representative of Hollywood on its way down from the golden era of the late Thirties and early Forties. George Raft, too, was past his prime as a box-office attraction, and shambles through this story of smuggling and chicanery. Jane Havoc does what she can with a 'dragon lady' sort of role, Helena Carter is a pretty if petulant heroine and the script, which runs like a newspaper comic strip, is a collection of oriental clichés almost as tired as the star. Director Edwin L Marin made some good Randolph Scott Westerns, but he can't do much with this.

Intruder, The ○
1953, UK, 84 mins, b/w
Dir: Guy Hamilton
Stars: Jack Hawkins, Dennis Price, Michael Medwin, George Cole
Rating: ★★★

Two films for the price of one: a wartime action adventure and a suspense drama, as ex-colonel Jack Hawkins hunts out old comrades in a bid to find out why one of them has turned to crime. Director Guy Hamilton, then just starting on a distinguished career, makes it all work well on both levels. Hawkins, too, gets well inside both the 'past' and 'present' personalities of the leading character. Michael Medwin gives just about his best film performance as the corporal turned criminal.

Intruder in the Dust ○
1949, US, 87 mins, b/w
Dir: Clarence Brown
Stars: David Brian, Juano Hernandez, Claude Jarman Jr, Porter Hall
Rating: ★★★

This adaptation of a William Faulkner novel is in low-key mode throughout, but holds up well both as a study of racial prejudice and as a murder thriller. The white teenager who tries to clear his elderly black friend (played with great dignity by Juano Hernandez) is portrayed by Claude Jarman Jr, one of the most appealing of Hollywood's child stars, who won a special Academy Award after his performance in *The Yearling* in 1946.

Invaders, The
See: *49th Parallel*

Invaders from Mars ○
1953, US, 78 mins, colour
Dir: William Cameron Menzies
Stars: Arthur Franz, Helena Carter, Jimmy Hunt, Leif Erickson
Rating: ★★

Although it aroused no great attention in its day, this garish, oddball science-fiction film has attained cult stature with the passing of the years. The Cinecolor process forces director/ production designer William Cameron Menzies to adopt a green-and-gold colour scheme which gives the film a distinctive, almost muddy look appropriate in particular to the sub-sandpit settings where the Martians carry on their fiendish work. The story is told from the view of a boy, played by Jimmy Hunt, who appeared as a police chief in the (inferior) remake 33 years later.

Invasion of the Body Snatchers ◑ ⓥ
1956, US, 80 mins, b/w
Dir: Don Siegel

Stars: Kevin McCarthy, Dana Wynter, Larry Gates
Rating: ★★★★

Lovers of the chiller-thriller should on no account miss this remarkable science-fiction film, which achieved tremendous and unexpected success on its first appearance. Fantasy is presented in its most terrifying form. There are no monsters – only the inhabitants of a small American town, their minds, wills and bodies 'taken over' by a weird form of life from outer space. Director Don Siegel brought an entirely new approach to the horror field. He proved himself master of the chilly clutch at the base of one's spine.

Invasion of the Body Snatchers ● ⓥ
1978, US, 111 mins, colour
Dir: Philip Kaufman
Stars: Donald Sutherland, Brooke Adams, Leonard Nimoy, Veronica Cartwright, Jeff Goldblum, Kevin McCarthy
Rating: ★★★

Although it coarsens the original classic 1956 version of the story, this remake of the chilling tale of alien possession is still a good thriller in its own right. Director Philip Kaufman pays homage to the first version of the yarn (in which a weird form of plant life descends on earth and takes over human beings when they fall asleep) not only in his use of the director (Don Siegel) and star (Kevin McCarthy) of the original in cameo roles, but by his use of angled shadow, reminiscent of Forties and Fifties film. Kaufman shows real skill in the way that everyday things are made to carry a sense of menace. And, for all its running length, this film moves along at an unflaggingly exciting pace. The ending carries a considerable shock charge. Further remake in 1993.

Investigation of Murder, An
See: *The Laughing Policeman*

Invisible Man, The ○
1933, US, 71 mins, b/w
Dir: James Whale
Stars: Claude Rains, Gloria Stuart, Henry Travers, William Harrigan
Rating: ★★★

Fine Hollywood version of H G Wells's story about the man whose invisibility creates havoc in an English village. The film made a star out of English-born actor Claude

Rains, even though his face is not seen until near the end of the film. But he quickly developed into one of Hollywood's most incisive character stars, and was nominated four times for Oscars (shamefully without winning once) in the best supporting actor category.

Invisible Ray, The ◑
1936, US, 81 mins, b/w
Dir: Lambert Hillyer
Stars: Boris Karloff, Bela Lugosi, Frances Drake, Frank Lawton
Rating: ★★★

This story of a scientist poisoned by radioactive ore, whose touch will kill after a daily antidote has worn off, was one of several grim yarns on which Boris Karloff and Bela Lugosi got together in the Thirties. Well directed by Lambert Hillyer, who made the underrated *Dracula's Daughter* in the same year as this picture.

Invisible Stripes ○
1939, US, 82 mins, b/w
Dir: Lloyd Bacon
Stars: George Raft, William Holden, Humphrey Bogart, Jane Bryan
Rating: ★★★

Seldom-seen (but good), strongly cast prison/crime story based on yet another book by Warden Lewis E Lawes, seemingly the source material for half the prison films in Hollywood's history. Humphrey Bogart's Chuck Martin is clearly related to his Baby Face Martin in *Dead End*, as he's still snapping, snarling and doing the things Bogey did all the time before he became a movie hero. Newcomer William Holden strengthened the cast even more when Warners cast him as ex-con George Raft's kid brother, but Britain's Flora Robson is uneasily cast as their ma. In-joke: when Bogart and moll Lee Patrick are seen leaving a film, it's *You Can't Get Away With Murder*. Not only is the title prophetic to this plot, but it starred Bogart and was based on yet another book by Lawes!

Invitation to a Gunfighter ○
1964, US, 92 mins, colour
Dir: Richard Wilson
Stars: Yul Brynner, George Segal, Janice Rule, Pat Hingle
Rating: ★★★

George Segal got his first leading role in this serious Western about a Union town which hires a notorious gunfighter to get rid of its only surviving

Rebel homesteader at the end of the American Civil War. Segal is very good as the dogged Reb, while Brynner's role is more or less a continuation of his Chris in the *Magnificent Seven* films.

In Which We Serve ○ ⊚
1942, UK, 110 mins, b/w
Dir: David Lean, Noel Coward
Stars: Noel Coward, John Mills, Bernard Miles, Celia Johnson, Richard Attenborough, Michael Wilding
Rating: ★★★★

Needing a co-director, Noel Coward gave David Lean his first chance behind the cameras on this inspiring, expertly-scripted war drama. The first British film to depict a naval war in all its grim reality, it proved the country's top moneymaker in the year of its release. Coward himself gave his best screen performance in the lead, and revived the film career of the young John Mills by casting him as Shorty Blake. With *We Dive at Dawn*, *This Happy Breed* and *Great Expectations* Mills' rise to the top in Britain would parallel that of his director. After Coward and Lean watched the finished film together, Coward turned to Lean and told him: 'Well, dear boy, from now on you can take anything I write and make a film of it.'

Ipcress File, The ○ ⊚
1965, UK, 109 mins, colour
Dir: Sidney J Furie
Stars: Michael Caine, Nigel Green, Guy Doleman
Rating: ★★★

This gruelling spy drama captured the imagination of the public to such a degree that star Michael Caine went on to star in two other (weaker) films about Len Deighton's Cockney crook turned secret agent Harry Palmer. If it seems to border on 007 territory, look no further than the production credits from the previous year's *Goldfinger* to see what they have in common – including co-producer Harry Salzman, editor Peter Hunt, production designer Ken Adam, assistant director Peter Murton and composer John Barry. Caine's anti-hero Palmer is a delightful creation, complete with thick spectacles, even thicker London accent, and a taste for Mozart and good food. The film was a huge international success for director Sidney J Furie, who demonstrated for the first time his panache for seeking out the strangest camera angles, in-

cluding shooting through a set of clashing cymbals and the top of a parking meter.

I Remember Mama ○
1948, US, 134 mins, b/w
Dir: George Stevens
Stars: Irene Dunne, Barbara Bel Geddes, Oscar Homolka, Philip Dorn
Rating: ★★★★

George Stevens' classic blend of humour and sentiment in the story of a Norwegian family, headed by a wise and indomitable mother, and their sometimes happy, sometimes tragic, always very human experiences, in San Francisco in 1910. Irene Dunne gives one of the best performances of her career (her Norwegian accent is impeccable) as Mama, while Oscar Homolka, as a bombastic uncle, creates minor havoc by his mere presence. The long running time is typical of Stevens' meticulous direction, where each scene is milked for every last drop of wonderful sentiment.

Irma La Douce ◑
1963, US, 146 mins, colour
Dir: Billy Wilder
Stars: Jack Lemmon, Shirley MacLaine, Lou Jacobi
Rating: ★★

Fairytale-style comedy which begins with a bang, and ends with a superbly-handled wedding scene, with the bride about to have a baby at any minute. Director Billy Wilder has taken the hit stage musical about a gendarme who falls for a prostitute, stripped it of its songs, and turned it into a pleasant, likeable comedy, with performances from Jack Lemmon and Shirley MacLaine (so memorable together in *The Apartment*) that are every bit as good as one might expect. Too long though; the songs instead of some of the dramatic padding might have made a difference.

Iron Eagle ◑ ⊚
1986, US, 119 mins, colour
Dir: Sidney J Furie
Stars: Louis Gossett Jr, Jason Gedrick, David Suchet, Tim Thomerson
Rating: ★★★

Leave logic behind and enjoy the surging action scenes in this gung-ho adventure film about a group of American fighter pilots attempting a perilous hostage rescue somewhere in the Middle East. The dialogue is mainly moronic, but the stars at least

I

look as though they believe in what they're doing and the aerial dogfights really set the adrenalin and blood bubbling. David Suchet is a caricature villain, but then most of this story could have sprung straight from a comic-strip.

Iron Eagle II ◖ ⓥ
1988, Canada, 101 mins, colour
Dir: Sidney J Furie
Stars: Louis Gossett Jr, Mark Humphrey, Stuart Margolin
Rating: ★★★

Naive and flag-waving, this is a very old-fashioned Hollywood-style 'war' film, with aerial action that edges out anything in *Top Gun*. The simplistic story of bomber pilots aiming to blow up an (unnamed) Arab nuclear base is given a novel tweak by mixing in a team of American and Russian pilots to do the job. But with dialogue like 'You got a discipline problem. I hear you find orders hard to swallow' and some exceptionally unlikely turns of events, director Sidney J Furie must rely on his special effects crew and aerial cameraman to deliver the goods. And so they do, in spectacular fashion, making this gung-ho action pic a very exciting 20th-century version of *Star Wars* as the pilots, by now maverick after discovering a high-up plot to sabotage the mission by assembling 'Dirty Dozen' misfits, home in on the missile base. Competent performances are, under the circumstances, all this international co-production requires.

Iron Glove, The ○
1954, US, 77 mins, colour
Dir: William Castle
Stars: Robert Stack, Richard Stapley, Ursula Thiess
Rating: ★★

Swashbuckling adventure based on a true event in 17th century history, when an adventurer called Charles Wogan was hired to protect the future bride of James, the Old Pretender, on a hazardous journey.

Iron Man, The ○
1951, US, 82 mins, b/w
Dir: Joseph Pevney
Stars: Jeff Chandler, Evelyn Keyes, Stephen McNally, Rock Hudson
Rating: ★★

Third screen version of the vigorous boxing novel of the same name by W R Burnett, who also wrote *Little Caesar*. Jeff Chandler is suitably

unrelenting as the miner who turns killer in the boxing ring, and there are good performances from Evelyn Keyes as his girl, Rock Hudson as the friend he ultimately has to fight, and Jim Backus as a sportswriter. The ring scenes are pretty authentic for their day, and director Joseph Pevney keeps the reliable old story going at a good clip.

Iron Maze ●
1991, US, 101 mins, colour
Dir: Hiroaki Yoshida
Stars: Jeff Fahey, Bridget Fonda, Hiroaki Murakami, J T Walsh
Rating: ★★

A turgid triangle running along *noir* lines, this is a drawn-out thriller comprising different accounts of an attempted murder – pretty obviously derived from the Japanese classic *Rashomon*. It isn't difficult to figure out the culprit, more difficult to figure out the attraction of moody bellboy Jeff Fahey for Bridget Fonda, the slight, plain American wife of the Japanese tycoon who's building an amusement park in the industrial town where Fahey used to work at the giant steel mill, now closed down. The atmosphere of the town's hopelessness is well established, but the unfolding of the slim plotline is slow and seems to take forever to reach its conclusion. J T Walsh, in a bigger role than usual, does a good turn as the local sheriff.

Iron Mistress, The ○
1952, US, 108 mins, colour
Dir: Gordon Douglas
Stars: Alan Ladd, Virginia Mayo, Joseph Calleia, Phyllis Kirk
Rating: ★★

Colourful adventure story which offers a sometimes exciting if often fanciful portrait of American Western folk-hero Jim Bowie, who invented the Bowie knife. The performances are a bit colourless, so the action is everything, especially when Bowie (Alan Ladd), armed only with a knife, takes on a swordsman in a darkened room.

Iron Petticoat, The ○
1956, UK, 96 mins, colour
Dir: Ralph Thomas
Stars: Bob Hope, Katharine Hepburn, James Robertson Justice, Robert Helpmann
Rating: ★★★

A sort of satirical *Ninotchka* refashioned as a Bob Hope comedy. Hope's bril-

liant comedy barbs are matched by Katharine Hepburn's acid wit. The script is by Ben Hecht, an Academy Award winner as far back as 1928.

Ironweed ● ⓥ
1987, US, 144 mins, colour
Dir: Hector Babenco
Stars: Jack Nicholson, Meryl Streep, Carroll Baker
Rating: ★★★

After the Oscar-winning success of his *Kiss of the Spider Woman*, this first American film from Brazilian director Hector Babenco was eagerly awaited. But despite two towering central performances from Jack Nicholson and Meryl Streep (reunited after the previous year's *Heartburn*), *Ironweed* was a disappointment. Dubbed 'a film without an audience' by one critic, it's a low life story set among the street bums of Manhattan during the great Depression, and based on a Pulitzer Prize-winning novel about a vagrant trying to get back into the society he dropped out of years earlier. Nicholson has an up-hill task to make you care about his character, while Streep has so little to do, it's a mystery why she accepted the role. Singer-turned-actor Tom Waits gives probably the film's most textured performance, which perfectly conveys the life he's sacrificed. But it's a slow and grimy journey that'll leave you wanting a bath.

Irreconcilable Differences ◖
1984, US, 113 mins, colour
Dir: Charles Shyer
Stars: Ryan O'Neal, Shelley Long, Drew Barrymore, Sam Wanamaker, Sharon Stone
Rating: ★★

Any movie is going to have problems recovering from an opening scene in which a (faintly obnoxious) nine-year-old child tells the judge: 'I wanna divorce my parents.' There are times, though, when this attempted screwball romantic drama gives it a fair go, thanks mainly to the efforts of Shelley Long as one half of the warring couple. The plot is full of nostalgia for older (and, alas, better) movies, within whose framework such a story might once have worked if our emotions had been engaged. But we aren't meant to take this one seriously, are we, especially with embryo film director Ryan O'Neal (as Long's other half) making a musical version of *Gone With the Wind* that goes over the top in every respect and must have been too horrendous in the first place to even contemplate? But the final courtroom 'tear-jerk', to say nothing of the slanging-match interludes, suggests that maybe this look at the spoilt rich who deserve a second chance represents the world at large and that we should coo in sympathy. Not in this day and age.

Isadora ◐
1968, US, 152 mins, colour
Dir: Karel Reisz
Stars: Vanessa Redgrave, James Fox, Jason Robards
Rating: ★★

Most people know the name Isadora Duncan, yet few could tell you what she actually did in life. So, if nothing else, this biopic does try to convey the flavour of an exceptional woman born wildly out of her time. Isadora was a free spirit, a dancer, and, if you like, a turn-of-the-century hippie. She believed in free expression and free love, and possessed an incredible magnetism which the film somehow fails to bring across, even given the benefit of Vanessa Redgrave's skilful and suitably extravagant interpretation of the title role. As a study of the lives and times of some of the more unusual inhabitants of English, French, Russian and American society in Edwardian times, however, the narrative remains gripping throughout its lengthy running time, originally more than three hours, but cut for subsequent general consumption. Jason Robards is terrific as Singer of the sewing maching family (by whom Isadora has a child) in one of the film's more amusing interludes.

I See a Dark Stranger ○ ◐
(aka: The Adventuress)
1946, UK, 111 mins, b/w
Dir: Frank Launder
Stars: Deborah Kerr, Trevor Howard
Rating: ★★★

Excellent wartime drama with a multiplicity of incident and some fascinating characters. Deborah Kerr is bewitching as the adventuress who, keen to join the IRA, becomes the pawn of Nazis instead. The writer-director team of Frank Launder and Sidney Gilliat, which had just had an enormous hit with *The Rake's Progress* and were shortly to have yet another with *Green for Danger* concocted, with the aid of Wolfgang Wilhelm and actor Liam Redmond

(who also plays a major part in the film) one of their cleverest and most incisive scripts.

I See Ice ☉
1938, UK, 81 mins, b/w
Dir: Anthony Kimmins
Stars: George Formby, Kay Walsh
Rating: ★★★

Wigan's cheeky comic George Formby became one of Britain's top box-office film stars in the Thirties. Here, he's on top form as a photographer who falls for a skater, lands himself in prison and ends up refereeing an ice hockey match. Uproarious, fast-moving comedy on and off the ice.

I Shall Return
See: An American Guerilla in the Philippines

Ishtar ○ ◐
1987, US, 107 mins, colour
Dir: Elaine May
Stars: Warren Beatty, Dustin Hoffman, Isabelle Adjani, Charles Grodin
Rating: ★★

Is it a road movie? Is it a sharp, witty comedy? Or is it a total turkey? Only a handful of films have been bad-mouthed by the movie industry , prior to release, to the extent of *Ishtar*. Despite the stories, the film was wrapped only a week behind schedule and only a million dollars or so over budget! It deserves a kinder look; director Elaine May is a true original and she coaxes performances of real, touching humour from the unlikely pairing of Dustin Hoffman and Warren Beatty. They play a pair of down-and-out songwriters who end up in a North African revolution (they actually did write one of the songs they perform – 'Half Hour Song'). Forget the gossip – remember the *Road* comedies and enjoy it!

Island at the Top of the World, The ☉
1974, US, 93 mins, colour
Dir: Robert Stevenson
Stars: Donald Sinden, David Hartman
Rating: ★★

A ripping adventure yarn in the best Victorian tradition, with only wobbly process work letting it down. When the son of an English lord goes missing on an expedition to the Arctic, his father is determined to find him, despite only having a curious map carved on whalebone and a rather

cryptic entry in a ship's journal. Donald Sinden amply fills the part of Sir Anthony Ross although David Hartman seems less comfortable as Professor Ivarsson, who accompanies him. But the adventure's the thing in this Boy's Own Paper saga, and there's plenty of that.

Island in the Sun ○
1957, US, 119 mins, colour
Dir: Robert Rossen
Stars: James Mason, Joan Fontaine, Dorothy Dandridge, Michael Rennie, Joan Collins, Harry Belafonte
Rating: ★★

Made on location in the sun-soaked Caribbean, this film portrayed one of the first black-white love affairs on screen. James Mason gives a fine performance as the weak, half-white and eventually homicidal son of a plantation owner, and is on record as saying it was one of the films he most enjoyed making. Generally, though, the all-star cast, perhaps sapped by the sunshine, is lacking in inspiration.

Island of Dr Moreau, The ●
1977, US, 95 mins, colour
Dir: Don Taylor
Stars: Burt Lancaster, Michael York, Barbara Carrera, Richard Basehart
Rating: ★★★

This later version of the H G Wells story, previously made in 1932 as *Island of Lost Souls*, has some superbly melodramatic dialogue and provides the screen with a splendid dose of grisly hokum, directed by Don Taylor at a pace that kills disbelief. You'll long remember mad scientist Burt Lancaster telling the victims of his experiments that 'He who breaks the law goes back to the House of Pain!'. 'I sleep better here,' mutters Nigel Davenport, in another vintage exchange. 'Not well, but better.'

Island of the Lost ☉
1968, US, 91 mins, colour
Dir: Ricou Browning, Richard Carlson
Stars: Richard Greene, Luke Halpin
Rating: ★★

Richard Carlson and Ricou Browning, who starred as scientist and monster in *The Creature from the Black Lagoon*, obviously developed a taste for watery weirdies. They are screenplay writer and co-director, respectively, on this adventure story about a voyage in search of uncharted islands. Richard Greene, in real life an enthusiastic yachtsman, proved an

I

ideal choice for the role of the bar-quentine skipper who encounters not only undersea perils but carnivorous ostriches and sabre-toothed wolves.

Island Rescue
See: Appointment with Venus

Isn't Life Wonderful! ⊙
1953, UK, 83 mins, colour
Dir: Harold French
Stars: Cecil Parker, Eileen Herlie, Donald Wolfit, Dianne Foster
Rating: ★★★

Comedy of a gentle order, in a charming romp about an Edwardian family. Director Harold French skil-fully milks the situations for all they are worth. One of the funniest sequences is that in which father, adamantly refusing advice or assis-tance, nearly kills himself trying to uncrate and assemble a bicycle. And another delightful piece of comedy is the railway trip which mother treats as a terrifying adventure. No big stars in this film, which makes it an unex-pected treat.

I Take This Woman ○
1940, US, 97 mins, b/w
Dir: W S Van Dyke II
Stars: Spencer Tracy, Hedy Lamarr, Kent Taylor, Laraine Day
Rating: ★★

This MGM romantic epic about a dedicated doctor who marries a glamour girl took so long to complete (Spencer Tracy, tired of reshooting scene after scene, went off and made another film in the middle) that the trade dubbed it *I Retake This Woman*. What eventually emerged is a routine soap opera, somewhat after the fashion of *The Citadel*, but enlivened by the presence of Tracy, Hedy Lamarr, Jack Carson and Laraine Day.

Italian Job, The ○ ⓥ
1969, UK, 100 mins, colour
Dir: Peter Collinson
Stars: Michael Caine, Noel Coward, Benny Hill, Raf Vallone, Rossano Brazzi
Rating: ★★★

Despite the talents of Michael Caine, Noel Coward and Benny Hill, the cars are the stars of this action-comedy in which Coward is the mastermind who from inside a prison cell organises the theft of four million dollarsworth of gold bullion. Michael Caine is the leader of a gang of comic crooks who carry out his plans. But it's the geta-way chase that you'll remember rather

than the robbery itself. It's brilliantly staged by director Peter Collinson, his second-unit director Phillip Wrestler, and a team of stunt drivers known as L'Equipe Remy Julienne. Together, they turn three Mini Coopers into acrobats and contortionists. One car jumps rooftops, while others career through sewers, arcades filled with diners, churches, stairways and other places that cars just aren't supposed to go. Skidding, scudding, screeching and scorching their tyres, they steal the show entirely, leaving scores of pur-suing vehicles wrecked in their wake.

It All Came True ○
1940, US, 97 mins, b/w
Dir: Lewis Seiler
Stars: Humphrey Bogart, Ann Sheridan
Rating: ★★

Warners' gangster comedies looked funnier when they came out, juxtaposed to the studio's own crime films, than they do now. Here it's Humphrey Bogart going for Damon Runyon-style comedy as a gangster who, hiding out in a theatrical board-ing house, becomes swept up in the atmosphere of the thing and even suggests turning it into a nightclub to solve everyone's financial problems. Sounds great, but the treatment here doesn't have the courage of the Bogart character's convictions and the script lacks real wit. Still, the atmosphere is jolly and seven songs make the movie feel at times almost like a musical.

It Always Rains on Sunday ○
1947, UK, 92 mins, b/w
Dir: Robert Hamer
Stars: Googie Withers, Jack Warner, John McCallum, Jimmy Hanley
Rating: ★★★

Well and truly installed in the cin-ema's Hall of Fame, this grimly gripping film flew in the vanguard of a revolution in the British cinema. For the first time, Ealing Studios took cameras out and about, into the city's back streets, and filmed their actors against markets, pubs and slums, alleyways and dock wharfs that were really there. The result was a brilliant new approach to the crime thriller – paralleled at the same time in America by *The Naked City*. The ac-tors slip into their parts like gloves, and the story of a man on the run, who has a way with women, assumes a semi-factual approach that adds to its power and excitement.

It Came from Beneath the Sea ○
1954, US, 80 mins, b/w
Dir: Robert Gordon
Stars: Faith Domergue, Kenneth Tobey
Rating: ★★

Ray Harryhausen, later to become responsible for the Dynamation process used in so many films, in-cluding the *Sinbad* adventures, got his second solo assignment on this sci-ence-fiction thriller about a giant octopus that goes on the rampage in San Francisco harbour. And it's an impressive creation. The creature is supposed to have been driven from the depths of the ocean by H-bomb experiments. Almost as impressive to watch is sultry Faith Domergue, once a Howard Hughes protégé at RKO, and as unlikely a scientist as ever was. Undeterred, she got mixed up in outer-space fantasy the following year in *This Island Earth*.

It Came from Outer Space ○
1953, US, 81 mins, b/w
Dir: Jack Arnold
Stars: Richard Carlson, Barbara Rush
Rating: ★★★

This tense science-fiction thriller – originally made for 3-D – has common assets with other films of its genre produced at Universal-International in the Fifties: a generous budget, a capable director (Jack Arnold, who made *Tarantula!* and *The Incredible Shrinking Man*) and some excellent source material, in this case a novel by Ray Bradbury. Arnold conducts the chills with a fine sense of mounting suspense and danger.

It Couldn't Happen Here ◑ ⓥ
1987, UK, 87 mins, colour
Dir: Jack Bond
Stars: Pet Shop Boys, Joss Ackland, Barbara Windsor
Rating: ★

Loved the music, but shame about the Pet Shop Boys' only film venture to date, which is no more than a series of videos – and a mixed bunch at that – masquerading as a movie. Unfortunately, the first quarter of the film is by far the worst and the whole enterprise never recovers. Director Jack Bond obviously has an eye for surrealistic visuals but some of the dialogue he co-wrote with James Dillon is embarrassingly bad. Such choreography as there is in the dozen or so musical numbers is mediocre at best. So to the songs: moody, well-written stuff with backgrounds that show great care and invention and are very interesting musically speaking, some of the most original sounds to emerge from the pop world since the Sixties. Pet Shop Boys fans will watch it anyway, but generally one's advice to the guys is to stick to the albums: emphasising their own moroseness hardly lends sparks to the laboured seaside postcard charades here.

It Happened in Brooklyn ○

1947, US, 105 mins, b/w
Dir: Richard Whorf
Stars: Frank Sinatra, Kathryn Grayson, Peter Lawford, Jimmy Durante, Gloria Grahame
Rating: ★★

A dispute with Technicolor laboratories led to this MGM musical being filmed in black-and-white instead of the usual lavish colour. Frank Sinatra's best showing as an actor in the early stages of his career, it also had a first-rate Jule Styne-Sammy Cahn score that includes 'Time After Time', 'I Believe', 'It's the Same Old Dream' and a smash-hit duet by Sinatra and veteran Jimmy Durante, 'The Song's Gotta Come from the Heart'. Gloria Grahame also scored an early success as the nurse who vies with singing teacher Kathryn Grayson for Sinatra's affections.

It Happened One Night ○ ⓥ

1934, US, 105 mins, b/w
Dir: Frank Capra
Stars: Clark Gable, Claudette Colbert, Walter Connolly, Roscoe Tarns, Jameson Thomas, Alan Hale
Rating: ★★★★

A delightful free-wheeling comedy that took the critics by surprise and subsequently became the first film to win all five major Oscars (film, director, actor, actress, screenplay), a feat rarely repeated since. The cross-country journey of Claudette Colbert and Clark Gable, she on the run from an arranged marriage, he on the lookout for a scoop, is still fresh, funny and enchantingly coated with sexual smoulder.

It Happened on 5th Avenue ○

1947, US, 115 mins, b/w
Dir: Roy Del Ruth
Stars: Victor Moore, Ann Harding
Rating: ★★

Millionaire Charlie Ruggles allows hobo Victor Moore to live in his plush New York apartment while he winters in Carolina. As you might imagine, Moore has a high old time, filling the place with friends and visitors. But two of those visitors are Ruggles and his daughter (Ann Harding) – heavily disguised . . . This musical comedy wears out its welcome eventually, but it's good-natured entertainment and the music's fun, too.

It Happened to Jane ⊙

(aka: That Jane from Maine)
1959, US, 98 mins, colour
Dir: Richard Quine
Stars: Doris Day, Jack Lemmon, Ernie Kovacs, Steve Forrest
Rating: ★★★

A fast-moving comedy with Doris Day as a small-town lobster-dealer who has a cargo ruined by the railway and is determined to get her own back. Beautiful colour photography and a furious finale involving trains, complement the likeable performances of Ms Day, Jack Lemmon and the apoplectic Ernie Kovacs, to make this one of the most enjoyable comedies in many a long day. The director is Richard Quine, who started his career at the age of 11 as a child actor, appeared in several musicals of the Forties as a juvenile lead, then turned director, his best films being *Operation Mad Ball*, *Bell, Book and Candle*, *The Notorious Landlady* and *How to Murder Your Wife*.

It Happened Tomorrow ⊙

1944, US, 84 mins, b/w
Dir: René Clair
Stars: Dick Powell, Linda Darnell, Jack Oakie, John Philliber
Rating: ★★★

French director René Clair made several excellent films during his enforced wartime stay in Hollywood, but none more delightful than this fantasy about a turn-of-the-century reporter. Dick Powell, just building a new career after saying goodbye to musicals, plays the newsman who understandably can't believe it when he meets an old man who gives him newspapers that 'foretell' events of the immediate future. Clair gets everything right, and the result is a film of much amusement and charm.

It's a Gift ⊙

1934, US, 73 mins, b/w
Dir: Norman Z McLeod

Stars: W C Fields, Kathleen Howard, Baby LeRoy, Jean Rouverol
Rating: ★★★★

An almost undiluted flask of W C Fields – one of the great man's finest comedies, casting him as a small-town shopkeeper beset by wife, family and customers alike. A whole barrage of masterly scenes includes the sequence where the blind man destroys Fields' shop with a few injudicious waves of his white cane; and the 'sleeping porch' segment where Baby LeRoy obligingly drops grapes into Fields' mouth ('Shades of Bacchus!' Fields gasps), but follows them with an ice-pick.

It's Always Fair Weather ○

1955, US, 101 mins, colour
Dir: Stanley Donen
Stars: Gene Kelly, Dan Dailey, Cyd Charisse, Dolores Gray
Rating: ★★★

Back on the town, three war buddies meet up again ten years after VJ day in this attractive Comden and Green musical. Excellent dancing from Gene Kelly, Dan Dailey and choreographer Michael Kidd; plenty of first rate numbers including the famous 'dustbin dance'. Good use of wide screen will be lost on television.

It's a Mad, Mad, Mad, Mad World ⊙ ⓥ

1963, US, 192 mins, colour
Dir: Stanley Kramer
Stars: Spencer Tracy, Milton Berle, Sid Caesar, Mickey Rooney, Ethel Merman, Phil Silvers
Rating: ★★

You can't keep all the people laughing all the time for three hours. But, to its eternal credit, this marathon comedy chase film does have a darned good try. And there are laughs galore in its giant story of 10 people (including Spencer Tracy, Mickey Rooney, Terry-Thomas and Phil Silvers) all after a case of thousand-dollar bills hidden in a certain area 'under a big W'. The bank robber, Jimmy Durante, gives them this enigmatic clue after they have seen his car crash off a mountain road. As he dies, he kicks a large bucket down the mountainside. It's that kind of film. Among those flashing across the screen in fleeting appearances, you may recognise Jerry Lewis, Buster Keaton, Leo Gorcey (without the Bowery Boys), Joe E Brown, Jack Benny and The Three Stooges.

I

It's a Wonderful Life ○ ⓥ
1946, US, 125 mins, b/w
Dir: Frank Capra
Stars: James Stewart, Donna Reed,
Lionel Barrymore, Thomas Mitchell,
Henry Travers, Gloria Grahame
Rating: ★★★★

This is Oscar-winning director Frank
Capra's finest film and could justifiably
lay claim to being one of the best
movies ever made. It's both a summation of Capra's own career and a
peak of achievement for a gentler kind
of American cinema which was to
fade in post-war years and disappear
altogether with the harshness and
violence of modern times. James
Stewart is at his best as the man asked
by an angel to reflect on his life when
he contemplates suicide. But it's in the
amazing depth of character and
incident, all immaculately conceived
and executed, that the film scores most
heavily. The ending is a real
tear-jerker and, if you don't agree
with Capra that life is really like this,
then you might go along with his
sentiments that it ought to be.

It's a Wonderful World ○
1939, US, 86 mins, b/w
Dir: W S Van Dyke II
Stars: Claudette Colbert, James
Stewart, Guy Kibbee, Frances Drake
Rating: ★★★

A big welcome for this screwball
comedy. A combination of *It
Happened One Night* and *The 39 Steps*,
with Claudette Colbert as a runaway
poetess and James Stewart as the man
just running – from the law. Very
funny, thanks to a pacy, witty script
from Ben Hecht and Herman J
Mankiewicz. The inspired story they
concocted makes room for several of
Hollywood's best character actors,
with even Nat Pendleton and Edgar
Kennedy funnier than usual as a
couple of comic cops in hot pursuit of
Colbert and Stewart.

It's a Wonderful World ○
1956, UK, 89 mins, colour
Dir: Val Guest
Stars: Terence Morgan, George Cole,
Kathleen Harrison, Mylene Nicole
Rating: ★★★

A rare British comedy-musical,
focussing on the efforts of two impoverished songwriters to break into
the world of pop music. Ted Heath
and his Music supply most of the
melody in this bright film, which
extracts every laugh possible from

odd-ball landladies, teenage pop fans,
highbrow music critics and Tin Pan
Alley in general. George Cole is on
good form as the scatterbrained half of
the writing duo, there's a good dream
sequence, and there's also some
tuneful songs from Mylene Nicole,
who became better known in films
under her real name of Mylene
Demongeot.

It's Great to be Young ⊙
1956, UK, 90 mins, colour
Dir: Cyril Frankel
Stars: John Mills, Cecil Parker
Rating: ★★★★

An exuberant comedy-musical, richly
shot in Technicolor by Gilbert Taylor
and full of fun and youthful bounce.
Though made in Britain, it's reminiscent of the Judy Garland-Mickey
Rooney let's-put-on-a-show films at
MGM in the early Forties. John Mills
is in tremendous form as the unorthodox school music master whose
sacking provokes a revolution and
with its tuneful score, the film was a
hit with critics and public alike. Top
songs: 'Marching Strings' and 'You
Are My First Love', with Ruby Murray providing Dorothy Bromily's
singing voice.

It Should Happen to You ○
1953, US, 100 mins, b/w
Dir: George Cukor
Stars: Judy Holliday, Peter Lawford, Jack
Lemmon
Rating: ★★★

Breezy romantic comedy featuring a
delightful performance by Judy
Holliday as an unemployed model
who changes her life by advertising
herself from a huge billboard
overlooking New York's Columbus
Circle. Jack Lemmon makes his film
debut and you may spot Constance
Bennett and Wendy Barrie as panel
game members, as well as John Saxon
(another film debut) as a boy on a park
bench.

It Shouldn't Happen to a
Vet ○
1976, UK, 94 mins, colour
Dir: Eric Till
Stars: John Alderton, Colin Blakely, Lisa
Harrow
Rating: ★★★

Another pleasant canter through the
laughs and heartbreaks of a country
vet in 1938. It's a sequel to *All Creatures Great and Small*, but with John
Alderton as the vet and Colin Blakely

as his senior partner instead of the
previous stars. Neither alteration does
any harm, with the result that this
romp, additionally enhanced by the
distinguished Yorkshire Moor
photography of Arthur Ibbetson, is a
slight improvement on its predecessor.
The delicious Lisa Harrow is again the
vet's wife, and supporting parts are on
the whole well-drawn, although the
county fair proves something of an
anti-climax. It's good lightweight fare.

It's Love Again ○
1936, UK, 83 mins, b/w
Dir: Victor Saville
Stars: Jessie Matthews, Robert Young,
Sonnie Hale
Rating: ★★★

The last, and critically most successful
of five films made by Britain's top
Thirties' musical star, Jessie Matthews,
with her favourite director Victor
Saville. Jessie sings and dances vivaciously in costumes that seem
sometimes amazingly scanty for the
time, and does her famous imitation of
Mrs Smythe-Smythe, a legendary
huntress from the east. Robert Young
was brought over from Hollywood to
give the film some clout in America,
and the Sam Coslow-Harry Woods
songs include 'It's Love Again' and
'Gotta Dance My Way to Heaven'.
The last highpoint of Jessie's film career.

It's Love I'm After ○
1937, US, 90 mins, b/w
Dir: Archie L Mayo
Stars: Leslie Howard, Bette Davis, Olivia
de Havilland
Rating: ★★

A rare romantic comedy for the great
Bette Davis, this film re-teams her
with Leslie Howard after their success
together in *The Petrified Forest*. Davis
and Howard play feuding Broadway
stars, with Olivia de Havilland forming the third point of the embattled
triangle as the heiress who develops a
crush on Howard's tarnished matinée
idol. Casey Robinson's script is full of
barbed wisecracks and wry-faced Eric
Blore almost steals the show as
(inevitably) a gentleman's gentleman.

It's Magic ⊙
(aka: Romance on the High Seas)
1948, US, 100 mins, colour
Dir: Michael Curtiz
Stars: Jack Carson, Janis Paige, Don
DeFore, Doris Day
Rating: ★★★

The film that launched the Hollywood career of Doris von Kappelhoff, a former singer with Les Brown's band, who would become a top box-office attraction under the new name of Doris Day. She was fourth billed here and only got the role as a last-minute replacement for Betty Hutton. Judy Garland had already turned it down. But 26-year-old Doris was the hit of the film, and cornered the market in succession of freckle-faced girl-next-door roles in light musicals and dramas. Her big musical numbers, 'It's Magic' and 'Put 'em in a Box, Tie 'em with a Ribbon and Throw 'em in the Deep Blue Sea', became king-sized hits in the dance halls. *It's Magic* — re-titled for Britain from *Romance on the High Seas* — was actually nothing more than a series of tired romantic situations, but it was pepped up with snappy songs and choreography from Busby Berkeley, who returned specially to Warners studio to create the dance sequences.

It's Never Too Late ○
1956, US, 95 mins, colour
Dir: Michael McCarthy
Stars: Phyllis Calvert, Patrick Barr
Rating: ★★

Bright and breezy family comedy with Phyllis Calvert, as the part-time author and full-time mum who suddenly has celebrity status thrust upon her, heading an accomplished cast of farceurs. Director Michael McCarthy keeps the amusing action bubbling over but does little to belie its stage origins.

It's Not Cricket ☉
1948, UK, 77 mins, b/w
Dir: Roy Rich
Stars: Basil Radford, Naunton Wayne, Susan Shaw
Rating: ★★★

Basil Radford and Naunton Wayne not for once as their most famous characters, Charters and Caldicott, but as bumbling private eyes Bright and Early. This is a consistently funny comedy which owes much to an amusing performance by Maurice Denham as a ubiquitous German spy and has a riotous climax whose inspiration may well have come from the 1935 Will Hay comedy *Boys Will Be Boys*. Diana Dors pops up in a cameo role.

It's Only Money ☉
1962, US, 84 mins, b/w
Dir: Frank Tashlin

Stars: Jerry Lewis, Zachary Scott
Rating: ★★★

Better than usual Lewis comedy (it's directed by Frank Tashlin), which casts Jerry as the unknowing heir to a fortune. Look out for 'The Attack of the Lawn Mowers': it's one of the funniest visual sequences in any Lewis comedy.

It Started in Naples ○
1960, US, 100 mins, colour
Dir: Melville Shavelson
Stars: Clark Gable, Sophia Loren, Vittorio de Sica
Rating: ★★★

Sophia Loren as a fiery cabaret entertainer in a charming comedy about a hardened 10-year-old Italian waif torn between her and a stiff American uncle. Easily the best comedy Sophia made for Hollywood — perhaps because she felt at home in Naples and its environs. The scenery — especially the harbour settings — is gloriously shot in colour, and there's a likeable performance by a little Italian boy called Manetto. Even Clark Gable, who tended to give rather staid performances in his later years, seems to unbend in the Neapolitan sunshine, to make this an altogether pleasurable experience. But it's Sophia's show. Just watching her flamenco dancing is worth it.

It Started with Eve ○
1941, US, 90 mins, b/w
Dir: Henry Koster
Stars: Deanna Durbin, Charles Laughton, Robert Cummings
Rating: ★★★

The captivating Deanna Durbin gets a chance to display a nice sense of comedy, and trills as prettily as ever, in this zany comedy, which was probably the zenith of her career. The story casts Charles Laughton as the millionaire head of a somewhat eccentric family.

Ivanhoe ○ ⓥ
1952, UK, 107 mins, colour
Dir: Richard Thorpe
Stars: Robert Taylor, Elizabeth Taylor, Joan Fontaine, George Sanders, Emlyn Williams, Robert Douglas
Rating: ★★★

All three of Robert Taylor's forays into English legend — the others were Knights of the Round Table and Quentin Durward — proved not able successes and this lively adaptation of Sir Walter Scott's novel by Noel

Langley was the first Taylor plays Wilfrid of Ivanhoe as a kind of Robin Hood in armour, doing his best to humiliate Prince John and his lieutenants — in this case George Sanders and Robert Douglas, later to take opposite sides in King Richard and the Crusaders — while waiting for King Richard to return from the Crusades. The jousting and other action scenes are magnificently handled by director Richard Thorpe.

Ivory Hunter
See: Where No Vultures Fly

Ivy ○
1947, US, 99 mins, b/w
Dir: Sam Wood
Stars: Joan Fontaine, Herbert Marshall, Patric Knowles, Cedric Hardwicke
Rating: ★★★

Joan Fontaine escaped her customary casting as a delicate damsel to play an Edwardian poisoness in this melodrama. Director Sam Wood endows the London settings with a nicely sinister atmosphere and the suspense is splendidly sustained. Wood had proved himself at MGM and other studios one of Hollywood's most versatile directors, his work including comedy (*A Day at the Races, A Night at the Opera*), drama (*Kitty Foyle, Kings Row, Our Town*), war epics (*For Whom the Bell Tolls, Command Decision*) and even epic weepies (*Madame X, Goodbye Mr Chips!*). He also completed *Gone With the Wind* when director Victor Fleming was taken ill. In *Ivy*, a rare visit for Wood to Universal studios, he had a classy ally in producer/production designer William Cameron Menzies, who strengthened the mediocre script with some splendid art direction and set design.

I Wake Up Screaming ○ ⓥ
(aka: Hot Spot)
1941, US, 82 mins, b/w
Dir: H Bruce Humberstone
Stars: Betty Grable, Victor Mature, Laird Cregar, Carole Landis
Rating: ★★★

One of Betty Grable's few non-musical roles of the war years, this thriller was remade 12 years later as *Vicki*. An early *film noir*, broodingly photographed by the talented Edward Cronjager, it allows room for rich character studies from burly Laird Cregar as an obsessive detective, Elisha Cook Jr as a twitchy liftboy, and suave Alan Mowbray as a big-headed ham

I

actor. The sense of threat surrounding the 'framed' hero (another serviceable performance from the undervalued Victor Mature) is very well sustained.

I Walk Alone ○
1947, US, 98 mins, b/w
Dir: Byron Haskin
Stars: Burt Lancaster, Kirk Douglas, Lizabeth Scott, Wendell Corey
Rating: ★★★

Burt Lancaster and Kirk Douglas were both at the beginning of their star careers when this grim, tough crime thriller was made. The plot is reminiscent of a couple of Cagney-Bogart vehicles of the late Thirties. And the action flows with a will. The screenplay is by Charles Schnee (not to be confused with Charles Schneer, producer of the Dynamation films). In 1952, Schnee won an Oscar for his script on *The Bad and the Beautiful*.

I Walked with a Zombie ◐
1943, US, 66 mins, b/w
Dir: Jacques Tourneur
Stars: Tom Conway, Frances Dee, James Ellison
Rating: ★★★

Much better than its title would indicate, this beautifully-made drama is a sort of Haitian voodoo offshoot of *Jane Eyre*. A little on the slow side, it nonetheless remained talented director Jacques Tourneur's favourite film, mainly becuse of its poetic qualities. It's very moody and sometimes quite chilly, with a commendably firm central performance by Frances Dee.

I Walk the Line ◐
1970, US, 95 mins, colour
Dir: John Frankenheimer
Stars: Gregory Peck, Tuesday Weld, Estelle Parsons, Ralph Meeker, Charles Durning
Rating: ★★

There's another magnetic performance from that underrated actress Tuesday Weld in this tale of moonshine whiskey runners and small-town scandal in America's Deep South. Nine songs by Johnny Cash provide a musical commentary on the hopeless passion of middle-aged sheriff Gregory Peck for Miss Weld's mountain girl.

I Want to Live! ◐
1958, US, 120 mins, b/w
Dir: Robert Wise
Stars: Susan Hayward, Simon Oakland
Rating: ★★★

Harrowing, very compelling dramatisation of the famous Barbara Graham case, with Susan Hayward giving an all-stops-out performance as the woman sentenced to the electric chair. Her showing won her an Academy Award, an honour she had just missed for her equally gripping portrayal of Lillian Roth three years earlier in *I'll Cry Tomorrow*.

I Want You ○
1951, US, 102 mins, b/w
Dir: Mark Robson
Stars: Dorothy McGuire, Dana Andrews, Farley Granger, Peggy Dow
Rating: ★★★

Nostalgically atmospheric slice of Americana, spotlighting the problems of small-town families whose menfolk are called away to (the Korean) war. Solid performances from Dorothy McGuire, Dana Andrews, Farley Granger and Peggy Dow.

I Was a Male War Bride ○
(aka: You Can't Sleep Here)
1949, US, 105 mins, b/w
Dir: Howard Hawks
Stars: Cary Grant, Ann Sheridan, Marion Marshall, Randy Stuart
Rating: ★★★★

Director Howard Hawks continued his successful theme of a series of abrasive battles-of-the-sexes between two people eventually destined to fall in love, begun in *Twentieth Century*, *Bringing Up Baby*, *His Girl Friday*, *Ball of Fire* and *To Have and To Have Not*. Ann Sheridan carries on splendidly in the tradition of Carole Lombard, Katharine Hepburn and Lauren Bacall, giving an unexpectedly sparkling performance as the American WAC lieutenant detailed to act as interpreter for a male chauvinist French officer, smoothly played by Cary Grant at his deftest. The series of misadventures suffered by the couple, on the way to an inn where Ann sees to it that Cary sleeps with the chickens, makes rollicking entertainment. Despite some amusing incidentals, in fact, the stars are the whole show.

I Was Monty's Double ○ ⓥ
(aka: Monty's Double)
1958, UK, 95 mins, b/w
Dir: John Guillermin
Stars: John Mills, Cecil Parker, Michael Hordern, Marius Goring
Rating: ★★★

A fascinating account of how an actor, M E Clifton-James (who plays himself in the film) passed as General Montgomery in an attempt to make the Germans believe that the invasion of Europe would come from North Africa. This amazing deception actually made Hitler hold a Panzer division in the South of France. The screenplay, a compact and compelling piece of work, was written by Bryan Forbes. The only point in his scenario which may annoy students of history is the fictional attempted kidnapping of 'Monty' by the Germans. The real ending was more amusing: James (he had been seconded from an Army office) returned to his base and was arrested as a deserter!

I Wonder Who's Kissing Her Now ☉
1947, US, 104 mins, colour
Dir: Lloyd Bacon
Stars: June Haver, Mark Stevens, Martha Stewart, Reginald Gardiner, Gene Nelson
Rating: ★★★

There's a certain freshness and verve that, added to its backstage insights and ultra-tuneful score, give this turn-of-the-century musical biopic the edge over many of its competitors. Hermes Pan's vaudeville routines carry an authentic smack of yesteryear and Ernest Palmer's Technicolor photography is as clear as crystal. The subject is a real-life composer called Joe Howard, breezily played by Mark Stevens, who like his predecessor in musicals at 20th Century-Fox, John Payne, later made his name in tough-guy roles. Here Stevens teams well with vivacious blonde June Haver (although his singing voice was dubbed by Buddy Clark) and their numbers together are charming. The toe-tapping musical numbers include 'What's the Use of Dreaming?', 'Honeymoon, Hello My Baby', 'I Wonder Who's Kissing Her Now?', 'Oh, Gee, Be Sweet to Me, Kid', 'Goodbye My Lady Love' and 'How'd You Like to be the Umpire?' Under the fizzy direction of Lloyd Bacon, who many years before had made the classic *42nd Street* with Busby Berkeley, the film made a profit of more than three million dollars, one of the biggest money-spinners of all the studio's many brightly-coloured musicals of the Forties.

J

Jabberwocky ◐ ⓥ
1977, UK, 105 mins, colour
Dir: Terry Gilliam
Stars: Michael Palin, Harry H Corbett, Max Wall, John Le Mesurier, Warren Mitchell
Rating: ★★

You may or may not find Terry Gilliam's medieval monster mayhem for the Monty Pythons a funny film, but it certainly is messy. It's full of people relieving themselves, flagellating themselves, rolling in mud or worse, fountaining blood and being chopped or chewed to pieces. Ugh! Amid all the grime and gore, it must be admitted, lurks (as well as the Jabberwock) the occasional snigger, mostly from Max Wall as King Bruno the Questionable. Gilliam's pictorial flair, however, was never seen to better advantage. Castles are silhouetted against sunsets, boats paddle silkily across stagnant, misty lakes, and the princess tiptoes towards the dazed hero (Michael Palin) through a flutter of nuns' handkerchiefs.

Jack Ahoy ☉
1934, UK, 82 mins, b/w
Dir: Walter Forde
Stars: Jack Hulbert, Nancy O'Neil, Alfred Drayton
Rating: ★★★

Long thought to be a lost film, this breezy if makeshift comedy features jolly Jack Hulbert as the latest in a long line of inept sailors. Naturally, this being a Jack Hulbert film, our hero gets to dance a hornpipe. He also accidentally terrorises the admiral to such an extent that that worthy, held hostage in the Far East and confronted by a rescuing Jack, tells him, 'Get out of here at once. If you don't I'll call the bandits!' The film has one big hit song, 'The Hat's on the Side of My Head', which it flogs remorselessly, and a rather limp leading lady in Nancy O'Neil, who is out-sparkled by a too-little-used Tamara Desni as an exotic spy. Surprisingly rough and ready at times, the film has an energetic performance by Hulbert (who endured four dips in cold waters off Weymouth Pier for a scene where he has to jump overboard) and some nice throwaway lines for those prepared to wait. It was re-

made 20 years later as a vehicle for Ronald Shiner and re-titled *Up to His Neck*.

Jack and the Beanstalk ☉
1952, US, 78 mins, colour
Dir: Jean Yarbrough
Stars: Bud Abbott, Lou Costello, Dorothy Ford, Buddy Baer
Rating: ★★

Don't expect too much from this Abbott and Costello pantomime. The team seems out of its element, even though the film does contain some of its most hilarious slapstick chases. One could do without the prince and princess and their songs too. Still the giant and his tall housekeeper are fun, as are the singing harp and the hen that lays the golden eggs. Begins in black and white, then bursts into SuperCinecolor when Jack (Lou) climbs the beanstalk into Cloudland.

Jack McCall, Desperado ○
1953, US, 76 mins, colour
Dir: Sidney Salkow
Stars: George Montgomery, Angela Stevens
Rating: ★★

One of a whole corral-full of Westerns which George Montgomery made for Columbia in the Fifties. This one tinkers with history a bit – Jack McCall is shown to be not so bad a guy, and doesn't actually shoot Wild Bill Hickok in the back – but the action is fast and furious and western fans won't complain.

Jacknife ● ⓥ
1988, US, 120 mins, colour
Dir: David Jones
Stars: Robert De Niro, Ed Harris, Kathy Baker, Charles Dutton, Loudon Wainwright III
Rating: ★★★

This is the type of romance that could at any moment tip over into tragedy. Robert De Niro stars as a Vietnam veteran who decides to take his wartime buddy (Ed Harris) on a fishing trip. An unlikely affair springs up between De Niro and Harris's sister (Kathy Baker) but is threatened by Harris, whose visions of Vietnam still torment him. Fine portrayals from the stars give the film a warmth it doesn't always deserve.

Jackpot, The ☉
1950, US, 87 mins, b/w
Dir: Walter Lang

Stars: James Stewart, Barbara Hale, James Gleason, Fred Clark
Rating: ★★★

One of the funniest Hollywood light comedies since the glossy, brittle romps of the late Thirties. The scene where Stewart gets stuck on the stairs, while trying to get to the 'phone and claim a huge quiz prize, matches anything he ever did in the world of comic cinema. The supporting cast is studded with rib-tickling performances, from old comedy hands Fred Clark and James Gleason, to a 12-year-old Natalie Wood as Stewart's precocious daughter. Stewart himself suffers exquisite agonies, especially when the prizes turn up, a white elephant every one. After all, what does one do with a giant steer carcass, or a three-year supply of frozen food (all at once)? To say nothing of the embarrassment inflicted by a twee interior decorator (superbly snooty Alan Mowbray) or an artist (glamorous Patricia Medina) commissioned to paint Stewart's portrait. The resulting chaos is hilarious.

Jack's the Boy ○
1932, UK, 89 mins, b/w
Dir: Walter Forde
Stars: Jack Hulbert, Cicely Courtneidge, Winifred Shotter
Rating: ★★★

This toe-tapping musical comedy-thriller, swung along at a fine pace by Walter Forde (who had directed the star in the previous year's *The Ghost Train*), was probably Jack Hulbert's greatest popular success. The plot's a simple comedy stand-by (the hapless son of a high-up policeman determines to follow in the steps of his father's size twelves), but Hulbert's cheerful energy and the likeable fooling of his real-life wife Cicely Courtneidge (here in a character role as a rambunctious old nurse) give it a style and rhythm all its own. Hulbert did his own choreography; the music and lyrics were by Vivian Ellis and Douglas Furber.

Jack the Bear ◐ ⓥ
1993, US, 101 mins, colour
Dir: Marshall Herskovitz
Stars: Danny DeVito, Robert J Steinmiller, Gary Sinise, Reese Witherspoon, Bert Remsen
Rating: ★★

There aren't many degrees of light and shade about this pretty miserable little piece about a 10-year-old boy's first

traumatic year in a new home after
the death of his mother – a pretty
jolting experience in itself as she died
in a car crash after storming out in a
row. The theme is lightened a little by
the fact that the father (Danny
DeVito) of the boy and his
three-year-old brother is the
black-lipped host of a late-night horror show on TV, and is always 'on' for
the local kids. What little comedy
there is, however, is soon firmly
squashed under the heel of tragedy.
The father is drinking heavily to forget, and the family falls out with the
local Nazi (Gary Sinise) and pays the
penalty when he finds ways to
blacken their lives. Just occasionally
the feeling of a community is captured, and there's a tensely exciting bit
towards the end when the older boy is
threatened with extinction at the
hands of the bad guy. Not terribly involving though: the cast probably
sheds more tears in this one than the
audience will.

Jack the Giant Killer ⊙

1962, US, 94 mins, colour
Dir: Nathan Juran
Stars: Kerwin Mathews, Judi Meredith,
Torin Thatcher, Don Beddoe
Rating: ★★★

More movie magic to delight (and in
some scenes frighten) the children,
from a wizard of special effects called
Howard Anderson, whose work
compares favourably with that of Ray
Harryhausen. Kerwin Mathews, previously seen as Gulliver and Sinbad in
Harryhausen films, battles various
monsters conjured up by a wicked
magician. Veteran character actor
Don Beddoe is pure delight as the
perverse Imp of the Bottle.

Jack the Ripper ◐

1958, UK, 85 mins, b/w
Dir: Robert S Baker
Stars: Lee Patterson, Eddie Byrne
Rating: ★★

To turn the story of Jack the Ripper
into a routine chiller is to do it an injustice. This film is guilty. Taken
simply as a police thriller, it's quite
enjoyable, although some of the
plot's shortcomings show through.
The period atmosphere is quite well
captured and the murders are effective
and realistic without being
unacceptably horrific. The vivid
black-and-white photography is a plus
factor.

Jacob's Ladder ● ⓥ

1990, US, 113 mins, colour
Dir: Adrian Lynne
Stars: Tim Robbins, Elizabeth Peña,
Danny Aiello, Matt Craven, Patricia
Kalember, Macaulay Culkin
Rating: ★★

With a screenplay by Bruce Joel
Rubin, subsequently to turn director
with *Ghost*, this is, for nine-tenths of
the way, a brilliantly constructed psychological thriller about a Vietnam
veteran (Tim Robbins) who is suffering a series of horrific
hallucinations. Struggling to hold on
to his sanity, he finds that several of his
old war buddies are experiencing
similar illusions . . . which may have
something to do with a mysterious
experiment performed in Vietnam.
Don't let anyone tell you the surprise
ending, especially as it pretty well
wrecks the entire film. Robbins is
first-rate as the tortured Jacob but
Macaulay Culkin is rather annoying in
a key supporting role.

Jacqueline ○

1956, UK, 93 mins, b/w
Dir: Roy Baker
Stars: John Gregson, Kathleen Ryan,
Richard O'Sullivan
Rating: ★★★

Comedy-drama-weepie about a
happy-go-lucky Irishman whose fear
of heights drives him to drink and
disgrace, especially in the eyes of his
children. These prove to be two enchanting moppets, in the forms of
Jacqueline Ryan (in the title role) and
Richard O'Sullivan, who grew up to
star in ITV comedy series such as *Man
About the House, Robin's Nest* and *Me
& My Girl*. It's a likeable little drama
with earnest performances and atmospheric background detail.

Jagged Edge ● ⓥ

1985, US, 108 mins, colour
Dir: Richard Marquand
Stars: Jeff Bridges, Glenn Close, Peter
Coyote, Robert Loggia, Leigh
Taylor-Young
Rating: ★★★

A tough-talking, clever courtroom
thriller of the kind that Hollywood
seems to produce every two or three
years. Just whether any lawyer would
get as involved with her client as
Glenn Close does with Jeff Bridges
during this messy murder trial is open
to conjecture. No matter, such
indelicacies never used to bother us
when we were cheering on Perry

Mason as he closed in on the killer at
the end, and neither should they here.
Despite the fashionable sex, violence
and bad language, this is a satisfyingly
old-fashioned sort of film, although
avid fans of the genre should guess the
solution to its ingenious plot at least a
reel before the end. None of the
characters is very sympathetic, but all of
them are well drawn (which is
more important here) – especially by
Close, Peter Coyote as the shady DA,
Robert Loggia as a foul-mouthed investigator and Marshall Colt as a
tennis-club stud.

Jailbirds
See: Pardon Us

Jailhouse Rock ○ ⓥ

1957, US, 96 mins, b/w
Dir: Richard Thorpe
Stars: Elvis Presley, Judy Tyler, Dean
Jones, Mickey Shaughnessy
Rating: ★

Elvis rocks, rolls and stands on other
people's blue suede shoes in this, his
third film, as a rebel hero who comes
out of prison to become (what else?) a
pop idol. The Presley pelvis (and lar-
ynx) work overtime on such numbers
as 'Treat Me Nice', 'Jailhouse Rock'
and 'You're So Square'; but for the
tragic Judy Tyler, it was her second
and last film. Shortly after completing
it she was killed in a car crash.

Jake Speed ○

1986, US, 100 mins, colour
Dir: Andrew Lane
Stars: Wayne Crawford, Dennis
Christopher, John Hurt
Rating: ★

There have been plenty of films about
comic-book heroes, but *Jake Speed*
rings the changes in that it's about one
that many of its other characters don't
believe exists. Only Grandpa (Leon
Ames, with lines he could never have
said as Doris Day's screen dad) thinks
that pulp-novel hero Jake is the man
to prise his daughter from the grip of
white-slave traders. No sooner has he
voiced his thoughts than his other
granddaughter (leggy Karen Kopins)
finds Jake (Wayne Crawford) and his
sidekick (Dennis Christopher) on her
doorstep with some hare-brained
scheme to rescue her sister. The adventure will be turned into a book,
they being the authors of their own
(real-life) exploits under a pseudonym.
So it's off to Africa where John Hurt
entertains us with a broad,
revue-sketch villain who takes 'great

pride in never having lived up to anything' and where there's more action than in the last 20 minutes of a Charles Bronson film. It's a nice idea that, with a lot of careful development and witty dialogue, might have been an unexpected delight. The fact that it doesn't begin to work on this level is largely the fault of Crawford himself, who co-scripted (heavily) and isn't really handsome or personable enough to play the hero.

Jamaica Inn ○
1939, UK, 108 mins, b/w
Dir: Alfred Hitchcock
Stars: Charles Laughton, Maureen O'Hara, Robert Newton, Leslie Banks, Emlyn Williams
Rating: ★★★

Villain Charles Laughton and hero Robert Newton had co-starred the previous year, in *Vessel of Wrath*, a Laughton role which Newton himself would play years later in *The Beachcomber*. And his Long John Silver doubtless owed something to Laughton's leering Captain Kidd. An array of British character actors is on hand to help them with full-blooded performances in this swaggering yarn. The results are a trifle lurid, but the film has plenty of thrills and, even as Hitchcock wrapped it up, Laughton and Maureen O'Hara were on their way to Hollywood to co-star in the classic *The Hunchback of Notre Dame*.

Jane Eyre ○
1944, US, 96 mins, b/w
Dir: Robert Stevenson
Stars: Orson Welles, Joan Fontaine, Henry Daniell, Margaret O'Brien
Rating: ★★★★

Despite Robert Stevenson's name as director on the credits, the influence of Orson Welles seems everywhere in this classic RKO version of Charlotte Bronte's broodingly romantic novel, in which Welles also co-stars as Mr Rochester. The early scenes in the monstrous Lowood are particularly effective, thanks in no little part to Peggy Ann Garner's plucky portrait of young Jane, and Elizabeth Taylor's heartrending account of her doomed companion, Helen. Following the arrival of Jane (now played by a rather too diffident Joan Fontaine) at Thornfield, however, thunder and lightning – and Orson Welles – take over.

January Man, The ●
1989, US, 97 mins, colour
Dir: Pat O'Connor
Stars: Kevin Kline, Mary Elizabeth Mastrantonio, Susan Sarandon, Rod Steiger, Harvey Keitel
Rating: ★★

This film doesn't quite know whether it's supposed to be a thriller, a comedy or a comedy thriller. So it never quite manages to be any of these things. Disgraced policeman Nick Starkey is brought back to the force by his brother (the police commissioner) to track down a serial killer. The fact that Nick was once involved with his brother's wife and proceeds to have an affair with the Mayor of New York's daughter tends to interfere with the main thrust of the plot and slow things down quite a bit. Still, despite the fact that this is a notably flawed and distinctly odd film, it's still quite fun, thanks to good performances from a seriously heavyweight cast – especially Kevin Kline and Rod Steiger, in a wonderfully OTT, scenery-chewing, upstaging role complete with hideous, ill-fitting curly wig.

Jason and the Argonauts ○ ⓥ
1963, UK, 104 mins, colour
Dir: Don Chaffey
Stars: Todd Armstrong, Nancy Kovack
Rating: ★★★

The DynaMation man, Ray Harryhausen, is associate producer on this mythological romp, and that means special effects run riot. During his quest for the Golden Fleece, Jason has to combat a giant iron man, whose only weakness is his heel; winged she-devils; and a seven-headed hydra (this battle is the highlight of the film). In *The 7th Voyage of Sinbad*, Harryhausen produced a sword-fighting skeleton. Here, we have a whole army of them for Jason and his men to fight at the climax.

Jassy ○
1947, UK, 102 mins, colour
Dir: Bernard Knowles
Stars: Margaret Lockwood, Patricia Roc, Dennis Price, Basil Sydney
Rating: ★★

A turbulent Technicolor tale from Gainsborough Pictures, with excellent production values, well photographed by Geoffrey Unsworth who went on to win an Oscar for *Cabaret*. The director, Bernard Knowles, was also once a cinema-

tographer and had already directed Margaret Lockwood twice in films when he made this moody Mallens-style melodrama which cast the star as a fiery gipsy.

Jaws ○ ⓥ
1975, US, 125 mins, colour
Dir: Steven Spielberg
Stars: Roy Scheider, Robert Shaw, Richard Dreyfuss, Lorraine Gary, Murray Hamilton
Rating: ★★★★

This monster success attacked the box-offices of the world with the same suddenness and ferocity with which the white killer shark of its title descends on the unsuspecting holidaymakers of an American beach paradise. The famous early sequence of the naked girl bather being eaten alive by the shark sets the tone for the swathe of blood and limbs that spreads across this nail-bitingly exciting story. Author Peter Benchley has a cameo as a journalist. Winner of Oscars for John Williams's score, editing and sound. Some of the shark violence may turn younger viewers a little green at the gills.

Jaws 2 ● ⓥ
1978, US, 115 mins, colour
Dir: Jeannot Szwarc
Stars: Roy Scheider, Murray Hamilton, Lorraine Gary
Rating: ★★

No one who thrilled to *Jaws* will want to miss this, although by the time it surfaced in cinemas three years after *Jaws*, shark adventures were two-a-penny and new ways of getting rid of a great white shark were running along similar lines to means of dispatching Dracula: you think up a new one with each succeeding sequel. Roy Scheider again gives a good performance as the police chief. Once more the citizens, again led by Murray Hamilton as the Mayor, won't believe him about the shark menace and even go as far as firing him. Director Jeannot Szwarc packs in as many teasing shots of swimmers taken from below the surface as the plot will decently allow before Scheider and the shark come to their final showdown.

Jaws 3 ○ ⓥ
1983, US, 99 mins, colour
Dir: Joe Alves
Stars: Dennis Quaid, Bess Armstrong, Simon MacCorkindale, Louis Gossett Jr,

J

Lea Thompson
Rating: ★★

The story, by Guerdon Trueblood, is
– so the credits tell us – suggested by
the novel *Jaws* by Peter Benchley.
Which is about as far as the similarity
between this shark shocker and the
two previous films goes, even though
co-scenarist Carl Gottlieb did work on
the script of Steven Spielberg's original
film. Instead, the action here takes
place in Florida (not Amity Island) but
there is still a great white shark or two
ready to snap their teeth at a cast that
includes Dennis Quaid, Bess
Armstrong and Britain's Simon
MacCorkindale and P H Moriarty.
The movie was originally shown in
cinemas in 3-D so be prepared for
sharks coming straight for the screen.

Jaws 4: The Revenge ① ⓥ
1987, US, 100 mins, colour
Dir: Joseph Sargent
Stars: Michael Caine, Lorraine Gary,
Lance Guest, Mario Van Peebles, Karen
Young
Rating: ★

Sean Brody, son of the police chief in
the original *Jaws*, is attacked and killed
by a great white shark. His mother is
convinced the shark has a grudge
against her family and looks to her
other son Michael, a marine biologist
in the Bahamas, for help. The shark
follows! The first film was tense,
exciting and credible, but by this time
the series had gone soft in the head.
How can Ellen Brody (Lorraine Gary)
imagine a fish can hold a grudge?
(Perhaps it swims along thinking
'that's the guy that harpooned my
brother'!). How did it find out that
she was going to the Bahamas? Even
assuming you swallow all this, the
fish itself is so obviously foam rubber
it doesn't exactly exude the kind of
menace that keeps you on the edge of
your seat. In what one can only assume was a moment of madness,
weakness or financial necessity, Michael Caine consented to appear in
this waterlogged slog as a dissolute
gambler who has taken a shine to the
widow Brody.

Jazzboat ○
1959, UK, 96 mins, b/w
Dir: Ken Hughes
Stars: Anthony Newley, Anne Aubrey,
James Booth, David Lodge
Rating: ★★

This madcap musical comedy was
made hot on the heels of *Idol on Pa-*

rade, the film which shot Anthony
Newley into the pop charts (with 'I've
Waited So Long') and enabled him to
carve out a whole new career. But,
apart from one number, 'Somebody to
Love', this film concentrates on
Newley's comedy talents, casting him
as an electrician who pretends to be a
big-time crook – and naturally gets
mixed up with the real thing. There's
quite a bit of dazzling dancing,
though, choreographed by the ubiquitous Lionel Blair, whose sister,
Joyce, plays Newley's girlfriend, and
backed by the music of Ted Heath
and his Orchestra. There is some
madcap humour from Bernie Winters
as a crook called Mugsy the Jinx, a
nickname which speaks for itself,
Lionel Jeffries (never better than
when, as here, he plays an inept detective), James Booth and David
Lodge. Ken Hughes' enthusiastic direction drives it along, and it was
successful enough to give rise to a sequel, *In the Nick*, in which Booth,
Winters and the delicious Anne
Aubrey all played the same characters
as in *Jazzboat*.

Jazz Singer, The ○
1953, US, 107 mins, colour
Dir: Michael Curtiz
Stars: Danny Thomas, Peggy Lee,
Mildred Dunnock
Rating: ★★

Colourful re-make by Warner Brothers of the classic early 'talkie' starring
Al Jolson. Danny Thomas assumes the
Jolson part of a Jewish boy torn between showbusiness and religion. The
tunes, including the catchy 'This is a
Very Special Day', are put across well,
especially by Peggy Lee. The period
has been brought up to date, and the
hero is a returned veteran of the Korean War. Thomas plays him with
plenty of personality, although his eccentric talent for telling a downbeat
yarn is hardly exploited.

Jean de Florette ○ ⓥ
1986, France, 122 mins, colour
Dir: Claude Berri
Stars: Gerard Depardieu, Yves Montand,
Daniel Auteuil, Elisabeth Depardieu
Rating: ★★★★

The first of a stunning double act of
films (the sequel, *Manon des Sources*, is
almost as good) shot simultaneously at
a cost of $17 million (a French record)
about life in a Provençal village in the
1920s. Showered with awards, this
first film is about the deceit and skulduggery involved in the fight for a

fertile piece of land and the efforts of
two farmers to ruin their neighbour.
The cast cannot be faulted (Gerard
Depardieu, as a simple hunchback, has
his real-life wife, Elisabeth, as his
screen partner) and the photography is
rich with the warmth of a French
countryside in summer. Highly
recommended.

Jennie
See: Portrait of Jennie

Jennifer Eight ● ⓥ
1992, US, 129 mins, colour
Dir: Bruce Robinson
Stars: Andy Garcia, Uma Thurman, Kathy
Baker, Lance Henriksen, John Malkovich
Rating: ★★

For the first 45 minutes, this threatens
to be a good serial-killer thriller – but
it just doesn't stick to the matter in
hand. It spends too much time instead
on the romance between burnt-out
detective Andy Garcia and beautiful
blind girl Uma Thurman – and on
Thurman's character in particular –
when it should be developing the
main thread of its story about a psycho
killer who has murdered and cut up
eight blind girls (so Garcia insists) and
is preparing to strike again. These
sideshoots act like suckers on a healthy
plant, and sap the tension from the
murder plot itself. An interrogation
sequence involving John Malkovich,
who is given an excessive proportion
of his pound of flesh as guest star, goes
on much too long, and the result of all
this is that a potentially tight
90-minute thriller stretched out to
well over two hours. The beginning,
though, is excellent – a rainsoaked
hunt for a grisly needle in a haystack
of garbage – and the last 10 minutes
are compulsive stuff.

Jeremiah Johnson ○ ⓥ
1972, US, 107 mins, colour
Dir: Sydney Pollack
Stars: Robert Redford, Will Geer
Rating: ★★★

The actor-director team of Robert
Redford and Sydney Pollack
(responsible for *Three Days of the
Condor, This Property is Condemned,
The Way We Were, The Electric Horseman* and *Out of Africa*) scores again
with this spectacularly shot yarn of a
mountain trapper and his adventures
near the America-Canada border in
the 1950s. Episodic in structure, the
film is kept constantly interesting by
its director who fills the screen with
colourful little anecdotes – like the

discovery of Hatchet Jack, frozen dead in the mountains, his last will and testament round his neck ('I, Hatchet Jack, being of sound mind and both legs broke'); or an eerie journey through an Indian burial ground. Supporting characters are minor, but richly delineated by the likes of Will Geer, Matt Clark, Charles Tyner and especially former musical star Allyn Ann McLerie as a 'crazy woman' who exists to tend the graves of her massacred family. Stunning snowscapes lend the action a primitive grandeur.

Jersey Girl ● ⓥ
1992, US, 95 mins, colour
Dir: David Burton Morris
Stars: Jami Gertz, Dylan McDermott, Sheryl Lee
Rating: ★★

If you fancy a straightforward version of a story you've seen a couple of hundred times before, there's nothing particularly wrong with this one. Toby (Jami Gertz), from across the river in downtown New Jersey, has a regular date with three (rather unattractive) girlfriends, but longs for something better. She stares at male models in *Elle*, asserting that 'this is the kind of guy who would remember your name'. Finding the man of her dreams (Dylan McDermott) in uptown New York, she pursues him relentlessly, survives getting him to crash his car and finally persuades him to date her. But he's eventually sucked back into his high-flying job and the society girlfriend (Sheryl Lee) with whom he'd had a tiff. But, McDermott being originally a downtown guy himself, and this being a *Cinderella* story, you don't need to flex your mental muscles to guess the ending. McDermott comes the Richard Gere act a bit heavy for Gertz, even though she's perhaps even more strident than she's meant to be, is winning enough to see it through. Easily-pleased romantics will like it.

Jesse James ○ ⓥ
1939, US, 106 mins, colour
Dir: Henry King
Stars: Tyrone Power, Henry Fonda, Nancy Kelly, Randolph Scott, Brian Donlevy, John Carradine
Rating: ★★★

First-rate, big-scale, splendidly directed (by Henry King) Western about the lawless career of the most famous outlaw of them all. There's a glimpse of Lon Chaney Jr just before he made

his name in *Of Mice and Men*, and a look at Randolph Scott when he was still playing supporting roles in top films. Tyrone Power's portrayal of Jesse James is remarkably similar in looks and mannerisms to that of Christopher Jones in the television series 30 years later.

Jesus Christ Superstar ○ ⓥ
1973, US, 107 mins, colour
Dir: Norman Jewison
Stars: Ted Neeley, Carl Anderson, Yvonne Elliman, Barry Dennen
Rating: ★★

Norman Jewison's brash big-screen version of the hit stage musical, which relates the last days of Christ from the viewpoint of Judas Iscariot (a powerhouse performance by Carl Anderson). Good use is made of the desert locations, but the treatment, complete with a camp Herod and military tanks, will not be everyone's religious cup of woe.

Jet Pilot ○
1950, US, 112 mins, colour
Dir: Josef Von Sternberg
Stars: John Wayne, Janet Leigh, Jay C Flippen, Paul Fix
Rating: ★

Allegedly directed by Josef von Sternberg, this film was held up for seven years before being finally released in 1957. With its comic-strip dialogue and one-dimensional heroics, it would sit well with Hollywood's more recent spate of 'Red-baiting' films. Janet Leigh is a cutie-pie Russian spy, while John Wayne shambles through the action with a permanent amiable grin. The flying scenes are flashily spectacular.

Jet Storm ○
1959, UK, 86 mins, b/w
Dir: Cy Endfield
Stars: Richard Attenborough, George Rose, Hermione Baddeley, Mai Zetterling, Diane Cilento, Stanley Baker
Rating: ★★

Arch-Goon Harry Secombe makes an effective appearance in a fairly straight dramatic role in this mid-air bomb-in-plane drama with some moments of tension, although not enough. Secombe joins an all-star cast that includes Stanley Baker, Diane Cilento, Mai Zetterling, Elizabeth Sellars, Marty Wilde and show business personalities Bernard Braden and Barbara Kelly. Richard Attenborough

gives another impassioned performance of a disturbed man, following his work in *The Man Upstairs*.

Jewel of the Nile, The ○ ⓥ
1985, US, 104 mins, colour
Dir: Lewis Teague
Stars: Michael Douglas, Kathleen Turner, Danny DeVito
Rating: ★★★

In some ways better than its predecessor *Romancing the Stone* (perhaps because it takes its villains more seriously), this is an enjoyable if never blood-surging romp that takes up the story of its two main characters six months after *Romancing*. In no time at all, Joan (Kathleen Turner) is in the middle of a desert war, with Jack (Michael Douglas) riding to the rescue. There are some good action sequences thereafter (especially a lengthy one on a fast-moving train) with both stars doing a lot of their own stuntwork, something that adds to the excitement. Turner and Douglas both ooze charisma and, in their relationship, strike all the right emotional sparks off each other. Danny DeVito, as their diminutive pursuer, is seen to rather better advantage than in the first film.

Jezebel ○ ⓥ
1938, US, 104 mins, b/w
Dir: William Wyler
Stars: Bette Davis, Henry Fonda, George Brent, Margaret Lindsay, Donald Crisp, Fay Bainter
Rating: ★★★

Bette Davis won her second Oscar for her performance as a wilful Southern belle in this handsomely-mounted melodrama which Warner Bros gave to the star as a consolation prize for not getting the coveted role of Scarlett O'Hara in *Gone with the Wind*. (*Jezebel*, incidentally, beat *GWTW* into the cinemas). Another Oscar, for best supporting actress, went to Fay Bainter as Davis' sympathetic aunt. Director William Wyler, borrowed from Samuel Goldwyn for the picture, does an excellent job although even he cannot make Davis' last-reel redemption through love convincing.

JFK ● ⓥ
1991, US, 191 mins, colour
Dir: Oliver Stone
Stars: Kevin Costner, Sissy Spacek, Tommy Lee Jones, Gary Oldman, John Candy, Kevin Bacon, Jack Lemmon
Rating: ★★★

J

Fascinating historically, persuasive and probably correct theoretically, but flawed dramatically, this account of New Orleans attorney Jim Garrison's pursuit of the Kennedy assassins raises the question as to why no-one has filmed it (been allowed to?) before. Far from the powerful document it might have been, the film still grips almost throughout because of the subject, and Garrison's examination and exploration of it. Even director Oliver Stone's pretentious beginning and end-piece can't deny the enormity of the tragedy and its consequences. Kevin Costner is not at his best as Garrison, seeming tired and lacking in conviction. And Sissy Spacek is poorly cast as his nagging wife, a part calling for a less sympathetic actress. The only thoroughly believable performance comes from Jack Lemmon as a private eye reluctant to turn informant even for the little he knows. No matter: the facts win out here. The deaths of many of those involved, including several key witnesses; the suppression or ignoring of evidence by others. A horror film it is for sure – but there's not a monster in sight, at least not of the conventional kind.

Jigsaw

1962, UK, 107 mins, b/w
Dir: Val Guest
Stars: Jack Warner, Ronald Lewis, Yolande Donlan
Rating: ★★★

From the moment director Val Guest's black-and-white camera zooms into a dark, open window, in sinister style, you are drawn chillingly into one of the most compulsive British murder thrillers in years. Jack Warner and Ronald Lewis really live the parts of the dogged investigators, and there are worthy contributions from Moira Redmond, John le Mesurier (in a rare dramatic role) and Michael Goodliffe.

Jimmy Reardon ●

(aka: A Night in the Life of Jimmy Reardon)
1987, US, 92 mins, colour
Dir: William Richert
Stars: River Phoenix, Ann Magnuson, Meredith Salenger, Ione Skye, Louanne, Paul Koslo
Rating: ★

This 'teenage rebel' film for the Eighties has a magazine cover cast but no likeable people. Director William Richert's own script endows his characters with no commendable

facets, allowing them only to sulk and scowl through the story of a working-class 17-year-old who has a rich girl on the hook but can't resist bonking everything else in sight while she keeps him waiting. Only Ann Magnuson, deservedly second-billed, as a Mrs Robinson of the blue-collar belt, brings any warmth and wistfulness to this would-be nostalgic tale. River Phoenix, playing like Mickey Rourke on heat, gives the worst performance of his too-brief career.

Jitterbugs ☉

1943, US, 74 mins, b/w
Dir: Malcolm St Clair
Stars: Stan Laurel, Oliver Hardy, Vivian Blaine, Bob Bailey
Rating: ★★

Another of Laurel and Hardy's Forties' comedies, in the years when they had switched without success from the Hal Roach Studio to MGM and 20th Century-Fox. As in *Way Out West*, they are out to protect the heroine (here Vivian Blaine) from the bad guy (splendid Douglas Fowley). Stan gets to dress up in drag, and Ollie has a nice Southern-style courtship scene with Lee Patrick. The trick ending is a 'gas'!

Joe Dakota

1957, US, 79 mins, colour
Dir: Richard Bartlett
Stars: Jock Mahoney, Luana Patten, Charles McGraw
Rating: ★★★

Mystery Western with an excellent story and some neat twists. Even though the direction is too slow, the plot is always intriguing enough to hold the interest. Former Disney child star Luana Patten has the leading feminine role and she's gorgeous. The supporting cast is bolstered by such good 'bad guys' as Charles McGraw, Claude Akins, Anthony Caruso and Lee Van Cleef. Another formidable screen villain, William Talman, once familiar as attorney Hamilton Burger in the Perry Mason TV series, co-wrote the film's screenplay.

Joe Kidd ◐

1973, US, 88 mins, colour
Dir: John Sturges
Stars: Clint Eastwood, Robert Duvall, John Saxon
Rating: ★★★

A strikingly handsome locomotive steals the attention from such hard

men of the screen as Clint Eastwood, Robert Duvall, John Saxon and Don Stroud in this typical Eastwood kill-them-all-and-come-back-alone Western. It's directed for once not by Eastwood himself but by the redoubtable John Sturges, who also made *Bad Day at Black Rock* and *The Magnificent Seven*.

Joe Macbeth

1955, UK, 90 mins, b/w
Dir: Ken Hughes
Stars: Paul Douglas, Ruth Roman, Bonar Colleano, Sidney James
Rating: ★★★

A blood-chilling modern gangster version of Shakespeare's play. Philip Yordan's screenplay is a bit arty at times, but retains the flavour of the original – and its moral: that power feeds upon itself, ultimately bringing self-destruction. Strong direction by Ken Hughes, powerful portrayals by Paul Douglas and especially Ruth Roman as Lady (here Lily) Macbeth.

Joe Versus the Volcano ○ ⓥ

1990, US, 100 mins, colour
Dir: John Patrick Shanley
Stars: Tom Hanks, Meg Ryan, Robert Stack, Lloyd Bridges
Rating: ★★

This is a peculiar number to come out of Hollywood in the 1990s and no mistake. Somewhere between a Frank Capra movie and a 'Road' film with Crosby, Hope and Lamour, the little parable that results almost never gets going, save for a few moments of high amusement towards the end. It does, however, have Tom Hanks and Meg Ryan enjoying themselves, which is just as well, as some of their stardust rubs off on the rest of the film. The idea is great: it's just the execution and pacing that drags it down. Hanks is a no-hoper stuck in a dead-end job with American Panascope, 'home of the rectal probe'. When an expensive doctor (Robert Stack) tells him he has a brain cloud, which is rare, spreading and limits his future to about six months, Hanks is easy prey to a hare-brained scheme that involves him sailing to a Pacific island and jumping into a volcano. There's a lovely sight gag involving two gongs on the island, but too few snappy lines and too little incident in the story development. Hanks and Ryan keep this scriptwrecked vessel afloat. But it's a waterlogged voyage most of the way.

Joey Boy ○
1965, UK, 91 mins, b/w
Dir: Frank Launder
Stars: Harry H Corbett, Stanley Baxter, Reg Varney
Rating: ★★

This wartime comedy about a wide boy who enjoys a profitable time in the army is a rather disappointing effort. Doubly so when one realises the usually-reliable Frank Launder is responsible for both the direction and the script. In the title role, Harry H Corbett tries his hardest with what he's given, but what passes for humour here is lowbrow and predictable. Also working hard to no worthwhile effect are Stanley Baxter, Bill Fraser, Reg Varney, Lance Percival and Derek Nimmo, among others. There are some bright moments, but not nearly enough to make up for the many dull ones.

Johnny Apollo ○
1940, US, 93 mins, b/w
Dir: Henry Hathaway
Stars: Tyrone Power, Dorothy Lamour, Edward Arnold, Lloyd Nolan
Rating: ★★★

Tyrone Power and Dorothy Lamour slipped away from swords and sarongs for this gangster and prison escape drama. It's fairly untypical of its studio (20th Century-Fox) at the time but, thanks to Henry Hathaway's firm direction, it's fast-moving and acceptable crime fare, with an outstanding performance from portly Edward Arnold. He shows he can handle a sympathetic role as well as dispense sneers as power-hungry villains.

Johnny Belinda ○
1948, US, 103 mins, b/w
Dir: Jean Negulesco
Stars: Jane Wyman, Lew Ayres, Charles Bickford, Stephen McNally
Rating:

Jane Wyman transformed her career with her portrayal of the deaf-mute girl and the depiction of her hard, and later tragic life in a coastal Nova Scotia fishing-farming community. The Academy Award she won for best actress set her up for a whole run of superior soap-operas that became known as The Wyman Weepies.

Johnny Come Lately ○ ⓥ
(aka: Johnny Vagabond)
1943, US, 97 mins, b/w
Dir: William K Howard
Stars: James Cagney, Grace George, Marjorie Main, Hattie McDaniel
Rating: ★★

One of James Cagney's most unusual films. He plays a wanderer – the film's British title was *Johnny Vagabond* – who comes to the aid of a newspaper proprietress (stage actress Grace George in her only film) being terrorised by the town's crooked boss. A little gunplay is thrown in to keep Cagney's Thirties' fans happy , but otherwise it's a mild character drama which doesn't quite fire on all cylinders.

Johnny Cool ○
1964, US, 103 mins, b/w
Dir: William Asher
Stars: Henry Silva, Elizabeth Montgomery, Sammy Davis Jr
Rating: ★★

This drama of a Sicilian assassin didn't shoot that excellent villain Henry Silva into the star bracket. Perhaps he was too cold and matter-of-fact, although that didn't hurt Alan Ladd in *This Gun for Hire*. Strong supporting cast includes Telly Savalas as a crime tsar.

Johnny Dangerously ○
1984, US, 90 mins, colour
Dir: Amy Heckerling
Stars: Michael Keaton, Marilu Henner
Rating: ★★

You can forgive this gangster comedy its flat spots and lapses into bad taste because the funny bits really are very funny. Too bad that there aren't enough of them. Michael Keaton plays the title role, a lad who turns to crime to pay his hypochondriac mother's medical bills. His life of crime keeps mum in pills and puts his kid brother through law school. A starry cast that includes Peter Boyle, Marilu Henner, Dom DeLuise, Griffin Dunne, Ray Walston and Danny DeVito works hard to keep things going but what could have been a delightful spoof on all those Warner Bros gangster films of the Thirties and Forties falls flat too often. Still, the gags there are are worth waiting for.

Johnny Eager ○
1942, US, 107 mins, b/w
Dir: Mervyn Le Roy
Stars: Robert Taylor, Lana Turner, Van Heflin
Rating: ★★★

An offbeat gangster thriller with a top-notch cast and an Oscar-winning performance from Van Heflin.

Robert Taylor plays the villain of the title, shrugging off his usual good-guy image to play a baddie with convincing nastiness. It is one of his finest roles, although given extra depth by the terrific acting of Heflin as his alcoholic friend. The 'Sweater Girl', Lana Turner, smoulders with sensuality – so much so that Taylor was drawn to her romantically in real life. MGM's publicity campaign made the most of their torrid on- and off-screen romance and they took out an ad which read 'TNT – Taylor 'n' Turner – Together, They're Terrific'.

Johnny Frenchman ○
1945, UK, 111 mins, b/w
Dir: Charles Frend
Stars: Francoise Rosay, Tom Walls, Patricia Roc
Rating: ★★★

Charming and very convincing story of the rivalry between Breton and Cornish fisherfolk, which benefitted considerably from location filming in Cornwall. The action includes a terrific fist fight between Ralph Michael and Paul Dupuis. And if you think the French accents are authentic, they should be. The film makers borrowed French refugees from the wartime hostilities to people some of the scenes.

Johnny Guitar ○
1953, US, 110 mins, colour
Dir: Nicholas Ray
Stars: Joan Crawford, Sterling Hayden, Scott Brady, Mercedes McCambridge, Ward Bond, Ernest Borgnine
Rating: ★★★★

A really heady Western, rife with symbolism and unusually boasting female protagonists. Joan Crawford's up there running the local gambling saloon, and psychotic cattle baron (or should it be baroness?) Mercedes McCambridge wants her run out of town or hanged, whichever can be arranged the sooner. The men, ostensibly in the forefront of the action, Sterling Hayden (in the title role), Scott Brady, Ernest Borgnine and Ward Bond, are really sideline attractions to this central issue, as Bond finds out towards the end, when he realises what's really been the driving force behind his posse. Everybody has the hots for someone else in this film; even Trucolor has never looked hotter than under Harry Stradling Jr's cameras. Crawford and McCambridge give strong, almost vicious performances; not surprisingly

J

they didn't get on, and director Nicholas Ray eventually had to shoot their scenes together separately. This is a one-of-a-kind Western. Only the minor *The Woman They Almost Lynched* even comes close.

Johnny Handsome ● Ⓥ
1989, US, 94 mins, colour
Dir: Walter Hill
Stars: Mickey Rourke, Ellen Barkin, Elizabeth McGovern, Morgan Freeman, Forest Whitaker, Lance Henriksen
Rating: ★★★

Here's a good old gangster flick in the modern manner. Director Walter Hill does his best job for some time on this story of a facially deformed robber (Mickey Rourke) double-crossed by fellow-thieves Ellen Barkin and Lance Henriksen, who kill Johnny's partners and make off with the loot. Near death after an attack by convicts hired by Henriksen, Johnny is offered a new face by plastic surgeon Forest Whitaker if he'll go straight. All this is taken with a pinch of salt by detective A Z Drones (Morgan Freeman) and by the audience, who know that Johnny Gruesome turned Handsome is hell-bent on revenge. Fast-moving and undemanding, the film is full of viciously dynamic action scenes and strong performances from all those mentioned. Elizabeth McGovern even manages to put punch and character into the role of the nice girl who almost keeps Johnny on the straight and narrow.

Johnny in the Clouds
See: The Way to the Stars

Johnny O'Clock ○
1946, US, 95 mins, b/w
Dir: Robert Rossen
Stars: Dick Powell, Lee J Cobb, Evelyn Keyes, Ellen Drew
Rating: ★★

It's a great title but otherwise this is one of Dick Powell's less interesting tough-guy roles, even though he and director Robert Rossen give the film a style that the typically shoddy Columbia production never approaches. Despite Powell's performance and a decent supporting cast that includes Jeff Chandler as a gunman in one of his first roles, the film never really engages your emotions and a sense of danger is noticeably lacking.

Johnny Reno ○
1965, US, 83 mins, colour
Dir: R G Springsteen

Stars: Dana Andrews, Jane Russell, Lyle Bettger
Rating: ★

It's reunion night at the old corral. The marshal with the chip on his shoulder is Dana Andrews. The crooked mayor is that meanest of villains, Lyle Bettger. The sheriff, simple but honest, is Lon Chaney Jr. The upright townsman is John Agar, hero of a dozen Western sagas. The young cowpuncher framed for murder is Tom Drake, once Judy Garland's trolley-bound beau in *Meet Me in St Louis.* And who's the gal in the saloon, swathed in crinoline? It can't be. Not after all these years. But it is. Jane Russell. Add Richard Arlen and Robert Lowery, and raise your glasses to the creaking cowboys' club.

Johnny Suede ● Ⓥ
1991, US/Switzerland, 95 mins, colour
Dir: Tom DiCillo
Stars: Brad Pitt, Catherine Keener, Calvin Levels, Tina Louise
Rating: ★

About the only original thing in this slice of minimalist cinema, filmed mostly in the corners of rooms, is the hero's mega-high bouffant hairdo. Otherwise, there are sparks in the dialogue and in the songs – 'I want to meet a model who's only got one name,' sings the hero (Brad Pitt), who idolises Sixties pop star Ricky Nelson – but not enough to suggest the film is going to build the cult reputation some critics thought. There must be better ways of spending even tiny budgets than having the hero encounter a few women, walk along a few streets, ride a few tube trains, amble around with his hand in his knickers, and arrive back at the point he started from. Lots of swearing though for those who like that kind of thing.

Johnny Tremain ☉
1957, US, 81 mins, colour
Dir: Robert Stevenson
Stars: Hal Stalmaster, Luana Patten, Sebastian Cabot, Richard Beymer
Rating: ★★★

This colourful adventure is Walt Disney's version of the start of the American Revolution as seen through the eyes of the title character. Johnny Tremain (Hal Stalmaster) embraces the revolutionary cause after suffering the rough edge of British justice when he is wrongly accused of theft. He joins the Sons of Liberty and

takes part in the imfamous (from our point of view) Boston Tea Party. Director Robert Stevenson (English, surprisingly enough) doesn't ignore the history but neither does he allow it to stop this being a ripping adventure yarn of appeal to all ages.

Johnny Vagabond
See: Johnny Come Lately

Joker Is Wild, The ○
1957, US, 127 mins, b/w
Dir: Charles Vidor
Stars: Frank Sinatra, Mitzi Gaynor, Jeanne Crain, Eddie Albert
Rating: ★★★

Solidly entertaining biopic of American nightclub entertainer Joe E Lewis, who started out in the Prohibition Twenties as a singer. After a gangster's razor put paid to any dreams of stardom in that direction, the bitter and disillusioned Lewis began an entirely new career as a sourly wisecracking comedian. Frank Sinatra gives a dramatic performance of total conviction in this demanding role, supported by a trio of lovely ladies in Mitzi Gaynor, Beverly Garland and Jeanne Crain. He also finds time to sing *All the Way* and *Chicago.*

Jokers, The ○
1966, UK, 126 mins, colour
Dir: Michael Winner
Stars: Michael Crawford, Oliver Reed, Harry Andrews, Daniel Massey
Rating: ★★★

Made in the middle of director Michael Winner's most fruitful period, long before he got bogged down in cool crime dramas with Charles Bronson, this is a thoroughly engaging comedy-thriller about two young rogues who hatch a plan to steal the Crown Jewels – and then give them back. The first part of the plan goes like clockwork. Michael Crawford and Oliver Reed are perfect as the amateur thieves.

Jolly Bad Fellow, A ◐
(aka: They All Died Laughing)
1964, UK, 94 mins, b/w
Dir: Don Chaffey
Stars: Janet Munro, Maxine Audley
Rating: ★★★

A black comedy in the Ealing manner, whose sometimes witty script, by Donald Taylor and Robert Hamer, cast Leo (Rumpole of the Bailey) McKern as a university don – thus the title – who proceeds to work his way to a fellowship award by eliminating those who stand in his way, after he discovers a poison that leaves no trace. Maxine Audley is most appealing as his wife, but Janet Munro seems miscast as the don's seductive laboratory assistant. The title of the original novel, by C E Vulliamy, is also fun: *Down Among the Dead Men*.

Jolson Sings Again ○ ⓥ
1949, US, 93 mins, colour
Dir: Henry Levin
Stars: Larry Parks, Barbara Hale, William Demarest
Rating: ★★★

The successor to *The Jolson Story* surprisingly turned out to be every bit as vivid, colourful, lively and entertaining as the original. Larry Parks once again mimes skilfully to Jolson's singing and Barbara Hale is warmth itself as his new wife. A multitude of songs includes 'Mammy', 'Swanee', 'Toot-Toot-Tootsie', 'Dixie', 'Carolina in the Morning' and 'Sonny Boy'.

Jolson Story, The ○ ⓥ
1946, US, 128 mins, colour
Dir: Alfred E Green
Stars: Larry Parks, Evelyn Keyes, William Demarest
Rating: ★★★

This story of Al Jolson's rise to fame was Columbia's biggest money spinner at that time and made a star of Larry Parks, even though Jolson himself provided the singing voice and did the long-shot dances. The musical sequences were directed by Joseph H Lewis, who made a name for himself among film fans for his fine handling of low-budget material in the Forties and Fifties.

Joseph Andrews ●
1976, UK, 98 mins, colour
Dir: Tony Richardson
Stars: Ann-Margret, Peter Firth, Michael Hordern, Beryl Reid, Jim Dale, Natalie Ogle
Rating: ★

Director Tony Richardson returns to the vein he mined so successfully in *Tom Jones*. Although this later costume romp cannot measure up to its illustrious Oscar-winning predecessor, it does have some very funny scenes. Much of it, though, has a tired feeling.

Josh and S.A.M. ○ ⓥ
1993, US, 97 mins, colour
Dir: Billy Weber

Stars: Jacob Tierney, Noah Fleiss, Martha Plimpton, Stephen Tobolowsky, Chris Penn
Rating: ★

Divided between divorced parents and feeling unwanted by both, 12-year-old Josh convinces his younger brother Sam that he has been 'programmed' by the Pentagon. After hearing at an airport stop between parents that their mother has remarried and thinking they've killed a man who menaced them, the boys run away together. A pretty slim premise on which to hang a road movie and indeed this is a pretty slim road movie at that, only barely interesting and tending to repetition. Jacob Tierney and Noah Fleiss are competent young actors, but none too charismatic and there's no emotional pull for the audience in staying around to see what happens to them. Martha Plimpton, Chris Penn and Udo Kier are some of the too-few people along the way, but only Stephen Tobolowsky as their father creates a character who seems to have a life outide the movie.

Journey Back to Oz ⊙
1971, US, 90 mins, colour
Dir: Hal Sutherland
Stars: Voice stars: Liza Minnelli, Mickey Rooney, Ethel Merman
Rating: ★★★

Nostalgia, nostalgia everywhere in this cartoon sequel to *The Wizard of Oz*. Based on L Frank Baum's own first sequel to his children's classic, it adds Dorothy to the plot of that and gives her the voice of Liza Minnelli, daughter of Judy Garland, the original Dorothy. Just for good measure, Margaret Hamilton, the original Wicked Witch, voices Aunt Em, and Mickey Rooney, Judy Garland's favourite dancing partner in films – they made nine together – provides the voice of the Scarecrow. Virtually completed in 1964, but tinkered around with for years before eventual release.

Journey of Natty Gann, The ○ ⓥ
1985, US, 101 mins, colour
Dir: Jeremy Kagan
Stars: Meredith Salenger, John Cusack, Ray Wise, Scatman Crothers
Rating: ★★★★

There's a return to the old values of the Disney studio here with the story of a 14-year-old girl who, tough as any boy, runs away from Depres-

sion-gripped Chicago to join her father, who has gone to Washington. She is befriended by a half-breed dog she calls Wolf and by a young drifter (John Cusack) for whom she feels the first stirrings of love. There's only one way to play Natty successfully, by going in there and giving it all you've got. Young Meredith Salenger does just that: she's never been as effective since. Director Jeremy Kagan conjured up an unfailing, exciting sense of period in creating the best family film the Disney people had turned out in more than a decade.

Journey to the Centre of the Earth ○ ⓥ
1959, US, 110 mins, colour
Dir: Henry Levin
Stars: Pat Boone, James Mason, Arlene Dahl, Diane Baker
Rating: ★★★

This spectacular adaptation of the Jules Verne adventure yarn is great fun, and was nominated for four Academy Awards, including special effects, art direction and set decoration. Highlights of the journey include prehistoric reptiles, a magnetic storm and a terrifying earthquake.

Joy Luck Club ● ⓥ
1993, US, 139 mins, colour
Dir: Wayne Wang
Stars: Tamlyn Tomita, Keiu Chinh, France Nuyen, Tsai Chin, Lisa Lu, Andrew McCarthy
Rating: ★★

A very well acted and presented story of Chinese-American life and the chequered histories that lead to the formation of a family network. But – and here comes the downside – it's also a story which makes it very difficult to keep track of its various threads. These are all enthralling and beautifully done – but not quite memorably enough so that we can keep a grip on its overall pattern. What with four daughters in America and their mothers in China and sometimes their mothers' mothers, it's hard to remember who has done what or had what done to them, and that deficiency strikes at the humanity so vital to the film's appeal. Still, nostalgia buffs will get a kick out of seeing Sixties stars France Nuyen, Lisa Lu, Tsai Chin and Kieu Chinh all delivering first-rate performances under Wayne Wang's direction.

J

Juarez ○
1939, US, 132 mins, b/w
Dir: William Dieterle
Stars: Paul Muni, Bette Davis, Claude
Rains, John Garfield, Donald Crisp
Rating: ★★

Everything about this mammoth historical epic was on a big scale; from the 1,000 extras and 54 massive sets – including 12 villages, four cities, and various castles and palaces – to the 3,000 bars of music composed by Erich Wolfgang Korngold. For all that (or perhaps because of it) the whiff of real life escapes it. Director William Dieterle certainly had his hands full with a set-ful of temperamental stars, but took precautions – he consulted his astrologer and demanded everyone to be on the set on a particular morning in 1938, a time when the planets indicated his personal destiny to be favoured. But they didn't help the box office figures and the film made a loss. Paul Muni is almost unrecognisable under tons of make-up as Mexican leader Benito Pablo Juarez, and Bette Davis goes to town as the unbalanced Empress Carlotta, offering a stone-faced tour-de-force of madness personified.

Jubal ○
1956, US, 101 mins, colour
Dir: Delmer Daves
Stars: Glenn Ford, Ernest Borgnine, Rod
Steiger, Charles Bronson
Rating: ★★★

Very tough Western, with a performance of integrity, depth and sincerity by Glenn Ford as Jubal, the cowhand who drifts into trouble with the boss's foreman and the boss's wife. A year later, Ford and director Delmer Daves combined again – on the classic Western, *3.10 to Yuma*. This film has a formidable combination of talent in its three leading players, of whom Rod Steiger, perhaps, has the plum role as a cowhand with a lemon-sour nature and a sadistic streak. The story is a strong one, and the picture is beautifully located against a background of the Montana mountains. In a featured role is Charles Bronson, quite some time before he developed into a top star. The feminine interest is supplied by Felicia Farr, who in real life is Jack Lemmon's wife.

Judge Hardy and Son ○
1939, US, 87 mins, b/w
Dir: George B Seitz

Stars: Lewis Stone, Mickey Rooney
Rating: ★★

One of the more sentimental entries in the Hardy family series, with Mother Hardy down with pneumonia, an elderly couple being evicted from their home and even Mickey Rooney's Andy less buoyant than usual when he gets weighed down with debts. Never mind, studio boss Louis Meyer was happy to see audiences crying with the Hardy family (his personal favourites) every step of the way. Meyer even personally wrote the prayer Andy offers up to God to spare Mother Hardy's life, after expressing dissatisfaction with what writer Carey Wilson had provided. The prayer became standard text for all similar situations in MGM movies for the next decade!

Judge Hardy's Children ○
1938, US, 78 mins, b/w
Dir: George B Seitz
Stars: Lewis Stone, Mickey Rooney
Rating: ★★★

The third of the Hardy films finds what was to become the regular cast almost in place, with peppy Ann Rutherford in for the first of many outings as Andy Hardy's girlfriend Polly. Spinster Aunt Milly is played by Betty Ross Clarke who would soon be replaced by Sara Haden. Solid family entertainment of its time.

Judgment at Nuremberg ○
1961, US, 190 mins, b/w
Dir: Stanley Kramer
Stars: Spencer Tracy, Burt Lancaster,
Richard Widmark, Marlene Dietrich,
Maximilian Schell, Judy Garland
Rating: ★★★

A graphic account of the Nuremberg Trials, in which members of the German judiciary were brought to book in the immediate post-war period. For his impassioned portrayal of the defending counsel, Maximilian Schell took an Academy Award as the year's best actor – but Spencer Tracy, Burt Lancaster and Co are also superb.

Judith ○
1965, US, 109 mins, colour
Dir: Daniel Mann
Stars: Sophia Loren, Peter Finch, Jack
Hawkins
Rating: ★

A moderately exciting drama set in strife-torn Israel in 1947. Sophia Loren looks eye-popping in sweater and short shorts but has little meaty acting

to do as a Jewess determined to kill her ex-Nazi husband. As a British officer, Jack Hawkins skilfully moulds the most sympathetic character in the film.

Juggernaut ○
1974, UK, 105 mins, colour
Dir: Richard Lester
Stars: Richard Harris, Omar Sharif,
Anthony Hopkins, David Hemmings, Ian
Holm
Rating: ★★★

This large-scale, water-bound thriller raises a fair amount of tension on its theme of seven bombs planted aboard a luxury liner. Richard Harris leads the team of men assigned to defuse them in the teeth of a howling gale while, back in England, Supt Anthony Hopkins, whose wife is aboard and whose son inadvertently costs two lives, races desperately to track down Juggernaut, the mad bomber. But Roy Kinnear steals the film as the ship]s social director – a memorably comic supporting portrayal. David Hemmings is also excellent and the suspense is good if not super-tense. A sub-plot involving Shirley Knight and Omar Sharif (as the ship's captain) is so negligible as to be simply not worthwhile.

Julia ◑
1977, US, 118 mins, colour
Dir: Fred Zinnemann
Stars: Jane Fonda, Vanessa Redgrave,
Jason Robards, Maximilian Schell, Hal
Holbrook
Rating: ★★★

This award-winning film is sensitive, atmospheric and often suspenseful. It recounts some early adventures in the life of American playwright Lillian Hellman (Jane Fonda), notably those concerning her childhood friend Julia, who became involved in resistance against the Nazis in the Thirties. Their story is painstakingly retold by director Fred Zinnemann, with assistance from one of the world's best colour cameramen, Douglas Slocombe. Vanessa Redgrave is exceptionally good as Julia, and certainly better than anyone could have expected in a part which creeps so uncomfortably close to her own political feelings. Jason Robards is a treat as Lillian's companion Dashiell Hammett – right back to his best form. Both performances were rightly rewarded with Academy Awards. In the supporting cast, you can see a future Oscar-winner, Meryl Streep, in her first film role.

Julia Has Two Lovers ● ⓥ
1990, US, 91 mins, colour
Dir: Bashar Shbib
Stars: Daphna Kastner, David Duchovny
Rating: ★

You could almost close your eyes and treat this story of seduction by phone as a radio play. Not that that would make its story any more believable. Julia (Daphna Kastner) is about to marry a man she doesn't love when along comes the voice of Daniel (David Duchovny) who specialises in making obscene phone calls to women to see if he can seduce them. He finds a willing participant in Julia and soon enough is knocking on her door and tumbling her into bed, only to have his lifestyle exposed by one of his previous conquests. There's very little to all of this save for the conversations: the budget apparently ran to about $25 and all of the acting apart from the leading players would discredit your local amateur dramatic society. Duchovny, though, has a lazy, laid-back charm that would subsequently be seen to advantage in bigger if not better films.

Julie ○
1957, US, 99 mins, b/w
Dir: Andrew Stone
Stars: Doris Day, Louis Jourdan, Barry Sullivan, Frank Lovejoy
Rating: ★★

This terrifying tale of a young widow who remarries, only to find that her new husband is a homicidal maniac, marked the beginning of Doris Day's complete breakaway from musicals, and her appointments with fear that continued with *Midnight Lace*. It was made by Andrew Stone, then a young director specialising in high-tension thrillers shot on location, such as *The Night Holds Terror*, *The Steel Trap*, *Cry Terror* and *The Last Voyage*. Later, he specialised in such panoramic musical blockbusters as *Song of Norway* and *The Great Waltz*.

Julius Caesar ○ ⓥ
1953, US, 120 mins, b/w
Dir: Joseph L Mankiewicz
Stars: Marlon Brando, James Mason, John Gielgud, Edmond O'Brien, Greer Garson, Deborah Kerr
Rating: ★★★

One of Hollywood's most prestigious Shakespearean productions, with an electrifying performance by Marlon Brando as Mark Antony, this is definitely the best film version available of the famous play. There are memorable performances from John Gielgud as Cassius and Edmond O'Brien as Casca, and the film's wealth of expert character-drawing extends right down to the minor roles, one of which is played by Edmund Purdom. Directed with imagination by Joseph L Mankiewicz, the film proved that the public would go for Shakespeare if the impact was strong and the performances attractive enough.

Julius Caesar ○
1970, US, 117 mins, colour
Dir: Stuart Burge
Stars: Charlton Heston, John Gielgud, Diana Rigg, Jason Robards, Richard Chamberlain, Christopher Lee
Rating: ★★

Charlton Heston stars in this not too well-known version – at any rate in comparison with the more famous Marlon Brando film of Shakespeare's play – made in Britain but with a few top American stars in leading roles somewhat at variance with an array of notable British acting talent. Jason Robards in particular seems ill-at-ease in the role of Brutus, but lovers of Shakespeare and good performances will find much that is rewarding. Robert Vaughn makes a superbly sneaky Casca.

Jumbo ⊙
(aka: Billy Rose's Jumbo)
1962, US, 125 mins, colour
Dir: Charles Walters
Stars: Doris Day, Stephen Boyd, Jimmy Durante, Martha Raye, Dean Jagger
Rating: ★★★

Pleasantly entertaining musical, Doris Day's last to date, about the rivalry between two circuses. The musical numbers are attractively staged, as one would expect with a combination of director Charles Walters and second-unit director Busby Berkeley who between them have made some of Hollywood's most invigorating musical entertainments. Nice, too, to see old-timers Martha Raye and Jimmy Durante in action again, even if one wishes the script gave the them more in which to sink their teeth.

Jumping Jacks ⊙
1952, US, 96 mins, b/w
Dir: Norman Taurog

Stars: Dean Martin, Jerry Lewis
Rating: ★★

Having created havoc in the Army (*At War With the Army*) and the Navy (*Sailor Beware*), Dean Martin and Jerry Lewis set about destroying the airborne infantry in this story of two song-and-dance men drafted into the paratroopers (which sounds suspiciously like Abbott and Costello's *Rookies*). But Robert Strauss is a delight as the ferocious sergeant who deals summarily with Jerry's request to tuck him up in bed at night. Mona Freeman is a resourceful and feminine heroine; and the film is quite a lot of fun.

Jumpin' Jack Flash ◐ ⓥ
1986, US, 120 mins, colour
Dir: Penny Marshall
Stars: Whoopi Goldberg, Jonathan Pryce, Jim Belushi, Carol Kane, Annie Potts
Rating: ★★★

The follow-up vehicle to Whoopi Goldberg's Oscar-nominated performance in Steven Spielberg's *The Color Purple* marked a dramatic change of pace and one more akin to her wacky, wisecracking, alternative comedy persona. An uneven comedy spy thriller, its main problem is that Whoopi's character, a hapless bank clerk who receives messages from a British spy trapped behind the Iron Curtain, is just too small for her personality. And Penny Marshall (later to make *Big*, but here in her debut as a director) was unable (or unwilling) to keep her star's wilder excesses in check. But there are still some comic gems, notably the scenes where Whoopi gatecrashes a ball at the British Embassy in New York by impersonating Diana Ross (watched with incredulity by British comedy actress Tracey Ullman, making a tiny US screen debut), and when her dress gets caught in an office shredder. A real curate's egg that leaves you wishing the rest of the film had matched its high points of hilarity. But with no less than five writers on the case, you're asking for trouble.

Jungle Book ⊙
1942, US, 109 mins, colour
Dir: Zoltan Korda
Stars: Sabu, Joseph Calleia, Rosemary deCamp, John Qualen
Rating: ★★★

After a number of successful films in Britain, teenage Indian star Sabu went to Hollywood with Alexander and

J

Zoltan Korda to complete *The Thief of Bagdad* and stayed with them to make this colourful adaptation of Kipling's classic tales. Because it tries to combine too many of the original tales the film tends to be a little muddled in places, but the sweep of the action and the fascination of the animals carries us through. Like many films of the period, it looks nothing like the real India but perhaps what it should look like, according to Hollywood. In fact, the exterior work was done at Lake Sherwood, just outside Los Angeles. The film is well up to the standards set by *The Thief of Bagdad* and makes vivid entertainment.

Jungle Book, The ⊙ ⓥ
1967, US, 78 mins, colour
Dir: Wolfgang Reitherman
Voice stars: Phil Harris,
Sebastian Cabot, George Sanders, Louis Prima, Bruce Reitherman
Rating: ★★★★

Coming up mint-fresh at each reissue, Disney's jazzed-up Kipling is brimming with marvellous characters: Baloo the bear, King Louie of the Apes, Colonel Hathi the elephant and Kaa the snake remaining triumphantly individual. And the whole film, apart from one or two very small dud patches, goes with a swing. Best of all is Shere Khan the tiger, but probably only because he's voiced by the silkily threatening tones of George Sanders. No actor's voice, surely, was ever more suited to a cartoon role. Only the quartet of Liverpudlian vultures are at all dated, although even they retain their inherent appeal. The Sherman Brothers' tuneful score – 'King of the Swingers', 'The Bare Necessities' and more – ensures that this one remains the king of the swingin' cartoons.

Jungle Fever ● ⓥ
1991, US, 132 mins, colour
Dir: Spike Lee
Stars: Wesley Snipes, Annabella Sciorra, Spike Lee, John Turturro, Anthony Quinn
Rating: ★

Man, this is long and heavy, and it really lays it on you like Spike Lee thinks it is. After delightful credits, pegged to street signs, and a stylish opening, this movie seems to go on for hours and hours. A savage film that sometimes resembles a silent, it's a mess of drugs, adultery, violence and murder and you're never quite sure that its characters' motivations are

what Lee thinks they are. The film's racist attitudes will sit uneasily with some audiences, and its characters – or, rather, caricatures, rarely ring true. Snipes stars as the upwardly-mobile accountant who eventually emerges unscathed from an affair with his temp secretary (Annabella Sciorra) brought on by late nights and takeaway suppers. Of course, he goes back to his wife, while Sciorra must crawl back to the father who beats her unmercifully and loses her boyfriend into the bargain. Black is beautiful, says Lee, and a white girl who wants an affair with a black man may get what she deserves. Subplots abound, if you can follow them, as the dialogue is screeched at ear-splitting level and seems to consist mostly of hysterically shouted four-letter words. If this is the fever, man, hand us the antidote.

Jungle Fighters
See: The Long and the Short and the Tall

Junior Bonner ◐ ⓥ
1972, US, 105 mins, colour
Dir: Sam Peckinpah
Stars: Steve McQueen, Robert Preston, Ida Lupino
Rating: ★★

A much quieter film than usual from *Straw Dogs* and *Bring Me the Head of Alfredo Garcia* director Sam Peckinpah, with Steve McQueen in excellent form as a rodeo rider who comes to realise that he can't go home on the range again. There's a lot to recommend in this study of a fish out of water, a man searching in a changing world for values that have long since disappeared. The rodeo footage is pretty exciting and Jerry Fielding's music is spot-on. Look out for the director's son, Matthew, as McQueen's son, Tim, and, in a small role, Donald 'Red' Barry. He had featured in Westerns since 1936 and for several years was voted one of the 'Top 10 Money-Making Western Stars'. He took his own life in 1980.

Jurassic Park ◐ ⓥ
1993, US, 126 mins, colour
Dir: Steven Spielberg
Stars: Sam Neill, Laura Dern, Jeff Goldblum, Richard Attenborough, Bob Peck, Martin Ferrero
Rating: ★★★

After a long and slow lead-in period, Steven Spielberg's dinosaur thriller explodes into the kind of action we've all been waiting for, as the ge-

netically engineered prehistoric animals go berserk after a renegade employee conveniently turns off all the electric fences penning them in, on their island home. It's at this stage that 90 per cent of the Jurassic Park staff seem to disappear, leaving only the principals to flee the predators and try to turn the current back on. But you can ignore the plot, such as it is, since not much of it makes any sort of sense you can grasp. Sam Neill and Laura Dern, along with kids Ariana Richards and Joseph Nazzello, give vigorous physical performances dodging the dinos, while Richard Attenborough (as the park's curator) and Jeff Goldblum offer rather actorly portrayals on the fringe of things. The dinosaurs themselves, of course, are the real stars, and they're marvellous – terrifyingly awesome and almost totally convincing. Enough to make even E.T. phone home.

Just Around the Corner ⊙
1938, US, 71 mins, b/w
Dir: Irving Cummings
Stars: Shirley Temple, Charles Farrell, Joan Davis
Rating: ★★★

Shirley Temple chirps her way through a typical Temple musical weepie, set in the Depression. This one contains what is probably her best production number in films – 'I Love to Walk in the Rain'. A good time for vintage-film fans: they can spot wide-mouthed comedienne Joan Davis, coloured dancer Bill 'Bojangles' Robinson, perfect-mannered, prissy Franklin Pangborn, and veteran vaudevillian Bert Lahr – to win everlasting fame a year later as The Cowardly Lion in *The Wizard of Oz*.

Just Ask for Diamond ○
1988, UK, 94 mins, colour
Dir: Stephen Bayly
Stars: Dursley McLinden, Colin Dale, Susannah York
Rating: ★★

The most inexplicable thing about this spoof *film noir* was the decision to drop the evocative title of screenwriter Adam Horowitz's novel, *The Falcon's Malteser*. But this was just one of a series of absurd misjudgements which mar this potentially entertaining children's film. The world of dark shadows and corruption could have been more convincingly realised and the humour might have been sharper too. Only a few early comic moments and Susannah York as the drink-sodden Lauren Bacardi make any impression.

Just Between Friends ◑
1986, US, 105 mins, colour
Dir: Allan Burns
Stars: Mary Tyler Moore, Christine Lahti, Ted Danson, Sam Waterston
Rating: ★★

This mega-weepie about the friendship between a wife and a mistress (not knowing at first who the other is) is heavy going at first, but gathers strength from the performances of Mary Tyler Moore and Christine Lahti, both perfectly cast. Later developments are not wholly believable, but these two powerhouse performers see it through.

Just For You ○
1952, US, 104 mins, colour
Dir: Elliott Nugent
Stars: Bing Crosby, Jane Wyman, Ethel Barrymore, Natalie Wood
Rating: ★★★

Pleasant musical about a composer, who doesn't spend enough time with his motherless son and daughter. Some splendid mountain scenery, able scene-stealing from a 13-year-old Natalie Wood as the daughter, tuneful songs and colourful dance sequences. There's also Ethel Barrymore, who dominates every scene in which she appears, and will leave you breathless with admiration, as the super-sophisticated headmistress of a superior girls' finishing school.

Just Like a Woman ● ⓥ
1992, UK, 109 mins, colour
Dir: Christopher Monger
Stars: Julie Walters, Adrian Pasdar, Paul Freeman
Rating: ★

Someone, somewhere, is due to write another good film soon for that most deserving of actresses, Julie Walters. But this isn't it. The sad thing about this whole, awful mess is that Julie is quite good, even affecting in it. Dreadfully mishandled so as to suggest appalling visual conflicts between the heterosexual transvestite and the effeminate way in which Adrian Pasdar, groping desperately, plays him, it's the story of a businessman who likes dressing up in women's clothes and the landlady who falls for him anyway. One of the problems with all this is that Pasdar never looks like anything but a man, which would be

all right in a docu-drama about transvestism, but makes nonsense of a plotline in which he's required to pass muster as a woman for all sorts of reasons.

Just My Luck ☉ ⓥ
1957, UK, 80 mins, b/w
Dir: John Paddy Carstairs
Stars: Norman Wisdom, Jill Dixon, Margaret Rutherford, Leslie Phillips
Rating: ★★★

Norman Wisdom's luck was just beginning to turn in the late Fifties, but this is still one of his better comedies, even if (or perhaps because) it's not tailored to his specific talents. Splendid support from Margaret Rutherford, Leslie Phillips, Edward Chapman and Joan Sims; the obligatory nice girl is Jill Dixon. The support cast is full of familiar faces from British films of the period: Sam Kydd scowls darkly, Michael Ward dithers, Bill Fraser splutters, and that's Marianne Stone serving behind the tea bar.

Just William ☉
1939, UK, 69 mins, b/w
Dir: Graham Cutts
Stars: Dicky Lupino, Jenny Laird, Fred Emney, Basil Radford
Rating: ★★

The first attempt to bring Richmal Crompton's infamous ragged rascal of a schoolboy to the screen. Likeable and good fun, the film makes the mistake that all 'William' films made, by trying to drag in too much of a 'thriller' plot to the exclusion of the plethora of little incidents that made the books so readable. Dicky Lupino, from the famous acting family, makes a spirited William, and his cohort Ginger is played by a wide-eyed Roddy McDowall, who would soon achieve far greater stardom in Hollywood.

Just William's Luck ☉
1947, UK, 92 mins, b/w
Dir: Val Guest
Stars: William Graham, Garry Marsh, Brian Roper, A E Matthews
Rating: ★★

First of two films made in the Forties featuring the scruffy schoolboy hero of Richmal Crompton's best-selling stories. Adapted from several *Just William* tales, it's a lively romp with a jolly knockabout climax in a house that William and his gang of 'outlaws' are trying to haunt.

Kaleidoscope ○
1966, UK, 104 mins, colour
Dir: Jack Smight
Stars: Warren Beatty, Susannah York, Clive Revill, Murray Melvin
Rating: ★★★

Jack Smight's feisty romantic thriller (with 'Swinging Sixties' trimmings) about a clever gambler. He's also found out as a clever cheat, hence his inability to refuse a police request to help trap a narcotics smuggler (icily played by Eric Porter). A fun film, with Warren Beatty and Susannah York sharing star billing and Clive Revill quite splendid as an unorthodox and faintly sinister Scotland Yard man. By far the funniest scene is that in which Revill and his assistant (Murray Melvin) play cards (for matchsticks) with a pack that they know to be marked. Revill asserts his authority by using a microscope to look at the backs of Melvin's cards – and still succeeds in losing.

Kalifornia ● ⓥ
1993, US, 118 mins, colour
Dir: Dominic Sena
Stars: Brad Pitt, Juliette Lewis, David Duchovny, Michelle Forbes
Rating: ★★

Any film with a leading character called Early Grayce has to be pretentious, allegorical, or both. This one also develops into an efficient bloodbath thriller in its last 40 minutes or so, but it's a long and languorous overture to this particular crescendo. David Duchovny plays stymied writer Brian, who has a fascination with serial killers, out of which he thinks he can create a bestseller by visiting the sites of their slaughter across America. His girlfriend (Michelle Forbes), who hopes to have her pornographic pictures accepted as art, goes along to do the illustrations. Unfortunately they take, as fuel-sharing travel companions, real multiple killer Earl (Brad Pitt, in yet another attempt to escape his pretty-boy looks) and his feeble-minded mistress (Juliette Lewis). Early is a genuine psychopath, although it takes Brian most of the journey to find out, leading to some interesting exchanges and shared experiences between the two men and the two girls before it all explodes. Pitt is genuinely menacing, but the strongest performance comes from Forbes in the least showy role.

Kangaroo ○
1952, US, 84 mins, colour
Dir: Lewis Milestone
Stars: Maureen O'Hara, Peter Lawford, Richard Boone, Chips Rafferty
Rating: ★★★

Photographed in blazing Technicolor by Charles G Clarke, this is an exciting, unusual and consistently dramatic action-adventure set in Australian pioneering days. The narrative rivets the interest, Finlay Currie and Maureen O'Hara contribute forthright performances as father and daughter ranchers, and Richard Boone's Gamble is an excellent study of cynical opportunism. Fresh, lively entertainment.

Kansas City Confidential
See: The Secret Four

Kansas Pacific ○
1952, US, 73 mins, colour
Dir: Ray Nazarro
Stars: Sterling Hayden, Eve Miller, Barton MacLane, Douglas Fowley
Rating: ★★

If trains fascinate you, then this vigorous Western has plenty to offer. The actors, headed by Sterling Hayden, aren't too well served by the dialogue, but the story's action shots pull it through. Director Ray Nazarro, an experienced hand at Westerns, ensures that this film has enough vitality and incident to keep the audience hooked throughout.

Karate Kid, The ◐ ⓥ
1984, US, 127 mins, colour
Dir: John G Avildsen
Stars: Ralph Macchio, Noriyuki 'Pat' Morita, Elisabeth Shue
Rating: ★★★★

After *Rocky*, it's Rocky Junior. Director John G Avildsen has taken the same basic elements that made his boxing film such a success and cunningly crafted them to a seven-stone-weakling-style yarn about Danny (Ralph Macchio), a 15-year-old whose meagre karate training is of no use against the local motorcycle gang, whose leader (the ex of the girl Danny fancies) doubles up as the school bully. As he and his friends are members of the 'no mercy' local karate school, Danny's education is proving a painful one until he meets

Mr Miyagi, the repair man at his flats, who proves, not unexpectedly, to be a karate expert and helps Danny train for the local championships. And guess who he meets in the final? Still, it all works very well, and will please younger audiences especially. Attractive Elisabeth Shue seems a trifle mature for our teenage hero, but the film is in any case stolen by veteran 'Pat' Morita as Miyagi, who makes the most of the film's good lines. Telling Danny to win back his girlfriend, he advises: 'To make honey, bee need young flower, not old prune.' Ah, Charlie Chan would have been proud of that.

Karate Kid Part II, The ○ ⓥ
1986, US, 113 mins, colour
Dir: John G Avildsen
Stars: Ralph Macchio, Noriyuki 'Pat' Morita, Tamlyn Tomita
Rating: ★★

The success of *The Karate Kid* meant there had to be a sequel — and here it is. As follow-ups go, this is a serviceable one, although it hardly eclipses the orginal. Danny (Ralph Macchio) again takes on the bad guys aided by his wise old tutor Miyagi ('Pat' Morita). The action then changes when the couple go to Miyagi's native Okinawa and Danny becomes involved in a duel. The balance between comforting familiarity and the new is struck fairly well and Morita obviously enjoys himself as he quotes pearls of eastern wisdom, like 'Best way to avoid punch — no be there!' There's a good storm sequence near the end, by which time you may be grateful for any touch of originality in such recycled twaddle. Still, even though it might largely be more of the same, box office takings showed that's just what *Karate Kid* fans wanted.

Karate Kid III, The ○ ⓥ
1989, US, 111 mins, colour
Dir: John G Avildsen
Stars: Ralph Macchio, Noriyuki 'Pat' Morita, Robyn Lively
Rating: ★

The relative failure of *Karate Kid Part II* should have taught its producers a thing or two. But no. This comic-book-style second sequel gives us another challenge, another girl-friend and another fight at the end that proves a complete anti-climax. The villains from the first *Karate Kid* (plus a bigger villain) swear vengeance on 'that old dojo and the punk kid' (that's still 'Pat' Morita and a now slightly

overweight Ralph Macchio). 'I'm gonna make them suffer for what they did to you,' swears villain number one. 'And suffer. And suffer. You know what the kid's gonna learn from me? Fear in his mind. And pain in his body.' All of which pain and suffering can be undergone by viewers subjecting themselves to this flabby and often laughable straggler in the series. A veritable seven-stone weakling of a film.

Katina
See: Iceland

Keep 'Em Flying ⊙
1941, US, 86 mins, b/w
Dir: Arthur Lubin
Stars: Bud Abbott, Lou Costello, Martha Raye, Dick Foran
Rating: ★★

Bud Abbott and Lou Costello, having given the Army (*Buck Privates*) and the Navy (*In the Navy*) a slapstick going-over, turned their attentions to the Air Force in this typical Forties farce. Martha Raye steals the film as twins, as well as singing a popular wartime hit called 'Pig Foot Pete'. The film cleaned up at the box-office and Bud and Lou found themselves the top box-office attractions in America by the end of the year.

Keeper of the Flame ○
1942, US, 100 mins, b/w
Dir: George Cukor
Stars: Spencer Tracy, Katharine Hepburn, Richard Wharf
Rating: ★★

The second Katharine Hepburn-Spencer Tracy film, and a very serious affair compared with the gaiety of their first, *Woman of the Year*. This is a straight dramatic story about famous people with feet of clay and has been justly neglected in favour of the comedies the famous pair made together. Glum.

Keep Fit ⊙
1937, UK, 82 mins, b/w
Dir: Anthony Kimmins
Stars: George Formby, Kay Walsh
Rating: ★★★

Comedian George Formby, still at his most popular when this comedy was made, plays a naive young barber who gets involved in a high-standard gymnastics competition to try and win the love of a glamorous manicurist. Guy Middleton, as Hector, George's rival in love, is a comic bounder in the finest Terry-Thomas tradition. It's a bouncy, confidently made comedy that's fun throughout and pretty hilarious in its boxing-ring conclusion.

Kelly and Me ⊙
1957, US, 86 mins, colour
Dir: Robert Z Leonard
Stars: Van Johnson, Piper Laurie, Martha Hyer, Onslow Stevens
Rating: ★★

Bright little musical about an untalented showman and the white alsatian who transforms his career. Mild, but colourful and enjoyable within its self-set limits. The dog, of course, outshines everyone, though that's not too difficult with most of this cast.

Kelly's Heroes ◐ ⓥ
1970, US, 143 mins, colour
Dir: Brian G Hutton
Stars: Clint Eastwood, Telly Savalas, Don Rickles, Carroll O'Connor, Donald Sutherland
Rating: ★★★

Troy Kennedy Martin's script neatly integrates the humour and the action as five American soldiers decide that there's more to World War Two than killing and being killed: instead they opt to steal 14,000 bars of gold from a bank in Occupied France. There's plenty of action, filmed with the co-operation of the Yugoslav Army, culminating in a head-on battle between six tanks in a small village. The action is in the capable hands of second unit director Andrew Marton, the man responsible for the chariot race in *Ben-Hur* while Brian G Hutton gets the best out of Clint Eastwood and friends. To quote a character played by Telly Savalas: 'That ain't an army, it's a circus!' A scene that apes Eastwood's own spaghetti Western showdowns is both unexpected and hilariously funny.

Key Largo ○ ⓥ
1948, US, 101 mins, b/w
Dir: John Huston
Stars: Humphrey Bogart, Edward G Robinson, Lauren Bacall
Rating: ★★★★

Under John Huston's skilful direction, Richard Brooks' adaptation of Maxwell Anderson's stage success proves cinematic enough not to look like a play and bristles with tension. The chemistry between Humphrey Bogart and Lauren Bacall is as cogent as ever as hotel occupants virtually

held hostage by gangsters, but it's the bad guys, notably snarling Edward G Robinson, back to his hateful best, and Claire Trevor, boozing and brazening her way to an Oscar as his mistress, who really catch the eye. Robinson happily accepted second billing to Bogart – his adversary in several past Warners crime classics – to do the part of the gang boss at bay. 'Why not second billing?' he told his agent. 'At 53 most actors are lucky to get billing at all.' The result is short-fused dynamite, right up to the moments when the film bursts into action in its fogbound climax.

Keys of the Kingdom, The ○
1944, US, 137 mins, b/w
Dir: John M Stahl
Stars: Gregory Peck, Thomas Mitchell, Vincent Price, Edmund Gwenn, Cedric Hardwicke, Rosa Stradner
Rating: ★★★

Long, elaborate, fairly faithful adaptation of A J Cronin's novel of a priest's adventures in China, which proved to be Gregory Peck's first major screen hit. The acting from a fine cast is solid and the story, which has some touching moments (and some exciting ones too), just about grips attention throughout.

Key to the City ○
1950, US, 101 mins, b/w
Dir: George Sidney
Stars: Clark Gable, Loretta Young, Frank Morgan, Marilyn Maxwell
Rating: ★★

A rather strained romantic comedy in which the two stars, Clark Gable and Loretta Young, are supported by a fine cast including Frank Morgan, Marilyn Maxwell, Raymond Burr and Lewis Stone, plus veteran James Gleason, who lends amusement to the edges of the film as a cop.

Khartoum ○
1966, UK, 134 mins, colour
Dir: Basil Dearden
Stars: Charlton Heston, Laurence Olivier, Richard Johnson, Ralph Richardson, Alexander Knox
Rating: ★★★

Massive epic about General Gordon, with Charlton Heston lending tremendous presence to the role of the stubborn Gordon, and Laurence Olivier in frighteningly ferocious form as the 'mad' Mahdi. The electrically-charged confrontation between the two is so well directed by Basil

Dearden that one can forgive that it never actually happened. Sharp Technicolor photography and battle scenes round off one of the best pictures of its kind that the Sixties produced.

Kickboxer ● ⓥ
1989, US, 105 mins, colour
Dir: Mark Disalle
Stars: Jean-Claude Van Damme, Dennis Alexio, Rochelle Ashana
Rating: ★

This is *The Karate Kid* for sadistic adults. Very predictable too. Take a big, ugly villain, get him to beat up the meek hero's brother/friend, then set our hero on a trail of revenge. If your idea of entertainment is a barbaric fight where the protagonists tie cords round their fists and dip them in glue and broken glass, this is probably the film for you. Van Damme, world champ at kickboxing (though not acting), is the milksop who trains under an inscrutable oriental and soon proclaims, 'I'm in the best shape of my life', which we can see he always was. The bad guys do their best: they rape Jean-Claude's girl, poison his dog, trap his trainer and kidnap his brother, the fighter that the villain crippled originally. What can poor Jean-Claude do? Don't strain yourself over the answer. It's all completely unconvincing, with previously invincible champions suddenly turning to jelly with one kick to the jaw.

Kid, The ⊙
1921, US, 52 mins, b/w
Dir: Charles Chaplin
Stars: Charlie Chaplin, Jackie Coogan
Rating: ★★★★

A Charlie Chaplin classic: a smash-hit dramatic comedy that mixes sentiment and slapstick with unerring accuracy in building up the touching relationship between Chaplin's fly-by-night and tiny Jackie Coogan's flop-haired kid, in a scene-stealing performance that set him up as a top child star for the ensuing decade. Especially well timed are the scenes in which Chaplin and Coogan 'operate' their window-fixing business, which involves the boy throwing a brick through a window which Chaplin subsequently offers to repair. A real winner, the film is genuinely charming throughout, with characters that tug at the heartstrings and tickle the funnybone in the next moment.

K

Kid ● ⓥ
1990, US, 92 mins, colour
Dir: John Mark Robinson
Stars: C Thomas Howell, Sarah Trigger, Brian Austin Green, R Lee Ermey
Rating: ★

Presumably a kind of junior league spaghetti Western was the idea here. At least, somebody has obviously seen a few Clint Eastwood films, as even the flashbacks explaining the mysterious stranger's mission are thrown in. For the teen-fan trade it's C Thomas Howell in the long coat and short cigarette amid a ludicrous plot about redneck villains who'd gun down defenceless innocent people if they didn't want them around. The action needs to be special to make it all work, but it's no more than routine and John Mark Robinson's direction could, even at 92 minutes, do with a deal of tightening up. Howell's about the best actor around and he's lucky he doesn't have too much to say, especially with dialogue penned by the same guy who not only wrote the songs, but provides only basic comic-strip characters to people his plot.

Kid Blue ◑
(aka: Dime Box)
1973, US, 100 mins, colour
Dir: James Frawley
Stars: Dennis Hopper, Warren Oates, Janice Rule, Ben Johnson, Peter Boyle, Lee Purcell
Rating: ★★

A romantic Western in which Dennis Hopper gives one of his warmest performances as the outlaw who, tired of failure at robbing trains, tries life in a tiny Texas town. Here he fails too – to keep jobs, to avoid seduction by his best friend's wife, to steer clear of the sheriff (Mean John), to keep his past from becoming public and, finally, to resist the temptation to rob the firm where he stokes the boiler. But he meets some rich characters on the way, and eventually makes his exit in a flying machine invented by a dotty 'preacher'. An old-fashioned film, swinging the cinematic pendulum back to the Fifties, and putting entertainment commendably before total authenticity.

Kid for Two Farthings, A ⊙
1955, UK, 96 mins, colour
Dir: Carol Reed
Stars: Celia Johnson, Diana Dors, David Kossoff, Brenda de Banzie, Jonathan

Ashmore
Rating: ★★★

Director Carol Reed's thoroughly enjoyable fairy-tale, set in London's East End, brought all sorts of unexpected pleasures. Blond bombshells Diana Dors and Vera Day both showed their acting ability in softer roles; the market of Petticoat Lane, and its environs, sprang vividly to life; and the Eastman Color photography of Ted Scaife was a delight. The best performance of all comes from David Kossoff as a kind of universal uncle.

Kid from Brooklyn, The ⊙
1946, US, 120 mins, colour
Dir: Norman Z McLeod
Stars: Danny Kaye, Virginia Mayo, Vera-Ellen, Steve Cochran, Eve Arden
Rating: ★★

One of Danny Kaye's Goldwyn films, casting him as a mild-mannered milkman credited with knocking out an unpleasant boxer. It's a remake of the 1936 Harold Lloyd comedy *The Milky Way*. Not too funny even in its day, it dates badly.

Kid from Spain, The ○
1932, US, 90 mins, b/w
Dir: Leo McCarey
Stars: Eddie Cantor, Lyda Roberti, Robert Young, Ruth Hall
Rating: ★★★

A big-budget musical extravaganza that has just about everything – romance, action, comedy, songs, Busby Berkeley dance routines and a galaxy of gorgeous Goldwyn Girls: not to mention the non-stop Eddie Cantor, singing another of his standards, 'What a Perfect Combination'. He plays a hapless college student who has to assume the identity of a bullfighter to escape the cops. The cops? Don't ask. Spot Betty Grable leading the girls in a chorus or two of 'The College Song'.

Kid from Texas, The ○
(aka: Texas Kid – Outlaw)
1950, US, 78 mins, colour
Dir: Kurt Neumann
Stars: Audie Murphy, Gale Storm, Will Geer, Albert Dekker
Rating: ★★

Audie Murphy's third film, and first Western, giving him more of a character than usual to work on, based as it is on the early life of Billy the Kid. He gets good support from a host of good character actors, including Will Geer, Albert Dekker, Paul Ford, William Talman, and – inevitably as a

sheriff – the moustachioed Ray Teal. British distributors changed the title to *Texas Kid – Outlaw*.

Kid Galahad ○ ⓥ
1962, US, 95 mins, colour
Dir: Phil Karlson
Stars: Elvis Presley, Gig Young, Lola Albright, Charles Bronson
Rating: ★★

A remake of the 1937 Humphrey Bogart film of the same title, which exposed the seamy side of the fight game in America. This time Elvis Presley plays the fighter who only becomes dangerous when he's soaked up enough punishment to make his eyes look like two fried eggs. And, of course, in his spare time he sings.

Kid Galahad ○ ⓥ
1937, US, 101 mins, b/w
Dir: Michael Curtiz
Stars: Edward G Robinson, Bette Davis, Humphrey Bogart
Rating: ★★★

Warner Brothers tough guys Edward G Robinson and Humphrey Bogart square off against each other as rival boxing promoters in this enjoyable fight film. Wayne Morris plays the title role – a bellhop with a sharp right hook whom Edward G thinks he can turn into a champ after Morris comes to the rescue of his girlfriend (Bette Davis). It's fast-moving and well-plotted, making you eager to watch the climactic fight between Morris and nasty William Haade, even though you know this is Hollywood in its heyday and there can only be one outcome. Edward G snarls around his cigar, Bogie sneers menacingly and Morris is charming as the naive boxer. Only Davis seems uncomfortable and out of place. It was another of those 'gangster's moll' roles Warner Brothers insisted on giving her despite her patent unsuitability for such parts.

Kid Millions ○
1934, US, 90 mins, b/w
Dir: Roy Del Ruth
Stars: Eddie Cantor, Ann Sothern, Ethel Merman, George Murphy
Rating: ★★★

Eddie Cantor goes east and nearly loses his head, committing the unpardonable sin of tramofatch which, roughly translated, means kissing a sheik's daughter while riding a camel. It's that kind of film, splashily produced by Sam Goldwyn with 11 production numbers. Lucille Ball is easily spottable among The Goldwyn Girls and the pop-eyed star (then the highest-paid entertainer in America) is given a good run for her money in the energy stakes by the young Ethel Merman, from the time she belts out the film's opening number 'An Earful of Music', which should perhaps have become her signature tune. The adrenalin really flows in 'I Want To Be a Minstrel Man' (with Cantor, Merman, George Murphy, Ann Sothern and The Nicholas Brothers maintaining a tremendous pace), but even this is topped by the spectacular finale (the only sequence in Technicolor), set in a monumental ice-cream factory.

Kidnapped ○
1938, US, 90 mins, b/w
Dir: Alfred Werker
Stars: Warner Baxter, Freddie Bartholomew, Arlene Whelan, John Carradine
Rating: ★★

Described by the *New York Times* as 'about as Scottish as a hot dog stand', this is Darryl F Zanuck's version of Robert Louis Stevenson's, which throws in a love interest called Jean MacDonald and jettisons Stevenson himself around the halfway mark. Freddie Bartholomew seems a little frail for the adventurous David Balfour but, if Warner Baxter is hardly ideal casting as Alan Breck, neither were Peter Finch and Michael Caine who followed him. Still, if you can stand a little literary vandalism in the course of action and intrigue, this story certainly hits the mark. The supporting cast looks as though it had strayed in from one of Basil Rathbone's Sherlock Holmes films.

Kidnapped ⊙
1960, UK, 100 mins, colour
Dir: Robert Stevenson
Stars: Peter Finch, James MacArthur, Bernard Lee, Peter O'Toole, John Laurie
Rating: ★★★

This Disney adaptation of Robert Louis Stevenson's tale (appropriately made by the studio's best director, who happened to be called Robert Stevenson!) is a little slow in the telling, mainly because of the stolid performance of James MacArthur in the leading role of David Balfour. But Peter Finch, though uneasily cast (as were Michael Caine and Warner Baxter in other versions) as Alan Breck, lends the part sufficient swash-

buckling gusto to make it work. Director Stevenson gives the story a vivid atmosphere, and John Laurie, normally seen in comedy roles, turns in a fine study of evil to give the adventure a lift just when it needs it most. Technicolor photography is excellent.

Kidnapped ○
1971, UK, 107 mins, colour
Dir: Delbert Mann
Stars: Michael Caine, Trevor Howard, Jack Hawkins, Donald Pleasence, Gordon Jackson
Rating: ★★

Film-makers do seem to choose the most unlikely actors to play Robert Louis Stevenson's adventurer Alan Breck. First American Warner Baxter, then Australian-raised Peter Finch, now Cockney Michael Caine. Still, Caine plays the role with dash and swagger, and the Scottish highlands are a treat in Technicolor.

Kidnappers, The ⊙
(aka: The Little Kidnappers)
1953, UK, 95 mins, b/w
Dir: Philip Leacock
Stars: Jon Whiteley, Vincent Winter, Duncan Macrae
Rating: ★★★

Child actors Jon Whiteley and Vincent Winter won special Oscars for their roles in this wonderful Ealing Studios family film, set in Nova Scotia, as two orphaned boys ruled over with a rod of iron by their stern, bigoted grandfather (Duncan Macrae). The boys steer just the right side of cuteness and deliver delightfully natural performances.

Killer of Killers
See: The Mechanic

Killer on a Horse
See: Welcome to Hard Times

Killers, The ○
1946, US, 105 mins, b/w
Dir: Robert Siodmak
Stars: Burt Lancaster, Ava Gardner, Edmond O'Brien, Albert Dekker, Sam Levene, William Conrad
Rating: ★★★★

First film version of Ernest Hemingway's thriller (remade 18 years later starring Lee Marvin), with its marvellously intricate plot, thundering drama throughout and a mighty punch in the final scene. A host of well-known players contribute to the

film's success and there's an excellent performance from Edmond O'Brien in the pivotal role. Other noteworthy portrayals come from menacing Jack Lambert and from Burt Lancaster, shooting to stardom in his first film. Two then newish actors, William Conrad (later to find television fame as Cannon) and Charles McGraw, register solidly as the killers of the title. The plot reveals surprise after surprise, while director Robert Siodmak, a German exile then at the peak of his Hollywood career, ensures that the nervous tension never lets up from the first moment that the killers move on to the scene.

Killers, The ◐
1964, US, 95 mins, colour
Dir: Don Siegel
Stars: Lee Marvin, John Cassavetes, Angie Dickinson, Ronald Reagan, Clu Gulager
Rating: ★★★

Based (very vaguely – but then so was the 1946 version) on a story by Ernest Hemingway, this is one of those 'how it really happened' stories, told in flashback. The clinically thrilling story revolves round two gunmen who are so puzzled as to why their victim calmly waits for his death that they decide to dig up his past. Lee Marvin gives a towering performance as the older hitman. Playing with great economy, he etches out a sharp character who is bad, but clearly understandable. Clu Gulager makes the younger gunman so repulsively likeable that you almost hope he won't get bumped off. All the more gripping for its sheer cold-bloodedness, The Killers is a fine film, directed in super-efficient style by Don Siegel. Oh yes, and Ronald Reagan is in there too, as a racketeer, in his final film role to date.

Killing, The ○
1956, US, 83 mins, b/w
Dir: Stanley Kubrick
Stars: Sterling Hayden, Coleen Gray, Vince Edwards
Rating: ★★★

Stanley Kubrick's breakthrough film. It's a hard-edged thriller along 'perfect robbery' lines, with a cluster of deeply-etched performances from a tight-knit group of Hollywood's best character stars. Elisha Cook Jr is first among equals here with his portrait of a downtrodden racetrack employee who can barely control his terror of being caught; and Marie Windsor

K

almost matches him as the avaricious wife whose duplicity ruins everything. A fascinating piece of filmmaking done in jigsaw style.

Killing Dad ○ ⓥ
1989, UK, 93 mins, colour
Dir: Michael Austin
Stars: Denholm Elliott, Julie Walters, Richard E Grant, Anna Massey
Rating: ★★

A strange black comedy – the sort that looks at life through a fish-eye lens. All of the characters are off kilter and one or two downright sinister. Definitely off his rocker – judging by the way he keeps thumping the side of his head and twitching – is Alistair (Richard E Grant), a failed hair-tonic salesman who reluctantly journeys to Southend to bring back the father he hasn't seen for 27 years. En route he resolves to kill him instead. Dad provides a prime part for the superbly rumpled Denholm Elliott, first encountered being sick into a plastic carrier (he hands it to Alistair), whose sole possessions seem to be a canary and a ventriloquist's dummy. Most of the laughs, though, come from Julie Walters as the glitzy but ageing seaside belle Dad currently has in tow. It's a bizarre brew and its pacing could do with a bit more frenzy. But relax a bit and you'll enjoy at least some of it.

Killing Fields, The ● ⓥ
1984, UK, 135 mins, colour
Dir: Roland Joffe
Stars: Sam Waterston, Dr Haing S Ngor, John Malkovich, Julian Sands, Craig T Nelson, Bill Patterson
Rating: ★★★

This Oscar-winning movie is ultimately a very moving experience – although it's a long time getting there. Almost two years in the making, this first major film about the Cambodian war is based on the true story of a friendship between an American war correspondent (Sam Waterston) and his Cambodian confederate. They are eventually separated at the time of the Khmer Rouge invasion of 1975, despite the guilt-ridden American's efforts to smuggle his friend out. A sad and angry plea for peace, and a successful attempt to engender revulsion at such wars, the film is also an account of the survival of the human spirit against all the odds. The atrocities of war are, however, piled on rather too much, and the pace in places rather too leisurely to rivet our attention to the central story, despite

the impassioned performances of Waterston and Haing S Ngor (who won an Oscar) in the leading roles. In the end, though, you can't help but be moved to tears at such a story, despite the shortcomings in its telling. That's only as it should be.

Killing of a Chinese Bookie, The ◐ ⓥ
1976, US, 113 mins, colour
Dir: John Cassavetes
Stars: Ben Gazzara, Timothy Agoglia Carey
Rating: ★★

You would expect a *film noir* by John Cassavetes to be a highly idiosyncratic addition to the genre, and here, at least, he does not disappoint. The moody, threatening atmosphere and the twists and turns of the convoluted plot have the unique Cassavetes stamp: an intense interest in the nuances of character and ambiguous relationships, a vivid use of light and colour, oddball humour, and powerful performances based partly on improvisation. Ben Gazzara dominates the film with his fine portrayal of the Los Angeles nightclub owner Cosmo Vitelli whose unsuccessful gambling spree leaves him with the obligation to despatch a troublesome Chinese bookie as payment in kind. There is a nice selection of gangsters and molls, with Timothy Agoglia Carey in danger of going over the top as the hit-man set on Gazzara's trail. Cassavetes fans will indulge the film's longueurs; others may not be so tolerant.

Killing of Sister George, The ● ⓥ
1968, UK, 138 mins, colour
Dir: Robert Aldrich
Stars: Beryl Reid, Susannah York, Coral Browne, Ronald Fraser
Rating: ★★★

Corrosive and powerful story about an ageing TV star (Beryl Reid brilliantly re-creating her stage role) whose affair with a younger woman is threatened by her own neurosis, the possible loss of her part in a long-running series, and finally by the intervention of a third party. If Lukas Heller's screenplay (he also wrote *What Ever Happened to Baby Jane?* for the same director, Robert Aldrich) extracts some of the humanity from Frank Marcus's original play, it lacks nothing in impact; and the performances en-

sure that the drama remains both engrossing, entertaining and highly amusing.

Kill Me Again ● ⓥ
1989, US, 99 mins, colour
Dir: John Dahl
Stars: Val Kilmer, Joanne Whalley-Kilmer, Michael Madsen, Jonathan Gries
Rating: ★★★

Despite some iffy performances, the direction and story make this a pretty good imitation of an RKO Radio *film noir* from 40 years earlier. Private eye Jack Andrews (Val Kilmer, miscast but reasonably effective) in debt to gamblers who have just broken his finger, is confronted with $10,000 by white-suited, sloe-eyed Fay (Joanne Whalley-Kilmer) if he will arrange for her fake death to put a murderous boyfriend off her trail. Well, 'tecs have to agree to this kind of thing, or we wouldn't have any stories, but one of the things Jack doesn't know is that Fay has almost a million dollars in Mafia money stolen from her boyfriend, who killed a mobster to get it. Big trouble for Jack, as you can see, from the police, from the Mob, from the boyfriend and not least from the distinctly unreliable Fay. Whalley-Kilmer looks good in the Jane Greer tradition but occasionally overdoes her femme Fay-tale. But Madsen is a knockout as the ruthless boyfriend, and director John Dahl moves the story doomily along without too much wasted footage, and has some nice touches with the inevitable cross and double-cross at the end.

Kill-Off, The ●
1989, US, 95 mins, colour
Dir: Maggie Greenwald
Stars: Loretta Gross, Andrew Lee Barrett, Jackson Sims
Rating: ★★★

This daring, grotesque murder thriller was the third in a trio of films based on cult Jim Thompson novels (the others were *The Grifters* and *After Dark*) to be released in 1990. Shot on a shoestring $1 million budget in only four weeks, and using New York stage actors with no film experience, it has a spartan, bleak look and feel which actually enhances its claustrophobic *film noir*-ish script. Director Maggie Greenwald, a former assistant sound effects editor for Walter Hill, among others, and film editor, proves to be happily at home in Thompson's regular milieu of bleak, corrupted low-life. All the characters are emotionally dead with little hope for the future, and yet their story is compulsive viewing. Loretta Gross, as the acid-tongued town gossip-monger, whose murder leaves many suspects, gives a strong central performance.

Kill or Cure ○
1962, UK, 86 mins, b/w
Dir: George Pollock
Stars: Terry-Thomas, Eric Sykes, Dennis Price, Lionel Jeffries, David Lodge
Rating: ★★★

A plethora of British funny-men in a rib-tickling comedy-thriller set in a bizarre health resort. Produced in 1962 by the team that made the Miss Marple comedy-thrillers, this film also comes up with such familiar television faces as Ronnie Barker, Derren Nesbitt and Peter Butterworth.

Kim ☉
1950, US, 112 mins, colour
Dir: Victor Saville
Stars: Errol Flynn, Dean Stockwell, Paul Lukas, Robert Douglas
Rating: ★★★

A robust screen adaptation of Rudyard Kipling's famous Indian tale. It takes a few liberties with the original, but provides some intense excitement, 'Boy's Own'-style, in the process. Stars Errol Flynn (the unlikeliest of Afghan horse dealers) and Paul Lukas actually got to film some of their scenes in India, but young Dean Stockwell, in the title role, never left California! The action, when it comes, is rousing enough, but there are too many stodgy patches for comfort.

Kindergarten Cop ◐ ⓥ
1990, US, 111 mins, colour
Dir: Ivan Reitman
Stars: Arnold Schwarznegger, Penelope Ann Miller, Pamela Reed, Linda Hunt, Carroll Baker
Rating: ★★★

Big Arnold ignores the advice about never acting with children or animals to form the centre piece of this artful concoction of a fistful of the elements most likely to make a box-office hit. How can you max-imise Arnie's muscular, awkward appeal? Drop him, like a fish out of water, into a crowd of screaming, uncontrollable, pre-school kids. Aces. They probably thought of the title, then Arnie, then the story. Naturally, there's some action to go with this, as a killer hunts his small son who is

somewhere at the school where Arnie has to go undercover as a teacher, after his partner (excellent Pamela Reed) falls ill. And romance appears in the shape of Penelope Ann Miller as an-other teacher whose son is in Arnie's class. Did we mention animals? Ah yes, Schwarzenegger has a pet ferret which helps him win over the kids after a nightmare first day in which he wishes he hadn't left his gun at home. It can't fail, can it? And it doesn't, even though the writer and director often use sentiment where charm and humour would have been better. Carroll Baker is chilling as the villain's domineering mother, a second fine performance in a film that doesn't call for great acting, and otherwise doesn't get it.

Kind Hearts and Coronets ○ ⓥ
1949, UK, 106 mins, b/w
Dir: Robert Hamer
Stars: Alec Guinness, Dennis Price, Valerie Hobson, Joan Greenwood, Arthur Lowe
Rating: ★★★★

A fiendishly funny satirical comedy from Ealing Studios. It treats murder as a joke, and gets away with it with elegant ease. Every time a character is killed off, you'll rock with laughter. Affectionately regarded as the best of many good things to come from Ealing in the post-war years, the film is also a 'tour-de-farce' for Alec Guinness and made his name as a comedy star. He plays all eight heirs standing between murderous Dennis Price and a dukedom – and does it with mind-boggling panache. Watch for Arthur Lowe in a small part at the end of the film as a reporter.

Kind of Loving, A ◐
1962, UK, 112 mins, b/w
Dir: John Schlesinger
Stars: Alan Bates, June Ritchie, Thora Hird, James Bolam, Leonard Rossiter
Rating: ★★★

A strong contender for box-office and critical acclaim in the bed-and-bosom environment of the British cinema of the early Sixties, this superbly acted downbeat romantic drama gave Alan Bates one of his biggest pushes towards stardom. His co-star, June Ritchie, alas, found her-self subsequently in too many inferior imitations, and it was some time be-fore she re-established herself as an actress of wide-ranging talent. Thora

Hird gives the outstanding perfor-mance of her career as Ritchie's mother.

Kindred, The ● ⓥ
1986, US, 92 mins, colour
Dir: Jeffrey Obrow, Stephen Carpenter
Stars: Rod Steiger, Kim Hunter, Amanda Pays, David Allen Brooks, Talia Balsam
Rating: ★★

This is a messy horror film with a monster that might be the derivation of the word slimebag. Quite what Professor Kim Hunter thought she was doing when she crossed a human skin graft with something like an oc-topus embryo one can't possibly imagine, but what she ended up with was something that has red eyes, hides in watermelons, lifts cars off the road and, not surprisingly, throttles people with its tentacles. Her son is under-standably concerned by what he finds at his mother's home after she has been killed off by even madder sci-entist Rod Steiger. 'She must have started calling it Anthony,' he mutters, 'after her favourite saint.' In Amanda Pays, the film discovers another great English non-acting looker, although with such lines as 'I had a theory that it might help bone disintegration in space' and 'Let's drink to memories that don't get made' Amanda probably deserves better than being turned into a relative of the Creature from the Black Lagoon. Still, the film is scary at the right moments and boasts a cellar that looks like something out of the Spanish Inquisition.

King and I, The ○ ⓥ
1956, US, 128 mins, colour
Dir: Walter Lang
Stars: Deborah Kerr, Yul Brynner, Rita Moreno, Martin Benson
Rating: ★★★

Following hard on the heels of *Carousel* and *Oklahoma!*, *The King and I* became the third Rodgers and Hammerstein musical within 12 months to break box-office records all over Britain and America. Yul Brynner (he won one of the film's five Academy Awards) and Deborah Kerr both recorded personal triumphs as the King of Siam and the governess whom he scorns at first but comes reluctantly to admire and respect. The score is Rodgers and Hammerstein at their most tuneful, including 'Getting to Know You' and 'Hello Young Lovers'.

K

King Arthur Was a Gentleman ⊙
1942, UK, 91 mins, b/w
Dir: Marcel Varnel
Stars: Arthur Askey, Evelyn Dall, Anne Shelton, Jack Train
Rating: ★★

A comedy with music that's a sort of very distant relative to *A Connecticut Yankee in King Arthur's Court*, with big-hearted Arthur Askey as a soldier in Africa (called Arthur King) who believes he has found King Arthur's magic sword. Some funny scenes and tuneful songs, but lots of missed opportunities as well.

King Creole ○ Ⓥ
1958, US, 116 mins, b/w
Dir: Michael Curtiz
Stars: Elvis Presley, Walter Matthau, Carolyn Jones
Rating: ★★★

Undoubtedly the best acting from Elvis Presley in a career in which most of his Hollywood efforts were purely mushy vehicles to sell record soundtracks (which they did in their millions). Much of the credit for this rests on the assured direction of Michael Curtiz (who will always be remembered for *Casablanca*) and who successfully put most of Hollywood's top male actors through their paces, including Humphrey Bogart, Errol Flynn (several times) and James Cagney. The plot is strong stuff for a musical, but there is a succession of now-familiar Elvis tracks for his fans. Film buffs should look out for a tiny cameo from silent screen actress Minta Durfee Arbuckle, the widow of the legendary Fatty Arbuckle. Both dynamic and dramatic by Elvis's later standards.

King David ◑ Ⓥ
1985, US, 114 mins, colour
Dir: Bruce Beresford
Stars: Richard Gere, Edward Woodward, Alice Krige, Cherie Lunghi
Rating: ★★

A good attempt to tell the Biblical story of David, with Richard Gere handsome and athletic in the title role. But director Bruce Beresford tries to cram too much of a colourful life into a film lasting less than two hours, which leads to some confusion if you haven't read the book! Edward Woodward comes out best of all as King Saul and the film also features Denis Quilley, Hurd Hatfield and Cherie Lunghi. She plays David's first wife in what could be termed a Second Division epic, unkindly known in Hollywood at the time as *An Israelite and a Gentleman*.

King in New York, A ○
1957, UK, 109 mins, b/w
Dir: Charles Chaplin
Stars: Charlie Chaplin, Dawn Addams
Rating: ★★

Charlie Chaplin's last starring film, a satire on America and its communist witchhunts. The film received only a limited release in its native Britain and wasn't seen at all in America until 1973. Yet it has many funny moments as the exiled European king, completely out of touch with the modern world, collides head-on with New York in the midst of the rock 'n' roll era. When the film goes serious towards the end, one longs for a return to these blissful interludes of slapstick, especially when the king chokes on an item he is advertising in front of the television cameras. Shani Wallis and Joy Nichols pop up as singers, and the invaluable Sidney James is one of Chaplin's supporting players.

King Kong ◑
1933, US, 100 mins, b/w
Dir: Ernest B Schoedsack, Merian C Cooper
Stars: Fay Wray, Robert Armstrong, Bruce Cabot
Rating: ★★★★

Very little one can add to the reams that have been written about this classic of the horror genre with its breathtaking trick work by Willis O'Brien. The story is about a giant gorilla brought to civilisation from a remote island: if you haven't seen it, don't miss the chance next time. Fay Wray is a genuinely touching heroine, and she and Kong himself combine to make this one of the few movies to induce real audience sympathy for its creature. The early part of the film, with the ship gliding through mists to Kong's island, is a splendidly atmospheric piece of cinema. It all still holds up well after more than 60 years.

King Kong ◑
1976, US, 136 mins, colour
Dir: John Guillermin
Stars: Jeff Bridges, Charles Grodin, Jessica Lange
Rating: ★★

Clodhopping remake of the imperishable original. Star Jessica Lange tried to shut it out of her mind: although it gave her a belated film debut at 27, she didn't film again for three years. The individual talents of Jeff Bridges and Charles Grodin are wasted, and the film's only major asset is the glittering Metrocolor photography by Richard H Kline, which won an Oscar nomination.

King Lear ○ Ⓥ
1987, France/US/Switzerland, 90 mins, colour
Dir: Jean-Luc Godard
Stars: Peter Sellars, Burgess Meredith, Molly Ringald, Woody Allen, Norman Nailer, Jean-Luc Godard

We can't wait to read the four-page review in some highbrow magazine describing this Jean-Luc Godard film as a masterpiece. Fragments from Shakespeare's *Lear* are spoken – when there is anything at all going on up there on the screen – by characters wandering around a continental coastal resort. They make marginally more sense than the rest of the film, which we think portrays young director looking for ideas for filming *King Lear*. Burgess Meredith blasts cantankerously through as Godard's version of Lear; Molly Ringwald sleepwalks Cordelia; Woody Allen speaks earnestly at the end. The rest is a meaningless shambles of bits and pieces assembled in haphazard fashion, as if from the cutting-room floor. But then again this may be a masterpiece.

King of Alcatraz ○
(aka: The King of the Alcatraz)
1938, US, 56 mins, b/w
Dir: Robert Florey
Stars: Gail Patrick, Lloyd Nolan, Harry Carey, Robert Preston
Rating: ★★

Fast and furious, and ranging from comedy to dramatic action without a blink, this is one of the most star-studded minor films ever made. There's a crackling script by Irving Reis, later to become a top director (of such films as *The Bachelor and the Bobby Soxer*), masterful direction by Robert Florey (who made *The Beast with Five Fingers*) and dynamic performances from Lloyd Nolan, Robert Preston (making a great team as rival radio operators), Anthony Quinn, Gail Patrick, Richard Denning, Dennis Morgan, Tom Tyler and especially J Carrol Naish as the escaped convict of the title. Perennial screen drunk Jack Norton appears as the first officer on board the ship where the action is. It all feels a bit rushed, though, which isn't surprising.

King of Comedy, The ○
1982, US, 109 mins, colour
Dir: Martin Scorsese
Stars: Robert De Niro, Jerry Lewis
Rating: ★★

This much-feted comedy of sarcasm is about a desperate, distinctly unbalanced would-be stand-up comedian. Robert De Niro makes this character as obnoxious as he can, while Jerry Lewis is quite endearing more or less playing himself. Admirable in some ways, but totally dislikeable and even quite annoying at times.

King of Jazz ○
1930, US, 93 mins, colour
Dir: John Murray Anderson
Stars: Paul Whiteman, John Boles, Laura la Plante, Bing Crosby
Rating: ★★★

Featured in this hugely entertaining early musical are roly-poly Paul Whiteman and his Orchestra and the singing trio The Rhythm Boys, one of whom, Bing Crosby, went on to bigger and better things. Very innovative: a veritable box of delights.

King of Kings ○
1961, US/Spain, 161 mins, colour
Dir: Nicholas Ray
Stars: Jeffrey Hunter, Hurd Hatfield, Harry Guardino, Rip Torn, Viveca Lindfors, Robert Ryan
Rating: ★★

It always seemed likely that the biggest weakness of Nicholas Ray's simply told and beautifully photographed Biblical epic would be the casting of the central role of Jesus. And so it proved to be, despite a dedicated effort at the role from Jeffrey Hunter. His performance had none of the nobility, subtlety and power that Max Von Sydow was to give the role four years later in *The Greatest Story Ever Told*. Far more memorable are Hurd Hatfield's Pilate, Siobhan McKenna's Virgin Mary and, surprisingly, Rita Gam as Herodias. Fine actor Robert Ryan seems too American (as did Charlton Heston) as John the Baptist, but Rip Torn is a splendidly shifty and furtive Judas. For once an actor accustomed to giving larger-than-life performances is cast in exactly the right role.

King of New York ● ⊙
1990, US, 104 mins, colour
Dir: Abel Ferrara
Stars: Christopher Walken, David Caruso, Larry Fishburne, Wesley Snipes
Rating: ★★★

A gangster film, with all the modern violence, sex, drug trade and bad language you'd expect. This one, however, is made in the style of the Thirties: straight, with no sideline issues, as one man shoots his way to the top, gunning down all those who stand in the way of his becoming crime czar of the city. Christopher Walken's icy and unsettling charm is well-suited to this role, a criminal mastermind with dangerous double standards. He wants to be a do-gooder and build schools and hospitals: to do it he must gain control of all the city's illegal activity, excusing the wholesale slaughter that results on the grounds that the crime lords he kills are squeezing the poor or peddling in teenage prostitution. Cops are reduced to vigilante action in efforts to stop him. Whether he needs to go as far as he does is open to question: so is the ease with which he and a few confederates with tommy-guns take over the city. The story, however, is deliberately streamlined to eliminate all side issues, and stylised so that everybody in it is dressed in black. Quite impressive, but also vaguely pretentious. Something a little different though for fans of *Godfather*-style drama.

King of the Grizzlies ⊙
1969, US, 93 mins, colour
Dir: Ron Kelly
Stars: John Yesno, Chris Wiggins
Rating: ★★★

A rousing Disney animal adventure based on Ernest Thompson Seton's *The Biography of a Grizzly*, with the usual musical comments and laconic Winston Hibler narration. Several bears seem to be used in the title role, but it hardly matters as children will love it anyway. Magnificently shot on location in the Canadian Rockies.

King of the Khyber Rifles ○
1953, US, 100 mins, colour
Dir: Henry King
Stars: Tyron Power, Terry Moore, Guy Rolfe, Michael Rennie
Rating: ★★

One of Tyrone Power's later pictures, but still within his tradition of making adventure films which spanned the

world. As the title indicates, the setting of this one is India in the turbulent late 19th century. The supporting cast includes some British stalwarts and also Richard Stapley, who was later to win Broadway musical fame as Richard Wyler.

King Ralph ○ ⊙
1991, US, 97 mins, colour
Dir: David S Ward
Stars: John Goodman, Peter O'Toole, John Hurt, Camille Coduri
Rating: ★★

Big John Goodman is a second-rate Las Vegas lounge singer who is distantly related to our royal family. When a (hilarious) disaster at a photocall wipes out all those above him, Britain finds itself with a decidedly different new king. A nice comic idea that works well in patches. Unfortunately, those patches are a little too widely spaced for the film's own good. Goodman is engaging as the gauche Yank who creates his own Berk's Peerage, while Peter O'Toole does his 'actor laddie' bit as the new king's imperious private secretary and John Hurt enjoys himself as the sneaky Lord Graves: watch the scene where he visits the heroine's flat – the inside pages of his newspaper are blank! No, this may not be a terribly good film – but it's fun in spurts and jolly king Goodman makes the most of his starring role.

King Rat ◑
1965, UK, 134 mins, b/w
Dir: Bryan Forbes
Stars: George Segal, James Fox, Tom Courtenay, Denholm Elliott, John Mills
Rating: ★★★

PoW camp-film fans will find plenty to get their teeth into in writer-director Bryan Forbes' cleverly-framed story of a corporal who gets away with everything – even selling the officers in the camp rat-meat as venison. George Segal gives a razor-sharp portrayal of Cpl King, the biggest scrounger in the camp, who eats fried eggs for breakfast while the others starve.

King Richard and the Crusaders ○
1954, US, 114 mins, colour
Dir: David Butler
Stars: Laurence Harvey, Rex Harrison, Virginia Mayo, George Sanders
Rating: ★★★

K

For once, the publicity says it all: 'A stirring saga of days of yore when bold knights rallied to the Christian cause.' This really is one of the best just-for -fun adventure stories Hollywood ever made. The storyline is so full of fights and thrills that there hardly seems time for noble hero Laurence Harvey to draw breath before the next battle. Never mind the script, just get an eyeful of that action.

Kings of the Sun ○
1963, US, 105 mins, colour
Dir: J Lee Thompson
Stars: Yul Brynner, George Chakiris, Shirley Anne Field, Richard Basehart, Brad Dexter
Rating: ★

Despite realistic location filming in Mexico, this historical drama about the ancient Mayan kingdom is sunk by uneasy casting, a superficial story and banal dialogue. Not even po-faced Yul Brynner, as chief of the local Indian tribe, can get away with lines as silly as 'And some day we will watch our babies lead buffaloes around by their noses.'

King Solomon's Mines ○
1937, UK, 80 mins, b/w
Dir: Robert Stevenson
Stars: Cedric Hardwicke, Paul Robeson, Roland Young, Anna Lee, John Loder
Rating: ★★★

Splendidly workmanlike version of Rider Haggard's famous jungle adventure yarn, full of action and with no time wasted. Paul Robeson gives a notable performance as Umbopa, the exiled native chief who guides the party of diamond-hunters, making the character more than just a noble savage.

King Solomon's Mines ○
1950, US, 102 mins, colour
Dir: Andrew Marton, Compton Bennett
Stars: Stewart Granger, Deborah Kerr, Richard Carlson, Hugo Haas
Rating: ★★★

This blockbuster jungle action yarn, based (though rather remotely) on Rider Haggard's famous story of a search for a missing man and the quest for the fabulous mines, was filmed in various parts of Africa. Its most striking feature is certainly the authentic location work of terrain, tribesmen and, above all, its spectacular animal footage, shot by co-director Andrew Marton. It was the first film to be made by Stewart

Granger following his departure from British films to fulfil a contract with MGM, launching him to international stardom.

King Solomon's Mines ○ ⦿ Ⓥ
1985, US, 100 mins, colour
Dir: J Lee Thompson
Stars: Richard Chamberlain, Sharon Stone, Herbert Lom, Ken Gampu
Rating: ★★★

Director J Lee Thompson has taken the old, much-filmed adventure classic and turned it into *Raiders of the Lost Mines*. H Rider Haggard it isn't, but it is fast, furious and fun, right down to the music: every time hero Richard Chamberlain swings into action, the theme tune trumpets forth. And, in Sharon Stone, whose previous roles had been strictly decorative, it has a heroine with a zany sense of humour and a willingness to give it all she's got. From the moment Chamberlain's Quartermain leads his African adventurers into a market-place and says, 'Here we are in beautiful downtown Tongola', we know that this is strictly spoofland. The plot moves rapidly from the incredible to the impossible, with poor Bernard Archard whipped unmercifully for the secret of the mines by Herbert Lom and John Rhys Davies who have clearly slipped in from a Pink Panther film and an Indiana Jones adventure respectively. Ms Stone's shorts shrink progressively along with the plot. An underrated romp.

King's Pirate, The ○
1967, US, 100 mins, colour
Dir: Don Weis
Stars: Doug McClure, Guy Stockwell
Rating: ★★★

Universal Studios are obviously happy on home ground with this agreeable pantomime, set in Madagascar, in 1700, with Doug McClure baring his chest obligingly in the sort of role once reserved for Tony Curtis. Rewards on the way include a former Miss America, Mary Ann Mobley, as an Indian with a Scots accent (!), and a dazzling display of swordplay from Jill St John in the finest Maureen O'Hara traditions. A light-hearted remake of Errol Flynn's *Against All Flags*.

King's Rhapsody ○
1955, UK, 93 mins, colour
Dir: Herbert Wilcox
Stars: Errol Flynn, Anna Neagle
Rating: ★★

Errol Flynn, in one of the last roles of his career, plays a European prince who chooses to abdicate to be with his mistress (Anna Neagle) but later takes the throne and learns to love his wife (played by Patrice Wymore, Flynn's third wife at the time of filming). Directed by Neagle's husband, Herbert Wilcox, this British-made, rusty Ruritanian romance with music (based on Ivor Novello's operetta) is a fairly threadbare affair with signs of a tight budget. The same scenes and effects are repeated again and again, the same extras line the cathedral steps for successive marriages and coronations and pasteboard is evident everywhere in the sets. Neagle, however, rises above the stilted script and pedestrian production with a sturdy assurance and great grace.

King's Row ○
1941, US, 127 mins, b/w
Dir: Sam Wood
Stars: Ann Sheridan, Robert Cummings, Ronald Reagan, Betty Field, Charles Coburn, Claude Rains
Rating: ★★★

The *Peyton Place* of its day and the reverse side of *Our Town* as Warners (in a startling movie for its day) portrays (in some cases for those who can read between the lines) sadism, incest, homosexuality and murder behind the neat-fronted Victorian houses of a small American town. Ronald Reagan, as a playboy, has never been better on screen (although he was only sixth choice for the role) and Ann Sheridan, as his girlfriend, is superb. Even Robert Cummings, as a brilliant medical student, managed acting beyond his usual low-key range (Warners originally wanted Fox to loan them Tyrone Power for the role). The production design is also worthy of note, with everything shot in the studio by master cinematographer James Wong Howe, even down to an orchard. The film's release was delayed for a year by a studio worried about showing such an unpatriotic view of American life during wartime.

Kipps ○
(aka: The Remarkable Mr Kipps)
1941, UK, 112 mins, b/w
Dir: Carol Reed
Stars: Michael Redgrave, Phyllis Calvert, Diana Wynyard, Arthur Riscoe
Rating: ★★★

Very respectable, detail-filled version of H G Wells' novel, directed by

Carol Reed after a string of successes: *Bank Holiday*, *A Girl Must Live*, *The Stars Look Down* and *Night Train to Munich*. Many years later Kipps would be made into the musical, *Half a Sixpence*, with Tommy Steele inheriting the role played here diffidently but engagingly by Michael Redgrave. Diana Wynyard and Phyllis Calvert are fresh and delightful as the girls involved.

Kismet ○
1944, US, 100 mins, colour
Dir: William Dieterle
Stars: Ronald Colman, Marlene Dietrich, James Craig, Edward Arnold
Rating: ★★

Another 'king of the beggars' role for Ronald Colman to follow *If I Were King* in this songless version of the yarn that later became more famous as a musical. This one does have sumptuous Technicolor, plus – preceding Shirley Eaton in *Goldfinger* by 20 years – a gold-painted Marlene Dietrich in an exotic dance routine.

Kiss, The ●
1988, US, 101 mins, colour
Dir: Pen Densham
Stars: Joanna Pacula, Meredith Salenger, Mimi Kuzyk
Rating: ★★

Apart from a spectacular climax in a swimming pool, nail-bitingly involving the destruction of various monsters, this Canadian opus is your average revolting horror film of today. It features Joanna Pacula (rhymes with Dracula?) as the African-born child afflicted by an aunt with the curse of the undead, and who must now pass it on to her teenage niece, played by the nubile Salenger, whose figure the director loses no chance to get into a revealing swimsuit. Opposing Pacula is one-time *Hill Street Blues* cop Mimi Kuzyk as the nurse next door with a yen for Meredith's dad, whose late wife was Pacula's first victim. Priests get devoured by fire, and various of Salenger's friends are cut away by Pacula's familiar, a kind of critter-cat, before the showdown at long last looms. The three stars at least give the rubbish no less than 100 per cent, and special effects are suitably repulsive.

Kiss Before Dying, A ●
1956, US, 89 mins, colour
Dir: Gerd Oswald

Stars: Robert Wagner, Jeffrey Hunter, Virginia Leith, Joanne Woodward
Rating: ★★★

Rather chilling thriller, with Robert Wagner surprisingly good as a psychopathic killer and Joanne Woodward and Virginia Leith as two of the girls on his list. It's the plot that counts here, rather than the acting, although Wagner dominates the film and George Macready and Mary Astor offer stiff competition for the older generation. The suspense is satisfactory, the climax exciting and the colour excellent. An unusual and rewarding film, still possibly the best thing Wagner has turned out.

Kiss Before Dying, A ● Ⓥ
1991, US, 90 mins, colour
Dir: James Dearden
Stars: Matt Dillon, Sean Young, Max von Sydow, Diane Ladd
Rating: ★★

A classy (if ultimately inferior) remake of the old Robert Wagner-Joanne Woodward thriller from Ira Levin's novel. Well-made, if not always well-acted, it features Dillon in the Wagner role, as Corliss, the baby-faced psycho determined to inherit the millions of one of the wealthiest families in America. Hooked up with one of its daughters (Sean Young), he murders her when she becomes pregnant and disinheritance looms. Her twin sister is his next target and, assuming a new identity (again by murder), he becomes a social worker and is soon shacked up with Ellen (also Young). Links with the past are ruthlessly eradicated as Corliss begins his climb to the top. Dillon does quite well in this kiss-me-kill-me role, but the murders themselves, though merciless, lack urgency. Young has her moments – and her lesser ones. Howard Shore's music does yeoman service in underlining the doomy qualities of the narrative.

Kiss Me Deadly ○
1955, US, 105 mins, b/w
Dir: Robert Aldrich
Stars: Ralph Meeker, Gaby Rodgers, Albert Dekker, Paul Stewart, Maxene Cooper, Jack Elam
Rating: ★★

Mickey Spillane and Mike Hammer, the bull-at-a-gate detective he created, could have found no more apt screen interpreter than director Robert Aldrich, as pace, punch and violence,

which saturate the Hammer novels, are present in almost all of Aldrich's film work, from *The Big Knife* to *The Choirboys*. Aggressive Ralph Meeker is perfectly cast as Hammer, adrift in the bleak streets and decaying buildings of the post-war New York and Los Angeles. Cloris Leachman makes her screen debut as a mystery girl.

Kiss Me Goodbye ●
1982, US, 101 mins, colour
Dir: Robert Mulligan
Stars: Sally Field, James Caan, Jeff Bridges, Paul Dooley, Claire Trevor, Mildred Nantwick
Rating: ★

The Hollywood of the Eighties developed an absolute mania for remaking sexy comedies from countries abroad that made it big at the English-speaking box-offices of the world. This is a rehash of the Brazilian smash *Dona Flor and Her Two Husbands*, but once again the recipe for success didn't travel too well, in spite of an attractive cast that includes Sally Field, James Caan, Jeff Bridges, Paul Dooley, Claire Trevor and Mildred Natwick. Director Robert Mulligan couldn't go altogether wrong with that collection, and there are indeed some nice moments, although the relaxed sexuality of the original isn't recaptured.

Kiss Me Kate ☉ Ⓥ
1953, US, 111 mins, colour
Dir: George Sidney
Stars: Howard Keel, Kathryn Grayson, Ann Miller, Keenan Wynn
Rating: ★★★★

Brilliant, fast-moving musical based on Shakespeare's *The Taming of the Shrew*. Howard Keel has never been more virile and Kathryn Grayson never gutsier (she's a real surprise here) as the feuding singers, while Ann Miller dances up a storm in the 'Tom, Dick or Harry' number, with the help of talented MGM hoofers Bob Fosse, Tommy Rall and Bobby Van. Add James Whitmore and Keenan Wynn as gangsters giving a priceless rendition of 'Brush Up Your Shakespeare' and you have almost the perfect show, marred only by things being thrown at the screen, a reminder that this was originally made in 3D.

Kiss of Death ○
1947, US, 98 mins, b/w
Dir: Henry Hathaway
Stars: Victor Mature, Brian Donlevy, Coleen Gray, Karl Malden, Richard

K

Widmark
Rating: ★★★

Victor Mature, revealing himself a more sensitive actor than many suspected, gave one of his best performances in this brisk thriller as a petty thief turned stoolpigeon. Even so, the acting honours went straight to Richard Widmark. Making his film debut as a psychopathic killer called Tommy Udo, and cackling hysterically as he tips one of his victims in a wheelchair down a flight of stairs, Widmark earned himself an Academy Award nomination in best supporting actor category – his only Oscar 'nod' to date. Director Henry Hathaway makes excellent use of a variety of well-chosen New York locations to add verisimilitude to the story. Good support comes from Karl Malden, Taylor Holmes, Millard Mitchell, Coleen Gray and Mildred Dunnock.

Kiss of Evil ●
(aka: Kiss of the Vampire)
1964, UK, 88 mins, colour
Dir: Don Sharp
Stars: Clifford Evans, Jennifer Daniel
Rating: ★★

It's business as usual for the men of Hammer here, in a story of a village of vampires. Director Don Sharp makes some of it pretty chilly (especially when Noel Willman first bites into Jennifer Daniel) with the help of some skilfully bleak colour camerawork.

Kiss of Fire ○
1955, US, 86 mins, colour
Dir: Joseph M Newman
Stars: Jack Palance, Barbara Rush
Rating: ★★

This unusual adventure story about a Spanish soldier-of-fortune escorting his country's princess through American Indian territory gave Jack Palance a rare romantic hero role, although he still endows the character of El Tigre with his customary ferocity. Nothing about this one, however, seems very relaxed or natural.

Kiss of the Spider Woman ● ⓥ
1985, US, 119 mins, colour
Dir: Hector Babenco
Stars: William Hurt, Raul Julia, Sonia Braga
Rating: ★★★

No webs are woven by female fiends here. Not that horror of a subtler kind is not implicit in the sometimes harrowing story of the relationship between two men in a prison cell. Molina (William Hurt in a totally effective, Oscar-winning performance) is a flagrant homosexual who has nothing in common with cell-mate Valentin (Raul Julia), a morose revolutionary imprisoned for political beliefs and awaiting only the next torture session. But Molina spins a gossamer web made up from the surface glitter of bad old films (especially one made by the Nazis) as he acts out their absurdly melodramatic plots for Valentin's benefit – and perhaps his own sanity. The drawing-together of the two men to the point where Molina bares all to become the heroine of one of his own films is only occasionally embarrassing, often touching and always absorbing. It's a pity that the film inserts themselves are just too daft to capture the spirit of the original. At the end, though, everything is satisfyingly resolved, showing that the protagonists have found a kind of peace, in the midst of angst, from their relationship. A pretty unusual film, it's uncompromising but never unsavoury.

Kiss of the Vampire
See: Kiss of Evil

Kiss the Blood Off My Hands ○
(aka: Blood on My Hands)
1948, UK, 80 mins, b/w
Dir: Norman Foster
Stars: Burt Lancaster, Joan Fontaine, Robert Newton
Rating: ★★

An early Burt Lancaster film, made two years after his sensational debut in *The Killers.* And that's what he plays in this turbulent thriller – a killer. It's a grim melodrama, with Lancaster as a man on the run. Good support comes from Joan Fontaine and Robert Newton. And there's wonderful black-and-white photography by Russell Metty, making the most of Lancaster's nocturnal flights from the law.

Kiss Tomorrow Goodbye ○
1950, US, 102 mins, b/w
Dir: Gordon Douglas
Stars: James Cagney, Barbara Payton, Luther Adler, Helena Carter, Ward Bond, Steve Brodie
Rating: ★★

One more time for James Cagney as the mobster on the run in this thriller, almost a reprise of this classic *White Heat* the previous year. Director Gordon Douglas stages one or two good chase sequences, and a strong supporting cast includes Ward Bond, Steve Brodie, Luther Adler, Helena Carter, William Frawley and Barton MacLane.

Kitchen Toto, The ●
1987, UK, 97 mins, colour
Dir: Harry Hook
Stars: Edwin Mahinda, Bob Peck, Phyllis Logan
Rating: ★★★

This grim reconstruction of events during the emergence of the Mau Mau terrorists in Kenya between 1950 and 1952 reminds us that, whatever else, we can rely on our latest generation of British filmmakers for accuracy, especially in the depiction of the mutual lack of understanding between white and black at the time, which merely made the bloodshed worse. There are few likeable people here, save for the title character, a young African seconded into white colonial service after his clergyman father is slaughtered for preaching anti-terrorist sermons. All too soon the youth himself is inducted into Mau Mau ranks and events fall swiftly towards darkness and tragedy. More penetrating, if less entertaining than such films of 30 years back as *Simba* and *Something of Value,* the film is decently acted by Edwin Mahinda, Bob Peck, Phyllis Logan, Robert Urquhart and Edward Judd and capably directed by its writer Harry Hook.

Kitty Foyle ○
1940, US, 100 mins, b/w
Dir: Sam Wood
Stars: Ginger Rogers, Dennis Morgan, James Craig
Rating: ★★★

No one could quite believe it when Ginger Rogers won the Best Actress Oscar, beating Bette Davis (for *The Letter*), Katharine Hepburn (*The Philadelphia Story*), Joan Fontaine (*Rebecca*) and Martha Scott (*Our Town*). This was Rogers' 40th film but her first starring dramatic role, playing a working girl who can't decide over rival suitors. Undeniably mushy in places, its success convinced Rogers that she didn't need to sing and dance to make movies. Co-star Katharine Stevens (who was billed as K T Stevens in future films) is the daughter of the film's director, Sam Wood.

Klute ● Ⓥ

1971, US, 114 mins, colour
Dir: Alan J Pakula
Stars: Jane Fonda, Donald Sutherland, Charles Cioffi, Roy Scheider
Rating: ★★★

Part thriller, part character study, this film focuses on Jane Fonda who is compelling as a New York call girl. She gives the role an emotional and dramatic depth not always apparent in the screenplay and deservedly took the Best Actress Academy Award for her performance. While Donald Sutherland is rather less lugubrious and mannered than usual (as the private detective involved in a somewhat obsessive romance with Fonda), he is overshadowed by his co-star. Alan J Pakula's often languorous direction tends to allow the narrative to slacken fatally at times, but there is no denying the overall impact of the movie or its more-adult-than-usual approach to its subject.

Knack . . . and How to Get It, The ◖

1965, UK, 84 mins, b/w
Dir: Richard Lester
Stars: Rita Tushingham, Ray Brooks, Michael Crawford, Donal Donnelly
Rating: ★★★

Hot on the heels of his first Beatles film, director Richard Lester made this way-out (or so it seemed at the time) modern farce. Quick-fire, sometimes Goonish, sometimes very satirical dialogue, lots of black-clothed players on white backgrounds, extensive use of rapid cross-cutting and the occasional burst into quick motion – these were the ingredients of Lester's art in 1965. The story is merely an excuse for a visual caper, involving Ray Brooks who has the Knack (of getting girls to the extent that he gives them Green Shield stamps) and Michael Crawford as a young teacher with two left feet, who most definitely has not got the Knack. Rita Tushingham has a delightful time sending up her own stock character of the wayside waif, as the girl who comes between them. Witty and inventive fun that gives sex its roughest, tongue-in-cheek handling on record.

Knickerbocker Holiday ○

1944, US, 85 mins, b/w
Dir: Harry Joe Brown
Stars: Nelson Eddy, Constance Towers, Charles Coburn, Shelley Winters
Rating: ★★

Pleasant musical, set in 17th century New Amsterdam (later New York), but uninspired in all but its Kurt Weill melodies, which include 'September Song' – sung in the stage version by Walter Huston but done here by Charles Coburn – and 'Indispensable Man'. Shelley Winters got her first big film chance as heroine Constance Dowling's sister.

Knight Moves ● Ⓥ

1992, US, 115 mins, colour
Dir: Carl Schenken
Stars: Christopher Lambert, Diane Lane, Tom Skerritt, Daniel Baldwin
Rating: ★

Busty beauties are falling victim to a serial killer and it seems chess may have something to do with it. On an island where thunder and lightning seemingly occur every night, the police (Tom Skerritt, Daniel Baldwin) close in on Grandmaster Christopher Lambert, whose protests that the killer is playing a chess-type game with him seem to be substantiated by the murderer's phone calls. 'You have to face the things you feel,' psychiatrist Diane Lane tells Lambert before leaping into bed with him. Yes, well, there's no answer to that. But at least the police could have faced up to putting a tail on Lambert, which would have saved them grilling him after every murder. Never mind: we, the audience, have been let in on the key to the plot in the first scene, so it's only poor Lambert (very bad in the emotional scenes) who has to suffer. Though, when he howls about 'going somewhere where the pain will finally stop', you wonder whether it's a hint to leave the film early. Director Carl Schenken has a few routine ideas about action and suspense, but with this ludicrous script, it's nowhere near enough: even the colour is rotten.

Knights of the Round Table ○

1953, UK, 115 mins, colour
Dir: Richard Thorpe
Stars: Robert Taylor, Ava Gardner, Mel Ferrer, Stanley Baker, Anne Crawford
Rating: ★★★

MGM's spectacular version of the King Arthur romance, involving such characters as Sir Lancelot, Queen Guinevere and Merlin, may take liberties with the legend but does compensate with plenty of rollicking action. The supporting cast includes Felix Aylmer (surprisingly but imaginatively cast as Merlin) and Stanley Baker, who makes a first-rate villainous character out of Sir Modred.

Knight Without Armour ○

1937, UK, 108 mins, b/w
Dir: Jacques Feyder
Stars: Marlene Dietrich, Robert Donat
Rating: ★★★

Marlene Dietrich looks absolutely ravishing in an Alexander Korda adaptation of James Hilton's novel about an idealistic young Englishman at large in Russia during its last Czarist years. The great French film-maker Jacques Feyder came to England to direct this atmospheric and splendidly-paced thriller.

K 9 ○ Ⓥ

1989, US, 102 mins, colour
Dir: Rod Daniel
Stars: James Belushi, Mel Harris, Kevin Tighe, Ed O'Neill
Rating: ★★★

Recent times have brought us a new spate of doggy pictures, and this one has James Belushi as the cop saddled with a canine partner while on the trail of a drugs lord (the ubiquitous Kevin Tighe). Quite fun and certainly suitable for 10-year-olds and upwards, as the dog refuses to obey, messes up the hero's love life, comes to the rescue, helps Belushi make a getaway, falls for a poodle and finally makes us all cry by getting shot. Director Daniel trails the action in exciting style, but seems less sure of what to do when it comes to head to head conversations. The dog of course is the star, but Belushi, whether exasperated, grateful or desperate about his 'partner', runs him close. The script is corny, but that shouldn't bother juvenile audiences.

Knock on Any Door ○

1949, US, 100 mins, b/w
Dir: Nicholas Ray
Stars: Humphrey Bogart, John Derek, George Macready
Rating: ★★★

One of Humphrey Bogart's first independent ventures away from the shelter of Warner Brothers, his studio for 14 years, this study of a young criminal was directed by Nicholas Ray. The following year, Ray and Bogart made *In a Lonely Place* together (Ray was later to make *Rebel Without a Cause*) and both films show the same uncompromising treatment of inherent violence smouldering just

K

below the surface of a seemingly calm personality. In this case, the dangerous element is not Bogart himself, but John Derek (in his first adult role) as the young hoodlum defended by lawyer Bogart on a charge of killing a policeman. The excitement and tension, both in and out of the courtroom, are crisply, cleanly captured in black-and-white by cameraman Burnett Guffey, many years later to win an Oscar for *Bonnie and Clyde*.

Knock on Wood ☉
1954, US, 103 mins, colour
Dir: Norman Panama, Melvin Frank
Stars: Danny Kaye, Mai Zetterling, David Burns, Torin Thatcher
Rating: ★★★

Danny Kaye, the ideal mixture of zany hero and coward, is here a ventriloquist running unintentional rings round a group of spies. And very funny it is, too. The highlights are Kaye's encounters with a gadget-ridden car and a super-twee ballet company.

Kotch ◐
1971, US, 114 mins, colour
Dir: Jack Lemmon
Stars: Walter Matthau, Deborah Winters, Felicia Farr
Rating: ★★★

Jack Lemmon's debut – and, to date, only effort – as a director won Oscar nominations for his old buddy Walter Matthau in the starring role and for the Marvin Hamlisch song 'Life Is What You Make It'. Through comedy, the film attempts to examine the plight of growing old in a society where it appears that only youth and beauty are treasured. Matthau has rarely been better cast or on better form than as the too-alert 72-year-old man keen to babysit his grandchildren but whose daughter-in-law resents his interference. But the film is a true family affair for Lemmon, who cast his real-life wife, Felicia Farr, used his press agent as producer and gave the daughters of four well-known actresses bit parts. A noble first effort and a real mystery why he didn't continue.

Krakatoa – East of Java ○
1968, US, 138 mins, colour
Dir: Bernard I Kowalski
Stars: Maximilian Schell, Diane Baker
Rating: ★★

It's surprising that no one had previously spun an adventure film around the 1883 Krakatoa volcanic explosion, which proved the most spectacular natural disaster in history. Small wonder, then, that this epic action saga has an old-fashioned feel, with its elements of sunken treasure in ancient shipwrecks, deep-sea divers in difficulties, mutiny and fire. The action blazes across the screen, although at rather infrequent intervals, especially since the dialogue and characters are strictly skin-deep. Originally shot in Cinerama, which heightened the action but magnified the film's faults.

Kramer vs Kramer ○ ⓥ
1979, US, 104 mins, colour
Dir: Robert Benton
Stars: Dustin Hoffman, Meryl Streep, Justin Henry, Jane Alexander, Howard Duff, JoBeth Williams
Rating: ★★★★

A searingly affecting weepie about a tug-of-love situation which became one of the big money-spinners of its year and walked off with the Academy Award for best picture. There were Oscars, too, for Dustin Hoffman and Meryl Streep, as the warring parents and for director Benton. Streep and Hoffman both give heartfelt performances, with the aid of some mordant and perceptive dialogue; but spare a thought for Jane Alexander, who is simply faultless as the woman perhaps waiting in the wings. Full of scorching scenes, this is riveting, touching entertainment of the highest quality.

Krays, The ● ⓥ
1990, UK, 119 mins, colour
Dir: Peter Medak
Stars: Billie Whitelaw, Tom Bell, Gary Kemp, Martin Kemp, Susan Fleetwood
Rating: ★★★

For its first hour this is a strong, chronological, extremely well-set reconstruction of the bloody careers of twin ganglords who ruled London's crime from East End to West End in the Fifties. In the second hour, the film rather loses its grip, as if suddenly conscious of its length, by telescoping and merging events and jumping a yawning time gap at the end. Also, by giving too much screen time to fringe characters, the film fails to create an impression of the building of a criminal empire – more that of a couple of psychos on the loose in London's clubland and its backstreets. A pity, this, since real-life brothers Martin and

Gary Kemp are startlingly good as the Krays, and Billie Whitelaw outstanding as their mother. Most of the other performances are good too (especially Jimmy Jewel as an inebriated uncle) and Susan Fleetwood has an excellent death scene as the twins' beloved Aunt Rose. Visually, the film has the right hard-as-ebony look and Michael Kamen's background score is one of the most musically inventive heard for some time in a British film. You expect violence to be an integral element, although it's not in fact intrusive to the story. Perhaps it would take three hours to bring the Krays properly to justice; here, a little less of their childhood and a little more of their murderous adulthood might have achieved a healthier balance.

Kremlin Letter, The ●
1969, US, 113 mins, colour
Dir: John Huston
Stars: Patrick O'Neal, Barbara Parkins, Orson Welles, George Sanders
Rating: ★

John Huston's vicious (and viciously complicated) espionage thriller in which few people are quite what they seem. An all-star cast includes Orson Welles, George Sanders, Richard Boone, Max Von Sydow, Barbara Parkins and Huston himself.

Krull ○ ⓥ
1983, US, 115 mins, colour
Dir: Peter Yates
Stars: Ken Marshall, Lysette Anthony, Freddie Jones, Francesca Annis, Bernard Bresslaw, Robbie Coltrane
Rating: ★★

The opening credits of this derivative British entry into the sci-fi genre promise a *Star Wars*-style space opera. But in the end the film settles for good old sword and sorcery in the Robin Hood tradition, no knowing tongue-in-cheek humour and very little blood-letting. Everything in it has been done before, in many cases better, and the lead characters are bland in the extreme. But for all that, it's hard not to like *Krull*. Bernard Bresslaw's Rell, a friendly giant who can throw a mean javelin, makes most impact, and well down the cast there for Robbie Coltrane in an small early role.

Kuffs ◐ ⓥ
1991, US, 102 mins, colour
Dir: Bruce A Evans

Stars: Christian Slater, Milla Jovovich, Bruce Boxleitner, Tony Goldwyn
Rating: ★

Tolerant Christian Slater fans, of which there must be a good few, might get something out of this asinine action comedy, which has the hero addressing the camera in *Alfie* style. Slater's a ne'er-do-well layabout who's currently proposing to leave his pregnant girlfriend (Milla Jovovich) but finds his life changed when his older brother, a precinct cop, is gunned down. Due to a rather bizarre Los Angeles law, Slater finds himself in charge of his brother's beat and tangling with the crooks who want to take over the neighbourhood. Though the action scenes are efficiently shot, the film's comic side hardly works at all, being strenuously over-directed by first time helmer Bruce A Evans. Slater's charisma helps a little bit but not much. And there's another of those flatulent dogs who became a tiresome staple of the early Nineties Hollywood comedy.

L

La Bamba ◐ �ⓥ
1986, US, 108 mins, colour
Dir: Luis Valdez
Stars: Lou Diamond Phillips
Rating: ★★★

The stuff of real life flows through this tribute to one of the youngest stars of the rock 'n' roll era, Ritchie Valens. The star's Mexican/Indian background promises to take this a little away from the run-of-the-mill and so it proves. Valens' meteoric rise to the top is perhaps taken in too low a key, but there's no doubting the emotional supercharge of his music, as launched from the screen by Phillips with the vocal assistance of Los Lobos. 'La Bamba' itself was quite unlike any other rock 'n' roll number and makes you wonder what someone of Valens' background might have achieved had his life run its full course. Phillips is pretty good as Valens, but the pick of a highly competent cast is Esai Morales as the handsome, glowering, misfit brother who proves an albatross around Ritchie's neck.

Labyrinth ○
1986, US, 97 mins, colour
Dir: Jim Henson
Stars: David Bowie, Jennifer Connelly
Rating: ★★

The Muppet version of *The Wizard of Oz*, with additional inspiration from the works of Lewis Carroll and Maurice Sendak. Teenager Sarah (Jennifer Connelly) accidentally says the words that will allow the King of the Goblins (David Bowie) to kidnap her baby brother. To get him back, she must find her way through the labyrinth that surrounds the goblin castle and face the king in his lair. There are some nice visual illusions (though the matte processing is sometimes rocky) along the way, and one vicious conundrum about truth and lies that might take you about 10 minutes to work out. The puppetry animation techniques impressively create a whole range of amusing characters, especially a jousting fox with Basil Brush voice, whose steed is an Old English sheepdog. But Bowie's songs are allowed to slow the film up badly and his speaking voice somehow doesn't fit the role of the goblin ruler. Connelly is, with her dark hair and eyes and the right aura of innocence,

visually perfect as the heroine, even if her lipstick comes and goes from shot to shot! Too slow for young children and too fey for teenagers, the film's ideal appeal lies somewhere in a narrow band of nine- to 13-year-olds.

La Cage Aux Folles ● ⓥ
1978, France/Italy, 91 mins, colour
Dir: Edouard Molinaro
Stars: Michel Serrault, Ugo Tognazzi
Rating: ★★★

This wildly successful French-Italian farce, which begat two sequels and gave a whole new lease of life to the play on which it was based, is really just the permissive cinema's variation on almost any cinematic frolic of misunderstandings, sexual and otherwise, from the 1930s onwards. A middle-aged gay couple, horrified when the son of one (no, don't ask) wants to marry a girl, get themselves into all sorts of trouble pending a confrontation with her parents. Funniest scene of all — when one of the couple miserably fails a crash course in heterosexual etiquette.

La Ciociara
See: Two Women

Ladies' Man, The ⊙
1961, US, 106 mins, colour
Dir: Jerry Lewis
Stars: Jerry Lewis, Helen Traubel, Jack Kruschen, Gloria Jean
Rating: ★★★

That erratic comedy genius Jerry Lewis wrote, produced and directed this zany, often very funny comedy about a chicken-hearted mother's boy who gets goose-pimples on his goose-pimples at the sight of a pretty girl. Naturally, when he takes a job as a houseboy at a Hollywood hotel, it proves to be full of them. That splendid female foil Kathleen Freeman has a good chance to parade her comedy talents and guest spots are filled by Gloria Jean, George Raft and Harry James. There seemed no good reason to film it in colour but, that said, the Technicolor photography, especially of interiors, is first-rate.

Ladies Who Do ○
1963, UK, 85 mins, b/w
Dir: C M Pennington Richards
Stars: Peggy Mount, Robert Morley, Harry H Corbett
Rating: ★

A comedy about a group of charwomen who find a bizarre way of making money on the Stock Exchange. Peggy Mount, Dandy Nichols, Avril Elgar and Miriam Karlin work hard as the chars. They have to – for the direction tends to lend leaden feet to what should be Ealing-style whimsy. Ron Moody and Nigel Davenport give great support.

Lady and the Tramp ⊙
1955, US, 76 mins, colour
Dir: Hamilton Luske, Clyde Geronimi, Wilfred Jackson
Rating: ★★★

He's a tramp – but you'll love him. Sentimental it may be, but Disney's doggy romance is a wonderful cure for the blues for people of all ages. Amazing animation – especially in the deadly duo of Siamese cats, Si and Am – highly singable tunes (including the mega-hit 'Bella Notte') and a sunshine atmosphere. All the characters are likeable, especially the blowsy Peg of the Pound (brilliantly voiced and sung by Peggy Lee), and only the end seems to have been watered down to conform to popular appeal. See it in a 'letterboxed' Cinemascope version if you can.

Lady Eve, The ○
1941, US, 93 mins, b/w
Dir: Preston Sturges
Stars: Henry Fonda, Barbara Stanwyck, Charles Coburn, William Demarest, Eugene Pallette
Rating: ★★★

Writer-director Preston Sturges, Hollywood's wonder boy of the wartime years, was at the top of his sparkling form with this romantic comedy in which 'clod' Henry Fonda ultimately turns the tables on cardsharps Barbara Stanwyck and Charles Coburn. Fonda's passion for reptiles ('Snakes are my life'), which probably explains his attraction to the sneaky Stanwyck, rivals, for sheer crazy fun, Cary Grant's obsession with bones in *Bringing Up Baby*. Sturges' breathless pacing steers the capers through to a riotous ending.

Lady from Shanghai, The ○
1948, US, 87 mins, b/w
Dir: Orson Welles
Stars: Orson Welles, Rita Hayworth, Everett Sloane, Glenn Anders, Ted De Corsia
Rating: ★★★

Orson Welles cast his own wife, Rita Hayworth, as the beautiful *femme fatale* in this outrageously baroque *film noir*.

But to the outrage of Columbia studio boss, Harry Cohn, Welles cut off her famous trademark red hair and dyed it blonde, portraying the sex siren as a cold, heartless manipulator. As a result, Cohn insisted on the film being extensively re-edited, delaying its release. When it finally saw the light of day, it was a resounding commercial flop. The film was shot under near-chaotic circumstances on locations in New York City, Mexico and on Errol Flynn's yacht off the shores of Acapulco. And Welles rewrote much of the script on a daily basis, putting a tremendous strain on his actors.

Lady Hamilton ○ ⓥ
(aka: That Hamilton Woman)
1940, US, 128 mins, b/w
Dir: Alexander Korda
Stars: Vivien Leigh, Laurence Olivier, Gladys Cooper, Alan Mowbray
Rating: ★★★

Sir Alexander Korda was more often producer than director, but this film, made in America and said to be Sir Winston Churchill's all-time favourite, was one he did direct himself. Starring Laurence Olivier as Nelson and Vivien Leigh as Lady Hamilton, it stands up remarkably well today, distinguished by some striking high-key photography by the Polish cinematographer Rudolph Maté, who later turned to directing. From the beginning, Korda had set out to make a quick pro-British propaganda film, whose messages (paralleling Napoleon and Hitler) would hit squarely home to America. One large set – Hamilton's villa in Naples – was utilised as much as possible, naval battle sequences were kept to a minimum, and the film was completed in six weeks. The scriptwriters, R C Sheriff, who had been brought over from England, and Austrian Walter Reisch, worked as shooting progressed. Even at the end of the six hectic weeks, there was a further crisis when the American censor refused to accept the film unless the script emphasised that adultery was not being condoned. To pacify him, Korda shot an extra scene showing Nelson realising his shame after a reprimand by his father. The scene was later deleted.

LadyHawke ○ ⓥ
1985, US, 118 mins, colour
Dir: Richard Donner
Stars: Matthew Broderick, Rutger Hauer, Michelle Pfeiffer, Leo McKern, John

Wood
Rating: ★★

A cross between sword-and-sorcery and *The Black Shield of Falworth*, this is a laborious adventure fantasy set in a medieval France where an evil bishop (John Wood) has cursed lovers Rutger Hauer and Michelle Pfeiffer – the blondest, bluest-eyed combo since Ladd and Lake – so that the one may turn into a wolf at night and the other into a hawk by day. Magnificent, imaginative set decoration and art direction, full of fires and torches against primeval battlements, and amazing sewer systems, are wasted here on a fatuous script and foolish story. The playing is surprisingly indifferent considering the cast, save for another whiskey priest from Leo McKern, and the action too frenziedly edited to set the pulses racing. The hawk and the wolf (or husky, or whatever), however, are both splendid – easily the most attractive things in a film whose modern English, often half-addressed to the camera, sits uneasily on its medieval characters' shoulders.

Lady Ice ◐
1973, US, 93 mins, colour
Dir: Tom Gries
Stars: Donald Sutherland, Jennifer O'Neill, Robert Duvall
Rating: ★★

An unusually straight role for Donald Sutherland, an actor who has specialised in the eccentric, as an insurance investigator who hijacks a priceless diamond necklace from a gang of jewel thieves. Perhaps it's not so surprising to find him in the part, however, as it followed directly on from his hugely successful detective in *Klute*. As to be expected from a film by the late Tom Gries, this thriller moves along in fine style, although the romantic comedy overtones refuse obstinately to blend with the rest of the film and nothing quite matches up to the slickly enjoyable opening sequence. Lucien Ballard's elegant Technicolor photography is a plus factor throughout, especially in the lushness of the scenes set in the Bahamas.

Lady in Cement ◐
1968, US, 93 mins, colour
Dir: Gordon Douglas
Stars: Frank Sinatra, Raquel Welch, Richard Conte, Joe E Lewis
Rating: ★★

Frank Sinatra returns as the hard-boiled Miami private eye he created in the previous year's *Tony Rome* for more lively mystery, mayhem and murder, well crafted, but with little style, by director Gordon Douglas. The slick, fast-moving screenplay is spiced with tart wisecracks smartly delivered by Sinatra who displays his shaggy, somewhat dangerous, charm to good effect. The sex and violence was considered to be quite tough for its time.

Lady in the Dark ○
1944, US, 100 mins, colour
Dir: Mitchell Leisen
Stars: Ginger Rogers, Ray Milland, Jon Hall, Warner Baxter
Rating: ★★

Ginger Rogers, making her first all-colour film, had one of the juiciest parts of her career in this heady (and heavy) mixture of music, romance and psychiatry. Strangely, although many of them were filmed, not all the Kurt Weill-Ira Gershwin songs from the stage original by Moss Hart (which had starred Gertrude Lawrence) made it into the release print. The movie was a hit for Paramount, who had paid the then record sum of $283,000 for the rights and spent $2 million making it.

Lady in the Lake ○
1946, US, 103 mins, b/w
Dir: Robert Montgomery
Stars: Robert Montgomery, Audrey Totter, Lloyd Nolan, Tom Tully
Rating: ★★★

Perhaps the most unusual film adaptation on record of one of Raymond Chandler's tough and tortuous thrillers. Star/director Robert Montgomery employs the highly original, and brilliantly successful device of telling the story entirely in the first person, through the eyes of the principal character, Phillip Marlowe (spelt here with two 'l's), who is rarely seen except in reflection. Additionally, the subjective camera records Marlowe's impressions while he listens to a character speak. For example, as he is interviewed by Adrienne Fromsett (Audrey Totter), her alluring receptionist enters the room and Marlowe follows her every move while she answers his 'stare' with seductive expressions. Not only does this technique increase visual interest, it also contrasts Adrienne's pretentiousness with Marlowe's more honest, albeit coarse, personality. 'I don't like your

manner,' says Adrienne, unimpressed by the down-to-earth detective. 'I'm not selling it,' replies Marlowe, indifferent to her appraisal. And, if you don't know the story, you'll be hard put to unravel its solution.

Lady in White ◐
1988, US, 105 mins, colour
Dir: Frank LaLoggia
Stars: Lukas Haas, Len Cariou
Rating: ★★★

When young Frankie (Lukas Haas) is locked into his class cloakroom by his classmates as a Hallowe'en joke, he sees the ghost of a young girl and a masked man. Are they connected to each other in some way? Frankie is determined to find out. Haas, the little Amish boy in *Witness*, is quite cute as the central character in this eerie supernatural thriller. The special effects are good and there's a nail-biting, if somewhat clichéd climax. All the elements here are familiar but writer/director Frank LaLoggia has mixed them well. Look out for Katherine (*Soap*) Helmond as a rather scary Miss Haversham-like eccentric.

Lady Jane ○ Ⓥ
1985, UK, 142 mins, colour
Dir: Trevor Nunn
Stars: Helena Bonham Carter, Cary Elwes, Michael Hordern, Jill Bennett, Jane Lapotaire
Rating: ★★★

This was former Royal Shakespeare Company director Trevor Nunn's second venture into movies (his first was the 1975 adaptation of Ibsen's *Hedda Gabler*, starring Glenda Jackson) and it's as wordy and weighty as you might expect. Playwright David Edgar has woven a story of political intrigue around Lady Jane Grey, who became queen in her teens but then was overthrown by Mary Tudor. His screenplay casts Jane in a new light, as a 16th century social reformer who takes pity on the downtrodden peasantry and returns their land to them. The period detail and lavish sets, including 11 Tudor castles, give an air of grandeur, but the real interest lies in the relationship between religious, reclusive Lady Jane (Helena Bonham Carter) and her enforced husband, the wild wastrel Guilford Dudley (Cary Elwes), son of the scheming Duke of Northumberland. Although it's decently acted, *Lady Jane* lacked the cinematic scope to make it a box-office success.

Lady Killer ○
1934, US, 74 mins, b/w
Dir: Roy Del Ruth
Stars: James Cagney, Mae Clarke, Henry O'Neill, Margaret Lindsay
Rating: ★★★

James Cagney is every bit as pugnacious as ever in this Thirties' gangster drama and once again Mae Clarke (who got the famous grapefruit in the face from Cagney in *The Public Enemy*) is on the receiving end of the rough treatment. This time he drags her across a room by her hair and throws her out into the corridor. Elsewhere, the star struts his familiar way through a staccato tale of crooks, bullets and blackmail. The twist that makes the film different is that the leading character escapes his environment to become a film star — after sending himself fan letters. Director Roy Del Ruth's films all moved at a rare pace, and this one is no exception.

Ladykillers, The ○ Ⓥ
1955, UK, 97 mins, colour
Dir: Alexander Mackendrick
Stars: Alec Guinness, Cecil Parker, Herbert Lom, Peter Sellers
Rating: ★★★★

Say 'Ealing Comedies' and this hilarious caper is one of the first films that springs to mind. Yet it isn't a typical Ealing offering, as it has a decidedly black edge. Alec Guinness is the seedy and sinister Professor Marcus who takes lodgings with the dithery Mrs Wilberforce in King's Cross. He is frequently visited by four equally shifty-looking friends, who, he says, are musicians. But they are really a gang of criminals planning a big robbery! The gang members (Peter Sellers, Herbert Lom, Cecil Parker and — seizing his best chance from a career of 'bit' parts — Danny Green) are perfectly cast and find a good balance between real villainy and farcical incompetence, while Guinness is at times genuinely menacing. But it is Katie Johnson as the delightfully dotty Mrs Wilberforce who manages to steal every scene she is in. Deservedly a classic.

Lady L ○
1966, US, 107 mins, colour
Dir: Peter Ustinov
Stars: Sophia Loren, Paul Newman, David Niven
Rating: ★★★

Peter Ustinov wrote and directed this richly entertaining *divertissement* about

L

the memoirs of an outrageous peeress, played by Sophia Loren. Set pieces include gendarmes on bicycles chasing a 'horseless carriage'; an army of umbrellas in pursuit of jewel thieves; and a dazzling party sequence, with dancers galloping through shadowed corridors like so many of Poe's revellers fleeing from the Red Death. An elegant film, with a devastating kick in the tail.

Lady Luck ○
1946, US, 97 mins, b/w
Dir: Edwin L Marin
Stars: Robert Young, Barbara Hale, Frank Morgan
Rating: ★★★

A divertingly dotty comedy with a Damon Runyon touch, as some of the character names (Happy Johnson, Little Joe, Sacramento Sam) would imply. Stars Robert Young and Barbara Hale are comfortably at home in this light romantic romp with a zany touch and confidently supply some pleasing entertainment with the help of a good few smart lines from Lynn Root and Frank Fenton's script.

Lady of Deceit ◖
(aka: Born to Kill)
1947, US, 95 mins, b/w
Dir: Robert Wise
Stars: Lawrence Tierney, Claire Trevor, Walter Slezak, Elisha Cook Jr
Rating: ★★★

A very dark, amoral thriller featuring Lawrence Tierney at his most psychopathic and full of characters whose hearts ruling their heads is the cause of their downfall. There are typical (but well-crafted) roles for Claire Trevor as the older woman furious with killer Tierney's fascination for her younger sister (Audrey Long), and Elisha Cook Jr as Tierney's sycophantic but more level-headed sidekick. Robert Wise's spare, head-on direction brooks no frills either in storyline or production. Film buffs will spot star-to-be Martha Hyer as a snoopy maid.

Lady of the Boulevards
See: Nana

Lady of the Tropics ○
1939, US, 92 mins, b/w
Dir: Jack Conway
Stars: Robert Taylor, Hedy Lamarr
Rating: ★★

The hot romantic combination of Robert Taylor and Hedy Lamarr

proved dynamite at the box-office in this sad little MGM concoction about a tropic love affair between a carefree playboy and a girl of mixed race. Reliable director Jack Conway made as many box-office hits for the studio as anyone else and, despite backdrops which now seem phoney, he gives the tragic affair a timeless quality, even though it seems longer than it is.

Lady on a Train ○
1945, US, 84 mins, b/w
Dir: Charles David
Stars: Deanna Durbin, Ralph Bellamy, Dan Duryea, Patricia Morison, Edward Everett Horton
Rating: ★★★

This comedy-thriller with music gave Deanna Durbin one of her greatest hits – 'Night and Day'. In true Miss Marple style, Deanna sees a murder from a train and gets herself into lots of danger trying to get the police to believe her and track down the killer. It was directed by Charles David – the man soon to become her husband. Don't guess too soon at the guilty party – you could be wrong.

Lady Sings the Blues ●
1972, US, 144 mins, colour
Dir: Sidney J Furie
Stars: Diana Ross, Billy Dee Williams, Richard Pryor
Rating: ★

Never mind the lurid, strident treatment this film gives to the tormented life of entertainer Billie Holiday, just listen to the way the lady, as impersonated by Diana Ross, sings the blues. The dialogue pulls no punches, and the story careers along on peaks of hysteria.

Lady Surrenders, A
See: Love Story [1944]

Lady Takes a Chance, A ○
(aka: The Cowboy and the Girl)
1943, US, 86 mins, b/w
Dir: William Seiter
Stars: Jean Arthur, John Wayne, Charles Winninger, Phil Silvers
Rating: ★★

The teaming of squeaky Jean Arthur and rumbling John Wayne in a romantic comedy works better than you'd expect, although not that much better. The stars do, however, extract some fun from the tall tale of a city girl who falls for a rodeo rider and uses all her wiles to rope him in.

Lady Vanishes, The ○
1938, UK, 98 mins, b/w
Dir: Alfred Hitchcock
Stars: Margaret Lockwood, Michael Redgrave, Dame May Whitty, Paul Lukas, Basil Radford, Naunton Wayne
Rating: ★★★★

A Hitchcock thriller which has become one of the few timeless classics from the British cinema of the Thirties, with its famous plot line of the little old lady who vanishes aboard the Transcontinental Express – one remembers especially Catherine Lacey as the 'nun' who proves to be wearing high heels – that almost became a trademark of the master's work once he moved to Hollywood. It also had his favourite setting – a train. Made during what Hitchcock later called his 'adventurous period', it features, besides unlimited tension and excitement, Margaret Lockwood ('delightful, uninhibited girl' recalled Hitchcock once) as the heroine who almost comes to believe that she didn't meet the elderly lady (Dame May Whitty) who has now vanished.

Lady Vanishes, The ○
1979, UK, 99 mins, colour
Dir: Anthony Page
Stars: Elliott Gould, Cybill Shepherd, Angela Lansbury, Herbert Lom, Ian Carmichael, Arthur Lowe
Rating: ★★★

You can't recreate an original by taking a new set of paintbrushes and doing it all over again. But, with a few deft touches of its own to complement the wise preservation of the best of the old, this new version of Ethel Lina White's classic thriller (first made by Hitchcock in 1938) does very nicely under its own steam. Rattled along at a fine pace by director Anthony Page, with superb supporting performances from Angela Lansbury – as the lady who disappears aboard a transcontinental express train in 1939 – Arthur Lowe and Ian Carmichael, this lady also has some literately witty dialogue from American George Axelrod. It includes one classic line (said by hero Elliott Gould of madcap heroine Cybill Shepherd) that perhaps sums up the whole film: 'Maybe that beautiful girl with the wild body and no brassiere is right!' In fact, there are few signal failures in this loving remake of an old masterpiece.

Lady With a Lamp, The ○
1951, UK, 110 mins, b/w
Dir: Herbert Wilcox

Stars: Anna Neagle, Michael Wilding, Gladys Young, Felix Aylmer
Rating: ★★★

The last of Anna Neagle's many portraits of famous ladies and one which her serenity and sincerity ideally qualified her to play. The film is not so much a biopic as episodes from the life of its subject, Florence Nightingale, and it tends to lack steel. But the period and its trappings are immaculate and Dame Anna's oft-time co-star Michael Wilding is there to provide elegant support.

Lady Without Passport, A ○
1950, US, 84 mins, b/w
Dir: Joseph H Lewis
Stars: Hedy Lamarr, John Hodiak, James Craig, George Macready
Rating: ★

A so-so thriller about illegal aliens trying to enter America, with Hedy Lamarr as a beautiful refugee. It was a brave attempt at a *film noir* thriller but didn't have enough *noir* to make it a film. Miss Lamarr needed better support than she received here, and the result was an unintended B-picture.

Lafayette Escadrille
See: Hell Bent For Glory

Lair of the White Worm, The ● Ⓥ
1989, UK, 94 mins, colour
Dir: Ken Russell
Stars: Hugh Grant, Peter Capaldi, Amanda Donohoe, Sammi Davis
Rating: ★

Ken Russell, that most mercurial of directors, managed to balance high camp and genuine horror modestly successfully in this, his own adaptation of Bram ('Dracula') Stoker's gothic novel. Amanda Donohoe is evily seductive as the wicked and often scantily-clad Lady Silvia Marsh and manages to dodge your laughter until near the end. By and large, though, the end-of-pier camp charade looks cheap and has acting to match. And its intentional jokes are feeble and fall pretty flat. It's certainly one of a kind though, with its streaks of humour, titillation and terror, coupled to some outrageous special effects. Purists will be outraged.

L'Amant
See: The Lover

Lamb ◑ Ⓥ
1985, UK, 110 mins, colour
Dir: Colin Gregg
Stars: Liam Neeson, Hugh O'Conor, Ian Bannen, Frances Tomelty
Rating: ★★★

Given director Colin Gregg's previous work, on *The Trespasser*, *To the Lighthouse* and *Remembrance*, there was little chance that *Lamb* would turn out to be a barrel of laughs. Yet, grim though the story is in many ways, there are both a few attractive lighter moments and a true poignancy to this tale of the doomed journey of a young priest and the foul-mouthed yet endearing 10-year-old epileptic boy he rescues from the (slightly improbable) tyranny of a remand home, run with callous lack of compassion by his fellow-priests. Although the naiveté of the priest stretches the credulity, persuasive performances by Liam Neeson (his first major impression) as the priest and Hugh O'Conor as the boy win the day. And Dudley Sutton is convincingly repugnant as a clammy pervert with a military manner. The harrowing tale also receives a constant boost from the excellence and clarity of Mike Garfath's noticeably good Eastman Color photography. *Lamb* may not cut deep enough to make you cry, but it will make you think.

Lancer Spy ○
1937, US, 84 mins, b/w
Dir: Gregory Ratoff
Stars: George Sanders, Dolores Del Rio, Joseph Schildkraut, Peter Lorre
Rating: ★★★

This exciting melodrama was Russian actor Gregory Ratoff's first try at directing a Hollywood film and a first-class job he made of it. The role of the young naval officer who undertakes a dangerous impersonation in Germany shot George Sanders, previously confined to supporting roles, to stardom. And Joseph Schildkraut, who won an Oscar in the same year as best supporting actor, in *The Life of Emile Zola*, is magnificent as a weakling prince. Ratoff's direction, always patient and at times inspired, leads to some thrilling moments, not least of which is the breathless final chase up to the Swiss border.

Land Before Time, The ⊙ Ⓥ
1988, US, 69 mins, colour
Dir: Don Bluth
Voice stars: Pat Hingle, Gabriel Damon, Helen Shaver, Candice Houston
Rating: ★

Only the very youngest children will suffer this animated dinosaur feature gladly. From the same team as *An American Tail*, it is weighed down by a lack of imagination and an overwhelming sense of cuteness. The film sets out to preach the message that surviving in a changing environment depends on achieving unity among the species. But the idea isn't strong enough to carry the tale which, at just over an hour long, is one of the slowest cartoon hours ever to plod across a screen.

Landfall ○
1949, UK, 88 mins, b/w
Dir: Ken Annakin
Stars: Michael Denison, Patricia Plunkett, David Tomlinson
Rating: ★★★

Adapted from Nevil Shute's novel, this is the story of a British wartime pilot acused of sinking one of his own submarines – although he's convinced it was a German U-boat. Excellent characterisations of people ranging from air raid wardens to admirals make the plot entirely plausible, even if it's never in the class of the book. Liquid-lipped Patricia Plunkett is most attractive as hero Michael Denison's resourceful girlfriend.

Land of the Pharaohs ○
1955, US, 105 mins, colour
Dir: Howard Hawks
Stars: Jack Hawkins, Joan Collins
Rating: ★★

Spectacle and epic are blended well in this epic if raggedly-scripted story of life in Egypt 5,000 years ago. Jack Hawkins, in his first American film, makes a statesmanlike Pharaoh, and Joan Collins' scheming princess could teach even Cleopatra a thing or two. This is a big film in every sense: director Howard Hawks used 9000 extras to build a pyramid, the immensity of which makes them look like ants. Hawks also had 100 boats built for scenes on the Nile and hired Nobel prizewinner William Faulkner to work on the screenplay – which makes you wonder what the dialogue must have been like in the first place.

L

Land Raiders ◐
1969, US, 100 mins, colour
Dir: Nathan Juran
Stars: Telly Savalas, George Maharis,
Arlene Dahl
Rating: ★

Blackly violent Western, with Telly
Savalas in rampaging form as a merciless bully who runs the whole
territory until his younger brother returns from exile to bring him to book.
It was made in Spain, despite the
dominance of English-speaking
actors (Jocelyn Lane, George
Couleris and Guy Rolfe are also
featured), and is the last film to date
directed by Nathan Juran, who won
an Oscar for art direction on *How
Green Was My Valley* in 1941.

Land That Time Forgot,
The ○ ⓥ
1974, UK, 91 mins, colour
Dir: Kevin Connor
Stars: Doug McClure, John McEnery,
Susan Penhaligon, Keith Barron
Rating: ★★★

Although Doug McClure, Susan
Penhaligon and John McEnery are its
leading actors, the real stars of this
prehistoric animal thriller are mon-
ster-maker Roger Dicken, editor John
Ireland and director Kevin Connor.
The pace is lively, the editing sharp
and the story on the whole believable.
Even the back-projection work is a
cut above Hollywood efforts of the
period. It's 1918 and German and
English mariners, forced to band together, use a submarine to enter an
underground river in Antarctica,
discovering a land where hot springs
bubble, allosauruses rear their ugly
heads and pterodactyls patrol the skies.
Some illogicalities in the plot and the
inadequacy of McClure as leading
man are more than compensated for
with the excitement provided by
Dicken's monsters, whether roaring
menacingly towards the camera,
shuddering against the impact of bullets or howling and weeping in defeat.
And the backgrounds are futuristic,
broodingly mysterious and brilliantly
realised.

Larceny Inc ○
1941, US, 95 mins, b/w
Dir: Lloyd Bacon
Stars: Edward G Robinson, Jane Wyman,
Broderick Crawford, Anthony Quinn, Jack
Carson, Edward Brophy
Rating: ★★★

A broad but mostly delightful crime
comedy about Edward G Robinson
buying a shop next door to the bank
he plans to rob, only to discover that
he's making more of a profit from that
than he ever did from crime. It's a pity
that it's played as outright farce.
Broderick Crawford's performance
makes Jack Carson's look subtle, but
watching Edward G wrap a suitcase in
about 10 yards of brown paper for a
customer is worth waiting for.

Lassie Come Home ⊙
1943, US, 88 mins, colour
Dir: Fred M Wilcox
Stars: Roddy McDowall, Donald Crisp,
Dame May Whitty, Elsa Lanchester
Rating: ★★★

The surprise box-office hit that
spawned many sequels as well as a TV
and radio series. Elizabeth Taylor had
only seventh billing, but with the
success of *National Velvet* was elevated
to star status for a sequel, *Courage of
Lassie*. Rising child star Roddy
McDowall was loaned from Fox to
MGM and he joined several other
London-to-Hollywood actors,
including Donald Crisp, Elsa
Lanchester, Nigel Bruce, Dame May
Whitty and Edmund Gwenn, to make
this thoroughly enjoyable family entertainment that won't leave a dry
eye in the sitting room in its closing
stages. Incidentally, the dog playing
Lassie was a male called Pal and cost
the studio ten dollars. He was originally hired as a stunt double for the
first-choice canine but stood in when
the female started shedding her coat
heavily.

Lassiter ◐
1983, US, 110 mins, colour
Dir: Roger Young
Stars: Tom Selleck, Jane Seymour,
Lauren Hutton, Bob Hoskins
Rating: ★★★

Tom Selleck chose a good script for
this cash-in on his *Magnum* success. It's
engagingly set in 1939 where
Lassiter, an American Raffles, is
strongarmed into stealing millions in
diamonds for the Nazis. Selleck is
backed by good performances from
both his leading ladies, Lauren
Hutton, who enjoys herself in a Mata
Hari role, and the underrated Jane
Seymour. Warren Clarke and Bob
Hoskins also register well as lethal in-
fluences in Lassiter's life, while Ed
Lauter's engaging Cockney
interpolations as Lassiter's chief cohort
clearly owe a lot to Dick Van Dyke's

interpretation of the chimney sweep
in *Mary Poppins*. This thriller certainly
is different, and Selleck's own performance in the title role is spot-on.

Last Action Hero ◐ ⓥ
1993, US, 130 mins, colour
Dir: John McTiernan
Stars: Arnold Schwarzenegger, F Murray
Abraham, Austin O'Brien, Robert Prosky,
Charles Dance, Anthony Quinn
Rating: ★★★

The idea of people jumping into films
is hardly new, but this treatment is
pretty inventive by the standards of
the genre, and allows Arnold
Schwarzenegger to play another
amusing variant on his own image: no
small achievement considering his
limited range. Wide-eyed Austin
O'Brien is the sub-teen film freak
given a magic ticket (invented by
Houdini!) to a preview of the latest
adventure of his favourite film
character Jack Slater. No sooner have
the first scenes unspooled than the kid
finds himself catapulted into the film.
Slater is baffled that the boy knows so
much about him – not to mention his
prior knowledge of the plot, which
has villains Charles Dance and
Anthony Quinn taking control of the
LA underworld. Later, the movie
neatly reverses everything when Slater
comes back to real life in pursuit of his
fictional enemies, and is puzzled to
find he's no longer invincible. The star
pokes fun at himself – Slater can't remember the name of the actor who
plays him and introduces himself as
Arnold Braunschweiger – and some
'real life' stars contribute cameos, including Schwarzenegger himself,
being nagged by his wife for relentlessly plugging his own chain of
restaurants. Underrated.

Last Boy Scout, The ● ⓥ
1991, US, 106 mins, colour
Dir: Tony Scott
Stars: Bruce Willis, Damon Wayans,
Chelsea Field, Taylor Negron, Danielle
Harris
Rating: ★★★

Bruce Willis returned to the *Die Hard*
formula here with the kind of tough
pulp fiction in which people will pay
to see him. Full of sadistic violence,
voluptuous undressed women,
tough-talking Willis wisecracks and so
much bad language they'll surely
never be able to screen it on network
TV. Bullets, blood and guts fly everywhere. Willis is a washed-up secret
service man turned shabby, unshaven

private eye. Handed a case by his partner, Willis drives home fast to find partner bedding Willis' wife. Partner exits in a car which promptly blows up, the first piece in the jigsaw of a multi-million dollar case involving legalising certain forms of gambling. Willis gets beaten up a lot, but (for once logically) never rubbed out, as the villains suspect he has something they want. One civilised nasty offers to effect introductions. 'Who cares?' asks Willis. 'You're the bad guy, right?' It's the kind of weary humour Willis was beginning to make his own. Somewhere in there is Willis' foul-mouthed 13-year-old daughter, played with great confidence by Danielle Harris, who more than once pulls daddy out of a hole. The action is terrific and the bad guys are pretty horrible.

Last Days of Pompeii, The ○
1935, US, 96 mins, b/w
Dir: Eernest B Schoedsack
Stars: Basil Rathbone, Preston Foster, Alan Hale, Louis Calhern
Rating: ★★

Despite special effects from Willis O'Brien and the team behind *King Kong*, this historical epic about the eruption of Mount Vesuvius lost $237,000 at the box office and didn't, in fact, start to make money until it was re-released on a double-bill with *She* 14 years later. The film actually bears no relation whatsoever to Sir Edward Bulwer-Lytton's novel, and much of the dialogue is of the wooden variety. Preston Foster is solid but uninspired in the lead role as an honest blacksmith caught up in the momentous events prior to eruption, but acting honours go to Basil Rathbone as Pilate, whose scenes were all shot in just seven days. Rathbone played the same role again 27 years later!

Last Detail, The ● ⓥ
1974, US, 105 mins, colour
Dir: Hal Ashby
Stars: Jack Nicholson, Randy Quaid, Carol Kane, Otis Young, Michael Moriarty
Rating: ★★★

A raw, raucous, grainy and grim story about two hard-cursing US Navy petty officers (Jack Nicholson and Otis Young) escorting an 18-year-old prisoner (Randy Quaid) half-way across America to serve an eight-year prison sentence for stealing 40 dollars from a polio collection box (it was a

favourite charity of the CO's wife). Jack Nicholson, who's in tremendous form as 'Bad Ass' Baddusky, and Randy Quaid were both nominated for Academy Awards.

Last Dragon, The ○
1985, US, 109 mins, colour
Dir: Michael Schultz
Stars: Taimak, Vanity
Rating: ★★

Billed as the first kung-fu musical, this is really a mish-mash of several kinds of film all fighting against each other. Director Michael Schultz displays a good sense of visual wit but the characters are nothing more than cartoon cyphers. It's not difficult to see, though, why the film did so well in America. It's bright and loud, full of 'impossible' action and has a crunching disco score: a pantomime of violence populated by beautiful people. The female lead, Vanity, was saddled as a glamorous sidekick in a series of tough action films, notably *Action Jackson*. Not many people know that she used to go by the name D D Winters, and can be glimpsed in the 1979 Canadian thriller *Terror Train*.

Last Embrace ●
1979, US, 97 mins, colour
Dir: Jonathan Demme
Stars: Roy Scheider, Janet Margolin, Sam Levene, Christopher Walken
Rating: ★★★★

A strong and complex thriller with classic ingredients: a hero with a weakness battles mysterious forces that are out to get him. Someone certainly has it in for Roy Scheider, as a government agent barely recovered from a nervous breakdown – after seeing his wife shot down by bullets meant for him. There's a mix-up over possession of his flat, someone tries to push him under a train – and he receives a mysterious death threat. Are his old colleagues (lead by Christopher Walken) out to get him, or has he become involved in some deeper nightmare? Jonathan Demme's tribute to Hitchcock includes the bell-tower from *Vertigo*, the street scene (and more) from *Marnie* and the climax straight from *Saboteur*, breathtakingly transferred from the Statue of Liberty to Niagara Falls. A pounding score from Miklos Rosza makes its presence felt at all the right times. The film was shunned by its British distributors for two years, perhaps because of the presence of the non-box office actress Janet Margolin as the anthropogist

who unintentionally shares Scheider's flat. Ironically, Miss Margolin is tremendous.

Last Emperor, The ○ ⓥ
1987, UK/Italy, 163 mins, colour
Dir: Bernardo Bertolucci
Stars: John Lone, Joan Chen, Peter O'Toole
Rating: ★★★★

Director Bernard Bertolucci built this fascinating story of China's last emperor on an epic scale, but in essence it is the very intimate tale of a man raised in glorious isolation who struggles to come to terms with a rapidly-changing world in which he is not equipped to live. Pu Yi became emperor of China at the age of three. Then, in 1912, China's new republic restricts him to the Forbidden City, the vast palace enclave, effectively creating the most opulent prison in history. His only connection with the outside world is his Scottish tutor, Reginald Johnson (Peter O'Toole). After eviction by a Chinese warlord, Pu Yi becomes a puppet of the Japanese, then, with the Mao revolution, becomes a prisoner in his own country. Although a long film, *The Last Emperor* never fails to fascinate, even when the pace seems decidedly leisurely. Four actors play the part of Pu Yi, but the move from one to the other as the character ages is seamless. Visually stunning, the picture's sheer scale is sometimes in danger of dwarfing the human tale it tells, but a strong cast and an intelligent script stop this happening. Maybe not the masterpiece Bertolucci hoped for, but a fine film not to be missed.

Last Exit to Brooklyn ● ⓥ
1989, US, 102 mins, colour
Dir: Ulrich Edel
Stars: Stephen Lang, Jennifer Jason Leigh, Burt Young, Jerry Orbach
Rating: ★★★

'Notorious' bestsellers don't normally make good movies, but this is a well-made, carefully composed film version of a prime piece of Fifties sleaze, the other side of the coin from such sentimental slices of Brooklyn life as *Wedding Breakfast* and *Marty*. Despite its blood, guts, four-letter words and fairly frank portrayal of a struggle for existence in Brooklyn's backstreets, this, too, is sentimental at heart, and even Jennifer Jason Leigh's raucous, breast-baring petty thief is looked on as a tart with a heart in search of a happy ending. German Director Edel

L

looks for, and sometimes finds, poetry in these squalid surroundings, even in the strikers' riot which results in mashed bones and cracked skulls. The use of classical music is a trifle over-done, but undeniably effective.

Last Flight of Noah's Ark, The ⊙
1980, US, 97 mins, colour
Dir: Charles Jarrott
Stars: Elliott Gould, Genevieve Bujold, Ricky Schroder
Rating: ★★

Charles Jarrott's direction largely keeps sentimentality at bay in this easy-going Disney offering, whose roster of performers includes two orphan children and a minor menag-erie of goats, assorted poultry, pigs, sheep, bulls and a cow. Faced with this array of two and four-legged potential scene-stealers, adults Elliott Gould and Genevieve Bujold hold their own ad-mirably. Attractive Hawaiian locations add decoration to the ad-venture.

Last Gangster, The ◯
1937, US, 81 mins, b/w
Dir: Edward Ludwig
Stars: Edward G Robinson, James Stewart, Rosa Stradner, Lionel Stander
Rating: ★★★

Spitting and snarling, Edward G Ro-binson, who became the talkies' 'first' gangster in *Little Caesar*, carries on in the same vein as Joe Krozac, an un-derworld boss who finds things have changed after he comes out of prison. Robinson was delighted with the part, which he saw as a farewell to his time in crime. But the typecasting was to dog him on and off for the rest of his career. Co-star James Stewart took another stride towards stardom, though he isn't flattered by a mous-tache and almost never wore one in films again.

Last Giraffe, The
See: Raising Daisy Rothschild

Last Grenade, The ◖
(aka: Grigsby)
1969, UK, 94 mins, colour
Dir: Gordon Flemyng
Stars: Stanley Baker, Alex Cord, Honor Blackman, Richard Attenborough
Rating: ★★

The action's the thing in this jun-gle-warfare thriller and there's plenty of it. A familiar crew of British actors, including John Thaw of *The Sweeney*,

add substance to a tale of revenge, played out against the background of the adventures of a group of merce-naries led by Stanley Baker. There are chases and explosions galore, good colour photography by Alan Hume and a forceful performance by Baker.

Last Hard Men, The ◖
1976, US, 103 mins, colour
Dir: Andrew V McLaglen
Stars: Charlton Heston, James Coburn, Barbara Hershey
Rating: ★★

Two big stars in a faintly unsavoury manhunt Western. Charlton Heston and James Coburn go through the paces that have served them well as the adversaries from way back who now engage in a final deadly duel, in-jecting much-needed personality into the catalogue of slow-motion violence that follows.

Last Holiday ◯
1950, UK, 88 mins, b/w
Dir: Henry Cass
Stars: Alec Guinness, Kay Walsh
Rating: ★★★

Although dating from a time when the famous Ealing comedies, with which Alec Guinness was then associated, were in full sway, this film is in an al-together gentler style. An affecting light drama with humorous insights, it comes from the pen of J B Priestley and features vivid supporting perfor-mances from Kay Walsh, Sidney James and Wilfrid Hyde White. But it's Guinness' quiet authority which lingers long in the memory.

Last Hunt, The ◯
1955, US, 108 mins, colour
Dir: Richard Brooks
Stars: Robert Taylor, Stewart Granger, Debra Paget, Lloyd Nolan
Rating: ★★

This story about two men on a buffalo hunt is quite grim by MGM Western standards. Lots of buffalo and a fair few Indians get killed one way and another and the two stars, Robert Taylor and Stewart Granger, fall out over a young Indian girl rescued by Taylor. Having said that, it's a pow-erful Western drama which holds your interest right through to the icy climax (to say more would be to give the ending away!). Taylor and Granger are solid (if a bit stolid) as the hunter and the rancher who join forces, and Lloyd Nolan, playing a

character called Woodfoot, looks as though he's thoroughly enjoying himself!

Last Hurrah, The ◯
1958, US, 121 mins, b/w
Dir: John Ford
Stars: Spencer Tracy, Jeffrey Hunter, Dianne Foster, Pat O'Brien
Rating: ★★★

Based on the career of Boston's con-troversial Irish-American mayor Jim Curley, a role that enables Spencer Tracy to dominate this John Ford film, this is an overlong but still strong po-litical saga. Tracy is surrounded by a veritable council of distinguished vet-eran stars, among them Basil Rathbone, Pat O'Brien, Donald Crisp, Ricardo Cortez, James Gleason and John Carradine.

Last Married Couple in America, The ●
1980, US, 100 mins, colour
Dir: Gilbert Cates
Stars: George Segal, Natalie Wood, Richard Benjamin, Valerie Harper, Dom DeLuise
Rating: ★

A sex comedy about a couple who question their own relationship when all their friends start getting divorced. It might well have come from the Sixties apart from the ribald dialogue, manfully coped with by a personable cast, all of whom play comfortably within their most familiar screen images. Funniest of the supporting players is Bob Dishy as a womanising divorce lawyer, although Valerie Harper (from television's *Rhoda*) and plumply likeable Dom DeLuise also provide good value.

Last Message from Saigon
See: Operation CIA

Last of England, The ●
1987, UK, 87 mins, colour
Dir: Derek Jarman
Stars: Tilda Swinton, Nigel Terry, Spencer Leigh, Derek Jarman, Spring
Rating: ★★

Told largely in subliminal flashes with a few grainy colour narrative sequences, this is a paean of despair for an England devastated by some nameless disaster. 'On every green hill,' intones narrator Nigel Terry (the film itself is virtually wordless) 'mourners stand and weep for the last of England.' On rubbish tips, waterfronts and in sewers too, according to director Derek Jarman, as the few (contaminated?) survivors are guarded by masked SAS-type figures who represent what is left of authority. Told like this, the film perhaps sounds more accessible than it is. Most audiences, though, won't know what to make of it. The 'flashes' are too repetitive to grip the interest all the time and only towards the end does the film find some of the poetry it seems to seek. The poetry of the gutter maybe: but here the film is at its most challenging. The more hopeful images seem echoes from other fantasies that equally flitted back and forth across the thin line between success and failure.

Last of Mrs Cheyney, The ○
1937, US, 98 mins, b/w
Dir: Richard Boleslawski
Stars: Joan Crawford, William Powell
Rating: ★★

Joan Crawford stars in this second version of Frederick Lonsdale's play. Although a moderate box office success, it's a cut below the original film (which starred Norma Shearer). A fake British aristocrat, Joan roams the parties of high-society London with her eyes on the jewelled necks and wrists of her so-called friends. Oozing charm, she and her trusted aide William Powell worm their way into a country mansion for a weekend party where her grace and charm have everyone fooled. Co-star Robert Montgomery has an unsympathetic role as a lord, but the comedy is well-handled and Joan, who hadn't played for laughs much at the time, took to it with unexpected aplomb. The film's making was marred by director Richard Boleslawski's death, his job being taken over by George Fitzmaurice.

Last of Sheila, The ◑
1973, US, 123 mins, colour
Dir: Herbert Ross
Stars: Richard Benjamin, Dyan Cannon, James Coburn, James Mason, Raquel Welch
Rating: ★★★

As twisty thrillers go, this conundrum can show even *Sleuth* a thing or two – and it's certainly a sight less stagey. The clues are all there, as the Ellery Queen books used to say. All you have to do is to sort the significant from the mass of insignificant. Not that one minds being told about the clues one missed – but it's rather humiliating to be actually shown them

in flashback. So many things that one should have seen! The plot, written by Stephen Sondheim and actor Anthony Perkins, is as ingenious as any original cinematic work for years – and played to the hilt by a cast that also includes Joan Hackett, James Mason, Dyan Cannon and Richard Benjamin. Director Herbert Ross tends to explain things one too many times, but the sheer intricacy of it all is amazing. As a whodunnit, it leaves *Murder on the Orient Express* standing in the station.

Last of the Badmen ○
1957, US, 75 mins, colour
Dir: Paul Landres
Stars: George Montgomery, Keith Larsen
Rating: ★★

Unusually for a Western, this action drama adopts a semi-documentary approach as Pinkerton-style detective George Montgomery trails a particularly callous ring of outlaws that 'springs' convicts, then kills them for the price on their heads. Nothing new apart from that, though the bounding music of Paul Sawtell provides spirited accompaniment to the proceedings. The effects of Ellsworth Fredericks' excellent CinemaScope and colour camerawork will be rather lost on the small screen.

Last of the Buccaneers ○
1950, US, 79 mins, colour
Dir: Lew Landers
Stars: Paul Henreid, Jack Oakie, Karin Booth, Mary Anderson
Rating: ★★

Another spectacular (but, apart from Mary Anderson, stiffly performed) story about pirate and adventurer Jean Lafitte, later to be given the epic treatment in De Mille's *The Buccaneer*. He's played by Paul Henreid, the Austrian leading man who came to Britain in the late Thirties and featured in such films as *Goodbye Mr Chips!* (1939) as Paul von Hernreid. But he is best remembered for his roles in such Warner Brothers films as *Casablanca*, *Now Voyager* and *Deception* before getting lost in an armada of 'easterns' like this one.

Last of the Comanches ○
(aka: The Sabre and the Arrow)
1953, US, 84 mins, colour
Dir: Andre De Toth
Stars: Broderick Crawford, Barbara Hale, Lloyd Bridges
Rating: ★★★

Make a thousand double-bill Westerns, and you must come up with one gem. Thus runs an ancient Hollywood proverb, which is proved to the hilt by this moving, exciting film. Director Andre De Toth pulls every trick and Broderick Crawford's tough Cavalry sergeant leads a parade of performances that make the characters live.

Last of the Fast Guns ○
1958, US, 82 mins, colour
Dir: George Sherman
Stars: Jock Mahoney, Gilbert Roland, Linda Cristal, Lorne Greene
Rating: ★★

Veteran Western director George Sherman keeps the action going at a good clip in this story of a gunfighter searching south of the border for his employer's long-lost brother.

Last of the Finest, The
See: Blue Heat

Last of the Mohicans, The ○
1936, US, 91 mins, b/w
Dir: George B Seitz
Stars: Randolph Scott, Bruce Cabot, Henry Wilcoxon, Binnie Barnes, Heather Angel
Rating: ★★★

James Fenimore Cooper's classic novel of the French and Indian war was brilliantly brought to the screen in this vintage but action-filled film directed by a veteran of early silent serials, George B Seitz. Two of Britain's brightest gifts to Hollywood in the Thirties, Binnie Barnes and Heather Angel, play the sisters who undertake a long and dangerous journey through hostile country.

Last of the Mohicans, The ◑ Ⓥ
1992, US, 112 mins, colour
Dir: Michael Mann
Stars: Daniel Day Lewis, Madeleine Stowe, Jodhi May, Russell Means, Eric Schweig, Steven Waddington
Rating: ★★★

James Fenimore Cooper's frontier Western, unfilmed for many years, gets a modern retelling, red in tooth and claw. Some stirring action scenes are the heart of the film's appeal, but director Michael Mann holds some of his carefully-composed shots far too long, trying to infuse the tale with a resonance and importance it doesn't really have. Daniel Day Lewis is a sort of Irish-American Hawkeye, but all

L

virility; and the fights are splendidly paced and edited, even if Day Lewis and his Indian pals' idea of combat seems to be to run at their opponents from a distance. Like the negotiations with the Indians towards the end, this remains somewhat puzzling. There doesn't seem to be much of a game plan going on at the climax, for example, to rescue Jodhi May from the bad guys. Whatever happened to good old Indian stealth in ambush? In the supporting cast, Steven Waddington is well on target as the unpleasant English officer who becomes Hawkeye's rival for the love of Madeleine Stowe.

Last of the Redmen ○
(aka: Last of the Redskins)
1947, US, 77 mins, colour
Dir: George Sherman
Stars: Jon Hall, Evelyn Ankers, Michael O'Shea, Julie Bishop, Buster Crabbe
Rating: ★★

Also known as *Last of the Redskins*, this is in fact another version of James Fenimore Cooper's Western classic *The Last of the Mohicans*. Two of the stars were crack swimmers – Jon Hall was champion swimmer of Tahiti and Buster Crabbe was an Olympic ace. Virile, solid, if cut-budget version of the story, with the good action scenes you'd expect from director George Sherman.

Last of the Redskins
See: *Last of the Redmen*

Last of the Renegades ○
1964, West Germany, 93 mins, colour
Dir: Harald Reinl
Stars: Lex Barker, Pierre Brice, Anthony Steel, Karin Dor, Klaus Kinski, Mario Girotti (Terence Hill)
Rating: ★★

German-made Western about Karl May's famous characters Old Shatterhand and his Indian friend, Winnetou the Warrior. English actor Anthony Steel turns up as the villain of the piece, and there's a well-staged shoot-out finale, in the depths of a labyrinth of caves and the heat of the desert.

L.A. Story ○ ⓥ
1990, US, 97 mins, colour
Dir: Mick Jackson
Stars: Steve Martin, Victoria Tennant, Richard E Grant, Marilu Henner, Sarah Jessica Parker
Rating: ★★

Pretty much a time-passer by Steve Martin's standards, this is partly Steve's equivalent of a Woody Allen film about Manhattan, and partly a reflection of his romance with real-life wife Victoria Tennant. There's a spot of parrot-juggling and skating in the art gallery but not quite as many zany moments as you'd expect in this sort of Martin movie. He's a TV weatherman bored with his romance with LA hipster Marilu Henner. He goes off on a wild weekend with bounding shop assistant Sarah Jessica Parker, in spite of the fact that he's fallen wildly for seemingly unobtainable Tennant as an unlikely London *Times* correspondent. The path of true love is helped by a Los Angeles freeway sign, but this touch of lunacy isn't enough to save the film from needing the big finish it doesn't get. Guest shots from Rick Moranis and Chevy Chase are more or less gratuitous and the funny moments get fewer as the film goes on.

Last Picture Show, The ○ ⓥ
1971, US, 118 mins, colour
Dir: Peter Bognanovich
Stars: Jeff Bridges, Cybill Shepherd, Timothy Bottoms, Ben Johnson, Ellen Burstyn, Cloris Leachman, Randy Quaid
Rating: ★★★★

Seldom if ever was the atmosphere of desolation, decay and despair in a small American town that has had its day better caught than in this classic study of dust-blown Texas life in the 1950s. Not much happens, but the characters' lives intertwine and develop, the screenplay by Larry McMurtry (author of the original novel) and Peter Bogdanovich himself creating a field day for the ensemble cast. From four acting nominations, Oscars were won by Ben Johnson (unforgettable as fading Westerner Sam the Lion) and Cloris Leachman. A return to the same territory 20 years later in *Texasille* is best forgotten.

Last Remake of Beau Geste, The ○
1977, US, 85 mins, colour
Dir: Marty Feldman
Stars: Marty Feldman, Ann-Margret, Michael York, Peter Ustinov
Rating: ★

There are a few chuckles in this expensive-looking comedy, written and directed by, as well as starring Marty Feldman as Digby Geste, twin brother of Michael York's Beau! Most of the

best laughs come towards the beginning, many of them supplied by Spike Milligan as the Gestes' ancient retainer, a performance that may owe something to a study of that remarkable old actor Wilfrid Lawson's butler Peacock in *The Wrong Box*. A confrontation between Feldman and a mirage of Gary Cooper from the 1940 film almost comes off, Cooper providing an oasis of class in this comic desert.

Last Rites ●
1988, US, 99 mins, colour
Dir: Donald P Bellisario
Stars: Tom Berenger, Daphne Zuniga, Chick Vennera
Rating: ★★

Tom Berenger is sadly miscast as a confused priest in this steamy drama about the dilemma of being an Italian-American Catholic priest and son of a top Mafioso. Because of that fact, nothing else about the glossy production is very convincing. Daphne Zuniga, whose career at this time appeared to be on the ascendent, is an attractive femme fatale, but she delivers a highly suspect Spanish accent at times. It's the brainchild of Donald P Bellisario, a longtime TV writer and producer and co-creator of the *Magnum* detective series. And that's about the level of it, in fact.

Last Starfighter, The ○
1984, US, 100 mins, colour
Dir: Nick Castle
Stars: Lance Guest, Dan O'Herlihy, Robert Preston, Catherine Mary Stewart
Rating: ★★★

More star wars, eminently suitable for all ages. Adults can relax, while the action will get the kids cheering. Robert Preston is terrific in his last film as Centauri, the alien inventor of the galaxy-wide Starfighter game, who recruits Alex, earthling whizzkid at the game, to be a real starfighter, the last galactic hope against alien marauders. The action's pretty much cut to pattern, with the exception of the 'robot' Alex, left behind to fool his fellow-earthmen, who gets involved in adventures of his own.

Last Summer ●
1969, US, 97 mins, colour
Dir: Frank Perry
Stars: Barbara Hershey, Richard Thomas, Bruce Davison, Cathy Burns
Rating: ★★★

Very highly-rated film about the violence that lurks beneath the skins of three holidaying teenagers, and the plain, teeth-braced girl who gets frighteningly caught up in their ever-darkening little circle. Compellingly spontaneous performances from the quartet of young actors – Barbara Hershey later changed her name to Barbara Seagull after the seagull her character kills in the film – and a terrifying ending.

Last Sunset, The ☾
1961, US, 112 mins, colour
Dir: Robert Aldrich
Stars: Kirk Douglas, Rock Hudson, Dorothy Malone, Joseph Cotten
Rating: ★★★

Director Robert Aldrich, the man who made *Whatever Happened to Baby Jane?* and *The Mean Machine*, goes down on the range and comes up with a typically weird Western. Rock Hudson and Kirk Douglas, who killed his brother-in-law, play a cat-and-mouse game on a cattle drive. But it's Joseph Cotten who picks up the cheese as an alcoholic rancher.

Last Tango in Paris ● ⓥ
1972, France/Italy, 129 mins, colour
Dir: Bernardo Bertolucci
Stars: Marlon Brando, Maria Schneider
Rating: ★★★

Director Bernardo Bertolucci's story of a vigorous (and sometimes violent) physical relationship between a middle-aged man and a young girl is a dark tale indeed, filled with sexual menace and foreboding. Paul, a middle-aged American, and Jeanne meet while viewing an empty apartment in Paris. They make love and from then on meet each day in the apartment to do the same. He then returns to the seedy hotel in which his adulterous wife has committed suicide, while she goes off to meet her fiancé, a filmmaker who is making a film about her. Despite an agreement that they won't talk about themselves, not even revealing names, Jeanne declares her love for Paul, news he greets with cynical indifference. A powerful, mesmeric central performance by Marlon Brando holds the attention here, despite the fact that the film is gloomy and laden with Paul's confusion and despair. This pain and passion are painted in sombre colours by Bertolucci and the film's harsh and shocking ending is, on reflection, inevitable. Although there

are no bright or uplifting moments to lighten its darkness, this is still a grimly fascinating film.

Last Train from Gun Hill ○ ⓥ
1959, US, 98 mins, colour
Dir: John Sturges
Stars: Kirk Douglas, Anthony Quinn, Carolyn Jones, Earl Holliman, Brad Dexter
Rating: ★★★

Kirk Douglas and Anthony Quinn, reunited from *Lust for Life*, are reluctant adversaries in this fiery Western directed in steamroller style by John Sturges and blazingly shot in Technicolor by Charles B Lang. Brian Hutton, who plays one of the killers of Douglas' wife, later became a director, and you may also glimpse Ty Hardin in one of his earliest roles. The rousing climax, as Douglas fights to get a killer on the train of the title, is justly famous.

Last Tycoon, The ☾
1976, US, 120 mins, colour
Dir: Elia Kazan
Stars: Robert De Niro, Tony Curtis, Robert Mitchum, Jack Nicholson, Jeanne Moreau
Rating: ★

An amazing all-star cast provide support to Robert De Niro in a dreadfully protracted and dreary movie about Hollywood in the late Thirties. A few mock-Thirties film clips which one hopes are intentionally funny provide much-needed light relief from the gloomy central tale of a 'boy wonder' producer (modelled on Irving Thalberg) and his *amour fou* for some boring girl who happens to look like his late wife. Ingrid Boulting is a stunning looker as the girl, but so dire a performer, in this role at least, as to make no sense at all of Harold Pinter's enigmatic dialogue. Much more interesting is Theresa Russell, here in her first film role but clearly bound for stardom. De Niro delivers a rare lacklustre performance, but at least you can keep awake by spotting the stars here: Robert Mitchum, Dana Andrews, Jack Nicholson, Anjelica Huston, Tony Curtis, Donald Pleasance, Jeanne Moreau, Peter Strauss, Ray Milland and John Carradine among them. What a waste! You can only think studio boss Mitchum is describing this film at the studio preview when he says it 'needs about 20 minutes out of it. Otherwise, it just lies there and goes to sleep.'

Last Unicorn, The ☉
1982, US, 85 mins, colour
Dir: Jules Bass
Stars: Voice stars: Angela Lansbury, Alan Arkin, Jeff Bridges, Mia Farrow
Rating: ★★★

A classy animated film based on the novel by Peter S Beagle about a unicorn's battle to save her kinfolk from an evil king. The pace is sprightly and animation highly colourful. The top-notch voice cast is headed by Angela Lansbury, Alan Arkin, Jeff Bridges and Mia Farrow.

Last Voyage, The ○
1960, US, 91 mins, colour
Dir: Andrew L Stone
Stars: Robert Stack, Dorothy Malone, George Sanders, Edmond O'Brien
Rating: ★★

One of the earliest examples of a true disaster movie, with the enterprising production team, Andrew L Stone and his then-wife Virginia, buying a real liner, the *Ile de France*, that was headed for the breaker's yard, and then sending it to the bottom. Everything in the film is geared to suspense, and quite a lot of it works.

Last Wagon, The ○
1956, US, 99 mins, colour
Dir: Delmer Daves
Stars: Richard Widmark, Felicia Farr, Susan Kohner, Tommy Rettig
Rating: ★★★

A red-blooded Western about the survivors of an Apache attack, and how they attempt to escape to freedom through rugged Indian territory. Richard Widmark is excellent as Commanche Todd, a primitive frontiersman whom the others believe to be a murderer but are forced to accept as leader. Directed by Delmer Daves in the middle of his best period – all Westerns – which included *Jubal* and *3.10 to Yuma*.

Last Wave, The ☾
1978, Australia, 106 mins, colour
Dir: Peter Weir
Stars: Richard Chamberlain, Olivia Hamnett, David Gulpilil
Rating: ★★★

A silly but stylish chiller by Australian director Peter Weir, who made *Picnic at Hanging Rock* and, more recently, *Witness*. Weir's confident direction of the bizarre material makes this a film to ponder upon. Richard Chamberlin is pretty good as the bemused lawyer, enmeshed in Aborigine tribal lore

L

which seems to be connected with a series of 'natural' disasters, and who finds the chilly hand of fate leading him and his family in a direction he'd rather not go.

Late Edwina Black, The ○
(aka: Obsessed)
1951, UK, 78 mins, b/w
Dir: Maurice Elvey
Stars: Geraldine Fitzgerald, David Farrar, Roland Culver
Rating: ★★

Geraldine Fitzgerald and Roland Culver, just back from stays in Hollywood, co-star with David Farrar, who was just about to go there, in a film version of the classic stage play. Jean Cadell steals the film from all three of them, as the housekeeper whose love for the late Edwina amounted to an obsession. Miss Cadell, a sharp-featured, soft-voiced Scottish character actress, was well used to stealing scenes in the cinema, having made her film debut during the very early days of the British cinema, as far back as 1912.

Late for Dinner ○ ⓥ
1991, US, 93 mins, colour
Dir: W D Richter
Stars: Brian Wimmer, Peter Berg, Marcia Gay Harden, Colleen Flynn, Kyle Secor, Peter Gallagher
Rating: ★★★

An unusual idea that shouldn't come off but nearly does. Two Texans, on the run after one has shot a man in self-defence, are cryogenically frozen, waking up unchanged 29 years later. The surprise – and pleasure – is that developments in the story are played for charm rather than farce or horror. The leader (Brian Wimmer) just wants his glamorous wife back, hardly thinking about her being over 50. His slow-witted brother-in-law (Peter Berg) is simply baffled by 1991. 'There's money in that wall, Willie,' he gasps as they pass a bank. The real bouquet of the film, though, goes to Marcia Gay Harden, as the wife who manages to look both 23 and 32 without apparent use of excessive makeup. Director W D Richter, despite the odd use of some comic names – the scientist who freezes them is called Doc Chilblains – treats this fragile fantasy with the gentility it deserves. Occasionally, the film strains to avoid falling off the fine line between conviction and foolishness. But Wimmer, Berg, Harden and

Colleen Flynn (as Willie's daughter) are all good and their sincerity sees it through.

Late George Apley, The ○
1947, US, 98 mins, b/w
Dir: Joseph L Mankiewicz
Stars: Ronald Colman, Peggy Cummins
Rating: ★★★

One of those light, frothy portrayals of American family life (this one set in 1912) at which Hollywood proved so expert in the Forties. John P Marquand's satirical play about a stuffy Bostonian family had much of its sting removed in this Hollywoodised version, although it's enjoyable on its own merits. Percy Waram steals the show (as he had done on stage) as Apley's level-headed and cynical brother-in-law.

Laughing Policeman, The ●
(aka: An Investigation of Murder)
1973, US, 111 mins, colour
Dir: Stuart Rosenberg
Stars: Walter Matthau, Bruce Dern, Lou Gossett, Anthony Zerbe
Rating: ★★

Why does a man massacre a bus full of people? What connection does it have with the two-year-old murder of a kinky prostitute? Why was a policeman on the bus? Where does the stripper with the amazing figure fit in? Can Walter Matthau and Bruce Dern find the killer before the chief (Anthony Zerbe) takes them off the case? This laughing policeman is no joke, but at least the Matthau-Dern combination saves it from being a routine blood-soaked urban thriller. You'll also like Lou Gossett as a hard black cop who tells a suspect, 'Whatever you're reaching for had better be a sandwich 'cos you're gonna have to eat it', and a gay bar called The Frolic Room.

Laughterhouse
See: Singleton's Pluck

Laughter in Paradise ○
1951, UK, 93 mins, b/w
Dir: Mario Zampi
Stars: Alastair Sim, Joyce Grenfell, Hugh Griffith, Fay Compton
Rating: ★★★

A reminder that George Cole was already making us laugh more than 40 years ago. He and Alastair Sim are the best things in this surefire British comedy about four people who have to do things totally out of character in

order to collect a fortune from the will of an eccentric relative. Director Mario Zampi's deft execution of this comedy of embarrassments doesn't leave many dull moments. But he has major help from Sim, richly larger than life as a penny-dreadful novelist who must become a petty thief, Cole as a meek cashier who must pretend to hold up his own bank and Joyce Grenfell as a gurglingly schoolgirlish ATS officer. Audrey Hepburn sparkles briefly as a cigarette girl in one of her earliest film appearances. The top moneymaking British film of its year.

Laura ○ ⓥ
1944, US, 88 mins, b/w
Dir: Otto Preminger
Stars: Dana Andrews, Gene Tierney, Clifton Webb, Vincent Price
Rating: ★★★

Superb dark thriller which made Otto Preminger's name as a director. It also clinched a sensational comeback for silent-screen actor Clifton Webb as the caustic radio star in love with the murdered Laura (Gene Tierney), and deservedly won an Academy Award for cameraman Joseph La Shelle, whose moody, ominously-shadowed photography dominates the film.

Laurel and Hardy's Laughing Twenties ⊙ ⓥ
1965, US, 90 mins, b/w
Dir: various
Stars: Stan Laurel, Oliver Hardy
Rating: ★★★★

One of the funniest films that is ever likely to come your way. Here are Stan Laurel and Oliver Hardy, wearing their angelic expressions, like small boys caught with catapults behind their backs. See them as musicians in 'You're Darn Tootin'', waiters in 'From Soup to Nuts' and housebuilders in 'The Finishing Touch'.

Lavender Hill Mob, The ⊙ ⓥ
1951, UK, 78 mins, b/w
Dir: Charles Crichton
Stars: Alec Guinness, Stanley Holloway, Sidney James, Alfie Bass
Rating: ★★★★

Probably the zenith of the Ealing Studios comedies. Although almost equalled by *The Ladykillers* a few years afterwards, *The Lavender Hill Mob* has certainly never been surpassed for sheer inventive merriment. Alec Guinness and Stanley Holloway revel in the witty script, bringing a feather-light comedy touch to the roles of the bank employee and his friend who plot a million-pound bullion robbery from their seedy boarding house. Even the small roles are immaculately played: one especially remembers Meredith Edwards (27th on the cast list!) as a harassed Welsh policeman. And there's a real bonus for star-spotters: the appearance of Audrey Hepburn (in her first year in British films) as a Brazilian señorita.

Law and Disorder ⊙ ⓥ
1958, UK, 76 mins, b/w
Dir: Charles Crichton
Stars: Michael Redgrave, Robert Morley, Elizabeth Sellars
Rating: ★★★

It's unusual to find Michael Redgrave in a comedy this broad, but the script – by 'Tibby' Clarke, Patrick Campbell and Vivienne Knight – ensures that there's a true Ealing flavour to this story of a confidence trickster who just can't stay out of trouble. Joan Hickson is a scream as the con-man's card-sharping sister.

Law and Order ○
1953, US, 80 mins, colour
Dir: Nathan Juran
Stars: Ronald Reagan, Dorothy Malone, Preston Foster
Rating: ★★

A rather free adaptation of *My Darling Clementine* (in which the real-life brothers Earp were the heroes), this vigorous Western has good performances from Ronald Reagan and Preston Foster who play the hero and the villain respectively. Ruth Hampton, the stunning one-time Miss Universe, plays a rare film role as the villain's stepdaughter. And Dennis 'McCloud' Weaver is a bad guy too.

Law and the Lady, The ○
1951, US, 104 mins, b/w
Dir: Edwin H Knopf
Stars: Greer Garson, Michael Wilding, Michael Wilding, Fernando Lamas
Rating: ★★

This comedy about two elegant tricksters (smoothly played by Greer Garson and Michael Wilding) who rob the rich to feed themselves is a remake of *The Last of Mrs Cheyney*. Marjorie Main scores as a garrulous woman.

Lawless Street, A ○
1955, US, 78 mins, colour
Dir: Joseph H Lewis
Stars: Randolph Scott, Angela Lansbury, Warner Anderson
Rating: ★★

This Randolph Scott Western is another powerful drama from the hands of Joseph H Lewis, who directed *7th Cavalry* and *Gun Crazy*. It fits in well with Scott's Fifties gallery of men with things they must prove and things they must do. This time, he's a town marshal whose wife leaves him because he refuses to quit the job when an influx of dangerous outlaws makes his town a grim place to live in. Badly shot up by hired killers, the marshal can't throw away his principles even if it means his death. Better value than many bigger films, with biting performances from Scott, Angela Lansbury, Warner Anderson, Wallace Ford, Jean Parker and James Bell.

Lawman ●
1970, US, 99 mins, colour
Dir: Michael Winner
Stars: Burt Lancaster, Robert Ryan, Lee J Cobb, Sheree North, Robert Duvall
Rating: ★★

Michael Winner's first American picture saw him taking Horace Greeley's advice 'Go West, young Man' and heading for New Mexico to make this tough and violent Western, which he directed with his usual vigour and rather too many zooms. A good cast work well with the British director, among them Burt Lancaster, Robert Ryan, Lee J Cobb (looking somewhat different without his usual toupee), Sheree North and one-time Bond villain Dr No, Joseph Wiseman.

Lawnmower Man, The ● ⓥ
1992, US, 105 mins, colour
Dir: Brett Leonard
Stars: Jeff Fahey, Pierce Brosnan, Jenny Wright, Geoffrey Lewis, Austin O'Brien, Jeremy Slate
Rating: ★★

Stunning computer-based graphic effects ('virtual reality') make you gasp while lines in the script make you giggle: pretty much a formula horror film then, but above par for a Stephen King adaptation. Men are dabbling once more in things Best Left Alone in a world where 'I have to run some tests' can have the most sinister implications. 'Goddam it Caroline,' snarls Pierce Brosnan at the start. 'Never unplug a programme while

I'm engaged.' He's just ratty 'cos the chimp at the lab has gone berserk and bumped off a couple of scientists. Brosnan blames the mind-blowing computer programmes he's subjected the chimp to: and he's right. But that doesn't stop him plucking a retarded man (Jeff Fahey) from lawnmowing duties to provide him with his first human subject. Unfortunately, the men behind the finance for the experiments ups the stakes, taking Fahey fairly rapidly into the ranks of Superbrains. All pretty ludicrous, with interest kept alive by state-of-the-art effects rather than the actors.

Law of the Lawless ○
1963, US, 88 mins, colour
Dir: William Claxton
Stars: Dale Robertson, Yvonne De Carlo, William Bendix, Bruce Cabot, Barton MacLane
Rating: ★★★

The first of a series of star Westerns made on tight budgets by producer A C Lyles at Paramount in the Sixties. They featured many well-known Hollywood names from the Fifties who had seemed to be fading from the scene with the removal of the studio double-feature schedules. In its quiet, occasionally actionful way, this story of a frontier judge (Dale Robertson) was one of the best films Lyles produced.

Lawrence of Arabia ○ ⓥ
1962, UK, 221 mins, colour
Dir: David Lean
Stars: Peter O'Toole, Alec Guinness, Anthony Quinn, Jack Hawkins, Omar Sharif, Anthony Quayle
Rating: ★★★★

David Lean's epic combination of physical deeds and mental agony. Peter O'Toole shot to first-rank stardom with his performance as T E Lawrence, the mystic, inscrutable young Army officer who started off by loving the desert and its way of life, and ended, two action-filled years later, half-demented and hating every grain of sand. O'Toole's strange, brooding portrait of Lawrence marked him out as an actor of the first magnitude. But there is also Anthony Quinn's very intelligently played Arab chief; I S Johar's marvellously human Gasim; Donald Wolfit's one-scene triumph as an army officer; and Alec Guinness' Feisal, almost as indefinable a character as Lawrence himself. Early scenes of the desert are especially

L

moving, as is Lawrence's relationship with a Bedouin who is shortly to be killed by a tribal chief.

Lawyer, The ●
1968, US, 117 mins, colour
Dir: Sidney J Furie
Stars: Barry Newman, Diana Muldaur, Robert Colbert, Kathleen Crowley
Rating: ★★★

Barry Newman gives a high-pressure performance as the young lawyer who antagonises the legal profession and, it seems, an entire town, in the course of defending an uncooperative client. Director Sidney J Furie's restless cameras bob and weave their way through a mass of intrigue in this diverting thriller. Newman later revived his character to form the basis for his successful *Petrocelli* series on TV.

Laxdale Hall ⊙
1953, UK, 77 mins, b/w
Dir: John Eldridge
Stars: Raymond Huntley, Ronald Squire, Kathleen Ryan, Sebastian Shaw
Rating: ★★

Whimsical, refreshing comedy, much along the lines of *Whisky Galore!*. Ronald Squire is in fine blustering form as the leader of the rebel Hebridean islanders who refuse to pay their road fund licences until a new road and pier are provided by officialdom.

League of Gentlemen, The ○
1959, UK, 114 mins, b/w
Dir: Basil Dearden
Stars: Jack Hawkins, Nigel Patrick, Richard Attenborough, Roger Livesey, Bryan Forbes, Kieron Moore
Rating: ★★★

No better tribute to the acting style of British bulldog Jack Hawkins could be screened than this stylish crime film which paces its laughs and thrills in equal proportions. This was one of Bryan Forbes' first big film breakthroughs as a writer. He also plays one of the 'gentlemen' who plan a well-devised raid on an army camp. Forbes' real-life wife, Nanette Newman, has a role as well; while the star line-up is impressively completed by Richard Attenborough, Nigel Patrick, Kieron Moore, Robert Coote, Roger Livesey, Patrick Wymark and Gerald Harper.

League of Their Own, A ○ Ⓥ
1992, US, 124 mins, colour
Dir: Penny Marshall
Stars: Geena Davis, Lori Petty, Madonna, Tom Hanks, Megan Cavanagh, Jon Lovitz
Rating: ★★★

Tom Hanks buries his clean-cut image to be suitably disgusting as the baccy-spitting, hard-drinking, unshaven ex-pro coach of one of the first all-girl baseball teams in this often entertaining comedy. The girls got their chance in 1943 because of the lack of wartime manpower and, although at first the public stayed away in droves, the women's game inevitably threw up front-page stars of its own. Tall Geena Davis is the team's ace catcher, Lori Singer as her kid sister is the pitcher, stand-up comedienne Megan Cavanagh the grim-looking star hitter and Madonna, of course, the team sex-bomb. Though the film seems forced and artificial in its earlier scenes, especially in the performance of Jon Lovitz, it gradually wins you over in the familiar progression of its story to the final game. There are too many characters here for the writers to sketch them in with any but the broadest lines. But, though the film drifts on too long in its sentimental ending, there are enough poignant and funny moments – especially in the final come-uppance of the too-bad-to-be-true fat kid of one of the players – to make this league a winner on points.

Leap of Faith ○ Ⓥ
1992, US, 107 mins, colour
Dir: Richard Pearce
Stars: Steve Martin, Debra Winger, Liam Neeson, Lolita Davidovich, Lukas Haas, Meat Loaf
Rating: ★★★★

It's not often that a film hits every nail on the head but this is one. Steve Martin stars in his best non-comedy role to this time as Jonas Nightengale, con-man turned fake faith healer and razzmatazz preacher. A story of 'faith, hope and fraud', the film centres on Nightengale's visit to Rustwater, Kansas, where the glitz of his show – clairvoyancy and fake miracles are laid on by his faithful team, headed by master technician Debra Winger, who feeds him information through an earpiece, almost rivals a Las Vegas nightclub. Winger is wooed by the sheriff (Liam Neeson), who is none-

theless determined to expose Martin as a ne'er-do-well. But some strange things are destined to happen in Rustwater before Jonas' 'circus' leaves town. Martin, a mass of nervous energy, whose eyes are always open to the main chance, is right on the money as Jonas, never putting a strutting foot wrong, even when cavorting on the catwalk of Christ. He dominates even such good actors as Winger and Neeson in this totally diverting and fizzingly paced light-hearted version of *Elmer Gantry*.

Lease of Life ○
1954, UK, 94 mins, b/w
Dir: Charles Frend
Stars: Robert Donat, Kay Walsh, Denholm Elliott, Adrienne Corri
Rating: ★★

Sincere if stilted melodrama with a sensitive performance by Robert Donat as the vicar with a year to live. In his impromptu sermon to a congregation of schoolboys, the performance of this remarkable actor, whose career was blighted by chronic asthma, gleams with emotion, excitement and truth.

Leather Boys, The ○ Ⓥ
1964, UK, 108 mins, b/w
Dir: Sidney J Furie
Stars: Rita Tushingham, Colin Campbell, Dudley Sutton
Rating: ★★★

Sensitive acting from Colin Campbell as a ton-up boy who marries young and regrets it. Rita Tushingham has a rare unsympathetic role as a bride who all too soon yearns for the bright lights – motorcycle headlamps, that is.

Leather Saint, The ○
1956, US, 86 mins, b/w
Dir: Alvin Ganzer
Stars: John Derek, Paul Douglas, Jody Lawrence, Cesar Romero
Rating: ★★★

Hollywood boxing films are almost always good value for money. And this solid story about a priest with a knock-out punch is no exception. John Derek is the KO curate and Paul Douglas puts in some good work as his adviser. Appearing as the curate's harassed superior is Ernest Truex, a diminutive character comedian popular on the British stage in the Twenties and Thirties, notably in *The Five O'Clock Girl*.

Leaving Normal ◐ ⓥ
1992, US, 110 mins, colour
Dir: Edward Zwick
Stars: Christine Lahti, Meg Tilly, Lenny Van Dohlen, Maury Chaykin, James Gammon
Rating: ★★★

Although its collection of adventures on the road don't give it the impetus of the contemporary *Thelma & Louise*, this is still a captivating female buddy road movie, starring Meg Tilly in one of her most beguiling turns as the sweet, innocent Marianne, running away from her unpleasant husband. She's partnered by Christine Lahti in an untypical role, subduing her natural warmth to play the tough, cynical, dislikeable Darly, fleeing from all of her unhappy past. How these two sad souls leave Normal, Wyoming, and become pals on the road as they try to find their own paths to joy forms a bittersweet tale that's well-acted, well-observed, well-directed (by Edward Zwick, who made the very different *Glory*) and certainly well worth watching.

Left Hand of God, The ○
1955, US, 87 mins, colour
Dir: Edward Dmytryk
Stars: Humphrey Bogart, Gene Tierney, Lee J Cobb, Agnes Moorehead, E G Marshall
Rating: ★★

Humphrey Bogart's second to last film provides him with the unusual role of an adventurer trying to escape, dressed as a priest, from the vengeance of a war lord – a role in which Lee J Cobb proves surprisingly effective. The hand of director Edward Dmytryk tends to weigh rather heavily on the proceedings, but Bogart sees it through, and Gene Tierney is as gorgeous as ever as the girl who believes she is falling in love with someone she can't marry.

Left, Right and Centre ○
1959, UK, 105 mins, b/w
Dir: Sidney Gilliat
Stars: Ian Carmichael, Patricia Bredin, Alastair Sim
Rating: ★★★

Frank Launder and Sidney Gilliat gleefully send up both British politics and the effect that television has on them in those dear distant days three decades ago when the swingometer wasn't even an electronic dot on the TV screen. Ian Carmichael and Alastair Sim combine to steal the show, while the then TV luminaries Gilbert Harding, Eamon Andrews and Josephine Douglas are on hand to add verisimilitude. Elsewhere on the hustings, there's a gallery of familiar faces that includes Richard Wattis, Eric Barker, Jack Hedley, Gordon Harker and George Benson.

Legacy, The ●
1978, UK, 100 mins, colour
Dir: Richard Marquand
Stars: Katharine Ross, Sam Elliott, John Standing, Roger Daltrey
Rating: ★

Up at the old mansion they're dying off like flies. Bloodcurdling shrieks in the middle of the night and the like. And they do say the house is full of cats . . . This grisly story has more loose ends than poor Hildegarde Neil seems to have pints of blood. But if your tastes run to Hammer Horror meeting *Carrie* and *Ten Little Niggers*, it could be right up your *Nightmare Alley*.

Legal Eagles ◐ ⓥ
1986, US, 116 mins, colour
Dir: Ivan Reitman
Stars: Robert Redford, Debra Winger, Daryl Hannah, Brian Dennehy, Terence Stamp
Rating: ★★★

This legal caper thriller is a bit like a highly superior TV movie. Robert Redford's at the centre of it, but has to concede the acting honours to Debra Winger. She is outstanding as a gutsy lawyer determined to root out the truth about the 18-year-old blaze that killed the painter father of the tall blonde (Daryl Hannah) currently on a murder charge. Good entertainment, not too demanding, directed with polish by Ivan Reitman of *Ghost Busters* fame. Although a shade light on credibility, the story's so craftily contrived around a few set-pieces that a lot of it works.

Legend ○ ⓥ
1985, US, 94 mins, colour
Dir: Ridley Scott
Stars: Tom Cruise, Mia Sara, Tim Curry
Rating: ★★

This is the film that Tom Cruise perhaps wishes he hadn't made. It took a whole year of his life, and he was labelled an insipid hero by critics. A fairy tale on a grand scale, the film is everything we have come to expect from Ridley Scott (*Alien, Thelma & Louise*), with stunning visuals, epic sets and a battle between good and evil. However, its major problems are with the script, where it borrows heavily from *Jack and the Beanstalk*, *A Midsummer Night's Dream* and *Peter Pan*, but has little wit or wisdom of its own. Still, Tim Curry is the most memorable Devil for decades.

Legend of Billie Jean, The ◐
1985, 95 mins, colour
Dir: Matthew Robbins
Stars: Helen Slater, Christian Slater, Peter Coyote
Rating: ★★

Helen Slater was unlucky with this follow-up to her starring debut in *Supergirl*. It wasn't as successful as it deserved to be, and co-star Christian Slater (no relation) not the major star he was soon to become. Both Slaters are good in a story of teens on the run from the law, but any message gets lost in the film's top-dressing and the adults, although played by good actors – Peter Coyote, Richard Bradford, Dean Stockwell – emerge as caricatures rather than characters.

Legend of the Lost ○
1957, US, 107 mins, colour
Dir: Henry Hathaway
Stars: John Wayne, Sophia Loren, Rossano Brazzi
Rating: ★★

Timbuktu is the background for this action yarn about the search for a lost city in the desert and a fabulous treasure. Made by that most adept director of adventure films, Henry Hathaway, who produced it as well, and photographed by Jack Cardiff. John Wayne swaps his horse for a camel, but otherwise remains very much the same Big John (complete with stetson) as a desert adventurer with the unlikely name of Joe January. There's a very exciting last reel as the characters battle for the treasure, and their lives, in a sandstorm.

Le Mans ○
1971, US, 108 mins, colour
Dir: Lee H Katzin
Stars: Steve McQueen
Rating: ★★

This is probably the most realistic film about motor racing ever made and also the most single-minded. Whereas most other racing films have had a sub-plot strong enough to keep the attention of those not interested in racing cars, the one here seems an afterthought. Race fans will find it an

L

irritating gap in the action and it doesn't have enough meat for anyone else. Steve McQueen is Delaney, a driver on the Porsche team determined to win the Le Mans 24-hour endurance race and beat his main rival, Ferrari driver Erich Stahler. He also forms a hesitant relationship with Lisa, widow of a driver killed during the previous year's race. The race scenes (of which there are many) are exciting, noisy and atmospheric – you really do get the feeling you are there. McQueen is pretty low-key, but armed with the knowledge that he did all his own driving, it's easy to figure where his heart was on this one. Advice for race fans: turn the sound up as loud as possible and just listen to those engines!

Lemon Drop Kid, The ○
1951, US, 91 mins, b/w
Dir: Sidney Lanfield
Stars: Bob Hope, Marilyn Maxwell, Lloyd Nolan, Jane Darwell
Rating: ★★★

Bob Hope works overtime at getting the gags in this racing comedy about a racetrack bookie, 'The Lemon Drop Kid', who gives a gangster a sure bet that loses. As the bad guys try to get the money back – or deliver Hope's head on a plate – the jokes come thick and fast. Based on a Damon Runyon and Edmund Beloin story, it has colourful characters with equally colourful names, such as Sam the Surgeon, No Thumbs Charlie and Gloomy Willie. Under Sidney Lanfield's zippy direction, it's anything but gloomy. Songs featured include 'Silver Bells', 'It Doesn't Cost a Dime to Dream' and 'They Obviously Want Me to Sing'.

Lemon Sisters, The ◑
1989, US, 93 mins, colour
Dir: Joyce Chopra
Stars: Diane Keaton, Carol Kane, Kathryn Grody, Elliott Gould
Rating: ★★

Although it's decidedly quirky and has some purple patches, this rather wan comedy (about three friends who formed a singing group that's breaking up as the movie starts), which is also occasionally irritating and endearing in turn, is unlikely to make you laugh a lot. The script is very sub-*Beaches* and the one really funny scene comes when Keaton's cats fight to eat her dinner while she's trying to hold a conversation. The men, Gould, Ruben Blades and Aidan Quinn, give

selfless, almost faceless support. And the bleakness of the Atlantic City coastline is flawlessly captured. Ultimately, though, this is a movie that promises much and never quite delivers. The actresses do their own singing, though the plot demands, unfortunately, that they don't do it very well.

Lenny ● Ⓥ
1974, US, 111 mins, b/w
Dir: Bob Fosse
Stars: Dustin Hoffman, Valerie Perrine, Jan Miner
Rating: ★★★

This close-up of the 'dirty' American night-club comedian Lenny Bruce is a hard-hitting film, but also one that proves difficult to watch. And too brief a glimpse is given of Lenny (edgily played by Dustin Hoffman) at his abrasive best on stage, giving the impression that, as a comedian, he was somewhat unfunny. Hoffman and the exquisite Valerie Perrine try their hardest as Lenny and his junkie-stripper wife: she is particularly heart-rending and shows, here at least, an impressive naturalistic acting style. Perhaps Lenny's environment, which gave birth to his humour, also did for him in the end. The thought is sad and depressing, rather like the film. Nominated for all four major Oscars (actor, actress, film, and director), it won none in the event.

Leon the Pig Farmer ◑ Ⓥ
1992, UK, 104 mins, colour
Dir: Vadim Jean, Gary Sinyor
Stars: Mark Frankel, Janet Suzman, Brian Glover, Connie Booth, Maryam D'Abo, Gina Bellman
Rating: ★★

This home-grown comedy about Leon (Mark Frankel), a Jewish boy who discovers he is really the son of a Yorkshire pig farmer, is more or less a one-joke film. But the joke is sustained to a degree both by its offbeat characters and by the amusing performances of Connie Booth and Brian Glover as Leon's Yorkshire parents, taking down the pigs' heads that adorn their walls and adopting Jewish mannerisms to make Leon feel at home. Despite Frankel's rather one-note and permanently bemused portrayal of the title character, this is a charmingly offensive little comic number and certainly an original.

Leopard, The ○
1963, Italy, 205 mins, colour
Dir: Luchino Visconti
Stars: Burt Lancaster, Alain Delon, Claudia Cardinale
Rating: ★★★

Historical film of great beauty, directed with care and superb understanding of the period and its people by Luchino Visconti. The period is 1860 in Sicily, the time of the revolt of Garibaldi's redshirts – which gives rise to spurts of action – and dynasties of noblemen dying out. In one superb scene, Visconti pans over one princely family sitting in church. Their days are numbered and they know it. Sitting in their pew, they already look enshrouded with dust. Avoid the shortened Hollywood version if possible.

Les Girls ○ Ⓥ
1957, US, 110 mins, colour
Dir: George Cukor
Stars: Gene Kelly, Mitzi Gaynor, Kay Kendall, Taina Elg
Rating: ★★★

With a starry cast headed by Gene Kelly, Mitzi Gaynor and Kay Kendall, songs by Cole Porter and direction by George Cukor, this colourful musical had all the winning ingredients. If it doesn't quite live up to *Singin' in the Rain* or *An American in Paris*, it's still a delightful piece of escapism. Kendall, a former dancer, ends up in court after publishing her memoirs about her days with Barry Nichols and Les Girls (herself, Kelly, Gaynor and Taina Elg). All the musical interludes are in flashback as each member of the troupe recalls their days in showbiz. Despite its delights, the film didn't do terribly well at the box office. Kay Kendall made a big impact in this, her first Hollywood film. Tragically, she was unable to capitalise on it, as she died of leukemia two years after it was made.

Les Miserables ○
1935, US, 109 mins, b/w
Dir: Richard Boleslawski
Stars: Fredric March, Charles Laughton, Cedric Hardwicke,
Rating: ★★★

A typical Hollywood historical classic, made with meticulous attention to detail, and with commanding leading performances from Fredric March as the hounded Valjean and Charles Laughton as the relentless Javert. Fine direction by Richard Boleslawski, who died two years later at only 48, ensures that not a second of the near two-hour actual running time is wasted.

Les Miserables ○
1952, US, 106 mins, b/w
Dir: Lewis Milestone
Stars: Michael Rennie, Robert Newton, Edmund Gwenn, Debra Paget
Rating: ★★

Middling rendition with a star-studded cast doing little more than going through the motions. Would-be poignant scenes are emotionally unimpressive, while the focus of the story is shifted too often from the plight of Jean Valjean (Michael Rennie) to the revolutionary ideas of student Cameron Mitchell. Newton for once chooses (wrongly) not to give a full-blooded performance as the obsessed Javert. But atmosphere, production values and photography (by Joseph La Shelle) are all top-notch. A bit of a trudge.

Less Than Zero ● ⊙
1987, US, 98 mins, colour
Dir: Marek Kanievska
Stars: Andrew McCarthy, Jami Gertz, Robert Downey Jr, James Spader, Tony Bill, Nicholas Pryor
Rating: ★★

This drugs movie is well-meaning and, in parts, well-performed, but its one-note march to death makes it a bit of a drag to watch. 'Have you seen Julian?' is both its theme and its most often used line, as nice young college student Andrew McCarthy tries to help junkie ex-schoolfriend Robert Downey Jr, who stole the girlfriend (Jami Gertz) who finds getting back together with McCarthy easier than giving up cocaine. Downey himself is well and truly in the clutches of the local pusher (James Spader, whose oily crocodile is the best thing he does) to the tune of $50,000 and soon reduced to becoming a rent boy to stay even on the debt. A sad tale and one told without too much spark. McCarthy is overly mannered as the hero, Gertz offers the best display of cleavage since Raquel Welch quit the screen and Downey, acting them both out of sight, is effectively pathetic and drug-ridden as the elusive Julian.

Let 'Em Have It ○
1935, US, 90m mins, b/w
Dir: Sam Wood

Stars: Richard Arlen, Virginia Bruce, Bruce Cabot
Rating: ★★★

The title of this vintage gangster movie was too strong for its first issue outside America and it was changed to *False Faces*. Some of the scenes are strong stuff, too, and very effective, particularly the famous sequences in which mobster Bruce Cabot 'silences' the surgeon who has changed his face by plastic surgery, only to find, on removing the bandages, that the man has carved the gangster's own initials on his 'new' face. Good supporting cast includes Virginia Bruce, Alice Brady, Eric Linden and Joyce Compton.

Let George Do It ○
1940, UK, 82 mins, b/w
Dir: Marcel Varnel
Stars: George Formby, Phyllis Calvert
Rating: ★★★

A wartime Formby comedy, with our ukulele-toting hero getting mixed up with naval spies. There's still time for a ditty or two in George's own inimitable style, including 'Mr Wu's a Window-Cleaner Now'. Bernard Lee, as a character called Slim, and Garry Marsh, as the villainous Mendez, provide poker-faced support. The fun and games were directed by French-born Marcel Varnel, the director who made countless comedy films in the Thirties and Forties (including *Oh! Mr Porter*), working with Formby, Arthur Askey, Will Hay, The Crazy Gang and others.

Lethal Weapon ● ⊙
1987, US, 110 mins, colour
Dir: Richard Donner
Stars: Mel Gibson, Danny Glover, Gary Busey, Mitchell Ryan
Rating: ★★★

Mel Gibson was never more lethal at the world's box-offices than in this typical Hollywood vigilante cop thriller with crackling dialogue, a protracted, exciting shoot-out climax, a few boring patches to pad it out and as many illogicalities in the plot as a James Bond film. He's a crack-shot, loner cop still broodingly suicidal after the death of his wife in a road accident. Gibson's John Wayne-style American accent seems appropriate for the kind of shoot-out film that has these days replaced the Western while retaining many of its key elements. Danny Glover also does quite well as the nearing-retirement cop who un-

willingly takes Mad Mel as his partner, and Gary Busey, a chameleon actor one can only recognise by his teeth, is a solid albino villain.

Lethal Weapon 2 ● ⊙
1989, US, 110 mins, colour
Dir: Richard Donner
Stars: Mel Gibson, Danny Glover, Joe Pesci, Joss Ackland, Patsy Kensit
Rating: ★★★

An all-action sequel to the blockbuster original, with Mel Gibson and Glover back as the unlikely partners-against-crime. This time they tangle with some evil South Africans running drugs under the shelter of diplomatic immunity. Thank goodness Mel goes berserk and flashes his smile at times: it adds a human element to the James Bond style thrills, staged in expert, polished fashion by director Donner, with more explosions than a gung-ho war film. Patsy Kensit is along to prove that all South Africans aren't bad, in what is marginally the best of the three *Lethal Weapon* movies to date.

Lethal Weapon 3 ● ⊙
1992, US, 118 mins, colour
Dir: Richard Donner
Stars: Mel Gibson, Danny Glover, Joe Pesci, Rene Russo, Stuart Wilson
Rating: ★★

This long-serving police vehicle has distinct signs of 'Running down, please pass' stamped all over it here. There's good action at either end of the third Mel Gibson/Danny Glover police thriller in the series, but not much of a story in between, to say nothing of a distinctly soft centre and a frantically joky approach which betrays the film's lack of real ideas. Gibson and Glover have done better: the second film, in particular, was fun because they developed their relationship; but the third reveals they have nowhere left to go. Joe Pesci supplies a few good laughs in the film's rapid-fire style. But overall a quick tow to the pound is called for: this 'weapon' has had its day.

Let Him Have It ● ⊙
1991, UK, 118 mins, colour
Dir: Peter Medak
Stars: Chris Eccleston, Paul Reynolds, Tom Courtenay, Tom Bell, Eileen Atkins
Rating: ★★★

Britain's Craig/Bentley case of 1952 was an emotive issue at the time, and it still is today. It seemed then that

L

everybody knew there had been a miscarriage of justice, even without the knowledge that the 19-year-old Bentley was an epileptic with a mental age of 11. This is largely a solid and careful reconstruction of Bentley's background and the events that led to his conviction. Bentley was much under the influence of 16-year-old tearaway Christopher Craig, and both were caught on the roof of a Croydon warehouse by police. Craig pulled a gun, the police told him to hand it over, Bentley allegedly shouted 'Let him have it, Chris', and a policeman was shot dead. The whole case for the murder charge against Bentley hinged on those words, and to this day their meaning looks as 50/50 as it did then. The acting, especially from Eccleston and Reynolds as the teenagers, couldn't be bettered. See it for sure, and shake your head that it ever happened.

Let's Dance! ⊙
1950, US, 112 mins, colour
Dir: Norman Z McLeod
Stars: Betty Hutton, Fred Astaire, Roland Young
Rating: ★★

No one should be surprised that Betty Hutton, at her peak when this musical was made, matches *Daddy Long Legs* Fred Astaire for vitality. She also proves adept at dogging his dance steps in their one full-scale routine together. And she provides the best piece of comedy in the film – getting herself, her son and two large suitcases trapped in a dog kennel with a Great Dane called Hamlet!

Let's Do It Again! ○
1953, US, 95 mins, colour
Dir: Alexander Hall
Stars: Jane Wyman, Ray Milland, Aldo Ray
Rating: ★★★

One of the more successful remakes of the Fifties, a champagne musical remodelling of the Cary Grant-Irene Dunne Oscar-winning 1937 comedy, *The Awful Truth*. Jane Wyman steps out in style after the gloom of *Johnny Belinda* and *The Blue Veil*, as a gay would-be divorcee off to Reno to sever all connections with her girl-chasing, jazz-mad husband. Good Technicolor photography by Charles Lawton and smooth support for Ms Wyman from Ray Milland and Tom Helmore.

Let's Do It Again ○
1975, US, 110 mins, colour
Dir: Sidney Poitier
Stars: Sidney Poitier, Bill Cosby, Calvin Lockhart
Rating: ★★

Quite a lively all-black piece that just gets by as a likeable lark. It's about a couple of working men who make a mint by hypnotising a useless boxer into winning a world championship. Director Sidney Poitier keeps it bouncing along well for most of its running time, even though it sags at the beginning and slumps at the end. His acting forte, though, isn't comedy, and his own over-playing compares badly with the laid-back performances of such experienced comedy men as Bill Cosby and Jimmie Walker. The dialogue is pretty variable, but fast and nutty at its best; what a pity this isn't a more consistent dose of laughter.

Let's Make Up
See: Lilacs in the Spring

Letter, The ○
1940, US, 95 mins, b/w
Dir: William Wyler
Stars: Bette Davis, Herbert Marshall, James Stephenson, Gale Sondergaard
Rating: ★★★

Easily the best of several film versions of Somerset Maugham's story of murder in Malaya, Bette Davis winning yet another Oscar nomination (and really unlucky to lose to Ginger Rogers for *Kitty Foyle*) with a smouldering, predatory performance, absolutely hypnotic in her account of the murder that occurs at the start of the film. The plantation atmosphere, elaborately re-created in the Warner studio, is entirely convincing, and English actor James Stephenson rose to stardom with his performance as Davis' defending counsel. Alas, a year later he was dead after a heart attack. Censorship of the day demanded a changed ending, but the new one, underplayed by director William Wyler, is effective nonetheless.

Letter to Brezhnev ● ⓥ
1985, UK, 94 mins, colour
Dir: Chris Bernard
Stars: Alexandra Pigg, Peter Firth, Margi Clarke, Neil Cunningham
Rating: ★★★

Forceful, lively, raunchy and full of imagination and creative energy, this is one of Film Four International's greatest successes to date on the cinema scene. The backdrop of Liverpool and its clubs is gaudy but vital, just like the two central characters: short-skirted, wisecracking, street-smart dollies unashamedly out for a good time. The girls are searingly well played in quite matter of fact fashion by Margi Clarke and Alexandra Pigg, neither of whom subsequently got the roles their talents deserved.

Letter to Three Wives, A ○
1949, US, 102 mins, b/w
Dir: Joseph L Mankiewicz
Stars: Jeanne Crain, Ann Sothern, Linda Darnell, Kirk Douglas, Jeffrey Lynn, Paul Douglas
Rating: ★★★

Biting comedy-drama that won Joseph L Mankiewicz Oscars both for his direction and his script about three small-town wives who spend an agonising time trying to guess with which one of their husbands their mutual best friend is running off. Fine ensemble acting too – not forgetting the acid voice of the malicious letter-writer, which belongs to Celeste Holm.

Leviathan ● ⓥ
1989, US, 98 mins, colour
Dir: George P Cosmatos
Stars: Peter Weller, Richard Crenna, Amanda Pays, Daniel Stern, Ernie Hudson, Lisa Eilbacher
Rating: ★★★

If you've seen *Alien*, *The Blob* and *DeepStar Six*, you've seen just about all this underwater horror film has to offer. But it's excitingly done under Cosmatos' fast-paced and intense direction, and the monsters are good enough for a scare or two. And with such lines as 'Oh my God it got the blood supply', it's almost like being back on Hammer's home ground, in the days when they used to write dialogue just like that for Peter Cushing. No prizes for guessing which of the crew here survives at the end, although excitement not unpredictability is the name of the game and it's done well enough to send us home happy. Peter Weller plays cowboy of the deep as the geologist in charge of the doomed silver-mining mission, and Amanda Pays gets to show off a pretty collection of knickers, although they really shouldn't have given her such lines as 'My astronaut training starts in two days'. Never mind, it's all good, heart-thumping stuff for addicts of the genre.

L'Homme de Rio
See: The Man from Rio

Liar's Moon ◐
1982, US, 107 mins, colour
Dir: David Fisher
Stars: Matt Dillon, Cindy Fisher, Christopher Connelly, Yvonne De Carlo
Rating: ★★

A star-studded love story set in small-town America in 1949. Corny but endearing, it features a charismatic performance from teen idol Matt Dillon as a farm boy very much from the wrong side of the Texas tracks, who not only upsets some influential people, but rattles an old skeleton out of the cupboard by falling for the daughter of land-rich parents. The plot may be unbelievable, but there's nothing trite about the burnished Metrocolor photography of the Texas settings by John Hora, which helps make the period spring to life.

Libeled Lady ○
1936, US, 98 mins, b/w
Dir: Jack Conway
Stars: William Powell, Jean Harlow, Spencer Tracy, Myrna Loy
Rating: ★★★★

One of the wildest, fastest and funniest of the Thirties' screwball farces, with four top stars working at full throttle. Editor Spencer Tracy is being sued by wealthy Myrna Loy and gets fiancee Jean Harlow and old enemy William Powell (who needs money) to help concoct a plan and get him off the hook. The fact that Harlow is actually married to Powell is only one of the many complications in this witty frolic, which pretty well has laughs in every scene. Sit back and enjoy.

Licence to Kill ◐ ⓥ
1989, UK, 133 mins, colour
Dir: John Glen
Stars: Timothy Dalton, Carey Lowell, Talisa Soto, Robert Davi, Anthony Zerber, Wayne Newton
Rating: ★★★

A royal Dalton performance, as a tougher James Bond assumes a lone wolf role to pursue a personal vendetta against the drugs baron who has maimed Bond's old pal Felix Leiter. But the girls in the case still bring out the other kind of wolf in Britain's fa-

vourite agent for over 30 years. Carey Lowell is quite a looker and a decent actress too as an adventurous charter pilot and CIA agent, while Talisa Soto provides somewhat less ability but stunningly exotic looks as the mistress of chief baddie Robert Davi. The ending provides 15 minutes of sustained excitement as Bond takes on the baddies aboard petrol tankers on a rocky roadway and the action throughout, although only spasmodic, is first-rate when it comes. Dalton and Davi both convince as dangerous men on opposite sides of the law and, if the villains miss their usual quota of chances to polish off Bond when they have him at their mercy, that's 007 showbiz for you.

Licensed to Kill ○
(aka: The Second Best Secret Agent in the Whole Wide World)
1964, UK, 96 mins, colour
Dir: Lindsay Shonteff
Stars: Tom Adams, Veronica Hurst, Karel Stepanek
Rating: ★

The Americans called this espionage thriller *The Second Best Secret Agent in the Whole Wide World*, which gives a good idea of who the leading character is based on. Here, the Bond figure is called Charles Vine, and he's just as adept with gun or girl. A pale copy of the original.

License to Drive ◐ ⓥ
1988, US, 88 mins, colour
Dir: Greg Beeman
Stars: Corey Haim, Corey Feldman, Carol Kane, Richard Masur
Rating: ★★

You can slip your brain into neutral for this busy but highly unoriginal teen car-chase comedy. Youngster Les (Corey Haim) flunks his driving test which blows his chances of a date with dream girl Mercedes (Heather Graham) and disappoints his buddies. So he steals his grandfather's pristine '72 Cadillac and goes out on the town anyway. You don't need to be told that the Caddy suffers a number of indignities before the end of the film. A shame, because it acts the pants off the rest of the cast. To be fair, director Greg Beeman keeps things moving at a terrific pace, which injects the film with a certain juvenile vitality.

Liebestraum ● ⓥ
1991, US, 112 mins, colour
Dir: Mike Figgis

Stars: Kevin Anderson, Pamela Gidley, Bill Pullman, Catherine Hicks, Kim Novak
Rating: ★

Deliberately slow-paced, this has little to do with reality and everything to do with filming for effect. Part ghost story, part thriller, part erotic drama and all jigsaw, it starts with a decades-old murder in a deserted building. Now, fascinated by its iron structure, architect Kevin Anderson, in town to see his dying mother, becomes equally fascinated with the wife (Pamela Gidley) of the old friend (Bill Pullman) in charge of the demolition. Given the way ex-model Gidley looks this isn't surprising. Alas, there follows some silly come-ons by women at parties, men pointlessly staring at each other, a ludicrous brothel scene, repeated lines and long shots of people sitting around: the kind of movie that seems in retrospect to have been shot in slow-motion. Anderson is dour, Pullman hangdog, Gidley just too available and Catherine Hicks just ridiculous. Old-timers Kim Novak (as Anderson's mother) and Taina Elg prove hazy figures in a plot which naturally interlocks all its elements and is much more than a romantic triangle. Stylish, though, to the point of sterility.

Life and Death of Colonel Blimp, The ○
1943, UK, 163 mins, colour
Dir: Michael Powell
Stars: Roger Livesey, Deborah Kerr
Rating: ★★★

This controversial portrait of a stuffy British officer was condemned by the British press as being 'disastrously bad propaganda' (because of the leading character's lifelong friendship with a Prussian officer). Believing the film undermined British confidence during WWII, Prime Minister Winston Churchill became enraged after a viewing and personally banned it from being exported. Because of this outrage, the film, completed in 1943, was not shown in the US until the war had ended and even then it was heavily edited to give the British a more favourable view. The central character, Colonel Blimp (played roisterously by Roger Livesey), stems from a cartoon strip which appeared in the *London Evening Standard*. Anton Walbrook is superb as his friend, and Deborah Kerr warmth itself as all of the several women in Blimp's life. Produced and directed by mavericks

L

Michael Powell and Emeric Pressburger, *Blimp* was re-released in pristine form in the early Nineties.

Life at the Top ◐
1965, UK, 117 mins, b/w
Dir: Ted Kotcheff
Stars: Laurence Harvey, Jean Simmons, Honor Blackman, Michael Craig
Rating: ★★

The blackly bitter drama that follows the career of Joe Lampton, 10 years after his ruthless ascent of the social ladder in *Room at the Top*. Jean Simmons takes over the Heather Sears part, as Susan, the girl Joe married, and catches exactly the right aura of disillusionment.

Life Begins at Eight Thirty ○
(aka: The Light of Heart)
1942, US, 85 mins, b/w
Dir: Irving Pichel
Stars: Monty Woolley, Ida Lupino, Cornel Wilde
Rating: ★★★

This sentimental comedy drama, based on Emlyn Williams' play *Yesterday's Magic*, hands a plum role to irascible Monty Woolley as the has-been star saddled with a crippled daughter and drowning in a sea of alcohol. Woolley makes the most of the well-rounded insults that his character is afforded by Nunnally Johnson's dialogue, but Ida Lupino, who was giving some superlative performances at this stage of her career, is more than a match for him as his daughter, creating a flesh-and-blood character with compassion, simplicity and, evidently, a great deal of forethought, in a portrayal that really tugs at your emotions.

Life Begins for Andy Hardy ○
1941, US, 101 mins, b/w
Dir: George B Seitz
Stars: Mickey Rooney, Judy Garland, Lewis Stone, Fay Holden, Ann Rutherford
Rating: ★★★

Judy Garland makes her third and most telling contribution to the Andy Hardy films in this family drama, which is the sport in the litter as far as the series is concerned and, in retrospect, the best of the series. Andy becomes involved with a divorcee and even his 'chats' with his father, Lewis Stone, show a maturity missing elsewhere in the series. And there's a fairly sombre suicide scene, the impact of which isn't ducked by director George B Seitz. Critics were cool when the film first appeared, and the National

League of Decency classified it as A2 – objectionable for children! To add to Garland's sensitive performance, Rooney also does his best, and certainly most well-considered work in any Andy Hardy film.

Lifeboat ○
1943, US, 96 mins, b/w
Dir: Alfred Hitchcock
Stars: Tallulah Bankhead, Walter Slezak, John Hodiak, William Bendix, Hume Cronyn, Canada Lee
Rating: ★★★

Not many directors would have dared to make an entire suspense film set on board a lifeboat, but Alfred Hitchcock did it during World War Two, and it comes off pretty well. He even squeezes in his customary guest appearance – via an advertisement for a lose-weight treatment on a newspaper floating past the boat. Forthright performances by Tallulah Bankhead, William Bendix and Walter Slezak (as the only German) keep the tension crackling.

LifeForce ● ⓥ
1985, US, 101 mins, colour
Dir: Tobe Hooper
Stars: Steve Railsback, Peter Firth, Frank Finlay
Rating: ★★★

Say what you like about Tobe (*Poltergeist*) Hooper's films – and the script of this one is pretty uneven – but they all career along like a runaway train. So it is with this *Quatermass*-like tale, made on a grand scale. A crew of astronauts that obviously hasn't seen *Alien* unwittingly brings terror from outer space back to earth, and we're set for a plot that – unusually for this kind of film – actually makes sense and gives us such gigantic and impressive set-pieces as London reeling under a veritable plague of vampirism. There are special effects to relish (the electric-blue 'lifeforce' is especially effective) and dialogue to treasure: 'The other two bodies,' orders Professor Frank Finlay sternly. 'Collect the pieces and watch them!'

Life for Ruth ○
(aka: Walk in the Shadow)
1962, UK, 91m mins, b/w
Dir: Basil Dearden
Stars: Michael Craig, Patrick McGoohan, Janet Munro
Rating: ★★★

'Problem' thriller about a father who denies his injured daughter a vital blood transfusion because of religious convictions. Patrick McGoohan gives one of his most controlled performances as a doctor and the tension rises to an agonising climax.

Lifeguard ◐
1976, US, 96 mins, colour
Dir: Daniel Petrie
Stars: Sam Elliott, Anne Archer, Stephen Young, Kathleen Quinlan
Rating: ★★

Offbeat drama about a husky, 32-year-old lifeguard, played by beefy Sam Elliott, trying to decide whether the time has come to settle for a conventional life. Interesting performances from the ladies, especially Kathleen Quinlan and Anne Archer.

Life Is Sweet ◐ ⓥ
1990, UK, 103 mins, colour
Dir: Mike Leigh
Stars: Alison Steadman, Jim Broadbent, Claire Skinner, Jane Horrocks, Timothy Spall
Rating: ★★★

Picking up awards at practically every film festival around the globe, this certainly ranks as one of independent British director Mike Leigh's biggest movie successes to date. Casting his real-life wife Alison Steadman in the lead role, he also provides a wonderful showcase for rising star Jane Horrocks, as her confused, anorexic daughter. As a precise observation of the British at work and play, the film is a knockout. Wonderful ensemble acting is the icing on the cake: Stephen Rea and David Thewlis, both now major stars in British films, have supporting assignments here.

Life of Emile Zola, The ○
1937, US, 116 mins, b/w
Dir: William Dieterle
Stars: Paul Muni, Joseph Schildkraut, Gale Sondergaard, Gloria Holden
Rating: ★★★

Less a biography of the celebrated French novelist than a dramatic reconstruction of the notorious Dreyfus affair when Zola took on the French Establishment to campaign on behalf of the wrongly-imprisoned army captain who was sentenced to be jailed in the hell-hole of Devil's Island. Muni, at his best in weighty roles, is an impressive Zola but the acting honours go to Joseph Schildkraut, whose performance won him the Oscar for Best Supporting Actor. The film, too, won an Oscar, as did the screenplay. Solid entertainment, solidly directed by William Dieterle.

Life of Her Own, A ◐
1950, US, 108 mins, b/w
Dir: George Cukor
Stars: Lana Turner, Ray Milland, Tom Ewell, Louis Calhern, Ann Dvorak
Rating: ★★

This dramatic epic, with Lana Turner as a ruthless model so hell-bent to get to the top that she can't see she is also careering down the path to self-destruction, originally ran for 150 minutes. The final release version was some 40 minutes shorter, but still contains fine performances from Ann Dvorak as a has-been model, riddled with drugs and alcohol, and Margaret Phillips as the neurotic cripple whose husband Miss Turner is out to steal. A glossy soap opera.

Life Stinks ◐ ⓥ
1991, US, 95 mins, colour
Dir: Mel Brooks
Stars: Mel Brooks, Lesley Ann Warren, Jeffrey Tambor, Howard Morris
Rating: ★★

Brooks in Frank Capra-land. He plays a billionaire businessman who makes a bet that he can live as a derelict for 30 days. Naturally he learns a lot more about life than from the top of his ivory tower, but the twist in the plot is that all his associates (he has no friends) double-cross him, and it seems he must remain a derelict for the rest of his life. More of a piece (and just slightly more serious) than most Brooks films, this is an entertainment where comedy often fails, but whose overall bitter-sweet mood is quite successfully sustained. We should all meet bag ladies as attractive as Lesley Ann Warren, but there are more credible sections of the film, involving Brooks' friendships with down-and-outs and his running rivalry with a man who thinks he's J Paul Getty.

Life With Father ☉
1947, US, 118 mins, colour
Dir: Michael Curtiz
Stars: William Powell, Irene Dunne, Elizabeth Taylor, Edmund Gwenn, ZaSu Pitts
Rating: ★★★

A tremendous box-office hit in its day, and the kind of film that Hollywood does so well. It's an amusing study, full of warmth and lushly photographed in colour, of a Victorian-style household in New York, its joys, sorrows and family crises. The characters are delightful, but Donald Ogden Stewart's script for them lacks bite and rambles a bit, while director Michael Curtiz, more at home with Errol Flynn action films, often seems to dull the edges of the fun. Still it's a handsome production and boasts one of Max Steiner's best music scores, plus a larger-than-life, Oscar-nominated performance by William Powell as Father.

Light at the Edge of the World, The ○
1971, US/Spain, 119 mins, colour
Dir: Kevin Billington
Stars: Kirk Douglas, Yul Brynner, Samantha Eggar, Fernando Rey
Rating: ★

A lighthouse off Cape Horn is the spectacular setting for this Jules Verne adaptation, searingly well photographed in colour by Frenchman Henri Decae. Kirk Douglas (who also produced the film) has always seemed at home with basic schoolboy heroics, and here he has a plum role as the mysterious American who takes on a whole crew of pirates (fiercely led by Yul Brynner) after they've taken over the lighthouse. The results, though, are alternately violent and laughable. Now available in a full-version print, it is to be hoped that it clears up much of the confusion that surrounded the cut version. This is, by the way, the only example of an American-Spanish-Liechtenstein co-production in the history of the cinema.

Lighthorsemen, The ○ ⓥ
1987, Australia, 115 mins, colour
Dir: Simon Wincer
Stars: Peter Phelps, Jon Blake, Tim McKenzie
Rating: ★★

Spurred on perhaps by the international success of *Gallipoli*, Australian filmmakers turned their attention to this epic war film about Australian cavalry fighting in the Palestinian desert of 1917. Overlength spoils it, but there's a spectacular charging battle sequence at the end which fires the adrenaline and makes the whole wait for action worthwhile. Personable performances in the leading roles from Peter Phelps (later to star in the first series of *Baywatch*) and John Waters do what they can to boost the rather insubstantial storyline.

Light of Heart, The
See: Life Begins at Eight Thirty

Lightship, The ◐ ⓥ
1985, US, 89 mins, colour
Dir: Jerzy Skolimowski
Stars: Robert Duvall, Klaus Maria Brandauer, Tom Bower, Badja Djola, Arliss Howard, William Forsythe
Rating: ★

On paper, the combination of Hollywood's Oscar-winning Robert Duvall and Austria's international star Klaus Maria Brandauer seems an explosive one. In fact, their clash between good and evil hardly raises even a fizzle, the two men reacting to each other like negative poles and never raising any tension in dramatic terms. It's a ponderous, almost incident-less story of three fugitives boarding a 1955 lightship whose German-born captain is haunted by an incident in the war that echoes the dilemma of Jack Hawkins in *The Cruel Sea*. Jerzy Skolimowski's direction, however, is so slack that none of this hits home, nothing solidifies to bolster the plot, and the dialogue, although it has its pretensions, lurches perilously close to clichés of long ago. Probably the two leading roles would have been better cast the other way round, but then Brandauer might have over-dominated the film. As it is Duvall is mannered without being menacing and Brandauer merely enigmatic – his final act of heroism scarcely quickening the pulse.

Light Sleeper ● ⓥ
1991, US, 103 mins, colour
Dir: Paul Schrader
Stars: Willem Dafoe, Susan Sarandon, Dana Delany, Mary Beth Hurt
Rating: ★

This story of a drug dealer suddenly reaching a crisis in his life doesn't amount to very much considering the talents involved. Film maker Paul Schrader offers a typically cold and atmospheric view of the city backstreets at night, but his writing of the story makes it seem hardly worth the effort. Willem Dafoe has the John Garfield role as the dealer. With his partners already considering changing their line of work, he runs into an old girlfriend – and trouble. Dana Delany is a fresh new face in this role, but most of the other performances are no

L

more than adequate, and Schrader almost tosses away what action there is. The moody soundtrack and its songs are terrific, but they may not be enough to prevent you copying the title.

Light that Failed, The ○
1939, US, 97 mins, b/w
Dir: William A Wellman
Stars: Ronald Colman, Walter Huston, Ida Lupino
Rating: ★★★

Sincere, moving and always gripping adaptation of the Rudyard Kipling novel about an artist going blind who hauls a girl from the gutters of London and makes her the subject of his last great masterpiece. Star Ronald Colman had wanted Vivien Leigh for the role of the guttersnipe, but it was grabbed (with both hands) by Ida Lupino who, fed-up with a series of milk-and-water roles, ripped in with a corrosive performance that jetted her to stardom in similar hard-bitten roles. Perhaps Colman was too busy feuding with director William A Wellman – 'We only agreed on one thing,' said Wellman, 'and that was that we didn't like each other' – to notice that Lupino was stealing the picture from under his nose. It's a good film, though, and one too long unseen.

Light Up the Sky ○
1960, UK, 90 mins, b/w
Dir: Lewis Gilbert
Stars: Ian Carmichael, Tommy Steele, Benny Hill
Rating: ★★

A mixture of high jinks and high drama with the members of a wartime searchlight unit. Experienced maker of war stories Lewis Gilbert directs. It's not surprising that the drama comes across equally effectively when one remembers that Gilbert also made *Albert RN*, *Reach for the Sky*, *Sink the Bismarck!* and *Carve Her Name with Pride*. Such efficient 'types' as Victor Maddern, Sydney Tafler, Johnny Briggs and Harry Locke do him yeoman service in support, while Dick Emery, and Cardew Robinson make, with Benny Hill, a trio of comedians in character roles.

Like Father, Like Son ○ ⓥ
1987, US, 98 mins, colour
Dir: Rod Daniel
Stars: Dudley Moore, Kirk Cameron, Margaret Colin
Rating: ★

Although made before *Big*, *Vice Versa* and *18 Again!*, this age-reversal comedy started, time-wise, from the back of the field in Britain and finished a distant fourth. Seen in isolation, this Dudley Moore comedy might not have looked too bad. As it was, three previous tellings of the tall tale only exposed its comic situations as merely embarrassing and its father-and-son characters more fun as themselves than when they switch bodies. Both Moore (as a famous surgeon) and Kirk Cameron (his truly average son) seem far too outspoken in their new identities; surely both would have been more cautious in the circumstances. Margaret Colin is on good form as a maneater who can't believe Moore's new-found enthusiasm for women, but the film's tiresome and illogical developments soon drain our interest, and there have been few, if any, entries into the genre since.

Likely Lads, The ◐
1976, UK, 90 mins, colour
Dir: Michael Tuchner
Stars: Rodney Bewes, James Bolam, Brigit Forsyth
Rating: ★★

Yet another TV spin-off that fell apart on the hazardous journey to the big screen. Philosophical comedy is the vein aimed at, but the dialogue is uneccessarily crude, and jars every time it steps out of key, which is often. It does best when indulging in quietly humorous nostalgia, or making the poker-faced Rodney Bewes the fall-guy for visual disasters. The uncertainty of much of the acting is no help, the only major success being Brigit Forsyth as Thelma.

L'il Abner ○
1959, US, 113 mins, colour
Dir: Melvin Frank
Stars: Peter Palmer, Leslie Parrish, Stubby Kaye, Stella Stevens
Rating: ★★

Bright, loud, bouncy cartoon-like musical based on Al Capp's famous comic-strip characters, who ran for years in American newspapers. Stella Stevens is an amazing Appassionata Von Climax and Stubby Kaye terrific as Marryin' Sam, especially when singing the show's big hit 'Jubilation T Cornpone'. But the romance is a bit drippy, the corny comedy pales after a while and the whole just lacks that vital spark that would put it among the classic film musical comedies.

Having said that, it's ten times better than the disastrous 1940 version – made without songs!

Lilacs in the Spring ○
(aka: Let's Make Up)
1954, UK, 94 mins, colour
Dir: Herbert Wilcox
Stars: Anna Neagle, Errol Flynn, David Farrar, Kathleen Harrison
Rating: ★★

This musical is not, as one might suppose, based on a stage hit by Ivor Novello but on one by Harold Purcell called *The Glorious Days*. It's very bright and inconsequential, with Anna Neagle tripping vivaciously through a series of old favourites that include 'Keep the Home Fires Burning', 'We'll Gather Lilacs' (which was written by Novello), Noel Coward's 'Dance Little Lady', 'Lily of Laguna', 'Tipperary' and 'Lilac Tango'. Much of the story is told in fantasies and flashbacks, which gives Dame Anna a chance to reprise her impressions of Nell Gwyn and Queen Victoria from earlier films, as well as fling herself with infectious abandon into some colourful period routines. And there's an intriguing glimpse of two old-time stars, actress Alma Taylor and singer Hetty King, as two richly-bejewelled theatregoers. A young Sean Connery is somewhere in the crowd of extras.

Lili ☉
1952, US, 81 mins, colour
Dir: Charles Walters
Stars: Leslie Caron, Mel Ferrer, Jean-Pierre Aumont
Rating: ★★★★

A warm and winning MGM musical with Leslie Caron as a French orphan who joins a travelling carnival and meets self-pitying puppeteer Mel Ferrer and sophisticated magician Jean-Pierre Aumont. Caron is convincingly ingenuous, the puppets are real scene-stealers and the score so enchanting it won Bronislau Kaper an Academy Award. A real charmer.

Lilith ◐
1964, US, 126 mins, b/w
Dir: Robert Rossen
Stars: Warren Beatty, Jean Seberg, Peter Fonda, Kim Hunter, Jessica Walter, Gene Hackman
Rating: ★★

A rather fey psychological drama-romance whose star-studded cast was not enough to prevent it dying a thousand deaths at the box-office. The pace is slow and the actors seem to take a long time to deliver their lines. As an oddity it's worth a look, though certainly not up to the stndards of Robert Rossen's previous film *The Hustler*. Unfortunately the writer-director died soon after *Lilith* was completed.

Lillian Russell ○
1940, US, 127 mins, b/w
Dir: Irving Cummings
Stars: Alice Faye, Don Ameche, Henry Fonda, Warren William, Edward Arnold, Leo Carrillo
Rating: ★★

Whitewashed but very watchable biography of an American stage star of the Gay Nineties, giving star Alice Faye no fewer than four leading men in Don Ameche, Henry Fonda, Warren William and Edward Arnold, the latter being in especially good form, repeating his earlier film characterisation of 'Diamond Jim' Brady. Director Irving Cummings began his career as a stage actor, with a company headed by – Lillian Russell.

Limelight ○ Ⓥ
1951, US, 144 mins, b/w
Dir: Charles Chaplin
Stars: Charlie Chaplin, Claire Bloom, Sydney Chaplin, Buster Keaton, Nigel Bruce
Rating: ★★★

The best of Chaplin's post-war films, and too rarely seen on television. It has a Pagliacci theme – Chaplin is the fading clown who helps a young girl from the brink of suicide to success as a ballerina – set against the London music-hall in the early 20th century that Chaplin himself had known in his youth. Although its plot is melodramatic and dated, Chaplin demonstrates his ability once more to wring a tear as well as a smile. And there are moments of high hilarity, not least from the climactic stage routine in which Buster Keaton plays Chaplin's piano accompanist. Another silent comic, Snub Pollard, can be glimpsed as a street musician.

Line-up, The ○
1958, US, 86 mins, b/w
Dir: Don Siegel
Stars: Eli Wallach, Robert Keith, Warner Anderson
Rating: ★★

Classy Don Siegel-directed, Stirling Silliphant-scripted crime thriller with Eli Wallach outstanding as an assassin. Based on a highly successful TV series (which also featured Warner Anderson), shown in Britain as *San Francisco Beat*. Forgettable stuff but sharply done.

Linguini Incident, The ● Ⓥ
1991, US, 99 mins, colour
Dir: Richard Shepherd
Stars: Rosanna Arquette, David Bowie, Eszter Balint, Marlee Matlin, Buck Henry
Rating: ★

What a difference a decent screenplay makes. The storyline to this foul-mouthed romantic comedy is pretty original and the settings delightfully gaudy. But the script is just so bad that the film never has a chance. Directorial mishandling doesn't help, while even the delectable Rosanna Arquette, as the cocktail waitress planning to be a female Houdini, comes across as irritating in this one. It does get a bit better towards the end: a case of too little, too late.

Lion, The ○
1962, US, 96 mins, colour
Dir: Jack Cardiff
Stars: William Holden, Trevor Howard, Capucine, Pamela Franklin
Rating: ★★

Sentimental, cleverly-acted drama, shot on location in East Africa. A young girl grows up there, and strikes up a friendship with a huge lion. Pamela Franklin, who plays the girl, later starred in such films as *The Prime of Miss Jean Brodie* and *David Copperfield*. Technicolor photography is as ravishing as one would expect from a film directed by former cameraman Jack Cardiff, who won an Oscar for his colour camerawork on the 1946 film, *Black Narcissus*.

Lionheart ●
(aka: AWOL)
1990, US, 110 mins, colour
Dir: Sheldon Lettich
Stars: Jean-Claude Van Damme, Harrison Page, Deborah Rennard, Lisa Pelikan
Rating: ★★★

Probably Jean-Claude Van Damme's best solo starring film to date, with more than a semblance of a decent story to go with kickboxing mayhem, in smoky backstreet rooms, or later, plusher joints. Van Damme's a French

Legionnaire who deserts to come to America where his drug-dealing brother has been torched by competitors. Soon, realising that his fighting skills are the only way to help his brother's widow and young daughter, he reluctantly ties in with black street hustler Harrison Page, and predatory, illegal-fight promoter Deborah Rennard, who turns against him when he fails to succumb to her advances. Although the story has its corny and woolly moments, first-time director Sheldon Lettich has an approach which now and again lends it freshness and shows he appreciates cinema. Rennard is just sufficiently over-the-top to be enjoyable without being silly and Van Damme shows his gentler side – wisely by sharing scenes with a kid who can't act. But he's also man enough to cast an actor like Page who can and does wipe the floor with him – more than any of his opponents manage in the ring.

Lion in Winter, The ○ Ⓥ
1968, UK, 135 mins, colour
Dir: Anthony Harvey
Stars: Peter O'Toole, Katharine Hepburn, Anthony Hopkins, Timothy Dalton, Jane Merrow
Rating: ★★★★

There can have been few bigger certainties in Academy Award history than James Goldman's Oscar for his screenplay on this brilliantly-written film, adapted from his own play. It's principally a game of verbal chess with a cutting edge, played out at Christmas 1183 between King Henry II and his estranged wife Eleanor of Aquitaine, whom he has shut away to stop her interference in affairs of state. In these plum roles, Peter O'Toole and Katharine Hepburn coat Goldman's coruscating dialogue in venom. The serious humour cuts deep as these two constantly hack away at each other, distant respect and attachment lurking behind years of bitterness as they amuse and stimulate us with the cut and thrust of it all. Add early appearances by Anthony Hopkins and Timothy Dalton and you have a rich pageant of entertainment for which Hepburn took her third Oscar.

Lion Is in the Streets, A ○
1953, US, 88 mins, colour
Dir: Raoul Walsh
Stars: James Cagney, Barbara Hale, Anne Francis, Warner Anderson
Rating: ★★

L

Although seemingly a change of pace for James Cagney – he plays a backwoods salesman who becomes a politician – this is still very much in the classic mould of the cocky little rebel. Very strikingly shot in Technicolor, with Cagney extremely effective in the 'young' scenes – even though he was 54 at the time! A good gallery of supporting players includes Cagney's real-life sister, Jeanne, as well as Lon Chaney Jr, Warner Anderson and John McIntire.

Lipstick ●
1976, US, 86 mins, colour
Dir: Lamont Johnson
Stars: Margaux Hemingway, Chris Sarandon, Anne Bancroft, Mariel Hemingway
Rating: ★

Out of 500,000 estimated cases of rape every year in California only 10,000 are reported and, of those cases brought to trial, just two per cent result in conviction. These shocking statistics are brought to light and then luridly expanded on in this notorious thriller. Margaux Hemingway plays the top model who brings just such a case after being raped by her psychotic teacher; and her younger (and more talented) sister Mariel plays the girl who introduces them without knowing the horrors around the corner. Strong stuff, this, but not good.

Lisa ○
(aka: The Inspector)
1962, US, 112 mins, colour
Dir: Philip Dunne
Stars: Stephen Boyd, Dolores Hart, Leo McKern, Hugh Griffith
Rating: ★★★

Sporadically interesting romantic melodrama based on Jan De Hartog's *The Inspector*. Handsomely photographed against authentic European backgrounds, the film flits from romance to action and mystery, with no one element dominating. Consequently, the final result is colourful, rambling and sometimes exciting. Leo ('Rumpole') McKern gives a sharp and bristling performance as a crochety old sea dog. And Hugh Griffith is on form as a Dutchman who swats bats with a tennis racquet.

Lisbon ○
1956, US, 90 mins, colour
Dir: Ray Milland
Stars: Ray Milland, Maureen O'Hara, Claude Rains
Rating: ★★

Actor Ray Milland made some interesting films as director, but there wasn't very much he could do with this dullish tale of international intrigue. The Portuguese settings look attractive even in Republic Studios' awful Trucolor, and a good cast, including Milland himself, Maureen O'Hara, Francis Lederer, Yvonne Furneaux and that old smoothie Claude Rains, does what it can to spark the stock situations. There are one or two good twists in the plot.

Listen, Darling ○
1938, US, 70 mins, b/w
Dir: Edwin L Marin
Stars: Judy Garland, Walter Pidgeon, Mary Astor, Freddie Bartholomew
Rating: ★★★

This vehicle for the teenage Judy Garland is very similar to early Deanna Durbin films. Judy brings much the same quality of freshness to her innocent, yet polished performance as the matchmaking daughter of widow Mary Astor, who was to play Judy's mum again six years later in *Meet Me in St Louis*. The film's big musical hit was 'Zing! Went the Strings of My Heart', sung by you-know-who.

Listen to Me ●
1989, US, 110 mins, colour
Dir: Douglas Day Stewart
Stars: Kirk Cameron, Jami Gertz, Roy Scheider, Amanda Peterson, Tim Quill, Anthony Zerbe
Rating: ★★

It's a pretty hard assignment to make an entertaining 110-minute film about a college for debating societies, but Columbia almost pulls it off in this passionately well-acted film. By pretending that debating is a life-or-death occupation (and 'a road straight into law school and politics') and plucking relentlessly at the heartstrings, director Douglas Day Stewart, aided by patriotic music swelling vaguely in the background, will draw a tear from the easily moved as junior debaters Jami Gertz and Kirk Cameron take on the mighty Harvard in the final. *Rocky* with words instead of fists: Gertz doesn't miss out on her big chance towards the end, Roy Scheider goes over the top for the team as their professor, and Tim Quill, a huskier version of Audie Murphy, is an interesting new face as the rich kid who seems to have it all, but . . .

List of Adrian Messenger, The ○
1963, US, 98 mins, b/w
Dir: John Huston
Stars: George C Scott, Dana Wynter, Kirk Douglas, Clive Brook, Herbert Marshall, Gladys Cooper
Rating: ★★★

Under the watchful and inventive eye of director John Huston, this eventful and atmospheric thriller proves to be great fun. Not only is there a killer on the loose who proves to be a gleeful master of disguise, but a number of famous guest stars appear (not that you can tell) under mounds of make-up to strew red herrings across the trail. Suspenseful moments, classy black and white photography and a thrilling chase climax.

Little Big Man ○ Ⓥ
1970, US, 147 mins, colour
Dir: Arthur Penn
Stars: Dustin Hoffman, Faye Dunaway, Martin Balsam, Richard Mulligan
Rating: ★★★

A fascinating, rather odd Western, with Dustin Hoffman playing an unlikely (and occasionally very funny) hero. Raised by Indians, he has to learn to live in white society but goes back to the Indian tribe who brought him up. But then comes General Custer and the Battle of Little Big Horn. Amusing and shocking, with a humanitarian message in the film somewhere.

Little Big Shot ⊙
1952, UK, 90 mins, b/w
Dir: Jack Raymond
Stars: Ronald Shiner, Marie Lohr
Rating: ★★

Another reminder of how much the world of British comedy has missed the abrasive Cockney wit of Ronald Shiner. Here he plays the soft-hearted son of a famous crook who tries to emulate his father. Alas, he's too nice to be a criminal, and the gang only keep him out of respect for his old man. Digby Wolfe, once a familiar television face on panel games and reviews, and later creator of *Laugh-In*, scores as an impecunious journalist ever on the look-out for a scoop.

Little Caesar ○ Ⓥ
1930, US, 80 mins, b/w
Dir: Mervyn Le Roy
Stars: Edward G Robinson, Douglas Fairbanks Jr, Ralph Ince, Glenda Farrell
Rating: ★★★★

This was the first talkie to glorify the gang wars of the Twenties and established Edward G Robinson as a star, pushing his minions around and spitting out dialogue like lead pellets in a pheasant. Robinson dominates the entire film, which grips consistently, never misses with its action and has no wasted footage in its 80 minutes.

Little Colonel, The ⊙
1935, US, 80 mins, b/w
Dir: David Butler
Stars: Shirley Temple, Lionel Barrymore, John Lodge
Rating: ★★★

Shirley Temple in the Deep South, and at her most beguiling. Lionel Barrymore inevitably has his heart of stone melted by the end; the talented tot also does the famous dance up and down the wooden steps with Bill 'Bojangles' Robinson. One sequence in colour.

Little Darlings ◐
1980, US, 92 mins, colour
Dir: Ronald F Maxwell
Stars: Tatum O'Neal, Kristy McNichol, Armand Assante, Matt Dillon
Rating: ★★

This is basically just another Hollywood 'summer camp' tale with a rather distasteful story about two girls involved in a bet about who will lose her virginity first. In this instance, however, the playing overcomes the formula development of Kimi Peck and Dalene Young's screenplay. In particular, Kristy McNichol (whose career has not progressed since as it should have done), as a tough teenager with a sleep-around divorcee mother, is so true, so natural in the conveying of inner feelings as to leave you gasping for more. All the sadness and cynicism of 15 years of rootless existence is expressed in these brown eyes. It's a performance deserving of the Oscar nomination it didn't get.

Little Drummer Girl, The ◐ ⓥ
1984, US, 130 mins, colour
Dir: George Roy Hill
Stars: Diane Keaton, Yorgo Voyagis, Klaus Kinski, David Suchet
Rating: ★★

Director George Roy Hill not only takes his time (well over two hours) with the film version of John Le Carré's best-seller, but doesn't do too well at getting us to believe that a pro-Palestinian American actress in

England could be recruited to the Israeli cause to help root out the very people whose cause she has espoused. Diane Keaton certainly has her moments in the title role, Klaus Kinski is fine as an Israeli counter-intelligence officer and there's some suspense towards the end. Otherwise Hill's treatment of a fine story lacks inspiration in too many departments.

Little Foxes, The ○
1941, US, 116 mins, b/w
Dir: William Wyler
Stars: Bette Davis, Herbert Marshall, Teresa Wright, Richard Carlson, Dan Duryea
Rating: ★★★★

Lillian Hellman's own adaptation of her Broadway stage success, brilliantly directed by William Wyler and full of classic scenes and images. Bette Davis gives one of her most unforgettable performances as Regina Giddens, a scheming, ruthless woman who alienates all those about her. Dan Duryea makes a notable screen debut, while Teresa Wright and Herbert Marshall do fine, unselfish work in support of the star. Nominated for eight Oscars, the film shamefully came away empty-handed.

Little Girl Who Lives Down the Lane, The ◐
1976, Canada, 90 mins, colour
Dir: Nicolas Gessner
Stars: Jodie Foster, Martin Sheen, Alexis Smith
Rating: ★★

With portraits of prostitutes and gangster's molls already behind her, the 13-year-old Jodie Foster handled her role as a disturbed teenager with amazing confidence in this Canadian thriller that reminds you of Hammer chillers of the mid Sixties. She's the whole show, especially with a plot that telegraphs every shock a few shivers in advance.

Little Hut, The ○
1957, US, 90 mins, colour
Dir: Mark Robson
Stars: Ava Gardner, Stewart Granger, David Niven, Walter Chiani, Finlay Currie
Rating: ★★

A pretty unrelaxed film version of a saucy stage farce, with Stewart Granger and Ava Gardner struggling in comedy that broad as two sides of a desert island triangle. David Niven is in raspingly good form as the rascally Brittingham-Brett, but there wasn't

much else for MGM to celebrate from what must have looked a sure box-office hit. Granger and Gardner, who had done scarcely better together with *Bhowani Junction*, were doomed at the studio from here on.

Little Kidnappers, The
See: The Kidnappers

Little Man Tate ◐ ⓥ
1991, US, 99 mins, colour
Dir: Jodie Foster
Stars: Jodie Foster, Dianne Wiest, Adam Hann-Byrd, Harry Connick Jr
Rating: ★★

'A Jodie Foster film' it says at the end, just in case we've missed the point that this simplistic fable (with its faint echoes of *Pinocchio*) about a seven-year-old genius is Jodie's directorial debut. Quite a nice little film too, even though it's a bit slow in parts, and it comes as something of a surprise at the end to find that it's purely a work of fiction. Jodie plays the kid's mother (the Geppetto figure), a waitress-dancer who's not as dim as she makes out. But she provides no sort of environment, thinks pain-in-the-butt professor Dianne Wiest (the Blue Fairy, sort of), in which to bring the kid up. She sweeps him off to bright kids' summer college where he shows amazing aptitude at maths, but gains most from the companionship of a human Lampwick (singer Harry Connick Jr in his acting debut) who teaches him how to play pool. But, this not being *Pinocchio*, the kids don't all turn into donkeys and, starved of affection, the kid heads for home and the life of a real little boy. It's a low-key film with some good laughs, the odd poignant moment and a tinkly piano score that sometimes makes the pace seem slower than it is. B plus for Jodie this time.

Little Mermaid, The ⊙ ⓥ
1989, US, 87 mins, colour
Dir: John Musker
Voice stars: Jodi Benson, Pat Carroll, Samuel E Wright, Buddy Hackett
Rating: ★★★

A liltingly enjoyable cartoon feature in the traditional Disney style. Though based on the Hans Andersen fairy-tale, it becomes, in Disney hands, a virtual remake of *Sleeping Beauty*, even to the final battle with the villainous sea-witch Ursula. The heroine is a teenage mermaid, Ariel, with a fascination with all things to do with humans. Rescuing a prince from a

L

shipwreck, she falls in love with him and sells her voice to the witch in return for three days as a human. If she fails to get the prince to give her a lover's kiss, she will turn back into a mermaid and forfeit her soul to Ursula as well. Ariel is quite a feisty heroine by Disney standards and her crab protector (a kind of West Indian Jiminy Cricket) and seagull sage are good characters too. Ursula is simply superb: an evil Mae West with eight tentacles instead of feet. There are three good songs – 'Part of This World', 'Under the Sea' and 'Kiss the Girl' – and children are certain to gasp, laugh and snivel in all the right places. It's too derivative to be a classic, but a nice lightweight goodie to add to the Disney hamper.

Little Miss Broadway ⊙
1938, US, 78 mins, b/w
Dir: Irving Cummings
Stars: Shirley Temple, George Murphy, Jimmy Durante
Rating: ★★★

A Shirley Temple vehicle with more music than usual, teaming her happily with both Jimmy Durante and George Murphy. Edna Mae Oliver also registers well as a crusty old landlady who relents in the end. Temple and Murphy both later went into politics and here they duet appropriately on 'We Should Be Together!', one of half a dozen tuneful songs that also include 'Be Optimistic', 'Hop, Skip and Jump' and 'If All the World Were Paper'. Nick Castle and Geneva Sawyer stage the dance routines with their usual flair, and Irving Cummings' direction avoids any dull moments, in what, helped by a snappy running time, is a pretty lively package.

Little Miss Marker ○
1980, US, 103 mins, colour
Dir: Walter Bernstein
Stars: Walter Matthau, Julie Andrews, Tony Curtis, Sara Stimson, Bob Newhart
Rating: ★★

Despite the fact that Damon Runyon's story about a little girl left with a bookie as 'security' was definitively annexed by Shirley Temple in 1934, producers have felt compelled to have several more tries at it since. Neither Mary Jane Saunders (in Bob Hope's *Sorrowful Jones*, 1949) nor Claire Wilcox (in Tony Curtis' *40 Pounds of Trouble*, 1962) laid a glove on the original and, in this most recent version, it's Sara Stimson struggling to make an impression as 'The Kid'.

Walter Matthau makes a dour Sorrowful and, strangely, it's Tony Curtis who this time round takes the role of the villain. Save your pennies and wait for Shirley's version to come round again.

Little Nellie Kelly ○
1940, US, 100 mins, b/w
Dir: Norman Taurog
Stars: Judy Garland, George Murphy
Rating: ★★★

Judy Garland received her first solo billing above the title of this little seen musical about a through-the-ages feud between two stubborn Irish-American families. Judy, stoutly supported by George Murphy and Charles Winninger, sings 'Nellie Kelly', 'It's a Great Day for the Irish', 'Pretty Girl Milking Her Cow' and believe it or not – 'Singin' in the Rain'. Her romantic interest is played by the promising young singer Douglas McPhail, who committed suicide a few years later.

Little Prince, The ○
1974, UK, 88 mins, colour
Dir: Stanley Donen
Stars: Richard Kiley, Steven Warner, Bob Fosse, Gene Wilder, Joss Ackland
Rating: ★

A musical treatment of Antoine de Saint Exupéry's fabulous fairy-tale about a little boy from outer space and his quest for knowledge and understanding. Director Stanley Donen plunges with both feet into a treacle well of sentiment and it requires all the efforts of Gene Wilder and Bob Fosse to pull him out. Wilder's a wily fox all in brown, but it's Fosse's snake, dressed entirely in black, hissing and bounding about, that really steals the film.

Little Princess, The ⊙
1939, US, 91 mins, colour
Dir: Walter Lang
Stars: Shirley Temple, Ian Hunter, Richard Greene, Cesar Romero
Rating: ★★

Shirley Temple's biggest (it cost $1.5 million) but by no means best film, this turn-of-the-century story, which was also her first in colour, has her as a girl haunting hospitals in search of her father, believed a victim of the Boer War. Shirley is as forthright and winning as ever, while Mary Nash is splendidly vindictive as the headmistress who has it in for her. Skilfully made by Walter Lang, one of 20th

Century-Fox's top directors for more than 20 years, but he can't stop you cringing at the ending.

Little Romance, A ○
1979, US, 108 mins, colour
Dir: George Roy Hill
Stars: Diane Lane, Theolonius Bernard, Laurence Olivier, Sally Killerman, Broderick Crawford
Rating: ★★★

An unlikely but fairly charming story about a 13-year-old French boy who lives in a world of films and a 13-year-old American girl who lives in a world (her mother's dizzy social whirl) from which her high IQ and sensible outlook leave her completely alienated. Their innocent affair culminates in a wild flight to Venice to kiss in a gondola under the Bridge of Sighs. The two youngsters (Diane Lane and Thelonius Bernard) are attractive but have their thunder stolen from them by the supporting cast. Broderick Crawford is splendid as himself, turning up at a party and growling, 'I figured what the hell, the booze is free and maybe I'll get laid.'

Little Shop of Horrors ◐ ⓥ
1986, US, 88 mins, colour
Dir: Frank Oz
Stars: Rick Moranis, Ellen Greene, Vincent Gardenia, Steve Martin, James Belushi, John Candy
Rating: ★★★

It's not often these days that producers gamble with a musical. So you can bet that when one does come along it has to be pretty special. This one is that its central character is a man-eating plant. And it sings, displaying iris-shaped tonsils! Playgoers will find the ending changed from the stage original, but it's a move neither for better nor worse, simply providing the film with a climactic battle between man and plant. Rick Moranis is the weedy assistant in a (very) downtown flower shop whose discovery of a little plant that grows on blood makes the shop and its owner (Vincent Gardenia) famous, and may even help Rick win his Monroeish co-worker (Ellen Greene) away from her sadistic dentist lover. This leading trio is so good that it's much to its credit not to be overshadowed by the array of guest stars. Dentistry may never be the same after Steve Martin's driller-killer (once seen from inside a patient's mouth). Bill Murray is very droll as his masochistic patient, while plump John Candy pops up as the livewire of Skid Row Radio and there's a glimpse of James Belushi as an opportunist eager to take cuttings from the far-from jolly green giant. Approach it with care when it cries 'Feed Me!'

Littlest Rebel, The ☉ ⓥ
1935, US, 70 mins, b/w
Dir: David Butler
Stars: Shirley Temple, John Boles, Jack Holt
Rating: ★★★

This was the film (the setting is the American Civil War) in which talented tot Shirley Temple was first teamed with her black dancing partner Bill Robinson. Get the children to have a handkerchief handy, 'cos Shirley's mother gets killed and Daddy, John Boles, looks like getting shot by Unionist Jack Holt.

Little Women ○
1933, US, 115 mins, b/w
Dir: George Cukor
Stars: Katharine Hepburn, Joan Bennett, Paul Lukas
Rating: ★★★

The definitive version of Louisa M Alcott's novel of four young women growing up is, in some ways, the other side of the coin from *Gone With the Wind*, in that it's set in New England at the time of the American Civil War. For one of the most successful adaptations of a difficult book ever brought to the screen, writers Victor Heerman and Sarah Mason were deservedly rewarded with Oscars. The production is as expensive as it is immaculate, and the four actresses flawless. Katharine Hepburn's bravura tendencies are beautifully kept in check by director George Cukor, enabling her to give a dominant but still sympathetic performance, and Frances Dee, Jean Parker (as the ailing Beth) and Joan Bennett are all appealing as her sisters. Spring Byington's marvellous 'Marmee' set her up for a whole run of engaging matrons and motherly types. Ironically she was, in real-life, a divorcee who never re-married.

Little Women ○
1949, US, 122 mins, colour
Dir: Mervyn Le Roy
Stars: June Allyson, Elizabeth Taylor, Janet Leigh, Margaret O'Brien, Mary Astor, Rossano Brazzi
Rating: ★★★

A cosy, sentimental, but atmospheric version of the Louisa M Alcott classic, looking like a series of Christmas card scenes in bright colours, but boasting sturdy performances from June Allyson as Jo, and Mary Astor as the beloved Marmee. MGM at its most family-minded.

Live and Let Die ○ ⓥ
1973, UK, 116 mins, colour
Dir: Guy Hamilton
Stars: Roger Moore, Yaphet Kotto, Jane Seymour, David Hedison
Rating: ★★★

The film that presented the world with its new James Bond. Roger Moore lacked Sean Connery's toughness, but made up for it in smoothness, dash and suavity. Although Moore joked about the role increasing his range of expressions from two to four, he confessed himself worried as never before over public identification of him as Bond, recognising it as a make-or-break stage in his career. But his success as 007 was such that he completed seven Bond films. The plot of *Live and Let Die* is wildly improbable and nearly incomprehensible – all about voodoo and black power. But it's the usual imaginative, expensive production, in this case whisking us from London to New York to New Orleans; from a lengthy but admittedly exciting speedboat pursuit to a glider-car chase; each stunt sequence stretched to its limit. Jane Seymour is a cool heroine, while Julius W Harris's sinister Tee Hee, whose right arm has been severed by an over-enthusiastic crocodile, is the best of the bad men.

Live It Up ☉
(aka: Sing and Swing)
1963, UK, 78 mins, b/w
Dir: Lance Comfort
Stars: David Hemmings, Veronica Hurst, Heinz Burt, Patsy Ann Noble
Rating: ★★★

A British echo-chamber musical with plenty of teenage attraction in such contemporary pop stars as Gene Vincent, Heinz and Sound Incorporated. The direction is smooth and the musical numbers on the whole are well staged. One of them, Vincent's 'Temptation Baby', is particularly good.

Live Now, Pay Later ◐
1962, UK, 104 mins, b/w
Dir: Jay Lewis

Stars: Ian Hendry, June Ritchie, John Gregson, Liz Fraser
Rating: ★★★

A blackly bitter satirical comedy which finds Ian Hendry in his element as the brash, fast-talking, womanising salesman who blights everybody's life including (eventually) his own. Jack Trevor Story's screenplay creates a series of dislikeable characters which gives the morality tale real bite, and there are unusual (but excellent) contributions from John Gregson and Liz Fraser, both effectively cast against type. Like Hendry's character as far as his acquaintances are concerned, the film outstays its welcome before the end, but this is British realist drama of the early Sixties at its most acerbic.

Lives of a Bengal Lancer, The ○
1935, US, 107 mins, b/w
Dir: Henry Hathaway
Stars: Gary Cooper, Franchot Tone, Richard Cromwell
Rating: ★★★

Rip-roaring, Oscar-winning adventure yarn set on India's North West frontier. Strong human values are not lost in director Henry Hathaway's successful search for great narrative drive and the vein of humour includes a marvellous snake-charming scene. Gary Cooper is in his element as the stalwart hero and there's a superbly sneaky minor performance by J Carrol Naish as a grand vizier. Douglas Dumbrille and Akim Tamiroff complete a classic trio of Hollywood character players you would rarely trust.

Living Daylights, The ○ ⓥ
1987, UK, 131 mins, colour
Dir: John Glenn
Stars: Timothy Dalton, Maryam D'Abo, Joe Don Baker, Jeroen Krabbe, John Rhys-Davies, Art Malik
Rating: ★★

Timothy Dalton – the fourth actor to play 007 agent James Bond – is neatly introduced in a suitably tongue-in-cheek pre-credits sequence in which three double-O agents (the other two bearing a remarkable similarity to Roger Moore and George Lazenby) parachute on to Gibraltar to see if they can penetrate the Rock's radar installation. Although Dalton proves to be a pale shadow of his predecessors, the film does see the return of Bond's trademark Aston Martin car, not the DB5 of the earlier

L

films but a more recent model, the Volante, souped up by 'Q' to carry laser beams that can cut a car in half, automatic missiles, and skis so that it can travel on snow and ice. The formula was looking very dated when this one finally made it to cinemas – especially with its story of a Russian agent defecting to the West.

Living Desert, The ☉
1953, US, 72 mins, colour
Dir: James Algar
Voice star: Winston Hibler
Rating: ★★★★

Although now often shortened for television, this was originally the first feature-length entry in Walt Disney's True Life Adventure series. It won an Academy Award and became the first nature documentary in years to attract worldwide queues. Purists complained about the brilliant orchestration of the material to fit with some highly original musical accompaniment, but the move helped to make the film immensely entertaining. The 'square dance' of the scorpions, contrived as it is, remains a classic.

Living Free ○
1972, UK, 92 mins, colour
Dir: Jack Couffer
Stars: Nigel Davenport, Susan Hampshire
Rating: ★★

Pleasant, leisurely sequel to *Born Free* and *The Lions Are Free*, gorgeously photographed in colour by Wolfgang Suschitzky. Susan Hampshire and Nigel Davenport romp with their leonine friends as to the manner born, and children will love every sentimental moment of it.

Living It Up ○
1954, US, 95 mins, colour
Dir: Norman Taurog
Stars: Dean Martin, Jerry Lewis, Janet Leigh, Sheree North, Edward Arnold
Rating: ★★★

The Dean Martin-Jerry Lewis team adds its own way-out comedy touch to this remake of the Fredric March-Carole Lombard laughter classic, *Nothing Sacred*. Jerry Lewis plays the man who is treated to a last fling by his doctor and a pretty girl journalist when an incorrect diagnosis reveals that he is dying of radiation poisoning. The misadventures they run into, the pitfalls they have to avoid, and the eventual showdown, are all fast,

furious and in the best traditions of slapstick. The snappy script comes from the combined pens of Melville Shavelson and Jack Rose, who worked a lot with that other great clown, Danny Kaye. The funniest situation they dream up here is one in which Jerry impersonates three foreign specialists who have been sent to examine him. He has knocked out his own doctor and substituted him as the patient. Happily, the script also makes room for delicious Sheree North – who started as a dancer but proved a durable actress – and that apoplectic mountain of a supporting comedy star, Fred Clark.

Lizzie ◑
1957, US, 81 mins, b/w
Dir: Hugo Haas
Stars: Eleanor Parker, Richard Boone
Rating: ★★

Although quite well written by Mel Dinelli, a veteran of RKO's *film noir* days, this story of a woman with three personalities ran a definite second-best to *The Three Faces of Eve*, the classic psycho-drama released the same year. The most ambitious film of morose Czech-born actor-director Hugo Haas (who usually, as here, played roles in his own movies), the film is hard-put to keep hysteria and sleazy melodrama at arms' reach, especially in the uncharacteristically undisciplined performance of Eleanor Parker in the title role. Richard Boone and Joan Blondell offer lower-key, more believable portrayals. Johnny Mathis makes a rare screen appearance, as a nightclub singer.

Lloyds of London ○
1936, US, 115 mins, b/w
Dir: Henry King
Stars: Tyrone Power, Madeleine Carroll, George Sanders, Freddie Bartholomew
Rating: ★★★

A good, solid piece of storytelling in the teemingly-detailed Hollywood style of the Thirties. Somehow the scriptwriters contrive to enliven the history of the famous English insurance and banking firm by pumping in romance, shipwrecks, conspiracies and even the Battle of Trafalgar. We watch little Freddie Bartholomew grow up to be Tyrone Power and they share the acting honours. Director Henry King keeps an impressive grip on his sprawling subject.

Local Hero ○ ⓥ
1983, UK, 110 mins, colour
Dir: Bill Forsyth
Stars: Burt Lancaster, Peter Riegert, Fulton MacKay, Denis Lawson, Peter Capaldi, Jenny Seagrove
Rating: ★★★

A leisurely, Scottish-set comedy in the old Ealing tradition, with wonderful coastal scenery and some marvellous laughs, mostly along blithely silly lines as an American gas-oil company bids to buy up a whole slice of the Scottish coast. The locals are only too willing to drive a hard bargain, until it's discovered that the old beachcomber who owns a section of the coastline just won't budge. If this has the outward appearances of such Ealing comedies as *Whisky Galore!* and *The Maggie*, the souls of *Airplane!* and *Monty Python* lurk not far under the surface. The black vicar is called Murdo Macpherson, the boss of the American company (Burt Lancaster) enjoys a manic relationship with his analyst, and a girl marine biologist turns out to have webbed feet. Director Bill Forsyth gets it all right, especially at the end, and there are inch-perfect performances from Lancaster, Peter Riegert (his young representative who falls under the spell of the place), Denis Lawson as the hotelier-lawyer-accountant-writer who heads up the villagers when not making love to his sultry wife (Jennifer Black), which isn't often, and Fulton MacKay, the latter priceless as the beachcomber.

Lock Up ● ⓥ
1989, US, 106 mins, colour
Dir: John Flynn
Stars: Sylvester Stallone, Donald Sutherland, John Amos, Darlanne Fluegel
Rating: ★★★

This is just the thing to see after a hard day at the office. Mindless, violent (but not that violent), well-made, professional entertainment: an entirely satisfactory vehicle for a star. Sylvester Stallone is the model prisoner with six months to serve who's suddenly and brutally transferred to a maximum security prison whose warden (Donald Sutherland) he once made a fool of in more ways than one. The plot's a joke, of course, but who cares? The mechanics of making a hard-hitting and effectively thrilling prison story, with all its stereotypes and clichés intact, are what matter here. Stallone does all that you could ask, and you can even understand some of his dialogue. Sutherland proves he's as effective as a psycho as in quieter roles. Forget your worries, sit back and let those brain cells not frazzled by the day just mop it up.

Lock Up Your Daughters! ◐
1969, UK, 102 mins, colour
Dir: Peter Coe
Stars: Christopher Plummer, Susannah York, Glynis Johns, Ian Bannen, Tom Bell, Jim Dale
Rating: ★★

Lusty comic entertainment along the lines of *Tom Jones*, actually adapted by Keith Waterhouse and Willis Hall from the stage musical which was in turn taken from the play *Rape Upon Rape* by Henry Fielding (who wrote *Tom Jones*) and Vanbrugh's *The Relapse*. Names such as Mr Squeezum, Lady Clumsey, Lusty, Hoyden and Lady Eager give an idea of the general tone, and the cast plunges in with a will. Jim Dale, Tom Bell and Ian Bannen are well contrasted as the three hot-blooded sailors desperate for wenches after months at sea; Susannah York is enchanting as the tomboy Hilaret; Fenella Fielding incredible as Lady Eager, uttering whispered cries for help when attacked by an attractive man; and Glynis Johns best of all in her lecherous observations on felons in the dock ('*Two* rapists? Indeed!').

Lolita ●
1962, US, 152 mins, b/w
Dir: Stanley Kubrick
Stars: James Mason, Sue Lyon, Peter Sellers, Shelley Winters
Rating: ★★

Director Stanley Kubrick was riding on the crest of a critical wave of applause, after *Paths of Glory* and *Spartacus*, when he persuaded Vladimir Nabokov to help make a film out of the novel – about a middle-aged man falling for a teenage temptress – that had delighted and scandalised the nation. He also got a formidable cast together, including Peter Sellers, who gives the best performance in what turned out to be a rather indigestible film, which did more for sunglasses (as worn by Sue Lyon's Lolita) than the cinema.

London Belongs to Me ○
(aka: Dulcimer Street)
1948, UK, 112 mins, b/w
Dir: Sidney Gilliat

Stars: Richard Attenborough, Alastair Sim, Fay Compton, Joyce Carey
Rating: ★★★

Absorbing Launder and Gilliat film about the denizens of a south London boarding house in 1939. A touchingly human drama with fine London atmosphere. Richard Attenborough has a familiar early role as a cocky but panicky young man involved in crime. Such expert character stars as Fay Compton, Joyce Carey and Alastair Sim are less cast to type but just as good. The settings are convincingly drab and the dialogue is believably written by Sidney Gilliat and J B Williams from a then-popular novel by Norman Collins.

London Kills Me ● Ⓥ
1991, UK, 105 mins, colour
Dir: Hanif Kureishi
Stars: Justin Chadwick, Emer McCourt, Naveen Andrews, Steven Mackintosh, Brad Dourif, Eleanor David
Rating: ★★

For the most part, this is a bizarre and unlovely film about homeless teenage drug dealers/users on the streets of London. Gaunt and dishevelled, Clint (Justin Chadwick), basically a dishonest charmer, is beaten up by men to whom he owes money. He resolves to get a proper job and gets a promise of work in a diner – if he can get a pair of new shoes. As Clint steals constantly from his immediate boss Muffdiver (Steven Mackintosh), a pair of shoes would seem an easy option. But apparently not. Despite many unappealing aspects, the film does quite a fair job of dividing its time between a portrait of the drug generation and the story of Clint looking for shoes to steal. Sometimes the tale becomes tedious, especially when its women are involved, but the upbeat ending helps, and Chadwick and Mackintosh are fresh, newish faces who perform with enthusiasm and a degree of conviction. Settings are suitably squalid, but in London these days that's not difficult: you just take your camera into its garbage-infested streets and shoot.

London Town ○
(aka: My Heart Goes Crazy)
1946, UK, 126 mins, colour
Dir: Wesley Ruggles
Stars: Sid Field, Petula Clark, Greta Gynt, Kay Kendall, Claude Hulbert
Rating: ★

This big Technicolor film was made as Britain's answer to Hollywood musicals, and to showcase successful stage comedian Sid Field whose one previous movie had been the 1940 comedy *That's the Ticket*. In fact, it was not very effective as either, although it did give an early leading role to Kay Kendall; and the 14-year-old Petula Clark is delightful as Field's daughter. The director is a Hollywood expert, Wesley Ruggles (brother of actor Charlie Ruggles), who made such early screen hits as *Cimarron, No Man of Her Own, I'm No Angel* and *Bolero*. Alas, he lost the Rank Organisation a fortune on this one.

Loneliness of the Long Distance Runner, The ◐ Ⓥ
1962, UK, 100 mins, b/w
Dir: Tony Richardson
Stars: Tom Courtenay, Julia Foster, Michael Redgrave, Alec McCowen
Rating: ★★★

A hard-edged drama filmed in stark black-and-white, this is the story of a poor working-class youth sent to Borstal. Fine acting and a good script keep this early Sixties 'angry young man' drama fresh-looking today. The ending, although structurally sound, remains unsatisfying.

Lonely Are the Brave ○
1962, US, 107 mins, b/w
Dir: David Miller
Stars: Kirk Douglas, Gena Rowlands, Walter Matthau
Rating: ★★★

Kirk Douglas turns in another fine performance as the old-fashioned cowboy out of step with and resistant to the modern world. He starts a brawl in a bar just to get jailed so he can see an old friend, Michael Kane. He then breaks out of jail, pursued by sheriff Walter Matthau. Douglas is on horseback, Matthau drives a jeep. To say any more would be to hint at the film's ending (and no, he doesn't get shot), but Douglas himself captured the mood of the picture when talking about why he took the role: 'The difficulty of being an individual today is what attracted me to the story.' Douglas' personality dominates the picture, but Matthau is convincing as the lawman who feels empathy for Douglas' cowboy.

Lonelyhearts ○
1962, US, 101 mins, b/w
Dir: Vincent J Donehue

L

Stars: Montgomery Clift, Robert Ryan, Myrna Loy
Rating: ★★

Unusual film drama about a hard-up reporter who becomes Miss Lonelyhearts of an agony column – and gets involved with his readers' problems. Good portrayals from Montgomery Clift, Robert Ryan and Myrna Loy, and especially Broadway actress Maureen Stapleton, who, in one of her rare screen appearances, gives an outstanding performance as the wife of a bitter cripple.

Lonely Passion of Judith Hearne, The ● ⓥ
1987, UK, 116 mins, colour
Dir: Jack Clayton
Stars: Maggie Smith, Bob Hoskins, Wendy Hiller, Prunella Scales, Ian McNeice
Rating: ★★

One of those films that makes you admire the quality of its acting, but offers much less in the way of entertainment. Maggie Smith etches to the last detail a repressed Irish spinster with a sideline in piano teaching and a weakness for the whisky. Moving in with a mealy-mouthed landlady and her bloated post-graduate son who spends his nights with the 16-year-old maid, the spinster soon conceives a hopeless passion for the landlady's brother (Bob Hoskins), back from America after 30 years. Riddled with religious guilt, the story's also frequently dull, despite the razor-sharp acting of a cast that also includes Wendy Hiller and Prunella Scales. Another great performance from Maggie Smith, though, that certainly commands your attention.

Lone Ranger, The ○
1956, US, 86 mins, colour
Dir: Stuart Heisler
Stars: Clayton Moore, Jay Silverheels
Rating: ★★

Feature-length version of the enormously popular television programme of the early Fifties, complete with the original stars. Husky voiced Lyle Bettger makes a stylish villain and former teenage star Bonita Granville is the heroine. Not great, but a lot better than the 1981 version though.

Lone Ranger and the Lost City of Gold, The ○
1958, US, 81 mins, colour
Dir: Lesley Selander

Stars: Clayton Moore, Jay Silverheels, Noreen Nash
Rating: ★★

Rousing action stuff for the children as the Lone Ranger and Tonto follow the trail of five medallions that lead to a fortune. Expert Western director Lesley Selander (a man, despite the spelling) keeps the rough-and-tumble brisk and uncomplicated. Noreen Nash, remembered as the freckled heroine from animal films of the Forties, gets a rare chance to play an all-out bad lot, and revels in the role.

Lone Wolf McQuade ● ⓥ
1983, US, 107 mins, colour
Dir: Steve Carver
Stars: Chuck Norris, David Carradine, Barbara Carrera
Rating: ★

An orgy of carefully-staged and edited violence. Chop-socky specialist Chuck Norris is the present-day Texas Ranger who's not certain to win until the bad guys hurt the things he loves: first the older Ranger he idolises, then his pet wolf, then his daughter. It's hard to know what the man of steel will run out of first: opponents or Achilles heels. Some well-known players, among them David Carradine, L Q Jones, R G Armstrong, Barbara Carrera and Leon Isaac Kennedy, are involved in the get-yourself-out-of-this situations. Action is heavily underlined by music in the Ennio Morricone mould.

Long and the Short and the Tall, The ●
(aka: Jungle Fighters)
1960, UK, 110 mins, b/w
Dir: Leslie Norman
Stars: Richard Todd, Richard Harris, David McCallum, Laurence Harvey
Rating: ★★★

A British patrol in Burma sows the seeds of its own destruction in this tougher-than-tough war film. The script, by Wolf Mankowitz from Willis Hall's play, burns through the screen like vitriol.

Long Arm, The ○
(aka: The Third Key)
1956, UK, 100 mins, b/w
Dir: Charles Frend
Stars: Jack Hawkins, John Stratton, Dorothy Alison
Rating: ★★★★

An excellent, intricately-plotted story of police work from Ealing Studios, with Jack Hawkins in towering form

as the inspector. He, Dorothy Alison and John Stratton build lifelike characters in the leading roles, while the exciting, well-knit plot has Hawkins and his men trekking across half of England on the trail of a master cracksman – and killer. A bit like *Dragnet* with British accents, the film piles on its excitement in fine style, making it streets ahead of Hawkins' other Fifties police story *Gideon's Day*. Even the cameo roles are well done in this, the last Ealing film actually to be made at Ealing studios.

Long Duel, The ○
1967, UK, 115 mins, colour
Dir: Ken Annakin
Stars: Yul Brynner, Trevor Howard, Harry Andrews, Andrew Keir, Charlotte Rampling
Rating: ★★

A British attempt to match the American action spectacles of the mid-Sixties, with Brynner and Howard as adversaries in the India of the British Raj of the Twenties. Three delectable actresses, Charlotte Rampling, Virginia North and Imogen Hassall, earn early film chances; and one can also spot Edward Fox and Patrick Newell (remember him as Mother in *The Avengers*?) among the supporting players. Long and dull.

Longest Day, The ○ ⓥ
1962, US/UK, 180 mins, b/w
Dir: Darryl F Zanuck, Ken Annakin, Andrew Marton, Gerd Oswald, Bernhard Wicki
Stars: John Wayne, Rod Steiger, Robert Ryan, Henry Fonda, Robert Mitchum, Richard Burton
Rating: ★★★

Just about the war film to end them all, with the participation of more than 50 star names. This is Darryl F Zanuck's – he produced and was one of the five directors – massive reconstruction of the events leading to, and happening on, 6 June 1944, when the Allied forces invaded Nazi Europe. It sticks closely to the known facts, photographs its events in a semi-newsreel manner (it was one of the last major films made in black and white) and relates countless stories of individual heroism and tragedy in its three hours-plus running time. To inject added realism, it also allows the Germans to speak their own language – with sub-titles. The first half of the picture, dealing with the events leading up to D-Day, is really only a warm-up, and a rather lengthy one at that, for the tremendous action on the Normandy beaches. When the action scenes do come, however, director Andrew Marton, deserves a large bouquet for his handling of them. How admirably he marshals his forces, taking our attention easily from one embattled group to another with a pan of the camera, or via the path of an aeroplane skimming low over the beach battlegrounds. Any number of small cameo scenes are skilfully woven into the larger patchwork of the D-Day operation, allowing room for small-scale but excellent performances from Henry Fonda, Robert Mitchum, John Wayne, Eddie Albert, Red Buttons and Curt Jurgens.

Longest Yard, The
See: The Mean Machine

Long Goodbye, The ● ⓥ
1973, US, 111 mins, colour
Dir: Robert Altman
Stars: Elliott Gould, Nina Van Pallandt, Sterling Hayden, Henry Gibson, Mark Rydell
Rating: ★

Raymond Chandler traditionalists who think private eye Philip Marlowe should wear a flap down hat and look like Humphrey Bogart or Dick Powell won't take to director Robert Altman's Seventies version. More to the point, this is a tedious and sometimes confusing film. Marlowe moves from the California of the Thirties to the California of the Seventies quite successfully, although he and his surroundings have changed considerably along the way. Altman's attention to character detail and slightly quirky direction coupled with bright colour photography soaked in the California sunshine are a world away from the monochrome Los Angeles through which Bogart and Powell walked unafraid. Elliott Gould's Marlowe is seedy and down-at-heel – and totally unconvincing. There is solid support from Sterling Hayden as a drunken writer and Henry Gibson as an evil doctor. And you can't miss a young Arnold Schwarzenegger, billed here as Arnold Strong! Watch out for the ending. For someone steeped in Chandler lore, it will be a culture shock – if you're still awake, that is.

Long Good Friday, The ● ⓥ
1979, UK, 114 mins, colour
Dir: John Mackenzie

Stars: Bob Hoskins, Helen Mirren, Dave King, Eddie Constantine
Rating: ★★★

In the early Sixties, there was *Hell is a City* and *The Criminal*; in the early Seventies *Villain* and *Get Carter*. Here the tough British crime film moves on another decade, revealing a yet blacker and more violent picture, as the over-complacent British gangster is ruthlessly brushed aside by interests from America and the new lawlessness from Ireland. As the Cockney kingpin of London crime, Bob Hoskins is best when roaring defiance at his enemies like a wounded, cornered animal. The scenes of violence are many, ugly and professional, and the film moves like a steamroller, heavy and relentless but ever onwards, greatly helped by the doomy background music of Francis Monkman. The acting does not always seem as relaxed as it might be, with the definite exception of Dave King's thoroughly bent policeman.

Long Gray Line, The ○
1955, US, 131 mins, colour
Dir: John Ford
Stars: Tyrone Power, Maureen O'Hara, Robert Francis, Ward Bond, Donald Crisp
Rating: ★★★★

Rolling along on a veritable flood of tears and nostalgia, this is John Ford's tribute to West Point, America's famous military academy, and to one Irishman who spent the greater part of his life there. Although the ending is protracted and over-sentimental (even by the film's own standards), most of it is a brilliant job of story construction by the director, who weaves many of his most personal themes into the piecemeal storyline, knitting it together and building a picture that packs a powerful emotional punch. If you're easily moved at the movies, keep a handkerchief or two safely by. Tyrone Power gives one of his better film performances as the central figure, but this is Maureen O'Hara's film. As the girl who becomes Power's wife, she has never been warmer or more winning.

Long Hot Summer, The ○
1958, US, 118 mins, colour
Dir: Martin Ritt
Stars: Paul Newman, Joanne Woodward, Orson Welles, Anthony Franciosa, Lee Remick, Angela Lansbury
Rating: ★★★

This fiery melodrama, based on two short stories and part of a novel by

William Faulkner, shot Paul Newman, Joanne Woodward, Lee Remick and Anthony Franciosa to stardom. Newman is the young opportunist who arrives in town, bringing with him a reputation for burning people's barns if they cross him. On the basis that guts get you places, he makes an impression on his landlord (a boisterous performance by Orson Welles), the town bigwig, and meets his match (in more ways than one – they fell in love on the set and married in the same year) in Joanne Woodward's sassy daughter. She is attracted to the newcomer but damned if she's going to marry him at her Dad's bidding. The scene is thus set for lots of incident and passion – and there's plenty of both. Newman and Woodward are first-class, and there's excellent support from Anthony Franciosa as Welles' wimpish son (who plans a dramatic revenge on his bully of a father), Lee Remick as his sweet-natured wife and Angela Lansbury as Welles' long-time mistress.

Long John Silver ○
1954, Australia, 109 mins, colour
Dir: Byron Haskin
Stars: Robert Newton, Kit Taylor, Grant Taylor, Rod Taylor
Rating: ★★

This was the second film that Robert Newton made in the character he created in *Treasure Island* – Long John Silver, the peg-legged scourge of the Caribbean. The film was produced in Australia, and many good Australian actors go miles over the top in a story that's simply crammed with incident, action and colour. A fair dinkum kid called Kit Taylor takes over from Bobby Driscoll as Jim 'awkins. And it's out with the telescopes, me hearties, to spot the actor lurking behind sightless eyes and a mass of stubble as bad old Israel Hands, waiting for Jim lad who blinded him those many years before. Yes, it's a youngster called Rodney (later Rod) Taylor, who went to America the following year and launched a star career that lasted 20 years. The film was made on location in the South Seas, and at Botany Bay, near Sydney, where one of the most expensive sets ever used in an Australian film was constructed: a typical 17th century seafaring town.

Long, Long Trailer, The ☉
1954, US, 103 mins, colour
Dir: Vincente Minnelli

L

Stars: Lucille Ball, Desi Arnaz
Rating: ★★★★

A totally side-splitting comedy about the misadventures of a newly-married couple taking their honeymoon in a giant caravan. Full of funny little individual scenes, the film, boosted by Lucille Ball and Desi Arnaz's success on TV, proved an absolute goldmine at box-offices on both sides of the Atlantic. There are nice little 'bits' for Keenan Wynn and Marjorie Main, but really the stars are the whole show. Vincente Minnelli directs it all at 60 mile-an-hour speed and Robert Surtees' Ansco Color photography is simply stunning.

Long Riders, The ● ⓥ
1980, US, 95 mins, colour
Dir: Walter Hill
Stars: Stacey Keach, David Carradine, Keith Carradine, Robert Carradine, Dennis Quaid, Randy Quaid
Rating: ★

The James-Younger gang rides again in yet another re-telling of their infamous bank-robbing career from Missouri to Minnesota (and the fateful Northfield raid), each version bloodier and gutsier than the last. The trump card here is the casting of four sets of acting brothers as the Jameses, Youngers, Millers and treacherous Fords. This acting fraternity equits itself well. Under Walter Hill's surprisingly lyrical direction (considering he made such stark thrillers as *Driver* and *The Warriors*), the film tries not to make heroes of the boys; but they come out that way anyway.

Long Ships, The ○
1964, UK, 125 mins, colour
Dir: Jack Cardiff
Stars: Richard Widmark, Sidney Poitier, Russ Tamblyn, Rosanna Schiaffino
Rating: ★

Richard Widmark and Sidney Poitier never seem anything but Hollywood stars in costume in this colourful adventure story about a Viking odyssey, actually shot on and along the rocky coastline of Yugoslavia. Decades later, the film set village still existed – although a bit dilapidated – and was regularly shown to parties of tourists. It's not half as decrepit as the script, though, and even Christopher Challis' colour camerawork seems below par.

Longtime Companion ● ⓥ
1990, US, 99 mins, colour
Dir: Norman René
Stars: Bruce Davison, Campbell Scott, Mary-Louise Parker
Rating: ★★★

This was Hollywood's first film to tell the story of how AIDS devastated America's homosexual community during the 1980s. A big hit at the Cannes Film Festival, it tells the stories of a group of friends whose lives are all affected in different ways by the deaths of lovers (the film's title comes from the euphemism given to gay partners in obituary columns) and friends. Made on a miniscule budget of $1.5 million, it skilfully weaves educational information with storyline and successfully avoids being at all mawkish during the more emotive scenes. Not without moments of great humour, the film does contain one truly outstanding performance from Bruce Davison (the father in the *Harry and the Hendersons* TV series) who was deservedly nominated for a Best Supporting Actor Oscar for his role as the lover of a TV soap scriptwriter who allows his friend to die with as much dignity as possible. A brave landmark film.

Long Voyage Home, The ○
1940, US, 120 mins, b/w
Dir: John Ford
Stars: John Wayne, Thomas Mitchell, Ian Hunter, John Qualen, Barry Fitzgerald
Rating: ★★★★

Great film that proves a major triumph for the John Ford/John Wayne partnership, then in its early days. In its story of seamen longing for a return home while going through hell and high water on the way, there are memorable performances from Thomas Mitchell and Ian Hunter, and the greasy, sweaty, smoky atmosphere of the tramp steamer in which the men live and toil is finely done. The story has a typical Eugene O'Neill air of futility about it (it's adapted from three of his one-act plays), but the tragedy-tinged ending, strongly reminiscent of a sequence in *Cavalcade*, only adds to the film's overall impact. There's great supporting acting from Ward Bond, Mildred Natwick and Arthur Shields, but all the cast sink themselves into the characters they play. A long, winding film, sometimes exciting, often touching, with some strongly descriptive black-and-white photography by Gregg Toland.

Look Back in Anger ◐ ⓥ
1959, UK, 99 mins, b/w
Dir: Tony Richardson
Stars: Richard Burton, Claire Bloom, Mary Ure, Gary Raymond, Edith Evans, Donald Pleasence
Rating: ★★★

This tough-talking film made an extraordinary impact on audiences in its day, and consolidated the arrival of new-wave realism – termed 'kitchen-sink' by some critics – begun by *Room at the Top*. The dialogue bristles with barbs – most of them from the lips of original angry young man Jimmy Porter, providing a prime role for Richard Burton.

Look for the Silver Lining ○
1949, US, 100 mins, colour
Dir: David Butler
Stars: June Haver, Ray Bolger, Gordon MacRae, Charlie Ruggles
Rating: ★★★

A typically cheerful Warner Bros. biopic – suitably fictionalised – with June Haver impersonating Twenties Broadway musical comedy star Marilyn Miller (a role previously played by Judy Garland in the 1946 film *Till the Clouds Roll By*). But it's Ray Bolger, playing Miller's mentor Jack Donohue, who steals the picture with some dazzling tap dancing, proving once again that he was one of the cinema's most shamefully underused dancers. Plenty of tuneful vintage songs (musical director Ray Heindorf received an Oscar nomination), LeRoy Prinz's smart choreography and David Butler's direction completing this lively package. The ending, very daring, actually hints at Miller's early death.

Looking Glass War, The ◐
1969, UK, 108 mins, colour
Dir: Frank R Pierson
Stars: Christopher Jones, Pia Degermark, Ralph Richardson, Anthony Hopkins, Susan George, Paul Rogers
Rating: ★

This espionage yarn from the bitter pen of John Le Carré is both an adventure story and a clinical portrayal of British Cold war espionage as a world apart, almost outdated in its approach and ideals. Christopher Jones plays the young Polish refugee sent on a dangerous mission into East Germany. The long training he undergoes is the most entertaining section of the film. After that, uncharacteristic acting and a wordy script sink all concerned.

Look Who's Talking ◐ ⓥ
1989, US, 96 mins, colour
Dir: Amy Heckerling
Stars: John Travolta, Kirstie Alley, Olympia Dukakis, George Segal, Voice of Bruce Willis
Rating: ★★

One of the big money-spinners of it's year, to the bafflement of many critics, this is a tolerable novelty romp if you care for cute comedies about babies. John Travolta's career certainly needed a break at this stage, but this was a mighty lucky one. An embarrassing beginning, giving a impression of a gang of sperms fertilising a human egg, is followed by a most unconvincing pregnancy in which unwed mum Kirstie Alley looks as though she is wearing a toilet seat under her dress. The tale is made partially palatable by the performance of the beautifully flat-faced Alley and by using the voice of Bruce Willis to give us the thoughts of the baby. Travolta is more or less along for the ride as the taxi-driver the baby wants to be his father, and George Segal and Olympia Dukakis don't make much impression in supporting roles. You'll enjoy some of it, though – also the continuity slip where our hero is 'driving' his cab, which is clearly being steered by a stuntman wearing dark glasses, while Travolta isn't wearing glasses at all! The sequel, *Look Who's Talking Too*, was cruder and quite without merit, as was a second sequel, *Look Who's Talking Now*.

Look Who's Talking Too ◐ ⓥ
1990, US, 77 mins, colour
Dir: Amy Heckerling
Stars: John Travolta, Kirstie Alley, Voices of Bruce Willis, Roseanne Arnold
Rating: ★

Good sense and good taste are certainly not on the menu for this typically crude Hollywood sequel to a wildly successful original. Lavatory humour, though, is well to the fore, emphasised by the use of Mel Brooks' voice as Mr Toilet Man, a loo-bowl come to life, spitting blue water and threatening irreparable damage to baby Mikey's private parts. Bruce Willis is as laconic as ever as the voice of Mikey, but Roseanne Arnold's contribution as the voice of his new baby sister is unexpectedly dull. Kirstie Alley and John Travolta still play

pleasingly as the parents, but the plotline is almost non-existent and the film, at well under 90 minutes, all too obviously a rush job.

Loot ◐ ⓥ
1970, UK, 101 mins, colour
Dir: Silvio Narizzano
Stars: Richard Attenborough, Lee Remick, Hwyel Bennett, Milo O'Shea
Rating: ★★

A really dark-hued black comedy, well adapted by *Hancock* and *Steptoe and Son* writers Ray Galton and Alan Simpson from Joe Orton's celebrated stage play. Silvio Narizzano's stylish direction and the neatly judged over-the-top performances perfectly complement the writers' sardonic view of life and death. Particularly effective are Lee Remick as a blond murderess and Richard Attenborough as the kind of policeman destined to give Scotland Yard a distinctly odd name.

Lord Jim ○
1965, US, 154 mins, colour
Dir: Richard Brooks
Stars: Peter O'Toole, James Mason, Curt Jurgens, Jack Hawkins, Eli Wallach, Daliah Lavi
Rating: ★★

Joseph Conrad's magnificent novel of high adventure in the 19th century Far East is translated faithfully to the screen in this film from the hands of writer-director Richard Brooks. The action is fierce and many of the characters are surely just as Conrad must have seen them, particularly Jack Hawkins as the narrator (Marlow) and James Mason, almost unrecognisable as the treacherous pirate Gentleman Brown. But Peter O'Toole completely misses the mystique of the central character, which he seems to see as a sort of Lawrence of Cambodia.

Lord Love a Duck ◐
1966, US, 103 mins, b/w
Dir: George Axelrod
Stars: Roddy McDowall, Tuesday Weld, Lola Albright
Rating: ★★★

Wild and bitingly funny sex comedy from George Axelrod, who wrote *The Seven-Year Itch* and *Breakfast at Tiffany's*. Roddy (*Planet of the Apes*) McDowall plays a collegiate who masterminds his fellow students' lives through hypnotism.

Lord of the Flies ◐ ⓥ
1963, UK, 90 mins, b/w

Dir: Peter Brook
Stars: James Aubrey, Tom Chapin, Hugh Edwards
Rating: ★★★

What would happen if a party of schoolboys were stranded on a desert island? This horrifying parable gives us the blackest possible answer. Their brittle society shatters, rules are broken and the boys become in turn arguers, hunters, idolaters, cannibals and murderers. The impact of director Peter Brook's film version of William Golding's novel is considerable, even though the acting of the minor roles is, in many cases, little more than a mechanical repetition of lines. But James Aubrey is solid as the sensible Ralph, and Tom Chapin excellent as the sullen, leering Jack, the head choirboy with a hyena's sneer, laugh and manners behind his public school veneer. Though his pace is slow in parts, Brook skilfully probes his way through the mounting horror, just as the camera weaves its grainy way through the undergrowth of the island.

Lord of the Rings ○ ⓥ
1978, US, 133 mins, colour
Dir: Ralph Bakshi
Stars: Voice stars: Christopher Guard, William Squire, John Hurt, Michael Sholes
Rating: ★★★

Director Ralph Bakshi's attempt to set down an animated version of J R R Tolkien's massive saga of Middle Earth (or at least the first half of it) must go down as a jolly good try at an almost impossible project. Certain sections – the mines of Moria; the Ringwraiths in the sky – are bitingly close to one's visualisation of the book. The voices of the hobbits seem a little too light and West Country at first but, like the rest of the voices – John Hurt makes a splendid Aragorn – they grow on you. The action is at times a bit jerky where so much has been telescoped into so little – don't miss the beginning or you'll lose the thread of it; but we should be grateful that Bakshi has tried so hard to be faithful to the original that its spirit and inspiration often shine through to stir the blood. Gandalf, Saruman (the good and evil wizards), Wormtongue and Legolas are particularly well realised, and the flowing music theme is of great assistance in lending the action momentum when it needs it most.

L

Lorenzo's Oil ❶ ⓥ
1992, US, 135 mins, colour
Dir: George Miller
Stars: Nick Nolte, Susan Sarandon, Peter Ustinov, Zack O'Malley Greenburg, Kathleen Wilhoite
Rating: ★★★

If we pardon its occasional lapses, this is a good, if very punishing account of one couple's struggle to find a cure for their son, stricken with ALD – a form of dystrophy which affects male children – which no boy had previously survived longer than 24 months. This is an inspiring story but the problem with the film, like so many modern ones, is that it goes on too long. By prolonging our agony as well as Lorenzo's, director George Miller dissipates the suspense and dissolves our emotional involvement. Matters are exacerbated near the end by a poorly-acted English scientist who tells us he has six months to retirement but looks more like 90. That said, Nick Nolte and Susan Sarandon, as the parents, and Zack O'Malley Greenburg, as the boy, give performances that deserved to be jostling at the Oscar queues that year (though only Sarandon's did). A pity their story is too intense and too repetitious for too long, but the achievements of the real-life people involved are beyond praise and even belief.

Loss of Innocence
See: The Greengage Summer

Lost ○
(aka: Tears for Simon)
1955, UK, 89 mins, colour
Dir: Guy Green
Stars: David Farrar, David Knight, Julia Arnall
Rating: ★★★

Carefully-made British thriller with a fair share of tension and excitement. Screenplay writer Janet Green made some useful contributions to the British cinema (*Sapphire*, *Life for Ruth* and Victim<I> were among her best) and here she fashions a tidy drama about a stolen toddler, which focuses both on the intricacies of the police hunt and the pressures faced by the distraught parents. As the mother, Austrian-born Julia Arnall, who was briefly under contract to Rank in the Fifties, gives her most effective screen performance. Character roles are more than capably filled by such stalwarts of the British cinema as Thora Hird, Anthony Oliver, Eleanor Summerfield and Marjorie Rhodes.

Lost and Found ○
1979, US, 112 mins, colour
Dir: Melvin Frank
Stars: George Segal, Glenda Jackson, Maureen Stapleton, Paul Sorvino
Rating: ★★

If George Segal taught Glenda Jackson a thing or two about the art of screen comedy in *A Touch of Class* (for which she won an Oscar), then the lesson was well and truly learnt. For it's George who comes out the loser in their second film together, flapping around while Glenda piles up the points with her tart and acerbic delivery. Most of the best fun comes in the first two reels when Glenda, on the run from her ex-husband's mistress ('Mona – age 22, bust 38, IQ indiscernible') and George, on the run from his late wife's memory, keep bumping into each other with devastating effect at a Swiss chalet resort.

Lost Boys, The ❶ ⓥ
1987, US, 98 mins, colour
Dir: Joel Schumacher
Stars: Jason Patric, Corey Haim, Dianne Wiest, Edward Herrman, Kiefer Sutherland, Jami Gertz, Corey Feldman
Rating: ★★★

A lively horror film that also crams in as many amusing lines as possible, this ends up as a kind of *Fangbusters*. Two boys and their mother move into a town where, as their grandpa puts it, 'if all the corpses in the churchyards were to stand up, we'd have one hell of a population problem.' Lured on by the comely Star (Jami Gertz), older brother Michael (Jason Patric) is soon inducted in to the society of The Lost Boys, led by the ghoulish David (Kiefer Sutherland). 'You're a vampire Michael,' squawks young Sam (Corey Haim). 'My own brother!' Enter Edgar and Allan, the real Fangbusters. 'We're almost certain,' says Edgar, 'that ghouls and werewolves are in high positions in City Hall.' So the scene is set for a special effects finale typical of today's cinema. The film drags a bit but it really gets motoring around the half-way mark. The British 15 certificate seemed harsh considering the blood-letting is mainly off-screen, there's little bad language and one 'PG' sex scene.

Lost Command ❶
1966, US, 130 mins, colour
Dir: Mark Robson
Stars: Anthony Quinn, Alain Delon, George Segal, Michelle Morgan, Claudia Cardinale
Rating: ★★

Scenes of incredibly tough paratroop training, and a sequence of bloodthirsty battles help to take your mind off thinking that the script of this blood-spattered story of France's war against Algeria is glorifying a messy war for the sake of entertainment. But, in more than two hours, surely some positive thinking on the whys and wherefores of this long and bitter affray could have replaced the devious sidetrack subjects which destroy any feeling of involvement with the characters. As it is, we have Anthony Quinn as a sort of Zorba the Sheep, who, after service in Indo-China, is deprived of his command, largely because he has no regard for higher authority, and is of peasant stock, a point the script loses no chance to ram home. 'I'd rather stand, sir,' Quinn tells a superior. 'It's a habit I developed as a shepherd boy.'

Lost Continent, The ❶
1968, UK, 98 mins, colour
Dir: Michael Carreras
Stars: Eric Porter, Hildegarde Knef, Suzanna Leigh
Rating: ★★★

Eerie atmosphere and decent monsters boost this rather bizarre piece of science-fantasy about a tramp steamer wandering into uncharted seas and discovering a lost civilisation. Eric Porter keeps a straight face and stiff upper lip; Dana Gillespie offers statuesque support.

Lost Horizon ○ ⓥ
1937, US, 130 mins, b/w
Dir: Frank Capra
Stars: Ronald Colman, Edward Everett Horton, H B Warner, Jane Wyatt, Sam Jaffe
Rating: ★★★★

Now almost completely restored to its original running time, this is Frank Capra's totally engrossing film version of the famous James Hilton novel. The brilliant opening, catching all the turmoil and panic of confused flight from a revolution, pitches us straight into the action. Once in the lost valley of Shangri-La, the film depends more on its acting and dialogue, but still Capra rarely puts a foot wrong. Ronald Colman is perfectly cast as the idealistic Robert Conway, Jane Wyatt quietly effective as his girl in Shangri-La and Sam Jaffe magnificent in yet another extraordinary characterisation (to set beside his water-carrier in *Gunga Din*) as the ancient High Lama. Thomas Mitchell and Isabel Jewell are as solid and genuine as ever in supporting roles, and the climax is brilliantly realised. Only the most cynical will fail to be moved.

Lost Horizon ○
1972, US, 143 mins, colour
Dir: Charles Jarrott
Stars: Peter Finch, Liv Ullmann, Sally Kellerman, George Kennedy, Michael York, Olivia Hussey
Rating: ★★

Imagine how James Hilton's famous story of Shangri-La would be remade as a musical by the producer of the Doris Day/Rock Hudson comedies, and you'll have a pretty fair idea of how this frothy farrago turned out. Liv Ullmann, so brilliant in Ingmar Bergman films, has never been very lucky with her choice of international roles. Here, she and Peter Finch seem singularly ill at ease with a tuneful Burt Bacharach score that includes the catchy 'The World Is a Circle'. But the scene-setting is extremely well done, and veteran actor Charles Boyer is excellent as the wise and ancient High Lama.

Lost in a Harem ○
1944, US, 89 mins, b/w
Dir: Charles Riesner
Stars: Bud Abbott, Lou Costello, Marilyn Maxwell, John Conte
Rating: ★★

Abbott and Costello on one of their two visits to Metro-Goldwyn-Mayer, which means better production values and a livelier overall drive. The boys have some nice scenes with wicked sultan Douglass Dumbrille whose idea of a hypnotising jewel was reprised by Bing Crosby and Bob Hope in *Road to Rio*.

Lost in America ◐
1985, US, 91 mins, colour
Dir: Albert Brooks
Stars: Albert Brooks, Julie Hagerty
Rating: ★★

A romantic road comedy directed by, co-written by and starring Albert Brooks who, although well-known for these talents in the US, will be better known to British audiences as the unphotogenic reporter in *Broadcast News*. Brooks plays nervy, anxious Los Angeles advertising executive David Howard, in debt and mortgaged to the hilt but living a full and yuppie

lifestyle with his successful personnel director wife (Julie Hagerty). When the big promotion he anticipates goes to an undeserving other and David is offered a transfer to New York, a stressed-out David persuades wife Linda to sell everything they own and invest in a motor home, the idea being to live a simple, carefree life on the road. Or so they think . . . The script is dotted with the occasional witty and insightful line and there are some sardonic sideswipes at 1980s materialism to lighten the hapless couple's clichéd voyage of discovery – although be warned, there is a cop-out ending. But if you can tolerate the manic over-acting of both Brooks and *Airplane!*'s Hagerty as you watch misfortune upon catastrophe befall them, you could well enjoy this journey.

Lost Patrol, The ○
1934, US, 74 mins, b/w
Dir: John Ford
Stars: Victor McLaglen, Boris Karloff, Wallace Ford
Rating: ★★★

One of John Ford's earliest classics, about a small group of soldiers trapped in the desert by marauding Arabs. Fierce, unrelenting tension, with ripe performances from Victor McLaglen as a tough soldier and Boris Karloff (memorably over the top) as a religious fanatic. Black and white photography by Harold Wendstrom catches exactly the oppressive combination of heat and fear that drives the men to the edge of insanity.

Lost Weekend, The ○
1945, US, 101 mins, b/w
Dir: Billy Wilder
Stars: Ray Milland, Jane Wyman, Howard da Silva
Rating: ★★★★

This striking study of alcoholism not only changed Ray Milland's career from lounge lizard leading man to personable star in both heroic and villainous roles, but shook the film colony by taking four of the year's major Academy Awards. Besides the almost inevitable award for Milland – the competition that year wasn't strong but Milland's performance would probably have won against almost anything – *The Lost Weekend* picked up statuettes for best film, best direction (Billy Wilder) and best screenplay (Wilder and Charles Brackett). And Frank Faylen should at least have been nominated in the best

supporting actor category for his frightening study of a male nurse in the film's most nightmarish and memorable sequence, when Milland lands up in the alcoholic ward of a hospital. Wilder's direction conveys a fine sense of frenzy, especially when Milland is hunting for the bottles his brother has removed from their hiding places.

Lost World, The ○
1960, US, 98 mins, colour
Dir: Irwin Allen
Stars: Michael Rennie, Jill St John, Claude Rains
Rating: ★★

Amusingly entertaining remake of an old 1924 classic, based on the story by Sir Arthur Conan Doyle. This one has some good battles between prehistoric beasts, even if most of the human cast seems miscast. Not exactly *Jurassic Park*, perhaps, but children will still have a whale (or a dinosaur) of a time.

Loudest Whisper, The
See: Children's Hour

Love and Bullets ◐
1978, UK, 103 mins, colour
Dir: Stuart Rosenberg
Stars: Charles Bronson, Rod Steiger, Jill Ireland, Strother Martin, Bradford Dillman
Rating: ★★

Charles Bronson does his worst, smearing blood over pretty locations as a cop who goes moll hunting for the FBI. Rod Steiger is wonderfully outrageous as a mobster nuts about MacDonald and Eddy.

Love and Pain and the Whole Damn Thing ○
1972, US, 110 mins, colour
Dir: Alan J Pakula
Stars: Maggie Smith, Timothy Bottoms
Rating: ★★

Alan J Pakula, who directed *All the President's Men* and *Klute*, reveals himself as the romantic one always suspected in this sumptuously photographed weepie with humour trailing in not far behind the tears. It has a breathtakingly good performance by Maggie Smith as the dying spinster who finds unlikely romance with a 20-year-old American boy. Whether getting stuck in the loo, gloriously drunk as she attempts suicide, or getting bedded by the boy – 'Think of

L

the generation gap!' she groans – Ms Smith is so good as to boggle the mind.

Love at First Bite ◐ ⓥ

1979, US, 96 mins, colour
Dir: Stan Dragoti
Stars: George Hamilton, Susan Saint James, Richard Benjamin, Dick Shawn
Rating: ★★★

'Here's blood in your eye,' says George Hamilton's Dracula in this fun-filled spoof of the old vampire legend. Evicted by authorities who plan to turn his castle into a gymnasium (they threaten him with 'parallel bars, trampolines, vaulting horses – and Nadia Comaneci'), the count emigrates to America, where he and devoted Renfield (irresistible Arte Johnson) are soon apologetically robbing a blood bank there, demanding, 'Give it to me in small bills – I mean bottles.' Dracula falls for a model (delightful Susan Saint James) whom he hopes will accept three bites and become his vampire bride. Hamilton happily plays it all dead straight. So, in a frenzied way, does Richard Benjamin, whom I can't ever remember laughing at before, as Saint James' on-off suitor who, confusing his masters, tries to kill Dracula with silver bullets. But the real winner is the screenplay by Robert Kaufmann that keeps the witty cracks and situations constantly flowing.

Love at Large ◐

1990, US, 97 mins, colour
Dir: Alan Rudolph
Stars: Tom Berenger, Elizabeth Perkins, Anne Archer, Ted Levine, Kate Kapshaw, Kevin J O'Connor
Rating: ★★

Trust director Alan Rudolph to make a detective story that isn't. Deliberately artificial, with oblique dialogue and story threads that turn to comic stylism, the film is really about people looking for love rather than people looking for people. Tom Berenger plays a detective, hired to follow a man, who picks the wrong man and finds himself in another case, followed by another detective (Elizabeth Perkins). The two eventually become partners in a story that never allows us the easy option, yet remains curiously unsatisfying. A cast of fine-looking women do unexpected things: the sophisticated Ms P plays a ragged embryo gumshoe; Anne Archer sings (well); Kate Capshaw subdues her usual bright glamour; Annette

O'Toole takes off Meryl Streep; Ann Magnuson takes off Shirley MacLaine. There's even the occasional line of smart dialogue. 'Ever want kids?' asks Berenger. 'Kids?' queries Perkins. 'Yeah,' growls Berenger. 'Little people running around with your face.' Maybe Bogart and Bacall could have made something of it all, though it might have baffled their fans as well.

Love Bug, The ☉

1969, US, 107 mins, colour
Dir: Robert Stevenson
Stars: Dean Jones, Michele Lee, Buddy Hackett, David Tomlinson
Rating: ★★★

This Walt Disney comedy about a Volkswagen with a mind – and life – of its own was an enormous box-office hit for the studio and gave rise to three sequels. None was as good as this extremely bright and funny romp, with breakneck direction from Robert Stevenson and personable degrees of heroism and villainy from Dean Jones, Michele Lee, Buddy Hackett and David Tomlinson.

Love Child, The ●

1987, UK, 96 mins, colour
Dir: Robert Smith
Stars: Sheila Hancock, Peter Capaldi, Percy Herbert, Voices of Alexei Sayle, Lesley Sharp
Rating: ★

A sometimes amiable, sometimes objectionable comedy in typical British late Eighties manner. Its adult-certificate sitcom style will look better on a small screen, but stands exposed and awkward on anything bigger. Charm and subtlety are clearly elements absent from the armoury of writer Gordon Hann, whose head-on humour demands, like a Clint Eastwood action film, that you either go with it or take a running jump. Consequently, the dislikeable characters ensure just a few felicitous moments in what could have been an enjoyable dose of mildly anarchic humour. Veterans Sheila Hancock – as the gran offered a new life to the chagrin of dull accounts clerk grandson Peter Capaldi, trying to live down his hippie parents' memory – and Percy Herbert adapt themselves awkwardly to the new style, like dolphins gliding uneasily through shark-infested waters.

Love Crazy ○

1941, US, 99 mins, b/w
Dir: Jack Cummings

Stars: William Powell, Myrna Loy, Gail Patrick, Jack Carson
Rating: ★★

A really wacky romantic comedy with the stars of the Thin Man series, William Powell and Myrna Loy, at the peak of their appeal. Catching his wife with a muscle-man teaching her the skills of a bow and arrow, Powell plans a divorce. In a flat spin when he realises his mistake, he launches all sorts of madcap schemes, including feigning madness and dressing up as his own sister, to set matters to rights. A bit too long, the film still has some very funny moments and a great supporting cast, including one of Florence Bates' famous grotesques. Contemporary audiences cheered when she gets pushed into a swimming pool.

Love Crimes ● ⓥ

1991, US, 89 mins, colour
Dir: Lizzie Borden
Stars: Sean Young, Patrick Bergin, James Read, Arnetia Walker, Ron Orbach
Rating: ★

Although at times dull, weird and ludicrous by turns, there are times when this very off-centre thriller comes close to being very interesting indeed. Sean Young is the DA whose childhood sexual terrors remain lodged in the back of her mind. Small wonder that she becomes obsessed with the case of a fake photographer (Patrick Bergin), who preys on vulnerable women and gets them to make sexually provocative poses before having sex with them. When he begins beating them up as well, and is obviously nearing the edge of violence, Young offers herself as the bait, only to become involved in a game of sexual cat-and-mouse from which she and her career may not recover. Rather too low-key for its own cause, the film gets within striking distance of hitting some disturbing chords. In the end, though, not good, and seeming much longer than it is.

Love Finds Andy Hardy ○

1938, US, 90 mins, b/w
Dir: George B Seitz
Stars: Mickey Rooney, Lewis Stone, Judy Garland
Rating: ★★

The second of Mickey Rooney and Judy Garland's ten films together, and Judy's first entry in the Andy Hardy series. Mickey was already the fourth most popular star at the American box-office, and Judy would soon join him in the top 10. Here she and glamorous Lana Turner provide hot competition for Mickey's regular series girlfriend Ann Rutherford. With the inevitable father-and-son chat between Lewis Stone, as Judge Hardy, and Rooney, as his tearaway teenage son who changes direction at the swirl of a skirt, everything is cosily in place in this polished family entertainment.

Love from a Stranger ○
1936, UK, 90 mins, b/w
Dir: Rowland V Lee
Stars: Ann Harding, Basil Rathbone
Rating: ★★★

After a slow beginning, suspense builds steadily as wealthy Ann Harding gradually, and only with anonymous help, cottons on to the fact that her sleek new husband (a menacingly plausible Basil Rathbone) may have married her with murder in mind. The film was made in Britain by a Hollywood director, Rowland V Lee: his inventive handling and skilful touches help tighten the tension to breaking point in the final cat-and-mouse game between the two protagonists.

Love from a Stranger ○
(aka: A Stranger Walked In)
1947, US, 81 mins, b/w
Dir: Richard Whorf
Stars: John Hodiak, Sylvia Sidney
Rating: ★★

This was the fourth in a little group of comeback films made by Sylvia Sidney after an absence from the screen of five years. But, although quite tense in parts, it did not lead to a permanent renewal of her once glittering movie career. Based on Frank Vosper's stage adaptation of an Agatha Christie thriller, the film (retitled *A Stranger Walks In* for British distribution) was a remake of the earlier version with Ann Harding and Basil Rathbone.

Love Happy ☉
1949, US, 85 mins, b/w
Dir: David Miller
Stars: Groucho Marx, Chico Marx, Harpo Marx, Vera-Ellen, Marilyn Monroe, Raymond Burr
Rating: ★★★

By no means the dud that Marx Brothers purists would have you believe, this is a fast-moving comedy that showcases Harpo and Chico (far

too little is seen of Groucho) close to their zaniest and best. Although the film is hampered by its slight story of a musical dancing troupe, it takes off every time the brothers are on screen. With the help of Vera-Ellen and an expert supporting cast, and especially a loony finish among the lights and signs high above the big city, the brothers bid a reasonably happy farewell to big-screen fame.

Love Hurts ●
1989, US, 115 mins, colour
Dir: Bud Yorkin
Stars: Jeff Daniels, John Mahoney, Cynthia Sikes, Cloris Leachman, Amy Wright
Rating: ★

This could have been called *A Wedding* if director Robert Altman hadn't already pinched the title as well as the theme. Bud Yorkin's comedy-drama is a much inferior version, full of morose, unpleasant characters and with far too few smartly funny lines. And it seems to go on for hours. The one bright spot is a nine-year-old actress called Mary Griffin, a relaxed child performer whose timing and natural delivery put some of her elders and betters here to shame. Jeff Daniels has the lead and the results don't say very much for his choice of scripts: he was playing far too many unsympathetic characters for his own good at this stage of his career.

Love Is a Many Splendored Thing ○
1955, US, 102 mins, colour
Dir: Henry King
Stars: William Holden, Jennifer Jones, Torin Thatcher
Rating: ★★

The chart-busting song is all that survives in most memories of this weepy love story set aginst some picturesque views of Hong Kong, ravishingly shot in colour by the Oscar-winning photographer Leon Shamroy. Jennifer Jones' exquisite portrayal of the real-life heroine, Han Suyin, rises above the basic stickiness of the situations. And the background of troubled times in the Orient – the film is set just before and during the Korean War – is handled well enough to make one realise what an intriguing and complex subject it was at the time.

Love Laughs at Andy Hardy ○
1946, US, 94 mins, b/w
Dir: Willis Goldbeck

Stars: Mickey Rooney, Lewis Stone
Rating: ★★

Andy Hardy came home from the war – and found that the great American public didn't want to know him anymore. This is no different to other films in the Hardy series, but the love affair between Mickey Rooney, for three years the number one box-office star, and the world's filmgoers was over. His career would struggle for years until he re-emerged as a pugnacious character star in the late Fifties.

Love Letters ○
1945, US, 101 mins, b/w
Dir: William Dieterle
Stars: Jennifer Jones, Joseph Cotten, Ann Richards, Gladys Cooper
Rating: ★★

A rarely-seen romantic drama, a sort of suspense weepie in which Jennifer Jones plays an amnesiac who has been tried for the manslaughter of her husband. Victor Young's beautiful theme music and William Dieterle's persuasive direction help Miss Jones and co-star Joseph Cotten to keep the tears flowing.

Love Letters ● ⓥ
1983, US, 98 mins, colour
Dir: Amy Jones
Stars: Jamie Lee Curtis, James Keach, Matt Clark, Amy Madigan
Rating: ★★★

A bit one-paced but touching at the end, this is, under the circumstances, a little miracle of a film from writer/director Amy Jones, made on the tiniest of budgets. Jamie Lee Curtis, working for next to nothing, throws herself whole-heartedly into some torrid love scenes, at the same time creating a movingly believable character who is an entirely true-life mixture of strengths and weaknesses. James Keach – brother of Stacy – is a bit of a bore as her paramour, but Amy Madigan and Matt Clark are useful supports in a slender but slightly off-beat drama that, thanks to the credible central performance, holds on to your interest to the end.

Love Lottery, The ○
1953, UK, 89 mins, colour
Dir: Charles Crichton
Stars: David Niven, Herbert Lom, Peggy Cummins
Rating: ★★

The film business laughs at itself in this joyous jibe at romantic star leads and

L

their hysterical fans. David Niven
smoothly plays the heart-throb actor
who, after being half-killed by his
admirers, suggests that he is put up for
a lottery, in which he will marry the
winner. Nonsense, of course, but
light and frothy with it. Niven plays
with the assurance that can come only
from an actor equally at home in both
comedy and drama. And Humphrey
Bogart puts in an unexpected guest
appearance.

Lovely Way to Die, A
See: A Lovely Way to Go

Lovely Way to Go, A ○
(aka: A Lovely Way to Die)
1968, US, 103 mins, colour
Dir: David Lowell Rich
Stars: Kirk Douglas, Sylva Koscina, Eli
Wallach, Sharon Farrell
Rating: ★★

This rather over-bright film, with its
irritatingly cheerful score, is a mixture
of high jinks, romantic comedy and
private-eye thriller that could only
have been made in the Sixties. Kirk
Douglas plays up archly to the
required mood, while Sylva Koscina is
an extremely decorative heroine. In
the supporting cast, Ralph Waite and
Philip Bosco have both made greater
impact in more recent times, Waite as
the father in *The Waltons* on TV, and
Bosco as the avuncular tycoon in the
film *Working Girl*.

Love Match, The ○
1954, UK, 86 mins, b/w
Dir: David Paltenghi
Stars: Arthur Askey, Shirley Eaton, Glenn
Melvyn, Thora Hird, James Kenney, Jill
Adams
Rating: ★★★

Arthur Askey made a highly successful
comeback to the cinema in this
north-country comedy with a soccer
flavour. The film also provides a rare
look at Robb Wilton, the famous
music-hall comedian, here in his
familiar role of Magistrate
Muddlecombe; and at Glenn Melvyn,
who also wrote the stage play on
which this lark was based. Askey's
daughter Anthea is in the supporting
cast.

Love Me or Leave Me ○
1955, US, 122 mins, colour
Dir: Charles Vidor
Stars: Doris Day, James Cagney,
Cameron Mitchell, Robert Keith
Rating: ★★★

Doris Day stars in this spirited,
acid-flavoured biopic of singer Ruth
Etting, from a producer best known
for glucose (Joe Pasternak). Etting's
fraught life gave Day a chance to
prove she was far more than a pretty
face and voice, though she has stiff
competition from James Cagney (as
Etting's gangster friend Marty the
Gimp). Full of vintage songs.

Love Me Tender ○ Ⓥ
1956, US, 95 mins, b/w
Dir: Robert Webb
Stars: Richard Egan, Elvis Presley,
Debra Paget, Neville Brand
Rating: ★★

Presley's debut is a civil war Western
about a southern family's three feuding sons and their love for sultry
Debra Paget. Elvis swings his hips to
'Let Me Be', 'Old Shep', 'Poor Boy'
and the smoochy title ditty. Stiff
Richard Egan is the nominal star. The
fans liked it and made it a hit.

Love Me Tonight ○
1932, US, 96 mins, b/w
Dir: Rouben Mamoulian
Stars: Maurice Chevalier, Jeanette
MacDonald, Charles Ruggles, Myrna Loy,
Charles Butterworth, C Aubrey Smith
Rating: ★★★★

Among the most memorable of Hollywood's early musicals, this Rodgers
and Hart song-feast is given added
charm by the inventive cinematic
treatment of director Rouben
Mamoulian and the vivacious, almost
mischievous performances of its two
stars, Jeanette MacDonald and Maurice Chevalier. The score includes
'Mimi', 'Lover (When You're Near
Me)', 'Isn't It Romantic?', 'Love Me
Tonight' and 'The Son of a Gun is
Nothing but a Tailor'.

Love on the Dole ○ Ⓥ
1941, UK, 100 mins, b/w
Dir: John Baxter
Stars: Deborah Kerr, Clifford Evans
Rating: ★★★

The 20-year-old Deborah Kerr gives a
beautiful performance in this sombre
but justly famous drama of life in
Lancashire during the Depression of
the Thirties.

Love on the Run ○ Ⓥ
1936, US, 80 mins, b/w
Dir: W S Van Dyke
Stars: Joan Crawford, Clark Gable,
Franchot Tone
Rating: ★★★

Fast and furious globe-trotting romance involving rival foreign
correspondents Clark Gable and
Franchot Tone dodging continental
spies as well as each other in the quest
for a scoop, romancing runaway
madcap heiress Joan Crawford on the
side. The plot's not much, but director
'Woody' Van Dyke wisely
concentrates on the personalities of the
stars, and there are good cameo roles
for bristling William Demarest and
incy-mincy Donald Meek. Tone gives
the stars unselfish support, and Gable
unbends with surprising style, especially in a daft sequence set in a castle.

Lover, The ● Ⓥ
(aka: L'Amant)
1992, UK/France, 110 mins, colour
Dir: Jean-Jacques Annaud
Stars: Jane March, Tony Leung, Voice of
Jeanne Moreau
Rating: ★★

Elaborately set, with some wonderful
views of Saigon, this ambitious sex
drama runs like a silent film with
erotic inserts. Based on a vignette of
her early life by writer Marguérite
Duras, the slight narrative has Jane
March as the 15-year-old Duras, restricted by her upbringing in France
and Vietnam, being seduced by a
handsome Chinaman (Tony Leung).
March has presence, but not much
acting ability at this stage of her
career, though the cast is not helped
by such lines as 'He's stolen at the
opium den again', which float up like
silent credit cards. Leung is well-cast,
but the sex scenes are nothing special
and quickly tedious, with March giving out with a few pouts too many
before the end. Thank goodness for
Saigon and for Jeanne Moreau's
marvellous voice-over narration.

Lover Boy ◑ Ⓥ
1989, US, 98 mins, colour
Dir: Joan Micklin Silver
Stars: Patrick Dempsey, Nancy Valen,
Kate Jackson, Carrie Fisher, Barbara
Carrera, Kirstie Alley
Rating: ★★★

What Warren Beatty did for hairdressing in *Shampoo*, Patrick Dempsey
does for pizza delivery here. This is a
conventional but cute and often
comic sex frolic, kept afloat by
Dempsey's own brand of charm and
clumsiness (he even dances!) as the
pizza boy who finds himself sexually
in demand by thirty-something
women customers, despite having the
kind of frame that, in the old mus-

cle-man adverts would be guaranteed to have sand kicked all over it. Time and again, Dempsey's energy – and Joan Micklin Silver's stylish direction – overcomes the clichéd conventionality of the situations, though his producers help a lot by surrounding him with a very good cast that includes Kate Jackson, Carrie Fisher (who made her debut in *Shampoo!*), Kirstie Alley, Barbara Carrera, Kim Miyori and Robert Ginty. Another winner from director Silver, whose record of consistency is superior to that of most of her female contemporaries.

Lover Come Back ○
1961, US, 102 mins, colour
Dir: Delbert Mann
Stars: Doris Day, Rock Hudson
Rating: ★★★

Dialogue as bright as the colour, misunderstanding piled on misunderstanding and production values as high as the unlikelihood of the story: battle-of-the-sexes comedies never came glossier than in the Doris Day-Rock Hudson sparring matches in the late Fifties and early Sixties, and this is one of the best. Advertising exec Rock has to invent a non-existent product to cover up his chicanery and rival Doris goes after it without realising that it doesn't exist. Smoothly, confidently made by Delbert Mann, the film has delightful supporting performances from Tony Randall, giving his usual impression of a demented flywheel, Edie Adams, delicious as a brainless chorus-girl, and Jack Kruschen as a bumbling inventor called in to give substance to the mythical product. Sheer enjoyment, sophisticated in technique and execution, and marred only by the insertion of a soupy song from Ms Day at quite the wrong moment.

Lovers!, The ○
1972, UK, 90 mins, colour
Dir: Herbert Wise
Stars: Paula Wilcox, Richard Beckinsale
Rating: ★★★

One of the most successful of TV comedy spin-offs, shot in excellent colour, and owing most of its better qualities almost entirely to the warmth and spontaneity projected by the two young leads, Paula Wilcox and Richard Beckinsale. They provide a relationship that, thanks to their portrayals and the script by Jack Rosenthal (who also wrote the series), is likeable, warm-hearted and funny.

Loves of Carmen, The ○
1948, US, 99 mins, colour
Dir: Charles Vidor
Stars: Rita Hayworth, Glenn Ford
Rating: ★★

Made by the same team responsible for the classic crime thriller *Gilda* (director Charles Vidor, plus stars Rita Hayworth and Glenn Ford), this romantic costume adventure – based on Mérimée's *Carmen* – strikes fewer sparks. Hayworth's tempestuous gipsy looks stunning but Ford's Spanish dragoon is merely silly. And Bizet's music might have helped a bit, rather than the tacky score that's provided by Mario Castelnuovo-Tedesco.

Loves of Joanna Godden, The ○
1947, UK, 85 mins, b/w
Dir: Charles Frend
Stars: Googie Withers, Jean Kent, John McCallum
Rating: ★★

A solid, well-acted rural drama with a human touch, the sort of thing you might have expected to find Barbara Stanwyck starring in on the other side of the Atlantic. In this Ealing Studios period saga, it's Googie Withers as the strong-willed Joanna in a well-crafted film that doesn't quite tug at the emotions as it might have done. The film's leisurely pace irked one contemporary reviewer who said that it was 'like watching a village cricket match on a lovely summer's day, nodding off now and then and waking to find Googie still batting away'.

Love Stinks
See: Only You

Love Story ○
(aka: A Lady Surrenders)
1944, UK, 104 mins, b/w
Dir: Leslie Arliss
Stars: Margaret Lockwood, Stewart Granger, Patricia Roc, Tom Walls
Rating: ★★

The second of Margaret Lockwood's really big hits of the wartime years, reuniting her with Stewart Granger (her co-star from *The Man in Grey*). The story – dying lady pianist falling for engineer going blind – is pure schmaltz, but it was solid gold at the box-office in Britain, proving to be one of the biggest financial winners of its year from any country. And the theme music, 'Cornish Rhapsody', was also massively popular.

Love Story ○
1970, US, 100 mins, colour
Dir: Arthur Hiller
Stars: Ryan O'Neal, Ali MacGraw, John Marley, Ray Milland, John Huston
Rating: ★★★

Totally resistible but phenomenally successful weepie about lovers from opposite ends of the social scale. Ali MacGraw expires as prettily (and from an unnamed disease) as any Hollywood star of the Thirties. But Ryan O'Neal will be okay since 'Love means never having to say you're sorry.' One way or another, you'll need a bucket.

Love with the Proper Stranger ○
1964, US, 100 mins, b/w
Dir: Robert Mulligan
Stars: Natalie Wood, Steve McQueen
Rating: ★★★

Romantic comedy, tinged with drama, set against the background of non-stop New York. Sometimes it seems as though Natalie Wood and Steve McQueen could do with rather more meaningful dialogue to get their teeth into, to help establish their growing relationship with each other. Nonetheless McQueen in particular still manages to give a performance that makes it easy to see why he was in the process of becoming a world box-office draw.

Loving You ○ ⓥ
1957, US, 101 mins, colour
Dir: Hal Kanter
Stars: Elvis Presley, Lizabeth Scott, Wendell Corey, Dolores Hart
Rating: ★★★

The second of Elvis Presley's 33 movies, nearly all of which were condemned by critics but profited at the box office. And it's always good to see the King in his pre-blobster days. This film is already the standard vehicle, tailor-made for his personality and talent. It cashed in on his appeal for the teen market at a time when the *Monthly Film Bulletin* could sniff: 'The phenomenon of Elvis Presley is one of the more puzzling and less agreeable aspects of modern music.' In this story Elvis the hillbilly singer is used as a gimmick to promote a waning cowboy band. Fame and romance await but not before much heartache and singing have taken place. One of the better King-flicks.

L

L-Shaped Room, The ◑
1962, UK, 142 mins, b/w
Dir: Bryan Forbes
Stars: Leslie Caron, Tom Bell, Bernard Lee
Rating: ★★★

Moving, tenderly-observed portrait of a lonely, pregnant French girl and the people she encounters in her cramped, crammed London boarding house. Written and directed by Bryan Forbes, whose wife Nanette Newman appears in a tiny part right at the end. And there are penetrating performances from Cicely Courtneidge, Patricia Phoenix and Emlyn Williams.

Lt Robin Crusoe USN ⊙
1966, US, 110 mins, colour
Dir: Byron Paul
Stars: Dick Van Dyke, Nancy Kwan
Rating: ★

This colourful comedy from the Walt Disney stable sounds a whole lot more fun than it is. The company had got some fine desert island action a few years earlier from their adaptation of *Swiss Family Robinson*, but here star Dick Van Dyke is given far too little to do, especially in the first half of the film. He tries valiantly to make us laugh and so does a talented chimpanzee called Floyd, but they get no help from the sluggish direction of Byron Paul. Very much later on things liven up considerably, with Van Dyke's Crusoe leading a suffragette army of native girls against the big bad cannibal chief.

Lucky Jim ○ ⊙
1957, UK, 95 mins, b/w
Dir: John Boulting
Stars: Ian Carmichael, Terry-Thomas, Hugh Griffith, Sharon Acker
Rating: ★★★

A Boulting Brothers' box-office blockbuster of its day, with Ian Carmichael scoring a big personal success as Jim Dixon, the accident-prone lecturer of the title. His final lecture on 'Merrie England' brings down the curtain on a riotous catalogue of disaster.

Lucky Nick Cain
See: I'll Get You for This

Lullaby of Broadway ○ ⊙
1951, US, 92 mins, colour
Dir: David Butler
Stars: Doris Day, Gene Nelson, Gladys George, S Z Sakall, Billy de Wolfe
Rating: ★★★

This was one of the earlier musical vehicles that Warner Brothers assembled for Doris Day in the days when she had just become their brightest new singing star. The story's not much, but who cares when Doris sings such standards as 'Just One of Those Things', 'Somebody Loves Me', 'Lullaby of Broadway' and 'You're Getting to be a Habit with Me'. Gene Nelson weighs in with 'Zing! Went the Strings of My Heart', and veteran star Gladys George is a knock-out as Doris's mother.

Lured ○
1947, US, 102 mins, b/w
Dir: Douglas Sirk
Stars: Lucille Ball, George Sanders, Charles Coburn, Boris Karloff
Rating: ★★★

Although it seems odd now to find Lucille Ball in a leading role as a lady in danger, this is an otherwise strongly-cast thriller, based on the 1939 French film *Pièges*, directed by Robert Siodmak just before he went to Hollywood. This version might have been creepier if Siodmak himself had directed it. Douglas Sirk, soon to make a name for himself with glossy weepies, gives it a handsome production and interesting London settings, but has trouble lending atmosphere to a routine script. There's no lack of suspects for policemen Charles Coburn (excellent, as usual), George Zucco and Alan Napier to sift through. George Sanders, Boris Karloff, Sir Cedric Hardwicke, Joseph Calleia and Alan Mowbray are all on hand to strew the plot with red herrings. Miss Ball's singing, incidentally, was dubbed by Annette Warren. Oddly, the British called both French and American versions of the story *Personal Column*.

Lure of the Wilderness ○
1952, US, 92 mins, colour
Dir: Jean Negulesco
Stars: Jean Peters, Jeffrey Hunter, Walter Brennan
Rating: ★★★

A really off-beat Western, which is about a man who strays into a swamp in 1910, and finds a man, living wild with his daughter, who has been hiding from the law for years. Good performances abound – and there's fine Technicolor photography on location in the Okefenokee Swamp Park by Edward Cronjager. His camerawork helps build up a fine sense of the claustrophobic menace conjured up by the oppressive green of the Everglades, and their sundry denizens, such as snakes and alligators. The film is a remake of the 1941 film *Swamp Water*, also known as *The Man Who Came Back*.

Lust for a Vampire ● ⓥ
1970, UK, 95 mins, colour
Dir: Jimmy Sangster
Stars: Ralph Bates, Yutte Stensgaard, Barbara Jefford
Rating: ★★★

Hammer horror films produced a number of hypnotic performances from vampire ladies, and Yutte Stensgaard, previously just a decorative actress, is extremely effective here as the finishing school girl who proves to be the reincarnation of the notorious Carmilla Karnstein from other Hammer blood feasts. It's easily Yutte's best film performance. Ralph Bates is also good as one of the men who falls under her deadly spell.

Lust for Gold ○
1949, US, 90 mins, b/w
Dir: S Sylvan Simon
Stars: Glenn Ford, Ida Lupino, Gig Young, William Price, Edgar Buchanan
Rating: ★★★

One often writes of underrated films, but surely *Lust for Gold* must now be one of the most neglected on record. A perfect little vignette about man's greed in the form of a Western, with the present-day story peripheral to the flash-back adventure yarn. It involves Glenn Ford in one of his best performances as a soulless émigré who discovers a fabulously wealthy mine, and is ruthless in his determination to keep sole possession. Very good performances also from Ida Lupino and Gig Young, and desperate suspense towards the end, make this a minor masterpiece.

Lust for Life ○ ⓥ
1956, US, 115 mins, colour
Dir: Vincente Minnelli
Stars: Kirk Douglas, Anthony Quinn
Rating: ★★★

Kirk Douglas (cruelly denied an Oscar) is artist Vincent Van Gogh to the very life in this long, rambling, but brilliantly photographed (credited to Metrocolor, but actually made in Ansco Color) story of the painter's life. Great pains have obviously been taken by director Vincente Minnelli to get the look and flavour of the film right, and it's a pity that an at-times magnificent movie outstays its welcome by at least half an hour. Anthony Quinn's sketchy Gauguin won the film's only Academy Award, while the brilliant, tigerish Douglas had to be content with a mere nomination. There's no justice!

Lust in the Dust ●
1985, US, 87 mins, colour
Dir: Paul Bartel
Stars: Tab Hunter, Divine, Lainie Kazan
Rating: ★

Paul Bartel's follow-up to his decidedly different *Eating Raoul* is a spoof Western that's too wild-eyed and knowing by half. The accent is on the wildly farcical, and the film saves its best moments for the climactic showdown around a grave, with a barrage of bullets, bluffs and revelations.

Lydia ○
1941, US, 90 mins, b/w
Dir: Julien Duvivier
Stars: Merle Oberon, Edna May Oliver, Alan Marshal, Joseph Cotten
Rating: ★★

Lush romantic trifle on the oft-tried theme of an elderly lady looking back on her love life. Director Julien Duvivier based it on his French success *Un Carnet de Bal* which he had made in his native France four years earlier, before World War Two forced him to take his talents to Hollywood. Merle Oberon (in the title role) and Joseph Cotten make a highly civilised romantic couple, and Miklos Rozsa earned an Oscar nomination for his liltingly dramatic score.

Lydia Bailey ○
1952, US, 89 mins, colour
Dir: Jean Negulesco
Stars: Dale Robertson, Anne Francis
Rating: ★★

Dale Robertson swaps his more usual cowboy clothes for the garb of a Negro field-hand in this romantic adventure story set in the jungles and plantations of Haiti in Napoleonic times. The studio, Fox, built up Robertson and Anne Francis as a big young romantic team at the time, though nothing further came of it. At the other end of the age scale, Hollywood's oldest supporting actress, Adeline De Walt Reynolds, has a strong featured role. She was 91 when the movie was made and lived to be 100.

M

M ◐
1931, Germany, 99 mins, b/w
Dir: Fritz Lang
Stars: Peter Lorre
Rating: ★★★★

Long since firmly established as one of the great classics of pre-war cinema (or of any other era, for that matter), the impact made by this film has hardly lessened at all over the years. Loosely based on the actual case of the Dusseldorf child murderer of the Twenties, it was Fritz Lang's first sound film, and later in life Lang himself regarded it as the most satisfying of all the films he had made. Its power is certainly tremendous, with striking imagery and visual qualities complemented by an often highly imaginative use of sound (like Alfred Hitchcock before him in *Blackmail*, Lang clearly took to the new medium like a duck to water). The film is equally famous now for marking the screen debut of Peter Lorre, who in the central role of the murderer, gave a performance so convincing and impressive that many found it frightening: he was never to get such a demanding role again.

Ma and Pa Kettle ○
1948, US, 75 mins, b/w
Dir: Charles Lamont
Stars: Marjorie Main, Percy Kilbride
Rating: ★★

Crow-voiced Marjorie Main, who was nominated for an Oscar when she played the harridan Ma Kettle in the hit comedy *The Egg and I*, was persuaded to return for a comedy series based on the hillbilly characters created by herself and Percy Kilbride. None of the nine Kettle films cost more than half a million dollars to produce, yet altogether they grossed close to $40 million for the studio, Universal, almost single-handedly saving it from bankruptcy in the early 1950s. This film got the series off to a rousing start.

Mac ● ⓥ
1992, US, 118 mins, colour
Dir: John Turturro
Stars: John Turturro, Michael Badalucco, Katherine Borowitz, Ellen Barkin
Rating: ★★

This is a kind of building industry equivalent of *The Godfather*. It must also rate as a rare film whose language is so bad it actually got it an 18 certificate from the British censor. Three Italian-American brothers get cheesed off working for a constructor building houses his way and decide to do it their way. Eventually they have some success and split up. That's the story, with star-director John Turturro as the elder brother and driving force behind their career, a man given to fits of anger and screaming (one of which brings on an early heart attack), a trait he must have inherited from his mother whose continual rants are mercifully only heard off screen. It's earthy, darkly photographed and its most meaningful lines of dialogue are often repeated – meaningfully. These people don't laugh a lot, but they do shout and screech and behave violently towards each other most of the time. Frankly their life, though like the film not without merit, is mostly heavy going.

Mac and Me ⊙
1988, US, 93 mins, colour
Dir: Stewart Raffill
Stars: Christine Ebersole, Jonathan Ward
Rating: ★

Loveable extra-terrestrial Mac finds himself stranded in suburban America but survives on a diet of Coca-Cola and the friendship of a disabled 10-year-old boy. A squirm-inducing children's film with more than a passing resemblance to Spielberg's *E.T.* but with the shameless product placement of the MacDonalds hamburger chain. Several scenes are set in branches of MacDonalds and children in the film wear clothing with the firm's logo. Young children won't notice this, of course, but it's a scandalous new form of advertising. Mercifully the film is so awful it doesn't much matter.

MacArthur the Rebel General ○
(aka: MacArthur)
1977, US, 130 mins, colour
Dir: Joseph Sargent
Stars: Gregory Peck, Dan O'Herlihy
Rating: ★★★

Although, even at 61, he looks absurdly young for the role, Gregory Peck does surprisingly well in this old-fashioned war film with an authoritative tang. Director Joseph Sargent wastes no time in getting on

M

with the action, from war in the Philippines in 1942 to MacArthur's final command in Korea in 1951. The general's own speeches are ringingly declaimed by Peck and the Technicolor photography, by Mario Tosi, is very good. The director's fondness for tracking shots, which seems likely to hinder the film at first, actually helps to keep things moving in the later stages.

Macbeth ○

1948, US, 89 mins, b/w
Dir: Orson Welles
Stars: Orson Welles, Jeanette Nolan, Dan O'Herlihy
Rating: ★★★

Orson Welles played around with Shakespeare's Scottish play to such an extent that it must have had The Bard spinning furiously in his grave. Shot in a mere 23 days with papier-maché rocks and sets so cardboard it's small wonder that the scenery-chewing antics of the cast didn't destroy them. Welles adopts similair oblique camera angles as in his masterful *Citizen Kane*, but here they are more of a distraction than anything else. Film fans should recognise the actor playing the second murderer, William Alland, who was the man who walked through *Citizen Kane* trying to uncover the secret of 'Rosebud'. He also gets a credit as dialogue director here, and later went on to become involved in film production, most notably with *The Creature from the Black Lagoon*. For all this, the visuals do have a certain weird fascination.

MacDonald of the Canadian Mounties

See: *Pony Soldier*

Macho Callahan ①

1970, US, 100 mins, b/w
Dir: Bernard L Kowalski
Stars: David Janssen, Jean Seberg, Lee J Cobb
Rating: ★★

David Janssen is as taciturn as ever in a rare Western role as a Civil War veteran, hunted by the widow of a man he has killed. The supporting cast is full of quality players, including Jean Seberg, Lee J Cobb and Britain's James Booth as a flashy gambler called 'King Harry' Wheeler and, as Crystal, Anne Revere, the veteran Hollywood actress who won an Academy Award as Elizabeth Taylor's mother in *National Velvet*. Watch also for David Carradine as a one-armed man who

gets gunned down by the main character early in the picture – something of an in-joke, perhaps, in reference to Janssen's hunt for the one-armed man in the long-running television series *The Fugitive*. The action is bold and powerful, although spoiled at times by director Bernard Kowalski's insistence on too many angles, which also negates much of the good work done by British cameraman Gerald Fisher, here working for the first time with the interesting Colour by Movielab.

MacKenna's Gold ○ ⓥ

1968, US, 136 mins, colour
Dir: J Lee Thompson
Stars: Gregory Peck, Omar Sharif, Telly Savalas, Keenan Wynn, Edward G Robinson, Julie Newmar
Rating: ★★

Another big adventure film from the same team – star Gregory Peck, writer/producer Carl Foreman and director J Lee Thompson – that made *The Guns of Navarone*. The girls tend to get in the way a bit more here, and Foreman's script is not of as high a calibre. But Omar Sharif is unexpectedly mobile and spirited as the ruthless Colorado and Gregory Peck reliably staunch as Sheriff MacKenna, who comes by accident into possession of a map pointing the way to fabulous hidden treasure. The rugged desert terrain is also impressive, thanks to the fine Technicolor photography of Joseph MacDonald. The voice of the narrator belongs to veteran actor Victor Jory.

Mackintosh Man, The ①

1973, US, 120 mins, colour
Dir: John Huston
Stars: Paul Newman, James Mason, Dominique Sanda, Harry Andrews, Ian Bannen, Michael Hordern
Rating: ★★

This thriller is not at all typical of its director John Huston or writer Walter Hill (who went on to direct hard action films like *The Streetfighter* and *Driver*). If it is reminiscent of anything, it's the stories of John Buchan, especially when Paul Newman's cover is blown and he flees from his enemies across the wilder parts of Ireland. A formidable battery of senior British actors – including Harry Andrews, Nigel Patrick, Niall MacGinnis, Roland Culver, Michael Hordern and Leo Genn – contribute cameos if not always conviction in the midst of Hill's studiedly intricate plot.

Mad About Men ○

1954, UK, 90 mins, colour
Dir: Ralph Thomas
Stars: Glynis Johns, Donald Sinden, Margaret Rutherford
Rating: ★★★

A sequel to 1948's *Miranda*, with Glynis Johns returning to her role as the man-mad mermaid. Despite the improbability of the plot (Miranda replaces her double with the aid of a wheelchair), this is a surprisingly amusing comedy, wittily scripted and played with fine relish, especially by Johns, Margaret Rutherford and Irene Handl, a formidable trio of female scene-stealers. Written by Peter Blackmore, who also co-scripted the first film from his own play, and brightly shot in Technicolor by Ernest Steward, one of Britain's best colour cameramen at the time.

Mad About Music ○

1938, US, 98 mins, b/w
Dir: Norman Taurog
Stars: Deanna Durbin, Herbert Marshall, Arthur Treacher
Rating: ★★★

Deanna Durbin's natural charm edges everybody else off the screen in this story of an orphan who goes to a Swiss school and invents a fictitious father. Deanna sings 'Ave Maria' (and more) and there's just about your only chance to see on screen Cappy Barra's Harmonica Band! They provide breezy backing for Durbin on another of her numbers, 'I Love to Whistle'. The story was remade by the same studio (Universal) without the songs 18 years later as *Toy Tiger*, a vehicle for now-forgotten child star Tim Hovey.

Madame Bovary ○

1949, US, 115 mins, b/w
Dir: Vincente Minelli
Stars: Jennifer Jones, James Mason, Van Heflin, Louis Jourdan
Rating: ★★★

With Vincente Minnelli directing and Louis Jourdan on the cast list you could almost be forgiven for expecting a Flaubert musical, and indeed the wonderfully well-organised ball sequence is one of the highlights of a film that, unlike many, has improved with age. There had been two earlier versions (Jean Renoir's in 1934 and a Hollywood 1932 attempt memorably entitled *Unholy Love*); this one framed the novel within the author's trial on a charge of corrupting morals by writing his book. Jennifer Jones makes a sedate Madame, but James Mason is noble as Flaubert himself. It has rather more bite than the recent Claude Chabrol version with Isabelle Huppert, but the Renoir version is still the best of all.

Madame Curie ○
1943, US, 124 mins, b/w
Dir: Mervyn LeRoy
Stars: Greer Garson, Walter Pidgeon, Robert Walker, Van Johnson, Henry Travers
Rating: ★★★

Film biographies had long been the province of Warner Brothers but Louis B Meyer wanted to change all that. His first attempt saw Spencer Tracy as Edison and despite the small box-office returns he decided to take a chance with a film based on Eve Curie's book about her scientist mother Marie – the Polish woman who discovered radium. Aldous Huxley and F Scott Fitzgerald both had a stab at the screenplay (Paul Osborn and Paul H Rameau eventually got the job) but it was abandoned when they couldn't get Greta Garbo to play the part. However, another G G was to step into the role – Irish-born Greer Garson, who had so successfully teamed up with Walter Pidgeon in *Blossoms in the Dust* and *Mrs Miniver*. Here, Pidgeon plays Marie's French husband Pierre Curie. The film itself stirred many hearts when it was released and stayed pretty close to the facts, something that many biographies failed to do in the Thirties and Forties.

Madame Sin ◑
1972, UK, 90 mins, b/w
Dir: David Greene
Stars: Bette Davis, Robert Wagner, Denholm Elliott
Rating: ★★

Bette Davis in James Bond territory: her Madame Sin in this unlikely espionage adventure is as exotic a villainess as stalked the screen since Gale Sondergaard played Spider Woman in a couple of Forties' thrillers. Co-star Robert Wagner also produced the film. Their British supporting cast is headed by Denholm Elliott, Gordon Jackson and Dudley Sutton. Originally made for US TV.

Madame Sousatzka ◑ ⓥ
1988, US, 122 mins, colour
Dir: John Schlesinger
Stars: Shirley MacLaine, Peggy Ashcroft, Navin Chowdhry, Twiggy, Leigh Lawson
Rating: ★★★

If you think they don't make 'em like they used to, this story of an eccentric piano tutor and her young star pupil will prove you wrong. Shirley MacLaine gives a fiery performance as Madame Sousatzka, living in a crumbling London house, obsessed with teaching her pupils good manners and good taste as well as the piano. Her young protege, Manek, is played by Navin Chowdhry and their scenes together are well observed and directed by John Schlesinger. The film is, if anything a little long, but for fans of classical music, it's a delight. In the supporting cast, Twiggy rises above typecasting (she plays a model and would-be pop singer) and her real-life husband Leigh (*Kinsey*) Lawson plays her music agent boyfriend who hears the young Manek play and offers him the chance to play a major concert.

Madame X ○
1966, US, 100 mins, colour
Dir: David Lowell Rich
Stars: Lana Turner, Keir Dullea, John Forsythe, Ricardo Montalban, Constance Bennett, Burgess Meredith
Rating: ★★★

Last but not least of the eight film versions of the story about that much-put-upon lady of the title, whose fortunes vary from rotten to worse. David Lowell Rich, here proving himself a strong and discerning director, holds it firmly and wisely to the spirit of the silent era, building up to an out-with-your-handkerchieves climax (Madame X being defended on a murder charge by her son, who knows her not) which is all the more effective being handled in a strictly old-fashioned manner. Russell Metty's beautifully-keyed colour photography also plays its part in the impact of the film which, once it hits its stride after the first 20 minutes, never misses a trick – the juvenile saying his prayers, the wicked stepmother framed in a window during a storm, Madame X collapsing in snow and contracting pneumonia. Yet still, a lot depends on the star and one can rarely remember a more affecting portrayal from Lana Turner, especially in the latter half of the film when she is so much more impressive than one would have thought possible that we're held almost entirely captive to a last reel in which she is utterly deglamorised and says much with brown eyes that seem old and fathomless. Along with *The*

Postman Always Rings Twice, this rates as one of the finest performances of her career.

Mad Dog and Glory ● ⓥ
1993, US, 95 mins, colour
Dir: John McNaughton
Stars: Robert De Niro, Uma Thurman, Bill Murray, David Caruso, Kathy Baker
Rating: ★★

Robert De Niro and company just barely squeeze a feature-length film out of this slim dreams-come-true story. De Niro's a loner police photographer noticeably lacking in bravado. But when he saves the life of a big-shot gangster (Bill Murray), he's rewarded with a live-in girl (Uma Thurman) for a week. Paying the crook back her brother's debts, she has to do as she's told. So she's a good girl, natch, even though it's only a couple of days before they're in the sack, and De Niro finds there's a heavy price to pay if he wants to keep his new love. Murray is intriguing casting as the gang boss who's also a stand-up comic, but it's the only spark of interest in a story where the leads just don't coalesce and where developments are strictly make-believe. The talented Kathy Baker is criminally wasted in a bit-part here, but then De Niro had already won her in *Jackknife* – a much more convincing partner than Thurman for whom he's obviously too old. She's nothing much and neither are most of the cast in this kill-time film.

Made in America ◑ ⓥ
1993, US, 110 mins, colour
Dir: Richard Benjamin
Stars: Ted Danson, Whoopi Goldberg, Nia Long, Will Smith, Jennifer Tilly
Rating: ★★

A pretty broad romantic comedy with some laughs in the right places, plus giggles and grimaces in the wrong ones. Whoopi Goldberg is a widow who runs an African bookshop and has a daughter who's not only drop-dead gorgeous, but about to win a major science award. The girl, conceived by using a sperm bank after her father's death, resolves to find her 'donor' father and discovers to her horror he's a loud-mouthed white car salesman (Ted Danson) who pulls sick-making advertising stunts with bears, elephants and monkeys on TV. Naturally Ted reforms and falls for Whoopi, giving rise to the usual sitcom misunderstandings and allowing Jennifer Tilly to steal the film as Ted's

M

squeaky live-in lover. The centrepiece is a funny sequence where Whoopi's bike-bell sends an elephant with Danson on it berserk through the town. Pretty long, though, for its content: when Whoopi gets knocked off her bike and the doctor warns that 'the next 48 hours could be crucial', you wonder if he's talking about the movie.

Made in Heaven ○
1952, UK, 78 mins, colour
Dir: John Paddy Carstairs
Stars: David Tomlinson, Petula Clark, Sonja Ziemann, A E Matthews
Rating: ★★

This soggy little romantic comedy, splendidly photographed in Technicolor by Geoffrey Unsworth, was typical of mainline British cinema in the early Fifties. The title has so many punning possibilities that is difficult to know where the real one lay, as a 'perfectly married' couple employ a Hungarian maid, whose statistics seem to be as much made in heaven as their marriage. Some fun, but it didn't make sparkling German actress Sonja Ziemann a star of the British cinema.

Made in Heaven ○ ⓥ
1987, US, 102 mins, colour
Dir: Alan Rudolph
Stars: Timothy Hutton, Kelly McGillis, Debra Winger, Maureen Stapleton, Don Murray, Mare Winningham
Rating: ★

This romantic fantasy is far from director Alan Rudolph's usual stamping ground of urban paranoia, which perhaps explains his failure to put any sort of personal stamp on the film. The story starts around 1946 when Mike (Timothy Hutton) is drowned and goes to Heaven where he falls in love with Annie (Kelly McGillis). She is an 'unborn soul' whom he marries but loses when she has to be 'born' to an earthling. Mike appeals to the heavenly supervisor – an unbilled Debra Winger completely stealing the film as the androgynous Emmett – who gives him 30 years to find Annie (now Ally) on Earth. Since the ending is always pretty obvious, the film depends heavily on the incidents that fill the lovers' journey along the way – but so little happens that it seems a very long and slow trip. The rest of the acting is forgettable, too, with the exception of a poignant performance by Ann Wedgeworth as Mike's mother. And the ending is anti-climactic, lacking all sense of joy.

Madeleine ○
1950, UK, 114 mins, b/w
Dir: David Lean
Stars: Ann Todd, Leslie Banks
Rating: ★★★

David Lean directed his then wife Ann Todd in this meticulous account of the events leading up to a famous murder trial in 19th-century Scotland. Miss Todd makes the enigmatic Madeleine such a cold fish that it's difficult to identify with her, but this is probably just what the situation orders here, and the case itself holds undeniable fascination. The final scene is handled in masterly style by both director and star.

Madhouse ○ ⓥ
1974, UK, 92 mins, colour
Dir: Jim Clark
Stars: Vincent Price, Peter Cushing, Adrienne Corri, Robert Quarry
Rating: ★★

The only horror film of the Seventies to unite those masters of menace, Vincent Price, Peter Cushing and Robert *Count Yorga* Quarry. Despite the presence of the other two, however, the film is specifically devoted to the particular talents of Price. Cushing and Adrienne Corri (the latter as a demented and disfigured crone brooding over a colony of spiders in her basement) also have a splendid time in this vivid tale of an actor's revenge.

Madhouse ○ ⓥ
1990, US, 90 mins, colour
Dir: Tom Ropelewski
Stars: John Larroquette, Kirstie Alley, John Diehl, Robert Ginty
Rating: ★★

'If we have a nuclear war,' says Kirstie Alley, in the course of this not unfunny comedy, 'the only things to survive will be house guests.' Mack and Jessie (John Larroquette and Kirstie) have a cosy home that suits them fine until other people move into it. These include an old friend with a pregnant wife who talks non-stop and commandeers the bathroom; Jessie's spendthrift sister who moves in with her massive boyfriend after being kicked out by her rich Arab husband; a cat with nine lives; the man next door and his awful kids after his house burns down; an elephant; the sister's cocaine-dealing son. Mack has nightmares about zombies moving in, and soon he and Jessie are living in a tent on the lawn.

It's not exactly frantically funny all the way through, but it does build to a fine pitch of madness towards the end. And there's always the nagging feeling that this could happen to you!

Madison Avenue ○
1961, US, 94 mins, b/w
Dir: Bruce Humberstone
Stars: Eleanor Parker, Dana Andrews, Jeanne Crain, Eddie Albert
Rating: ★★

A strange drama, which in cast and approach looks more like a film from the early Fifties. A downbeat story of cross and double-cross in New York's big business jungle, it's directed by Bruce Humberstone, best known for Forties' musicals. But perhaps his best film was a thriller – the Betty Grable/Laird Cregar drama, *Hot Spot*, made in 1941.

Mad Little Island
See: Rockets Galore

Mad Love ○
1935, US, 70 mins, b/w
Dir: Karl Freund
Stars: Peter Lorre, Frances Drake, Colin Clive
Rating: ★★★

Peter Lorre was never more striking, visually at least, than in this now seldom-seen version of *The Hands of Orlac* in which, shaven-headed (which makes his baby-faced looks more evil than ever), he plays a surgeon infatuated to the point of madness with a beautiful young actress, played by the gorgeous Frances Drake. His chilling presence smooths the film over passages which, in lesser hands, might seem absurdly melodramatic. Master cameraman Karl Freund, in one of his rare assignments as a director, crowds the film with low-key lighting, gloomy settings and bizarre camera angles which heighten Lorre's sidestep into madness. And May Beatty also scores as a drunken housekeeper (her cockatoo plays a memorable role in the climax) whose hobby is feeding flies to her carnivorous plant.

Mad Magician, The ○
1954, US, 72 mins, b/w
Dir: John Brahm
Stars: Vincent Price, Mary Murphy, Eva Gabor
Rating: ★★

For his title role in this horror film about a vengeful illusionist, Vincent Price swotted up on a dozen real magician's tricks, and became quite accomplished at such things as making a stream of water run out of a sword, producing a girl from a flower pot, and making a man disappear through a wall. Patrick O'Neal makes his film debut as the goodie.

Mad Max ❶ Ⓥ

1979, Australia, 93 mins, colour
Dir: George Miller
Stars: Mel Gibson
Rating: ★★★

One of the most successful Australian films of all time, this is the first of the trilogy of *Mad Max* action movies starring one of Australia's hottest box office properties, Mel Gibson. All three were made in Australia, but this first one was dubbed with American accents for a wider audience. A weird, desolate, violent atmosphere prevails in all three, and this one tells us why Max became mad in the first place. There's plenty of exciting action on the road and some great stunts in this, director George Miller's impressive feature debut. Deservedly a cult favourite.

Mad Max 2 ● Ⓥ

1981, Australia, 95 mins, colour
Dir: George Miller
Stars: Mel Gibson, Bruce Spence, Vernon Wells, Mike Preston
Rating: ★★

This is the movie to see if you like watching cars exploding or being blown to bits. The scene is the future in the Australian desert and the action reminiscent of American bike movies of the late Sixties in which Peter Fonda used to star. Max (Mel Gibson again) is a 'road warrior', a former pursuit cop embittered by the past who teams up, reluctantly, with a group of gasolene people protecting their wares against desert renegades. There are a lot of pretentious close-ups, rather like those begrimed Western faces Sergio Leone gave us in the 'Dollars' films. Nearly everyone gets blown up in the end, except a boy who kills people with steel boomerangs, but is meant to be lovable and the symbolic future leader of his people. Utter rubbish this, done without style or polish (but carrying undoubted impact), a destructive millionaires amateur dramatics piece. The villains are all bald or mohawk-haired, or anything, in fact, but normal. Even 'hero' Gibson has a yellow streak in his hair to signify the

punk influence in this orgy of death and destruction. The best of the series, though, was yet to come.

Mad Max Beyond Thunderdome ❶ Ⓥ

1985, Australia, 107 mins, colour
Dir: George Miller, George Ogilvie
Stars: Mel Gibson, Tina Turner, Angela Russitto, Helen Buday
Rating: ★★★★

This third chunk of the adventures of an Australian desert warrior (still Mel Gibson) a few years after the nuclear apocalypse is a superior, well-crafted flight of the imagination. Bartertown, the centre of its action, is worthy of a Germanic science fiction film of the Twenties – a swarming, repulsive temple of thieves. And lording over this cesspit of humanity is Tina Turner as Aunty Entity, into whose voracious clutches Max falls. The dialogue, though sparse, always has something constructive or funny to say and the action is devastatingly well staged.

Mad Miss Manton, The ○

1938, US, 77 mins, b/w
Dir: Leigh Jason
Stars: Barbara Stanwyck, Henry Fonda, Sam Levene, Frances Mercer, Stanley Ridges
Rating: ★★

A tiresome screwball comedy-cum-murder mystery that wastes the talents of a great cast, headed by Barbara Stanwyck and Henry Fonda, and including Penny Singleton in one of a number of Thirties' roles she played before becoming the screen's Blondie. Only those who like spotting a whole battery of character actors from the era are likely to sit through this one till the end. Stanwyck and Fonda give the professional performances you'd expect in this fast but flimsy frolic, though even here the strain shows at times.

Madness of the Heart ○

1949, UK, 105 mins, b/w
Dir: Charles Bennett
Stars: Margaret Lockwood, Paul Dupuis, Maxwell Reed, Kathleen Byron
Rating: ★★

This unrestrained melodrama was Margaret Lockwood's last major success for the British cinema. She falls in love, goes blind, flees a convent and undergoes fierce romantic and acting competition from Kathleen Byron in her best *Black Narcissus* mood. It was pure gold-dust at the box-office.

Mad Room, The ●

1969, US, 92 mins, colour
Dir: Bernard Girard
Stars: Stella Stevens, Shelley Winters
Rating: ★★

A Grand Guignol shocker, from a story by Garrett Fort, who wrote the original screenplays for such vintage Thirties chillers as *Dracula* and *Dracula's Daughter* and also had a hand in the 1931 *Frankenstein*. Here, the delicious Stella Stevens is for once allowed some acting rope, and the audience's nerves are not the only things that get hacked to pieces. A good performance also comes from the Queen of B pictures, Beverly Garland.

Mad Wednesday! ☉

1946, US, 90 mins, b/w
Dir: Preston Sturges
Stars: Harold Lloyd, Frances Ramsden, Jimmy Conlin
Rating: ★★

Originally known as *The Sin of Harold Diddlebock*, this was the last film made by Harold Lloyd, renowned (especially in silent days) for his comedy capers on dizzy heights: almost everyone knows the famous 'big clock' scene in his 1923 masterpiece *Safety Last*. High-ledge antics recur in the climax of *Mad Wednesday!*, which was written and directed by another great comedy talent, Preston Sturges. Unfortunately, by far the funniest part of this film is the beginning, which is lifted almost whole from Lloyd's 1925 classic *The Freshman*. It was a nice idea to look at what might have happened to the character from that film but here, like Sturges, Lloyd was past his prime and only a few mild smiles result as both men try too hard.

Maggie, The ☉

(aka: High and Dry)
1953, UK, 95 mins, b/w
Dir: Alexander Mackendrick
Stars: Paul Douglas, Alex Mackenzie
Rating: ★★★

Ealing Studios comedy that's as refreshing as a dram of fresh air. Paul Douglas is a delight as the pushy American businessman who falls foul of an old puffer boat, *The Maggie*, and her crew of rascally Scottish seamen.

Magic ❶ Ⓥ

1978, US, 106 mins, colour
Dir: Richard Attenborough

M

Stars: Anthony Hopkins, Ann-Margret, Burgess Meredith, Ed Lauter
Rating: ★★

Director Richard Attenborough's story of a ventriloquist taken over by his dummy, *Dead of Night*-style, aims to be a classic chiller. Anthony Hopkins conjures cleverly and sweats mightily as the possessed entertainer, also sporting a splendid backstreets American accent. But it's Ann-Margret, radiating warmth, who gives the best performance in the film. Burgess Meredith is also firmly in character as Hopkins' agent. Suspense, however, is a notably missing ingredient in the chilly proceedings.

Magic Bow, The ○

1947, UK, 106 mins, b/w
Dir: Bernard Knowles
Stars: Stewart Granger, Phyllis Calvert, Dennis Price, Jean Kent
Rating: ★★

Stewart Granger as the famous musician Paganini? Well thanks to a lot of off-camera help, Granger at least looks convincing on the violin, while Yehudi Menuhin plays on the sound track. If you forget the story and enjoy the music, the film is a treat. The director is Bernard Knowles, whose second movie this was after a distinguished career as a film cameraman, much used in particular by Alfred Hitchcock.

Magic Box, The ○ ⓥ

1951, UK, 118 mins, colour
Dir: John Boulting
Stars: Robert Donat, Margaret Johnston, Maria Schell
Rating: ★★

Robert Donat oozes dignity as William Friese-Greene, inventor of the movie camera, whose life was, otherwise, full of hardships and disaster. The film, which was the industry's contribution to the Festival of Britain, has an appropriately stellar cast of actors who pop in for a few seconds in a well-mounted drama. Laurence Olivier, for example, has a highly amusing cameo as a policeman. Maria Schell and Margaret Johnston play Donat's two wives.

Magic of Lassie, The ○

1978, US, 100 mins, colour
Dir: Don Chaffey
Stars: Mickey Rooney, Stephanie Zimbalist, James Stewart, Alice Faye, Pernell Roberts
Rating: ★★

A game attempt to make a 1946 movie 32 years on. If only the pace weren't so slow, it might have come close to success. The colour photography mightn't be as lush as it was in the MGM days, but every possible ingredient to make the picture cute and lovable is thrown into the pot. The doggy star is immaculately trained, and, while the children are crying buckets over Lassie coming home after another incredible journey, for us adults there's always James Stewart, acting his heart out (and ridiculously losing star billing to Mickey Rooney) as if he thought he were in some other, better film. Mike Mazurki and Alice Faye are around to add to the nostalgia quotient, but it's Stewart's film: he even out-acts the dog and that's saying something.

Magnificent Ambersons, The ○

1942, US, 88 mins, b/w
Dir: Orson Welles
Stars: Joseph Cotten, Dolores Costello, Agnes Moorehead, Tim Holt, Anne Baxter, Ray Collins
Rating: ★★★★

Engrossing study by Orson Welles of a mid-western American family in terminal decay, set against a series of crowd scenes and backdrops that look like black and white etchings from an earlier era. Imposing performances from Joseph Cotten, Tim Holt and especially Agnes Moorehead, the film is full of scenes of thudding impact. To its undying shame, RKO tacked a new ending on to the film behind Welles' back and almost ruined it, leaving us with an unsatisfactory conclusion. In its original form, it could almost have been the equal of Welles' previous film *Citizen Kane*. The perfect narration is by Welles himself.

Magnificent Doll ○

1946, US, 95 mins, b/w
Dir: Frank Borzage
Stars: Ginger Rogers, David Niven, Burgess Meredith
Rating: ★★

Universal probably wasn't the best studio in the immediate post-war years for the mounting of this ambitious biography about Dolly Payne, a widow in Washington from 1796 on, who was wooed by several prominent politicians and eventually won by a man destined to become president. Ginger Rogers looks fabulous in

gowns designed by Travis Banton and Vera West, but seems a little overawed by long speeches about democracy, which take her a step too far off the dance floor. David Niven, although miscast, at least performs with spirit. As usual with Hollywood at the time, any resemblance between the events of the plot and the accepted facts of American history is purely coincidental.

Magnificent Obsession ○

1954, US, 108 mins, colour
Dir: Douglas Sirk
Stars: Jane Wyman, Rock Hudson, Barbara Rush, Agnes Moorehead
Rating: ★★★

Douglas Sirk's glossy remake of the 1935 film of the same title, with Jane Wyman and Rock Hudson succeeding the original co-starring team of Irene Dunne and Robert Taylor. Basically the material is of the magazine-fiction school, though the novel on which both films were based was written by Lloyd C Douglas, author of *The Robe*. Playboy Hudson inadvertently causes Wyman to be knocked down by a car and blinded. Stricken with remorse, he takes the only way out: he becomes a brain surgeon and cures her. Simple really. Wyman takes it in her stride; Hudson looks a touch bewildered but toughs it out; Barbara Rush underplays effectively; and Agnes Moorehead steals the film. Lush colour, doleful glances, tasteful clothes, nothing nasty: another world.

Magnificent Seven, The ○ ⓥ

1960, US, 138 mins, colour
Dir: John Sturges
Stars: Yul Brynner, James Coburn, Steve McQueen, Horst Buchholz, Charles Bronson, Robert Vaughn, Brad Dexter
Rating: ★★★★

A truly thunderous Western, with its wonderful ensemble cast and Elmer Bernstein's stirring music. The build-up is tremendous, the dialogue studded with memorably quotable lines, and director John Sturges' early action sequence in a graveyard as impressive and blood-surging as anything in the film. Charles Bronson, James Coburn, Steve McQueen and Robert Vaughn etch moving, unforgettable characters in a Hollywood remake (of the Japanese *Seven Samurai*) that for once doesn't disgrace the original.

Magnificent Showman, The ○ ⓥ

(aka: Circus World)
1964, US, 135 mins, colour
Dir: Henry Hathaway
Stars: John Wayne, Claudia Cardinale, Rita Hayworth, John Smith, Lloyd Nolan, Richard Conte
Rating: ★★

If you like circuses, John Wayne or Claudia Cardinale, then this merry, gaudy and faintly numbing panorama of circus life is the film for you. It's certainly a handsome show with the accent on spectacle and sentiment, even if it tends to sit back and say, 'Aren't I a wonderful show?' and let the audience do the rest. Miss Cardinale, all bosom and sparkling teeth, has never used her native Italian charm to greater effect, and puts poor Rita Hayworth (at some disadvantage from the start in playing her mother) in the shade. But the film is really one big circus from start to finish. Wayne did much of his own stuntwork in the fire scenes and spent several days in bed for his trouble.

Magnificent Two, The ○

1967, UK, 96 mins, colour
Dir: Cliff Owen
Stars: Eric Morecambe, Ernie Wise
Rating: ★★

The Rank Organisation's third and last attempt to make film stars out of TV masterclowns Morecambe and Wise. The laughter measure is high in parts in this, the most successful of the three (Eric and Ernie get mixed up in a revolution), though there are vague and unsettling undercurrents of nastiness running through the story. And people get killed. In a Laurel and Hardy comedy, a lift could fall on a man from 60 feet and he got up. He got up as a dwarf, but he got up. Still, there's always Eric, bespectacled and bewildered and as deadpan as ever. 'I will always be the woman behind you,' Major Carla (Margit Saad) reminds him. Remarks Eric, looking perplexed: 'You'll come round the front now and again, won't you?'

Magnum Force ● ⓥ

1973, US, 124 mins, colour
Dir: Ted Post
Stars: Clint Eastwood, Hal Holbrook, Mitchell Ryan, David Soul
Rating: ★★

Inspector Harry Callahan takes on a gang of hijackers, a band of store robbers, a mad bomber and even, in the storyline's main theme, a group of vigilantes who are conducting their own private massacre of the city's underworld. None of those characters is any match for tall, tough, taciturn Harry, as you can imagine, played with all the finesse of a Magnum .44 revolver by Clint Eastwood. The screenplay is written by John Milius (who subsequently directed *Dillinger* and *The Wind and the Lion*) and Michael Cimino (who also turned director with *The Deer Hunter*).

Mahler ◑ ⓥ

1974, UK, 115 mins, colour
Dir: Ken Russell
Stars: Robert Powell, Georgina Hale, Richard Morant
Rating: ★★★

Ken Russell's highly individual biography of the famous composer is an essay in style, image and effect. But what style! What eye-popping images! And what dazzling effect! Russell has virtually done no more than set Mahler's exciting music to his own visual interpretations, against a background of flashbacks on a train journey when the composer – strikingly well played by Robert Powell – has only a few days to live. A naked girl escapes from a chrysalis; a child dies; a conversion to Catholicism turns into a cross between 'The Ride of the Valkyries' and a Busby Berkeley routine; a girl performs a striptease with SS men; and there's a ride on a white horse through moonlit woods. You can see that there's no lack of riches; that certainly it's outrageous; and that occasionally Russell overreaches himself. But Mahler's life story is there at the back of it all; and Robert Powell is exceptionally good at catching, besides the various ages, the man's uncertainties, determination, eccentricities and fear of death. Above all, the music makes you want to go out and buy the records!

Major and the Minor, The ○

1942, US, 100 mins, b/w
Dir: Billy Wilder
Stars: Ginger Rogers, Ray Milland, Rita Johnson, Robert Benchley
Rating: ★★★

An enchantingly amusing comedy in which, posing as a 12 year-old schoolgirl, Ginger Rogers finds herself in the middle of a boys' military school. Diana Lynn is equally good as her impish sister. A big box-office and critical hit that sent the team of writer-director Billy Wilder and co-writer Charles Brackett on their way to a decade of fabulous success.

Major Barbara ○

1941, UK, 121 mins, b/w
Dir: Gabriel Pascal, Harold French, David Lean
Stars: Wendy Hiller, Rex Harrison, Robert Morley, Robert Newton, Emlyn Williams, Deborah Kerr
Rating: ★★★

An efficient and entertaining screen version of Bernard Shaw's satirical play about a wealthy girl who becomes a major in the Salvation Army. Wendy Hiller and Rex Harrison are the leading players, while Robert Newton's performance in support made him a star of the British cinema.

Major Dundee ○

1964, US, 120 mins, colour
Dir: Sam Peckinpah
Stars: Charlton Heston, Richard Harris, James Coburn, Senta Berger
Rating: ★★★

A big Sam Peckinpah Western about a mixed bag of Unionists and Confederates hunting renegade Indians in the last months of the Civil War. The action is stirring, and the Metrocolor photography splendid in set pieces, particularly with one shot of Charlton Heston and Senta Berger on the outskirts of a small Mexican town. As a one-armed scout, James Coburn gives a portrayal which lifts an ordinary supporting role into one of compelling stature. Jim Hutton and Michael Anderson Jr show up well as younger soldiers, while R G Armstrong also does well as a fire-eating, rifle-swinging priest. There's a glorious final battle sequence in which Dundee's rabble army not only ambushes and attacks a tribe of murderous Indians, but fights a splendid rearguard action against what seems to be the entire French Army.

Majority of One, A ○

1961, US, 153 mins, colour
Dir: Mervyn LeRoy
Stars: Alec Guinness, Rosalind Russell
Rating: ★★

A sentimental drama that fires on most tearducts thanks to the moving performances of the two stars, Alec Guinness and Rosalind Russell, as a Japanese gentleman and a Jewish lady falling in love. Lushly photographed in Technicolor and less successful at the box-office than it deserved to be, it

M

was the beginning of a gentle down-swing in Guinness' phenomenally successful film career.

Major League ◐ ⓥ
1989, US, 107 mins, colour
Dir: David S Ward
Stars: Tom Berenger, Charlie Sheen, Corbin Bernsen, Margaret Whitton, Rene Russo, Wesley Snipes
Rating: ★★

This okay baseball comedy is the usual Hollywood sporting stuff about the bunch of no-hopers who turn out to be world-beaters. Well put together, it's not as funny as its publicity and reputation would have you believe. Plotwork is by the numbers and characters are stereotypes. But the acting from an all-star cast lends the enterprise an extra dimension, especially from Charlie Sheen as the short-sighted demon pitcher who becomes known as Wild Thing. A sequel followed five years later.

Make Mine Mink ☉
1960, UK, 100 mins, b/w
Dir: Robert Asher
Stars: Terry-Thomas, Athene Seyler, Hattie Jacques, Billie Whitelaw
Rating: ★★★

A rib-tickling comedy in which Terry-Thomas, Athene Seyler and Hattie Jacques ham it up delightfully as members of a genteel gang of fur thieves, while Billie Whitelaw's warm-hearted portrait of the maid with a police record almost steals the film. Lots of amusing sketch-like incidents carry the fun along in style, aided by a well above-par comedy cast that also includes Kenneth Williams, Ron Moody, Sydney Tafler, Raymond Huntley and Irene Handl.

Making Mr Right ◐ ⓥ
1987, US, 98 mins, colour
Dir: Susan Seidelman
Stars: Ann Magnuson, John Malkovich, Glenne Headly, Ben Masters, Polly Bergen, Laurie Metcalf
Rating: ★★

A bright-*looking* misfire on the now-familiar theme of the android who develops human feelings. It's quite difficult to say why Susan Seidelman's film doesn't quite work, except that its leading performers do lack individuality. Ann Magnuson, for example, is nothing special and never quite hits the mark as the high-powered, highly sexed hype consultant hired to humanise a new space mission

android, Ulysses (John Malkovich) for the benefit of the media. She looks like a supporting actress just slightly out of her depth. Malkovich also plays the robot's alter-ego scientist, who shows rather less in the way of emotions (surprisingly) than his creation. The fun and games that result from this situation are rather limited and not too inspired or involving. Okay for video, though, where attention is less demanding; and Glenne Headly is good as the heroine's dizzy friend.

Malaga
See: Moment of Danger

Malaya ○
(aka: East of the Rising Sun)
1949, US, 98 mins, b/w
Dir: Richard Thorpe
Stars: Spencer Tracy, James Stewart, Sidney Greenstreet, John Hodiak, Valentina Cortesa
Rating: ★★★

Big-scale, two-fisted adventure story set during World War Two. The film's action comes in frequent bursts once Spencer Tracy and James Stewart (playing an ex-jailbird and a newspaperman respectively) are put ashore behind enemy Japanese lines. The entire cast, in fact, is quite breathtakingly formidable and, unsurprisingly, strike a good many sparks off one another, despite the inferior script and direction. Down in the credits, you may spot one for 'Music Conductor'. The name: Andre Previn, then only 21.

Malcolm X ● ⓥ
1992, US, 201 mins, colour
Dir: Spike Lee
Stars: Denzel Washington, Angela Bassett, Spike Lee, Al Freeman Jr, Theresa Randle, Lonette McKee
Rating: ★★★

Director Spike Lee's powerful portrait of the controversial black American leader gave Denzel Washington a great acting opportunity, and for his electrifying portrayal of Malcolm X's rise from teen thug to street preacher and political activist he was nominated for an Academy Award. Full of passionate ideas and inflammatory speeches, and with a powerful message, this is an extraordinary true story – but at over three hours it does take some watching, particularly since its most memorable moments are dotted in little bright bursts throughout the

film. Nelson Mandela makes a cameo appearance; the talented Angela Bassett is sadly underused.

Malice ● ⓥ
1993, US, 107 mins, colour
Dir: Harold Becker
Stars: Alec Baldwin, Nicole Kidman, Bill Pullman, Anne Bancroft, George C Scott
Rating: ★★★

If you're at home with the lights down and there's a storm raging outside, this might give you a creep or two. Set in an America when people leave doors, back and front, open (as you do) and an address like 36 Hedges Lane proves to be on the edge of a cliff, this is one of those plots where very little is likely to end up being what it seemed in the first place. Without wishing to betray the plot . . . well, given that Nicole Kidman collects $20 million for surgeon Alec Baldwin cutting out a healthy ovary and walks out on husband Bill Pullman for letting Baldwin do it, and given that we're less than half way through the film, it won't take avid thriller fans long to figure that something is Going On. Nor are they likely to pause long before pouncing on the identity of the serial killer who just happens to be raping and murdering girls from Prof Pullman's college at the same time. Well-made and enjoyable rubbish, this, if a touch on the unpleasant side. Anne Bancroft and George C Scott are among those given time for supporting cameos.

Malta Story ○
1953, UK, 103 mins, b/w
Dir: Brian Desmond Hurst
Stars: Alec Guinness, Jack Hawkins, Flora Robson
Rating: ★★★

The direction is sharper than the script in this sincere and clear-eyed story of the siege of Malta by the Germans and Italians in World War Two. Director Hurst brings the hot, rocky Malta scene brilliantly to life, and creates such moments to remember as close-ups of authentic Maltese faces, and shots of children at play during an air-raid. Muriel Pavlow is delicately touching as a young Maltese girl in love with part-time pilot Alec Guinness (slightly uncomfortable outside his normal comedy roles), and there are workmanlike service types from Jack Hawkins, Anthony Steel and – particularly good – Ralph Truman.

Maltese Falcon, The ○ ⓥ
1941, US, 101 mins, b/w
Dir: John Huston
Stars: Humphrey Bogart, Mary Astor, Peter Lorre, Sydney Greenstreet, Barton Maclane
Rating: ★★★★

Humphrey Bogart's first major starring role, gripping from start to finish in its account of various eccentric criminals and their hunt for a fabulous statuette, in which detective Bogart becomes embroiled. Indelible performances from Bogart and especially the perfumed Peter Lorre and the hulking Sydney Greenstreet as two of the oiliest and most treacherous conspirators in film history: the public loved them together and they co-starred in several more films thereafter. Original author Dashiell Hammett based the Greenstreet character on a real-life rogue, Maundy Gregory, a corpulent British detective who turned in his badge and became involved in numerous intrigues including a hunt for a lost treasure not unlike the plot Hammett constructed for *The Maltese Falcon*.

Mambo Kings, The ① ⓥ
1992, US, 101 mins, colour
Dir: Arne Glimcher
Stars: Armand Assante, Antonio Banderas, Cathy Moriarty, Maruschka Detmers, JT Taylor, Desi Arnaz Jr
Rating: ★★

Apart from the sex scenes, this is an old-fashioned film that reflects the Fifties in which it's set and catches well the cultural flavour of its central characters. Other characters and situations are pretty stereotyped, though, as Cuban musician brothers Armand Assante and Antonio Banderas flee from gangsters in their native land and set out to become the mambo kings of the USA. Complications are provided by Banderas not being able to forget his true love in Cuba (now married to a gangster) and Assante falling heavily for the girl his brother marries on the rebound. The music is hot to begin with, but one mambo sounds much like another, and the film's key song, though lovely, is repeated rather too many times. As the older brother, Assante is excellent: this is probably the best performance of his career to date, in a film where everything else is pretty middling. Roscoe Lee Browne is the nasty villain who gets the brothers banned from his clubs.

Mame ○ ⓥ
1974, US, 131 mins, colour
Dir: Gene Saks
Stars: Lucille Ball, Robert Preston, Beatrice Arthur
Rating: ★

The hit Broadway musical transferred to the screen with Lucille Ball in Angela Lansbury's place (shot in close-up through a thousand gauze filters) as Auntie Mame, the eccentric socialite forced to take in her orphan nephew. There's a notable lack of singing talent involved. But Beatrice Arthur (later better known as Dorothy in TV's *The Golden Girls*) re-creates her stage success as Mame's actress friend Vera Charles. The best songs are Mame and Vera bitching at each other through 'Bosom Buddies' and 'The Man in the Moon is a Lady' sequence from Vera's latest stage success, which Mame manages to wreck in spectacular fashion. As a film musical it's a lumbering, static affair, but a must for lovers of high camp.

Man Alive ○
1945, US, 70 mins, b/w
Dir: Ray Enright
Stars: Pat O'Brien, Adolphe Menjou, Ellen Drew, Rudy Vallee, Fortunio Bonanova
Rating: ★★★

An amusing change of pace for tough-guy Pat O'Brien as a man who, presumed dead, likes the idea until someone else makes a play for his wife. Then he becomes a 'ghost' to scare the suitor off. Entertaining comedy.

Man Alone, A ○
1955, US, 96 mins, colour
Dir: Ray Milland
Stars: Ray Milland, Mary Murphy, Ward Bond, Raymond Burr
Rating: ★★★

Ray Milland is a gunfighter on the run wrongly accused of murder in this well-plotted Western which was also Milland's directing debut. The sheriff's daughter (Mary Murphy) helps him prove his innocence and hides him from a lynch mob. Ward Bond gives good support as the town sheriff and there are two good baddies in Raymond Burr and a young, snake-eyed Lee Van Cleef. Milland's first try at directing himself. It's deliberate and humourless, but the tension is well concentrated.

Man and a Woman, A
See: Un Homme et une Femme

Man at the Top ○ ⓥ
1973, UK, 87 mins, colour
Dir: Mike Vardy
Stars: Kenneth Haigh, Nanette Newman, Harry Andrews
Rating: ★

After starring in the long running television series of the same title, Kenneth Haigh gave a ruthless abrasiveness to the famous character of Joe Lampton, created in John Braine's best-seller and incarnated originally in the cinema by Laurence Harvey. In this spin-off from the TV series, Haigh is the newly appointed managing director of a pharmaceutical company: he finds out just why his predecessor killed himself and then uses the knowledge to blackmail his way to the top, showing that Lampton still has some nastiness left in him.

Man, a Woman and a Bank, A ○
(aka: A Very Big Withdrawal)
1979, Canada, 101 mins, colour
Dir: Noel Black
Stars: Donald Sutherland, Brooke Adams, Paul Mazursky
Rating: ★★★

This is better than most bank robbery capers, if only because of the determinedly light mood, skilfully maintained by director Noel Black, whose best-known film is *Pretty Poison*. Otherwise it's a routine job, involving a computerised heist executed by Donald Sutherland and Paul Mazursky. Little Mazursky shows as much talent here as a character actor as he does as the director of such films as *An Unmarried Woman*. Sutherland and Brooke Adams, reunited from *Invasion of the Body Snatchers*, work pleasingly well together and, although there are a few lulls, and a silly 10-minute interlude which serves little better purpose than the foreground for a song, this remains pleasing, undemanding entertainment with a few clammy-handed thrills thrown in.

Man Between, The ○
1953, US, 100 mins, b/w
Dir: Carol Reed
Stars: James Mason, Claire Bloom, Hildegarde Neff
Rating: ★★

Carol Reed moved from the Vienna of *The Third Man* to Berlin, and from racketeers to refugees in this cold-war

M

thriller which has echoes of *The Spy Who Came In From the Cold*. Although the script is generally disappointing, Reed and his cameraman Desmond Dickinson conjure up some brilliant atmospheric moments and a tense climax.

Man Called Horse, A ◑ ⓥ
1970, US, 114 mins, colour
Dir: Elliot Silverstein
Stars: Richard Harris, Judith Anderson, Jean Gascon
Rating: ★★★

One of Richard Harris's mightiest box-office successes. He's in terrific form as the English aristocrat who falls into the clutches of a tribe of Sioux Indians. Fascinated by his fair skin and blond hair, they take him prisoner and proceed to inflict terrible torture by ritual (turn your eyes away at the 'Sun Vow' scene where our hero is suspended by horsehair ropes from bones inserted into holes made in his chest by eagle claws) before they will accept him. Obviously, this and other scenes make this far more brutal than Kevin Costner's *Dances With Wolves*, but it remains a fascinating, if slightly gauche, variation on the 'man living wild' theme, bluntly addressing both anthropological differences, and the inevitable contempt that ignorance of different cultures engenders.

Manchurian Candidate, The ◑ ⓥ
1962, US, 126 mins, b/w
Dir: John Frankenheimer
Stars: Frank Sinatra, Laurence Harvey, Janet Leigh, Angela Lansbury
Rating: ★★★★

Chilling, suspenseful, right-on-target adaptation of Richard Condon's novel about a soldier back from the Korean War who has been brainwashed and primed to kill at the release of a certain code. Electrifying direction by John Frankenheimer, good work from Frank Sinatra, Janet Leigh and Laurence Harvey (never better cast) and an outstanding performance by Angela Lansbury, far from her cosy Jessica Fletcher image, as a woman ambitious for political power.

Mandy ⊙
(aka: The Crash of Silence)
1952, UK, 93 mins, b/w
Dir: Alexander Mackendrick
Stars: Phyllis Calvert, Jack Hawkins, Mandy Miller, Terence Morgan
Rating: ★★★

A dramatic, exciting film about the problems facing a young couple whose child is unable to speak or hear. Mandy Miller, as the little girl who lives in a silent world, gives an affecting performance which won the hearts of millions. A Venice Film Festival prize winner, the film's subject might have seemed too serious for a director like Alexander Mackendrick since his previous two full-length films had been comedies (*Whisky Galore!* and *The Man in the White Suit*). Yet his background in documentary films stood him in good stead. He also proved to have a sure way with child stars, as shown by his later films – *The Maggie*, *Sammy Going South* and *A High Wind in Jamaica*.

Man for All Seasons, A ○ ⓥ
1966, UK, 120 mins, colour
Dir: Fred Zinnemann
Stars: Paul Scofield, Wendy Hiller, Leo McKern, Robert Shaw, Orson Welles, Susannah York
Rating: ★★★

Fred Zinnemann's handsome film of Sir Thomas More's trials under the whims of King Henry VIII scores in every department except its senior school history book dialogue. It won six Academy Awards, including Oscars for Paul Scofield as Sir Thomas, and for Ted Moore, whose colour photography would have won in almost any year. All the other performances are good, notably Orson Welles' plotting Cardinal Wolsey, Wendy Hiller's understanding, very human wife, and John Hurt's weak and waspish Richard Rich.

Man Friday ○
1975, UK, 115 mins, colour
Dir: Jack Gold
Stars: Peter O'Toole, Richard Rountree
Rating: ★★

This colourful film plays a novel variation on Defoe's classic tale of life on a desert island. It supposes that Friday (Richard Roundtree), instead of being taught by Robinson Crusoe (Peter O'Toole), contrives, by craft and patience, to reverse the situation so that Crusoe learns a basic way of life from him, each assimilating the best of one another's culture. The setting is attractive, the performances appealing and the situations, particularly a sports day, are often amusing. Only in the last 10 minutes does it veer off line and seem to go a bit to pieces.

Man from Bitter Ridge, The ○
1955, US, 80 mins, colour
Dir: Jack Arnold
Stars: Lex Barker, Stephen McNally, Mara Corday
Rating: ★★

Lex Barker, then still escaping from his Tarzan image, is the hero of this Western, as an undercover agent after stagecoach bandits. But all the acting class comes from Stephen McNally, who did such yeoman service in countless Universal Westerns.

Man from Colorado, The ○
1948, US, 99 mins, colour
Dir: Henry Levin
Stars: Glenn Ford, William Holden, Ellen Drew, Edgar Buchanan
Rating: ★★★

Lively Western in good Technicolor, with Glenn Ford in a very different role from his other co-starring Western with William Holden, *Texas*, in 1941. Here he plays an army officer with a streak of brutal violence, who is made a federal judge, and clashes with Holden, as his oldest friend. Ford does well as the totally dislikeable Devereaux, and the supporting cast is filled with Columbia regulars. They include chubby Edgar Buchanan (who had also appeared in *Texas*); lean-featured Jim Bannon, who starred in the Red Ryder Western series; fresh-faced Jerome Courtland, who later turned director with the Disney studio; benevolent Ray Collins, who went on to win fame as Lt Tragg in the *Perry Mason* series on television; and character actor Denver Pyle.

Man from Dakota, The ○
(aka: Arouse and Beware)
1940, US, 75 mins, b/w
Dir: Leslie Fenton
Stars: Wallace Beery, John Howard, Dolores Del Rio
Rating: ★★

A tough-edged but rousing Western made as a vehicle for big, brawling Wallace Beery, here as a bullying sergeant contemptuous of the youthful officer (John Howard) with whom he escapes from a Confederate prison camp during the American Civil War. The plot doesn't develop quite as you might expect, thanks to its basis – a novel by Mackinlay Kantor – and makes room for the soulfully lovely Dolores Del Rio as a woman who helps the escapees.

Man from Del Rio, The ○

1956, US, 83 mins, b/w
Dir: Harry Horner
Stars: Anthony Quinn, Katy Jurado
Rating: ★★

An unusual, thoughtful, and decidedly worthwhile Western. There's not a lot of action, apart from a fierce gun-fight at the start and a tense climax. But the performances of the principals more than make up for it. Photographed by the great Stanley Cortez.

Man from Laramie, The ○ Ⓥ

1955, US, 104 mins, colour
Dir: Anthony Mann
Stars: James Stewart, Arthur Kennedy, Donald Crisp, Cathy O'Donnell, Alex Nichol, Aline MacMahon
Rating: ★★★

Superior Western with a famous theme tune, and James Stewart going through hell and high water to track down the man who sold Indians rifles that led to the death of Stewart's brother. There are two excellent performances from old-stagers Donald Crisp and Aline MacMahon, but delicate Cathy O'Donnell seems a little lost among the film's many fights. Jack Elam scores in a small but sinister role, and colour, music and action all hit the mark well in this tautly-strung outdoor whodunnit.

Man from Nevada, The

See: The Nevadan

Man from Snowy River, The ○ Ⓥ

1982, Australia, 104 mins, colour
Dir: George Miller
Stars: Kirk Douglas
Rating: ★★

More like bargain basement Disney than a John Ford Western, this Australian saddle saga takes its cue from the successful *Wilderness Family* films. A growing pains melodrama, it suffers through the inexperience of its young leads – Tom Burlinson and Sigrid Thornton – and the cheap gimmick of casting Kirk Douglas as both a reclusive mountain man who helps the boy overcome his sudden state as an orphan and the girl's stubborn father. Even so, it was a huge hit Down Under. Incidentally, director George Miller is not the same as the George Miller who directed Mel Gibson's *Mad Max* trilogy.

Man from the Diners' Club, The ⊙

1963, US, 96 mins, b/w
Dir: Frank Tashlin
Stars: Danny Kaye, Martha Hyer, Telly Savalas, George Kennedy
Rating: ★★★

In the late Forties, Danny Kaye's popularity was such that it was a major feat to get tickets for one of his stage appearances at the London Palladium. By 1963, his best films and his peak of fame were certainly behind him, but this funny film didn't get its just deserts at the time. It was directed by comedy specialist Frank Tashlin, who earlier had written for Bob Hope and, especially, Jerry Lewis. It's unusual to find a Kaye comedy in black-and-white (20 years earlier his films were already in colour). But the great man will soon get you laughing with impersonations of a dotty masseuse, or an unwittingly-brilliant gymnast, out-manoeuvring a gang of crooks led by a bewigged Telly Savalas. And the final half-hour includes a wild and wacky chase on the freeway.

Manhattan ○ Ⓥ

1979, US, 96 mins, b/w
Dir: Woody Allen
Stars: Woody Allen, Diane Keaton, Michael Murphy, Mariel Hemingway, Meryl Streep
Rating: ★★★

Considered by many Woody Allen fans to be his best film, *Manhattan* is more thoughtful and less obviously funny than the similar but Oscar-laden *Annie Hall*. Allen is a successful television writer who wants to do something more worthwhile. He also feels guilty about his relationship with a teenage girl (Mariel Hemingway) who dotes on him. His ex-wife (Meryl Streep) is a lesbian and he hesitantly starts an affair with Diane Keaton. It all sounds more complicated than it is, and Allen's excellent script and deceptively simple direction make *Manhattan* a joy to watch. The fact that it is shot in black and white entirely on location in Allen's home town adds to its quirky appeal.

Manhattan Melodrama ○

1934, US, 93 mins, b/w
Dir: W S Van Dyke
Stars: Clark Gable, William Powell, Myrna Loy, Leo Carrillo, Mickey Rooney
Rating: ★★★

Clark Gable gained useful practice for the 1936 blockbuster *San Francisco* (in both cases he's a gambling house proprietor called Blackie) in this familiar but oh-so-well-done story of two orphaned kids, one of whom grows into an upright citizen, the other into a smooth-talking racketeer and gambler. Although he's uncredited on the MGM handout, you may notice that the boy playing Gable as a lad is Mickey Rooney. Arthur Caesar's screenplay won an Academy Award, and the crisp black-and-white photography is by James Wong Howe, who had to wait 21 years for an Oscar of his own – for *The Rose Tattoo*. *Manhattan Melodrama* was the film 'public enemy number one' John Dillinger had just seen when he was gunned down by federal agents.

Manhattan Murder Mystery ○ Ⓥ

1993, US, 109 mins, colour
Dir: Woody Allen
Stars: Woody Allen, Diane Keaton, Alan Alda, Anjelica Huston
Rating: ★★★

Something different from Woody with lots of smiles and rarely a neurosis in sight: a comedy-thriller that balances the comedy and thrills in the right ratio, a formula that seems to have eluded Hollywood for several decades. A bit annoying at first (and its hand-held camera wavers remain so), but increasingly enjoyable, it casts Woody Allen and Diane Keaton as a middle-aged couple indulging each other's pastimes of ice hockey (his) and opera (hers). 'Every time I hear Wagner,' he grumbles, 'I feel I should invade Poland.' Keaton is longing to do something with her life, and her curiosity runs wild when her fairly elderly neighbour drops dead. She feels sure the gossipy woman would have mentioned her heart condition. And why are her ashes hidden under the sink? Didn't her husband mention they'd bought twin cemetery plots? We share Woody's sceptical view of her suspicions, but amazingly it seems there *is* something going on – though not quite what Keaton thinks – especially when the woman turns up alive. Stir in Alan Alda as Keaton's old flame who still has a yen for her, and publisher Allen's ace author Anjelica Huston, who fancies a mystery almost as much a man, and you have a feisty brew that actually has one or two exciting, stylish and creepy moments

M

amidst the modish comedy. You should find this mystery worth investigating.

Manhattan Project, The ○ Ⓥ

1986, US, 117 mins, colour
Dir: Marshall Brickman
Stars: John Lithgow, Christopher Collet, Jill Eikenberry, Cynthia Nixon, John Mahoney, Robert Sean Leonard
Rating: ★★

It's amazing what you can do while you're studying for your chemistry exam. Take young Paul, for example. Seeing his mother's getting pally with a nuclear scientist and recognising bottles of plutonium during a tour on which the scientist generously takes him, Paul decides to break into the lab, steal some and make his own atomic bomb. Well, this is America, so you can at least believe it if you take a heavy swallow. Although overlong, the film is a neat enough comedy-thriller offshoot of *WarGames*, with (thank goodness) a personable and accomplished quartet of leading portrayals from mighty John Lithgow (the scientist), Christopher Collet (the boy), Jill Eikenberry (his mother) and Cynthia Nixon (his – rather mature – girlfriend). Some tension is generated towards the end, although not about the bomb itself, which we know won't explode in a film of this timbre. The four-letter word which gives the film its 'grown up' rating is presumably to keep sub-teens from getting similar ideas.

Manhunt

See: From Hell to Texas

Man Hunt ○

1941, US, 98 mins, b/w
Dir: Fritz Lang
Stars: Walter Pidgeon, Joan Bennett, George Sanders, John Carradine, Roddy McDowall
Rating: ★★★

This now little-known Fritz Lang film, about a man who almost kills Hitler, contains some of the most exciting chase sequences ever made. After years of minor films at MGM, Walter Pidgeon was loaned to 20th Century-Fox for two pictures, this and *How Green Was My Valley*. He returned to MGM a star. Another powerful performance is given by John Carradine, in frightening form as the man who hunts Pidgeon down.

Manhunter ● Ⓥ

1986, US, 118 mins, colour
Dir: Michael Mann
Stars: William L Petersen, Kim Greist, Brian Cox, Joan Allen, Dennis Farina
Rating: ★★

The character of Hannibal the Cannibal makes its first film appearance in this blood-spattered but slow psychological thriller, with bursts of action including the inevitable confrontation between cop and killer at the climax. A full-moon killer (this one known as the Tooth Fairy) is on the loose again, and only an ex-FBI agent (William L Petersen), who is slightly deranged himself, seems likely to catch him. Quite a brooding performance from Petersen and some mildly interesting psychological overtones, but overall this thriller, though strong meat, is pretty routine.

Maniac ○

1963, UK, 86 mins, b/w
Dir: Michael Carreras
Stars: Kerwin Mathews, Nadia Gray, Donald Houston
Rating: ★★

Kerwin Mathews is most commonly associated with the Dynamation films (he was in *The Three Worlds of Gulliver*, *The 7th Voyage of Sinbad* and *Jack the Giant Killer*), but this time he's up to some very non U-certificate goings-on in this eerie Hammer suspense story, set in the Camargue marshlands of France. Liliane Brousse stirs up some genuine Gallic sex appeal in the steamy settings in a Jimmy Sangster-scripted story – mostly shot at night – of a mad axe-murderer on the loose.

Maniac Cop ● Ⓥ

1988, US, 85 mins, colour
Dir: William Lustig
Stars: Tom Atkins, Bruce Campbell, Laurene Landon, Richard Roundtree
Rating: ★

Even though he didn't direct it, the hand of writer-director Larry Cohen (*It's Alive!* was his biggest hit) puts its dabs all over this horror film masquerading as a police thriller. A vengeful brain-dead cop rises from the grave, dons his uniform and initiates a mass slaughter of the city's night-time population. A detective smells a (dead) rat and contacts a TV friend to break the ban on the story. 'You gotta make it bigger than AIDS,' he says. The unfortunate consequence of his action is that while the maniac cop

goes on killing innocent people, citizens start killing innocent cops. The rest is pretty lively if rudimentary B-movie stuff, sketchily acted with the exception of Sheree North and sickeningly violent throughout. Most unsuitable for children.

Maniac Cop 2 ● Ⓥ

1990, US, 85 mins, colour
Dir: William Lustig
Stars: Robert Davi, Claudia Christian, Bruce Campbell, Laurene Landon, Leo Rossi
Rating: ★

The psycho policeman is back on the beat(ing), and this time he has a signature tune: 'You'd better watch out when you hear that sound.' It means that the maniac cop's around.' Fun huh? The first film was not without interest, but this sequel is pure pulp. The hero and heroine from *Maniac Cop* (Bruce Campbell, Laurene Landon) are soon despatched by Cordell, the disgraced (and framed) cop risen from the dead, and he's confronted by a new star duo (Robert Davi, Claudia Christian), as he teams up with a serial killer (Leo Rossi) and kills the innocent to protect the guilty. The trail eventually leads back to Sing Sing prison where Cordell was bumped off by three inmates, paid with public money. Cynically cut to the formula its public will expect, the film also makes a miserable attempt to forge a bond of friendship between the cop and the killer along the lines of Frankenstein's creature and the blind hermit from *Bride of Frankenstein*. If only this had a tenth of that film's flair and style.

Maniacs on Wheels

See: Once a Jolly Swagman

Man in a Cocked Hat

See: Carlton-Browne of the F.O.

Man in Grey, The ○

1943, UK, 116 mins, b/w
Dir: Leslie Arliss
Stars: Margaret Lockwood, James Mason, Phyllis Calvert, Stewart Granger
Rating: ★★★

This period adventure yarn was the film that really started the box-office clicking for Gainsborough Films, soon to become Britain's most successful company in the 1940s. All four stars – Margaret Lockwood, Stewart Granger, Phyllis Calvert and especially James Mason, as the evil Marquis of

Rohan – gave fine performances which assured their popularity for years to come.

Man in Love, A ● ⊙
1987, France, 110 mins, colour
Dir: Diane Kurys
Stars: Peter Coyote, Greta Scacchi, Peter Riegert, Jamie Lee Curtis, Claudia Cardinale
Rating: ★★★

I suppose it would take Greta Scacchi, if anything, to drag one away from Jamie Lee Curtis; but Peter Coyote certainly is a lucky man to have the two to choose between in this moody romantic piece. A bit long, but with a nice overall feel, the film has some really effective atmospheric shots of European cities in summer and the affair between movie star Coyote and starlet Scacchi is accompanied by sweeping music from Georges Delarue in the grand manner. Claudia Cardinale looks magnificent as Scacchi's mother and she, Coyote, Peter Riegert and Curtis steal the acting honours, while Scacchi offers frequent displays of skin that will have her devotees drooling in the aisles.

Man in the Attic ○
1953, US, 82 mins, b/w
Dir: Hugo Fregonese
Stars: Jack Palance, Constance Smith
Rating: ★★★

Jack Palance adds a portrait of Jack the Ripper to his gallery of screen grotesques in this gripping and at times quite frightening thriller. The Victorian atmosphere rings true, and there are two good supporting performances from Rhys Williams and Frances Bavier as the parents of one of the Ripper's would-be victims.

Man in the Dark ○
1953, US, 71 mins, colour
Dir: Lew Landers
Stars: Edmond O'Brien, Audrey Totter, Ted De Corsia
Rating: ★★

The credentials of this tense and sometimes frightening crime thriller make it worth watching. The director, Lew Landers, was responsible for some interesting horror films in the Thirties and Forties. And the action is hair-raisingly photographed, especially a chase on a roller-coaster, by Hollywood veteran Floyd Crosby, who worked on all of the Sixties' film adaptations of Edgar Allan Poe stories.

Man in the Grey Flannel Suit, The ○
1956, US, 153 mins, colour
Dir: Nunnally Johnson
Stars: Gregory Peck, Jennifer Jones, Fredric March, Marisa Pavan, Lee J Cobb
Rating: ★★

Compelling, if overlong, account of a man fighting to find hope in the future and save his marriage. Dominated by a brilliant performance from Fredric March, although Marisa Pavan also registers well as the girl in Gregory Peck's past.

Man in the Iron Mask, The ○
1939, US, 110 mins, b/w
Dir: James Whale
Stars: Louis Hayward, Joan Bennett, Joseph Schildkraut, Alan Hale
Rating: ★★★

The amazing atmosphere in this brooding version of Dumas' classic tale of intrigue and derring-do is achieved in masterly style by skilful lighting and can chiefly be attributed to the director, James Whale, whose last great film this was, following a series of horror classics that had included *The Invisible Man* and *Bride of Frankenstein*. One cannot imagine an actor more able than Louis Hayward to suggest the separate natures – one foppish and treacherous, the other straightforward and gallant – of the twins who between them must decide the fate of the throne of France. Unfortunately, the role type-cast Hayward in swashbucklers, and he was unable to escape them. Watch for a very young Peter Cushing in a walk-on role.

Man in the Middle ○
1964, UK, 94 mins, b/w
Dir: Guy Hamilton
Stars: Robert Mitchum, Trevor Howard, Keenan Wynn, Barry Sullivan, France Nuyen
Rating: ★★

One thing stops this film from being just another surprise witness courtroom thriller: here, the last-minute surprise is provided by the masterly Trevor Howard. The climax is the last and best of the three scenes in which Howard appears. As he gives his vital evidence, chewing on every word, as if the rather ordinary script were something to be relished, one views the story subjectively for the first time, at last with the characters, rather than merely watching what is going on. And it takes a master actor to achieve

that. Robert Mitchum goes through his sleepy paces willingly enough as the defending officer in an army court martial in India in 1944. He has to prove the defendant (an effectively ranting performance by Keenan Wynn) insane, if he is not to hang for the murder of a British soldier. In support, Alexander Knox and Sam Wanamaker are excellent as two doctors unwilling to give evidence.

Man in the Moon ○ ⊙
1961, UK, 110 mins, b/w
Dir: Basil Dearden
Stars: Kenneth More, Shirley Ann Field, Michael Hordern, John Phillips
Rating: ★★

William Blood, human guinea-pig, was virtually the last of the cheerfully comic characters – from Richard Grimsdyke in *Doctor in the House*, through *The Admirable Crichton* to *The Sheriff of Fractured Jaw* – with which Kenneth More added colour and life to the British cinema of the Fifties and Sixties. This comedy from the Michael Relph-Basil Dearden team was co-written by Bryan Forbes and is given spice by the splendidly nasty, aristocratic performance of Charles Gray, as one of a snooty trio of astronauts with whom Blood becomes involved. Although the film's ideas are often superior to director Dearden's execution of them, the screenplay by Relph and Forbes keeps up a good quota of drily witty lines, from which More and Gray benefit in particular. Amusing cameos come from bewhiskered Irish actor Noel Purcell, as a prospector, and from Danny Green and Jeremy Lloyd, as two motorists from opposite ends of the social scale.

Man in the Moon, The ◐ ⊙
1991, US, 100 mins, colour
Dir: Robert Mulligan
Stars: Sam Waterston, Tess Harper, Gail Strickland, Reese Witherspoon, Jason London
Rating: ★

Well-meant and sincerely performed, this is nonetheless what some would call a real snoozeroo. The scripts of this kind of film have to be amazingly good for them to hold interest, and most of the dialogue here is moderate at best. It's packed with lines you've heard before – 'Maybe life's not supposed to make sense' – and lines that go too far – 'You're growing up like a weed' a 'kindly' neighbour tells the central character, a 14-year-old girl

M

Dani (Reese Witherspoon) living in rural Louisiana of the Fifties. Dani falls heavily for the new boy at the waterhole, but a promising friendship is blunted when he claps eyes on her ravishing 17-year-old sister. The resultant triangle is resolved in melodramatic rather than sympathetic fashion, resulting in scenes poised somewhere between *East Lynne* and *The Archers*. Director Robert Mulligan has proved expert at warming up slices of Americana, but he has too little to chew on here. 'Call me if anything happens,' says Dani at one point. Viewers might be justified in lodging a similar request.

Man in the Saddle ○
(aka: The Outcast)
1951, US, 87 mins, colour
Dir: Andre De Toth
Stars: Randolph Scott, Joan Leslie, Alexander Knox, Ellen Drew, Richard Rober, Cameron Mitchell
Rating: ★★

This Randolph Scott Western is by no means run-of-the-mill, and includes such excellent actors as Alexander Knox, Richard Rober and Cameron Mitchell among the villains. The longer running time gives a clue that the script has more bite than most of Scott's Westerns of the early Fifties. Scott is a rancher caught between the love of two girls, and the jealousy of a rich cattleman who has married one of them. Fans needn't worry: there's still plenty of gunplay amid the romance.

Man in the White Suit, The ○ ⓥ
1951, UK, 81 mins, b/w
Dir: Alexander Mackendrick
Stars: Alec Guinness, Joan Greenwood, Cecil Parker, Michael Gough
Rating: ★★★★

Highly original Ealing comedy about a young factory worker who invents a white fabric that won't wear out. Down the cast-list Mandy Miller makes her debut at the age of seven – a year before her tremendous success in *Mandy*. She was no problem – but the producers did have a snag. Guinness's white suit, supposedly dirt resistant, became so easily soiled on set that 13 replicas had to be made to keep him looking whiter than white. It races along like the paraphernalia in Guinness's laboratory, with their unforgettable, symphonic gurgling. A classic.

Man Is Ten Feet Tall, A
See: Edge of the City

Man Made Monster ●
(aka: The Electric Man)
1940, US, 57 mins, b/w
Dir: George Waggner
Stars: Lon Chaney Jr, Lionel Atwill
Rating: ★★

Lionel Atwill and Lon Chaney Jr slip easily into their familiar film personalities of mad scientist and genial, dumb, doomed ox in this story of an incredible hulk who develops a super-immunity to electricity but inevitably finds his 'gift' being used for evil ends. George Waggner, who directed Chaney to his triumph in *The Wolf Man*, is again in the director's chair.

Mannequin ○
1937, US, 95 mins, b/w
Dir: Frank Borzage
Stars: Joan Crawford, Spencer Tracy, Alan Curtis, Ralph Morgan
Rating: ★★

This rags-to-riches story was the sole screen coupling of MGM's top stars Spencer Tracy and Joan Crawford, so it's disappointing that their material is on the thin side. No matter how great her acting, nothing can convince you that Crawford's character comes from the downtrodden Hester Street area of New York, populated almost totally by East European and Jewish. However, Leo Gorcey, as her younger brother, is far more believable because he was actually born in that area. As Crawford's double-crossing husband, former male model Alan Curtis catches the eye, but his career was eventually cut short when he died following a kidney operation at the age of 43.

Mannequin ○ ⓥ
1987, US, 90 mins, colour
Dir: Michael Gottlieb
Stars: Andrew McCarthy, Kim Cattrall, Estelle Getty, James Spader, G W Bailey
Rating: ★★★

Extremely well performed, scripted, edited and directed, this batty comedy doesn't waste a second in telling its tall story. In other words, this department store romp offers you a real bargain. It's a fantasy-farce about a mannequin that, possessed by the wandering spirit of a wayward Egyptian princess (Kim Cattrall), comes to life and helps a loser (Andrew McCarthy) become an ace window-dresser. The script bulges

with original comic characters: Carole Davis as McCarthy's fickle black girlfriend; James Spader as the smarmy store director ready to sell out to a rival from under the tiny feet of owner Estelle Getty; G W Bailey from the *Police Academy* films, as the hawkish store cop whose bulldog Rambo has a yellow streak right down his brindle back; and, best of all, Meshach Taylor as a gay black window-dresser called Hollywood who's sympathetic to every crisis. 'You know what works best for me?' he tells McCarthy. 'Crying shamelessly.' You may find yourself laughing shamelessly at this cornball slice of fun that's never lost for a bright idea.

Mannequin on the Move ○ ⓥ
1991, US, 95 mins, colour
Dir: Stewart Raffill
Stars: William Ragsdale, Kristy Swanson, Meshach Taylor, Terry Kiser
Rating: ★

The original *Mannequin* was a lively screwball romp. This stupefying unfunny follow-up has Kristy Swanson, a great looker who doesn't show much personality or acting talent here, as a medieval princess turned to wood by a cursed necklace. A thousand years later, she turns up in the same store where the original *Mannequin* took place. Dressed in bottom-hugging, bust-bulging minis, Swanson doesn't exactly cut a dewy-eyed or sympathetic figure, and the relentlessly overplayed 'fun' that follows will have you shaking your head in disbelief. Director Raffill has made some great *Wilderness Family*-style outdoors adventures, but his flat handling here proves comedy is definitely not his forte. And, with this script (by four people), the cast seems to be going through the motions; the store lights are on but, in this picture at least, there's no-one at home.

Man of a Thousand Faces ○
1957, US, 122 mins, b/w
Dir: Joseph Pevney
Stars: James Cagney, Dorothy Malone, Jane Greer
Rating: ★★★

The 'Man of a Thousand Faces' was, of course, the gifted master of movie disguise Lon Chaney, here played energetically by James Cagney. Like most Hollywood biopics, facts are suitably coloured for dramatic purposes, but the film, a solid job if not especially inspired, provides much to admire. Chaney used to do his own make-up (he even contributed a piece on the art to the *Encyclopaedia Britannica*), but here the credit goes to Universal's Bud Westmore and Jack Kevan.

Man of La Mancha ○ ⓥ
1972, US, 132 mins, colour
Dir: Arthur Hiller
Stars: Peter O'Toole, Sophia Loren, James Coco, Harry Andrews
Rating: ★★★

The score here by Darion and Leigh is one of the all-time Broadway bests, and provides a super-emotive film musical based on *Don Quixote*, whose high spots all survive Arthur Hiller's flat direction. Peter O'Toole and Sophia Loren sing with fervour, although they have a little help on the high notes from other sources.

Man of the Moment ○
1955, UK, 85 mins, b/w
Dir: John Paddy Carstairs
Stars: Norman Wisdom, Lana Morris
Rating: ★★★

This is possibly the best of Norman Wisdom's comedies of embarrassment which brought millions to British cinemas in the Fifties. The story for once is highly original and studded with inventive and hilarious moments. Lana Morris charms as the 'nice girl' in the story and Belinda Lee is every inch the foreign spy in a cast which includes several Rank starlets of the time (Julia Arnall, Susan Beaumont, Lisa Gastoni, Beverly Brooks) and such on-form character comics as Harold Kasket, Jerry Desmonde, Garry Marsh and Charles Hawtrey. Wisdom himself is in uproarious form as the hapless Foreign Office clerk who becomes an international figure; contemporary audiences roared at the sequence in which a chase through the TV studios interrupts several well-known programmes.

Manon des Sources ○ ⓥ
1986, France, 120 mins, colour
Dir: Claude Berri
Stars: Yves Montand, Daniel Auteuil, Emmanuelle Beart
Rating: ★★★

The sequel to *Jean de Florette*, which takes up the story of greed and deception in 1920s rural France. The action switches 10 years on and Manon (Emmanuelle Beart), daughter of Gerard Depardieu's hunchback

farmer, seeks revenge for what happened to her father. Daniel Auteuil is once again superb as the rat-like nephew, Ugolin, but Hippolyte Girardot is unconvincing as the local schoolmaster. On the whole this is a rougher, less involving effort than its predecessor but together they make up an imposing achievement.

Man on Fire ○
1957, US, 95 mins, b/w
Dir: Ranald Macdougall
Stars: Bing Crosby, Inger Stevens
Rating: ★★

One of the rare occasions Bing Crosby played a completely straight role. He gives a sincere performance as the father in a tug-of-love case. Inger Stevens made her film debut, and, for a while, the headlines, when she had a short-lived romance with the star.

Man on Fire ● ⓥ
1987, US/Italy, 92 mins, colour
Dir: Elie Chouraqui
Stars: Scott Glenn, Jade Malle, Brooke Adams, Jonathan Pryce, Paul Steiner, Joe Pesci
Rating: ★★

Quite watchable for most of the time, this is all too often a ponderous and portentous thriller, with an exaggerated sense of its own weight, that looks like a Chuck Norris cast-off. Scott Glenn even assumes the Norris mien of bearded unkemptness as the soldier of fortune whose relationhip with the 12-year-old daughter of a rich American family in Italy leads him into a crazed vendetta when she is kidnapped for a million dollar ransom. Jade Malle (daughter of director Louis) is quite winning as the girl, but the film is weakly scripted and put together in such a way as to remind you that directors in films no longer have a studio at their shoulder to tactfully suggest, at some stage in the rushes, that they might be making a hash of what is basically a quite workable concept. The opening and kidnap scenes are striking, but Glenn has little chance to impress his personality on the vengeance-seeker and little else in the film suggests the imagination necessary to bring the project to life.

Manpower ○
1941, US, 105 mins, b/w
Dir: Raoul Walsh
Stars: George Raft, Edward G Robinson, Marlene Dietrich, Alan Hale, Frank

McHugh, Eve Arden
Rating: ★★★

In between turning down *High Sierra*, *The Maltese Falcon* and *Casablanca* (all inherited by Humphrey Bogart) because his character either died or didn't get the girl, George Raft did accept this highly-charged account of two high-wire 'linemen' in love with the same woman. Raft may have missed out on the big ones, but this rip-roaring drama is pretty good for all that, with Edward G Robinson and Marlene Dietrich providing star wattage as the other two points of the triangle.

Man's Best Friend ● ⓥ
1993, US, 87 mins, colour
Dir: John Lafia
Stars: Ally Sheedy, Lance Henriksen, Robert Costanzo, Fredric Lehne
Rating: ★

This demon doggie movie could almost be called *Mad Max 4*. And Max is mad all right, but then so would you be if you'd been made the subject of genetic experiments that gave you all the 'best' traits of other animals. When Max breaks loose so, consequently, does All Hell. Postmen have their throats ripped out and cats are swallowed whole. Not that Max ever kills without provocation – probably the reason he's so lovable to heroine Ally Sheedy, who hides him from the authorities. 'If I don't get him tonight,' grates chief scientist Lance Henriksen 'he's going to go through a psychotic episode.' Boldly treading in the footsteps of George Zucco and a whole string of Hollywood scientists and doomed medical ventures, Henriksen appears to be enjoying himself even more than Max. 'What about my dog,' he asks the head-scratching coppers. 'Any leads?' 'Ruff' stuff this, an enjoyably bad movie in the good old style.

Man's Favourite Sport? ☉
1963, US, 120 mins, colour
Dir: Howard Hawks
Stars: Rock Hudson, Paula Prentiss
Rating: ★★★

Gangling, treacle-voiced comedienne Paula Prentiss came close (but alas not close enough) to stardom in this lazy-paced comedy about fishing which is, after all, a lazy-paced sport. Still, Prentiss and Rock Hudson keep us nicely amused for a couple of hours, which is not bad considering they spend most of their time falling in

M

the lake. The plot is simple. Hudson plays an ace angling salesman who is forced to enter a big fishing competition, despite the fact that he has never fished before in his life. With the help of Paula, he lands some big fish – but in rather unorthodox ways. Pleasant entertainment, this is easy to take: you'll especially enjoy Prentiss trying the remove a plaster cast from Hudson's arm with the aid of a power saw, and a droll performance by Norman Alden as a very up-to-date native American called John Screaming Eagle.

Man Trouble ◑ ⓥ
1992, US, 99 mins, colour
Dir: Bob Rafelson
Stars: Jack Nicholson, Ellen Barkin, Beverly D'Angelo, Harry Dean Stanton, Viveka Davis
Rating: ★★

There are some bright spots, if fewer than you'd expect from the star teaming, in this too-seldom-feisty romantic comedy (with some sinister undertones). It involves Jack Nicholson as a sort-of-detective who loans out alsatians to protect people, and Ellen Barkin as an opera star frightened of her own shadow, concerned about the Hillside Strangler, and absolutely *terrified* when her apartment is burgled. That's when Nicholson, the dog and unlikely romantic entanglement come in, with all the complications in the plot being provided by Barkin's sister Beverly D'Angelo's memoirs, which notably blacken the name of mega-rich crook Harry Dean Stanton (in for an overdone cameo near the end of the film). Nicholson delivers his dialogue in low, deliberate tones as if to reassure us that less is more. On this occasion, however, it would seem that less is less and Nicholson's approach only underlines the dull, low quality of director Bob Rafelson's treatment of the Doris Day-style caper. Barkin, though, whether sweetly sultry or scared stiff, is really quite good.

Man Who Came to Dinner, The ○
1941, US, 112 mins, b/w
Dir: William Keighley
Stars: Bette Davis, Ann Sheridan, Monty Woolley, Jimmy Durante, Reginald Gardiner
Rating: ★★★

Despite a longish film career, big, bluff, bearded Monty Woolley scored his greatest success in this, his first

major starring role, in which he repeated his pain-in-the-neck lecturer character from the equally funny stage play of the same title. The hilarious screenplay is by the talented Epstein brothers, Philip and Julius, who won an Oscar the following year for a very different kind of script: *Casablanca*. Beaky Mary Wickes made a notable comic debut as Woolley's nurse, and Bette Davis' role was especially expanded in accordance with her star status. To find out how four penguins and an octopus get into the plot, you'll just have to watch this priceless piece of fun.

Man Who Could Cheat Death, The ◑
1959, UK, 83 mins, colour
Dir: Terence Fisher
Stars: Anton Diffring, Christopher Lee, Hazel Court
Rating: ★★

Hammer horror at its grimmest – with a gruesome transformation scene for its climax. Anton Diffring breaks away from nasty Nazis, but keeps the sneer on his face, in the Dorian Gray-type role. Hazel Court is suitably terrified (and a treat in colour) as the girl who only just cheats death, while Christopher Lee, usually the source of screams, is for once a good sort. It's a remake of the 1942 Hollywood film, *The Man in Half Moon Street*.

Man Who Could Work Miracles, The ○
1936, UK, 82 mins, b/w
Dir: Lothar Mendes
Stars: Roland Young, Ralph Richardson
Rating: ★★★

This hilarious comedy sees H G Wells in his most light-hearted fantasy vein, in a story of a man who suddenly finds all objects animate and inanimate, obey his command. The film contains some brilliant trick photography, genuine crackling wit and a riotous climax.

Man Who Fell to Earth, The ●
1976, UK, 135 mins, colour
Dir: Nicolas Roeg
Stars: David Bowie, Rip Torn, Candy Clark
Rating: ★★★

An alien comes to Earth, takes human form and, with his superior technical knowledge, soon amasses a fortune. His aim is to find water for his arid home planet. David Bowie's somewhat other-worldly and ambiguous

persona means he's perfectly cast as the enigmatic alien in this curious and adult sci-fi fantasy and he is ably supported by Rip Torn, Candy Clark and Buck Henry. A little odd in places but always fascinating: director Nicolas Roeg created an unusual film which still has a strong cult following. As befits a former cinematographer (he worked on *Lawrence of Arabia*), Roeg's film is also visually arresting. Science-fiction it may be, but *The Man Who Fell to Earth* is light years away from *Buck Rogers*.

Man Who Haunted Himself, The ○
1970, UK, 90 mins, colour
Dir: Basil Dearden
Stars: Roger Moore, Anton Rodgers, Olga Georges-Picot, Hildegarde Neil
Rating: ★★★

Roger Moore gives perhaps his best screen performance in this interesting chiller-thriller about a man who finds that his life is being taken over by his 'double'. Director Basil Dearden mixes dull stretches with some palm-sweating suspense. Freddie Jones' twitching, pill-swallowing psychiatrist steals the supporting honours from a gallery of colourful minor characters.

Man Who Knew Too Much, The ○ ⓥ
1956, US, 120 mins, colour
Dir: Alfred Hitchcock
Stars: James Stewart, Doris Day, Bernard Miles, Brenda de Banzie
Rating: ★★★

This underrated suspense-builder is a remake by Alfred Hitchcock of his own 1934 film, whose brooding tension made it an instant classic. James Stewart and Doris Day play the American couple whose son's kidnap involves them unwittingly in an assassination plot. Miss Day's song 'Que Sera, Sera' won an Academy Award. The climax in the concert hall is as nail-biting as ever.

Man Who Loved Women, The ○
1983, US, 122 mins, colour
Dir: Blake Edwards
Stars: Burt Reynolds, Julie Andrews, Kim Basinger, Marilu Henner
Rating: ★★

This loose remake of the 1977 French film of the same title has some nice ideas of its own, even if central character Burt Reynolds spends rather too much screen time discussing his obsession about women with psychiatrist Julie Andrews. It's just as well the stars give subtle and appealing performances in these roles, leaving the histrionics to co-star Kim Basinger as a voracious harpy who eats men for breakfast and spits out the pieces, then shoots her husband and jumps bail!

Man Who Never Was, The ○
1956, UK, 103 mins, colour
Dir: Ronald Neame
Stars: Clifton Webb, Gloria Grahame, Robert Flemyng, Stephen Boyd
Rating: ★★★

Ronald Neame's persuasive version of Ewen Montagu's book about the famous wartime deception, which involved planting fake documents on a corpse clothed in the uniform of a British officer, which was then 'washed ashore' at a spot which made it bound to come to the attention of the Nazis. Good work by Clifton Webb as Montagu, and some first-class colour photography as well.

Man Who Shot Liberty Valance, The ○
1962, US, 122 mins, b/w
Dir: John Ford
Stars: James Stewart, John Wayne, Vera Miles, Lee Marvin, Edmond O'Brien, Lee Van Cleef
Rating: ★★★

John Ford's last tribute to the values that he liked to remember both about the Old West and about America itself. The fact that it was shot in black and white and that John Wayne (taking second billing – a real rarity and a sign of his affection for the director) looks, with his huge white stetson, every inch the silent Western hero, are only two of the signs indicating a nostalgic tribute to times past. The film is beautifully structured – the key twist is cleverly concealed until the moment it happens – and the shoot-outs are thrillingly staged. The bad guys are Lee Marvin and Lee Van Cleef, both just before they became big box-office stars. This, incidentally, is the film in which the famous phrase 'When the legend becomes fact, print the legend' was heard for the first time.

Man Who Would Be King, The ○ Ⓥ
1975, UK, 129 mins, colour
Dir: John Huston
Stars: Sean Connery, Michael Caine,

Christopher Plummer, Saeed Jaffrey, Shakira Caine
Rating: ★★★

This spirited yarn, set first in India and then in a country north of the North-West Frontier, is based on a story by Rudyard Kipling and is generally regarded as among the best of director John Huston's latter-day films. And it gives splendid acting opportunities to Sean Connery and Michael Caine, who are compelling and amusing (though you may think the parts would have been better cast the other way round) as the roguish central characters of the story who get involved with warring tribesmen. The background gives rise to plenty of local colour and exotic settings, thanks to splendid location work in Morocco.

Man With a Cloak, The ○
1950, US, 81 mins, b/w
Dir: Fletcher Markle
Stars: Leslie Caron, Joseph Cotten, Barbara Stanwyck, Louis Calhern
Rating: ★★

Canadian director Fletcher Markle builds up suspense and atmosphere in fascinating style in this mystery story set in the New York of the mid-1900s. Joseph Cotten is impressive as the mystery figure in the plot, which involves Leslie Caron in her first acting role, and blends its ingredients – such as a mysterious house, a poison ring and a missing will – with a fine sense of high drama. There's a devastating twist in the final few frames.

Man With a Million
See: The Million Pound Note

Man With Bogart's Face, The ○
(aka: Sam Marlow Private Eye)
1980, US, 106 mins, colour
Dir: Robert Day
Stars: Robert Sacchi, Franco Nero, Michelle Phillips, Olivia Hussey, Herbert Lom
Rating: ★★

This comedy-thriller is a real treat – as star-studded as it's engagingly nutty. Robert Sacchi is an American actor who bears a remarkable resemblance to the great Humphrey Bogart and here the gimmick is happily milked for all it's worth, with Sacchi as a private eye who's forever relating incidents and personalities to films and stars of yesteryear. Franco Nero, Herbert Lom, Victor Buono and Jay Robinson

are a splendid quartet of villains and there's one particularly funny sequence at the hall of mirrors in the Hollywood Wax Museum. Misty Rowe, who once played Marilyn Monroe, also scores as the hero's dumb blonde secretary.

Man with One Red Shoe, The ○ Ⓥ
(aka: Mischief)
1985, US, 95 mins, colour
Dir: Stan Dragoti
Stars: Tom Hanks, Dabney Coleman, Lori Singer, Charles Durning, Carrie Fisher, Jim Belushi
Rating: ★★

Director Stan Dragoti's other comedies – *Mr Mom, Love at First Bite, She's Out of Control* – have all had their moments, but here he's working on a Hollywood remake of a French original that wasn't funny in the first place. A terrific cast – Tom Hanks, Lori Singer, Dabney Coleman, Carrie Fisher, Jim Belushi, Charles Durning – works a bit too hard to make something of it, and even Hanks' fall-guy hero isn't as likeable as he should be. Some fun, though, from the odd good line and a couple of well-paced action sequences.

Man Without a Face, The Ⓓ Ⓥ
1993, US, 110 mins, colour
Dir: Mel Gibson
Stars: Mel Gibson, Nick Stahl, Margaret Whitton, Geoffrey Lewis, Richard Masur
Rating: ★★★★

Mel Gibson's directorial debut is a tale of man's inhumanity to man and readiness to believe the worst. Gibson himself stars as a disfigured recluse shunned by the nearby townsfolk but reluctantly drawn into tutoring a troubled 12-year-old boy (Nick Stahl), who believes his only chance to escape the grasp of a mother about to embark on her fourth husband is to go to military academy like his dad. But there are secrets from their pasts that will threaten the relationship between man and boy that gradually grows into something special. Although at times the tutoring borders on the tedious, Gibson pushes his key plot developments through at just the right time, and ties everything together in an emotive ending that may have you punching the air. Young Stahl's dialogue is occasionally difficult to hear, yet he, like Gibson, still creates an unforgettable figure of

M

alienation and isolation. A memorable movie from Mel. More please.

Man Without a Star ○
1955, US, 89 mins, colour
Dir: King Vidor
Stars: Kirk Douglas, Jeanne Crain, Claire Trevor, William Campbell
Rating: ★★

The plot of this range-war Western, prefaced by another of Frankie Laine's throbbing theme songs, is conventional enough. But the fierce performance of Kirk Douglas as the drifter at its centre and the individual style of director King Vidor – who made such milestone movies as *The Big Parade*, *Billy the Kid* and *Northwest Passage* – make it all very watchable. Jeanne Crain isn't too happy as a good/bad girl and loses out to Claire Trevor.

Man with the Golden Arm, The ◑ ⓥ
1955, US, 119 mins, b/w
Dir: Otto Preminger
Stars: Frank Sinatra, Kim Novak, Eleanor Parker, Darren McGavin
Rating: ★★★

A hot potato for the censor in its time, this is a savage indictment of drug-trafficking in which Frank Sinatra gives one of his most powerful performances as a junkie trying to 'kick the habit' – finally in a harrowing 'cold turkey' cure. In 1955 it was considered very daring for addiction and its resultant miseries to be so graphically portrayed. Eleanor Parker makes the most of her role as Sinatra's crippled wife and Kim Novak turns in one of her most dramatically effective performances as a sympathetic girl who stands by Sinatra when he's accused of killing a dope peddler.

Man with the Golden Gun, The ○ ⓥ
1974, UK, 125 mins, colour
Dir: Guy Hamilton
Stars: Roger Moore, Christopher Lee, Britt Ekland, Maud Adams
Rating: ★★

Film fans familiar with Christopher Lee only as the cinema's greatest Dracula may be surprised that the master of menace so effortlessly takes the acting honours in this James Bond thriller, prowling his island mansion like some suave but deadly lizard as arch-villain Scaramanga. Midget actor Herve Villechaize (later seen in the TV series *Fantasy Island*) is personable

as another of those out to exterminate Bond, while the Swedish-born actress-model Maud Adams, in for a brief appearance here as Andrea, was later seen as the leading lady in the Roger Moore 007 adventure, *Octopussy*.

Man With the Gun, The ○
(aka: The Trouble Shooter)
1955, US, 88 mins, b/w
Dir: Richard Wilson
Stars: Robert Mitchum, Jan Sterling, Angie Dickinson
Rating: ★★

Robert Mitchum in rough mood, as a westerner brought in to clear up a lawless town. The film was the first independent production venture of Sam Goldwyn Jr, son of the famous movie mogul. The younger Goldwyn was determined not to be outdone by his famous father when it came to realism, and a huge fire was one of the scenes he staged. Watch out for Angie Dickinson in a tiny role as a saloon girl as well as this fire sequence: Mitchum started such a blaze that it got out of hand and nearly burned down the entire set.

Man With Two Brains, The ◑ ⓥ
1983, US, 93 mins, colour
Dir: Carl Reiner
Stars: Steve Martin, Kathleen Turner, David Warner, Paul Benedict
Rating: ★★★

Feminists should be well pleased with the central premise of this hilarious comedy – Steve Martin falls not for a woman's body but for her mind or, rather, her brain (voiced by Sissy Spacek) which is conveniently portable in its glass jar. What could simply have been another horror movie spoof in the style of Mel Brooks' *Young Frankenstein* is turned by Martin and his director and co-writer Carl Reiner into a magnificently surreal movie which offers the star plenty of well-taken opportunities to display his unique brand of verbal and visual foolery. Mind you, while he steals the film, Kathleen Turner, in what appears to be a wicked send-up of her man-eating character from *Body Heat*, gives him a good run for his money and demonstrates that she is as skilled at comedy as she is at drama. As with the best comedy, good taste is largely kept at bay and the result is a genuine if rude treat.

Map of the Human Heart ◑ ⓥ
1992, Australia/Canada/France/UK, 121 mins, colour
Dir: Vincent Ward
Stars: Jason Scott Lee, Anne Parillaud, Patrick Bergin, Annie Galipeau, Robert Joamie, Jeanne Moreau, John Cusack
Rating: ★★★

Although it goes on too long, and sometimes falters towards the end, there are moments in this epic love story that are as good as anything the cinema had produced for some time. If you're looking for the unusual, you'll certainly find it here. A young Arctic boy, half-Eskimo, half-white, is befriended in 1931 by a young mapper/surveyor (Patrick Bergin) who, seeing the boy is suffering from tuberculosis, takes him to a sanitarium in the city. Here he becomes friends with another 'outcast', a half-white, half-Cree Indian girl. The close nature of their friendship is frowned on by the nuns there, who split them up. Years later the boy (now Jason Scott Lee) runs into Bergin again, and asks him to help find the girl. Later still, serving with other Canadians in the RAF, he meets her (Anne Parillaud) again, only to find she is romantically involved with Bergin himself . . . Subsequent developments don't entirely convince, but scenes of the children's friendship and, later, the wartime bombing of Dresden, are wonderfully well staged. Also available in a recut 95 minute version.

Maracaibo ○
1958, US, 88 mins, colour
Dir: Cornel Wilde
Stars: Cornel Wilde, Jean Wallace, Francis Lederer, Abbe Lane, Michael Landon
Rating: ★★

Colourful drama of the lives and loves of oil fire-fighters in Venezuela. Cornel Wilde, whose wife, Jean Wallace, co-stars, also directed, a habit he was to pursue with some success (notably in *Lancelot and Guinevere*). Here, he gives us some exciting fire sequences that are masterpieces of stage management.

Marathon Man ● ⓥ
1976, US, 126 mins, colour
Dir: John Schlesinger
Stars: Dustin Hoffman, Laurence Olivier, Roy Scheider, William Devane, Marthe Keller
Rating: ★★★

Director John Schlesinger has tried with great intelligence to suggest that the plot of this thriller – Nazi war criminals after a fortune in diamonds – is more ingenious than it is, while William Goldman's elliptical screenplay, based on his own novel, also hints at depths not justified in the exposition. Dustin Hoffman is the marathon runner whose endurance stands him in good stead when he is caught up in the web of intrigue that his brother (Roy Scheider) is weaving on behalf of a CIA offshoot. The plot moves with a fair share of excitement along tried and true lines, to a carefully-staged climax in which Hoffman and the arch-villain (Laurence Olivier) come face to face. By far the best performance comes from William Devane as a double-agent with a voice and a line that is all too plausible for the innocent fish to swallow.

March of the Wooden Soldiers
See: Babes in Toyland

March or Die ◐
1977, US, 104 mins, colour
Dir: Dick Richards
Stars: Gene Hackman, Terence Hill, Catherine Deneuve, Max von Sydow, Ian Holm
Rating: ★

Aux armes, mes braves, those Arabs are revolting again. And our bold Legionnaires must try to defeat them in the desert, or perish in the attempt. Armed with a plot about Legionnaires defiling ancient Moroccan tombs and incurring the wrath of the Arabs in the post-World War One period, director Dick Richards (who recaptured the Old West in *The Culpepper Cattle Co*) tries to show the Foreign Legion warts and all, without completely destroying its myth. A pity, then, that the dialogue, cliched from the start (a woman starts singing La Marseillaise as battered Legionnaires return from the war, and Major Gene Hackman grunts 'There are no heroes in war – only survivors'), gives him only rubber bullets for ammunition. Terence Hill, Max Von Sydow, Ian Holm (improbably blacked up as an Arab chief) and Catherine Deneuve (as the inevitable mystery woman) are among those making a last stand against the assaults of David Zelag Goodman's script.

Margie ○
1946, US, 94 mins, colour
Dir: Henry King

Stars: Jeanne Crain, Glenn Langan, Alan Young, Lynn Bari
Rating: ★★★

This potent dose of Americana, glowingly evoking the late 1920s, was made by director Henry King, monarch of the genre. King also made the original *State Fair* in 1933, as well as *Maryland* (1940) and *Wait 'Till the Sun Shines, Nellie* (1952). Bathed in Technicolor by Charles Clarke, the film contains Jeanne Crain's most charming performance as the brainbox who thinks herself unattractive to men. Since she's wrong, matters are easily resolved, but in a highly tuneful and entertaining way.

Maria's Lovers ● Ⓥ
1984, US, 100 mins, colour
Dir: Andrei Konchalovsky
Stars: Nastassja Kinski, John Savage, Robert Mitchum, Keith Carradine, Bud Cort
Rating: ★★★

John Savage keeps himself alive in a Japanese Prisoner-of-War camp with the powerful mental image of his childhood sweetheart Maria (Nastassja Kinski). But when he returns to Pennsylvania and marries her, he finds that he cannot consummate the marriage with his idealised Maria. There's plenty to admire along the way as the subsequent drama is played out: there are good performances from the leads, with Savage in another of his offbeat choices of roles. Ms Kinski, glowingly photographed (by Juan Ruiz Anchia), is stunning to watch. Keith Carradine brings a weasely charm to the part of one of Maria's lovers and Robert Mitchum has a smaller, but telling role as Savage's lecherous father. Atmospheric, superior soap.

Marie ◐ Ⓥ
1985, US, 106 mins, colour
Dir: Roger Donaldson
Stars: Sissy Spacek, Jeff Daniels, Morgan Freeman
Rating: ★★★

The David and Goliath battle between the individual and the state/big business (take your pick) is now a familiar theme in films, so to make another variation on that well-worn theme takes courage. It also takes a good script if the film is to succeed. *Marie* succeeds thanks to a good script and good director (Roger Donaldson) and a strong cast in Sissy Spacek, Jeff Daniels and Morgan Freeman. Spacek

is a parole board chairman who, when asked to speed a few parolees through by an aide of the state governor, refuses. She is promptly sacked, but fights her case in court, opening up a big can of corrupt officialdom worms. Spacek as the parole chairman is excellent and Jeff Daniels makes a convincingly smooth aide. Based on a true story, and that adds to the drama, making it a very watchable piece.

Marie Antoinette ○
1938, US, 149 mins, b/w
Dir: W S Van Dyke II
Stars: Norma Shearer, Tyrone Power, John Barrymore, Robert Morley, Gladys George, Anita Louise
Rating: ★★★

Goodness knows what this sumptuous, near-three-hour spectacle would have cost if MGM had filmed it in colour. As it is, the budget still went close to the $2 million mark. Robert Morley, who was making his screen debut, hated all the opulence and razzmatazz and referred to the film as 'Marie and Toilette', but his performance as King Louis XVI still earned him an Oscar nomination, as did the work of Norma Shearer in the title role. Finally, though, all the cast is dwarfed by the stunning sets of Cedric Gibbons – halls, ballrooms and chambers simply dripping with period artefacts, and peopled by hundreds of cast and extras in authentic costumes of the period. This is Hollywood spectacle at its peak – and certainly at its most extravagant.

Marines, Let's Go ○
1961, US, 104 mins, colour
Dir: Raoul Walsh
Stars: Tom Tryon, David Hedison
Rating: ★★

Director Raoul Walsh attempts a difficult double: realistic war sequences coupled with the comic adventures of the Marines in, around and under the bars of Tokyo. The result: a sprawling, brawling colourful adventure romp.

Marjorie Morningstar ○
1958, US, 121 mins, colour
Dir: Irving Rapper
Stars: Natalie Wood, Gene Kelly, Claire Trevor, Everett Sloane, Ed Wynn
Rating: ★★

In its day, this fairly faithful adaptation of Herman Wouk's huge novel was a major disappointment. Natalie Wood, at 19, proved not quite up to the demands of the central role as the starstruck teenager, fleeing from a

M

Jewish background she sees as claustrophobic, who becomes obsessed with a holiday resort entertainer twice her age (shades of *Dirty Dancing!*). As the self-centred showman, Gene Kelly is simply too classy to play a song-and-dance man whose ambitions to the highest class are torpedoed by his second-class talent. The story, as somewhat restructured by Everett Freeman from Wouk's original, with the family background largely glossed over in favour of the show business angles, was described by one aggrieved critic as 'about as Jewish as *The Seven Samurai.*'

Marked for Death ● ⓥ
1990, US, 94 mins, colour
Dir: Dwight H Little
Stars: Steven Seagal, Basil Wallace, Keith David, Joanna Pacula
Rating: ★

'Try to find a gentle self inside you,' the priest tells a troubled Steven Seagal. No chance. Though an affable-looking chap with a pony-tail, Mr S is in the business of dealing out death and, when the bad guys shoot his niece, you can bet there's plenty of that to come. The trade-marks of Seagal action films are drugs, topless women, crunching bones and severed limbs, plentifully supplied and usually roughly in that order. This one adds a touch of voodoo, and about all you can say is that it isn't actually dull, though fearfully unimaginative. Director Dwight H Little does try to do something with it, but always going for the entirely expected, though Seagal fans are hardly likely to notice. Joanna Pacula is second-billed in the opening credits, but scarcely in the film at all.

Mark of the Vampire ◗
1935, US, 61 mins, b/w
Dir: Tod Browning
Stars: Lionel Barrymore, Elizabeth Allan, Bela Lugosi
Rating: ★★★

As much a teasing puzzle as a horror film – the atmosphere engendered by James Wong Howe's photography and Tod Browning's direction is even creepier than on Browning's original *Dracula*. This is a remake of another Browning picture *London After Midnight* (1927) which starred Lon Chaney Jr. Devotees of the genre say that Carol Borland's female vampire is the definitive interpretation of the role.

Mark of Zorro, The ○
1940, US, 94 mins, b/w
Dir: Rouben Mamoulian
Stars: Tyrone Power, Linda Darnell, Basil Rathbone, Gale Sondergaard, Eugene Pallette
Rating: ★★★

Dashing remake of the silent swashbuckling classic with Douglas Fairbanks, whose role of Zorro, a Western equivalent of *The Scarlet Pimpernel*, here goes to Tyrone Power, athletically setting female hearts a-flutter as the masked righter-of-wrongs in early California. Rhythmically directed by Rouben Mamoulian, it has a rousing music score by Alfred Newman, an early appearance by Linda Darnell at her loveliest, and the famous final duel between Power and Basil Rathbone, that for sheer skill and exhilaration, rivals the one between Rathbone and Errol Flynn at the end of *The Adventures of Robin Hood*.

Marlowe ○
1969, US, 95 mins, colour
Dir: Paul Bogart
Stars: James Garner, Gayle Hunnicutt, Carol O'Connor, Rita Moreno, Bruce Lee
Rating: ★★

It can't have been just coincidence that MGM hired a director called Bogart (Paul) for a story about the character made famous by another Bogart (Humphrey), and actually based on Raymond Chandler's novel *The Little Sister*. The result is the most muted Marlowe to appear on the screen. Its weakness is James Garner, miscast in the title role (as was Elliott Gould in *The Long Goodbye*). For compensation there's a tortuous plot, and the first film appearance of Bruce Lee as an oriental bad guy who demolishes Marlowe's entire office by use of martial arts, as a grim warning. Lee, in fact, steals the film. It's strange that his potential was ignored for so long.

Marnie ◗ ⓥ
1964, US, 130 mins, colour
Dir: Alfred Hitchcock
Stars: Tippi Hedren, Sean Connery
Rating: ★★★

Alfred Hitchcock's sly psychological study of a compulsive thief – played by Tippi Hedren – marked a change of pace for her co-star Sean Connery, then solidly established as superspy James Bond. The film contains much for Hitchcock fans to admire, but one

cannot help wondering why the director settled for so many poor process shots and some highly unconvincing backdrops. Evan Hunter worked on an early version of the screenplay which was finally (and solely) credited to Jay Presson Allen. The efforts of writer and director persuade us to follow Marnie's adventures with sympathy and attention. And the moments when her past life starts to come to light are among the best in the film. Diane Baker gives excellent support as Connery's spiteful, scheming, jealous sister-in-law.

Maroc 7 ◐
1967, UK, 91 mins, colour
Dir: Gerry O'Hara
Stars: Gene Barry, Cyd Charisse, Elsa Martinelli, Leslie Phillips, Denholm Elliott
Rating: RB

There's lots of high-fashion clothes and an attractive cast in this vaguely Bond-style thriller. The trouble is that too many of the cast are miscast, including co-producer Leslie Phillips, who obviously fancied a villainous role as a change from the comedy parts that had made him famous. Slowly directed by Gerry O'Hara (who was more at home with intimate drama), the film stars a languorous Gene Barry, in the wake of his *Burke's Law* fame, and proves that even exotic locations and a string of glamorous models can prove more of a hindrance to a film than an asset. A notable misfire.

Marriage on the Rocks ○
1965, US, 109 mins, colour
Dir: Jack Donohue
Stars: Frank Sinatra, Deborah Kerr, Dean Martin, Cesar Romero, Hermione Baddeley, Nancy Sinatra
Rating: ★★★

A scintillating light comedy that takes an hilarious look at the Great American Marriage gone sour. Dean Martin is very funny as the lifelong bachelor who suddenly finds himself married and doesn't like it, Hermione Baddeley a riot as Frank Sinatra's (later Martin's) ferocious Scottish mother-in-law. Beset for the umpteenth time by the bag-playing harridan, Martin says he'll take the dog out for a walk. But they don't have a dog, says his wife. That's all right, says Martin, he'll find one. Cy Howard's script is mostly delightful stuff. Martin is at his best when he wears his worried look, and the girls (Joi Lansing, Davey Davidson, Nancy Sinatra and Tara Ashton) all have acting talent.

Married to It ● ⓥ

1991, US, 112 mins, colour
Dir: Arthur Hiller
Stars: Beau Bridges, Stockard Channing, Ron Silver, Cybill Shepherd, Mary Stuart Masterson, Robert Sean Leonard
Rating: ★★

A starry cast and a well-written script are the highlights of this entertaining-enough slice-of-married-life that's not as black as most critics painted it, even though it sat on the shelf for two years before release. The story follows the complex relationships of three very different New York couples who become the unlikeliest of firm friends, and the dramatic events that unfold will hold great interest for fans of such 'old pals' movies as *The Big Chill* and *Grand Canyon*. Absorbing and involving thanks to its cast (especially Mary Stuart Masterson and Stockard Channing), but let down by characters that are often annoying, and by a cloying, too-good-to-be-true ending.

Married to the Mob ◐ ⓥ

1988, US, 103 mins, colour
Dir: Jonathan Demme
Stars: Michelle Pfeiffer, Matthew Modine, Dean Stockwell, Mercedes Ruehl, Alec Baldwin, Joan Cusack, Nancy Travis
Rating: ★★★

An offbeat comedy about a Mafia widow attempting to sever her connections with the Mob after her husband is assassinated in the bathtub for dallying with a crime boss's girlfriend. Michelle Pfeiffer is a total delight in a very different portrait of a mobster's wife to the one she gave in *Scarface*. Director Jonathan Demme cooks up a manic stew so bright and exaggerated that it jumps cartoon-like out of the screen. Throughout the film he takes delight in creating as many unexpected oppositions and goofy juxtapositions as possible. Look out for singer Chris Isaak as a hitman disguised as a fast food restaurant clown.

Marrying Kind, The ○

1952, US, 93 mins, b/w
Dir: George Cukor
Stars: Judy Holliday, Aldo Ray
Rating: ★★

Although there are plenty of good laughs in this, Judy Holliday's second film working with director George Cukor, there are also moments of sadness and drama. She and Aldo Ray are in the divorce court and the story of their marriage, the good and the bad times, is shown in flashback. The beefy Ray, in his first major role, makes a good foil for Holliday and the script is sharp and witty. Watch out for a young Charles Bronson (billed as Charles Buchinski) as a work buddy of Ray's.

Marrying Man, The
See: Too Hot to Handle

Marty ○

1955, US, 91 mins, b/w
Dir: Delbert Mann
Stars: Ernest Borgnine, Betsy Blair
Rating: ★★★

Hollywood moguls were shocked by the critical and commercial success of this perceptive story about a lonely man in his mid-thirties who hesitantly finds love. With wide screen and Technicolor in full swing, a studio-bound black-and-white film based on an admittedly successful television play hadn't seemed such a great idea. But Ernest Borgnine showed an acting depth not hinted at in previous 'villain' roles, and his performance earned him an Oscar. The film also won for Best Director (Delbert Mann), Best Picture, and Best Screenplay (Paddy Cheyefsky, adapting his own TV script). Borgnine makes the most of the part of his life and Esther Minciotti, as his mother, gives fine support. Betsy Blair, as the plain girl he falls in love with, is, although too attractive, delicately effective. The film looks decidedly dated now, as do many British 'kitchen sink' films of the same era, but Borgnine's affecting performance is not to be missed.

Maryland ⊙

1940, US, 92 mins, colour
Dir: Henry King
Stars: Walter Brennan, Fay Bainter, Brenda Joyce, John Payne
Rating: ★★

Somewhere between *National Velvet* and *Now, Voyager*, this was Darryl Zanuck's tribute to the Great American Outdoors and specifically its horses. Walter Brennan is at his most endearing, but Fay Bainter also gets a look in as a tyrannical mother, with John Payne as her son. Early use of

lush Technicolor by George Barnes and Ray Rennahan celebrates the sumptuous natural landscapes, which are the real stars here, and not the script which, besides formula dialogue, provides such now-contentious issues as foxhunts and demeaning portraits of black servants.

Mary, Mary ○

1964, US, 126 mins, colour
Dir: Mervyn LeRoy
Stars: Debbie Reynolds, Barry Nelson, Michael Rennie
Rating: ★★

An adaptation of the stage comedy success about a separated couple trying to get together again. Barry Nelson gives a magnificent, non-stop comic performance as the husband, the highlight being his efforts to keep awake with three sleeping pills inside him. Miss Reynolds copes well as the chain-smoking, wise-cracking wife, and still manages to look teenager-cute in pyjamas and an outsize overcoat. The only drawback is that it still looks like a stage play.

Mary of Scotland ○

1936, US, 123 mins, b/w
Dir: John Ford
Stars: Katharine Hepburn, Fredric March, Donald Crisp, Florence Eldridge, John Carradine
Rating: ★★

This historical drama proved that John Ford was more in his element with male orientated subjects. A financial dud despite its starry cast, including Katharine Hepburn (as Mary Stuart). Ford's direction of it was interesting and experimental with different lighting and camera angles for each character. A real curio.

Mary Poppins ⊙ ⓥ

1964, US, 139 mins, colour
Dir: Robert Stevenson
Stars: Julie Andrews, Dick Van Dyke, David Tomlinson, Glynis Johns, Hermione Baddeley, Ed Wynn
Rating: ★★★★

Unjustly ignored for the film version of *My Fair Lady*, Julie Andrews bounced back to win an Oscar as the magical mystery nanny who changes the lives of the Banks family for the better. Perhaps the last great original Hollywood musical, with joyous dance routines – especially the chimney sweeps on rooftops – and a whole nursery full of hit songs. Andrews, Ed Wynn (as the uncle who floats when

M

he laughs), Glynis Johns and David Tomlinson are delightful. And Dick Van Dyke, as Bert, pavement artist, sweep and one-man band, sang and danced his way to film stardom (in spite of a pawky cockney accent). Don't forget to stay tuned for the last line of the credits. It's definitely supercalifragilisticexpialidocious.

Mary, Queen of Scots O
1971, UK, 128 mins, colour
Dir: Charles Jarrott
Stars: Vanessa Redgrave, Glenda Jackson, Patrick McGoohan, Timothy Dalton, Nigel Davenport, Trevor Howard
Rating: ★★

Although it's not particularly accurate as a history lesson, this colourful period drama features something that similar films can't hope to boast – a dynamic acting battle between two of the foremost British female talents of the time, Vanessa Redgrave, as Mary, and Glenda Jackson, raspingly repeating her TV portrait of Elizabeth I. All credit, therefore, to Timothy Dalton, Patrick McGoohan and Nigel Davenport for bringing charisma and understanding to supporting roles.

M*A*S*H O C V
1969, US, 116 mins, colour
Dir: Robert Altman
Stars: Donald Sutherland, Elliott Gould, Tom Skerritt, Sally Kellerman, Robert Duvall
Rating: ★★★

This blood-soaked black comedy gave new dimension to the word irreverence, and has perhaps been undeservedly eclipsed in memory by the outstanding TV series that stemmed from it. The film boosted several star careers, including those of Elliott Gould and Donald Sutherland, while Robert Altman's direction of their capers as surgeons in an ill-equipped mobile army service hospital (thus the title) in Korea brings home with full force the desperation behind the humour. The football match at the end is the funniest of its kind since the one enjoyed by the Marx Brothers in *Horse Feathers*. Screenwriter Ring Lardner Jr won an Academy Award.

Mask C V
1985, US, 120 mins, colour
Dir: Peter Bogdanovich
Stars: Cher, Eric Stoltz, Sam Elliott, Estelle Getty, Laura Dern
Rating: ★★★

After *The Elephant Man* comes the 'Elephant Boy'. Rocky (Eric Stoltz) was born with a kind of dysplasia – a one-in-22 million chance – which deformed his face to an alarming degree. His biker mother, nicely played by Cher, sent him to a normal school, where he proved extremely bright. The story of Rocky's fight to live a normal life is told with a large amount of tender loving care by director Peter Bogdanovich, even though it's draped in an extremely tough exterior. Good performances, too, from Stoltz as the boy and Sam Elliott as his mother's charismatic on-off lover.

Mask of Dimitrios, The O
1944, US, 95 mins, b/w
Dir: Jean Negulesco
Stars: Peter Lorre, Sidney Greenstreet, Zachary Scott, Faye Emerson
Rating: ★★★

Zachary Scott, one of Hollywood's best portrayers of sneering villainy, made his film debut as the mysterious international criminal Dimitrios in this shadow-strewn thriller gem. Acting honours, though, go almost inevitably to Sydney Greenstreet and little Peter Lorre, reunited from *The Maltese Falcon* and *Casablanca*. Their highly enjoyable teamwork established them as the Laurel and Hardy of the mystery movie world. Among the film's many additional pleasures is the appearance of what seems almost the complete roster of Warner Brothers character actors of the wartime years, including Florence Bates, Steve Geray, Eduardo Ciannelli, John Abbott, Victor Francen and Kurt Katch.

Mask of Fury
See: First Yank into Tokyo

Masque of the Red Death, The ● V
1964, US, 89 mins, colour
Dir: Roger Corman
Stars: Vincent Price, Hazel Court, Jane Asher, David Weston, Patrick Magee
Rating: ★★★

Highly stylish, imaginative Roger Corman adaptation of the Edgar Allan Poe tale, although a touch disappointing compared with some of his earlier work in the same field. Gone are the cold, clammy sets Corman worked with in America. This one was made in England, against warm, rich tapestries. Somehow, Corman hasn't quite the same control of crowd scenes that he musters with lone people fumbling their way along dank corridors. The horror is still ever-present, but the icy finger up the spine is missing. We all know what these characters fear: it's the Red Death, a plague which has swept through villages and now menaces the castle of the rich Prince Propero (Vincent Price), a sort of medieval Faust who has sold his soul to the Devil. In the sub-plot (based on another Poe story, *Hop Frog*), a romance between two dwarfs is touchingly, tactfully done, and one of them, Skip Martin, reveals himself as rather a good actor in a little scene with Patrick Magee that's loaded with evil. But the final coming of the Red Death to the castle isn't as effective as it might have been, especially to those who have read Poe's story.

Masquerade O
1965, UK, 101 mins, colour
Dir: Basil Dearden
Stars: Cliff Robertson, Jack Hawkins, Marisa Mell
Rating: ★★★

A good comedy-thriller full of twists and turns in a complicated plot which gives hero Cliff Robertson a headache in more ways than one. He's knocked on the head (twice), beaten up, thrown in a wine vat, lassoed and dragged along the ground, imprisoned in an animal cage, and nearly falls over a 100ft dam. About the only thing he temporarily gets the better of is a vulture called Charlie. Given that the film sets out to puzzle its audience from the word Go, most of the twists are obvious, but one or two still spring quite a surprise. Jack Hawkins revels in a part that is tailor-made for him, and Robertson fits equally well into a role for which he does not seem naturally equipped.

Masquerade ● V
1988, US, 87 mins, colour
Dir: Bob Swaim
Stars: Rob Lowe, Meg Tilly, Kim Cattrall, Doug Savant, John Glover
Rating: ★★★

Film murder mysteries aren't exactly two-a-penny these days, so this throwback to the *film noir* is very welcome, even with all its 18-certificate trimmings. The story could equally well have been called *Suspicion*, *Charade*, or almost any of those fashionable one-word titles bestowed on romantic suspense thrillers since Hitchcock first got into his Hollywood stride. Not that this film can stand comparison with the classics: although it's just about possible to work out at the end who is doing what to whom, far too many loose ends are left dangling elusively to fully satisy fans of the genre. Yachtsman Rob Lowe, having a steamy romance with boss's wife Kim Cattrall, soon steers himself into the calmer waters of an equally sensual romance with heiress Meg Tilly. She's loved from afar by local policeman Doug Savant, and hated by stepfather John Glover. You may think you can safely unravel the plot from here on, although you could find the final link in the chain of crime is a knot that writer Dick Wolf is not too willing to untie. Performances are adequate, especially from the dreamlike Tilly and the predatory Glover, and John Barry's music helps a lot.

Masques ●
1987, France, 100 mins, colour
Dir: Claude Chabrol
Stars: Philippe Noiret, Robin Renucci, Monique Chaumette, Anne Brochet, Bernadette Lafont
Rating: ★★

Thrillers in which no one is exactly what he seems are usually quite fun, and Claude Chabrol's country-house game of cat and mouse, although somewhat lacking in dramatic tension and variety of developments, proves, on the whole, no exception. Philippe Noiret is affable TV personality Christian who hosts a squirmy geriatric talent contest and has invited writer Wolf (Robin Renucci) to his country home to work on a ghosted autobiography. Such an avuncular figure can't be up to any good in a Chabrol film and, once in the lion's den, Wolf finds that Christian's granddaughter (Audrey Hepburn-lookalike Monique Chaumette) is bearing signs of undernourishment and has recently had treatment that accidentally (?) paralysed her legs. You'll probably have sorted out the goodies from the baddies by half-way, especially as Chabrol is not as interested in concealment as in duels of wit and words, but personable performances by Noiret and Bernadette Lafont (as his in-house masseuse) keep the interest afloat and the tension pricking.

Massacre in Rome ●
1973, Italy/France, 103 mins, colour
Dir: George Pan Cosmatos

Stars: Richard Burton, Marcello Mastroianni, Leo McKern
Rating: ★★

The story of a resistance action during World War Two that provoked a 10-for-one reprisal on the part of the Nazis. Richard Burton is the Nazi commanding officer and Marcello Mastroianni the priest who tries to prevent the reprisals. Both are very good in flashes; at other times each falls victim to a script that is 60 per cent literacy and 40 per cent platitudes, and sometimes huffs and puffs to little effect. Leo McKern gives one of his rare bad performances as the senior Fascist officer, but it's interesting to see former British matinee idol Anthony Steel in a minor role. The film is a little too long, but it does have its moments of truth, especially towards the end.

Mass Appeal ●
1984, US, 100 mins, colour
Dir: Glenn Jordan
Stars: Jack Lemmon, Zeljko Ivanek, Charles Durning
Rating: ★★

The title is as contrived as everything else in this effectively emotive tear-jerker about a happy-go-lucky, wine-tippling priest (Jack Lemmon) with a touch of showbiz razzamatazz in his sermons. He finds himself taking on a young rebel deacon whose abrasive behaviour and admission of relations with both sexes threatens to have him thrown out on his ear. Naturally both men have a lot to learn from one another and they do. Most of the other characters, including Charles Durning's bigoted monseigneur, are too rigidly stereotyped to do much with, but the dialogue is truthful enough to make some of its lessons hit home. Young Zeljko Ivanek, as the deacon, probably learned a thing or two about acting, too, by watching yet another of Lemmon's expertly anguished performances.

Master of Ballantrae, The ○
1953, UK, 86 mins, colour
Dir: William Keighley
Stars: Errol Flynn, Roger Livesey, Anthony Steel, Beatrice Campbell, Felix Aylmer
Rating: ★★★

Master of swashbuckling, Errol Flynn could hardly have found a better vehicle for his talents than this colourful version of Robert Louis Stevenson's

famous story of mystery and adventure. As the forceful Jacobite Jamie Durisdeer, his sword flashes as often as his smile and his winning ways win fair ladies. Despite the British material, setting and cast, the film was made under the aegis of Warner Brothers, the Hollywood studio where both Flynn and director William Keighley spent the greater part of their careers.

Master of Lassie
See: The Hills of Home

Masters of the Universe ○ ⓥ
1987, US, 106 mins, colour
Dir: Gary Goddard
Stars: Dolph Lundgren, Frank Langella, Meg Foster, Jon Cypher, Chelsea Field
Rating: ★★

Swedish muscle mountain Dolph Lundgren certainly looks the part of bestselling children's action toy He-Man, in this would-be epic in the *Star Wars* mould. But he doesn't have enough charisma – or acting ability – to carry the film in which nothing less than the future of the universe is at stake. The evil Skeletor's 'Darth Vader' clones have no eyes – which explains their appalling aim with laser guns.

Mata Hari ○
1932, US, 95 mins, b/w
Dir: George Fitzmaurice
Stars: Greta Garbo, Ramon Novarro, Lionel Barrymore
Rating: ★★★

Not many actresses in screen history have had a stab at playing the infamous lady spy of World War One. Magda Sonja was a silent Mata, then along came Greta Garbo with her smouldering allure and exotic temple dance. More recently, Jeanne Moreau has done well in the part and there was a disastrous Eighties version with Sylvia Kristel once more baring her all. This Garbo version is a pictorial stunner under the elegant guidance of cultured director George Fitzmaurice.

Matchmaker, The ○
1959, US, 97 mins, b/w
Dir: Joseph Anthony
Stars: Shirley Booth, Paul Ford, Shirley MacLaine, Anthony Perkins
Rating: ★★★

Well-staged version of Thornton Wilder's famous comedy play, which was later made into the smash-hit

M

Broadway and film musical *Hello Dolly!*. Shirley Booth is nearer the right age for the part than was Barbra Streisand, and Paul Ford is in fine, spluttering form in the part played by Walter Matthau in the later film. Rich in supporting talent, the film has many rewarding moments – not least of which is the sight of a very young Robert Morse masquerading as an elderly lady. This was Morse's first film and, surprisingly, his talent went unnoticed. He went back to the stage, and it was another five years before he returned as a star in his next film *Honeymoon Hotel*.

Matewan ◑ ⓥ
1988, US, 132 mins, colour
Dir: John Sayles
Stars: Chris Cooper, Mary McDonnell, Kevin Tighe, James Earl Jones
Rating: ★★

'Worthy' and 'admirable' are words that spring easily to mind to describe this account of the West Virginia miners' strike of the 1920s culminating in what became known as the Battle of Matewan. Compassion drips from every frame; yet the brutal truth is that *Matewan* is a very slow film that, for all its brilliant re-creation of period and hardship, makes severe demands on our patience. Excellent performances by Chris Cooper, as the travelling union organiser, Mary McDonnell, as the widow with whom he rooms, Kevin Tighe, as the repugnant union-breaker hired by the mining company, David Strathairn as the down-the-line local sheriff, James Earl Jones as the leader of the black miners, and many more, can't paper over the fatal lack of pace that John Sayles brings to this slice of history sprung to life.

Matinee ○ ⓥ
1993, US, 98 mins, colour
Dir: Joe Dante
Stars: John Goodman, Cathy Moriarty, Simon Fenton, Jesse White, Dick Miller
Rating: ★

Dull, over-acted and very slow to start, this is a fun-sounding idea that in fact only livens up towards the end. The twin story threads – the Cuban missile crisis of 1962, and the visit of a film showman to Key West to plug his new horror film *Mant!* ('Half man, half ant, all terror!') – are obviously destined to intertwine, but John Goodman as the cigar-chomping movie mogul is kept out of the action far too long for the film's comfort. Drippy sub-teens

dominate too much of the storyline, but the climax is just about worth hanging in there for. Pop out to the pub in the middle of this Matinee.

Mating Season, The ○
1951, US, 101 mins, b/w
Dir: Mitchell Leisen
Stars: Gene Tierney, John Lund, Miriam Hopkins, Thelma Ritter
Rating: ★★★

A comedy from one of Hollywood's more underrated directors, Mitchell Leisen, about a rich girl who falls in love with a man whose mother owns a hamburger shop. Thelma Ritter gives a show-stopping performance, as the mother and Gene Tierney's high-class society girl is both exquisite and likeable.

Matter of Life and Death, A ○
(aka: Stairway to Heaven)
1946, UK, 104 mins, colour & b/w
Dir: Michael Powell, Emeric Pressburger
Stars: David Niven, Marius Goring, Roger Livesey, Kim Hunter, Raymond Massey, Richard Attenborough
Rating: ★★★★

The first Royal Command Performance film is one of Britain's most famous movies: bizarre, beautiful, poignant and exciting, with a plot – about a pilot (David Niven) caught in limbo between Heaven and Earth – that is unique. Impressive portrayals from David Niven, Kim Hunter (five years before her Oscar in *A Streetcar Named Desire*) and Roger Livesey, fresh from his triumph in *The Life and Death of Colonel Blimp*, giving a tremendous performance as a psychoanalyst involved in the strange affair, whose events are played out at a high pitch of tension. Partly in Technicolor, partly in black and white.

Maurice ● ⓥ
1987, UK, 140 mins, colour
Dir: James Ivory
Stars: James Wilby, Denholm Elliott, Rupert Graves, Hugh Grant, Simon Callow, Billie Whitelaw
Rating: ★★

This poignant Merchant-Ivory film is a story of homosexuality in pre-war England based on the semi-autobiographical novel by E M Forster, not published until after the author's death because of its controversial nature. It has excellent, sustained portrayals by James Wilby and Hugh Grant, whose unconsum-

mated university affair takes them ultimately in very different directions. Director James Ivory lets it run on for a bit too long, but the film is sumptuously well set in period and has some distinguished players acting to their strengths in supporting roles, if for once Ben Kingsley seems all at sea as an American quack psychiatrist trying to rid our hero of his 'affliction'. The script is carefully, literately composed, although you may giggle at the odd jarring line of dialogue, such as: 'Since I was here, I went wrong with the gatekeeper.'

Maverick Queen, The ○
1956, US, 86 mins, colour
Dir: Joe Kane
Stars: Barbara Stanwyck, Barry Sullivan
Rating: ★★★

This Western has acquired something of a cult following along the lines of Joan Crawford's *Johnny Guitar*, perhaps because it comes from the same studio (Republic), has another Hollywood legend, Barbara Stanwyck, in a similar role, and Scott Brady again, as the Sundance Kid (he played the Dancin' Kid in the Crawford film). This isn't as good as *Guitar*, although it does have some rousing acting and a splendidly dominating performance from Stanwyck. Virtually the studio's last major production before it lurched towards extinction.

Maxie ○
1985, US, 90 mins, colour
Dir: Paul Aaron
Stars: Glenn Close, Mandy Patinkin, Ruth Gordon
Rating: ★★

One of the low points in the career of five-times Oscar-nominated Glenn Close. She has dual roles in this unashamedly old fashioned romantic comedy – a hard-working secretary and the ghost of a flamboyant jazz era flapper, who inhabits her body to grab one last chance of fame in films. Harry Hamlin of *L A Law* fame makes an unbilled appearance as himself, and the film contains Ruth Gordon's last screen appearance, as yet another in a long line of dotty neighbours. Production values look penny-pinching on screen, which doesn't help its B-movie feel. Only Glenn makes *Maxie* even a close call with success.

Maybe Baby ◑ ⓥ
(aka: For Keeps?)
1987, US, 98 mins, colour
Dir: John G Avildsen

Stars: Molly Ringwald, Randall Batinkoff, Kenneth Mars, Conchata Ferrell, Larry Drake
Rating: ★

Although technically very competent, this one really does prove a bit of a drag. It's hard to get involved in the problems of high school teenagers Molly Ringwald and Randall Batinkoff when they discover she's pregnant, especially with a script that runs the gamut of predictable situations – rejection of abortion, hasty marriage, struggles to make ends meet, money worries, constant bickering and moving in with mom – and fails to find anything penetrating or poignant about any of them. Ringwald's acting with a perpetual pout is less tolerable than usual. She looks as though she'd be happier in a comedy and indeed the film's best sequence is the Thanksgiving dinner at which she announces her pregnancy to the two families. Some tart dialogue winds its way through this scene, but the thread fails to reappear elsewhere and the film disappears up its own tear duct of gloom, doom and inevitable reconciliation.

Maytime ○
1937, US, 132 mins, b/w
Dir: Robert Z Leonard
Stars: Jeanette MacDonald, Nelson Eddy, John Barrymore
Rating: ★★★

MGM began making this Jeanette MacDonald-Nelson Eddy musical in Technicolor. But frightened by the cost, they got cold feet one-third of the way through and, abandoning all the colour footage, re-shot the entire film in black-and-white. Even so the film, with its stagey but uniquely emotive ending, remained MacDonald's favourite. No wonder: it drips with fine music, and includes one of the peerless pair's finest duets: 'Will You Remember?'

Maytime in Mayfair ○
1949, UK, 96 mins, colour
Dir: Herbert Wilcox
Stars: Anna Neagle, Michael Wilding, Peter Graves
Rating: ★★

Despite its coat of Technicolor, this post-war romp has worn less well than most of the box-office champions turned out by Anna Neagle and Michael Wilding. Perhaps it's because the romantic hijinks are set in a fashion house. Still, the stars play off one another as elegantly as ever.

McCabe and Mrs Miller ● Ⓥ
1972, US, 120 mins, colour
Dir: Robert Altman
Stars: Warren Beatty, Julie Christie, Rene Auberjonois, William Devane, Shelley Duvall, Keith Carradine
Rating: ★★★

Director Robert Altman cast his usual idiosyncratic gaze upon the West and came up with this adult view where the men are men and the women are available. In this case the most available is Julie Christie as Mrs Miller, the ambitious English whore who goes into partnership with McCabe (Warren Beatty) to set up a lavish brothel for the sex-starved citizens of a frontier town called Presbyterian Church. Altman is determined to show the West as it really was. The bit part players contribute as much to the film as Beatty and Christie, who seem content to play within their screen images. Among the Altman regulars are Shelley Duvall, who has appeared in several of his films, Rene Auberjonois, from *M*A*S*H*; and Keith Carradine, star of Altman's *Thieves Like Us* and *Nashville*. And William Devane has a small but flashy role as a lawyer.

McKenzie Break, The ○
1970, UK, 106 mins, colour
Dir: Lamont Johnson
Stars: Brian Keith, Helmut Griem, Ian Hendry
Rating: ★★

A taut, well executed World War Two drama about a plan by Nazi PoWs to escape from a Scottish camp, and the efforts of an Irish intelligence officer to foil the attempt. It succeeds largely because of particularly strong characterisations by Brian Keith, as the special troubleshooter, and Helmut Griem as a hard-drinking U-boat captain suspected of being the mastermind behind the plot.

McMasters, The ●
1970, US, 90 mins, colour
Dir: Alf Kjellin
Stars: Burl Ives, Brock Peters, Nancy Kwan, David Carradine
Rating: ★

A violent Western with Jack Palance as a bigoted Confederate determined to drive out an elderly rancher and his negro partner. The result is an orgy of murder, rape and sundry mayhem. There's a very good performance from David Carradine as a Red Indian supporter of the embattled duo, and a good one from Dane Clark (in a return to the screen after 10 years) as a liberal-minded rancher also sympathetic to their cause.

McQ ◐ Ⓥ
1974, US, 111 mins, colour
Dir: John Sturges
Stars: John Wayne, Eddie Albert, Clu Gulager
Rating: ★★

One of John Wayne's last films but a more workaday assignment than most. Stepping out of his Western togs and into the role of a Seattle police detective (a modern-day role as in *Brannigan*), big John goes in search of vengeance on the gangster who killed his friend. John Sturges directed this plain man's thriller with its ragbag of narcotics, corruption and shotguns. It rambles a bit, but then it does have plenty of plot.

McVicar ● Ⓥ
1980, UK, 112 mins, colour
Dir: Tom Clegg
Stars: Roger Daltrey, Adam Faith, Cheryl Campbell, Steven Berkoff, Ian Hendry
Rating: ★★

A muscular crime drama offering two pop stars-turned-actors for the price of one. Roger Daltrey takes the title role of the now rehabilitated and respectable criminal John McVicar, Adam Faith is his accomplice in a prison break-out, Walter Probyn. As one might expect, the film is somewhat sanitised but, despite that, the prison scenes carry conviction. Tom Clegg, more used to the confines of small screen series such as *The Sweeney*, provides efficient if anonymous direction.

Mean Machine, The ◐
(aka: The Longest Yard)
1974, US, 123 mins, colour
Dir: Robert Aldrich
Stars: Burt Reynolds, Eddie Albert, Ed Lauter, Michael Conrad
Rating: ★★★

A bit like a Laurel and Hardy film with an X certificate or the Marx Brothers' *Monkey Business* with brass knuckles. It's *Cool Hand Luke* prison fare all over again – except that the name of the game is not escaping but

M

American football. It all works very happily indeed, mixing its modern violence with pleasant old-fashioned dialogue and some hard-nut humour.

Mean Season, The ◐
1985, US, 100 mins, colour
Dir: Phillip Borsos
Stars: Kurt Russell, Mariel Hemingway, Richard Jordan, Richard Masur, Joe Pantoliano
Rating: ★★

Kurt Russell plays a reporter who hits the headlines himself when he becomes the mouthpiece for a serial killer in this tense and atmospheric thriller. As the only person the killer (Richard Jordan) will talk to, Russell's journalist begins to enjoy his own media celebrity, losing sight of the implications of his unusual position. The inevitable showdown comes when the killer abducts Russell's girlfriend. Both Russell and Jordan give strong performances and there's also solid support from Richard Masur, Joe Pantoliano and, in a small role, Andy Garcia. Tension and excitement go hand-in-hand to create a watchable thriller set in a very sultry midsummer Miami.

Mean Streets ● Ⓥ
1973, US, 110 mins, colour
Dir: Martin Scorsese
Stars: Harvey Keitel, Robert De Niro, Amy Robinson, Richard Romanus
Rating: ★★★

New York's Little Italy district has never looked seedier or tougher than in this gripping slice-of-Mafia-life drama, the first of Martin Scorsese's many descents onto the grimier streets of the Big Apple. Shot on a shoestring budget of $600,000 with two weeks' rehearsal and six days on location in New York (the rest of the filming was done in Los Angeles to save money), it has been hailed as a masterpiece by Scorsese's most ardent fans, and gave Harvey Keitel an early leading role. All the other roles are astutely cast with special praise reserved for Robert De Niro in the difficult role of a mercurial loner constantly in debt to a slimy loan-shark (a bravura performance from Richard Romanus). The film also boasts a terrific rock score that actually heightens the effect of its dynamic images. Look out for the director in a cameo as Shorty – the killer in a car.

Mechanic, The ●
(aka: Killer of Killers)
1972, US, 100 mins, colour
Dir: Michael Winner
Stars: Charles Bronson, Jan-Michael Vincent, Jill Ireland, Keenan Wynn
Rating: ★

A thriller that's as cold, calculating and passionless as its central character – a hired assassin, philosophically played by Charles Bronson, teaming again with director Michael Winner who made the *Death Wish* films. The director's well-oiled techniques generate some explosive excitement as usual, although one cannot help but think the makers should have heeded the advice given by Bronson to protege Jan-Michael Vincent when he tells him: 'You've been watching too many late-night movies.' No doubt, though, Bronson and Winner could churn out these violent morality plays in their sleep.

Medicine Man ○ Ⓥ
1992, US, 105 mins, colour
Dir: John McTiernan
Stars: Sean Connery, Lorraine Bracco, Jose Wilker, Rodolfo de Alexandre
Rating: ★★★★

A bit talky, but definitely different, this is an ecological adventure set deep in the Brazilian jungle. Lorraine Bracco is the Brooklyn girl whose brains have taken her to the top of the scientific tree. What she doesn't reckon on is swarming up to the top of the tallest tree in the Brazilian forest. Deep in the greenery works Dr Campbell, a scientist who has 'gone native', played by a pigtailed Sean Connery. Already feeling responsible for the death of a village, he's now doubly shaken: having found a cure for cancer, he has been unable to duplicate it. As he searches desperately for the missing ingredient, the bulldozers clearing the jungle move closer. And now Bracco has arrived to tell him his time is running out. This is another super performance by Connery, giving us the whole man without portraying him as too much of a saint, or making him too unsympathetic. Bracco is raucous at first, but finally moving. And, although stuntmen are credited, it's obvious that the stars are doing a lot of their own aerial work among the trees. Plot-spotters will probably get the twist of the tale before Connery and Bracco stumble on it, but that won't detract from your enjoyment of

a well-told story, where elements of fun, sadness, drama and action blend into good medicine.

Medusa Touch, The ◐
1978, UK, 109 mins, colour
Dir: Jack Gold
Stars: Richard Burton, Lee Remick, Lino Ventura, Harry Andrews
Rating: ★

'I am the man with the power to create catastrophe,' booms Richard Burton in this horror-style story. Burton's character has the power to move objects, to cause the death of anyone who stands in his way. Like his nanny, his parents, or all the passengers in a jumbo jet. When he turns his attention to cathedrals, atomic research establishments and moonshots, it's obvious the authorities have to step in. Fans of horrific hokum will enjoy themselves while cynics chuckle. Ironically, the film's most effective patches come with dialogue that is actually meant to be funny, especially Burton's scathingly vitriolic dissection of his faithless wife.

Meeting Venus ● Ⓥ
1991, Hungary/France, 119 mins, colour
Dir: Istvan Szabo
Stars: Glenn Close, Niels Arestrup
Rating: ★★

Films about opera and ballet have enjoyed success in the past: *The Great Caruso* and *The Red Shoes* are two famous examples. But they have not been much at the box-office for the past 40 years, and this one hardly breaks through the 'culture barrier'. As a movie, it has its moments: a Hungarian conductor (Niels Arestrup) arrives in Paris to helm a polyglot production of Wagner's *Tannhäuser*. Apart from walking into a Tower of Babel where not everyone understands a common language let alone each other's, he finds the inter-relations of the whole company akin to a TV soap. Affairs are rife, union demands disrupt every rehearsal as do tea and coffee breaks. There are disputes over scenery, choreography and whose duty it is to do what. Pretty soon, he himself is engulfed in a torrid affair with his leading lady (Glenn Close). Though Arestrup is good and Close lip-synchs superbly to Kiri Te Kanawa's singing, the film is too often not quite believable. But the ending is marvellous, and occasionally the passion of the performances – especially Close's – transcends the essentially cheapjack quality of the material.

Meet John Doe ○

1941, US, 123 mins, b/w
Dir: Frank Capra
Stars: Gary Cooper, Barbara Stanwyck, Edward Arnold, Walter Brennan
Rating: ★★★

A crowd-pleasing Frank Capra film that provides biting social comment and good entertainment at the same time. A bit slow in parts, with too many long speeches, but marvellously well cast and acted, with a sensational ending. Barbara Stanwyck is outstanding as the reporter who thinks up the idea of a made-up figure writing in to complain about injustice and finds that she has caught a tiger by the tail, as the 'complaints' take a nation by storm. Gary Cooper's natural sincerity lends quiet authority to the title role, although Walter Brennan as his sceptical friend steals all their scenes together.

Meet Me After the Show ○

1951, US, 88 mins, colour
Dir: Richard Sale
Stars: Betty Grable, Macdonald Carey, Rory Calhoun, Eddie Albert
Rating: ★★★

To compensate for the absence of regular partner Dan Dailey, Fox provided Betty Grable with three 'second league' leading men, Macdonald Carey, Rory Calhoun and Eddie Albert, in this musical about a Broadway star who loses her memory. As well as those Million Dollar Legs, look for acid comedian Fred Clark as Tim, and a couple of sizzling speciality dancers called Steve Condos and Jerry Brandow. Their routine benefits, as does the whole show, from scintillating choreography by the highly talented Gwen Verdon (who can also be seen on screen with Grable in the 'I Feel Like Dancing' number) and Jack Cole. This movie, with its vacuous plot and a waning star, had all the makings of a flop – but its dazzling dancing saved it.

Meet Me in St Louis ⊙ ⓥ

1944, US, 113 mins, colour
Dir: Vincente Minnelli
Stars: Judy Garland, Margaret O'Brien, Mary Astor, Tom Drake, Leon Ames
Rating: ★★★★

Vincente Minnelli directs his wife-to-be Judy Garland in one of the best and warmest period musicals ever filmed. It was his first colour film – and the Technicolor photography is Christmas card bright. The film follows a year in the lives of the Smith family. Nothing much happens, except that two of the daughters fall in love and the father faces a difficult job relocation decision. But the attention to ordinary detail made it a big success. Judy had to be persuaded against her will to star, but the finished film contains one of her best roles, her tear-jerking rendition of 'Have Yourself a Merry Little Christmas' and the show-stopping five-minute song and dance routine for 'The Trolley Song'. Child star Margaret O'Brien steals every scene she's in.

Meet Me Tonight ○

1952, UK, 85 mins, colour
Dir: Anthony Pelissier
Stars: Kay Walsh, Ted Ray, Stanley Holloway
Rating: ★★★

Alternately warmly witty and cuttingly cruel, this is typical Noel Coward fare, consisting of three short stories based on his stage presentation *Tonight at 8.30*. Things get off to a rousing start with Kay Walsh and Ted Ray as the 'Red Peppers', supposedly a second-rate song-and-dance team but in fact just as enjoyable in harmony on stage as wrangling off it. The other tales have Stanley Holloway as a worm who takes rather too long to turn and (most dated but still quite funny) Valerie Hobson and Nigel Patrick as social butterflies living off rich Riviera friends.

Meet Mr Lucifer ○

1953, UK, 77 mins, b/w
Dir: Anthony Pelissier
Stars: Stanley Holloway, Peggy Cummins, Gordon Jackson
Rating: ★★

Based on a play by Arnold Ridley, best remembered as one of the stars of *Dad's Army*, this amiable Ealing comedy takes some enjoyable sidewipes at television, and gives Stanley Holloway a good opportunity to flex his comic muscles in a dual role. Also on view: Ian Carmichael as Man Friday in a pantomime, Kay Kendall as a 'lonely hearts' singer and (briefly) star comic Norman Wisdom.

Meet the Applegates ◑ ⓥ

1990, US, 89 mins, colour
Dir: Michael Lehmann
Stars: Ed Begley Jr, Stockard Channing, Dabney Coleman, Bobby Jacoby
Rating: ★★

The Applegates are your average American family. They even look average. But their new neighbours think there's something weird about them and they're right: the A's are really mutated forms of six-foot high cockroaches from the rain forest of Brazil. They've come to America to destroy man's nuclear capacity – 'You must pronounce it nucular,' Pa (Ed Begley Jr) warns the kids – and millions of humans at the same time. Alas, the four Applegates soon fall victim to all the evils to which man has become heir. Ma (Stockard Channing) goes on a shopping spree with credit cards, Junior (Bobby Jacoby) becomes a hophead, and the nubile girl Applegate (Cami Cooper) gets pregnant on her first date. Needless to say, this is a comedy, but one with a thoroughly adult and sometimes stomach-churning content. Though high in the cinema's canon of mad movies, *Applegates* is just not mad enough, nor light enough, to make you laugh like a bug. You will smile though, when Pa complains: 'There's not a spark of trash about the house; the kids and I had to eat the morning paper!'

Melba ○ ⓥ

1953, UK, 120 mins, colour
Dir: Lewis Milestone
Stars: Patrice Munsel, John McCallum, Robert Morley, Sybil Thorndike
Rating: ★★★

Producer Sam Spiegel (under his alias of S P Eagle) and director Lewis Milestone, with lavish assistance from art director Andre Andrejew, make a spectacular job out of this highly coloured, immensely fictionalised biography of the famous Australian-born opera singer of Victorian times. Patrice Munsel gives a sterling performance as the rancher's daughter who becomes a world star, and sings a good selection of arias quite beautifully. The men in the film fare less well, but there are memorable performances from two dowager duchesses of British acting: Sybil Thorndike, as Queen Victoria, and Martita Hunt, as the famous singing teacher who comes out of retirement to help the heroine attain her ambitions. In the story's hectic two-hour running time, Milestone's direction remains sensitive,

M

dramatically effective, and full of imaginative little touches that raise the film out of the conventional class.

Melody ○
(aka: S.W.A.L.K.)
1971, UK, 103 mins, colour
Dir: Waris Hussein
Stars: Jack Wild, Mark Lester, Tracy Hyde
Rating: ★★★

A teenage comedy-drama reuniting Mark Lester and Jack Wild after their success as Oliver Twist and The Artful Dodger respectively in the musical *Oliver!* Despite its title, *Melody* is not a musical. Wild and Lester play school chums at a London comprehensive school whose friendship is threatened when Lester falls for a pretty girl in their class. Her name is Melody (Tracy Hyde). This film marks an early collaboration of David Puttnam (producer) and Alan Parker (screenplay) who were tp become major forces in the cinema.

Melody Time ⊙
1948, US, 75 mins, colour
Dir: Hamilton Luske, Clyde Geronimi, Jack Kinney, Wilfred Jackson
Rating: ★★★★

A delightful Disney cartoon compilation. Children will be charmed by the sagas of Pecos Bill, Johnny Appleseed and Little Toot (a tugboat) and Donald Duck makes a guest appearance. The classical motifs of *Fantasia* are carried over into 'Trees' and, best of all, 'Bumble Boogie', based on Rimsky Korsakov's 'Flight of the Bumble Bee', with a panic-stricken bee dodging various musical menaces. A real gem in which Disney's animators are allowed the full range of their creative abilities.

Melvin and Howard ◐ ⓥ
1980, US, 95 mins, colour
Dir: Jonathan Demme
Stars: Paul Le Mat, Jason Robards, Mary Steenburgen, Michael J Pollard, Dabney Coleman, Gloria Grahame
Rating: ★★★

Episodic but extremely engaging escapade dealing with a true meeting between a milkman called Melvin and the film and business tycoon Howard Hughes. Like other films by director Jonathan Demme (*Last Embrace* and *Citizen's Band*), it is full of fascinating characters; as Melvin's wife Lynda, Mary Steenburgen won an Oscar.

Memed My Hawk ○
1983, UK, 101 mins, colour
Dir: Peter Ustinov
Stars: Peter Ustinov, Herbert Lom, Denis Quilley, Michael Elphick
Rating: ★

Hard to tell whether star-writer-director Peter Ustinov intended this unlikely tale of Turkish bandits in 1923 as a whimsical action film or an outright satirical comedy. With its deliberately unreal performances, it tends to come across as the latter.

Memoirs of an Invisible Man ◐ ⓥ
1992, US, 99 mins, colour
Dir: John Carpenter
Stars: Chevy Chase, Daryl Hannah, Sam Neill, Michael McKean, Stephen Tobolowsky
Rating: ★

We always did find invisibility thrillers resistible stuff, and the lost art of the comedy-thriller is hardly revived by this thin script, hopefully written in invisible ink. Not fast enough, tight enough, or good enough, the slackly-constructed story finds director John Carpenter struggling outside his usual horror genre. Chevy Chase is the indolent businessman who finds he has to move faster than for years when a laboratory accident renders him not only invisible, but the target for a nest of rogue CIA agents led by Sam Neill. Lots of tedious conversation between Chase and girlfriend Daryl Hannah follows, punctuated by special effects that are remarkably clumsy by modern standards and seem not to have moved on much since Claude Rains' day nearly 60 years earlier. Neill would make a good villain with better material, but Chase is given little opportunity for his famous wisecracks, and can't seem to make up his mind here whether he wants to be Bob Hope or Cary Grant.

Memphis Belle ◐ ⓥ
1990, UK, 102 mins, colour
Dir: Michael Caton-Jones
Stars: Matthew Modine, Eric Stoltz, Tate Donovan, D B Sweeney, Billy Zane, Sean Astin, Jane Horrocks
Rating: ★★

The story of the 25th and final mission of the Memphis Belle, the most celebrated of the US Air Force B-17 bombers, based in Britain. In the hands of director Michael Caton-Jones, who went on to make *Scandal*, it ends up a highly romanticised view of wartime heroics and just the sort of unashamedly commercial popcorn fodder that had Forties audiences cheering in the aisles for the likes of Errol Flynn and Jimmy Cagney. The plane is crewed by the freshest faces Hollywood could muster, with acting honours going to Eric Stoltz as the romantic Danny and Billy Zane's suave Val, whose bravado hides a guilty secret. The photography of sweeping landscapes is stunning and the model work in the aerial fight scenes is flawless. Film fans may notice original footage from the 1944 documentary *Memphis Belle*, by William Wyler, father of this film's co-producer, Catherine Wyler, used for tear-jerking effect with letters from parents of dead soldiers read over it by David Strathairn's commanding officer. A genuine crowd-pleaser of the old school of filmmaking.

Menace II Society ● ⓥ
1993, US, 97 mins, colour
Dir: The Hughes Brothers
Stars: Jada Pinkett, Tyrin Turner, Larenz Tate
Rating: ★★

If 23-year-old John Singleton made a stunning directorial debut with *Boyz N the Hood*, then what of this film from 20-year-old twin directors The Hughes Brothers? It's not as good as *Boyz*, but still a remarkable first feature, full of venom, passion and raw energy. Some of its directors' work lacks control, and their story is a series of scenes with predictable outcomes but, unlike Caine, their leading character, they surely have a bright future. Caine (Tyrin Turner) is a decent sort considering his upbringing with hop-headed parents, but still he sells drugs and runs with the local boyz. After he leaves school, his life soon enters a downward spiral: his running mate O-Dog (Larenz Tate) casually kills a Korean shopkeeper over some imagined insult, making Caine an accessory. When his cousin is killed by rival gangsters, Caine seeks and takes revenge. While O-Dog continues his rampage, Caine is offered a route out of the ghetto via his relationship with Ronnie (Jada Pinkett) and her young son . . . Fluently told, the film is not for the faint-hearted or easily offended.

Men Are Not Gods ○
1936, UK, 92 mins, b/w
Dir: Walter Reisch

Stars: Miriam Hopkins, Rex Harrison, Gertrude Lawrence, Sebastian Shaw
Rating: ★★★

Wittily contrived comedy-drama which plays an interesting variation on the *Othello* theme. Miriam Hopkins is a delight as the girl who makes an actor playing Othello want to murder his wife, and other bright contributions come from A E Matthews, as a drama critic, and Rex Harrison. The film also offers a rare opportunity to see the legendary Gertrude Lawrence, as the wife of the Othello actor, who's played by Sebastian Shaw. Nearly half a century later, Shaw was to appear as Mark Hamill's father in *Return of the Jedi.* Impresario Val Gielgud plays – a producer. Excellent black and white camerawork by Hollywood's Charles Rosher.

Men at Work ◐ ⓥ
1990, US, 97 mins, colour
Dir: Emilio Estevez
Stars: Emilio Estevez, Charlie Sheen, Leslie Hope, John Getz
Rating: RB

Films like this shouldn't be allowed. A feckless farce from brothers Charlie Sheen and Emilio Estevez, this is a waste of (anybody's) money that wouldn't have got past first base in the old studio days. Way over the top playing and direction decorates a vapour-thin story about two garbage men who become involved with a murder and vital tape that incriminates those behind a scandal concerning the dumping of toxic waste. Sound promising? Forget it: Estevez wrote it as well and he didn't do a good job – the dialogue is more likely to send you to sleep than make you laugh. And what happened to the vital tape at the end? No-one seemed to care. Credit Leslie Hope with being the fastest movie mover in a short, tight skirt and you've said it all. Garbage is right.

Men Don't Leave ◐ ⓥ
1990, US, 115 mins, colour
Dir: Paul Brickman
Stars: Jessica Lange, Chris O'Donnell, Charlie Korsmo, Arliss Howard, Joan Cusack, Kathy Bates
Rating: ★★★

Yet another Hollywood movie based on a French original, this well-made weepie still has Gallic whiffs about its moods of melancholia. And, though it occasionally goes over the top, you will find yourself affected by the plight of Jessica Lange, suddenly widowed by a husband who leaves her with two sons, $63,000 in debts and insufficient insurance. Some of the editing seems a bit rough, doubtless in the effort to keep the film under two hours, but there's a multitude of incidents, well handled by director Paul Brickman, who creates a believable flat-dwellers' atmosphere while his star acts her socks off having a nervous breakdown, trying strainedly to enjoy herself, coping with her older son's love affair with an older woman (superb Joan Cusack) and tackling her small son's traumas and petty thieving. Go, enjoy and have a good cry.

Men in War ○
1956, US, 104 mins, b/w
Dir: Anthony Mann
Stars: Robert Ryan, Aldo Ray, Robert Keith, Vic Morrow
Rating: ★★

An ambitious film set in the Korean war. It was unusually realistic for its time, but finally found little new to offer. Rugged, uncompromising performances from Robert Ryan and Aldo Ray: in fact, all the cast come across as individuals in spite of a script that often requires them to do little but look miserable and unshaven.

Men of Boys' Town ○
1941, US, 106 mins, b/w
Dir: Norman Taurog
Stars: Spencer Tracy, Mickey Rooney, Lee J Cobb, Mary Nash
Rating: ★★

Somehow, MGM managed to assemble pretty well all the original cast of *Boys' Town,* including Spencer Tracy and Mickey Rooney, for this sentimental sequel. Such was the power of the studio contract system! The plot is more of the same, without the inspiration of the first film.

Men of Sherwood Forest, The ○
1954, UK, 77 mins, colour
Dir: Val Guest
Stars: Don Taylor, Eileen Moore
Rating: ★★

One of two lively, good-natured adventure films about Robin Hood to come from Hammer Films, mainly known for their horror products. This one has a genial American Robin, in the form of Don Taylor (who later met and married the British actress Hazel Court), and an excellent Friar Tuck in Reginald Beckwith. Attrac-

tive Eastman Colour photography by the experienced Jimmy Harvey adds the finishing gloss to the rousing yarn.

Men's Club, The ● ⓥ
1986, US, 105 mins, colour
Dir: Peter Medak
Stars: Roy Scheider, David Dukes, Harvey Keitel, Stockard Channing, Jennifer Jason Leigh
Rating: RB

A thinking man's porno movie. Hard to believe, though, that voyeurs wouldn't be bored to tears by the first half, in which seven affluent men, at least three of them dangerously unbalanced, meet for their first 'club' meeting and end up gleefully wrecking their host's home (with his connivance), casually kicking the furniture around, smashing the kitchen door and shattering priceless ornaments in a wild knife-throwing competition. Even so, it's a little tough to believe that the host's wife (Stockard Channing, inevitably wasted) on arrival home would actually go so far as to fracture her husband's skull with a broiling pan, or that the doctor member would offer no better advice that to stem the flow of blood with a handkerchief. The remaining six 'boys' end up at an opulent brothel with just enough Playboy centrefolds to go round. A good cast, also including Craig Wasson, Frank Langella, Richard Jordan and Treat Williams, presumably saw something about the meaning of life in all this. Wrong, guys.

Mephisto Waltz, The ●
1971, US, 109 mins, colour
Dir: Paul Wendkos
Stars: Alan Alda, Jacqueline Bisset, Curt Jurgens, Barbara Parkins
Rating: ★★★

A highly-effective devil-worship chiller directed by the underrated Paul Wendkos. Here he makes the most of terror that creeps up on one in luxurious surroundings, with some nerve-jangling use of Liszt's title music.

Mermaids ◐ ⓥ
1990, US, 110 mins, colour
Dir: Richard Benjamin
Stars: Cher, Bob Hoskins, Winona Ryder, Christina Ricci, Michael Schoeffling
Rating: ★★★

A mother and daughter fable. And, this being the movies, these are no ordinary mother and daughter.

M

Rachel Flax (Cher) is sexy, sassy, brassy and on the move from town to town, and man to man. Her idea of a solid meal is a marshmallow kebab. Her motto is: 'Life is change, and death is dwelling in the past or staying in one place too long.' Daughter Charlotte (Winona Ryder) thinks she wants to be a nun (no mean feat as they're Jewish) but finds she has too many of mother's hormones floating around and falls heavily for the hunky caretaker (Michael Schoeffling) out at the nunnery instead. There's also a younger daughter (Christina Ricci) who wants to be a swimming champ. The film really revolves round Cher and Ryder and they keep it flowing warmly along in spite of the fact that deceptively little actually happens. Bob Hoskins is sweetly blue-collàr as the man who may make momma settle down, but he's kept pretty much on the sidelines as the mermaids try to sort out a life together, via a rather contrived emotional climax.

Merrill's Marauders ○

1962, US, 98 mins, colour
Dir: Samuel Fuller
Stars: Jeff Chandler, Ty Hardin
Rating: ★★★

Jeff Chandler leads a band of US Marines through the Burmese jungle in this characteristically rugged World War Two action adventure directed and co-scripted by Samuel Fuller, an ebullient, cigar-chewing American who has become something of a cult figure in the film world. Shot in soft and very distinctive Technicolor (with the Philippines standing in for Burma), the film has some striking and moving sequences, not least of which is a desperate pitched battle at a railhead, culminating in Stockton (Ty Hardin) walking desolately through piles of twisted bodies. For rugged Jeff Chandler, who plays Hardin's CO, the Merrill of the title, it was to be his last film role. Even before it was released Chandler was dead, a victim of blood poisoning following a seemingly minor operation on the spine.

Merry Christmas Mr Lawrence ● Ⓥ

1982, UK, 124 mins, colour
Dir: Nagisa Oshima
Stars: Tom Conti, David Bowie, Ryuichi Sakamoto, Takeshi, Jack Thompson
Rating: ★★★

What happens, please, when Japanese director make international co-production about Allied prisoners

in Jap World War Two prison camp? I tell you: you get velly stlange film. But, though *Mr Lawrence* has some slow and dreamy passages, it also possesses a fascination you can't deny: one that shows the original cinematic mind of Nagisa Oshima, who made *Empire of Passion* and *Empire of the Senses*. David Bowie is nicely cast as the enigmatic prisoner who arrives at the camp at the same time as the Japanese officer who seems hypnotised by his personality. Tom Conti gives a very civilised performance as the Japanese-speaking Allied officer who tries to keep the camp's atrocities within bounds, while Jack Thompson is excellent as the far less cerebral group captain in charge of the prisoners. Probably best of all is Takeshi as the master-sergeant only beginning to understand what human relationships are all about. For all its faults, this is a film you won't easily forget. And the insistent theme tune (written by co-star Ryuichi Sakamoto) is equally haunting.

Merton of the Movies ○

1947, US, 82 mins, b/w
Dir: Robert Alton
Stars: Red Skelton, Virginia O'Brien, Gloria Grahame
Rating: ★★

This is the third film to be culled from the popular play by George S Kaufman and Marc Connelly, the first being a silent version in 1924 and then another in 1932 under the title *Make Me a Star*. The eponymous hero here is played by Red Skelton, who rises from being a humble theatre usher to stardom. The premise of this version was to recapture the atmosphere of the early days of Hollywood and it does exude some of that good-time spirit, but not enough enthusiasm or *joie-de-vivre*. The producers employed Buster Keaton to give Skelton lessons in slapstick technique.

Message to Garcia, A ○

1936, US, 86 mins, b/w
Dir: George Marshall
Stars: Barbara Stanwyck, Wallace Beery, John Boles
Rating: ★★★

Barbara Stanwyck as a Cuban freedom fighter? Well, she's a feisty lady and, although the accent is distinctly strange, she goes at her role with gusto in this period adventure set in the last century during the Spanish-American war. It's only loosely based on a real

incident (as described in Lieutenant Andrew Rowan's 1898 book), since Fox felt compelled to leaven the fact with a massive dose of fiction. Handsome, dependable John Boles plays Lieutenant Rowan, charged with getting a vital message from US President McKinley through to Cuban rebel leader General Garcia (Enrique Acosta). Needless to say, the terrain is tricky, and so is Wallace Beery as the maverick US marine Sgt Dory who is supposed to be aiding Rowan in his quest. It's all good traditional action fare, helmed by that prolific comedy and Western director George Marshall, who made *Destry Rides Again* and *The Ghost Breakers*.

Meteor ○

1979, US, 103 mins, colour
Dir: Ronald Neame
Stars: Sean Connery, Natalie Wood, Karl Malden, Brian Keith, Martin Landau, Trevor Howard
Rating: ★★★

The ultimate in disaster movies. To pump up a rather slender story-line about a massive meteor headed for Earth, which must be deflected by a combination of Russian and American missiles, a tidal wave, an avalanche and the destruction of a city are thrown in, via convenient splinters from the meteor. Sean Connery has a few aptly acerbic lines as the scientist-in-chief, and the Russian spoken by Natalie Wood and Brian Keithis most impressive – perhaps partly the reason why they walk away with the film. Special effects, with the exception of the avalanche scenes, are acceptably done.

Metropolis ◑

1984 [1926], Germany, 87 mins, b/w
Dir: Fritz Lang
Stars: Brigitte Helm, Gustav Frolich
Rating: ★★★★

Composer and musician Giorgio Moroder is responsible for the re-editing, colourising and futuristic score of this version of Fritz Lang's silent sci-fi classic. At just over 80 minutes long, Moroder's 1984 version is 40 minutes shorter than the original cinema release, but it's not just a cutting job. He has edited in footage from the original German 150-minute version to add clarity to the narrative. 'Colourising' simply means that many scenes are given an overall tint in different colours, presumably to heighten the mood of a particular sequence. It's a fascinating variation and tightens the rambling narrative of the original. Having said that, the ramblings are pretty good and add to what is still considered a cinematic masterpiece.

Metropolitan ◐ ⓥ
1989, US, 98 mins, colour
Dir: Whit Stillman
Stars: Edward Clements, Carolyn Farina, Christopher Eigeman
Rating: ★★★

Whit Stillman, a 37-year-old New Yorker, sold his Manhattan apartment and persuaded friends to come up with the rest of the money to finance this low budget and engagingly quirky comedy of manners. His personal sacrifice was vindicated at the Cannes Film Festival when *Metropolitan* proved to be the must-see event of the entire festival. The story centres on a group of East Side yuppies who dub themselves the Sally Fowler Rat Pack, after the girl whose sprawling Park Avenue flat is their meeting place, or the UHBs, short for Urban Haute Bourgeoise. Their self-deluding world, inspired by F Scott Fitzgerald's *This Side of Paradise*, is both attractive and repulsive to newcomer Tom (Edward Clements, giving the best performance). This talkative picture succeeds on many levels, offering intelligent arguments and dialogue, fully rounded characters and a welcome look behind the door of a seldom-seen milieu.

Miami Blues ● ⓥ
1989, US, 97 mins, colour
Dir: George Armitage
Stars: Fred Ward, Alec Baldwin, Jennifer Jason Leigh, Charles Napier
Rating: ★★★

A consistently engrossing thriller whose extreme violence and quite funny dialogue blend unexpectedly well. The plot carries echoes of *Shadow of a Doubt*: Junior (Alec Baldwin) is a vicious and daring thief who steals from those who steal and is not above the odd murder to help him evade the law or change identities. He sets up home with a little hotel hooker (Jennifer Jason Leigh) of whom he remains strangely fond, even when he decides to add her nest egg of $10,000 to his coffers. Hot on their trail is a veteran cop (Fred Ward) trying to cope with a massive workload as well as a new set of upper dentures. After a heavy interview, Junior decides said cop would be better in hospital for a while. Beating him up, he steals his

gun, badge and – for added humiliation – teeth. Baldwin creates a memorable portrait of this lethal Jack the Lad and, while Ward is a touch over the top as the grimacing cop, some of his exchanges with his partner (Charles Napier) are spot on target with their rough-edged but comradely banter. Leigh is perfect as the vulnerable call girl still chasing the American dream. Lots of little scenes contribute to the momentum of a film with very little wasted footage in its 97 minutes.

Mickey's Christmas Carol ⊙
1983, US, 26 mins, colour
Dir: Burny Mattinson
Rating: ★★★

Disney's first pantomime is a delightful cartoon featurette version of Dickens' famous story. It brings together almost every well-known Disney character, including Mickey and Minnie Mouse as the Cratchits and Goofy as Marley's Ghost. Ratty and Mole collect for the poor, Toad appears as Mr Fezziwig and the three little pigs rush breathlessly along the sidelines. Only Pluto is sadly missing. A treat for Disney fans of all ages – although it's all too short, and could surely have used a song or two.

Micki + Maude ◐
1984, US, 118 mins, colour
Dir: Blake Edwards
Stars: Dudley Moore, Amy Irving, Ann Reinking, Richard Mulligan
Rating: ★★★

Cuddly Dudley Moore, whose Hollywood films have scaled the heights and plumbed the depths, is firing on all cylinders in this fast-moving farce. He is teamed up with director Blake Edwards, whose film *10* made Dud a star, and this is just the kind of broad, slightly wacky comedy that Edwards does so well. Dud plays Rob, who longs to be a dad. But wife Micki (Ann Reinking) is an ambitious lawyer, with no time for family life. Then he meets Maude (Amy Irving), a cellist, and they have an affair. When she tells him she is pregnant, Rob marries her, even though he's still married to Micki – who also proves to be pregnant! This, as you can see, is a recipe for complete chaos, as Rob tries to keep his two lives separate. Not easy when both ladies have the same gynaecologist! A furiously-paced comedy that's great fun, although it does peter out a bit towards the end.

Midas Run ○
(aka: A Run on Gold)
1969, US, 106 mins, colour
Dir: Alf Kjellin
Stars: Richard Crenna, Anne Heywood, Fred Astaire, Ralph Richardson, Roddy McDowall
Rating: ★★

Caper film concerning a gang planning to hijack a bullion shipment. It's enlivened by some piquant vignettes, notably by Sir Ralph Richardson, and by Karl Alberty as a German ex-fighter pilot who, asked to force down an English plane, responds with relish: 'Gott in Himmel, I haven't done that for years!' In a small role: Jacques Sernas, a French actor who 14 years earlier went to Hollywood to make *Helen of Troy* and *Jump into Hell*.

Middle of the Night ○
1959, US, 118 mins, b/w
Dir: Delbert Mann
Stars: Fredric March, Kim Novak
Rating: ★★

A film for romantics, with Fredric March fine as the middle-aged widower who falls for a divorcee 20 years younger, played by Kim Novak in one of her firmest performances. Talented supporting cast includes Albert Dekker, Lee Grant, Glenda Farrell and Martin Balsam which helps to guarantee quality. It's a hard-shelled film with a splendidly soft centre, and Paddy Chayefsky's observant, thoroughly believable script mounts a prodigious attack on the tear ducts. A pity it's so slow-moving.

Midnight ○
1939, US, 90 mins, b/w
Dir: Mitchell Leisen
Stars: Claudette Colbert, Don Ameche, John Barrymore, Frances Lederer, Mary Astor
Rating: ★★★

Claudette Colbert and Don Ameche spar delightfully as director Mitchell Leisen demonstrates his stylish gift for sophisticated comedy to the full. Brilliantly scripted by Billy Wilder and Charles Brackett, it's marvellous entertainment, always lively and wittily funny. In its day, it was even considered somewhat 'naughty'.

Midnight Clear, A ● ⓥ
1992, US, 108 mins, colour
Dir: Keith Gordon
Stars: Ethan Hawke, Kevin Dillon, Arye Gross, Frank Whaley, Gary Sinise
Rating: ★★

M

One more time for the futility of war, and at least the issues of World War Two are clearer in the snowbound Ardennes forest, than those of Vietnam. A patrol of six young Americans, holed up in December '44 at a chateau filled with art treasures, encounters seven Germans who, after snowball fights and singsongs round the Christmas tree, just want to surrender. A fake skirmish is arranged (for no seemingly viable reason except dramatic effect). This being the moralising, ironic kind of film it is, it all goes inevitably and messily wrong. Not much here, really, to keep you hanging around for nearly two hours. Decently acted and told, it would look better as an hour-long play on television. None of the cast is exactly charismatic, but then that was perhaps what the director wanted.

Midnight Cowboy ● ⓥ
1969, US, 113 mins, colour
Dir: John Schlesinger
Stars: Jon Voight, Dustin Hoffman, Sylvia Miles, John McGiver
Rating: ★★★★

It was quite a shock when British director John Schlesinger's portrait of the grime and slime of New York's underbelly took the best film Oscar because it was the first to be honoured having an 'X' certificate. Today its subject matter looks pretty tame, but there was no denying its shock value more than 20 years ago. Jon Voight and Dustin Hoffman are both brilliant as the odd couple of drifters who try to eke out a meagre living as hustlers on the streets of the Big Apple. Sylvia Miles is also memorable as one of gigolo Voight's many unsuccessful liaisons. The material was such a downer that no-one thought for a minute that it would take off as the success it was. Cinematographer Adam Holender wrung the last bit of atmosphere out of the locations, hitting a high spot with an absurd Andy Warholesque party scene.

Midnight Lace ○
1960, US, 108 mins, colour
Dir: David Miller
Stars: Doris Day, Rex Harrison, John Gavin, Myrna Loy, Roddy McDowall, Herbert Marshall
Rating: ★★★

Based on Janet Green's stalwart seaside-rep murder mystery of the 1950s, *Matilda Shouted Fire*, which in itself was a modernised variant on *Gaslight*, this is a flossy Ross Hunter murder movie with Doris Day as the wife of wealthy Rex Harrison being terrified by eerie voices through the London fog. The special-effects boys went completely overboard with the pea-soup fog effects and Grosvenor Square is barely visible at all as rich American wife Doris Day (dressed in some of former top MGM designer Irene's most fabulous gowns) is pursued by the would-be killer.

Midnight Movie Massacre ●
1986, US, 86 mins, colour & b/w
Dir: Mark Stock
Stars: Robert Clarke, Ann Robinson
Rating: ★★

An affectionate spoof horror film about people in a mid-Fifties American cinema being devoured by a tentacled monster while they sit watching an opus called *Space Patrol*. The gory modern effects sit uneasily both with the sub Carry On-style comedy and with the affable re-creation of an old-time science-fiction serial. But fantasy fans will be pleased with the presence of genre veterans Robert Clarke and Ann Robinson in an episode from the serial.

Midnight Run ● ⓥ
1988, US, 122 mins, colour
Dir: Martin Brest
Stars: Robert De Niro, Charles Grodin, Yaphet Kotto, John Ashton, Joe Pantoliano
Rating: ★★★

Looking leaner than in many of his recent films, Robert De Niro's in good form here as a modern-day bounty hunter intent on capturing his biggest prize in years – bail-jumping embezzler Charles Grodin – in New York and taking him across country to Los Angeles. It should be an easy job, a 'midnight run', but the accountant has robbed the Mafia. Soon enough the FBI, the Mob and a rival bounty hunter are all in pursuit. Subsequent developments run like a slightly darker *Planes, Trains and Automobiles*, with enough action to keep the plot in a state of perpetual motion. *Beverly Hills Cop* director Martin Brest handles the action with elan and the by-play between odd couple De Niro and Grodin produces genuine comic sparks. The film belongs firmly to the hangdog fugitive, a part in which Grodin gives his best performance in years, creating a funny/sad, canny/grumbling character who never sheds our sympathy.

Midnight Sting ●
(aka: Diggstown)
1992, US, 97 mins, colour
Dir: Michael Ritchie
Stars: James Woods, Louis Gossett Jr, Bruce Dern, Oliver Platt, Heather Graham, Randall 'Tex' Cobb
Rating: ★★★

The sting in this lively tale is the con set up by hustler James Woods to relieve a rich but evil businessman (Bruce Dern) of his wealth. And the method is to entice him to bet that ageing boxer 'Honey' Roy Palmer (Louis Gossett) can't knock out 10 men in successive bouts in a prize fight bonanza. The tournament is loaded with skulduggery, as Woods and Dern attempt to out-con each other, and the boxing action is first-class – although there's rather a lot of it for those of a more sensitive disposition. Sparkling entertainment, though, and not just for fans of the sport.

Midnight Story, The ●
1957, US, 89 mins, b/w
Dir: Joseph Pevney
Stars: Tony Curtis, Marisa Pavan, Gilbert Roland, Ted de Corsia
Rating: ★★

Exciting, crisply-paced thriller, formerly known in Britain as *Appointment with a Shadow*. Tony Curtis is a traffic cop who plays a lone hand in tracking down the murderer of a priest.

Midsummer Night's Dream, A ☉
1935, US, 117 mins, b/w
Dir: William Dieterle, Max Reinhardt
Stars: James Cagney, Olivia de Havilland, Mickey Rooney, Dick Powell, Victor Jory
Rating: ★★★

Quirkily fantastic Hollywood version of Shakespeare's play, with Mickey Rooney a quicksilver Puck, James Cagney a truculent Bottom, Victor Jory a splendidly sinister Oberon and Dick Powell a delightfully miscast Lysander. Anita Louise and Olivia de Havilland (as Titania and Hermia) were just about Hollywood's prettiest young actresses at the time, but the real star of the film is Hal Mohr's glistening, mystical black and white camerawork – a deserved Academy Award winner.

Midsummer Night's Sex Comedy, A ○ ⓥ
1982, US, 88 mins, colour
Dir: Woody Allen

Stars: Woody Allen, Mia Farrow, Jose Ferrer, Julie Hagerty, Mary Steenburgen
Rating: ★★

This Woody Allen frolic is exactly what it says it is. There are a few laughs, much pictorial beauty in the photography of the New England countryside, and a fair attempt at catching the spirit of Shakespeare. Three couples pair off, re-pair, part, come together and air their neuroses within the comedy of anxiety familiar to Woody's fans, who will also be amused by his attempts to take to the air (the period is the early 1900s) in his newly-invented flying machine.

Mighty Barnum, The ○
1934, US, 95 mins, b/w
Dir: Walter Lang
Stars: Wallace Beery, Virginia Bruce, Adolphe Menjou
Rating: ★★

Wallace Beery (who had taken the role before in 1930's *A Lady's Morals*) plays the legendary American showman P T Barnum to the hilt (and often further) in this entertainingly fictionalised biopic. And there's a memorable slice of scene-stealing from Adolphe Menjou as the amiable drunk who eventually adds his name to Barnum's to form the celebrated Barnum and Bailey Circus.

Mighty Joe Young ○
1949, US, 94 mins, b/w
Dir: Ernest B Schoedsack
Stars: Terry Moore, Ben Johnson, Robert Armstrong, Frank McHugh
Rating: ★★★

This is the film on which the great Willis H (*King Kong*) O'Brien handed over the reins of monster magic to Ray (Dynamation) Harryhausen, who worked as his assistant on this enjoyable story about a giant but lovable gorilla. The orphanage fire scene, in which Joe rescues several children from certain death, was originally tinted.

Mighty Quinn, The ●
1989, US, 98 mins, colour
Dir: Carl Schenkel
Stars: Denzel Washington, James Fox, Mimi Rogers, M Emmett Walsh
Rating: ★

This ill-conceived affair tries to mix police mystery thriller elements with social comment about race relations in the Caribbean. On both scores it fails miserably. Denzel Washington is an island police chief under pressure to

charge a childhood friend with the murder of a white businessman, who's been decapitated in a hotel jacuzzi. But his acting is all on the surface and the rest of the cast are criminally wasted, especially Mimi Rogers, who surely took the role because she fancied a holiday in a beautiful hot spot. The villains are pretty transparent – in fact the principal villain of the piece is Swiss-born director Carl Schenkel for believing he had talent or ability as a director. Probably the only way to get any enjoyment out of the cornball affair is to treat it like a holiday report on Jamaica, where it was filmed. And yes, the film is named after the Bob Dylan-penned song, which gets several plays whenever the action lapses, which is often.

Milagro Beanfield War, The ○ ⓥ
1987, US, 118 mins, colour
Dir: Robert Redford
Stars: Ruben Blades, Richard Bradford, Sonia Braga, John Heard, Melanie Griffith
Rating: ★★★★

Robert Redford's second film as director following *Ordinary People* is a suitably ecologically friendly story about the rights of citizens versus the might of the dollar and the preservation of a cultural heritage. The story of how one poor Mexican bean farmer's decision to cultivate land needed by outside developers leads to a stand-off between the down-trodden community and big business, it's a whimsical allegory that pits rich bad guys against poor good guys and never leaves any doubt about which side will win. Glowing location photography, a fistful of likeable characters and a lush score won Dave Grusin an Oscar. Despite the draw of Redford's name and a cast that includes such familiar faces as Melanie Griffith and Christopher Walken, it was an undeserved box-office flop.

Mildred Pierce ○
1945, US, 109 mins, b/w
Dir: Michael Curtiz
Stars: Joan Crawford, Jack Carson, Zachary Scott, Eve Arden, Ann Blyth
Rating: ★★★

Michael Curtiz, who made *Casablanca*, directed Joan Crawford to an Oscar as the tragic Mildred Pierce in another classic of what is now regarded as cinema's highest camp. Wonderfully well constructed, the film also has memorable portrayals from Zachary

Scott as the worthless Monte, and Ann Blyth as the self-seeking Veda, both carving out repellent characters that equalled anything they subsequently did in the cinema.

Miles from Home ● ⓥ
1988, US, 120 mins, colour
Dir: Gary Sinise
Stars: Richard Gere, Kevin Anderson, Brian Dennehy, Penelope Ann Miller, John Malkovich, Laurie Metcalf
Rating: ★★

Richard Gere goes back to the farm for the first time since *Days of Heaven* for this think-piece about two brothers on the run, having burned down the farm whose fortunes have crumbled since they took it over from their father. The film reaches for pain and bitter irony but just misses them.

Milky Way, The ⊙
1936, US, 88 mins, b/w
Dir: Leo McCarey
Stars: Harold Lloyd, Helen Mack, Adolphe Menjou
Rating: ★★★

Remade with Danny Kaye as *The Kid From Brooklyn*, this is the hilarious Harold Lloyd original, with Lloyd as the meek milkman mistaken for a potential world boxing champion. Probably Lloyd's last classic comedy, it features great supporting performances from Adolphe Menjou and gravel-voiced Lionel Stander.

Millennium ○ ⓥ
1989, US, 108 mins, colour
Dir: Michael Anderson
Stars: Kris Kristofferson, Cheryl Ladd, Daniel J Travanti, Robert Jory
Rating: ★

Well dressed science-fiction claptrap about time travellers lifting deathbound passengers from crashing planes. There are some interesting ideas here but, with stiff performances, tatty effects, indifferent direction and a script full of such lines as 'It's incredible' that beg the viewer to agree, the whole thing runs like an uninspired TV mini-series. Kris Kristofferson looks too old and tired for the role of the crash investigator, Cheryl Ladd (as the time traveller) shows why she's never really broken out of television and poor Daniel J Travanti hams in frenzied fashion in an impossible role as the professor who suspects not divine but alien intervention. At the predictably fiery climax, the time

M

travellers open the gate for escape to safety. Audiences may rush for an earlier exit.

Miller's Crossing ● Ⓥ
1990, US, 115 mins, colour
Dir: Joel Coen
Stars: Gabriel Byrne, Albert Finney, Marcia Gay Harden, John Turturro, Jon Polito
Rating: ★★★★

A perfect Twenties' gangster film beautifully written and scored and full of studied scenes. The flawlessly paced plot is crammed with darkness, menace and violence but is faultlessly constructed and makes absolute sense. Tom Reagan (Gabriel Byrne) is the brains behind the throne of Irish ganglord Leo O'Bannon (Albert Finney): when they fall out, Reagan sets a complex plan in motion – and it's a joy to see the pieces of the jigsaw here fitting together towards the end. The dialogue is Bogart and Bacall crossed with a gangster relative of the Marx Brothers. 'Intimidatin' helpless women is my business,' drawls Byrne to Harden. 'Then find one,' she snaps, 'and intimidate her.' Armed with this gem of a script, the actors give perfectly-weighted performances. The expressions on their faces are never misjudged, shadow and angle adding emphasis to dilemma and resolution. The action blazes in bursts between the workings of the plot. And the violence is relentlessly real, earning a film without sex or any bad language an adult certificate on its own. Joel Coen's direction never puts a foot wrong.

Millionairess, The ○
1960, UK, 90 mins, colour
Dir: Anthony Asquith
Stars: Sophia Loren, Peter Sellers
Rating: ★★★

No more delightful version of Shaw's play has been made than this. Sophia Loren and Peter Sellers are perfect foils for each other as the millionairess and the impoverished Indian doctor she sets out to enmesh.

Million Dollar Duck ☉
1971, US, 92 mins, colour
Dir: Vincent McEveety
Stars: Dean Jones, Jack Kruschen, Sandy Duncan
Rating: ★★★

Sandy Duncan is a smart little American actress-comedienne who never quite made it in the movies. Here's

her best try, in a funny Disney comedy about a duck that lays eggs with solid gold yolks. It's hard not to be charmed by her bright-eyed, fizzy performance, especially when she is trying to deposit one of the eggs in her bank account. Personable support from a whole roster of Disney stalwarts, including Dean Jones, Edward Andrews, Joe Flynn, Jack Kruschen, Arthur Hunnicutt and Vaughn Taylor and a hectic chase that culminates in a rooftop rescue add to the winning brew.

Million Pound Note, The ○
(aka: Man With a Million)
1953, UK, 91 mins, colour
Dir: Ronald Neame
Stars: Gregory Peck, Jane Griffiths, Ronald Squire, Joyce Grenfell
Rating: ★★★

Witty, intelligent and charming, this film adds zest and zip to Mark Twain's famous story about a penniless seaman who finds himself living like a lord as a result of being in possession of a million pound note. Gregory Peck is in excellent form as the man lifted from the high seas to high society without spending a cent, and the appealing story is given an extremely attractive coat of Technicolor by cameraman Geoffrey Unsworth.

Mind Benders, The ◑
1962, UK, 101 mins, b/w
Dir: Basil Dearden
Stars: Dirk Bogarde, Mary Ure, John Clements
Rating: ★★★

One of director Basil Dearden's psychological thrillers, with Dirk Bogarde as the scientist who submits himself to the ultimate in mental stress, and a rare latter day appearance from John Clements as the government security officer who tracks Bogarde's gradual disintegration under pressure.

Mine Own Executioner ○
1947, UK, 108 mins, b/w
Dir: Anthony Kimmins
Stars: Burgess Meredith, Dulcie Gray, Kieron Moore
Rating: ★★★

Tense, exciting and wholly absorbing, this psychological thriller was the best film of director Anthony Kimmins' career. Burgess Meredith's intense performance, given before his portrayals began to descend from character to caricature, provides the

film with a strong central pillar. And Kieron Moore's tortured portrait of the man being treated by Meredith's psychiatrist is a credit to actor and director alike.

Ministry of Fear ○
1943, US, 85 mins, b/w
Dir: Fritz Lang
Stars: Ray Milland, Marjorie Reynolds, Dan Duryea, Carl Esmond
Rating: ★★★

Director Fritz Lang was still at his Hollywood peak when he made this suspense classic, bulging with sinister atmosphere (especially in the splendid opening sequences) and full of marvellous little touches worthy of Alfred Hitchcock. Ray Milland and Marjorie Reynolds have the leading roles, but most of the attention is taken by the performances of Carl Esmond – a handsomely menacing Austrian actor – and whining Dan Duryea, one of Lang's favourite villains. He takes part in one of the film's most gripping sequences, involving a stabbing with a pair of scissors.

Miniver Story, The ○
1950, US, 104 mins, b/w
Dir: H C Potter
Stars: Greer Garson, Walter Pidgeon, John Hodiak, Leo Genn, Cathy O'Donnell
Rating: ★★

Tragedy once again stalks the Miniver family in this stodgy sequel to the six-Oscar success *Mrs Miniver*. Greer Garson gives another sensitive performance as the mother of the family, and her young son, Toby, is played by William Fox, later to win adult acting fame as James Fox. Watch also for Peter Finch in a small role as a Polish army officer.

Miracle, The ○
1959, US, 121 mins, colour
Dir: Irving Rapper
Stars: Carroll Baker, Roger Moore, Walter Slezak
Rating: ★★

Handsomely mounted if basically empty romance glossily set against the Napoleonic wars in 19th century Spain. Director Iving Rapper moves it along so persuasively that he almost makes us believe its story of a nun (Carroll Baker) who falls in love with a handsome dragoon (Roger Moore) and runs away from her convent. Such professionalism is hardly surprising, coming from the man who directed *Now, Voyager*, *The Corn Is Green* and *Forever Female*.

Miracle, The ● ⓥ
1990, UK, 97 mins, colour
Dir: Neil Jordan
Stars: Beverly D'Angelo, Donal McCann, Niall Byrne, Lorraine Pilkington
Rating: ★★★

Irish filmmaker Neil Jordan returns to his home town of Bray on the coast of County Wicklow for this gentle, romantic fantasy-drama. Visually, it's a delight, with Philippe Rousselot's shimmering photography, and there's a haunting score (saxophone solos played by Courtney Pine). A pair of 15-year-olds, Jimmy and Rose (charmingly played by Niall Byrne and Lorraine Pilkington), wander the streets (he to escape his drunken dad, she to avoid her uncommunicative parents), living in their own world, creating stories about the people they see. But the arrival of a smartly dressed American woman (Beverly D'Angelo) at the railway station is to send ripples across the waters of their fantasy life. No prizes for guessing that D'Angelo turns out to be closely connected to Jimmy in this variation on the Oedipal theme. It's a highly attractive, many-layered film which is reminiscent of *Night in Tunisia* and *The Company of Wolves* as it mixes fantasy, romance, dream and reality to tell its rite-of-passage story.

Miracle in the Rain ○
1956, US, 107 mins, b/w
Dir: Rudolph Maté
Stars: Jane Wyman, Van Johnson, Fred Clark, Peggie Castle, Josephine Hutchinson, Alan King
Rating: ★★

One of the last in the long line of 'Wyman weepies' which deluged audiences with tears in the Forties and Fifties. Beginning memorably with *Johnny Belinda* (which won Jane Wyman an Oscar), and including *Magnificent Obsession* and *All That Heaven Allows*, they progressed through to this story of a plain girl in love with a soldier in wartime, in which Heaven does indeed allow Jane a semi-happy ending. Her performance and the location filming on New York streets are big plus factors, and there's a bumper collection of the best Hollywood character people in the supporting cast, including Fred Clark, Eileen Heckart, Halliwell

Hobbes, Barbara Nichols, William Gargan, Marcel Dalio and Minerva Urecal.

Miracle of Fatima, The ⊙
(aka: The Miracle of Our Lady of Fatima)
1952, US, 102 mins, colour
Dir: John Brahm
Stars: Gilbert Roland, Frank Silvera, Angela Clarke, Sherry Jackson
Rating: ★★★

Gentle, unaffected film about three children who witness a miracle in a small Portuguese village in the early years of this century. The film has its share of action, too, as well as a sensitive performance by Gilbert Roland, and beautifully-toned Warnercolor photography. It did rather better than expected at the box-office, where such subjects usually die the death, and it is well worth a look. John Brahm, the director, was a German (real name: Hans Brahm) who followed such distinguished colleagues as Billy Wilder and Fritz Lang to Hollywood in the mid-Thirties.

Miracle of Morgan's Creek, The ⊙
1943, US, 99 mins, b/w
Dir: Preston Sturges
Stars: Betty Hutton, Eddie Bracken, Diana Lynn, William Demarest
Rating: ★★★★

Frantic, fast-paced, outrageous comedy written and directed by Preston Sturges, with lunatic sub-plots going off everywhere. Betty Hutton was never funnier than as Trudy Kockenlocker, pregnant in wartime by a vanished soldier husband whose name she recalls vaguely as Ratzkiwatzki; the family of Kockenlockers discussing the unlikelihood of the name Ratzkiwatzki is itself hilarious. William Demarest is a tower of bewilderment as her father, Diana Lynn delightfully brattish as her kid sister and Eddie Bracken a riotously twitching rag doll as the idiot who loves her from afar (though not far enough for Trudy's liking).

Miracle of the White Stallions ⊙
(aka: Flight of the White Stallions)
1962, US, 117 mins, colour
Dir: Arthur Hiller
Stars: Robert Taylor, Lilli Palmer, Eddie Albert, Curt Jurgens
Rating: ★★

Robert Taylor keeps a stiff upper lip as the director of the Spanish Riding School in Vienna, trying to smuggle his priceless white horses out of Austria in 1938 from under the noses of the Nazis. It's a little long and slow, but there's some fitful excitement and the colour is excellent. So, too, is the acting of Lilli Palmer.

Miracle on 34th Street ⊙
(aka: The Big Heart)
1947, US, 93 mins, b/w
Dir: George Seaton
Stars: Maureen O'Hara, John Payne, Edmund Gwenn, Natalie Wood
Rating: ★★★★

Heartwarming piece of Hollywood comedy-fantasy which won three Academy Awards, one each for screenplay and original story and one for Edmund Gwenn's performance as the lovable old store Santa Claus who is all too convincing in the role. The child whose suspicious nature he has to conquer is played by an eight-year-old Natalie Wood – already a film veteran of some four years' experience. Scrape-voiced Thelma Ritter makes her screen debut as one of the mothers visiting the store; and Maureen O'Hara, as the store supervisor, takes a pleasant break from glamour and swashbuckling to prove herself an accomplished light comedienne, skilfully complementing Gwenn's eye-catching performance. Remade in 1994.

Miracles ○ ⓥ
1985, US, 88 mins, colour
Dir: Jim Kouf
Stars: Tom Conti, Teri Garr, Paul Rodriguez, Christopher Lloyd, Jorge Russek
Rating: RB

A pretty desperate comedy-adventure photographed in mucky colour that reminded us of those frantic Jean-Paul Belmondo capers of the mid-Sixties that took in several countries while putting hero and heroine through hell and high water. Here it's divorcees (from each other) Teri Garr and Tom Conti who lurch from a car crash in America through kidnap by Central American revolutionaries to crash-landing in the desert, storm at sea and capture by natives in the South American jungle. Ms Garr's makeup does gradually disappear but not her nail varnish, which sustains nary a chip to the bitter end. Everybody in the cast mugs like mad and Jim Kouf directs his own screenplay at breakneck pace but to no avail: it's still terrible.

M

Miracles for Sale ○
1939, US, 71 mins, b/w
Dir: Tod Browning
Stars: Robert Young, Florence Rice, Henry Hull
Rating: ★★★

The last film directed by Tod Browning, who made *Dracula* (1931) and *Freaks*, is a strange thriller, in which magicians are murdered. Robert Young plays an illusionist who tries to protect Florence Rice after two of her friends have died while dabbling in the occult. Were their deaths magic or murder? Browning's well-paced direction keeps us guessing right up to the end.

Miracle Worker, The ◑
1962, US, 106 mins, b/w
Dir: Arthur Penn
Stars: Anne Bancroft, Patty Duke
Rating: ★★★

This powerful dramatic film about Helen Keller, the deaf, dumb and blind girl who triumphed over adversity, won Oscars for its two leading ladies, Anne Bancroft and Patty Duke. The director was Arthur Penn, later to make *Bonnie and Clyde*.

Mirage ○
1965, US, 109 mins, b/w
Dir: Edward Dmytryk
Stars: Gregory Peck, Diane Baker, Walter Matthau, Kevin McCarthy, Jack Weston, George Kennedy
Rating: ★★★

A splendid star trio head the cast of this intriguing thriller which, if it doesn't quite live up to the promise of its appetizing early sequences, nevertheless remains very entertaining and will keep you guessing. The plot (written by Peter Stone, who scripted *Charade*) has so many twists and turns that not even Edward Dmytryk's heavy-handed direction can muff everything; and he really lets his hair down in the film's best scene, when Gregory Peck finds an old acquaintance brutally done to death.

Miranda ○
1947, UK, 80 mins, b/w
Dir: Ken Annakin
Stars: Glynis Johns, Googie Withers, Griffith Jones
Rating: ★★★

A superb comedy cast in the classic tale of *Miranda the Mermaid*. It's the film role, according to star Glynis Johns, for which people remember her most. Glynis plays to perfection as the amorous mermaid who leaves a string of lovesick men floundering on dry land before returning to the briny. And there's a richly comic performance from Margaret Rutherford as Nurse Cary, who aids and abets Miranda in her intrigues. Also in the cast: Miss Rutherford's real-life husband Stringer Davis, as a museum attendant.

Mirror Crack'd, The ○ ⓥ
1980, UK, 105 mins, colour & b/w
Dir: Guy Hamilton
Stars: Elizabeth Taylor, Kim Novak, Angela Lansbury, Rock Hudson, Tony Curtis, Geraldine Chaplin
Rating: ★

Producers before John Brabourne have tried the theory that putting a cluster of veterans together creates a box-office success. Not here it didn't. Under Guy Hamilton's leaden direction, far too little is seen of Angela Lansbury as Miss Marple in this Agatha Christie mystery about a murder within the confines of an American film unit visiting Britain. For once, Ms Christie's elaborate plot scarcely holds water; neither do the performances, with the exception of Geraldine Chaplin's as the director's secretary. Don't blame the actors too much: directorial flair is sadly lacking. In fact, we preferred the mock-Fifties movie, *Murder at Midnight*, that begins the film. The storyline of the 'real' film is too subservient to stardom. Liz Taylor looks like a younger version of the Queen Mother.

Mischief
See: The Man With One Red Shoe

Misery ● ⓥ
1990, US, 107 mins, colour
Dir: Rob Reiner
Stars: James Caan, Kathy Bates, Richard Farnsworth, Frances Sternhagen, Lauren Bacall
Rating: ★★★

Caught in a blizzard on the way back from the wilds of Colorado after finishing his new novel, Paul (James Caan) is rescued from certain death after his car crashes down a hill into the snow. Legs badly broken, Caan awakes in the warmth and comfort of a bed in a house in the countryside. But he still has a survival problem: his saviour (Kathy Bates) is as nutty as a fruitcake. A former nurse given to fits of frenzy in which she could kill or maim, his hostess is not only the 'dragon lady' of past headlines, but unfortunately his number one fan. Now she has him to herself she has no intention of returning him to civilisation. Worse still, she turns into a fury when she reads his new novel and finds out that he has killed off Misery Chastain, the heroine of all the rest. This is a fine old two-hander in traditional shocker style, well played by Caan and particularly Bates, who won an Oscar: she's really frightening as the seemingly dowdy, frumpish spinster-sinister. None of it is exactly unpredictable, but director Rob Reiner does it well within its limitations, and gets well-observed supporting portraits from Richard Farnsworth and Frances Sternhagen as the local sheriff and his wife.

Miss Firecracker ○ ⓥ
1989, US, 103 mins, colour
Dir: Thomas Schlamme
Stars: Holly Hunter, Mary Steenburgen, Tim Robbins, Alfre Woodard, Scott Glenn, Trey Wilson
Rating: ★★

Beth Henley's plays – *Crimes of the Heart* was another – are southern states nostalgia pieces that haven't transferred too well to the screen. This one is about a magnolia-county beauty contest that the leading character's beautiful older cousin won a few years back. The younger sister (Holly Hunter), though plainer and less prepossessing, decides to try to emulate her cousin's achievement – but learns by the end how empty it was, and finds herself instead. Well, okay, I guess, but *Miss Firecracker* just barely justifies its existence as a film, with a screenplay that only occasionally rubs away its drabness to reveal the gleam of truth. There's one outstanding performance, from Mary Steenburgen, as the spoiled older cousin. The rest of the acting is as humdrum as the movie and Hunter is harsh and unsympathetic in the central role.

Miss Grant Takes Richmond ⊙
(aka: Innocence Is Bliss)
1949, US, 87 mins, b/w
Dir: Lloyd Bacon
Stars: Lucille Ball, William Holden, Janis Carter, James Gleason
Rating: ★★★

A wild and wacky comedy starring Lucille Ball as a dimwit secretary and William Holden as her bookmaker who's having trouble with the syndicate. They land up promoting low cost housing for the homeless when

Ball thinks she's working for an estate agent. The original story is credited to Everett Freeman (older brother Devery helped write the screenplay) but there is a startling resemblance to the tales of Damon Runyon – the gambler with the heart of gold, the gal who's smarter than she looks, the characters who hang out with the bookie. Holden had, up to now, been known as a dramatic actor, but here displays a talent for comedy, even though he has to play second-fiddle to Ball, whose sense of visual clowning was really apparent here for perhaps the first time. It's side-splittingly funny at times.

Missing Pieces ○ ⓥ
1991, US, 93 mins, colour
Dir: Leonard Stern
Stars: Eric Idle, Robert Wuhl, Lauren Hutton
Rating: ★

A comedy of ineptitudes featuring the one-off team of Robert Wuhl and Eric Idle, failed musician and failed poet respectively, who become involved with a mysterious inheritance which keeps threatening their lives. It's old-fashioned stuff where bodies keep turning up around open doors and in the boots of cars, and has a running gag about the name Hoo that dates back to Abbott and Costello. Lots of simple slapstick in the Three Stooges tradition, a bit of which is almost funny, including Idle's prolonged encounter with an electric mouthwash and a telephone in that order; and Idle's hiding in a vat of wine, a gag that dates back even further – to Laurel and Hardy. Wuhl, a Robert Preston lookalike, is notably less successful with a script that runs like a Gene Wilder–Richard Pryor reject and has an incongruous Broadway show-style score by Marvin Hamlisch. The film is bad, but not that bad: it will play better on video.

Mission, The ○ ⓥ
1986, UK, 128 mins, colour
Dir: Roland Joffe
Stars: Robert De Niro, Jeremy Irons, Ray McAnally, Liam Neeson, Aidan Quinn, Ronald Pickup
Rating: ★★★★

Roland Joffe's film of Spanish and Portuguese oppression in 18th-century South America is all that the Cannes Festival thought it was when they awarded it the supreme Palme D'Or. It is brilliant, it is breathtakingly spectacular, it is

packed with action and thought-provoking dialogue, it is heartbreaking at the end, and it is certainly one of the most unusual stories ever put on screen. At what cost, in both monetary and physical terms, one can only guess. Perhaps it's as well that such obviously Herculean labours have reaped their just rewards. As it is, thanks to the talents of Joffe and screenwriter Robert Bolt, the film remains a graphic monument of what madnesses and atrocities have been committed in the pursuit of 'progress' or, as in this case, religious persecution. Jeremy Irons plays the leader of the Jesuit brethren who risks life and limb climbing a massive falls to reach and convert a fierce and remote jungle tribe. The towering scenery is never allowed by Joffe to dwarf the drama; rather, he uses it to emphasise the issues at stake, as with impressive shots of the 'enemy' soldiers swarming up massive cliffs on their ropes, a little miracle of 'mise-en-scene'. *The Mission* is a rarity – a great film that will entertain you as well.

Missionary, The ○ ⓥ
1981, UK, 90 mins, colour
Dir: Richard Loncraine
Stars: Michael Palin, Maggie Smith, Trevor Howard, Denholm Elliott, Michael Hordern
Rating: ★★

This kind of sideshoot from Michael Palin's *Ripping Yarns* is a black comedy about missionary Palin becoming (all too) involved with 'fallen women' in London's dockside. The film is quirkily entertaining, although fatally sentimental at its centre. It never quite seems to know where it's going. Michael Hordern's doddering butler is by far the most joyous thing in the film – forever losing his way in his employers' vast mansion and serving dinner in one of the bedrooms.

Mississippi Burning ● ⓥ
1988, US, 125 mins, colour
Dir: Alan Parker
Stars: Gene Hackman, Willem Dafoe, Frances McDormand, Brad Dourif
Rating: ★★★★

British director Alan Parker always favours a sledgehammer to crack a nut and a lingering moment of agony rather than just the hint of violence. This horrifying study of racial violence allows him free rein to indulge in both practices, but not even his countless shots of burning crosses and

frequent lynchings can detract from two powerful central performances from Willem Dafoe and Gene Hackman as FBI agents. Hackman should have won an Oscar for his portrait of a man who feels powerless to act to change things for blacks in America's Deep South but who knows how to wheedle information out of the locals. Frances McDormand also gives a standout performance as the wife of the local sheriff, who finds herself attracted to Hackman with terrifying consequences for herself. Peter Biziou's fabulous photography was a worthy Oscar winner.

Mississippi Masala ○ ⓥ
1991, US, 113 mins, colour
Dir: Mira Nair
Stars: Denzel Washington, Sarita Choudhury, Roshan Seth
Rating: ★★★

This is an attractive romantic drama with dashes of comedy on a familiar theme – racial prejudice – with a slightly different twist, directed by Mira Nair. Jay (Roshan Seth), a prosperous Asian lawyer, is forced to leave Idi Amin's Uganda with his wife Kinnu (Sharmila Tagore) and small daughter. In 1990, nearly 20 years later, in Mississippi, the family runs a liquor store and young Mina (Sarita Choudhury) has become thoroughly American. She also falls in love with a carpet cleaning operative, Demetrius (Denzel Washington). Not only is he black, but he comes from a distinctly humble background. The story is nicely told, with attractive performances from Choudhury and Washington as the illicit lovers, but examination of the real issues involved here remains rather superficial. More convincing is the depiction of Jay's loss of status in his adopted country and his inability, superbly conveyed by Seth, to let go of his old homeland. The camera captures his dilemma neatly, with witty juxtapositions of Jay's beautiful property in old Uganda and the unattractive clutter of the average American small town.

Miss Mary ● ⓥ
1986, Argentina, 102 mins, colour
Dir: Maria Luisa Bemberg
Stars: Julie Christie, Nacha Guevara, Luisina Brando, Sofia Virnboff, Barbara Bunge
Rating: ★

A very slow, poorly constructed Argentinian film with all the elements

M

of a continental sexploitation film of a decade earlier. The comely governess succumbs to her 15-year-old charge, while her employer helps to drive his family round the bend by laying a nubile widow across the snooker table. The film's pretensions to class lie in its setting – Argentina from 1938 to 1945 – and in the presence of Julie Christie as the governess. Christie, however, is not exactly ideally cast, and the rest of the acting is nowhere quite passable. Not even especially good to look at, it leans heavily on its attention to period – which its own fragmented structure works against – and on the performances of its younger players, of whom Sofia Virnboff and Barbara Bunge do show some aptitude, perkiness and individuality.

Missouri Breaks, The ● ⊙
1976, US, 126 mins, colour
Dir: Arthur Penn
Stars: Marlon Brando, Jack Nicholson, Randy Quaid, Frederic Forrest, Harry Dean Stanton
Rating: ★★

Marlon Brando and Jack Nicholson add star power to this mud-strewn film about a bounty hunter after an obstinate rustler; but basically it's just another Western. Director Arthur Penn decks up the action with a few new tricks, and Brando tries everything he knows to spark the role of the 'regulator', from a variety of accents to dressing up as a woman to shoot one of his victims.

Miss Robin Hood ⊙
1952, UK, 78 mins, b/w
Dir: John Guillermin
Stars: Margaret Rutherford, Richard Hearne, James Robertson Justice, Sidney James, Michael Medwin
Rating: ★★

With Dame Margaret Rutherford at the helm, you can't go far wrong. *Miss Robin Hood* is a robust comedy of the Ealing school about an eccentric adventure story fan who becomes involved in a crazy plot to rescue a secret whisky formula. Dame Margaret is in fine form, especially when storming a newspaper office with a regiment of children. Watch for Reg Varney in a tiny role.

Miss Sadie Thompson ⊙
1954, US, 91 mins, colour
Dir: Curtis Bernhardt

Stars: Rita Hayworth, Jose Ferrer, Aldo Ray
Rating: ★★

Based (though rather remotely) on Somerset Maugham's *Rain*, this torrid drama features the gorgeous Rita Hayworth in the title role, following such stars as Joan Crawford and Gloria Swanson as Sadie Thompson, an 'entertainer' who finds herself on a tropical island, surrounded entirely by burly US marines. Among the soldiers crowding like moths around Miss Hayworth's flame-red hair, look out for the craggy features of Charles Bronson.

Mister Cory ⊙
1957, US, 92 mins, colour
Dir: Blake Edwards
Stars: Tony Curtis, Martha Hyer, Charles Bickford
Rating: ★★★

Universal were still grooming Tony Curtis as a big dramatic star when Blake (*Pink Panther*) Edwards directed him in this good, meaty story, with Curtis ideally cast as a crooked Chicago slum gambler. Charles Bickford donates his usual polished performance and there's forthright acting, too, from young Kathryn Grant, a sensitive and witty actress who later married Bing Crosby. Solid, underrated drama extremely well photographed in Eastman Colour by Russell Metty.

Mister 880 ⊙
1950, US, 90 mins, b/w
Dir: Edmund Golding
Stars: Burt Lancaster, Dorothy McGuire, Edmund Gwenn, Millard Mitchell
Rating: ★★★

Wicked scene-stealer Edmund Gwenn is cast as an endearing old forger in this whimsical, winning comedy. The rest of the cast includes Burt Lancaster, Dorothy McGuire and some very good character players, but they just don't stand a chance. There's a good script by Robert Riskin and Edmund Goulding's discreet direction sews the package up nicely. Good for children too.

Mister Frost ● ⊙
1990, France/UK, 103 mins, colour
Dir: Philip Setbon
Stars: Jeff Goldblum, Alan Bates, Kathy Baker, Jean-Pierre Cassel, Daniel Gelin
Rating: ★★

This very strange brew is an up-market chiller about a mass-murderer who may be the devil in-

carnate and can bend people and objects to his will. Jeff Goldblum (as the devil), Alan Bates (as his pursuer) and Kathy Baker (as the psychiatrist unwise enough to take him on) keep the story afloat with very little help from the largely wooden acting of their international supporting cast. Just so that you can tell when Frost has got to his victims, they have crosses in their eyes: just about the director's only concession to the conventional horror movie. His general approach, however, is far from sharp and it's left to hollow-eyed character actor Vincent Schiavelli to briefly enliven the proceedings as the cigar-chewing manager of a seedy boarding house.

Mister Johnson ◐ ⊙
1990, UK, 102 mins, colour
Dir: Bruce Beresford
Stars: Maynard Eziashi, Pierce Brosnan, Edward Woodward, Beatie Edney, Denis Quilley
Rating: ★★★

This colonial tale of the 1920s finds director Bruce Beresford on sound ground. His central character is Johnson, a native wheeler dealer engagingly played (but not overdone) by stocky Nigerian actor Maynard Eziashi. Johnson wears a suit, tie and solar topi, thinks of himself as English and works for the district officer (Pierce Brosnan). Johnson's trouble is that, besides the deals and personal cuts that find their way into his pocket, he is not above a little embezzlement (and eventually theft). It's these incursions across the thin line between chicanery and crime that eventually prove this likable, always-in-debt rascal's undoing. Not, however, before he has helped with the seemingly impossible task of building a road that will connect his little outpost with the main highway and civilisation. Beresford establishes period and atmosphere immaculately, though his pacing is a shade too deliberate, if in keeping with the stumbling qualities of the natives' pidgin English. A nicely-made film that rewards the patient viewer.

Mister Moses ⊙
1965, UK, 103 mins, colour
Dir: Ronald Neame
Stars: Robert Mitchum, Carroll Baker, Ian Bannen
Rating: ★★

Robert Mitchum as a modern-day Moses – actually a gin-swigging adventurer who is lured on a strange pilgrimage by a missionary's daughter – in an African-set action yarn which runs ingeniously parellel to the Biblical story, including a novel parting of the waves.

Mister Roberts ○
1955, US, 123 mins, colour
Dir: John Ford, Mervyn LeRoy
Stars: Henry Fonda, James Cagney, William Powell, Jack Lemmon, Ward Bond
Rating: ★★★

Henry Fonda recreates his Broadway role as a war-hungry officer aboard a cargo ship captained by a small-time Hitler (James Cagney, in his 44th movie for Warners). But it was a far from happy occasion. Fonda rowed on set with director John Ford, even getting involved in a punch-up at one stage, and Ford was replaced by Mervyn LeRoy. Jack Lemmon won the Best Supporting Actor Oscar as a sex-crazed ensign, but the film is an uneasy blend of slapstick and long boring passages. Despite its variable quality, the film was a big popular success.

Mitchell ●
1975, US, 96 mins, colour
Dir: Andrew V McLaglen
Stars: Joe Don Baker, Martin Balsam, Linda Evans, John Saxon
Rating: ★★

An ultra-tough thriller, one in a long line of hard-boiled detectives from Joe Don Baker. If the thought of seeing a maverick cop beating up the bad guys, slamming a crook's hand in a car door and bashing another repeatedly over the head with a rock is your cup of tea, then this by-the-numbers crime tale will fit the bill. But it has real problems with a storyline that spends its first half on endless, uninteresting scene-setting. Mitchell is a cop with a nose for trouble. And he gets a deadly whiff of past-sell-by-date red herrings about a wealthy lawyer claiming self-defence over the savage murder of a burglar at his house. But before he can beat up his suspect, Mitchell is ordered off the case. Not that that stops him getting to the facts! Dynasty fans should look out for Linda Evans in an early role, cast against type as Greta, a $1000-a-night call girl.

Mob, The ◐
(aka: Remember That Face)
1951, US, 90 mins, b/w
Dir: Robert Parrish
Stars: Broderick Crawford, Richard Kiley, Ernest Borgnine, Neville Brand, Charles Bronson
Rating: ★★★

A tough crime film, pretty violent for its day, filled not only with sordid, fascinating characters but with early performances from soon to be well-known players, such as Neville Brand, Ernest Borgnine and Charles Bronson, here still acting under his real name, Charles Buchinsky. Broderick Crawford is as hard as nails in the lead of this tale of waterfront corruption, in which it's sometimes hard to differentiate between the law and the lawless.

Mo' Better Blues ● ⓥ
1990, US, 127 mins, colour
Dir: Spike Lee
Stars: Denzel Washington, Spike Lee, Wesley Snipes, Robin Harris, John Turturro, Cynda Williams
Rating: ★★

Despite a big, glossy production, that diminutive dynamo Spike Lee doesn't quite do the right thing by the jazz world here. The film opens brilliantly, giving rise to hopes that it will open out into a gritty social drama in the Bird tradition, giving us insight into a jazz man's life. Instead, the film is soon marching to the beat of a different drum, with Denzel Washington providing star presence, but not enough depth, as the selfish New York horn player who freezes everyone out of his life. Even with prickingly individual supporting work from Lee himself, Wesley Snipes, Giancarlo Esposito (as the delightfully named Left Hand Lacey) and Ruben Blades (as Lee's Spanish-speaking bookie), plus some enticing love scenes and witty dialogue, this is a 'Bird' that never quite takes wing.

Mobsters ● ⓥ
(aka: Mobsters – The Evil Empire)
1991, US, 104 mins, colour
Dir: Michael Karbelnikoff
Stars: Christian Slater, Patrick Dempsey, Richard Grieco, Costas Mandylor, Anthony Quinn
Rating: ★★★

'It ain't enough Pop!' grates the young 'Lucky' Luciano (Christian Slater) in this moody portrait of the friendship of four of the gangland legends from America's prohibition era, setting the scene for their rise to the top in the world of crime. Nothing if not efficient, even though it rolls out most of the clichés in the gangsters' book, the film fiddles with the facts to create a sort of Young Machine Guns. Slater is first-rate as Luciano: dangerous and yet still sympathetic. Patrick Dempsey, Richard Grieco and Costas Mandylor are well in character as his cohorts Meyer Lansky, Bugsy Siegel and Frank Costello, while F Murray Abraham, Anthony Quinn and Michael Gambon are the gang bosses they must elbow past. Nicholas Sadler also makes a strong impression as the maniac killer 'Mad Dog' Coll. Despite the formula script, director Michael Karbelnikoff achieves a sense of imminent danger and death about almost every scene. Not a classic, but a well-crafted addition to what in modern days seemed to be filmdom's most popular genre.

Moby Dick ○ ⓥ
1956, UK, 116 mins, colour
Dir: John Huston
Stars: Gregory Peck, Richard Basehart, Orson Welles
Rating: ★★★

The full power of Herman Melville's classic tale of Captain Ahab's obsessive hunt for the white whale that crippled and scarred him is brought vividly to the screen by director John Huston. The seemingly wayward casting of Gregory Peck as Ahab works well, although Huston had wanted to make the film 20 years earlier and star his father Walter. The mystery and romance of the sea is fully captured and the climactic battle with the whale is as epic a piece of cinema as you are likely to see. A roster of fine English and American stars that fills out the supporting cast includes Orson Welles, Leo Genn, Richard Basehart, Bernard Miles, Harry Andrews and James Robertson Justice. Huston, together with sci-fi writer Ray Bradbury, wrote a script that was pretty faithful to the book, stamping this film as one of the most enduring and exciting sea sagas ever made. Oswald Morris' unusual colour photography vividly conveys the bleaker qualities of the hunt.

Model Murder Case, The
See: Girl in the Headlines

Modern Romance ◐
1981, US, 89 mins, colour
Dir: Albert Brooks
Stars: Albert Brooks, Kathryn Harrold, Bruno Kirby
Rating: ★★

M

Albert Brooks' fate in his film career has been a bit like that of the character he played in *Broadcast News*: talented but never quite making it on the big occasion. His other films, such as *Real Life* and *Lost in America*, were critical but not popular successes, and *Modern Romance*, too, built up a cult following but not a pile of box-office takings. Alternately uncomfortable and very funny, this is a typically Brooksian view of an on-off romance, benefitting from the comedian's wry eye for the follies of modern life.

Moderns, The ● Ⓥ
1988, US, 121 mins, colour
Dir: Alan Rudolph
Stars: Keith Carradine, Linda Fiorentino, Genevieve Bujold, Geraldine Chaplin
Rating: ★★

Strong on atmosphere but less interesting in content, this is a skilful and elaborate evocation of Paris in the 1920s, or more accurately its artists' quarter at that time. Although skilfully structured, the results still run more like a TV mini-series than a film. One admires director Alan Rudolph's beginning, with real-life Paris 1926 footage speeded up, to indicate people hurrying and scurrying about and getting nowhere, but, of the performances thereafter, only Keith Carradine's rises above the ordinary. Evocation can only go so far in itself, and these artistic butterflies and barnacles grow tiresome before the film is half-way through.

Modern Times ☉ Ⓥ
1936, US, 87 mins, b/w
Dir: Charles Chaplin
Stars: Charlie Chaplin, Paulette Goddard, Chester Conklin
Rating: ★★★

'Modern times' buffet Charlie Chaplin's tramp in this classic, much in the fashion that sound films offended his pantomimist's sensibilities. But the little man, moving from hapless factory worker to singing waiter, triumphs over adversity just as Chaplin the film-maker proved victorious over sound, his only dialogue being a song in gibberish Italian. There is, however, also Chaplin's own music, which includes the 'Smile' theme. His wife-to-be Paulette Goddard is charming in the feminine lead, and her younger sister is played by a bubbly 12-year-old called Gloria De Haven, who grew up to become a star of MGM musicals and comedies of the Forties.

Modesty Blaise ○
1966, UK, 119 mins, colour
Dir: Joseph Losey
Stars: Monica Vitti, Dirk Bogarde, Terence Stamp, Harry Andrews
Rating: ★★

Director Joseph Losey makes no pretence at reality in his colourful adaptation of Peter O'Donnell's famous strip-cartoon thriller. Fantasy, or perhaps phantasmagoria, is the keynote of the proceedings. Monica Vitti is hardly ideal casting in the title role, and far from O'Donnell's (and Jim Holdaway's) original image. Terence Stamp is a dark-haired brawny Willie Garvin. But the best of the characters is Dirk Bogarde's cool villain, with his endless collection of parasols – a man who only sheds his perfumed wig when the going gets hot. The best individual moment also belongs to Bogarde: staked out in the desert, he croaks 'Champagne, champagne . . .' Also good are Clive Revill, as his twitching Scots assistant, and Rossella Falk as a villainess who kills her victims on the stoat and rabbit principle. The action is punctuated with op-art effects – there's even an op-art cell for Modesty when she's captured by the enemy. And there are many comic asides and interludes for song parodies.

Mogambo ○
1953, US, 116 mins, colour
Dir: John Ford
Stars: Clark Gable, Ava Gardner, Grace Kelly, Donald Sinden, Eric Pohlmann
Rating: ★★

John Ford directed this jungle romance and Clark Gable, Ava Gardner and Grace Kelly star in it, which should guarantee a high quality entertainment. But it doesn't. It's not that *Mogambo* is such a bad film, it's just that, with so much going for it, it should have been a whole lot better. Gable is a white hunter in Kenya, Ava Gardner is a wisecracking showgirl who falls for him. But along comes Grace Kelly, with husband Donald Sinden in tow and Gable goes for her. Yes, the old eternal triangle. If all this sounds a mite too familiar, it's because the film is merely a remake of the 1932 Gable/Jean harlow vehicle *Red Dust*. Only the names and locations have been changed to fool the unwary. *Mogambo* looks better thanks to good location photography in Africa, but the original film had a sharper script and a steamier atmosphere.

Mohawk ○
1956, US, 79 mins, colour
Dir: Kurt Neumann
Stars: Scott Brady, Rita Gam, Neville Brand, Lori Nelson, John Hoyt, Allison Hayes
Rating: ★★

Take about 100 Western cliches all in the same film, superb Pathecolor photography, fine action scenes, pallid acting (with the notable exception of Rita Gam) and an unusually inventive music score and you have this bizarre mixture of good and bad, which is, in turn exciting and unintentionally hilarious. Most of the well-known cast (including Ted De Corsia and Mae Clarke as Red Indians!) seem to lack interest in the project. In view of the corny ending they knew they were coming to, you probably can't blame them.

Molly and Lawless John ○
1972, US, 97 mins, colour
Dir: Gary Nelson
Stars: Vera Miles, Sam Elliott, Clu Gulager, John Anderson
Rating: ★★

This rugged Western, which was described by one American reviewer as 'almost a love story', features a fine role for Vera Miles, one of Hitchcock's favourite actresses. She plays a much put-upon wife who forsakes her sheriff husband to flee to Mexico with a wanted outlaw. John Anderson has some powerful moments as the sheriff, and so does the redoubtable Clu Gulager as his obnoxiously cocky sidekick.

Molly Maguires, The ○
1968, US, 123 mins, colour
Dir: Martin Ritt
Stars: Richard Harris, Sean Connery, Samantha Eggar, Frank Finlay, Anthony Zerbe
Rating: ★★★

Probably Martin Ritt's most consistently underrated film – a grippingly dramatic story of unrest and sabotage in the grim Pennsylvania coal mines during the second half of the 19th century. The claustrophobic atmosphere of oppression and poverty is vividly caught, and the emotions of the major characters ripped gut-raw, with Richard Harris and Sean Connery each giving one of their strongest and most moving performances.

Mom and Dad Save the World ○ ⓥ
1992, US, 88 mins, colour
Dir: Greg Beeman
Stars: Teri Garr, Jeffrey Jones, Jon Lovitz, Eric Idle, Wallace Shawn, Kathy Ireland
Rating: ★★★

You'll have to be in a really silly mood to enjoy this one. Wholesome American couple Madge and Dick Nelson (Teri Garr, Jeffrey Jones) head for Santa Barbara for a rare romantic weekend. Some weekend! In no time at all, they find themselves whisked off to the planet Spengo by its evil emperor, who plans to make Madge his bride before he destroys the Earth with his all-consuming death ray! It's up to Madge and Dick to save the cosmos, and the whole cast has at least as much fun as the audience in this supremely daft but often captivating *Flash Gordon*-style space pantomime.

Moment By Moment ●
1978, US, 102 mins, colour
Dir: Jane Wagner
Stars: Lily Tomlin, John Travolta
Rating: ★

An unashamedly romantic film spun around the hopefully body beautiful John Travolta. But the best performances in this beautifully-coloured animated postcard from the beaches of California come from the women: comedienne Lily Tomlin, playing it straight as Travolta's toy-woman, and Debra Feuer, the ex-Mrs Mickey Rourke, as Stacie. Not good, but perhaps not quite as bad as you've been led to believe.

Moment of Danger ○
(aka: Malaga)
1960, UK, 87 mins, b/w
Dir: Laslo Benedek
Stars: Trevor Howard, Dorothy Dandridge, Edmund Purdom, Michael Hordern
Rating: ★★

A chase thriller directed by Laslo Benedek, who made Marlon Brando's famous film *The Wild One*. The only assets of this sluggish drama, though, are a gritty portrayal by Trevor Howard and good location photography in Spain (the film's American title was *Malaga*).

Mommie Dearest ◐
1981, US, 129 mins, colour
Dir: Frank Perry

Stars: Faye Dunaway, Diana Scarwid, Steve Forrest, Howard Da Silva
Rating: ★★

A fairly grim and unrelenting film about the relationship between Joan Crawford and her adopted daughter Christina. The star is depicted as a vicious, self-serving monster who beat her child for petty reasons. Doubtless many of the actual events are true but, of course, we only see one side of the story – Christina's. Although one longs for the other point of view, the result is certainly a very effective case history, with hard-driving Faye Dunaway at times looking uncannily like Crawford. Little Mara Hobel offers a very forthright and clearly delineated portrait of Christina as a child but Diana Scarwid's interpretation of the adult Christina is less certain.

Mo' Money ● ⓥ
1992, US, 91 mins, colour
Dir: Peter Macdonald
Stars: Damon Wayans, Marlon Wayans, Stacey Dash, John Diehl, Joe Santos
Rating: ★★

Damon and Marlon Wayans, brothers in real life, play a pair of lovable rogues in this frantic, romantic action comedy. Damon not only stars but also wrote the screenplay and co-executive produced. So he gives himself lots of chances to show off his range of Eddie Murphy-style comic skills as Johnny, a sharp-talking, small-time conman who meets the girl of his dreams (Stacey Dash) and decides to go straight – with sometimes hilarious and often dangerous results. Fresh, fast and funny, but also unnecessarily violent in parts: an enormous public success, though, in its native land.

Mona Lisa ● ⓥ
1986, UK, 104 mins, colour
Dir: Neil Jordan
Stars: Bob Hoskins, Cathy Tyson, Michael Caine, Robbie Coltrane
Rating: ★★★

It isn't just Bob Hoskins' terrific, Oscar-nominated performance that makes *Mona Lisa* one of the more memorable British films in recent years. His role of George, fresh out of prison and working as chauffeur for a gangland boss' prize call-girl, certainly dominates the film but there's also much else to savour. Director Neil Jordan adopts a rich visual style that turns London's underbelly (including

Soho sex dives and the Kings Cross red light district) into a garish and nightmarish hell-on-earth. Michael Caine, hair slicked back, turns up in a couple of key sequences as seedy crime czar Mortwell, oozing false bonhomie, while Cathy Tyson hypnotically combines slinky aloofness with bruised vulnerability as the up-market hooker, Simone. Still, it's Hoskins' touching portrayal of unrequited love that so splendidly fills the screen; and the pathos of his sad situation is beautifully underlined by the use of Nat King Cole's aching ballads 'Unforgettable' and, of course, the title song.

Money Mania ○ ⓥ
1987, US, 95 mins, colour
Dir: Richard Fleischer
Stars: Eddie Deezen, Wendy Sherman, Tom Bosley
Rating: ★

When a dying conman gives a cryptic clue to four separate hidden stashes, each of $1 million, the chase is on to find them. If the plot of this chase comedy sounds a lot like *It's a Mad, Mad, Mad World*, you're right. There's one fundamental difference, though: this one isn't funny. When you see that the two main characters are called Rollie and Lollie, warning bells should ring. *Variety* summed it up: 'The film has no momentum, no thrust, no continuity and, ultimately, nothing to recommend it.' Don't complain you weren't warned!

Money Pit, The ○ ⓥ
1985, US, 91 mins, colour
Dir: Richard Benjamin
Stars: Tom Hanks, Shelley Long, Alexander Godunov, Maureen Stapleton, Joe Mantegna, Philip Bosco
Rating: ★★★

This is a sort of yuppie version of Cary Grant's *Mr Blandings Builds His Dream House*. Tom Hanks and Shelley Long are the city couple who buy their dream house, but the restoration turns into a nightmare. Some of the horrors will strike familiar notes with anyone who has been at the mercy of builders and plumbers, and some scenes are genuinely funny. Where the whole thing parts company with reality is with the house itself. It looks about the size of Buckingham Palace and you keep asking: 'How can they afford it?' Still, Hanks and Long, both likeable personalities, work extra hard to keep things bubbling and, for the most part, they succeed.

M

Monkey Business ⊙ ⓥ
1931, US, 81 mins, b/w
Dir: Norman Z McLeod
Stars: Groucho Marx, Chico Marx, Harpo Marx, Zeppo Marx, Ruth Hall
Rating: ★★★★

The Marx Brothers stow away on board a ship, pour themselves tea and coffee while living in 'kippered herring' barrels and try to get through customs all disguised as Maurice Chevalier. The scene where Harpo joins a Punch and Judy show is a gem of sustained comic invention.

Monkey Business ○ ⓥ
1952, US, 97 mins, b/w
Dir: Howard Hawks
Stars: Cary Grant, Ginger Rogers, Marilyn Monroe, Charles Coburn
Rating: ★★★

This very funny comedy, directed by the incomparable Howard Hawks, is about a monkey that accidentally invents a chemical potion that makes everyone who takes it 20 years younger. Cary Grant and Ginger Rogers display a delightful sense of comic absurdity. And Marilyn Monroe is in sparkling form as a non-typing, non-shorthand secretary. 'Ah well,' says her boss (portly Charles Coburn). 'Anyone can type.'

Monkey on My Back ○
1957, US, 93 mins, b/w
Dir: Andre De Toth
Stars: Cameron Mitchell, Dianne Foster, Jack Albertson
Rating: ★★

Cameron Mitchell gives one of his finest screen portrayals in this compelling story of champion boxer (Barney Ross – 'the man with the million-dollar legs') whose greatest fight is against drug addiction. The fight scenes are excellent, and Mitchell's anguished, harrowing performance is complemented by those of Canadian actress Dianne Foster as his wife, and Jack Albertson – years later to win an Oscar in *The Subject Was Roses* (1968) – as his friend.

Monkeys, Go Home! ⊙
1966, US, 101 mins, colour
Dir: Andrew V Mclaglen
Stars: Maurice Chevalier, Dean Jones, Yvette Mimieux, Jules Munshin
Rating: ★

Disney whimsy, with Maurice Chevalier beaming benignly, Dean Jones looking harassed and Jules *On the Town* Munshin making a rare lat-ter-day appearance. It's nice to see Marcel Hillaire (the village mayor) playing something other than a head-waiter, but Andrew V McLaglen, noted for his big action films, seems a strange choice as a director and, as a result, the enterprise lacks sparkle.

Monkey Shines ● ⓥ
1988, US, 113 mins, colour
Dir: George A Romero
Stars: Jason Beghe, John Pankow, Kate McNeil
Rating: ★★★

There's monkey business here all right, and it's no joke. A mad scientist (well, hopped-up on drugs) is injecting human brain serum into monkeys, but goes too far with Ella, one capuchin that he gives as helper to quadriplegic Alan (Jason Beghe), rendered near helpless in a road accident. All goes well at first, with the beast even learning to work the telephone. Trouble is, the scientist keeps up the dosage and the monkey, forming some kind of mind bond with her wheelchaired master, acts out his deepest hate desires, like wanting to dispose of the girlfriend who left him for, of all people, the surgeon who operated after the accident. Murder and mayhem follow in a film that gets progressively more exciting towards the end, when nail-biters may be down to the quick.

Monkey's Uncle, The ○
1964, US, 87 mins, colour
Dir: Robert Stevenson
Stars: Tommy Kirk, Annette Funicello
Rating: ★★

This Disney studio sequel to *The Misadventures of Merlin Jones* was made with an eye to television judging by the fact that it consists of two separate stories, both concerning the exploits of Merlin (Tommy Kirk) and his pet chimpanzee. The children will enjoy the special effects and flying machine of the second story. Annette Funicello – billed here as Annette – has co-star billing, though she does little more than hold the chimp.

Mon Oncle ⊙
1956, France, 126 mins, colour
Dir: Jacques Tati
Stars: Jacques Tati
Rating: ★★★

Jacques Tati's famous comic bungler Monsieur Hulot takes on the world of gadgetry and the results are gently hilarious; joke follows joke in miraculously timed sequences. A distant relative of Chaplin's *Modern Times* this, but with an engaging personality all its own – and a lasting reminder of a unique comic talent.

Monsieur Beaucaire ○
1946, US, 93 mins, b/w
Dir: George Marshall
Stars: Bob Hope, Joan Caulfield, Joseph Schildkraut, Patric Knowles
Rating: ★★★

The success of *The Princess and the Pirate*, made by Bob Hope on loan-out to Goldwyn, encouraged his home studio, Paramount, to go for period costume again in this Hope romp based very loosely on the Rudolph Valentino film of 1924. He's a bumbler sent on a suicidal masquerade to the court of Louis XV of France, but the gags are strictly Forties Hollywood.

Monsieur Hulot's Holiday ⊙ ⓥ
1951, France, 114 mins, b/w
Dir: Jacques Tati
Stars: Jacques Tati
Rating: ★★★

Delightful first appearance of Jacques Tati's pipe-smoking, disaster-prone blunderer whose well-meaning efforts constantly bring chaos to order, especially when that order involves modern contrivances. Here, the mood is delightfully all-of-a-piece and full of wordless gems of comedy. Who, for example, could forget the rocket flying in through the open window at the fireworks display?

Monsieur Verdoux ○ ⓥ
1947, US, 125 mins, b/w
Dir: Charles Chaplin
Stars: Charlie Chaplin, Martha Raye, Isobel Elsom
Rating: ★★

Charlie Chaplin shocked some of his fans with this sinister black comedy about a mass murderer. By now shaken and disillusioned by the antagonism shown towards him in America which, in the panic waves emanating from the Communist witch hunts, seemed to want to be rid of him, Chaplin mingled his black humour with some rather bitter pacifist statements. 'Mass killing,' Verdoux remarks when arrested. 'Does the world not encourage it? I'm an amateur by comparison.' Scenes between

Chaplin and wide-mouthed Martha Raye are the highlights of the film. Audiences, however, laughed nervously at such goings-on, and the film was not a great success.

Monsignor ◐

1982, US, 122 mins, colour
Dir: Frank Perry
Stars: Christopher Reeve, Genevieve Bujold, Fernando Rey, Jason Miller
Rating: ★

A change of pace for Christopher Reeve from his skyward swoopings as Superman sees him playing a Catholic priest with a past and a degree in finance charged with solving the Vatican's cash crisis. Genevieve Bujold is one of the more attractive temptations put in his way by the odd screenplay, co-written by once blacklisted Abraham Polonsky. An interesting cast includes Fernando Rey, former Bond villain Adolfo Celi as a Cardinal and Robert J Prosky, now a regular Hollywood character player.

Monster of Terror

See: *Die Monster Die*

Monster Squad, The ◐ ⓥ

1987, US, 83 mins, colour
Dir: Fred Dekker
Stars: Andre Gower, Robby Kiger, Stephen Macht, Duncan Regehr, Tom Noonan
Rating: ★★

Discarding modern film fiends, director Fred Dekker goes back to the traditional Hollywood gang of monsters for this junior league version of *Ghost Busters*, as Dracula and company stir from the depths to fight for possession of an amulet that controls the balance between good and evil. Once every century, the amulet becomes vulnerable to attack, and the moment for Drac and the gang has arrived. As well as Frankentein's creature, the Wolf-Man and the Mummy, Old Fangface has also inherited the Gill-Man from the somewhat more recent *Creature from the Black Lagoon*. Although their opponents are a gang of sub-teens who believe in monsters, time-honoured traditions are not neglected. Thus Frank's creature befriends the five-year-old junior girl member of the M Squad and is soon converted to its cause. The rest is average spoof hokum, apart from a spectacular beginning, 100 years ago (with vet

British actor Jack Gwillim as Van Helsing) and an even more spectacular ending as tots and grots battle to the death.

Monte Carlo or Bust ☉ ⓥ

(aka: Those Daring Young Men in Their Jaunty Jalopies)
1969, UK, 120 mins, colour
Dir: Jack Davies
Stars: Tony Curtis, Susan Hampshire, Peter Cook, Terry-Thomas, Dudley Moore, Eric Sykes
Rating: ★★

As the American title would indicate, this is a sort of sequel to that flying-machine comedy, with Terry-Thomas again in dastardly form as an English nobleman who plans to sabotage all his rivals in the Monte Carlo Rally. Ken Annakin's direction finds most fun in the sequences where the cars Terry-Thomas has sabotaged start coming apart.

Monte Walsh ◐

1970, US, 108 mins, colour
Dir: William A Fraker
Stars: Lee Marvin, Jack Palance, Jeanne Moreau
Rating: ★★

Melancholy, elegiac, dusty-looking Western with Lee Marvin as a veteran cowboy who finds himself a dinosaur in an old west that's dying out. First film as director for award-winning cinematographer William Fraker; his debut has a nice nostalgic feel, but the pace is too slow to keep a good grip on the interest. But there's a touching performance by Jack Palance in an unusual 'good guy' role.

Monty Python and the Holy Grail ◐ ⓥ

1974, UK, 90 mins, colour
Dir: Terry Gilliam, Terry Jones
Stars: Graham Chapman, John Cleese, Terry Gilliam, Terry Jones, Michael Palin, Eric Idle
Rating: ★★★

A grubby, muddy and vile picture of the Middle Ages, told in the inimitable, anarchic style of the Monty Python team. The funniest scenes involve a Trojan rabbit, Robin and his minstrels, a crazed bridgekeeper and a fight between King Arthur (Graham Chapman) and the Black Knight (John Cleese) in which Arthur has to sever all his rival's limbs, leaving only a head that rants for him to come back and fight like a man. Made on a tight budget in a way that only adds to its

lunatic charm, such as scenes where knights don't have horses but are followed around by servants knocking coconut shells together.

Monty Python's Life of Brian ◐ ⓥ

1979, UK, 93 mins, colour
Dir: Terry Jones
Stars: John Cleese, Michael Palin, Graham Chapman, Terry Gilliam, Eric Idle, Terry Jones
Rating: ★★★

Irreverent was for once the right word for this Monty Python pastiche of the New Testament, which provoked a furious outcry from religious organisations. Far be it for us to join the debate here: suffice to say the results are very funny. Director Terry Jones and his team confessed themselves baffled at the protests and petitions. 'We didn't have any quarrel with Christ himself,' he said at the time. 'My feelings towards Christ are that he was a bloody good bloke, even though he wasn't as funny as Margaret Thatcher.'

Monty Python's The Meaning of Life ○ ⓥ

1983, US, 91 mins, colour
Dir: Terry Jones
Stars: John Cleese, Terry Gilliam, Eric Idle, Michael Palin, Terry Jones, Graham Chapman
Rating: ★★

Touted by some as the film with something to offend everyone. Well, not in this day and age perhaps, although 90 per cent of the content is about sex and bodily functions and sometimes the film seems more intent on portraying taboos than being funny, which is a shame. Even so, some of the material undoubtedly achieves its intention of being offensively funny, especially in a sex lesson by teacher John Cleese to his boys, which goes into graphic detail about stimulation and foreplay before Cleese and his wife demonstrate the sexual act while at the same time ticking off the class for not paying attention. One gets the feeling that this is the film the Monty Python gang needed to make because the BBC would never have let them. One just wonders whether they're chiefly hoping you'll be shocked at what naughty boys they are – or be too busy laughing to care.

M

Monty's Double
See: I Was Monty's Double

Moonfleet ○
1955, US, 90 mins, colour
Dir: Fritz Lang
Stars: Stewart Granger, George Sanders, Joan Greenwood, Viveca Lindfors
Rating: ★★★

One of director Fritz Lang's last films, this is a stylish adaptation of J Meade Falkner's classic story of 18th century smuggling and derring-do on and around the Dorset coast. Joan Greenwood is in fine, astringent form as the snooty Lady Ashwood; and young Jon Whiteley – the older of the two small boys from *The Kidnappers* – turns in a very real portrayal of the fatherless boy who forms an affectionate bond with a likeable rogue (Stewart Granger), the leader of an adventurous band of freebooters. The plot, in which man and boy chase after a fabulous lost diamond, is full of narrow escapes from revenue men, slashing sword duels and wild chases over fen and moor. And there's one terrific fight between Granger and a halberd-swinging smuggler. Mark this one down as splendid entertainment.

Moon Is Blue, The ◑
1953, US, 95 mins, b/w
Dir: Otto Preminger
Stars: William Holden, David Niven, Maggie McNamara
Rating: ★★

A really not very naughty sex comedy for which director Otto Preminger harvested enormous publicity by getting it refused a Seal of Decency in America rather than delete such words as 'virgin', 'mistress' and 'seduction'. It was some years before the film was released in Britain. It did, however, herald the first signs of crumbling in the bastions of the infamous Hollywood Production Code, and marked a major step forward (or backward, depending on your point of view) on what could be seen and heard on screen.

Moonlighting ○
1982, UK, 97 mins, colour
Dir: Jerzy Skolimowski
Stars: Jeremy Irons, Eugene Lipinski
Rating: ★★

Rather a nice little movie, ideally suited to the television screen in its intimate drama, about four Polish workmen sent to England to 'do up' a house for a quarter of what their boss would have to pay English workmen. Jeremy Irons plays their leader with an expression of permanent alarm on his face, trying desperately to make ends meet and keep papers (with news of the Solidarity suppression) away from his workmates, presumably on account of the pictures, as none of them speaks a word of English. Soon he is reduced to shoplifting, an occupation at which, although he develops a naive cunning, he bears a charmed life. These escapades, both tense and amusing, prove the most entertaining part of this interesting film.

Moon Over Miami ○ ⓥ
1941, US, 91 mins, colour
Dir: Walter Lang
Stars: Betty Grable, Don Ameche, Robert Cummings, Carole Landis
Rating: ★★★

A kind of forerunner of *On the Town*, with two gold-digging sisters on the loose on a millionaire-finding Miami holiday. Made with irresistible verve and energy by its stars (especially Betty Grable, Carole Landis and Charlotte Greenwood) and by director Walter Lang, who films include *State Fair, Tin Pan Alley, Call Me Madam, There's No Business Like Show Business* and *The King and I*. Quite a musical record!

Moon Over Parador ◑ ⓥ
1988, US, 106 mins, colour
Dir: Paul Mazursky
Stars: Richard Dreyfuss, Raul Julia, Sonia Braga
Rating: ★★★

Richard Dreyfuss excels as a small-time actor who spends a deliciously dangerous year impersonating the newly-killed president of the island republic of Parador. A bit over-the-top at times, but fun to be with and, thanks to his central performance, you really do care what happens to Dreyfuss in the end. Raul Julia is a little more restrained than usual as the power behind the throne and all the company takes the comedy seriously enough for you to enjoy it. Especially relishable is Dreyfuss' first speech to the nation when he calls on lines from *Man of La Mancha* in his hour of need. Only minus: a noisy music score by Maurice Jarre.

Moonraker ○ ⓥ
1979, UK, 126 mins, colour
Dir: Lewis Gilbert
Stars: Roger Moore, Lois Chiles, Michael Lonsdale, Richard Kiel, Bernard Lee
Rating: ★★

Each new James Bond film was a bit like an annual outing to a pantomime: comforting old characters and familiar situations where credibility and logic play second fiddle to the wonders that delight the eye. The plot relies alternately on the inconceivable and the impossible and all the proven ingredients are here, with the customary quota of mechanical marvels, including a jet-propelled gondola that converts into a hovercraft, plus an impressive outer-space battle at the end.

Moonshine War, The ◑
1970, US, 95 mins, colour
Dir: Richard Quine
Stars: Patrick McGoohan, Richard Widmark, Alan Alda
Rating: ★★

Deep in whisky-still country (Kentucky, to be precise) for an action film faintly reminiscent of Mitchum's *Thunder Road*, and with echoes from *Bonnie and Clyde*. It's a pity that the leading character doesn't have a stronger actor than Alan Alda, and the music seems inapt considering the serious tenor of the plot. But Richard Widmark, Patrick McGoohan and singer Lee Hazlewood are first-rate portraying varying degrees of corruption and repulsiveness.

Moon Spinners, The ○
1964, US/UK, 119 mins, colour
Dir: James Neilson
Stars: Hayley Mills, Eli Wallach, Peter McEnery, Joan Greenwood, John le Mesurier, Pola Negri
Rating: ★★

Hayley Mills, Eli Wallach, Peter McEnery, Joan Greenwood and silent star Pola Negri. What are the odds against finding that line-up in one film? Walt Disney somehow got them all together for this Hitchcock-style caper about smuggling in Crete. The story's a little long for its weight, but there's lots of local colour, Hayley gets her first screen kiss and Wallach and Negri enjoy themselves with the riper roles. The honeyed tones of the much-missed Joan Greenwood are always to be treasured.

Moonstruck ○ ⓥ
1987, US, 102 mins, colour
Dir: Norman Jewison

Stars: Cher, Nicolas Cage, Vincent Gardenia, Olympia Dukakis, Danny Aiello
Rating: ★★★

A romantic farce set in New York's Little Italy, but totally free of the Mafia, and criss-crossing several couples who all seem to be affected by a huge full moon. A young widow (Cher) accepts a proposal, but falls for her fiance's estranged brother, the loving couple encountering her father and his mistress at the opera, while his wife finds herself dining with a man who has been jilted by his young student, just as he was before in an incident witnessed by the young widow . . . a sort of *Il Rondo*, as you can see, although director Norman Jewison and the film's music rather overdo the amore and Italian openess. Still, there are winning performances from Cher (collecting an Oscar), Nicolas Cage as the hairy ape who sweeps her off her feet, and Olympia Dukakis and Vincent Gardenia as her parents. A little slow at times the film becomes more amusing as it goes on and the personalities of the actors begin to make an impact on their roles. As the theme song says: 'When the moon hits the sky like a big pizza pie, that's amore.' This film sets out to prove no more than that.

Moonwalker ○ ⓥ
1988, US, 93 mins, colour
Dir: Colin Chilvers, Jerry Kramer
Stars: Michael Jackson
Rating: ★★

A spectacular fantasy film telling the story of Michael Jackson's phenomenal success. It includes recent concert footage and a remake of his 'Bad' video, this time starring eight year-olds. But the eye-popping highlight is the seduction based on his hit 'Smooth Criminal', directed by Colin Chilvers, who created the *Superman* effects and using Oscar-winning make-up guy Rick Baker (who transformed Michael into a werewolf in 'Thriller') who this time changes him into a gleaming silver robot. This sequence alone contains as many special effects shots as Steven Spielberg's *Close Encounters of the Third Kind*. Unmissable if you're a Jackson fan, with Oscar-winning Joe Pesci as a fiendish villain.

Morgan – A Suitable Case for Treatment ○ ⓥ
(aka: Morgan)
1965, UK, 97 mins, b/w
Dir: Karel Reisz

Stars: Vanessa Redgrave, David Warner, Robert Stevens, Irene Handl, Bernard Bresslaw
Rating: ★★★

Raw-boned actor David Warner made his first big impact in this with-it comedy about a young man with a passion for Trotsky, Marx (Karl, not the Brothers) and all furry animals. In his fantasies, he likens the people he knows to various four-footed beasts. Not surprisingly, perhaps, he sees himself as an ape-man – the cue for some nostalgic footage of Tarzan (Weissmuller version) and the incomparable King Kong. These Tarzan/ape-man sequences, which include Morgan invading his ex-wife's remarriage reception dressed as a gorilla, are the best in the film. 'I've gone all furry,' says Morgan, with a simple, but satisfied smile on his face at one stage; and, at another, with a certain amount of relish: 'I shall be hunted down from Wapping to Wimbledon.' He's also the proud possessor of a stuffed gorilla, which gives rise to the film's biggest laugh when he tries to save it from a fire. 'My God,' gasps his father-in-law, as Morgan staggers out of the smoke with an indistinct figure slung over his shoulder, 'he's got my wife.' A trio of believable eccentrics in the supporting cast comprises Irene Handl as Morgan's Stalinist mum, Bernard Bresslaw as a harassed, hopscotch-happy policeman and Arthur Mullard as a wrestler called Danny the Gorilla. No wonder Morgan has an affinity with him.

Morituri
See: Saboteur – Code Name Morituri

Morning After, The ◖ ⓥ
1986, US, 103 mins, colour
Dir: Sidney Lumet
Stars: Jane Fonda, Jeff Bridges, Raul Julia
Rating: ★★

Alcoholic Jane Fonda wakes up to find she's lying next to a brutally murdered soft-porn photographer. With a history of alcoholism and blackouts and an assault conviction, she decides that calling the police may not be a good idea. Luckily for her, she runs into Jeff Bridges, an ex-cop who decides to help her solve the murder. Quite a tense thriller results from this beginning, although it loses steam a bit towards the end. Fonda and Bridges are very good, but increasingly the film focuses on their growing rela-

tionship rather than the murder, which is what slows it down. Still, the dialogue is good and you've got to keep watching to find out whodunnit.

Morning Departure ○
1949, UK, 115 mins, b/w
Dir: Roy Baker
Stars: John Mills, Helen Cherry, Richard Attenborough, Nigel Patrick
Rating: ★★★

This British marine drama has all the stiff-upper-lip characteristics typical of the period, with submarine commander John Mills giving a virtual repeat of his performance in the 1943 Gainsborough drama *We Dive at Dawn*, but fine for all that. Richard Attenborough, as the stoker who becomes hysterical, also gives a solid performance, in line with many of his weak, blustery characters of the period. And Helen Cherry makes an effective, if brief, appearance. There are lots of other British stalwarts here – Nigel Patrick, Lana Morris, James Hayter (providing some light relief to the intense, life-or-death proceedings), George Cole and Kenneth More. The film was typical fare for director Roy Baker, who relished dramas involving people being tested to their limits, *The One That Got Away* and *A Night to Remember* being two excellent later examples.

Morocco ○
1930, US, 92 mins, b/w
Dir: Joseph Von Sternberg
Stars: Gary Cooper, Marlene Dietrich, Adolphe Menjou
Rating: ★★★

Marlene Dietrich's first American film cast her as the singer and adventuress Amy Jolly, ensnaring then being ensnared by legionnaire Gary Cooper. Brilliantly shot by Lee Garmes, whose work was nominated for an Oscar, *Morocco* is a film of shadows and shimmering heat, painstakingly directed for maximum effect by Dietrich's mentor Josef von Sternberg. Marlene never looked more alluring, and sings three songs, including 'What Am I Bid for My Apples?' A trail-blazing box-office success.

Morons from Outer Space ◖
1985, UK, 91 mins, colour
Dir: Mike Hodges
Stars: Mel Smith, Griff Rhys Jones, Dinsdale Landen, James B Sikking, Joanne Pearce
Rating: ★

M

Alas indeed that wonderful Mel Smith and Griff Rhys Jones should have got involved in this fifth-form farce about four low-IQ aliens at large on earth. Fortunately, both they and Jimmy (*Spender*) Nail have moved on to more suitable fare since. Best gag has Mel rescued from spacedrift by a repulsive alien who gives him the galactic heave-ho after finding that he isn't the right sex. Don't stay awake waiting for further laughs: there aren't any.

Mortal Thoughts ● Ⓥ

1991, US, 104 mins, colour
Dir: Alan Rudolph
Stars: Demi Moore, Glenne Headly, Bruce Willis, Harvey Keitel, John Pankow
Rating: ★★

A slick, flashback-framed psychological thriller which the director can't resist making too complex, with surges of slow-motion and an ending that is not only loaded with a creel-full of red herrings but doesn't play fair with what's gone before. By and large, though, this is a slickly-produced thriller starring real-life husband-and-wife Bruce Willis and Demi Moore, he cast as the no-good husband of Glenn Headly playing Moore's best friend. When Willis is murdered, the two women weave a web of deceit – and dogged detectives Havey Keitel and Co must root out the truth. Good performances in an offbeat, unsettling film.

Moscow on the Hudson ◐ Ⓥ

1984, US, 117 mins, colour
Dir: Paul Mazursky
Stars: Robin Williams, Maria Conchita Alonso, Cleavant Derricks, Alejandro Rey
Rating: ★★

This episodic account of the adventures of a Russian musician (Robin Williams) who defects to America in the middle of Bloomingdale's department store has some amusing moments but rather lacks charm. And it seems (no doubt deliberately on the part of director Paul Mazursky) that none of the people Vladimir comes into contact with is actually American. His lawyer is Cuban, his doctor Indian, his girlfriend Italian and so forth. This is partly because he lives in a ghetto district, although there would be sufficient novelty value in a Russian saxophonist to get him showbiz dates. Mazursky himself helped to write the script, which is peppered with sardonically amusing lines and situations. Interesting fare, though you may find it hard to get involved.

Mosquito Coast, The ◐ Ⓥ

1986, US, 117 mins, colour
Dir: Peter Weir
Stars: Harrison Ford, Helen Mirren, River Phoenix
Rating: ★★

Fans of Harrison Ford's action films will be sorely disappointed by this wordy, downbeat ecological drama. He's a father who rants and raves against pre-packaged, mass consumed American culture, and packs his unquestioning family off to the Mosquito Coast of Central America in search of a Utopian lifestyle. But as Ford's character begins to unravel, so does this film, even though scriptwriter Paul Schrader makes the anti-hero more attractive and likeable than he was in Paul Theroux's original novel. Helen Mirren has little to do in the underwritten role of his wife, but River Phoenix successfully started to branch out from teen pictures as the eldest son who reflects his father's complex character and also acts as narrator. It's yet another brave attempt by Australian director Peter Weir to explore an unfriendly culture caught in a moment of decision, but in the end the miserable ending is the film's undoing.

Mosquito Squadron ○

1968, UK, 90 mins, colour
Dir: Boris Sagal
Stars: David McCallum, Suzanne Neve, David Buck
Rating: ★★

It seems strange that anyone should still have wanted to make a standard World War Two action film in the late Sixties but, within the limited budget, experienced director Boris Sagal turns in a good job, with an exciting bombing raid at the end and sturdy performances.

Moss Rose ○

1947, US, 83 mins, b/w
Dir: Gregory Ratoff
Stars: Peggy Cummins, Victor Mature, Ethel Barrymore, Vincent Price
Rating: ★★★

Absorbing and well-acted Edwardian thriller that will keep most viewers busily guessing until the final reel. Peggy Cummins's cockney accent has to be heard to be believed, but Ethel Barrymore gives a splendid, full-blooded performance as a domineering old dowager. Vincent Price is at his best and most restrained as the policeman on the case.

Most Dangerous Game, The ○

(aka: The Hounds of Zaroff)
1932, US, 63 mins, b/w
Dir: Irving Pichel, Ernest B Schoedsack
Stars: Fay Wray, Joel McCrea, Leslie Banks, Robert Armstrong
Rating: ★★★

A classic, chilling chase story which has been remade and imitated many times since. It provided a showy debut role in the cinema for British actor Leslie Banks as the sadistic count. Badly wounded in World War One, Banks had bravely resumed his career that was to be dogged by illness in its later years. Among the stars he menaces here is the lustrous Fay Wray who was to fall into the clutches of an even bigger monster the following year when she starred in *King Kong*.

Mother, Jugs and Speed ○

1976, US, 95 mins, colour
Dir: Peter Yates
Stars: Bill Cosby, Raquel Welch, Harvey Keitel, Larry Hagman
Rating: ★★

One of those films that goes off in all directions. It's a case of love me, love my moods in this black comedy about rival ambulance services. And, while the funny bits are often very funny, the serious stuff works less well. Bill Cosby pulls the twin shafts of the plot with most success, and you have to admire a film that can make you fall about – Raquel Welch proves surprisingly adept with some of Tom Mankiewicz's wittier dialogue – after a couple of dramatic disasters.

Mother's Boys ● Ⓥ

1993, US, 95 mins, colour
Dir: Yves Simoneau
Stars: Jamie Lee Curtis, Peter Gallagher, Joanne Whalley-Kilmer, Vanessa Redgrave, Joss Ackland
Rating: ★

A laughably ludicrous, if not entirely unenjoyable chiller starring Jamie Lee Curtis as an unbalanced woman who walked out on her husband and three boys a few years ago. Now that hubby (Peter Gallagher) has fallen in love with a teacher (Joanne Whalley-Kilmer), and sues for a divorce, his ex-wife decides she wants her family back. None of what follows is soundly enough based to have any impact beyond making you giggle, leading to a quite preposterous climax, with a car balanced on a tree overhanging a chasm. Jamie Lee tries hard in a blonde wig to be bad, and Joanne tries hard to be good, but both are wildly cast against type and arouse the wrong sort of reaction. Gallagher is just lost open-mouthed in the middle. Vanessa Redgrave is in for a few lines as granny and to give her stunt girl a chance to fall spectacularly down a flight of stairs.

Mother Wore Tights ○
1947, US, 107 mins, colour
Dir: Walter Lang
Stars: Betty Grable, Dan Dailey, Mona Freeman
Rating: ★★★

Probably the best of the post-war Betty Grable-Dan Dailey musicals at Fox, with superior direction by Walter Lang and dazzling colour camerawork by Harry Jackson. Alfred Newman won an Oscar for the best scoring of a musical and the film was a tremendous public success. The voice of the narrator is that of Oscar-winning actress Anne Baxter, who ironically co-starred with Dailey the following year in a not dissimilar musical called *You're My Everything*.

Moulin Rouge ○ ⓥ
1952, UK, 120 mins, colour
Dir: John Huston
Stars: Jose Ferrer, Colette Marchand, Zsa Zsa Gabor, Christopher Lee
Rating: ★★★

This stunningly beautiful film was director John Huston's second picture in a British studio; he had filmed interiors for *The African Queen* at Isleworth Studios the previous year. He and Antony Veiller did a strong job of adapting Pierre La Mure's fictionalised biography of the famed French artist Toulouse-Lautrec for the screen. Jose Ferrer's extraordinary performance earned him an Academy Award nomination. The film, too, was nominated as Best Picture, Huston received an Oscar nomination as director and Colette Marchand, playing Marie, also received an Oscar nomination. The superb colour cinematography by Oswald Morris and Paul Sheriff's art direction created an impressive evocation of 19th century Montmartre. Film buffs will be pleased to see the Peter 'Frankenstein' Cushing and Christopher 'Dracula' Lee make pre-horror stardom appearances, although not in the same scene.

Mountain, The ○
1956, US, 105 mins, colour
Dir: Edward Dmytryk
Stars: Spencer Tracy, Robert Wagner, Claire Trevor, William Demarest
Rating: ★★

Beautifully photographed tale of selflessness and greed which maintains a high degree of suspense. Spencer Tracy, as usual, displays a quiet dignity that take one's attention away from the plot's shortcomings. At times Tracy looks as imposing as the mountain with his crevasse-lined face capped by snowy hair, while Robert Wagner has winning but ruthless charm – although the disparity in their ages (they play brothers) is rather disconcerting.

Mountains of the Moon ● ⓥ
1989, US, 135 mins, colour
Dir: Bob Rafelson
Stars: Patrick Bergin, Iain Glen, Richard E Grant, Fiona Shaw, Anna Massey
Rating: ★★★

The story of explorers Burton and Speke and their search for the source of the Nile in the 1800's gains new life in this handsomely produced account. It has the added trimmings of some spicy sex scenes between Burton (Patrick Bergin) and his wife-to-be (the interesting Fiona Shaw) and red-blooded violence in which steel is quite often seen to penetrate flesh in one way or another – whether slowly, or with the speed of the spear that splits Burton (who survives) from cheekbone to cheekbone in one of the action's early skirmishes. Although the film's final segment telescopes a few years, director Bob Rafelson can certainly be excused such licence in view of the dramatic effect it achieves. Overall, the narrative is a little long, and contains a number of minor scenes which could have been trimmed more ruthlessly. The performance, though, are unquestionably 'on the money', especially Richard E Grant's unctuous Oliphant, using both Speke's homosexual nature and his own cunning persuasion to set the explorers at odds with one another for his own publishing gain.

Mouse and his Child, The ☉
1977, US, 83 mins, colour
Dir: Chuck Swenson
Rating: ★

Too much talk and not enough action sinks this dullish cartoon, which sets

out to be a sort of *Pinocchio* of the mouse world. The film's dialogue and sentiments will be over the heads of most children, despite the efforts of a talented voice cast that includes Peter Ustinov, Cloris Leachman, Andy Devine (his last work in films, appropriately as the voice of a frog), Neville Brand and Sally Kellerman.

Mouse on the Moon, The ○
1963, UK, 85 mins, colour
Dir: Richard Lester
Stars: Margaret Rutherford, Bernard Cribbins, Ron Moody, June Ritchie
Rating: ★★★

A sequel to the Peter Sellers comedy hit, *The Mouse that Roared*. This time, the tiny Duchy of Great Fenwick joins the space race! Ron Moody's crafty prime minister, and Margaret Rutherford's Grand Guignol-style Queen Gloriana make it well worth watching.

Mouse that Roared, The ○ ⓥ
1959, UK, 85 mins, colour
Dir: Jack Arnold
Stars: Peter Sellers, Jean Seberg
Rating: ★★★

Peter Sellers is at his sparkling, zany best in this comedy satire with a Richard Lester touch (in fact, Lester directed the sequel *The Mouse on the Moon*) about a tiny European kingdom which declares war on the United States. Sellers plays Tully Bascombe, who leads his country's chain-mailed 'army' in its invasion, launched so that Grand Fenwick won't have to go bankrupt. Besides Tully, Sellers also plays the Prime Minister of Grand Fenwick and also its decaying queen, Gloriana. Director Jack Arnold, mostly associated with chillers such as *The Incredible Shrinking Man*, puts the fun across in free and easy style, and the visual gags include one great belly-laugh built around the television series *Robin Hood*.

Move Over Darling ○ ⓥ
1963, US, 103 mins, colour
Dir: Michael Gordon
Stars: Doris Day, James Garner, Polly Bergen, Chuck Connors, Thelma Ritter
Rating: ★★★

This comedy about a wife who returns from the dead (actually a desert island) was the film on which Marilyn Monroe was working just before she died. It was re-modelled for Doris Day and right from the outset she seems

M

determined to make the star part her own creation, attacking it with tremendous verve, and turning what could have been a routine sex comedy into a gay and amusing occasion. Thelma Ritter has too little to do, but 'nervous' comedian Don Knotts has a few acid moments as a shoe salesman; crusty Edgar Buchanan makes his mark as a divorce judge; and waspish comic actor Fred Clark is so good as a hotel manager that it's a pity we couldn't have seen more of him. The plot has been filmed twice before: as *My Favourite Wife* in 1940, and as *Three for the Show*, in 1955.

Movers and Shakers ◐
1985, US, 80 mins, colour
Dir: William Asher
Stars: Walter Matthau, Charles Grodin, Steve Martin, Gilda Radner, Tyne Daly
Rating: RB

Could you believe that a comedy film with the above cast could, even at 80 minutes, be a total waste of time? You wouldn't? Then you have a reason for seeing one of the few films we've ever watched in which almost nothing seems to happen. 'It looks very nice,' says one of the characters early on, about a stone dinosaur. 'But it just doesn't move.' Yes, well, there's no answer to that. The 'plot', written by Charles Grodin whose talent with the pen is usually much sharper than this, is about a film company that buys the title of a best-selling sex manual and tries to conjure a movie therefrom. They fail, and so does the film, which has powder-puff dialogue, rooted camerawork and performances in search of a director.

Moving Target, The
See: Harper

Mr & Mrs Bridge ◐ Ⓥ
1990, US, 124 mins, colour
Dir: James Ivory
Stars: Paul Newman, Joanne Woodward, Robert Sean Leonard, Kyra Sedgwick, Blythe Danner, Simon Callow
Rating: ★★★

Both a pleasant study of upper-class American life 50 years ago and a scrutiny of repressed womanhood, this is an opportunity for Paul Newman and Joanne Woodward to shine, with performances that, though not always naturalistic, are carefully presented for our inspection, reflection and pleasure. The story spans roughly the years 1930 to 1945. Mrs Bridge, though secure in her family, remains a totally subjugated housewife whose conse-

quently disturbed nature gives rise to occasional tearful outbursts. Husband Walter is a stuffy lawyer with rigid principles who is desirous of his wife, as he puts it, but not always affectionate as he might be. Although rather heavily preoccupied with sexual relations, this is nonetheless rather a gentle and old-fashioned film by to-day's standards, with one or two particularly fine sequences, such as the scene in which the Bridges sit firm at their dinner table while a tornado howls outside and the rest of the restaurant customers cower in the cellar. Inevitably, the film is also a little dull at times and the ending, with its explanatory captions, is strange: almost as if the producers had run out of money.

Mr and Mrs North ○
1941, US, 67 mins, b/w
Dir: Robert B Sinclair
Stars: Gracie Allen, William Post Jr
Rating: ★★

Gracie Allen without George Burns seems pretty strange, and indeed it's difficult to see why George couldn't have played Mr North in this story of a couple of amateur sleuths. The results are sometimes funny, sometimes strained, but there's a good supporting cast, including Tom Conway, Virginia Grey, Rose Hobart, Porter Hall, Millard Mitchell, Jerome Cowan and Felix Bressart. William Post Jr is a rather nebulous Mr North, while Paul Kelly is the Norths' harassed police adversary. Also in there somewhere is Keye Luke, famous as Charlie Chan's meddlesome son. The Norths first became famous on American radio; in a long series on British radio, they were played by Bernard Braden and Barbara Kelly.

Mr and Mrs Smith ○
1941, US, 95 mins, b/w
Dir: Alfred Hitchcock
Stars: Carole Lombard, Robert Montgomery, Gene Raymond, Jack Carson
Rating: ★★

Alfred Hitchcock's single stab at screwball comedy teams Carole Lombard and Robert Montgomery successfully as a couple discovering their marriage wasn't legal. Hitch makes his customary guest appearance, this time as a down and out cadging money for drink. Miss Lombard directed this scene, making the director do it over and over again, demanding more and more powder to

cover his reddening face. It was her way of getting back at him for all the practical jokes he'd perpetrated on set.

Mr Arkadin
See: Confidential Report

Mr Ashton Was Indiscreet
See: The Senator Was Indiscreet

Mr Baseball ◐ Ⓥ
1992, US, 113 mins, colour
Dir: Fred Schepisi
Stars: Tom Selleck, Ken Takakura, Dennis Haysbert, Aya Takanashi
Rating: ★★

Given that one nation can see as strengths the qualities that another nation sees as weaknesses, that America is as culturally different to Japan as chalk to cheese, and that popular Tom Selleck barges bear-like through his role as a fading baseball player transferred from the US to Japan, we could have had the makings of a marvellously funny culture-clash comedy. Sadly, there is just not enough originality in this formula frolic, every development signposted from Selleck's initial smart-Alec stance to his conversion to a human being thanks to the love of a Japanese girl. Selleck is engaging as the head-in-the-clouds hero, but it's not enough to make this any more than pleasant fun.

Mr Belvedere Rings the Bell ○
1951, US, 87 mins, b/w
Dir: Henry Koster
Stars: Clifton Webb, Joanne Dru, Hugh Marlowe, Zero Mostel
Rating: ★★

The last of the three Belvedere comedies which began with the character's unforgettable appearance in *Sitting Pretty*, when he poured a bowl of breakfast food over an errant baby's head. This time it is the other end of the age scale: Belvedere, the self-styled genius, once again played by crusty Clifton Webb is let loose on an old folks' home.

Mr Billion ○
1977, US, 93 mins, colour
Dir: Jonathan Kaplan
Stars: Terence Hill, Valerie Perrine, Jackie Gleason, Slim Pickens
Rating: ★★★

This light-hearted action romp is fast, furious and fun. Italian leading man Terence Hill, simply bursting with star quality (although previously best known in spaghetti Westerns) made a belated Hollywood debut as the garage mechanic who suddenly comes into a fortune and is immediately beset by homicidal vultures who will stop at nothing to get their hands on it. Hill and Valerie Perrine (she's the femme fatale who falls for her intended victim) do all that could be asked of them. But it's a writer's and director's film. Both script and treatment are full of quirky little touches that mark the film as above average of its kind. 'Wait,' pleads a rapist cornered by Hill, 'perverts are people too.' But Hill is undoubtedly the man to watch – and watch him you do, every incident-filled step of the way.

Mr Blandings Builds His Dream House ○
1948, US, 84 mins, b/w
Dir: H C Potter
Stars: Cary Grant, Myrna Loy, Melvyn Douglas, Jason Robards
Rating: ★★★★

Cary Grant and Myrna Loy delight, and H C Potter directs with immense good humour, in this lovable tale of two city people who have a house built in the country to their own special and somewhat extravagant specifications, and get taken for a ride by every country trickster in sight. The plot was re-worked nearly 40 years later for Tom Hanks and Shelley Long as *The Money Pit*.

Mr Deeds Goes to Town ○
1936, US, 118 mins, b/w
Dir: Frank Capra
Stars: Gary Cooper, Jean Arthur, George Bancroft, Lionel Stander
Rating: ★★★★

Country bumpkin Gary Cooper inherits $20 million and finds himself the centre of curious attention in sophisticated New York. Jean Arthur is the hard-nosed reporter sent by an equally hard-nosed editor to ridicule Cooper and his honest country ways. As you might expect, she falls in love with him. Even in 1936, this plot wasn't exactly fresh, but the perfect casting and delightful playing of Cooper and Arthur, coupled with Frank Capra's light but observant directional touch, made this an instant hit and a lasting classic. The character of Deeds is not particularly real, but Capra's trick is making you want to believe people like him exist (a device he used in all his films). So sit and watch honesty and sincerity win the

day against the smart guys and the cynics – you won't often see it happen in real life!

Mr Denning Drives North ○
1951, UK, 93 mins, b/w
Dir: Anthony Kimmins
Stars: John Mills, Phyllis Calvert, Sam Wanamaker
Rating: ★★★

This vehicle for John Mills at the height of his success as the most popular star of British cinema walks the tightrope between suspense and comedy with varying degrees of success. A difficult subject (Mills' character accidentally kills his daughter's blackmailing lover) to treat as a comedy-thriller and director Anthony Kimmins and writer Alec Coppel, even though working from Coppel's own novel, don't quite pull it off. There are some good performances, notably from Mills himself, and from Herbert Lom, as the crook he kills.

Mr Drake's Duck ☉
1950, UK, 85 mins, b/w
Dir: Val Guest
Stars: Douglas Fairbanks Jr, Yolande Donlan, Wilfred Hyde White, A E Matthews
Rating: ★★★

This fast-moving city-couple-down-on-the-farm comedy was a widespread favourite in its day and was pretty much along the successful furrows ploughed by *George Washington Slept Here* and *The Egg and I*. Yolande Donlan is a scatterbrained delight as the wife who (accidently) buys a duck that lays uranium eggs, and the situations come up fresh and funny. A good laugh.

Mr Hobbs Takes a Vacation ○
1962, US, 110 mins, colour
Dir: Henry Koster
Stars: James Stewart, Maureen O'Hara, Fabian, John Saxon, Reginald Gardiner, Marie Wilson
Rating: ★★

The first of James Stewart's three 'harassed father' comedies at 20th Century-Fox in the early Sixties. Here he tries to cope with a nightmare holiday home as well as a difficult family, whose members include Lauri Peters, whose next role took her to Britain as Cliff Richard's leading lady in *Summer Holiday*. There are some amusing anecdotes involving plumbing and the like, but the

enterprise is rather a long way from such previous Stewart comic glories as *The Jackpot*.

Mr Lucky ○
1943, US, 98 mins, b/w
Dir: H C Potter
Stars: Cary Grant, Laraine Day, Charles Bickford, Gladys Cooper
Rating: ★★★

An engaging comedy drama with lots of sharp little cameo performances, this story of a gambler reformed by love was later remade (very loosely) as *Gambling House*. Cary Grant's charisma in the title role ensured that the film, though nothing special, took more than $2 million at the box-office, a healthy return in Hollywood's wartime years.

Mr Majestyk ◐
1974, US, 103 mins, colour
Dir: Richard Fleischer
Stars: Charles Bronson, Al Lettieri, Linda Cristal
Rating: ★★★

If you can actually believe in Charles Bronson as a simple watermelon farmer who won't bow down to the local syndicate, you could find this more exciting than the average latter-day Bronson thriller. Nifty direction by Richard Fleischer makes the most of the action set-pieces. Good supporting work by Al Lettieri and Paul Koslo as two sneering bad guys, plus a script by Elmore Leonard that's surprisingly witty as well as hard-hitting.

Mr Music ○
1950, US, 108 mins, b/w
Dir: Richard Haydn
Stars: Bing Crosby, Nancy Olson, Charles Coburn, Ruth Hussey
Rating: ★★★

Tuneful Bing Crosby musical, additionally enlivened by the appearance of such guest stars as Peggy Lee, Dorothy Kirsten and, in particular, Groucho Marx. Bing plays a lazy songwriter whose friends hire a super-efficient secretary (the gorgeous Nancy Olson) to keep him on his toes. Richard Haydn, who plays a featured role, also directed.

Mr Nanny ○ ⓥ
(aka: Rough Stuff)
1993, US, 84 mins, colour
Dir: Michael Gottlieb

M

Stars: Terry 'Hulk' Hogan, Austin Pendleton, David Johansen
Rating: ★

After the modest success of *Suburban Commando*, wrestler Hulk Hogan crashes to the canvas with a resounding thump in this almost unbearable action-comedy about a wrestler hired as bodyguard to two hell-raising kids who have got rid of more nannies than Jane and Michael Banks in *Mary Poppins*. The plot, apart from the traps the kids set for the unwary Hulk, has them as offspring of a genius scientist (Austin Pendleton) who's invented a microchip that the bad guys, led by manic mastermind David Johansen (who happens to be Hulk's old nemesis) are dying to get their hands on. Johansen proves to be a madly mugging villain, whose OTT rants are allowed to stop the plot (such as it is) in its tracks far too often. And parents should be advised that many of the pranks the children play are potentially lethal. In fact, while dad is dozing off in this one, the kids may be taking notes for a surprise on his next trip downstairs.

Mr North ○ Ⓥ
1988, US, 93 mins, colour
Dir: Danny Huston
Stars: Anthony Edwards, Lauren Bacall, Robert Mitchum, Anjelica Huston, Mary Stuart Masterson, Harry Dean Stanton
Rating: ★★★

Danny Huston, son of John, sadly hasn't directed another film since this gentle, inoffensive tale of a young traveller whose bedside manner and soothing healing ways make him the toast of decadent Rhode Island society in 1926. Though the film meanders and occasionally falters, it's kept afloat by the class of the acting and the maintenance of an even pace and tenor, as Mr North brushes aside his detractors and paddles across the tricky waters of the *nouveau riche* with scarcely a ripple impeding his progress. The dog charm of Anthony Edwards is perfectly placed in the central role, and there's sympathetic support from players who hit exactly the note required, especially Robert Mitchum, Mary Stuart Masterson, Harry Dean Stanton (as a fake English butler!) and the delicious Virginia Madsen. The music (David McHugh) too never puts a note out of place in its tuneful elegance, even when Mr North is being pursued across town by dozens of would-be patients hoping for his healing touch.

Mr Peabody and the Mermaid ○
1948, US, 89 mins, b/w
Dir: Irving Pichel
Stars: William Powell, Ann Blyth, Irene Hervey
Rating: ★★

William Powell was well into his avuncular period when he made this mermaid comedy hot on the tail of the earlier British success with *Miranda*. This American copy isn't as effective, but Powell is always watchable and has one glorious scene when he buys the top half of a swimsuit and tries to explain its purpose to the mermaid, coyly played by Ann Blyth. 'Prissy' comedy actor Clinton Sundberg also has a good role, as the press agent of the holiday resort where Powell encounters the finny charmer.

Mr Perrin and Mr Traill ○
1948, UK, 92 mins, b/w
Dir: Lawrence Huntington
Stars: David Farrar, Marius Goring, Greta Gynt
Rating: ★★★

Penetrating study of the way that resentment can eat away inside a man until it makes him do something quite out of character. Marius Goring is excellent as the middle-aged schoolmaster whose idiosyncratic but secure little world begins to crumble beneath his feet when a younger teacher chips away both at his authority and his aspirations to romance. Absorbing, unusual and worthwhile drama.

Mr Saturday Night ○ Ⓥ
1992, US, US mins, colour
Dir: Billy Crystal
Stars: Billy Crystal, Julie Warner, David Paymer, Jerry Lewis, Jerry Orbach, Ron Silver
Rating: ★★

A curious mixture of good and not-so-good, this is the kind of film that looked better 30 years ago. Billy Crystal is the nightclub comedian who abuses those about him and whose nasty streak shows through everything he does. But he is funny: on and off. Only his wife (Julie Warner) and brother (David Paymer) stand by him for long and at the outset of the film we find him in his 60s, with a career that has long since gone down the toilet. 'You took every bad break you ever had – and made it worse,' Paymer tells him in a rare break from their jokey, but always

master-and-servant-like relationship. Cue for a flashback, of which there should be more: the film carries too much of Crystal in unconvincing old-age makeup (Paymer ages much more gracefully and deserved his Oscar nomination) and too many downbeat scenes involving his vitriolic if occasionally poisonously funny outbursts against those around him. Still, there are funny moments here and there and moving ones, too. Jerry Lewis does a guest-turn as himself and proves he's still capable of turning on the 'idiot' voice that won him fame.

Mrs Doubtfire ○ Ⓥ
1993, US, 125 mins, colour
Dir: Chris Columbus
Stars: Robin Williams, Sally Field, Pierce Brosnan, Harvey Fierstein
Rating: ★★★

Too much sentiment and not enough fun blemish this great idea which gives Robin Williams – an actor of enormous comic talent if limited charm – a dream role as the divorced husband who disguises himself as a Scottish housekeeper (who keeps saying she comes from England) to be near his three beloved kids. Whether the disguise is good enough to pull the wool over ex wife Sally Field's eyes, especially as Williams slips and snarls his way out of character too often, is another matter. But there are a good many bright patches around here, especially when Williams, out of drag, demonstrates his mastery of a string of famous voices in a session with his social worker. Pierce Brosnan has a thankless role as the other man in Field's life but comes through it pretty well. And Harvey Fiersten is quite a laugh as Williams' gay brother. Not much of the film pays attention to logic – what out-of-work father could afford an entire children's zoo for a party or cough up $140 on the spot for fast-food meals? – but then the rules aren't quite the same for comedy. Parents should note a sprinkling of bad language and suggestive dialogue: it underlines that subtlety is not one of this film's strengths. A field day, though, for fans of the star.

Mr Skeffington ○
1944, US, 127 mins, b/w
Dir: Vincent Sherman
Stars: Bette Davis, Claude Rains, Walter Abel, Richard Waring, George Colouris
Rating: ★★★

The inimitable Bette Davis was perfectly cast as the vain and selfish young woman who marries for money in this lavish melodrama which progresses from the turn of the century through to 1944. This was Davis's 53rd picture and she was nominated for an Oscar for the role, but lost to Ingrid Bergman (for *Gaslight*). A soap opera to end them all, it's heartrending stuff and Davis is finely complemented by her distinguished co-star, Claude Rains, as the long-suffering Skeffington. The whole is deftly directed by Vincent Sherman, one of Warners' leading directors, who extracted one of Davis's most complex performances.

Mrs Mike ○
1949, US, 98 mins, b/w
Dir: Louis King
Stars: Dick Powell, Evelyn Keyes
Rating: ★★

Tough stuff, this turn-of-the-century romantic drama set in the wilds of the Canadian northwest and based on a true story. Evelyn Keyes is Boston girl Kathy O'Fallon, who marries Canadian mounted policeman Dick Powell and swaps the comforts of urban life for the hardships of pioneering. Predictably, every imaginable hazard is encountered, with laughter and tears thrown in. Joseph Biroc's camera captures very effectively the great Canadian outdoors, Keyes and Powell are both sympathetic in their roles, and Powell even gets the chance to sing!

Mr Smith Goes to Washington ○ ⓥ
1939, US, 129 mins, b/w
Dir: Frank Capra
Stars: James Stewart, Jean Arthur, Claude Rains, Edward Arnold, Thomas Mitchell, Guy Kibbee
Rating: ★★★★

Nominated for eight Oscars, Frank Capra's magnificently corny epic of the 'little man' taking on corrupt politicians remains one of the cinema's enduring clasics, with splendid performances all round. Young James Stewart, perfectly cast as the heart-breakingly sincere country boy, is delightfully teamed with lovely Jean Arthur, a city slicker secretary with a well concealed heart of gold. Edward Arnold and Claude Rains make a formidable pair of villains, but Harry Carey's late appearance (as the Senate president) almost steals the whole show. Be prepared, though, for an over-hasty climax.

Mrs O'Malley and Mr Malone ○
1950, US, 69 mins, b/w
Dir: Norman Taurog
Stars: Marjorie Main, James Whitmore, Ann Dvorak, Fred Clark
Rating: ★★

Despite a tasty supporting cast, character stars Marjorie Main – she of the steely gaze and rasping voice – and James Whitmore are really the whole show in the energetic MGM programme-filler about a widow and a lawyer involved with murders on a train. No great shakes, but worth it just to hear Main singing 'Possum Up a Gum Stump'.

Mrs Parkington ○
1944, US, 124 mins, b/w
Dir: Tay Garnett
Stars: Greer Garson, Walter Pidgeon, Edward Arnold, Dan Duryea, Agnes Moorehead, Cecil Kellaway
Rating: ★★★

Fifth teaming of Greer Garson and Walter Pidgeon in a typical grand-scale MGM vehicle for their popular talents, chronicling the fortunes over 60 years of a maid who becomes a great lady. Great supporting roles from pompous Edward Arnold and shifty Dan Duryea as two of the dowager Garson's grasping relations. The epic stature to which the film aspired is effortlessly reached by director Tay Garnett and a great production team, entirely overcoming an indifferent script to bring a lump to the throat at the end.

Mrs Soffel ◐ ⓥ
1984, US, 110 mins, colour
Dir: Gillian Armstrong
Stars: Diane Keaton, Mel Gibson, Matthew Modine
Rating: ★★

In 1901, the wife of the warden of Pittsburgh Prison sneaked hacksaws to two convicted murderers she believed innocent and deserted hearth and home (and four children) to run off with them through snow-covered countryside towards Canada. This film by Australian director Gillian Armstrong, who made *My Brilliant Career*, examines at some length the all-consuming passion that led to such a hopeless action. In casting Diane Keaton as the 35-ish Bible-pushing wife and Mel Gibson as the main object of her obsession, Armstrong cheats to a degree, since the physical attraction of Miss Keaton at her most

luminous and Mr Gibson at his most casually charming is all too obvious. Even so, one is drawn along to the story's inevitable end in fairly hypnotic fashion. The dingy backgrounds outside of the prison scenes fairly creak with Victorian trappings and indeed Kate Soffel's family life is sketched in with rather too much warmth for our ease in accepting her flight from it. But Keaton lightens this strain by skilfully steering Mrs Soffel from soberly loving mother to faintly zany fugitive. Gibson's American accent is again amazingly good and fans of the stars will enjoy them in these slightly offbeat roles.

Much Ado about Nothing ◐ ⓥ
1993, US/UK, 113 mins, colour
Dir: Kenneth Branagh
Stars: Kenneth Branagh, Emma Thompson, Michael Keaton, Denzel Washington, Keanu Reeves, Robert Sean Leonard
Rating: ★★

Kenneth Branagh's second joust with the Bard is a bit of a mixed bag. Most successful in its comedy content, especially the dialogue shared by Branagh and Emma Thompson, it fares less well with the plot's heavier melodrama, while the musical interludes have much the same effect as one of Harpo Marx's solos or a Bing Crosby ballad in a *Road* film: yup, just time to get the popcorn. The main interest lies in seeing stars more familiar in other kinds of film: Denzel Washington (very good) as the noble Don Pedro – here depicted as a kind of John Wayne loner; Michael Keaton, rather too obnoxious as the constable, Dogberry; and Keanu Reeves, working hard on his sneer as the dastardly Don John. There are nice supporting performances from Phyllida Law (Emma's mum) and from Richard Clifford as one of Reeves' henchmen. Branagh and Thompson invent some tasty bits of comic business (especially one involving Branagh's trying to erect a medieval deck chair) and it all runs along like a roistering and raunchy pantomime. On balance the best bits are worth waiting for.

Much Too Shy ○
1942, UK, 92 mins, b/w
Dir: Marcel Varnel
Stars: George Formby, Eileen Bennett, Jimmy Clitheroe
Rating: ★★

M

A George Formby wartime lark, notably for the appearance of diminutive Lancashire comedian Jimmy Clitheroe, then only 20 but later to become phenomenally popular as star of the radio comedy series The Clitheroe Kid. The cameraman is Arthur Crabtree, who successfully turned director two years later with *Madonna of the Seven Moons* and *They Were Sisters*. Formby's ukelele-accompanied ditties in this one include 'I'm Delivering the Morning Milk' and 'They Laughed When I Started to Play'.

Mudlark, The ○
1951, UK, 98 mins, b/w
Dir: Jean Negulesco
Stars: Irene Dunne, Alec Guinness, Andrew Ray, Anthony Steel, Finlay Currie, Wilfred Hyde White
Rating: ★★★

Thank goodness Hollywood resisted what must have been an overwhelming desire to call this fascinating and charming piece of whimsy something like 'The Queen and the Kid'. Irene Dunne makes rather hard work of being Queen Victoria, and loses out along the line to Andrew Ray – son of Ted – in the title role, and to Alec Guinness' brilliant Disraeli.

Mummy, The ◑
1932, US, 72 mins, b/w
Dir: Karl Freund
Stars: Boris Karloff, Zita Johann
Rating: ★★★

Boris Karloff's make-up as the mummy, layered on to his face filament by filament, is masterly in this vintage shocker – really giving the impression of having been hidden away for centuries; you can almost smell the must and dust. Bramwell Fletcher gives one of his best film portrayals as one of the men he frightens, and the visuals are most impressive under the direction of Karl Freund, an expert cinematographer who made too few appearances in the director's chair.

Mummy, The ◑
1959, UK, 88 mins, colour
Dir: Terence Fisher
Stars: Peter Cushing, Christopher Lee, Yvonne Furneaux,
Rating: ★★

Director Terence Fisher's remake of *The Mummy's Hand* completed a Hammer/Fisher trilogy after their

versions of the Frankenstein and Dracula stories. Christopher Lee is almost unrecognisable beneath layers of skilful make-up as the mummy who avenges himself on those who have defiled his tomb. Boris Karloff's original had first appeared in 1933. The trouble with it, and practically every other mummy film since, is that, although the initial appearance of the mummy, re-awakening after thousands of years, was suitably terrifying, writers rapidly ran out of ideas as to what to do with him once he was on the loose.

Munster Go Home! ○
1966, US, 90 mins, colour
Dir: Earl Bellamy
Stars: Fred Gwynne, Yvonne De Carlo, Al Lewis
Rating: ★★★

Remember the Munsters? They're a whole family of movie monsters, headed by Frankenstein's little creation, and here they are in their own film comedy. Representing the less familiar English branch of the family are Hermione Gingold (as Lady Effigie!), Terry-Thomas and Jeanne Arnold, constituting a terrible trio much agin' their American relatives. Watch, too, for a cadaverous John Carradine in a supporting role as Cruikshank.

Muppet Christmas Carol, The ⊙ ⓥ
1992, US/UK, 86 mins, colour
Dir: Brian Henson
Stars: Michael Caine, The Muppets
Rating: ★★★

If you can imagine that Charles Dickens was ever blue and furry and hung around with a rat, you are half-way to enjoying this irreverent Muppet version of the author's classic seasonal story. The Great Gonzo appears as Dickens, who narrates the tale with his sidekick Rizzo the Rat, quipping and wisecracking to keep both kids and adults amused. Michael Caine, the only human member of the cast as the miserly Scrooge, blends so well with the Muppet characters that Muppet and human are indistinguishable. Paul Williams' songs are apt and tuneful in a lively, colourful and witty show which Caine may well remember with affection as perhaps the highpoint of the latter stages of his checkered career.

Muppet Movie, The ⊙ ⓥ
1979, US, 97 mins, colour
Dir: James Frawley
Stars: Mel Brooks, Bob Hope, Telly Savalas
Rating: ★★★

Make way for the Muppets! Jim Henson and his personable puppet performers hit the big screen, with Kermit at his rightful place at the centre of things seeking his fame and fortune in Hollywood, and proving a wistful and appealing character in the process. Even though there's much original thought in the story, this remains a film primarily for children and aficionados – although there are guest stars galore for the unconverted, including Mel Brooks, Bob Hope and James Coburn.

Muppets take Manhattan, The ⊙ ⓥ
1984, US, 94m mins, colour
Dir: Frank Oz
Stars: Dabney Coleman, Art Carney, James Coco, Gregory Hines
Rating: ★★★

Kermit and company really do turn Manhattan into an isle of joy in this, the best of the Muppet films. Good story, witty script, inventive use of New York locations, and some very snappy verbal exchanges between Kermit and Miss Piggy. Kermit loses his memory and wanders the streets of New York. Miss Piggy is mugged in Central Park. Yes, all Muppet life is here. And there's even the big finish to end them all, with two of the main characters getting married on stage. It seemed that this might be the last of the Muppets on film, but happily they re-emerged years later with their version of *A Christmas Carol*.

Murder! ○
1930, UK, 100 mins, b/w
Dir: Alfred Hitchcock
Stars: Herbert Marshall, Norah Baring, Edward Chapman, Miles Mander
Rating: ★★★

This Hitchcock film is the rarely-seen follow-up to *Blackmail* and like most of the Master's most famous films, having a one-word title. *Murder!* contains some brilliant composition of scenes, as well as innovative devices that soon became cinema cliches, such as 'voice over' thoughts of a character seen in tight-lipped close-up; Hitchcock would still be working variations on this as late as *Psycho*. Herbert Marshall provides a reassuring star presence as the juror determined to prove a convicted girl's innocence. Norah Baring is sometimes quite touching as the girl, and the story is full of well-cast character stars who may or may not be the killer. Impressionistic sound is again used (as in *Blackmail*) proving particularly effective in the jury sequences.

Murder Ahoy ○

1964, UK, 74 mins, b/w
Dir: George Pollock
Stars: Margaret Rutherford, Lionel Jeffries
Rating: ★★★

The last of MGM's quartet of Miss Marple thrillers, with Margaret Rutherford tripping delightfully through a series of murders with a naval flavour. A number of familiar television faces – Francis Matthews, William Mervyn and Derek Nimmo among them – decorate the mayhem, but even Lionel Jeffries, as a snuff-taking seadog, is no match for Dame Margaret, who deservedly dominates the film. Her achievements here include a joyous sword-fight with the villain that runs the length and breadth of a ship. Her opening remark in this sequence is delicious.

Murder at the Gallop ○

1963, UK, 81 mins, b/w
Dir: George Pollock
Stars: Margaret Rutherford, Robert Morley, Flora Robson
Rating: ★★★

Agatha Christie's spinster detective Miss Marple rides again, literally, in a jolly little murder mystery which, apart from being set at a riding stable, sticks closely to the established Christie whodunnit formula: we open with one murder, witness another among the suspects, and finally see Miss Marple setting herself up as bait to catch the killer. Dame Margaret Rutherford's Miss Marple is at least twice as good as anything else in the film. Her double chin quivers with anticipation as she makes an important find or waits for the murderer to come into her room, and her extraordinarily mobile face expresses fiendish glee as she tells the hapless inspector (Charles Tingwell) that she has deduced who the murderer is. And, if it had nothing else to offer, the film would still be worth a look to see Dame Margaret doing the twist. Incidentally, one of the murder

weapons used is a hat-pin – so watch out for that maiden aunt next time you visit.

Murder at the Vanities ○

1934, US, 95 mins, b/w
Dir: Mitchell Leisen
Stars: Victor McLaglen, Carl Brisson, Jack Oakie, Kitty Carlisle
Rating: ★★

Acceptable mixture of murder and music with detective Victor McLaglen suspecting everyone in sight and songs that include 'Cocktails for Two' and 'Sweet Marijuana'. See if you can spot future star Ann Sheridan in the chorus.

Murder by Death ○

1976, US, 94 mins, colour
Dir: Robert Moore
Stars: Eileen Brennan, Alec Guinness, David Niven, Peter Sellers, James Coco, Maggie Smith
Rating: ★★

Neil Simon took time off from writing his hard-shelled, soft-centred romantic comedies set in the big city to pen this popular charade in which a fistful of well-known stars have the time of their lives playing famous detectives at large in a sinister country mansion. Although the script is not of Simon's highest quality, you'll enjoy the impersonations of legendary sleuths of fiction and the cinema. It's not too difficult to work out on which crime-solvers each of them is modelled.

Murder by Decree ●

1978, US, 112 mins, colour
Dir: Bob Clark
Stars: Christopher Plummer, James Mason, Genevieve Bujold, Donald Sutherland, David Hemmings
Rating: ★★★

Sherlock Holmes meets Jack the Ripper again. Despite a stellar cast, the real star of this gaslit chiller is production designer Harry Pottle, who creates narrow, grimy streets, vaguely welcoming taverns, gaunt wharves and battered Victorian slums with all the flair of the old Hollywood. The film itself does its job well as a baffling thriller until the superfluous last half-hour.

Murderers' Row ○ ⓥ

1966, US, 108 mins, colour
Dir: Henry Levin

Stars: Dean Martin, Ann-Margret, Karl Malden
Rating: ★★

The second screen adventure of singing spy Matt Helm (Dean Martin at his most relaxed), pitting him against villain Karl Malden, who plays superbly tongue-in-cheek. Some of the gadgetry is outrageously ingenious, although you may find Helm's backward-firing gun a little too nasty comfort

Murder, He Says ○

1945, US, 93 mins, b/w
Dir: George Marshall
Stars: Fred MacMurray, Helen Walker, Marjorie Main
Rating: ★★★

Fred MacMurray encounters a family of hayseed murderers in a kind of hillbilly version of *The Old Dark House*. The plot is as daft as it's devious but the situations are often very funny under the direction of George Marshall, who made Bob Hope's *The Cat and the Canary* and *The Ghost Breakers*.

Murder in Reverse ○

1945, UK, 88 mins, b/w
Dir: Montgomery Tully
Stars: William Hartnell, Chili Bouchier, Jimmy Hanley, Dinah Sheridan
Rating: ★★★

Age hasn't dulled the edge of this excellent British thriller about a man who serves 15 years for a murder he didn't commit. Made on a low budget, it's full of atmosphere and tension.

Murder in the Private Car ○

(aka: Murder on the Runaway Train)
1934, US, 63 mins, b/w
Dir: Harry Beaumont
Stars: Mary Carlisle, Charlie Ruggles, Una Merkel
Rating: ★★★

Director Harry Beaumont made his name with Jazz Age romps featuring Joan Crawford and Clara Bow. This is an uncharacteristic mystery thriller about a threatened heiress. A thoroughly enjoyable time-passer with some good character actors in the cast, among them Charlie Ruggles, Porter Hall, Una Merkel and Berton Churchill.

Murder in Thornton Square, The

See: Gaslight [1944]

M

Murder Man, The ○

1935, US, 70 mins, b/w
Dir: Tim Whelan
Stars: Spencer Tracy, Virginia Bruce, Lionel Atwill, James Stewart
Rating: ★★★

A snappy little thriller with Spencer Tracy at full throttle as a hard-drinking reporter who specialises in homicide scoops. James Stewart makes his film debut as another reporter, inaptly nicknamed Shorty. Said Tracy later of the man who was to become a lifelong friend: 'In his very first scene on film he showed he had all the good things.'

Murder Most Foul ○

1964, UK, 91 mins, b/w
Dir: George Pollock
Stars: Margaret Rutherford, Ron Moody, Charles Tingwell, Andrew Cruckshank, Dennis Price, Francesca Annis
Rating: ★★★

Agatha Christie's Miss Marple tackles a series of murders in a travelling repertory company. Charles Tingwell is again the long-suffering inspector, one of whose men is almost allowed to beat Miss Marple in an hilarious game of draughts. Margaret Rutherford, of course, is the film. Her triumph here includes a remarkable rendition of 'The Shooting of Dan McGrew' that has to be seen and heard to be believed. Dame Margaret won an Oscar for the glossy *The VIPs* of 1964. But it was for her eccentric lady sleuth and her superb stage work – in such plays as *The Importance of Being Earnest* – that she was most loved.

Murder, My Sweet

See: Farewell, My Lovely [1945]

Murder on Monday

See: Home at Seven

Murder on the Orient Express ○ ⓥ

1974, US, 131 mins, colour
Dir: Sidney Lumet
Stars: Albert Finney, Lauren Bacall, Martin Balsam, Ingrid Bergman, Sean Connery, Vanessa Redgrave
Rating: ★★

This star-studded, if laborious and deliberate, thriller has Albert Finney as Agatha Christie's detective Hercule Poirot, trying to find out who murdered tycoon Richard Widmark on the Orient Express in December 1935. There is a glitttering cast of

suspects to choose from and their performances range from great to ghastly. Bergman won an Oscar for her missionary lady forever muttering about 'little brown babies'.

Murder She Said ○

1961, UK, 86 mins, b/w
Dir: George Pollock
Stars: Margaret Rutherford, Arthur Kennedy, James Robertson Justice
Rating: ★★★

Dame Margaret Rutherford's first outing as Agatha Christie's spinster sleuth Miss Marple is a workmanlike adaptation of the novel *4.50 to Paddington*. The star has no trouble dominating her motley cast of suspects, even though they include Arthur Kennedy and James Robertson Justice. For a Christie mystery, the killer is fairly obvious. The success of this film gave rise to three more Miss Marple mysteries, usually featuring Charles Tingwell as the dogged Inspector Craddock, who never quite gets the better of Miss Marple, and with cameo roles for Dame Margaret's real-life actor husband, Stringer Davis.

Murders in the Rue Morgue ◐

1932, US, 62 mins, b/w
Dir: Robert Florey
Stars: Bela Lugosi, Sidney Fox
Rating: ★★★

John Huston had a hand in the writing of this expressionistic horror film, only distantly related to the Edgar Allen Poe story on which it's based. Bela Lugosi's eyes glitter as he invites prospective victims up for coffee. Pretty, diminutive Sidney Fox is an ideal frightened heroine. Silly but fun.

Murders in the Rue Morgue ●

1971, US/Spain, 87 mins, colour
Dir: Gordon Hessler
Stars: Jason Robards, Herbert Lom, Lilli Palmer, Christine Kaufmann, Adolfo Celi
Rating: ★★★

Gordon Hessler's most stylish horror film, baroque in effect, and reminiscent of the work of another director, Roger Corman, in its conception and execution. Poe addicts should be told right away that the only connection with the famous story of the same name is that it is being the enacted by the travelling company around whom the grisly plot revolves. But Hessler's sole aim is to shock and shock he does, by constantly edgy di-

rection and intelligent use of a recurring dream sequence that fascinates, entertains and skilfully maintains the theme. Ingeniously, the dream is partly explained, partly made to come true, before a down-beat ending which it would be spoiling your post-mid-night shivers to reveal. But I think that Poe would have approved of the climax and of the film.

Murders in the Zoo ○

1933, US, 64 mins, b/w
Dir: Edward Sutherland
Stars: Charles Ruggles, Lionel Atwill, Randolph Scott
Rating: ★★★

Strong stuff in its time, when short but grisly horror films were giving censors nightmares in more ways than one, *Murders in the Zoo* opens with mad Lionel Atwill sewing up the mouth of one of his wife's lovers before feeding him to one of the creatures in the zoo and almost never lets up, save for Charles Ruggles' comic relief. When the wife asks if her friend left a message, Atwill replies grimly, 'He didn't say anything.' A feast for horror fans (as well as the pythons and crocodiles), the film has fine cast that also includes Randolph Scott and Gail Patrick.

Murphy's Law ● ⓥ

1986, US, 100 mins, colour
Dir: J Lee Thompson
Stars: Charles Bronson, Kathleen Wilhoite, Carrie Snodgress
Rating: ★★★

A not-so-bad latter-day Charles Bronson thriller with lots of vivid action and a plot that works through to a logical and well-staged climax. It also allows good actress Carrie Snodgress to enjoy herself as the psycho who's bumping off all Bronson's friends because of a 10-year-old conviction. Bronson's whisky-cop, Jack Murphy, thinks it's the brother of a Mafia hood he's just gunned down who's framing him for the killings. And there's a fellow-cop who'd like nothing more than to see Murphy fry in the hot chair. All he's got to help him is a tough-talking street-criminal waif who keeps crossing his path. Newcomer Kathleen Wilhoite does what she can with this difficult and underwritten role, while director J Lee Thompson's prowling camera sometimes makes a striking setpiece out of a molehill of violence that isn't unpalatable by today's standards. The dialogue is marginally the right side of risibility and most of the performances only serviceable, save for the excellence of Snodgress, and Lawrence Tierney as a puffy private eye who's not destined to last long into the film. Hardened Bronson fans will like it; it doesn't do them wrong.

Murphy's Romance ◐
1985, US, 102 mins, colour
Dir: Martin Ritt
Stars: Sally Field, James Garner, Brian Kerwin, Corey Haim
Rating: ★★★

There's an old-fashioned haze to this Arizona romance that provides James Garner with his most 'character-full' leading role in a long while, and won him an Oscar nomination. Sally Field plays another of her now-familiar gutsy women of the outdoors as the divorcee who heads west to start a horse-training ranch (and a new life) with her 12-year-old son. She's befriended by widower Garner and has trouble with her ex-husband. It all works well enough, with Garner's laid-back charm making you wonder why the cinema always allowed him to slip back to the small screen. There's a nice running gag, too, about him refusing to reveal his age and the dialogue provides a few more warm chuckles along similar lines.

Murphy's War ◐
1970, UK, 108 mins, colour
Dir: Peter Yates
Stars: Peter O'Toole, Sian Phillips, Philippe Noiret, Horst Jansen
Rating: ★★★

Excellent colour photography on tropical locations and some stirring action scenes (especially in the last reel) put the fizz into this unusual war story. Peter O'Toole excels as the sole survivor of a German U-boat raid who carries on his own war from a settlement on the banks of the Orinoco River.

Music Box ◐ ⓥ
1989, US, 123 mins, colour
Dir: Costa-Gavras
Stars: Jessica Lange, Armin Mueller-Stahl, Frederic Forrest
Rating: ★★

A lawyer defends her father on charges of being a Nazi war criminal in his native Hungary. As the case veers one way, then the other, the audience is asked to share her doubts as to his innocence or guilt. Despite the subject matter, and the excellence of Jessica Lange's acting as the lawyer, though,

you'll find this only mildly involving, perhaps because of undynamic direction and the too-quiet performance of Armin Mueller-Stahl as the accused man. Well-made, if a mite overlong, the film doesn't match up to the excellence of other Costa-Gavras socio-political movies such as *Z, The Confession* and *Missing.* Most of the other portrayals are good, and Frederic Forrest gives one of his best performances as the prosecuting attorney. Although the story does remain interesting to the end, the outcome is never seriously in doubt, which perhaps accounts in part for the film's curiously muffled impact.

Music Lovers, The ● ⓥ
1971, UK, 122 mins, colour
Dir: Ken Russell
Stars: Richard Chamberlain, Glenda Jackson, Christopher Gable
Rating: ★

Controversial portrait of the life of Tchaikovsky, written by Melvyn Bragg and directed by the bad boy of British cinema, Ken Russell, who offers another full-frontal view of Glenda Jackson to follow the one in *Women in Love:* would that this film were anywhere near as good. Its scenes of sexual excess, however, at least ensured it of notoriety. The director really kicks over the traces in this lurid biography of the famous composer, who lived a short but gay life in Tsarist Russia before expiring of cholera (a scene in which Russell revels). Richard Chamberlain struggles gamely with the composer while Jackson nobly does her pieces as a nymphomaniac who can be relied on to go spectacularly mad in the end. Only the '1812' sequence works consistently well in a film that fails to endow its catalogue of depravities and deformities with any kind of depth. If only the composer's music had been allowed to speak for itself.

Music Man, The ☉ ⓥ
1961, US, 151 mins, colour
Dir: Morton Da Costa
Stars: Robert Preston, Shirley Jones, Buddy Hackett, Hermione Gingold
Rating: ★★★

A big, brassy, rumbustious musical packed with hummable tunes. Robert Preston repeats his Broadway triumph as the travelling swindler who breezes into River City, Iowa in 1912, and tells its citizens they 'have trouble with a capital T and that rhymes with P and that stands for Pool' – planning to

woo the youngsters away from playing pool and sell the citizens a fortune's worth of musical instruments to form a boys' band. Hermione Gingold also excels as a mayor's wife with an astonishing collection of hats and a firm conviction that all literature is smut.

Music of Chance, The ◐ ⓥ
1993, US, 95 mins, colour
Dir: Philip Haas
Stars: James Spader, Mandy Patinkin, Charles Durning, M Emmet Walsh, Joel Grey
Rating: ★★

There's something strange going on here all right. But be warned: debut director Philip Haas is not about to let us in on the secret. Driver Mandy Patinkin picks up a battered, bloodied roadside refugee James Spader (as you would) and gives him a ride. Spader proves to be a gambler, and Patinkin, whose inheritance appears to be on its last legs and who has mysteriously driven 97,000 miles in a year in his new car, has a proposition. Spader will take on two rich old pushovers at poker, and they'll share the proceeds. The pushovers (Charles Durning, Joel Grey) naturally win, and their opponents find themselves landed with a strange forfeit: they must build a huge wall on the estate to pay for their debts. When these are 'cleared' in 50 days, they are handed a bill for food and other 'expenses' and must work on. There is no escape, either, over high walls and barbed wire. This has a 'circular' kind of feel to it, as in the best chillers: the men seem to be trapped in some kind of descending spiral – but the problem is that nothing is ever explained. The ending is a surprise all right, but not very likely the kind you'll welcome. Christopher Penn and Samantha Mathis also have roles in this, so the acting is more competent that the director's grip on the plot.

Mutiny on the Bounty ○
1935, US, 135 mins, b/w
Dir: Frank Lloyd
Stars: Charles Laughton, Clark Gable, Franchot Tone
Rating: ★★★

In the days when there were so many films (especially from MGM) that attractions at London's Empire Cinema (Metro's English showcase) hardly ever ran longer than seven days, this great sea story packed them in for three weeks, and was sold out every

M

night. Frank Lloyd's direction captures the feel of the sea, and the harshness of the times, putting the film well ahead of the (nonetheless underrated) Marlon Brando remake of 27 years afterwards. It won an Academy Award for best film. Its highlight of course, is Charles Laughton's rigid and inhuman Bligh, ruthless in his treatment of the seamen. Remembered, imitated, caricatured, but never bettered, it stays indelibly in the mind long after the film is over.

Mutiny on the Bounty ○ ⓥ
1962, US, 185 mins, colour
Dir: Lewis Milestone
Stars: Marlon Brando, Trevor Howard, Richard Harris, Hugh Griffith, Richard Haydn
Rating: ★★★

Two of the screen's finest actors star in this giant-sized, stunningly-mounted remake of the 1935 classic, based on one of history's greatest true-life sea adventures. Marlon Brando and Trevor Howard each bring their own powerful individualism to contrasting roles in the spectacular drama of two men with opposing attitudes and opposite ideals whose inevitable clash is set against the barbaric cruelty of life aboard a Royal Navy Ship in the 18th century. Good action, spectacular colour photography, and many moving moments. It was directed by veteran Lewis Milestone, who became famous with *All Quiet on the Western Front*.

My Beautiful Laundrette ● ⓥ
1985, UK, 97 mins, colour
Dir: Stephen Frears
Stars: Gordon Warnecke, Daniel Day Lewis, Saeed Jaffrey, Roshan Seth, Shirley Anne Field
Rating: ★★★

An example of low-budget British film-making at its most abrasive, this little gem also did well in America where it grossed more than $5 million. Hanif Kureishi's award-winning script is funny, sexy, violent and perceptive by turn and treats its central homosexual love story in an honest and low-key way. The gutsy pivotal performances of Daniel Day Lewis (remarkable as a blond punk) and Gordon Warnecke (as his business partner and lover) are complemented by Saeed Jaffrey's deliciously underhand uncle – a sort of Pakistani South London Arthur Daley – and by Shirley Anne Field as his white mistress.

My Blue Heaven ● ⓥ
1990, US, 95 mins, colour
Dir: Herbert Ross
Stars: Steve Martin, Rick Moranis, Joan Cusack, Melanie Mayron, William Irwin
Rating: ★★★

It's good to see Steve Martin back in outright comedy and this one is a lot of fun. He's a laugh from the start as a Mafia gangster with loo-brush hair and sheer silk suits, transplanted by FBI agent Rick Moranis to Anytown America as part of the witness relocation programme. Naturally the Mafioso can't keep his fingers out of crime, not that he's fazed when DA Joan Cusack keeps arresting him: he knows Moranis will keep him out of jail and well protected from the hitmen who will try to bump him off. Dotty dialogue and a myriad of actional incidents make this one of the snappiest and cleanest Martin comedies in years. The highspot is a wild dance sequence in the middle of the film, when Martin teaches Moranis the marenga. And the fun escalates when the gangster discovers many of his old criminal associates, all living under aliases in the same area. Funny supporting turns from Melanie Mayron and William Irwin steal scenes from even these stars in a barrage of non-stop fun whose pace is dictated by its Latin-American beat.

My Bodyguard ○
1980, US, 96 mins, colour
Dir: Tony Bill
Stars: Chris Makepeace, Adam Baldwin, Matt Dillon, Ruth Gordon, John Houseman, Martin Mull
Rating: ★★★

A heartwarming teen drama about school bullying that leads to a touching relationship between two boys. It's a modest film that never lets its message get in the way of the story. Among the cast of then-unknowns is Matt Dillon as the school bully, while Adam Baldwin is a true find as the silent brooding hulk who instils terror in every boy, but turns out to be a gentle giant. The screenplay is honest, the teens talk the way teens do, and first-time director Tony Bill (himself an actor) strikes not one false note. Dave Grusin's brooding score adds immeasurably to the atmosphere.

My Brother Jonathan ○
1947, UK, 107 mins, b/w
Dir: Harold French
Stars: Michael Denison, Dulcie Gray
Rating: ★★★

An honest and entertaining piece of work about a doctor's life, this film made Michael Denison a British box-office star. The atmosphere of the old-time slum areas of the Black country is very well sustained. Watch out for a young Pete Murray in a supporting role.

My Cousin Rachel ○
1952, US, 98 mins, b/w
Dir: Henry Koster
Stars: Olivia de Havilland, Richard Burton
Rating: ★★★

Atmospheric and compelling film of Daphne Du Maurier's best-seller, a perfect example of the way they just don't make 'em any more. It was Richard Burton's first film in Hollywood and although, understandably, he didn't register too well in a slightly weak role which is always subsidiary to Olivia de Havilland's splendid Rachel, his next two performances (in *The Robe* and *The Desert Rats*) established him as powerful actor of the widest range. The mood of *My Cousin Rachel* is magnificently all of a piece, achieved by the combined efforts of director Henry Koster, composer Franz Waxman and photographer Joseph La Shelle. With few equals in the art of black and white camerawork, La Shelle already had an Oscar under his belt for his superb work in another film about a mystery woman – *Laura*.

My Cousin Vinny ● ⓥ
1992, US, 119 mins, colour
Dir: Jonathan Lynn
Stars: Joe Pesci, Ralph Macchio, Marisa Tomei, Fred Gwynne
Rating: ★★

An enormously overlong comedy that runs like a 50-minute TV play expanded to two hours. Joe Pesci in a funny wig is Vinny, a forty-something Brooklyn boy, newly graduated from law school with amazingly little knowledge of legal procedure and absolutely no qualifications in social graces. Vinny's all at sea when called on to defend his nephew (Ralph Macchio) and a friend on a murder charge, and it looks like the boys are for the chair. Such fun as is to be had in the first hour stems from the constant flow of bad language from Vinny and his fiancee (the stunning Marisa Tomei in an Oscar-winning performance) and his fruitless efforts to find a hotel where he can actually get some sleep. Things liven up a bit when Vinny starts turning into a Columbo of the court-room, but the meat of the film takes little more than 10 minutes to unfold. Big Fred Gwynne is drolly funny as the judge, while most of the actors around him are going over the top; Macchio is wasted in a nothing role.

My Darling Clementine ○ ⓥ
1946, US, 100 mins, b/w
Dir: John Ford
Stars: Henry Fonda, Victor Mature, Linda Darnell, Walter Brennan, Ward Bond
Rating: ★★★★

Though by no means acclaimed in its day, this John Ford Western about Wyatt Earp and the gunfight at the OK Corral has now become accepted as a classic of the genre. 'This is not a film to rave about,' muttered the British *Monthly Film Bulletin* rebelliously, 'The story is not particularly good.' A true one, however, and good enough to form the axis of several other sturdy Western films. Decorated by the twin themes of camaraderie and action that were to dominate Ford films of the first post-war decade as never before, the film has black and white photography of amazing depth by Joe MacDonald and memorable portrayals by Henry Fonda (as Wyatt Earp), the underrated Victor Mature, coming up trumps as Doc Holliday, and Walter Brennan, the epitome of evil (even when not saying anything) as Old Man Clanton. John Ireland is again on the side of the Clantons, just as he was to be 10 years later in *Gunfight at the OK Corral*. But Ford's movie, studded with memorable individual scenes and shots, is the definitive version of the story.

My Fair Lady ○ ⓥ
1964, US, 175 mins, colour
Dir: George Cukor
Stars: Rex Harrison, Audrey Hepburn, Stanley Holloway, Wilfrid Hyde White, Gladys Cooper, Jeremy Brett
Rating: ★★★

With $17 million invested in transferring the monster stage musical to the screen, producer Jack L Warner was to rue the day he cast Audrey Hepburn over the stage actress Julie Andrews. Although she was yet to make it big as a household name, Andrews went on to stardom in *Mary Poppins* and *The Sound of Music* all within 12 months. In another ironic twist, Marni Nixon, who dubbed the vocals for Audrey Hepburn (and did the same job for Natalie Wood in *West Side Story*), went on to appear

alongside Andrews in *The Sound of Music*. Warner wanted Cary Grant to play Professor Higgins and James Cagney over Stanley Holloway as dustman Alfred Doolittle. But for all the casting disappointments, the film was a triumph and went on to win eight Oscars, including Best Film and for Cecil Beaton's amazing costumes, especially the stunning black and white Edwardian numbers as worn in the famous 'Ascot Gavotte' scene.

My Father the Hero ○ ⓥ
1994, US, 90 mins, colour
Dir: Steve Miner
Stars: Gerard Depardieu, Katharine Heigl, Dalton James, Lauton Hutton
Rating: ★

A one-joke comedy (the US version of a French frolic also starring Gerard Depardieu) about a divorced father who takes his very advanced 14-year-old daughter (Katharine Heigl) for a holiday in the Bahamas. Fancying the nearest all-American hunk on the beach (Dalton James), the girl declares father Depardieu to be her lover (don't ask for logic) and some awkward and often embarrassing (not to mention boring) misunderstandings are set in motion for the next hour before the film livens up a bit towards the end as father and daughter gang up to net her the hunk. Highlight: Depardieu emptying the hotel restaurant (for more reasons than one) with a stirring rendition of 'Thank Heaven for Little Girls'. Lowpoint: a speedboat stunt sequence that goes on for ages. A running gag has Depardieu constantly phoning his never-seen love, who turns out to be a surprise guest star: alas one with a voice so familiar that few won't guess who she is.

My Favorite Blonde ○
1942, US, 78 mins, b/w
Dir: Sidney Lanfield
Stars: Bob Hope, Madeleine Carroll, Gale Sondergaard, George Zucco
Rating: ★★★

Nearly all of Bob Hope's films in the comedy-thriller vein were successful, and this was one of the best. It began the 'favourite' series which continued with *My Favorite Brunette* and *My Favorite Spy* and would surely have contained *My Favorite Redhead* if Hope's script-writers could have dreamed up a plot in which Paramount's Rhonda Fleming could profitably have been employed as leading lady. She did appear with him

in *The Great Lover*, but the material wasn't quite in the same mode. The presence of a gang of evil spies puts Hope into plenty of situations that expose the yellow streak running right down his character's back, especially when encountering dangers on a train with Madeleine Carroll as the blonde of the title. It also gives his writers (here including three of the best, Melvin Frank, Norman Panama and Don Hartman) the opportunity to provide 'Old Ski Nose' with the kind of 'cowardly wisecracks' his fans loved. Stony-faced Gale Sondergaard and oily George Zucco, who menaced Hope in his first great success, *The Cat and the Canary*, are on hand to lead the spies; but all concerned are upstaged in spectacular fashion by a talented penguin called Percy.

My Favorite Brunette ○
1947, US, 84 mins, b/w
Dir: Elliott Nugent
Stars: Bob Hope, Dorothy Lamour, Peter Lorre, Lon Chaney
Rating: ★★★

A really well-sustained Bob Hope comedy that plays to all his strengths. There's an inventive story (baby photographer Hope gets mistaken for the detective in the office next door and is pitched headlong into a complex and dangerous adventure), lots of big laughs, Dorothy Lamour as the femme who almost proves fatale to Hope, and a wonderful cast of civilised and un-civilised heavies that includes Peter Lorre, Jack LaRue, Lon Chaney, Frank Puglia, Charles Dingle and John Hoyt. Alan Ladd's cameo as Hope's private eye pal is really good – played dead straight and right on the mark. And a certain 'old groaner' makes an inevitable and very amusing guest appearance almost at the end of the film.

My Favorite Spy ○
1951, US, 93 mins, b/w
Dir: Norman Z McLeod
Stars: Bob Hope, Hedy Lamarr, Francis L Sullivan
Rating: ★★★

The third in Bob Hope's *Favorite* series of comedies gives him another delicious leading lady (Hedy Lamarr) to follow Madeleine Carroll and Dorothy Lamour. It casts him as a vaudeville comic compelled to impersonate the ruthless international spy who just happens to be his double, a trusty comedy situation on which Danny Kaye and Norman Wisdom, among

M

others, would play variations in later years. Bob's wisecracks are in rattling good form (three men worked on the screenplay). Asked to assume the spy's identity, he croaks: 'That ain't my line of work. I tell jokes. That's dangerous enough.'

My Favorite Wife ○
1940, US, 80 mins, b/w
Dir: Garson Kanin
Stars: Irene Dunne, Cary Grant, Randolph Scott, Gail Patrick
Rating: ★★★★

The original version of the famous comedy (since remade as *Three for the Show, Move Over Darling* and *Three's a Crowd*) about a wife who returns from being shipwrecked on a desert island to find that her husband is about to get married again. The direction was taken over by writer Garson Kanin after the original director, Leo McCarey, had been involved in a road accident. And a really slick, sophisticated, rib-tickling job Kanin turned in, with Cary Grant and Irene Dunne at the top of their form. Make yourself a pot of coffee and settle down for laughs galore.

My Favorite Year ○ Ⓥ
1982, US, 92 mins, colour
Dir: Richard Benjamin
Stars: Peter O'Toole, Mark Linn-Baker, Jessica Harper, Joseph Bologna
Rating: ★★★

A funny, nostalgic reminder of the days of live television, directed with warmth and affection by Richard Benjamin. Mark Linn-Baker makes an impressive feature debut as Benjy Stone, the eager young writer placed in charge of stylish, swashbuckling movie legend Alan Swann (Peter O'Toole), who is scheduled to guest star on the live TV show 'Comedy Cavalcade' – if he can stay sober for long enough. There is some cringingly hilarious mayhem, such as when Swann visits Benjy's Jewish Brooklyn family for dinner, and some inspired moments such as when Benjy tries to teach his girlfriend (Jessica Harper) the art of telling a good joke. The finale, with O'Toole swashing his buckle joyously, is truly heartwarming.

My Foolish Heart ○
1949, US, 98 mins, b/w
Dir: Mark Robson
Stars: Susan Hayward, Dana Andrews
Rating: ★★★

This was the big weepie of its year, boosted by the romantic musical theme by Victor Young, which was to become a world-wide best-seller. As the girl who is tempted to pass the responsibility for the pregnancy from a wartime romance on to a new admirer, Susan Hayward suffers nobly, as she was to do in a dozen films over the next decade, culminating in an Academy Award for her portrait of a condemned murderess in *I Want to Live!*.

My Friend Flicka ⊙
1943, US, 89 mins, colour
Dir: Harold Schuster
Stars: Roddy McDowall, Preston Foster, Rita Johnson
Rating: ★★★

The teenage Roddy McDowall enjoyed one of his best Hollywood roles in this enormously popular story of a boy and his horse, stunningly shot in Technicolor on Utah locations by Dewey Wrigley. Director Harold Schuster, who made Britain's first Technicolor feature *Wings of the Morning* (also about a horse) shows a sure touch for this kind of outdoor adventure with a family background. The horse is the star, but Preston Foster and Rita Johnson skilfully and unobtrusively supply warmth and authority as McDowall's parents.

My Gal Sal ○
1942, US, 103 mins, colour
Dir: Irving Cummings
Stars: Rita Hayworth, Victor Mature, Carole Landis, James Gleason
Rating: ★★★

The career of Paul Dreiser (brother of the novelist Theodore) forms the basis for this charming and beguiling musical set in the 1890s. Dreiser, who changed his name to Dresser, is played rather well by Victor Mature, but the real stars of the show are Rita Hayworth (although the singing voice she uses belongs to Nan Wynn) and a whole string of nostalgic song hits.

My Geisha ○
1962, US, 120 mins, colour
Dir: Jack Cardiff
Stars: Shirley MacLaine, Yves Montand, Edward G Robinson
Rating: ★★

This comedy about a director's wife (Shirley MacLaine) who whites up as a geisha girl to win the leading role in his next picture was produced by Miss MacLaine's real-life husband, Steve

Parker, who lived in Japan for several years. Sadly it's a one-joke idea stretched to almost two hours.

My Girl ○ Ⓥ
1991, US, 105 mins, colour
Dir: Howard Zieff
Stars: Dan Aykroyd, Jamie Lee Curtis, Macaulay Culkin, Anna Chlumsky, Richard Masur, Griffin Dunne
Rating: ★★

Rather pointlessly set in the Seventies, this is a merciless tear-jerker about the 12th summer of the daughter of an undertaker. A hypochondriac tomboy with a crush on her English teacher, her world comes crashing down when her widower father (Dan Aykroyd) takes on a beautician (Jamie Lee Curtis) to make up the corpses' faces and falls in love with her. The plot is slightly stiffened by the girl's aged grandma, who never says anything, but occasionally bursts vigorously into song, and by her friendship with a bespectacled fellow-student (Macaulay Culkin) who's very down-to-earth despite his fragile appearance. The film constantly strives not to be dull, but never quite succeeds, the dialogue needing to be sharper to make up for the lack of variety in the plot. But only the hardest of hearts will resist its massive attack on the tear-ducts in the last 20 minutes. Performances are okay. A poor sequel followed three years later.

My Girl Tisa ○
1948, US, 95 mins, b/w
Dir: Elliott Nugent
Stars: Lilli Palmer, Sam Wanamaker
Rating: ★★★

Lilli Palmer did rather better than her then husband Rex Harrison out of Hollywood during their stay there in the late 1940s, making some excellent films which also included *Cloak and Dagger* and *Body and Soul*. This charming period drama, with its strong romantic flavour, featured her appeal at its best. Allen Boretz's perceptive script takes some gentle but amusing sideswipes at politicians and red tape. Oddly, enough, the film's happy ending was changed on its British release to an unhappy one – a rare occurrence for the time.

My Heart Goes Crazy
See: London Town

My Hero
See: A Southern Yankee

My Left Foot ◐ ⓥ
1989, UK, 98 mins, colour
Dir: Jim Sheridan
Stars: Daniel Day-Lewis, Ray McAnally, Brenda Fricker
Rating: ★★★★

Don't miss Daniel Day-Lewis' Oscar-winning portrait of the Irish writer Christy Brown, afflicted from childhood with cerebral palsy. Quite apart from his crippling disability, Brown was also a witty, eccentric, difficult man, and Day-Lewis expresses the combination amazingly, sometimes frighteningly well, as does young Hugh O'Conor (from *Lamb*), playing Brown as a boy. Not an easy film from director Jim Sheridan but certainly a rewarding one.

My Life ◐ ⓥ
1993, US, 117 mins, colour
Dir: Bruce Joel Rubin
Stars: Michael Keaton, Nicole Kidman, Haing S Ngor
Rating: ★★

Skilfully sentimental, at least on the surface, this study of a man, who, dying of cancer, decides to leave a video history of himself for his unborn child, is just about prevented from sinking into a sea of tears by the multi-faceted performance of Michael Keaton, who's allowed to show he can still be funny as well as dramatic – and just as well. Writer-director Bruce Joel Rubin seems to have no deeper objective than making his audience cry and his script, though competently written with some warmly amusing dialogue for the star, lacks the ambition to lend its story greater stature and contains too few surprises along the way. Nicole Kidman is competent in a quieter role than usual, but seems, like most of the cast, to be crying out to contribute something more meaningful.

My Little Chickadee ○
1939, US, 83 mins, b/w
Dir: Edward Cline
Stars: Mae West, W C Fields
Rating: ★★★

'Is this a game of chance?' asks an innocent suckered by W C Fields into a card game. 'Not the way I play it, no,' replies Fields in this zany burlesque of Westerns which united his immoveable force with Mae West's irresistible object in a comedy battle that finally emerges as an entertaining draw. The two stars wrote the screenplay between them, delivering some of their most memorable lines. West, asked if she is trying to show contempt for the court, confides that she is trying to hide it. And Fields ends the film by inviting West to 'C'mon up and see me some time.' Not as funny as it might have been, the film's best sequences still make it a pleasure to be with.

My Little Girl ● ⓥ
1986, US, 118 mins, colour
Dir: Connie Kaiserman
Stars: Mary Stuart Masterson, Geraldine Page, James Earl Jones, Anne Meara, Peter Gallagher, Page Hannah
Rating: ★★

This parable about a 16-year-old trainee social worker at a centre for homeless girls is almost as naive as its central character, a poor little rich girl played with some appeal by Mary Stuart Masterson. Overlong and with a script that doesn't cut deep enough, it's nonetheless sufficiently involving to make you want to learn a bit more about the ultimate fate of its characters. James Earl Jones gives a characteristically highly-charged performance as the centre's director – one of the few characters that isn't overdrawn – and Geraldine Page does what she can with the cameo role of the heroine's gran.

My Man Godfrey ○
1936, US, 90 mins, b/w
Dir: Gregory La Cava
Stars: William Powell, Carole Lombard
Rating: ★★★

Sparkling screwball comedy, made during the Depression, about a tramp adopted as a butler by a millionaire's eccentric family. Peerless playing by William Powell (urbane even in rags) and the delightful Carole Lombard, both earning Oscar nominations.

My Man Godfrey ○
1957, US, 92 mins, colour
Dir: Henry Koster
Stars: David Niven, June Allyson
Rating: ★★★

A spirited remake of the classic original 1937 comedy film, which starred Carole Lombard and William Powell. Adroit playing from David Niven as Godfrey the butler complements clever direction by Henry Koster. Better than its reputation would have you think.

My Name Is Julia Ross ○
1945, US, 70 mins, b/w
Dir: Joseph H Lewis
Stars: Nina Foch, George Macready, Dame May Whitty
Rating: ★★★

This moody little thriller about a girl who finds herself losing her identity is enthralling from beginning to end, and helped to make a cult figure of its director Joseph H Lewis. It looks less convincing today, with the villainy of George Macready and Dame May Whitty more amusing than chilling. Nina Foch, though (as Julia), was never better.

My New Gun ● ⓥ
1992, US, 99 mins, colour
Dir: Stacy Cochran
Stars: Diane Lane, James LeGros, Stephen Collins, Tess Harper
Rating: ★★

A strange, semi-surrealist, almost *Twin Peaks*-like film about the bizarre consequences of a husband (Stephen Collins) believing his wife (Diane Lane) needs a gun for protection. He ends up in hospital, they part, and she ends up with the strange youth next door (James LeGros), whose pixilated mother (Tess Harper) is possibly a former country and western star in failing health . . . who seems to be threatened by someone or something. Hardly food and drink to the run-of-the-mill cinemagoer, it's one of those films with rather poor sound, lots of odd pauses and indecisive action and dialogue that sometimes sounds improvised. People move and act as if in a dream world. And you may not grasp what the film's about even when it's over. Downright peculiar.

My Own Private Idaho ● ⓥ
1991, US, 104 mins, colour
Dir: Gus Van Sant
Stars: River Phoenix, Keanu Reeves, James Russo, William Richert
Rating: ★★★

This unusual and highly original road movie looks at the mixed fortunes of a couple of street hustlers: River Phoenix, as a sex-for-hire male prostitute, who suffers from narcolepsy – falling asleep at a second's notice – and Keanu Reeves as the wealthy son of Portland's mayor, and the object of Phoenix's unrequited love. It was a brave choice of role for Phoenix, despite the credentials of the director, Gus Van Sant, who had already transformed the career of fellow

M

teen pin-up Matt Dillon with *Drugstore Cowboy*, and he brought to the role his trademark honesty and simplicity. The critical acclaim he received boded well for a long and fruitful career, but that was not to be. Actually, for a film about two gay hustlers, *Idaho* contains very little sex. But the unsavoury milieu might be enough to have more sensitive viewers reaching for the channel switch. Those who stick with it will discover a highly personal vision brimming over with passages of intriguing hallucinatory effects, and even a flirtation with Shakespeare's *Henry IV, Part 1* in the entertaining screenplay.

My Sister Eileen ○

1955, US, 108 mins, colour
Dir: Alexander Hall
Stars: Janet Leigh, Jack Lemmon, Betty Garrett, Bob Fosse
Rating: ★★★

Columbia certainly pulled out a plum with this musical remake of their own comedy success of a dozen years earlier. A bright, cheerful frolic full of vitality, the film is dominated by Janet Leigh – always surprisingly good when given the chance – and Betty Garrett (even better) as singing sisters. The comedy is joyously funny, the dancing scintillating and the singing delightful. All this and a singing Jack Lemmon too: no wonder this one leaves a warm glow behind.

My Six Convicts ○

1952, US, 104 mins, b/w
Dir: Hugo Fregonese
Stars: Millard Mitchell, Gilbert Roland, John Beal
Rating: ★★★

Under a novel prison rehabilitation scheme, a group of six prisoners become 'trustys'. A first-rate and heart-warming semi-documentary produced by Stanley Kramer and featuring Swedish actor Alf Kjellin, Marshall Thompson and, lurking way down the cast-list under the anonymity of his real name, Charles Bronson, billed as Charles Buchinsky. The situations produce some very funny moments and a few tellingly dramatic ones, while the best performances come from veteran Millard Mitchell, and much-wasted actor John Beal.

My Stepmother Is an Alien ○ ⊙

1988, US, 107 mins, colour
Dir: Richard Benjamin

Stars: Dan Aykroyd, Kim Basinger, Jon Lovitz
Rating: ★★★

In the first roles ideally suited to Marilyn Monroe and Tom Ewell since *The Seven Year Itch*, Kim Basinger has never been sexier and Dan Aykroyd never funnier than in this Frankenscience comedy. Kim's alien is simply sensational, whether stripping for Aykroyd's pleasure, or doing an impression of Jimmy Durante learned from television. When widower Aykroyd first meets her, he's hooked: he hopes he isn't boring the pants off her. With an extra-terrestrial twist, Basinger checks it out and looks up her own skirt. No, she announces, they're still there. Actually, it's his secret she's after – an extra-galactic probe that can save her planet. Aykroyd has other probes in mind and, after Kim has learned about kissing and sex from her 'living' handbag, he's down on his knees proposing. 'Boy,' gasps Dan, 'I spend my whole career trying to find life on another planet and when I do I end up marrying it'. The situations bubble and the laughs come fairly thick and fast, with Basinger a dizzy delight.

Mysterious Island ○

1961, UK, 101 mins, colour
Dir: Cy Endfield
Stars: Michael Craig, Joan Greenwood, Herbert Lom
Rating: ★★★

This action-filled adventure film, based on a book by Jules Verne, provides a field day for the special effects boys, once again headed by the ubiquitous Ray Harryhausen. Here he provides a battery of giant beasts, birds, crabs and bees. Top composer Bernard Herrmann, one of Alfred Hitchcock's favourites for background music, weighs in with a characteristically full-blooded score. A good cast, which includes Gary Merrill, Nigel Green and Herbert Lom as the ever-present Captain Nemo, puts the hokum across with spirit.

Mystery of Edwin Drood, The ○ ⊙

1993, UK, 100 mins, colour
Dir: Timothy Forder
Stars: Robert Powell, Finty Williams, Jonathan Phillips, Rupert Rainsford, Nanette Newman, Michelle Evans
Rating: ★

Various versions of Charles Dickens' last, unfinished story lead one only to conclude that the great CD had, by this time, lost it. The first hour of this story of foul deeds and unrequited passion is as dull as ditchwater and even includes, as its lowpoint, a long, inane discussion on why the sexton Durdles is nicknamed Stoney. Photographed in black and brown, this section of the film is about as interesting as paint drying and has much the same pace. Only when writer/director Timothy Forder is able to break free of Dickens does he, in the words of Laurel and Hardy, start to get some place. If the last 40 minutes are more Victorian Gothic (with a touch of Hammer horror), they do seem to be closer to what Dickens' work was about than those parts of the story contributed by the novelist himself. Robert Powell isn't exactly right for John Jasper but does well when the script allows; but Finty Williams is poor as Rosa: an undistinguished film debut indeed for Judi Dench's daughter.

Mystery of the Wax Museum, The ⦿

1933, US, 77 mins, colour
Dir: Michael Curtiz
Stars: Lionel Atwill, Fay Wray, Glenda Farrell, Frank McHugh
Rating: ★★★

Director Michael Curtiz's macabre classic builds up an atmosphere of brooding evil that puts it several points ahead of the 1953 remake *House of Wax*. Lionel Atwill is the disfigured and vengeful wax-modeller who captures the delicious Fay Wray (the two had co-starred in another chiller classic, *Dr X*, the previous year) in an alarming and disturbing climax. The film was thought to be totally lost until a perfect print turned up in a collection a few years ago. Now it can be shown in the original, and rare two band Technicolor. This colour process, primitive by modern standards, was achieved by an amalgam of two films, one shot in 'red and blue' the other in 'green'. Although the results here are remarkably successful, adding a strange, eerie quality to Anton Grot's spectacular art direction, the lighting involved during shooting produced such an intense heat that the wax figures used in the museum sequences were forever starting to melt, to say nothing of the poor actors. Glenda Farrell provides Miss

Wray with some hot competition in the acting stakes with her intrepid, wisecracking reporter.

Mystery Street ○
1950, US, 93 mins, b/w
Dir: John Sturges
Stars: Ricardo Montalban, Sally Forrest, Bruce Bennett, Jan Sterling
Rating: ★★★

A fascinating account of a criminal case solved almost entirely by science. Director John Sturges gives a wealth of detail about painstaking police work, employing semi-documentary techniques similar to those in the British classic of crime detection, *The Blue Lamp*. Good acting from a cast that includes Ricardo Montalban, Bruce Bennett, Betsy Blair, Elsa Lanchester – in viciously fine form as the victim's avaricious landlady – and Jan Sterling.

Mystery Submarine ○
(aka: Decoy)
1962, UK, 92 mins, b/w
Dir: C M Pennington-Richards
Stars: Edward Judd, James Robertson Justice
Rating: ★★

A British war film that seems to have strayed into the 1960s from at least 10 years earlier. Resolute Edward Judd is fine as the commander of a wolf in sheep's clothing – a Nazi submarine with a British crew – and James Robertson Justice is in typically fiery form as Rear-Admiral Rainbird.

Mystery Train ● Ⓥ
1989, US, 110 mins, colour
Dir: Jim Jarmusch
Stars: Screamin' Jay Hawkins, Nicoletta Braschi, Joe Strummer
Rating: ★★

The first colour film by the cult American director, Jim Jarmusch, composed of three tales featuring out-of-place foreigners who all end up in a seedy Memphis hotel on the same night. Certain details reappear, linking the three tales: a gunshot, a DJ's patter (the voice of Tom Waits) on the radio, the night clerk and bellhop at the hotel (played by veteran R&B singer Screamin' Jay Hawkins and Spike Lee's brother Cinque) who keep up a deadpan double act. The three sets of protagonists never meet and nothing much happens, which may frustrate viewers used to more mainstream American films. Fans of Jarmusch's offbeat style of filmmaking, however,

will relish his familiar trademarks, all present here – long takes, lots of lateral tracking shots, elliptical dialogue, and full of quirky details, like the plum the Japanese girl gives as a tip to the hotel bellhop. Newcomers to Jarmusch may find *Mystery Train* maddening but given half a chance it is oddly rewarding.

Mystic Pizza ● Ⓥ
1988, US, 104 mins, colour
Dir: Donald Petrie
Stars: Annabeth Gish, Julia Roberts, Lili Taylor, Vincent D'Onofrio
Rating: ★★

Another in the still-popular line of female buddy movies, this time about three waitresses working at a pizza house in the New England fishing town of Mystic. They're all part of the local Portuguese fishing community, which explains their restlessness at the all-too-real possibilities of becoming trapped for life in one small township. Lili Taylor, Annabeth Gish and Julia Roberts deliver knockout performances in these three roles and it's a shame their efforts aren't supported by a better script. Believable dialogue and logical plot and character developments are not, alas, on the menu at the Mystic Pizza, though there are some foolish sex scenes for those with a taste for them. Never mind, our dynamite girl trio serves up a feast of fine acting between courses to help you forget that the main meal has fallen flat.

My Teenage Daughter ○
(aka: Teenage Bad Girl)
1956, UK, 100 mins, b/w
Dir: Herbert Wilcox
Stars: Anna Neagle, Sylvia Syms
Rating: ★★

Teenage dramas were all the rage when Sylvia Syms made her debut in this tearful but absorbing drama, which never fails to hold attention. Kenneth Haigh also made an excellent debut as her boyfriend, but seemed afterwards to prefer the stage. Norman Woolland brings the right touch of masculine comfort as the suitor of harassed Dame Anna Neagle. But poor Wilfrid Hyde White, billed as co-star, gets so few lines that he might as well have stayed at home.

My Wife's Family ○
1956, UK, 76 mins, colour
Dir: Gilbert Gunn

Stars: Ronald Shiner, Ted Ray, Diane Hart, Greta Gynt, Robertson Hare
Rating: ★★

Broad comedy, with Ronald Shiner and Ted Ray extracting the maximum number of laughs (not many) out of the mother-in-law-coming-to-stay situation. Fabia Drake gives a sharply-observed portrait of the old battleaxe.

M

N

Nadine ○ Ⓥ
1987, US, 83 mins, colour
Dir: Robert Benton
Stars: Jeff Bridges, Kim Basinger, Rip Torn
Rating: ★★★

A lightweight, enjoyable comedy, entirely atypical of writer–director Robert Benton, and more like a TV movie with an above-average script. Though the plot doesn't have any situations that aren't familiar, Benton's script has enough life in it to make them seem, if not mint-new, at least acceptable. In the title role, Kim Basinger, radiant in Fifties costumes, and obviously in control of her material, has never looked better.

Nails ● Ⓥ
1992, US, 100 mins, colour
Dir: John Flynn
Stars: Dennis Hopper, Anne Archer, Tomas Milian, Keith David, Cliff De Young
Rating: ★★

Slam-bang action all the way, with Dennis Hopper as Detective Harry 'Nails' Niles, a good cop with a bad attitude (well, being Hopper he would have wouldn't he?). When his partner gets killed in an ambush while working on Something Big, dirty Harry sets out to foil the baddies and administer his own brand of vigilante-style justice. A well-plotted film whose endearing quirkiness is mainly down to Hopper's own offbeat personality. Director John Flynn, who made *The Outfit*, *Best Seller* and *Lock Up*, knows how to steamroller this sort of action crime thriller along and, like his leading character, doesn't allow too many sideline issues to get in his way. If you like Hopper, the odds are on you liking this. Don't expect subtlety though.

Naked ● Ⓥ
1993, UK, 126 mins, colour
Dir: Mike Leigh
Stars: David Thewlis, Katrin Cartlidge, Lesley Sharp
Rating: ★

Loved by 99 per cent of the world's critics, but not this one nor I fancy quite a fair proportion of the video-watching public, this is appalling minimalist cinema from director Mike Leigh which might well have shared the title of one of his previous films *Bleak Moments*. Shot to all intents and purposes in black and white (actually colour with the shades drained), this has little to do with entertainment or cinema. A drifter (David Thewlis) turns up at his ex girlfriend's ramshackle flat and proceeds to couple with her gothic friend and anyone else who comes within range, all of whom are quite ready for instant sex. As a portrait of deadbeats, this is charmless, clumsy, cramped and only occasionally amusing. It could, in fact, be a cure for insomnia – but if you've had a hard day and feel like putting your head in the gas oven, these mannered manic depressives will give you a shove.

Naked Alibi ○
1954, US, 85 mins, b/w
Dir: Jerry Hopper
Stars: Sterling Hayden, Gloria Grahame
Rating: ★★★

Described by *Picturegoer* as 'one of the best cop-crook thrillers of the year', this is a really tight melodrama about a policeman obsessed with proving an acquitted man guilty of murder. It starts off ordinarily, then gets better and better: every line of its sparse dialogue has a point, every spurt of action a punch. Sterling Hayden and Gloria Grahame both give gutsy portrayals in this gripping drama – but Gene Barry, in the best performance of his career, is outstanding as the man the policeman is after. Hair-raising climax.

Naked City, The ○
1948, US, 96 mins, b/w
Dir: Jules Dassin
Stars: Barry Fitzgerald, Howard Duff, Don Taylor
Rating: ★★★★

Filmed almost entirely on location on the streets of New York City, this thrilling crime film deservedly took Oscars for best editing (Paul Weatherwax) and best black-and-white photography (William Daniels) in its story of a hunt for a killer (one of the 'eight million stories in the naked city', according to its narrator). It also has a marvellously dry performance by Barry Fitzgerald, as the detective in charge of the investigation, some exciting action and chase sequences, and a famous climax on Brooklyn Bridge. One of the best films of its type ever made.

Naked Gun, The: From the Files of Police Squad! ● Ⓥ
1988, US, 85 mins, colour
Dir: David Zucker
Stars: Leslie Nielsen, Priscilla Presley, Ricardo Montalban, George Kennedy, O J Simpson
Rating: ★

David Zucker takes over from Jim Abrahams as director of the *Airplane!* team's comedy films, and the result is a laugh drought that may have fans screaming for half-an-hour of sitcom on the telly. The jokes are mostly elaborately telegraphed and clumsily executed; most of them will make you wince, grimace or pull any expression other than a smile. Lesley Nielsen heads an all-too-undistinguished cast as a cop on the trail of a mob kingpin (Ricardo Montalban); he could have hit him over the head with a sledgehammer – it would have been well in keeping with the tenor of these disastrously unfunny proceedings. The Queen of England somehow gets dragged into the monumentally humourless affair that follows, but certainly to no-one's advantage. One funny scene: when the outline of a corpse is drawn on water at a murder scene; every cloud has a silver lining.

Naked Gun 2½, The: The Smell of Fear, ● Ⓥ
1991, US, 85 mins, colour
Dir: David Zucker
Stars: Leslie Nielsen, Priscilla Presley, George Kennedy, O J Simpson, Robert Goulet
Rating: ★★★

Altogether more agreeable than its predecessor, this sequel to *The Naked Gun* is more akin to *Airplane!* in its humour. Sometimes there are so many gags going on in the background to a scene that it's hard to keep up, especially if you're trying to follow the plot about Lt Frank Drebin (Nielsen) uncovering a dastardly attempt to influence the energy policy of the US government. At the same time, he attempts to rekindle the fading embers of his affair with Jane (Presley) who just happens to be involved. Drebin's capacity for catastrophe is definitely rivalling that of Peter Sellers' Clouseau and is used to the full in a wildly successful running gag involving the misfortunes of then-First Lady Barbara Bush. Watch quickly for Zsa Zsa Gabor in a fleeting but funny guest appearance.

Naked Jungle, The ○
1954, US, 90 mins, colour
Dir: Byron Haskin
Stars: Eleanor Parker, Charlton Heston,
William Conrad
Rating: ★★★

Ernest Laszlo's Technicolor photography makes the most of an unusual setting – a turn-of-the-century cocoa plantation in the South American jungle – in this combination of romantic drama and suspense thriller. Lots of tension and excitement towards the end as a massive army of soldier ants marches towards plantation owner Charlton Heston and his new bride. The script is less effective, but this deficiency becomes insignificant once the ants take charge of the story. Producer George Pal and director Byron Haskin, who also made *The War of the Worlds* together, conjure up some amazing special effects involving ants that are guaranteed to make you itch, and imported millions of the creatures for close-up work actually filmed during production.

Naked Lunch ● ⊙
1991, US, 115 mins, colour
Dir: David Cronenberg
Stars: Peter Weller, Judy Davis,
Ian Holm, Julian Sands, Roy
Scheider
Rating: ★

A film about drugs, hallucinations and cockroaches, which sets out to disgust us and succeeds admirably. Writer William Lee moonlights as a bug exterminator, but becomes hooked on his own bug powder, shooting his wife (or does he?) and hallucinating himself into an 'inner zone', where he imagines all the typewriters turn into cockroaches with talking orifices, or gooey monsters with phallic appendages in their heads. Sex and the drive to write, together with the drugs, sends the poor guy on the trip to end them all, but might provide a cure for insomnia for the rest of us. Peter Weller plays Lee morosely; Judy Davis as his wife leers like Glenda Jackson on one of her off days. Just don't ask us what the title means, or we'll catch you a fourpenny one with our cockroach – sorry, we mean typewriter. On balance, Weller could reflect that even *Robocop 3* might have been better.

Naked Runner, The ○
1967, UK, 104 mins, colour
Dir: Sidney J Furie

Stars: Frank Sinatra, Peter Vaughan,
Nadia Gray
Rating: ★★

Frank Sinatra's only British film has him cast as an ordinary businessman caught up in international intrigue. Sidney Furie directs tricksily, but the action is explosively effective and there are some good twists. In transferring Francis Clifford's best-selling book to the screen, Stanley Mann doesn't quite manage to iron out the illogicalities (how does a businessman happen to have his gun with him on an apparently routine trip to a trade fair?) or the confusions. But there's little doubt he succeeds in keeping events coming at a cracking pace.

Naked Spur, The ○
1953, US, 91 mins, colour
Dir: Anthony Mann
Stars: James Stewart, Janet Leigh,
Robert Ryan
Rating: ★★★

Drawling James Stewart unhitches his lower lip and hits the trail to capture Robert Ryan, playing a picture of leering dishonesty called Ben Vandergroat. The result is an excellent Western, taut, tense and exciting, with a brilliant climax on a high cliff, which was one of director Anthony Mann's best. The classic dramatic framework – three men trying to bring another back to justice – is superbly maintained, and Mann gets excellent portrayals from each one of his four men (Millard Mitchell and Ralph Meeker are the others) as well as from Janet Leigh, pretty much deglamorised here and sporting a new cropped haircut. The screenplay was nominated for an Academy Award.

Naked Street, The ○
1955, US, 84 mins, b/w
Dir: Maxwell Shane
Stars: Anthony Quinn, Farley Granger,
Anne Bancroft
Rating: ★★

Tough thriller with Anthony Quinn as a gangster resorting to desperate measures to save his sister's lover from the death penalty. *The Naked Street* is one of the films Anne Bancroft made in the mid-Fifties, when struggling to establish herself as a dramatic actress following a series of milk-and-water roles at Fox. All of these films take on new significance in the light of Miss Bancroft's subsequent performances in

The Miracle Worker (for which she won an Oscar), *The Pumpkin Eater* and *The Graduate*.

Naked Truth, The ⊙
(aka: Your Past Is Showing)
1957, UK, 92 mins, b/w
Dir: Mario Zampi
Stars: Terry-Thomas, Peter Sellers,
Peggy Mount
Rating: ★★★

Terry-Thomas and Peter Sellers, fresh from playing the robbers in *tom thumb*, are both on top form in this zany comedy of errors about a scandal magazine publisher (Dennis Price at his smoothest) and the intended 'victims' who turn on him in various hilarious ways. The screenplay by Michael Pertwee gives Sellers some delightfully Goonish dialogue, and an opportunity to demonstrate his mastery of disguises.

Name of the Rose, The ● ⊙
1986, US, 130 mins, colour
Dir: Jean-Jacques Annaud
Stars: Sean Connery, Christian Slater,
F Murray Abraham
Rating: ★★★

Too many grotesques almost spoil the broth in this impressively well-made film version of Umberto Eco's massive best-seller. And the motivation and resolution of the murders that plague an isolated 14th century Italian monastery are never quite sharp enough to focus our attention whole-heartedly on a story that struggles manfully to pull its disparate elements together. Sean Connery is admittedly a great help as the investigator, a sort of Franciscan Sherlock Holmes; and production designer Dante Ferretti deserves high praise for his amazing monastery with its clutter of medieval bric-a-brac and the labyrinth that lies within its tower. Visually memorable then, if dramatically dense, the film is on the whole an enjoyable experience.

Namu the Killer Whale ⊙
1966, US, 88 mins, colour
Dir: Laslo Benedek
Stars: Robert Lansing, Lee Meriwether
Rating: ★★

An odd film to come from Laslo Benedek, who made Brando's *The Wild One*. But children will enjoy this beautifully photographed story of a killer whale which became a gentle pet.

N

Nana ○
(aka: Lady of the Boulevards)
1934, US, 89 mins, b/w
Dir: Dorothy Arzner
Stars: Anna Sten, Phillips Holmes,
Lionel Atwill
Rating: ★★

This adaptation of the Emile Zola
classic was Samuel Goldwyn's attempt
to make a new Garbo out of the
beautiful Russian actress Anna Sten.
She hadn't Garbo's mystique, though,
and after a few more films was
relegated to lesser roles.

Nana ◐
1955, France/Italy, 96 mins, colour
Dir: Christian-Jacque
Stars: Martine Carol, Charles Boyer
Rating: ★★

An opulent French-Italian version of
Emile Zola's classic novel about a
courtesan at the time of Napoleon
III. Blonde sex symbol Martine Carol
was well at home in such surroundings, having also played Caroline
Cherie, Lola Montes, Lucrezia Borgia
and Madame DuBarry. Her gowns
here are extraordinarily elaborate and,
if the harsh realism and acute social
observation of Zola's original goes
largely by the board, the production
design and evocative music by
Georges van Parys provide some
compensation.

Nancy Steele Is Missing ○
1937, US, 86 mins, b/w
Dir: George Marshall
Stars: Victor McLaglen, Peter Lorre,
June Lang, Walter Connolly
Rating: ★★★

Slightly unusual kidnap melodrama
with an interesting cast. Censorship
restrictions had meant very few such
films since the real-life Lindbergh
kidnapping case, and this one was
particularly lucky to get through, in
that it showed a kidnapper in a sympathetic light. Victor McLaglen's
personality infuses this character with
life, and there's distinctive support
from June Lang, Jane Darwell, Walter
Connolly, John Carradine and especially Peter Lorre as McLaglen's
devious cellmate.

Nanny, The ◐ ⓥ
1965, UK, 93 mins, b/w
Dir: Seth Holt
Stars: Bette Davis, Wendy Craig
Rating: ★★★

The suspense is so well built up in this
chilly drama that it's a pity the end is

something of an anti-climax. No fault
of the direction or actors: Jimmy
Sangster's otherwise impeccable
screenplay must shoulder the blame.
Sitting perfectly poised on the suspense fence, the film asks the question:
is Nanny (Bette Davis at her
tightest-lipped) really the deranged
and dangerous old woman that
10-year-old Joey (William Dix)
alleges? Once or twice, the film descends on the ridiculous, but mostly
the audience is kept well strung up
awaiting the next development, to
the accompaniment of some dramatic
background music.

Narrow Margin, The ○
1952, US, 71 mins, b/w
Dir: Richard Fleischer
Stars: Charles McGraw, Marie Windsor
Rating: ★★★★

Tense, taut, sharply-acted low-budget
thriller about a detective assigned to
guard an important witness on a train
journey. Charles McGraw, in one of
a number of credibly tough performances he gave at this time, is
first-rate as the witness's reluctant,
hard-boiled protector who must save
her from deadly strangers on a train.
Marie Windsor is also strong as the
gangster's widow he hates to have to
keep alive. Richard Fleischer's
fast-paced direction builds the suspense by the minute. A cracker.

Narrow Margin ◐ ⓥ
1990, US, 97 mins, colour
Dir: Peter Hyams
Stars: Gene Hackman, Anne Archer
Rating: ★★★

This thrilling chase thriller, set mostly
aboard – and on top of – a speeding
train hurtling through the stark Canadian wilderness, is a remake of one
of the most successful B-movies in the
history of RKO. *The Narrow Margin*,
starring Charles McGraw, turned in a
fantastic profit on a modest budget of
$230,000 for the studio in 1952. This
updated remake cost $21 million, and
every cent of it is on the screen in the
shape of spectacular stunts and
breathtaking action set pieces. Gene
Hackman turns in another reliable
performance as a deputy district
attorney charged with delivering key
Mafia killing witness Anne Archer to
testify at a trial and having to keep
them both safe from a gang of armed
heavies in a pursuing helicopter and
on the train. Peter Hyams, who cut
his action genre teeth with the likes of
Capricorn One, Outland and *The Pre-*

sidio, is virtually the only Hollywood
director since Josef von Sternberg who
doubles as his own cinematographer.
Here he uses interior wide angle shots
for unusual views of the carriages and
breathtaking Panavision aerial shots
of the Canadian lakes and forests along
the route. It's also nice to see James B
Sikking (Lt Howard Hunter from *Hill
Street Blues*) cast against type as the
lead heavy.

National Health, The ◐
1973, UK, 97 mins, colour
Dir: Jack Gold
Stars: Lynn Redgrave, Donald Sindén,
Jim Dale
Rating: ★★

Jim Dale gets all the best lines in Peter
Nichols' skilful adaptation of his own
hit play in which the scandalous conditions of a ramshackle national health
hospital are contrasted with the comic
cavortings in the medical soap opera
being shown on the ward television.
A beguiling, perceptive and sometimes
funny black comedy.

National Lampoon's Animal House ● ⓥ
1978, US, 109 mins, colour
Dir: John Landis
Stars: John Belushi, Tim Matheson,
John Vernon, Verna Bloom
Rating: ★

Several of the people associated with
this hugely successful exercise in bad
taste campus comedy – costing less
than $3 million to make, it soon
grossed more than a $100 million –
moved on to greater fame. For chubby
star John Belushi, who plays the gross
Bluto, however, there was no happy
ending; he was found dead from a
drug overdose in 1982.

National Lampoon's Christmas Vacation ◐ ⓥ
(aka: National Lampoon's Winter
Holiday)
1989, US, 103 mins, colour
Dir: Jeremiah Chechik
Stars: Chevy Chase, Beverly D'Angelo,
Randy Quaid, Diane Ladd, E G Marshall,
Juliette Lewis
Rating: ★★★

A welcome return to form for the
hapless Griswold family, back on
native soil after the hapless *European
Vacation*. Chase is superbly
straight-faced as the father whose
grandiose schemes for a 'Griswold
family Christmas' inevitably lead to
disaster, including the funniest

rooftop antics since Laurel and Hardy tried to erect an aerial. The Christmas dinner scene, and the expression of those participating, is also a priceless piece of film farce.

National Lampoon's European Vacation ❶ ⓥ
1985, US, 94 mins, colour
Dir: Amy Heckerling
Stars: Chevy Chase, Beverly D'Angelo, Eric Idle
Rating: ★

With Chevy Chase's comedy *National Lampoon's Vacation* scoring a surprise $30 million hit, it was perhaps predictable that a second serving was on the cards. But this graceless affair – a sort of American *Carry On* farce – is a sorry sequel. The starting point is pink-faced Chicago suburbanite Chase and his obnoxious family winning a holiday in England, France, Italy and Germany, on a TV game show called Pig-in-a-Poke, which could well sum up the finished film. Celebrity look-alike Jeanette Charles takes off the Queen on screen once more, and even Charles and Diana are dragged into the tiresome plot. The best thing in it, though, is the opening sequence. Director Amy Heckerling falls into the same trap as her biggest hit to date, *Look Who's Talking*, by getting carried away with physical humour. But with the script providing just the sketchiest of character details, perhaps that was to be expected. Look out for fleeting cameos by British comedy stalwarts Mel Smith, Robbie Coltrane and Maureen Lipman.

National Lampoon's Loaded Weapon 1 ❶ ⓥ
1993, US, 83 mins, colour
Dir: Gene Quintano
Stars: Emilio Estevez, Samuel L Jackson, Tim Curry, William Shatner, Whoopi Goldberg
Rating: ★★

The hero rises from the heroine's bed and walks off, ripplingly naked, down the corridor. 'What are you doing?' she asks. Emilio Estevez turns his head. 'Just taking one of those un-motivated butt-in-movie walks,' he replies. Yes, this is Hollywood in Lampoonland, a popular venue, already visited by *Airplane!*, *Hot Shots!* and others. This example is a very busy movie at 83 minutes, taking pot shots at *Lethal Weapon*, *Basic Instinct*, *The Silence of the Lambs*, *Star Trek* and even *Teenage Mutant Ninja Turtles*. Samuel L Jackson has the Danny

Glover role while villains William Shatner and Tim Curry are not so far over the top that we don't enjoy them. Shatner's *Star Trek* engineer Scotty turns up trying to stop the police station coffee machine from blowing apart and there are amusing guest appearances from Whoopi Goldberg, Bruce Willis, F Murray Abraham (very good as Hannibal Lecher) and Erik Estrada, and a silly one from Charlie Sheen. Although it is often jolly rather than funny, at least this one doesn't tax your brain – or outstay its welcome.

National Lampoon's Vacation ❶ ⓥ
1983, US, 95 mins, colour
Dir: Harold Ramis
Stars: Chevy Chase, Beverly D'Angelo, Randy Quaid
Rating: ★★★

Let's face it: any holiday where a maiden aunt *dies* in the back of your car has *got* to be a disaster. And catastrophe is virtually guaranteed with the hapless Griswold family, especially with Chevy Chase's know-it-all dad at the helm. He shows up well in this change-of-pace role as the father who drives his wife and kids thousands of miles to Walley World (a close relative of Walt Disney World) in Florida. En route they have the car stolen when they misroute into a ghetto district, enjoy a chaotic stay with poor country cousins ('Eddie says that after the baby comes I can quit one of my night jobs'), get lost in the desert and are thrown off a vibrating bed in a motel. That's just for starters! Beverly D'Angelo is a real little scene-stealer as Chase's wife, while the two kids, Anthony Michael Hall and Dana Barron, seem as near natural and un-spoilt as it's possible for movie kids to be.

National Lampoon's Winter Holiday
See: National Lampoon's Christmas Vacation

National Velvet ☉ ⓥ
1944, US, 120 mins, colour
Dir: Clarence Brown
Stars: Elizabeth Taylor, Mickey Rooney, Donald Crisp, Angela Lansbury
Rating: ★★★★

One of the greatest tear-jerkers that MGM ever made: a warm-hearted piece of escapism about an 11-year-old girl and her horse, who take on the world's best steeplechasers

in the Grand National. Elizabeth Taylor had already made a big impression in her first major film, *Lassie Come Home*, the previous year. Here her moving portrayal of Velvet, the girl determined to ride in the National, made millions reach for their handkerchieves, and shot her to stardom. Mickey Rooney gives her energetic support as the cynical jockey 'with a secret past' and Anne Revere won an Academy Award as her mother. It all adds up to an outsize dose of nostalgia for film fans, and a treat for children – and you'll notice Miss Taylor does much of her own horse-riding. During filming she took one particularly bad fall, injuring her back to such an extent that she has suffered pain from it throughout her career.

Natural, The ❶ ⓥ
1984, US, 137 mins, colour
Dir: Barry Levinson
Stars: Robert Redford, Robert Duvall, Glenn Close, Kim Basinger
Rating: ★★

A talented 19-year-old baseball player is shot in a hotel room by a mysterious woman. Fifteen years later Roy Hobbs, in his mid-thirties, tries out for an ailing major league team and impresses with his exceptional skills. With Roy, the team prospers, but not everybody is happy. Director Barry Levinson has given this baseball film an air of mystery and the supernatural that, although quite fun (every time there's a flash of lightning, you know Redford's going to hit the ball about two miles) doesn't sit comfortably in this framework. Even so, with a cast that, headed by Robert Redford, also includes Robert Duvall, Kim Basinger, Glenn Close, Barbara Hershey, Richard Farnsworth and Joe Don Baker, it's still good entertainment. Set in the 1930s, the film has a good sense of period and the story is reminiscent of films of that time. There are times when everything seems to be moving rather slowly, but despite the long running time it's enjoyable enough. Redford fans won't be disappointed and others shouldn't allow themselves to be put off by the baseball theme – especially as the sports sequences are excitingly done.

Naughty Marietta ○
1935, US, 106 mins, b/w
Dir: W S Van Dyke II

N

Stars: Jeanette MacDonald, Nelson Eddy
Rating: ★★★

Ah, sweet mystery of life! It's the film that brought Nelson Eddy and Jeanette MacDonald together. She's a French princess running off to America. He's the Indian scout she falls in love with. Pleasing period operetta with a Victor Herbert score.

Navigator, The ⊙

1924, US, 63 mins, b/w
Dir: Donald Crisp
Stars: Buster Keaton
Rating: ★★★★

One of Buster Keaton's most successful full-length films, which made $2 million on its initial release. The 'business' on board the good ship Navigator is often priceless.

Navy S.E.A.L.S. ● ⓥ

1990, US, 113 mins, colour
Dir: Lewis Teague
Stars: Charlie Sheen, Michael Biehn, Joanne Whalley-Kilmer, Bill Paxton
Rating: ★

This gung-ho American action film in the tradition of *Sands of Iwo Jima* and *The Wild Geese* is just fine until any of its characters has to open his mouth. Outdated in attitudes by a good 40 years, it presents us with a US land/water squad in the SAS tradition that has to destroy stolen US missiles somewhere in Lebanon. No problem, of course. 'You're dealing with extremists,' the squad is told. 'You're dealing with the Navy Seals,' is the reply. Ha!! With men like this, we could be off on World War 3 at any moment, especially hothead Charlie Sheen, who shoots a man for speaking disrespectfully of his mother. Michael Biehn is the caring skipper ('Are you all right?' he asks an obviously dying man) and Joanne Whalley-Kilmer gives a career-worst performance as a half-Lebanese reporter in love with him. Mind you, some of these cast members over-act even when they have no dialogue. The action is competently staged and constant, making this an enjoyably awful movie.

Near Dark ● ⓥ

1987, US, 94 mins, colour
Dir: Kathryn Bigelow
Stars: Adrian Pasdar, Jenny Wright, Lance Henriksen, Bill Paxton, Tim Thomerson
Rating: ★★

In contrast to its contemporary, *The Lost Boys*, this represents the darker side of the vampire coin. Its vampires are made to expire in a painfully protracted way as opposed to a clean stake through the heart and the doomy theme music by Tangerine Dream indicates that director Kathryn Bigelow intends few smiles to be had in this one. Old Hollywood might have called it *The Fiends Who Walked the West.* 'They ain't normal,' growls hero Adrian Pasdar's father (Tim Thomerson), trying to rescue his son from their clutches after he has been seduced into the pack by a slinky lady vamp (Jenny Wright). 'Normal people don't spit out bullets when you shoot 'em.' Well, very true but then normal people weren't around as far back as the American Civil War. There are times when the film's obsession with gore makes it hard to come to terms with, but the performances are solid and the director throws in a few genuine chills as well as liberally catering for more blood-hungry fans of the genre.

Nearest and Dearest ○

1972, UK, 93 mins, colour
Dir: John Robins
Stars: Hylda Baker, Jimmy Jewel
Rating: ★★★

Pledge's Purer Pickles ride again with Hylda Baker not only starring, but also singing the title song. The script is a kind of bumper bundle of seaside postcard jokes, with acting honours going to Jimmy Jewel, underrated as a character actor, and Yootha Joyce, who pops up as Mrs Rowbottom. It's based on the British TV series by Vince Powell and Harry Driver, although the screenplay here is supplied by two other TV comedy stalwarts, Tom Brennand and Roy Bottomley.

Nearly a Nasty Accident ○

1961, US, 94 mins, b/w
Dir: Don Chaffey
Stars: Jimmy Edwards, Kenneth Connor, Shirley Eaton, Richard Wattis
Rating: ★★

Frantic black-and-white farces proliferated in the British cinema of the 1958–1963 period, no doubt inspired by the box-office success of *Carry On Sergeant.* Not all of them were as funny as that, but they did give starring opportunities to such comedians as Bob Monkhouse, Alfred Marks, Spike Milligan and Jimmy Edwards. Here it's Edwards

co-starring with diminutive, bumbling Kenneth Connor, who plays the 'erk' whose antics irk the Air Force.

Necessary Roughness ① ⓥ

1991, US, 105 mins, colour
Dir: Stan Dragoti
Stars: Scott Bakula, Harley Jane Kozak, Robert Loggia, Hector Elizondo, Jason Bateman, Kathy Ireland
Rating: ★

Who would want to make a movie – especially about American football – that had nothing new to offer? Well, not quite. This one does have a girl goal kicker, although she barely gets a look in. Otherwise, this numbskull sports comedy soon wastes whatever potential it had. The comic elements – especially the dean who hates football and will do anything to scupper the team – are pitifully over the top. The serious elements come close to making you laugh, especially the romance between 34-year-old Scott Bakula (brought back to college education he never had to make winning passes) and journalism teacher Harley Jane Kozak. Commiserations to them both: even Tom Cruise and Michelle Pfeiffer couldn't have done anything with these characters. 'Take 'em out,' says the coach to Bakula at the (anti) climactic game. 'It's your team, son.' Such dialogue might have worked 50 years ago. We only said might.

Needful Things ● ⓥ

1993, US, 120 mins, colour
Dir: Fraser C Heston
Stars: Ed Harris, Bonnie Bedelia, Max Von Sydow, J T Walsh, Amanda Plummer
Rating: ★★

The Devil comes to the little American town of Castle Rock (coincidentally the name of this film's distributors) and, considering all this is based on a Stephen King novel, the results are pretty much as you'd expect. In return for their heart's desire (from the depths of Satan's antique shop), the 'good' citizens of Castle Rock are only too keen to go about the Devil's bidding. In no time at all people are chopping each other up into little bits. All this is rather perplexing for Sheriff Ed Harris who thought he was in for the quiet country life when he quit the big-city force, but now finds himself in the middle of a holocaust. Subsequent developments allow that usually good character actor J T Walsh to go right over the top while Max Von Sydow's

Satan abandons his antique shop owner guise and chuckles happily at the mayhem. Pretty silly but well-enough done and certainly never dull.

Neighbors ◑ ⓥ
1981, US, 94 mins, colour
Dir: John G Avildsen
Stars: John Belushi, Kathryn Walker, Dan Aykroyd, Cathy Moriarty
Rating: ★★

This follow-up comedy by John Belushi and Dan Aykroyd to their successful *The Blues Brothers* was never shown in Britain, despite the fact that it's often funny in an outrageous way, and both Belushi and Aykroyd give the best of their film portrayals. If you like modern comedies of insult and embarrassment, in fact, you'll be in clover here.

Neither the Sea nor the Sand ●
1972, UK, 116 mins, colour
Dir: Fred Burnley
Stars: Susan Hampshire, Michael Petrovitch, Frank Finlay
Rating: ★★

Adapted from his own novel by TV newscaster Gordon Honeycombe, this is a most unusual combination of amour fou and horror story, with thoughtful performances from Susan Hampshire and Frank Finlay. If it doesn't quite capture the chilliness of the book, it's a brave try.

Nell Gwyn ○
1934, UK, 85 mins, b/w
Dir: Herbert Wilcox
Stars: Anna Neagle, Cedric Hardwicke
Rating: ★★★

This well-produced slice of history proved a popular vehicle for Anna Neagle as the famous orange-seller who competes with the Duchess of Portsmouth (Jeanne de Casalis) for King Charles II (an unusually jovial Sir Cedric Hardwicke). It was one of the earliest of Neagle's historical heroines, providing a solid centre to Herbert Wilcox's rollicking costume romp which maintains a good sense of period. Written by chubbily jowled Miles Malleson, who gave himself a part as Chaffinch.

Neptune's Daughter ○
1949, US, 93 mins, colour
Dir: Edward Buzzell

Stars: Esther Williams, Red Skelton, Betty Garrett, Ricardo Montalban
Rating: ★★★

One of the most successful of MGM's Esther Williams aqua-musicals, with a handful of Frank Loesser songs spearheaded by the Oscar-winning 'Baby, It's Cold Outside', sung not only by Miss Williams and Ricardo Montalban, but also by Betty Garrett and Red Skelton, who stole the show with some amiable and enthusiastic fooling in their mistaken-identity romance. Director Edward Buzzell made sure that the production was full of Technicolor slickness and Xavier Cugat rhythm, plus the obligatory Williams water ballet.

Network ● ⓥ
1976, US, 121 mins, colour
Dir: Sidney Lumet
Stars: Faye Dunaway, Peter Finch, William Holden, Robert Duvall
Rating: ★★★

Black satire with a vengeance, if ultimately a little wearing, taking a savage bite at American television and the ratings that rule the people who work in it. Peter Finch, winning an Oscar in his last film, is the ranting newscaster who flips his lid and announces that he is going to commit suicide on the air – which boosts the ratings to such an extent that he finds his salary doubled for prophesying gloom and doom. Faye Dunaway's strident performance, though it threatens to overbalance the film, was also rewarded with an Oscar, as was Beatrice Straight's magnificent one-scene tour-de-force as William Holden's neglected wife. Sidney Lumet's direction is at times devastating, especially in a magnetic scene where people come to the windows of their block of flats in a thunderstorm.

Nevadan, The ○
(aka: The Man from Nevada)
1949, US, 81 mins, colour
Dir: Gordon Douglas
Stars: Randolph Scott, Dorothy Malone
Rating: ★★

Very much in the 'a-man's-gotta-do-what-a-man's-gotta-a-do' mould of Randolph Scott's later Westerns. Our grim-faced hero has to bring in both an outlaw (Forrest Tucker) and stolen gold to the value of $200,000. A rancher – expertly played by George Macready – and his disenchanted wife (Dorothy Malone) also become involved. Scott, who has to team up with Tucker at one point in one of

the script's inventive little quirks, is sobriety itself as the hero, and Frank Faylen registers well in a supporting role.

Nevada Smith ○ ⓥ
1966, US, 135 mins, colour
Dir: Henry Hathaway
Stars: Steve McQueen, Karl Malden, Suzanne Pleshette, Janet Margolin
Rating: ★★★

An epic Western that stems from the character created by Harold Robbins in *The Carpetbaggers*. John Michael Hayes wrote both films and this is how you would imagine he would tackle a Western – lengthy, packed with characters, blood, action and veiled moralising, with a dash of sex thrown in. Stir well and hope it turns out tasty. And, in fits and starts, it does: the odds are that you'll enjoy watching Steve McQueen as a country boy on a long, long hunt for the trio of vicious killers who tortured and killed his parents. Star actors fill all the many main parts, although only Arthur Kennedy's convict on the run sticks for any length of time in the memory. Familiar faces in the supporting cast include those of Lyle Bettger and Howard Da Silva, and the hunt is photographed in splendidly detailed colour by Lucien Ballard, who proves just as adept at following a night-time knife-fight as portraying a lone rider in panoramic daytime view.

Never a Dull Moment ○
1967, US, 95 mins, colour
Dir: Jerry Paris
Stars: Dick Van Dyke, Edward G Robinson, Dorothy Provine, Henry Silva
Rating: ★★

A frisky comedy crime caper that never quite adds up to the sum of the talents involved. With Dick Van Dyke and Dorothy Provine as leads, Edward G Robinson as a mob boss with a penchant for art (Robinson's sideline in real life) and such flavoursome character actors as Jack Elam, Henry Silva, Slim Pickens and Mickey Shaughnessy around, it could have been a comic chase classic. As it is, Jerry Paris' pacing doesn't always live up to the title of the film.

NeverEnding Story, The ○ ⓥ
1984, UK, 94 mins, colour
Dir: Wolfgang Petersen
Stars: Barret Oliver, Tami Stronach
Rating: ★★★

N

A combination of *The Wizard of Oz* and *The Dark Crystal* as a young bullied schoolboy discovers a fantasy world in which he can be a hero for once when he opens up a musty old book. Director Wolfgang Petersen, away from the claustrophobic underwater submarine world of *Das Boot*, displays a rare talent for children's storytelling. And the British special effects team of Brian Johnson (*Alien*) and Bruce Nicholson (*The Empire Strikes Back*) have created deadly swamplands and spooky woods and special effects on the vast sound stages of the West German Bavaria Studios that match anything from George Lucas's Industrial Light & Magic. Basically it's a message film about a generation who have spurned the fantastic imaginary worlds of books in favour of the bland and mundane on TV. The film was a monster smash in Germany and led inevitably to a sequel. Pop fans will recognise the dulcet tones of five-minute wonder Limahl, ex-lead singer with Kajagoogoo, singing the catchy Giorgio Moroder theme tune.

Never Give an Inch ◐
(aka: Sometimes a Great Notion)
1971, US, 130 mins, colour
Dir: Paul Newman
Stars: Paul Newman, Henry Fonda, Lee Remick, Michael Sarrazin
Rating: ★★★

The title is the motto of a logging family in this formidably cast Paul Newman, Henry Fonda, Lee Remick, Michael Sarrazin – adaptation of a massive novel by Ken Kesey, who also wrote *One Flew Over the Cuckoo's Nest*. But the outstanding performance, if a supporting one – by long-time Hollywood character player Richard Jaeckel, who was nominated for an Academy Award.

Never Give a Sucker an Even Break ◯
(aka: What a Man!)
1941, US, 71 mins, b/w
Dir: Edward Cline
Stars: W C Fields, Margaret Dumont, Gloria Jean, Leon Errol
Rating: ★★★

W C Fields fans will be helpless with laughter at this, zany by even his standards – he wrote the story under the name Otis Criblecoblis – in which he plans to sell nutmegs to Russians in Mexico, but falls out of a plane and lands on a mountain-top where he meets Margaret Dumont. *What Was*

That? would be a good title for the film (which was actually called *What a Man!* in Britain). It all ends in a typically Fieldsian car chase.

Never Let Go ◐
1960, UK, 91 mins, b/w
Dir: John Guillermin
Stars: Richard Todd, Peter Sellers, Elizabeth Sellars
Rating: ★★★

This nail-biting thriller has been all-too-rarely seen since its first release. Peter Sellers had his first truly unsympathetic part as the hard-cursing crook who imagines himself as England's answer to Little Caesar. Sellers is out-gunned in more ways than one, however, by Richard Todd, who gives a tremendous performance as the down-at-heel salesman who, although beaten, battered and bruised by the gang who have stolen the car that is more important to him than life itself, won't give up. The director ensures that tension remains on a high level throughout, and the drama really packs a punch.

Never Let Me Go ◯
1953, UK, 92 mins, colour
Dir: Delmer Daves
Stars: Clark Gable, Gene Tierney
Rating: ★★

Similar in theme to the loudly-hailed British film *The Young Lovers*, which it preceded by a few months, this drama of east-west romance was made entirely in Britain by an American director, Delmer Daves, mainly on location in Cornwall. Stalwart British based cast includes former ice star Belita, Bernard Miles, Richard Haydn and Kenneth More (just before he shot to stardom in *Genevieve*) and such reliable Slavonic types as Theodore Bikel and Karel Stepanek.

Never Say Die ◯
1939, US, 80 mins, b/w
Dir: Elliott Nugent
Stars: Bob Hope, Martha Raye
Rating: ★★★

The best of several late Thirties comedies Bob Hope made with chasm-mouthed Martha Raye, and something of a rarity. The wisecracks fly thick and fast as Hope (playing John Kidley 'the big bean man') goes for what he thinks are his dying days to Bad Gaswasser, a European health spa. Having nothing to lose, he proceeds to marry Martha, playing a Texas oil heiress called Mickey, to

save her from a loveless marriage to a lecherous prince. A sequence in which the prince (Alan Mowbray) tries to insult Hope into fighting a duel is particularly funny. And the supporting cast is relishable, including stony Gale Sondergaard, who menaced Hope in several other films, Andy Devine, Sig Rumann and Monty Woolley. As well as two of Hope's usual writers, the great Preston Sturges also had a hand in the roller-coaster screenplay. This film contains the original inspiration for the famous 'Chalice from the Palace' routine from the Danny Kaye classic *The Court Jester*.

Never Say Goodbye ◯
1956, US, 96 mins, colour
Dir: Jerry Hopper
Stars: Rock Hudson, Cornell Borchers, George Sanders
Rating: ★★

Not to be confused with the Errol Flynn-Eleanor Parker film of the same title ten years earlier, this is a typically glossy Universal romantic melodrama of the mid-Fifties, with Hudson as a man who tries to re-marry his long-estranged wife. Shelley Fabares, later to star several times with Elvis Presley, makes her screen debut as Hudson's daughter. Other faces to look out for belong to George Sanders, David Janssen, once *The Fugitive*, and, in a very small role, Clint Eastwood.

Never Say Never Again ◯ ⓥ
1983, UK, 137 mins, colour
Dir: Irvin Kershner
Stars: Sean Connery, Klaus Maria Brandauer, Kim Basinger
Rating: ★★★

The original Bond returns, and it's quite a comeback. The lengthy exposition to this remake of *Thunderball*, in fact, merely detracts from the excellence of Sean Connery, purring lethally as 007, but given hot competition in the acting department by Klaus Maria Brandeur, who makes Largo a memorable smiling psychotic. Kim Basinger and Barbara Carrera are extremely well cast as heroine and villainess, and respond wholeheartedly to the demands of their roles. The action is staged with all the mechanical efficiency of the Roger Moore Bond films, but with a bit more bite. The machines aren't quite allowed to take over from this Bond. Lorenzo Semple's script cuts down on the smut and beefs up the wit – or maybe it's just the way Connery delivers the lines. Whether wearing a variety of brown and grey wigs, bedding a variety of pink and dusky girls, or outwitting rather than out-gunning the heavies, this monarch of mayhem strides easily back into his kingdom.

Never So Few ○

1959, US, 124 mins, colour
Dir: John Sturges
Stars: Frank Sinatra, Gina Lollabrigida, Peter Lawford, Steve McQueen
Rating: ★★

There's a bit of everything in John Sturges' drama about wartime Burma – serious political talk, pretty scenery, and Gina Lollobrigida. The film proved once and for all that Frank Sinatra looks silly with a goatee, but it helped advance Steve McQueen's career: the following year he was one of the *Magnificent Seven*. This one, though, is pretty stolid stuff by Sturges' standards.

Never Take No for an Answer ⊙

1951, UK/Italy, 95 mins, b/w
Dir: Maurice Cloche
Stars: Vittorio Manunta, Denis O'Dea
Rating: ★★★

This charming British-Italian co-production is a real heart-breaker; word of mouth made it an unexpected box-office hit in its day. Vittorio Manunta gives a totally winning performance as the little ragged scrap called Peppino, who stops at nothing to get his sick pet donkey to the crypt of St Francis of Assisi, where he is sure she will be cured. Watch for a young John le Mesurier in a small supporting role.

Never Too Late ○

1965, US, 105 mins, colour
Dir: Bud Yorkin
Stars: Paul Ford, Connie Stevens, Maureen O'Sullivan, Jim Hutton
Rating: ★★★

Happy transference of the hit stage play to screen, with character actor Paul Ford wondrously well cast as the middle-aged businessman, who finds that his wife, played by old screen star Maureen O'Sullivan (Mia Farrow's mother and once Tarzan's Jane) is expecting another baby, 20 years after the last. One of the funniest scenes is that in which Ford and his daughter's new husband (Jim Hutton) totter out together to get drunk after being

given the brush-off by their respective wives. Miss O'Sullivan and another Thirties' star, Jane Wyatt, are as pretty a pair of 50-year-olds as ever graced the screen, and even Connie Stevens has her moments as the buxom blond bombshell who suddenly finds herself the family drudge.

New Adventures of Don Juan, The

See: The Adventures of Don Juan

New Centurions, The ◐

(aka: Precinct 45: Los Angeles Police)
1972, US, 105 mins, colour
Dir: Richard Fleischer
Stars: George C Scott, Stacy Keach, Jane Alexander, Scott Wilson
Rating: ★★

'Laws change, people don't,' says one of the characters in this black thriller that takes another pretty gloomy look at the police – this time at the role they play in the violence-ridden America of the Seventies. Despite the customary excellence of George C Scott, it never really catches fire or makes us care about the characters who, Scott's apart, are indifferently acted. One can only blame director Richard Fleischer for not exercising tighter control. But he does raise the excitement in the chases.

New Face In Hell ◐

(aka: P J)
1969, US, 108 mins, colour
Dir: John Guillermin
Stars: George Peppard, Raymond Burr, Gayle Hunnicutt
Rating: ★★★

In America the title of this lively thick-ear thriller was the rather more sober *P J*, the initials of the sub-Philip Marlowe private detective played to the tough, laconic hilt by George Peppard. Sample dialogue: 'You know what I like about you? You're all armpit.' John Guillermin's first Hollywood movie shows him in splendid command of the requirements of this kind of hard-boiled action-cum-mystery movie.

New Interns, The ○

1964, US, 123 mins, b/w
Dir: John Rich
Stars: Michael Callan, Dean Jones, Barbara Eden, Stefanie Powers
Rating: ★

Sequel to *The Interns*, another hospital epic with sentiment unlimited, crises

in the clinic and hysterics in the ward. Side-attractions include the tightest nurses' uniforms ever invented, a 'wild' party as-it-were below stairs and a surgeon who visits the children's ward with a funny face painted on his mask. The girls, Stefanie Powers, Barbara Eden and Inger Stevens, are all very appealing.

New Jack City ● Ⓥ

1991, US, 97 mins, colour
Dir: Mario Van Peebles
Stars: Wesley Snipes, Ice T, Mario Van Peebles, Judd Nelson, Vanessa Williams
Rating: ★★★

The rise and fall of a black ganglord provides another very different central role for the versatile Wesley Snipes. This is a very violent, but crisp and cleanly made narcotics thriller, nicely put together in an old-fashioned style by director Van Peebles, who also plays (not very well, alas) one of its featured roles. Good playing all round otherwise, lots of action and dialogue you can hear. Nothing new here but incisively presented with punch and precision.

New Kind of Love, A ○

1963, US, 110 mins, colour
Dir: Melville Shavelson
Stars: Joanne Woodward, Paul Newman, Thelma Ritter
Rating: ★★★

This romantic romp, with its amusing dream sequences, made a pleasant change from heavy drama for Mr and Mrs Paul Newman (Joanne Woodward), and at its best is reminiscent of Hollywood's best light comedies of the Thirties and Forties. Unfortunately, that standard isn't often reached, although its husband-and-wife team play it impeccably, and the acid tongued Thelma Ritter offers valuable support.

New Leaf, A ○

1971, US, 102 mins, colour
Dir: Elaine May
Stars: Walter Matthau, Elaine May
Rating: ★★★★

Elaine May made Hollywood history with this wickedly funny throwback to the screwball comedies of the 1930s, as the first female star-writer-director. But Paramount were unhappy with her final version running to a weighty three hours and took the film out of her hands and cut it by 78 minutes. Despite her understandable fury and (unsuccessful) attempt to have

N

her name removed from the credits, the film was still a delight and went down well with critics and paying public alike. There are laughs-a-plenty from star Walter Matthau's attempts to stave off destitution by marrying a wealthy woman, and it makes several excellent observations on greed. Spare a thought, however, for actor William Hickey, whose blackmailer character was deleted completely in the revised version of the film.

New Moon ○
1940, US, 105 mins, b/w
Dir: Robert Z Leonard
Stars: Jeanette MacDonald, Nelson Eddy
Rating: ★★★

The rousing score keeps this creaky old operetta afloat, as Jeanette MacDonald and Nelson Eddy flee strife-torn France in 1788 and set sail for a new life in Louisiana USA. Never mind the acting, often pretty wooden, just feel the surge of adrenalin from such stirring numbers as 'Stout-Hearted Men', 'Lover Come Back to Me', 'Softly as in a Morning Sunrise', 'One Kiss' and 'Wanting You'. Good stuff, drivingly directed by Robert Z Leonard, and tightly edited down to a bare hour and three-quarters actual film, trimming that left several roles on the cutting-room floor, including Buster Keaton's cameo as a prisoner on the good ship Lulu. Shimmering photography and nicely-orchestrated crowd scenes make this one of the most spirited of musical action films.

Newsfront ○
1978, Australia, 110 mins, colour
Dir: Phillip Noyce
Stars: Bill Hunter, Wendy Hughes, Chris Haywood
Rating: ★★★

Phillip Noyce's fascinating, fine look at the lives of newsreel cameramen in the Fifties. Gripping throughout, especially in its re-creation of a flood disaster. A most unusual and rewarding film which deservedly put its director on the map.

New York Confidential ○
1955, US, 86 mins, b/w
Dir: Russell Rouse
Stars: Broderick Crawford, Richard Conte, Anne Bancroft, Marilyn Maxwell
Rating: ★★★

This allegedly fact-based gangster thriller, in which the police hardly get a look in, was black and violent enough in its day to get an 'X' certificate. Certainly the last reel contains enough bodies to decorate a production of *Hamlet*. Tough-guy actors Broderick Crawford and Richard Conte are completely at home in their mobster roles, but the best performance of all comes from a young Anne Bancroft as Crawford's daughter, hopelessly trying to escape her father's gangland environment.

New York, New York ○ Ⓥ
1977, US, 164 mins, colour
Dir: Martin Scorsese
Stars: Robert De Niro, Liza Minnelli, Lionel Stander, Barry Primus, Mary Kay Place
Rating: ★★

Martin Scorsese's epic Big Band film is a hit-and-miss love story about a singer (Liza Minnelli) and a saxophonist (Robert De Niro). Forget the Frank Sinatra version of the theme tune; it was written specially for Liza and her rendition at the end of the film is one of the cinema's great show-stoppers. The complete version of the film was reissued in 1981 with the show-stopping finale intact.

New York Stories Ⓒ Ⓥ
1989, US, 125 mins, colour
Dir: Woody Allen, Francis Coppola, Martin Scorsese
Stars: Nick Nolte, Rosanna Arquette, Woody Allen, Julie Kavner, Talia Shire
Rating: ★★

The good news about this three-story, three-director portmanteau view of New York life is that, in it, Woody Allen at last reaffirms his talent for wildly original comedy with a laugh around every other street corner. The bad news is that you have to sit through two really draggy episodes to get to the Allen part. They should re-lease Woody's 40-minute wonder on its own and forget the other two stories altogether. In the first story, temperamental artist Nolte will go to any lengths to prevent untalented bimbo painter Arquette from leaving him; the second concerns a small girl whose personality and quick thinking helps reconcile her parents. Brother, forget it. These anecdotes, directed by Scorsese and Coppola, are much ado about nothing. In Woody's tale, *Oedipus Wrecks*, he's a lawyer beset by the Jewish mother to end them all. Imagine his joy when he takes her to

a magic show and she disappears in the Chinese box. No-one sees her for days and he's a changed man. But retribution beckons. This segment is funny all the way through, but perhaps at its best in Woody's misadventures with a clairvoyant.

Next Man, The Ⓒ
1976, US, 107 mins, colour
Dir: Richard C Sarafian
Stars: Sean Connery, Cornelia Sharpe
Rating: ★★★

Sean Connery triumphs over offbeat casting as an Arab politician who is the target of a glamorous assassin, played by attractive newcomer Cornelia Sharpe. Connery's authoritative performance dominates the film. Although the plot is rather confusing, director Richard C Sarafian stages much of it, especially the scenes at the United Nations, with considerable impact and conviction. Connery and Italian actor Adolfo Celi, old adversaries from *Thunderball* a decade earlier, clash again here.

Next of Kin ● Ⓥ
1989, US, 109 mins, colour
Dir: John Irvin
Stars: Patrick Swayze, Liam Neeson, Adam Baldwin, Helen Hunt, Bill Paxton
Rating: ★

As cut to formula as they come, this Patrick Swayze popcorn action yarn establishes his character as a hillbilly cop in Chicago in a prologue, then kills off his brother to set up the revenge plot. When it becomes apparent towards the end that he needs some help, his country cousins come storming in from the wilds of Kentucky, armed with snakes and bow-and-arrows, to take on the local branch of the Mafia. Guess who wins? Director Irvin is hard put to stop the audience giggling at all this, and settles for a bunch of vaguely comic crooks, one of whom, when thrown through plate glass, remarks: 'That hurt!' The acting is, to say the least, rudimentary, although twitchy Michael J Pollard overacts most enjoyably as the shabby-motel owner who surveys the arsenal imported by Swayze's brother with amusing calm. The dialogue is sometimes difficult to catch: but then it's the kind of film where the hero mutters: 'If Ahm not back b'mornin', call m'keen' and it takes you a few seconds to work out he's not talking about his boss.

Next to No Time! ○
1958, UK, 93 mins, colour
Dir: Henry Cornelius
Stars: Kenneth More, Betsy Drake,
Roland Culver
Rating: ★★

This whimsical comedy, beautifully
shot in colour by the Oscar-winning
cameraman Freddie Francis, was the
last film to be made by the talented
director Henry Cornelius before his
early death at 45. Among Cornelius's
greatest successes were *Passport to
Pimlico*, *The Galloping Major* and
Genevieve, all of them, like *Next to No
Time*, comedies which found their fun
in aspects of the English character.
Here the *Genevieve* star, Kenneth
More, is caught up in a series of
rib-tickling adventures on board the
liner Queen Elizabeth, as he tries to
pluck up the nerve to approach a
millionaire in the hope of getting
finance to help his engineering firm.
Roland Culver, as the millionaire, and
the delightful Betsy Drake play neatly
in support of the star.

Niagara ○ ⓥ
1952, US, 89 mins, colour
Dir: Henry Hathaway
Stars: Marilyn Monroe, Joseph Cotten,
Jean Peters, Casey Adams
Rating: ★★

The film that caused world-wide
queues as the full impact of Marilyn
Monroe's sexual appeal burst for the
first time on the public. Looked at
again through unsteamed glasses,
Niagara can be seen to be a very
moody, rather good thriller, extremely
well directed by Henry Hathaway.
Monroe's erotic charge and Jean
Peters' simpler appeal make equally
striking impacts. Miss Peters' husband
is played by Casey Adams who now
acts under his real name of Max
Showalter.

Nice Girl? ○
1941, US, 95 mins, b/w
Dir: William A Seiter
Stars: Deanna Durbin, Franchot Tone,
Robert Stack, Robert Benchley
Rating: ★★★

Deanna Durbin was just beginning to
lose her unique freshness when she got
an early kiss (from Robert Stack!) in
this standard Hollywood frolic, with a
plot predictably based almost entirely
on misunderstandings. Franchot Tone
and Robert Benchley supply polish

and good humour and the star finds
time to sing 'Thank You America' and
'Love At Last'.

Nice Girl Like Me, A ○
1969, UK, 91 mins, colour
Dir: Desmond Davis
Stars: Barbara Ferris, Harry Andrews
Rating: ★★

Baby-faced blond Barbara Ferris
rocketed about the screen scene for
several years from 1963 onwards,
before concentrating on a stage career.
In this quirky comedy, she's a
warm-hearted (unmarried) girl who
just can't stop having babies!

Nicholas and
Alexandra ○ ⓥ
1971, UK, 189 mins, colour
Dir: Franklin J Schaffner
Stars: Michael Jayston, Janet Suzman,
Laurence Olivier, Jack Hawkins, Tom
Baker
Rating: ★★

Even a film as long as this can only
scratch the surface of its subject – the
fall of Imperial Russia and the rise of
the revolution. And this is perhaps it's
failing. It tries to cover too much
historical ground, which means you
get a little bit of everything but not
enough to sink your teeth into. Having said that, the central tale, that of
the last Tsar, Nicholas, and his wife
Alexandra, holds everything together.
We are watching the fall of a dynasty
and the pressures inside a family which
you know is doomed. In the broad
sweep of history, the problems of one
family, even a Royal one, don't add
up to much, so you find yourself
wanting the film to concentrate more
on what is happening outside the palace walls. Despite its faults, the film
holds your interest thanks largely to
Michael Jayston and Janet Suzman in
the title roles, supported by a cast that
looks like a British theatre roll call.
Special mention must go to Tom
Baker, gloriously evil as Rasputin, and
Michael Bryant, looking firm-jawed
and determined as Lenin.

Nicholas Nickleby ○ ⓥ
1947, UK, 108 mins, b/w
Dir: Alberto Cavalcanti
Stars: Derek Bond, Cedric Hardwicke,
Sally Ann Howes, Bernard Miles
Rating: ★★★

Made when Dickens films were all the
go in the British cinema – *Great Expectations*, *The Pickwick Papers*, *Scrooge*
and *Oliver Twist* were all filmed be-

tween 1946 and 1952 – this Ealing
Studios film is directed with great care
and feel for the period by their distinguished Brazilian veteran, Alberto
Cavalcanti. Despite the star-studded
cast, the film doesn't exactly grab the
attention throughout, although the
Dotheboys Hall sequences spring vividly to life. You can spot three ladies
who were to become stalwarts of TV
comedy, Hattie Jacques, Patricia
Hayes and Dandy Nichols, in their
younger days.

Nick Carter, Master
Detective ○
1939, US, 60 mins, b/w
Dir: Jacques Tourneur
Stars: Walter Pidgeon, Rita Johnson
Rating: ★★★

The stylish Jacques Tourneur cut his
directing teeth on this, the first of
three Carter thrillers made with Walter Pidgeon, battling against the
villains, in the starring role. Loses
momentum in its later stages.

Nickelodeon ○ ⓥ
1976, UK/US, 122 mins, colour
Dir: Peter Bogdanovich
Stars: Ryan O'Neal, Burt Reynolds,
Tatum O'Neal, Brian Keith
Rating: ★

Throughout all its zany situations, this
crazy comedy about early silent
movies only rarely manages to raise a
laugh. Director Peter Bogdanovich's
pacing seems at fault and his actors
might as well be in plastic bags as they
thrash about trying to register as real
live characters. Only Stella Stevens
breaks out of the clutches of the script
to provide us with some genuine
spark. Ryan O'Neal, Burt Reynolds,
Brian Keith and Tatum O'Neal give
sub-par performances; inexperienced
leading lady Jane Hitchcock is a
washout. Even photographer Laszlo
Kovacs is less than his admirable self.
At least it's a genuine family movie; if
only it were a good one too.

Nicky and Gino ◑ ⓥ
1988, US, 109 mins, colour
Dir: Robert M Young
Stars: Tom Hulce, Ray Liotta, Jamie Lee
Curtis, Todd Graff
Rating: ★★★

There's a lot of sincerity if not many
laughs in this story of a 26-year-old
aspiring doctor (Liotta) and his
brain-damaged brother, played by
Hulce with one silver tooth rather
uneasily underlining the idiot image.

N

But, though the story is gloomy and slow at the start, director Robert M Young has knitted a good pattern out of it by the finish, thanks to a subplot that works wonders at bolstering the basic storyline, as Liotta battles with himself over the decision to leave Pittsburgh and Hulce (whose garbage-truck money has put him through college) and pass his finals in far-away California. Jamie Lee Curtis is her usual sterling self as Liotta's girlfriend and Todd Graff puts in a good job as Hulce's drug-dealing, hair-slicking workmate. There's also a dog called O'Malley, whose talent at heading a ball some struggling soccer clubs could surely use.

Nico

See: Above the Law

Night Ambush

See: Ill Met by Moonlight

Night and Day ○ ⓥ

1946, US, 132 mins, colour
Dir: Michael Curtiz
Stars: Cary Grant, Alexis Smith
Rating: ★★

Although this song-strewn tribute to the great composer Cole Porter obviously had to steer clear of his bisexuality, it does in other respects, and with the undervalued help of Cary Grant, capture something of the restrained, distant air which made Porter at the same time charismatic and sometimes difficult. Mary Martin is on hand to sing (brilliantly) 'My Heart Belongs to Daddy', and the film would have been better off handing this Broadway legend the leading singing role actually played by band vocalist Ginny Simms. Nice orchestrations by Ray Heindorf, however, can't disguise the fact that this film is, even just as a musical tribute, not the movie it might have been.

Night and the City ○

1950, UK, 91 mins, b/w
Dir: Jules Dassin
Stars: Gene Tierney, Richard Widmark, Googie Withers, Francis L Sullivan
Rating: ★★★

Director Jules Dassin, whose previous three films had been *Brute Force*, *Naked City* and *Thieves' Highway*, continued his look at world-wide criminal life with this strongly atmospheric thriller set in London. The dark, sleazy, foggy Thameside setting is splendidly evocative and Richard Widmark's shifty,

slippery weasel is one of his best early performances. The film opens as it means to continue, with Widmark's character hunted, fearful, out of breath and frantically trying to avoid being cornered. Past dark buildings and through alleyways, he is stalked by unseen feet, and by the insistent, frenetic chords of a memorable score by Franz Waxman.

Night and the City ● ⓥ

1993, US, 105 mins, colour
Dir: Irwin Winkler
Stars: Robert De Niro, Jessica Lange, Cliff Gorman, Jack Warden, Eli Wallach
Rating: ★★

This low-life urban drama is a remake of the Hollywood-funded, British-based 1950 thriller with Richard Widmark. In the Nineties, the hustler, Harry Fabian, is played by Robert De Niro and has become a lawyer straight out of the Marx Brothers' Shyster, Flywheel and Shyster. Typical advice to a client is: 'If you want to walk in Central Park, leave the baseball bat at home.' Becoming involved with mobsters, an affair with his barman's wife (Jessica Lange) and the shadier end of the boxing world, Harry Fabian is clearly not destined for a dull, long or happy life. Despite De Niro's non-stop performance, however, and a veritable barrage of street language, this version of his downfall lacks dramatic weight and punch, and is further weakened by a softening of the original ending, which was unusually bleak by Fifties' standards.

Night at the Opera, A ○ ⓥ

1935, US, 92 mins, b/w
Dir: Sam Wood
Stars: Groucho Marx, Chico Marx, Harpo Marx, Margaret Dumont, Allan Jones
Rating: ★★★★

Modestly described by its studios' publicists as 'A thirty-ring circus of laughs, songs, girls, spectacle', this wild extravaganza of inspired lunacy is easily the best of the Marx Brothers' MGM movies, crammed with comic gems. See director Sam Wood cram more people into a tiny ship's cabin than British Rail manage to stuff into a commuter carriage! Marvel at the classic encounters between Groucho and Margaret Dumont's immoveable object! Watch and hear as Harpo introduces 'Take Me Out To The Ball Game' into Verdi's score for 'Il Trovatore'! And wonder at Jewish Chico's Italian accent! All this, and more, is on offer

in a comedy that wears its age with great charm and effect. And remember: there ain't no sanity clause!

Night Boat to Dublin ○

1945, UK, 91 mins, b/w
Dir: Lawrence Huntington
Stars: Robert Newton, Raymond Lovell, Guy Middleton, Muriel Pavlow
Rating: ★★★

Crisply-photographed (by Otto Hestler) spy thriller, developed by director Lawrence Huntington as a catalogue of breathless excitements. Several performers seized chances to establish themselves as stars of the post-war British cinema, among them Muriel Pavlow; and Robert Newton, quite unusually cast as the heroic secret agent thwarting Nazi plans, provides a sturdy central pillar around whom the film's tense action revolves.

Nightbreed ● ⓥ

1990, US, 101 mins, colour
Dir: Clive Barker
Stars: Craig Sheffer, David Cronenberg, Anne Bobby, Charles Haid
Rating: ★★★

Good fare for horror fans: noisy, full-blooded and slightly off the beaten track. A society of freaks and monsters (they're the heroes, by the way) lives beneath the Midian cemetery and Boone (Sheffer) finds himself drawn there, even after death – though to reveal quite why would be to unlock a key element in writer-director Clive Barker's plot. The first couple of reels are a bit wearisome, but the sheer expense and spectacle of the rest, even given the repulsive nature of some of the 'creatures', is quite overwhelming. The 'human' actors have an unenviable task in a film like this, but Sheffer, Bobby (his girl) and director Cronenberg (as Sheffer's psychiatrist) all infuse a creditable amount of personality into their characters under the circumstances – although why the villain has to dispatch a policeman near the end is something of a mystery. But Barker's bizarre imagination and a pretty high budget provides some demented tableaux that even outdo Hieronymous Bosch. Non-horror fans may find it quite disgusting.

Night Creatures ◐

(aka: Captain Clegg)
1962, UK, 82 mins, b/w
Dir: Peter Graham Scott
Stars: Peter Cushing, Oliver Reed
Rating: ★★

A Hammer studios' mystery yarn, also known as *Captain Clegg*, in which the legendary 'phantoms' of Romney Marsh are used as cover for 18th-century smugglers. Based on Russell Thorndike's *Dr Syn*, with Oliver Reed leading the supporting cast.

Night Hair Child ●

1971, UK, 89 mins, colour
Dir: James Kelly
Stars: Mark Lester, Britt Ekland, Hardy Kruger, Lilli Palmer
Rating: ★★

Child star Mark Lester startled many of his fans from *Oliver!* with his performance in this shocker, as a psychotic 12-year-old, who preys on his new stepmother. Harry Andrews and Lilli Palmer contribute moments of cultured calm to the fevered proceedings that follow.

Night Has a Thousand Eyes ○

1948, US, 80 mins, b/w
Dir: John Farrow
Stars: Edward G Robinson, Gail Russell, John Lund
Rating: ★★★

One more time for the story of the mind-reader whose gift of foreseeing the future brings him nothing but torment and tragedy. This version certainly has the right fatalistic feel about it, plus a strong central performance from Edward G Robinson as the man who can flee the future but cannot escape his own destiny.

Nighthawks ● ⓥ

1981, US, 99 mins, colour
Dir: Bruce Malmuth
Stars: Sylvester Stallone, Billy Dee Williams, Lindsay Wagner, Rutger Hauer
Rating: ★★★

Sylvester Stallone took time out from his series of *Rocky* movies to play a tough New York policeman seconded to Interpol to join in the hunt for a ruthless terrorist. And he's rather good, well supported by Billy Dee Williams, as his partner, and Nigel Davenport, as the man who trains the cops in anti-terrorist tactics. But the film is dominated by Rutger Hauer as their quarry: his powerful performance took the blond Dutch actor into the big league of international screen actors.

Night Holds Terror, The ○

1955, US, 85 mins, b/w
Dir: Andrew Stone

Stars: Jack Kelly, Vince Edwards, John Cassavetes, Hildy Parks
Rating: ★★★

Hailed as an outstanding second-feature in its day, this hostage thriller keeps tension on high throughout, and was a boost to the careers of its stars, who include Jack Kelly, Vince Edwards and John Cassavetes. Director Andrew Stone, who specialised in fast-moving, hard-hitting, location-shot thrillers, based his script on incidents from two real-life ransom cases.

Night in Casablanca, A ⊙

1946, US, 85 mins, b/w
Dir: Archie Mayo
Stars: Groucho Marx, Harpo Marx, Chico Marx
Rating: ★★★

The film that brought The Marx Brothers and their zany magnificence back to the screen after a five-year absence. The humour is almost undiluted Marx lunacy, from the cork so huge that it leaves no room for wine, to the crashing collapse of a wall that Harpo has insisted he is holding up. Chico baffles his companions with double-talk while Groucho lopes across the screen as the manager of the Hotel Casablanca. 'I'm Bea,' remarks a shapely guest. 'I stop at the hotel.' 'I'm the hotel manager,' Groucho leers. 'I stop at nothing.'

Nightingale Sang in Berkeley Square, A

See: The Biggest Bank Robbery

Night in Heaven, A ◗ ⓥ

1983, US, 80 mins, colour
Dir: John G Avildsen
Stars: Christopher Atkins, Lesley Ann Warren, Robert Logan, Andy Gacia
Rating: ★★

Not an angelic comedy, as the title might suggest, but rather a sex romp through the world of Chippendale-style male exotic dancers. Christopher Atkins, the fresh-faced moppet from *The Blue Lagoon*, hardly looks old enough to be stripping to his assets as Rickey Rocket at the Heaven ladies-only night-club. Lesley Ann Warren is his college teacher who is dragged to the club by her thrill-seeking sister and ends up having the groin of the student she's just failed from her course thrust into her shocked face. You can guess the rest as student and teacher 'reawaken'

long-suppressed physical longings. The director is John G Avildsen, who won an Oscar for the original *Rocky*.

Night in the Life of Jimmy Reardon, A

See: Jimmy Reardon

Nightmare ○

1956, US, 88 mins, b/w
Dir: Maxwell Shane
Stars: Edward G Robinson, Kevin McCarthy, Connie Russell
Rating: ★★

Clearly writer-director Maxwell Shane liked the plot of this ingenious thriller since he had filmed it before, in 1947, as *Fear in the Night*. Here, aided by Joseph Biroc's moody monochrome photography, he creates an effective atmosphere of mystery and menace and gets a good performance from Kevin McCarthy as the man who believes he's a murderer. But the acting honours go to Edward G Robinson's tough detective with a soft heart who discovers that all is not what it seems. The music is very effective and is provided by Billy May and his Band, with May taking a brief dramatic role.

Nightmare ◗

1963, UK, 82 mins, b/w
Dir: Freddie Francis
Stars: Jennie Linden, David Knight, Moira Redmond
Rating: ★★

An early Hammer chiller-thriller about a girl with a recurring nightmare, directed by Freddie Francis, an Oscar-winning cameraman (he photographed *The Innocents*). In common with that film, this drama is creepily shot in black-and-white, and has Clytie Jessop again as a 'ghost woman'.

Nightmare Alley ○

1947, US, 111 mins, b/w
Dir: Edmund Goulding
Stars: Tyrone Power, Joan Blondell, Coleen Gray, Mike Mazurki
Rating: ★★★

A strange and fascinating thriller-drama set against a background of carnival freaks and sideshows. It originally sprang from the equally strange mind of writer William Lindsay Gresham, who was obsessed by the darker corners of the entertainment world, and ended his days by committing suicide. Tyrone Power tackles, for him, a most unusual role as the fake spiritualist whose decline is as

N

sudden as his success. For the making of the film, a huge carnival was rented for the 10 weeks' shooting and re-erected in 10 acres of the 20th Century-Fox backlot.

Nightmare on Elm Street, A ● ⓥ
1984, US, 91 mins, colour
Dir: Wes Craven
Stars: Robert Englund, Heather Langenkamp, Johnny Depp
Rating: ★★

'One, two, Freddy's comin' for you; three, four, better lock your door; five, six, grab your crucifix; seven, eight, gonna stay up late; nine, ten, never sleep again.' This haunting, twisted nursery rhyme launched one of the most successful horror film series since Universal launched *The Mummy* and *Frankenstein* on an unsuspecting public in the Thirties. Five sequels have followed and a spin-off TV series, *Freddie's Nightmares*. Pity creator and director Wes Craven, who signed away the lucrative rights to his bogeyman villain Freddy Krueger (billed as Fred in the original film). But the series proved to be a goldmine for Robert Englund – originally only ninth billed as the child-killer horrifically burned alive by his victims' parents, and who now wreaks revenge on their children through their dreams. There's a nice homage to Hitchcock's *Psycho*, in that Craven, like Hitchcock 30 years earlier, kills off in early scenes the person the audience is led to believe is the main character. Look out for rising star Johnny Depp in an early role as one of Freddy's victims. Five sequels to date, all inferior to this.

'Night Mother ◐
1986, US, 96 mins, colour
Dir: Tom Moore
Stars: Sissy Spacek, Anne Bancroft, Ed Berke, Carol Robbins
Rating: ★★

Director Tom Moore, whose only previous movie experience was the disastrous *Return to Boggy Creek* horror film in 1978, seems a strange choice to film this gruelling but ultimately stagebound version of the Pulitzer Prize-winning play. But it is a small triumph on its own terms for Moore, who directed the original stage version. Sissy Spacek is intensely moving as the daughter who wants to end her own life and whose logic about that

decision confounds her hysterical mother (Anne Bancroft). However, this was yet another example of Hollywood casting glamorous young stars over established Broadway actors. Kathy Bates played Miss Spacek's part in the original production just as she played Michelle Pfeiffer's role in *Frankie and Johnny*. And that's a crying shame!

Night Moves ●
1975, US, 95 mins, colour
Dir: Arthur Penn
Stars: Gene Hackman, Jennifer Warren, Edward Binns
Rating: ★★

Though it's highly rated in many circles, there are too many unanswered questions at the end of director Arthur Penn's detective story to make it a classic of the genre. Good though Gene Hackman is as the sleuth, you may not be prepared to work out his problems for him as the director seems to be asking. Complex it certainly is, though, with a bravura climax, and very early screen appearances from James Woods and Melanie Griffith. But this is the disillusioned detective syndrome taken to its ultimate extreme, and you may feel that it finally disappears up its own nightmare. See it and decide for yourself.

Night Must Fall ◐
1964, UK, 105 mins, b/w
Dir: Karel Reisz
Stars: Albert Finney, Susan Hampshire, Mona Washbourne, Sheila Hancock, Michael Medwin
Rating: ★★

A remake of the 1937 chiller about a mad young man (then Robert Montgomery, now Albert Finney) who kills a woman with an axe and pops her head in a hat-box. Montgomery whistled 'Danny Boy' to send shivers up our spines; Finney goes round the house in canvas shoes, a maniacal smile hovering at the corners of his lips. The suspense thus engendered, and grisly results, may well startle those who haven't seen the earlier version, although this one is more shocking than sinister. There's masterly black-and-white photography from Freddie Francis, and especially good acting from Mona Washbourne, who conveys well the pitiful vulnerability of old Mrs Bramson, who looks set fair to become Danny's next victim. But even so, it's not half as good as the rarely-shown original.

Night My Number Came Up, The ○
1955, UK, 94 mins, b/w
Dir: Leslie Norman
Stars: Michael Redgrave, Sheila Sim, Alexander Knox
Rating: ★★★

Ingenious thriller concerning a nightmare (about an air crash) which seems to be coming true. Within a few minutes of the opening, one knows exactly what is going to happen. The surprising thing is that the cast manages to sustain a high degree of suspense right up to the end. The whole thing is apt to send a shiver down your spine. Michael Redgrave, as an air marshal who scoffs at the dream at first, then finds himself enacting it, looks suitably perturbed.

Night of the Demon ◐
(aka: Curse of the Demon)
1957, UK, 82 mins, b/w
Dir: Jacques Tourneur
Stars: Dana Andrews, Peggy Cummins
Rating: ★★★

This famous chiller opens with an attack on the nerves and sustains it right to the end. Evil, raised up by a professor of the occult, raises its head in such seemingly innocuous settings as the British Museum's library, the grounds of an English country home and in a railway carriage. The edgy direction by veteran Hollywood horror-man Jacques Tourneur makes the bizarre events seem spinechillingly real.

Night of the Eagle ◐ ⓥ
(aka: Burn, Witch, Burn)
1961, UK, 87 mins, b/w
Dir: Sidney Hayers
Stars: Janet Blair, Peter Wyngarde, Margaret Johnston
Rating: ★★★

Director Sidney Hayers, one of the hardest-working British film-makers, who eventually went to Hollywood in the late Seventies, turned in one of his finest jobs in this genuinely frightening witch-craft thriller. Aided by menacing black and white photography by Reginald Wyer, director Hayers proves remarkably successful at suggesting an atmosphere of super-natural dangers, rather than relying simply on overt horror.

Night of the Following Day, The ◐ ⓥ
1968, US, 93 mins, colour
Dir: Hubert Cornfield

Stars: Marlon Brando, Richard Boone
Rating: ★★

Brando has appeared in some strange films in his time, and this bizarre thriller is no exception. Its circular plot construction has more than a little in common with that classic of the macabre, *Dead of Night*.

Night of the Generals ◐ Ⓥ
1966, UK, 148 mins, colour
Dir: Anatole Litvak
Stars: Peter O'Toole, Omar Sharif, Joanna Pettet
Rating: ★★

A whodunnit of epic proportions, set in Nazi-occupied Paris during World War Two. Peter O'Toole and Omar Sharif are the big star guns, but Tom Courtenay contributes the most controlled performance in a formidable cast that also includes Donald Pleasence, Christopher Plummer, John Gregson and Joanna Pettet. A steamroller of a movie that falls between several stools.

Night of the Grizzly ○
1966, US, 102 mins, colour
Dir: Joseph Pevney
Stars: Clint Walker, Martha Hyer, Keenan Wynn
Rating: ★★★

A decidedly different action Western – Clint Walker plays an ex-lawman trying to forge a new life in wild country – in which normal human lives are intertwined skilfully with just that proportion of natural tragedy that must have haunted families in the old west. And the fights involving a marauding grizzly bear have a savage realism. The photography catches exactly the feel of the countryside, and swoops like a big cat on the odd object, such as a pumpkin head at Hallowe'en or, in a very funny scene, a drunken cockerel. The cast is a gold mine of vignette parts. You'll remember Nancy Kulp, as the horse-faced store-keeper; Don Haggerty as Walker's grizzled sidekick; and Jack Elam as the handyman (reformed town drunk!).

Night of the Hunter, The ● Ⓥ
1955, US, 93 mins, b/w
Dir: Charles Laughton
Stars: Robert Mitchum, Shelley Winters, Lillian Gish
Rating: ★★★★

The only film directed by actor Charles Laughton – he called it 'a nightmarish sort of Mother Goose tale' – contains the performance of his life from lugubrious Robert Mitchum, as a psychopathic killer in search of hidden money. A *film noir* classic, *The Night of the Hunter* was, surprisingly, not a hit on original release and Laughton was never again offered the chance to get behind the cameras. Laughton's masterly direction drew heavily from German directors Fritz Lang and Josef von Sternberg in its use of shadows and darkness to create mood, apprehension and terror. The film's cinematographer, Stanley Cortez, was the brother of Ricardo Cortez, one-time Latin lover of the silent screen. Stanley's work also included *The Magnificent Ambersons* for Orson Welles.

Night of the Iguana, The ◐
1964, US, 118 mins, b/w
Dir: John Huston
Stars: Richard Burton, Ava Gardner, Deborah Kerr, Sue Lyon
Rating: ★★★

Typically overheated Tennessee Williams melodrama, although with rather more humour than one usually associates with that playwright, co-directed with a full head of steam by John Huston on location in the remote Mexican fishing village of Mismaloya. Richard Burton enjoys himself as a defrocked priest now reduced to working as a courier to a party of American teachers and finding himself locked into a sexual square dance with Sue Lyon (in her first role since her debut as a pouting nymphet in *Lolita*), Ava Gardner as a widow running the remote seaside hotel where he and his party end up, and Deborah Kerr, superb as a spinster with hidden depths. The performances match the ripeness of the writing and the locations add to the impact of an always watchable – if rarely credible – star movie.

Night of the Living Dead ● Ⓥ
1969, US, 96 mins, b/w
Dir: George A Romero
Stars: Duane Jones, Judith O'Dea
Rating: ★★★★

A genuinely frightening, edge-of-seat suspense horror film, this made the reputation of its director, George A Romero, and led to two Romero-directed sequels, *Zombies – Dawn of the Dead* and *Day of the Dead*. All are good, but this is the pick of the bunch, uncomfortably made in black and white. A plague of zombies in the American countryside leads to some truly terrifying scenes, with the main protagonists trapped in a house. The shock moments are very skilfully done, and the horror presented head-on, leaving the viewer with no escape. Remade in 1993.

Night of the Living Dead ● Ⓥ
1990, US, 96 mins, colour
Dir: Tom Savini
Stars: Patricia Tallman, Tony Todd, Tom Towles, McKee Anderson
Rating: ★★

A pointless colour remake of the George A Romero classic, which gained immense power from being in black and white. This one, scripted by Romero but directed by Tom Savini, is just your standard zombie movie, with a few good moments and a lot of chuckles. An excellent, hard-driving performance by Patricia Tallman, going from nervous wreck to intense, knife-edge gun girl, is unfortunately the only good one in the film. Tony Todd, later much more effective in *Candyman*, is particularly disappointing as the hero, though he's by no means the worst performer in the film. The living dead themselves are always ludicrous rather than threatening, in a film that unsurprisingly sat on the shelf for three years before its British release in 1993.

Night on Earth ● Ⓥ
1991, US, 120 mins, colour
Dir: Jim Jarmusch
Stars: Winona Ryder, Gena Rowlands, Béatrice Dalle, Roberto Benigni
Rating: ★

Five cities, five stories, five dreary taxi journeys. Jim Jarmusch's pointless cab drive around the world does catch some of the bleaker qualities of the cities visited, and is briefly enlivened by Robert Benigni's Roman scandals when he confesses (to his priestly passenger) his sexual encounters with pumpkins, sheep and his brother-in-law's wife. Béatrice Dalle is quite effective as a French blind girl, and Winona Ryder and Gena Rowlands act hard in one of the two American sections. At two hours, though, this ride has so little to say that's entertaining that it's hardly worth the fare. Probably a cult movie in the making.

Night on the Town, A ◐ Ⓥ
(aka: Adventures in Babysitting)
1987, US, 93 mins, colour
Dir: Chris Columbus

N

Stars: Elisabeth Shue, Maia Brewton, Keith Coogan
Rating: ★★

An old Disney trunk item dusted up with a few four-letter words and trotted out under the company's adult Touchstone banner. Elisabeth Shue is the babysitter who lurches into a kind of junior-grade *After Hours* when her best friend calls up in trouble and she's forced to take her mother's car, her young charge and two 15-year-olds in a ride into the big city that turns into a nightmare of often barefaced contrivance, with some very annoying characters. The talented Shue, who's been unlucky with her career, tries very hard to make something of it, and the film spurts into life when she's forced to break into an impromptu 'Babysitting Blues' after bursting on to a nightclub stage hotly pursued by a couple of comic gangsters led by old sad-eyes John (Davis) Chandler. Shue carries the sequence through with delightful verve. Otherwise you can only sympathise as she yelps, 'This is not funny,' during one of her misadventures. An old-fashioned Disney night on the town, then, but alas no longer one for the family.

Night Passage ○
1957, US, 88 mins, colour
Dir: James Neilson
Stars: James Stewart, Audie Murphy, Dan Duryea, Dianne Foster
Rating: ★★

The mouth-watering Western combination of James Stewart, Audie Murphy, Dan Duryea and Brandon de Wilde doesn't quite produce the fireworks you'd expect in this railroad Western, in spite of Murphy doing well with his unusual casting as a good-bad guy. The treatment sorely misses the touch of Stewart's normal Western director, Anthony Mann. Even so, this remains a workmanlike action picture, with Stewart contributing his usual double dose of sincerity, and Duryea just walking away with the film as the blink-eyed, double-dyed Whitey Harbin.

Night People ○
1954, US, 93 mins, colour
Dir: Nunnally Johnson
Stars: Gregory Peck, Broderick Crawford, Anita Bjork, Rita Gam
Rating: ★★★

Drama of espionage and counter-espionage in post-war Berlin. Broderick Crawford is especially ef-fective as the man whose son has been kidnapped by the Communists. Attractive Rita Gam, usually seen in more sultry roles, appears as Colonel Gregory Peck's poker faced secretary; and Swedish actress Anita Bjork plays an East German double-agent. For any suspense going Nunnally Johnson deserves all the praise. He not only produced the film, but wrote and directed it. 20th Century-Fox's selling line for the film was: 'We didn't say "Nice People", we said "Night People"!'

Night Shift ◐
1982, US, 105 mins, colour
Dir: Ron Howard
Stars: Henry Winkler, Michael Keaton, Shelley Long
Rating: ★★★

Delightfully macabre comedy which takes a series of tasteless elements and fashions them into a tasty romp about a wimpish type (Henry Winkler) who takes a job at the local morgue, where his sharpie assistant embroils him in a wild scheme involving a prostitution racket. The two leading roles are feistily played by Winkler and Michael Keaton, Shelley Long from *Cheers* is also there somewhere, and the film represented a big step forward in the directorial career of former child star Ron Howard, who has since made *Splash*, *Cocoon* and *Backdraft*.

Night Song ○
1947, US, 101 mins, b/w
Dir: John Cromwell
Stars: Dana Andrews, Merle Oberon
Rating: ★

A really drippy and unbelievable weepie about a pianist blinded in an accident, but given the will to compose by the love of a clever woman. Dana Andrews and Merle Oberon haven't the sympathetic personalities needed to make this work, even if the script gave them any help. Best moment: pianist Arthur Rubinstein performing with the New York Philharmonic.

Night They Invented Striptease, The
See: The Night They Raided Minsky's

Night They Raided Minsky's, The ○
(aka: The Night They Invented Striptease)
1967, US, 99 mins, colour
Dir: William Friedkin

Stars: Jason Robards, Britt Ekland, Norman Wisdom
Rating: ★★★★

The complicated plotline culminates in Britt Ekland (improbably cast as a naive, stage-struck Amish girl) inventing striptease by accident and bringing the era of American burlesque to an end. But the story takes place to the film's entertaining evocation of the old burlesque shows and Norman Wisdom, in his only American film, shows his co-stars, notably Jason Robards, just how variety acts were done. Bert Lahr, best remembered for his Cowardly Lion in *The Wizard of Oz*, makes his final screen appearance: his role is truncated since he died during filming and a double had to be used in some scenes.

Night to Remember, A ○
1942, US, 91 mins, b/w
Dir: Richard Wallace
Stars: Loretta Young, Brian Aherne
Rating: ★★★

Nice little wartime frolic about a mystery writer and his wife who get a real-life murder puzzle to solve. Nothing new in this, for sure, but a vivid array of character players, including Gale Sondergaard, Sidney Toler, Lee Patrick and Blanche Yurka, ensures the right atmosphere for the not-too-serious thrills and chills.

Night to Remember, A ○ Ⓥ
1958, US, 123 mins, b/w
Dir: Roy Baker
Stars: Kenneth More, Ronald Allen, Honor Blackman
Rating: ★★★

A tense, dramatic, watchable reconstruction of what happened on the disastrous night in 1912 when the liner Titanic sank. It has everything from stiff upper lips to panic, from high drama to low comedy, plus a first-rate performance from Kenneth More as the Second Officer, a role played in the 1953 Hollywood version (simply called *Titanic*) by Edmund Purdom.

Night Train
See: Night Train to Munich

Night Train to Munich ○
(aka: Night Train)
1940, UK, 95 mins, b/w
Dir: Carol Reed
Stars: Margaret Lockwood
Rating: ★★★

The affinities of this lively spy thriller with Hitchcock's *The Lady Vanishes* are obvious. That's not surprising, however, since it was scripted by that film's writers, Frank Launder and Sidney Gilliat who also reintroduced the cricket enthusiasts Charters and Caldicott, played by Basil Radford and Naunton Wayne, and Margaret Lockwood once again stars. Carol Reed's direction is suitably tense and he stages excellent chase sequences. Notable among the set pieces is the cable-car shootout at the climax, much imitated in later films, including 1969's *Where Eagles Dare*.

Night Walker, The ◐
1965, US, 86 mins, b/w
Dir: William Castle
Stars: Barbara Stanwyck, Robert Taylor
Rating: ★★

A strange film to reunite Barbara Stanwyck and Robert Taylor on screen after 20 years, this twisty, chilly thriller comes from the 'showman of shock', William Castle. It's a frightening tale he unfolds, at its creepiest and best in the first 20 minutes. Ms Stanwyck, who was married to Taylor from 1939 until 1952, proved she could still come out of a searching close-up with as many honours as actresses half her age.

Night Watch ◐
1973, UK, 98 mins, colour
Dir: Brian G Hutton
Stars: Elizabeth Taylor, Laurence Harvey, Billie Whitelaw
Rating: ★

Did Elizabeth Taylor really see a man with his throat cut in the window opposite her bedroom? Is she going mad after a nervous breakdown? Are her husband (Laurence Harvey in his last major film performance) and best friend (Billie Whitelaw) having an affair and plotting against her? By pitching his suspense at hysteria level throughout, director Brian G Hutton makes sure that no one dozes off in this film, even if we don't believe a word of it.

Night We Dropped a Clanger, The ○
1959, UK, 86 mins, b/w
Dir: Darcy Conyers
Stars: Brian Rix, Cecil Parker
Rating: ★

A fine cast of comedy performers all at sea in a typically rickety British farce of the late Fifties, a time when the

Carry On films were gaining their first foothold. Brian Rix has a field day in a dual role and William Hartnell gives his comic all as a barking sergeant.

Night We Got the Bird, The ○
1960, UK, 82 mins, b/w
Dir: Darcy Conyers
Stars: Brian Rix, Ronald Shiner, Dora Bryan
Rating: ★★

A fast and furious farce about a man reincarnated as a parrot, with the regulars from the Brian Rix Theatre of Laughter well to the fore. And there are some priceless cameo performances from the supporting cast, including Robertson Hare as a dithering doctor, John Le Mesurier as a long-suffering court clerk and Kynaston Reeves, hilarious as a deaf magistrate.

Night We Never Met, The ● ⓥ
1993, US, 99 mins, colour
Dir: Warren Light
Stars: Matthew Broderick, Annabella Sciorra, Kevin Anderson, Jeanne Tripplehorn, Louise Lasser, Justine Bateman
Rating: ★★

Matthew Broderick gives a bright, chirpy performance as New York bachelor Sam in this engaging if underwritten and highly predictable comedy of mistaken identity. Sam shares an apartment in the city with two other tenants, sensitive painter Ellen (Annabella Sciorra) and yuppie party animal Brian (Kevin Anderson). But as each uses the apartment on separate days, none of the tenants ever meets up. Before long, some farcical misunderstandings escalate to gigantic proportions. An old-fashioned sex comedy for cynical romantics, just about kept afloat to the end by its bright young cast.

Nine Hours to Rama ○
1962, US, 125 mins, colour
Dir: Mark Robson
Stars: Horst Buchholz, Jose Ferrer, Valerie Gearon
Rating: ★★★★

So Indian, you can almost taste the curry, was how one critic described this tensely dramatic account of the events in Delhi, India, on the day of Mahatma Gandhi's assassination. Director Mark Robson's nationwide search to find an actor to play Gandhi was rewarded by the discovery of J S

Casshyap, who bore such a striking resemblance as to make some of the film look almost like a newsreel. Horst Buchholz is suitably wide-eyed as the religious fanatic assigned the assassination, and there are good performances from Diane Baker and Don Borisenko. The whole thing is amazingly tense considering one is aware of the outcome, and the colour photography conveys exactly the heat, dust and dirt of the country.

976 EVIL ● ⓥ
1988, US, 100 mins, colour
Dir: Robert Englund
Stars: Stephen Geoffreys, Patrick O'Bryan, Jim Metzler, Sandy Dennis, Lezlie Deane
Rating: ★

Robert 'Freddy Krueger' Englund turns film director, but on the evidence of this one he was wise to return to Elm Street. A horror film in which almost nothing happens for 50 minutes, it eventually develops into a sort of *Little Phone of Horrors*, with a hero in direct descent from Rick Moranis' Seymour. Dial 976 EVIL and, before you know it, your mind has been consumed with evil thoughts and you start developing green toenails and looking like Dorian Gray's portrait in the attic. Clearly this state of affairs can't last, and towards the end Englund does stage some nice tableaux with visions of Hell breaking out all over the place. But it's too little evil and too late. Just about worth a look for horror fans, if only to spot Englund's own cameo, and for Sandy Dennis' extraordinary performance as Aunt Lucy.

Nineteen Eighty Four ◐ ⓥ
1984, UK, 115 mins, colour
Dir: Michael Radford
Stars: John Hurt, Richard Burton, Suzanna Hamilton
Rating: ★★★

John Hurt, the screen king of torture, torment, anguish and suffering, is at it again in this version of George Orwell's bleak vision of the future. And nobody does it better, whether the suffering is mental or, in the harrowing latter part of the film, physical, as interrogator Richard Burton (underplaying too much) sticks electricity through the thin-framed Hurt like a butcher skinning a carcass of meat. Hurt also has his hair chopped off again, and his fans must be wondering what it's like to see him smile. Cyril Cusack scoops up what

N

acting scraps Hurt (and the film's ubiquitous rats) leaves around, as the treacherous junk dealer, but the ultimate result of Michael Radford's downbeat direction is a sombre and depressing film. After this one, you may not be able to look a rat in the eye for some time!

1969 ● Ⓥ
1988, US, 96 mins, colour
Dir: Ernest Thompson
Stars: Robert Downey Jr, Kiefer Sutherland, Bruce Dern, Mariette Hartley, Winona Ryder
Rating: ★

A whole crew of good actors is shipwrecked in a sea of precious dialogue in this look at 1969, flower power, Vietnam protests and all that. Mind you, Sutherland, Ryder and Mariette Hartley look good even when speaking these lines. Robert Downey has to tackle yet another bag-eyed loner pressing the self-destruct button, while Dern and Joanna Cassidy fare even less well trying to express an adulterous relationship the whole town know about. The plot, alas, never flows with any fluency, and did anyone really say, especially back then: 'This is the last year of our innocence'? And would anyone have wanted to know them if they did? No matter. Not even this script could prevent Sutherland and Ryder becoming major stars of the Nineties.

Nine to Five ○ Ⓥ
1980, US, 110 mins, colour
Dir: Colin Higgins
Stars: Jane Fonda, Dolly Parton, Lily Tomlin, Dabney Coleman, Sterling Hayden
Rating: ★★★

Fast, furious and unusual comedy that gave rise to the successful TV series. For most of its running time, it proves to be fun to have around, tripping a zany light fantastic round three lady office workers: the brains (Lily Tomlin), the bust (Dolly Parton) and the bewildered (Jane Fonda in an offbeat role – especially funny when trying to cope with a computer filing system). The main villain, however, is not the machine age but the girls' intolerable, grind-the-employees-into-the-ground sexist employer. This is a thankless but well-played role for Dabney Coleman, who at least gets star billing for his pains. How the girls keep Coleman prisoner in his own home while proving fraudulent conversion against him is every

henpecked clerk's dream. Wish-fulfilment to be sure but of the happiest kind, with hallucination sequences, madcap encounters with a corpse on a trolley and even cartoon characters on the way. Lily Tomlin is delightful as Violet but subsequent suitable roles for both her and Dolly Parton have proved difficult for the cinema to provide.

99 ⁴⁴⁄₁₀₀ % Dead
See: Call Harry Crown

99 River Street ○
1953, US, 83 mins, b/w
Dir: Phil Karlson
Stars: John Payne, Evelyn Keyes, Brad Dexter
Rating: ★★★

This was the first of a series of really good, fast-moving and extremely tough thrillers made by director Phil Karlson in the mid-Fifties, years that took in such highly-praised films as *Tight Spot*, *The Phoenix City Story* and *The Secret Four*. Here, former song-and-dance man John Payne plays a taxi-driver framed for murder.

Ninotchka ○ Ⓥ
1939, US, 110 mins, b/w
Dir: Ernst Lubitsch
Stars: Greta Garbo, Melvyn Douglas
Rating: ★★★★

Greta Garbo's first comedy role – the film was advertised as 'Garbo Laughs' – and her penultimate film before self-imposed retirement. She brings out all the nuances of her role, and her stunning performance earned her a fourth Oscar nomination, but she was squeezed out by Vivien Leigh and *Gone With the Wind*, which swept the board that year. The film was quite daring for its day because of the fact that it made fun of Communism for the first time in a major American film. The film's title caused MGM major headaches, and executives came up with more than dozen suggestions before settling on *Ninotchka*, with the selling line: 'What makes Garbo blush and laugh in *Ninotchka*? Don't pronounce it . . . See it.' The great star's scenes with Ina Claire were particularly electric, not surprising since Claire was the widow of John Gilbert, who had been Garbo's longtime lover on and off screen.

Ninth Configuration, The ●
1979, US, 118 mins, colour
Dir: William Peter Blatty

Stars: Stacy Keach, Scott Wilson
Rating: ★★

Psychological sideshow that runs like a play but strangely never was, its source being a novel by writer-director William Peter Blatty, whose most recent film in these capacities was *The Exorcist Part III*. Stacy Keach plays the slow-speaking psychiatrist colonel – it's apparent there's something odd about him from the start – caring for a group of demented 'Nam veterans at a grotesque castle in northwest America. Blatty tries in his usual fashion to grab his audience's attention any way he can, with violence and nudity thrown in at the end, but can't disguise the surface bag of tricks as anything but a pageant run by an entrepreneur who plays for effect rather than depth, show rather than substance. All the same, this rates highly in the canon of cinema curiosities and at least tries to be stimulating and thought provoking at the same time. There's a stupendous barroom fight scene. Keach (a long way from Mike Hammer here) and Scott Wilson show sincerity, but the film's best performances comes from the ever-reliable Ed Flanders.

No Blade of Grass ○
1970, UK, 97 mins, colour
Dir: Cornel Wilde
Stars: Nigel Davenport, Jean Wallace
Rating: ★★★

Another of Cornel Wilde's primitive parables as director, to follow the success of *The Naked Prey* and *Beach Red*. For the first time here, Wilde wisely forewent the difficult double of acting and directing, leaving the leading role in the capable hands of Nigel Davenport as a man trying to take his family to safety through an English countryside devastated by a deadly virus. Wilde's real-life wife, Jean Wallace, co-stars.

Nobody Lives Forever ○
1946, US, 95 mins, b/w
Dir: Jean Negulesco
Stars: John Garfield, Geraldine Fitzgerald, Walter Brennan, Faye Emerson
Rating: ★★★

You could almost sketch out the plot developments for this crime drama from films you'd seen before. But never mind, the acting glitters, especially from John Garfield with another of his embittered loners, and from Geraldine Fitzgerald as a widow

whose fortune Garfield is after.
Humphrey Bogart was originally slated
to play the leading character, but it fits
Garfield to a T. Completed in November 1944, the film was considered
by Warners to be too downbeat for
audiences still bogged down in war,
and they didn't release it until two
years later.

Nobody Runs Forever ○
(aka: The High Commissioner)
1968, UK, 101 mins, colour
Dir: Ralph Thomas
Stars: Rob Taylor, Christopher Plummer,
Lilli Palmer
Rating: ★

After 12 years of Hollywood stardom,
Rod Taylor reverted to his native
Australian accent in this thriller about
a detective trying to foil an assassi-
nation bid. You'll spot Franchot
Tone in his last film and, maybe, Leo
McKern (unbilled) as the Premier of
New South Wales. The best perfor-
mance comes from the ever-reliable
Lilli Palmer, but somehow the whole
enterprise lacks zest.

Nobody's Fool ◐
1986, US, 105 mins, colour
Dir: Evelyn Purcell
Stars: Rosanna Arquette, Eric Roberts,
Mare Winningham
Rating: ★★

A kooky comedy that continued to
prove that Rosanna Arquette is a poor
picker of scripts. She hasn't had a
sizeable hit since *Desperately Seeking
Susan*, and it's not hard to see why.
This flat romance fails to sparkle as
small town waitress Arquette has to
choose between a life of drudgery and
regret or take a chance on a new Mr
Wonderful in town played with
craggy immobility by Eric Robot,
sorry, Roberts. Nobody much fancied
it, and they were no fools.

Nocturne ○
1946, US, 88 mins, b/w
Dir: Edwin L Marin
Stars: George Raft, Lynn Bari, Virginia
Huston
Rating: ★★★

The detective fascinated by the
lifestyle of someone in a murder case
dates back to *Laura*, and has been seen
as recently as 1987 in *Black Widow*.
Here it's George Raft as the loner
envious of the libertine's life enjoyed
by the murder victim. The result is a
taut thriller, even if it never matches

the brilliance of the opening sequence.
Perhaps the best of Raft's post-war
ventures.

No Deposit, No Return ☉
1976, US, 125 mins, colour
Dir: Norman Tokar
Stars: David Niven, Darren McGavin,
Don Knotts
Rating: ★★

Although this Walt Disney comedy
makes you wait a long time for a
laugh, it finally delivers the goods in a
hectic wharfside chase. The story's
about two children (personable Kim
Richards and obnoxious Brad Savage)
who, with their pet skunk, persuade
two petty thieves to hold them to
ransom so the crooks can pay their
debts. The skunk is the best thing in
the film, and David Niven is not noticeably stretched by his role as the
kids' grandfather.

No Highway in the Sky ○
1951, UK, 99 mins, b/w
Dir: Henry Koster
Stars: James Stewart, Marlene Dietrich,
Glynis Johns, Jack Hawkins
Rating: ★★★

Mid-air suspense was always a good
bet to bring the best out of cast writer
and director, and here a fine cast miss
few of the opportunities presented by
the array of interesting characters in
this tense and likeable adaptation of
Nevil Shute's novel *No Highway* (the
film's British title). James Stewart was
still very much at his peak (which
lasted from 1939–1958) when he
played the mild-mannered professor
who insists that a new plane will crack
up after it has flown a specific number
of hours. The plot uncannily predicted
the cause of the Comet crashes of the
Fifties.

Noises Off ◐ ⊛
1992, US, 104 mins, colour
Dir: Peter Bogdanovich
Stars: Carol Burnett, Michael Caine,
Denholm Elliott, Julie Hagerty,
Christopher Reeve
Rating: ★★

A gallant but doomed attempt by director Peter Bogdanovich to film an
unfilmable stage farce about a group of
ham actors trying to put on a new
British stage farce along traditional,
trouser-dropping lines. Half a dozen
irresistibly funny moments burst
through the tedium of the rest, and
remind you how hilarious the original
was. Michael Caine and a distin-

guished company give frantic
endeavour in their efforts to raise the
few laughs going up to hysteria pitch.
It certainly is fast but not, alas, too
funny.

No Limit ○
1935, UK, 80 mins, b/w
Dir: Monty Banks
Stars: George Formby, Florence
Desmond
Rating: ★★★

Just to see George Formby on his
black-and-white checkered motor-bike marked 'George Shuttleworth
– Speed Demon' is to start giggling,
and audiences went for this sporty
comedy in a big way. It was the lad
from Lancashire's first big studio
comedy, and he also sang one of his
greatest hits, 'Riding at the TT
Races'. The antics are directed at a
fine pace by Monty Banks, himself a
famous screen comedian who knew
the art of comedy inside out, and are
spiced up with footage from the actual
1935 TT event.

No Love for Johnnie ◑
1960, UK, 111 mins, b/w
Dir: Ralph Thomas
Stars: Peter Finch, Stanley Holloway,
Mary Peach, Donald Pleasence
Rating: ★★★

A solid, downbeat drama based on a
posthumous novel by MP Wilfred
Fienburgh, who was killed in a car
crash. Peter Finch is the MP who
wrecks his private life to reach the top
in politics; Mary Peach, Billie
Whitelaw and Rosalie Crutchley are
the unlucky ladies he discards on the
way. And you'll catch a glimpse of
Oliver Reed as a rowdy party guest.
Donald Pleasence makes a rather more
lasting impression as a shifty politico.

No Man of Her Own ○
1949, US, 98 mins, b/w
Dir: Mitchell Leisen
Stars: Barbara Stanwyck, John Lund
Rating: ★★

Strung out emotionally as usual,
Barbara Stanwyck is well on form in
this cross of weepie and *film noir*, based
on a book by Cornel Woolrich, writing under the pseudonym of William
Irish. Her blackmailing lover is very
effectively played by Lyle Bettger,
making his screen debut after a string
of stage successes. The fair-haired actor with the evil grin was to fill his 25
film years with a whole gallery of bad
men. Watch too for a brief appearance

N

by Dooley Wilson, once Sam of 'play it again' fame, as a waiter in the dining-car of a train. Quite a comedown after taking the spotlight at Rick's Café Americain!

No Man's Land ● ⓥ

1987, US, 105 mins, colour
Dir: Peter Werner
Stars: Charlie Sheen, D B Sweeney, Lara Harris, Randy Quaid, Bill Duke, M Emmet Walsh
Rating: ★★★

This is the one about the policeman who goes undercover with a gang, is attracted to the leader's charm and falls in love with the bad guy's sister. As old as the hills then, right down to the ritual shoot-out climax. Still this version is quite well done, with the youth of D B Sweeney, as the cop, and Charlie Sheen, as the crook, lending an uncomfortable edge to the familiar tale. Sheen in particular catches the eye in a compelling portrayal of the mask of reckless boyishness which hides a deadly core. Randy Quaid takes a more mature role than hitherto as Sweeney's police chief contact. Car chase excitements punctuate the theme of cat and mouse and the story (souped up to hypertension by such tactics), though never memorable, entertains all the way.

No Mercy ● ⓥ

1986, US, 105 mins, colour
Dir: Richard Pearce
Stars: Richard Gere, Kim Basinger
Rating: ★★

For the most part darkly photographed and slow-moving, this New Orleans-set cop thriller does have a tremendous shoot-out climax, to which the whole film seems geared from the start. It's good that Richard Gere presents a more vulnerable character than, say, Stallone or Schwarzenegger would under similar circumstances, an element which lends a keener edge of tension to the fiery *High Noon*-type finish at a Western-style saloon in the centre of town. The villain (Jeroen Krabbé) has a pigtail, which makes him extra bad, but he's also extra foolish, killing one of his own men off at the end and shortening the odds against Gere's lone wolf hero. Gere and Kim Basinger do their best with the rest of the movie, but there's little chemistry between them, and it's the kind of

film where you could pop out and make the coffee without missing a thing any time but the last 15 minutes.

Nora Prentiss ○

1947, US, 117 mins, b/w
Dir: Vincent Sherman
Stars: Ann Sheridan, Kent Smith, Bruce Bennett, Robert Alda
Rating: ★★

Although the twists and turns of this flashback melodrama take some swallowing, solid performances by Ann Sheridan and the underrated Kent Smith buoy up this glossy cross between a *film noir* and what was known then as a 'woman's picture'. The camerawork and direction neatly emphasises the plight of the two leading characters, trapped by circumstances and their own weaknesses.

Norma Rae ⓒ

1979, US, 114 mins, colour
Dir: Martin Ritt
Stars: Sally Field, Beau Bridges, Ron Leibman, Pat Hingle
Rating: ★★★★

Another triumph for Martin Ritt, surely one of the most consistent directors who ever worked in Hollywood. The performances of Sally Field (winning an Oscar), Beau Bridges – never better – and Ron Leibman are beyond reproach, but this is above all a director's film, so brilliantly organised and constructed that if the last 20 minutes don't bring a lump to your throat, nothing in the cinema ever will. The tiny, gritty Field has the title role as the best-looking gal in the mill factory: she has two children who live with her and her parents, one the daughter of her dead husband, the other illegitimate. The theme of the film, though, concerns the advent of a union man (Leibman) to the southern town where events are set, and the conversion of the bright but downtrodden Norma Rae to a fierce force 100 per cent behind the union cause. Ritt builds this activity to an enormous emotional impact by the climax, and the writers play an ace card by having Field marry a run-of-the-mill widower (Bridges) and then not sleeping with the union man as their friendship strengthens, making an altogether different story of their farewell scene at the end.

North ○ ⓥ

1994, US, 91 mins, colour
Dir: Rob Reiner

Stars: Elijah Wood, Bruce Willis, Jon Lovitz, Dan Aykroyd, Kathy Bates, John Ritter
Rating: ★

A dumb comedy-fantasy about a boy, North (Elijah Wood) who, tired of his selfish parents, wins a court action against them and is given a limited period to circumnavigate the world in search of a new family. The school genius (Mathew McCurley) meanwhile uses North's fame and influence to establish his own power base whose Macchiavellian proportions will be ruined if North returns home. Following this unpromising beginning, all the episodes of North's search are cut to the same formula: initial enthusiasm for prospective parents in Texas, Hawaii, Alaska, China, Zaire and France, then disillusionment, plus a homily on the values of life from Bruce Willis, who turns up as everything from an Easter bunny to a nightclub comedian called Joey Fingers. The name 'Bedford' crops up once or twice as a town, but any comparison with Frank Capra's *It's a Wonderful Life* (set in Bedford Falls) is wishful thinking on the part of the director, whose film has none of the charm or subtlety of the best Hollywood moonshine.

North Avenue Irregulars, The

See: Hill's Angels

North by Northwest ○ ⓥ

1959, US, 136 mins, colour
Dir: Alfred Hitchcock
Stars: Cary Grant, Eva Marie Saint, James Mason
Rating: ★★★★

There are strong echoes of *The 39 Steps* in this, perhaps Alfred Hitchcock's most famous suspense thriller on a chase theme. The attack on Cary Grant by the crop-duster plane in the middle of a desolate prairie has now passed into film folklore. But the film has many other fine moments, notably the tense scenes on board a train (one of Hitchcock's favourite locations), the assassination at the United Nations building, and the climax at Mount Rushmore.

North Dallas Forty ●

1979, US, 114 mins, colour
Dir: Ted Kotcheff
Stars: Nick Nolte, Mac Davis, Charles Durning, Dayle Haddon
Rating: ★★★

If this tough and funny film is a true picture of the way American football is run and played – most of its players must surely end physically damaged for life – then thank heavens for other varieties of the game. Its main weakness has dogged countless similar Hollywood movies: the star player is sent on at the end of the game to try to win it for his side. It's the stuff of which dreams not dramas are made. But Nick Nolte is extremely good as the player beginning to have doubts about it all, and he is almost matched by G D Spradlin as the fanatical coach, a portrayal that brilliantly skirts the pit of caricature into which several members of the cast plunge headlong.

North Sea Hijack ○
(aka: ffolkes)
1979, UK, 100 mins, colour
Dir: Andrew V McLaglen
Stars: Roger Moore, James Mason, Anthony Perkins
Rating: ★★

Rufus Excalibur ffolkes, the eccentric hero of this action-thriller, hates women, dresses in tweed suits, loves cats and has his own private underwater army of saboteurs. Not exactly James Bond, but he's just the man the government need when an oil drilling rig and platform is hijacked and a £25 million ransom demanded. The cast, with Roger Moore as the dotty ffolkes, James Mason as an admiral and Anthony Perkins as No 1 villain, have some fun with a formula story, but considering the calibre of the cast and the behind-the-scenes team, the film's a bit of a disappointment; it needed some of those spectacular Bond stunts to liven things up.

North Star, The ○
1943, US, 105 mins, b/w
Dir: Lewis Milestone
Stars: Anne Baxter, Farley Granger
Rating: ★★

This decently made WWII propaganda film, produced at the request of US President Franklin D Roosevelt at the time when his son James was the president of the Samuel Goldwyn Studios, was all about a Soviet village resisting the Nazi onslaught. The credits were impeccable: Lewis Milestone (*All Quiet on the Western Front*) directed, Lillian Hellman wrote the script, James Wong Howe was the cinematographer and Aaron Copland supplied the score. In addition, there was a clutch of stars: Anne

Baxter, Farley Granger (in his first starring role), Jane Withers, Eric Roberts and Dana Andrews in the roles of the Ukrainian villagers at the centre of the story; Walter Huston as the village doctor and Erich von Stroheim as, inevitably, the Nazi doctor. Unfortunately, the film never rises above tub-thumping and Lillian Hellman made public her disappointment at what had happened to her script. Ironically, in the Fifties, the House Un-American Activities Committee called upon the film-makers to explain why they had made the film . . .

North to Alaska ○ ⓥ
1960, US, 122 mins, colour
Dir: Henry Hathaway
Stars: John Wayne, Stewart Granger
Rating: ★★★

John Wayne in action – and how! This rumbustious knockabout Western, with Wayne and Stewart Granger as partners in Gold Rush days, seems in retrospect to be one long fist fight. It certainly does have the bar-room brawl to end them all, plus rich colour photography, a memorable theme song by Johnny Horton and stout support from a whole saloon-full of Western character players.

North West Frontier ○ ⓥ
(aka: Flame Over India)
1959, UK, 129 mins, colour
Dir: J Lee Thompson
Stars: Kenneth More, Lauren Bacall
Rating: ★★★

One of Kenneth More's best films: an exciting, old-fashioned action adventure set (mostly aboard a train) in 1905 India and blazingly shot in unusually rich Eastman Colour by Oscar-winning cameraman Geoffrey Unsworth. It's adventure all the way as More and cool governess Lauren Bacall try to get a young prince to safety through 300 miles of rebel-held country. The story races along and there are personable supporting performances from Herbert Lom, Wilfrid Hyde White, and especially I S Johar as a feisty engineer. This was the year in which More was voted the most popular British star in a nationwide poll.

North West Mounted Police ○
1940, US, 125 mins, colour
Dir: Cecil B DeMille
Stars: Gary Cooper, Paulette Goddard, Madeleine Carroll, Robert Preston,

Preston Foster
Rating: ★★★

'Blood will run like water!' exclaims the villain, gleefully surveying his new Gatling gun. 'You won't notice it much,' grins his associate. 'The Mounted Police wear red coats.' Well, the Cecil B DeMille adventure spectacles never were noted for their dynamic dialogue, but the action and colour in this one more than make up for the winces in the script. Gary Cooper is perfect as the tall, taciturn Texas Ranger who helps the Mounties clear up the Riel Rebellion of 1885 and the film made Paramount a mint despite their penny-pinching on the cost, which included their refusing to allow DeMille to shoot in Canada, and planting 300 pine trees in the studio backlot instead. The supporting cast gives you the chance to spot several stars of the future, including Robert Ryan, Richard Denning and Rod Cameron. But it doesn't offer solace to those who have trouble telling Preston Foster from Robert Preston: they're both in it.

Northwest Passage ○
1940, US, 125 mins, colour
Dir: King Vidor
Stars: Spencer Tracy, Robert Young, Walter Brennan
Rating: ★★★★

The Technicolor MGM classic (actually intended to be the first of a two-part epic) which paved the way for new standards of realism in open-air spectaculars. Horror and heroism, combined with action and battle scenes remarkable even by today's standards, stamp the film with the hallmark of greatness. Urged on by King Vidor's uncompromising direction, Spencer Tracy gives a magnificent performance. Heartbreaking and blood-surging in turn, this is a winner all the way.

No Sex Please, We're British ◐ ⓥ
1973, UK, 91 mins, colour
Dir: Cliff Owen
Stars: Ronnie Corbett, Beryl Reid, Arthur Lowe, Ian Ogilvy
Rating: ★★

A film version of the epic-running British stage farce, with a cast of funsters more formidable than ever the theatre could muster. Ronnie Corbett – in fine dithering form – and Ian Ogilvy are the quiet bank clerks suddenly deluged with pornographic

N

literature and other roles are filled by such familiar faces as Arthur Lowe (skilfully underplaying the moralising bank manager), Michael Bates, Robin Askwith, Michael Robbins, Deryck Guyler, Michael Ripper, Beryl Reid, Brian Wilde, Frank Thornton and Sydney Bromley. Cliff Owen directs at a helter-skelter pace throughout.

Nothing But the Best ◑

1963, UK, 99 mins, colour
Dir: Clive Donner
Stars: Alan Bates, Denholm Elliott, Millicent Martin, Pauline Delany
Rating: ★★★

Room at the Top played for laughs, as Jimmy Brewster, anti-hero and stop-at-nothing rogue, drags his way to the top of the firm by means strictly foul, and wins the boss's daughter. All the performances are attractive with Alan Bates superbly amoral as Jimmy, and Denholm Elliott establishing his latter-day seediness for the first time.

Nothing But the Night ●

1972, UK, 90 mins, colour
Dir: Peter Sasdy
Stars: Christopher Lee, Peter Cushing, Diana Dors
Rating: ★★

Christopher Lee here departs from the traditional style of horror film with which he has been most associated – and indeed, his traditional role, as he plays a Special Branch chief in this unsuccessful but occasionally unsettling mixture of mystery and the uncanny, with fantasy and even science-fiction overtones. The story, which concerns the strange deaths of various people who were all trustees of an orphanage, is adapted from an intriguing novel by John Blackburn.

Nothing But the Truth ☉

1941, US, 90 mins, b/w
Dir: Elliott Nugent
Stars: Bob Hope, Paulette Goddard, Edward Arnold, Leif Erickson
Rating: ★★★

Bob Hope wartime comedy, with Hope as a wimp who makes a foolish wager to tell nothing but the truth for 48 hours. Filmed twice before, the film provides surefire fun for Hope fans, centring on a lavish houseboat party in which the complications for Hope with his bet become increasingly not only precarious but hilarious. Seldom seen these days, this Hope

rarity, which teams him with Paulette Goddard for the third time, remains timeless fun and well worth catching.

Nothing But Trouble ○ ⓥ

1991, US, 93 mins, colour
Dir: Dan Aykroyd
Stars: Chevy Chase, Dan Aykroyd, John Candy, Demi Moore
Rating: ★

This may not be the laugh-a-minute comedy that you expect from director Dan Aykroyd and his fellow graduates from the *National Lampoon* school of lunacy, Chevy Chase and John Candy. 'An absolute failure as a comedy,' thundered one British critic. But it's an oddly satisfying film if only because it lets loose a real sense of the bizarre. Aykroyd plays a 106-year-old judge who dispenses medieval justice in an oddball corner of rural America. It's the sort of place where speeders are fed into a fairground device called 'Mr Bonestripper'. Chase plays the innocent New Yorker who gets trapped in the hell of Valkenavia and Candy plays, among other parts, the judge's deaf-mute granddaughter . . . May become a cult movie in years to come.

Nothing in Common ◑ ⓥ

1986, US, 119 mins, colour
Dir: Garry Marshall
Stars: Tom Hanks, Jackie Gleason, Eva Marie Saint, Hector Elizondo, Bess Armstrong, Sela Ward
Rating: ★★

A generation gap comedy-drama that on the whole goes nowhere in particular, although it does have a few inspired moments of comedy, as you would expect from this director and these stars. In more dramatic moments, however, the script too often has that phoney ring – smart scripters writing lines for people who just wouldn't communicate like this, if they communicated at all. Chief non-comunicators here are the parents (Jackie Gleason, Eva Marie Saint) of advertising whiz Tom Hanks, completely wrecking his hip, well laid-out (like his girls) life. Director Garry Marshall encourages the whole cast, Saint especially, to shout a lot, while the wry-faced Hanks is such a natural comedian that he's wasted on the poignant or emotional parts where the script is giving him so little help. Bess Armstrong is appealing as the college crush of his past, and Sela Ward glamorous in the Gene Tierney tradition as the career woman who

sees herself and Hanks as a high-flying duo. Not bad, but you'd be hard put to find reasons to recommend people to actually see it.

Nothing Sacred ○

1937, US, 77 mins, colour
Dir: William Wellman
Stars: Carole Lombard, Fredric March
Rating: ★★★

A scathing satirical romp about a girl from the sticks who is given the time of her life in New York simply because a reporter there is mistakenly under the impression that she's dying from radiation poisoning. Carole Lombard, Frederic March and Walter Connolly (as the reporter's long suffering publisher) work like demons to keep things moving at firecracker pace, Ben Hecht's inventive script not only bristles with wit, but its packed array of incidents enable director William Wellman to create some treasurable moments – especially the fist-fight between Lombard and March, and the scene where March ventures into a hostile small town and is attacked in a manner which has to be seen to be believed. The film is very attractively shot in Technicolor by W Howard Greene, a master of the colour cinematographer's art. He shot many early colour classics, finally winning an Oscar in 1944 for his work on *Phantom of the Opera*.

Notorious ○ ⓥ

1946, US, 101 mins, b/w
Dir: Alfred Hitchcock
Stars: Cary Grant, Ingrid Bergman, Claude Rains, Louis Calhern
Rating: ★★★

One of Alfred Hitchcock's most edge-of-seat films is this famous suspense thriller in which Cary Grant plays a US government agent after big and very dangerous fish in South America. The camera angles which heighten the tension were not surpassed until *Psycho*. The photography is by Ted Tetzlaff, who is said to have got tired of Hitchcock's fussiness on getting shape and shadow exactly right – although Tetzlaff used both to great effect in *Riff Raff* and *The Window* when he himself turned director shortly afterwards. Ingrid Bergman lends her star presence as a refugee half-reluctantly in league with Grant, and Claude Rains is superb as the spy.

Not Quite Jerusalem ◐
1984, UK, 114 mins, colour
Dir: Lewis Gilbert
Stars: Joanna Pacula, Sam Robards
Rating: ★

It isn't too easy to see why anyone would want to make a film about life on an Israeli kibbutz, but at least director Lewis Gilbert strengthened this film's appeal by unearthing a new star in sultry Joanna Pacula. Otherwise Paul Kember's script straitjackets its characters into revue-sketch stereotypes, complete with an Australian girl who declares herself so hungry that 'Gosh, I could eat a dingo'. Small wonder, then, that the scenes without words are those that Gilbert makes work the best, especially in a well-staged fire sequence, and a couple of camp(us) romances, which include a touching Japanese-Jewish/American exchange of languages.

No Tree in the Street
See: No Trees in the Street

No Trees in the Street ◐ ⓥ
(aka: No Tree in the Street)
1958, UK, 96 mins, b/w
Dir: J Lee-Thompson
Stars: Sylvia Syms, Herbert Lom, Stanley Holloway
Rating: ★★

Sylvia Syms' sensitive and poignant performance is the glittering prize in this otherwise stale, dreary and and unconvincing portrait of London slum life which falls rather heavily betwen the Ealing realism of post-war years and the 'kitchen sink' dramas which had started with *Room at the Top*.

Not Without My Daughter ◐ ⓥ
1990, US, 115 mins, colour
Dir: Brian Gilbert
Stars: Sally Field, Alfred Molina, Sheila Rosenthal, Roshan Seth
Rating: ★★★★

True stories about courage in the face of massive adversities are always guaranteed to tug at our emotions: this one has the edge on heart-on-sleeve pieces like *Born on the Fourth of July* in that it deliberately under-emphasises the horrors of the situation in which the central character finds herself. Betty (a typically pugnacious performance by Sally Field) is happily married to Moody (Molina), an Iranian-born doctor who has lived in America for 20 years. They have a five-year-old daughter. Very reluctantly, Betty agrees to a two-week holiday in Iran. Whether this is a ruse, or whether Moody very quickly reverts to the traditions of his native Islam, the film doesn't make clear, but the result is the same – a living nightmare for Betty and her daughter. Moody decides to stay in Iran and his wife finds herself watched day and night, confined to her quarters and beaten for disobedience. Field never overplays her hand as the terrorised wife and Molina, not batting an eyelid, achieves a seamless transfer from loving, gentle husband, to ranting wife-beating tyrant.

No Way Out ● ⓥ
1987, US, 116 mins, colour
Dir: Roger Donaldson
Stars: Kevin Costner, Gene Hackman, Sean Young, Will Patton, George Dzunda
Rating: ★★★

A very loose remake of the classic 1948 Ray Milland/Charles Laughton *film noir* thriller *The Big Clock*, with Kevin Costner as the Pentagon man investigating the death of his goodtime girlfriend Sean Young (who was also the lover of his boss, Gene Hackman). The thriller element comes in when Costner's character slowly realises that he has been set up as the fall guy and the men beneath him are on the verge of identifying him as the killer. The ending is a dramatic departure from the original film, and a little hard to swallow. But the rollercoaster journey to the final reel will leave you breathless. Well down the cast you might spot Tia Maria commercial model, Iman.

No Way to Treat a Lady ◐
1968, US, 108 mins, colour
Dir: Jack Smight
Stars: Rod Steiger, Lee Remick, George Segal
Rating: ★★★

This comedy about a serial killer who is a master of disguise is of the deepest black: in fact it's quite gruesome in places. Rod Steiger is a theatre owner who takes out his mother-hatred and misogyny on a number of innocent victims. George Segal is the Jewish cop put on the case who has a typically Jewish mother. Steiger enjoys himself enormously going right over the top as the looney impresario. In one of his disguises he even plays a woman (Rod Steiger in drag? You'd better believe it). The film is rattled along at an exciting pace by director Jack Smight right up to the climactic showdown between killer and cop. A wicked sense of humour makes this film great fun – and watch out for Steiger getting the chance for a dry run at his W C Fields impression, which he would carry into a full-blown biopic a few years later.

Nowhere to Go ○
1958, UK, 87 mins, b/w
Dir: Seth Holt
Stars: George Nader, Maggie Smith
Rating: ★★

There's some interesting casting against type in this morose Ealing drama. Hollywood's mild-mannered George Nader, for example, is an escaped convict who had cheated a rich woman out of thousands, and Bernard Lee, who almost always played reliable coves, is an even more despicable crook who double-crosses him. Maggie Smith, in one of her earliest roles, plays a woman much milder and less flavoursome than those she depicted in coming years. The screenplay is intelligently written, but the inter-relationship of characters, too few of whom are sympathetic, never really takes off.

Nowhere to Run ● ⓥ
1993, US, 95 mins, colour
Dir: Robert Harmon
Stars: Jean-Claude Van Damme, Rosanna Arquette, Ted Levine, Joss Ackland
Rating: ★

Another attempted breakthrough into mainstream cinema from Jean-Claude Van Damme, this action-drama–romance gives us the Muscles from Brussels as a warm-hearted escaped convict who proves, among other things, a whiz with motorcycles. Alas, the vehicle that results here misfires on all cylinders except the action. Jean-Claude's acting style remains what you might call taciturn, while his heavy romance with Rosanna Arquette, a widow farmer (with two small children) menaced by landgrabbing Joss Ackland, founders on the rocks of such dialogue as (she) 'Would you like to sleep in my room tonight?' He: 'You're a very special woman. See you tomorrow', raising more giggles than sighs. The final fistfight with villain Ted Levine, however, really delivers, pitchforkng us (literally) into the thick of things, and only slightly hampered by some intervening slow motion. Arquette, as usual, looks as though she could be

N

good in a decent film, but Ackland is pretty ludicrous as the villain and the kids are not too hot by today's demanding standards.

Now, Voyager ○ ⓥ
1942, US, 117 mins, b/w
Dir: Irving Rapper
Stars: Bette Davis, Paul Heinreid, Claude Rains
Rating: ★★★★

Bette Davis' portrayal of the repressed spinster Charlotte Vale in this magnificent weepie completed a remarkable run of seven Academy Award nominations for her in nine years. As full of memorable images and lines as any film in cinematic history: the farewell on the railway station, the lighting of two cigarettes at once, and 'Don't ask for the moon when we have the stars.' Some of the dialogue was inserted into the script by Davis herself using quotes from the original novel. Chock-full of successfully emotive moments and directed for maximum impact by Irving Rapper, with top-notch support from Gladys Cooper, Claude Rains and Bonita Granville, it's a classic that will have you furtively brushing away a tear at the end.

Now You See Him, Now You Don't ⊙
1972, US, 88 mins, colour
Dir: Robert Butler
Stars: Kurt Russell, Cesar Romero
Rating: ★★★

This follow-up to the successful *The Computer Wore Tennis Shoes* has a young Kurt Russell again starring as smart student Dexter Riley. This time Dexter stumbles upon a serum that causes invisibility, which comes in very useful in the battles between his hard-up college and the baddies who want to take it over. Good fast-moving fun with nice comic performances from Russell, Jim Backus (the voice of Mr Magoo) and verteran star Cesar Romero, and well-realised special effects.

Number Seventeen ○
1932, UK, 64 mins, b/w
Dir: Alfred Hitchcock
Stars: Anne Grey, John Stuart, Garry Marsh, Barry Jones
Rating: ★★★

This early Hitchcock thriller marked the real beginning of his obsession with trains as settings for suspense. There's a first-rate chase sequence

dazzlingly photographed by Jack Cox, and skilfully edited, at the end of a story about jewel thieves hiding out in a deserted railwayside house.

Nuns on the Run ◑ ⓥ
1990, UK, 89 mins, colour
Dir: Jonathan Lynn
Stars: Eric Idle, Robbie Coltrane
Rating: ★★

Eric Idle and Robbie Coltrane play two petty crooks on the run, with two suitcases full of money, from gang bosses who'd like them back in this fast-moving and farcical comedy. They hide out in a convent school disguised as nuns, and therein lies the source of much of the saucy humour. Pragmatic Sister Superior Janet Suzman sees the money as a cure for the school's financial problems so tolerates the two rather strange new nuns. Writer/director Jonathan Lynn keeps things moving at a fair pace. The situations and one-liners are rude rather than crude and are delivered with gleeful panache by Idle and Coltrane. Good fun.

Nun's Story, The ○ ⓥ
1959, US, 151 mins, colour
Dir: Fred Zinnemann
Stars: Audrey Hepburn, Peter Finch
Rating: ★★★★

Luminous Audrey Hepburn chalked up another major success in this long but always absorbing story based on Kathryn Hulme's bestselling book. Director Fred Zinnemann struck a perfect balance of pace and sensitivity in the tale of a young Belgian girl who becomes a nun and is sent to the Belgian Congo to work in a hospital under the atheistic eye of surgeon Peter Finch. With an excellent script, fine performances and intellegent direction, it's amazing that the film didn't win any of the six Oscars it was nominated for. But the blockbusting and admittedly visually impressive *Ben-Hur* overshadowed it at awards time. A shame, as there's a strong argument for the contention that this is the better film.

Nurse Edith Cavell ○
1939, US, 93 mins, b/w
Dir: Herbert Wilcox
Stars: Anna Neagle, Edna May Oliver, George Sanders
Rating: ★★★

The first of several real-life war-torn heroines Dame Anna Neagle would play in the later stages of her career.

This film was made in America and cast her as the British nurse who helped thousands of World War One refugees to escape from Belgium to Holland. Its director, Herbert Wilcox, was soon to become her husband.

Nurse on Wheels ○
1962, UK, 86 mins, b/w
Dir: Gerald Thomas
Stars: Juliet Mills, Ronald Lewis, Joan Sims
Rating: ★★

Thanks largely to Juliet Mills' chirpy performance in the leading role, this is an engaging comedy in sub-*Carry On* style, about the misadventures of a young and much mistrusted by veteran villagers, district nurse. Miss Mills' warm sense of fun, only really seen to its full advantage in Billy Wilder's *Avanti!* some years later, permeates the whole film, making the most farcical of developments seem amusingly possible. Veteran Irish character actor Noel Purcell enjoys himself as one of her more reluctant patients.

Nutcracker ●
1982, UK, 101 mins, colour
Dir: Anwar Kawadri
Stars: Joan Collins, Carol White, Paul Nicholas
Rating: ★

A mild little comedy-drama, glossed over with some soft-core sex, about a Russian ballerina defecting to the West. In other words, an archetypal Joan Collins vehicle of the Eighties – although one would have hardly thought that 'Russian ballerina breaks ankle' was worth a banner headline in the *Daily Mirror*. Finola Hughes is quite personable as the young dancer.

Nuts ● ⓥ
1987, US, 115 mins, colour
Dir: Martin Ritt
Stars: Barbra Streisand, Richard Dreyfuss, Karl Malden, Eli Wallach, James Whitmore, Leslie Nielsen
Rating: ★★★

A good, solid courtroom yarn, full of enough incidental humour to lighten the drama, and old-fashioned in all but the language. Streisand gives her best-balanced dramatic performance to date as the high-class, mid-thirties hooker who has withdrawn to such an extent after killing one of her clients that the authorities are convinced she is mentally unfit to plead and should be put away. Enter her knight in shining armour (Richard Dreyfuss) in the shape of a pugnacious legal-aid lawyer (she has broken her previous lawyer's nose) who is determined to root out some causes. Before long, in traditional Hollywood style, skeletons are not only out of cupboards but cascading all over the court-room floor. Director Ritt has a few problems keeping it going at a lively enough pace, but a veteran cast has seen this kind of thing on the *Perry Mason* show and has the know-how to bring it through to an emotional conclusion.

Nutty Professor, The ○
1963, US, 107 mins, colour
Dir: Jerry Lewis
Stars: Jerry Lewis, Stella Stevens, Kathleen Freeman
Rating: ★★★

Wild, spasmodic but mostly very funny comedy, produced by, directed by, and starring that wayward comic genius Jerry Lewis. It's a comic variation on the Jekyll and Hyde story (shades of Abbott and Costello!) with Jerry cleverly going through a series of highly-coloured transformations that skilfully combine the fright with the fun, in his change from meek little professor to dashing debonair Hyde. In the supporting cast, watch for Stella Stevens, surely the most glamorous student any professor ever had. Jerry invents some side-splitting sight gags in this one, and even does a wicked impersonation of his old partner Dean Martin in what proved to be one of his greatest successes as a solo comic. Lewis has been threatening for years to make a sequel, but to date it's never happened.

O

Objective, Burma ○ Ⓥ
1945, US, 142 mins, b/w
Dir: Raoul Walsh
Stars: Errol Flynn, James Brown, George Tobias
Rating: ★★★

Errol Flynn gives a performance all the stronger for its restraint in this much-maligned but actually very well made story of an American paratroop contingent struggling to get back to safety through the Burmese jungle after carrying out a sabotage mission behind enemy lines. Director Raoul Walsh offers a succession of fluid action scenes, especially early on, when the claustrophobic atmosphere of jungle warfare is skilfully built up, and he maintains suspense throughout the film's lengthy running time.

Object of Beauty ◐ Ⓥ
1991, UK, 103 mins, colour
Dir: Michael Lindsay-Hogg
Stars: John Malkovich, Andie MacDowell
Rating: ★★

Originally made for the television, this film and *Truly Madly Deeply* were deemed good enough to warrant a cinema release. Of the two efforts, this is definitely the weaker article. Imported American leads John Malkovich and Andie MacDowell are rather miscast and find the lightweight romantic comedy material beyond their grasp. The plot revolves around a missing Henry Moore miniature, which Malkovich and MacDowell planned to use to make a false insurance claim to pay their extravagant London hotel bill and prop up his ailing business. A sub-plot about a deaf-mute chamber maid and her punk brother sits uneasily with the rest of the proceedings. *Object of Beauty* is a throwback to the escapist British cinema of the Sixties, but fails to recreate its frenetic energy.

Oblong Box, The ● Ⓥ
1968, UK, 95 mins, colour
Dir: Gordon Hessler
Stars: Vincent Price, Christopher Lee, Hilary Dwyer
Rating: ★★

Another of director Gordon Hessler's very sinister essays on the theme of retribution claiming long-delayed victims, and reaching out even from

beyond the grave. Lots of blood, though mostly spilled at night, not a little style and the eye-opening climax (just when one thought the evil was over) that was to become a Hessler trademark. That personable leading lady Hilary Dwyer became involved with several creepy films at this time, including *The Body Stealers*, *Witchfinder General* and *Cry of the Banshee*.

Obsessed
See: The Late Edwina Black

Obsession ○ Ⓥ
(aka: The Hidden Room)
1948, UK, 95 mins, b/w
Dir: Edward Dmytryk
Stars: Robert Newton, Sally Gray, Wayne Naughton
Rating: ★★

A sombre drama about a man who keeps his wife's lover in an underground room, planning a grim death for him after prolonging his agony. Robert Newton is the 'jailer' bent on revenge, but acting honours in the film are taken by Phil Brown as the lover, and by Naunton Wayne as the policeman trying to trace the missing man.

Obsession ◐ Ⓥ
1976, US, 98 mins, colour
Dir: Brian De Palma
Stars: Cliff Robertson, Genevieve Bujold, John Lithgow
Rating: ★★

Hollywood's king of suspense in the Seventies and Eighties, director Brian De Palma strikes again with this basically silly but skilfully presented thriller. Cliff Robertson plays a businessman whose wife and daughter are killed in a blazing car after a police attempt to trap their kidnappers has backfired. The bodies are never recovered. Sixteen years later, Robertson goes to Italy with his partner, and meets a girl who looks exactly like his dead wife. But when he brings her back to America, she seems possessed by the wife's spirit. The partner calls in a psychiatrist, and if avid armchair detectives haven't got it after watching thus far, they should throw away their Crime Club memberships. De Palma gives the film a deliberately old-fashioned treatment – hazes, flashbacks, heavenly choirs and a tremendous, thundering background score by Bernard Herrmann.

O

Robertson looks baffled throughout: but he should have guessed it, he really should.

Ocean's 11 ○
1960, US, 128 mins, colour
Dir: Lewis Milestone
Stars: Frank Sinatra, Dean Martin, Sammy Davis Jr, Peter Lawford, Angie Dickinson
Rating: ★★★

A glossy, sophisticated blend of comedy and thrills, this is the first and best of the Frank Sinatra 'Rat Pack' films, as he heads a gang of 11 ex-paratroopers planning to lift the entire Christmas takings from Las Vegas' five biggest casinos. The whole affair is a highly-coloured chuckle from beginning to end, with a most satisfactory, if somewhat obvious climax. There are some bright guest appearances, especially that by Shirley MacLaine, and a galaxy of star names, with Sammy Davis Jr making the most impression, especially when standing idly by, while gang members are blacking their faces in preparation for the raid, making reference to the fact that he has already been prepared by nature. Director Lewis Milestone gives us some poignant moments, too, supplied (with impeccable taste, in the midst of the razzmatazz planning for the robbery) by Richard Conte in one of his most sympathetic performances.

October Man, The ○
1947, UK, 98 mins, b/w
Dir: Roy Baker
Stars: John Mills, Joan Greenwood
Rating: ★★★

A first-class thriller. John Mills gives a memorable performance as a man haunted by his past and director Roy Baker, in his first major assignment, uses shape and shadow highly effectively. Direction, set design and photography combine very well to conjure up the interiors of the awful, seedy, middle-class hotel in which the pressures of the past catch up on the central character in violent fashion.

Octopussy ○ ⓥ
1983, UK, 130 mins, colour
Dir: John Glen
Stars: Roger Moore, Maud Adams, Louis Jourdan
Rating: ★★★

James Bond up to more of what his colleague 'Q' describes as 'adolescent antics' – although this Bond adventure

has the edge on most other Roger Moore entries in the series and 007's battles with the baddies are meatier affairs than usual. Perhaps mindful of the competition offered by Sean Connery's *Never Say Never Again*, Moore looks more as though he means business, throwing himself energetically into an adventure that takes him to India and East Berlin. Bondian ripostes have multiplied, so that few situations are allowed to pass without witticisms of varying quality. But there are some good set-pieces too, among them a chase through an Indian market area in which, to defend himself, Moore whips a sword from a sword-swallower, filches a flaming torch from a juggler and sees to it that beds of nails and hot coals are also put to use. The supporting cast is lightweight but the action's the thing and there's plenty of variety in that.

Odd Couple, The ○
1968, US, 105 mins, colour
Dir: Gene Saks
Stars: Jack Lemmon, Walter Matthau, Monica Evans, Carole Shelley
Rating: ★★★

One of the rollicking situation comedies with which Neil Simon made his name. This is the one about two divorcees of contrasting character sharing a flat. Jack Lemmon and Walter Matthau play off each other to perfection in these roles, and Simon's clever screenplay is a constant source of amusement. Lemmon is fastidious Felix, who insists on cleaning up his friend Oscar's cluttered flat, much to the disgust of Oscar (Matthau) who says Felix is the kind of man who 'wears a seat belt at a drive-in movie' and is driven mad by his friend's myriad messages ('It took me two hours to work out that F U meant Felix Ungar'). A word for Monica Evans and Carole Shelley, also delightful as the giggly English girls who live upstairs.

Odd Job, The ① ⓥ
1978, UK, 83 mins, b/w
Dir: Peter Medak
Stars: David Jason, Graham Chapman, Diana Quick
Rating: ★

Refugee from Monty Pythonland Graham Chapman turns up in this dotty comedy as a man who hires an eccentric assassin to kill him – then changes his mind. David Jason features as the hapless assassin in this film adapted from a short television play.

It's the sort of sketch granny used to laugh at on her visits to the end of the pier.

Odd Man Out ○
1947, UK, 110 mins, b/w
Dir: Carol Reed
Stars: James Mason, Robert Newton, Kathleen Ryan
Rating: ★★★★

Carol Reed's haunting, suspenseful study of an IRA gunman on the run in the Twenties, through a Belfast permanently pelted by rain or coated with snow. James Mason broke right away from his run of regency cads in the title role, and there are memorable supporting performances from Kathleen Ryan, as his tragic girlfriend, F J McCormick, as the little man who tries to sell him for money and Cyril Cusack as his hot-headed fellow-rebel. Fortunately, Robert Newton only appears in the last half-hour, as his extravagant performance almost unbalances the film. Robert Kracker's black-and-white photography adds greatly to the mounting tension, as events build up to an exciting and agonising finale. Krasker was nominated for an Oscar that year, but had to wait two years before he actually won one – for another Reed classic, *The Third Man*.

Odds Against Tomorrow ○
1959, US, 96 mins, b/w
Dir: Robert Wise
Stars: Harry Belafonte, Robert Ryan, Shelley Winters, Ed Begley
Rating: ★★

A carefully-constructed thriller about a bank robbery, and the conflicting motives and ideals behind it. Another strong drama from the hands of writer-director team Nelson Gidding and Robert Wise, of *I Want to Live!*, *The Haunting* and *The Andromeda Strain* fame. The least effective part of their story here is the sub-plot about the racial problem, although that does give us an early glimpse of Cicely Tyson, the remarkable black actress who was to win such praise 15 years later for her performances in *Sounder* and *The Autobiography of Miss Jane Pittman*. *Odds Against Tomorrow* is based on a first-rate crime novel by William P McGivern, the corking climax to which is brilliantly recreated by Gidding and Wise in this film. Robert Ryan, excellent as always, runs away with the acting honours.

Odessa File, The ⓞ ⓥ
1974, US/UK, 128 mins, colour
Dir: Ronald Neame
Stars: Jon Voight, Maria Schell,
Maximilian Schell, Mary Tamm, Derek
Jacobi
Rating: ★★

This was never the most vivid of
Frederick Forsyth's novels and director
Ronald Neame and his scriptwriters,
Kenneth Ross and George Markstein,
have worked hard to pep up the
thinnish plot with bits of narrative
addenda that bolster the action
content, as well as a changed ending
that reflects the same intention. Of the
German accents with which the cast
battle, the best is undoubtedly that of
star Jon Voight, dourly playing against
the baby-faced charm he displayed in
his earlier roles.

Odette ○
1950, UK, 123 mins, b/w
Dir: Herbert Wilcox
Stars: Anna Neagle, Trevor Howard
Rating: ★★★

One of Anna Neagle's best performances as the famous war heroine in
an otherwise fairly routine war film,
based on the best-selling book by
Jerrard Tickell. Once more Herbert
Wilcox is in the director's chair, his
best handling of the film coming in its
big emotional scenes.

Offbeat ○
1960, UK, 72 mins, b/w
Dir: Cliff Owen
Stars: William Sylvester, Mai Zetterling
Rating: ★★★

Co-stars William Sylvester and Mai
Zetterling impress, as does Australian
actor John Meillon, in a tense story
about a cleverly-planned bank robbery. Much better than most of its
kind.

Off Beat ○
1986, US, 88 mins, colour
Dir: Michael Dinner
Stars: Judge Reinhold, Meg Tilly,
Cleavant Derricks
Rating: ★★★

Silly but endearing, and pacily directed
by Michael Dinner, this screwball
comedy refreshingly has a beginning,
middle and end, with the faintly ineffectual hero proving himself to the
heroine. You won't believe the plot
for a moment, but you can't help enjoying it for all that. The amiable
Judge Reinhold is right on the money

as the librarian forced to impersonate a
cop friend when that worthy is drafted
to take part in a police dance show.
Not only does Reinhold get hooked
on the dancing, but falls for a feisty
lady cop (Meg Tilly) who's as likely to
lay him out with a left hook as kiss
him. It's a lightweight lark, but almost
everything about it is fun and some
of it funny as well. Harvey Keitel turns
up as a bank robber and Austin
Pendleton does a very amusing cameo
as a gun shop salesman. Shame on the
makers for not having the courage of
their convictions and only showing us
the climactic dance show under the
closing credits.

**Officer and a Gentleman,
An ● ⓥ**
1981, US, 125 mins, colour
Dir: Taylor Hackford
Stars: Richard Gere, Debra Winger,
David Keith, Louis Gossett Jr, Robert
Loggia, Lisa Eilbacher
Rating: ★★★

One of the oldest plots in Hollywood's book – perhaps that's why it
works so well. Officer recruits are
taken to their limits on a training
course, and a lot of it is pretty abrasive
stuff. Yet we can cheerfully defy you
not to be moved by the scene in
which Richard Gere blows his
chances of a record in the obstacle
course to stay and shout the only female recruit over the high wall that
has always defeated her; or by the
highly emotive ending. Strongly
effective performances by Gere, Debra
Winger, David Keith, Lisa Blount and
– winning an Oscar as the tough sergeant – Louis Gossett Jr round off a
cunningly wrapped package of commercial ingredients.

Off Limits
See: Saigon

Of Human Hearts ○
1938, US, 100 mins, b/w
Dir: Clarence Brown
Stars: Walter Huston, James Stewart,
Beulah Bondi
Rating: ★★★

The direction, by Clarence Brown, of
this poignant melodrama set in the
Ohio Valleys before and during the
American Civil War, is sensitive and
pictorially very imaginative; and he
extracts superb performances from
Walter Huston, James Stewart and
Beulah Bondi. The plot, about the
resentful son of a martinet clergyman
who becomes determined to make a

go of his life as a doctor despite abject
poverty, is often syrupy but Brown
overcomes the storyline faults with a
lively eye and sprightly visuals.

Of Love and Desire ⓞ
1963, US, 97 mins, colour
Dir: Richard Rush
Stars: Merle Oberon, Curt Jurgens,
Steve Cochran, John Agar
Rating: ★★

A good cast does its best to salvage
something from this frantically
overheated melodrama about a nymphomaniac's search for happiness.
Merle Oberon (whose own lavish
home is one of the film's exotic
Mexican settings) swivels her eyeballs
and looks distraught as the woman
with a rack of male swimming trunks
as trophies of past conquests. Steve
Cochran, Curt Jurgens, John Agar and
Steve Brodie are among the men who
battle to put their wardrobe on a
more permanent basis. Unbelievably,
writer-director Richard Rush came
back many years later to make the
award-winning Peter O'Toole film
The Stunt Man.

Of Mice and Men ○
1939, US, 107 mins, b/w
Dir: Lewis Milestone
Stars: Burgess Meredith, Lon Chaney Jr,
Betty Field, Charles Bickford
Rating: ★★★

Directed with taste and realism by
Lewis Milestone, this excellent,
moving film is still the best available
version of John Steinbeck's play. The
casting is without fault, with Burgess
Meredith as the wily George, Betty
Field as the farmstead flirt and, in the
performance of his career, Lon
Chaney Jr as the simple, hulking
Lennie. Streets ahead of the decent
1992 remake.

Of Mice and Men ⓞ ⓥ
1992, US, 110 mins, colour
Dir: Gary Sinise
Stars: John Malkovich, Gary Sinise,
Sherilyn Fenn, Alexis Arquette, Casey
Siemaszko, Ray Walston
Rating: ★★★

A forthright new version of John
Steinbeck's classic novel about the
friendship between two men – one of
them mentally backward and innocent
(John Malkovich), and the other (Gary
Sinise) his guardian. As they travel
Depression-hit America in the 1930s
working the land, their lives are
changed forever by the arrival of a

O

beautiful young woman (Sherilyn Fenn) in their unconventionally well-ordered lives. There's some stunning photography here, as well as first-rate performances from Malkovich and Sinise, who also directs. Not as good, though, as the classic 1939 version. Despite Kenneth MacMillan's splendid colour work on the heat-baked landscapes here, it's the black and white atmosphere of the original that sticks in the memory.

O'Hara's Wife ○

1982, US, 87 mins, colour
Dir: William S Bartman
Stars: Edward Asner, Mariette Hartley, Jodie Foster
Rating: ★★

The talented Mariette Hartley gets one of her rare leading roles in a cinema film in this sentimental romantic comedy drama. She plays a wife who returns from the dead in spectral form to help widower Edward (*Lou Grant*) Asner through the first few months without her.

O Henry's Full House ○

(aka: Full House)
1952, US, 117 mins, b/w
Dir: Howard Hawks
Stars: Marilyn Monroe, Richard Widmark, Anne Baxter, Farley Granger, Jeanne Crain
Rating: ★★★

A nap hand from the stories of O Henry. Comedy comes off best here, especially in *The Cop and the Anthem*, a delicious little sketch played with relish by Charles Laughton and David Wayne as a couple of tramps. Also funny is *The Ransom of Red Chief*, in which Fred Allen and Oscar Levant are suitably perplexed as two confidence tricksters hopelessly browbeaten and out-tricked by the small boy they are supposed to have kidnapped. Marilyn Monroe and Richard Widmark are among many other stars in the cast.

Oh! For a Man

See: Will Success Spoil Rock Hunter?

Oh, God! ○ ⓥ

1977, US, 104 mins, colour
Dir: Carl Reiner
Stars: George Burns, John Denver, Teri Garr, Donald Pleasence
Rating: ★★★

Overlong but generally amiable reversion to the supernatural farces of the Forties: its success seems to show

that people again need this kind of comfort. George Burns's dry delivery and perfect timing boost this inoffensive comedy about a supermarket manager visited by God. His thoughts on ostriches, avocados and TV prove irresistible and undeniably funny.

Oh, God! Book II ○ ⓥ

1980, US, 90 mins, colour
Dir: Gilbert Cates
Stars: George Burns, Suzanne Pleshette
Rating: ★★

A mild follow-up to the enormous success of *Oh, God!*, with George Burns repeating his portrayal of a benign but salty God. There's too little of Burns and too much of child actress Louanne, but there's some strong talent in minor roles (including Howard Duff, Hans Conried and Wilfrid Hyde White) and a good sequence involving a motorcycle and sidecar.

Oh, God! You Devil ○ ⓥ

1984, US, 92 mins, colour
Dir: Paul Bogart
Stars: George Burns, Ron Silver
Rating: ★★

This light and often amusing canter through the Faust legend enabled George Burns to end his three-film stint as God on a relatively celestial note and play The Devil into the bargain. A bargain, of course, is just what hapless hero Ted Wass makes when he sells his soul (for a way out of financial ruin) to a Devil who drives around in a red sports car with the licence number HOT. Not, as Burns points out, that Satan needs the work, as Heaven is only half full and has had to close down its main dining hall. Good support from Ron Silver as a fast-talking executive with a record company.

Oh, Men! Oh, Women! ○

1957, US, 86 mins, colour
Dir: Nunnally Johnson
Stars: David Niven, Ginger Rogers
Rating: ★★★

Outstanding light comedy performances from David Niven, Dan Dailey, Barbara Rush and particularly Tony Randall (in his screen debut) illuminate this madcap, if inconsequential comedy with lush trimmings. Even the credit titles are presented in a novel way; it's a bright beginning the film lives up to. You've seen funnier farces, but this

psychiatric caper scores high marks for originality and Charles G Clarke's colour photography is luscious.

Oh! Mr Porter ⊙

1937, UK, 84 mins, b/w
Dir: Marcel Varnel
Stars: Will Hay, Moore Marriott, Graham Moffatt
Rating: ★★★★

Blustering Will Hay finds himself the stationmaster of a railway station where no trains stop, in this classic British comedy. His staff, a doddery old clerk and a fat porter, are Moore Marriott and Graham Moffatt, who appeared to great comic effect in most of Hay's films. He spruces the station up and books a train to transport the local football team. But the train and its passengers disappear. There are foul deeds afoot and it's down to Will and his not terribly brave lads to save the day. Not very sophisticated by today's standards perhaps, with its music hall roots very much in evidence, but still great fun, and including Marriott's classic line: 'The next train's gone!' A chase at the climax of the film is, surprisingly, quite exciting.

O.H.M.S. ○

(aka: You're in the Army Now)
1936, US, 86 mins, b/w
Dir: Raoul Walsh
Stars: Wallace Ford, John Mills
Rating: ★★

This flag-waving action adventure is well up to all but the top Hollywood standards – not surprising as it was made in Britain by American director Raoul Walsh, who built a whole career out of such films, especially in vehicles for Errol Flynn, Humphrey Bogart and James Cagney. Here he has a somewhat lesser light in burly Wallace Ford, a Hollywood star who had been raised in a London orphanage and now made headlines when seeking and finding his real parents while in England to make this film. The young John Mills gives him brisk support.

Oh! What a Lovely War ○

1969, UK, 144 mins, colour
Dir: Richard Attenborough
Stars: John Mills, Laurence Olivier, Susannah York, Maggie Smith
Rating: ★★★

The film that began Richard Attenborough's phenomenally successful new career as a director, following years of success as an acting star. Although he has difficulty in overcoming the unwieldy structure of Joan Littlewood's stage original, Attenborough conjures many vivid and poignant moments from this panoramic look at World War One from the end of Brighton Pier. Amid an enormous star cast, John Mills is outstanding as Sir Douglas Haig, and viewers will have fun spotting a multitude of stars in very tiny roles.

Oh, You Beautiful Doll ⊙
1949, US, 94 mins, colour
Dir: John Stahl
Stars: June Haver, Mark Stevens
Rating: ★★★

June Haver and Mark Stevens, two of 20th Century-Fox's young talents of the time, received top billing in this bright and breezy musical, set in New York's Tin Pan Alley of 1910. Beautifully shot in Technicolor by Harry Jackson, the film has a gem of a part for 'Cuddles' Sakall as a striving but luckless 'serious' composer who everywhere lugs around with him the score of his monumental but unperformed opera. On top of this there's the delightful Charlotte Greenwood, here not only long-legged but long-suffering as the composer's wife.

Okay for Sound ⊙
1937, UK, 85 mins, b/w
Dir: Marcel Varnel
Stars: Bud Flanagan, Chesney Allen
Rating: ★★★

One of the Crazy Gang's earliest film comedies. Not surprisingly, it contains most of their funniest stage routines (including slow motion wrestling, a TV commentary skit and a chaotic ballet) as the Gang turn a film studio upside down. The production is on the same lavish scale as the Gang's successful London Palladium show of the same name, but – horror of horrors! – the 'blue' jokes (well, they were blue then) and scantily clad chorus girls got the film an 'A' certificate!

Oklahoma! ○ ⓥ
1955, US, 145 mins, colour
Dir: Fred Zinnemann
Stars: Gordon MacRae, Shirley Jones, Rod Steiger, Gloria Grahame
Rating: ★★★

This sweeping Western musical contains probably the best score that Rodgers and Hammerstein ever wrote, from the breeziness of 'Kansas City' through the brashness of 'All 'Er

Nuthin' and the sly humour of 'Poor Jud is Dead', to the dreamy lilt of 'Surrey with the Fringe on Top'. Talented director Fred Zinnemann's approach brought a joyous freshness to the genre, resulting in one of the cleanest, most enjoyable musicals ever to come out of Hollywood.

Oklahoma Crude ⓒ
1973, US, 111 mins, colour
Dir: Stanley Kramer
Stars: George C Scott, Faye Dunaway, John Mills, Jack Palance
Rating: ★★★

Stanley Kramer has become a disappointing director since the late Sixties, but this is the best of his films since then, a raw rugged, amoral but oddly likeable story of conflict in the Oklahoma oilfield just before World War One. The plot is the one about the Cavalry and Indians besieging the fort, welded winningly to an account of a lone woman fighting to hang on to her wild-cat oil-rig against the 'heavy mob' employed by the state-wide oil trust to get her out. The stars all play very acceptably within their own images: George C Scott as the gruff, independent loner with a rough sense of humour; Faye Dunaway as the self-willed Lena, determined to give as good as any man; Jack Palance, back in *Shane* mood as the contemptuous, humourless heavy; and John Mills, almost stealing the film as Dunaway's dog-eared father, belatedly trying to help her make a mark on life.

Oklahoma Kid, The ○
1939, US, 85 mins, b/w
Dir: Lloyd Bacon
Stars: James Cagney, Humphrey Bogart, Rosemary Lane
Rating: ★★★

In the same year they made the classic crime picture *The Roaring Twenties*, Cagney and Bogart again played mortal enemies in this rousing Western. Neither looks at home in Western gear: Cagney's the Kid, Bogey the bad guy all-in-black, but their fans will love seeing them in unfamiliar guise.

Oklahoman, The ○
1956, US, 76 mins, colour
Dir: Francis D Lyon
Stars: Joel McCrea, Barbara Hale
Rating: ★★

A Western full of wide vistas and clear-cut issues, sparklingly shot in

colour by Carl Guthrie. Joel McCrea's shambling, too-old hero is the only hindrance to a fast-moving tale of racial prejudice and disputes over oil, with nicely-judged performances from Barbara Hale, Brad Dexter and Gloria Talbott. More incisive action would have sparked the story more, but writer Daniel B Ullman's screenplay still gives us some telling moments. Saturnine Australian actor Michael Pate is once again cast as a Red Indian!

Old Acquaintance ○
1943, US, 110 mins, b/w
Dir: Vincent Sherman
Stars: Bette Davis, Miriam Hopkins
Rating: ★★★★

The film that reunited Bette Davis and Miriam Hopkins, the latter fast approaching the end of her major film days, after 1939's *The Old Maid*. Warners hoped that the off-screen friction and enmity between the two stars would help the plot about two childhood friends who become deadly rivals. Davis, in particular, relished the scene in the film when Hopkins' character becomes hysterical and Bette has to slap her across the face. It would have been a great picture if director Vincent Sherman hadn't alowed it to run on too long towards the end; even so, the last scene makes up for a lot. Remade (badly) as *Rich and Famous* in 1981.

Old Dark House, The ⓒ
1932, US, 75 mins, b/w
Dir: James Whale
Stars: Charles Laughton, Melvyn Douglas, Boris Karloff, Gloria Stuart, Raymond Massey
Rating: ★★★★

Director James Whale's famous tongue-in-cheek horror film, alive with atmosphere as travellers are stranded for the night at an old mansion which one almost expects to crumble to pieces at any moment. Based on J B Priestley's book *Benighted*, the film has a marvellous cast that, besides Boris Karloff as the great hulking butler, includes Charles Laughton, Gloria Stuart, Ernest Thesiger, Melvyn Douglas and Raymond Massey. Full of quotable lines and creepy moments, it's a must for fans of the genre.

Old Fashioned Way, The ○
1934, US, 74 mins, b/w
Dir: William Beaudine

O

Stars: W C Fields, Judith Allen
Rating: ★★★★

W C Fields in prime form, heading a Victorian acting troupe in performances of *The Drunkard*, doing his juggling act and having some classic encounters with Baby LeRoy. Fields' most underrated film and perhaps even his best.

Old Gringo ◐ ⓥ

1989, US, 119 mins, colour
Dir: Luis Puenzo
Stars: Jane Fonda, Gregory Peck, Jimmy Smits
Rating: ★★★★

Only the fact that the motivations of its characters are often obscure keeps this well-writen and extremely well-directed film from being among the best of the cinema's sprawling romantic adventures. But it will still bring a gasp and a tear to your throat. Fonda, looking amazingly young, is the spinster governess who breaks clear of her severe old mother at last, travelling to Mexico at Revolution time, where she becomes involved with the fortunes of a charismatic young general (Jimmy Smits) and an old writer (Gregory Peck) seeking an honourable death. Both the action and dialogue scenes are directed in such a way by Puenzo as to make characters and events spring to life and stir the emotions. Performances are not outstanding, but all good, making *Old Gringo* the cinematic equivalent of a good read.

Old Maid, The ○

1939, US, 95 mins, b/w
Dir: Edmund Goulding
Stars: Bette Davis, Miriam Hopkins, George Brent
Rating: ★★★★

By the time she made this incredibly powerful film, set during the American Civil War, Bette Davis had already won two Oscars, for *Dangerous* in 1935 and *Jezebel* in 1938, and she was coming into her prime as a Hollywood star. She showed herself capable of even greater emotional depth in the role of Charlotte, the sweet young woman who has an illegitimate child by her cousin's jilted fiancé and has to hide the fact by running an orphanage. It was the third film that she made with British-born director Edmund Goulding (the first two being *That Certain Woman* and the highly successful *Dark Victory*) and one of seven films she made with

handsome nice guy George Brent. It's a story that tugs at the heartstrings and one of Davis's great star turns. The ending won't leave a dry eye in the house.

Old Man and the Sea, The ○

1958, US, 86 mins, colour
Dir: John Sturges
Stars: Spencer Tracy
Rating: ★★

Director John Sturges captures the near Biblical simplicity of Hemingway's classic story about an old Cuban fisherman who vows to make a great catch. In the lead, Tracy, as ever, is superb. Dimitri Tiomkin's music score won an Academy Award. Tracy and cinematographer James Wong Howe were both nominated. For all their efforts, though, this is a dull film that will have you looking at your watch.

Old Yeller ○ ⓥ

1957, US, 81 mins, colour
Dir: Robert Stevenson
Stars: Dorothy McGuire, Fess Parker, Tommy Kirk, Chuck Connors
Rating: ★★★

Both an exciting adventure and an effective tear-jerker, this was the Disney Studio's first film about a boy and his dog, adapted from the novel by Fred Gipson. It's photographed in warm, clear Technicolor by Charles Boyle and this, together with sturdy performances from Fess Parker and Dorothy McGuire as the boy's ranching father and his wife, and brisk, no-nonsense direction by Robert Stevenson, builds a convincing picture of life in the Texas countryside in the mid-1850s. The title dog is heartily well played by an animal called Spike, who lives up to the well-remembered song tribute from the film as 'the best doggone dog in the west'.

Oliver! ○ ⓥ

1968, UK, 146 mins, colour
Dir: Carol Reed
Stars: Mark Lester, Ron Moody, Oliver Reed, Jack Wild, Hugh Griffith
Rating: ★★★

Carol Reed's multiple Oscar-winner, with claims to being one of the best British film musicals ever made, still comes up looking good thanks to Ron Moody's wistful Fagin and Bart's one totally successful score. Note Leonard Rossiter as 'undertaker' and Harry Secombe as the definitive Beadle.

Oliver Twist ○ ⓥ

1948, UK, 116 mins, b/w
Dir: David Lean
Stars: Robert Newton, Alec Guinness, John Howard Davies, Kay Walsh
Rating: ★★★★

The definitive version of the Dickens classic about an orphan boy struggling to escape the underbelly of London in the early 1800s. Made in the middle of director David Lean's richest period, the film teems with detail and imaginatively-realised characters, particularly Alec Guinness's Fagin, piggy eyes gleaming as his rat's-nest beard dangles over some new plunder secured by his under-age army of pickpockets. Robert Newton makes a glowering, fearful Bill Sikes and Guy Green's sharp photography of the mainly dingy settings is a triumph of the black-and-white cameraman's art, bringing the London streets as alive with atmosphere as they are with predators.

Olly Olly Oxen Free

See: The Great Balloon Adventure

Omar Khayyam ○

1957, US, 101 mins, colour
Dir: William Dieterle
Stars: Cornel Wilde, Michael Rennie, Debra Paget, John Derek
Rating: ★★

They don't make them like this any more. A typical Hollywood *Arabian Nights* adventure, all action and colour, with a literate and faintly tongue-in-cheek script by Barre Lyndon and a good cast that also includes eight-octave Peruvian singer Yma Sumac in one of her few film roles. It was the last film directed by the great German William Dieterle, who came to Hollywood at the advent of sound, and stayed to make some of its most polished entertainments, including *Juarez*, Laughton's *The Hunchback of Notre Dame*, *The Life of Emile Zola* and *The Story of Louis Pasteur*. Cornel Wilde, who stars as the poet Omar, seeking fame and fortune in 11th-century Persia, had himself just made his first film as director (*Storm Fear*) and was later to direct several more.

Omega Man, The ● ⓥ

1971, US, 98 mins, colour
Dir: Boris Sagal
Stars: Charlton Heston, Anthony Zerbe, Rosalind Cash
Rating: ★★★

This post-nuclear apocalypse sci-fi drama has firm-jawed Charlton Heston as one of the few survivors who hasn't been turned into a pale-skinned mutation. The mutants, led by nasty, sneering Anthony Zerbe, want to eradicate what is left of the culture they feel is responsible for the nuclear disaster — and this, of course, includes Chuck. Not a bad film, but strangely dated now and seemingly clichéd, although it wasn't at the time it was made.

Omen, The ● Ⓥ

1976, US, 111 mins, colour
Dir: Richard Donner
Stars: Gregory Peck, Lee Remick, David Warner, Billie Whitelaw
Rating: ★★

During the Seventies, there were several key movies which brought an individual slant and startling new concepts to horror-style films, completely different from the familiar, traditional idiom which had drawn enthusiastic audiences for years. *The Exorcist* was a notable example and, undoubtedly, so was *The Omen*. Fundamentally, it centres on the re-birth of the anti-christ, Damien. Several of the characters come to a sticky end in scenes which range from the bizarre to the genuinely (and quite frighteningly) eerie, while the most famous 'shock' scene is a stunning and horrifying example of first-rate special-effects work.

Omen II

See: Damien – Omen II

Omen III – The Final Conflict ● Ⓥ

(aka: The Final Conflict)
1981, US, 108 mins, colour
Dir: Graham Baker
Stars: Sam Neill, Rossano Brazzi, Don Gordon, Lisa Harrow
Rating: ★

The final part of *The Omen* trilogy runs a bit like a Macnee-Rigg episode of *The Avengers*, but its predictability is redeemed in part by the charismatic performance of Sam Neill, the New Zealand-born actor, as Damien the Antichrist. Poor old Damien is getting like Dracula, with his stake, and the werewolf, with his silver bullets, as he can now only be killed by one of seven ornate daggers, the significance of which escaped us.

On an Island with You ○

1948, US, 107 mins, colour
Dir: Richard Thorpe
Stars: Esther Williams, Peter Lawford, Ricardo Montalban
Rating: ★★

Esther Williams was at her peak when she made this aqua-musical, and MGM had to look no further than the box-office takings for the proof. Worldwide, the film was one of the top 10 moneymakers of the year and the following year Esther appeared in the 10 most popular film stars list for the first time. This one, though no great shakes in the story department, is splashy in more ways than one, and the studio sold it with lots of moody shots of Esther in slinky, shiny bathing suits. Peter Lawford and Ricardo Montalban mooned over her, Hawaiian backgrounds were lush and tropical, and producer Joe Pasternak's budget even allowed him to throw in Cyd Charisse, Jimmy Durante and ever-beaming Cuban-raised (Spanish-born) band-leader Xavier Cugat. Durante ripped into one of his speciality numbers, 'I Can Do Without Broadway', but even he couldn't upstage Esther. The story got itself un-waterlogged every time she hit the waves.

On Borrowed Time ○

1939, US, 99 mins, b/w
Dir: Harold S Bucquet
Stars: Lionel Barrymore, Sir Cedric Hardwicke
Rating: ★★★

Today it seems almost incredible that, when this film first appeared in Britain, it was given an 'H' (for horror) certificate. It's a fantasy and contains a vein of whimsy — an old man who isn't ready to die traps Death (who has come to collect him) up a tree! — but certainly not 'horror'. Lionel Barrymore and Cedric Hardwicke lead a fine cast of reliable character actors under the direction of Harold S Bucquet, a genial Londoner who worked for MGM in Hollywood from 1934, most notably on the famous *Dr Kildare* and *Dr Gillespie* films. This is undoubtedly Bucquet's most untypical work, worth seeing for the bizarre dream sequences alone.

Once a Jolly Swagman ○

(aka: Maniacs on Wheels)
1948, UK, 100 mins, b/w
Dir: Jack Lee

Stars: Dirk Bogarde, Bill Owen, Renee Asherson, Bonar Colleano
Rating: ★★★

With a plot that rather rambles through its 13-year span, this is nonetheless a graphic and hard-edged portrait of the thrills and spills of a dangerous sport. Dirk Bogarde serves early notice of his promise of being more than just a matinee idol, giving depth and dimension to the speedway rider who starts as a cocky young ace and graduates to fighting for riders' rights through a union. The action scenes are, for their time, vividly done. The supporting case abounds in notable character actors from the post-war British cinema, including Bill Owen, Sidney James, Cyril Cusack, Thora Hird, James Hayter and Cyril Chamberlain.

Once Around ◖ Ⓥ

1990, US, 110 mins, colour
Dir: Lasse Hallstrom
Stars: Richard Dreyfuss, Holly Hunter, Danny Aiello, Laura San Giacomo, Gena Rowlands
Rating: ★

A romantic comedy of embarrassment that's almost unbearable to watch is bad news. This one is in-and-out for a little while, but completely falls apart in the last hour. One of its major problems is that you just can't see what's so wrong with the character played by Dreyfuss, who's supposed to tear an Italian-American family apart when he marries its older daughter (Holly Hunter). He's alleged to be crass and arrogant, though he's certainly no more vulgar than the family he joins. And, as Dreyfuss is rather a charming actor, it's difficult to understand why Papa (Danny Aiello) would want to throw him out. Dreyfuss is good, as usual. The others try their best with what they've got. It isn't much.

Once in a Lifetime ○

1932, US, 90 mins, b/w
Dir: Russell Mack
Stars: Jack Oakie, Sidney Fox, Aline MacMahon, ZaSu Pitts
Rating: ★★★

Another satire on Hollywood, this time angled on the panic that quickly envelops the film capital as it tries to convert to sound. Larger than life studio types are well delineated by Jack Oakie, Aline MacMahon, ZaSu Pitts, Louisa Fazenda and, best of all, Gregory Ratoff as Herman Glogauer.

Once Is Not Enough ●
1975, US, 121 mins, colour
Dir: Guy Green
Stars: Kirk Douglas, Deborah Raffin,
David Janssen
Rating: ★

Based on Jacqueline Susann's brazen
bestseller, this is a glossy saga of love
and lust in the American millionaire
belt. Tolerably well acted, especially
by the gravel-voiced David Janssen
and Brenda Vaccaro, with Deborah
Raffin just about adequate as the sweet
young thing who gets her heart broken several times over.

Once Upon a Crime ○ ⓥ
(aka: Criminals)
1992, US, 94 mins, colour
Dir: Eugene Levy
Stars: John Candy, James Belushi, Cybill
Shepherd, Sean Young, Richard Lewis,
Ornella Muti
Rating: ★

John Candy's co-star from *Armed and
Dangerous* and *Speed Zone*, Eugene
Levy, somehow managed to persuade
the big guy (and a lot of other
unfortunates) to star in this atrociously
written, strenuously over-performed
farce, directed by Levy in a unique,
in-your-face fashion which may have
you reaching for the earplugs. A furious farce involving a lost dog, a
compulsive gambler, a jilted lover, an
actor, a gigolo and a murder, it does
at least ensure you're not starved of
familiar faces to recognise: besides
the list above, there's George Hamilton, Joss Ackland, Elsa Martinelli and
even Giancarlo Giannini, attempting a
Herbert Lom-style police inspector
amid the raucous comic chaos. Despite good intentions, it's a star-
strangled bummer.

Once Upon a Forest ⊙ ⓥ
1993, US, 68 mins, colour
Dir: Charles Grosvenor
Voice stars: Michael Crawford,
Ben Vereen, Ellen Blain, Paige Gosney,
Ben Gregory
Rating: ★★

Tinies will be enchanted by this ecologically friendly cartoon, ideal for
children of nursery school age. In
similar fashion to *FernGully*, disaster
overtakes the forest (here in the form
of an overturned tanker full of poison
gas) and it's up to three 'furlings'
(animal children) to raise the medicine
necessary to save a friend, after all
other animals die or flee the forest.
These prove to be a girl mouse

(unusual to have a female lead character under these circumstances but it
works rather well), a boy mole and a
boy hedgehog, and their adventures
form the core of the entertainment.
Backgrounds are poor, but whizzy
adventures of a home-made flying
contraption almost make up for it. A
fearsome one-eyed owl may frighten
some of the smallest members of the
family. Michael Crawford provides
the voice of the victim's granddad and
gets the chance to sing a song too.

Once Upon a Honeymoon ○
1942, US, 116 mins, b/w
Dir: Leo McCarey
Stars: Cary Grant, Ginger Rogers, Walter
Slezak
Rating: ★★

Very entertaining movie from Leo
McCarey (who won Oscars for *The
Awful Truth*, *Going My Way* and *Love
Affair*). It's hard to categorise: perhaps
thriller-cum-romantic comedy-
melodrama would be about the nearest one could get. At any rate, Cary
Grant and Ginger Rogers play delightfully against one another, and
Walter Slezak is in fine form as the
oily aristocrat who marries Ms Rogers,
and then turns out to be a traitor of his
country and a menace to her life. The
ending is delightful.

Once Upon a Time in the West ○ ⓥ
1969, Italy, 165 mins, colour
Dir: Sergio Leone
Stars: Henry Fonda, Charles Bronson,
Jason Robards, Claudia Cardinale
Rating: ★★★

The film that belatedly made a superstar of Charles Bronson after
nearly 20 years of tough-guy roles.
Ironically, he was actually billed
fourth in the original cast (although his
character is clearly the main one), the
same as Alan Ladd when he made his
breakthrough to stardom 26 years
earlier as another cool killer in *This
Gun for Hire*. The film is a typical
Sergio Leone Western – long, languorous, punctuated with emphatic
action, and full of close-ups of sweaty,
grimy faces which go towards painting
an atmospheric picture of a hot, desolate part of the west where life was
hard, tempers could frequently explode and the weak were ruthlessly
weeded out by the strong. Don't miss
the first 10 minutes of the film – a
protracted pre-credit shoot-out which
established Bronson in his Clint
Eastwood-type role of silent avenger,

and sees three of the featured cast
mown down before the film proper
has started. Henry Fonda contributes a
first-rate, fully rounded portrait of the
villainous Frank, completing a trio of
similar characters he had played in
Warlock and *Firecreek*.

On Dangerous Ground ○
1951, US, 82 mins, b/w
Dir: Nicholas Ray
Stars: Ida Lupino, Robert Ryan, Ward
Bond, Ed Begley
Rating: ★★★

Moody romantic thriller from director
Nicholas Ray, with Robert Ryan well
at home as the embittered cop who
reassesses his values when sent on a
case that takes him away from the
mean streets of his city environment.
A good supporting cast is full of familiar Hollywood faces from the
Fifties, and there's a tiny appearance
by A I Bezzerides (he plays Gatos)
who also wrote the script. Bernard
Herrmann contributes an especially
melodic background score, but it's
Ryan – snarling 'Why do you punks
make me do it?' as he smashes into a
shady suspect – that you'll remember.

On Deadly Ground ● ⓥ
1994, US, 102 mins, colour
Dir: Steven Seagal
Stars: Steven Seagal, Michael Caine,
Joan Chen, R Lee Ermey, John C
McGinley
Rating: ★

An action movie that also has to be
seen to be green, this breaks new
ground all right – a new low even for
Steven Seagal and Michael Caine,
who have both made a fair number of
turkeys in recent times, even if
Seagal's have been comparatively successful. 'What does it take to change
the soul of a man,' asks Seagal, in one
of the film's highly resistible bursts of
pious philosophy. Broken bones,
direst agony and long periods of un-
consciousness will do the trick,
judging by this film, in which Seagal
casts himself as an oil rigger whose
conscience is pricked by the plight of
Eskimos in Alaska at the mercy of big
business interests, headed up by Caine
in a dark wig that makes him look like
Robert Maxwell. The action scenes
are nastily well done, but Seagal is on
shaky ground here compared with the
relative splendours of *Under Siege*,
especially with the cringe-making final
speech. Caine tries hard to scowl and
sneer, but remains basically engaging

(and therefore miscast), while Seagal is uncomfortably unsympathetic as the hero.

One Born Every Minute
See: *The Flim-Flam Man*

One-Eyed Jacks ○ ⓥ
1961, US, 141 mins, colour
Dir: Marlon Brando
Stars: Marlon Brando, Karl Malden
Rating: ★★★

Marlon Brando's one-man-band film: he also produced and directed this lovely-to-look-at Western (it was shot along the California coastline) with himself as a bandit hunting down the former partner who betrayed him and netted him a stiff jail sentence. Look for a telling cameo portrayal from Elisha Cook Jr as a frightened bank cashier.

One False Move ● ⓥ
1990, US, 106 mins, colour
Dir: Carl Franklin
Stars: Bill Paxton, Cynda Williams, Billy Bob Thornton, Michael Beach
Rating: ★★

Aside from its language, the casual violence and black atmosphere of this modern *film noir* ties it to gangster films of the late 1950s when mid-west villains like Pretty Boy Floyd were shown in their unglamorous true colours. Two lethal criminals mercilessly slaughter two households, one of innocent partygoers, the other of drug holders that leads them to $15,000 in cash and a massive stash of narcotics. Their front girl is the impassive, drug-hyped Fantasia (Cynda Williams): on the run, the trip heads for her home ground, the territory of brash but efficient Arkansas sheriff Dale Dixon (Bill Paxton), who soon finds himself with two LA cops to deal with as well as the impending showdown with the criminals, and even darker revelations from his own past. *One False Move* works fine while its killers are on the run and the relationship between country and city cops is swaying to and fro. But director Carl Franklin's command of the pace falters when Dixon's past comes to the fore; Paxton, though, is right on the money as the small-town lawman with big ambitions.

One Flew over the Cuckoo's Nest ● ⓥ
1975, US, 134 mins, colour
Dir: Milos Forman

Stars: Jack Nicholson, Louise Fletcher, Christopher Lloyd, Danny DeVito
Rating: ★★★

The first winner of all five major Oscars (actor, actress, film, direction and screenplay), this is an immensely skilful attempt to make a commercially enjoyable film out of life in a mental institution. The opening scenes – Hollywood-style shots of imbecilic inmates and the symbolic squirrel outside the wall (freedom) – signal the facile approach the film feels forced to adopt to get its message across. Fortunately, it has at its centre Jack Nicholson's brilliant performance as R P McMurphy, the sane patient who improbably brings a shaft of sunlight into the lives of his less sane fellows by holding a fateful all-night drinking spree and by taking them on a joyous fishing expedition. There are excellent supporting performances by Louise Fletcher (another Oscar-winner), Brad Dourif (Oscar-nominated) and the massive Will Sampson, and early appearances from Christopher Lloyd and Danny DeVito.

One Foot in Heaven ○
1941, US, 108 mins, b/w
Dir: Irving Rapper
Stars: Fredric March, Martha Scott
Rating: ★★★

The easily moved will cry a pulpit full of tears at this family drama about the life of an inspirational Methodist minister, constructed in Hollywood's finest heartwarming style. Fredric March and Martha Scott are at their most sincere as the minister and his wife in a film that looks a bit over-the-top today, but still works if you're in an indulgent mood. Directed by Irving Rapper who, used to directing Bette Davis weepies, extracts the maximum from your emotional reactions. Gene Lockhart and Laura Hope Crews supply two of several three-dimensional cameos in the supporting cast.

One Foot in Hell ○
1960, US, 90 mins, colour
Dir: James B Clark
Stars: Alan Ladd, Don Murray, Dan O'Herlihy
Rating: ★★

Alan Ladd plays an embittered man who resolves to take revenge on the townsfolk who refused to help him when his wife was dying in this rather offbeat Western. Feeling guilty, they

offer him the job of deputy sheriff. Ladd kills the sheriff, takes his job and then gathers an unruly gang to help him rob the town bank and kill those who earlier didn't come to his aid. It's unusual and interesting to see Ladd as a baddie, and it's a shame the film itself turns out to be trite, implausible and hamstrung by the leaden direction of James B Clark. The real villains of the piece, though, were scriptwriters Aaron Spelling and Sydney Boehm. Luckily for him (and us!), one-time actor Spelling discovered a greater talent as a producer and became one of the richest men in Hollywood.

One Good Cop ● ⓥ
1991, US, 105 mins, colour
Dir: Heywood Gould
Stars: Michael Keaton, Rene Russo, Anthony LaPaglia, Rachel Ticotin
Rating: ★★

You can sympathise with Keaton in the impossible attempt to find a follow-up to *Batman*, but he blew it here. Impossibly schmaltzy and of very dubious ethical value, it casts Keaton as a cop whose partner gets killed, leaving Keaton and his wife with the dead man's three small daughters. To avoid losing the girls, and to buy a house for them, Keaton robs a drug dealer of his stake money. Generally, the film lacks strength in most departments, and Keaton's supporting cast is weak by the standards of modern cinema. Consequently, the film never whacks hard at the emotions, builds to a climax, or gives you the impression that it really knows where it's going. *One Good Cop* is one mediocre movie.

One Hour to Doomsday ○
(aka: City Beneath the Sea)
1971, US, 98 mins, colour
Dir: Irwin Allen
Stars: Stuart Whitman, Robert Wagner, Rosemary Forsyth
Rating: ★★★

Irwin Allen, the man responsible for the film (and subsequent TV series) *Voyage to the Bottom of the Sea*, came up here with a fast, exciting undersea comic-strip that resembles *Stingray* with real people. Stuart Whitman certainly has the eyebrows for the Troy Tempest part as the only man who can save the scientific city of Pacifica, beneath the ocean, from destruction by a huge, flaming meteorite headed straight for it. Told about the meteorite, with a density three

O

million times that of earth, Whitman exclaims, with commendable understanding: 'Good God! Casualties could run into millions.' Robert Wagner enjoys himself immensely as Whitman's villainous brother, while the exquisite Rosemary Forsyth, so memorable in *The War Lord*, actually manages to contribute an acting performance that rivals the special effects (the meteorite, when it comes, is very convincing). Children, especially those between seven and 12, will love every minute of it.

One Hour with You ○
1932, US, 75 mins, b/w
Dir: Ernst Lubitsch, George Cukor
Stars: Maurice Chevalier, Jeanette MacDonald, Roland Young
Rating: ★★★

Like *Love Me Tonight*, this is another scintillating vehicle for the delectable co-starring team of Maurice Chevalier and Jeanette MacDonald. Also similarly, it was notable at the time for its risqué elements which Hollywood could get away with in the early Thirties. It is not a musical as such, rather a dramatic comedy with music (largely written by the operetta composer Oscar Straus, noted particularly for *The Chocolate Soldier*). A remake of Ernst Lubitsch's silent success *The Marriage Circle*, it is generally accepted as a Lubitsch film and certainly looks like one. However, the picture was started by George Cukor who had disagreements with Lubitsch (then production supervisor at Paramount) with the result that Lubitsch completed the film himself with Cukor at the time credited merely as 'dialogue director'. Unusual features included its use of rhyming dialogue and the device of having Chevalier address the audience directly to introduce characters and comment on situations. One way and another, it's a treat for vintage film fans.

One Hundred and One Dalmatians ⊙
1961, US, 79 mins, colour
Dir: Wolfgang Reitherman, Hamilton S Luske, Clyde Geronimi
Voice stars: Rod Taylor, Lisa Davis, Cate Bauer, J Pat O'Malley, Betty Lou Gerson, Tom Conway, Mary Wickes
Rating: ★★★

Innovative animation, an uncluttered storyline, a tremendous villainess and hilariously action-packed chase sequences all combined to make this a hugely popular feature cartoon from the Disney stable. Fifteen Dalmatian puppies are stolen from their home by the horrendous Cruella De Vil, or to be exact her henchmen Jasper and Horace Badun, who whisk the pups off to Cruella's home, Hell Hall, where they will go with dozens of other dogs to make Cruella an amazing black and white dreamcoat. She reckons, however, without the 'Twilight Bark', a series of cross-country messages that culminates in a rescue bid by the pups' parents, Pongo and Perdita, a crafty cat called Sergeant Tibs, a haughty sheepdog known as The Colonel and sundry allies. Delightful characters and an unrelenting pace make this a film that will enchant all children.

100 Men and a Girl ⊙
1937, US, 84 mins, b/w
Dir: Henry Koster
Stars: Deanna Durbin, Adolphe Menjou
Rating: ★★★

The film in which Deanna Durbin's freshness and spontaneity really burst on the cinemagoing public like a breath of spring. No doubt about it, Deanna is delightful as the bouncy teenager who charms a world-famous musician into conducting a symphony played by her father's orchestra of unemployed musicians. Good support from Eugene Pallette, Billy Gilbert and Mischa Auer, but it's the little girl's show all the way. Deanna's ditties include 'It's Raining Sunbeams'.

One Man Mutiny
See: Court-Martial of Billy Mitchell

One Man's War ●
1990, UK, 87 mins, colour
Dir: Sergio Toledo
Stars: Anthony Hopkins, Norma Aleandro, Ruben Blades
Rating: ★★

There's material for a grim and gripping film here. And, given Anthony Hopkins as his leading man, director Sergio Toledo really should have done better. But, taking everything at a snail's pace, he muffles much of the impact of this depressing tale of military repression in 1976 Paraguay – then lets the story slide into an abrupt and unsatisfying conclusion. Where professional polish would have added punch, Toledo allows the Hopkins character too often to drift away from being a resolute centre and gets an uncharacteristically theatrical performance from Norma Aleandro and an unexpectedly halting one from Ruben Blades as Hopkins' lawyer. Even with all its faults, though, the film's to be commended for opening a window on little-known but no less horrifying violations of human rights. Tough talk and details of torture mean it should be kept away from sub 15-year-olds, though older teenagers as well as adults may find it food for thought and an education too. Slow and sombre stuff.

One Million Years BC ○ ⓥ
1966, UK, 100 mins, colour
Dir: Don Chaffey
Stars: Raquel Welch, John Richardson
Rating: ★★★

With Raquel Welch in her famous fur-trimmed bikini and special effects by the legendary Ray Harryhausen, Hammer could hardly fail with this, their '100th film' and the movie duly cleared up at the box-office. All the monsters look superb, and special effects are first-rate, especially in the final, earth-splitting volcanic eruption. But it's Raquel you'll remember.

One More Train to Rob ○
1971, US, 108 mins, colour
Dir: Andrew V Mclaglen
Stars: George Peppard, Diana Muldaur, John Vernon, France Nuyen
Rating: ★★

One is so used to seeing either John Wayne or James Stewart as the star of Andrew McLaglen's Westerns that it comes as something of a surprise to find George Peppard leading the cast of *One More Train to Rob*. He plays an ex-jailbird bent on revenge on the double-crossing partner who is now wealthy. Sounds familiar? It should: Brando used the same plot basis for his *One-Eyed Jacks*. Keep an eye open for former stars France Nuyen and Ben Cooper, down the cast as a Chinese girl and a deputy sheriff.

One of Our Aircraft Is Missing ○
1941, UK, 102 mins, b/w
Dir: Michael Powell, Emeric Pressburger
Stars: Godfrey Tearle, Eric Portman, Hugh Williams, Googie Withers
Rating: ★★★

Gripping war film from the Powell-Pressburger team – later to make *A Matter of Life and Death* and *The Red Shoes* – about six airmen shot down over Nazi-occupied Holland.

One of Our Dinosaurs Is Missing ⊙
1975, US, 94 mins, colour
Dir: Robert Stevenson
Stars: Peter Ustinov, Helen Hayes, Clive Revill, Derek Nimmo
Rating: ★★★

There's this army of nannies being pursued by fiendish Chinese spies because they've stolen a dinosaur. There are also two boys with a snake, and the police, and a microfilm, to say nothing of a Mayfair sharpshooter who's trying to bag the dinosaur. But the nannies, driving a steam-engine on and off a train, have stolen the wrong dinosaur. Consequently, they have to take on the Chinese kung-fu experts in a free-for-all. It could only happen at the Disney Studios in the Seventies, and *Dinosaurs* was the merriest, most madcap comedy to surface there in a decade. The inspired lunatic who thought it all up was Bill Walsh, who wrote many Disney comedy hits. Sadly, this was his last script before he died.

One-Piece Bathing Suit, The ○
1952, US, 115 mins, colour
Dir: Mervyn LeRoy
Stars: Esther Williams, Victor Mature, Walter Pidgeon
Rating: ★★

That phenomenon of the Forties and Fifties – the aqua-musical. This one is far more tolerable than most, being based on the inspiring life story of Australian swimming star Annette Kellerman. The original title, *Million Dollar Mermaid*, was as appropriate for Esther Williams – voted one of the 10-box office attractions in America in the previous two years – as it was for Annette. Victor Mature takes over from Van Johnson and Ricardo Montalban as Esther's leading man. Pug-faced Jesse White is also featured.

One Step to Hell ○
1967, Spain/US, 90 mins, colour
Dir: Sandy Howard
Stars: Ty Hardin, Pier Angeli, Rossano Brazzi, Helga Line, George Sanders
Rating: ★

Spanish-American co-production set in Africa! Ty Hardin has the requisite brawn as the policeman chasing a group of escaped convicts through the jungle, while Rossano Brazzi and George Sanders have not much more

than walk-on roles, leaving the Spanish supporting cast to do most of the donkey work.

One That Got Away, The ○
1957, UK, 110 mins, b/w
Dir: Roy Baker
Stars: Hardy Kruger
Rating: ★★★

An interesting and unusual war story with a nail-biting ending. It is, in fact, the climax which lifts a goodish film into another class altogether. It's a really fine sequence, staged against a brilliantly photographed St Lawrence Seaway in Canada. Hardy Kruger's excellent performance as the German PoW determined to escape his British captors set him up for further international roles after 15 years journeyman work in the German cinema. And Terence Alexander registers well in a small part. But the grip of this film is almost entirely accounted for by its fascinating true story.

One-Trick Pony ◑
1980, US, 98 mins, colour
Dir: Robert M Young
Stars: Paul Simon, Blair Brown, Rip Torn
Rating: ★★

Paul Simon plays a past-it pop singer trying to repair his career and his relationship with his ex-wife (Blair Brown) in this interesting if not terribly good rock drama. The story (scripted by Simon) moves along familiar lines, which is a minus, but the music is a definite plus (especially if you're a fan of the man). You've got to admire Simon's guts because after amply demonstrating his profound lack of acting ability in *Annie Hall*, a lesser man than Simon would have gone back to what he is good at with his tail between his legs. But no, our vertically-challenged star decided to give it another go and although he's still no actor, he shows a marked improvement. The music's good, though and there's an interesting and varied collection of guest stars which includes The Lovin' Spoonful (remember them?), the B52's, Sam and Dave and Tiny Tim (!).

One, Two, Three ○
1961, US, 104 mins, b/w
Dir: Billy Wilder
Stars: James Cagney, Horst Buchholz, Pamela Tiffin, Lilo Pulver
Rating: ★

A raucous modern farce, played at breakneck pace by both star James Cagney and director Billy Wilder, although this is not quite such a happy visit to Berlin for Wilder as in his 1948 comedy, *A Foreign Affair*. There are some nice in-jokes, however, especially Cagney's threat to squash a grapefruit in Horst Buchholz's face.

One Way Passage ○
1932, US, 69 mins, b/w
Dir: Tay Garnett
Stars: William Powell, Kay Francis
Rating: ★★★

Said *Variety* on the first release of this weepie: 'Not a big box-office picture.' How wrong can you be? The film not only brought Warner Brothers some of its biggest returns of the year, but became one of the enduring classics of its genre. The romance between execution-bound criminal William Powell and ailing beauty Kay Francis, on board a ship bound from China to America, ensured that the cinema was a sea of handkerchiefs when the house lights went up at the end. Sharp supporting cameos by Frank McHugh, Aline MacMahon and Warren Hymer add the finishing touches. Robert Lord cocked a further snook at the poor unfortunate *Variety* reviewer by winning an Academy Award for the best original story of the year.

One Way Pendulum ○
1964, UK, 90 mins, b/w
Dir: Peter Yates
Stars: Eric Sykes, George Cole, Julia Foster, Jonathan Miller
Rating: ★★★

The Groomkirbys look like an ordinary family. But come into their home. They are all, if James Thurber will excuse the theft, as crazy as jay birds. Mr G reconstructs the Old Bailey in his living room, even to knocking a hole in the ceiling to get the Statue of Justice in. Gran imagines she boarded a train at St Pancras and landed up in the Outer Hebrides. Mrs G pays a neighbour to eat up scraps of food left by the family. Daughter Sylvia has paid so many visits to the apes at the zoo she thinks her arms are too short. But the prize loon is son Kirby, teaching a choir of speak-your-weight machines to 'sing' by putting different weights on them. You need a Goonish (not to say ghoulish) sense of humour to appreciate the laughs in this film version of N F Simpson's madcap play. And the film slips in veiled acidities about human nature

O

and racial prejudice that are still valid today. Jonathan Miller (Kirby) is really funniest without saying anything. Eric Sykes is delightfully bemused as Mr G And the choir of weighing machines alone make it worth seeing. If you think the world is round, however, better leave the Groomkirby family alone.

One Way Street ○
1950, US, 80 mins, b/w
Dir: Hugo Fregonese
Stars: James Mason, Marta Toren
Rating: ★★

Fairly routine action thriller with some exciting patches, but not really worthy of James Mason, then striving to establish himself in Hollywood after years as Britain's number one box-office star. Here he plays a crooked physician on the run with some stolen loot. There's a first rate supporting quintet of bad guys – Dan Duryea, William Conrad, King Donovan, Jack Elam and Rudolfo Acosta – that adds character to the thrills. And you'll also spot Rock Hudson who, in one of his earliest roles, makes a small appearance as a truck driver.

One Woman's Story
See: The Passionate Friends

On Golden Pond ○ ⓥ
1981, US, 109 mins, colour
Dir: Mark Rydell
Stars: Katharine Hepburn, Henry Fonda, Jane Fonda
Rating: ★★★★

A great Hollywood mogul used to say: 'If it makes you cry, it must be good.' It didn't necessarily follow, but he would have been proud of *On Golden Pond*. It does make you cry and it is superb. After a sticky beginning, both Katharine Hepburn and Henry Fonda relax into their roles of a crusty 79-year-old professor and his 10-years-younger wife, spending their 48th summer together at their holiday fishing lake. Jane Fonda, in a poignant piece of casting, has what amounts to little more than a cameo role as the daughter with whom the old man has failed to communicate for 40 years. Subsequent development, involving the son she leaves with the old couple for a month, could easily have been mawkish, but are very persuasively written by Ernest Thompson, on whose play the film is based. Billy Williams' colour photography of menacing skies and sun-flecked water is quite flawless and helps to catch the

mood of the piece, a last fling, perhaps, for Hollywood's vintage years, in which Hepburn and Henry Fonda (both Oscar-winners for their roles) are finally unbearably touching. Critics, on the whole, hated it; the public responded with its feet.

On Her Majesty's Secret Service ○ ⓥ
1969, UK, 140 mins, colour
Dir: Peter Hunt
Stars: George Lazenby, Diana Rigg, Telly Savalas
Rating: ★★★

Sent to foil arch-villain Blofeld's plan for world domination by spreading a plague through ten beautiful women infected with a deadly virus, George Lazenby steps athletically into Sean Connery's 007 role. Director Peter Hunt, who edited earlier Bond films, directs pacily, keeping the action moving and staging an exciting snow chase with one villain torn to pieces in a snow plough.

Onion Field, The ● ⓥ
1979, US, 126 mins, colour
Dir: Harold Becker
Stars: John Savage, James Woods, Ted Danson, Priscilla Pointer
Rating: ★★★

There are very few shafts of light in this black, bitter and violent true-life case study, involving the shooting of a young policeman and the gradual mental disintegration of his partner. Strong performances by John Savage, James Woods, Ronny Cox and Ted Danson help alleviate the fact that the film does go on a bit. But the central sequence – the nighttime killing in the onion field of the title – is chillingly well realised by director Harold Becker. Tough stuff.

Only Game in Town, The ○
1969, US, 113 mins, colour
Dir: George Stevens
Stars: Elizabeth Taylor, Warren Beatty
Rating: ★★★

Elizabeth Taylor is gorgeously gowned in this bitter-sweet story of the affair between a gambler and a chorus girl stranded in Las Vegas. Directed by double Oscar-winner George Stevens, it is the direction which lifts the rather old-fashioned story, based on a stage play, out of the ordinary. Stevens evokes the night-life of Las Vegas to perfection with the aid of only a few scenes – neon signs, coloured fountains, the dazzling

brightness of the gambling casinos. And the persuasive performances of Warren Beatty and Ms Taylor makes us believe that the cattiness of their own private sex war could melt to the final realisation that marriage really is 'the only game in town'.

Only the Lonely ◐ ⓥ
1991, US, 104 mins, colour
Dir: Chris Columbus
Stars: John Candy, Maureen O'Hara, Ally Sheedy, Anthony Quinn, James Belushi
Rating: ★★★

The moral of this *Marty*-style romance is: never co-star with 70-year-old actresses making a come-back. They will wipe the floor with you. This should be Candy's film and, in a straight romantic role, the 20-stone comedian has probably never been better. But it's O'Hara as the overbearing Irish mother who has stifled his romantic chances, who walks away with the film. Candy is a plump cop who falls for mortician's plain daughter Sheedy. But his own concern for his mother (her opinion and her welfare) seemingly dooms the romance from the start. There's not much to the ensuing story, and some of it is pretty silly; but it does contain perhaps the best performance of O'Hara's career. Unlucky one, John.

Only the Valiant ○ ⓥ
1951, US, 100 mins, b/w
Dir: Gordon Douglas
Stars: Gregory Peck, Barbara Payton, Gig Young, Ward Bond, Lon Chaney
Rating: ★★

Action galore but that's all for Western fans in this disappointingly written adaptation of Charles Marquis Warren's classic novel about a cavalry officer (stalwart Gregory Peck) who goes to hell and back to regain the respect of his men and his girl. Not the first classic Western novel Hollywood has messed up, nor the last. Only one of their mistakes here was not to make the film in colour.

Only Two Can Play ◐
1962, UK, 106 mins, b/w
Dir: Sidney Gilliat
Stars: Peter Sellers, Mai Zetterling, Virginia Maskell
Rating: ★★★

Peter Sellers' first real attempt to move outside the realms of straightforward farce. But it's still the farcical bits – mainly attempted seductions which end in disaster – that come off best, in this black comedy about a Welsh librarian and would-be lecher who is constantly frustrated in his attempts to get girls into bed. Sellers is admirably backed by Mai Zetterling, as the centre of his attentions, and by Richard Attenborough and Kenneth Griffith.

Only When I Larf ○
1968, UK, 103 mins, colour
Dir: Basil Dearden
Stars: Richard Attenborough, David Hemmings
Rating: ★★

David Hemmings, Richard Attenborough and Alexandra Stewart play confidence tricksters who cross and double-cross each other in a bewildering series of events, following an amusing opening sequence. Based on a novel by Len Deighton, who wrote the Harry Palmer spy thrillers.

Only You ◐ ⓥ
(aka: Love Stinks)
1992, US, 88 mins, colour
Dir: Betty Thomas
Stars: Andrew McCarthy, Kelly Preston, Helen Hunt, Daniel Roebuck, Kid Creole, Reni Santoni
Rating: ★★

You'll be at least one step ahead of the hero all the way in this formula and totally predictable romantic frolic about a hot-blooded young man (Andrew McCarthy) trying to find the perfect mate. It's written to a well-tried Hollywood recipe: pretty airhead in a tropical paradise setting is the object of the male's desire, while his true love – the good-hearted, plain Jane type – lurks unnoticed in the background. Please! Despite the stereotyping, McCarthy carries it all quite well, whether fighting with feisty Helen Hunt (who has personality to spare) or swooning over brainless blonde Kelly Preston. Undemanding entertainment, but nicely stitched together by Betty Thomas, once the formidable Sergeant Bates in TV's *Hill Street Blues*.

On Moonlight Bay ○
1951, US, 95 mins, colour
Dir: Roy Del Ruth
Stars: Doris Day, Gordon MacRae
Rating: ★★★

Stuck for a musical vehicle for the fast-rising Doris Day, Warners took the *Penrod* stories that had been filmed before and (making the central character Day's younger brother) crossed them with *Meet Me in St Louis*,

added period songs and set the whole thing in a small Indiana town around 1917. Day and Gordon MacRae are more than pleasant company, but it's the supporting cast (and colour photography) that really make this one glow: Leon Ames (especially good) as the father suspected of drunkenness; Rosemary deCamp as mother; Ellen Corby as the schoolma'am; Mary Wickes as the acid family maid; and Billy Gray as the rumour-spreading brother.

On the Avenue ○
1937, US, 86 mins, b/w
Dir: Roy Del Ruth
Stars: Dick Powell, Madeleine Carroll, Alice Faye, The Ritz Brothers
Rating: ★★★

A smashing Irving Berlin score, three stars on top form and Roy Del Ruth's brisk direction make this one of the most enjoyable 20th Century-Fox musicals of the Thirties. Alice Faye sings 'This Year's Kisses' and duets with Dick Powell on 'I've got My Love to Keep Me Warm'. Top marks to her vocalising and to the zany antics of the Ritz Brothers, one of whom, Harry, appears in drag in an imitation of Faye in the novelty number 'O Chi Chornia'. And yes, musical buffs, Irving Berlin did write a title number called 'On the Avenue' for the film – but for some reason it was deleted before the movie's release. Very strange.

On the Beat ☉ ⓥ
1962, UK, 100 mins, b/w
Dir: Robert Asher
Stars: Norman Wisdom, Jennifer Jayne
Rating: ★★

Norman Wisdom gets a chance to play a dual role. He's Norman Pitkin, who longs to join the police force but can't fill his father's size 12 boots, and Giulio Napolitani, Neapolitan king of London's underworld of crime. Best segment: Norman pursued over the fences of a long row of back gardens in a sequence which comes to resemble a human Grand National.

On the Black Hill ● ⓥ
1987, UK, 117 mins, colour
Dir: Andrew Grieve
Stars: Mike Gwilym, Robert Gwilym, Bob Peck, Gemma Jones
Rating: ★★

Based on the award-winning novel of the same name by Bruce Chatwin, this is a dour diatribe, beautifully photo-

graphed in Welsh border country by Thaddeus O'Sullivan, that sets out to prove the old maxim that the answer lies in the soil. The land, in fact, is the silent but dominant character in this saga of twins (played by real-life brothers), their work, their loves, their quarrels and their makings-up over an 80-year period that proves a trifle too much for the film's structure. The episodes, though effective in their own right, fail to build up a single theme, but the performances are as dedicated as the twins themselves, especially from Bob Peck and Gemma Jones as their ill-matched parents.

On the Buses ○
1971, UK, 88 mins, colour
Dir: Harry Booth
Stars: Reg Varney, Doris Hare, Michael Robbins
Rating: ★★

The popular TV series transferred to the cinema, complete with the original cast: Doris Hare as Mum, Michael Robbins as Arthur, Anna Karen as Olive, Bob Grant as Jack, Reg Varney as Stan and Stephen Lewis as Blakey. The story is about Blakey trying to introduce women drivers to the bus company. It was Hammer Films' first comedy for 10 years.

On the Riviera ☉
1951, US, 89 mins, colour
Dir: Walter Lang
Stars: Danny Kaye, Gene Tierney, Corinne Calvet
Rating: ★★

Brightish entertainment that will please Danny Kaye fans though probably not win any converts to his brand of fun. Like *Hans Christian Andersen*, the story (a remake of 1935's *Folies Bergere*) isn't much, but the score is delightful, including 'Popo the Puppet', 'On the Riviera', 'Happy Ending' and 'Ballin' the Jack'. And there are lovely girls all over the place, including Gene Tierney, Corinne Calvet, Mari Blanchard and dancer Gwen Verdon, here billed as Gwyneth.

On the Threshold of Space ○
1955, US, 96 mins, colour
Dir: Robert D Webb
Stars: Guy Madison, Virginia Leith, John Hodiak, Dean Jagger
Rating: ★

This was one of Fox's big prestige movies at the time when Cinema-

O

Scope was still all the rage. Guy Madison plays a young air force doctor who agrees to take part in a dangerous experiment involving a new ejector seat. They should have tried the script on it instead.

On the Town ⊙ ⓥ

1949, US, 98 mins, colour
Dir: Gene Kelly, Stanley Donen
Stars: Gene Kelly, Frank Sinatra, Vera-Ellen, Ann Miller, Betty Garrett, Jules Munshin
Rating: ★★★★

The catchy songs and dazzling on-location dancing made this one of the best and most talked-about song-and-dance films ever to come out of Hollywood. With its scintillating rooftop routines and brilliant colour photography, this wonderfully-paced tale of three sailors on brief leave in New York set new standards for musicals for years to come. And it still comes up fresh each time.

On the Waterfront ⊙ ⓥ

1954, US, 108 mins, b/w
Dir: Elia Kazan
Stars: Marlon Brando, Karl Malden, Lee J Cobb, Eva Marie Saint
Rating: ★★★★

Powerful drama set on New York's waterfront, where gangsters control the longshoremen's union and stevedore Terry Malloy (stunningly played by Marlon Brando) faces the terrible dilemma of whether or not to turn informer. Full of dynamic performances (Brando, Malden, Cobb, Saint, Rod Steiger), quotable, pungent lines and with a memorable climax, this, highly-charged throughout, is a winner all the way. The film won eight Oscars, including Best Picture, Director, Actor (Marlon Brando), Supporting Actress (Eva Marie Saint), Cinematography (Boris Kaufman) and Art Director (Richard Day).

Operation Amsterdam ○

1958, UK, 104 mins, b/w
Dir: Michael McCarthy
Stars: Peter Finch, Eva Bartok, Tony Britton
Rating: ★★

Tony Britton, now best known as a smooth comedy actor from his work in TV series, turns to high dramatics in this true story of wartime derring-do in Holland. Another capable actor, Canadian-born Alexander Knox, gives a fine portrayal as a Dutch patriot, and Peter Finch is a solid lead.

Director McCarthy's last film: the following year he was dead at the age of only 42.

Operation Bullshine ○

1959, UK, 84 mins, colour
Dir: Gilbert Gunn
Stars: Donald Sinden, Barbara Murray, Ronald Shiner
Rating: ★★

Well, they couldn't call this formula army comedy anything stronger in the late Fifties. Watch out for former Olympic swimming champion Judy Grinham as a PT instructress. She's part of a formidable cast that also includes Barbara Murray, Carole Lesley, Joan Rice, Ronald Shiner, Daniel Massey and Naunton Wayne.

Operation CIA ○

(aka: Last Message from Saigon)
1965, US, 90 mins, b/w
Dir: Christian Nyby
Stars: Burt Reynolds, Danielle Aubry
Rating: ★

Burt Reynolds as a CIA agent dispatched on a dangerous mission in the Far East. Although it took him another four years to climb to the top, one would have thought that his star quality was obvious, even in such minor thrillers as this one.

Operation Daybreak ○

1975, UK, 119 mins, colour
Dir: Lewis Gilbert
Stars: Timothy Bottoms, Martin Shaw, Nicola Pagett, Anthony Andrews
Rating: ★★

Well-made and suspenseful, this war film doesn't involve the emotions as much as Lewis Gilbert's best work in the genre, such as *Carve Her Name with Pride* and *Reach for the Sky*, although the ending is undeniably moving. Timothy Bottoms, Anthony Andrews and Martin Shaw don't lend much personality to the three Czech saboteurs out to kill Czech Nazi leader Heydrich, a role in which Anton Diffring is as marvellously hateful as ever. The action scenes are all well-staged.

Operation Mad Ball ○

1957, US, 105 mins, b/w
Dir: Richard Quine
Stars: Jack Lemmon, Ernie Kovacs, Mickey Rooney, Kathryn Grant
Rating: ★★★

Before Jack Lemmon went serious and Ernie Kovacs was killed in a car crash, they were involved in a delightful and

often very funny series of zany comedies at Columbia Studios in the Fifties. Others in which one or both of them appeared included *Bell, Book and Candle, It Happened to Jane, Phffft, Sail a Crooked Ship* and *The Notorious Landlady*. But *Operation Mad Ball* is probably the wildest of them all. Lemmon is right at the top of his form in this wild farce about an army private who breaks all the rules in order to hold a 'mad ball'. Stores are pinched, timetables tampered with, and regiments re-routed. All these happenings bring purple apoplexy to the face of disciplinarian Captain Lock – the cigar-chewing Kovacs, making a big hit in his screen debut.

Operation Pacific ○

1950, US, 109 mins, b/w
Dir: George Waggner
Stars: John Wayne, Patricia Neal, Philip Carey, Ward Bond
Rating: ★★★

There are some roaring battle scenes, well assembled by director George Waggner (best known for such horror films as *The Wolf Man*), in this large-scale John Wayne war film. No doubt Wayne was impressed by the production values the Warner Brothers were able to inject into their action movies, compared with those at Wayne's usual studio (Republic), as he made several more for them. Patricia Neal makes a cool and believable love interest in this story of the varied activities – attack, interception and rescue – of a submarine in the Pearl Harbor area.

Operation Petticoat ○

1959, US, 124 mins, colour
Dir: Blake Edwards
Stars: Cary Grant, Tony Curtis
Rating: ★★★

Those masters of comedy, Cary Grant and Tony Curtis – Curtis always preferred playing comedy and Grant was his hero in the genre – make the most of their material in this World War Two navy lark about the operation mounted to rescue a sunken American submarine. Grant is the sub's commander who experiences a certain amount of confusion at the unconventional methods used by his first officer (Tony Curtis), involving lots of lovely ladies whose lingerie is put to some unusual uses. Although the humour remains pretty obvious and the script could have been snappier, Blake

Edwards directs with pace and the whole is a happy and at times hilarious vehicle for its stars' talents.

Opposite Sex, The ○
1956, US, 117 mins, colour
Dir: David Miller
Stars: June Allyson, Ann Sheridan, Joan Collins, Joan Blondell
Rating: ★★

Three great stars of MGM musicals, June Allyson, Ann Miller and Dolores Gray, are mixed with Joan Collins and Ann Sheridan in a musical remake of the Norma Shearer/Joan Crawford comedy classic, *The Women*. Some good numbers enliven the original plot, which still retains much cattiness in the in-fighting. Another change is that men are this time seen, though not to any great effect.

Optimists of Nine Elms, The ○ ⓥ
1973, UK, 110 mins, colour
Dir: Anthony Simmons
Stars: Peter Sellers, Donna Mullane
Rating: ★★★

This charming and touching story of life by the slums of London's industrial riverside represents Peter Sellers' best work in the Seventies. He plays an old busker with music-hall memories and a sick dog for company. The two children who befriend him are played with Cockney freshness by Donna Mullane and John Chaffey. And the script by Anthony Simmons (who also directed) and Tudor Gates, based on Simmons' novel, makes some perceptive observations about the futility and despair involved in moving from a shabby basement to a hardly more attractive tower-block flat where the kids can't even keep a dog.

Oracle, The ○
(aka: The Horse's Mouth)
1952, UK, 84 mins, b/w
Dir: C M Pennington Richards
Stars: Robert Beatty, Mervyn Johns, Michael Medwin, Virginia McKenna
Rating: ★★

A clever, enjoyable British comedy featuring Robert Beatty as a reporter who goes on holiday to a little island off the coast of Ireland. There he finds an Oracle that lives at the bottom of the well and can foretell any future event. Persuading the Oracle to give him accurate weather forecasts, the reporter cables the information to his boss – and is promptly sacked for id-

iocy. But when, with the Oracle's help, he starts to forecast racing winners, matters rapidly begin to escalate.

Orchestra Wives ○
1942, US, 98 mins, b/w
Dir: Archie Mayo
Stars: George Montgomery, Glenn Miller, Lynn Bari, Carole Landis
Rating: ★★

One of television's most-requested films, with Glenn Miller and his band (thinly disguised as Gene Morrison and his band) giving out with a whole string of Miller pearls, including 'At Last', 'Serenade in Blue' and 'I've Got a Gal in Kalamazoo'.

Ordeal by Innocence ◐
1984, UK, 87 mins, colour
Dir: Desmond Davis
Stars: Donald Sutherland, Faye Dunaway, Sarah Miles, Christopher Plummer, Ian McShane
Rating: ★

Agatha Christie has continued down the decades to be an irresistible magnet for film-makers with star casts in mind, even if the essence of the lady continues to elude many of them. Donald Sutherland and Michael Elphick (although the latter is uncomfortable with a Scottish accent) lend their distinctly offbeat presences to this tale of murder in Fifties' Devon. Faye Dunaway and Sarah Miles are seen to less advantage, but sex appeal is so piquantly provided by Phoebe Nicholls and Cassie Stuart that one is rather sorry to see one of them get bumped off in the course of the plot. Although Dave Brubeck's obtrusive jazz score seems to belong to some other movie, Billy Williams conjures up some atmospheric Eastman Colour photography on location in Dartmouth. On the whole, though, ordeal is right.

Orders Are Orders ☉
1954, UK, 78 mins, b/w
Dir: David Paltenghi
Stars: Margot Grahame, Brian Reece
Rating: ★★

Today the cast of this comedy looks colossal, although in its time it wasn't exactly a major film. But it did give a first comedy character role to Peter Sellers, who plays batman to Brian Reece (whom vintage-radio fans will remember in *The Adventures of PC 49*). In a contemporary interview, Sellers confessed himself torn between Goonery and character parts and

thought that *Orders Are Orders* had set his career off on a new and profitable course. How right he was. It proves to be a spasmodically side-splitting army-based comedy that is faintly reminiscent of *The Amorous Prawn*. All its importance in retrospect, however, lies in that first appearance of Sellers in a character part.

Ordinary People ◐ ⓥ
1980, US, 124 mins, colour
Dir: Robert Redford
Stars: Donald Sutherland, Mary Tyler Moore, Timothy Hutton, Judd Hirsch
Rating: ★★★

Robert Redford's auspicious debut behind the camera earned him an Academy Award as Best Director for this overwrought study of a well-heeled American family in crisis. The picture took the Best Film Oscar and young Timothy Hutton's passionate performance as the teenage son eaten up by guilt over his brother's death earned him the Best Supporting Actor statuette. Mary Tyler Moore also excels as the cold-hearted mother – a role very much against type. She too was hotly tipped to win an Academy Award, but lost to Sissy Spacek in *Coal Miner's Daughter*.

Oregon Trail, The ○
1959, US, 86 mins, colour
Dir: Gene Fowler Jr
Stars: Fred MacMurray, Gloria Talbott, John Carradine
Rating: ★★

A Western that wanders as much as the wagon train carrying ace reporter Fred MacMurray from Missouri to Oregon in 1846. A good cast, a much-needed battle with the Indians at the end, primitive colour photography (don't adjust your sets) and a couple of good singalong Western songs. Typical late Fifties fare.

Orphans ●
1987, US, 120 mins, colour
Dir: Alan J Pakula
Stars: Albert Finney, Matthew Modine, Kevin Anderson
Rating: ★★

This grim and unpalatable morsel was once a successful stage play and still looks like one. You may find it worth wading through the boredom of the first half-hour to reach the meat of the performances by Matthew Modine and Kevin Anderson as primevally reclusive brothers and especially by

O

Albert Finney as the gangster they kidnap. How retribution catches up with them all is unconvincingly contrived, but there are some good individual scenes, particularly the one in which Finney tries to teach Modine to keep his explosive temper in check.

Oscar, The ◐
1966, US, 120 mins, colour
Dir: Russell Rouse
Stars: Stephen Boyd, Elke Sommer, Eleanor Parker, Joseph Cotten, Broderick Crawford, Walter Brennan, Ernest Borgnine
Rating: ★

Another knife in Hollywood's back, although the cast of this meretricious melodrama boasts as many stars as the script has reference to famous names. Joseph Cotten wins out over all of them – by cleverly underplaying his role as a movie studio boss. Stephen Boyd is the actor who will tread on any friend to win the coveted Academy Award. Five actors in the cast have actually won Oscars: Broderick Crawford, Ed Begley, Walter Brennan (who won three times as Best Supporting Actor), Ernest Borgnine and James Dunn.

Oscar ○ Ⓥ
1991, US, 110 mins, colour
Dir: John Landis
Stars: Sylvester Stallone, Ornella Muti, Kirk Douglas, Don Ameche, Peter Riegert, Tim Curry, Marisa Tomei, Eddie Bracken
Rating: RB

This is as stunningly bad an all-star movie as you could find. Totally over-played, and directed with cameras seemingly riveted to the floor, it's about a gangster (Sylvester Stallone), who's promised his dying father (Kirk Douglas!) that he'll go straight. His efforts to proceed in this direction and become a banker are hampered by trying to marry off his daughter to several different people in a single day. The distinguished cast is encouraged to move stiffly and mug gracelessly by director Landis, who deserves some kind of onion for the worst direction of a major film in ages. Stallone's wife and daughter (Ornella Muti, Marisa Tomei) look about the same age: the least of the worries of a film that's so awful you'll probably find the design of the cinema (or living-room) ceiling more interesting.

Oscar Wilde ◐
1960, UK, 96 mins, b/w
Dir: Gregory Ratoff
Stars: Robert Morley, Phyllis Calvert, John Neville, Ralph Richardson
Rating: ★★

The first out (by a few days) of two films both based on Oscar Wilde's last few years, this one was the loser at the box-office, chiefly through being made in black-and-white, while its rival, *The Trials of Oscar Wilde* (with Peter Finch) was in splashy colour. More slowly-paced than the Finch version, this look at Wilde's tragic obsession with the young Lord Alfred Douglas benefits from brilliant performances by Robert Morley as Wilde and Ralph Richardson as Sir Edward Carson. The film really comes alive in the cut and thrust of the courtroom scenes towards the end.

Osterman Weekend, The ●
1983, US, 102 mins, colour
Dir: Sam Peckinpah
Stars: Rutger Hauer, John Hurt, Burt Lancaster
Rating: ★★★

An everybody-is-corrupt thriller which involves a TV exposé man inviting three old friends for a reunion weekend knowing them all to be Russian agents. But beware: this plot is so fiendish it baffled even critics at the time. The film itself is a bit slow but quite fun when it gets going with its killing spree towards the end, although I wish the TV man's wife had been allowed to kill everyone with her bow and arrow. Rutger Hauer is adequate as the TV man, John Hurt good as the warped CIA agent, and Burt Lancaster familiar doing his corrupt older statesman bit as the CIA chief. Director Sam Peckinpah's last film.

Othello ○
1965, UK, 166 mins, colour
Dir: Stuart Burge
Stars: Laurence Olivier, Maggie Smith, Frank Finlay, Derek Jacobi
Rating: ★★★

Laurence Olivier's towering stage portrayal of Shakespeare's Moor of Venice is sewn together for the screen by director Stuart Burge. The result is a remarkable experience. And, even if Maggie Smith doesn't seem quite right for Desdemona, she's a whole lot better than some previous interpreters of the role.

Other People's Money ○ Ⓥ
1991, US, 101 mins, colour
Dir: Norman Jewison
Stars: Danny DeVito, Gregory Peck, Penelope Ann Miller, Piper Laurie, Dean Jones
Rating: ★★

This has a beautiful idea, but it doesn't quite work. For that, blame the burgeoning romance between Danny DeVito and Penelope Ann Miller, as two opposing sharpsters. This not only hurts the film by being an unconvincing attraction but slows it up considerably. Things would have been much more entertainingly played here as a no-holds-barred fight to the finish between DeVito's side and Gregory Peck's. It's true that the central character, a piranha of the takeover world, is perfectly suited to DeVito's talents for abrasive blue-collar comedy. 'I like dogs, doughnuts and money,' he beams at the beginning. 'But best of all I like money. It doesn't make you fat and it doesn't poop on your carpet.' But he's fatally softened in the telling of the story, and even the result of the final confrontation is swept under the carpet in a cavalier climax. When Danny's being a shark, though, he's great. Peck is stiff but sincere. Miller seems miscast. The best performances come from Piper Laurie and Dean Jones, the latter especially good on his return to the screen as a small-time corporate chief losing sleep over deciding whether or not to sell out.

Otley ○
1968, UK, 91 mins, colour
Dir: Dick Clement
Stars: Tom Courtenay, Romy Schneider, Alan Badel, James Bolam
Rating: ★★★

Tremendously entertaining comedy-thriller from the talented team of Dick Clement (who also directed) and Ian La Frenais. Tom Courtenay, one of the cinema's great underrated actors, creates a sympathetic character out of the cowardly, workshy 'hero'. The sardonic dialogue and brisk pace are spot-on the mark throughout.

Our Betters ○
1933, US, 80 mins, b/w
Dir: George Cukor
Stars: Constance Bennett, Gilbert Roland, Anita Louise
Rating: ★★★

Spiky Constance Bennett (sister of Joan), in one of the best roles she ever had, sloughs off her philandering husband and gets by in London society of the Thirties with, in her own words, 'strength of character, wit and un-scrupulousness'. Source material by Somerset Maugham, elegant production by David O Selznick, and sardonic direction by the masterly George Cukor: this is a film with pedigree, polish, pacing and pezzazz, as Constance kicks over the traces and wears black to the ball. The only really dated note is struck by Tyrell Davis' mincing dance instructor.

Our Girl Friday ○ ⓥ
(aka: The Adventures of Sadie)
1953, UK, 87 mins, colour
Dir: Noel Langley
Stars: Joan Collins, Kenneth More, George Cole, Robertson Hare
Rating: ★★

This fast and sometimes funny desert-island farce was the first film in Eastman Colour. Very attractive the settings look, too, though no more than a very young Joan Collins as the girl shipwrecked with three men. Kenneth More scores as the ill-bred Irishman who bides his time while the other two (George Cole, Robertson Hare) make fools of themselves making passes at the girl; for More, it was one of the final steps upwards on the ladder to stardom.

Our Little Girl ○
1935, US, 64 mins, b/w
Dir: John Robertson
Stars: Shirley Temple, Joel McCrea
Rating: ★★

Almost songless (just the title number) Shirley Temple vehicle about a tug-of-love. On the set of this weepie in which Shirley plays a little girl whose parents' marriage seems headed for the rocks, co-star Joel McCrea earned the ultimate Temple accolade: 'I love you,' she told him.

Our Man Flint ○
1966, US, 107 mins, colour
Dir: Daniel Mann
Stars: James Coburn, Lee J Cobb, Gila Golan, Edward Mulhare
Rating: ★★★

Meet the computer spy. Derek Flint may be superbly entertaining, but he's also the most inhuman hero the spy wave has thrown up since Batman. The difference, though, is that no sex was allowed to poor old Batman, while Flint has a well-stocked harem and wins his battles by gadgetry as opposed to wizardry. However, the

good old sock on the jaw – mostly with the hero's feet – is not entirely forgotten. As played by the cheetah-like James Coburn, Flint is certainly faster on those feet than any spy on celluloid, and a shade more invincible than Bond into the bargain. Visually, his adventures are lively, ingenious and amusing. And ridiculous, of course. But what marvellous, breath-taking stuff it is to be sure.

Our Man in Havana ○
1959, UK, 112 mins, b/w
Dir: Carol Reed
Stars: Alec Guinness, Burl Ives, Maureen O'Hara, Ralph Richardson
Rating: ★★★★

Graham Greene's cutting satire about the vacuum cleaner salesman who, in need of extra cash, joins the British Secret Service. The dialogue for Noel Coward as the suave spy chief might easily have been written by the Master himself. 'Have you got an electric kettle?' he asks an agent. 'You'll need it to steam open letters.'

Our Mother's House ◑
1967, UK, 105 mins, colour
Dir: Jack Clayton
Stars: Dirk Bogarde
Rating: ★★

Sombre, sinister drama of seven children living together after their mother dies, but suddenly threatened by their long-missing father – a performance of great menace by Dirk Bogarde. The entire movie was shot on location at a real, rambling old house in Croydon, Surrey, the gloom of which is well captured by director Jack Clayton and adds much weight to the doomy atmosphere. Pretty Sarah Nicholls, who plays one of the children, later made an adult career as an actress as Phoebe Nicholls.

Our Relations ⊙ ⓥ
1936, US, 65 mins, b/w
Dir: Harry Lachman
Stars: Stan Laurel, Oliver Hardy
Rating: ★★★

The feature film in which Stan and Ollie play not only respectable citizens much beset by nagging wives, but also their twin brothers, Alf and Bert, the black sheep of the families, who have become sailors. This is the cue for much mistaken identity, all building to a hilarious wharfside climax, with one pair of twins, having fallen foul to gangsters, rocking to and fro like

Subbuteo figures, their feet encased in concrete, on the edge of a thirty-foot drop into the river. The film also contains the last of their escalating battles with their old enemy Jimmy Finlayson, here cast as their ship's chief engineer; and an appearance, as a rascally ship's captain, by veteran actor Sidney Toler, soon to take over the role of oriental detective Charlie Chan, and play it in more than 20 films.

Our Town ○
1940, US, 90 mins, b/w
Dir: Sam Wood
Stars: William Holden, Martha Scott, Frank Craven, Thomas Mitchell
Rating: ★★★

A brilliant evocation of American small-town life over a 40-year period. This was always the kind of thing Hollywood did well, but few examples are better than this. The cast, headed by William Holden, sinks itself totally into the role of the two small-town families who are the subject of the film's all-pervading eye. Rich in detail, it is full of unexpected glimpses of everyday things that form a solid backcloth to the story. And it even has something extra: a mystical, timesliding last reel (as the heroine hovers between life and death in childbirth) that was far advanced for its time.

Our Very Own ○
1950, US, 93 mins, b/w
Dir: David Miller
Stars: Ann Blyth, Farley Granger, Joan Evans, Jane Wyatt, Ann Dvorak
Rating: ★★

Ace producer Samuel Goldwyn almost always had his finger on the public pulse. So this was a rare miscalculation on his part. Even fresh, appealing performances from Ann Blyth, Joan Evans and Natalie Wood are no match for F Hugh Herbert's saccharine script, especially in Miss Blyth's squirm-making final speech extolling the virtues of the American family. And the story, set in an upper middle-class American suburb where the most important thing in the world seems to be the love problems of teenagers, found few sympathetic ears on this side of the Atlantic. For all that, there was a promising debut by pretty Phyllis Kirk as the girl who eventually sets Miss Blyth to rights.

O

Outback ●
1970, Australia, 109 mins, colour
Dir: Ted Kotcheff
Stars: Donald Pleasence, Gary Bond
Rating: ★★

An unpalatable, unpleasant but curiously hypnotic look at the underbelly of life in the outback Down Under, hardly likely to go down well with the Australian tourist board. Donald Pleasence is at his nastiest as the seedy doctor who subjects the young hero to some of the numerous humiliations he undergoes on an alcohol-induced stay in bush country where life veers towards the primitive. Not for the squeamish.

Outcast, The ○
(aka: The Fortune Hunter)
1954, US, 90 mins, colour
Dir: William Witney
Stars: John Derek, Joan Evans, Jim Davis, Ben Cooper
Rating: ★★

This was one of the last films made by director William Witney for Republic, the studio where he laboured for many years churning out a series of Westerns starring Roy Rogers. John Derek is a rancher who fights to win his rightful inheritance of his uncle's ranch, but he's almost too macho to play the role, constantly fingering his gun or battering his knuckles. The supporting cast features Jim Davis, later to play Jock Ewing in *Dallas*.

Outcast, The
See: Man in the Saddle

Outcast of the Islands ○
1951, UK, 102 mins, b/w
Dir: Carol Reed
Stars: Trevor Howard, Ralph Richardson, Kerima
Rating: ★★★

The culmination of director Carol Reed's brilliant quartet of post-war films, following *Odd Man Out*, *The Fallen Idol* and *The Third Man*. It's based on a typical Joseph Conrad novel that has a lot in common with the also-filmed Conrad story *Lord Jim*, in that it deals with a 'lost' man wandering the ports of Far Eastern seas – a role in which Trevor Howard gives a haunting performance, although most of the film's publicity headlines were won by Kerima as the sultry and highly desirable native girl who proves his downfall. Reed directs with great sympathy, and some outstanding

location photography by John Wilcox adds immeasurably to the atmosphere. The climax, although different to the ending of the book (in which the story goes on quite a bit further) is admirably suited to Conrad's conception of the character. The only Reed work comparable with these early films from his later period, *Our Man in Havana*, is strangely also about an individual adrift in tropical surroundings.

Outcasts of Poker Flat, The ○
1952, US, 81 mins, b/w
Dir: Joseph M Newman
Stars: Anne Baxter, Dale Robertson, Miriam Hopkins, Cameron Mitchell
Rating: ★★

Absorbing, downbeat Western, about four assorted ne'er-do-wells, driven out of town by the local citizenry, and subsequently marooned in an old cabin in a snowstorm. Adapted from a novel by Bret Harte, the suspenseful plot gains considerably from the tight acting performances, particularly from the three ladies. The black-and-white photography adds to the claustrophobic tension in and around the cabin.

Outfit, The ◐
1973, US, 103 mins, colour
Dir: John Flynn
Stars: Robert Duvall, Karen Black, Joe Don Baker, Robert Ryan
Rating: ★★★★

In some respects, this crime thriller is like *Charley Varrick*, except that it's more basic, more excitingly directed, and cunningly fitted together with pieces, each of which piles on the tension. Here, as in *Varrick*, the central figure's crime lies in knocking over a bank belonging to the Outfit. Macklin (Robert Duvall) and his brother Ed get three years for the bank job, but the Outfit is still waiting for them when they come out. Ed is dispatched by an assassin, but Macklin turns the tables on his hit-man and determines to bleed the Outfit for all he can get. Enlisting the aid of another bank-raid confederate (Joe Don Baker), he embarks on a ruthless and skilful game of skinning the syndicate. The raids that follow are accomplished with staggering precision by director John Flynn, but the core of the film's appeal is that the non-action scenes are enthrallingly memorable. The cast is knee-deep in class, and the scenes between Duvall and Baker have an abrasive but close camaraderie that

brings about an audience identification with the characters too often missing from today's impersonal thrillers.

Outland ● Ⓥ
1981, US, 105 mins, colour
Dir: Peter Hyams
Stars: Sean Connery, Peter Boyle, Frances Sternhagen
Rating: ★★★

A version of *High Noon* set in outer space as marshal Sean Connery stands alone against a planet-wide drug ring. Connery is just right as the flawed hero and Frances Sternhagen first-rate as the doctor who ultimately risks death to give him a hand.

Outlaw Josey Wales, The ○ Ⓥ
1976, US, 135 mins, colour
Dir: Clint Eastwood
Stars: Clint Eastwood, Chief Dan George, Sondra Locke
Rating: ★★★★

Parts of this tremendous and unusual Western, directed by as well as starring Clint Eastwood, are so good as to make one reluctant to admit that it actually goes off the boil towards the end. The script is almost all dry, laconic, amusing and literate, bolstering good performances by Paula Trueman as a dauntless octogenarian pioneer and Sam Bottoms as the boy soldier who is Josey's first trail partner. But the best lines go to Chief Dan George as an Indian as sardonic as he's ancient. The Chief, treating them all to the same deadpan delivery, just walks off with the film.

Out of Africa ○ Ⓥ
1985, US, 162 mins, colour
Dir: Sydney Pollack
Stars: Meryl Streep, Robert Redford, Klaus Maria Brandauer
Rating: ★★★★

Overall a magnificent nostalgic romance about a Danish woman (Meryl Streep) who finds herself running a farm in Africa from 1913 after her husband (Klaus Maria Brandauer) decides to opt out for the life of a hunter. The first half is brilliantly paced and immaculately acted, but the greatness rather drifts away from the film in the second half, somewhat aided by a misfit Robert Redford, who just doesn't seem to fit with the rest of the film. Streep and her Danish accent are amazing, while Brandauer, Suzanna Hamilton, Michael Kitchen and Michael Gough offer really first-rate support. Intelligently scripted and beautifully shot on location by David Watkin, *Out of Africa* proves a moving, stimulating and entertaining experience. Winner of seven Oscars, including best film and best director.

Out of the Clouds ○
1954, UK, 88 mins, colour
Dir: Michael Relph, Basil Dearden
Stars: Anthony Steel, Robert Beatty, David Knight, Margo Lorenz
Rating: ★★★

This catalogue of crisis incidents in the lives of people stranded at a fogbound airport makes surprisingly good entertainment, with an array of second-line British stars all giving of their best, some nice cameos from such people as Sidney James and attractive Eastman Colour photography by Paul Beeson. Margo Lorenz not only looks beautiful, but gives her best screen performance.

Out of the Fog ○
1941, US, 86 mins, b/w
Dir: Anatole Litvak
Stars: Ida Lupino, John Garfield
Rating: ★★

Well thought of in its time, this now looks a very stage-bound version of Irwin Shaw's play *The Gentle People*, darkly photographed virtually on a single set, and with a broodingly charismatic performance by John Garfield as the gangster who's the terror of the Brooklyn waterfront. Good work in support by that consistent actress Aline MacMahon; and it's interesting to see little tough guy Leo Gorcey outside his normal Dead End Kids/Bowery Boys milieu.

Out-of-Towners, The ○
1969, US, 97 mins, colour
Dir: Arthur Hiller
Stars: Jack Lemmon, Sandy Dennis
Rating: ★

More than Jack Lemmon's urban angst, with he and Sandy Dennis staggering from bad to worse in Neil Simon's very black comedy about a small-town couple getting torn to pieces in the big city. But these are dislikeable characters, and their catastrophes accumulate rather than develop, robbing the tale of some of its momentum. Simon's script though, is consistently witty and portrays the couple's trials and tribulations with acid humour.

Outpost in Malaya
See: The Planter's Wife

Outrageous Fortune ◐ Ⓥ
1987, US, 100 mins, colour
Dir: Arthur Hiller
Stars: Shelley Long, Bette Midler, Peter Coyote
Rating: ★★★

A hard-cursing but outrageously funny comedy-thriller with Shelley Long and Bette Midler working wonderfully well together as aspiring actresses duped by Romeo teacher Peter Coyote who turns out to be an international double-agent. Savour some very funny dialogue mostly delivered by Midler as a bit-part film player who has just appeared in a movie called *Ninja Vixens*.

Outriders, The ○
1950, US, 93 mins, colour
Dir: Roy Rowland
Stars: Joel McCrea, Arlene Dahl, Barry Sullivan, Claude Jarman Jr
Rating: ★★

Rousing Western about a trio of Civil War Confederates on the run. The colour photography is excellent throughout: seldom have horses on the move been so excitingly pictured, and shots of a wagon train moving through Indian territory are also exceptional. Barry Sullivan steals the acting honours as bad Jesse Wallace.

Out West With the Hardys ○
1938, US, 90 mins, b/w
Dir: George B Seitz
Stars: Lewis Stone, Mickey Rooney
Rating: ★★

Another episode in the money-spinning Hardy series, chiefly notable for the duel of wit and muscle between Mickey Rooney's teenage Andy, who fancies himself as the 'terror of the plains', and 10-year-old cowgirl Virginia Weidler, a tiny terror who not unexpectedly wipes the floor with him. Weidler played many other juvenile roles in the late Thirties and early Forties, usually as a homely-looking kid told to scram because she bothered the adults.

Overboard ○ Ⓥ
1987, US, 112 mins, colour
Dir: Garry Marshall
Stars: Goldie Hawn, Kurt Russell, Edward Herrmann
Rating: ★★★

Here's a romantic comedy that's both romantic and a comedy without

being sticky about either. Rich bitch Goldie Hawn, married to boring Edward Herrmann, falls off her luxury yacht and surfaces in the home of handyman Kurt Russell suffering from amnesia. Having endured her overbearing manner while working on the yacht, Russell claims her as his missing wife and sets her to work raising his four unruly sons. Needless to say, Goldie, initially repelled by the squalor around her, eventually makes herself indispensable in these five male lives. That all this doesn't make you squirm owes a lot to a script by Leslie Dixon (who also wrote *Outrageous Fortune*) that's clear-eyed and buzzing with incident and inbuilt pace. Off-screen couple Hawn and Russell spark well together in this enchanting thirties-style movie directed by Garry Marshall, who went on to make *Beaches* and *Pretty Woman* to create a hat-trick of hits. Good for Goldie too: this is something a bit different for her and she brings it off.

Over Her Dead Body ◐ Ⓥ
(aka: Enid Is Sleeping)
1991, US, 101 mins, colour
Dir: Maurice Phillips
Stars: Judge Reinhold, Elizabeth Perkins, Jeffrey Jones, Rhea Perlman, Maureen Mueller
Rating: ★

This is the familiar black comedy about the couple who have to dispose of a dead body but find fate conspiring against them. Under this treatment by Maurice Phillips, almost none of it works, despite strenuous (at times too strenuous) efforts by Elizabeth Perkins and Judge Reinhold. The sheer accumulation of events does achieve a certain wild grandeur towards the end, but by then we're looking at a lost cause, thanks to directorial handling that's as leaden as the corpse that just won't lie down. Such extravagant character players as Michael J Pollard, Brion James, Henry Jones and Charles Tyner are also on hand, but the cameos they supply are, like the film, largely tedious and heavy-handed.

Overlanders, The ○
1946, UK/Australia, 91 mins, b/w
Dir: Harry Watt
Stars: Chips Rafferty, Daphne Campbell
Rating: ★★★

The first of the highly successful series of Ealing Studios action and adventure films set in Australia. It was to be followed by such notable dramas as

O

Eureka Stockade and *Bitter Springs*. The
outstanding score is by John Ireland
– the only music the great composer
wrote directly for the cinema. Tremendous scenes of cattle on the move
complete a dust-rousing package.

Over the Edge ●
1979, US, 95 mins, colour
Dir: Jonathan Kaplan
Stars: Michael Kramer, Matt Dillon,
Pamela Ludwig, Vincent Spano
Rating: ★★★

A disturbing American classic about
alienated teenagers, in the tradition
of *Blackboard Jungle* and *Rebel Without a
Cause*. Not seen outside America (and
only given a minor showing there)
until 1984, the film eventually
reached the wider audience it deserved
thanks to the increasing popularity of
one of its 14-year-old stars, Matt
Dillon. A strong, violent and pretty
bleak chronicle of the criminal lives of
kids with nowhere to go, it's directed
by Jonathan Kaplan with a surprisingly
keen sense of the American pre-teen's
eye-view of modern suburban life.

Over the Top ○ Ⓥ
1987, US, 93 mins, colour
Dir: Menahem Golan
Stars: Sylvester Stallone, Robert Loggia,
David Mendenhall, Susan Blakely, Rick
Zumwalt
Rating: ★★

A pretty cunning departure from style
from Sly Stallone, this offers his fans
the action they'll expect while allowing the star the chance to play
slight variations on the working-class
characters that have made his name.
And, although the script and situations
are repetitive and prolonged to the
point of irritation, their simple-
minded appeals to the emotions
work at least some of the time.
Arm-wrestling (whatever next?) is the
name of the game here, but the
Rocky-style build-up is given an interesting twist by Stallone's
bicep-bulging trucker's battle for the
heart and custody of his 10-year-old
son, played with old-fashioned charm
by David Mendenhall. The relationship that springs up between them
ensures that even though the film lays
everything on a bit thickly, you'll be
cheering for Sly on both custody and
arm-wrestling fronts at the finale. David Garfinkel's photography is ever
alert to bright clear composition and
his remarkably good use of
Metrocolor gives the film a crisp,
natural look.

Oxford Blues ◑
1984, US, 97 mins, colour
Dir: Robert Boris
Stars: Rob Lowe, Ally Sheedy, Amanda
Pays, Julian Sands
Rating: ★★

A thinly-veiled remake of the 1938
film *A Yank in Oxford*, with Rob
Lowe in the Robert Taylor role as the
upstart American who tries to use his
rowing prowess to impress the aristocratic English beauty on whom he's
set his heart. There's a nice college
atmosphere, and some engaging
performances, notably from Ally
Sheedy (as the American lady cox
Lowe seems destined to end up with)
and Julian Sands. Otherwise the conventions of the Hollywood teen
movie are strictly adhered to in spite
of the picturesque English settings.

P

Pacific Heights ● Ⓥ
1990, US, 104 mins, colour
Dir: John Schlesinger
Stars: Melanie Griffith, Matthew Modine,
Michael Keaton, Laurie Metcalf
Rating: ★★★

A good thriller that could have been
called *The Tenant* if someone hadn't
already used the title. Keaton and
Griffith both deliver spot-on performances in the offbeat, unsettling tale
of a couple (Melanie Griffith, Matthew Modine), who spend every cent
to rent an apartment building (with
the intention of leasing two of its
three flats), then fall foul of a sitting
tenant (Michael Keaton) who stalls on
paying the rent. They soon find out
that, as the lease has been signed by
both parties, the law is on the squat-
ter's side. But this is no ordinary
tenant; and this aspect of the plot
makes for some suspenseful and exciting later developments. The fact
that almost none of this holds water,
but still grips our attention, is a tribute
to John Schlesinger's direction of it,
and to the performances of the stars,
although Modine is a little bland in
the least interesting of the three main
roles. Carl Lumbly makes his mark as
the tenant they should (and, but for an
accident, would) have taken on
before Keaton arrives and Griffith's
mother Tippi Hedren is in for a
cameo.

Package, The ◑ Ⓥ
1989, US, 108 mins, colour
Dir: Andrew Davis
Stars: Gene Hackman, Joanna Cassidy,
Tommy Lee Jones, Dennis Franz
Rating: ★★★

Although its tale of cold warfare and
secret police in East Berlin was
overtaken by events, this is a very efficient thriller of its type. There's a
plot to assassinate both the American
president and the Soviet general
secretary and only Gene Hackman can
stop it. Yes, we've been here before,
but scenes between high-up
conspirators are mercifully sidelined in
favour of the thriller aspects of the
plot, its interlocking pieces falling
nicely into place before the end.
Dennis Franz, looking as though he
never left *Hill Street Blues*, turns up as a
Chicago policeman, Tommy Lee
Jones is fine as the assassin, and di-

rector Davis keeps it moving to a predictable but briskly staged finale. Above all, it's Hackman's grit and integrity as an actor and a personality that keeps it marginally believable as well as exciting.

Pack Up Your Troubles ○ ⓥ
1932, US, 65 mins, b/w
Dir: George Marshall, Raymond McCarey
Stars: Stan Laurel, Oliver Hardy
Rating: ★★★

This early Laurel and Hardy feature film is now best remembered for the scene in which Stan reads a small girl a story to send her to sleep and succeeds in sending himself to sleep instead. Oliver Hardy was originally to have played this scene, but generously decided it would be funnier with Stan. Watch for the film's co-director George Marshall, playing a homicidal chef.

Pagan Love Song ○
1950, US, 76 mins, colour
Dir: Robert Alton
Stars: Esther Williams, Howard Keel, Rita Moreno
Rating: ★

Despite the title, don't expect anything more exotic than the MGM backlot in this musical vehicle for swim star Esther Williams, then tops at the box-office. Director Robert Alton, better known as a choreographer, only really scores here in the inevitable Williams water ballets. Producer Arthur Freed also wrote some of the songs, and did his best to suggest an atmosphere with the titles: 'Tahiti', 'The Sea of the Moon', 'Pagan Love Song' and 'The House of Singing Bamboo'. At least you can't accuse it of going on too long.

Paid in Full ○
1950, US, 105 mins, b/w
Dir: William Dieterle
Stars: Lizabeth Scott, Diana Lynn, Robert Cummings
Rating: ★★

Familiar story about two sisters, one of them nice, the other unscrupulous, who fall in love with the same man. Tragedy, unrequited love, honeymoons, death and insanity are dealt with in that order. It's left to that brilliant comedienne Eve Arden, as the hard-boiled Tommy Thompson, to inject some much-needed comic relief into this triple-handkerchief weepie.

Paint Your Wagon ○ ⓥ
1969, US, 164 mins, colour
Dir: Joshua Logan
Stars: Lee Marvin, Clint Eastwood, Jean Seberg, Harve Presnell
Rating: ★★★

The film that put Lee Marvin's gravel voice at the top of the charts, with the million-selling 'Wandrin' Star'. The setting for this hard-shelled musical Western is the California Gold Rush, rendered very pretty to look at by director Joshua Logan's picture-postcard approach to history. The story concerns a lady pioneer (Jean Seberg) who takes two husbands, but its quality scarcely matters, given that the husbands are played by Marvin and Clint Eastwood, and that there's a supremely tuneful score. The other vocal highlight: Harve Presnell's spectacular rendition of 'They Call the Wind Maria'.

Pajama Game, The ○ ⓥ
1957, US, 101 mins, colour
Dir: Stanley Donen
Stars: Doris Day, John Raitt
Rating: ★★★★

One of the most exhilarating of all Hollywood musicals, with a clutch of performances as nearly perfect as one could wish to see. Doris Day – who else more fitted to the part of Babe Williams? – gives a more extrovert performance than one would have thought possible. The score includes such hits as 'Hey There', 'The Pajama Game', 'Once a Year Day', 'I'm Not at All in Love' and the spirited Day-John Raitt duet 'There Once Was a Man', one of the best performed musical numbers of all time. Like the film, it's enormous fun.

Paleface, The ○
1948, US, 90 mins, colour
Dir: Norman Z McLeod
Stars: Bob Hope, Jane Russell
Rating: ★★★

This glorious romp was the first of Bob Hope's four spoof Westerns, and also a much-needed hit for his co-star Jane Russell, who joins him in the Academy Award-winning song 'Buttons and Bows'. One of the film's best comedy routines harks back to Hope's duel scene in *Never Say Die* (and forward to Danny Kaye's in *The Court Jester*) as Hope faces a feared gunman in the main street while attempting to remember advice like 'He moves to the right, so shoot to

the left' and trying to calculate the direction of the wind. Richly enjoyable stuff, fun to the final scene.

Pale Rider ◐ ⓥ
1985, US, 115 mins, colour
Dir: Clint Eastwood
Stars: Clint Eastwood, Michael Moriarty, Carrie Snodgress
Rating: ★★

Although not acknowledged as such in its credits, Clint Eastwood's first Western since *The Outlaw Josey Wales* is a virtual remake of *Shane*, that classic Western from the Fifties in which a mysterious stranger (then Alan Ladd, now Eastwood) helps a band of farmers (now gold prospectors) against the ruthless land grabbers (and their hired gunman) who threaten to blow them off the face of the earth. Michael Moriarty is very good in the part originally played by Van Heflin, Carrie Snodgress is his 'fiancée' and Sydney Penny the teenager who storms on to do the 'Come back, Shane' bit at the end. *Pale Rider* works well as a kind of latter-day *Dollars*-style adventure, with a blazing action showdown at the end, but it can't quite fill *Shane*'s boots, partly because the writing isn't strong enough and partly because the Eastwood character is so invincible there is no chance of him losing, and only the vaguest of hints about his past. However, as a clever fusion of the spaghetti and American prairie Westerns, it'll do nicely for Eastwood fans. And *L.A.Law* fans will enjoy seeing Richard Dysart (alias Leland McKenzie) in a very different role.

Pal Joey ○ ⓥ
1957, US, 111 mins, colour
Dir: George Sidney
Stars: Frank Sinatra, Rita Hayworth, Kim Novak
Rating: ★★★

Splashy, garishly entertaining, perfectly-cast musical, with Frank Sinatra ideal as the singing con-man who finds hell hath no fury like a rich mistress scorned when true love comes along. One of Rodgers and Hart's best scores includes 'Bewitched, Bothered and Bewildered', 'The Lady Is a Tramp', 'Small Hotel', 'I Didn't Know What Time It Was' and 'Funny Valentine'. Rita Hayworth and Kim Novak both have some good moments as the contrasting women in Joey's life, but the songs are the thing.

P

Palm Beach Story, The ○
1942, US, 90 mins, b/w
Dir: Preston Sturges
Stars: Claudette Colbert, Joel McCrea, Mary Astor, Rudy Vallee
Rating: ★★★

Romantic comedy crossed with moments of sheerest lunacy as straw-brained wife Claudette Colbert deserts husband Joel McCrea in order to find someone who will give her 99 thousand dollars – to finance McCrea's daft invention. Decorated with pleasing idiocies as only director Preston Sturges knows how, plus the treasurable Ale and Quail Club, and one of the earliest of one-time singing idol Rudy Vallee's appearances as a wistfully comic character star. Here, as the world's wealthiest bachelor, he's allowed to give vent to his famous complaint that 'one of the tragedies of this life is that the men most in need of a beating-up are always enormous.'

Palmy Days ○
1931, US, 80 mins, b/w
Dir: A Edward Sutherland
Stars: Eddie Cantor, Charlotte Greenwood, George Raft
Rating: ★★★

This farcical musical, a cute follow-up to Samuel Goldwyn's production of *Whoopee!*, had the benefit of Busby Berkeley's choreography just as the master was beginning to develop his inimitable style. The storyline is fairly ordinary, but lots of pretty girls, plenty of songs and the incredible energy of Eddie Cantor make it well worthwhile. Look hard at the Goldwyn Girls and you will spot Betty Grable, legs 'n' all, in her seventh film appearance. George Raft is also on board, but he added little to the picture.

Palooka ○
1934, US, 86 mins, b/w
Dir: Benjamin Stoloff
Stars: Jimmy Durante, Lupe Velez, Stuart Erwin, Robert Armstrong
Rating: ★★★

In the long-running American comic strip, Joe Palooka was a big, gormless, hopeful boxer who somehow succeeded every time in spite of his own lack of pugilistic ability. The role of his scheming manager, Knobby Walsh, was a gift for Jimmy Durante in his first real starring role and 'The Great Schnozzle' (coincidentally that was the British title of the film) even gets to sing his famous novelty number 'Inka Dinka Doo'. A good time is had by all in this fast-moving romp, not least the viewer!

Pancho Villa ◐
1972, Spain, 93 mins, colour
Dir: Gene Martin
Stars: Telly Savalas, Clint Walker, Anne Francis, Chuck Connors
Rating: ★★

Telly Savalas as the infamous Mexican bandit chief takes some swallowing, but director Eugenio (Gene) Martin, who also directed the actor in *Horror Express*, has it that his head is shaven by the authorities 'to make him look like the convict he is'. The film itself's a routine Western, but full of noise and fury and with a head-on train crash for a spectacular climax.

Pandora and the Flying Dutchman ○
1951, UK, 120 mins, colour
Dir: Albert Lewin
Stars: James Mason, Ava Gardner
Rating: ★★

A rum kettle of fish and no mistake. A long, ornate, dry, lovely-to-look-at Technicolor fantasy that split the critics and died at the box-office. Ava Gardner never looked more ravishing as Pandora, James Mason never more agonised as the Dutchman doomed to roam the seas for ever. Gardner also sings two songs, including 'How Am I to Know?' Strange is the word.

Panic in Echo Park ○
1977, US, 74 mins, colour
Dir: John Llewellyn Moxey
Stars: Dorian Harewood, Catlin Adams, Robin Gammell
Rating: ★★

This drama tells the story of a black doctor – played by Dorian Harewood, who portrayed Simon Haley in *Roots* and here also sings a background song – involved in an epidemic that threatens to jeopardise his career. Despite tight direction from Britain's John Llewellyn Moxey, this 'pilot' film for TV failed to spawn the intended series.

Panic in the Parlor
See: Sailor Beware!

Panic in the Streets ○
1950, US, 96 mins, b/w
Dir: Elia Kazan
Stars: Richard Widmark, Paul Douglas, Barbara Bel Geddes, Jack Palance
Rating: ★★★

Elia Kazan's extremely exciting and splendidly paced (in recollection it seems like one long chase) thriller about two killers on the run in New Orleans, carrying with them pneumonic plague. Edna and Edward Anhalt won an Oscar for best original story, and there are powerful performances from Jack Palance and Zero Mostel, both getting their first big film chances. The film deserved one Academy Award it didn't win: for Joe MacDonald's great location photography of the back alleys, low bars and wharfs of New Orleans.

Papa's Delicate Condition ⊙
1963, US, 98 mins, colour
Dir: George Marshall
Stars: Glynis Johns, Jackie Gleason
Rating: ★★★

Gentle, sometimes very funny comedy, lushly shot in Technicolor, about a man living in Texas at the turn of the century, whose 'delicate condition' is almost perpetual inebriation. Jackie Gleason revels in his role as portly Papa.

Paper, The ● ⓥ
1994, US, 112 mins, colour
Dir: Ron Howard
Stars: Michael Keaton, Glenn Close, Marisa Tomei, Robert Duvall, Randy Quaid, Jason Robards
Rating: ★★★

Apart from the salty modern language, this is a solid, comfortingly familiar story of hard-pressed newspapermen and the traditional 24-hour sweat to produce a front page. Sweat, in fact, is something people do a lot in this film, from Michael Keaton as the 'metro editor' (No.3) through Glenn Close as the managing editor (No.2) to Robert Duvall (No.1) as the chain-smoking editor who's just been told he's got prostate cancer. There's lots of shouting and hard-boiled humour, plus, of course, the inevitable story to be chased: two black youths arrested for a double murder they didn't commit. Director Ron Howard hardly lets the pace drop, so you won't have too much time to ponder the near-impossibility of Keaton's achievements on the trail of the truth. Drily humorous lines, or remarks that the audience finds funnier than the characters, take the place of jokes in David and Stephen Koepp's script, and keep you willing the right story to land on the town's doorsteps in the morning.

Paperhouse ● ⑨
1988, UK, 92 mins, colour
Dir: Bernard Rose
Stars: Charlotte Burke, Jane Bertish
Rating: ★★★

The heroine of this film is in a lot of danger in a house of her worst nightmares. And she's only 11. An original chiller with not a drop of blood, *Paperhouse* is about a schoolgirl who draws a house and finds herself going to it in her dreams. When she draws a face at a window, it becomes a boy, trapped in the house and unable to walk, whom the girl realises, as she is taken to bed with glandular fever, is just like the boy her doctor is treating for muscular dystrophy. But there is more danger around, from a figure familiar in her life, than just the fight for the boy's survival. Fascinating stuff, directed with many a frisson by Bernard Rose, who conjures up just the kind of world one might imagine in a fever, and grips our attention almost throughout. One could have done with a more natural child actress, though, than young Charlotte Burke who, though visually interesting in her interpretation of emotions, is less convincing once she opens her mouth. Rose employs the interesting device of giving the story two or three false endings before finishing on an unexpected upbeat note.

Paper Mask ● ⑨
1990, UK, 105 mins, colour
Dir: Christopher Morahan
Stars: Paul McGann, Amanda Donohoe, Tim Wilkinson
Rating: ★★★

Thriller fans will be familiar with the situation: you can't see the expression on the face behind the surgeon's mask as he reaches for the scalpel. But what if he were not even a doctor? Even though some of its developments – especially a man falling hundreds of feet down Cheddar Gorge and surviving – take a lot of believing, this remains a suspenseful thriller about a bogus doctor who gets away with murder. Close enough to reality to be pretty chilling, the film stars Paul McGann as the hospital porter who longs to escape his mundane existence and afford holidays in far-away places. He gets his chance when, packing the effects of a young doctor killed in a car crash, he comes across a letter confirming an interview at a hospital in Bristol. McGann is stickily-palmed plausible as the man always on the edge of being found out, Wilkinson

excellent as a suspicious superior and Donohoe effective, if not at her best as the gullible nurse who mistakes incompetence for inexperience. Recommended to all except those with a mortal fear of hypodermic needles.

Paper Moon ●
1973, US, 100 mins, b/w
Dir: Peter Bogdanovich
Stars: Ryan O'Neal, Tatum O'Neal, Madeline Kahn, John Hillerman
Rating: ★★★

Tatum O'Neal became the youngest ever winner of a best supporting actress Oscar (she was 10 when the film was made) in this winning fable, although her subsequent career, as with so many child stars, has not lived up to expectations. She proves more than a match for father Ryan O'Neal, who's a bible-selling con-man at large in the American mid-west of the mid-Thirties. Jut-jawed comedienne Madeline Kahn was also nominated for an Oscar for her portrayal of fading floozie Trixie Delight.

Paper Tiger ○ ⑨
1975, US, 99 mins, colour
Dir: Ken Annakin
Stars: David Niven, Toshiro Mifune
Rating: ★

A rather awkwardly-contrived parable about an English tutor (David Niven) whose title of major, and tales of military heroism, are equally fraudulent. Niven is persuasive in the title role (which has echoes of his Oscar-winning character in *Separate Tables*). He offers a performance far superior to the script, which fatally compromises itself between comedy, adventure and socio-political statement.

Papillon ● ⑨
1973, US, 150 mins, colour
Dir: Franklin J Schaffner
Stars: Steve McQueen, Dustin Hoffman, Victor Jory
Rating: ★★

This could have been the film of a lifetime. As it is, it just seems to last that long. Tiring, rather than inspiring, is this story of Papillon (Steve McQueen), the French prisoner sent in the Thirties to a horrendous prison establishment in French Guiana, from which his attempts to escape land him with various periods of solitary confinement. But he never gives up. The dialogue between McQueen and

Dustin Hoffman, as his fellow-prisoner, is a shade too joky, though, for such desperate situations, and the film's doses of philosophy are somehow hard to swallow. McQueen works tremendously hard, but the situations are so banal – there's even an idyllic interlude with a native girl – that all but a few of them defeat him. If only this had settled for being harrowing drama, or high adventure, it might have been a more powerful document against the monstrous – and now departed – system it indicts.

Paradine Case, The ○ ⑨
1947, US, 115 mins, b/w
Dir: Alfred Hitchcock
Stars: Gregory Peck, Ann Todd, Charles Laughton
Rating: ★★★

Another Alfred Hitchcock-David O Selznick production to follow *Rebecca* and *Spellbound*. Riveting stuff, underrated in its time, when everything Hitchcock made was being judged by an impossibly high standard. Valli plays the beautiful adventuress who is accused of the murder of her wealthy husband. Gregory Peck is the lawyer who defends her and falls under her hypnotic spell.

Paradise ○ ⑨
1992, US, 110 mins, colour
Dir: Mary Agnes Donoghue
Stars: Melanie Griffith, Don Johnson, Elijah Wood, Thora Birch
Rating: ★★

A Hollywood retread of a much better French film, *Le Grand Chemin*. A 10-year-old boy (Elijah Wood) is shunted off by his heavily pregnant mother (whose husband may have deserted her) to stay the summer with friends in the country. The friends (Melanie Griffith, Don Johnson) have problems of their own: they're hardly on speaking, let alone touching terms since the death of their three-year-old son in an accident four years before. At first the boy spends much of his time up trees with his nine-year-old neighbour (Thora Birch). But then Ben (Johnson) takes an interest and takes the boy shrimp fishing: the prelude to a summer both idyllic and traumatic. Writer-director Mary Agnes Donoghue also wrote *Beaches*, but her treatment of this story makes it hard to care about any of the people, and the narrative, despite its emotive elements, proves dull and boring.

P

Birch is appealing as the girl, but Wood lacks warmth in the central role.

Paradise Alley ◐

1978, US, 104 mins, colour
Dir: Sylvester Stallone
Stars: Sylvester Stallone, Lee Canalito, Armand Assante
Rating: ★★★

The phrase 'sensitive and intelligent film-maker' and the name Sylvester Stallone don't mix in most people's minds, but this story proves the two *can* go together to produce an entertaining and well made film. Stallone wrote, directed and starred in this story about three slum brothers who try to make some money by encouraging the youngest (and by far the biggest) brother (Lee Canalito) to become a wrestler. For a change Stallone isn't the monosyllabic brute, he's the fast-talking sharp guy. Canalito is endearing as the slow but powerful Victor and Armand Assante is effective as the bitter, war-wounded elder brother. With an intelligent story and some well-staged action, supported by a solid cast, this is a film that was undeservedly overshadowed by *Rocky II*, a significantly inferior film. It's a shame the *Rocky* and *Rambo* films were so successful: if they hadn't been, we might have had more films like this from Mr Stallone.

Paradise – Hawaiian Style ○ ⓥ

1966, US, 91 mins, colour
Dir: Michael Moore
Stars: Elvis Presley, Suzanna Leigh, James Shigeta, Donna Butterworth, Marianna Hill
Rating: ★

Elvis's off-screen high living was beginning to show when he made this rather sad and fey attempt to recapture the feeling of his earlier *Blue Hawaii*. Here he's overweight and puffy – rather like the storyline – and it's numbing to see the 'King' reduced to singing such ineffectual numbers as 'A Dog's Life' and 'Bill Bailey, Won't You Please Come Home?' 'I've changed,' he says at one point in the 'action' here. But he hasn't: it's still the same tired old stuff that was soon to see him get out of movies altogether.

Paradise Lagoon

See: The Admirable Crichton

Parallax View, The ◐

1974, US, 102 mins, colour
Dir: Alan J Pakula
Stars: Warren Beatty, Paula Prentiss, Hume Cronyn
Rating: ★★★

The Manchurian Candidate taken a stage further: this black thriller from director Alan J Pakula opens with the assassination of a presidential candidate and proceeds along familiar, if nightmare roads – the 'assassin' is swiftly dispatched and material witnesses disappear faster than a tub of butter under the grill. Can crusading reporter Warren Beatty penetrate the 'Parallax Corporation' and bring them to book? Stylish and persuasive, this is a much more consistent film than Pakula's earlier *Klute* and infinitely more complex than it first appears. Hume Cronyn almost steals Beatty's acting thunder as an editor who seems to produce his paper single-handed.

Paranoiac ◐

1963, UK, 80 mins, b/w
Dir: Freddie Francis
Stars: Janette Scott, Oliver Reed, Liliane Brousse, Alexander Davion, Maurice Denham
Rating: ★★

Hammer chilling and thrilling, with melodrama given full rein in the story of a girl whose dead brother 'returns' from the past. Reed enjoys himself as the heroine's brutal second brother, and there's a suitable holocaust to tidy things up at the end.

Pardners ☉

1956, US, 88 mins, colour
Dir: Norman Taurog
Stars: Dean Martin, Jerry Lewis, Lon Chaney Jr, Lori Nelson
Rating: ★★

That excellent comedy craftsman Norman Taurog directed this spoof Western loosely based on the 1936 Bing Crosby vehicle *Rhythm on the Range* (which was also directed by Taurog). Jerry Lewis as the simple-minded son of a rich mother is the centre of the film and his fans will enjoy some bouts of inspired clowning. 'Young' cowhand Dean Martin croons away in a splendid parody of backwoods music, Lori Nelson is a charming heroine and Agnes Moorehead is in fine fettle as the formidable Mrs Kingsley. A terrific

cast of heavies, including Lon Chaney Jr, Jack Elam and Lee Van Cleef, wildly exaggerates the villainy.

Pardon Mon Affaire ◐

1977, France, 105 mins, colour
Dir: Yves Robert
Stars: Jean Rochefort, Claude Brasseur, Victor Lanoux, Daniele Delorme
Rating: ★★★

Several of French director Yves Robert's Gallic farces have travelled well abroad. This one was one of his biggest international successes (and was remade badly in Hollywood by Gene Wilder as *The Woman in Red*). Jean Rochefort has some nice moments as the middle-aged man with a roving eye, while the lovely Daniele Delorme (a star of French films 20 years earlier) is still so attractive that it makes Rochefort's amorous excursion just a little hard to believe.

Pardon My Sarong ☉

1942, US, 85 mins, b/w
Dir: Erle C Kenton
Stars: Bud Abbott, Lou Costello, Virginia Bruce, Robert Paige
Rating: ★★★

This Abbott and Costello South Seas romp makes a nice change from their taking on city crooks and military might, and there are good supporting turns from Lionel Atwill as a jewel thief-cum-pirate, William Demarest as a flat-footed detective and Leif Erickson as the big-headed islander Whaba ('I biggest stinker of them all'). There's a volcano, an island, a yacht race, hidden treasure, a jungle pursuit, a performing seal, musical numbers and native girls by the lagoon-full, including a rare on-camera appearance by Nan Wynn, best known in films as the singing voice of Rita Hayworth.

Pardon Us ☉

(aka: Jailbirds)
1931, US, 55 mins, b/w
Dir: James Parrott
Stars: Stan Laurel, Oliver Hardy
Rating: ★★★

Stan and Ollie fall foul of Prohibition and are sent to prison where their bumbling protests about a pending hunger-strike foil an escape plot. Originally intended as a two-reeler, it was expanded for economic reasons when the prison set proved too expensive to build.

Parenthood ◐ ⓥ
1989, US, 124 mins, colour
Dir: Ron Howard
Stars: Steve Martin, Mary Steenburgen, Dianne Wiest, Jason Robards
Rating: ★★★

Only a quasi-comedy, this Steve Martin film examines a uniquely American upbringing of angst and pain that people elsewhere can only barely comprehend. A nine-year-old in therapy is obviously a fairly normal experience there, while the three sets of parents involved, and those around them, insist on making a crisis out of every drama. At the end, the film settles for unconvincing reconciliation to basic values: it's a cop-out and the makers clearly know it. Only comfortably-off middle-class American parents could get into messes like these and the implications of it all fill you with unease. Martin and wife Mary Steenburgen (she gives the film's best performance) are told that their son – absolutely normal to British eyes – must attend a special school, Rick Moranis drills his three-year-old daughter into becoming a genius (a little more believable) and Dianne Wiest has a pregnant daughter who hides her in-house lover under the bed (doesn't everyone?). One doesn't give a cent for the future chances of any of these people and it's kind of frightening that we should be asked to care. Martin fortunately supplies a few characteristic laughs along the way.

Parent Trap, The ☉
1961, US, 124 mins, colour
Dir: David Swift
Stars: Hayley Mills, Maureen O'Hara, Brian Keith
Rating: ★★★

'Hayley Mills and Hayley Mills' boasted the posters for this Disney frolic, in which the Sixties' most popular child star plays twin sisters intent on reuniting their parents, a story filmed before (but far less successfully) 10 years previously in Britain as *Twice Upon a Time*, with real-life twins playing the girls. This version gave the Disney boys the chance to show their expertise at trick photography by putting the two Hayleys in one scene at the same time. And Hayley's personality and popularity was such that, despite being no great singer, she took the film's song hit, 'Let's Get Together', high into the

charts. Three TV movie sequels, all pretty average, followed nearly 30 years later.

Paris, Texas ◐ ⓥ
1984, US, 150 mins, colour
Dir: Wim Wenders
Stars: Harry Dean Stanton, Nastassja Kinski, Dean Stockwell
Rating: ★★★

Ry Cooder's haunting guitar music sets the mood and the pace of a film that is fascinating, dramatic, amusing and touching by turns. As the man found wandering in the Mojave Desert, refusing to say a word, the laconic Harry Dean Stanton shows how well he could have handled leading roles long before this if he had been given the chance. The film is very well made, terrifically acted, flawlessly photographed and . . . well . . . a bit boring, especially towards the end.

Paris Trout ● ⓥ
1991, US, 110 mins, colour
Dir: Stephen Gyllenhaal
Stars: Ed Harris, Barbara Hershey, Dennis Hopper
Rating: ★★

Dennis Hopper creates a monster more frightening than anything in *The Silence of the Lambs* as Paris Trout, a psychotic white bigot making a living as a storekeeper in the Georgia of 1949. When he feels gypped by a black sharecropper who's pranged the dud car Paris sold him and wants to claim the insurance (on which Paris intends to welch), Trout storms out to his home with a friend, both armed. There Trout goes berserk, shooting the man's kid sister dead and severely wounding his mother. When his wife (Barbara Hershey) expresses her horror, he attacks and humiliates her sexually, in a revoltingly graphic scene. She flees to the arms of his lawyer (Ed Harris) who is already becoming uneasy at defending Paris. Unrelentingly grim, the film is full of dingy, dust-filled rooms that make you wonder if the sun ever shone in this part of the post-war American South.

Paris When It Sizzles ○
1964, US, 110 mins, colour
Dir: Richard Quine
Stars: William Holden, Audrey Hepburn
Rating: ★★

Some nice moments in this comedy about a screenplay writer and his sec-

retary acting out the weird and wonderful ideas they dream up for a film script, with diversions into *Dracula*, spy stories and jungle epics on the way. Guest stars Tony Curtis, Noel Coward, Mel Ferrer and (for two seconds) Marlene Dietrich. Although the film, scripted by George Axelrod, who wrote *The Seven Year Itch*, tends to be an hour of unadulterated fun and 50 minutes of rather tiresome talk, it's well worth a look for its high quota of madcap moments. One is an early chase sequence, when William Holden, as a fictitious secret agent, is pursued by dozens of trench-coated spies; and another is a second, even more hilarious pursuit through Paris, with Tony Curtis and Gregoire Aslan, guest-starring as two comic policemen, chasing the fictitious Holden, who is this time attired as the Lone Ranger. Audrey Hepburn is a delight, too: what a shame the script had to lace its champagne with flat beer.

Party, The ○
1968, US, 94 mins, colour
Dir: Blake Edwards
Stars: Peter Sellers, Claudine Longet, Marge Champion, Steve Franken, Fay McKenzie
Rating: ★★★

Consistently funny comedy from the team responsible for the *Pink Panther* series – star Peter Sellers and director Blake Edwards. Sellers plays an Indian actor who is an absolute walking disaster. Sight gags abound.

Party Girl ○
1958, US, 98 mins, colour
Dir: Nicholas Ray
Stars: Robert Taylor, Cyd Charisse, Lee J Cobb, John Ireland
Rating: ★★★

The best of Robert Taylor's later films, this crime drama comes across like a black-and-white movie suddenly converted into CinemaScope and colour. Pushily, vividly directed by Nicholas Ray, it makes a few salient points about the morals of the law and the underworld having a lot in common, before settling for a formula action finale. Co-star Cyd Charisse has a couple of well-staged dances, and you may spot future TV star Barrie Chase among the showgirls.

Pascali's Island ◐ ⓥ
1988, UK, 104 mins, colour
Dir: James Dearden

P

Stars: Ben Kingsley, Charles Dance, Helen Mirren
Rating: ★★

This good-looking, but slow moving drama, set in the early years of the 20th century and based on Barry Unsworth's novel, was James Dearden's first screenplay following *Fatal Attraction*. Here he directs as well, though he keeps the drama too much at a distance for the audience to get very involved. Ben Kingsley gives an eye-catching, if mannered central performance as a small-time spy operating from an Aegean island, Charles Dance repeats his *White Mischief* portrayal of the bronzed, womanising adventurer and Helen Mirren brings some much-needed warmth to the story as the object of both their desires. Lushly shot by Roger Deakins on the Greek islands of Rhodes and Simi.

Passage, The ◐
1978, US, 98 mins, colour
Dir: J Lee Thompson
Stars: Anthony Quinn, James Mason, Malcolm McDowell, Patricia Neal
Rating: ★

An intended tribute to the strength of the human spirit in adversity during World War Two. Stuck in France, James Mason and his family need to escape the Nazis and the only way out, as for the von Trapps before them, is over the mountains. Selected by the underground to guide them is a big, gruff, sheep-loving man of the mountains. It has to be Anthony Quinn and it is. Malcolm McDowell, eyes gleaming madly, gives an extraordinary performance as the Nazi pursuing them.

Passage Home ○
1955, UK, 102 mins, b/w
Dir: Roy Baker
Stars: Peter Finch, Diane Cilento, Anthony Steel, Cyril Cusack
Rating: ★★★

Director Roy Baker creates an exciting action film here – no mean feat considering he has a basic plot that has seen service in a dozen other previous films. Diane Cilento sparkles as the hub of the yarn – one girl among a shipload of seamen on a perilous 30-day voyage. The sea scenes have an authentic ring, the story moves along not only rapidly but even plausibly, and the acting, especially from Peter

Finch as the captain and Geoffrey Keen as the bosun, has a lusty, gritty feel.

Passage to India, A ○ ⱱ
1984, UK, 163 mins, colour
Dir: David Lean
Stars: Judy Davis, Victor Banerjee, Peggy Ashcroft, James Fox, Alec Guinness, Nigel Havers
Rating: ★★★

David Lean's pleasing if typically overlong account of E M Forster's novel set in India in the 1920s. Judy Davis gives an intriguingly enigmatic performance as the young English woman who goes to India with her fiancé's mother (Peggy Ashcroft). Dazed by the heat, the erotic influence of a love temple and the more immediate impact of a bizarre echo cave, she brings a charge of rape against the hapless Dr Aziz (Victor Banerjee), a friendly if over-subservient young doctor who has accompanied Davis and Ashcroft on a somewhat ambitious and costly trip to the mountains. Dame Peggy is excellent and deservedly won an Oscar, although Lean's old ally Alec Guinness never quite escapes caricature as the Brahmin mystic professor who believes that fate decides all. Still, all in all this is a worthwhile passage, distinguished by the fascination of the story and the richness of its flavour.

Passage to Marseille ○ ⱱ
1943, US, 110 mins, b/w
Dir: Michael Curtiz
Stars: Humphrey Bogart, Michele Morgan, Claude Rains, Sydney Greenstreet, Peter Lorre
Rating: ★★★

What seems like half the cast of *Casablanca* is reunited in this rugged wartime adventure story that has won rather undeserved notoriety as the only film with flashbacks within flashbacks within flashbacks within the main story. If you feel confused already, don't worry. Director Michael Curtiz (also from *Casablanca*) packs the complex scenario with tense action scenes, from an escape from Devil's Island, through a mutiny on board an Atlantic freighter, to a night-time raid of Free French bombers over Germany. Michele Morgan isn't quite Ingrid Bergman, but comes creditably close; and there are the flavour-filled performances you'd expect from Humphrey Bogart (intelligently shedding his semi-toupée in later scenes to make himself look older), Claude

Rains, Sydney Greenstreet, Peter Lorre, and practically Hollywood's entire collection of European emigrés. Fluid camerawork by James Wong Howe often ups the tempo of the action.

Passed Away ◐ ⱱ
1992, US, 96 mins, colour
Dir: Charlie Peters
Stars: Bob Hoskins, Maureen Stapleton, William Peterson, Nancy Travis, Jack Warden, Pamela Reed, Tim Curry, Blair Brown
Rating: ★★

A talented cast is largely sold down the river by director Charlie Peters script here. 'We'll give Dad a wake he'll never forget,' declares doting son Bob Hoskins (whose American accent is not quite so on-the-ball as usual) at the start of this quirky lightweight black farce set over one weekend in the lives of a distinctly oddball Irish-American family. Besides Maureen Stapleton giving good value to the role of the new widow, and Nancy Travis playing commendably straight as a mysterious stranger at the funeral, the cast also includes Peter Riegert, Teri Polo and Frances McDormand. All of them capture well their characters' eccentricities. Expect gently humorous, but not side-splitting entertainment from this offbeat caper.

Passenger 57 ● ⱱ
1992, US, 84 mins, colour
Dir: Kevin Hooks
Stars: Wesley Snipes, Bruce Payne, Alex Datcher, Tom Sizemore, Marc Macaulay
Rating: ★★

This brief but very violent action film is, in all but name, *Die Hard, Sky High*, with Wesley Snipes nearly but not quite a match for Bruce Willis. Wesley plays a security chief who, still haunted by the death of his wife in a supermarket robbery, finds himself on the same plane as the world's most wanted hijack terrorist, now a captive, but whose men are planted aboard ready to extract him from FBI custody (a bullet between the eye is the preferred method) and take over the plane. Snipes, trapped in the john just like Willis, or as Steven Seagal in the freezer in *Under Siege*, soon starts cutting down the odds, together with a very curvy stewardess (Alex Datcher) who is obviously going to help him get over his wife's death in the course of time. Although the pace of the film varies, a lot of incident is packed into its 84 minutes, which even throws in action in a fairground when the plane is forced to land and the terrorists attempt getaway on foot. The dialogue has moments of high lunacy: 'It's Charles Rane: the sophisticated British aristocrat known as the Rane of Terror', but action fans won't find much to complain about.

Passion ○

1954, US, 84 mins, colour
Dir: Allan Dwan
Stars: Cornel Wilde, Yvonne De Carlo, Raymond Burr
Rating: ★

Not a love story but a poorly-written Western vendetta thriller into which co-stars Cornel Wilde and Yvonne De Carlo put plenty of spirit. The action scenes whip up some excitement and supporting cast includes Raymond Burr, Lon Chaney Jr and veteran John Qualen. Directed by Allan Dwan, whose career spanned 50 years and some 400 films.

Passionate Friends, The ○

(aka: One Woman's Story)
1949, UK, 100 mins, b/w
Dir: David Lean
Stars: Ann Todd, Claude Rains, Trevor Howard
Rating: ★★★

Pitched somewhere between *Brief Encounter* and *Ryan's Daughter*, this romantic drama, enormously popular in its day, gives further evidence of director David Lean's fascination with women caught up in circumstances over which they seem to have no control, and which alter the lives of those around them. Here, it's Ann Todd as the married woman whose innocent day out with a former lover leads to a tangled sequence of events. Claude Rains is masterly as the husband, while the story itself develops swiftly and incisively in a way that Lean's films failed to do in later times.

Passionate Summer ○

1958, UK, 104 mins, colour
Dir: Rudolph Cartier
Stars: Virginia McKenna, Bill Travers, Yvonne Mitchell
Rating: ★★

Tangled love tale which should prove especially satisfying to all women who like a good-going romance with tons of complications. Bill Travers really makes one feel for him as the man caught in the middle of it all. And it seems only natural that of the three ladies vying for his affections he should plump for Virginia McKenna – after all, in real life, they had just been married.

Passion Fish ● ⓥ

1992, US, 135 mins, colour
Dir: John Sayles
Stars: Mary McDonnell, Alfre Woodard, David Strathairn, Vondie Curtis-Hall, Angela Bassett, Sheila Kelley
Rating: ★★★

Handed the role of a lifetime, the underrated Mary McDonnell deservedly notched up an Oscar nomination for her portrayal of the sour soap star who, paralysed in a car crash, returns to her childhood home in Louisiana. Various nurses desert her because of her bitchiness, until Chantelle (Alfre Woodard) appears, with problems of her own, but more than able to stand up to her new employer. Writer-director John Sayles has come up with a touching and gently funny story of the unlikely friendship that springs up between two people who feel they deserve better out of life. The supporting cast gleams with class and, if the piece drifts on just too long in the final reckoning, its visual qualities and emotional appeal more than make up for that.

Passport to Fame

See: The Whole Town's Talking

Passport to Pimlico ⊙ ⓥ

1949, UK, 84 mins, b/w
Dir: Henry Cornelius
Stars: Margaret Rutherford, Stanley Holloway, Basil Radford, Hermione Baddeley
Rating: ★★★★

Possibly the best film Ealing Studios made, a delightfully inventive comedy, brilliantly executed by director Henry Cornelius and a dazzling cast headed by Margaret Rutherford and Stanley Holloway. Pimlico's inhabitants find documents saying they belong to Burgundy, and promptly secede from the UK. Subsequent developments bring a chuckle a minute.

Pat and Mike ○

1952, US, 90 mins, b/w
Dir: George Cukor
Stars: Spencer Tracy, Katharine Hepburn
Rating: ★★★

Spencer Tracy and Katharine Hepburn play off against each other with immense pleasure in this constantly entertaining comedy about a lady who's a whiz at several sports (a role tailor-made for Hepburn) but who seizes up when her boyfriend's around. Several well-known sports stars of the day appear as themselves, one of the highlights of the action being a tennis match between Hepburn (quite a tennis enthusiast in real life) and 'Gorgeous' Gussie Moran. Possibly the most enjoyable of all the Tracy-Hepburn films, with a debut role for Chuck Connors and an early appearance by Charles Bronson under his real name, Charles Buchinsky.

Patch of Blue, A ◑

1965, US, 105 mins, b/w
Dir: Guy Green
Stars: Sidney Poitier, Shelley Winters, Elizabeth Hartman
Rating: ★★★

Blindness in films tends to be a subject on which most directors fail to avoid dipping their fingers into the sticky jar of over-sentiment. Guy Green is an exception to the rule, as he proves in this touching story of an 18-year-old girl who falls in love with a coloured reporter without knowing the colour of his skin. Shelley Winters won an Oscar as the sluttish mother who still knocks the girl around despite the fact that it was she who accidentally blinded her daughter at the age of five with acid (in a brilliantly-handled flashback scene). Elizabeth Hartman is excellent as the girl, giving the kind of intense performance often given by a young actress at the beginning of her career, and often never repeated. But perhaps best of all is the Ol' Pa of Wallace Ford. His last role, it also proved his meatiest for many years. The director tops it all off by not skipping any detail of the girl's everyday life, so that her joys really do seem joyous.

Paternity ◑

1981, US, 90 mins, colour
Dir: David Steinberg
Stars: Burt Reynolds, Elizabeth Ashley
Rating: ★★

There was much conjecture that this romantic comedy echoed star Burt Reynolds' real life in that he plays a man called Buddy (his own nickname) who wants to father a baby though he isn't married. Easy enough? Not the way Burt goes about it in a fun film which steers clear of the rocks of reality and contains some witty exchanges between Reynolds and

P

Juanita Moore as his sardonic house-keeper. 'What does the name Erasmus mean?' he asks her. 'That means your child won't have friends,' she answers.

Pat Garrett and Billy the Kid ◐ ⓥ
1973, US, 106 mins, colour
Dir: Sam Peckinpah
Stars: James Coburn, Kris Kristofferson, Bob Dylan, Jason Robards, Rita Coolidge
Rating: ★★

Director Sam Peckinpah's version of the Billy the Kid legend is a moody and atmospheric Western which, despite the wide open spaces, is almost claustrophobic. There's enough action to keep things moving, though, although it's not as overtly violent as some of Peckinpah's other films. The friendship between Billy and Sheriff Pat Garrett is really only hinted at, which reduces the drama of the final scenes. There are strong central performances from James Coburn as Garrett and Kris Kristofferson as Billy, supported by Jason Robards, Jack Elam and Bob Dylan – who also wrote the soundtrack music.

Paths of Glory ○
1957, US, 86 mins, b/w
Dir: Stanley Kubrick
Stars: Kirk Douglas, Wayne Morris, Adolphe Menjou, Ralph Meeker
Rating: ★★★

Stanley Kubrick's prize-winning film about man's folly in World War One, when three young soldiers are picked at random to be tried and shot for cowardice. The idea is to instil fear into their comrades. Kirk Douglas, as the young colonel who tries to defend the three men, gives one of his best performances in a sad and angry film that puts its message across without compromise.

Patriot Games ◐ ⓥ
1992, US, 116 mins, colour
Dir: Phillip Noyce
Stars: Harrison Ford, Patrick Bergin, Anne Archer, James Fox, Thora Birch, Sean Bean
Rating: ★★★

This thriller, exciting stuff towards the end, imagines that a rogue faction of the IRA (led by Patrick Bergin) might try to kill members of the British royal family, and that ex-CIA analyst Jack Ryan (Harrison Ford) might find himself caught up in one such attempt. 'Having a go' in the midst of the mayhem, Jack shoots dead the

brother of fanatical Sean Miller (Sean Bean), who subsequently escapes to make life a living nightmare for Jack and his family. There are holes galore in a plot that grows progressively less pacy until it gets down to business in the last 15 minutes, as Ryan and a visiting royal (James Fox) are besieged in a house (guarded by only three security men!) in a thrilling game of cat and mouse that ends up in speeding boats. Bean is every inch the merciless IRA man, and it's a pity his ultimate downfall is signposted so needlessly. Anne Archer has warmth as Ford's wife and Thora Birch is first-rate as their daughter. Don't get too logical about this thriller and you'll enjoy most of it.

Patsy, The ☉ ⓥ
1964, US, 101 mins, colour
Dir: Jerry Lewis
Stars: Jerry Lewis, Ina Balin
Rating: ★★

Another of star Jerry Lewis' inspired ideas half-ruined by director Lewis' own laborious treatment. A group of Hollywood technicians, all experts in their fields, takes a goofy bellboy under their wing and vows to mould him into a famous comedy star. Fecklessly and sometimes embarrassingly, he wrecks all their efforts to do so. How funny this might have been. But always there is too much 'space' on screen. Too long with nothing doing. To have such talented performers as Peter Lorre, Keenan Wynn, Everett Sloane and John Carradine walking around a vast, multi-coloured Hollywood apartment saying nothing for most of the time seems a criminal waste of talent. When director Lewis gives comic Lewis a chance, the picture bursts with fun – as with the superbly-staged scene where the music teacher (Hans Conried) finds both himself and his apartment gradually torn apart when he tries to teach Lewis how to sing. The rest is prime evidence why comedians shouldn't direct their own pictures.

Patterns ○
(aka: Patterns of Power)
1956, US, 83 mins, b/w
Dir: Fielder Cook
Stars: Van Heflin, Everett Sloane, Ed Begley, Beatrice Straight
Rating: ★★★

Based on a television hit play by Rod Serling, this film takes a candid and unusually discerning peep into the

executive suites of the world of big business in America. The cut and thrust of the business giants' tactics is thrilling and the dialogue diamond-hard and brilliant. The film was praised to the skies by critics, but thrown away by distributors and practically ignored by the public. One of its best scenes comes when Van Heflin and Everett Sloane slug it out together in a verbal battle about the film's central theme. Is big business, they argue, a good or an evil thing? Finding the answer poses a lot of problems for the characters involved.

Patterns of Power
See: Patterns

Patton
See: Patton: Lust for Glory

Patton: Lust for Glory ◐ ⓥ
(aka: Patton)
1970, US, 171 mins, colour
Dir: Franklin J Schaffner
Stars: George C Scott, Karl Malden
Rating: ★★★

Now mainly remembered as the film for which George C Scott was awarded, and refused, an Oscar, this is an intimate war film, in the sense that it concentrates on the complex character of Patton himself, with the help of some tremendous work by Scott. The battle scenes themselves are exciting enough, but it's the character conflicts you'll remember.

Patty Hearst ● ⓥ
1988, US, 108 mins, colour
Dir: Paul Schrader
Stars: Natasha Richardson, William Forsythe, Ving Rhames, Dana Delany, Frances Fisher
Rating: ★

Patty's is one of the most fascinating and extraordinary stories of our violent times. A pity it's made such a boring film. Hard to see what director Paul Schrader could have done about it, apart from not stylising the bank robberies involved, presumably to eliminate vicarious excitement. Well, we could have done with some vicarious excitement to liven up the re-telling of the story of rich girl Patty's kidnap and brainwashing by an obscure liberation army who seem to do little apart from indoctrinate their members, think about robberies to raise money, and have sex with each other. Schrader's liking for darkened rooms and nighttime scenes ensures that we can grasp details of the squalid saga only by aural contact with the screenplay, which consists mainly of four-letter words. Natasha Richardson, looking exactly like mum Vanessa Redgrave, puts heart and soul into Patty and is the only thing that comes close to holding the movie together. Great American accent too, Natasha; shame about the film.

Paula
See: Framed

Pay Day ⊙ ⓥ
1922, US, 21 mins, b/w
Dir: Charles Chaplin
Stars: Charlie Chaplin
Rating: ★★★

Charlie Chaplin's last short film, this contains a marvellous sequence of comic events that begins when workman Charlie staggers home drunk in the pouring rain.

Pay Or Die! ○
1960, US, 111 mins, b/w
Dir: Richard Wilson
Stars: Ernest Borgnine, Zohra Lampert, Alan Austin, Murvyn Vye
Rating: ★★★

Ernest Borgnine's best post-Marty role, as a detective who wages a one-man war against the Mafia, in this interesting, exciting and forceful crime thriller set in the early 1900s. Borgnine's honest-to-goodness performance gives the drama just the grittiness it needs, and Zohra Lampert makes a pleasing debut as his wife. Other good performances come from Alan Austin and Murvyn Vye, as two characters very much on different sides of the law.

Payroll ○
1961, UK, 105 mins, b/w
Dir: Sidney Hayers
Stars: Michael Craig, Françoise Prevost, Billie Whitelaw, William Lucas
Rating: ★★★

For more than 20 years, filmgoers have been familiar with the type of crime thriller on the 'caper' theme. The idea had been used in the cinema before, certainly, but it is hard to escape the feeling that it was Jules Dassin's famous French film *Rififi*, with its celebrated, virtually soundless robbery sequence, which really set the fashion for so many films of this ilk – a fashion which has continued almost ever since. The 'robbery which

goes wrong' is a favourite theme and *Payroll* is a variation which is a well-knit thriller tale.

Pearl of the South Pacific ⊙
1955, US, 80 mins, colour
Dir: Allan Dwan
Stars: Virginia Mayo, Dennis Morgan, David Farrar
Rating: ★

Technicolor tales of the South Seas really got under way with Dorothy Lamour and her sarong in the mid-Thirties. This tiresome yarn limped in right at the end of the cycle but contains all the familiar elements: beautiful girl, dashing hero, hot-headed tribal chief and even the octopus that guards the sunken treasure. No treasure here, though.

Peeping Tom ●
1959, UK, 109 mins, colour
Dir: Michael Powell
Stars: Carl Boehm, Moira Shearer
Rating: ★★★

Producer-director Michael Powell, usually associated with get-away-from-it-all films, such as *A Matter of Life and Death*, *Age of Consent* and *They're a Weird Mob*, here made one of the most horrifying contributions to the cinema of the macabre since World War Two. Written by Leo Marks, who co-scripted *Twisted Nerve*, it tells of a psychopathic young cameraman who photographs his victims' terrified death agonies. The murders themselves are horrifyingly tense, and Carl Boehm couldn't be bettered as the psychopath. It makes gripping, adult entertainment: not recommended for the nervous.

Pee-wee's Big Adventure ○ ⓥ
1985, US, 91 mins, colour
Dir: Tim Burton
Stars: Paul Reubens, Elizabeth Daily
Rating: ★★★

The feature debut of Pee-wee Herman, the on-screen persona of cult comedian Paul Reubens, is a most stylish affair. From the start, when the childlike Pee-wee awakens in a room filled with Heath Robinson-style contraptions on the traumatic day his beloved red bicycle is stolen, we know we're in for a visual treat. There's not really much of a story. But Pee-wee, with his comical white pan-sticked face, rosy cheeks and red painted lips, offers us the perfect opportunity to re-experience our own

innocent wonder as we see things through his eyes. Director Tim Burton, whose later work was to include *Beetlejuice*, *Batman* and *Edward Scissorhands*, paints a colourful canvas, and the overall effect is rather like a huge box of brightly coloured toys being spilled onto the screen. Don't be fooled into thinking that this film is just for kids – adults will find it inventive, imaginative and totally engaging.

Peggy Sue Got Married ◐ ⓥ
1986, US, 104 mins, colour
Dir: Francis Coppola
Stars: Kathleen Turner, Nicolas Cage
Rating: ★★

Although its cast has strength in depth, this is a tedious and inexplicably overrated fantasy which comes across as a romance-orientated version of *Back to the Future*. Middle-aged Kathleen Turner (unconvincing as a teenager) magically returns to high school and gets a second chance with her boyfriend (Nicolas Cage, overacting) and future husband. There are plenty of faces to look out for in the supporting cast, including director Francis Coppola's daughter Sofia as Turner's kid sister, stars-to-be Joan Allen, Catherine Hicks, Kevin J O'Connor and Helen Hunt and such personable veterans as Maureen O'Sullivan, Don Murray, Barbara Harris, John Carradine and Leon Ames. There's even a rare glimpse of Shirley MacLaine's acting daughter Sachi Parker. A pity Coppola couldn't conjure up something more worthy of such a starry gathering.

Pelican Brief, The ◐ ⓥ
1993, US, 141 mins, colour
Dir: Alan J Pakula
Stars: Julia Roberts, Denzel Washington, Tony Goldwyn, John Heard, Sam Shepard, John Lithgow
Rating: ★★

Dodging killers while bodies are dropping all about her, Julia Roberts made a high-profile return to film leading roles after a couple of years away, as the young law student whose intelligence and nose for suspicious detail gets her into all sorts of trouble. Based on John Grisham's best-seller (reputedly written with Roberts in mind), it's a little too similar in flavour to Grisham's other blockbuster *The Firm*; the plot is even more complex and assuredly leaves you no time to go out and make the coffee unless you

P

stop the film. Denzel Washington is competent in the co-starring role as the determined reporter who proves to be Roberts' only reliable ally in her flight from powerful and deadly forces, but like hers, his role is underwritten so that these people, like their opponents, remain little more than cyphers, albeit of good against evil. Action scenes keep the pulse racing; but don't bank on remembering the plot if anyone asks you.

Pendulum ◐
1968, US, 106 mins, colour
Dir: George Schaefer
Stars: George Peppard, Jean Seberg
Rating: ★★

Routine tough American detective thriller, somewhat after the style of Don Siegel, but here integrating the various aspects of its plot together with the same panache. Good performances from Charles McGraw, as a rugged chief of detectives, and Robert F Lyons, as a psychopathic killer. Razor-sharp colour photography by Lionel Linden is another distinct asset to the violent parable.

Penny Princess ○
1952, UK, 92 mins, colour
Dir: Val Guest
Stars: Yolande Donlan, Dirk Bogarde
Rating: ★★★

Given a storyline that is not so much slim as positively anorexic, the film has to rely on the charm of the actors and the pace of their playing and, in this respect, Yolande Donlan comes through with flying colours, putting over her lines wth genuine fizz. Dirk Bogarde supports nobly and spent most of the film in his pyjamas but, since it had a 'U' certificate, everything was naturally proper and above board. Donlan's husband Val Guest wrote and directed.

Penny Serenade ○
1941, US, 120 mins, b/w
Dir: George Stevens
Stars: Cary Grant, Irene Dunne
Rating: ★★

Well thought of in many quarters, George Stevens' over-extended weepie about a will-they-won't-they-part? couple looks rather stiff and maudlin today: only stars like Irene Dunne and Cary Grant could see material like this through, but even they are unlikely to stop you drifting off to make the coffee half-way through.

People That Time Forgot, The ○
1977, UK, 96 mins, colour
Dir: Kevin Connor
Stars: Patrick Wayne, Sarah Douglas, Doug McClure, Dana Gillespie
Rating: ★★

This sequel to *The Land That Time Forgot* is a funny (sometimes intentionally) and altogether rather smashing pantomime adventure which the kids will swallow whole while adults sit convulsed in an adjoining armchair. The beginning of the picture, with Captain Tony Britton – apparently strayed in from a British war film of the Fifties – piloting his icebreaker into the wilder Antarctic regions through which Doug McClure was seen plodding at the end of the previous film – is definitely weak. But, once away from exteriors, director Kevin Connor finds his touch. Among the more spectacular of his visuals are: a party of scarlet-pennoned horsemen riding out from Skull Mountain across the horizon; and a deeply-shrouded cavern, walled with tiny skulls, where the explorers are kept captured. A little tableau compromising a grotesque executioner and his grubby dwarf familiar is also splendidly imaginative. A bouquet to Shane Rimmer, whose comic relief is well-timed and funny; while the tall and willowy Sarah Douglas, (the villainess in *Conan the Destroyer*), is obviously a lady to be reckoned with. The action scenes are brilliantly edited and carry bite and conviction.

People Vs Dr Kildare, The ○
1941, US, 78 mins, b/w
Dir: Harold S Bucquet
Stars: Lew Ayres, Lionel Barrymore
Rating: ★★

More of the action takes place in the courtroom than in the hospital in this Kildare drama which has the good doctor defending himself against a malpractice suit. The supporting cast is fairly extraordinary, with former child star Bonita Granville as the girl whose skating career seems to have ended under Kildare's knife, comic Red Skelton as a hospital janitor, tough-guy star Grant Withers as a policeman and silent leading lady Anna Q Nilsson on the jury. The foreman of these 12 good and true people is Dwight Frye, remembered as the hunchback from *Frankenstein* and the insect-eating Renfield in *Dracula*. Who would trust him with a verdict?

People Will Talk ○
1951, US, 110 mins, b/w
Dir: Joseph L Mankiewicz
Stars: Cary Grant, Jeanne Crain, Hume Cronyn, Walter Slezak
Rating: ★★

Joseph L Mankiewicz's follow-up to the Oscar-winning successes of his *All About Eve* the previous year leans to a similar degree on dialogue for its impact, but lacks the venom that so distinguished the previous film. Cary Grant smoothly plays the eccentric medico whom all the 'talk' is about, but Mankiewicz did not get on with leading lady Jeanne Crain, thrust upon him by the studio after his original choice Anne Baxter had to withdraw because she was expecting a baby. At least the film is hard to categorise. It belongs in the cinema's bulging vaults of 'one-off' near misses.

Pepe ○
1960, US, 157 mins, colour
Dir: George Sidney
Stars: Cantinflas, Shirley Jones, Dan Dailey, Ernie Kovacs
Rating: ★★

Colourful musical trip around Hollywood, with many stars appearing as themselves. The song-and-dance numbers are sparklingly shot in colour and well worth watching. The slim story-line revolves around Cantinflas – the Mexican comic actor who made such a name for himself as Passepartout in *Around the World in 80 Days* – as a simple peasant whose horse is bought by a film director. Those who like to play star-spotting should look for Tony Curtis, Frank Sinatra, Bing Crosby, Debbie Reynolds, Kim Novak, Greer Garson, Edward G Robinsin, Janet Blair, Donna Reed, Jack Lemmon, Janet Leigh, Judy Garland, Maurice Chevalier, Bobby Darin, Jimmy Durante, Sammy Davis Jr, Andre Previn and several more only slightly less famous. Seems to go on forever though.

Percy ● ⓥ
1971, UK, 103 mins, colour
Dir: Ralph Thomas
Stars: Hywel Bennett, Denholm Elliott, Elke Sommer, Britt Ekland
Rating: ★

This is a one-joke film and the joke isn't that funny. Hywel (*Shelley*) Bennett is the recipient of the world's first penis transplant after a freak accident. He spends most of the film trying to discover the identity of

Percy's (his pet name for his new organ) owner. It's not simply that this is all in rather bad taste, it's not very good either. Positively limp, in fact. You're not shocked by the humour or the naff music hall phallic references, but you are embarrassed for all the talented people who obviously spent so much time producing so little. Unbelievably, they made a sequel, *Percy's Progress*. Believably, it was worse.

Perfect ● Ⓥ
1985, US, 119 mins, colour
Dir: James Bridges
Stars: John Travolta, Jamie Lee Curtis, Laraine Newman, Marilu Henner, Anne de Salvo
Rating: ★★★

The cast of this drama (with yet another pre-sold disco soundtrack), about an investigative reporter doing a smut story on aerobic clubs being the singles bars of the Eighties, is so charismatic as to make you quite like a story of which you can hardly believe a word. John Travolta as the journalist does his best to carve a likeable centrepoint to the drama, although the screenplay hardly helps. And, if the whipcord Jamie Lee Curtis is on her best form, she is certainly given very tough competition by all three of the other femmes in the cast – Laraine Newman and Marilu Henner as ladies of the club and Anne de Salvo as Travolta's sometime photographer colleague. All three catch the exact essence of the characters they play – and Newman and Henner both convey the vulnerability behind the banter and pushiness behind the man-mad swingers they portray.

Perfect Couple, A Ⓞ
1979, US, 110 mins, colour
Dir: Robert Altman
Stars: Paul Dooley, Marta Heflin
Rating: ★★

A well-crafted, engagingly acted but basically silly story about a romance (by computer dating) between two people from weird and absurdly exaggerated family units. If you think her 'pop' commune is off beat, wait until you see his martinet Greek family, ruled over with a rod of iron by a father who conducts gramophone records while a family of all ages sits and watches. If the story fails by and large to take off, its music is most attractive. In fact, the soundtrack may be a better bargain than the film itself, despite the gauche charm with which

it's endowed by stars Paul Dooley and Marta Heflin. A Robert Altman original!

Perfect Friday Ⓞ
1970, UK, 94 mins, colour
Dir: Peter Hall
Stars: Ursula Andress, Stanley Baker, David Warner
Rating: ★★

Bank robbery thriller, given light-hearted treatment by director Peter Hall and especially by John Dankworth's racy music score. Ursula Andress is always worth watching, in and out of clothes, the robbery itself is quite tensely staged, and the whole caper never outstays its welcome. The sugar-coated spoof is delightfully easy to swallow and makes for thoroughly diverting entertainment.

Perfect Furlough, The Ⓞ
(aka: Strictly for Pleasure)
1958, US, 93 mins, colour
Dir: Blake Edwards
Stars: Tony Curtis, Janet Leigh, Keenan Wynn
Rating: ★★

Comedy written round the talents of Tony Curtis and Janet Leigh when they were still Hollywood's ideal young couple. Talented supporting cast includes television superstar Elaine Stritch. Curtis, though, was never as good in comedy as he liked to think, with the honourable exception of *Some Like It Hot*.

Perfectly Normal ● Ⓥ
1990, Canada, 107 mins, colour
Dir: Yves Simoneau
Stars: Michael Riley, Robbie Coltrane, Deborah Duchene, Kristina Nicholl
Rating: ★

Although slow-moving and over-long, this comedy piece has a certain slight charm. Renzo (Michael Riley) is an Italianate Canadian who inherits his mother's spacious home, but carries on working at a drink factory, secretly singing opera in the shower and keeping goal for the local ice hockey team. Renzo's life begins to change when he meets Alonzo Lafayette Turner (Robbie Coltrane), a porky failed restaurateur, who moves in. Renzo is also lusted after by Deborah Duchene, the dishy dinette at the rink. Riley is too low-key for words as the shy, harassed and uncommunicative Renzo. You can believe the works foreman who tells him: 'This is some new territory you've entered here.

You've gone past dull.' Too many of Renzo's qualities rub off on the film too, although the climactic fight in Alonzo's operatic diner has a certain nutty grandeur.

Perfect Woman, The Ⓞ
1949, UK, 89 mins, b/w
Dir: Bernard Knowles
Stars: Patricia Roc, Stanley Holloway, Nigel Patrick
Rating: ★★

A scatterbrained comedy about a professor who invents a robot woman. That delicious ditherer Miles Malleson plays the inventor and, as another professor, you may spot Noel Howlett, later to become well known as headmaster Cromwell in TV's popular comedy series *Please Sir!*

Perfect World, A Ⓞ Ⓥ
1993, US, 138 mins, colour
Dir: Clint Eastwood
Stars: Kevin Costner, Clint Eastwood, Laura Dern, T J Lowther
Rating: ★★

This manhunt thriller has some of the best performances in a Hollywood action drama for some little time past but suffers from severe credibility problems at crucial stages of its plot. Kevin Costner is the man on the run with a boy (T J Lowther) as hostage – even the circumstances of the initial kidnapping themselves are somewhat unconvincing – Clint Eastwood the pursuing Texas Ranger and Laura Dern a criminologist assigned to the case. All four of these performances are first-class, and the ending, when it comes, is quite emotive, but drags on far too long and, like much of the plot, is bedevilled by a failure to dodge any contrivance or cliché you might expect (and hope to avoid) in this kind of film. An imperfect world, then, but heaven maybe for fans of the stars, who are well up to their own best standards.

Performance ● Ⓥ
1970, UK, 105 mins, colour
Dir: Donald Cammell, Nicolas Roeg
Stars: James Fox, Mick Jagger, Anita Pallenberg
Rating: ★★

Nicolas Roeg, up till then a distinguished cinematographer, advanced his career by co-directing this ugly but compelling mood piece about a gangster on the run who finds a hideout in the mansion of a reclusive pop star. Glowingly photographed by

P

Roeg himself, who went on to continue his career in often unpalatable adult themes with such films as *Walkabout, Don't Look Now, Bad Timing* and *Eureka*, the film is tough and sometimes violent, with personable performances from James Fox and Mick Jagger in the two leading roles.

Perils of Pauline, The ○

1947, US, 96 mins, colour
Dir: George Marshall
Stars: Betty Hutton, John Lund, Billy de Wolfe, William Demarest
Rating: ★★★

It's laughter, tears and songs again with Betty Hutton, and another of her larger-than-life heroines (she also played Annie Oakley, Texas Guinan and Blossom Seeley). This time around, it's Pearl White, queen of the silent serial world, getting the Hutton treatment. Doyenne screen actress Constance Collier heads the supporting cast, which also includes William Demarest, Frank Faylen and Billy de Wolfe.

Personal Services ● ⓥ

1987, UK, 105 mins, colour
Dir: Terry Jones
Stars: Julie Walters, Alec McCowen, Danny Schiller, Shirley Stelfox
Rating: ★★

The story of London 'madam' Cynthia Payne. Or, according to the credits of the film, entirely fictitious and nothing to do with her, even though she was technical consultant and the central character is called Christine Paynter. Ah, what a tangled legal web we weave when things are still *sub judice*. Alternately bright and grim and occasionally amusing in its desperate way, the result is about what you'd expect: lots of earthy language and 'late-night' wit, with a salty if rather variable performance by Julie Walters which, like the story, gets wearing after a while. Generally, the film falls between vulgar low-life humour and St Trinian's titillation but, if you like that sort of thing, it's all good clean dirty fun, both the film and its characters being in the good old British tradition. Indeed the last two reels could have come straight out of *Carry On Whoring*. 'You'll go down for this,' scowls the police sergeant after the final raid on Christine's suburban brothel. 'I only go down for a price dear,' retorts Walters, 'and I

doubt whether you can afford it.' You can just see Joan Sims saying the same thing to Kenneth Williams.

Pete Kelly's Blues ○

1955, US, 95 mins, colour
Dir: Jack Webb
Stars: Jack Webb, Janet Leigh, Edmond O'Brien, Lee Marvin, Peggy Lee, Ella Fitzgerald
Rating: ★★★

Only a contrived ending mars Jack Webb's forceful drama of gangsters and musicians in the Jazz Age of the Twenties. The jazz is brassy and basic, and the story has a cutting edge of realism that gives it a gritty feel. There's good support from Andy Devine and Lee Marvin (cast for once as the hero's wisecracking friend) and a solid story, plus a few unconventional directorial tricks from Webb, who also has the sense to surround himself with such real jazz people as singers Peggy Lee (her striking performance got her nominated for an Oscar) and Ella Fitzgerald, plus musicians Dick Cathcart, Matty Matlock, Moe Schneider and George Van Eps. And you can't miss Jayne Mansfield as a cigarette girl! It's hard-hitting and well on the beat.

Peter Ibbetson ○

1935, US, 91 mins, b/w
Dir: Henry Hathaway
Stars: Gary Cooper, Ann Harding, John Halliday, Ida Lupino
Rating: ★★

This fey, not to say bizarre romantic fantasy baffled most critics of the mid-Thirties, who were accustomed to a cinema that went in for realism. Gary Cooper struggles with a role to which he seems not entirely suited, but Ann Harding is fine as the childhood sweetheart with whom he is reunited in dreams, and that sharp character star John Halliday excels in the rather too small role of Miss Harding's screen husband.

Peter No-Tail ☉

1981, Sweden, 75 mins, colour
Dir: Stig Lasseby
Rating: ★★★

This Swedish feature cartoon was so successful internationally that a sequel, *Peter No-Tail in America*, appeared two years later. Its hero, a cat born without a tail, has been a favourite of Scandinavian children since stories about him (written first by Gosta Knutsson, later by Leif Krantz) first appeared in the Thirties. Almost

three million books have since been sold relating the adventures of Peter, who was based on a cat that Knutsson had encountered as a child: that animal, however, Knutsson learned, had had its tail bitten off by a rat! This first film's good entertainment, with vivid animation, a resourceful hero and an eventful story.

Peter Pan ☉ ⓥ

1952, US, 77 mins, colour
Dir: Hamilton Luske, Clyde Geronimi
Voice stars: Bobby Driscoll, Kathryn Beaumont, Hans Conried, Bill Thompson, Heather Angel, Tom Conway
Rating: ★★★

Cruelly underrated in its day, this sees the Disney studio close to its best in a cleverly-detailed fairy-tale adventure of great charm, spun round J M Barrie's play about the boy who never grew up, lives in a faraway island with The Lost Boys and engages in duels of wits and sword-play with the dastardly Captain Hook. There are memorable songs – 'I Can Fly', 'The Second Star to the Right' – although they take second place to the action. You might be surprised to find that one of the most popular songs from the film, 'Never Smile at a Crocodile', was actually cut from the film and only survives as a musical theme when the crocodile appears to menace his old enemy Hook. Younger children will be enthralled and excited at this one, and rightly so.

Peter's Friends ● ⓥ

1992, UK, 103 mins, colour
Dir: Kenneth Branagh
Stars: Kenneth Branagh, Emma Thompson, Stephen Fry, Hugh Laurie, Rita Rudner, Imelda Staunton
Rating: ★★

The kind of modish ensemble piece that may look woefully dated in years to come, enabling a group of Britain's ageing bright young things to portray university friends 10 years on. The story of their reunion has moments of wit and perception but, after a delightful and often funny first 40 minutes, it becomes increasingly heavy going, dominated by a torrent of four-letter words and unlikely sexual shenanigans, and going right over the top with Kenneth Branagh's drunken rant at the end. A credibility problem exists here right from the start (could any university footlights revuers really have performed for an audience that sat with their backs to them, ignored them, or went to sleep?) and continues right through the film. The Branagh and Emma Thompson characters – she's initially delightful as a bookish spinster worried about the welfare of her cat – are especially inconsistent and hard to take, and only Stephen Fry achieves the right blend of wit and melancholy the piece requires.

Pete's Dragon ⊙
1977, US, 134 mins, colour
Dir: Don Chaffey
Stars: Helen Reddy, Jim Dale, Mickey Rooney, Shelley Winters
Rating: ★★

This Disney musical fantasy combines live action and animation and very young children will love it. Purists will notice that foregrounds do occasionally wobble, and the songs are largely undistinguished. But the cast has its moments, especially in a vertigo-inducing trio sung by Helen Reddy, Mickey Rooney and youngster Sean Marshall at the top of a lighthouse. And it really is them hauling themselves up and dancing round the top. At such times, *Pete's Dragon* almost spreads its wings and flies.

Pet Sematary ● ⓥ
1989, US, 103 mins, colour
Dir: Mary Lambert
Stars: Dale Midkiff, Fred Gwynne, Brad Greenquist
Rating: ★

Screen adaptations of Stephen King's best sellers have been mainly disappointing, but for this atrocity the author has only himself to blame. He wrote the screenplay, as well as appearing in a rather incongruous bit part. Even to begin with, it's hard to sympathise with a family who, with two kids and a cat, move to a home about six yards away from a dangerous, unguarded motorway. But they do, or we wouldn't have a story, such as it is, which involves an Indian burial ground (actually beyond the 'pet sematary') which brings the dead back to life in fiendish form. King could never be accused of good taste, but here logic deserts him as well. People behave in impossibly idiotic fashion in order to sustain the horror, and the dialogue all too often matches the plot developments for sheer lunacy. Bury this turkey in the 'pet sematary' – but don't let it come back.

Petticoat Pirates ○ ⓥ
1961, UK, 87 mins, colour
Dir: David MacDonald
Stars: Charlie Drake, Anne Heywood, Cecil Parker, John Turner
Rating: ★★

A laugh on the ocean wave with Charlie Drake among the Wrens. Charlie's antics include dressing up as a girl and – in the funniest sequence – taking part with the Wrens in a chaotic exercise at sea. By no means great, but offbeat, bright and breezy.

Petulia ◐ ⓥ
1967, UK, 105 mins, colour
Dir: Richard Lester
Stars: Julie Christie, George C Scott, Richard Chamberlain, Joseph Cotten
Rating: ★★★

Richard Lester directed this highly individual and thoroughly entertaining film after making those delightfully inconsequential Beatles pictures and the different but equally amusing *The Knack*. Julie Christie plays Petulia, the unorthodox heroine, one of whose actions is to steal a tuba at night from a pawnshop! The film's considerable supporting cast also includes Richard Chamberlain, Joseph Cotten and Shirley Knight. The film drew mixed reactions from critics on its release, but in our book it is classified only fractionally below the top class. It is certainly Lester's best performance as director.

Peyton Place ◐ ⓥ
1957, US, 157 mins, colour
Dir: Mark Robson
Stars: Lana Turner, Lee Philips, Arthur Kennedy, Hope Lange, Lloyd Nolan, Diane Varsi
Rating: ★★★

The original film version of Grace Metalious's best-selling book about the sores that lurk beneath the respectable facade of a small American town. William Mellor's brilliant colour photography – especially notable in the passing of the seasons – complements Mark Robson's deft direction of this lusty slice of Americana. The cast also includes Lee Philips, Terry Moore and Russ Tamblyn; but it's the more experienced hands – Lana Turner, Leon Ames and Mildred Dunnock – who takes the acting honours.

Phantasm II ● ⓥ
1988, US, 97 mins, colour
Dir: Don Coscarelli
Stars: James LeGros, Reggie Bannister, Angus Scrimm, Paul Irvine, Kenneth Tigar
Rating: ★★★

A drive-in movie that gets sillier and sillier as it goes along or more and more fun, according to your inclinations. Spot the name 'Sam Raimi' (another horror film-maker) on a dead man in the mortuary, and you know that Don Coscarelli, who made the first *Phantasm*, is only playing fun and games. There'll be an ending in which the forces of evil are vanquished, but then a tailpiece paving the way for yet another sequel. Angus Scrimm is back as the Tall Man, a thinking man's Freddie Krueger, along with his deadly flying spheres and demon dwarfs. Poor grandma is dragged off almost before she can get into the plot and we're into an imaginatively grisly game of Tom and Jerry, climaxing in a lengthy all-action finale as the Tall Man and his black legions try to consign our heroes to a space-age limbo or permanent dwarfdom or both. Lots of blood, both red and yellow, is spilt, but sufficient pace, imagination and lightness of tone ensure that we don't take it all too seriously. Horror fans can confidently swallow the grisly dose in one gulp: just watch out for the flying sphere.

Phantom Lady ○
1944, US, 87 mins, b/w
Dir: Robert Siodmak
Stars: Ella Raines, Franchot Tone, Alan Curtis, Thomas Gomez
Rating: ★★★★

This top-flight *film noir* about a missing witness in a murder case was directed by Robert Siodmak, second only in the Forties to Alfred Hitchcock as a purveyor of suspense and claustrophobic terror. His use of camera angles, sound effects and sequences without dialogue is remarkably effective and moody monochrome cinematography by Woody Bredell serves to underline the growing atmosphere of tension and unease. There's a fine performance by Elisha Cook Jr as a frightened little man (amazing in his final scene) and Aurora Miranda, the sister of Brazilian Bombshell Carmen Miranda, appears briefly as the star of a musical show and sings 'Chick-Ee-Chick'.

Phantom of the Opera, The ○
1925, US, 94 mins, b/w
Dir: Rupert Julian
Stars: Lon Chaney, Mary Philbin
Rating: ★★★

P

The first and still most famous screen version of Gaston Leroux's lurid tale of the mad music master who haunts the secret corridors of the Paris Opera House. Lon Chaney, the 'man of a thousand faces', took the title role and achieved another triumph in make-up when the face beneath the mask was finally revealed (heightened by the film's bursting into colour), to the horror of the heroine, played by the bewitching, birdlike Mary Philbin. Amazing sets, splendid atmosphere.

Phantom of the Opera, The ○ Ⓥ
1943, US, 92 mins, colour
Dir: Arthur Lubin
Stars: Nelson Eddy, Claude Rains, Susanna Foster
Rating: ★★★

Despite some critics' cynical reservations about any version of *The Phantom of the Opera* in which the actor playing the Phantom was billed beneath Nelson Eddy, this was a huge money-spinner for Universal Films in spite of its nine million dollar budget, a big outlay for the studio at the time. Claude Rains gives a fine, sympathetic performance as the man behind the mask. This was one of a fine actor's finest hours. The stunning Technicolor photography of Hal Mohr and W Howard Greene won an Academy Award as did the opulent art direction by John B Goodman and Alexander Golitzen.

Phantom of the Opera ● Ⓥ
1989, US, 92 mins, colour
Dir: Dwight H. Little
Stars: Robert Englund, Jill Schoelen, Alex Hyde White, Bill Nighy, Stephanie Lawrence
Rating: ★★

It's a nightmare at the opera house! Yes, Robert Englund, alias Freddy Kruger, takes his turn as the masked master of murder and music, and the results make the Hammer horror rendition of 1962 look a model of restraint. This isn't a modernised version, simply the old chestnut with a silly modern framing story which makes no sort of sense, in which the heroine discovers Freddy's – sorry, Erik's – old manuscripts and history and gasps, 'Gee, isn't that weird – composer by day and serial killer by night!' The script, in fact, is a bigger villain than the Phantom, although the settings are opulently, painstakingly stylish. Englund is actually all right as the Phantom, when he's al-

lowed to do more than skin his victims alive and peel layers of bloody guck off his face. But Schoelen seems all wrong as a flat-chested opera singer with little sense of dramatic timing. The last two reels do contain some bravura moments and the enterprise, though disappointingly trite and silly, is by no means a bore.

Phantom of the Paradise ●
1974, US, 91 mins, colour
Dir: Brian De Palma
Stars: Paul Williams, William Finley, Jessica Harper
Rating: ★★

This film, which started director Brian de Palma on an eye-catching orgy of violence and suspense that, to date, has included *Carrie*, *The Fury*, *Blow Out* and *Dressed to Kill*, is a cheeky rock-music remake of *Phantom of the Opera*. That diminutive dynamo of the pop world, Paul Williams, not only stars as the megalomaniac impresario Swan, who callously steals the hero's songs, but also wrote the music and lyrics for the film himself. Among the minor credits, you'll notice the name of Sissy Spacek, taking time out from acting, as set decorator. Her real-life husband Jack Fisk was production designer on the film.

Phantom of the Rue Morgue ◐
1954, US, 84 mins, colour
Dir: Roy Del Ruth
Stars: Karl Malden, Claude Dauphin, Patricia Medina, Steve Forrest
Rating: ★★

One of the few big-scale adaptations of stories by Edgar Allan Poe not to star Vincent Price. This time it's Karl Malden dispensing the sneers in the story of a grisly series of murders in turn-of-the-century Paris. Poe's storyline is followed quite faithfully, sombre Warnercolor photography plays up the creepy scenes, and there are good performances from Malden, Claude Dauphin and Allyn McLerie, plus an appealing one from blond stage star Dolores Dorn, who unfortunately ends up as one of the killer's victims.

Phantom Tollbooth, The ☉
1970, US, 90 mins, colour
Dir: Abe Levitow, David Monahan
Stars: Butch Patrick
Rating: ★★★

A charming part-live action but mostly animated version of Norton Justin's children's book which marked

the debut as a feature film director of Chuck Jones. Jones was the Warners animator who helped create such classic cartoon characters as Bugs Bunny, Porky Pig, Daffy Duck, Tweetie Pie and Road Runner, and his early work was notable for speed, violent action and side-splitting sight gags. This film combines some fairly sophisticated ideas, such as demons from the 'Mountains of Ignorance' with cute and likable characters that will grab a young child's attention. The principal voice talent is the late and much lamented Mel Blanc, the 'voice' of Bugs Bunny, Porky Pig and Daffy Duck.

Phar Lap ○ Ⓥ
1984, Australia, 118 mins, colour
Dir: Simon Wincer
Stars: Tom Burlinson, Martin Vaughan
Rating: ★★★

It's 1928. Struggling Australian racehorse trainer Harry Telford (Martin Vaughan) buys a horse, sight unseen, from New Zealand. Mockingly called Phar Lap (Siamese for Lightning), the horse comes last in his first five races. But an inspired change of diet and an intense training programme turns Phar Lap into a winner. Eventually, pressure from the Racing Commission forces Telford and Phar Lap's owner Dave Davis (Ron Leibman) to take the horse to America, where it is entered for the 'Richest Race in the World'. The true story of Phar Lap has now become part of Australian folk history and this film captures the spirit of the time and the sport. There are engaging performances from Vaughan, Leibman and Tom Burlinson and the whole thing is a kind of cross between *Chariots of Fire* and *National Velvet*. If that sounds like a put-down, it's not meant to – *Phar Lap* is a thoroughly enjoyable film.

Phase IV ●
1973, US, 86 mins, colour
Dir: Saul Bass
Stars: Nigel Davenport, Lynne Frederick, Michael Murphy
Rating: ★★

If you're a victim of formication – someone who suffers a prickly sensation, as of ants crawling over the skin – you're not likely to enjoy this visually brilliant – courtesy of director Saul Bass and photographer Dick Bush – but tricky-to-follow story of scientists trying to discover why colonies of normally antagonistic ants are banding together and attacking as a collective force. Nigel Davenport, Lynne Frederick and Michael Murphy are the humans in danger. Bush's colour camerawork is the best thing in the film.

Phffft! ○
1954, US, 91 mins, b/w
Dir: Mark Robson
Stars: Judy Holliday, Jack Lemmon, Kim Novak, Jack Carson
Rating: ★★★

Columbia got much publicity mileage from the title of this (then) saucy comedy romp, one of a series of very bright comedies from the studio made throughout the Fifties and early Sixties, starring any or all of the formidable trio of Judy Holliday, Jack Lemmon and Kim Novak. All three are in this story of a marriage breaking apart (giving rise to the sound in the title). Add Jack Carson as Holliday's new beau and a sparkling script by George Axelrod, and you had the formula for a surefire laughter success.

Philadelphia ● ⓥ
1993, US, 122 mins, colour
Dir: Jonathan Demme
Stars: Tom Hanks, Denzel Washington, Mary Steenburgen, Jason Robards, Antonio Banderas, Joanne Woodward
Rating: ★★★

A real tear-jerker this, and professionally done, with a strong directorial focus on emotive performances from the leading actors. Gay lawyer Tom Hanks believes he has been sacked by his plush leather firm because they found out he has AIDS, and gets wheeler-dealer counsel Denzel Washington to bring suit against them. Director Jonathan Demme makes sure sympathies are not weighted too blatantly by making Washington a man who dislikes homosexuals, but whose love of the law impels him to take the case. Jason Robards and Mary Steenburgen (she going for the Anthony Hopkins school of understatement) get a chance to show their sharper side as the bigoted head of the law firm and his chief counsel – although one might question a man of Robards' perspicacity sacking Hanks when it's obvious from the time-span of the scenario that he would have had to resign in a matter of weeks. But the principle is the thing here; our support is solicited and indeed assured as Hanks – whose Oscar-winning performance rises to a carefully-choreographed crescendo when he describes his love of opera –

rivets our attention to his dying countenance. At heart, of course, it is a courtroom drama in which we are invited to root for the underdog – and do so.

Philadelphia Story, The ○ ⓥ
1940, US, 112 mins, b/w
Dir: George Cukor
Stars: Cary Grant, Katharine Hepburn, James Stewart
Rating: ★★★★

Pungently witty classic which was re-made 15 years later as *High Society*. The original is still the best. James Stewart scooped two Oscars for this superb piece of escapism. Stewart, then only 31, was acclaimed 1940's best actor for his performance as Mac. Donald Ogden Stewart deservedly took the writer's award for the best screenplay of the year. Katharine Hepburn, too, was nominated for an Academy Award (she lost it to Ginger Rogers in *Kitty Foyle*) in her role as Tracy Lord, the poor little rich girl dissatisfied with the men in her life. This film belongs in a now extinct highly-polished and sophisticated, light Hollywood comedy style in which a thin story was made to race along beautifully on the wings of excellent dialogue and excellent stars. These days Hollywood is still turning out comedies with featherweight scripts and acting talent to balance the scales. This breezy masterpiece with three big stars reminds us what we're missing.

Phobia ●
1980, US, 90 mins, colour
Dir: John Huston
Stars: Paul Michael Glaser, John Colicos, Susan Hogan
Rating: ★

John Huston playing with his audience within a whodunit framework as in *The List of Adrian Messenger*, although not as effectively. The plot isn't really believable, and takes too long unwinding to the (expected) unexpected ending. But Huston's enjoyable professional juggling of his narrative just about keeps you watching to find out just how unlikely the ending is going to be.

Physical Evidence ●
1988, US, 99 mins, colour
Dir: Michael Crichton
Stars: Burt Reynolds, Theresa Russell, Ned Beatty, Kay Lenz
Rating: ★★

The latter half of the 1980s wasn't a particularly good time for Burt Reynolds. He increasingly found himself in tough cop roles, most of which weren't very good. This film, in which Burt plays an ex-cop accused of murder, is better than most. Even so, the film is rather slow and disjointed and doesn't come across as very credible, although Burt turns in a creditable performance, given the run-of-the-mill script. Theresa Russell, not convincingly prim and efficient, is badly miscast as his lawyer – she's much more fun when she's bad. A lady lawyer defends a discredited cop on a murder charge? Sounds familiar and it is, just like the film, routine and truly average right down the line. There's a bit of action and some decent stalking through city streets, with Toronto standing in for the States, but all concerned, especially director Michael Crichton, should have done better.

Piano, The ● ⓥ
1993, New Zealand/UK/US, 120 mins, colour
Dir: Jane Campion
Stars: Holly Hunter, Sam Neill, Harvey Keitel, Anna Paquin
Rating: ★★★

An unusual erotic drama with some striking visual moments (but rather too little story and dramatic movement) about a strong-willed but mute Scottish widow (Holly Hunter) who travels to 19th century New Zealand to fulfil an arranged marriage with a landowner (Sam Neill). He refuses to bring her beloved piano up from the beach and it falls into the hands of Baines (Harvey Keitel), his construction manager who has 'gone native'. Neill proves a cold husband who can't bring himself to touch his wife while Keitel can't wait to get his hands on her, exacting progressive sexual favours in return for her earning back the piano key by key. All this is pretty weird and only marginally convincing, especially with Keitel attempting an all-purpose Limey accent to cope with dialogue that, like most of the rest, sounds fascinating but not like things people would actually say. After a slow start, the film picks up and unreels like a silent drama, producing some stunning images towards the end when the murky Eastman Color process work will allow. Oscar-winning Hunter is wonderfully expressive and does her own piano playing, which is just fine. Sexually direct, the film has

P

some very explicit scenes. Young Anna Paquin, as Hunter's daughter, also received an Oscar.

Piccadilly Jim ○
1936, US, 100 mins, b/w
Dir: Robert Z Leonard
Stars: Robert Montgomery, Frank Morgan, Madge Evans, Billie Burke
Rating: ★★★

P G Wodehouse's book filmed as elegantly as only MGM knew how. Robert Montgomery and Madge Evans provide the appropriate light comedy touch, while Frank Morgan and Billie Burke bumble and dither in the expected manner. But the film is stolen from all of them by Eric Blore as Bayliss the butler who seems mercifully for the slightly overlength screenplay to be everywhere at once.

Piccadilly Third Stop ○
1960, UK, 90 mins, b/w
Dir: Wolf Rilla
Stars: Terence Morgan, Yoko Tani, Mai Zetterling, Dennis Price
Rating: ★★

No one can accuse Leigh Vance's screenplay of being devoid of incident, including as it does theft, blackmail, smuggling and adultery. It's all directed with pace and polish by Wolf Rilla, and the climactic chase in the underground sizzles with excitement. The cast, too, is not without interest and there's some good support from Mai Zetterling, Yoko Tani and, in particular, William Hartnell, who gives one of his excellent portrayals of smarmy villainy.

Pickup Alley
See: Interpol

Pick-Up Artist, The ○ ⓥ
1987, US, 79 mins, colour
Dir: James Toback
Stars: Molly Ringwald, Robert Downey, Dennis Hopper, Harvey Keitel
Rating: ★

Molly Ringwald, who was *Pretty in Pink*, proves pesky in purple in this dialogue-heavy romantic comedy. Robert Downey (who moved on to grander things five years later with *Chaplin*) is the girl-chaser who is more than somewhat surprised when his seasoned approaches are so successful with Ringwald that she jumps him as soon as his car has ground to a halt. Unfortunately, Downey has leapt straight into bed with a nest of vipers, as her alcoholic father (it has to be

Dennis Hopper and it is) is heavily in debt to a cabal of dangerous gamblers led by a scowling Harvey Keitel. The odds are that you won't care how the plot's confusions sort themselves out, since the script never touches the right emotions. Hopper does his familiar wild-eyed, unshaven act and veteran Mildren Dunnock crops up in a rare role as Downey's diabetic gran. But neither gets a chance to extend their character beyond the one-dimensional. Despite its short running time, the film contrives to cram 12 songs on to its inevitable pop soundtrack.

Pickwick Papers, The ○
1952, UK, 115 mins, b/w
Dir: Noel Langley
Stars: James Hayter, James Donald, Alexander Gauge,
Rating: ★★★

Director Noel Langley scripted this effective adaptation of Charles Dickens' comic novel and filled it with plenty of entertaining incident. He filled it, too, with an excellent cast headed by James Hayter as a splendidly jovial Pickwick. Lively playing all round, especially from Nigel Patrick and Donald Wolfit.

Picnic ○
1955, US, 113 mins, colour
Dir: Joshua Logan
Stars: William Holden, Kim Novak
Rating: ★★★

Superb colour photography by James Wong Howe and splendid acting highlight this striking and unusual film, which is something between a comedy-drama and a love story. Full marks to the writer, Daniel Taradash (adapting William Inge's play to the screen), and congratulations to the players, particularly Rosalind Russell as the town's spinster teacher and William Holden as the drifter who sets everyone's emotions on edge. Also good though are Kim Novak, Susan Strasberg and Cliff Robertson. The ending may take you (happily) by surprise, and even the music (notably the 'Moonglow' theme) is great in this memorable and delightful film.

Picnic at Hanging Rock ⓓ
1975, Australia, 110 mins, colour
Dir: Peter Weir
Stars: Rachel Roberts, Dominic Guard, Helen Morse
Rating: ★★★

After a rather ordinary beginning, in which events are somewhat overtly staged, this richly-textured piece develops into a haunting, extremely good ghost-horror story played out in broad daylight. A group of Australian schoolgirls and teachers in 1900 go for a picnic to the towering, primeval Hanging Rock deep in the desert – an excursion from which three of them are never to return. It's only after things start to happen, which is rather a long time, that Weir's film really hits its stride, with the director always keeping the explanation of the horrors tantalisingly out of reach. It was certainly the best film from Down Under for some time, and gave the native industry a deserved boost.

Picture Mommy Dead ⓓ
1966, US, 88 mins, colour
Dir: Bert I Gordon
Stars: Don Ameche, Martha Hyer, Susan Gordon
Rating: ★★

Fascinating cast-from-the-past (it also includes Wendell Corey, Zsa Zsa Gabor, Maxwell Reed and Signe Hasso) in a lurid shocker only weakened by the central casting of Susan Gordon as the young girl still suffering from hallucinations in dead mummy's mansion. Superb Pathecolor photography makes the most of shocks.

Picture of Dorian Gray, The ○
1945, US, 110 mins, b/w & colour
Dir: Albert Lewin
Stars: George Sanders, Hurd Hatfield, Donna Reed, Angela Lansbury
Rating: ★★★

Elaborately produced version of Oscar Wilde's famous story of the bizarre, elegantly shot in black and white, with a startling burst into vivid Technicolor at the climax. Harry Stradling won the Oscar for his cinematography. Hurd Hatfield made a tremendous impression in this, being admirably suited to his role as the coldly sardonic Victorian gentleman whose portrait in the attic grows hideous with age and sin while he himself alters not a whit. Hatfield's subsequent film career, however, was less successful.

Picture Snatcher ⓓ
1933, US, 73 mins, b/w
Dir: Lloyd Bacon
Stars: James Cagney, Ralph Bellamy, Patricia Ellis
Rating: ★★

James Cagney is perpetual motion in this typically fast-paced Warners action film based rather uneasily on real-life events. His occupation – snapping sensational pictures of unsavoury events – paralleled the real-life activities of a New York Daily News photographer who captured a death-cell execution on film. Two well-rehearsed fight sequences that went wrong left Alice White (at the hands of Cagney) and Cagney himself (at the hands of Ralph Bellamy) nursing sore jaws. 'I sure was sorry,' said Cagney of the White accident, 'to hit that cute little kisser.'

Pied Piper, The ○
1942, US, 86 mins, b/w
Dir: Irving Pichel
Stars: Monty Woolley, Roddy McDowall, Peggy Ann Garner
Rating: ★★★

A winning Hollywood version of Nevil Shute's novel, which provides a tailor-made role for Monty Woolley as the child-hating Englishman forced to shepherd a handful of kids through occupied France during the Nazi occupation. The film catches the story's delicately tender feel and holds it well. Suspense is built-in, but the movie also has warmth and jollity – and keeps strictly within the fragile mood it creates. Roddy McDowall and Peggy Ann Garner head the youngsters.

Pied Piper, The ○
1972, UK, 90 mins, colour
Dir: Jacques Demy
Stars: Donovan, Donald Pleasence, Jack Wild
Rating: ★★★

The title character of this quaint musical fantasy, based on Browning's famous poem and set in 14th-century Germany, gave popular folk singer Donovan his only film role. Frenchman Jacques Demy directed, bringing a picture-book prettiness to the olde-worlde settings.

Pigeon That Took Rome, The ○
1962, US, 101 mins, b/w
Dir: Melville Shavelson
Stars: Charlton Heston, Elsa Martinelli
Rating: ★★

Charlton Heston got a chance to break away from his 'Mr Epic' image, and exercise his considerable talent for light-comedy in this amiable romp about two American agents getting

messages out of wartime Italy by pigeon post. Plump Italian comedy actor Salvatore Baccaloni adds to the fun.

Pigskin Parade ○
1936, US, 93 mins, b/w
Dir: David Butler
Stars: Stuart Erwin, Patsy Kelly, Jack Haley, Betty Grable, Judy Garland
Rating: ★★★

Judy Garland fans will really appreciate this rarely-seen college football musical. It was the 14-year-old Judy's feature film debut (three years before 1939's *The Wizard of Oz*). She's billed ninth down the cast, playing the kid sister of hunky young quarterback Amos Dodd (Stuart Erwin, Oscar-nominated for his performance), who, based on his reputation for hurling melons, leads a Texan hillbilly team invited to play against Yale up in snooty New England. It's all jolly college stuff and you can forget the plot and concentrate on an interesting cast: the snappy Patsy Kelly as the coach's wife, cheery Jack Haley as the coach (he would go on to be the Tin Man in *Wizard*), Betty Grable (the million-dollar legs had not yet reached the top rung of stardom) and, would you believe, toughie Alan Ladd as a student, singing with The Yacht Club Boys! There are some nice songs that actually have something to do with the story: 'You Do the Darndest Things', 'Baby', 'Down With Everything', and 'Woo! Woo!' among them. The pigskin, of course, refers to the football itself.

Pilgrim, The ○
1922, US, 48 mins, b/w
Dir: Charles Chaplin
Stars: Charlie Chaplin, Edna Purviance, Mack Swain
Rating: ★★★

Charlie Chaplin's films, once so plentiful, were beginning to become few and far between in comparison by the time *The Pilgrim* came out in January 1923, five months after its completion. It opens in similar style to *The Adventurer*, with Chaplin as a convict on the run, and ends with the classic image of the fugitive with a foot in each country, an ironic pointer to the wanderer he would later become.

Pillow Talk ○ ⓥ
1959, US, 100 mins, colour
Dir: Michael Gordon
Stars: Doris Day, Rock Hudson
Rating: ★★★

Doris Day and Rock Hudson's first comedy together, this battle-of-the-sexes romp was one of the box-office blockbusters of its day and was followed by more Day/Hudson pairings, such as the hilarious *Lover Come Back* (1961) and the black comedy *Send Me No Flowers* (1964). The film marked quite a change of style for director Michael Gordon, who was then better known for well-made thrillers and such meaty dramas as *An Act of Murder*. It also enabled Day to lose a little of her virginal girl-next-door image and Hudson to prove that he was more than just a handsome hunk. Directed with verve, it's dotty, witty and highly entertaining. Writers Stanley Shapiro and Maurice Richlin won that year's Oscar for Best Screenplay, and the film's Oscar nominations included Best Actress, Best Supporting Actress (for Thelma Ritter as Day's cynical maid, Alma), Best Art Direction and Best Music.

Pimpernel Smith ○
1941, UK, 121 mins, b/w
Dir: Leslie Howard
Stars: Leslie Howard, Francis L Sullivan, Mary Morris
Rating: ★★★

Known in America as *Mister V*, which rather defeated the object of the exercise, this was an updating of Baroness Orczy's French Revolution hero to World War Two. Leslie Howard (who had starred in the original version of *The Scarlet Pimpernel* seven years earlier) directed and also gave one of his best-ever performances as the archaeology professor helping Jewish refugees escape from Hitler in the period just before the outbreak of war.

Pink Panther, The ○ ⓥ
1963, US, 113 mins, colour
Dir: Blake Edwards
Stars: David Niven, Peter Sellers, Claudia Cardinale, Robert Wagner
Rating: ★★★

Gay, warm and amusing comedie-desriches that introduced the bungling French detective Clouseau, as personified by Peter Sellers. Everything Clouseau touches turns to dust. He can't even get his wife sleeping pills without spilling them all over the floor. The screen is filled with his wife's disgusted expression, and the sound of crunching as Clouseau treads a bedward path. Naturally, when such a man comes to grips with a master criminal known as The Phantom, it's

P

long odds on him coming to grief, and on our doubling up with mirth watching him. After a while, of course, one knows what is going to happen. It becomes no longer necessary to show Sellers falling to the floor, dropping things, or draping a blanket over his head while trying to put it on the bed. A noise, a crash, a clatter, together with the lugubrious face of Sellers, is sufficient to convince us that disaster has struck again. He even finds time for a Goon-style joke or two: 'They have stolen my Surete-type overcoat' or (in a suit of armour) 'Gad, it's hell in here.' Not that the visual gags are lost as, when Sellers accidentally brings the thieves to book, he tells them in their cell: 'You'll get 20 years for this,' firmly planting his hands in their bowls of porridge.

Pink Panther Strikes Again, The ○ ⓥ
1976, UK, 103 mins, colour
Dir: Blake Edwards
Stars: Peter Sellers, Herbert Lom, Leonard Rossiter, Lesley-Anne Down
Rating: ★★

Sellers' bungling Inspector Clouseau encounters (as he would put it) more hurmps and burmps, plus Herbert Lom's marvellous ex-Inspector Dreyfuss, who has escaped from his asylum and laid hands on a doomsday machine with which he threatens to extinguish the whole world unless it gives him Clouseau. Brilliantly inventive titles by Richard Williams Animation are followed by the usual spasmodically funny Sellers shenanigans, with the peripheral characters coming off better as laughter-raisers than Clouseau himself. Particularly good is a running joke about then-President Ford falling over things, plus Lom's relishable pop-eyed maniac who sets up his new headquarters in a Dracula-style castle. Omar Sharif and Robert Beatty make unbilled cameo appearances and Lesley-Anne Down is a suitably glamorous Russian spy.

Pink String and Sealing Wax ○
1945, UK, 89 mins, b/w
Dir: Robert Hamer
Stars: Googie Withers, John Carol, Mervyn Johns, Gordon Jackson
Rating: ★★★

Love, murder and blackmail are the ingredients of this classic British thriller, one of several fine films directed by Robert Hamer at Ealing Studios in the mid-Forties. Others were *Kind Hearts and Coronets*, *Dead of Night* and *It Always Rains on Sunday*. Here he has Googie Withers (Britain had no one better at being bad) as the evil-hearted landlady of a seaside pub, who blackens all the lives she touches. A young Gordon Jackson has a co-starring role.

Pinocchio ⊙
1940, US, 88 mins, colour
Dir: Ben Sharpsteen, Hamilton Luske
Rating: ★★★★

Still perhaps Disney's best single-story cartoon, this tale of a little wooden boy is vividly related and crammed with adventures (some a little frightening for the very young). Memorable characters abound: Geppetto the woodcarver; Jimmy Cricket; Figaro and Cleo (a cat and a goldfish); and the villains J Worthington Foulfellow (a fox), Gideon (an alleycat), Stromboli the showman, and the terrifying coachman. Teeming with detail, it even had an Oscar-winning song: 'When You Wish Upon A Star'.

Pin Up Girl ○ ⓥ
1944, US, 85 mins, colour
Dir: Bruce Humberstone
Stars: Betty Grable, John Harvey, Martha Raye, Joe E Brown
Rating: ★★

A pretty obvious title for a pretty obvious Betty Grable wartime vehicle which makes up in zest and high spirits for what it lacks in the way of plot. Martha Raye and Joe E Brown provide the comedy, Hermes Pan provides some lively choreography. The flag-waving finale seems to go on forever.

P.I. Private Investigations ○
1987, US, 91 mins, colour
Dir: Nigel Dick
Stars: Clayton Rohner, Talia Balsam
Rating: ★★★

Writer-director Nigel Dick came to fame with a string of pop videos, famously 'Do They Know It's Christmas'. Here he's come up with a cheerful, love-and-bullets caper that rushes forward at a tremendous pace. It's from the 'Yuppie-almost-gets-it-but-learns-to-be-a-regular-guy-in-time' school of movies but is packed with zest. There are nice performances from newcomers Clayton Rohner and Talia Balsam (daughter of Martin, who also appears).

Piranha ●
1978, US, 92 mins, colour
Dir: Joe Dante
Stars: Bradford Dillman, Heather Menzies, Kevin McCarthy
Rating: ★★★

Swimming in on the tail of *Jaws*, but with teeth firmly in cheek, this is both an enjoyable story in its own right and an amusing take-off of fishy disaster stories. The horrific parts are all very well done, and the dialogue often scores too. Our favourite line: 'But sir, they're eating the guests.'

Pirates ◑
1986, France, 124 mins, colour
Dir: Roman Polanski
Stars: Walter Matthau, Cris Campion
Rating: ★★

Pirate adventures, are, by their very nature, over the top, so it's pretty difficult to overplay your hand when making one. Roman Polanski managed it, though, in this colourful buccaneering romp. Walter Matthau is notorious sea-dog Captain Red, cast adrift on a raft with only a treasure chest and 'The Frog' (Cris Campion) for company. They are rescued when a Spanish ship picks them up, but the treasure is lost in the rescue. Still, never mind, there's a priceless golden Inca throne on board, but how can the wily Captain steal it? Matthau obviously enjoyed himself as Captain Red, but all the other players seem merely caricatures. Nevertheless, it's an enjoyable, if occasionally vulgar yarn. It's not in the same class as Burt Lancaster's *The Crimson Pirate* as a pirate parody, but it's good lightweight fun. Keep your eyes peeled for Michael Elphick and rock singer Ian Dury in small roles.

Pirates of Blood River, The ○
1961, UK, 87 mins, colour
Dir: John Gilling
Stars: Kerwin Mathews, Glenn Corbett
Rating: ★★

An interesting attempt by Hammer films in the early Sixties to widen their range beyond the horror film. In this story of piracy in the Caribbean, they tried, with considerable success, to match the pace and technical standards of the best Hollywood action films. Although two American stars were imported to boost the film's chances in the US, all the acting quality comes from Christopher Lee and Oliver Reed, who have a high old time as two really villainous buccaneers. And, as a young boy, you may also spot Dennis Waterman, who played *Just William* in the television series, and later achieved adult stardom in *The Sweeney* and *Minder*.

Pirates of Tortuga ○
1961, US, 97 mins, colour
Dir: Robert D Webb
Stars: Ken Scott, Leticia Roman, Dave King, John Richardson
Rating: ★★

Two Britons – comedian Dave King, and husky John Richardson – share the fencing honours with American hero Ken Scott, in this sparky pirate thriller. Another British actor, Robert Stephens, turns up as the famous buccaneer, Sir Henry Morgan. Action abounds, and it's a sure bet to keep the children quiet if it's a wet day.

Pirates of Tripoli ○
1955, US, 72 mins, colour
Dir: Felix Feist
Stars: Paul Henreid, Patricia Medina
Rating: ★★

A bright and lively swashbuckler. Henry Freulich's admirable Technicolor photography is effective particularly in an exciting naval battle scene. Paul Henreid maintains the immobile expression he also used for such trifles as *Thief of Damascus*, *Siren of Baghdad* and *Last of the Buccaneers*, but Patricia Medina (in real life married to Joseph Cotten) is given the opportunity to show both spirit and a handsome wardrobe.

Pistolero of Red River, The ○
1967, US, 90 mins, colour
Dir: Richard Thorpe
Stars: Glenn Ford, Angie Dickinson, Chad Everett, Gary Merrill
Rating: ★★

One more time for one of the oldest Western stories in the book: it's the yarn about the young gunslinger who has to prove himself against the older man. But a good cast all turn in fine performances, and veteran director Richard Thorpe brings it in with a fresh lick of paint, and just a suspicion of a surprise about the ending. Glenn Ford endows the lawman with an air of rugged authority; there's a peach of a performance from Jack Elam, as a hired, but tired assassin who just isn't quite good enough; and you may spot

blond British actress Delphi Lawrence, once prominent in crime thrillers made in this country in the Fifties.

Pit and the Pendulum, The ● Ⓥ
1961, US, 82 mins, colour
Dir: Roger Corman
Stars: Vincent Price, John Kerr, Barbara Steele
Rating: ★★★

Directed by Roger Corman, master of the cut-price horror saga, this chiller is more Price than Poe, but our Vincent is in great form showing off his Spanish Inquisition torture chamber – 'This room was my father's life . . .' Barbara Steele is in typically fierce form, proving an ideal foil for Price's very slightly tongue-in-cheek performance and the sets are wonderful. Pretty spooky too, as its characters creep along cobwebbed corridors clutching flickering candles, and, with stunning shock moments, this is altogether the best of the earlier Corman horror films made in America.

Pitfall ○
1948, US, 85 mins, b/w
Dir: Andre De Toth
Stars: Dick Powell, Lizabeth Scott, Raymond Burr, Jane Wyatt
Rating: ★★★

More than just a thriller, *Pitfall* is also a far-seeing film in that it takes an early look at a man's disillusionment with the American dream of secure job, home and family, none of which prevent insurance agent Dick Powell from falling into the clutches of predatory Lizabeth Scott and a world of violence, suspicion and death. An exciting film that also makes you think.

Pit of Darkness ○
1961, UK, 76 mins, b/w
Dir: Lance Comfort
Stars: William Franklyn, Moira Redmond
Rating: ★★★

William Franklyn had one of his best film roles (as an amnesia victim) in this black little thriller. You'll recognise many of the supporting cast, including Anthony Booth, later a regular in *Till Death Us Do Part*, Nanette Newman in a rare bad-girl role, Nigel Green, Leonard Sachs (the ebullient chairman of *The Good Old Days*) and veteran actor John Stuart.

Pittsburgh ○
1942, US, 90 mins, colour
Dir: Lewis Seiler

Stars: Marlene Dietrich, Randolph Scott, John Wayne
Rating: ★★★

This lusty mixture of romance and melodrama, seasoned with flag waving World War Two propaganda, reunited the stars of the same year's *The Spoilers* and once again found John Wayne and Randolph Scott as rivals for the favours of Marlene Dietrich. Scott may get the girl but Wayne has the more substantial role and does well as a man who is ready to ride roughshod over everyone to get to the top but finally comes to see the folly of his ways. The director, Lewis Seiler, stages some vigorous action scenes but tends to take much of the film at rather too sedate a pace. The stars, however, carry all before them.

P J
See: *New Face in Hell*

Place in the Sun, A ○
1951, US, 122 mins, b/w
Dir: George Stevens
Stars: Montgomery Clift, Elizabeth Taylor, Shelley Winters
Rating: ★★★

A powerful version of Theodore Dreiser's story *An American Tragedy*, filmed 20 years previously under its original title in a now-forgotten version. Director George Stevens made sure his would be the film everyone would remember, by getting vivid performances from a cast headed by Montgomery Clift as the poor-born young man anxious to climb the social ladder. The film was made in the same year (1951) as *A Streetcar Named Desire* and *An American in Paris*, and there was hot competition for Oscars. But it came away with six, including one for Stevens as best director. It hasn't worn too well by today's standards, but isolated moments still catch the breath.

Place of One's Own, A ○
1945, UK, 92 mins, b/w
Dir: Bernard Knowles
Stars: Margaret Lockwood, James Mason, Barbara Mullen, Dennis Price
Rating: ★★★

'A fine piece of work . . . gripping, marvellous, outstanding, eerie, perky, beautiful, lovely and different.' Thus was how the film was described on its first appearance by no less a critic than C A Lejeune. It's an elegant ghost story that will raise the hackles on your neck, but without any of today's

P

obligatory trimmings of sex and gore. James Mason is first-rate in the leading role.

Places in the Heart ◐ ⓥ

1984, US, 111 mins, colour
Dir: Robert Benton
Stars: Sally Field, Lindsay Crouse, Ed Harris, John Malkovich, Danny Glover
Rating: ★★

Nice to see Sally Field in her best form, in this rather meandering rural drama, set in 1935 Texas, which won her a second Oscar. She's a widow who has somehow to fend for herself and ward off the bank whose first thought is to foreclose on the mortgage. With a few companions – the black handyman who she saves from the law when he steals from her, the sister whose husband is having an affair with his best friend's wife, the blind man foisted on her by his conniving banker relative – she plants fields of cotton and scrapes up a living while learning the hard facts of commercial life through the black man's seasoned eyes. All these elements are entertaining in themselves, as is the tornado scene in their midst, but they never quite pull together. And the ending, though 'different', just doesn't work: the structure of the film demands a big emotional climax which it doesn't get. Also, the film walks a tightrope between sentiment and common sense from which it frequently falls. Writer-director Robert Benton has failed to give his material, however affectionately or rationally observed, the vital emotional surge to reach out to a general audience – even with the admirable Field at the head, and a sturdy supporting cast that includes Lindsay Crouse, Terry O'Quinn, John Malkovich, Ed Harris, Amy Madigan and Danny Glover.

Plague Dogs, The ◐

1982, US, 103 mins, colour
Dir: Martin Rosen
Voice stars: John Hurt, James Bolam, Judy Geeson
Rating: ★★★

Don't expect a cheerful or light-hearted time from this animated feature. It's a good but gloomy story with a real tear-jerker ending (changed from the one in Richard Adams' book) that will leave you needing a bucket to cry in. The central characters are two dogs who, neither of them fully fit in mind and body, escape from a horrendous experimental station in England's Lake

District. But the film is entirely stolen, probably at the intention of the film-makers, by The Tod, the fell-wise fox they meet out on the moors. The dogs have scant regard for the self-serving fox, yet he twice saves their hides and finally . . . but that would be telling. Suffice to say that, in a world where, in contrast to Disney, total realism is demanded of the animations, The Tod survives such a personality draining approach to become a definitive character in his own right. Like the film, which is a little slow and could benefit from trimming, he worms his way into your affections. Not suitable for younger children.

Plague of the Zombies, The ● ⓥ

1966, UK, 91 mins, colour
Dir: John Gilling
Stars: Andre Morell, John Carson, Diane Clare, Jacqueline Pearce
Rating: ★★★

An enjoyable Hammer horror film for late night fiends. It strives to be a little different and shows some original thought in Peter Bryan's screenplay, which has some interesting new ideas. There's one excellent nightmare sequence when the dead rise from their graves and for comic relief, the irreplacable Michael Ripper as the village policeman. 'It doesn't need me to tell you,' huffs Ripper at the start of the mayhem (you can almost see his hands on his braces), 'that there's something strange going on in the village.' Later he asks the hero, in hushed tones: 'In Heaven's name, where are they?' after all the graves in the local churchyard are found to be empty. Chief assets of the suspense are André Morell's very human, strong and identifiable sexagenarian hero, and John Carson's villainous squire, with a James Mason voice full of silky menace. Jacqueline Pearce is also good as the dying girl who turns into one of the zombies of the title.

Plainsman, The ○

1936, US, 92 mins, b/w
Dir: Cecil B DeMille
Stars: Gary Cooper, Jean Arthur, James Ellison
Rating: ★★★

As big as you would expect a Western from Cecil B DeMille to be, *The Plainsman's* spectacle is balanced by the astringent, off-beat relationship between Gary Cooper, playing Wild Bill Hickok, and the delightfully

squeaky-voiced Jean Arthur as Calamity Jane. The supporting cast includes those stalwart Western 'sidekicks' of the Forties and Fifties, George 'Gabby' Hayes and Fuzzy Knight, and you'll also spot Anthony Quinn as a Cheyenne Indian. Lots of action, too.

Plan 9 from Outer Space ◐

1958, US, 79 mins, b/w
Dir: Edward D Wood Jr
Stars: Bela Lugosi, Tor Johnson, Vampira, Lyle Talbot
Rating: RB

This ultra-cheap, ultra-ridiculous science-fiction 'shocker' won a nationwide poll in America as the worst film of all time. A bold claim you may think: but then you haven't seen the paper plates which stand in for flying saucers; or the director's wife's friend who stood in for star Bela Lugosi who died after three days of shooting; or heard director Edward D Wood's unique screenplay. Probably funniest of all is the commentator who asks the audience at the end: 'My friends, you have seen this incident based on sworn testimony. Can you prove it didn't happen?' No answers, please.

Planes, Trains and Automobiles ◐ ⓥ

1987, US, 92 mins, colour
Dir: John Hughes
Stars: Steve Martin, John Candy, Michael McKean
Rating: ★★★

A rollercoaster ride of accidents and disasters. Frazzled ad executive Steve Martin finds he's stuck with slobby salesman John Candy when his flight is cancelled and he tries to get home to his family in time for Christmas. An outrageously funny film in which Martin is the straight man to Candy's loudmouthed and uncouth buffoon. Whatever can go wrong, does, and the film is a catalogue of comic chaos. Martin is marvellous and Candy also very funny (and, at the end, quite touching) in what is arguably his best film to that time. Nice ending too.

Planet of the Apes ○ ⓥ

1967, US, 112 mins, colour
Dir: Franklin J Schaffner
Stars: Charlton Heston, Roddy McDowall, Kim Hunter
Rating: ★★★

Although its impact has perhaps been lessened by four sequels, *Planet of the*

Apes was at the time of its release regarded as the most outstanding science-fiction film in years. Its director, Franklin Schaffner, had already caught critical attention with such films as *The Best Man* and *The War Lord*. Here he succeeded in making a powerful allegory out of a book which even original author Pierre Boulle had thought unfilmable. Leon Shamroy, a veteran cinematographer who had won three Oscars, assisted him greatly, taking his cameras on location to desolate areas of Utah and Arizona to create superbly the cold, unfriendly, barren atmosphere of the planet on which Charlton Heston and his doomed fellow space-travellers crash-land at the beginning.

Planter's Wife, The ○
(aka: Outpost in Malaya)
1952, UK, 91 mins, b/w
Dir: Ken Annakin
Stars: Claudette Colbert, Jack Hawkins, Anthony Steel
Rating: ★★

Unusual drama about a plantation owner and his wife in Malaya of the early Fifties, facing up to the probability of a terrorist attack on their home. Although the plot lacks dramatic cohesion, the treacherous jungle atmosphere is well conjured up. Jack Hawkins is forthright and virile as the planter and Claudette Colbert competent as his wavering wife, while Ram Gopal's native servant is a skilfully drawn portrait.

Platinum Blonde ○
1931, US, 92 mins, b/w
Dir: Frank Capra
Stars: Loretta Young, Robert Williams, Jean Harlow, Reginald Owen
Rating: ★★★

Director Frank Capra's comedy about a culture clash between newspapers and high society. Loretta Young is top-billed but, as one contemporary critic put it 'runs third on footage', leaving the show to be stolen by Jean Harlow, as the 'blonde' of the title, and Robert Williams, whose bumbling, laconic personality is well-suited to the reporter who marries in haste and repents at (too much) leisure. Both Harlow and Williams were destined to die tragically young. The screenplay creates lots of likeable characters, and bluff character star Halliwell Hobbes is delightful as a snooty butler, a role in which he tended to find himself type-cast.

Platoon ● ⓥ
1986, US, 120 mins, colour
Dir: Oliver Stone
Stars: Tom Berenger, Willem Dafoe, Charlie Sheen
Rating: ★★★

The first part of director Oliver Stone's planned Vietnam War trilogy – the second was the award-winning *Born on the Fourth of July*, starring Tom Cruise – is a bloody, brutal vision of the conflict as witnessed first hand by the ordinary foot soldiers, or 'grunts'. Forget all previous, blindly patriotic Hollywood Vietnam films such as John Wayne''s *The Green Berets*, this is the reality of the conflict with no-one shown as right or wrong. A stickler for accuracy, Stone – himself twice decorated in the conflict – put the actors through a punishing physical rehearsal period at the hands of a retired Army sergeant. It made a star out of Charlie Sheen, as the central figure through whose shell-shocked eyes we see the atrocities, and Stone cast him in his follow-up film *Wall Street*. Well down the cast you'll spot stars-in-waiting Johnny Depp and Kevin (brother of Matt) Dillon. It won Oscars for Best Picture and Best Director.

Playboys, The ◐ ⓥ
1992, US, 108 mins, colour
Dir: Gillies MacKinnon
Stars: Albert Finney, Aidan Quinn, Robin Wright, Milo O'Shea, Niamh Cusack
Rating: ★★

A drop o' the Oirish – old-fashioned style. Credit director Gillies MacKinnon for wanting to get away from a) the IRA and b) an avalanche of swearing in this tinker's tale of a nubile unmarried mum who falls for a travelling carnival man while the local police sergeant, who lusts after her, threatens to ensure everything ends in tragedy. Aidan Quinn's Irish accent passes muster as the carny; rather shakier on the old brogue are Robin Wright as the girl and Albert Finney as the ruddy-cheeked sergeant. Still at least they don't stick out like sore thumbs from an otherwise genuinely Irish cast, and their film is okay in a meandering, TV drama-ish sort of way. It has a real feel of country life, and appealing performances from Milo O'Shea as the chief of the travelling 'Playboys' and Niamh Cusack as Wright's sister.

Play Dirty ○
1968, UK, 115 mins, colour
Dir: Andre De Toth
Stars: Michael Caine, Nigel Davenport
Rating: ★★

Serviceable war adventure along the lines of *The Dirty Dozen*, with Michael Caine leading a unit of ex-convicts on an 'impossible' mission in World War Two North Africa. Strong performances from Nigel Green and Nigel Davenport in this rugged offering.

Player, The ● ⓥ
1992, US, 123 mins, colour
Dir: Robert Altman
Stars: Tim Robbins, Greta Scacchi, Fred Ward, Whoopi Goldberg, Richard E Grant, Peter Gallagher
Rating: ★★

Long, rambling, critically-applauded black comedy which, like most Robert Altman films, starts very well and has the enticing main setting of a Hollywood studio and its surrounds. When the film sticks to the plot, it's an intriguing little number in *noir* style, but interest gradually drains away and you may even get tired before the end of trying to spot all the 65 famous guest stars who flit in and out of the real scenario (only Patrick Swayze actually ended up on the cutting-room floor). Tim Robbins is a pretty irritating lead and the original offbeat casting of Chevy Chase might have worked better. Lots of amusing in-jokes about the Hollywood scene, but most of these will undoubtedly fly right over the head of the average viewer. There's a corker of a 65-minute thriller battling to get out here, but Altman smothers it in top-dressing before the end.

Playing for Time ◐
1980, US, 130 mins, colour
Dir: Daniel Mann
Stars: Vanessa Redgrave, Jane Alexander
Rating: ★★★

This grim but compelling true-life story of a woman's orchestra in Auschwitz, whose members played literally to keep themselves alive, was scripted by famous author Arthur Miller, who won a Pulitzer Prize for his fine play *Death of a Salesman*. Despite all the controversy which surrounded the selection of Vanessa Redgrave to play the central character, Jewish cabaret singer Fania Fenelon on whose memoirs the film is based, there was no dispute that her perfor-

P

mance was a remarkable one. And Jane Alexander's account of the orchestra's leader, a niece of the great composer Mahler, also attracted much praise. In a generally admirable cast, there is a forceful performance, too, from Shirley Knight as the Nazi in charge of the women. There is little doubt that *Playing for Time* emerged as one of the most striking and important TV movies of its year.

Play it Again, Sam ○ Ⓥ

1973, US, 86 mins, colour
Dir: Herbert Ross
Stars: Woody Allen, Diane Keaton, Tony Roberts, Jerry Lacy
Rating: ★★★★

This Woody Allen comedy, adapted from his stage hit but directed for once not by Woody but by Herbert Ross, is a very funny, very endearing film on Allen's recurring theme, lifelong failure. His wife has walked out and his two best friends Dick and Linda try to encourage him to score with somebody else. But Allan, nervous and weedy, is mostly at home watching old Bogart movies, and the only advice he heeds is from a fantasised Bogey, played to the hilt by Jerry Macy. 'Don't you cook anything but those frozen TV dinners?' asks Dick. 'Who cooks 'em?' replies a despondent Allen, 'I suck 'em.' When he does get to take a girl out, she's quickly snatched off him by a couple of ageing rockers. Allen staggers back to Dick and Linda, who can see he's been in a fight. 'I snapped my chin down on one guy's fist,' he explains, 'and hit the other one in the knee with my nose.' Falling for Linda only leads to another attack of nerves – about telling Dick. 'If you want me,' he tells Linda, as they go to do the deed, 'I'll be home on the floor, having an anxiety attack.' Telling the plot isn't likely to spoil your enjoyment of a film whose incidental touches – and they are numerous – mark it out as one of the most unusual as well as one of the funniest of its year. The ending restages *Casablanca* with great panache.

Play Misty for Me ● Ⓥ

1971, US, 100 mins, colour
Dir: Clint Eastwood
Stars: Clint Eastwood, Jessica Walter, Donna Mills
Rating: ★★★★

Hold tight to the edge of the armchair for as jumpy and chilling a thriller as there's been since *Psycho*. Indeed, there are many comparisons between

that film and Clint Eastwood's impressive directorial debut, although it would be unfair to the plot to go into detail. Eastwood the actor unselfishly hands the spotlight to Jessica Walter, an actress much underused by the cinema, who turns in a frightening, virtuoso performance as the unbalanced young girl who starts the chills rolling by ringing up disc jockey Eastwood insistently with her requests for 'Misty'. Eastwood's regular cameraman Bruce Surtees handles the night-time photography especially well, combining with the director to extract maximum impact from the spine-jolting scenes towards the end.

Plaza Suite ○

1971, US, 110 mins, colour
Dir: Arthur Hiller
Stars: Walter Matthau, Maureen Stapleton, Barbara Harris
Rating: ★★

That lovable grouch Walter Matthau and his famous lived-in face crop up not once but three times in this mildly amusing romp (from Neil Simon's play) with three different segments. He's very good (even though miscast) in the first episode, about a middle-aged wife (marvellous Maureen Stapleton) whose wisecracks hide her insecurities. 'Everyone cheats with their secretaries,' she chides Matthau. 'I expected something better from my husband.'

Please Sir! ○

1971, UK, 101 mins, colour
Dir: Mark Stewart
Stars: John Alderton, Deryck Guyler, Joan Sanderson
Rating: ★★

More warm-hearted high jinks at Fenn Street Secondary School, with John Alderton, Deryck Guyler and the unruly pupils of 5C. To one who thought the TV series of this title the funniest and most original show in years, this film version was more than welcome. The performances of Alderton, Guyler and Joan Sanderson are models of comic timing.

Please Turn Over ○

1959, UK, 87 mins, b/w
Dir: Gerald Thomas
Stars: Julia Lockwood, Ted Ray, Jean Kent, Lionel Jeffries
Rating: ★★

A kind of *Return to Peyton Place* – played for laughs, *Carry On* style. A young girl writes a book in which – so

her fellow-townspeople believe – their intimate secrets are exposed in scandal-sheet fashion. Fairfun.

Pleasure of His Company, The ○

1961, US, 114 mins, colour
Dir: George Seaton
Stars: Fred Astaire, Debbie Reynolds, Lilli Palmer, Tab Hunter
Rating: ★★★

Underrated comedy film which gives Fred Astaire full play for his dazzling dancing and sophisticated humour. Reminiscent of the British film *Quiet Wedding* with Astaire as the black sheep of the family, whose daughter (Debbie Reynolds) is about to get married. Astaire worked out his dance routines in collaboration with Hermes Pan, the dance director who masterminded almost all of his classic film dances of the Thirties with his most famous partner, Ginger Rogers. Not that the ladies in this witty comedy are forgotten. Ms Reynolds gets the chance to wear 30 different costumes.

Plenty ● Ⓥ

1985, UK, 124 mins, colour
Dir: Fred Schepisi
Stars: Meryl Streep, Charles Dance, Tracey Ullman, John Gielgud, Sting, Sam Neill
Rating: ★★★

This ambitious film, scripted by David Hare from his hit play, charts the growing social malaise in Britain in the years following World War Two. Meryl Streep gives a tour de force performance as the central character, a neurotic young woman who moves from idealism to frustration and madness in her passage through a succession of bleak political and personal events. Director Fred Schepisi, who reteamed with Streep for *A Cry in the Dark*, about the dingo baby case, here coaxed a dazzling if cold performance from her. Top marks too for another of her brilliant accent jobs. The rest of the (mostly British) cast are well up to their roles. All it lacks is passion.

Ploughman's Lunch, The ● Ⓥ

1983, UK, 100 mins, colour
Dir: Richard Eyre
Stars: Jonathan Pryce, Tim Curry, Rosemary Harris, Frank Finlay
Rating: ★★★

Hailed in some quarters as a *Room at the Top* for the Eighties, this renews the collaboration between writer Ian McEwan and director Richard Eyre who had earlier worked together on *The Imitation Game* for television. It features a stunning leading performance from Jonathan Pryce as the central character, a self-seeking, hardly laudable writer who is prepared if need be to rewrite history.

Pocketful of Miracles ○

1961, US, 130 mins, colour
Dir: Frank Capra
Stars: Glenn Ford, Bette Davis
Rating: ★★

Frank Capra's swansong was a re-working of his earlier *Lady for a Day*. Based on a Damon Runyon story, its gangsters, as always, talk tough but underneath are real pussycats. Helen Hayes was first choice to play 'Apple Annie', a drunken fruit salesperson who tries to convince her long lost daughter that she's a grand, moneyed lady, but she was on a State department tour of Russia, so Bette Davis stepped in. But the real star of the film is Peter Falk, stealing every scene he lurches through as 'Joy Boy', the chauffeur of a New York gangster. The role changed Falk's career, taking him away from the world of hoodlums and into the exalted ranks of film stardom.

Point Blank ● ⑰

1967, US, 92 mins, colour
Dir: John Boorman
Stars: Lee Marvin, Angie Dickinson, Keenan Wynn
Rating: ★★★

Fresh from his debut success, *Catch Us If You Can* starring pop group The Dave Clark Five, British director John Boorman was grabbed by Hollywood to direct two thrillers starring Lee Marvin, of which *Point Blank* was the first. In this first film, Boorman appears obsessed with vertical lines, with much of the film being shot through Venetian blinds, prison bars, concrete slats and metal grids. The picture opens with crook Marvin shot and left for dead in the deserted Alcatraz island prison. Just how he manages to swim ashore while injured – a feat that defeated the fit and active characters in Clint Eastwood's *Escape from Alcatraz* – is just one of the more bizarre plot twists that will either intrigue or leave you cold, although Boorman keeps it coming at a cracking pace.

Point Break ① ⑰

1991, US, 125 mins, colour
Dir: Kathryn Bigelow
Stars: Patrick Swayze, Keanu Reeves, Gary Busey, Lori Petty, John C McGinley
Rating: ★★

Full of philosophizing in between its action scenes, this is the surfers' guide to high crime. Four surfin' nuts spend their spare time robbing banks as the 'Ex-Presidents Gang', wearing Carter, Reagan, Johnson and Nixon masks. The reason? Says their leader Patrick Swayze, blue eyes misting over: 'It's about the human spirit . . . we show them that the human spirit is still alive.' But they never shoot anyone, and never go into the banks' vaults (and if you don't think these are clues to the denouement, you've not seen many highly-contrived thrillers). Enter sharp young FBI man Johnny Utah (Keanu Reeves), fresh off the shooting-range. He's hot on the trail, but sucked into the cool mysticism of the surfin' guru. 'If you want the ultimate,' Swayze tells him, 'you've got to pay the ultimate price.' (This is another clue). Best not to ask such questions as what Reeves is doing in the FBI with a gammy leg, or why he goes back to the beach when his cover is blown, or why Swayze chooses to go for the vault on his ultimate raid. Director Kathryn Bigelow patches over script and story deficiencies here by giving us action on land, sea and in the air, including the screen's first freefall fistfight!

Point of No Return

See: The Assassin

Poison Ivy ● ⑰

1992, US, 90 mins, colour
Dir: Katt Shea Rubin
Stars: Drew Barrymore, Tom Skerritt, Sara Gilbert, Cheryl Ladd
Rating: ★★

A polished, adult performance by Drew Barrymore as the poisonous Ivy – a sleazy, sexy teenager who wheedles her destructive way into the lives of lonely Cooper (*Roseanne*'s Sara Gilbert), Cooper's ailing mother (an uneasily cast Cheryl Ladd) and rich celluloid father – will be the main reason for watching this rather nasty thriller. Gilbert does well in her Bohemian misfit role, in a sometimes gripping tale of obsession, manipulation and murder, which would work better if its characters were more clearly fleshed out – and without the sledgehammer direction

of Katt Shea Ruben. Barrymore's quite a number in this one, though: the right role for this talented gal must be out there somewhere.

Police Academy ● ⑰

1984, US, 95 mins, colour
Dir: Hugh Wilson
Stars: Steve Guttenberg, Kim Cattrall, G W Bailey, Bubba Smith
Rating: ★★★

As a cross between *Animal House* and *Airplane!*, this comedy along *Carry on Copper* lines has one big advantage over most of its kind: it's funny. Especially good is George Gaynes as the vague, even slightly touched commandant of a police academy which receives more than its fair share of misfit recruits when a local lady mayor decides to abandon all restrictions on eligibility for joining the force. Director Hugh Wilson probably knows you could write the script and character developments for him, but that doesn't stop him doing the best he can with his material. His knack of getting the most out of characters and situations without ever going over the top makes for some very big laughs. You'll enjoy Bubba Smith as the tree-like black recruit who used to be a florist, G W Bailey as the sneering sergeant and of course the ever-beaming Steve Guttenberg at the centre of things. But Gaynes is the icing on this comic cake. Followed by five sequels, all markedly inferior to this.

Police Academy 2: Their First Assignment ○ ⑰

1985, US, 87 mins, colour
Dir: Jerry Paris
Stars: Steve Guttenberg, Colleen Camp
Rating: ★★

A predictable sequel to the first film in the series, with the accent on sight gags – a store manager has a cardboard cut-out of Clint Eastwood on show to deter robbers – and humour that stems from the characters established in the first film. Cheap-looking but very, very cheerful, the film also has some nice by-play in its script, especially between the laid-back police captain and his power-hungry lieutenant.

Police Academy 3: Back in Training ○ ⑰

1986, US, 82 mins, colour
Dir: Jerry Paris
Stars: Steve Guttenberg, Bubba Smith
Rating: ★★

P

Anyone who does not know what to expect when the motley band of misfits strap on their truncheons for another madcap adventure has been walking the Himalayas for the last six years. The team that makes the *Carry Ons* seem as subtle and sophisticated as Noel Coward are back again making the streets safe to walk. The jokes come as thick and fast, hit and miss as usual and it is all done in good spirit if not always in good taste. An improvement on *Police Academy II*, if not as good as the original.

Police Academy 4: Citizens on Patrol ○ Ⓥ

1987, US, 87 mins, colour
Dir: Jim Drake
Stars: Steve Guttenberg, Sharon Stone
Rating: ★

Predictable lunacy from the boys in blue of Washington Police Academy. The main failing of this, and in fact all five sequels, is that they neither expand upon nor exploit the characters established in the original. Instead, they offer more of the same Keystone Kops-style chaos which, while avoiding all Academy Awards for excellence, nevertheless managed, as a series, to take over a billion dollars at box offices worldwide. Steve Guttenberg's last appearance in the series, though the principal interest for Nineties' filmgoers is that new superstar Sharon Stone's in it too.

Police Academy 5: Assignment Miami Beach ○ Ⓥ

1988, US, 90 mins, colour
Dir: Alan Myerson
Stars: Bubba Smith, David Graf
Rating: ★

Without Steve Guttenberg, star of the four previous *Police Academy* movies, who had wisely decided that enough was enough, the charm level in this story of the blunderers in blue manages to fall even lower. Locating the action in Miami provides a pretty picture postcard setting, but a serious lack of decent script and plot substance means that the law and order goofballs have to rely more than ever on tasteless sight gags. One funny moment when someone's hat is set alight is about the highspot; other routines make The Three Stooges look like The Marx Brothers.

Police Academy 6: City Under Siege ◐ Ⓥ

1989, US, 83 mins, colour
Dir: Peter Bonerz

Stars: Bubba Smith, David Graf
Rating: ★

More law and disorder with the asinine antics of those Police Academy underachievers. And it's more of the same with this their sixth outing. Same situations, same gags – well you get the picture. The formula is looking decidedly tired now and you may find yourself nodding off, too. You might get a couple of laughs out of it, but none you haven't had before.

Pollyanna ⊙

1960, US, 134 mins, colour
Dir: David Swift
Stars: Hayley Mills, Richard Egan, Nancy Olson, Karl Malden, Adolphe Menjou
Rating: ★★★

Somewhere in a small American town that never was, we encounter Hayley Mills as one of the do-gooders of all time, melting hearts of stone and winning a special Oscar in this massive money-spinner from the Disney studio. David Swift's easy-going direction and well-written script coat the old-fashioned exercise with a lot of charm. Jane Wyman and Nancy Olson resolutely refuse to let Hayley's urchin appeal hog the limelight, dispensing laughter and tears with a practised grace. Despite the thick sugar coating, the story is at times very entertaining.

Poltergeist ● Ⓥ

1982, US, 114 mins, colour
Dir: Tobe Hooper
Stars: Craig T Nelson, JoBeth Williams, Heather O'Rourke, Beatrice Straight
Rating: ★★★★

If this film doesn't scare you, nothing ever will. Somewhere in the middle of a night of terror for a suburban American family, their cute little daughter seems to have been sucked into the TV, which has been left on by dozing (and dozy) Dad. This is only the beginning of the most sensational ghost story since *The Haunting*. If your nerves can stand the pounding director Tobe Hooper and producer/co-writer Steven Spielberg give them in the last hour of this, they're up to anything. And JoBeth Williams, as Mum, braving monsters, corpses, poltergeists and even the jaws of hell with shrieks of 'Take your hands off my babies!' will tear you right apart. The film is one superbly-engineered shock upon another; from writhing wraiths to gaping ghouls and sinister spectres,

the story is an orgy of horrific action that never lets up for a moment. Truly frightening, even if it ends with a delightful chilly smile. The moral: never leave your TV on at night.

Poltergeist II: The Other Side ● Ⓥ

1986, US, 86 mins, colour
Dir: Brian Gibson
Stars: JoBeth Williams, Craig T Nelson, Heather O'Rourke
Rating: ★★

A sequel was inevitable to Tobe Hooper's film about possession in suburbia, which scared up terrific box office takings. If you've seen that, you'll understand that it's just another of those nights for the Freeling family. So please be understanding when father is possessed by a caterpillar in his tequila, mother sees armies of 19th-century religious fanatics and daughter talks to her her dead granny on a toy phone. To the Freelings, it's just one of those Things – even if it is after their daughter. After all, they can simply enlist the aid of a passing Indian medicine man and battle it out with Satan's lot between the underground caverns of the dead and the jaws of hell. I mean, you'd do the same yourself. All the original cast are back in harness (which is always a good indicator of a sequel's potential) although Craig T Nelson, as Dad, unfortunately gets most screen time as a soppy drunk and ghoulie-spewing monster. The denouement is a bit of a let down, but the special effects and shocks up to that point are top-notch. Sadly it was the last film in the illustrious career of Indian actor Will Sampson, who made his debut as the towering silent giant in *One Flew Over the Cuckoo's Nest*.

Poltergeist III ● Ⓥ

1988, US, 97 mins, colour
Dir: Gary Sherman
Stars: Tom Skerritt, Nancy Allen, Heather O'Rourke, Zelda Rubinstein
Rating: ★★

This third entry in the popular and increasingly derivitive horror series carries a tribute to its young star, Heather O'Rourke, who died soon after filming was completed. When Craig T Nelson and JoBeth Williams (sensibly) called a halt to playing the exasperated parents of poltergeist-prone Carol Anne (O'Rourke) after episode two, the writers came up with the wheeze of sending her to plague the living daylights out of other relatives. And sure enough, as soon as she moves into the spanking new Chicago high-rise home of Nancy Allen and Tom Skerritt, mirrors crack, smoke follows her down corridors and she can hear noises in her bedroom – not to mention the ice in the swimming pool (one of the best of a bad, cheap group of special effects). Various friends and lovers get bumped off and there's a lot of mumbo-jumbo spouted by mystics and psychics, but director Gary Sherman has no interest in supplying any meaning or motivation for what occurs in his own screenplay. Disappointing.

Pony Express ○
1953, US, 101 mins, colour
Dir: Jerry Hopper
Stars: Charlton Heston, Rhonda Fleming, Jan Sterling, Forrest Tucker
Rating: ★★

Charlton Heston, in his pre-Moses days, sits massively in the saddle in this big-scale frontier Western as Buffalo Bill Cody. Vigorous performances from Heston, Forrest Tucker and Jan Sterling and a neat study in hawk-cruel villainy from mean-featured Henry Brandon. Sturdy action fare, only just short of the top class.

Pony Soldier ○
(aka: MacDonald of the Canadian Mounties)
1952, US, 82 mins, colour
Dir: Joseph M Newman
Stars: Tyrone Power, Cameron Mitchell, Thomas Gomez, Penny Edwards
Rating: ★★

Attractively photographed in pale but pretty Technicolor by Harry Jackson, this is a story of the early days of the Mounties and their relationships with the Indians. Penny Edwards, who spent many years languishing in Roy Rogers Westerns, is the heroine. Very minor stuff by Tyrone Power's standards.

Pool of London ○
1950, UK, 85 mins, b/w
Dir: Basil Dearden
Stars: Bonar Colleano, Susan Shaw, Earl Cameron
Rating: ★★★

Another of the thrillers – started by the success of *It Always Rains on Sunday* – that Ealing Studios made against natural backgrounds, in this case London's dockland. The theme of a friendship between black man and

white girl is boldly treated for the time (and honestly acted by Earl Cameron and Susan Shaw) and leads to a moving and suspenseful twist ending. Leslie Phillips has a featured role.

Poor Cow ●
1967, UK, 104 mins, colour
Dir: Kenneth Loach
Stars: Carol White, Terence Stamp, John Bindon, Kate Williams
Rating: ★★★

Director Kenneth Loach made his name with a series of socially committed plays for television, making his feature film debut with this production in the same style: aggressively realistic but with a soft centre that ultimately tends to diffuse the drama. *Poor Cow* – whose principal characters happily accept lying, thieving and sexual promiscuity as a way of survival – seems very much a period piece now, but a fascinating one, with a script (Loach and Nell Dunn, from Dunn's novel) and direction that veer between small-screen compromises and big-screen lyricism. What still holds the attention is Carol White's vital and beautifully conceived performance as the much put-upon heroine.

Poor Little Rich Girl ⊙
1936, US, 79 mins, b/w
Dir: Irving Cummings
Stars: Shirley Temple, Alice Faye, Jack Haley
Rating: ★★★★

Little Miss Hollywood, in one of her biggest successes, with such co-stars as Jack Haley (Tin Man in *The Wizard of Oz*) and Alice Faye and big production numbers. Shirley plays a millionaire's runaway daughter who teams up with two vaudevillians – giving her the chance to sing 'But Definitely', 'Oh My Goodness' and 'When I'm with You'. It was previously filmed with Mary Pickford in 1917!

Pope Must Die, The ◐ ⊙
(aka: The Pope Must Diet)
1991, UK, 97 mins, colour
Dir: Peter Richardson
Stars: Robbie Coltrane, Beverly D'Angelo, Herbert Lom, Peter Richardson
Rating: ★★

In all but name, another 'Comic Strip' film. The boys are on uneasy territory here, and there's an amateurish edge to their crude satire of Catholicism.

Except from this the 20-stone Robbie Coltrane who achieves pretty well the only real character in the film as the ex-mechanic priest who, through a clerical (!) error, finds himself elevated to the Papacy. The subsequent farce needed to carry a sharper cutting edge and a shade more seriousness to hit the mark. Lom plays a twitching Godfather to follow his twitching Dreyfuss in the *Pink Panther* films; like the other characters, he's drawn strictly in one dimension. There are a few funny lines – the TV commentator says, 'We're gonna see the Pope get buried live here on CNN' – but four-letter words, nudity and bloody violence make Coltrane's down-to-earth Pope seem positively at home in the Vatican by comparison. The film's cardinal sin is that it has something to offend most people, but not enough laughs to convert them to its cause.

Pope Must Diet, The
See: The Pope Must Die

Popeye ⊙
1980, US, 114 mins, colour
Dir: Robert Altman
Stars: Robin Williams, Shelley Duvall, Ray Walston
Rating: ★★

Out with the videotape, parents, for this is simple, spring-heeled fun for tiny tots, much along the lines of the famous cartoons. It's very well cast – Robin Williams looks and sounds like Popeye, Shelley Duvall is enchanting as Olive Oyl, Paul Dooley and Paul Smith are visually perfect as Wimpey and Bluto – but there are drawbacks for adults: the score is poor and there are dull patches, especially when Williams and Duvall sing two mawkish songs in a row. But the settings are charming and, although the film tends to substitute noise for pace, most children of six and under will love it. It's exuberant, ebullient and ingenuous enough to appeal to all tinies – and the young at heart.

Pork Chop Hill ○
1959, US, 97 mins, b/w
Dir: Lewis Milestone
Stars: Gregory Peck, Rip Torn, George Peppard, Harry Guardino
Rating: ★★★

Bitter story of the last days of the Korean War, brought to the screen with harrowing and uncompromising clarity by Lewis Milestone who directed *All Quiet on the Western Front*. That

P

film's tremendous success in 1930 had the effect of landing Milestone with war films – not, oddly enough, immediately after making it, but later in his career. *Pork Chop Hill* was his seventh essay in the field and to it Milestone brought his characteristic striving for realism. 'One scene alone must have cost twice as much as the actual combat,' he commented. 'Unlike war, Hollywood demands re-takes.' Gregory Peck leads a cast which includes a number of actors who at the time were in the early phases of their careers but who subsequently became very well known – among them George Peppard, Rip Torn, Robert Blake, Woody Strode, Harry Guardino and Martin Landau.

Porky's ● ⓥ

1982, US, 98 mins, colour
Dir: Bob Clark
Stars: Dan Monahan, Mark Herrier, Wyatt Knight, Roger Wilson
Rating: ★

A raucous, rowdy, bawdy college comedy with randy collegiates as its heroes and redneck night-clubbers as its villains. Although crude in its sentiments, dialogue and 'story' content (complete with the famous shower scene), it certainly isn't dull – thanks to the pacily-crafted direction of Bob Clark. A huge success at box-offices worldwide. Two inferior sequels with much the same cast followed.

Port Afrique ○

1956, UK, 91 mins, colour
Dir: Rudolph Mate
Stars: Pier Angeli, Phil Carey
Rating: ★★

An unusual role for the late Pier Angeli as a woman of mystery, in this modern-day adventure story set in Morocco. Partly made on location, partly in Britain, where Ms Angeli made one of her best-ever films, *The Angry Silence*. In the supporting cast here: a jaunty Anthony Newley and a suave Christopher Lee, for whom fame and *Frankenstein* were still four films away. This sounds good, but proves plodding in the telling.

Portrait of Alison

See: *Postmark for Danger*

Portrait of Jennie ○

(aka: *Jennie*)
1948, US, 86 mins, b/w
Dir: William Dieterle

Stars: Jennifer Jones, Joseph Cotten, Ethel Barrymore
Rating: ★★★

A haunting, compelling fantasy about an artist who meets a young girl off and on through the years and begins, chillingly, to realise that she is an apparition. Excellent acting, especially from Joseph Cotten and veterans Ethel Barrymore and Lillian Gish; breathtaking black and white photography by Joseph August.

Poseidon Adventure, The ○ ⓥ

1972, US, 117 mins, colour
Dir: Ronald Neame
Stars: Gene Hackman, Ernest Borgnine, Roddy McDowall, Shelley Winters, Red Buttons
Rating: ★★★

The film that started a whole wave of disaster movies in the 1970s and still one of the best, though you may find it hard to take it seriously with Leslie Nielsen as the ship's captain. Nevertheless, it's one of the most human and believable of its kind, once you accept the idea that an ocean liner could flip over quickly enough to trap a huge reservoir of air under its upturned hull. Another point in its favour is that there are no Hollywood heroes, although the central characters are heroic. Gene Hackman is a Catholic priest who leads the survivors to the bottom of the ship (upturned = top, remember) hoping to break through to a rescue team. Good tense action keeps things moving, without letting you know if rescue is at hand.

Posse ◐

1975, US, 94 mins, colour
Dir: Kirk Douglas
Stars: Kirk Douglas, Bruce Dern
Rating: ★★

A Western that reverses all the traditions. Audience sympathy is invited for the outlaw (Bruce Dern), although he has shot a sheriff. And the marshal (Kirk Douglas) who heads the posse in pursuit is seen as a man consumed by ambition for high office. The killer ultimately buys all the posse men but one, by offering them money they have robbed a town to get, thinking it was to save the marshal. It's an unusual action film that nearly works. One never quite believes it all, but Kirk Douglas's direction, coupled with tight editing, almost suspends our dis-

belief, even if Douglas is bested in the acting stakes by Dern's steely scoundrel.

Posse ● ⓥ

1993, US, 111 mins, colour
Dir: Mario Van Peebles
Stars: Mario Van Peebles, Stephen Baldwin, Salli Richardson, Billy Zane, Pam Grier, Richard Jordan, Blair Underwood
Rating: ★

A thoroughly pretentious black spaghetti western, complete with old-timer Woody Strode topping and tailing the film. It has swirling camera angles, filters to make the old west look golden, an embarrassing would-be erotic love scene, and a story that's deadly dull in between the admittedly frequent bursts of violent, savage but heavily stylised action. Jesse Lee (haltingly played by Mario Van Peebles, who even ends the film on a close-up of his own face) escapes, gold-laden from the Spanish–American war, with renegade colonel Billy Zane in hot pursuit. Jesse Lee aims to revenge himself on those who burned his preacher father, whose dream of black Fremantown has now been realised. But the town still lives under the shadow of nearby Sheriff Bates (Richard Jordan) . . . The whole thing does end in a good old-fashioned shootout, by which time the tale has taken nearly two hours to unfold. As a document on the black experience in the old West, the film isn't nearly as interesting as it might be, thanks to the tiresome treatment. That needs to be told in a less angry and more considered way.

Posse from Hell ○

1961, US, 85 mins, colour
Dir: Herbert Coleman
Stars: Audie Murphy, John Saxon, Vic Morrow
Rating: ★★★

A high quality Audie Murphy Western, distinguished by the playing of Murphy and John Saxon, as leaders of a posse chasing four killers. Their characters strike up a credible and likeable association of opposites to track the killers down. Clair Huffaker's adaptation of his own novel is sharp and literate for a Western, and the bad-guy department is also good value, comprising Vic Morrow, Rudolfo Acosta, James Bell and Lee Van Cleef.

Possessed ○
1947, US, 108 mins, b/w
Dir: Curtis Bernhardt
Stars: Joan Crawford, Van Heflin,
Raymond Massey, Geraldine Brooks
Rating: ★★★

Highly watchable melodrama that
earned Joan Crawford an Oscar nomination, two years after she won the
award for *Mildred Pierce*. The director,
Curtis Bernhardt, had a penchant for
psychological dramas, notably in
Conflict and *The High Wall*, and he
skilfully evokes the events and
surroundings which chip away at the
Crawford character's mental control.
The result, right from the dreamlike
opening sequences, is absorbing from
start to finish.

Postcards from the
Edge ① ⓥ
1990, US, 101 mins, colour
Dir: Mike Nichols
Stars: Meryl Streep, Shirley MacLaine,
Dennis Quaid, Gene Hackman, Richard
Dreyfuss
Rating: ★★★★

It's a pity that Carrie Fisher's real talent – for writing, which far outshines
her acting abilities – had to come to
light in such a cathartic and traumatic
way. For, despite the usual disclaimers
in these *romans a clef*, this is essentially
the story of her relationship with her
mother, musical superstar Debbie
Reynolds. Fortunately, their shouting
matches are punctuated with stretches
of wickedly funny humour that makes
you relish the thought of Fisher writing an out-and-out comedy. Streep, a
little too old but great anyway, is the
daughter whose wisecracks for every
occasion thinly veil an inner bitterness
and confusion. 'Do you always talk in
bumper stickers?' she asks her detox
doctor, after being hauled back from a
drug overdose. MacLaine matches her
as the mother who tells her 'Sing me
one of your old numbers from my
act.' She gets the very best of a script
that drips with gems of wit and pearls
of wisdom. And who's that singing for
Streep in the musical numbers? Ha!
Who would dare dub Meryl? It's her
of course – and terrific too.

Postman Always Rings Twice,
The ○
1946, US, 113 mins, b/w
Dir: Tay Garnett
Stars: Lana Turner, John Garfield
Rating: ★★★★

A brilliant *film noir* smouldering with
sexual sparks in an era when
Hollywood could hardly film James M
Caine's steamy novel in its original
form. Lana Turner in white is the angel from hell who seduces John
Garfield's grubby drifter into a nightmare world of attempted murder, as
he strives to get rid of Turner's unwanted husband (a performance of
pathetic brilliance by Cecil Kellaway).
Turner was rarely better and Hume
Cronyn gives superb support in the
film's later stages. A classic *film noir*,
stylishly, purposefully directed by Tay
Garnett, and simply streets ahead of
the sweaty, oversexed remake with
Jack Nicholson and Jessica Lange
many years later.

Postman Always Rings Twice,
The ●
1981, US, 123 mins, colour
Dir: Rob Rafelson
Stars: Jack Nicholson, Jessica Lange
Rating: ★★

A no-holds-barred, steamy remake of
the classic 1946 MGM film, based on
the controversial and once-banned
novel by James M Cain. Jack
Nicholson is nothing less than his
typically audacious best, but the
film's real find is Jessica Lange (in the
role made famous by Lana Turner).
Nothing in the remake of *King Kong*
or Bob Fosse's *All That Jazz* prepared
us for her amazing acting range, which
director Bob Rafelson skilfully
exploits. Here, David Mamet's script
piles on the twists and ends up too
plot-heavy for its own good. But the
power and passion of the central
performances just about bring this
deeply unpleasant film home.

Postmark for Danger ○
(aka: Portrait of Alison)
1955, UK, 84 mins, b/w
Dir: Guy Green
Stars: Robert Beatty, Terry Moore,
William Sylvester
Rating: ★★

As with so many British co-features of
the Fifties, the producers of this neat
thriller imported an American star – in
this case Terry Moore – to give their
film appeal at the box-office in the
United States. Moore, who much later
bared all at the age of 50 in *Playboy*
magazine, acquits herself well in this
screen version of a television serial by
the prolific Francis Durbridge, creator
of detective Paul Temple. Cinema-

tographer-turned-director Guy
Green handles the twists and red herrings effectively.

Powder River ○
1953, US, 78 mins, colour
Dir: Louis King
Stars: Rory Calhoun, Cameron Mitchell,
Corinne Calvet, Penny Edwards
Rating: ★★

Cameron Mitchell walks away with
the acting honours in this rousing
Western from the 20th Century-Fox
stable. It's full of all the best ingredients, including gunfights that shatter
the mirror behind the bar, and fist
fights that threaten to shatter the jaws
of the participants. But characterisation is not ignored in Louis King's
fresh and vigorous direction and Edward Cronjager's bright Technicolor
photography brings the small mining
town of the title to vivid life.

Power ① ⓥ
1985, US, 111 mins, colour
Dir: Sidney Lumet
Stars: Richard Gere, Julie Christie, Gene
Hackman, Denzel Washington
Rating: ★

This trite and often downright embarrassing tale of politics and media
manipulation marked a real low point
in the career of Richard Gere. He's an
amoral image-maker whose services
packaging politicians for a TV-
orientated society guarantees success.
His offices, wardrobe, and fee of
$25,000 a month are witness to his
ability. But things go wrong when he
takes on a new client. All the plot
twists are well telegraphed in a script
that doesn't come anywhere near director Sidney Lumet's corrosive exposé
of television in *Network*. Julie Christie
and Kate Capshaw add love interest,
but their characters are bland cyphers.

Powwow Highway ●
1988, US, 87 mins, colour
Dir: Jonathan Wacks
Stars: A Martinez, Gary Farmer, Amanda
Wyss, Graham Greene
Rating: ★★

Americans do love their road movies –
long-held shots of cars travelling along
the highway to twangy musical accompaniment. This story of modern
Indians trying to fight for their rights
is not too bad once it gets going, but
it does take a long time for its events
to gain momentum. A Martinez is the
political activist whose sister is jailed
on a trumped-up charge in far-away

P

Santa Fe, as soon as he shows sign of throwing a spanner in the works of unscrupulous whites seeking to do the native Americans down over the riches of their lands. The bad guys reckon without his man-mountain friend (Gary Farmer), who buys a clapped-out Buick and sets out with Martinez for Santa Fe, discovering himself as a spirited warrior on the way. Once the Indians hit town the film takes wing, but that's in the last half-hour and it's a heap long trek, my braves, till then.

Prayer for the Dying, A ● ⓥ
1987, UK, 108 mins, colour
Dir: Mike Figgis
Stars: Mickey Rourke, Bob Hoskins, Alan Bates, Sammi Davis, Liam Neeson, Alison Doody
Rating: ★★

Streaks of reverence and sentimentality, plus uncertainties of casting, fatally flaw this often interesting, well paced and rarely boring thriller about an IRA hit-man on the run. Fallon (Mickey Rourke), sickened by the killing of innocent people in Northern Ireland, has come to England where he is sought by the IRA, the police and an underworld kingpin (Alan Bates), who wants a killing from Fallon in return for a passport and money. It seems strange that a man with nowhere to run should go for such a deal but the execution is duly carried out, triggering off the rest of the plot in which a priest (Bob Hoskins) witnesses the murder, only to be silenced by Fallon's admissions in the Confessional. Rourke, sporting a decent Irish brogue, makes a good job of the lonely Fallon, while a bizarrely cast Hoskins works perhaps too hard (his dialogue isn't up to the passion he puts into it) and it's sad to see Bates so over-the-top in an unworthy role. Action scenes are toughly, sharply staged and the film rarely seems its length.

Precinct 45: Los Angeles Police
See: The New Centurions

Predator ● ⓥ
1987, US, 107 mins, colour
Dir: John McTiernan
Stars: Arnold Schwarzenegger, Carl Weathers, Elpidia Carrillo
Rating: ★★★

A semi-remake of *Alien*, told in terms of jungle warfare, this is a violent, brutal and exciting science-fiction thriller that scales new heights of sav-

agery even by the standards of previous Arnold Schwarzenegger films. It would be nice not to be able to forecast the ending of one of these crescendoes of death, but we all know that Big Arnie will triumph in the end, even over an eight-foot-tall, nearly invisible alien with an armoury of sophisticated weapons that tear you apart. So we must sit through the dispatch of his comrades one by one before the final showdown comes, leaving the sheer mechanics of the thing to keep our interest buzzing, which they do, especially the semi-invisibility which is very well realised. *Predator 2* was in production almost before the blood was dry on this one.

Predator 2 ● ⓥ
1990, US, 107 mins, colour
Dir: Stephen Hopkins
Stars: Danny Glover, Kevin Peter Hall, Gary Busey, Ruben Blades, Maria Conchita Alonso, Robert Davi
Rating: ★★★

What with Colombian and Jamaican drug dealers ruling the streets, and police getting mown down by the precinct-full, the last thing the city's finest of the near future needs is an alien predator on the loose. Yet that's just what it gets and street cop Glover is out to nail his hide, even if it means getting in the way of a special unit led by Busey, who knows the alien's on the loose but wants him alive. The result is a thoroughly unpleasant but undeniably thrilling action film, with a strong cast giving sweatily good value to their abrasive roles. The last 15 minutes, with a just-one-thing-after-another structure, is particularly exciting stuff even though it makes no great sense. The film's closing lines promise us *Predator 3* one day if we can stand the pace.

Prelude to a Kiss ○ ⓥ
1992, US, 106 mins, colour
Dir: Norman René
Stars: Meg Ryan, Alec Baldwin, Kathy Bates, Ned Beatty, Patty Duke, Stanley Tucci
Rating: ★★

After a whirlwind romance, Meg Ryan and Alec Baldwin get hitched. But things start to go seriously wrong at the wedding when the bride is kissed by a mysterious old man. Suddenly, she isn't herself any more. A neat twist makes this amusing story that little bit different, with Baldwin trying to figure out what on earth (or

elsewhere?) has happened. An enjoyable romp, this, although it does leave a lot of questions unanswered. Since Ryan is as enchanting as ever, it's just a pity they couldn't have done more with such a highly original idea. Mysteriously unreleased in Britain where it went straight to video.

Presenting Lily Mars ○
1943, US, 104 mins, b/w
Dir: Norman Taurog
Stars: Judy Garland, Van Heflin
Rating: ★★★

Joe Pasternak's second vehicle as producer for MGM is a budget-conscious black-and-white musical with a good crop of songs and the ineffable advantage of Judy Garland as star. The legendary Judy was not yet 21 when she made the film, but had already starred in such enduring classics as *The Wizard of Oz*, *Babes in Arms*, *Strike Up the Band* and *Babes on Broadway*. They had even given her a special Oscar after her triumph in the *Oz* film in 1939. Judy's name now sold tickets on its own, and, when she sang, a film came alive. As Lily Mars, a small-town girl who makes it to the big time on Broadway, Judy sings a lot. The score includes 'Broadway Rhythm', 'Tom Tom the Piper's Son', 'Sweethearts of America', 'Where There's Music', 'Is It Love?' and 'Three O'Clock in the Morning'. But one song is special – a duet sung by Judy with veteran character actress Connie Gilchrist. Beautifully staged by director Norman Taurog, the number, 'Every Little Movement', is a combination of acting, singing and choreographed movement that brings a tear to the eye. There's a big finish too, in the MGM style – but only because studio boss Louis B Mayer insisted on it. They called in dance director Charles Walters, threw what they had in the dustbin, and re-shot the last few minutes from top to bottom.

President's Analyst, The ○
1967, US, 107 mins, colour
Dir: Theodore J Flicker
Stars: James Coburn, Joan Delaney
Rating: ★★★★

This brilliantly funny and inventive satire was ahead of its time (and therefore failed to find an audience) and remains by far and away the best film that director Theodore J Flicker ever made. The script (also by Flicker) is sharp and witty and the film, with the panther-like James Coburn at the centre of its action, rollicks along from one outrageous incident to another with a never-slackening pace. Stay tuned for the glorious finale involving the Telephone Company. The whole enterprise is an unexpected treat.

Presidio, The ● ⓥ
1988, US, 98 mins, colour
Dir: Peter Hyams
Stars: Sean Connery, Mark Harmon, Meg Ryan, Jack Warden
Rating: ★★

The well-worn cop thriller theme of two opposites having to work together despite not liking each other is given a military/civilian twist in this well-paced film. A military policeman is shot checking out a break-in at the officers' club and civilian cop Jay Austin (Mark Harmon) is called in to investigate. An ex-soldier, he has to team up with his old commanding officer (Sean Connery). Austin was discharged from the service for trying to arrest an officer, who (surprise, surprise) is a suspect in the murder case. Strong performances from Connery and Meg Ryan as his daughter Donna lift this film from the average that it would otherwise be. Harmon, on the other hand, is a little bland and doesn't quite carry conviction.

Press for Time ⊙
1966, UK, 102 mins, colour
Dir: Robert Asher
Stars: Norman Wisdom, Derek Bond, Angela Browne
Rating: ★

The last in Norman Wisdom's long string of madcap comedies for the Rank Organisation, this one casts him as a hapless reporter and gives him the chance to do a mini Alec Guinness by playing four different parts. Pretty nearly laughless: the star and studio called it a day after this one.

Presumed Innocent ● ⓥ
1990, US, 126 mins, colour
Dir: Alan J Pakula
Stars: Harrison Ford, Greta Scacchi, Brian Dennehy, Raul Julia, Bonnie Bedelia
Rating: ★★★

While other genres come and go in cycles, the court-room drama marches on. Every couple of years, Hollywood throws up a lengthy, well-scripted legal labyrinth that engrosses everyone, right up to the

twist surprise ending. This was the 1990 offering, given additional clout as the guy presumed innocent until proven guilty is played by harassed-looking Harrison Ford. Twist number one is that Ford is a top prosecuting attorney himself and his alleged murder victim a beautiful, self-serving attorney in his own department. That's the trigger for the plot and, if red herrings are rather strenuously spread across our path in the cause of one suspect, the identity of the killer will baffle almost everyone until at best a couple of minutes before it's revealed. Occasional dull patches, loose ends and improbabilities can't prevent the thing from exercising a grip and a fascination to the very end. Good performances from Ford, Julia (his lawyer), Bedelia (his wife), Scacchi (the mistress) and others.

Pretty Baby ○
1950, US, 92 mins, b/w
Dir: Bretaigne Windust
Stars: Betsy Drake, Dennis Morgan, Zachary Scott, Edmund Gwenn
Rating: ★★★

Delightful romantic comedy with the enchanting Betsy Drake as the girl whose blanket-wrapped doll brings her a whole new life. Edmund Gwenn is his engaging self as the crusty old tycoon who takes a shine to her, unaware that her 'baby' is a doll she uses to get her a seat on the subway. The screenplay by Everett Freeman and Harry Kurnitz has lots of laughs and funny situations and ensures comedy fans of good value for their money. A pity the talented Ms Drake, later to be the third wife of Cary Grant, didn't make more films.

Pretty in Pink ◑ ⓥ
1986, US, 99 mins, colour
Dir: Howard Deutch
Stars: Molly Ringwald, Harry Dean Stanton, Andrew McCarthy, Jon Cryer, James Spader
Rating: ★★

A pretty weird (but hugely successful) movie from the John Hughes factory, in that it's odd anyone would still want to make a poor-girl-being-asked-to-the-prom-by-rich-boy film that didn't amount to any more than that. Given that its elements have been used in countless other films, though, there's a lot of Acting going on here with a capital A, especially from Molly Ringwald and Andrew McCarthy as the couple concerned, both shifting and twitching away like mad, but

failing to avoid being upstaged both by Jon Cryer as her unrequited Teddy-Boy-style love, and by Harry Dean Stanton as the heroine's disarming father, his five o'clock shadow as permanent as his unemployment.

Pretty Maids All in a Row ●
1971, US, 95 mins, colour
Dir: Roger Vadim
Stars: Rock Hudson, Angie Dickinson, Telly Savalas
Rating: ★

It's not surprising that Angie Dickinson seems sexier than ever before in this campus murder thriller – the director is Frenchman Roger Vadim, who moulded the careers of Brigitte Bardot, Catherine Deneuve and other French femme fatales. The film itself is the usual Vadim jumble, effective only in flashes. But Ms Dickinson's the girl to watch: she almost sets the screen on fire. The casting of Telly Savalas as the policeman on the case seems all too inevitable today, when he is known world-wide as Kojak. But, when this film was made, the part of police captain Surcher got him away from a run of psychopathic villains.

Pretty Poison ◑
1968, US, 89 mins, colour
Dir: Noel Black
Stars: Anthony Perkins, Tuesday Weld
Rating: ★★★★

A very chilly psycho-drama with Anthony Perkins as an arsonist who joins forces with a young blond thrill-seeker (Tuesday Weld) on his latest sabotage mission, only to find that her fluffy exterior conceals an unbalanced mind of pure evil. Very soon she has spiralled out of control. A one-of-a-kind movie with a very effective performance by Perkins and a simply amazing one by Weld, who rarely got the parts she deserved in the movies, but really rose to the occasion when she did. A very disturbing movie in which things keep going from bad to worse, especially for Perkins. The best film of director Noel Black, who never made anything half as good again. Here he rounds the story off with a beautifully conceived and highly satisfactory tailpiece.

Pretty Woman ◑ ⓥ
1990, US, 117 mins, colour
Dir: Garry Marshall
Stars: Richard Gere, Julia Roberts,

P

Ralph Bellamy, Laura San Giacomo,
Hector Elizondo
Rating: ★★★★

Romantic comedy makes a
comeback in style – even with a few
tears at the end. Hollywood hooker
meets millionaire wheeler-dealer. At
first he's just amused, she's bemused.
But then – wham! It is, as a character
reminds us at the end, only the stuff
that dreams are made of. But here it's
wrapped round a script, by J F
Lawton that, 30 years ago, Rock
Hudson and Paula Prentiss would
have killed to lay hands on: immaculately tailored to be funny, dramatic
or touching as to the moment.
Roberts is just adorable as the hooker:
a star-making performance in the old
tradition. Opposite her, Gere
unexpectedly blossoms as a light romantic comedian of the very deftest
touch. And there are wonderful supporting roles: Elizondo as the
manager of the hotel where the action
is, Patrick Richwood as the ogling
night elevator boy who can't believe it
all, and Jason Alexander, a real
slimebag as Gere's oily lawyer. Okay,
so the sex is a little raunchier than the
genre's used to, the language a bit
saltier and the ending a tiny bit
muffed. But the whole thing's so
warm and funny you'll cry.

Prick Up Your Ears ● Ⓥ
1987, UK, 108 mins, colour
Dir: Stephen Frears
Stars: Gary Oldman, Alfred Molina,
Vanessa Redgrave, Julie Walters
Rating: ★★★

One feels that this scabrous comedy-drama is the kind of biography
that grinning satyr Joe Orton would
have liked. A rampant homosexual
and diamond-sharp literary talent, he
lived, despite the wealth his brilliant
plays brought him, in a cramped bedsit
with his one-time lover, failed ac-
tor-writer Kenneth Halliwell – a
relationship that inevitably led to
tragedy. Alan Bennett's script, which
intersperses their crises with the kind
of cruel humour in which Orton revelled, keeps the story from becoming
too tawdry and grim. The production,
though, is a bit too tarted up in places,
and the storyline rather too slight to
sustain the film's length. Slightly more
emphasis on Orton's writing achievements and less on his private life might
have helped, as well as emphasising
the excellent performances of Gary
Oldman and Alfred Molina as Orton
and Halliwell, very well supported by

Vanessa Redgrave, Frances Barber and
Julie Walters as Orton's agent, sister
and mother, all of whom seem to be
having fun with their roles. If
anything, the film underplays the natural vulgarity that gave the waspish
Orton so much pleasure and provided
the acid edge to his all-too-few plays.

Pride and Prejudice ○
1940, US, 118 mins, b/w
Dir: Robert Z Leonard
Stars: Greer Garson, Laurence Olivier,
Mary Boland, Edmund Gwenn
Rating: ★★★

An elegant, marvellously well-
produced version of Jane Austen's
book, liberally laced with charm, humour and style. Delightfully acted by a
very strong cast, it's full of good
things. Clark Gable, Robert Donat,
Norma Shearer and Vivien Leigh were
all in the running at one time for
Elizabeth Bennet and Mr Darcy, the
roles played eventually by Greer
Garson and Laurence Olivier. But
Garson and Olivier had played *Romeo
and Juliet* together in an early TV
transmission of Shakespeare's play,
and they make a first-class team.

Pride and the Passion, The ○
1957, US, 131 mins, colour
Dir: Stanley Kramer
Stars: Cary Grant, Frank Sinatra, Sophia
Loren
Rating: ★★

Stanley Kramer's version of C S Forester's Napoleonic adventure *The Gun*
is packed with action and spectacle –
and gave Sophia Loren her first English-speaking role. But Cary Grant and
Frank Sinatra are uncomfortably cast
and Edna and Edward Anhalt's script
below par.

Pride of the Yankees, The ○
1942, US, 128 mins, b/w
Dir: Sam Wood
Stars: Gary Cooper, Teresa Wright,
Walter Brennan
Rating: ★★★

Gary Cooper stars as the doomed
baseball star Lou Gehrig, struck down
by illness at the peak of his notable
career. There's a beautifully
understated performance by Cooper
himself, given shortly after he had
won his first Academy Award, for
Sergeant York. Many baseball 'greats'
of the era, including the famous Babe
Ruth, appear as themselves in what,
tactfully and intelligently directed by
Sam Wood, remains one of the best

tributes to a sporting hero ever made.
Keep a very large handkerchief ready
for the ending.

Prime Cut ●
1972, US, 91 mins, colour
Dir: Michael Ritchie
Stars: Lee Marvin, Gene Hackman,
Sissy Spacek, Angel Tompkins
Rating: ★★

A strange kettle of fish and no mistake.
A gangster thriller with a Seventies
touch or two, it has a poor script and
variable performances but is very
well directed (by Michael Ritchie) and
photographed in colour at
Oscar-winning level by Gene Polito.
Lee Marvin plays a cool Chicago
gunman sent to collect half a million
dollars in unpaid 'rakeoff' money from
Kansas big shot Gene Hackman.
Previous messengers have come back
in parcels as sausage meat. There's a
sleazy sub-plot involving Sissy Spacek
in her major film debut, and everything builds of course to the final
shoot-out. This is superbly realised, as
Marvin battles his way through the
bad guy's gunmen, in a vast field of
sunflowers, under thunder-filled skies.

Prime of Miss Jean Brodie, The ● Ⓥ
1968, UK, 116 mins, colour
Dir: Ronald Neame
Stars: Maggie Smith, Gordon Jackson,
Robert Stephens, Pamela Franklin, Celia
Johnson
Rating: ★★★

A remarkable encapsulation of character by Maggie Smith as an eccentric
schoolteacher in the Edinburgh of the
Thirties earned her an Academy
Award for this film version of the famous stage success. It's Smith you'll
remember long after the fadeout, despite doughty support from Celia
Johnson (excellent as her headmistress), Robert Stephens and real-life
husband-and-wife Gordon Jackson
and Rona Anderson.

Prince and the Pauper, The ⊙
1962, UK, 89 mins, colour
Dir: Don Chaffey
Stars: Guy Williams, Sean Scully,
Donald Houston, Jane Asher
Rating: ★★★

A zestful, well-staged and un-
justly-neglected Walt Disney version
of the Mark Twain classic, also filmed
in 1937 (with Errol Flynn and the
Mauch Twins) and again in 1977
(with Oliver Reed and Mark Lester).

Photographed in excellent colour by
Paul Beeson, this is certainly the equal
of the Flynn film and some way ahead
of the Reed version. Director Don
Chaffey has always done well at the
Disney studio with adventure films
aimed at younger audiences and he
grips the attention throughout here,
even with the old familiar story of the
beggar boy who swaps places with his
double, who happens to be Edward
Tudor, the future king of England.
Vigorous performances from the pre-
dominantly British cast, notably
Donald Houston as the pauper's scurrilous father. Jane Asher makes a
fetching Lady Jane Grey and Guy
Williams (then a big star for Disney on
TV in the *Zorro* series) acquits himself
pretty well as the boys' dashing and
unlikely protector.

Prince and the Pauper, The ○
(aka: Crossed Swords)
1977, UK, 121 mins, colour
Dir: Richard Fleischer
Stars: Oliver Reed, Raquel Welch, Mark
Lester, George C Scott
Rating: ★★

Mark Twain's classic story of twin
boys, one a prince, the other a pauper,
in the time of King Henry VIII, is a
rattling good yarn, and has been
filmed several times before. Sumptuously staged, this version cost $8
million to make and the money, as
they say in the business, is all there on
the screen. It really does look magnificent. George MacDonald Fraser's
screenplay, however, is somewhat less
splendid, and the star cast meets its
coy and often awkward phraseology
with varying degrees of success. Oliver
Reed, in the part once played by Errol
Flynn, fares quite well as the pauper's
mentor, a nobleman usurped of his
castle and his woman (Raquel Welch)
by his treacherous brother. George C
Scott gives an extraordinary account
of the King of the Beggars in a scene
in which one expects the assembled
cast at any moment to burst into a
chorus of 'Gotta Pick a Pocket or
Two'. The film's best performance is
given by a little lady called Lalla Ward
(later to star in the TV series *Doctor
Who* and marry the programme's lead
actor Tom Baker), all fire and steel as
Young Bess.

Prince and the Showgirl,
The ○ ⓥ
1957, US, 117 mins, colour
Dir: Laurence Olivier

Stars: Laurence Olivier, Marilyn Monroe,
Sybil Thorndike, Jeremy Spenser
Rating: ★★

Playwright Terence Rattigan wrings a
few laughs and a tear or two from this
screen version of his stage success *The
Sleeping Prince*. The performances are
delightful, especially Marilyn
Monroe's sophisticated innocent and
Sybil Thorndike's dotty dowager.
Laurence Olivier provides an unselfish
foil to Monroe's breathy charm, but
his heavy direction puts too many
brakes on the film's pace.

Prince of Darkness ● ⓥ
1987, US, 101 mins, colour
Dir: John Carpenter
Stars: Donald Pleasence, Jameson
Parker, Lisa Blount
Rating: ★★

Slightly above average of its type, John
Carpenter's onrush of horrors is a
quite successful grafting together of
several genres – the youngsters-in-
peril film, the AntiChrist film and the
10 Little Niggers thriller. Carpenter's
own, doomy, basso profundo music
sets the tone for the story of a group
of scientists and graduate students who
gather together in an abandoned
church surrounded by zombie-like
tramps, to learn the secret of a mysterious, centuries-old canister whose
whirling green contents seem to be
generating new life from within. Not
a pretty can of worms (creatures
which, along with others, swarm
across the screen from time to time)
but quite well realised, with an unusually understated performance from
Donald Pleasence. The graduates
aren't much on the whole, but then
most of them are turned into zombies
anyway.

Prince of Foxes ○
1949, US, 107 mins, b/w
Dir: Henry King
Stars: Tyrone Power, Orson Welles,
Wanda Hendrix, Katina Paxinou,
Marina Berti, Everett Sloane
Rating: ★★

Tyrone Power pageantry, in a fictional
episode from the life of the Italian
Renaissance despot, Cesare Borgia.
Hold on tight for the scene in which
Power has his eyes gouged out by
Everett Sloane. But be prepared for a
surprise. Pretty fiery stuff, this, with
not too many dull moments and
amazingly detailed photography by
the awesome Leon Shamroy.

Prince of Pennsylvania,
The ● ⓥ
1988, US, 87 mins, colour
Dir: Ron Nyswaner
Stars: Keanu Reeves, Fred Ward,
Bonnie Bedelia, Amy Madigan
Rating: ★★★

A cross between a rites of passage film
and a black comedy – and even that
doesn't quite get it. Keanu Reeves
plays an angry young man who should
have walked out months before on
macho father Fred Ward, unfaithful
mum Bonnie Bedelia and faceless
younger brother. It takes an affair with
café owner Amy Madigan and a lunatic
kidnap scheme to help him see the
attraction of the broad white highway.
Slow to start, the film does get to you
later on with its mixture of oddball
characters, funny one-liners and
emotional pull. Ward reveals a talent
for dry comedy with his portrait of a
man whose outlook is as limited as his
word power. 'Sometimes', yells his
wife, 'I feel I married Jimi Hendrix
and woke up with Oliver North'.

Prince of Pirates ○
1953, US, 81 mins, colour
Dir: Sidney Salkow
Stars: Barbara Rush, John Derek
Rating: ★★

Spectacular action picture, with battles
on sea and land, as Spain and Holland
get all tangled up during the 17th
century. Pretty Barbara Rush joins in
the sword fights with welcome vigour.
She and John Derek share the action
honours as a spirited pair of Dutch
patriots, and help give pace and point
to the energetic pantomime.

Prince of Shadows ● ⓥ
1991, Spain, 114 mins, colour
Dir: Pilar Miró
Stars: Terence Stamp, Patsy Kensit,
Geraldine James
Rating: RB

Drained of both colour and interest,
this is no horror film (well, not in that
sense) but a tired espionage thriller
briefly enlivened by Patsy Kensit's
quite passable impression of Rita
Hayworth doing 'Put the Blame on
Mame' in a nightclub scene. Terence
Stamp toplines as a former hitman
drawn back into the world of subter-
fuge to eliminate another 'traitor' (to
an unnamed cause) somewhere in
Spain. The story, such as it is, unfolds
slowly (revealing Stamp's past
assassination of an innocent man for
whose wife he had fallen), but at least

avoids being silly until a quite ludicrous climax which will leave you falling around the sitting-room. Poor acting and stilted, vaguely pretentious dialogue torpedo the ship beyond repair: director Pilar Miró even manages to get a rare bad performance from Geraldine James. Scarcely in colour to speak of, the film hardly even engages the interest, although it will tax your patience.

Prince of the City ●
1981, US, 160 mins, colour
Dir: Sidney Lumet
Stars: Treat Williams, Jerry Orbach, Richard Foronjy
Rating: ★★

Director Sidney Lumet's epic treatise on police corruption makes his earlier film on a similar subject, *Serpico*, seem like a flyweight fantasy. Realist drama at its most compelling, this is the true story of NYPD detective Bob Leuci (played with intense sincerity by Treat Williams), who acceded to pressure and informed for the notorious King Commission into corruption on the force. Falling into a classic trap, Leuci (rechristened Danny Ciello in the movie) tangles with powerful forces believing that he can manipulate and control them. The results are catastrophic: from a body of 70 men Leuci considered to be his friends and compatriots, 52 are indicted, two commit suicide and one goes insane. The viewer is filled with a sense of impotent rage as the complex story unfolds, showing the American legal system to be on the verge of total collapse. But there's no doubt that Lumet views Leuci/Ciello not only as a victim but also a hero. It's just a pity his film goes on so damned long, diluting its own power in progressive fashion.

Prince of Tides, The ● ⊙
1991, US, 132 mins, colour
Dir: Barbra Streisand
Stars: Barbra Streisand, Nick Nolte, Blythe Danner, Kate Nelligan, Jeroen Krabbé, Melinda Dillon
Rating: ★★★

A much more impressive turn in the director's chair from Barbra Streisand compared with her first, *Yentl*. This is a finely crafted, beautifully shot voyage of self-discovery. Streisand hands the spotlight to Nick Nolte's excellent, Oscar-nominated performance in the difficult role of Southern boy Tom Wingo who, when summoned to New York by his sister's psychiatrist (Streisand) after the sister has attempted suicide, must learn to reveal his repressed emotions and face the horrors in his past. You may find the only problem with this film is Streisand's own performance; she continues to impress less in straight drama than in musicals or comedies, and perhaps should have limited herself to the director's chair here. Otherwise, it's a high class weepie.

Princess and the Pirate, The ○
1944, US, 94 mins, colour
Dir: David Butler
Stars: Bob Hope, Virginia Mayo, Walter Brennan, Victor McLaglen
Rating: ★★★

One of Bob Hope's early Technicolor outings, this one made on loan from Paramount to Samuel Goldwyn. Hope plays Sylvester the Great, a conceited actor with the familiar yellow streak running right down the middle of his back, trying to save a princess (Virginia Mayo) from being kidnapped. Guess which famous guest star whisks the girl from under Hope's ski-nose at the end of the film.

Princess Bride, The ○ ⊙
1987, US, 98 mins, colour
Dir: Rob Reiner
Stars: Cary Elwes, Mandy Patinkin, Chris Sarandon, Peter Falk
Rating: ★★

'Not just your average ho-hum fairy tale' promised the publicity for this movie. The problem is that all too often, despite some Pythonesque shafts of humour, it is your average ho-hum fairy tale, and sometimes its only interest lies in trying to recognise well-known stars beneath mounds of make-up: Billy Crystal and Carol Kane, for example, will surely defeat all but those in the know. The playing, though, is on the whole extremely good, especially from Chris Sarandon's James Mason-like villain. 'I've got my country's 500th anniversary to arrange,' he complains, 'my wife to murder and Guilder (a neighbouring kingdom) to blame for it. I'm swamped.' Heroine Robin Wright's English accent is good, though she's otherwise negligible, hero Cary Elwes has his moments and Peter Falk's storyteller does Grandpa Columbo. But Rob Reiner's direction and William Goldman's screenplay finally fall fatally between fairy tale, Flynn fantasy and outright satirical comedy.

Prince Valiant ○
1954, US, 100 mins, colour
Dir: Henry Hathaway
Stars: Robert Wagner, James Mason, Janet Leigh, Debra Paget, Sterling Hayden, Victor McLaglen, Brian Aherne
Rating: ★★

This period adventure was based on a famous comic strip, and was itself parodied in a subsequent Bugs Bunny cartoon called *Prince Violent*. James Mason easily steals the acting honours as the villainous Sir Brack, leaving Janet Leigh with little to do but look chastely desirable as usual. It took *Psycho* to prove what a good actress she really is. Robert Wagner (with a page-boy bob) plays the spirited young Valiant, and the whole cast is far too distinguished to be appearing in this sort of nonsense. In any case, the real heroes are director Henry Hathaway and his cameraman Lucien Ballard: they make the jousting scenes and the burning of a Viking stronghold colourful and vividly exciting.

Prince Who Was a Thief, The ○
1950, US, 88 mins, colour
Dir: Rudolph Maté
Stars: Tony Curtis, Piper Laurie
Rating: ★★

The totally unexpected box-office success of this slight romantic *Arabian Nights* adventure shot Bernie Schwartz, alias Mr Curtis, and Rosetta Jacobs, alias Ms Laurie, to stardom. Both proved themselves capable actors in later days, Curtis notably in *Sweet Smell of Success* and Laurie in *The Hustler*. Another look at *The Prince Who Was a Thief* today, reveals it to be a bit short on action, but Piper really was a pretty package, and it was worth the price of admission to see her slithering through a maze of iron bars. Former cameraman Rudolph Mate directs it all in stylish Technicolor.

Prison ● ⊙
1987, US, 102 mins, colour
Dir: Renny Harlin
Stars: Lane Smith, Viggo Mortensen, Chelsea Field, Lincoln Kilpatrick
Rating: ★★★

There can't be too many horror films set inside a prison. Director Renny Harlin and writer C Courtney Joiner give both styles of film full value here, combining the toughest possible elements from both genres. The sadistic warden (Lane Smith, a Richard Nixon lookalike hidden for years in character roles) is the villain of the piece, a man who had an innocent prisoner sent to the chair for an 'inside' killing he didn't commit. The hero is his victim, returning supernaturally from the grave when the prison in which they clashed is reopened years later. The inevitable deaths that start to happen once the avenging force is released are ingeniouly contrived and staged with considerable panache. Horror fans can look forward to a thoroughly grisly night out on the town, while prison-film aficionados will find that this film contains all the fondly remembered clichés tightly wrapped within some (literally) electrifying special effects. Performances are appropriately full throttle in this vivid dose of horrific hokum.

Prisoner, The ○
1955, UK, 91 mins, b/w
Dir: Peter Glenville
Stars: Alec Guinness, Jack Hawkins
Rating: ★★★

This gripping drama was inspired by the real-life case of Hungarian Cardinal Mindszenty who was jailed by the Nazis in 1944 for not allowing his Catholic parishoners to say a mass and sing a Nazi-ordered 'Te Deum' for 'the liberation of Budapest from the Jews'. Then, in 1948, he rebelled against Communist domination and was put in solitary confinement, an act that led to the action shown in this film. Although it remains very much a filmed stage play, Alec Guinness as the Cardinal and Jack Hawkins as a police state psychologist, are never less than compulsively watchable. It ranks as one of the finest films in both actors' distinguished careers. The film caused waves wherever it was shown: the French banned it from the Cannes Film Festival as 'anti-Communist', and the Italians did the same at the Venice Film Festival.

Prisoner of Second Avenue, The ○
1975, US, 98 mins, colour
Dir: Melvin Frank
Stars: Jack Lemmon, Anne Bancroft, Gene Saks
Rating: ★★

Jack Lemmon plays an advertising executive who has a nervous breakdown after losing his job and Anne Bancroft his supportive wife in this Neil Simon comedy. Replete with typical Simon one-liners and sharp dialogue, this is only slightly

better than the strangely similar (in tone, anyway) *The Out-of-Towners*, which also starred Lemmon. Nevertheless, there's still plenty to enjoy, with Lemmon and Bancroft on top form. Sharp eyes will spot Sylvester Stallone in a very minor role in a scene set in Central Park. Superstardom as Rocky was only a year away . . .

Prisoner of Zenda, The ○
1937, US, 101 mins, b/w
Dir: John Cromwell
Stars: Ronald Colman, Madeleine Carroll, Douglas Fairbanks Jr, Mary Astor
Rating: ★★★★

This Selznick production, a blockbuster of its day, is vastly superior to the MGM remake of 1953, even though the final duel in that (between Stewart Granger and James Mason) was almost as good as the one here between Ronald Colman and Douglas Fairbanks Junior. Colman plays the commoner forced to impersonate a king in a mythical European country, a situation that gives rise to some moments from which director John Cromwell manages to extract the maximum of tension. And the ingenious lighting of award-winning cameraman James Wong Howe adds great style to the fight scenes. There had been two silent versions of Anthony Hope's famous novel of swordplay, intrigue and derring-do, but this justly eclipsed them both. And, in Fairbanks as Rupert of Hentzau, and Raymond Massey as Black Michael, it produced two of the outstanding villains of Thirties' action films. The rest of the casting is exemplary and with good reason the film has never lost its reputation of being one of the most outstanding adventure-romances ever made.

Prisoner of Zenda, The ○ ⊗
1952, US, 100 mins, colour
Dir: Richard Thorpe
Stars: Stewart Granger, Deborah Kerr, James Mason, Louis Calhern
Rating: ★★★

The fifth of six film versions of Anthony Hope's famous adventure story of royal impersonation is more swish-buckler than swashbuckler. Stewart Granger and Deborah Kerr can't hold a castle candle to the poignant performances of Ronald Colman and Madeleine Carroll in the 1937 version, and James Mason is miscast as Granger's adversary, Rupert

of Hentzau, with a Rommel haircut and a penchant for heel-clicking. Nonetheless, the story still carries its own excitement, and the final duel scene is every bit as good as the origional betwen Colman and Douglas Fairbanks Jr. Lewis Stone, who played the dual leading role in a silent version made in 1922, has a small cameo here as the Cardinal. The action scenes are safely in the hands of MGM regular Richard Thorpe, who specialised for over 33 years at MGM in escapist entertainment.

Prisoner of Zenda, The ○ ⊗
1979, UK, 105 mins, colour
Dir: Richard Quine
Stars: Peter Sellers, Lynne Frederick, Lionel Jeffries, Elke Sommer
Rating: ★★★

A spoof by Dick Clement and Ian La Frenais of the famous old swashbuckler by Anthony Hope about the commoner forced to impersonate a weak and beleaguered king. Here it's Peter Sellers in the dual role, but Hope who has the last laugh, for the thrills work better than the comedy. Sellers is not too funny as the foppish king, but good as the London cabby who steps into his shoes. Stuart Wilson, whose Rupert of Hentzau is a very well-modulated parody of Douglas Fairbanks Jr, and Jeremy Kemp are stylishly over the top as the villains, while Lynne Frederick, Elke Sommer and Catherine Schell (even though the latter two roles could have been telescoped into one) are as pretty a trio of doll-faced, well-bosomed but animated ladies fayre as you could wish to collect. Richard Quine's direction works well with most of the action scenes, but he seems less at home with the comedy, although Gregory Sierra is tolerably amusing as Sommer's cuckolded husband. Pleasant entertainment then: just don't expect to laugh too much.

Prisoners of the Sun
See: Blood Oath

Private Benjamin ◐ ⊗
1980, US, 110 mins, colour
Dir: Howard Zieff
Stars: Goldie Hawn, Eileen Brennan, Armand Assante, Sam Wanamaker
Rating: ★★★

A comedy-drama-romance that packs all its fun in the first half, when Goldie Hawn as a fairly scatterbrained Jewish girl who enlists in the army. The basic training she undergoes provides good

P

fun in the Abbott and Costello tradi-tion, and Goldie's triumph against the odds is both funny and uplifting. The second half of this film is rather a different kettle of fish. From the mo-ment Colonel Robert Webber tries to force himself on our heroine in an aircraft after she has (somewhat unconvincingly) chickened out of jumping, the film dips into a romantic nosedive. With Goldie's involvement with a French doctor, the story, sud-denly shot in pastel colours, loses the spirit of adventure that has sustained it so well. Still, for the fun of the first 50 minutes, it remains well worth watching, and won Goldie an Oscar nomination.

Private Function, A ◐ ⓥ

1984, UK, 94 mins, colour
Dir: Malcolm Mowbray
Stars: Michael Palin, Maggie Smith, Denholm Elliott, Richard Griffiths
Rating: ★★★

Only the best ingredients are used in this feast of a film. There is the prize-winning screenplay by Alan Bennett, Malcolm Mowbray's sharply observant direction, and, tastiest of all, a hand-picked cast headed by the de-licious Maggie Smith and spiced with the talents of such character stars as Denholm Elliott, Richard Griffiths, Liz Smith and Alison Steadman. The result is a comedy in the tradition of Ealing at its prime in which the quirks and eccentricities of the English mid-dle-classes are gently, always affectionately but neverless sharply lampooned. Never act with animals and children is the clichéd advice of-fered to actors but in this case, in spite of a memorable porcine appearance, the humans put the pig at the centre of this shaggy dog story (to mix a metaphor) firmly in its place.

Private Hell 36 ○

1954, US, 81 mins, b/w
Dir: Don Siegel
Stars: Ida Lupino, Steve Cochran, Howard Duff, Dorothy Malone
Rating: ★★

Despite an excellent cast, director (Don Siegel) and director of photog-raphy (Burnett Guffey), this independent production (looking as if it cost no more than a handful of dol-lars) comes through as just an average crime drama. Ida Lupino is good, as usual. She also helped to write the script.

Private Life of Henry VIII, The ○ ⓥ

1933, UK, 97 mins, b/w
Dir: Alexander Korda
Stars: Charles Laughton, Robert Donat, Merle Oberon, Binnie Barnes, Elsa Lanchester, Wendy Barrie
Rating: ★★★

Classic Alexander Korda-directed, sa-tirical dissection of Tudor court life. Laughton gives probably his finest performance on screen as the lusty king, particularly in the section con-cerning the marriage to Anne of Cleves. Perhaps the reason for its suc-cess was that Anne was played by Elsa Lanchester, Laughton's wife in real life.

Private Life of Sherlock Holmes, The ○ ⓥ

1969, UK, 125 mins, colour
Dir: Billy Wilder
Stars: Robert Stephens, Colin Blakely, Genevieve Page, Christopher Lee
Rating: ★★★

Director Billy Wilder's personal and rather melancholy look at the Baker Street sleuth comes at you in sections and indeed was originally a much longer film running close to three and a half hours. Robert Stephens is whimsical as Holmes, Irene Handl priceless as Mrs Hudson. Lyrical interludes don't work as well as the parts that owe most to Conan Doyle, but the enterprise sparkles with wit and polish and the ending is as excit-ing as it is preposterous.

Private Lives of Elizabeth and Essex, The ○ ⓥ

1939, US, 100 mins, colour
Dir: Michael Curtiz
Stars: Bette Davis, Errol Flynn, Olivia de Havilland, Vincent Price
Rating: ★★★

A talky slice of history with Bette Davis, in her first Technicolor film, as the Virgin Queen, Elizabeth I, whose love affair with the Earl of Essex led to his downfall and execution. Davis, the reigning queen of the Warners studio with no less than three films on release in 1939, wanted Laurence Olivier to play her suitor, but was overruled by boss Jack L Warner in favour of the studio's swashbuckling champ Errol Flynn. Seeking the utmost authen-ticity, Davis shaved the front of her head and her eyebrows and insisted on ugly bags under her eyes. Flynn, attempting to flex his box office clout, insisted the film be called *The Knight*

and the Lady, but lost the argument. In the final anaysis, Davis stole the acting honours with one contemporary critic noting, 'Bette Davis's Elizabeth is a strong, resolute, glamour-skimping characterisation against which Mr Flynn's Essex has about as much chance as a beanshooter against a tank.'

Privates on Parade ◐

1982, UK, 100 mins, colour
Dir: Michael Blakemore
Stars: John Cleese, Denis Quilley, Nicola Pagett
Rating: ★★

An *Oh! What a Lovely War* of the Malayan jungle in 1948. The stage version was a smash. The film, despite enjoyable individual performances, snappy choreography and a good many bright moments, never quite works. Being an Eighties' product, it tries to be all things to all filmgoers, injecting real drama, real sex and real blood into the central theme of a camp (in more ways than one) con-cert. So what with trying to be *Lovely War*, *The Virgin Soldiers* and *It Ain't Half Hot Mum* all at the same time, it's no wonder the film never finds an identity. But there are great compensations, notably John Cleese, presenting Basil Fawlty in uniform as the God-fearing, high-stepping major, and Denis Quilley, richly pleasurable as the perfumed Queen of the Boards – a really expert performance that never puts a crooked finger wrong. Perhaps the most unexpected hit of the show is Nicola Pagett, absolutely bursting with talent as the Welsh-Indian (difficult accent but she just about gets it) 'black velvet' girl who keeps the camp's few hetero-sexual boys in line (waiting). The interludes from the unit's show are so good that the fringe drama could be better than it is and still not stand up to them!

Private's Progress ○

1955, UK, 97 mins, b/w
Dir: John Boulting
Stars: Richard Attenborough, Dennis Price, Ian Carmichael
Rating: ★★

The unexpected success of this army comedy started – and set the pattern for – a whole rush of popular Boulting Brothers capers – a run that included *Brothers-in-Law* and *Lucky Jim*. Ian Carmichael, playing the first of his several dithering heroes, and Terry-Thomas getting the opportunity to call his men 'an absolute shower', both established distinct comic personalities that saw them through several years of crowd-pulling comedy films. It's not actually all that funny – but nearly all of the Boulting comedies that followed it were.

Private War of Major Benson, The ⊙

1955, US, 105 mins, colour
Dir: Jerry Hopper
Stars: Charlton Heston, Julie Adams
Rating: ★★★

Credit Charlton Heston with a largely successful attempt to do something different here as the martinet commander of a military school, guying his own tough image and allowing tiny Tim Hovey to steal scenes from him left, right and centre. You'll enjoy the scene where Heston, thundering at the mite, asks him how tall he thinks he (Heston) is, and Hovey quavers about 10 feet. A film whose bright ideas come off, this will give a lot of pleasure to family audiences. Heston makes it seem as though he were made for the part of the gruff Major Benson, Julie Adams is a capable heroine, and Hovey does admirably as the boy in a role that thrust him into the public eye for a short while as a new child star. Heart-warming laughter all the way.

Prize of Arms, A ○

1961, UK, 105 mins, b/w
Dir: Cliff Owen
Stars: Stanley Baker, Helmut Schmid, Tom Bell
Rating: ★★★

One of a long line of tough thrillers made by Stanley Baker in the Sixties. All of them had good casts and here, in small roles, you'll spot Fulton Mackay, Glynn Edwards, Patrick Magee, Roddy McMillan, Rodney Bewes and two familiar faces from the *On the Buses* TV series and films, Michael Robbins and Stephen Lewis.

Prize of Gold, A ○

1954, UK, 98 mins, colour
Dir: Mark Robson
Stars: Richard Widmark, Mai Zetterling, Nigel Patrick, George Cole
Rating: ★★

The plot of this film may be none too convincing but, under the direction of Mark Robson, it provides both entertainment and excitement in generous proportions. George Cole is very good as the British sergeant in-volved with tough-guy Widmark in a plan to steal a fortune in gold bullion from occupied Berlin.

Prizzi's Honor ● ⓥ

1985, US, 129 mins, colour
Dir: John Huston
Stars: Jack Nicholson, Kathleen Turner, Robert Loggia, Anjelica Huston
Rating: ★★★

An outrageous black comedy about two very different hitmen for the Mafia. Jack Nicholson's street-tough assassin for the Prizzi family is not the brightest of men. When his girlfriend (Anjelica Huston, deservedly winning an Oscar) tells him about Art Deco, he responds 'Art who?' Kathleen Turner's svelte blonde hired killer, on the other hand, is as different as chalk from cheese. But the mixture is pure dynamite. The air fairly crackles with sexual tension whenever Turner and Nicholson spar verbally, but the best scenes were claimed by Huston, daughter of the film's director, John Huston. Film fans will relish an appearance by B-movie actor of old, Lawrence Tierney (who took the title role in *Dillinger* in 1945) as a bald-headed (and predictably tough) cop on the take. The production values are top-drawer, led by a script that credits its audience with intelligence.

Problem Child ◑ ⓥ

1990, US, 80 mins, colour
Dir: Dennis Dugan
Stars: John Ritter, Michael Oliver, Jack Warden, Amy Yasbeck
Rating: ★

Or: how not to make a comic variation on *The Bad Seed*. This repulsive comedy will turn your stomach over rather than tickle your ribs. Michael Oliver is obscenely awful as the monstrous kid Ritter and Yasbeck are unwise enough to adopt. It begins quite well, but subsequent scenes are so crude as to make the *Carry On* films seem a tower of good taste. But then, if you like seeing cats tortured, this could be for you. Amazingly, practically the entire cast signed on for a sequel.

Problem Child 2 ◑ ⓥ

1991, US, 88 mins, colour
Dir: Brian Levant
Stars: John Ritter, Michael Oliver, Jack Warden, Laraine Newman, Amy Yasbeck, Ivyann Schwann
Rating: RB

If you have a fondness for 'adult' comedies that delight in the disgusting, there could be something here for you. For most tastes, though, this is an unbelievably bad sequel to a gruesome original, a flatulent farce about an awful child who blows up his teacher in the toilet, accelerates a merry-go-round to a crazy rate and makes everybody sick, and swaps medical cards on a woman he doesn't like so that she'll have plastic surgery to make her nose bigger. You may say that all this surreal, but this is a nasty, thoroughly ill-natured film that makes *Porky*'s look like a comedy classic. There are jokes about the bowel movements of dogs, and any other bodily function the writers can think of. One step forward has been made, though: instead of a custard pie fight, the characters have a pizza fight. Boy actor Michael Oliver gives another dreadful, camera-hogging performance.

Prodigal, The ○

1955, US, 114 mins, colour
Dir: Richard Thorpe
Stars: Lana Turner, Edmund Purdom
Rating: ★★

Another lavish Hollywood excursion into the stories of the Bible, this was Edmund Purdom's second film venture into the realms of ancient history. And it has similar virtues to the first, *The Egyptian*. The sets and costumes are magnificent, and the supporting cast is full of interesting faces. Notable among them is that of Francis L Sullivan, one of filmland's finest fat men, as a villain, Bosra. And Louis Calhern, Neville Brand, Audrey Dalton, Taina Elg, Cecil Kellaway and Henry Daniell also have prominent roles. Quite empty though.

Producers, The ○ ⓥ

1967, US, 88 mins, colour
Dir: Mel Brooks
Stars: Zero Mostel, Gene Wilder
Rating: ★★★

Down-and-out theatrical producer Zero Mostel and his naive accountant Gene Wilder plan to make a fortune by finding rich backers for a flop show and running off with the money. The result is *Springtime for Hitler*, a rabid musical written by a fanatical Nazi! The show is so bad, it's a roaring success. This cult classic was director Mel Brooks' first film. A vulgar and broad farce, it has something to offend everyone – and it's outrageously funny, with Mostel on top eyeball-rolling

P

form. The scenes from the musical –
goose-stepping Nazis singing the
show's title song – are displays of gross
bad taste that will either offend or
have you helpless with laughter. Great
stuff.

Professionals, The ○
1966, US, 117 mins, colour
Dir: Richard Brooks
Stars: Burt Lancaster, Lee Marvin, Robert
Ryan, Jack Palance, Claudia Cardinale
Rating: ★★★

One of the best action-adventure films
of the Sixties, epitomised, perhaps, by
Burt Lancaster, biting on a cigar butt
and wriggling through enemy lines
with a fistful of explosive and a fuse
timed to burn to the exact second.
Gunfights, train ambushes and
night-time raids are equally well handled as the action thunders on its way.
Lancaster's deadly charm impresses –
like an iron fist in a velvet glove. And
director Richard Brooks' adaptation
of a Frank O'Rourke novel pares the
dialogue to a terse minimum, letting
action and the fierce Nevada desert
locations speak eloquently of the
dangers facing the quartet of
adventurers.

Professor Beware ○
1938, US, 87 mins, b/w
Dir: Elliott Nugent
Stars: Harold Lloyd, Phyllis Welch,
Raymond Walburn
Rating: ★★

Harold Lloyd, in one of his last major
pictures, as the archaeologist in search
of the rare tablet which will explain
the mystery of a 3,000-year-old romance; the classic top-of-the-train
sequence is here, and a great deal of
this train sequence was for real. The
inscription on his 1952 special Oscar
reads, incidentally, 'master comedian
and good citizen'.

Projectionist, The
See: The Inner Circle

Project X ○ ◐ ⓥ
1987, US, 103 mins, colour
Dir: Jonathan Kaplan
Stars: Matthew Broderick, Helen Hunt
Rating: ★★★

Cunningly contrived to make the
maximum appeal to the emotions in
its last 30 minutes, this is an escape
story with a difference. An intelligent
chimp, trained for three years by a
university researcher (Helen Hunt),
somehow ends up with a dozen other
chimps at a USAF secret project base

where, under the tutelage of Jimmy
(Matthew Broderick), he learns to fly
a simulated aircraft. It wouldn't be fair
to the plot to reveal more; suffice to
say that the time comes when, with
the chimps' lives at stake, Broderick
and Hunt meet up and resolve to do
something about it. Slow in parts
this picks up a good deal in the last
three reels, the emotive charge
of James Horner's music cleverly
reinforcing the impact of the escalating action. Broderick and Hunt
are good enough, and supporting
characters nicely drawn by Robin
Gammell, Bill Sadler and Jonathan
Stark. The chimps are simply amazing,
especially Willie, the one trained in
sign language and flying, Karanja and
Luke, who play three of the leading
animals. They'll draw many a tear
from those of sentimental inclination
before and during the silly but
touching climax.

Promised Land ● ⓥ
1987, US, 102 mins, colour
Dir: Michael Hoffman
Stars: Jason Gedrick, Kiefer Sutherland,
Meg Ryan, Tracy Pollan
Rating: ★

Slow motion. Dark photography.
Flashbacks to the big game and golden
days. Yes folks, the great American
masterpiece bites the dust again –
especially with a tragic ending plain
from the first few moments of its
scene. Disillusionment runs riot: can
the American Dream be as nightmarish as this? Depressing and
predictable throughout, the film fails
to enliven familiar characters and
shows no subtlety. Meg Ryan's personality, though, shines through,
even in a ridiculously obvious role.
This would be an attractive performance in a good film; in a bad one,
it's outstanding. And Kiefer Sutherland is also convincing in a poorly
written role.

Promise Her Anything ○
1966, US, 97 mins, colour
Dir: Arthur Hiller
Stars: Warren Beatty, Leslie Caron, Bob
Cummings, Hermione Gingold
Rating: ★★

Zany, freewheeling comedy about a
blue-movie maker (Warren Beatty)
with a French widow in his room in
the shape of Leslie Caron. It's pleasant,
lightweight and occasionally
gratifyingly lunatic. Spot Warren
Mitchell, silent star Bessie Love and
Donald Sutherland in small roles; be-

moan the waste of comediennes
Hermione Gingold and Libby Morris;
and applaud Keenan Wynn, who deservedly gets all the best lines as a
super-salesman.

Promoter, The
See: The Card

Prospero's Books ● ⓥ
1991, Netherlands/France/Italy,
120 mins, colour
Dir: Peter Greenaway
Stars: John Gielgud
Rating: ★★

Prospero's Books is difficult to assess
because it is a visually bold film, filled
with stunning images that live long in
the memory – images often as powerful and persuasive as the words of
the Bard that accompany them. Director Peter Greenaway deserves
much credit for the courage to bring
Shakespeare's *The Tempest* to the
screen in his own uncompromising
fashion. So it's a pity to say that it is
ultimately a deeply unsatisfying film.
John Gielgud's central performance as
Prospero dominates to such a degree
that all the other players seem mere
cyphers. This feeling is heightened by
the fact that Sir John speaks the majority of the dialogue, which, even if
you know the play, causes no small
amount of confusion. Almost every
scene contains some nudity (although
no sex), often simply there as background. As this neither helps the story
nor provides any kind of worthwhile
titillation, the question arises: 'what's
the point?' That question could be
used to sum up the whole film, were
it not for the rich photography and
the vivid visual invention Greenaway
shows in almost every scene.

Protocol ○ ⓥ
1984, US, 95 mins, colour
Dir: Herbert Ross
Stars: Goldie Hawn, Chris Sarandon
Rating: ★★

A movie specifically designed for its
star, in this case Goldie Hawn. It plays
to all her strong points – daffiness,
endearing vulnerability and resilience
under pressure. Not surprisingly its
executive producer is one Goldie
Hawn and the plot structure bears a
passing resemblance to that of a
previous Hawn success, *Private Benjamin*. Starting off as a sort of lunatic
comedy of the Sixties (with a few
sharply funny lines), it ends up more as
Miss Smith Goes to Washington, with
Goldie telling a Congressional hearing

that to which it is not accustomed – the truth (including her age). She's a cocktail waitress pitched into the public eye when foiling an assassination attempt on an eastern emir, and subsequently winning the hearts of TV millions with her slightly scatterbrained frankness. Subsequent developments provide rich pastures for Goldie Hawn fans, though others may regret that the more biting wit drifts out of the film in favour of patriotic sentiment.

Proud Ones, The ○
1956, US, 94 mins, colour
Dir: Robert D Webb
Stars: Robert Ryan, Virginia Mayo, Jeffrey Hunter, Walter Brennan
Rating: ★★★

A first-rate Western of the kind that was already close to hitting the dust in the then-changing climate of Hollywood. Robert Ryan and Jeffrey Hunter both give honest-to-goodness, hard-biting performances in the two leading roles of this suspenseful piece, although Virginia Mayo, more used to working her way through college in Warners musicals, seems miscast as the girl. The climax of the film, expertly staged by director Robert D Webb, may stay with you for some while, as could the whistled theme tune.

Proud Rebel, The ○
1958, US, 103 mins, colour
Dir: Michael Curtiz
Stars: Alan Ladd, Olivia de Havilland
Rating: ★★★

Alan Ladd's last film of any stature: a well-made (by Michael Curtiz) Western about a Southerner and his mute son roaming the countryside after the Civil War. Olivia de Havilland submerges her natural beauty to play a tough spinster farmer.

Providence ●
1977, France/Switzerland, 107 mins, colour
Dir: Alain Resnais
Stars: Dirk Bogarde, Ellen Burstyn, David Warner, John Gielgud
Rating: ★

This bizarre, one-of-a-kind film from Alain Resnais is a kind of obscene sideshoot from *Citizen Kane*, only with John Gielgud as the dislikeable, dying old man, effing and blinding away to himself in his lonely mansion as the pain gets worse. We see his offspring as he sees them in fantasy, crude daydreams that reflect his bit-

terness. David Mercer's script is flamboyant, if a crass criss-cross of role-play and Freudian puzzles, with Gielgud as both tormentor and victim. The director's treatment of all this is pretty unsubtle, but Mercer finds worthier allies in photographer Ricardo Aronovitch and composer Miklos Rosza, who both make major contributions to the film.

Prudence and the Pill ◐
1968, UK, 98 mins, colour
Dir: Fielder Cook
Stars: Deborah Kerr, David Niven, Judy Geeson
Rating: ★

The much-teamed David Niven and Deborah Kerr – this was their fourth film together – are backed by Joyce Redman, Judy Geeson, Keith Michell, Robert Coote, Vickery Turner, Edith Evans and Irina Demick in this comedy about contraceptives, in which doors open and close in true Feydeau fashion. There's one incredible scene in which Edith Evans (actually a stunt woman, of course) walks across the track at Brands Hatch while a race is on, with Formula 3 cars doing 100mph missing her by inches. No trick photography took place here – the scene took place exactly as shot. But motor racing fans may notice that the cars are going the wrong way round the track – a concession to the cameraman in order to get sunlight from the right direction.

Psyche 59 ◐
1964, UK, 94 mins, b/w
Dir: Alexander Singer
Stars: Patricia Neal, Curt Jurgens, Samantha Eggar, Ian Bannen
Rating: ★

Ever since this psychological sex drama came out, we have been trying to fathom the significance of the title. The plot concerns a nymphomaniac who sets her cap at her blind sister's husband, doing her tempting in front of her sister's sightless eyes. Patricia Neal and Samantha Eggar deserve credit for acting it so well. Walter Lassally's black and white photography also gives it some style.

Psycho ● ⓥ
1960, US, 109 mins, b/w
Dir: Alfred Hitchcock
Stars: Anthony Perkins, Janet Leigh, Vera Miles, John Gavin
Rating: ★★★★

Psycho is now rightly regarded as a masterpiece and probably Alfred Hitchcock's most accomplished and consistently sustained film. So it's a surprise, perhaps, to discover that the film was heavily panned by most critics on its initial release. But, of course, a few years later, they were hailing the picture as a classic, now right after the event and in the wake of cinema audiences who made *Psycho* a massive box-office hit right from the start. What may have unsettled reviewers was the fact that not only was the film a genuinely sweatily suspenseful shocker and not simply another of the director's polished thrillers but that it was also filled with delicious black humour that was even more concentrated than in Hitchcock's equally misunderstood *The Trouble With Harry* a few years previously. There's a great deal more to the movie than simply the justly celebrated set pieces, most memorably the legendary murder in the shower, shot by Saul Bass. For a start, there is the inventive and superbly-constructed screenplay by Joseph Stefano, based on Robert Bloch's novel; John L Russell's fine black and white cinematography; art director Joseph Hurley and Robert Clatworthy's haunting Gothic mansion which lowers over the cabins of the Bates Motel; and Bernard Herrmann's sinister and screeching score. Add to that Hitchcock's impeccable control of every scene, casting and performances that could hardly be bettered and you have a not-to-be-missed cinema experience to be savoured time and time again. Some parts are still hard to watch. Leigh's Oscar nomination was the only one of her career.

Psycho II ● ⓥ
1983, US, 125 mins, colour
Dir: Richard Franklin
Stars: Anthony Perkins, Vera Miles, Meg Tilly
Rating: ★★★

Just when you thought it was safe to go back into the shower, Anthony Perkins returned as Norman Bates, 22 years after he first operated the Bates Motel under Alfred Hitchcock's management. Unlike most sequels, this one comes off remarkably well. Perkins is in fine, twitchy form, developing the character with some sly touches of black humour rather than simply reprising it. Nice to see Vera Miles back too, still pursuing Norman over her sister's death.

P

Psycho III ● ⓥ

1986, US, 93 mins, colour
Dir: Anthony Perkins
Stars: Anthony Perkins, Diana Scarwid,
Jeff Fahey
Rating: ★★★

Good news for horror fans. The Bates
Motel is back in business. 'Could you
tell me – is there an inexpensive place
to spend the night around here?' asks
runaway nun Diana Scarwid, fleeing
from the desires of the flesh right into
the arms of Hollywood's favourite
psychopath (still Anthony Perkins)
until Freddy Krueger came along.
Scarwid is even made up to look like
Janet Leigh (complete with the same
character initials) – but 'momma'
don't allow . . . and, as the Perkins
features assume the familiar twitch,
the corpse count soon piles up. 'Can't
have that sort of thing happening in
my motel,' Perkins chides Scarwid,
after finding her, wrists slashed, in the
bath, rather pre-empting his 'mother's'
intention of murdering her. 'I guess I
did leave the bathroom in a mess,' she
apologises. Perkins smiles. 'I've seen it
worse,' he says. Such black irony sits
well with Perkins' own direction,
which piles on the gore with a tactful
hand of which even Hitchcock might
not have disapproved.

Psychomania ●

(aka: The Death Wheelers)
1972, UK, 95 mins, colour
Dir: Don Sharp
Stars: George Sanders, Beryl Reid,
Nicky Henson
Rating: ★★

Considering Don Sharp's reputation as
a fine director of action scenes and
horror films, it's not surprising that
the scenes without dialogue work best
in this black horror comedy about a
gang of Hell's Angels motorcyclists.
They make a pact with the Devil in
return for the secret of immortality,
then commit suicide and return from
the grave. Sounds silly and it is, but
Sharp ensures that you'll jump out of
your armchair on at least one occasion
and maybe more.

P'tang, Yang, Kipperbang ○

1982, UK, 93 mins, colour
Dir: Michael Apted
Stars: Alison Steadman, Robert
Urquhart, John Albasiny
Rating: ★★★

This touching, gently comic account
of a schoolboy's obsession with a girl
in his class, skilfully drawn by Jack

Rosenthal, centres on Alan, perfectly
played by John Albasiny, whose secret
torment is as pure as the idyllic
post-war setting. Young Alan's seething mass of schoolboy desire is, in fact,
as chaste as the private life of his
teacher (Alison Steadman) is unchaste.
The suspense involved in Alan's attempts to get his girl is beautifully
drawn out. So serious a quest does this
become that it even overrides his
passion for cricket. He relives John
Arlott's commentaries word for word,
amusingly applying the action to his
imaginary struggle to win not the
Ashes but his beloved Ann. As the
elusive heroine, Abigail Cruttenden,
in the role of the prettiest girl in the
class, expresses all the boredom and
smugness that third form girls tend to
adopt in such circumstances. As Alan's
cohorts, Mark Brelsford and Chris
Caballis commendably display the
more unsavoury nature of rampant
schoolboys (short of hair but long on
curiosity), leaving their more
sensitive friend to suffer alone those
first steps along the rocky road from
word games to women.

Public Enemy, The ○ ⓥ

1931, US, 84 mins, b/w
Dir: William A Wellman
Stars: James Cagney, Jean Harlow,
Edward Woods, Joan Blondell
Rating: ★★★

James Cagney's blazing performance
in this classic Warner Bros gangster
film confirmed him as a major star and
endeared him to all the grapefruit
growers of America when he found a
new use for their product by pushing
one into Mae Clarke's face. (He was
later to continue his screen assault on
her by hurling her out of bed and
throwing her across a corridor in *Lady
Killer*). The story of the rise and fall of
a crime czar may have been something
of a cliché through over-use but here,
under William A Wellman's pacy
direction, it fizzes across the screen
with excitement, and Cagney's death,
wrapped like a mummy and delivered,
bullet-ridden to his mother's door,
still retains its power.

Public Enemy's Wife ○

1935, US, 69 mins, b/w
Dir: Nick Grindé
Stars: Pat O'Brien, Margaret Lindsay,
Cesar Romero, Dick Foran
Rating: ★★★

Pat O'Brien and Robert *King Kong*
Armstrong are G-Men (the film,
somewhat confusingly, was shown in

Britain as *G-Man's Wife*) and Margaret
Lindsay takes the title role of the
much put-upon heroine who is saddled not only with gangster Cesar
Romero as a husband, but also a fake
marriage that turns out to be the real
thing, plus the kind of merry melodrama typical of Warner Bros
co-features of the period. Slick direction by Nick Grindé covers up the
less credible moments.

Public Eye, The ● ⓥ

1992, US, 98 mins, colour
Dir: Howard Franklin
Stars: Joe Pesci, Barbara Hershey,
Stanley Tucci, Jerry Adler, Jared Harris
Rating: ★★★

An unusual film for crime
connoisseurs, appropriately set in
1942. There hasn't been a film about a
sensation-hungry photographer in
many a year: this darkly-shaded example spotlights Joe Pesci as the
shutterbug with pretensions to recognition, a sad little whippet of a
man who's always first on the scene at
fires, killings, car crashes and other
tragedies. Human suffering is stamped
on all his work but no one will pub-
lish his portfolio of front-page
sensations. Depressed, Pesci is putty in
the hands of femme fatale Kay
(Barbara Hershey) who runs her late
husband's nightclub but is worried
about his Mob connections. When
one of them turns up dead when Pesci
knocks on his door on Kay's behest,
the little man opens up a whole well
of worms that looks as if it might suck
him right down inside. Pesci catches
exactly the vulnerability beneath the
camera hotshot's cockiness. Hershey is
particularly good as the flame to his
moth, no better than she ought to be
but no worse. It's an impressive piece
of work on an offbeat but constantly
absorbing theme.

Pufnstuf ⊙

1970, US, 98 mins, colour
Dir: Hollingsworth Morse
Stars: Jack Wild, Billie Hayes, Martha
Raye, Mama Cass
Rating: ★★

H R Pufnstuf is the friendly dragon on
that faraway island who, more than
anyone, paved the way for the
success of the Muppets. Here, his TV
series is extended into a full-length
feature film whose only weakness is
that the human characters come across
more stongly than the puppets, led by
Pufnstuf himself. Mama Cass especially
makes a splendidly impressive first

appearance, sitting in a gaudily-painted hip bath, surrounded by fruit, and singing 'Different', the best of a very tuneful score. The in-human characters sometimes come into their own, however, particularly with the advent of a cigar-smoking stove that talks like James Cagney.

Pulp ◐
1972, US, 95 mins, colour
Dir: Mike Hodges
Stars: Michael Caine, Mickey Rooney, Lizabeth Scott
Rating: ★★

Second-rate crime writer Michael Caine finds himself involved in murder and political intrigue when he is invited to write the biography of a has-been Hollywood movie gangster (Mickey Rooney) in this spoof thriller. Director Mike Hodges obviously enjoyed making this fun but uneven film; having said that, his scattergun tactics mean that many of his targets were missed. Michael Caine seems somewhat detached from all the goings-on, but Mickey Rooney gets his teeth into what was one of his best roles for years. There are also some delightful cameo roles, especially one from Dennis Price. Any sideswipe at gangster films and thrillers is somewhat obscured by the script and the sunny Mediterranean setting.

Pumping Iron ○
1976, US, 85 mins, colour
Dir: George Butler, Robert Fiore
Stars: Arnold Schwarzenegger, Lou Ferrigno
Rating: ★★

This beautifully made documentary on the unique world of bodybuilders presaged, in its way, the new interest in 'muscle-man' films. Once populated by Steve Reeves and Gordon Scott in the late Fifties and early Sixties, they have been given a fresh lease of life in the Eighties by the popularity of Lou Ferrigno as the green half of *The Incredible Hulk* and of Arnold Schwarzenegger in a host of macho roles. Both men are 'on show' here, Schwarzenegger proving particularly personable in his articulate and humorous approach to his 'art', in this unexpectedly winning and agreeable film.

Pumpkin Eater, The ◐
1964, UK, 110 mins, b/w
Dir: Jack Clayton

Stars: Anne Bancroft, Peter Finch, James Mason
Rating: ★★

'Perceptive' and 'lacerating' are among the adjectives which have been used to describe this powerful drama dealing with the disintegration of a marriage. The three stars (Peter Finch and James Mason are the others) all give excellent performances, and Anne Bancroft won a British Oscar for her interpretation of the role of the inward looking wife. The film was a landmark in the British cinema of the Sixties. Its excellent supporting cast includes Sir Cedric Hardwicke (superb in his last role), Richard Johnson, Maggie Smith and Yootha Joyce, who has a small but telling role as a woman in a hairdressing salon.

Pump Up the Volume ● ⓥ
1990, US, 100 mins, colour
Dir: Allan Moyle
Stars: Christian Slater, Scott Paulin, Ellen Greene, Samantha Mathis, Annie Ross
Rating: ★★★

It's obvious from the outset of this story of a teenage radio pirate that the star has to be something special to make it work. Well, the brooding Slater is something special here and, after a fairly tedious couple of reels, this film gets a grip on you. The purpose of Slater's 10 o'clock broadcasts, which somehow remains a mystery to his parents (he makes them from home) is to expose the corruption at his own school; and this he eventually does. It's always nice to see injustice stood on its head and there's a special irony here in that Slater's father is the school commissioner who needs his eyes opened by his own son. Slater is fine, and he's virtually the whole show, although there's a nice turn from singer Ellen Greene in a straight role as a conscientious teacher. Annie Ross is slightly over the top as the corrupt headmistress of the school, and one or two other performers as similar figures of authority, trying hard for comedy, tend to undercut the basic values of the film.

Punch and Judy Man, The ○
1962, UK, 90 mins, b/w
Dir: Jeremy Summers
Stars: Tony Hancock, Sylvia Syms
Rating: ★★

Struggling to establish a film career, Tony Hancock should have stuck with his TV writers Ray Galton and

Alan Simpson, even though their first movie script for him, *The Rebel*, had proved less than a total success. Slow, self-indulgent and far too lugubrious to be a hit with the millions who had switched on to 'the lad 'imself' on TV, this second effort flattened Hancock's movie career at a swoop. Yet it has some incidental pleasures, not least in the opening sequence of Hancock dressing and morosely eating breakfast, and in the performances of Hancock himself and John le Mesurier as the melancholy Sandman who instructs him obliquely about the obligations of marriage.

Punchline ◐ ⓥ
1988, US, 128 mins, colour
Dir: David Seltzer
Stars: Sally Field, Tom Hanks, John Goodman
Rating: ★★

They say that by and large comedians are rather sad people. You can well believe it after watching this cuttingly well acted, out-of-the-ordinary but rather dislikeable picture about the stand-up comics of a downtown American nightclub. Naturally, they all long to leap from the part-time to the big time, and this story focuses on two particular cases: the brilliant but unstable Steven (Tom Hanks) and the housewife (Sally Field) who just likes making people laugh, but whose husband (John Goodman) doesn't understand. No prizes for guessing that a contest at the club for a TV spot will come down to a battle between them. Hanks is at times brilliant, even memorable, and Field tries hard for sympathy in her familiar puppy-dog fashion. But it's difficult to get close to these people, or to root for them at the end. The film does catch some of the roar of the greasepaint and the smell of the crowd, though you can't see any of these melancholy funny-people enjoying it for long. Hanks took some real-life success, though, when his performance won an Oscar nomination.

Punisher, The ● ⓥ
1990, US, 89 mins, colour
Dir: Mark Goldblatt
Stars: Dolph Lundgren, Louis Gossett Jr, Jeroen Krabbé, Kim Miyori
Rating: ★

There are surely too many martial arts avengers with vaguely foreign accents around for the genre to last. You feel it's only a matter of time before Lundgren, Van Damme and Co are

P

joining forces to meet Dracula and
the Werewolf. In the meantime,
here's Dolph as a *Marvel* comic-strip
hero, an ex-cop who knocks off a few
dozen gangsters a year and lurks in the
sewers with only an arsenal of weapons for company, brooding over the
death of his wife and children these
five years before. It's a pretty unpleasant exercise in which the main
object seems to be to impale those
parts of the body that haven't already
been sliced off. The language is hardly
that of *Marvel* comics, unless they've
changed since our teenage days – not
that that will worry fans of this sort of
thing. Nancy Everhard has a fresh appeal as one of the cops pursuing The
Punisher and the action scenes are
well-edited and directed with ruthless
efficiency. Pretty nasty.

Puppet on a Chain ○
1970, UK, 98 mins, colour
Dir: Geoffrey Reeve
Stars: Sven-Bertil Taube, Barbara
Parkins, Alexander Knox
Rating: ★

A breathtaking speedboat chase
through the canals of Amsterdam is
the highlight of this Alistair MacLean
thriller about a gang of heroin
smugglers. The acting and the action
are formula Seventies' stuff, but that
waterbound sequence – made, incidentally, not by director, Geoffrey
Reeve, but by another director, Don
Sharp – will jolt you right out of your
seats.

**Pure Hell of St Trinian's,
The** ○
1960, UK, 94 mins, b/w
Dir: Frank Launder
Stars: Cecil Parker, George Cole, Joyce
Grenfell
Rating: ★★

The *St Trinian*'s cycle was beginning
to run down a little, but while George
Cole (as Flash Harry) and Joyce
Grenfell (as Sgt Ruby Gates) are
around, there are still some laughs to
be squeezed out of the little horrors,
who are discovered at the outset busy
at their usual occupation of burning
down the school.

Pure Luck ○ ⊙
1991, US, 96 mins, colour
Dir: Nadia Tass
Stars: Martin Short, Danny Glover,
Sheila Kelley, Sam Wanamaker, Scott
Wilson
Rating: ★

Another French success, *Le Chèvre*, gets
the Hollywood treatment, and the
result is pure disaster. Some guys have
all the luck. Eugene Proctor (the
manic Martin Short) isn't one of them.
When an accident prone heiress goes
missing in Mexico, disaster-magnet
Eugene is chosen to find her: the
theory apparently is that, as his fatal
attraction for mishaps mirrors hers, so
he will retrace her steps. Hmm. Sent
to search with him is a humourless
detective (Danny Glover), rapidly to
realise how lethal a weapon his new
partner can be. Slapstick pure and
simple with Short at his most resistible. A long 96 minutes.

Purple Mask, The ○
1955, US, 83 mins, colour
Dir: Bruce Humberstone
Stars: Tony Curtis, Colleen Miller, Gene
Barry, Angela Lansbury
Rating: ★★★

Tony Curtis enjoys himself as a kind
of Napoleonic Scarlet Pimpernel, in
an adventure story with a polish and
literacy that places it several grades
above such early Curtis swashbucklers
as *Son of Ali Baba*. Here he has some
sizzling duels, notably with Dan
O'Herlihy, and with two familiar television faces: Gene Barry, once of
Burke's Law , and George Dolenz,
who cut a fair dash himself as *The
Count Of Monte Cristo*.

Purple Plain, The ○
1954, UK, 100 mins, colour
Dir: Robert Parrish
Stars: Gregory Peck, Win Min Than,
Bernard Lee, Brenda de Banzie
Rating: ★★★

Harrowing, exciting war film, set
largely in the Burmese jungle, with
Peck as a nerve-shot pilot trying to get
himself and his wounded navigator
back to safety after their plane has
been downed in a dogfight. Eric Ambler's screenplay agonisingly recreates
the novel by H E Bates, and Maurice
Denham gives an awesomely good
account of an out-and-out coward.
Excellent photography in Technicolor
by Geoffrey Unsworth includes a
first-rate crash sequence.

Purple Rain ● ⊙
1984, US, 111 mins, colour
Dir: Albert Magnoli
Stars: Prince, Apollonia Kotero, Morris
Day, Olga Karlatos, Clarence Williams III,
Jerome Benton
Rating: ★★

In his first major movie, the purple
popinjay of pop, Prince, comes
across as a kind of coffee-coloured
Elvis Presley for the Eighties, complete with a story that might have
been ripped from one of The King's
earlier films. Short of stature, but with
an eager contempt for his audience
and an obvious confidence in his own
entertaining ability, Prince
dominates the show. Subtlety, as you
might expect, is hardly the keynote of
a film that is crude in every sense of
the word, overdrawn and archly
written in such time-honoured movie
phrases as (Prince's mother to his father) 'You don't let me have any fun.'
A strange and violent film this, but
true to its own lights and shamelessly
aimed at a teenage disco-dancing
public. Prince has a nice casual way
with the odd humorous line – the
very few, that is, that don't contain
four-letter words.

**Purple Rose of Cairo,
The** ⊙ ⓥ
1985, US, 82 mins, colour
Dir: Woody Allen
Stars: Mia Farrow, Jeff Daniels, Danny
Aiello, Dianne Wiest
Rating: ★★★

Woody Allen's fascination with technical wizardry continued with this
delightful comedy about a 1930s
waitress (Mia Farrow) who falls in
love with a fictional hero (Jeff Daniels)
in the latest attraction, *The Purple Rose
of Cairo*, at her local cinema. One day
he steps out of the movie screen and
into reality and literally sweeps her off
her feet. 'I just met a wonderful man,'
she confides to a friend. 'He's fictional
but you can't have everything.' It's the
kind of inventive, ingenious, romantic, endearingly silly fantasy that
scriptwriters once turned out for
Hollywood at regular intervals. This
one bears the imprint of Allen's own
wistful, sense-of-loss comedy. Farrow
is quite outstanding as the amazed
Cecilia and Daniels more mobile and
personable that any movie star of his
type would have been (or allowed to
be) in the mid-Thirties.

Pursuit of the Graf Spee
See: The Battle of the River Plate

Pushover ○
1954, US, 88 mins, b/w
Dir: Richard Quine
Stars: Fred MacMurray, Phil Carey,
Dorothy Malone
Rating: ★★★

The cynical detective in this thriller, which shot Kim Novak to stardom, might well be Fred MacMurray's character from *Double Indemnity* 10 years on. A decade older and wearier, but no wiser than his earlier character, MacMurray falls for the ample charms of Novak and turns against his own kind to get the girl and the proceeds of the robbery with which she was involved. The script comes up with some nice ironies, and MacMurray is perfect in the kind of shallow but not dislikeable character he always played wonderfully well.

Pygmalion ○
1938, UK, 96 mins, b/w
Dir: Leslie Howard, Anthony Asquith
Stars: Leslie Howard, Wendy Hiller, Wilfrid Lawson
Rating: ★★★★

The original, now classic 'straight' version of Bernard Shaw's play, long before it was set to music to emerge as *My Fair Lady*. It's a well-known fact that Shaw himself didn't care at all for the casting of Leslie Howard as Professor Higgins, though in the event Howard's account of the role won acclaim. Nonetheless, the show was stolen by Wendy Hiller, who scored a major triumph in the part of Eliza Doolittle and as a result soared to film stardom. Even today, many regard her performance as the yardstick by which successive Elizas have been judged. Enjoyable, too, is Wilfrid Lawson as Eliza's father, Doolittle the dustman. Those who like a story to be neatly rounded off could well feel that in his play Shaw somewhat evaded resolving the problem he'd set himself: the film opts for a different, more conclusive if not altogether convincing ending. Witty, entertaining and thoroughly delightful, this remains one of the great British films of the late Thirties.

Pyrates ● Ⓥ
1991, US, 95 mins, colour
Dir: Noah Stern
Stars: Kevin Bacon, Kyra Sedgwick, Bruce Payne, Deborah Falconer
Rating: ★

A very rude sex comedy about a couple who set things alight when they make love. It's also a very bad sex comedy. The script runs like a Woody Allen throw-out, with such lines as 'You realise that memories are not your own but shared by someone else.' There's the spark (!) of a fun idea here, but Kevin Bacon can't play

comedy this broad and his real-life wife Kyra Sedgwick is way over the top as his fiery friend. The best things in this film are the impressive clips of cities on fire from such vintage movies as *In Old Chicago*.

Q

Q & A ● Ⓥ
1990, US, 132 mins, colour
Dir: Sidney Lumet
Stars: Nick Nolte, Timothy Hutton, Armand Assante, Patrick O'Neal
Rating: ★★

A good formula detective story on everybody's-corrupt lines, its impact muffled in the telling. Director Lumet has only himself to blame: he wrote it as well. A cop called Brennan (Nolte), as maverick as he's crooked, takes it on himself to gun down an underworld figure. The DA (who, being played by Patrick O'Neal, you wouldn't trust as far as the next room) hires assistant DA Al Reilly (Hutton) to investigate. Reilly's green, inexperienced: and that's the idea. He'll wrap the case up neatly and quickly. We've seen too many of these movies, of course, to think it will turn out like that. But it takes Lumet a long time to reach his expected conclusion: minor bad guys are expendable, but you never get the ones at the top. What attracted Nolte to play your run-of-the-mill psychopathic cop is hard to fathom – the role has no depth at all. Other performances are generally unattractive. The action is brutal but sluggish – Lumet should perhaps ask himself why, when it starts so snappily, this little crime thriller should run 132 minutes.

Q Planes ○
1939, UK, 80 mins, b/w
Dir: Tim Whelan
Stars: Laurence Olivier, Valerie Hobson, Ralph Richardson
Rating: ★★★

Exciting film about British bomber planes disappearing on test flights. The story was written by American writer Brock Williams (although four people worked on the eventual screenplay). Williams was called into Alexander Korda's office and told of a newspaper article about a plane that went up but never came down. Williams asked what happened, and Korda said: 'How should I know? It's for you to write the rest of the story!' This he did, capturing both thrills and the mood of the period.

Q – The Winged Serpent ●
1982, US, 100 mins, colour
Dir: Larry Cohen

Stars: Michael Moriarty, David Carradine, Candy Clark
Rating: ★★

Older cinemagoers who have seen *The Giant Claw* will know what to expect from this piece of mumbo jumbo about a pterodactyl-type monster. Brought to life by an ancient Aztec prayer, it lays an egg in a feathery-looking tower and proceeds to pluck nubile maidens from every rooftop swimming pool and lilo in New York. All this is coupled with the story of a smalltime crook (a busy, eye-catching performance by Michael Moriarty) who finds the creature's lair and feeds it the two associates menacing him for the diamonds he has lost after a robbery.

Quackser Fortune Has a Cousin in the Bronx ○

1970, US, 90 mins, colour
Dir: Waris Hussein
Stars: Gene Wilder, Margot Kidder
Rating: ★★★

American stars Gene Wilder and Margot Kidder, both at the beginning of distinguished careers, head an otherwise Irish cast in this pleasing regional comedy, with Wilder ideally cast (and sporting a fruity Irish accent) as the happy-go-lucky horse-manure salesman whose life is changed by an American girl he meets in Dublin. A good script by Gabriel Walsh and sensitive direction by Waris Hussein bring out both the fun and the embarrassment of the hero's futile attempts to become part of student society.

Quadrophenia ● ⓥ

1979, UK, 120 mins, colour
Dir: Franc Roddam
Stars: Phil Daniels, Sting, Leslie Ash, Toyah Wilcox
Rating: ★★★

An adrenalin-high film which successfully explores the Sixties Mod culture. Its source material is the rock album by The Who, whose film company produced *Quadrophenia*. The violent centrepiece is a well-staged Bank Holiday seaside riot. Director Franc Roddam brings it all down to human terms through the emotional and social conflicts of the central character Jimmy (a meaty role for Phil Daniels). Stylish, angry, loud – just like the era it recreates – the film also features the acting debut of singer Sting.

Quality Street ○

1937, US, 80 mins, b/w
Dir: George Stevens
Stars: Katharine Hepburn, Franchot Tone, Fay Bainter
Rating: ★★

Flimsy 19th-century whimsy from Hollywood, a typical Katharine Hepburn performance of the Thirties, and you'll find her radiant or annoying according to your tastes. Fay Bainter, soon to move on to mother roles (and an Oscar for *Jezebel*) is excellent as Hepburn's level-headed older sister and Joan Fontaine has a minor role.

Quantez ○

1958, US, 80 mins, colour
Dir: Harry Keller
Stars: Fred MacMurray, Dorothy Malone, Sydney Chaplin, John Gavin
Rating: ★★★

Tough and gripping Western about a group of fugitives from justice, holed up in a ghost town near the Mexican border. Fine performances, especially from John Gavin and Dorothy Malone. Ms Malone had won an Oscar two years previously for *Written on the Wind*, and she shows clearly here that that was no flash in the pan. The ending packs a powerful impact. The pace is a bit stodgy, but the strength of the acting sees it through.

Quantrill's Raiders ○

1958, US, 68 mins, colour
Dir: Edward Bernds
Stars: Steve Cochran, Leo Gordon, Diane Brewster, Gale Robbins
Rating: ★

Westcott, a Confederate spy, enlists the help of Quantrill, a lawless raider, in a poor, unsubtle (but action-packed) Western adventure with Steve Cochran sitting comfortably in the saddle as the hero. In the proverbial black hat is Leo Gordon as Quantrill, an effective baddie. Colour and music are good but the script isn't: every ragged cliché in the Western hall of fame is trotted out here.

Quatermass and the Pit ● ⓥ

(aka: Five Million Miles to Earth)
1967, UK, 100 mins, colour
Dir: Roy Ward Baker
Stars: James Donald, Barbara Shelley
Rating: ★★

Despite muddy colour and occasionally laughable effects, the air of foreboding and evil that hangs over this third of the *Quatermass* films gives it an atmosphere that makes it a worthy addition to the series. Although not as suspenseful as the TV original, this film version contains forthright performances from James Donald, Andrew Keir (as Quatermass) and Barbara Shelley, offering the last in her long line of Hammer heroines.

Quatermass Experiment, The ○

(aka: The Creeping Unknown)
1955, UK, 82 mins, b/w
Dir: Val Guest
Stars: Brian Donlevy, Jack Warner, Margia Dean, Gordon Jackson
Rating: ★★★

A nail-biting chiller based on the television serial that kept millions glued to their screens. As a film, it owes a lot to the tremendously powerful performance of Richard Wordsworth as the former space pilot now possessed by he knows not what. He brings horror, loneliness and helplessness to the role. Special effects are as good as one could possibly expect and the film encouraged its studio, Hammer, to go on to become Britain's foremost purveyor of horror for the next 20 years.

Quatermass 2 ○

(aka: Enemy from Space)
1957, UK, 85 mins, b/w
Dir: Val Guest
Stars: Brian Donlevy, John Longden, Sidney James
Rating: ★★

The sequel to the legendary *The Quatermass Experiment* doesn't recapture the bleakness, originality and excitement generated by the original. Still, it has a fascinating cast, including Brian Donlevy, Bryan Forbes, Sidney James and John Longden. American distributors ditched poor old Quatermass again and called it *Enemy from Space*.

Queen Bee ○ ⓥ

1955, US, 95 mins, b/w
Dir: Ranald MacDougall
Stars: Joan Crawford, Barry Sullivan
Rating: ★★★

Totally tailored to the talents of Joan Crawford, Hollywood's queen of post-war melodrama, this gives her a chance to dominate her supporting cast as a villainess you'll love to hate. One American critic wrote when the film came out that 'Miss Crawford plays her role with such silky villainy that we long to see her dispatched'.

Writer-director Ranald MacDougall turns in a thoroughly adept slice of lush film melodrama, and Crawford's vicious, neurotic Eva is magnificently gowned throughout by Jean Louis.

Queen Kelly ○
1928, US, 96 mins, b/w
Dir: Erich Von Stroheim
Stars: Gloria Swanson, Seena Owen, Walter Byron, Wilhelm von Brincken, Madge Hunt, Wilson Benge
Rating: ★★★

This much troubled film was undertaken by Gloria Swanson against all advice, especially when she hired profligate director Erich Von Stroheim to direct the screen version of his own story. A typical Von Stroheim yarn about debauched royalty and aristocracy (with a degenerate prince that he must have created with himself in mind), it received the usual Von Stroheim extravagance. Close to a million dollars had already been spent with no end in sight when Swanson phoned her backers to report that 'There's a madman in charge here. The scenes he's shooting will never get past the censor.' Production was shut down. Much later, Swanson and director Edmund Goulding shot an ending completely different from the one originally envisaged. Their film was a flop, and it was nearly 60 years before a restored version was pieced together. There are some striking sequences, but others (such as Kelly's marriage in Africa) are prolonged to ridiculous lengths. Swanson's a little old and sophisticated for the adorable orphan, as her plentiful close-ups emphasise. Still, she makes a fair stab at the role. Seena Owen, who later became a respected screenwriter, is particularly effective as the possessive monarch who blights Kelly's chances of romance with the prince, and Tully Marshall absolutely odious as the dissolute ruffian who enters Kelly's life late in the story.

Queen of Destiny
See: *Sixty Glorious Years*

Queen of Spades, The ○
1948, UK, 96 mins, b/w
Dir: Thorold Dickinson
Stars: Anton Walbrook, Edith Evans
Rating: ★★★

An outstanding film from a particularly productive period in British cinema, *The Queen of Spades* is a macabre fantasy set in Russia in 1806. The leading role is played by Aus-

trian-born Anton Walbrook, a popular star of the day (he had earlier made another British success, *Gaslight*, for the same director, Thorold Dickinson). As the old Countess, Edith Evans gives one of her most memorable screen portrayals in a baroque chiller that remains one of a kind.

Quentin Durward
See: *The Adventures of Quentin Durward*

Quest for Love ○
(aka: Quest)
1971, UK, 90 mins, colour
Dir: Ralph Thomas
Stars: Joan Collins, Tom Bell, Denholm Elliott
Rating: ★★★

One of the narrowest near-misses in the realm of highly original science-fiction to be recorded in recent years. There's a lot to admire, not least in the performances of Tom Bell and Joan Collins, in this Ralph Thomas-directed version of a strange little short story by John Wyndham, who wrote *The Midwich Cuckoos* and *Day of the Triffids*. The initial stages of the film are chillingly well realised and the final chase comes off heartwarmingly well. Only in the middle stages does it all not quite work. But give this unusual film a try: you could find that you like it a lot.

Quick Before It Melts ○
1965, US, 98 mins, colour
Dir: Delbert Mann
Stars: George Maharis, Robert Morse, Anjanette Comer, Yvonne Craig
Rating: ★★★

Bright, if sporadic comedy, with rubber-faced Robert Morse mugging gamely as the reporter from *Sage* – 'the magazine that thinks for you' – sent out to cover life at the South Pole, although he and George Maharis are rather hampered by having their faces covered by huge bears most of the time. Pretty Yvonne Craig keeps the feminine flag flying bravely and the script does come up with one gem. While Morse is flirting with Ms Craig (his fiancée and the boss's daughter), the boss rings up. 'What are you doing?' he barks. 'Well,' replies Morse happily, 'I'm trying to seduce your daughter.' 'How're you making out?' demands the boss. (Pause) 'Oh, yeah, I know. I had the same trouble with her mother.' Better comedies would have given their right arm for less.

Quiet American, The ○
1957, US, 120 mins, b/w
Dir: Joseph L Mankiewicz
Stars: Audie Murphy, Michael Redgrave, Claude Dauphin
Rating: ★★

Joseph L Mankiewicz's adaptation of Graham Green's *The Quiet American* is elegant and also scrupulously faithful – until the end. Green's story is basically anti-American, but the climax here – as the naive American seeks an end to the war in Saigon – shifts all the blame onto the Communists. Audie Murphy is audaciously cast as the (un-named) American, but the acting honours are shared by Michael Redgrave's memorably cynical journalist and Claude Dauphin's wary police chief. Perhaps not surprisingly, disappointingly little is made of the few bursts of action – Mankiewicz was very much a man of words.

Quiet Man, The ○ ⓥ
1952, US, 129 mins, colour
Dir: John Ford
Stars: John Wayne, Maureen O'Hara, Barry Fitzgerald
Rating: ★★★

Director John Ford and his favourite leading man John Wayne transfer the fisticuffs of the Old West to the West of Ireland in this love story with bloody knuckles. It is one of Ford's finest hours, painstakingly constructed as if he were at work on an oil painting, and highlighted by a terrific knock-down fight between Wayne and Victor McLaglen. The whole thing has a wonderful fresh-air feel.

Quiet Please, Murder ○
1942, US, 70 mins, b/w
Dir: John Larkin
Stars: George Sanders, Gail Patrick, Richard Denning
Rating: ★★

A most unusual little crime drama, with an excellent study in sardonic degeneracy from George Sanders as Fleg – one of his admirable gallery of villains from Hollywood's early Forties. A well-made thriller.

Quiet Wedding ○
1941, UK, 80 mins, b/w
Dir: Anthony Asquith
Stars: Margaret Lockwood, Derek Farr, A E Matthews, Peggy Ashcroft
Rating: ★★★

Classic farce of pre-nuptial chaos, much imitated but rarely bettered, not

Q

even by the lively remake *Happy is the Bride!* 16 years later. This version, full of kindly caricature and spiky wit, allows room for splendid cameo performances by, among others, Peggy Ashcroft, David Tomlinson, Bernard Miles and Margaret Rutherford.

Quiet Weekend ○
1946, UK, 93 mins, b/w
Dir: Harold French
Stars: Derek Farr, Marjorie Fielding, George Thorpe
Rating: ★★

A sequel to *Quiet Wedding*, this comedy is based on a hit play by Esther McCracken, and again has the Royd family well to the fore, this time (unsuccessfully) seeking peace and quiet in a country cottage. Some fun is had, and the weekend cottage is a beautiful piece of the production designer's art, with its antique plumbing and 'Mind your head' signs beside low doorways. Only in comparison with the original, in fact, does the material here look a bit thin.

Quigley Down Under ○ ⓥ
1990, Australia, 116 mins, colour
Dir: Simon Wincer
Stars: Tom Selleck, Alan Rickman, Laura San Giacomo, Chris Haywood, Ben Mendelsohn
Rating: ★★

Or: *A Fistful of Dingos*, as Selleck's Australian Western proves to have a distinct flavour of spaghetti. Although the music is sub-Elmer Bernstein, the pacing and treatment of this long film is strictly Sergio Leone, with a nod to the horses on the move and towering outback mountainscapes that always feature strongly in director Wincer's films. Selleck is a 19th century Yank adventurer who travels hundreds of miles in response to rancher Rickman's ad for a crack long shot, only to find that all Rickman wants him to do is shoot Aborigines from a distance. Selleck throws Rickman out of his ranch-house window, which earns him and the 'crazy woman' (San Giacomo) who has attached herself to him, a one-way ticket to the middle of the desert. Or, at least, it should be one way. But this being a Western where the hero never misses and the villain has expendable henchmen by the ranchful, you can guess the rest, down to the final shoot-out when the bad guys have Selleck at their mercy but decide to give him a gun. San Giacomo, rather overshadowed by Julia Roberts in *Pretty Woman*, is terrific.

Quiller Memorandum, The ◑
1966, UK, 100 mins, colour
Dir: Michael Anderson
Stars: George Segal, Alec Guinness, Max Von Sydow, Senta Berger
Rating: ★★★

George Segal had one of his best parts to date in this taut, sometimes very exciting spy thriller set in present-day Berlin. Segal, hunted by low-key camerawork on the one hand, and a neo-Nazi group of killers on the other, is perfectly cast as the dogged special agent – humorous as the hunter, defiant in defeat as the hunted. To this chilly and compelling spy thriller, writer Harold Pinter contributed a faintly mocking, faintly menacing collection of words that gives the characters identities all their own, and raises the stealthy, nervy prowlings-around to a high level of suspense. Alec Guinness has all the most acid lines but Segal does particularly well. John Barry wrote the haunting background music, delicately clangorous and underlining the tension.

Quintet ◑
1979, US, 110 mins, colour
Dir: Robert Altman
Stars: Paul Newman, Vittorio Gassman, Bibi Andersson, Brigitte Fossey
Rating: ★★★

Director Robert Altman's best work since *Images* eight years earlier. A sort of sciene-fiction Western, with hints of *10 Little Niggers*, it's ingenious, imaginative and rare for an Altman film – at times even exciting. The time is the future, and the setting is a remote colony near one of the poles, where mankind seems to be in the painful process of dying out. The only game in town is Quintet, deadly offshoots of which have developed into 'tournaments', in which the players really try to kill one another. And it is in just such a tournament that 'hero' Paul Newman becomes involved. Absolute hocus-pocus, this, of course, but carried off with some style. The sub-arctic settings are splendidly realised, and Jean Boffety's icy camerawork does these imaginatively bleak surrounds full justice, without ever sinking into dreariness.

Quo Vadis ○ ⓥ
1951, US, 171 mins, colour
Dir: Mervyn LeRoy
Stars: Robert Taylor, Deborah Kerr, Leo Genn, Peter Ustinov
Rating: ★★★

The famous film with dramatic scenes of combat between Christians and lions in the arena, and many other spectacular sequences that include the burning of Rome. Deborah Kerr became the first Christian martyr to go to the stake in diaphonous blue chiffon. Peter Ustinov scene-steals as Nero while Rome burns: they should have thrown the sermonising script in as well.

R

Race for Your Life, Charlie Brown ⊙
1977, US, 75 mins, colour
Dir: Bill Melendez
Rating: ★★

A brainless cartoon feature which does little justice to the *Peanuts* gang of comic strip fame. It chronicles their adventures, together with Snoopy the dog and Woodstock the canary, on a raft race during a summer camp. No story, no characterisation, zero. And the humour of the newspaper strip remains obstinately on the other side of the screen. Harmless enough for kids, but a major disappointment for Snoopy fans.

Racers, The ○
(aka: Such Men Are Dangerous)
1955, US, 112 mins, colour
Dir: Henry Hathaway
Stars: Kirk Douglas, Bella Darvi, Gilbert Roland
Rating: ★★

A motor-racing drama made by Henry Hathaway, a master of action and adventure since the mid-Thirties when he made *The Lives of a Bengal Lancer*. The main character, well played by Kirk Douglas, who revels in such casting, is as unpleasant a 'hero' one could hope to find before the days of angry young men. And the hair-raising routine of the dedicated driver's life, always wondering whether the next race will be his last, is perfectly captured. Gilbert Roland and Cesar Romero, two 'Latin lovers' from Hollywood's golden days of the Thirties, are both impressive as two drivers who are almost over the hill. Even so, it's Katy Jurado, so good in a small role as a driver's wife, who steals the show from the stars

Race to the Yankee Zephyr ◐
(aka: Treasure of the Yankee Zephyr)
1981, Australia/New Zealand, 108 mins, colour
Dir: David Hemmings
Stars: Ken Wahl, Lesley Ann Warren, Donald Pleasence, George Peppard
Rating: ★★★

It's non-stop action all the way in actor David Hemmings' fifth film as director. Shot on location in the rugged terrain of New Zealand's South Island, it puts mean and moody Ken Wahl (later to hit the big time as star of the *Wiseguy* TV series) and Donald Pleasence (just moody) as the good guys chasing a $50 million payroll hidden since 1944 in the wreck of the 'Yankee Zephyr' plane. George Peppard is the snarling villain (a throwback to a 1960's spoof) on their tails. There's no denying the energy in the frantically paced production, but it remains unfocussed, and the helicopter chases seemingly go on forever.

Rachel Papers, The ● ⓥ
1989, UK, 95 mins, colour
Dir: Damian Harris
Stars: Dexter Fletcher, Ione Skye, Jonathan Pryce, James Spader
Rating: ★★

This film of the bestselling Martin Amis novel will annoy anyone who read and loved the original and confuse newcomers to it, who will only be mystified by the novel's cult status. Dexter Fletcher treads water as the film's hero, Charles Highway, a precocious 19-year-old who embarks on a steamy affair with a beautiful American girl (Ione Skye), tires of her and ends up single again. End of story. End of film. In the end Fletcher is too self-conscious in the role (especially given his endless monologues to camera) and first-time director screenplay-adaptor Damian (son of Richard) Harris can't decide whether his characters belong in the swinging Sixties or the up-to-date Nineties. Skye, on the other hand, gives such a sensual, glowing performance that you can't understand why Charles grows bored with her. *The Rachel Papers* is a lost opportunity in more ways than one.

Racing with the Moon ●
1984, US, 108 mins, colour
Dir: Richard Benjamin
Stars: Sean Penn, Elizabeth McGovern, Nicolas Cage
Rating: ★★

This teen film about two boys about to be drafted into World War Two is a nostalgia picture but nothing special. Although competently and occasionally amusingly written, it doesn't make us care about its characters and, however hard the cast tries, the movie remains superficial. Sean Penn and Nicolas Cage certainly look the parts, but Cage's accent jars, as it would when he went on to star in *Peggy Sue Got Married*, and only Elizabeth McGovern seems really of the period. An onion too to director Richard Benjamin for not spotting that the 'contemporary' Paramount newsreel logo he uses bears a copyright date of 1927!

Racket, The ○
1951, US, 88 mins, b/w
Dir: John Cromwell
Stars: Robert Mitchum, Lizabeth Scott, Robert Ryan
Rating: ★★★

An exciting crime thriller that's decidedly different from the usual run. Based on a play previously filmed as an early talkie in 1928, it features Robert Mitchum as a city cop, and Robert Ryan as a mobster, both dinosaurs in their respective worlds, doing things the old way and refusing to listen to superiors. In their way, both are pawns of modern-style corruption above them. Although Samuel Fuller and Nicholas Ray also worked on the film, John Cromwell directed the vast majority of the footage, and a hard-hitting job he made of it, even if it still looks slightly like a play and the lack of background music does it no favours. A star-studded cast all get a fair share of the acting cake, and down-the-cast Robert Hutton actually gets to walk off with heroine Lizabeth Scott!

Radio Days ○ ⓥ
1987, US, 85 mins, colour
Dir: Woody Allen
Stars: Julie Kavner, Seth Green, Dianne Wiest
Rating: ★★★★

The Woody Allen film that hits the nostalgia jackpot. This is everything that an evocation of childhood should be but rarely is. It has warmth, many shafts of humour, a setting perfect in look and feel and a title that is no cover of convenience, the theme of radio running richly through an immensely enjoyable story about a childhood in a central American town around the years 1939 to 1944. Allen's own anecdotes (he narrates but doesn't appear) enliven and enrich the narrative, which runs separate stories of a poorish Jewish family from the backstreets, and a cigarette girl (Mia Farrow) who narrowly avoids being shot by a gangster, gains a precarious living as a radio 'chantoose' and ends up becoming a lioness among Hollywood gossip columnists. Farrow, whether squeaking bronchial Bronx or clambering over rounded vowels

R

when she takes elocution lessons, has never been better; even her singing isn't bad.

Radio Flyer ◐ ⓥ

1992, US, 120 mins, colour
Dir: Richard Donner
Stars: Lorraine Bracco, Adam Baldwin, Elijah Wood, John Heard, Joseph Mazzello, Ben Johnson
Rating: ★★

Much re-filmed in a checkered production, this is a disturbing drama with strong performances from intelligent young actors Elijah Wood and Joseph Mazzello as two brothers forced to retreat into a world of fantasy to escape their living nightmare. When their mother (Lorraine Bracco) remarries, young Mike and Bobby find themselves at the mercy of a brutal and unpredictable new stepfather (Adam Baldwin, a decade on from his more friendly hulk in *My Bodyguard*). Seeking refuge in a world of their imagination, they dream of building a flying machine. There are some pretty simplistic, uneasy, sub-Spielberg views afloat in all this, and it remains hard for the viewer to accept its concepts, in spite of the thoroughly engaging portrayals of the two boys. Tom Hanks is the unbilled narrator.

Rage in Harlem, A ● ⓥ

1991, US, 110 mins, colour
Dir: Bill Duke
Stars: Forest Whitaker, Gregory Hines, Robin Givens, Zakes Mokae, Danny Glover, Badja Djola
Rating: ★★

Today's black romantic comedy-crime-thriller: that is to say, laced with extreme violence and language, with most of the dialogue pitched at top-decibel level. The action starts in the sticks, with a black-white shootout that ends with sweet trick Givens hotfooting it out of a charnel-house full of bodies clutching a suitcase full of crude gold. Once in town, she latches on to plump, religious, virginal Whitaker as a prospective meal-ticket, falls in love with him and involves him with various literally cutthroat factions out to get the gold. Whitaker is quite sympathetic, and Givens seductive enough to kill for all right, but Glover has the only interesting role as a gangster who trusts only his beloved Pomeranian dog.

Raggedy Man ○

1981, US, 94 mins, colour
Dir: Jack Fisk
Stars: Sissy Spacek, Eric Roberts, Sam Shepard
Rating: ★★

A well-made, low-key drama which ends, not unexpectedly, in violence. Its most charismatic performance is given by Sissy Spacek as a divorcee with two sons who works as sole telephone operator at a small American town almost as forsaken as the one in *The Last Picture Show*.

Raggedy Rawney, The ◐ ⓥ

1988, UK, 102 mins, colour
Dir: Bob Hoskins
Stars: Bob Hoskins, Dexter Fletcher, Zoe Nathenson, Ian MacNeice
Rating: ★★★

A good film, unusual too – but downbeat and quite unpleasant to sit through: aspects of Bob Hoskins' debut as director/star which harmed its prospects at the box-office. The rawney of the title is a deserter from an unnamed war in an unknown country. He stumbles, dressed as a woman, into an encampment of gypsies also on the run from the war, and is sheltered by a girl, who knows he's a man and subsequently has his baby. To the gypsies, he remains a rawney, a mad woman, and brings them magical luck before turning into a jinx. Though Hoskins himself never really convinces as a gypsy, the film is full of super performances, especially Ian MacNeice as a friendly farmer and Zoe Nathenson as the girl. The ending is smashing, just right and, unlike some of the film, not over-protracted.

Raging Bull ● ⓥ

1980, US, 119 mins, b/w
Dir: Martin Scorsese
Stars: Robert De Niro, Cathy Moriarty, Joe Pesci, Burt Young
Rating: ★★★

The boxing sequences occupy only some 12 minutes but they rank among the most realistic and painful ever put on film: one thanks the fact that director Martin Scorsese chose to film this searing account of life and times of world middleweight champion Jake La Motta in black and white. The dramatic scenes are no less searing, carrying an emotional power and impact far in excess of the usual conventions of the Hollywood biopic. The movie is adult, both in its frank language and its characterization and narrative and, like its central character, pulls few punches. It is also completely compelling. Robert De Niro, who went as far for his art as to gain 50 pounds for the scenes where La Motta is on the way down, gives a commanding performance that more than deserved the Oscar it won. And Cathy Moriarty, as his wife, is no less impressive. You'll rock with every punch in the boxing scenes.

Raiders of the Lost Ark ○ ⓥ

1981, US, 115 mins, colour
Dir: Steven Spielberg
Stars: Harrison Ford, Karen Allen, Denholm Elliott, Paul Freeman, Alfred Molina, Ronald Lacey
Rating: ★★★

A 1941-style high adventure made in the James Bond manner and driven along with tremendous panache by director Steven Spielberg. It's the kind of film where the hero can say 'Meet me at Oscar's' while parting from a friend in the middle of the desert and no-one seems to think it amiss. Harrison Ford is the intrepid archaeologist transformed into a man of action at the drop of his spectacles; Karen Allen more than matches him as the feisty heroine who follows him through fire, water and – in one especially hackle-raising sequence – a pit of writhing snakes.

Raid on Entebbe ○

1976, US, 144 mins, colour
Dir: Irvin Kershner
Stars: Charles Bronson, Peter Finch, Horst Buchholz
Rating: ★★★

Considering the haste with which it was made – a rival version of the famous attack held by Israeli forces to rescue hostages held at Uganda's Entebbe Airport, *Victory at Entebbe*, was in production at the same time – the quality of this film surprised many critics. Cool, detached, exciting and well directed by Irvin Kershner, the film recreates the whole nightmare situation with chilling conviction. Nothing is overstated, people are drawn as real characters with no false heroics and the suspense builds remorselessly up to the raid itself.

Raid on Rommel ○ ⓥ

1971, US, 99 mins, colour
Dir: Henry Hathaway
Stars: Richard Burton, John Colicos, Clinton Greyn, Wolfgang Preiss
Rating: ★★

A war adventure, made in Mexico, aimed at boys of all ages. As in *The Desert Rats*, almost 20 years before, Richard Burton plays a British Army captain (then MacRoberts, here Foster) who crosses swords with the legendary Rommel in the North African desert. That talented German actor Wolfgang Preiss sensitively matches James Mason's classic portrayal of Rommel from earlier films, but the rest of the acting, from an assorted crew of British and Continental players, simply isn't in the same class. Coincidentally, it was director Henry Hathaway, usually to be found in realistic crime stories or John Wayne Westerns, who made both this film and *Rommel – Desert Fox*, in which Mason first etched his brilliant portrait of the German field marshal. The action is plentiful and explosive but – a common Hollywood ploy – extensive sections of it are taken from an earlier Universal desert warfare epic, the Rock Hudson film *Tobruk*.

Rails into Laramie ○

1954, US, 81 mins, colour
Dir: Jesse Hibbs
Stars: John Payne, Mari Blanchard, Dan Duryea, Lee Van Cleef
Rating: ★★

Rousing Western action, one of the many genre pictures made at Universal during the Fifties, with a neat line in sneering villainy from Dan Duryea. The brisk direction is by Jesse Hibbs, who made 11 films in the Fifties before moving to television and working on series such as *Wagon Train, Rawhide, Laramie* and *Perry Mason*.

Railway Children, The ⊙ Ⓥ

1970, UK, 108 mins, colour
Dir: Lionel Jeffries
Stars: Dinah Sheridan, Jenny Agutter, Bernard Cribbins, William Mervyn, Iain Cuthbertson, Sally Thompsett
Rating: ★★★

The wife and three children of a Foreign Office employee falsely accused of treason have to start a new life in Yorkshire. The girls soon get used to their new home and befriend a neighbour who says he will try to clear their father's name. A well-acted and scripted film from E Nesbit's much-read book, with lots of warmth and lovingly accurate attention to period detail (it's set in Edwardian times). Comic actor Lionel Jeffries directs effectively to produce a drama that holds attention right to the end.

Acting kudos go to a young Jenny Agutter as the older daughter, and Bernard Cribbins as Perks, the porter at the local railway station.

Rainbow, The ● Ⓥ

1988, UK, 104 mins, colour
Dir: Ken Russell
Stars: Sammi Davis, Paul McGann, Amanda Donohoe, Glenda Jackson
Rating: ★★

Russell returns to the works of D H Lawrence with this prequel to *Women in Love* and, at least in fits and starts, to his best form. The film does, though, suffer from typical Russellian excesses, especially in the nude scenes, and from a rather strained central performance by Sammi Davis as Ursula. More relaxed portrayals come from Amanda Donohoe, as her lesbian seducer, and inevitably from Glenda Jackson as her mother, not given quite sufficient screen time to walk off with the film. The most successful sequences are those set in junior teacher Davis's first school, a veritable workhouse of a place presided over with Dickensian intensity by Jim Carter. Particularly effective is the scene where Davis's worm turns and literally gets up off the floor to thrash a recalcitrant troublemaker within an inch of his life. The music by Carl Davis and Technicolor photography by Billy Williams catch the required mood exactly – often more successfully than Russell himself.

Raining Stones ● Ⓥ

1993, UK, 90 mins, colour
Dir: Ken Loach
Stars: Bruce Jones, Julie Brown
Rating: ★★

Director Ken Loach returns to showing life as it is, and this is a depressing look at the workless (though not workshy) working-class of Oldham. Bob (Bruce Jones) will turn his hand to anything from sheep-stealing to drain-cleaning to make a few bob for his family. Of course he gets into trouble after going to the local loan shark. But it's hard to feel as much sympathy for the guy as Loach wants us to. While resorting stubbornly to illegal activities to pay £100 for his daughter's Confirmation outfit, Bob still finds plenty for a profuse amount of smoking and drinking, plus an occasional flutter on the nags. Character inconsistencies and poor continuity, coupled with inadequate acting in minor roles (although Julie Brown is excellent as the long-suffering wife),

all conspire to drain your interest in this one, however commendable its intentions.

Rain Man ● Ⓥ

1988, US, 140 mins, colour
Dir: Barry Levinson
Stars: Dustin Hoffman, Tom Cruise, Valeria Golino, Jerry Molen, Jack Murdock
Rating: ★★★

When a film goes through four directors and the same number of possible stars in as many years, it's usually a sign that something is badly wrong with the leading actor, the idea, the script or the budget – or all four. But director Barry Levinson (*Tin Men* and *Good Morning, Vietnam*) struck box office gold in choice of star, Dustin Hoffman, and script, by Barry Morrow and Ronald Bass, with the finished film winning Oscars for both Best Actor and Best Original Screenplay. On the surface, the idea of a young hustler (Tom Cruise) kidnapping his autistic savant (a person extremely limited in some mental areas and extremely gifted in others) brother (Hoffman) because he's been left a bigger share of their father's inheritance, doesn't sound like blockbuster material. But it was. The scenes where the relationship between the brothers changes are raw and touching. Cruise displays a new maturity as an actor but is simply outclassed by Hoffman in what is admittedly a more sympathetic and showy role.

Raintree County ○

1958, US, 166 mins, colour
Dir: Edward Dmytryk
Stars: Elizabeth Taylor, Montgomery Clift, Eva Marie Saint, Lee Marvin
Rating: ★★

A sweeping romance with Elizabeth Taylor and Montgomery Clift, set against the backcloth of the American Civil War, and on a similar grandiose scale. It was MGM's costliest film when originally made – small wonder, with such crowd scenes, and a cast that also includes Eva Marie Saint, Lee Marvin, Nigel Patrick, Rod Taylor, Tom Drake, Agnes Moorehead and DeForest Kelley. The burning of Atlanta, Sherman's march through Georgia and the lavish scenes of life in the Deep South are all impressively spectacular. Yet, strangely, the most memorable scene is a small one: an hilarious sequence in which

R

Montgomery Clift defeats Lee Marvin in a foot race, despite a plot to get him drunk.

Raise the Titanic! ○
1980, US, 112 mins, colour
Dir: Jerry Jameson
Stars: Jason Robards, Anne Archer, Alec Guinness
Rating: ★★

An adaptation of Clive Cussler's best-selling novel about the greatest salvage operation of all time. The final scenes are exhilaratingly exciting, although it takes rather long time to get to them. Alec Guinness is along for the splash to provide a touch of acting class.

Raising a Riot ○
1955, UK, 91 mins, colour
Dir: Wendy Toye
Stars: Kenneth More, Shelagh Fraser, Mandy Miller, Jan Miller
Rating: ★★★

Sunny, fun-filled comedy that soon happily settles down into a series of domestic mishaps as Kenneth More tries to cope with his three kids (while the wife's away) at his father's ramshackle country home. A refreshing romp, carefree and uninhibited. Jan Miller is a bright leading lady, while sister Mandy plays one of the children.

Raising Arizona ◐ ⓥ
1987, US, 92 mins, colour
Dir: Joel Coen
Stars: Nicolas Cage, Holly Hunter, Trey Wilson, John Goodman
Rating: ★★

Romantic action farce from the *Blood Simple* and *Miller's Crossing* director Joel Coen. The criminal of *Raising Arizona* however – a role in which Nicolas Cage is perfectly cast – is strictly second-rate. A habitual cornerstore hold-up man, he falls in love with lady cop (Holly Hunter), who takes his picture each time he goes to jail. When she finds she can't have children, the solution seems easy: steal one of the quins recently born nearby. Now is that a dumb idea or what? It's a fiercely flaky film with charmless characters but lots of inspiration: the notion of a bounty hunter (called in by the distraught father of the kidnapped child) called the Lone Biker of the Apocalypse is very funny, and an extended chase scene involving a rapid tracking camera and pack of dogs is also worth a smile or two.

Raising Cain ● ⓥ
1992, US, 91 mins, colour
Dir: Brian De Palma
Stars: John Lithgow, Lolita Davidovich, Steven Bauer
Rating: ★★★

Big husky men dressing as women; bodies in cars disappearing into lakes; multiple personalities; dreams; people returning from the dead; the sudden shock at the end; yes, this is Brian De Palma's version of a black comedy. And, as De Palma's films are always at a remove from reality, it proves quite successful. John Lithgow is the child psychologist sorely in need of psychiatric help, and seemingly collecting babies (after killing their mothers) to satisfy some whim of his dead father. But the old guy may be alive, or just another of the several further personalities unleashed when Lithgow sees his wife (Lolita Davidovich) making love with an old flame just a few hours after he's come back into her life. All the De Palma trademarks are here: tracking camera, slow-motion, over-prolonged suspense, set pieces. The over-the-top performances of the three stars sit nicely within the film once you gauge the mood. It's De Palma at his least visceral and most playful.

Raising Daisy Rothschild ○
(aka: The Last Giraffe)
1979, UK, 93 mins, colour
Dir: Jack Couffer
Stars: Susan Anspach, Simon Ward
Rating: ★★

Backed by several TV favourites, Susan Anspach and Simon Ward play the Melvilles in this beautifully filmed animal story about rare giraffes.

Raising the Wind ○ ⓥ
(aka: Roommates)
1961, UK, 91 mins, colour
Dir: Gerald Thomas
Stars: Paul Massie, Jennifer Jayne, Leslie Phillips, Kenneth Williams, James Robertson Justice
Rating: ★★

A *Carry On* film in all but name, this is a farcical comedy set in a music academy, where six young students run through the gamut of musical jokes under the baton of Sir Benjamin Boyd, world famous conductor. Sir Benjamin is played by James Robertson Justice, in an extension of his Sir Lancelot Spratt creation for the *Doctor* series. Among the music stu-

dents, watch out for a young Jim Dale (later to take star roles in *Carry On* comedies) in a very small role playing a very large musical instrument.

Rally Round the Flag, Boys ○ ⓥ
1958, US, 106 mins, colour
Dir: Leo McCarey
Stars: Paul Newman, Joanne Woodward, Joan Collins
Rating: ★★

It's surprising to find Paul Newman and Joanne Woodward in a bedroom farce this broad, and Newman's strenuous over-playing in it gave such contemporaries as Cary Grant and David Niven little to worry about. Joanne Woodward makes a game shot at a role that needed a Carole Lombard, and Joan Collins is cast to type as a man-hungry neighbour with designs on Newman. Two of Hollywood's most talented men, Leo McCarey and Claude Binyon, wrote the script; that only suggests that this romp about a small American town menaced by military installations was never a good idea in the first place.

Rambling Rose ● ⓥ
1991, US, 113 mins, colour
Dir: Martha Coolidge
Stars: Laura Dern, Robert Duvall, Diane Ladd, Lukas Haas
Rating: ★★

Passion drums in the Deep South, and beats in the hearts of all men who meet Rose (Laura Dern). Quite happy to open up her petals to anyone who catches a whiff of her scent, this little nymphomaniac of the magnolia belt is devastating to the small community into which she's taken as a maid by the Hillyer family during the Depression. Before a few weeks are out, she's thrown herself at Daddy (Robert Duvall), popped into bed with the family's 13-year-old son (Lukas Haas) who helps himself to an impromptu sex lesson, and teeters around town in a dress that reveals more than it covers. Surprisingly, the film of Rose's misadventures aims at charm and atmosphere rather than titillation. Laura Dern is quite good as Rose, but Diane Ladd and Duvall are rather mannered and artificial as her employers. Nonetheless, Dern and Ladd were both nominated for Academy Awards, making them the first real-life mother and daughter to be so.

Rambo: First Blood Part II ● ⓥ

1985, US, 96 mins, colour
Dir: George P Cosmatos
Stars: Sylvester Stallone, Richard Crenna, Julia Nickson, Charles Napier, Steven Berkoff
Rating: ★★★

Again played by Sylvester Stallone, by now assuming the proportions of a mini Schwarzenegger, war veteran John Rambo is extracted from prison and sent back to Vietnam to locate missing American PoWs in this dazzling dose of jungle mayhem. When Rambo realises he has been set up as a sacrificial goat to appease a complaining American public, to be shot down in search of non-existent (the opposite of the truth) prisoners, the mission becomes one of revenge as well as rescue. The resultant hell-let-loose is breath-taking rubbish that entertains every foot of the way. For adventure fans, Rambo's trek provides action on a first-class ticket: never mind reality, feel the speed and power, and the skill of the editing. Not since the days of Errol Flynn has there been such a one-man army as this – and why not? Today's too-down-to-earth screen needs more like him. Followed by the exciting, but even less credible *Rambo III* in 1987.

Rambo III ● ⓥ

1987, US, 101 mins, colour
Dir: Peter MacDonald
Stars: Sylvester Stallone, Richard Crenna
Rating: ★★

Spectacularly topping its predecessors with a magnitude of panoramic action pyrotechnics, here are the further adventures of Rambo (Sylvester Stallone), the muscular monosyllabic warrior, and his mission into Soviet occupied Afghanistan. The battle scenes are explosive and terrifying with Rambo, as usual, gloriously and inhumanly impervious to fear and danger (who else could outrun a bullet-spitting helicopter?). Stallone, to his credit, makes the insane single-mindedness of Rambo believable in its fantastical context, but not surprisingly, the screenplay gives short shrift to the complexities of the Afghan war.

Rampage ○

1963, UK, 98 mins, colour
Dir: Phil Karlson

Stars: Robert Mitchum, Jack Hawkins, Elsa Martinelli
Rating: ★

Fine colour photography, a foot-tapping musical score by Elmer Bernstein and the sense of pace about Phil Karlson's direction, all contribute towards compensating for the holes in the script of this jungle adventure yarn. The object of the safari is to catch the 'enchantress' – 'half tiger, half-leopard' boasts the film – but when she does appear, it's rather a disenchantment, as she proves to be a sad-looking leopard with her coat partially dyed pink. Far more exciting are scenes of a tiger hunt, when two of the animals are caught in nets at the same time. Robert Mitchum and, particularly, Jack Hawkins, struggle manfully to extract some sense from their cardboard characters. Elsa Martinelli, with wardrobe by Oleg Cassini, looks a dream as the inevitable girl torn between the two men.

Ramrod ○

1947, US, 94 mins, b/w
Dir: André De Toth
Stars: Veronica Lake, Joel McCrea
Rating: ★★★

A somewhat underrated Western that looks rather more interesting now than when it first appeared – and vanished quickly, partly because of the declining box-office fortunes of its star, Veronica Lake. She's actually quite well cast as a headstrong spitfire in Barbara Stanwyck mould who takes the law into her own hands when her spineless rancher father knuckles under to a big-shot cattleman, nastily well played by Preston Foster. Strongly cast (Joel McCrea, Charles Ruggles, Arlene Whelan, Lloyd Bridges, Don DeFore and Donald Crisp are also in it), the film fairly gallops along under André de Toth's hard-driving direction.

Rancho Notorious ○

1952, US, 89 mins, colour
Dir: Fritz Lang
Stars: Marlene Dietrich, Arthur Kennedy, Mel Ferrer
Rating: ★★★

For all those who love moody, singing-commentary Westerns, there's only one better than this, and that's *High Noon*. Arthur Kennedy wears his 'twisted' expression to great effect as the embittered cowboy hunting the man who killed his fiancée, following the trail to an outlaws' roost run by

Marlene Dietrich at her slinkiest – triggering off a story, in the words of the song, 'of hate, murder and revenge'. Tightly, seethingly directed by the great Fritz Lang.

Random Harvest ○

1942, US, 126 mins, b/w
Dir: Mervyn LeRoy
Stars: Ronald Colman, Greer Garson
Rating: ★★★★

Charles Rainer (Ronald Colman), a British officer in the First World War, loses his memory and is being cared for in a sanitorium. Eluding the staff, he wanders off and starts a new life for himself and becomes a successful businessman, with the help of his devoted secretary. A delightful period piece that is lifted above mere soap opera by the performances of Colman and Greer Garson. A weepie with a happy ending, it was a Best Picture Oscar nomination. They don't make sentimental dramas like this anymore (not successfully anyway), which is a shame.

Randy Rides Alone ○ ⓥ

1934, US, 54 mins, b/w
Dir: Harry Frazer
Stars: John Wayne, Alberta Vaughan, George 'Gabby' Hayes
Rating: ★★

Here's a real rarity – an early John Wayne film with George 'Gabby' Hayes as the villain! Gabby's as nasty as he can manage as a character appropriately called Matt Black, but doubtless he was glad to get back to playing sidekicks who made up in whiskers for what they lacked in the way of teeth.

Ransom ○

1955, US, 109 mins, b/w
Dir: Alex Segal
Stars: Glenn Ford, Donna Reed, Juano Hernandez
Rating: ★★★

Following on *Blackboard Jungle* and *Trial*, this was the third of Glenn Ford's famous 'anguished' roles all within the same year, in which he revealed his new 'Method' style of acting after a spell with the Actors' Studio. Here, he is cast as a rich industrialist who incurs public wrath when he decides not to pay a massive ransom demand after his small son has been kidnapped. Good though Ford is, he has the acting honours stolen from under his nose by veteran black actor Juano Hernandez. The movie

R

itself, fraught with tension, is streets ahead of the usual Hollywood kidnap thriller. It was adapted by the writers, Cyril Hume and Richard Maibaum, from their television play *Fearful Decision*, and a fine job they made of doubling the length without losing any of the suspense. As Ford's hysterical wife, Donna Reed had her best film role since winning an Academy Award for *From Here to Eternity*.

Ransom ○

1977, UK, 97 mins, colour
Dir: Richard Compton
Stars: Oliver Reed, Deborah Raffin, Stuart Whitman, John Ireland
Rating: ★★

Cat-and-mouse Oliver Reed-Stuart Whitman thriller also known as *Assault on Paradise* and *Maniac*. Paradise is the name of the Arizona town subjected to a ransom demand as unusual as it is terrifying. Some serviceable suspense by the efforts to trap the fiend who is responsible.

Rapid Fire ● ⓥ

1992, US, 95 mins, colour
Dir: Dwight H Little
Stars: Brandon Lee, Powers Boothe, Nick Mancuso, Kate Hodge, Raymond J Barry
Rating: ★★

Enter the baby dragon: Brandon Lee, son of Bruce, is the Chinese American with a short fuse who demolishes people and objects alike if they come within three feet of him. After displaying the quieter side of his character – he draws a detailed likeness of a killer after a fleeting glimpse through a doorway – he gets down to the wisp of a plot and destroying the drug barons of east and west who are still operating through the same Chinese laundry such ne'er-do-wells ran in films of the Thirties. The film is almost nothing but action – well choreographed by Lee, director Dwight H Little and Jeff Imada – and nearly everyone gets killed but the star. Powers Boothe has some charisma, but delivers dialogue harshly as the lawman who becomes Lee's father figure; Kate Hodge is the obligatory curvy cop with the hots for our hero. 'Jake,' says Boothe, in an in-joke that may draw a groan or two, 'why don't you take those fists of fury of yours outside?' Fists of fury, flashing feet: Lee fans will love it.

Rare Breed, The ○

1966, US, 97 mins, colour
Dir: Andrew V McLaglen
Stars: James Stewart, Maureen O'Hara
Rating: ★★★

Fresh from his triumph with *Shenandoah*, director Andrew V McLaglen strengthens his reputation for creating warm, human characters and genuine wide-open-spaces atmosphere, in this engaging, richly-coloured yarn. His star, as in *Shenandoah*, is James Stewart, here as an ageing cowhand still looking for a dream. Gradually, unwillingly at first, Stewart acquires a fanatical belief in the potential of one Hereford breed bull, brought to America by prissy Englishwoman Maureen O'Hara. Stewart, blue eyes blazing with determination, especially when searching for the Hereford in a blizzard – is ideally matched by Brian Keith's red-bearded, extravagantly Scots-accented rancher, who has a whisky bottle in his bath instead of a cake of soap. And Jack Elam's bit-part villain sticks in the mind long after he is rather precipitously killed off.

Rashomon ● ⓥ

1950, Japan, 88 mins, b/w
Dir: Akira Kurosawa
Stars: Toshiro Mifune, Machiko Kyo, Masayuki Mori
Rating: ★★★★

Deservedly taking the Oscar for Best Foreign Language Film, this compelling drama ranks among director Akira Kurosawa's finest works. Using the story of the rape of a woman and the murder of her samurai husband, recounted in various versions by different eye witnesses, Kurosawa came up with a haunting, poetic and totally riveting study of the nature of truth and experience. His grouping and fluid visuals make the film a feast for the eye and superb performances – particularly by Toshiro Mifune as the violator and Machiko Kyo as the wife – engage the imagination. A masterpiece.

Rasputin and the Empress ○

1933, US, 123 mins, b/w
Dir: Richard Boleslawski
Stars: John Barrymore, Ethel Barrymore, Lionel Barrymore
Rating: ★★★

The only screen teaming of the three famous Barrymores. The film was called *Rasputin – The Mad Monk* in this country, a title used again many years later for a British version of the story made by Hammer Studios and featuring Christopher Lee. Strangely, although John Barrymore had already starred in *Svengali* and *The Mad Genius*, it's Lionel, the character actor of the family, who plays the flamboyant Rasputin in this film, with Ethel as the Empress fascinated by his evil charm. Treatment is tense, lavish and exciting, but the real treat for film fans is seeing the three Barrymores on screen together.

Rasputin – The Mad Monk ◐

1965, UK, 92 mins, colour
Dir: Don Sharp
Stars: Christopher Lee, Barbara Shelley
Rating: ★★

The legend of Rasputin, the monk who exerted a powerful and mysterious influence on the Russian royal family during the last days before the revolution, is a good basis for a thrilling drama. This Hammer offering doesn't quite make the most of its opportunities, though, despite a powerful and pretty frightening central performance from Christopher Lee as Rasputin. As you might expect from Hammer, the film is highly-coloured and quite bloody at times. Unfortunately, apart from the tense final scenes, director Don Sharp doesn't give the film the pace to make it truly gripping.

Rat Race, The ○

1960, US, 105 mins, colour
Dir: Robert Mulligan
Stars: Tony Curtis, Debbie Reynolds
Rating: ★★★

One of the few films to make the proper demands on Debbie Reynolds' undervalued acting ability, this is a heartwarming and thoroughly entertaining study of struggling showbusiness hopefuls in the garrets of New York. Tony Curtis and Ms Reynolds succeed in striking up a relationship of real warmth, involving us in all their ups and downs – mostly downs. And Jack Oakie gives them splendid support in his part as the barman-confidant. This was director Robert Mulligan's second film. He went on to such later successes as *To Kill a Mockingbird* and *Summer of '42*. Here, in addition to the performances of his cast, he's helped by a screenplay by Garson Kanin that is warmly rich in its observation of human behaviour. Kanin is best remembered today for his scripts on such Tracy-Hepburn successes as *Adam's Rib* and *Pat and Mike*. This script is more down to earth, but no less enjoyable.

Rattle of a Simple Man ◐ ⓥ
1964, UK, 95 mins, b/w
Dir: Muriel Box
Stars: Harry H Corbett, Diane Cilento, Michael Medwin, Thora Hird
Rating: ★★

A rather touching and at times richly amusing extended playlet about an 'innocent' football fan from the north, and the night he spends talking to a London prostitute in her flat. Not very plausible, perhaps, but winningly done. As Cyrenne, the streetwalker, Diane Cilento is persuasive and just right. And Harry H Corbett was able to break away completely from his *Steptoe* image. Michael Medwin is also very good as Corbett's big-talking friend. It was the last film directed by Muriel Box, wife of producer Sydney.

Raven, The ◐
1935, US, 61 mins, b/w
Dir: Lewis Friedlander
Stars: Boris Karloff, Bela Lugosi
Rating: ★★★

Director Lew Landers was a specialist in quickfire films that rarely ran longer than 70 minutes. This was his first feature (made under his real name, Lewis Friedlander) and among his fastest and most forceful, thanks mainly to a fortuitous teaming of horror kings Boris Karloff and Bela Lugosi. The plot has very little to do with Edgar Allan Poe, although the writers do manage to squeeze in his pendulum torture from *The Pit and the Pendulum*.

Raven, The ○
1963, US, 86 mins, colour
Dir: Roger Corman
Stars: Vincent Price, Peter Lorre, Boris Karloff, Hazel Court, Jack Nicholson
Rating: ★★★

Horror has rarely been more skilfully spoofed than in this delightful Roger Corman-directed spree. Vincent Price excels as a retired magician who needs to change a raven into human (Peter Lorre) form by a mixture of dead man's hair, jellied spiders and bat's blood – 'Dried or dehydrated?' Price asks the talking bird. But the cauldronful is not enough – Lorre still has his wings and Price has run out of dead man's hair. So down they trot to the family vault. 'I'm sure Dad

wouldn't mind,' smiles Price. It gets funnier, too, ending up with our two friends pitting their magical wits against the wickedest wizard of all (dear old Boris Karloff) in a storm-surrounded castle. Despite the original 'X' certificate, most children will enjoy this hugely. Jack Nicholson's in it too, though you'd never guess he'd end up a superstar from his performance here.

Raw Deal ○
1948, US, 85 mins, b/w
Dir: Anthony Mann
Stars: Dennis O'Keefe, Claire Trevor, Marsha Hunt, Raymond Burr
Rating: ★★★

The last (and probably best) of an excellent quartet of tough, medium budget thrillers made by director Anthony Mann before he moved on to a memorable series of Westerns with James Stewart. There are few likeable characters in this story of a framed gangster's ruthless revenge. Claire Trevor scores heavily as his moll (as well as providing the laconic narration), Dennis O'Keefe makes a good job of the 'hero' who cynically uses people for his own ends, and Raymond Burr is an excellent, sadistic heavy. The excitement of the climax is underlined by the skilful, shadow-laden photography of cameraman John Alton.

Raw Deal ● ⓥ
1986, US, 105 mins, colour
Dir: John Irvin
Stars: Arnold Schwarzenegger, Kathryn Harrold, Sam Wanamaker, Darren McGavin, Robert Davi
Rating: ★★

The problem with Schwarzenegger, Norris and Stallone's Eighties' movies like this is that, however polished and persuasive the build-up of the plot, we know that our heroes will eventually take a machine-gun and mow down the entire syndicate of bad guys just like shelling peas. Pieces of furniture to hide behind? Forget it. Only the hero does that. A pity, for much of *Raw Deal* is held firmly in the *film noir* tradition by John Irvin even if the hero is not quite the alienated loner the genre customarily demands. The theme of the undercover man being trapped into doing things he doesn't want to do to keep his cover intact has been around for more than half a century, and it works well enough here on a pulp fiction level, with a burnished performance by Harrold as

the gangster's moll with whom good ol' Arnold won't sleep 'cos he's married – even though his wife thinks he's dead. But then you know he can get out of the tightest corner just because he's Arnold. No vulnerability, you see. That's what made you grip your chairs for the safety of the agents of yore.

Raw Edge ○
1956, US, 76 mins, colour
Dir: John Sherwood
Stars: Yvonne De Carlo, Rory Calhoun, Mara Corday, Rex Reason
Rating: ★★

A very unusual Western, set in the wilds of Oregon. For a principal ingredient in its action-packed story, it makes use of an old pioneer custom which decreed that a widow goes to the first man who claims her. The central character is played by the glamorous Yvonne De Carlo, so it's understandable that competition is pretty fierce. The supporting cast includes Neville Brand and Emile Meyer, who acted together with brilliant effect in that outstanding prison drama film, *Riot in Cell Block 11*. Ms De Carlo herself gets plenty of competition in the spitfire stakes from sultry Mara Corday.

Rawhide ○
1950, US, 86 mins, b/w
Dir: Henry Hathaway
Stars: Tyrone Power, Susan Hayward
Rating: ★★

Rawhide is the name of the trail station at which Tyrone Power and Susan Hayward are trapped by outlaws in this Henry Hathaway-directed Western which gave a first sizeable role to Jack Elam as one of the bandits. Hathaway sustains the claustrophobic tension well and stages a couple of exciting gunfights.

Rawhide Years, The ○
1955, US, 84 mins, colour
Dir: Rudolph Mate
Stars: Tony Curtis, Arthur Kennedy
Rating: ★★★

Western fans shouldn't miss this well-plotted, firmly characterised but little-seen action film. Arthur Kennedy gives another of his nicely done, double-shaded portrayals as a genial ruffian who helps a riverboat gambler clear himself of a murder charge. Earl Felton's screenplay, from an excellent novel by Norman A Fox, gives Kennedy and Tony Curtis (as

R

the gambler) many opportunities to score off one another, as well as keeping the story going at a lively pace.

Razor's Edge, The ○ Ⓥ
1946, US, 146 mins, b/w
Dir: Edmund Goulding
Stars: Tyrone Power, Gene Tierney, John Payne, Anne Baxter
Rating: ★★★

Hollywood had a brave stab here at filming Somerset Maugham's famous philosophical novel, and the results ran well over the two-hour mark. It did, however, win an Oscar for Anne Baxter, cast against type as the dipso-maniac Sophie. Tyrone Power is the restless aviator searching for meaning in his life; Herbert Marshall plays Maugham himself, and there are spar-kling supporting performances from Clifton Webb and Elsa Lanchester. For all its faults, the film is far more absorbing than the 1984 remake with Bill Murray and Theresa Russell.

Razor's Edge, The ◐
1984, US, 128 mins, colour
Dir: John Byrum
Stars: Bill Murray, Theresa Russell, Denholm Elliott
Rating: ★★

Remaking a classic film is a dangerous business usually doomed to failure and so it proved here. It's doubly difficult when the original film is based on an equally classic novel. Bill Murray, good though he is, can't fill Tyrone Power's shoes as the tormented man who doesn't want to settle down. He becomes involved in the First World War then travels to India to 'find himself'. Murray's persona makes Somerset Maugham's central character something of a lightweight, robbing it of a lot of credibility. On the plus side, Theresa Russell, as the girl Murray tries to rescue from a life of sin and degradation, gives a very strong performance, as does the ever-reliable Denholm Elliott. The film also looks quite impressive, apart from the battle scenes, but it's ultimately an unsatis-fying experience, poorly edited and stuffed to the gills with stilted dialogue that seems to belong to another era.

Reach for the Sky ○
1957, UK, 135 mins, b/w
Dir: Lewis Gilbert
Stars: Kenneth More, Muriel Pavlow
Rating: ★★★

Written and directed by Lewis Gil-bert, this is based on Paul Brickhill's book about Douglas Bader, the air ace who lost both legs but was determined to overcome his disability and fly again. Kenneth More's legs were encased in aluminium and he spent hours with Bader himself an adviser to the film – perfecting the stiff-legged gait of a man with artificial legs. There was also a galaxy of British character actors in the supporting cast, which included Michael Gough, Dorothy Alison, Sydney Tafler, Jack Watling, Nigel Green and Eric Pohlmann. More inevitably dominates and takes a lion's share of the limelight, although Ms Alison sneaks it from him for a while with her sympathetic portrayal of Nurse Brace. The film stays the course smoothly and seems but half its length.

Real Genius ●
1985, US, 106 mins, colour
Dir: Martha Coolidge
Stars: Val Kilmer, Michelle Meyrink
Rating: ★

This attempted satirical comedy about scientists being corrupted in the search for *Star Wars*-type weapons misfires in all directions. After *Top Secret!* and *Top Gun*, this was distinctly bottom-drawer for star Val Kilmer, and relies on below-the-belt humour for what impact it can muster. Best of the cast is Michelle Meyrink as a curva-ceous, non-stop, engineering student. Director Martha Coolidge has done much better work since, including the Oscar-winning *Rambling Rose*.

Real Glory, The ○
1939, US, 95 mins, b/w
Dir: Henry Hathaway
Stars: Gary Cooper, Andrea Leeds, David Niven
Rating: ★★★

Unjustly neglected Hollywood action film, directed with dash by Henry Hathaway, staging some excellent ac-tion scenes as Doctor Gary Cooper tries to save Philippine patriots from murderous insurgents just after the Spanish-American war. 'Coop', David Niven and Broderick Crawford form a *Soldiers Three*-style triumvirate and battle scenes explode all over the screen. Even if you saw the film long ago, you'd be hard put to remember the name of the actress who shares top billing with the star: it was Andrea Leeds. Far more interesting though is Vladimir Sokoloff, playing the

sneaky, treacherous Datu, with the skin and eyes of a reptile.

Reality Bites ◐ Ⓥ
1994, US, 99 mins, colour
Dir: Ben Stiller
Stars: Winona Ryder, Ethan Hawke, Ben Stiller
Rating: RB

Director Ben Stiller chooses to give us quite a chunk of this dose of post-graduate blues on home videos shot by the characters, trying to the eyes and hardly cinema either. Not that you'll want to trouble yourself with the unconvincing problems of a dishevelled quartet of wannabes, who share a cluttered bedsit. Two of them, Winona Ryder and Ethan Hawke, are obviously destined to end up together and it seems an eternity be-fore they realise what the rest of us could have told them during the opening credits. These are tiresome twentysomethings from the start and they don't get any better. See it for the stars if you must, but you could pack your bags and go home 10 min-utes from the end when the dialogue reaches an all-time low as Hawke declares he has 'a planet of regret sit-ting on my shoulders'. We know what he means.

Real McCoy, The ◐ Ⓥ
1993, US, 100 mins, colour
Dir: Russell Mulcahy
Stars: Kim Basinger, Val Kilmer, Terence Stamp
Rating: ★★

One more time for the caper thriller about the robbery of the impregnable bank. There's nothing new here and the only twist is that the gang is led by a woman, fresh out of prison and blackmailed into the job by the kidnap of her son. Kim Basinger is pretty good in the role and she's about all the dullish film has going for it. Val Kilmer is not much of anything as the guy who helps her double-cross the raiders, and Terence Stamp attempts an American accent as the gang boss that just doesn't pass muster by today's high standards. Even the robbery itself is pretty routine: there are one or two tense moments, but not enough to keep the eyelids from drooping before the end. At least it has a professional gloss and for that and Basinger, a two-star rating is just about justified.

Real Men ◐
1987, US, 93 mins, colour
Dir: Dennis Feldman

Stars: James Belushi, John Ritter, Barbara Barrie
Rating: ★

A distinctly unfunny spy spoof comedy about aliens battling with the CIA over some kind of big gun that can blow up an entire planet. Scenes fail to hang together as a cohesive whole and James Belushi and John Ritter mug their embarrassed way through it by the skin of their teeth, no doubt justifiably thinking that their talents deserved better. Even United Artists, who backed it, didn't think much of the finished film, releasing it only in the Kansas City and St Louis areas!

Rear Window ○ ⓥ
1954, US, 112 mins, colour
Dir: Alfred Hitchcock
Stars: James Stewart, Grace Kelly, Raymond Burr
Rating: ★★★

Hitchcock suspense classic about a press photographer who, housebound with his leg in plaster, becomes obsessed with the notion that his neighbour across the way (a white-haired Raymond Burr in pre-*Perry Mason* and *Ironside* days) has done away with his wife. Besides the mounting suspense (especially of the 'will they or won't they get away with investigations before the 'murderer' comes back to catch them?' variety), there's the famous love scene where Hitch's camera circles hero James Stewart and girlfriend Grace Kelly as they kiss. All this plus prime performances from Stewart (no mean feat to achieve such emotion and conviction in such an immobile role) and from sandpaper-voiced Thelma Ritter as his nurse. John Michael Hayes and Hitchcock were Oscar-nominated for screenplay and direction, as was the excellent Robert Burks for his very skilful handling of the Technicolor photography which called for an equal amount of carefully-composed long shots and huge close-ups. Hayes actually based his screenplay on a story by Cornell Woolrich although the finished product differs markedly from the original, and Hitchcock freely admitted to having borrowed some of the more grisly aspects of the plot from the real-life murder cases of Patrick Mahon and Dr Crippen!

Rebecca ○ ⓥ
1940, US, 130 mins, b/w
Dir: Alfred Hitchcock

Stars: Joan Fontaine, Laurence Olivier, Judith Anderson, George Sanders
Rating: ★★★★

Hitchcock's first work in Hollywood, a brilliantly realised and atmospheric adaptation of Daphne du Maurier's enduring novel, won Oscars for Best Film and for George Barnes' fine camerawork. Joan Fontaine made her breakthrough to stardom as the (nameless) young bride haunted by the memory of husband Laurence Olivier's first wife, the enigmatic Rebecca of the title, who died in mysterious circumstances. In later years, Hitchcock rather mischievously dismissed Rebecca as a novelette, 'a woman's picture' lacking in humour. But its virtues are simplicity, superb performances and a richly textured visual style that compels attention. And just one of the many typical touches by the Master is his representation of Manderley's creepy housekeeper Mrs Danvers: in her unforgettable portrayal of this key role, Judith Anderson is almost never shown in motion but seems to materialise in rooms and doorways, standing perfectly still, as if from nowhere.

Rebel, The ○
(aka: Call Me Genius)
1960, UK, 105 mins, colour
Dir: Robert Day
Stars: Tony Hancock, Paul Massie, Irene Handl, George Sanders
Rating: ★★★

Despite being attacked by the British critics at the time, Tony Hancock's first starring venture is a minor comedy classic. The scribes, too familiar with Hancock's cosy half-hour TV and radio format, vented their spleen on this superb piece of buffoonery from the Lad Himself. Admittedly, Hancock's gloomily truculent persona was stretched wider by the big screen, but his shabby splendour, his conviction of unrecognised grandeur and his whole down-at-heel veneer of respectability, all shine through to make his frustrated insurance clerk with visions of artistic excellence a thoroughly sympathetic and loveable figure. *The Rebel* is scripted by the creators of the pompous denizen of *23 Railway Cuttings*, Alan Simpson and Ray Galton, and although one misses Tony's streetwise anchor-man Sidney James (he was soon to be jettisoned by Hancock from his TV series), doughty support is given by Irene Handl, as the awful landlady Mrs Crevette, and

George Sanders, in the opening scene which beautifully conveys the soul-destroying grind of the commuter's lot, despite its glaring piece of cinematic licence – it is impossible to move from one train to another parked alongside as both doors open outwards. A treat for all lovers of this fine British funnyman.

Rebel ◑ ⓥ
1985, Australia, 91 mins, colour
Dir: Michael Jenkins
Stars: Matt Dillon, Debbie Byrne, Bryan Brown
Rating: ★★

Matt Dillon has a name to match his screen persona, even if he's badly miscast in this Australian musical romance. As Rebel, a US marine who has gone AWOL in Sydney in 1942, Dillon hasn't the dramatic depth to carry off a character whose motives are ambiguous to say the least. Craggy Bryan Brown, who went on to leading man status in Hollywood with *Gorillas in the Mist*, *Cocktail* and *F/X*, is a sharp profiteer, while there is a startling cameo from Ray Barrett as a flamboyant club pianist. But it is left to pretty Debbie Byrne, as the married singer in an all-girl showband, to sweep all before her as she belts out a clutch of songs written specially for the film.

Rebel Without a Cause ◑ ⓥ
1955, US, 111 mins, colour
Dir: Nicholas Ray
Stars: James Dean, Natalie Wood, Sal Mineo, Dennis Hopper
Rating: ★★★★

James Dean, the legendary idol of the 1950s, starred in just three feature films. This powerful work gave him the role with which he is most associated – the troubled and delinquent youth misunderstood by his parents and society. His highly charged, very personal portrayal of Jim helped create the cult which has persisted around his name ever since. Natalie Wood (in one of her best performances) and Sal Mineo are fellow rebels; action and colour photography are excellent, and the script full of well-remembered lines. The only weakness is the ending, which doesn't seem to prove very much at all.

Reckless ○
1935, US, 92 mins, colour
Dir: Victor Fleming

R

Stars: Jean Harlow, Franchot Tone, William Powell
Rating: ★★

Producer David O Selznick severely and unnecessarily dented Jean Harlow's confidence here by casting her in the completely unsuitable role of a song-and-dance star. Joan Crawford, who could at least dance, had originally been slated for the role of a showgirl who marries the wrong man, but the plot probably carried too many echoes of her own *Dancing Lady* two years earlier (complete with Franchot Tone as the wrong man). So Harlow was uncomfortably straitjacketed into a role where her singing had to be dubbed and her dancing heavily edited. A good supporting cast, including Tone, William Powell, Rosalind Russell, Allan Jones and Henry Stephenson (and, in much smaller roles, Mickey Rooney and Akim Tamiroff), provides consolation for film buffs, along with a score that includes 'Trocadero', 'Cyclone', and the Kern-Hammerstein title number. Harlow's songs are dubbed by vocalist Virginia Verrill.

Reckless Moment, The ○
1949, US, 82 mins, b/w
Dir: Max Ophuls
Stars: Joan Bennett, James Mason, Geraldine Brooks
Rating: ★★★

James Mason scored his first major Hollywood success as a reluctant blackmailer in this tautly-made melodrama about a woman who falls into the clutches of ne'er-do-wells while trying to protect her errant daughter. Good local detail, sadly ironic ending. Joan Bennett co-stars as the woman in a thriller/drama that still looks good today.

Reckoning, The ◐
1969, UK, 111 mins, colour
Dir: Jack Gold
Stars: Nicol Williamson, Rachel Roberts
Rating: ★★

Nicol Williamson's sexual bull on the rampage was much in vogue in the late Sixties and early Seventies but, somehow, he couldn't extend the characterisation into fully-fledged stardom. Here, he's in typical stop-at-nothing mood as a rough diamond climbing to the top of London's social ladder. The film is distinguished by Rachel Roberts' very erotic account of a sensual northern landlady, and by the

ravishing Technicolor photography of Geoffrey Unsworth, who, three years later, won an Oscar for his work on *Cabaret*, just reward for many years of consistently fine colour camerawork. Ann Bell, a constantly underrated actress, is also good as Williamson's much put-upon wife.

Red Badge of Courage, The ○ ⓥ
1951, US, 69 mins, b/w
Dir: John Huston
Stars: Audie Murphy, Bill Mauldin
Rating: ★★★

More has been written about this John Huston film than almost any other movie, including a whole book! Huston shot Stephen Crane's novel about a young soldier's baptism of fire in the American Civil War in painstaking, poetic style. The film, made in black and white, is full of swirling mists and smoke of battle, but Huston's fast-moving cameras, tracking the action and charging with the soldiers, ensure that there's plenty of excitement as well. MGM saw the finished product, got cold feet about the meaning and impact of its anti-war sentiments and hacked it down to a mere 69 minutes of cinema running time. The original was probably a masterpiece; even these tattered remnants are full of striking moments, with actors chosen for the characters they can express rather than their abilities. Audie Murphy plays the youth, Bill Maudlin (later a Pulitzer Prize-winning cartoonist) is his friend. In Britain the film was originally released in a double-bill with the Spencer Tracy/Katharine Hepburn comedy *Pat and Mike*. Some programme!

Red Beret, The ○
1953, UK, 88 mins, colour
Dir: Terence Young
Stars: Alan Ladd, Leo Genn, Susan Stephen
Rating: ★★

There was much alarm when Ladd came to Britain to make this film about the Paratroopers, for fear it should show him winning the war for the Americans in the same way as did Errol Flynn eight years earlier in *Objective Burma*. But it's a straight forward and exciting war film, with fine colour photography, and Ladd backed by a strong British cast.

Red Dust ○
1932, US, 89 mins, b/w
Dir: Victor Fleming
Stars: Clark Gable, Jean Harlow, Mary Astor
Rating: ★★★

A sturdy and enjoyable romantic melodrama set in Indo-China where Clark Gable romances sexy floozie Jean Harlow and meanwhile married Mary Astor falls for him. The triangular relationship reappeared in 1940 as *Congo Maisie* and again in 1954 as *Mogambo*, in which Gable – now in Africa – repeated his original role with Ava Gardner in the Harlow part and Mary Astor's role taken by Grace Kelly. This one is still the best version, with all three stars in top form.

Red Fury, The ○
1985, US, 90 mins, colour
Stars: Katherine Cannon, William Jordan
Rating: ★★

Hardly an original story – boy loves horse and, naturally, makes good in the final reel. But, given the somewhat old-fashioned plot, which also delves into the realms of racial intolerance, the drama makes its way pleasantly to its upbeat conclusion. Familiar faces in the cast include Alan Hale Jr – the son of the great Hollywood character actor Alan Hale in one of his last screen roles – and Diane McBain. Hardly another *Black Stallion*, although horse-loving children and teenagers will doubtless be enthralled by the vivid tracking shots of horses on the move.

Redhead from Wyoming, The ○
1953, US, 80 mins, colour
Dir: Lee Sholem
Stars: Maureen O'Hara, Alex Nicol
Rating: ★★

Alex Nicol, fair-haired contract player from several Universal-International films of the Fifties, landed his biggest role in this Grade A Western, opposite fiery Maureen O'Hara as Kate (the redhead of the title) who runs a gambling casino that's also a hideaway for wanted men.

Red Heat ○ ⓥ
1988, US, 106 mins, colour
Dir: Walter Hill
Stars: Arnold Schwarzenegger, James Belushi, Peter Boyle
Rating: ★★

Poor old Arnold Schwarzenegger. No matter how different the plot they

give him, it still comes out the same.
Arnie walks in, demolishes the bad
guys and walks out again. No sweat.
Just the odd bruise or two for effect.
He almost smiles in this one. But not
quite. The smiles came later, in *Twins*
and *Kindergarten Cop*. Here the thud of
fist on bone is much the same in any
language, even when big Arnie is a
Soviet policeman come to Chicago to
bring home the Russian drugs dealer
who shot his comrade cop. 'I now
vork undercover,' growls Arnie,
which presumably means he takes his
shirt off less in this one. At any rate,
multiple mayhem in the States, with
local lawman James Belushi in tow,
results. There is a lot of shouting,
swearing, killing, and knocking over
cars and other convenient obstacles.
It's all fair video entertainment and
Belushi even gets the odd good line:
'I'd like to break this up,' he tells the
incredible hulk, 'but we're parked in
a red zone – no offence.'

Red Mountain ○
1951, US, 84 mins, colour
Dir: William Dieterle
Stars: Alan Ladd, Lizabeth Scott, Arthur
Kennedy
Rating: ★★

This fast-paced, if dramatically stodgy,
Western was made on the Paramount
lot by veteran Hollywood director
William Dieterle and blazingly
photographed in Technicolor by colour specialist Charles B Lang. Alan
Ladd and Lizabeth Scott make a fine
fair-haired, blue-eyed partnership but
the film is stolen by John Ireland, fresh
from the Oscar-winning *All the King's
Men*, contributing a full-blooded portrayal of the rebel General Quantrell.

Red Pony, The ⊙
1949, US, 90 mins, colour
Dir: Lewis Milestone
Stars: Myrna Loy, Robert Mitchum
Rating: ★★★

Outdoor adventure stories about boys
and horses held great appeal in Hollywood in the Forties, so John
Steinbeck's short novel about a chestnut colt seemed a natural for filming.
All credit to Republic Studios who
hired a good cast, top photographer
Tony Gaudio (whose Technicolour
camerawork is wonderful) and noted
composer Aaron Copland to provide
the score. The results are poignant and
winning; Peter Miles, who plays the
boy, later became a screenwriter and
author.

Red River ○ ⓥ
1948, US, 133 mins, b/w
Dir: Howard Hawks
Stars: John Wayne, Montgomery Clift,
Joanne Dru
Rating: ★★★★

Howard Hawks was at his pinnacle
when he directed this grand-scale
movie which stars John Wayne, has a
first-rate screenplay and dazzling
black-and-white photography, and
features Montgomery Clift giving one
of his most attractive and least complicated performances. The sprawling
story, about the epic first cattle drive
from Texas to Abilene, along the
Chisholm Trail, first appeared as a
Saturday Evening Post serial by top
Western writer Borden Chase, who
helped turn it into a film with the aid
of the experienced, award-winning
screenwriter Charles Schnee. Wayne's
towering performance as Thomas
Dunson foreshadowed many of the
larger-than-life Westerners he would
in fact be playing two decades later.
And he dominates even a cast of this
quality, including as it does John
Ireland, Joanne Dru, three-time
Academy Award winner Walter
Brennan and Western veteran Harry
Carey Senior, whose last film this was,
and to whom it is dedicated. Music
composer Dmitri Tiomkin's rousing
score underlines the width and depth
of a drama that frequently raises the
dust without ever becoming dusty,
and no more so than in the magnificent final flat-out scrap between the
two stars at the end of the trail. The
story was recently (unwisely) remade
as a movie for television. A strange
decision. How can you compete
with a legend?

Red Rock West ● ⓥ
1992, US, 98 mins, colour
Dir: John Dahl
Stars: Nicolas Cage, Dennis Hopper,
Lara Flynn Boyle, J T Walsh
Rating: ★★★

Another journey into director John
Dahl's world of *noir* duplicity: hired
killers, lovers trapped by circumstance
and women you can't trust. Nicolas
Cage is the Texas drifter whose
gammy leg costs him a job in
Wyoming and forces him to drive on
to the town of Red Rock, where he's
almost immediately mistaken by
Wayne (J T Walsh) as the killer he's
hired to dispatch his faithless wife
(Lara Flynn Boyle). Taking the
money, Cage hotfoots it to warn the

wife who immediately gives him more
money to kill her husband. Stocking
up with provisions, Cage goes for the
sensible course and drives off with all
the money. Circumstances in these
films being what they are, however, he
soon finds himself driving in and out
of Red Rock like a yo-yo, always on
the run from someone, most notably
the real hitman (Dennis Hopper).
Doomy, tightly shot and with a suitably desperate hero, *Red Rock* is all
that this kind of film should be, down
to the bitter climax. The characters are
cold and passionless, oblivious till the
last moment that fate is closing in on
them all.

Reds ○ ⓥ
1981, US, 200 mins, colour
Dir: Warren Beatty
Stars: Warren Beatty, Diane Keaton,
Jack Nicholson, Maureen Stapleton
Rating: ★★★

A story of epic proportions, set in
America and Russia in the 1915-1921
period. And it is also a love story – on
a scale to match *Doctor Zhivago* and
Gone With the Wind. Warren Beatty
plays an idealistic Communist in
America, Diane Keaton the
free-thinking writer who joins his
semi-underground movement. Together, they are caught up in
momentous events in world history
which culminate in her trekking across
frozen wastes to find him in Finland,
after he has fled the Bolsheviks. When
it concentrates on people and not
politics, in fact, this film is a winner.
Diane Keaton is superb – a tribute to
the direction of Beatty, for which he
won an Academy Award.

Red Shoes, The ○
1948, UK, 136 mins, colour
Dir: Michael Powell, Emeric Pressburger
Stars: Moira Shearer, Anton Walbrook
Rating: ★★★★

One of the very few successful films
about ballet, this movie was helped by
striking design and ravishing
Technicolor, with the result that it
was a delight to the eye. Many a bal-
let-mad schoolgirl went crazy about
the film in general and the 20-year-old
red-haired Ms Shearer in particular.
The highlight of it all was The Red
Shoes Ballet, perhaps the most effective and entertaining thing of its kind
ever put on film, the music for which
was especially composed by Brian
Easdale.

R

Red Skies of Montana ○
1952, US, 90 mins, colour
Dir: Joseph M Newman
Stars: Richard Widmark, Jeffrey Hunter, Constance Smith
Rating: ★★

An action-filled account of the work of the parachute firefighters of the US Forest Rescue service. A cast of some of America's most rugged actors, including Richard Widmark, Jeffrey Hunter, Richard Boone, Richard Crenna and Charles Bronson, does sterling work under the direction of Joseph M Newman, whose film career petered out sooner than it should have, despite constant accolades from certain critical quarters. The script of this one is pretty average, but Newman splices in some superb action sequences involving forest fires, some of them doubtless inspired by his previous documentary film, *Smoke Jumpers*.

Red Sonja ● ⓥ
1985, US, 89 mins, colour
Dir: Richard Fleischer
Stars: Brigitte Nielsen, Arnold Schwarzenegger
Rating: ★

Although the statuesque Brigitte Nielsen gets top billing in this sword and sorcery epic, it is pumped-up Arnold Schwarzenegger who steals the attention. As a mythical warrior who declares 'Danger is my trade', he certainly looks the part, but his big problem is that he has to talk too much. About every 15 minutes or so! Arnie fights to get his thick Austrian accent around the most banal dialogue (written by Clive Exton and George MacDonald Fraser, both of whom obviously had an off day) and mispronounces Red Sonja's name as 'Sony-uh' at every turn. To her credit, Nielsen never seems to listen to a word he says. But despite the presence of such testosterone giants of the cinema and Arnie's earlier success as *Conan the Barbarian*, the film flopped at the box-office. Schwarzenegger should have worried: he would soon be Hollywood's most powerful star, and leave such junk as this far behind.

Red Sun ◑
1971, Italy, 112 mins, colour
Dir: Terence Young
Stars: Charles Bronson, Toshiro Mifune, Alain Delon, Ursula Andress
Rating: ★★

A blood-and-guts adventure film that's not so much a spaghetti Western (actually a Franco-Italian-Spanish-American co-production) as a Samurai Western, as Japanese warrior Toshiro Mifune stalks the Wild West with unlikely partner Charles Bronson in search of a fabulous jewel-encrusted sword. The sword has been stolen by Bronson's treacherous ex-partner, a New Orleans gambler played by Alain Delon (sporting one silver tooth amid the white). The heroine is Ursula Andress who, with her habit of stripping to the waist in every film, reminds me of those beefcake heroes of a couple of decades ago (such as Victor Mature) who couldn't appear without taking off their shirts at least once. In the acting stakes, though, Ursula loses out to Capucine, who makes the most of an almost non-existent part. The action will satisfy the most blood-thirsty Western fan.

Red Sundown ○
1955, US, 82 mins, colour
Dir: Jack Arnold
Stars: Rory Calhoun, Martha Hyer, Robert Middleton, Dean Jagger
Rating: ★★★

In pace and uncompromising toughness, this blood-spattered Western was years ahead of its time. Not surprising, as its director, Jack Arnold, was at the peak of his form, and was to combine a year later with one of the stars, Grant Williams, to make the outstanding science-fiction thriller *The Incredible Shrinking Man*. Here, he has Rory Calhoun as the gunfighter who discovers the life of a deputy sheriff is not all patrolling the streets and throwing drunks in jail, when fat and influential Rufus Henshaw (Robert Middleton) tries taking over the town. Martha Hyer is remarkably successful as the nice girl, there are good performances from Williams and Dean Jagger, and sandy-haired James Millican is outstanding as Bud Purvis. Tragically he died later the same year, at the age of 45.

Red Tent, The ○
1969, UK, 121 mins, colour
Dir: Mikhail K Kalatozov
Stars: Peter Finch, Sean Connery, Claudia Cardinale, Hardy Kruger
Rating: ★★

In between his last two assignments as James Bond, Sean Connery gave some fine performances for the cinema, and this portrait of the Norwegian explorer Amundsen is one of them. This is not an account of his race with Scott to reach the South Pole, but a later episode in his exciting career, dealing with his bid to rescue the survivors of an airship which crashed in a blizzard near the North Pole. The pictorial qualities of the film are strong, but the rest of the cosmopolitan cast, which includes British, German, Italian and Russian players, has to struggle hard to come to terms with the occasional inconsistencies in the dialogue.

Red Tomahawk ○
1966, US, 82 mins, colour
Dir: R G Springstein
Stars: Howard Keel, Broderick Crawford, Scott Brady
Rating: ★★

This Western about the aftermath of the Custer massacre provided a nostalgic return to Dodge City for its star Howard Keel, who had first ridden through the town in the Doris Day musical *Calamity Jane*. Betty Hutton was slated to make a comeback in this film, but quit soon after shooting began. Another Paramount star of the Forties, Joan Caulfield, replaced her.

Reflections in a Golden Eye ● ⓥ
1967, US, 105 mins, colour
Dir: John Huston
Stars: Marlon Brando, Elizabeth Taylor, Brian Keith, Julie Harris
Rating: ★★

One of John Huston's most bizarre ventures. Brando gives one of the more interesting of his latter performances as the repressed homosexual soldier whose wife has to turn to another officer (Brian Keith) for affection. Elizabeth Taylor is beautifully cast as Brando's desirable but insensitive wife. Huston also picked two newcomers for his cast – New York hairdresser Zorro David, as Taylor's Filipino houseboy, and untried actor Robert Forster as another soldier to whom Brando finds himself attracted. Although neither has made much impact since, both proved excellent in their roles. Huston confessed himself angered by the studio's refusal to carry out his original plan to desaturate the print to a duo-tone of pinks and golds – but he did use severely under-exposed stock, giving the picture the dull sepiatone look of an old photograph. He made much of the film in Italy, in countryside around Rome, although the unit did spend a fortnight on Long Island, New York, to get authentic army base backgrounds.

Regarding Henry ○ ⓥ
1990, US, 116 mins, colour
Dir: Mike Nichols
Stars: Harrison Ford, Annette Bening, Bill Nunn, Mikki Allen
Rating: ★★★

Excellent performances by Ford and Bening help keep sentimentality largely at bay in this manipulative but successful movie about a hard-nosed lawyer who changes for the better after being brain-damaged by a bullet in a liquor-store raid. Slowly recovering the powers of speech and movement, he returns to his wife and family, unaware that his daughter lives in fear of him, and that he and his wife had drifted apart and were both having affairs. His wife finds herself with a new man – and likes what she finds, even if Henry has become simple, slow-witted and methodical rather than his sharp, soulless and sharklike former self. His former associates can offer him only pity, and precious little of that. 'One minute you're an attorney, the next an imbecile,' they joke at a party. You'll be able to find plenty of sympathy for Henry, however, and enjoy his redemption and rehabilitation, not to mention righting a few wrongs along the way. Although it over-simplifies its case history, this is another winner from consistent director Mike Nichols.

Reivers, The ◖
1969, US, 107 mins, colour
Dir: Mark Rydell
Stars: Steve McQueen, Sharon Farrell
Rating: ★★★★

A gentle, rambling tale of a young boy's adventures in the Deep South, which start when his grandfather's hired hand Boon (Steve McQueen) 'borrows' his boss's new 1905 Winton car and takes the lad to Memphis. There they visit a bordello, lose the car and try to win a horserace. The episodic tale is taken from the book by William Faulkner (his last and probably most difficult to read) and given rhythm by Burgess Meredith's narration. It's beautifully photographed, has a strong sense of period, and the rite-of-passage elements of the story avoid the usual mawkish pitfalls. McQueen is excellent as is young Mitch Vogel as the boy. Having said that, they have strong competition from Robert

Crosse as McQueen's black workmate who tags along for the ride: he manages to steal many of the scenes he's in. A delightful film, full of the fun of being alive.

Reluctant Debutante, The ○
1958, UK, 94 mins, colour
Dir: Vincente Minnelli
Stars: Rex Harrison, Kay Kendall, Sandra Dee
Rating: ★★★

A sparkling romantic romp that shows Rex Harrison at his elegant and witty best. Both he and his wife Kay Kendall supply accurate but offhand comedy timing to a diamond-sharp script by William Douglas-Home that also brings a career-best performance from Sandra Dee as the deb of the title. Polished, accomplished, relaxed yet fast-moving, the whole enterprise is a delight. Angela Lansbury supplies the icing on the cake as a designing society mother.

Reluctant Dragon, The ⊙
1941, US, 72 mins, colour
Dir: Alfred Werker, Jim Handley, Ford Beebe, Erwin Verity, Jasper Blystone
Stars: Robert Benchley
Rating: ★★★

This film mixes live action and animation, using the arrival of the popular humorist Robert Benchley at the Disney Studio (watch for Alan Ladd as an animator) as the excuse for a behind-the-scenes look at the magic of animation. Disney fans will enjoy glimpses of some of their favourite characters as well as some fascinating footage of how artists drew an elephant from life for *Dumbo*, the recording of a duet for Donald Duck and Clara Cluck, and sound men creating thunder and talking railway trains. The dragon of the title is of course a delight, but, as a peaceable fellow who thinks jaw is better than war, he was out of step with the public mood at the time.

Remains of the Day, The ○ ⓥ
1993, UK, 135 mins, colour
Dir: James Ivory
Stars: Anthony Hopkins, Emma Thompson, James Fox, Christopher Reeve, Peter Vaughan, Hugh Grant, Tim Pigott-Smith
Rating: ★★★★

This beautifully crafted film is a very English piece, full of unspoken emotions. Anthony Hopkins is per-

fectly cast as Stevens, the butler in a stately home of the 1930s whose noble owner (James Fox) talks appeasement with the Germans and who will, with the coming of war, be reviled as a traitor. Also among his ancestral home's many servants is the housekeeper, Miss Kenton (Emma Thompson), whose relationship with Stevens develops into one of mutual respect and affection, if the butler ever permitted himself such an emotion. The fact that he does not, and despises relationships among servants, is a fatal flaw in his makeup, and one that is to cost him dear. Ruth Prawer Jhabvala's screenplay, pretty faithful to the book by Kazuo Ishiguro, arrows unerringly to a heartrending conclusion. Brilliant performances by the principals; good support from Fox, Tim Pigott-Smith and Christopher Reeve. Peter Vaughan is a touch over the top but still memorable as Stevens' father, whom he employs as an under-butler even though he knows the old man is past it.

Remarkable Mr Kipps, The
See: Kipps

Rembrandt ○
1936, UK, 85 mins, b/w
Dir: Alexander Korda
Stars: Charles Laughton, Gertrude Lawrence, Elsa Lanchester
Rating: ★★★★

This biography of the 17th-century Dutch painter has been described as Alexander Korda's greatest film, and through it he won over some of his most severe critics. Korda, who produced and directed the film, concentrates on the later, poverty-stricken years of Rembrandt, when his work was no longer appreciated. The sets (by Korda's brother Vincent) and costumes were based on Dutch paintings of the period. Korda's ambition was to interpret, by camera and film, the scenes which Rembrandt had captured with paint and canvas. The critics felt he had succeeded, and praised film and performances – especially Charles Laughton and his wife Elsa Lanchester – highly.

Remember? ○
1939, US, 83 mins, b/w
Dir: Norman Z Mcleod
Stars: Robert Taylor, Greer Garson, Lew Ayres
Rating: ★★

A loss-of-memory comedy from director Norman Z McLeod, whose

R

zany sense of fun contributed largely some of the best efforts in the genre, from W C Fields to Bob Hope. This offering, however, is not in the *Paleface* class. Great dramatic actors do not necessarily make very deft comics and perhaps the starry cast of Robert Taylor, Greer Garson and Lew Ayres is a bit overpowering for such a slight vehicle: like putting a Formula 1 engine in a go-kart.

Remember My Name ◐

1978, US, 96 mins, colour
Dir: Alan Rudolph
Stars: Anthony Perkins, Geraldine Chaplin
Rating: ★★★

A kind of avant-garde *film-noir*, with Geraldine Chaplin perfectly cast as the enigmatic ex-convict clearly determined on vengeance for some past miscarriage of justice. Anthony Perkins proves almost equally well-suited to the role of the man whose life she bedevils, which gives him the opportunity to offer another of his expert studies in personal torment.

Remember the Day ○

1941, UK, 85 mins, b/w
Dir: Henry King
Stars: Claudette Colbert, John Payne
Rating: ★★★

This weepie isn't much remembered today, although it's actually compulsive viewing. It's very well directed by Henry King, who was a master at pulling the tear strings from the silent days (*Tol'able David, Stella Dallas*) right up to the late Fifties (*Carousel, Love is a Many-Splendoured Thing*) and impeccably structured throughout. It also gave John Payne a chance to break away from musicals, and Claudette Colbert the opportunity to escape from glamour into character, as an elderly schoolteacher journeying to see one of her former pupils.

Remo – Unarmed and Dangerous ○ ⓥ

(aka: Remo Williams – The Adventure Begins)
1985, US, 110 mins, colour
Dir: Guy Hamilton
Stars: Fred Ward, Joel Grey, Wilford Brimley
Rating: ★★

Typical mid-Eighties Hollywood hokum, with a streetsmart cop (Fred Ward) being 'killed off' so that he can start life afresh as Remo Williams, su-preme righter of wrongs for a secret syndicate. Director Guy Hamilton's job is to dress this up so that it doesn't seem too preposterous, at least while we're watching, and he doesn't do a bad job of it. Remo is trained in martial arts by an ancient Korean, then pitted against a corrupt armaments manufacturer whose weapons, great and small, are not quite what they're cracked up to be. There's a fair-enough dice with death around the Statue of Liberty and an amazing encounter with three lethal and intelligent Doberman dogs in the film's serial-like developments on the way to the bad guys meeting a demise that seems tame by the Eighties' exacting standards of violence. Most of the cast seem to be in need of acting rather than combat lessons, although Joel Grey enjoys himself as Ward's Korean mentor.

Remo Williams – The Adventure Begins

See: Remo – Unarmed and Dangerous

Renegades ○

1946, US, 88 mins, colour
Dir: George Sherman
Stars: Evelyn Keyes, Willard Parker, Larry Parks
Rating: ★★★

Although Larry Parks (he later fell foul of the Un-American Activities Committee) is best remembered for his film portrayals of Al Jolson, he never gave a better performance than in this rousing, unexpectedly good Western. Nominally, Parks gets third billing on the cast list. But the film is his from the moment he appears on the screen. This was his last film before *The Jolson Story*, and his acting here probably helped him win the part. Those he outplays include such seasoned Western heroes as Willard Parker, Jim (Red Ryder) Bannon, Forrest Tucker and Edgar Buchanan. Director George Sherman manoeuvres the action with a fine grasp of dramatic action and the Technicolor photography is sheer delight.

Renegades ● ⓥ

1989, US, 102 mins, colour
Dir: Jack Sholder
Stars: Kiefer Sutherland, Lou Diamond Phillips, Jami Gertz
Rating: ★★★

Hollywood was running out of variations for its cycle of buddy action films around this time, but this one has a thread that at least gives a slightly different slant to its parade of icy killers, undercover cops, car chases and violent action set pieces. The title might suggest it's a modern Western and indeed Lou Diamond Phillips' impassive native American might have ridden straight out of the past as, in pursuit of a stolen sacred spear, he time and again rescues faintly inefficient maverick cop Sutherland from his own poor judgment. You couldn't really give a nickel for the chances of the duo surviving in this world of corruption and instant death, but as usual the killers and their henchmen are bad shots and our heroes make it through to the well-staged climax involving a blazing barn, a handy motorcycle, a cat-and-mouse hunt through woods and, of course the Final Vengeance of the spear. Leave your thinking caps in the hall and enjoy.

Repo Man ● ⓥ

1984, US, 92 mins, colour
Dir: Alex Cox
Stars: Emilio Estevez, Harry Dean Stanton, Tracy Walter
Rating: ★★★

Unemployed Emilio Estevez learns to steal cars from Harry Dean Stanton, but it's all legal: Stanton is a finance company repossession man. Then they pick up a car with a dangerous 'box of tricks' in the boot. The film, set in the urban sprawl of Los Angeles, looks great and the ending, coming as it does after a long chase sequence, is unexpected and great fun. Estevez and Stanton obviously had great fun in this, British director Alex Cox's debut film. It has now become a cult film and not without reason, although bits of it do drag.

Repossessed ● ⓥ

1990, US, 93 mins, colour
Dir: Bob Logan
Stars: Linda Blair, Leslie Nielsen, Ned Beatty, Anthony Starke
Rating: ★

Blair has had a chequered film career since she first sprang to public attention as the possessed pre-teen in *The Exorcist*. But whatever 'possessed' her to make this simply appalling comedy can only be guessed at. That the public would briefly flock to see it has to be the answer, as script and treatment are so fourth-formish that anyone could tell at a glance that the results would be deadeningly unfunny. Director Bob Logan's sense of comic timing is non-existent, his idea of an

the two stars are on the screen, the movie, carefully directed by Daniel Petrie, catches fire dramatically, while Mario Tosi's cinematography adds an attractive sheen.

Return from the River Kwai ◐ Ⓥ

1988, US, 100 mins, colour
Dir: Andrew V Mclaglen
Stars: Edward Fox, Denholm Elliott, Christopher Penn, George Takei
Rating: ★★

The original *Bridge on the River Kwai*, however spurious, was a classic war film. This much belated follow-up attempts to tell a true story from the same period but, sadly lacking charismatic players, comes over as no more than a routine war saga. Edward Fox and George Takei are both so stilted as the humane English and Japanese commanders that you long to stick a pin in them to make them behave naturally. Christopher Penn looks mighty overweight for an American pilot going through hell and high water, and it's left to Denholm Elliott (killed too soon) and Nick Tate (as the Australian PoW commander) to inject the briskness, conviction and down-to-earth life the film needs. And, though handed a routine character, Tatsuya Nakadai is also good as the tightly fanatical Japanese camp supervisor. The action scenes carry some excitement, but Andrew V McLaglen's direction, perhaps blunted by too many TV movies, lacks a certain edge and vitality.

Return from Witch Mountain ○

1978, US, 95 mins, colour
Dir: John Hough
Stars: Kim Richards, Ike Eisenmann, Bette Davis, Christopher Lee
Rating: ★★

Undemanding fun from the Disney Studio, with Christopher Lee and Bette Davis as villains who might have stepped straight out of a silent serial, and a plot pitched on the level of an *Our Gang* comedy. Endearing young heroes Kim Richards and Ike Eisenmann return from the first film, *Escape to Witch Mountain*, where their material was certainly more original.

Return of Frank James, The ○

1940, US, 92 mins, colour
Dir: Fritz Lang
Stars: Henry Fonda, Gene Tierney
Rating: ★★★

One of the rare occasions in the cinema when a sequel is as good as the original. The reason lies mostly in the direction – by master craftsman Fritz Lang. The action is fast and fierce and the colour photography first-rate. Henry Fonda provides an authoritative and intensely sympathetic portrayal of Frank James, and proves no slouch at the gunplay game either. The opening sequence shows Jesse's death from the end of the previous film, *Jesse James*, made in 1939. The actor playing Jesse is Tyrone Power.

Return of Swamp Thing, The ◐ Ⓥ

1989, US, 89 mins, colour
Dir: Jim Wynorski
Stars: Louis Jourdan, Heather Locklear, Sarah Douglas, Dick Durock
Rating: ★★

This is a literal transplantation of a horror comic to the screen with the accent on the comic – but it's hard to know whether to laugh at it or with it. 'Where do you come from?' gasps one of two very tiresome children. 'From the bog,' chortles the jolly green giant of the title, though he turns serious when romanced by healthily curvy Heather Locklear. 'Please don't,' he admonishes. 'This will never work.' That's OK, she reassures him: she's a vegetarian. Well folks, there's also a plot about mad scientist Louis Jourdan (originally responsible for the hero's state of vegetation) who plays the organ in between creating horrific mutants in his search for eternal life. 'You sold your soul to the Devil,' Locklear accuses him. He smiles: 'Let's just say he has a lease with an option to buy.' DC comics have a lot to answer for but at least their monstrous offspring, though badly acted, is never dull.

Return of the Fly ◐ Ⓥ

1959, US, 80 mins, colour
Dir: Edward L Bernds
Stars: Vincent Price, Brett Halsey, David Frankham, Danielle De Metz
Rating: ★★

The second of three horror films about the Delambre family and their obsession with 'teleporting' human beings through space, from one country to another. In the first film, *The Fly*, André Delambre became half-man, half-fly. This sequel has Vincent Price back in his original role as André's brother François, with his now grown-up nephew Philippe (Brett Halsey) undergoing some nasty

but predictable disasters in the teleportation chamber. Scowling Dan Seymour, one of the most memorable of the cinema's fat, ugly and menacing villains, notably as Captain Renard of the Vichy Police in *To Have and Have Not*, plays Max Berthold.

Return of the Jedi ○ Ⓥ

1983, US, 133 mins, colour
Dir: Richard Marquand
Stars: Mark Hamill, Harrison Ford, Carrie Fisher, Billy Dee Williams
Rating: ★★★

Delightful finish to the trilogy that George Lucas always said was intended for children but ended up, because of its scale, style and imagination, as fabulous entertainment for all. Some marvellous new creations, especially Jabba and the Ewoks, and the unbeatable special effects more than make up for a slightly tired storyline. Though it is more sentimental than its predecessors, it's no less enjoyable or uplifting, and the fireworks at the end restore it to the realm of super-pantomime to which it belongs.

Return of the Living Dead Part II ● Ⓥ

1988, US, 89 mins, colour
Dir: Ken Wiederhorn
Stars: James Karen, Thom Mathews, Dana Ashbrook, Michael Kenwortky
Rating: ★★

Another one of those radiation waste disposal canisters has fallen off the back of a lorry and before you can say 'Aargh!' zombies by the thousand are scissoring up through the earth and advancing on the local population. This seems to be quite a problem in America, although box-office returns indicate it'll be with us for some time. 'Symptoms,' says the boozy doctor (Phillip Bruns) inspecting an infected patient, 'suggest chronic intractible rigor mortis!' 'My God,' says his co-hort, 'is it serious?' Yes, folks, this is a (very gruesome) horror comedy, quite hilarious in spots, epecially the zombie who, pranged by the heroes, complains: 'Get this goddam screwdriver out of my head.' The zombies advance with cries of 'Fresh brains!' but never fear: the heroine is 'Junior state sharpshooter champion' and her younger brother grabs a hefty pistol, crying: 'Make my night!' Excessive it's true, the film runs out of steam (or something) before the end, but you can forgive it a lot for its sense of humour.

Return of the Musketeers, The ○ ⓥ
1989, UK, 100 mins, colour
Dir: Richard Lester
Stars: Michael York, Oliver Reed, Frank Finlay, C Thomas Howell, Kim Cattrall
Rating: ★★

York, Reed, Richard Chamberlain and Frank Finlay all return for more swash and buckle in this sequel to the *Musketeers* stories, an adaptation of Dumas's *Twenty Years After*. As an action yarn it works quite well. As a comedy, though, it doesn't work at all, which is a pity, as the vein of humour is clearly meant to be its trump card. The problem is that director Lester doesn't treat this as a comedy of character, making fun of the heroes' ageing bones, rather as one of incidental (and very heavy-handed) humour, with peripheral characters rhubarbing away to themselves as they comment on the action. Never mind, Kim Cattrall enjoys herself lustily as the villainous Justine, snapping, fighting and leaping with an energy unparalleled since the days of Maureen O'Hara. And Geraldine Chaplin is delightful as a feather-headed, flibbertigibbet Anne of Austria. The best acting performance, though, is Alan Howard's cool and calculating Cromwell. Although Finlay appears to be killed in the final fight, he is magically resurrected for the triumphant brotherly fadeout!

Return of the Pink Panther, The ○ ⓥ
1974, UK, 113 mins, colour
Dir: Blake Edwards
Stars: Peter Sellers, Christopher Plummer, Catherine Schell, Herbert Lom
Rating: ★★

He is defeated by a door-bell, tricked by a telephone, routed by a radio, beset by a bath and vanquished by a vacuum cleaner. Mechanical contrivances confound him; 'apparati' assail him. In short, Inspector Clouseau is back, as, for a third time, Peter Sellers assumes his most famous role in *The Return of the Pink Panther*. Again the famous diamond known as the Pink Panther has been stolen. Ostensibly, the thief is once more The Phantom (formerly David Niven, now Christopher Plummer, who registers well). Clouseau, first encountered haranguing an organ-grinder in a Paris street while a bank robbery takes place in the window behind them, is assigned to break the case much to the chagrin of his

superior (Herbert Lom) whose mental control of the Clouseau situation is rapidly slipping. Some of the comedy is a little crude, especially at first, and slow-motion gags generally don't work. But the film is awash with inventive comic touches; Clouseau giving his hat, coat and gloves to a man at the hotel only to realise that the fellow is no clerk but a thief; Clouseau instructing a cab driver 'Follow that car,' only for the man to . . . well, no, we won't give that one away, but there are many more besides, plus the reappearance of Clouseau's homicidal oriental manservant Cato, again played by Burt Kwouk. This Pink Panther may not be a priceless jewel – it needs cutting. But it certainly is bright.

Return of the Scarlet Pimpernel, The ○
1937, UK, 94 mins, b/w
Dir: Hans Schwartz
Stars: Barry K Barnes, Sophie Stewart, Margaretta Scott, James Mason
Rating: ★★

James Mason, who made his screen debut in the first Pimpernel film, has a much bigger role in this sequel, as a French partisan. It's based on Baroness Orczy's *The Elusive Pimpernel*. Barry K Barnes made his film debut in this film, in the role previously played by Leslie Howard. Barnes' elegant performance made him a star. But ill-health curtailed his later career and he died in 1965, at the age of 58. Another actor whose acting span was brief was David Tree, who can be seen as Lord Harry Denning. From a famous acting family, Tree seemed set for a bright future, but lost an arm in war service, and left the profession.

Return of the Seven ○
1966, US, 95 mins, colour
Dir: Burt Kennedy
Stars: Yul Brynner, Robert Fuller, Warren Oates
Rating: ★★

A sequel to *The Magnificent Seven*, with Yul Brynner again, as the leader of a new septet of crusading gunmen. The theme – defence of a village against marauding outlaws – is similar to that in the original film. Here the cast includes Claude Akins and Warren Oates, and the director is Burt Kennedy, one of Hollywood's best-respected makers of Westerns. The screenplay is written by Larry Cohen, who later wrote and directed his own distinctive films, often in horror vein.

This is very ordinary fare compared to the first film, and shot in muddy colour to boot.

Return to Oz ○
1985, US, 110 mins, colour
Dir: Walter Murch
Stars: Nicol Williamson, Jean Marsh, Piper Laurie, Fairuza Balk, Matt Clark
Rating: ★★★

More tales of derring-do along the yellow brick road as the Disney people mix up incidents and characters from L Frank Baum's second and third Oz books in an adventure that has good special effects (notably the rock-men who provide little Dorothy Gale's principal opposition), looks expensive and shows lots of imagination. Some early bits may prove a little scary for nervous toddlers.

Return to Paradise ○
1953, US, 85 mins, colour
Dir: Mark Robson
Stars: Gary Cooper, Roberta Haynes, Barry Jones, Moira MacDonald, John Hudson
Rating: ★★

Gary Cooper moves from the Wild West to the South Seas, but remains as much the man of action as ever, in this adaptation of a James (Hawaii) Michener story, in which a beachcomber has to pit himself against a fire-breathing missionary for control of an island in the South Pacific. Leading lady Roberta Haynes, a sultry beauty of her day, later became a film producer.

Return to Peyton Place ○
1961, US, 135 mins, colour
Dir: Jose Ferrer
Stars: Jeff Chandler, Carol Lynley, Eleanor Parker, Mary Astor
Rating: ★★

The second Peyton Place film shares one virtue with the original – fine colour photography. Actor Jose Ferrer, who directed, was not auspiciously successful on the other side of the camera – *The Great Man* was perhaps his best. Here veteran actresses Eleanor Parker and Mary Astor offer him stout support. Carol Lynley plays Allison, who has now written a scandalous book about her home town, turning the wheel full circle.

Return to the Blue Lagoon ◑ ⓥ
1991, US, 105 mins, colour
Dir: William A Graham

R

Stars: Milla Jovovich, Brian Krause, Lisa Pelikan
Rating: ★

A truly unnecessary sequel to the Brooke Shields remake of the old classic. All the old plot lines are trotted out and, after a fair beginning – with two new children shipwrecked on a desert isle with a guardian who'll conveniently die when they are old enough to fend for themselves – the movie becomes completely expend-able as soon as the kids grow up. The teenagers – Brian Krause, who looks like a tennis pro, and Milla Jovovich, a genuine, sun-kissed Californian maid – simply aren't up to it. Monsoon rains, a few tame natives, underwater kissing scenes and a mangy-looking shark. That's about it, and it'll bore you stiff.

Reunion ◐ ⓥ
1988, US, 101 mins, colour
Dir: Jerry Schatzberg
Stars: Jason Robards, Christien Anholt, Samuel West, François Fabian
Rating: ★★

There were a number of films about the Nazi rise in Germany around in the late Eighties, but this one, though over-leisurely, is off the beaten track. In 1932, an unlikely friendship springs up between two 16-year-old boys: Konradin, a member of the German aristocracy and Hans, the son of a Jewish doctor. Much welcomed by both youths, neither gregarious by nature, their time together can only be numbered in months, as Hitler rises to power and the oppression of the Jews begins. But, though they part in bitterness, each has opened the other's eyes. The film opens as Hans (Jason Robards) prepares to return to Germany after 55 years to discover what happened to his friend. The film is competently acted by Anholt and West as the boys and more than competently by Robards, though the physical disparity between himself and Anholt, as his younger self, is rather disturbing. The ironic twist ending is well-worked – and works well.

Revenge ● ⓥ
1989, US, 123 mins, colour
Dir: Tony Scott
Stars: Kevin Costner, Anthony Quinn, Madeleine Stowe, Sally Kirkland, Miguel Ferrer
Rating: ★

Given that rugged Costner is a di-vorced flier who's just quit the US armed forces and gone to see his aged friend Quinn, a ruthless Mexican power broker and man of violence, with a beautiful, unhappy wife (Stowe), would you need over two hours to tell the ensuing story? Indeed would you tell it at all? 'A woman like that .....' mutters Quinn. 'I do almost anything to keep her. 'I do almost anything to keep her.' The biggest mystery, though, is not that the film got made, but that the two leading characters ever thought they could get away with a love affair un-der the nose of such a man. It needs a special chemistry, giving off heatwaves of passion, to overcome these improbabilities, but every time Costner and Stowe are together on screen, the film goes to sleep. The violence and sleaze that vein the film are more successful than the eroticism, though, with good support work from Ferrer (son of Jose), Kirkland, James Gammon and Joe Santos. Be warned: after more than two hours, the film still doesn't really have much of an ending.

Revenge of Frankenstein, The ●
1958, UK, 89 mins, colour
Dir: Terence Fisher
Stars: Peter Cushing, Francis Matthews, Eunice Gayson
Rating: ★★

Another Jimmy Sangster-written, Terence Fisher-directed film with the excellent colour photography that distinguished their earlier entries into the genre. The police inspector in the case (another Frankenstein creature has gone berserk) is played by former matinee idol John Stuart, whose debut in films was as long ago as 1920, and who went on to become a star in such Hitchcock films as *Number Sev-enteen*.

Revenge of the Pink Panther ○ ⓥ
1978, UK, 98 mins, colour
Dir: Blake Edwards
Stars: Peter Sellers, Herbert Lom, Dyan Cannon, Robert Webber, Robert Loggia
Rating: ★★★

But for the untimely death of Peter Sellers, one imagines that the *Pink Panther* series would have gone on for years with him at the helm, very much like the James Bond films. Here Clouseau is believed dead, which prompts his now-mad ex superior Dreyfuss (marvellous Herbert Lom) to leave his mental home and rejoin the force, and his houseboy Cato to turn their apartment into what Clouseau terms a 'Chinese nookie factory'. The usual inept disguises, fights with Cato and triumph over self-inflicted disasters follow in this, the last fully fledged Panther film.

Revengers, The ◑
1972, US, 108 mins, colour
Dir: Daniel Mann
Stars: William Holden, Susan Hayward, Woody Strode
Rating: ★

The Western was in decline by the early Seventies, but the producers of this one decided there was still some mileage to be gained in re-teaming William Holden and Ernest Borgnine, co-stars in one of the last great West-ern successes, *The Wild Bunch*. Susan Hayward is wasted as an unlikely Irish frontier nurse, though her ravishing looks totally belie her 55 years at the time. The film itself is formula stuff for tiring stars, redeemed in part by a set of nicely varied locations.

Reversal of Fortune ● ⓥ
1990, US, 110 mins, colour
Dir: Barbet Schroeder
Stars: Glenn Close, Jeremy Irons, Ron Silver, Annabella Sciorra, Fisher Stevens
Rating: ★★

Some fine acting can't stop this being a fairly comprehensively tedious re-construction of the Claus Von Bulow trial and subsequent appeal. Von Bulow was accused of the attempted murder of his wife Sunny by administering insulin to kill her and gain possession of her fortune. The defence counsel (Ron Silver), a professor, was helped by a gaggle of associates and students who found serious holes in the prosecution's case. Director Schroeder elects not to show us the trial itself, a serious mis-calculation since it involves far too many static conversations between Silver and Jeremy Irons (winning an Oscar) as Claus (who, though clearly no Santa, may well have been inno-cent) as well as slow and lengthy reconstructions of various crises in the Von Bulows' lives. Glenn Close's Sunny delivers a deadpan narration from the depths of her hospital bed, assuring the viewer that they should be in no hurry to find out the truth. By the end, she's preaching to the converted.

Revolution ◐ ⓥ
1985, UK, 123 mins, colour
Dir: Hugh Hudson

Stars: Al Pacino, Donald Sutherland, Nastassja Kinski, Joan Plowright
Rating: ★

Condemned by the critics and shunned by the paying public, this rambling American Independence film helped to sink the British production company Goldcrest that backed it. Not even the presence of Al Pacino, then in a career low point, could create enough box-office interest. Director Hugh Hudson certainly has a great visual style (witness his earlier *Chariots of Fire* and *Greystoke*) but a ludicrous script with huge moments of incoherence delivers the death-blow here. Among the more bizarre castings are pop singer Annie Lennox and comedian Robbie Coltrane.

Rhapsody ○
1954, US, 116 mins, colour
Dir: Charles Vidor
Stars: Elizabeth Taylor, Vittorio Gassman, John Ericson
Rating: ★★

If you have tears, prepare to shed them as poor little rich girl Elizabeth Taylor (MGM gowned and groomed) vacillates between violinist Vittorio Gassman and pianist John Ericson with appropriate musical passion. Charles Vidor had a way of dressing up clichés as though they were eternal truths and this triangular love story takes strength from him. Look out for the young Stuart Whitman in one of his biggest roles before Fox groomed him for contract stardom.

Rhapsody in August ◐ ⓥ
1990, Japan, 104 mins, colour
Dir: Akira Kurosawa
Stars: Sachiko Murase, Hisashi Agawa, Richard Gere
Rating: ★★

This is not the greatest film you ever saw by Japanese master director Akira Kurosawa – far from it. It allows an obsession with the Nagasaki A-bomb to get fatally in the way of a delicate observation of four children staying with their grandmother for the summer holidays. There are some nicely composed shots, and winning performances from the children and granny. But it's very slow (more of a drawback here than in some Japanese films) and some of its attitudes may be less acceptable to western eyes, with its characters made to talk in such simplistic phrases as 'People do anything just to win a war.' Holly-

wood's Richard Gere is in for a cameo and must be congratulated on his seemingly competent Japanese: for such a big star, though, his journey to the east seemed hardly necessary.

Rhapsody in Blue ○
1945, US, 139 mins, b/w
Dir: Irving Rapper
Stars: Robert Alda, Joan Leslie, Charles Coburn, Alexis Smith, Oscar Levant
Rating: ★★★

The usual tuppence-coloured Hollywood version of a famous composer's life, in this case that of George Gershwin, and almost wholly redeemed by the quality of the music involved. Robert Alda, father of Alan, made his screen debut as Gershwin, but the film didn't make him into the superstar it might have done. Joan Leslie is very appealing as the early love of his life and the treatment, however fast-and-loose it may play with the facts, does capture some of Gershwin's genius and the conflicts he faced within his own world of music.

Rhinestone ○
1984, US, 111 mins, colour
Dir: Bob Clark
Stars: Dolly Parton, Sylvester Stallone
Rating: ★★

Although the corn is as high as an elephant's eye in the script of this comedy-musical with a country and western flavour, Dolly Parton proves again her facility for mocking her own image, and her songs (15 of them) make the film much more lively musically than *The Best Little Whorehouse in Texas*. Sylvester Stallone also sings acceptably as the loudmouthed Bronx cab driver whom Dolly tries to turn into a singing star for a bet. Still, it's Dolly's show, whether deflating the male macho image by the lift of an eyebrow, or moving into more positive action by flooring an antagonist with a single punch. 'Who are you?' Stallone gasps. 'Jane Wayne?'

Rhino! ○
1964, US, 91 mins, colour
Dir: Ivan Tors
Stars: Harry Guardino, Robert Culp, Shirley Eaton
Rating: ★

Another colourful animal film from the hands of Ivan Tors, creator of *Flipper* and *Daktari*. The film, which was made entirely on location in Zululand, features within its fictional plot an entire cross-section of African

wild life, but concentrates on the white rhino, perhaps the most remarkable of all animals remaining on Earth. This giant beast, standing six feet tall and weighing up to five thousand pounds, traces its ancestry back 75 million years to the age of the stegosaurus. Its massive horn is capable of smashing a truck. Its hoof can crush a man to pulp. It's certainly more interesting than the human cast here, who battle to no avail with a formula jungle plot.

Rhodes of Africa ○
1936, UK, 92 mins, b/w
Dir: Berthold Viertel
Stars: Walter Huston, Oscar Homolka
Rating: ★★★

A major British film of its time, for which the famous American actor, Walter Huston, then a major screen personality, was invited to come to Britain to play the 19th-century pioneer Cecil Rhodes. Oscar Homolka plays Rhodes' dangerous adversary, President Paul Kruger of South Africa. Peggy Ashcroft makes a rare and welcome appearance and there's also an early screen role for Bernard Lee, later to become famous as James Bond's boss 'M'.

Rhubarb ○
1951, US, 95 mins, b/w
Dir: Arthur Lubin
Stars: Ray Milland, Jan Sterling
Rating: ★★★

Riotous comedy that may well make the children fall out of their armchairs. A dotty millionaire leaves his entire fortune to a ferocious ginger cat who inherits a baseball team and proves its indispensable mascot. The cat out-acts everyone in sight, no mean feat considering the cast, which includes Ray Milland, Jan Sterling, Gene Lockhart and William Frawley. In an hysterically comic climax, it looks as though all is lost. But the cat deservedly has the last miaow! In a cast packed with Damon Runyon-style character actors, watch quickly for Paul Douglas (husband of Sterling) as a man in the park, and a young Leonard Nimoy as one of the baseball players.

Richard III ○ ⓥ
1955, UK, 161 mins, colour
Dir: Laurence Olivier
Stars: Laurence Olivier, Ralph Richardson, Claire Bloom, John Gielgud
Rating: ★★★★

R

Not even in the same actor-director's *Henry V* has Shakespeare ever made such dazzling, hypnotic screen entertainment as in Laurence Olivier's *Richard III*. And Olivier's power-hungry Richard Crookback is unforgettable – a ruthless, dominant, unstoppable gross black spider of a figure that devours or possesses everything in its path. Tremendous colour photography and stunning dramatic impact in one of the most successful Shakespeare films ever made.

Richest Cat in the World, The ○
1986, US, 92 mins, colour
Dir: Gregg Beeman
Stars: Ramon Bieri, Steven Kampmann, Caroline McWilliams, George Wyner
Rating: ★★★

Above average on all counts, this is a refreshing dose of lunacy from the Disney studio, very much along the lines of *The Cat from Outer Space*, with a talking feline called Palmer who may well rank towards the top of the all-time great cat actors. Fun all the way.

Rich in Love ○ ⓥ
1992, US, 106 mins, colour
Dir: Bruce Beresford
Stars: Albert Finney, Jill Clayburgh, Kyle MacLachlan, Suzy Amis, Piper Laurie, Kathryn Erbe, Ethan Hawke
Rating: ★★

One of those lovingly photographed films drenched in nostalgia, warmth and the scent of magnolias, this is also a portrait of a time when life changes irrevocably for one South Carolina family. Mother (Jill Clayburgh) takes off for a second life and 17-year-old daughter Lucille (Kathryn Erbe) is left not only to cope with leaving school, drifting away from her boyfriend and trying to get her father (Albert Finney) to survive the blow, but face the arrival of her pregnant, newly married sister (Suzy Amis) and a husband (Kyle MacLachlan) whom Lucille soon begins to fancy. For its first hour, this film is nearly as beguiling as its teenage heroine, although her forwardness with men seems at odds with her character as established in earlier scenes. No matter, the film runs out of steam towards the end and is of little account after Clayburgh returns to hearth and home, upsetting Finney who has taken up with widder-

woman Piper Laurie. Laurie's appropriately sassy in this role, but some of the other acting isn't up to much.

Rich Kids ○
1979, US, 101 mins, colour
Dir: Robert M Young
Stars: Trini Alvarado, Jeremy Levy
Rating: ★★★

The name of Robert Altman on this film's credits, albeit only as executive producer, leads us to expect something out of the ordinary. The film, directed by Robert M Young, is certainly that, for its leading characters are only 12 years old. Through their eyes, the film takes a perceptive look at the effect on young teenage children of that frequent occurrence in American upper-middle-bracket life – the marriage break-up. It develops ultimately into a mixture of astringent observation and more routine situation comedy, with bright performances by Trini Alvarado and Jeremy Levy as the 'rich kids' involved.

Ricochet ● ⓥ
1991, US, 110 mins, colour
Dir: Russell Mulcahy
Stars: Denzel Washington, John Lithgow, Ice T, Kevin Pollak, Lindsay Wagner
Rating: ★★

A familiar sort of action thriller, this Denzel Washington vehicle begins savagely but well. It gets increasingly fatuous after half-way, though, ending on a note of James Bond spoof. You've sat through these plot developments and characters before. Washington is the hotshot cop who brings down hit-man John Lithgow on the verge of his breakthrough to big-time crime. Lithgow nurses an insane desire for revenge while behind bars. By the time he escapes seven years later, Washington has risen to assistant DA. But it's seven years' bad luck when Lithgow's evil plotting turns his life upside down and makes him the wanted man. Russell Mulcahy tries hard to make us credit that no-one would believe Washington's story of a madman bent on framing him, but he never quite succeeds, nor convinces us that Washington's underworld childhood friends (led by Ice T) would come to his rescue at the end. Lithgow's an excellent menace when the script doesn't make him look silly; Washington has his moments and seemingly does much of his own stuntwork.

Riddle of the Sands, The ○ ⓥ
1978, UK, 102 mins, colour
Dir: Tony Maylam
Stars: Michael York, Jenny Agutter, Simon MacCorkindale
Rating: ★★

When Erskine Childers' classic novel was first published in 1903, its theme was to underline the vulnerability of England's eastern coast to foreign invasion – and this handsomely-mounted film retains the theme to good effect. Its two well-bred heroes, Michael York and Simon MacCorkindale, are in the best tradition of the gifted amateur caught up in mystery and intrigue and coming up trumps against sinister foreign villains, in this case led by urbane Alan Badel, who gives the film's most stylish and enjoyable performance. Director (and co-writer) Tony Maylam moves things along smoothly and, with considerable assistance from cinematographer Christopher Challis, admirably captures the timeless attraction of small-boat sailing that provides the backcloth to the clean-cut heroics.

Ride a Crooked Trail ○
1959, US, 87 mins, colour
Dir: Jesse Hibbs
Stars: Audie Murphy, Gia Scala, Walter Matthau, Henry Silva
Rating: ★★

Man-sized Audie Murphy Western, casting him for once as a bad guy, directed with great punch by Jesse Hibbs, and featuring one of the early screen performances of Walter Matthau, here as the judge of a frontier town, who was already stealing scenes even at this stage of his career. Cold-eyed Henry Silva also adds quality to the supporting cast.

Ride Clear of Diablo ○
1954, US, 80 mins, colour
Dir: Jesse Hibbs
Stars: Audie Murphy, Dan Duryea, Susan Cabot
Rating: ★★★

Audie Murphy's Westerns, with a strong humorous content and a *Destry*-like plot. Murphy gives a mild, but finely-timed performance as the railroad surveyor who brings in a notorious outlaw, and Dan Duryea is a laconic knock-out as the not-so-bad villain. Fine Technicolor location photography by Irving Glassberg, who shot so many Universal action films.

Ride 'em Cowboy ⊙
1941, US, 82 mins, b/w
Dir: Arthur Lubin
Stars: Bud Abbott, Lou Costello
Rating: ★★

One of the earliest and most energetic of the Abbott and Costello comedies, made in a year when they had four big box-office hits. It's also one of Ella Fitzgerald's rare film appearances (she sings 'A Tisket, A Tasket'); and another bonus comes in the friendly shape of Johnny Mack Brown, who once starred with Garbo before becoming one of America's favourite film cowboys. Villainy is in the hissworthy hands of Douglass Dumbrille, as a character called Jake Rainwater!

Ride in the Whirlwind ◐
1966, US, 85 mins, colour
Dir: Monte Hellman
Stars: Jack Nicholson, Cameron Mitchell, Millie Perkins
Rating: ★★

Jack Nicholson was a busy man in this somewhat offbeat Western. Not only did he star in it, he also co-produced it and wrote the screenplay. He and Cameron Mitchell are two cowboys wrongly pursued as outlaws by a relentless posse. Slammed by the critics when it was first released in America (it never had a cinema release in Britain), it has now become a minor cult film. Different but not nearly as good as the Western filmed back-to-back with this, *The Shooting*.

Rider on the Rain ●
1969, France, 119 mins, colour
Dir: Rene Clement
Stars: Marlene Jobert, Charles Bronson
Rating: ★★★★

The highlights of distinguished French director René Clément's career (*Bataille du Rail*, a story of the French Resistance, and *Forbidden Games*, about two small children in wartime) were far behind him when he turned his hand to this extraordinary melodrama, one of whose many oddities is the habit of the leading character (Charles Bronson) of throwing walnuts at windows, and breaking the nuts but not the glass. Ms Jobert is delicious, but faint hearts should be warned that the beginning is rather nasty.

Riders of the Storm
See: The American Way

Ride the High Country
See: Guns in the Afternoon

Riding High ○
1950, US, 112 mins, b/w
Dir: Frank Capra
Stars: Bing Crosby, Coleen Gray, Charles Bickford, Frances Gifford
Rating: ★★★★

Much underrated remake by Frank Capra of his 1934 hit *Broadway Bill*, full of skilful character players (nine of them repeating their roles from the earlier film) and with a real lump-in-the-throat finale. Particularly memorable are Harry Davenport as a drunken butler, Oliver Hardy as the betting man taken for a ride by con-men and William Demarest as Happy, perfectly countering Bing Crosby's 'How's your wallet' with 'I know. I ate it yesterday.' Songs include the Oscar nominated 'Sunshine Cake'. Richly enjoyable.

Riff-Raff ○
1935, US, 90 mins, b/w
Dir: J Walter Ruben
Stars: Jean Harlow, Spencer Tracy, Joseph Calleia
Rating: ★★

Platinum-blond bombshell Jean Harlow is pretty unrecognisable here in a brown wig as a tuna cannery worker who falls in love with big-headed fisherman Spencer Tracy, leading to tragedy. While not the pair's most memorable film, it does contain snappy, hard-boiled dialogue from two of Hollywood's top female writers; Frances Marion (who won Oscars for *The Champ* and *The Big House*) and Anita Loos (best remembered for the screenplay for Marilyn Monroe's *Gentlemen Prefer Blondes*.

Riff-Raff ● Ⓥ
1990, UK, 95 mins, colour
Dir: Ken Loach
Stars: Robert Carlyle, Emer McCourt, Ricky Tomlinson
Rating: ★★★

Director Ken Loach, who has recently won fresh acclaim with *Raining Stones*, pushes his politics right into the background for this gritty comedy very much based on real life on a building site. Writer Bill Jesse was himself a building worker and his colourful, wisecracking script is a joy. Loach insisted that all the actors

should have had building site experience, and this pays off in some strong performances, particularly from Robert Carlyle as Stevie, Ricky Tomlinson (a founder-member of the *Brookside* cast as Bobby Grant), Willie Ross as the hard-bitten foreman Gus, and Derek Young as the black guy keen to search for his roots in Africa. Comedy and real life at the bottom of the heap mix well in this entertaining film (which was selected for the Directors' Fortnight at Cannes) but you will have to concentrate hard to understand some of the richer regional accents.

Right Stuff, The ◐ Ⓥ
1983, US, 193 mins, colour
Dir: Philip Kaufman
Stars: Sam Shepard, Scott Glenn, Ed Harris, Barbara Hershey, Lance Henriksen, Dennis Quaid, Fred Ward
Rating: ★★★

There are some great moments in this story of the first Americnan astronauts and let that not be forgotten. The special effects work and aerial photography, for example, could hardly be bettered. And the film tries hard to tell the story of human beings as well as hardware. But, at more than three hours, you long for the excision of unnecessary material and an earlier splashdown. The film attempts to tell parallel stories, although it never quite successfully integrates them. Yeager (perhaps Sam Shepard's best film performance) is a test pilot of the old breed, breaking the sound barrier and scorching his plane though Mach 2. He wants nothing to do with the 'suicide squadron' who volunteer for astronaut training, although he stares a little wistfully at their trail of glory in the sky. He remains, you feel, what the film's makers really consider the 'right stuff'. Creditable performamnces from a long star cast bolster this film of enough inspired sequences to make it linger in the memory.

Ring of Bright Water ⊙ Ⓥ
1969, UK, 107 mins, colour
Dir: Jack Couffer
Stars: Bill Travers, Virginia McKenna
Rating: ★★★

A fair British attempt to emulate the success of Walt Disney's family-orientated animal films. Bill Travers is the London gent who starts a new life with a loveable but destructive otter in the Scottish Highlands. His real-life wife and *Born Free* co-star Virginia McKenna is on hand and Val

R

Doonican contributes the title song. Director Jack Couffer went on to specialise in heart-tugging wildlife family films, including *Living Free* (the second *Born Free* sequel) and *Raising Daisy Rothschild*. The film is perfect family entertainment, and only contains one brief incident of violence that may upset very small children.

Rio Bravo ○ Ⓥ
1961, US, 140 mins, colour
Dir: Howard Hawks
Stars: John Wayne, Dean Martin, Ricky Nelson, Angie Dickinson, Walter Brennan, John Russell
Rating: ★★★

Director Howard Hawks made several good Westerns with John Wayne – others were *Red River* and *El Dorado* – and here's one of the best-regarded, on Hawks' favourite theme of a tightly-knit group of goodies, beset by their own failings as much as anything else, taking on a whole nest of baddies. Long but involving, with an unexpectedly good performance from Dean Martin.

Rio Conchos ○
1964, US, 107 mins, colour
Dir: Gordon Douglas
Stars: Richard Boone, Stuart Whitman, Tony Franciosa
Rating: ★★★

A Western in the old 20th Century-Fox tradition, with towering scenery, truly De Luxe colour, and men who are as tough and hard-hitting as the action that frequently punctuates the story. Richard Boone, a favourite actor of mine from his pre-television days when he played nasty villains very well, is a bitter ex-Rebel army major whose wife and children have been killed by the Apache (it beats me how these desert wanderers always get the money to survive). He agrees to lead a hazardous expedition through Apache territory. The object is to find another ex-Confederate (splendid Edmond O'Brien) who is about to sell hundreds of stolen rifles to the Indians.

Rio Grande ○ Ⓥ
1950, US, 107 mins, b/w
Dir: John Ford
Stars: John Wayne, Maureen O'Hara, Ben Johnson
Rating: ★★★

The third in director John Ford's Cavalry trilogy (following *Fort Apache*

and *She Wore a Yellow Ribbon*) and the first of John Wayne and Maureen O'Hara's five films together. Wayne is larger than life in his role as an embattled fort commander and he did all his own riding and stunts as usual. He even persuaded Ford to cast his son Patrick in a cameo role. It's a powerful portrait of the wild and far southwest during the Indian wars.

Rio Lobo ○ Ⓥ
1970, US, 110 mins, colour
Dir: Howard Hawks
Stars: John Wayne, Jennifer O'Neill, Jack Elam
Rating: ★★★

Both star John Wayne and director Howard Hawks – whose last film this was – were getting a bit long in the tooth and saddlesore when they churned out this enjoyable but derivative Western. It's a virtual retread of their previous two horse operas, *Rio Bravo* and *El Dorado*, with wronged soldier Wayne ending up in a showdown in a dusty town. Events run like a door-slamming Feydeau farce ensuring plenty of laughs between the bullets. The technicolor camerawork is top drawer and the film is finally lifted out of the rut by veteran Jack Elam's marvellously Gothic performance as a half-crazed old rancher, whose finger itches demonically on the trigger every time he gets a bad guy in his sights. Jennifer O'Neill got her first starring role here, and became an established star the following year with *Summer of '42*.

Rio Rita ☉
1942, US, 91 mins, b/w
Dir: S Sylvan Simon
Stars: Bud Abbott, Lou Costello, Kathryn Grayson, John Carroll, Tom Conway
Rating: ★★

For Abbott and Costello's first visit to MGM, the studio decided to revamp the hit stage musical that had provided a successful feature debut for another comedy team, Wheeler and Woolsey, in 1929. The plot is almost entirely changed, to make room for a gang of Nazi agents. And only a few of the songs were retained, although enough for young singer Kathryn Grayson to make an impression on the critics: she would go on to become one of Metro's biggest stars in the next decade. The Abbott and Costello bits are much as their fans will expect – the apple-changing routine, the 'mirage' that turns out to be real, the talking dog, the spinning car at the

garage and the tequila stew scene, most of them borrowed from old radio and vaudeville routines.

Riot in Cell Block 11 ○
1954, US, 80 mins, b/w
Dir: Don Siegel
Stars: Neville Brand, Emile Meyer
Rating: ★★★

This was America's first X film – a gritty harsh and forceful thriller, which, under the pin-point direction of double Oscar-winner Don Siegel, broke new grounds in realism, and looked at the root of trouble from both sides. It also opened up a whole new career for Neville Brand as the leader of the rioters, a tough but thinking man who keeps the convicts just sufficiently under control to ensure that the better conditions they are fighting for are not threatened by their own behaviour. And such less familiar faces as Emile Meyer, Frank Faylen, Robert Osterloh, Leo Gordon, Whit Bissell, Dabbs Greer, James Anderson and Alvy Moore, were all able to show themselves as fine actors.

Riptide ○
1934, US, 90 mins, b/w
Dir: Edmund Goulding
Stars: Norma Shearer, Herbert Marshall, Robert Montgomery
Rating: ★★

Norma Shearer, she of the flawless complexion, and debonair Robert Montgomery, so successful together in the film version of Noel Coward's *Private Lives*, were paired again in this piece of frou-frou in which their performances are far superior to director Edmund Goulding's screenplay. The charm and elegant playing of the stars pulls it through, although there must have been times when they didn't know whether to play scenes for laughs, tears or dramatic effect.

Rising Damp ○
1980, UK, 96 mins, colour
Dir: Joe McGrath
Stars: Leonard Rossiter, Frances de la Tour, Don Warrington, Christopher Strauli, Denholm Elliott
Rating: ★★★

The film version of the television success about the lecherous landlord (a role which rightly made a star of Leonard Rossiter) and his incredibly seedy boarding-house wisely sticks to the 'sketch' formula. If it succeeds only in fits and starts, that's because Joe McGrath's direction seems to be

working against the efforts of the
excellent Rossiter and the adorable
Frances de la Tour, as the wallflower
tenant who finally succumbs to the
advances of the wolfish lodger
(Denholm Elliott at the top of his
form) who really covets her Post Office Saving Books. One could have
done with a little more fun at the expense of the conditions which
Rossiter's tenants suffer; even so, there
are some very funny lines, and Ms de
la Tour's description of her father's
death remains the laugh of a lifetime.

Rising Sun ● ⓥ
1993, US, 129 mins, colour
Dir: Philip Kaufman
Stars: Sean Connery, Wesley Snipes,
Cary-Hiroyuki Tagawa, Tia Carrere,
Harvey Keitel, Ray Wise
Rating: ★★★

Despite the backdrop of Japa-
nese-American business competition
in LA (little more than window-
dressing), this is really a mystery
thriller about a videotape recording of
a murder: what it tells detectives, what
it doesn't tell them, and what it
conceals from them. A high-priced
mistress is strangled on a boardroom
table (it seems) while having sex with
her lover (it seems), but the identity of
the killer is hidden on the missing disk
taken by a security camera (or is it?).
Sean Connery is the cop with the
know-how to penetrate the Japanese
community; Wesley Snipes is the cop
who's officially on the case. Together
they have to wade through layers of
deceit that conceal – what? More
deceit? With the help of a beautiful
video expert (Tia Carrere), they soon
discover that even the truth can lie.
Parts of this are intriguing, parts exciting and parts drag a bit. Harvey
Keitel is rather wasted as another bad
lieutenant, but Connery's cool
authority and the intrigue of video-
trickery keep you watching this
complex whodunnit to the end.

Risky Business ● ⓥ
1983, US, 95 mins, colour
Dir: Paul Brickman
Stars: Tom Cruise, Rebecca DeMornay,
Richard Masur
Rating: ★★

It's the old, old story of a teenage
boy's initiation into manhood, but in
this case given a whole new and potentially hilarious slant – besides
providing Tom Cruise with his initiation into stardom. Joel (Cruise) is
cornered into calling a call girl while

his parents are away. After the inevitable night of bliss, he gets involved
in her running away from a pimp,
then incurs thousands of dollars worth
of damage when he plunges his father's car into Lake Michigan. The girl
(Rebecca DeMornay) turns out to
have quite a head for business, and
suggests that he can make a mint by
inviting all her 'friends' over for a
night if he'll invite his fellow students.
This isn't quite the end of a story
which has some beautifully funny
moments, but doesn't carry its basic
idea through with enough conviction;
it sets up a nice theme and then pussy-
foots around with it. Still, you'll be
glad about the upbeat ending the
scriptwriters have managed to devise
to round it off.

Rita, Sue and Bob Too ● ⓥ
1986, UK, 95 mins, colour
Dir: Alan Clarke
Stars: Siobhan Finneran, Michelle
Holmes, George Costigan, Lesley Sharp
Rating: ★

An ugly, sad, tedious four-letter farrago about life as it is lived in the
backstreets of Bradford. Rita and Sue
are two 16-year-old tarts well on their
way to becoming slum mums, even
though their school days are not quite
over. They babysit for Bob who drives
them home over the moors. The girls
casually comply with his leering
request for a double lay and a permanent liaison is soon forged. 'He
certainly knows how to give a girl a
good time,' remarks Rita, pathetically,
after 30 seconds in the reclining seat
of Bob's car. When Bob's frayed wife
throws him out, he takes in pregnant
Rita, and Sue's forced to move in
with a Pakistani boyfriend. The film's
idea of twists in the plot is pretty well
limited to Bob's failure to 'make it'
on one occasion and the song 'Gang
Bang' is well in keeping with its spirit.
The acting is fair, given that the characters have little to do but yell
expletives at each other.

River, The ○
1951, UK, 87 mins, colour
Dir: Jean Renoir
Stars: Nora Swinburne, Esmond Knight
Rating: ★★

Jean Renoir's touching film about
adolescent love among the English
community in India is simply ablaze
with vivid, contrasting colours. Its
storyline encompassing death, birth
and a girl's journey into womanhood
is devoid of any emotional highpoints

and flows gently along as seamlessly as
the river Ganges, on whose banks the
action is set. Thomas Breen is well
cast as the ex-US soldier to whom
three girls lose their hearts, but the
standout performance is by Radha,
who dances enchantingly and plays the
part of a half-caste girl with memorable intensity.

River, The ◐
1984, US, 122 mins, colour
Dir: Mark Rydell
Stars: Mel Gibson, Sissy Spacek, Scott
Glenn
Rating: ★★★

Mel Gibson is living dangerously
again, although the evils that face him
in this back-to-the-land drama are
drought, flooding and the efforts of
bad guy Scott Glenn to drive him off
his farm. Sissy Spacek follows along
the trail blazed by Sally Field and
Jessica Lange as the wife who tends
the farm (and nearly loses her life in a
tractor accident which provides the
film's most agonising scene) when her
man is forced to go away to earn
money – as a 'scab' at a striking steel
works. The combination of Gibson
and Spacek should have been dynamite but, though both are good, a
unifying element between them seems
to be missing, so that the scene-stealers
are little Becky Jo Lynch as their
daughter, and Glenn, coming on like
a younger James Coburn as Spacek's
high-school beau, now bent on
flooding the valley he grew up in.
Colour photography is splendid,
whether in summer sunshine, winter
floods or the interior of the steel-
works. The ending may choke you up
a bit and reveals director Mark Rydell
however practical his view of the
modern Mid-West may be, as a sen-
timentalist at heart.

River of No Return ○ ⓥ
1954, US, 91 mins, colour
Dir: Otto Preminger
Stars: Robert Mitchum, Marilyn Monroe,
Rory Calhoun
Rating: ★★★

Almost a classic, as Marilyn Monroe
and Robert Mitchum fight the rapids,
greasy villain Rory Calhoun and
themselves in a spectacular Western
that also gives Marilyn time to sing
'One Silver Dollar', 'River of No
Return' and 'I'm Gonna File My
Claim'. Even if they're in the studio
tank, the stars' ride on the raft looks

R

pretty hairy, and the second half of the film, brightly shot in colour by Joseph LaShelle, is terrific all through.

River Runs Through It, A ◐ ⊙

1992, US, 123 mins, colour
Dir: Robert Redford
Stars: Craig Sheffer, Brad Pitt, Tom Skerritt, Emily Lloyd, Brenda Blethyn
Rating: ★★★

Robert Redford's third film as director is a poetic tale of a Montana childhood. Mention that it's also about fly-fishing and you might run a mile. But you would be mistaken. For, although this film never savages the emotions, it certainly stirs them through its tale of the sons of a fishing preacher. One is destined for an academic life and, on a return to Montana, tries to look after the life of his wilder, charismatic and clearly doomed younger brother. Brad Pitt not unnaturally steals the film in this latter role, with his flashing smile and star personality, though one hoped (to no avail) that there might be an Oscar nod for the long-serving Tom Skerritt for his deeply-etched and never overstated portrait of their father.

Roadgames ◐

1981, Australia, 100 mins, colour
Dir: Richard Franklin
Stars: Stacy Keach, Jamie Lee Curtis
Rating: ★★★★

Director Richard Franklin, who also made *Psycho II*, is a self-confessed Hitchcock fanatic, and this scary thriller is full of references to the Master. Truck driver Stacy Keach has in his cab a magazine called *Hitchcock*, and the leading female character is not only called Hitch but is played by Jamie Lee Curtis, daughter of Janet *Psycho* Leigh. The resulting mix of murder and mystery, seen entirely from Keach's point of view, is a combination of *Duel* and *Rear Window*. The device of Keach talking aloud to himself (and being answered by his own thoughts) is faultlessly done, and the two leading performances perfectly balanced. The audience is continually kept guessing, but Franklin finds time for one or two demonstrations of flair; such as the flashing lightning that suddenly reveals the 'killer' van and its owner, as if from nowhere, or a suspicious Keach, training binoculars on the van-driver, only to turn away again

just as the man looks up and straight at him. The climax is a nerve-grinding affair and includes a glorious twist when everyone who suspects Keach closes in on him while the actual killer begins to recede into the crowd.

Road House ○

1948, US, 105 mins, b/w
Dir: Jean Negulesco
Stars: Ida Lupino, Cornel Wilde, Richard Widmark, Celeste Holm
Rating: ★★★

Smokily atmospheric triangle melodrama, with a typically hard-boiled performance from Ida Lupino as the roadhouse chanteuse whose cigarettes burn grooves in her piano, and about whom one character says: 'She does more without a voice than anyone I've ever heard.' Richard Widmark is chillingly effective as the roadhouse owner whose obsession with Lupino turns him into a psychotic villain.

Road House ● ⊙

1988, US, 114 mins, colour
Dir: Rowdy Herrington
Stars: Patrick Swayze, Kelly Lynch, Ben Gazzara, Sam Elliott
Rating: ★

A beefcake vehicle for Patrick Swayze, this is a modern version of the spaghetti Western, full of heavy sex and even heavier violence, as Swayze takes on the job of marshal – sorry I mean 'cooler' (head bouncer) – at a rowdy midwest road house. 'It's the kind of place,' explains owner Kevin Tighe, 'where they sweep the eyeballs up after closing.' 'It's my way or the highway,' growls Swayze in response, although he doesn't say that to the local medico, played by tanned, long-legged Kelly Lynch, who's no match for harum-scarum Kathleen Wilhoite in the personality stakes. Soon, Swayze finds he has to take on the whole lawless town, especially local big shot Gazzara and his formidable gang of heavies. No problem. Blood, sweat and tears are here in plenty, but originality is nowhere in sight.

Road to Bali ○

1952, US, 90 mins, colour
Dir: Hal Walker
Stars: Bing Crosby, Bob Hope, Dorothy Lamour
Rating: ★★

The only *Road* comedy in colour, this hasn't the joie-de-vivre of some of Hope, Crosby and Lamour's earlier efforts, although there are funny guest

spots from Jane Russell (right at the end), Dean Martin and Jerry Lewis and (on film) Katharine Hepburn and Humphrey Bogart. The most popular song was Bing and Bob's duet 'Chicago Style'. The humour here seems more forced than before and Hope and Crosby (though not Lamour) too old to be cavorting in such capers any more. The next road (to Hong Kong) was to be the last and Crosby's death robbed the two old stagers of the film they were planning, *The Road to the Fountain of Youth*.

Road to Denver, The ○

1955, US, 90 mins, colour
Dir: Joseph Kane
Stars: John Payne, Mona Freeman, Lee J Cobb, Lee Van Cleef
Rating: ★★★

A vigorous, satisfying Western, well adapted from Bill Gulick's good novel *Man from Texas*, and with as strong a cast as Republic Studios could muster on the budget. The leading roles are well played by John Payne and Mona Freeman while, in support, glowering Lee J Cobb, leering Skip Homeier, snarling Lee Van Cleef and grizzled Andy Clyde all catch the eye. The studio's colour process, Trucolor, had greatly improved since it was first introduced some years earlier, and cameraman Reggie Lanning was able to achieve some rich photography with it. Although the film is set in Texas and Colorado, a lot of the location shooting was done in Utah! Sturdy stuff.

Road to Hong Kong, The ⊙

1961, UK, 100 mins, b/w
Dir: Norman Panama
Stars: Bing Crosby, Bob Hope, Joan Collins, Dorothy Lamour
Rating: ★★

The last of the *Road* comedy films, and the formula's now looking as tired as veteran stars Bing Crosby and Bob Hope as they chase a drug to cure amnesia and end up on another planet. The plot's enlivened by some funny guest appearances (from Frank Sinatra, Dean Martin, David Niven, Jerry Colonna and especially Peter Sellers) and zingy songs that include 'Teamwork', 'Road to Hong Kong', 'It's the Only Way to Travel' and 'Warmer Than a Whisper'. Joan Collins is the leading lady, but it should really have been Dorothy Lamour, here shamefully relegated to a guest appearance.

Road to Morocco ⊙
1942, US, 83 mins, b/w
Dir: Victor Schertzinger
Stars: Bing Crosby, Bob Hope, Dorothy Lamour, Anthony Quinn
Rating: ★★★

The third of the *Road* comedies that were as sure-fire box-office bets in the war years as a *Rambo*, *Rocky* or *Dirty Harry* films would be today. As usual Hope loses Lamour to Crosby, who also sings ('Time to get the popcorn folks,' laments Hope) 'Moonlight Becomes You', the film's big hit, although nowadays it's the title duet that people seem to remember. This is also the one with the camel who complains that this is 'the screwiest picture I was ever in.'

Road to Rio ⊙
1947, US, 100 mins, b/w
Dir: Norman Z McLeod, Jack Rose
Stars: Bing Crosby, Bob Hope, Dorothy Lamour
Rating: ★★★

The last of the really funny *Road* comedies with Bing Crosby, Bob Hope and Dorothy Lamour. The Wiere Brothers, a zany musical comedy trio, are a big hit as Brazilian musicians hired by Bing and Bob to make up a quintet of Americans and given the briefest of crash courses in American slang; villainess Gale Sondergaard hypnotises Dorothy Lamour into hating Bing and Bob at inconvenient moments; and Crosby and the Andrews Sisters had a big hit with 'You Don't Have to Know the Language'. And how come Hope manages to land Lamour at the end instead of Crosby getting her? You'll have to watch the last few feet of the film to find out the answer to that one.

Road to Singapore ⊙
1940, US, 84 mins, b/w
Dir: Victor Schertzinger
Stars: Bing Crosby, Bob Hope, Dorothy Lamour, Charles Coburn
Rating: ★★★

Who could have guessed that this modest Paramount comedy-musical could have ignited the world with laughter under the complementary talents of Bing Crosby and Bob Hope and lead to nationwide queues for the most successful comedy series of its time. In this one, the 'patty-cake' routine is invented and songs include 'Sweet Potato Piper', 'Captain Custard' and 'The Moon and the Willow Tree'.

Road to Utopia ⊙
1945, US, 90 mins, b/w
Dir: Hal Walker
Stars: Bing Crosby, Bob Hope, Dorothy Lamour, Robert Benchley
Rating: ★★★★

Or, more properly, *Road to Alaska*. Drily narrated by that ineffable wit Robert Benchley, it has Bing Crosby, Bob Hope and Dorothy Lamour skating all over the Klondike in search of a lost gold mine. All this and dancing bears, talking fish and a very funny twist-ending. An absolute riot of wit and invention.

Road to Zanzibar ⊙
1941, US, 92 mins, b/w
Dir: Victor Schertzinger
Stars: Bing Crosby, Bob Hope, Dorothy Lamour
Rating: ★★★

The second *Road* film, a bungle through the jungle that's possibly the wildest of the lot. Said the publicity: '152 more laughs (count 'em) than *Road to Singapore*.' Bob Hope's Fearless Frazier has some terrific one-line gags, while Bing Crosby and Dorothy Lamour parody their romantic duets in 'You're Dangerous'. Burly Charles Gemora gets inside a gorilla suit, just as he did in Laurel and Hardy's *Swiss Miss*.

Roaring Twenties, The ○ ⓥ
1939, US, 106 mins, b/w
Dir: Raoul Walsh
Stars: James Cagney, Humphrey Bogart, Priscilla Lane, Jeffrey Lynn
Rating: ★★★

Spinning madly through a plot that would take today's directors twice the time to tell, Raoul Walsh vividly sets out a panorama not only of the violent decade under survey, but of the whole gangster-film product of his studio (Warner Brothers) throughout the Thirties. James Cagney, Humphrey Bogart, Priscilla Lane and Gladys George all give, in their different veins, what the American press of the time might have dubbed 'socko' performances. The final scene is a classic of Hollywood cinema.

Robbers of the Sacred Mountain ○
1983, US, 90 mins, colour
Dir: Olaf Pooley
Stars: John Marley, Simon MacCorkindale
Rating: ★★

Clearly inspired by the success of *Raiders of the Lost Ark*, this is an effective low-budget update of traditional serials, spliced with frequent action sequences, treachery and twists. Britain's Simon MacCorkindale is the Indy-type lead; Blanca Guerra and Louise Vallance provide him with striking female company.

Robbery ○
1967, UK, 114 mins, colour
Dir: Peter Yates
Stars: Stanley Baker, Joanna Pettet, James Booth, Frank Finlay
Rating: ★★★

Thriller that follows up a successful raid on a night train from Glasgow, loaded with millions of banknotes. The film caused quite a stir on its initial release, particularly as its theme had an obvious parallel in real life. And Hollywood star Steve McQueen was so taken by Peter Yates' snappy direction that he insisted on having the Englishman helm the following year's *Bullitt*. Yates, of course, went from strength to strength and is still turning out hit films today.

Robe, The ○ ⓥ
1953, US, 135 mins, colour
Dir: Henry Koster
Stars: Richard Burton, Jean Simmons, Victor Mature, Michael Rennie, Dean Jagger
Rating: ★★★

This dignified pageant of Ancient Rome, dealing with the events following the Crucifixion, has the appropriate cast of thousands and a literate script by Philip Dunne, from the mammoth novel by Lloyd C Douglas. Richard Burton and Jean Simmons are both good but the best performance for my money – and, indeed, the best portrayal of his career – comes, surprisingly, from Victor Mature as Demetrius. The 'beefcake' star gives a sensitive performance which adds more to the reality of the story than anything else. The exciting photography of Leon Shamroy – particularly in the action sequences – makes a brilliant backcloth to a story that reaches a moving peak.

Roberta ○
1935, US, 105 mins, b/w
Dir: William A Seiter

R

Stars: Irene Dunne, Fred Astaire, Ginger Rogers
Rating: ★★

In their third film together, Fred Astaire and Ginger Rogers played second fiddle to Irene Dunne, as a Russian princess, sparring in and out of love with American footballer Randolph Scott, and get to perform four inspired dance routines. Look out for new RKO girl Lucille Ball in the lineup of mannequins in the extended fashion show sequence. Swathed in ostrich feathers, she descended a staircase onto the runway, making the most of what she later called 'halfway between an extra and a bit.'

Robin and Marian ○ ⓥ
1976, UK, 106 mins, colour
Dir: Richard Lester
Stars: Sean Connery, Audrey Hepburn, Robert Shaw, Nicol Williamson
Rating: ★★

Sherwood Forest 20 years after, and it's hardly the Nottingham of Errol Flynn's day that we are in here. It's a land of mud and grime, but the wicked sheriff (Robert Shaw) is still in there oppressing the peasants, as Robin Hood (Sean Connery) and Little John return from the Crusades. Director Richard Lester's how-it-really-was style, coupled with typical surrealist comic touches, somehow leaves the film struggling to find a rhythm. The only performance which suggests Lester's theme while proving attractive in its own right is Nicol Williamson's Little John. But the final battle between Connery and Shaw is gruelling, pulsating and bloody stuff.

Robin Hood ○ ⓥ
1973, US, 83 mins, colour
Dir: Wolfgang Reitherman
Voice stars: Peter Ustinov, Terry-Thomas, Brian Bedford
Rating: ★★

Coloured in pastel shades, this is a pleasant if unexceptional (by Disney standards) cartoon version of the story made live by the studio 20 years earlier. The voices of Peter Ustinov and Terry-Thomas are amusingly employed as cowardly lion and sneaky snake, but the music of the Sherman Brothers (*Mary Poppins* etc) is much missed.

Robin Hood ○ ⓥ
1991, US, 104 mins, colour
Dir: John Irvin

Stars: Patrick Bergin, Jeroen Krabbé, Edward Fox, Uma Thurman, Jurgen Prochnow
Rating: ★★

This is the kind of film that looks absolutely marvellous until the actors have to open their mouths. The credit sequence of lights on a hillside, followed by a thrillingly shot and cunningly edited manhunt sequence, promises a stylish slice of Sherwood – until the dialogue begins, a strange mixture of vulgarity and Richard Greenery. Bergin and Thurman as Robin and Marian show enough spirit to get the better of it at times, but Prochnow and Krabbé are bludgeoned into ludicrous over-acting, only half-trying to make sense of such lines as 'Sometimes, you're so wet one could shoot snipe off you', and even conceding the laurels for worst supporting actor to Edward Fox's Prince John, who bags the honour in one short appearance.

Robin Hood: Men in Tights ① ⓥ
1993, US, 102 mins, colour
Dir: Mel Brooks
Stars: Cary Elwes, Amy Yasbeck, Richard Lewis, Roger Rees, Tracey Ullman, Dom DeLuise, Mel Brooks
Rating: ★★

Mel Brooks runs wild in a Sherwood Forest that's more blue than green. Subtlety dies a thousand deaths, as Brooks' lavatorial arrows find the mark time and again in this skit (satire is definitely too strong a word) on the Hood legend, already targeted by Brooks in his TV series *When Things Were Rotten*. Cary Elwes and Amy Yasbeck wisely play this straight as Robin and Marian, letting Brooks have his head as Rabbi Tuckman, who's given a good run for his money by Roger Rees' snivelling Sheriff of Rottingham and Tracey Ullman's cackling hag Latrine. Brooks, never a man to let good taste stand in his way, steals shamelessly from past successes in what resembles nothing more than an English countryside version of *Blazing Saddles*.

Robin Hood: Prince of Thieves ① ⓥ
1991, US, 128 mins, colour
Dir: Kevin Reynolds
Stars: Kevin Costner, Morgan Freeman, Mary Elizabeth Mastrantonio, Christian Slater, Alan Rickman, Sean Connery
Rating: ★★

Credit this version of the Sherwood legend with trying to be something different, then ask what it is that it's trying to be. There's a tongue-in-cheek Robin (Kevin Costner) with an American accent. A thoroughly modern Marian, played by Hollywood's Mastrantonio with an English accent. A comic Sheriff of Nottingham (Alan Rickman) who gets lines like, 'Cancel the kitchen scraps for lepers and orphans. And cancel Christmas!' And a collection of English yokels as the merrie men, mustering as much cursing and crudity as they think a PG-13 (or in the UK, 12) certificate will take. The end product looks as though the cast read the script and decided the best thing to do was have a good time and enjoy themselves. So at least this is less stilted than some Robins. And it unexpectedly comes up with one memorable character in the form of Morgan Freeman as a Moor, brought back by Robin from the Crusades. As a classic adventure, though, it scarcely gets out of the starting-gate. The action is reasonably well-staged, though some of it is so unlikely as not to be thrilling.

Robinson Crusoe on Mars ○
1964, US, 110 mins, colour
Dir: Byron Haskin
Stars: Paul Mantee, Adam West
Rating: ★★★

Remarkably successful transition of Daniel Defoe's classic castaway novel to a futuristic setting. While sticking quite close to the incidents in the original, it transports its hero to outer space, as the first American astronaut to land on Mars – albeit unwillingly. The oppressively desolate Martian landscapes are well conceived in splendid Technicolor and Byron Haskin's direction is impressively imaginative, making this fine fun for boys from five to 85. Adam West, who plays the spaceman who is killed early on in the film, became much better known shortly afterwards as television's comic book hero *Batman*.

RoboCop ● ⓥ
1987, US, 103 mins, colour
Dir: Paul Verhoeven
Stars: Peter Weller, Nancy Allen, Dan O'Herlihy, Ronny Cox, Ray Wise
Rating: ★★★

Looking like a vehicle tailor-made for Arnold Sch-you know who, this is a technician's dream of a film, set in the near future with crime rampant on the streets of 'old' Detroit. Robot policemen are a fledgling idea, but inclined to go haywire at the drop of a connection. So when cop Murphy (Peter Weller) is drilled to bits by the local mob, Morton (Miguel Ferrer), a brainbox as obsequious as he is obnoxious, reassembles him electronically to become the world's first RoboCop. After preliminary skirmishes, in which RoboCop cleans up a few local hoodlums, the nub of the plot comes into play. He starts to have recollections of the gang who obliterated him, who are in turn the henchmen of Jones (Ronny Cox) who controls the city's crime as well as being second-in-command of the company which built RoboCop, and now runs the local police. Although scarcely plausible at several key junctures, and aimed at producing the maximum grievous bodily damage, this is an entertaining adult romp with the villains, Cox and Kurtwood Smith, coolly stealing the show. The firepower around here is tremendous – the blood and gore (one villain disintegrates in toxic waste) splatters all over the screen. But there are one or two subtler comic moments too, such as the futuristic family playing a game of Nukem (together with fake explosion) in their sitting room.

Robocop 2 ● ⓥ
1990, US, 116 mins, colour
Dir: Irwin Kershner
Stars: Peter Weller, Nancy Allen, Daniel O'Herlihy, Tom Noonan
Rating: ★★

Number Two certainly delivers the action, even if its plot is impossible to follow. The city is wide open to criminals and looters, the police are on strike and unscrupulous private interests plan to take over. The chief criminal having been hospitalised by Robocop, his henchmen plan to make a deal with the mayor: they'll deliver a crime-free city in return for a 'nuke' (Futuristic drug) market at lower cost and safer substances. Private interests cannot allow such a devil's contract. And that's where *Robocop 2* comes in. Although the way is left clear for *Robocop 3*, this sequel lacks the humour and originality of the first film, often running like an old-time serial. Weller and Allen, though both looking a bit long in the tooth, resume their roles with straight-faced gusto. Weller also gets the only line of any real wit, but unfortunately it's the last

one in the film. The beginning, too, with a guest shot from John Glover, is quite amusing.

Rob Roy – The Highland Rogue ⊙
1953, UK, 85 mins, colour
Dir: Harold French
Stars: Richard Todd, Glynis Johns, James Robertson Justice, Jean Taylor-Smith
Rating: ★★

Adventure has fine old fling in these Highland fun and games from the Disney studio. It may merit a dunce's cap as a history lesson, but as a lively, colourful, action-filled yarn with something of a 'Western' feel, it belongs near the top of the class.

Rock-a-Doodle ⊙
1990, US, 74 mins, colour
Dir: Don Bluth
Stars: Phil Harris, Glen Campbell, Christopher Plummer, Sandy Duncan
Rating: ★

Children's entertainment is always to be welcomed but, though teenies will surely love it, accompanying adults are likely to give a thumbs down to this dumb, dim cartoon feature based on the story of Chanticleer. Cock of the roost on his farm, he's forced to leave when the animals discover that his crow doesn't actually make the sun rise. This is all the work of the owls (led by the Duke of Owl) who love the dark and don't want the sun to come up any more at all. The animals, flooded out by storms, decide to make for the city and bring Chanticleer back from his career there as a rock star. Despite a good voice cast, director Bluth has failed to create any interesting characters here, with the possible (unintentional) exception of a magpie who seems to think he's a woodpecker. The innovation of owls as villains is at least a novelty, but the rooster hero and his pheasant heroine are particularly unprepossessing, and the effects work in mixing live characters with cartoon pretty unimpressive.

Rock Around the Clock ○
1956, US, 74 mins, b/w
Dir: Fred F Sears
Stars: Bill Haley and the Comets, Johnnie Johnston, The Platters
Rating: ★★

This was the one that really set the Rock movement alight. As Bill Haley and his saxophone descended slowly

to the floor, teenagers of all shapes and sizes on both sides of the Atlantic left their cinema seats and bopped it up in the aisles. Parents: look in on this and remember what it was like when you were misunderstood teenagers. You'll find that the slight story looks even slighter today and that now, as then, it's only the music that matters.

Rock Around the World
See: The Tommy Steele Story

Rocketeer, The ⊙ ⓥ
1991, US, 108 mins, colour
Dir: Joe Johnston
Stars: Bill Campbell, Jennifer Connelly, Alan Arkin, Timothy Dalton
Rating: ★★★

Pretty stylish by strip-comic-epic standards and with something a little different to offer, this is an adventure (set in 1938) about a revolutionary rocket pack that, when strapped to man's back, can jet him around the skies. We seem to remember that Sylvester the Cat went awfully wrong with one of these in a Warner Brothers cartoon, but hero Bill Campbell can just about steer the damn thing well enough to effect a daring aerial rescue when a pal gets into trouble. Unfortunately, this attracts the attention not only of the FBI, and of aviation pioneer Howard Hughes, but also a group of Nazi infiltrators led (in a sly dig at Errol Flynn) by a swashbuckling movie star, expertly played by Timothy Dalton. For good measure, there's an almost-too-voluptuous heroine (Jennifer Connelly) a lovable old inventor sidekick (Alan Arkin) and a hulking assassin made up to look like Forties' film villain Rondo Hatton. Director Johnston, who made *Honey, I Shrunk the Kids*, pitches us straight into the action from the start and there's no lack of it. Acting, apart from Dalton who's on a subtler level, is fairly rudimentary.

Rockets Galore ⊙
(aka: Mad Little Island)
1958, UK, 94 mins, colour
Dir: Michael Relph
Stars: Donald Sinden, Jeannie Carson
Rating: ★★

Ealing Studios first turned their attention to Sir Compton Mackenzie's whimsical tales of the Scottish highlands and islands in the memorable *Whisky Galore!*. This sequel brings the island of Todday into the nuclear age and proves a spotty successor to the original, with the islanders fighting to

R

stop a rocket base being built there. Gordon Jackson and Ian Hunter have featured roles, and you'll also spot Ronnie Corbett.

Rocking Horse Winner, The ○
1949, UK, 90 mins, b/w
Dir: Anthony Pelissier
Stars: Valerie Hobson, John Howard Davies, Ronald Squire, Susan Richards
Rating: ★★★

John Howard Davies, later the producer of TV's *Fawlty Towers*, plays the sinister child who, once aboard his rocking horse, can predict the winner in any given race. As might be expected from the star of *Oliver Twist*, Master Davies brings this version of a D H Lawrence novella to chilling, disturbing, but fascinating life.

Rocky ○ ⓥ
1976, US, 119 mins, colour
Dir: John G Avildsen
Stars: Sylvester Stallone, Talia Shire, Burt Young, Carl Weathers, Burgess Meredith
Rating: ★★★★

Sylvester Stallone's career-making film is a cross between *Marty* and *Somebody Up There Likes Me*. Rocky, a boxer, is 30 and, although a winner of 44 of his 64 fights, is already considered a bum by his local gym manager (Burgess Meredith) who hates him 'because he had the talent to become a good fighter' but has let his chance slip away and now fights for two-bit purses in smoky halls. Out of the blue, the world champion decides to offer a chance to an unknown home town boy. Of course, the choice is Rocky. The nice thing about the film from then on – that allows it to build cleanly to the grandstand finish – is, of course, that no one will try to nobble the challenger, or get him to take a dive, since they don't think he has a chance. The fight itself is quite superbly done, all thud and blood, and pace, adrenalin and noise. Like the movie, it never relaxes its grip. Stallone does well and the character is utterly believable. In his screenplay, he also reveals an ear for a funny line, dropped delightfully into unexpected, mid-conversational places. James Crabe's photography is outstanding, especially in the night-time scenes which evoke the grimy night-life of Philadelphia in a mellow fashion which melds with the mood of the film. A knock-out.

Rocky II ○ ⓥ
1979, US, 119 mins, colour
Dir: Sylvester Stallone
Stars: Sylvester Stallone, Talia Shire, Burt Young, Burgess Meredith
Rating: ★★★

Stallone does it again. Against all the odds, he brings home his *Rocky* sequel as another winner – even if it's a notch below its predecessor in every respect. Even so, if your knees aren't trembling at the end of the inevitable re-match for the World Heavyweight Championship, then your adrenalin must have dried up and gone away. The early scenes of Rocky hitting the skids after blowing his money are sticky and predictable, and only the luminous performance of Talia Shire as his wife keeps it going at this stage. Rocky's dry, throwaway, semi-dim humour improves things still further, and the music, photography and boxing 'choreography' really come into their own in the build-up to the big fight. But Ms Shire's conversion to wanting Stallone to fight again (despite the risk to his eyesight) is hardly more convincing than the result of the fight itself.

Rocky III ○ ⓥ
1982, US, 99 mins, colour
Dir: Sylvester Stallone
Stars: Sylvester Stallone, Talia Shire, Burt Young, Burgess Meredith, Carl Weathers, Mr T
Rating: ★★★

Sylvester Stallone's boxing saga rolls on in this predictable but effective third segment. Rocky is now world champ. His manager (Burgess Meredith) has set him up with 10 hand-picked opponents in a row – only Rocky doesn't know it. What we need to psych us (and Rocky) up is a defeat that has to be avenged. Conveniently, it comes along in the shape of Clubber Lang (Mr T), a fearsome and hungry black fighter who wants Rocky's guts in a sling. After Rocky bites the inevitable dust, his old opponent Apollo Creed (Carl Weathers) comes back into the picture . . . as his new trainer. The fights here don't measure up to those from the two previous films, but the series retains its likeability and stays afloat on the personalities of its performers: Stallone is again the grunting Rocky to the life; Talia Shire as his wife only has one big scene this time and she doesn't muff it. Even if the contrivances are beginning to show, and Rocky's 'relapse' into the soft life

doesn't convince for one moment, serious fans can have little to complain about from this third round in the contest.

Rocky IV ○ ⓥ
1985, US, 110 mins, colour
Dir: Sylvester Stallone
Stars: Sylvester Stallone, Talia Shire
Rating: ★★

The spiralling improbabilities of the Rocky saga reached their pinnacle with this moronically jingoistic episode. The Russians have biologically engineered a huge fighting machine, Ivan Drago (Dolph Lundgren), and former world heavyweight champ Apollo Creed challenges him to an exhibition bout in Las Vegas. Drago fells him with his left hook and he dies. Rocky Balboa (Sylvester Stallone) gives up his title to fight the Russian in an unauthorised bout in the Soviet Union. What we get here is Rocky (looking decidedly pebble-like compared with the giant Lundgren) defending the American way against the dark evils of communism. With the dismantling of the USSR, most films that display Russia as an eternally evil empire look pretty silly now – *Rocky IV* particularly so, as its pro-US anti-Russian stance is so simplistic. That said, the fight sequences are stunningly well done and the split-screen sequence where you see both protagonists training is also very effective. The odd thing is, although you know this is all rubbish, you still find yourself rooting for the good guy. There's a lesson there somewhere, and Stallone's astute enough to have learned it.

Rocky Horror Picture Show, The ◐
1974, UK, 95 mins, colour
Dir: Jim Sharman
Stars: Tim Curry, Susan Sarandon, Barry Bostwick, Richard O'Brien, Jonathan Adams, Little Nell
Rating: ★★

After the comedy horror film came this hugely successful musical comedy horror, which is pretty far out even for the mid-Seventies. An all-American couple, unwise enough to stop at a castle to use the phone, are both seduced by its occupant, a transsexual transvestite Transylvanian intent on creating a superman for his own pleasures. The best performance comes from Richard O'Brien (who also wrote it) as the obligatory hunchback; his first appearance at a window is a sensationally striking moment that the rest of the film never quite matches.

Roger and Me ●
1989, US, 91 mins, colour
Dir: Michael Moore
Rating: ★★★

A bitingly funny documentary on the collapse of an American town – Flint, Michigan – following the decision of General Motors and its chairman Roger Smith to throw 23 per cent of its people out of work by closing the auto factory there. Director Moore describes not only his own battle to interview Smith, but also the descent of Flint into a living hell where half the population are on general welfare. Many of the car workers are in the new huge prison there, many others are guards in the same grim structure. An idiotic attempt to attract tourism by building a Hyatt Regency Hotel, the Water Street Pavilion and the Auto World Theme Park founders within a few months, the deserted places just joining the crumbling heart of Flint, where evictions run at several a day. The film has scenes that some viewers may find upsetting; the story is not a downbeat one, though, thanks to Moore's telling it with bitter sarcasm and a prowling camera that catches the funny side as well as the tragic. He also reveals that America has some spooky people. Some of them even live in Flint . . .

Rogues of Sherwood Forest ☉
1950, US, 75 mins, colour
Dir: Gordon Douglas
Stars: John Derek, Diana Lynn, George Macready
Rating: ★★

John Derek as the son of Robin Hood in a typical Columbia action film of its time in which reality is kept at arm's length. Diana Lynn, former child actress, who was one of the sweetest Hollywood heroines, makes a beautiful lady fair, George Macready is as sleek a villain as you could wish for, and old-time silent comedian Billy Bevan pops up as Will Scarlett. The action, ravishingly photographed in Technicolor by ace cameraman Charles Lawton Jr, provides a new slant on why King John signed the Magna Carta.

Rogues' Regiment ○
1948, US, 86 mins, b/w
Dir: Robert Florey

Stars: Dick Powell, Marta Toren, Vincent Price, Stephen McNally
Rating: ★★

Typically tough Dick Powell post-war thriller with Powell as an American intelligence officer at large in the Foreign Legion, trying to ferret out a Nazi war criminal.

Rollerball ● ⊽
1975, US, 129 mins, colour
Dir: Norman Jewison
Stars: James Caan, John Houseman, Maud Adams, Ralph Richardson
Rating: ★★

The futuristic society of 2018 is rather vaguely realised but there's no doubting the ferocious power of the actual Rollerball sequences. This savage spectator sport is brought to life in a powerful series of brutally exciting scenes. James Caan and John Beck are well teamed as Rollerball stars while John Houseman scores as the seemingly benign Bartholomew.

Rollercoaster ○
1977, US, 115 mins, colour
Dir: James Goldstone
Stars: George Segal, Richard Widmark
Rating: ★★★

Fancy a ride on a scenic railway? The chances are that you'll be off them for some time after you've seen this good old-fashioned entertainment thriller about a cool young bomber (Timothy Bottoms) who blew one up, and threatens to do it again unless America's amusement park chiefs come up with a million dollars. Bottoms contributes his best film work for some time as the icy assassin, but it's George Segal who dominates the film by making the leading role (that of the safety inspector after the saboteur) seem tailor-made for his own attractive blend of cynicism and sincerity. Despite the massacre at the beginning, this is one the children could safely watch as well. And, for spotters of movie stars of 25 years ago, there are brief appearances by William Prince, Monica Lewis and – looking no different from his Warner contract days of the early Fifties – Dick Wesson.

Rollover ●
1981, US, 118 mins, colour
Dir: Alan J Pakula
Stars: Jane Fonda, Kris Kristofferson
Rating: ★

From director Alan J Pakula, who made *All the President's Men* and *The Parallax View*, comes another

convoluted study of the underside of American public life. This time, the subject is its financial world. Although you may not understand all the ins and outs of the plot, you're still likely to be hooked on its enticing mystery element which has banking wizard Kris Kristofferson and heiress widow Jane Fonda uncovering each other and a plot to undermine the world money market.

Romance in the High Seas
See: It's Magic

Romancing the Stone ○ ⊽
1984, US, 105 mins, colour
Dir: Robert Zemeckis
Stars: Michael Douglas, Kathleen Turner, Danny DeVito
Rating: ★★★

A colourful slice of escapism that's so likeable and fast-moving that you often forget how silly it all is. Kathleen Turner, Michael Douglas and Danny DeVito all boosted their careers with larger than life performances in the kind of film that French director Philippe de Broca used to make with that stunt-minded actor Jean-Paul Belmondo 20 years ago. These days, all pretences towards reality and conviction have been tossed away in this kind of romp, but Turner's sympathetic performance as the beleaguered authoress helps a lot as she is hauled out to a sea of mud and the tropical storms in the Colombian outback to rescue a kidnapped sister, by yielding up the treasure map sent to her by her sister's dead husband. In South America, she's rescued by Jack Colton (Michael Douglas) who, while having an eye on the treasure map, is the amalgam of all the romantic heroes of her own fiction. Their subsequent hunt for the treasure might be even more fun if the villains weren't so intentionally comic, but we should still be grateful to director Robert Zemeckis and his actors for such non-stop action entertainment.

Roman Holiday ○ ⊽
1953, US, 118 mins, b/w
Dir: William Wyler
Stars: Gregory Peck, Audrey Hepburn, Eddie Albert
Rating: ★★★★

This is William Wyler's enchanting romantic comedy (in which Audrey Hepburn won an Oscar) about a princess who spends 24 hours incognito in Rome, squired by a reporter and photographer, who are well

R

aware of her real identity, and out for a scoop for their paper. A series of small, but delightful incidents subtly builds up our identification with the characters, lending a great charm and making the climax a truly moving movie moment. Eddie Albert offers a richly humorous account of the photographer, and Gregory Peck's casual romantic style is ideally suited to the role of the reporter. As the princess, Hepburn brought a unique blend of naive charm, refinement and elegance to the part that justly made her Hollywood's newest star.

Roman Scandals ○
1933, US, 92 mins, b/w
Dir: Frank Tuttle
Stars: Eddie Cantor, Ruth Etting
Rating: ★★★

Quite a few funny things happen to pop-eyed Eddie Cantor on his way to the forum in this lavish Goldwyn musical comedy. Cantor's co-star is torch singer Ruth Etting, whose life story was later told in Doris Day's *Love Me or Leave Me*. There are some wild dance numbers organised by the ubiquitous Busby Berkeley and director Frank Tuttle gives it lots of joie de vivre. The hit of the show is undoubtedly 'Keep Young and Beautiful'.

Roman Spring of Mrs Stone, The ○
1961, US, 104 mins, colour
Dir: Jose Quintero
Stars: Vivien Leigh, Warren Beatty
Rating: ★★★

This adaptation of a Tennessee Williams novel about a middle-aged actress falling for a young Italian gigolo has a bizarre, rather chilling charm. Vivien Leigh and Warren Beatty give interesting performances in these roles, but the film is stolen from both of them by Lotte Lenya as the widow's wasp-tongued friend.

Romantic Comedy ◑
1983, US, 103 mins, colour
Dir: Arthur Hiller
Stars: Dudley Moore, Mary Steenburgen
Rating: ★★

Cuddly Dudley Moore tried to reverse his fortunes after two box office bombs (*Six Weeks* and *Lovesick*) with this film version of Bernard Slade's Broadway play. With this tale of two playwrights who team up with varying personal and professional success he unfortunately scored a hat-trick, as the

end product, although enjoyable in parts, and with a good performance by Mary Steenburgen, ends up being neither very romantic nor very funny. Steenburgen plays the other writer and she and Moore battle hard against a script and pacing that lack the snap and crackle this type of comedy needs.

Romantic Englishwoman, The ● ⓥ
1975, UK, 116 mins, colour
Dir: Joseph Losey
Stars: Glenda Jackson, Michael Caine, Helmut Berger, Kate Nelligan
Rating: ★

Director Joseph Losey's answer to *Last Year in Marienbad*; it's only his direction that makes this puzzle picture an occasionally fascinating, if too often ludicrous cinematic exercise. Certainly, he has little help from the screenplay. In fact, it's hard to tell which is more trite – the film's script, or the pulp books written in the attic by author Michael Caine while downstairs he is losing his wife (Glenda Jackson) to narcotics-smuggling gigolo Helmut Berger. Or is he? That's just one of the riddles you have to tackle. The background music by Richard Hartley is some of the loveliest heard in a British film for quite a while.

Romeo and Juliet ○
1936, US, 126 mins, b/w
Dir: George Cukor
Stars: Leslie Howard, Norma Shearer
Rating: ★★★

Although it sports a pair of over-age lovers in Norma Shearer and Leslie Howard, this is in all other respects a perfectly splendid version of Shakespeare's classic, still the best available on film. Sensitive direction by George Cukor brings out all the passion of the play, with a last great flamboyant performance by John Barrymore as Mercutio. Howard at first insisted that he was too old for Romeo but, after the part had been turned down by Fredric March, Clark Gable, Errol Flynn and Robert Donat, the studio went back to its original choice and persuaded him to play the role.

Romeo and Juliet ○ ⓥ
1968, UK/Italy, 138 mins, colour
Dir: Franco Zeffirelli
Stars: Olivia Hussey, Leonard Whiting, Michael York
Rating: ★★

The brilliance of the supporting cast and the haunting music by Nino Rota more than compensate for the inexperience of the young leading players in Franco Zeffirelli's version of Shakespeare's tragic romance. It's a delight to the eye if not always to the ear.

Romeo Is Bleeding ● ⓥ
1993, US, 112 mins, colour
Dir: Peter Medak
Stars: Gary Oldman, Lena Olin, Annabella Sciorra, Juliette Lewis
Rating: ★

Gary Oldman lurches through the grunge once again for the sake of his art in this bloodsoaked story that's described as a black comedy, but isn't much like any comedy you ever saw, and a sight more difficult to follow. Oldman's a cop on the make who hoards his Mob bribes in a hole in his yard, is fond of his wife (Annabella Sciorra, good in thankless role) and his mistress (Juliette Lewis), but comes unstuck when he becomes involved with a ruthless hit-girl (Lena Olin). There's also the matter of the Mob don (Roy Scheider) cutting off one of his toes, when one of his tip-offs goes wrong. Yes Oldman's in a mess. And it gets worse. Unlike the film, which actually gets a bit better (though not much) towards the end. Olin does her best to be bad, Lewis does her mindless bimbo act, and Oldman, looking like Dick Powell, kills or nearly gets killed by everyone. Very slow, doomy and full of unnecessary excesses, the film demands your devotion to the star to see it through.

Rommel – Desert Fox ○ ⓥ
(aka: The Desert Fox)
1951, US, 88 mins, b/w
Dir: Henry Hathaway
Stars: James Mason, Cedric Hardwicke, Jessica Tandy
Rating: ★★★

James Mason's performance as the famous World War Two German field-marshal established him as a star in Hollywood after a tentative start to his career on the other side of the Atlantic. This story involves not so much Rommel's North Africa campaign as his involvement in a plot to assassinate Hitler (played by Luther Adler who took on the role a year later in *The Magic Face*). Under Henry Hathaway's cool, detached direction, the plot grips throughout.

Rookie, The ● Ⓥ
1990, US, 121 mins, colour
Dir: Clint Eastwood
Stars: Clint Eastwood, Charlie Sheen,
Sonia Braga, Raul Julia
Rating: ★★

Tough cop Clint Eastwood and his
new partner Charlie Sheen (the rookie
of the title) go on an orgy of destruction to catch baddie Raul Julia in
this crash bang wallop cop thriller.
Lots of action rattled along at a rapid
pace by Eastwood wearing his director's hat doesn't cover the fact that
The Rookie is formula stuff poorly
served by an indifferent script. It's as if
Eastwood got fed up with everyone
else making second-rate *Dirty Harry*
rip-offs, so made one himself.
Eastwood's cop is the grim avenger
you would expect, but Sheen is pretty
unconvincing and the usually
excellent Julia is a dreadfully clichéd
baddie, complete with indefinable
(and bad) foreign accent. To cap it all,
even Eastwood's normally sound directing skills seem to have deserted
him. Slip your brain into neutral and
you may enjoy this mindless slice of
mayhem.

Rookie of the Year ○ Ⓥ
1993, US, 100 mins, colour
Dir: Daniel Stern
Stars: Thomas Ian Nicholas, Gary
Busey, Daniel Stern, John Candy
Rating: ★

Actor Daniel Stern positively does not
seem set for a shining career as a director after this fairly agonising debut
behind the cameras. It's a sporting
fantasy about a 12-year-old kid
(Thomas Ian Nicholas) who becomes
a dynamite baseball pitcher after a
broken-arm accident 'fuses his
tendons with his humerus'. Subsequent developments are quite
ingeniously worked out, but director
Stern encourages all the cast to mug
shamelessly, setting them an example
himself with some painfully rampant
over-acting in an all-too-high profile
cameo role. Gary Busey, looking just
like Nick Nolte in this one, does his
best to calm things down a bit as the
veteran pitcher who takes the kid
under his wing, and John Candy appears unbilled (one of the film's few
wise decisions) as an excitable commentator. Pretty bad.

Rookies
See: Buck Privates

Room at the Top ◐
1958, UK, 117 mins, b/w
Dir: Jack Clayton
Stars: Laurence Harvey, Simone
Signoret, Heather Sears, Donald Wolfit
Rating: ★★★★

The powerful drama that brought a
new freedom to the British cinema. It
also introduced audiences to Joe
Lampton who later became the
anti-hero of the television series *Man
at the Top*. Simone Signoret won an
Academy Award for her performance
in this film, as did Neil Paterson for
his biting screenplay, adapted from
John Braine's original novel.

Roommates
See: Raising the Wind

Room Service ○ Ⓥ
1938, US, 78 mins, b/w
Dir: William A Seiter
Stars: Groucho Marx, Chico Marx, Harpo
Marx
Rating: ★★

RKO paid a then-record $225,000 for
the film rights to the hit Broadway
play *Room Service* and lured The Marx
Brothers from MGM as stars, then sat
back and expected a box-office smash.
But it proved to be a paragon of miscasting and misdirecting. A snail
could crawl quicker than the storyline
and it was almost devoid of the usual
Marx Brothers lunacy and verbal
jousting. Even Groucho admitted, 'It
was the first time we had tried doing a
play we hadn't created ourselves. And
we were no good. We've got to
originate the characters and the
situations ourselves. Then we can do
them.' Groucho is a theatrical con
man trying to stage a hit Broadway
play while hanging on to his hotel
room, which he hasn't the money to
pay for. RKO contract players Lucille
Ball and Ann Miller – the hoofer with
the million-dollar legs – are woefully
underused with only a walk-on role
for Lucy and little chance allowed for
Ann to display her wonderful singing
and dancing talents.

Room With a View, A ○ Ⓥ
1985, UK, 115 mins, colour
Dir: James Ivory
Stars: Maggie Smith, Helena Bonham
Carter, Denholm Elliott, Julian Sands,
Daniel Day-Lewis, Simon Callow
Rating: ★★★

A film which pleases the eye, if not
the soul, *A Room With a View* is reminiscent of a Claude Monet painting
– beautiful to look at, but hardly passionately afire. The production/
direction team of Ismail Merchant and
James Ivory seems to have taken it
upon itself to present the English at
their most English in this triple Oscar-winning adaptation of E M
Forster's rather fey novel. It is a sop-
orifically gentle film about manners
but the viewer clamours for some
outrageous behaviour and it takes a
street fight from some unruly Italians
to convince young Lucy
Honeychurch (Helena Bonham
Carter) that there is more to life than
poetry, decorum and cucumber
sandwiches. When a headstrong Englishman (Julian Sands) plants a kiss on
her unsullied lips it's regarded as an
apocalyptic scandal. Subsequently,
more and more social restraints are
subtly breached by a superb British
cast.

Rooney ○
1958, UK, 88 mins, b/w
Dir: George Pollock
Stars: John Gregson, Muriel Pavlow,
Barry Fitzgerald
Rating: ★★★

It's not often that a dustman is the
central character in a film, but here is
an exception – rejoicing in the delightful name of James Ignatius
Rooney. It's an enjoyable if relatively
little known British comedy film,
based on a book by that highly popular and widely read novelist
Catherine Cookson.

Rooster Cogburn ○ Ⓥ
1975, US, 108 mins, colour
Dir: Stuart Millar
Stars: John Wayne, Katharine Hepburn
Rating: ★★

There are echoes of *The African Queen*
in this Western adventure, what with
Katharine Hepburn as a fire-breathing
(and sharpshooting) missionary, and
John Wayne as the crusty old lawman
who's forced to take her along on a
manhunt – not to mention the river
setting which dominates most of the
film. Worth a look for the way in
which Wayne and Hepburn deliver
their dialogue, for the superb scenery
and for a good cruel villain from
Richard Jordan. Wayne reprises the
character that won him an Oscar in
True Grit, but the script here is not in
the same class.

R

Rope ○ ⓥ

1948, US, 80 mins, colour
Dir: Alfred Hitchcock
Stars: James Stewart, Farley Granger,
Sir Cedric Hardwicke
Rating: ★★

It's a plot right up Alfred Hitchcock's
macabre street: two college boys
murder a friend, just for kicks, and
hide his body in a trunk which they
then use as a drinks table for a party
attended by the dead man's parents
and fiancée. James Stewart is the
school-teacher who begins to smell a
rat. For this, his first film in colour,
Hitchcock used a technique of long
takes to give a smooth feel to the
story, which is all set in one
claustrophobic room. The same
real-life case was used as the script for
the more recent highly praised *Swoon*,
which emphasised the homosexual
relationship between the killers, a
point Hitchcock had to exclude.

Rope of Sand ○

1949, US, 105 mins, b/w
Dir: William Dieterle
Stars: Burt Lancaster, Paul Henreid,
Peter Lorre, Claude Rains, Corinne
Calvet
Rating: ★★★

This rugged adventure yarn, set in
South Africa, is a replica of the kind of
Bogart thriller that held audiences to
their seats throughout the Forties and
early Fifties. The Bogart-style
supporting cast is headed by Claude
Rains, Paul Henreid and Peter Lorre,
and the only change is Burt Lancaster
for Bogey in the leading role. The plot
concerns a search for a cache of
diamonds and the action is enough to
satisfy fans of the toughest thriller.

Rosalie Goes Shopping ○ ⓥ

1989, US, 95 mins, colour
Dir: Percy Adlon
Stars: Marianne Sagebrecht, Brad
Davis, Judge Reinhold, William Harlander
Rating: ★★

Rosalie is a Bavarian hausfrau transplanted to Arkansas by the simple-
minded, crop-dusting husband
she calls Liebling. Rosalie has seven
children and a nifty line in shoplifting
and major credit card fraud that keeps
her family in the style to which she
has accustomed them. That means
gourmet dinner materials for her
trainee chef son, wardrobes of clothes
for herself and the kids, trampolines
and slides in the garden and the latest
gadgets which she throws away if they

show the slightest signs of not working. Financial problems with the bank
or cheque card companies? Rosalie
just reports her card stolen and goes
out on a spree with it. But a $11,000
computer almost proves her undoing.
This is basically a half-hour anecdote
stretched out to 95 minutes and so
only amusing every now and again.
But plump Sagebrecht is winning as
Rosalie and Reinhold on the mark as
the priest bewildered by the extent of
her confessions.

Rose, The ● ⓥ

1979, US, 134 mins, colour
Dir: Mark Rydell
Stars: Bette Midler, Alan Bates, Frederic
Forrest
Rating: ★★★

The initial impact of singer Bette
Midler as a performer and actress is
undoubtedly sensational in the
opening sequences of *The Rose*. It
must be added that, at well over two
hours of film, you may find Ms Midler
at full throttle a trifle wearing, as with
the film, a powerful no-holds-barred
portrait of a rock star of the Sixties
(supposedly modelled on Janis Joplin).
She's on the run from drink and drugs
and vainly seeking either stability in
her life or respite from the constant
strain. Little concession is made to the
period, particularly in the star's frothy
hairdo, yet the film remains an unforgettable experience, thanks to its
supercharged (and Oscar-nominated)
star.

Roseanna McCoy ○ ⓥ

1949, US, 100 mins, b/w
Dir: Irving Reis
Stars: Farley Granger, Joan Evans,
Charles Bickford, Raymond Massey
Rating: ★★

A sort of *Romeo and Juliet* of the hillbilly world, with young lovers from
the Hatfields and McCoys sparking up
embers from the legendary family
feud of the 1880s. Charles Bickford
and Raymond Massey are the unlikely
leaders of the two clans, with the title
role going to Joan Evans, a striking
young actress Goldwyn hoped to turn
into a big star. That never quite happened, though she worked steadily in
the industry for another 12 years.

Rosebud ○

1974, US, 126 mins, colour
Dir: Otto Preminger
Stars: Peter O'Toole, Richard
Attenborough
Rating: ★

Topical suspense tale of wealthy girls
kidnapped by Arabs, best regarded as
an outrageous attempt at smart entertainment. A dramatic exposition
with a curious mixture of panache and
laughable heavy-handedness, making
it look increasingly like a cut-price
Frederick Forsyth thriller. Star performance by Peter O'Toole.

Rose-Marie ○

1936, US, 113 mins, b/w
Dir: W S Van Dyke II
Stars: Jeanette MacDonald, Nelson
Eddy
Rating: ★★★

Despite the occasional artificial backdrop, location filming at Lake Tahoe
lends a fresh, breezy feel to the old
story (first seen on stage in 1924)
about the backwoods singer (in this
version a Canadian opera star) and the
Mountie who gets his woman.
Jeanette MacDonald and Nelson
Eddy, then the screen's hottest romantic singing team, were surefire
box-office in these roles. But there's
additional interest for film buffs today
in early appearances by James Stewart
(as the heroine's villainous brother!),
singer Allan Jones (who would rise to
fully-fledged co-star with Ms
MacDonald in *The Firefly*) and a very
young-looking David Niven (billed as
Nivens). It couldn't miss and it didn't:
MGM made a mint. Remade (without
the same zest) in 1954.

Rosemary's Baby ●

1968, US, 137 mins, colour
Dir: Roman Polanski
Stars: Mia Farrow, John Cassavetes,
Ruth Gordon, Ralph Bellamy
Rating: ★★★

Roman Polanski's famous film about
modern witchcraft on the loose in an
ordinary-looking New York apartment building, where new tenant
Rosemary (Mia Farrow) plunges
deeply, giddily into a nightmare world
which enfolds her in evil. Polanski,
who had already demonstrated his
talent for the bizarre and stomach-
churning in *Repulsion*, uses every
throat-clutching trick in the book to
compel his audience into total belief
of what is basically a rather preposterous tale. At times he is so
persuasively nasty that it needs strong
nerves to see him out as he opts for a
(then smart) open-ended climax. Mia
Farrow grips every ounce of sympathy every
inch of the way as the beleaguered
Rosemary, in spite of occasionally
banal snatches of script: 'I've been to

Vidal Sassoon,' she tells her jobless husband (another thankless role for John Cassavetes) after she must have already spent a fortune on clothes. As the witch who ensnares her, veteran Hollywood writer and actress Ruth Gordon took an Academy Award. Charles Grodin makes his screen debut as a doctor.

Rosencrantz and Guildenstern are Dead ○ ⓥ
1990, US, 117 mins, colour
Dir: Tom Stoppard
Stars: Gary Oldman, Tim Roth, Richard Dreyfuss, Iain Glen, Ian Richardson
Rating: ★

Playwright (and here writer-director) Stoppard has taken two never-seen characters from Shakespeare's *Hamlet*, and given them a story of their own. However, the results, on screen at least, are such that we venture to suggest a run round the block would be more entertaining. Oldman and Roth, exchanging dialogue like a medieval Abbott and Costello, are the hapless pair recalled to Denmark where they become involved in a plot as potty as it's soporific, in which a group of strolling minstrels (led by Richard Dreyfuss, in the role illness prevented Sean Connery playing) depict the events in *Hamlet* before they happen. Photographed in atrocious colour, this is about as much fun as it sounds (although it worked much better on stage), the proceedings dragging on for nearly two hours. 'I've had enough,' says Oldman (who gives the film's only watchable performance) at one stage, and he's right. Connery was lucky.

Rose of Washington Square ○
1939, US, 86 mins, b/w
Dir: Gregory Ratoff
Stars: Tyrone Power, Al Jolson, Alice Faye
Rating: ★★★

Or, the original *Funny Girl*. This vintage 20th Century-Fox musical is loosely based on the life of Fanny Brice, with Alice Faye and Tyrone Power in the roles later filled by Barbra Streisand and Omar Sharif. The songs include 'My Man' and 'Toot, Toot, Tootsie'.

Rose Tattoo, The ○
1955, US, 117 mins, b/w
Dir: Daniel Mann
Stars: Anna Magnani, Burt Lancaster, Marisa Pavan, Ben Cooper
Rating: ★★★

Although the story isn't very strong, the sheer weight and quality of the acting pull it through in style in this screen version of the play by Tennessee Williams. It's headed by a deservedly Oscar-winning performance by Anna Magnani as the Sicilian peasant woman transported by her (now dead) husband to the gulf coast of America. Burt Lancaster, as the man who comes physically into her life, and Jo Van Fleet are excellent in support, while Marisa Pavan (also Oscar-nominated), Virginia Grey, Ben Cooper and Sandro Giglio all give career-best performances under Daniel Mann's direction. Despite its characters' fits of bad temper, this is, in fact, for the most part a happy, friendly, intimate film, well-made, well-photographed (James Wong Howe won another of the movie's Oscars) and superbly acted.

Rough Company
See: The Violent Men

Rough Shoot ○
(aka: Shoot First)
1952, UK, 87 mins, b/w
Dir: Robert Parrish
Stars: Joel McCrea, Evelyn Keyes, Herbert Lom
Rating: ★★★

Hollywood stars Joel McCrea and Evelyn Keyes made a worthwhile trip across the Atlantic to make this polished British thriller. Eric Ambler's highly professional script provides some comedy amidst the excitement and clever plot developments. Herbert Lom and Roland Culver excel as two rather quirky secret agents.

Rounders, The ○
1965, US, 85 mins, colour
Dir: Burt Kennedy
Stars: Glenn Ford, Henry Fonda
Rating: ★★

Pleasing comedy Western about two veteran cowhands, played by Henry Fonda and Glenn Ford, forever trying to tame the same bucking bronco. Try to see this in its full 85-minute form, compared with the 73 minutes to which it was cut in British cinemas.

'Round Midnight ◑ ⓥ
1986, France/US, 131 mins, colour
Dir: Bertrand Tavernier
Stars: Dexter Gordon, François Cluzet, Christine Pascal
Rating: ★★

A loving homage to jazz musicians and their world from French director Bertrand Tavernier. The story of an ageing and burned-out American jazz musician and a passionate French admirer is very loosely based on the real-life relationship between Bud Powell and Francis Paudras in the Paris of the late 1950s. Paris of that era was a haven for many jazz musicians because the interest in jazz didn't fade in France as it did in America. Tavernier cast a real jazz musician – tenor sax great Dexter Gordon – rather than an actor in the central role and Gordon fills the part well, perhaps giving it an authenticity an actor would have struggled to achieve. In fact all the well-known names in this film are musicians. Jazz fans will have a good time listening to the music (of which there is plenty) and spotting Herbie Hancock, Ron Carter, Freddie Hubbard and Wayne Shorter, to name but a few. All the music was recording live while filming, not dubbed over afterwards, as is usual. It must have been a nightmare for the sound engineers, but did create the club sound and atmosphere Tavernier was aiming for.

Roustabout ○ ⓥ
1964, US, 101 mins, colour
Dir: John Rich
Stars: Elvis Presley, Barbara Stanwyck, Joan Freeman, Leif Erickson
Rating: ★

With Barbara Stanwyck as co-star, there were high hopes for this Elvis Presley film. Alas, the King hit a new low instead, saddled with the oldest story in showbusiness – and some of the oldest dialogue to go with it. The story can be cut to a few words: wild motorcycle youth rides into carnival, and is tamed by lovely young girl (Joan Blackman). Girl: 'Everyone needs somebody to worry about them.' Driven away by the girl's oafish father, the youth returns when the carnival cannot do without him. Oafish father: 'Let's go on with the show.' That's all folks, and, this time round, even the songs, apart from 'Little Egypt', are unmemorable. Enough to make you join the Rudy Vallee Revival Society.

Rover Dangerfield ☉ ⓥ
1991, US, 74 mins, colour
Dir: Jim George, Jim Seeley
Voice stars: Rodney Dangerfield, Susan Boyd, Ronnie Schell, Ned Luke, Dana Hill
Rating: ★★

R

A cute-for-a-while cartoon comedy written by twitchy US comic Rodney Dangerfield, who also provides the voice of the canine star. Streetwise Rover is snatched from his big city life and dumped on a backwater farm. But this wisecracking hound's bone idle, and soon Rover's in the doghouse. Lively animation – just watch that opening sequence – lovable characters and lavish songs (listen to the instant classic love song 'I'd Give Up a Bone for You') make this fun for the whole family, although adults may tire of it after the half-way mark. Dangerfield is, however, funnier when you don't have to look at him!

Roxanne ○ ⓥ
1987, US, 107 mins, colour
Dir: Fred Schepisi
Stars: Steve Martin, Daryl Hannah, Rick Rossovich, Shelley Duvall
Rating: ★★★

Steve Martin always said he had a nose for comedy. But this is carrying the notion rather too far! Steve's had a nose job all right, and the result is on the whole a delightful reworking of the classic *Cyrano de Bergerac*, which remains surprisingly faithful to the original 19th-century play – although this version is never quite as funny or touching as it might be. Steve plays a fire chief who's the most easy-going of chaps unless someone insults his pronounced proboscis. Then he tends to take them to pieces. But when leggy astronomer Daryl Hannah sashays into town, Steve's eyes pop out of his head – well, at least as far as the end of his nose. The boy's in love. Alas, Daryl has a yen for the latest recruit to Steve's Keystone Kops fire brigade. And pretty soon the fire chief finds himself standing in on literacy for the bone-headed Romeo. 'I guess I mistook sex for love,' moans Daryl, wise after the event. 'I did that once,' confidante Shelley Duvall tells her. 'It was great.' Sadly, such gems in Martin's own script aren't as many as you'd like. This, though, is a film that's almost always fun to be with.

Roxie Hart ○
1942, US, 75 mins, b/w
Dir: William A Wellman
Stars: Ginger Rogers, Adolphe Menjou, George Montgomery
Rating: ★★★

Ginger Rogers' second great success from 1942 following *The Major and the* *Minor*, this was much later made into a hit stage musical called *Chicago*. Ginger portrays a showgirl who agrees to go on trial for murder for the publicity she'll reap (naturally she didn't do it). The trial itself turns into something of a carnival, with the photographers crying, 'The knees, Roxie, the knees.' Rogers and Adolphe Menjou are well matched as defendant and shyster lawyer, and play it to the hilt.

Royal Wedding ⊙ ⓥ
(aka: Wedding Bells)
1951, US, 93 mins, colour
Dir: Stanley Donen
Stars: Fred Astaire, Jane Powell, Peter Lawford, Sarah Churchill
Rating: ★★★

This slim musical is decorated by two classic Fred Astaire numbers – his brilliant solo dance with a hatstand as a partner and his mind-boggling routine in which he dances not just on the floor but on the walls and ceiling as well. Also contains a dynamic Astaire-Powell duet with one of the longest song titles in history: 'How Could You Believe Me When I Said I Loved You When You Know I've Been a Liar All My Life?'

Ruby ● ⓥ
1992, US, 110 mins, colour
Dir: John Mackenzie
Stars: Danny Aiello, Sherilyn Fenn, Arliss Howard, David Duchovny, Marc Lawrence
Rating: ★★

The success of *JFK* begat a little flurry of movies leading to Dallas 1963. Writer Stephen Davis here has quite a lot more to say on the subject. He may come to the same conclusion as Oliver Stone, but, in its way, his movie stands just as solidly on its own. Jack Ruby, of course, was the small-time Dallas nightclub owner who earned his place in history by shooting Kennedy's alleged assassin Lee Harvey Oswald. Vaguely clinging to connections with both the Mafia and the CIA, Ruby (Danny Aiello) is close to closure when he runs into Candy Cane (Sherilyn Fenn) who becomes his premier stripper and goes with him to Cuba when he travels to help free a Mafia boss. Told to hit the man instead, Ruby turns on the assasin. It seems loyal, but is probably a big mistake, as he becomes embroiled at the edges of a Mafia/CIA con- spiracy which he thinks is to assassinate Castro, but realises too late is to assassinate Kennedy instead. It's the relationship between Ruby and Candy, though, solidly done by Aiello and Fenn who come alive as people, that saves the enterprise from going stale before it starts. Though the story sags in the middle, its fascinating to see its bits and pieces falling together.

Ruby Cairo ● ⓥ
1992, US, US mins, colour
Dir: Graeme Clifford
Stars: Andie MacDowell, Liam Neeson, Viggo Mortensen
Rating: ★★

A pretty intriguing plot (at least to begin with) is set adrift here by wishy-washy treatment that turns it into something of an extended travelogue. Andie MacDowell is the mother-of-three seemingly left with nothing but a grateful of bills when her chauvinistic husband, struggling to keep his airplane salvage business afloat, is killed in a Mexican air crash. However, in this kind of film, as soon as the local authorities tell her that he was 'burned from head to toe', you can smell a live rat. When Andie finds a pack of baseball cards and cracks the codes on the backs of them (only one of the film's unlikely premises), the trail leads her to a cache of secret bank accounts across the world. Now you and I would pocket the $840,000 and live in the lap of luxury. But if Andie did the same, we'd only have half a film. So she follows the trail on to Egypt where the extent of her husband's nefarious activities is revealed. MacDowell is appealing and keeps her credibility intact; but a lighter, more skilful directorial hand was needed to lend impact to this particular flight of fancy.

Ruby Gentry ○ ⓥ
1952, US, 82 mins, b/w
Dir: King Vidor
Stars: Jennifer Jones, Charlton Heston, Karl Malden
Rating: ★★

Down in the Carolina swamplands, where they have names like Boake, Jud, Jewel (a man) and Cullen, springs yet another overheated Hollywood melodrama about a doomed damsel from the wrong side of the swamp. Jennifer Jones tosses her hair tempestuously, making the sultry most of a thoroughly artificial role, even if it sometimes looks like a re-run from her earlier *Duel in the Sun*. Earlier in

1952, the girl who had made her name as the saintly heroine of *The Song of Bernadette* played another tarnished tramp with romantic ideals in *Carrie*.

Rude Awakening ◑ ⓥ
1989, US, 101 mins, colour
Dir: Aaron Russo, David Greenwalt
Stars: Eric Roberts, Cheech Marin, Robert Carradine, Julie Hagerty
Rating: ★

Supposing two hippies had lived wild in the jungles of Central America for 20 years, growing and smoking marijuana and eating fish, only to suddenly re-emerge into the world when they stumble across a CIA plot to start a war in their new-found paradise. The possibilities for fun are practically endless; alas, directors Russo and Greenwalt have missed almost all of them in this tiresome film whose budget seems barely to extend beyond the sparsely furnished interiors of people's flats. Its people, too, are no fun to be with – stolid Roberts, whining Hagerty, bland Carradine and irksome Marin, once of the equally resistible Cheech and Chong. Supporting players fare better, notably Andrea Martin as a progressively drunker social climber who shares a Laurel and Hardy relationship with tight-lipped husband Buck Henry when it comes to putting on jackets. The film's impassioned pleas for conservation, though, are likely to fall on deaf ears as well as sleepy eyes.

Ruggles of Red Gap ○
1935, US, 92 mins, b/w
Dir: Leo McCarey
Stars: Charles Laughton, Mary Boland
Rating: ★★★

Heartwarming comedy about an English butler taken to Red Gap in America where he becomes a celebrity. Charles Laughton in very spritely form, never puts a foot wrong as the manservant who becomes his own master, and shares the film's best sequence with Charlie Ruggles and James Burke when the three go out on a boozy binge together.

Rumble Fish ● ⓥ
1983, US, 100 mins, b/w
Dir: Francis Ford Coppola
Stars: Matt Dillon, Mickey Rourke, Diane Lane, Dennis Hopper
Rating: ★★

This bizarre and visually arresting film was shot back-to-back with director Francis Ford Coppola's other S E Hinton novel adaptation about teen alienation, *The Outsiders*, with much the same cast and crew. It's a case of a youth (Matt Dillon) living under the shadow of his older, idolised brother (Mickey Rourke). But don't go looking for Freudian messages in the screenplay which answers few questions. *Rumble Fish* is an exercise in style over content. Terrific black-and-white photography (with Technicolor sequences) is matched with a pounding, impressionistic score by Stewart Copeland of The Police. But for all that it looks good, it leaves the viewer cold and uninvolved. Look out for S E Hinton in the bit-part of a hooker.

Runaway ◑
1984, US, 100 mins, colour
Dir: Michael Crichton
Stars: Tom Selleck, Cynthia Rhodes, Gene Simmons
Rating: ★★★

Specialist policeman Tom Selleck is the man they call when there's a rogue robot on the loose in this well-made and exciting sci-fi thriller. A criminal genius is reprogramming robots to use for his own illegal ends and it's Selleck and his new partner Cynthia Rhodes' job to catch him. Despite the sci-fi theme, the film keeps its feet firmly on the ground, making it completely believable. This is thanks both to the underrated Selleck, who gives a thoughtful and intelligent performance, and director Michael Crichton, who wrote *Westworld* and *Coma*. This is perhaps less thought-provoking, but it's a well-rounded story with an exciting, vertigo-inducing climax. Watch out for Kirstie Alley in a pre-*Cheers* role and the baddie is played by Gene Simmons, formerly the lead singer of outrageous rock band Kiss.

Runaway Bus, The ○
1954, UK, 80 mins, b/w
Dir: Val Guest
Stars: Frankie Howerd, Petula Clark, Belinda Lee
Rating: ★★

Frankie Howerd's thunder is rather stolen by his female co-stars in this, his first starring vehicle (if you'll pardon the pun). He plays a coach driver lost in the fog, with a fortune in stolen bullion in the boot. Dame Margaret Rutherford steals the film as surely as

she stole Norman Wisdom's first starring comedy film, *Trouble in Store*. Belinda Lee runs her a very close second as a dumb-belle who reads thrillers ad infinitum and is genuinely funny in the process.

Runaway Train ● ⓥ
1985, US, 111 mins, colour
Dir: Andrei Konchalovksy
Stars: Jon Voight, Eric Roberts, Rebecca DeMornay, John P Ryan
Rating: ★★★

Visually, this is a dynamite action film, with a driverless train thundering across the snow-covered Alaskan wastes. The engineer has died from a heart attack and the only people on board, unbeknown to the authorities, are two long-term escaped convicts (Jon Voight, Oscar-nominated) and an unlikely female railway worker played by Rebecca DeMornay. The action is hammer-hard and never less than gripping, while all the train scenes are brilliantly handled by director Andrei Konchalovsky, and his actors and stuntmen. The dialogue, unsurprisingly, isn't in the same class; it never quite rings true, and occasionally ascends to the highly fanciful considering the semi-literate nature of the characters. In the end the film matches Voight's description of Roberts: 'more guts than brains.' But those guts make it well worth watching.

Run for Cover ○
1954, US, 92 mins, colour
Dir: Nicholas Ray
Stars: James Cagney, Viveca Lindfors, John Derek
Rating: ★★★

Good, solid Western with ultra-sharp Technicolor photography by Daniel Fapp. John Derek is excellent as the embittered young man who provides the axis for the action, and James Cagney, although clearly ageing, is his usual tough self as the youth's ex-jailbird friend, now a sheriff. Fight scenes are effectively done and, if the denouement seems rather improbable, there's compensation in the vigorous playing of the bad guys, notably Grant Withers and Ernest Borgnine.

Run for the Sun ○
1956, US, 95 mins, colour
Dir: Roy Boulting
Stars: Richard Widmark, Jane Greer, Trevor Howard
Rating: ★★★

R

This re-working of *The Hounds of Zaroff* makes exciting popular entertainment. Richard Widmark and Jane Greer (both on good form) are the intrepid hero and game heroine being pursued through various arduous trials by nasty villains who, in this kind of action thriller, are reassuringly bound to come to a sticky end. It's a go-ey, gory adventure, directed at a rare pace by Britain's Roy Boulting, and with a brilliant performance by Peter van Eyck as chief villain Trevor Howard's cohort. There are more than enough thrills along the way and the ending is quite startling. The odds are you'll enjoy every moment of this adventurous hokum.

Run for Your Money, A ○
1949, UK, 83 mins, b/w
Dir: Charles Frend
Stars: Alec Guinness, Moira Lister, Donald Houston, Joyce Grenfell, Hugh Griffith
Rating: ★★★

Another fast and funny comedy from the Ealing Studios stable. Released in their peak year, 1949, it's about two Welsh miners who win a trip to London to see the Wales v England rugby match. Alec Guinness uses a rapier-like wit to keep the laughs coming, leaving Donald Houston and Meredith Edwards as the miners to raise the broad guffaws. The final chase through the streets of London rates as one of the most hilarious and best edited since Keystone days.

Running Brave ○
1983, US, 106 mins, colour
Dir: D S Everett
Stars: Robby Benson, Pat Hingle, Claudia Cron
Rating: ★★

The punning title (it's about an American Indian athlete) heralds a sort of *Wigwams of Fire* with Robby Benson as Billy Mills, the half-Sioux who unexpectedly qualified to run the 10,000 metres for the United States at the 1964 Japan Olympics. The reconstruction of Mills' road to Tokyo doesn't entirely escape soap-opera conventions – the script sees to that – but it scores points for being true. Benson – becoming another blue-eyed Hollywood Indian – does the running stuff well, and his fellow-Indians are mostly made out to be the pitiable figures they were. Denis Lacroix is excellent here as one of Billy's most tragic comrades. Claudia Cron makes a pretty but nebulous

heroine, and down the cast is Graham Greene, who gave such a distinguished performance much later in *Dances With Wolves*.

Running Man, The ○
1963, UK, 100 mins, colour
Dir: Carol Reed
Stars: Laurence Harvey, Lee Remick, Alan Bates
Rating: ★★★

The late Carol Reed's underrated film about a couple (Laurence Harvey and Lee Remick) who try to bring off a giant insurance fraud, and the mysterious man who appears to be dogging their footsteps. A good story well told, with a high proportion of suspenseful moments, thanks partly to John Mortimer's edgy script.

Running Man, The ● ⓥ
1987, US, 101 mins, colour
Dir: Paul Michael Glaser
Stars: Arnold Schwarzenegger, Maria Conchita Alonso, Yaphet Kotto, Jim Brown, Richard Dawson
Rating: ★★★

Another extended comic-strip adventure with Big Arnie, perhaps the most literal translation of comic image from page to screen since the 1966 *Batman*. You can see the picture come alive and visualise Schwarzenegger's shameless sub-Bond puns in 'balloons', as each villain is dispatched in turn. Earlier in this futuristic frolic (based on a book by Stephen King, although vaguely recalling a French film called *The Prize of Peril*), there are signs of seriousness in Schwarzenegger's escape from prison, following his arrest on trumped-up charges after failing, in his time as a helicopter cop, to massacre unarmed civilians when ordered to do so. The overall view of an American police-state city of 2019 is quite imaginative but, once the game show of the title starts – criminals run for their lives on video before a live audience – we're on familiar Schwarzenegger ground, with our hero (and a few friends) taking on a series of massive opponents armed with flame throwers, spiked scythes, chain-saws and anything else the scriptwriter can lay hands on. Good stuff of its kind and heroine Alonso looks great in the jump-suit the 'contestants' wear.

Running on Empty ◐
1988, US, 117 mins, colour
Dir: Sidney Lumet

Stars: Christine Lahti, River Phoenix, Judd Hirsch, Martha Plimpton
Rating: ★★

Whatever the qualities of his movie, at least director Lumet has a new idea here. A family of activists, forever on the run since bombing a napalm lab many years before (a man who shouldn't have been there was blinded and paralysed), meets its inevitable crisis of conscience when the elder of its two sons reaches 17 and feel other tugs of loyalty. These come for the boy (snub-nosed, slight River Phoenix, a most unlikely offspring of hook-nosed Hirsch and steeple-tall Lahti) in the form of a girlfriend (the Jodie Foster-ish Martha Plimpton) and the chance of a scholarship to improve his already impressive talents on the piano. It's a film of effective moments which just about outweigh the patches of tedium. Lahti is excellent as the mother, especially when meeting her father for the first time in 14 years and telling him she's 'sorry for having caused you so much pain.' Not all of the film's emotive moments, though, strike as true as this one.

Running Scared ◐ ⓥ
1986, US, 106 mins, colour
Dir: Peter Hyams
Stars: Billy Crystal, Gregory Hines, Darlanne Fluegel, Steven Bauer, Joe Pantoliano, Jimmy Smits
Rating: ★★

A totally typical Hollywood buddy-buddy cop movie, but so well made by photographer-director Peter Hyams that, for all its routineness, it does keep you watching, albeit in a slightly detached way, right through to the end. Billy Crystal and Gregory Hines (no reason, I suppose why you shouldn't pick a comic and a dancer to play policemen) are the partners who joke their way through the pursuit of a king drug dealer (Jimmy Smits) who always seem to be slipping away from justice, if for no other reason than to allow further developments, chases and shoot outs in the plot. You couldn't describe this as a bad movie, nor say you didn't get your money's worth in the way of action and excitement. But any episode of such classic US cop shows as *Hill Street Blues* or *NYPD Blue* would supply more humanity, wit and delicacy of touch in the acting. Still, if it's a rainy evening and *Running Scared*'s on TV, you could do a lot worse.

Run Wild, Run Free ○ ⓥ

1969, UK, 98 mins, colour
Dir: Richard C Sarafian
Stars: John Mills, Mark Lester, Gordon Jackson
Rating: ★★★

Children will enjoy this fairly charming tale of a mute boy and a white colt, picturesquely set on Dartmoor. The fog-bound climax is highly effective.

Rush ● ⓥ

1991, US, 120 mins, colour
Dir: Lili Fini Zanuck
Stars: Jason Patric, Jennifer Jason Leigh, Sam Elliott, Max Perlich, Gregg Allman, William Sadler
Rating: ★

Whoever thought the idea of two narcotics cops becoming addicts themselves in pursuit of their prey was surefire reckoned without this treatment of the theme. Decked out with mournful music by Eric Clapton, the story is slow to the point of abstraction. Leading man Jason Patric mumbles unattractively even when not on drugs, while Jennifer Jason Leigh, in a rare below-par performance, sounds as though she has a stone in her mouth in her efforts to effect a Texas accent. Unbelievable, poorly written and filled with extraneous stretches of repetitive and meaningless dialogue to pad out some slow action scenes, the film is difficult to watch in more ways than one. First-time director Lili Fini Zanuck really blew it with this one and at time of writing hasn't yet had a second chance. You can take your choice of sentiments you want to echo, from Leigh's 'I just want it to end' to Patric's 'Feels like a long ride to nowhere'. Unintentional smiles are the only ones you'll get from this one.

Russia House, The ● ⓥ

1990, US, 117 mins, colour
Dir: Fred Schepisi
Stars: Sean Connery, Michelle Pfeiffer, Roy Schneider, James Fox, Klaus Maria Brandauer
Rating: ★★

Very slow to get going, but mercifully sparked by the performances of Connery and Pfeiffer, this is hopefully about the last we'll see of cold-war thrillers full of tired CIA, M15 and KGB men trying to outwit each other, while others undergo the physical danger. Connery, as reliable as ever as the jazz-playing publisher caught up in

the espionage game, and Pfeiffer, with a convincing-sounding Russian accent, create characters that evolve into the only believable or interesting people in the film. A strong cast otherwise does not acquit itself with distinction, director Schepisi spends far too long touring the sights of his locations, and Tom Stoppard's script (from John Le Carré's novel) is routine even by the standards of this genre. Trust Connery to find the few gems in it and polish them up bright enough to bring tears to our eyes.

Russian Roulette ○

1975, Canada, 93 mins, colour
Dir: Lou Lombardo
Stars: George Segal, Christina Raines
Rating: ★★

The Falcon lives! At least in spirit. For those who remember that suave Forties' screen sleuth, this is just the kind of exciting espionage nonsense that Hollywood was turning out with such success in the period, but doesn't seem to make any more. The story, about a plot to kill Russian premier Kosygin, is pure moonshine. But director Lou Lombardo keeps it careering crazily along and throws in a nerve-grinding climax on the acutely-slanting roof of the Royal Canadian Mounted Police headquarters in Vancouver. George Segal and Christina Raines play it with gusto while the villans are just as badly acted as they were in Tom Conway's day. Despite some marginally nasty violence, children could safely watch (and enjoy) this thriller, cleaner and sharper as it is than the mid-Seventies' average.

Russians Are Coming, the Russians Are Coming, The ☉

1966, US, 126 mins, colour
Dir: Norman Jewison
Stars: Carl Reiner, Eva Marie Saint, Alan Arkin, Brian Keith
Rating: ★★★★

You'll find many extraordinarily funny moments in this gem of a comedy about a Russian submarine that runs aground off America. It's in the Russians' panic that the fun chiefly lies. Lots of face-twitching, grunting and the Russians' broken English helps build a mountain of laughter. Seldom has a comic jigsaw had so many perfectly fitting pieces. There's a magnificent little cameo involving a garrulous old woman captured by the Russians. Her husband, old, doddery and deaf, comes down and eats his

breakfast, blissfully unaware that the old harridan is making frantic efforts to free herself from a position on top of the wardrobe just over his right shoulder. One feels it's probably the first morning's peace the old man's ever had in his life.

Rustler's Rhapsody ⓒ

1985, US, 88 mins, colour
Dir: Hugh Wilson
Stars: Tom Berenger, Marilu Henner, G W Bailey
Rating: ★★

Good guys in white hats and bad guys in black hats are what this comedy Western is all about. *Rustlers' Rhapsody* is an affectionate parody of those adorably dreadful Saturday morning Westerns serials. Unfortunately, the parody is too well done and the film itself outstays its welcome and becomes the victim of its own joke. Tom Berenger, in a rare comic role, is our firm-jawed hero, while Marilu Henner is a feisty heroine. The advantage of the original serials is that although they were embarrassingly bad, they at least only lasted 20 minutes an episode.

Ruthless ○

1948, US, 104 mins, b/w
Dir: Edgar G Ulmer
Stars: Zachary Scott, Louis Hayward, Diana Lynn, Sydney Greenstreet
Rating: ★★★

A stylish *film noir* that hardly deserved its famous one-line dismissal by British film critic C A Lejeune, who wrote: 'I'd find *Ruthless* far more winning if it could end at the beginning.' Time has brought a well-merited re-assessment, with Zachary Scott playing the archetype of all his roles as sharks in wolf's clothing: you'll love to hate him as he steps on everyone as if they were bothersome bugs on the rungs of his ladder to the top. Sydney Greenstreet is excellent as a Southern tycoon, and the girls – Diana Lynn (in a dual role), Martha Vickers and Lucille Bremer – are no mere ciphers. Directed by cult favourite Edgar G Ulmer, who had slightly more than his usual shoestring budget to work on, but had to put up with a contrived 'tidy' ending imposed by the studio.

Ruthless People ● ⓥ

1986, US, 93 mins, colour
Dir: Jim Abrahams, David Zucker, Jerry Zucker

R

Stars: Danny DeVito, Bette Midler, Judge Reinhold, Helen Slater
Rating: ★★

A broad blue-collar farce about a kidnapped wife who is so gross her husband is only too pleased not to pay the ransom, especially as he was planning to bump her off anyway. The film gets funnier as it goes on, due mostly to the increasing role played by Bette Midler as the wife. For her, it's a triumph.

Ryan's Daughter ◐ ⓥ

1970, UK, 206 mins, colour
Dir: David Lean
Stars: Sarah Miles, Robert Mitchum, Trevor Howard
Rating: ★★★

David Lean's epic story of a self-willed Irish girl at the time of World War One, her unsuccessful marriage to a quiet teacher, and the consequences of her passionate affair with a shell-shocked English army officer. The film won two Academy Awards, one for its photography and one for John Mills who moved totally out of character as the misshapen village idiot. It also has outstanding performances by Robert Mitchum and Trevor Howard as teacher and priest, respectively.

S

Saadia ○

1953, US, 85 mins, colour
Dir: Albert Lewin
Stars: Cornel Wilde, Rita Gam
Rating: ★★★

Underrated in its time, this is an extremely exciting story set in Morocco, about a girl, smoulderingly played by Rita Gam, who believes she brings bad luck to those who know her. Good stuff for children, who won't notice the vague literary pretensions of maverick director Albert Lewin, a Hollywood scriptwriter from the silent days, who also directed *The Moon and Sixpence*, *The Picture of Dorian Gray* and *Pandora and the Flying Dutchman*. Gam and Mel Ferrer share acting honours: Cornel Wilde seems less happy as the French-educated nobleman who battles the local witch doctor and native superstition. Burningly photographed in ultra-rich Technicolor by Christopher Challis.

Sabotage ○ ⓥ

(aka: The Woman Alone)
1937, UK, 76 mins, b/w
Dir: Alfred Hitchcock
Stars: Sylvia Sidney, Oscar Homolka
Rating: ★★★★

In view of the bomb attacks that these days punctuate life in Britain's major cities, this Hitchcock thriller about an anarchist plotting to blow up Piccadilly Circus has acquired fresh topicality. It's based on Joseph Conrad's novel *The Secret Agent* and has splendidly seedy locales, a brooding, doom-laden atmosphere and the usual crop of memorable sequences, including the meeting of spies in an aquarium.

Saboteur ○ ⓥ

1942, US, 108 mins, b/w
Dir: Alfred Hitchcock
Stars: Robert Cummings, Priscilla Lane, Otto Kruger
Rating: ★★★★

Hitchcock's story of wartime sabotage, beginning and ending memorably, with the factory fire and the scenes in and on the Statue of Liberty. The trek in between, as hero Robert Cummings flees from the web of circumstantial evidence threatening to entrap him, is sometimes a bit wearing, but Priscilla Lane, as always, is a personable heroine, and Hitchcock 'touches' constantly boost the suspense.

Saboteur – Code Name Morituri, The ○

(aka: Morituri)
1965, US, 122 mins, b/w
Dir: Bernhard Wicki
Stars: Marlon Brando, Yul Brynner, Janet Margolin, Trevor Howard
Rating: ★★★

A tense spy thriller, set at sea during World War Two. Marlon Brando is a saboteur sent to steer a vital cargo of rubber into Allied hands, while at the same time preventing the captain (Yul Brynner) from scuttling the ship. For Brynner, it was the best role he'd had in years. With plenty to get his teeth into – he plays an anti-Nazi German who takes to drink when he hears of his once-gentle son sinking a hospital ship – and no worries about his dialogue, he's a more relaxed and therefore more effective actor. Bernhard Wicki directs always to a purpose, and keeps the high tension smouldering in a film that we fancy will have stood the test of time better than most – despite the cumbersome title.

Sabre and the Arrow, The

See: Last of the Comanches

Sabrina

See: Sabrina Fair

Sabrina Fair ○

(aka: Sabrina)
1954, US, 113 mins, b/w
Dir: Billy Wilder
Stars: Humphrey Bogart, Audrey Hepburn, William Holden
Rating: ★★★★

A slick, witty and immensely charming Billy Wilder comedy, set among the Long Island homes of some of America's wealthiest families. Audrey Hepburn, in a Cinderella-type role, is at her most impish and even William Holden seems more relaxed and dashing than usual. But the hit of the show is undoubtedly Humphrey Bogart as Holden's grumpy older brother who tries to arrange a marriage for him. The kind of film where you know what's coming but, because of the treatment, enjoy it all the same.

Saddle the Wind ○

1958, US, 84 mins, colour
Dir: Robert Parrish

Stars: Robert Taylor, John Cassavetes
Rating: ★★★

This thoughtfully-written Western, the best film of Robert Taylor's later work, hardly received its fair due when it first appeared, both the star and genre being past their peak of popularity. As well as making plenty of sense, Rod Serling's screenplay provides an abundance of action and colour, setting itself against the magnificent backdrop of the Colorado Rockies. John Cassavetes catches the eye as gunfighter Taylor's reckless young brother, a mannered but imaginative performance. And the ending is dynamically and poignantly unexpected.

Saddle Tramp ○
1950, US, 77 mins, colour
Dir: Hugo Fregonese
Stars: Joel McCrea, Wanda Hendrix, John Russell
Rating: ★★

Veteran film cowboy Joel McCrea offers one of his most likeable characterisations as the hobo on horseback in this well-made Western about a drifter reluctantly involved with a large family of children and their problems. Character-full supporting cast includes John Russell, John McIntire, Jeanette Nolan, Ed Begley and former silent screen idol Antonio Moreno.

Safari ○
1956, UK, 91 mins, colour
Dir: Terence Young
Stars: Victor Mature, Janet Leigh, Roland Culver
Rating: ★★

One of several lively, all-action colour adventure films produced by Britain's Warwick Films – usually with Victor Mature or Robert Taylor as star – in the late Fifties. It's rich, robust, hell-for-leather stuff, with the animals out-acting the cast.

Safety Last ⊙
1923, US, 70 mins, b/w
Dir: Fred Newmeyer
Stars: Harold Lloyd, Mildred Davis
Rating: ★★★★

The Harold Lloyd comedy that everyone seems to remember, with Harold hanging on to the hands of a clock in an attempt to carry out a daredevil stunt. Lloyd did nearly all the dangerous climbing scenes himself, no mean feat considering that, earlier in the picture, he had lost the thumb

and half a finger from his right hand, after a 'fake' bomb he had been holding exploded. He was forced to go through the rest of his films wearing a special glove. Lloyd did work above a platform – though it was three storeys below – and made good use of camera angles and careful editing. Even so the climbing sequence, which occupies half an hour of the film, still remains the greatest – and funniest – of its kind ever put on film. But the whole film is beautifully made and full of cleverly funny moments. Said one contemporary critic: 'Even Lloyd's worst enemy will have to laugh.' The girl in the film is played by Mildred Davis, Lloyd's wife in real life.

Sahara ○
1943, US, 97 mins, b/w
Dir: Zoltan Korda
Stars: Humphrey Bogart, Dan Duryea, Bruce Bennett
Rating: ★★★

This exciting war yarn was originally seen as a Russian film, *The Thirteen*. Britain also made a variation on the story, called *Nine Men*. But this version – thanks largely to a dominating performance by Humphrey Bogart at his taciturn best – became the most famous. Directed by Zoltan Korda, it transfers the action of the story, with great effect to the Western desert, and throws in some of Hollywood's most penetrating performers, including Dan Duryea, Lloyd Bridges, Rex Ingram and J Carrol Naish.

Sahara ○
1984, US, 104 mins, colour
Dir: Andrew V Mclaglen
Stars: Brooke Shields, Lambert Wilson, Horst Buchholz, John Mills
Rating: ★

A sort of modern-day version of *The Perils of Pauline*, with Brooke Shields as the girl posing as a man and competing in a no-holds barred cross-country car race in the Sahara Desert and getting herself kidnapped by a desert sheik. John Mills turns up in the cast, but not even actionman director Andrew V McLaglen can rescue this one from the quicksands.

Saigon ● ⓥ
(aka: Off Limits)
1987, US, 102 mins, colour
Dir: Christopher Crowe
Stars: Willem Dafoe, Gregory Hines, Fred Ward, Scott Glenn, Amanda Pays
Rating: ★

Remember the crime thriller where the suspects keep getting bumped off as they're about to talk? Someone had the bright idea of transferring the locale to 1968 Vietnam in the middle of *that* war. Prostitutes are being murdered by someone who is evidently a high-ranking officer and US Army CI (criminal investigation) men Willem Dafoe and Gregory Hines are given the case – which gradually becomes an obsession. The resolution of the plot doesn't make any sense, but the screenplay is the real killer to this film's chances and even Dafoe and Hines' efforts to weld a buddy-buddy relationship are destroyed by lines devoid of literacy, humour or even sense. 'I'm sorry, sister – this world is so insane,' Dafoe solemnly tells the nun who helps them (a laughable performance by Amanda Pays and not, in fairness, the only one in this film). The sanest person here is probably guest star Scott Glenn, who jumps out of a plane without a parachute. Perhaps he, at least, read the script.

Sailor Beware ⊙
1952, US, 108 mins, b/w
Dir: Hal Walker
Stars: Jerry Lewis, Dean Martin
Rating: ★

Dean Martin and Jerry Lewis's enlistment in the Navy proves even less funny than their army manoeuvres. The plot is a predictable series of skits, with a running gag of Jerry Lewis taking up a bet to kiss real-life actress Corinne Calvet. The French-born actress never hit the big time and was just as unhappy in her private life, where she was married numerous times.

Sailor Beware! ○
(aka: Panic in the Parlor)
1956, UK, 80 mins, b/w
Dir: Gordon Parry
Stars: Peggy Mount, Cyril Smith, Shirley Eaton, Ronald Lewis
Rating: ★★

In this screen version of the wildly successful stage farce, Peggy Mount shot to stardom by repeating her characterisation of Emma Hornett, the world's most formidable mother-in-law. Most of her co-players seem not surprisingly over-awed, but look out for some amusing cameos from Thora Hird, Geoffrey Keen (as a vicar), Gordon Jackson and Henry McGee (as a milkman).

S

Sailor of the King ○
1953, UK, 84 mins, b/w
Dir: Roy Boulting
Stars: Jeffrey Hunter, Michael Rennie, Wendy Hiller
Rating: ★★★

A remake of the famous C S Forester story, *Brown on Resolution*, the 1935 version of which (first shown under that title but reissued as *For Ever England*) gave John Mills his first big critical film success. Here, it's Jeffrey Hunter as the young seaman whose bravery and resourcefulness keep a German battleship pinned down. Stirring, sturdy stuff.

Sailors Three ○
(aka: Three Cockeyed Sailors)
1940, US, 86 mins, b/w
Dir: Walter Forde
Stars: Tommy Trinder, Claude Hulbert, Michael Wilding
Rating: ★★

Tommy 'You lucky people' Trinder is the fulcrum of this Ealing wartime propaganda comedy about three drunken sailors who stumble on to a German ship and capture it. Slow to get under way, but pretty funny in the end. Star-spotters might like to decide whether or not there's a fleeting glimpse of a young Anton Diffring in this one.

Saint in New York, The ○
1938, US, 71 mins, b/w
Dir: Ben Holmes
Stars: Louis Hayward, Kay Sutton, Jack Carson
Rating: ★★★

A real treat for lovers of Thirties' detective fiction: the original *Saint* film, based on the character created by Leslie Charteris, in turn immortalised by Roger Moore on television. Louis Hayward handed the role over to George Sanders in the late Thirties, but played the Saint again 15 years later – in a British film variously called *The Saint's Return* and *The Saint's Girl Friday*. He brought a certain mocking humour to the role that none of his successors could match.

Saint Jack ◐
1979, US, 112 mins, colour
Dir: Peter Bogdanovich
Stars: Ben Gazzara, Denholm Elliott, James Villiers
Rating: ★★

Director Peter Bogdanovich finds himself deep in Graham Greene country in this study of disillusionment and moral disintegration, qualities which the stars, Ben Gazzara and Denholm Elliott, have proved themselves expert in projecting over the years. Robby Muller, a West German cinematographer who has worked on several of the films of Wim Wenders, really brings the teeming streets of Singapore to colourful life. Elizabeth Gazzara, production assistant and wardrobe mistress on the film, is Ben's daughter.

Saint's Girl Friday, The ○
(aka: The Saint's Return)
1953, UK, 73 mins, b/w
Dir: Seymour Friedman
Stars: Louis Hayward, Naomi Chance, Sydney Tafler
Rating: ★★

Louis Hayward, the screen's best Simon Templar (he was the first film *Saint* in 1938), returned to the role in this fair British thriller. Charles Victor is perfectly cast as the long-suffering Inspector Claude Eustace Teal and steals even Hayward's thunder. Thomas Gallagher is an acceptable Hoppy Uniatz and Diana Dors makes a brief appearance. The film's low budget cramps its style, but the plot and Hayward's charm just about see it through. The last *Saint* film to date, although the character has made numerous appearances since on British TV.

Saint's Return, The
See: The Saint's Girl Friday

Salaam Bombay! ● ⓥ
1988, UK/India, 113 mins, colour
Dir: Mira Nair
Stars: Shafiq Syed, Aneeta Kanwar
Rating: ★★

A poignantly-made and vividly-drawn (if consistently depressing) tale of the life of an urchin on the streets of Bombay. Its continuity is not too hot, but the terrific, sun-soaked colour photography reflects both the climate and the burnt-out quality of the character's lives. And the immediacy is such that we cannot help but be drawn into parts of the story. Overall, an impressive debut feature film from director Mira Nair, even if the portrait it paints of homelessness in India is such a very miserable one.

Salem's Lot ● ⓥ
1979, US, 112 mins, colour
Dir: Tobe Hooper
Stars: David Soul, James Mason, Bonnie Bedelia, Lance Kerwin
Rating: ★★★

Tobe Hooper's scary version of the Stephen King bestseller retains its visceral power – and even has a few extra frames of added gore for good measure in the video version. David Soul is not ideally cast as a writer but James Mason displays creepy authority as a sinister antiques dealer who is actually the ruthless watchdog for one of the most frightening vampires on film – Reggie Nalder's haunting appearance terrifyingly recalls the original *Nosferatu*.

Salome ○
1953, US, 104 mins, colour
Dir: William Dieterle
Stars: Rita Hayworth, Stewart Granger, Charles Laughton
Rating: ★★

Spectacular, certainly, if far from faithful, the Bible according to Columbia Pictures finds Rita Hayworth sinuously shedding her Seven Veils while Alan Badel (giving the film's best performance as John the Baptist) loses his head. Director William Dieterle stages some vivid large-scale scenes, Charles Laughton makes a memorable meal of a licentious King Herod, well supported by Judith Anderson as his Queen and Stewart Granger heads a strong British contingent which includes Cedric Hardwicke and Basil Sydney.

Salome's Last Dance ● ⓥ
1988, UK, 88 mins, colour
Dir: Ken Russell
Stars: Glenda Jackson, Stratford Johns, Nickolas Grace, Imogen Millais-Scott
Rating: ★

Decadence there certainly is, in this version of Oscar Wilde's banned *Salome*. But director Ken Russell has stretched Wilde's playlet interminably to 88 minutes when it should charitably run no more than 45, a slot admittedly destined for late-night TV. Glenda Jackson and Stratford Johns play up, play the game and keep their clothes on. Elsewhere, beautiful boys and bounteous boobs abound in the traditional Russell manner, as Wilde lounges around a brothel watching a production of his work. Once again, Russell, the old reprobate, has produced something here to offend everyone. Unfortunately, this time, he has offended our powers of endurance as well.

Salsa ❶ Ⓥ
1988, US, 97 mins, colour
Dir: Boaz Davidson
Stars: Robby Rosa, Magali Alvarado,
Rodney Harvey, Miranda Garrison
Rating: RB

In decades gone by, when turkeys
were turkeys, a really bad film could
make you laugh until you couldn't
stop. Most bad films today are merely
boring. But not *Salsa*, a kind of
Puerto Rican *Saturday Night Fever*.
The music is hot, the dancing's dynamic and the rest of the film is
wonderfully, gloriously awful. The
dialogue, ludicrous throughout, tries
to run through the standard musical
cliché's but can't even string those together. Unintentionally funny lines
drop, rat-a-tat, like dud grenades,
from the mouths of the youthful and
unskilled players. Gems abound: 'He's
growing up so fast, but in so many
ways he's just a little boy.' 'You
wanted to be blood brothers but I was
afraid of blood'. 'When I was a kid my
dad said: "Rico, I'm gonna take you
to Puerto Rico, Rico." And then he
died.' It's the way they tell 'em! 'Rico
has a lot of problems,' observes one
character, omitting to point out that
one of them is that Bobby Rosa, as
Rico, can only pose and not act. Even
so, he's a Brando compared to
Rodney Harvey as his pal, whose
declaration of blood brotherhood
towards the end almost had the audience on the floor.

Saludos Amigos ☉
1943, US, 42 mins, colour
Dir: Jack Kinney, Hamilton Luske,
Wilfred Jackson
Rating: ★★★

Don't let the children miss this little
-seen short animated feature from
Walt Disney which shook away the
wartime blues on a cartoon-strewn
tour of South America. Something of
a dry run for *The Three Caballeros*,
which was to follow two years later,
the film resulted from a tour of Central and South America by Disney and
some of his colleagues, and was largely
based on their experiences. Some
live-action footage leads into four
main cartoon sequences, mingling
such established favourites as Donald
Duck and Goofy, with such popular
newcomers as the cigar-puffing,
samba-dancing parrot José 'Joe' Carioca
and, in one of the best novelty cartoons Disney ever made, Pedro the
little mail plane. Pedro's adventures
feature some vivid and inspired

animation, as he makes his first solo
flight across the Andes, braving freak
air currents and thunderstorms to get
the mail through.

Salute of the Jugger ● Ⓥ
1990, Australia, 92 mins, colour
Dir: David Peoples
Stars: Rutger Hauer, Joan Chen, Vincent
Phillip D'Onofrio, Anna Katarina
Rating: ★★

Or: *Mad Max Meets Rollerball*. It's year
two thousand-and-something in the
South Australian outback where teams
of wandering 'juggers' engage in a
kind of gladiatorial version of American football played with a dog's skull
that has to be stuck on a post. Broken
bones and scar tissue are the orders of
the day but, although it's all pretty
idiotic, the Australians are good at
this kind of movie, especially when it
comes to the underground city at the
end, where spectators are 'caged' and
the combatants play in leagues. Hauer
and his men are just another bunch of
nomadic bonecrushers until they
acquire a new 'quick' in the form of
oriental Joan Chen. That's when
Hauer, a former league player who fell
from grace, decides to issue a challenge to a league team. The film is
slow in between games, but then it has
nowhere to go except the final
bloodfeast. Chen gives her all in the
arena, with some great individual
somersaults: she really does impress as
a likely league player. Hauer looks as if
he would give his all for a glass of
Guinness, which is what some exhausted viewers may feel in need of at
the end.

Salute to the Marines ○
1943, US, 101 mins, colour
Dir: S Sylvan Simon
Stars: Wallace Beery, Fay Bainter,
Reginald Owen
Rating: ★★★

MGM crossed a typical rumbustious
Wallace Beery vehicle with a
flag-waving war film and came up
with this rip-snorting rough diamond
of a film about a retired sergeant major
who organises a 'peace settlement
force' on a Pacific island, then finds
himself heading his rag-tag army to
delay the Japanese advance. Keye
Luke, familiar as Charlie Chan's
number one son, has a rather different
role here as a character called Flashy.

Salvador ● Ⓥ
1986, US, 123 mins, colour
Dir: Oliver Stone

Stars: James Woods, James Belushi,
John Savage, Michael Murphy, Elpedia
Carrillo
Rating: ★★

A rather determinedly grim exposé of
the atrocities of the El Salvador civil
war of the early Sixties, and the part
played by America in the reinstate-
ment of an allegedly oppressive
regime. The body count piles up, mass
open graves are graphically portrayed
and the blood flows through mouth
and limb. But the film never really
grips us in a narrative, despite the
(perhaps over) committed performances of James Woods, John Savage
and Michael Murphy, leaving James
Belushi to linger longest in the mind
as a hard-cursing American abroad
floating bewildered on a sea of booze
and blood. Unpleasant, depressing and
angry, the film finally falls victim to
its own viscera-thumping rhetoric in
failing to convert us to a probably
worthy cause. The end product is rather more of an ordeal than an
entertainment. Woods performance
was Oscar-nominated.

Salvation! ● Ⓥ
1987, US, 80 mins, colour
Dir: Beth B
Stars: Stephen McHattie, Dominique
Davalos, Rockets Redglare, Viggo
Mortensen, Exene Cervenka
Rating: RB

These pointless pyrotechnics from
underworld darling director Beth B
seemed unlikely to inject her into the
mainstream of film-making, and so it
proved. Her splashy style unnecessarily
maroons Stephen McHattie's quite
compelling central performance as
the TV Bible-thumper invaded by a
demonic group of people which, with
the help of the sister (Dominique
Davalos) of one, he eventually rejects.
Underneath all the glitz and flashy
editing, something very trite is being
said here. Whatever happened to
plots?

Sam Marlow Private Eye
See: The Man With Bogart's Face

Sammy and Rosie Get Laid ●
1987, UK, 100 mins, colour
Dir: Stephen Frears
Stars: Shashi Kapoor, Frances Barber,
Claire Bloom, Ayub Khan Din, Roland
Gift
Rating: ★

Not a sex film (though there's plenty
of that) but a fiercely political diatribe
about the evils of racial hatred at large

S

in Britain today, to which writer Hanif Kureishi offers no solutions. What he presents us with (within the framework of an Indian returning, horrified, to the London he once knew) is the shooting of Cherry Groce, the Brixton riots, police brutality, oppression of squatters and street and tube muggings – laid end to end, as if this were everyday life in urban Britain. Authority and government are, without exception, uncaring fiends. 'Buy yourself a house in a part of England that is not twinned with Beirut,' remarks Sammy's father (Shashi Kapoor), in one of the film's best black comedy lines. Whether haunted by the past, or squashing the latest Pinteresque harangue of his deserted love (Claire Bloom) with earthy realism, Kapoor is excellent throughout. In fact, he and young American actress Wendy Gazelle, as Sammy's mistress, give considerably more relaxed performances than any of the British contingent.

Sammy Going South ○
(aka: A Boy 10 Feet Tall)
1963, US, 118 mins, colour
Dir: Alexander Mackendrick
Stars: Edward G Robinson, Fergus McClelland
Rating: ★★★

In that it's a Michael Balcon production directed by Alexander Mackendrick, this colourful, absorbing and engaging picture is an Ealing film in all but name. You'll be gripped throughout to the adventures of 10-year-old Sammy (Fergus McClelland) as he journeys down the length of Africa to find his only surviving relation. Edward G Robinson steals the film as a rascally but friendly diamond smuggler.

Sammy the Way-out Seal ○
1962, US, 92 mins, colour
Dir: Norman Tokar
Stars: Jack Carson, Robert Culp, Patricia Barry
Rating: ★★★

Charming, amusing, light-hearted comedy, brightly photographed in Technicolor by Gordon Avil, and featuring the last screen appearance of Jack Carson, in heartily blustering form as the small-town entrepreneur who wants to turn a pet seal into the local attraction, much to the chagrin of his two small owners. Sammy causing chaos in a supermarket with the help of a pack of dogs is a genu-

inely funny sequence and the fun never outstays its welcome. In the supporting cast is angular Renie Riano, once the popular star of the low-budget 'Jiggs and Maggie' comedies. Incidentally, it should be pointed out that Sammy is actually played by a sea-lion!

Samson and Delilah ○ ⓥ
1949, US, 128 mins, colour
Dir: Cecil B DeMille
Stars: Victor Mature, Hedy Lamarr, George Sanders, Angela Lansbury
Rating: ★★

This Cecil B DeMille epic was described by one waspish critic as 'the most expensive haircut in history.' But the showman/director had the last laugh when the film grossed more than $12 million, becoming the then biggest money-making film in Paramount's 34 years. The temple pulled down by Samson at the end actually took five months to build and eight days to demolish. Victor Mature and Hedy Lamarr (a slightly mature Delilah!) provide the brawn and the beauty, but the acid acting of George Sanders and Angela Lansbury outshines the stars.

Sam Whiskey ○
1969, US, 96 mins, colour
Dir: Arnold Laven
Stars: Burt Reynolds, Angie Dickinson, Clint Walker
Rating: ★★

This lightweight but amusing comedy Western has our hero Burt Reynolds breaking into a bank to put back a gold consignment stolen by someone else. Widow Angie Dickenson hires Burt to do the job as she doesn't want her husband's crime to be discovered, thereby soiling the family name. The lively plot has Burt, with help from Clint Walker and Ossie Clark, scheming to get into the bank while trying to avoid outlaw Rick Davis, who wants the bullion for himself. It's all good fun, although lacklustre direction from Arnold Laven fails occasionally to keep the humour on the boil. Still, Burt is on good form and good fun to be with.

San Antonio ○ ⓥ
1945, US, 111 mins, colour
Dir: David Butler
Stars: Errol Flynn, Alexis Smith
Rating: ★★★

This was Errol Flynn trying to pick up where he left off in 1941, when a series of war films succeeded the superbly-organised Westerns and swashbucklers that had made his name. The production is elaborate, and there's a splendid battle between Flynn and villain Paul Kelly at the finish. Nonetheless, the hand of director Michael Curtiz, who made almost all of Flynn's best action films before their wrangling grew too much for either man to take, is sorely missed; and Flynn's subsequent vehicles at Warners confirmed the beginning of his decline. Glowingly good Technicolor photography makes this always a handsome film.

San Demetrio, London ○
1943, UK, 105 mins, b/w
Dir: Charles Frend
Stars: Walter Fitzgerald, Robert Beatty
Rating: ★★★★

Classic, unforgettable Ealing Studios war film guaranteed to bring a lump to your throat. A petrol tanker's crew are forced to abandon ship, drift for two days, then sight the still-burning, still-floating remains of their own ship. Totally inspiring, uplifting, exciting epic of the sea. A whole crew of then less than well-known film faces helps to prove that truth can indeed by stranger – and stronger – than fiction. Don't miss this rarity if it comes your way.

Sand Pebbles, The ○
1966, US, 193 mins, colour
Dir: Robert Wise
Stars: Steve McQueen, Richard Attenborough, Candice Bergen, Richard Crenna
Rating: ★★

A three-hour action epic, set in China 50 years ago, that Robert Wise made hard on the heels of the two musicals for which he won Academy Awards, *West Side Story* and *The Sound of Music*. As usual with Wise's films, there's no lack of star appeal in the cast. Steve McQueen plays Jake, a seaman who is a newcomer to the crew of an old gunboat now doing duty on the Yangtze River; and Richard Attenborough is the only other member of the crew with whom Jake, essentially a 'loner', forms any real attachment. Also featured are Richard Crenna as the Captain, and Candice Bergen as an American girl who has arrived in China to teach at a mission.

Sands of Iwo Jima ○ ⓥ
1949, US, 109 mins, b/w
Dir: Allan Dwan
Stars: John Wayne, John Agar, Forrest Tucker, Adele Mara
Rating: ★★★

'Before I'm through with you, you're gonna move like one man and think like one man,' growls Sergeant John Wayne to the new recruits in this flag-waving but strong and believable war film. When an old hand tells the newcomers that Wayne 'knows his business', the recruit retorts: 'So did Jack the Ripper.' Full of this kind of mildly tough humour, and very decent action scenes that convey well the confusion of war, the film brought Wayne his only Oscar nomination before his triumph in *True Grit* 20 years later.

Sands of the Desert ○ ⓥ
1961, UK, 92 mins, colour
Dir: John Paddy Carstairs
Stars: Charlie Drake, Sarah Branch
Rating: ★★

That tiny bundle of energy, Charlie Drake, capers across the desert wastes in a quick-fire series of comic escapades. He plays a shy little clerk in a travel agency who finds himself involved in foreign intrigues once he's transferred to the desert. Valentino himself would have shed glycerine tears at Peter Arne's amusing portrait of a woman-chasing sheik.

Sands of the Kalahari ◐
1964, UK, 119 mins, colour
Dir: Cy Endfield
Stars: Stanley Baker, Stuart Whitman, Susannah York
Rating: ★★★

A really blood-thirsty picture on a survival-in-the-desert theme, with some brilliant desert cinematography by Erwin Hillier. The camerawork reaches an early highpoint with a view of the co-pilot's grave (the action starts with a plane crash) against the background of a giant arrow, fashioned from the fragments of the wrecked aircraft, and pointing the way the survivors have gone. Susannah York copes bravely with a character that is unexplainedly puzzling and takes a shower without getting her hair wet. Scenes of apparent animal cruelty are terrifyingly done.

San Francisco ○
1936, US, 110 mins, b/w
Dir: W S Van Dyke
Stars: Clark Gable, Jeanette MacDonald, Spencer Tracy
Rating: ★★★

Nostalgia sweetens one's memories of this, the film with the famous, extremely impressive and really magnificently edited reconstruction of the San Francisco earthquake of 1906. In fact, the earthquake is tacked on to a rather trite story about a selfish gambling-house proprietor, his infatuation with a poor but lovely singer, and his lifelong friendship with the local priest. In other words, an excuse for the stars to go through their familiar paces but pulled through in style by the sheer professionalism of Woody Van Dyke's direction, and the slickness and sincerity, respectively, of the performances by Clark Gable and Spencer Tracy.

San Quentin ○
1946, US, 66 mins, b/w
Dir: Gordon M Douglas
Stars: Lawrence Tierney, Barton MacLane
Rating: ★★

Inmates in San Quentin prison organise an Inmates Welfare League to help order in the prison and prepare prisoners for life back on the outside. But when Nick (Barton MacLane) breaks out and goes on a crime spree, the scheme is in danger of being scrapped. The prisoners send a former founding member (Lawrence Tierney), already out, to track Nick down. Although this all sounds a little far-fetched (which it is), there's enough action in this short sharp RKO drama to make you forget the fact. Some way down the cast list there's a prisoner who became a solid cornerstone of the law as Perry Mason and Ironside – Raymond Burr.

Santa and the Three Bears ☉
1970, US, 60 mins, colour
Dir: Tony Benedict
Rating: ★★★

Enchanting little American feature, mainly animated, with a live-action framework combining two folk legends in one. The principal part of the story concerns two baby bears who put off their hibernation so that they can stay awake and see Father Christmas. Their mother's plans to make sure they're not disappointed go somewhat awry. Highly original entertainment with children in mind.

Santa Claus ☉ ⓥ
1985, US, 105 mins, colour
Dir: Jeannot Szwarc
Stars: Dudley Moore, John Lithgow, David Huddleston
Rating: ★★

After convincing the world that they could make a man fly in the *Superman* series, producers Alexander and Ilya Salkind poured $50 million into this (unintentional) Christmas turkey. David Huddleston comes across as a department store Santa, while Dudley Moore chases around manically (rather like in his Tesco chicken commercials) as Santa's go-ahead elf helper Patch. Nothing quite lives up to the magical opening scenes, and it's not surprising that the film was less successful than expected at the box office. Called *Santa Claus: The Movie* (as opposed to what?) on all publicity, although those last words don't appear on screen.

Santa Fe Trail ○
1940, US, 110 mins, b/w
Dir: Michael Curtiz
Stars: Errol Flynn, Olivia de Havilland, Raymond Massey
Rating: ★★

Another blockbuster action film from the team of star Errol Flynn and director Michael Curtiz, who also made *Captain Blood*. This one is a minor *Gone With the Wind* with the obligatory cast of thousands, some splendidly-staged battle scenes, and Ronald Reagan as the young Custer, whose last years would ironically be portrayed by Flynn himself the following year in *They Died With Their Boots On*.

Santiago
See: The Gun Runner

Saphead, The ○
1920, US, 70 mins, b/w
Dir: Herbert Blache
Stars: Buster Keaton
Rating: ★★★

Buster Keaton's first feature film is a fascinating example of his unique talent in embryo. There's too much plot for Keaton really to break out, but he gives a memorable display of vaudeville acrobatics in the Stock Exchange and the movie's rarity value makes it unmissable.

Saps at Sea ☉
1940, US, 60 mins, b/w
Dir: Gordon Douglas

S

Stars: Stan Laurel, Oliver Hardy
Rating: ★★★

The last feature comedy that Stan and Ollie made for the Hal Roach studio. Here, they're off on an ocean cruise, with an escaped convict stowed away on board. Some good sight gags include several during a medical inspection of Mr Hardy by Dr James Finlayson; and the famous sequence where they make a feast for the convict without using anything that's actually edible . . . see it to believe it.

Saraband
See: Saraband for Dead Lovers

Saraband for Dead Lovers ○
(aka: Saraband)
1948, UK, 96 mins, colour
Dir: Michael Relph
Stars: Stewart Granger, Joan Greenwood, Flora Robson
Rating: ★★★

Stewart Granger and Anthony Quayle have to concede the acting honours to Flora Robson in this splendidly-mounted costume adventure-tragedy set in 17th-century Germany. Dame Flora is superb, especially in a horrifying scene where she burns Granger's face with a curling iron. He and Quayle do at least have a splendid sword duel.

Saracen Blade, The ○
1954, US, 78 mins, colour
Dir: William Castle
Stars: Ricardo Montalban, Betta St John, Rick Jason, Carolyn Jones
Rating: ★★★

A sprawling novel by the prolific Frank Yerby is condensed into a full-blooded costume action film, typical of Hollywood's sword and sandal sagas of the early Fifties, full of clichéd but effective dialogue and stirring action scenes. Enthusiastic performances by Ricardo Montalban, Betta St John, Michael Ansara, Rick Jason and especially Carolyn Jones, whose minxish portrayal steals the film, ensure you'll be cheering the hero on through a slew of improbable adventures. An underrated film: very entertaining.

Sarafina! ◐ ⊛
1992, US/South Africa, 118 mins, colour
Dir: Darrell James Roodt
Stars: Leleti Khumalo, Whoopi Goldberg, Mariam Makeba, John Kani
Rating: ★★★

Most people will find this semi-musical about South Africa's apartheid years deeply disturbing. And, because it is a passionately committed enterprise, its dramas are more affecting than those of such better-acted African stories as *Cry Freedom* and *A Dry White Season*. Sarafina (Leleti Khumalo) is a teenage pupil at a Soweto school where rebellious talk costs lives and oppression by the military is the order of the day. Her teacher Mary (Whoopi Goldberg) teaches national pride mixed with history which is too heady a brew for the authorities who soon have her in their sights. What follows is an all too familiar story of massacre, beating, kidnap and torture, only slightly relieved by the surging songs that drive the story along. Well-shot and edited and just well enough acted to get by, this is a harrowing, moving and entertaining history lesson in itself, although, alas, surely not the beginning of the end to racial oppression in the world.

Sarah ⊙
(aka: The Seventh Match)
1981, US, 71 mins, colour
Dir: Yoram Gross
Rating: ★★

An unusual, inventive cartoon feature from the prolific Australian animator Yoram Gross, whose best-known work to date is probably *Dot and the Kangaroo*. This is more serious than most of his films, concerning a small girl befriended by the animals of the forest while on the run from the Nazis in World War Two. Mia Farrow gives Sarah a suitably delicate yet determined voice.

Satanic Rites of Dracula, The ● ⊛
1973, UK, 88 mins, colour
Dir: Alan Gibson
Stars: Christopher Lee, Peter Cushing, Freddie Jones, Joanna Lumley
Rating: ★★

A modern-dress entry into the Dracula series, which gives a new, if rather improbable method of disposing of vampires and presents the bad count as a property speculator with a cellar full of nubile girl vampires. Peter Cushing and Christopher Lee play with their usual aplomb.

Satan's Skin
See: Blood on Satan's Claw

Saturday Night and Sunday Morning ◐ ⊛
1960, UK, 90 mins, b/w
Dir: Karel Reisz
Stars: Albert Finney, Rachel Roberts, Shirley Anne Field
Rating: ★★★

This was a significant milestone in British cinema since the film not only took a highly (for the time) adult attitude towards sex, but also treated working class people without any attempt either to patronise or to mock them. Much of its still considerable power derives from Allan Sillitoe's honest and abrasive screenplay – based on his own novel – and Karel Reisz's impressive direction in his first film in this capacity. He succeeded in getting quite superb performances from Finney as an archetypal angry young man forced to face up to his responsibilities, Rachel Roberts as his married mistress, and from music hall comedienne Hylda Baker whose portrayal of a working class woman gave her career a major boost. And the fine use of locations – marvellously photographed by Freddie Francis – gives an almost documentary view of an English industrial town.

Saturday Night Fever ◐ ⊛
1977, US, 119 mins, colour
Dir: John Badham
Stars: John Travolta, Karen Lynn Gorney
Rating: ★★★

Never mind the quality of the script, feel the vibrations that made John Travolta a star in this famous and really rather bitter story of life in the slums of Brooklyn. The teenagers slave away in thankless jobs, and only come to life on Saturday nights at the spectacular local disco. Brilliant photography by Ralph D Bode makes the most of the sequences in which Travolta proves he's the dancing king.

Saturn 3 ○ ⊛
1980, US, 87 mins, colour
Dir: Stanley Donen
Stars: Kirk Douglas, Farrah Fawcett
Rating: ★★★

A not unexciting variant on a formula science-fiction theme, as a space station (manned by Kirk Douglas and Farrah Fawcett) is invaded by a killer and the robot he constructs. Director Stanley Donen gives it a gutsy pace, lots of pounding chases up and down the station and a spectacular climax. The film is good to look at, its effects as competent as anything in *Star Wars*. The editing wisely relies as little as possible on the dialogue to provide the thrills.

Savage Innocents, The ○
1959, UK, 107 mins, colour
Dir: Baccio Bandini
Stars: Anthony Quinn, Yoko Tani, Peter O'Toole
Rating: ★★★

A bizarre offering from cult director Nicholas Ray, who is better known for the James Dean classic *Rebel Without a Cause*. Anthony Quinn and Yoko Tani star as Eskimos battling to survive against nature – and the onset of civilisation, in the shape of white traders, Christianity and rock 'n' roll! Not surprisingly, it ends in tears. The film was a troubled international co-production and co-star Peter O'Toole was later dubbed into Americanese by another actor. But it does contain some striking location photography (as well as dodgy back projection at Pinewood studios). Animal lovers should be prepared for the savagery of the Eskimo lifestyle, with close-up scenes of caribou eyes and crawling maggots as food and the ripping open of a dog's belly so that frozen hands can be thawed in the entrails.

Savage Islands ○
1983, US, 100 mins, colour
Dir: Ferdinand Fairfax
Stars: Tommy Lee Jones, Michael O'Keefe, Jenny Seagrove
Rating: ★★

Like *The Scarlet Buccaneer*, this is a doomed attempt to duplicate the Hollywood pirate picture of the Fifties. It starts well, but becomes progressively less spirited and well-organised as the story progresses. Made in New Zealand with an American, British and Australasian cast.

Save the Tiger ●
1972, US, 100 mins, colour
Dir: John G Avildsen
Stars: Jack Lemmon, Jack Gilford
Rating: ★★

Although this is rather an unpalatable film, it has a typical Jack Lemmon performance of full-throttled intensity, revelling in another portrait of modern angst, chewing the role voraciously before swallowing it

whole. For his performance as the snarlingly harassed Harry, Lemmon was rewarded with an Oscar.

Saving Grace ○
1986, UK, 112 mins, colour
Dir: Robert M Young
Stars: Tom Conti, Fernando Rey
Rating: ★

A gentler affair than Robbie Coltrane's irreverent *The Pope Must Die*, although nowhere near as well-paced. This comedy casts Tom Conti as a Pope who runs away from office to live among ordinary people for a while to re-learn his trade. Actually, he not so much runs away as locks himself out of the Vatican garden while dressed in civvies, and just takes his time in getting back in! Scriptwriter David S Ward captures well the naive spirit of Italian English (in spite of the plot taking place in Italy) while Conti uses a heavy Italian accent! He makes an owlishly smiling Pope in a role he would probably have lost to Peter Sellers had the latter lived, while sawn-off Angelo Evans is excellent as the sub-teen wide boy who becomes his first convert. Pretty dull though.

Say Anything ◐ ⓥ
1989, US, 104 mins, colour
Dir: Cameron Crowe
Stars: John Cusack, Ione Skye, John Mahoney
Rating: ★★★

A teenage drama with a difference. The excellent John Cusack is the average Joe graduating from college who falls in love with the lovely school brainbox (Ione Skye) who has an incredibly close relationship with her adoring father. But all is not quite what it seems, and this is what strikes the spark that sets the movie apart from the average teenage romance. That, plus excellent performances – the film is all but stolen by John Mahoney as Skye's dad – and the fact that the story is about people with feet of clay. An uplifting film for teenagers to see, it proves that you can do anything if you think clearly and keep the major relationships in your life intact at the same time.

Say It With Flowers ○
1933, UK, 71 mins, b/w
Dir: John Baxter
Stars: Mary Clare, Ben Field, George Carney
Rating: ★★

Many 'greats' of the old-time music-hall appear in this affectionately-made film about two street traders who fall on hard times. Directed by John Baxter, portrayer par excellence of the British working classes through three decades of the cinema.

Sayonara ○ ⓥ
1957, US, 147 mins, colour
Dir: Joshua Logan
Stars: Marlon Brando, Miiko Taka, Patricia Owens
Rating: ★★★

Marathon tear-jerker about American servicemen in love with Japanese girls at the time of the Korean War, and the sometimes tragic consequences. Brando puts on a convincing Southern States accent, and develops his character nicely. But acting honours went to Red Buttons, previously known only as a comic actor, and Miyoshi Umeki as the Japanese girl he marries. Both players deservedly won Oscars. The film also took Academy Awards for art direction and sound recording, and deserved one which it did not get – for the very high quality Technicolor photography by Ellsworth Fredericks. The atmosphere is authentic and the story wholly absorbing.

Scalawag ◉
1973, US, 93 mins, colour
Dir: Kirk Douglas
Stars: Kirk Douglas, Mark Lester
Rating: ★

As well as being the star, Kirk Douglas made his debut as a director on this pirate yarn based on a story by Robert Louis Stevenson. Douglas' wife Anne was co-producer. Douglas became an enthusiastic balloonist – a balloon figures prominently in the action – when he filmed the story on locations along the Yugoslavian coast. In the film, Douglas, like everyone else, strenuously over-plays, as a one-legged rogue called Peg, in a story whose strongest asset is Jack Cardiff's sunny Technicolor photography. Children will enjoy the simple blood-and-thunder Douglas provides. Adults may just stay awake long enough to spot Danny DeVito in one of his earliest roles.

Scalphunters, The ◐
1968, US, 102 mins, colour
Dir: Sydney Pollack
Stars: Burt Lancaster, Shelley Winters, Telly Savalas, Ossie Davis
Rating: ★★★

S

An uncharacteristic film for both Burt Lancaster (in his later years, at any rate) and director Sydney Pollack. This is a rip-roaring adventure story about a tough fur trapper 'landed' with a runaway slave for company, during a dangerous few days in which they get involved with a gang of scalphunters, and a tribe of Kiowa Indians. Shelley Winters is splendidly fiery and surprisingly glamorous in a throwback to the kind of role she was playing 15 years earlier. And, as one of the scalphunters, there's Dan Vadis, who played the lead in countless Italian muscle-man epics, but only made this one American film.

Scam ● ⓥ
1992, US, 102 mins, colour
Dir: John Flynn
Stars: Christopher Walken, Lorraine Bracco, Miguel Ferrer
Rating: ★

Something that has more twists than a corkscrew ought to grip all right, but this 'scam' doesn't even bite into the cork. The plot dodges this way and that and changes course several times in the last few minutes, but all to no avail; the odds are that you won't care too much about who's doing what to whom. Lorraine Bracco's con-girl in cahoots with Miguel Ferrer, coming on to rich pick-ups, drugging their drinks and relieving them of their bankrolls and Rolexes. Along comes Christopher Walken, who abducts her, may or may not be an FBI man and enlists her in a scheme to rob the bad guys of computer disk information – or maybe a few million in banknotes. Jamaican backgrounds supply some colourful padding as director John Flynn allows the plot to ramble on in its tired and outmoded way. Walken and Bracco give pat performances that smack of insufficient enthusiasm for the project: you won't care much what happens to either of them at the end.

Scandal ● ⓥ
1989, UK, 106 mins, colour
Dir: Michael Caton-Jones
Stars: Joanne Whalley-Kilmer, John Hurt, Bridget Fonda, Ian McKellen
Rating: ★★

Despite a script culled from no less than five books on the subject, this film of the notorious Profumo case – 'The Minister, the Model, and the Russian Spy' – is a sadly whitewashed affair. With most of its characters still alive and the libel minefield to nego-

tiate, it is perhaps not surprising that the filmmakers played safe. Joanne Whalley-Kilmer certainly looks the part of 'showgirl' Christine Keeler, whose affairs with a Russian official and British Cabinet minister helped bring down the Conservative government of the day. But the film's revelation is American actress Bridget Fonda (daughter of Peter and niece of Jane) who perfectly captures the capricious nature and British accent of fellow goodtime girl Mandy Rice-Davies, famous for her 'Well, he would say that' line during the famous court case. John Hurt is excellent as the sad establishment fall guy, Dr Stephen Ward. But this scandal resembles nothing more than a storm in a china tea-cup.

Scandal at Scourie ○
1952, US, 91 mins, colour
Dir: Jean Negulesco
Stars: Greer Garson, Walter Pidgeon
Rating: ★★

Scandal at Scourie was the end of an era: it was the last film the famous Greer Garson-Walter Pidgeon team made together in 12 years which included such colossal hits as *Mrs Miniver* and *Madame Curie*. This is a typical Garson-Pidgeon mixture of laughter and tears, with cute and clever Donna Corcoran as a little orphan girl who causes no end of trouble to her foster-parents. An irresistible and highly enjoyable piece of sheer sentiment, with Canadian backgrounds richly photographed in Technicolor.

Scandal Sheet ○
(aka: The Dark Page)
1951, US, 82 mins, b/w
Dir: Phil Karlson
Stars: Broderick Crawford, John Derek, Donna Reed
Rating: ★★★

Broderick Crawford is in typical scowling, hard-hitting form as the ruthless editor of a gutter newspaper, who finds himself pursued by his own reporters when he accidentally puts an end to his ex-wife. This last scene is the best in the film, filled with an atmosphere of doom. There are fine performances from Crawford and from Rosemary De Camp, usually cast in cosy mother roles, but here in splendidly vengeful form as the long-deserted wife. Director Phil Karlson ensures that the pace is fast and the action crackles. His cast also includes Harry Morgan and Henry O'Neill.

Scanners ● ⓥ
1981, Canada, 103 mins, colour
Dir: David Cronenberg
Stars: Jennifer O'Neill, Patrick McGoohan
Rating: ★★★

This was director David Cronenberg's best film to date and deservedly put him on the international map. Scanners are superior if tormented beings who can kill by thought transference. Literally, they blow your mind. Consequently, Cronenberg predictably interested not so much in the story as in the opportunity it provides for special effects. These are exceptionally good, especially the scene of a head blowing apart, and in the final duel between two master scanners. The ending is cryptic in the way the best of Roger Corman's films were and, if the acting is not too hot, the subject matter remains fascinating to the end.

Scapegoat, The ○
1958, UK, 92 mins, b/w
Dir: Robert Hamer
Stars: Alec Guinness, Bette Davis, Nicole Maurey
Rating: ★★★

Brilliant thriller – based on the novel by Daphne du Maurier – in which an English schoolmaster (Alec Guinness) finds himself in desperate trouble after meeting his 'double' in France. The nerve-wracking closing scenes in which Guinness once more confronts his lookalike will keep you guessing up to the last moment.

Scar, The
See: Hollow Triumph

Scaramouche ○
1952, US, 110 mins, colour
Dir: George Sidney
Stars: Stewart Granger, Eleanor Parker, Mel Ferrer, Janet Leigh
Rating: ★★★★

One of Stewart Granger's best films at MGM: a remake of the famous Rafael Sabatini swashbuckler set in 18th-century France, with Granger as the rake who turns avenger when his best friend is murdered. The climax is one of the most dazzling and longest duel scenes ever filmed, between Granger and Mel Ferrer, that bettered even the one Granger was to have with James Mason in another spectacular MGM remake, *The Prisoner of Zenda*.

Scared Stiff ○
1953, US, 108 mins, b/w
Dir: George Marshall
Stars: Dean Martin, Jerry Lewis, Lizabeth Scott, Carmen Miranda
Rating: ★★

A remake – and a pretty funny one – of the old Bob Hope classic *The Ghost Breakers*, with Dean Martin and Jerry Lewis jointly taking the Hope role of a cowardly entertainer dodging zombies on a mist-enshrouded island. Lewis pulls some incredible faces and gives a passable impression of Brazilian bombshell Carmen Miranda, whose last film appearance this was. Two of Dean and Jerry's comedy rivals at Paramount at the time make surprise guest appearances in this enjoyable show that seamlessly blends chuckles and chills.

Scarface ○ Ⓥ
1932, US, 90 mins, b/w
Dir: Howard Hawks
Stars: Paul Muni, Ann Dvorak, Karen Morley, Boris Karloff
Rating: ★★★★

This landmark gangster movie is strong stuff, indeed too strong for America in 1932, where it had to be sub-titled *The Shame of a Nation*. The film is dominated by the tenacious performance of Paul Muni as the gangster of the title, who shoots his way venomously to the top. The film is drivingly well directed by Howard Hawks, although it took later critics to pick out the 'cross' motif which accompanies most of the deaths in the film – a parallel to the crosslike scar on Muni's face.

Scarface Mob, The ○
1959, US, 102 mins, colour
Dir: Phil Karlson
Stars: Robert Stack, Neville Brand, Pat Crowley, Keenan Wynn
Rating: ★★

This fast-moving gangster story hearkened back to the vintage years of tommy-gun thrillers at Warner Brothers and triggered off the long-running television series *The Untouchables*. Neville Brand plays famous gangster Al Capone for the first of several times for film and television. Pretty Pat Crowley makes an appealing heroine, providing a welcome gentle touch amid the 'macho' machine-gun mayhem of the rest of the movie.

Scarlet Angel ○
1952, US, 80 mins, colour
Dir: Sidney Salkow
Stars: Yvonne De Carlo, Rock Hudson
Rating: ★★

This colourful romantic adventure was Rock Hudson's last step up the ladder before becoming a fully-fledged star. He was billed above the title, in type almost as big as the lead, Yvonne De Carlo, who plays an adventuress called Roxy, at large in New Orleans waterfront saloons – and later high society – in the early 1800s. Television fans with long memories will recognise the actress playing Susan Caldwell. She's Amanda Blake, later Miss Kitty in the long-running *Gunsmoke* series.

Scarlet Buccaneer, The ○
(aka: Swashbuckler)
1976, US, 100 mins, colour
Dir: James Goldstone
Stars: Robert Shaw, James Earl Jones, Peter Boyle, Genevieve Bujold
Rating: ★★

Pirate films seek no logic. Therefore, it's not surprising that, with a mild nod to modern times in the form of the villain's bisexuality, director James Goldstone has chosen to make a swashbuckler in the truest Errol Flynn – well, at any rate, Burt Lancaster – tradition. Unfortunately, Goldstone is no Michael Curtiz when it comes to marshalling crowded action scenes and the dialogue plays the whole thing a shade too tongue-in-cheek. Robert Shaw's brighter buccaneer of the title is really the only good performance, but if Genevieve Bujold is a mite short on acting strength, she shows herself handy with a sword and pitches into her fiery heroine with genuine Maureen O'Hara spirit. The whole thing is noisy, violent and, especially in the early stages, moves at a rare old clip.

Scarlet Empress, The ○
1934, US, 110 mins, b/w
Dir: Josef von Sternberg
Stars: Marlene Dietrich, John Lodge
Rating: ★★★

The story almosts drowns in a sea of lushness and exoticism in this version of the rise to power in Russia of Catherine the Great – very different to that being made in Britain at the same time with Elisabeth Bergner as Catherine. There, the emphasis was on character creation; here, it is wholly on costume, spectacle and camerawork, Bert Glemmon excelling in this last department with his ultra-mobile black and white cameras (later he would become an acknowledged expert in colour as well). Marlene Dietrich is fine as the shy young princess, but less effective when a figure of power. The film itself, which nowadays would be described as high camp is, under Josef von Sternberg's dedicated direction, a treat to the eye. And there's an amazing performance by Sam Jaffe.

Scarlet Pimpernel, The ○
1934, UK, 98 mins, b/w
Dir: Harold Young
Stars: Leslie Howard, Merle Oberon, Raymond Massey
Rating: ★★★★

Best-remembered of the many films about the adventures of Baroness Orczy's famous chameleon Sir Percy Blakeney, the soldier of fortune who confounds the French revolutionaries who seek him here, there and everywhere. Originally, Charles Laughton had been chosen for the title role, but the public protested that he didn't match up to the popular conception of the Pimpernel – and Leslie Howard was chosen. His Pimpernel remains the archetypal performance, catching exactly the false foppishness and underlying steel, as well as the mythical qualities which make the character seem so invincible. James Mason can be spotted, standing around rather stiffly in his first film, in a non-speaking role. Three years later, he was to star in the sequel, called *The Return of the Scarlet Pimpernel*. Howard popped up again in 1941, in an updated version of the story, called *Pimpernel Smith*.

Scarlet Pimpernel, The ○
1982, UK, 144 mins, colour
Dir: Clive Donner
Stars: Anthony Andrews, Jane Seymour, Ian McKellen
Rating: ★★★

It took London Films 47 years to repeat the ideal casting of their 1935 version of this swashbuckling classic (which starred Leslie Howard as Sir Percy and Merle Oberon as his wife), but they did it to perfection: Anthony Andrews and Jane Seymour fit the roles like elegant gloves.

Scarlet Street ○
1945, US, 103 mins, b/w
Dir: Fritz Lang

S

Stars: Edward G Robinson, Joan Bennett, Dan Duryea
Rating: ★★★★

Fine seedy thriller, with a perfect performance by Edward G Robinson as the meek cashier ensnared by trollop Joan Bennett into providing her with the luxuries she craves. Dan Duryea's sleek straw-hatted con-boy completes the same trio of stars from director Fritz Lang's other great Forties' crime drama, *The Woman in the Window*. This one is a remake of Jean Renoir's early French sound classic *La Chienne*. An amazingly intense *film noir*.

Scars of Dracula, The ● Ⓥ
1970, UK, 96 mins, colour
Dir: Roy Ward Baker
Stars: Christopher Lee, Dennis Waterman
Rating: ★★

Dennis Waterman is less at home here battling the vampire count (Christopher Lee) than he was soon to become in TV's *The Sweeney* and *Minder* series. Roger Dicken's special effects are excellent, but there's too little of Lee in this one.

Scenes from a Mall Ⓒ Ⓥ
1991, US, 85 mins, colour
Dir: Paul Mazursky
Stars: Bette Midler, Woody Allen, Bill Irwin
Rating: ★

Midler and Allen together. It's an idea good enough to start you laughing while you're still in the queue. And, for a while, it works. The trouble is that the scripters have no idea what to do with the terrible two once they get them inside a massive shopping mall. It was certainly not a great notion, either, to cast them as long-term husband and wife who, after they've told each other about their recent affairs, just make up and bicker, make up and bicker, through the rest of the film. There are occasional good moments (but not many) in the last hour of a film that mercifully is at least short. What a waste of these two tiny titans of talent to have them go even semi-serious on us under circumstances like these.

Scenes from the Class Struggle in Beverly Hills ● Ⓥ
1989, US, 104 mins, colour
Dir: Paul Bartel

Stars: Jacqueline Bisset, Ray Sharkey, Mary Woronov, Ed Begley Jr
Rating: ★★

Director Bartel made *Eating Raoul* and lots of similarly outrageous stuff. So you can guarantee that his idea of a sexploitation comedy is not going to be quite like anyone else's. Lunatic? You got it. And, even though Bartel himself said at the time that 'if this doesn't offend anybody, it isn't working', it isn't actually as rude and crass as its reputation would have you believe. In a Hollywood mansion couples couple compulsively and without compunction. It's light, lusty and luxuriously lewd; and occasionally funny too.

Scent of a Woman ● Ⓥ
1992, US, 157 mins, colour
Dir: Martin Brest
Stars: Al Pacino, Chris O'Donnell, Gabrielle Anwar, James Rebhorn
Rating: ★★

You know the one about opposites having something to learn from each other and forging the unlikeliest of friendships. *Beaches* somehow made it work; here writer Bo Goldman and director Martin Brest show us how to go right over the top with the idea. Chris O'Donnell (not half firm enough) is a 17-year-old prep student saddled for the weekend with irascible, unreasonable, unmanageable, blind retired Lt Col Slade (a notably mannered performance from Al Pacino which took an Oscar). The kid finds himself whisked off to New York, where the colonel has in mind spending his disability pension on one hell of a time, followed by blowing his brains out. The adventures of this unlikely if somewhat unlovable couple have a certain charm, and sequences involving a dance and a madcap car drive work winningly. But it's 92 minutes' worth spread out to more than 150. The climax piles our disbelief into a sandwich of sentiment, and opportunities for meaningful dialogue between the two protagonists are all wasted.

Schindler's List ● Ⓥ
1993, US, 195 mins, b/w
Dir: Steven Spielberg
Stars: Liam Neeson, Ben Kingsley, Ralph Fiennes, Caroline Goodall, Embeth Davidtz
Rating: ★★★

Steven Spielberg's very worthy (although *very* long) and sometimes moving Oscar-winning account of the wartime exploits of Oskar Schindler, an Austro–German businessman and profiteer who made a fortune from a Polish pots-and-pans factory using Jewish labour he didn't have to pay – except in kind. To those Jews in the Krakow ghetto, work for Schindler was infinitely preferable to anything else. Concerned only with making money, he was basically a kind of sharp wheeler-dealer who treated his staff fairly. Hobnobbing with the Germans, he bought Nazi friendship with money and black market goods, even beguiling his psychotic local commandant (Ralph Fiennes) whose hobby was taking pot shots at passing Jews. But the high-living, womanising Schindler inevitably became drawn to the deprivations of his workforce. As the man who became an unlikely hero and the saviour of a race not his own, Liam Neeson is excellent all the way through, only faltering in an out-of-character breakdown at the end. The direction is often fine – especially in the Auschwitz scenes when 300 Schindler Jews are mistakenly taken to the death camp – but sometimes a bit flashy, especially in the use of colour to highlight a candle flame or a girl's red coat: it seems merely intrusive and adds nothing.

School for Scoundrels ⊙
1959, UK, 95 mins, b/w
Dir: Robert Hamer
Stars: Ian Carmichael, Terry-Thomas, Alastair Sim, Janette Scott
Rating: ★★★

A fitting and hilarious tribute to the late Stephen Potter, on whose incomparable books *Gamesmanship*, *Lifemanship* and *Oneupmanship* this comedy film was based. One remembers with particular pleasure the snooker and tennis confrontations between Ian Carmichael and Terry-Thomas, and Alastair Sim is perfect casting as the author himself. The supporting cast includes Janette Scott, Dennis Price, Peter Jones – especially funny as a car salesman – and Hattie Jacques.

School Ties Ⓒ Ⓥ
1992, US, 107 mins, colour
Dir: Robert Mandel
Stars: Brendan Fraser, Chris O'Donnell, Andrew Lowery, Amy Locane, Zeljko Ivanek
Rating: ★★

This drama of racial prejudice at a senior college for the sons of rich men lies somewhere between so-so and quite good. Though not without merit or food for thought, it's by no means as gripping as landmark films in the genre. David (Brendan Fraser) comes from a working-class Jewish family and is at the college on a football scholarship. On his father's (and coach's) advice, he doesn't tell his roommates he's a Jew, which with hindsight proves a grave mistake, and one which is to have serious repercussions. As with many of these dramas, this is simplistic in treatment and its issues are fairly black and white, with characters either basically sympathetic to David or total bigots. Nonetheless, it doesn't always opt for the obvious, as in David's attitude to authority, which is barely respectful and although prepared to talk frankly to his seniors, rarely having anything really telling to say. Fraser has a difficult role in this not entirely sympathetic part, but does it well.

Scorchers ● ⓥ

1991, US, 88 mins, colour
Dir: David Beaird
Stars: Faye Dunaway, Denholm Elliott, Emily Lloyd, James Wilder, Jennifer Tilly, James Earl Jones
Rating: RB

This strange kettle of catfish down in the Bayou is one of those films that makes it glaringly obvious that it started life as a play. It seems to be about young brides losing their inhibitions through a) imagined contact with a dead mother and b) positive contact with the town whore. 'I'm scared, daddy,' wails Emily Lloyd. 'I'm not woman enough to please my man,' pouts Jennifer Tilly. Both are better actresses than you could possibly guess from this very badly directed (by its writer) film that has an all-too-distinguished cast embarrassingly and stiltedly over-acting to the extent that it simply turns an audience off. The movie starts with a rambling rigmarole by Leland Crooke (who?) as Lloyd's father, which seems to have no more point than lengthening the film by five minutes – and ominously sets the 'unreal' tone of things to come. You get the feeling that here and there the film is meant to be affecting and amusing, but it isn't either. Son of a gun, it's just no fun on this Bayou.

Scorpio ◐

1972, UK, 114 mins, colour
Dir: Michael Winner
Stars: Burt Lancaster, Alain Delon, Paul Scofield, Gayle Hunnicutt
Rating: ★★

Tough espionage thriller awash with unsympathetic characters, good action scenes, sharp dialogue and a pretty confusing plot. Burt Lancaster is at his most taciturn as the hit-man who wants to turn it in, but inevitably cannot shake himself free of the spider's web cast by his organisation, and finds another hit-man (played by Alain Delon) on his heels.

Scott of the Antarctic ○ ⓥ

1948, UK, 111 mins, colour
Dir: Charles Frend
Stars: John Mills, Derek Bond, James Robertson Justice, Kenneth More, Harold Warrender, Reginald Beckwith
Rating: ★★★

John Mills has the lead role in this moving screen monument to the men of the ill-fated trek to the South Pole. Derek Bond plays Oates, the man who surrendered his own life to give his colleagues a better chance of survival. Much of the shooting was done on arduous locations in Switzerland and Norway, where packed lunches froze solid, and several crewmen were sent back to base with frostbite. Of the other actors doing yeoman work under such conditions, Harold Warrender is Wilson, Reginald Beckwith plays 'Birdie' Bowers and James Robinson Justice is the ill-fated Evans, the first to die. An honest account, but still inspiring, with fantastic Technicolor camerawork from three of Britain's finest cameramen – Jack Cardiff, Osmond Borrodaile and Geoffrey Unsworth.

Scrooge ○

1935, UK, 79 mins, b/w
Dir: Henry Edwards
Stars: Sir Seymour Hicks, Donald Calthrop, Athene Seyler, Oscar Asche, Barbara Everest, Maurice Evans
Rating: ★★★

A good early version of the cast-iron Dickens classic *A Christmas Carol*, with convincing Victorian atmosphere and settings. The famous actor-manager and comedy character star Sir Seymour Hicks is in topnotch form in the title role. This remained the top film account of the story until eclipsed by the Alastair Sim version of 1951.

Scrooge ○ ⓥ

(aka: A Christmas Carol)
1951, UK, 86 mins, b/w
Dir: Brian Desmond Hurst
Stars: Alastair Sim, Kathleen Harrison, Jack Warner, Michael Hordern
Rating: ★★★★

Alastair Sim was born to play Charles Dickens' supernaturally reformed miser from *A Christmas Carol* and he relishes every moment of his time on screen to provide a performance to treasure. Kathleen Harrison, Mervyn Johns and a splendidly sepulchral Michael Hordern, as the ghost of Jacob Marley, offer sterling support and Brian Desmond Hurst's solid direction is complemented by the work of two directors-to-be, cinematographer C Pennington Richards and editor Clive Donner. The definitive screen version of the story.

Scrooge ○

1970, UK, 113 mins, colour
Dir: Ronald Neame
Stars: Albert Finney, Alec Guinness, Edith Evans, Kenneth More
Rating: ★★★

A great victory over poor material is enjoyed by Albert Finney as Scrooge, in this lively and lavish version. Alec Guinness and Edith Evans enjoy themselves as, respectively, Jacob Marley and the spirit of Christmas Past, but the screenplay is only middling and the music and lyrics by Leslie Bricusse fairly forgettable. It's left to Finney, whether scowling behind iced-up windows, or jigging for joy when converted by the Spirits, to bring this Christmas treat home in triumph.

Scrooged ◐ ⓥ

1988, US, 101 mins, colour
Dir: Richard Donner
Stars: Bill Murray, Karen Allen, John Forsythe
Rating: ★★★

Bill Murray's first star comedy in four years since *Ghost Busters* is an updating of *A Christmas Carol* with him cast in the Scrooge role as an utterly venal TV chief whose taste lies well and truly in the gutter. Attacked in some quarters for its questionable humour – a Richard Pryor flambé joke is particularly tasteless – it remains a top drawer production, with sumptuous sets and costumes, and some impressive special effects. Its comic highlight is unquestionably Carol Kane's appearance as the Ghost of Christmas

Present. She looks like the Good Witch of the North from *The Wizard of Oz*, but dispenses verbal and physical punishment with sadistic glee.

Sea Chase, The ○
1955, US, 117 mins, colour
Dir: John Farrow
Stars: John Wayne, Lana Turner, David Farrar, Lyle Bettger
Rating: ★★

John Wayne takes an unusual role in this vigorous war drama, as a skipper determined to steer his ship back to Germany despite a British blockade. The Wayne-Lana Turner combination doesn't quite ignite the sparks you'd expect, but there's a colourful supporting cast that includes David Farrar, Lyle Bettger, Tab Hunter, James Arness, John Qualen, Paul Fix and Claude Akins.

Sea Devils ○
1937, US, 88 mins, b/w
Dir: Ben Stoloff
Stars: Victor McLaglen, Preston Foster, Ida Lupino
Rating: ★★

Only Victor McLaglen or Wallace Beery could have played a character called Medals Malone and here it's McLaglen in a typically rough-and-ready vehicle about coastguards who seem to spend more time feuding with each other than carrying out their duties. The idea of ice patrols and daring sea rescues should make a good film story, but here the originality is all but stifled by the treatment. The performances, even from such experienced campaigners as McLaglen, Preston Foster and Ida Lupino, are rather too spirited for comfort.

Sea Devils ○
1953, UK, 91 mins, colour
Dir: Raoul Walsh
Stars: Yvonne de Carlo, Rock Hudson, Bryan Forbes
Rating: ★★

British-made action film about smuggling and espionage in the Napoleonic era, directed by American Raoul Walsh. One can only admire the untroubled gusto with which stars Rock Hudson and Yvonne de Carlo enter the fray. Events move at such a cracking pace it hardly seems to matter that so many of them are inexplicable. As the much-in-evidence friend of the hero, Britain's Bryan Forbes gets all the best lines and makes the most of them.

Sea Hawk, The ○ ⓥ
1940, US, 127 mins, b/w
Dir: Michael Curtiz
Stars: Errol Flynn, Brenda Marshall, Claude Rains, Flora Robson
Rating: ★★★★

This is Errol Flynn swashing his buckle as only he knows how. Although every bit as good as *The Adventures of Robin Hood*, *The Sea Hawk* hasn't achieved the same classic status. One possible explanation for this is that it isn't in colour. This doesn't stop the film being one of the most exciting adventure yarns ever made. Flynn is a privateer, robbing and sinking Spanish ships during the reign of Elizabeth I. Flora Robson is regal as Elizabeth, while Claude Rains is rascally as the cunning Spanish ambassador to the English court. Brenda Marshall is his beautiful daughter, whom Flynn falls for. Directed by Michael Curtiz, an action specialist who had already directed most of Flynn's other adventures, the film is fast-moving and thrilling right up to the almost balletic climactic duel between Flynn and traitor Henry Daniell. Wonderful stuff.

Sea of Grass, The ○
1947, US, 131 mins, b/w
Dir: Elia Kazan
Stars: Spencer Tracy, Katharine Hepburn, Robert Walker, Melvyn Douglas
Rating: ★★

The great Spencer Tracy-Katharine Hepburn team has the acting honours whisked from under its nose in this rather talky piece, and the culprit is that distinctive actor Robert Walker. Elia Kazan directs with his customary force, Robert Armstrong of *King Kong* fame, is effective in support.

Sea of Love ● ⓥ
1989, US, 108 mins, colour
Dir: Harold Becker
Stars: Al Pacino, Ellen Barkin, John Goodman
Rating: ★★★

This tightly scripted thriller about a killer who places romantic rhyming ads in newspaper personal columns and the Fifties' hit *Sea of Love* on the record player at the scenes of the crimes, marked a triumphant return to movies by Al Pacino four years after his disastrous flop, *Revolution*. His rivetting performance as a burned-out New York cop clutching at a second chance at love with chief suspect Ellen Barkin is the highlight of this glossy

film noir that will have you guessing to the final double twist ending. The sexual chemistry between the two leads is a big plus, as is the atmospheric photography of British cinematographer Ronnie Taylor. Patricia Barry also scores as a much older woman who heartbreakingly picks up the wrong vibes from Pacino over lunch after answering one of his own phony ads to catch the killer. Strong, adult and good.

Sea of Sand ○
(aka: Desert Patrol)
1958, UK, 97 mins, b/w
Dir: Guy Green
Stars: Richard Attenborough, John Gregson, Michael Craig
Rating: ★★★

Gruelling location filming in Libya paid off handsomely here, giving this gritty World War Two drama a compelling sense of the heat and desolation of the desert. The story is a moving and exciting one of a dangerous mission by the Long Range Desert Group to destroy a vital German petrol dump behind enemy lines in North Africa, strongly acted by the all-male cast. Director Guy Green stages tank battles, machine-gun duels and desperate crossings of minefields with great realism.

Searchers, The ○ ⓥ
1956, US, 119 mins, colour
Dir: John Ford
Stars: John Wayne, Jeffrey Hunter, Natalie Wood, Vera Miles
Rating: ★★★

Ethan (John Wayne) spends five years searching for his two nieces, abducted by Indians, in this lengthy Western, with some first-rate VistaVision photography rather dominating the acting of the leading players, what with Wayne sort of playing himself and Vera Miles being a bit disappointing. Jeffrey Hunter, though, is excellent and Ward Bond solid, while a great featured-role performance by veteran Antonio Moreno leads some eye-catching supporting acting, which includes a surprisingly small, if key role for the star-billed Natalie Wood. Action is pretty good, story first-rate and powerfully told too. You'll find the ending haunting, or overmelodramatic according to your tastes, although it's lovingly composed by director John Ford, who really picks up the pace towards the end. Full of wide open spaces and interesting characters, this may not be Ford or

Wayne's best Western, as many would claim, but it's still head and shoulders above most big-scale adventure films.

Sea Shall Not Have Them, The ○

1954, UK, 91 mins, b/w
Dir: Lewis Gilbert
Stars: Michael Redgrave, Dirk Bogarde, Anthony Steel
Rating: ★★

One of the most star-studded of all films, this harrowing tale of air-sea rescue was made by former boy actor Lewis Gilbert, soon to have a smash success on his hands with *Reach for the Sky*. Unfortunately, the scriptwriters set the film itself adrift in a sea of repetitious situations – but the cast itself brings redemption, from such megastars of the time as Michael Redgrave, Dirk Bogarde and Anthony Steel to a crew of familiar faces that includes Bonar Colleano, Nigel Patrick, Jack Watling, Anton Diffring, Guy Middleton, Griffith Jones, Paul Carpenter and Joan Sims.

Season of Passion
See: Summer of the Seventeenth Doll

Sea Wife ○ Ⓥ

1957, UK, 82 mins, colour
Dir: Bob McNaught
Stars: Richard Burton, Joan Collins, Basil Sydney, Cy Grant
Rating: ★★★

Four assorted shipwreck survivors – one of them a nun – are thrown together in an open boat in this adaptation of J M Scott's novel, *Sea Wyf and Biscuit*, which boasted explosive star power in Richard Burton and Joan Collins. Director Bob McNaught, who took over after Italian film-maker Roberto Rossellini had resigned from the production, shot the film in and around Jamaica. The four stars – Basil Sydney and Cy Grant were the other two – didn't have too much time to enjoy the local beauty spots: they spent long hours on and in the Caribbean. Commented Joan Collins at the time: 'When I made my first island picture (*Our Girl Friday*), I could hardly swim at all. Now I'm almost a second Esther Williams.'

Sea Wolf, The ○ Ⓥ

1940, US, 90 mins, b/w
Dir: Michael Curtiz
Stars: Edward G Robinson, Ida Lupino, John Garfield, Alexander Knox
Rating: ★★★

The studio's fog machines work overtime on this dark and moody adaptation of Jack London's famous story. Edward G Robinson again demonstrates his versatility, this time playing the tyrannical captain of the bad ship Ghost. It obviously wasn't too much for supporting cast members Barry Fitzgerald and Howard da Silva. They switched studios a few years later and signed up for *Two Years Before the Mast*.

Sea Wolves, The ○ Ⓥ

1980, UK, 120 mins, colour
Dir: Andrew V Mclaglen
Stars: Gregory Peck, David Niven, Roger Moore, Trevor Howard
Rating: ★★★

A spectacular war film about a crew of veteran saboteurs recruited to blow up a ship. The chief fascination about the film, as far as hardened film fans are concerned, will lie in the appearance, some of them with no more than a line or two to say, of such stalwarts of post-war British cinema as Patrick Allen, Patrick Holt, Percy Herbert, Donald Houston, Michael Medwin, Kenneth Griffith and several more besides. Most of them play members of the semi-retired group of saboteurs – they're not the 'Sea Wolves' of the title, by the way: that refers to the German U-boats that are doing the damage. Gregory Peck, Roger Moore, David Niven and Trevor Howard are the actual stars of the film and they all offer professionally competent performances, as does the director Andrew V McLaglen on the action sequences.

Sebastian ○

1967, UK, 95 mins, colour
Dir: David Greene
Stars: Dirk Bogarde, Susannah York, Lilli Palmer, John Gielgud
Rating: ★★★

Stylish, inventive comedy-thriller, with Dirk Bogarde as a super-brain, involved in code-breaking and dodging double-agents. Director David Greene, responsible for such diverse entertainments as *The Shuttered Room* and *Godspell*, sets the right note from the beginning, spicing the thrills with sophisticated laughs – notably in Sebastian's army of girl secretaries, all with pencils poised to put down his thoughts – and setting it all in motion at a cracking pace. You can spot Ann Sidney (former Miss World), Donald Sutherland and disc jockey Alan Freeman in minor roles.

Second Best Secret Agent in the Whole Wide World, The
See: Licensed to Kill

Second Chance ○

1953, US, 82 mins, colour
Dir: Rudolph Maté
Stars: Robert Mitchum, Jack Palance, Linda Darnell
Rating: ★★★

Vividly-shot thriller, with a climactic fight in a cable car, hundreds of feet above the ground, between those two big men of the screen – Robert Mitchum, as a prizefighter on the run from killing a man, and Jack Palance as a gangster. The ending must have been even more hair-raising in the 3-D for which the film was originally made.

Seconds ◑

1966, US, 110 mins, b/w
Dir: John Frankenheimer
Stars: Rock Hudson, Salome Jens, John Randolph
Rating: ★★

An exciting piece of science-fiction that only just failed to make the grade. The storyline bulges with originality. A middle-aged man, convinced that he has nothing left to live for, is offered a new life by a strange firm, employing bright-eyed plastic surgeons. A body, he is told, will be found; a death certificate will be issued. So far, so very good. John Randolph comes incredibly close to the life of the hollow man who is offered substance of a sort. And director John Frankenheimer holds a Hitchcock-like grip on the opening scenes, which leaves one's mouth dry with suspense. The macabre under-thoughts, too, are subtly implanted. The offer seems unbelievable if wondrous. But where do the bodies come from, for certification of death? Later, when Randolph has been transformed into Rock Hudson, the dialogue becomes less persuasive, the pace less positive. But the blood-chilling ending fully restores the film to its former high plane. And, although it's not the most effective or meaningful part of the story, a grape-orgy scene made the film famous.

Second Time Around, The ○

1961, US, 99 mins, colour
Dir: Vincent Sherman
Stars: Debbie Reynolds, Andy Griffith, Steve Forrest
Rating: ★★

S

In spite of a really strong supporting cast, this rambunctious romp soon turns into another one-woman show by Debbie Reynolds, who's all over the scenery as the winsome widow out west in 1912 who foils a bank raid and gets herself elected sheriff. A good-natured film with likeable characters (including one of the last of Thelma Ritter's treasurable cameos, almost inevitably as a character called Aggie), energetic fight scenes and smartly-paced direction by Vincent Sherman.

Secret Admirer ◐ Ⓥ
1985, US, 98 mins, colour
Dir: David Greenwalt
Stars: C Thomas Howell, Lori Loughlin, Kelly Preston, Fred Ward, Dee Wallace Stone, Casey Siemaszko
Rating: ★★

Above the average in ideas and general good humour for the high-school comedy of the mid-Eighties, this film's *raison d'etre* lies in the letters a lovestruck girl pens to the boy next door. In turn, she decides to rewrite the letters he's written to the nubile 17-year-old of his dreams. Certain letters get into certain other hands and in no time at all the boy's mother is on the verge of an affair with the sexbomb's father while the boy's father is responding to the overtures of the sexbomb's mother. There are genetic improbabilities in all this (a blonde daughter of parents with raven-dark hair for openers) but some funny lines too. 'What'd you think I should wear?' asks the sexbomb. 'Oh,' says her friend, the letter-writing cause of all the trouble, 'something demure'. 'Oh,' says the sexbomb. 'Christian Demure. I got tons of her stuff.' The inept Romeo duly gets his date with her. 'What should I do?' he gasps. 'Grow a moustache,' suggests the girl next door. 'Well,' he considers, 'if you can do it, I can.'

Secret Agent ○
1936, UK, 83 mins, b/w
Dir: Alfred Hitchcock
Stars: John Gielgud, Madeleine Carroll, Peter Lorre
Rating: ★★★

Following the previous year's *The 39 Steps*, Hitchcock again cast Madeleine Carroll as a feisty leading lady with considerably more get-up-and-go than the hero – here, the young John Gielgud as a spectacularly languorous spy reluctantly recruited to kill a foreign agent. Some fine set pieces –

including a climactic chase through a Swiss chocolate factory – and a scene-stealing performance from Peter Lorre.

Secret Beyond the Door, The ○
1948, US, 98 mins, b/w
Dir: Fritz Lang
Stars: Joan Bennett, Michael Redgrave
Rating: ★★★

Weird and wonderful movie from director Fritz Lang and star Joan Bennett, not as strong as their previous films together, *Man Hunt, The Women in the Window* and *Scarlet Street*, but definitely not your run-of-the-mill thriller. Bennett at her most beautiful and Michael Regrave at his most tormented just manage to suspend our disbelief through a mind-boggling tale of murder, jealousy, hallucination and mental disorder, set in a mansion of rooms that are replicas of famous murder sites, and mistily photographed in black and white by the great Stanley Cortez. If it had all worked, and had a stronger script, it might even have been a masterpiece of macabre.

Secret Four, The ○
(aka: Kansas City Confidential)
1954, US, 98 mins, b/w
Dir: Phil Karlson
Stars: John Payne, Coleen Gray
Rating: ★★★

This tough, tense study of a robbery is directed with fine ruthlessness of purpose by Phil Karlson. The 'four' all give good portrayals, not surprising when the actors are Preston Foster, Lee Van Cleef, Jack Elam and Neville Brand. Karlson was just hitting his stride at about this time, into a five-year period in which he made a series of films that are still considered his best work. Tough, hard-hitting action films, sometimes exposing actual scandals and criminal activities, they remain a slice of American cinema to be remembered. Titles include *99 River Street, Five Against the House, Tight Spot, The Phenix City Story* and *The Brothers Rico*.

Secret Friends ● Ⓥ
1992, UK, 98 mins, colour
Dir: Dennis Potter
Stars: Alan Bates, Gina Bellman, Tony Doyle, Frances Barber
Rating: RB

If you manage to make head or tail of Dennis Potter's enormously self-indulgent study of imaginary

friends, fantasies and a disordered mind you'll be a lot wiser than we were after seeing the whole film. Flower-painter Alan Bates, haunted by a repressed past, is going off his rocker. Ex high-class hooker Gina Bellman has been unwise enough to marry him. Well, probably not. This is more likely to be one of the many manifestations of a fevered brain shown in the film. You keep waiting for something coherent to happen: but this is not Potter's plan, which appears to be to bore the hide off his audience rather than let them get any sort of grasp on anthing approaching a plot. Bates is annoying; Bellman looks like Ava Gardner but hasn't the talent; Frances Barber hovers lasciviously on the fringes of the film waiting for something to do. Others strike poses as required by the director.

Secret Garden, The ⊙
1949, US, 92 mins, b/w
Dir: Fred M Wilcox
Stars: Margaret O'Brien, Herbert Marshall, Dean Stockwell, Gladys Cooper
Rating: ★★★

The awesomely-talented Margaret O'Brien steals the acting honours in this well-made film of Frances Hodgson Burnett's suspenseful novel. It proves to be richly atmospheric under the direction of Fred M Wilcox, who made his name with a string of immensely successful *Lassie* films, and later produced a masterpiece of the sci-fi genre in *Forbidden Planet*. Here he elicits a sensitive, attractive performance from O'Brien (not difficult, admittedly), who is joined by another child star of the Forties, Dean Stockwell. Don't adjust your set when the screen suddenly blazes into Technicolor.

Secret Garden, The ⊙
1987, UK, 96 mins, colour
Dir: Alan Grint
Stars: Gennie James, Michael Hordern, Billie Whitelaw
Rating: ★★★

Visually handsome adaptation of Frances Hodgson Burnett's popular children's novel, turned by MGM into a charming vehicle for Margaret O'Brien in 1949. This remake remains steadfastly faithful to the book, and is similarly disinclined to shy away from the serious subject of bereavement. It also benefits from some top-notch character acting by Michael Hordern (as the curmudgeonly gardener Ben) and Billie Whitelaw (perfectly cast as the Dickensian housekeeper Mrs Medlock). An engrossing couple of hours for adults and youngsters alike. Remade again in 1993.

Secret Garden, The ⊙ ⓥ
1993, UK, 100 mins, colour
Dir: Agnieszka Holland
Stars: Kate Maberly, Maggie Smith
Rating: ★★

A competent new version of the undentable Frances Hodgson Burnett novel about a spoiled (but unloved) 10-year-old girl, Mary, whose parents live in India and get killed in an earthquake there. Brought to the forbidding and loveless mansion of her widowed uncle and his hidebound housekeeper and servant, Mary soon proves more than a match for the lot, discovering hidden passageways, her sickly cousin Colin (who has never walked) and, of course, the secret garden of the title, where her uncle's wife died, giving premature birth to Colin, after falling off a swing. A lot depends on the central performance and Kate Maberly, although no great actress, is just right for the role. 'Everybody thinks I'll die,' wails Colin. 'Humph,' says Mary, arms akimbo. 'If people thought that of me, I wouldn't do it!' Maggie Smith has fun as the purse-lipped housekeeper, her best line coming when she tells the ailing boy 'You could be clotting.' It's a bit halting in pace, though, and the ending is on the weak side.

Secret Life of Walter Mitty, The ⊙
1947, US, 104 mins, colour
Dir: Norman Z McLeod
Stars: Danny Kaye, Virginia Mayo, Boris Karloff
Rating: ★★★

An extension of James Thurber's famous story of a man who lives in a world of daydreams, this is a custom-built vehicle for Danny Kaye's much-admired talents in the field of comedy and mimicry. The villains' roles are rather disappointingly ordinary, especially that given to old horror master Boris Karloff, leaving Kaye as the whole show. His impressions of fearless gunman, air ace, miracle surgeon, riverboat gambler (and many more) are topped off with his virtuoso rendition of 'Anatole of Paris'.

Secret of My Success, The ○
1965, UK, 112 mins, colour
Dir: Andrew L Stone
Stars: James Booth, Lionel Jeffries, Shirley Jones, Honor Blackman
Rating: ★★

Pleasing comedy about an inept policeman who unwittingly helps three lovely but lethal ladies of crime. Lionel Jeffries does a mini-Alec Guinness by playing four parts.

Secret of My Success, The ○ ⓥ
1987, US, 110 mins, colour
Dir: Herbert Ross
Stars: Michael J Fox, Helen Slater, Richard Jordan
Rating: ★★

Hick from the sticks Michael J Fox wants the ultimate yuppie dream – a penthouse in New York, jacuzzi, a beautiful girlfriend and a private jet to go home in. Setting up in an abandoned office, his life becomes ever more complicated by the attentions of his uncle's neglected wife and the fact that the girl of his dreams is his uncle's mistress. A nice twist on the classic screwball farces of the 1930s, but given a leaden treatment and suffering from the lightweight central performance and the Eighties' vogue to replace dialogue and speed up the action. The film does capture well New York as a city of gleaming steel and concrete – but too often the characters seem to be made of the same stuff.

Secret of NIMH, The ⊙
1982, US, 82 mins, colour
Dir: Don Bluth
Voice stars: Derek Jacobi, Dom DeLuise, Shannen Doherty, Wil Wheaton
Rating: ★★★

This was the first film from Don Bluth and fellow Disney animators who tired of the way the American studio was penny pinching on their feature length films and set up in exile in Ireland. The story of a mother mouse desperately trying to save her family from a farmer's plans to plough over their home, is beautifully animated but strangely uninvolving because of a weak script. The assembled voice cast is outstanding, including Derek Jacobi, Dom DeLuise, Shannen Doherty and Wil Wheaton.

Secret of the Incas, The ○
1954, US, 103 mins, colour
Dir: Jerry Hopper

Stars: Charlton Heston, Nicole Maurey, Robert Young, Thomas Mitchell
Rating: ★★

Rugged, if unsubtle, jungle thriller – the kind of stuff that Steven Spielberg nowadays turns into an extravaganza. Charlton Heston is very good as the ruthless adventurer hunting a priceless Inca jewel. And he gets good support from veteran Hollywood character actor Thomas Mitchell. Colour and scenery are excellent and the plot has a neat twist at the end.

Secret Partner, The ○
1961, UK, 91 mins, b/w
Dir: Basil Dearden
Stars: Stewart Granger, Haya Harareet
Rating: ★★★

A tightly-written thriller starring Stewart Granger which keeps the suspense going until the last reel. Norman Bird is excellent as a seedy, blackmailing dentist. Another unheralded, low-key winner from the consistent Basil Dearden.

Secret Rapture, The ● ⓥ
1993, UK, 96 mins, colour
Dir: Howard Davies
Stars: Juliet Stevenson, Neil Pearson, Joanne Whalley-Kilmer, Penelope Wilton
Rating: ★

Heavy drama, cheerless people: this is a doleful piece from the Film on Four stable which has an interesting performance from Juliet Stevenson (though she takes her clothes off too often) but little else to bring a smile in any sense. Not least of its deficiencies is a budget apparently so low that no-one ever wants to turn the light on. As bleak as the stone cottage whose elderly owner's death triggers the drama, the story concerns his young alcoholic widow (Joanne Whalley-Kilmer) and the foisting of her, via embittered sister Penelope Wilton and husband Alan Howard, on to Stevenson and her lover Neil Pearson, whose graphic design business has previously kept them happy. Pearson's *volte-face* in agreeing to sell the business to Wilton for expansion is only one of the things insufficiently validated by David Hare's screenplay, which too often speaks in disconnected phrases which seem couched for theatrical effect rather than advancing the characters. The ending is at least in character with the rest, although those in a depressed mood are advised to stay clear.

S

Seekers, The ○
1954, UK, 90 mins, colour
Dir: Ken Annakin
Stars: Jack Hawkins, Glynis Johns
Rating: ★★

Rip-roaring saga of pioneers trying to forge new frontiers in 19th-century New Zealand against all the odds. An uncertain attempt to match the power and sweep of the American covered-wagon epics, with Maoris doing the marauding Injuns bit and the British settlers standing in for the cowboys. It has its exciting moments and, thanks to Geoffrey Unsworth's handsome colour photography, the unfamiliar locations are always good to look at.

See No Evil
See: Blind Terror

See No Evil, Hear No Evil ● ⓥ
1989, US, 107 mins, colour
Dir: Arthur Hiller
Stars: Richard Pryor, Gene Wilder, Joan Severance
Rating: ★

Getting a blind man and a deaf man to be each other's eyes and ears against a gang of crooks sounds like a great comic idea. But with Wilder and Pryor offering overpitched performances (especially when giving painful impersonations of foreign doctors), the results are pretty feeble – except for a couple of bright sequences here and there. The female lead, Joan Severance, must have been hired for her stunning looks rather than acting ability and the only highspots are blind Pryor being asked to help another blind man across the road, and two blind men stalking each other with revolvers. Parents might also note that this has an amazingly high ration of four-letter words for a comedy. Still, if you want a comedy-adventure that's frantic if not funny, this could pass a couple of hours without too much pain.

See You in Hell, Darling ◑
1966, US, 103 mins, colour
Dir: Robert Gist
Stars: Stuart Whitman, Janet Leigh, Eleanor Parker
Rating: ★★

A harsh amoral gangster yarn, adapted from Norman Mailer's novel *An American Dream.* The theme and its treatment are reminiscent of Hollywood thrillers of the Forties, with Whitman as an anti-gangster television crusader who falls into the clutches of the underworld through the death of his wife. In a small part as a maid, who, clad only in towel and shower-water, tries to seduce the hero, Austrian actress Susan Denberg, with sulky stare, flaxen tresses and eyes like opaque green marble, quite walks away with the film.

See You in the Morning ◑ ⓥ
1988, US, 119 mins, colour
Dir: Alan J Pakula
Stars: Jeff Bridges, Alice Krige, Farrah Fawcett, Drew Barrymore, Macaulay Culkin
Rating: ★

It's hard to know what to say about a film as dull as this. Of two marriages in 1984, one breaks up, the other leaves the wife a widow. The husband of the first (Jeff Bridges) marries the widow (Alice Krige), misses his two children and has a few minor problems with his two stepchildren. This all takes two hours to unfold and the best the film can do in the way of a spanner in the works is having the husband sleeping with his ex-wife (Farrah Fawcett) the night after his mother dies. The script never gives the players a chance to pluck the heartstrings and even gets mawkish at times. You can see that director Pakula was trying to make a valid human document here, but his writers have let him down by the sheer ordinariness of their script.

Sellout, The ◑
1975, UK/Italy, 102 mins, colour
Dir: Peter Collinson
Stars: Richard Widmark, Oliver Reed, Gayle Hunnicutt
Rating: ★

This espionage thriller must have seemed an attractively downbeat drama during its conception although, as it turns out, the screenplay gives it very little character. Oliver Reed plays an ex-CIA agent who defected to Moscow, and is now lured to Israel where he is the target for both CIA and KGB killers. The stunt driving is by Remy Julienne, so effective on *The Italian Job,* although here the object seems only to be for the cars to knock down as many unnecessary obstacles as possible.

Semi-Tough ◑
1977, US, 103 mins, colour
Dir: Michael Ritchie
Stars: Burt Reynolds, Kris Kristofferson, Jill Clayburgh
Rating: ★★

Jill Clayburgh, the delightful Hollywood actress who sounds as though she gargles honey, makes a silk purse out of a sow's ear in this freewheeling comedy. The film, mainly about the relationship between Ms Clayburgh, Burt Reynolds and a miscast Kris Kristofferson, tries very, very hard to be outrageous. That it succeeds in being merely quite funny is to our advantage. Reynolds' natural charm supplies most of the laughs – more, in fact, than the aimless script has any right to expect.

Senator Was Indiscreet, The ○
(aka: Mr Ashton Was Indiscreet)
1947, US, 81 mins, b/w
Dir: George S Kaufman
Stars: William Powell, Ella Raines, Peter Lind Hayes
Rating: ★★★

Don't miss the chance to see this rare screwball comedy, written by Charles MacArthur (late husband of Helen Hayes and father of James MacArthur) whose Hollywood career was harmed by the McCarthy blacklist. His witty script is anarchic without being too satirical, pitching William Powell's asinine senator, up for President, into a series of splendidly ridiculous situations. Especially funny is the sequence where Powell takes on a bunch of kids in an IQ test – and loses.

Send Me No Flowers ○
1964, US, 1964 mins, colour
Dir: Norman Jewison
Stars: Rock Hudson, Doris Day
Rating: ★★★

You'll get a good quota of laughs from this grey comedy (it isn't really sinister enough to be called black) about a hypochondriac (Rock Hudson) who believes, through a misunderstanding with his long-suffering doctor, that he is dying from a heart condition. Doris Day was probably the only Hollywood actress of the time who could have handled this brand of light, bright comedy-with-kinks in such expert fashion. Tony Randall is even better than usual as the inevitable sidekick of the hero, and toothsome Paul Lynde also scores as a funeral director with a lugubrious leer, giving away green stamps with his plot reservations. But the real winner is Julius Epstein's screenplay, full of funny lines and situations which enable the actors to make the most of themselves.

Separate Tables ○
1958, US, 98 mins, b/w
Dir: Delbert Mann
Stars: Deborah Kerr, Rita Hayworth, David Niven, Burt Lancaster
Rating: ★★★

This fine, enjoyable film about the hidden weaknesses of the guests at an English seaside hotel (adapted from his own play by Terence Rattigan) provides absorbing entertainment and a feast of fine acting. For their sensitive portrayals, David Niven, as the fake major, and Wendy Hiller, as the hotel proprietress, both won deserved Academy Awards. Niven's last few scenes in the film are especially moving.

September ○ ⓥ
1987, US, 83 mins, colour
Dir: Woody Allen
Stars: Mia Farrow, Denholm Elliott, Sam Waterston, Elaine Stritch, Dianne Wiest, Jack Warden
Rating: ★

Woody Allen shot this script with one set of actors, then decided to scrap the results and do it all over again with a completely different cast. He should have quit while he was ahead. Boring is the word and only Britain's Denholm Elliott in an elegant, low-key performance, can handle Allen's overwrought romantic dialogue with the appropriate kid gloves. The lives of these artificial characters of fiction, and of Mia Farrow's mother and stepfather (Elaine Stritch, Jack Warden), whose past is clearly copied from Lana Turner's, are only of the vaguest interest and if your attention is gripped at all by this sexual merry-go-round, it will be by how the actors handle their key emotional scenes: Farrow best, Dianne Wiest whiningly worst and so on. The film is largely photographed in brown and yellow except for scenes involving a pool table for which such filters would clearly be inappropriate.

September Affair ○
1950, US, 104 mins, b/w
Dir: William Dieterle
Stars: Joan Fontaine, Joseph Cotten, Francoise Rosay
Rating: ★★★

Exceptionally well-made weepie about a couple who decide to seize their

chance for love late in life, when they are reported killed in an air crash. Director William Dieterle steers it on its romantic way with tremendous pictorial flair. He had been responsible in previous years for such richly varied entertainments as *A Midsummer Night's Dream, The Life of Emile Zola, Juarez, The Hunchback of Notre Dame, Kismet, Portrait of Jennie* and *Salome.* Although many of his films took Academy Awards, Dieterle himself never won one.

Sergeant, The ●
1968, US, 107 mins, colour
Dir: John Flynn
Stars: Rod Steiger, John Phillip Law, Ludmila Mikael
Rating: ★★

John Flynn's first feature film – he later directed *The Jerusalem File* and the brilliant crime thriller *The Outfit* – is one of the most powerful portrayals of a man destroyed by his own homosexuality to be put on screen. Rod Steiger pours everything into his portrait of Master-Sergeant Callan and it hurts to watch the man's disintegration. It isn't a likeable film, nor exactly an enjoyable one. If it were a book, however, you would find it hard to put it down.

Sergeant Rutledge ●
1960, US, 111 mins, colour
Dir: John Ford
Stars: Jeffrey Hunter, Woody Strode, Constance Towers
Rating: ★★

This was truly a landmark film, as it marked a rare occasion when a movie from a major studio (Warner Brothers) depicted a black actor as the central heroic figure. Woody Strode gives a moving performance as a sergeant accused of the murder of his commanding officer and rape and murder of the dead man's daughter. While the film's stance on tackling racism is laudable, the courtroom setting proves too claustrophobic for director John Ford, and the master of the unspoken emotion has to rely on long speeches to get his points across. Strode, who was quite an inexperienced actor in terms of major roles, was tricked by Ford for the filming of his pivotal final speech. Ford threw a drinks party for him and told him the next day's shooting was cancelled. Then he had him dragged from bed at six the next morning, groggy and very hung over. But the wily director got the result he wanted. Former silent

star Mae Marsh, who was one of D W Griffith's regular heroines and retired in 1925, made one of her rare latter-day appearances in a small role.

Sergeant York ○ ⓥ
1941, US, 134 mins, b/w
Dir: Howard Hawks
Stars: Gary Cooper, Walter Brennan
Rating: ★★★

One of Gary Cooper's finest roles, as a true-life peace-loving farmer who becomes a hero of World War One. The film's patriotic sentiments were immensely popular in the dark early days of World War Two and Cooper's sensitive and caring performance was rightly rewarded with an Oscar. There's a nice balance between rural and combat sequences and simply superb black-and-white photography by Arthur Edeson. Too long, perhaps, but that's partially justified by the atmosphere the movie builds.

Serpico ●
1973, US, 129 mins, colour
Dir: Sidney Lumet
Stars: Al Pacino, John Randolph, Cornelia Sharpe
Rating: ★★★

Al Pacino gives a very edgy and intelligent performance as Frank Serpico, the honest and idealistic cop who sees corruption all around him. Based on a true story, director Sidney Lumet's intense and hard-hitting thriller hits all the right notes and maintains its dramatic tension from beginning to end. Although Pacino's portrayal dominates the film, all the supporting roles are finely cast, particularly Tony Roberts, who plays an officer close to the mayor's investigating committee. Sharp eyes will spot Oscar winner F Murray Abraham in a small role as a detective.

Servant, The ● ⓥ
1964, UK, 110 mins, b/w
Dir: Joseph Losey
Stars: Dirk Bogarde, James Fox
Rating: ★★★

An illogical ending is the only sin committed by Joseph Losey's otherwise splendid black-and-white investigation into the treachery and power of evil. Dirk Bogarde does brilliantly as the calculating servant, especially in the lighter scenes after Tony (James Fox) has re-engaged him, when for a few moments he becomes more akin to a nagging housewife. For the most part, however, the perfor-

S

mance is more likely to make your flesh creep than to tickle your funnybone.

Set Up, The ○
1949, US, 72 mins, b/w
Dir: Robert Wise
Stars: Robert Ryan, Audrey Totter
Rating: ★★★★

Powerful, thrilling and very moving in turn, this fine film is now universally recognised as one of the two or three best boxing movies ever made. It was directed by Robert Wise long before he won Oscars for *West Side Story* and *The Sound of Music*, and contains one of the screen's great perfomances from Robert Ryan as an ageing boxer whose manager hasn't bothered to tell him that he is supposed to take a dive. Cleverly, the action takes place within the same time span as the movie, which underlines the tension.

Seven Chances ⊙
1925, US, 69 mins, b/w
Dir: Buster Keaton
Stars: Buster Keaton
Rating: ★★★

Lovely, cleanly-made Buster Keaton comedy, directed by the star. It's the one in which Buster has but a few hours to find a bride and ends up getting pursued by a veritable army of ferocious women. He is also pursued, in another scene, by an avalanche of rocks – yet another sequence that reflects Keaton's unshowy mastery of comic timing.

Seven Cities of Gold ○
1955, US, 103 mins, colour
Dir: Robert D Webb
Stars: Richard Egan, Anthony Quinn, Michael Rennie, Rita Moreno
Rating: ★

20th Century-Fox took their De Luxe Color cameras, helped by ace cameraman Lucien Ballard, on location to make this action and adventure yarn about Spanish explorers in 18th-century Mexico and California. A sincere religious theme fails to lift this history book Western from the routine class, although it provides Michael Rennie with the plum role, as the priest along on the expedition. Acting with great feeling, he's streets ahead even of such spirited company as Rita Moreno and Anthony Quinn.

Seven Days in May ○
1964, US, 120 mins, b/w
Dir: John Frankenheimer

Stars: Burt Lancaster, Kirk Douglas, Fredric March, Ava Gardner
Rating: ★★★

John Frankenheimer's powerful thriller about a coup d'etat in the United States. Burt Lancaster plays the grim-faced leader of the military conspirators, Fredric March the President who uses advance warning of the take-over to try and prevent it. The film is admirable for its brisk efficiency. March is particularly good as the President, but it's in Edmond O'Brien's senator and Martin Balsam's presidential aide and life-long friend that one sees the breath of life. Ava Gardner is better here than for years past. For Lancaster and Kirk Douglas, it seems too often an exercise in acting technique – but Rod Serling's crackling screenplay keeps their performances rooted in reality.

Seven Days to Noon ○
1950, UK, 93 mins, b/w
Dir: John Boulting
Stars: Barry Jones, Olive Sloane, André Morell, Joan Hickson
Rating: ★★★

A classic thriller from the Boulting Brothers in the days before they turned their talents to comedy. Barry Jones has the best part of his career as the unbalanced scientist who threatens to blow up the Houses of Parliament unless his demands are met. The suspense grows almost unbearable in the subsequent search for the scientist and the bomb he has planted. One of the screen's most reliable character actors, Victor Maddern, makes his screen debut as a soldier.

Seven Faces of Dr Lao ○
1964, US, 95 mins, colour
Dir: George Pal
Stars: Tony Randall, Barbara Eden, Arthur O'Connell, John Ericson
Rating: ★★

That expert light comedian Tony Randall enjoys himself hugely in a very different characterisation as a Chinese magician – at large in a turn-of-the-century America – who can turn himself into anything. Barbara Eden, nowadays better known as a singer, proves she can act as well, and the special effects – when the magician changes himself into all kinds of creatures, natural and mythical – are admirable. Pleasing supporting cast includes John Qualen, Lee Patrick and Noah Beery Jr.

Seven Hills of Rome ○
1957, US/Italy, 104 mins, colour
Dir: Roy Rowland
Stars: Mario Lanza, Marisa Allasio, Peggie Castle
Rating: ★★

Made a year before Lanza's death, this musical might well have been titled *An American in Rome*. But, in keeping with the trends of the time, the waif-like Continental girl, as personified by Leslie Caron, was replaced by a busty Italian charmer, in this case Marisa Allasio, who had already built up a reputation in some torrid melodramas. Lanza, cast as a successful singer revisiting the land of his fathers, offers a liberal display of tonsils and interesting impressions of Dean Martin, Perry Como, Frankie Laine and even Louis Armstrong! Ms Allasio offers a liberal helping of daring decolletage hardly in keeping with her role as a sweet Italian working girl. But the film is stolen from both of them by impish Italian comedian Renato Rascel.

Seven Little Foys, The ○
1955, US, 95 mins, colour
Dir: Melville Shavelson
Stars: Bob Hope, Milly Vitale
Rating: ★★★

Based on a true story, this musical-whimsical-sentimental look at the life of renowned vaudeville performer Eddie Foy cramps Bob Hope's style by casting him in an unsympathetic and uncomic role. It's left to James Cagney, recreating his Oscar-winning role from *Yankee Doodle Dandy* of song-and-dance man George M Cohan, to steal the show. Together he and Hope hoof their way through 'Mary's a Grand Old Dame' and 'Yankee Doodle Dandy' and momentarily the screen lights up.

Seven Nights in Japan ○
1976, UK, 104 mins, colour
Dir: Lewis Gilbert
Stars: Michael York, Hidemi Aoki, James Villiers
Rating: ★

A truly sticky romance about an English prince who falls for a Japanese geisha girl who doubles as a tour-bus conductress. It does have one very funny line, when tourist Yolande Donlan (in for a brief cameo) asks her husband, with regard to a statue: 'How many concubines did he have?' Replies hubby, with some logic: 'I guess he had 'em all.'

Seven Samurai ○ ⊽
1954, Japan, 208 mins, b/w
Dir: Akira Kurosawa
Stars: Takashi Shimura, Toshiro Mifune
Rating: ★★★★

Akira Kurosawa took an elemental
Western 'good guys versus bad guys'
plot and turned it into a classic epic
which is still probably the best-known
– and one of the best – films to come
from Japan where, at the time of its
making, it was that country's most
expensive picture ever. Kurosawa's
pacing is immaculate and allows for
periods of calm in which to establish
character, punctuated by viscerally
exciting bursts of action which culminate in the extraordinary climactic
battle between the samurai and the
bandits which ranks among the very
finest combat sequences ever put on
film. Unlike John Sturges' remake,
The Magnificent Seven, the characters
grow originally from the action and
are not conveniently established by
star-castings. And the performances –
even those of the bit players – are superb, with Toshiro Mifune's portrait
of the harebrained but courageous
young warrior dominating the proceedings.

Seven Sinners ○
(aka: Doomed Cargo)
1936, UK, 70 mins, b/w
Dir: Albert De Courville
Stars: Edmund Lowe, Constance
Cummings
Rating: ★★★

A vintage thriller with a clever plot,
likeable characters and an express
train as one of its settings (as in
Hitchcock's *The Lady Vanishes* two
years later). Both films were written
by that distinguished duo, Frank
Launder and Sidney Gilliat. Their
plot developments here may well have
you struggling to identify the guilty
party.

Seven Sinners ○
1940, US, 86 mins, b/w
Dir: Tay Garnett
Stars: Marlene Dietrich, John Wayne
Rating: ★★★

'We don't need her around,' someone
complains, 'the Navy already has
plenty of destroyers.' The reference is
to Marlene Dietrich, singing siren of
the South Seas, who takes John
Wayne's mind away from ships. Spirited entertainment, made in the wake
of *Destry Rides Again*, with three
songs, much fisticuffs, and a jolly cast.

7th Cavalry ○
1956, US, 75 mins, colour
Dir: Joseph H Lewis
Stars: Randolph Scott, Barbara Hale
Rating: ★★★

This Western is just a shade different,
thanks to Peter Packer's screenplay,
and especially to the direction of Joseph H Lewis. He never really rose
above the second feature, but turned
in some fine work within the genre,
notably in *So Dark the Night*, *The
Swordsman* and *The Undercover Man*.
The story is about a cavalry officer
accused of cowardice who is placed in
charge of misfits and 'ne'er-do-wells'
detailed to bury the dead after the
massacre of the Little Big Horn. Good
cast of 'misfits' includes Jay C Flippen
and Denver Pyle.

7th Dawn, The ○
1964, US, 123 mins, colour
Dir: Lewis Gilbert
Stars: William Holden, Susannah York,
Capucine, Tetsuro Tamba, Sydney Tafler
Rating: ★

A colourful adventure-romance set in
the terrorist-torn Malaya of the 1950s.
The story is the old reliable of two
men, friends in the war against the
Japanese who, years later, find
themselves on opposite sides. It's all
quite exciting, although the ending is
a disappointing anti-climax. Of the
four stars, Capucine is the only one
who gives her role any real feeling, as
the other three – William Holden,
Susannah York and Tetsuro Tamba –
go through absolute hell in rain, mud
and undergrowth to save her from
hanging for a crime she did not
commit. Sydney Tafler is very good in
support as a sympathetic police chief.
Director Lewis Gilbert drives his
players hard, although his efforts are
often stunted by Karl Tunberg's clichéd
script. Sample: Ms York (discovered
swimming in the nude): 'I'm in
excellent condition.' Holden: 'Yes,
you look in good shape.'

Seventh Heaven ○
1937, US, 102 mins, b/w
Dir: Henry King
Stars: Simone Simon, James Stewart
Rating: ★★

This wartime romance is a tearstrewn
remake of the 1927 classic, with
James Stewart and Simone Simon in
the roles created by Charles Farrell and
Janet Gaynor. This time, however,
acting honours are secured by screen
schemer Gale Sondergaard as the cru-

elly dominant Nana. She was unlucky
not to be nominated for an Oscar, the
year after she actually won the award,
for her performance in *Anthony
Adverse*.

Seventh Match, The
See: Sarah

Seventh Seal, The ○ ⊽
1957, Sweden, 96 mins, b/w
Dir: Ingmar Bergman
Stars: Max Von Sydow, Bengt Ekerot
Rating: ★★★★

One of Ingmar Bergman's most brilliant and approachable films, as a
knight returning from the Crusades
plays chess with Death for the lives of
his companions while the plague rages
all around. Full of images that stay in
the mind (especially in the final sequence), *The Seventh Seal* ranks with
The Silence and *Wild Strawberries* as the
best of Bergman's films, but is probably the one you should see above all
others. As the knight, Max Von
Sydow made his first major impact on
international audiences.

Seventh Sign, The ● ⊽
1988, US, 97 mins, colour
Dir: Carl Schultz
Stars: Demi Moore, Michael Biehn,
Jurgen Prochnow, Lee Garlington, John
Heard
Rating: ★★

This preposterous poppycook,
mumbo-jumbo in the *Omen* mould, is
stylishly and emotively made and
benefits from an impassioned
performance by Demi Moore in the
leading role. She's a pregnant
American wife who alone can prevent
the Apocalypse, the destruction of the
world. You see, we've already had the
rivers of blood, the desert village
frozen in ice, an eclipse, the death of
the oceans and all that. The birth of
the first baby without a soul (Demi's),
due to the emptying of the celestial
Guf (no comment) is the final sign –
and that's what she has to prevent. It's
to the credit of the actors and
technicians that this arrant nonsense –
'It was written by the prophets as poetry not a laundry list', one character
says but that's a bit how the film treats
it – keeps our attention if not our belief. Michael Biehn is sincere as
Moore's husband, Peter Friedman fun
as the priest who turns out to be
Pilate's gatekeeper (yes he does) and
Manny Jacobs amusing as a knowl-
edgable young Jew who has trouble

S

helping Demi with quotations from the New Testament because it's 'not my book'.

Seven Thunders ○
(aka: The Beasts of Marseilles)
1957, UK, 100 mins, b/w
Dir: Hugo Fregonese
Stars: Stephen Boyd, Tony Wright, Anna Gaylor
Rating: ★★★

A good Marseilles setting lifts this prisoner-of-war escape film out of the rut. The tensions of the occupied town, outwardly unruffled, inwardly seething with intrigue, are effectively suggested. James Robertson Justice is colourfully improbable as a French man who offers freedom but deals in double-cross. Anna Gaylor, a French actress with looks, charm and style, and Kathleen Harrison (miscast but great fun as Madame Abou) add body to a supporting cast in which Rosalie Crutchley, Marcel Pagliero and Eugene Deckers give the settings a believable smack of wartime Marseilles life. Director Hugo Fregonese's skilful handling of the suspense reaches a nailbiting peak when the two English heroes are forced to make a desperate bid for freedom after the Germans begin a systematic destruction of their quarter of the city. Steely-eyed Anton Diffring is inevitably cast as a Nazi officer.

7th Voyage of Sinbad, The ○
1958, US, 87 mins, colour
Dir: Nathan Juran
Stars: Kerwin Mathews, Kathryn Grant
Rating: ★★★

The film that started the DynaMation craze and made the reputation of the system's creator, Ray Harryhausen, who provides monsters galore to thrill children and adults alike. A snake-woman, a dragon, a man-eating Cyclops, two-headed rocs and living skeletons (to become Harryhausen's favourite 'characters' in later films) are all impressive.

Seven-ups, The ◐
1973, US, 103 mins, colour
Dir: Philip D'Antoni
Stars: Roy Scheider, Tony Lo Bianco
Rating: ★★★★

Philip D'Antoni, who produced *The French Connection*, turned director himself with this even-darker, hard-driving detective yarn, with spectacularly successful results. The set-pieces, especially the nerve-grinding mid-film sequence in a carwash which becomes a chamber of doom, are hard, uncompromising and right on target. Roy Scheider contributes a performance of almost frightening power in the pivotal role of the senior detective hunting down a group of loan-sharks: no soft-centred detective this. The sharp, low-key colour photography of Urs Furrer is absolutely right, and the final dialogue between Scheider and Tony Lo Bianco forms a devasting and brilliantly-fashioned coda to a very cinematic crime thriller.

Seven Ways from Sundown ○
1960, US, 87 mins, colour
Dir: Harry Keller
Stars: Audie Murphy, Barry Sullivan, John McIntire
Rating: ★★★

Better-than-average Audie Murphy Western, with an excellent performance from Barry Sullivan as a wily outlaw whom a young lawman – his name is Seven-Ways-from-Sundown Jones and thus the title – has to escort back to justice. Clair Huffaker's inventive screenplay has the vein of humour that keeps this sort of film going well: the continual element of surprise and turning-of-the-tables, deft acting from all concerned and of course, the shoot-out – here with a subtle difference. Exciting stuff.

7 Women ◐
1964, US, 80 mins, colour
Dir: John Ford
Stars: Anne Bancroft, Eddie Albert, Mike Mazurki, Flora Robson, Margaret Leighton
Rating: ★★★

John Ford forsook Westerns, but stayed with action, to make this absorbing adventure film about a mission on the violent Chinese-Mongolian border in 1935. Anne Bancroft has the John Wayne role as a cigarette-smoking, jackbooted, stetsoned doctor, and plays it superbly, while the Metrocolor photography is absolutely splendid. Eddie Albert and Mike Mazurki lead the male contingent.

Seven Year Itch, The ○ ⓥ
1955, US, 105 mins, colour
Dir: Billy Wilder
Stars: Marilyn Monroe, Tom Ewell
Rating: ★★★

Always entertaining, at times vastly amusing, this famous comedy has

Tom Ewell at the top of his form as a fortyish husband left alone while his wife and son go off on holiday. Soon, he forms the famous but abortive liaison with the blond upstairs (Marilyn Monroe), his wolfish dreams coming to nothing in the face of her brick-solid ingenuousness and his own ineptitude. Clever performances by the stars, with the funniest sequences of all being those in which Ewell dreams of himself as the great lover.

Severed Head, A ●
1970, UK, 96 mins, colour
Dir: Dick Clement
Stars: Lee Remick, Richard Attenborough, Ian Holm, Claire Bloom
Rating: ★

Determinedly smart and sophisticated comedy about partner-swapping in the supertax belt. Adapted by Frederic Raphael from the hit play, which was in turn taken by J B Priestley and Iris Murdoch from Ms Murdoch's blackly funny novel of the early Sixties. Director Dick Clement accentuates the glossiness a shade too much, but the ladies in the cast, Lee Remick, Claire Bloom, Jennie Linden and Ann Firbank, all acquit themselves admirably.

Sex and the Single Girl ○
1964, US, 114 mins, colour
Dir: Richard Quine
Stars: Tony Curtis, Natalie Wood, Henry Fonda, Lauren Bacall
Rating: ★★

A sex comedy that's as crisp and polished as the thin ice over which it so skilfully skates. In an hilarious last 20 minutes, the starry cast are all outshone by Larry Storch as a hatchet-faced motor-cycle cop with cars stamped on his machine. At other times, Henry Fonda and Lauren Bacall show their experience in coolly outpointing Tony Curtis and Natalie Wood. Mel Ferrer, Edward Everett Horton and even Count Basie and his Orchestra are all in there somewhere as Helen Gurley Brown's book (allegedly the source material) is pushed aside in favour of sex 'n' slapstick capers.

sex, lies and videotape ● ⓥ
1989, US, 100 mins, colour
Dir: Steven Soderbergh
Stars: James Spader, Andie MacDowell, Peter Gallagher, Laura San Giacomo
Rating: ★★★

Although this piece is not exactly ideal cinema material, its deliberate pace, carefully considered acting and doomy background music do sneak under your guard after a while. The catalyst to the action, such as it is, is James Spader as a drifter majoring in weirdness who looks up an old friend (Peter Gallagher) whose affair with his wife's sister (Laura San Giacomo) is on the verge of writing finis to his crumbling yuppie marriage to Andie MacDowell. Spader's occupation is interviewing women about their sex lives, and in the course of the next few days, some 'trapped' people are freed and 'free' people deservedly trapped. Despite its foul language and sombre approach to the eponymous items, this is a film which champions, in the end, all the traditional values of love and happiness. Spader is perfectly cast as the alienated soul who can only 'get on' with his tapes, and MacDowell gives a glowing account of the wronged wife who, clearly going round the bend at the start of the film, is accidentally and miraculously gifted with a chance to repair her life.

Shadowlands ○ ⓥ
1993, UK, 131 mins, colour
Dir: Richard Attenborough
Stars: Anthony Hopkins, Debra Winger, Edward Hardwicke, Michael Denison, Joseph Mazzello, John Wood
Rating: ★★

Impeccable performances by Anthony Hopkins, Debra Winger and especially Edward Hardwicke (as Hopkins' brother) illuminate this story of the initially unspoken love affair between the academic and children's author C S Lewis and the Jewish Communist American poet Joy Gresham. It's their efforts that touch the heart in this otherwise dusty account of a dying woman that might almost be called *A Stately Way to Go*. Director Richard Attenborouh has not so much filmed William Nicholson's fine play as embalmed it. But the dialogue, as literate as Lewis himself, and with a welcome sense of gallows humour, proves a sturdy ally to the actors' efforts. 'See what it takes to make me see sense,' smiles Hopkins, as he tells Winger he loves her (following a marriage of 'convenience' to help her stay in Britain) after learning she has cancer. 'Think I've overdone it?' she replies. A film that will bore children, though patient adults will find the dialogue and acting enough to sustain them.

Shadow Makers ◐ ⓥ
(aka: Fat Man and Little Boy)
1989, US, 127 mins, colour
Dir: Roland Joffe
Stars: Paul Newman, Dwight Schultz, Bonnie Bedelia, John Cusack
Rating: ★

Immaculately set in its period, this film about the making of the first atomic bomb by the Americans is not a bad movie, merely a dull one. But, at 127 minutes, that's almost as grievous a sin. Almost nothing happens until near the end, when one of the main characters gets burned by radiation, and there's very little that Newman (as the military head of the project), Schultz (as Oppenheimer, the brains behind it), Bedelia, Cusack, Laura Dern, Natasha Richardson and the rest of a very distinguished cast can do to enliven it. A film that talks itself out of being any good.

Shadow of a Doubt ○
1943, US, 108 mins, b/w
Dir: Alfred Hitchcock
Stars: Teresa Wright, Joseph Cotten, MacDonald Carey
Rating: ★★★★

Perceptive as well as suspenseful, this is one of Alfred Hitchcock's best all-round films. The thread of unease is skilfully woven into the narrative, gradually becoming stronger as Young Charlie (Teresa Wright) begins to suspect that her beloved Uncle Charlie (Joseph Cotten) may not be the sunny, uncomplicated figure she always thought. Further developments ensure engrossing viewing and a chilling climax.

Shadow of the Thin Man ○
1941, US, 95 mins, b/w
Dir: Major W S Van Dyke II
Stars: William Powell, Myrna Loy
Rating: ★★

The fourth *Thin Man* film and pretty thin it is too, even if the teaming of William Powell and Myrna Loy is still a joy to behold. This time the sleuthing socialites are visiting a racetrack when a jockey is murdered. MGM used the occasion to show off its latest contract players, in this case Donna Reed and Barry Nelson.

Shadows and Fog ◐ ⓥ
1991, US, 86 mins, b/w
Dir: Woody Allen
Stars: Woody Allen, John Malkovich, Mia Farrow, John Cusack
Rating: ★★

Woody Allen's black-and-white pastiche offers expressionistic frolics with a few light laughs for those in the mood. In a mittel-European town of the 1920s, a killer lurches through the fog strangling his victims. Woody's Kleinmann (little man, get it?) staggers in bewilderment between vigilante factions while seeking to evade the long arm of the law and the clutches of the killer. Mia Farrow, of course, is in it too as the sword-swallower who flees from her adulterous clown lover (John Malkovich) and likewise wanders the streets two footfalls ahead of the killer. Waiting for guest appearances by Madonna, Lily Tomlin, Jodie Foster, Kate Nelligan and others helps to stave off tedium from time to time, though authentic Allen one-liners are as thin on the ground as the dry ice is thick. 'You're not really a coward, a yellow-belly, a worm?' asks a colleague. Woody gulps. 'No, but you're in the right column.' The best line, though, goes to Jodie Foster. 'I've never paid for sex in my life,' Woody protests. But she is much wiser. 'Oh,' she says lightly, 'you just think you haven't.'

Shag ◐ ⓥ
1988, US, 100 mins, colour
Dir: Zelda Barron
Stars: Phoebe Cates, Annabeth Gish, Bridget Fonda, Page Hannah, Scott Coffey, Shirley Anne Field
Rating: ★

Shag is a drag. It's difficult to understand what made director Zelda Barron, who specialises in stories of close-knit girl friendships, actually want to re-create a 1963 beach film, unless she discerned some qualities in the script that don't make themselves apparent on screen. The story follows pretty much familiar lines – four teenage girls escape parental control to set up a fun weekend on the beach – except that, unlike the similarly coiffed Phoebe Cates here, Annette Funicello would never have gone 'all the way'! The girls show about as much talent as the strictly one-dimensional script will allow, although Annabeth Gish does invest her role – the pudgy wallflower – with a special glow that the others (even Bridget Fonda, at this early stage of her career) don't have. Another famous scion, Tyrone Power Jr, is desperately wasted in the role of the stuffy suitor Cates rejects for the slow-burning

Robert Rusler. Shag, by the way, is the name of a dance supposedly all the rage at the time.

Shaggy DA, The ☉

1976, US, 91 mins, colour
Dir: Robert Stevenson
Stars: Dean Jones, Tim Conway, Suzanne Pleshette
Rating: ★★★

This Disney canine caper is based on a book by Felix Salten, the author of *Bambi*, and is a follow-up to the studio's 1959 film *The Shaggy Dog*. Dean Jones has the role originally played by Tommy Kirk as a young lawyer running for the office of District Attorney, but whose past catches up with him in the shape of an ancient curse that turns him into a dog at the most unfortunate moments. Especially funny are scenes in a dog-pound that hark back to those in *Lady and the Tramp*.

Shakedown

See: Blue Jean Cop

Shakiest Gun in the West, The ☉

1967, US, 101 mins, colour
Dir: Alan Rafkin
Stars: Don Knotts, Barbara Rhoades, Jackie Coogan, Don Barry
Rating: ★★

Knotts, a bumbling, 'nervous' American comedian who shot to fame on television, was so good in his early films – *Move Over, Darling* and *The Incredible Mr Limpet* – that Universal decided to build a whole series of big colour comedies around him in the late Sixties. This one is a remake of the Bob Hope/Jane Russell classic *The Paleface*, with Knotts as Jesse Heywood (Painless Potter in the original) and the personable Barbara Rhoades rather good value in the Calamity Jane part, here called Bad Penny Cushings. Movie veterans Don 'Red' Barry, who has a fine time as a fake vicar, and Jackie Coogan, the former child star, fill the villains' shoes with easy skill.

Shaking the Tree ☉ ⓥ

1990, US, 107 mins, colour
Dir: Duane Clark
Stars: Arye Gross, Doug Savant, Courteney Cox, Steven Wilde, Gail Hansen
Rating: ★

Director Duane Clark has related how he and co-writer Steven Wilde had

trouble interesting studios in this script; on seeing the film, that causes no surprise. A second-rate story of four guys (who have been friends since college 10 years ago and now rally round when one has problems), it needs a much stronger screenplay to give it any chance of working. Though their story is brightly shot in Astro Color, these are dull, unattractive characters and their problems don't seem to amount to a hill of beans in terms of entertainment. The best Clark can come up with by way of a climax is the quartet assembling for the birth of the married one's baby. 'Don't worry,' they console him, 'we're with you as long as it takes.' 'Congratulations, it's a boy,' pronounces the over-bright nurse. Commiserations, fellas, you've only given birth to a turkey.

Shalako ◐

1968, UK, 118 mins, colour
Dir: Edward Dmytryk
Stars: Sean Connery, Brigitte Bardot, Stephen Boyd, Jack Hawkins
Rating: ★★

Sean Connery turned his back on James Bond and the offer to star in (the forgettable) *On Her Majesty's Secret Service* for this so-so big budget British Western. His beautiful French co-star, Brigitte Bardot, who hadn't made a film for two years, also rejected an offer to be George Lazenby's Bond girl in *OHMSS* and pocketed a cool £350,000 for going topless here, which in turn allowed her to sunbathe on the Riviera without having to work for a further year. A further Bond conection comes in the shapely form of Honor Blackman, who played Pussy Galore opposite Connery in *Goldfinger*. Henry Fonda was first choice of the producers here for the lead character, a wandering cowboy whose Indian name means 'he who brings rain'. But no-one could have pumped much life into the arid script. It is left to the picturesque location filming of Spain, standing in for New Mexico, to stay in the mind long after the plot has faded to grey.

Shall We Dance ○

1937, US, 116 mins, b/w
Dir: Mark Sandrich
Stars: Fred Astaire, Ginger Rogers
Rating: ★★★

Ginger Rogers accepted Fred Astaire's invitation to trip the light fantastic for the seventh time in four years. But this time they were just rehashing old

plots and the film got a thumbs down from critics. Just as well that George and Ira Gershwin delivered the goods in their second film as composers (the first was *Delicious*, six years earlier) and only collaboration with Rogers and Astaire. The highlight is the roller-skating sequence, 'Let's Call the Whole Thing Off', against a Central Park setting.

Shampoo ● ⓥ

1975, US, 110 mins, colour
Dir: Hal Ashby
Stars: Warren Beatty, Julie Christie, Goldie Hawn, Lee Grant, Jack Warden
Rating: ★★★

An immensely succesful film in which the vein of strong black humour disguises its criticisms of American morals and society. Warren Beatty is the hairdresser, determined to set up his own business, who preys on those wealthy female clients whom he knows won't upset his diet of shampoo and sex with wails about marriage and divorce. But it is that formidable actress Lee Grant, as Beatty's first big catch, who won an Academy Award. Carrie Fisher, later to gain fame as the heroine in the *Star Wars* movies, makes her debut as Grant's sexy daughter.

Shamus ◐

1972, US, 106 mins, colour
Dir: Buzz Kulik
Stars: Burt Reynolds, Dyan Cannon
Rating: ★★

Private-eye thriller that promises rather more than it delivers, especially given Burt Reynolds, as a 'gumshoe' who sleeps on a pool table, showing early signs of the Reynolds comedy touch, and doing most of his own, bone-crunching stuntwork. It was this film, in fact, that brought the star's long-standing feud with Hollywood insurance men to a head, when he injured his back in one flying leap, and production was held up while he recovered. One other coup: the casting of opera singer Giorgio Tozzi as a gourmet gangster who 'snitches' on his fellow criminals over a four-course lunch. The film takes some sly digs at *The Big Sleep* on the way, and its plot is every bit as complicated.

Shane ○ ⓥ

1953, US, 118 mins, colour
Dir: George Stevens
Stars: Alan Ladd, Jean Arthur, Van Heflin, Jack Palance
Rating: ★★★

Even though it's about as slow as you'd expect of a two-hour film adapted from a novelette, George Stevens' Western caught the public imagination in no uncertain fashion. Its gunplay is magnetically powerful and the camerawork superb. The only surprise was that Loyal Griggs' award for Technicolor photography was the only Oscar the film received. Alan Ladd found that *Shane* revived a faltering career, in a role similar in some respects to the one that originally shot him to stardom in *This Gun for Hire*, and provided Jean Arthur with a suitable swan song to her career, as the rancher's wife half in love with the gunman. There's tremendous support from a mightily sinister Jack Palance as a sadistic gunslinger.

Shanghai Express ◐
1932, US, 81 mins, b/w
Dir: Josef von Sternberg
Stars: Marlene Dietrich, Clive Brook, Anna May Wong, Eugene Pallette
Rating: ★★★★

'It took more than one man to change my name to Shanghai Lily,' drawls Marlene Dietrich in one of cinema's classic lines, and the scene is set for a visually stunning melodrama that was the third film she made in Hollywood with director Josef von Sternberg. It's one of his finest films, a kind of *Grand Hotel* on wheels. Lee Garmes' amazing photography won an Academy Award and Dietrich's sultry siren is enough to make even Clive Brook's stiff upper lip quiver.

Shanghai Surprise ◐ ⓥ
1986, US, 97 mins, colour
Dir: Jim Goddard
Stars: Sean Penn, Madonna
Rating: ★

Watching Madonna trying (unsuccessfully) to play a Thirties' missionary lady called Gloria is one of the few reasons to bother with this adventure film that never fulfils its eastern promise. Her then-husband Sean Penn portrays too sleazy a character for him to fill Indiana Jones's boots, and the film moves along at the pace of a waterlogged rat negotiating a paddy-field. There are a few compensations, notably Maurice Binder's Bond-like credit sequence and some spry supporting players, especially Clyde Susatsu as a baseball-crazy opium-buyer called Joe Go. Executive producer George Harrison makes a brief singing appearance.

Shark! ◐
1967, US, 92 mins, colour
Dir: Samuel Fuller
Stars: Burt Reynolds, Barry Sullivan
Rating: ★★

In making this underwater adventure yarn a stuntman was killed by a shark. Freak weather conditions drove hundreds of the huge fish down the California coast into the Mexican waters, where star Burt Reynolds and director Samuel Fuller were filming. Famous underwater explorer Jacques Cousteau commented that despite its name, he had never before known a white killer shark attack a man in so vicious a manner which was little consolation for the relatives of Jose Marco.

Sharkfighters, The ○
1956, US, 76 mins, colour
Dir: Jerry Hopper
Stars: Victor Mature, Karen Steele, James Olsen
Rating: ★★

Mighty Mature is given every opportunity to flex his muscles in this story of a team of scientists in World War Two, struggling to perfect a shark-repellent in the Pacific. The underwater photography is splendid, and James Olsen, since a star in *Rachel, Rachel*, makes his film debut in a featured role.

Sharky's Machine ● ⓥ
1981, US, 117 mins, colour
Dir: Burt Reynolds
Stars: Burt Reynolds, Vittorio Gassman, Rachel Ward
Rating: ★★★

A very, very tough Burt Reynolds thriller about crime, cops, corruption and all that. Blood runs down the walls and people get blown away, but Reynolds, who also directed the film, still finds time for an intelligently-presented obsessive affair with a high-class hooker, played by the British actress Rachel Ward. She's used to better advantage and clearly given more help by her director than in any previous film. As a director, in fact, Reynolds is full of ideas, even if, like his character (who also loses a couple-your-eyes torture scene), he occasionally loses his cool. But it's good to see Henry Silva back in the role he does best – a cold-blooded killer – while the rest of the cast is full of familiar faces doing their thing and relishing the chance to give vent to fusillades of four-letter words as well

as bullets. The action goes on and on: no fan of blood-soaked cop thrillers could ask for more.

Shattered ● ⓥ
1991, US, 106 mins, colour
Dir: Wolfgang Petersen
Stars: Tom Berenger, Bob Hoskins, Greta Scacchi, Joanne Whalley-Kilmer, Corbin Bernsen
Rating: ★★

Sometimes amnesia thrillers can still be good, but here's one that's not as good as it thinks it is. The makings are here, but neither the execution, nor the twists that should make you gasp with surprise. Given that things are not what they appear to be for car crash victim Tom Berenger, there's only one other likely explanation, and most viewers are likely to get it early on. Some of the performances are good (Greta Scacchi as Berenger's wife, Bob Hoskins as the part-time detective he hires), but most are ordinary, and one or two poor, notably veteran Theodore Bikel in an inauspicious return to films, and Debi A Monahan as the voluptuous secretary who's a ludicrous and swiftly discarded red herring. Berenger looks as though he can't make up his mind what to do with his role: fatal vacillation at the centre of a well-scored, stylish thriller that's finally just not intricate enough.

She ○
1935, US, 95 mins, b/w
Dir: Lansing C Holden, Irving Pichel
Stars: Helen Gahagan, Randolph Scott, Helen Mack, Nigel Bruce
Rating: ★★★

Thought at one time to be a lost film, this is an impressively-set first sound version (there had been several silents) of Rider Haggard's yarn about a legendary, ageless female ruler of a city, situated in Africa in the book but here transferred to the Arctic. Excellent photography by J Roy Hunt and music by Max Steiner help stir up atmosphere you can almost grasp. The title role is played by Helen Gahagan, who later married Melvyn Douglas, and became a Congresswoman. This was her only film.

She ◐
1965, US, 105 mins, colour
Dir: Robert Day
Stars: Ursula Andress, Peter Cushing, Bernard Cribbins, John Richardson, Christopher Lee, Rosenda Monteros
Rating: ★★

S

Hammer version of H Rider Haggard's oft-filmed novel, with Ursula Andress (more magnificent than when she rose out of the sea and into stardom in *Dr No*) as 'She Who Must Be Obeyed'. It's all done with great tongue-in-cheek zest by director Robert Day (who later made a name for himself with Hollywood TV movies) and Hammer's stalwarts, Peter Cushing and Christopher Lee, are on hand to support Ms Andress. But the most striking performances come from Bernard Cribbins (who has all the best lines) and Rosenda Monteros as a native girl.

She-Devil ◗ Ⓥ
1989, US, 99 mins, colour
Dir: Susan Seidelman
Stars: Meryl Streep, Roseanne Barr, Ed Begley, Linda Hunt
Rating: ★★

TV's scorching trilogy by Fay Weldon is well and truly revamped by Hollywood into a scatty romantic comedy which serves as a vehicle for Barr (now Arnold) to expand her popular TV image and Streep to let her hair down. Ed Begley Jr is nicely cast, being equally believable as a desirable man and a figure of fun, as the husband Barr loses to romantic novelist Streep. Deserted, the frumpy housewife turns she-devil to exact a tortured (and tortuous) revenge. Streep and Barr have fun and so, to a degree, do we, even if the enterprise lacks a certain vital spark. As a wet weather time passer, it does the job. Lovers of the TV serial, though, may be advised to stay away.

She Didn't Say No! ○
1958, UK, 97 mins, colour
Dir: Cyril Frankel
Stars: Eileen Herlie, Niall MacGinnis, Ian Bannen
Rating: ★★

The dangers of playing alongside scene-stealing child actors have rarely been more evident than in this charming comedy about an unmarried mother with six children. Little Raymond Manthorpe, as Toughy, manages to steal every scene in which he appears.

She Done Him Wrong ○
1933, US, 66 mins, b/w
Dir: Lowell Sherman
Stars: Mae West, Cary Grant, Gilbert Roland, Owen Moore
Rating: ★★★★

Mae West proving for the first time the truth of her famous maxim that 'When women go wrong, men go right after them.' She also has the benefit of Cary Grant as leading man, plus such songs as 'Frankie and Johnny', 'Easy Rider' and 'I Like a Man Who Takes His Time'. Slyly salty dialogue makes Mae sexy and side-splitting at the same time. It was her first big film hit, short and very sharp and based on her self-written stage success *Diamond Lil*. The film made a star of Grant and a fortune for its studio, Paramount, which was stunned to rake in a three million dollar profit on an outlay of $200,000. It contains some of Mae's finest gems of dialogue, including 'I was once so poor I didn't know where my next husband was coming from', 'When women go wrong, men go right after them' and 'Why don't you come up sometime, see me', plus the famous no-claws-barred fight between Mae and dagger-eyed Rafaela Ottiano.

Sheena – Queen of the Jungle ○
1984, US, 117 mins, colour
Dir: John Guillermin
Stars: Tanya Roberts, Ted Wass, Donovan Scott
Rating: ★

Shades of *Tarzan* in a spectacular jungle adventure which, with a script straight out of the early Forties, may remind older viewers of a Saturday morning serial. Tanya Roberts, with her bleached blond hair, spectacular figure, coral-pink lipstick, eye make-up and shaved armpits, is every curvy inch Hollywood's idea of the title role. John Guillermin and his second unit director Jack Couffer do a great job in capturing the breathtaking Kenyan locations, so that the highly-coloured yarn is alternately good for a gasp and a giggle.

Sheepman, The ○
1958, US, 86 mins, colour
Dir: George Marshall
Stars: Glenn Ford, Shirley MacLaine, Leslie Nielsen
Rating: ★★★

A charmingly natural Western, photographed in glowing Metrocolor by Robert Bronner. It has laughs, action and a lot of attractive characters, not least Shirley MacLaine's copper-haired tomboy heroine and Mickey Shaughnessy's Jumbo McCall. Glenn Ford has the title role as the sheepman fenced in by cattle ranchers

but determined to stay put, and *Naked Gun* fans will be surprised to find a young Leslie Nielsen turning up as the treacherous villain. Good stuff this, genial, fresh and likeable, with a little gentle satire on the conventional Western thrown in for good measure.

She'll Be Wearing Pink Pyjamas ◗
1984, UK, 90 mins, colour
Dir: John Goldschmidt
Stars: Julie Walters, Anthony Higgins
Rating: ★★★★

An excellent emotive outdoor drama about eight very varied women tackling an adventure course. Naturally it's their souls as well as their soles that get bared. Julie Walters, as the brassy northerner whose feelings as well as feet are really the most vulnerable in the octet, is the only star name and indeed comes over as the most clearly defined character. But several of her fellows acquit themselves more than adequately in roles that, like the course, stretch women far more than the average film. A lot of the dialogue is very frank, but the relaxed delivery of the players keeps it from being offensive. And the ending brings a lump to the throat without resorting to high dramatics. An unusual film that is, by its own standards, right on target.

Shenandoah ○
1965, US, 101 mins, colour
Dir: Andrew V McLaglen
Stars: James Stewart, Doug McClure
Rating: ★★★★

This is director Andrew V McLaglen's best film by a country mile. The story of a farming family that tries to keep out of the American Civil War, it's unpretentious, very much to do with real life and absolutely beautifully made. And it gives James Stewart, as the father of the family, the kind of role that actors of his potential and maturity must dream about. He plays it so well that the performance has to be seen to appreciate its closeness to life. Every inch of the way, the film, while punctuated with imaginative action scenes, has something to say that is sensible, thought-provoking or humorous. At the birth of his eldest son's first child, Stewart's youngest son asks for a glass of celebration liquor. 'I only want a taste,' he pleads. 'Boy,' replies Stewart, 'some men have drunk it all their lives and never tasted it.'

She Played with Fire
See: Fortune Is a Woman

Sheriff of Fractured Jaw, The ○
1958, UK, 103 mins, colour
Dir: Raoul Walsh
Stars: Kenneth More, Jayne Mansfield
Rating: ★★★

The unlikely combination of Kenneth More and Jayne Mansfield shouldn't really have worked, but under Raoul Walsh's rousing direction, most of the difficulties were ironed out. The result is a sunny and fun-filled spoof Western, with More as the tweedy English gunsmith who finds himself the most feared gunman in the Wild West. Such familiar Hollywood faces as Henry Hull, William Campbell and Bruce Cabot are on hand to lend a touch of authenticity to the atmosphere. Sid James totters in and out as the town drunkard. Mansfield's singing voice comes courtesy of Connie Francis.

Sherlock and Me
See: Without a Clue

Sherlock Holmes and the Spider Woman ○ ⓥ
1944, US, 63 mins, b/w
Dir: Roy William Neill
Stars: Basil Rathbone, Nigel Bruce
Rating: ★★★

Basil Rathbone is in cracking form as Sherlock Holmes in this adaptation of a Conan Doyle short story, as he adopts his usual disguise and undergoes some pretty harrowing experiences to solve the case. He is finely matched in a battle of wits and wills by that mistress of menace, Gale Sondergaard, whose character survived to make a sequel (without Rathbone), *Spider Woman Strikes Back*.

Sherlock Holmes in New York ○
1976, US, 94 mins, colour
Dir: Boris Sagal
Stars: Roger Moore, John Huston, Patrick Macnee
Rating: ★★★

Bond-man Roger Moore joins the illustrious ranks of actors who have assumed deerstalker and violin as Conan Doyle's famous Victorian sleuth. But this classy romp has Holmes far from his usual haunts and chasing the evil Professor Moriarty (a dastardly John Huston) through the streets of turn-of-the-century New

York. For once Moore gets material that requires a little more than the customary raised eyebrows! 'What I like most about playing Holmes,' he once confided, 'is that in one speech I have more dialogue than I ever had in 120 Saint shows or my Bond movies.'

Sherlock Junior ☉
1924, US, 46 mins, b/w
Dir: Buster Keaton
Stars: Buster Keaton
Rating: ★★★★

One of the most enjoyable of Buster Keaton's silent feature films. He ends up outwitting the crooks in a marvellous sequence involving a falling sword, poison and an exploding pool ball.

She's Gotta Have It ● ⓥ
1986, US, 84 mins, b/w
Dir: Spike Lee
Stars: Tracy Camila Johns, Tommy Redmond Hicks, John Canada Terrell, Spike Lee
Rating: ★★★

Spike Lee, the driving force behind this off-the-wall sexual sparring match with jokes, is a kind of babbling black Woody Allen. He wrote, directed, edited and ultimately had the good sense to cast himself as the 'funny one' of the three lovers of the girl to whom the provocative title refers. The script is sharp and witty, but Lee's pacing is not all it might be, and the film only comes to life when he and his ideas are around. Tracy Camila Johns has a certain raw sexuality as the girl with three men in tow, none of them surely a permanent prospect, even though the film tries to sustain itself on the possibility that she might end up with one of them. Lee himself is obviously buzzing with talent and cinematic ideas and has since made the big time.

She's Out of Control ◑ ⓥ
1990, US, 95 mins, colour
Dir: Stan Dragoti
Stars: Tony Danza, Catherine Hicks, Wallace Shawn, Ami Dolenz
Rating: ★

A dated but occasionally amusing farce about the pains of a father with a teenage daughter. There was a rash of these about 20 years before, with such veteran stars as James Stewart and David Niven. At least here Tony Danza is the right age, making a very young-looking 37-year-old, as daughter Dolenz does all the things

that teenage girls with pretty faces and curvy figures are wont to do in these films. The best sequence comes in the middle, when Danza attempts to fit in with his daughter's lifestyle and befriend her associates. Otherwise it's pretty tired and painful – and not too well performed either, with some strenuous 'reacting' from most of the cast. Its contrived charm is easily resistible.

She's Working Her Way Through College ○
1952, US, 101 mins, colour
Dir: Bruce Humberstone
Stars: Virginia Mayo, Ronald Reagan, Gene Nelson, Phyllis Thaxter
Rating: ★★

Although it bears little resemblance to *The Male Animal*, the James Thurber-Elliott Nugent play (and later film) on which it's allegedly based, this is nonetheless a bright, snappy Technicolor musical, produced at the Warner studio in the early Fifties when such stars as Virginia Mayo and Gene Nelson (as well as Doris Day and Gordon MacRae) were the resident attractions. Here the plum role goes to Mayo as a burlesque queen who aspires to a writing career, re-enrols (incognito) at her old college and soon replaces the annual Shakespeare play with a musical written by herself which, as usual, proves a more elaborate show than any educational establishment could afford to stage. If this sounds zany, it certainly is, and the 'plot' is just a peg on which to hang a series of zippy song-and-dance numbers with room for a witty cameo by Roland Winters, fresh from being Hollywood's last Charlie Chan, as a college governor with a murky past. As the stuffy English teacher, Ronald Reagan looks suitably discomfited at such goings-on (as might befit a future US president) and Gene Nelson again steals the film from everyone with his acrobatic dancing.

She Wore a Yellow Ribbon ○ ⓥ
1949, US, 103 mins, colour
Dir: John Ford
Stars: John Wayne, Joanne Dru, John Agar, Ben Johnson, Victor McLaglen
Rating: ★★★★

One of John Wayne's best performances, as an ageing cavalry officer trying to drive Indians off lands they regard as their own. This is the second of what has now come to be regarded as John Ford's unofficial

S

cavalry trilogy, completed by *Fort Apache* and *Rio Grande*. What particularly distinguishes it is its feel for those early pioneer days of wide open spaces, especially well captured in Ford's sensitive direction, and in Winton C Hoch's breathtaking colour photography, which deservedly won an Oscar. The film's quiet power – only the comedy scenes involving Victor McLaglen seem out of key – makes it an unchallenged classic in its field.

Shinbone Alley ⊙
1971, US, 86 mins, colour
Dir: David Detiege
Voice stars: Eddie Bracken, Carol Channing, John Carradine
Rating: ★★

A full-length cartoon, not shown in Britain's cinemas, based on the famous *Archy and Mehitabel* stories by Don Marquis, about a cat and a cockroach. Voices to be heard behind the characters include those of Carol Channing, Eddie Bracken and John Carradine. Second-class animation, maybe, compared to that from the Disney studio, but top-class tunes and colourful characters make this a pleasure to be with.

Shining, The ● ⓥ
1980, US, 119 mins, colour
Dir: Stanley Kubrick
Stars: Jack Nicholson, Shelley Duvall, Danny Lloyd
Rating: ★★★★

Stanley Kubrick's underrated chiller, adapted from Stephen King's novel, is one of those films that makes you check under the bed to see there's no-one there after you've finished watching it – especially if you imagine Jack Nicholson and his axe could soon be after you. This is grim and grisly ghost-story telling with a vengeance, as Nicholson, his wife (Shelley Duvall) and son (Danny Lloyd), who is endowed with extra-sensory perception (the 'shining' of the title) and can see the horrors in store for them, take on the caretakership of a Rocky Mountain hotel for the winter. Somewhere in the past a previous caretaker has gone berserk and axed his wife and daughters to death, and it isn't long before the house is exercising an evil influence on Nicholson. His language becomes foul, he works like a demon and starts consorting with the ghosts that infest the hotel. Kubrick paces the symphony of horror with masterly

precision, using tracking cameras a lot to heighten the fright and emphasise the terror of a pursued victim. Nicholson has a wonderful time, while Shelley Duvall registers a fine line in hysteria. You shouldn't really see it alone.

Shining Through ◑ ⓥ
1991, US, 133 mins, colour
Dir: David Seltzer
Stars: Michael Douglas, Melanie Griffith, Liam Neeson, Joely Richardson, John Gielgud
Rating: ★

A real Mills and Boon of a film about a World War Two heroine. The preposterous cock-and-bull story has Melanie Griffith as one of the more inept wartime agents. She's recruited chiefly, it seems, for her ability to speak German (badly) and her knowledge of Hollywood films, which isn't up to much since she thinks Cary Grant and Brenda Marshall were in *The Fighting 69th* (they weren't). The film itself, indeed, could come from the Forties, were it not for the fact that Griffith is required to bare her breasts in the course of her affair with equally incompetent spymaster Michael Douglas, who sends her off on a mission that requires her to cook for a Nazi. The story that follows has lots of silliness, but no dramatic tension and very little subtlety. A key to a room filled with secrets is on a ledge over the door, and the secrets themselves have vital spots marked in red to enable the heroine to do a quicker job. This is a rotten part, but at least Griffith seems daft enough for the heroine as presented here, who, when injured, thinks a roll of film hidden in her glove will be found by a doctor but not an SS Officer. A ludicrous framing interview by 'the BBC' is even more embarrassing than the story it surrounds.

Ship Ahoy ⊙
1942, US, 91 mins, b/w
Dir: Edward Buzzell
Stars: Eleanor Powell, Red Skelton, Bert Lahr, Virginia O'Brien
Rating: ★★

Lots of talented people decorate this very silly MGM musical, whose ragged editing makes it look like a patchwork quilt. Even though it was obviously cobbled together in a hurry to provide patriotic war fare, there's plenty of entertainment value: Tommy Dorsey's trombone work, Eleanor Powell's dancing, Frank

Sinatra's singing and Buddy Rich's devastating drumming. Red Skelton's addled fooling is put in the shade by vaudeville veteran Bert Lahr, here making one of his too-rare movie appearances outside of his immortal Cowardly Lion in *The Wizard of Oz*.

Ship of Fools ○
1965, US, 149 mins, b/w
Dir: Stanley Kramer
Stars: Vivien Leigh, Simone Signoret, Lee Marvin, Oskar Werner
Rating: ★★★

Stanley Kramer's allegorical drama of passengers aboard a transatlantic ship in 1933. Noteworthy for the doomed love affair memorably carved out by Simone Signoret and Oskar Werner, for Vivien Leigh's bored divorcee, breaking indecorously into a solo Charleston below decks when no-one is looking, and for Lee Marvin's retired baseball player who could never hit 'a curving ball on the outside corner.' Although the voyage is a long one, a lot of its drama is good, meaty stuff. You'll also like Michael Dunn's dwarf, moralising though he is, while Jose Greco's acting surprisingly shows the same snap and fire as his flamenco dancing. Only George Segal and Elizabeth Ashley, as a young artist and his fiancée, obstinately refuse to develop into real people.

Ship Was Loaded, The
See: Carry On Admiral

Shipwreck! ⊙
1978, US, 98 mins, colour
Dir: Stewart Raffill
Stars: Robert Logan, Mikki Jamison-Olsen
Rating: ★★

Another of the man-against-nature films made by director Stewart Raffill and likeable star Robert Logan, best known for their *Wilderness Family* series and for the splendid *Across the Great Divide*. The title tells you all you need to know about the story, although the site of the shipwreck may be a surprise: it's not a desert island but the coast of Alaska. Cuteness threatens, but is skilfully kept at bay, and the scenes involving animals are exceedingly well done.

Shirley Valentine ◑ ⓥ
1989, UK, 108 mins, colour
Dir: Lewis Gilbert
Stars: Pauline Collins, Tom Conti, Alison Steadman, Julia McKenzie,

Joanna Lumley, Bernard Hill
Rating: ★★★

This delightful romantic comedy started life as a one-woman stage show, but you'd never know it, as it took to the big screen like a duck to water. Following their success with *Educating Rita*, director Lewis Gilbert and writer Willy Russell teamed up again for this film. Pauline Collins reprised the role she filled so sucessfully on stage and, inevitably, dominates the film. She plays a bored housewife who dreams of drinking 'a glass of wine in a country where the grape is grown' and eventually takes off for a Greek island, leaving a note to her husband in the kitchen! The fine supporting cast includes Tom Conti, Bernard Hill, Julia McKenzie and Joanna Lumley, but it's Pauline's show. It's something a little different and fun too.

Shock! ◐
1945, US, 70 mins, b/w
Dir: Alfred Werker
Stars: Vincent Price, Lynn Bari
Rating: ★★

When he made this film, Vincent Price's screen career had been in a variety of roles, and he had not yet become a specialist in horror films which were later to make him so famous. He co-stars with Lynn Bari, an actress who appeared in numerous pictures from her debut in 1933 until about 1954, when she virtually retired. Perhaps she never reached the top rank of stardom, but she was one of those personable and very reliable performers without whom Hollywood's golden years would have been distinctly the poorer. One critic once described her quite deliciously as 'the Paulette Goddard of the B feature'.

Shock to the System, A ◐ ⓥ
1990, US, 87 mins, colour
Dir: Jan Egleson
Stars: Michael Caine, Peter Riegert, Elizabeth McGovern, Will Patton
Rating: ★★

This is a minor black comedy, but the art of Michael Caine turns it into an enjoyable if forgettable lark. The story is *Kind Hearts and Coronets* meets *Columbo*, set in America, with Caine as the good-natured, efficient, henpecked businessman tipped over the edge by his failure to clinch a long-expected promotion within his

firm. After accidentally pushing a tramp under a subway train without recrimination, he does what 90 per cent of the world's population dream about. He murders the ruthless, obnoxious and ambitious yuppie who has leap-frogged him at the firm. Then, of course, there's the nagging wife. She'll have to go too. And there's the detective on his trail (Patton, with apologies to Peter Falk). And the managing director. And even the mistress who could betray him. Caine keeps it all jogging nicely along, with only token help from his script and director. Just watch his face as his wife's ashes blow back over him at her funeral. And Riegert proves he can play a nasty blowhard as well as unassuming nice guy.

Shoes of the Fisherman, The ○
1968, US, 157 mins, colour
Dir: Michael Anderson
Stars: Anthony Quinn, Laurence Olivier, Oskar Werner, David Janssen
Rating: ★★★

Impressive, strikingly coloured epic about a fighting Russian bishop. This was not a popular with the critics when it first appeared, even though Quinn was tipped at the time for an Oscar. But it has several moving scenes, beautiful photography by Erwin Hillier and an eye-catching performance by Leo McKern. It also uncannily predicted the emergence of a Pope from Eastern Europe.

Shoot First
See: Rough Shoot

Shooting, The ○
1966, US, 82 mins, colour
Dir: Monte Hellman
Stars: Warren Oates, Millie Perkins, Jack Nicholson
Rating: ★★

A cult Western, set against the parched backdrop of the desert, that will fascinate some viewers and severely try the patience of others. A few people play out destinies from which none of them seems fated to escape. Enigmatic to the last, the film will certainly keep you guessing as to who is doing what to whom and why. Co-produced by Jack Nicholson, who also plays a featured role as the hired gunman on the trail of bounty hunter Warren Oates.

Shootist, The ○ ⓥ
1976, US, 95 mins, colour
Dir: Don Siegel

Stars: John Wayne, Lauren Bacall, Ron Howard, James Stewart, Richard Boone
Rating: ★★★★

Well may this finely-crafted film use clips of John Wayne shoot-outs through the years under its credits. For it is both a summation of the Wayne legend and an ending to it – a tying, if you like, of all the ends in one knot. Wayne plays a gunfighter – the name is unimportant, he is Wayne – who comes to an elderly doctor friend to be told he has cancer: there is no escape. Spending his dying days in the embryo Carson City, he is surrounded – as Wayne is surrounded in the film by star acting friends – by those who come to sponge on him, those who come to mock or pity him, and those who come to kill him. Around all this, director Don Siegel has delivered a beautiful job of work. If the pace leaves a little to be desired, never mind: it may be argued that is the pace of an old man making the most of his winter years. And, in a notable achievement, Siegel has elicited fine performances from people who might have been considered past giving them, especially Wayne (quieter and more effective than in the Oscar-winning *True Grit*) Stewart and Lauren Bacall. This concise, caring and lovingly-photographed (by Bruce Surtees) film makes a not inconsiderable headstone beneath which to bury the Wayne Western legend.

Shoot to Kill
See: Deadly Pursuit

Shopping ● ⓥ
1993, UK, 107 mins, colour
Dir: Paul Anderson
Stars: Jude Law, Sadie Frost, Sean Pertwee, Jonathan Pryce
Rating: ★★

The British 'B' crime movie of long ago updates itself here to the near future. It begins well: in a *noir*-lit backstreets world of gleaming grime, anarchy rules and teenage gangs roam unchecked. Crime of the month is ram raiding: the smashing through shop windows by cars which load up with goods and flee into the night. The police are an endangered species. Billy (Jude Law), released from prison, and greeted by his Irish girl (Sadie Frost, with a mostly credible accent) in a stolen car, is resolved to re-establish himself as a joy-riding, ram-raiding kingpin. Tommy (Sean Pertwee), current black market boss, is set on defending his territory. On the fringes,

S

Inspector Conway (Jonathan Pryce) waits like a patient wolf for one to dump the other into his jaws. Looking good, the film's poorly paced in between its bursts of action: the only thing that's constantly on the move is the camera which doesn't help a lot. The actors give the predictably foul-mouthed dialogue their best shot, right up to the equally predictable ending.

Shopworn Angel ○
1938, US, 82 mins, colour
Dir: H C Potter
Stars: Margaret Sullavan, James Stewart
Rating: ★★★

This dated but still touching vehicle for Margaret Sullavan and James Stewart (the second of their four films together) is a remake of an even older weepie that starred Nancy Carroll and Gary Cooper as the showgirl and the soldier who enjoy a mad fling in New York the night before he is due to be shipped overseas for wartime service. In keeping with the sweetness of her image, Sullavan's angel isn't quite as shopworn as Carroll's was in 1928, but Stewart's gangly charm is every inch the equal of Cooper's and there will be few dry eyes in the house as Sullavan goes on stage to sing 'Pack Up Your Troubles in Your Old Kit Bag' at the end.

Short Circuit ○ ⓥ
1986, US, 98 mins, colour
Dir: John Badham
Stars: Ally Sheedy, Steve Guttenberg, Fisher Stevens, Austin Pendleton, G W Bailey, Brian McNamara
Rating: ★★★

A pleasant and occasionally very funny caper about a runaway robot that, having been struck by lightning, reprogrammes itself to believe it's alive. And, assimilating all the knowledge it can find and imitating any human function it can cope with, Number Five does become alive – as near as dammit. Unfortunately, it's also armed with an annihilating laser weapon. So the authorities want the escapee back and, with the help of an animal-hoarding girl (Ally Sheedy), Number Five must hide, run dodge and fight with all the capacity it can find in its brainbox. The robot is really the whole show, especially when dancing with Sheedy in imitation of a Travolta video, and most of the fun stems from the information it 'gathers' from watching TV, especially when it

reprogrammes three enemy robots to behave like The Three Stooges. Excellent for children, who will enjoy the odd rude word, Sheedy's house of animals and Number Five making mincemeat of the opposition.

Short Circuit 2 ○ ⓥ
1988, US, 110 mins, colour
Dir: Kenneth Johnson
Stars: Fisher Stevens, Cynthia Gibb
Rating: ★★

So often follow-ups are doomed to failure, if only because they are merely warmed-over copies of the original. Unfortunately, this is true of *Short Circuit 2*. The stars of the original film, Steve Guttenberg and Ally Sheedy, obviously saw it coming, as they ducked the sequel, leaving their co-star Fisher Stevens to take the lead (and the can!) The robot, Number Five, insists on being called Johnny Five and, mysteriously, Stevens' character's name has changed from Ben Jabituya to Ben Jahrvi. Stevens' Indian accent is so awful it's embarrassing, making him sound like an extra from *It Ain't Half Hot, Mum*. The kids will love it, though.

Short Cuts ● ⓥ
1993, US, 188 mins, colour
Dir: Robert Altman
Stars: Anne Archer, Tim Robbins, Jennifer Jason Leigh, Madeleine Stowe, Andie MacDowell
Rating: ★★

Rather a long cut at more than three hours, this proves, after an excellent beginning – as pesticide-dropping 'copters drone over the city – to be a pretty aimless amble through the sub-strata of Los Angeles by director Robert Altman, as a score or more lives criss-cross and sometimes come to climaxes or watersheds. These are mostly deeply unpleasant people who often have no patience with one another and to stay in their company for this length of time certainly demands stamina to savour the occasional rewarding moment. An all-star cast appears willingly in various stages of undress; for Altman is a master, is he not, and so it is all in the cause of art.

Short Time ◐ ⓥ
1990, US, 97 mins, colour
Dir: Gregg Champion
Stars: Dabney Coleman, Matt Frewer, Teri Garr, Joe Pantoliano, Xander Berkeley
Rating: ★★

For the first half-hour, it seems that this tale of a long-serving cop (Dabney Coleman) who thinks he's about to die is going to strike out. It's frenetic, over-played and awkward too. As soon as Coleman starts trying to get himself killed, though, the film moves into another gear. Never wildly funny, but consistently chucklesome, the main body of the film is packed with chase and mindlessly enjoyable. Divorced and depressed, Coleman is saddled with a partner who looks like Clint Eastwood and sounds like Kermit the Frog and a career that has eight days to run before retirement. Then there's a mix-up at the hospital and Coleman's told he has Wexler's Curtain: his retirement will be permanent in about 20 days. The only thing he can do is die in the line of duty and get $300,000 insurance for his young son. He doffs his gun and bullet-proof vest and becomes a fearless vigilante cop, only to find himself bearing a charmed life. Teri Garr is, not for the first time, the best thing in the show as the wife bewildered by her ex-husband's sudden realisation of what's really important in life.

Shot in the Dark, A ○ ⓥ
1964, US, 101 mins, colour
Dir: Blake Edwards
Stars: Peter Sellers, Elke Sommer, Herbert Lom, Burt Kwouk, Graham Stark
Rating: ★★★

Like the Mounties, Inspector Clouseau (alias Peter Sellers) always gets his man. He just has a little more trouble than they do. Take his problem here. A murder has been committed at a millionaire's mansion. Clouseau is assigned. No sooner has he picked himself out of the lake in the grounds than he falls head over heels for the chief suspect (Elke Sommer). He determines to prove her innocence. But, alas, in addition to being accident-prone, the defective detective becomes corpse-prone. Three more murders turn up at the mansion. And 10 more people are killed (accidentally) as an unseen hand goes after Clouseau himself. 'Ah well, it is all part of life's rich pageant,' as Clouseau says, after setting his raincoat on fire with his own lighter. Sellers is supremely funny as Clouseau. And Herbert Lom proves superbly comic as the superior whom Sellers gradually reduces to a nervous wreck. Series regulars Lom, Burt Kwouk and Graham Stark all started in this one.

Shoulder Arms ☉
1918, US, 35 mins, b/w
Dir: Charles Chaplin
Stars: Charlie Chaplin
Rating: ★★★

Charlie Chaplin took so long to make this three-reel comedy – his longest to that date – that it finally premiered only three weeks before the end of the World War One. Still, the public loved it, especially the scenes where Charlie kicks the Kaiser in the seat of his pants, disguises himself as a tree – he still looks like a tramp – or eats the cheese from a mousetrap.

Shout at the Devil ○
1976, UK, 119 mins, colour
Dir: Peter Hunt
Stars: Lee Marvin, Roger Moore, Barbara Parkins
Rating: ★★

As with the previous collaboration between star Roger Moore and director Peter Hunt, the action is everything in this explosive account of two Zanzibar-based mercenaries in 1913 making ivory-poaching forays against what seems to be half the German armed forces. The technical skill with which the set-pieces are filmed – a biplane going down in flames, a David-and-Goliath duel between contrasting boats, an exploding battleship, and a free-for-all fist fight between Moore and Lee Marvin – is of a high order. Only the love interest, between Moore and Barbara Parkins, as Marvin's daughter, is dull and redundant. Otherwise, extravagant and enjoyable adventures for viewers of all ages.

Show Boat ○
1936, US, 113 mins, b/w
Dir: James Whale
Stars: Irene Dunne, Allan Jones, Paul Robeson, Helen Morgan
Rating: ★★★★

Possibly the most famous version of the Kern-Hammerstein musical about life and love on a Mississippi show boat in the early 1900s. Skilful direction by James Whale, best known for his Universal horror films, milks the story for every emotional moment, while Irene Dunne's vivacious performance – she's an absolute delight singing 'Can't Help Loving That Man' – should have alerted producers to her possibilities long before they were fully realised. The songs, all beautifully staged, also include the Dunne-Allan

Jones duet 'Only Make Believe', Paul Robeson's famous rendition of 'Ol' Man River', sung while the camera sweeps a circle around him, and Helen Morgan's 'My Bill'.

Show Boat ○ ⓥ
1951, US, 107 mins, colour
Dir: George Sidney
Stars: Kathryn Grayson, Ava Gardner, Howard Keel, William Warfield, Marge Champion, Gower Champion
Rating: ★★★★

Most critics will tell you that this marvellous musical doesn't compare with James Whale's 1936 version: but don't believe a word of it. Certainly the earlier film is smashing too. But this MGM remake, with all their technical departments working at full throttle and George Sidney in the director's chair, is much underrated. And how the stars shine. Howard Keel, especially, acts and sings well as the gambling Gaylord; Kathryn Grayson, in one of her best performances, is charming (and very pretty) as Magnolia and more vivacious than one could credit from some of her other roles. Old-time comic Joe E Brown deserves special mention for his superb playing as her father, while Ava Gardner and Agnes Moorehead also tug skilfully at the emotions in their big scenes. Charles Rosher's camerawork is the quintessence of all that was best about the peak days of Hollywood Technicolor photography and the only surprise is that neither version of this hugely entertaining film won a single Oscar. Indeed the 1936 film wasn't even nominated for one!

Showdown ○
1963, US, 79 mins, b/w
Dir: R G Springsteen
Stars: Audie Murphy, Kathleen Crowley, Charles Drake, Harold J Stone
Rating: ★★

Slowdown might be a better title for this Audie Murphy Western, made at a time when Murphy's fortunes at Universal were on the wane and the studio were no longer even prepared to splash out colour on his vehicles. But his old (real-life) friend Charles Drake is there to support him, just as he had been on *Gunsmoke!*, *To Hell and Back* and *No Name on the Bullet*. Together the two conjure up some action and one or two moments that touch the emotions.

Showdown ○
1972, US, 99 mins, colour
Dir: George Seaton
Stars: Rock Hudson, Dean Martin, Susan Clark
Rating: ★★★

A pity Hudson and Martin were past their box-office peak when this film was issued in 1973, for it's above-average of its kind, thanks to thoroughly professional direction by George Seaton and an intelligent script by Theodore Taylor that's full of drily witty dialogue exchanges. You feel that if the two stars had intended it as their cinematic swan-song they could not have chosen much better: you may be reminded at times of another Western, *Guns in the Afternoon*, in which Randolph Scott and Joel McCrea virtually said goodbye to the cinema. The two films also share remarkably good colour photography of the Western countryside among their assets, in this case by the ever-excellent Ernest Laszlo. There's some exciting action, too, but that versatile and talented actress Susan Clark is again wasted, here as Hudson's wife.

Showdown at Abilene ○
1956, US, 80 mins, colour
Dir: Charles Haas
Stars: Jock Mahoney, Martha Hyer, Lyle Bettger
Rating: ★★

This story of a gun-shy sheriff was a favourite Western plot at Universal, who filmed it several times up to 1967, when Bobby Darin featured in *Gunfight in Abilene*. This version features Jock Mahoney who, a couple of years later, became one of the screen's many Tarzans. The splendid, husky-voiced Lyle Bettger is the villain, heading a supporting cast which also includes Martha Hyer, Grant Williams, David Janssen and Ted de Corsia.

Show Goes On, The ○
1937, UK, 93 mins, b/w
Dir: Basil Dean
Stars: Gracie Fields, Owen Nares
Rating: ★★

Gracie was well established as one of Britain's top box-office stars when this tearful musical was made. She was cast opposite silent screen matinee idol, Owen Nares, a young Patrick Barr, and that hearty actor, Cyril Richard. Helping to lighten the gloom of the story are Olsen's Sea

S

Lions and, of course, Our Gracie, who stands on the topmost deck of the Queen Mary, and sings 'Smile When You Wave Goodbye' to a troopship.

Shuttered Room, The ◐

1966, UK, 110 mins, colour
Dir: David Greene
Stars: Gig Young, Carol Lynley, Oliver Reed, Flora Robson
Rating: ★★

'Things' locked away in shuttered rooms, villagers frightened by goings-on at the old mill, and strange webbed footprints. A sound horror formula and, with a screenplay based on a story by that master of the macabre H P Lovecraft, a chilly one at that. Oliver Reed is splendidly menacing in a glowering key role.

Shy People ● ⓥ

1987, US, 119 mins, colour
Dir: Andrei Konchalovsky
Stars: Jill Clayburgh, Barbara Hershey, Martha Plimpton, Mare Winningham, Merritt Butrick, Don Swayze
Rating: ★

Every so often, film-makers suffer a mental aberration which causes them to go down to the American swamplands. Few of the resulting movies have proved less than ludicrous and most, as here, are about people who seem to be as potty as the films themselves. Shy's hardly the word, for sure, for Barbara Hershey and her sons, a less civilised version of Ma Barker and her killer brood. Mentally deranged from too much time in the swamps, perhaps, but hardly shy. The catalyst that turns their bizarre lives into a series of violent confrontations is a visit from civilised cousin Jill Clayburgh and her nymphet daughter Martha Plimpton, who seduces the son who's kept in a cage in the yard. Yes he is and she does. What can have attracted Hershey and Clayburgh to two equally unsuitable roles in this frenzied farrago is a matter for them and their agents to ponder. The scenes in the swamps have a predictably weird beauty, though, even if they add layers of lethargy to an already slow-moving film.

Sibling Rivalry ◐ ⓥ

1990, US, 88 mins, colour
Dir: Carl Reiner
Stars: Kirstie Alley, Bill Pullman, Carrie Fisher, Jami Gertz, Scott Bakula, Sam Elliott
Rating: ★★

The modern equivalent of a Feydeau farce, this is mostly a limp affair in spite of its top-flight cast. Alley is unhappily married to granite-jawed Bakula, one of a family of doctors who treat her as something the pathologist dragged in. A casual hot affair with a man (Sam Elliott) who dies at the end of an epic love-making session triggers off one of those games of consequences that only happen under the covers of fiction. Kirstie's lover was her husband's long-lost brother, but he's discovered by an inept salesman (Bill Pullman) who thinks he's killed him. Pullman's brother (Ed O'Neill), a top cop, calls on Kirstie because she made a panic phone call about the dead man, and falls for Alley's sister Jami Gertz. This goes on (and on) but, despite a few nice moments, is directed without verve by Carl Reiner, who could definitely do with some kind of wild climax to round it off. His screenwriter, presumably, didn't give him the chance.

Sicilian Cross ◐

1976, Italy, 102 mins, colour
Dir: Maurizio Lucidi
Stars: Roger Moore, Stacy Keach
Rating: ★★

Unquenchable British nonchalance marks Roger Moore's characterisation of a Sicilian peasant somehow transformed by an English education into a crooked American lawyer, in this loosely-constructed Mafia thriller. A scenic tour of Sicily, ominous statements about family honour, and the vulture-like presence of an ageing 'godfather' would seem to underline the film's ancestry. But the odd-ball pairing of Moore and Stacy Keach suggests that director Maurizio Lucidi was thinking more along the lines of a crooked *Starsky and Hutch*. Ernest Tidyman's name heads an amazingly long list of screeplay writers – and the best thing about the film is a very funny car sequence, which apes the classic automobile-subway chase in Tidyman's previous film, *The French Connection*.

Sid and Nancy ● ⓥ

1986, UK, 107 mins, colour
Dir: Alex Cox
Stars: Gary Oldman, Chloe Webb, Drew Schofield, David Hayman, Debby Bishop
Rating: ★★

This exceptionally well-made film about the rise and fall of punk rocker Sid Vicious and his groupie love

Nancy Spungen is about as comfortable an evening as spending an hour and three quarters sitting on barbed wire. Hardly entertainment and that's a fact – but not to be thrust aside either. The performances of Gary Oldman and Chloe Webb, who live their roles to a frightening degree, are just amazing; and at least a small feeling of obsessive romance, even beneath layers of drug-induced stupor, does filter through. Certainly a film of the Eighties' generation and one that you hope won't have to be repeated.

Siege at Red River, The ○

1954, US, 81 mins, colour
Dir: Rudolph Maté
Stars: Van Johnson, Joanne Dru, Richard Boone, Milburn Stone
Rating: ★★

Well-photographed Western from the short-lived Panoramic Productions. The story is set at the time of the American Civil War, and concerns the battle for the first Gatling gun. It's a good plot, well unfolded, with action all the way, and plenty of suspense for good measure. Richard Boone and Jeff Morrow are strong villains; but Edward Cronjager's Technicolor photography is the real star.

Siege of Pinchgut, The ○

(aka: Four Desperate Men)
1959, UK, 104 mins, b/w
Dir: Harry Watt
Stars: Aldo Ray, Heather Sears
Rating: ★★★

This cliff-hanging thriller was the last film to come out of Ealing Studios, which produced many of Britain's most famous films, from *The Blue Lamp* and *The Ladykillers* to *Kind Hearts and Coronets* and *The Man in the White Suit*. Gravel-voiced American giant Aldo Ray glowers and Heather Sears cowers as the bullets whiz around them. Director Harry Watt makes good use of an unusual location – Australia's Sydney Harbour, long before the Opera House.

Siege of the Saxons ○

1963, UK, 85 mins, colour
Dir: Nathan Juran
Stars: Ronald Lewis, Janette Scott
Rating: ★★★

Broadswords flash and arrows whistle in a busy slice of Arthurian history, made by an American company on location in Britain, with an all-British cast. Showing scant respect for legend, the film kills Arthur off at an early stage, leaving a Robin Hood-style woodsman (Ronald Lewis) and Arthur's hoyden daughter (Janette Scott's best role in ages) to ward off the claims of the treacherous Duke of Cornwall (Ronald Howard) to the throne. Certainly it has an unintentional laugh or two – as when Scott, bouncing up and down on the throne, declares, 'I'll be a good queen, I know I will' – but such quibbles are largely irrelevant when the end product is well-acted, colourful, exciting and whose constant tongue-in-cheek aim is to entertain. Lewis obviously enjoys every moment of his role as the dashing hero in this rip-roaring stuff.

Sierra ○
1950, US, 83 mins, colour
Dir: Alfred E Green
Stars: Wanda Hendrix, Audie Murphy, Dean Jagger, Burl Ives
Rating: ★★

One of Murphy's first Westerns, casting him as a young cowboy whose father has been in hiding for years from the law and the one on which he met and married the star, Wanda Hendrix. It was up-and-coming Tony Curtis's fourth movie role. A big break, too, for fast-rising villain actor, Richard Rober. But Rober didn't have the luck of the others. Two years later, he was killed in a car crash.

Siesta ● ⓥ
1987, US, 104 mins, colour
Dir: Mary Lambert
Stars: Ellen Barkin, Gabriel Byrne, Jodie Foster, Julian Sands, Martin Sheen, Isabella Rossellini
Rating: RB

Poor Ellen Barkin: this irredeemably potty farrago looks like a Brigitte Bardot reject from 30 years before. And it's filled with people of striking talent who have often proved bad choosers of scripts; all of them are adrift here in a ludicrous screenplay that provides quotable bad lines by the pageful. Barkin plays a skydiver who, fearful of her latest stunt and hungry for former lover Gabriel Byrne, flees hubby Martin Sheen and flies to Spain, where she throws herself at her ex-paramour. 'Do you remember,' she gasps, 'at the circus, when we crept into the cage and made love with the lions still inside?' Byrne remembers: 'We didn't even know they were there.' Julian Sands is so awful that he deserves such lines as: 'To me, the only falling that doesn't mean failing is falling in love.' At least Jodie Foster

contributes a grand English aristocratic accent and isn't quite as wasted as the rest. The plot structure has a potentially intriguing puzzle framework, but the dialogue and treatment by the director sink it without trace. Not dull, though; just a disaster.

Sign of Four, The ○
1983, UK, 103 mins, colour
Dir: Desmond Davis
Stars: Ian Richardson, David Healy, Cherie Lunghi, Thorley Walters
Rating: ★★

The excellent Ian Richardson emphasises Sherlock Holmes' haughty intellect and steely arrogance in this accomplished adaptation of the Arthur Conan Doyle story. Good support too, from blustering Thorley Walters, sinister Joe Melia and waspish Clive Merrison, while Cherie Lunghi makes a most fetching damsel in distress.

Sign of the Pagan ○
1954, US, 92 mins, colour
Dir: Douglas Sirk
Stars: Jeff Chandler, Jack Palance
Rating: ★★

Having learned something, perhaps, from Anthony Quinn's portrayal of Attila the Hun the previous year, Jack Palance ferociously dominates this 5th-century adventure yarn about the Hun chieftain and his (fictitious) battle of wits and wills with a Roman centurion, grumpily played by Jeff Chandler. Scenes of the Huns on the move are impressively done but, as you'd expect from Universal-International at the time, the film just lacks that extra something. Rita Gam, Eduard Franz and Alexander Scourby provide some solid support, and there are the usual bit-parts for the studio's starlets, including Allison Hayes (later to win fame in *Attack of the 50-foot Woman*) and Sara Shane.

Silence of the Lambs, The ● ⓥ
1990, US, 119 mins, colour
Dir: Jonathan Demme
Stars: Jodie Foster, Anthony Hopkins, Scott Glenn, Ted Levine, Diane Baker
Rating: ★★★

To hit the crime jackpot today, you need something that will churn the stomachs of all but those whose hunger for nightmare thrillers is insatiable. The particular brand of gore and psychiatry on offer here is highly effective in its best scenes, even though it does go on a bit. And what

better method of mayhem could you devise than a serial killer who skins his victims alive? And what better help than from America's most feared prisoner, a psychiatrist turned mass murderer called Hannibal the Cannibal from his habit of eating parts of his victims? Hopkins makes Hannibal at once a frightening and almost sympathetic character, locked away from the world until interviewed by fledgling agent Foster, looking for a clue to the Buffalo Bill murders. Writer Ted Tally inserts another key element into the plot by having 'Bill' kidnap each of his victims for three days before killing and skinning them, for a foul purpose that becomes clear later – this giving brainy Foster time to work out Hopkins' enigmatic clues to the killer, in return for which she must tell him details of her own past life. Director Demme can now sit back and let the story unwind to a scary confrontation climax in the cellars of a house which seem to have endless doors and patches of darkness. Hopkins and Foster won Oscars.

Silencers, The ○
1966, US, 103 mins, colour
Dir: Phil Karlson
Stars: Dean Martin, Stella Stevens
Rating: ★★★

Dean Martin became the screen's first singing super-spy in this splendidly entertaining action film. Victor Buono hams it up gloriously as the oriental villain. And a Martin crack about Sinatra brings back memories of the Crosby-Hope screen 'feud'. With Cyd Charisse and Nancy Kovack out of the way in the first half-hour, Dean is torn between the rosebud lips of Stella Stevens and the escalating eyebrows of Daliah Lavi as to who is the double-agent. Ms Stevens wins the acting battle from her rivals – but she does have the best lines.

Silent Enemy, The ○
1958, UK, 112 mins, b/w
Dir: William Fairchild
Stars: Laurence Harvey, Dawn Addams, Michael Craig, John Clements
Rating: ★★

An exciting war film based freely on the adventures of Britain's most famous frogman, 'Buster' Crabb. Filled with action, suspense and deeds of derring-do, it also has a vein of humour and a thread of wartime romance, provided by Dawn Addams.

S

Silent Movie ○ ⓥ

1976, US, 87 mins, colour
Dir: Mel Brooks
Stars: Mel Brooks, Marty Feldman, Dom DeLuise
Rating: ★★

One of those comedies that's fun without being very funny. Made almost entirely without words, it tells of three lunatic film-makers who save a major studio by making a silent movie in 1976. Several big stars come on and play themselves, and most of them show a much more precise sense of comedy than the central trio of Mel Brooks, Marty Feldman and Dom DeLuise, whose frantic mugging is entirely alien to the style of comedy to which the film is presumably taking a bow. The jokes are mainly telegraphed so far in advance that you can forecast a punchline (on silent credit cards, that is) about five seconds before it comes. Even a funny running gag about a newspaper vendor being struck by a bundle of papers isn't really carried through. Pleasant, lightweight and good for a giggle, the film falls some way short of the standards you feel it's setting itself.

Silent Running ○

1971, US, 90 mins, colour
Dir: Douglas Trumball
Stars: Bruce Dern, Cliff Potts
Rating: ★★★★

A beautiful, gentle, constantly entertaining science-fiction film, ahead of its time as far as ecology is concerned. Bruce Dern gives perhaps his best screen performance as the outer-space gardener who refuses to terminate his floating greenhouse and goes to any lengths, including the murder of his colleagues, to ensure its continuance. Not even two delightful robots called Huey and Dewey can steal Dern's show here. One of a kind, with lovely, crystal-clear colour pgotography by Charles F Wheeler.

Silk Stockings ○ ⓥ

1957, US, 111 mins, colour
Dir: Rouben Mamoulian
Stars: Fred Astaire, Cyd Charisse, Peter Lorre
Rating: ★★★

Elegant, long-legged Cyd Charisse was cast opposite Fred Astaire in this delightful Cole Porter musical set in Paris. It was a remake of Ernst Lubitsch's glittering dour-communist-East-meets-decadent-West comedy of 1939 that starred Greta Garbo as the

Soviet ice-maiden melted by romance. Charisse may be no match for Garbo in the acting department, but no matter: in the dance numbers she is stunning. Hermes Pan and Eugene Loring provided some fine choreography to match Porter's toe-tapping score and witty lyrics, all briskly directed by Rouben Mamoulian. Numbers to relish include Astaire and Charisse in 'All of You' and 'Fated to be Mated', Astaire and Janis Paige in a delightful Gene Kelly spoof, 'Stereophonic Sound', Astaire in the extraordinary 'The Ritz Roll and Rock', and Peter Lorre, Jules Munshin and Joseph Buloff as a trio of emininently corruptible communists (their number 'Siberia' is a hoot). Astaire was in excellent form, but it was to be his last MGM musical until he co-hosted the compilation *That's Entertainment* in 1974.

Silkwood ● ⓥ

1983, US, 131 mins, colour
Dir: Mike Nichols
Stars: Meryl Streep, Kurt Russell, Cher
Rating: ★★

Long and slow, but interesting and well-acted (as you would expect from a cast headed by Meryl Streep, Kurt Russell and Cher), this film revolves around the real-life Karen Silkwood, the plutonium worker who set out to expose contamination risks and other irregularities at her plant. This would make a fascinating subject for an hour-long TV documentary and, despite Streep's charismatic performance (which brought another deserved Oscar nomination) re-creating the flyaway character Karen must have been as well as her rather goofy lifestyle, there are times when you long to jump up with a huge pair of scissors and cut great chunks out of the film, as director Mike Nichols drifts dream-like through the story. Streep's performance, though, is something else: see it for that alone. And modern-day star-spotters will have a field day catching early appearances by Fred Ward, Ron Silver, Will Patton, Tess Harper and others.

Silverado ◑ ⓥ

1985, US, 132 mins, colour
Dir: Lawrence Kasdan
Stars: Kevin Kline, Kevin Costner, Scott Glenn, Jeff Goldblum, Danny Glover, John Cleese
Rating: ★★★

Although the Western was later given the kiss of life by Kevin Costner's

Dances With Wolves and Clint Eastwood's *Unforgiven*, it was little more than a sad corpse when brothers Lawrence and Mark Kasdan penned this entertaining homage to the best in the west (and ironically co-starring Costner). All the classical Western themes, including loyalty and friendship and the need of social misfits to find their niche in the great landscape, are explored, and there's an all-star cast, including Kevin Kline, Scott Glenn, Danny Glover, Jeff Goldblum and Linda Hunt, that any Hollywood producer today would give his right arm for if he had the budget. The women fare worst – but then they always did in Westerns – but Hunt, as the midget saloon owner, comes off better than Rosanna Arquette, whose character is either woefully underwritten or had its scenes drastically cut. John Cleese has a scene-stealing cameo as an English sheriff who knows when not to cross state boundaries and Brian Dennehy is a pugnacious villain.

Silver Bears ○ ⓥ

1977, US, 113 mins, colour
Dir: Ivan Passer
Stars: Michael Caine, Cybill Shepherd, Louis Jourdan
Rating: ★★

A light-hearted caper thriller that makes adequate entertainment but hardly comes up to the standard of the same writer's *Charade*. The story is something about crooks involved with banking and silver mines, but the film's approach is scarcely calculated to make you want to keep track of it. There are a few double-crosses, Cybill Shepherd does her kooky act (which is amusing at first but wears thin) and there are familiar characterisations from Michael Caine, Louis Jourdan and David Warner. It is, above all, a rather mechanical exercise in the art of making an international movie in the Seventies: local charm, a 'money' theme, ingratiating characters, colourful backrounds – the kind of film that has become increasingly less commercial in recent times.

Silver Chalice, The ○

1954, US, 144 mins, colour
Dir: Victor Saville
Stars: Paul Newman, Pier Angeli, Virginia Mayo, Jack Palance
Rating: ★★

Paul Newman made his film debut in this spectacular slice of Biblical Hollywoodiana about the silver chalice used at the Last Supper. In its way, it was Warner Brothers' answer to *The Robe*. The supporting cast includes Virginia Mayo, Jack Palance, Joseph Wiseman, Albert Dekker, Lorne Greene and a 15-year-old Natalie Wood, who plays Virginia Mayo's character when younger. Only flashes of the brilliance to come emerge from Newman's performance.

Silver City ○
(aka: High Vermilion)
1951, US, 90 mins, colour
Dir: Byron Haskin
Stars: Yvonne De Carlo, Barry Fitzgerald, Edmond O'Brien
Rating: ★★★

Three fine film old-timers, Barry Fitzgerald, Richard Arlen and Gladys George, give solid supporting performances in this Western about a mine-owner trying to trick a girl out of her ownership of a rich vein of silver. Director Byron Haskin injects a lot of fierce action which keeps the plot moving along like a racing stagecoach, and there's an exciting chase sequence along the top of a moving train. Producers William Pine and William Thomas ensure the production has a satisfyingly expensive look. They produced a whole string of adventure movies in the Fifties.

Silver Dream Racer ○
1980, UK, 111 mins, colour
Dir: David Wickes
Stars: David Essex, Beau Bridges, Cristina Raines
Rating: ★

Pop star David Essex's third foray into film stardom (after *That'll Be the Day* and *Stardust*) is the type of adolescent motorbike racing yarn that almost writes itself. Fighting the script's clichés and David Wickes' determinedly flashy direction are such reliable British performers as Lee Montague, Diane Keen and Harry H Corbett, and the American actor Beau Bridges who was, at the time, no stranger to motor racing circuits, having already appeared in *Heart Like a Wheel* and *Greased Lighting*.

Silver Lode ○
1954, US, 80 mins, colour
Dir: Allan Dwan
Stars: John Payne, Lizabeth Scott, Dan Duryea
Rating: ★★★

The impact of this crackerjack Western was totally unexpected when it was first released as the lower half of a double-bill with a very moderate adventure yarn called *Passion*. The story has echoes of *High Noon*: John Payne is very good as the man against whom the whole town gradually turns when an alleged posse shows up to arrest him for murder. The direction by veteran Allan Dwan, colour photography by John Alton and art direction by Van Nest Polglase all go towards making the most of the action and tension that result. The final scenes − following an agonisingly exciting shoot-out in a bell tower − are extremely moving. Dan Duryea, excellent as always, and Lizabeth Scott contribute strong support.

Silver Streak ○ ⓥ
1976, US, 130 mins, colour
Dir: Arthur Hiller
Stars: Gene Wilder, Jill Clayburgh, Richard Pryor, Scatman Crothers, Ned Beatty, Patrick McGoohan
Rating: ★★★

A train full of crooks, a bemused hero and a heroine in distress. It's a sure-fire formula for a successful comedy thriller, and one used all too seldom in recent years. Gene Wilder's wide-eyed and unbelieving George is just right and Jill Clayburgh makes the most of her too-few chances as a smouldering blond. Only Arthur Hiller's rather sluggish direction lags behind the other elements in the film, but he doesn't muff much of Colin Higgins' sparkling script, and Wilder's delivery of some of its comic gems would have even had Cary Grant's nod of approval. Staring at a newspaper headline with himself as a murder suspect he exclaims: 'That's my driving licence picture. I hate that picture!'

Simba ○
1955, UK, 99 mins, colour
Dir: Brian Desmond Hurst
Stars: Dirk Bogarde, Donald Sinden, Virginia McKenna
Rating: ★★★

Pretty nearly the full force of the Mau Mau terror in the Kenya of the Fifties is brought vividly to the screen in this intelligent, moving and at times terrifying film. Although not all the characters interest us as they might, the action builds up to a terrific climax and the film wisely offers no solution to what was a horrifying situation in its time. Geoffrey Unsworth's photography is a model lesson in how to make the most of the not always brilliant Eastman Colour process and director Brian Desmond Hurst's intelligent camera placements help heighten the drama.

Sinbad and the Eye of the Tiger ○
1977, US, 113 mins, colour
Dir: Sam Wanamaker
Stars: Patrick Wayne, Taryn Power, Jane Seymour
Rating: ★★

More magical adventures from the fertile imagination and painstaking creativity of special-effects genius Ray Harryhausen. This time, however, Sinbad's escapades are more padded out than usual, so you may find the children shifting restlessly in their armchairs waiting for the good parts. And Harryhausen's colleagues let him down a little with their back-projection work on the enchanted country Sinbad visits at the North Pole, which might well have been called the Land of the Wobbly Lines. Harryhausen's own work is well up to standard, especially in the swarm of flying devils.

Sinbad the Sailor ☉
1947, US, 117 mins, colour
Dir: Richard Wallace
Stars: Douglas Fairbanks Jr, Maureen O'Hara, Walter Slezak, Jane Greer
Rating: ★★★

Colourful extravaganza which has Douglas Fairbanks Junior flying in the footsteps of his fabulous father in the title role. Maureen O'Hara is a spirited heroine, and Walter Slezak contributes another of his famous studies in leering villainy as the conniving barber aboard Sinbad's ship. Amazing art direction is the last word in Hollywood 'eastern' taste.

Since You Went Away ○
1944, US, 172 mins, b/w
Dir: John Cromwell
Stars: Claudette Colbert, Jennifer Jones, Joseph Cotten
Rating: ★★★

Tremendously professional three-hour epic of the American way of life, as patriotic film-makers liked to see it, during World War Two. Memorable scenes include family gatherings; an instant nostalgia dance held in a deserted aircraft hangar, before the men go off to fight; and a lovers' farewell at a railway station.

S

Sing ○

1989, US, 98 mins, colour
Dir: Richard Baskin
Stars: Lorraine Bracco, Peter Dobson, Patti LaBelle
Rating: ★★★

Somewhere between *Dirty Dancing*, *Fame*, *Blackboard Jungle* and *42nd Street* lies *Sing*, as good a bad film as you'll see. The kids are putting on a show, but the adults are closing down the school. Nice Jewish Hannah is pitched in with Italianate delinquent Dominic as co-organisers of the Brooklyn school's last-ever 'sing' and guess what happens? No kidding! Hannah's hard-hearted mamma won't come to the concert, but will she relent at the last moment? Is the Pope still a Catholic? The clichés are deeper than the songsheets in this one, but it's richly enjoyable, pumped full of *joie-de-vivre* with tuneful music and brilliantly executed production numbers. The New York critics who thought it was performed without enthusiasm must have rocks for brains. Lorraine Bracco top-stars as the dynamo teacher who puts on the show, and she can dance as well as act. And the emotive surge of the musical climax will surely bring a tear to the eye in this glitzy, supercharged package.

Sing and Swing
See: Live It Up

Singapore ○

1947, US, 79 mins, colour
Dir: John Brahm
Stars: Fred MacMurray, Ava Gardner
Rating: ★★

One of the films that helped Ms Gardner's rise to stardom, this well-mounted but lifeless thriller features MacMurray as an adventurer searching for a priceless pearl, and English actor Roland Culver in one of the parts he played during a prolonged stay in Hollywood – as a Dutchman!

Sing As We Go ○

1934, UK, 80 mins, b/w
Dir: Basil Dean
Stars: Gracie Fields, John Loder
Rating: ★★★

Gracie Fields' most famous comedy-musical (also the title of her autobiography). It was especially written for her by J B Priestley. Gracie seems to be enjoying herself

more than in any other film, Stanley Holloway scores as a policeman, and you'll have to look fast and hard to spot 13-year-old Muriel Pavlow in the van of a crowd of cheering schoolgirls.

Singin' in the Rain ⊙ ⓥ

1952, US, 102 mins, colour
Dir: Stanley Donen
Stars: Gene Kelly, Donald O'Connor, Debbie Reynold, Jean Hagen
Rating: ★★★★

This famous MGM musical about the adventures of a matinee idol (Gene Kelly) in the early days of sound films is perhaps the most enduring ever to roll off the Hollywood production line. And while nothing in it can top the brilliant foot-tapping sequence to the title song, with Kelly joyously dancing in a California downpour – 'an irrepressible ode to optimism' according to the screenwriters – every other number was still head and shoulders above most musicals of the 1950s. Jean Hagen gives the best performance as a dim star who has endless difficulties with concealed microphones but knows the value of a contract. And a sequence where Cyd Charisse dances in a veil taxed Kelly's abilities as a choreographer and required no less than three aircraft engines to give the veil the right flow. The whole thing probably runs neck and neck with Kelly's *On the Town* for the most joyous musical of all time.

Singles ◐ ⓥ

1992, US, 100 mins, colour
Dir: Cameron Crowe
Stars: Bridget Fonda, Campbell Scott, Kyra Sedgwick, Matt Dillon, Bill Pullman, Jim True
Rating: ★

This modish film about the single life in Seattle has no good characters and is practically devoid of interest. Boring is the word, and you might find youself sleepy in Seattle long before the end. Little warmth is generated by the people played by Bridget Fonda, Kyra Sedgwick, Campbell Scott and Matt Dillon (not that the script gives them much chance) and their future as couples doesn't seem to hold too much promise. Sheila Kelley (taking time out from her *L A Law* duties on TV) is a little more interesting as the 'single' looking for her opposite number via a videotape dating agency.

Singleton's Pluck ○

(aka: Laughterhouse)
1984, UK, 93 mins, colour
Dir: Richard Eyre
Stars: Ian Holm, Penelope Wilton, Bill Owen
Rating: ★★★★

Red River with geese. All this laughter and tears film needs in fact, is a stampede. But, with geese, that would be difficult. The story and its execution, however, would not disgrace Ealing Studios at their best. Faced with transport and union problems, after one of his men loses a finger in the plucking machine, farmer Singleton (Ian Holm) sets out to drive his flock of several hundred geese all the way from Norfolk to London in time for the Christmas market. He is pursued not only by TV crews – who at one stage let the geese loose simply to provide a story – but by a goose-loving fox whom Singleton calls Basil, but whose feathery prey lies forever just beyond his dripping jaws. The human element in this chronicle struggles to make itself felt but gradually rises triumphant against a background of Constable-like landscapes lovingly photographed by Clive Tickner. Holm, Penelope Wilton and Stephanie Tague as their (too tall?) daughter are excellent in their roles, but the picture is stolen by Bill Owen as the Jethro Larkin-type goosehand who gets all the juiciest lines.

Single White Female ● ⓥ

1992, US, 107 mins, colour
Dir: Barbet Schroeder
Stars: Bridget Fonda, Jennifer Jason Leigh, Stephen Tobolowsky, Steven Weber
Rating: ★★

This is the one about the unsuspecting hero/heroine who hires a psycho as servant/housekeeper/babysitter/flatmate. Perm heroine and flatmate from these possibilities and you have Bridget Fonda and Jennifer Jason Leigh as the protagonists in a tale of terror adapted from the novel *Single White Female Seeks Same* by John Lutz. The story's nicely set up, the last 15 minutes superbly edited and very exciting with a final duel to the death, predictably in the spooky underbelly of the apartment block we've been shown at the beginning. In between, though, it goes on a bit and gets tedious, moving in fits and starts when it should be tightening the tension. Tiny Jason Leigh is tough to take as a ferocious fiend but she really does give it her best shot, as does Fonda in one of the most effective roles of her career. Stephen Tobolowsky contributes yet another of his slimebags, but this is the girls' show and they make the most of it.

Sink the Bismarck! ○ ⓥ
1959, UK, 97 mins, b/w
Dir: Lewis Gilbert
Stars: Kenneth More, Dana Wynter, Carl Mohner
Rating: ★★★

Although this World War Two action film is based on fact, there have been complaints that it is most inaccurate. Be that as it may, this – one of the last great British films about wartime naval action – is a most exciting account of the quest for the formidable German battleship *Bismarck*. As the withdrawn officer directing operations, Kenneth More has one of his most interesting roles and is well supported by a whole fleet of the best British character actors.

Sins of Rachel Cade, The ○
1960, US, 123 mins, colour
Dir: Gordon Douglas
Stars: Angie Dickinson, Peter Finch, Roger Moore
Rating: ★★

A poor man's version of *The Nun's Story*, with Angie Dickinson delivering one of her best performances as the medical missionary who finds the call of the flesh stronger than the call of duty. Peter Finch, left over from *The Nun's Story*, provides quiet authority, and Roger Moore handsome egotism as the pilot who leads Ms Dickinson astray during this episode drama set in the then Belgian Congo.

Sirens ● ⓥ
1994, Australia, 94 mins, colour
Dir: John Duigan
Stars: Hugh Grant, Tara Fitzgerald, Sam Neill, Elle MacPherson
Rating: ★

A silly Australian sex frolic that could have come from West Germany 25 years ago and ended up in porno cinemas. Coming from Australia rather than Austria, perhaps this kind of thing now qualifies as art. At any rate Hugh Grant and Tara Fitzgerald amusingly and skilfully do what they can as the cleric and wife who come to interview painter Sam Neill (under-used) about his crude nude

pictures. She is soon seduced by the exotic atmosphere of this household of nude models, not to mention the convenient and muscular blind handyman. Titillating garbage, derivative and completely unbelievable.

Sister Act ○ ⓥ
1992, US, 102 mins, colour
Dir: Emile Ardolino
Stars: Whoopi Goldberg, Maggie Smith, Harvey Keitel, Mary Wickes, Kathy Najimy
Rating: ★★★

Hollywood's been making films like this ever since they put gangster James Cagney in charge of the reformatory in *The Mayor of Hell* nearly 60 years before. Not that Whoopi Goldberg is actually a bad guy here. She's Dolores, a Reno lounge singer who's forced into the witness protection programme after accidentally barging in on a hit by her gangster boyfriend (Harvey Keitel). Her hideout proves to be a convent – and her 'cover' is just that. 'Look at me,' she wails. 'I'm a nun. I'm a penguin.' Inevitably, Dolores comes to be affected by her surroundings, notably in organising the convent choir into an enlargement of Diana Ross and the Supremes. So, when her cover is blown, with a concert before the Pope by the now-famous choir just hours away, she doesn't want to leave. This all gets a bit over-the-top towards the end, even for a farce, but very enjoyable for all that. Whoopi is pretty well the whole show, with the eminent Dame Maggie Smith a little lost as the waspish Mother Superior who disapproves of modern methods.

Sister Act 2: Back in the Habit ○ ⓥ
1994, US, 107 mins, colour
Dir: Bill Duke
Stars: Whoopi Goldberg, Maggie Smith, James Coburn, Kathy Najimy, Mary Wickes, Barnard Hughes
Rating: ★★

Soul sister Whoopi Goldberg is back in wimple and designer sunspecs, but fails to make quite as much Whoopi on her second visit to the convent. This time the action switches from a rundown parish church to a rundown high school, where motormouth Whoopi is soon transforming the local tearaways into a choir to save the place from closure. Kathy Najimy as Sister Mary Patrick and veteran Mary Wickes as sourpuss Sister Mary Lazarus steal the best laughs again,

with Maggie Smith more peripheral this time as the 'mother of all mother superiors'. Even disco diva Sheryl Lee Ralph gets in on the act with a straight acting role. But the film strikes a bum note with its hardly magical choreography and several confusing, stodgy sub-plots to the main action. Overall, it's a case of sequelitis with limited mass appeal. The trailer's great, though: don't let it make you expect too much.

Sisters ●
(aka: Some Girls)
1988, US, 94 mins, colour
Dir: Michael Hoffman
Stars: Patrick Dempsey, Jennifer Connelly, Lila Kedrova
Rating: ★

A boring film with human dynamo Patrick Dempsey would seem a contradiction in terms, but here it is. A downright peculiar Gothic comedy romance, it exists principally for one more virtuoso performance by veteran European star Lila Kedrova, as the grandmother whose dying spirit dominates a weird family whose three daughters all enjoy an on/off romantic entanglement with Dempsey when he comes to stay with the youngest (Jennifer Connelly) for Christmas. There's a lot of wandering around the richly brocaded trappings of the house, which gives the cameraman opportunities to photograph everything in varying shades of brown. As things develop (or fail to), you may soon feel like donning Dempsey's nightshirt and nightcap and joining this latter-day Eddie Bracken in slumber.

Sitting Bull ○
1954, US, 106 mins, colour
Dir: Sidney Salkow
Stars: Dale Robertson, Mary Murphy
Rating: ★

Custer's Last Stand gets another airing in this big action film originally made as one of the early CinemaScope spectacles. J Carrol Naish plays Sitting Bull for the second time in films. Shot in blurred colour, the results are overlong, melodramatic, unconvincing and at times even boring. Dull and uninspired then, adjectives which can certainly also be applied to Naish as the great Indian warrior, although Dale Robertson shows up well as the hero. Only real bright spot: an excellent, dignified song, 'Great Spirit'.

S

Sitting Pretty ○
1948, US, 84 mins, b/w
Dir: Walter Lang
Stars: Robert Young, Maureen O'Hara, Clifton Webb
Rating: ★★★

It's probably fair to say that Clifton Webb was a shooting star in the Hollywood of the late Forties. He had been a film actor (and a dancer) since the silent days, but it wasn't until he was about 50 and had gone to 20th Century-Fox as a character actor that he quite suddenly became famous. He attracted attention in films such as *Laura* and *The Razor's Edge*, but it was this comedy, *Sitting Pretty*, that really launched him into popularity. For here he essayed what has rightly been called his 'waspish' speciality, playing for the first time the role of Lynn Belvedere, the testy but unconventional babysitter who stolidly maintains he's a genius. He did it with such success that Fox followed it with two sequels, *Mr Belvedere Goes to College* and *Mr Belvedere Rings the Bell*. The film is great fun throughout and includes the classic scene in which Belvedere fulfils the wishful thinking of thousands of frustrated parents by pouring a bowl of porridge over a fractious toddler's head, leaving the bowl stuck on top.

633 Squadron ○ ⓥ
1964, UK, 94 mins, colour
Dir: Walter E Grauman
Stars: Cliff Robertson, George Chakiris
Rating: ★★

The rousing music composed by Ron Goodwin is the thing most people remember about this sporadically exciting but ultimately indifferent war film. It centres on a plan to bomb and destroy a Nazi V2 rocket factory in Norway, with the aid of the Norwegian Resistance. Cliff Robertson is firm-jawed as the American leader of the British squadron assigned to the task and George Chakiris is the resistance leader involved. Those with memories long enough objected to the idea of a Yank showing us how to win the war in this one, but in any event, the story was ill-served by a poor script and the film only comes to life during the well-realised battle scenes.

Sixty Glorious Years ○
(aka: Queen of Destiny)
1938, UK, 95 mins, colour
Dir: Herbert Wilcox
Stars: Anna Neagle, Anton Walbrook, C Aubrey Smith
Rating: ★★★

A companion film to *Victoria the Great*. This time, the whole film is in Technicolor. Producer director Herbert Wilcox, who five years later married the star, Anna Neagle, obtained special permission to film much of it at Windsor Castle. The result was an immense popular success at the box-office.

Skin Deep ● ⓥ
1989, US, 101 mins, colour
Dir: Blake Edwards
Stars: John Ritter, Vincent Gardenia, Alyson Reed, Chelsea Field
Rating: ★

A few years before this, the prolific Edwards made a movie called *The Man Who Loved Women*. It would have exactly fitted this one, too, with Ritter as a compulsive womaniser and all-round pain in the butt. The film's overall tedium is lightened by a couple of very funny scenes, including one outrageous sequence involving luminous condoms, and another in which Ritter accidentally sits on his hated mother-in-law's pet dog. Alas, his character plays too much of a one-note samba to appeal to audience sympathy for long. And Alyson Reed is dull as the wife he's trying to win back. Interesting, though, to see veterans Gardenia, Don Gordon, Nina Foch and Michael Kidd in the supporting cast.

Skin Game ○
1971, US, 102 mins, colour
Dir: Paul Bogart
Stars: James Garner, Lou Gossett, Susan Clark
Rating: ★

An overrated, squirmingly unfunny Western comedy with James *Maverick* Garner shamelessly over the top as a con-man travelling the American south 'selling' his black partner (Lou Gossett) as a slave. The latter subsequently escapes and the men share the spoils. Gossett supplies what few smiles are going, while Andrew Duggan at least tries to play it straight as a cruel plantation owner. Subtlety is not in the script's vocabulary, however, allowing us to have little feeling for any of the characters, as the plot limps laughlessly along. The underlying message about the evils of slavery and human greed is, of course, serious, and enhances the film – a little.

Skull, The ◐
1965, UK, 83 mins, colour
Dir: Freddie Francis
Stars: Peter Cushing, Patrick Wymark, Christopher Lee, Jill Bennett
Rating: ★★★

A fine cast of horror-mongers adds gloss to this beautifully-mounted horror film, directed with a nerve-jangling edge by Freddie Francis, who endows everything with a chilly sense of menace, even though the special effects occasionally wobble. Black candles smoke evilly; browns and yellows give flickering light to moments of horror; and Peter Cushing gives a fine study in bewildered terror as the ultimate owner of the skull. Other moments to remember include an eerily effective dream sequence; and an aged doctor, marked for doom, seen through the eyes of . . . the skull.

Skullduggery ○
1969, US, 101 mins, colour
Dir: Gordon Douglas
Stars: Burt Reynolds, Susan Clark, Edward Fox
Rating: ★

Reynolds brings his own tongue-in-cheek approach to this unlikely but attractively photographed tale of an archaeological expedition to New Guinea that ends up finding what might be the missing link, that unexpected gap in evolution between anthropoid apes and man. Engaging performances also from Susan Clark as a sniffy lady scientist, Roger C Carmel, Edward Fox and, in almost his last film, Australian veteran Chips Rafferty. In the supporting cast are any number of interesting people, including Britain's avuncular Wilfrid Hyde White; diminutive actress Pat Suzuki, who played the lead in the original stage version of *Flower Drum Song*; William Marshall, powerful black character actor; and Paul Hubschmid, the German-born actor who was from 1949 to 1956 a Hollywood star under the name Paul Christian.

Skyjacked ○
1972, US, 100 mins, colour
Dir: John Guillermin
Stars: Charlton Heston, Yvette Mimieux, James Brolin
Rating: ★★

Skyjackings were particulary rife at the time this mid-air suspense epic was rushed out by the capable hands of John Guillermin, later to make *The Towering Inferno* and *King Kong*. Given that there's a maniac with a bomb aboard Charlton Heston's airliner, characters, situations and developments are highly predictable, and the main interest lies in guessing Who Planted It. Guillermin ensures that what suspense he can muster is capped by a suitably explosive ending. Three years later, Heston was back in high-altitude tension with *Airport*.

Sky Murder ○
1940, US, 72 mins, b/w
Dir: George B Seitz
Stars: Walter Pidgeon, Kaaren Verne
Rating: ★★

Urbane Walter Pidgeon possessed many good qualities as an actor, but dynamism wasn't one of them. Thus he was somewhat uneasily cast as Nick Carter, the 'dime novel' detective whose exploits had been thrilling Americans since his first appearance in print in 1886. In this, the third of Pidgeon's three stabs at the role, Carter is inevitably involved with Axis spies, out to perpetrate dastardly deeds against poor Uncle Sam. Leading lady Kaaren Verne (briefly married to Peter Lorre) flourished in Hollywood for a while in the early war years but what acting honours there are in this film go to sparky Joyce Compton, and to smooth Tom Conway (real-life brother of George Sanders), who was to make a bigger mark than Pidgeon in screen detective fiction by playing The Falcon in several low-budget adventures.

Sky West and Crooked ○
(aka: Gypsy Girl)
1965, UK, 102 mins, colour
Dir: John Mills
Stars: Hayley Mills, Ian McShane, Laurence Naismith, Geoffrey Bayldon
Rating: ★★

This rather fey attempt to broaden Hayley Mills' image toward adult roles was directed by her father, John Mills, and co-written by her mother, Mary Hayley Bell. It's the kind of film where everyone speaks in Mummerset but Hayley gives a spirited performance as the retarded 17-year-old daughter of a gin-sodden mother and the English countryside is prettily photographed in Eastmancolor by Arthur Ibbetson.

Slamdance ◐
1987, US, 101 mins, colour
Dir: Wayne Wang
Stars: Tom Hulce, Mary Elizabeth Mastrantonio, Virginia Madsen, Adam Ant
Rating: ★

With a weak script to start with, director Wayne Wang obviously decided to take the 'style over content' route with this thriller. Unfortunately, that didn't work either. Tom Hulce (who played Mozart in *Amadeus*) is a cartoonist who has an affair but then finds the lady murdered and that he is the prime suspect. Hulce is wild-eyed and slightly psychotic as usual, which is irritating, while Mary Elizabeth Mastrantonio is given little to do but look lovely. Harry Dean Stanton is wasted as a shady detective and Adam Ant once again proves that he couldn't act startled if you set his trousers alight. A deeply unsatisfying film on every level.

Slap Shot ● ⓥ
1977, US, 122 mins, colour
Dir: George Hill
Stars: Paul Newman, Michael Ontkean, Lindsay Crouse
Rating: ★★

A blood-and-guts action drama that takes us into a world of low-grade, free-for-all ice hockey, where brawls are more frequent than goals and the really bad mauler-with-a-stick 'has been known to carve a man's eye out with a flick of his wrist.' You can believe it, too, when Paul Newman and his team of no-hopers become the Bad News Boars as they fight and claw their way up to the top of their game by playing dirty. Like their game, the film is sometimes a bit too abrasive to take. But it does have its moments of apocalyptic joy, notably when three backward, bespectacled colts turn into fighting furies as Newman sends them out on the ice; or when one player decides that a solo spotlight is better than a mass punch-up and does a mildly successful striptease to the delight of the crowd and the chagrin of the fighting players.

Slattery's Hurricane ○
1951, US, 83 mins, b/w
Dir: Andre De Toth
Stars: Richard Widmark, Veronica Lake, Linda Darnell
Rating: ★★

One of the earliest of Richard Widmark's part-good-bad roles: here he plays war hero and smuggler. Good storm sequences but the film did little at the box-office and signalled a sadly early end to Veronica Lake's career in mainline films. Director De Toth was her husband at the time this film was made.

Slaughter on 10th Avenue ○
1957, US, 103 mins, b/w
Dir: Arnold Laven
Stars: Richard Egan, Julie Adams, Walter Matthau, Jan Sterling
Rating: ★★

A cast that's only a little short of terrific, in a grimly-told crime thriller that's only a little better than routine. A sort of *On the Waterfront* seen from the police point of view, it features Walter Matthau in one of his earliest cinema roles, giving a memorable portrayal of a pig-mannered, odiously self-assured union chief. Dan Duryea has a disappointingly small role towards the end, but there are good performances from Julie Adams, Jan Sterling, Mickey Shaughnessy, Charles McGraw and Sam Levene. Director Arnold Laven does manage one brilliantly jumpy moment that may jerk you from the armchair.

Slaughter Trail ○
1952, US, 78 mins, colour
Dir: Irving Allen
Stars: Brian Donlevy, Gig Young
Rating: ★★

A singing commentary is the principal attraction of this Western in woozy Cinecolor, but, as a device, it doesn't work as well as in, say, *Cat Ballou* or *Rancho Notorious*. Brian Donlevy boosted the cast when he replaced blacklisted Howard Da Silva, but the interiors have a cramped look, and the whole project could have had more style with an injection of funds from stingy RKO boss Howard Hughes. The occasional bursts of 'Injun' action are more than welcome.

Slaves of Babylon ○
1953, US, 82 mins, colour
Dir: William Castle
Stars: Richard Conte, Linda Christian
Rating: ★

Surprising to find Richard Conte in this, one of a series of 'easterns' made by Columbia in the early Fifties. Resident stars included, more predictably, Rhonda Fleming, Paul Henreid and Maureen O'Hara. This one tells the story of Cyrus, young shepherd, who turn out to be the

S

rightful heir to the throne of Persia. Cyrus is played by Terence Kilburn, a Hollywood child star of a decade before, notably in *A Christmas Carol*, *Goodbye Mr Chips* – as four generations of schoolboys in the Colley family – *The Swiss Family Robinson* and *National Velvet*. The story of Daniel in the Lions' Den is also thrown in by director William Castle, to accentuate the Biblical flavour.

Slaves of New York ◑
1988, US, 126 mins, colour
Dir: James Ivory
Stars: Bernadette Peters, Mary Beth Hurt, Chris Sarandon, Mercedes Ruehl
Rating: ★★

There's more than a touch of eccentricity in this film about the struggling denizens of the artists' quarter in downtown Manhattan. Bernadette Peters is excellent in the pivotal role (and thank God there is one) of the near-normal 'working girl' hat designer who can't get over her crush on her live-in lover, a batty artist whose petty jealousies are hardly compatible with his own double standards in matters of the heart. She's a much better person than him, but her grasshopper mind can't take the concept. Offered drugs at a party, she parries with 'No thanks, I have enough trouble with regular reality.' For the rest, it's what original author Tama Janowitz says it is: 'Everyone pursuing everyone else in a desperate quest for – something intangible, the pursuit of happiness and a better apartment.' A bit of a jumble, the resultant trip through the artistic jungle, but with Ms Peters to guide us, the safari is at least rarely dull.

Sleeper ○ ⓥ
1973, US, 88 mins, colour
Dir: Woody Allen
Stars: Woody Allen, Diane Keaton, John Beck
Rating: ★★★

No Woody Allen comedy is funny all the way through, but this one comes closer than most. Woody's been frozen alive and awoken by scientists 200 years later, only to find that nothing has changed except clothes, buildings and sex (it's automatised). He also has a robot dog, which disturbs him. 'Is he housebroken?' he asks, 'or will he leave little batteries all over the floor?' Diane Keaton was never funnier as a female clown than here, and she and Woody go together like Laurel and Hardy. Ultimately,

they join the revolution, which makes Woody remember another female acquaintance. 'Yes,' he sighs, 'she was arrested for selling pornographic join-the-dots books.'

Sleepers, The ○
1988, US, 77 mins, colour
Dir: Richard Benjamin
Stars: Sidney Poitier, River Phoenix, Richard Jenkins, Caroline Kava, Richard Bradford, Richard Lynch
Rating: ★★

This much foreshortened version of a film known in its native America as *Little Nikita* adds further staccato impetus to an already fast-paced if formula thriller. The idea is clever and the story starts strongly. But, even in the full version, implausibilities and disjointed events soon overwhelmed our sympathy with the leading characters. Sidney Poitier and River Phoenix bond together quite well as the FBI agent and prospective Air Force trainee who become involved in a dangerous situation as society spies, but acting honours are stolen from both of them by Richard Bradford (once TV's *Man in a Suitcase*) as a dangerous KGB agent. Like Poitier's, his performance is loaded with controlled intensity.

Sleeping Car to Trieste ○
1948, UK, 95 mins, b/w
Dir: John Paddy Carstairs
Stars: Jean Kent, Albert Levien
Rating: ★★★

In this skilful remake of the Thirties suspense classic *Rome Express*, Albert Lieven takes the part originally played by Conrad Veidt–Zurta, the criminal mastermind tracking down the petty crook who's double-crossed him. The familiar faces of Finlay Currie, Alan Wheatley and Hugh Burden appear in a strong supporting cast. Lively thriller from the confident British cinema of the post-war years.

Sleeping Tiger, The ○
1954, UK, 89 mins, b/w
Dir: Joseph Losey
Stars: Dirk Bogarde, Alexis Smith, Alexander Knox
Rating: ★★★

Foolish but full-blooded stuff in the highest Warner Brothers melodramatic style. But this is a British film made by blacklisted Hollywood talents. Screenwriter Derek Frye is really Carl Foreman, and director Joseph Losey lurks under the

pseudonym of Victor Hanbury, who actually produced the film. It was the beginning of Losey's profitable association with Dirk Bogarde that was ultimately to lead to *The Servant*, *King and Country* and *Accident*. Alexis Smith revels in the kind of part she could never have won at Warners where Bette Davis had first choice of such red meat.

Sleeping With the Enemy ◑ ⓥ
1991, US, 100 mins, colour
Dir: Joseph Ruben
Stars: Julia Roberts, Patrick Bergin, Kevin Anderson
Rating: ★★★

This vehicle for the talents of Julia Roberts is a suspense chiller that does its job pretty well. The action starts off by establishing Roberts as a wife beaten by her affluent but unbalanced husband (Patrick Bergin) and continues with a very effective midnight storm at sea, in which she escapes to a new life. The rest of the film is a slow build-up to the last reel, as Bergin finds out she's alive and tracks her down. The climax is chock full of false shocks as director Ruben shamelessly plays on his audience's nerves. Where will Bergin jump out from, to make us, and Roberts, collapse with fright? The middle-section romance between Roberts and small-town drama teacher Anderson is predictably soppy but, nonetheless, this is a seat-gripper from which fans of the genre will not come away disappointed.

Sleepless in Seattle ○ ⓥ
1993, US, 105 mins, colour
Dir: Nora Ephron
Stars: Tom Hanks, Meg Ryan, Bill Pullman, Ross Malinger, Victor Garber, Rosie O'Donnell
Rating: ★★★

It's amazing that a film can sustain a theme of two people not destined to meet until its final scenes. French director Claude Lelouch used to help this mixture go down with a tablespoonful of sugar, but this sweet and funny movie just about makes it on its own – aided by romantic songs from unlikely sources Louis Armstrong and Jimmy Durante. And it has Tom Hanks and Meg Ryan. Especially Ryan, more appealing than ever as a journalist about to marry snuffly suitor Bill Pullman (also very good) – until, on the car radio, she hears Hanks pouring out his heart (to the agony aunt his young son Jonah has rung) over the death of his beloved wife 18 months before. Like women all over America, Ryan is hooked. But, as we know, this one is different. Jonah (Ross Malinger) knows it too: he picks out Annie's letter from the rest, because of a simpatico reference to baseball. Hanks tries to date, but Jonah doesn't approve. 'He's eight,' says Hanks. 'He's good at it,' remarks the date. So will they ever meet? It doesn't seem like it, but director/co-writer Nora Ephron knows she can't string us this far without a happy ending. One for a smile and a furtive tear, rather than a good cry.

Sleep My Love ○
1948, US, 96 mins, b/w
Dir: Douglas Sirk
Stars: Claudette Colbert, Robert Cummings, Don Ameche
Rating: ★★★

When she made this film, Claudette Colbert had been a top star for over 20 years and had been an Oscar-winner in 1934 for her performance in Frank Capra's evergreen comedy *It Happened One Night*. Highly popular throughout the Thirties and maintaining her popularity in the following 10 years, she was now approaching the end of the main, uninterrupted part of her career. Here she plays a woman who is a victim of amnesia, unable to remember why she left New York on a train to Boston. The film, which includes an early appearance by Raymond Burr, was directed by the long-neglected, now esteemed, Douglas Sirk.

Sleepwalkers ● ⓥ
1992, US, 89 mins, colour
Dir: Mick Garrick
Stars: Mädchen Amick, Brian Krause, Alice Krige
Rating: ★★

An unintentionally funny but still lively Stephen King horror film about a family of furless werecats that can change their shape to look like human beings. They also possess superhuman powers and, so that the horror content of the story is not neglected, have to drain the lifeforce from virgins to survive, though you would have thought a good fat steak would do them more good. Somehow the nearest local virgin (Mädchen Amick) manages to survive the attempts of the werecat son (Brian Krause) to deprive her of said force so as to feed mum (Alice Krige), while all about her are meeting grisly deaths. The werecats'

only natural enemies are real cats, which converge on their house in hordes, although even some of these turn out to have less than nine lives, and it's left to a police cat called Clovis to keep Amick's lifeforce intact. In fairness, King's script occasionally goes for real gallows humour, but never settles for one brand of horror and emerges as an uneasy if action-packed mix for fans of the genre.

Slender Thread, The ○
1965, US, 98 mins, b/w
Dir: Sydney Pollack
Stars: Sidney Poitier, Anne Bancroft, Telly Savalas
Rating: ★★

Director Sydney Pollack, who has since gained critical acclaim with *They Shoot Horses, Don't They?* and *Three Days of the Condor*, made his big-screen bow with this essay in suspense, about the fight to locate a woman (Anne Bancroft) who is threatening to commit suicide. Pollack and Oscar-winning writer Stirling Silliphant (he won it for *In the Heat of the Night*) cast the star of the film, Sidney Poitier, as the young worker at a 'crisis clinic' (an American equivalent of The Samaritans) and he responds with a performance that radiates sincerity and fervour. Silliphant based the story of the film on real-life characters and incidents.

Sleuth ◑ ⓥ
1972, US, 133 mins, colour
Dir: Joseph L Mankiewicz
Stars: Laurence Olivier, Michael Caine
Rating: ★★★

Multi-Oscar-winning director Joseph L Mankiewicz ended his cinema career on a high note with this virtuoso version of the famous stage play. The two central roles have provided prime acting material for a number of actors down the years, and Laurence Olivier (in particular) and Michael Caine enjoy themselves enormously with them here. Both they and Mankiewicz earned Academy Award nominations, but that was the year in which *The Godfather* swept the Oscars board. The only problem with a cinema version of the play's famous puzzle plot is that the film camera has a penetrating and enquiring eye, so that some of the story's deceptions, disguises, decoys and detours appear more transparent than when viewed from the safer distance of the theatre stalls. But the film is richly enjoyable

for all that, and Ken Adam's inventive production design is a marvel in itself.

Slight Case of Murder, A ○
1938, US, 85 mins, b/w
Dir: Lloyd Bacon
Stars: Edward G Robinson, Jane Bryan
Rating: ★★★

Of all the great gangster stars who rose to fame at Warner Brothers in the Thirties, none was better at guying his own image than Edward G Robinson. This wonderful Damon Runyon comedy (remodelled 14 years later for Broderick Crawford as *Stop, You're Killing Me*) stands alongside *Brother Orchid* as one of the most joyously successful parodies of the genre. Beer baron Robinson tries to go straight as Prohibition wanes, but suddenly starts to find dead bodies all over his swish country mansion. This needs to be seen after seeing a 'straight' Warner crime film to appreciate how funny it really is.

Slipper and the Rose, The ○ ⓥ
1976, UK, 146 mins, colour
Dir: Bryan Forbes
Stars: Richard Chamberlain, Gemma Craven, Annette Crosbie, Edith Evans, Michael Hordern
Rating: ★★

'There's someone in the room!' booms Edith Evans' vague and deaf Dowager Queen in this sumptuous but ultimately empty reworking of the *Cinderella* story. The joy in Evans' performance comes from the fact that director Bryan Forbes has tailored each role perfectly to the stock company of the cream of British acting talent he has assembled. Richard Chamberlain is a suave prince and Gemma Craven the servant girl he falls for. The opening snowbound shots filmed in Austria add to the atmosphere.

Slipstream ○ ⓥ
1989, UK, 101 mins, colour
Dir: Steven Lisberger
Stars: Bill Paxton, Mark Hamill, Bob Peck, Kitty Aldridge, Ben Kingsley, F Murray Abraham
Rating: ★

The producer of this science-fantasy about a planet dominated by its 'slipstream' is Gary *Star Wars* Kurtz, the director the man who made *Tron*. But lightning doesn't strike twice in these weird waters and this

S

loop-the-loopy aerial 'trip' is no mega-hit. It took me a while to work out the difference between Ben Kingsley and F Murray Abraham in two cameos that amount to no more than a cough and a spit. And even longer to figure out that Mark Hamill was the villain. But that's the least of the film's problems since, although it possesses some bizarre notions that might prove absorbing on the printed page, there's almost no action or incident to back them up, with the dialogue gradually falling away to the point where it produced titters from the audience. Bob Peck's oddball reading of the android-on-the-run doesn't really work; Hamill has little to do; and hero (or so, in the end, it proves) Bill Paxton can't quite fill Harrison Ford's boots.

Slither ◐

1973, US, 96 mins, colour
Dir: Howard Zieff
Stars: James Caan, Peter Boyle, Sally Kellerman
Rating: ★★★★

Written by W D Richter, creator of some thoroughly off-beat entertainments down the years, this crime comedy-thriller proves conclusively that an ingeniously constructed story, with carefully made individual scenes and twist after twist, can be as strong a winner as it ever was – and perhaps still the most entertaining genre of all. The plot is like a Bogart film gone haywire. James Caan plays an ex-convict on the trail of an embezzled $300,000, with the help (and hindrance) of kooky Sally Kellerman, who holds up restaurants when she needs money. Soon Dick and his contact are being pursued by two sinister black Dormobiles half-way across California. Who is doing what to whom? It's all lovely jigsaw-puzzle stuff, with one masterly scene from director Howard Zieff, as Caan tries desperately to escape four would-be assassins in a bingo tent.

Sliver ● ⓥ

1993, US, 106 mins, colour
Dir: Phillip Noyce
Stars: Sharon Stone, William Baldwin, Tom Berenger, Martin Landau, Polly Walker
Rating: ★

A poor, slow thriller, its impoverished plot overwhelmed by its erotic content. Sharon Stone is the new tenant in a high-rise block whose denizens have a habit of falling to their deaths

from a great height. Very soon she's involved with William Baldwin, the young owner of the building, whose control-room houses myriads of screens that enable him to spy on all the occupants. Also in the frame for Sharon's affections as well as a murder rap is poor Tom Berenger (what a comedown) as a dried-up author. There's about 30 minutes of plot here, but time enough to completely waste Martin Landau, Nina Foch, Colleen Camp and other talented players in peripheral roles. Don't hang around for the 'climax': it isn't worth it. The usually reliable Phillip Noyce, who made *Dead Calm*, must take the blame for some of this soporific claptrap masquerading as a stylish chiller. Stone is dull: whatever happened to the feisty actress from *King Solomon's Mines*?

Slow Dancing in the Big City ○

1978, US, 101 mins, colour
Dir: John G Avildsen
Stars: Paul Sorvino, Anne Ditchburn
Rating: ★

'Dancing she's a star – talking she ain't.' Let's paraphrase the famous comment on Esther Williams and apply it to Anne Ditchburn, the brilliant Canadian dancer who made her film debut in this rocky (if director John G Avildsen will excuse the in-pun) weepie about a reporter with a heart condition who falls in love with a ballet dancer who learns she will never dance again. Unlikely it is and yet it almost works towards the end, thanks to Paul Sorvino's hard-grafting performance as the reporter. And, though Ms Ditchburn is patently no actress, her dancing's a delight. No marks, though, for the scene where she arrives covered in sweat from rehearsal and changes into her clothes without so much as a shower. Pooh!

Small Back Room, The ○

(aka: Hour of Glory)
1948, UK, 106 mins, b/w
Dir: Emeric Pressburger, Michael Powell
Stars: David Farrar, Kathleen Byron, Jack Hawkins
Rating: ★★★

Tight, tense and fascinating drama about a crippled scientist battling both with his own problems and a new kind of German bomb which he and his fellow boffins are studying. A star-studded cast includes Sidney James and Bryan Forbes (his first film) in

minor roles. The direction of Michael Powell and the black and white camerawork of Christopher Challis heighten the claustrophobically compelling scenes of the difficult conditions under which boffins worked in wartime London.

Smallest Show On Earth, The ⊙

1957, UK, 80 mins, b/w
Dir: Basil Dearden
Stars: Virginia McKenna, Bill Travers, Peter Sellers, Margaret Rutherford
Rating: ★★★

All too short, this is a quite delightful comedy about a young couple who inherit a ramshackle old cinema – together with its equally ramshackle staff. With Margaret Rutherford as the cashier, Bernard Miles as the commissionaire, Peter Sellers as the drunken projectionist who gets hilariously entangled in thousands of feet of film, Leslie Phillips and Sidney James to support stars Virginia McKenna and Bill Travers, it just can't miss.

Smashing Time ○

1967, UK, 96 mins, colour
Dir: Desmond Davis
Stars: Rita Tushingham, Lynn Redgrave, Michael York
Rating: ★★

Although there are many chuckles in this custard pie comedy about two northern lasses on the loose in swinging London, the film has one fault: it tries too hard to be funny. With such a cast – Anna Quayle and Irene Handl contribute invaluable cameos – a screenplay by George Melly and direction by Desmond Davis, it is hard not to expect too much. Incidentally, the names of many of the characters are taken from poems by Lewis Carroll, principally *Jabberwocky*.

Smokey and the Bandit ○

1977, US, 96 mins, colour
Dir: Hal Needham
Stars: Burt Reynolds, Sally Field
Rating: ★★★

Another smash-'em-up chase movie, set in America's Deep South. But this one shows enough humour in the dialogue to make one wish there had been a few more words and a little less crashing of cars. The action is *Road Runner*-style stuff. Bandit (Burt Reynolds), the hero, is brilliant, and the 'smokeys' (cops), led by Jackie

Gleason, are all clods. Their cars are forever landing in streams, canals or bridges or the backs of other vehicles, as they hurtle in fruitless pursuit of Bandit's car. Followed by several increasingly resistible sequels.

Smokey and the Bandit II ○
1980, US, 104 mins, colour
Dir: Hal Needham
Stars: Burt Reynolds, Jackie Gleason, Sally Field
Rating: ★★

There are some nice comic moments in this sequel to *Smokey and the Bandit.* Notably the 'It'll Be All Right on the Night' section right at the end, when things that went wrong during filming of this hell-for-leather comedy can be seen between the end credits. Jackie Gleason is again the Sheriff, forever prusuing The Bandit in hair-raising car chases, although he is rather outpointed by ex-Tarzan Mike Henry, playing his son. Emptying his own gun and grabbing his son's, Gleason is told by his giant-sized son: 'When I put bullets in it, Daddy, it gets too heavy.' The film's British title was *Smokey and the Bandit Ride Again.*

Smokey and the Bandit III ○
1983, US, 88 mins, colour
Dir: Dick Lowry
Stars: Jackie Gleason, Jerry Reed, Colleen Camp, Mike Henry
Rating: ★

Although the sense of fun that so distinguished the first entry in this series of comedy chase films is less in evidence, director Dick Lowry decided to return to the non-stop car-to-car destruction derby of the original. Jackie Gleason and Mike Henry are still around as the sheriff and his son, Jerry Reed takes over as the Bandit, and Burt Reynolds puts in a brief guest appearance as 'the Real Bandit'. Gleason remains as funny as ever at the centre of this patchwork of arbitrary mayhem. Brothel sequences makes it unsuitable for younger children.

Smoky ○
1946, US, 87 mins, colour
Dir: Louis King
Stars: Fred MacMurray, Anne Baxter, Burl Ives
Rating: ★★★

A cowboy captures and trains a wild horse which he calls Smoky. A special bond is formed between the two, but

Smoky is lost during a cattle raid. This blatantly sentimental film was quite a hit in its day and is the best of the three versions of the story made. Luckily it manages to avoid wallowing in the mire of mawkishness it could so easily have slipped into even though it occasionally brings a lump to the throat. This is thanks to fine playing by Fred MacMurray, Anne Baxter and (in his first film) Burl Ives, and director Louis King's firm grip on the story. You'll cheer for Smoky and hiss bad old Bruce Cabot as he ill-treats the horse in a scene that may upset some younger children.

Smooth Talk ◑
1985, US, 92 mins, colour
Dir: Joyce Chopra
Stars: Treat Williams, Laura Dern
Rating: ★★

The relationship Mary Kay Place has with teenage daughter Laura Dern in this bizarre film will gladden the hearts of mothers and daughters who believe theirs couldn't be worse. Both living their lives on a hair-trigger, they fling insults at each other for little apparent reason, in the manner of long-lost enemies. Virgin-on-the-verge Dern simmers in the summer of a small American town, beset by Mom, indecisive Dad and the goody-goody older sister she used to love. Well, something's gotta happen, right? And it does, in the form of smooth-talking stranger Treat Williams, who lures Laura out of the house and into a ride in his car, after which everything in her life seems okay. There should be some kind of prize to anyone who can guess what the last two reels of the film are all about, although you won't find us taking part: we hadn't a clue. Puzzle pictures are rare in modern times; those you can't be bothered to unravel are even rarer – even though this is sumptuously photographed by James Glennon and contains a very promising performance by Dern.

Smuggler's Island ○
1951, US, 74 mins, colour
Dir: Edward Ludwig
Stars: Jeff Chandler, Evelyn Keyes, Philip Friend
Rating: ★★

Jeff Chandler and Evelyn Keyes star in this exotic adventure yarn about gold-running and deep-sea diving off the coast of China. One of several colourful films that British star Philip Friend – who perhaps looked a little too much like Richard Greene –

made in Hollywood at the time, other examples being *Panther's Moon, Buccaneer's Girl, Sword in the Desert* and *The Highwayman.*

Snake Pit, The ○
1948, US, 108 mins, b/w
Dir: Anatole Litvak
Stars: Olivia de Havilland, Mark Stevens, Celeste Holm, Leif Erickson
Rating: ★★★

Gruelling film about life in an outdated mental asylum. Olivia de Havilland came close to winning her second Oscar in three years (she made up for it a year later in *The Heiress*) with her portrayal of the gentle but tormented woman pitched into a horrifying and barbaric environment.

Sneakers ◑ ⓥ
1992, US, 125 mins, colour
Dir: Phil Alden Robinson
Stars: Robert Redford, Dan Aykroyd, Sidney Poitier, River Phoenix, Ben Kingsley, Mary McDonnell
Rating: ★★

The title characters in this star-heavy film are code-crackers or, as the script has it, 'People you hire to break into their places to make sure no one can break into their places.' The more intriguing possibilities of such a set-up are largely ignored by writer-director Phil Alden Robinson in favour of a straightforward jokey 'caper' film, as the sneakers mount a plan to break into the mega-security building run by leader Robert Redford's old college partner Ben Kingsley. Kingsley has a master code-breaking device that the sneakers stole, gave to the 'government' and now want back. It's all quite good fun, although it gets very silly at the end, as a group of agents bargain with the sneakers when they could just as easily gun them down. An ageing Redford looks ill-at-ease; Sidney Poitier is better on both counts as his ex-FBI aide, and Dan Aykroyd has a few good lines as their comrade, 'Mother'. You wonder, though, if a lightweight film like this would ever have got made without them.

Sniper ● ⓥ
1992, US, 97 mins, colour
Dir: Luis Llosa
Stars: Tom Berenger, Billy Zane, J T Walsh
Rating: ★★★

Inconsequential but exciting, this 'hit'-strewn movie is about two US

S

soldiers on a covert mission in the
South American jungle. Their orders:
to kill a rebel general and a drugs
overlord with simultaneous shots. It's
a sort of hard man's buddy–buddy
movie, except that the two snipers are
at war with each other more often
than they engage the enemy. Tom
Berenger, in yet another jungle picture, is the kill-hardened veteran
taking on a new partner in supe-
rior-ranked Billy Zane, who has never
even killed a man. They reach a kind
of understanding by the end, but only
after thoughts of killing each other
have been interrupted by more immediate danger. The dialogue, blunt
and to the point, has little new to say,
but does introduce action audiences to
a new phrase: 'just a click away'. Shots
of bullets coming towards you are
nastily effective, though oddly
reminiscent of 3D effects that never
were. On target, though, this one, as
far as action fans are concerned.

Snoopy, Come Home ☉
1972, US, 77 mins, colour
Dir: Bill Melendez
Rating: ★★

Although the script is by the redoubtable Charles M Schulz himself,
much of the epigrammatic quality of
the *Peanuts* strip cartoon seems to be
missing from this animated feature
based on its characters. Still, if there is
too little wit and too many songs, it's a
pleasant exercise which at least
acknowledges Snoopy the beagle to be
the star of the show. And an occasional flash of the real *Peanuts* flavour
breaks through in such comments as
Lucy's on learning that Snoopy has a
previous owner. 'Huh,' she snaps,
'you got a used dog, Charlie Brown!'

Snowball Express ☉
1972, US, 99 mins, colour
Dir: Norman Tokar
Stars: Dean Jones, Nancy Olson, Harry
Morgan, Keenan Wynn
Rating: ★★★

The Baxters escape the New York rat
race when they inherit a dilapidated
hotel in the Rockies – but their plans
to create a ski resort go dreadfully
wrong in this often very funny Disney
family film. Dean Jones is particularly
good as the harassed father and there
are some very amusing sequences
(especially the final chase scene) and
valuable comedy contributions from
Harry Morgan, Keenan Wynn and

Mary Wickes, still going strong today
as one of America's funniest character
actresses.

Snowbound ○
1948, UK, 87 mins, b/w
Dir: David Macdonald
Stars: Robert Newton, Dennis Price,
Stanley Holloway
Rating: ★★★

Director David Macdonald sustains the
claustrophobic menace well in this
story of a group of men gathered in an
isolated ski-hut, ostensibly to make a
film but in fact for some much darker
purpose, which is revealed only in the
last reel. Guy Middleton is splendid as
Gilbert Mayne, cleverly allying his
usual bluff characterization with a hint
of real steely evil. An exciting thriller,
it should keep you guessing.

**Snows of Kilimanjaro,
The** ○ ⓥ
1952, US, 117 mins, colour
Dir: Henry King
Stars: Gregory Peck, Susan Hayward,
Ava Gardner
Rating: ★★

20th Century-Fox had several attempts at the works of Ernest
Hemingway in the Fifties, and despite
high technical standards – Leon
Shamroy's colour photography here is
particularly fine – never really came
to grips with the great man. It's not so
much the studio's insistence on altering the original ending that's at fault
here, more the screenplay of Casey
Robinson, which expands
Hemingway's story so much as to blur
its impact. But there are some solid
performances, plus excellent
background music by Bernard
Herrmann.

Soapdish ◑ ⓥ
1991, US, 97 mins, colour
Dir: Michael Hoffman
Stars: Sally Field, Kevin Kline, Robert
Downey Jr, Whoopi Goldberg, Carrie
Fisher
Rating: ★★

If only it had been more consistent,
this broad comic satire on US daytime soap TV could have been a
riot. Field throws herself whole-
heartedly into the role of the veteran
soap queen who finds younger wolves
snapping at her heels, and skeletons
from the cupboard of her past tumbling out on set. 'This place is
crawling with sub-plots,' grumbles
one executive, while the head of

programming (director Garry
Marshall in a rare acting role) is more
concerned with the content of the
studio's top soap *The Sun Never Sets*.
'That's cute,' he snaps at chief writer
Goldberg, 'but when are we gonna
put someone in a coma?' Fast-moving,
scattershot, and more miss than hit,
the movie wastes Goldberg completely, leaving her a bemused
sidelines observer. Even that beats the
fate suffered by Carrie Fisher, whose
character disappears after about 10
minutes. Just when your attention's
wandering, though, the script comes
up with one of its gems again.

S.O.B. ● ⓥ
1981, US, 121 mins, colour
Dir: Blake Edwards
Stars: Julie Andrews, Richard Mulligan,
William Holden
Rating: ★

Director Blake Edwards' rudely satirical bite at the Hollywood hand
that fed him. Richard Mulligan, alias
Burt from the *Soap* series, plays the
director who tries to retrieve a
disastrous film by turning it into a sex
saga. Crude, rude and – most unfor-
givable of all – squirmingly unfunny.

So Dark the Night ○
1946, US, 71 mins, b/w
Dir: Joseph H Lewis
Stars: Steven Geray, Micheline Cheirel
Rating: ★★★

An intelligently made psychological
thriller, outstanding by 'B-feature'
standards. In almost his only leading
role, the Russian-Czech actor Steven
Geray delivers the performance of a
lifetime as the Simenon-like detective
who becomes involved in murder
while on holiday in the country. It's a
pity the rest of the cast is weak by
comparison. Even so, the film is
justly renowned for Burnett Guffey's
photography, 'trapping' characters
by shooting through windows, using
'framing' devices and making
astoundingly effective use of light,
shadow, rain and darkness.

So Evil My Love ○
1948, UK, 109 mins, b/w
Dir: Lewis Allen
Stars: Ann Todd, Ray Milland, Geraldine
Fitzgerald, Leo G Carroll
Rating: ★★

Hollywood director Lewis Allen, who
made those fine Forties' chillers *The
Uninvited* and *The Unseen*, came back
to his native England to make this in-

tricately detailed portrait of evil, with Ann Todd giving a perfectly-judged performance that's streets more effective than her portrayal of the maybe-murderess in *Madeleine*.

So Fine ●
1981, US, 91 mins, colour
Dir: Andrew Bergman
Stars: Ryan O'Neal, Jack Warden
Rating: ★★★

A splendidly silly farce which gives Ryan O'Neal his happiest role in years, repeating his *What's Up Doc?* persona as a bespectacled college professor forced to help out with the family clothing business when his father (Jack Warden) falls in debt to a seven-foot gangster (who else but Richard Kiel?). When Ryan falls in bed with the gangster's wife (sexy Italian star Mariangela Melato), everything is set for a sublimely scatty operatic finale with the cast acting out the last act of Verdi's *Othello* for real on the stage of the campus theatre. The stars perform heroically, with Andrew Bergman directing at a pace faster than Ms Melato can get her clothes off, or Warden can cut the million pairs of see-through jeans that save his bacon. Even so, cavern-voiced Fred Gwynne, once Herman Munster of TV fame, steals it from all of them with a wickedly funny impersonation of the self-centred state university chairman.

Soft Beds, Hard Battles ●
(aka: Undercovers Hero)
1973, UK, 94 mins, colour
Dir: Roy Boulting
Stars: Peter Sellers, Lila Kedrova
Rating: ★

Peter Sellers plays seven roles in this Roy Boulting comedy about a war-time brothel. There are a couple of good jokes, but most of the capers are crashingly leaden. A good cast (including Rula Lenska and Windsor Davies in the minor roles) gives its all, but it is as if each had a ball and chain around his leg. Not exactly one of Sellers' best films!

Soft Top Hard Shoulder ◐ ⓥ
1992, UK, 90 mins, colour
Dir: Stefan Schwartz
Stars: Peter Capaldi, Elaine Collins, Simon Callow, Frances Barber, Phyllis Logan
Rating: ★★

Shafts of wry Scottish wit brighten this meandering road movie, as a failed graphic artist (Peter Capaldi, who also wrote the screenplay) attempts to drive from London to Glasgow in his clapped-out car in a bid to claim a share of the family inheritance. Along the way, he picks up Wendy (Elaine Collins, the real-life Mrs Capaldi), who clearly has some dark secret by the way she hides from the police. Still, she proves adept at making the car go when it conks out and convinces him to hand back a found credit card (they get a reward which compensates for the loss of his wallet). The film's major problem is that it's too full of 'just as if' situations, especially a silly interlude where the couple tries to buy bus tickets, which seems inserted for the sake of some rather arch humour. The ending's nice, though, even if it's the one you expect from such a gently humorous film. Capaldi goes at his self-penned hero full throttle; Collins is a bit mature but refreshingly unglamorous as the girl; Simon Callow does a nice guest shot.

So I Married an Axe Murderer ◐ ⓥ
1993, US, 92 mins, colour
Dir: Thomas Schlamme
Stars: Mike Myers, Nancy Travis, Anthony LaPaglia, Amanda Plummer, Brenda Fricker, Charles Grodin
Rating: ★★★

This anarchic comedy, an uneasy mixture of Monty Python, Grand Guignol horror and the deadpan humour of someone like Bill (*Gregory's Girl*) Forsyth, was Mike Myers' eagerly awaited follow-up to the comedy hit *Wayne's World*. And, despite rumours of frantic re-editing before the film was released, it's a laughter winner. Myers' puppy-dog eagerness and naive charm are perfect ingredients for the man with a fear of commitment who soon comes to suspect his new bride (Nancy Travis) is a husband killer. Wry-faced Amanda Plummer enjoys herself in yet another oddball role as Travis' sister. There are lots of quite successful comic ideas dotted around the plot, and the only failure is Myers' attempt to play his own Scottish father.

Solarbabies ◐
(aka: Solarwarriors)
1986, US, 94 mins, colour
Dir: Alan Johnson

Stars: Richard Jordan, Jami Gertz, Jason Patric, Lukas Haas, Charles Durning, Adrian Pasdar
Rating: ★

On a futuristic planet earth where every drop of water is precious, heroine Gertz and her roller-skating 'solarwarrior' cohorts battle a tyrannical enemy with the aid of an ancient mystical force. Filmed on location in a drought-stricken Spain, and using the country's national roller hockey players, by (Mel) Brooks Films. Too violent for younger children.

Solarwarriors
See: Solarbabies

Soldier in the Rain ○
1963, US, 88 mins, b/w
Dir: Ralph Nelson
Stars: Steve McQueen, Jackie Gleason, Tuesday Weld, Tony Bill, Ed Nelson
Rating: ★★

A rare comedy film for both Steve McQueen and director Ralph Nelson, who made *Soldier Blue*. McQueen plays the arch scrounger in an army camp, and Jackie Gleason contributes a gem of a performance as the master-sergeant who reaps the benefit of McQueen's labours.

Soldier of Fortune ○
1955, US, 96 mins, colour
Dir: Edward Dmytryk
Stars: Clark Gable, Susan Hayward, Michael Rennie, Gene Barry
Rating: ★★

Director Edward Dmytryk's later films tended to be on the sluggish side. This one looks like being no exception until it finds its feet about half-way through when Clark Gable, as a smuggler hunting a missing man in Hong Kong, becomes involved with an impressive collection of unsavoury underworld figures. There's an exciting escape climax, but Susan Hayward has a role less dynamic than those she was used to at the time, and it's a surprise to find Thirties' glamour star Anna Sten in a small role of a middle-aged woman. The story bristles with clichés, but there's plenty of action to keep adventure fans happy. And Leo Tover's probing colour camera really makes the teeming streets and waterways of Hong Kong spring to life.

Soldier's Story, A ●
1984, US, 101 mins, colour
Dir: Norman Jewison

S

Stars: Howard E Rollins Jr, Adolph Caesar, Denzel Washington
Rating: ★★★

This electrifying and totally absorbing whodunnit/social drama runs like an offshoot of *In the Heat of the Night*, as a black military attorney from the north arrives to investigate the murder of a black master-sergeant stationed in Louisiana. The mystery element grips throughout, while your brain cells will be exercised in different directions by the screenplay's incisive probe into racism within black ranks. Solid performances from a (then) little-known cast that includes Denzel Washington (who went on to win an Oscar for *Glory*) as one of the suspects. Adapted by Charles Fuller from his own Pulitzer Prize-winning play.

Soldiers Three ○

1951, US, 87 mins, b/w
Dir: Tay Garnett
Stars: Stewart Granger, Walter Pidgeon, David Niven
Rating: ★★

Boisterous Indian Army romp, reminiscent of *Gunga Din*, and featuring Stewart Granger, Robert Newton and Cyril Cusack as the three brawling privates forever in hot water. Their broad comedy playing just about keeps the antediluvian antics afloat.

Solid Gold Cadillac, The ○

1956, US, 99 mins, b/w
Dir: Richard Quine
Stars: Judy Holliday, Paul Douglas, Fred Clark
Rating: ★★★

One of a series of delightful comedies made by Judy Holliday in the Fifties, offering her the kind of material that Goldie Hawn would love to get her hands on today. Here, in a reworking of a hit Broadway play, she's the small stockholder who makes life deservedly miserable for the crooked board of directors of a vast company eventually forced to employ her to try and hush her up. This hapless bunch of crooks is beautifully drawn by Fred Clark, Ray Collins, Ralph Dumke and John Williams, insincerity dripping delightfully from their jaws. It's a hilarious plot, smartly developed and propelled along by a gorgeously witty script. You'll recognise the voice of the narrator: it's George Burns.

Solomon and Sheba ○

1959, US, 142 mins, colour
Dir: King Vidor

Stars: Gina Lollobrigida, Yul Brynner
Rating: ★★

This is the epic that Tyrone Power was making when he collapsed on set with a heart attack. Soon afterwards he was dead, at the age of 44. Yul Brynner took over the part of Solomon, opposite Gina Lollobrigida's fiery Sheba. It was the first Hollywood epic to be made away from America. Director King Vidor chose Spain to stand in for the plains of the Middle East in Israel's battle against the Egyptian hordes; and several Spanish actors take prominent roles. Harry Andrews and David Farrar are included in the British contingent.

So Long at the Fair ○

1950, UK, 86 mins, b/w
Dir: Terence Fisher, Antony Darnborough
Stars: Jean Simmons, Dirk Bogarde, Honor Blackman, David Tomlinson
Rating: ★★★

A good old film plot stand-by that hardly ever fails: someone disappears, and everyone denies all knowledge of the missing party, while their friend/wife/lover spends the rest of the film trying to trace them. All a diabolical plot of course, but at least this time there's a nice young artist on hand to help pretty Jean Simmons when her brother mysteriously disappears at the Paris Exhibition of 1889. Directors Terence Fisher – later to do the initial Hammer horror films – and Anthony Darnborough don't miss many tricks, and keep the suspense mounting nicely.

Somebody Killed Her Husband ○ Ⓥ

1978, US, 97 mins, colour
Dir: Lamont Johnson
Stars: Farrah Fawcett-Majors, Jeff Bridges
Rating: ★★

Romance, mystery and murder, with Farrah Fawcett-Majors (as she was then) and Jeff Bridges uneasily cast together in Reginald Rose's rather zany comedy-thriller. The final fight amid the giant toys of Macy's store works better than anything else in the film.

Somebody Loves Me ○

1952, US, 97 mins, colour
Dir: Irving Brecher
Stars: Betty Hutton, Ralph Meeker, Adele Jergens, Robert Keith
Rating: ★★

Colourful (and highly-coloured!) account of the life of singer Blossom Seeley makes a typical Betty Hutton helping of songs, laughter and tears. As well as Blossom's career and love life, the movie throws in the San Francisco earthquake – and happily makes room for a guest spot from master comedian Jack Benny. Could have been better though.

Somebody Up There Likes Me ○

1956, US, 112 mins, b/w
Dir: Robert Wise
Stars: Paul Newman, Pier Angeli
Rating: ★★★★

After a disastrous start to his film career as a Greek sculptor in *The Silver Chalice*, Paul Newman quickly recovered. His first step up the ladder to star status was here as boxer Rocky Graziano, a role originally written for James Dean, before his car-crash death. Newman adopted a range of Brando-style mannerisms as the rebellious East Side delinquent, who rose through reform school, jail and army detention to become middleweight boxing champion of the world. The film proved a knockout with both the public and the annual Oscars voters, who awarded it two statuettes, for Best Cinematography (Joseph Ruttenberg's third Academy Award after *The Great Waltz* and *Mrs Miniver*) and Best Art Direction. Look closely among the supporting players and you'll spot Steve McQueen making his film debut, as well as a young Robert Loggia.

Some Came Running ○

1959, US, 136 mins, colour
Dir: Vincente Minnelli
Stars: Frank Sinatra, Dean Martin, Shirley MacLaine
Rating: ★★★

Madison, Indiana, 73 miles from Cincinnati, suddenly found itself elevated to more than just an insignificant spot on the American map, when Frank Sinatra, Dean Martin and 80 actors and location workers moved in overnight to make the film of James Jones' massive novel about snobbishness in small-town America. Madison had been picked out as 'the most typical US town'. It also bore a fine resemblance to Jones' description of the fictional town of Parkman, where returning serviceman Dave Hirsh (Frank Sinatra) meets all sorts of problems and prejudices. The best performance, in the sprawling, brawling film that results, comes surprisingly from Dean Martin as a gambler.

Some Girls Do ◐
1968, UK, 93 mins, colour
Dir: Ralph Thomas
Stars: Richard Johnson
Rating: ★

Here come the bikini assassins again in the sequel to Johnson's first Bulldog Drummond film, *Deadlier Than the Male*. Robert Morley makes an all-too-brief excursion into the mayhem as a cookery expert with one earring, and the girls – Daliah Lavi, Beba Loncar, Adrienne Posta, Virginia North, Vanessa Howard, and especially heroine Sydne Rome – are almost enough to take one's mind off the absurdities of the plot. Another of the girl robots in the story is played by Yutte Stengaard, soon to make a delectable lady vampire for Hammer Films in *Lust for a Vampire*.

Some Kind of Wonderful ◐ ⓥ
1987, US, 93 mins, colour
Dir: Howard Deutch
Stars: Eric Stoltz, Mary Stuart Masterson, Lea Thompson
Rating: ★★

Writer/director John Hughes has enjoyed a prolific Hollywood career spanning angst-ridden teen-dramas – *Pretty in Pink*, *The Breakfast Club*, *16 Candles* – and screwball comedies for Chevy Chase and Steve Martin – *Planes, Trains and Automobiles*, *National Lampoon's Christmas Vacation* – and family comedies – *Uncle Buck* and the hugely successful *Home Alone*. *Some Kind of Wonderful* falls into the first category, and confirms Hughes' standing as one of the most insightful writers around on contemporary American youth. Eric Stoltz is the focus of attention here. He's a rather fey youth chasing the most popular girl in school, unaware that his tomboy best friend also has the hots for him. The bond between him and Mary Stuart Masterson (in her most assured performance to that date) as the tongue-tied best friend is nicely etched out, and for once the adult characters have shape and depth rather than emerging as mere caricatures.

Some Like It Hot ○ ⓥ
1959, US, 122 mins, b/w
Dir: Billy Wilder
Stars: Marilyn Monroe, Tony Curtis, Jack Lemmon, George Raft, Joe E Brown, Pat O'Brien
Rating: ★★★★

The legendary comic masterpiece from director Billy Wilder. Marilyn Monroe parades sexily in her role as singer Sugar Kane, object of pursuit by musicians Tony Curtis and Jack Lemmon (who cannot reveal their lust for her because they are dressed as women in order to escape from murderous mobsters). The performances by Lemmon and Curtis are sensational, and the script, by Wilder and I A L Diamond, simply sizzles with wit – listen for Joe E Brown's now-classic closing line. A milestone comedy to see and see again.

Someone to Watch Over Me ● ⓥ
1987, US, 102 mins, colour
Dir: Ridley Scott
Stars: Tom Berenger, Mimi Rogers, Lorraine Bracco
Rating: ★★

Good to look at but lethargic in development, this is yet another thriller about a cop who falls for the witness he's trying to protect. And there's not much logic to its sketchy story about a murderer who corners the witness in a powder room but threatens her with disfigurement rather than bumping her off. Tom Berenger is suitably dewy-eyed as the besotted cop, and strong when he should be. The abrasive Lorraine Bracco as his wife wins the personality battle hands down over Kathleen Turner-lookalike Mimi Rogers who has about as much charisma as a slab of marble. It's all nicely shot and beautifully dressed but, despite its explosive showdown, this is, on the whole, too slow to set our pulses racing.

Something Big ○
1971, US, 108 mins, colour
Dir: Andrew V McLaglen
Stars: Dean Martin, Brian Keith, Honor Blackman
Rating: ★★★

A spirited spoof Western with some inspired patches of dialogue by the distinguished Western writer James Lee Barrett. Director Andrew V McLaglen sets a rousing pace, Dean Martin's lazy charm makes him a disarming rogue, and there's even room for two British actresses, Honor Blackman and Carol White, in this slice of the wild west. Character actors from the world of McLaglen's mentor, John Ford, abound in the supporting cast, and Barett gives them some richly comic lines to deliver. Particularly good is the character who, asked if he intends to bury a recently-deceased comrade, replies: 'Naw. Perhaps somethin'll come down out of the hills tonight and drag him off.'

Something of Value ◐
1956, US, 113 mins, b/w
Dir: Richard Brooks
Stars: Rock Hudson, Dana Wynter
Rating: ★★★

Richard Brooks' strong drama about the Mau Mau terror, well-acted and not for the squeamish. Wendy Hiller is excellent as a doomed wife. The suspense plot maintains a strong grip throughout.

Something Wicked This Way Comes ◐
1983, US, 94 mins, colour
Dir: Jack Clayton
Stars: Jason Robards, Jonathan Pryce
Rating: ★★

Or: A nostalgic nightmare. Ray Bradbury's story of a boy's dream of evil in early 20th-century America is quite well realised in this rare film from Jack Clayton, whose previous movie had been *The Great Gatsby* in 1974. Although somewhat slow at times, this is a work of much imagination that at least deserves a minor place in the hall of fame of film fantastique. To music that surely owes something to *A Night on the Bare Mountain*, a carnival and freak show rolls into a small American town. Two small boys soon sniff out the supernatural behind the razzmatazz as Mr Dark and his cohorts grant the dearest wishes of those who come at a heavy price. The fact that the film leaves a lot to the imagination adds to its shivery air of mystery. And Britain's Jonathan Pryce is a formidable Mr Dark indeed.

Something Wild ● ⓥ
1986, US, 113 mins, colour
Dir: Jonathan Demme
Stars: Jeff Daniels, Melanie Griffith, Ray Liotta
Rating: ★★★

This nightmare comedy became the cult success of the year, and deservedly so. Its theme of a clean-cut yuppie hero being dragged kicking and screaming into dark and dangerous terrain by a woman and the lure of dangerous sex, and the fear of the unknown, was a popular one at the time, surfacing again in *After Hours* and *Blue Velvet*. Director Jonathan Demme – who later achieved mainstream success with *The Silence of the Lambs* – never allows his audience to relax for a minute as he constantly shifts style and throws in more twists than a corkscrew. Melanie Griffith boosted her own career as the kinky Lulu, who starts events moving by handcuffing hapless Jeff Daniels to her motel bed; so did *Goodfellas* star Ray Liotta, in his first major film, as her menacing, psychotic husband. But the greater fun in early Demme films can be found in the incidental characters and details – the soundtrack music ending when Lulu switches off the radio in her car, a dog in a crash helmet riding motorcycle pillion passenger, an off-licence owner with a bulldog and an overstated pipe, and the owners of 'Mom and Dad's' restaurant answering phone enquiries with 'Mom and Dad's: Dad here'.

Sometimes a Great Notion
See: Never Give an Inch

Somewhere I'll Find You ○
1942, US, 108 mins, b/w
Dir: Wesley Ruggles
Stars: Clark Gable, Lana Turner, Robert Sterling
Rating: ★★

The Clark Gable/Lana Turner partnership set up in 1941 for *Honky Tonk* was such a box-office hit that MGM just had to bring them together again – striking while the iron was hot, so to speak – and they certainly knock sparks off each other in this romance-cum-war story. Gable is at his commanding best as a fast-talking newsman, but Lana doesn't have any trouble at all getting a word in edgeways.

Somewhere in France
See: The Foreman Went to France

Somewhere in the Night ○
1946, US, 108 mins, b/w
Dir: Joseph L Mankiewicz
Stars: John Hodiak, Nancy Guild, Lloyd Nolan, Richard Conte
Rating: ★★★

Joseph L Mankiewicz's second film as director provides John Hodiak with one of his best roles in a fascinating thriller about an amnesia victim's attempts to uncover his true identity . . . a search that brings him into contact with gangsters, a beautiful night-club singer – and sudden death.

A well-worn theme, perhaps. But at least Mankiewicz concentrates on the mystery angle of the plot – partwritten by him – and doesn't digress into any phoney psychological prattle. Lloyd Nolan, best known at the time for his portrait of screen private eye Michael Shayne, steps over to the official side of the law as a tough police lieutenant, and, in a supporting role, Richard Conte took another pace towards stardom. Three years later, Mankiewicz emerged a double Oscar-winner for his writing and direction on *A Letter to Three Wives*.

Somewhere in Time ○ Ⓥ
1980, US, 103 mins, colour
Dir: Jeannot Szwarc
Stars: Christopher Reeve, Jane Seymour, Christopher Plummer
Rating: ★★★

This delicately-crafted movie offers us a chance, rare in modern cinema, to have a good cry. The story – about time-travel and a great love affair – doesn't quite hang together under close inspection, but the immense fondness with which director Jeannot Szwarc (with a little help from music by Rachmaninov) treats it, sees it through. Jane Seymour gets a real acting chance and proves herself a player of no mean ability. But the real triumph belongs to Christopher Reeve, who not only dominates the film, but shows great power to reach out and affect the emotions of an audience. A pity that the otherwise excellent ending goes too far: you may have to suppress a giggle through the tears.

Some Will, Some Won't ○
1969, UK, 90 mins, colour
Dir: Duncan Wood
Stars: Ronnie Corbett, Thora Hird, Michael Hordern, Leslie Phillips
Rating: ★

A host of faces familiar from TV, splashy use of colour and a nudging title mark this remake of the classic 1951 comedy *Laughter in Paradise*. The foolproof plot – an eccentric practical joker places embarrassing obstacles in the way of relatives grasping for his will – provides a steady stream of amusing situations, but the tone (like the title) is rather strained compared to the original.

Sommersby ○ Ⓥ
1993, US, 112 mins, colour
Dir: Jon Amiel
Stars: Richard Gere, Jodie Foster, Bill Pullman, James Earl Jones
Rating: ★★

After the American Civil War, Jack Sommersby (Richard Gere) returns to his wife (Jodie Foster) and son a changed man, following six years away. He is, says his wife, 'so much better it scares me.' But is he really Sommersby at all? All might be well under these circumstances, with Foster happy to love her greatly-improved husband whether he be Jack or no. But in films there is always a spanner in the works. It duly arrives in the form of Orin (Bill Pullman), a flop-haired farmer embittered by the disablement of his foot, who figures that he smells a rat and that the rat is the 'new' Sommersby. Gere, Foster and director Jon Amiel only seem to be operating a seven-eighths throttle here and that's not quite enough to convince us of the validity of a resolution that doesn't hold up for reasons you couldn't go into without spoiling the story. But the writers must hope we won't question the options obviously open to Foster and Gere without taking the course they do. There are lots of good moments in *Sommersby* but, perhaps because it tries so hard to touch the heart, it doesn't quite succeed.

Song Is Born, A ○
1948, US, 113 mins, colour
Dir: Howard Hawks
Stars: Danny Kaye, Virginia Mayo, Benny Goodman, Steve Cochran
Rating: ★★

An almost scene-for-scene musical remake of *Ball of Fire*, itself a variation on *Snow White and the Seven Dwarfs*. Danny Kaye (in the Gary Cooper part) is more restrained than usual, and there's no room even for one of his tongue-twisting songs. But there is lots of music from a gaggle of jazz greats, including Louis Armstrong, Benny Goodman, Lionel Hampton and Charlie Barnet. Tommy Dorsey and His Orchestra also pitch in with 'I'm Getting Sentimental Over You'. Other numbers include 'Muskrat Ramble', 'Bach Boogie', 'Stealin' Apples', 'Flying Home' and 'Redskin Rhumba'. Virginia Mayo plays the Barbara Stanwyck part, her last role for Goldwyn, the man who raised her from chorus girl to star.

Song of Bernadette, The ○ Ⓥ
1943, US, 156 mins, b/w
Dir: Henry King
Stars: Jennifer Jones, William Eythe, Charles Bickford, Vincent Price
Rating: ★★★

Although it's overlong and cries out for a more colourful treatment, this reverently made story of the simple French girl who saw visions at Lourdes is at times very moving, and won four Academy Awards: for Jennifer Jones, rocketing to stardom as Bernadette, and for its photography, art direction and music. It lost out on the best film competition, though – to *Casablanca*.

Song of Norway ○
1970, US, 142 mins, colour
Dir: Andrew L Stone
Stars: Toralv Maurstad, Florence Henderson, Harry Secombe, Robert Morley, Edward G Robinson
Rating: ★★

The fjords are alive with the sound of music . . . as producer-director Andrew L Stone forsook the action thrillers that made him famous and went for a big-scale musical biopic of Edvard Greig. The scenery is magnificent, the music too, the script a rather dismal third. Harry Secombe, Robert Morley, Edward G Robinson and Oscar Homolka are in there somewhere, although even they cannot compete with the film's pictorial values. This kind of film certainly wasn't foreign to Stone, though, whose first successes in his early days had been *There's Magic in Music*, *The Great Victor Herbert* and *Stormy Weather*.

Song of the Islands ○
1942, US, 75 mins, colour
Dir: Walter Lang
Stars: Betty Grable, Victor Mature, Jack Oakie, Thomas Mitchell
Rating: ★★

Lavish and colourful dose of musical escapism for fun-starved wartime audiences, even if it did cause *Variety* to complain that it had taken four writers to create a 'semblance of a plot' which their reviewer was 'practically unable to find'. Most of the film seems to have been staged by dance director Hermes Pan, in fact, with Betty Grable no doubt increasing her GI fan mail after twitching through her grass-skirt dance routines.

Song of the South ⊙
1946, US, 94 mins, colour
Dir: Wilfred Jackson, Harve Foster
Stars: Bobby Driscoll, James Baskett
Rating: ★★★★

An almost wholly delightful Disney combination of cartoon and live-action which won two Oscars and pulled post-war audiences into cinemas in droves. James Baskett, as the tale-telling Uncle Remus (he won a special Oscar), and Bobby Driscoll and Luana Patten as the children all give winning performances, the cartoon segments involving the crafty Brer Rabbit are among Disney's sharpest and the songs (of which 'Zip-a-Dee-Doo-Dah' took another Academy Award) caught the imagination of millions.

Song to Remember, A ○
1945, US, 113 mins, colour
Dir: Charles Vidor
Stars: Cornel Wilde, Paul Muni, Merle Oberon
Rating: ★★★

And how could we forget Cornel Wilde coughing photogenic blood on the piano keys, Paul Muni acting his head off as the old music master, or Merle Oberon's glacially seductive George Sand, all in this memorable Hollywood biopic of Chopin? Of course, Sidney Buchman's script has more than its share of unintentionally funny lines, but Jose Iturbi's playing (and Wilde's first-class finger-matching) of Chopin's music has a glorious sweep, and Tony Gaudio's Technicolor photography was worthy of the Academy Award nomination it received.

Song Without End ○
1960, US, 141 mins, colour
Dir: Charles Vidor
Stars: Dirk Bogarde, Capucine, Genevieve Page
Rating: ★★

Having prettied up Chopin's life in *A Song to Remember*, Columbia decided to do some further tampering with history and gloss up the Franz Liszt story. Patricia Morison makes a viperish George Sand and the music (the scoring won an Oscar) is lovely. Star Dirk Bogarde, confronted with a script of awesome banality, must have wished he had stayed at home. Director Charles Vidor died during the making of the film, which was completed by George Cukor.

Son of a Gunfighter ○
1965, Spain, 93 mins, colour
Dir: Paul Landres
Stars: Russ Tamblyn, Kieron Moore
Rating: ★

Ex-dancer Russ Tamblyn finds little time for fancy footwork in this lively 'vendetta' Western made in Spain. The cast is nothing if not cosmopolitan and Britain's Kieron Moore turns up as a Mexican-Texan half-breed who ends his days staked out in the sun by a ruthless Mexican outlaw, played by that Bunuel stalwart, Fernando Rey. Maria Granada is a pretty heroine who looks exactly like American actress Annette Funicello, and James Philbrook is good enough as the hero's outlaw father to make one wonder why the role wasn't built up a little more. The climax raises the dust effectively, and there's the usual MGM bonus of attractive Metrocolor photography.

Son of Ali Baba ⊙
1952, US, 75 mins, colour
Dir: Kurt Neumann
Stars: Tony Curtis, Piper Laurie
Rating: ★★

Action and spectacle, *Arabian Nights*-style, with Tony Curtis and Piper Laurie a photogenic pair in one of four popular films they made together in the Fifties. This film followed their initial impact in *The Prince Who Was a Thief* a year earlier. Both were to enjoy great sucess in the following decade. If you're struggling to put a name to the young actor playing Mustafa, it's William Reynolds, later Tom Colby in the long-running TV series *The FBI*.

Son of Dracula ◐
1943, US, 80 mins, b/w
Dir: Robert Siodmak
Stars: Lon Chaney Jr, Louise Allbritton
Rating: ★★

Hollywood's third entry into the Dracula syndrome certainly whips up some chilling moments, and a well-staged climax. The eerie effectiveness of its more sinister scenes isn't surprising: the director was Robert Siodmak, who, two years later, was to direct a notable essay in claustrophobic suspense called *The Spiral Staircase*.

Son of Frankenstein ◐
1939, US, 99 mins, b/w
Dir: Rowland V Lee

Stars: Boris Karloff, Basil Rathbone, Bela Lugosi
Rating: ★★★

Third in the Frankenstein series keeps up a good standard, with imposing sets, steamroller direction by Rowland V Lee and the introduction of Bela Lugosi's best film character, Ygor the mad shepherd. For Boris Karloff, this was also the third – and last – time he stomped in his asphalt spreader's boots for Universal as the Creature: he should have stayed away from pits of boiling sulphur. Watch for an amusingly different performance by Lionel Atwill as a police inspector.

Son of Fury ○

1942, US, 110 mins, b/w
Dir: John Cromwell
Stars: Tyrone Power, Gene Tierney, George Sanders, Frances Farmer
Rating: ★★

Adapted from one of Edison Marshall's huge swashbuckling romantic novels, this gave Tyrone Power one of the last of his dashing early roles before he enlisted in war service. Set in the late 18th century, it provides solid escapist fare. The central section in the Polynesian islands sags a bit, but there's always Gene Tierney's glamorous native charmer for compensation.

Son of Kong ○

1934, US, 70 mins, b/w
Dir: Ernest B Schoedsack
Stars: Robert Armstrong, Helen Mack
Rating: ★★

A semi-comic sequel to the great *King Kong* with a rather endearing, if somewhat smaller 'son' of Kong, good creatures by Willis O'Brien on a very limited budget and the return of several characters (headed by Robert Armstrong as Denham) from the original. Helen Mack is a feisty and interesting heroine and, though the film takes a long while to get going, it has some touching, tense and amusing moments.

Son of Lassie ⊙

1945, US, 100 mins, colour
Dir: S Sylvan Simon
Stars: Peter Lawford, Donald Crisp
Rating: ★★★

Laddie, son of Lassie, the collie that made MGM millions, goes to war in this enormously popular entry to the Lassie series, blazingly shot in Technicolor by Charles Schoenbaum. The dog almost seems to be more

hindrance than help to master Peter Lawford, attracting Nazis like some dogs attract fleas while trying to reach safety after being shot down over Norway. No matter: it makes for a tense and exciting film. Young Helen Koford, who plays Thea, grew up to be adult actress Terry Moore.

Son of Monte Cristo, The ○

1940, US, 102 mins, b/w
Dir: Rowland V Lee
Stars: Louis Hayward, Joan Bennett, George Sanders
Rating: ★★★

Lively swashbuckler whose stylish presentation can be chiefly attributed to its director, Rowland V Lee, who also made the original *The Count of Monte Cristo* with Robert Donat a few years earlier. Lee had an imaginative visual sense which had already reflected itself in such varied films as *Zoo in Budapest, Son of Frankenstein* and *Tower of London*. Here, he got Louis Hayward away from a run of smiling detectives and into a run of swashbucklers that was to last for 15 years. Hayward has the title role, as a masked avenger who fights to free his country from the shackles of a dictator's rule.

Son of Paleface ⊙

1952, US, 95 mins, colour
Dir: Frank Tashlin
Stars: Bob Hope, Jane Russell, Roy Rogers, Bill Williams
Rating: ★★★

All three of Bob Hope's comic Westerns were among his funniest films, and this one is a sequel to his first *The Paleface*. Hope's gags perhaps lack the snap and crackle of 10 years earlier, but even so most of the material is bright. Told that co-star Jane Russell is 'tops in California' Hope retorts that she's not so bad in North and South Dakota either. And, as the director is the cartoon-trained Frank Tashlin, sight gags abound, including the one where Hope shoots a stuffed moose which consequently pours out coins like a jackpot. Songs include 'Wing Ding Tonight', 'Am I in Love', 'Four-Legged Friend' (by Roy Rogers) and a reprise of 'Buttons and Bows' from the earlier film. There are one or two guest stars to spot too. Shivering as a photographer takes a picture of him in a towel, Hope snaps, 'Hurry Up! Who do you think you are – Cecil B DeMille?' It *is* Cecil B DeMille.

Son of Robin Hood ⊙

1958, UK, 77 mins, colour
Dir: George Sherman
Stars: June Laverick, Al Hedison, David Farrar, Marius Goring
Rating: ★★

Not so much Son as Daughter of, with trim British blond June Laverick swashing many a buckle as the off-spring of the famous Sherwood outlaw. The Hollywood influence is pronounced in the presence of veteran Western director George Sherman and American star Al Hedison, fresh from playing *The Fly*, ensuring that 20th Century-Fox financing reaped the rewards on both sides of the Atlantic. David Farrar (as the Black Duke!) and Philip Friend had also spent some years in Hollywood. The hearty features of George Woodbridge make a robust Little John, although staring-eyed villain George Coulouris is somewhat rum casting as Alan A'Dale. Otherwise characterisation is in the best, full-blooded, comic-strip tradition, as is the action, handled in highly professional style by the director.

Son of Sinbad ○

1955, US, 88 mins, colour
Dir: Ted Tetzlaff
Stars: Sally Forrest, Lili St Cyr, Vincent Price, Dale Robertson
Rating: ★★

This wittily-scripted *Arabian Nights* spoof proffers a scene-stealing part to that most suave master of menace, Vincent Price. He really relishes his role here as Omar Khayyam, composing love poems for Dale Robertson's Sinbad as they stroll through this burlesque 'eastern', and in which sharp eyes may pick out Kim Novak as one of the Kahlif's harem girls. Novak can't have been much amused: *Pushover*, which she made subsequently, had already been released, making her a star.

Sons and Lovers ◑

1960, UK, 103 mins, b/w
Dir: Jack Cardiff
Stars: Trevor Howard, Wendy Hiller, Dean Stockwell, Mary Ure
Rating: ★★★★

One of the most successful attempts to translate a work by D H Lawrence to the screen, with Trevor Howard (nominated for an Oscar) and Dean Stockwell (the finest English accent ever done by an American actor at that time) in conflict as father and son, over whether the latter shall go into the pits or become a painter. Wendy Hiller is also fine as the mother; while Freddie Francis did win an Academy Award for his black-and-white photography in this absorbing, entertaining film.

Sons of Katie Elder, The ○
1965, US, 122 mins, colour
Dir: Henry Hathaway
Stars: John Wayne, Dean Martin, Martha Hyer, George Kennedy
Rating: ★★★

Films about brothers or heroes banded together in a common cause have always been among the cinema's most successful and usually work very well – especially if some of the heroes get killed, putting subtle pressure on our emotions. Nowhere does this apply more than in the Western, and this John Wayne film is well in the tradition of *My Darling Clementine* and *The Magnificent Seven*, with the story about about four brothers out to avenge their father's death. Background music by Elmer Bernstein that's much in the mould of *The Magnificent Seven* and the cultured direction of Henry Hathaway (later to make Wayne's Oscar-winning *True Grit*) both help to shunt the story along in cracking style. The action is dashingly violent, giving a foretaste of the spaghetti Westerns to follow, with gunman George Kennedy falling victim to one of the most devastating blows ever struck on the cinema screen.

Sons of the Desert ⊙ ⓥ
1933, US, 69 mins, b/w
Dir: William A Seiter
Stars: Stan Laurel, Oliver Hardy, Charley Chase, Mae Busch
Rating: ★★★★

Stan Laurel and Oliver Hardy in one of their finest feature films, the one in which they deceive the dreaded wives in order to attend a riotous fraternal convention. Many laughs, wonderful ending and Ollie singing 'Honolulu Baby!' Bliss.

Sons of the Musketeers ○
(aka: At Sword's Point)
1952, US, 75 mins, colour
Dir: Lewis Allen
Stars: Maureen O'Hara, Cornel Wilde, Robert Douglas
Rating: ★★

This entertaining if hardly inspired costume drama set in medieval France pits the children of the original Three Musketeers (who are now too old and doddery) against the sinister Duke Lavalle. Fiery Maureen O'Hara, who does her own stuntwork, steals the acting honours as a female swordsman who proves herself just as deadly with a rapier as her male counterparts. Moroni Olsen, who played Porthos in RKO's original *Three Musketeers* in 1935, plays Elderly Porthos here. Good swashbuckling fun if occasionally a trifle clumsy.

Sophie's Choice ● ⓥ
1982, US, 145 mins, colour
Dir: Alan J Pakula
Stars: Meryl Streep, Kevin Kline, Peter MacNicol
Rating: ★★★

Meryl Streep learned Polish and German in order to speak authentically, and her English accent is impeccable in this grim but gripping post-Holocaust drama. Her gut-wrenching performance was duly rewarded with a Best Actress Oscar – her second statuette following *Kramer Vs Kramer*. For a full three quarters of the film's running time, it appears that the choice facing Streep's character is between the two love rivals (Broadway musical star Kevin Kline, in his film debut, and young Peter MacNicol) in the boarding house where they live. But the truth is far more horrifying. Some of the war footage is hard to watch and the language is fairly abrasive. Marvin Hamlisch took an Oscar for the score.

Sophie's Place
See: Crooks and Coronets

Sorcerer
See: The Wages of Fear

SOS Titanic ○
1979, US, 140 mins, colour
Dir: William Hale
Stars: David Janssen, Cloris Leachman, Susan Saint James, Helen Mirren
Rating: ★★

TV movie on a favourite screen theme. Like *Mayerling,* the Titanic story seems to offer everything – great wealth, tragic death, the end of an era, plus the added thrill of its having actually happened. Stylish; good performances; a bit long.

So This Is New York ○
1948, US, 79 mins, b/w
Dir: Richard Fleischer
Stars: Henry Morgan, Rudy Vallee, Bill Goodwin
Rating: ★★★

A smartly-written comedy about country bumpkins 'at the mercy' of city slickers. It was one of the films that helped establish director Richard Fleischer's reputation as a young film-maker capable of handling all types of story. The funny screenplay by Carl Foreman and Herbert Baker is based on Ring Lardner's Runyonesque novel *The Big Town*.

So This Is Paris ○
1954, US, 96 mins, colour
Dir: Richard Quine
Stars: Tony Curtis, Gloria de Haven, Gene Nelson, Corinne Calvet, Paul Gilbert, Mara Corday
Rating: ★★★

A slick, lively musical in *On the Town* style, this tuneful trifle gave Tony Curtis the chance to prove he could be a song-and-dance man. The songs are hummable, and the dance routines acrobatically excellent. Paul Gilbert is especially impressive in his one solo number, 'I Can't Do a Single, But I'll Try'. But it's teamwork and verve that pulls this one up high in the entertainment ratings.

Soul Man ◐ ⓥ
1986, US, 104 mins, colour
Dir: Steve Miner
Stars: C Thomas Howell, Arye Gross, Rae Dawn Chong, James Earl Jones
Rating: ★★

Too trite by half to be anything like the classic of satirical comedy for which half the American critics took it, this attempt to make fun out of a white man posing as black still has some ingratiating moments, especially in the relationship between the central protagonist (C Thomas Howell), the black girl (Rae Dawn Chong) whose scholarship he has inadvertently usurped and her four-year-old son, very winningly played by little Jonathan 'Fudge' Leonard. But its straighter scenes tend to be embarrassing rather than effective, with the consequence that the film has laughs in the wrong as well as the right places. And its plot often mistakes high farce for gentle, biting humour, especially in the scenes involving the formidable James Earl Jones, whose intelligent performance is deserving of something rather better. Most successful funny scene comes when the tall Howell reveals himself as the world's most inept black basketball player.

S

Souls at Sea ○
1937, US, 92 mins, b/w
Dir: Henry Hathaway
Stars: Gary Cooper, George Raft,
Frances Dee, Robert Cummings
Rating: ★★★

Rousing 19th-century seafaring tale
made on a fairly lavish scale, and given
plenty of guts by action specialist
Henry Hathaway. Gary Cooper is the
ex-slaver who finds himself wielding
the power of life and death in a maritime disaster with not enough
lifeboats to go round. He's more than
matched, unexpectedly, by George
Raft, who offers one of his best performances as his fellow adventurer.
Some vivid minor scenes round out
this colourful and seldom-seen film.
The stirring music by Milan Roder
and W Franke Harling was nominated
for an Academy Award.

Sound and the Fury, The ◐
1958, US, 115 mins, colour
Dir: Martin Ritt
Stars: Yul Brynner, Joanne Woodward,
Margaret Leighton
Rating: ★★

Rather dreary drama from the foetid
pen of William Faulkner, who takes
yet another look at an old-established
family in the southern states of
America. A tremendous cast, led by
Yul Brynner in a toupée, works very
hard to retract some life from the yarn
and Joanne Woodward and Margaret
Leighton really give acting enthusiasts
value for money.

Sound Barrier, The ○
(aka: Breaking the Sound Barrier)
1952, UK, 109 mins, b/w
Dir: David Lean
Stars: Ralph Richardson, Ann Todd,
Nigel Patrick
Rating: ★★★

A dynamic British film about the air
pioneers who tried to break the sound
barrier in the post-war years. Director
David Lean conjures up not only tremendous tension in the flying scenes,
but forceful performances, especially
from Ralph Richardson, John Justin,
Nigel Patrick, Dinah Sheridan and
Denholm Elliott, that really make
their characters spring to life. Lean's
approach to his subject is unmelo-
dramatic and, at times, likely to
make the viewer miss a heartbeat or
two. The technical side of the picture
is dealt with swiftly and with en-
lightening simplicity, making the
purpose and ultimate achievement of

the project to beat the 'barrier' lucid
to the layman. Among its most effective dramatic moments is the scene
where a test pilot's pregnant wife tries
to persuade her husband not to risk his
life in a dangerous experimental flight.

Sounder ○
1972, US, 105 mins, colour
Dir: Martin Ritt
Stars: Cicely Tyson, Paul Winfield, Kevin
Hooks
Rating: ★★★

A beautiful, throat-gripping film that
deserves to be seen much more often
than it is. Its story of black share-
croppers' struggles during the
American depression gets its blend of
hope and tragedy exactly right, as you
would expect from the caring direction of Martin Ritt, a firm confronter
of oppression and injustice in such
films as *A Man is 10 Feet Tall*, *The
Molly Maguires*, *The Front* and *Norma
Rae*. Cicely Tyson gives a flawless,
completely natural portrayal of the
mother of the family.

Sound of Music, The ○ ⓥ
1965, US, 174 mins, colour
Dir: Robert Wise
Stars: Julie Andrews, Christopher
Plummer, Eleanor Parker
Rating: ★★★

Although it fails to avoid sentimentality (unlike the stage show) and
even abbreviates the original score,
this epic musical, about a postulant
nun who comes as governess to seven
Austrian children in the late Thirties,
is saved time and again by Julie Andrews' own special brand of sincerity.
Julie, the true-life story, and the popular Rodgers and Hammerstein score
ensured massive box-office success.
She's really the only genuine character
in sight, even if, when she sings
'Confidence in Me' (one of two songs
written specially for the film), like
some mischievous vagabond, it's so
Poppins-ish that you almost expect her
to jump on her brolly and sail back to
the Abbey. For the rest, the children
are well-drilled and sing pleasantly
(though their acting is pretty appalling) and the scenery is, apart from
one obvious backcloth, beautifully
caught in Technicolor by Boris Leven.
At the end, it's the overwhelming
impact of those magnificent tunes that
sweeps aside your resistance to the
cloying sentiment, even though not a
treacly trick is missed. For the purists,
though, it's especially sad that such a
simple and beautiful duet as 'An

Ordinary Couple' should be replaced
by something much triter in the same
scene. The film won the Academy
Award for Best Picture.

Soursweet ◐
1988, UK, 107 mins, colour
Dir: Mike Newell
Stars: Sylvia Chang, Danny Dun, Jodi
Long
Rating: ★★★

In days gone by, Hollywood stars
would have given their matchsticks
and makeup to play the role here
taken by Hong Kong megastar Sylvia
Chang in this saga of an oriental couple struggling to make a go of life in
England. She, the daughter of an ace
martial artist, wants to run their own
restaurant; he (Danny Dun) is happy
to work in a Chinatown kitchen. The
upshot is a kind of Chinese *This
Happy Breed*, dominated by Chang and
interrupted slightly implausibly by a
story-thread of gang warfare in Central London's Chinese community. This
whole side of the plot, in fact,
hangs on the hero's inability to stop
gambling after obtaining the money
to clear his father's Hong Kong debts.
Frankly it's out of character, and only
underlines what would have been the
wisdom of sticking to the central
theme. The family's gradual ascent to
financial stability, the son's problems
at school, Chang's sister's pregnancy
by a passing truck-driver and the eccentricities of Grandpa are handled
tenderly, build nicely and have sufficient dramatic weight to stand by
themselves. Chang is faultless and,
even though a lot of the acting is only
serviceable (including another
overbalanced performance from Hollywood's Soon Teck-Oh), a sense of
community and lifetime struggle is
caught. Recommended with regretful
reservations.

Southern Comfort ●
1981, US, 100 mins, colour
Dir: Walter Hill
Stars: Keith Carradine, Powers Boothe
Rating: ★

A tough but foolish action thriller on a
Ten Little Niggers theme, in which the
characters stupidly go and do all the
things most likely to get them killed.
A squad of nine National Guardsmen
goes on exercise in the Louisiana
swamps and so stirs up the local trappers that those worthies kill the
Guardsmen one by one. The initial
incident – the soldiers steal three
canoes to get across the swamp – is

believable enough. But the trigger to the subsequent violence (a soldier 'machine-guns' the shorebound trappers with blanks) is far less likely, and the film gets more unpleasant and incredible by the minute. Keith Carradine and Powers Boothe give personable performances as the ultimate leaders of the beleaguered group.

Southern Star, The ○
1968, US/UK, 105 mins, colour
Dir: Sidney Hayers
Stars: George Segal, Ursula Andress, Orson Welles, Ian Hendry
Rating: ★★★

Set in French West Africa just prior to World War One, this lively film, based on a story by Jules Verne, is a combination of action and adventure, blood and thunder, animal interest (ranging from snakes to stampeding elephants) and tongue-in-cheek humour. The title refers to a large diamond. The gem is found by George Segal, as a geologist who has a taste for teach-yourself banjo-playing. The diamond is, nevertheless, the property of a big business magnate, played by Harry Andrews, with whose daughter (Ursula Andress) the geologist is in love. Ian Hendry, as the head of the tycoon's private army, would like to get his hands on both the diamond and Ursula, and he tries to effect a frame-up with Segal as his victim. Meanwhile, Orson Welles has a whale of a time as Hendry's confederate, drilling his native troops to a record of a bugle. Another vital character in the drama is, of all things, a kleptomaniac ostrich! One way and another, it's great stuff for schoolboys – of all ages.

Southern Yankee, A ⊙
(aka: My Hero)
1948, US, 90 mins, b/w
Dir: Edward Sedgwick
Stars: Red Skelton, Arlene Dahl, Brian Donlevy, John Ireland
Rating: ★★★

This is probably Red Skelton's funniest film outing. That's hardly surprising, as it was directed by Edward Sedgwick, and many of its visual gags were devised by Buster Keaton. Sedgwick and Keaton combined on two of Buster's best comedies, *The Cameraman* and *Spite Marriage* in the last days of the silent era, and *A Southern Yankee* would have made a wonderful Keaton vehicle in itself. As it is the rubber-faced Skelton does

well enough in this Civil War spoof, especially in Keaton-inspired routines when, in one instance, he escapes through a forest of legs and, in another, where he rides between Confederate and Unionist lines wearing a uniform dark blue on one side and grey on the other.

South of Pago Pago ○
1940, US, 96 mins, b/w
Dir: Alfred E Green
Stars: Victor McLaglen, Jon Hall, Frances Farmer
Rating: ★★★

This rip-roaring South Seas adventure is unjustly more famous today for the beginning of the downswing of the career of the tragic Frances Farmer, as she was forced to play roles unworthy of her talent. In its own right, though, this is a hard-hitting adventure movie with a swaggering performance from Victor McLaglen as the improbably named Bucko Larson, and first-class black-and-white photography by John Mescall.

South of St Louis ○
1949, US, 88 mins, colour
Dir: Ray Enright
Stars: Joel McCrea, Alexis Smith, Zachary Scott, Dorothy Malone
Rating: ★★

A good cast, fast-paced direction by Ray Enright (who had just finished a spate of eight good Westerns with Randolph Scott) and classy colour camerawork by Karl Freund all help strengthen this routine Western about three Texans (Joel McCrea, Zachary Scott, Douglas Kennedy) who get tangled up with gun-runners and Civil War renegades. The plot is pretty complicated, and most of it, despite the title, takes place *west* of St Louis! Victor Jory and Bob Steele (once himself a Western hero) make a thoroughly unpleasant pair of bad guys and Alan Hale, in one of his last film roles, etches a vivid portrait of the local bartender. Alexis Smith and Dorothy Malone have some splendid costumes as the girls involved.

South Pacific ○ ⓥ
1958, UK, 151 mins, colour
Dir: Joshua Logan
Stars: Mitzi Gaynor, Rossano Brazzi, John Kerr, Juanita Hall
Rating: ★★

Successful both on stage and on screen, with a score that includes 'Some Enchanted Evening', 'Happy

Talk', 'Younger Than Springtime', 'There is Nothing Like a Dame', 'I'm Gonna Wash That Man Right Outa My Hair' and 'Bali Ha'i'. The stage show was a smash success, but the film, with its tremendous colour photography (including the use of colour filters) and dazzling musical scenes actually shot on location amid sea and sand, offered even more to converted fans: the performances, though, from Mitzi Gaynor, Rossano Brazzi and John Kerr, are by and large disappointing.

Souvenir ●
1987, UK, 93 mins, colour
Dir: Geoffrey Reeve
Stars: Christopher Plummer, Catherine Hicks, Michael Lonsdale, Christopher Cazenove
Rating: ★

This flashback drama has an absorbing and initially fascinating idea, but proves boring in its progressive exposition and over-melodramatic towards the end. Touching early scenes – between Christopher Plummer as an ex-German soldier just retired from his Canadian butcher's shop, and Susannah York-lookalike Catherine Hicks as his daughter – go for nothing once the action reaches the French rural community where Plummer fell in love with a young French housewife in World War Two. The village, however, has a subsequent history of which he is unaware. Michael Lonsdale's character as the English-speaking mayor, who knows 'ambush' and 'skirmish' but not the English for 'chest', is, with Christopher Cazenove's stereotype English reporter abroad, the most flawed character. Despite civilised performances neither can do much with these types and a sideline romance between Cazenove and Hicks is risibly handled. Hicks and Plummer both have their moments, without much apparent help from director Geoffrey Reeve. Amélie Pick is very attractive as Plummer's lost love, and Tony Kinsey's music has that haunting quality that so much of *Souvenir* lacks.

Soylent Green ◑
1973, US, 97 mins, colour
Dir: Richard Fleischer
Stars: Charlton Heston, Edward G Robinson, Leigh Taylor-Young
Rating: ★★★

This ecologist science-fiction thriller, set in the year 2022, bulges with originality and imagination.

S

Charlton Heston gives his usual sincere and impassioned performance as the detective who investigates assassination in high places and stumbles across a horrendous secret. And Edward G Robinson is tremendous in his last film as the aged researcher with whom Heston shares a precious flat while the vast majority of New Yorkers live on the green-befogged streets or on the filthy stairways of grossly overcrowded tenement buildings. In the background, there are one or two gratifyingly large sets that take one back to the Hollywood of 15 years ago; and director Richard Fleischer uses them well. The 'poor hospital' is particularly well assembled so as to take on the aspect of a Renaissance painting, in which uniformed killer Chuck Connors looks just the intruder he is. And 20th-century buildings that stand in for 21st-century ones are as skilfully used by Fleischer as by Lang or Godard before him. The extermination centre, probably some ordinary New York skyscraper by day, becomes a forbidding tomb of light with a gaping mouth at its base, that dominates the wide, dusty, waste-ravaged avenue that stands before it.

Spaceballs ◐ ⓥ
1987, US, 96 mins, colour
Dir: Mel Brooks
Stars: Mel Brooks, John Candy, Rick Moranis, Bill Pullman
Rating: ★★

There are half-a-dozen brilliant comic ideas in this Mel Brooks parody of a space movie: e.g. John Hurt repeating his chest-expanding bit from *Alien*. The sad thing is that they're lost in a downpour of puerile jokes, feeble puns and idiotic gags – 'Beam me down, Snotty'! is a fair example.

SpaceCamp ○ ⓥ
1986, US, 108 mins, colour
Dir: Harry Winer
Stars: Lea Thompson, Kate Capshaw, Leaf Phoenix, Kelly Preston, Tom Skerritt, Terry O'Quinn, Tate Donovan
Rating: ★★

Let's give a hoot and a holler for good old-fashioned teamwork. Because that's what this Disneyish teenage adventure is all about. Initially believable, but finally ridiculous, especially with some bargain-basement special effects, the film still has bits that work on the emotions in the way that was obviously intended, especially

with a stirring and well-thought performance by Lea Thompson. She plays the girl who eventually has to fly a space shuttle after the only professional pilot on board is badly injured. The first third of the film is really a non-event as four teenagers and a space-mad sub-teen assemble for holiday 'training' to be astronauts at NASA's SpaceCamp. A friendly robot takes the youngest at his word about really going into space and – hey presto! – gains access to all the right buttons to make it happen. Once aloft, the film gains both momentum and emotional tug, although the tatty effects badly undercut scenes of the tiro astronauts making a life or death mission to get more oxygen from a floating space station.

Spaced Invaders ○
1990, US, 100 mins, colour
Dir: Patrick Read Johnson
Stars: Douglas Barr, Royal Dano, Adriana Richards, J J Anderson
Rating: ★★

'Well, Jim,' says the old-timer to his dog. 'It looks like you and me is the Earth's only hope. Kinda sad, isn't it?' Kinda sad, too, that poor delivery spoils most of the funny lines in this overlong space-age pantomime in which little green men from Mars storm down to Earth after hearing an anniversary broadcast of Orson Welles' famous radio programme about the landing of Martians. A granny and grandpa are recalling how he put a bucket on his head when the original *The War of the Worlds* was broadcast, when a spaceship hurtles past the house. 'I'll get the bucket,' she says. A pity that the treatment by and large means adults will find the antics tedious, but tinies should get a lot of fun out of it.

Spacehunter: Adventures in the Forbidden Zone ◐ ⓥ
1983, US, 85 mins, colour
Dir: Lamont Johnson
Stars: Peter Strauss, Molly Ringwald, Ernie Hudson, Michael Ironside
Rating: ★★★

Originally in 3D, this comic strip sci-fi *Star Wars* clone has lots of action, large, complex and very impressive sets, a good monster or two, and dislikable performances from the leading players. Ingenuity, however, wins the day, as Spacehunter (Peter Strauss) searches for three simpering maidens kidnapped by an aged megalomaniac (Michael Ironside) kept

alive by artificial means on a distant and inhospitable planet. 'Are they missing any limbs?' grumbles Ironside, in one of the script's few flashes of genuine humour. 'I hate it when they're missing limbs.' Fair enough.

Spaceman and King Arthur, The ☉
(aka: Unidentified Flying Oddball)
1979, UK, 93 mins, colour
Dir: Russ Mayberry
Stars: Dennis Dugan, Jim Dale, Ron Moody, Kenneth More
Rating: ★★★

A jolly shenanigan from the Disney people, which transposes Mark Twain's tale of the *Connecticut Yankee at King Arthur's Court* into the space age, with an astronaut jetting back through time and landing in Camelot. Dennis Dugan differentiates nicely between the astronaut and his robot twin and there are some ingenious laughs from the timewarp situation. Kenneth More and John le Mesurier are both treasurable as King Arthur and Sir Gawain, each in turn more fey and fuddled than the other, 'Can I have a word with you after the burning?' enquires Dugan, as he goes to the stake. 'Very well,' sighs More to le Mesurier. 'If he feels up to it.'

Spaceways ○
1953, UK, 76 mins, b/w
Dir: Terence Fisher
Stars: Howard Duff, Eva Bartok
Rating: ★

Adapted from a radio play, this British entry into the major league of science-fiction films fails to stir the blood in spite of having Terence Fisher in the director's chair, a Hollywood star (Howard Duff) in the lead, and smart photography by Reginald Wyer. A lame script is the chief culprit, although the actors do their best.

Spanish Gardener, The ○
1956, UK, 97 mins, colour
Dir: Philip Leacock
Stars: Dirk Bogarde, Jon Whiteley, Michael Hordern
Rating: ★★★

Rank didn't purchase many class properties for Dirk Bogarde when he was their most popular star, but this was definitely one of them. Adapted from the novel by A J Cronin, it reunites Bogarde with Jon Whiteley, the talented boy actor who had previously starred with him in *Hunted*.

And the director Philip Leacock was renowned for eliciting brilliant portrayals from child players; he also directed Jon Whiteley and Vincent Winter in the classic Ealing success *The Kidnappers*. The result of all this talent is not surprisingly a fresh and entertaining film.

Spanish Main, The ⊙
1945, US, 100 mins, colour
Dir: Frank Borzage
Stars: Paul Henreid, Maureen O'Hara, Walter Slezak, Binnie Barnes
Rating: ★★★

A really big pirate adventure story from RKO-Radio, clips from which turned up in the studio's action pictures for years afterwards. Chiefly notable for Binnie Barnes' spirited contribution as the lady pirate Ann Bonny (the character later reappeared in Cecil B DeMille's *The Buccaneer*) and for getting Henreid away from a series of women's pictures at Warners. He subsequently became equally typed in swashbucklers, appearing in *Last of the Buccaneers*, *Thief of Damascus* and *Pirates of Tripoli*. The director of this stirring saga is Frank Borzage, who won the first-ever director's Oscar in 1927 for *Seventh Heaven*.

Spare a Copper ○
1941, UK, 75 mins, b/w
Dir: John Paddy Carstairs
Stars: George Formby
Rating: ★★★

George as a gormless war reserve policeman, in a comedy formula that couldn't miss with British wartime audiences. Some inimitable Formby songs including 'I'm Shy' and 'On the Beat'.

Spare the Rod ○
1961, UK, 93 mins, b/w
Dir: Leslie Norman
Stars: Max Bygraves, Donald Pleasence, Betty McDowall
Rating: ★★★

Max Bygraves, who plays an idealistic schoolmaster in this story of life in a tough London school, staked nearly £50,000 of his own money to bring Michael Croft's controversial novel to the screen. One film company dropped the project when the censor threatened an 'X' certificate, but Max stuck to his guns, determined to bring this angry swipe at corporal punishment before a viewing public. No punches are pulled, even though the school's problems may look minor

compared with some of those today. There are savage thrashings, administered mainly by hardliner Geoffrey Keen, and a riot in which pupils wreck furniture and windows and scream slogans of hate. 'The final irony,' said Michael Croft, when the film escaped with an 'A' certificate, 'is that the canings were more brutal, the attitude to teachers less sympathetic, than anything in the original script!' The results ring true right to the final scene, helped by good performances from all the youngsters, headed by Claire Marshall and Richard O'Sullivan.

Spartacus ① ⓥ
1960, US, 184 mins, colour
Dir: Stanley Kubrick
Stars: Kirk Douglas, Laurence Olivier, Jean Simmons, Tony Curtis, Charles Laughton, Peter Ustinov
Rating: ★★★★

The sole surprise about Stanley Kubrick's marvellous epic is that it only won four Oscars. They included awards for Peter Ustinov's clever and finally greatly moving performance as Batiatus and for Russell Metty's breathtaking colour photography, at its very best in the final tableau of a sea of crosses silhouetted against a sunset. Kubrick's control of the massive battle scenes is commendable. But it is in the observation of human detail, and in many memorable little scenes that the film scores most heavily over other epics, and in which it finds an inner strength. It has at least half a dozen flawless portrayals. Ustinov, Kirk Douglas, Jean Simmons and Tony Curtis and John Ireland all do commendably craftsmanlike work. Topping them all is Charles Laughton as the wily old senator Gracchus. With a flicker of the corner of his mouth, or the raising of an eyelid, Laughton conveys more in an instant than others might in an hour.

Special Delivery ○
1955, US, 86 mins, b/w
Dir: John Brahm
Stars: Joseph Cotten, Eva Bartok, Niall MacGinnis
Rating: ★★

Here's a novel angle on an old plot. The suspense and thrills take place behind the Iron Curtain of the Fifties, but it isn't the theft of confidential plans or a swap of double-agents that sparks off the excitement – it's a baby. Filmed in Germany and the impressive

settings give the sentimental story some stylish weight. Eva Bartok makes a charming and touching heroine.

Special Delivery ①
1976, US, 99 mins, colour
Dir: Paul Wendkos
Stars: Bo Svenson, Cybill Shepherd
Rating: ★★★

An action caper that skilfully steers its way between thriller, romance and black comedy. A breathless opening, when four ex-marines rob a bank posing as toy salesmen, gives way to some nice dark jokes and acceptable romantic comedy, building to a suspenseful climax in which all interested parties close in warily on a mailbox containing the proceeds of the robbery. Sleekly directed by the talented Paul Wendkos, it's the best film of granite-jawed Bo Svenson's prolific career.

Spellbinder ●
1988, US, 94 mins, colour
Dir: Janet Greek
Stars: Timothy Daly, Kelly Preston, Rick Rossovich
Rating: ★

When young lawyer Jeff Mills (Timothy Daly) rescues a young girl from a savage beating he suddenly gains a girlfriend and a whole load of supernatural trouble. The girl (Kelly Preston) is the intended victim of a coven of diabolists and you know how these types hate to let a good victim slip through their fingers. If this all sounds pretty daft, it's because it is. Even by second-division horror standards, this film doesn't make much sense and was a poor choice for debut director Janet Greek. Special effects are good and the film has pace, but plot and dialogue leave a lot to be desired.

Spellbound ○ ⓥ
1945, US, 111 mins, b/w
Dir: Alfred Hitchcock
Stars: Gregory Peck, Ingrid Bergman
Rating: ★★★

Dazzling Hitchcock suspense film about an amnesiac, brilliantly written and directed, with a shock revelation around every corner. There's also a breathtaking – and very relevant – dream sequence designed by Salvador Dali. During the Forties, Ingrid Bergman was a favourite actress for the heroine of Hitchcock films. *Spellbound* was the first of three she did for Hitchcock (*Notorious* and *Under*

S

Capricorn followed). Here she plays a psychiatrist trying to help a man who is suffering from amnesia – and who might be a murderer too.

Spencer's Mountain ⊙

1963, US, 110 mins, colour
Dir: Delmer Daves
Stars: Henry Fonda, Maureen O'Hara, James MacArthur
Rating: ★★

This rose-tinted American rural drama, about a talented farm boy desperate to get a college education, proved too twee for British critics. But the home-spun wisdom and hillbilly memories of its source novel, by Earl Hamner Jr, struck gold almost a decade later when the location was changed from Spencer's Mountain to Walton's Mountain for the long-running TV series *The Waltons*. Director Delmer Daves, a former actor who studied civil engineering and law, only made two more films before retiring from Hollywood in 1965 to lecture on cinema.

Sphinx ○

1980, US, 117 mins, colour
Dir: Franklin J Schaffner
Stars: Lesley Anne-Down, Frank Langella, Maurice Ronet
Rating: ★

Easy-on-the-eye, easier-on-the-mind adventure hokum with Lesley-Anne Down facing more perils than Pauline as she searches for the long-lost tomb of an ancient Pharaoh. The direction, by Franklin J Schaffner, is lively enough to cover most of the holes in the story-line; Frank Langella is a suitably ambivalent hero, and John Gielgud turns up, rather surprisingly, as the Egyptian owner of an antique shop – probably the same one where the script was purchased. Ernest Day's attractive cinematography makes the most of the seductive locations.

Spider Woman Strikes Back ○

1946, US, 59 mins, b/w
Dir: Arthur Lubin
Stars: Gale Sondergaard, Brenda Joyce, Kirby Grant, Rondo Hatton
Rating: ★★

Fresh from her encounter with Sherlock Holmes, the Spider Woman (formidable Gale Sondergaard) is now slaughtering cattle with a poison distilled from carniverous plants which she feeds with blood and spiders. Rather a devious way of doing it, but it makes for a suitably shuddery shocker.

Spies Like Us ○ ⓥ

1985, US, 109 mins, colour
Dir: John Landis
Stars: Dan Aykroyd, Chevy Chase, Donna Dixon
Rating: ★★

A comedy of funny moments rather than consistent achievement, this update of the Hope and Crosby *Road* films has Chevy Chase and Dan Aykroyd off on the road to Afghanistan and bound for trouble. Many filmic in-jokes and guest appearances by famous directors will probably fly over the head of the average cinema-goer who will, however, recognise Ronald Reagan, Steve Forrest, Terry Gilliam and Bob Hope. But the plot and script – both co-written by Aykroyd – are endearingly silly enough to keep viewers chuckling happily enough for most of the way.

Spin of a Coin ○

(aka: The George Raft Story)
1961, US, 106 mins, b/w
Dir: Joseph M Newman
Stars: Ray Danton, Jayne Mansfield, Julie London, Neville Brand
Rating: ★★

A field day for Hollywood's gangster-type character actors in this incident-packed film biography of George Raft, the famous tough-guy star. Ray Danton endows Raft with cool charm, Neville Brand plays Al Capone for the second time, and the whole thing is fascinating for those who know little of how Raft started his career, as a dancer. The movie's also packed with gorgeous girls; dancer Barrie Chase, Fred Astaire's partner in many television shows; husky-voiced songstress Julie London; and the one and only Jayne Mansfield as the actress Raft gets a crush on. The film spotlights Raft's continual fight against criticism of his underworld associations.

Spinout

See: *California Holiday*

Spiral Staircase, The ☾

1945, US, 83 mins, b/w
Dir: Robert Siodmak
Stars: Dorothy McGuire, George Brent, Ethel Barrymore
Rating: ★★★★

Under Robert Siodmak's expert direction the potentially creaky plot – defenceless mute girl in mortal danger in an old dark house during a thunderstorm – is genuinely gripping, the suspense piled on to chilling effect. As the put-upon heroine unable to scream, Dorothy McGuire suffers gracefully, with telling support from Ethel Barrymore, Elsa Lanchester and Sara Allgood. The men are less effective (Kent Smith is an unusually stiff hero), but in any case the real stars are that magnificently malevolent house and the utterly relentless thunderstorm. Vastly superior to the 1975 re-make starring Jacqueline Bisset.

Spirit of St Louis, The ☾ ⓥ

1957, US, 138 mins, colour
Dir: Billy Wilder
Stars: James Stewart, Patricia Smith, Murray Hamilton
Rating: ★★

A gripping, if rather long, reconstruction of Charles Lindbergh's epic solo flight from New York to Paris in 1927. Honest and sincere and intelligently acted, especially by James Stewart (as Lindbergh) and Patricia Smith (an actress who unaccountably missed top stardom), there are times when true inspiration is lacking. But the climax is wonderfully emotive and the account of Lindbergh's early exploits as stunt pilot and mail flyer fascinatingly provides the film with an extra dimension. The period reconstructions are admirable.

Splash ○ ⓥ

1984, US, 110 mins, colour
Dir: Ron Howard
Stars: Tom Hanks, Daryl Hannah, John Candy
Rating: ★★★

It was certainly about time we had another mermaid film (it being nearly 30 years since Glynis Johns splashed her way through the sequel to *Miranda*). That might help explain the huge success of this comedy, which heralded a profitable new era for Disney's Touchstone Pictures unit, now one of the most successful in the world. This romp takes a while to get going (until the appearance of the mermaid, in fact), but when it does it has some funny lines, amusing characters and an engagingly funny heroine in Daryl Hannah as the amorous Madison. Though insufficient thought is given to technical details,

Spot Marks the X 671

the film is never less than fun to be with. These days you can't ask for much more than that.

Splash, Too ○
1988, US, 100 mins, colour
Dir: Greg Antonacci
Stars: Todd Waring, Amy Yasbeck
Rating: ★★

Another fishy comedy-adventure for Madison the mermaid, with Amy Yasbeck as the girl whose legs turn into a fishtail at the touch of water. Humour is laid on thick but, despite the familiar treatment, the story stays afloat and the family audience at whom it's aimed should enjoy it. Originally made for TV.

Splendor ○
1935, US, 77 mins, b/w
Dir: Elliott Nugent
Stars: Miriam Hopkins, Joel McCrea, Paul Cavanagh, David Niven
Rating: ★★

Miriam Hopkins, best known for her bitchy roles, was not ideally cast in this quiet romantic tear-jerker, routinely adapted by Rachel Crothers from her own play. A notable supporting cast includes comedienne Billie Burke, 'the perfect butler' Arthur Treacher and a dashing young David Niven. Dated but interesting.

Splendor in the Grass ◐
1961, US, 124 mins, colour
Dir: Elia Kazan
Stars: Natalie Wood, Warren Beatty
Rating: ★★★

Warren Beatty made his film debut in this heated drama of teenage sexuality, which was specially written for him by playwright William Inge after the actor had appeared in Inge's stage play *A Loss of Roses*. Inge, who has a small role in the film as a minister, won a Best Screenplay Oscar. And Natalie Wood has seldom involved us more with one of her performances.

Split, The ○
1968, US, 91 mins, colour
Dir: Gordon Flemyng
Stars: Jim Brown, Ernest Borgnine, Diahann Carroll, Julie Harris
Rating: ★★★

Director Gordon Flemyng may not have known it, but he had a star-studded cast of the future on his hands when he made this brutal robbery thriller, based on a novel by Richard Stark, who also wrote *Point Blank*. Photographer Burnett Guffey,

who had won an Oscar the previous year on *Bonnie and Clyde*, again dazzles us with the splendour of his colour camerawork – from sunny scenes of Southern California, through a shattering car smashing 'initiation test', to a night-time shoot-out on the cargo-crammed wharfside.

Split Second ○
1953, US, 85 mins, b/w
Dir: Dick Powell
Stars: Stephen McNally, Alexis Smith, Jan Sterling, Keith Andes
Rating: ★★★

A routine suspense movie from first-time director Dick Powell, former crooner and tough guy actor. Stephen McNally is rough and mean as the escaped convict holding hostages in an atomic testing area.

Split Second ● ⓥ
1991, UK, 90 mins, colour
Dir: Tony Maylam
Stars: Rutger Hauer, Kim Cattrall, Neil Duncan, Michael J. Pollard, Ian Dury
Rating: ★★

A silly but watchable horror thriller starring Rutger Hauer in his familiar garb of long topcoat and shotgun. This time Rutger's a cop in waterlogged, rat-infested London of 2008. A mutant monster is going around ripping out people's hearts (as monsters do) and Rutger's after its alien guts. It's already dispatched his partner, causing Rutger, who was having an affair with said partner's wife (Kim Cattrall) to go on the sauce. By 2008 the only black stuff he's on is constant coffee, but he's still one step behind the monster, who's taunting him by leaving him messages and ripping out a fresh heart every full moon. Saddled with be-spectacled partner Neil Duncan, Rutger marches masterfully through murky mush in a bid to end the reign of terror of the fiend, which has the familiar breathing difficulties beloved of the screen's sound effects boys. At the final show-down, the monster becomes the first thing in years to show up on time at a London railway station. Lots of unintentionally funny lines – 'It looks like an astrological symbol,' gasps Duncan, looking at an incomprehensible mass of blood on the ceiling – and gruesome, well-edited, well-shot action indicate a long life on video shelves.

Spoilers, The ◐
1942, US, 87 mins, b/w
Dir: Ray Enright

Stars: Marlene Dietrich, John Wayne, Randolph Scott
Rating: ★★

Rex Beach's famous adventure yarn set in Alaska of the Gold Rush era has been filmed several times and, despite the presence of Marlene Dietrich in this version, is most famous for the tremendous fist fight at the end between its two male protagonists. The one here, between John Wayne and Randolph Scott, is perhaps the daddy of them all. A very strong supporting cast includes Margaret Lindsay, Harry Carey and, as The Bronco Kid, that romantic idol of the silent screen Richard Barthelmess.

Spoilers, The ○
1955, US, 84 mins, colour
Dir: Jesse Hibbs
Stars: Jeff Chandler, Anne Baxter, Rory Calhoun, Barbara Britton
Rating: ★★

Fifth screen version of Rex Beach's classic action story, set in the Yukon. A terrific fist fight between Jeff Chandler and Rory Calhoun leaves both participants needing a bath or two. The old chestnut was showing its age, though (so was Anne Baxter), and hasn't been remade to date.

Spooks Run Wild ○
1941, US, 69 mins, b/w
Dir: Phil Rosen
Stars: Bela Lugosi, Leo Gorcey, Huntz Hall
Rating: ★★

Once *The Cat and the Canary* had proved that you could successfully mix chuckles with chills, there was no lack of takers jumping on the band wagon. The original sound Dracula, Bela Lugosi, was roped in for this East Side Kids (later The Bowery Boys) romp, and he has rather too much class for the Kids to handle. Pity about the tame ending, otherwise it's good clean fun.

Spot Marks the X ○
1986, US, 90 mins, colour
Dir: Mark Rosman
Stars: Barret Oliver, Natalie Gregory, David Huddleston, Geoffrey Lewis
Rating: ★★

Mike the dog, who all but stole the hit movie *Down and Out in Beverly Hills*, as tramp Nick Nolte's pooch, dognaps the limelight again in this Disney TV movie which casts him as a gangsters' mutt who becomes the pet of some youngsters who help him 'go straight'.

S

Barret Oliver, the boy from *The NeverEnding Story*, is his young master, and expert character actors Geoffrey Lewis and David Huddleston bolster the supporting cast. The first genuine canine star since Benji, Mike has almost single-handedly blazed a trail for troublesome dogs in films, most recent examples being *K-9* and *Turner and Hooch*, with James Belushi and Tom Hanks the stars upstaged by their doggy partners. In *Spot Marks the X*, Mike goes through his paces in fine style, helping to eradicate his criminal past by bringing a gang of bank-robbers to book.

Spotswood ○ ⓥ
1991, Australia, 93 mins, colour
Dir: Mark Joffe
Stars: Anthony Hopkins, Russell Crowe, Ben Mendelsohn, Rebecca Rigg, Toni Colette
Rating: ★★★

Anthony Hopkins took time off from the big league in 1991 to star in this small-scale, pleasing Australian film as an English time-and-motion expert in the late 1960s, faced with the difficult task of estimating possible redundancies at a moccasin factory in a small Melbourne suburb. The factory is pretty well the lifeblood of the town, so Hopkins, failing in an initial attempt to preserve his anonymity, is guaranteed hostility from the locals. What makes this film spring to life though, is the variety of characters flitting in and out of Hopkins's life. Ball, the boss, played with immense sympathy by Alwyn Kurtz; Carey, the nerdish dispatch clerk (Ben Mendelsohn), lovelorn for the boss's daughter (Rebecca Rigg); Wendy, Carey's unglamorous friend (an exceptionally honest performance by Toni Colette); Kim (Russell Crowe), the smart-ass opposite side of the coin to Carey; and the workmen and women at Ball's, the men indulging in a passion for slot-car racing (toy-car stuff on a grand scale) in which Hopkins finds himself beguilingly embroiled. A wise choice by Hopkins, this, choice being the operative word for a quietly effective film that wears its heart on its sleeve in the old-fashioned way.

Spring and Port Wine ○
1970, UK, 101 mins, colour
Dir: Peter Hammond
Stars: James Mason, Diana Coupland, Susan George, Rodney Bewes
Rating: ★★★

Phlegmatic, rather patronising, story of a Bolton family dominated by the patriarchal James Mason (himself a northerner, but from the White Rose county). The fulcrum of the tale is the reluctance of his younger daughter (a pert, teenaged Susan George) to eat a herring for supper and the subsequent plot centres around the tortuous ritual imposed by her father of serving up the hapless fish at every meal until she devours it.

Springfield Rifle ○ ⓥ
1952, US, 92 mins, colour
Dir: Andre De Toth
Stars: Gary Cooper, Phyllis Thaxter, David Brian, Lon Chaney Jr, Paul Kelly, Phil Carey
Rating: ★★

Filmed on location at altitudes of up to 9,500 feet on the slopes of California's Mount Whitney, and breathtakingly shot in WarnerColor by Edwin DuPar, this is a spasmodically exciting account of espionage and counter-espionage during the American Civil War. Gary Cooper makes an impassive hero. Good supporting cast largely hangs around waiting for something decent to do.

Spring in Park Lane ○
1948, UK, 92 mins, b/w
Dir: Herbert Wilcox
Stars: Michael Wilding, Anna Neagle
Rating: ★★★★

This brightest and wittiest of all the Anna Neagle-Michael Wilding films which boosted British box-office takings in post-war years. A brilliant script by Nicholas Phipps embellishes a lightweight plot about a footman in a high-society household who is not quite what he pretends to be. In this role, Wilding steals this particular film from under Dame Anna's delightful nose.

Springtime in the Rockies ○ ⓥ
1942, US, 85 mins, colour
Dir: Irving Cummings
Stars: Betty Grable, John Payne, Carmen Miranda, Cesar Romero
Rating: ★★★

The Fox musical stock company moved from Cuba and *A Week-End in Havana* to the Canadian rockies for this zingy song-and-dance feast with a whistle-worthy Mack Gordon-Harry Warren score that includes 'I Had the Craziest Dream', 'Run Little Raindrop Run' and the slam-bang fi-nale 'Pan-American Jubilee'. John Payne, Carmen Miranda – weighing in with 'Chattanoogo Choo-Choo' as well as her usual South American tongue-twister – and Cesar Romero, displaying a nifty line in dancing, were along for the ride, and, as the icing on the cake, Fox top-billed their newest musical sensation, Betty Grable, for the first time. For vitality and vivacity, it's one of Betty's brightest performances. Ace trumpeter Harry James made a guest appearance in the film and, a year later, he and Grable were man and wife. Charlotte Greenwood and Edward Everett Horton add their own brands of vitality and waspish wit and even get to dance a step or two at the finale.

Spy in Black, The ○
1939, UK, 82 mins, b/w
Dir: Michael Powell
Stars: Conrad Veidt, Sebastian Shaw, Valerie Hobson
Rating: ★★★

Alexander Korda's participation in this tense, romantic melodrama is tenuous and uncredited. His name does not appear on the titles (Irving Asher produced at Denham Studios for Columbia-British release), but several of his contract artists were involved, his brother Vincent was supervising art director and, according to one biographer 'Korda couldn't keep his fingers out of it.' The American title was *U-Boat 29* and has under-water sequences directed by Vernon Sewell, who was to direct over 200 films himself. Vivien Leigh was originally scheduled to play the schoolteacher spy eventually portrayed by Valerie Hobson.

Spy Who Came in From the Cold, The ○
1965, UK, 112 mins, b/w
Dir: Martin Ritt
Stars: Richard Burton, Claire Bloom
Rating: ★★★

The first film to show the dirty, squalid side of spying, as opposed to the luxury world of James Bond. Twist piles upon twist as a British agent Alec Leamas (Richard Burton at his most world weary) becomes involved in a fiendishly complicated plot to get an ex-Nazi spy chief, a plot that's more monstrously twisted than he imagines it to be. The script by Guy Trosper and Paul Dehn, from the novel by John Le Carré, is razor sharp and especially acute in its observations of human nature. Claire Bloom gives a stand-out performance in a film as ingenious as it is bitter.

Spy Who Loved Me, The ○ ⓥ

1977, UK, 125 mins, colour
Dir: Lewis Gilbert
Stars: Roger Moore, Barbara Bach, Curt Jurgens, Richard Kiel, Caroline Munro
Rating: ★★★

Roger Moore's third and best outing as James Bond is an enjoyable mixture of hectic action, big set-pieces and tongue-in-cheek humour. Richard Kiel makes his first appearance as the monstrous 'Jaws' and Carly Simon sings one of the more memorable Bond themes, 'Nobody Does it Better'. A ski sequence (culminating in a good visual joke) gets the action off to a fine start and tense, underwater scenes have a vital bearing on the plot.

Square Dance ① ⓥ

1986, US, 112 mins, colour
Dir: Daniel Petrie
Stars: Jason Robards, Jane Alexander, Rob Lowe, Winona Ryder, Deborah Richter
Rating: ★★

A moderate script is lit from within by the performances of its four leading player in this story of a 13-year-old girl who leaves her elderly father's egg farm to live with her gadabout mother in the bright lights of Texas's Fort Worth. Rob Lowe, in a showy but difficult role, is better than one could have ever expected as the retarded boy who becomes the object of her affection and Winona Ryder (as the girl), Jane Alexander and Jason Robards all play far above the level of the lines they are asked to read.

Square Peg, The ⊙ ⓥ

1958, US, 89 mins, b/w
Dir: John Paddy Carstairs
Stars: Norman Wisdom, Honor Blackman, Edward Chapman
Rating: ★★

One of the better films made by Norman Wisdom, the little big man of British comedy of the Fifties and Sixties. As Norman the road-mender, he is accidentally parachuted behind enemy lines in 1943 with his tetchy boss, Mr Grimsdale. Fortunately, he turns out to be the double of a German general, whom he impersonates and, after singing an operatic aria with

Hattie Jacques in the funniest scene in the film, manages to circumvent a firing squad, rescue his friends and become a war hero. The film gave Oliver Reed one of his earliest screen opportunities.

Ssssnake ●

1973, US, 99 mins, colour
Dir: Bernard L Kowalski
Stars: Strother Martin, Dirk Benedict
Rating: ★★★

An archetypal mad scientist movie that cheerfully recalls the heyday of such films in the Fifties with Strother Martin giving a zestful performance as the man who decides to turn luckless Dirk Benedict into a reptile. The film was produced by Richard Zanuck and David Brown, who were also responsible for *Jaws*, and the brisk direction is by Bernard L Kowalski who made such other genre chillers as *Attack of the Giant Leeches* and *Night of the Blood Beast*. Great grisly fun but not for snake lovers!

Stagecoach ○ ⓥ

1939, US, 99 mins, b/w
Dir: John Ford
Stars: Claire Trevor, John Wayne, George Bancroft, John Carradine, Thomas Mitchell
Rating: ★★★★

John Ford's supreme triumph and perhaps even the greatest Western of all time. John Wayne, then laguishing on the tiny backlots of Poverty Row studios, became a major star as an escaped prisoner who joins a stagecoach packed with an odd assortment of individuals for a journey through Apache territory that none of them will ever forget. Ford had not directed a Western for 13 years, and the public were startled by its use, for the first time ever, of the remote Monument Valley, with its arid plains 4000 feet above sea level and jutting buttes, some reaching 1500 feet. It was the first 'adult' Western to portray in-depth characters with allegorical themes running just beneath the surface plot of their life and death stuggles. Most Westerns that followed owed it a great and undying vote of thanks and its influence continues to this day. Ford had a tough job persuading any major studio to cast Wayne, and Claire Trevor received top billing. But the film's $392,000 budget looked money well spent when *Stagecoach* earned more than one million dollars on first release.

Stagecoach ○

1966, US, 114 mins, colour
Dir: Gordon Douglas
Stars: Ann-Margret, Alex Cord, Bing Crosby
Rating: ★★

Not the John Wayne/John Ford classic, nor even the Kris Kristofferson TV movie, but the 20th Century-Fox remake, too long for its content, but still good for some thrills as the stagecoach load of passengers, mostly fleeing from their own pasts, rattles its way through Indian territory, bringing each to his own destiny. Some roles are miscast, but Bing Crosby does well as the drunken Doc Boone, the role originally played by Thomas Mitchell. Overall, though, it underlines the motto: 'If it ain't broke, don't fix it.'

Stage Door ○

1937, 92 mins, b/w
Dir: Gregory La Cava
Stars: Katharine Hepburn, Ginger Rogers, Adolphe Menjou, Lucille Ball
Rating: ★★★★

This has to be one of the best films about show business ever made, and was, in fact, nominated for several Oscars, including Best Film, Best Screenplay and Best Director for Gregory La Cava. Katharine Hepburn is a society debutante who defies her father by becoming a Broadway hopeful. The luck of the draw sees her sharing a room in a New York boarding house with Ginger Rogers, a tough cookie who heckles everyone. The feuding actresses are equally determined to make it to the top. Hepburn had been in several costume epics and was beginning to be typecast, but this outing showed her as someone who could play comedy and pathos equally convincingly. The film is a totally absorbing treat to the eyes and the ears, especially seeing such stars-to-be as Lucille Ball, Jack Carson, Eve Arden and Ann Miller all grabbing early chances.

Stage Fright ○

1949, UK, 106 mins, b/w
Dir: Alfred Hitchcock
Stars: Jane Wyman, Richard Todd, Marlene Dietrich, Michael Wilding
Rating: ★★★

A Hitchcock thriller in which the murderer of a famous actress's husband remains unidentified until the final, hectic moments. It's based on a novel by Selwyn Jepson – the Special

S

Operations major who recruited many wartime agents including Violette Szabo GC – with Jane Wyman uneasily cast as a student actress who helps Richard Todd, the man on the run from a murder rap. Alastair Sim's own special brand of humour (as Ms Wyman's father) is given fair play as he begins to diagnose the cause of foul play. The rest of the cast, though, could have easily been better chosen. It also includes Marlene Dietrich (singing 'The Laziest Gal in Town') and Sybil Thorndike, each apparently determined to act the other off the screen.

Staircase ◐

1969, UK, 101 mins, colour
Dir: Stanley Donen
Stars: Richard Burton, Rex Harrison, Cathleen Nesbitt, Beatrix Lehmann
Rating: ★★

An opening-out by playwright Charles Dyer of his own hit play about two middle-aged homosexuals living above a barber's shop. This film version is tailored to the acting talents of its two leading players, although it seems almost wilfully perverse to cast two of filmland's most married actors, Richard Burton and Rex Harrison, in these roles. The music score for this curio is by Dudley Moore.

Stairway to Heaven

See: A Matter of Life and Death

StakeOut ◐ ⓥ

1987, US, 115 mins, colour
Dir: John Badham
Stars: Richard Dreyfuss, Emilio Estevez, Aidan Quinn, Madeleine Stowe
Rating: ★★★

The plot for this film is both improbable and unoriginal – a cop on a surveillance job falls in love with the woman he is spying on – but that doesn't stop *StakeOut* being a thoroughly enjoyable picture. This is principally thanks to Richard Dreyfuss and Emilio Estevez as the two cops on surveillance and some sharp dialogue. They make such a good double act, you're left hoping they'll make more films together.

Stalag 17 ○ ⓥ

1953, US, 120 mins, b/w
Dir: Billy Wilder
Stars: William Holden, Don Taylor, Otto Preminger
Rating: ★★★

William Holden in his Oscar-winning performance as a World War Two PoW camp scrounger, whose rackets include a peep-show by telescope into the women's barracks, horse races with mice competitors and distilling home-brewed gin. Naturally, he's number one on his fellow-prisoner's list of suspects when deaths of would-be escapers make it plain than an informer is at work. Billy Wilder's film strikes several different notes – it's comic, dramatic, suspenseful and touching in turn. But most notable is the comedy vein, in which character actor Robert Strauss had his biggest film success as Animal, a neolithic type who shuffles around in underwear that no washday mum could be proud of. If Holden's gritty, forceful portrait is the film's lynchpin, then Strauss, Harvey Lembeck, Otto Preminger, Neville Brand and Peter Graves all contribute materially to its success.

Stalking Moon, The ○

1968, US, 109 mins, colour
Dir: Robert Mulligan
Stars: Gregory Peck, Eva Marie Saint
Rating: ★★

Off-beat Western, ravishingly photographed in colour by Charles Lang (who won an Academy Award as long ago as 1933 for his photography on *A Farewell to Arms*). Peck plays a veteran cavalry scout trying to protect a young widow and her son from a marauding Indian who sees himself as the boy's rightful father. It's an unusual film to come from director Robert Mulligan, more a specialist in human drama. His sure touch in the interior scenes is very much in evidence, especially in a charming sequence where Peck's half-breed friend teaches the boy to count by initiating him into the rules of poker. There's also a quota of excitement when Peck and his friends try to kill the Indian before he kills them, and look like losing.

Stamboul Quest ○

1934, US, 88 mins, b/w
Dir: Sam Wood
Stars: Myrna Loy, George Brent, Lionel Atwill, C Henry Gordon
Rating: ★★★

An early Hollywood stab at a fact-based World War One story much later filmed in Britain as *Fraulein Doktor*. In this stylish and exciting version, scripted by Herman J Mankiewicz, it's Myrna Loy as the conscience-torn German spy falling in love with an enemy in Turkey. Sam

Wood, one of MGM's top directors, keeps the heady combination of romance and intrigue moving along well.

Stampeded

See: The Big Land

Stand and Deliver ◐

1988, US, 107 mins, colour
Dir: Ramon Menendez
Stars: Edward James Olmos, Lou Diamond Phillips, Rosana De Soto, Andy Garcia
Rating: ★★★★

A totally inspirational film whose cumulative emotional impact is such that it may have you weeping like a child in the last few minutes. In fact, the only criticism you could level against it, that it stretches credulity to the limits, is totally invalidated by the fact that it's a true story. Edward James Olmos lives the role of the sly, humorous, seemingly laid-back maths teacher at a Los Angeles ghetto school, who takes a class of ragged, rebellious, tough Mexican-American girls and boys on the verge of juvenile delinquency and lives of drudgery and turns them into dedicated students. Ace performances, cleverly written screenplay: don't miss it.

Stand by for Action

See: Cargo of Innocents

Stand by Me ◐ ⓥ

1986, US, 89 mins, colour
Dir: Rob Reiner
Stars: Wil Wheaton, River Phoenix, Corey Feldman, Kiefer Sutherland, Richard Dreyfuss
Rating: ★★

A group of young friends search for the body of a missing teenager after one of them overhears his older brother, who claims to have seen it. A simple plot, but there's a lot more to the film than the basic storyline. The search for the body becomes something of an odyssey for the boys and more of an adventure than even they expected. Unusually, the tale is narrated by one of the boys, now in middle age. Not always a device that works, it succeeds here, as it doesn't interfere with or slow down the story. It's also a very nostalgic film, which is heightened by the late Fifties songs used in the soundtrack.

Stand-in ○

1937, US, 90 mins, b/w
Dir: Tay Garnett

Stars: Leslie Howard, Joan Blondell, Humphrey Bogart
Rating: ★★★

A high-grade comedy on Hollywood low-life and an absolute treat for fans of Leslie Howard and Humphrey Bogart to see them step outside their normal genres and play such an intelligently-made blend of satire, sentiment and farce. Howard is delicious as the head-in-the-books accountant sent to save Colossal Studios from financial ruin and Bogart quite amazing as a drunken director.

Stanley & Iris ◑ ⓥ
1989, US, 102 mins, colour
Dir: Martin Ritt
Stars: Jane Fonda, Robert De Niro, Swoosie Kurtz, Martha Plimpton
Rating: ★★★

It sounds unkind to say it in these harsh times, but the characters in *Stanley & Iris* are really too nice for words. Fonda is a widow with a pregnant daughter, scraping up a living in a bakery. De Niro is a cook with the same firm. He helps her when she gets mugged, but gets fired because he can't read or write. Yes, we know, you can tell us the rest (given that De Niro's an inventor, too), but it's pleasantly done, without too much incident or bite, but rarely boring to be with and leisurely rather than slow, as the two characters tentatively and uncertainly build their relationship.

Stanley and Livingstone ○
1939, US, 101 mins, b/w
Dir: Henry King
Stars: Spencer Tracy, Nancy Kelly, Richard Greene
Rating: ★★★

Always absorbing account of newspaperman Henry Stanley's endeavours to find the missionary doctor David Livingstone in the depths of then–darkest Africa of 1869. Spencer Tracy and Walter Brennan both foreshadow the roles they played in the following year's *Northwest Passage*, with the locale changed from Africa to the Canadian wilderness. The ending is stirring stuff.

Star! ○
1968, US, 175 mins, colour
Dir: Robert Wise
Stars: Julie Andrews, Richard Crenna, Michael Craig
Rating: ★★

A feast of brilliantly-recreated Twenties' and Thirties' songs is the main attraction of this mammoth musical biopic about Gertrude Lawrence, with Julie Andrews in the title role. On stage the film's a hit; off-stage it never quite catches fire, in spite of Daniel Massey's delightful impersonation of Noel Coward, which was rightly rewarded with an Academy Award nomination.

Star Chamber, The ●
1983, US, 109 mins, colour
Dir: Peter Hyams
Stars: Michael Douglas, Hal Holbrook, Yaphet Kotto, Sharon Gless
Rating: ★★

Vicious criminals are getting off on technicalities thanks to the smartness of their lawyers. Under these circumstances, talented writer-director Peter Hyams would have us believe, a group of high court judges might set up their own court of no appeal, where sentences are carried out by a hit-man. It sounds reasonable enough and the only dubious part of the plot is why newest judicial recruit Michael Douglas would really want to do anything about it when he finds that two homicidal crooks 'sentenced' to death didn't commit the actual murders of which they have been accused. Hyams craftily hypes up the action, but pat performances make this an occasionally routine urban thriller.

Stardust ● ⓥ
1974, US, 105 mins, colour
Dir: Michael Apted
Stars: David Essex, Adam Faith, Larry Hagman
Rating: ★★

It's surprising that the weak link in this powerful and provocative follow up to *That'll Be The Day* should prove to be the music. It wouldn't have lifted the Beatles to stardom, let alone Jim MacLaine (David Essex), the subject of this bitter and harrowing morality play about the sorrows and solitude of stardom. Limply acted by Essex and by Ines de Longchamps as his moll, the film is rescued and dominated by Adam Faith as the star's manager. Even given that Essex meekly hands him centre stage, Faith takes it like a lion, giving a magnetic portrayal of seemingly innocuous evil that creates a memorable movie character.

Stardust Memories ○
1980, US, 88 mins, b/w
Dir: Woody Allen

Stars: Woody Allen, Charlotte Rampling, Jessica Harper
Rating: ★★

Or: Woody Allen strikes back. Setting out all the things of which his detractors have accused him, he creates an entire film (of fragments) around them. Allen is Sandy, a movie-maker accused of 'trying to document his private suffering and fob it off as art'. Woody obviously doesn't agree (at least, perhaps, as to whether it's art) so he offers us more of the same. The resulting film has its good moments, mostly in the too-few scenes from the comedy films Sandy has made in the past, but is sometimes equally likely to send you to sleep. It also doesn't have Diane Keaton or Mia Farrow, and Charlotte Rampling (although quite effective), Jessica Harper and the charmless Marie-Christine Barrault are simply no substitute. Viewers may find that, as people keep telling Woody in the film, they 'prefer his earlier, funny comedies' to this. The background score, though, is a vintage-jazz enthusiast's delight, Louis Armstrong's rendition of 'Stardust' creating an especially memorable few moments.

Starflight One ○
1982, US, 155 mins, colour
Dir: Jerry Jameson
Stars: Lee Majors, Hal Linden
Rating: ★

They really should have called this one *Airplane III*. Hypersonic Starflight One, piloted by iron-jawed Cody Briggs (Lee Majors) goes into orbit trying to avoid a rogue rocket. Some good players are caught up in the events that follow; Ray Milland grits his teeth and wades through the dialogue like a man eating chalk. One-time rising star Michael Sacks (lead roles in *Slaughterhouse Five* and *Sugarland Express*) has a supporting role as the navigator (at least he takes the quick way out as guinea-pig for a failed rescue bid) and even lower in the cast is Robert Englund, now enshrined in the minds of a whole generation of horror film fans for his portrayal of evil Freddie Krueger in the *Nightmare On Elm Street* shockers.

Star Is Born, A ○
1937, US, 111 mins, colour
Dir: William A Wellman
Stars: Janet Gaynor, Fredric March, Adolphe Menjou, Andy Devine
Rating: ★★★

First of three versions of the classic Hollywood drama about the tempestuous star couple whose show careers are going in opposite directions: hers up, his down. Janet Gaynor and Fredric March shine in the parts later played by Judy Garland and James Mason (in 1954), and by Barbra Streisand and Kris Kristoffrson (in the 1976 rock music version). Written by Dorothy Parker, Alan Campbell and Robert Carson, from a story by Wellman and Carson, but based in part on the 1932 film *What Price Hollywood?*. Splendidly filmed in early Technicolor, *A Star Is Born* won Oscars for W Howard Green's cinematography and for Best Original Story. On the film's release the New York Times described it as the 'the most accurate mirror ever held before the glittering, tinselled, trivial, generous, cruel and ecstatic world that is Hollywood.'

Star Is Born, A ○ Ⓥ
1954, US, 154 mins, colour
Dir: George Cukor
Stars: Judy Garland, James Mason, Charles Bickford
Rating: ★★★★

The best of three versions of the story about a rising actress (Judy Garland – never better) and her sinking, alcoholic fading star husband (James Mason). An artistic and personal triumph for Garland, who took her character through an emotional gamut, pulling a heart-rending performance from the depths of her own. And Mason is magnificent: thank goodness Cary Grant, Humphrey Bogart and Frank Sinatra failed to win the part. The show stopping 'Born in a Trunk' sequence was only added at a later date to show how the character became a star. Garland was nominated for a Best Actress Oscar but lost out on the night to Grace Kelly for *The Country Girl*, leading Groucho Marx to comment that her loss 'was the biggest robbery since Brink's.' A later 'restored' version lasted 170 minutes.

Star Is Born, A ● Ⓥ
1976, US, 140 mins, colour
Dir: Frank Pierson
Stars: Barbra Streisand, Kris Kristofferson, Gary Busey
Rating: ★

Modern remake of the famous musical about love, fame and tragedy – as you can tell by the proliferation of four letter words, which tend to distract your attention from the story of a rock idol on the way down who marries a pop singer on the way up to international stardom. In the Fredric March/James Mason role, Kris Kristofferson does best with the quieter moments, seeming sometimes too intense; too often director Frank Pierson appears to be allowing his players to act the scene as they think fit rather than under his guidance. Barbra Streisand sings a good variety of showy songs which her fans should enjoy. As well as star, executive producer and part composer of two of the film's songs, she also gets a credit for 'Ms Streisand's clothes from . . . her closet'! Even so, the film trails in a dismal third of the three versions, causing some carpers to call it *A Bore is Starred*.

Starman ◖ Ⓥ
1984, US, 115 mins, colour
Dir: John Carpenter
Stars: Jeff Bridges, Karen Allen, Charles Martin Smith, Richard Jaeckel
Rating: ★★★

This story about a human *E.T.* – or at least an alien in human form – is a built-in success for a director who can pull the right emotional chords at the right time. John Carpenter isn't the sort to miss easy opportunities, and the result is a fairly old-fashioned mix of emotion, excitement and enjoyment – although we could have done with a little more extra-terrestrial activity and a little less earthly romance, even if Starman's miracles seem limited to the number of 'magic marbles' he carries on his person. Jeff Bridges gives a clever performance as the alien who learns about human emotions through the young widow (appealing Karen Allen) whose dead husband he has fashioned himself to resemble. Charles Martin Smith does well as the only other human interested in saving Starman rather than destroying him, and the perennial Richard Jaeckel, pushing 60 but still looking 45, is in fine, snapping form as the chief governmental bad guy. No big surprises about this film, but, despite one or two script lapses that provide unintentional smiles, it offers solid entertainment along reassuring lines.

Star of India ⊙
1953, UK, 97 mins, colour
Dir: Arthur Lubin
Stars: Cornel Wilde, Jean Wallace, Herbert Lom
Rating: ★★

Cornel Wilde and his wife, Jean Wallace, came to Britain to make this cheerfully ingenuous swashbuckler, as did their Hollywood director, Arthur Lubin. The best performance comes from Herbert Lom as the villain of the piece and C Pennington Richards, later to turn to direction, provides some attractive colour photography.

Stars and Bars ◖ Ⓥ
1988, US, 94 mins, colour
Dir: Pat O'Connor
Stars: Daniel Day-Lewis, Harry Dean Stanton, Martha Plimpton, Joan Cusack, Will Patton, Glenne Headly
Rating: RB

Superstardom was around the corner for Daniel Day-Lewis but you could never have guessed it from this atrocious hillbilly comedy with a misbegotten central idea. It features Day-Lewis as an Englishman in America given the task of buying a newly-discovered Renoir from an eccentric Southerner, played by Harry Dean Stanton. All of the performances are bad (quite a feat with this cast) but script and direction are worse. Day-Lewis's dedication in dragging his bag-of-bones body through the rain in the altogether is painful to behold and probably led to him beefing up his physique for subsequent roles. A complete shambles.

Stars Are Singing, The ○
1953, US, 99 mins, colour
Dir: Norman Taurog
Stars: Rosemary Clooney, Anna Maria Alberghetti, Layritz Melchior
Rating: ★★★

Bright, tuneful musical about a teenage refugee with a glorious soprano voice. It introduced filmgoers to Rosemary Clooney and, in the role of the refugee, gave a big singing chance to Anna Maria Alberghetti, for whom suitable subsequent roles proved hard to find. But the show is stolen by a droll comedian called Bob Williams, and his even funnier 'trick' dog, Red Dust, who makes a hilarious hash of every command he receives.

Stars Look Down, The ○
1939, UK, 110 mins, b/w
Dir: Carol Reed
Stars: Michael Redgrave, Margaret Lockwood, Emlyn Williams
Rating: ★★★

This solidly-crafted film of A J Cronin's pre-war best-seller set in a mining community in the North of England placed director Carol Reed in the forefront of young British directors. Co-written by Cronin, it's finely acted by a strong cast headed by Michael Redgrave, Margaret Lockwood and Emlyn Williams. Ms Lockwood is shrewishly effective in the first of her many famous film bad girls.

Star-spangled Rhythm ○
1942, US, 99 mins, b/w
Dir: George Marshall
Stars: Eddie Bracken, Betty Hutton, Bob Hope, Dorothy Lamour
Rating: ★★★

One of five films that Betty Hutton and Eddie Bracken made together at Paramount in the war years, the best-remembered of which is *The Miracle of Morgan's Creek*. In post-war times, their stars exploded, and both were out of Hollywood by the early Fifties. Their roles here are as nominal stars to one of those marvellous wartime studio extravaganzas in which pretty well every contractee was bound to turn up; in this case that meant Bob Hope, Bing Crosby, Dorothy Lamour, Alan Ladd, Veronica Lake, William Bendix, Fred MacMurray, Ray Milland, Susan Hayward, Paulette Goddard, Dick Powell and many more, with some well-known studio directors popping in for good measure. Betty Hutton plays the studio's scatterbrained telephone operator involved in putting on a show for her sailor boyfriend (Bracken) and his pals, and the songs include 'That Old Black Magic' (nominated for an Oscar) and 'Time to Hit the Road to Dreamland'.

Starting Over ◐
1979, US, 93 mins, colour
Dir: Alan J Pakula
Stars: Burt Reynolds, Jill Clayburgh, Candice Bergen, Charles Durning
Rating: ★★★

A funny-sad comedy-romance that has Burt Reynolds trying to decide between the respective attractions of ex-wife Candice Bergen and new lady Jill Clayburgh. As Bergen is no match for Clayburgh in both acting and charm departments, you can guess the outcome, but, though there are a few dead patches on the way, the script offers some nice laughs and a sniffle or two as well. The wry-faced Reynolds gives a peerless performance, again belying his muscleman image and even stealing the film from the luminous Clayburgh. Austin Pendleton also does a very nice job as Reynolds' bespectacled friend at the

almost convincing men's divorce circle. Director Alan Pakula's efforts at making a charming film seem a little calculated, but they work quite a lot of the time.

Star Trek: The Motion Picture ○ ⓥ
1979, US, 132 mins, colour
Dir: Robert Wise
Stars: William Shatner, Leonard Nimoy, DeForest Kelley, James Doohan
Rating: ★★

Robert Wise, who made such science fiction classics as *The Day the Earth Stood Still* and *The Andromeda Strain*, returned to the genre for this film. Glamorous Persis Khambatta joins the Star Trek regulars, as a bald-headed Deltan beauty who forms part of a desperate Earth bid to reunite the original crew of the Starship Enterprise and stop an irresistible force travelling towards our planet. Special effects are good, as well they might be in the hands of Douglas Trumbull of *2001* and *Silent Running* fame. So are the set designs and Jerry Goldsmith's music. But the cast often seems undecided as to whether the venture should be played straight or tongue-in-cheek. 'Dammit, Bones,' growls William Shatner at one stage to DeForest Kelley, 'I need you – badly.' Not as badly, Admiral Kirk, as you needed some better lines in the script.

Star Trek II: The Wrath of Khan ○ ⓥ
1982, US, 113 mins, colour
Dir: Nicholas Meyer
Stars: William Shatner, Leonard Nimoy, DeForest Kelley, Kirstie Alley
Rating: ★★★

Trekkies will not be disappointed with this second feature film from the famous TV series, even though it seems to deprive them of one of their favourite characters. Kirk (William Shatner) once again says, 'Don't mince words Bones, what do you really mean?' and the whole legend is cleverly camped up by the actors (and director Nicholas Meyer) with many an arched eyebrow and amused twitch of the corner of the mouth. Kirk's adversary is Khan (played by Ricardo Montalban as the Demon King of Space: so much so that you almost expect him to appear in a puff of smoke), a renegade out for revenge for his casting away on a desert planet these 15 years before. But the plot concentrates on character rather than

action, although there's enough of that too. Effects are limited but well done and James Horner's Tchaikovsky-style music captures the spirit of the thing with tongue-in-cheek panache.

Star Trek III: The Search for Spock ○ ⓥ
1984, US, 105 mins, colour
Dir: Leonard Nimoy
Stars: William Shatner, Leonard Nimoy, DeForest Kelley
Rating: ★★

There's a glorious innocence about the continuing adventures of the Starship Enterprise, though this one is more routine than its theme promises. Spock 'died' in the last adventure, but you can bet your last Klingon coin that Captain Kirk (still William Shatner) and his trusty crew will not allow him to rest in peace for long. Add a Klingon warlord out to wrest the secret of 'Genesis' (the regeneration of a dead planet) from its inventor (Kirk's son) and you have a simple mixture which goes down at a rather leisurely pace for the next hour and three quarters. Shatner continues to grow younger while all about him look ready to draw their old-age pensions: an offshoot from the 'Genesis' project perhaps. A giggle a minute for the rest of us while Trekkies remain spellbound.

Star Trek IV
See: The Voyage Home

Star Trek V: The Final Frontier ○ ⓥ
1989, US, 100 mins, colour
Dir: William Shatner
Stars: William Shatner, Leonard Nimoy, DeForest Kelley
Rating: ★★

This fifth attempt to boldly venture where no man has gone before is an improvement on one or two of the others, even though it sags in the middle when batty Vulcan Lawrence Luckinbill holds forth on the state of God, pain and the Galaxy. Just as well there's a ship full of hostile Klingons to contend with as well, so, at the beginning and end at least, the sci-fi pot is kept bubbling with a good deal of action. The direction (by star William Shatner) is serviceable enough and, if things sometimes get too deliberately silly, there's still a deal of amusement to be gained from the banter between the old comrades. 'Please, Captain,' chides Spock

S

(Leonard Nimoy), as Kirk is about to embrace him, 'not in front of the Klingons.'

Star Trek VI: The Undiscovered Country ○ ⓥ
1991, US, 109 mins, colour
Dir: Nicholas Meyer
Stars: William Shatner, Leonard Nimoy, DeForest Kelley, James Doohan, Nichelle Nichols
Rating: ★★★

Sentiment over what's ostensibly the last of the Star Trek films, nicely rounded off with the signatures of the cast, can't cloak the fact that it isn't actually the finest entry in the captain's log. Kirk's old enemies the Klingons are faced with extinction and agree to attend a world conference relevant to their survival. Faced with the unthinkable – peace and retirement – Kirk and his men are perhaps more relieved than they'd care to admit that certain elements are determined to destroy the conference and ensure the continuation of war. The film's centre-piece is the imprisonment of Kirk and Dr McCoy (William Shatner, DeForest Kelley) in the mines beneath a planet of icy wastes. Here as elsewhere, though, the pace is pretty lethargic, and a sense of urgency only grows towards the end – almost as if the crew were reluctant to say farewell. 'Once again,' smirks Shatner, tongue-in-cheek, at the end, 'I've saved civilisation as we know it.' And so he has. But perhaps the bigger miracle is that the entire cast is still alive after 25 years on board with the series.

Start the Revolution Without Me ◐
1969, US, 95 mins, colour
Dir: Bud Yorkin
Stars: Gene Wilder, Donald Sutherland
Rating: ★★★★

Lively, underrated swashbuckling spoof. Fred Freeman and Lawrence J Cohen's screenplay gives the French Revolution the runaround and casts Gene Wilder and Donald Sutherland as two sets of twins – The Corsican Brothers (master swordsmen) and a couple of feckless peasants, who of course get mistaken for them. The fun lies chiefly in the by-play between Wilder and Sutherland ('I'll run him through.' 'You'd be lucky to run the girl through.'). But the giant ballroom scene is also a hysterical success, with a surfeit of notes, most of them hinting at assassination plots, passing bewilderingly from dancer to dancer, until Wilder receives one (from a man) saying 'Hello, handsome'. The scene ends in masterly fashion, as the comic king (Hugh Griffith), dressed as a cockerel under the mistaken impression that the ball was fancy dress, weaves his way slowly back through the revellers to the royal chamber. Though director Bud Yorkin pulls every trick in the book, gales of laughter thereafter are strictly spasmodic.

Star Wars ○ ⓥ
1977, US, 116 mins, colour
Dir: George Lucas
Stars: Mark Hamill, Harrison Ford, Carrie Fisher, Alec Guinness
Rating: ★★★

This super-colossal science-fiction pantomime smashed box-office records all over the world. And, like most pantomimes, it's a lot of fun. There are monsters, robots and battles galore, and an endearing pair of androids, C-3PO and R2-D2, that accompany the hero (Mark Hamill) on his exploits. Alec Guinness and Peter Cushing are there to provide the class, and Carrie Fisher makes a practical heroine, even if her ancestry seems closer to Brooklyn than outer space. The film's adrenalin-raising drive makes it well-nigh irresistible.

State Fair ⊙ ⓥ
1945, US, 100 mins, colour
Dir: Walter Lang
Stars: Jeanne Crain, Dana Andrews, Dick Haymes, Vivian Blaine
Rating: ★★★★

Warm-hearted musical in marvellous colour made by that unsung hero of film musicals, Walter Lang, who also directed *Coney Island*, *Mother Wore Tights*, *Call Me Madam*, *There's No Business Like Show Business*, *The King and I* and many others. Lilting Rodgers and Hammerstein score includes, as well as the title number, 'That's for Me', 'It's a Grand Night for Singing' and 'It Might As Well Be Spring', the latter winning an Oscar as the year's best song. Louanna Hogan 'ghost' sings for Jeanne Crain, who makes a charming heroine. Vivian Blaine and Dick Haymes contribute their own tonsil work. The songs put it ahead of the 1993 original with Will Rogers and Janet Gaynor.

State Fair ○
1962, US, 113 mins, colour
Dir: Jose Ferrer

Stars: Pat Boone, Ann-Margret, Bobby Darin, Alice Faye, Tom Ewell
Rating: ★★

Jose Ferrer directed this re-make of the famous Rodgers and Hammerstein musical about a country family who all come up for the huge state fair. Sultry Ann-Margret offsets the pure charm of Mr Boone, but it is the older generation who steals the honours – Tom Ewell and Alice Faye, herself making a comeback as the mother and looking just as trim and lovely as in the days when she starred in such musicals as *Alexander's Ragtime Band*, *Rose of Washington Square*, *Tin Pan Alley*, *Hello Frisco Hello* and *The Gang's All Here*. Not as good as the Forties' version, but the score is still enchanting.

State of Grace ● ⓥ
1990, US, 134 mins, colour
Dir: Phil Joanou
Stars: Sean Penn, Ed Harris, Gary Oldman, Robin Wright, John Turturro, Burgess Meredith
Rating: ★★

A long and gruelling film about the Irish gangsters of New York's *Hell's Kitchen*. The script is only marginally compelling and all of the performances have moments when melodrama takes over from conviction. Penn is a young man who escaped the Kitchen and now, it seems, has returned. He renews acquaintance with Jackie (Gary Oldman) and his brother Frankie (Ed Harris), now the neighbourhood protection boss – and rekindles his steamy affair with their sister (Robin Wright). The Irish gangsters are dinosaurs at the mercy of the modern technology of the Mafia, but they still kill people. It's a desperate and dangerous way to earn a living and you don't exactly get the idea that any of these guys are happy or secure in their work. And, street warfare being what it is, most of the cops' work is done for them in the end, more effectively than they could do it themselves. It's a harsh and familiar tale of executions and betrayals, somewhat hampered in the telling by the fact that the characters, even the girl, are cold and unsympathetic throughout.

State of the Union ○
(aka: The World and His Wife)
1948, US, 110 mins, b/w
Dir: Frank Capra

Stars: Spencer Tracy, Katharine Hepburn, Van Johnson, Angela Lansbury
Rating: ★★★

Another Spencer Tracy/Katharine Hepburn vehicle, this Frank Capra-directed dissection of political chicanery, has an excellent script by Anthony Veiller and Myles Connolly. Although basically an emotive drama, the screenplay is veined with marvellous wisecracks and the moral brought home strongly in the approved Capra style. Angela Lansbury has an excellent 'bitch' role which she plays icily and to the hilt, while Tracy's outburst at the end reminds one of the speech he was to make nearly 20 years later, at the end of his last film *Guess Who's Coming to Dinner*.

State Secret ○
(aka: The Great Manhunt)
1950, UK, 104 mins, b/w
Dir: Sidney Gilliat
Stars: Douglas Fairbanks Jr, Glynis Johns, Jack Hawkins, Herbert Lom
Rating: ★★★

A superior, stylish, fast paced thriller, absolutely alive with atmosphere, as a surgeon played by Douglas Fairbanks Jr goes on the run from the state police of an East European country after he has failed to save their dictator on the operating table. Its sheer panache and excitement, together with excellent performances from all four principals, made this film a classic.

Static ● ⓥ
1985, US, 93 mins, colour
Dir: Mark Romanek
Stars: Keith Gordon, Amanda Plummer, Bob Gunton, Barton Heyman
Rating: ★★

Now Ernie Blick is what you and I would call a weirdo. With his parents dead in a car crash, this mechanical maniac has invented a machine that will show him a picture of Heaven so that he can find and talk to them. Director Mark Romanek, whose first film this was, and who wrote the script with star Keith Gordon, gets marks for originality here, but the film is played out at a halting, deliberate pace that renders it much too slow for the average viewer, stop-starting to an ending that just isn't believable. Gordon is every inch the nut who may just have something, but Amanda Plummer is too downbeat to make an impact as the girl who comes back into his life after time away. You can see the wires working in her perfor-

mance – an accusation that can't be levelled at Lily Knight as the waitress who'd like to make Gordon a father to her young son.

Station West ○
1948, US, 92 mins, b/w
Dir: Sidney Lanfield
Stars: Dick Powell, Jane Greer, Agnes Moorehead
Rating: ★★★

A very sharply written sort of Western *film noir*, with tough guy Dick Powell donning cowboy duds and going undercover in pursuit of a gang of gold robbers. Powell shares some smart exchanges of dialogue with a blonde (but still dangerous) Jane Greer as a casino owner who may or may not be involved with it all. 'Have you ever made love to a woman?' she asks, in a scene worthy of Mae West. 'Only from the doorway,' replies Powell cryptically. 'You haven't made love to me,' purrs Jane, to which Powell's reponse is, 'Come over to the doorway.' Crisp, confident stuff from RKO Radio in the purple patch of its immediate post-war years. A superior supporting cast includes Agnes Moorehead, Burl Ives, Steve Brodie and Raymond Burr.

Staying Alive ○ ⓥ
1983, US, 96 mins, colour
Dir: Sylvester Stallone
Stars: John Travolta, Cynthia Rhodes, Finola Hughes
Rating: ★★

John Travolta's second appearance as dancer Tony Manero is, under Sylvester Stallone's direction, actually better than his first in *Saturday Night Fever* – though not all of this sequel matches up to the original so well. Manero's now a dance instructor in Manhattan but, at nighttime, like Dustin Hoffman in *Tootsie*, he fails auditions for Broadway shows. The Bee Gees' driving music and the sweat gland-bursting dances should get teenagers clapping everywhere. Travolta is first-rate and Cynthia Rhodes as his long-suffering girl (doing all her own singing and dancing as well as proving a definite personality) also has lots of talent. Keep your eyes peeled if you want to spot a fleeting guest appearance by director Stallone.

Stay Tuned ○ ⓥ
1992, US, US mins, colour
Dir: Peter Hyams

Stars: John Ritter, Pam Dawber, Jeffrey Jones
Rating: ★★

This comedy, that gets A for invention and B for execution, shows what might happen to *you* if you watch too much television. Sold a massive set with a garden dish the size of a ferris wheel, compulsive goggler Roy Knabel (John Ritter) is sucked into the dish with his wife (Pam Dawber) who was about to leave him, and lands in Hellvision, a multi-channel nightmare in which the Knables are zapped from programme to programme by Mr Spike (Jeffrey Jones), a Be'elzebub of the box, who sold Roy the set in the first place. The Knables' electrical genius son – can you see the ending coming? – watches in disbelief as his parents fall through 'screens' to their next adventure, sequences they must survive for 24 hours to return to the other side of the screen. Thus Roy finds himself in many of the things he has watched most: a gameshow, a Western, a swashbuckler, a black-and-white detective movie, a cartoon – entertainingly done by the legendary Chuck Jones – an Arctic adventure, a *Star Trek* episode and others. These are sketched in with varying degrees of success, but don't miss the brief clip from Hellvision's *Three Men and Rosemary's Baby*.

Steamboat Bill Jr ☉
1928, US, 71 mins, b/w
Dir: Charles F Reisner
Stars: Buster Keaton, Ernest Torrence
Rating: ★★★

One of Buster Keaton's last great silent comedies, memorable particularly for the hilarious scene in which Keaton tries to smuggle a file to his father in jail, and for the climactic cyclone which sweeps Keaton along the streets of the town in his hospital bed. The antics are crisply directed by Charles F 'Chuck' Reisner, a Hollywood comedy expert. Reisner began his film career as a knockabout comic in early two-reelers but progressed to assist Chaplin on four films and later made vehicles for W C Fields, Abbott and Costello and The Marx Brothers.

Steaming ●
1985, UK, 95 mins, colour
Dir: Joseph Losey
Stars: Vanessa Redgrave, Sarah Miles, Diana Dors, Patti Love, Brenda Bruce
Rating: ★★

S

Steaming was a highly successful play on both sides of the Atlantic, but it loses something in its translation to the big screen. Director Joseph Losey's reverential treatment of playwright Nell (*Up The Junction*) Dunn's play has sapped the original's wit and pace. It does have its lighter moments, though, thanks to a strong cast headed by Vanessa Redgrave, Sarah Miles and especially Diana Dors. It's set in a bath house, where Violet (Diana Dors) has to deal with both the emotional ups and downs of her customers and the threat of closure from the local council. A sad footnote to the film was that both Losey and Diana Dors died soon after it was made.

Steel ◐
1979, US, 101 mins, colour
Dir: Steve Carver
Stars: Lee Majors, Jennifer O'Neill, Art Carney, Harris Yulin
Rating: ★★★

This is cheerfully old-fashioned Hollywood hokum in Universal-International 1950 style, with Jennifer O'Neill in the Ann Sheridan role as the lady thrust into heading a race against time to erect a gigantic building and Lee Majors as the ramrod she hires despite his having lost his nerve for heights. The credibility barrier is nearly breached at times, but Michel Colombier's rousing music drives it along. Majors has said that it was a most dangerous film to work on and one can quite see his point. Back projection hadn't been invented as far as this unit was concerned, and it adds bags to the realism of an enterprise on which one stuntman was killed.

Steel Magnolias ○ Ⓥ
1989, US, 115 mins, colour
Dir: Herbert Ross
Stars: Sally Field, Dolly Parton, Shirley MacLaine, Daryl Hannah, Olympia Dukakis, Julia Roberts
Rating: ★★★

A really big all-girl weepie for which you'll require a bucket rather than a handkerchief. Fortunately, its tears and tragedy are deliberately leavened with some funny dialogue, mainly stemming from the relationship of the six main characters within the confines of a hairdressing salon. Sally Field is the loving mother whose only daughter (Julia Roberts) is trying to get married while their father (Tom Skerritt) shoots at birds in the trees and local granny-grump Ouiser

(Shirley MacLaine) is upsetting everyone. It transpires that Roberts is a diabetic and despite all medical advice, decides to have a baby. You won't need a diagram of the rest of the plot, but the film stays afloat on its sea of tears through a series of treasurable one-liners. You'll sympathise with MacLaine at Christmas, when she asks Field (whose character's frankly a bit of a pain): 'What's wrong with you these days? You got a reindeer up your butt?' Some excellent performances, especially from MacLaine, Skerritt and, surprisingly, Daryl Hannah. You may find the characters a shade too nice, but it's this quality that gives the film some backbone and helps see it through.

Stella ● Ⓥ
1990, US, 114 mins, colour
Dir: John Erman
Stars: Bette Midler, Trini Alvarado, John Goodman, Marsha Mason, Stephen Collins
Rating: ★

This 'classic' weepie was creaky even in Barbara Stanwyck's day. So there was little chance that even Bette Midler could pull a new version of this old chestnut out of the fire. And so it proves, although the new *Stella* (*Dallas*, that is) is actually worse than you might fear. Would a better script have helped? It's certainly hard to believe that Robert Getchell, who wrote *Alice Doesn't Live Here Anymore*, also penned this garbage whose nightmare, *Dynasty*-style dialogue would make buffoons out of a better cast than this. Collins, as the man who makes Stella pregnant, actually achieves the unwelcome distinction of being as bad as John Boles in the original, although, required to keep telling Alvarado, 'I don't know about you, but I need you to put your head right here' (on his shoulder), he can be partially excused the glazed look and slack-jawed disbelief. There remain a few Midler whiplash wisecracks but, over 114 minutes, they fade like drops of water in a desert. Even with everything right, this remake would still have been a mistake. As it is, it's a disaster.

Stella Dallas ○
1937, US, 106 mins, b/w
Dir: King Vidor
Stars: Barbara Stanwyck, John Boles, Anne Shirley
Rating: ★★★

One of the great weepies of the screen, filmed before in 1925, but here

in a definitive version directed by King Vidor. Barbara Stanwyck suffers memorably (she was nominated for an Academy Award) as the woman dedicated to her daughter's happiness at her own expense. Wonderfully well made; keep a couple of handkerchiefs at the ready for the end.

St Elmo's Fire ● Ⓥ
1985, US, 108 mins, colour
Dir: Joel Schumacher
Stars: Emilio Estevez, Rob Lowe, Andrew McCarthy, Demi Moore, Judd Nelson, Ally Sheedy
Rating: ★★

This is one of those films, like *Silverado* which, years after its heyday, proves to be knee-deep in stars. A nostalgic look at school friendships thrown into the big wide world, it has so many good points that you wish you could say they amounted to more. The framework of intertwining relationships among the seven contrasting 22-year-olds who congregate in the noisy St Elmo's Bar, filled with music and smoke, is handled with warmth, compassion and skill by director Joel Schumacher and his players. And every time the contrived and often archly unreal dialogue threatens to swamp their efforts, David Foster's magnificent score, one of the best composed for an Eighties' film, comes to their rescue, giving the relationships an emotional depth not always justified by the script. Without the players and the music, it's doubtful if the story would involve us enough: they're the elements which set *St Elmo's* if not on fire then at least constantly glowing with their talents.

Stepfather, The ● Ⓥ
1986, US, 93 mins, colour
Dir: Joseph Ruben
Stars: Terry O'Quinn, Shelley Hack, Jill Schoelen, Stephen Shellen, Charles Lanyer
Rating: ★★★

Good for a giggle and a grip of the arm of your seat is this chiller that doesn't take itself seriously for a second longer than it takes to make an audience jump. Terry O'Quinn is splendidly nutty as the schizo killer who sets up home with fatherless families, then slaughters the lot when his authority is challenged. Shelley Hack and Jill Schoelen, the latter particularly natural, are the latest hapless stones on to which this lethal barnacle has battened itself. It's to the film's credit that it keeps the interest mounting in spite of the foregone conclusion the plot rolls inexorably towards from then on. First-class editing – not a scene is held too long – has a lot to do with it. So do the personalities of the leading actors and the precision direction of Joseph Ruben. The music janglingly fits the mood, and those who prefer a chuckle (unintentional or otherwise) with their chills may find the whole meal just their bowl of blood. Two inferior sequels followed.

Stepford Wives, The ◑
1974, UK, 115 mins, colour
Dir: Bryan Forbes
Stars: Katharine Ross, Paula Prentiss
Rating: ★★

Walter and Joanna (Peter Masterson and Katharine Ross) tire of the rat race and move to the sleepy Connecticut town of Stepford. Joanna meets the local wives, but finds them rather odd – they seem to delight in moronic conversation and are cheerfully subservient to their husbands. But the truth about the wives is more shocking than their lives . . . A nice idea given a light touch, with a neat twist at the end. It's just a shame that the first hour or so of this film is so slow. Director Bryan Forbes should really have spent less time setting things up before getting to the meat of the story. Ross and Paula Prentiss are good and Forbes gave his wife Nanette Newman a part as one of the strange wives. The little girl in the film is a seven-year-old Mary Stuart Masterson (son of star Peter) in her first film role. Not a bad film, but not one that does justice to Ira Levin's enjoyable book.

Stepkids ○ ⓥ
(aka: Big Girls Don't Cry . . . They Get Even)
1992, US, 104 mins, colour
Dir: Joan Micklin Silver
Stars: Hillary Wolf, Griffin Dunne, David Strathairn, Patricia Kalember, Adrienne Shelly, Margaret Whitton, Dan Futterman
Rating: ★

An interminable tale about a 13-year-old misfit girl lost in a sea of stepfathers, stepbrothers and stepsisters. By running away from home, she brings everyone back together again. Harmless but pointless, the film is a wry comedy that hardly makes you laugh at all. Hillary Wolf is so annoying as the girl that it's no wonder everyone else finds her such a drag.

Step Lively ○
1944, US, 88 mins, b/w
Dir: Tim Whelan
Stars: Frank Sinatra, George Murphy, Gloria DeHaven
Rating: ★★★

Frank Sinatra, the biggest vocal star in showbusiness in the year this film was made, took top billing and did quite well in this musical version of *Room Service*, a not-so-good Marx Brothers offering from five years earlier. He plays a country yokel from upstate New York who has written a play and sends it, along with his savings, to Miller (George Murphy), a New York producer. Twists abound when his money is used to stage a different production, which Miller offers him a part in. The romantic interest is added when Sinatra meets showgirl Gloria DeHaven – with whom he has his first screen kiss! The songs, which include 'Other Time', 'As Long As There's Music' and 'Where Does Love Begin?', add a great deal to an otherwise slim story, even if they do interfere with its flow.

Stepping Out ○ ⓥ
1991, US, 110 mins, colour
Dir: Lewis Gilbert
Stars: Liza Minnelli, Shelley Winters, Bill Irwin, Ellen Greene, Julie Walters
Rating: ★★★

Cynics may scoff, but there are some good bad films you just can't help enjoying and this one is pretty near the top of the list. Failed hoofer Mavis Turner (Liza Minnelli) runs a dance class downtown in a church hall and has a motley class of no-hopers and a pianist (Shelley Winters) who looks like a bag lady. Mavis has her own problems, as do her pupils whose ages range from 20 to 40; not half of them, however, measure up to the dance floor, and these are given a new edge with the 'opportunity' to perform in a charity show. Thanks to Liza, one of the great wasted talents of our generation, and her perfectly-cast oddball chorus line, this proves to be a movie with heart. Even a poor script and clumsy direction can't kill it; and the chances are you'll cry your eyes out on the night of the big show. It's a triumph of talent and personality over everything else.

Steptoe and Son ◑
1972, UK, 98 mins, colour
Dir: Cliff Owen
Stars: Wilfred Brambell, Harry H Corbett
Rating: ★★

TV comedy spinoffs proliferated in the early Seventies; this example is brighter than most, thanks to the basic strength of Galton and Simpson's original series. Directed by Cliff Owen, a neglected talent.

Steptoe & Son Ride Again ◑
1973, UK, 98 mins, colour
Dir: Peter Sykes
Stars: Wilfrid Brambell, Harry H Corbett
Rating: ★

The tone of this big screen version of the hit TV series about the sparring rag-and-bone father and son is firmly set by buxom co-star Diana Dors. Bending over a drinks cabinet to reveal her knickers, she purrs, as only she can, 'Can you see anything you like?' It's strictly below the belt material, with plenty of references to lavatories, booze, breasts and the hilarity of death. Sadly, the sharply observed class distinctions and the perfect turn of phrase of the small screen series are sacrificed in preference for a crude and lewd series of loosely linked sketches.

Stevie ○ ⓥ
1978, UK, 102 mins, colour
Dir: Robert Enders
Stars: Glenda Jackson, Mona Washbourne, Trevor Howard
Rating: ★★★★

'Who or what is Stevie Smith? Is she woman or is she myth?' wrote Ogden Nash. Robert Enders' beautifully-balanced film of Hugh Whitemore's play about the spinster English poet who shocked many with her work shatters the mirror of the myth and shows us the woman standing behind it. Initially, you may resist the treatment of one-room action and addressing the camera. But soon, very soon, you'll be drawn into the web of poor Stevie Smith (Glenda Jackson) and her sad, determinedly lonely existence in suburban London, initially with her 'lion aunt' (superb Mona Washbourne) and later alone. 'I was too far out for most of my life, and not waving but drowning': thus Stevie on that existence and her preoccupation with death, whom she called Black March, even when he promised her, in her visions, 'a breath of fresh air' and she attempted suicide. But the film can be funny and knowing as well as sad and bitter, and one anecdote where Stevie meets the Queen to receive an award is rich in dry and deadly wit. Ms Jackson's delivery here, as everywhere, is perfection. As the narrator and her latter-day friend, Trevor Howard offers his best portrayal in ages. And Ms Washbourne, cruelly denied even an Oscar nomination (although she did win a British Oscar), is brilliant in her last great performance.

Sting, The ◐ Ⓥ
1973, US, 129 mins, colour
Dir: George Roy Hill
Stars: Paul Newman, Robert Redford, Robert Shaw
Rating: ★★★

This fortuitous re-teaming of Paul Newman and Robert Redford (from *Butch Cassidy and The Sundance Kid*) drew seven Oscars and worldwide queues. The Thirties' settings, in the hands of cameraman Robert Surtees, costume designer Edith Head and art director Henry Bumstead, veterans all, vividly recreate conditions of the period, and the humorous playings of the stars is immensely winning. The film also revived the ragtime music of Scott Joplin, arranged here by Marvin Hamlisch. Amusing, exciting, ingeniously plotted and very entertaining.

Sting II, The ◐
1983, US, 102 mins, colour
Dir: Jeremy Paul Kagan
Stars: Jackie Gleason, Mac Davis, Teri Garr, Oliver Reed
Rating: ★★

Ten years after Paul Newman and Robert Redford fleeced Robert Shaw in *The Sting*, for which screenwriter David M Walsh won an Oscar, Walsh struck back with the inevitable sequel. But now Shaw was dead and, presumably, Newman and Redford passed up the opportunity to return to the scene of their former triumph. Given the unenviable task of following on are Jackie Gleason and Mac Davis as the conmen and Oliver Reed as their victim. Teri Garr scoops the acting honours under Jeremy Paul Kagan's direction.

Stir Crazy ● Ⓥ
1980, US, 110 mins, colour
Dir: Sidney Poitier
Stars: Gene Wilder, Richard Pryor
Rating: ★★

This salty, offbeat comedy has a few nice ideas rattling around in its story of two drifters wrongly imprisoned on bank robbery charges – such as Gene Wilder coming up trumps after each new torture, more horrendous than the last in turn, to make him ride in the annual inter-prison rodeo. Co-star Richard Pryor mugs dreadfully, but Wilder's natural off-centre charm is proof even against director Sidney Poitier's crowd-the-screen technique and the uneven quality of the script. Make sure you see the movie from the start and don't miss the pre-credits scene where a woman gets her shoe caught in a grating.

St Ives ●
1976, US, 93 mins, colour
Dir: J Lee Thompson
Stars: Charles Bronson, John Houseman, Jacqueline Bisset, Maximilian Schell
Rating: ★

'Every time we find a stiff, you're around.' This snatch of Forties-style dialogue gives you an idea of what to expect from this confusing and poorly-acted cloak-and-dagger story. It starts off well enough as a routine tough thriller, but long before the end you're left wondering just what's going on, and why they keep showing the same clip of film at the drive-in movie where a 'drop' is being made. Mark this down as for hardened Charles Bronson fans only, despite a good cast which has Elisha Cook, Daniel J Travanti, Robert Englund, Jeff Goldblum and Michael Lerner in brief roles.

St Louis Blues ○
1958, US, 90 mins, b/w
Dir: Allen Reisner
Stars: Nat 'King' Cole, Eartha Kitt, Pearl Bailey
Rating: ★★

Suitable film roles for the great Nat 'King' Cole proved sadly few and far between. However, half the jazz greats in the Hollywood vicinity were in this all-black musical about the famous blues composer W C Handy and Cole has the star role, although it arrived too late, at 39, to set him up for a film career. Even so, his singing andd piano playing is, as always, a delight. Of the 'real' actors, Juano Hernandez (as Handy's father) and Ruby Dee put in sterling work, while a string of blues standards includes 'Yellow Dog Blues', 'Careless Love', 'St Louis Blues', 'Chantez Les Bas', 'Aunt Hagar's Blues', 'Beale Street Blues', 'Steal Away', 'Hesitating Blues' and 'Morning Star'.

St Martin's Lane ○
1938, UK, 85 mins, b/w
Dir: Tim Whelan
Stars: Charles Laughton, Vivien Leigh, Rex Harrison
Rating: ★★★

One of Charles Laughton's most likeable and at the same time moving performances: he plays a busker entertaining on the streets of London. Vivien Leigh's vivacious performance as the guttersnipe pickpocket, who becomes part of Laughton's grubby little group is said to be the one that first attracted the attention of Hollywood producers. American director Tim Whelan really does capture some of the atmosphere of London's West End streets of the time, one of the few film-makers of his era to do so. Sadly, his career after 1940 was wasted on mediocre Hollywood offerings.

Stockade ◐ Ⓥ
1990, US, 98 mins, colour
Dir: Martin Sheen
Stars: Martin Sheen, Charlie Sheen, F Murray Abraham, Larry Fishburne, Michael Beach
Rating: ★★

This combined effort from the ubiquitous Sheen family – Charlie's brother Ramon Estevez is also in it – is almost, but not quite a good film. This is about as pleasant a tale of life in a military stockade as you're ever likely to see, and you'll undoubtedly warm to the growing friendship of hardcase Charlie Sheen and his five even-harder-case black prisoners. At heart, though, you've got to admit that Charlie's character is a whinger steeped in self-pity and you can't quite side with him when he tells psychotic sergeant-major Martin Sheen that 'You're on me' or 'You're a bully and I hate everything you stand for' any more than you could believe Sheen Sr wouldn't have had him on treble duties for a week for insubordination. Too simplistic a narrative, then, yet the performances are pretty good and Sheen Sr's own direction competent and solid. If the film occasionally makes you smile when you should be tearful, there are enough good moments to balance the scales and make the whole thing at least worth a look.

Stolen Face ○
1952, UK, 72 mins, b/w
Dir: Terence Fisher
Stars: Lizabeth Scott, Paul Henreid, Andre Morell, Susan Stephen
Rating: ★

Paul Henreid and Lizabeth Scott came to Britain to make this thriller which proves to be a melodramatic variation on Bogart's *Dark Passage*. Henreid is the surgeon who operates on lady criminals to improve their looks and he gets grim-faced support from Ms Scott, Mary Mackenzie and Andre Morell. Pretty Susan Stephen, who later married cinematographer director Nicolas Roeg, shows up well in a supporting role. The fevered plot developments are handled by the experienced Terence Fisher, some years before he got to grips with Frankenstein and Dracula for Hammer Films.

Stolen Hours ○
1963, UK, 100 mins, colour
Dir: Daniel Petrie
Stars: Susan Hayward, Michael Craig, Diane Baker
Rating: ★★★

This is a real tear-jerker, although there is often great charm about its story (a remake of 1939's *Dark Victory*, for which Bette Davis nearly won a third Oscar) of a rich socialite who, with a year to live and a wasted life behind her, grabs her chance of happiness while she may. And one cannot imagine anyone being better than Ms Hayward in the leading role.

Stolen Life, A ○
1946, US, 107 mins, b/w
Dir: Curtis Bernhardt
Stars: Bette Davis, Glenn Ford, Dane Clark
Rating: ★★★

A stolen idea, too, as six years previously this story of twin sisters falling for the same fellow, with the nasty one initially getting him, had been filmed with Elisabeth Bergner playing the two sisters. Admittedly, this version, with Bette Davis as the two sisters, is better. Glenn Ford is the chap they both fall for and there's solid support from Walter Brennan, Dane Clark and Charles Ruggles. Bette, obviously, dominates the film with two fine and distinct characterisations. It's pure melodrama and deservedly popular in its day. A double (or even triple) success for Bette, as she was also the film's producer.

Stone Killer, The ◐
1973, US, 96 mins, colour
Dir: Michael Winner
Stars: Charles Bronson, Martin Balsam
Rating: ★★

Formula tough-cop stuff in the *Dirty Harry* mould. Under Michael Winner's professional but passionless direction, the film emerges as a series of violent set-pieces, each perfectly executed and as cold and clinical as a gun-barrel. The best of these is saved until last – an exciting multiple shoot-out staged in a remote desert fortress. Charles Bronson is the star, and sharp eyes may pick out John Ritter in a minor role.

Stooge, The ☉
1951, US, 100 mins, b/w
Dir: Norman Taurog
Stars: Dean Martin, Jerry Lewis
Rating: ★★★

A song-and-dance man finds his act a success when he acquires a seemingly moronic stooge. This often funny and strangely affecting film is a real must for connoisseurs of Martin and Lewis, and rightly considered about the best thing they ever did as a team. The situations may be old, but under the skilled direction of Norman Taurog, both comedy and pathos prove effective.

Stop! or My Mom Will Shoot ○ ⓥ
1992, US, 92 mins, colour
Dir: Roger Spottiswoode
Stars: Sylvester Stallone, Estelle Getty, JoBeth Williams, Roger Rees
Rating: RB

Even after the debacle of *Oscar*, Sylvester Stallone still had the idea he could play comedy. This deplorable caper clearly proves him wrong – even if the script gives him no help at all. Stallone's a cop whose 4ft 11in mother (Estelle Getty – terrible) sets his career in reverse gear from the moment of her arrival at his apartment. Overplayed by everyone, the ensuing plot is trying in the extreme. 'This whole thing is just ridiculous,' laments Stallone at one point, and you really just have to agree. Even *Rocky 6* or *Rambo 4* would be better than this, and the star wisely returned to well choreographed action with *Cliffhanger*.

Stopover Tokyo ○ ⓥ
1957, US, 95 mins, colour
Dir: Richard L Breen
Stars: Robert Wagner, Joan Collins, Edmund O'Brien
Rating: ★★

Director Richard L Breen's adaptation of John P Marquand's espionage story

is attractively photographed against some picturesque backgrounds and Robert Wagner is, as always, likable and efficient. However, the tale fails to deliver much eastern promise in the way of real suspense or excitement. Only stop over here if you've nothing better to do.

Storm Boy ☉
1976, Australia, 89 mins, colour
Dir: Henri Safran
Stars: Greg Rowe, Peter Cummins, David Gulpilil
Rating: ★★★

This Australian film, winner of the Aussie Academy Award as Best Picture, is the sort of wholesome family entertainment at which Disney excels. You'll need the tissues handy for the tear-jerking story of a boy and his relationship with a baby pelican. Ten-year-old non-professional Greg Rowe is a natural in the title role, while first-time Paris-born director Henri Safran captures perfectly the bleak, grim environment of the rugged South Australian coastline with beautiful, atmospheric photography.

Storm Over the Nile ○
1955, UK, 107 mins, colour
Dir: Zoltan Korda
Stars: Anthony Steel, Laurence Harvey, Mary Ure, Ian Carmichael
Rating: ★★

A remake of *The Four Feathers*, with its vivid action scenes and breathtaking Technicolor locations intact. Although the story is jingoistic and full of *Boy's Own* heroics, the treatment teems with detail that puts it not too far behind the original. And there are fine supporting performances from James Robertson Justice and Christopher Lee. It was the fourth screen version of A E W Mason's famous full-blooded adventure novel. A fifth version appeared with Robert Powell more than 20 years later, and the story still wore well.

Stormy Monday ● ⓥ
1988, UK, 93 mins, colour
Dir: Mike Figgis
Stars: Melanie Griffith, Tommy Lee Jones, Sting, Sean Bean
Rating: ★★★

A sturdy little *film noir* from Film Four International that takes full advantage of its Newcastle and jazz backgrounds, using both to give a smoky local edge to its story of a crooked American wheeler-dealer

S

(Tommy Lee Jones) moving in on Tyneside. Sean Bean (more recently the villain in *Patriot Games*) makes an impressive star debut as the young drifter who becomes involved in all this when he both strikes up a relationship with the part-time hooker (Melanie Griffith) who works for the big shot, and obtains employment at the jazz club the American hopes to take over, presumably as a front for his nefarious activities. Sting is more effective than for several films past, reverting to his native Geordie accent as the club owner whose friendship proves useful to the hero – even though it's always slanted towards his own interests. Forty years ago, this material would have made a classy Hollywood second-feature. Substituting Newcastle for New York gives it new life.

Stormy Weather ○
1943, US, 77 mins, b/w
Dir: Andrew Stone
Stars: Lena Horne, Bill Robinson
Rating: ★★★

Dazzling, all-black musical that purports to tell the life story of Bill 'Bojangles' Robinson, whom most people associate with Shirley Temple in those wounderfully intricate dances of the Thirties. Robinson stars as himself, and star supporting turns include Lena Horne singing the title number, brilliant dancing by The Nicholas Brothers, and Fats Waller playing and singing 'Ain't Misbehavin'.

Story of Alexander Graham Bell, The ○
1939, US, 97 mins, b/w
Dir: Irving Cummings
Stars: Don Ameche, Loretta Young, Henry Fonda, Charles Coburn
Rating: ★★★

A typically professional Hollywood biopic of the late Thirties, this was the film that dogged its star, Don Ameche, for years to come. In later years, he would complain that many people thought that Don Ameche had invented the telephone and not Mr Bell! Henry Fonda surprisingly takes a subordinate role as Bell's co-worker.

Story of Dr Wassell, The ○
1944, US, 140 mins, colour
Dir: Cecil B DeMille
Stars: Gary Cooper, Laraine Day, Signe Hasso, Dennis O'Keefe
Rating: ★★

A Cecil B DeMille war epic with a cast of thousands and a budget of millions. It also contains just about every war-film cliché in the book, but the patriotic wartime public didn't seem to mind, and swallowed the familiar mixture whole. Gary Cooper's solid sincerity gives the lengthy adventure the bulwark it needs, and Dennis O'Keefe, as one of the wounded men he treats on Java, soared finally to stardom after years of patient extra work. Nominated for Academy Awards for its sound recording and photographic effects.

Story of Esther Costello, The ◑
(aka: Golden Virgin)
1957, UK, 103 mins, b/w
Dir: David Miller
Stars: Joan Crawford, Rossano Brazzi, Heather Sears
Rating: ★★

The film that shot the talented and sensitive Heather Sears to stardom, although subsequent roles (such as *Room at the Top* and *Sons and Lovers*) proved rather too similar for her career's good. She plays a beautiful mute girl, all too soon the victim of ruthless promoters who exploit her as the front for what seems charitable work, but is in fact a scurrilous swindle. Joan Crawford emotes in mournfully melodramatic style as her 'benefactor'.

Story of Gilbert and Sullivan, The ○
1953, UK, 109 mins, colour
Dir: Sidney Gilliat
Stars: Robert Morley, Maurice Evans, Eileen Herlie, Dinah Sheridan
Rating: ★★★

There's some glowing Technicolor camerawork by Christopher Challis in this biopic, plus a generous ration of the famous G and S operettas. A feast for fans of their music, with Robert Morley in particularly good form as the irascible Gilbert.

Story of Louis Pasteur, The ○
1935, US, 85 mins, b/w
Dir: William Dieterle
Stars: Paul Muni, Josephine Hutchinson, Anita Louise, Donald Woods
Rating: ★★★

The film that made biography box-office in the Hollywood of the Thirties. Paul Muni won an Academy Award as the distinguished French chemist of the title, director William Dieterle wastes not a second in racing

through the more interesting aspects of his career battling infection and disease, and writers Pierre Collings and Sheridan Gibney also took an Oscar for their screenplay

Story of Mankind, The ○
1957, US, 100 mins, colour
Dir: Irwin Allen
Stars: Ronald Colman, Vincent Price, Peter Lorre
Rating: ★

Human history served up in about an hour and a half. Such is the scope of this quite extraordinary star-studded film. Indicative of its quality and conviction is the casting of Hedy Lamarr as Joan of Arc, Peter Lorre as Nero and Harpo Marx as Isaac Newton.

Story of Robin Hood and His Merrie Men, The ⊙
1952, UK, 83 mins, colour
Dir: Ken Annakin
Stars: Richard Todd, Joan Rice, Peter Finch, James Hayter
Rating: ★★★

Another cheerful romp through Sherwood Forest in the company of Robin and his band of outlaws, made in England by Walt Disney. Attractively photographed by director-to-be Guy Green, it was directed by Ken Annakin who staged the action set pieces with verve, if little originality. Richard Todd as Robin Hood and Joan Rice as Maid Marion are serviceable rather than inspired and the most enjoyable performances come from James Hayter as Friar Tuck, Hubert Gregg as a sly Prince John and Elton Hayes who is in pleasant voice as Allan-a-Dale. Peter Finch also catches the eye as Sheriff of Nottingham.

Story of Vernon and Irene Castle, The ○
1939, US, 93 mins, b/w
Dir: H C Potter
Stars: Fred Astaire, Ginger Rogers
Rating: ★★★

Fred Astaire and Ginger Rogers were the perfect pair to portray Vernon and Irene Castle, the vaudeville entertainer and the doctor's daughter whose carefree glamour had captivated Europe and America in those magic years just before World War One. They created a complete dance revolution, making the new syncopated dances stylish and socially acceptable to all. This film, directed by H C Potter, is full of delightful pastiches (choreographed by Hermes Pan) of the dances that the Castles made popular and packed with favourite songs of the period, but underplays the social and personal history. Even if Astaire and Rogers were ever so slightly past their peak, this final picture that they made with RKO is a must for dance fans. Watch out in particular for that famous montage when they dance their way across a huge map of America. And stand by to shed a tear at the end. The film undeservedly lost money and signalled the end of the Astaire-Rogers partnership for 10 years.

Stowaway ⊙
1936, US, 86 mins, b/w
Dir: William A Seiter
Stars: Shirley Temple, Robert Young, Alice Faye
Rating: ★★★

One of Shirley Temple's most charming movies. As a little girl brought up in China, she gets a chance to speak some bewildering pidgin Chinese, and sing a rickshaw-full of hits including 'That's What I Want for Christmas Love', 'You Gotta S-M-I-L-E to be H-A-double-P-Y' and 'I Wanna Go to the Zoo'. She also impersonates (with great confidence) Al Jolson and Eddie Cantor and does a Ginger Rogers routine with a Fred Astaire doll. Okay Shirley, we're convinced you have talent! Luminous black-and-white photography by Arthur Miller, and self-effacing back-up for the star from Alice Faye (who also sings a couple of numbers), Robert Young, Eugene Pallette, Helen Westley and Arthur Treacher. Definitely a stowaway to get on board with.

Straight On Till Morning ●
1972, UK, 96 mins, colour
Dir: Peter Collinson
Stars: Rita Tushingham, Shane Briant, Tom Bell
Rating: ★★

Made hard on the heels of his other tale of terror, *Fright*, director Peter Collinson's second Seventies' chiller is again pitched on one sustained note: hysteria. Rita Tushingham, in a rare latter-day film role, is again cast as an ugly duckling from the north of England, but this time one in love with a psychotic killer. Subsequent plot developments are hardly credible, but at least Collinson gallops through the mayhem with singular aplomb.

Straight Talk ○ ⓥ
1992, US, 91 mins, colour
Dir: Barnett Kellman
Stars: Dolly Parton, James Woods, Griffin Dunne, Michael Madsen, Teri Hatcher, Jerry Orbach
Rating: ★★

Soft-hearted comedies needed to be way sharper than this to succeed in the early Nineties. Even Doris Day might have blinked at taking on this Dolly Parton vehicle in which the star is allowed to pour southern treacle all over a story about a dance instructress who, fired for discussing too many of her customers' problems with them, accidentally ends up as 'Dr Shirlee', an agony aunt on a Chicago radio station. Her southern fried advice, though there's nothing very special about it, soon makes her a citywide celebrity, bringing her to the attention of a scoop-hungry reporter (James Woods) who worms his way into her life, then, match, falls in love with her. Dolly squeaks unconvincingly through a role that Doris or Judy Holliday would at least have made you believe. Woods tries not to look embarrassed and squirms around doing it. There are a few funny lines from Griffin Dunne, a sort of chain-store Dudley Moore, but no-one seems at ease with the star.

Straight to Hell ● ⓥ
1987, US/UK, 86 mins, colour
Dir: Alex Cox
Stars: Sy Richardson, Joe Strummer, Dick Rude, Dennis Hopper, Elvis Costello, Grace Jones
Rating: RB

They said that director Alex Cox could write his own ticket after *Repo Man* and *Sid and Nancy*. The trouble is, they let him do it. And this is the result. Three bandits bungle a killing, somehow reap a suitcase full of money and hide out in a Mexican desert town where they are fired upon by a group of British and American actors and actresses wearing false beards and corselettes. Presumably intended to be surrealistic, this never grips the interest for a moment. Appallingly self-indulgent, it's a waste of everybody's time and money. Music by The Pogues and Pray for Rain.

Straitjacket ◐
1964, US, 89 mins, b/w
Dir: William Castle
Stars: Joan Crawford, Diane Baker, Leif Erickson, George Kennedy
Rating: ★★★

Vivid, gruesome melodrama, with Joan Crawford as a woman jailed for two particularly grisly axe murders – a type of killing that begins all over again when she is released from jail 15 years later. Down go the lights, bang goes the door on the victim, up screams the music and there, sure enough, is that shadowy figure on the wall, axe aloft. Appropriately the screenplay was written by Robert Bloch, who wrote *Psycho*. Much of the time, director William Castle tips the suspense over into melodrama and doesn't keep in touch with reality; but at least it can never be accused of not being lively. Whether you die giggling or of fright is a matter between you and your nerves.

Strange Cargo ○
1940, US, 113 mins, b/w
Dir: Frank Borzage
Stars: Clark Gable, Joan Crawford, Ian Hunter, Peter Lorre
Rating: ★★★

This unusual and exciting film about a group of prisoners escaping from a South American penal colony, directed by Frank Borzage (winner of the first-ever director's Academy Award in 1928) and produced by Joseph L Mankiewicz, featured the then-explosive box-office team of Joan Crawford and Clark Gable. But it is in the supporting acting that the real riches lie – particularly from Peter Lorre as a creepy character called M'Sieu Pig. One of the film's highlights is a terrific fight between the characters played by Gable and Albert Dekker. It takes place in the surf beside a boat and, although it lasts only two minutes on screen, it look two days to film, divided up into 'rounds' because the action proved so exhausting to the two actors.

Strange Deception
See: The Accused

Strange Invaders ○ ⓥ
1983, US, 94 mins, colour
Dir: Michael Laughlin
Stars: Paul LeMat, Nancy Allen, Diana Scarwid
Rating: ★★

Striking special effects and scary scenes when the bug-like aliens return to their proper shape made one blink at the British censor's decision to let this well-made pastiche of Fifties horror films off with a 'PG' certificate. By and large, though, director and co-writer Michael Laughlin succeeds

S

in his aim of 'recapturing a sense of fun characteristic of Hollywood in the Fifties', though the separate elements of light comedy and heavy horror don't always mix readily, even with the engagingly offbeat performances of stars Paul LeMat and Nancy Allen. But the whole thing is made with such pace and affection that one can't really complain.

Strange Love of Martha Ivers, The ○

1946, US, 117 mins, b/w
Dir: Lewis Milestone
Stars: Barbara Stanwyck, Van Heflin, Kirk Douglas, Lizabeth Scott
Rating: ★★★

A pity that – mainly because of war service – Kirk Douglas didn't make his film debut until he was 28, in this typical Forties black drama, directed in this case by the veteran director Lewis Milestone, who had made *All Quiet on the Western Front* and *Of Mice and Men*, and here skilfully handles a flashback tale of blackmail and murder. Barbara Stanwyck is in her element as the poisonous Miss Ivers, but critics quite rightly picked out Douglas's magnetic performance as the beginning of a long star career.

Stranger Among Us, A

See: Close to Eden

Stranger in Between, The

See: Hunted

Stranger on the Third Floor ◑

1940, US, 64 mins, b/w
Dir: Boris Ingster
Stars: Peter Lorre, John McGuire, Margaret Tallichet
Rating: ★★★

Classic RKO thriller where menace lurks in every shadow and staircase. Sets, photography, an amazing dream sequence and Peter Lorre all contribute to the bizarre Germanic atmosphere. A most rewarding oddity.

Strangers All ○

1935, US, 70 mins, b/w
Dir: Charles Vidor
Stars: May Robson, Preston Foster
Rating: ★

This family drama about a mother and her four self-centred and unappreciative kids really doesn't have a lot going for it. Flat and uninvolving with a weak storyline, it's indifferent even by the standards of RKO's

programmers of the Thirties. Serious film buffs can at least note its early starring role for Preston Foster.

Strangers Kiss ●

1983, US, 94 mins, colour
Dir: Matthew Chapman
Stars: Peter Coyote, Victoria Tennant, Richard Romanus
Rating: ★★★

There are some interesting bits and pieces about this story, and they just need one or two more elements integrated into them to make a really fascinating movie. Presumably based on director Stanley Kubrick's early career, it's about the making of a film in 1955, in which a shady character puts up the money so that his mistress can play the lead. Peter Coyote displays an attractive personality as the director and has happily been seen more often since. But Blaine Novak is surely nobody's idea of a leading man, although his co-scripting does show talent.

Strangers on a Train ○ ⓥ

1951, US, 101 mins, b/w
Dir: Alfred Hitchcock
Stars: Robert Walker, Farley Granger, Ruth Roman
Rating: ★★★★

Co-scripted by Raymond Chandler, *Strangers on a Train* is a roller-coaster ride of suspense with actor Robert Walker gleefully creating an extravagant killer who hatches a bizarre, psychopathic scheme to 'swap' murder victims with an understandably bemused Farley Granger. The locations are chosen with Hitchcock's customary care in this taut adaptation of Patricia Highsmith's novel and the climactic chase through a fairground is a triumph of photography, editing and direction. It was the film that served as a blueprint for Danny DeVito's recent comedy hit *Throw Momma from the Train*.

Strangers When We Meet ○

1960, US, 117 mins, colour
Dir: Richard Quine
Stars: Kirk Douglas, Kim Novak, Ernie Kovacs, Barbara Rush
Rating: ★★

A searching look at love and life in an upper-class American suburb. Adapted by Evan Hunter from his own best-seller, it finds Kirk Douglas understandably torn between Kim Novak and Barbara Rush while trying to find himself as an architect. Douglas

looks pained, Novak expresses pent-up desire quite well, Rush is poignantly pretty and Ernie Kovacs has a few waspishly funny lines though not enough. Walter Matthau, not unexpectedly, steals it from them all with his skilful portrait of a callous neighbour. Charles Lang's lush Technicolor photography expertly complements the characters' high-flying lifestyle.

Stranger Waits, A ◑

1987, US, 100 mins, colour
Dir: Robert Lewis
Stars: Suzanne Pleshette, Justin Deas
Rating: ★★

Wealthy widow Suzanne Pleshette really shouldn't have insisted on living out at The Cliffs, a swanky house hanging over the water and the site of the death of her former caretaker. And when good-looking handyman Justin Deas applies for the vacant job, she really should have checked out his references rather than ogling his biceps. But, of course, she does everything she shouldn't if she wants to stay alive. Produced by *Murder, She Wrote* star Angela Lansbury's brothers Edgar and his twin, Bruce, this TV movie chiller has more holes than a sieve, but still manages to pack a few genuine shocks.

Stranger Wore a Gun, The ○

1953, US, 83 mins, colour
Dir: Andre De Toth
Stars: Randolph Scott, Joan Weldon
Rating: ★★

A hard-riding, fast-shooting, grim-faced hombre (Randolph Scott, of course) helps the pretty owner of a stagecoach line to beat off bandits. But not before some well-staged gunfights and a splendid fire. The Academy Award-winning actress Claire Trevor completes a formidable supporting cast, in which the three villains are played by George Macready, Lee Marvin and Ernest Borgnine.

Strapless ● ⓥ

1988, UK, 97 mins, colour
Dir: David Hare
Stars: Blair Brown, Bruno Ganz, Bridget Fonda
Rating: RB

Endless in both senses, David Hare's trying film gives us dialogue that exists only on the printed page for people who surely never were. This is highlighted in the ludicrous scene in which, in an idyllic country cottage setting, a genteel English lady and her teenage son communicate with each other almost entirely in four-letter words. Who are these people and would we be interested even if we believed in them? The central character is an American nurse working in Britain who finds herself swept off her feet by the persistence of a West German 'businessman' who, it turns out, believes only in the ideal of romantic love, and disappears over the horizon as soon as a woman indicates she'd like to settle down. There's a message in there somewhere about taking responsibility for your feelings – but it gets lost in the welter of Hare's strange, unbelievable script that only exists two paces away from reality. Blair Brown tries hard as the nurse, Bruno Ganz looks puzzled as the eternal lover. Bridget Fonda is hardly in it as the heroine's sloppy sister, but the chances are that you'll lose patience with these shadow people long before the end.

Strategic Air Command ○
1955, US, 114 mins, colour
Dir: Anthony Mann
Stars: James Stewart, June Allyson
Rating: ★★

James Stewart and June Allyson had already had one smash-hit at Universal with *The Glenn Miller Story*. Here the human drama they provide is intermingled with an engrossing study of men in their magnificent flying machines, in this case the B-36 bomber and its post-war development. Reliable supporting cast includes Henry Morgan, Bruce Bennett, Frank Lovejoy, Alex Nicol, Jay C Flippen, Barry Sullivan and that underrated actor James Millican. Scorching Technicolor photography both on the ground and in the wild blue yonder.

Stratton Story, The ○
1949, US, 106 mins, b/w
Dir: Sam Wood
Stars: James Stewart, June Allyson, Agnes Moorehead
Rating: ★★★

This sports biography, well directed by Sam Wood, was strengthened by the fact that it stuck more closely to the facts than was usual for its time. Athletic James Stewart was well cast in the role of baseball pitcher Monty Stratton, as was archetypal dutiful wife June Allyson as the girl Stratton marries. As Stratton's mother, Agnes

Moorehead contributes a calm and restrained performance, and the film also benefits from the appearance of several baseball greats as themselves: Eugene Bearden, Bill Dickey and Chicago White Sox manager Jimmy Dykes. Even if you know nothing about baseball, the film tells an inspiring human story, with Stratton battling against incredible odds after a tragic accident. The picture won an Oscar for screenplay writer Douglas Morrow.

Streetcar Named Desire, A ○
1951, US, 122 mins, b/w
Dir: Elia Kazan
Stars: Vivien Leigh, Marlon Brando, Kim Hunter, Karl Malden
Rating: ★★★★

Brilliant ensemble performances won Academy Awards for Vivien Leigh, Kim Hunter and Karl Malden, plus a nomination for Marlon Brando in this explosive film version of Tennessee Williams' uncomfortably powerful play. Leigh is unforgettable as a fading southern belle who is forced to stay with her sister (Kim Hunter) and her heavy-drinking husband (Marlon Brando) in their rattrap New Orleans 'apartment' (really too grand a word for it). Although sordid and gloomy throughout, Elia Kazan's film fascinates rather than alienates the viewer, thanks to the unpredictability of the plot, the hypnotic qualities in the acting, and art direction and set decoration (you can almost feel the damp and hear the cockroaches) that were both also rewarded with Oscars. Brando's sweaty, animalistic Stanley Kowalski shot him to superstardom and brought forth a million imitators of his earthy, vaguely slurred delivery. Only reservation: all the characters with the exception of Hunter are just faintly unbelievable, though the strength of the performances more than compensates.

Street Corner ○
(aka: Both Sides of the Law)
1953, UK, 93 mins, b/w
Dir: Muriel Box
Stars: Peggy Cummins, Terence Morgan, Anne Crawford, Rosamund John,
Rating: ★★

Director Muriel Box offers one excellent chase sequence in this tribute to the work of women police. It's a down-to-earth study, without any of the glamour of Angie Dickinson's

Police Woman world. And there are fine character roles for Thora Hird and Dora Bryan.

Streetfighter, The ○ ⓥ
(aka: Hard Times)
1975, US, 97 mins, colour
Dir: Walter Hill
Stars: Charles Bronson, James Coburn, Jill Ireland, Strother Martin
Rating: ★★★

Although the plot of this gritty film follows a well-worn theme, it is carefully and economically made, and distinguished by some of the best colour photography in a very long while. Charles Bronson has the title role, a man who drifts into New Orleans in 1936 with six dollars and the knowledge that he can fight: that he can avoid a swinging blow where others would assimilate it and hope to give better – and that he has a hammer punch in his own right hand. Not for him the small purses of the boxing ring. He has trained himself hard while still unknown, and seeks a nest-egg from the richest game of all: bare-knuckle streetfighting. Philip Lathrop's photography shows masterly composition in catching the dingy darkness of the era and its back streets, keying his scenes perfectly without ever sacrificing clarity or true colours. The warehouses in which the fights are held, in a netted arena where tiers of yelling gallery fans clamour for blood, seem cold and clammy, or bright and oppressive; and one can almost smell the night air at the stockyards in the perfect final scene. Under Walter Hill's firm and assured direction, both Bronson and Jill Ireland give their best performances in ages. Nothing is over-emphasised, and the thud of fist on bone speaks for itself. The British censor at the time chose to give this little gem an 'AA' certificate but, despite peripheral scenes in a brothel, there is very little not suitable to the average tough and intelligent 11-year-old. As for adults, only those with a dislike of boxing can fail to enjoy it, although even they may appreciate the finer qualities of a movie as tough, clean and without flab, as the streetfighter himself.

Streets of Fire ○
1984, US, 94 mins, colour
Dir: Walter Hill
Stars: Michael Paré, Diane Lane, Rick Moranis, Willem Dafoe
Rating: ★★★

S

A 'rock 'n' roll fable', says the credits, and that's what Walter Hill's film is – its action is there merely to entertain and not convince. And entertain it does, in this kind of spaghetti street film with Diane Lane as the singer kidnapped by bikers, Michael Paré as the ex-lover/ex-soldier called in to get her back, and husky-voiced Amy Madigan, given a part that enables her to walk off with the film, as another ex-soldier who becomes Paré's strong right arm. Rick Moranis and Willem Dafoe complete a striking cast.

Streets of Gold ◐ Ⓥ

1986, US, 95 mins, colour
Dir: Joe Roth
Stars: Klaus Maria Brandauer, Adrian Pasdar, Wesley Snipes
Rating: ★★

The great Klaus Maria Brandauer hasn't quite had the roles he deserves in Hollywood; here he plays a Russian emigre ex-boxer who was denied a chance of world glory in the Soviet Union because he was Jewish. Now, in America, he trains boxers for a Golden Gloves side to fight a Russian team managed by his own ex-manager. There are no surprises in this film, but it will please *Rocky* fans, if not dialogue purists, who will moan about the number of clichéd lines and situations. The boxing sequences are smartly staged, and Brandauer is always worth watching as he bobs and weaves around the worst the script can throw at him.

Streets of Laredo ○

1949, US, 88 mins, colour
Dir: Leslie Fenton
Stars: MacDonald Carey, William Holden, William Bendix, Mona Freeman
Rating: ★★★

A solid remake of the 1936 version of *The Texas Rangers*, with William Holden, William Bendix and Macdonald Carey this time around as the three bandits who end up on different sides of the law. Carey, handsomely moustachioed, steals every scene he's in as the really bad apple of the three (it's his best screen performance) and Mona Freeman is a most attractive spitfire heroine. The action could have done with a more sparkling script to back it up, but the film's burnishingly shot in Technicolor by Ray Rennahan and a hit theme song did it no harm at the box-office.

Street With No Name, The ⊙

1948, US, 100 mins, b/w
Dir: William Keighley
Stars: Mark Stevens, Richard Widmark, Lloyd Nolan, Barbara Lawrence, Ed Begley
Rating: ★★★

Although taciturn Mark Stevens is the nominal star of this hard-hitting crime drama, based on a real case, the film belongs to Richard Widmark who plays the gang leader with a fine collection of neuroses and hinted perversions. Actual FBI personnel were used in supporting roles.

Strictly Ballroom ○ Ⓥ

1992, Australia, 94 mins, colour
Dir: Baz Luhrmann
Stars: Paul Mercurio, Tara Morice, Bill Hunter, Barry Otto, Gia Carides, Pat Thompson
Rating: ★★★

This sweet-natured, lively, colourful, stylised Australian comedy musical about the brittle world of ballroom dancing was a hit around the world, and it's not hard to see why. Innovative young dancer Paul Mercurio dreams of winning the Australian ballroom championship, even after his flighty partner leaves him when he refuses to conform to tradition. Along comes dance school wallflower Tara Morice who persuades him to take her on as a partner and (no, really?) takes off her glasses and transforms an ugly duckling into a swinging swan. Although the often funny comedy-romance that results soon ditches credibility in favour of caricature and coincidence, the film remains winning throughout: low in budget but high in returns, thanks to the talent and enthusiasm of all concerned.

Strictly for Pleasure

See: The Perfect Furlough

Strike Me Pink ○

1936, US, 100 mins, b/w
Dir: Norman Taurog
Stars: Eddie Cantor, Ethel Merman
Rating: ★★

The last of the five comedy-musicals that pop-eyed Eddie Cantor made in the Thirties for Samuel Goldwyn, although he rarely had a co-star as dynamic as Ethel Merman, who's involved in three of the movie's four big song numbers. Not quite in the same class as *Kid Millions* or *Roman Scandals*, the film still has some snappy dialogue (supplied by four writers) and plenty

of zest. Making one of her earliest appearances is peppy brunette Rita Rio (real name: Rita Nivella) who led her all-girl band in several shorts and features of the time. But she didn't attract leading roles until she hit the *Road to Morocco* in 1942 with Bing Crosby, Bob Hope and Dorothy Lamour, under a new name – Dona Drake.

Striking Distance ● Ⓥ

1993, US, 101 mins, colour
Dir: Rowdy Herrington
Stars: Bruce Willis, Sarah Jessica Parker, Dennis Farina, Tom Sizemore, Brion James
Rating: ★★

Stripping him of much of his laconically humorous dialogue, this routine thriller hardly showcases Bruce Willis at his best. A 'B' movie in flimsy 'A' feature coating, it has Willis as a cop whose life has gone down the tubes since he denounced his own partner (who jumped off a bridge) and challenged police conclusions over the identity of a serial killer who also murdered Willis's cop father. Now, two years on, Willis works for the river police, and it seems that the serial murders have started again, bumping off women Willis has known. He believes the killer is a cop – but no one on the force even wants to speak to him. To use the film's own background, none of this holds water for a minute: how on earth could the killer track down so many of Willis's old flames in so short a time? A decent leading lady might help, but Sarah Jessica Parker, admittedly miscast as Willis's river partner, is limp and unconvincing. Rowdy Herrington's direction offers efficent action, but no more. Careless, too: don't look too closely at the first body being dumped in the river, or you might identify the killer. *Die Hard* afloat it isn't.

Stripes ◐ Ⓥ

1981, US, 102 mins, colour
Dir: Ivan Reitman
Stars: Bill Murray, Harold Ramis, Warren Oates, John Candy
Rating: ★★

This army comedy from the *Ghost Busters* team has a few modern trimmings and original laughs, but it is otherwise pretty much like every other army comedy from Abbott and Costello and Bob Hope to Goldie Hawn's *Private Benjamin*. The laconic Bill Murray is in his element as the wise guy who joins up just for something to do, riles the sergeant, gets double-duty, finds himself in a misfit platoon, flops all over the obstacle course and wins comic glory in the last reel. Most of the visual jokes are telegraphed in advance but it really doesn't matter – the film remains mildly amusing throughout, apart from one genuine belly laugh early on involving a football. Warren Oates is the suffering sergeant and John Candy scores an early hit as the platoon's obligatory fat man, in a fine comedy cast that also includes Judge Reinhold, Sean Young and John Larroquette.

Stroker Ace ○
1983, US, 91 mins, colour
Dir: Hal Needham
Stars: Burt Reynolds, Ned Beatty
Rating: ★

Never shown in this country's cinemas, this is one of the more recent offerings from crash-'em-up race-and-chase specialist director Hal Needham who made the *Cannonball Run* and *Smokey and the Bandit* films. Burt Reynolds is again on hand with his laid-back charm, this time as a stock-car driver who at one time turns up in a chicken suit – well in context with the film's cartoon-like structure and standard 'good ol' boy' hijinks.

Stronger than Fear
See: Edge of Doom

Strongest Man in the World, The ☉
1975, US, 92 mins, colour
Dir: Vincent McEveety
Stars: Kurt Russell, Joe Flynn, Eve Arden
Rating: ★★★

The third film in Disney's college comedy trilogy, and pretty nearly as funny as the first two, *The Computer Wore Tennis Shoes* and *Now You See Him, Now You Don't*. Kurt Russell (though by now 24) is still the accident-prone student Dexter Riley, Joe Flynn is back as the opportunistic Dean Higgins and bizarre mishaps are still occurring in the science labs of Medfield College. This time Dexter accidentally invents a cereal that gives the eater superhuman strength. Phil Silvers is in there too, providing his own brand of humour, but it's Flynn who steals many of the biggest laughs.

Strong Man, The ◐
1926, US, 75 mins, b/w
Dir: Frank Capra

Stars: Harry Langdon, Priscilla Bonner, Gertrude Astor, William V Mong
Rating: ★★★★

Harry Langdon was at his butter-innocent, baby-faced best when directed by the young Frank Capra. Delights of this enchanting comedy include Langdon trying to carry a golddigger up a long flight of stairs and trying to make a reputation as a weightlifter when his strongman friend gets drunk.

Stud, The ◐ ⓥ
1978, UK, 90 mins, colour
Dir: Quentin Masters
Stars: Joan Collins, Oliver Tobias, Sue Lloyd
Rating: ★

Solidly backed with a pre-sold pop soundtrack, this dislikeable version of Jackie Collins' lurid bestselling novel proved to be just what the public wanted in the late Seventies and revived Joan Collins' star career. The best thing in it, however, is the performance of Doug Fisher as the best friend of Oliver Tobias, playing the title role. The girls are pretty and they and their sex scenes are attractively photographed. The rest, apart from some flashes of native wit, is preposterous, pretentious and very pseudo-sophisticated.

Student Prince, The ☉
1954, US/UK, 107 mins, colour
Dir: Richard Thorpe
Stars: Ann Blyth, Edmund Purdom, Mario Lanza (voice)
Rating: ★★★

A joyous musical featuring the throbbing tenor of Mario Lanza – but not his acting! Feuding with his studio, MGM, Lanza recorded the songs for this remake of Sigmund Romberg's famous operetta but, because of the dispute and his continuing weight problem, never showed up on set. Later, it looked as though studio and star had made peace, and Lanza began work, but there were arguments over the interpretation of the role and he walked out, this time for good. English actor Edmund Purdom, who played a supporting role in the studio's *Julius Ceasar*, was called in to act the title role and mime the songs to Lanza's voice. Purdom's excellent performance made him an MGM star, but his popularity only lasted a few years. Ann Blyth, who had co-starred with Lanza in *The Great Caruso*, is in excellent form (and voice)

as the love of the prince's life, and Lanza songs include 'The Drinking Song', 'Deep in My Heart' and 'Serenade', as well has his very popular renditions of two new songs written for the film, 'I'll Walk with God' and 'Beloved'.

Study in Terror, A ●
(aka: Fog)
1965, UK, 94 mins, colour
Dir: James Hill
Stars: John Neville, Donald Houston, John Fraser
Rating: ★★★

Sherlock Holmes gets to grips with Jack the Ripper as he was to do 14 years later in *Murder by Decree*. Director James Hill's all-stops-out style ensures that the results here are both thrilling and frightening, with lurid killings, sparkling photography and some nail-biting suspense. The last murder in particular is improbably, but successfully, drawn out to set one's teeth right on edge.

Stunt Man, The ◐ ⓥ
1979, US, 129 mins, colour
Dir: Richard Rush
Stars: Peter O'Toole, Barbara Hershey, Steve Railsback, Sharon Farrell
Rating: ★★★

Director Richard Rush cut his teeth on low-budget exploitation films and then worked for a reported nine years on this extraordinary project, an outrageous black comedy that brought Oscar nominations both for Rush and for his leading man Peter O'Toole as a dictatorial film director who hires a man on the run as a stuntman on his latest picture. Packed with first-rate action and sly wit, the film demands close attention from its viewer – but proves worth the effort in the end.

St Valentine's Day Massacre, The ◐
1966, US, 100 mins, colour
Dir: Roger Corman
Stars: Jason Robards, George Segal, Ralph Meeker
Rating: ★★

Director Roger Corman's body-strewn look at the feud between gangsters Al Capone and Bugs Moran is as coldly clinical as a gun barrel. The supporting cast is a mine of Brooklyn-type menaces and film fans can have fun picking out such familiar faces as Bruce Dern, Jack Nicholson, John Agar, Ralph Meeker, Joseph Campanella and Richard Bakalyan.

S

Submarine X-1 ○

1968, US, 89 mins, colour
Dir: William Graham
Stars: James Caan, Norman Bowler
Rating: ★★

A brisk, if routine World War Two action film with American star James Caan heading a cast of British performers under the competent direction of fellow-American William Graham. The underwater climax is well staged and the film always succeeds in holding one's interest.

Suburban Commando ○ Ⓥ

1991, US, 91 mins, colour
Dir: Burt Kennedy
Stars: Hulk Hogan, Christopher Lloyd, Shelley Duvall, Larry Miller
Rating: ★★★

Wrestler Hulk Hogan takes on a new guise as a space warrior in a science-fiction action comedy that shows his wrestling days to have taught him the full range of facial expressions, especially anguished looks – being less successful here spouting such dialogue as 'I spend more time saving worlds than living in them' than as a kind of inter-galactic straight man. It's a comment on Hogan's way-out presence and appearance that the wild-haired, wild-eyed Christopher Lloyd is allowed to represent the essence of normality as the head of the suburban family upon whom Hogan descends. Lloyd's character can't quite grasp the concept of alien bounty hunters being out to get the incredible Hulk. 'A couple of leeches,' growls Hogan by way of explanation, 'they make their living off the blood of others.' 'You mean,' gasps Lloyd, 'investment bankers?' It's in keeping with this kind of humour that not many things in this film turn out the way you'd expect, in a comedy that, though by no means great, is more fun than most.

Subway ◑ Ⓥ

1985, France, 104 mins, colour
Dir: Luc Besson
Stars: Christopher Lambert, Isabelle Adjani
Rating: ★★

Modernised French fatalism. In fact, substitute the Quai des Brumes or some top-floor hideout for the subway here and we might almost (apart from the language of course) be back in pre-war days. Possibly veteran art director Alexandre Trauner makes his presence felt here. Star Christopher Lambert, looking here more like Jean-Paul Belmondo than Tarzan of the Apes, is the safeblower who escapes via a street-ripping car chase to the subway. Below the underground system he meets a weird mob of subterranean denizens who protect him from police and pursuers while bored rich wife Isabelle Adjani is falling in love with him. But, just as with Jean Gabin and Michele Morgan in *Quai des Brumes*, you know it can't last. The film's sense of the idiotic sits ill-at-ease with its gutter language, but it's definitely different, and welcome for that alone.

Such Men Are Dangerous

See: The Racers

Sudden Fear ○

1952, US, 111 mins, b/w
Dir: David Miller
Stars: Joan Crawford, Jack Palance
Rating: ★★★

Engrossing all the way is this story of a woman marrying a man she gradually begins to suspect may be planning to murder her. Spot-on performances by Crawford, Palance and Gloria Grahame. Good control of the mounting suspense by director David Miller. This is one film that's much better than its reputation.

Suddenly It's Spring ○

1946, US, 87 mins, b/w
Dir: Mitchell Leisen
Stars: Fred MacMurray, Paulette Goddard, Macdonald Carey
Rating: ★★

A lightly comic variation on the British film *Perfect Strangers*, in that it deals with the problems faced by husbands and wives separated for months, even years, by war. Realistic characters and some, if not enough, amusing dialogue. Competent performances by leading players Paulette Goddard and Fred MacMurray.

Suddenly Last Summer ● Ⓥ

1959, UK, 114 mins, b/w
Dir: Joseph L Mankiewicz
Stars: Elizabeth Taylor, Katharine Hepburn, Montgomery Clift
Rating: ★★★

Three Oscar-winning ladies (Elizabeth Taylor, Katharine Hepburn and Mercedes McCambridge) compete for the acting honours in this headily absorbing suspense drama, based on Tennessee Williams' strong play about a girl committed to an institution after witnessing the violent death of her cousin. Hepburn wins the acting battle, while the film is so powerfully written by Gore Vidal and Williams himself that it's almost frightening.

Sudden Terror

See: Eyewitness

Suez ○

1938, US, 104 mins, b/w
Dir: Allan Dwan
Stars: Tyrone Power, Loretta Young, Annabella, Henry Stephenson
Rating: ★★★

How the Suez Canal was built, according to Hollywood. Lavishly mounted, the film's best sequence is a thrilling game of real tennis between Tyrone Power and Joseph Schildkraut. The story is so well structured and full of action that it's a pity it has so little to do with the truth.

Sugarfoot ○

(aka: Swirl of Glory)
1951, US, 80 mins, colour
Dir: Edwin L Marin
Stars: Randolph Scott, Raymond Massey, Adele Jergens
Rating: ★★

Very much a formula Randolph Scott Western of the period, slightly enhanced by the presence of Raymond Massey as the villain, and by some sparkling Technicolor photography by Wilfrid M Cline. It did inspire a TV series, also called *Sugarfoot* – that ran for 69 episodes between 1957 and 1960, starring Will Hutchins in the Scott role. Massey came back for more in a second Scott Western, *Carson City*, the following year. Pretty ordinary.

Sugarland Express, The ◐

1974, US, 110 mins, colour
Dir: Steven Spielberg
Stars: Goldie Hawn, Ben Johnson, Michael Sacks, William Atherton
Rating: ★★

Movie Brat Steven Spielberg was just 26 when he made this first feature (he'd already done *Duel* for television and had been making movies since winning a contest at the age of 13 with a 40-minutes war film). Later he was to make his name with *Jaws* and *Close Encounters*, but here, using a true story of 1969 Texan jailbreakers, he first began to develop his favourite theme of ordinary people pursued by extraordinary forces.

Suicide Squadron
See: Dangerous Moonlight

Sullivan's Travels ○
1941, 91 mins, b/w
Dir: Preston Sturges
Stars: Joel McCrea, Veronica Lake
Rating: ★★★★

Brilliant picaresque comedy about a film director tired of making comedies and looking for meaning in life. Some might see it as a portrait of director Preston Sturges' own state at the time. Whatever the conclusions to be drawn from the plot, the end results are delightfully amusing, with Veronica Lake at her most bewitching as 'The Girl' and Joel McCrea as the director who becomes a tramp in his quest for the truth. Sturges was over time and over budget on this one, but its tricky blend of slapstick and sadness never jars and the studio forgave him when it made a mint.

Summer and Smoke ◑
1961, US, 118 mins, colour
Dir: Peter Glenville
Stars: Laurence Harvey, Geraldine Page, Una Merkel, John McIntire, Rita Moreno, Thomas Gomez
Rating: ★★★

One of the least violent of all Tennessee Williams' stories, although, in this story of a spinster and a gambler, some of the dialogue is explosive enough. The British director, Peter Glenville, gets fine performances ·from Geraldine Page as the spinster, and from Una Merkel: both were nominees.

Summer Holiday ☉
1962, UK, 105 mins, colour
Dir: Peter Yates
Stars: Cliff Richard, Lauri Peters, The Shadows
Rating: ★★

With the title song proving a massive number one hit for star Cliff Richard, the distributors of this tuneful, if slightly wishy-washy musical could start counting the takings even before it opened. They also had the fortune to have a dynamic young director, Peter Yates, and an inventive choreographer, Herbert Ross, both of whom would go on to become major directors in international cinema. Another plus is the engagingly chirpy personality of the young Una Stubbs, who rather puts the pallid leading lady, Lauri Peters, in the shade.

Summer Madness ○
(aka: Summertime)
1955, UK, 99 mins, colour
Dir: David Lean
Stars: Katharine Hepburn, Rossano Brazzi, Isa Miranda, Darren McGavin
Rating: ★★★

Memorable, bitter-sweet love affair, directed by David Lean. He coaxes a fine performance from Katharine Hepburn, endearingly vulnerable as the plain, middle-ageing secretary who goes to Venice on holiday and finds herself improbably caught up in an idyllic romance with a (married) antiques dealer. Jack Hildyard's majestic Eastman Colour photography of Venice and its environs adds immeasuringly to the flavour. There's an endearing waif who follows Hepburn everywhere, and her famous tumble into the canal. It's a film that has in abundance what most of Lean's bigger-scale films, however excellent, lack: charm.

Summer of the Seventeenth Doll ◑
(aka: Season of Passion)
1960, Australia, 94 mins, b/w
Dir: Leslie Norman
Stars: John Mills, Ernest Borgnine, Anne Baxter, Angela Lansbury
Rating: ★★★

Super fine – changed by those insensitive Americans to *Season of Passion* – for the film version of a fine Australian play about the sweet life of two cane cutters turning sour. The script was written by John Dighton, author of the great stage and screen success *The Happiest Days of Your Life*. As a film writer since the mid-Thirties, he was particularly associated with Ealing Studios and had worked on a wide range of scripts, from George Formby farce to Dickens adaptation, by way of the celebrated Ealing comedy *Kind Hearts and Coronets*.

Summer Stock ○
1950, US, 109 mins, colour
Dir: Charles Walters
Stars: Judy Garland, Gene Kelly, Eddie Bracken, Gloria DeHaven
Rating: ★★★

This farmyard frolic was Judy Garland's last big musical for MGM, and her on-off weight problems can clearly be spotted from scene to scene. But she puts plenty of bounce into a film that reunites her with Gene Kelly from *The Pirate* and gives her a chance

to sing two of her best-known numbers, 'If You Feel Like Singing, Sing' and 'Get Happy'.

Summertime
See: Summer Madness

Sun Also Rises, The ○
1957, US, 129 mins, colour
Dir: Henry King
Stars: Tyrone Power, Ava Gardner, Mel Ferrer, Errol Flynn
Rating: ★★

Ernest Hemingway's paean of hope and dissillusionment to the lost generation in the wake of World War One may be the most faithful of all his transcriptions to the screen. While the film has many flaws, producer Darryl F Zanuck was determined to follow the novel as closely as possible. He admired Hemingway greatly, once saying: 'If I could have been anybody else, I'd like to have been Ernest Hemingway.' Indeed they were great friends, but their relationship had been affected by the author's reaction to Zanuck's production of *The Snows of Kilimanjaro* which, the author maintained, should have been called *The Snows of Zanuck*. Here, Tyrone Power is in the lead as Jake Barnes, a man rendered impotent by a war-wound. At 43, many thought Power was too old for the part, but the criticisms seemed somewhat churlish in light of the fact that this proved to be his second-to-last film. He died the following year of a heart attack. This was also Errol Flynn's penultimate picture, but his self-parodying performance is the best thing in the film which also stars Mel Ferrer and Juliette Greco, who was making her American movie debut.

Sunburn ○
1979, US, 94 mins, colour
Dir: Richard C Sarafian
Stars: Farrah Fawcett, Charles Grodin, Art Carney, Joan Collins
Rating: ★★

Identikit movie stitches together dozens of familiar film elements in a blandly exciting story of a $5 million insurance fraud. Farrah Fawcett Majors (who has since dropped the Majors and proved herself a capable actress) acts with her teeth, and a mighty supporting cast includes Charles Grodin, Eleanor Parker, Art Carney, Keenan Wynn – and Joan Collins! The action is drenched in sunshine and there's a zingy pop soundtrack.

S

Sunday Bloody Sunday ●
1971, UK, 110 mins, colour
Dir: John Schlesinger
Stars: Glenda Jackson, Peter Finch, Murray Head, Peggy Ashcroft
Rating: ★★

This film really shows its age now, through no fault of its own. In the AIDS aware 1990s no-one would make this story of a slightly unusual menage à trois, with Glenda Jackson and Peter Finch sharing the same lover, Murray Head. It was critically acclaimed for its low-key approach to its subject. Jackson and Finch were nominated for Oscars, as were director John Schlesinger and screenplay writer Penelope Gilliatt. The three main characters are terribly modern and civilized about the situation which is perhaps the film's biggest downfall as none of them display any great amount of emotion. Given the time and the subject this may have been the best way of presenting the story in acceptable form, but I'm afraid it doesn't make for particularly gripping cinema. With such a strong cast (and Peggy Ashcroft, Tony Britton, Maurice Denham and Frank Windsor give sterling support) and a director of Schlesinger's calibre the result could and should have been better.

Sunday Too Far Away ●
1975, Australia, 94 mins, colour
Dir: Ken Hannam
Stars: Jack Thompson, Phyllis Ophel
Rating: ★★★

This thoroughly enjoyable visit to the hard-drinking hard-working world of Australian sheep shearers heralded international recognition for the Australian film industry and garnered great critical acclaim. Following on its heels came such films as *Breaker Morant* and *Mad Max*. Star Jack Thompson won a Best Actor prize at the Australian Film Awards for his portrayal of a shearer who leads a strike while managing to hold onto his own job. If there are shades of Fred Zimmerman's *The Sundowners*, that's no bad thing and, in fact, the shearing scenes were shot in the same shed!

Sundowners, The ○
1960, Australia, 133 mins, colour
Dir: Fred Zinnemann
Stars: Deborah Kerr, Robert Mitchum
Rating: ★★★★

Tender story of the travels of a happy-go-lucky Australian sheep farmer, with a wife who desperately wants to settle down. Director Fred Zinnemann captures a whole panorama of Australian outdoor life, and his commonplace tapestry is enriched by a whole series of wonderful character studies from Ronald Fraser, Mervyn Johns, and especially Glynis Johns as a faintly blowzy widow with sights firmly set on Peter Ustinov's rascally Venneker. Robert Mitchum's Australian accent is impeccable and his portrayal one of his finest achievements. It's a film that really makes one feel for the characters it presents.

Sunflower ○
1969, Italy, 101 mins, colour
Dir: Vittorio De Sica
Stars: Sophia Loren, Marcello Mastroianni
Rating: ★★

One of the more effective of director Vittorio De Sica's later films, this epic romantic melodrama, described by one contemporary critic as 'gloriously batty' gives Sophia Loren full rein for some unrestrained emotional acting in a story positively soaked in one of Henry Mancini's lushest scores. The Technicolor photography of Giuseppe Rotunno and David Vinitsi is truly ravishing, helping more than anything else to approach realisation of the director's obvious ambition: to make a classic love story.

Sunset ◑ Ⓥ
1988, US, 107 mins, colour
Dir: Blake Edwards
Stars: Bruce Willis, James Garner, Mariel Hemingway, Kathleen Quinlan, Malcolm McDowell
Rating: ★★

Cowboy star Tom Mix meets Western legend Wyatt Earp in Hollywood – and they solve a murder together. Very much fiction, very much a concoction: if only they'd set it 15 years earlier than 1929, everything would have been right, not least the ages of the two men as portrayed here by Bruce Willis and James Garner (Earp died in 1928). As it is, not much of it is believable, especially with the casting of a Charlie Chaplin-type comedian (Malcolm McDowell) as the villain. And, although Willis and Garner carry the TV-style plot comfortably enough, it isn't often in a major film that you come across three main female performances as weak as those given here by Mariel Hemingway, Jennifer Edwards and Patricia Hodge. The chameleon Kathleen Quinlan is better company, but what the film needs is dynamism, pace and a sense of period. Not only does the director not supply these in sufficient quantities, but he has to cope with a corny musical score by Henry Mancini that intrudes on the action rather than underlining it. At least Willis and Garner give the venture a sense of grace.

Sunset Boulevard ○ Ⓥ
1950, US, 110 mins, b/w
Dir: Billy Wilder
Stars: William Holden, Gloria Swanson, Erich von Stroheim, Nancy Olson
Rating: ★★★

There's a superbly doom-laden atmosphere about this abrasively distinctive portrait of a reclusive Hollywood star and the writer enmeshed in her web, which clinched a sensational comeback to films for the silent superstar Gloria Swanson and won Oscar nominations for all four stars. William Holden, Nancy Olson and Erich von Stroheim were the three others. Holden and Ms Olson give impressive performances but cannot help but be overshadowed by the magnetic, powerful portrayal of the faded actress by Ms Swanson and the playing of the other veterans of a Hollywood gone by – represented by one scene where legendary director Cecil B DeMille is visited on the set where he is making his epic film *Samson and Delilah*.

Sun Valley Serenade ○
1941, US, 86 mins, b/w
Dir: H Bruce Humberstone
Stars: Sonja Henie, John Payne, Glenn Miller, Milton Berle
Rating: ★★★

This toe-tapping musical was one of Glenn Miller's rare acting roles in a short Hollywood career before his ill-fated flight across the English Channel. Set in the famous Idaho ski resort, it was the brainchild of Fox studio boss Darryl F Zanuck, who had recently enjoyed a holiday there and thought it would be a lovely setting for a musical. World champion ice skater Sonja Henie gets to smile more than skate, and her final showstopping number, skated on ice sprayed black, dissolves into a rendition of 'Chattanooga Choo Choo' because she fell during shooting and Zanuck refused to pay for an extra day's filming. The Glenn Miller Band have too little to do, but the film does include such killer Miller standards as 'In the Mood'. The cinematography and music were nominated for Oscars.

Supergirl ○ ⓥ
1984, US, 124 mins, colour
Dir: Jeannot Szwarc
Stars: Helen Slater, Faye Dunaway, Peter O'Toole, Peter Cook, Mia Farrow
Rating: ★★

The lifeblood, or whatever it is that flows through the veins of superpeople, is clearly thinning in this episode from the 'super' series and, although Helen Slater and Faye Dunaway give their all to Supergirl and her sorceress adversary, the plot and situations that surround them are strictly one-dimensional. Slater is actually more fun in her schoolgirl disguise than as Supergirl herself and it would have been nice to see more of the film spun round this side of her life. However, the demands for bigger-and-better decree that she shall combat the forces of evil, the Phantom Zone, the Alien Storm, the Fearful Fireball and all that sort of thing. Ms Dunaway and especially Brenda Vaccaro as her cigarette puffing confidante, plotting nothing less than world domination from a room in a funfair ghost house, make the most of their roles. Special effects are good and young children should enjoy it thoroughly, while their parents can use the romantic interludes to make the coffee.

Superman ○ ⓥ
1978, US, 143 mins, colour
Dir: Richard Donner
Stars: Christopher Reeve, Margot Kidder, Gene Hackman, Marlon Brando, Trevor Howard, Terence Stamp
Rating: ★★★

After a very impressive first 20 minutes, this develops into predictable comic-strip action. But in those stunning opening scenes, there are enough brilliant special effects to satisfy the most avid science-fiction fan. Christopher Reeve is actually rather good as Superman, getting away nicely with being both bespectacled newspaperman and wrong-righting wonder, without making you ask why no one spotted the similarity.

Superman II ○ ⓥ
1980, US, 127 mins, colour
Dir: Richard Lester
Stars: Christopher Reeve, Gene Hackman, Margot Kidder
Rating: ★★★

The best and certainly the most refreshing of the three *Superman* films, given a witty approach by director Richard Lester, another clever dual-identity characterisation by Christopher Reeve and slam-band action that boasts both a joyous zing and a wicked sense of humour. The script has a good sprinkling of funny lines: 'When will these dummies learn to use a doorknob?' mutters one character watching the bad guys break down walls to get at hapless Jackie Cooper (once again as the editor-employer of Superman in his Clark Kent guise). Sparkling Technicolor photography lends the top-dressing to a fast-moving (apart from the expendable romantic interludes when Superman – horrors! – actually gets to go to bed with Lois Lane) piece of first-class entertainment.

Superman III ○ ⓥ
1983, US, 123 mins, colour
Dir: Richard Lester
Stars: Christopher Reeve, Richard Pryor, Jackie Cooper, Pamela Stephenson
Rating: ★★★

Superman falls temporarily from grace in this inventive third film in the high-flying series. Poisoned by synthetic Kryptonite containing nicotine tar, he blows out the Olympic torch, straightens up the Tower of Pisa and pollutes the oceans with oil, just for starters. Christopher Reeve gives the whole thing a human element some actors wouldn't manage, and excels in the battle between good and bad Supermen. The start is riotously good, the main plotline rather less so with Richard Pryor not at his best as a crooked computer genius. Special effects are well up to the mark, especially when Superman uses a frozen lake to put out a raging fire.

Superman IV – The Quest for Peace ○ ⓥ
1987, US, 90 mins, colour
Dir: Sidney J Furie
Stars: Christopher Reeve, Gene Hackman, Margot Kidder, Jackie Cooper
Rating: ★★

This fourth and last (to date) outing for Christopher Reeve as the Man of Steel has him ridding the world of nuclear armaments and battling against Nuclear Man, a super-baddie created by Superman's arch-enemy Lex Luthor (Gene Hackman). Although marginally better than *Superman III*, it's still a long way from

the first two films. The special effects look decidedly cut-rate, the direction is flaccid and the script (based on a story by Reeve) is pretty poor, too. Hackman gets most of the best lines and he has to work hard for those. Still, the scene where Superman disposes of all the world's nuclear weapons by tossing them into the sun and the final battle on the moon with Nuclear Man are both enjoyable. The undemanding will probably enjoy this, but if you really liked *Superman* and *Superman II*, you'll be disappointed with this.

Super Mario Brothers ○ ⓥ
1993, US, 104 mins, colour
Dir: Rocky Morton, Annabel Jankel
Stars: Bob Hoskins, John Leguizamo, Dennis Hopper, Samantha Mathis, Fisher Stevens, Fiona Shaw, Lance Henriksen
Rating: ★★

Take a few dinosaurs. Add state-of-the-art special effects. Stir in an old-fashioned 'save the world from evil' story in a modern computer-game setting, and you have a recipe for success – at least with kids who love the game and its characters, while their parents sit bewildered in adjoining armchairs. Bob Hoskins and John Leguizamo play a pair of intrepid plumbers who answer a call from a maiden in distress and enter a nether world full of slimy monsters. Dennis Hopper has a field day as the monsters' tyrannical leader in a fantasy-adventure for teens and under that entertains but could have been so much better. We yield to no one in our admiration for the directors' critically panned version of *DOA*, but they have pretty well blown a promising premise here with this over-charged, OTT ear-blaster.

Support Your Local Gunfighter ○ ⓥ
1971, US, 92 mins, colour
Dir: Burt Kennedy
Stars: James Garner, Suzanne Pleshette, Jack Elam, Chuck Connors, Joan Blondell, Harry Morgan
Rating: ★★★

A surprisingly successful follow-up to *Support Your Local Sheriff!*, in which James Garner's rogue gambler jumps train at a small gold-mining town of Purgatory and is immediately taken to be the feared gunman Swifty Morgan. Garner's determined to take the town for everything he can get, but naturally the real Swifty turns up

S

towards the end and there's a fast and furious finale. Excellent support from Suzanne Pleshette, as a feisty dame whose aggression belies her intentions of running a ladies' finishing school, from a whole Main Street full of colourful Hollywood characters, and best of all from scowling Jack Elam as the town drunk who becomes Garner's sidekick. His on-train monologue at the end just grabs the film its third star.

Support Your Local Sheriff! ○ ⓥ
1968, US, 89 mins, colour
Dir: Burt Kennedy
Stars: James Garner, Joan Hackett, Walter Brennan, Harry Morgan, Bruce Dern, Jack Elam
Rating: ★★★

Wonderfully funny and likeable spoof Western, with James Garner guying his Maverick image as the tall dark stranger who prefers the use of brains to brawn, and cleans up a lawless town in his own highly individual way. William Bowers' screenplay, besides having more than its fair share of amusing lines, throws up any number of rich characters. There's Joan Hackett as the accident-prone heroine, forever falling on her bustle; Jack Elam as the drunken brawler whom Garner makes deputy sheriff; and Walter Brennan, clearly relishing his comic villain.

Sure Thing, The ◑ ⓥ
1985, US, 94 mins, colour
Dir: Rob Reiner
Stars: John Cusack, Daphne Zuniga, Boyd Gaines, Anthony Edwards, Tim Robbins, Viveca Lindfors
Rating: ★★

A sharp comedy from the director of *Misery, When Harry Met Sally* and *Stand by Me*. A pleasant mix of road movie and teen drama, it stars John Cusack as the fast-food junkie youth ready to clear the last hurdle in coming-of-age and Daphne Zuniga as a prim and proper fellow student who thinks that spontaneity is a social disease. Thrown together on a car journey to California, the couple start out as sparring opposites but gradually come to see that their oil and water mix could be complimentary. It's a familiar theme – witness such classic comedies as *It Happened One Night* – but Reiner casts a refreshing eye at the clichéd goings-on and gives events a nice twist.

Surrender ◑ ⓥ
1987, US, 110 mins, colour
Dir: Jerry Belson
Stars: Sally Field, Michael Caine, Steve Guttenberg, Peter Boyle
Rating: ★★★

As battle-of-the-sexes comedies go, this is only a little above the average at base, but writer/director Jerry Belson gets such crackerjack performances from Michael Caine, Sally Field, Steve Guttenberg and Peter Boyle that his film is a constant pleasure to be with. Caine plays a successful writer with a weakness for women who systematically take him to the cleaners. Once the despair of his lawyer (Boyle), Caine now has a sign on the gates of his mansion banning women. Then along comes failed painter Sally Field and, tied up to her during a robbery, Caine soon gets that mating urge again. The film is full of chuckles, and a few big laughs too, such as when Caine tells Boyle that he's 'getting rid of all the parasites in my life.' 'You mean,' gasps Boyle, 'that you're firing me?' Curiosity note: model/actress Iman could be the first person ever to achieve star billing on the strength of two fleeting appearances and lines.

Susannah of the Mounties ○
1939, US, 78 mins, b/w
Dir: William A Seiter
Stars: Shirley Temple, Randolph Scott, Margaret Lockwood
Rating: ★★

One of Shirley Temple's last big films. Two years later she finished as a child star, and her mother sent her to a full-time school for two years before she resumed her career (less successfully) as a teenager. One of her co-stars in this spectacular action film about Mounties and Indians was a full-blooded Blackfoot Indian boy called Martin Good Rider.

Susan Slept Here ○
1954, US, 98 mins, colour
Dir: Frank Tashlin
Stars: Dick Powell, Debbie Reynolds
Rating: ★★★

Just about the madcap blend of musical and wacky comedy you'd expect from ex-cartoonist Frank Tashlin, this bright, light-hearted frolic has near-perfect performances from a smooth Dick Powell and a sparky Debbie Reynolds, excellent colour and even flashes of genuine wit. Anne Francis is excellent as Powell's

cold-hearted fiancée and wisecracking Glenda Farrell superb as the secretary who knows all the answers.

Suspect, The ○
1944, US, 84 mins, b/w
Dir: Robert Siodmak
Stars: Charles Laughton, Ella Raines, Henry Daniell, Rosalind Ivan
Rating: ★★★

Superbly directed by Robert Siodmak, who made *Phantom Lady*, this is the absorbing story of a vaguely Crippen-like murder (although Charles Laughton's reluctant killer is really quite a sympathetic character) committed in the gaslit London just after the turn of the century. Siodmak tightens the tension much in the manner of Hitchcock and extracts a string of first-rate performances from his cast. Laughton is memorable as the henpecked worm who finally turns, but he is extremely well supported by Ella Raines as the lonely girl who impels him to strive for a divorce, Stanley Ridges as the dogged inspector determined to nail the killer, Rosalind Ivan (never better) as Laughton's vicious wife and Henry Daniell, supremely smarmy as his drunken, blackmailing, thoroughly unpleasant neighbour. And Molly Lamont, a South African-born actress who starred in British films before going to Hollywood with only moderate success, gives her best film performance as Daniell's long-suffering wife. A beautifully-made thriller, one of the best from the war years.

Suspect ○
(aka: The Risk)
1960, UK, 81 mins, b/w
Dir: Roy Boulting
Stars: Tony Britton, Peter Cushing, Virginia Maskell
Rating: ★★

A gripping comedy-thriller that's as full of twists as the Boulting Brothers can make it. Good performances from Tony Britton, Ian Bannen and Virginia Maskell in a story of research chemists tempted to betray their country to get their findings on a plague serum published.

Suspect ◑ ⓥ
1987, US, 101 mins, colour
Dir: Peter Yates
Stars: Cher, Dennis Quaid, Liam Neeson, John Mahoney, Joe Mantegna, Philip Bosco
Rating: ★★★

As this is a nicely made courtroom whodunnit, it would be a kindness not to dwell too deeply on its plot. Suffice to say that, despite a central performance by Cher that's only adequate, and a screenplay that definitely does not bear close inspection, director Peter Yates, helped a great deal by Michael Kamen's tense music score, hooks us on to the action throughout. A supreme court justice hands a package to a female court official. Soon after, both are dead, he a suicide, she murdered. A deaf-and-dumb vagrant (well played by Liam Neeson) is brought to trial on strong circumstantial evidence. Of course, there's more to it, as his floundering defence counsel discovers, especially when helped out by an inquisitive juror (Dennis Quaid). Just as well, too, for, as written and played, the lady doesn't seem able to prove her way out of a paper bag. Never mind, the continuation of the suspense is the thing. That's where Yates and his lieutenants do a fine job out of making a silk purse out of a sow's ear.

Suspicion ○
1941, US, 99 mins, b/w
Dir: Alfred Hitchcock
Stars: Cary Grant, Joan Fontaine
Rating: ★★★★

This second American film from Alfred Hitchcock has an all-British cast except for Joan Fontaine, who was born in the Far East to British parents, and who won an Oscar for her role here. Many considered that the Academy gave her it to make up for losing the statuette the previous year (when she starred in Hitchcock's *Rebecca*) to Ginger Rogers in *Kitty Foyle*. Cary Grant is the fortune hunting cad who woos a spinster into marriage. She then begins to suspect that he is a murderer who wants to kill her next. The film's denouement isn't worthy of the moody build-up, but that can be blamed on the studio, RKO, who demanded an upbeat ending in the days before Hitchcock had absolute control of his material. Shame.

Svengali ○
1931, US, 83 mins, b/w
Dir: Archie Mayo
Stars: John Barrymore, Marion Marsh, Bramwell Fletcher
Rating: ★★★

This classic melodrama is dominated by an extraordinary performance from John Barrymore as the mesmerist of the title. The expressionistic sets by Anton Grot add to the film's considerable atmosphere, and the photography by Barney McGill, especially a tight shot that begins on Barrymore's face, then tracks across the roofs of Paris to end on a close-up of his hypnotised victim, is a tour-de-force.

Svengali ○
1954, UK, 82 mins, colour
Dir: Noel Langley
Stars: Donald Wolfit, Hildegarde Neff, Terence Morgan, Derek Bond
Rating: ★★

A lavish, if rather bizarrely coloured version of George du Maurier's hoary old yarn about the singer and the hypnotist in old-time Paris. It seemed somewhat unwise of the producers to hire a German actress (Hildegarde Neff) who has to attempt an Irish accent – it's a brave try, even so – but the film is dominated by Donald Wolfit's Svengali, at once horrifying and pathetic. The production is handsomely and authentically dressed, but the script fails to give the yarn the lift it needs, and it's left to Wolfit to provide the film's strength single-handed.

Svengali ○
1983, US, 93 mins, colour
Dir: Anthony Harvey
Stars: Peter O'Toole, Jodie Foster
Rating: ★★

John Barrymore and David Wolfit, *outre* performers both, have each had their wicked way with George du Maurier's famous creation, the mad artist-teacher who completely dominates his youthful pupil. Now the story is updated, none too convincingly, to allow Peter O'Toole's haughty imperiousness full range as a voice teacher training a young rock singer (Jodie Foster retaining her puppy fat in the Trilby role). Clearly relishing the script's ample opportunities for over-playing, O'Toole gleefully describes Ms Foster's voice as being 'like raw meat'. He hasn't been as enjoyably successful as this since his marvellous portrayal of the dictatorial film director in *The Stunt Man* four years before.

S.W.A.L.K.
See: Melody

Swallows and Amazons ⊙
1974, UK, 92 mins, colour
Dir: Claude Whatham
Stars: Virginia McKenna, Ronald Fraser
Rating: ★★★

The Lake District looks lovely in this delightful, traditional children's adventure yarn adapted from Arthur Ransome's novel and involving boats, an island, a cross uncle and a burglary. There's rather a lot of obvious scene-setting, but the island sequences are great fun and the film is attractively acted by all the children involved. There are also personable performances from Virginia McKenna, Ronald Fraser and Brenda Bruce as the adults.

Swamp Thing ◑ ⓥ
1982, US, 90 mins, colour
Dir: Wes Craven
Stars: Louis Jourdan, Adrienne Barbeau, Ray Wise
Rating: ★★

Is it a man? Is it a compost heap? No, it's Swamp Thing! This pretty well sums up director Wes (*Nightmare on Elm Street*) Craven's monster movie parody of Fifties creature 'B' films. At least this green giant is jollier than The Incredible Hulk, and the script has a sense of humour too, even if it's more knowing than its counterparts from the Fifties.

Swanee River ○
1939, US, 84 mins, colour
Dir: Sidney Lanfield
Stars: Don Ameche, Andrea Leeds, Al Jolson
Rating: ★★★

Lavish biography of the famous American composer Stephen Foster, resplendent in early Technicolor and bursting with drama, sentiment and such famous ditties as 'Oh! Susanna', 'Jeannie with the Light Brown Hair', 'Camptown Races' and 'The Old Folks at Home'. Director Sidney Lanfield keeps a firm hold on the thread of the story (and even on the histrionics of Al Jolson, playing the famous minstrel man E P Christy). The photographer who brings such warmth and atmosphere to the Deep South setting is Bert Glennon, a distinguished cameraman who started in the early silent days. Later he proved equally adept with black-and-white (in *Stagecoach*) and colour (*Hurricane* and *Drums Along the Mohawk*).

S

Swashbuckler
See: The Scarlet Buccaneer

Sweeney! ◐
1976, UK, 89 mins, colour
Dir: David Wickes
Stars: John Thaw, Dennis Waterman,
Barry Foster
Rating: ★★

The first spin-off film from the TV
series that brought a whole new
toughness to the police genre. It established a gritty and amusing
camaraderie between its two major
characters (played by John Thaw and
Dennis Waterman) which, coupled
with a *Z Cars* pattern of small scenes,
made it among the most fluid and
hard-hitting thrillers seen on television. The action still packs a punch
here, even though it serves up a
B-feature plot about oil sheiks and
blackmail in high places. Michael
Coles, as the leader of an unlikely
squad of assassins, is the best of the
supporting cast.

Sweeney 2 ◐
1978, UK, 108 mins, colour
Dir: Tom Clegg
Stars: John Thaw, Dennis Waterman
Rating: ★★

Action, tough, rugged and plentiful, is
the order of the day in this second film
to stem from the famous TV crime
series. The story – Regan and Carter
pursuing the perpetrators of a long and
clever series of armed bank robberies
from London to Malta – works very
well apart from one episode involving
a bomb scare which is not only poorly
done but superfluous. John Thaw and
Dennis Waterman make their farewell
appearances as Regan and Carter,
roles that fitted them like gloves.

Sweet Charity ○
1969, US, 149 mins, colour
Dir: Robert Fosse
Stars: Shirley MacLaine, Sammy Davis
Jr, Ricardo Montalban
Rating: ★★★

Shirley MacLaine is the tart with the
heart of gold who falls in love with a
naive young man who doesn't know
about her 'profession' in this lively
adaptation of the successful stage
musical. Directed by choreographer
Bob Fosse, there are some great
routines and some memorable songs –
'Big Spender', 'If My Friends Could
See Me Now' and 'The Rhythm of
Life'. Peter Stone wrote the script,
based on Neil Simon's play, which it-

self is an adaptation of Fellini's film
Notte di Cabiria. If the third-hand story
doesn't quite hold up in places, it really doesn't matter, Ms MacLaine's
exuberance and a fine supporting cast
– Sammy Davis Jr, Stubby Kaye,
dancers Chita Rivera and Paula Kelly
– keep things moving along in fine
style.

Sweethearts ○
1938, US, 114 mins, colour
Dir: W S Van Dyke II
Stars: Jeanette MacDonald, Nelson
Eddy, Frank Morgan, Ray Bolger
Rating: ★★★

One of the longest of the Jeanette
MacDonald-Nelson Eddy musicals,
which is good news for their fans –
and in Technicolor, too. The Victor
Herbert melodies are really the whole
show, especially the lilting title number. The script is certainly above-
average for a MacDonald-Eddy musical, and the songs also include
'Wooden Shoes', 'Every Lover Must
Meet His Fate' and 'Little Gray Home
in the West'.

Sweet Liberty ◐
1986, US, 107 mins, colour
Dir: Alan Alda
Stars: Alan Alda, Michael Caine,
Michelle Pfeiffer, Bob Hoskins
Rating: ★★★

Alan Alda wrote, directed and stars in
this swipe at films and film-making.
He's the writer of a serious book
about the American Revolution,
which is to be filmed. Screenwriter
Bob Hoskins wants to liven it up; and
temperamental stars Michael Caine
and Michelle Pfeiffer cause their own
problems. The plot meanders a bit
but the stars hold the film together and
it remains a witty tale with some
genuinely funny moments.

Sweet November ○
1968, US, 114 mins, colour
Dir: Robert Ellis Miller
Stars: Sandy Dennis, Anthony Newley
Rating: ★★

Sandy Dennis is one of those mannered but unusual actresses whom one
either finds hard to take or likes very
much. She has a good part here as a
Brooklyn girl with advanced ideas.
The film is a bitter-sweet romance,
directed by Robert Ellis Miller, in
between two very good ones, *Any
Wednesday* (known in Britain as
Bachelor Girl Apartment) and *The Heart
is a Lonely Hunter*. There are some

witty lines in Herman Raucher's
script, mostly for Anthony Newley –
who also sings the title song – as a
prosperous young tycoon who
moves in with Ms Dennis, the girl
who takes on a different lover each
month. Like all Miller's films, the crisp
black edges conceal a soft centre, but
it would be unfair to the storyline to
reveal just what.

Sweet Rosie O'Grady ○
1943, US, 74 mins, colour
Dir: Irving Cummings
Stars: Betty Grable, Robert Young,
Adolphe Menjou
Rating: ★★

Described by the New York Times as
'pretty as a bowl of wax fruit . . . in
luscious Technicolor . . . with Betty
Grable in some low-necked ensembles
that resemble an Italian wedding cake',
this musical, although rather on the
short side for such a classy item, was
just the ticket for wartime audiences
gasping for escapism. Ms Grable is the
songbird who moves from high-kicks
in a Brooklyn beer garden to high society in London. Nice period feel, as
always in these Fox 'Gay Nineties'-type musical marshmallows.

Sweet Smell of Success ○
1957, US, 96 mins, b/w
Dir: Alexander Mackendrick
Stars: Burt Lancaster, Tony Curtis
Rating: ★★★★

A fine American film, directed by
Britain's Alexander Mackendrick,
who learned his trade in Ealing
comedies. Burt Lancaster, wearing a
pair of owlish spectacles for his role, is
frighteningly sinister as the
newspaperman who glories in the
cringing servility of those who seek his
favours; and Tony Curtis gives a
magnificent performance as the
crawling press agent, Sidney Falco,
who would – and does – sell his soul
for a paragraph in Lancaster's column.
Susan Harrison plays Lancaster's sister,
in a permanent state of white-faced
fear, and Marty Milner is her upright,
incorruptible boyfriend. Clifford
Odets and Ernest Lehman dipped their
pens in acid to write the screenplay;
the black (and blacker) photography is
superb and the whole package is
backed up by the haunting jazz of
Chico Hamilton.

Sweet William ●
1979, UK, 90 mins, colour
Dir: Claude Whatham

Stars: Sam Waterston, Jenny Agutter, Anna Massey
Rating: ★★

A loveable rogue who loves them and leaves them, 'Sweet' William speeds around on his bike from conquest to conquest without his live-in girlfriend Ann knowing much about it – until it's too late and she's pregnant. It's basically a sex comedy-drama of the old school, but handled with delicacy and sensitivity by director Claude Whatham. The best sequence is an episode involving Ann's visit to her father (superb Arthur Lowe) and awful mother by the seaside, which says more in a few glances than the rest of the script in its entirety. Sam Waterston is quite nicely cast as the freewheeling William and Jenny Agutter pretty good as the bedded, bothered and bewildered Ann.

Swimmer, The ○
1968, US, 94 mins, colour
Dir: Frank Perry
Stars: Burt Lancaster, Janet Landgard, Janice Rule
Rating: ★★

Fascinating evocation of schizophrenia, with Burt Lancaster offering a thoughtful performance as the man who attempts a swim across the county via his friends' pools, encountering increasing hostility on the way. Location filming in Connecticut perfectly recaptures the mood of the interesting John Cheever short story on which the film is based. Watch for chat show hostess Joan Rivers in a minor role.

Swing Kids ◐ ⊛
1993, US, 112 mins, colour
Dir: Thomas Carter
Stars: Robert Sean Leonard, Christian Bale, Frank Whaley, Barbara Hershey, Kenneth Branagh
Rating: ★★★

Quite well done but awfully familiar, and we're once again with the rise of Nazism in Germany in the Thirties. Based on real events, it's the spirited story of a group of rebellious German teenagers. By embracing the American swing music and dancing, forbidden by their Führer, the Swing Kids openly demonstrate their dedication to freedom of expression. But before long the propaganda machines of the Hitler Youth are in motion and some of the youngsters prove to be more dedicated to their ideals than others. It starts stickily, but builds in character

and atmosphere as it goes along. A moving eye-opener in some ways, it will certainly make you cheer for the Swing Kids as they spit dangerously in the eye of authority. Okay performances really needed to be special to lift this film to excellence.

Swing Shift ◐ ⊛
1984, US, 100 mins, colour
Dir: Jonathan Demme
Stars: Goldie Hawn, Kurt Russell, Christine Lahti, Fred Ward
Rating: ★★

Surprisingly anti-feminist for a Goldie Hawn film, and much-troubled in the making (three reels were apparently re-shot at the star's insistence), this wartime drama is much better than you might expect from all its production problems. There are sterling performances from a very strong cast, but what really gives the film its credibility is the work of its production designer, costume designer and photographer. Together they create an evocative period (the early 1940s) that brims with patriotism and feeling for a lifestyle and values worth defending. It's just a pity that the actual characters and their actions are not more likeable.

Swing Shift Maisie ○
1943, US, 87 mins, b/w
Dir: Norman Z McLeod
Stars: Ann Sothern, James Craig, Jean Rogers
Rating: ★★

An experienced comedy director, Norman Z Mcleod, adds some brighter moments than usual to this *Maisie* romp, in which, it being wartime, our girl takes a job at the local defence factory, and works the anti-social hours of the swing shift. That would have meant little to British audiences, so the title was changed to *The Girl In Overalls*, hardly more of an invitation to view. In the supporting cast, there's a good role for little, huffly-snuffly character player John Qualen, as the owner of a troupe of performing dogs who looks a bit like one of his own charges.

Swing Time ○ ⊛
1936, US, 103 mins, b/w
Dir: George Stevens
Stars: Fred Astaire, Ginger Rogers
Rating: ★★★★

The sixth pairing of Fred Astaire and Ginger Rogers. He blacks up for 'Bojangles of Harlem' in tribute to Bill

Robinson and she croons 'Pick Yourself Up'. There are only six songs and the first isn't heard for almost 30 minutes (a big mistake) but 'The Way You Look Tonight' won the Oscar. A smart, hip movie that recreates the nightclub era of the 'Roaring Twenties' with superb sets.

Swiss Family Robinson ⊙
1959, US, 128 mins, colour
Dir: Ken Annakin
Stars: John Mills, Dorothy McGuire, James MacArthur, Janet Munro
Rating: ★★★

This roistering Disney version of the Johann Wyss novel, filmed on location in Tobago, is all action and colour. John Mills enthusiastically leads the Robinsons in their adventures on a desert island, where they dispatch a gang of cutthroats in splendidly entertaining style.

Swiss Miss ⊙
1938, US, 73 mins, b/w
Dir: Hal Roach
Stars: Stan Laurel, Oliver Hardy, Della Lind, Walter Woolf King
Rating: ★★★

A Laurel and Hardy 'comic opera' which is particularly notable for two famous sequences. One of these is Stan's hilarious attempts to rob a Saint Bernard dog of the barrel of brandy round its neck. The other is a scene in which the boys try to move a piano across a suspension bridge high above the ground, encountering a gorilla halfway across. The gorilla makes another appearance in the riotously funny climax.

Switch ● ⊛
1991, US, 114 mins, colour
Dir: Blake Edwards
Stars: Ellen Barkin, Jimmy Smits, Lorraine Bracco, JoBeth Williams, Perry King, Tony Roberts
Rating: ★

Shades of *Goodbye Charlie!* In this case, it's goodbye Steve, as a sleazy sexist of that name is murdered by a trio of angry lovers. His womanising life, however, ensures that Heaven's gates remain firmly closed. He's sent back to earth to mend his wicked ways, but there's a twist: Steve now has the body of a beautiful blond female (Ellen Barkin). Much of the humour is deadeningly heavy-handed, in typical latter-day Blake Edwards style, with the only real entertainment provided by Barkin's slinky sexiness – voted

S

'Sexiest Man Alive' by *U.S. Magazine*. Not for the first time she's the only good thing in a film, which doesn't say a lot for her choice of scripts.

Switching Channels ○ Ⓥ
1987, US, 97 mins, colour
Dir: Ted Kotcheff
Stars: Kathleen Turner, Burt Reynolds, Christopher Reeve, Ned Beatty
Rating: ★

Look out, here comes *The Front Page* again. One of the cinema's most-filmed plots switches its leading reporter role from male to female, and its setting from a newspaper to a TV newsroom. But no amount of switching can crank the hoary old vehicle into life, especially with a script that almost totally lacks wit and sparkle. Kathleen Turner, Burt Reynolds and Christopher Reeve play over-brightly; Ted Kotcheff's direction is faceless if occasionally frenzied. Perhaps after this and the disappointing Billy Wilder version of the previous decade, they'll now let *The Front Page* rest in peace.

Sword and the Rose, The ⊙
1953, UK, 93 mins, colour
Dir: Ken Annakin
Stars: Glynis Johns, Richard Todd
Rating: ★★

Colourful, fast-moving, if thoroughly inaccurate slice of Disney history with Glynis Johns a first rate spitfire Mary Tudor and James Robertson Justice a witty, athletic Henry VIII. Polished sword-and-cloak stuff, it has the expert touch.

Sword and the Sorcerer, The ● Ⓥ
1982, US, 100 mins, colour
Dir: Albert Pyun
Stars: Lee Horsley, Kathleen Beller, Simon MacCorkindale, Richard Lynch
Rating: ★★

Remember Tony Curtis and Piper Laurie in *The Prince Who Was a Thief*? It was what Hollywood used to call an eastern. Special effects and the popularity of musclemen heroes have given the genre a new lease of life in recent times and *The Sword and the Sorcerer* runs along familiar lines, with Lee Horsley as the prince out to reclaim his rightful position and Kathleen Beller the spitfire princess who has who rashly promised him a night of love for rescuing her brother.

'Buccaneer! Slave! Rogue! General!' raves the script about its hero. Unfortunately, Horsley's rather negative personality allows us to believe little of this build-up and the film is entirely stolen by its villains – gimlet-eyed Richard Lynch, impassive George Maharis (dead sneaky) and Richard Moll as the sorcerer, a gentleman who seems to have trouble preventing his face from liquefying. Kathleen Beller is allowed to do little more than heave a heroic bosom which is rather a pity, as we know from other films that she can act as well. Many of the other characters wear beards that make them look like refugees from the *Planet of the Apes*. Special effects are often shimmeringly good, and nowhere more so than the opening scene when a creature rises from the dead and plucks out a witch's heart; definitely not for the squeamish. This, like most of the action, is photographed through a permanent brown haze which, we think, is intended to give a medieval feel. The ending promises a sequel – *Tales from the Ancient Empire* – but to date we haven't seen it.

Sword in the Stone, The ⊙
1963, US, 80 mins, colour
Dir: Wolfgang Reitherman
Voice Stars: Rickie Sorenson, Sebastian Cabot
Rating: ★★★

Much underrated on first release, this delightful Disney feature was described as 'whiz-bang wizard of whimsy!'. It's about the young days of King Arthur – although the story is just an excuse for a series of extraordinarily ingenious situations. Children will delight in a whole range of inventive characters: Archimedes, the wizard's owl; a ferociously funny pike which chases 'Wart' when Merlin changes him into a fish; and the self-described 'marvellous, mad, mad, mad Madame Mim', a Gingold-like witch with pink hair. Our personal favourite is a beautifully-drawn scraggy wolf who lurks around in the forest for the titbit that always seems to just evade his rat-trap jaws. Despite the somewhat ineffectual songs by the Sherman brothers, it's a dazzling show, with one scene that really stands out – the marvellous wizards' duel between Merlin and the evil Madame Mim, who transform themselves into a variety of animals as they seek to gain the upper hand.

Sword of Monte Cristo, The ⊙
1951, US, 80 mins, colour
Dir: Maurice Geraghty
Stars: George Montgomery, Paula Corday, Bearry Kroeger, William Conrad
Rating: ★★

Set in early 19th-century France, this is a swashbuckler with a slight difference. The masked avenger and righter of wrongs who is by day a member of Napoleon III's court is a woman. It is she who has the valuable sword which once belonged to the Count of Monte Cristo and holds the key to his hidden fortune. Despite this variation, this is a formula adventure with stereotyped characters, which hardly does justice to Alexandre Dumas' novel. Still, it rattles along at a fair pace and Paula Corday is an attractive heroine, although George Montgomery is a rather stiff hero. Lurid colour photography helps to take your mind off the plot deficiencies.

Sword of Sherwood Forest ○ Ⓥ
1961, UK, 80 mins, colour
Dir: Terence Fisher
Stars: Richard Greene, Peter Cushing
Rating: ★★

This was the film that sprang from the long-running television series, with Richard Greene following in the footsteps of such famous Hoods as Douglas Fairbanks Sr, Errol Flynn and Richard Todd. Faces to watch out for include that of Oliver Reed (fresh from playing a werewolf for the same studio, Hammer) as a vicious villain called Melton, who takes part in a smashing sword battle in the last reel. And Derren Nesbitt, once of *Special Branch*, plays a nice young outlaw who gets a fatal taste of arrow in the first part of the film. It's fine action fare for children and adults alike.

Swordsman, The ○
1947, US, 81 mins, colour
Dir: Joseph L Lewis
Stars: Larry Parks, Ellen Drew, George Macready
Rating: ★★★

First-rate action film about a blood feud in the Scottish highlands, that owes a lot to the spirit of the Western. Rarely, too, was CineColor ever better used, and there are superb chase sequences through forests and across streams. Director Joseph H Lewis has, in fact, done a fine job, which has been compared by some writers to the style of the best of the Japanese action films. Larry Parks and George Macready are as personable as you could wish as hero and villain.

Sylvia ◐

1964, US, 115 mins, b/w
Dir: Gordon Douglas
Stars: Carroll Baker, George Maharis, Edmond O'Brien
Rating: ★★

The question isn't Terence Rattigan's, but that of an understandably suspicious millionaire who can't resist asking Maharis' private eye to investigate the background of his seemingly perfect fiancée. Sylvia – prize rose-grower, poetess and bookworm – is revealed through a series of jigsaw flashbacks to have had a tough time in her younger days, turned on to prostitution by a brutal rape. Sydney Boehm's screenplay shades in the scarlet past without too much purple prose. Though melodrama is really rampant, Boehm steers a careful course on the right side of bathos. Even when Sylvia goes joylessly back on the game to pay for her best friend's hospital bills, credibility is maintained. Much is owed to Carroll Baker's spirited rendering of the title role, emerging finally from the years of Harlow-like promotion (ironically, she was to play that legendary star the following year). There is uncommonly strong support from Joanne Dru as Sylvia's best friend; Viveca Lindfors, as a guardian angel librarian; and Nancy Kovack as a tall, myopic showgirl.

T

Table for Five ○

1983, US, 122 mins, colour
Dir: Robert Lieberman
Stars: Jon Voight, Richard Crenna
Rating: ★★★

The Royal Performance Film of its year, this is a calculated (and calculating) tear-jerker that ultimately does its job with clinical efficiency. Jon Voight has a lot of speeches to make as the absentee father and lifelong failure whose decision to take the children he deserted on a once-in-a-lifetime cruise to Egypt has far-reaching consequences. This rose-coloured look at the 'ideal' solution to his problems obviously expects us to swallow the glutinous dose in one gulp.

Take a Girl Like You ◐

1970, UK, 101 mins, colour
Dir: Jonathan Miller
Stars: Hayley Mills, Oliver Reed
Rating: ★★

Ms Mills again cast as a virgin-on the-verge in a sex comedy directed by Jonathan Miller. Oliver Reed does very well in an unusual (for him) light comedy role. He imagines he's irresistible to women (and isn't too far out). George Melly wrote the screenplay from the novel by Kingsley Amis, and in a supporting part you'll spot Penelope Keith, who later proved her worth in star roles.

Take Her, She's Mine ○

1963, US, 98 mins, colour
Dir: Henry Koster
Stars: James Stewart, Sandra Dee, Audrey Meadows, Robert Morley
Rating: ★★

This generation-gap comedy is cheerfully recommended to all fans of James Stewart. Whether fuming over the courting of his blossoming daughters, or accidentally getting arrested at a students' sit-in, Stewart's deceptively funny performance gives the shenanigans a lift they barely deserve. Stewart himself deserves much better, and would mercifully receive it with his next films, *Cheyenne Autumn* and, especially, *Shenandoah*. In the featured cast, Charla Docherty's fresh approach outshines the limited talent of Sandra Dee as her sister.

Take It Easy

See: American Anthem

Take Me High ○

1973, UK, 90 mins, colour
Dir: David Askey
Stars: Cliff Richard, Debbie Watling, George Cole, Anthony Andrews
Rating: ★

Cliff Richard makes an unlikely merchant banker in this breezy romantic comedy, his last screen musical to date. Hugh Griffith provides some welcome light relief as a rumbustious eccentric and the remarkable cast also includes the delicious Debbie Watling and Madeline Smith, George Cole, Richard Wattis and a very young Anthony Andrews as Richard's chief competitor. The bright colour photography of Birmingham (which gets almost as many close-ups as the star) is by Norman Warwick.

Take Me Out to the Ball Game ○ ⓥ

1948, US, 93 mins, colour
Dir: Busby Berkeley
Stars: Gene Kelly, Frank Sinatra, Esther Williams, Betty Garrett
Rating: ★★★★

This Busby Berkeley musical is a period baseball romp that finds Sinatra and Kelly in dynamic form and even Esther Williams (as the team manager) much livelier than usual. There's a tremendous fun finale, while two novelty songs, 'O'Brien to Ryan to Goldberg', and 'The Hat My Father Wore on St Patrick's Day', provide the musical highspots.

Take One False Step ○

1949, US, 94 mins, b/w
Dir: Chester Erskine
Stars: William Powell, Shelley Winters, Marsha Hunt
Rating: ★★★

Although writer-producer-director Chester Erskine specialised in tightly-knit thrillers like this one, his biggest hit (two years earlier) was, oddly, a comedy, *The Egg and I*. William Powell excels here as a college professor unwittingly involved in murder, while a strong supporting cast includes Marsha Hunt, James Gleason, Dorothy Hart and Sheldon Leonard.

Take the Money and Run ○ ⓥ

1969, US, 90 mins, colour
Dir: Woody Allen

Stars: Woody Allen, Janet Margolin
Rating: ★★★

Woody Allen's first film as his own director is a hotch-potch comedy about a bungling criminal who spends more time behind bars than on the outside. But forget the uneven storyline and enjoy it for what it is: a non-stop cavalcade of sight gags and inspired one-liners. Especially good is the sequence where Woody tries to break out of jail with a gun made of soap.

Take the Stage
See: Curtain Call at Cactus Creek

Taking Care of Business
See: Filofax

Taking of Pelham One Two Three, The ●
1974, US, 104 mins, colour
Dir: Joseph Sargent
Stars: Walter Matthau, Robert Shaw, Martin Balsam
Rating: ★★★

A fast and stylish, if slightly mechanical thriller about a gang that hijacks a subway car and its passengers with a juicy million dollar ransom in mind. Walter Matthau is invaluable as the railway security chief, and Peter Stone's snappy screenplay hardly needs to resort to the tough language it sometimes uses. Best of the rest: Tony Roberts as a straight-talking deputy mayor determined to pay the money and get things over.

Taking the Heat ◐ ⓥ
1993, US, 91 mins, colour
Dir: Tom Mankiewicz
Stars: Tony Goldwyn, Lynn Whitfield, Alan Arkin, George Segal, Will Patton, Peter Boyle
Rating: ★

This one must have dropped on a few stars' doorsteps before they finally found any takers. Tony Goldwyn and Lynn Whitfield ended up playing the lead roles in an action comedy where only the action scenes show any sign of working at all. It's the kind of thing that was considered high fashion in the Seventies, where the hero (a material witness) and heroine (a feisty cop) go by truck, taxi, speedboat and car, running, swimming and riding their way to a vital court hearing in between dodging the villain's sextet of hit-men (well, you would need six assassins to bump off one man, wouldn't you?). Years before, and

with a better script, it might have starred George Segal and Jane Fonda. Here, ironically, it's poor Segal who has the worst role of all as the prosecutor, mugging even more frantically than fellow-unfortunates Alan Arkin, Will Patton and Peter Boyle, who play bad guy, defence counsel and judge. The dated antics are padded out to feature length with deejays on the soundtrack and panoramic views of New York City.

Tale of Two Cities, A ○
1935, US, 128 mins, b/w
Dir: Jack Conway
Stars: Ronald Colman, Elizabeth Allan
Rating: ★★★★

The definitive version of Charles Dickens' classic story. Made by David O Selznick in 1935, the film superbly captures the period atmosphere and is splendidly held together by Colman's dominating performance as Sydney Carton. The Revolutionary sequences were 'arranged' – and seldom have crowd scenes been better staged – by Val Lewton and Jacques Tourneur. Six years later, they became producer and director on one of the very best sequences of horror films in film history, including *Cat People*, *The Leopard Man* and *I Walked with a Zombie*.

Tale of Two Cities, A ○ ⓥ
1958, UK, 117 mins, b/w
Dir: Ralph Thomas
Stars: Dirk Bogarde, Dorothy Tutin, Cecil Parker, Athene Seyler
Rating: ★★★

Steady, interesting British version of Dickens' novel. There are no crowd scenes to compare with the Hollywood 1935 film, but the story is forthrightly acted and simply told. Dirk Bogarde gives one of the best performances of his career as Sidney Carton, and there's a beautiful, gentle performance by Marie Versini, who unfortunately only appears towards the end of the film. Christopher Lee also makes a vivid impression as the evil Marquis St Evremonde. Character roles are ably filled by such reliable British stalwarts as Athene Seyler, Donald Pleasence and Leo McKern.

Tales From the Crypt ●
1972, UK, 92 mins, colour
Dir: Freddie Francis
Stars: Ralph Richardson, Joan Collins, Ian Hendry, Peter Cushing
Rating: ★★

Another of the Amicus Films horror compilations, taking in five tales of terror for the price of one. As usual, it proves to be a mixture of good and bad, with the best episode – nerve-janglingly directed by Freddie Francis – rightly reserved until last.

Tales of Beatrix Potter ⊙
1971, UK, 90 mins, colour
Dir: Reginald Mills
Rating: ★★★

Brilliantly costumed ballet film based on such Beatrix Potter characters as Mrs Tiggy-Winkle, Peter Rabbit and Jeremy Fisher. Fine dancing, imaginative choreography (recognisably by Sir Frederic Ashton) and some super animal masks. Fun for all the family, even if you dislike ballet: endearing and entertaining, this is one of the most successful films of its kind ever made.

Talk of a Million ○
1951, UK, 78 mins, b/w
Dir: John Paddy Carstairs
Stars: Jack Warner, Barbara Mullen
Rating: ★★

A typical British comedy film from the late Forties/early Fifties period, a time which produced such gems as *Whisky Galore*, *A Run for Your Money* and *Another Shore*, all finding fun from England's neighbours in the United Kingdom. This time in the Emerald Isle, with Jack Warner improbably cast as a carefree hobo who will do anything to avoid work. Besides Milo O'Shea as a signwriter, other familiar faces in the supporting cast belong to Alfie Bass, as a townsman, and Sidney James as an American lawyer. Both were to appear together three years later in another vintage comedy – *The Lavender Hill Mob*.

Talk of the Town, The ○ ⓥ
1942, US, 118 mins, b/w
Dir: George Stevens
Stars: Cary Grant, Jean Arthur, Ronald Colman
Rating: ★★★

It's unusual to find two stars of the magnitude of Cary Grant and Ronald Colman in the same film (especially with the delightful Jean Arthur sandwiched between them) and indeed the script only just manages to give all three leading players a fair crack of the whip in this enjoyable manic comedy leavened with a tablespoonful of social satire. Grant is a treat in the urbanely bewildered mood he also displayed in *Arsenic and Old Lace*, and his timing is as immaculate as ever.

Talk Radio ● ⓥ ★★
1988, US, 108 mins, colour
Dir: Oliver Stone
Stars: Eric Bogosian, Alec Baldwin, Ellen Greene, Leslie Hope
Rating: ★★

Barry Champlain is that new phenomenon – a 'shock jock'. A master of talk-insult on air whom most people hate but find compulsive. A user, never a giver, he feeds off people's fears, hatreds and prejudices. An expert on the callous putdown and the cutoff button alike, he lets callers vent their spleen and then flushes them down the radio waves and out of his system. 'Why do you hurt so many people?' asks an angry caller. The answer is that it gives him a charge and earns him a living. 'We reap what we sow,' Barry patly tells a listener, and so the ending of *Talk Radio* will surprise no-one (it's partly based on a real-life personality). Although the movie sometimes comes close to talking itself to death, moments to admire in the script (co-written by Bogosian) come thick and fast, making it often compulsive stuff. Just don't expect to like anyone in this story.

Tall Guy, The ● ⓥ
1989, UK, 94 mins, colour
Dir: Mel Smith
Stars: Jeff Goldblum, Emma Thompson, Rowan Atkinson
Rating: ★★

Although there aren't too many outright laughs in comedian Mel Smith's debut as film director, it's a jolly and lively romp with some highly original ideas. Directorially, it's a bit of a mess, sloppily edited and shapeless. But there are compensations. A musical monstrosity based on *The Elephant Man*, for example, is such a hoot that you'd like to see the whole show! The same goes for the musical follow-up, *Dirty Dick*, inspired by Shakespeare's *Richard III*. Hollywood's Jeff Goldblum is suitably laconic in the title role, as a 'bit' actor desperate for a break, Emma Thompson shows off her offbeat personality (and a lot else) as the uninhibited heroine and Rowan Atkinson is wonderfully obnoxious as the comedian for whom Goldblum has to stooge at the beginning of the story. The director himself makes a rather predictable guest appearance as a belching drunk.

Tall in the Saddle ○
1944, US, 87 mins, b/w
Dir: Edwin L Marin
Stars: John Wayne, Ella Raines
Rating: ★★

This hard-hitting but overly plotted oater was a labour of love for star John Wayne, who tried unsuccessfully to persuade John Ford to direct. It was written by Paul Fix, a personal friend of the Duke, and a frequent acting co-star (he also had a bit part here). Wayne starts out in the film as a virtual misogynist, but is tamed by frisky Ella Raines, who not only shoots at him but also flings a knife in his direction. There's sterling support from Wayne's regular sidekick, George 'Gabby' Hayes, as a stagecoach driver, complete with trademark croak. Not a film to compare with the lofty heights of Wayne's earlier *Stagecoach* and *The Long Voyage Home*, but it still made a very healthy $4 million profit.

Tall Man Riding ○
1955, US, 83 mins, colour
Dir: Lesley Selander
Stars: Randolph Scott, Dorothy Malone, Reggie Castle, John Dehner
Rating: ★★

The tall man is sharp shooting Randolph Scott involved in a vendetta with cattle baron Robert Barrat, whose daughter Dorothy Malone he has set his sights on. Sturdy cowboy fare, lifted slightly out of the rut by its theme of greed during the land-granting to the Montana settlers. Directed by Lesley Selander, whose countless credits include *Buck Jones* and *Hopalong Cassidy*.

Tall Men, The ○
1955, US, 122 mins, colour
Dir: Raoul Walsh
Stars: Clark Gable, Jane Russell, Robert Ryan, Cameron Mitchell
Rating: ★★★

Rugged enjoyable Western which furnished meaty roles for Clark Gable and Jane Russell when both had been going through a patch of bad films. Their initial meeting provides some rich dialogue: 'I want a man with great, big dreams,' pouts Jane (coming on like Mae West), 'who's goin' places an' has room for a passenger.' Replies Gable: 'Help me pull off this boot.' Good photography, tough action and a real feel for the wide open spaces of the west, for which veteran director Raoul Walsh must take most of the credit. Gable seems to enjoy himself a

lot, whether picking off Indians, bandying words with Jane, rushing barricades or, in one especially handsome sequence, stampeding a herd of cattle.

Tall T, The ○
1957, US, 78 mins, colour
Dir: Budd Boetticher
Stars: Randolph Scott, Maureen O'Sullivan, Richard Boone
Rating: ★★

A very tough, adult and bloody Western for its time, about a rancher and a newly married couple held captive by outlaws at a stagecoach relay station. The ending, a crescendo of violence, foreshadowed Italian Westerns to come. One of a series of Westerns made by Scott with director Budd Boetticher, now rated in many critical circles as among their best work. This one, though, is not as good as some people think it is.

Tall Target ○
1951, US, 78 mins, b/w
Dir: Anthony Mann
Stars: Dick Powell, Paula Raymond, Adolphe Menjou
Rating: ★★★

Hyper-tense suspense thriller set in 1861, and centring on an attempted presidential assassination on board a train. For director Anthony Mann, it bridged the gap between his tough thrillers of the Forties (such as *T-Men*) and his brilliant series of James Stewart Westerns in the Fifties. Here, Dick Powell is the star.

Tamahine ○
1963, UK, 95 mins, colour
Dir: Philip Leacock
Stars: Nancy Kwan, John Fraser, Dennis Price
Rating: ★★

Fast-pace frolic, rather similar in style to the Boulting Brothers' *A French Mistress* a couple of years earlier, featuring Nancy Kwan as the nut-brown Polynesian maiden who not only disrupts life at a boy's public school, but beats them out of sight at the school sports. Ms Kwan bounds around with suitable abandon, and smiles and undresses attractively; while a small crowd of unbelievably 18-year-old sixth-formers, led by John Fraser and James Fox, slaver suitably in return.

Tamarind Seed, The ○
1974, UK, 125 mins, colour
Dir: Blake Edwards
Stars: Julie Andrews, Omar Sharif, Anthony Quayle, Daniel O'Herlihy, Sylvia Syms, Oscar Homolka
Rating: ★★

There's an interesting idea in this romantic drama which would have been more effective if someone like Alfred Hitchcock could have got to work on it. Omar Sharif turns on the famous charm to some effect as the Russian diplomat who falls in love with cool Julie Andrews, playing a girl who can somehow afford a Dior wardrobe on a Home Office salary. She provides an additional motive for him to defect when his liberal views make him a target for KGB suspicions. All very promising, though the dialogue makes the stars labour mightily to make anything of the situations. Anthony Quayle, Daniel O'Herlihy, Oscar Homolka and Bryan Marshall are among the reliable players giving them stalwart support. There are one or two moments of high suspense, especially towards the end, but not enough to keep tedium at bay throughout.

Taming of the Shrew, The ○ ⓥ
1967, US/Italy, 126 mins, colour
Dir: Franco Zeffirelli
Stars: Elizabeth Taylor, Richard Burton, Michael York, Cyril Cusack, Michael Hordern
Rating: ★★

This really spectacular version of Shakespeare's comedy owed much of its impact to Franco Zeffirelli's fizzing direction and the dazzling colour camerawork of Oswald Morris. Elizabeth Taylor's shrew and Richard Burton's tamer are at their best in the extraordinarily funny wedding scene.

Tanganyika ○
1954, US, 81 mins, colour
Dir: Andre De Toth
Stars: Van Heflin, Ruth Roman, Howard Duff, Jeff Morrow
Rating: ★★

One of the colourful all action features that Universal-International trotted out with such regularity and polish in the Fifties, this jungle thriller features Van Heflin as a white hunter battling against a mercenary army in the forests of British East Africa. Relentlessly routine.

Tango & Cash ● ⓥ
1989, US, 106 mins, colour
Dir: Andrei Konchalovsky
Stars: Sylvester Stallone, Kurt Russell, Jack Palance, Teri Hatcher
Rating: ★

Times were when Konchalovsky made acclaimed movies in his native Russia. His Hollywood career showed a certain integrity with *Maria's Lovers* and *Runaway Train*, but then he slipped into pulp fiction, and heaven knows what attracted him to this sloppily-scripted variation on Sixties' superspy movies like *Our Man Flint*. There are two heroes for the price of one. Stallone (the best thing in the film) is the pinstriped, market-playing Tango. Kurt Russell is the T-shirted Cash. Both are super-cops, rapidly getting under the skin of super drugs baron Palance who, with the help of henchman Brion James (with a misbegotten 'British' accent that will afford considerable amusement in the UK), railroads our heroes most unconvincingly into prison, from where they escape and blast the bad guys out of existence. End of story. Despite quite imaginative sets and burst of action – the prison scenes are particularly vividly staged – this is a fitfully boring film with perished elastic in its would-be whiplash dialogue.

Tank Force ○
(aka: No Time To Die!)
1958, UK, 102 mins, colour
Dir: Terence Young
Stars: Victor Mature, Leo Genn, Anthony Newley, Luciana Paluzzi
Rating: ★

'C'mon, let's hit the road,' says Victor Mature at one stage in this exciting, if implausible, *Boy's Own*-style World War Two adventure. But you really can't blame Sergeant Mature for his idiomatic choice of command to his fellow escapees from an Italian prison camp in the Libyan desert. Because he is playing that almost inevitable character in British movies of the Fifties, the token Yank. Director Terence Young (who was to put 007 through his paces in the first bond movie *Dr No*) set up his production headquarters in Tripoli for *Tank Force* and his cast and crew of 88 were filming in the Libyan desert for eight weeks. The film was released in Britain as *No Time To Die!* By the time the plentiful action and incident get under way, there's not much time to relax either.

Tap ◑
1988, US, 110 mins, colour
Dir: Nick Castle
Stars: Gregory Hines, Suzzanne Douglas, Sammy Davis Jr
Rating: ★★

You've got to hand it to Gregory Hines for single-handedly forwarding the cause of dancing – and tap, in particular – in the face of indifference from the Hollywood studios and public alike. Undeterred by the lack of success of his earlier *White Nights* and *The Cotton Club*, he puts his heart and soul into this rich blend mixing dance and a tale of urban struggle. The story is certainly no great shakes but the dancing is sensational (Hines is credited for 'improvography'). This ranges from a 'challenge' contest between tap greats Sandman Sims, Bunny Briggs, Jimmy Slyde, Steve Condos, Pat Rico, Arthur Duncan and Harold Nicholas to Hines' own 'Tap-Tronics' finale, in which his taps are connected with synthesizers to make rhythmic and melodic music. The director and screenwriter is Nick Castle, whose father choreographed Fred Astaire and Gene Kelly in their heyday.

Taps ○ ⓥ
1981, US, 126 mins, colour
Dir: Harold Becker
Stars: George C Scott, Timothy Hutton, Sean Penn, Tom Cruise
Rating: ★★

Tom Cruise was originally signed to just a small cameo role as one of the recruits at a military academy taken over by its students in this gripping siege drama. But director Harold Becker spotted his potential and on the second day of filming elevated him to play the third lead, as the gung-ho right-hand lieutenant of Timothy Hutton's maverick gun-toting lead recruit. Fellow Brat Pack star Sean Penn adds his menacing presence, but a central fault lies in the fact that despite a military crew cut and serious swagger, Hutton is just too nice to be believable as the ruthless renegade who leads the students in armed revolt at plans to close their academy and sell off the land for land development. George C Scott scores in a brief cameo as a slightly deranged academy principal, who acts as Hutton's role model.

Tarantula! ○
1955, US, 77 mins, b/w
Dir: Jack Arnold

Stars: John Agar, Mara Corday, Leo G Carroll, Nestor Paiva
Rating: ★★★★

A pulsating thriller and technically superb horror film, which is probably the best 'giant creature' film since *King Kong*. The director is Jack Arnold, who made a whole parcel of quality chillers in the mid-Fifties including *The Incredible Shrinking Man*. This one is about a giant spider that escapes from a laboratory in Arizona. Watch out for Clint Eastwood as the leader of the bomber pilots who try to put paid to the hairy horror.

Taras Bulba ○
1962, US, 124 mins, colour
Dir: J Lee Thompson
Stars: Tony Curtis, Yul Brynner
Rating: ★★

Tony Curtis among the Cossacks in J Lee Thompson's spectacular epic set in the 16th century. He's every inch the all-American boy, leaving the film to be entirely stolen by Yul Brynner's dynamic account of the title character. The action is exciting and occasionally even stylish. But scenes of Cossack home life seem phony and there's too much singing and dancing hereabouts to pad out the running time. Only in its scenes of plague in a besieged city and in the battle scenes towards the end does the film come to life and approach the achievement of its own ambitions. Time and again, though, Curtis' indifferent showing as Brynner's son drags it down.

Target ○ Ⓥ
1985, US, 118 mins, colour
Dir: Arthur Penn
Stars: Gene Hackman, Matt Dillon, Gayle Hunnicutt
Rating: ★★

Surprise! Surprise! – for young Chris (Matt Dillon) when his mother is kidnapped in Paris. It turns out that years ago Daddy (Gene Hackman) was a CIA agent. Now someone is out to settle an old score. Actually, it's only the father-and-son relationship – as they dodge bullets, glamorous spies and double-agents in their hunt for Mama (Gayle Hunnicutt) that sets this film above any run-of-the-mill spy thriller of the Sixties. Even here, though, it doesn't dig deep enough, a shame as the theme is especially well handled in Hackman's thoughtful performance. Disappointing to find a director of Arthur Penn's standing associated with a film that manages its

routine chases, shoot-outs and explosions well enough, but is otherwise strictly for fans of the stars.

Targets ○
1967, US, 90 mins, colour
Dir: Peter Bogdanovich
Stars: Boris Karloff, Tim O'Kelly, Nancy Hsueh
Rating: ★★★

A very unsettling film which not only put Peter Bogdanovich right on the map as a director but gave ageing horror star Boris Karloff a welcome meaty role as – an ageing horror star. But its concern over American gun laws, voiced through the story of a sniper who has already killed his own family, went largely unheeded. Ingeniously constructed, hard-hitting stuff.

Tarka the Otter ○ Ⓥ
1978, UK, 90 mins, colour
Dir: David Cobham
Stars: Peter Bennett, Edward Underdown
Rating: ★★★

Enormous care has been taken to keep this film version faithful to spirit of Henry Williamson's fine novel. The visuals are as evocative as they are brilliant. The wild-life photography is phenomenal. The film is full of memorable images – none more so than the owl's feather drifting down on to the nose of the mother otter in the old oak they share at the start of the film. Wildlife documentary-maker David Cobham handles the material with skill and respect. Filmed in Devon.

Tartu
See: The Adventures of Tartu

Tarzan and the Amazons ○
1945, US, 75 mins, b/w
Dir: Kurt Neumann
Stars: Johnny Weissmuller, Brenda Joyce
Rating: ★★

One of Tarzan's most desperate adventures, with a sturdy supporting cast and a nail-biting climax in the best traditions of Saturday morning serials. The story involves a lost tribe of woman warriors.

Tarzan and the Great River ○
1967, US, 88 mins, colour
Dir: Robert Day
Stars: Mike Henry
Rating: ★★

Tarzan's up to his loincloth in trouble again, this time in South America. Manuel Padilla, who played Jai in the subsequent TV series, pops up here as a character called Pepe. Bright colour photography by Irving Lipman does an attractive job with a mass of lush tropical vegetation.

Tarzan and the Huntress ○
1947, US, 70 mins, b/w
Dir: Kurt Neumann
Stars: Johnny Weissmuller, Brenda Joyce
Rating: ★★

Tarzan becomes involved with a lady trapper, and a group of villainous hunters out to assassinate the heir to a native kingdom. Glamorous singing star Patricia Morison slums it a bit here as the huntress.

Tarzan and the Jungle Boy ○
1966, US, 90 mins, colour
Dir: Robert Day
Stars: Mike Henry, Alizia Gur, Rafer Johnson
Rating: ★★

This brightly-made American-Swiss co-production sees Mike Henry playing Tarzan for the third and last time. Directed by Robert Day, who had made several other entries in the series, the adventure makes the most of its lush tropical locations.

Tarzan and the Leopard Woman ○
1946, US, 70 mins, b/w
Dir: Kurt Neumann
Stars: Johnny Weissmuller, Acquanetta
Rating: ★

Jungle adventure thriller, with Weissmuller once again in the loincloth, and Burmese-born Acquanetta – in the Forties the poor man's Dorothy Lamour – as the villainess.

Tarzan and the Lost Safari ○
1957, US, 84 mins, colour
Dir: Bruce Humberstone
Stars: Gordon Scott, Robert Beatty, Betta St John
Rating: ★★

The second of Scott's five films as Tarzan (and the first in colour) as our hero tries to guide the survivors of an air crash through dangerous jungle country. Robert Beatty enjoys himself enormously as a villainous white hunter called Tusker Hawkins. Remarked one contemporary critic: 'Screaming heroines may come and dastardly hunters may go, but Tarzan,

T

Cheta and that murderous jungle tribe with the funny head-gear go on for ever.'

Tarzan and the Mermaids ⊙
1947, US, 70 mins, b/w
Dir: Robert Florey
Stars: Johnny Weissmuller, Brenda Joyce
Rating: ★★

Johnny Weissmuller's last film as Tarzan after a jungle reign of 17 years. That sinister British actor George Zucco takes a break from horror films to provide suave villainy.

Tarzan and the She-Devil ⊙
1953, US, 76 mins, b/w
Dir: Kurt Neumann
Stars: Lex Barker, Joyce MacKenzie, Monique Van Vooren, Tom Conway
Rating: ★★

Jungle adventure, with famous fictional detectives Raymond (*Ironside*) Burr and Tom (*The Falcon*) Conway supporting Lex Barker in his last outing as Tarzan.

Tarzan and the Slave Girl ⊙
1950, US, 71 mins, b/w
Dir: Lee Sholem
Stars: Lex Barker
Rating: ★★

A distinguished supporting cast in this jungle adventure includes Robert Alda, who portrayed Gershwin in *Rhapsody in Blue*; Hurd Hatfield, who was Gray in *The Picture of Dorian Gray*; French actress Denise Darcel; and Arthur Shields, brother of screen actor Barry Fitzgerald. Brenda Joyce had retired from the role of Jane after five films, and pretty Vanessa Brown took over. The story is about a mysterious band of kidnappers and Lex Barker it is who dons the loincloth for this tolerable entry in the series.

Tarzan and the Trappers ○
1957, US, 70 mins, b/w
Dir: Charles Haas
Stars: Gordon Scott, Eve Brent
Rating: ★

A film with a fascinating history. After Scott's first film as Tarzan, producer Sol Lesser decided to sell half-hour Tarzan adventures to television. *Tarzan and the Trappers* was made, as an introduction to the proposed series, in three half-hour segments. But, in the same year, came the crash of Lesser's studio, RKO, and the deal was never completed. The three segments were edited into this (poor) feature film.

Tarzan and the Valley of Gold ⊙
1966, US, 87 mins, colour
Dir: Robert Day
Stars: Mike Henry, Nancy Kovack
Rating: ★★★

There are some good South American scenes, lushly captured by Irving Lipman, in this jungle adventure taking Tarzan to a lost Aztec valley. Thanks to Clair Huffaker's inventive, sophisticated ('One of your aircraft is missing,' Tarzan informs the villain on a stolen walkie-talkie, having blown up one of his helicopters) and enjoyable screenplay, along with Robert Day's crisp, no-nonsense direction, this proves to be one of the best of the latter-day Tarzan films. Mike Henry is a more than usually mobile Tarzan, making good use of his witty, jet-age dialogue, and he is well matched with the gorgeous Nancy Kovack – excellent as the villain's discarded mistress. (She was, during her career, the tallest actress in the movies, at exactly six feet.) He also has a formidable adversary in the tree-like Don Megowan who, appropriately, plays a character called Mr Train. He's the henchman of gold-hungry Vinaro – a rich study in sub-*Goldfinger* villainy from David Opatoshu.

Tarzan Escapes! ⊙
1936, US, 95 mins, b/w
Dir: Richard Thorpe
Stars: Johnny Weissmuller, Maureen O'Sullivan
Rating: ★★★

Finally released three years after the previous Tarzan film, this adventure was greatly re-shot, after being considered too violent, frightening and daring for younger audiences. Maureen O'Sullivan's costume as Jane was considerably enlarged and many of the action scenes were cut, re-edited or just re-done. The only 'shocking' scene left in is the one in which tribesmen's victims are tied to bent trees, which are then released, hurling the ripped-up unfortunates to all parts of the jungle. The results, though, are pretty good considering the film's teething problems.

Tarzan Finds a Son! ⊙
1939, US, 90 mins, b/w
Dir: Richard Thorpe
Stars: Johnny Weissmuller, Maureen O'Sullivan
Rating: ★★★

The fourth of former Olympic swimming gold-medallist Johnny Weissmuller's six Tarzan adventures with Maureen O'Sullivan as his mate, Jane, is by far the most logical of the bunch. The African location footage was among the best used in a Hollywood picture at that time, and underwater footage – shot in Florida – of Tarzan, his new-found orphan son and a baby elephant, adds to the fun. It fairly zips along, thanks to the energetic directing of Richard Thorpe, who after 33 years became the longest-serving director in the history of MGM (he was also responsible for *Ivanhoe*) earning a reputation as the studio's 'one take' specialist.

Tarzan Goes to India ⊙
1962, US, 86 mins, colour
Dir: John Guillermin
Stars: Jock Mahoney, Mark Dana, Leo Gordon
Rating: ★★

Former Western star Jock Mahoney – he had the title role in the television series *The Range Rider* – donned the loincloth for the first time in this modern-day Tarzan adventure, as the lord of the jungle is jetted to the forests of Mysore to help save a giant herd of elephants from extinction. Pretty Eastman Colour photography, and brisk direction from John Guillermin.

Tarzan's Desert Mystery ⊙
1943, US, 70 mins, b/w
Dir: William Thiele
Stars: Johnny Weissmuller, Nancy Kelly
Rating: ★★

One of Johnny Weissmuller's less convincing entries. He has to deal sternly with a group of Nazis stirring up trouble in the Sahara, as well as confronting sundry dinosaurs and a giant spider.

Tarzan's Fight for Life ⊙
1958, US, 85 mins, colour
Dir: Bruce Humberstone
Stars: Gordon Scott, Eve Brent
Rating: ★★

With this film, the Tarzan series, which had just burst into colour, featured Jane, Tarzan's mate, for the last time to date, Eve Brent taking over from Joyce MacKenzie. And Tarzan has to fight to save her from a fate worse than death . . . There's also a wicked-looking snake fight and some authentic African wildlife. This one may be a bit scary for very young children.

Tarzan's Greatest Adventure ○
1959, US, 90 mins, colour
Dir: John Guillermin
Stars: Gordon Scott, Anthony Quayle
Rating: ★★★

One of the best Tarzan films, with a spare, literate script by Berne Giler and director John Guillermin, and good performances in the bad-guy department from 29-year-old Sean Connery, as a villainous Irishman, and Anthony Quayle, as Tarzan's principal adversary. The girls are worth seeing, too. America's Sara Shane is the girl who once had a picture of herself printed in two halves (waist-up and waist-down) in successive issues of a magazine, as a (very successful) publicity stunt; Italy's Scilla Gabel is a poor man's Sophia Loren.

Tarzan's Hidden Jungle ○
1955, US, 73 mins, b/w
Dir: Harold Schuster
Stars: Gordon Scott, Jack Elam, Vera Miles, Peter Van Eyck
Rating: ★★

This was ex-lifeguard Gordon Scott's debut in the role of the jungle hero, and he showed due gratitude to the studio for giving him Vera Miles as his leading lady – by marrying her.

Tarzan's Magic Fountain ⊙
1949, US, 70 mins, b/w
Dir: Lee Sholem
Stars: Lex Barker, Brenda Joyce, Albert Dekker, Evelyn Ankers
Rating: ★★

Evelyn Ankers, heroine of countless Forties' horror films, takes a rest from creepie-crawlies as an aviatrix who finds the secret of eternal youth from the waters of a natural fountain deep in the jungle. It was Lex Barker's first appearance as Tarzan and Brenda Joyce's last as Jane. There's a bit more story to this adventure, although, in spite of a good cast (Albert Dekker, Charles Drake, Henry Brandon, Alan Napier), it soon moves from the sublime to the ridiculous.

Tarzan's Peril ⊙
1951, US, 75 mins, b/w
Dir: Byron Haskin

Stars: Lex Barker, Virginia Huston, George Macready, Dorothy Dandridge
Rating: ★★★

This jungle thriller, the best of Lex Barker's five films as the eponymous lord of the jungle, was known in Britain as *Tarzan and the Jungle Queen*. A pre-*Carmen Jones* Dorothy Dandridge is the queen, and George Macready makes a really bad hat of the villain, running guns galore and getting the surly Yorango tribe to attack the peace-loving Ashubas, an enterprise that's obviously doomed to failure once Tarzan gets wind of it. Stirring entertainment for undemanding kids.

Tarzan's Revenge ○
1938, US, 70 mins, b/w
Dir: D Ross Lederman
Stars: Glenn Morris, Eleanor Holm
Rating: ★

This decidedly second-rate Tarzan adventure stars Glenn Morris, one of a number of pretenders to Johnny Weissmuller's jungle crown in the Thirties. Morris, an Olympic decathlon champion, looked the part, but his acting abilities were limited. Having said that, he's in good company here. This film includes a rare appearance by bitchy Hollywood columnist and bad actress Hedda Hopper. Her move from acting to gossip writing may not have been much fun for everyone in Tinseltown, but for the rest of us it was a blessed relief.

Tarzan's Savage Fury ⊙
1952, US, 80 mins, b/w
Dir: Cyril Endfield
Stars: Lex Barker, Dorothy Hart, Patric Knowles, Charles Korvin
Rating: ★

There's nothing very savage or furious about this dim and dull addition to the jungle series, which heralds the first appearance of a jungle boy (Tommy Carlton) since Johnny Sheffield outgrew the role of Tarzan's son. Directed by, of all people, Cyril (Cy) Endfield, who later made some very respectable action films in Britain, including *Hell Drivers* and *Zulu*.

Tarzan's Secret Treasure ⊙
1941, US, 80 mins, b/w
Dir: Richard Thorpe
Stars: Johnny Weissmuller, Maureen O'Sullivan
Rating: ★★★

Former Olympic swimmer Johnny Weissmuller's fifth vine-swinging adventure in a loin cloth and Maureen O'Sullivan's fourth, co-starring as his mate, Jane. This one is efficient rather than exceptional as Tarzan repels yet another group of gun-toting explorers intent on shattering the peace of the jungle.

Tarzan's Three Challenges ○
1963, US, 90 mins, colour
Dir: Robert Day
Stars: Jock Mahoney, Woody Strode, Woody Strode
Rating: ★★

Spirited Tarzan adventure, shot in colour on location in India. The exciting climax has Jock Mahoney and Woody Strode battling on a net over a pit of burning coals. Children will be thrilled by the action in this one.

Tarzan the Ape Man ⊙
1932, US, 95 mins, b/w
Dir: W S Van Dyke
Stars: Johnny Weissmuller, Maureen O'Sullivan
Rating: ★★★

The 'Garbo speaks!' headline could have been followed by 'Tarzan talks!' when this first sound Tarzan film hit the screens. Ex-Olympic swimmer Johnny Weissmuller, longer-haired and slimmer than in later efforts, became the definitive screen ape man in this, the first and arguably the best of his jungle adventures. This pre-Hays Office picture also had Weissmuller and Maureen O'Sullivan (as Jane) more scantily-clad than in subsequent outings. Despite production values that make the film look almost as primitive as its central character, this 1932 film is still an exciting and adventurous yarn. Even the 'Me Tarzan, you Jane' line doesn't sound bad when heard in context! Fresh, fast fun, and very much in the spirit (if not the letter) of the original Edgar Rice Burroughs books.

Tarzan the Ape Man ○
1959, US, 82 mins, colour
Dir: Joseph Newman
Stars: Denny Miller, Joanna Barnes
Rating: ★★

This colourful Tarzan jungle remake gave muscular blond basketball star Denny Miller his finest hour as an actor. The 12th screen incarnation of the ape man, Miller went on to play small bit parts in films as diverse as *The Vikings* and *The Party*. His Jane, who is

T

attacked by cannibals, angry elephants, a rhinoceros and a tarantula, is played by Californian blond Joanna Barnes, who as well as acting, wrote several steamy novels based on life in Hollywood. The film is a rehash of every previous Tarzan effort, with predictable incidents, colour tinting of stock black and white footage, and even the placing of fake large ears on the smaller ears of performing Asiatic elephants.

Tarzan, the Ape Man ● ⓥ
1981, US, 112 mins, colour
Dir: John Derek
Stars: Bo Derek, Richard Harris
Rating: ★

Over the years many cinematic liberties have been taken with Edgar Rice Burroughs' jungle hero, but none were more flagrant than this shoddy excuse to get Bo Derek frolicking naked at every opportunity. In fact Burroughs' estate filed a lawsuit against John Derek, Bo's mentor, husband and director of this dreadful film. The ape man himself is relegated to third billing behind the nubile Bo and Richard Harris, who rises to the occasion here and produces a ham performance stunning in both its vigour and ineptitude. Bo, for her part, also managed a unique distinction. Admittedly very attractive, she's also bland and boring. To walk around naked and yet be uninteresting is a curious achievement, but one Bo achieves with charmlessness to spare.

Tarzan the Magnificent ⊙
1960, US, 88 mins, colour
Dir: Robert Day
Stars: Gordon Scott
Rating: ★★★

The last of Scott's five films as Tarzan. Playing the villain: Jock Mahoney, the man who took over Scott's part!

Tarzan Triumphs ⊙
1943, US, 78 mins, b/w
Dir: William Thiele
Stars: Johnny Weissmuller
Rating: ★★

A wartime Tarzan adventure, with Weissmuller tangling with Nazi paratroopers. No Jane this time, but pretty Frances Gifford does very nicely as Zandra.

Task Force ○
1949, US, 116 mins, colour & b/w
Dir: Delmer Daves

Stars: Gary Cooper, Jane Wyatt, Wayne Morris, Walter Brennan
Rating: ★★

A typically splashy Warner biopic from the Forties, made in black and white, but with some Technicolor newsreel footage added in to spice up the impact. Gary Cooper gives his usual solid and sincere performance, even if he has difficulty in looking in his late twenties when the story begins. Jane Wyatt is delightful (and acts well too) as the widow he eventually marries. Very well produced by Jerry Wald, the film looks terrific and went down like a bomb with the public.

Taste of Fear ◐
1961, UK, 81 mins, b/w
Dir: Seth Holt
Stars: Susan Strasberg, Ronald Lewis, Ann Todd, Christopher Lee
Rating: ★★★

A lonely house with creaking shutters. Flickering candles. A piano playing in an empty room – apparently of its own accord. A disappearing corpse. A girl scared to the point of hysteria. The archetypal formula for a Hammer nightmare thriller and this is one of the best, full of red herrings and unexpected twists. Definitely not for the nervous, it's like a masquerade where the players only take off their masks at the end.

Taste of Honey, A ◐ ⓥ
1961, UK, 100 mins, b/w
Dir: Tony Richardson
Stars: Rita Tushingham, Dora Bryan, Robert Stephens
Rating: ★★★

Fashioned from Shelagh Delaney's successful play, this poignant film about an unloved, ugly duckling teenage girl brought Rita Tushingham to stardom, and marked Dora Bryan's breakaway from comic character roles. She's first-rate, as the heartless, tart-ish mother heedlessly setting her daughter up for a lifetime of misery. Murray Melvin gives his finest screen performance as the homosexual who proves to be the girl's only real friend.

Taste the Blood of Dracula ● ⓥ
1969, UK, 95 mins, colour
Dir: Peter Sasdy
Stars: Christopher Lee, Geoffrey Keen, Gwen Watford, Linda Hayden
Rating: ★★

In this addition to Hammer Films' celebrated *Dracula* cycle, the action takes place in England instead of Europe. The reactivating process for the dreaded vampire is a quantity of red powder contained in a phial. Innocent enough looking in itself, but once mixed with human blood – up pops the dreaded Drac. The film differs from its predecessors in that Dracula himself, here in a vengeful frame of mind, remains substantially an onlooker while others accomplish the death and destruction. Director Peter Sasdy stages some effective shock moments, particularly in scenes shot inside a church.

Tatie Danielle ◐ ⓥ
1990, France, 112 mins, colour
Dir: Etienne Chatiliez
Stars: Tsilla Chelton, Catherine Jacob, Eric Prat, Isabelle Nanty
Rating: ★★★

Tatie Danielle is a horrible old woman who makes life hell for those she despises and who pussy-foot to her every demand – most notably her great-nephew and his well-meaning wife. Only when her family goes on holiday and a strong-willed teenager is assigned to care for her does Tatie Danielle meet her match. Blackly funny, if not for all tastes, this French film is a dire warning to all those planning to bring granny home to live. Stage star Tsilla Chelton is splendidly appalling and malevolent in the title role.

Taxi Driver ● ⓥ
1976, US, 110 mins, colour
Dir: Martin Scorsese
Stars: Robert De Niro, Cybill Shepherd, Jodie Foster, Harvey Keitel
Rating: ★★★★

This brilliant film is enough to put you off New York for life. This is strong, strong meat and no mistake, its jet-black theme underlined by Bernard Herrmann's tremendous music. The film is both a damning indictment of the conditions that so easily beget violence in so many ways and from so many different directions, and a tremendous conjuring up of the nighttime atmosphere of downtown New York. All the night scenes are powerful, sombre, affecting stuff. There are one or two passages that are near-dull, or don't fit the general tenor, but the ending is brilliant, restoring the film to the black plane to which it so often soars. If there are any reservations with the acting, they have to rest with the central performance of Robert De Niro, as the psychotic taxi driver whose environment and insomnia combine to drive him berserk. It is a splendid performance on the surface, but there doesn't seem to be too much going on behind the eyes. Jodie Foster is quite amazing as a 12-year-old prostitute, and just saunters away with the film.

Taza, Son of Cochise ○
1954, US, 75 mins, colour
Dir: Douglas Sirk
Stars: Rock Hudson, Barbara Rush
Rating: ★★

The last of Jeff Chandler's three appearances as the Apache chief Cochise. He's briefly glimpsed as a dying man at the beginning of this action saga, handing over the reins of power to Rock Hudson. The director is Douglas Sirk, later to make the most successful of Hudson's Fifties' films, including *Magnificent Obsession* and *Written on the Wind*.

Tchin Tchin
See: A Fine Romance

Teachers ●
1984, US, 106 mins, colour
Dir: Arthur Hiller
Stars: Nick Nolte, JoBeth Williams, Judd Hirsch, Ralph Macchio
Rating: ★

Low grades for this story of a horrendous American ghetto school – the old story of one honest man bucking the whole rotten system. The execution of it here is often embarrassing, especially in the screenplay. But its single, emotional appeal almost works towards the end.

Teacher's Pet ○
1958, US, 120 mins, b/w
Dir: George Seaton
Stars: Clark Gable, Doris Day, Gig Young
Rating: ★★★

A slickly funny comedy that enables both Clark Gable and Doris Day to show a sure sense of tongue-in-cheek humour. Gig Young is a bonus as the rival for Ms Day's hand, whom Gable continually outwits. Funniest scene: when the two men try to slip each other knock-out drops at a nightclub. Young and the script (by Fay and Michael Kanin) were both nominated for Academy Awards.

Tea for Two ○
1950, US, 97 mins, colour
Dir: David Butler
Stars: Doris Day, Gordon MacRae, Gene Nelson, Eve Arden
Rating: ★★★

More than any other, this musical set Doris Day up for her run of success at Warners in the Fifties. It's a bright, lively and tuneful version of *No, No, Nanette* (first filmed with Anna Neagle in 1940) in which Doris, as the girl who has to say 'No' to everything for 24 hours, danced on screen for the first time. She also duetted so well with Gordon MacRae on the title number that they made two further films together. Other songs include 'Crazy Rhythm', 'I Only Have Eyes for You' and 'I Want to Be Happy'.

Tears for Simon
See: Lost

Teenage Bad Girl
See: My Teenage Daughter

Teenage Mutant Ninja Turtles ○ ⓥ
1990, US, 93 mins, colour
Dir: Steve Barron
Stars: Judith Hoag, Elias Koteas, Michael Turney, Raymond Serra, James Saito, Jay Patterson
Rating: ★★

Darkly photographed fantasy adventure that created four new high-kicking heroes and blitzed box offices everywhere. What's afoot? The Foot Clan, that's what, terrorising the New York streets (as if they weren't terrorised enough) and incurring the wrath of the sewer-dwelling, pizza-eating, giant-sized (mutated by radioactive waste) turtles, who swing into action, demolishing scores of Oriental extras with a degree of violence that alarmed guardians of the children at whom the film is aimed. The head-banded amphibians also prove better actors than most of the human cast, although that's not too difficult. Their constant stream of in-lingo wisecracks amuses or annoys according to taste in this hardly awesome, but passably bodacious slice of tongue-in-cheek, half-shelled action.

Teenage Mutant Ninja Turtles II: The Secret of the Ooze ○ ⓥ
1991, US, 87 mins, colour
Dir: Michael Pressman

Stars: Paige Turco, David Warner, Ernie Reyes Jr
Rating: ★

For turtle fans only is this rather tired first sequel to the hit original, which runs like a Three Stooges feature with violent action scenes added on. Not many people will be frightened by the monster-villains and you keep expecting the turtles to take their heads off and show that they're really human after all. David Warner comes on as the mad scientist in charge of the dreaded Ooze. Unfortunately, he makes off with it again at the end, probably paving the way for a future Oozy farrago with the fearsome four, who here have lost whatever personality they might once have possessed. *Turtles I* and *III*, it must be said, are both a little better than this.

Teenage Mutant Ninja Turtles III ○ ⓥ
1992, US, 92 mins, colour
Dir: Stuart Gillard
Stars: Paige Turco, Stuart Wilson, Elias Koteas, Sab Shimono, Vivian Wu
Rating: ★★

The combative amphibians travel back in time to 1603 Japan where, not surprisingly, they are regarded as demons. They intervene in a battle between feudal lords and village warriors who all covet the very magic sceptre that has whisked the Turtles and their reporter friend April (still Paige Turco, now looking too mature for the part) nearly 400 years back in time. Their efforts to save the day at least score more success than teaching the 17th-century Orientals to make pizza. Stuart Wilson's villain has style and swagger in the manner of Captain Hook (motto: 'Places to go, people to kill'). But the adventure never really takes off in a way that might excite any but the youngest children. Other members of the cast overact, while Oriental extras wander into background shots, seemingly with no idea what to do. There are isolated moments of satirical fun, though, as when Samurai warriors, whisked forward in exchange to New York, watch ice hockey on TV. Invited to have the kind of game they've just seen, they simply start to fight each other.

Teen Wolf ○ ⓥ
1985, US, 90 mins, colour
Dir: Rod Daniel
Stars: Michael J Fox, James Hampton, Susan Ursitti
Rating: ★★★

T

It had been a decade or so since we'd had a werewolf comedy, when this simple but effective vehicle for the appropriately named Michael J Fox arrived to surprise us pleasantly as a follow-up (actually shot earlier) to his smash-hit *Back To The Future*. He's almost the whole show in this romp as a college kid who starts growling when annoyed, gets an itchy feeling round the neck and arms and hears high pitched whistles no-one else can. He goes for advice to his basketball coach (Fox playing basketball? Never mind, somehow they make it work). The coach, however, has only three rules to follow: never miss 12 hours' sleep, never play cards with a man whose first name is a state, and never go near a woman with a dagger tattoo. Werewolves? No problem. The tail, sorry tale, climaxes with a very well choreographed basketball game as the ghoul-in-school fights to go straight and avoid a lifetime of biting the mailman and dodging silver bullets.

Teen Wolf Too ⊙ ⓥ
1987, US, 93 mins, colour
Dir: Christopher Leitch
Stars: Jason Bateman, Kim Darby, John Astin, Paul Sand, Kathleen Freeman
Rating: ★

Nice title, shame about the film. Sequels to comedy successes are always a problem, but this one gives itself unnecessary feet of lead by substituting the charmless Jason Bateman for the Michael J Fox of the original. Otherwise the elements are much as before, with special effects on the meagre side, emphasis shifted to college stereotype and the 'wolf's' sport changed from basketball to boxing. John Astin overdoes it (as usual) as the dean, Kim Darby is wasted (again) as the wolf's biology teacher, and veteran Kathleen Freeman turns in a nice little job as an unrelenting admissions clerk. Even with all the film's familiarity, the final boxing match carries some excitement. Sure makes the original look good though: any future teen wolves had better learn some new tricks.

Telefon ◑ ⓥ
1977, US, 103 mins, colour
Dir: Don Siegel
Stars: Charles Bronson, Lee Remick, Tyne Daly, Donald Pleasence, Patrick Magee
Rating: ★★

Something rather out of the ordinary run of spy thrillers, this film also covers a lot of territory so far as locations are concerned. The story moves with pace from Russia (actually shot in Finland) to a wide variety of places in the US. Charles Bronson stars as a KGB agent named Borzov assigned to stop the nefarious activities in America of a hard-line Stalinist agent (played by Donald Pleasence) who has practical – and very sinister – plans of his own to reinstigate the Cold War. The star is partnered by attractive Lee Remick, another double agent; Patrick Magee and Alan Badel are effective as high officials in the Russian secret police; and the dynamic Tyne Daly who made such an impression in one of the Clint Eastwood *Dirty Harry* movies – *The Enforcer* – almost steals the show as a CIA computer analyst.

Tempest ○
1959, Italy, 123 mins, colour
Dir: Alberto Lattnada
Stars: Van Heflin, Silvana Mangano, Viveca Lindfors
Rating: ★★

Van Heflin as the Russian rebel Pugachev, taking on Catherine the Great (Viveca Lindfors). Based on stories by Pushkin, this impressively-mounted epic has some of the biggest battle scenes ever filmed. It also has Agnes Moorehead, in superb form as a pipe-smoking wife of the Steppes.

10 ◑ ⓥ
1979, US, 122 mins, colour
Dir: Blake Edwards
Stars: Dudley Moore, Julie Andrews, Bo Derek
Rating: ★

Julie Andrews in an 'X' certificate film? It certainly seemed a surprise at the time, but then poor Julie is hardly ever in this wish fulfilment sex frolic which made hot box-office properties of her co-stars, Dudley Moore and Bo Derek. This is the kind of thing director Blake Edwards might have done, a little less outspokenly, perhaps, with his favourite star Peter Sellers some years before. But here it's cuddly Dudley as the fortyish bachelor who finds his perfect girl (the '10' of the title) and follows her everywhere only to discover in the end that looks can be all too deceptive. Edwards finds a few funny situations in all this, mostly in his familiar Clouseau vein, such as the doddery old maidservant who tries to serve drinks to a chimney in a very amusing sequence.

Ten Commandments, The ○
1956, US, 219 mins, colour
Dir: Cecil B DeMille
Stars: Charlton Heston, Yul Brynner, Anne Baxter, Yvonne De Carlo, Edward G Robinson, John Derek
Rating: ★★★

Cecil B DeMille's last film (he made his first in 1913) is a remake of the Biblical epic he first directed in 1923. Even then the parting of the Red Sea (in early colour) was impressive, but, with the benefit of more modern special effects, DeMille was able to turn in a really spectacular job, and the sequence won the film an Oscar. The movie was also nominated as best picture of the year, but surprisingly lost out to *Around the World in 80 Days*. The writing of the tablets in the wilderness is also a highlight of a film that remains a supreme example of vivid Hollywood story-telling at its best, with Charlton Heston in towering form as Moses. Financially, too (unlike some of today's free-spending directors) DeMille knew exactly what he was about. The film cost $13 million, and grossed almost four times that amount.

Tender Comrade ○
1943, US, 101 mins, b/w
Dir: Edward Dymtryk
Stars: Ginger Rogers, Robert Ryan
Rating: ★★

When the McCarthy anti-Communist witch-hunts were in full flow, Senator McCarthy branded this Ginger Rogers film as red-tinged throughout. Its story of four women during wartime setting up in a commune-style home was not surprising, considering the film's director (Edward Dmytryk) and scriptwriter (Dalton Trumbo) would later be jailed for a year as two of the 'Hollywood Ten'. Co-star Kim Hunter also saw her career take a nosedive after her name appeared in a Red-scare pamphlet *Red Channels*. But none of that could detract from the fact that *Tender Comrade* was a weak affair, with Ms Rogers offering a stagey performance. RKO tried to spice things up with a new ending but then ditched that in favour of re-editing the original final shots. The film's star later claimed that she had felt so strongly that some of the dialogue in the picture 'had struck at the heart of America's democratic ideals' that she refused to speak the lines on camera and they had to be re-assigned to supporting characters.

Tension at Table Rock
Tender Is the Night ○

1961, US, 146 mins, colour
Dir: Henry King
Stars: Jennifer Jones, Jason Robards Jr, Joan Fontaine, Tom Ewell
Rating: ★★

Although the film lacks pace and atmosphere the polished performances of Jennifer Jones and Joan Fontaine see this disappointing version of Scott Fitzgerald's novel through. But spectacular locations and a feel for the period can't compensate for director Henry King and writer Ivan Moffat failing to get to grips with Fitzgerald's coruscating (and corrosive) characters.

Tender Mercies ○ ⓥ

1982, US, 90 mins, colour
Dir: Bruce Beresford
Stars: Robert Duvall, Tess Harper, Wilford Brimley, Ellen Barkin
Rating: ★★★

Robert Duvall won an Oscar for his portrayal of a down-on-his-luck country singer in this low-key domestic drama. After the break-up of his marriage, Mac Sledge (Duvall) takes a job working for Rosa Lee (Tess Harper), a religious widow who owns a motel and gas station. They fall in love and Sledge tries to make a comeback as a singer. Although Duvall plays his part well, this is a very talky film with no action to spice it up and give it tension. Australian director Bruce Beresford perhaps should have let an American direct this quintessentially American story, although he succeeded later with *Driving Miss Daisy*.

Tender Trap, The ○

1955, US, 111 mins, colour
Dir: Charles Walters
Stars: Frank Sinatra, Debbie Reynolds
Rating: ★★★

Sinatra comedy has him as the swinging New York bachelor on the trail of winsome Debbie Reynolds, though the best things here are the title song and the more acid support of Celeste Holm (a year later to partner Sinatra herself in *High Society*) and David Wayne.

Ten Gentlemen from West Point ○

1942, US, 104 mins, b/w
Dir: Henry Hathaway
Stars: George Montgomery, Maureen O'Hara, Laird Cregar
Rating: ★★

Though not too close to the real facts, this spirited film about the establishment of West Point as a military academy in the early 1800s is, under Henry Hathaway's direction, an exciting adventure story in its own right. George Montgomery – who had started in films four years earlier as a stuntman – stars as the backwoodsman who doesn't fit in with his fellow cadets. But the film is stolen by burly Laird Cregar, in commanding form as the major in charge of the raw recruits. Two years later Cregar was dead at 28, killed by a heart condition following a crash diet.

Ten Little Niggers

See: And Then There Were None

Tennessee's Partner ○

1955, US, 87 mins, colour
Dir: Allan Dwan
Stars: John Payne, Ronald Reagan
Rating: ★★★

Although it was nearing the end of its life, RKO Radio produced some remarkably good action pictures in its last few years – mainly directed, as here, by the veteran Allan Dwan. It's a lavishly produced version of Bret Harte's Western novel, with surprisingly effective performances from Ronald Reagan and Rhonda Fleming. The climax is extremely moving and, overall, the film reaches and maintains a very high entertainment value.

10 Rillington Place ●

1970, UK, 106 mins, colour
Dir: Richard Fleischer
Stars: Richard Attenborough, Judy Geeson, John Hurt, Pat Heywood
Rating: ★★★

Director Richard Fleischer's occasional preoccupation with bizarre murder cases (one remembers *Compulsion*, about the Leopold-Loeb murders, and *The Boston Strangler*), brought him to England in 1970 to make this grim reconstruction of the case of John Reginald Christie, who murdered seven people between 1944 and 1952 in his dingy North London home. Richard Attenborough sinks himself frighteningly well into this role, which has echoes of his earlier performance in *Seance on a Wet Afternoon*. Even so, he is more than matched by the splendid John Hurt, whose pathetic Timothy Evans, convicted of two of the murders committed by Christie, compels total sympathy. The case itself is brought to life with harrowing authenticity,

sparing little of the horrifying and gruesome detail involved, and never sensationalising its subject. Clive Exton's screenplay is soundly constructed, using recorded dialogue wherever possible. The result is a thoroughly engrossing and fluid version of one of the most compellingly nasty cases of mass murder on record: warmly recommended to all but those of nervous disposition.

Ten Seconds to Hell ○

1960, US, 93 mins, b/w
Dir: Robert Aldrich
Stars: Jeff Chandler, Jack Palance, Martine Carol
Rating: ★★

A strange and sometimes exciting film of mixed origins, dealing with German demolition workers in Berlin after World War Two. It was made by the English Hammer company, directed by American Robert Aldrich, shot on location in Berlin, and with English, French and American actors in the cast. Jeff Chandler enjoys himself thoroughly in a rare villain role, in a film where character development plays second fiddle to inbuilt suspense.

Tension ○

1949, US, 91 mins, b/w
Dir: John Berry
Stars: Richard Basehart, Audrey Totter
Rating: ★★★

A downbeat, curiously unrelaxed *film noir* with a typically alienated hero in Richard Basehart's unassuming chemist, pushed over the edge when his virago of a wife (a splendidly spiteful performance by diminutive but curvy Audrey Totter) decides to leave him for another man. Being an MGM film, this is treated rather less darkly than similar stuff being made across the road at RKO and Columbia but writer Allen Rivkin's sharpish script doesn't allow John Berry to fudge the issues involved. The inane narration, though you get used to it, does do some harm to the film, but there's an unexpectedly good performance by Cyd Charisse who makes the most out of a dull role as the girl who steers Basehart away from his murder plan.

Tension at Table Rock ○

1956, US, 89 mins, colour
Dir: Charles Marquis Warren
Stars: Richard Egan, Dorothy Malone, Cameron Mitchell, Billy Chapin
Rating: ★★★

T

Another Western with a theme song (what Western hadn't in those days?), as well as echoes of *High Noon* and *Shane*. It's adapted from Frank Gruber's novel *Bitter Sage* and directed by Charles Marquis Warren, himself a distinguished author of wild west yarns. Richard Egan is impassive as the friendless gunman, Edward Andrews impressive as a sneaky villain. Dorothy Malone is a bit too good to believe in a pokey town like Table Rock, but she should worry; her next film, *Written on the Wind*, would bring her an Oscar. The colour photography by Joseph Biroc is extremely fine and the credits nicely done. *Star Trek*'s De Forest Kelley is first-class in a cameo as another gunman.

Ten Tall Men ○

1951, US, 97 mins, colour
Dir: Willis Goldbeck
Stars: Burt Lancaster, Gilbert Roland, Kieron Moore, Jody Lawrance
Rating: ★★

Burt Lancaster was still in his all-action mould when he turned out this superficially exciting Foreign Legion story, in between making *The Flame and the Arrow* and *The Crimson Pirate*. The formidable features of Mike Mazurki loom large in support, and you can spot up-and-coming star Mari Blanchard in a small role. A good sandstorm sequence and some frisky editing can't really disguise the fact that this is typical Columbia oriental mutton dressed up as lamb.

10.30pm Summer ◑

1966, US/Spain, 85 mins, colour
Dir: Jules Dassin
Stars: Melina Mercouri, Peter Finch, Romy Schneider
Rating: ★★

Three international stars form the points of this torrid emotional triangle. This was the fourth of five films that Greek-born Melina Mercouri made for her director husband, Jules Dassin, a partnership which produced such classics as *Phedra*. Her co-stars are Britain's Peter Finch, who initially made his name in Australian films, and Austrian actress Romy Schneider. It's a tangled web their characters weave in the sun-baked square of a small Spanish town in which they have been stranded, ironically by floods. When night falls, Dassin captures the heat and tension with camerawork that sears the screen in reds, yellows and dark browns. And there's a wild flamenco dancing scene towards the

end which plays its part in releasing the pent-up feelings the characters have towards each other.

10 to Midnight ●

1983, US, 95 mins, colour
Dir: J Lee Thompson
Stars: Charles Bronson, Lisa Eilbacher, Andrew Stevens
Rating: ★★★

Don't ask us to explain the title, but, as blood-soaked vigilante cop thrillers go, this is a fairly good example. Not very believable perhaps, but thrashed along by veteran director J Lee Thompson (and well edited by his son Peter) with plenty of emphasis on the characters involved, and on the pace of the action. Feminists may complain that the story exploits women since the killer seems to aim his knife at some of the most nubile girls in town! To add to the film's sensational aspect, the killer (disturbing newcomer Gene Davis) also does his bloody work in the altogether (save for gloves). This is logical in the sense that he avoids bloodstains on his clothes, but does raise the query about how he manages to both get his clothes off and sneak into buildings without anyone seeing him. Still, the treatment bears a very professional stamp, the scenes of menace are skilfully exploited for suspense and excitement and individual people are clearly drawn in three dimensions.

Ten Wanted Men ○

1955, US, 80 mins, colour
Dir: Bruce Humberstone
Stars: Randolph Scott, Jocelyn Brando, Richard Boone
Rating: ★

Though the situations move through well-trodden pastures, there's plenty of fire-power in this gritty Western about a peacable rancher – Randolph Scott, forced to protect his woman and property against hired killers imported by a jealous rancher. In the role of Corinne, Marlon Brando's sister Jocelyn makes one of her rare screen appearances. And the bad guys include a whole crop of faces you love to see bite the dust – including Lee Van Cleef's.

Tequila Sunrise ● ⊛

1988, US, 108 mins, colour
Dir: Robert Towne
Stars: Mel Gibson, Michelle Pfeiffer, Kurt Russell, Raul Julia
Rating: ★★

This flashy thriller is a strange kettle of tequila and no mistake. You'll have as hard a time following the plot as figuring out when it's meant to be taken seriously. Robert Towne, who scripted *Chinatown*, wrote and directed this multi-mooded drug-bust drama set near the California-Mexico border. Mel Gibson is the ex-cocaine king whom the script tries hard to convince us should be allowed to go free after getting out of the business and falling for a good woman (Michelle Pfeiffer in an interesting portrayal). It's Kurt Russell, though, who gives the film's best performance, as the cop who also beds Pfeiffer and has a long-term friendship with Gibson, although he too has problems with the screenplay's declarations of love, clumsily directed by Towne. Raul Julia, playing a devious Mexican 'coke king', gives an extraodinarily misjudged performance that bears comparison with some of Orson Welles' less restrained cameos. There's some good smart dialogue in all this, but the film's constant switches of mood and pace do it no good at all. It's a scenario on which the sun never does quite rise.

Terminator, The ● ⊛

1984, US, 108 mins, colour
Dir: James Cameron
Stars: Arnold Schwarzenegger, Linda Hamilton, Michael Biehn, Paul Winfield, Lance Henrikseon
Rating: ★★★

Good for a laugh and a thrill and pounded along in typical style by director James Cameron, who gets an 'A' for cinema-craft from the opening scene. This was a cult hit that set Arnold Schwarzenegger on the road to super-stardom after a stuttering start in *Conan*-type films. Schwarzenegger and Michael Biehn come back from the future: Arnie's an android who starts killing women called Sarah Connor. The one he wants, of course, is bound to be last on the list, or we wouldn't have any suspense, and Cameron makes sure there's plenty of that, as well as electrifying action – as Biehn, who's returned from the future to save the relevant Sarah, has to find a way to stop The Terminator – and that's not easy. Schwarzenegger dominates the film as Mr T, and his famous line 'I'll be back' has passed into film legend. The prolonged climactic sequence is one of the most nail-biting and brilliantly-edited of the Eighties. There are a few dull patches and poor supporting performances; however,

Cameron made sure there were none of either in the sequel seven years later.

Terminator 2: Judgment Day ● Ⓥ
1991, US, 136 mins, colour
Dir: James Cameron
Stars: Arnold Schwarzenegger, Linda Hamilton, Edward Furlong, Robert Patrick
Rating: ★★★★

If big Arnold was well cast as the bad Terminator sent back to the future to kill the mother of the future world leader, then he's perfectly cast as the good Terminator sent back to protect the now 10-year-old boy against bad Terminator 2. The twists and turns of logic and time will amaze you almost as much as the 'liquid metal' effects and the highway chases of this 10-years-later sequel, as Arnie develops sufficient human traits and command of slang to bring additional veins of humour to the almost non-stop action. If he was paid around $15 million, then Hamilton, appropriately beefed up as befits the world's toughest lady, is worth every cent of the one million she is said to have got to repeat her role. Notable assists come from Edward Furlong as her son and Robert Patrick as T2, who has the edge on Arnie as he's a more advanced model. There's a welcome sprinkling of deadpan humour to give you relief from the bludgeoning action, too. 'Were you gonna kill him?' the boy asks Arnie of one victim. 'Of course I was,' snaps the big man. 'I'm a Terminator.'

Term of Trial ◑
1962, UK, 113 mins, b/w
Dir: Peter Glenville
Stars: Laurence Olivier, Simone Signoret, Sarah Miles, Terence Stamp
Rating: ★★

Controversial drama about a schoolteacher accused of assaulting a teenage pupil. Laurence Olivier is sternly superb as the teacher, while Sarah Miles, in her film debut, oozes sex appeal as the precocious girl.

Terms of Endearment ● Ⓥ
1983, US, 132 mins, colour
Dir: James L Brooks
Stars: Shirley MacLaine, Debra Winger, Jack Nicholson, Jeff Daniels
Rating: ★★★

What starts out as a finely balanced mixture of comedy and drama, about a mother-daughter relationship and its ups and downs over the years, slips uncomfortably at the midpoint into unadulterated soap-opera as the daughter contracts cancer. Even so, there wasn't a dry eye as the film topped the box-office the world over and then cleaned up at the Oscars, taking statuettes for Best Film, Director (James L Brooks), Actress (Shirley MacLaine), Supporting Actor (Jack Nicholson) and Screenplay (Brooks, again). Only Nicholson could get away with playing an ex-astronaut called Garrett Breedlove, and he almost steals the film from under the noses of MacLaine and Debra Winger, as her daughter. Filming was not a happy experience for the leading actresses, however, and today MacLaine still refuses to talk about – let alone ever work again with – the younger star. The supporting cast includes Danny DeVito (who worked with the director on *Taxi*) and Jeff Daniels – and there's a wealth of foot-tapping hit songs on the soundtrack.

Terry Fox Story, The ○
1983, Canada, 97 mins, colour
Dir: Ralph L Thomas
Stars: Robert Duvall, Eric Fryer, Christopher Makepeace, Rosalind Chao
Rating: ★★★

A modern-day, true-life story of real heroism. Director Ralph L Thomas presents a heartwarming biography of a young man with cancer who, after having his leg amputated, finds enough of the right stuff to undertake a one-man marathon across Canada to raise money to help other cancer sufferers. This film follows the marathon of hope undertaken by Terry (played by real amputee Eric Fyer). The scenes where Terry courageously runs into Toronto, and is met by thousands of adoring admirers, are handled with much inspiration. It's an altogether uplifting experience.

Tex and the Lord of the Deep ○
1985, US, 90 mins, colour
Dir: Duccio Tessari
Stars: Giuliano Gemma, William Berger, Isabel Russinova
Rating: ★★

One of the greatest of comic-book heroes on the continent, Tex was created in 1948 by Giovanni Luigi Bonelli, who makes a cameo appearance in this fantasy Western adventure as an old witch-doctor. The action is fast and furious, but curiously uninvolving, as our three heroes escape from one impossible situation after another with the regularity of an old-fashioned serial. But Riccardo Petrazzi is a colourful villain, a hooded alchemist who manufactures a deadly, glowing-green rock from the depths of his headquarters in a volcano.

Texas Kid – Outlaw
See: The Kid from Texas

Texas Rangers, The ○
1936, US, 95 mins, b/w
Dir: King Vidor
Stars: Fred MacMurray, Jack Oakie, Jean Parker, Lloyd Nolan
Rating: ★★

Strongly-mounted Western about three outlaws, two of whom join the Texas rangers and eventually, inevitably, have to bring in the third. Fred MacMurray, Jack Oakie and Lloyd Nolan are quite well contrasted as the three guys, with Nolan stealing the acting honours just as did Macdonald Carey in the same role in the rather more memorable 1949 remake *Streets of Laredo*.

Texas Rangers, The ○
1951, US, 74 mins, colour
Dir: Phil Karlson
Stars: George Montgomery, Gale Storm, Jerome Courtland, Noah Beery
Rating: ★★★

Rudimentary but rousing Western, ferociously paced by director Phil Karlson, who gives us battles on land, horseback and train as well as grouping together several famous Western outlaws who have to be corralled by upright rangers George Montgomery and Jerome Courtland. Rather uncertainly shot in SuperCinecolor and very routinely scripted, the film has a feisty heroine in Gale Storm and a good cast of outlaws that includes William Bishop, Douglas Kennedy, John Dehner and Ian MacDonald. Action fans won't complain either: there are more fights and gun battles here than in many a longer Western.

Texasville ○ Ⓥ
1990, US, 126 mins, colour
Dir: Peter Bogdanovich
Stars: Jeff Bridges, Cybill Shepherd, Cloris Leachman, Timothy Bottoms, Eileen Brennan, Randy Quaid
Rating: ★

T

Although it has a few good moments and a touching ending, this is a largely pointless sequel to the Oscar-winning *The Last Picture Show* from the same director and with much the same cast, now 20 years older. Alas, these are characters who no longer have anywhere to go. Duane (Jeff Bridges) has seen his oil-wells run as dry as his marriage to Karla (Annie Potts). Lester (Randy Quaid) is the town barber, in financial trouble of his own. Sonny (Timothy Bottoms) retreats into the movie shows of the past and towards a gentle madness, his affair with Ruth (Cloris Leachman), now Duane's ageing secretary, almost forgotten. Lusty waitress Genevieve (Eileen Brennan) is now disabled on the sidelines. Jacy (Cybill Shepard), Duane's high school crush, returns to the town for its centenary celebration after the collapse of her marriage and death of her son. With all these elements of tragedy running through, it's surprising that *Texasville* tries so hard to be a comedy. The strain shows in over-acting by the players, Quaid especially, in scenes that stretch for humour. It's a long, slow and boring prowl across fields of past glory.

Texican, The ○
1966, US/Spain, 91 mins, colour
Dir: Lesley Selander
Stars: Audie Murphy, Diana Lorys, Broderick Crawford
Rating: ★★

A gritty Western, made in Spain, with American director Lesley Selander (a man, despite the spelling) making sure the action stays fast and lively. Audie Murphy is his poker-faced self as the man hunting the murderer of his brother, after escaping from a chain gang. Red-haired Diana Lorys, decorated several such Westerns in the Sixties.

Thank God It's Friday ○
1978, US, 90 mins, colour
Dir: Robert Klane
Stars: Donna Summer, Chick Vennera, Jeff Goldblum, Debra Winger
Rating: ★

A piledriving beat infuses this disco movie that follows the events in a Hollywood disco-cum-nightclub over a single evening. Director Robert Klane gives the episodic structure pace and visual excitement, abetted by a splendid score which includes the Oscar-winning song 'Last Dance', performed by star Donna Summer. The Commodores appear as them-

selves, and there's a neat performance by Chick Vennera who was to score the following year in *Yanks*.

Thanks a Million ○
1937, US, 87 mins, b/w
Dir: Roy Del Ruth
Stars: Dick Powell, Ann Dvorak, Fred Allen, Patsy Kelly
Rating: ★★★

A satirical musical romp that still looks smart today. Dick Powell has one of the breeziest and brightest of his early roles as the singer who finds himself running for governor because his personality is such a hit with the public. But there's one big snag: he's honest. Powell gets plenty of help with the musical numbers (sometimes from such unexpected quarters as Ann Dvorak and Patsy Kelly) and the script by Nunnally Johnson has more wit, bite and insight (not to mention good laughs) than any musical has a right to deserve.

Thank You All Very Much
See: A Touch of Love

Thank You, Mr Moto ○
1937, US, 68 mins, b/w
Dir: Norman Foster
Stars: Peter Lorre, Pauline Frederick, Sidney Blackmer, John Carradine
Rating: ★★★

The oriental sleuth, (played by Peter Lorre) as cunning as he is courteous, first appeared in serial stories in the popular *Saturday Evening Post*, and very quickly became a cult hero. Unfortunately, the series was terminated with the emergence of the Japanese as American enemies in World War Two.

That Certain Age ○
1938, US, 100 mins, b/w
Dir: Edward Ludwig
Stars: Deanna Durbin, Melvyn Douglas, Jackie Cooper, Irene Rich
Rating: ★★

Deanna Durbin, allowed by Universal to grow up (but not too much), develops a teenage crush on sophisticated older man Melvyn Douglas, to the understandable annoyance of her young screen boyfriend, Jackie Cooper. Despite this daring romantic innovation, the film is the same cheerfully innocent mixture of sentiment and comedy as before, decorated by Durbin's attractive

singing. She and Douglas give light and charming performances that give the frothy tale just the lift it needs.

That Certain Feeling ○
1956, US, 103 mins, colour
Dir: Melvin Frank, Norman Panama
Stars: Bob Hope, Eva Marie Saint, George Sanders, Pearl Bailey
Rating: ★★

There are some delightful moments in this Bob Hope comedy from the experienced team of Melvin Frank and Norman Panama, which a year earlier had been responsible for Danny Kaye's classic *The Court Jester*. Hope gets a chance to build a genuine character, Pearl Bailey enhances every scene in which she appears, and Eva Marie Saint exploits an unsuspected comedy talent to good effect in the film's best musical sequence, a drunken dance romp. Songs include the title number, 'Zing Went the Strings of My Heart' and 'Time to Hit the Road to Dreamland'.

That Darn Cat! ⊙
1965, US, 116 mins, colour
Dir: Robert Stevenson
Stars: Dean Jones, Hayley Mills, Roddy McDowall
Rating: ★★★

This stylish comedy-thriller is the best of all the films Hayley Mills made for the Disney studio. She's the owner of DC (Darn Cat, supposedly the Siamese from *The Incredible Journey*) who, in-between stealing duck dinners and outwitting bulldogs, stumbles, through his nose for fish, across the hideout of two bank-robbers holding hostage a woman teller from the bank they've just robbed. The teller substitutes her watch for DC's collar and, in no time at all, Hayley has grabbed the best-looking FBI agent she can lay hands on, and a tail (!) is put on DC, in the hope that he will lead the law to the lair. The cast, ankle-deep in star names, all give perfectly-judged performances. Ed Wynn, fresh from *Mary Poppins*, had a hilarious few minutes as a querulous clockmaker petrified by the FBI saying they 'won't forget him'.

That Forsyte Woman ○
(aka: The Forsyte Saga)
1948, US, 114 mins, colour
Dir: Compton Bennett
Stars: Greer Garson, Walter Pidgeon, Errol Flynn, Janet Leigh
Rating: ★★★

Metro-Goldwyn-Mayer's lavish, colourful version of the first part of Galsworthy's Forsyte odyssey, concentrating on the fortunes of Irene. This is not surprising, as Greer Garson, who plays her, was one of the studio's biggest stars of the time.

That Hamilton Woman
See: *Lady Hamilton*

That Jane from Maine
See: *It Happened to Jane*

That'll Be the Day ◐
1973, UK, 91 mins, colour
Dir: Claude Whatham
Stars: David Essex, Ringo Starr, James Booth
Rating: ★★

A curiously flat rendition of the Fifties, with David Essex manfully shouldering a lead role that isn't always sympathetic. Good cameo work from Ringo Starr and Keith Moon, both hinting at the excesses which were to feature in the (much inferior) sequel, *Stardust*, the following year. In supporting roles are two major stars of TV comedy series: Robert Lindsay and Karl Howman.

That Lucky Touch ○
1975, UK, 90 mins, colour
Dir: Christopher Miles
Stars: Roger Moore, Susannah York, Shelley Winters, Lee J Cobb
Rating: ★

Director Christopher Miles' location scenes in Brussels here recall his earlier work in *Time for Loving*. That was a film with great feel for romantic atmosphere, and indeed it is the romantic moments that work best in this comedy about an arms dealer and a crusading journalist. It really needs Cary Grant and Katharine Hepburn to make it work properly (here the leads are Roger Moore and Susannah York) and the plot is so thin that the dialogue needs to be as slick, smart and steely as possible to make it stand up. Shelley Winters has the best lines, but it's Raf Vallone who gets the closest to hitting the right note with his performance as an amorous Italian brass-hat.

That Man from Rio ○
(aka: *L'Homme de Rio*)
1964, France, 120 mins, colour
Dir: Phillippe De Broca
Stars: Jean-Paul Belmondo, Francoise Dorleac
Rating: ★★★

This hectic French comedy-thriller was one of the first, and best, spoofs of the James Bond films. Hero Jean-Paul Belmondo is pitched from crisis to crisis in a style of which Pearl White would have been proud.

That Midnight Kiss ○
1949, US, 96 mins, colour
Dir: Norman Taurog
Stars: Mario Lanza, Kathryn Grayson, Jose Iturbi, Ethel Barrymore
Rating: ★★

Mario Lanza made his starring screen debut (he had appeared in the chorus of the 1944 film of the show *Winged Victory*) in this sugary MGM musical produced by Joe Pasternak, the man behind Deanna Durbin's successes at Universal in the Thirties. The plot is the standard one of an unknown making good, well used as a showcase for Lanza's singing talents, solo and with his co-star Kathryn Grayson, offering a musical feast for his fans. Even Keenan Wynn gets in on the act, leading a quartet with 'Down Among the Sheltering Palms'.

That Riviera Touch ○
1966, UK, 98 mins, colour
Dir: Cliff Owen
Stars: Eric Morecambe, Ernie Wise
Rating: ★★

Eric Morecambe and Ernie Wise never seemed to hit it off on the big screen, where producers unsuccessfully tried to open out their intimate style of humour. Much the same sort of thing happened to Laurel and Hardy in the early Forties. This is the best of the three Morecambe and Wise films, with a comic cliff-hanger climax in finest Harold Lloyd traditions. Fired from their humdrum jobs in a chocolate-making factory, Eric and Ernie decide to splash their (well, actually Eric's) savings on a glorious spree on the French Riviera.

That's Entertainment ☉ ⓥ
1974, US, 122 mins, colour
Dir: Jack Haley Jr
Stars: Fred Astaire, Bing Crosby, Gene Kelly, Peter Lawford
Rating: ★★★

The history of MGM musicals gives us rather too much of its commentators and rather too little of the actual films, but it's a small quibble at a magnificent spectrum of musical entertainment, with such inevitable gems as Gene Kelly 'Singin' in the Rain' being balanced by such amusing oddities as

Cary Grant, James Stewart and Clark Gable exercising their tonsils in rare bursts of song. The film is also a feast for Judy Garland fans. It seems to take in something from almost every MGM film she made.

That's Entertainment – Part II ☉ ⓥ
1976, US, 121 mins, colour
Dir: Gene Kelly
Stars: Doris Day, Gene Kelly, Fred Astaire
Rating: ★★★

Criticised at the time it came out for not being quite as good as *That's Entertainment* (how could it be? – that was la crème de la crème), this sequel is still a glorious wallow in mainly musical nostalgia, featuring literally scores of clips from MGM films spanning the years 1929 to 1958. Our personal favourites from a good crop of musical numbers include Leslie Caron singing 'Hi Lili Hi Lo', 'Now You Has Jazz' by Bing Crosby and Louis Armstrong from *High Society* and Fred Astaire and Judy Garland dressed as tramps singing 'A Couple of Swells' from *Easter Parade*. Comedy gets its fair share of the limelight, too, with Laurel and Hardy sinking into roadworks in their car from *Leave 'Em Laughing*, the cabin sequence from the Marx Brothers' *A Night at the Opera*, and W C Fields letting David Copperfield in on the perils of high finance.

That Sinking Feeling ○ ⓥ
1979, UK, 92 mins, colour
Dir: Bill Forsyth
Stars: Robert Buchanan, John Hughes, Janette Rankin
Rating: ★★★

A delightful early comedy from director Bill Forsyth (who subsequently made *Gregory's Girl* and *Local Hero*) about a group of young Glaswegians on the dole who come to the conclusion that there must be something more to life than contemplating suicide and decide to do something (a trifle illegal) about it. Fresh and funny.

That's Life! ◐ ⓥ
1986, US, 102 mins, colour
Dir: Blake Edwards
Stars: Jack Lemmon, Julie Andrews, Sally Kellerman, Robert Loggia
Rating: ★★

The character of Harvey Fairchild could have been written for Jack Lemmon. Harvey's acute hypochondria begets the kind of comedy

T

of desperation in which Lemmon's expertise has become a byword. Approaching his 60th birthday, Harvey thinks he has blood pressure, heart trouble, impotency and allergies galore and his doctor can't find a thing wrong with him. Harvey doesn't exactly seem a true-life character but, if he were, Lemmon wouldn't be able to get so much anguished fun out of him. What he doesn't know is that his wife (Julie Andrews) really does have something to worry about – a throat tumour that may be malignant or benign. If all this sounds less than a barrel of laughs, there are times when that's true. But, in between, the script is peppered with enough amusing scenes and one-liners to pull it through. Particularly nice are Lemmon's story about how to make a lobster die happy, and his anguish over a dream where 'I built the world's tallest building so's I could jump off it.' The film's a family affair – Lemmon's son and Andrews' daughter are in it and her husband, Blake Edwards, directed. But it's the seniors' show, with Lemmon's wife Felicia Farr enjoying a nice little vignette as a voraciously seductive fortune-teller.

That's My Boy ⊙

1951, US, 98 mins, b/w
Dir: Hal Walker
Stars: Jerry Lewis, Dean Martin
Rating: ★★

This football-flavoured comedy was the second major film vehicle for Martin and his then-partner Jerry Lewis. The film isn't terribly good, but the public totally ignored critical opinion and had made the team America's top film attractions by the following year. Much of their thunder is stolen here by raucous Eddie Mayehoff, as Lewis' domineering father, but the comedy routines drop to earth with a dull thud and, as with the boys' *The Stooge* a year later, it's the sentimental aspects of the plot which work best.

That Was Then, This Is Now ● Ⓥ

1985, US, 100 mins, colour
Dir: Christopher Cain
Stars: Emilio Estevez, Craig Sheffer, Kim Delaney, Jill Schoelen, Barbara Babcock, Morgan Freeman
Rating: ★

The appeal of American teenage angst, a popular subject in the early Eighties as well as in James Dean's day, was

noticeably wearing thin here, where it became apparent that the novels of S E Hinton, once the hottest properties around, were played out as acceptable film material. Although there are moments when you feel for the characters and want their story to go on, there are rather more when you just want to close your eyes and forget about them. Emilio Estevez wrote it as well as starring as the maybe-psychotic, maybe-homosexual, but for sure confused friend of hero Craig Sheffer, whose acquiring of a girlfriend is something he can't accept. Estevez even gives off some reverberations of a young Kirk Douglas in this role, but the film is stolen from everybody by that earthy actress Barbara Babcock as Sheffer's mother.

Thelma & Louise ● Ⓥ

1991, US, 130 mins, colour
Dir: Ridley Scott
Stars: Susan Sarandon, Geena Davis, Harvey Keitel, Michael Madsen, Brad Pitt
Rating: ★★★

A road movie with female companions is quite unusual. Quite how Thelma and Louise go off on a fishing holiday and end up cornered by dozens of police cars in the Grand Canyon takes some explaining and some hard-to-swallow turns of the plot. And it often seems a long, long day's journey into this particular night. Fortunately, the performances of Sarandon and Davis (both Oscar-nominated) keep this vehicle, as well as their '66 Cadillac, on the road, despite a sight too many 'travelling' shots and little scenes that could have been lost altogether. But if you can believe in: the girls taking a gun (not too difficult), Davis encountering a rapist at their first motel (a bit less easy), Sarandon shooting the man (for a motive explained later), their happening to encounter a travelling bandit, and Davis robbing a store and disarming a policeman, to say nothing of Sarandon phoning the pursuing police chief (Harvey Keitel) to discuss the case, then you're in for a fine time. But surely not even Davis's Thelma would be ditzy enough to leave $67,000 in a motel room with a lover who's just confessed he's a hold-up man? 'Thelma,' says Sarandon, 'You are disturbed.' 'Yes,' beams Davis, 'I believe I am.' Thank goodness they create such character-full and companionable ladies out of Thelma and Louise.

Thelma Jordon
See: The File on Thelma Jordon

Them! ●

1954, US, 95 mins, b/w
Dir: Gordon Douglas
Stars: James Whitmore, Edmund Gwenn
Rating: ★★★

This famous science-fiction thriller was so good (and popular) that it started a whole new syndrome of giant-animal horror films. Even the performances are solid down the line: James Whitmore, as a heroically tough policeman, takes most of the honours, but little Sandy Descher is excellent as the terrified little girl who appears at the beginning and big James Arness, as an FBI agent, as much the man of action as in his TV days as Matt Dillon. Excellent trick photography and ingenious special effects add to the excitement. The tableau of the 'monsters' in their collective lair at the end is unpleasant but unforgettable. Star-spotters will notice Leonard Nimoy in a very minor role.

There's a Girl in My Soup ○ Ⓥ

1970, UK, 95 mins, colour
Dir: Roy Boulting
Stars: Peter Sellers, Goldie Hawn
Rating: ★★

Terence Frisby's long-running comedy play was obviously a must for a film with two stars, and eventually Peter Sellers and Goldie Hawn landed the roles. Hawn is in especially good form as the dumb blond who confounds Peter Sellers with a unique blend of corruption and innocence.

There's No Business Like Show Business ○ Ⓥ

1954, US, 117 mins, colour
Dir: Walter Lang
Stars: Ethel Merman, Donald O'Connor, Marilyn Monroe, Dan Dailey, Mitzi Gaynor, Johnnie Ray
Rating: ★★★

Big, gaudy Irving Berlin musical, awash with clichés and saving the biggest of all for a tearful reunion scene at the end. Of its six major stars, Mitzi Gaynor shows up best; she gives her role any amount of bounce and vitality. Dan Dailey's also good while Marilyn Monroe weighs in with two of her best-remembered songs, 'Heatwave' and 'After You Get What You Want You Don't Want It'. Ethel Merman is, as usual, larger than life as the mother hen with greasepaint in her veins, and there's also 'crying' crooner Johnnie Ray in one of his very rare film roles.

There Was a Crooked Man . . . ○
1970, US, 125 mins, colour
Dir: Joseph L Mankiewicz
Stars: Kirk Douglas, Henry Fonda, Hume Cronyn
Rating: ★★★

Kirk Douglas playing one of the smiling rogues that he did so well. He dominates this Western film as Paris Pitman Junior, a scurrilous but immensely likeable master thief making plans to escape from an impregnable territorial prison. It's a richly entertaining yarn, very enjoyably directed by Joseph L Mankiewicz. And there's some fine Technicolor photography by Harry Stradling Jr.

These Thousand Hills ○
1960, US, 96 mins, colour
Dir: Richard Fleischer
Stars: Don Murray, Richard Egan, Lee Remick
Rating: ★★

Firmly directed by Richard Fleischer this well characterised Western is about two cowboys who antagonise a flashy rancher/gambler, and pay a heavy price. Richard Egan enjoys himself in a rare villain role. Don Murray and Lee Remick also take advantage of a satisfying and well-structured script by Alfred Hayes.

These Three ○
1936, US, 93 mins, b/w
Dir: William Wyler
Stars: Miriam Hopkins, Merle Oberon
Rating: ★★★

As controversial themes were strictly taboo in the Hollywood of the Thirties, it was plain that there would have to be some changes made to *The Children's Hour*, Lillian Hellman's successful play about a latently lesbian affair and the consequences when a vicious schoolgirl spills the beans. Fortunately, as so often happened in those studio-dominated days, the revised version that appeared on screen made just as strong, if different, entertainment. Hellman herself brilliantly adapted her play into a straightforward romantic triangle, and there's a scene-stealing performance from Bonita Granville as the nasty teenager. Director William

Wyler got unusually low-key performances from both his highly-strung female stars, Miriam Hopkins and Merle Oberon, that heightened one's sympathy for their characters. Many years later, he was to film the original play, equally successfully, as *The Loudest Whisper*, with Audrey Hepburn and Shirley MacLaine.

They All Died Laughing
See: A Jolly Bad Fellow

They Call Me MISTER Tibbs! ◐
1970, US, 108 mins, colour
Dir: Gordon Douglas
Stars: Sidney Poitier, Martin Landau, Barbara McNair, Anthony Zerbe
Rating: ★★

The second of three films featuring Sidney Poitier as tough city cop Virgil Tibbs, this time investigating the violent murder of a prostitute. The prime suspect is Tibbs' close friend, an activist priest, played by Martin Landau. While the character of Tibbs is hardly fleshed out at all, Landau does a magnificent job at creating a well-rounded figure of a guilt-ridden cleric. Poitier was allowed to direct several scenes that he didn't appear in, but it's hardly a distinguished affair in the same class as the earlier Tibbs outing, *In the Heat of the Night*.

They Came to Cordura ○
1959, US, 123 mins, colour
Dir: Robert Rossen
Stars: Gary Cooper, Rita Hayworth, Van Heflin, Tab Hunter
Rating: ★★★

Rugged and punishing action film about seven people on an arduous Mexican desert trek in 1916.

They Died With Their Boots On ○ ⊙
1941, US, 140 mins, b/w
Dir: Raoul Walsh
Stars: Errol Flynn, Olivia de Havilland, Arthur Kennedy, Anthony Quinn
Rating: ★★★

Rousing if historically inaccurate picture of General George Armstrong's career – culminating in a thrilling portrayal of the battle of Little Big Horn. As a long-haired, hippie-type Custer, fighting Indians and red tape with equal dash, Errol Flynn was the embodiment of every boy's idea of a Western hero, and every girl's dream. Expertly directed by Raoul Walsh, and packed with splendidly staged

battles, it remains one of the screen's more impressive epic Western adventures.

They Drive By Night ○
1938, UK, 84 mins, b/w
Dir: Arthur Woods
Stars: Emlyn Williams, Anna Konstam, Ernest Thesiger
Rating: ★★★

Not to be confused with the George Raft/Humphrey Bogart film of the same name, this is an excellent atmospheric black thriller directed by Arthur Woods, a promising British director killed during World War Two. Emlyn Williams gives a dominant performance as the man just released from prison who finds himself in desperate straits when he comes under suspicion of murders committed by a psychotic strangler. Pacy direction from Woods makes the film's 80-odd minutes fly by; good photography, too, from Basil Emmott, most of it at night.

They Drive By Night ○
1940, US, 93 mins, b/w
Dir: Raoul Walsh
Stars: George Raft, Ann Sheridan, Humphrey Bogart, Ida Lupino
Rating: ★★★

This trucking drama (later developing into a courtroom thriller) has a formidable Warners star quartet in George Raft, Ann Sheridan, Humphrey Bogart (his last film before stardom at last overtook him in *High Sierra*) and Ida Lupino. Lupino's unforgettable performance as a psychotic wife (following on her startling portrayal of an equally unbalanced artist's-model in *The Light That Failed*, the previous year) puts the other stars well in the shade, and established the British-born actress as one of Hollywood's most powerful portrayers of neurotic women.

They Got Me Covered ○ ⊙
1943, US, 95 mins, b/w
Dir: David Butler
Stars: Bob Hope, Dorothy Lamour, Otto Preminger
Rating: ★★★

Hailed at the time of its release as Bob Hope's best film, this comedy has Hope as the Moscow correspondent of an American agency who achieves journalism's greatest reverse scoop by missing the German invasion of Russia. Muscling in on the act are a sarong-less Dorothy Lamour plus Otto

T

Preminger, Edward (Eduardo) Cianelli and Philip Ahn, who give neat burlesques of enemy agents as Hollywood used to see them.

They Live! ● ⓥ
1988, US, 95 mins, colour
Dir: John Carpenter
Stars: Roddy Piper, Keith David, Meg Foster
Rating: ★★

A lively science-fiction adventure somewhat after the lines of *Invasion of the Body Snatchers*. Aliens have taken over, but the man in the street doesn't know it – until he puts his dark glasses on. How the freedom fighters could have found out that a certain kind of glass revealed an alien to them is only one of the many holes in the plot – but the tale is fun while it lasts. Roddy Piper is a hero far too dozy to ever expose the aliens nationwide – he can't twig one enemy agent even after she throws him out of a window when he offers her the dark glasses – then convinces him she didn't realise he was 'in the know'. Lots of stuntmen fling themselves around as Piper closes in on the alien transmission: mindless but enjoyable, it'll be popular on video.

They Made Me a Criminal ○ ⓥ
1939, US, 92 mins, b/w
Dir: Busby Berkeley
Stars: John Garfield, Claude Rains
Rating: ★★★

This, John Garfield's third starring film, confirmed his status as Warner Brothers' new tough guy. He plays a boxer who, believing he has killed a reporter in a drunken brawl, goes on the run. He ends up in Arizona, working on a farm which is also a rehabilitation centre for New York slum kids. As you might expect, helping the kids reforms the boozy, womanising, selfish Garfield. He is on good form as the central character but is given a run for his money by the Dead End Kids as the young offenders. Although miscast, Claude Rains is enjoyable as the police detective on Garfield's trail. The director, perhaps surprisingly, is Busby Berkeley, more famous for his extravagantly staged musicals. Berkeley pleaded with Warners to give him something other than a musical to direct and this was the result. His skills as a choreographer are still evident in the well-staged and (for the time) realistic boxing scenes.

They Met in Bombay ○
1941, US, 100 mins, b/w
Dir: Clarence Brown
Stars: Clarke Gable, Rosalind Russell, Peter Lorre
Rating: ★★★

An opulent adventure story set in the troubled Far East shortly before Pearl Harbor. Given their biggest action star, Clark Gable, MGM predictably spared no expense in making the film. They even went to the extent of reconstructing the most lavish annual event of British India: the celebration of Empire Day. And thousands of splendidly-dressed extras swarm through the streets of Bombay, from which jewel thieves Gable and Rosalind Russell flee when the going gets too hot – straight into the arms of rascally Peter Lorre, who not only threatens to turn them in, but steals the film as well. It's no great movie, but the stars are fun to be with, and you'll spot Alan Ladd in a minor role.

They Might Be Giants ○
1971, US, 98 mins, colour
Dir: Anthony Harvey
Stars: Joanne Woodward, George C Scott, Jack Gilford
Rating: ★★★

Fiction's most famous detective, the Baker Street sleuth Sherlock Holmes, has figured in many a motion picture – but never before in quite the way he's involved in this film. In James Goldman's adaptation of his own stage play, the central figure (George C Scott) is a man who, facing an emotional crisis, retreats into a private fantasy world, becoming a replica in outlook and behaviour of the immortal Holmes. He finds his Dr Watson in a psychiatrist of that name (played by Joanne Woodward in one of her best, superbly controlled performances) whom he persuades to help him in his quest for Holmes's dreaded arch-enemy Moriarty. The film, which in fact won critical acclaim when it was first shown in Britain in 1972, was co-produced by Paul Newman. It was directed by Anthony Harvey, who directed *The Lion in Winter*. Watch for F Murray Abraham playing a tiny role in his first film.

They Rode West ○
1954, US, 97 mins, colour
Dir: Phil Karlson
Stars: Robert Francis, Donna Reed, Phil Carey, May Wynn
Rating: ★★★

A thinking man's Western, directed in the John Ford manner by Phil Karlson. Richly photographed in Technicolor by the experienced Charles Lawton, it has strong performances from Robert Francis, as the caring young doctor out west, Donna Reed and Phil Carey. Francis, a most promising leading man, was killed in 1955 in a plane crash.

They Shoot Horses, Don't They? ◑ ⓥ
1969, US, 129 mins, colour
Dir: Sydney Pollack
Stars: Jane Fonda, Michael Sarrazin, Susannah York, Gig Young, Bruce Dern, Red Buttons
Rating: ★★★

Gig Young got his Oscar for playing the promoter of a Thirties dance marathon. We are given a depressing view of humanity, but it's fascinating.

They Were Expendable ○
1945, US, 135 mins, b/w
Dir: John Ford
Stars: Robert Montgomery, John Wayne, Donna Reed
Rating: ★★★

John Ford's moving salute to the American torpedo crews in the Pacific during World War Two is an episodic but passionate drama that shows the pain, loneliness and sacrifice of war. Ford packed one poignant and powerful scene after another into this film and got so carried away that he fell from scaffolding and broke a leg. Star Robert Montgomery, who also gives the best performance, took over the directing chores for the last two weeks of filming. The movie's battle scenes are particularly impressive, but it's now a little dated in places and generally difficult to follow. The officer played by John Wayne sued and got $4,000 from MGM but the nurse portrayed by Donna Reed hit the jackpot and picked up $290,000 in damages.

They Who Dare ○
1953, UK, 107 mins, colour
Dir: Lewis Milestone
Stars: Dirk Bogarde, Denholm Elliott, Akim Tamiroff, Kay Callard
Rating: ★★

A distant wartime ancestor of *Who Dares Wins*, as men of the special Boat Service launch a daring expedition to blow up German-held Aegean airfields. Dirk Bogarde, Denholm Elliott and Akim Tamiroff provide plenty of personality behind the sweat and grime, and the action is brilliantly photographed in Technicolor by Wilkie Cooper. The director is Hollywood's Lewis Milestone, adding one more war film to a famous list that by this time already included *The Purple Heart*, *A Walk in the Sun* and *Halls of Montezuma*, as well as the famous 1930 version of *All Quiet on the Western Front*.

They Won't Believe Me ○
1947, US, 95 mins, b/w
Dir: Irving Pichel
Stars: Robert Young, Susan Hayward, Jane Greer, Rita Johnson
Rating: ★★★

And you won't believe the ending, either, to this otherwise fine dark thriller about a man involved with three women. It was essentially a cop-out to skirt around the then severe censorial requirements. Jane Greer, Susan Hayward and Rita Johnson give vivid portrayals which unfortunately put a somewhat miscast Robert Young rather in the shade.

Thief
See: Violent Streets

Thief of Bagdad, The ⊙ ⓥ
1924, US, 155 mins, b/w
Dir: Raoul Walsh
Stars: Douglas Fairbanks
Rating: ★★★

Acclaimed at the time as 'the furthest and most sudden advance films have made', this was Douglas Fairbanks' most ambitious production, wildly and wonderfully extravagant, and filled with magical special effects far ahead of their time.

Thief of Bagdad, The ⊙
1940, US/UK, 109 mins, colour
Dir: Michael Powell, Tim Whelan
Stars: Conrad Veidt, Sabu, June Duprez, John Justin
Rating: ★★★★

This spectacular *Arabian Nights* fantasy provided plum parts for Conrad Veidt, as the wicked Grand Vizier, and black actor Rex Ingram, as the giant djinn. John Justin and June Duprez make a striking romantic team in this magical adventure whose special effects have rarely been equalled.

Thief of Baghdad, The ⊙
1961, Italy, 90 mins, colour
Dir: Arthur Lubin

Stars: Steve Reeves
Rating: ★★

Third screen version of the famous *Arabian Nights* tale of a thief who falls in love with a princess, and has to brave all sorts of dangers to win her. It was Reeves' attempt at a breakaway from pure musclemen roles. And although it's not as good as the Douglas Fairbanks Sr (1924) or Sabu (1940) versions, the trick photography is clever, and the children will enjoy every minute of the fun.

Thief of Baghdad, The ○
1978, UK, 100 mins, colour
Dir: Clive Donner
Stars: Roddy McDowall, Terence Stamp
Rating: ★★

The most recent film version of the famous *Arabian Nights* story, complete with such ingredients as the magic carpet, the wicked wazir, the All-Seeing Eye and the Temple of Truth. Peter Ustinov does a variation on his baffled panda act as the cuddly caliph. Terence Stamp's wazir, flapping in on his black cloak like a living corpse, is clearly a dry run for his villains in the *Superman* movies and the stage version of *Dracula*. French actor Daniel Emilfork also scores with his mischievously grinning genie. The juvenile leads, as in previous versions, are good looking but negligible.

Thief Who Came to Dinner, The ○
1973, US, 105 mins, colour
Dir: Bud Yorkin
Stars: Ryan O'Neal, Jacqueline Bisset
Rating: ★★★

With one of her most delicious performances, Jill Clayburgh entirely steals this entertaining comedy-thriller about a computer analyst turned jewel thief – whose plot might itself have rolled out of a computer. Clayburgh makes the most of some nice throwaway lines in a film whose disparate elements are all permitted by director Bud Yorkin to pursue their own course at their own pace. Ryan O'Neal is the thief. Superficial but pleasing entertainment.

Thieves' Highway ○
1949, US, 94 mins, b/w
Dir: Jules Dassin
Stars: Richard Conte, Valentina Cortesa, Lee J Cobb
Rating: ★★★

Rough, tough, no-holds-barred story of California truckers battling against

corrupt wholesalers quite happy to stoop to murder to get things done their way. This was shot against genuine locations, in this case arterial roads in and around San Francisco. The sense of imminent threat is well-maintained by director Jules Dassin throughout the film, and there's a wagonload of tension and excitement on the roads.

Thieves Like Us ◐
1973, US, 123 mins, colour
Dir: Robert Altman
Stars: Keith Carradine, Shelley Duvall, John Schuck
Rating: ★

A long and very protracted film from Robert Altman (about three bank robbers in the Thirties) whose very length robs it of much of it's intended impact. Keith Carradine is too impersonal as the youngest robber, Shelley Duvall better as his backwoods moll and John Schuck horrifyingly homicidal as the drinker of the three. It has it's excitements and the Thirties' radio programmes used as background are fascinating.

Thing, The ● ⓥ
1982, US, 108 mins, colour
Dir: John Carpenter
Stars: Kurt Russell, A Wilford Brimley
Rating: ★★

John Carpenter's visceral remake of the famous 1951 horror film, about an alien at large in the Antarctic that takes the form of those it destroys. Carpenter's aim is to make you jump out of your seat and maybe hide behind it as well. Watch out!

Thing Called Love, The ◐ ⓥ
1993, US, 114 mins, colour
Dir: Peter Bogdanovich
Stars: River Phoenix, Samantha Mathis, Dermot Mulroney
Rating: ★★

Once upon a time, there would have been a rush to release the final film of a newly deceased teen idol star. After River Phoenix's death, though, this was barely released in America and went straight to video elsewhere, an odd decision, since Peter Bogdanovich's Country and Western romance, though not without flaws, has a good deal of charm. The story's plain but sweet: four aspiring young Country and Western singer-songwriters descend on Nashville's famous Bluebird Café for auditions – but get bogged down by the thing

T

called love. A cast of rising Hollywood stars does quite well with this innocuous but charmingly played romance.

Thing (From Another World), The ◑
1951, US, 95 mins, b/w
Dir: Christian Nyby
Stars: Margaret Sheridan, Kenneth Tobey, James Arness
Rating: ★★

The great Howard Hawks supervised production (and, it is said, direction) on this classic science-fiction thriller. The film is so well made, in fact, that even its more absurd implausibilities carry some measure of conviction under the guidance of Hawks, director Christian Nyby and screenplay writer Charles Lederer. And Dimitri Tiomkin contributes a notable music score. The 'Thing' itself is played by 6ft 8in James Arness, later to win fame as Marshal Matt Dillon in *Gunsmoke*.

Things Change ○ ⓥ
1988, US, 96 mins, colour
Dir: David Mamet
Stars: Don Ameche, Joe Mantegna, Robert Prosky
Rating: ★★

A gentle, amusing, well-played but slow gangster comedy from writer-director David Mamet who has made such an impact on the Hollywood scene since his *House of Games*. The games in this film begin when Gino (Don Ameche), a shoe repairer who happens to resemble a notorious Mafia hit-man, is persuaded to confess to a gangland killing in return for money, security on release and the fulfilment of his dream – a boat. Now the bad guys don't exactly intend to stick to their end of the bargain, but Gino doesn't know this, and neither does Jerry, a gangster (Joe Mantegna) whose 'probationary' assignment after a bungled job is to look after Gino for a few days before the trial. Fed up, and taking pity on the shoeshop 'Mafioso', Jerry sweeps him off to Lake Tahoe for a couple of days, where things change . . . and dramatically alter what would otherwise have been the logical ending of the film. Ameche and Mantegna are excellent, but the treatment of their story is too low-key and far too leisurely to make this outstanding entertainment.

Things to Come ○
1936, UK, 97 mins, b/w
Dir: William Cameron Menzies

Stars: Raymond Massey, Cedric Hardwicke, Edward Chapman, Ralph Richardson
Rating: ★★★

H G Wells' classic science-fiction saga translated to the screen with superb sets and great imagination by director William Cameron Menzies' team. Cedric Hardwicke, brought in to replace another British actor, as Theotocopulos, is reported to have said: 'My work in *Things to Come* was completed with such speed and lack of ceremony, that the actor I had replaced had no idea that his entire performance lay on the cutting room floor . . . until he went to the premiere with a party of expectant friends.'

Thin Ice ○
1937, US, 78 mins, b/w
Dir: Sidney Lanfield
Stars: Sonja Henie, Tyrone Power
Rating: ★★

With this, her second (and best) film, skating champion Sonja Henie briefly became Hollywood's highest-paid female star, with earnings in excess of $200,000 for the year. The fun-filled romantic musical (based on a Viennese operetta) contains an excellent role for rubber-faced comedienne Joan Davis, later to win star comedy roles of her own, as well as the TV series *I Married Joan*. Here she makes a big hit with the film's great novelty number 'I'm Olga from the Volga'. The movie was first shown in Britain as *Lovely to Look At*.

Think Dirty
See: Every Home Should Have One

Thin Man, The ○
1934, US, 93 mins, b/w
Dir: W S Van Dyke
Stars: William Powell, Myrna Loy
Rating: ★★★★

Nick Charles and his wife Nora (personified by William Powell and Myrna Loy) were the most sophisticated sleuths the screen had seen – a clue in one hand and a champagne cocktail in the other. Nick, in fact, seemed to be in a permanent state of semi-inebriation, but that didn't stop him from bringing a number of murderers to book between 1934 and 1947, the dates of the first and last of the *Thin Man* films. The Thin Man himself is a character from this first adventure – but the soubriquet gradually became attached to Powell himself, who was hardly slim enough

to warrant it. Myrna Loy, however, was pencil-slim, and the role of Nora Charles got her away from a string of oriental temptresses and well up the ladder towards becoming the Queen of Hollywood, a title she won in a nationwide poll.

Thin Man Goes Home, The ○
1944, US, 100 mins, b/w
Dir: Richard Thorpe
Stars: William Powell, Myrna Loy
Rating: ★★★

This later adventure of sophisticated sleuths Nick and Nora Charles suffers from the demands of wartime on the plot, and from the fact that Woody Van Dyke, who had directed previous films in the series, had just died. And the dialogue for Myrna Loy as Nora is flat champagne compared with previous scripts. But William Powell is in his usual smooth form as Nick, and a whole gallery of familiar character actors from the period enjoy themselves immensely as the various suspects in the case of the murdered painter.

Third Key, The
See: The Long Arm

Third Man, The ○ ⓥ
1949, UK, 104 mins, b/w
Dir: Carol Reed
Stars: Joseph Cotten, Alida Valli, Orson Welles, Trevor Howard, Wilfrid Hyde White
Rating: ★★★★

Welles' last great Forties' role, as Harry Lime, master-criminal at large in a post-war Vienna of fairs and ruins, shapes and shadows. They seek him here, they seek him there. Harry Lime is presumed dead, but there can be few filmgoers now who don't know that he turns out to be alive, and ultimately pursued through the sewers of the city by Joseph Cotten, Trevor Howard, Bernard Lee, and Anton Karas' insistent zither music, which hooked itself into the minds of the world. There's devastating photography by Robert Krasker (deservedly winning an Oscar), and inspired direction by Carol Reed. Not to be missed.

Third Party Risk ○
(aka: The Deadly Game)
1955, UK, 70 mins, b/w
Dir: Daniel Birt
Stars: Lloyd Bridges, Finlay Currie
Rating: ★★

An unimaginative British thriller from the Hammer studio, lifted by a number of capable performances, notably from American Lloyd Bridges as a Yank in Spain accused of killing an old Army buddy to obtain microfilm.

Third Time Lucky ○
1949, UK, 91 mins, b/w
Dir: Gordon Parry
Stars: Dermot Walsh, Glynis Johns
Rating: ★★

Glynis Johns, as a girl who brings her gambler boyfriend good luck, is the main reason for watching this otherwise routine British crime drama. Sharp eyes will spot Ballard Berkeley, the old duffer major from *Fawlty Towers*, and even further down the cast list is that famous fly fisherman and acting knight Michael Hordern.

Thirty-Nine Steps, The ○ ⓥ
1935, UK, 87 mins, b/w
Dir: Alfred Hitchcock
Stars: Robert Donat, Madeleine Carroll, Godfrey Tearle, Peggy Ashcroft
Rating: ★★★★

Outstanding Alfred Hitchcock version of the John Buchan thriller which subsequent remakes have struggled in vain to emulate. Excitement and suspense are skilfully maintained by the director, whose stitching together of a pattern of telling individual scenes makes for a memorable film. Atmospheric black-and-white photography by Bernard Knowles provides a compelling backcloth to alert, witty performances by Robert Donat and Madeleine Carroll, with vivid supporting contributions from Godfrey Tearle, Wylie Watson (as Mr Memory), Peggy Ashcroft and Lucie Mannheim.

39 Steps, The ○
1959, UK, 93 mins, colour
Dir: Ralph Thomas
Stars: Kenneth More, Taina Elg
Rating: ★★

When John Buchan wrote *The 39 Steps* at the outbreak of World War One, he could hardly foresee that it would eventually lead to a governor-generalship of Canada and a peerage (although he showed his gratitude by knighting his hero, Richard Hannay, in a subsequent book). Hannay's unintentional forays into the world of espionage first attracted the attention of suspense master Alfred Hitchcock in 1935 and the resultant film was acclaimed as a

classic. This later production, starring Kenneth More as Hannay, is an ambitious attempt to improve it still further. Wonderful Scottish scenery complements exciting sequences showing the first aerial manhunt – in fiction at any rate.

Thirty Nine Steps, The ○
1978, UK, 102 mins, colour
Dir: Don Sharp
Stars: Robert Powell, Karen Dotrice, John Mills
Rating: ★★★

This exciting version of the famous thriller is closer to John Buchan's original novel than any other, even if the Hitchcock 1935 film remains the best. Robert Powell again advanced his star career with his portrayal of Richard Hannay, and there's some lovely colour photography of the Scottish countryside. The action set-pieces, if sometimes a little preposterous, are excitingly done by director Don Sharp, especially the climax on the face of Big Ben. There's a nice supporting performance from John Mills.

Thirty Seconds Over Tokyo ○
1944, US, 138 mins, b/w
Dir: Mervyn Leroy
Stars: Spencer Tracy, Van Johnson, Robert Walker
Rating: ★★★

Quasi-documentary re-creation of the events which took place 131 days after the Japanese bombing of Pearl Harbor, the incident which brought the USA into World War Two in December 1941. The story is based on the account of one of the survivors of the retaliatory American bombing raid on the Japanese cities of Tokyo and Yokohama – Captain Ted W Lawson. He is played here by Van Johnson. Spencer Tracy gives his usual exemplary performance as the leader of the mission and look out for a young Robert Mitchum and, well down the cast, Blake Edwards, director of the *Pink Panther* series and *10*.

37°2 le Matin
See: Betty Blue

36 Hours ○
1964, US, 104 mins, b/w
Dir: George Seaton
Stars: James Garner, Eva Marie Saint, Rod Taylor
Rating: ★★★

Unusual war thriller about an American officer who is made to believe that the war is over so that he will talk of the Normandy invasion plans to his Nazi captors. James Garner and Eva Marie Saint turn in solid performances under George Seaton's workmanlike direction. But the really great performance in the film comes from Rod Taylor, unusually cast but memorable as an American-speaking dedicated German doctor.

This Above All ○
1942, US, 110 mins, b/w
Dir: Anatole Litvak
Stars: Tyrone Power, Joan Fontaine, Thomas Mitchell
Rating: ★★★

This stylish World War Two morale-booster has Tyrone Power as a lower-middle-class Englishman who deserts from the army because he does not believe in fighting for a country dominated by the upper class. But, naturally, he turns out to be a hero in the end, redeemed by his romance with Joan Fontaine. The screenplay was by English playwright R C Sherriff. Anatole Litvak directed in a studio-bound Hollywood version of Britain which won an Oscar for art directors Richard Day and Joseph Wright; another went to set decorator Thomas Little.

This Boy's Life ● ⓥ
1993, US, 115 mins, colour
Dir: Michael Caton-Jones
Stars: Robert De Niro, Ellen Barkin, Leonardo Di Caprio
Rating: ★★

Thank goodness there's an upbeat ending to what is mostly a deeply unpleasant and depressing film about the teenage years of the writer Tobias Wolff. Toby (Leonardo Di Caprio) and his mother Caroline (Ellen Barkin) are discovered at the outset of the film on the run from her latest ill-chosen lover after the break-up of her marriage (which has left Toby's older brother with her ex). Once in Seattle, Toby is soon on the verge of juvenile delinquency and, to provide a stable background, Caroline marries rough but seemingly benevolent and courteous Dwight Larsen (Robert De Niro). The wedding ring on, Dwight proves to be a ranting, bullying tyrant, determined to bestow Caroline no more favours and to knock her son into shape. The rest of the movie is a catalogue of oppression, repression and suppression, punctuated by Toby's exploits on the streets and at school. Barkin gives the best performance in this film by some little way, and the scene where she outshoots her new husband at a target contest, summing up her basic superiority, is one of the few moments of subtlety in the film.

This Gun for Hire ○
1942, US, 125 mins, b/w
Dir: Frank Tuttle
Stars: Veronica Lake, Robert Preston, Laird Cregar
Rating: ★★★★

Although clearly having the central role, Alan Ladd was actually billed fourth, after Veronica Lake, Laird Cregar and Robert Preston, in this adaptation of a Graham Greene thriller. However, the role of the expressionless killer of the title made the fair-haired, pint-sized Ladd a big star. A whole series of larger-than-life characters help director Frank Tuttle move the story along in gripping style, although the photographer John Seitz can take all the credit for one of the film's most atmospheric sequences – a chase through freight yards.

This Happy Breed ○
1944, UK, 114 mins, colour
Dir: David Lean
Stars: Robert Newton, Celia Johnson, John Mills, Kay Walsh, Stanley Holloway
Rating: ★★★

This sentimental and nostalgic look at the lives of an average British working-class family between the two world wars was David Lean's debut as a solo director and his first in Technicolor. Although not his greatest critical success, the film was hugely popular with the public; by toning down the more patronising aspects of Noel Coward's original play, Lean really captured the spirit of the people. And, to his great credit, he obtained one of Robert Newton's rare understated performances as the father of the family. The much-praised photography by Ronald Neame (himself later to become a noted director) actually lent warmth to the subject, and really showed Hollywood a thing or two about the subtler uses of Technicolor.

This Happy Feeling ⊙
1958, US, 92 mins, colour
Dir: Blake Edwards
Stars: Curt Jurgens, Debbie Reynolds, Alexis Smith, John Saxon
Rating: ★★★

An engaging cast is in good form in this zippy romantic comedy, one of the earliest films directed by Blake Edwards. Veteran actress Estelle Winwood is particularly noteworthy as an eccentric housekeeper. The chirpy title song is by three-time Oscar-winners Ray Livingston and Jay Evans.

This Island Earth ○
1955, US, 86 mins, colour
Dir: Joseph M Newman
Stars: Jeff Morrow, Faith Domergue, Rex Reason
Rating: ★★

A rare piece of imaginative, genuine science-fiction that's gradually allowed to slide into juvenile space opera. Something for everyone in this, though, the only Technicolor sci-fi film Universal-International ever made. There's some intricate gadgetry, a gorgeous heroine menaced by forces unknown, special effects ahead of their time and a super mutant monster. Rex Reason is quite good, but Faith Domergue is given little to do but scream lustily and look gorgeous. Technical details are presented in convincing enough fashion.

This Is My Affair ◐
1937, US, 101 mins, b/w
Dir: William A Seiter
Stars: Robert Taylor, Barbara Stanwyck, Victor McLaglen
Rating: ★★

Not the full-blown romance the title would suggest (especially as stars Robert Taylor and Barbara Stanwyck were a steady twosome in real life and would marry two years later), but more of a melodrama with elements of excitement, suspense, romance and ingenious plot twists. Well set (at the turn of the century) and skilfully directed by the always workmanlike William A Seiter, it deals with an undercover agent on a presidential mission to root out a gang of bank robbers.

This Is My Life ◐ ⊙
1992, US, 95 mins, colour
Dir: Nora Ephron
Stars: Julie Kavner, Samantha Mathis, Dan Aykroyd, Carrie Fisher, Gaby Hoffman
Rating: ★★

Nice performances, good one-liners, shame about the film: the story of a Jewish mother who, after years of looking after two daughters, comes

into some money and becomes famous as a stand-up comic. Despite the wisecracks – mom (Julie Kavner) tells the girls she only had one detour into folly 'but we'll leave your father out of this' – the tale just isn't particularly interesting. Kavner is on the mark, if somewhat uncharismatic, as the mom who is always 'on'. Dan Aykroyd lends considered support as the impresario – 'the Moss' – for whom she falls and Samantha Mathis is quite superb as the older daughter – emotions conveyed in the clenching of a fist or the tightening of a lip. Gaby Hoffman is mercifully uncute as her sister. But you just can't imagine anyone actually paying a cent to share an hour and a half with these people.

This Is My Love ◐
1954, US, 91 mins, colour
Dir: Stuart Heisler
Stars: Linda Darnell, Rick Jason, Dan Duryea, Faith Domergue
Rating: ★★★

The best of the later films of director Stuart Heisler, who made his name with the Alan Ladd version of *The Glass Key*. This is a powerful, tragic drama with haunting theme music by Franz Waxman, a throbbingly true performance from Linda Darnell which carries great impact, and a pathetically brilliant portrayal of an embittered cripple by Dan Duryea. The film is also richly photographed in Pathecolor by Ray June.

This Is My Street ◐
1963, UK, 94 mins, b/w
Dir: Sidney Hayers
Stars: Ian Hendry, June Ritchie
Rating: ★★

Although this film does cash in on the backstreets bedroom drama popular in Sixties' British cinema, director Sidney Hayers has at the same time contrived a very interesting drama from a rather middling English *Peyton Place*-type novel by Nan Maynard. A strong, magnetic story, and genuinely sympathetic characters are the best things about a film that sees Ian Hendry giving a performance of compelling brilliance as an alley-cat charmer, turning laughter to menace and back in the flicker of an eyelid. As the working wife he seduces, June Ritchie's vocal delivery is somewhat short of her range of facial emotions.

This Is Spinal Tap ● ⊙
1984, US, 82 mins, colour
Dir: Rob Reiner

Stars: Christopher Guest, Michael McKean
Rating: ★★★

A spoof 'rockumentary' chronicling the adventures of an English rock band while on tour in America. Director Rob Reiner amusingly takes a subsidiary role as a 'movie-brat'-type filmmaker and you'll also spot Anjelica Huston, who two years later was the deserved winner of a best supporting actress Oscar for her role in *Prizzi's Honour*. The flat, South London accents of the group members (who are actually American and Canadian actors) are uncannily and hilariously accurate. Bruno Kirby, Ed Begley Jr and Billy Crystal also contribute cameos in the supporting cast.

This Land Is Mine ○
1943, US, 103 mins, b/w
Dir: Jean Renoir
Stars: Charles Laughton, Maureen O'Hara
Rating: ★★

A forceful, poignant war drama marred by a script that takes some believing, even in the midst of Hollywood's most flagwaving years. The camera-hogging Charles Laughton plays a seemingly mild teacher who becomes a local hero when the occupying Nazis arrest him for murder. But then there are so many eye-catching performances in this movie, passionately well directed by wartime refugee Jean Renoir, that one contemporary critic thought it should have been called *This Film Is Mine*!

This Man's Navy ○
1945, US, 100 mins, b/w
Dir: William A Wellman
Stars: Wallace Beery, Tom Drake
Rating: ★★

And this is a man-sized World War Two action film from the MGM stable, with overwhelming Wallace Beery making life difficult for Tom Drake as a rookie sailor Beery treats as a son. The combat scenes are sturdy and noisy, as to be expected from enthusiastic war-film director William A Wellman, who also made *Wings*, *The Story of G I Joe*, *Hell Bent for Glory* and *Battleground*.

This Property Is Condemned ◐
1966, US, 110 mins, colour
Dir: Sydney Pollack

Stars: Natalie Wood, Robert Redford, Charles Bronson
Rating: ★★★

There's a formidable trio of stars in this turbulent love story (adapted from a play by Tennessee Williams) which is played out against a background of violence and industrial strife. Robert Redford and Natalie Wood give impressive portrayals; but the really great performance comes from Mary Badham, as an ugly 12-year-old, worldly-wise beyond her years. Director Sydney Pollack keeps a tight grip on the sentimentality until towards the end, and James Wong Howe's colour camerawork is superb, capturing a hot Southern-states night, or making a breathtaking pan over the muddy, sun-flecked Mississippi River.

This Sporting Life ◐ ⓥ
1963, UK, 134 mins, b/w
Dir: Lindsay Anderson
Stars: Richard Harris, Rachel Roberts, Alan Badel
Rating: ★★★

Richard Harris broke through to big-time stardom in this gritty study of a coal-miner who becomes a professional rugby player. In many ways the highpoint of the British 'kitchen sink' movement that had begun five years earlier, it gave Rachel Roberts an eye-catching 'good-hearted tart' type of role that she was to play, with variations, for the rest of her career. Unflinching direction (and dissection) of the characters by Lindsay Anderson draws us right into their high-pressure world. Watch out for Glenda Jackson (her screen debut) in a miniscule role as one of a group of people singing around a piano.

Thomas Crown Affair, The ◐ ⓥ
1968, US, 102 mins, colour
Dir: Norman Jewison
Stars: Steve McQueen, Faye Dunaway
Rating: ★★★

Thirty years before, this would have starred Kay Francis and been called *Undercover Girl*. In 1968, with the stars making psychedelic love, it seemed a glitzy fuss about not very much. The plot is too slight to allow Steve McQueen and Faye Dunaway to expand their roles enough for us to identify fully with them, although the bank raid scenes are tautly effective

and there's a nice chess/seduction scene reminiscent of the eating orgy in *Tom Jones*.

Thoroughly Modern Millie ○
1967, US, 138 mins, colour
Dir: George Roy Hill
Stars: Julie Andrews, Mary Tyler Moore, James Fox
Rating: ★★★

One of Julie Andrews' most successful vehicles; the star gives one of her sprightliest performances in the title role of this Twenties' musical spoof and there's a delicious turn by Beatrice Lillie as the white-slaving Mrs Meers. A bit long, but the score is tuneful (Elmer Bernstein won an Oscar for it) and director George Roy Hill keeps the idiotic plot going at a nice pace.

Those Daring Young Men in Their Jaunty Jalopies
See: Monte Carlo or Bust

Those Magnificent Men in Their Flying Machines ☉ ⓥ
1965, US/UK, 133 mins, colour
Dir: Ken Annakin
Stars: Sarah Miles, James Fox, Terry-Thomas, Robert Morley, Eric Sykes, Benny Hill
Rating: ★★★

It's a sure-fire bet that, sooner or later, one of the 1910 aviators in this crazy all-star comedy will crash into the local sewage farm. These gigantic splashes provide the most side-splitting moments in a film whose greatest assets are the animated Ronald Searle cartoons at the beginning, middle and end. There's rather too much romance and too little of Terry-Thomas, as a dastardly Victorian villain, and Eric Sykes – his downtrodden manservant. Hilarious compensations include a Keystone Kops fire brigade bossed by Benny Hill.

Thousands Cheer ○
1943, US, 126 mins, colour
Dir: George Sidney
Stars: Gene Kelly, Kathryn Grayson, Mary Astor
Rating: ★★★

Probably the biggest of all wartime musical extravaganzas. Being made at MGM, it was in Technicolor and had a cast no other studio could match, with Gene Kelly (doing his famous 'mop' dance) and Kathryn Grayson singing 'The Joint is Really Jumpin' at Carnegie Hall', Red Skelton and little Margaret O'Brien competing to

T

see who can eat the most ice-cream, Virginia O'Brien's famous deadpan rendition of 'In a Little Spanish Town' and Lena Horne's showstopping 'Honeysuckle Rose'. Thousands cheered all right: the film was a massive box-office hit.

¡Three Amigos! ○ ⓥ
1986, US, 105 mins, colour
Dir: John Landis
Stars: Chevy Chase, Steve Martin, Martin Short
Rating: ★

This comedy Western spoof is like a plate of Mexican refried beans in bad need of a dose of red hot chillis to spice it up. The idea of having three wimpy silent cowboy movie heroes coming to the aid of downtrodden Mexicans in a sort of affectionate spoof of *The Magnificent Seven* is a great one, especially with Steve Martin, Chevy Chase and Martin Short in the title roles. But the execution by director John Landis is unexpectedly ham-fisted, and the script weak and illogical. Why is there a medieval dungeon beneath one of the houses? But a funny scene where the Three Amigos sit singing a corny cowboy bedtime song in front of a matte painting of Monument Valley, where they are joined by a mountain lion, a turtle, a coyote, an owl and other desert creatures, shows the film's potential in the hands of better writers.

Three Caballeros, The ◐
1944, US, 71 mins, colour
Dir: Norman Ferguson
Stars: Aurora Miranda, Carmen Molina
Rating: ★★★★

Donald Duck sings! If Mickey Mouse had soared to a career peak as The Sorcerer's Apprentice, then the spluttering duck enjoys his finest hour vocalising with Joe Carioca the parrot and Panchito the rooster, and dancing with Aurora Miranda in this brilliant Disney cartoon/live-action compilation that ends (next week) with a whizzbang tour of Mexico. Earlier cartoon sequences introduce such memorable characters as Pablo the Cold-Blooded Penguin and The Flying Donkey. And, just as you are starting to yawn at the antics of the live actors, Disney peps you up again with such brilliant cartoon images as a little train chugging through gardens of flowers against a background of black. Altogether, it's a quacker.

Three Cockeyed Sailors
See: Sailors Three

Three Coins in the Fountain ○ ⓥ
1954, US, 102 mins, colour
Dir: Jean Negulesco
Stars: Clifton Webb, Dorothy McGuire, Jean Peters, Louis Jourdan, Rosanno Brazzi
Rating: ★★

Famous romantic weepie about the love affairs of three American girls in Rome whose storyline follows very much the same path as Jean Negulesco's earlier *How to Marry a Millionaire*. Remembered now chiefly for the theme song and for its lyrical colour photography which won an Oscar, although the travelogue elements almost swamp the story. The actresses concerned, Dorothy McGuire, Jean Peters and Maggie McNamara, give the formula material rather more than it deserves.

Three Days of the Condor ◐
1975, US, 118 mins, colour
Dir: Sydney Pollack
Stars: Robert Redford, Faye Dunaway, Cliff Robertson
Rating: ★★★

A *39 Steps*-type spy thriller in which bookish Robert Redford finds himself the only survivor when his CIA section is massacred. But this bookworm is a clever man. He wriggles off the hook of further assassination attempts and noses his way towards the rotten core of an organisation where sides change constantly and one's friend may be forced to become one's enemy in the space of a phone call. Will Redford survive? The suspense is killing. Apart from its fashionably enigmatic ending, this is a film with much to recommend it, with its atmospheric nighttime sequences, Redford's own edgy performance (peering nervously from behind gold-rimmed spectacles and putting his brain to dreadful tortures to try to stay alive) and Owen Roizman's clever but subtle colour photography – far above average for a modern location film.

Three Faces of Eve, The ◐
1957, US, 95 mins, b/w
Dir: Nunnally Johnson
Stars: Joanne Woodward, David Wayne, Lee J Cobb
Rating: ★★★

This was the early highpoint of Joanne Woodward's distinguished acting career, in a portrait of a split personality woman said to be based on a real-life case. The actress's clever differentiation between the three faces of Eve (and then some) marked her out as a dramatic star of most skilful talents. She was nominated for an Oscar alongside Deborah Kerr, Anna Magnani, Elizabeth Taylor and (rather unexpectedly) Lana Turner and, when it came to awards night, Joanne was announced as the winner. The voice of the narrator in *The Three Faces of Eve* will be familiar to radio listeners: it belongs to Alastair Cooke. Writer-director Nunnally Johnson, whose distinguished scripting career included *The Grapes of Wrath, The Moon is Down, The Keys of the Kingdom, The Dark Mirror* and *Oh Men! Oh Women!* makes this story a compelling casebook history. And David Wayne? He made his indelible mark on screen history with his superb performance as the small-town barber in *Wait 'Til the Sun Shines Nellie*, in 1952.

Three Fugitives ◐ ⓥ
1989, US, 93 mins, colour
Dir: Francis Veber
Stars: Nick Nolte, Martin Short, James Earl Jones
Rating: ★★★

Lord knows why weedy bank robber Martin Short chooses hulking Nick Nolte as a hostage during his one-man bank raid. I mean, you'd pick a little old lady, wouldn't you? Never mind, we wouldn't have a film otherwise, so we must allow writer-director Francis Veber this little quirk in an otherwise feisty comedy that almost seamlessly blends fun, action and sentiment. Nolte, you see, is a man just out of jail after committing 14 armed robberies himself. And he's determined to go straight – until Short skitters on to the scene, a bundle of nerves but determined to hijack the bank for enough money to keep his six-year-old daughter (who hasn't spoken since her mother died) in her special school. You won't need to be told that, despite his best intentions, Nolte becomes hopelessly embroiled with Short and his problems, not least because the police investigator (James Earl Jones) figures that such an all-time loser had to be in on the robbery himself. There are few dead patches in the ensuing flight of the ill-assorted duo (later with little girl in tow) and some quite funny interludes, including Nolte's being treated (after Short accidentally shoots him in the leg) by a doddering old vet (Kenneth McMillan) who thinks he's a dog, feels his nose and even puts him down a bowl of food. Nolte's tough guy is the best thing in the film – his down-the-line playing raising more laughs than most current offerings from full-time funnymen.

3 Godfathers ○
1948, US, 106 mins, colour
Dir: John Ford
Stars: John Wayne, Harry Carey Jr, Ward Bond, Pedro Armendariz
Rating: ★★★★

If you're prepared to let its liberal doses of sentiment get to you, this is a brilliant John Wayne-John Ford Western, their first together in colour, about three bank raiders (Wayne, Pedro Armendariz, Harry Carey Jr) who become saddled with a baby when its mother dies in the desert. From then on the film maintains a wonderful balance between suspense, sentiment and some grim humour. 'The best and surest way of feeding the baby,' Carey reads from a manual, 'is the one which nature has provided.' 'Well,' growls Wayne, 'that's out!' Ford took pleasure in goading young Carey (to whose father, early Western star Harry Carey, the film is dedicated) to a fine, moving performance, by telling him every time he did something wrong that he wished he had hired Audie Murphy for the part. Breathtakingly shot in Technicolor by Winton C Hoch, this underrated film deserves to stand with the best of the Ford-Wayne Westerns from the Forties and Fifties.

Three Lives of Thomasina, The ⊙
1964, UK, 97 mins, colour
Dir: Don Chaffey
Stars: Patrick McGoohan, Susan Hampshire, Karen Dotrice
Rating: ★★★

The Scots have always been easy prey for animal sob-stories and the Disney studio wrings the tears from this one with practised ease. The children, Karen Dotrice and Matthew Garber (the pair from Disney's *Mary Poppins*) have a natural appeal which puts them among the better grade of screen tots, while Susan Hampshire scores a big personal success as the 'witch' who tends to sick animals. The storyline itself is wrong, although there's one amusing howler early on when Thomasina (the ginger cat of the title)

says her family called her Thomas at first until they 'got to know her better'. And her master a vet? Pull the other one, Disney.

3 Men and a Baby ○ ⓥ
1987, US, 98 mins, colour
Dir: Leonard Nimoy
Stars: Tom Selleck, Steve Guttenberg, Ted Danson, Nancy Travis
Rating: ★★

The old film maxim 'Never act with children or animals' seems not to have scared Tom Selleck, Ted Danson and Steve Guttenberg. Otherwise, none of them would have taken on this airy romp about three macho bachelors in their 30s who get landed with a baby girl by Danson's decamping ex-mistress. Selleck and Guttenberg look after the infant while Danson's away and soon become doting foster-fathers, handling more nappies than women. Fortunately, this somewhat gooey narrative is injected with a subplot involving drugs which supplies some much-needed action and variation in theme. The three stars all have their moments in a tolerable toddle through triteness that turned into a bundle of box-office joy for its producers.

Three Men and a Cradle ○
(Trois Hommes et un Couffin)
1985, France, 106 mins, colour
Dir: Coline Serreau
Stars: Roland Giraud, Michel Boujenah, Andre Dussollier
Rating: ★★

Charm, amusement and tedium mingle in equal parts in this very Gallic comedy, subsequently remade by Hollywood into a smash-hit called *3 Men and a Baby*. Three macho bachelors in their thirties are suddenly burdened with the illegitimate infant daughter of one. The actual father being away on a trip, the remaining two take cack-handed charge of the baby – played by two real charmers – and, taking endless time off work, soon get used to the routine of nappy days and sleepless nights. Their instant devotion does take some swallowing – especially when, on the very first day, their landlady offers to change the baby and is met with a refusal! Nice performances, particularly by Michel Boujenah (who won a French Oscar) and Roland Giraud; the overrated remake robbed it of what charm it possessed in the first place.

3 Men and a Little Lady ○ ⓥ
1990, US, 103 mins, colour
Dir: Emile Ardolino
Stars: Tom Selleck, Steve Guttenberg, Ted Danson, Nancy Travis
Rating: ★★★

It's five years on and the bachelor guys from *3 Men and a Baby* are still living together in harmony with baby Mary (now Robin Weisman) whose actress mother Sylvia (Nancy Travis) returned several years back, and is secretly adored by Selleck, who can't find the words to tell her. You know what we mean: silly characters and situations, but fun anyway. Even when the trio pursues Sylvia to England, where she plans to marry, there's still some merriment to be had, although most of it seems to stem from a study of British comedies of the Fifties. This is especially true of Fiona Shaw's portrait of a man-hungry headmistress which, scene-stealing though it is, reminds you of one of Joyce Grenfell's old cameos which when she did them. With the American scenes, everyone's on firmer ground: Selleck again recalls Clarke Gable, but proves himself better at light comedy than the King ever was. Danson has the showiest role, and carries it off with great confidence and panache: he's the real laughter-getter here, and a 'rap' lullaby the three men do to send Mary to sleep is a genuine show-stopper. By and large, this is more fun than the original.

Three Musketeers, The ⊙
1938, US, 73 mins, colour
Dir: Allan Dwan
Stars: Don Ameche, The Ritz Brothers, Binnie Barnes, Gloria Stuart
Rating: ★★★

A film comedy based – more or less – on Dumas' famous story! The Ritzes – zany nightclub comedians of the Thirties whose stature at one time rivalled that of the brothers Marx – collide head-on with Alexandre Dumas in this pastiche of the famous swashbuckling story. Villainy is in the capable hands of Binnie Barnes, Lionel Atwill, John Carradine, and Douglas Dumbrille, and the Oscar-winning Joseph Schildkraut complete an excellent supporting cast.

Three Musketeers, The ○ ⓥ
1948, US, 125 mins, colour
Dir: George Sidney

T

Stars: Gene Kelly, June Allyson, Lana Turner, Vincent Price
Rating: ★★★

MGM spared no expense in this spectacular Technicolor version of Dumas' classic tale of intrigue, romance, derring-do, and treachery in 17th-century France. It's every bit as star-studded as the two new films made from Dumas' novels. A fine cast is headed by Gene Kelly, taking a rest from his dancing duties, and turning D'Artagnan into a balletic athlete; Vincent Price, as evil as ever, as Cardinal Richelieu; and Lana Turner, contributing one of her best screen portrayals as the poisonous Milady de Winter. Angela Lansbury, Lana's rival for the part at MGM, eventually lost out, and had to be content with portraying Queen Anne. Suave Gig Young plays Porthos, and portly Robert Coote is Aramis. Strange: one would have thought these two parts better cast the other way round.

Three Musketeers, The ○ ⓥ
1993, US, 106 mins, colour
Dir: Stephen Herek
Stars: Chris O'Donnell, Charlie Sheen, Kiefer Sutherland, Rebecca DeMornay, Tim Curry, Oliver Platt
Rating: ★★

Almost inevitably dubbed *Young Swords*, this fiercely-paced version of the Dumas classic, full of crashing, clangorous action, suffers from its players, with Charlie Sheen and Kiefer Sutherland equalling MGM's old pairing of Van Heflin and Robert Coote in making the 1973 Athos and Aramis, Oliver Reed and Richard Chamberlain, seem positive gems of casting. Like the latter film, a vein of humour is evident here and, as director Stephen Herek previously made *Bill and Ted's Excellent Adventure* and *Don't Tell Mom the Babysitter's Dead*, the blame for its falling flat can be levelled at some pretty stolid performances. Never mind, there are compensations: Rebecca DeMornay is well cast as the icy Milady de Winter, and Oliver Platt cheerfully steals the show as a brawling, sprawling, carousing young Porthos. For the film itself, though, colourful and energetic are about the best adjectives you could think of to describe its attractions.

Three Musketeers: The Queen's Diamonds, The ○
1973, UK, 107 mins, colour
Dir: Richard Lester

Stars: Michael York, Oliver Reed, Raquel Welch, Faye Dunaway
Rating: ★★★

Immeasurably the better of Richard Lester's two *Musketeers* films, this actually seems funnier on a second viewing. So if you've seen it in the cinema, take another look. Although the cutting and editing might have been tighter, the director's visual style provides comedy and drama in equal proportions. The stars are largely left to their own devices, and those who play the straightest succeed the most, notably Raquel Welch and Simon Ward. Michael York's D'Artagnan is rather wetter than I suspect even Lester intended and although Richard Chamberlain is elegantly cast as Aramis, Oliver Reed's rapidly increasing proportions reveal him as more suitable to Porthos (actually played by Frank Finlay) than to Athos.

Three of Hearts ● ⓥ
1992, US, 110 mins, colour
Dir: Yurek Bogayevicz
Stars: William Baldwin, Sherilyn Fenn, Kelly Lynch, Joe Pantoliano, Gail Strickland
Rating: ★★

'Any woman, any time, any place. Guaranteed.' That's the motto of Joe (William Baldwin), an up-market male prostitute or, as he prefers to be called, escort for hire. So who more suitable for getting back the girlfriend (a brunette Sherilyn Fenn) of Connie, a lesbian (Kelly Lynch), and sending her running back to Connie. Now you don't need a crystal ball to see that Baldwin and Fenn are going to fall in love but there's a bit more to the story than that, although not enough to stretch the film to 110 minutes without a few lulls. Under its conventional facade (Joe works for a man who also runs a kinky sex phone line), this is a very conventional movie in structure – and Lynch has some endearingly goofy moments as Connie who, perhaps unfortunately for the film's emotional centre, turns out to be the most likeable character in the film. Baldwin exercises his charismatic grin to good effect, but overall the film doesn't quite engage the emotions, though it's better than you might expect from seeing the terrible trailer!

Three Ring Circus ☉
1954, US, 103 mins, colour
Dir: Joseph Pevney

Stars: Dean Martin, Jerry Lewis, Joanne Dru, Zsa Zsa Gabor
Rating: ★★★

Although not as side-splittingly funny as some of their films together, this is about as colourful and entertaining a show as Dean Martin and Jerry Lewis ever put on screen. Jerry is a natural for the assistant lion tamer who wants to be a clown and Dean's lazy charm and melodious warble hits it big with a song called 'It's a Big, Wide, Wonderful World'. A rare Martin-Lewis duet, 'Hey, Punchinello', is also a highlight of the film.

Three Smart Girls ○
1936, US, 84 mins, b/w
Dir: Henry Koster
Stars: Deanna Durbin, Charles Winninger, Binnie Barnes, Ray Milland
Rating: ★★★

Deanna Durbin was never more delightful than this, her feature debut, as a matchmaking teenager out to keep her (divorced) errant father on the straight and narrow path back to mother. Songs include 'My Heart is Singing' and 'Someone to Care for Me'. As always in her pre-war films, the Durbin kid is like a breath of fresh air.

Three Smart Girls Grow Up ○
1939, US, 90 mins, b/w
Dir: Henry Koster
Stars: Deanna Durbin, Charles Winninger, Nan Grey
Rating: ★★

The sequel to 1937's *Three Smart Girls*, again directed by Henry Koster. Little Deanna matchmakes for her sisters, sings 'Because' and wins over every crusty heart in sight. Very refreshing.

3.10 to Yuma ○ ⓥ
1957, US, 80 mins, b/w
Dir: Delmer Daves
Stars: Glenn Ford, Van Heflin
Rating: ★★★

Very high-quality suspense Western which will have you biting your nails right up to the memorable climax. It seemed that every other Western in the Fifties had a theme song by Frankie Laine and this is no exception. Other bonuses are tight performances by Ford as the outlaw and Van Heflin as the poor farmer who tries to bring him in against all the odds, and Charles Lawton's crisp black and white photography. Of the supporting cast, Henry Jones and Richard Jaeckel both etch sharp portrayals of gentlemen on opposite sides of the law, but the finest performance in the film is given by Leora Dana as Heflin's wife.

3 Women ●
1977, US, 125 mins, colour
Dir: Robert Altman
Stars: Sissy Spacek, Shelley Duvall, Janice Rule
Rating: ★

Downright peculiar film from Robert Altman that you will find totally compelling or heavy going according to taste. The 'plot' is about three women who metamorphose into identities other than their original ones. There is certainly more to its events than meets the eye, although quite what is sometimes hard to fathom. And everything is so stylised that the characters simple aren't believable – although Altman devotees aren't likely to find that a hindrance to fascination or enjoyment.

Three Worlds of Gulliver, The ☉
1960, UK, 100 mins, colour
Dir: Jack Sher
Stars: Kerwin Mathews, Jo Morrow, June Thorburn
Rating: ★★★

Master of DynaMation Ray Harryhausen allows that perennial hero of mythical magic, Kerwin Mathews, to wander among Lilliputians and giants. There's no sign of Gulliver's other two voyages or Swift's satire – but it's all very entertaining and pleasant.

Three Young Texans ○
1954, US, 78 mins, colour
Dir: Henry Levin
Stars: Mitzi Gaynor, Keefe Brasselle, Jeffrey Hunter
Rating: ★★

An exuberant Western which gave the sparkling Mitzi Gaynor her only outdoors role. Director Henry Levin makes the most of a good train robbery sequence, and the Technicolor photography is first-rate throughout.

Thrill of a Romance ○
1945, US, 105 mins, colour
Dir: Richard Thorpe
Stars: Van Johnson, Esther Williams, Frances Gifford
Rating: ★★

MGM obviously figured in this plush musical-comedy that with Esther Williams swimming, Van Johnson smiling, opera star Lauritz Melchior

singing and Tommy Dorsey, Xavier Cugat and their orchestras playing away like billy-o, they didn't need to bother too much about story or script. How right they were. The film proved to be one of the big money-spinners of its year. And it had two huge song hits: 'I Should Care' and 'Don't Say No, Say Maybe'.

Thrill of it All, The ○
1963, US, 108 mins, colour
Dir: Norman Jewison
Stars: Doris Day, James Garner
Rating: ★★★

Producer Ross Hunter's luxurious world of make-believe receives another comic twist in this story of housewife Beverley Boyer (Doris Day) who becomes a national celebrity through selling soap on TV. All this upsets her husband (James Garner) not a little, especially when he becomes known as 'Mr Beverley' and finds himself driving into the swimming pool the TV sponsors have made out of his wife's garage. Day, as genuinely nice as ever, and Garner make a perfect team together in this pleasant entertainment with a good few laughs.

Throne of Blood ◐ ⓥ
1957, Japan, 108 mins, b/w
Dir: Akira Kurosawa
Stars: Toshiro Mifune, Isuzu Yamada
Rating: ★★★★

Japanese master Akira Kurosawa's version of Shakespeare's *Macbeth*, impressively transferred to a Samurai setting. As with *Ran*, Kurosawa's more recent version of *King Lear*, the film's most powerful performance is provided by the leading lady, in this case Isuzu Yamada, in fierce and frightening form as the film's equivalent of the Lady Macbeth character. The redoubtable Toshiro Mifune, Kurosawa's usual protagonist, has the leading role in this graphic film, bulging with imagination and with a brilliant, unforgettable finale.

Throw Momma from the Train ◐ ⓥ
1987, US, 88 mins, colour
Dir: Danny DeVito
Stars: Danny DeVito, Billy Crystal, Anne Ramsey, Kim Greist
Rating: ★★

Directors seem to have developed a fine art in today's comedy cinema of making films that are fun without actually being funny. A fine line, per-

haps, but one that can make the difference between staggering off holding your sides or having been mildly amused. That gripe apart, this black romp, nicely performed and well produced, has a lovely basic idea. Failed writer-teacher Billy Crystal hates the wife who stole his only publishable novel. Danny DeVito, who also directed, is his dimwit pupil (with an ogre of a mother) who conceives the idea of a 'swap' murder after watching Hitchcock's *Strangers on a Train*. The film has too many semi-climaxes thereafter, but both DeVito and Crystal give it their all and a bit more, and Anne Ramsey cuts a horrendous figure as the fiend who yells and cuffs her middle-aged son into frequent cowering submission.

Thunderball ○ ⓥ
1965, UK, 140 mins, colour
Dir: Terence Young
Stars: Sean Connery, Claudine Auger, Adolfo Celi, Luciana Paluzzi
Rating: ★★

Regular Bond devotees won't be disappointed with this, his fourth film adventure, although it's the weakest of his early capers and underwater battles don't somehow carry the same charge as adventures on terra firma. There's the usual preliminary fencing with the main adversary (splendid Italian actor Adolfo Celi), a welter of fantastic gadgets – plus the famous Aston Martin again – and a plentiful array of Bond beauties. In this department, the two girls with lesser roles – flashing-eyed Martine Beswick as an agent, and sultry Molly Peters as a physiotherapist – rather outshine the leading ladies, Claudine Auger and Luciana Paluzzi. This is the story which was profitably (and slightly more sharply) remade by star Sean Connery as *Never Say Never Again*.

Thunder Bay ○
1953, US, 102 mins, colour
Dir: Anthony Mann
Stars: James Stewart, Joanne Dru, Dan Duryea
Rating: ★★

James Stewart and Anthony Mann took a break from their great series of rugged Westerns (*Winchester 73*, *Where the River Bends*, *The Naked Spur*, *The Far Country*, *The Man from Laramie*) to make this equally action-filled, ahead-of-its-time story of wildcatters drilling for oil under the sea. There's much of the spirit of the Western here, though, especially in a rich sup-

T

porting cast which includes old reliables Gilbert Roland, Dan Duryea, Jay C Flippen and Henry Morgan. Joanne Dru and Marcia Henderson are less effective as the girls. There's a hurricane, a killing, a near-lynching and plenty of free-for-alls. Does Stewart complete the winning formula by getting covered in oil at the end? See the picture to find out.

Thunderbolt and Lightfoot ● Ⓥ

1974, US, 114 mins, colour
Dir: Michael Cimino
Stars: Clint Eastwood, Jeff Bridges, George Kennedy, Gary Busey
Rating: ★★★

This fast-moving crime caper – director Michael (*The Deer Hunter*) Cimino's debut film – starts off in high spirits but ends in a black mood. Clint Eastwood is a bank robber who is trying to keep one step ahead of two former cronies who believe he cheated them out of their share of a robbery. Jeff Bridges is a young drifter who latches onto Eastwood. The cronies (George Kennedy and Geoffrey Lewis) eventually catch up with Eastwood and are persuaded to pull another caper. Although Eastwood is the central character, Bridges, Kennedy and Lewis all fill their roles impressively, collectively overshadowing the star. In fact Bridges was nominated for a Best Supporting Actor Oscar. The film picks up momentum as it goes along and the robbery and getaway scenes are well done and exciting. But Cimino never allows the action to dwarf the characters, who are all well drawn. The grim turn towards the end of the film gives it a somewhat downbeat ending, but it's on the whole an excellent action thriller.

Thunderhead – Son of Flicka ☉

1945, US, 78 mins, colour
Dir: Louis King
Stars: Preston Foster, Roddy McDowall
Rating: ★★★

Dog-fever in the Hollywood of the Forties, after MGM struck it rich with Lassie, was quickly followed by horse-fever. A colt called Flicka, the creation of author Mary O'Hara, spearheaded a whole host of vigorous, colourful outdoor adventures, guaranteed to thrill animal-lovers and wring a tear from the most hardened animal-hater around. This is the sequel to the original Flicka film (*My Friend Flicka*), with Preston Foster and

Roddy McDowall again as the McLaughlins, ranch folk of America's mid-west. It was made by Louis King (brother of another director, Henry King), who was a real expert in the genre. Louis' output also included *Smoky*, *Bob*, *Son of Battle*, *Green Grass of Wyoming* (from another novel by Mary O'Hara) and *The Lion and the Horse*.

Thunderheart ◐

1992, US, 119 mins, colour
Dir: Michael Apted
Stars: Val Kilmer, Sam Shepard, Graham Greene, Fred Ward, Ted Thin Elk
Rating: ★★

You'll have reservations about this modern American Indian murder thriller – one of which will probably be that it's overlong. When it comes together in the last half-hour, though, the film becomes engrossing and enjoyable, topped with a stunning overhead shot at the action climax and one of those emotive endings you thought Hollywood had forgotten how to make. A young FBI agent (Val Kilmer) of Indian ancestry is uprooted from his Washington DC patch and dispatched to the South Dakota badlands, where murders of native Americans there need to be solved and, as usual in these films, cloak some far more sinister goings-on. The film builds up some interesting characters along its rather plodding course. And, like the film, the script gets more interesting towards the end. But you'll need patience to extract heap good medicine from this one.

Thunder in the Valley ☉

(aka: Bob, Son of Battle)
1947, US, 103 mins, colour
Dir: Louis King
Stars: Peggy Ann Garner, Lon McCallister, Edmund Gwenn
Rating: ★★★

An American film, set in the Scottish Highlands, from a book by an Englishman, Alfred Ollivant; *Owd Bob* is one of the most famous animal stories in the English language. And Hollywood gave it the full treatment. Edmund Gwenn is at his crusty best as the embittered old shepherd who owns one of the two dogs suspected of being a sheep-killer; and the exhilarating scenery is handsomely photographed in Technicolor. Two of filmland's brightest stars of the Forties, Lon McCallister and Peggy Ann Garner, give sympathetic performances in the lead roles. The dogs,

of course, are magnificent. The children should keep a handkerchief ready for the scenes in which the dogs come close to getting killed; and when McCallister's treasured violin is broken by the ill-tempered Edmund Gwenn.

Thunder of Drums, A ○

1961, US, 97 mins, colour
Dir: Joseph M Newman
Stars: Richard Boone, George Hamilton, Luana Paten, Charles Bronson
Rating: ★★★

This tough Western will please all fans of Cavalry-versus-Indians adventures, and gives the commendable Richard Boone a role he can sink his teeth into. He's the battle- and memory-scarred commander of a grossly under-manned desert garrison, who gets saddled with three young and inexperienced lieutenants with whom to fight the Indians. The most aggressive of them is played by George Hamilton, in one of his more mobile and thoughtful portrayals. In addition to its tough action and rich colour camerawork, the film is a real bonanza for star-spotters. Besides Richard Chamberlain in his first major role as another of the lieutenants, there are pop guitarist Duane Eddy (his only straight part) and that granite-faced man of action Charles Bronson, who later moved on to star roles. James Douglas's performance as Lt Gresham won the young actor a plum role in the television series *Peyton Place*, which was in the planning stage at the time. Veteran cavalrymen are played by Arthur O'Connell and Slim Pickens, and the leading lady is former Disney child star Luana Patten.

Thunder Over Arizona ○

1956, US, 72 mins, colour
Dir: Joe Kane
Stars: Skip Homeier, Kristine Miller
Rating: ★★

A minor Western from Republic that is instantly forgettable but proves to be a pleasant enough time filler, thanks mainly to its attractive landscapes captured in the studio's Naturama and Trucolor processes. The directing chores are in the capable hands of Joe Kane, the former cellist-turned filmmaker, who churned out dozens of low budget action pictures for Republic, including many starring John Wayne, Gene Autry and Roy Rogers, and was rewarded for his efforts in the mid-Fifties by being elevated to handling many of the studio's medium-budget pictures.

THX 1138 ● ⓥ

1970, US, 95 mins, colour
Dir: George Lucas
Stars: Robert Duvall, Donald Pleasance, Maggie McOmie
Rating: ★★★

Director George Lucas' first film, and just as good as either of his two subsequent hits, *American Graffiti* and *Star Wars*. This is a more serious, very *1984*-like science-fiction thriller, although the director shows the same schoolboy relish at unveiling the special effects in his cinematic box of tricks, the same enthusiasm for entertaining his audience, that made his later features so enjoyable. And the final flight from robot police is as exciting as anything in *Star Wars*.

Tiara Tahiti ○

1962, UK, 100 mins, colour
Dir: William T Kotcheff
Stars: John Mills, James Mason, Claude Dauphin, Herbert Lom
Rating: ★★

Engaging battle of wits between the two stars, as an ex-officer and a beachcomber, against the magnificent backdrop of Tahiti. James Mason is a raking beachcomber, crossing wits with John Mills, who offers an amusing variation on his pompous vulnerable officer from *Tunes of Glory*.

Ticket to Tomahawk, A ⊙

1950, US, 90 mins, colour
Dir: Richard Sale
Stars: Dan Dailey, Anne Baxter, Rory Calhoun, Walter Brennan
Rating: ★★★

A riotous comedy-musical, directed at a brisk pace by Richard Sale, and set aboard a train in the Old Wild West, where passengers are besieged by bad guys and Indians. Down among Les Girls in the theatrical troupe involved, watch out for Marilyn Monroe in one of her early film parts. In the same chorus line are Marion Marshall and Joyce Mackenzie who, while not in the Monroe bracket, also became stars. In another small role, wall-eyed Jack Elam was just starting out on a very profitable career in film villainy. See if you can figure out who Dailey has named his daughters after in the final scene.

Tiger Bay ○ ⓥ

1959, UK, 105 mins, b/w
Dir: J Lee Thompson
Stars: Hayley Mills, Horst Buchholz, John Mills
Rating: ★★★★

The brilliant thriller, both tense and touching, in which Hayley Mills burst on the film world with her superb portrayal of a hoydenish nine-year-old Welsh girl who becomes involved with a murderer. Hayley and her co-star, Horst Buchholz, both give tremendously human performances. John Mills is a steady foil as the determined police inspector. Atmosphere is excellent, and the suspense generated is tremendous. You'll be held to every second.

Tigers Don't Cry ○

(aka: African Rage)
1976, SA, 102 mins, colour
Dir: Peter Collinson
Stars: Anthony Quinn, John Phillip Law
Rating: ★

An eventful story of attempted assassination, told in the helter-skelter grasshopper style that director Peter Collinson stamped on all his films before his early death at 44 in 1980. Although one could have done without most of the intrusive music score, Anthony Quinn gives a typically gutsy performance as the kidnapper looking for a big ransom to assure his daughter's future, and Simon Sabela has an interesting if clumsily developed role as Quinn's target — an educated black president given to quoting Shakespeare alongside *The Wind in the Willows*. The film, made in South Africa, is based on Jon Burmeister's novel *Running Scared*.

Tiger's Tale, A ◐ ⓥ

1992, US, 97 mins, colour
Dir: Peter Douglas
Stars: Ann-Margret, C Thomas Howell, Charles Durning, Kelly Preston
Rating: ★★

Common sense tells me that this story of a spring-autumn affair isn't a terribly good film, basically because its screenplay (by the director, Peter Douglas) doesn't cut deep enough to affect the emotions. But it's hard to be objective about any film that gives that neglected talent Ann-Margret as many chances as this. Lucky C Thomas Howell. Every 19-year-old should have an affair with a lady in her forties who looks this good. Typical Hollywood wish-fulfillment, of

course, and with spots of tedium along the way; but the animals in the movie – Howell's father (Charles Durning) is a retired vet – are an unusual added attraction, and Howell, while his acting lacks depth, romps most courageously with the two tigers who double the role of his pet. Pardon me while I don my teenager disguise and book a flight to California.

Tiger Warsaw ◐ ⓥ

1987, US, 92 mins, colour
Dir: Amin Q Chaudhri
Stars: Patrick Swayze, Barbara Williams, Lee Richardson, Piper Laurie
Rating: ★

All-American angst, dull and depressing and scripted in such a way that the actors' big emotional scenes are liable to make you laugh rather than cry. Tiger (Patrick Swayze) is the prodigal son, the black sheep of the Warsaw family exiled these many years since he shot daddy following a row when he was discovered spaced out on drugs and peeping on sister. Now Tiger's back, unaware that his sister cancelled her marriage plans and is about to marry again, or that his father is a mental and physical shell. 'Is it really true you can't go home again?' wails Tiger, a sentiment which a suffering audience may well endorse. Amin Chaudhri's direction is slow and meaningful and the film is heavily edited for effects. Under the circumstances, Piper Laurie is pretty good, even when having to hide Tiger in the closet. Everyone else stinks. It's a tiger totally without teeth.

Tight Little Island

See: Whisky Galore!

Tightrope ● ⓥ

1984, US, 114 mins, colour
Dir: Richard Tuggle
Stars: Clint Eastwood, Genevieve Bujold
Rating: ★★★

A tough, exploitative Clint Eastwood crime film that looks like a latter-day vehicle for Charles Bronson. Prostitutes were surely never as dishy as the crew who make up the hit-list in this urban thriller which casts Eastwood as Dirty Harry with problems, alias Wes Block, a cop who finds himself under suspicion and his family and friends in danger as a result of his consorting with hookers after his wife has left him. Eastwood's own daughter Alison is the 12-year-old who waits at home while her father first goes out on his midnight prowls, then hunts a killer who seems to be playing cat and mouse with him. The thrills and kills are efficiently stage-managed by debutant director Richard Tuggle who steers clear of gore until the final scene.

Tight Spot ○
1955, US, 97 mins, b/w
Dir: Phil Karlson
Stars: Ginger Rogers, Edward G Robinson, Brian Keith, Lorne Greene
Rating: ★★★

A thriller that will have you rooted to your armchair for nearly two hours. Ginger Rogers is in dynamic form as the woman convict pressured to testify against a gangland czar and Brian Keith's terrific (the best performance of an undervalued career) as the detective assigned to protect her. Katherine Anderson is also very good in a supporting role. Terse dialogue, interspersed at just the right intervals with bursts of action by director Phil Karlson, ensures that the claustrophobic suspense engendered by the film becomes almost unbearable towards the end. Thrilling and moving at once, this was one of the best three crime films of its year, crisply photographed in black-and-white by Burnett Guffey, who 12 years later won an Academy Award for his camerawork on *Bonnie and Clyde.*

Till the Clouds Roll By ○
1946, US, 137 mins, colour
Dir: Richard Whorf
Stars: Robert Walker, Judy Garland, Van Heflin, Lucille Bremer
Rating: ★★

Never mind the quality of the script, feel the width of these Jerome Kern songs, more than 20 of them, in this potted MGM biography of the composer's life, awash with guest stars (of whom June Allyson is the liveliest), plus Judy Garland as Marilyn Miller and an earnest performance from Robert Walker as Kern himself. And just get a look at the young Frank Sinatra in that pink dinner suit.

Tim ◑ ⊗
1978, Australia, 108 mins, colour
Dir: Michael Pate
Stars: Mel Gibson, Piper Laurie
Rating: ★★★

The talents of a youthful Mel Gibson and a Piper Laurie slimmed down from her comeback in *Carrie* two years earlier are just enough to make us care about the outcome of the slow-building romance between a retarded man in his twenties and the fortysomething woman who teaches him to read and opens his eyes to the world. A thoughtful romantic drama based on a book by Colleen McCullough, who wrote *The Thorn Birds,* and directed by Michael Pate, an Australian actor who spent many years in Hollywood.

Timberjack ○
1954, US, 94 mins, colour
Dir: Joseph Kane
Stars: Sterling Hayden, Vera Ralston
Rating: ★

A trite script and acting as wooden as the lumber that's felled during the action sequences sink this tiresome story of inter-family rivalry in the woods of western Montana. The only diversion comes from laconic jazzman Hoagy Carmichael, who tinkles the ivories as the local saloon pianist. An unusually generous Republic poured money down the drain on this one with good production values and better-than-usual Trucolor.

Time After Time ◐ ⊗
1979, US, 112 mins, colour
Dir: Nicholas Meyer
Stars: Malcolm McDowell, David Warner, Mary Steenburgen
Rating: ★★★

The clever premise of this fantasy thriller is that H G Wells builds the time machine of his stories and that Jack the Ripper, being one of Well's associates, escapes in it to the future. As he hasn't the retainer key, the machine returns (without him) to its Victorian resting-place. Wells, anguished that he has loosed the Ripper on what he has always imagined to be a Utopian future, determines to pursue. Writer-director Nicholas Meyer has constructed an ingenious and highly-original thriller on this basic theme, whose every piece falls into its proper place before the end, leaving no loose ends. The raging music of Miklos Rosza is a fine asset to the atmosphere; and the performances, especially that of Mary Steenbergen — who gives off strong echoes of the early Shirley MacLaine — create the believable characters so vital to this kind of science-fiction. The author's own treatment of his work eschews frills and is all the better for it.

Time Bandits ◐ ⊗
1980, UK, 110 mins, b/w
Dir: Terry Gilliam

Stars: Craig Warnock, David Rappaport, John Cleese, Sean Connery, David Warner, Ralph Richardson
Rating: ★★

For most of its length a cross between a sword and sorcery adventure and *Monty Python and the Holy Grail,* this fantasy from director Terry Gilliam (later to make *Brazil*) becomes exciting and really imaginative in cinematic terms only when our six dwarf heroes reach the fortress of Ultimate Darkness; otherwise it's a comic-strip trip through time and space. Devotees of Python humour, however, will undoubtedly savour John Cleese's Robin Hood.

Time Bomb ○
1984, US, 100 mins, colour
Dir: Paul Krasny
Stars: Billy Dee Williams, Morgan Fairchild, Joseph Bottoms, Merlin Olsen
Rating: ★★

Morgan Fairchild, star of *Flamingo Road* and *Falcon Crest,* has long been cast as a super-bitch bombshell. But here she takes her man-killer reputation one stage further as a ruthless terrorist attempting to hijack a load of plutonium. Even she was mindful of the strange casting when she spoke of the role. 'I hope it doesn't seem too Hollywood,' she told *Time* magazine. 'I have this little porcelain face and short of taking a hammer to it there's nothing you can do.' But she did confess to killing burly Merlin Olsen – 'It was like the ant who took Chicago.' The comic book action is a natural for director Paul Krasny, after early work on series such as *Mission Impossible, Hawaii Five-O* and *Chips.*

Time Flies ⊙
1944, UK, 88 mins, b/w
Dir: Walter Forde
Stars: Tommy Handley, Evelyn Dall, George Moon
Rating: ★★

One of the great radio comedian Tommy Handley's few feature films, this sends him to Elizabethan London in a time machine. Unseen now for many years, the film features guest appearances (as a soothsayer and his nephew) by those stalwarts of Will Hay comedies, plump Graham Moffatt and wheezy Moore Marriott. Despite the subject and the cast, the treatment lacks vivacity.

Time for Giving, A ◐
(aka: Generation)
1969, US, 104 mins, colour
Dir: George Schaefer
Stars: David Janssen, Kim Darby, Pete Duel
Rating: ★★★

Tenderly-observed, often amusing and ultimately moving human drama about a young couple who want to deliver their own baby and resent the well-meaning interference of the girl's father. It's far from being as cloying as it sounds, and David Janssen, who didn't have much luck with his film roles, delivers a fine performance as the father. Making his screen debut in a supporting role is Sam Waterston, who later played Nick Carroway in *The Great Gatsby* and is still a busy leading actor today.

Time Gentlemen Please! ○
1952, UK, 83 mins, b/w
Dir: Lewis Gilbert
Stars: Eddie Byrne, Edie Martin
Rating: ★★

This is a charming little comedy from the all-too-short-lived Group 3 Productions (formed to boost British independent film-making). Its story, which involves the village drunk-cum-layabout coming into a fortune, clearly shows the influence of the Ealing Studios school of fun, and gives Irish character star Eddie Byrne an opportunity for a richly comic characterisation as the idler. The best of any number of amusing performances in support (Ian Carmichael has a tiny role as a public relations man) comes from little Edie Martin as a blood-and-thunder prophetess.

Time Lock ○
1957, UK, 73 mins, b/w
Dir: Gerald Thomas
Stars: Robert Beatty, Betty McDowall
Rating: ★★

That talented child star Vincent Winter, who first came to prominence in *The Kidnappers*, is at the heart of this tense thriller made by Peter Rogers and Gerald Thomas before they turned their attention to making *Carry On* comedies. Vincent plays a little boy who gets accidentally locked in a bank vault; and the suspense mounts steadily as attempts to rescue him become increasingly desperate. Spot the young Sean Connery in a brief role as a welder.

Time Machine, The ○
1960, US, 103 mins, colour
Dir: George Pal
Stars: Rod Taylor, Yvette Mimieux
Rating: ★★★

Special effects wizards Gene Warren and Tim Baar took an Academy Award for their visual trickery in this adaptation of the H G Wells fantasy classic. Comic-strip action, but some eerily effective moments too.

Time of Destiny, A ◐
1988, US, 117 mins, colour
Dir: Gregory Nava
Stars: William Hurt, Timothy Hutton, Melissa Leo, Francisco Rabal, Stockard Channing
Rating: ★★

This very slow war-romance-family-vendetta epic offered the first evidence that not even the Oscar-winning William Hurt was director-proof. Very old-fashioned in its execution (and set in the 1943-45 period), the plot hands Hurt a rare villainous role as the GI who has vowed to kill his sister's new husband, whom he holds responsible for the death of the family father who tried to prevent the marriage. Gregory Nava's direction is top-heavy with symbolism and has no pace, hampered a bit perhaps by the film's complex flashback and flash-forward structure. The script isn't bad, although it has one or two laughable lines even Hurt can't cope with. The best thing in the film is Melissa Leo's utterly sincere portrayal of the beleaguered but strongly-characterised heroine. The climax in a bell-tower is enjoyably badly staged and at least gives the movie a lively final reel.

Timescape ◐ ⓥ
(aka: Grand Tour: Disaster in Time)
1991, Canada, 98 mins, colour
Dir: David N Twohy
Stars: Jeff Daniels, Ariana Richards, Jim Haynie, Emilia Crow
Rating: ★★

An intriguing idea is never quite carried out with sufficient urgency by writer-director David Twohy to put this in the top flight of fantasy. Innkeeper Jeff Daniels, battling the booze and the memory of leaving his wife to die, finds his hotel housing a group of strange tourists who turn out to be time travellers visiting earthly disasters. Can he prevent one happening in 1991 and rescue a child from her vengeful grandfather at the same time? Watch this space!

Timeslip ○
1955, UK, 93 mins, b/w
Dir: Ken Hughes
Stars: Gene Nelson, Faith Domergue
Rating: ★★★

The plot of this thriller takes some believing. But director Ken Hughes makes it so fast and exciting that you won't have time to work out the deficiencies. Hollywood players Gene Nelson and Faith Domergue head the cast, but Britain's Peter Arne steals the film in the dual role that provides the key to the story.

Timetable ○
1955, US, 79 mins, colour
Dir: Mark Stevens
Stars: Mark Stevens, Felicia Farr
Rating: ★★★

Star Mark Stevens also directed this taut, fast-moving thriller about a big train robbery. As a director, he was much sharper than as an actor, as he showed in such other films as *Cry Vengeance!* Here, he keeps the action going like the train that is robbed in a well-planned and brilliantly executed raid. Jack Klugman makes his screen debut as a frightened witness, and it's a notable first film performance.

Time Travellers, The ○
1964, US, 82 mins, colour
Dir: Ib Melchior
Stars: Preston Foster, Philip Carey, Merry Anders
Rating: ★★★

An interesting piece of science-fiction which had a limited release in British cinemas. An uneven film, it has good performances from Merry Anders – one of those great unsung Hollywood actresses who work steadily for 20 years without really becoming stars – and John Hoyt. The ending is unexpected and rather chilling.

Tina – What's Love Got to Do with It ● ⓥ
1993, US, 118 mins, colour
Dir: Brian Gibson
Stars: Angela Bassett, Lawrence Fishburne
Rating: ★★★★

River deep and mountain high, sang Tina Turner in one of her greatest hits. That was about how low she sank and how high she had to climb to survive and escape a marriage to her

T

stage partner Ike Turner from which her music was the only relief. Subjected to a savage 15-year campaign of beating by a husband who, flirtatious and self-centred by nature, was unable to cope with his wife taking the limelight. Tina only divorced him as late as 1977, making a sensational solo comeback three years later. In two Oscar-nominated performances, Angela Bassett mimes superbly to Turner's songs and Lawrence Fishburne is excellent as Ike, moving convincingly from smooth Romeo with deep bass singing voice into a drug-sniffing, short-fused monster and ageing believably at the same time. Yet the strength of the performance is that he never quite loses all our sympathy. Bassett conveys well the transformation in Tina when she takes to the stage, and it was possibly a mistake for Turner to come on as herself on stage at the end; this is rightly Bassett's show (audiences cheered when she hits back for the first time in 15 years) and it's wrong to deprive her shining performance of its final bow.

Tin Drum, The ◐
1979, West Germany/France, 142 mins, colour
Dir: Volker Schlondorff
Stars: David Bennent, Mario Adorf, Angela Winkler
Rating: ★★★★

Brilliant West German movie which deservedly won an Oscar as the best foreign film of its year. Director Volker Schlondorff races through a complex but coherent narrative at a good rhythm, and the film never sags in its look at 20th century German history through the rather scary gaze of a boy who has stunted his own growth because he has decided not to grow up. Some scenes are memorably unsettling; semi-surrealistic details may be too much for the squeamish.

Tin Men ● ⓥ
1987, US, 112 mins, colour
Dir: Barry Levinson
Stars: Richard Dreyfuss, Danny DeVito, Barbara Hershey, John Mahoney
Rating: ★★★

A sad, oddly touching and well-acted slice-of-life story which would be even more effective if you didn't have the feeling that it's meant to be a comedy. Richard Dreyfuss and Danny DeVito are 'aluminium siding' salesmen, door-to-door hustlers who find their livelihoods under threat

from the Home Improvement Commission. As if this weren't enough, the two men are involved in a collision in their new cars which very rapidly escalates into a tit-for-tat war of ridiculously ugly proportions. As the coup de grâce, Dreyfuss beds DeVito's wife (Barbara Hershey). But – you've guessed it – he falls in love with her. Nice, lived-in dialogue by director Barry Levinson, with the occasional acidly amusing line cloaking the wretchedness in the lives of these smooth-moving losers. Hershey is exceptionally good as the wasted wife, Dreyfuss spot-on as the rustproof Romeo. DeVito fits round his oily, four-letter character like a well-worn glove. These are bad-tempered, sweaty people, but they have the whiff of life. I warn you, though, you may never let another salesman in the house again. As for laughs, you'll get more from an episode of *EastEnders*.

Tin Pan Alley ⊙
1940, US, 94 mins, b/w
Dir: Walter Lang
Stars: Alice Faye, Betty Grable, John Payne, Jack Oakie
Rating: ★★

The only major teaming of Fox's two big musical blonds of the early Forties, Alice Faye and Betty Grable, is a bright, bustling musical set in the early years of the 20th century, against America's music publishing business. Director Walter Lang fizzes the story along, the teeming streets of 'Tin Pan Alley' are vividly captured, and there's a tuneful score. The highlight is probably 'The Sheik of Araby', danced and sung by Grable and Faye, with plump Billy Gilbert as the sheik. One of the few big Fox musicals of the time not to be shot in colour – a pity, as the story cries out for the Technicolor treatment.

Tin Star, The ○
1957, US, 93 mins, b/w
Dir: Anthony Mann
Stars: Henry Fonda, Anthony Perkins, Betsy Palmer
Rating: ★★★

Despite the absence of his usual star, James Stewart, this is probably Anthony Mann's best Western. It's a classic re-telling of the one about the inexperienced lawman helped by an older, embittered gunman. It provided Henry Fonda with one of a series of meaty Western roles in the Fifties and Sixties. In this film, there's one stand-out scene, superbly caught in

black-and-white, as the doctor's black carriage rattles back into town after he has gone missing. And the showdown climax is in the best tradition of the Western, while Anthony Perkins gives an especially sensitive performance as Fonda's very agreeable foil.

Titanic ○
1953, US, 97 mins, b/w
Dir: Jean Negulesco
Stars: Clifton Webb, Barbara Stanwyck, Robert Wagner
Rating: ★★★

One of two Fifties' films on the great 1912 maritime disaster that are superior to any other film on the subject before or since. Clifton Webb and Barbara Stanwyck provide more depth to their roles than the script really deserves while Richard Basehart gives a quietly striking performance as a drunken, unfrocked priest. Edmund Purdom makes one of his earliest screen appearances as Lightoller, the role played by Kenneth More in the other famous 'Titanic' film *A Night to Remember*.

Titfield Thunderbolt, The ⊙ ⓥ
1953, UK, 84 mins, colour
Dir: Charles Crichton
Stars: Stanley Holloway, George Relph, Naunton Wayne
Rating: ★★★

Sunny, enjoyable Ealing Studios fun about the fight to preserve a 'one-horse' railway. The first Ealing comedy in colour, and the gorgeous Technicolor photography of darkest Surrey is quite splendid. It's in similar vein to *Passport to Pimlico* and *The Lavender Hill Mob*, with the usual stock Ealing characters tilting at local windmills. George Relph stands out as an engine-loving cleric and Stanley Holloway offers another of those amiable drunks who are always pleasingly littered around Ealing pictures.

T-Men ○
1947, US, 87 mins, b/w
Dir: Anthony Mann
Stars: Dennis O'Keefe, Mary Meade, Charles McGraw
Rating: ★★★

Dynamic, documentary-style thriller about US Treasury agents in great danger while tracking down a gang of counterfeiters. Its hard-hitting style made the reputations of director Anthony Mann and cinematographer

John Alton, who close in on the action like hired assassins stalking their victim and create an urgent atmosphere of high tension throughout. Star Dennis O'Keefe, whose previous star career had been mainly in comedy, found himself with a new image as a screen tough guy and, as a new member of the T-Men, a little-known actor called Alfred Ryder makes an especially strong impression.

Toast of New Orleans, The ○
1950, US, 97 mins, colour
Dir: Norman Taurog
Stars: Mario Lanza, David Niven
Rating: ★★★

Mario Lanza's second film was one of the biggest musicals that even MGM had ever mounted. A cast of thousands swarms across 35 sets – including complicated construction jobs for the fishing village and the opera house. Magnificent Technicolor photography makes the most of it all, the supporting cast is full of character and Lanza (with Kathryn Grayson) sings perhaps his biggest film hit – 'Be My Love'.

Tobacco Road ○
1941, US, 84 mins, b/w
Dir: John Ford
Stars: Charley Grapewin, Marjorie Rambeau, Gene Tierney, Dana Andrews
Rating: ★★

Charley Grapewin added another to his gallery of wheezy old codgers (notable previous examples have occurred in *Ah, Wilderness!*, *The Petrified Forest* and *The Grapes of Wrath*) with the idle Jeeter Lester in this somewhat bowdlerised version of a notorious novel and play, one of the earliest about steamy goings-on in the American deep South. John Ford's direction and Arthur Miller's photography lend the film poetic touches which help balance its portrait of degradation and despair.

To Be or Not to Be ○
1942, US, 99 mins, b/w
Dir: Ernst Lubitsch
Stars: Carole Lombard, Jack Benny, Robert Stack
Rating: ★★★

Three months after completing this, probably her best film, that so-talented Hollywood funny lady Carole Lombard was killed in a plane crash. The story, which revolves round second-rate Polish actors on the run from the Nazis, was thought in bad taste at the time, but is now seen as a black comedy classic. Jack Benny's soliloquy from *Hamlet* stops the show. The film was remade with Mel Brooks and Anne Bancroft as the stars.

Tobruk ○
1966, US, 110 mins, colour
Dir: Arthur Hiller
Stars: Rock Hudson, George Peppard
Rating: ★★

A straightforward World War Two action film, with an exciting beginning (a night raid by frogmen), an explosive ending and a pretty routine middle. Rock Hudson is surprisingly effective as the British major who does everything from conversing in the vernacular with a passing Tuareg tribesman to destroying the German fuel installations at Tobruk. The screenplay is by veteran Hollywood 'heavy' Leo Gordon, who also plays a supporting role. George Peppard plays a German-born Jew working for the Allies.

To Catch a Thief ○ ⓥ
1955, US, 106 mins, colour
Dir: Alfred Hitchcock
Stars: Cary Grant, Grace Kelly, Jessie Royce Landis, John Williams
Rating: ★★★

Like any work by the master of suspense, Alfred Hitchcock, this thriller – about a jewel thief trying to track down his impersonator – has its fair share of mystery. But it is also the one in which Hitchcock plays some jokes (some of them at the expense of the audience), with plentiful red herrings and dead-end trails. Distinctive Hitchcockian touches are here too, in plenty: one remembers especially Jessie Royce Landis stubbing out her cigarette in an egg, and a bizarre costume ball with policemen awkwardly masquerading in fancy dress. And there's a splendid car chase along the Grand Corniche (a Riviera hilltop road), filmed from a helicopter. Cary Grant is smooth, if improbable, as the jewel thief while Grace Kelly is icily effective as the high society girl whose reserve is gradually melted by the prospect of a romance tinged with excitement.

To Each His Own ○
1946, US, 122 mins, b/w
Dir: Mitchell Leisen
Stars: Olivia de Havilland, John Lund, Mary Anderson, Roland Culver
Rating: ★★★

Olivia de Havilland finally achieved the recognition she craved as an actress with her fine performance in this very classy weepie, notable for its well-constructed script and remarkably un-starry cast. The star's leading man was an unknown from Broadway, John Lund, who does well here, but never achieved true front-rank stardom in the cinema. But Olivia went on to greater glories. She won her first Oscar here, for her performance as the embittered spinster, and it was not long before she would win another, for *The Heiress*.

To Have and Have Not ○ ⓥ
1944, US, 100 mins, b/w
Dir: Howard Hawks
Stars: Humphrey Bogart, Walter Brennan, Lauren Bacall
Rating: ★★★★

An absolute screen classic, brimming over with razor-sharp dialogue, first-rate direction and acting as good as it comes. Warners wanted another *Casablanca* from this tale of WWII intrigue in exotic Martinique – and found the perfect foil to Humphrey Bogart in 18-year-old New York model Betty Bacall. Virtually unknown in Hollywood, she was spotted on the cover of Vogue magazine by the wife of the film's director, Howard Hawks. Her name was changed to Lauren, she was whisked off her feet in real life by her co-star and the rest, as they say, is movie history. Bacall was so nervous during the early days of filming that she had to keep her trembling chin down almost to her chest and flick her eyes upwards to look at Bogey. In an instant 'The Look' was born and it launched her smouldering beauty into a succession of hit films.

To Hell and Back ○ ⓥ
1955, US, 106 mins, colour
Dir: Jesse Hibbs
Stars: Audie Murphy, Marshall Thompson, Charles Drake
Rating: ★★★

Remarkably successful film of Audie Murphy's book about his early life, and the wartime heroics which made him the most decorated American soldier of World War Two. Very exciting, too. Murphy gives a commendably modest portrayal without being too self-effacing.

To Kill a Mockingbird ⓒ ⓥ
1962, US, 129 mins, b/w
Dir: Robert Mulligan

T

Stars: Gregory Peck, Mary Badham, Philip Alford, Robert Duvall
Rating: ★★★

Gregory Peck finally won a coveted Best Actor Oscar at the fifth time of being nominated for his compassionate performance in this classic race-hate drama. Peck gives a fine character reading of the lawyer and widowed father of two children who has to defend a black man accused of raping a white girl in a Deep South town in the 1930s. But it's the child actors who steal every scene in which they appear. Mary Badham, a nine-year-old who had never acted before, is truly charming as the tough little sister who tries to keep pace with her brother, but ends up having to wear a dress, however embarrassing it is to her. Still Peck's favourite film from a varied career.

To Kill a Priest ● Ⓥ
1988, UK, 119 mins, colour
Dir: Agnieszka Holland
Stars: Christopher Lambert, Ed Harris, Joanne Whalley-Kilmer Cherie Lunghi, Peter Postlethwaite
Rating: ★

Something went dramatically wrong with this film about the young Solidarity priest murdered by Polish secret agents in 1984. Too great an attempt has been made, for one thing, to *dramatise* the story, causing a bevy of good British actors to overact like mad. And Agnieszka Holland has, in her sincerity as a Polish patriot, allowed the enterprise to go on for far too long. Christopher Lambert is adequate if not terribly charismatic as the priest. Hollywood's Ed Harris strives mightily to pull it all together as the tortured secret policeman who yearns to kill him and spare him at the same time, but Tim Roth and Timothy Spall as his associates give garish performances more suited to a *Carry On* film. The sad thing about the whole sorry business is that it's such a limp and laboured tribute to a genuine martyr.

To Live and Die in L.A. ● Ⓥ
1985, US, 116 mins, colour
Dir: William Friedkin
Stars: William L Petersen, Willem Dafoe, John Pankow, Debra Feuer
Rating: ★

This violent police thriller with all the ingredients you'd expect from an adults-only Eighties film was described in its publicity as 'sophisticated'. But

believe me there is *nothing* in the least sophisticated in this story about a cop (William L Petersen) who swears to break all the rules to avenge the death of his partner at the hands of a killer. Despite a a a great cast (including Willem Dafoe, John Turturro, Dean Stockwell and Robert Downey Jr), the film is hard to follow and harder still to get involved in when its characters on both sides of the law are so dislikeable. Stockwell gives easily the best performance as a lawyer with one money-grabbing foot on either side of the legal fence. The rock soundtrack (by Wang Chung) is as raucous and aggressive as most of the characters in the film.

Tomahawk ○
(aka: Battle of Powder River)
1950, US, 82 mins, colour
Dir: George Sherman
Stars: Van Heflin, Yvonne De Carlo, Jack Oakie
Rating: ★★

Election day gets off to a rousing start with this colourful saga about Cavalrymen and Indians.This was one of the earliest of the vivid 80-minute co-features for which Universal-International was to become famous in the Fifties. Several of the actors in this adventure – Alex Nicol, Yvonne De Carlo, Rock Hudson and Susan Cabot among them – were to become staple elements of these action films, while the cast here is considerably boosted by the presence of such experienced Hollywood stars as Van Heflin, Jack Oakie and Preston Foster.

Tom and Jerry The Movie ⊙ Ⓥ
1992, US, 84 mins, colour
Dir: Phil Roman
Voice stars: Richard Kind, Dana Hill, Henry Gibson, Charlotte Rae
Rating: ★★

The famous cat and mouse's first feature film is a lively enough caper which can't begin to compare with the classic MGM cartoons, but might please modern tots who have somehow missed these on TV. The story – in which Tom and Jerry save a young orphan from her evil guardians (a well-worn cartoon theme) – works well enough, but there are a few shocks for vintage T & J fans. The first is that they speak! This makes their normal rough-and-tumble antics seem merely gratuitously violent. The second is that they become pals! Still, the

cat-and-mouse slapstick that results will please simple minds, although younger viewers may find the darker side, which includes kidnap and death threats, slightly upsetting. Although it has more lowspots than highpoints, the caper will still give rise to the occasional guffaw. There's life in the old cat and mouse yet.

Tomb of Ligeia, The ●
1964, US, 81 mins, colour
Dir: Roger Corman
Stars: Vincent Price, Elizabeth Shepherd, John Westbrook
Rating: ★★★★

Director Roger Corman's second film in Britain, and the last and best of his series of horror tales based on the works of Edgar Allan Poe. Corman hardly puts a foot wrong in this one, which is not only quite faithful to the Poe original (a short story), but adds its own conclusion to Poe's unfinished scenario. It's very literate, frightening in parts and very well acted, particularly by Vincent Price and by Oliver Johnston as his manservant. And the plot has as many twists and turns as the black cat which plays such a vital part in its disentanglement. Some of the earlier scenes – notably one in which the heroine is lured by the cat into a bell-tower – are especially well-staged. A minor classic of its genre.

Tom Brown's Schooldays ⊙
1951, UK, 95 mins, b/w
Dir: Gordon Parry
Stars: John Howard Davies, Robert Newton, Diana Wynyard, Hermione Baddeley
Rating: ★★★

Less well-paced than the 1940 Hollywood version of Thomas Hughes' famous school story, but more solidly acted, this British version was directed by Gordon Parry and proved an immense success at the box-office. A young Max Bygraves makes an early film appearance aboard a coach, and John Howard Davies, reunited with his *Oliver Twist* co-star Robert Newton (who plays the headmaster) is ideal as Tom Brown.

Tom, Dick and Harry ○
1941, US, 86 mins, b/w
Dir: Garson Kanin
Stars: Ginger Rogers, George Murphy, Alan Marshal, Burgess Meredith
Rating: ★★★

A deliciously scatty comedy about a girl who has three suitors on the go at one time, but tends to get them and their financial status mixed up. Director Garson Kanin shot the ending three ways, so that none of the actors concerned would know who got the girl. Highly original stuff, much less pretentious than star Ginger Rogers' faintly similar film called *Lady in the Dark*, three years later.

Tom Horn ○ ⓥ
1980, US, 98 mins, colour
Dir: William Wiard
Stars: Steve McQueen, Linda Evans, Richard Farnsworth, Slim Pickens
Rating: ★★★

There's certainly a touch of the genuine old west about Steve McQueen's second-last film, picturesquely set and lovingly photographed. The first half is packed with rugged action, the second brings us down to earth as frontiersman Horn is laid low. One would have liked to have seen more of the character's colourful early life, especially his involvement in the Indian wars. That said, it must be added that John Alonzo's colour cinematography is not only beyound fault, but also imaginative and the work of a real stylist.

Tom Jones ❶ ⓥ
1963, UK, 129 mins, colour
Dir: Tony Richardson
Stars: Albert Finney, Susannah York, Hugh Griffith, Edith Evans, Diane Cilento
Rating: ★★★★

A deserved Academy Award winner, this lusty, magnificent period comedy deservedly gave the British their first 'best picture' Oscar for 15 years. Director Tony Richardson (who has never equalled his achievements here), takes Henry Fielding's famous story of a foundling's amorous adventures and, with incredibly cheeky sleight-of-hand, including quick motion, freezeframe, and characters addressing the audience, enriches the screen with earthy entertainment played for laughs at breakneck speed. Five members of the cast were Oscar nominees, including Albert Finney, endowing Tom with a drive and a lust for life that is irresistible, and Hugh Griffith as the squire. Red-cheeked, debauched, leering at his farmgirls, or angrily pushing away his farm animals while he is trying to think, his is a richly comic performance. Best of all, though, is Edith Evans, as the haughty Miss Western. 'Stand and deliver!' cries a highwayman. 'Sir,' retorts Dame Edith. 'I am no travelling mid-

wife. Coachman, drive on!' But Oscars were won by Richardson, by John Osborne for his script, and by John Addison for his devastatingly witty 18th-century-style musical accompaniment to the ribald goings-on.

Tommy ● ⓥ
1975, UK, 111 mins, colour
Dir: Ken Russell
Stars: Ann-Margret, Oliver Reed, Roger Daltrey, Elton John
Rating: ★★★

A bizarre, full-blooded and drivingly powerful version of the rock opera by The Who. The story is of a boy – struck deaf, dumb and blind by seeing his father killed by his stepfather – who becomes the king of the pinball wizards and, on recovery of his full faculties, a Messiah-like figure for the young. Director Ken Russell's typically pile-driving approach ensures that you'll be swept away in the film's tide of dazzlingly entertaining obscenities. And you must admire the tremendous singing and uninhibited verve of Ann-Margret and the sardonic subtlety of Oliver Reed's hilarious teddy boy. Tina Turner is something else as the Acid Queen. It's wicked but it's wizard, the *Gone With the Wind* of the pop-video era.

Tommy Steele Story, The ○ ⓥ
(aka: Rock Around the World)
1957, UK, 82 mins, b/w
Dir: Gerard Bryant
Stars: Tommy Steele, Lisa Daniely
Rating: ★★★

There can't be many film biopics that were made when their subject (and star) was still only 21. Even Keaton and Jolson had to wait until they were well into middle age. But already Tommy Steele had packed enough incident into his young life to make the conception of a tune-filled life story well worthwhile. It's rather a quiet film for a period when Bill Haley and his Comets were breaking records and eardrums at every theatre in Britain and America. Even so, it's packed with songs – 18 of them. There are guest artists of the day, such as Humphrey Lyttelton, Charles McDevitt and Nancy Whiskey, while Tommy himself sings a wide variety of songs, the best of which is 'Butterfingers'. An engaging entertainment, dominated by the star's own chirpy personality.

Tommy the Toreador ○ ⓥ
1959, UK, 86 mins, colour
Dir: John Paddy Carstairs
Stars: Tommy Steele, Janet Munro, Sidney James
Rating: ★★★

No time at all for a siesta in this enjoyably lightweight comedy with music, a British version of the type of family fare Elvis Presley turned out in the early Sixties. Tommy Steele's energetic performance is nicely offset by comedy cameos from a host of familiar funny men (including Sidney James, Eric Sykes, Bernard Cribbins, Kenneth Williams and Warren Mitchell) and by Janet Munro's attractive presence.

Tomorrow Is Forever ○
1945, US, 105 mins, b/w
Dir: Irving Pichel
Stars: Claudette Colbert, Orson Welles, George Brent
Rating: ★★★

Natalie Wood appears here in her first major film, at the age of six. It's a big weepie about a man (Orson Welles) returned from the dead to find his wife has re-married. The director is Irving Pichel, a former actor who brought considerable bulky presence to such horror films as *Dracula's Daughter*.

Tomorrow We Live ○
(aka: At Dawn We Die)
1942, UK, 82 mins, b/w
Dir: George King
Stars: John Clements, Godfrey Tearle, Hugh Sinclair, Greta Gynt
Rating: ★★★

An eventful war film about French freedom fighters, 'made with the official co-operation of General de Gaulle'. Good performances from Greta Gynt, Judy Kelly, Yvonne Arnaud and Karel Stepanek, all of whom outshine the nominal stars of the film headed by John Clements. It may look a bit stiff by today's standards, but it was food and drink to the British wartime box-office and didn't do badly in America either, the February 1943 première being treated as an important social event.

tom thumb ⊙
1958, US, 98 mins, colour
Dir: George Pal
Stars: Russ Tamblyn, Peter Sellers, Terry-Thomas
Rating: ★★★

A delightful children's entertainment, with Russ Tamblyn a sprightly inch-high hero and Peter Sellers and

T

734 Tonight's the Night

Terry-Thomas stealing all their scenes as the roguishly comic villains. The scene where they count and share out their ill-gotten gains is hilarious. Hummable tunes (especially 'The Yawning Song'), good puppet animation and notable contributions from Jessie Matthews and Bernard Miles as Tom's foster-parents complete a delightful entertainment.

Tonight's the Night
See: Happy Ever After

Tony Rome ○
1967, US, 110 mins, colour
Dir: Gordon Douglas
Stars: Frank Sinatra, Jill St John, Richard Conte, Gena Rowlands
Rating: ★★

Tired-eye private eye Tony Rome, who tackles his cases from a houseboat, was Frank Sinatra's first stab at playing detective in a career stretching back 25 years. He promptly proceeded to make two more films in the same vein, *Lady in Cement* and *The Detective*. All three were directed by Sinatra's old friend Gordon Douglas and all feature the maximum feminine distraction and a collection of weird characters in the finest Bogart tradition. This one, set in Miami, was highly thought-of in some critical circles and involves our weary hero in a rather nasty mystery concerning drugs and, of course, murder.

Too Hot to Handle ○ ⓥ
(aka: The Marrying Man)
1991, US, 117 mins, colour
Dir: Jerry Rees
Stars: Kim Basinger, Alec Baldwin, Robert Loggia, Elisabeth Shue, Armand Assante
Rating: ★★

On the face of it (and everywhere else), Basinger would seem to have everything: looks, talent, sex appeal and even singing ability, as she proves here. But most of it doesn't come across in this one. And the problems of Kim and the equally charmless Alec Baldwin just don't seem to amount to a hill of beans, when they should be carrying us through two hours of on-off love-hate-love. Neil Simon has fashioned a very corny over-the-years romance which starts in 1948 when playboy Baldwin, about to marry a film magnate's daughter, becomes a heap of quivering lust at one sighting of sultry songbird Basinger, who just happens to be the mistress of gangster Bugsy Siegal. Strangely, this situation

doesn't qualify the duo for concrete overcoats, but instead triggers a plot in which Baldwin marries Basinger four times over. If only he'd left it at one! Among several anachronisms in its script, the film uses the word 'bimbo' a lot, which we can't believe was around 40 years ago. This plot, however, was – and it looks its age.

Too Late for Tears ○
1949, US, 99 mins, b/w
Dir: Byron Haskin
Stars: Lizabeth Scott, Don DeFore, Dan Duryea, Arthur Kennedy
Rating: ★★

Lizabeth Scott excels as a particularly deadly femme fatale in this dark thriller that casts her as a hard-bitten blonde only too ready to stoop to murder to keep her hands on $60,000 in cash that has accidentally come her way, in her anxiety to 'move out of the ranks of the middle-class poor'. Even Dan Duryea's slimy, corrupt detective pales besides the pure evil of the Scott character. Good, unsettling use of Los Angeles locations by director Byron Haskin adds the finishing touch to an efficient, if slightly unpleasant thriller.

Too Late the Hero ○ ⓥ
1969, US, 144 mins, colour
Dir: Robert Aldrich
Stars: Michael Caine, Cliff Robertson, Ian Bannen, Denholm Elliott
Rating: ★★

A tense and exciting war drama set in the Pacific, with Michael Caine and Cliff Robertson sent behind enemy lines to destroy a Japanese observation post which monitors allied shipping. Almost as violent but nowhere near as gung-ho as director Robert Aldrich's earlier war adventure *The Dirty Dozen*. Perhaps this has something to do with the fact that it has a largely British cast, although there is nothing stiff-upper-lipped about Caine's performance as Cockney tough Tosh Hearne. Robertson gives good value, as usual, and there are also strong portrayals by Ian Bannen and Denholm Elliott. Thrilling stuff, with a few twists and turns before the final reel.

Too Many Crooks ⊙
1958, UK, 87 mins, b/w
Dir: Mario Zampi
Stars: Terry-Thomas, George Cole, Brenda De Banzie
Rating: ★★

British film comedy, currently rather in the doldrums, was going through one of its richest periods when director Mario Zampi made this very funny farce about a bunch of bungling burglars. Zampi's previous comedies included *Laughter in Paradise*, *Happy Ever After* and *The Naked Truth* – all winners. His early death in 1963 was a great loss to the British cinema.

Tootsie ○ ⓥ
1982, US, 116 mins, colour
Dir: Sydney Pollack
Stars: Dustin Hoffman, Jessica Lange, Teri Garr, Dabney Coleman, Bill Murray
Rating: ★★★

Dustin Hoffman acts both his male and female co-stars off the screen as an out-of-work actor who 'drags' up as a woman he names Dorothy Michaels to land a job on a daytime soap opera. And he was so convincing as a woman that industry wags suggest that Hoffman should have been nominated for a Best Actress Oscar as well as the Best Actor statuette. He himself wasn't convinced that he could pull off the deception and spent a year and thousands of dollars on screen tests. He even fooled actor friend Jon Voight by making a pass at him in a lift at the studio! But he was sad that although he was believable, he didn't make an attractive woman. On Oscars night, it was Jessica Lange who scooped the Best Supporting Actress Award as the girl Hoffman fancies and who Hoffman as 'Dorothy' gets to sleep with as best girlfriends, causing no end of comic complications. The film's director, Sydney Pollack, plays Hoffman's agent, Geena Davis makes her first screen appearance, and well down the cast you'll find Estelle Getty (Sophia from *The Golden Girls*) billed in a cameo as a middle-aged woman.

Topaz ○
1969, US, 127 mins, colour
Dir: Alfred Hitchcock
Stars: Frederick Stafford, John Forsythe, Karin Dor
Rating: ★★

Underrated Hitchcock thriller based on the best-selling book by Leon Uris, author of the (also filmed) *Exodus*. Keep your thinking caps on for the incredibly complicated plot and you'll be gripped throughout.

Top Gun ○ ⓥ
1986, US, 110 mins, colour
Dir: Tony Scott

Stars: Tom Cruise, Kelly McGillis, Val Kilmer, Anthony Edwards, Tom Skerritt, Meg Ryan
Rating: ★★

The searing aerial action in this thunderous action film took the filmgoing world and especially younger filmgoers by storm on its first appearance, pushing Tom Cruise and Kelly McGillis into the megastar bracket at a single step. Movie buffs from way back, though, will have seen its like before. It's the one about the maverick fighter pilot who bucks authority, proves he's the best, cracks up on the death of a friend, but comes good in the end to claim the glory or the girl. In other years, it could have starred James Cagney and Tony Curtis and been part of an action double-bill; here it's Cruise, flashing his teeth a lot and oozing charisma, and McGillis, with multiple under-lid looks, who keep us watching, with the aid of lots of noisy action and a synthesised pop score. The rest of the characters are such cardboard cut-outs that they could be wheeled on and off the set without affecting the plot. And, this being the computer age, that thing on Cruise's shoulder is presumably a microchip!

Top Hat ○ ⓥ
1935, US, 100 mins, b/w
Dir: Mark Sandrich
Stars: Fred Astaire, Ginger Rogers
Rating: ★★★★

This effervesent Fred Astaire and Ginger Rogers musical was the perfect panacea for Depression-era audiences. Every one of Irving Berlin's five songs from the film was a hit and the movie was the second highest grossing of the year after *Mutiny on the Bounty*, and proved to be RKO's biggest moneymaker of the decade. Astaire and Berlin were on a percentage, so they were happy men. Look out for the scenes where Astaire flies off to Venice – it's outtakes from *Flying Down to Rio*!

Topkapi ○ ⓥ
1964, US, 120 mins, colour
Dir: Jules Dassin
Stars: Melina Mercouri, Maximilian Schell, Peter Ustinov, Robert Morley
Rating: ★★★

Thieves as ingenious as those in this thriller really do deserve to get away with it. Unfortunately, in films at least, they rarely do. Their target here is the Topkapi jewels, four fabulous emeralds in an Istanbul museum. The only way to get at the gems is to lower someone down to the case from above. Husky-voiced Melina Mercouri is the boss of the gang. But it's Peter Ustinov's film as the seedy, down-at-heel Englishman, Arthur Simpson, who makes a living selling blue postcards to tourists. He stumbles into the plot by mistake, and soon becomes a conscript. A sequence where he tries to drive a grenade-loaded car into Istanbul, and falls foul of the Customs and the police, is one of the funniest in the film. Ustinov won an Oscar for the performance. Robert Morley is bewitching too, as the craftsman of the gang, whose home is crammed with toys and gadgets that make it look like something out of James Bond. In spite of the dazzling array of dresses and nail-varnishes, Mercouri isn't entirely at home in her role, but the film really whips up the suspense when three of the crooks clamber dizzily across Istanbul roof tops to reach the museum.

Top of the Form ⊙
1952, UK, 75 mins, b/w
Dir: John Paddy Carstairs
Stars: Ronald Shiner, Anthony Newley, Harry Fowler
Rating: ★★

Ronald Shiner was at the peak of his popularity when he made this broad comedy – a remake of the Will Hay film *Good Morning, Boys* – casting him as a bogus professor (in reality a horse tipster) who finds himself working as a real teacher. Anthony Newley, Harry Fowler and Gerald Campion are among the overgrown schoolboys in his bizarre classroom, and you may spot Ronnie Corbett (at the age of 22) as the 'titch' of the form.

Topper ○
1937, US, 97 mins, b/w
Dir: Norman Z Mcleod
Stars: Constance Bennett, Roland Young
Rating: ★★★

Another of Thorne Smith's novels about mischievous ghosts (he also wrote *I Married a Witch*) is turned into a film comedy classic. Constance Bennett not only revived her entire career as the vivacious (if ethereal) Marion Kerby, but also starred in a sequel, *Topper Returns*. She and Cary Grant make a totally delightful duo, but great credit must also be given to Roy Seawright's special effects, which allow them to materialise at will in their efforts to help a harassed bank president overcome the malevolent machinations of his shrewish wife – two memorable performances by Roland Young (as Topper) and Billie Burke. Briefly glimpsed as an elevator boy is Arthur Lake, whose career was going through a bit of a lull. A year later, he would hit a financial jackpot when cast as Dagwood Bumstead in the long-running *Blondie* series.

Topper Returns ○
1941, US, 88 mins, b/w
Dir: Roy del Ruth
Stars: Joan Blondell, Roland Young, Billie Burke, Dennis O'Keefe
Rating: ★★★

In the famous series of fantasy comedies which began with *Topper* in 1937, full of humorous ghostly adventures, this was the third and last. It's seldom that a sequel or follow-up measures up to the original, but here is an exception. And, despite the success of the first two, it had a different director – Roy Del Ruth instead of Norman Z McLeod. Absolutely scatty, delightful comedy entertainment.

Topper Takes a Trip ○
1939, US, 85 mins, b/w
Dir: Norman Z McLeod
Stars: Constance Bennett, Roland Young, Billie Burke
Rating: ★★★

The second of the three original highly successful *Topper* films about two ghosts interfering in the life of Cosmo Topper, the timid, henpecked little banker hero of Thorne Smith's novels. Throughout the short-lived series, the ghosts changed, but the central character was always played by Roland Young, adding yet another whimsical, bemused character to his collection. He was actually nominated for an Oscar for the original film, which co-starred Cary Grant.

Top Secret! ◑ ⓥ
1984, US, 90 mins, colour
Dir: David And Jerry Zucker
Stars: Val Kilmer, Lucy Gutteridge, Jeremy Kemp, Christopher Villiers
Rating: ★★

Not so many outright guffaws this time around from the *Airplane!* team, but it's fun identifying all the old movies parodied in this spoof on spy/espionage films, set in the rock 'n' roll (well, surfin') era. Aficionados will assuredly recognise *The Conspirators* (a whole sequence), *The Blue Lagoon*, *Gidget*, *Jailhouse Rock*, *The Great Escape* and *The Wizard of Oz*, but there are countless more besides. There's a briskly confident performance from Val Kilmer as the rock star on the run.

Tora! Tora! Tora! ○ Ⓥ
1970, US/Japan, 144 mins, colour
Dir: Ray Kellogg, Toshio Masuda, Kinji Fukasaku
Stars: Martin Balsam, Soh Yamamura, Joseph Cotten, Jason Robards
Rating: ★★★

Long, lavish and meticulous re-creation of the Japanese invasion of Pearl Harbor, which attempts to tell the true story from both sides, took four years to make and cost 20th Century-Fox the enormous (for the time) sum of $25 million to make. It must be the first time that one-time antagonist countries ever got together to tell their respective war stories. It proves to be an impressively impartial account of the events, and the special effects are superb, but the film as a whole turns out to be one-paced and worthy rather than inspired. Perhaps it might have been better had the distinguished director Akira Kurosawa not had to withdraw from the project part-way through. Jason Robards, who plays an American general in the film, was actually in the navy at Pearl Harbor, on 7 December 1941, the day of the attack, and won the Navy Cross. Best performances in the piece, however, come from James Whitmore, as America's Admiral Halsey, Soh Yamamura, as a conscience-stricken Japanese admiral, and Takahiro Tamura, as the man who led the actual attack.

Torch Song ○
1953, US, 90 mins, colour
Dir: Charles Walters
Stars: Joan Crawford, Michael Wilding, Gig Young
Rating: ★★

Near-laughable in parts, but pretty enjoyable as a whole, this all-out melodrama casts Joan Crawford as a bitchy Broadway star who unexpectedly meets her match in the form of a blind pianist, played by Britain's Michael Wilding in the best of his not-very-impressive bunch of Hollywood roles. Strangely, Crawford's singing is dubbed in all but one number – 'Tenderly'. The 'clumsy' dancer with her in the film's opening sequence is in fact the director of the movie, Charles Walters, a musical expert who also made *Easter Parade*, *Lili* and *High Society*. Amazingly, it was Crawford's first starring role in a colour film.

Torch Song Trilogy ● Ⓥ
1988, US, 120 mins, colour
Dir: Paul Bogart
Stars: Harvey Fierstein, Anne Bancroft, Matthew Broderick, Karen Young
Rating: ★★

As full of smart Jewish humour as it is, this film version of Harvey Fierstein's stage hit, complete with the author as star (ludicrous to bill himself third in the credits), still makes pretty heavy going as a film. In spite of the humour, tragedy is perhaps kept too much to the fore in this story of a gay drag queen and his life from 10 to 40. The central character, who seemed so touchingly human in Antony Sher's London stage interpretation, comes across on screen as harsh, unsympathetic and self-centred. And the one-paced direction of Paul Bogart tends to underline the inevitably stagy quality of many of the scenes outside of the club where Arnold (Fierstein) works as an entertainer. Worth sitting through, though, if only to watch Arnold's hefty black transvestite friend hold up a gold ladies' shoe in a dress shop and ask the assistant if she has it in a 16.

Torn Curtain ◐
1966, US, 128 mins, colour
Dir: Alfred Hitchcock
Stars: Paul Newman, Julie Andrews
Rating: ★★

This was the most un-Hitchcock-like Hitchcock in a decade. Despite a nail-bitingly grisly murder scene, in which Hitchcock demonstrates how difficult it really is to kill someone, there are no twists, shocks or surprises to speak of in this conventional spy thriller with some arch dialogue. 'We're sending you out,' whispers an underground worker, 'in the costume bags of a Czech ballet company.' A subdued Paul Newman is the scientist who, apparently defecting to East Berlin, couldn't act more suspiciously if he tried. Small wonder the secret police are soon on his trail, or that fiancée/secretary Julie Andrews treats him like Jane and Michael Banks rolled into one. The film picks up once the couple go on the run from Iron Curtain police and encounter Lila Kedrova as a refugee Polish countess. Her extravagant portrayal is in a completely different world – a Hitchcock world in fact – from the rest of the film.

Torrid Zone ○
1940, US, 88 mins, b/w
Dir: William Keighley
Stars: James Cagney, Ann Sheridan, Pat O'Brien
Rating: ★★★

Robust action and ready wisecracks are the order of the day in another typical Warners vehicle of the early war years, although the setting – a plantation in Central America – is quite unusual for the time. Ann Sheridan steals the show with her honest-to-goodness torch singer, James Cagney and Pat O'Brien exchange banter and double-cross each other with practised ease. Bouquets also to photographer James Wong Howe, art director Ted Smith and set decorator Edward Thorne for first-rate jobs.

To Sir, With Love ○ Ⓥ
1966, UK, 105 mins, colour
Dir: James Clavell
Stars: Sidney Poitier, Suzy Kendall, Judy Geeson
Rating: ★★

This brightly coloured look (through rose-tinted glasses) at the trials and tribulations of an idealistic black teacher at a tough London school made a mint in its day. If it looks more than a little dated and simplistic today, there are good performances from Sidney Poitier, Suzy Kendall, Faith Brook and Adrienne Posta to carry it through its stickier patches. Pop star Lulu seems happier performing the film's hit song than in acting tough with the classroom rebels.

Total Recall ● Ⓥ
1990, US, 109 mins, colour
Dir: Paul Verhoeven
Stars: Arnold Schwarzenegger, Rachel Ticotin, Sharon Stone, Ronny Cox, Michael Ironside
Rating: ★★★

Though perhaps not quite 'the ride of your life' promised by its posters, this action yarn is still a lively sci-fi thriller about a man who has had his memory erased for a purpose other than that which he imagines. It's the distant future. Mars is colonised and Schwarzenegger's Doug Quaid is haunted by nightmares about life there. This is somewhat surprising as he's a building worker who lives on Earth. But Quaid soon becomes convinced he must get back to Mars and end the despotic reign of the men in charge there. From here on, the action hardly stops, with space machine-guns chattering, Schwarzenegger and heroine Rachel Ticotin diving everywhere and special effects running riot, especially in the creation of a colony of mutants who prove to be the hero's allies rather than his enemies. Ironside and Cox are excellent tight-lipped villains, one snapping to the other: 'You should have killed Quaid on Mars!' Well, yes, but they all say that. Actually, there's a special reason why they didn't, but that would be giving too much away of a plot that's above-average in complexity for this kind of film. Those seeking blood, guts and even a little brain-matter that isn't splashed all over the screen will find it all here.

To the Devil a Daughter ● Ⓥ
(aka: To the Devil – A Daughter)
1976, UK/Germany, 95 mins, colour
Dir: Peter Sykes
Stars: Richard Widmark, Christopher Lee, Denholm Elliott, Nastassja Kinski
Rating: ★★

Not the first time that the house of Hammer had dabbled with Dennis Wheatley's diabolic books, but unfortunately the last. After this British-West German co-production, Hammer concentrated on TV work. The hero is an American occult novelist (Richard Widmark, displaying commendable conviction), the villain an ex-communicated priest (the redoubtable Christopher Lee). Their point of contention: a beautiful young girl whose soul is up for grabs. Nastassja Kinski is well cast in this pivotal role, a beguiling mix of innocence and malevolence. A strong supporting cast, glittering photography by David Watkin, and Les Bowie's expert special effects all help to off-set the sometimes confusingly fragmented development of the plot. And the shivers come thick and fast at the end.

To the Ends of the Earth ○
1948, US, 109 mins, b/w
Dir: Robert Stevenson
Stars: Dick Powell, Signe Hasso
Rating: ★★★

A great thriller from the Forties: suspenseful, brilliantly lit and

photographed, grittily acted and with a splendid twist at the end. Dick Powell holds the whole thing together with strength and great skill as the agent who pursues a narcotic ring halfway around the world. But don't go out to make the tea or you may lose the thread of the cleverly-plotted story.

To the Shores of Tripoli ○
1943, US, 86 mins, colour
Dir: Bruce Humberstone
Stars: John Payne, Randolph Scott, Maureen O'Hara
Rating: ★★

It's almost bizarre these days to see Randolph Scott's face not beneath a stetson. This was one of his last non-Western roles as a rival for the hand of the delicious Maureen O'Hara in a story of life in a Marine training camp in wartime. Shot in vivid Technicolor, and giving Henry Morgan his first screen role, it's not to be confused with *Tripoli*, a period adventure made eight years later, which also starred John Payne and O'Hara. Pretty Nancy Kelly provides additional decoration.

Touch of Adultery, A
See: *A Fine Romance*

Touch of Class, A ◐
1972, US, 106 mins, colour
Dir: Melvin Frank
Stars: George Segal, Glenda Jackson
Rating: ★★★

For the first half of its running time, this delightful comedy is quite the best of its kind since the heyday of such witty cat-and-dog forays into sexual sparring, some 30 years earlier. Although Glenda Jackson doesn't seem entirely happy in comedy at first, she reacts superbly to the brilliant timing and deft underplaying of her co-star, making their early scenes together comparable with similar Tracy-Hepburn encounters in the past. Things do run down a bit towards the end, when the script forgoes wit for sarcasm and abrasiveness for sentimentality. Still, there is much that is memorable and much to enjoy in this story of a love affair that turns alternately sweet and sour. For it, Jackson won her second Academy Award.

Touch of Evil ◐
1958, US, 114 mins, b/w
Dir: Orson Welles

Stars: Charlton Heston, Orson Welles, Janet Leigh, Joseph Calleia
Rating: ★★★★

Now generally recognised as one of Orson Welles' masterpieces, this broodingly menacing film was originally intended to feature Welles just as an actor. But when megastar Charlton Heston became involved under the (then-mistaken) impression that Welles was to direct, the seeds were sown for the creation of an unforgettable cinema classic full of warped, tormented, unpleasant characters who litter the paths of Heston and his screen wife Janet Leigh as they become dangerously involved on honeymoon with narcotics and murder down Mexico way. Despite being recut by a studio that didn't understand its structure, it still picked up international awards, accepted by a somewhat bemused Welles who was convinced Universal had almost ruined his film. Among the guest stars who fell over themselves to appear once word got around that Welles was making a new film, you'll spot Marlene Dietrich, Joseph Cotten, Zsa Zsa Gabor and Keenan Wynn.

Touch of Larceny, A ○
1959, UK, 93 mins, b/w
Dir: Guy Hamilton
Stars: James Mason, Vera Miles, George Sanders
Rating: ★★★

James Mason is cast as a naval officer in this entertaining and enjoyable comedy – a role vastly different from the types he played in his earlier days in such films as *The Seventh Veil* and *Odd Man Out* when perhaps only the more perspicacious could foresee what a wide-ranging actor he would soon become. He demonstrates how deftly he can handle comedy as he organises a scheme to get libel damages.

Touch of Love, A ◐ Ⓥ
(aka: Thank You All Very Much)
1969, UK, 102 mins, colour
Dir: Waris Hussein
Stars: Sandy Dennis, Ian McKellen
Rating: ★

Four talents who venture all too rarely into the cinema – actors Sandy Dennis and Ian McKellen, writer Margaret Drabble (here adapting her own novel *The Millstone*) and director Waris Hussein – are involved in this story of a young graduate and the decisions she has to make on finding herself pregnant. The characters

T

remain strangely unsympathetic and don't involve one despite Sandy Dennis' delicate portrayal.

Touch of Scandal, A ●
1984, US, 93 mins, colour
Dir: Ivan Nagy
Stars: Angie Dickinson, Tom Skerritt, Jason Miller, Don Murray
Rating: ★

Nostrils flaring and eyes ablaze, Angie Dickinson emotes at full throttle throughout this lurid blackmail thriller. The relentless synthesizer score determinedly apes the Giorgio Moroder/Jan Hammer school of dramatic impetus while the director Ivan Nagy, taking a break from the *Miami Vice* beat, is very much at home with the garish neon-chic of Los Angeles at twilight.

Tough Guys ●
1986, US, 120 mins, colour
Dir: Jeff Kanew
Stars: Burt Lancaster, Kirk Douglas, Charles Durning, Alexis Smith
Rating: ★★★

It was a sweet idea, teaming Kirk Douglas and Burt Lancaster as two elderly bank robbers returning to life on the outside after 30 years in jail. And, by and large, it works. The action-comedy that results is hardly a blockbuster and its laughs and thrills are amiable rather than dynamic, but it's made with affection – their probation officer is 40 years younger than they are – and its veteran performers do at least come across as real people, half-way between snarling gangsters and Hope and Crosby in a *Road* film. These tough guys may be small-time in terms of today's megamovies, but their act has class and style.

Towering Inferno, The ○ ⓥ
1974, US, 165 mins, colour
Dir: Irwin Allen
Stars: Steve McQueen, Paul Newman, William Holden, Faye Dunaway
Rating: ★★★

Amazingly suspenseful disaster epic, given that British director John Guillermin was presented with a cast top-heavy with major stars. It was such a major undertaking, it took two rival studios, 20th Century-Fox and Warners, to finance the project and the script was culled from two weighty books. In fact, the setting up of the disaster – a fire that traps civic dignitaries near the top of a new 138-storey skyscraper – is far more

interesting than later rescue attempts. An Oscar winner for cinematography, editing and theme song, 'We May Never Love Like This Again', sung by Maureen McGovern.

Tower of London ●
1939, US, 92 mins, b/w
Dir: Rowland V Lee
Stars: Basil Rathbone, Boris Karloff, Vincent Price
Rating: ★★★

Extremely well-produced and atmospheric film about Richard III, which gave Boris Karloff one of his best roles as the shaven-headed executioner who looks like a forerunner of Fester in *The Adams Family* films. Basil Rathbone provides an incisive Richard III, a role taken over in the 1962 sequel by Vincent Price, who coincidentally appears here as the doomed Duke of Clarence.

Town Like Alice, A ○
1956, UK, 107 mins, b/w
Dir: Jack Lee
Stars: Virginia McKenna, Peter Finch
Rating: ★★★

Grim, moving, mud bespattered account of a group of refugee Englishwomen in World War Two Malaya who cannot find a place to stay. They trek hundreds of miles through jungle and swamp simply because no Japanese officer will take responsibility for their welfare. Virginia McKenna and Peter Finch (as an Australian soldier-prisoner who tries to help the women) reach near-brilliance in their harrowing portrayals. No effort is spared to make the story ring true to life, and only the contrived ending is off-key.

Town on Trial! ●
1956, UK, 96 mins, b/w
Dir: John Guillermin
Stars: John Mills, Charles Coburn
Rating: ★★★

A formidable list of suspects for Supt Halloran (John Mills) to sort through in this sinister adaptation of Francis Durbridge's story *The Nylon Murders*. Mills digs deeper into the character than the script has any right to expect, and director John Guillermin conjures up some genuine excitement, particularly in the initial murder sequence where poor Magda Miller 'gets hers', as the killer and the camera stalk through a shadowy wood. The ending – a pursuit up a church steeple – is equally nail-biting.

Toys ● ⓥ
1993, US, 121 mins, colour
Dir: Barry Levinson
Stars: Robin Williams, Michael Gambon, Joan Cusack, Robin Wright, LL Cool J, Donald O'Connor
Rating: ★★

Coming to life in its last 20 minutes with a pitched battle between wind-up toys and modern war toys for control of the factory, this is a fey fantasy with elements of coarse language, a sex scene, and a slow pace that all mark it out as unsuitable for younger children. Robin Williams toplines as the son his dying father (Donald O'Connor) considers too immature to leave in charge, though O'Connor himself scarcely seems to live in the adult world. Enter, as the new boss, O'Connor's megalomaniac military brother (Michael Gambon) who sees real-life possibilities for miniature tanks and helicopters and shuts off most of the factory for his own nefarious purposes. Sounds like a great idea, and indeed brightness and invention are everywhere, but the film is nowhere near fleet enough of foot, light enough of hand or innocent enough of mind to succeed on almost any level. The attraction of the settings soon pales and tedium overtakes the film for long stretches when it seems that director Barry Levinson needs someone to wind up the clockwork key in his back.

Toys in the Attic ●
1963, US, 90 mins, b/w
Dir: George Roy Hill
Stars: Geraldine Page, Wendy Hiller, Dean Martin, Yvette Minieux
Rating: ★★★

George Roy Hill (he went on to direct *Butch Cassidy and the Sundance Kid* and *The Sting*) brought a deftness of touch to Lillian Hellman's adaptation of her own play. Dean Martin is on top form as the gadabout who comes home to spinster sisters Geraldine Page and Wendy Hiller with a child bride.

Toy Soldiers ● ⓥ
1991, US, 112 mins, colour
Dir: Daniel Petrie
Stars: Lou Gossett, Sean Astin, Wil Wheaton, Keith Coogan, Denholm Elliott, Jerry Orbach
Rating: ★

Gung-ho Americana of the lowest kind as, to stirring music, prep school boys soften up the Colombian drug runners holding them hostage before the military move in to mop up. These, one must add in fairness, are teenagers with behavioural problems, all from rich families, which accounts for the Colombians moving in to try to get their leader released in exchange for the boys' lives. There's some suspense along the way as the boys' rebel leader (Sean Astin) attempts various acts of escape and sabotage without being found out; by and large, though, it's like a TV movie (and not a good one) with bad language (lots of it) added, and it's a measure of the film's failure to appeal that your sympathies remain largely with the Colombians. Dean Lou Gossett takes a bullet through the heart but survives to wave cheerily to his boys: in flag-waving, rose-coloured Hollywood corners like this, some things never change.

Traces of Red ● ⓥ
1992, US, 104 mins, colour
Dir: Andy Wolk
Stars: James Belushi, Lorraine Bracco, Tony Goldwyn, William Russ
Rating: ★

Nubile corpses, hardboiled cops ever-ready to be seduced, a plot in which little is what it seems: *Traces of Red* runs like a Hank Janson pulp novel. Yet, despite a generally inept script and a poor performance by (an admittedly miscast) Lorraine Bracco, there's a good little thriller struggling to get out here. James Belushi's performance in the lead might be quite acceptable, for example, if other events in the movie were in working order. His laconic narration, begun over his own dead body, tells us he and those around him all seem to be involved in the case of the psycho who murders girls, smears their faces with lipstick and leaves not a trace of their clothing behind. Andy Wolk's direction of the subsequent twists is often very competent, although even he can't convince us about the climax which, although inventively done, simply isn't believable. The music, though bluesy and *noir*-ish, is just the kind of accompaniment this kind of soft-porn, soft-cover fiction demands.

Track 29 ● ⓥ
1987, UK, 90 mins, colour
Dir: Nicolas Roeg
Stars: Theresa Russell, Gary Oldman, Christopher Lloyd, Colleen Camp
Rating: ★★★

Director Nicholas Roeg in playful mood, toying with his audience as he describes the hallucinations of a mind in breakdown. Linda (Theresa Russell) contemplates suicide, but demons torment her, chiefly the vision of her son (Gary Oldman, doing a satanic variation on Norman Wisdom) returned from her past to give her some fleeting happiness. Oldman is the dynamo that galvanises this bizarre comedy into life. See it, be manipulated and enjoy it: this is Roeg at his most Roegish.

Track of the Cat ○
1954, US, 102 mins, colour
Dir: William A Wellman
Stars: Robert Mitchum, Teresa Wright, Tab Hunter, Diana Lynn
Rating: ★★★

Sadly neglected in its time, this is one of the most important location-shot films of the Fifties. Director William A Wellman experimented with colour photography in striking fashion in this story of a ranch menaced by a giant mountain lion. The snowbound ranch and its environs are confined almost entirely to sharp, crisp black-and-white, the only splashes of colour being the bright clothes and the green of the trees. William Clothier's photography is complemented by Roy Webb's distinctive music and some striking directorial set-pieces, including a mother guarding her son's body like a vulture and a burial scene from inside the open grave. The screenplay, from a novel by Walter Van Tilburg Clarke, who wrote *The Ox-Bow Incident*, is given full value by the players, especially Robert Mitchum, and Beulah Bondi and Philip Tonge as his mother and father.

Trade Winds ○
1938, US, 120 mins, b/w
Dir: Tay Garnett
Stars: Fredric March, Joan Bennett, Ralph Bellamy, Ann Sothern
Rating: ★★★

Not quite the South Seas idyll you might imagine from the title, this rarely-seen Hollywood movie is a crisply-scripted mystery-romance whose stars, despite the varying Far Eastern backgrounds, never left the studio! Fredric March takes himself a little less seriously than usual as the cynical sleuth tracking murder suspect Joan Bennett on a round-the-world hunt.

Trading Hearts ○
1988, US, 88 mins, colour
Dir: Neil Leifer

Stars: Raul Julia, Beverly D'Angelo
Rating: ★★

This is one of those would-be romantic charmers where a child tries to find a new father/mother for its single parent. In this case, 11-year-old Jenny Lewis is such a sassy charmer that she does manage to bring a little extra fun to the tired old formula, which here involves her trying to net over-the-hill baseball star Raul Julia for her divorced mum (Beverly D'Angelo) who is having an uphill struggle making ends meet. D'Angelo also sings nicely on a couple of songs (remember her as singer Patsy Cline in *Coal Miner's Daughter*?) but the whole thing makes you wonder why the stars and filmmakers bothered with it all in the first place.

Trading Places ● ⓥ
1983, US, 116 mins, colour
Dir: John Landis
Stars: Dan Aykroyd, Eddie Murphy, Ralph Bellamy, Don Ameche, Jamie Lee Curtis, Denholm Elliott
Rating: ★★★

Reminiscent at times of a Preston Sturges film, this bright comedy is director John Landis' best (and most popular) film to date. And when the good guys hit back at the bad guys who have been doing them down all evening, it stands to reason that the audience is in for some fun. Dan Aykroyd is the stuck-up white blueblood who wheels and deals in stocks and shares for the aged Duke brothers, Eddie Murphy (shooting to stardom) the failed black conman whose wheelings are confined to his efforts to convince the populace he's a legless veteran and whose dealings are mainly with the police. On a bet, the (crooked) Dukes swop them round, and everything goes to plan – until the two men understand what's happened. Then the fun really begins. Jamie Lee Curtis weighs in as a tart with a nest-egg of gold and Denholm Elliott's butler gets the best lines in the film, delivered with just the right bite.

Traffic ○
1970, France, 96 mins, colour
Dir: Jacques Tati
Stars: Jacques Tati
Rating: ★★

Jacques Tati's famous comic creation Monsieur Hulot let loose on the French motorway system. Much of the fun in this particular catalogue of hilarious disasters stems from Tati's

T

treatment of cars as creatures with wills of their own, liable to seize up, or even turn on their masters, if they feel they are being treated badly.

Trail of the Pink Panther ○ Ⓥ

1982, UK, 97 mins, colour
Dir: Blake Edwards
Stars: Peter Sellers, David Niven, Herbert Lom, Joanna Lumley
Rating: ★★

The first half of this Blake Edwards venture is a coy, affectionate look at the late Peter Sellers' famous creation Inspector Clouseau, with the help of footage not previously used in *Pink Panther* films. Later developments are less interesting, but the film is briefly enlivened by the performance of Richard Mulligan (helped by a talented dog) as Clouseau's father, the original stumbling block from which the chip was fashioned.

Trail of the Vigilantes ○

1940, US, 78 mins, b/w
Dir: Allan Dwan
Stars: Franchot Tone, Warren William, Broderick Crawford
Rating: ★★★

Wild and wacky Comedy-Western that moves along like a stagecoach pursued by Indians. Matinee idol Franchot Tone, a lounge-suit actor if ever there was one, had never made a Western before. But the script of this one – written by Harold Shumate, a Texas-born writer who contributed over 100 movie screenplays and had his first accepted in 1916 – lured him into the wide open spaces for the first time.

Trail Street ○

1947, US, 84 mins, b/w
Dir: Ray Enright
Stars: Randolph Scott, Robert Ryan
Rating: ★★

This modest little Western plays out the familiar tale about the conflict between ranchers and crop farmers but is lifted by its two stars – Randolph Scott and Robert Ryan. Scott plays Western legend Bat Masterson who rides into town to help land agent Ryan sort out the bad guys. The script's a bit clichéd but the action's good and the film sets a fair pace. There's also Roy Rogers' long-time sidekick George 'Gabby' Hayes around for a bit of light relief.

Train, The ○ Ⓥ

1964, US, 140 mins, b/w
Dir: John Frankenheimer
Stars: Burt Lancaster, Paul Scofield, Jeanne Moreau
Rating: ★★★

Gripping action film concerning the attempts of the French Resistance movement to save art treasures from the Nazis. Burt Lancaster, who also collaborated with director John Frankenheimer on *Bird Man of Alcatraz*, *The Young Savages* and *Seven Days in May*, got his first all-action part for almost a decade when he was cast as Resistance leader Labiche. Lancaster captures the spirit of this fighting man with relish and feeling. The three German officers involved bring outstanding performances from Paul Scofield (in one of his rare film roles), Wolfgang Preiss and Howard Vernon.

Train of Events ○

1949, UK, 85 mins, b/w
Dir: Charles Crichton
Stars: Jack Warner, Valerie Hobson, John Clements, Irina Baronova
Rating: ★★

Trains are always good for an hour-and-a-half of meaty drama and this film, though not up to Ealing Studios' previous compilation chiller *Dead of Night*, holds our attention throughout by offering us several train stories for the price of one. Various people on board the train of the title have their problems resolved in one way or another by the end of their journey, with the story switching from humour to icy drama as different characters appear. Don't blink too much while you're watching: you might miss someone like Leslie Phillips or John Gregson in a minor role. Jack Warner is the train driver, and there's a very youthful Peter Finch as an actor who has strangled his wife.

Train Robbers, The ○ Ⓥ

1973, US, 92 mins, colour
Dir: Burt Kennedy
Stars: John Wayne, Ann-Margret, Rod Taylor, Ricardo Montalban
Rating: ★★

The characters in this Western will be old friends to those familiar with Wayne's work in the last 20 years. The hardened gunfighter (Wayne), the kid (usually a pop star, and in this case Bobby Vinton), the co-star (here Rod Taylor) and the veteran (Ben Johnson) against a mob of gunmen who far

outnumber them. Burt Kennedy's script contains some amusing exchanges of dialogue (and a running joke that parallels the one in *Big Jake*, where everyone tells Wayne they thought he was dead). But his direction, although pitching one nicely into the core of the action, asks little more of the star than that he be John Wayne, which is rather a pity, as Siegel's *The Shootist* later showed.

Trancers ◐ Ⓥ

(aka: Future Cop)
1984, US, 85 mins, colour
Dir: Charles Band
Stars: Tim Thomerson, Helen Hunt, Michael Stefani
Rating: ★★★

Inspired by those classics of the futuristic genre *Blade Runner* and *The Terminator*, Charles Band – once dubbed the Eighties' answer to Roger Corman – produced and directed this clever science fiction thriller. Comedian Tim Thomerson is well cast as a low-budget version of Harrison Ford who is sent back in time some 300 years to 1985 Los Angeles. He has to inhabit the body of one of his ancestors and change history to prevent a totalitarian state from coming to power. The satire is well observed and the film is visually arresting.

Trap, The ○

1966, UK, 106 mins, colour
Dir: Sidney Hayers
Stars: Oliver Reed, Rita Tushingham
Rating: ★★★

In the depths of some of the most beautiful rugged scenery in the world, director Sidney Hayers creates a tough-but-tender love story that often keeps you on the very edge of the seat and riveted to the characters of the black-bearded trapper who survives in the heart of the wilds, and the mute bondmaiden whom he buys as a bride, for two bags of gold dust. The very best of the film is its mid-section when, following a hair-raising fight with wolves, with the girl racing to save the trapper from ending as fox in the grip of hounds, she has to call on all her courage and strength of character to keep him alive. As the trapper, Oliver Reed has never been better.

Trapeze ○

1956, US, 105 mins, colour
Dir: Carol Reed

Stars: Burt Lancaster, Gina Lollobrigida, Tony Curtis
Rating: ★★

You can almost smell the elephant droppings in this popular film that captures the fun, danger and excitement of life under the Big Top. The script is actually a lacklustre affair but that didn't seem to bother audiences of the day who flocked to see former acrobat Burt Lancaster in a milieu he loved as a famous circus trapeze artist. The high wire work, as Lancaster and Curtis train to perform the impossible, a triple somersault in mid-air off the trapeze, is very exciting to watch, compensating for script shortcomings once the action returns to the ground.

Travelling North ○
1986, Australia, 98 mins, colour
Dir: Carl Schultz
Stars: Leo McKern, Julia Blake
Rating: ★★★

This well-written, occasionally funny but ultimately sad Australian film about old age gives Leo McKern a powerful central role which he lives up to by giving a remarkable performance. He plays Frank, a widower who retires at 70 and plans to move from Melbourne to Northern Queensland where he has bought a spectacular clifftop house. The well observed script was based by David Williamson on his own successful stage play. Sharp dialogue and fine acting all round make this an absorbing and affecting drama and director Carl Schultz has created a film that belies its stage origins.

Travels With My Aunt ◐
1972, US, 109 mins, colour
Dir: George Cukor
Stars: Maggie Smith, Alec McCowen
Rating: ★★

Graham Greene's novel, brought to the screen with Maggie Smith in the role originally intended for Katharine Hepburn – the eccentric lady adventurer who introduces her staid nephew, a bank manager, to a world of intrigue and chicanery. George Cukor directs briskly and divertingly without ever quite drawing us into Aunt Augusta's own bizarre lifestyle, despite admirable support from John Box's stylised settings and Douglas Slocombe's garish but attractive (and suited to the subject) photography.

Treasure Island ○ ⓥ
1934, US, 105 mins, b/w
Dir: Victor Fleming

Stars: Wallace Beery, Jackie Cooper
Rating: ★★★

A solid version of Robert Louis Stevenson's tale of high seas adventure, and, of the many movies made from it, a respectable second-best after the classic Robert Newton version. Long John Silver is played by a relatively subdued Wallace Beery, and the whole piece teems with action, atmosphere and period detail. Cultured Douglass Dumbrille is a strange choice to play the murderous Israel Hands, though.

Treasure Island ○
1950, UK, 96 mins, colour
Dir: Byron Haskin
Stars: Robert Newton, Bobby Driscoll, Basil Sydney
Rating: ★★★

Full-blooded Disney version of the classic story, with the definitive portrait of Long John Silver from an eyeball-rolling Robert Newton and an appealing performance as Jim Hawkins from rosy-cheeked Bobby Driscoll: you'll be on the edges of your seats as he flees up the mast from kill-crazed Israel Hands.

Treasure of Lost Canyon, The ⊙
1952, US, 82 mins, colour
Dir: Ted Tetzlaff
Stars: William Powell, Julie Adams, Rosemary DeCamp, Tommy Ivo
Rating: ★★

William Powell returned to movies after a three-year break for this family Western, but although pleasant, sunny fare, it lacks bite. Based on a story by Robert Louis Stevenson, but hardly the high adventure that might promise, its finest asset is the customary high-quality photography by Russell Metty, an Oscar-winning master of his trade. Powell's co-star is rising child actor Tommy Ivo, whose career didn't go much further.

Treasure of Pancho Villa, The ○
1955, US, 96 mins, colour
Dir: George Sherman
Stars: Rory Calhoun, Shelley Winters
Rating: ★

Modestly well-made, routine action drama. Interesting to watch the Mexican Revolution being turned into double-feature fodder. Scriptwriter Niven Busch attempts some long words and deep thoughts, though the film seems happier once the guns start blazing and the dynamite exploding.

Treasure of the Golden Condor ○
1953, US, 93 mins, colour
Dir: Delmer Daves
Stars: Cornel Wilde, Constance Smith, Finlay Currie, Anne Bancroft
Rating: ★★

Some rugged scenery, magnificently photographed in Technicolor by Edward Cronjager, on location in Guatamala, highlights this period action film from Delmer Daves, best known for such Westerns as *Jubal*, *Three-Ten to Yuma* and *Broken Arrow*. Cornel Wilde portrays the young Frenchman hunting treasure in the Central American forests, but all the acting class comes from the supporting cast, which includes Anne Bancroft, George Macready, Fay Wray and Leo G Carroll.

Treasure of the Sierra Madre, The ○ ⓥ
1948, US, 126 mins, b/w
Dir: John Huston
Stars: Humphrey Bogart, Walter Huston, Tim Holt, Bruce Bennett
Rating: ★★★★

Thought by many to be John Huston's finest film, this is a tale of greed, fear and murder in Mexico as three men fall out over the gold they have clawed out of the inhospitable and bandit-ridden mountains. Humphrey Bogart gives a riveting portrait of an increasingly unhinged prospector, but the kudos went to the Huston clan with John receiving Oscars for screenplay and direction and his father Walter best supporting actor. The first post-war film to be shot entirely on location, its budget spiralled crazily out of control to $3 million. Studio boss Jack Warner, who had been conned into believing it was just a cheap Western, went berserk, but it was a huge hit with the public and made its costs back several times over.

Treasure of the Yankee Zephyr
See: Race to the Yankee Zephyr

Tree Grows in Brooklyn, A ○
1945, US, 128 mins, b/w
Dir: Elia Kazan
Stars: Dorothy McGuire, James Dunn, Joan Blondell, Lloyd Nolan
Rating: ★★★

Brilliant Hollywood adaptation of Betty Smith's novel about life in the slums of an American city in the early 1900s. The film is beautifully scripted

T

and photographed and tellingly observed in its loving depiction of a little girl's joys and sadnesses growing up in this environment. It has extremely attractive performances from Dorothy McGuire, Joan Blondell, James Dunn (a marvellous comeback performance as the drunken father) and wistful Peggy Ann Garner as the child. Dunn and Garner won Oscars.

Tremors ○ ⓥ
1990, US, 96 mins, colour
Dir: Ron Underwood
Stars: Kevin Bacon, Fred Ward, Finn Carter, Reba McEntire
Rating: ★★★

Another creature feature that's pretty exciting once it hits its stride. Its monsters, sort of underground alien slugs 10 times the size of humans, are far more intelligent than your average slug – the beasties even dig a trap for our human heroes when they try to escape in a bulldozer. It's all set in a remote part of the Nevada desert, although you're still inclined to ask why creatures that have presumably been around for zillions of years have only just started gobbling people up. There's no shortage of excitement, though – the executive producer is Gale Anne Hurd, who was associated with *Aliens* – and heroes Kevin Bacon and Fred Ward give 100 per cent to their unlikely exploits in blowing the sons o' bitches to pieces.

Trent's Last Case ○
1952, UK, 90 mins, b/w
Dir: Herbert Wilcox
Stars: Margaret Lockwood, Michael Wilding, Orson Welles, John McCallum
Rating: ★★

The famous novel by E C Bentley gets the full Herbert Wilcox polish in this adaptation, co-produced by the director's wife, Anna Neagle. Her producing chores presumably meant that she was unable to take on the leading role, of a woman suspected of complicity in the murder of her husband. But it's one that Margaret Lockwood handles coolly and capably, even if the screenplay gives her few highspots to hit. Despite the efforts of Michael Wilding (as Trent, the detective), John McCallum and such experienced scene stealers as Miles Malleson, it's Orson Welles who dominated proceedings with a sinister flashback account of the murdered man. Kenneth Williams makes his debut as the gardener.

Trespass ● ⓥ
1992, US, 101 mins, colour
Dir: Walter Hill
Stars: Bill Paxton, William Sadler, Ice T, Ice Cube, Art Evans
Rating: ★★★

'A billion dollars in gold – just laying there waitin' for us.' Famous last cinematic words, and so it proves once again in Walter Hill's all-go action thriller. Bill Paxton and William Sadler are two Arkansas firemen who have undiscovered treasure apparently handed to them on a plate when they attend a fire and receive a map and solid gold cross from a demented old man who staggers off into the flames. Seems like it's the key to the whereabouts of the loot from a fabled 50-year-old robbery. But, once arrived on the scene, the pair soon become involved with the local underworld kingpin (Ice T) and his gang, who corner them in the abandoned building that the treasure's hiding-place has now become. Hill doesn't waste any footage in the subsequent game of violent cat-and-mouse, although he misses a chance to put a kick in the tail after the principal protagonists have bitten the dust. Action fans won't complain though: they get a full ration here as rival factions and splinter groups from all sides blast the daylights out of one another.

Trial ○
1955, US, 105 mins, b/w
Dir: Mark Robson
Stars: Glenn Ford, Dorothy McGuire, Arthur Kennedy, John Hodiak
Rating: ★★★

Fine, tense courtroom thriller about a university instructor in criminal law who undertakes to defend a young Mexican on a charge of murder, but finds himself made the dupe of political factions. Glenn Ford plays the instructor in suitably tormented fashion.

Trial by Combat ○
(aka: Dirty Knight's Work)
1976, UK, 90 mins, colour
Dir: Kevin Connor
Stars: John Mills, Donald Pleasence, Barbara Hershey, Peter Cushing
Rating: ★

A wildly eccentric comedy-thriller that fails on some levels and succeeds on others. The plot, completely potty, concerns a group of titled Englishmen who dress up as knights and do to death wrongdoers who have escaped

the police. Some of the action that follows is genuinely exciting, some plain silly. None of it, however, is even remotely credible. John Mills even seems to play on two levels, sometimes straight, sometimes for obvious comic effect. And the dialogue veers from unspeakable – 'I didn't do it, master John,' gasps gamekeeper Neil McCarthy. 'I was feedin' the pheasants' – to quite amusing. The script is credited to three writers, and I'm quite prepared to believe they were writing three different films. At one time, Mills is chained to the cellar wall, Barbara Hershey is driving a car pursued by men on horseback, the new police commissioner is turning out to be a homicidal maniac, David Birney is fighting with the gamekeeper and Donald Pleasence, dressed in full armour, is pursuing an East End crook through a castle greenhouse. Whatever else, this film certainly is extraordinary.

Trials of Oscar Wilde, The ○
1960, UK, 123 mins, colour
Dir: Ken Hughes
Stars: Peter Finch, Yvonne Mitchell, John Fraser, Lionel Jeffries
Rating: ★★★

Gripping historical drama portraying the downfall of the great dramatist and wit Oscar Wilde following his unsuccessful libel action against the Marquis of Queensberry. Peter Finch, in what was seen at the time as a curious casting decision, plays the writer. Written and directed by Ken Hughes, the film was shot at the same time as another film treating the same events, *Oscar Wilde*, starring Robert Morley.

Trio ○
1950, UK, 88 mins, b/w
Dir: Harold French
Stars: James Hayter, Nigel Patrick, Jean Simmons, Michael Rennie
Rating: ★★★

Three stories, each very different, from the work of W Somerset Maugham. Although they seem a little more stretched, understandably, than the tales in *Quartet* (the first of the Maugham films, made two years earlier), each remains a fine example of the author's craftsmanship and observation of life. Character star James Hayter, just entering his most profitable period in the British cinema (he was soon to play Mr Pickwick) revels in his leading role as the illiterate verger who makes a mint.

Triple Cross ○
1966, UK/France, 126 mins, colour
Dir: Terence Young
Stars: Christopher Plummer, Romy Schneider, Yul Brynner, Trevor Howard
Rating: ★★

World War Two spy yarn based on fact, with Christopher Plummer as the cunning safecracker who works for both sides. Gert (*Goldfinger*) Frobe gives the best performance as a disillusioned German officer.

Triple Echo, The ●
1972, UK, 100m mins, colour
Dir: Michael Apted
Stars: Glenda Jackson, Oliver Reed
Rating: ★

Although Michael Apted is best known as a director of television plays, the few films that he has made have all been powerful, striking and unusual. This is another of H E Bates' rural tragedies, a companion to the previous year's *Dulcima*, although considerably less successful and progressively more turgid and unlikely.

Trip to Bountiful, The ○ ⓥ
1985, US, 105 mins, colour
Dir: Peter Masterson
Stars: Geraldine Page, John Heard, Rebecca DeMornay
Rating: ★★★

For those who fancy a good, old-fashioned howl, this tear-jerker will fit the bill nicely. In her Oscar winning performance (following eight unsuccessful nominations), Geraldine Page plays a feisty, sentimental, hymn-singing old southern lady with a slightly dicky heart and a grasping sourpuss of a daughter-in-law who makes her life hell and has the Indian sign on the old girl's submissive son. After one bitter row, Page packs up and makes one of her occasional attempts to get back to her home town of Bountiful, now all but deserted. Somehow, this time she evades pursuit, with a small assist from a friendly fellow traveller, and begins the long bus journey to the nearest town. That's really the whole story, although incidentals, dialogue and the central performance all count for a lot, even if they don't quite prevent a yawn sometimes sneaking in between

the tears: the truth behind the basic situations sometimes cuts too deep for comfort.

Triumph of the Spirit ● ⓥ
1989, US, 120 mins, colour
Dir: Robert M Young
Stars: Willem Dafoe, Robert Loggia, Edward James Olmos, Costas Mandylor
Rating: ★★

Or: *A Boxer in Auschwitz*. Decently made, this is the true story of a Greek boxing champion who, being Jewish, was shipped off to a German concentration camp in World War Two. Here, while all his fellows gradually dropped away, he kept alive by undergoing 200 bouts and winning every one. Though somewhat sanitised, this is still horrific enough for most tastes, with heartfelt performances from Willem Dafoe (the boxer), Robert Loggia (his father) and Edward James Olmos, that Gary Merrill lookalike, as their 'gypsy' guard. The Jenny Agutter-like Wendy Gazelle is a poignant heroine who makes the most of her few scenes.

Trois Hommes et un Couffin
See: Three Men and a Cradle

Troll ● ⓥ
1985, US, 83 mins, colour
Dir: John Carl Buechler
Stars: Michael Moriarty, Shelley Hack, Noah Hathaway, Sonny Bono, June Lockhart
Rating: ★★

Gremlins, ghoulies and other beastly offspring of modern special effects were bound to give birth to all manner of evil creatures of mythology and here it's the turn of the troll. Like most of the rest, he's small and smart, drips with saliva, has teeth that would keep a dentist in bridgework for life and is out to rule the world by a combined action of transmogrification and extermination. The best lines in this stop-start catalogue of his attempts to take over a modern apartment building all go to June Lockhart as the witch assigned to stop him. When youthful hero Noah Hathaway, out to save his 'taken over' younger sister, pays her a visit, he asks her how she knew it was him. 'I recognise the knock,' she tells him. 'It's pre-pubescent.' Michael Moriarty gives another quirky performance as the boy's father whose miming to pop music keeps him from realising the truth until a forest crops up outside his apartment with a spellbound witch in

the middle of it telling him to close the door. 'What's going on?' asks his wife, vapidly played by Shelley Hack. 'I don't know,' gasps Moriarty, 'but *I'm* listening to the tree.'

Tron ○ ⓥ
1982, US, 96 mins, colour
Dir: Stephen Lisberger
Stars: Jeff Bridges, Bruce Boxleitner, David Warner
Rating: ★★★

The Disney Studio comes up with a new way to play cops and robbers in this innovative thriller about a man who finds himself inside a computer game fighting for his life. David Warner is a splendidly hateful villain who could hold you, adding, in the same breath: 'Bring in the laser probe!'

Troopship
See: Farewell Again

Trouble Bound ● ⓥ
1993, US, 89 mins, colour
Dir: Jeffrey Reiner
Stars: Michael Madsen, Patricia Arquette, Seymour Cassel, Florence Stanley
Rating: ★★

There's a bad guy lurking around every corner in this clone of the far better *Something Wild*. Michael Madsen, a student of the Bruce Willis school of charm in this one, plays Harry, an ex-convict who wins a car in a poker game little realising that its trunk contains a dead body, the victim of a Mafia assassination. And when he meets wacky Kit (Patricia Arquette), out for revenge on the Mob for the murder of her father, Harry's troubles double. Madsen still looks more powerful as a top supporting bad guy than a leading man, but at least he and the spunky Arquette manage to lift these black frolics out of the rut from time to time – although there are far too many chases when the director's lack of imagination is all too evident.

Trouble Brewing ○
1939, UK, 90 mins, b/w
Dir: Anthony Kimmins
Stars: George Formby, Googie Withers
Rating: ★★★

Toothy George Formby was Britain's top box-office star when this comedy film was made. He plays a compositor involved with a gang of counterfeiters. The Formby vocal chords work overtime on such ditties

T

as 'Fanlight Fanny' and 'Hitting the Highspots Now', and the climax is a hectic pursuit through a brewery.

Trouble in Mind ● ⓥ
1985, US, 111 mins, colour
Dir: Alan Rudolph
Stars: Kris Kristofferson, Keith Carradine, Lori Singer, Genevieve Bujold, Divine
Rating: ★★

Love them or loathe them, most of director Alan Rudolph's films are unlike those by anyone else, and this science-fiction thriller/comedy/philsophical drama is certainly no exception. Kris Kristofferson is perfectly cast as the loner ex-cop trying to prevent a drifter and his wife from falling in with the underworld of Rain City. Stylish it certainly is and some scenes have a wonderfully bleak feel, but Rudolph's computer mind finally overloads (and explodes) in a semi-slapstick finale.

Trouble in Paradise ○
1932, US, 83 mins, b/w
Dir: Ernst Lubitsch
Stars: Miriam Hopkins, Herbert Marshall
Rating: ★★★

Feather-light, delightfully naughty Ernst Lubitsch comedy classic about cross and double cross among international jewel thieves, as they move from Venice to Paris and other European society spots with rich pickings. It's among the most cultured and sophisticated films ever made, although Lubitsch does leave room for a very funny running gag involving Kay Francis and that delightful ditherer, Edward Everett Horton. The first voice you hear while watching the scene in Venice is that of the famous tenor Enrico Caruso.

Trouble in Store ⊙ ⓥ
1953, UK, 85 mins, b/w
Dir: John Paddy Carstairs
Stars: Norman Wisdom, Margaret Rutherford
Rating: ★★★

Norman Wisdom's first starring comedy, a side-splitting romp which has him falling over his own feet all over a large department store. Margaret Rutherford is at her hilariously imperious best as a shoplifter, whose top coat seems to be able to hold more goods than that of Harpo Marx.

Trouble in the Glen ○
1953, UK, 91 mins, colour
Dir: Herbert Wilcox
Stars: Margaret Lockwood, Orson Welles
Rating: ★

Herbert Wilcox's tartan turkey trots out Orson Welles as a monstrously bewigged Highland laird being unpleasant to local tinkers and incurring the wrath of a little girl crippled with polio. So, predictable comedy about Scots and treacly sentimentality are guaranteed. Margaret Lockwood, Forrest Tucker, Victor McLaglen and John McCallum are wasted. And, what's more, the film is a truly awful example of the Trucolor process.

Trouble in the Sky
See: Cone of Silence

Trouble Shooter, The
See: The Man With the Gun

Trouble with Angels, The ⊙
1966, US, 112 mins, colour
Dir: Ida Lupino
Stars: Rosalind Russell, Hayley Mills
Rating: ★★★

A most effective dose of funnery in the nunnery, persuasively directed by Ida Lupino, with a delightful collection of individual nuns gracing a story of two high-spirited teenagers at a convent school. There's the elderly nun, always asleep; the shy one, having to go out with girls to choose bras; the ungainly games nun, forced to dive in to save non-swimmers who have got out of swimming lessons for three years. And the death of a nun one has come to know is a genuinely moving moment. Hayley Mills produces one of her best performances while Rosalind Russell is gloriously in control of her dialogue as the Mother Superior, and has some classic moments when operating on a student unable to get her head out of a plaster cast.

Trouble with Harry, The ○ ⓥ
1955, US, 99 mins, colour
Dir: Alfred Hitchcock
Stars: Shirley MacLaine, John Forsythe, Edmund Gwenn, Mildred Natwick
Rating: ★★★

This is Alfred Hitchcock's zany, offbeat suspense comedy about a corpse that very definitely won't lie down. Endearing portrayals by John Forsythe, Shirley MacLaine, Edmund Gwenn and Mildred Natwick, filled

both with impishness and dramatic sense, key in perfectly with the black hijinks. And Robert Burks' colour photography of autumnal settings is some of the best ever seen. The dialogue is surprisingly risqué for a Fifties' film, but Hitchcock's brilliant handling of a corpse being buried and dug up six times in all makes the film a triumphant and very unusual laughter-raiser. A winner – and no trouble.

True Confessions ●
1981, US, 108 mins, colour
Dir: Ulu Grosbard
Stars: Robert De Niro, Robert Duvall, Charles Durning
Rating: ★★★

The cinematic equivalent of a good read, a rarity in modern cinema. De Niro is very good as a wheeler-dealer priest and Duvall even better as his blunt and bitter policeman brother. Together they become involved in a grisly murder hunt that leaves scars on them both - and on several of those around them.

True Glory, The ○
1945, US/UK, 90 mins, b/w
Dir: Garson Kanin, Carol Reed
Rating: ★★★

Breathtakingly good wartime documentary, made by Britain's Carol Reed and America's Garson Kanin, who assembled a vividly personal picture of the last 18 months of World War Two from newsreel records shot by more than 1,400 cameramen. The commentary, spoken by men from different advancing armies, is outstanding in the way it clarifies situations but at the same time provides them with an intensely human realism.

True Grit ○ ⓥ
1969, US, 128 mins, colour
Dir: Henry Hathaway
Stars: John Wayne, Glen Campbell, Kim Darby
Rating: ★★★

Taking on a gang of badmen who include Dennis Hopper and Robert Duvall, John Wayne roared into Western history with an Oscar under his belt. More than any other of his post-war films, this and his last film *The Shootist* summed up the man and his career. 'It was the first really decent role I'd had in 20 years,' he growled, clutching his Academy Award – a reference to his only previous Oscar nomination, for *The Sands of Iwo Jima* in 1949. The film deserved one other Oscar – for Lucien Ballard's Technicolor photography.

True Identity ● ⓥ

1991, US, 93 mins, colour
Dir: Charles Lane
Stars: Lenny Henry, Frank Langella, Andreas Katsulas, Charles Lane, James Earl Jones
Rating: ★★

Comedy star Lenny Henry literally changes his face for this, his Hollywood debut. He plays Miles, a budding actor who hears the confession of a Mafia hitman on an out-of-control plane, then has to use the help of a friend who's a movie makeup genius to disguise himself as a white man to stay alive when the plane lands safely. A fair showcase for Henry who does at least allow him full scope for his talent for mimicry and impersonation. The humour is pretty obvious, and it's uncomfortable in parts; even so, you'll find it hard not to chuckle on several occasions.

True Love ● ⓥ

1989, US, 104 mins, colour
Dir: Nancy Savoca
Stars: Annabella Sciorra, Ron Eldard, Aida Turturro, Roger Rignack, Star Jasper
Rating: ★

Think it would be tedious, eavesdropping on stag and hen parties and the dogfights in the 48-hour run-up to an Italian-American wedding? Think right! A colleague thought the piece well-observed and that may well be true: the film is certainly well thought of in some quarters. But a well-observed portrait of a boring lifestyle and klutzy characters still makes for a boring film. The bridegroom (Ron Eldard) is a deli assistant who even wants to party with the boys on his honeymoon night. It's the height of his ambition. The bride (Annabella Sciorra, in her first big leading role) is a foul-mouthed, angel-faced sweetie understandably having doubts about the whole thing. The ending is obvious right from the beginning but, even so, I still hoped someone might gets hot and liven things up a bit.

True Romance ● ⓥ

1993, US, 118 mins, colour
Dir: Tony Scott
Stars: Christian Slater, Patricia Arquette, Dennis Hopper, Christopher Walken,

Gary Oldman, Brad Pitt
Rating: ★

To be stuffed with extreme violence and still be boring takes some doing, but this offbeat action farce-thriller does it in style. A star-studded cast, including cameos from Brad Pitt, Val Kilmer, Dennis Hopper, Gary Oldman, Chris Penn and Christopher Walken, all presumably saw something in the raucous and sometimes embarrassing script that doesn't manifest itself on the screen. You could fear the worst from the opening. 'To this day,' drones heroine Patricia Arquette, 'the events that followed seemed like a distant dream. They changed our lives forever.' When new hubby Christian Slater comes back from blasting her pimp to hell and stealing millions in cocaine, she tells him 'I think what you did was so romantic.' It gets less romantic when the Mafia gets on the trail, headed by Walken (who disappears after one scene) while the happy couple has dreams of selling their booty to a hophead Hollywood producer. The orgy of sadism and violence that follows is like an old-fashioned Disney comedy with an adult certificate. The characters are all dislikeable and their performances pitched at high-decibel level.

True Story of Jesse James, The ○

1956, US, 92 mins, colour
Dir: Nicholas Ray
Stars: Robert Wagner, Jeffrey Hunter, Hope Lange
Rating: ★★

Hollywood has filmed the Jesse James saga at least half-a-dozen times, each time trying to analyse why the James Brothers turned outlaw. Some have claimed they were victims of circumstance; others have painted their characters black. This film, which professes to have the facts, shows them to be a bit of both. Robert Wagner as Jesse and Jeffrey Hunter as Frank – they really do look like brothers – handle their roles with veteran-like authority.

Truly Madly Deeply ○ ⓥ

1990, UK, 107 mins, colour
Dir: Anthony Minghella
Stars: Juliet Stevenson, Alan Rickman, Bill Paterson
Rating: ★★★

This romantic – and funny – ghost story received huge critical acclaim as

well as *Evening Standard* British Film Awards for Alan Rickman (Best Actor), Juliet Stevenson (Best Actress) and writer/director Anthony Minghella (Most Promising Newcomer) in his directorial debut. Early on, you suspect that you are in for some heavy stuff about the psychology of grief, but when Rickman appears in ghost form, the tone of the film lightens. Stevenson gives a performance of great charm and is well complemented by Rickman, so that you can happily forget that the joke – how does one actually live day-to-day with a ghost? – is a little overworked, especially when Rickman invites a number of his friends. 'Are you telling me,' asks an incredulous Stevenson, 'that there are dead people in my living-room watching videos?' A strong support cast includes Bill Paterson as Stevenson's sympathetic boss and David Ryall in a delightful cameo as a philosophical pest control officer.

Trust ● ⓥ

1990, UK/US, 106 mins, colour
Dir: Hal Hartley
Stars: Adrienne Shelly, Martin Donovan
Rating: ★★

Based firmly on unreality, this is silly low-budget nonsense and the only surprise is that the actors and director actually manage to make something of it. Director Hal Hartley, who made the critically-successful *The Unbelievable Truth* with much the same cast, has only himself to blame for the material he has to work with here: he wrote it. And, while such phrases as 'A family's like a gun – you point in the wrong direction, you're going to kill somebody' sound as if they have something to say, they're actually pretty daft. If one warms to the film as it goes on, this is due to the affecting performances of Adrienne Shelly and Martin Donovan as the two losers, seemingly set for a lifetime of unhappiness, who touch each other's lives and make them better.

Truth About Spring, The ⊙

1965, UK, 102 mins, colour
Dir: Richard Thorpe
Stars: Hayley Mills, John Mills
Rating: ★★

A tolerably enjoyable adventure romp which casts Hayley Mills as the tomboy daughter of a roguish old sea-dog, played by father John Mills. Such British film stalwarts as Lionel Jeffries, Harry Andrews and Niall MacGinnis have a high old time rolling their eyes

T

and pretending to be piratical. This, the third co-starring film for father and daughter, following *Tiger Bay* and *The Chalk Garden*, was shot on location in the Costa Brava, providing the stars with a working holiday in the sun.

Truth About Women, The ○

1957, UK, 98 mins, colour
Dir: Muriel Box
Stars: Laurence Harvey, Julie Harris, Derek Farr
Rating: ★★★

Rather rambling and slapdash but very enjoyable period drama in which an aristocrat (Laurence Harvey) relates sundry romantic adventures from his past. The cinematic equivalent of a good book, the film is very attractively photographed in Eastman Colour by Otto Heller, and its ladies stunningly costumed by Cecil Beaton: they include Julie Harris, Jackie (later Jocelyn) Lane, Elina Labourdette, Mai Zetterling, Diane Cilento, Eva Gabor and Catherine (later Katie) Boyle. The art direction by George Provis is also striking – often opulent, it presents the period most convincingly.

Tucker – The Man and His Dreams ○ Ⓥ

1988, US, 107 mins, colour
Dir: Francis Ford Coppola
Stars: Jeff Bridges, Joan Allen, Frederic Forrest, Martin Landau, Dean Stockwell, Christian Slater
Rating: ★★★

As beautifully crafted as one of the revolutionary cars of its title, *Tucker* is like a Frank Capra film in an age when America finally recognises that the good guys rarely won in real life. Jeff Bridges is the ever-smiling post-war inventor whose affable exterior envelops a nervous system as tightly wound as a clockwork coil. Capra would have let him win, but this is the real world where big business interests crush private initiative with the ruthlessness of a bulldozer, and you'll clench your fists in frustration at the realisation that Tucker stood no chance against them. Though its pace is sometimes on the stately side, Coppola's film comes alive in the final courtroom scenes when Bridges' performance rivals that of James Stewart in *Mr Smith Goes to Washinton*. The dialogue is well-written and is a shade cautious, and gives its best line to Martin Landau's elderly adviser: 'Don't get too close to people – you'll catch their dreams.' 44

Tucker cars, a coda tells us, are still in working order: they must be worth a fortune.

Tudor Rose ○

(aka: Nine Days a Queen)
1936, UK, 79 mins, b/w
Dir: Robert Stevenson
Stars: Sir Cedric Hardwicke, Nova Pilbeam, John Mills, Sybil Thorndike
Rating: ★★★

A forcefully impressive and affecting piece of history, rich in period detail and photographed with great skill by Mutz Greenbaum. There are biting performances from Sir Cedric Hardwicke and Felix Aylmer in this story of Lady Jane Grey (played with touching vulnerability by teenage star Nova Pilbeam). The juvenile lead is a fresh-looking young chap called John Mills.

Tugboat Annie ☉

1933, US, 87 mins, b/w
Dir: Mervyn LeRoy
Stars: Marie Dressler, Wallace Beery
Rating: ★★★

Marie Dressler and Wallace Beery, reunited from *Min and Bill*, in which she took an Oscar (he won an Academy Award that same year – 1931 – for *The Champ*), climb all over the scenery as feuding river-dwellers in this immensely popular MGM comedy. It must have been a relaxing chore for director Mervyn LeRoy, following on his work on the much grimmer *Five Star Final*, *Two Seconds* and *I Am a Fugitive from a Chain Gang*.

Tumbleweed ○

1953, US, 79 mins, colour
Dir: Nathan Juran
Stars: Audie Murphy, Lori Nelson, Chill Wills, Lee Van Cleef
Rating: ★★★

Nice-looking Western (as one would expect from the director, Nathan Juran, a former art director who won an Oscar in that capacity for *How Green Was My Valley*) with Audie Murphy as a wagon train guard unjustly (of course) accused of desertion. A warm and sometimes wryly humorous script makes the film a pleasure to listen to as well as watch, although Murphy's thunder is well stolen by K T Stevens (actress daughter of director Sam Wood) and a personable white horse. The mean features of Lee Van Cleef make an early appearance as one of the bad guys.

Tunes of Glory ◐

1960, UK, 106 mins, colour
Dir: Ronald Neame
Stars: Alec Guinness, John Mills, Dennis Price, Kay Walsh
Rating: ★★★

Scathingly memorable drama about two contrasting army officers who drive each other to the brink of madness. Ronald Neame directs the powerful clash of wills in uncompromisingly frank fashion, and Susannah York makes her film debut. Alec Guinness gives a fine character reading of the hard-drinking Scots officer replaced by a British martinet. But John Mills, playing from deep within and giving the performance of a lifetime, wins this acting duel by a whisker.

Tunnel of Love, The ○

1958, US, 98 mins, b/w
Dir: Gene Kelly
Stars: Doris Day, Richard Widmark, Gig Young
Rating: ★★

A rare comedy role for Richard Widmark in this Gene Kelly-directed frolic about a couple trying to adopt a baby. Complications ensue, with Widmark getting involved with a glamorous 'other woman' from the adoption agency, played by the late Gia Scala. Giving Widmark and Doris Day stalwart backing is Gig Young, who played the hero's friend dozens of times before his adept acting was rewarded by a 1970 Oscar for *They Shoot Horses, Don't They?*

Turk 182! ◐ Ⓥ

1985, US, 98 mins, colour
Dir: Bob Clark
Stars: Timothy Hutton, Robert Urich, Kim Cattrall
Rating: ★★★

Everybody likes to see injustice be made to stand on its head, so there should be a lot of people cheering for this unlikely but vigorous and mildly enjoyable spot of escapism. Timothy Hutton is the 20-year-old who heeds the famous advice 'Go fight City Hall' after his older brother, a fireman (a role that gives Robert Urich rather more acting opportunities than the star), is badly injured when, off-duty and slightly the worse for drink, he rescues a child from a tenement blaze. After Urich is denied private treatment, and then a disability pension, because he'd been drinking, Hutton goes to work as a kind of plain-clothes caped crusader, humiliating the vaguely corrupt New York mayor (a sharkishly-smiling Robert Culp) at every opportunity. If the thrills are cheap and the lines occasionally cheaper, the enterprise still has the surefire appeal of a non-league side taking on Liverpool in the Cup. Hutton is in (though several levels below such screen heroes as Jefferson Smith and Longefellow Deeds). The American dream lives!

Turkey Time ☉
1933, UK, 73 mins, b/w
Dir: Tom Walls
Stars: Tom Walls, Ralph Lynn, Mary Brough
Rating: ★★★

The Aldwych farces kept audiences of the late Twenties and early Thirties laughing. The Tom Walls-Ralph Lynn-Robertson Hare trio are supported here by such stalwarts as Mary Brough and Norma Varden and there are Christmas carols for good measure.

Turner & Hooch ○ ⓥ
1989, US, 97 mins, colour
Dir: Roger Spottiswoode
Stars: Tom Hanks, Mare Winningham, Craig T Nelson
Rating: ★★★

This amiable movie is hardly likely to rate highly in Tom Hanks' career, yet Hanks' inventive comedy sense and an incredibly ugly (and talented) dog give it enough extra life to make it worthwhile. Hanks is a police officer in a quiet coastal town who's acquainted with the local derelict (John McIntire) and his fearsome dog. Pinned down by the pooch, Hanks is reassured by McIntire that 'He didn't even break the skin. He loves you boy.' And so he does, after McIntire has been murdered and Hooch has reduced Hanks' house to rubble before knuckling down to crack the case. Hanks is beautiful as the house-proud snooper who hoovers his new partner's shirtfront in the car as he's eating a muffin; the dog is almost (but not quite) too slobby to be lovable and, like all canine heroes, does what a dog has to do in the end. The rest of the cast isn't much, but then this gruesome twosome would probably show them up anyway.

Turning Point, The ○
1977, US, 119 mins, colour
Dir: Herbert Ross

Stars: Shirley MacLaine, Anne Bancroft, Mikhail Baryshnikov
Rating: ★★★

An interesting, although not wholly successful film about careers, regrets, love, applause and envy, set against the unusual backcloth of ballet. The story is treated with great delicacy by director Herbert Ross, as are its two stars: Shirley MacLaine as the ballerina who married and gave it all up, and Anne Bancroft as the one who went on, and must now face the inevitability of getting too old. There are several good performances in support of their histrionics, notably from Tom Skerritt as MacLaine's husband and Mikhail Baryshnikov who, besides being a brilliant dancer, projects a pleasing personality. As MacLaine's daughter, Leslie Browne is a pretty dancer but hard and unsympathetic as a character. The first hour of the film is exceptionally good, but leaves too little room for expansion of the plot. It must be added that there is rather a lot of splendid ballet.

Turn the Key Softly ○
1953, UK, 83 mins, b/w
Dir: Jack Lee
Stars: Yvonne Mitchell, Joan Collins, Terence Morgan
Rating: ★★

Unusual melodrama about three women convicts and their attempts to come to terms with freedom. Although realism scarcely gets a look in, the plot rattles along with all the self-confidence of a driver making speed along a familiar road. Joan Collins draws the tart to the life, tight of skirt and loose of eye. Kathleen Harrison's pathetic little shop-lifter offers a fresh slant on old age and poverty. But the best performance is given by Yvonne Mitchell, giving a sensitive lift to the classy lady unable to break away from her criminal lover. The film got an added boost in its day from the huge success of its title song, recorded by Ruby Murray.

Turtle Beach ● ⓥ
1992, Australia, 88 mins, colour
Dir: Stephen Wallace
Stars: Greta Scacchi, Joan Chen, Art Malik, Jack Thompson, Norman Kaye
Rating: ★★

Beginning with vivid violence, including an amazing shot of a head being sliced off, this story of unrest in Malaysia has moments of poignancy, but at the same time seems designed as

an exercise to allow Greta Scacchi and Joan Chen to take their clothes off. Not very well acted – Scacchi is about the best of a mediocre bunch – the film examines the plight of Vietnamese and other boat people, trying to land in a Mayalsia where they are hated, and where, on Turtle Beach, an army of extras waving knives emerges on cue, like some kind of demon chorus, every time a refugee boat heaves into view. Lots of local colour here, but not much story. But the hazardous state of the Vietnamese is genuinely moving and, with a little more quality in all departments, this could have been a good film that brought that home to the world.

Turtle Diary ○
1985, UK, 97 mins, colour
Dir: John Irvin
Stars: Glenda Jackson, Ben Kingsley, Richard Johnson
Rating: ★★★★

Ben Kingsley creates one of the most fully-rounded everyday men you're ever likely to meet in this excellent film, full of sudden changes of expression and nervous smiles that could spring from real emotions. It's an amazing performance that even develops as the character careers through a basically crazy adventure. In fact, if we told you that the film was about two cranks who steal three turtles from the zoo and let them loose in the sea, you'd probably turn the other way. But the everyday, incident-filled world that writer Harold Pinter creates around these two rush-of-blood-to-the-heads conservationists will make you cry a little and laugh a lot. Pinter's ear for commonplace dialogue, full of embarrassing pauses, has never been better, especially when used to create the seedy milieu of the boarding house where divorced bookshop assistant Kingsley lodges with people as lonely as himself. There's not a false note in this eccentric slice of everyday life. Warmly recommended.

12 Angry Men ○ ⓥ
1957, US, 95 mins, b/w
Dir: Sidney Lumet
Stars: Henry Fonda, Lee J Cobb, Ed Begley, E G Marshall, Jack Warden, Martin Balsam
Rating: ★★★★

Surely the finest ensemble picture ever made, as 12 jurors sweat it out to decide the guilt or innocence of a teenager accused of murdering his father. It was director Sidney Lumet's first film – and what a debut. Virtually the entire film is set in one room, as the doughty dozen play cat and mouse with a man's life. It seems to be an open and shut case, as 11 jurors give the metaphorical thumbs down to the accused. His only hope lies with the sole holdout – liberal Henry Fonda, who was also co-producer of this ambitious but brilliant work. Meticulously analysing the facts as he heard them in court, Fonda tries to convince his colleagues that there might be room for reasonable doubt. But he's working against deeply-ingrained prejudices and dubious priorities. Creating an excruciatingly stifling atmosphere, Lumet delivers as powerful a drama as you're likely to see on screen. The film won three Oscar nominations, for best picture, best director and best screenplay (Reginald Rose, who adapted his own TV play). Miss it at your peril. For the record, here are the angry 12: Fonda, Lee J Cobb, Jack Klugman, Martin Balsam, Robert Webber, Jack Warden, Ed Begley, E G Marshall, Joseph Sweeney, John Fielder, Edward Binns and George Voscovec.

Twelve Chairs, The ○
1969, US, 94 mins, colour
Dir: Mel Brooks
Stars: Ron Moody, Dom DeLuise, Mel Brooks
Rating: ★★

Another zany comedy from Mel Brooks (who also makes an acting appearance), made between *The Producers* and *Blazing Saddles*. Based on the same Russian story from which Jack Benny and Fred Allen derived their famous Forties' hit *It's in the Bag!*, about a fortune hidden away in a presumably worthless old armchair. Some typical Brooks bursts of lunacy liven up a basically rather soggy story.

Twelve O'Clock High ○ ⓥ
1949, US, 132 mins, b/w
Dir: Henry King
Stars: Gregory Peck, Hugh Marlowe, Gary Merrill
Rating: ★★★★

This memorable study of men in war and under stress won an Academy Award for Dean Jagger as best supporting actor of the year, and produced deserved queues at box offices all round the world. It combines action and penetrating dialogue with a

long line of well-rounded characters in its story of an American air unit based in Britain during World War Two.

Twentieth Century ○
1934, US, 91 mins, b/w
Dir: Howard Hawks
Stars: John Barrymore, Carole Lombard
Rating: ★★★

Matinee idol John Barrymore said of his sassy co-star Carole Lombard after completing this screwball comedy: 'She is perhaps the greatest actress I ever worked with.' And Barrymore plus Lombard equals dynamite in this fast-paced, frantic entertainment about a harum-scarum impresario trying to talk his ex-mistress into acting in one of his plays. There are fights, histrionics, and even a fake suicide in a film that thunders along like the train of the title.

Twenty Mule Team ○
1940, US, 84 mins, b/w
Dir: Richard Thorpe
Stars: Wallace Beery, Leo Carrillo, Marjorie Rambeau, Anne Baxter
Rating: ★★★

A typical Wallace Beery vehicle of its time, when he had ceased to be one of the studio's major stars, but still had a solid fan following. Often in these action comedies, he was teamed with horse-faced Marjorie Main; but here brisk Marjorie Rambeau is his vis-à-vis (with Anne Baxter making her film debut as her daughter) in a lively tale of borax bandits. Borax? It was a kind of salt crystal much mined in old California. The vigorous melodramatics are directed by MGM stalwart Richard Thorpe, just getting bigger films after 12 years as a director, and later to gain a reputation with spectacular action dramas.

Twenty One ● ⓥ
1990, UK, 100 mins, colour
Dir: Don Boyd
Stars: Patsy Kensit, Jack Shepherd, Patrick Ryecart
Rating: ★★

This sleazy little number is one of those fashionable British films still swimming in the wake of the swinging Sixties. Patsy Kensit tries to crack her milk-and-water image as the girl involved with a junkie and a married man and her loser father, but she still emerges as a sweet young suburban thing, talking dirty but enraged by her own mother's infidelity. Kensit has her moments –

especially when, after bereavement, singing along to a Nina Simone record – but there isn't much enjoyment to the film: if this is the life of the average secretary, you think, then Heaven help her. Despite its graphic portrait of sex, drugs and violence, the film surprisingly got a 15 certificate in Britain. Competently acted (just), it will probably look better on late-night TV. Maybe.

20,000 Leagues Under the Sea ⊙ ⓥ
1954, US, 125 mins, colour
Dir: Richard Fleischer
Stars: Kirk Douglas, James Mason, Paul Lukas, Peter Lorre
Rating: ★★★

James Mason is a memorably brooding Captain Nemo in Disney's handsomely-produced film of the Jules Verne classic. There were Oscars for art direction and special effects, the latter featuring an exciting underwater fight with a huge octopus. Direction by Richard Fleischer whose father Max, was Disney's only major rival in the field of full-length cartoons in the Thirties and Forties. There aren't many films, either, in which you can hear Kirk Douglas sing, but this is one of them!

20,000 Years in Sing Sing ○
1932, US, 77 mins, b/w
Dir: Michael Curtiz
Stars: Spencer Tracy, Bette Davis
Rating: ★★★

A rare unsympathetic role for Spencer Tracy in a role that looks hand-tailored for James Cagney and was: Cagney priced himself out of the running and Tracy's career got a big boost from his skilful handling of the cocky criminal sent 'up the river'. The first of several films based on accounts of prison life by real-life Sing Sing warden Lewis Lawes, who acted as technical adviser on this film. Bette Davis' rather flashy portrayal of Tracy's moll is not one of her best.

Twice in a Lifetime ◑
1985, US, 117 mins, colour
Dir: Bud Yorkin
Stars: Gene Hackman, Ann-Margret, Ellen Burstyn
Rating: ★★★

I suppose that if there's one thing that might make a man leave the super Ellen Burstyn, it could be the delicious Ann-Margret. On those grounds, this family drama about an extreme case of the 30-year itch could at least be said to be well cast. And none of the players could be bettered: Burstyn, Margret, Ally Sheedy, Amy Madigan, Brian Dennehy and Gene Hackman as the father at the centre of it all. They combine to bring warmth and understanding to a film that could have gone home laden with Oscars with a better script. Madigan gives an outstanding performance as the daughter who simply can't forgive dad his desertion. The ending doesn't make it clear which woman Hackman's going back to: but we should all have such a choice.

Twice Round the Daffodils ○
1962, UK, 89 mins, b/w
Dir: Gerald Thomas
Stars: Juliet Mills, Donald Sinden, Ronald Lewis, Donald Houston
Rating: ★★

An unlikely setting for a comedy – a TB sanatorium – in this film from the *Carry On* team: producer Peter Rogers, director Gerald Thomas and writer Norman Hudis. It's in slightly more serious vein and the title refers to the ritual in which patients do a double turn round the flower bed before being discharged. Juliet Mills is charming as an efficient, selfless nurse nicknamed Catty and Donald Sinden, a busy screen star of the Fifties and Sixties, scores as a patient with frustrated sex urges. Also in the cast are *Carry On* stalwarts Kenneth Williams and Joan Sims. Based on a play by actor Patrick Cargill called *Ring for Cathy*

Twilight for the Gods ○
1958, US, 120 mins, colour
Dir: Joseph Pevney
Stars: Rock Hudson, Cyd Charisse
Rating: ★★

Writer Ernest K Gann (who also penned *The High and the Mighty*) had only himself to blame for this messy and sluggish version of his great best-selling novel, since he did the screenplay. Gann and director Joseph Pevney (an ex-actor who directed numerous big-budget films for Universal without making much of any of them) flagrantly waste exotic South Seas settings, a decent storyline and an excellent cast that includes Rock Hudson, Cyd Charisse and Arthur Kennedy. A shame.

Twilight of Honor
See: The Charge is Murder

Twilight's Last Gleaming ◐
1977, US/Germany, 146 mins, colour
Dir: Robert Aldrich
Stars: Burt Lancaster, Richard Widmark, Charles Durning
Rating: ★★

Nothing wrong from a directorial point of view with this action thriller, even though its story of a thinking madman who holds America to ransom by 'kidnapping' atomic missiles is familiar to the point of contempt. Robert Aldrich's direction keeps the action sharp, tense and exciting, his extended use of split screens working to a large degree in tightening the suspense. The film's weakest point is the script. 'Perhaps it might be a midget,' suggests saboteur Paul Winfield as an enemy sniper scuttles behind a tank. Head saboteur Burt Lancaster thinks for a moment. 'There are no midgets,' he snaps, 'in the United States Air Force!' They and the rest of the cast – Richard Widmark, Richard Jaeckel, Joseph Cotten, Melvyn Douglas, Charles Durning and Charles McGraw – are certainly more distinguished that their material.

Twilight Zone – The Movie ◐ ⓥ
1983, US, 102 mins, colour
Dir: Steven Spielberg, Joe Dante, George Miller, John Landis
Stars: Vic Morrow, Scatman Crothers, Bill Quinn, Selma Diamond
Rating: ★★★

This series of bizarre journeys into an unknown dimension is very much a curate's egg. Its four stories are all made by different directors, the best effort being a gentle little tale from Steven Spielberg about a group of old folk made young again by a roguish old black man. But the last episode is the most exciting, with John Lithgow going splendidly to pieces as the only passenger who can see a malign and destructive gremlin on the wing of his plane in mid flight. Despite the original '15' certificate, the highly-coloured 'trip' could cheerfully be recommended for all sturdier children of secondary school age. Just be prepared for the odd monster or two.

Twin Beds ○
1942, US, 85 mins, b/w
Dir: Tim Whelan

Stars: George Brent, Joan Bennett, Mischa Auer
Rating: ★★

This rather faded farce (it first appeared on stage in 1914) wouldn't amount to much without the participation of that pop-eyed, Russian-born Hollywood character star Mischa Auer. Auer chose this film to give one of his most memorable performances, especially when heavily involved in the comic pandemonium at the end of the film. He's quite irresistible, playing an eccentric slavic musician called Cherubin who's infatuated with heroine Joan Bennett.

Twinky ●
(aka: Lola)
1969, UK, 98 mins, colour
Dir: Richard Donner
Stars: Charles Bronson, Susan George, Trevor Howard
Rating: ★

This story of a middle-aged author in love with a nubile nymphet was titled *Lola*, presumably to cash in on the Lolita image. The combination of rugged Charles Bronson and prettily pouting Susan George would, I suspect, be irresistible in an action film, but seems faintly bizarre in this early offering from director Richard Donner, who, not long after, hit the big time with such hits as *The Omen*, *Superman* and *The Goonies*. Here Donner resorts to a full bag of cinematic tricks – freeze frames, a clangorous pop score, slow-motion action and speeded-up bicycle ride – to pep up his picture of London at the end of the allegedly swinging Sixties. Honor Blackman raises a smile as the absent-minded mum who drops the breakfast kippers on the dining-room carpet and Trevor Howard plays all stops out as the grandpa with a roving eye and a penchant for potting foreigners with a shotgun. Television comedy hosts Jimmy Tarbuck and Norman Vaughan appear as themselves.

Twin Peaks: Fire Walk with Me ● ⓥ
1992, US, 135 mins, colour
Dir: David Lynch
Stars: Sheryl Lee, Kyle MacLachlan, Moira Kelly, David Bowie, Harry Dean Stanton, Kiefer Sutherland
Rating: ★

A surrealistic comment on a prequel to the cult TV series, this seems, at

T

two and a quarter hours, a long indulgence. The wanton Laura Palmer (Sheryl Lee) is duly bumped off by her possibly incestious father (Ray Wise) but who cares? David Bowie appears and says nothing, while other stars appear and may wish they had said nothing. Subliminal shots, strobe lights, half-seen things, pictures coming to life and not much sense: just the film, I'm sure, that David Lynch wanted to make – not forgetting the sex and titillation that are high on his agenda. Somewhere, we're certain, there are people waiting to see this.

Twins ○ Ⓥ
1988, US, 112 mins, colour
Dir: Ivan Reitman
Stars: Arnold Schwarzenegger, Danny DeVito, Chloe Webb, Kelly Preston
Rating: ★★★

Inspirational casting is the basis for success in this unlikely action comedy. You couldn't imagine two actors less alike than hairy, strapping Arnold Scwarzenegger and little, barrel-shaped Danny DeVito. Casting them as twins is so ridiculous it just has to pay off in terms of laughs. And so it proves, even if they seem to be having slightly more fun than the audience. 'I hate violence,' groans Arnie, throwing the bad guys 'through' a lift. 'But you're so good at it,' beams Danny, amazed to have a protective twin whose back 'looks like a map of North Dakota.' There's a bit of a plot too, but it's only an excuse for Arnie and Danny to fool around to some effect in identical costumes, whether wooing Chloe Webb and Kelly Preston or dancing with each other.

Twisted Nerve ●
1968, UK, 115 mins, colour
Dir: Roy Boulting
Stars: Hywel Bennett, Billie Whitelaw
Rating: ★★★

There hadn't been a film as jumpy as this in quite a while. Is that the killer's shadow on the door as Hayley Mills tries to call up her boyfriend? The Boulting Brothers prove that most of the old suspense tricks are still the best, in this story of a psychotic youth who kills his stepfather and landlady on his way to mental disintegration. Barry Foster scores as a bawdy lodger with an eye on landlady Billie Whitelaw.

Two-faced Woman ○
1941, US, 94 mins, b/w
Dir: George Cukor

Stars: Greta Garbo, Melvyn Douglas, Constance Bennett, Roland Young
Rating: ★★★

Notorious as the film which caused Greta Garbo to leave MGM and end her screen career, this romantic comedy turns out to be an entertaining and frothy confection. Perhaps it was because the star deliberately abandoned her image of aloofness and mystery that the film was reviled by contemporary critics. Garbo proves in fact to be a dab hand at light comedy as a woman who poses as her own sister in order to win back her philandering husband, played by her *Ninotchka* partner Melvyn Douglas. She has a classic tipsy scene, dances a lively variation of the rumba, the 'chica-choca', and even, more surprisingly, gets to appear in a one-piece bathing suit.

Two Faces of Dr Jekyll, The ○
(aka: House of Fright)
1960, UK, 88 mins, colour
Dir: Terence Fisher
Stars: Paul Massie, Dawn Addams, Christopher Lee
Rating: ★★

Hammer horror meets Robert Louis Stevenson. In this generous adaptation – by noted author and playwright Wolf Mankowitz – of R L S's classic tale of double identity and murder, the colour photography gives a good impression of bright Victorian decadence. Christopher Lee looks distinctly uncomfortable at having to play a straightforward 'good guy' in a horror film, Paul Massie plays the hapless Jekyll and, in a small part, you can spot a young Oliver Reed as a bully.

Two Flags West ○
1950, US, 92 mins, b/w
Dir: Robert Wise
Stars: Joseph Cotten, Linda Darnell, Cornel Wilde, Dale Robertson,
Rating: ★★

Director Robert Wise, one of the most respected senior film-makers in the business, had just left RKO where he had made his name editing *Citizen Kane* and directing *The Body Snatcher* and *The Set-Up*, and started up at Fox, where his career would reach its high point 15 years later with *The Sound of Music*. In *Two Flags West*, Wise augmented a formidable cast with some spectacular battles between cavalry and Indians.

Two for the Road ○
1967, UK, 112 mins, colour
Dir: Stanley Donen
Stars: Audrey Hepburn, Albert Finney, Eleanor Bron, William Daniels
Rating: ★★

Centred on one particular car journey through France, but mixed with numerous scenes set in various times in the past, this comedy concerns the superficial changes that come over a young married couple. The dialogue is incisively accurate on the moods, manners and morals of modern life but, despite the problems of the couple involved, it's very much a 'pro-marriage' story. Author Frederic Raphael admitted that he first hit on the idea while on a drive through France with his wife, but resisted the suggestion that it might be any more autobiographical than any of his other writing. Fine acting by Albert Finney and Audrey Hepburn, with some scene-stealing by Eleanor Bron and the ineffably fussy William Daniels.

Two Girls and a Sailor ○
1944, US, 124 mins, b/w
Dir: Richard Thorpe
Stars: Van Johnson, June Allyson
Rating: ★★

A really swinging musical packed full of songs and speciality numbers which deservedly swamp a typically weak June Allyson-Van Johnson MGM plot about . . . well, two girls and a sailor. Tom Drake and Gloria De Haven are in there to ensure misunderstandings are sorted out by a double happy ending, but the music's the thing. Jimmy Durante reprises one of his greatest numbers, 'Inka Dinka Doo', Lena Horne gives a classic rendition of 'Paper Doll', and Allyson, De Haven and Helen Forrest help Harry James and His Music Makers swing into 'Sweet and Lovely'.

Two Jakes, The ● Ⓥ
1990, US, 137 mins, colour
Dir: Jack Nicholson
Stars: Jack Nicholson, Harvey Keitel, Meg Tilley, Madeleine Stowe, Eli Wallach, Frederic Forrest
Rating: ★★

The problem with this lacklustre sequel to *Chinatown* is that it never really goes anywhere. There are no great revelations at the end of a story that is immensely difficult to follow and way too long in the telling. As director as well as star, Jack Nicholson, repeating his role as Jake Gittes, is obviously responsible for the stately and rather suffocating feel of the piece. It is, however, marvellously well set in period and written with great literary bite by Robert Towne, who also penned the original. In fact, you want it to be better than it is: after all, the initial elements of the story sound interesting even if they don't eventually amount to much. Alas, even Nicholson, now roly-poly and flat-footed, no longer seems ideal casting for the private eye fallen on better times, who finds ghosts from the past rising to haunt him during a seemingly straightforward case of revenge killing. There are some good moments here, but they just don't fuse together; and the acting, considering the strength of the cast, is not that great.

Two Minute Warning ○
1976, US, 115 mins, colour
Dir: Larry Peerce
Stars: Charlton Heston, John Cassavetes, Martin Balsam, Beau Bridges, David Janssen
Rating: ★★

The all-star disaster movie was nearing the end of its useful life when Universal put Charlton Heston at the head of the cast, and a sniper on a tower overlooking a football stadium and hoped that that would be enough to shore up a shaky plot. Full of sound and fury, but signifying very little, the film provides good actors like Gena Rowlands, John Cassavetes, Jack Klugman, David Janssen and Brock Peters with hackneyed characters they do their best to enliven. Walter Pidgeon makes one of his last film appearances as an aged pickpocket, and you may also spot Robert *Exterminator* Ginty as a vendor.

Two Mules for Sister Sara ○ ○
1969, US, 105 mins, colour
Dir: Don Siegel
Stars: Shirley MacLaine, Clint Eastwood
Rating: ★★★

Set in Mexico, this is an American-made film but one which resembles – in some of its content and most of its style – the so-called 'spaghetti' Westerns which were being turned out in Italy at the time, achieving such popularity over here. Perhaps the similarity is heightened by the fact that the music was composed by that specialist in Italian Westerns, Ennio Morricone. Despite its quite lengthy running time, the film is a

lively one with considerable outbursts of action, a story which has more than one surprise up its sleeve and magnetic performances by its stars, Clint Eastwood and Shirley MacLaine.

Two of a Kind ○ ○
1983, US, 87 mins, colour
Dir: John Herzfeld
Stars: John Travolta, Olivia Newton-John, Oliver Reed, Charles Durning
Rating: ★

It might have seemed like a bright idea to reunite John Travolta and Olivia Newton-John after the huge success of *Grease*, but whoever dreamt up this load of nonsense must have had an oil slick on the brain. God is so angry at the human race that he's about to destroy the Earth until four angels persuade him to give humanity one more chance. Salvation is in the hands of inventor-turned-robber Travolta and bank teller Newton-John. If they can be nice to each other . . . Sharp eyes may spot Kathy Bates way down the cast list, long before her Oscar-winning success in *Misery*.

2001: A Space Odyssey ○ ○
1968, UK, 141 mins, colour
Dir: Stanley Kubrick
Stars: Keir Dullea, Gary Lockwood
Rating: ★★★

Stanley Kubrick's visually stunning sci-fi epic is something of a space oddity and one that has confused and confounded almost everyone who has seen it. Arguments about what it all means still continue, 25 years after the film was released. The story starts four million years ago when a group of cavemen discover a mysterious monolith. The moment they touch it, they turn from peaceful vegetarians into war-like carnivores. Four million years later the monolith is discovered on the moon and a spaceship is on a mysterious mission to Jupiter. Things become curiouser and curiouser and if you manage to keep up with it, you'll be doing better than most. It all looks fantastic, even though special effects have improved greatly since the film was made. Very much a curate's egg, *2001*'s delights compensate for its confusions.

2010 ○
1984, US, 111 mins, colour
Dir: Peter Hyams
Stars: Roy Scheider, John Lithgow, Helen Mirren
Rating: ★★★

Boldly going where few men would have dared to tread, writer-director Peter Hyams has fashioned an entirely respectful sequel to Stanley Kubrick's influential science-fiction classic *2001: A Space Odyssey*. Overcoming the slight hiccup of its wordy scene-setting opening, *2010* develops into a fascinating space saga in its own right as American Roy Scheider (inheriting William Sylvester's role from Kubrick's film) joins a Russian team to solve the mystery of Discovery's disappearance. The tension between these reluctant colleagues is keenly felt, and the state-of-the-art effects culminate in a climactic revelation that's as eerie as it is wonderful.

Two-Way Stretch ○ ○
1960, US, 87 mins, b/w
Dir: Robert Day
Stars: Peter Sellers, Wilfrid Hyde White, Lieonel Jeffries, Beryl Reid, David Lodge
Rating: ★★★

Probably the funniest and most consistently riotous of all Peter Sellers' British comedies, a short head in front of *The Wrong Arm of the Law*. Sellers, David Lodge and Bernard Cribbins are a trio of unholy jailbirds, but Lionel Jeffries steals the show as a would-be vicious warder called Sidney Crout. Jeffries tries to prevent Sellers and Co from carrying out a million pound robbery (while technically still in prison) but succeeds only in falling hilariously foul of their nefarious schemes. Maurice Denham, Wilfrid Hyde-White (in his element as an educated, plausible, ever-smiling con-man), Irene Handl, Liz Fraser and Beryl Reid round out a hand-picked supporting cast.

Two Women ○
(aka: La Ciociara)
1961, Italy, 110 mins, b/w
Dir: Vittorio De Sica
Stars: Sophia Loren, Eleanora Brown
Rating: ★★★

Sophia Loren's Oscar-winning tour-de-force in an Anna Magnani-type role that few believed she was capable of playing. But Sophia was superbly moving as a wartime widow with a teenage daughter. Their survival after horrendous rape at the hands of Moroccan soldiers makes for an involving and emotional story. The desolate atmosphere of war-torn Italy is superbly captured by director Vittorio de Sica.

T

Two Years Before the Mast ○
1946, US, 98 mins, b/w
Dir: John Farrow
Stars: Alan Ladd, Howard Da Silva,
Brian Donlevy, William Bendix
Rating: ★★

Round the Horn, me hearties, in the
days of wooden ships and iron men.
Some of the acting is a little wooden,
too, in this catalogue of maritime
brutality based on a rather more
literate book by Richard Henry Dana.
Used to the night-time world of Paramount's crime dramas, Alan Ladd,
Howard da Silva, Brian Donlevy and
William Bendix look a little pale
around the gills, or maybe it was just
the rocking of the ship in the studio
tank. Da Silva has a high old time as a
martinet captain who makes Captain
Bligh and Ahab seem positively
avuncular by comparison. Several of
the cast are lashed to the mast and
mercilessly flogged – a treatment that
should have been reserved for the
writers.

Tycoon ○
1947, US, 129 mins, colour
Dir: Richard Wallace
Stars: John Wayne, Laraine Day
Rating: ★★

A relatively lesser-known John Wayne
film from the Forties, although there's
no reason why it should be, apart from
having been made by a studio in
difficulties (RKO Radio). It's no
stodgy boardroom drama, either, but a
spectacular action adventure story
with some hair-raising storm scenes,
brilliantly photographed in
Technicolor. Wayne and co-star
Laraine Day reputedly didn't get on
together, and it shows in the stiffness
of their romantic scenes.

Ugly Dachshund, The ⊙
1965, US, 93 mins, colour
Dir: Norman Tokar
Stars: Dean Jones, Suzanne Pleshette,
Charlie Ruggles
Rating: ★

Flimsy Disney whimsy about a
filthy-rich young couple who adopt a
Great Dane puppy as a brother for
their four dachshund bitches. 'You've
got a boy puppy,' he tells his wife.
'That's what you always wanted.'
Dean Jones and Suzanne Pleshette
coat the treacle with their winning
brands of charm.

Ulysses ○
1954, Italy, 104 mins, colour
Dir: Mario Camerini
Stars: Kirk Douglas, Silvana Mangano,
Anthony Quinn, Rossana Podesta
Rating: ★★

No fewer than seven writers, including Irwin (*The Young Lions*) Shaw,
worked on creating a film script from
Homer's *Odyssey*. They managed to
condense the epic poem into four
main incidents: the clash between
Ulysses and the Cyclops, and his
encounters with Circe, the Sirens and
Nausicaa. This telescoping of events
enabled Mario Camerini to gradually
increase the pace until the hectic
climax in which Ulysses takes on his
wife's suitors. The mistily beautiful
photography of the sea scenes
greatly enhances the film.

Ulzana's Raid ●
1972, US, 103 mins, colour
Dir: Robert Aldrich
Stars: Burt Lancaster, Bruce Davison,
Torge Luke, Richard Jaeckel
Rating: ★★★

World-weary but wise scout Burt
Lancaster helps callow and naive
cavalry officer Bruce Davison track
down a renegade Apache in this violent Western from director Robert
Aldrich. Exciting though it is, the film
isn't without its thoughtful side. Lancaster, while not justifying Ulzana's
actions, has sympathy for the Indians,
and indeed has an Indian wife.
Davison believes them all to be
savages, little more than animals, until
he sees the savagery of his own men.
Lancaster gives a fine performance as

the scout and Davison is also very
good as the young lieutenant fresh
from an Eastern military academy.
Well-scripted by Alan Sharp, this
powerful Western has drama and
action in equal measure.

Umbrella Woman, The
See: The Good Wife

Uncanny, The ●
1977, UK/Canada, 85 mins, colour
Dir: Denis Heroux
Stars: Peter Cushing, Ray Milland,
Donald Pleasence
Rating: ★

Three horror stories about cats very
much in the style established by the
British outfit Amicus Films in the
Sixties. This picture, however, was
made in Canada with a star-studded
cast. Special effects are rather below
par and the light-heartedness of the
last episode (somewhat after the humour of *The Raven*) comes as a
welcome relief.

Uncle Buck ○ ⊗
1989, US, 94 mins, colour
Dir: John Hughes
Stars: John Candy, Jean Louisa Kelly,
Gaby Hoffman, Macaulay Culkin, Amy
Madigan
Rating: ★★★

For Buck, read schmuck. That's how
bulbous John Candy's cast in this
simplistic but rather enjoyable comedy. Fat, out-of-work and 40, and
forever evading marriage to his
long-suffering girlfriend (Amy
Madigan), Buck suddenly finds himself
temporarily in charge of his
brother's kids, two wild juves and Tia,
a teenager who shows all the signs of
getting herself pregnant at an early
age. Buck is a sausage-fingers who
breaks everything and cooks enormous
breakfasts consisting of eggs on onions,
but the kids' problems appeal in no
time to his innate sense of adulthood
and, in a few weeks, he proves himself
a better parent than his brother ever
was. It all sounds too predictable to be
much fun, but in fact it works pretty
well, giving Candy a chance to show
what he can do, playing a variant on
the slob who comes good that he
played in *Planes, Trains and
Automobiles*. Not a great film, but one
that makes you feel better for having
seen it.

Uncle Silas ○
1947, UK, 103 mins, b/w
Dir: Charles Frank
Stars: Jean Simmons, Katina Paxinou
Rating: ★★★

This creepy thriller was the film that consolidated Jean Simmons' position as a new young star of the British cinema, coming only months after her outstanding supporting performance in *Black Narcissus*. Here, she plays a plucky Victorian miss who refuses to knuckle under to the sinister uncle and strange governess into whose chilly care she has been placed following the death of her father. The combination of screenplay writer Ben Travers (more famous for his Aldwych stage farces) and J Sheridan Le Fanu, the Victorian master of the chiller on whose story Travers based his script, couldn't have seemed too promising. But in the hands of Simmons and her cohorts, plus the edgy direction of Charles Frank, the time-honoured old plot generates fresh suspense around every shadowy corner and down each dark stairway.

Uncommon Valor ◑
1983, US, 105 mins, colour
Dir: Ted Kotcheff
Stars: Gene Hackman, Robert Stack, Fred Ward, Patrick Swayze
Rating: ★★★

Searching for its battered self-esteem after Vietnam, America welcomed a rash of 'let's rescue our boys' action films, the worst of which was the idiotic *Rambo*. This one, starring Gene Hackman, was one of the better ones (Hackman also made another – *Bat*21*). He stars as a colonel whose son is missing in action. Despairing of the slow-moving 'usual' channels, he gathers together a group of hardened veterans and goes to find him. The politics behind this (and similar films) may be a bit questionable, but it's exciting and fast-moving. Hackman gives his character a bit more emotional depth and motivation than is usually found in such films and director Ted Kotcheff moves it at a pace that maintains the tension.

Unconquered ○
1947, US, 146 mins, colour
Dir: Cecil B DeMille
Stars: Gary Cooper, Paulette Goddard, Howard Da Silva, Boris Karloff
Rating: ★★

Cecil B DeMille spent a reported $4 million to bring this epic story of colonial America to the screen. Most of it shows up on the screen, although, to judge from some of the contemporary reviews, only a small part of the budget went to the screenplay. This combines melodrama with improbability and garnishes it with enough hokum to fill three regulation-size films. Not that it matters because DeMille's speciality was spectacle and he certainly provides a full measure here – splendidly staged Indian attacks and an edge-of-the-seat escape by Gary Cooper and Paulette Goddard over treacherous rapids are most notable among the set pieces. And, being DeMille, he even arranged a scene in which Goddard took a tantalising bath on camera! The heroic derring-do of Cooper is in the best tradition of the genre, Howard Da Silva is an eminently hissable villain and Boris Karloff makes a rather surprising appearance as an Indian chief. Subtlety is not its strong point but Saturday serial-style thrills certainly are.

Undefeated, The ○ ⓥ
1969, US, 119 mins, colour
Dir: Andrew V McLaglen
Stars: John Wayne, Rock Hudson, Tony Aguilar, Bruce Cabot
Rating: ★★

Director Andrew V McLaglen carried his interest in the American Civil War a stage further on from *Shenandoah*, in which a peace-loving family was drawn into the conflict, to look at the first days following the war. After a moving opening, the theme of bitterness lingering on gradually disappears beneath the action and the spectacle for which McLaglen later became famous. John Wayne is the Unionist and Rock Hudson the Confederate, compelled to join forces against bandits, Emperor Maximilian's agents and a troop of French cavalry, across 2,000 miles of adventure to the wilds of Mexico.

Under Capricorn ○
1948, UK, 117 mins, colour
Dir: Alfred Hitchcock
Stars: Ingrid Bergman, Joseph Cotten, Michael Wilding, Margaret Leighton
Rating: ★★

After *Spellbound* and *Notorious*, Alfred Hitchcock cast around in vain for another major hit until his dazzling run

of success in the Fifties. For *Under Capricorn*, he even had the star of those two great Forties hits, Ingrid Bergman, working with him again. And the plot included such surefire Hitchcock elements as the dominant housekeeper, the skeleton in the cupboard and the confession of guilt towards the end. But, as he admitted himself, basic mistakes were made in the preparation of the movie which contributed to its box-office and critical failure at the time. Hitchcock enlisted James Bridie, a playwright, and Hume Cronyn, an actor, to help him with the screenplay, but neither was suited to turning Helen Simpson's novel or the play that sprung from it into a Hitchcock-style picture. Then there was the ludicrous miscasting of the principals, Bergman (as an aristocratic Irish girl!) and Joseph Cotten, plus the expensive decision to shoot the film in (unnecessary) Technicolor. 'If I'd been thinking clearly,' said Hitchcock ruefully afterwards, 'I'd have never tackled a costume picture at all.' Still, the film was ineffably romantic, and Jack Cardiff's colour photography did make it beautiful to look at. Margaret Leighton easily took the acting honours.

Undercover Blues ◑ ⓥ
1993, US, 90 mins, colour
Dir: Herbert Ross
Stars: Kathleen Turner, Dennis Quaid, Fiona Shaw
Rating: RB

Whatever happened to Kathleen Turner and Dennis Quaid? Two of the brightest stars of the mid-Eighties, their careers slid downwards and downwards until they ended up in this stunningly inept farce, played so far over the top by its cast as to be an embarrassment. The only hint of subtlety in the whole enterprise is the title: Quaid and Turner are Mr and Mrs Blue, undercover FBI (or something, who cares?) agents working on a case to deport a continental mastermind. The villains are quite ludicrously comic, and you can't help puzzle why, even at this low point in their careers, Turner and Quaid ever became involved in it all. It makes the contemporary *Cop & ½* seem a gem of wit and action. Blues is right.

Undercovers Hero
See: Soft Beds, Hard Battles)

U

Undercurrent ○
1946, US, 116 mins, b/w
Dir: Vincente Minnelli
Stars: Katharine Hepburn, Robert Taylor, Robert Mitchum, Edmund Gwenn
Rating: ★★★

This was the first film which Robert Taylor made after his return to Hollywood from three years' wartime service in the US Navy. And his choice of role surprised many fans who were used to seeing him play heroes of unblemished character. Here he takes the part of a man who outrageously swindles his own brother, then sweeps a scientist's daughter off her feet, marries her and takes her off to an isolated home in Virginia Woods. Katharine Hepburn is cast as the bride who finds that behind her husband's pleasant facade is a seething mass of fears and hatreds. Worse, she realises that he is a psychopath with her in mind as his victim. Strong dramatic entertainment.

Under Fire ● ⓥ
1983, US, 128 mins, colour
Dir: Roger Spottiswoode
Stars: Gene Hackman, Nick Nolte, Joanna Cassidy, Ed Harris, Jean-Louis Trintignant
Rating: ★★★

This fine, raw film is reminiscent of Peter Weir's *The Year of Living Dangerously* and would have been made decades earlier with more razzmatazz, plus Clark Gable, Spencer Tracy and Myrna Loy. Here it's Nick Nolte, Gene Hackman and Joanna Cassidy as the three roving war correspondents found at the start in the process of moving from Chad to Nicaragua in 1979. In the Central American melting-pot, the three newshounds – Nolte is a photojournalist, the others news reporters – become all too heavily involved as the revolution boils over into fighting in the streets. Few of the horrors of such a situation are spared us, but at the same time there is more personality-building than in the Weir film. Besides the leading trio, all giving solid portrayals, Jean-Louis Trintignant as a mysterious French 'spy', Ed Harris as a grinning mercenary killer and Alma Martinez as a girl guerilla all make their marks. Some rather trite points about exchanging one set of tyrants for another – so that the film can wave its white flag of impartiality – cannot obscure the tension dripping from every frame of such reconstructed

immediacy. Jerry Goldsmith's haunting panpipe-type music is his best score in some while.

Under Milk Wood ○
1971, UK, 90 mins, colour
Dir: Andrew Sinclair
Stars: Richard Burton, Elizabeth Taylor, Peter O'Toole, Glynis Johns
Rating: ★★

A star-heavy film version of Dylan Thomas' famous 'radio play for voices'. But the big names, Elizabeth Taylor, Richard Burton, Peter O'Toole and Glynis Johns, have to yield best to Rachel Thomas, a joy as Mary Ann Sailors, and Talfryn Thomas, quietly hilarious as Pugh the Poisoner. Most of the other players (and director Andrew Sinclair) seem to approach Thomas' material with too much respect, leaving it on the fringes of some picturesque rural images.

Under Siege ● ⓥ
1992, US, 98 mins, colour
Dir: Andrew Davis
Stars: Steven Seagal, Tommy Lee Jones, Gary Busey, Erika Eleniak, Patrick O'Neal, Nick Mancuso
Rating: ★★★

A team of trained saboteurs has taken over a US nuclear warship. The outlook for mankind looks bleak. 'Wake up the President,' growls the admiral. But when master cook Steven Seagal sums up the situation and swallows hard, you know the bad guys have had it. Armed only with a chopping knife and accompanied by busty centrefold playmate Erika Eleniak, he sets about decimating the opposition in the most painful possible way. Swiftly in touch with defence HQ, he's asked how many saboteurs there are. About 30, he says. He's swiftly picked off that number but, fortunately for his fans there are still lots left, all dispatched in (agonisingly) different fashions. It gets progressively more ludicrous but remains thoroughly entertaining, apart from going right over the top at the end when villain Tommy Lee Jones, in finest movie tradition, gets the drop on Seagal, but chooses not to finish him off. Seagal actually gets to make a joke or two and, thanks to J F (*Pretty Woman*) Lawton's script, shows up better as an actor than on previous assignments. Gary Busey enjoys himself hugely as Jones' 'inside man' on the ship, an extravagant performance (including a wild drag act) that almost steals the show.

Under Suspicion ● ⓥ
1991, US/UK, 100 mins, colour
Dir: Simon Moore
Stars: Liam Neeson, Laura San Giacomo, Kenneth Cranham
Rating: ★★

A full-blooded British attempt at a *film noir* thriller, complete with a seemingly watertight murder case with a detective (disgraced cop Liam Neeson) as number one suspect, who just happens to be having an affair with the number two suspect. Is one of them setting the other up to take the rap? Is neither of them guilty? They certainly both look and act as if they are, but that's just two of the possible red herrings floating around. Kenneth Cranham is the detective on the case and looks as if he doesn't believe a word he has to say. American Laura San Giacomo, fresh from her success in *sex, lies and videotape* and as Julia Roberts' hooker girlfriend in *Pretty Woman*, acts like the British cold weather has frozen her joints. The illusion of sinful Brighton in the 1950s is ruined by a modern telephone box in one scene. By the final prison gallows scene, you'll either be on the edge of your seat with excitement or rolling around the floor in uncontrolled mirth.

Under 10 Flags ○
1960, US/Italy, 92 mins, b/w
Dir: Duilio Coletti, Silvio Narizzano
Stars: Van Heflin, Charles Laughton, Mylene Demongeot
Rating: ★★

Producer Dino de Laurentiis was really aiming for the international market when he made this war film in four different languages. The cast includes American, British, French, German and Italian players!

Under the Clock ○
(aka: The Clock)
1945, US, 90 mins, b/w
Dir: Vincente Minnelli
Stars: Judy Garland, Robert Walker
Rating: ★★★

In a rare and successful non-singing role, Judy Garland re-teamed with director Vincente Minnelli for their second box-office smash in a row after *Meet Me In St Louis*. Soon after the release of *The Clock*, as it was titled in the US, she married the director and the following year their daughter, Liza Minnelli, was born. But while audiences flocked to see Garland and co-star Robert Walker portray one of Hollywood's best-matched young screen couples, presenting an image of pure and innocent first-love, both stars were well on the road to personal tragedy.

Under the Volcano ●
1984, US, 111 mins, colour
Dir: John Huston
Stars: Albert Finney, Jacqueline Bisset, Anthony Andrews
Rating: ★★

Director John Huston's sombre, ultra-gloomy, but well-acted piece about a British ex-consul in Mexico who cannot live with or without the wife who has had an affair with his half-brother. Albert Finney's highly-mannered performance as the permanently stoned-into-oblivion diplomat takes a while to get attuned to, but Huston extracts the best performance from Jacqueline Bisset in quite a while as the wife. James Villiers contributes an amusing few minutes as an 'Englishman abroad' who almost runs over a Finney finally felled by alcohol. The tragic ending is rather too contrived to compel total belief, and emotionally the film remains at a distance.

Under the Yum Yum Tree ○
1963, US, 110 mins, colour
Dir: David Swift
Stars: Jack Lemmon, Carol Lynley, Dean Jones
Rating: ★★★

Jack Lemmon in top comedy form as a lothario landlord who lives in an apartment that might have been designed by Edgar Allan Poe, and whose tenants are all female. One of them (Carol Lynley) is living platonically with her fiancé, and Lemmon tries all sorts of spying tricks to see how the battle of the bedroom is getting on. But an enchanting ginger cat – the one from *Breakfast at Tiffany's* – keeps upsetting his applecart as he climbs on to the roof/patio balustrade, and Lemmon somehow always ends up in the bushes below. This is that modern-day rarity: a good adult comedy. Lynley wins over with a charming portrayal, while Dean Jones is excellent as the fiancé. In support, Paul Lynde and Imogene Coca grab what chances are going with eager hands. Even so, Lemmon is almost the whole show on his own.

Under Two Flags ○
1936, US, 111 mins, b/w
Dir: Frank Lloyd
Stars: Ronald Colman, Claudette Colbert, Victor McLaglen, Rosalind Russell
Rating: ★★★

Rousing *Boy's Own* stuff here, with handsome Ronald Colman joining the Foreign Legion after being accused of a crime his brother committed. Camp follower Claudette Colbert takes a shine to him in a big way which arouses the jealousy of Legion commander Victor McLaglen, who proceeds to make Colman's life a misery. Unfair, really, as Colman has fallen for Rosalind Russell. It all comes to a head when Colman is captured by Arabs and only Colbert, now feeling the anger of a woman scorned, can save him. If not quite up to *Beau Geste*, this fast moving adventure yarn isn't far behind. All the ingredients are mixed thoroughly and baked to perfection to the classic Hollywood recipe. Colman is a firm-jawed hero and McLaglen plays the nasty to the hilt. Colbert is a little too refined to be a true tart-with-a-heart (Jean Harlow would have been better), but she looks the part and of course rescues our hero in the end.

Underwater ○
1955, US, 99 mins, colour
Dir: John Sturges
Stars: Jane Russell, Richard Egan
Rating: ★★

Howard Hughes and RKO Radio poured $3 million into this adventure story, made mainly as a vehicle for Jane Russell, and it shows, particularly in the technical excellence of the underwater scenes. Russell fans will ask no more than the sight of their idol in a swimsuit, although Lori Nelson comes across as the more likeable of the two girls involved in a fast-moving sunken-treasure yarn.

Unfaithfully Yours ○
1948, US, 105 mins, b/w
Dir: Preston Sturges
Stars: Rex Harrison, Linda Darnell, Rudy Vallee, Lionel Stander
Rating: ★★★

A classic black comedy from Hollywood's fun king of the Forties, writer-director Preston Sturges. Rex Harrison is the orchestra conductor who visualises various fiendish demises for his wife (gorgeous Linda Darnell) while he is in the middle of a concert. Very good support from bandleader Rudy Vallee who proved himself an admirable comedy foil when his days as a musical star were over.

Unfaithfully Yours ◑
1983, US, 105 mins, colour
Dir: Howard Zieff
Stars: Dudley Moore, Nastassja Kinski, Armand Assante, Albert Brooks
Rating: ★★★

A likeable remake of the classic 1948 Preston Sturges comedy, with Dudley Moore inheriting the role played by Rex Harrison in the original. Like Harrison before him, Moore ably captures the main character's dual personality: a world-famous conductor who's both obnoxiously arrogant and insecure enough to doubt his beautiful wife's fidelity. As the wife in question, Nastassja Kinski pouts prettily but the laughs belong to Moore (who envisages an elaborate murder plot to do away with his wife and her mysterious lover) and a gallery of comic turns in support: Albert Brooks as Moore's manager, Richard Libertini as the devoted valet and Richard B Shull as the excessively eager detective who sets in motion the chaos that ensues. Directed with brio by Howard Zieff and co-written by Barry Levinson, who himself won critical plaudits for directing *Diner* and *Tin Men*.

Unforgiven, The ○
1960, US, 125 mins, colour
Dir: John Huston
Stars: Burt Lancaster, Audrey Hepburn, Audie Murphy, John Saxon
Rating: ★★★★

Magnificent John Huston Western that compares in tension to *High Noon* or *Shane*. The claustrophobic atmosphere of the tiny ranch under siege by the Kiowa Indians is splendidly conveyed by director and cameraman. And there are excellent performances from Burt Lancaster, Audrey Hepburn, Audie Murphy and veteran screen queen Lillian Gish.

Unforgiven ● ⓥ
1992, US, 130 mins, colour
Dir: Clint Eastwood
Stars: Clint Eastwood, Gene Hackman, Morgan Freeman, Richard Harris, Frances Fisher, Jaimz Woolvett
Rating: ★★★

U

In what may be his swan song to the Western, Clint Eastwood plays a character who could be 'The Man With No Name' 20 years on. An infamous gunslinger tamed by the love of a woman who has since died, he now farms pigs with his two children. Hatred of his new life, coupled with a need for money, impels him to ride out in search of a reward offered by a brothel, one of whose girls was cut up by two cowhands who got off with little more than a fine. The sadistic sheriff, Gene Hackman (who handed out the 'penalty'), deals more summarily with bounty hunters, but all might still have been straightforward were it not for an event that finally makes Eastwood reach for both bottle and gun and turns him back into 'The Man With No Name' for the last 15 minutes of the film. Too slow at times, the film is redeemed not by its realistic view of the old west (what else is new?), but by its rich array of characters: not only Eastwood and Hackman (building his own home, but the world's worst carpenter), but Morgan Freeman as Eastwood's old partner, Richard Harris as an English bounty killer and Saul Rubinek as Harris' travelling biographer. Appropriately, the survivor of the final shootout rides not into the sunset, but through mud and a night-time rainstorm. The film won a saddle full of Oscars at the 1993 Academy Awards.

Unholy, The ● Ⓥ
1988, Spain/US, 104 mins, colour
Dir: Camilo Avila
Stars: Ben Cross, Jill Carroll, William Russ, Trevor Howard, Hal Holbrook, Ned Beatty
Rating: ★★

A routine horror tale of demonology and a priestly temptation, this chiller has all the expected ingredients of the genre: passable special effects, oodles of gore, nubile maidens in flimsies and bags of dry ice floating up from the ground. Very sub-John Carpenter, but quite good fun for fans of this sort of thing, if a bit nasty for the average cinemagoer. Ben Cross is the priest who must do battle with a demon from Hell and makes rather a meal of it (all he has to do, for God's sake, is call it by name) and Trevor Howard, Hal Holbrook and Ned Beatty do their bit as the usual grim-faced priests and detectives. Only William Russ, as the sub-Brando owner of a devil-worship club, is a character away from the ordinary in this kind of thing.

Unholy Partners ○
1941, US, 95 mins, b/w
Dir: Mervyn LeRoy
Stars: Edward G Robinson, Edward Arnold, Laraine Day, Marsha Hunt, Marcel Dalio, Frank Faylen
Rating: ★★

Another little-known goodie from the Edward G Robinson collection. Vaguely based on the exploits of a real-life pressman who worked for the *New York Mirror*, it's an entertaining newspaper melodrama which takes Robinson and director Mervyn LeRoy back to their *Five Star Final* setting. But, being made at MGM, rather lacks the sinew that Robinson's home studio, Warner Brothers, might have brought to the story. Still, Robinson and Edward Arnold are both rock-solid as the newspaperman and the underworld Czar who become the unholy partners of the title.

Unholy Wife, The ○
1957, US, 94 mins, colour
Dir: John Farrow
Stars: Rod Steiger, Diana Dors, Tom Tryon, Beulah Bondi, Marie Windsor, Arthur Franz
Rating: ★★

This was Diana Dors' first Hollywood picture and she plays a typical man-hungry woman who plots no good to get what she wants. Justice, of course, prevails but no matter how good a film, it hardly lives up to its own advertising line, 'Half Angel, Half Devil, She Made Him Half a Man'. It was actually a rather insipid remake of the 1940 film *They Knew What They Wanted*. Rod Steiger, as Dors' long-suffering husband, is hampered by a bad dose of Method-actingitis, and it is left to Tom Tryon, as her no-good seducer, to bring any conviction to the proceedings. But it looks better today than it did then.

Un Homme et une Femme ● Ⓥ
(aka: A Man and a Woman)
1966, France, 102 mins, colour
Dir: Claude Lelouch
Stars: Jean-Louis Trintignant, Anouk Aimee
Rating: ★★★★

This is a stylish bitter-sweet romance between a racing driver and a film script girl. Her husband died in a stunt accident, his wife committed suicide and they meet because their children go to the same boarding school. Like all those Sixties British films set in swinging London, the film is set very firmly in its own time and therefore looks rather dated now. Unlike those British films, it's not a squirming embarrassment to watch, although some of the pretty-pretty scenes now look a bit naff and the theme song gets on your nerves after a while. The performances of Anouk Aimee and Jean-Louis Trintignant are strong, if not entirely convincing, and hold the film together.

Uninvited, The ● ℂ
1944, US, 98 mins, b/w
Dir: Lewis Smith
Stars: Ray Milland, Ruth Hussey, Donald Crisp, Gail Russell
Rating: ★★★

A real surprise in its day, this is one of Hollywood's best ghost stories, which should send some genuine shivers up your spine. Hauntingly beautiful Gail Russell is just right on her screen debut for the role of the girl who holds the key to the mystery of the haunted house that brother and sister Ray Milland and Ruth Hussey have bought on the English coast. British-born director Lewis Allen keeps you guessing every step of the way and the ending is a real chiller.

Union Pacific ○
1939, US, 135 mins, b/w
Dir: Cecil B DeMille
Stars: Barbara Stanwyck, Joel McCrea
Rating: ★★★

Cecil B DeMille's epic Western is one of his most enjoyable films, full of sprawling, brawling adventure, the highlight of which is a spectacular train crash. Barbara Stanwyck's gutsy daughter of a railroad engineer (she has a becoming Irish Brogue), more than holds her own with a virtually all-male cast, and there's one of the screen's great fist fights for good measure – between Joel McCrea and Robert Barrat. All this and Indians too.

Union Station ○
1950, US, 80 mins, b/w
Dir: Rudolph Mate
Stars: William Holden, Nancy Olson, Barry Fitzgerald
Rating: ★★★★

Tight, hard-hitting thriller about the kidnap of a blind girl by a vicious gang. William Holden and Barry Fitzgerald create likeable and contrasting characters as the policemen on the case; Nancy Olson is a pretty and resourceful heroine who enlists our sympathies from the outset; Allene Roberts is touchingly true as the hapless kidnap victim; and Lyle Bettger and Jan Sterling carve memorably nasty portraits of those on the wrong side of the law. Rudolph Maté's taut and skilful direction doesn't miss a thrill. The suspense builds irresistibly to a nail-biting underground climax.

Universal Soldier ● ⓥ
1992, US, 104 mins, colour
Dir: Roland Emmerich
Stars: Jean-Claude Van Damme, Dolph Lundgren, Ally Walker, Ed O'Ross, Jerry Orbach
Rating: ★★

Just about the ultimate in muscular violence, this overrated, futuristic saga gives us two invincible icons of the screen for the price of one. Dolph Lundgren (who at least gets to enjoy himself playing a thoroughly bad lot) and Jean-Claude Van Damme are a couple of military corpses revived to become perfect fighting machines (just like *RoboCop*, devoid of memory (just like *Robcop*) but one of whom accidentally starts recalling pieces of the past (yes, just like *RoboCop*) which sets them off on a collision course and eventual battle to the death. Don't let the plot (and certainly not the weak leading lady) detract from the real thing – the non-stop, muscle-ripping action. And remember: Lundgren is 'all ears' . . .

Unlawful Entry ● ⓥ
1992, US, 111 mins, colour
Dir: Jonathan Kaplan
Stars: Kurt Russell, Madeleine Stowe, Ray Liotta
Rating: ★

Developments are heavily signalled in this thriller of menace, in which psychotic policeman Ray Liotta develops a fixation on the beautiful wife (Madeleine Stowe) of businessman Kurt Russell, and determines to ruin Russell's life and take her away from him. From here on in, you'd better be prey to the easy thrill as the plot goes strictly by the numbers. Showers are on while phones ring; the family cat is good for several attempts to make us

jump; and people do the usual silly things they do in such films. Liotta's partner tells him he'll turn him in if he doesn't get help: no prizes for guessing his fate. Stowe's friend goes straight to the door and dismantles the burglar alarm after she's persuaded Liotta, who frightens her, to leave his 'groceries' outside the door. Curtains again! And Russell, framed by Liotta on a drugs charge, can't get bail because of some mysterious long-past misdemeanour. Deprived of any touch of originality or surprise, director Jonathan Kaplan does the best he can with what's left, giving us lots of violent action and a modicum of suspense.

Unmarried Woman, An ◖
1978, US, 124 mins, colour
Dir: Paul Mazursky
Stars: Jill Clayburgh, Alan Bates
Rating: ★★★★

It was high time in 1978 that someone dedicated a film to the wide-ranging talents of Jill Clayburgh – and director Paul Mazursky did just that in this perceptive and penetrating study of a woman in her mid-thirties whose husband suddenly and her unexpectedly leaves her and her 15-year-old daughter. Jill Clayburgh is flawless in the title role and Michael Murphy also offers a well-considered account of the husband. Alan Bates seems less at ease as the artist who offers the heroine a somewhat unlikely second chance at happiness, but it's an under-written part and he makes the most of what's there. It is what once might have been termed a 'woman's picture' – but this one plays fair with both sexes, gently but firmly.

Unseen, The ◖
1945, US, 81 mins, b/w
Dir: Lewis Allen
Stars: Joel McCrea, Gail Russell
Rating: ★★★

A follow-up by star Gail Russell and director Lewis Allen to their previous chiller success *The Uninvited*. The plot, even though you may guess the solution of its mystery early on, remains interesting, as Russell's limpid beauty comes under threat from strange goings-on in a mysterious boarded-up house that's next door to the one owned by her employer (Joel McCrea), a withdrawn figure still under suspicion himself following the death of his wife two years before. John F Seitz's black-and-white cam-

eras skilfully cloak the mystery in shape and shadow and provide some effectively jumpy moments. Richard Lyon, son of Bebe Daniels and Ben Lyon, does well as McCrea's young son.

Unsuspected, The ○
1947, US, 103 mins, b/w
Dir: Michael Curtiz
Stars: Claude Rains, Joan Caulfield, Audrey Totter, Constance Bennett, Hurd Hatfield, Michael North
Rating: ★★★

One of the best of Hollywood's black Forties' thrillers, with Claude Rains in superb form as the deadly sophisticate whose lust for a fortune leads him into a feverish dance with murder as his partner. Writer Ranald MacDougall and director Michael Curtiz, who collaborated on the Oscar-winning *Mildred Pierce*, spin a beguiling web of dark streets, shrieking trains and black-mirrored mansions. Especially memorable is the glimpse of an intended poison victim, seen through the bubbles in a glass of champagne.

Untamed ○
1955, US, 111 mins, colour
Dir: Henry King
Stars: Tyrone Power, Susan Hayward, Agnes Moorehead, Richard Egan
Rating: ★★

A spectacular period adventure, with wagon train travellers fighting to establish the Dutch Free State in 19th-century South Africa. Tyrone Power plays the leader of a commando group, while Susan Hayward, who excelled herself in all kinds of melodrama, is outrageously superb as what one critic called 'a kind of Scarlett O'Hara of the veldt'. In a way, the picture is similar in vein to a Western, but transplanted to an African setting. It was directed by Henry King, a reliable and versatile director of general entertainment movies, and for many years associated with 20th Century-Fox. My favourite line comes when Power tells Hayward: 'You, here in South Africa, fighting Zulus. I can't believe it.'

Untamed Heart ◖
1993, US, 102 mins, colour
Dir: Tony Bill
Stars: Christian Slater, Marisa Tomei, Rosie Perez, Kyle Secor, Willie Garson
Rating: ★★★

U

This is a boy-meets-girl story with a difference, though not one for the cynical or hard-hearted. Waitress Marisa Tomei is a loser in love. Loner busboy Christian Slater is a loser in life: an orphan convinced by convent custodians that his diseased heart is that of a baboon. It's inevitable, of course, that they should end up together, even though Slater is, by most people's standards, a bit of a weirdo. His habit of following Tomei home (and, it turns out, sometimes getting into her house and watching her sleep) pays off when he saves her from rape on a wintry night. It's obvious from developments that their subsequent relationship can't have too happy an ending, but director Tony Bill lets us down easy on the tears and, if the story will be too silly and simplistic for some, at least Slater and Tomei, two of the most talented of Hollywood's younger stars in the early Nineties, give it 101 per cent.

Until the End of the World ● ⓥ

1991, Germany/France/Australia, 158 mins, colour
Dir: Wim Wenders
Stars: William Hurt, Solveig Dommartin, Sam Neill, Max Von Sydow, Jeanne Moreau
Rating: ★

Originally over three hours long, Wim Wenders' trip around the world is still a hard slog at its present length, and with Sam Neill narrating to help you follow the plot. Did we say plot? Well, there's about enough to fill the back of an envelope. The first half of the film consists of a 'road' movie in which heroine Solveig Dommartin (not destined to become an international star) follows William Hurt from France on to China, America and Australia in pursuit of some money he's stolen, which she in turn was holding for the bank robbers who caused her to crash her car into them in the middle of nowhere. The second half is set in South Australia, where Hurt's father (Max Von Sydow) is conducting experiments in an underground laboratory that will help his blind wife (Jeanne Moreau) see. When that's accomplished, they use computers to project the images from dreams on to a screen. All this seems to go on for more than four hours let alone nearly three; Hurt and Von Sydow offer unattractive, occasionally overwrought performances.

Until They Sail ◑

1957, US, 95 mins, colour
Dir: Robert Wise
Stars: Jean Simmons, Joan Fontaine, Paul Newman
Rating: ★★

Robert Wise's observant portrait of women in war – four sisters in New Zealand during World War Two. Watch for a startling performance by Piper Laurie, previously seen in 'sweet spitfire' roles, but here pretty good as a pretty bad lot. Laurie did nothing else of great note until another excellent portrayal as Paul Newman's girlfriend in *The Hustler*, which she made four years later, and after that vanished from sight until the 1970s. The other sister is played by Sandra Dee.

Untouchables, The ● ⓥ

1987, US, 119 mins, colour
Dir: Brian De Palma
Stars: Kevin Costner, Sean Connery, Robert De Niro, Andy Garcia, Charles Martin Smith
Rating: ★★★

Whatever you might have expected from director Brian De Palma's account of the 1931 battle of wills between clean-cut law enforcer Eliot Ness (Kevin Costner) and gangland czar Al Capone (played by Robert De Niro), it couldn't have been a re-run of the old Robert Stack TV series. Yet that's more or less what you get only done with some style, and the addition of blood (lots of it) and expletives. And there's a further dimension in the welcome shape of Sean Connery's veteran cop who joins and mentors the Untouchables; this fully-rounded portrait deservedly won Connery an Academy Award. Otherwise, there's the same vacuum feeling about the periods between the action, and the same slow build-up to the action set-pieces themselves, which are hard-hitting, but only rarely anything but predictable. Only once does De Palma use the element of surprise, turning a suspense scene involving a mother and her baby into a tribute to Hitchcock and Eisenstein. Costner, steely-eyed and distant, vaguely echoes Stack in the original; De Niro makes Capone just a blustering, if dangerous bully. Like him, this bumper bundle of guns and gangsters (gals hardly get a look in) doesn't quite punch its weight.

Up in Arms ☉

1944, UK, 83 mins, colour
Dir: Elliott Nugent

Stars: Danny Kaye, Dinah Shore
Rating: ★★★

After years of struggle in vaudeville, Danny Kaye enjoyed a career surge engineered by his talented wife, Sylvia Fine, who wrote most of the tongue-twisting songs that helped to make him such a success. This was his feature-film debut and, if a story about a hypochondriac who joins the US Army in World War Two and is captured and tortured doesn't sound a likely basis for comedy, you haven't got the Goldwyn spirit. The whole troopship, for example, is festooned with sunbathing Goldwyn Girls, who include Virginia Mayo, soon to become Danny's leading lady.

Up in Central Park ○

1948, US, 88 mins, b/w
Dir: William A Seiter
Stars: Deanna Durbin, Dick Haymes, Vincent Price
Rating: ★★

This lavishly produced but otherwise routine musical was Deanna Durbin's penultimate picture. Durbin is in fine voice and there's an attractively staged skating routine performed by William Skipper and Nelle Fisher. Albert Sharpe hams happily as Durbin's dad.

Up in the World ☉

1956, US, 106 mins, b/w
Dir: John Paddy Carstairs
Stars: Norman Wisdom
Rating: ★★★

In his seventh film, Norman Wisdom the window cleaner breaks many panes, falls off ladders, goes to jail, sings songs, and keeps a hamster called Harold. The laughter quotient is roughly one belly laugh for each of the three writers involved. Even so, this film is a vast improvement on some Wisdom comedies, and this one has just enough chuckles to keep it going.

Up Periscope ○

1958, US, 111 mins, colour
Dir: Gordon Douglas
Stars: James Garner, Edmond O'Brien
Rating: ★★

A routine submarine drama with rebellious demolition expert James Garner assigned to serve on Edmond O'Brien's by-the-book ship. There's plenty of suspense in the final action scenes, and keep your eyes peeled for a very young Warren Oates as a sailor always to be found in the mess hall eating.

Up Pompeii ◖
1971, UK, 90 mins, colour
Dir: Bob Kellett
Stars: Frankie Howerd, Michael Hordern
Rating: ★★

The first of three big screen spin-offs from Frankie Howerd's Roman TV comedy. The jokes are not only similar to those in the sitcom penned by Talbot Rothwell, many are exactly the same – although this script is credited to Sid Colin! But the cast has more star quality, with the addition of Michael Hordern, Roy Hudd and Adrienne Posta. Howerd runs his usual gamut of grunts, exclamations and wheezes, but his thunder is somewhat stolen by Patrick Cargill's accomplished portrayal of boredom as Emperor Nero. All but ardent fans of these Roman scandals will be in complete agreement.

Upstairs and Downstairs ○
1959, UK, 101 mins, colour
Dir: Ralph Thomas
Stars: Michael Craig, Anne Heywood, Mylene Demongeot
Rating: ★★

This lightweight domestic comedy about a young middle-class couple who have trouble finding suitable servants manages to misfire on all cylinders. Such problems were outdated and outmoded even when it was made and certainly look unreal today. A witty script would have offset these problems, but one wasn't forthcoming. Michael Craig and Anne Heywood can't find reliable servants. Ahh, ain't life tough! Mylene Demongeot as a Swedish maid and Daniel Massey as the man who falls in love with her are bright points. But they're really not enough.

Up the Chastity Belt ◖
1971, UK, 94 mins, colour
Dir: Bob Kellett
Stars: Frankie Howerd, Graham Crowden, Bill Fraser
Rating: ★★

Frankie Howerd as a serf called Lurkalot? It must be funny, surely? Alas, it's not so much a case of lurkalot as laugh a little. And, considering Alan

Galton and Ray Simpson were two of the writers on this Crusades charade, it's all the sadder that it proves that all great comics are at the mercy of their writers. Even in such a relentless essay in sexual innuendo, though, Howerd's Lurkalot still contrives some delicious moments, notably in his confrontation with Rita Webb's amazingly gross Maid Marian. 'Who is this fragile wood nymph?' he gasps.

Up the Creek ◖
1958, UK, 83 mins, b/w
Dir: Val Guest
Stars: David Tomlinson, Peter Sellers
Rating: ★★

This Val Guest romp is firmly in the tradition of British naval farces, but given a big boost by the presence of Peter Sellers as the wily Irish bo'sun who operates a black-market laundry, grocery, bakery and general stores to the nearest village from the depths of his mothballed ship.

Up the Down Staircase ◖
1967, US, 124 mins, colour
Dir: Robert Mulligan
Stars: Sandy Dennis, Eileen Heckart
Rating: ★★★

Sandy Dennis and Eileen Heckart, Oscar-winners both, in Robert Mulligan's penetrating school story of a young teacher's struggle to help her tough pupils to realise their potential and, if possible, escape their ghetto environment. A sort of *Blackboard Jungle* 12 years on, with welcome nods to the humour of *Please, Sir!*

Up the Junction ●
1967, UK, 119 mins, colour
Dir: Peter Collinson
Stars: Suzy Kendall, Dennis Waterman, Adrienne Posta, Susan George
Rating: ★★

It was hard to imagine anyone bettering the biting television original of this look at Battersea life with all its warts and sores. But director Peter Collinson decided to have a try, and turned out a colour film which slants its story towards the adventures of an upperclass girl in a working-class district of London. Screen writer Roger Smith has fashioned a script which holds the episodic structure of Nell Dunn's original together with some skill, thanks to the central relationship between the girl and her cockney boyfriend, which benefits from the understated performances of Suzy Kendall and Dennis Waterman. These

two emerge as real characters, as opposed to the rest of the cast, which verge on caricature and include a young Susan George as one of the girls in the sweet factory where the heroine goes to work. The music score by Mike Hugg and Manfred Mann is both apposite and attractive.

Uptown Saturday Night ◖
1974, US, 104 mins, colour
Dir: Sidney Poitier
Stars: Sidney Poitier, Bill Cosby, Harry Belafonte
Rating: ★★

Sidney Poitier and Bill Cosby hit a profitable vein of broad, black-slanted comedy with this farcical tale of two innocents entering the lion's den of crooks and Godfathers. As director, Poitier showed more control in the sequels *Let's Do It Again* and *A Piece of the Action*, but the film's silliness is engaging.

Urban Cowboy ◖
1980, US, 135 mins, colour
Dir: James Bridges
Stars: John Travolta, Debra Winger, Scott Glenn
Rating: ★★

John Travolta plays a saloon-bar rodeo rider on an automated bucking bronco here – but both he and the film bite the dust. Travolta's acting in this one is as over-melodramatic as John Gilbert's seemed with the coming of sound. Far more worth watching are Debra Winger as his barroom bride and Scott Glenn as the bad guy. But their story, crazily overlong at two and a quarter hours, takes a lot of swallowing.

Used Cars ◖
1980, US, 115 mins, colour
Dir: Robert Zemeckis
Stars: Kurt Russell, Jack Warden, Jack Warden
Rating: ★★

A fascination with cars has certainly been profitable for Hollywood writers Bob Gale and Robert Zemeckis (who also directed this comedy about the used car business). Kurt Russell and Jack Warden (in a dual role) give feisty, energetic performances, and Al Lewis (Grandpa in *The Munsters*) has a nice stand-out cameo as an imposing judge. But the ropy script lets the proceedings down, choosing to find humour in the various characters' hu-

U

miliation, embarrassment and even death. 'Tasteless' humour, brief nudity and bad language make this one unsuitable for most younger children.

Used People ◐ ⓥ

1992, US, 126 mins, colour
Dir: Beeban Kidron
Stars: Shirley MacLaine, Marcello Mastroianni, Kathy Bates, Marcia Gay Harden, Jessica Tandy
Rating: ★★

The winning, sweetness-and-light ending to this story of love the second time around tends to obscure the fact that parts of the tale are quite tediously told. The Bermans, mother Pearl (Shirley MacLaine) and daughters Nora (Marcia Gay Harden) and Bibby (Kathy Bates), are angry, ill-tempered, almost tragic figures always shouting at each other in public. Joe (Marcello Mastroianni), a long-time admirer of Pearl's, must certainly be an ardent suitor not only to ask her out for dinner at her husband's funeral (exceptionally unlikely!) but to want to jump in with this nest of vipers. Joe, however, a widower, is a true Italian and even snakebites, though they may annoy him, can't deter his passion. Jessica Tandy and Sylvia Sidney do good work as MacLaine's mother and her equally aged confidante – the scene where they visit a nursing home straight out of *Metropolis* is one of the best in the film – but these used people are not likeable people and it's hard to share their joys and (mostly) sorrows.

Utu ◐ ⓥ

1983, New Zealand, 100 mins, colour
Dir: Geoff Murphy
Stars: Bruno Lawrence, Anzac Wallace, Kelly Johnson, Kuki Kaa
Rating: ★★★

This epic drama, about British colonial presence in New Zealand in the 1870s, was at the time the most expensive film in New Zealand's history. Bruno Lawrence, star of two of the other big Kiwi movie successes, *Smash Palace* and *Quiet Earth*, is totally believable as a man driven to seek revenge against the Brits. The film's title actually translates from the Maori word for 'Retribution', and action fans will not be disappointed by director Geoff Murphy's slam-bang style of delivery. He has subsequently moved on to a Hollywood career with such action films as *Freejack* and *Young Guns II*.

U2 – Rattle and Hum ◐ ⓥ

1988, US, 99 mins, colour
Dir: Phil Joanou
Stars: Bono, The Edge, Adam Clayton, Larry Mullen, B B King
Rating: ★★★

At a cost of $5 million, this concert film of Irish rock group U2 ranks as the most expensive music documentary ever. It captures the group during a period when lead singer Bono and the lads explored American music and culture following the blockbuster commercial and critical success of their seventh album, 'The Joshua Tree'. Director Phil Joanou (who did much to foster Madonna's raunchy image through daring pop promo videos) pulls off his task thanks to the use of black-and-white footage, using grainy blow-ups of 16mm film to create a gritty 'street' feel. And strobelight-style editing gives the ghostly impression that the band are flashing spirits during the concert sequences. But the film's momentum drops when it switches to colour and scenes of the group visiting Elvis's Graceland mansion are as awkward as the band appear to be at mugging in front of the camera. But, on the whole, *Rattle and Hum* emerges as an exhilarating celebration of one of the greatest rock bands still on the go.

V

Vagabond King, The ○

1956, US, 86 mins, colour
Dir: Michael Curtiz
Stars: Kathryn Grayson, Oreste, Rita Moreno
Rating: ★★

This bright and colourful version of Friml's famous stage musical was supposed to have made a star of Oreste (Kirkop), when he stepped into one of the many singing roles vacated by an overweight Mario Lanza. Although Oreste projected an attractive personality and warm tenor voice, the public didn't take to him as a cinema personality. And the film itself lacks sparkle, apart, that is, from Rita Moreno's flashing-eyed portrait of Huguette.

Valachi Papers, The ● ⓥ

1972, France/Italy, 125 mins, colour
Dir: Terence Young
Stars: Charles Bronson, Jill Ireland
Rating: ★★

This crime thriller, based on a bestselling book by Peter Maas, gives Charles Bronson an unusual role in that he's an elderly gangster looking back on the time he started as a young petty thief. The film could use some humour and individuality, but there's no lack of action. The feeling of the underworld is well caught in this treatment, which is annoyingly inattentive to detail and seems most interested in letting blood flow all over the screen.

Valdez Is Coming ○

1970, US, 86 mins, colour
Dir: Edwin Sherin
Stars: Burt Lancaster, Susan Clark
Rating: ★★

Murkily shot in the dreaded Colour by De Luxe, this is a revenge Western in which Burt Lancaster's stoical Valdez takes a mighty long time in arriving to get his own back on those who humiliated him. The cast includes early roles for Jon Cypher (Chief Daniels from *Hill Street Blues*), Hector Elizondo (most recently seen as the hotel manager in *Pretty Woman*) and Richard Jordan. In a minor part you may spot Roberta Haynes, who 18 years earlier had been Gary Cooper's leading lady in *Return to Paradise*.

Vampire's Kiss 761

Valentino ● Ⓥ
1977, US, 127 mins, colour
Dir: Ken Russell
Stars: Rudolf Nureyev, Leslie Caron, Michelle Phillips
Rating: ★

Ken Russell's 'pop' version of the career of the unique silent film idol is colourful, outrageous and keeps on the move and, even if we never really get to know the man himself, presents us with a vivid picture of the free-for-all life of New York and Hollywood in the Twenties. Nureyev is not actually asked to do much beyond look and seem like Valentino on the surface, and enact scenes from some of his most famous films, but there is a wealth of striking acting in support, especially from Leslie Caron (as Nazimova), Huntz Hall (as Jesse Lasky) and Felicity Kendal as Valentino's agent June Mathis.

Valley of Fury
See: Chief Crazy Horse

Valley of Gwangi, The ○
1968, US, 95 mins, colour
Dir: James O'Connolly
Stars: James Franciscus, Gila Golan, Richard Carlson
Rating: ★★

More magic from Ray Harryhausen's box of monsters, which here include a tiny prehistoric horse, a styrocosaurus, and an allosaurus (the giant Gwangi of the title) in a story of early 20th-century cowboys exploring a forbidden valley in Mexico.

Valley of the Dolls ●
1967, US, 123 mins, colour
Dir: Mark Robson
Stars: Barbara Parkins, Patty Duke, Sharon Tate, Susan Hayward
Rating: ★★

The film version of Jacqueline Susann's notorious novel about drug abuse on the showbiz scene was a built-in success, thanks in part to Susann's own constant publicity campaigning. Susan Hayward took over the role of Helen Lawson from an ailing Judy Garland (after it had been rejected by Ginger Rogers as 'too smutty') and stormed away with the picture.

Valley of the Kings ○
1954, US, 86 mins, colour
Dir: Robert Pirosh
Stars: Robert Taylor, Eleanor Parker
Rating: ★★

The first Hollywood film ever shot on location in Egypt proves to be a workmanlike and sometimes exciting story that just lacks the surges of real excitement that might have turned it into an adventure classic. The natural backdrops are fascinating, and look mighty hot, leaving Eleanor Parker's cool beauty to add a refreshing touch to those parched desert sands. On the whole it's pretty good fun, and a scene where hero Robert Taylor shows a Bedouin swordsman that a blade and buckler are no match for a good American right hook may well have influenced Steven Spielberg when he came to film a similar scene with Harrison Ford for *Raiders of the Lost Ark*.

Valmont ● Ⓥ
1989, UK/France/US, 140 mins, colour
Dir: Milos Forman
Stars: Annette Bening, Colin Firth, Meg Tilly, Fairuza Balk, Sian Phillips, Jeffrey Jones, Henry Thomas
Rating: ★★

Held up for two years, but finally released on the strength of Annette Bening's then-rising fame, this is yet another version of *Dangerous Liaisons*. While quite an effective satirical look at the sexual mores of the 18th-century French upper class, it doesn't have the same impact as the Glenn Close-Michelle Pfeiffer starrer which had already pinched all the kudos. Bening and Meg Tilly are exceptionally good in these roles, it's true, but the film, stretched out to 140 minutes, doesn't exactly grip you all the way through. Nor is Colin Firth quite as rakish and amoral as you might expect as the corrupt seducer Valmont; and Fairuza Balk, although actually the right age, seems a little young for the all-too-easily-deflowered convent maid. Veteran actress Fabia Drake, though, is tremendous in her last film role. The dread Eastman Color makes the look of the film pretty drained in comparison with its competitor.

Value for Money ○
1955, UK, 89 mins, colour
Dir: Ken Annakin
Stars: John Gregson, Susan Stephen, Diana Dors, Derek Farr
Rating: ★★

Robust, regional comedy along traditional British lines, but made with tremendous confidence by director Ken Annakin for the Rank Organisation at a time when they were

prepared to splash out on Technicolor and VistaVision for their brighter products. Diana Dors is at her best as a brass-digging blond who sets her cap at Yorkshire millionaire John Gregson, there's some music thrown in and you may catch glimpses of Leslie Phillips, Donald Pleasence, Ferdy Mayne, Joan Hickson, Molly Weir and a teenage Oliver Reed.

Vamp ● Ⓥ
1986, US, 94 mins, colour
Dir: Richard Wenk
Stars: Grace Jones, Chris Makepeace
Rating: ★★★

'You get the feeling we're not in Kansas any more?' trembles one of three out-of-town, wet-behind-the-ears college kids as they first stumble on the neon-lit lair of disco vampire Grace Jones. First time writer/director Richard Wenk has taken a tired horror genre and injected new blood, ensuring this contemporary bloodsucking black comedy carries plenty of bite. It's also the perfect vehicle for disco diva Jones and her wide-eyed dangerous persona. Just as it suggests it is going to jump on the teen sexploitation comedy bandwagon, *Vamp* does a swift U-turn and ends up being a camp, wisecracking, breathless chase.

Vampire Circus ●
1971, UK, 87 mins, colour
Dir: Robert Young
Stars: Adrienne Corri, Laurence Payne, Thorley Walters
Rating: ★★

Another creep in the crypt from Hammer who took two scripts, one about vampire depredations and the other about a sinister circus – and cobbled them together quite successfully. There are some good sequences in a hall of mirrors, and film buffs will no doubt recognise the village of Schtettel from *Twins of Evil*.

Vampire's Kiss ● Ⓥ
1989, US, 103 mins, colour
Dir: Robert Bierman
Stars: Nicolas Cage, Maria Conchita Alonso, Jennifer Beals, Elizabeth Ashley
Rating: ★

Not content with being one of the most foul-mouthed movies of even these modern times, this is an amazingly miscalculated spoof horror/black comedy, with a wildly miscast Nicolas Cage (looking like British TV host Jonathan Ross) as a young executive

V

who compulsively bites bar-girls and goes completely round the bend when one of them bites him in the neck. The fire of madness in his diminished marbles is further fuelled by the appearance of a bat in his flat. Before you can say Nosferatu, Cage is lurching around the New York streets eating insects and pigeons, biting people in the neck, and inviting passers-by to kill him with a stake through the heart. Viewers will find it hard to tell when the film is trying to be funny and the repulsive and violent nature of Cage's affliction will, in any case, make laughter hard to summon. Cage is grotesque: come to think of it, Jonathan Ross could probably have done it better.

Vampires of Venice ●
1988, US, 92 mins, colour
Dir: Augusto Caminito
Stars: Klaus Kinski, Barbara De Rossi, Donald Pleasance
Rating: ★★

A follow-up to *Nosferatu the Vampire*, this has the same kind of eerie atmosphere, but less credibility. Klaus Kinski is back as the man with the miniature tusks, while Christopher Plummer and Donald Pleasance lend additional star value as ineffectual vampire hunters. The ending is annoyingly inconclusive, but Kinski's performance and a screeching score by Vangelis and Luigi Ceccarelli do their best to bolster the chills.

Vanishing, The ● ⓥ
1993, US, 110 mins, colour
Dir: George Sluizer
Stars: Jeff Bridges, Kiefer Sutherland, Nancy Travis, Sandra Bullock, Lisa Eichhorn
Rating: ★★★

If you haven't seen the even more chilling Dutch original, you should enjoy this suspense yarn about a girl who mysteriously disappears – and her lover's obsessive search for her over a three-year period. It becomes apparent rather earlier this time that the girl has been kidnapped (during a service station stop) by professional nutcase Jeff Bridges, who has just saved a girl from drowning and is now anxious to prove to his beloved daughter that he is as capable of evil as of heroism (!) But is the victim (Sandra Bullock) alive or dead? Bridges just keeps the right side of idiocy as the learned madman and Kiefer Sutherland's role tends to dwindle as the film goes on, though he's already getting hot com-

petition from the strong performance of Nancy Travis (as his new girlfriend) before she rises admirably to the challenge of ferocity and a battle of wits with Bridges at the end. A bit long and dawdling at times, but director George Sluizer (who made the original) has a baited hook to keep us snapping to the end of the film.

Vanishing Point ◑
1971, US, 107 mins, colour
Dir: Richard C Sarafian
Stars: Barry Newman, Cleavon Little, Dean Jagger
Rating: ★★★

Perhaps more so even than *Bullitt*, this was the film that started a craze for car-chase movies. Richard C Sarafian takes his carefully-plotted story (an embittered ex-war hero driving all out from Colorado to California for the sheer hell and exhilaration of it) and endows it with a crude raw energy that sustains it throughout its fast-moving running time. The film is very much an *Easy Rider* of the four-wheel world. Its theme of individuality in a uniform society is vividly put across with the help of a powerful performance from the rugged Barry Newman; and it concerns itself almost exclusively with people on the fringes of society. In general, it treats them all sympathetically and, in pointing up the instant community bond that exists between them and the driver, gives the story a continuity it might not have found.

Variety Girl ○
1947, US, 83 mins, b/w
Dir: George Marshall
Stars: Bing Crosby, Bob Hope, Dorothy Lamour, Alan Ladd
Rating: ★★★

One of those marvellous all-star cocktails that are no longer possible in today's cimena, this one offering the entire 1947 roster of Paramount players with the exception of Betty Hutton who was pregnant at the time. Highlights are a couple of duets – 'Friendship' by Bing Crosby and Bob Hope and 'Tallahassee' by the less likely combination of Alan Ladd and Dorothy Lamour. The juvenile lead proves to be DeForest Kelley, years later to become Doc McCoy of the *Star Trek* series.

Vault of Horror ●
1973, UK, 87 mins, colour
Dir: Roy Ward Baker

Stars: Dawn Addams, Tom Baker, Michael Craig, Denholm Elliott
Rating: ★★

Another melange of five horror stories from the gore-minded lads at Amicus Films. The better episodes involve firstly Glynis Johns and Terry-Thomas, and then Curt Jurgens and Dawn Addams in the story of a rope with a mind of its own. The rest of the cast is no less impressive, including Michael Craig, Denholm Elliott, Anna Massey, Edward Judd, Daniel Massey, Mike Pratt and, in a rare excursion to the world of horror, Robin Nedwell, alias the disaster-prone Duncan Waring from the TV series *Doctor on the Go*.

Venetian Bird ○
(aka: The Assassin)
1952, UK, 95 mins, b/w
Dir: Ralph Thomas
Stars: Richard Todd, Eva Bartok, John Gregson, George Coulouris
Rating: ★★

Written by Victor Canning from his own novel, this thriller is something of a reworking of *The Third Man*, with Richard Todd caught up in mystery and intrigue as he tries to find an Italian partisan in Venice. John Gregson scores as a sly but engaging villain, Sidney James is a somewhat improbable Italian (although, why not, since this archetypal British movie cockney was actually a South African?) and Eva Bartok is decorative. Nice cinematography from Ernest Steward, who makes some dazzling use of the Venetian locations. Ralph Thomas directs in his usual efficient but prosaic manner.

Vengeance ●
1962, UK, 82 mins, b/w
Dir: Freddie Francis
Stars: Anne Heywood, Peter Van Eyck, Cecil Parker
Rating: ★★

Third screen version of Curt Siodmak's classic science-fiction shocker *Donovan's Brain*. This time round (it was Erich von Stroheim in 1944 and Lew Ayres in 1953), it's Peter Van Eyck as the scientist convinced that a dead man's brain can be kept alive. But the brain has a strange effect on him. This was one of the earliest shockers directed by Freddie Francis, who has won Oscars for his work as a cameraman on *Sons and Lovers* and *Glory*.

Vengeance of She, The ○

1967, UK, 101 mins, colour
Dir: Cliff Owen
Stars: John Richardson, Olinka Berova, Edward Judd, Colin Blakely
Rating: ★

Czech actress Olinka Berova takes over from Ursula Andress as 'She Who Must Be Obeyed' in this sequel by Hammer Films to their own 1964 version of H Rider Haggard's famous fantasy yarn. For those ready to jump up and point out that Andress died at the end of the previous adventure, let us hasten to point out that it's her spirit that possesses the busty Berova in this risibly-scripted romp, played with enthusiasm by a largely British cast that includes Colin Blakeley, George Sewell, Andre Morell and Noel Willman.

Vengeance Valley ○

1951, US, 83 mins, colour
Dir: Richard Thorpe
Stars: Burt Lancaster, Robert Walker, Joanne Dru
Rating: ★★

A sombre, very serious and gripping Western on the theme of the good and the bad brother. Burt Lancaster puts on a more sober face than his fans were used to seeing in such films as *The Flame and the Arrow*, although he still gets plenty of chance to show his athleticism, but Robert Walker steals the film as his slimy brother. The compact plot, based on a novel by Luke Short, could do with some more action, but gets by with the help of ravishing colour camerawork by George Folsey.

Venom ●

1981, UK, 98 mins, colour
Dir: Piers Haggard
Stars: Klaus Kinski, Oliver Reed, Nicol Williamson, Sarah Miles
Rating: ★★

A startlingly good cast should perhaps have heeded the famous film maxim about never appearing with children and animals in this chiller about a kidnapped boy (engaging Lance Holcomb) and an elusive black mamba. Klaus Kinski, Sarah Miles and Susan George are among those fleeing its fangs, and you'll long treasure the expression on Oliver Reed's face as the snake crawls up his trouser leg.

Venus Peter ○

1989, UK, 100 mins, colour
Dir: Ian Sellar

Stars: Ray McAnally, David Hayman, Sinead Cusack
Rating: ★★

In many ways, this tangy tale can be seen as a companion piece to *When the Whales Came*. This one is set in the Orkney Islands, again concerns children growing up in a fishing community and, yes, there's a stranded whale to heighten the comparison. Mostly, the smack of salt is almost tangible enough to taste, nowhere more so than in Ray McAnally's measured portrayal of the boy's grandfather. To spice up the plot, there's the island mad woman, the awakening of the boy's interest in poetry by his new teacher (Sinead Cusack), the return of the boy's prodigal father and the war over the family boat. But the script shies away from too close an inspection of the complex issues involved.

Vera Cruz ○

1954, US, 94 mins, colour
Dir: Robert Aldrich
Stars: Gary Cooper, Burt Lancaster, George Macready, Ernest Borgnine, Charles Bronson
Rating: ★★★

Riotous, big-scale Gary Cooper Western that never lacks excitement, and gives Burt Lancaster (of the flashing teeth and villainous smile) one of his most colourful characters. It is reputed to have cost $3 million to make (in 1954) – a figure that looks from the stars and the sets to be no exaggeration. The bad guys in this vivid and virile yarn of old Mexico include Jack Elam, Ernest Borgnine, Charles Bronson (billed as Charles Buchinsky) and George Macready.

Verdict, The ◑ Ⓥ

1982, US, 129 mins, colour
Dir: Sidney Lumet
Stars: Paul Newman, Charlotte Rampling, Jack Warden, James Mason
Rating: ★★★

It's an old Hollywood chestnut, of course – the drunken lawyer winning back his self-respect in a case that proves not as straightforward as everyone thought. But, under the guidance of such skilful manipulators of our emotions as director Sidney Lumet and star Paul Newman, and with the help of an immaculately-structured screenplay by David Mamet (later to write and direct *House of Games*), this film plays fair and square with its audience and emerges

as gripping, old-style entertainment. James Mason is as smoothly persuasive as ever as Newman's courtroom opponent, but what really gives the film a lift is Newman's grip on the central character. This piece of exemplary filmcraft, rather than *The Color of Money*, is surely the movie for which he should have won an Oscar.

Vertigo ○ Ⓥ

1958, US, 128 mins, colour
Dir: Alfred Hitchcock
Stars: James Stewart, Kim Novak, Barbara Bel Geddes
Rating: ★★★★

A classic in suspense from Alfred Hitchcock, pitching us right into the action from the start, and baffling most of us to the finish. There is much for The Master's fans to savour in his smooth and atmospheric handling of the complex tale (based on a story by the authors of *The Fiends*). James Stewart is as assured as ever as the obsessed hero battling against his fear of heights, and Kim Novak's lack of expression in a difficult role strangely adds depth to her performance. The tense key scenes in a bell-tower are brilliantly staged.

Very Big Withdrawal, A

See: A Man, a Woman and a Bank

Very Important Person ○

1961, UK, 100 mins, b/w
Dir: Ken Annakin
Stars: James Robertson Justice, Leslie Phillips, Stanley Baxter
Rating: ★★★

First and best of the four comedies made by its star trio of James Robertson Justice, Leslie Phillips and Stanley Baxter, set in a PoW camp. Funniest of a talented supporting cast is Eric Sykes, as an escape fanatic nicknamed The Mole.

Vibes ◑ Ⓥ

1988, US, 99 mins, colour
Dir: Ken Kwapis
Stars: Cyndi Lauper, Jeff Goldblum, Peter Falk, Julian Sands, Elizabeth Peña, Michael Lerner
Rating: ★

There are some endearingly goofy moments in this comedy about psychics hired to find a world-changing 'McGuffin' high in the Ecuador mountains. In the end, though, they don't add up to much without solid direction, decent special effects or a script that needs to back its barbs

V

with some character and story development. You couldn't get a much more unorthodox hero and heroine than bug-eyed Jeff Goldblum and squeaky rock star Cyndi Lauper, but neither of them wins our sympathy and it's left to Peter Falk's unscrupulous rogue to give the affair some heart. 'You should have slept with me,' he tells Lauper after she's rebuffed Goldblum at altitude. 'What good would that have done?' she squawks. Falk considers. 'Well,' he replies, 'it would have done me a lot of good.' Elizabeth Peña also scores briefly as a local *femme fatale* who strips off and asks Goldblum, 'You like?' 'Parts of me,' he pants, 'are already applauding.' Scraps of gold, these, though, from a film that muffs pretty well all its chances.

Vice Squad ○
(aka: The Girl in Room 17)
1953, US, 88 mins, b/w
Dir: Arnold Laven
Stars: Edward G Robinson, Paulette Goddard
Rating: ★★★

A good solid little thriller, the kind that would probably these days be labelled with the overworked 'gritty'. No real suprises here, but Edward G Robinson gives it a boost as the hard-pressed police captain, and there are good supporting performances from Lee Van Cleef, Paulette Goddard, Porter Hall and, especially, Mary Ellen Kay as a frightened hostage.

Vice Versa ⊙
1947, UK, 111 mins, b/w
Dir: Peter Ustinov
Stars: Roger Livesey, Kay Walsh, Anthony Newley, Petula Clark
Rating: ★★

Peter Ustinov wrote and directed this tale of an Edwardian identity switch between father and son. Fascinating to see Petula Clark and Anthony Newley (who both have leading roles) as teenagers.

Vice Versa ○ ⓥ
1988, US, 100 mins, colour
Dir: Brian Gilbert
Stars: Judge Reinhold, Fred Savage, Corinne Bohrer, Swoosie Kurtz
Rating: ★★★

Another of the late Eighties' 'role reversal' comedies in a period that could have been called the invasion of the body switchers. Judge Reinhold

holds centre stage in this one (a loose remake of the 1947 British film of the same title). In this version the fun is a little less naive and sex rears its head along with other foreseeable complications. Reinhold clowns around like mad, but it's young Fred Savage from *The Wonder Years*, stuck in school as a 35-year-old, who gets the best stuff to do. Corinne Bohrer is a sweet love interest, and the film is pleasant to have around if pretty forgettable – sometimes amusing, occasionally embarrassing.

Vicki ○
1953, US, 85 mins, b/w
Dir: Harry Horner
Stars: Jeanne Crain, Richard Boone, Jean Peters
Rating: ★★

Suspense thriller, centred on the murder of a model (played by Jean Peters), with plenty of red herrings along the way. In its way, it's quite an ingenious whodunnit, told in flashback, and with a good characterisation from Richard Boone as a vindictive detective with a grudge against one of the suspects. A web of suspense is intriguingly spun, and it's comparable to the Betty Grable-Victor Mature *I Wake Up Screaming*, from which its plot is derived. If it had a stronger leading man than benign Elliott Reid, this might have been a winner.

Victim ◐
1961, UK, 100 mins, b/w
Dir: Basil Dearden
Stars: Dirk Bogarde, Sylvia Syms, Dennis Price
Rating: ★★★

Forthright and fascinating British film on the hitherto taboo subject of homosexuality, which also turns out to be a good thriller in its own right. Dirk Bogarde is fine as the successful and now-married barrister threatened by spectres from the past. And Norman Bird is especially good as a frightened small-time bookseller.

Victoria the Great ○
1937, UK, 118 mins, b/w & colour
Dir: Herbert Wilcox
Stars: Anna Neagle, Anton Walbrook
Rating: ★★★

Anna Neagle's performance in this film about Queen Victoria won such tremendous popular acclaim that it was followed by a companion story – *Sixty Glorious Years*, made in the fol-

lowing year. *Victoria the Great*, which was made in black and white, with a burst into colour in the climactic Diamond Jubilee scenes, was directed by Herbert Wilcox (whom Dame Anna married in 1943), and led to a whole series of Neagle-portrayed great ladies, such as *The Lady With a Lamp* (Florence Nightingale) and *They Flew Alone* (Amy Johnson).

Victory Through Air Power ○
1943, US, 65 mins, colour
Dir: Jack Kinney, James Algar
Rating: ★★★

During the Second World War, Walt Disney set up a department for propaganda and information films. Even the likes of Mickey Mouse and Donald Duck became involved, notably Donald in the Oscar-winning *Der Fuehrer's Face*, a wild mixture of broad comedy and surrealism, seen here as a prelude to *Victory Through Air Power*, a unique combination of humour, deadly seriousness, detailed maps and highly imaginative animation, that treads a fine line between entertainment and realism. The humorous 'History of Aviation' animation sequence gives way to a rather wooden major going into detail about bombing. But do wait for the extraordinary animated climax as the American eagle dive-bombs the Japanese octopus in the South Pacific!

View to a Kill, A ○ ⓥ
1985, UK, 121 mins, colour
Dir: John Glen
Stars: Roger Moore, Christopher Walken, Tanya Roberts, Grace Jones
Rating: ★★

Roger Moore, selected 12 years earlier to take over Sean Connery's position in the 007 shirt (George Lazenby had popped up for one appearance in 1969), makes his seventh and last showing as everyone's favourite hit-man in this extravagant Bondian escapade packed with 'he'll-never-get-out-of-this, surely' situations. The gamut of apocalyptic scenarios is run (the denouement involves an airship hitched up to the Golden Gate Bridge); there's a stylish villain (Christopher Walken); and the beauties are really beautiful (Tanya Roberts, Grace Jones, Alison Doody and Fiona Fullerton). But for all these typically glossy ingredients, Moore looks a tired old warhorse, resorting to double entendres, which might have been cast-offs from a *Carry On* script.

Duran Duran supply the rather mechanical theme song, a big hit at the time.

Vigil ◑ ⓥ
1984, New Zealand, 90 mins, colour
Dir: Vincent Ward
Stars: Bill Kerr, Fiona Kay, Gordon Shields, Penelope Stewart, Frank Whitten
Rating: ★★

Life for a family on a remote sheep farm is dramatically changed when the farmer is killed in a hunting accident and his body is brought home to his wife and daughter by a mysterious stranger. This strange story is told from the pubescent daughter's viewpoint as she watches the stranger's influence on her mother and eccentric grandfather. New Zealand director Vincent Ward has created a visually arresting and stylish film, but the poor script and obscure storyline don't live up to the way it looks.

Viking Queen, The ○
1966, UK, 91 mins, colour
Dir: Don Chaffey
Stars: Don Murray, Carita, Donald Houston, Adrienne Corri
Rating: ★

'See: Bladed chariots of death! Men roasted alive in the cage of hell! Mighty legions of Rome! Barbarism of the mad emperor! Savage rites of the Iceni!' blazed the original publicity. If you're careful, you'll also see a watch on the wrist of one of the actors in this Roman Britain epic. Finnish beauty Carita plays the title role.

Vikings, The ○
1958, US, 116 mins, colour
Dir: Richard Fleischer
Stars: Kirk Douglas, Tony Curtis, Janet Leigh, Ernest Borgnine
Rating: ★★★

Kirk Douglas and Tony Curtis have the times of their acting lives in Richard Fleischer's Norse opera about the battle-loving Vikings of the 10th century, spectacularly shot by Jack Cardiff on locations in Brittany and Norway (Hardangerfjord). Eileen Way makes a distinct Agnes Moorehead-style impression as an old crone, and some fierce hand-to-hand combat scenes will have you on the edge of your armchair. Britain's James Donald is also good as a treacherous informer.

Village of Daughters ○
1961, UK, 86 mins, b/w
Dir: George Pollock
Stars: Eric Sykes, Scilla Gabel
Rating: ★★

Sparky comedy about a salesman asked to judge an Italian beauty contest – with a difference. In a rare leading role, lucky Eric Sykes is surrounded by some of Britain's loveliest young starlets of the time.

Village of the Damned ◑
1960, UK, 79 mins, b/w
Dir: Wolf Rilla
Stars: George Sanders, Barbara Shelley
Rating: ★★★

Edgy, eerie and effective, this is a fine screen adaptation of John Wyndham's classic science-fiction novel *The Midwich Cuckoos*, about demon children born during a short period when life in an English village appears to have come to a stop. Director Wolf Rilla's discreetly incisive handling of the mounting suspense evokes some quite frightening moments.

Villain ● ⓥ
1971, UK, 98 mins, colour
Dir: Michael Tuchner
Stars: Richard Burton, Ian McShane, Nigel Davenport, Fiona Lewis
Rating: ★★★

Richard Burton's choice of roles in his last years was not always the happiest, but this is one of his most striking and intense portrayals: a homosexual East End gang leader who treads people down like insects. A thriller as tough as its central character. Ian La Frenais and Dick Clement – more usually associated with comedy series – contribute a script that drips venom.

Villain, The
See: Cactus Jack

Villa Rides! ○
1968, US, 125 mins, colour
Dir: Buzz Kulik
Stars: Yul Brynner, Robert Mitchum, Charles Bronson, Grazia Buccella
Rating: ★★

There's not much to test the brain cells but a feast of action for the eyes in this story about the Mexican patriot-bandit who flourished in the early part of this century. Jack Hildyard's Technicolor photography helps director Buzz Kulik to milk the maximum impact from a succession of battles, explosions, raids, duels and chases. Charles Bronson, giving one of

the last of his sadistic tough-guy portrayals before being promoted to stone-faced superstar, breathes life into his role.

Violent Men, The ○
(aka: Rough Company)
1955, US, 96 mins, colour
Dir: Rudolph Mate
Stars: Glenn Ford, Barbara Stanwyck, Edward G Robinson
Rating: ★★★

Columbia's much-trumpeted first film in wide-screen CinemaScope is a Western that sets out to be another *Shane* with its 'greed for land' theme but misses the mark. Polish-born director Rudolph Mate who, as a cinematographer, captured co-star Barbara Stanwyck in one of her best films, *Stella Dallas*, produces several thrilling action shots but is less sure-footed when marshalling his actors. In fact, Edward G Robinson picked out *The Violent Men* in his autobiography as one of the movies that marked his decline from stardom. In Britain, it was released as *Rough Company*, the title of the novel by Donald Hamilton on which the film is based.

Violent Playground ○
1957, UK, 108 mins, b/w
Dir: Basil Dearden
Stars: Stanley Baker, Anne Heywood, David McCallum, Peter Cushing
Rating: ★★

A tough-minded British thriller about a detective's hunt for an arsonist. Its semi-documentary style and good location shots of the Liverpool slums lend authority to a polished script. It's a well-paced film which builds up to a tension-filled climax.

Violent Saturday ○
1955, US, 91 mins, colour
Dir: Richard Fleischer
Stars: Victor Mature, Richard Egan, Stephen McNally, Virginia Leith
Rating: ★★★

Richard Fleischer's forceful thriller about three bank-raiders who indirectly bring to the surface all the sores, weaknesses and suspicions of the small town whose bank they are about to rob. The bank robbers are exceptionally well played by Stephen McNally, Lee Marvin and, particularly, J Carrol Naish.

V

Violent Streets ●
(aka: Thief)
1981, US, 126 mins, colour
Dir: Michael Mann
Stars: James Caan, Tuesday Weld, Willie Nelson
Rating: ★★

An uncompromising thriller about a professional robber who makes one of the few mistakes in his meticulous career when he allies himself with organised crime for what he thinks is one job. Tuesday Weld is, as usual, wasted as his wife, and James Belushi makes a notable debut as Caan's skilful associate. The ending splatters bodies all over the pavement, somewhat compensating for the snail-like pace of much of the film.

Virgin and the Gypsy, The ◐
1970, UK, 95 mins, colour
Dir: Christopher Miles
Stars: Joanna Shimkus, Franco Nero, Honor Blackman, Mark Burns
Rating: ★★

Direction (by Christopher Miles) and photography (by Robert Huke) come very close to capturing the brooding atmosphere of the original in this adaptation of an earthy short novel by D H Lawrence. Joanna Shimkus (who later married Sidney Poitier) shines as the gentle Yvette who is emancipated from her surroundings through her friendship with, and love for, a gypsy who calls, selling his wares, at the north of England rectory which is her home. The gypsy is played by Franco Nero, but generally the acting honours go to the ladies in the cast.

Virginia City ○
1940, US, 121 mins, b/w
Dir: Michael Curtiz
Stars: Errol Flynn, Randolph Scott, Humphrey Bogart, Miriam Hopkins
Rating: ★★★

They couldn't afford stars such as Errol Flynn, Humphrey Bogart and Randolph Scott in the same film today – not unless the producers had millions in the bank. Not unexpectedly the resulting movie, directed by Michael Curtiz (who made Flynn's best films and three years later won an Oscar for *Casablanca*), is a Western par excellence. Nor will action fans be disappointed: the film is packed with battles of one kind or another. As a Rebel spy, the acerbic Miriam

Hopkins steals the acting honours from under the noses of the eminent trio.

Virgin Island ○
1958, UK, 94 mins, colour
Dir: Pat Jackson
Stars: John Cassavetes, Virginia Maskell, Sidney Poitier
Rating: ★★

The stars of *A Man is 10 Feet Tall* reunited in a far gentler film about a young couple starting a new life on a far-from-civilised island. Directed by Pat Jackson, who distinguished himself on the wartime documentary *Western Approaches*, and later, in contrast, proved best at 'women's pictures'.

Virgin Queen, The ○ ⓥ
1955, US, 92 mins, colour
Dir: Henry Koster
Stars: Bette Davis, Richard Todd, Joan Collins
Rating: ★★

Bette Davis' second interpretation of the role of Elizabeth I, and considered by many critics to be even better than her first essay in *The Private Lives of Elizabeth and Essex*. Richard Todd plays Sir Walter Raleigh, and Joan Collins gives a spirited performance as the lady-in-waiting with whom he falls in love.

Virgin Soldiers, The ● ⓥ
1969, UK, 96 mins, colour
Dir: John Dexter
Stars: Lynn Redgrave, Hywel Bennett, Nigel Davenport, Nigel Patrick
Rating: ★★

Popular film version of Leslie Thomas' best-seller with raw recruits learning about the birds and battles in the Far East. A good performance from Lynn Redgrave, as usual, but the message about the uselessness of war and National Service is largely submerged by the *Carry On* style. However, this does make the best shock moments all the more telling.

Vivacious Lady ○
1938, US, 90 mins, b/w
Dir: George Stevens
Stars: Ginger Rogers, James Stewart
Rating: ★★★

Here's another dancing lady – in the shape of Ginger Rogers as the nightclub entertainer whom mild professor James Stewart falls for in this one-joke but still fairly sparkling romantic comedy. Penny-pinching RKO

allowed Ginger only one dance, but the personalities of the stars save the day.

Viva Villa! ○
1934, France/Italy, 125 mins, b/w
Dir: Jack Conway
Stars: Wallace Beery, Leo Carrillo, Fay Wray
Rating: ★★★

Rowdy, roistering, well-scripted account of the famous Mexican bandit's exploits. Its episodic quality might be partly due to the fact that director Howard Hawks left half-way through, and was replaced by Jack Conway, who is credited with the final version of the film. But it was assistant director John Waters who took the film's only Academy Award, although Ben Hecht's script contains some pungent exchanges, particularly the final dialogue between Wallace Beery (as Villa) and Stuart Erwin as the reporter who chronicles his career.

Viva Zapata! ○ ⓥ
1952, US, 113 mins, b/w
Dir: Elia Kazan
Stars: Marlon Brando, Jean Peters, Anthony Quinn
Rating: ★★★

One of Marlon Brando's earliest screen roles, as the famous bandit of Mexican history. Although his brooding portrait proved him capable of a wide range of roles, he is outgunned both by Jean Peters as his fiercely ambitious wife, and by Anthony Quinn as his roistering brother, the latter winning an Oscar which established him as a serious actor after 17 years' hard labour on the Hollywood scene – and also setting the pattern for the remainder of his career. Under Elia Kazan's direction, the action and treatment are fierce and uncompromising.

V.I. Warshawski ● ⓥ
1991, US, 89 mins, colour
Dir: Jeff Kanew
Stars: Kathleen Turner, Jay O Sanders, Charles Durning, Angela Goethals
Rating: ★★★

This female private-eye film runs like tough pulp fiction from another era. The heroine always has a ready wisecrack (with a literacy rather above her station in life), the mystery she has to solve is mighty murky and, of course, it involves a woman. 'I've just told you everything I know,' gasps V I's sometime lover/reporter friend. 'Tut,

tut,' she chides, 'you always did suffer from premature articulation.' When a villain boasts of having had 500 women, she has an answer for that too. 'Can't get the hang of it, huh?' Yes, this Warshawski is tough all right. An aikido expert, she's inclined to beat up on thugs sent to work her over and almost always has the last word. Kathleen Turner plays her about right: the story she's involved with has something to do with three brothers feuding over selling their shipping concern. When one of them is killed, and Warshawski is left holding his daughter, the case becomes her concern. Despite its awful background music, this film was underrated by public and critics alike.

Vogues ○
1937, US, 108 mins, colour
Dir: Irving Cummings
Stars: Warner Baxter, Joan Bennett, Helen Vinson, Mischa Auer
Rating: ★★

Amazing fashions, a smooth script and pretty indifferent musical numbers make up the mix for this archetypal slice of lavish late-Thirties entertainment, Hollywood-style, chiefly remarkable for its innovative use of early Technicolor under the skilled camera of Ray Rennahan. Experienced smoothie Warner Baxter, used to putting on shows since *42nd Street*, here mounts a fashion show to remember, while The Wiere Brothers, underused by films, steal the comedy honours. And just cast an eye over Miss Chesterfield, Miss Pepsodent, Miss Lux Soap and Miss Lucky Strike!

Voice in the Night, A
See: Freedom Radio

Volunteers ◐ ⓥ
1985, US, 107 mins, colour
Dir: Nicholas Meyer
Stars: Tom Hanks, John Candy
Rating: ★★

Hollywood's Mr Nice Guy, Tom Hanks, and Tinseltown's tub of fun, John Candy, teamed up only a year after they played brothers in the hugely successful *Splash* for this lightweight comedy. The premise – compulsive gambler (Hanks) escapes from his creditors and inadvertently ends up on a Peace Corps mission to Thailand – is promising but considering the combined talents of Hanks and Candy, the end product is largely disappointing. However, in

their distinctly different ways, both leads prove worth watching here, and went on to greater glories.

V1
See: Battle of the V1

Von Richthofen and Brown ○
1971, US, 97 mins, colour
Dir: Roger Corman
Stars: John Phillip Law, Don Stroud
Rating: ★★

After working his way up through crab monsters, wasp women, Poe stories and gangsters, Roger Corman climaxed his directing career with this highly personal treatment of von Richthofen and Brown – aerial combat stars of the First World War. The dog-fights are splendidly staged for poetic effect while the script pays due attention to motivation and values. 'My ancestors were Teutonic knights,' says John Phillip Law's von Richthofen. 'I merely exchanged the horse for the aeroplane.'

Von Ryan's Express ○ ⓥ
1965, US, 117 mins, colour
Dir: Mark Robson
Stars: Frank Sinatra, Trevor Howard, Brad Dexter
Rating: ★★★★

A very successful mixture of *The Train* and *The Great Escape*, dealing with a group of Allied prisoners-of-war who capture the train taking them to Berlin, and set off full steam for Switzerland. And, incorporating the tenser situations from each film, it has the edge on both for sheer excitement. Frank Sinatra and Trevor Howard turn in thoroughly workmanlike performances, and in support Italian actors Sergio Fantoni and Adolfo Celi, as Allied-sympathiser and Nazi-sympathiser respectively, are outstanding. And Edward Mulhare gives a delicately wry portrayal of the padre forced to pose as a German officer – because he is the only one of the prisoners who can speak the language fluently. But the action is everything. And nowhere more so than in the edge-of-seat ending.

Vote for Huggett ○
1949, UK, 95 mins, b/w
Dir: Ken Annakin
Stars: Jack Warner, Kathleen Harrison, Susan Shaw, David Tomlinson
Rating: ★★

The third in the series about the adventures of a Cockney family (other

titles were *Holiday Camp*, *Here Come the Huggetts* and *The Huggetts Abroad*). All were directed by Ken Annakin, and were a kind of throwback to the hearty humour purveyed in the British cinema of the Thirties by such comedians as Leslie Fuller. The cast, too, was constant: Jack Warner as Dad, Kathleen Harrison (with an epithet for every occasion) as Mum, Susan Shaw as daughter Sue, Petula Clark as daughter Pet, and Peter Hammond as the perennial boyfriend. Here the cast also includes David Tomlinson, Diana Dors and Anthony Newley.

Voyage Home – Star Trek IV, The ○ ⓥ
1986, US, 119 mins, colour
Dir: Leonard Nimoy
Stars: William Shatner, Leonard Nimoy, DeForest Kelley, Catherine Hicks
Rating: ★★

Half a science-fiction adventure and half a timely plea for whale conservation, this adventure of the Starship Enterprise shows the formula wearing pretty thin despite four credited writers. Returning to earth to face court martial, Kirk and Co find the planet in a state of panic thanks to the presence high above of a paralysing probe trying to communicate with a species of whale that's extinct. Kirk and his crew travel back in time (conveniently to 1986) when the whales still existed and find a pair in a San Francisco aquarium that are about to be booted off to Alaska where whale-hunters abound. This makes for a reasonably tense, if slightly over-extended climax and, if not much is made of the invaders' bemusement in 20th-century America, the camaraderie of the cast does produce some nice lines and reactions. Catherine Hicks, a spirited American version of Susannah York, is a refreshing younger face among the collection of affectionately remembered friends.

Voyage of the Damned ○
1976, UK, 155 mins, colour
Dir: Stuart Rosenberg
Stars: Faye Dunaway, Max Von Sydow, Oskar Werner, Malcolm McDowell, Orson Welles
Rating: ★★

The movie equivalent of a good, long read, this is an epic drama, based on fact. The all-star cast includes Orson Welles as a wily Cuban industrialist, Faye Dunaway, Max Von Sydow

V

(whose sterling performance holds the disparate dramas together), Oskar Werner, James Mason, Malcolm McDowell and Ben Gazzara. Director Stuart Rosenberg keeps his huge cast and sprawling narrative steadily in control.

Voyager ● Ⓥ
1991, Germany/France, 117 mins, colour
Dir: Volker Schlöndorff
Stars: Sam Shepard, Julie Delpy, Barbara Sukowa
Rating: ★

Gloom and doom are draped all over this journey into grace, especially as we can guess very well what hero Sam Shepard doesn't know – that the pert teenager (Julie Delpy) he plans to bed is his own daughter. 'Do you believe in chance?' asks Shepard. And you'd better. Because Max Frisch's bestseller, on which this glum number is based, depends entirely on it. Solemn Sam is ideally cast in this sort of thing, as the man without belief in life, or a future. You just have to feel sorry for his character, even though it's hard to sympathise with a man who comes out with things like 'Three or four days with a woman is my maximum. After that, I start to dissimilate.' Even the few moments of humour seem forced and unreal.

Voyage to the Bottom of the Sea ○ Ⓥ
1961, US, 105 mins, colour
Dir: Irwin Allen
Stars: Walter Pidgeon, Joan Fontaine, Peter Lorre
Rating: ★★

Special effects are top-notch in this exciting, colourful and fluid piece of science fiction, on which the TV series was based. Here, it's Walter Pidgeon leading the star-studded cast as Admiral Nelson (the part played by Richard Basehart in the series), battling against giant octopi and melting Polar ice-caps in his huge submarine, *Seaview*. Older film fans may recognise Regis Toomey (as Dr Jamieson). Toomey was in scores of films in the Thirties and Forties, as pugnacious policemen, wisecracking reporters, or 'squealers' who inevitably 'bought it' in the final reel.

W

Wabash Avenue ☉
1950, US, 92 mins, colour
Dir: Henry Koster
Stars: Betty Grable, Victor Mature, Phil Harris
Rating: ★★★

If you have a feeling of déjà vu, don't be surprised – this bright and brash musical is a remake of 1943's *Coney Island*, with the same producer (William Perlberg) and the same star, Betty Grable. This time Victor Mature (all teeth and bogus charm) and Phil Harris are the two men with Grable on their minds when they are not trying to swindle each other, but the film belongs firmly to its leading lady, million-dollar legs enjoyably in evidence as she performs a series of lively musical numbers. Easy on the eye (20th Century-Fox's Technicolor was never lovelier) and on the mind, with engaging support from James Barton as an Irish drunk and Margaret Hamilton as a crusading reformer. A good show.

Wackiest Ship in the Army, The ☉
1960, US, 99 mins, colour
Dir: Richard Murphy
Stars: Jack Lemmon, Ricky Nelson
Rating: ★★

Jack Lemmon as a yachtsman with a crew of novices on a dangerous wartime mission. It is one of his sunniest comedies. Patricia Driscoll, one-time Maid Marian in the *Robin Hood* TV series, has the main female role.

Wages of Fear, The ◑
(aka: Sorcerer)
1977, US, 122 mins, colour
Dir: William Friedkin
Stars: Roy Scheider
Rating: ★★

William Friedkin, director of *The French Connection* and *The Exorcist*, made this $21 million remake of the famous suspense movie, the first version of which starred Yves Montand in the role now grittily played by Roy Scheider. The remainder of the characters remain less well developed than in the original, which so entrapped us in following the fortunes of the four men desperate enough to undertake a suicidal journey with a cargo of nitro-glycerine along the dangerous jungle and cliffside roads.

Wagonmaster ○
1950, US, 86 mins, b/w
Dir: John Ford
Stars: Ben Johnson, Joanne Dru, Harry Carey Jr, Ward Bond
Rating: ★★★

Brimming with atmosphere, this John Ford Western is resplendent with all the Ford trademarks: breathtaking scenery, dancing, songs and a warm sense of humour. Ben Johnson takes over as star from Ford's ever-present, John Wayne, though in fairness Wayne is too big a personality to fit into this small, intimate story about two drifter cowhands joining a Mormon wagon train. Ford's son, Patrick, co-wrote the screenplay, and it remained a personal favourite throughout Ford Sr's career. 'Along with *The Fugitive* and *The Sun Shines Bright* it came closest to what I had wanted to achieve,' he once told fellow director Peter Bogdanovich. *Wagonmaster* is pure poetry, eschewing plot twists and rugged action for a bird's eye view of ordinary people going about their ordinary lives. In short, it's an uplifting film about life which affirms that anyone can achieve the ultimate dream.

Waiting for the Light ○ Ⓥ
1990, US, 102 mins, colour
Dir: Christopher Monger
Stars: Shirley MacLaine, Teri Garr, Clancy Brown, Vincent Schiavelli, Hillary Wolf
Rating: ★★

A family film of lightweight charm, with Shirley MacLaine as an eccentric aunt whose magic first gets her niece's children into trouble, then proves their salvation when she provides the 'miracle' that brings people to their little cafe in the middle of nowhere. Not much to stir the blood here, but MacLaine deservedly assumes centre stage and there are good, pleasant performances from Teri Garr, Clancy Brown, Vincent Schiavelli, John Bedford Lloyd and especially Hillary Wolf as Garr's daughter. Some amusingly staged special effects make MacLaine's miracle magic seem real enough for the gullible.

Wait 'Til the Sun Shines, Nellie ○
1952, US, 108 mins, colour
Dir: Henry King

Stars: David Wayne, Jean Peters, Hugh Marlowe, Albert Dekker
Rating: ★★★★

One of director Henry King's warmest pieces of nostalgia. In fact, if this had starred a high-profile star like Spencer Tracy in the leading role it might now be regarded as a classic – not that David Wayne is anything but excellent as the small-town barber looking back over half a century of his life. It rambles a bit, but the acting, direction and glowing colour photography of Leon Shamroy more than make up for that. Not to be missed.

Wait Until Dark ◑

1967, US, 108 mins, colour
Dir: Terence Young
Stars: Audrey Hepburn, Alan Arkin, Richard Crenna
Rating: ★★★

Don't be put off: sit through the first hour or so of stagey, confined melodrama to see the petrifying last 40 minutes of this jolting thriller, as blind girl Audrey Hepburn (one character describes her as the World's Champion Blind Lady and he's right) smashes all the lights and takes on two baddies and one very evil psycho who are after a doll stuffed with heroin, which is in her basement flat. One moment of fright in particular, near the end, is terrifyingly sudden.

Wake Island ○

1942, US, 88 mins, colour
Dir: John Farrow
Stars: Brian Donlevy, Robert Preston, MacDonald Carey
Rating: ★★★

Exciting and typically flag-waving American film of the early war years. In this case, there really was something to wave the flag about – the heroic defence of a Pacific island by a few hundred Marines against 10,000 Japanese that lasted for 15 days. Brian Donlevy is very good as the island commander.

Wake of the Red Witch ○ ⓥ

1948, US, 106 mins, b/w
Dir: Edward Ludwig
Stars: John Wayne, Gail Russell, Gig Young
Rating: ★★

High adventure with a richly-detailed story (made rather too complicated by flashbacks) that's vaguely reminiscent of the work of Joseph Conrad, though actually based on a novel by Garland

Roark. It kicked off a three-year period for star John Wayne in which he made some of his best films, including *Three Godfathers*, *Red River*, *Fort Apache*, *Sands of Iwo Jima*, *She Wore a Yellow Ribbon* and *Rio Grande*. This film gives him a chance to play a more complex character than usual and Wayne responds with one of his most haunting performances. It's an East Indies seafaring yarn that takes in fist-fights, storms, romance, friendship, treachery and the pursuit of sunken treasure, and has a climax that should have you gripping the armchair. Wayne was so fond of the film that he took the name of his production company, Batjac, from its shipping line. Hawaiian sporting star Duke Kahanamoku appears in a supporting role.

Wake Up and Live ○

1937, US, 91 mins, b/w
Dir: Sidney Lanfield
Stars: Walter Winchell, Ben Bernie and His Band, Alice Faye, Jack Haley
Rating: ★★★

An excellent satire on the world of radio which was big time showbusiness when this was made. Newspaper columnist Walter Winchell and bandleader Ben Bernie, as themselves, play 'feuding' radio show hosts (not unlike the real-life Jack Benny-Fred Allen 'feud' which was a complete fabrication) in this slap-happy comedy musical which fairly bounces along. Alice Faye also stars as a kind of radio agony aunt. Winchell actually had his own Sunday night broadcast which became cult listening for Americans in the Thirties. He was a powerful character and allegedly the model for Burt Lancaster's J J Hunsecker in *Sweet Smell of Success*. As anyone who has seen that film will recall, this was hardly a man overflowing with the milk of human kindness: so see how convincing you find Winchell's performance here!

Walkabout ◑

1970, Australia, 100 mins, colour
Dir: Nicolas Roeg
Stars: Jenny Agutter, David Gumpilil
Rating: ★★★

Cameraman Nicolas Roeg made a new reputation as an innovative director with this exciting and sad moral tale about two children marooned in Australia's alien outback, strikingly captured in burnished colour.

Walk, Don't Run ○

1966, US, 114 mins, colour
Dir: Charles Walters
Stars: Cary Grant, Samantha Eggar, Jim Hutton
Rating: ★★★

This story was originally used in the 1943 Charles Coburn-Jean Arthur hit *The More the Merrier*. But the setting is here transferred from wartime Washington to Tokyo's 1964 Olympics. Grant is on top comedy form as a match-making diplomat, raising laughs often without saying a word. Watch his face and listen to his Bluto-like grunts as he potters around Samantha Eggar's kitchen (he has become her flat-mate through sheer gift of the gab) trying to find things.

Walking My Baby Back Home ⊙

1953, US, 95 mins, colour
Dir: Lloyd Bacon
Stars: Donald O'Connor, Janet Leigh, Buddy Hackett
Rating: ★★★

A bright, colourful musical that didn't quite come off as a star vehicle. Probably it's because Donald O'Connor was better playing second fiddle to people like Gene Kelly and Bing Crosby, and because Janet Leigh, although she dances gracefully, sings pleasantly and looks gorgeous, isn't really a musical star. 'Scatman' Crothers scores in a support as a jazz-loving pianist, the dance numbers are expertly, if slightly mechanically, staged and the music takes in everything from a hot version of Liszt's 'Liebestraum' to some good old New Orleans blues. Second-grade, but undemandingly enjoyable, even though Universal couldn't make this sort of musical like MGM, or even 20th Century-Fox.

Walk in the Shadow

See: *Life for Ruth*

Walk in the Spring Rain, A ○

1969, US, 100 mins, colour
Dir: Guy Green
Stars: Anthony Quinn, Ingrid Bergman, Fritz Weaver
Rating: ★★

Spring romance in their Autumn years for middle-agers Anthony Quinn and Ingrid Bergman, who had previously appeared together in the starkly contrasted *The Visit*. Bergman's husband is played by Fritz Weaver, the authoritative American actor who first

W

sprang to prominence as the colonel who cracked up in Sidney Lumet's *Fail Safe*. Weaver has more recently come back into the limelight with the lead in the mammoth television series *Holocaust*. Set in the mountainous but attractive countryside of Tennessee, *A Walk in the Spring Rain* is exquisitely shot in colour by the distinguished Hollywood cameraman Charles B Lang, whose many awards include an Oscar as far back as 1933 for the first version of *A Farewell to Arms*.

Walk in the Sun, A ○
1945, US, 117 mins, b/w
Dir: Lewis Milestone
Stars: Dana Andrews, Richard Conte, Sterling Holloway
Rating: ★★★

One of the most highly regarded World War Two movies, with an unsentimental screenplay by Robert Rossen (later to turn director with such films as *All the King's Men* and *The Hustler*) plus concentrated direction by Lewis Milestone, who made the classic World War One pacifist movie *All Quiet on the Western Front*.

Walk the Proud Land ○
1956, US, 88 mins, colour
Dir: Jesse Hibbs
Stars: Audie Murphy, Pat Crowley, Anne Bancroft, Charles Drake
Rating: ★★★

This excellent true-life story of the first Apache agent was Audie Murphy's follow-up to the great success of the autobiographical *To Hell and Back*. Murphy dominates the film, with the usually sparky Pat Crowley rather subdued, leaving Anne Bancroft free to take the feminine acting honours as an Apache widow woman. Supporting acting is sturdy, especially from Charles Drake, as a friendly sergeant, and Robert Warwick, as the resigned and noble old Apache chief.

Wall Street ● Ⓥ
1987, US, 124 mins, colour
Dir: Oliver Stone
Stars: Michael Douglas, Charlie Sheen, Martin Sheen, Daryl Hannah, Terence Stamp, Sean Young
Rating: ★★★

Director Oliver Stone's swift follow-up to the Oscar-winning *Platoon* takes him from the battlefields of Vietnam to the battlefields of the New York financial markets. Charlie Sheen, who played the central character in *Platoon*, is again the youngster through

whose eyes Stone shows the ugly underbelly of life. As an ambitious young broker, he achieves the ultimate yuppie dream of a huge salary, high-powered car, glamorous girlfriend and luxury penthouse. But there's a terrible personal cost to him as he crosses the line of legality in providing his corporate raider idol Gordon Gekko with illegal insider information on Sheen's father's airline business. There is a nice touch in the casting of real-life father Martin Sheen as Charlie's screen dad, but it was Michael Douglas, as the monstrous Gekko – motto: 'Greed is good' – who scooped the Best Actor Oscar (a feat never achieved by his father Kirk). Sean Young, as Gekko's wife, clashed continually on the set with Stone and her role was cut in the final print. Sylvia Miles has a wonderful scene-stealing cameo as an estate agent, and future star of *sex, lies and videotape* James Spader, can be spotted in one of his first screen roles.

Waltz of the Toreadors ○
1962, UK, 105 mins, colour
Dir: John Guillermin
Stars: Peter Sellers, Margaret Leighton, Dany Robin, John Fraser.
Rating: ★★★

Peter Sellers excels as an ageing general with an eye for the ladies in this happy and successful, sometimes touching, adaptation of Jean Anouilh's famous play. And the excellent Technicolor photography fairly sparkles, especially in a scene of lovers meeting in a cornfield. Many familiar television faces decorate the supporting cast, including those of Denise Coffey, who starred in the series *Do Not Adjust Your Set*, *Girls About Town* and *Hold the Front Page*, Jean Anderson, the mother of *The Brothers*, and John Le Mesurier, famous for his role of Sgt Wilson in *Dad's Army*.

Wanted Dead or Alive ● Ⓥ
1987, US, 104 mins, colour
Dir: Gary Sherman
Stars: Rutger Hauer, Gene Simmons, Mel Harris, Robert Guillaume
Rating: ★★

Massive blows, explosions and assassinations are the order of the day in this assembly-line vehicle about a modern-day bounty hunter, supposedly the grandson of the character played by Steve McQueen in the TV Western series of the same title. Dutch actor Rutger Hauer, already

sporting a near-perfect American accent, plays the ex-CIA agent recruited by his old bosses to stop an Arab terrorist who plans to blow up half of Los Angeles. Remaining developments are cut to formula, with bludgeoning sentiment, corny situations and a brave attempt by Robert Guillaume to make something out of his cornball dialogue. But like his character, nothing in this film ever quite comes to life.

War and Peace ○
1956, US, 208 mins, colour
Dir: King Vidor
Stars: Henry Fonda, Audrey Hepburn, Mel Ferrer
Rating: ★★★

This impressive – and a little overwhelming – Hollywood version of Leo Tolstoy's Napoleonic saga suffers from too much peace and too little war, especially given that the battle scenes are tremendously staged by Mario Soldati, helping out credited director King Vidor. Henry Fonda, though miscast and too old, is still amazingly good as Pierre, and there are excellent contributions from Mel Ferrer, Herbert Lom, Anita Ekberg and especially Oscar Homolka. Although developments in the drama are signalled heavily, this is still a commendable stab at a mammoth undertaking.

WarGames ○ Ⓥ
1983, US, 113 mins, colour
Dir: John Badham
Stars: Matthew Broderick, Dabney Coleman, Ally Sheedy, Barry Corbin, John Wood
Rating: ★★★

Another computer-age thriller, though a pretty exciting one about a teenage computer freak who accidentally plugs into America's nuclear defence system and finds the computer playing a war game with him that may very well be for real. Though you may not understand the ending, you'll appreciate the tension that leads up to it, as the boy and his girlfriend (he's won her over by programming the school computer to give her an A in biology instead of an F) fight desperately to a) convince the authorities and b) find the thought-dead scientist who may be able to stop it all. Matthew Broderick, Dabney Coleman, John Wood and Juanin Clay are convincingly distraught: but then it's only a game. Or is it? From January 1979 to June 1980, some 147 such full-scale alerts had their grim scenarios played out in earnest before America and Russia pulled back from the brink.

Warlock ○
1959, US, 123 mins, colour
Dir: Edward Dmytryk
Stars: Richard Widmark, Henry Fonda, Anthony Quinn, Dorothy Malone
Rating: ★★

Over 200,000 rounds of blank ammunition – the script calls for 47 people to bite the dust – were fired during the making of this epic Western. Director Edward Dmytryk initially wanted Henry Fonda to play the hero, and Richard Widmark the villain. But after they had read the screenplay, each actor wanted to play the other's role. And that's the way it ended up, setting Fonda on a course that culminated memorably in his bad guy in *Once Upon a Time in the West*.

Warlock ● ⓥ
1988, US, 102 mins, colour
Dir: Steve Miner
Stars: Richard E Grant, Julian Sands, Lori Singer
Rating: ★★

There's a laugh and a thrill to be had in this witch's brew which has Julian Sands as a 17th-century warlock who escapes to 1988 to avoid being hanged and burned. But he's pursued by the spirit of his sworn enemy (Richard E Grant) who rises from the grave to protect the heroine (Lori Singer) – which is just as well as Sands has put a spell on her which ages her at the rate of 20 years a day. 'Nothing can be worse than this,' she howls, presumably referring to her 60-year-old makeup. So she sets out to trek with Grant to prevent Sands putting three parts of a book together (the Grand Grimoir), find out God's real name and reverse the Creation. There's the inevitable race to get to the third part of the book, which lies in a tomb with a hex-mark on it. Hex, you see, marks the spot. All this, plus good 'hex' music by Jerry Goldsmith, some good lines, pretty variable special effects and enjoyable unintentional humour.

War Lord, The ○
1965, US, 122 mins, colour
Dir: Franklin Schaffner
Stars: Charlton Heston, Richard Boone
Rating: ★★★★

Moody and magnificent (even after studio interference), this is one of the most impressive pieces of medieval drama that Hollywood ever made. Charlton Heston heightens the sense of period by his skilful handling of the dialogue as an embittered, war-hardened Norman noble who invokes his feudal right and steals a bride in his Belgian territory on her wedding night. He's matched by Rosemary Forsyth, who never bettered her blazingly sincere portrait of the girl. But the film's aces in the hole are Jerome Moross's melodic, mood-invoking music, and Russell Metty's amazing colour photography. He gives us beautiful portraits of all kinds of skies, outdoor scenes like old prints and interiors that use and blend colour – gold, turquoise and blood-red against sullen backgrounds – in masterly style. And there's a classic little cameo in black-and-white that profiles Heston and Forsyth against a thunderstrewn sky while they talk quietly together on a castle turret. Whatever your tastes, be they for action, romance or sheer technical perfection, you'll find something to savour here.

Warlords of Atlantis ○
1978, US, 96 mins, colour
Dir: Kevin Connor
Stars: Doug McClure, Peter Gilmore
Rating: ★★

The fourth, least likely and probably most colourful adventure film from the John Dark/Kevin Connor team (who made the *Time Forgot* movies). Again, its chief attribute is the monsters created by Roger Dicken. The story is laughable, but the effects better than ever and the film, crammed with action, should appeal both to the young and the young at heart.

Warning Shot ○
1967, US, 95 mins, colour
Dir: Buzz Kulik
Stars: David Janssen, Eleanor Parker, George Sanders, Joan Collins
Rating: ★★★

This big police thriller was David Janssen's reward for doing so well on *The Fugitive*. It casts him as a dedicated law officer accused of murder. Good supporting performances from Eleanor Parker and Lillian Gish, in a corker of a plot. Janssen and Keenan Wynn play off well against each other as police partners. A few years later,

they repeated the partnership, this time as truckers, in an excellent TV movie, *Hijack*.

War of the Roses, The ● ⓥ
1989, US, 111 mins, colour
Dir: Danny DeVito
Stars: Michael Douglas, Kathleen Turner, Danny DeVito, Marianne Sagebrecht
Rating: ★★★

A truly vicious black comedy about a divorce that escalates into a war. The story of the Roses (Michael Douglas and Kathleen Turner) is told as a cautionary tale by a megabuck lawyer (Danny DeVito) to a divorce-bent client. As DeVito points out: 'When a $450-an-hour lawyer advises you for nothing, you'd better listen.' The problem with the Roses is that they really have nothing in common but sex. The cracks soon star to appear, aggravated by the husband's stifling of his wife's individuality and undermining her confidence. What follows, although perhaps over the top, is a horrifying lesson to us all and pretty good entertainment as well. Turner, Douglas and DeVito are all good, DeVito especially, and the later action, as the Roses go for the jugular in a house of horrors, is staged with the appropriate touch of *Grand Guignol* by DeVito himself, doubling as director.

War of the Wildcats ○
(aka: In Old Oklahoma)
1943, US, 102 mins, b/w
Dir: Albert S Rogell
Stars: John Wayne, Martha Scott, Albert Dekker
Rating: ★★

The wildcats of the title are oil-drilling pioneers, with John Wayne and Albert Dekker as rivals in the oilfields of old Oklahoma. Songthrush Dale Evans, soon to marry cowboy star Roy Rogers and appear exclusively in his films, plays a character called Cuddles and gets to sing 'Put Your Arms Around Me, Honey'. Red-headed glamour star Rhonda Fleming is supposed to have made her debut in this film, but little if any of her role seems to have been left in the finished version. Lots of vigour, little subtlety.

War of the Worlds, The ◐ ⓥ
1953, US, 85 mins, colour
Dir: Byron Haskin
Stars: Gene Barry, Ann Robinson
Rating: ★★★

W

This film version of H G Wells' science fiction classic won an Academy Award for its special effects, and was justly acclaimed by the critics. The imaginative treatment by producer George Pal and director Byron Haskin does full justice to Wells' nightmare vision of an inter-planetary war, and is full of telling little touches. If you are struggling to recognise the voice of the narrator – it belongs to Cedric Hardwicke.

Warpath ○
1951, US, 95 mins, colour
Dir: Byron Haskin
Stars: Edmond O'Brien, Dean Jagger, Forrest Tucker
Rating: ★★

A rousing Western on the revenge theme. The opening reel is, in fact, reminiscent of another Western, *Rancho Notorious*: the hero's fiancée is murdered by outlaws and he sets out to hunt them down. Edmond O'Brien is just fine in the central role, and there's lots of action against the Indians, after O'Brien joins the Cavalry in pursuit of his prey. Ray Rennahan's Technicolor photography paints an attractive background to the drama.

Warriors, The
See: *Dark Avenger*

War Wagon, The ○
1967, US, 101 mins, colour
Dir: Burt Kennedy
Stars: John Wayne, Kirk Douglas
Rating: ★★★

Here come John Wayne and Kirk Douglas as the fastest guns in the territory in a Western that sits well with such other big hits of the Sixties for Wayne as *The Comancheros* and *El Dorado*. Douglas is hired to kill Wayne but you know he won't and soon the two are happily in harness against the hired guns. 'Mine hit the ground first!' claims Douglas as two of their enemies bite the dust. 'Huh,' grunts Wayne. 'Mine was taller.' Add Howard Keel, bizarrely cast as a renegade Redskin who calls his brethren 'dumb Indians' and a succulent cast of villains that includes Bruce Cabot, Bruce Dern and Gene Evans and you have a Western with humour that director Burt Kennedy keeps solidly and comfortably in the best traditions.

War Zone ● ⓥ
1988, West Germany/Israel, 100 mins, colour
Dir: Nathaniel Gutman

Stars: Christopher Walken, Hywel Bennett
Rating: ★★★

War-torn cities infested with rival factions have always been popular locations for movie-makers and Beirut in the late 1980s was an obvious candidate. Taking advantage of its setting, this is quite a good little movie, full of the sense of imminent danger that must have the words 'Don't shoot!' leaping into the mouths of foreign journalists at the appearance of anything that looks like a uniform. Christopher Walken contributes a thoughtful performance as the opportunistic American journalist dragged from the fireside comfort of 'reporting' with the help of old cassettes to a real-life interview with a Palestinian leader who wants to advocate diplomacy instead of violence. Or, is he being made a gullible dupe? In the end, Walken's Steven, forced by circumstance to become a real reporter, is as bewildered as he is involved. As an English reporter (Hywel Bennett) tells him: 'Here you don't kill who you want. You kill who you can.'

Watch It, Sailor! ○
1961, UK, 81 mins, b/w
Dir: Wolf Rilla
Stars: Dennis Price, Liz Fraser, Irene Handl, Frankie Howerd
Rating: ★★

Broad comedy about the world's most fearsome mother-in-law – no, not Peggy Mount but that similarly formidable lady, Marjorie Rhodes. John Meillon, now a distinguished and frequent performer in Australian films, is the lad who has to put up with Ma Rhodes if he wants to marry pretty Vera Day.

Watch Your Stern ○
1960, UK, 100 mins, b/w
Dir: Gerald Thomas
Stars: Kenneth Connor, Joan Sims
Rating: ★★

A broad but fairly rollicking British comedy produced by the *Carry On* team. Kenneth Connor stars as an Ordinary Seaman who is called upon to impersonate a scientist, summoned to help correct a top secret torpedo called The Creeper which has a disconcerting habit of returning to base when fired. Hectically involved are such other *Carry On* stalwarts as Sid James, Hattie Jacques and Joan Sims.

Water ◐
1985, UK, 95 mins, colour
Dir: Dick Clement
Stars: Michael Caine, Valerie Perrine, Brenda Vacarro, Leonard Rossiter, Billy Connolly, Maureen Lipman
Rating: ★★★

Although it has its share of embarrassing moments when things go over the top, this throwback to Ealing comedies (with some dialogue Michael Balcon would never have condoned) has more funny lines than most British comedies of the previous decade put together. The setting is Cascara, a very small British island in the Caribbean (its features include Desolation Bay, Point Peril and Calamity Cove and it has no beaches) where the local industry is largely confined to the governor's (Michael Caine) cultivation of marijuana. The British government, led by Leonard Rossiter as a ministerial buffoon under the lash of a superb impersonation of Margaret Thatcher by Maureen Lipman, decides to evacuate Cascara and turn it into the rubbish-tip of the Empire. Meanwhile an oil company has struck mineral water, exciting the local rebels led by Billy Connolly wielding a guitar. All it lacks are Basil Radford and Naunton Wayne as the local drunks and cricket fans, but it does have Fulton Mackay as a wavering whisky priest who appears to have sired half the local population in 'moments of weakness'. Pretty dotty all round, but with some very good one-liners, including a scandalous put-down of Mahatma Gandhi by Lipman's Thatcher.

Water Babies, The ☉
1978, UK, 92 mins, colour
Dir: Lionel Jeffries
Stars: James Mason, Billie Whitelaw, Tommy Pender
Rating: ★★

Not as successful as *The Railway Children*, which was actor Lionel Jeffries' first stab at directing, this charming story is part-animated. The Polish animation is not particularly inspired but the performances of James Mason, Bernard Cribbins and Billie Whitelaw are some compensation. Young children will be entertained but anyone over eight years may be less than gripped.

Waterdance, The ● ⓥ
1991, US, 106 mins, colour
Dir: Neal Jimenez, Michael Steinberg

Stars: Eric Stoltz, Wesley Snipes, Helen Hunt, William Forsythe, Elizabeth Peña
Rating: ★★

'Good thing we're already paralysed,' gasps one of the escaping paraplegics, as they break out of their 'rehab' hospital in an ambulance, and narrowly avoid an accident. Reaching their destination, a strip club, who should they encounter but their charge nurse, whom they gently blackmail into funding the evening. The film could do with even more of this black humour, as it follows the forging friendships and sexual problems of the rather deliberately disparate residents of one particular ward. Eric Stoltz, portraying wheelchaired writer-director Neal Jimenez's alter ego (the film is partially autobiographical) isn't the strongest of leads, and one grows rather tired of him, but there are compensations in Helen Hunt, as his confused (and married) girlfriend, Wesley Snipes as the black philanderer whose wife refuses to stand by him and William Forsythe as the biker whose aggression hides a desire for macho friendship with his fellows. On the whole, a worthy addition to the cinema's studies of the disabled and their attempts to come to terms with what life now holds.

Waterland ● ⓥ
1992, UK, 93 mins, colour
Dir: Stephen Gyllenhaal
Stars: Jeremy Irons, Sinead Cusack, Ethan Hawke, John Heard, Grant Warnock
Rating: ★

A sad tale in more ways than one. This picturesquely-set nostalgia piece is tedious when it should be poignant and, though it has some original ideas, doesn't weld them together in such a way as to glue us to its story. Jeremy Irons play a professor of history with a wife whose mind is cracking under the strain of the memories of their collective past. As bored as his American pupils with the routine of the classroom, Irons begins telling them about his own past life in the East Anglian fenlands of England. Unfortunately, this is almost entirely concerned with sex and incest and has so little story content that it would surely send most American schoolchildren to sleep.

Waterloo ○ ⓥ
1970, Italy/Russia, 132 mins, colour
Dir: Sergei Bondarchuk

Stars: Rod Steiger, Christopher Plummer, Orson Welles, Virginia McKenna, Jack Hawkins
Rating: ★★

An enormously expensive epic, culminating in an hour-long battle scene. Unexpectedly, it's Christopher Plummer's Wellington who steals the attention and the acting honours, from Rod Steiger's Napoleon, the one an understatement in suavity and wit, always cool and collected, the other all exaggeration, never stating anything simply where a whisper or a shout will do.

Watership Down ○ ⓥ
1978, UK, 92 mins, colour
Dir: Martin Rosen
Voice stars: John Hunt, Richard Briers, Ralph Richardson, Zero Mostel, Roy Kinnear, Denholm Elliott
Rating: ★★★

Red in tooth and claw (but not unsuitable for family viewing) this is an appropriately dark adaptation of Richard Adams' novel about an itinerant rabbit colony, tailored to the talents of an impressive voice cast whose characters tend to take on the identities of such familiar actors as John Hunt, Richard Briers, Ralph Richardson and Zero Mostel, whose seagull proves the liveliest character in the film. Older kids may get restless in the dull bits, but the action towards the end is genuinely nail-biting stuff and the animation of the rabbits amazing in its accuracy.

Watusi ○
1958, US, 85 mins, colour
Dir: Kurt Neumann
Stars: George Montgomery, David Farra
Rating: ★★

MGM go back to their old hunting grounds in this sequel to *King Solomon's Mines* but don't quite strike the same riches. George Montgomery, David Farra and Taina Elg see the thrills along in fair enough fashion, but some of the dialogue seems a little tarnished and the stampede of wild animals had already begun to outlive its function as a useful plot element. Against this, James Clavell's screenplay rightly brooks no interruption from side issues and Harold E Wellman's lush Technicolor photography is well above average for jungle melodrama.

Wayne's World ○ ⓥ
1992, US, 95 mins, colour
Dir: Penelope Spheeris

Stars: Mike Myers, Dana Carvey, Rob Lowe, Tia Carrere
Rating: ★★★

Or: Wayne and Garth's Excellent Adventures. The shades of *Bill and Ted* ride again in this endearingly silly tale of two all-American goofballs who broadcast a weekly cable TV show from the basement of a private house. Major networks reach out for them in the shape of all-American slimebag Rob Lowe, but – surprise, dudes! – Wayne and Garth not only refuse to conform, but even tack their own ending on the film when it looks as though Lowe is going to snatch Wayne's singer girlfriend (Tia Carrere). Carrere is a stunning-looking Eurasian girl who can really sing and darned nearly steals this idiot's delight of a show. The fun could have been more sustained, but party-on-ers will find it quite excellent anyway.

Wayne's World 2 ○ ⓥ
1993, US, 95 mins, colour
Dir: Stephen Surjik
Stars: Mike Myers, Dana Carvey, Tia Carrere, Christopher Walken
Rating: ★★

Partied out, guys: *Wayne's World 2* has little of the freshness which made the original so endearingly amusing, and only one really funny scene – when Wayne and his friends break into an impromptu version of 'YMCA' when trapped in a gay club by bad guy Christopher Walken. Mike Myers mugs madly as Wayne. Dana Carvey's Garth comes on as a wizened Norman Wisdom and is forced to act out a coy sex comedy with Kim Basinger in scenes which embarrass both of them. Spotting guest stars like Basinger, Drew Barrymore and Charlton Heston is, though, more fun than most of the script, which involves Wayne trying to organise a vast pop concert called Waynestock in which everyone proves supremely disinterested. It's all harmless fun but here's a cult that's definitely on the Wayne.

Way Out West ☉ ⓥ
1937, US, 65 mins, b/w
Dir: James Horne
Stars: Stan Laurel, Oliver Hardy
Rating: ★★★★

Laurel and Hardy classic that is probably most people's favourite. Stan and Ollie go to Brushwood Gulch to deliver the deed to a gold mine, do the most famous of their dances, sing

W

'Trail of the Lonesome Pine' and have riotous encounters with a mudhole, Jimmy Finlayson and a mule, in that order. Packed with comic gems and splendidly idiotic Laurel one-liners. 'What did he die of?' he's asked. 'I think he died of a Tuesday,' says Stan.

Way to the Stars, The ○
(aka: Johnny in the Clouds)
1945, UK, 109 mins, b/w
Dir: Anthony Asquith
Stars: Michael Redgrave, John Mills, Rosamund John
Rating: ★★★★

Crafted with typical British understatement, and exquisitely structured, this is one of the greatest war films from any country. As well as a string of fine performances from such familiar names as Michael Redgrave, Trevor Howard and John Mills, and a sensitive one from the American Douglass Montgomery (whose film career was over before the decade was out), the film contains early appearances by Jean Simmons and Bill Owen (here billed under his real name, Bill Rowbotham). Anthony Asquith's direction is inspired, and the story is greatly enhanced by the poetry of John Pudney and the uplifting music by Nicholas Brodzsky.

Way West, The ○
1967, US, 122 mins, colour
Dir: Andrew V McLaglen
Stars: Kirk Douglas, Robert Mitchum, Richard Widmark
Rating: ★★

Epic Western about a wagon train of pioneers bound from Missouri to Oregon. Robert Mitchum plays Dick, the taciturn scout who leads them over hazard after hazard, including one massive cliff. 'D'you think we could maybe go round, Dick?' asks one of the emigrants. They don't of course, which results in some breathtaking excitement. Good performances by the trio of masculine stars are supplemented by those of leading lady Lola Albright and well-known featured players including William Lundigan, Jack Elam and Harry Carey Jr. Adding lustre is the breathtaking sweep of William Clothier's glorious colour photography.

Way We Were, The ○ ⓥ
1973, US, 118 mins, colour
Dir: Sydney Pollack

Stars: Barbra Streisand, Robert Redford, Bradford Dillman, Viveca Lindfors
Rating: ★★

This superstar tearjerker chronicles the romance – from the late Thirties to the early Fifties – between two irreconcilable opposites. She is Barbra Streisand, outspoken, aggressive Jewish activist; he is Robert Redford, the all-American, golden haired college boy who becomes a successful novelist and then goes to Hollywood as a screenwriter. The movie equivalent of a good read, it's fascinating to see how expertly director Sydney Pollack succeeds in making the stars' very different acting styles – Streisand's vigour and Redford's shallow reliance on his good looks – work so well together. The title song took one of the film's two Oscars.

Web, The ○
1947, US, 87 mins, b/w
Dir: Michael Gordon
Stars: Edmond O'Brien, William Bendix, Vincent Price
Rating: ★★★

Typical *film noir* of the post-war years, more shadow and style than substance, but given strength by the powerful ensemble playing of a personable cast. Edmond O'Brien, Vincent Price, Ella Raines and William Bendix have the leads. But shifty John Abbott and dependable Fritz Leiber also enjoy two of their juiciest roles. It's thanks to the personalities involved that this is a satisfying thriller.

Wedding Bells
See: Royal Wedding

Wedding Breakfast, The
See: The Catered Affair

We Dive at Dawn ○ ⓥ
1943, UK, 92 mins, b/w
Dir: Anthony Asquith
Stars: Eric Portman, John Mills
Rating: ★★★

Not quite so well-known as some classic British war films, this is a clever and claustrophobic study in mounting excitement, focusing first on the shore-leave lives of the crew of a submarine, then on their secret mission to torpedo a Nazi battleship before she can reach the Kiel Canal. John Mills and Eric Portman are excellent (years later they would co-star in another war classic, *The Colditz Story*) and the original script was re-tailored (very tightly) by Frank

Launder. Launder remembered in more recent times that the Royal Navy had decided the screenplay 'lacked authenticity' and he found himself despatched to a submarine base to gather first-hand knowledge. Here Launder was lucky enough to meet a submarine officer with writing talent, who wrote a rough draft of the final attack sequence 'most authentically with a lot of human touches'. In the end, neither Launder nor the officer received official screen credit!

Weekend at Bernie's ◑ ⓥ
1989, US, 97 mins, colour
Dir: Ted Kotcheff
Stars: Andrew McCarthy, Jonathan Silverman, Catherine Mary Stewart
Rating: ★★★

It's party time at Bernie's beach house, but the host is late. Murdered that is. But the world refuses to admit that Bernie has passed away, and life goes on as before. Naturally his first guests (Andrew McCarthy, Jonathan Silverman) should report the corpse to the cops, but when they cop a look at Bernie's weekend lifestyle, they decide to delay matters just a wee while. The problem is that, in creating the impression that Bernie's alive, they fool the departing killer (a sort of demented Ken Dodd) as well. All this makes for a jolly, occasionally over-energetic jape with some fast and furious fun towards the end, and a staggering performance as Bernie by Terry Kiser who, through thick and thin, never bats an eyelid. They should strike a special Oscar for best supporting stiff. A disappointing sequel followed in 1994.

Weekend with Lulu, A ○
1961, UK, 91 mins, b/w
Dir: John Paddy Carstairs
Stars: Bob Monkhouse, Leslie Phillips, Shirley Eaton, Alfred Marks
Rating: ★★

Bob Monkhouse, Leslie Phillips and Alfred Marks mug furiously in the cause of comic entertainment in this breezy farce spiced with salty wisecracks and additionally decorated with such members of the *Carry On* team as Kenneth Connor and Sidney James. Irene Handl is wonderful as the interfering busybody who accompanies her daughter (Shirley Eaton) on what was supposed to be a romantic weekend, and then-popular Russ Conway pops up as a French pianist.

Weird Science ◐ ⓥ

1985, US, 94 mins, colour
Dir: John Hughes
Stars: Kelly LeBrock, Anthony Michael Hall, Ilan Mitchell-Smith, Robert Downey Jr, Bill Paxton
Rating: ★

Two high school no-hopers are unable to attract girls, so they decide to create one, with the help of a home computer, a Barbie doll and a fistful of centrefolds. What they end up with is Kelly LeBrock. Not bad for two physically unattractive and intellectually underdeveloped 15-year-olds. As is usual with such high-school high jinks, they then go on a series of adventures which involve getting drunk, driving fast cars and having wild and destructive parties. They also chase girls, despite having the sultry LeBrock in tow. Throw in some mutant bikers and LeBrock's unexplained magical powers and you end up with a confusing hotch-potch of asinine American schoolboy sex humour. Kelly LeBrock and her incongruous English accent (also unexplained) is the only reason for watching this.

Welcome to Hard Times ◐

(aka: Killer on a Horse)
1966, US, 105 mins, colour
Dir: Burt Kennedy
Stars: Henry Fonda, Janice Rule, Keenan Wynn, Janis Page
Rating: ★★

Welcome indeed to this fascinating mixture of the psychological, symbol-laden Western and the basic cowboy action yarn. Henry Fonda (aged 62) is exactly right as a leading citizen of the rundown town of Hard Times who at first doesn't stand up to crazed gunman Aldo Ray (wonderfully wicked). Written and directed by Burt Kennedy from a novel by E L Doctorow (author of *Ragtime*). And just look at that support cast: Warren Oates, Edgar Buchanan, Lon Chaney, Elisha Cook).

Welcome To L. A. ●

1976, US, 106 mins, colour
Dir: Alan Rudolph
Stars: Keith Carradine, Sally Kellerman, Geraldine Chaplin, Harvey Keitel
Rating: ★★

A cinema curiosity made by Alan Rudolph, a disciple of Robert Altman. It turns out to be a kind of tragi-comic *La Ronde*, set against the free-living music business of Los Angeles. Keith

Carradine has the central role of the composer back in L A for the recording of a pop cantata he has composed. Despite (or perhaps because of) a goatee beard and a deerstalker hat, he hardly displays the charisma one would have thought necessary to attract such personable ladies as Sally Kellerman, Sissy Spacek, Geraldine Chaplin, Diahann Abbott, Viveca Lindfors and Lauren Hutton into his bed.

Went the Day Well ○

(aka: 48 Hours)
1942, UK, 92 mins, b/w
Dir: Alberto Cavalcanti
Stars: Leslie Banks, Basil Sydney, Frank Lawton, Elizabeth Allan
Rating: ★★★

Intriguing Ealing Studios wartime film, somewhat akin to the later *It Happened Here*. The theme – not surprisingly the subject of a few outcries in its time – was the infiltration of an English village by a group of Nazis. Thora Hird plays a land-girl and briefly glimpsed is her real-life toddler daughter – Janette Scott.

We're No Angels ○

1954, US, 106 mins, colour
Dir: Michael Curtiz
Stars: Humphrey Bogart, Aldo Ray, Peter Ustinov, Joan Bennett
Rating: ★★★

A really exquisite comedy which gives Humphrey Bogart a rare chance to lean to the lighter side, as one of three French convicts on the run from Devil's Island, who choose to sort out the problems of some friends in their own way. Most of the screenplay's gems go to Peter Ustinov, as a roly-poly convict who pretends to be strait-laced but covets secret memories of the fleshpots of Marseilles. There's also a pearl of a performance from Basil Rathbone as the ruthless cousin of the nice family with whom the jailbirds are hiding.

We're No Angels ◐ ⓥ

1989, US, 106 mins, colour
Dir: Neil Jordan
Stars: Robert De Niro, Sean Penn, Demi Moore, Hoyt Axton, Bruno Kirby, Ray McAnally
Rating: ★★

Based – but only in theme – on the Bogart film of 1954, this romp gives Robert De Niro and Sean Penn a chance to play for laughs as two (unwillingly) escaped convicts in 1935

who, in the course of attempting to flee to Canada, disguise themselves as priests and gradually become involved in affairs at the Sanctuary of the Weeping Virgin. De Niro mugs ferociously in his worst film performance to date, but Penn is better and Demi Moore excellent as a rough-tongued single mum. The film itself is not too bad when not straining for laughs, though the violence at the beginning is a bit excessive for a comedy. The last 20 minutes, though, do score with a good blend of laughs, sentiment and thrills, and show the virtue of playing comedy straight, as opposed to the strenuous facial contortions employed by De Niro and Penn for much of the film.

Werewolf of London ◐

1935, US, 75 mins, b/w
Dir: Stuart Walker
Stars: Henry Hull, Valerie Hobson, Warner Oland
Rating: ★★★

The first Hollywood film centred totally round the idea of a man who became a werewolf at the time of the full moon, this predated the famous wolf man series by six years. Although the first transmogrification of man into werewolf is achieved by having the character pass behind a series of heavy pillars, the acting by Henry Hull fills one with sympathy for the plight of the good doctor afflicted with the curse of the werewolf. The photography, especially in the moonlit sequences, is reminiscent of the best of the great pre-war German films, and altogether this little-known horror film is one to catch if you can.

Westbound ○

1959, US, 72 mins, colour
Dir: Budd Boetticher
Stars: Randolph Scott, Virginia Mayo
Rating: ★★

Director Budd Boetticher has a rather overinflated cult reputation, but his Westerns with Randolph Scott were always better than their second-feature status. This is one of the best of the bunch, pacy and attractively photographed by J Peverell Marley and with a commanding performance by the star as a Northern captain trying to keep gold deliveries running by stage from California during the Civil War. Look out for Australian actor Michael Pate, who, after a sturdy career in Hollywood, often playing

Indians, returned Down Under to become a surprisingly good producer and director.

Westerner, The ○
1940, US, 100 mins, b/w
Dir: William Wyler
Stars: Gary Cooper, Walter Brennan, Doris Davenport
Rating: ★★★

This outdoor epic about a range war gave Gary Cooper one of the best of his strong, laconic roles as the drifter caught between opposing factions. A shrewd piece of villainy as Judge Roy Bean brought Walter Brennan's total of 'best supporting actor' Oscars up to three.

West of Zanzibar ○
1954, UK, 94 mins, colour
Dir: Harry Watt
Stars: Anthony Steel, Sheila Sim
Rating: ★★

Sequel to the 1951 Royal Film Performance movie *Where No Vultures Fly*, retaining the same director and producer, Harry Watts and Leslie Norman, and having Anthony Steel once again as the game warden Bob Payton. He shares the Hollywood hero's ability to come through the most vicious fight with no more than a spotless handkerchief tied around one bulging bicep.

West Point Story, The ○
1950, US, 107 mins, b/w
Dir: Roy Del Ruth
Stars: James Cagney, Virginia Mayo, Gordon MacRae, Doris Day
Rating: ★★

Bright, breezy backstage musical which gave James Cagney his first song-and-dance role since his great success in *Yankee Doodle Dandy*. The plot is the old stand-by about the two partners who come together again. But a star-studded cast, including Doris Day in one of her very early musical roles, does it more than justice. The director is Roy Del Ruth, former Sennett gag writer, who cut his teeth on such Thirties musicals as *Kid Millions*, *Broadway Melody of 1936* and *On the Avenue*.

West Side Story ○ ⊙
1961, US, 151 mins, colour
Dir: Robert Wise, Jerome Robbins
Stars: Natalie Wood, Richard Beymer, George Chakiris, Rita Moreno, Russ Tamblyn
Rating: ★★★★

The dazzling and devastating dancing set new standards for the film musical in this wildly successful transition of Leonard Bernstein's stage musical to the screen. George Chakiris and Rita Moreno were never sharper and their performances won them two of the film's 10 Oscars, which also included best film and best director for Robert Wise. As the star-crossed lovers, Natalie Wood and Richard Beymer do touching work in this New York ghetto update of *Romeo and Juliet*, even if their singing voices belonged to other people. And the tragic finale will leave few eyes dry: such emotive moments in musicals are rare indeed. Prepare to be both moved and exhilarated.

Westward Ho, the Wagons ○
1956, US, 90 mins, colour
Dir: William Beaudine
Stars: Fess Parker, Kathleen Crowley, Jeff York
Rating: ★★

This lightweight Western looks great, thanks to impressive Technicolor photography, but generates very little tension and excitement. Fess (*Davy Crockett*) Parker is our firm-jawed hero but this Walt Disney view of the West is sanitised even by the standards of the 1950s. Doc Grayson (Parker) is a scout helping a wagon train on its way to Oregon which meets both hostile and friendly Indians en route. As far as plot goes, that's about it really, which means there isn't enough adventure to keep you interested. Even the well staged action scenes, created by second-unit director Yakima Canutt, aren't enough to lift this bland pioneer saga.

Westward Passage ○
1932, US, 73 mins, b/w
Dir: Robert Milton
Stars: Ann Harding, Laurence Olivier
Rating: ★★

A lightweight romance with Ann Harding and Laurence Olivier as the two young lovebirds. Olivier is a poverty-stricken, struggling author, but his love for Harding sustains him through the hard times. They marry, have a child and get on with life. But as time goes by, his patience wears thin and the marriage breaks up. Harding marries again on the rebound . . . but that's not the last twist in a story that, although prone to be overly theatrical at times, does manage to engage and entertain the whole way through.

Westward the Women ○
1951, US, 118 mins, b/w
Dir: William Wellman
Stars: Robert Taylor, Denise Darcel, Henry Nakamura
Rating: ★★★

This story of 140 women bound for California through Indian country is vintage MGM action. And they had the ideal director in William Wellman, a devoted chronicler of the west who already had two classic Westerns, *The Ox-Bow Incident*, from 1942, and *Yellow Sky*, from 1948, to his name.

Westworld ○ ⊙
1973, US, 89 mins, colour
Dir: Michael Crichton
Stars: Yul Brynner, Richard Benjamin, James Brolin
Rating: ★★★

Director Michael (*Jurassic Park*) Crichton's sci-fi thriller about robots in a futuristic theme park running out of control comes across as suprisingly fresh considering the basic idea of the tale wasn't new even then. The robot-turning-on-its-master theme goes right back to Fritz Lang's *Metropolis*. With *Westworld*, though, Crichton has created an entirely believable scenario which makes the whole thing pretty frightening. Yul Brynner is chilling as the android gunslinger who can't be gunned down and who inexorably pursues resort guests Richard Benjamin and James Brolin. Fast-moving and exciting – and you get the feeling that it all so easily could happen.

Wetherby ●
1985, UK, 97 mins, colour
Dir: David Hare
Stars: Vanessa Redgrave, Ian Holm, Judi Dench
Rating: ★

What really happened in a Yorkshire town to cause a young man to blow his brains out? Director David Hare's screenplay will certainly keep you guessing; its elliptical dialogue has the characters uttering disconnected phrases like unrelated sections of a Pinter play. There's a touching performance by Joely Richardson, daughter of the film's star, Vanessa Redgrave.

Whales of August, The ○ ⊙
1987, US, 90 mins, colour
Dir: Lindsay Anderson

Stars: Bette Davis, Lillian Gish, Vincent Price
Rating: ★★★★

A fitting tribute to Lillian Gish, this is a little gem about two elderly sisters living on an island off the coast of New England. Not only is Lindsay Anderson to be congratulated on directing his best film in quite a while, but in achieving the almost impossible in getting legends Gish and Bette Davis to play the sisters. Gish edges out her rival by a whisker with her intuitive warmth, but that isn't to say Davis doesn't have some striking, subtle and emotive moments. Also good are Ann Sothern, as the well-meaning lifelong friend of the sisters and Vincent Price as the Russian emigré who tries to batten on to the sisters before confessing that 'I have spent my life visiting friends.' Full of poignant moments, the film has an ending that is certain to have you on the verge of tears. Gish is simply a marvel, Davis as cantankerously indomitable as ever. Together, they carve out a memorable movie memorial in roles for once worthy of their own greatness.

What About Bob? ○ ⓥ
1991, US, 99 mins, colour
Dir: Frank Oz
Stars: Bill Murray, Richard Dreyfuss, Julie Hagerty, Charlie Korsmo
Rating: ★★★

This is the one about the psychiatric patient who proves so persistent that he finally drives the psychiatrist mad. Bob (Bill Murray) is a walking nightmare who has a phobia about touching things and going places, and thinks his bladder is about to explode. Leo (Richard Dreyfuss) is a shrink wallowing in self-control, self-satisfaction and self-glory who sees all three gradually disintegrate when Bob pursues him to his holiday home by a New Hampshire lake. The trouble with Bob is not that he's dangerous, just that he won't go away. The habits that Leo finds so annoying perversely only endear Bob to others, including Leo's family, especially when he 'rescues' (actually destroys) Leo in a TV interview about the shrink's new book. Delightfully manic performances from Murray and Dreyfuss help us forget that this is little more than an anecdote, and keep us happily chuckling towards the climax, and Leo's last desperate attempt to send Bob where he feels he belongs – eternity.

What a Carve-Up! ○
(aka: Home Sweet Homicide)
1961, UK, 88 mins, b/w
Dir: Pat Jackson
Stars: Kenneth Connor, Sidney James
Rating: ★★★

Although it begins and ends weakly, this comedy-chiller is great fun as long as it's going at full throttle, which is most of the time once Kenneth Connor and Sidney James have arrived at spooky Blackshaw Towers for the reading of Connor's uncle's will. Supposedly based on *The Ghoul* (filmed straight in the Thirties with Boris Karloff), but owing more to another Karloff starrer, *The Old Dark House*, this is fast and furious fun, thanks to Pat Jackson's inventive direction and the straight-faced playing of a supporting cast that includes Shirley Eaton, Dennis Price, Michael Gough and Donald Pleasence. Any subtlety in British comedy in the early Sixties was as unexpected as it was welcome.

What a Man!
See: Never Give a Sucker an Even Break

What a Way to Go! ○
1964, US, 145 mins, colour
Dir: J Lee-Thompson
Stars: Shirley MacLaine, Paul Newman, Dean Martin, Robert Mitchum
Rating: ★★

Shirley MacLaine stars in this frivolity as Louisa, an unwittingly lethal lady. Much of the fun in this colourful, star-studded romp lies in waiting to see how Louisa's various husbands meet their doom. Funniest of all is probably Gene Kelly, as a dancer who gets trampled to death by his own fans. There's also Dean Martin, Robert Mitchum, Bob Cummings, Dick Van Dyke and Reginald Gardiner to watch for, not to mention the Marx Brothers' great foil Margaret Dumont.

What Ever Happened to Baby Jane? ① ⓥ
1962, US, 132 mins, b/w
Dir: Robert Aldrich
Stars: Bette Davis, Joan Crawford
Rating: ★★★

Robert Aldrich's classic of the chilly grotesque, with Bette Davis and Joan Crawford a convincingly gruesome twosome as ex-silent stars living together – and hating each other – in a gloomy mansion.

What Price Glory? ○ ⓥ
1952, US, 111 mins, colour
Dir: John Ford
Stars: James Cagney, Dan Dailey
Rating: ★★

John Ford's remake of the raucous army comedy about a feuding officer and sergeant, previously filmed by Victor McLaglen and Edmund Lowe (who made a whole series out of it) but here with James Cagney and Dan Dailey. The honours are quietly sneaked from them, though, by Robert Wagner and Marisa Pavan as young lovers.

What's Eating Gilbert Grape ① ⓥ
1993, US, 117 mins, colour
Dir: Lasse Hallstrom
Stars: Johnny Depp, Juliette Lewis, Leonardo Di Caprio, Mary Steenburgen, Kevin Tighe
Rating: ★★

Johnny Depp continues to make the oddest films. Hollywood's Mr Solemn followed *Edward Scissorhands* and *Benny & Joon* with this sweet-natured but rather slow goofball of a film that casts him as the senior son in a decidedly different rural household. Father hanged himself and mother has ballooned to 35 stone. There are two sisters but it's Gilbert (Depp) who's responsible for the safe keeping of his 17-year-old mentally handicapped brother Arnie (a miraculous performance by Leonardo Di Caprio that was Oscar nominated). Gilbert is also having an affair with a housewife (Mary Steenburgen) whose simple-minded husband (Kevin Tighe) wants to sell Gilbert insurance – that is until strange new girl Becky (Juliette Lewis) blows into town in her granny's trailer. Yes, this is odd all right, but so haltingly paced that your attention wanders. Yet its heart's in the right place, and you may remember these characters longer than those from your average mainline movie. Though you may have trouble digesting it all, in fact, there are no sour grapes here.

What's New Pussycat? ①
1965, US, 108 mins, colour
Dir: Clive Donner
Stars: Peter Sellers, Peter O'Toole, Romy Schneider, Woody Allen
Rating: ★★

Definitely the kinkiest comedy of its year, *Pussycat* has a screenplay by Woody Allen that varies from sheer

W

smut to sheer genius and casts Peter O'Toole as a playboy journalist who's irresistible to women – whose clothes come apart at his touch. As he, too, is coming apart at the seams, he consults Peter Sellers – a long-haired Viennese psychiatrist who's more of a couch case than he is. Sellers' trouble is the reverse of O'Toole's, in that he attacks women on sight – and they scream in terror. (Funny? Well, it is the way Sellers plays it.) All, that is, except his mountainous wife. 'Pretty?' he asks her. 'I am prettier than you!' Sellers is highly comical, so is Paula Prentiss when given the chance. Edra Gale does Sellers' Wagner-spouting wife to a hilarious T. Credit Woody Allen with writing funny dialogue for everyone else and leaving himself with a role that proves rather ineffectual.

What's the Matter with Helen? ●
1971, US, 101 mins, colour
Dir: Curtis Harrington
Stars: Debbie Reynolds, Shelley Winters, Dennis Weaver
Rating: ★★★

Another expert chiller from Curtis Harrington, who made *Games* for the cinema, *Killer Bees* for TV, and several other sinister stories. This one, with its echoes of *Whatever Happened to Baby Jane?*, is (very well) set in the Thirties and lavishly photographed in colour by Lucien Ballard. Debbie Reynolds (very good) and Shelley Winters (somewhat over the top) play two middle-aged ladies on the run from their past which, naturally, catches up with them, preying on their sanity as Harrington steers the story skilfully to a bravura climax.

What's Up Doc? ○ ♥
1972, US, 94 mins, colour
Dir: Peter Bogdanovich
Stars: Barbra Streisand, Ryan O'Neal
Rating: ★★★

Director Peter Bogdanovich's tribute to those great screwball comedies of the Thirties is a sort-of remake of the Katharine Hepburn–Cary Grant classic *Bringing Up Baby*. And pretty funny it is, too, with Barbara Streisand doing what she does best – being funny in a loveable, uncomplicated way, and singing too – and some hilarious chase sequences involving split-second timing such as we haven't seen since Mack Sennett's days.

What's Up, Tiger Lily? ○
1966, US, 80 mins, colour
Dir: Senkichi Taniguchi
Stars: Tatsua Mihashi, Mie Hama, Akiko Wakabayashi, Tadeo Nakamuru, Susumu Kurobe, Woody Allen
Rating: ★★

Woody Allen has taken a disastrous Japanese comedy-thriller in the James Bond vein and spoofed it up with dubbed American dialogue that bears no relation to what the oriental actors are saying. Thus fights are punctuated by cries of 'Roman cow!', 'Russian snake!', 'Spartan dog!', 'Spanish fly!' or 'Turkish taffy!' There are a dozen good chuckles here, but one is left with a sneaking suspicion that the original might have been (unintentionally) even funnier.

When a Stranger Calls ● ♥
1979, US, 97 mins, colour
Dir: Fred Walton
Stars: Charles Durning, Carol Kane, Tony Beckley, Rachel Roberts
Rating: ★★

After carefully building up a palpable sense of claustrophobic tension in its lengthy opening sequence, this baby-sitter-in-peril thriller goes somewhat off the rails by concentrating on the psychopath's inconclusive relationships with a psychiatrist and a female barfly. Good to see that valuable character actor Charles Durning centre stage for once, even if his role of a vengeance-driven detective isn't particularly rewarding.

When Dinosaurs Ruled the Earth ◐
1969, UK, 100 mins, colour
Dir: Val Guest
Stars: Victoria Vetri, Robin Hawdon
Rating: ★★

The visual effects are predictably the best things in this prehistoric pot-boiler. The bronzed Victoria Vetri, once better-known under her real name, Angela Dorian, is an excellent physical successor to Raquel Welch, star of Hammer's previous extravaganza *One Million Years BC*. The men behind the monsters include Roger Dicken, who subsequently created those in *The Land That Time Forgot*.

When Eight Bells Toll ○ ♥
1971, UK, 94 mins, colour
Dir: Etienne Perier

Stars: Anthony Hopkins, Jack Hawkins, Robert Morley
Rating: ★★

As usual with Alistair MacLean's thrillers, there are no unnecessary embellishments to this rousing story of bullion robbers off the coast of Scotland. It's just scenery and action and plenty of both. However, there's a good role for Robert Morley, who's in splendid form as an Intelligence boss whose major worry lies in the fact that the chief suspect may be on his club's wine committee. The character of Philip Calvert gives Anthony Hopkins a rare straightforward leading man role.

When Harry Met Sally . . . ◐ ♥
1989, US, 95 mins, colour
Dir: Rob Reiner
Stars: Billy Crystal, Meg Ryan, Carrie Fisher, Bruno Kirby
Rating: ★★★

This offbeat romantic comedy is rather protracted but kept afloat by some very good individual lines. Billy Crystal and Meg Ryan play the couple for whom (at college) it's indifference at first sight. This mutual non-attraction is followed by an on-off 12-year period as friends despite his assertion that 'Men and women can't be merely friends, because sex always gets in the way.' He's right in this case, of course, and we know it too, but Nora Ephron's script makes it worthwhile staying the course to see the maxim proved. Crystal, Ryan, Bruno Kirby and especially Carrie Fisher are all fine, and Ryan's famous 'fake orgasm' scene in a restaurant remains the funniest thing in the film.

When I Fall in Love ●
(aka: Everybody's All American)
1989, US, 127 mins, colour
Dir: Taylor Hackford
Stars: Jessica Lange, Dennis Quaid, Timothy Hutton, John Goodman
Rating: ★

Despite solid (if not great) performances from a good cast, practically everything else is wrong with this down-the-years story of embattlement and disillusionment. Direction, script and treatment (including too-dark camera work) all make the narrative far too fragmentary and never dig below the surface to stir our emotions – or those of the characters. Dennis Quaid is the star footballer whose life and career gradually but surely go down the tubes. He's the best thing in the film, although somewhat mysteriously second-billed below Jessica Lange, who doesn't give much to the role of the blonde cheer-leader who becomes his wife. Quaid's appearance at the end – bloated, thick-limbed and near alcoholic – is brilliant, but, even with his enthusiasm for the role, the storyline never holds your attention for more than a minute or two at a time.

When Knights Were Bold ○
1936, UK, 75 mins, b/w
Dir: Jack Raymond
Stars: Jack Buchanan, Fay Wray, Garry Marsh, Moore Marriott
Rating: ★★

Thirties tomfoolery along the lines of a British *A Yankee at King Arthur's Court* with Jack Buchanan as the man who imagines himself back in the Middle Ages after a suit of armour falls on him. Buchanan is allowed his usual polished tap-dance and warbles a tune or two, and the film is fun to be with, especially when Moore Marriott, as a trombone-playing tramp, is around. Hollywood's Fay Wray is a classy leading lady and there are funny supporting turns by Garry Marsh as a blusterer called Brian, and Kate Cutler and Martita Hunt as the hero's maiden aunts.

When Strangers Marry
See: *Betrayed* [1944]

When the Daltons Rode ○
1940, US, 80 mins, b/w
Dir: George Marshall
Stars: Randolph Scott, Kay Francis, Brian Donlevy, George Bancroft
Rating: ★★★

This was a more straightforward Western for director George Marshall, coming, as it did, hard on the heels of his famous *Destry Rides Again*. More than any other film, it can be said to have set the pattern for the majority of Randolph Scott's later roles. Like most of those latter Scott Westerns this has fast-moving, convincing action and a splendid supporting cast, including Brian Donlevy, Frank Albertson, Broderick Crawford and Andy Devine.

When the Legends Die ○
1972, US, 105 mins, colour
Dir: Stuart Millar
Stars: Richard Widmark, Frederic Forrest
Rating: ★★★

Although it didn't do well at the box-office, director Stuart Millar had the satisfaction of hearing resounding critical applause for his film about a young American Indian in modern times who becomes, in his search for 'the new ways', a great rodeo star. Richard Widmark gives a dominating, unforgettable performance as the ex-rodeo rider, sinking into an alcoholic haze, who becomes the hero's guardian and friend.

When the Whales Came ○ ⓥ
1989, UK, 100 mins, colour
Dir: Clive Rees
Stars: Helen Mirren, David Suchet, Paul Scofield, David Threlfall
Rating: ★★

This prestigious British film is picturesquely set in the Scilly Isles, 1914, and tells of the effect of war on the islanders (they hide driftwood from the authorities, à la *Whisky Galore!*), the growing-up of two friendly children and the expiation of a curse relating to narwhals (horned aquatic mammals). The film's emotive ending works well and the children are charming. Elsewhere, Paul Scofield's old man of the sea is King Lear with weatherbeaten cheeks; Helen Mirren tries hard to look unglamorous as a fisher-wife; and John Hallam's lascivious child-beater might have stepped from the pages of a Scilly *Mallens*. Costumes are carefully ragged and dirty, and the animatronic narwhal is brilliant.

When Time Ran Out . . . ○
1980, US, 121 mins, colour
Dir: James Goldstone
Stars: Paul Newman, Jacqueline Bisset, William Holden, Veronica Hamel, Red Buttons, Ernest Borgnine
Rating: ★

The disaster movie reaches new heights of lunacy (despite a script penned by Oscar-winners Carl Foreman and Stirling Silliphant) in this old pals' reunion from *The Towering Inferno*, as producer Irwin Allen and stars Paul Newman and William Holden from that film face fresh catastrophe. Here, it's crisis time on that volcanic island again – a new towering inferno indeed that produces the biggest bang since Krakatoa exploded east of Java. There's plenty of glamour in the picture – among those fleeing the molten lava are sultry Jacqueline Bisset, Veronica (*Hill Street Blues*) Hamel, and exotic Barbara Carrera.

When Worlds Collide ○
1951, US, 82 mins, colour
Dir: Rudolph Mate
Stars: Richard Derr, Barbara Rush, John Hoyt
Rating: ★★★

Producer George Pal won the second of five Academy Awards for the special effects in this particular piece of science fiction about a planet on a collision course with the Earth. It's also a very exciting film in its own right. It set pretty Barbara Rush up for a long screen career in which she was able to prove herself a capable actress in such films as *Magnificent Obsession* and *Bigger Than Life*.

Where Angels Fear to Tread ⓒ ⓥ
1991, UK, 118 mins, colour
Dir: Charles Sturridge
Stars: Helena Bonham Carter, Rupert Graves, Judy Davis, Helen Mirren
Rating: ★★

Beautifully staged, set and costumed, as destinies flit between England and Italy, this is a typical product of early Nineties, prestige, TV-backed cinema in Britain. Yet another adaptation of the work of E M Forster, it's acted with bare competence by such familiar faces in these period dramas as Helena Bonham Carter, Rupert Graves and Judy Davis, and written with tact and some literacy but no inspiration. The pace is stately for, after all, the piece must run towards the two-hour mark, even though the novella on which it's based is slim indeed. Only Helen Mirren of the cast (and she disappears all too soon) commands our attention in a film which above all lacks any excitement, physical or cerebral.

Where Angels Go . . . Trouble Follows ⊙
1968, US, 95 mins, colour
Dir: James Neilson
Stars: Rosalind Russell, Stella Stevens
Rating: ★★

Well, well, it's television's Sally McMillan, alias Susan Saint James, taking over from Hayley Mills as the chief mischief-maker at St Francis Convent School, in the sequel to *The Trouble with Angels*. Rosalind Russell carries on as the Mother Superior.

Where Does It Hurt? ⓒ
1971, US, 88 mins, colour
Dir: Rod Amateau

W

Stars: Peter Sellers, Jo Ann Pflug, Rick Lenz
Rating: ★

The medical profession takes another torpedo amidships in this rudely irreverent comedy. A treasured memory is of Peter Sellers, as the money-mad, nurse-mad head of the hospital, inspecting the coke machine, which doesn't actually give out coke but vomits the money into his private office. 'A dollar twenty-five,' he muses, looking at the 'take' . . . 'I'll have to put more salt in the water.'

Where Do We Go From Here? ○
1945, US, 77 mins, colour
Dir: Gregory Ratoff
Stars: Fred MacMurray, June Haver, Joan Leslie, Gene Sheldon
Rating: ★★

One of Hollywood's more extraordinary ventures, a piece of wartime escapism in which Fred MacMurray's efforts to get into the army with the help of a genie only result in him visiting various episodes of American history. The score by Kurt Weill and Ira Gershwin includes 'Christopher Columbus' and 'The Nina, the Pinta and the Santa Maria', both of which come from the film's best section – an operatic version of Columbus's adventures. June Haver and Joan Leslie are sweetly decorative; Anthony Quinn looks bewildered as a comic Indian chief.

Where Eagles Dare ○ Ⓥ
1968, US, 158 mins, colour
Dir: Brian G Hutton
Stars: Richard Burton, Clint Eastwood, Mary Ure, Michael Hordern, Patrick Wymark
Rating: ★★★

A great piece of *Boys' Own* derring-do, this World War Two adventure is immensely enjoyable. Its star Richard Burton, after a series of intense roles (*The Spy Who Came in From the Cold, Who's Afraid of Virginia Woolf?, Doctor Faustus, Boom!*) was seeking a starring role in a more 'popular' genre. So producer Elliott Kastner contacted ace thriller writer Alistair MacLean and six weeks later MacLean came up with the screenplay – which he subsequently turned into a novel. MacLean obviously had fun with this one: what with a nasty Nazi enclave in a medieval castle perched high on a mountain (actually the

11th-century Schloss Hohenwerfen in Austria), devious double-agents and all manner of extraordinary exploits. Burton is fine, Clint Eastwood is suitably gritty as his second-in-command, Allied agent Mary Ure remains impeccably groomed, a host of British stalwarts do their bits for their countries and Anton Diffring does what is expected of him. But the real stars are the special effects directed by the legendary stuntman Yakima Canutt, who in 1966 received a special Oscar for 'creating the profession of stuntman as it exists today and for the development of many safety devices used by stuntmen everywhere.' It all looks pretty dangerous all the same!

Where No Vultures Fly ⊙
(aka: Ivory Hunter)
1951, UK, 107 mins, colour
Dir: Harry Watt
Stars: Anthony Steel, Dinah Sheridan, Harold Warrender
Rating: ★★★

A colourful African adventure, full of fights with lions and leopards, chosen for the 1951 Royal Film Performance. As with most such choices, the film took a greater mauling from the critics than any big cat could provide. But the public adored the picture, and turned it into Britain's biggest box-office smash of the year, at the same time establishing Dinah Sheridan and Anthony Steel as major British stars.

Where's Charley? ○
1952, UK, 97 mins, colour
Dir: David Butler
Stars: Ray Bolger, Allyn McLerie, Mary Germaine
Rating: ★★★★

This sunny musical version of *Charley's Aunt* resulted in a tour-de-force for visiting American star Ray Bolger in the title role. Bolger's dazzling dancing, combined with his deceptively casual handling of the tuneful score (which includes 'Once in Love with Amy') makes his performance a joy to watch. And he throws himself into the slap-stick situations with unbridled enthusiasm, creating the most convincing 48-year-old undergraduate ever seen! A word also for Erwin Hillier's Technicolor photography. It is, like Bolger's performance, a treat. Allyn McLerie is delightful as Charley's girl-friend Amy, and the whole thing

makes for relaxing, and sometimes very funny entertainment for the whole family.

Where's Jack? ○
1968, UK, 119 mins, colour
Dir: James Clavell
Stars: Tommy Steele, Stanley Baker
Rating: ★★★

Tommy Steele's first non-musical in a curiously sporadic cinema career. He plays a young lad, forced into a life of crime by an unscrupulous 'thief-taker', who becomes a legend in his own lifetime through his ability to escape from prison, bring off daring thefts and elude the law. Crowd scenes, particularly the one at the climactic hanging, are brilliantly handled by director James Clavell, while John Wilcox's fluorescent colour photography has a quality all its own. Two thoroughly enjoyable supporting performances are contributed by Dudley Foster and Noel Purcell, as scurrilous a pair of rogues as ever stalked the screen.

Where's That Fire? ○
1939, UK, 73 mins, b/w
Dir: Marcel Varnel
Stars: Will Hay, Moore Marriott, Graham Moffatt
Rating: ★★★

This Will Hay comedy is ideal for children as, although not among his best films, it relies more than usual on slapstick for its laughs. Hay's cohorts, whiskery Moore Marriott and tubby, belligerent Graham Moffatt, are on hand to help with the frolics, which are all (just about) under the control of Hay's best director, the French-born Marcel Varnel.

Where There's a Will ⊙
1936, UK, 81 mins, b/w
Dir: William Beaudine
Stars: Will Hay, Hartley Power, Gina Malo, Graham Moffatt
Rating: ★★★

This lesser-known Will Hay comedy treasure, with the star as an incompetent lawyer, was made between *Good Morning, Boys* and *Windbag the Sailor*. The great man is as delightful as ever and there are plenty of complications and misunderstandings, with a policeman's carol party forming part of the wild climactic chase. Famous fat boy Graham Moffatt adds to the fun, playing the office boy.

Where the River Bends ○
(aka: Bend of the River)
1952, US, 90 mins, colour
Dir: Anthony Mann
Stars: James Stewart, Arthur Kennedy, Julia Adams
Rating: ★★★

This excellent Western has top grade written all over it. One of a series made by star James Stewart with director Anthony Mann (*Winchester 73* and *The Man from Laramie* were others), it features stunning Western vistas, fierce fist fights, impressively busy crowd scenes and a show-stealing performance by Arthur Kennedy as the good-bad guy who must be bested in the end. And it provided almost the final step up the ladder to stardom for Rock Hudson, here as a gambler.

Where the Spies Are ○
1965, UK, 113 mins, colour
Dir: Val Guest
Stars: David Niven, Françoise Dorléac, Nigel Davenport
Rating: ★

A spy comedy thriller about Dr Jason Love, the reluctant agent created by novelist James Leasor, on whose novel *Passport to Oblivion* this film was based. Deep in trouble from the word go, Jason fumbles his way through the case: the trail includes a wide-eyed blond, a foiled assassination and a high-flying climax aboard a Soviet plane. Françoise Dorléac, brunette sister of Catherine Deneuve, was headed for a big star career at this time. But two years later, she was killed in a car crash at only 25.

Where Were You When the Lights Went Out? ○
1968, US, 94 mins, colour
Dir: Martin Melcher
Stars: Doris Day, Robert Morse, Terry-Thomas
Rating: ★★★

Manic comedy of the misadventures that befall various people in the famous New York blackout a few years ago. Doris Day guys her own image and displays superb comic timing, especially in a drunk scene. Terry-Thomas and Robert Morse have some splendidly lunatic moments, but no one tops veteran vaudeville comic Ben Blue as a man continually trying to finish a shave.

While the City Sleeps ○ ⊙
1956, US, 100 mins, b/w
Dir: Fritz Lang
Stars: Dana Andrews, Vincent Price, Ida Lupino
Rating: ★★★

With this film, German director Fritz Lang completed 20 memorable years in Hollywood after a distinguished early career in the German cinema that included such classics as *Metropolis*. The film is both a jaded look at the morals of big-city newspapermen and a slick, smooth crime yarn, which has a memorable subway chase climax, and suffers only from having too many characters, which throws meat to a hungry all-star cast but also lends the film a certain disjointedness in its storytelling. Good work from Dana Andrews, Sally Forrest, Thomas Mitchell, Vincent Price and John Barrymore Jr.

Whipsaw ○
1935, US, 83 mins, b/w
Dir: Sam Wood
Stars: Spencer Tracy, Myrna Loy
Rating: ★★★

Crisp romantic crime thriller which gave Myrna Loy just about the last of her screen 'bad girl' roles, unsuspectingly leading G-man Spencer Tracy to the lair of the gang of criminals with whom she's associated. A routine plot but, under the direction of Sam Wood, one of MGM's finest – it thrills, amuses and entertains all the way. The pace is kept up right through to the punchy fade-out.

Whirlpool ○
1949, US, 97 mins, b/w
Dir: Otto Preminger
Stars: Gene Tierney, Richard Conte, Jose Ferrer, Charles Bickford
Rating: ★★★

This tense thriller dates from a time when Otto Preminger was really coming to the fore as a major director. Jose Ferrer delivers a fine portrayal as the evil Korvo in what was his third film. Beautiful Gene Tierney plays the woman who falls foul of Ferrer's Svengaliesque villain.

Whisky Galore! ⊙ ⓥ
(aka: Tight Little Island)
1948, UK, 82 mins, b/w
Dir: Alexander Mackendrick
Stars: Basil Radford, Joan Greenwood, James Robertson Justice
Rating: ★★★★

The Ealing Studios comedy masterpiece that took the world by storm. The joyous story concerns a Hebridean island whose inhabitants confiscate a cargo of whisky which founders on the rocks, and find the most unlikely places to hide it.

Whisperers, The ○
1966, UK, 106 mins, b/w
Dir: Bryan Forbes
Stars: Edith Evans, Eric Portman
Rating: ★★★

One of the few films to study closely the problem of old age, this Bryan Forbes film gained immensely in stature from the performance of Dame Edith Evans, which deservedly won a British Academy Award. She plays old Mrs Ross, whose only friends are the 'whisperers' – the voices that she insists she hears in her dank and dingy old flat. There's good support from Eric Portman as her errant husband, and especially Gerald Sim as a friendly Assistance Board man who tries to help her.

Whispering Ghosts ○
1942, US, 75 mins, b/w
Dir: Alfred Werker
Stars: Milton Berle, Brenda Joyce, John Carradine
Rating: ★★

Popular television comedian Milton Berle played one of his earliest film roles in this comedy-thriller about a menaced heiress and missing diamonds.

Whispering Smith ○
1948, US, 88 mins, colour
Dir: Leslie Fenton
Stars: Alan Ladd, Robert Preston, Brenda Marshall
Rating: ★★★

A blazing railroad Western that provides an ideal companion piece for Alan Ladd's other classic Western, *Shane*. Brilliantly shot in Technicolor by Ray Rennahan, this constantly exciting film has Ladd, Robert Preston and Frank Faylen playing characters loosely based on real-life westerners Joe Lefors, Butch Cassidy and Harvey Logan. Good performances from all three charge the film with emotional tension, creating fine entertainment for Western enthusiasts.

Whispers in the Dark ● ⓥ
1992, US, 102 mins, colour
Dir: Christopher Crowe
Stars: Annabella Sciorra, Alan Alda, Anthony LaPaglia, Jamey Sheridan, Jill Clayburgh, Deborah Unger
Rating: ★★

W

The whispers are the shocking secrets told to psychiatrist Ann Hecker (Annabella Sciorra). And the dark, you might say, is the trouble she gets into when, after she has an affair with a man who turns out to be the lover of one of her patients, the patient is murdered. Plagued by erotic dreams and hounded by a dogged detective (Anthony LaPaglia), Dr Ann runs to her old friend and mentor Alan Alda. But is even he to be trusted? Everyone's a suspect in this intelligently written, strongly cast, *Jagged Edge*-style adult thriller. Unfortunately, Christopher Crowe's direction of it is characteristically sluggish and tends to take the edge off the suspense. Sciorra, LaPaglia and Alda are all spot-on.

Whistle Blower, The ◐ ⓥ
1986, UK, 107 mins, colour
Dir: Simon Langton
Stars: Michael Caine, James Fox, Nigel Havers
Rating: ★★

Skilfully handled but slightly tired British spy thriller full of character stars playing grim-faced government/security types who know that the hero's investigation is doomed to fail. Familiar territory this, since the beginning of John le Carré's popularity as a writer, yet with excellent performances by Michael Caine and Nigel Havers that score by understatement.

Whistle Down the Wind ○ ⓥ
1961, UK, 99 mins, b/w
Dir: Bryan Forbes
Stars: Hayley Mills, Alan Bates, Bernard Lee
Rating: ★★★★

This brilliant, totally convincing British film was the first directed by Bryan Forbes. It's about three young farm-children who find a man on the run in their barn, and believe him to be Jesus Christ. Hayley Mills follows up solidly her success in *Tiger Bay*, and little Alan Barnes is unbelievably good. The last five minutes remain among the most moving ever seen.

Whistling in Brooklyn ○
1943, US, 87 mins, b/w
Dir: S Sylvan Simon
Stars: Red Skelton, Ann Rutherford, Jean Rogers
Rating: ★★

The third in the series of scatter-brained comedies featuring Red Skelton as the radio sleuth 'The Fox'

who turns to jelly when confronted by a real mystery. The character is clearly inspired by those that made Bob Hope a star, but nonetheless effective. Co-star Ann Rutherford and director S Sylvan Simon carry on from the first two films.

Whistling in Dixie ○
1942, US, 74 mins, b/w
Dir: S Sylvan Simon
Stars: Red Skelton, Ann Rutherford
Rating: ★★

This fairly bright comedy is one of three wartime MGM capers revolving round the adventures of a radio 'detective' called 'The Fox', embodied by the rubber-faced Red Skelton, who finds himself mixed up in real-life crime capers. Here he's in deep trouble in the Deep South.

Whistling in the Dark ○
1941, US, 77 mins, b/w
Dir: S Sylvan Simon
Stars: Red Skelton, Conrad Veidt, Ann Rutherford
Rating: ★★

Red Skelton – here in his first starring role – was compared by contemporary critics with Bob Hope, which was not too surprising since MGM had provided him with a plot for this lively comedy-thriller very much in the vein of Hope's *The Cat and the Canary*, complete with a creepy mansion replete with sliding panels and hidden passages. The film was the first of Skelton's three outings as radio criminologist 'The Fox' (*Whistling in Dixie* and *Whistling in Brooklyn* followed in 1942 and 1943) and packs in plenty of good gags under S Sylvan Simon's brisk direction.

White Cargo ○
1942, US, 90 mins, b/w
Dir: Richard Thorpe
Stars: Hedy Lamarr, Walter Pidgeon, Frank Morgan
Rating: ★★

First made as an early British sound film, this Hollywood version of a hoary old classic, which silent vamps would surely have given their eye teeth to star in, features a suitably tall and taciturn Walter Pidgeon – a top box-office star thanks to his screen partnership with Greer Garson. He is the plantation owner trying to fend off the advances of a (literally) poisonous native charmer who seems to have vamped half the white men within 50 miles of the Equator. The delicious

Hedy Lamarr was never more exotic and effective than as Tondelayo, luring men to destruction from under her dusky lids.

White Christmas ○ ⓥ
1954, US, 120 mins, colour
Dir: Michael Curtiz
Stars: Bing Crosby, Danny Kaye, Rosemary Clooney, Dean Jagger, Vera-Ellen
Rating: ★★

A slam-bang Christmas classic that grossed $12 million on its first release and became the top money-making film of its year. The first full-length feature in the new VistaVision process, its combination of Bing Crosby and Danny Kaye – the latter a last-minute replacement for Donald O'Connor, who broke his leg – and an enchanting score by Irving Berlin proved irresistible. The boys are a song and dance team who organise a Christmas benefit concert for their ex-army general, whose ski resort is going bankrupt due to the lack of snow. Of the songs, 'Sisters', sung by both Rosemary Clooney and Vera-Ellen and then mimed to the girls' voices by Crosby and Kaye, stands out above the rest – save the title song, of course.

White Feather ○
1955, US, 104 mins, colour
Dir: Robert Webb
Stars: Robert Wagner, John Lund, Debra Paget, Jeffrey Hunter
Rating: ★★★

Spectacular Western with Robert Wagner in good form as a peace-maker between cavalry and Indians. And it has some superb scenery, beautifully shot in colour by Lucien Ballard. At the time the film was made, Debra Paget, Wagner and Jeffrey Hunter were regularly appearing in 20th Century-Fox pictures. In fact, all three were Fox discoveries and had made their film debuts at much the same time. Here, they all do well in a film which, although filled with action, is notable as an early example of Hollywood's more sympathetic and respectful attitude to what we would soon come to call native Americans.

White Heat ○ ⓥ
1949, US, 114 mins, b/w
Dir: Raoul Walsh
Stars: James Cagney, Edmond O'Brien, Virginia Mayo, Steve Cochran
Rating: ★★★★

The last fling of the Warners gangster film and of James Cagney's roles therein. Raoul Walsh, who made Cagney's famous *The Roaring Twenties* 10 years earlier, is again in charge of the snarling mayhem and few ardent film fans can be unaware that it all ends in an explosive gun battle with Cagney making his famous 'Made it, Ma – top of the world' speech from high up on the gasholder. Margaret Wycherly's brooding portrait of his obsessed mother also makes an indelible impression on the film. Walsh's zestful direction reaches its peak in the scene in the prison dining-hall where his cameras track feverishly along the prisoners as events conspire to send Cagney berserk.

White Hunter, Black Heart ① Ⓥ
1990, US, 112 mins, colour
Dir: Clint Eastwood
Stars: Clint Eastwood, Jeff Fahey, George Dzundza, Marisa Berenson
Rating: ★★

Clint Eastwood's account of the traumas undergone in trying to get director John Huston to make *The African Queen* in 1951 makes interesting, if hardly stimulating screen fare, shimmeringly shot on location in Zimbabwe. You imagine that the Peter Viertel book on which it's based is rather more engrossing. Viertel, screenwriter on the film, is played as a narrator figure by the arrestingly good-looking Jeff Fehey as a cross between James Mason and Audie Murphy. Eastwood does a kind of Burt Lancaster impersonation as the Huston character, here called John Wilson: like Eastwood's direction of this one, it's on the stodgy side. Timothy Spall and Mel Martin make good supporting appearances as a bush pilot and a white bigot, and the impersonations of Bogart, Hepburn and Co are close enough to provoke a smile.

White Lions, The ⊙
1981, US, 110 mins, colour
Dir: Mel Stuart
Stars: Michael York, Glynnis O'Connor
Rating: ★★

Michael York stars in this pretty well-worn story of a naturalist in the African bush who fights to preserve the wildlife there. The African locations make this enjoyable viewing, despite the familiar simplicity of the story. York didn't win any awards for

this one, you won't be surprised to hear, but the animals are the stars, and its fair to assume he realised that.

White Men Can't Jump ● Ⓥ
1992, US, 114 mins, colour
Dir: Ralph Shelton
Stars: Wesley Snipes, Woody Harrelson, Rosie Perez, Tyra Ferrell, Ernest Harden Jr
Rating: ★★

A shouting-and-screaming film about hustling in the backstreets basketball courts of Venice, California. Moulded along the lines of a buddy-buddy comedy film, it features Wesley Snipes and Woody Harrelson as a black/white combination that will lull the opposition into a false sense of security, then take all their money in the subsequent game. Director Ralph Shelton leaves nothing to chance here: there are gangsters, four-letter words and steamy sex scenes galore. Wesley's sensuous spouse wants to get away from the ghetto. Woody's voluptuous Puerto Rican girlfriend – hey, let's get another ethnic group in, guys – has a different ambition: she's stuffing her head full of knowledge for the day she gets on to the TV quiz show *Jeopardy*. That's the whole plot, and it has a few streetwise smiles along the way, although, like its characters, it gets a bit tiresome towards the end and you, too, may grow weary at making the effort to keep up with its screeching, squeaking, high-velocity dialogue.

White Mischief ● Ⓥ
1987, UK, 107 mins, colour
Dir: Michael Radford
Stars: Greta Scacchi, Charles Dance, Joss Ackland, Sarah Miles
Rating: ★★★

A beautifully shot tale of lust and murder among a hedonistic group of ex-patriate Britons living in Nairobi, Kenya, during World War Two. Stylishness, elegance and decadence ooze from the very pores of Michael Radford's interesting if leisurely treatment of the cause célèbre that resulted from the murder of one of the 'Happy Valley' sophisticates, whose high society resembles nothing more than Berlin at the time of *Cabaret*. Greta Scacchi, in and out of period costume, certainly does look well worth dying for, as a couple of characters do before the end. And her Forties' 'look', as with everything else in the film, is impeccable. The murder suspects line up as if in an Agatha Christie tale, and though the real killer

was never brought to book, the filmmakers leave the viewer in no doubt as to their own solution of the crime. The film gets slower as it goes, but it never quite loses its overall fascination.

White Palace ● Ⓥ
1990, US, 110 mins, colour
Dir: Luis Mandoki
Stars: Susan Sarandon, James Spader, Jason Alexander, Kathy Bates, Eileen Brennan
Rating: ★★★

If you've been saving up your tears for a really sloshy romance, this is it – an ace love story where you really get to know the characters. Widower James Spader is a 27-year-old high flyer of immaculate (Jewish) breeding. Susan Sarandon is a 43-year-old, foul-mouthed, sloppy, failed Catholic ('Confession made me jumpy') waitress. They get the hots for each other and if you can't guess subsequent developments, or the final outcome, then you haven't seen too many romantic movies. Sarandon and Spader (she especially) are great; as for the film itself, apart from the frankness of its dialogue, it could have been made 20, 30, even 40 years ago. Some things, including Hollywood wish-fulfilment, thankfully never change!

White Sands ● Ⓥ
1992, US, 101 mins, colour
Dir: Roger Donaldson
Stars: Willem Dafoe, Mickey Rourke, Mary Elizabeth Mastrantonio, M Emmet Walsh
Rating: ★★★

Such a nicely-made thriller that it's a shame that, from start to finish, you haven't a clue what's going on. Sheriff Willem Dafoe discovers a body, a gun and a suitcase full of banknotes in remote New Mexico ruins and from here on in you're on your own. The FBI, the CIA and a couple of arms dealers are in there somewhere but the thrill of the chase is the thing. You can see director Roger Donaldson's mind ticking as he gives us a mobile shot of Dafoe taking a gun from the glove compartment of his car, a time-saving, pace-setting device that sums up the tempo of the whole plot. Dafoe is particularly good as the resourceful, likeable, laid-back lawman. Not far behind are Mary Elizabeth Mastrantonio, Mickey Rourke, M Emmett Walsh, J E Freeman and (uncredited) Mimi Rogers,

W

John Ryan and Fred Dalton Thompson. Royce Applegate is also noteworthy in a one-scene role as a motel owner. Never mind the plot, feel the quality: it's the real stuff.

White Tie and Tails ○
1946, US, 81 mins, b/w
Dir: Charles Barton
Stars: Dan Duryea, Ella Raines, William Bendix
Rating: ★★★

This breezy comedy of embarrassment gives those film tough guys Dan Duryea and William Bendix a chance to lean to the lighter side. The plot, an old standby (here based on a novel called *The Victoria Docks at Eight* by Rufus King and Charles Leakon), is about menials taking over a household while their employers are away.

White Witch Doctor ○
1953, US, 96 mins, colour
Dir: Henry Hathaway
Stars: Susan Hayward, Robert Mitchum, Walter Slezak
Rating: ★★

African missionary nurse meets rugged white hunter in one of 20th Century-Fox's wilder excursions into the jungle, not dissimilar from another Robert Mitchum film, *Mister Moses*, made 12 years later. Susan Hayward offers sensitive acting above and beyond the call of duty as the inhibited Ellen, but not enough happens to sustain the film through its running time, although the Technicolor photography of Leon Shamroy, including some exciting animal shots, is masterly. Oily villainy is in the hands of Walter Slezak and Timothy Carey.

White Zombie ◑
1932, US, 74 mins, b/w
Dir: Victor Halperin
Stars: Bela Lugosi, Madge Bellamy
Rating: ★★★

This cult movie has an eerie atmosphere all its own. Bela Lugosi gives one of his best performances as Murder, the Haitian sorcerer who commands an army of zombies. The film's out-of-this-world quality makes it seem dated even by Thirties' standards, but this somehow only adds to its fascination. And director Victor Halperin achieves some remarkable tableaux that could be removed from the film and hung in art galleries

alongside the work of Hieronymous Bosch. The film, too, is bosh, but bosh with sinister style.

Who Dares Wins ◑ Ⓥ
1982, UK, 140 mins, colour
Dir: Ian Sharp
Stars: Lewis Collins, Judy Davis, Richard Widmark
Rating: ★★

The exploits of the SAS, with their masks, machine guns and deadly efficiency, here gave British filmmakers the chance to reply in kind to the increasingly tough thrillers from Hollywood. On TV, *The Sweeney* and *The Professionals* had shown the way and it can be no coincidence that Lewis Collins, a star from the second of these, features here as the SAS man who goes undercover to undermine a terrorist organisation planning to hold top politicians hostage. The action is a long time coming, but is brilliantly staged in an explosive last 20 minutes when it does. Something about it remains intractibly British: after all, it's dining-room windows the bullets are spraying through here, not ghetto slums.

Who Done It? ○
1942, US, 75 mins, b/w
Dir: Erle C Kenton
Stars: Bud Abbott, Lou Costello, William Bendix, William Gargan, Thomas Gomez
Rating: ★★★

This tongue-in-cheek thriller, about a murder committed on a mystery show broadcast, has one of the best casts of any Abbott and Costello film. It's full of such experienced Hollywood heavies as William Bendix, William Gargan and Thomas Gomez. Vintage-film fans may also spot Jerome Cowan (Humphrey Bogart's partner in *The Maltese Falcon*), Don Porter and horse-faced Mary Wickes. The fun comes fast and furious. One of Bud and Lou's snappiest numbers; funny finish too.

Who Done It? ⊙
1955, UK, 85 mins, b/w
Dir: Basil Dearden
Stars: Benny Hill, Belinda Lee, David Kossoff, Garry Marsh
Rating: ★★★

Although something of a rough diamond, this Ealing Studios comedy vehicle for Benny Hill is so funny as to make one wonder why the star didn't make more such films. A bloodhound called Fabian and

Belinda Lee, as a strongarm showgirl, both give Benny (who gives a likeable performance) a run for his money in the laughter-raising stakes. Down the cast – as a mere PC – you'll spot Stratford Johns, soon to be promoted to higher office in television's *Z Cars*.

Who Framed Roger Rabbit ○ Ⓥ
1988, US, 103 mins, colour
Dir: Robert Zemeckis
Stars: Bob Hoskins, Christopher Lloyd, Joanna Cassidy
Rating: ★★★★

Humans and cartoon characters have been intermixed before, but never so noisily, inventively or abrasively as in this raucous romp which casts Bob Hoskins as a drunken Californian gumshoe hired to dig the dirt on the seductive human-toon wife of a cartoon rabbit. It all runs deeper than that, of course, and Hoskins' Eddie Valiant soon finds himself reluctantly drawn back towards Toontown to help Roger Rabbit beat a murder rap, and the the toons from being wiped off the face of the earth. Besides playing fair by the rules of its own game, the film allows room for pretty well all the Disney and Warners cartoon characters. Daffy and Donald Duck appear for positively the only time together in a piano duet, Mickey Mouse and Bugs Bunny team to baffle Hoskins with cartoon logic, Betty Boop regrets being in black and white and Frank Sinatra provides the voice of the Singing Sword. Talking of voices, Kathleen Turner's brings even more dimension (the characters all have a '3D' effect) to the voluptuous Jessica Rabbit, assuring Hoskins that 'I'm not really bad – I'm just drawn that way.'

Whole Town's Talking, The ○
(aka: Passport to Fame)
1934, US, 95 mins, b/w
Dir: John Ford
Stars: Edward G Robinson, Jean Arthur, Wallace Ford
Rating: ★★★

Director John Ford gave Jean Arthur her big break in 1923 in *Cameo Kirby*, but her career failed to take off. Twelve years later, he finally made her a star with this excellent combination of farce and melodrama that was a huge box-office hit. Edward G Robinson has great fun playing dual roles, as a timid white collar clerk and his 'double', 'Killer Mannion', a notorious gangster. And as the girlfriend with a smart lip, Arthur (who dyed her hair blond for the role) firmly established her screen persona as a wisecracking, cynical woman who would usually start taking advantage of an idealist, eventually fall in love with him, and then use her wordly knowledge to help him beat the bad guys by the end of the picture.

Wholly Moses! ◐
1979, US, 109 mins, colour
Dir: Gary Weis
Stars: Dudley Moore, Laraine Newman, James Coco, Richard Pryor
Rating: ★

A sort of unholy sideshoot to Monty Python's *Life of Brian*, this Hollywood comedy, little seen in this country's cinemas, has Dudley Moore as Herschel, who fondly imagines that it was he, and not Moses, who was chosen to lead his people out of bondage. Guy Thomas's script is peppered with amusing puns and clever situations, although director Gary Weis's pacing is too often slow to take advantage of them all. Laraine Newman has a nicely offbeat personality as the heroine, and James Coco is a delight as Herschel's father.

Whoopee! ○
1930, US, 93 mins, colour
Dir: Thornton Freeland
Stars: Eddie Cantor, Eleanor Hunt
Rating: ★★★

This early two-colour Technicolor musical has Eddie Cantor singing such hits as 'Makin' Whoopee' and 'My Baby Just Cares for Me' and established him as a star of screen as well as stage. It also provided a foothold in films for the young Broadway dance director Busby Berkeley, who would go on to become the foremost man in his field in Thirties' musical films. The Goldwyn Girls include an allegedly 14-year-old Betty Grable leading the chorus in the opening cowboy number. But it's Cantor's clowning that holds centre stage in this early musical treat.

Whoops Apocalypse ● ⓥ
1986, UK, 91m mins, colour
Dir: Tom Bussmann
Stars: Loretta Swit, Peter Cook, Michael Richards, Rik Mayall
Rating: ★

Whoops – a laugh eclipse. British satire hits rock bottom with a cavernous clang in this awful attempted comedy whose sex, nudity, gore and

four-letter words are possibly marginally more entertaining than the – er – jokes. Loretta Swit as the US president, is, under impossible circumstances, one of the few performers not highly over the top in this story of Britain taking back a Central American colony by force, then threatening a nuclear strike when the invaders kidnap a British princess in retaliation. More suffering might have been pre-empted by a nuclear strike on the whole idea. The sequence depicting the SAS is probably the most over-extended film joke since Pinocchio's nose.

Whore ● ⓥ
1991, US, 80 mins, colour
Dir: Ken Russell
Stars: Theresa Russell, Antonio Fargas, Benjamin Mouton
Rating: ★

Ken Russell's idea of a docudrama on prostitution runs like a lurid but old-fashioned sexploitation film, with raunchy Nineties dialogue and a theme song called 'I Want to Bang Her'. Theresa Russell (no relation) tries hard, but isn't very good, in the title role; Antonio Fargas is rather more effective as the black hobo who eventually proves that a friend in need is a friend in deed. Penny dreadful and tuppence coloured, the gaudy parable is calculated only to titillate, not to be informative or teach a moral lesson.

Who's Afraid of Virginia Woolf? ◐ ⓥ
1966, US, 129 mins, b/w
Dir: Mike Nichols
Stars: Elizabeth Taylor, Richard Burton, George Segal, Sandy Dennis
Rating: ★★★

Elizabeth Taylor won her second Oscar for this abrasive four-hander about an embattled middle-ageing couple, living on a college campus. 'You are cordially invited to George and Martha's for an evening of fun and games,' said the publicity at the time. But George and Martha's idea of fun and games is a marathon, macabre shouting match, in which the young couple who are their guests for the evening become semi-willing participants. The film depends almost entirely for its effect on its very powerful dialogue, the creation of playwright Edward Albee, admirably translated for the screen in Ernest Lehman's screenplay, which tinkers little with the original, leaving

sufficient strong language to preserve the flavour of the thing, without alienating the more general cinema-going public. Alex North's music offsets the mood in exactly the right proportion. As Martha and George, Taylor and Richard Burton never quite get away from being Elizabeth Taylor and Richard Burton, although Taylor, de-glamourised at least about the face, and looking most unlike her usual self, is every bit as good as we have any right to expect in such a demanding part.

Who's Been Sleeping in My Bed? ○
1963, US, 103 mins, colour
Dir: Daniel Mann
Stars: Dean Martin, Elizabeth Montgomery
Rating: ★★

Dean Martin is surrounded by lovely girls in this comedy about a television personality forced to live up to his own amorous image. But the honours are entirely stolen by a performance of non-stop verve from comedienne Carol Burnett.

Who's Got the Action? ○
1962, US, 93 mins, colour
Dir: Daniel Mann
Stars: Dean Martin, Lana Turner
Rating: ★★★

A talented cast make the most of Jack Rose's consistently funny script and Daniel Mann's direction moves the fun along at an irresistible pace, in this comedy about a wife who becomes her own husband's bookie in order to try and cure him of the betting craze. Of course, his horses begin to win . . . and win . . . and . . .

Who's Harry Crumb? ◐ ⓥ
1989, US, 98 mins, colour
Dir: Paul Flaherty
Stars: John Candy, Jeffrey Jones, Annie Potts, Shawnee Smith
Rating: ★

You wanna hear a joke? Here it is. 'I am from Budapest.' 'Ah, Hungary.' 'No, I filled up before I got here.' Yes folks, alas for poor John Candy, this is the kind of script every comedian has nightmares about getting for his first solo vehicle. The plot, which runs like a Norman Wisdom reject from 1966, casts Candy as an inept private eye called in to investigate a kidnapping because his boss has masterminded the crime himself and needs the worst operative in the country. Ham-fisted

W

Harry knocks over every priceless object and wall in sight and is called on not to apologise, just look pained. Director Paul Flaherty's execution is as clumsy as Harry, but then this script must have given him migraines from the start. Candy survived this, but mercifully not the character. Don't call us Harry – we certainly won't call you.

Who's Minding the Store? ⊙
1963, US, 90 mins, colour
Dir: Frank Tashlin
Stars: Jerry Lewis, Jill St John, Agnes Moorehead, John McGiver, Ray Walston
Rating: ★★★

Under Frank Tashlin's skilful direction, Jerry Lewis gives one of his zaniest performances in this very entertaining comedy. Watch him trying to paint the tip of a flagpole, selling shoes to a female wrestler, and demonstrating a vacuum cleaner that sucks up everything, including a customer's chihuahua dog. And Jill St John as the glamorous Barbara is everyone's idea of a dream lift-girl.

Who's That Girl ○ ⓥ
1987, US, 94 mins, colour
Dir: James Foley
Stars: Madonna, Griffin Dunne, John Mills
Rating: ★

Madonna's first mainline solo starring vehicle is, alas for the lass, a wretchedly unfunny, woefully mistimed comedy with one of those plots you thought had gone out in the Sixties. Comic heroes flee comic crooks who are in turn pursued by comic police. Everybody's in on the joke except the audience. Madonna's okay as the squeaky streetgirl jailbird, out to clear herself of the frame that gave her four years inside. But Griffin Dunne is highly resistible as her hapless hero, waylaid from marrying the inevitable rich girl. And what is John Mills doing in all this? Very little, mercifully. But not, he might think on seeing the results, little enough.

Why Bother to Knock?
See: Don't Bother to Knock

Why Me? ◑ ⓥ
1989, US, 87 mins, colour
Dir: Gene Quintano
Stars: Christopher Lambert, Christopher Lloyd, Kim Griest
Rating: ★

On top of everything else, this feebly written and directed caper comedy is saddled with a completely meaningless title! The stars, as a trio of safecrackers, show a little, but not much enthusiasm for a story about one of those fabulous *Pink Panther*-style jewels that passes from hand to hand as several factions strive to gain possession of it. J T Walsh has one or two funny moments as the local police chief, but most of the acting has the desperate air of players going resolutely over the top. Old-timers Michael J Pollard and Lawrence Tierney make nominal appearances in the supporting cast of this ill-fated enterprise.

Wichita ○
1955, US, 81 mins, colour
Dir: Jacques Tourneur
Stars: Joel McCrea, Vera Miles
Rating: ★★

Joel McCrea pins on a tin star to play legendary lawman Wyatt Earp in this surpisingly stylish Western. He's hired to clean up the town and starts by banning firearms – not a popular decision. But when the wife of the town banker is killed it's down to Earp to track down the outlaw responsible. An all-too familiar plot and an indifferent script could have condemned this horse opera to oblivion, but director Jacques Tourneur created a fast-moving action-filled tale whose pace gallops over any plot deficiencies. In a very strong cast, watch out for a young Lloyd Bridges as a gunslinger and Peter Graves (the pilot in *Airplane!*) in an early role. The familiar menacing figures of Jack Elam and Robert Wilke are also among those members of the supporting cast waiting to shoot McCrea in the back. And, yes – there's a theme song, too, sung by the *High Noon* man Tex Ritter.

Wicked As They Come ○
1956, UK, 94 mins, colour
Dir: Ken Hughes
Stars: Arlene Dahl, Phil Carey, Herbert Marshall
Rating: ★★

A British attempt to catch up on the American *film noir* of the late Forties. Arlene Dahl is the girl who will stop at nothing to get what she wants out of life. Men fall at her feet, and soon she's covered in diamonds and mink, to say nothing of dirt. Retribution is just around the corner . . . but wait, there's a twist in the tail. Very pro-

fessionally directed by Ken Hughes, whose other films include *The Internecine Project* and *Alfie Darling*.

Wicked Lady, The ○
1945, UK, 104 mins, b/w
Dir: Leslie Arliss
Stars: Margaret Lockwood, James Mason
Rating: ★★

The definitive Margaret Lockwood vehicle, this Lime Grove-shot film scandalised wartime London when it first appeared. Plunging necklines (which had to be re-shot for American audiences) and a racy story about a 17th-century married lady who carries on with a highwayman combined to spell pure box-office. And something else pulled them in: the sheer star quality of Lockwood and James Mason. In all honesty, it's little more than lurid melodrama, but still streets ahead of the ill-advised Eighties' remake with Faye Dunaway.

Wicked Lady, The ●
1983, UK, 99 mins, colour
Dir: Michael Winner
Stars: Faye Dunaway, Alan Bates, John Gielgud, Denholm Elliott
Rating: ★

Mighty are the depths to which the wicked Lady Barbara sinks in this hoary old period tale of a woman with a thirst for danger and adventure, revamped for the modern cinema by director Michael Winner, with Faye Dunaway in the old Margaret Lockwood role. Some of photographer Jack Cardiff's colour compositions are so good, catching the period flavour in their crowd scenes especially, that they might grace a masterpiece.

Wicker Man, The ●
1973, UK, 110 mins, colour
Dir: Robin Hardy
Stars: Edward Woodward, Christopher Lee, Britt Ekland
Rating: ★★★

One of the most unusual British horror films since Hammer pumped new blood into the genre in the mid-Fifties. *The Wicker Man* was treated somewhat unfairly by its distributors, being sent out as a second-feature to *Don't Look Now*, which meant that it was hardly noticed, and, indeed, half-missed by many. It turns out to be a chilling relative of *The Dark Secret of Harvest Home*, all about pagan worship on a Scottish offshore island, and very persuasively written by Anthony Schaffer, author of *Sleuth* and other big stage-into-film hits. A very good, unsettling performance from Edward Woodward is far removed from his famous portrait of Callan in the long-running TV series.

Wide Sargasso Sea ● ⓥ
1992, UK/Jamaica, 98 mins, colour
Dir: John Duigan
Stars: Karina Lombard, Nathaniel Parker, Rachel Ward, Casey Robinson
Rating: ★★

An erotic prequel to *Jane Eyre*: whatever next? The idea is inspired, the tropical Jamaican settings lush and colourful. But the (attempted) eroticism overwhelms it, to the extent that there seems to be virtually no story, especially as John Duigan's direction is so slow. And it would take better actors than Karina Lombard and Nathaniel Parker (as Rochester) to survive this script as written. She at least emerges with pride intact, but he is made to look a little foolish by what must be the foreshortenings of plot in Jean Rhys's acclaimed last novel. Still, it all has a certain touch of the bizarre, that's for sure. Rachel Ward is quite good as the heroine's mad mother and there are moments of poetry – the parrot consumed by flames is a gruesome masterpiece of special effects – that sparkle like jewels in the paste of the rest.

Widows' Peak ○ ⓥ
1993, UK, 101 mins, colour
Dir: John Irvin
Stars: Mia Farrow, Joan Plowright, Natasha Richardson, Adrian Dunbar, Jim Broadbent
Rating: ★★★

Here's one film it's difficult to discuss without giving too much of the plot away. A sparkling comedy with undertones of mystery, it's set in a 1920s Irish community ruled by a formidable colony of widows that might have even put the fear of God into the witch from *The Wizard of Oz*. Witchcraft of a sort seems to be somewhere on the menu, especially with the arrival of Edwina Broom (Natasha Richardson), a war widow whom Peak residents, led by Joan Plowright, see as a most suitable asset to the community, even with her American accent (not clear why English Richardson has to be an American, but no matter) and glamorous appearance. All, that is, save Miss O'Hare (Mia Farrow), a spinster

whose quiet existence and deference to other residents may owe something to a scarlet past. Thus begins a feud that, via dance hall brawls, regatta shunts, acts of mutual revenge and mysterious letters, spirals rapidly out of control . . . We can say no more in deference to Hugh Leonard's plot which is of a higher calibre than the Irish accents attempted by those members of the cast who aren't. Entertaining.

Wife Vs Secretary ○
1936, US, 88 mins, b/w
Dir: Clarence Brown
Stars: Clark Gable, Jean Harlow, Myrna Loy, James Stewart
Rating: ★★★

Never mind the plot, a frothy trifle of marital misunderstandings, just savour the teaming of Clark Gable, Jean Harlow, Myrna Loy and James Stewart, the intelligent direction by Clarence Brown and the witty dialogue exchanges supplied by Norman Krasna, Alice Duer Miller and John Lee Mahin. Gable's a publisher and Harlow his firecracker assistant, with both Loy (Gable's wife) and Stewart (Harlow's boyfriend) wrongly suspicious of the relationship. Stewart, in his fourth feature film, revelled in his scenes with Harlow. 'Clarence,' he recalled, 'wasn't too pleased by the way I did the smooching. He made us go over it several times. I botched it up on purpose, of course. That Jean Harlow sure was a good kisser!'

Wild and the Innocent, The ○
1959, US, 84 mins, colour
Dir: Jack Sher
Stars: Audie Murphy, Joanne Dru, Gilbert Roland, Sandra Dee
Rating: ★★★

Something of a departure for Audie Murphy, and almost a throwback to his first Western, *Sierra*. It's a well-made adventure story, which creates instantly sympathetic characters. Down the cast: Strother Martin, typed even then as the uncouth villain, a mould which took him to good parts in *Cool Hand Luke* and *Butch Cassidy and the Sundance Kid*.

Wild at Heart ● ⓥ
1990, US, 127 mins, colour
Dir: David Lynch
Stars: Nicolas Cage, Laura Dern, Diane Ladd, Willem Dafoe, Isabella Rossellini, Harry Dean Stanton
Rating: ★★★★

Imagine a combination of *Twin Peaks* and *Bonnie and Clyde*, with touches of *Rambo* and *The Wizard of Oz*, and you're perhaps half-way to catching the flavour of this love-it-or-leave-it 'on the road' movie. It's a jet-black comedy that's unmistakably the work of maverick Hollywood director David Lynch (*Blue Velvet*, *The Elephant Man*). Nicolas Cage, released from jail after serving time for manslaughter, is reunited with tearaway sweetheart Laura Dern. Her vengeful mother (Diane Ladd), who once fancied Cage herself, is determined to separate them. Cage is 'wild at heart', wears a snakeskin jacket to demonstrate his individuality, sings Elvis Presley songs – and kills people. Brace yourself for the ensuing journey. Violent, adult, alienating and compelling all at the same time.

Wild Bunch, The ◑ ⓥ
1969, US, 134 mins, colour
Dir: Sam Peckinpah
Stars: William Holden, Ernest Borgnine, Robert Ryan, Warren Oates, Ben Johnson
Rating: ★★★

This famous Western epic was one of a group of much-imitated movies (*Bonnie and Clyde* and *Easy Rider* were others) which changed the face and concept of their particular genre, each bent on disproving a popular myth, yet tinged with the sadness of an impending and inevitable tragic ending. And, although the Clint Eastwood spaghetti Westerns were visually violent, only *The Wild Bunch* truly brought home the horrors of a violent death. Its climactic orgy of annihilation is justly famous, writing *finis* both to its characters and to the old-style Western. It also proved that William Holden, in his best performance since winning an Academy Award for *Stalag 17*, was a much stronger actor when being something darker than a straightforward hero.

Wildcats ◑ ⓥ
1986, US, 107 mins, colour
Dir: Michael Ritchie
Stars: Goldie Hawn, James Keach, Swoosie Kurtz, M Emmet Walsh
Rating: ★★★

Goldie Hawn has a happy facility of choosing scripts that showcase her particular brand of charm, feistiness and vulnerability, and once again she's virtually the whole show in this predictable but enjoyable tale of a teacher who becomes coach to a

W

football team at an unspeakable Chicago ghetto school. Nothing unexpected happens, but there are a few good laughs and you'll be rooting for the school team at the climax. There are some interesting names down the cast, too, notably Woody Harrelson and Wesley Snipes (later co-stars in another sports romp, *White Men Can't Jump*), L L Cool J, M Emmet Walsh and, for fans of old late-night movies, Ann Doran and Gloria Stuart.

Wild Country, The ⊙
1970, US, 100 mins, colour
Dir: Robert Totten
Stars: Steve Forrest, Vera Miles, Jack Elam, Ron Howard
Rating: ★★★

A warm-hearted, incident-filled combination of Western and pioneering drama from the Disney studio, based on the conventional opposition between might and right. The mountain locations are stunning, and veteran character star Jack Elam gets a chance to create a real character instead of being a mean villain or a figure of farce. Ron Howard, who plays the son of the family trying to make a go of farming in the wilds of Wyoming in the 1880s, is the same Howard who later turned director with such effect on *Splash*, *Cocoon* and *Backdraft*.

Wild Geese, The ○ Ⓥ
1978, UK, 134 mins, colour
Dir: Andrew V McLaglen
Stars: Richard Burton, Roger Moore, Richard Harris
Rating: ★★

This explosive adventure film produced huge queues at the box office. Its plot is as predictable as the coming of Christmas and doesn't contain half as many surprises. However, it is also crammed with incident, noise, movement and action. Richard Burton, Roger Moore and Richard Harris play the leaders of a group of hand-picked mercenaries flown to Africa to rescue an African politician from the clutches of his enemies. Burton, as the hard-drinking mercenary-in-chief, gives one of his better performances. You'll have fun (but not much difficulty) keeping one jump ahead of the scriptwriter and in identifying a whole parade of stalwart supporting players.

Wild Geese II ◑ Ⓥ
1985, UK, 125 mins, colour
Dir: Peter Hunt

Stars: Scott Glenn, Barbara Carrera, Laurence Olivier, Edward Fox
Rating: ★★

Although dedicated to Richard Burton, this is only a sequel to *The Wild Geese* in the loosest possible way. Dealing with a much darker kind of espionage (with its attendant element of betrayal), the story is closer to Harry Palmer territory than it is to the Burton film. Scott Glenn provides a muscular and laconic performance in the lead, but co-star Barbara Carrera is understandably defeated by such dialogue as 'With a man like you, surely nothing is impossible?'

Wild Heart, The ○
(aka: Gone to Earth)
1950, UK, 82 mins, colour
Dir: Emeric Pressburger
Stars: Jennifer Jones, David Farrar, Cyril Cusack
Rating: ★★

Jennifer Jones as one of those tempestuous country girls – this one is a kind of English equivalent to Ruby Gentry and a forerunner of *Ryan's Daughter* – that she played in between portraying saints and martyrs. Jones tries to save her beloved fox cub from pursuing hunters, and herself from pursuing men, notably the local squire, brutishly played by David Farrar.

Wild in the Country ○ Ⓥ
1961, US, 114 mins, colour
Dir: Philip Dunne
Stars: Elvis Presley, Hope Lange, Tuesday Weld
Rating: ★★

A curiosity among Elvis Presley films, portraying him as a rebellious country boy with the talent to become a literary giant. A strong cast does doughty battle with an overblown Clifford Odets screenplay, Elvis sings five songs, and there's a glimpse of Joan Crawford's daughter Christina in a small acting role.

Wild North, The ○
1951, US, 97 mins, colour
Dir: Andrew Marton
Stars: Stewart Granger, Wendell Corey, Cyd Charisse
Rating: ★★

Hardly distinguished in itself, *The Wild North* is nonetheless a noteworthy film in several respects. It was MGM's first film in AnscoColor – an attractive process which they developed themselves. The new colour coped

particularly well with the snowbound scenery. It was also Stewart Granger's first Western, the fore-runner of many in the later stages of his career. The director was Andrew Marton, the Budapest-born filmmaker who came to Hollywood with the great Ernst Lubitsch in 1923. Marton was noted for the quality of his action scenes in such films as *The Longest Day*.

Wild One, The ○ Ⓥ
1953, US, 80 mins, b/w
Dir: Laslo Benedek
Stars: Marlon Brando, Lee Marvin, Mary Murphy
Rating: ★★★

This shatteringly forceful film about mob-rule (produced by noted filmmaker Stanley Kramer) was banned by the British Board of Censors on its initial appearance, in 1953, because its smouldering atmosphere was considered too conducive to teenage violence. In today's climate, when such films as *Quadrophenia* paint an even more graphic picture of teenage gang violence, *The Wild One* seems a less frightening, if no less powerful film.

Wild Orchid ● Ⓥ
1989, US, 112 mins, colour
Dir: Zaeman King
Stars: Mickey Rourke, Carre Otis, Jacqueline Bisset, Bruce Greenwood
Rating: ★

Welcome to Brazil, where they party all day and party all night. Or so director Zaeman King, master of well-dressed erotic claptrap, would have us believe. Leggy young lawyer Carre Otis is overwhelmed by the eroticism of the place, what with voluptuous couples having sex around every corner and even in the back seat of a car next to her. Small wonder that when she can't get frigid wheeler-dealer Mickey Rourke to respond to her, the virginal Otis, breathing heavily, goes off for a steamy session with an American who thinks she's a hooker. He subsequently proves to be her opponent in a land deal being negotiated by her decadent boss (Jacqueline Bisset). All this is probably giving the film credit for more plot than it has, especially when you consider it runs 112 minutes. Rourke, underplaying, and Otis, wide-eyed, do what they can to play the Rio sex-and-soap opera straight. Bisset over-acts with relish, probably just as well with dialogue that has Dallas

licked all the way. It's like an old
Warners melodrama, only feverishly
overheated and running completely
out of control.

Wild River ○
1960, US, 110 mins, colour
Dir: Elia Kazan
Stars: Montgomery Clift, Lee Remick, Jo
Van Fleet, Albert Salmi
Rating: ★★★

Apart from the fact that it comes
across in a curiously cool way, this Elia
Kazan film is one of the finest
examples in films of an evocation of a
particular time and place, in this case
the Tennessee Valley area of the early
Thirties. Brilliantly controlled
performances from Montgomery Clift,
nicely edgy as the water authority
agent sent to deal with a difficult
situation; Lee Remick, creating
touching moments as the widow who
falls for him; Albert Salmi, making a
superb smiling sadist of the local
bully; and consummate character actress Jo Van Fleet, as usual playing a
woman years beyond her own age, as
the matriarch who refuses to budge
from her property so that the land
might be flooded. A rare example of a
film adapted from two novels: William
Bradford Huie's *Mud on the Stars*, and
Borden Deal's *Dunbar's Cove*.

Wild Strawberries ◐ ⓥ
1957, Sweden, 93 mins, b/w
Dir: Ingmar Bergman
Stars: Victor Sjöström, Bibi Andersson
Rating: ★★★★

Bergman put one of his own recurring
dreams (the coffin falling from the
hearse) into this rich tapestry of
memories and fears. Film director
Victor Sjöström – Swedish cinema's
best-known pioneer (best known for
his silent work) – gives an astonishingly moving performance as the aged
scientist who embarks on a sentimental journey; he died three years
later, aged 81. Beautifully paced and
acted, it's an occasionally over-
symbolic work, but is filled with richly
observed characters and a real feeling
for the joys of nature and youth; one
of Bergman's warmest, and therefore
finest, films.

Wild Target ● ⓥ
1992, France, 87 mins, colour
Dir: Pierre Salvadori
Stars: Jean Rochefort, Marie Trintignant,
Guillaume Depardieu
Rating: ★★

This black comedy about a hired assassin (lugubrious Jean Rochefort)
starts in hilariously funny style and
ends brightly too. In between some
nicely timed shoot-outs, though, it
sags more than a bit when the plot
involves Marie Trintignant as a forgery
fence whom Rochefort is ordered to
hit but ends up protecting. The beginning, though, when he almost
silences a parrot which he subsequently gives to his mother (a retired
assassin who *does* silence the bird) is
just the funniest few moments in ages.

Wild West ◐ ⓥ
1992, UK, 85 mins, colour
Dir: David Attwood
Stars: Naveen Andrews, Sarita
Choudhury, Ronny Jhutti, Ravi Kapoor
Rating: ★★★

This engaging if rough-hewn film
about a Pakistani Country-and-Western
band is a kind of low-key Asian
equivalent of *The Commitments*.
Despite the rough language, casual
violence and smattering of sex, it's at
heart a gentle sort of film in which
three brothers from Southall led by
Zaf (Naveen Andrews) try to get away
from their suburban semi as the
Honky Tonk Cowboys. Zaf seems to
find it impossible to hold down a job
for longer than a day, and is in trouble
with a local gang of white toughs after
taking a shine to the battered wife
(Sarita Choudhury) of their leader.
When she proves to be the kind of
vocalist Zaf is dreaming of, hope
burns anew for the Honky Tonk
Cowboys. Unfortunately Mother,
whose house is their haven, wants to
move back to Pakistan. The ending is
upbeat and downbeat at the same
time, but the film is more interested in
capturing the spirit of people more
than anything else: that and the cosmopolitan atmosphere of Southall,
with its attendant dangers, is flavour-
fully caught.

Will Any Gentleman . . . ? ⊙
1953, UK, 84 mins, colour
Dir: Michael Anderson
Stars: George Cole, Veronica Hurst, Jon
Pertwee
Rating: ★★★

Madcap comedy about a meek little
man who is transformed into a tiger by
a hypnotist. Typical of George Cole's
film roles of the time, with a nicely
dotty script, good colour photography
and contributions from such jesters as
Sid James, Jon Pertwee and Lionel
Jeffries.

Willard ●
1971, US, 95 mins, colour
Dir: Daniel Mann
Stars: Bruce Davison, Ernest Borgnine,
Elsa Lanchester
Rating: ★★★

This scary film was a runaway success
when it first came out. Bruce Davison,
whose subsequent career has not quite
fired on all cylinders, plays the lonely
young man of the title who makes
friends with a pack of rats, one of
whom proves particularly devious and
intelligent, rather like Napoleon the
pig in *Animal Farm*. The results of this
alliance moved publicists to advise
that 'this is the one movie you should
not see alone'. A sequel, *Ben*, followed.

William at the Circus ⊙
(aka: William Comes to Town)
1948, UK, 90 mins, colour
Dir: Val Guest
Stars: William Graham, Brian Roper
Rating: ★★

He's back! Richmal Crompton's ragged rascal springs to tousled life again
in the third and last of his three screen
adventures. The supporting cast has
Brian Roper as an excellent Ginger,
and Marquis the chimpanzee, who
steals every scene he's in.

William Comes to Town
See: William at the Circus

Willie & Phil ○
1980, US, 116 mins, colour
Dir: Paul Mazursky
Stars: Michael Ontkean, Margot Kidder,
Ray Sharkey
Rating: ★★

On paper, the concept of a homage to
François Truffaut's *Jules et Jim* must
have seemed a non-starter, with Michael Ontkean and Ray Sharkey so in
love with the French film that they
model their personal relationships on
its two male characters. On the screen,
however, it works surprisingly well,
thanks to charming and unforced
performances by Ontkean and
Sharkey and by Margot Kidder as the
third person in their decade-long
ménage à trois. Writer-director Paul
Mazursky infuses the film with a nice
line of humour, wth the occasional
satirical bite and Sven Nykvist's
colour photography gives the whole
affair an attractive gloss.

W

Willow ○ ⓥ

1988, US, 125 mins, colour
Dir: Ron Howard
Stars: Val Kilmer, Joanne Whalley-Kilmer, Warwick Davis, Jean Marsh
Rating: ★★★

This epic fantasy has more than a few elements in common with *Lord of the Rings*, in that it's about little people (played by dwarf actors) who set out, in a time long ago, to destroy the power of evil, by shepherding an abandoned baby on a journey to fulfil its destiny as a saviour for good. The trek's sometimes a bit slow, but the screen is alive with adventure most of the time and the final duel of magic and muscle provides an exciting climax. Not recommended for very young children, who might find a fearsome two-headed monster the stuff of which nightmares are made.

Will Penny ◑

1967, US, 109 mins, colour
Dir: Tom Gries
Stars: Charlton Heston, Joan Hackett, Donald Pleasence, Quentin Dean
Rating: ★★★

There is a magnificent cast in this elegiac Western that was the best thing writer-director Tom Gries ever made. Charlton Heston is a middle-ageing cowboy offered a rewarding but dangerous new life with a frontier widow and her son. Joan Hackett as the widow forms a strong axis for the action in a touching and warm relationship with Heston. Donald Pleasence is memorably over-the-top as the psychotic preacher who menaces their happiness. The fight scenes are red-blooded and raw, and the ending will leave all but the hardest pretty misty-eyed.

Will Success Spoil Rock Hunter? ○

(aka: Oh! For a Man)
1957, US, 94 mins, colour
Dir: Frank Tashlin
Stars: Tony Randall, Jayne Mansfield
Rating: ★★★

Zany, good-natured and packed with inventive gags, writer-director Frank Tashlin's adaptation of George Axelrod's Broadway hit provided Jayne Mansfield with her best film. From the opening sequence, combining credits with a skit on TV commercials, the fun hardly ever lets up, and there are delightful contributions from Tony Randall, Betsy Drake and Henry Jones, plus a

'surprise' appearance from Groucho Marx. Two stars of comedy films from a much earlier era, Minta Durfee and Benny Rubin, appear in cameo roles.

Willy Wonka and the Chocolate Factory ⊙

1971, US, 100 mins, colour
Dir: Mel Stuart
Stars: Gene Wilder, Jack Albertson, Peter Ostrum
Rating: ★★★★

Pure magic: the only filmed version of a Roald Dahl story written by Dahl himself and not the other by a mile. Foot-tapping songs, especially 'Oompa Loompa Doompadee Doo', amazing Heath Robinson-type settings in the chocolate factory and, enjoying his finest hour, Gene Wilder as the charmingly devious Wonka himself. Julie Dawn Cole is wonderfully horrid as the most obnoxious of the five children who go on a tour of the factory, several of them destined for appallingly appropriate fates.

Wilt ◑ ⓥ

1989, UK, 91 mins, colour
Dir: Michael Tuchner
Stars: Griff Rhys Jones, Mel Smith, Alison Steadman, Diana Quick
Rating: ★★

An adult comedy only in the sense that there's a lot of coarse comic business with an inflatable doll, this vehicle for Mel Smith and Griff Rhys Jones leans more towards the world of a lewder *Carry On* humour than that of *Lucky Jim*, out of which its leading character, Henry Wilt (Rhys Jones), seems to have stepped. Murder and mayhem ensue, but mirth is largely absent, notably in a bungled ending which should have been hilarious. Smith and Jones do their things, Alison Steadman is gorgeous. Bright and breezy, and the team's best film work to date, *Wilt* still seriously lacks the roots in reality that all quality comedy needs.

Winchester 73 ○

1950, US, 92 mins, b/w
Dir: Anthony Mann
Stars: James Stewart, Shelley Winters, Dan Duryea, Stephen McNally
Rating: ★★★

First-rate picturesque Western which was a major springboard for the revival of the genre in the Fifties, with a fine leading performance from James Stewart, taut direction by Anthony

Mann and superb photography by Greta Garbo's favourite cameraman, William Daniels. Rock Hudson and Tony Curtis, both then-newcomers, have small featured roles (Hudson plays a Red Indian) and there are sharply-etched portraits of Western characters on either sides of the law from such reliable players as Dan Duryea, Shelley Winters, Stephen McNally, Millard Mitchell, Jay C Flippen, Will Geer and John McIntire.

Wind ◑ ⓥ

1992, US, 125 mins, colour
Dir: Carroll Ballard
Stars: Matthew Modine, Jennifer Grey, Cliff Robertson, Jack Thompson, Rebba Miller
Rating: ★★

'Winning is everything,' is the message in this often exhilarating, always superbly shot (by John Toll) yachting drama, which sometimes hits the doldrums away from its action scenes. The prize at stake here is the America's Cup, for which American sailor Matthew Modine and his girlfriend (Jennifer Grey) have to take on the forces of nature as well as an arrogant Australian (but of course) rival. The plot is a bit clichéd and the emotional elements are bland, but the stars seem to be giving it all they've got on board the yacht, and the spectacular racing action, paricularly at the breathtaking climax of this patriotic American tale, will keep you near the edges of your seats. Another outdoors action drama from Carroll Ballard: a specialist in the genre, he also made *Never Cry Wolf* and *The Black Stallion*.

Wind and the Lion, The ○

1975, US, 119 mins, colour
Dir: John Milius
Stars: Sean Connery, Candice Bergen, Brian Keith, John Huston
Rating: ★★★★

Seldom has a story been so stylishly, colourfully, excitingly and movingly captured as in John Milius's saga of action in Morocco in 1904. The pace, the action and the spirit of pre-war adventure rush across the screen in a never-slackening surge. At the centre of it sits the formidable figure of Sean Connery, wildly miscast as a sort of whimsical Scottish Berber, but giving a brilliantly understated performance that overcomes all and will leave you cheering for him before the end; and Candice Bergen could not be bettered as the cool and gutsy American widow he kidnaps from Tangier, with her two children, aiming to exchange them for money, rifles and his rightful place in the country's aristocracy. President Teddy Roosevelt (Brian Keith's best performance in ages) agrees to the bargain, but plans to assert his authority with force if necessary. Add German intervention and Moroccan intrigue and it is thrillingly inevitable that the pot should boil over in the last reel. The participation of the two children will have watching youngsters living the saga with them.

Windbag the Sailor ⊙

1936, UK, 85 mins, b/w
Dir: William Beaudine
Stars: Will Hay, Moore Marriott
Rating: ★★★

Will Hay himself helped to write this priceless comedy about a bogus sea captain shipwrecked on a cannibal isle. Hay, bewhiskered Moore Marriott and tubby Graham Moffatt enjoy some hilarious scenes, especially those revolving around the compass.

Wind Cannot Read, The ○

1958, UK, 115 mins, colour
Dir: Ralph Thomas
Stars: Dirk Bogarde, Yoko Tani, Ronald Lewis
Rating: ★★★

Simple, touching story of a doomed romance between an RAF officer and a delicately lovely Japanese girl during World War Two. Sensitive acting from Dirk Bogarde and Yoko Tani ensures that you'll need a handkerchief long before the end. Author Richard Mason provided a perceptive screenplay from his own novel, a far superior piece to that other east-west romance *The World of Suzie Wong* which Mason also wrote. And there's some beautiful photography by Ernest Steward – the Eastmancolour process has surely never looked better.

Window in London, A ○

1939, UK, 76 mins, b/w
Dir: Herbert Mason
Stars: Michael Redgrave, Sally Gray, Paul Lukas, Patricia Roc
Rating: ★★★

This absorbing film, translated from the original French, has a real sting in the tail. It was also the last British film made by Paul Lukas before he went back to Hollywood where, four years later, he won an Academy Award in *Watch on the Rhine*.

Wings ○

1927, US, 143 mins, b/w
Dir: William Wellman
Stars: Clara Bow, Richard Arlen, Jobyna Ralston, Gary Cooper
Rating: ★★★

The flying sequences in the first winner of Hollywood's best film Oscar are still among the most breathtaking ever put on screen, with the infantry battle scenes not far behind. Despite some extremely poignant moments, however, the story is really too slight for this sort of running time. It's a pity, as the action stuff is unmissable: all that you see on screen was actually shot by dedicated daredevil director William Wellman for the film, with scores of photographers positioned in planes and cameras largely positioned on gun mounts. Clara Bow, Buddy Rogers and Richard Arlen head the cast (with a young Gary Cooper getting a moving cameo – and lots of fan mail): but the planes are still the stars.

Wings of Eagles, The ○

1957, US, 110 mins, colour
Dir: John Ford
Stars: John Wayne, Maureen O'Hara
Rating: ★★

Epic John Ford film, beautifully constructed and with its fair share of action. It's based on the life of one of America's greatest air heroes, Frank 'Spig' Wead, a kind of American equivalent to Douglas Bader. The real-life Wead, despite being crippled by a fall after some spectacular Twenties' exploits in the Schneider Cup air races, made a substantial contribution to America's war effort in the Pacific in World War Two. He also wrote plays about the war. And one of them – *They Were Expendable* – was filmed by Ford in 1945, ironically with Wayne in the starring role. Ward Bond, another of Ford's favourite actors, does sterling, unobtrusive work as Wead's right-hand man and Maureen O'Hara gets well into the character of Mrs Wead and grows old, as always, beautifully.

Wings of Fame ◐ Ⓥ

1990, Holland, 109 mins, colour
Dir: Otakar Volocek
Stars: Peter O'Toole, Colin Firth, Marie Trintignant
Rating: ★★

Films about people who die and find themselves in some kind of staging post for the dead have enjoyed sporadic popularity with film-makers

since the success of *Outward Bound* more than 60 years ago. *Wings of Fame* is not destined to join the greats of the genre, although it does get better – a lot better – towards the end. For the most part, although the idea is nice, the execution is poor, full of clumsily staged scenes and actors talking at the tops of their voices. And the notion of blending real famous dead people with fictitious ones in the vast hotel on a fog-shrouded island, is one that works against the film rather than in its favour. Towards the end, director Otakar Volocek seems to get the hang of it, and things come together to rather better effect. Peter O'Toole and Colin Firth star as the matinee idol actor and his youthful murderer and the idea of it all, I think, is that fame is fleeting.

Wings of the Apache ◐ Ⓥ

(aka: Fire Birds)
1990, US, 89 mins, colour
Dir: David Green
Stars: Nicolas Cage, Tommy Lee Jones, Sean Young
Rating: ★★★

Down-the-line Hollywood combat film of the old school, with American Apache helicopters in aerial action against new foes: Colombian drug dealers and the ace pilot who protects them. Nicolas Cage is the young hot-shot US pilot, Tommy Lee Jones the older instructor who wishes he were back in the action. And, in these days of equality, Sean Young is no wilting violet waiting back at the base, but a 'scout pilot' who helps the boys out of trouble at the end. Shortish, noisy and incident-filled, the film has a serviceable script and keeps you hopping, if hardly guessing. Cliffhanging stuff for action fans and an unusually straightforward role for Cage that his fans will like.

Winnie the Pooh and a Day for Eeyore ⊙ Ⓥ

1983, US, 26 mins, colour
Dir: Wolfgang Reitherman
Rating: ★★★

If anything, the Disney series of adaptations from the stories of A A Milne gained in charm as it went along. There's a definite woodland feel as well as a nostalgic tug as the stories of Poohsticks and Eeyore's holiday interweave and unravel deep in the Hundred Acre Wood. Eeyore has a wonderful laconic voice and his tribulations are always pleasing and sometimes amusing.

W

Winnie the Pooh and the Blustery Day ⊙ ⓥ

1968, US, 26 mins, colour
Dir: Wolfgang Reitherman
Rating: ★★★

Chronologically the second of the charming Disney featurettes from the works of A A Milne, in which Tigger arrives in the forest and Owl's house is blown down in a storm. A nightmare ballet involving pink and blue elephants seems to have strayed in from *Fantasia* via *Dumbo*!

Winnie the Pooh and the Honey Tree ⊙ ⓥ

1965, US, 26 mins, colour
Dir: Wolfgang Reitherman
Rating: ★★★

Apart from the intrusion of a character called Gopher (who hastens to tell us that he isn't in the books), this is a delightful Disney featurette from stories by A A Milne. The drawing, for example, is quite beautiful and faithful to a rare stage of delicacy to Ernest Shepard's original illustrations. Much of the stories' text, too, has been retained. The catchy songs are by the Mary Poppins men, Oscar-winners Richard and Robert Sherman.

Winnie the Pooh and Tigger Too ⊙ ⓥ

1974, US, 26 mins, colour
Dir: John Lounsbery
Rating: ★★★

The third in the series of Walt Disney cartoon featurettes from the books of A A Milne. Charming, amusing and refreshingly close to the spirit of the original.

Winslow Boy, The ○ ⓥ

1948, UK, 117 mins, b/w
Dir: Anthony Asquith
Stars: Robert Donat, Margaret Leighton, Cedric Hardwicke
Rating: ★★★

Terence Rattigan's stage success, based on a real-life *cause célèbre*, is the very stuff that drama, suspense and audience appeal are made of. After it proved equally effective as a radio play, the playwright himself helped translate the piece into a film, the screen version getting a boost from the powerful portrayal of Robert Donat, as the QC who defends a young naval cadet accused of a theft which, although minor, could ruin his career. The plot is brilliantly constructed, with a highly satisfying climax, and directed with a keen insight into English character by

Anthony Asquith, who keeps tension on high throughout, especially in the climactic courtroom scenes. A highly superior cast includes fully-rounded characterisations from Margaret Leighton, Cedric Hardwicke, Frank Lawton, Basil Radford, Kathleen Harrison, Francis L Sullivan and Stanley Holloway.

Winter Kills ●

1979, US, 97 mins, colour
Dir: William Richert
Stars: Jeff Bridges, John Huston, Anthony Perkins, Dorothy Malone
Rating: ★

Very complex film about a presidential assassination mystery that makes the John F Kennedy killing, as one critic put it, 'look like a connect-the-dots puzzle'. Jeff Bridges achieves a believable characterisation of a man caught up in a situation he can't grasp, a situation with which the audience might well sympathise. 'It's a conundrum,' growls Richard Boone. 'A riddle within a riddle.' He can say that again. Elizabeth Taylor pops in for a brief wordless cameo role as a former movie star who served as procuress for the late president.

Winter People ○ ⓥ

1988, US, 111 mins, colour
Dir: Ted Kotcheff
Stars: Kurt Russell, Kelly McGillis, Lloyd Bridges
Rating: ★

Another of those backwoods/hillbilly feuding families dramas where a good beginning and better intentions are soon submerged beneath a morass of rampant melodrama. John Ehle's book may well have the 'beauty and depth of feeling' that screenwriter Carol Fobieski described in interviews, but if it does then she has made a hash of it. Kelly McGillis acts her socks off as the unwed mother who lives alone and nurses a guilty secret (pretty obvious that her baby's father is one of the rival clan), but she's fighting a losing battle against this script and the miscasting of Kurt Russell as the wandering clockmaker for whom she falls after he and his eight-year-old daughter stumble on her cottage. The daughter (Amelia Burnette) is a real charmer, but has too little to do in further proceedings, which are strictly along East Lynne lines and become progressively more ludicrous.

Wired ● ⓥ

1989, US, 108 mins, colour
Dir: Larry Peerce
Stars: Michael Chiklis, Patti D'Arbanville, J T Walsh
Rating: ★★

Tubby, high-living John Belushi was a film star, comedian and drug addict, and in the end his habit killed him. Ultimately, this is all that director Larry Peerce's biopic (based on Bob Woodward's best-selling biography) can say, despite a bright beginning, and adopting the unusual approach of having the dead Belushi rise from the morgue and relive parts of his past with the help of his guardian angel. A wonderful life it's not, and the film doesn't paint it that way. But it's too one-note to grip and fascinate, despite the excellent impersonation of Belushi by 25-year-old Michael Chiklis, and the entertainingly accurate re-creation of some of Belushi and Dan Aykroyd's *Blues Brothers* routines.

Wisdom ● ⓥ

1987, US, 109 mins, colour
Dir: Emilio Estevez
Stars: Emilio Estevez, Demi Moore, Tom Skerritt, Veronica Cartwright
Rating: ★★

A distinctly quirky latter-day *Bonnie and Clyde*, with Clyde coming in the form of John Wisdom, played rather glumly by Emilio Estevez. Wisdom has a record – he stole a car in a drunken spree when 19. Now that conviction disqualifies him from all but the most menial jobs. Inspired by a TV programme about banks foreclosing on farmers and small businessmen unable to maintain their mortgage payments, Wisdom decides to do something positive with his life. He buys a powerful automatic rifle with the money he has saved for a car, and starts to hold up banks – not to steal money, but to burn their mortgage records. His girlfriend (Demi Moore), at first his unsuspecting getaway driver, soon begins to believe in his cause while, to half the population of America, Wisdom becomes some kind of folk hero.

Wise Blood ◐

1979, US/Germany, 108 mins, colour
Dir: John Huston
Stars: Brad Dourif, Ned Beatty, Amy Wright, John Huston
Rating: ★★★

John Huston's very black comedy about the exploits of the atheist son of a hellfire preacher in America's southern states' 'Bible belt', a character whom Brad Dourif makes both funny and frightening. It's a disturbing sermon on gullibility and greed, sometimes quite horrifying, but at its funniest in the sequences where a fake gorilla visits the town to promote a film.

Wish You Were Here ● Ⓥ
1987, UK, 92 mins, colour
Dir: David Leland
Stars: Emily Lloyd, Tom Bell
Rating: ★★★

This famous film lifts elements from every avant-garde British film you've seen in the past 25 years. And, like his central character, a 'difficult' teenager, writer-director David Leland is out to impress. His work, though, pales by comparison with sassy, delightful newcomer Emily Lloyd as the girl, whose top-notch performance made her Britain's youngest international star at 16. Her character, Lynda, is cocky, rude, sexually aware and can't wait to get on with life. As played by the piquant Lloyd, she's also quite delightful, even if enough to make all fathers of teenage daughters wince. And she's also got a ready quip for every occasion. 'Your mother would have shown you the door,' her father grates. 'I've seen it,' she replies. The film, set in the early Fifties, is, although not credited as such, based on the early life of Cynthia (*Personal Services*) Payne. Stanley Myers' music to accompany Lynda's high and low jinks is as quirkily individual as ever.

Wistful Widow of Wagon Gap, The ○
1947, US, 78 mins, b/w
Dir: Charles Barton
Stars: Bud Abbott, Lou Costello, Marjorie Main
Rating: ★★★

Bud and Lou go west, and get saddled with a fearsome widow (Marjorie Main, later famous as Ma Kettle) and numerous children. One of the bad guys is played by 6ft 4in Glenn Strange, who also appeared in the following Abbott and Costello film comedy – as the Frankenstein monster! The screenplay is by Robert Lees, Fred Rinaldo and John Grant who did so much of Abbott and Costello's best work in the Forties.

Witchcraft ◑
1964, UK, 79 mins, b/w
Dir: Don Sharp

Stars: Lon Chaney Jr, Jack Hedley, Jill Dixon
Rating: ★★★

A witch rises from the dead and strange and fatal things begin to happen to the descendants of those who had buried her alive. Director Don Sharp (who made *Rasputin* and *Kiss of the Vampire*) is an old hand at this sort of thing and conjures up bags of creepy atmosphere with the aid of good black and white photography.

Witches, The ○ Ⓥ
1989, UK, 90 mins, colour
Dir: Nicolas Roeg
Stars: Anjelica Huston, Mai Zetterling, Rowan Atkinson, Jasen Fisher
Rating: ★★★★

There's a witches' convention going on in Newquay and it's the decision of the Grand High Witch to use an evil potion (via sweet shops) to turn the children of Britain into mice. You can tell witches by the glint of purple in their eyes; their feet have square ends, and they're bald, scratching their heads because of the irritation of their wigs. Nothing can stop the cackling fiends and their evil plans – except perhaps a cigar-smoking Swedish granny and the grandson the High Witch has turned into a mouse. What is it about Roald Dahl's stories that makes such excellent cinema? Who can say, but this is a truly delightful children's film in which real mice and 'mice' from Jim Henson's Creature Workshop blend almost seamlessly as the battle between good and evil maintains a fevered pace. Huston is magnificently malevolent as a witch as fearsome as anything from Disney, and Zetterling excellent as the fearful but determined grandma. There's loads of green and purple smoke and action galore. Tinies, though, should have a parent standing by.

Witches of Eastwick, The ● Ⓥ
1987, US, 118 mins, colour
Dir: George Miller
Stars: Jack Nicholson, Cher, Susan Sarandon, Michelle Pfeiffer
Rating: ★★★

Fast-moving and fun (once the scene is set), this black erotic fantasy has 'witches' Cher, Susan Sarandon and Michelle Pfeiffer trying to conjure up their perfect man. Enter Jack Nicholson who with the right blend of charm, bravado and promises manages to seduce all three. Director

George (*Mad Max*) Miller is a master of pace and keeps the ball rolling here, which disguises the fact that the plot is a bit thin in places. In addition to this, Jack Nicholson goes wildly over the top in a demonic role that is perfect for his kind of histrionics. His manically gleeful portrait of Daryl Van Horne, the lover unwisely and mystically summoned by the three ladies, dominates the whole film, almost eclipsing his female co-stars. The last reel is an overblown special effects triumph entirely in keeping with Nicholson's performance.

Witchfinder-General ● Ⓥ
1967, UK, 98 mins, colour
Dir: Michael Reeves
Stars: Vincent Price, Ian Ogilvy, Patrick Wymark
Rating: ★★★

The third and last horror film made by the talented young director Michael Reeves, who died soon after at the age of 25. This one deals with religious persecution in England at the time of Cromwell. Reeves made his first film, *Revenge of the Blood Beast*, with Barbara Steele, in Italy. But he returned to his native Britain in 1967 to direct veteran horror star Boris Karloff in *The Sorcerers*. *Witchfinder-General* has been accused of painting too bloody and violent a picture of the times, but its power is undeniable.

With a Song in My Heart ○
1952, US, 117 mins, colour
Dir: Walter Lang
Stars: Susan Hayward, Rory Calhoun, David Wayne, Thelma Ritter
Rating: ★★★

Susan Hayward, who seemed to be forever being nominated for an Oscar until she finally won it in 1958 for *I Want to Live!*, contributes another attention-grabbing performance in this musical biopic about singer Jane Froman, who lost the use of both legs after a wartime plane crash. Hayward is really the whole show, although the young Robert Wagner has a few effective moments as a GI, and Froman herself makes a notable contribution by supplying the rich, melodic singing voice to which Hayward mimes so well.

Withnail & I ● Ⓥ
1986, UK, 107 mins, colour
Dir: Bruce Robinson
Stars: Richard E Grant, Paul McGann, Richard Griffiths, Michael Elphick
Rating: ★★

W

This comic chronicle of the hazardous times of two out-of-work actors holidaying at a farm in Penrith, the one pursued by the 25-stone gay uncle of the other, is a successor in its comedy of desperation to such TV series as *Hancock* and *The Likely Lads*. With a few dozen four-letter words added, of course. Despite well-drawn characters, though, the film remains as bogged in tedium as the actors' flat is in dirty dishes until the boys hit the road to the country. Here their efforts to keep body and soul together are often more than mildly amusing, especially when suffering the attentions of Richard Griffiths as the puffing billy gourmet uncle, and Michael Elphick as the local poacher with a chicken in his coat and eels down his trousers. The two leading actors, Paul McGann and Richard E Grant, work well together, Grant suggesting perfectly the wasted Thespian with classic voice, hollow eyes and talent that will forever go unappreciated.

Without a Clue ○ Ⓥ
(aka: Sherlock and Me)
1988, UK, 106 mins, colour
Dir: Thom Eberhardt
Stars: Michael Caine, Ben Kingsley, Jeffrey Jones
Rating: ★

It's a lovely idea, to spin a Sherlock Holmes adventure around the notion that the real crime-solver was Dr Watson but, at least in this treatment, it doesn't work. The simple-minded script supposes that Holmes is in fact a ham actor whom Watson is forced to employ in order to hide his own activities from the medical profession. But the vein struck is *Carry On Holmes*, with Michael Caine as Holmes given the thankless task of incarnating a character who's just too idiotic to be true. It's impossible to identify with such a farcical blunderer and so, in spite of Ben Kingsley's cerebral medical mastermind and Lysette Anthony's spirited lady in distress, who has an amusing role to play in the finale, the charade never holds our interest until the set-piece of the final 20 minutes, a showdown in and below a deserted theatre.

Without a Trace ◐
1983, US, 120 mins, colour
Dir: Stanley R Jaffe
Stars: Kate Nelligan, Judd Hirsch, David Dukes, Stockard Channing
Rating: ★★★

Kate Nelligan was fast bidding to become the queen of screen anguish when she made this heartrending film. After the controversial TV movie *Victims*, in which she waged a lone battle to get a rapist convicted, she's out on her own again in this three-handkerchief drama as a mother whose six-year-old son disappears without trace on a short journey to school one morning. The subsequent drama is too strung-out, especially in the closing stages, when director Stanley Jaffe's treatment of the story robs it of some of its inherent tension. Still, Nelligan, looking very Lilli Palmer-ish in this role, holds it together, intelligently conveying a literate woman holding hard to her sanity and only giving way to pity when it doesn't matter. And the ending will make most viewers reach for at least one tissue to wipe away a tear.

Without Love ○
1945, US, 111 mins, b/w
Dir: Harold S Bucquet
Stars: Spencer Tracy, Katharine Hepburn, Lucille Ball
Rating: ★★

Philip Barry's plays (and Donald Ogden Stewart's adaptations of them) had made successful films twice before for Katharine Hepburn (in *Holiday* and *The Philadelphia Story*) so, especially selecting Spencer Tracy as her leading man, she was obviously on to another winner here in a comedy about a 'platonic' marriage. The stars, though, have scenes stolen from under their noses by Lucille Ball and Keenan Wynn. But Tracy, too, has his comic moments, especially in the scenes where he walks in his sleep and encounters a dog that has been trained to stop him.

With Six You Get Eggroll ○
1968, US, 95 mins, colour
Dir: Howard Morris
Stars: Doris Day, Brian Keith
Rating: ★★

A wholesome if rather obviously-plotted comedy about the disaster-prone romance of a widow (with three sons and an enormous Old English sheepdog) and a widower with a teenage daughter and a French poodle. Their numerous troubles seem largely of their own making, but nonetheless it's fun, with a good chase sequence, and some nice comic 'bits' from Alice Ghostley (as a nutty housekeeper), Pat Caroll (as heroine Doris Day's wisecracking sister) and George Carlin as a smart-Alec hamburger stand operator.

Witness ◐ Ⓥ
1985, US, 112 mins, colour
Dir: Peter Weir
Stars: Harrison Ford, Kelly McGillis, Lukas Haas, Danny Glover, Alexander Godunov, Josef Sommer
Rating: ★★★★

A high-tension thriller that won an Oscar for its editing, and was unlucky not to take several more. Remarkably sensitive performances from Harrison Ford and Kelly McGillis, still among the best either has done, and wide-eyed boy actor Lukas Haas, plus a thrilling *High Noon*-style shootout at the climax. One of the villains is played by Danny Glover before he became part of the *Lethal Weapon* team.

Witness for the Prosecution ○ Ⓥ
1957, US, 114 mins, b/w
Dir: Billy Wilder
Stars: Tyrone Power, Marlene Dietrich, Charles Laughton
Rating: ★★★★

Now you think you've solved it, now you haven't, is the theme of this Agatha Christie-inspired suspense classic directed by Billy Wilder, with Charles Laughton giving his last great screen performance as the eccentric barrister who uses a monocle to reflect sunlight into the eye of a hostile witness. Based on Christie's hit play, the story, of a man on trial for murder, is vastly entertaining with many twists and blind turnings. But Laughton's real-life wife, Elsa Lanchester, almost steals his thunder as nurse Miss Plimsoll — always ready to administer yet another injection or pop another series of pills down his throat — and her delightful performance earned her an Oscar nomination.

Wiz, The ⊙ Ⓥ
1978, US, 133 mins, colour
Dir: Sidney Lumet
Stars: Diana Ross, Michael Jackson, Richard Pryor
Rating: ★★★

A hip, black, Motown *Wizard of Oz*. Diana Ross couldn't have seemed further from the concept of Dorothy: but, apart from being entirely the wrong age, she is unexpectedly excellent. So is the choreography and especially Tony Walton's production design. The first sight of the Emerald City and scenes of Dorothy and friends dancing away down the yellow-brick road are all eye-catchingly successful. The ensemble scenes are mostly good too – especially Brand New Day – and the make-up for Tin Man and Lion quite superb. The script, alas, is the film's weak link and there is too much of it. Oswald Morris' colour photography is exceptionally skilful. The film's disparate elements can't quite fuse into a whole entertainment though. Nonetheless, this trip up the yellow-brick road has something to please almost everyone.

Wizard of Oz, The ⊙ ⓥ
1939, US, 101 mins, colour
Dir: Victor Fleming
Stars: Judy Garland, Frank Morgan, Ray Bolger, Bert Lahr
Rating: ★★★★

Pure, vintage magic. The most fabulous fairy-story ever filmed – and a triumph for MGM's decision to make L Frank Baum's story as a live-action musical and not a cartoon. And, when Shirley Temple proved unavailable, Judy Garland was an inspired choice as Dorothy, breaking everyone's hearts with her simple rendition of 'Over the Rainbow', which nearly got cut out of the finished film. Several directors played their part. George Cukor got rid of Judy's blond wig and doll-like makeup, Victor Fleming took over for the body of the film, and King Vidor shot the monotone framing scenes. Over the years, the film has lost none of its original charm, and several of its actors – Margaret Hamilton (Wicked Witch), Ray Bolger (Scarecrow), Jack Haley (Tin Man) and Bert Lahr (Cowardly Lion) achieved immortality in a single performance.

Wolfen ●
1981, US, 110 mins, colour
Dir: Michael Wadleigh
Stars: Albert Finney, Diane Venora, Gregory Hines, Edward James Olmos
Rating: ★★

A horror film with pretensions. People are getting their throats torn out in New York City, and Michael Wadleigh's prowling cameras, plus killings 'seen' in negative give you a pretty good idea of what's going on. Albert Finney, with a ragged American accent left over from *Annie*, is the detective hauled off suspension to investigate, running into a lot of mumbo-jumbo about hunting grounds, families and killing to survive. There's a Red Indian who seems to think he's a wolf, but he proves to be more of a Red Herring. With all its creeping around, frank dialogue and bits of people flying through the air when the 'wolfen' attack, it's not a film for the nervous or easily shocked. Director Wadleigh tries hard to cover the film with an other-worldly quality and a feeling of something outside our understanding, and Gregory Hines scores nicely on his film debut as a hip coroner with a disarming sense of humour.

Wolf Man, The ◖
1940, US, 70 mins, b/w
Dir: George Waggner
Stars: Lon Chaney Jr, Claude Rains, Bela Lugosi
Rating: ★★★

Werewolves, unlike Dracula and Frankenstein, have no literary origin. So, for Universal's second stab at lycanthropy, writer Curt Siodmak concocted a slice of instant mythology in the form of the old Romany rhyme: 'Even a man who is pure at heart and says his prayers by night, can become a wolf. When the wolfbane blooms and the moon is full and bright.' The movie, set in an improbable Hollywood version of Wales, gave Lon Chaney Jr his chance – excellently taken – to join the pantheon of movie monsters as the reluctant victim of the bite of the werewolf. Helped by make-up wizard Jack Pierce and his painfully applied yak hairs and by splendid special effects from John P Fulton, Chaney gives a memorable and quite moving performance which was to typecast him in horror movies for much of his subsequent career.

Wolves of Willoughby Chase, The ◖ ⓥ
1988, UK, 93 mins, colour
Dir: Stuart Orme
Stars: Stephanie Beacham, Mel Smith, Geraldine James, Richard O'Brien
Rating: ★★

Stephanie Beacham took time out from crossing verbal swords with Joan Collins in *Dynasty* to jet to Prague to play monstrous Victorian governess, Letitia Slighcarp, whose twisted schemes put Disney's Cruella DeVille to shame. She and Mel Smith, as rotund Dickensian sidekick, Mr Grimshaw, are the best things in this very dark children's fantasy from the superb Joan Aiken novel. It's a familiar story of two adventurous girls from different social backgrounds who are abandoned into a nightmare world of the workhouse and poverty. All the elements are in place for a classic children's film along the lines of *The Railway Children*; but somewhere down the line they refused to gel, even though the settings are brilliant. As to the wolves of the title, they look more like Alsatian pets and never likely to devour our young heroines.

Woman Alone, The
See: Sabotage

Woman in a Dressing Gown ○
1957, UK, 93 mins, b/w
Dir: J Lee Thompson
Stars: Yvonne Mitchell, Anthony Quayle, Sylvia Syms
Rating: ★★★

An adult and unsentimental drama, one of a wave of British realist dramas of its time. Putting a marriage on the rocks under a magnifying glass, it brings into focus the faults on both sides. Anthony Quayle and Yvonne Mitchell are magnificent as the couple under scrutiny, Mitchell especially deserving praise for allowing the make-up department to turn her into such a spectacular drab.

Woman in Question, The ○
(aka: Five Angles on Murder)
1949, UK, 88 mins, b/w
Dir: Anthony Asquith
Stars: Jean Kent, Dirk Bogarde
Rating: ★★★

Absorbing whodunnit with the accent on character. The victim, a fairground fortune teller, is viewed in different lights by each of five acquaintances; their recollections make up the thread of the story – but which, if any, shows her in the true light? An interesting experiment which doesn't quite work, but Anthony Asquith's clever handling of the mounting suspense ensures that you'll stay watching to the end to discover the answer.

Woman in Red, The ◖ ⓥ
1984, US, 87 mins, colour
Dir: Gene Wilder
Stars: Gene Wilder, Kelly LeBrock, Gilda Radner, Joseph Bologna, Charles Grodin
Rating: ★

Hollywood has had considerable success with remakes of such French successes as *3 Men and a Baby*. But

W

Gene Wilder came a coinsiderable cropper with this revised version of *Pardon Mon Affaire*, which flattens the delicate Gallic naughtiness and fails to come up with anything funny by way of compensation. Wilder does bring some warmth and his own zany charm to the minor executive obsessed with a girl in red (Kelly LeBrock, a great looker of limited acting ability) but the talents of Joseph Bologna and Charles Grodin as his friends are wasted.

Woman in the Window, The ○ Ⓥ

1944, US, 99 mins, b/w
Dir: Fritz Lang
Stars: Edward G Robinson, Joan Bennett, Raymond Massey, Dan Duryea
Rating: ★★★

Tremendous thriller made by the German director Fritz Lang at the end of a very profitable decade in Hollywood, years which had already yielded *Fury, You Only Live Twice, The Return of Frank James* and *Hangmen Also Die*. Edward G Robinson gives a fine study in increasingly anguished desperation as the mild professor who becomes enmeshed in violence, murder and blackmail after a little innocent flirtation with a woman who resembles a portrait that has fascinated him. Robinson and co-stars Joan Bennett and Dan Duryea, here at his silkily treacherous best as the blackmailer, teamed again the following year with Lang for the equally remarkable *Scarlet Street*.

Woman Obsessed, A ○

1959, US, 102 mins, colour
Dir: Henry Hathaway
Stars: Susan Hayward, Stephen Boyd
Rating: ★★

Triple-handkerchief weepie, with Susan Hayward as the courageous widow carving out a new life for herself and her seven-year-old son. Beautiful colour photography of the Canadian Rockies. Arthur Franz can be seen in a small role as Hayward's husband, killed in a forest fire early on.

Woman of Straw ○

1964, UK, 117 mins, colour
Dir: Basil Dearden
Stars: Gina Lollobrigida, Sean Connery, Ralph Richardson
Rating: ★★★

This electrifying thriller with a fistful of twists provided a respite from 007 for Sean Connery. He plays the

ne'er-do-well nephew of a wheel-chair-bound millionaire and talks the old man's nurse (Gina Lollobrigida) into a marriage of convenience. The question of inheritance is greedily anticipated until the poor man's untimely death complicates matters. La Lollo and Connery play the situations crisp and tight, in direct contrast to the flamboyant cackle of Ralph Richardson's millionaire. Director Basil Dearden sometimes shows a tendency to pull Hammer horror tricks to enliven the suspense, but the acting keeps things going smoothly, the colour photography is nicely in tune with the surroundings, and the love scenes have genuine passion. Only the ending is weak and flaws the film's impact.

Woman of the Year ○

1941, US, 115 mins, b/w
Dir: George Stevens
Stars: Spencer Tracy, Katharine Hepburn
Rating: ★★★★

A great start to the Spencer Tracy-Katharine Hepburn screen partnership. It's a real pleasure to see two big stars indulging in barbed-wire banter in such a relaxed way, as Tracy's down-to-earth sports reporter tames Hepburn's current affairs hotshot. Watching her trying to cope with his pugilistic friends and her first game of baseball are only two of the delights in this sophisticated, witty, highly enjoyable film. Ring Lardner Jr and Michael Kanin deservedly won an Oscar for Best Original Screenplay. William Bendix makes his screen debut.

Woman's Face, A ○

1941, US, 105 mins, b/w
Dir: George Cukor
Stars: Joan Crawford
Rating: ★★★

The film that set the pattern for Joan Crawford's decade of suffering. She plays a badly-scarred woman set for a life of crime until a skilful surgeon restores her looks and changes her attitudes to the world. This is a trace tougher than director George Cukor's usual elegant film fare, but he makes it a most exciting thriller with a human touch and some striking visual moments. Conrad Veidt is especially good as Crawford's former partner in blackmail who is naturally reluctant to let her go.

Woman's Secret, A ○

1949, US, 85 mins, b/w
Dir: Nicholas Ray
Stars: Maureen O'Hara, Melvyn Douglas, Gloria Grahame
Rating: ★

A half-baked *film noir* written by Herman J Mankiewicz, who co-authored *Citizen Kane* with Orson Welles. RKO rued the day it agreed to finance it – they lost a whopping $760,000 (at 1940 prices!) A series of criss-cross flashbacks jolt rather than help the story along, and (a miscast) Maureen O'Hara's confession to murder in the opening scenes is a mystery. Just why did she confess at all? We will never know . . . All very peculiar.

Woman Times Seven ◐

1967, US, 99 mins, colour
Dir: Vittorio De Sica
Stars: Shirley MacLaine, Peter Sellers, Rossano Brazzi
Rating: ★★

Very ambitious seven-part comedy that's almost inevitably hit-and-miss, the best episodes involving Shirley MacLaine as (a) a plain, neglected housewife who resolves to turn herself into husband Lex Barker's Super Girl fictional character and (b) with Alan Arkin in a double-suicide pact that backfires at every turn.

Woman Without a Face ○

1965, US, 100 mins, b/w
Dir: Delbert Mann
Stars: James Garner, Jean Simmons, Suzanne Pleshette
Rating: ★★

James Garner gets a rare old going over in the acting stakes as his four female co-stars all turn in eye-catching performances in this variation on one of Hollywood's most durable plots: the man who has lost his memory. Garner is a man who wakes up on a bench in Central Park minus his memory. His encounters with four women bring back fragments of the past, of past women – or just one woman. The plot is so satisfying that it's a pity the solution to it all isn't more of a climax. Delbert Mann directs in an efficient, if old-fashioned, way, and there's some splendid black and white photography of New York by Ellsworth Fredericks. Suzanne Pleshette is as warmly real as she always is – whenever she has a character to work on – while Angela Lansbury and Jean Simmons play to the gallery to great effect as floozies from opposite ends of the social scale.

Women, The ○
1939, US, 132 mins, b/w
Dir: George Cukor
Stars: Norma Shearer, Joan Crawford, Rosalind Russell, Paulette Goddard
Rating: ★★★

George Cukor, almost every Hollywood actress's favourite director in the Thirties, was the ideal man to direct this all-woman show about a wife coerced by her catty circle of friends into seeking a divorce she doesn't really want. A starry cast takes full advantage of the bitchy dialogue, adapted by Anita Loos and Jane Murfin from Clare Boothe's original play. The all-claws-out approach is led by Norma Shearer, Joan Crawford, Rosalind Russell, Paulette Goddard, Mary Boland and Hedda Hopper.

Women in Love ● Ⓥ
1969, UK, 130 mins, colour
Dir: Ken Russell
Stars: Alan Bates, Oliver Reed, Glenda Jackson, Jennie Linden
Rating: ★★★★

Ken Russell's most disciplined film, a clever and atmospheric adaptation of D H Lawrence's classic novel of two turbulent love affairs in a small Midlands colliery town in the Twenties. Glenda Jackson won her first Oscar and there are fine performances, too, from Alan Bates, Jenny Linden and a perfectly-cast Oliver Reed. Only Eleanor Bron seems ill-at-ease. Evocative colour photography by Billy Williams decorates this almost perfect film.

Women on the Verge of a Nervous Breakdown ● Ⓥ
1988, Spain, 89 mins, colour
Dir: Pedro Almodovar
Stars: Carmen Maura, Antonio Banderas, Julieta Serrano
Rating: ★★

Mysteriously Oscar-nominated as best foreign film, this much over-praised film is an innocuous, if foul-mouthed, comedy that looks like a stage adaptation. Fairly tedious for most of its exposition, it does come together a bit (like its characters) at the end. Carmen Maura is a lively and interesting leading lady, and there are one or two amusing, if irreverent touches, such as the soap powder ad on TV in which a murderer's mother

shows pride in getting the bloodstains out of his clothes. Fashionable Spanish director Almodovar sees to it that doors open and close at the requisite moments in the best of farcial traditions. But an Oscar nomination? That's a bigger laugh than anything on display here.

Wonder Bar ○
1934, US, 84 mins, b/w
Dir: Lloyd Bacon
Stars: Al Jolson, Kay Francis
Rating: ★★★

A rare treat for fans of Hollywood musicals of the Thirties in this Busby Berkeley-staged musical with numbers including the eye-popping 'Goin' to Heaven on a Mule'. Directed by Lloyd Bacon, who was especially good at comedy (although he could turn his talents to anything) and whose contribution to such other Berkeley-choreographed musicals *42nd Street, In Caliente* and *Gold Diggers of 1933* has been unjustly neglected.

Wonderful Life ⊙
1964, UK, 108 mins, colour
Dir: Sidney J Furie
Stars: Cliff Richard, Walter Slezak, Susan Hampshire
Rating: ★★

In the desert, Cliff slows down. This Cliff Richard musical is pleasant, sunny entertainment, but a bit yawn-inducing at times. There's too much pre-planning here and too little of the youthful exuberance that the same star and director (Sidney J Furie) showed in *The Young Ones*. Cliff and Susan Hampshire compete with each other in upturned noses, but not in the acting stakes (she wins hands down). One or two of the dance routines are lively, particularly those featuring Una Stubbs, and other points to note include Cliff being dragged 200 yards by a runaway camel and getting up without a grain of sand on him, and a rather sharp take-off of The Marx Brothers.

Wonderful Things ○
1958, UK, 85 mins, b/w
Dir: Herbert Wilcox
Stars: Frankie Vaughan, Jeremy Spenser, Jackie Lane, Wilfrid Hyde White
Rating: ★★★

If you can believe in Frankie Vaughan and Jeremy Spenser as Gibraltar fishermen, you'll enjoy this Anna Neagle-produced trifle about love and

life, Latin-style. Fiery Jackie Lane eclipses model Jean Dawnay's screen debut.

Wonderful World of the Brothers Grimm, The ⊙
1962, US, 134 mins, colour
Dir: Henry Levin
Stars: Laurence Harvey, Karl Boehm, Claire Bloom
Rating: ★★

With Laurence Harvey and Karl Boehm miscast as the Grimms (too cool and charmless), all the best moments in this fanciful biopic come from Oscar-winning George Pal's presentation of the fairy-tales themselves: Russ Tamblyn's bounding woodsman and Jim Backus's Magoo-voiced king in *The Dancing Princess*; Buddy Hackett's battle with a cleverly animated dragon in *The Singing Bone*; and the brilliant 'Puppetoon' sequence in *The Cobbler and the Elves*. Originally a long-runner in Cinerama, the rest of its drama looks pretty faded today.

Wonder Man ⊙
1945, US, 98 mins, colour
Dir: Bruce Humberstone
Stars: Danny Kaye, Virginia Mayo, Vera-Ellen
Rating: ★★

Danny Kaye gets plenty of scope for his own individual brand of fooling in this Goldwyn comedy which very successfully blends elements of a musical, a gangster spoof and ghost-comedy thriller to provide lavishly zany entertainment. The film won an Academy Award for its special effects (photographic and sound) and remains one of Kaye's most satisfying and colourful vehicles. Songs include the famous tongue-twister 'Ochitchorna'.

Won Ton Ton, the Dog who Saved Hollywood ⊙
1975, US, 92 mins, colour
Dir: Michael Winner
Stars: Bruce Dern, Madeline Kahn, Art Carney
Rating: ★★★

With some 75 former Hollywood stars making cameo appearances, this is an affectionate satire on *Rin Tin Tin*. Bruce Dern and Madeline Kahn are pleasant leads, and the canine is talented enough to have been given more of the film. Certainly the funniest sequence is when the dog, down on his luck and taken to drink, tries to

W

commit suicide. It only remains to say that Ann Miller, Cyd Charisse, Gloria De Haven and Rhonda Fleming still look quite dazzling.

Wooden Horse, The ○ Ⓥ
1950, UK, 101 mins, b/w
Dir: Jack Lee
Stars: Leo Genn, Anthony Steel, David Tomlinson
Rating: ★★★

An exciting ingenious prisoner-of-war camp story that set the pattern for several such films to come. It also made Anthony Steel a major star of the British cinema while, in a small supporting role, Peter Finch was soon to attain similar status.

Woodstock ◑ Ⓥ
1969, US, 184 mins, colour
Dir: Michael Wadleigh
Rating: ★★★

There has never been a pop music festival to compare with (to give it its full title) The Woodstock Music and Art Fair, held over 72 tumultuous hours in some fields outside the tiny township of Bethel in up-state New York. The music itself is now legendary, and the film treatment of it, directed by Michael Wadleigh with the assistance of the now-famous Martin Scorsese and editing from Thelma Schoonmaker, set new standards for the filming of pop concerts. Outstanding contributions come especially from Joan Baez, Jimi Hendrix, The Who, Sly and the Family Stone and Country Joe MacDonald. The nudity, from spectators removing wet and muddy clothes (the torrential rain quickly turned the concert grounds into a quagmire) is almost completely inoffensive. Altogether, a remarkable record of a unique occasion.

Woo Woo Kid, The ◑ Ⓥ
1987, US, 100 mins, colour
Dir: Phil Alden Robinson
Stars: Patrick Dempey, Beverly D'Angelo, Talia Balsam, Michael Constantine
Rating: ★★

A fetching little comedy about a teenager, Sonny 'Woo Woo' Wisecarver, who grabbed headline notoriety in wartime America by running off with a couple of married women. His ingenuous odyssey needed a Preston Sturges or Woody Allen, though, to turn it into a rollicking oddity. It has a good star in

the Eddie Bracken-like Patrick Dempsey but what it lacks is outright laughs. Dempsey's one-liners mainly consist of repeat lines like 'It'll be great' or 'That's the saddest thing I've ever heard'. They don't quite give the picture the sweep of madness it needs. But Talia Balsam is particularly appealing as Sonny's first love, and there are good cameos from raucous Kathleen Freeman as the kid's landlady and mournful Michael Constantine as his father. Glenn Miller tunes give the piece a familiar period feel. The real Sonny Wisecarver appears as a mailman.

Words and Music ○
1948, US, 120 mins, colour
Dir: Norman Taurog
Stars: Mickey Rooney, Tom Drake, Janet Leigh, Judy Garland
Rating: ★★★

Known as *The Works* when it first came out, this ludicrously fictionalised biography of Rodgers and Hart cost MGM one of its biggest-ever salary bills. Mickey Rooney, who could hardly have portrayed Hart as the homosexual he was, at least had a good stab at the mercurial nature of the man, and sometimes seems to be asking his audience to be reading between the lines. But you can forget about the story (pure Hollywood schmaltz, expertly produced and melodramatic to the last reel) and wallow instead in the glorious music of the composers. Almost every song, every dance routine is a highspot in the film. But watch out especially for Lena Horne, scorching the screen with 'Where or When'; Cyd Charisse's dazzling dancing dexterity in 'On Your Toes'; Judy Garland – surely the only singer who could be heard above the brass on 'Johnny One Note'; and the razor-slick version of 'Slaughter on 10th Avenue' from Gene Kelly and Vera-Ellen.

Working Girl ◑ Ⓥ
1988, US, 125 mins, colour
Dir: Mike Nichols
Stars: Harrison Ford, Melanie Griffith, Sigourney Weaver, Alec Baldwin, Joan Cusack
Rating: ★★★

A solid entertainment picture from director Mike Nichols with a plum role for Melanie Griffith as the breathy but brainy secretary who has a business degree but not the right background for success. Escaping the clutches of one lecherous boss after another, she

goes to work for a woman (Sigourney Weaver), an outwardly friendly broker but a treacherous piranha of a woman who swallows competitors whole and ruthlessly steals the first bright idea Griffith sets in front of her. Griffith finds out about the deception and determines to put through the deal involved herself. This being a warm-hearted sort of film, with few lapses into bad taste, you can guess subsequent developments; but the cast handle their roles with panache and skill, especially Griffith, Weaver (a vivacious villainess), Harrison Ford (an unexpectedly subtle comedian), and Philip Bosco as the big fish Griffith hopes to hook. Griffith is terrific, whether determined, dampened, drunk, dejected or radiant. And Weaver, as the businesswoman who views marriage as a merger ('I've indicated I'm receptive to an offer') is ripely enjoyable in a decidedly different role. Not a great film, but one to enjoy.

World According to Garp, The ●
1982, US, 136 mins, colour
Dir: George Roy Hill
Stars: Robin Williams, Mary Beth Hurt, Glenn Close, John Lithgow
Rating: ★★

A very serious film about life, masquerading as a black comedy, this a very weird kettle of fish. Robin Williams' Garp, the son of a woman who chose a dying serviceman as his father because she wanted to owe no allegiance to a man, lives a life filled with pain, both mental and physical; his story is far-fetched in the manner of the blackest farce, with all the crises in his life revolving round sex in one way or another. All this is perhaps an allegory about the way modern man lives a life of agony searching for the greener grass on the other side of the fence only to discover, like Dorothy in *The Wizard of Oz*, that there's no place like home. Williams and Mary Beth Hurt as his wife often look puzzled, as well they might, and are outshone by Glenn Close, in her major film debut, bringing an inner glow even to such an unlikely person as Garp's mother, and by John Lithgow, who gently brings real character to the sex-change lady who becomes Garp's confidante. Both these performances received Oscar nominations.

World and His Wife, The
See: State of the Union

World Apart, A ○ ⓥ
1988, US, 113 mins, colour
Dir: Chris Menges
Stars: Jeroen Krabbe, Barbara Hershey, Jodhi May, David Suchet, Tim Roth
Rating: ★★

This horrendous portrait of the beginnings of repression in South Africa in 1961, when the 90-day custody law was introduced, is well-meant and extremely well-acted and occasionally even heartbreaking. Director Chris Menges' sympathy with his actors is obvious, but otherwise his treatment is unnecessarily laborious, unable to resist stretching the true story out and driving every anti-Apartheid point home. A script that paid more attention to literary persuasion and wore its heart less obviously on its sleeve would also have helped the film's impact. Still, there are great performances from Barbara Hershey and young Jodhi May (as his daughter) and from Nadine Chambers as Hershey's friend, not strong enough to leap the gulf of ostracism. Worth seeing then for the acting and for its vitally important and tragic theme.

World in His Arms, The ○
1952, US, 104 mins, colour
Dir: Raoul Walsh
Stars: Gregory Peck, Ann Blyth, Anthony Quinn, John McIntire
Rating: ★★★

Gregory Peck isn't the sort one naturally associates with high adventure, although this boisterous period yarn about a 19th-century adventurer who wants to buy Alaska was a natural follow-up for him to the naval heroics of *Captain Horatio Hornblower RN.* The rousing action scenes are in the capable hands of veteran director Raoul Walsh. A race between the hero's ship and that of the rascally Portugee (Anthony Quinn) is especially well done.

World's Greatest Athlete, The ⊙
1973, US, 93 mins, colour
Dir: Robert Scheerer
Stars: Jan-Michael Vincent, Tim Conway, Roscoe Lee Browne, Dayle Haddon
Rating: ★★★

Some decent trick photography and a scene where the Tarzan-like hero's myopic landlady fails to see that his 'roommate' is a tiger enliven this otherwise standard Disney comedy with a lively pace but a dismally unfunny supporting comedy team in Tim Conway and John Amos.

World's Greatest Lover, The ○
1977, US, 89 mins, colour
Dir: Gene Wilder
Stars: Gene Wilder, Carol Kane, Dom DeLuise
Rating: ★★

For his second foray into direction Gene Wilder, who also scripted, sends up Hollywood in the Twenties, although his satirical barbs take second place to wild slapstick in the style of his mentor Mel Brooks. Carol Kane is excellent as Wilder's wife, who goes off with Rudolph Valentino while her husband attempts to win a contest to find a screen star to outshine The Great Lover. Dom DeLuise is entertainingly over the top as an explosive studio head.

Wrecking Crew, The ○
1969, US, 105 mins, colour
Dir: Phil Karlson
Stars: Dean Martin, Elke Sommer
Rating: ★★

The last of the four films about Donald Hamilton's super-agent Matt Helm, and better than the second and third, if not quite up to the first of the series, *The Silencers.* The director is Phil Karlson, which at least guarantees that the screen will be busy 100 per cent of the time. The action, as a result, fairly buzzes along. Once more Helm proclaims he's through with ICE, the super-secret organisation out to conquer an enemy organisation known as Big O; but soon he's involved in a hunt for a billion dollars in gold which has been hi-jacked in Denmark.

Written on the Wind ○
1956, US, 99 mins, colour
Dir: Douglas Sirk
Stars: Lauren Bacall, Rock Hudson
Rating: ★★★

Although not perhaps director Douglas Sirk's best film, this was the one that caught the critics' eye, and won Dorothy Malone an Oscar for her barnstorming portrayal of a nymphomaniac Texan.

Wrong Arm of the Law, The ○
1962, UK, 94 mins, b/w
Dir: Cliff Owen
Stars: Peter Sellers, Lionel Jeffries, Bernard Cribbins, Bill Kerr
Rating: ★★★

Irresistibly funny comedy, thanks to a screenplay that simply never lets up for a minute. The fun and games are full of moments to treasure: Bill Kerr as the leader of the Australian gang who pose as policemen in order to 'confiscate' the loot from robberies committed by other crooks; Lionel Jeffries as the impossibly inept Inspector 'Nosey' Parker; Bernard Cribbins as a nervous crook who wears a seat belt in the back seat of his car and Peter Sellers as 'Pearly' Gates, whose suave French accent slips deliciously into snarling Cockney when the Law appears on the scene.

Wrong Box, The ○
1966, UK, 105 mins, colour
Dir: Bryan Forbes
Stars: Michael Caine, Nanette Newman, Peter Cook, Dudley Moore
Rating: ★★★

A rich black comedy, set in London just before the turn of the century, and concerning the last two (elderly) survivors of a bizarre lottery. The fun gets increasingly wilder, with Grandpa John Mills, superbly made up, and rushing about in a nightshirt like an aged imp, makes frenzied attempts to assassinate Grandpa Ralph Richardson and collect the money. Also very funny are Peter Sellers, as a doctor who has cats around his house the way some people have mice; and Wilfrid Lawson, in his last film, as the family's decrepit butler.

Wrong Man, The ○ ⓥ
1957, US, 105 mins, b/w
Dir: Alfred Hitchcock
Stars: Henry Fonda, Vera Miles, Anthony Quayle
Rating: ★★★

A taut, moving Hitchcock suspense film, much underrated in its day, told in semi-documentary style and based on a true story. Henry Fonda is just right as the sensitive musician bewildered by the way circumstantial evidence piles up against him on a robbery count. Vera Miles gives the finest performance of her career as his mentally fragile wife. The film was also one of the first to employ the talents of British actor Anthony Quayle in a major role; but he quickly established himself on the international scene.

W

WUSA ◐
1970, US, 117 mins, colour
Dir: Stuart Rosenberg
Stars: Paul Newman, Joanne Woodward, Anthony Perkins, Laurence Harvey
Rating: ★★

Great things were expected from this film because director Stuart Rosenberg was teamed again with star Paul Newman for the first time since *Cool Hand Luke*. But *WUSA* and their two further films together, *Pocket Money* and *The Drowning Pool*, were all commercial flops. *WUSA*, taking its name from the ultra-right wing New Orleans radio station where drunkard Newman talks his way into a job, is a political satire, but a dire and pretentious one at that. At times it looks like a travelogue as Newman and real-life wife Joanne Woodward, as the girl he picks up, exchange predictable dialogue while walking hand in hand through the city streets. Anthony Perkins is the redeeming factor, delivering a twitching, nervous performance as a trendy liberal/revolutionary in the guise of Norman Bates from *Psycho*.

Wuthering Heights ○
1939, US, 104 mins, b/w
Dir: William Wyler
Stars: Laurence Olivier, Merle Oberon, David Niven
Rating: ★★★★

Easily the most memorable version of Emily Brontë's romantic novel, with haunting characterisations by Laurence Olivier and Merle Oberon as Heathcliff and Cathy. Olivier had wanted Vivien Leigh for the role, but, under William Wyler's persuasive direction, Oberon gave the best performance of her career. The film was nominated for numerous Academy Awards but on the night won only one: it went, however, to the most deserving of all nominees – Gregg Toland, whose evocative black-and-white photography in this film has been seldom equalled.

Wuthering Heights ○
1970, UK, 105 mins, colour
Dir: Robert Fuest
Stars: Timothy Dalton, Anna Calder-Marshall, Harry Andrews
Rating: ★★

Remake of the story of the famous doomed love affair between Catherine and Heathcliff on their beloved Yorkshire moors. Director Robert Fuest and his talented cameraman John Coquillin capture the ghastly bleak beauty of Emily Brontë's powerful novel. But the script is much less spirited than in the famous 1939 Olivier film, and only Anna Calder-Marshall (as Catherine) and the ever-excellent Judy Cornwell remain for long in the memory.

Wuthering Heights ○ ⊛
1992, US, 106 mins, colour
Dir: Peter Kosminsky
Stars: Ralph Fiennes, Juliette Binoche, Janet McTeer, Sophie Ward, Simon Ward, Jennifer Daniel
Rating: ★

This stickily cast, TV-style version of Emily Brontë's passionate novel of obsessive love in the 18th century runs more like a Gothic horror story than a romance. Ralph Fiennes, though unorthodox casting, at least looks and sounds the part as the wild-eyed, rugged Heathcliff, descending into madness at the loss of his love. But Juliette Binoche's Cathy is a total disaster and she tries in vain to conceal her French accent, or makes risible attempts at a sort of Parisian Yorkshire. The windswept, barren Yorkshire moors are the only stars of this dark and doomy costume piece, directed in TV commercial style by debutant director Peter Kosminsky and scored for a thoroughly annoying collection of screeching violins by Ryuichi Sakamoto. Alas, poor 'Eathcleef, we knew 'eem well.

W W and the Dixie Dancekings ◐
1975, US, 94 mins, colour
Dir: John G Avildsen
Stars: Burt Reynolds, Art Carney, Connie Van Dyke, Ned Beatty
Rating: ★★★

Little known off-beat Burt Reynolds comedy in which he plays W W Bright, an ex-garage hold-up artist who accidentally takes charge of a sleazy band known as Dixie and the Dancekings. John G Avildsen's film is marvellously light handed, using Fifties Presley hits by Leiber and Stoller to recapture a lost world of 1950s Country and Western.

Wyoming Mail ○
1950, US, 87 mins, colour
Dir: Reginald Leborg
Stars: Stephen McNally, Alexis Smith, Ed Begley
Rating: ★★

A rough, tough Western, dazzlingly photographed in Technicolor by Oscar-winning cameraman Russell Metty. Stephen McNally is suitably forceful as the boxer on a dangerous undercover mission for the government, and a fine supporting cast includes Ed Begley, Alexis Smith, Howard Da Silva, Richard Jaeckel, Gene Evans, James Arness and Richard Egan.

Wyoming Renegades ○
1955, US, 73 mins, colour
Dir: Fred F Sears
Stars: Phil Carey, Martha Hyer
Rating: ★★

Butch Cassidy and The Sundance Kid ride again – but here, as in so many Westerns before Newman and Redford made the characters folk heroes, they're the villains of the piece. This is a vigorous Western in good Technicolor, one of innumerable colour horse-operas turned out at Columbia in the Fifties, all of them moving along at a rattling pace, and hardly one over 80 minutes. Here Phil Carey's the hero (though he showed in another Columbia Western, *Gun Fury*, that he could be a fine villain), but burly Gene Evans as Butch Cassidy has no trouble acting the rest of the cast clear off the screen.

X

Xanadu ○ ⓥ
1980, US, 96 mins, colour
Dir: Robert Greenwald
Stars: Olivia Newton-John, Gene Kelly, Michael Beck, James Sloyan
Rating: ★★★

Vivid musical fantasy remake of *Down to Earth* (the old Rita Hayworth musical) which has one drawback – its leading lady, Olivia Newton-John, as a goddess helping to put on an earthly show. Fortunately production designer John Corso and director Robert Greenwold demonstrate great flair for colour, composition and movement, with the result that *Xanadu* is as dazzling to the eye as any of the vintage Hollywood musicals. Story? Well, hardly any, but it's engagingly surrealistic in a pop-glitter way, and Gene Kelly's there to help Newton-John shine in her most successful scene when they dance together in his memories of the Forties. Expect a super de luxe version of *Top of the Pops* and you won't be disappointed.

X the Unknown ◐
1956, UK, 80 mins, b/w
Dir: Leslie Norman
Stars: Dean Jagger, Edward Chapman
Rating: ★★

Pretty nasty and effective by 1956 standards, this early Hammer horror film has the benefits of sinister black and white photography by Gerald Gibbs and such sterling players as Dean Jagger, Edward Chapman, Leo McKern and William Lucas. There is also an interesting performance from the less well known John Harvey, and the familiar faces of Michael Ripper and Anthony Newley crop up as two of the soldiers battling a mysterious 'something' that creeps up from a bottomless fissure created by an atomic explosion on the Scottish moors. Leslie Norman's direction misses few chances to point up the shock moments – and there are plenty.

X, Y and Zee ●
1971, UK, 110 mins, colour
Dir: Brian G Hutton
Stars: Elizabeth Taylor, Michael Caine, Susannah York
Rating: ★

A strident and sometimes effective dissection of a marriage on the rocks, of mutual dislike and the eternal triangle. It certainly has star value, with Elizabeth Taylor, Michael Caine and Susannah York as the embattled trio. The film is often abrasive and occasionally funny, although you may find it, like the raucous Zee (a super professional performance by Elizabeth Taylor), just a little wearing.

Y

Yakuza, The ●
1975, US, 112 mins, colour
Dir: Sydney Pollack
Stars: Robert Mitchum, Takakura Ken, Brian Keith
Rating: ★★★

Those with no stomach for blood are advised to steer clear of this well-made gangster film in which limbs are sliced off (sometimes by their owners) here, there and everywhere, while other parts of the body are slit open or blasted apart. Robert Mitchum and Takakura Ken give excellent performances as two men who hate each other (it's a woman, of course) but come to deep mutual respect through a body-strewn battle against a common enemy. The action with swords is sometimes hard to watch, but the code of honour, and its burden of obligation, in the world of the yakuza (Japanese mobster) comes across strongly under the sensitive direction of Sydney Pollack. Recommended for those with constitutions strong enough to take it.

Yangtse Incident ○
1956, UK, 110 mins, b/w
Dir: Michael Anderson
Stars: Richard Todd, William Hartnell
Rating: ★★★

Stirring account of the real-life suspense saga of HMS Amethyst, held virtual prisoner by the Chinese on the Yangtse River in 1949 until a sensational and daring escape plan was devised. Richard Todd is in his element as the forthright captain; below decks, Bernard Cribbins plays one of his earliest screen roles.

Yank at Oxford, A ○
1938, US/UK, 100 mins, b/w
Dir: Jack Conway
Stars: Robert Taylor, Lionel Barrymore, Maureen O'Sullivan, Vivien Leigh
Rating: ★★★

Considering that it underwent almost a year of writing and re-writing, this was – and is – a remarkably entertaining and successful story about English university life knocking the rough edges off of a brash American and teaching him some real values. Robert Taylor studies with Maureen O'Sullivan, dallies with Vivien Leigh (one of her best performances) and (in a marvellous scene) bandies words with an old English gent (Morton Selten) on a train. When Taylor boasts that the whole of Britain could be put into the state of Nebraska, his companion replies: 'Doubtless – but with what object?' The exchange was contributed by Sidney Gilliat, one of eight writers credited in one capacity or another. Many others worked uncredited on the project, among them John Paddy Carstairs, Angus Macphail, Frank Wead, Harold Goldman and F Scott Fitzgerald!

Yankee Buccaneer ○
1952, US, 86 mins, colour
Dir: Frederick De Cordova
Stars: Jeff Chandler, Scott Brady, David Janssen
Rating: ★★

One of those colourful action-packed 90 minute adventure stories which Universal-International rolled out with such regularity and expertise in the Fifties. The story moves along in aggressive style, and the Technicolor photography of Russell Metty makes the film a constant pleasure to look at. In the supporting cast, you can spot a very young David Janssen.

Yankee Doodle Dandy ○
1942, US, 126 mins, b/w
Dir: Michael Curtiz
Stars: James Cagney, Joan Leslie, Walter Huston
Rating: ★★★

Even James Cagney was rarely as dominant as he is in this musical biography of George M Cohan, awash with music, sentiment and patriotic fervour. Cagney swept triumphantly to an Academy Award, and the film took two other Oscars, including one for the best scoring of a musical. It remained the star's favourite throughout the remainder of his career. The songs include 'Over There', 'Yankee Doodle Boy' and 'Give My Regards to Broadway'. Its highlight remains Cagney's dazzling cross-stage strutting dance, involving 'climbs' on either side.

Yankee Pasha ○
1953, US, 84 mins, colour
Dir: Joseph Pevney
Stars: Jeff Chandler, Rhonda Fleming, Lee J Cobb
Rating: ★★

One of the major wonders of Fifties' cinema is how Universal-International managed to take Edison Marshall's enormous novel *Yankee Pasha*, and compress it into 84 minutes without actually losing much of the plot. Not surprisingly, there's incident and excitement a-plenty in their version of Marshall's extravagant yarn about an American fur-trapper in the 1800s (played by Jeff Chandler), who sets out to recover his lost love from Moroccan pirates and ends up as arms adviser to the Sultan of Morocco. No film that casts Lee J Cobb as an eastern sultan can be taking itself entirely seriously, and proceedings are very much on the light-hearted side. Bart Roberts, who plays the treacherous Omar-Id-Din, made most of his films under his real name – Rex Reason.

Yank in the RAF, A ○
1941, US, 98 mins, b/w
Dir: Henry King
Stars: Tyrone Power, Betty Grable
Rating: ★★★

Tyrone Power winning the Battle of Britain in a Hollywood war film that strangely raised fewer hackles than Errol Flynn's subsequent (and lower-key) exploits in *Objective, Burma*. The British are in there somewhere, though, and there *are* some fine aerial combat scenes. It's persuasively put together, too, by Henry King who, after years with 20th Century-Fox, was nothing if not versatile. He could be relied upon for anything from musicals such as *Alexander's Ragtime Band* to something out-of-the-rut like the classic Western *The Gunfighter*.

Yanks ◑ ⓥ
1979, US, 141 mins, colour
Dir: John Schlesinger
Stars: Vanessa Redgrave, Richard Gere, William Devane, Lisa Eichhorn, Tony Melody, Rachel Roberts
Rating: ★★★

There are many pleasurable things in this long John Schlesinger film, not least the way in which it flawlessly recreates the life of an English town in 1943. Schlesinger directs with great affection for the time and place (the north of England) and a keen eye and ear for the right sights and sounds. And he gets well-sustained performances from his principal players, Richard Gere, Lisa Eichhorn, William Devane and Tony Melody. Vanessa Redgrave and Rachel Roberts are less consistent, though they have their affecting moments, Rachel Roberts really looking painfully close to death

when she is supposed to be. Scenes of a ballroom dance, a children's party and a mass farewell on a station (could one small town boast quite so many girls?) are reminiscent of such American films of that time as *Since You Went Away*: in this respect at least, and greatly helped by the thoughtful colour photography of Dick Bush, the director has preserved the moment in time to perfection.

Yearling, The ☉
1946, US, 134 mins, colour
Dir: Clarence Brown
Stars: Gregory Peck, Jane Wyman, Claude Jarman Jr
Rating: ★★★

Based on a book by Marjorie Kinnan Rawlings (whose own story was told in *Cross Creek*), this is a lovingly made, glowingly photographed (Technicolor was never richer than in Charles Rosher and Leonard Smith's hands) and completely unforced study of a backwoods boy and his love for a tame fawn that must eventually, inevitably, be returned to the wild. Gregory Peck and Jane Wyman exude sympathy and understanding as the boy's parents, and the story is compellingly told through a series of small but enthralling incidents by Clarence Brown, still at MGM, where he had been for many years and who was once Garbo's favourite director. Oscars for photography and art direction, plus a special award to Claude Jarman Jr (the boy) as outstanding child actor of the year.

Year of Living Dangerously, The ◑ ⓥ
1983, Australia, 115 mins, colour
Dir: Peter Weir
Stars: Mel Gibson, Sigourney Weaver, Linda Hunt, Michael Murphy, Bill Kerr
Rating: ★★★

Director Peter Weir catches all the tension and turmoil of an impoverished and oppressed country (in this case 1965 Indonesia under Sukarno) as it overheats and boils over into revolution. The atmosphere and seething background to this is captured down to the last bead of sweat; but what Weir has largely failed to do is tell an exciting story to go with it. Mel Gibson is too cool and dispassionate here as the Australian correspondent coming to prominence in the last days of Sukarno's regime. Other casting is weird, but more successful, especially Linda Hunt as the native photographer Billy: as a woman playing a man she adds to the enigmatic qualities of the character, and the performance won her an Oscar. The music score, based partly on native themes, is most effective. Even so, the richness of all the film's teeming detail pales after a while, and you long for something more: involvement.

Year of the Gun ● Ⓥ
1991, US/Italy, 111 mins, colour
Dir: John Frankenheimer
Stars: Andrew McCarthy, Valeria Golino, Sharon Stone, John Pankow
Rating: ★

These days, an international co-production like this seems dated before it hits the screen. The players act loudly and strenuously, the director focuses on them with lenses that pick out every pock-mark, characters look grim or compliant according to the tenor of their role, and the colour has those washed-out shades that make greenery take on tinges of blue. The acting by Andrew McCarthy, Sharon Stone and Valeria Golino is hardly top-notch, either, in this tedious story of undercover saboteurs in Italy's Red Brigade of the late Seventies, but then the dialogue and this treatment would make Streep and Hoffman look silly at times. Director John Frankenheimer's long career has gradually slid downhill since the heady days of *Birdman of Alcatraz* and *The Manchurian Candidate*. The city of Rome, too, is hardly made the most of. Ah, for the days when Carol Reed turned Vienna into a character by itself in *The Third Man*.

Years Without Days
See: Castle on the Hudson

Yellow Balloon, The Ⓒ
1952, UK, 80 mins, b/w
Dir: J Lee-Thompson
Stars: Andrew Ray, Kenneth More, Kathleen Ryan
Rating: ★★★

This was Britain's first X-rated film: a suspense thriller about a little boy involved with a murderer. Andrew Ray (son of Ted) was, at the age of 12, already an established star when he made this, and his role as Frankie Palmer endeared him further to the critics. There is a frighteningly effective climax, as a killer lures him into a disused tube station, planning to throw him down a lift shaft. The silence is broken only by the panting of hunter and hunted, and the eerie clatter of trains. The star gets lots of

quality support in this one, from a cast that includes Kenneth More, Kathleen Ryan, William Sylvester, Sandra Dorne, Sidney James, Bernard Lee, Veronica Hurst and Hy Hazell.

Yellowbeard ● Ⓥ
1983, US, 101 mins, colour
Dir: Mel Damski
Stars: Graham Chapman, Peter Boyle, Peter Cook, Marty Feldman
Rating: ★

Pirate spoofs got a bad name in the 1980s, what with Roman Polanski's *Pirates* and this directionless jumble of comic sketches. The film was actually the brainchild of Keith Moon, drummer with The Who; hence one of the main characters, an evil bosun, being called Moon.

Yellow Rolls Royce, The ○
1964, UK, 122 mins, colour
Dir: Anthony Asquith
Stars: Ingrid Bergman, Rex Harrison, Omar Sharif, Shirley MacLaine
Rating: ★★

Multi-story film about the love affairs – and adventures – that start in the back seat of a vintage car. With a sizzling international cast, the team of Anthony Asquith (director), Anatole de Grunwald (producer) and Terence Rattigan (writer) have produced a sleek bit of entertainment.

Yellow Sky ○
1948, US, 98 mins, b/w
Dir: William Wellman
Stars: Gregory Peck, Anne Baxter, Richard Widmark
Rating: ★★★

Set in an Arizona ghost town, director William Wellman, expert purveyor of man-sized action, makes this Western of confrontation a gritty, suspenseful and exciting affair. There are sharp-edged portraits from Gregory Peck (always best when cast against his seemingly natural gentle type), Anne Baxter (also enjoying a change of pace, as a rifle-toting tomboy) and John Russell. But no one out-acts Richard Widmark, offering another of the smiling psychopaths that decorated his early years in films.

Yellow Submarine ☉
1968, UK, 87 mins, colour
Dir: George Dunning
Stars: The Beatles
Rating: ★★★

Moving from live-action comic-strip in *Help!*, The Beatles became even

more animated in this lively 'day-glo' feature-length animation film. The first full-length cartoon from a British studio since *Animal Farm* 13 years earlier, it was based on one of the group's biggest hits. It took no less than four writers – including Erich Segal of *Love Story* fame – to fashion a storyline full of such bizarre characters as the Blue Meanies (who want to rid the world of music and happiness), a sea of monsters and a super-intellectual pendant called Boob (voice courtesy of Dick Emery). Its hippie theme that L-O-V-E conquers all may be a bit too twee in this day and age, but there's no denying the film's stunning animation, in particular the weird and wonderful 'kinky boot beasts'.

Yentl ○ Ⓥ
1983, US, 134 mins, colour
Dir: Barbra Streisand
Stars: Barbra Streisand, Mandy Patinkin, Amy Irving
Rating: ★★

Barbra Streisand's first film as star and director is a bizarre cross-dressing story of a Jewish girl who disguises herself as a man to beat limitations her society imposes on her. Songs have been added to bolster the doubts that soon begin to creep in, but nothing can shore up the crumbling structure of the central situation: few actresses would be believable as a man and Streisand isn't one of them. Even ignoring the stature, the feminine gestures and the tiny feet, there's the voice . . . 'How could I have been so blind?' asks Avigdor (Mandy Patinkin) when she finally tells him. And we can but agree. Its major achievement in the middle of the expected razzle-dazzle of a Streisand musical is that moments of quiet observation and reflective wisdom are given their due, and that Streisand manages to play the scenes requiring her to be discreetly demure with surprising success.

Yol ◐ Ⓥ
1982, Switzerland, 111 mins, colour
Dir: Serif Goren
Stars: Tarik Akan
Rating: ★★★

An extraordinary film from the brain of Yilmaz Guney, once Turkey's most popular film star, but later a director who fell out with the authorities and spent a large proportion of his later life in prison or in hiding. This harrowing and unrelenting portrait of the hard life endured by Kurds, and others, in Turkey in the Eighties had to be

Y

smuggled into western Europe, where it took practically every prize going at the 1982 Cannes Film Festival. It will make many wince, not only at the grim lives of the main characters – prisoners allowed a brief period of freedom, spelling doom to most – but also at the treatment of women who stray from the law. There were to be no more films from Guney, who died from cancer in 1984 – still in exile in France.

You Can't Sleep Here
See: I Was a Male War Bride

You Can't Take It with You ⊙
1938, US, 127 mins, b/w
Dir: Frank Capra
Stars: Jean Arthur, James Stewart, Lionel Barrymore
Rating: ★★★

Although it's worn less well than some Frank Capra classics, this is still a charming and amusing study of a carefree, eccentric family and their tangles with the authorities. It gave Capra his third Academy Award for best director and his second for best picture. And there were five other nominations. Lionel Barrymore, who plays the head of the family, was suddenly crippled at the outset of the film by the arthritis that had been troubling him for years. He had doubts about continuing his career, but Capra insisted on having him as Grandpa Vanderhof. He put a plaster cast on Barrymore's foot, had him hop around on crutches and explained it by having Vanderhof say that he has sprained his ankle after his granddaughter dared him to slide down the banisters – wholly in keeping with the character! Capra added Jean Arthur and James Stewart for the romantic leads, plus one character who hadn't been in the original play, a Mr Poppins, who makes ingenious toys for fun, and is delightfully portrayed by gnomish Donald Meek. The results are wonderful and warm, or faintly irritating, according to your tastes!

You Can't Win 'em All ◐
1970, US, 95 mins, colour
Dir: Peter Collinson
Stars: Charles Bronson, Tony Curtis, Michele Mercier
Rating: ★★

There can't be many films set against the Turkish Civil War in 1922, but it crops up here as the backcloth to a rousing comedy adventure story set mainly on board a train carrying a shipment of treasure from Turkey to Egypt. Charles Bronson and Tony Curtis are the two American adventurers hired to guard the train, and the treasure, against the constant attacks of a band of determined hijackers. Pretty Michele Mercier, who played Angelique, of historical novel fame, in several lavish films, is the governor's daughter who's also under their care. Veteran Hollywood heavy Leo Gordon brings his familiar mean features to a supporting role – and reveals an unexpected side to his talent. He also wrote the screenplay for the film.

You'll Never Get Rich ○
1941, US, 88 mins, b/w
Dir: Sidney Lanfield
Stars: Fred Astaire, Rita Hayworth
Rating: ★★★

A brisk, good-humoured combination of backstage musical and wartime romance, with Rita Hayworth proving a delightful (and likeable) new partner for Fred Astaire after Ginger Rogers had quit the team for high drama. Cole Porter's score, hamstrung by patriotic necessities, isn't exactly his best, but the stars dance impressively together and Astaire goes solo on the memorable 'A-Stairable Rag'.

Young Americans, The ● Ⓥ
1993, UK, 104 mins, colour
Dir: Danny Cannon
Stars: Harvey Keitel, Iain Glen, Thandie Newton, Viggo Mortensen, Craig Kelly
Rating: ★★

A New York cop comes to Britain and soon gets in the British law's hair: a familiar movie theme from time immemorial. Seeing that it's Harvey Keitel as the cop, we get a performance of typical clamped-down intensity – a man doing his job despite the weight of the world (and a broken marriage) on his shoulders. No bad lieutenant this, though: he's even willing to go out on a limb for the young informer (Craig Kelly) who's resolved to trap criminals he grew up with after they become involved with the death of his father. And there's another American: Fraser (Viggo Mortensen), a big drug-dealing fish Keitel's been after for years. Thandie Newton is appealing as Kelly's girl, while Terence Rigby, Keith Allen and others give traditional British portrayals of nightclub crooks. Iain Glen and John Wood are the men in macs who soon come to respect Keitel's ability to crack crimes it nor- mally takes British bobbies months to bring to book. Traditionalists will know what we mean when we say that this is B dressed up as A.

Young and Innocent ○ Ⓥ
1937, UK, 80 mins, b/w
Dir: Alfred Hitchcock
Stars: Nova Pilbeam, Derrick De Marney
Rating: ★★★

This rarely-seen Alfred Hitchcock suspense thriller was adapted from Josephine Tey's novel *A Shilling for Candles*. It was made at the newly opened Pinewood Studios, which had stages big enough to allow Hitchcock to indulge in some spectacular crane shots in a story of two young people on the run trying to clear the man of murder, as in *The 39 Steps*. Hitchcock himself makes his usual cameo appearance: watch out for him in the crowd outside a courthouse. A scene in which fugitives try to get away from a party is priceless.

Young at Heart ○ Ⓥ
1954, US, 117 mins, colour
Dir: Gordon Douglas
Stars: Doris Day, Frank Sinatra
Rating: ★★★

Frank Sinatra lends his own touch of moody melancholy to a musical remake of the 1938 John Garfield film *Four Daughters*. Playing a loner who thinks he's a loser, his character's grudge against the world isn't settled even when he falls for a homely girl from a small Connecticut town. Some good songs include 'Someone to Watch Over Me', 'Just One of Those Things', 'One for My Baby' and 'Young at Heart'.

Young Bess ○
1953, US, 112 mins, colour
Dir: George Sidney
Stars: Jean Simmons, Stewart Granger, Charles Laughton
Rating: ★★★

Close that history book and settle back for Hollywood's version of the childhood and first great romance of Queen Elizabeth I. Never mind the facts, there's a feast of good acting on show here, from Jean Simmons as the rebellious Bess, Charles Laughton repeating his Oscar-winning triumph of 20 years before as Henry VIII, Deborah Kerr as a dignified and kindly Catherine Parr, Guy Rolfe and Kathleen Byron as nasty as you could wish as Bess's enemies and young Rex Thompson, endearingly first-class as

Edward VI, the boy king. Thanks to Charles Rosher's rich Technicolor camerawork, one of the earliest examples of photography making scenes look like old paintings, it's also one of the best-looking films even MGM ever made.

Young Billy Young ○
1969, US, 89 mins, colour
Dir: Burt Kennedy
Stars: Robert Mitchum, Angie Dickinson, Robert Walker, David Carradine
Rating: ★★

Sheriff Robert Mitchum and killer Robert Walker team up to find the murderer of Mitchum's son. They become lawmen in the town of Lordsburg, as Mitchum hopes to track down the killer there. There's really nothing new in this Western, but it's a good yarn told with style by director Burt Kennedy. There are also good performances from Mitchum, Walker, David Carradine and Angie Dickinson – as the dance hall girl who falls for the sheriff.

Youngblood ● Ⓥ
1986, US, 110 mins, colour
Dir: Peter Markle
Stars: Rob Lowe, Cynthia Gibb, Patrick Swayze
Rating: ★

A truly dreadful ice hockey film depicting the Canadian variety of the sport as a cross between hockey, boxing and unlawful wounding. The entertainment value of the sporting scenes is zero and the film is naively scripted and badly acted into the bargain. Brat Pack front runner Rob Lowe leans heavily on his shyly cocky smile, but apart from the maelstrom of four-letter words, this would look more at home as a TV movie. Sin-bin penalties all round.

Youngblood Hawke ○
1964, US, 137 mins, b/w
Dir: Delmer Daves
Stars: James Franciscus, Suzanne Pleshette, Genevieve Page
Rating: ★

James Franciscus plays a young author who loses his ideals in the high society jungle. Adapted from a huge novel by Herman Wouk, with a good supporting role for Don Porter, this is another slice of romantic melodrama from the hands of Delmer Daves, who made all those Troy Donahue films in the Fifties. The supporting cast – Suzanne Pleshette, Mary Astor, Lee

Bowman, Eva Gabor – work hard to cover up a non-performance by Franciscus in the lead.

Young Cassidy ○
1964, UK, 110 mins, colour
Dir: Jack Cardiff, John Ford
Stars: Rod Taylor, Flora Robson, Maggie Smith, Julie Christie
Rating: ★★

Begun by John Ford and completed by cameraman-turned-director Jack Cardiff, this atmospheric drama recounts the early struggles of the Irish playwright Sean O'Casey, here known as Johnny Cassidy. Rod Taylor is hardly ideally cast in the title role, but he has stout support from the distinguished ladies in the cast, among them Maggie Smith, Julie Christie, Flora Robson, Edith Evans and Sian Phillips.

Young Dr Kildare ○
1938, US, 81 mins, b/w
Dir: Harold S Bucquet
Stars: Lew Ayres, Lionel Barrymore
Rating: ★★

This is the first 'official' entry of MGM's *Dr Kildare* series, although the first film adaptation of author Max Brand's characters came a year earlier with *Interns Can't Take Money*. Lew Ayres, who stars as the idealistic medic, said of his first attempt at the role: 'Frankly, I thought it was terrible.' However, Ayres went on to appear in eight more films alongside Lionel Barrymore as his mentor, Dr Leonard Gillespie. Barrymore remained with the series until its completion in 1947. The characters were rejuvenated in the Sixties with Richard Chamberlain and Raymond Massey in the leading roles.

Young Einstein ○ Ⓥ
1988, Australia, 90 mins, colour
Dir: Yahoo Serious
Stars: Yahoo Serious
Rating: ★★★

The wacky, wild-haired Yahoo Serious was already something of an Australian phenomenon when he made this startlingly successful screen debut at 26. Writer, director, singer, comedian and dancer: how's that for a start? As an actor, he's not much yet, but as a filmmaker he proves full of way-out comedy ideas. Indeed, the biggest laughs in this amiable romp stem from its incidental scenes: Einstein's mother contentedly knitting wool unravelling from an uncon-

cerned (talking) sheep, or the cook in the lunatic asylum making a pie with several live kittens in it (not as awful as it sounds!) Serious also takes some inspired pratfalls, and, if there aren't many more outright laughs around, the lark remains good-natured and watchable throughout. The plot really does concern *the* Albert Einstein – as a Tasmanian outbacker, inventing the theory of relativity in 1906 and falling for Marie Curie at the same time! He also invents bubbles in beer, the first electric guitar and rock 'n' roll.

Young Frankenstein ◑ Ⓥ
1974, US, 105 mins, b/w
Dir: Mel Brooks
Stars: Gene Wilder, Peter Boyle, Marty Feldman, Madeline Kahn
Rating: ★★

It's a pity that Mel Brooks' films always sound much funnier than they turn out. This black-and-white monster mix is one of the better ones. It is, of course, a pastiche on the Frankenstein legend. Or, to be more precise, the first few Universal films on that subject in the Thirties. The most successful scene is a masterpiece of comic business between the Monster (Peter Boyle) and the blind hermit (an unbilled Gene Hackman). Gene Wilder has the thankless task of carrying the lion's share of both the less funny bits – apart from a glorious song-and-dance with the Monster – and the film's slightly more serious side. Madeline Kahn, Teri Garr and Cloris Leachman are nice though under-used, and neither is proper use made of Marty Feldman as the hunchback, apart from his first memorable appearance ('Hump? What hump?'). A pity that this misses so many opportunities, if only by a narrow margin, because it still has enough laughs to keep you entertained.

Young Guns ● Ⓥ
1988, US, 107 mins, colour
Dir: Christopher Cain
Stars: Emilio Estevez, Kiefer Sutherland, Lou Diamond Phillips, Charlie Sheen
Rating: ★★★

Some people thought the Hollywood Western was in trouble – until the Brat Pack rode to the rescue. And a pretty reasonable job, too, they made of these early adventures of Billy the Kid. Personable performances by Emilio Estevez as the kid and Kiefer Sutherland as his poetic sidekick Doc help offset a slight overlength in the telling, and inevitable 'Wild Bunch'

Y

slow-motion at the climactic shootout. Not that slow motion plays any part in the rest of the action, of which there's a lot. Terence Stamp is the Englishman who harbours young fugitives and helps civilise them while they work on his ranch, but old Jack Palance sets the young guns on a killing spree when he becomes jealous of Stamp's growing influence and has him eliminated. The rest of it is tough and bloody, but varied in content and rarely dull. Estevez's chirpy charisma as Billy helps the film from becoming too dark in tone, although Sutherland gets most of the best lines, including the classic riposte: 'I used to ride with the dirty underwear gang.' Tom Cruise and Brooke Shields supposedly make brief guest appearances in a saloon-bar scene towards the end of the film.

Young Guns II ◐ ⊚
1990, US, 104 mins, colour
Dir: Geoff Murphy
Stars: Emilio Estevez, Kiefer Sutherland, Lou Diamond Phillips, Christian Slater
Rating: ★★★

This gunfire-packed sequel turns its back on what we learned at the end of *Young Guns* about the fates of its characters and tells another, darker, maybe truer story of Billy the Kid and his merry men. Director Geoff Murphy, a New Zealander, brings an Antipodean look to the wild west – all browns, golds and searing blues, with scarcely a patch of green in sight. Against this backdrop, he gives us vividly-rounded portraits of the characters involved, emphasised by frequent close-ups: Emilio Estevez, cackling maniacally as Billy – still very much the kid: 'I aim to play the game,' he says, meaning only partly to see things through. Kiefer Sutherland's Doc, reluctantly dragged back to outlawry by a federal dragnet, Lou Diamond Phillips' superstitious Mexican Indian, William Peterson's tortured turncoat Pat Garrett and Viggo Mortensen's nasty, sardonic Irish John Poe are all sharply sketched. James Coburn is in it too, as land boss John Chisum: only a 'bit', but as authoritatively Coburn as ever. And Christian Slater's headstrong, self-centred Arkansas Dave Rudabaugh lends a cutting edge to the gang's constant flight from the law. A major new Western that's pretty much in the old style, with a strikingly rousing score by Alan Silvestri.

Young Guns of Texas ○
1962, US, 84 mins, colour
Dir: Maury Dexter
Stars: James Mitchum, Alana Ladd, Jody McCrea
Rating: ★★

Boisterous Western about four young people forced to go on the run after one of them has killed a man in a gunfight. Its chief attraction lies in the fact that the offspring of three famous Hollywood stars play the leading roles. James Mitchum and Jody McCrea went on to become minor leading men in their own right, but little more was heard of Alana Ladd. Director Maury Dexter, who made a couple of good horror films in the early Sixties, throws in a mixed bag of ingredients, including marauding Apaches, renegade Confederates, buried gold and even Calamity Jane (played by Barbara Mansell) to keep the going lively, and has Western veterans Chill Wills and Robert Lowery to help him along. The Technicolor photography is fine.

Young in Heart, The ○
1938, US, 95 mins, b/w
Dir: Richard Wallace
Stars: Janet Gaynor, Douglas Fairbanks Jr, Paulette Goddard, Roland Young
Rating: ★★★

A delightful romantic comedy about a family of confidence tricksters who are reformed by a rich old lady. At the heart of its success is a witty script by Paul Osborn and Charles Bennett from the story *The Gay Banditti* by I A R Wylie. The banditti in question are headed by Roland Young and Billie Burke as the parents, with Janet Gaynor and Douglas Fairbanks Jr as their children. Richard Carlson made his screen debut as Gaynor's suitor. Sharp and funny, expertly handled by director Richard Wallace.

Young Lions, The ○ ⊚
1958, US, 167 mins, b/w
Dir: Edward Dmytryk
Stars: Marlon Brando, Montgomery Clift, Dean Martin
Rating: ★★★

Edward Dmytryk's powerful film from Irwin Shaw's novel of three young soldiers – two American, one German – during World War Two. Marlon Brando and screenwriter Edward Anhalt remoulded the central character of the young Nazi, Christian. The brute of the book was changed to a dedicated but humane officer whose

conscience troubles him more and more until he can no longer shut his eyes to atrocities committed in the name of the Reich. Three more outstanding performances – by Maximilian Schell as the officer whose wife becomes Christian's mistress, Parley Baer, as Christian's friend and, surprisingly, Dean Martin, as the brasher of the Americans – make this a film to stay in the memory. The black and white photography by Joe MacDonald is also outstanding.

Young Lovers, The ○
1954, UK, 96 mins, b/w
Dir: Anthony Asquith
Stars: Odile Versois, David Knight
Rating: ★★★

American boy falls for Russian girl in London in this fine, moving film, delicately handled by director Anthony Asquith. Towards the end it becomes both a love story and a tense thriller in its own right, as the couple battle to stay together.

Young Man of Music ○
(aka: Young Man with a Horn)
1949, US, 112 mins, b/w
Dir: Michael Curtiz
Stars: Kirk Douglas, Lauren Bacall, Doris Day, Hoagy Carmichael
Rating: ★★

Adapted from the Dorothy Baker book *Young Man with a Horn*, this musical biopic was inspired by the life of trumpet player Bix Beiderbecke. Kirk Douglas gives a typically fierce and intense performance as the young man of the title, but Hoagy Carmichael almost steals the film as his laconic sidekick Smoke. Although written by the formidable team of Carl Foreman and Edmund H North, the screenplay, which is rather a long way from the real facts, tends to be overwrought and contains the classic line: 'Put down your trumpet, jazz man, I'm in the mood for love.' Lauren Bacall performs a thankless task well as a girl who lures Douglas away from the musical freeway, and Doris Day is the singer who tries to put him back there, while adoring him from afar. An absorbing dose of Hollywood moonshine, thanks not least to the professional polish applied by director Michael Curtiz.

Young Man with a Horn
See: Young Man of Music

Young Mr Lincoln ○
1939, US, 100 mins, b/w
Dir: John Ford
Stars: Henry Fonda, Alice Brady, Marjorie Weaver, Arleen Whelan
Rating: ★★★

A finely-detailed piece of Americana from director John Ford with a sterling performance by Henry Fonda, playing the young Abraham Lincoln as a travelling lawyer of the 1880s. There's a fine supporting performance by Alice Brady (an appealing leading lady of silent times), who had won an Academy Award the previous year for her moving performance in *In Old Chicago*. Unfortunately *Young Mr Lincoln* was to be her last film, before her early death from cancer.

Young Ones, The ⊙ Ⓥ
1960, UK, 104 mins, colour
Dir: Sidney J Furie
Stars: Cliff Richard, Carole Gray, Robert Morley
Rating: ★★★

Music, comedy and drama are combined with an unquenchable get-up-and-go zippy story which raised the level of the British musical to a new high. The song-and-dance routines are brilliantly staged within the framework of a story about a group of teenagers fighting to save their youth club.

Young Sherlock Holmes ○ Ⓥ
(aka: Young Sherlock Holmes and the Pyramid of Fear)
1985, US, 109 mins, colour
Dir: Barry Levinson
Stars: Nicholas Rowe, Alan Cox, Sophie Ward
Rating: ★★★

A fun adventure with a schoolboy Sherlock hot on the trail of a strange Egyptian cult who kill anyone who gets in their way. Lively performances from Nicholas Rowe as Holmes and Alan Cox as Watson go a long way towards making up for the silliness of the plot, which kicks off like an old episode of *The Avengers*. Its adventurous spirit is certainly more in keeping with a schoolboy romp than the adult Holmes' more cerebral investigations. The only jarring notes in the narrative are some hallucination

scenes, which don't add anything to the story. Stay tuned to the end of the credits – there's an extra scene!

Young Sherlock Holmes and the Pyramid of Fear
See: Young Sherlock Holmes

Young Soul Rebels ● Ⓥ
1991, UK, 105 mins, colour
Dir: Isaac Julien
Stars: Valentine Nonyela, Mo Sesau, Dorian Healy
Rating: ★★

You have to hand it to Britain's BFI and Film Four International. There can't be any other companies who would make a film about the black homosexual experience set against the Queen's silver jubilee in 1977. Not only that, but the film also portrays the racial prejudice that prevents even black DJs from making progress in the London of the late Seventies, and tries (not very successfully) to be a murder thriller as well. Performances are rough-edged but good, and the characters have an infectious energy that doesn't let your attention drop. This is no great movie but, given its elements (and its budget), this is probably about as good as it could get. The Metrocolor photography by Nina Kellgren is excellent throughout. Just don't try fathoming the thriller elements of the plot. You'll guess 'who done it' but still wonder why.

Young Tom Edison ○
1939, US, 82 mins, b/w
Dir: Norman Taurog
Stars: Mickey Rooney, Fay Bainter, George Bancroft
Rating: ★★★

Mickey Rooney was America's top box-office star, ahead of even Clark Gable, when this biography of the inventor's youth was made. It's a surprisingly effective and entertaining picture, relying less on Rooney's personality and mannerisms than almost any other of his star vehicles.

Young Winston ○ Ⓥ
1971, UK, 157 mins, colour
Dir: Richard Attenborough
Stars: Robert Shaw, Anne Bancroft, Simon Ward, Anthony Hopkins
Rating: ★★★

Don't be deceived into thinking that this is a political drama unworthy of your attention. From the opening battle scenes, in strife-torn India

before the turn of the century, to Winston Churchill's hair-raising adventures as a correspondent caught up in the Boer War, the exploits of the great man's youth are rousingly recalled by director Richard Attenborough and a stalwart British cast. Simon Ward's portrayal of the young Winston is quite faultless, even if it lacked the magnetism to make him a superstar. But there are colourful characterisations from Anne Bancroft (as Jennie, Lady Churchill), Robert Shaw (as Randolph Churchill), Anthony Hopkins (as David Lloyd George) and especially Pat Heywood as Winston's loving nanny – while the spectacularly-shot scenes of desert warfare offer John Mills the chance of a sharp little cameo as General Kitchener.

Young Wives' Tale ○
1951, UK, 78 mins, b/w
Dir: Henry Cass
Stars: Joan Greenwood, Nigel Patrick, Derek Farr, Helen Cherry
Rating: ★★

Fast-paced, incident-filled and very British comedy about two young couples who share a home to beat the housing shortage. Some households seem made for mishaps. In this one, baths overflow, kettles vainly whistle and the neighbour's dog steals the Sunday joint. The house's three bedrooms are occupied by the two married couples and a man-hungry girl lodger, played by Audrey Hepburn in one of her earliest film roles, before she went to Hollywood. Anne Burnaby puts plenty of comic business into her adaptation of Ronald Jeans' stage hit, and director Henry Cass keeps the plot bowling along through an endless series of compromising situations, giving a new twist to the 'not in front of the servants' theme. There are fine comic performances from Joan Greenwood, Nigel Patrick and the moustache-twirling Guy Middleton, who never quite got the roles he deserved in British films.

You Only Live Once ○
1937, US, 85 mins, b/w
Dir: Fritz Lang
Stars: Henry Fonda, Sylvia Sidney
Rating: ★★★

A superb early variation on a *Bonnie and Clyde* theme, this consolidated German director Fritz Lang's Hollywood career following his shattering debut with *Fury*. The feeling of

Y

the inevitability of doom was never more poignantly captured than in the story of Henry Fonda's ex-convict trying fruitlessly to keep on the straight and narrow. The evocative black and white photography is by Leon Shamroy, later to become master of the colour camera. Especially memorable here is a masterly shot of a rain-drenched street in front of a bank, where pedestrians scurry by beneath a canopy of black umbrellas.

You Only Live Twice ○ Ⓥ
1967, UK, 117 mins, colour
Dir: Lewis Gilbert
Stars: Sean Connery, Donald Pleasence
Rating: ★★★

James Bond goes east, anticipating future film trends as usual: five years later, martial arts thrillers would be all the rage. Lewis Gilbert directs the plentiful action in fine style, and Ken Adam and his crew of Pinewood technicians did everyone especially proud on this one, creating at a cost of more than half a million pounds the largest interior set ever constructed in Europe. The set represents the inside of a volcano (headquarters of villain Donald Pleasence) and houses a working monorail, a heliport and a 66-foot space rocket that actually fired 50 feet above the staging gantry. Adam's masterpiece makes the extras (300 of them, as SPECTRE minions) look like ants. It's definitely the mechanical marvels that hold sway in this adventure. They also include a deadly rocket that uses a cigarette as its firing tube, and a speedy one-seat autogiro in which Bond does battle with a fleet of SPECTRE helicopters. The most amusing item though, is a helicopter equipped with an electro-magnet – for removing unwanted cars from the highway.

You're a Big Boy Now ◑
1966, US, 96 mins, colour
Dir: Francis Ford Coppola
Stars: Elizabeth Hartman, Geraldine Page, Peter Kastner
Rating: ★★★

This adult comedy about a youth's induction to manhood was a huge critical success at the time. Only one of its stars has progressed notably in the film world since, however: young Karen Black, who was nominated for an Oscar in Five Easy Pieces. But the director did go places. His name was Francis Ford Coppola, and he subsequently made The Godfather.

You're in the Army Now
See: O.H.M.S.

You're My Everything ○
1949, US, 94 mins, colour
Dir: Walter Lang
Stars: Dan Dailey, Anne Baxter
Rating: ★★★

Tuneful and sharply-scripted variation on the backstage marriage theme, this Dan Dailey movie also takes an amusing look at the Hollywood scene of the Twenties and Thirties. Oscar-winning actress Anne Baxter shows she can go through a dance routine with the best of them, Shari Robinson is a sweet tot in the best Shirley Temple tradition and Buster Keaton has a few wildly funny moments as a delightfully improbable butler.

You're Never Too Young ○
1955, US, 102 mins, colour
Dir: Norman Taurog
Stars: Dean Martin, Jerry Lewis
Rating: ★★★

Another remake, as were many of the Dean Martin-Jerry Lewis comedies, this time of The Minor and the Major, a 1942 hit, in which Ginger Rogers played the Jerry Lewis role of the woman/man who dresses as a child on a train to avoid a murderer. This time round, it's Raymond Burr, now thoroughly moulded as a television goodie, who plays the villain.

You're Only Young Twice! ○
1952, UK, 81 mins, b/w
Dir: Terry Bishop
Stars: Duncan MacRae, Diane Hart, Joseph Tomelty
Rating: ★★

Actor Reginald Beckwith, who plays the small role of a BBC commentator, also had a hand in the screenplay of this adaptation of a James Bridie play, What Say They? Bushy-haired Joseph Tomelty is his usual whimsical self as the porter who surveys some riotous goings-on at a Scottish university.

You're Telling Me ⊙
1934, US, 67 mins, b/w
Dir: Erle C Kenton
Stars: W C Fields, Larry Buster Crabbe
Rating: ★★★

'Dear Mr Fox,' wrote W C Fields to the production manager at Universal in 1940, 'If you'd like to see what I do with family stories, you might care to run You're Telling Me. This doubtless prompted such series as The Hardy

Family and contains some of the best material I wrote first for the Follies of 1924. Stick a nickel in me and I keep talking all day.' The great golfing sequence is probably the best of his many old routines.

Your Past Is Showing
See: The Naked Truth

Yours, Mine and Ours ○
1968, US, 111 mins, colour
Dir: Melville Shavelson
Stars: Lucille Ball, Henry Fonda, Van Johnson
Rating: ★★★

A throwback to the Hollywood family comedy, this pleasing story portrays the sometimes very funny courtship of a widow with eight children, by a widower with 10. A heartwarming comedy that provided Lucille Ball with the best of her latter-day Hollywood roles.

Youth Runs Wild ○
1944, US, 67 mins, b/w
Dir: Mark Robson
Stars: Bonita Granville, Kent Smith, Glenn Vernon
Rating: ★★

One of the few non-horror films produced by Val Lewton (creator of The Curse of the Cat People and other important Forties tales of terror). It was intended as a socially important drama about working class teenagers who get involved in petty crime while their parents were away at war. But the film ended up as a clichéd, turgid drama when studio chiefs insisted on re-cutting and adding some new scenes. Lewton tried to have his name removed from the credits, but his request was denied.

Z

Zandalee ● Ⓥ
1990, US, 104 mins, colour
Dir: Sam Pillsbury
Stars: Nicolas Cage, Judge Reinhold, Erika Anderson, Viveca Lindfors, Joe Pantoliano, Aaron Neville
Rating: ★

Nicolas Cage has made some pretty loony movies in his time, and this sex-filled Southern States steamer is so off-kilter as to be almost round the bend. It's not so much *Wild Orchid* as *Wild Magnolia*, as Cage's painter drifts into New Orleans, and into the life of leggy Zandalee (the seldom-clad Erika Anderson) whose mind seldom strays off sex and whose husband (Judge Reinhold), a poet turned enforced-businessman, just happens not to be giving her any. This is the kind of sleazy subject European soft-porn filmmakers were flooding the market with in the Seventies, dressed up here with some ragin' Cajun music and vapidly coloured Louisiana locations which exec producer Reinhold presumably afforded by saving on Anderson's wardrobe. A death-dance sequence between the two men is daft enough to seem inspired by comparison with the rest, as the clichés roll out like millstones round the necks of the cast. It seems amazing that a couple of fairly major stars could find nothing better to do than make this overcooked kettle of catfish pie

Zarak ○
1956, UK, 99 mins, colour
Dir: Terence Young
Stars: Victor Mature, Michael Wilding, Anita Ekberg
Rating: ★★

Although never quite credible, this is a colourful adventure yarn, set in old India, but in fact shot on location in Spanish Morocco! The realism of the battle scenes was such that the first-aid unit was kept as busy as the crew and cast. In the charging mêlées, dozens of extras came a cropper, Michael Wilding cracked three ribs and Victor Mature suffered concussion from an ill-timed blow. The film was a hit with the public although not kindly received by the critics. The writer, producers and director had the last

laugh, though, six years later, when they made an even more successful film – *Dr No*.

Zardoz ●
1973, UK, 105 mins, colour
Dir: John Boorman
Stars: Sean Connery, Charlotte Rampling
Rating: ★★

A sort of *2001: A Space Oz-yssey.* But the basic concept of this adult fable, set in the 23rd century, is *The Wizard of Oz* – as the title indicates. Some critics thought the resultant work (directed by John Boorman) was tinged with genius, while others condemned it as pretentious drivel. Whatever your verdict, you'll agree that Sean Connery compels attention as the 'Brutal' who finds himself betrayed by his masters and vows vengeance – especially on the 'Eternals' who live for ever.

Zebra in the Kitchen ☉
1965, US, 93 mins, colour
Dir: Ivan Tors
Stars: Jay North, Martin Milner, Andy Devine
Rating: ★★

Animal film directed by Ivan Tors, creator of the television series *Flipper* and *Daktari*. It's a riotous comedy set in the city, about a boy who lets all the animals out of his local zoo.

Zelig ◑ Ⓥ
1983, US, 79 mins, b/w
Dir: Woody Allen
Stars: Woody Allen, Mia Farrow
Rating: ★★★

A highly original comedy that restored Woody Allen's stature in the genre after some early Eighties' lapses. He plays a mysterious figure from the past, traced by 'contemporary' newsreel, whose longing for friendship and companionship gave him the power to turn himself into likenesses of those whom he was with. More clever than funny, but marvellously hypnotic to watch, and with a few typically goofy Allen asides. As well as marrying several wives in various identities, his character is accused of 'performing unnecessary dental extraction'! His story is related (in a dig at *Reds*) by 'witnesses', including a couple of aged reporters. 'You just told the truth,' says one, 'and it sold papers. It never happened before!'

Zeppelin ○
1971, UK, 101 mins, colour
Dir: Etienne Perier
Stars: Michael York, Elke Sommer, Peter Carsten, Marius Goring
Rating: ★

World War One adventure fiasco with Michael York as an Allied spy trying to pinch the Zeppelin plans from the Germans. The glamorous Elke Sommer is an unlikely aviatrix, and Marius Goring pops up as her professor husband. The rest of the cast includes such reliable German 'types' as Anton Diffring and Peter Carsten and the director is the Frenchman Etienne Perier, whose later work included the Alastair MacLean thriller *When Eight Bells Toll.*

Ziegfeld Follies ○ Ⓥ
1944, US, 110 mins, colour
Dir: Vincente Minnelli
Stars: Fred Astaire, Lucille Ball, Judy Garland, Kathryn Grayson, William Powell, Gene Kelly
Rating: ★★★

The third and last of MGM's Ziegfeld musicals is a straight-forward revue directed by Vincente Minnelli who had worked on some of the Great Flo's stage extravaganzas.

Zigzag
See: False Witness

Zorba the Greek ○ Ⓥ
1964, US, 131 mins, b/w
Dir: Michael Cacoyannis
Stars: Anthony Quinn, Alan Bates
Rating: ★★★

A long and patiently-made picture with a two-fold aim. It tells both of the rites and customs of a small Cretan village, and of a young Englishman (Alan Bates) who comes to the village to reopen the disused mine that belonged to his late father. His major domo is Zorba, a real character, played with careful relish by Anthony Quinn, who has his own madcap schemes for re-working the mine. Full of long, lingering pans from the artistic camera of Walter Lassally, who took one of the film's three Academy Awards, *Zorba* is, at its best, both human and amusing. It also has its horrifying moments, such as a throat-slitting, and the looting of a dead woman's house by old crones who look like so many black cockroaches. The performances are topped by that of Lila Kedrova

Z

(another Academy Award winner) with her brilliant, almost gruesome portrait of the fading countess.

Zorro, the Gay Blade ◐

1981, US, 93 mins, colour
Dir: Peter Medak
Stars: George Hamilton, Lauren Hutton, Brenda Vaccaro
Rating: ★

Spoof variation on the Zorro legend, but the pacing is all wrong for high voltage laughter. George Hamilton mugs frantically as the foppish son of the famous swordsman and his look-alike gay brother Bunny.

Zulu ○ ⓥ

1963, UK, 138 mins, colour
Dir: Cy Endfield
Stars: Stanley Baker, Jack Hawkins, James Booth, Michael Caine
Rating: ★★★

This is that rarity in films – an all-action, no-frills, straightforward re-creation of an heroic moment in history. On this occasion, the action concerns the Zulu wars in South Africa and, in particular, the electrifying Battle of Rorke's Drift in 1879, where little more than 100 men of the South Wales Borderers made a staggeringly brave stand against 4,000 yelling Zulu warriors, who had just massacred a force of over 1,000 British troops. It is in the supporting roles that the film finds its own strength. James Booth, as the malingering Private Hook, Nigel Green, as the colour-sergeant, Ivor Emmanuel (in his only film appearance) and Kerry Jordan (the camp cook) all give exemplary service. And then-newcomer Michael Caine is so impressive it's amazing he wasn't snapped up for more star roles long before *The Ipcress File*. The last few scenes of *Zulu*, as rank after rank of the last defenders pour leaden defiance at the Zulus from a few yards' range, are pulsatingly thrilling.

Zulu Dawn ○

1979, US, 121 mins, colour
Dir: Douglas Hickox
Stars: Burt Lancaster, Peter O'Toole, Simon Ward
Rating: ★★★

This spectacular account of the events leading up to those shown in the famous film *Zulu* is an outstanding piece of movie-making craftsmanship, especially in its deployment of the vast forces used in its epic battle scenes. Burt Lancaster has a key role as Colonel Durnford, a one-armed veteran of numerous African campaigns, and Peter O'Toole plays General Lord Chelmsford in command of the British forces.